YUGOSLAVIA •3,940 20°E 25°E R.Danube 30°E Black 35°E Sea

Sofia •5,036 Varna Sinop Samsun

•9,524 BULGARIA Istanbul Zonguldak

Skopje Thessaloniki Ankara

•ALBANIA •9,573 •5,807 T U R K E Y 7,352 Kayseri

Tirane GREECE Aegean Afyenkarahisar

7,594 Izmir Adana

Athens •10,125 Aleppo

•7,903 Rhodes Nicosia SYRIA

Iraklion Crete CYPRUS 6,403 Famagusta LEBANON

e a n Beirut Damascus

S e a ISRAEL

Benghazi Tobruk Damietta Amman Jerusalem Dead Sea

•Sidra Rosetta Port Said Gaza

Alexandria Suez Canal Aqaba

El'Alamein Cairo Ismailia Eilat

Libyan Plateau •289 Pyramids Suez Sinai

Siwa Qattara Memphis 8,652 7,710

Depression El Faiyûm

E G Y P T

Qasr Farâfra Barrage Asyut 7,175

L I B Y A Girga Thebes

Dakhla Oasis Luxor

El Kharga Isna

Kufra Oasis

•85 1st. Cataract Aswan •6,486 Foul B.

Aswan Dam

•3,550 L. Nasser 4,439

•6,256 2nd. Cataract Wadi Halfa 7,271

•10,334 Nubian Desert

R. Nile •4,068

•3,015 3rd. Cataract Port Sudan

•4,298 Suakin

•Emi Kussi 4th. Cataract 5,226

•1,969 5th. Cataract Berber 9,121

Atbara 8,446

Ed Damer R. Atbara Massawa

6th. Cataract Kamaran Is.

•3,076 Omdurman Khartoum Agordat (YEMEN P.D.R.)

Jebel Aulia Dam Kassala Tessenei Asmara

•6,411 •3,698 El 1,680

S U D A N Gezira Wad Medani Aduwa

El Fasher El Obeid Sennar Dam 15,158 Gondar

J. Marra •10,131 •4,636 •13,747

3,412 Er Roseires 10,272 Lake Tana 13,042

Nyala •7,999 13,451

•2,693 Bahr el 'Arab Ethiopian

CENTRAL •4,183 •4,409 Bahr el Ghazal Malakat Addis Ababa Harar

•2,171 Wau R.Sobat ETHIOPIA 5,984 Awash

N REPUBLIC Sudd Plateau Ginir

•2,059 •2,559 Jonglei 14,131

Mobaye 5,710 13,780

R.Oubangui Bondo Juba 5,811

R.Uele Nimule Lake Rudolf Mega Moyale

Z A I R E Mungbere UGANDA 30°E 35°E Obbia

R.Congo (R.Zaire) Lake Albert L.Kyoga Tororo K E N Y A R.Juba Equator

© Oxford University Press

Africa Countries (inset)

ALGERIA LIBYA EGYPT MOROCCO

SPANISH SAHARA MAURITANIA MALI NIGER CHAD SUDAN

SENEGAL UPPER VOLTA NIGERIA ETHIOPIA SOMALIA

GUINEA GHANA TOGO DAHOMEY CAMEROON CENTRAL AFRICAN REPUBLIC UGANDA KENYA

SIERRA LEONE LIBERIA IVORY COAST GABON CONGO (P.R.) ZAIRE TANZANIA

ANGOLA ZAMBIA MALAWI MADAGASCAR

SOUTH WEST AFRICA RHODESIA MOZAMBIQUE BOTSWANA SWAZILAND REPUBLIC OF SOUTH AFRICA LESOTHO

AFRICA
Countries

1 THE GAMBIA
2 GUINEA-BISSAU
3 EQUATORIAL GUINEA
4 RWANDA
5 BURUNDI

AFRICA
Aden to Dakar
Scale 1:19,000,000 approx.

ONE INCH TO 300 MILES

0 Miles 150 300 450

▨ Towns over 1 million people

◉ Towns over 100,000 people

Boundaries - international

Canal Marsh

Sand desert Salt pan

SA'UDI ARABIA

Jidda Mecca

Red Sea

YEMEN Sa'na A.R. YEMEN P.D.R. 15°N

Assab 10,720 G. of Aden C.Guardafui

Bab el Mandeb As Shaab Aden

6,760 FR. TERR Djibouti Zeila Berbera 7,218

AFARS ISSAS •7,900

Diredawa 3,668 6,014 Hargeisa Erigavo 10°N

S O M A L I A •3,379

Haud

O g a d e n 640

R.Shibeli •1,230

5°N

S0-BUW-986

AFRICA SOUTH OF THE SAHARA
1973

AFRICA
SOUTH OF
THE SAHARA
1973

EUROPA PUBLICATIONS LIMITED
18 BEDFORD SQUARE LONDON WC1B 3JN

First Edition 1971
Second Edition 1972
Third Edition 1973

REF 960.32 Af835
1973

Africa South of the
Sahara.

73 29

SAN FRANCISCO PUBLIC LIBRARY

© EUROPA PUBLICATIONS LIMITED 1973

ISBN 0 900 36252 9

Library of Congress Catalog Card Number 78-112271

AUSTRALIA AND NEW ZEALAND
James Bennett (Collaroy) Pty. Ltd., Collaroy, N.S.W., Australia

INDIA
UBS Publishers' Distributors Pvt. Ltd., P.O.B. 1882, 5 Ansari Road, Daryaganj, Delhi 6

JAPAN
Maruzen Co. Ltd., Tokyo

Printed and bound in England by
STAPLES PRINTERS LIMITED
at The Stanhope Press, Rochester, Kent, establishment

Foreword

THIS third edition of AFRICA SOUTH OF THE SAHARA has been thoroughly revised in order to keep pace with the changes which have taken place during the past year in the states and territories of the continent outside North Africa.

Wherever possible, the articles on the Background to the Continent and on the recent history and economy of each country have been completely updated by their authors, acknowledged as experts on the problems, countries and areas involved. Where this has not been possible, the services of other similarly qualified writers have been obtained, or extensive research and revision has been carried out by experienced editors.

This edition incorporates several important new items. A highly informative article by Timothy Curtin on Africa and the European Economic Community appears for the first time in Part I. New articles on the recent history of Burundi and Rwanda have been written by Professor René Lemarchand, author of the standard history of these countries and widely recognized as the leading authority. Dr. David Dalby has expanded his section on African Languages by the addition of a map showing languages having over one million speakers. This year, particular attention has been paid to the statistical surveys, which have been greatly extended in an attempt to provide more comprehensive data and to facilitate direct comparisons between countries. In addition, the directory sections have been subjected to close examination and thorough revision. Each chapter truly reflects the developments of a year which saw racial troubles and border conflict in Uganda, *coups d'état* in Ghana and Dahomey, tribal massacre in Burundi, a report on African opinion in Rhodesia, settlement of the political crisis in Madagascar, and the achievement of peace in Sudan.

January 1973

Acknowledgements

The editors gratefully acknowledge the interest and co-operation of all the contributors to this volume, and of many national statistical and information offices in Africa and embassies and high commissions in London, Paris or Brussels, whose kind assistance in updating the material contained in AFRICA SOUTH OF THE SAHARA is greatly appreciated.

We are particularly indebted to the Food and Agriculture Organization of the United Nations for permission to reproduce statistics from its various publications, most notably the *Production Yearbook 1971*, and to the International Institute for Strategic Studies, 18 Adam Street, London, WC2N 6AL, for the use of defence statistics from *The Military Balance 1972–1973*.

The articles on St. Helena, Ascension, Tristan da Cunha and Seychelles are largely based on material from *A Year Book of the Commonwealth*, with the kind permission of the Controller of Her Majesty's Stationery Office.

We are grateful to authors and publishers for permission to reproduce the following maps:

p. 3 from Basil Davidson, *East and Central Africa to the late Nineteenth Century*, Longmans, 1967; after R. Oliver, "Bantu Genesis", *Journal of the Royal Society of Arts*, September 1966.

p. 5 from Merrick Posnansky (Ed.), *Prelude to East African History*, Oxford University Press, 1966.

p. 8 from Basil Davidson, *A History of West Africa 1000–1800*, Longmans, 1965.

p. 9 from Basil Davidson, *East and Central Africa to the late Nineteenth Century*, Longmans, 1967.

p. 11 adapted from Basil Davidson, *A History of West Africa 1000–1800*, Longmans, 1965.

p. 13 from Roland Oliver and Anthony Atmore, *Africa since 1800*, Cambridge University Press, 1967.

p. 15 from J. D. Fage, *An Atlas of African History*, Edward Arnold, 1958.

Contents

PART ONE
Background to the Continent

PART TWO
Regional Organizations

PART THREE

Country Surveys*

CONTENTS

CONTENTS

CONTENTS

CONTENTS

PART FOUR

Other Reference Material

---

* The Directory section of each chapter is arranged under the following headings, where they apply:

THE CONSTITUTION

THE GOVERNMENT
  HEAD OF STATE
  CABINET/COUNCIL OF MINISTERS/POLITICAL BUREAU OF PARTY

DIPLOMATIC REPRESENTATION

PARLIAMENT

POLITICAL PARTIES

DEFENCE

JUDICIAL SYSTEM

RELIGION

THE PRESS

PUBLISHERS

RADIO AND TELEVISION

FINANCE
  CENTRAL BANK
  STATE BANKS
  DEVELOPMENT BANKS
  COMMERCIAL BANKS
  FOREIGN BANKS
  STOCK EXCHANGE
  INSURANCE

TRADE AND INDUSTRY
  PUBLIC CORPORATIONS
  CHAMBERS OF COMMERCE AND INDUSTRY
  COMMERCIAL AND INDUSTRIAL ORGANIZATIONS
  TRADE FAIRS
  EMPLOYERS' ORGANIZATIONS
  TRADE UNIONS
  CO-OPERATIVES
  MAJOR INDUSTRIAL COMPANIES

TRANSPORT
  RAILWAYS
  ROADS
  SHIPPING
  CIVIL AVIATION

POWER

TOURISM

EDUCATION
  ACADEMY
  LEARNED SOCIETIES
  RESEARCH INSTITUTES
  LIBRARIES
  MUSEUMS AND ART GALLERIES
  UNIVERSITIES
  COLLEGES

† Translated from French.

Maps

The Contributors

Abdel Rahim, Muddathir. UNESCO Senior Expert in Public Administration and Social Sciences; formerly Visiting Professor of Political Science, Makerere University, Kampala, Head of Department of Political Science, University of Khartoum, Lecturer, University of Zambia. Author of *Imperialism and Nationalism in the Sudan: a Study in Constitutional and Political Development, 1899–1956* (1969).
(Recent History of Sudan, p. 850.)

Aboyade, Ojetunji. Economic Development Institute, International Bank for Reconstruction and Development, Washington; formerly Professor of Economics, University of Ibadan; has on occasion advised Nigerian Government on economic development; member of International Association for Research in Income and Wealth. Author of *Foundations of an African Economy—A Study of Growth and Investment in Nigeria* (1966); "The Nigerian Economy", in Robson, P. and Lury, D. A. (Eds.): *The Economies of Africa* (1969); and a number of articles. Editor of *Nigerian Journal of Economic and Social Studies* since 1962.
(Economy of Nigeria, p. 612.)

Aduamah, E. Y. Writer on African culture. Author of articles in *West Africa*, and unpublished work on Volta Basin and Ewe traditions.
(Recent History of Togo, p. 928.)

Ajayi, J. F. Ade. Vice-Chancellor, University of Lagos; formerly Professor of History, University of Ibadan. Author of *Christian Missions in Nigeria 1841–91* (1965); *Milestones in Nigerian History* (1962). Co-author of *Yoruba Warfare in the Nineteenth Century* (1964). Co-editor of *A Thousand Years of West African History* (1965).
(Recent History of Nigeria, p. 607.)

Amer, John. Head of Geography Department, Ledbury Grammar School, Herefordshire; formerly teacher, examiner and broadcaster in Malawi. Author of "Industry in Malawi", in Agnew, Lady S., et al.; *Malawi in Maps*; and several papers and articles.
(Physical and Social Geography of Botswana, p. 176, Lesotho, p. 461, Malawi, p. 512, South Africa, p. 759, South West Africa, p. 833, Swaziland, p. 883.)

Amin, Samir. Director, African Institute for Economic Planning and Development, Dakar; formerly Research Fellow with the Economic Development Organisation, Cairo, Technical Adviser to the Government of Mali. Author of *Trois expériences africaines de développement: le Mali la Guinée et le Ghana* (1965); *L'Economie du Maghreb* (1966); *Le Maghreb moderne* (1970) (English translation: *The Maghreb in the Modern World*, 1970); *Le développement du capitalisme en Côte d'Ivoire* (1967) (English edition forthcoming); *Le monde des affaires sénégalaises* (1968); *L'Accumulation à l'échelle mondiale—critique de la théorie du sous-développement* (1970) (English Italian and Swedish editions planned); and several papers and contributions to collective works. Co-author of *Histoire économique du Congo 1880–1968* (1969).
(Economy of Dahomey, p. 288, Guinea, p. 397, Ivory Coast, p. 415, Mali, p. 538, Mauritania, p. 552, Niger, p. 592, Senegal, p. 710, Togo, p. 931, Upper Volta, p. 973.)

Anstey, Roger. Professor of Modern History, University of Kent at Canterbury; formerly Lecturer, University of Ibadan, Reader, University of Durham, Visiting Professor, University of British Columbia. Author of *Britain and the Congo in the Nineteenth Century* (1962); *King Leopold's Legacy: The Congo under Belgian Rule, 1908–1960* (1966); and a number of articles.
(Recent History of Zaire, p. 990.)

Austin, Dennis. Professor of Government, University of Manchester; formerly Reader in Commonwealth Studies, University of London. Author of *West Africa and the Commonwealth* (1957); *Politics in Ghana 1946–60* (1964); *Britain and South Africa* (1966); *Malta and the End of Empire* (1971).
(Recent History of Ghana, p. 366.)

Berry, L. Professor of Geography and Director of Bureau of Resource Assessment and Land Use Planning, University of Dar es Salaam.
(Physical and Social Geography of Sudan, p. 849, Tanzania, p. 897.)

Boateng, E. A. Principal, University College of Cape Coast, Ghana; formerly Lecturer in Geography, University College of Ghana, Dean, Faculty of Social Studies; has held Visiting Professorships in University of Pittsburgh and U.C.L.A.; Smuts Visiting Fellow, University of Cambridge, and Foundation Fellow, Ghana Academy of Arts and Sciences. Author of *A Geography of Ghana* (1959) and various articles in learned journals and encyclopaedias.
(Physical and Social Geography of Ghana, p. 365.)

Brown, Richard. Lecturer in History, University of Sussex; formerly Lecturer, University College of Rhodesia. Author of a number of articles in the *Journal of Commonwealth Political Studies, Current History*, etc. Co-editor of *The Zambesian Past* (1966), and contributor to *African Societies in Southern Africa* (1969).
(Recent History of Rhodesia, p. 653.)

Clarke, John I. Professor of Geography, University of Durham; previously Professor, Fourah Bay College, University of Sierra Leone. Author of *Population Geography* (1965); *Population Geography and Developing Countries* (forthcoming). Part-author of *Africa and the Islands* (1964); *A Geography of Africa* (1969). Editor of *Sierra Leone in Maps* (1966); *Population of the Middle East and North Africa*.
(Physical and Social Geography of Cameroon, p. 203.)

Cornevin, R. Director, Centre d'Etude et de Documentation sur l'Afrique et l'Outre-Mer; formerly Administrator in Senegal, Dahomey, Cambodia and Togo. Author of *Histoire du Togo* (1962); *Histoire des peuples de l'Afrique noire*; *Histoire du Dahomey* (1962); *Les Bassari du nord Togo* (1962); *Histoire du Congo-Léopoldville* (1963); *Togo, nation pilote* (1963); *Histoire de l'Afrique* (1964); *Histoire de la colonisation allemande*.
(Recent History of Central African Republic, p. 229, Chad, p. 248, Congo (Brazzaville), p. 265, Gabon, p. 339.)

Crowder, Michael. Professor of History and Director, Institute of African Studies, University of Ife, Ile-Ife, Nigeria. Author of *Senegal: a Study in French Assimilation Policy* (1962); *The Story of Nigeria* (1966); *West Africa under Colonial Rule* (1968); etc.

(Recent History of Dahomey, p. 282, Guinea, p. 396, Ivory Coast, p. 537, Mali, p. 413, Mauritania, p. 551, Niger, p. 591, Senegal, p. 709, Upper Volta p. 972.)

Curtin, Timothy. Director, Maxwell Stamp Africa Ltd., Kenya; formerly Economic Adviser with the East African Community at Arusha in Tanzania, Lecturer in Economics at the universities of York and Rhodesia. Co-author of *Economic Sanctions and Rhodesia* (1967). Author of articles in *African Affairs*, the *Journal of Commonwealth Political Studies*, etc.

(Africa and the European Economic Community, p. 61, Economy of Rhodesia, p. 657.)

Dalby, David. Reader in West African Languages, School of Oriental and African Studies, University of London. Editor of *African Language Review*.

(Two maps on African Languages, pp. 26 and 27.)

Davidson, Basil. Writer and Historian; formerly on staff of *The Economist, The Times, New Statesman, Daily Mirror*. Has travelled widely in Africa since 1951, and has made a special study of the Portuguese territories. His books on Africa have been published in many languages and include *Report on Southern Africa* (1952); *The African Awakening* (1955); *Old Africa Rediscovered* (1959); *Black Mother* (1961); *The African Past* (1964); *Which Way Africa?* (1964); *A History of West Africa, 1000–1800* (1965); *Africa: History of a Continent* (1966); *East and Central Africa to the Late Nineteenth Century* (1967); *Africa in History: Themes and Outlines* (1968); *The Liberation of Guiné* (1969); *The Africans: an Entry to Cultural History* (1970); *In the Eye of the Storm* (1972).

(Africa in Historical Perspective, p. 3; Recent History of Portugal's African Territories, p. 150.)

Davies, D. Hywel. Formerly Professor of Geography, University of Zambia; formerly Senior Lecturer, University of Cape Town. Author of *The Central Business District of Cape Town: a Study in Urban Geography* (1965); and articles in *South African Geographical Journal, Economic Geography*, etc. Editor of *Zambia in Maps* (1970).

(Physical and Social Geography of Zambia, p. 1022.)

Dommen, E. C. Member of the Commonwealth Secretariat Technical Assistance Group; formerly Head of the Mauritius Economic Planning Unit, Professor of Economics, University of Mauritius.

(Physical and Social Geography of Mauritius, p. 565, Economy of Mauritius, p. 567.)

Ewing, A. F. Permanent Staff Member, UN Secretariat; at present UNDP Resident Representative and Co-ordinator of External Aid, Prek Thnot (power and irrigation) project, Khmer Republic; formerly on the Secretariat, UN Economic Commission for Europe (Director, Steel, Engineering and Housing Division), Secretariat, UN Economic Commission for Africa (successively—1961–68—Director, Industry, Transport and Natural Resources Division, Special Adviser to Executive Secretary and Director of ECA Sub-regional Office for Central Africa). Author of

Industry in Africa (1968) (French edition 1970), *Planning and Policies in the Textile Finishing Industry* (1972); and articles and contributions to the *Journal of Modern African Studies, Jeune Afrique*, various symposia, etc.

(Problems of Industrialization, p. 41.)

First, Ruth. Author and Journalist; trained as sociologist in South Africa and later worked there as editor and journalist on publications associated with the African opposition movement until leaving for Britain in 1964. Author of *South West Africa* (1963); *117 Days* (1965); *The Barrel of a Gun: Political Power in Africa and the Coup d'Etat* (1970). Editor of *No Easy Walk to Freedom* by Nelson Mandela (1965). Co-author of *The South African Connection* (1972).

(Political and Social Problems of Development, p. 17, Recent History of South West Africa, p. 834, Economy of South West Africa, p. 836.)

Foster, Philip. Professor, Department of Education and Sociology, and Assistant Director of Comparative Education Center, University of Chicago. Formerly teacher in Uganda. Author of *Education and Social Change in Ghana* (1965); *The Fortunate Few: A Study of Secondary Schools and Students in Ivory Coast* (1966) (with Remi Clignet).

(Problems of Educational Development, p. 72.)

Fyfe, Christopher. Reader in African History, Centre of African Studies, University of Edinburgh; formerly Government Archivist, Sierra Leone. Author of *A History of Sierra Leone* (1962), *A Short History of Sierra Leone* (1962), *Sierra Leone Inheritance* (1964), *Africanus Horton* (1972). Editor of *Christianity, Islam and the Negro Race* by E. W. Blyden (1968).

(Recent History of Sierra Leone, p. 728.)

Giles, B. D. Senior Lecturer in Economics, University of Bristol; formerly Economic Adviser to the Government of Lesotho, Consultant on Customs to the Government of Lesotho, Temporary Director of Planning, Swaziland. Author of "Principles of Economic Development", in *Symposium Intercoloniale* (1952); "Agriculture and the Price Mechanism", in *Oxford Studies in the Price Mechanism* (1951).

(Economy of Lesotho, p. 465, Economy of Swaziland, p. 887.)

Gourou, Pierre. Professor of Geography, Université Libre de Bruxelles and Collège de France, Paris; did research in Indo-China until 1935, and in tropical Africa in 1945, 1949, 1955, 1958 and 1959. Author of *La densité de la population au Congo belge* (1951); *La densité de la population au Ruanda-Urundi* (1953); *L'Afrique* (1970).

(Physical and Social Geography of Rwanda, p. 690, Zaire, p. 989.)

Green, Reginald Herbold. Honorary Professor of Economics at the University of Dar es Salaam and Economic Adviser to the Tanzania Treasury; has worked mainly in west Africa 1960–65 and in east Africa 1965–70. Author of *Unity or Poverty? The Economics of Pan-Africanism* (with A. Seidman, 1968) and "Political Independence and the National Economy" in *African Perspectives* (1970).

(Economy of Cameroon, p. 207.)

Halpern, Jack. Author and Journalist; formerly Editor and Information Officer, South African Institute of Race Relations, Editor, *Central African Examiner*, Salisbury, Central African Correspondent *The Observer*, African Correspondent *New Statesman* (as James Fairbairn). Author of *South Africa's Hostages: Basutoland, Bechuanaland and Swaziland* (1965).

(Recent History of Botswana, p. 176, Economy of Botswana, p. 180, Recent History of Lesotho, p. 461, Recent History of Swaziland, p. 883.)

Harrison Church, R. J. Professor of Geography, London School of Economics; has been interested in west Africa for nearly forty years, and has visited all its countries on many occasions; has lectured on Africa in five continents. Author of *West Africa* (1957—now in its sixth edition); and other works in collaboration.

(Physical and Social Geography of Dahomey, p. 282, The Gambia, p. 353, Guinea, p. 395, Ivory Coast, p.413, Mali, p. 537, Niger, p. 591, Senegal, p. 709, Togo, p. 928, Upper Volta, p. 972.)

Hilling, David. Lecturer in Geography, Bedford College, University of London; formerly Lecturer, University of Ghana; travelled widely in west and equatorial Africa and developed particular interest in port development and economic growth. Author of "Politics and Transportation—the problems of West Africa's landlocked states", in Fisher, C. A. (Ed.): *Essays in Political Geography* (1968); and articles in *Geography, Geographical Journal, Geographical Magazine*, etc. Co-editor of *Seaports and Development in Tropical Africa* (1970).

(Physical and Social Geography of Central African Republic, p. 229, Chad, p. 247, Congo (Brazzaville), p. 264, Gabon, p. 339, Mauritania, p. 551.)

Hopkins, A. G. Lecturer in Economic History, Centre of West African Studies, University of Birmingham. Author of articles in *Economic History Review, Past and Present, African Historical Studies, Journal of the Historical Society of Nigeria, Tarikh*, etc.

(Recent History of The Gambia, p. 353.)

Jolly, Richard. Director of Institute of Development Studies, University of Sussex; has twice worked for the Government of Zambia, first as Adviser on Manpower, then as senior economist in Development Division, Ministry of Development and Finance; has taught or researched in development problems in Universities of Cambridge, Sussex, Yale University and Makerere College. Author of *Planning Education for African Development* (1969); Editor of *Education in Africa: Research and Action* (1969) and Co-Chief of ILO mission to Kenya report *Employment incomes and Equality* (1972).

(Economy of Zambia, p. 1026.)

Karsten, Detlev. Universitätsdozent, University of Stuttgart; formerly Associate Professor of Economics, Haile Sellassie I University, Addis Ababa. Author of *Wirtschaftsordnung und Erfinderrecht* (1964), *The Economics of Handicrafts in Traditional Societies* (1972). Co-author of *Industrial Development of Ethiopia*, Report for the UN (1965).

(Economy of Ethiopia, p. 313.)

Katzen, L. Senior Lecturer in Economics, University of Leicester; formerly Senior Lecturer in Economics, University of Cape Town. Author of *Gold and the South African Economy* (1964); and articles in *South African Journal of Economics, Optima, International Migration*, etc.

(Economy of South Africa, p. 773.)

Kay, George. Professor of Geography, University College of Rhodesia. Author of *Changing Patterns of Settlement and Land Use in the Eastern Province of Northern Rhodesia* (1965); *A Social Geography of Zambia* (1967).

(Physical and Social Geography of Rhodesia, p. 651.)

Kyesimira, Y. Reader in Economics, Makerere University, Kampala, and Chairman, National Grindlays Bank, Uganda.

(Economy of Uganda, p. 949.)

Lacroix, J. L. Professor, Institut de Recherches Economiques et Sociales, Université Lovanium, Kinshasa. Author of *Industrialisation au Congo: la transformation des structures économiques* (1966); *Les pôles de développement industriel dans le Congo* (1967).

(Economy of Zaire, p. 996.)

Lamb, Douglas. Senior Lecturer and Vice-Principal, Institute of Public Administration, University of Malawi.

(Economy of Malawi, p. 516.)

Langlands, B. W. Professor of Geography, Makerere University College, Kampala.

(Physical and Social Geography of Uganda, p. 945.)

Last, G. C. Adviser, Imperial Ethiopian Ministry of Education and Fine Arts; has spent 15 years in Ethiopia as teacher and adviser to the Ministry. Author of a number of school texts on geography. Part-author and editor of *Unesco Source Book for Teaching the Geography of Africa*.

(Physical and Social Geography of Ethiopia, p. 305.)

Lemarchand, René. Professor of Political Science at the University of Florida; formerly Director of the African Studies Center at the same university. Author of *Political Awakening in the Congo: The Politics of Fragmentation* (1964), *Rwanda and Burundi* (1970).

(Recent History of Burundi, p. 192, Rwanda, p. 690.)

Le Vine, Victor T. Professor and Head of Department of Political Science, University of Ghana (1969–71) and Professor of Political Science, Washington University (St. Louis, U.S.A.); has also conducted research in French-speaking Africa. Author of *The Cameroons from Mandate to Independence* (1964), *Political Leadership in Africa* (1968), *The Cameroon Federal Republic* (1971); and articles for various books and periodicals.

(Recent History of Cameroon, p. 204.)

Lewis, I. M. Professor of Anthropology, London School of Economics. Author of *A Pastoral Democracy* (1961); *The Modern History of Somaliland* (1965). Editor of *Islam in Tropical Africa* (1966); *History and Social Anthropology* (1968).

(French Territory of the Afar and Issa, p. 336, Physical and Social Geography of Somalia, p. 744, Recent History of Somalia, p. 744, Economy of Somalia, p. 747.)

Livingstone, Ian. Reader in Economics, University of Newcastle upon Tyne; formerly Research Professor, Economic Research Bureau, University of Dar es Salaam, Lecturer in Economics at Sheffield University, Lecturer and Reader at Makerere College, Kampala, Director of the Economic Research Bureau at the University College, Dar es Salaam. Author of *Economics for East Africa* (1968); *West African Economics* (with H. W. Ord) (1969) and *Economics and Development* (with A. Goodall) (1970) and journal articles on economic theory and economic development, including several on agricultural marketing in East Africa. Editor of *Foreign Aid and Rural Development in Tanzania* (1970), *The Teaching of Economics in African Universities* (1970) and *Economic Policy for Development*, Penguin Modern Readings in Economics (1971).

(Agriculture in African Economic Development, p. 30.)

Lonsdale, John. Lecturer and Director of Studies in History, Trinity College, Cambridge; formerly carried out research in Kenya, Lecturer, University College, Dar es Salaam. Author of *A Political History of Western Kenya, 1883–1958* (in press) and articles in *Journal of African History*, *African Affairs* and *Race*.

(Recent History of Kenya, p. 432, Tanzania, p. 898, Uganda, p. 946.)

Loxley, John. Senior Lecturer in Economics, University of Dar es Salaam; formerly Lecturer, Makerere University College, Kampala, Uganda; Research Manager, National Bank of Commerce, Tanzania. Author of articles on monetary affairs and public finance in eastern Africa.

(Economy of Tanzania, p. 902.)

Luling, Virginia. Social Anthropologist; has carried out research in the Somali Republic. Author of *A South Somali Community* (1973).

(Revisions to French Territory of the Afar and Issa, p. 336, Recent History of Somalia, p. 744, Economy of Somalia, p. 747.)

Mabogunje, Akin L. Professor of Geography, University of Ibadan. Author of *Yoruba Towns* (1962); *The City of Ibadan* (1967); *Urbanization in Nigeria* (1968); *Regional Mobility and Resource Development in West Africa* (1972).

(Physical and Social Geography of Nigeria, p. 605.)

McCracken, John. Lecturer in History, University of Stirling; formerly Lecturer in History, University College, Dar es Salaam.

(Recent History of Malawi, p. 513.)

Mitchell, Peter K. Lecturer, Centre of West African Studies, University of Birmingham.

(Physical and Social Geography of Sierra Leone, p. 727.)

Morgan, William Thomas Wilson. Lecturer, Department of Geography, University of Durham; formerly Lecturer in Geography, Royal Technical College of East Africa, Professor of Geography, University College, Nairobi; member of Royal Geographical

Society South Turkana Expedition 1968–70. Author of *Nairobi: City and Region* (1967); *Population of Kenya: distribution and density* (1966) (with N. M. Schaffer); *East Africa* (in press). Editor of *East Africa: its Peoples and Resources* (1970).

(Physical and Social Geography of Kenya, p. 431.)

O'Brien, Donal Cruise. Department of Economic and Political Studies, School of Oriental and African Studies, University of London; has done research in Senegal. Author of *Mourides of Senegal* (1971) and articles on French West Africa in various journals.

(Recent History of Dahomey, p. 282, Guinea, p. 396, Ivory Coast, p. 413, Mali, p. 537, Mauritania, p. 551, Niger, p. 591, Senegal, p. 709, Upper Volta, p. 972.)

Omer-Cooper, J. D. Professor of History, University of Zambia. Author of *The Zulu Aftermath* (1966).

(History of South Africa, p.761.)

Pankhurst, R. Professor of Economic History and Director, Institute of Ethiopian Studies, Haile Sellassie I University, Addis Ababa. Author of *The Ethiopian Royal Chronicles* (1938); *An Introduction to the Economic History of Ethiopia* (1961); *Travellers in Ethiopia* (1965); *Economic History of Ethiopia* (1968). Co-editor of *Journal of Ethiopian Studies* and *Ethiopia Observer*.

(Recent History of Ethiopia, p. 308.)

Parrinder, Geoffrey. Professor of the Comparative Study of Religions, University of London. Author of *West African Religion* (1961); *Religion in a West African City* (1963); *Religion in Africa* (1969).

(Religions of Africa, p. 78.)

Pélissier, René. Author and Journalist specializing in contemporary Spanish-speaking and Portuguese-speaking Africa. Author of *Los territorios espanoles de África* (1964); *Campagnes militaires au sud-Angola 1885–1915* (1969); *Etudes hispano-guinéennes* (1969).

(Physical and Social Geography of Angola, p. 149, Economy of Angola, p. 157, Physical and Social Geography of Cape Verde Islands, p. 226, Economy of Cape Verde Islands, p. 227, Physical and Social Geography of Equatorial Guinea, p. 298, Recent History of Equatorial Guinea, p. 299, Economy of Equatorial Guinea, p. 300, Physical and Social Geography of Guinea (Bissau), p. 410, Economy of Guinea (Bissau), p. 411, Physical and Social Geography of Mozambique, p. 578, Economy of Mozambique, p. 579, Physical and Social Geography of São Tomé and Príncipe, p. 705, Economy of São Tomé and Príncipe, p. 706, Physical and Social Geography of Spanish Sahara, p. 845, Recent History of Spanish Sahara, p. 845, Economy of Spanish Sahara, p. 846.)

Rake, Alan. Editor of *African Development* magazine; formerly editor of East and West African editions of *Drum*; has lived in Kenya, Nigeria, Ghana and South Africa for several years; broadcasts regularly on Africa and specializes in the economics of Africa. Author of *Tom Mboya: Young Man of New Africa* (1963). Editor of *Africa 1969–70* and *1970–71*. Contributor to *The Times* and *Financial Times* African surveys.

(Revisions to Economy of Zaire, p. 996.)

Rimmer, Douglas. Senior Lecturer, Centre of West African Studies, University of Birmingham; formerly Lecturer, University of Ghana. Author of articles in various journals; at present working on a book on the economics of social change with reference to west Africa in the 1950s and 1960s.

(Economy of The Gambia, p. 355, Ghana, p. 371, Sierra Leone, p. 730.)

Roberts, Andrew. Lecturer in African History, School of Oriental and African Studies, University of London; formerly Research Fellow in History, University of Zambia; has also carried out research in Uganda. Author of *A History of the Bemba* (*N.E. Zambia*). Editor of *Tanzania before 1900* (1968). Has contributed numerous articles to books and journals.

(Recent History of Zambia, p. 1023.)

Robson, Peter. Professor of Economics, University of St. Andrews; has worked for several years in Africa both as economist in government service and as academic economist, and has travelled widely throughout the continent. Author of *Economic Integration in Africa* (1968). Co-editor of *The Economies of Africa* (1969).

(Economy of Central African Republic, p. 233, Chad, p. 249, Congo (Brazzaville), p. 267, Gabon, p. 341, Kenya, p. 435.)

Schulze, Willi. Professor of Geography, University of Giessen, German Federal Republic; formerly a lecturer in Chile and Colombia, and at the University of Liberia. Author of about 20 papers on west Africa, especially Liberia; and of a book on the geography of Liberia.

(Physical and Social Geography of Liberia, p. 475, Recent History of Liberia, p. 476, Economy of Liberia, p. 478.)

Simmons, Adele. Dean of Student Affairs and Lecturer, Department of History, Princeton University, Princeton, New Jersey; formerly Assistant Dean, Jackson College for Women, Tufts University, Massachusetts.

(Recent History of Mauritius, p. 565.)

Suliman, Ali Ahmed. Acting Head, Department of Economics, University of Khartoum. Member, editorial board of *Eastern Africa Economic Review*. Author of articles in Sudanese, African and UN journals. Co-author of "The Economy of Sudan", in Robson, P., and Lury, D. A. (Eds.); *The Economies of Africa* (1969).

(Economy of Sudan, p. 857.)

Thompson, Virginia. Lecturer in Political Science, University of California, Berkeley, and Research Associate for The Hoover Institution, Stanford University. Author of *West Africa's Council of the Entente* (1972). Co-author of *French West Africa* (1958); *The Emerging States of French Equatorial Africa* (1960); *The Malagasy Republic: Madagascar Today* (1965); *Djibouti and the Horn of Africa* (1968); *The French Pacific Islands* (1971).

(Physical and Social Geography of Madagascar, p. 493, Recent History of Madagascar, p. 494, Economy of Madagascar, p. 497.)

Van Arkadie, Brian. Fellow of the Institute of Development Studies at the University of Sussex; formerly Economic Adviser, Ministry of Economic Affairs and Development, Tanzania; Chief Planning Economist, Central Planning Bureau, Uganda; Economic Adviser, U.K. Ministry of Overseas Development. Author (with C. Frank) *Economic Accounting and Development Planning* (1965, 1969).

(Financing African Development, p. 48.)

White, F. Reader, Commonwealth Forestry Institute, University of Oxford. Editor of *AETFAT/UNESCO Vegetation Map of Africa*.

(Vegetation Map of Africa, p. 28.)

Whiteman, Kaye. Deputy Editor, *West Africa* magazine. Contributor to several papers and magazines on African affairs, and to *Nigerian Politics and Military Rule: Prelude to Civil War*.

(Revisions to Recent History of Dahomey, p. 282, Guinea, p. 396, Ivory Coast, p. 413, Mali, p. 537, Mauritania, p. 551, Niger, p. 591, Senegal, p. 709, Upper Volta, p. 972, Zaire, p. 990.)

Abbreviations

Acad.	.. ..	Academician, Academy
accred.	.. ..	accredited
ADB	.. ..	Asian Development Bank
adm., admin.	..	administration
A.E.F.	.. ..	Afrique équatoriale française
AfDB	.. ..	African Development Bank
A.G.	.. ..	Aktien-Gesellschaft
a.i.	.. ..	ad interim
Amb.	.. ..	Ambassador
A.O.F.	.. ..	Afrique orientale française
approx.	.. ..	approximately
apptd.	.. ..	appointed
Ass.	.. ..	Assembly
Asscn.	.. ..	Association
Assoc.	.. ..	Associate
asst.	.. ..	assistant
A.T.E.C.	..	Agence Transéquatoriale des Communications
Aug.	.. ..	August
auth.	.. ..	authorized
Av.	.. ..	Avenue
Avda.	.. ..	Avenida (Avenue)
b.	.. ..	born
Bd., Blvd., Bld.		Boulevard
B.E.A.	.. ..	British European Airways
Benelux	..	Belgium-Netherlands-Luxembourg Union
Biol.	.. ..	Biology, Biological
BIS	.. ..	Bank for International Settlements
Bldg.	.. ..	Building
B.O.A.C.	..	British Overseas Airways Corporation
br.(s)	.. ..	branch(es)
Brig.	.. ..	Brigadier
C., cen.	..	central
c, ca.	.. ..	circa
cap.	.. ..	capital
Cape	.. ..	Cape Province
Capt.	.. ..	Captain
C.A.R.	.. ..	Central African Republic
CCCE	.. ..	Caisse Centrale de Coopération Economique
CEAO	.. ..	Communauté Economique de l'Afrique de l'Ouest
CEUCA	..	Customs and Economic Union of Central Africa (UDEAC)
CFA	.. ..	Communauté Financière Africaine
Chair.	.. ..	Chairman
Cie.	.. ..	Compagnie
c.i.f.	.. ..	cost, insurance and freight
C.-in-C.	..	Commander-in-Chief
circ.	.. ..	circulation
c/o	.. ..	care of
Co.	.. ..	Company, County
Col.	.. ..	Colonel
Coll.	.. ..	College, Collège
Comm.	.. ..	Commission
Commdr.	..	Commander
Commdt.	..	Commandant
Commr.	..	Commissioner
Conf.	.. ..	Conference
Confed.	..	Confederation
Cons.-Gen.	..	Consul-General

Corpn.	.. ..	Corporation
corresp.	.. ..	corresponding
C.P.	.. ..	Cape Province
CPSU	.. ..	Communist Party of the Soviet Union
CSIRO	..	Commonwealth Scientific and Industrial Research Organization
Cttee.	.. ..	Committee
cu.	.. ..	cubic
curr.	.. ..	current
cwt.	.. ..	hundredweight
Dec.	.. ..	December
Del.	.. ..	Delegate, Delegation
Dep.	.. ..	Deputy
dep.	.. ..	deposits
Dept.	.. ..	Department
Devt.	.. ..	Development
Dir.	.. ..	Director
Div.	.. ..	Division
Dott.	.. ..	Dottore
D.Phil.	..	Doctor of Philosophy
Dr., Doc.	..	Doctor
dr.(e)	.. ..	drachma(e)
D.Sc.	.. ..	Doctor of Science
d.w.t.	.. ..	dead weight tons
E.	.. ..	East, Eastern
EAC	.. ..	East African Community
ECA	.. ..	Economic Commission for Africa
Econ.	.. ..	Economic(s)
ECOSOC	..	Economic and Social Council (UN)
ECSC	.. ..	European Coal and Steel Community
Ed.	.. ..	Editor
ed.	.. ..	educated
EDF	.. ..	European Development Fund
edn.	.. ..	edition
Educ.	.. ..	Education
EEC	.. ..	European Economic Community
e.g.	.. ..	exempli gratia (for example)
Eng.	.. ..	Engineer, Engineering
Esc.	.. ..	Escuela, Escudos
est.	.. ..	established, estimate, estimated
etc.	.. ..	etcetera
excl.	.. ..	excluding
Exec.	.. ..	Executive
f.	.. ..	founded
FAC	.. ..	Fonds d'Aide et Coopération
FAO	.. ..	Food and Agriculture Organization
Feb.	.. ..	February
Fed.	.. ..	Federal, Federation
FG	.. ..	Guinea Franc
FIDES	..	Fonds d'Investissement et de Développemont Economique et Social
F.M.	.. ..	Frequency Modulation
FMG	.. ..	Malagasy Franc
fmr(ly)	..	former(ly)
f.o.b.	.. ..	free on board
Fr.	.. ..	Franc
ft.	.. ..	foot (feet)

GATT	.. ..	General Agreements on Tariffs and Trade
G.D.P.	.. ..	Gross Domestic Product
Gen.	.. ..	General
G.m.b.H.	.. ..	Gesellschaft mit beschränkter Haftung (Limited Liability Company)
G.N.P.	.. ..	Gross National Product
Gov.	.. ..	Governor
Govt.	.. ..	Government
g.r.t.	.. ..	gross registered tons
GWh	.. ..	Gigawatt hours
ha.	.. ..	hectare
h.c.	.. ..	honoris causa
H.E.	.. ..	His Eminence, His Excellency
hl.	.. ..	hectolitre
H.M.	.. ..	His (or Her) Majesty
Hon.	.. ..	Honorary (or honourable)
HQ	.. ..	Headquarters
H.R.H.	.. ..	His (or Her) Royal Highness
H.S.H.	.. ..	His Serene Highness
IBRD	.. ..	International Bank for Reconstruction and Development (World Bank)
I.D.	.. ..	Independence Decoration
IDA	.. ..	International Development Association
IDEP	.. ..	African Institute for Economic Development and Planning
IFC	.. ..	International Finance Corporation
ILO	.. ..	International Labour Organisation
IMF	.. ..	International Monetary Fund; International Metalworkers' Federation
in. (ins.)	.. ..	inch (inches)
Inc., Incorp., Incd.		Incorporated
incl.	.. ..	including
Ing.	.. ..	Ingenieur
Inst.	.. ..	Institute
Int.	.. ..	International
Is.	.. ..	Islands
ISIC	.. ..	International Standard Industrial Classification
ISVS	.. ..	International Secretariat for Volunteer Service
Jan.	.. ..	January
Jt.	.. ..	Joint
K	.. ..	Kwacha (Malawi and Zambia currency)
kg.	.. ..	kilogramme
kHz	.. ..	kilohertz
km.	.. ..	kilometre
kWh.	.. ..	kilowatt hours
kW.	.. ..	kilowatt(s)
lb.	.. ..	pounds
Le.	.. ..	Leone (Sierra Leone currency)
Legis.	.. ..	Legislative
Lt., Lieut.	.. ..	Lieutenant
Ltd.	.. ..	Limited
m.	.. ..	million
Maj.	.. ..	Major
Man.	.. ..	manager, managing
m.b.H.	.. ..	mit beschränkter Haftung (limited liability)
Mc/s	.. ..	megacycles per second

mem.	.. ..	member
Mfg.	.. ..	Manufacturing
mfrs.	.. ..	manufacturers
Mgr.	.. ..	Monseigneur; Monsignor
MHz	.. ..	Megahertz
Mil.	.. ..	Military
Min.	.. ..	Minister, Ministry
M.L.A.	.. ..	Member of the Legislative Assembly
M.P.	.. ..	Member of Parliament
MSS	.. ..	Manuscripts
m.t.	.. ..	metric tons
MW	.. ..	megawatt(s)
N.	.. ..	North, Northern
n.a.	.. ..	not available
Nat.	.. ..	National
no.	.. ..	number
Nov.	.. ..	November
nr.	.. ..	near
n.r.t.	.. ..	net registered tons
OAMPI	.. ..	Office Africain et Malgache de la Propriété Industrielle
OAU	.. ..	Organization of African Unity
OCAM	.. ..	Organisation Commune Africaine, Malgache et Mauricienne
Oct.	.. ..	October
OECD	.. ..	Organisation for Economic Co-operation and Development
OERS	.. ..	Organisation des Etats Riverains du Sénégal
O.F.S.	.. ..	Orange Free State
OMVS	.. ..	Organisation pour la Mise en Valeur du Fleuve Sénégal
OPEC	.. ..	Organization of the Petroleum Exporting Countries
Org.	.. ..	Organization
p.a.	.. ..	per annum
Parl.	.. ..	Parliament(ary)
Perm.	.. ..	Permanent
Phil.	.. ..	Philosophy
pl.	.. ..	place
P.O.B.	.. ..	Post Office Box
polit.	.. ..	political
Pres.	.. ..	President
Prof.	.. ..	Professor
Propr.	.. ..	Proprietor
Prov.	.. ..	Province
p.u.	.. ..	paid up
publ.	.. ..	publication
q.v.	.. ..	quod vide
R	.. ..	Rand
R.A.F.	.. ..	Royal Air Force
reg., regd.	.. ..	register, registered
Rep.	.. ..	Representative
Repub.	.. ..	Republic
reorg.	.. ..	reorganized
res.	.. ..	reserve
retd.	.. ..	retired
Rev.	.. ..	Reverend
Rs	.. ..	Rupees (Mauritius currency)
Rt.	.. ..	Right
Rt. Hon.	.. ..	Right Honourable

ABBREVIATIONS

S.	.. ..	South, Southern, San.
S.A.	.. ..	Société anonyme (Limited Company)
S.Af.	.. ..	South Africa
Sec.	.. ..	Secretary
Secr.	.. ..	Secretariat
Sen.	.. ..	Senior
Sept.	.. ..	September
SITC	.. ..	Standard International Trade Classification
Soc.	.. ..	Society
S.p.A.	.. ..	Società per Aziono (Joint Stock Company)
sq.	.. ..	square
St.	.. ..	Saint; Street
stds.	.. ..	standards (timber measurement)
subs.	.. ..	subscriptions
Supt.	.. ..	Superintendent
techn.	.. ..	technical
Treas.	.. ..	Treasurer
Tvl.	.. ..	Transvaal
UAMPT	..	Union Africaine et Malgache des Postes et Télécommunications.
U.A.R.	.. ..	United Arab Republic
UDEAC	..	Union Douanière et Economique de l'Afrique Centrale
UDEAO	.. ..	Union Douanière des Etats de l'Afrique de l'Ouest
UEAC	.. ..	Union des Etats de l'Afrique Central
U.K.	.. ..	United Kingdom

UN	.. ..	United Nations
UNCTAD	..	United Nations Conference on Trade and Development
UNDP	.. ..	United Nations Development Programme
UNESCO	..	United Nations Educational, Scientific and Cultural Organisation
UNHCR	..	United Nations High Commissioner for Refugees
UNICEF	..	United Nations Children's Fund
UNIDO	..	United Nations Industrial Development Organizations
UNITAR	..	United Nations Institute for Training and Research
Univ.	.. ..	University
UNRISD	..	United Nations Research Institute for Social Development
UNTSO	..	United Nations Truce Supervision Organization
U.S.A. (U.S.)	..	United States of America (United States)
U.S.S.R.	..	Union of Soviet Socialist Republics
VHF	.. ..	Very High Frequency
viz.	.. ..	videlicet
Vol(s).	.. ..	Volume(s)
W.	.. ..	West, Western
WHO	.. ..	World Health Organization
yr.	.. ..	year

LATE INFORMATION

Comoro Islands (*see* p. 263): A new Council of Government has been formed under the presidency of AHMED ABDALLAH.

Congo (Brazzaville) (*see* p. 276): A government reshuffle was announced on January 8th. The new Council of State contains seven new ministers.

Guinea (Bissau) (*see* p. 411) and **Cape Verde Islands** (*see* p. 228): Dr. AMÍLCAR CABRAL, leader of the PAIGC, was assassinated on January 20th in Congkry, Guinea.

PART ONE

Background to the Continent

Africa in Historical Perspective

Basil Davidson

EARLY MAN

Remotely ancestral types of mankind appeared in Africa during the Lower Pleistocene, some two or three million years ago, having evolved from *hominidae* of the late Miocene. It is possible—on present evidence even probable—that they were the earliest types of mankind to appear anywhere. Most of these types were not in the direct ancestry of true man, *homo sapiens*, but continued to evolve along their own lines in Africa and in the other continents through which they spread. They proved "unsuccessful departures", however, and gradually died out; the last of them, a type widely spread in Africa and elsewhere and known as Neanderthal Man, after a site in Europe where its fossil remains were first identified, is thought to have vanished from the scene by about 12,000 years ago.

Meanwhile there were other types standing in the direct ancestry of *homo sapiens*, notably an east African type identified as *homo habilis*. These types resulted in the evolution of *homo sapiens* in Africa and elsewhere in a period broadly around 40–50,000 years ago. Little is known about this evolution, although it seems likely that *homo sapiens* at a very remote period,

and probably during his early evolution, was already sub-divided into a number of distinctive physical types, each with its own characteristics of height, head-shape, pigmentation and so on. There is as yet no clear agreement on the classification of these types. However, it would appear probable that towards the end of the African Middle Stone Age—conventionally ending around 12,000 years before the present—there were at any rate three types completely indigenous to Africa. These were respectively the ancestors of the Bushmen and of their partly-related Khoikhoi (Hottentot) neighbours; of the Pygmies; and, most important, of the much taller and generally darker-skinned peoples whom Europeans have usually called "Negroes". As well as these there were in Africa two other types, a north African/Mediterranean type and a north-east African/west Asian type, which were similarly African but which had evolved partly through mixture with exterior peoples. The former developed the Berber language variants spoken throughout the Maghreb and the Sahara, as well as in Libya, before the much later spread of Arabic; while from the latter is thought to have derived the Cushitic family of languages, spoken today by such peoples as the Somali.

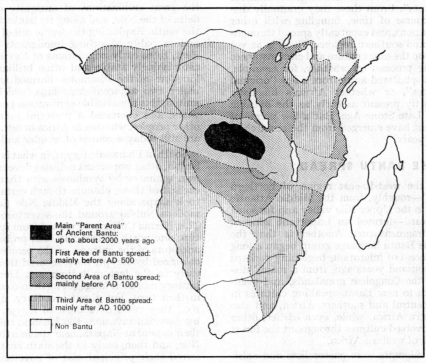

Main "Parent Area" of Ancient Bantu: up to about 2000 years ago

First Area of Bantu spread: mainly before AD 500

Second Area of Bantu spread; mainly before AD 1000

Third Area of Bantu spread: mainly after AD 1000

Non Bantu

Supposed stages in the spread of Bantu-speaking peoples.

3

Subsequent mixture and further evolution have gone far to confuse and complicate this neat picture, though it may still have some schematic value. Peoples originally of the Berber language group remain dominant in north Africa and the Sahara, but most of them have long since adopted Arabic as their native tongue and Islam as their culture. A few Cushitic-speaking peoples have continued to develop in north-eastern Africa, though with much mingling with non-Cushitic neighbours. Pygmy groups survive in the Congo forests, few in numbers and likewise influenced culturally by their non-Pygmy neighbours; while similarly sparse Bushman groups and somewhat more numerous Khoikhoi groups are still to be found in the regions of the far south-west. South of the Sahara, however, the main history of human development has long been concerned with the growth and evolution of the "Negroes"—a term that is quite unsatisfactory, given the wide differences among these peoples in culture as well as in appearance, yet one that is still in common use outside the continent.

It is the "Negroes", evolving a thousand languages and cultural variants over the past several thousand years, who have been responsible for the peopling of Africa with most of its modern inhabitants. Almost certainly they were dominant among the Late Stone Age pastoralists of the Saharan regions before the area began to become desiccated around 2000 B.C.; thus they formed or helped to form the early populations of Pharaonic Egypt and other peripheral areas along the Nile. South of the Sahara they appear to have flourished during the Late Stone Age at a number of "growing points". From these they gradually dispersed in the course of time, mingling with other Stone Age populations, and eventually spread throughout the central and southern regions. There is as yet little agreement on the exact nature and circumstances of this spreading process: on whether, for example, many languages splintered away from a few "original mother languages", or whether Africa's linguistic richness was partly present as early as the opening centuries of the Late Stone Age. But a few points of general agreement have emerged from the research of the last twenty years.

THE BANTU SPREAD

One is that the west-to-east region of northern "Middle Africa"—roughly, from the Middle Atlantic Coast (Senegal) to the Upper Nile valley and for some distance southward—formed an important zone of early cultural fragmentation. Another is that the "Negroes" of the Bantu language group began a long and complex process of migration, beginning perhaps around three thousand years ago, from a main "dispersal area" in the Congolese grasslands, and eventually gave birth to new Bantu-speaking cultures in many lands of central and southern Africa, and also in parts of eastern Africa, while, even earlier, other "Negroes" had evolved cultures throughout the forest and coastal zone of western Africa.

These Bantu migrants were pastoralists and cultivators, and understood how to obtain iron and smelt and use it for hoe heads and weapons. They had moved into the southern grasslands (Zambia, Rhodesia and neighbouring areas) by the beginning of the Christian era, and, forming small village communities that were increasingly stable in settlement, they repeatedly produced a surplus population which pushed on southward in search of new land for grazing and cultivation. Their first pioneering groups crossed the Limpopo into the present territory of South Africa during the last centuries of the first millenium A.D. By the fourteenth century A.D. they had evolved throughout the eastern half of south Africa large and stable communities, speaking languages of the Southern Bantu group. These southernmost Bantu communities were still slowly expanding in numbers, sometimes at the cost of Bushman and Khoikhoi neighbours, when, during the eighteenth century, the first Dutch settlers began encroaching on their lands, in what afterwards became the eastern part of Cape Province. By that time their ancestors had been in south Africa for the best part of a thousand years.

EARLY CIVILIZATIONS

For most of Africa the effective time-span of history, in so far as it can now be understood, reaches back over about two millenia, and is divided from prehistory—along a line that is always faint and sometimes arbitrary—by the development of iron-working and cultivation, as early populations dispersed and spread through the plains, hills and forests south of the Sahara. There had, of course, been some earlier exceptions. During the fourth millenium B.C. one of the great civilizations of antiquity emerged in the delta of the Nile, and along its banks for some way to the south. Exploiting the fertile soil of the Nile banks, and probably absorbing immigrants from the Near East, these early populations of Egypt developed the astonishingly stable and often brilliantly innovating kingdom of the Pharaohs. Formed around 3500 B.C. under two adjacent kingships, which then became united, this remarkable civilization persisted for 3,000 years, and exercised a powerful influence on many other peoples, whether in Africa or not. Its monuments are still today a source of wonder and admiration.

South of Pharaonic Egypt, in what is now the eastern Sudan, other important cultures developed out of their own genius or by symbiosis with that of Egypt. The earliest of these, obscure though certainly influential, took shape along the Middle Nile (in and south of modern Nubia) around the seventeenth century B.C. This Kerma Culture, so named from its archaeological type-site north of Dongola, was probably among the ancestors of the cultures of the people of Kush. Long colonized by Egypt, these secured their independence early in the last millenium B.C. During the eighth century B.C. their kings set forth to conquer northward in their turn. For about a century, up to about 660 B.C., they ruled over most of Egypt. Defeated then by Assyrian invasion, the Kushite rulers returned to their capital at Napata, near the fourth cataract of the Nile, and then, early in the sixth century B.C., transferred their principal seat of government southward to Meroë, lying about a hundred miles north of modern Khartoum.

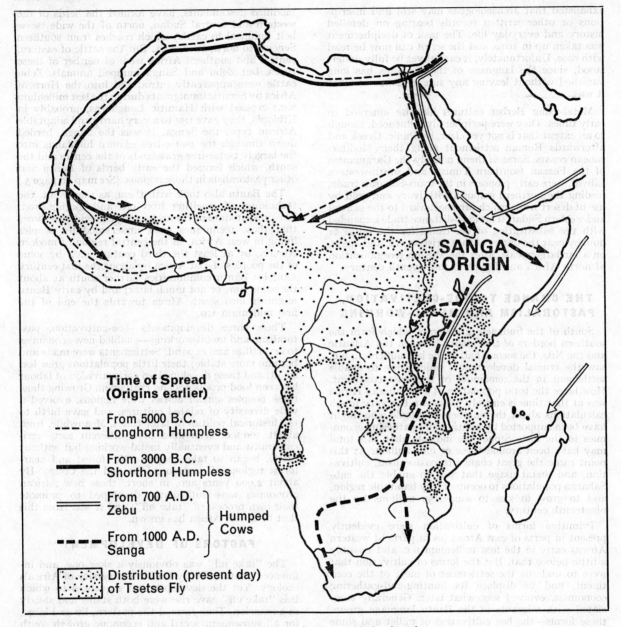

SANGA
ORIGIN

**Time of Spread
(Origins earlier)**

From 5000 B.C.
Longhorn Humpless

━━━
From 3000 B.C.
Shorthorn Humpless

═══
From 700 A.D.
Zebu

╌╌╌
From 1000 A.D.
Sanga

} Humped
Cows

Distribution (present day)
of Tsetse Fly

Early movements of different kinds of cattle.

Here at Meroë, and at neighbouring stone-built towns in what is now the Butana Desert, as well as in towns established in lower Nubia (near the modern U.A.R.-Sudan frontier), the Kushites built another civilization of great originality and some splendour. Though long retaining a Pharaonic overlay, Kushite culture took its own road. From the fourth century B.C. it continuously developed its own architecture in masonry, the cult of its own gods, its own skilled

handicrafts (notably in painted pottery) and its own interests in long-distance trade. Not the least of its achievements was the invention of its own alphabet, inspired possibly by demotic Egyptian and the Greek script of Ptolemaic Egypt, yet entirely original in form. Consisting of twenty-three signs, including vowels and a sign for word division, this script was widely used in Kush for grave and other inscriptions through at least five centuries; and the hope is not yet exhausted that archaeologists may still find inscriptions or other written records bearing on detailed history and everyday life. The task of decipherment was taken up in 1910, and the script can now be read with ease. Unfortunately, it cannot yet be fully understood, since the language of the Kushites has long vanished without leaving any sure evidence of what it was.

Metal-using Berber cultures likewise emerged in early times. They were peripherally influenced, though to an extent that is not yet clear, by Punic, Greek and afterwards Roman settlement along their Mediterranean coasts. Some of them, notably the Garamantes of the Fezzan (southern Tunisia and south-western Libya), were early pioneers in the trans-Saharan trade, feeding the northern emporia with ivory and gold by use of desert trails which ran southward to the central and western Sudan. This long-distance trade expanded with the substitution of the camel for the horse or donkey near the outset of the Christian era, and again, on a far larger scale, after the Muslim reorganization of north Africa and Egypt in the seventh century.

THE CHANGE TO HOE-CULTIVATION, PASTORALISM AND METAL-WORKING

South of the Sudanese grasslands, which form the southern borders of the Sahara between the Atlantic and the Nile, the second half of the last millenium B.C. saw the crucial developments which were to enable settlement in the remainder of this vast continent. How large the total population of sub-Saharan Africa was at that time is entirely unknown, but very rough calculations about the numbers of people who might have been supported by hunting-and-gathering economies in the Late Stone Age indicate that this total may have been around three or four million. At this point came the great change to pastoralism, cultivation, and metal usage that was to enable the sub-Saharan populations to occupy every habitable region, and to grow in size to some 150 millions by the nineteenth century.

Primitive forms of cultivation were evidently present in parts of east Africa (as in parts of western Africa) early in the first millenium B.C. and possibly a little before that. But the forms of cultivation that were to underlie the settlement of most of the continent, and to displace its hunting-and-gathering economies, evolved somewhat later. Generally associated with migrants of the Bantu language group, these forms—the hoe cultivation of millet and some varieties of sorghum—appeared in eastern and central Africa some two thousand years ago, and spread gradually southward with the extension of early Bantu cultures.

These were also pastoralist cultures. Pastoralism had been present in the pre-desiccated Sahara from at least 3500 B.C., the earliest domesticated cattle there being the so-called Hamitic Longhorn (which had come into Egypt from the Near East around 5000 B.C.). These were later joined by a shorthorned type, *Brachyceros*, also of Egyptian and ultimately Near Eastern origin. These two types, or rather their

modified descendants, have formed the herds of the western and central Sudan, north of the wide tsetse belt (inimical to cattle) which reaches from southern Senegal to northern Kenya. But the cattle of eastern, central and southern Africa were of neither of these types, but Zebu and Sanga humped animals. Zebu cattle were apparently introduced into the Horn of Africa by Semitic immigrants during the last millenium B.C.; crossed with Hamitic Longhorns, probably in Ethiopia, they gave rise to a very hardy and adaptable African type, the Sanga. It was the Sanga, herded down through the tsetse-free eastern highlands into the largely tsetse-free grasslands of the centre and the south, which formed the early herds of Bantu and other pastoralists in those regions. (*See* map on page 5.)

The Bantu also took with them, as they went, the techniques of smelting iron ore and forging iron. The present state of the archaeological evidence shows that these techniques were understood by peoples living in west Africa, in the central region of modern Nigeria, by at least the third century B.C.; by some of the peoples of east Africa by about the first century A.D.; by Bantu communities farther south at about the same time or not much later; and by early Bantu migrants into south Africa towards the end of the first millenium A.D.

These three developments—hoe-cultivation, pastoralism, and metal-working—enabled new economies to crystallize and expand. Settlements were made and became more stable; their little populations grew less small; and these developed an early division of labour between food producers and craftsmen. Growing thus, these peoples spread across wide regions, evolved a wide diversity of related cultures, and gave birth to the historical polities of later times. Meanwhile, from about 500 B.C. economies of a different sort, agriculturalist and eventually metal-working but without cattle, began to take shape in the forest and near-forest regions of western Africa and the Congo. By about 2,000 years ago, in short, these new African economies were sufficiently developed to promote their own process of "take off"; and it was from this that historical Africa has grown.

FACTORS OF DEVELOPMENT

The "take off" was obviously a slow one, and influenced continually by the wide diversity of Africa's ecology. Yet the developmental sequences to which this "take off" gave rise were both stable and steady in expansion. They formed the pattern, by and large, for all subsequent social and economic growth south of the Sahara until the nineteenth century. Capable of great flexibility of adaptation, they evoked a bewildering variety of socio-structural responses, and nourished the evolution of a correspondingly wide variety of cultures. It is, of course, the nature of these developmental sequences, and their economies, that explain the consistent success of Africans in populating and domesticating their often harshly hostile continent, as well as the limitations of their technology and productive systems.

On the one hand, Africans were able to solve every major problem with which they were faced, so that their populations could and did expand in measure with the slow but steady expansion of their productive capacity. With some local exceptions, it was not until the twentieth century that Africa was to be faced with any great crisis of "over-population"—of a critically widening gap, that is, between the upward curve of population growth and the now much flatter upward curve of indigenous production of food and other necessities.

On the other hand, this very success proved an obstacle to inventive change. If the peoples living north of the Sahara were repeatedly influenced by the Mediterranean and west Asian world about them, and moved as repeatedly into new processes of technology and corresponding changes of culture, those to the south of the Sahara (again with some peripheral exceptions) had little or no incentive to invent new methods of production, transport or exchange. They developed their own systems, from the "take off" of about 2,000 years ago, with a continuous and sometimes remarkable success, but seldom or never felt any need to depart from those systems. This served them well enough until the nineteenth century. Then, suddenly, they found themselves exposed to a world which had developed quite different systems and, with these, a far greater technological power.

Several perceptibly crucial factors of growth may be traced from late in the first millenium A.D. Itself the product of earlier technological advance—of the processes already indicated—the size of Africa's populations continued to grow, and, as it grew, to induce new political and social problems. These were solved in ways which have remained characteristic of African cultures, and their profound influence is indeed still evident even in the greatly changed circumstances of today.

Patterns of Rule

The very small hunting-and-gathering communities of Stone Age Africa could remain content with the minimal forms of self-rule by family leaders. But long-term settlement soon outgrew such simple types of authority. Extending and modifying early patterns of rule by "senior kin", African societies entered upon a history of social and political development which, while almost always tracing its roots back to the early patterns of Stone Age origin, in time produced a profusion of village governments, chiefdoms, kingships, and, here and there, large and powerful empires. Departing as they did from the same roots, these many forms of self-rule—modified again by the varying influence of ecology—differed greatly in detail and customary appearance but retained, none the less, an essential similarity of basic attitude and belief. The political development of Africa over the past fifteen centuries or so is thus a consistent demonstration of unity within diversity. It is this that may to some large extent enable one to speak of "African civilization", in the singular, with the same broad meaning as one speaks of "European civilization".

Overseas Crops

Africa was initially poor in food crops, but its capacity for supporting community life was considerably increased with the arrival of useful plants, roots and fruits from overseas. One of the most nutritious of the African bananas, *musa paradisiaca*, may have come from Indonesia during the first centuries A.D. Asian rice undoubtedly came in from India at about the same time, though an indigenous type of rice was apparently being harvested in the western Sudan as early as the second millenium B.C. But the principal gains of this kind came from America during the sixteenth century with the introduction, by way of European ships, of maize, cassava, pineapples, sweet potatoes and some other foods. Among these it is likely that cassava proved the most valuable: resistant to heat and disease, though of comparatively low food content, the cassava root had become a staple crop among a wide range of African cultivators by the end of the seventeenth century, and may have considerably enhanced the growth of population.

New Technologies

African farmers developed new techniques and insights so as to accommodate these new crops. Other technologies similarly developed. In parts of west Africa, for example, the growing, spinning and high-quality dyeing of cotton became an industry that was widely practised, possibly from about A.D. 1000. In the late fifteenth and sixteenth centuries the Portuguese and other European maritime traders found that some of these west African textiles (and especially the fast-colour dyeing of them) were superior to anything then being made in Europe. Meanwhile, a large number of peoples, whether in west Africa or other regions, had become skilled in locating mineral ores—iron, tin, copper, gold and some others; their extraction, crushing and smelting in small blast furnaces; and their forging and use for tools, weapons, ornaments and trading ingots. It is estimated that Africans had exported several thousand tons of gold by A.D. 1500 (and more in later centuries). They, or at least some of them, were capable of producing metal sculpture of a very high quality by a date which, according to the latest archaeological evidence, was as early as the ninth or tenth centuries A.D.

THE INFLUENCE OF TRADE

These technologies were stimulated by the needs of societies which were now of growing complexity and wealth, but they were also promoted by long-distance trade. Local trade—short-distance trade between neighbouring communities—no doubt goes back to the earliest times of settlement. Villages capable of supporting metalsmiths or other artisans would have developed early forms of exchange of food for tools and the like. Gradually goods would have been traded over longer distances. Here and there, too, exterior peoples arrived with trading ends in mind. The Carthaginians, and after them the Romans, undoubtedly drew their gold and ivory, and some other African products, from coastal trade or from overland trade by way of the Berbers of the Sahara. A Greek-Egyptian mariners' guide to the Red Sea and the

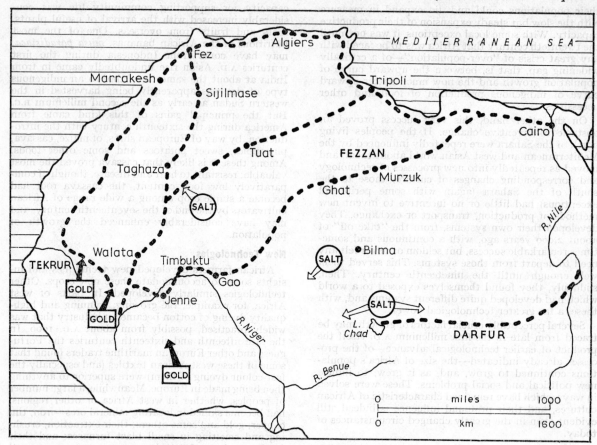

Trade and trading-routes across the Sahara in early times.

north-western Indian Ocean, written around A.D. 120, tells of a regular trade between Red Sea ports and the coasts of what are now Somalia, Kenya and Tanzania.

The Trans-Saharan Complex

The main formative development of long-distance African trade occurred after the expansion of Muslim civilization in northern Africa, and in two main regions: one in the west and the other along the Indian Ocean seaboard. The Arab leaders, having conquered Egypt and the northern Berber states during the seventh century, at once turned their attention to the trans-Saharan trade, from which Byzantium, after Rome and Carthage, had gained. Early Arab military expeditions towards the south were defeated by the desert, but traders soon succeeded where the soldiers had failed. The key to success for these traders lay in the fact that they were, for the most part, Berbers who had accepted a form of Islam—derivative from the Kharidjite heresy—which, because of its egalitarian attitudes, seems to have been especially acceptable to the men of the desert and its confines.

In the eighth century there arose in the Maghreb a series of linked Berber Muslim polities, with Tāhert and Sijilmāsa at their head, which rapidly made themselves masters of the trans-Saharan trade, and, acting through Desert Berbers (Tuareg), forged new and fruitful links with the peoples of the western and central Sudan. Their traders were welcomed by the states which had now taken shape in these grasslands. Soon the old trails were being used by many more caravans every year. In this way the peoples of the western and central Sudan, and, indirectly, other peoples farther south in the near-coastal forest lands of west Africa, were drawn into a wide network of trade with north Africa, with Muslim Spain (and thus with western Europe), with Egypt, and with the Near East. This great "western network" proved of steadily growing value for several centuries. Through it the peoples of Europe were fuelled with their needs in gold—the earliest gold currencies of late medieval Europe, beginning with the *fiorentino* or florin of the thirteenth century, were almost certainly struck in west African gold; while at the same time there developed a steady export in west African captives

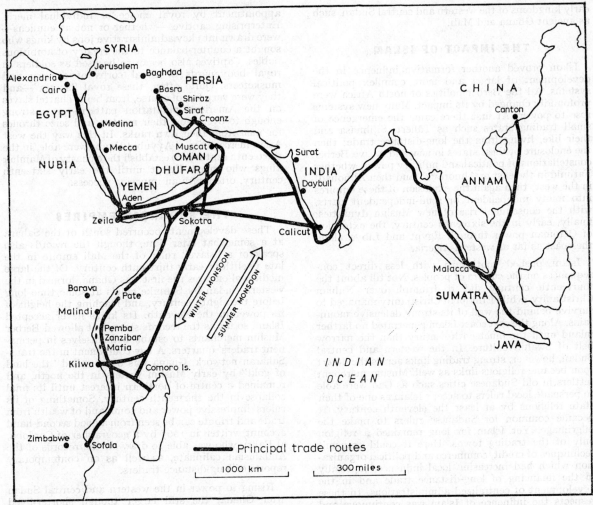

The Indian Ocean and its trade in about A.D. 1200.

for domestic use, military service, and craftsmanship. On their side, Africans of the grasslands imported manufactured metalware, horses, salt from the Sahara, other useful commodities, and also some occasional captives for domestic use.

Indian Ocean Trade

A comparable long-distance network developed in some of the eastern and south-central regions. Having established trading stations along the coasts of India, south-east Asia and southern China, Arabs from the Persian Gulf states began to enlarge a long existing but hitherto minor interest in African trade. Founded early in the ninth century, trading stations along the east coast soon grew into substantial ports. Some of these, whether on the coast itself or on nearby islands, became fine stone-built cities after A.D. 1200. Here lay the origins of Swahili culture—Bantu in its basis and ethnic composition but Muslim and Arabic in much

of its cultural overlay. Enterprising in the long-distance trade, these Swahili cities acted as intermediaries between the oversea traders of the Indian Ocean and the overland traders of the interior.

Here again, as in the Sudanese-Saharan-Mediterranean network, gold and ivory were staple African exports, while imports consisted mainly of textiles and metalware, as well as luxury goods such as Persian pottery and Chinese porcelain for rich men's houses. And once more, here as in the west, the long-distance trade proved a spur to political development, whether along the seaboard or far inland among the gold producers of the central-southern plateau. Thus the kingdoms of the Shona—since famous for the ruins of their palaces and shrines, such as those at Great Zimbabwe, Khami, Dhlo Dhlo and other sites—appear to have taken shape in partial response to the opportunities of the long-distance trade, just as did the early kingdoms of the western and central Sudan, such as ancient Ghana and Mali.

THE IMPACT OF ISLAM

Islam proved another formative influence in the development of larger and more complex political systems. All the Berber polities of north Africa were profoundly changed by its impact. Many new systems rose to power. At first there came the emergence of small trading states such as Tāhert, Sijilmāsa and their like, living from the long-distance trade; then the enclosure of these states in new and native Berber constellations of political and military power, whether Fatimid in the east or Almoravid (and then Almohad) in the west; then again the explosion of these empires into many independent or semi-independent parts, with the consequent rise of new Muslim dynasties; finally, early in the sixteenth century, the extension of Ottoman power through Egypt and Libya along the coast as far as western Algeria.

Islam pushed southward with less direct consequences on the culture of peoples. Not till about the fourteenth century did it triumph over Nubian Christianity, while Ethiopian Christianity managed to survive behind the wall of its strong defensive mountains. Along the east coast Islam penetrated no farther inland until the nineteenth century than the narrow belt of Swahili culture. In the western and central Sudan, however, strong trading links across the desert soon became religious links as well. Muslim merchant settlers in old Sudanese cities such as Gao were able to persuade local rulers to accept Islam as one of their state religions by at least the eleventh century. It became common for Sudanese rulers to make the pilgrimage. Yet Islam for long remained a religion only of the trading towns. Here it could transmit techniques of credit, commerce and political organization which had increasing local influence, especially in the financing of long-distance trade and in the development of centralized administrations. In these respects the influence of Islam was continuous and pervasive.

EARLY AFRICAN KINGDOMS

Kingdoms emerged in several African regions during the first millenium A.D. At first, so far as the slender evidence goes, they were little more than enlarged chiefdoms whose rulers or main representatives were at once senior lineage leaders and persons charged with ritual powers concerned with their people's general welfare. The ritual powers survived, as in kingdoms outside Africa, and were duly enshrined in complex ceremonials and rules designed to safeguard the king's (and hence the kingdom's) spiritual *persona*, as distinct from the king's mortal person. But ritual powers were buttressed by secular powers whose importance gradually increased under the influence of political and economic development.

As these secular powers increased, so too did the need for central bureaucracies detached from traditional lineage-groups. There came a shift from appointment to positions of authority by right of birth to appointment by royal choice or individual merit. Enterprising captives—whether or not as eunuchs—were drawn into key administrative jobs by kings who sought a counter-balance to the rivalry of ambitious nobles. Captives also began to be used as soldiers in royal bodyguards or royal corps of cavalry and musketeers. Quite often, these royal "slaves"—and they were very far, of course, from being chattel slaves on the American plantation pattern—grew strong enough to overthrow their masters and seize thrones for men from their own ranks. In this way the west Asian mercenaries of Ayyubid Egypt were able, in the thirteenth century, to establish the dynasty of Mamluk kings who ruled Egypt until the early sixteenth century, often with an imposing success.

THE SUDANESE EMPIRES

These developments occurred south of the Sahara at a somewhat later date, though the records also speak of a "slave" ruler of the Mali empire in the late twelfth or early thirteenth century. Of the large mediaeval empires the first was Ghana, formed in the western Sudan by Soninke chiefs at some time long before the eighth century, and reaching the height of its power in the eleventh. Its kings never accepted Islam, so far as the records show, but allowed Berber Muslim merchants to establish themselves in permanent traders' quarters. A key component in the trans-Saharan network, Ghana was often called "the land of gold" by early Muslim writers in the north, and remained a centre of northern interest until its final collapse in the thirteenth century. Something of its rulers' impressive power and command of wealth from trade and tribute can be seen from a good second-hand account written in 1067 by a geographer of Cordoba, al-Bakri, who was able to draw on the records of the Andalusian caliphate, as well as on contemporary reports of long-distance traders.

Rising to power in the western and central Sudan after Ghana, the still larger though shorter-lived empire of Mali likewise became dominant over the southern terminals of the trading network of the west. Its Mandinka kings appear to have accepted Islam as early as the eleventh century, and several of them made the pilgrimage. But the triumph of Islam in Mali really came with the reign of its most famous ruler, *Mansa* Kankan Musa (reg. 1312–1337), who brought most of the western Sudan, the westerly portions of the central Sudan, and much of the southern Sahara under his general control; who made a pilgrimage in 1324 that was long remembered in Cairo for the splendour of its spending in gold; and who, upon returning, introduced Muslim patterns of administration into his court and government structure.

Even so, the shift from "ascription to appointment" in the royal service came not with the growth of Mali but with that of the next large Sudanese empire, Songhay, centred on the Songhay people of the middle Niger, and, in respect of trading centres, on Gao, Timbuktu and Jenne. This strengthening of centralized government in Songhay is associated particularly with the emperor Askia Muhammad (reg. 1493–1528).

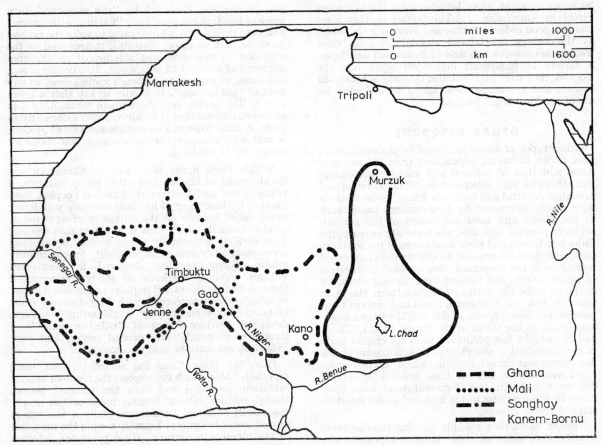

The Sudanese empires at their largest extents: Ghana (in the eleventh century), Mali (under Kankan Musa), Songhay (under Askia Muhammad) and Kanem-Bornu (*c.* 1550).

At much the same time a similar development was occurring in a fourth empire, that of Kanem-Bornu on either side of Lake Chad. By 1500 both empires had evolved administrations in which "king's men"—mainly soldiers or eunuchs of captive origin—were systematically balanced in the structure against title-holders of noble birth. These changes in turn influenced the political systems of the Hausa states, lying between them. Emerging around 1000, these Hausa states grew by trade and tribute, as well as by their handicraft industries, notably weaving and agriculture. Prominent among them were Kano, Katsina and Zaria, all of which survive today as cities of Nigeria.

THE KINGDOMS OF GUINEA

Comparable developments took place elsewhere, beyond the range of Muslim influence. The coastal region of west Africa—known to Europeans after the fifteenth century as upper and lower Guinea, the word Guinea being of Berber origin—saw the emergence of a large number of kingdoms at a point generally before about A.D. 1400. Notable among these were early kingdoms of the Yoruba (western Nigeria), of the Edo (mid-western Nigeria), of the Akan (central Ghana), and of the Wolof (Senegal). The kingdoms of the Yoruba appear to have evolved from a process of cultural symbiosis, between existing indigenous peoples and intrusive migrants from the central Sudan, at some time not long before A.D. 1000. They developed a rich cultural life, some outstanding skills in handicraft production, a characteristic but rare pattern of large urban settlements, and complex political systems. Generally disunited, except in religious loyalty and ethnic solidarity, many of these Yoruba kingdoms were later drawn together in the Oyo empire (*c.* 1650–1810).

The Edo city and empire of Benin took shape in the same general period as the Yoruba kingdoms. Acquiring strong central government around A.D. 1400, Benin repeatedly impressed visiting Europeans (first arriving there at the end of the fifteenth century) with its trading wealth, political order, and urban comfort. "As you enter it," wrote a Dutch visitor around 1600, "the town appears very great: you go into a great broad street, not paved, which seems to be seven or eight times broader than the Warmoes Street in Amsterdam. . . . The houses in this town stand in good order, one close and even with the other, as the houses in Holland stand. . . ." Like their Yoruba neighbours, the Edo of Benin had developed a variety of handicraft industries; again like the Yoruba, they were highly skilled in working brass and bronze, and in casting these alloys for sculpture by use of the "lost wax" process.

OTHER KINGDOMS

Other types of kingship, basically the same as in west Africa in having crystallized from the needs of ritual and then of political and military leadership, but otherwise very divergent in detail, were formed in eastern, central and southern Africa. Some of them were deeply influenced by long-distance trade, such as the Shona and their neighbours of the central-southern plateau, and, after the sixteenth century, the Luba and Lunda and their neighbours of the southern Congolese-Angolan grasslands. Others were concerned mainly with the command, defence and distribution of cattle pasture and farming land: among these, for example, were the states of the southern Bantu in what are now the Transvaal, Natal and eastern Cape provinces of South Africa, and in neighbouring areas— among others the states of the Swazi, Venda, Xhosa and Ngoni (the last producing the Zulu empire early in the nineteenth century). Others, again, were stratified "conquest kingdoms" in which cattle-owners ruled over cultivators on lines marked by ethnic difference, and with ties of mutual dependence compared by some writers to the lord-and-vassal relationships of feudal Europe.

Though based on a steadily growing class or caste stratification, none of these kingdoms evolved the hierarchical rigidities of Europe or, indeed, of Asia, if only because there was no private ownership of land but only private ownership of its fruits, and of cattle. With some exceptions in north Africa and Egypt, the vertical divisions of lineage membership and loyalty generally remained as important as any of the horizontal divisions introduced and promoted by divisions of labour. This, no doubt, affords another explanation for the long persistence, however modified by circumstance, of economies of merely handicraft production. The very success of these economies—of this limited technology—induced a conservatism hostile to inventive change.

"Stateless Societies"

This conservatism was the more marked among that large number of African societies which developed neither central governments with kings, nor even, sometimes, any form of politically-endowed chiefship. The systems of these "stateless societies", as they have been somewhat misleadingly labelled, were certainly not uninventive. On the contrary, many of them evolved a highly complex balance of intra-group power and interest, enshrining this balance in beliefs and rites of continuous retaining strength. They became, in other words, embraced in a conservatism drawn from the success of their patterns of community life

and production. Achieved by "the ancestors" in a more or less timeless past, their "balance with nature" and thus their social balance came to seem the highest good, so that whatever disturbed it appeared as the intrusion of evil, and was interpreted as the consequence of malevolent witchcraft. To say this is not, of course, to suggest that these societies lived in any kind of "golden age". It is only to say that a given way of life, having brought a given community into existence and enabled it to survive and sufficiently to prosper, came to seem a way of life sanctioned by God, or rather by the spirits of the ancestors who spoke for the spirits of the land.

Within these limits there was an almost endless development of kinship and other group patterns of political and social authority. Pastoral peoples, fragmented by their way of life into annually wandering units, relied heavily on the authority of age-groups, of structures in which men (and sometimes women) were divided horizontally across society by age and corresponding degrees of responsibility for community affairs. Forest peoples, clustered in permanent villages, evolved methods of village government through lineage elders and popular assemblies. Others, especially those concerned with long-distance trade or marginally influenced by neighbouring kingships, developed various forms of "titled societies"—of structures in which titles carried power, and were gained by seniority or skill in commerce.

Many of these "stateless societies", but more especially those which lay beyond the reach of outside intrusion, persisted well into the colonial period, though seldom without bearing more or less deeply the marks of colonial influence. Quite a few others moved towards forms of kingship during the pressures of the nineteenth century. These pressures, whether internal to African growth or resulting from non-African intrusion, raised a common demand for a stronger community leadership such as could afford better self-defence or more effective participation in long-distance trade. Ritual leaders now tended to become kings, or "proto-kings"—though colonial invasion was soon to halt the process of autonomous development—while weak chiefships tended to become stronger ones. The same process of power-concentration pushed a number of kingships towards autocracy.

WHITE INTRUSION

Here and there, at least along the seaboard, earlier pressures had produced something of the same effect. Notable among these was the Atlantic slave trade, beginning in the 1440s, vastly expanding after the early European settlement of the Americas, and coming to a final halt only in the 1880s. (The overland slave trade to the north, or the Asian slave trade from the east coast, began much earlier and persisted even longer, but its general impact on African life was undoubtedly far smaller than that of the Atlantic trade.) How profoundly the Atlantic trade influenced African society remains a modern controversy. There was much suffering; at least ten million Africans were landed in the Americas, not counting all those who

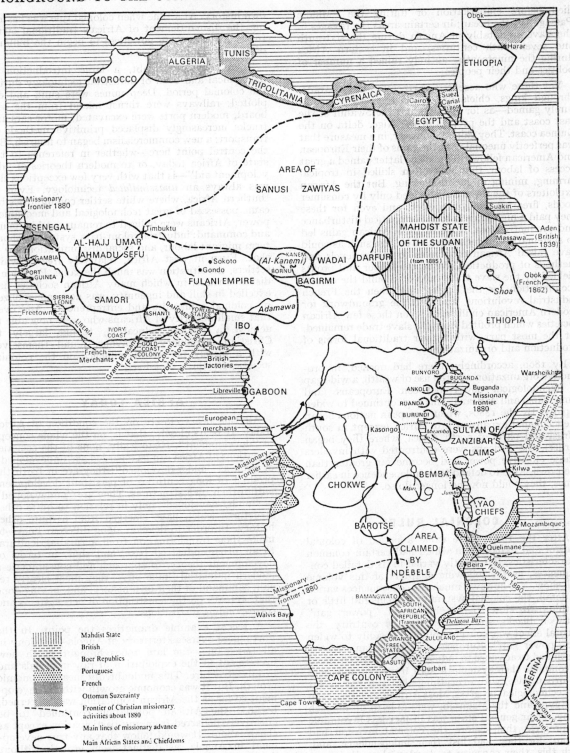

Africa on the eve of colonial partition: African states and European settlements.

died before embarkation or during the "Middle Passage" of the ocean; in certain areas the ravages of the slavers—notably in Angola during the sixteenth and seventeenth centuries, and in eastern Africa during the nineteenth—entirely ruined a number of polities and their peoples.

Yet those who accepted partnership in the trade, through kings, chiefs or "titled societies", just as surely gained—as for example did the Swahili of the east coast and the peoples of the Niger delta on the Guinea coast. They gained, however, in a measure that was perfectly unequal with the gains of their European and American fellow-traders. The latter gained a great access of labour that was often skilled in tropical farming, mining or metal-working. But the African exploiters of the slave trade gained only by consumer goods, firearms and gunpowder, and even for these they paid a high price in social or political disturbance and productive loss. None of these African gains led to systematic and technological change such as could have raised African economies to higher levels and methods of production. While the labour and profits yielded by the slave trade helped to build the capital accumulation for the English and then the French industrial revolutions, and laid the groundwork for modern American civilization, even those few African societies which profited from the slave trade remained, for the most part, within their traditional forms of production and organization.

By 1800, accordingly, there had opened, in productive organization and the use of wealth, a wide gap in technological power between Europeans (and Americans) and Africans. This gap continued to widen rapidly. By the 1880s, when European nations began their colonial expansion into Africa (except in south Africa and parts of north Africa, where they began earlier), the Africans were confronted with invaders whose effective power had become far greater than their own. Able to defend their independence in earlier times, they could now no longer do so.

COLONIAL RULE

After the 1880s there came a period of colonial control and exploitation which had certain common characteristics, but greatly varied in its detailed consequences, as the following chapters of this volume will show. Yet however much the consequences varied in detail, the colonial system or systems did little or nothing to close the technological "power gap" between blacks and whites. On the contrary, the general effect was considerably and steadily to widen the "power gap". European and American societies continued to advance to industrialism; they continued to complete their systematic shift from a rural base to an urban base, with everything that this has meant for technological progress. Most African societies, even in Egypt and the Maghreb, were able to do no such thing. Their general state was in fact less favourable to progress than before the colonial invasion had begun: for they had lost their independence, and, with this, their capacity to develop along their own lines. They had lost, in short, the command of their

own history. At a time when colonial rule was hastening the dismantlement of Africa's traditional structures, Africans were powerless to begin the building of new structures.

There was, no doubt, a large introduction of mechanical and even of industrial technology during the colonial period. Deep mines were sunk and exploited; railways were thrust inland from the seaboard; modern ports were excavated; motor cars and trucks increasingly displaced primitive methods of transport; a new commercialism began to flourish. But the central point here—whether in reference to the state of Africa today, or to modern theories of "development aid"—is that with very few exceptions this was always an *unassimilated* technology. Even in southern Africa, where white settler communities became possessed of great technological and mechanical power, Africans were obliged to remain outside its use and command: industrial colour-bars, systems of short-term migrant labour, and social discrimination saw to that. Even in west Africa, relatively free of white settlers, the situation was much the same. Even long-distance trade, in which many African societies had excelled in skill and ingenuity, was now monopolized by colonial companies and entrepreneurs. And even that small minority of Africans who were now able to achieve a modern education, thanks largely to Christian missionary endeavour, found themselves with a merely peripheral influence on the colonial societies in which they lived.

AFRICA TODAY

All this bears closely on the condition of Africa today. It bears closely, that is, on the whole concept of "development". Historically, none of the societies or nations of Africa can be regarded as "undeveloped" or even as "under-developed": they are in truth the product of long centuries of persistent development within their own structures. They are "undeveloped" or "under-developed" only in relation to quite other structures which have emerged from a quite other history. In order to develop along different lines—to make their transformation from a rural-agricultural to an urban-industrial base, and thus, in terms of development theory, to approach and consummate a modern industrial "take off"—they must clearly regain command of their own history, and, having done that, embark on the construction of new systems and corresponding institutions.

A recent example dramatizes the point. In the Portuguese overseas territory of Angola—a colony in all but name—the late 1960s brought much new investment in the exploitation of raw materials and in infrastructure. This undoubtedly meant economic growth. But it was economic growth without development so far as the African population was concerned, because the African population continued to be effectively debarred from any participation except as cheap labour. It would follow that any true development in Angola, as distinct from growth without development, must depend on a new system of society, implying an end to colonial rule and, after that

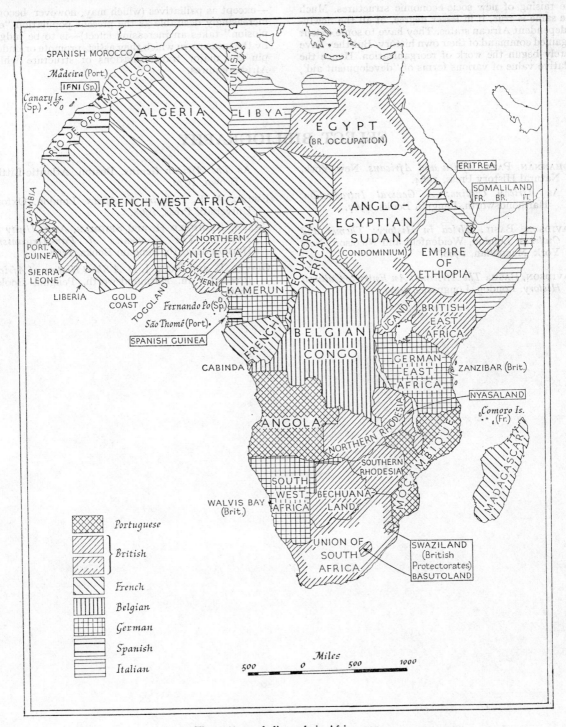

SPANISH MOROCCO

Madeira (Port.)

IFNI (Sp.)

Canary Is. (Sp.)

MOROCCO

RIO DE ORO

TUNISIA

ALGERIA

LIBYA

EGYPT
(BR. OCCUPATION)

ERITREA

SOMALILAND
FR. BR. IT.

GAMBIA

FRENCH WEST AFRICA

ANGLO-
EGYPTIAN
SUDAN
(CONDOMINIUM)

EMPIRE
OF
ETHIOPIA

PORT.
GUINEA

SIERRA
LEONE

LIBERIA

GOLD
COAST

TOGOLAND

NORTHERN

NIGERIA

SOUTHERN

KAMERUN

Fernando Po (Sp.)

São Thomé (Port.)

SPANISH GUINEA

EQUATORIAL AFRICA

FRENCH

CABINDA

BELGIAN
CONGO

UGANDA

BRITISH
EAST
AFRICA

ZANZIBAR (Brit.)

GERMAN
EAST
AFRICA

NYASALAND

Comoro Is.
(Fr.)

ANGOLA

NORTHERN RHODESIA

MOZAMBIQUE

SOUTHERN
RHODESIA

MADAGASCAR

SOUTH
WEST
AFRICA

WALVIS BAY
(Brit.)

BECHUANA-
LAND

UNION OF
SOUTH
AFRICA

SWAZILAND
(British
Protectorates)
BASUTOLAND

Portuguese

British

French

Belgian

German

Spanish

Italian

Miles

500   0   500   1000

The pattern of alien rule in Africa, 1914.

the raising of new socio-economic structures. Much the same is true, if in lesser degree, of all the newly-independent African states. They have to some extent regained command of their own history. But they have barely begun the work of reorganization. Hence the relative value of various forms of "development aid", —except as palliatives (which may, however, become increasingly desirable as the present population "explosion" takes an increasing effect)—is to be judged by the measure in which they assist, promote or underpin the major transformations of structure which Africa requires.

SELECT BIBLIOGRAPHY

BOHANNAN, PAUL. *Africa and Africans*. New York, Natural History Press, 1964.

As *African Outline: A General Introduction*. Harmondsworth, Penguin Books, 1967.

DAVIDSON, BASIL. *Africa in History: Themes and Outlines*. London, Weidenfeld and Nicolson; New York, Macmillan, 1968.

DAVIDSON, BASIL. *The Africans: An Entry to Cultural History*. London, Longmans, 1969.

As *The African Genius*. Boston, Atlantic-Little, Brown, 1970.

EWING, A. F. *Industry in Africa*. London, Oxford University Press, 1968.

GREEN, REGINALD H. and SEIDMAN, ANN. *Unity or Poverty? The Economics of Pan-Africanism*. Harmondsworth, Penguin Books, 1968.

OLIVER, R. and FAGE, J. D. *A Short History of Africa*. Revised Edn. Harmondsworth, Penguin Books, 1966.

Political and Social Problems of Development

Ruth First

A decade and a half have seen dramatic changes on the continent of Africa. In the mid-1950s the independent states could be counted on the fingers of one hand. They were Ethiopia and Liberia, Egypt and Libya. At the beginning of the 1970s, there were 42 independent African states. The latest to attain political sovereignty were The Gambia and Equatorial Guinea in west Africa and Botswana, Lesotho and Swaziland in southern Africa. The latter three, though among the newest to gain independence and among the poorer of the African states, are important in terms of continental issues. All three are enclaves of independence encircled by the white minority régimes that lie south of what has been termed Africa's Mason-Dixon Line. While the flow of independence has thus run far southwards, the conflict between black- and white-ruled Africa has been brought into increasingly sharp focus by the continuing state of guerrilla war, especially in the Portuguese colonies of Angola and Mozambique and, in west Africa, in Guinea (Bissau). If proof were needed of the threat to the security of the independent régimes of Africa by the intransigence of the remaining colonial strongholds, this was demonstrated in November 1970 by the invasion of Guinea by a group of Portuguese mercenaries acting together with disaffected Guineans. The attack was repulsed by a counter-action in which the liberation forces of the PAIGC (African Independence Party of Guinea) played a prominent part. In the south, on the one side, the governments of South Africa (and the annexed territory of South West Africa or Namibia), Rhodesia and Portugal increasingly pursue common defence and economic strategies in the interests of the maintenance of white minority rule; on the other side the independent states and the OAU are committed to the liberation of the African populations still under white colonial-type rule. Zambia lies along the north of this line of conflict and very much in its front line; and it is significant that her capital of Lusaka was chosen as the venue of the Third Conference of Non-Aligned States in September 1970. Thus of the two principal sets of problems which preoccupy the continent one arises from the contronfation between the two Africas.

The second set of problems absorbing African states consists in the dilemmas thrown up by the need of the continent to advance from political sovereignty to full-scale economic independence, and the search not only for economic strategies to this end, but for the political means and institutions to achieve it. The formal accession to independence—the entry of new states into the United Nations and the establishment of sovereign political forms—is the beginning, not the end of the act of independence. The increase of the continent's rate of growth, currently as low as 1 per cent per annum according to the OECD, is proving more arduous by far. The development problems of the continent reveal themselves not only in economic but also in political forms, most dramatically in the political crises in which governments and politicians have fallen, often precipitately, and new ones risen. In this, Africa is by no means distinct from other countries and continents in which régimes rise and fall, but her crises have been characteristic of the continent's current problems of under-development.

Of the politicians who led their countries to independence in 1960, the watershed independence year for Africa, over half were unceremoniously ousted by *coups d'état*. Since 1960 African armies have intervened against their governments in 17 African countries, this tally not including the abortive army plots in countries like Gabon, Ethiopia and Morocco. The *coups* themselves have differed one from the other in motive and course. What they have served to illustrate is a basic instability of a widely differing range of political systems and government.

FORMS OF GOVERNMENT

In the initial years of independence it seemed that African forms of government could easily be grouped into identifiable categories. Some régimes installed Westminster-type parliamentary systems with accommodation for government and opposition (Kenya, Nigeria and Ghana, initially). By contrast with these multi-party systems there were the single-party systems, under which highly concentrated presidential régimes generally operated (Ghana after 1960, the Ivory Coast and most of the former French colonies). As the experience of independence lengthened, the single-party system became the predominant pattern. And, with the monopoly of power held by a single party, that party asserted its control over other organs of government: legislature, executive, judiciary and local administration.

In the former French colonies, strongly influenced by Gaullist forms, the tendency towards presidentialism meant that the president, both as head of state and head of government, possessed overriding powers. There was the dominant governing party, with the president the dominant figure in it and in government, and often the constitution itself reflected the domination of the state not only by a single party but by a single man. So, for instance, in the Ivory Coast, Dahomey, Niger and Upper Volta, there were virtually identical constitutions and the President was the exclusive holder of executive power. In Ghana the President's powers were as great, if not greater.

With the development of the dominant-party system and the style of government and leadership that accompanied it, there grew a fluently enunciated ideology. It argued that the single-party system reflected a basic consensus of opinion among the

African population, of single countries and of the continent as a whole, in the face of the tasks of national reconstruction. In the anti-colonial period the mass nationalist party had been an expression of the united needs of the African people to struggle against colonialism. In the post-colonial era, once the colonialists had gone, there was no remaining division between rulers and ruled, and therefore no need for conflicting parties. Provision in the political system for a formal "opposition" would have meant straining to find a real basis of opposition for the sake of preserving an imported model of democracy. Therefore, it was argued, the parties should attempt to retain their pre-independence character of broad-based national movements, representative of all shades of opinion. The multi-party system was repudiated as open to manipulation and misuse by regional or tribal interests or by neo-colonialist pressures.

Towards the middle of the first decade of independence the modal type of régime was the one-party system. Governing parties saw the institutions of government as designed to serve the interests of the party, which were at the same time the interests of the political governing élite and, it was claimed, of the people as a whole. However, not all the single-party states had identical types of party or identical social aims. The one-party systems ranged from that of the True Whig Party of Liberia on the one hand to the "mobilization" régimes of Mali, Ghana and Guinea on the other. Some were élite parties involving relatively small and privileged groups; others were mass parties seeking to mobilize the mass of the people behind efforts not simply to modify colonial structures but to transform them altogether by restructuring the economy. The élite parties expressed conservative and traditionalist tendencies; the mass parties espoused more radical ideologies, and in the case of Kwame Nkrumah in Ghana, Sekou Touré in Guinea and Modibo Keita in Mali advocated "scientific" as against "African" socialism. These ideological divisions were carried into the pan-African alignments of the moderate Monrovia bloc on the one hand and the more radical Casablanca bloc on the other.

COUPS D'ETAT

The wave of *coups d'état* proved to be no respecter of the political distinctions between differing African régimes and their social policies or professed range of popular support. The *coups* happened with little regard to types of political structure or ideology, and were also unrelated to the size and effectiveness of the armies. When contingents of soldiers struck against government, some of the best-vaunted mobilization parties turned out to be weak reeds. Régimes displaced ranged from those in the smallest countries (Dahomey, Congo (Brazzaville) and Togo) to those in the largest (Congo (Kinshasa) and Nigeria). They included those governed by conservative patronage parties (Upper Volta and the Central African Republic), some committed to western-type parliamentary government (Nigeria and Sierra

Leone), and the régimes most committed to social revolution (Algeria, Ghana and Mali). The wave of *coups d'état* and the range of governments affected by them suggested that political instability was the expression of profound and generalized economic problems and social conflict, and that many seemingly dissimilar political systems shared an incipient state of crisis because political independence alone had not enabled Africa to break the circle of dependence that was the condition of colonialism.

The *coups* were not all the same. Some were fairly simple pay strike actions: the army acted rather like a trade union of soldiers and struck to defend its immediate interests, often on issues of pay or promotion or the status of the army. Togo, for instance, experienced in 1963 a relatively simple army strike which resulted in the death of President Olympio and the collapse of his government. In Sudan in 1958, during the early *coups* in Dahomey, and in Sierra Leone, when political disputes made imminent the defeat of the governing party, the army acted as an extension of the régime and stepped into office to shore it up. Other *coups* in turn have been actions by sections of the army identifying with sections of the political spectrum and invading government to further the cause with which they identify (the Nigerian *coups* in January and July 1966).

Many strains of motive combine in any single army take-over of government. The armies are themselves amalgams of different interest groups which are sometimes politically and sometimes regionally based. Thus in Nigeria regional cleavages in the political system were also present in the officer corps; and in some countries, Togo and Congo (Brazzaville) among them, the largely northern officer corps has asserted the claims to political leadership of the neglected north as against the élites of the more privileged southern coastlines, which at independence were entrenched in both politics and administration.

The striking feature of army take-overs of government is that to almost every *coup d'état* there has been a counter-*coup*. This is an expression of the conflicting interests within the body of the army, not least tension within the officer corps between senior and junior officers which sometimes extends into the ranks of non-commissioned officers. Frequently the interests of senior officers and the régime in power coincide, whereas the junior officers tend to identify with reforming or opposition tendencies.

But whether the army stages a *coup* as an arbitrator of political disputes, or as guardian for an existing government, or as political partisan itself, it is liable to become a competitor for power in the furtherance of its corporate interests. Thus, while in Ghana and Mali the army seized power in sympathy with a generalized political disaffection at a time of economic dislocation and hardship, the army was largely prompted into action by the fear that its own interests were being undermined by the formation of popular militia (in Ghana, the presidential guard). Attempts by government to build a countervailing force against the monopoly of the means of violence held by the professional army have proved to be a sure provocation to army usurpation of government.

Once in power the African armies have acted to assert their own immediate interests. A growing proportion of the state's revenues begins to accrue to the defence budget; the army is smartened up and new equipment bought; and army pay rises, often dramatically. Like the politicians, the army officers and the civil servants—whom the armymen lean heavily upon when they take over government, so that the administrators achieve an influence and a prominence in political decision-making that they never enjoyed under the politicians—regard themselves as the heirs to independent government, and they act to protect and assert their interests.

By the beginning of the 1970s the wave of *coups* showed little sign of abating. Apart from the abortive inner-army *coup* attempts in Togo in 1970, in Congo (Brazzaville) in 1969, 1970 and again in February 1972 when President Ngouabi claimed that leading members of the governing party involved in party reorganization had resorted to conspiratorial means, and in Morocco in July 1971, the most recent successful *coups* have occurred in Mali (1968), Sudan (May 1969 and an abortive and harshly suppressed counter-coup in July 1971), Uganda (January 1971), Ghana (January 1972) and Dahomey (October 1972), both of which had only recently returned to civilian rule following earlier *coups*. The 1969 *coups* in Sudan and Libya, both led by young officers in their late twenties, installed Revolutionary Command Councils committed to domestic programmes of nationalization of foreign assets and internal reform, and to foreign policies based on anti-imperialism and pan-Arabism. The balance between the northern, Arab-speaking states of Africa had thus been radically changed. Tunisia, pursuing cautious foreign policies, found herself wedged between Algeria and the new Libyan régime, and Morocco, under King Hassan II, felt equally uncomfortable. The position of Egypt on the other hand, flanked by Sudan to the south and Libya in the west, was strengthened, so much so that Egypt and Libya are now partners in a federation with Syria, and Sudan is a potential member.

In Morocco King Hassan narrowly escaped overthrow and death in the abortive army *coup* when a dozen highranking officers raided the Palace with a force of troops. The régime was steadied when loyalist troops turned the table on the coup-makers and Morocco reverted to the mixture much as before: a fairly large moderate left-wing opposition with virtually no influence over the political system and a royal autocracy which after the *coup* framed a new constitution which somewhat lessened the powers of the King and strengthened a partly-elected Parliament, but which left the monarch the ultimate seat of power. In the Sudan an abortive *coup d'état* in July 1971 was due to a conflict over the nature of the political system of a rather different kind. The army régime under President Nemery was instituting a Nasserite political system under which the armed forces play the leading role and all political groupings, including the trade unions, are required to merge their interests in a state-created Arab Socialist Union. In the Sudan a large and influential left movement including the unions and the Communist Party was pressing for the retention of the popular organizations as the mass base of the revolution. The dispute culminated in the crisis of mid-1971 when an abortive left wing *coup* against Nemery was crushed and widespread reprisals resulted in the execution of the leaders of the short-lived revolutionary régime, and of leading members of the Sudanese Communist Party. Alienated both from the traditional conservative forces of the country and the mass-based left and in its urgent need to consolidate itself, the Sudanese régime then bent to the problem of the south where civil war had flared intermittently since independence. A peace agreement reached at Addis Ababa in March 1972 resulted in a ceasefire and an agreement for the creation of a provisional government for the southern region, and the integration into the standing army of Anyanya rebel forces. Northern and southern interests thus agreed to accept the framework of a single national identity. The most formidable task remained that of the economic revival of the long-neglected southern areas, and the stability of the Nemery régime, like that of its predecessors, would clearly be deeply bound up with the success of the southern policy. When Egypt and Libya together with Syria launched their Federation of Arab Republics (based on the Tripoli Agreement of December 1969) it was above all the sensitive southern question which kept the Sudan out. By August 1972 Egypt and Libya had agreed to advance from the loose links between the three partners to full political merger of their two states. This was to be achieved by September 1973 when the issue goes before a referendum in the two countries.

In Uganda the *coup* in which General Idi Amin overthrew President Milton Obote was prompted largely by the fear of imminent presidential control over part of the army command. The *coup* was followed by several weeks of internecine fighting in the army where support for the new and old heads of state divided partly along ethnic lines. General Amin's highly idiosyncratic style of rule, based principally on the army but with civil servants posted to ministries, was climaxed by his visit to Tripoli to see Libya's head of state Colonel Muammar al Gaddafi. It was this encounter which led to Uganda's order to Israel, which had been the most significant foreign influence in Uganda certainly since the *coup*, to withdraw her personnel, and to Uganda's establishment of consultative relations with the Federation of Arab Republics, and to the signing of a defence pact between Uganda and the Sudan. Libya's attempt to use her resources to build a bridgehead across Africa to counter Israel's influence—seen in her closer relations with Uganda but also with Chad—was among the initiatives that bore fruit in the OAU's Middle East resolution which affirmed support for Egypt and called on Israel to withdraw from occupied territories in accordance with the UN Security Council resolution.

In Ghana the much-vaunted civilian régime under Dr. K. Busia, which had inherited power from the army régime which in 1966 displaced Kwame Nkrumah's CPP government, lasted less than eighteen months. In January 1972 a *coup* led by Colonel Acheampong displaced Dr. Busia's government and installed a National Redemption Council under army control. The *coup* was a response to dismissals from the armed forces and the retrenchment of the civil service, but also to pressing economic problems aggravated by the revaluation of the cedi by the Busia régime. Parliament was dissolved and political parties were banned, but the army régime restored the Trade Union Congress. The new government repudiated part of Ghana's external debt, notably to British companies whose contracts it alleged were "tainted with corruption", and embarked on a programme of part nationalization of business. Ghana also reversed the previous policy of dialogue with South Africa. If some aspects of the régime's policy seemed reminiscent of the Nkrumah period this was more a reaction against its immediate predecessor, the Busia régime, than any concerted assertion of principle, and Colonel Acheampong has been quick to deny any affinity with Nkrumahism.

In Madagascar President Tsiranana was forced to hand executive powers to his army chief of staff General Gabriel Ramanantsoa as a result not of a direct *coup d'état* but of a month of riots and demonstrations which had shaken his government and made it impossible for him to rule without the army. Half of the new Cabinet consisted of military men and President Tsiranana was reduced to titular head of state. This development followed a crisis of more than two years duration during which the trade unions, the students and the coastal peoples who were not identified with the absolute rule of the Tsiranana government which represented only one of the island's 18 ethnic groups, had been increasingly alienated by the régime's domestic failings and also by its foreign policy of close co-operation with France and with South Africa.

These *coups* apart, Dahomey experienced its fifth successful *coup* in October 1972 ending less than two years of civilian rule under a Presidential Council; there had already been an attempted *coup* by a score of soldiers in February 1972. Upper Volta, on the other hand, has introduced a draft constitution for a staggered programme of return to civilian government.

The most durable military régime has proved to be the one presided over by President Mobutu in Zaire. This has been achieved by a systematic policy of incorporating into government or—as in the case of Pierre Mulele—effectively disposing of political dissenters; and by scrupulous attention to the needs of the army which brought the régime to power. But even these measures might not have been effective without the Congo's reconciliation with Belgium, and the special budgetary support given to the Congo by the United States to ensure internal stability. Following a less easy economic situation caused by the slump in the world price of copper which was approximately halved in a year, Zaire embarked upon a vigorous programme of "authenticity", or in the words of President Mobutu who, under the programme of

name-changing, became Mobutu Sese Seko, "upsurge of authentic nationalism". If it did nothing else, this would undoubtedly be a useful diversion from hardening economic problems, an increasingly authoritarian political system, and a conspicuous division between rich politicians, civil servants, army men and businessmen and the rest.

Many of the other military governments proved no more stable in office than the civilian régimes they displaced. Some were shaken or even displaced as the result of counter-*coups*. Others proved no better able than the civilian governments in power before them to grapple with the problem facing one African economy after another: the problem of achieving self-sustaining economic growth.

ECONOMIC GROWTH PROBLEMS

There is no easy solution. In the years 1965–67 agricultural production growth in independent Africa was only 1.4 per cent a year compared with 2.6 per cent in the first half of the decade. Per caput agricultural production which had remained more or less constant in the early 1960s declined by almost 1 per cent between 1964–66 and 1966–68. In addition the composition of Africa's agricultural exports remains very restricted: two products, coffee and cocoa, contributed 44 per cent of the total value of the trade in 1968. Such a dependence on a limited range of exports makes African economies dangerously vulnerable to price fluctuations on the world market. Though mining, the fastest growing sector, increased its share of the total G.D.P. from 1960 to 1968 and mineral processing industries have expanded, ECA statistics suggest that Africa's overall per caput G.D.P. is growing very slowly indeed, and some economies are slipping backwards. States like Zambia, Mauritania and Libya, where mineral or oil deposits have attracted heavy foreign investment, are exceptions to the generally sombre picture, but here foreign ownership in growth sectors leads to the heavy repatriation of profits and to a reduction in the propensity for reinvestment. As for those countries which placed great store by international aid, the Pearson Report warned of a crisis in development assistance, and recent figures confirm this. In 1968, for instance, official aid flows provided by governments actually declined from the previous year's totals. Further, the terms of loan commitments have hardened, and a growing percentage of aid is tied, a factor which imposes severe restraints on the ability of the recipient countries to use the money effectively, and in any case reduces the real value of aid.

The low rate of the continent's economic growth is part of the colonial legacy of unbalanced development, and it is perpetuated by the constantly deteriorating terms of trade for the poor as compared with the rich world. Its consequence is that in one African country after another public expenditure on current items—largely government and administrative salaries—is vastly outstripping rises in production, thus leaving little capital for investment in new economic projects. Even as countries have found themselves overwhelmed with this problem, governments have grown more profligate, and administrations, which preserved inflated colonial salary structures—and are a powerful magnet for the younger educated élites as one of the profitable sources of employment in otherwise sluggish economies—have grown larger and more extravagant. The result has been a massive gap in living standards between the political and administrative élites and the common people. René Dumont was one of the first observers to draw attention to this. "For too many African élites independence has meant taking the place of the whites and enjoying the privileges, often exhorbitant, hitherto accorded to colonials," he wrote. A peasant of the Cameroon countryside told him in 1961: "Independence isn't for us, it's for the people in the towns." More and more in Africa the question is coming to be asked: who governs and to whose ends?

CONTESTING CLAIMS

The existence of the one-party state has been found in itself to be no guarantee of the successful reconstruction of the economy, and the systems of government based on western forms have proved no more effective. This is in part because political power, whatever its constitutional form in Africa, has proved to be more than political office; it has also given access to direction of the economy, and increasingly resources have been expended on a conspicuously consumptionist élite. This has placed a major brake on development efforts, for the benefits of economic growth are being concentrated in the hands of a relatively small group. It has also proved a source of dispute and conflict between contesting claims for the disposal of those resources that are available in the new states.

In some countries the contest has taken the form of the *coup d'état*, with army officers and civil servants lodging their objection to the rule of the politicians and their corruption of office. In other countries where resources have been unevenly available or unevenly allocated between different regions and ethnic groups, the contest has taken on a "tribal" form, not necessarily because tribal antagonism is in itself deep-rooted, but because different sections of the élite have fortified their own claims by identifying with and rallying regional or communal bases of support. This appeared to be the case in Burundi where a deep-running conflict between the minority Tutsi oligarchy and the majority Hutu resulted during 1972 in an alleged *coup* attempt followed by grotesquely large-scale killings of civilians. In other countries still it has been the demands of the trade unions which have precipitated political crises, and often directly, army interventions.

While Africa's wage-earning force is small, often less than 5 per cent of the population, and the numbers of unionized workers even smaller, the unions have significant bargaining power gained by their association with the nationalist movement in the pre-independence days, and also by the fact that because government and public corporations are the largest employers of labour, the trade unions often occupy

strategic positions in the economy and the administration (the powerful unions are often of civil servants, railway and port workers). In Congo (Brazzaville), Dahomey and Upper Volta general strikes against austerity drives—initiated rather unconvincingly by governments not remarkable for their own austerity—brought down unpopular régimes, but the unions were not strong enough to assume power themselves, and having invited the army to do so, their role subsided. In many countries in Africa governments have limited the autonomy and freedom of action of the trade unions by attaching them to the party apparatus or to the administration; this is said to be in the interests of development and so that the government can monitor the wage claims of workers and their demands on the economy. In other countries, as in Kenya and Tunisia, there is legislation for compulsory wage and dispute arbitration. In several countries, among them Senegal, Ivory Coast, Ghana, Nigeria and Mauritania, there have been recent trials of strength between trade unions and government. In Mauritius a general strike towards the end of 1971 led to a state of emergency in essential services and the suspension of the trade unions by the government.

EGALITARIAN SOLUTIONS

Several countries have sought solutions to political dissent and the contests between interest groups by skilfully handled personal and political alliances, major cabinet reshuffles and constitutional reform. Senegal and Tunisia are examples. Tanzania, on the other hand, is seeking to evolve egalitarian policies and an economic programme which will minimize corruption and restrict the accumulation of wealth by a small governing and administrative élite. President Nyerere's memorandum to the TANU National Executive in June 1966 argued that in a poor country like Tanzania, where there was little attraction for capital investment, "development depends primarily on the efforts and hard work of our people, and on their enthusiasm and belief that they and their country will benefit from whatever they do. How could anyone expect this enthusiasm and hard work to be forthcoming if the masses see that a few individuals in the society get very rich and live in great comfort, while the majority continue apparently for ever in abject poverty?" This memorandum was the prelude to the Arusha Declaration six months later. This demanded that the self-reliance of the peasant be matched by the self-sacrifice and socialist commitment of the leadership, and it stressed internal capital accumulation rather than dependence on loans as the major instrument of development.

In the continent-wide debate about directions in economic planning and the balance between agriculture and industry it is once again Tanzania that has evolved a policy which, by encouraging *ujamaa vijijini* (literally "familyhood villages"), emphasizes communal, though technologically developed, modes of agricultural production. The stress on socialized forms of production in the countryside was in part devised as an answer to the growth in the countryside of vested interest groups of the more prosperous farmers, who constitute a rural oligarchy and possess strong family and political links with the governmental and administrative élites in power. A subsequent policy elaboration resulted in the March 1971 Mwongozo guidelines which urged a change in leadership method from the individualistic to the collective in the spheres of government and administration and also in the management of enterprises, and which reflected something of the tussle which was growing between Tanu-roused grassroot forces and the bureaucracy. The mainland's concentration on the unfolding of a development strategy was interrupted by the assassination in April 1972 of Sheikh Abeid Karume, the first vice-president and head of the Zanzibar régime, in what appeared to be a struggle by young men in the army and associated at one time with left-wing UMMA Party circles which had grown critical of the authoritarian tendencies that had developed in government under Karume's Afro-Shirazi Party.

Thus, whereas the seminal issue for Africa in the early years of independence seemed to be the form of political power and the structure of parties, in the later years it has been the emergence of stratified interests and differing approaches to the management of the economy. Numbers of countries have introduced wide-scale nationalizations (Tanzania, Zambia and Algeria). Others like Senegal pursue a more cautious path: President Senghor's policy is to "Senegalize that which is Senegalizable", in other words, what is realistic, taking into account the power bases of the political system and relations with France.

Whatever the national policy towards foreign investment, the continent's economic problem remains the need to generate development from within, and to do this for Africa's own markets. Africa is heavily dependent on trade but this is for the most part trade with the rest of the world and is almost entirely the exchange of primary products for manufactures. Intra-African trade is less than ten per cent of total trade and is also mainly in primary products.

ECONOMIC CO-OPERATION

In theory Africa is agreed that there should be a break with small-scale economic organization and a move towards continental co-operation. But this has been difficult because the colonial Anglophone-Francophone divisions in trade and economic organization remain, not least in the existence of two currency areas. France's special relationship with her former colonies remains especially close and she exerts strong leverage over their economies through the closely knit franc zone, based on Paris centralization.

There have been some bilateral agreements for co-operation, and some attempts at sub-regional planning; there are also several regional organizations. It is principally the former French colonies, together with the other Francophone countries and Somalia, 19 states in all, which are party through the Yaoundé Convention to the European Economic Community.

The Senegal River States Organization, which was created in 1968 to harmonize the development programmes of Mauritania, Senegal, Mali and Guinea and to build common projects, collapsed and made way for the Senegal River Development Organization (OMVS), which links Senegal, Mali and Mauritania, but not Guinea. Also in 1968 the Economic Commission for Africa—which, in a series of studies designed to aid African economic integration, delineated four regional groups—initiated a meeting of heads of state of fourteen countries to prepare a West African Economic Community. A group of eight west African states which made up the Customs Union of West African States (UDEAO) met in 1970 to adopt a protocol for a West African Economic Community (CEAO). The CEAO Treaty was signed by seven West African countries at Bamako in June 1972, shortly after the Senegal-Guinea reconciliation. There have been some fluctuations in the fortunes of attempted central African groupings. United States influence was charged with having detached Chad and the Central African Republic from UDEAC (the Central African Customs and Economic Union); and France was blamed in turn for detaching the Central African Republic from UEAC (the Union of Central African States), which the breakaway states from UDEAC had formed together with Zaire. In east Africa the East African Community with headquarters at Arusha came into existence at the end of 1967, committed, among other aims, to promote industrial development, including the processing of primary products, and to give Uganda and Tanzania preference in view of Kenya's headstart. There is also a Maghreb sub-regional economic organization.

PAN-AFRICANISM

The continent's movement towards political pan-Africanism, expressed in numbers of pan-African conferences in the pre-independence years, culminated in the founding in 1963 of the OAU. The moderate Monrovia bloc and the more radical Casablanca grouping combined within the single body, though their concepts of unity differed. The more conservative powers saw the new body as an alliance for limited inter-African co-operation and the more radical group wanted a movement committed to the revolutionary transformation of the continent. Their combination in one organization made for some years of uneasy compromise, but after the fall of Nkrumah the differences between the two groups largely lost their edge. While these two groupings dissolved in the interests of the new body, OCAM (*Organisation commune africaine et malgache*) did not, and this Francophone group (now the *Organisation commune africaine, malgache et mauricienne*) has at times been a running source of discord within the OAU, most recently on the issue of *apartheid*. (After some years within this grouping Zaire withdrew from OCAM during 1972 as part of her pursuit for Central African leadership rather than association with a regional group of the former French colonies.)

Two strands of agreement have formed the basis of OAU unity in the years since its formation. One is the decision taken in 1964 that the OAU should uphold the frontiers inherited with independence. This issue of sovereignty and denial of the right of secession was put to its sharpest test during the Nigerian civil war when four OAU member-states supported Biafra, and the OAU was unable to resolve the conflict through its own offices. Other internal conflicts in African states have been studiously ignored in accord with the 1964 decision. These include the demand of Eritreans for independence from Ethiopia; and the armed revolt in Chad. The June 1972 summit meeting of the OAU at Rabat showed rather more unity than its predecessors due in part to the OAU's successful mediation of the border dispute between Morocco and Algeria and the reconciliation between Guinea and Senegal.

The other basis of pan-African unity has been the commitment of the OAU to the total liberation of the continent, especially the south. The policy of the African states is to isolate white-ruled southern Africa through the use of boycotts and sanctions and at the same time to channel aid to the liberation movements through the OAU Liberation Committee. The issue dominates successive heads of state conferences and pan-African deliberations, and, as in the issues of sanctions against Rhodesia and the supply of arms to South Africa, preoccupies individual African states in their relations with the west. A sharp departure from this policy of furthering the southern African liberation struggle was augured by the attempt by the Ivory Coast—supported by some of the former French colonies—to initiate "dialogue" with the South African government, but this approach received a sharp setback after changes of régime in Ghana and Madagascar and the reversal of those states' previous support of the "dialogue" policy. Madagascar had previously been one of the main links in Pretoria's chain of co-operation with African states for the purposes of undermining OAU unity against apartheid.

THE WHITE-RULED SOUTH

Of the southern territories Angola is not only Portugal's principal foreign currency earner through the production of diamonds, iron ore, coffee and, recently, oil; this territory is also of decisive value in the overall strategic balance of southern Africa. In Angola the guerrilla war is in its twelfth year. The MPLA (*Movimento Popular de Libertação de Angola*) is sustaining offensives along the eastern front bordering Zambia. In the north GRAE (*Governo Revolucionário de Angola no Exílio*) under Holden Roberto is quiescent despite the favour of the Gen. Mobutu's government of Zaire which, by contrast, denies access through its territory to MPLA fighters. Hopes of a change in this policy were expressed by a meeting between MPLA's Agostinho Neto and GRAE's Holden Roberto in Congo (Brazzaville) and their commitment at the OAU's Rabat summit in 1972 to explore co-operation between the two movements. In Mozambique FRELIMO (*Frente de Libertação de Moçambique*) is entrenched in the two northern provinces of Niassa and Cabo Delgado, and is now fighting an offensive in Tete Province, which is an important agri-

cultural area and also the site of the projected Cabora Bassa Dam. Following U.D.I. in Rhodesia in November 1965, the Rhodesian ZAPU (Zimbabwe African Peoples' Union) and the South African ANC (African National Congress) launched combined guerrilla offensives in Rhodesia, intensifying co-operation between the white minority régime headed by Mr. Ian Smith and that of South Africa, which rushed security reinforcements into Rhodesia after 1967 against their common enemy. During 1972 ZAPU and ZANU announced the formation of a unified military command. Attempts by Britain and the white minority régime in Rhodesia to solve the crisis created by U.D.I. resulted in constitutional proposals that, in accordance with the five principles enunciated by a previous British government, were put to the test of majority African opinion by the British Government's Pearce Commission. The Commission recorded an African veto against the proposed basis for independence, which had retreated from the principle of unimpeded progress towards majority rule. The African National Council (ANC) which had been formed to campaign for a "No" vote urged a National Convention of all race groups to resolve the constitutional deadlock; this was rejected by the Smith government, which proceeded to take control measures against the ANC. By mid-1972 a solution which accommodated African claims seemed as remote as ever. The OAU reasserted its call for mandatory sanctions to isolate the illegal white régime. In South West Africa, SWAPO (the South West African People's Organization) has launched actions from the Caprivi Strip.

Increasingly the régimes of South Africa, Rhodesia and Portugal are devising concerted policies to hold the line across the Zambezi. There is evidence of close defence and intelligence planning between them. Central to their combined economic strategy in the region are two hydroelectric schemes, one spanning the Kunene River between Angola and South West Africa, and the larger in Tete Province in Mozambique at the strategic conjunction of Zambia, Malawi and Rhodesia. The plan is to hook the countries of the south into an integrated power-using region dominated by the economic strength of South Africa. The Cabora Bassa Dam in Mozambique is to be financed and built by a giant international consortium of South African, French, West German and some British capital. It will be the second largest hydroelectric generating station on the continent (double the size of Kariba and 70 per cent larger than Aswan) and will provide irrigation schemes, interlocking projects for mining and industrial development and new road and railway networks. But it is planned to be a centre not only of hydroelectric power but also of white settler power, for Portugal has announced a scheme to settle white immigrants along the Zambezi to strengthen the manpower resources of the white minority régimes of the south.

Apart from her part in long-term economic planning in the region, South Africa's response to the escalation of guerrilla warfare in the sub-continent has been the evolution of a new "outward-looking" foreign policy. By contrast with her previous policy of isolationism towards black Africa, she has of late made repeated offers of co-operation to African states on the grounds that differences in domestic policy need be no bar to joint economic projects and trade. There are clearly two principal reasons for the changed policies of the *apartheid* state. One is a defensive reaction to the growing co-operation between the liberation movements of the different territories; the second is the need of the thriving South African economy for larger markets and fields of investment. Plans for the formation of a Southern African Common Market have been mooted for some time. In any such regional grouping South Africa's formidable economic strength could readily reduce her partners to satellite economies adopting a set of policies and priorities not for their own economic independence but in tune with the needs of the dominant partner, South Africa. This has already been the experience of Botswana, Lesotho and Swaziland, all virtually economic hostages of South Africa in their dependence on her customs union, currency area, transport system and industrial labour market.

Malawi has forged close links with South Africa and other states in the region notably Madagascar and Mauritius are being urged to follow her example. On the other hand the joint TanZam railway project of Zambia and Tanzania to give Zambia's copper an outlet to the sea other than through Salisbury and Mozambique and Botswana's scheme for a road north to link her with Zambia through the narrow Caprivi Strip, are both attempts by these independent states to disengage from the economic grip of the white-dominated south.

The 1970 Non-Aligned Conference which called for the total isolation of the white régimes was no sooner over than South Africa's Premier, Mr. B. J. Vorster, offered a non-aggression treaty to African states and warned in the course of the same statement that any large guerrilla incursions into South Africa would not only be met with appropriate force but would also be followed back into the country from which they had come. This makes the conflict readily exportable north into the continent. One serious indication of South African earnestness arose when a para-military group crossed briefly into Zambia from the Caprivi Strip where South West Africa guerillas had been active. Zambia, as the buffer zone between the white south and the black independent north, has grown increasingly vulnerable not only to an assertive South African foreign policy but also to the plunging price of copper which has provoked a serious foreign exchange crisis in that country and has also aggravated domestic political tensions. A long war of attrition lies ahead in the south and it is the outcome of this struggle which may well be the crucible of Africa's future.

SELECT BIBLIOGRAPHY

AMIN, S. *Trois expériences africaines de développement: le Mali, la Guinée et le Ghana*. Paris, Presses universitaires de France, 1965.

ARRIGHI, GIOVANNI, and SAUL, JOHN S. "Nationalism and Revolution in Sub-Saharan Africa, in Ralph Miliband and John Saville (Eds.) *The Socialist Register* 1969, Merlin Press.

FIRST, RUTH. *The Barrel of a Gun: Political Power in Africa and the Coup d'Etat*. London, Allen Lane, The Penguin Press, 1970.

GIBSON, RICHARD. *African Liberation Movements*. London, Oxford University Press for the Institute of Race Relations, 1972.

LONSDALE, JOHN. "The Tanzanian Experiment" in *African Affairs*, Vol. 67, No. 268, October 1968.

MORTIMER, ROBERT. "Senegal Seeks a Broader Political Base" in *Africa Report*, June 1970.

POST, KEN. *The New States of West Africa*. Harmondsworth, Penguin Books, 1968.

ZOLBERG, A. R. *Creating Political Order: The Party States of West Africa*. Chicago, 1966.

Dates of Independence of African Countries

(in Chronological Order of Independence—Post-War)

Libya	24 Dec.	1951
Sudan	1 Jan.	1956
Morocco	2 March	1956
Tunisia	20 March	1956
Ghana	6 March	1957
Guinea	2 Oct.	1958
Cameroon . . .	1 Jan.	1960
Togo	27 April	1960
Mali	20 June	1960
Senegal	20 June	1960
Madagascar . . .	26 June	1960
Democratic Republic of Congo (now Republic of Zaire) .	30 June	1960
Somalia	1 July	1960
Dahomey . . .	1 Aug.	1960
Niger	3 Aug.	1960
Upper Volta . . .	5 Aug.	1960
Ivory Coast . . .	7 Aug.	1960
Chad	11 Aug.	1960
Central African Republic .	13 Aug.	1960
People's Republic of Congo (Brazzaville) . . .	15 Aug.	1960
Gabon	17 Aug.	1960
Nigeria	1 Oct.	1960
Mauritania . . .	28 Nov.	1960
Sierra Leone . . .	27 April	1961
Tanzania (as Tanganyika) .	9 Dec.	1961
Rwanda	1 July	1962
Burundi	1 July	1962
Algeria	3 July	1962
Uganda	9 Oct.	1962
Zanzibar	10 Dec.	1963
Kenya	12 Dec.	1963
Malawi	6 July	1964
Zambia	24 Oct.	1964
The Gambia . . .	18 Feb.	1965
Botswana	30 Sept.	1966
Lesotho	4 Oct.	1966
Mauritius	12 March	1968
Swaziland . . .	6 Sept.	1968
Equatorial Guinea . .	12 Oct.	1968

African Languages
David Dalby

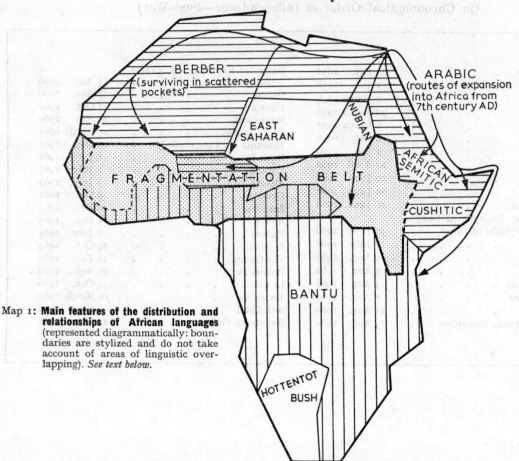

Map 1: **Main features of the distribution and relationships of African languages** (represented diagrammatically: boundaries are stylized and do not take account of areas of linguistic overlapping). *See text below.*

MAP 1

Linguistically Africa is one of the most complex areas in the world, with a total of around 1,000 languages. If closely related languages are counted together, then this number may be reduced to nearly 100 "groups" (of one or more languages each). The vast majority of these groups are situated within the sub-Saharan "Fragmentation Belt", a band of extreme linguistic fragmentation extending from Senegal in the west to Ethiopia and Kenya in the east (stippled on Map 1 *above*). Outside the Fragmentation Belt linguistic relationships are more straightforward and may be expressed in terms of eight language-groups plus Arabic (as named on the map).

Wider relationships among African languages and language-groups have been the subject of much debate, but there is general agreement on the existence of two major "areas of wider affinity": the so-called HAMITO-SEMITIC languages of northern Africa (horizontal hatching on the map) and the NIGER-CONGO languages of western, central and southern Africa (vertical hatching on the map). Traditionally these have been referred to as "families", implying that the languages involved have descended from a single common ancestor in each case. Although such regular relationships are far from proven, it is clear that

the existence of these two areas of wider affinity is of historical significance. The HAMITO-SEMITIC languages extend into Asia, but within Africa they comprise the *African Semitic* (including Amharic and Tigrinya), *Cushitic* (including Somali and Galla) and *Berber* language-groups, together with the so-called *"Chadic"* languages (including Hausa) of the northern Fragmentation Belt. In the east there is some doubt about how far the HAMITO-SEMITIC affinity extends into the Fragmentation Belt (dotted boundary on the map). Since the seventh century A.D. a further HAMITO-SEMITIC language (Arabic) has spread into Africa by a number of routes (shown by arrows on the map). The NIGER-CONGO languages comprise the *Bantu* language-group, the most extensive in Africa (including Swahili) and a large number of smaller groups in the southern and western segments of the Fragmentation Belt. In the west the precise boundary of the NIGER-CONGO affinity is also in doubt (dotted boundary on map). The areas of the map without horizontal or vertical hatching indicate languages which cannot be assigned readily to either of the two major areas of wider affinity: outside the Fragmentation Belt, these include the *East Saharan* (including Kanuri) and *Nubian* language-groups of north-central Africa and the so-called *Hottentot* and *Bush* (or *Bushman*) language-groups of south-western Africa. These

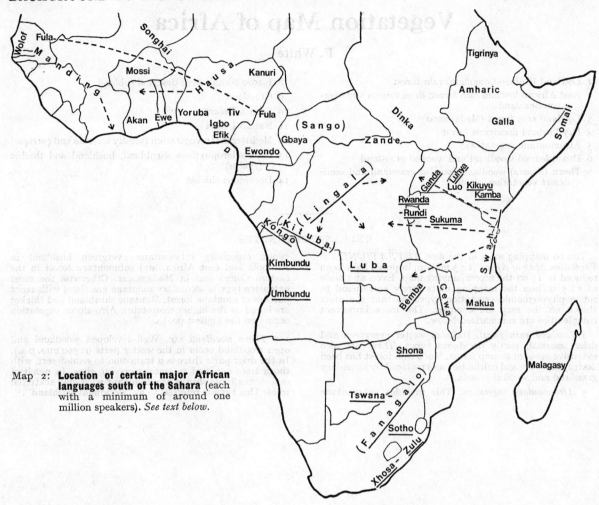

Map 2: **Location of certain major African languages south of the Sahara** (each with a minimum of around one million speakers). *See text below.*

latter groups have receded in recent centuries from the area of the Cape, where languages of European origin have become established (Afrikaans and English). Such languages of European origin (including also Creole English and Creole Portuguese in West Africa), together with the *Indonesian* dialects of Madagascar (Malagasy), have been excluded from this diagrammatic map of African languages.

MAP 2

Although almost 50 major African languages are each spoken by one million or more speakers, they represent only one-twentieth of the total number of languages spoken in the continent. Since these major languages have been selected for the above map on demographic criteria, they tend to be clustered together in areas of relatively high population (such as Nigeria, East Africa and South Africa), whereas in several less densely populated areas (such as South-West Africa and Gabon) no language approaches a total of one million speakers. Major languages spoken entirely or primarily as second languages (i.e. as a means of inter-ethnic communication in mixed language areas) are bracketed on the map, and arrows indicate the directions in which the use of certain languages has spread—or is still spreading—among speakers of other languages (i.e. Manding and Hausa in West Africa, Lingala in Zaire, and

Swahili in East Africa). The scattered spread of Fula from west to east across the West African savannah (as the language of a pastoralist people) is represented diagrammatically by a broken line. The drawing of linguistic boundaries has not been attempted on the above map, since there is often much fluidity and overlap between areas occupied by adjacent languages.

Languages underlined on Map 2 are members of the Bantu language-group, comprising approximately half the major languages of sub-Saharan Africa. Hyphens linking pairs of major Bantu languages (i.e. Rwanda-Rundi, Tswana-Sotho and Xhosa-Zulu) indicate an especially close relationship between them, so that for practical purposes each pair may be regarded as dialects of the same language. In other cases also, individual languages are often known by different names in different areas (especially when spoken by a number of distinct ethnic groups and/or in different dialectal forms). Hence Akan comprises Twi, Ashanti and Fante, Manding comprises Mandinka, Bambara and Dyula, Ewe covers also Fon, Efik also Ibibio, Sukuma also Nyamwezi, and Cewa also Nyanja. Zulu may also be taken to include Swazi (spoken further north in South Africa and in Swaziland) and Ndebele (in Rhodesia).

Vegetation Map of Africa

F. White

1. Lowland (Guineo-Congolian) rain forest
2. East African lowland rain forest, drier forests and evergreen bushland
3. Lowland rain forest (Madagascar)
4. Dry lowland deciduous forest
5. Afromontane vegetation
6. Broad-leaved woodland and wooded grassland
7. Thorn (*Acacia*) woodland, wooded grassland and semi-desert vegetation

8. Karoo-Namib semi-desert shrubland
9. Grassland
10. Sahara Desert
11. Namib Desert
12. Mediterranean vegetation (mostly *macchia* and *garrique*)
13. Cape sclerophyllous shrubland, bushland and thicket (*fynbos*)
14. Deciduous thicket

EXPLANATORY NOTES

The 60 mapping units of the new *AETFAT/UNESCO Vegetation Map of Africa* (1 : 5 million, in press) have been reduced to 14 on the accompanying map. Even at a scale of 1 : 5 million the mapping units rarely correspond to single physiognomic vegetation types, so that the units shown on the map are complex. The more important complexities are summarized below.

1 *Lowland rain forest*. Includes wetter evergreen and drier seasonal, partly deciduous types. There are also extensive areas of swamp forest. Much rain forest has been destroyed by fire and cultivation and replaced by secondary grassland and wooded grassland.

5 *Afro-montane vegetation*. This includes submontane types, especially submontane evergreen bushland in Ethiopia and east Africa, and submontane forest in the eastern Congo and in Madagascar. Otherwise the most extensive type is secondary montane grassland with relict patches of montane forest. Montane shrubland and thicket are found on the higher mountains. Afro-alpine vegetation occurs on the highest peaks.

7 *Thorn woodland* etc. Well-developed woodland and open woodland occur in the wetter parts (*c.* 500 mm. p.a.). In the drier parts there is a transition to semi-desert, with thorn trees confined to water-receiving sites. In much of east Africa large shrubs are dominant with only scattered trees. This type is referred to as "deciduous bushland".

28

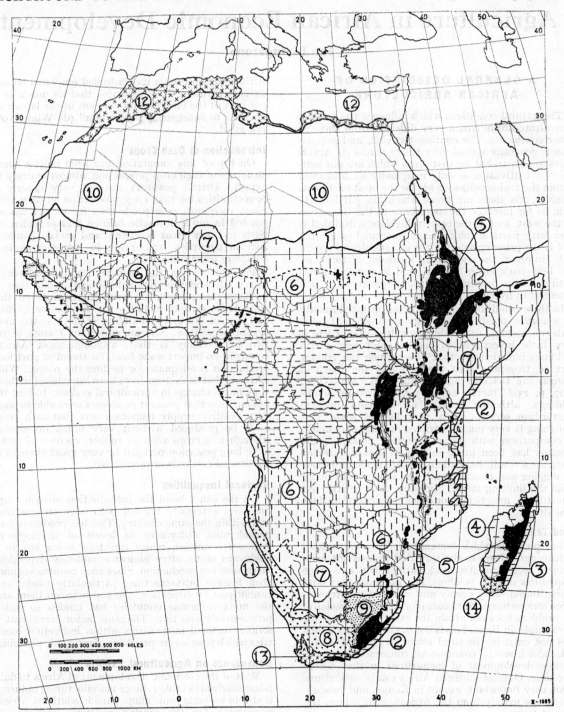

Vegetation Map of Africa

(See notes opposite)

Agriculture in African Economic Development

Ian Livingstone

A GENERAL DESCRIPTION OF AFRICAN AGRICULTURE

The natural conditions which influence the form of agriculture are in Africa very different from those in other continents. The continent is vast, and population is generally spread very thinly across it. Arable areas are separated by vast areas which are not suitable for cultivation or only marginally so, and even within the arable belts soils are for the most part poor. Against this there are areas which are particularly rich, as for instance the mountains of the Cameroon in the west, and of the eastern highlands. Rainfall is over large parts of the continent marginal or erratic, and is the primary determinant of agricultural potential. However, the widespread incidence of tsetse fly has held back entire regions, and in particular has until recently prevented the development of a rich potential in livestock.

In these conditions agriculture has operated mainly on a very extensive and apparently inefficient basis with considerable use of shifting cultivation. There is very little investment in capital equipment—farm buildings included—so that "over much the greater part of tropical Africa the hoe and the machete (panga) are the only agricultural tools" (de Wilde, 1967, p. 23). Tractors are very little used on smallholdings, although certain governments operate tractor-hire services on a very limited scale. Ox-ploughing is very much restricted in use, particularly in comparison with Asian countries, though great progress has been made in certain areas in recent years. As a result, heavy demands are made on labour for digging and clearing land, and labour is in many areas the limiting factor. Similarly there is little use of fertilizers, insecticides, or other elements of modern agriculture.

Land Tenure

One problem which fortunately does not bedevil African agriculture in the way that it does the agricultural sectors in Asia and Latin America is huge inequalities in land holdings. For the most part land is distributed fairly evenly and in those countries in which serious inequality exists (north Africa especially) the problem does not attain the same proportions as, for example, in India. This is not to say that inequality does not exist in the rural sector in tropical Africa and, indeed, several countries are concerned about the possible development of inequalities in that sector over time. Outside southern Africa estate agriculture is not very important, except in Kenya, and production comes mainly from the African smallholder, the peasant farmer.

Subsistence Production

Subsistence production continues to provide the foundation for agriculture. More specifically it has been stated that "A prominent characteristic of African agriculture is its continued emphasis on subsistence farming. It is probable that as much as 70 per cent of the land and 60 per cent of the labour are devoted to subsistence production" (de Wilde, 1967, pp. 21–2).

Introduction of Cash Crops

On top of this foundation has been built a superstructure of cash crop production, almost entirely for export. African peasants respond very eagerly to opportunities for cash crop production as they arise. Since 1900 cash crop production for export has expanded in quite dramatic fashion and provided the basis for very great economic and social change in African countries, amounting in many cases to a complete transformation.

For this reason the picture described above of heavy dependence on subsistence production is perhaps exaggerated. It must be remembered that subsistence output includes the production of food and, for instance, the building of houses, the most urgent necessities. Also an important feature of the African economy is that, although most African countries do import some food, for the most part food production is adequate for feeding the people. What is true is that cash crops have been introduced without very much change in agricultural *systems*. Indeed the main reason that peasant producers were able to show very positive supply responses was that cash crops *could* be produced without very much investment (though tree crops such as rubber, cocoa and coffee have long gestation periods) or very great changes in traditional methods of production.

Regional Inequalities

On the other hand the introduction of cash crops has been extremely uneven both between countries and within the same country. This has produced very considerable differences in levels of development between countries, many countries being left in a backward state, often almost completely dependent on subsistence production. Since such countries cannot then finance infrastructure, particularly roads, and cannot pay for education, the gap between them and the more fortunate countries has tended to widen progressively over time. The same factors have created serious regional inequalities within individual countries which pose severe problems of economic planning.

Dependence on Agricultural Exports

Most of the economic development of Africa to date is summarized in table 1. Since manufacturing industry is still in an embryonic stage outside southern Africa, production for the market consists especially of primary products, agricultural and mineral. From the table it can be seen that the important minerals in Africa north of the Zambezi are petroleum, copper, diamonds, iron ore and phosphates, sited in 13 or 14 fortunate countries.

[continued on p. 33

Table 1

COUNTRIES DEPENDENT ON ONE, TWO OR THREE MAJOR EXPORT COMMODITIES

	ONE MAJOR EXPORT	%
1. Libya[1]	Crude petroleum	99.9
2. Zambia[1]	Copper	95.7
3. Mauritius[1]	Cane sugar	91.0
4. Mauritania	Iron ore	87.0
5. Chad	Raw cotton	82.1
6. Réunion	Sugar	82.1
7. The Gambia[1,2]	Groundnuts and groundnut oil	80.7
8. Liberia[1]	Iron ore	71.9
9. Sierra Leone	Diamonds	71.0
10. Algeria	Crude petroleum	66.3
11. Zaire	Copper	66.1
12. Niger	Groundnuts, groundnut oil and cake	64.5

	TWO MAJOR EXPORTS		%
13. Sudan[1]	Cotton	Oilseeds, etc.	82.0
14. Somalia	Animals, incl. camels	Bananas and plantains	81.0
15. Rwanda	Coffee	Tin ores	77.6
16. Uganda[1,3]	Coffee	Cotton	73.8
17. Central African Republic	Diamonds	Cotton	69.9
18. Ethiopia[1]	Coffee	Hides and skins	69.6
19. Ghana	Cocoa	Aluminium	68.9
20. Upper Volta	Animals	Cotton	64.8
21. Nigeria[1]	Petroleum	Oilseeds, etc.	64.7
22. Togo	Cocoa	Phosphates	64.6
23. Congo (Brazzaville)	Logs	Diamonds	64.4
24. Gabon	Petroleum	Logs	64.2

	THREE MAJOR EXPORTS			%
25. Ivory Coast	Cocoa	Coffee	Logs	79.3
26. Malawi[1]	Tobacco	Tea	Groundnuts	75.9
27. Egypt[1]	Cotton	Textiles	Rice	75.3
28. Mali	Animals	Fish	Oilseeds, etc.	73.9
29. Senegal	Oilseeds, etc.	Phosphates	Fish	69.6
30. Cameroon	Cocoa	Coffee	Aluminium	67.7
31. Angola	Coffee	Diamonds	Iron ore	65.8

OTHER COUNTRIES: MOST IMPORTANT EXPORTS

32. Dahomey	Food, palm kernel oil, oilseeds, cotton
33. Kenya[1,3]	Coffee, tea, petroleum products
34. Madagascar	Coffee, spices, rice
35. Morocco	Phosphates, oranges, vegetables
36. Mozambique[4]	Cotton, cashew nuts, sugar
37. Rhodesia[1,5]	Tobacco, food, asbestos, machinery
38. South Africa[6]	Gold, food, diamonds, wool, copper
39. Tanzania[1,3]	Coffee, cotton, diamonds, sisal
40. Tunisia	Petroleum, olive oil, phosphates, fertilizers, fruit and vegetables

Source: United Nations, *Yearbook of International Trade Statistics 1969.*

NOTE: Figures give the percentage of total export earnings accounted for in 1969 (except where otherwise stated) by one, two or three major export commodities.

[1] Excluding re-exports.
[2] 1968.
[3] Excluding inter-trade between Kenya, Tanzania and Uganda in local produce and locally manufactured goods.
[4] Excluding exports of gold.
[5] 1965.
[6] Including Botswana, Lesotho, Swaziland and South West Africa (Namibia).

AFRICA: MAIN AGRICULTURAL and NON-AGRICULTURAL EXPORTS

PERCENTAGE SHARE OF MAJOR COMMODITIES IN TOTAL EXPORT EARNINGS, 1969

NORTH AFRICA

Algeria
Crude petroleum	66.3
Wine	14.0
Other	19.7

Egypt[1]
Raw cotton	40.4
Textile yarn, fabrics, etc.	17.9
Rice	17.1
Other	24.7

Libya[1]
Crude petroleum	99.9
Other	0.1

Morocco
Natural phosphates	22.4
Oranges	15.8
Vegetables	15.7
Other	46.1

Sudan[1]
Raw cotton	57.8
Oilseeds, oil and cake	24.3
Gum Arabic	10.1
Other	7.8

Tunisia
Crude petroleum	24.3
Olive oil	12.1
Natural phosphates	10.6
Other	53.0

WEST AFRICA (NORTHERN)

Central African Republic
Diamonds	44.8
Raw cotton	25.1
Coffee	15.3
Other	14.8

Chad
Raw cotton	82.1
Other	17.9

The Gambia[1,2]
Groundnuts	56.7
Groundnut oil	24.0
Food	16.8
Other	2.5

Mali
Live animals	48.2
Fish	14.1
Oilseeds, cake and meal	11.6
Raw cotton	10.0
Other	16.1

Mauritania
Iron ore	87.0
Other	13.0

Niger
Groundnuts, oil and cake	64.5
Live Cattle	12.3
Other	23.1

Senegal
Oilseeds, oil and cake	54.1
Other	45.9

Upper Volta
Live animals	36.9
Raw cotton	27.8
Oilseeds, oils and cake	17.9
Other	17.3

WEST AFRICA (SOUTHERN)

Cameroon
Cocoa	38.0
Coffee	20.2
Aluminium	9.5
Other	32.3

Dahomey
Food	26.4
Palm kernel oil	21.6
Oilseeds	13.8
Raw cotton	11.6
Other	26.5

Ghana
Cocoa	55.7
Aluminium	13.2
Logs and lumber	11.8
Other	19.3

Ivory Coast
Cocoa	27.2
Coffee	26.6
Saw and veneer logs	25.5
Other	20.7

Liberia[1]
Iron ore	71.9
Natural rubber	16.2
Other	12.0

Nigeria[1]
Crude petroleum	42.5
Oilseeds, oils and cake	22.2
Cocoa	16.5
Other	18.8

Sierra Leone[1]
Diamonds	71.0
Iron ore	11.3
Other	17.7

Togo
Cocoa beans	35.4
Calcium phosphates	29.2
Coffee	15.2
Other	20.1

CENTRAL AFRICA

Angola
Coffee	34.4
Diamonds	19.6
Iron ore	11.7
Other	34.2

Congo (Brazzaville)
Saw and veneer logs	49.6
Diamonds	14.8
Food	12.2
Veneer sheets	11.3
Other	12.1

Gabon
Petroleum	34.2
Saw and veneer logs	30.0
Manganese ores	20.2
Other	15.6

Rwanda
Coffee	46.5
Tin ores	31.1
Tungsten ores	10.9
Other	11.4

Zaire
Copper	66.1
Other	33.9

EASTERN AFRICA

Ethiopia[1]
Coffee	59.6
Hides and skins	10.0
Fruit and vegetables	9.9
Other	20.5

Kenya[1,3]
Coffee	26.7
Tea	17.9
Petroleum products	12.3
Other	43.1

Madagascar
Coffee	28.4
Spices	15.1
Other	56.5

Malawi[1]
Tobacco	34.6
Tea	26.0
Groundnuts	15.3
Other	24.1

Mauritius[1]
Cane sugar	91.0
Other	9.0

Mozambique[4]
Raw cotton	19.5
Cashew nuts	19.1
Raw sugar	13.4
Other	48.0

Réunion
Sugar	82.1
Essential oils	9.9
Other	8.0

Somalia
Live animals	56.9
Bananas and plantains	24.0
Other	19.0

Tanzania[1,3]
Coffee	15.5
Raw cotton	14.1
Diamonds	10.7
Sisal, etc.	9.6
Other	50.1

Uganda[1,3]
Coffee	55.8
Raw cotton	18.0
Other	26.2

Zambia[1]
Copper	95.7
Other	4.3

SOUTHERN AFRICA

Rhodesia[1,5]
Tobacco	33.0
Food	10.3
Other	56.7

South Africa[6]
Gold	33.7
Food	12.2
Diamonds	11.3
Other	42.7

For notes, *see* Table 1 on page 31. *Source:* United Nations, *Yearbook of International Trade Statistics 1969.*

continued from p. 30]

Since international trade in agricultural produce within Africa is comparatively unimportant, the production of cash crops for export outside Africa dominates the pattern of international trade, together with the minerals mentioned.

This pattern is shown in table 1. African countries are not only dependent on the export of primary products: they depend on a small number of such export commodities. The table shows twelve countries dependent on one major export; another twelve on two major exports; and seven more on three major exports. The figures in the table give the percentage of total exports accounted for by one, two, or three major exports in 1969. Extreme cases of dependence on a single export crop are Mauritius, on sugar, and Chad, on cotton.

THE USE OF AGRICULTURAL INPUTS IN AFRICAN AGRICULTURE

We now examine in more detail the use of agricultural inputs in African agriculture and how far inputs such as fertilizers, insecticides, new varieties of crop, and capital equipment may be expected to raise output.

Table 2
USE OF FERTILIZERS IN AFRICA AND ELSEWHERE
(1969–70)

	CONSUMPTION PER HECTARE OF ARABLE LAND (kg.)
Europe (excl. U.S.S.R.) . . .	158
U.S.S.R.	34
North and Central America . .	66
Oceania	33
South America	14
Africa	7
Asia (excl. China) . . .	20
WORLD TOTAL (excl. China . .	45

Source: FAO, *Annual Fertilizer Review* 1970, Table 12.

Fertilizers

By and large the African farmer makes little use of fertilizers. Table 2 shows that fertilizer consumption per hectare of arable land is minute in absolute terms and very low relative even to other developing areas. There has been a relatively rapid rate of increase in the levels of usage in the Near East and Africa, 17 per cent in 1967–68 compared to 7 per cent for the developed countries (FAO, 1969), but this rate has not matched the very rapid increases in Latin America (24 per cent in 1967–68) and the Far East (31 per cent). However, of the nine less developed countries that made particularly rapid progress at this time, only one, Senegal, was an African country. In fact fertilizer usage is very concentrated, Senegal and Morocco, significantly both countries where fertilizers

are manufactured locally, being outstanding. Morocco's *Opération engrais* for the application of fertilizers made a major contribution to a record wheat crop in 1968.

It is difficult to assess how far this neglect of fertilizers represents lack of economic rationality. It must be remembered firstly that the labour/land ratio is very low *on average* throughout Africa, and that where land is the abundant factor maximization of yield per acre is not desirable. There are on the other hand a number of particular areas and even regions subject to considerable population pressure and land shortage where this does not hold. Secondly, given the poor quality of the soils over much of Africa the responsiveness of arable land to fertilizer inputs is uncertain, and it cannot be said that adequate research on returns has been carried out. In particular, thirdly, there is a whole range of other factors—rainfall especially and pests and timing of operations by the farmer—which make yields of food and cash crops fluctuate widely from year to year, so that returns of fertilizer expenditure must be heavily discounted for risk. Generally speaking effective use of fertilizers depends on a number of agricultural practices being simultaneously adopted by the farmer, which has further limited their use.

There is, however, ample evidence of high returns from fertilizer use in particular situations and of positive response from African farms. For example, a fertilizer subsidy scheme was launched in the early 1960s in northern Nigeria for use in groundnut production: usage increased rapidly from 4,000 tons in 1962 to 35,000 tons in 1967.

Insecticides

Like fertilizers, insecticides are not used on a wide scale, despite research indicating very high returns in particular circumstances. We may take the spraying of cotton in Uganda as a case study. Laker (Bunting, 1970, p. 611) refers to a survey which showed that where farmers sprayed four times during the season (the third and fourth sprays protect the crop in a particularly critical period), yields were up on average by 425 lb. per acre. In fact the average number of sprays by farmers surveyed was 2.3, increasing yield by 174 lb. This represents both a very economic rate of return on investment and a significant shortfall on the potential rate of return with four sprays.

The insecticides in question were provided under a government subsidy scheme which was started in 1961. The response, shown in table 3, is interesting. Farmers accepted insecticides for only 25,000 acres in 1964, when they were made to pay 5s. per tin, still representing a very large subsidy, after having taken insecticides for 475,000 acres the previous year, when they were completely free. While there was no doubt considerable waste in 1963, and while in 1964 it was no doubt possible to use stocks of insecticide, it is difficult to explain why usage took four years to recover to the 1961 level despite demonstrated high returns. Clearly improvidence in setting aside cash and reluctance to divert cash to the purchase of inputs must have played a role. We may note, however, that by 1967, six years after the scheme started, usage had moved up to a much higher level, indicating a distinct response, if a delayed one, to the opportunity offered.

Table 3
AREA OF COTTON SPRAYED IN UGANDA, 1961–67 (BASED ON INSECTICIDE SALES) AND LEVEL OF SUBSIDY ON INSECTICIDE

	Area (acres)	Subsidy (%)
1961 . . .	104,000	83–100
1962 . . .	111,200	100
1963 . . .	475,000	100
1964 . . .	25,076	92
1965 . . .	54,000	92
1966 . . .	95,281	92
1967 . . .	173,225	n.a.

Source: J. S. Laker in Bunting, Ed., 1970, Table 1.

This is probably indicative of the position in Africa as a whole with respect to the adoption of improved methods of cultivation: not widespread, but many hopeful developments. In the case of cotton, spraying is much more usual now in Africa. Zambia is one country in which an organized spraying campaign has been successful in developing cotton production recently.

New Crop Varieties

How far can the "green revolution" be expected to affect Africa? In most parts of Africa the use of high-yielding cereal varieties is still at an experimental stage—maize in Kenya is the main exception—but developments in other parts of the developing world are very promising.

Very high-yielding varieties of rice have been developed through the research programme of the International Rice Research Institute in Manila, and the potential of the new rice hybrids has already been demonstrated in Cameroon and in Madagascar. This could have a major impact in west Africa in particular.

Hybrid varieties of millet and sorghum have been developed in the U.S.A. and in India, where they have increased yields by 60–80 per cent. In wheat production new varieties have doubled yields over local varieties in Pakistan, and under special irrigation conditions with progressive farmers yields have been increased as much as seven-fold in Pakistan. In the Near East the FAO Near East Wheat and Barley Improvement Project was started as long ago as 1952; developments in this crop should benefit north Africa in particular, and one or two other countries such as Tanzania where wheat is less important.

The potential of new varieties of groundnuts has also been shown in Senegal and in Uganda. Given the importance of oilseed production in Africa this could be of very great significance.

The main breakthrough in Africa has been in Kenya, in maize production. There was previously a great

deal of experience in the U.S.A. and since the early 1940s in Mexico, but interest in Kenya was not focused in this direction until the mid-1950s, when European large-scale farmers became interested, and

Table 4
ADOPTION OF HYBRID MAIZE IN KENYA BY LARGE- AND SMALL-SCALE FARMERS (ACREAGE)

	Area on Large-Scale Farms (ha.)	Area on Small-Scale Farms (ha.)	%	Total Area (ha.)
1963 .	156	4	(3)	160
1964 .	11,300	700	(6)	12,000
1965 .	21,900	8,000	(27½)	29,000
1966* .	25,200	15,100	(37½)	40,300
1967 .	52,100	53,900	(51)	106,000

* Seed supply limited by drought in 1965.

Source: G. F. Sprague in Bunting, 1970.

local hybrids were developed. However, the rapidity with which small-scale African farmers followed their examples, illustrated in table 4, is extremely instructive. The adoption of new varieties here was very much helped by a well organized system of demonstration plots and agricultural extension, as well as by the existence of an efficient system of marketing. Yields of as much as eight times those common in the area have been obtained in trials, and already a substantial increase in marketed production has occurred. Tanzania, next door, is hoping to expand maize production also and attempts are being made to introduce new hybrids in limited areas.

With these possibilities for maize, millets, rice, groundnuts and wheat, one or other of which provides a staple part of diets over the bulk of the continent, prospects appear reasonably good for substantial increases in food supply in the future. Considerable research is still needed, however, in the African situation and many countries are not well prepared in order to organize the widespread adoption of improvements as research demonstrates the possibilities.

Capital Equipment

The limited use of animal or tractor power in African agriculture has already been noted. Table 5 indicates how poorly Africa compares to other parts of the Third World in this respect.

Calculations by agricultural economists and the use of tractors in many African countries indicate that in the *typical* African farming situation tractors are very uneconomic, particularly in comparison with ox-ploughing. This is apart from the question of foreign exchange costs arising from having to import tractors. Most schemes show a very low rate of utilization of equipment, partly related to the existence of small plots.

As a result, for instance, plans for increased use of tractors in Sierra Leone have been reviewed. Mechanization, which was to play a prominent role in Tanzania's village settlement programme, is not to be a significant element in the new *ujamaa* village programme. In Ghana the whole programme for mechanization and for state-corporation farming is being

Table 5
USE OF ANIMAL AND TRACTOR POWER IN THE LESS-DEVELOPED COUNTRIES

Regions and Countries	Power Units per 1,000 of Agricultural Population
Africa	21
Far East	53
Near East	64
Latin America	133
Morocco	59
India	76
Japan	104
U.S.A.	2,864

NOTE: Tractor power expressed as mechanical horsepower divided by five, animal power converted to horse equivalents.

Source: FAO (1969).

reorganized. In Kenya tractor use is being left mainly to private initiative, except on specific schemes. And in Uganda the programme for group farms, which was based on mechanization, has run into serious difficulties. Government tractor hire services have proved very expensive and have either been abandoned or have required heavy subsidy on a continuing basis.

A particular feature has been the poor maintenance of machinery, which can have serious effects on cost. This has been a feature of both large schemes—such as the Ghana state farm programme and the *Office du Niger* scheme in Mali—and of small schemes. The Gezira Scheme in Sudan has managed to avoid this. Where tractors are used on a large scale—except in a non-viable or poorly organized scheme—it is, of course, easier to provide efficient maintenance services.

Another aspect of the use of tractors in Africa is that the existence of small plots creates the problem of organization of sharing of machinery, if not actual co-operative production. These problems of managerial and social organization have not been tackled well, and have not been approached with caution as they should have been.

This is true also because the overhead costs of mechanization call for an intensification of production if it is to pay. Irrigation schemes provide the best opportunity, where there is a high-priced crop or where several crops a year may be raised.

Intensification also means an *increased* demand for labour with mechanization, rather than a reduced one, partly because of increased acreage—requiring increased weeding for example—and partly because the use of fertilizers, pesticides, and improved seeds in-

volved in more commercialized farming all imply labour demands. Baldwin (Niger) and Joy (Uganda) have pointed to evidence on both sides of Africa of reluctance to supply the additional labour required, with the result that the use of tractors has not been accompanied either by increased acreage per family farmed or by increased yields, which would have helped to cover mechanization costs (quoted in de Wilde, 1967, Vol. 1, pp. 97 and 98).

ATTEMPTS AT AGRICULTURAL TRANSFORMATION

There has been a whole host of agricultural schemes in Africa aimed at promoting agricultural progress or solving serious agricultural problems. There is also a wide range of types of settlement scheme. Some schemes involve the planned relocation of population and others do not: a major difference. Some schemes have aimed at the sedenterization of nomadic peoples. Irrigation schemes generally imply the relocation of people on empty land, and constitute a special model of settlement scheme (Apthorpe, 1968, p. 5).

The purpose of the Kenya settlement schemes was first to relieve population pressure in overcrowded African farming areas and second to take the opportunity provided by the availability adjacently of vacated or underutilized land in the former "White Highlands", a programme involving the transfer of population on a substantial scale. The problem here was not the availability of willing settlers, as has occurred in some major schemes, but rather the administrative problem of organizing a smooth transfer at a rapid rate, and the maintenance of efficient farming with high yields per acre after the switch from large-scale commercial farmers to small-scale peasant farmers.

In contrast the group farms in West Nigeria during the early 1960s were aimed at solving another aspect of the population problem, that of providing a livelihood for school-leavers. There has been a similar scheme in Uganda (described by C. Hutton in Apthorpe, 1968).

The success of settlement schemes may depend not only on how severe the population pressure is—severe in the Kenya case but less so in respect of the Tanzania village settlement programme of the 1960s or in the *Office du Niger* scheme—but also on how far the resettled population is expected to move, again much greater in the latter two schemes than in the Kenya example.

Success depends not only on the pressure of forces pushing people into the scheme, but also on the pull of the scheme itself—the relative level of incomes it can offer. Irrigation may provide the opportunity for great increases in incomes relative to other areas; and, if this is combined with the opportunity to grow a particularly valuable cash crop, as in the case of the Gezira cotton scheme, we have the most favourable conditions. The *Office du Niger* scheme in particular lacked the same commercial "pull" as Gezira.

Finally, settlement schemes may incorporate a programme of mechanization or not, just as mechanization schemes may or may not involve some resettlement of population.

Some Specific Settlement Schemes

The West Nigerian settlement schemes of the early 1960s were, as we have said, aimed at locating on the land some of the vast number of school-leavers being produced every year. It was hoped to emulate the success of the *moshavim* of Israel, but the possibility of doing this within a different social structure was not adequately considered. The cost of establishing one settler was planned at the fantastically high level of £4,000 (income per head in Nigeria being around £25); by the end of 1966 1,200 settlers had been installed on 19 settlements at a cost of £7 million, amounting in fact to £4–5,000 per family (de Wilde, 1967). The costs include generous allowances to settlers over the long period before tree crops matured, not to mention two years' training at a farm institute. Not surprisingly school-leavers were found not to be motivated towards a hard farming life, particularly after having been subsidized for so long. Staff to administer the scheme was inadequate. Yields and costs were not forecast accurately.

In Kenya at the time of independence in 1963 some 7 million acres were owned by European farmers many of whom wished to sell up; within five years 2 million acres had been taken over by African farmers, by no means all in an orderly fashion. There were to be three types of assisted settler, corresponding to different levels of planned income, but the most important category was that of landless and unemployed Africans with little or no capital or agricultural knowledge. Each settlement was to be of about 300 or 400 settlers, with about 30 acres per family. The planned level of income was modest, about £25–70 per annum, and unlike the West Nigerian scheme, realistic in relation to the rest of the economy. Already by June 1966 70 schemes had been established covering 0.7 million acres and employing nearly 24,000 settlers. The ultimate target of a million acres—the scheme was referred to as the One Million Acres Settlement Scheme —was well within reach. Costs of settlement were modest, apart from purchase of the land itself.

The village settlement programme was set up in Tanzania in the early 1960s following the recommendation of the World Bank Report on Tanganyika in 1961 of a transformation approach in agriculture, in view of the pessimistic outlook for agricultural improvement within the more densely populated (backward?) peasant farming areas. Transformation would transplant settlers to newly-cleared areas, and make use of more modern methods of cultivation, including mechanization, than in the traditional farming areas. The scheme failed, and was replaced within five years. And agricultural output in the traditional areas increased substantially within the same period without much assistance.

Large-scale Schemes

We can also distinguish between settlement schemes on the basis of the *scale* of the scheme, Africa in particular having witnessed some of the most ambitious agricultural transformation schemes.

The Tanganyika groundnut scheme is perhaps the most famous failure. This was put forward in a British White Paper in 1947. The anxiety to reach a breakthrough in development is reflected in the plan's statement that: "No significant increase in the present output of oilseeds can be achieved . . . by the existing methods of peasant production. Nothing but the most highly mechanized agricultural methods on a vast scale never previously envisaged will result in any appreciable amelioration of the present disastrous food position" (quoted by Kamarck, 1967, p. 119).

The statement shows clearly the pessimism regarding peasant methods and over-optimism regarding large-scale mechanical methods. The scheme cost some $80 million, most of which was lost.

The Gambia poultry scheme was launched by the British Colonial Development Corporation at about the same time for the large-scale raising of chickens. A million dollars was lost here.

Francophone Africa had its "groundnut scheme", perhaps in the shape of the *Office du Niger* scheme in Mali. In fact this was a very much bigger scheme, which was launched in 1930 and has been continuing since, absorbing something approaching $200 million.

The schemes had much in common in that in each case forward planning was wholly inadequate. Technical factors such as soils and rainfall were wrongly assessed, as were the physical and economic possibilities for mechanization. The human factors involved in recruiting and establishing settlers were underestimated and administrative apparatus to cope with the dimensions of the projects was not provided.

The Gezira scheme in Sudan is the success story of agricultural transformation based on irrigation. We have already discussed factors favouring this success. It should be added that, although the Gezira Board, which runs the scheme, was set up in 1950, the scheme itself developed out of irrigation experience in the area going back more than 25 years. Its success shows that large-scale transformation is not impossible where there is careful planning, through knowledge in advance of technical and economic factors, avoidance of over-centralization, and high potential incomes.

Socialist Transformation Schemes

A great number of African countries have experimented at one time or another with socialist schemes of different kinds. There have been two kinds of motivation behind these. For some the main aim has been to raise productivity to new levels through mechanization: it was considered necessary, in order to tap economies of scale from mechanization, to work the land in large units, either through state farms or more commonly collective or group farms, rather than through individual African smallholders. For others mechanization has not been the main aim, but rather the socialization of agriculture as such: the *ujamaa* village programme of Tanzania is the best and most current example. This is aimed at reducing inequalities in the rural sector, avoiding the development of a rural wage-earning proletariat which could be "exploited" by large farmers, and deliberately organizing social as well as economic life on a communal rather than competitive basis. Mechanization is to play a minimal part in this programme, since, as already mentioned, Tanzania has had previous disillusioning experiences in this direction.

State Farms

The main countries to experiment with state farms have been Ghana and Guinea. Apart from the ideological attractiveness of state organization *per se*, the motivation has been a feeling of impatience with tradition-bound peasant farming as compared to modern and supposedly high-productivity methods. Thus in Ghana the state farms were expected "to show the advantages of large-scale mechanized socialist farming over small-scale peasant farming" (First Biennial Report, State Farms Corporation, quoted by Gordon in Bunting, 1970).

Farms were established in Ghana from 1962 under the Ghana State Farms Corporation. The programme was launched in an incautious manner, the number of farms increasing from 26 in 1962 to 107 in 1963 and rising to 135 farms with 20,800 workers in February 1966, at the time of the *coup*. A number of basic errors were made: peasants were antagonized by the brutal manner in which their land was seized without compensation to be turned over to state farming; there was gross over-ordering and misuse of tractors and other expensive equipment; the farms were not well-managed, with over-centralization of decisions in Accra; and finally the land probably did not have such a high potential yield as to easily cover high running costs.

State farms were also launched on a wide scale in Guinea, and these too failed badly. Again poor management and failure to cover heavy costs of mechanization were to blame.

Ironically enough there were great similarities in the motivation behind these socialistic projects and the large-scale transformation schemes of the colonial period, such as the groundnut scheme: in both cases a pessimistic view was taken of the possibilities for progress through conservative or "backward" peasant farmers, there was impatience with attempts to cajole small farmers, through agricultural extension and other means, to higher levels of productivity, and a desire to take a short cut through direct state action with minimal involvement by peasants in decision-making. The failure of state farms so far have been for the same kind of reasons: inadequate technical/economic preparation; incautiously rapid rates of implementation; and lack of consideration of the human factor involved in labour supply or settler participation.

As with transformation schemes in general, therefore, this experience does not prove state farms to be inherently unworkable—after all estate agriculture, which is similarly organized, has proved highly successful in many parts of Africa—but that a more careful and selective approach is required. Thus Tanzania, for example, plans currently to establish only a limited number of state farms in wheat production and cattle ranching, where economies of scale are deemed to exist.

Co-operative Production

The more appealing form of socialist production in African countries has, however, been communal farming by co-operative groups. Hopes for this form of development have been raised by the existence of traditional forms of co-operation in African society—communal grazing, for example, on the production side, and the extended family on the side of distribution of benefits. Moreover, co-operatives have been extremely successful in Africa at the marketing level, which is held to indicate possibilities for extension into production.

It is probable, however, that the extent of real co-operation in the traditional system has been exaggerated by western observers with only superficial knowledge of African societies. Even if individual land titles do not exist, land is largely worked on an individual basis, and, as one observer has pointed out, even "within African polygamous families it seems so necessary to get direct responsibilities and incentives for labour that usually each wife has her separate plots" (Raeburn, 1959, p. 49). The most fundamental problem in co-operative production is, of course, that of incentives, together with the peasant's desire for the security associated with having his own piece of land. This is the reason, no doubt, why, although a number of countries in each of east, west and north Africa have experimented with group farming, the results to date have been uniformly disappointing with very few exceptions.

Group Cotton Farms in Central Nyanza, Kenya

These farms, which apparently grew up spontaneously (de Wilde, 1967), were based on a component of traditional society, the kinship group known as *jokokwaro*, and have apparently been viable and successful in improving methods of cultivation to some extent. The farms, which started on a basis of sugar cane production, are now based on cotton production. There were about 90 farms in 1964.

The champs collectifs in Mali

In Mali the government encouraged farmers to move in the direction of co-operative production by encouraging groups to work common fields, *champs collectifs*, as well as their own individual holdings. As has happened elsewhere in this situation, less attention was given by farmers to these communal fields than to their own holdings, and there has been no apparent interest in expanding the size of the co-operative fields relative in individual holdings.

Group Farms in Uganda

Although earlier attempts at co-operative farms in Uganda in the 1950s had come to nothing, a major programme for group farms was launched in 1963. These had no strong ideological motivation, however, and were essentially schemes for mechanization. As an official statement at the time said (*see* Charsley in

Apthorpe, 1968, p. 57), the scheme was "designed to enable modern machinery to be applied" in cotton production. The first three group farms were established in 1963, and 20 more added in 1964. The second five-year plan, 1966–71, gave a major role within the agricultural sector to an expanded programme of group farms. Detailed information on performance is not readily available, but one farm, which is described as typical, has been analysed in detail (see Charsley in Apthorpe, 1968). Land is cultivated on a "block" basis, block cultivation of cotton in this case, with each member each year allocated a different piece within the block. A central area is provided for settlement and food crop production.

A number of factors have contributed to what has eventually been the disintegration of the programme. The most fundamental one lies in the economics of mechanization, where despite earlier negative experience and research demonstrating the costliness of tractors, the costs were higher than expected. In addition, however, there was poor settlement planning, giving rise to a reluctance to live on site and incomplete commitment to the group farm. There was a failure to specify what the form of management and organization would be: in some cases responsibility would be with the District Agricultural Officer, who was too busy with other duties; in others, responsibility lay with the committee of the Co-operative Marketing Society, although only a percentage of society members were participants in and thus had a direct interest in the group farm. Finally, where a manager was provided, he was generally a very junior and inexperienced expatriate who had problems of communication with farmers.

Ujamaa Vijijini (Socialist Villages) in Tanzania

The ultimate purpose of the *ujamaa* village programme in Tanzania, launched in 1967, is to put the entire rural sector on to a socialist basis. The aims are both social and economic. On the social side the disadvantages of a competitive individualistic system are pointed out: the development of inequality, the creation of a work-force of landless labourers dependent on others for employment, and other forms of rural differentiation and stratification. In contrast communal working of the land is considered to provide a better way of life for all, and to be desirable *per se*, independently of any economic advantage. The case has been precisely put by Nyerere himself (1967):

" . . . the moment such a man extends his farm to the point where it is necessary for him to employ labourers in order to plant or harvest the full acreage, then the traditional system of ujamaa has been killed" (p. 7) . . . "as land becomes more scarce we shall find ourselves with a farmers' class and a labourers' class, with the latter being unable either to work for themselves or to receive a full return for the contribution they are making to the total output. They will become a 'rural proletariat' depending on the decisions of other men for their existence, and subject in consequence to all the subservience, social and economic inequality, and insecurity, which such a position involves" (p. 8).

The second aim, however, is directly economic in that this form of organization could lead to direct increases in output. First joint work by villagers in clearing land, putting up buildings, and so on could be more effective. Secondly, since rural population in Tanzania is so scattered, there are advantages in bringing them closer together—in villagization in fact —because economies can be effected in the supply of infrastructural services, such as schools and water supplies. Most important, it is hoped that agricultural extension can be rendered much more effective when addressing itself to more concentrated settlements organized in the *ujamaa* spirit.

The method is essentially voluntary, although there are incentives in the form of favouritism in the provision of government services, and considerable political exhortation. By September 1970 there were already 1,500 designated *ujamaa* villages, though a large proportion had not changed much except in name. Since the policy is one of gradual change throughout the whole rural sector, it is far too early to pass judgment. The major problems include the highly individualistic behaviour of peasant farmers in the richer cash-crop areas and that of organizing nomadic cattle peoples in the drier areas. Critics certainly need to come up with alternative answers to the problem of inequality where a person's means of livelihood are closely tied to his having access to land, and to the problem of changing traditional attitudes and methods on a broad front.

The opposite policy is, of course, that of encouraging the progressive farmer, which has been the usual one in the past. The promotion of the progressive farmer, the *Chikumbe* in Malawi, who might lead by example, is for instance currently stressed in that country. What is not certain is how effective such example really is, or what the long-term effects on stratification are.

THE ROLE OF AGRICULTURE IN AFRICAN ECONOMIC DEVELOPMENT

While agriculture in Africa faces a whole range of serious problems, and the promotion of rural development in Africa will be an extremely hazardous affair, it remains true that agriculture will continue to provide the foundation for development as a whole, as most African governments have generally recognized.

Agriculture and Industry

In the first place agriculture provides an overwhelming part of gross domestic product in all African countries outside South Africa, and a large proportion of people are employed, or rather self-employed in this sector. It follows that high rates of growth in national income will not be attainable unless the agricultural sector contributes in a major way. This is particularly so because there is a finite limit to the amount of new industry which can be established in any given period, depending on the industrial base so far achieved, the supply of entrepreneurship, the growth of administrative capacity within government departments and agencies, and the development of general technical education. A rate of growth for manufacturing industry of 10 to 15 per cent per annum is probably a ceiling, and by itself can contribute only 1 or 1½ per cent to total national income growth per annum at the most.

A stronger case for rapid industrialization exists where there is land shortage due to pressure of population, resulting in diminishing returns on effort in the agricultural sector. As we have pointed out, population pressure sufficient to cause acute land shortage currently exists in Africa only in localized areas, even if high rates of population growth imply a threat for the future.

In countries with population surplus industrialization becomes urgent as a means of employment creation to absorb surplus workers. Due especially to the fairly rigid capital/labour ratios which have existed in manufacturing industry so far, however, the latter has not been a very effective employment creator. To take two examples, total paid employment in Uganda has stayed almost constant at around 230,000 since 1952, despite considerable expansion of industry. Paid employment in Ghana increased somewhat faster, from 267,000 in 1956 to 362,000 in 1965; but the figures are tiny fractions compared to the total work-force of the country.

Moreover, income distribution considerations, which should be even more important at low levels of income than high, also suggest a strong agricultural emphasis in the development effort. This is the main reason for the rural development emphasis in socialist Tanzania, for example (Nyerere, 1967). Additional industries may directly increase the incomes of only a tiny fraction of the population: to increase the incomes of the mass of the population at all rapidly, agricultural development is essential. The only way to develop a backward region, as we have seen, may be to find a suitable cash crop.

Innovation in Agriculture

Many economists who have favoured a heavy industrial emphasis have done so because of their extreme pessimism regarding the possibilities for rapid change in the rural sector, with all its conservatism and backwardness. This view, as we have seen, does not do justice to the very great economic and social change which has taken place in the last fifty years and particularly in the last twenty. However inadequate his methods of cultivation, the peasant farmer has not been slow to take up the opportunities as they have arisen for the production of cash crops for export.

Clearly there is need for research into the best methods of agricultural extension, which in most African countries needs complete rethinking and reorganization, but there is evidence that a frontal assault on the problem, combining extension advice with agricultural credit and other forms of assistance, can bring increasing returns. The expansion of African agriculture in Kenya under the Swynnerton Plan illustrates the possibilities for concerted action, even if opportunities vary greatly in different parts of

Africa. Thus in 1956 African farmers in Kenya received £5.86 million in gross revenue from cash crops, and in 1964 £14 million. Political independence appears to provide the possibilities for a considerable fresh momentum, where the new governments are prepared to make strenuous attempts at mobilizing the rural development effort.

Significant technical advances are not confined to manufacturing industry either. Whereas the "green revolution" has not yet reached much of Africa, there are clear indications already, as we have seen, of the possibilities for dramatic increases of the yield of foodcrops, for example.

Marketing being a serious constraint on agricultural production over much of Africa, the development of transport and of marketing facilities will most likely permit considerable expansion of output.

Africa's High Export Dependence

Another case for industrialization arises from the high dependence of less developed countries on exports, and a very small number of export commodities at that, exposing these countries to short-term instability as the world prices of these commodities fluctuate. Table 1 above described the position of Africa in this respect.

As a recent study (Macbean, 1966) has clearly demonstrated, it is not necessarily true that less developed countries do have a greater dependence on foreign trade; or that export instability has been greater for these countries; or that the instability which has occurred has had much effect on development. Some of the explanation lies in the fact that exports should be calculated as a percentage of gross domestic product *including* the large subsistence sector; and secondly that the prices of many primary products are in fact quite stable.

Moreover, while dependence on a limited number of export commodities indicates an urgent need for diversification—particularly where market prospects for individual commodities are poor—this need not imply industrialization. Diversification within the agricultural sector may be not only possible but easier: table 1 above shows eight African countries (plus the South African customs union) which do not have strong export concentration (and are only partially assisted by mineral exports). To diversify the source of incomes for a large number of people agriculture will be more effective.

The Terms of Trade

The strongest case for pushing ahead as fast as possible with industrialization is based on the behaviour of the terms of trade between primary products (exported by the less developed countries) and manufactured products (imported by them), or rather between agricultural products and manufactured goods. The evidence in this direction is not at all clear, however, at least until the post-war period. Bhagwati, for example, has recently examined the behaviour of the terms of trade between 1950 and 1967 and found that "the average terms of trade for food and agricultural non-food items have indeed remained sluggish recently instead of tending to improve; but they do not compare too unfavourably with levels in the pre-Korean War and pre-1939 periods . . . " (J. Bhagwati, "Agriculture and international terms of trade", in Bunting, 1970). In Africa sisal is one product which has been badly hit by falling prices (affecting Tanzania, which managed, however, to maintain export revenue by increasing and diversifying other *agricultural* output). The market prospects for coffee, an important crop in nine or ten African countries, will not permit much further expansion to more countries or within existing producing countries. But for many other

agricultural export commodities market prospects are reasonably firm.

The greatest constraint on industrial expansion in Africa is the generally low level of incomes. Agricultural development by increasing local purchasing power can permit a faster rate of industrialization, and provide the quickest route to an industrialized state. In this respect, even if a decline in the terms of trade robs the less developed countries of a *part* of the revenue from increased agricultural output, industry may still be capable of a faster eventual rate of increase through emphasis on a major effort in the agricultural sector now.

REFERENCES

DE WILDE, J. C. *Experiences with Agricultural Development in Tropical Africa.* Vols. I and II, Johns Hopkins University, 1967.

FAO. *The State of Food and Agriculture* (annual). Rome.

BUNTING, A. H. (Ed.). *Change in Agriculture.* Duckworth, 1970; especially: J. BHAGWATI, "Effects of international terms of trade on change in agriculture; G. F. SPRAGUE, "Factors affecting the adoption of hybrid maize in the United States and Kenya"; W. ROIDER, "Nigerian farm settlement schemes"; J. GORDON, "State farms in Ghana"; J. S. LAKER, "The campaign against cotton diseases and pests in Uganda".

APTHORPE, R. (Ed.). *Land Settlement and Rural Development in Eastern Africa.* Nkanga Editions, Makerere University, Kampala, 1968; especially:

R. APTHORPE, "Planned Social Change and Settlement"; C. HUTTON, "Making Modern Farmers"; S. CHARSLEY, "The Group Farm Scheme in Uganda".

KAMARCK, A. M. *The Economics of African Development.* London, Pall Mall, 1967.

RAEBURN, J. R. "Some Economic Aspects of African Agriculture", *East African Economic Review,* January, 1959.

NYERERE, J. K. *Socialism and Rural Development.* Dar es Salaam, Government Printer, 1967.

MACBEAN, A. I. *Export Instability and Economic Development.* London, 1966.

LIVINGSTONE, I. "Agriculture versus Industry in Economic Development", *Journal of Modern African Studies,* 6/3, 1968.

Problems of Industrialization

A. F. Ewing*

Africa started on the road toward industrialization considerably later than the other under-developed regions of the world. Much of Latin America has been accustomed to some industry for decades, even though in many countries of the sub-continent progress has been relatively slow. There are poor countries in Asia whose industrial map is little different from that of Africa, but others whose incomes per head are as low as in Africa although a start in industrial development was made many years ago. India is the leading case, but there are others, admittedly smaller, who have made steady industrial progress since the Second World War: Pakistan, Thailand, the Philippines, Taiwan, South Korea, Hong Kong, Singapore. Until the war Africa, excepting South Africa, and to a very limited extent Egypt, was essentially a continent of primitive agriculture and a producer for export of unprocessed mining products and tropical agricultural items such as coffee, cocoa, groundnuts, palm oil and hardwoods. Egypt's serious industrial development began in the early 1950s. Beyond a certain range of simple consumer goods, the rest of Africa, for the most part, became industry-conscious for the first time with the coming of political independence in the late 1950s and early 1960s. Since then, although there have been serious efforts towards development and considerable progress in many countries, the handicap of a late start means that the industrial map is still much blanker in Africa than in most of the other parts of the under-developed world. An assessment of the situation at the beginning of the 1970s without recourse to extensive statistics—in any case still far from comprehensive—is not easy. In this respect, as in many others in this chapter, the principal source of information is the work of the United Nations Economic Commission for Africa.

THE PRESENT STATE OF INDUSTRIALIZATION

To assess the present state of industry and later to examine the development perspectives, it is convenient to use a broad economic classification: first, consumer goods, mainly food and textiles (including allied products such as footwear); second, intermediate goods: metals, non-metallic minerals, forest products and chemicals (including fertilizers); third, capital goods: metal products, mechanical engineering, electrical engineering and transport equipment. The building and civil engineering industry is of a somewhat different nature, ranging from artisanal methods to highly organized and mechanized jobs such as large dams, power stations, bridges, factories and offices, which are capital goods, and houses, which are durable consumer goods. The metal manufacture categories above also include consumer goods of varying durability, from transistors to refrigerators and passenger cars, but such industry will not be widespread in Africa for some time.

Most African industry at present is in the consumer goods category. Nearly all countries produce soft drinks and beer. All of them process cereals in one form or another. Production of meat and fish and associated products on an industrial scale is determined in the first instance by resource patterns, and is limited in extent. The same is true of fruit and fruit juices, and vegetables. Countries which have made a start in one or other of these areas are actual or potential exporters, e.g. Tunisia, Kenya, Madagascar and Ivory Coast. The big producers and exporters of vegetable oil also produce some oils for domestic consumption, for example, Zaire, Nigeria and Senegal. The pattern of sugar production is still specialized, with among major producers Mauritius, Uganda, Ethiopia, Congo (Brazzaville), Nigeria and Ivory Coast. Africa is still a large-scale importer of food but this reflects underdevelopment of agriculture rather than of processed food industry, for which the domestic demand is at present limited.

Textile and clothing industries are widespread, although there are still substantial imports of these goods from outside the continent. All the cotton-growing countries carry out ginning but, excepting Egypt and, to a lesser extent, Nigeria, Ethiopia and the East African Community countries, spinning, weaving and finishing facilities, based overwhelmingly on cotton, are relatively primitive. Almost all countries produce footwear, often basically rubber (grown in a few countries) or plastic (which is imported).

In the intermediate goods category, almost all countries produce simple metal products, mainly from imported steel. Apart from North Africa, iron and steel production is confined to re-rolling in a few countries, e.g. Ghana. Aluminium metal is produced in Cameroon and will shortly be in Egypt, but several countries produce simple products from imported metal, such as domestic utensils. Iron ore and non-ferrous ores are almost all exported, mainly in unprocessed form. Timber is produced for export, mainly in the form of logs, but all countries produce furniture and builders' joinery, and the big timber exporters in west and central Africa also produce plywood and veneers, e.g. Gabon. Pulp and paper is so far confined to north Africa. North, east and central Africa, as sub-regions, are approaching self-sufficiency in cement but there are still substantial imports into west Africa. Concrete and clay products are produced by relatively primitive methods almost everywhere. Production of glass bottles is widespread. That of chemicals, apart from North Africa, is virtually confined to soap, liquid air, sulphuric acid and, in the mining countries, explosives, and final preparation of pharmaceuticals and perfumes. Nitro-

* Although the author is a Permanent Staff Member of the UN Secretariat, the views he expresses here are entirely his own.

gen fertilizers are produced in Egypt and Algeria, phosphate fertilizers in Egypt, Morocco, Tunisia and Uganda, and potash in Congo (Brazzaville). In capital goods, the industrial map is almost blank except in Egypt and, to a limited extent, the Maghreb. This is particularly true of mechanical and electrical engineering. In the transport equipment category there is limited assembly of cars on the basis of imported components, mainly in north Africa, and production of coastal and river craft, as well as ship repair, in, for example, North Africa, Zaire and Nigeria.

The broad picture is one of concentration on simple consumer goods through import substitution, and limited production of intermediate goods, with capital goods confined to very few countries. In much of the existing industry the value added locally is low.

AFRICA'S ADVANTAGES AND DISADVANTAGES

In the approach to industrialization Africa starts with certain natural advantages. The natural resources endowment, even on the basis of far from sufficient surveying and prospection, is rich: abundant high-grade iron ore, non-ferrous metals, phosphates, potash, marine salt, oil and natural gas, limestone, cotton, timber, the natural potential for meat and fish production on an industrial scale and vast cheap hydro-power potential.

The obstacles are also evident. Much of the climate is hostile. If the population pressure is not for the most part serious, there is a dearth of management and middle-grade personnel and skilled labour. The distances are vast and despite recent progress, the transport and communication system is geared to the needs of a colonial system, with the lines running to former metropolitan countries. Although, again, there has been much recent progress, energy is still mainly potential. The agricultural base is weak. It is now well understood that industrial growth is soon arrested without parallel agricultural development to provide food and raw materials to meet a growing demand, just as agricultural development depends partly on inputs from industry, tools and chemicals, and partly on the stimulus of increased demand from the industrial sector. Finally, most African markets are small. On the basis of World Bank GNP estimates for 1968 (which show higher and more realistic figures than those derived from conversion of national currency figures to US dollars at the official exchange rate), there are only ten countries with a GNP of more than US $200 a head (three in North Africa); and 18 with less than US $100. Including the off-shore islands only six countries have a population of more than ten million; there are 32 with less than four million, 23 with less than 2 million and 18 with less than one million.

THE STRATEGY

The need for industrialization starts from the pattern of the international economy. Africa exports primary products, for which the income elasticity of demand is low (with limited exceptions such as oil and copper); and imports industrial goods for which the income elasticity of demand is high. If its economies are to grow, more and more industrial goods have to be produced within Africa. Moreover, it is only through industrialization that the structure of an economy is changed and can grow, since the productivity of labour in industry is higher than in agriculture, and although, as already indicated, the agricultural sector must also grow, the industrial sector has to do so still faster. Again, not any kind of industry will do. The tendency is to start with consumer goods through import substitution. But the limits of this process are soon reached, as has been experienced in Latin America and much of Asia. More intermediate and capital goods have to be imported, leading quickly to a foreign exchange constraint, unless these industries are laid down progressively. Consumer goods are often produced at high cost behind tariff barriers and they do nothing to change the structure of the economy. Their production is a drain on the necessarily scarce investment resources, which could be applied to the installation of intermediate and capital goods capable of promoting cumulative benefits.

It is capital goods which are the motor—above all machinery which produces more machinery and raises the productivity of labour everywhere. This is a pattern through which virtually all economies which are now advanced have passed. The time-scale in the application of this strategy can vary from country to country, partly as a result of natural resource endowment. as in the Maghreb, and partly as a result of historical factors, as in Zaire, Ghana, Kenya, Senegal and Ivory Coast. There are other countries, such as Tanzania and Cameroon, which are still mass importers of consumer goods, yet which possess appropriate raw material bases favouring a mixed strategy including continued import substitution of consumer goods.

In Africa there is another vital element in the strategy. Most markets are small and much industry in the intermediate and capital goods categories is restricted to a minimum size below which production is not economic, benefiting with corresponding cost advantages at levels above this. African countries will, therefore, have to group their markets and combine their efforts to make possible production of, for example, iron and steel, fertilizers, basic chemicals, machine tools, industrial equipment, earth-moving equipment, turbines and generators, and electric motors.

Some examples can be given of minimum scales of output in tons per annum, together with an indication of what this means in African market terms. Light steel requires a minimum output of 500,000 to one million tons, using conventional processes, and 300,000, if very cheap electric power is available. West Africa's estimated consumption of all steel products by 1980 is about 2 million tons. The economic size of a multi-product integrated works is about 3.5 million tons. The minimum scale for ammonia. the basis of nitrogen fertilizer, is 50,000 tons, though costs fall considerably at higher figures. Two to three plants in west and one in central Africa would be justified by the prospective market. The scale of output for the main acids and caustic soda is 5,000 to 10,000 tons, which means that about two per sub-region would be feasible. For pulp and paper it is 40,000 tons, justified in present African conditions only if overseas markets can be found. The whole Maghreb market would support one flat glass plant of 10,000 tons It is estimated that the whole east African market would support one each of the following industries: ropes, cables, tyre wires (40 to 50,000 tons); wire drawing for fencing, netting and wire gauze (30,000); drilling tools (2,000); metal cutting saws (1,000); lathes (3,000); and two each of the following: milling tools (4 to 5,000) and internal combustion engines (9 to 10,000).

Needless to say, not all industries are technologically inflexible, thus requiring a minimum size to be economic. Wherever there is a choice between a more and a less capital-intensive technique, it is frequently in a poor country's interest to choose the less intensive one, e.g. in a wide range of construction, in internal transport and handling within a factory and in many industries at the packaging stage. But it has to be remembered that the whole purpose of industrialization is to raise the productivity of labour throughout the economy and thus incomes too. Widespread use of primitive industrial methods would be self-defeating. As Myrdal has shown from his detailed study of Asian conditions, industry is not for a long time to become an employment creator; new employment outlets have to be sought elsewhere in the economy.

Economies of scale, generally becoming ever more important under the impetus of technological change, explain why, under the leadership of the Organization of African Unity and the UN ECA, Africa is promoting sub-regional groupings to plan and execute major industrial development projects on the basis of rational specialization. Furthermore, the exploitation of linkage effects with external economies, which are part of and reinforce the industrialization process, becomes possible on the basis of the wider markets to which such groupings give rise.

In the process of industrializing Africa along these lines the earnings of traditional exports will be insufficient to produce the growing amount of foreign exchange required. The principal way out is through increased trade among African countries, itself only possible by a diversification of the structure of production through industrialization. But there should also be industries capable of exporting beyond Africa. These not only have to be competitive but they also require the same concessions from the wealthy countries as other developing countries—the reduction and elimination by the advanced countries of tariff and other barriers to the import of semi-manufactures and manufactures. Products Africa should eventually be able to export include meat and fish in frozen and processed form, tinned fruit, fruit juices and vegetables, timber manufactures, pulp and paper and some textiles and clothing (in a limited number of countries which may be able to install a modern industry, e.g. Egypt and perhaps Morocco, Nigeria and the emerging economic group based on Kenya, Uganda and Tanzania). It should also be possible to export fertilizers

(particularly where there is abundant natural gas) and possibly at a later stage semi-finished steel and copper and aluminium manufactures.

The final point, which tends to be left out of account in an industrial strategy and one which is of course the most important of all, is the encouragement of a climate, the adoption and the putting into practice at all levels of a policy which will promote the actual establishment of industries. This means entrepreneurs, private or public, domestic, foreign or mixed, who will undertake and produce industrial goods, and a sufficiency of managers, technicians, foremen and skilled workers who know how to do the producing. These and other practical aspects of industrialization are considered later.

AFRICAN PERSPECTIVES

Illustrative perspectives have been worked out, derived originally from Surendra Patel's analysis of economic distance between countries, which showed that provided Africa succeeds in putting into practice a strategy along the lines described, it would take about four decades to reach average levels of national income comparable to those in western Europe at about the middle of this century. To do this, the annual rates of growth of the gross domestic product required are 6 per cent for two decades and 7 per cent for the next two. The agricultural growth rates need to reach respectively 5.2 and 4.7 per cent and the industrial growth rates respectively 7.9 and 8.9 per cent, with capital and intermediate goods growing faster than consumer goods. The consequence of achieving such growth rates would be to double agricultural production per head and multiply 25 times industrial production per head. These ideas seemed utopian to many people when they were first expressed by the UN ECA in the early 1960s. But the actual experience of the decade now ending is more encouraging than is generally realized. The Pearson report points out that during the decade the combined G.D.P.s of the underdeveloped countries have been increasing at an annual rate of 5 per cent. Despite their late start, African countries, accounting for 92 per cent of combined G.D.P. (excluding South Africa) have grown at 4 per cent. For the Second United Nations Development Decade a target of 6 per cent has been adopted; if this is achieved, most under-developed countries will attain self-sustained growth by the end of the century.

The prospects opened up may be summarized briefly, following the division into two periods of 20 years adopted here. Iron and steel would be produced in all the countries on the north African coast, in Uganda, Zambia, Zaire, Gabon, Nigeria, Mali and Liberia; aluminium metal in Cameroon, Congo (Brazzaville), Ghana and Guinea; and copper (including manufactures) in Zambia, Zaire and Mauritania. Forest industries would develop mainly in the rich timber-growing areas of central and parts of west Africa; much of the market would be within Africa for builders' joinery and furniture, and there are also potential markets overseas for veneers, plywood, pulp and paper. Self-sufficiency could be attained at an early date in cement, with some degree of specialization among countries, based largely on the availability of suitable limestone. The starting point of a chemical industry would be fertilizers: the main producers of phosphate fertilizer are already becoming established in north Africa and will be joined later by Uganda, Togo and Senegal. Congo (Brazzaville) would become the main producer of potash, followed perhaps by Ethiopia; and Algeria, Libya and Nigeria major producers of nitrogen fertilizer from natural gas. Caustic soda/chlorine would be produced in north Africa, Kenya, Zaire, Ghana, Senegal and Guinea. Petrochemicals would follow in the countries already cited where ample natural gas occurs.

Metal products form a field where small-scale industry is both feasible and genuinely useful to a growing economy, and the range, including, for instance, wire products, steel work for construction, tool grinding and agricultural implements and ploughs, would be extended in all African countries. Greater specialization is essential in mechanical and electrical engineering, and growth would inevitably be in those countries which have already started effectively on the road towards industrialization. Commercial vehicles, railway rolling stock, coastal and river craft normally start through the assembly of imported components, but to be economic there has to be progressive manufacture of the components themselves. Consequently, close co-operation among groups of countries is essential, and already overdue in, for example, the Maghreb and west Africa.

Increasingly, Africa could move toward self-sufficiency in processed foods. Countries particularly well placed for increasing production of sugar are Ethiopia, Magadascar, Congo (Brazzaville) and the Senegal River Basin countries. Africa is also a major potential producer of meat. Apart from Kenya, an already established producer, there is potential in Ethiopia and in the inland countries of central and west Africa which in turn could generate industries based on processed meat and its by-products. Much more could be done with Africa's resources of fish, both sea and fresh water.

It would be logical, in terms of harmonized industrial development, to increase textile production primarily in the cotton-growing countries; here the scope for specialization arises partly from the variety of end products. Increased manufacture of leather products would be associated with the meat industry. The principal manufacturers of rubber products would be Zaire, Cameroon, Nigeria and Liberia.

Provided the perspectives for the first 20 years or so are realized and both the overall and industrial growth rates are achieved, the African region as a whole might well, by the end of the century, be producing from between 80 to 100 million tons of iron and steel, which would be widely dispersed. Aluminium and copper would be major industries serving markets throughout the continent as well as overseas. Africa would be a major net exporter of timber manufactures. Cement production would be around 100 million tons. Sulphuric acid production would be about 15 million tons. There would be several major caustic/chlorine

complexes. Production of nitrogen and phosphate fertilizer would be of the order of, respectively, 3 million and 20 million tons. There would be two or three well-developed petrochemical complexes providing, *inter alia*, the raw material for a widely dispersed plastic manufactures industry. Metal products would be produced throughout the region; and mechanical and electrical engineering and transport equipment would be well established in a considerable number of countries, with some of them producing specialized industrial machinery.

By then, although there should be a high degree of self-sufficiency, Africa would be entering into world trade on equal terms and, though still a major exporter of primary products and importer of specialized capital equipment, would be able to follow the trade patterns of the developed world, so that the main emphasis in the twenty-first century would be exchange of manufactures between Africa and its trading partners overseas. In the intervening period Africa, unlike some of the Latin American countries and the more advanced of the developing countries in Asia, cannot expect to be a major exporter of industrial manufactures. North Africa, already farther along the road to development, should become a significant exporter of industrial goods well ahead of the others, partly because it is geographically well placed to enter into close trading relations with Mediterranean Europe, and partly because of the immense petrochemical possibilities opened up by oil and natural gas. Tropical Africa should be able to move steadily in the direction of increasing export of manufactures based on fish, meat and timber.

SOME PRACTICAL PROBLEMS

The starting point has to be the right strategy of industrialization, including the pattern and the pooling of effort, resources and markets. But this is not enough.

The physical infrastructure is still inadequate, particularly for an industrial policy based primarily on Africa producing a growing range of industrial goods for its own markets. Transport links between countries —road, rail and water—have to be much improved. New connexions cannot be justified economically without more traffic, and new industrial plants cannot be built unless they can serve neighbours with whom they have adequate communications. This vicious circle has to be broken. Joint industrial planning is the only solution. Meanwhile, progress is being made. Examples are the TanZam railway, construction of which has recently started, and which will make possible a connexion between Dar es Salaam and Lusaka, opening up the hinterland of Tanzania; the extension of the trans-Cameroon railway, which will make possible the development of the central and northern territories of Cameroon and eventually connect Chad and the Central African Republic to the sea; a trans-Saharan link, now being studied, to connect the Maghreb with Niger, Mali and ultimately much of west Africa; and studies, still at an early stage, to connect up by rail the countries bordering on the Great Lakes, east Africa, Sudan and Zaire.

The cheap hydropower potentially available in much of sub-Saharan Africa from, for example, the Senegal, Niger, Congo and Nile rivers can be harnessed only if there are sufficient industrial users. Here again, progress is being made, with the construction of the Akosombo and Kainji projects and active study of power connexions between Nigeria, Ghana, Dahomey, Togo and the Ivory Coast; the extensive study of the Senegal River Basin with two major projects in view, Gouina in Mali, and Konkouré in Guinea; the construction of the first stage of the Inga project in Zaire; the completion of the Aswan Dam in Egypt; the construction of the Kafue project in Zambia; and the study of the Rufiji project in Tanzania. Most of these projects are of actual or potential interest to more than one country.

The technological gap between the advanced countries and Africa is constantly growing. What is needed to counteract this is the grouping of Africa's scientific research efforts, with assistance from outside, and mechanisms for the transfer and, where appropriate, adaptation of modern technology.

Almost all African countries have adopted national plans of the indicative variety, for the most part with weak instruments for their execution. But whatever the professed ideology, some form of mixed economy is practised, with state or joint state-private enterprise, and inducements to foreign private enterprise. Belief in the possibility of genuine indigenous private enterprise is comparatively rare, exceptions being Morocco, Kenya, Nigeria and, in principle (although not so far very much in practice), Ivory Coast and Liberia. If the basic strategy advocated here is to be carried out, more effective national planning, including comprehensive industrial programming, is evidently essential, including increasing harmonization of national plans —lip service is paid to this but not much more. However, there is every reason to advocate an empirical approach to the methods of execution of industrial projects. The emphasis has to be on genuine enterprise and it is of small importance if this is private, public or mixed.

Much more is needed to prepare properly industrial projects. There is now a wealth of preliminary studies, indicators of potential opportunities, but insufficient recognition of the need for patient, time-consuming and often expensive feasibility and engineering studies. Here outside help is needed, both to carry out this pre-investment work and train Africans in the techniques, and the United Nations Development Programme is playing an important part.

The amount of finance required is large, but this need not be a major constraint. Pearson has shown that the achievements of the developing countries in the last decade have been financed to the extent of 85 per cent from their own savings, and that these countries as a group are now saving 15 per cent of their G.D.P. Africa has done less well, though there are exceptions: Gabon, Mauritius, Tanzania and Zambia have saved more than 15 per cent; and Zaire, Morocco, Nigeria, Tunisia and Egypt between 10 and 15 per cent. Continuing foreign aid is needed (not least in Africa), and Pearson shows that this should not require serious sacrifice on the part of the rich countries. But the essence of the matter in Africa is a higher rate of saving and this should now be possible.

There remain two more points, both of major importance. The first is the lack of qualified people. This is true not only of Africa but of much of the under-developed world and is the real reason why, in different ways, there has recently been rapid industrial growth in several Latin American countries, in Hong Kong, in Singapore, in Taiwan and more recently in the Philippines and South Korea, since industrial skills have emerged or are emerging in these countries. To say "leave it to private enterprise" is not enough, although the genuine article should be fully encouraged. It is understandable and proper that Africans, as with other developing countries, should not want to leave their industries mainly in foreign hands; but the concept of the mixed enterprise and the progressive training of nationals to take-over is now well established. What is not yet sufficiently understood is that the State industry formula does more harm than good unless there is attention to efficiency and a competitive product. This may be evident enough where export is involved but it is also necessary even in the domestic market. Too often an "infant industry" is kept alive by the doctor (or the pharmacist) when an early death would be in the interest of all concerned and especially the family.

The root of the problem, of course, starts with the education system, so far ill adapted to encouraging its products to enter the industrial world, whether to become entrepreneurs, managers, industrial technologists, shop foremen or skilled workers. But beyond the restructuring of formal education, there is a need to reform non-formal education and to multiply training arrangements at all levels, through management courses, vocational training centres and trade schools and through in-plant training. Most of this has to be organized within Africa, though it can be supplemented abroad on a selective basis.

The second point is that the success of a rapid industrial development programme depends not only on people but on the political will of the nations and their leaders. Inevitably, in the early post-independence period much time has been spent on consolidating, sometimes defending, newly established nations. This has diverted attention from economic development and, as is crucial in the case of industry, practical measures for furthering the kind of permanent economic co-operation required among countries.

Africa is tackling this problem on a sub-regional basis. One group is based on the Maghreb: Algeria, Morocco and Tunisia. Another is in east Africa, initially Kenya, Tanzania, Uganda, where negotiations are proceeding towards a wider eastern African grouping in which the present members of the East African Community, Kenya, Tanzania and Uganda, would be joined by Zambia, and perhaps also Ethiopia and Somalia. (Malawi and Rhodesia are turning for the time being towards South Africa.) In the central African group Cameroon, the Central

African Republic, Chad, Congo (Brazzaville) and Gabon have for a number of years been associated in the *Union douanière et économique de l'Afrique centrale* (UDEAC), and there have been attempts to associate also Zaire. Efforts are also being made to group the countries of west Africa.

The essential principles underlying such groupings have been recognized. There must be an agreed programme of multinational development in which each country finds some reasonably equitable benefits. Possible joint programmes have to be studied in sufficient economic and technical detail to enable binding commitments on specific projects to be made. There has to be a programme covering long periods of time, and an order in which the programme is to be executed, so that the members can see what they are conceding and receiving and their cohesiveness is retained. Finally, permanent institutions have to be established and staffed to plan and execute the programmes.

Efforts among the Maghreb countries which started with the establishment of permanent institutions have now been in progress for nearly a decade. Although there has been a real advance in several economic sectors, there has not yet been much in the direction of industrial co-operation. In east Africa the form of association which originated under British rule broke down because the main benefit accrued to one country, Kenya. The arrangements were completely renegotiated in the mid-1960s, a real achievement on the part of all concerned. They are now not only equitable but more comprehensive, covering virtually the whole economic spectrum. Moreover, as pointed out, the geographical scope of the East African Community is likely to be progressively enlarged. In central Africa the UDEAC has recently been in difficulty, since the benefits of the grouping proved to be unequally distributed, favouring Gabon, Cameroon and, to a lesser extent, Congo (Brazzaville) at the expense of Chad and the Central African Republic. The sheer economic weight of Zaire has also been an obstacle to closer association with its natural partners. In this part of the world there have also been political problems, not least between the two Congos. In west Africa the sheer extent of the area, range of size of countries, geographical dispersion and the criss-crossing of former French and British territories have all made progress slow. The way forward may well be first in smaller groupings, e.g. among the four states of the Senegal River Basin—Senegal, Mali, Mauritania and Guinea—and between Ghana and its neighbours. Setting up practical and permanent forms of economic co-operation will require time and patience. Much of the detailed technical work is being done with the help of the UN ECA. But to bring it to fruition also requires enduring political decisions at the highest level.

The perspectives for the industrialization of Africa began to be worked out nearly a decade ago. It would be idle to deny that subsequent progress has been disappointing. Just as the concentration of attention of African leaders on other issues has handicapped the progress towards multi-national co-operation, essential for industrial development in Africa's particular situation, so, for the same reason, economic performance generally and especially in the agricultural and industrial sectors has been below the potential available and less than Africans and their friends had hoped. A pattern is emerging where States with interesting exportable natural resources, oil and minerals such as ferrous and non-ferrous metal ores, are prospering, at least in financial terms, though there is little progress towards the structural transformation of their economies: Zaire, Zambia, Gabon, Mauritania, Libya, for example; where Egypt, until 1967 the most encouraging of African countries from the point of view of industrialization and structural change, is caught up in a political and military confrontation; where a limited number of others which had adopted promising policies, for themselves and in association with their neighbour countries, continue to be involved in internal political and social conflict; where one country—Nigeria—despite more than its own share of internal conflict, is large enough and has a dynamic people so that there is industrial progress; but where most of the rest are small countries whose economies remain rather stagnant and continue to be mainly dependent, directly or indirectly, on the outside world. The only alternative policy is an industrialization strategy along lines outlined in this chapter; this is not a sufficient condition for economic and social progress but it is a necessary one.

SELECT BIBLIOGRAPHY

ARON, R. *Dix-huit leçons sur la société industrielle.* Paris, Ed. Le Livre de poche, 1962.

AMIN, S. *Trois expériences africaines de développement: le Mali, la Guinée et le Ghana.* Paris, Presses universitaires de France, 1965.

L'Economie du Maghreb: les perspectives de l'avenir. Paris, Editions de Minuit, 1967.

Le développement du capitalisme en Côte d'Ivoire. Paris, Editions de Minuit, 1967.

BRYCE, M. *Industrial Development.* New York, McGraw-Hill, 1960.

DE BERNIS, G. "Industries lourdes et industries légères", in *Industrialisation au Maghreb.* Paris, Maspero, 1963.

EWING, A. F. *Industry in Africa.* London, Oxford University Press, 1968 (see Notes for detailed sources, especially UN ECA documents).

GREEN, R. H. and SEIDMAN, A. *Unity or Poverty? The Economics of Pan-Africanism.* Harmondsworth, Penguin Books, 1968.

KILBY, P. *Industrialisation in an Open Economy: Nigeria 1945-1966.* Cambridge University Press, 1969.

LACROIX, J. L. *Industrialisation au Congo.* Paris, Ed. Mouton, 1967.

LITTLE, I. M. D. and MIRRLEES, A. R., *Manual of Industrial Project Analysis in Developing Countries,* Vol. II, "Social Cost Benefit Analysis", Paris, OECD, 1969.

MADDISON, A. *Economic Progress and Policy in Developing Countries.* London, Allen and Unwin, 1970.

MAIZELS, A. *Industrial Growth and World Trade.* London, Cambridge University Press, 1963.

PATEL, S. J. *Essays in Economic Transition.* Bombay, Asia Publishing House, 1965.

PEARSON, LESTER B. and associates. *Partners in Development.* London, 1969.

PERROUX, F. *L'Economie des jeunes nations.* Paris, Presses Universitaires de France, 1962.

SEERS, D. "The Stages of Economic Development of a Primary Producer in the Middle of the 20th Century". *Economic Bulletin,* 7/3, Ghana, 1963.

UN *Study of Industrial Growth.* (Sales No. 62.II.B.2), New York, 1963.

UN *Patterns of Industrial Growth, 1938-1958.* (Sales No. 5.9.XVII.6), New York, 1959.

UN *Towards Accelerated Development:Proposals for the Second United Nations Development Decade.* Report of the Committee for Development Planning (Sales No.:E.70.11.A.2), New York, 1970.

UN ECA *Industrial Development in Africa.* (Sales No. 66.II.B.24), New York, 1966.

UN ECA *Industrial Growth in Africa.* (Sales No. 63.II.K.3), New York, 1963.

UN ECA *Economic Development of Zambia.* N'Dola, 1964.

UN ECA *Report of the West African Industrial Co-ordination Mission* (E/CN.14/246). Addis Ababa, 1964.

UN ECA *Report of the Industrial Co-ordination Mission to East Africa* (E/CN.14/247). Addis Ababa, 1964.

UN ECA *Report of the Industrial Co-ordination Mission to Algeria, Libya, Morocco and Tunisia* (E/CN.14/248). Addis Ababa, 1964.

UN ECA *Report of the ECA Mission on Economic Co-operation in Central Africa.* (Sales No. 66.K.11), New York, 1966.

Financing African Development

Brian Van Arkadie

In a brief account of development finance within a continental perspective the dangers of misleading generalizations are great, both because of the diversity between countries and because of the inherent bias in much of the available data. Continental aggregate estimates of private foreign investment, for example, would be heavily influenced by South Africa, and, even if South Africa were excluded, the picture emerging would be particularly dependent on investment in those few countries especially endowed with mineral wealth. Generalizations derived would therefore be of little meaning for the many countries in which the mining sector is of little importance.

INVESTMENT IN SMALLHOLDER AGRICULTURE

The most important source of bias in the available data on development finance derives from the measurement of capital formation. Financing development is often identified with financing capital formation. Development mobilization is frequently gauged by the achievement in raising the rate of investment. The economies of many African countries, however, represent the classic characteristics of the "dual economy". The large majority of the population of sub-Saharan independent Africa is engaged in economic activity outside the so-called "modern sector". Such activity not only involves subsistence farming and house building, but also involves production of food and other agricultural products both for domestic and export markets. Such activity is not only important as the source of livelihood for the majority of the people of Africa, but has even been the major source of expansion of monetary gross domestic product and of export earnings in those economies without substantial mining activity. Capital formation in such African smallholder farming is characteristically in the form of application of labour to land, often by the smallholder and his family, or of the expenditure of small sums of cash which typically would not be recorded as investment items. In this situation discussion of "investment" too often concentrates on large-scale infrastructural investment and on investment in urban activities, ignoring what is often the most important source of expanding productive capacity. This is unfortunate not only because it misrepresents the real situation but also because it can lead to bias in the formulation of policy, which can become overcommitted to measures to raise investment in the "modern sector", sometimes through policies resulting in unrecognized but still very real reductions in capital formation in the "traditional sector".

In practice investment of this type can be inferred, after the event, from the performance of smallholder output. The expansion of smallholder tree crops, such as coffee, cocoa, cashew nuts and oil palms, involves an investment of labour and time in post-poning consumption of the benefits of that labour over the years in which the trees grow to full production. The amount of such investment activity can be estimated from the eventual growth in output.

Actual financial contributions to such developments will take the form of infrastructural investment directly required by such activities, the provision of credit facilities to farmers, and the finance of new seeds, extension advice and other agricultural services. Traditionally the main external form of such support has been through finance for infrastructure and through technical assistance support. In recent years, however, finance of rural credit and general financial support for intensive schemes of smallholder development have become a fit object of external finance. Notably the World Bank, through the agency of the IDA, has changed its position and taken an increasing interest in financing smallholder development, both in providing support for multi-purpose credit schemes and in funding intensive crop development programmes (e.g. tea and tobacco in eastern Africa).

However, such external finance still touches but a small part of smallholding activity. Most expansion in productive capacity results from the input of labour and savings from within the sector itself.

In the past, although the smallholder has not been an important user of financial resources from other domestic sectors or from abroad, he has been an important source of funds. In terms of domestic resource mobilization smallholder farming has provided an important part of the tax base in many African countries. During periods of export boom large surpluses were also extracted through the agency of marketing boards and similar arrangements. This was most notably the case during the colonial period, but has been less true during the 1960s, partly because of the mediocre export price situation during most of that period. The smallholder has been the main source of foreign exchange earnings in many African economies. In such situations the import of capital equipment to build up non-agricultural activities has been made possible in part through the export production of the smallholder. It is important to emphasize this to counter the impression that African development either has been or must be largely dependent on external finance. As smallholder agriculture is the largest sector, indeed at the outset almost the total of economic activity, and as new economic activities (e.g. industry) do not have their own source of funds, the domestic development finance problem may be viewed in simple terms as the problem of transferring resources from smallholder agriculture to finance other sectors without, by so doing, undermining rural development.

Because of the unreliable coverage of capital formation in rural activities, interpretation of the sort of data shown in table 1 is tricky. This is not only because, in general, the rate of capital formation may in many cases be underestimated, but also because the variation in investment from year to year and country to country may well be misrepresented.

In most cases changes in so-called "capital formation" represent changes in the limited urban and large-scale infrastructural sectors and do not reflect behaviour in the more important rural sector. The figures shown should not necessarily be interpreted as pessimistically as might be suggested by comparisons with norms expected for high growth in more industrial economies. Nevertheless the general picture does suggest that higher rates of capital formation of this type will be required if rates of structural change are to be achieved sufficient to boost growth in income per capita above the 1–2.5 per cent per annum experienced by African countries in the 1960s.

FOREIGN PRIVATE INVESTMENT IN THE MODERN SECTOR

Investment outside the smallholder agriculture sector includes economic and social infrastructure, mining, industry, tourism, plantation agriculture and urban housing and office building. Investment activity in much of this range of activities typically has been dependent upon international support.

The nature of this external involvement may be seen as depending upon a number of factors in addition to the purely financial:

(i) *Machinery:* Africa does not produce capital equipment. Investment in transport equipment, industrial equipment, electrical generating equipment, etc., therefore involves the utilization of real resources from abroad, but not necessarily external finance.

Table 1

FIXED CAPITAL FORMATION

COUNTRY	YEAR	PERCENTAGE OF GROSS DOMESTIC PRODUCT IN PURCHASERS' VALUES	COUNTRY	YEAR	PERCENTAGE OF GROSS DOMESTIC PRODUCT IN PURCHASERS' VALUES
Botswana	1964–65	16	Niger	1963	12
(July 1st to June 30th)	1968–69	21		1966	11
Cameroon	1963	11	Nigeria	1960–61	11
	1968	13	(April 1st to March 31st)	1963–64	12
Chad	1963	11		1967–68	15
Dahomey	1963–64	17	Réunion	1965	23
(July 1st to June 30th)	1966–67	13		1969	25
Egypt	1960–61	15	Sierra Leone	1963–64	11
(July 1st to June 30th)	1963–64	20	(July 1st to June 30th)	1968–69	13
	1969–70	12	South Africa	1960	20
Ethiopia	1963	12	(incl. Namibia)	1963	20
	1969	12		1970	25
Ghana	1960	20	Southern Rhodesia	1960	22
	1963	18		1963	14
	1969	10		1970	16
Ivory Coast	1960	14	Sudan	1960–61	11
	1963	14	(July 1st to June 30th)	1963–64	16
	1969	18		1968–69	12
Kenya	1964	13	Swaziland	1966–67	19
	1970	20	(July 1st to June 30th)	1967–68	21
Lesotho	1964–65	9	Tanzania	1964	11
(April 1st to March 31st)	1967–68	11	(excl. Zanzibar)	1968	17
Libya	1962	34		1970	21
	1968	24	Togo	1963	10
Madagascar	1960	10		1966	14
	1970	14	Tunisia	1963	22
Malawi	1963	13		1969	22
	1969	17		1966	12
Mauritius	1963	16	Upper Volta	1966	14
	1970	14	Zaire	1966	14
Morocco	1960	10		1968	15
	1963	12	Zambia	1960	18
	1969	14		1963	16
				1969	20

Source: United Nations, *Statistical Yearbook 1971.*

(ii) *Markets:* the project may require access to external markets for the end-product to ensure viability.

(iii) *Foreign contractors:* large-scale construction in many cases involves foreign contractors, although local labour and materials may be utilized. Again, this does not necessarily imply external finance.

(iv) *Expertise:* often the constraining factor in a development project is not financial or physical but rather the absence of available competence in the line in question. Promoting development is then not so much a matter of *financing* development as *designing, organizing* and *managing.*

On the African side of the bargain foreign private investment is often sought because of the facilities offered by the foreign firm in addition to finance. This may be managerial expertise, technical knowledge, or access to a foreign market. In practice the specific initiatives for private investment tend to be promoted by the overseas investor. On his side of the bargain he is likely to be meeting the competition of rivals, or seeking to guarantee a source of supply. Naturally in such cases private investors often seek a high degree of leverage, aiming to achieve the desired control or access with a minimum commitment of resources. The relative significance of private investment is therefore difficult to judge from aggregate financial data.

Alternatively, the provision of short-term finance may ensure the sale of machinery, or the completion of a construction contract.

The capital funds aspect is, therefore, only one facet of a bargain struck in which the real concern on either side may not be directly related to the ostensible finance involved.

In terms of sectoral allocation throughout the continent the extractive industries have proved to be of by far the greatest interest to foreign private investors. By the end of 1967, for example, U.S. direct investment in Africa amounted to $2.3 billion (a relatively minor part—about 4 per cent—of total U.S. direct investments abroad) of which some 54.1 per cent was in petroleum and 17.5 per cent was in mining and smelting. Interestingly enough, of the $667 million going to make up the total invested in South Africa, nearly half was in manufacturing. British and French investment is certainly more diversified, with much more substantial investments in commerce, banking and agriculture.

During the 1960s the most significant change in the pattern of private foreign investment was the increasing interest in manufacturing based on import substitution. Overseas manufacturing enterprises were typically interested in investment to ensure access to markets in a situation in which the independent African governments were introducing much higher tariffs than those of the colonial period. In some cases the existing foreign trading companies extended their activities into manufacturing to ensure an expanding base in the face of the growth of local private and state trading activities and the potential creation of domestic manufacturing capacity in lines which they currently imported.

Government Policy

In principle two extreme strategies relating to foreign investment can be identified. At one end is the open encouragement of foreign investment with maximum inducement and few, if any, controls. The plan, if it exists, and the government economic agencies invite investors to play the major role in industrial and mining development. At the other end of the scale governments prevent foreign equity holdings, at least in the strategic sectors of the economy, nationalize existing enterprises and allocate the promotional function to the state development corporation. Ivory Coast, Liberia and Nigeria on the west coast and Kenya on the east coast would be identified with the first category, Guinea, Tanzania and possibly Zambia with the second.

However, in practice, such neat categories do not fit exactly. Thus we find even Liberia seeking to participate in the ownership and control of her iron ore industry, while Kenya is readily accepting the possibility of participating in the ownership of one of the foreign-owned commercial banks, National and Grindlays, and engages in a number of public sector ventures in industry and agriculture. On the other hand governments which have nationalized continue to do active business with foreign investing concerns, sometimes seeking out new joint ventures, sometimes offering management contracts.

From the point of view of the African governments, there is a dilemma to be overcome in weighing the need to gain access to foreign resources against the dangers of excessive dependence with the possible resulting domination by foreign economic interests. The need to fashion a strategy which achieves the required access to the means of structural change, while avoiding the very real dangers of neo-colonialism is, therefore, the critical task facing economic policy makers.

The lack of indigenous entrepreneurs with experience in large-scale economic activity is an important contributory factor to the dependent situation, which suggests the need for state action to achieve national economic goals, even in the absence of a commitment to state-directed development. In recent years, therefore, there has been a pattern of active intervention by governments and public development corporations in areas attractive to foreign investors. This has ranged from efforts to ensure some degree of public corporation participation in major new ventures to outright nationalization of existing foreign-owned activities.

A full account of the efforts of African governments to redefine the terms on which private foreign business operates within their economies—and the response of foreign business to their actions—would be worthy of a substantial study. In some instances such a study would not yet be possible, as the full implications of recent policy initiatives are not yet apparent. This is so in the case of nationalization measures announced during 1970 in Uganda and Sudan, for example. In other cases, while the broad terms on which new bargains have been struck are known, the ultimate consequences are still very unclear; for example, the full consequences of management contracts and various kinds of joint-ownership arrangements are very difficult to evaluate.

Amongst nationalization moves in the last three years the largest enterprises involved have probably been the copper concerns in Zambia. However, with a continuing ownership interest on the part of the companies, with elaborate compensation arrangements and management contracts with the companies, the full consequences of the nationalization for Zambia are particularly difficult to discern. The companies do not seem to have suffered from the deal. On the Zambian side there may be short-term benefits from associated adjustments in a rather inefficient mining tax system; the longer-term benefits are likely to come only as a specifically Zambian managerial and technical expertise is created.

The Tanzanian nationalizations from 1967 on, although quite thorough-going in terms of taking over the large-scale foreign-owned interests, did not involve such large investments as in the Zambian case. Indeed the very poverty of Tanzania made for a certain freedom of manoeuvre in that it was never a major centre for foreign investment, and nationalization did not threaten any really substantial economic interests. From the development finance point of view the nationalization of the commercial banks is of especial interest. The Tanzanian government took over 100 per cent control of the commercial banking system in 1967. As the three largest banks withdrew their top level management soon after, the change of ownership also involved an immediate change of managerial control. As experience increases, it will be interesting to see if the new management branches out in more venturesome directions. The British commercial banks operating in Africa have frequently come under criticism for favouring expatriate interests, having a traditional and not too relevant loans policy and, in general, not being well attuned to the need for innovation in banking practice.

For some types of industry adjustments to taxes and royalties may be a more appropriate tool than nationalization in order to gain access to a greater share of the national resources for the nation. This is apparently the strategy being pursued, for example, by Libya and Algeria in relation to the exploitation of their oil deposits.

Faced with nationalist developments on a continental scale (and, indeed, reflecting developments elsewhere in the Third World) international business is becoming increasingly sophisticated in its strategies. Understandably enough, of course, investing companies still maintain a preference for conservative régimes with openly sympathetic policies. There may well be a contradiction in this, for it may prove to be the governments which are conservative and too openly sympathetic to foreign investors which will create the most unstable social situations—but such

foresight may involve a time horizon beyond that used by investors in making their decisions. To deal with situations far from their ideal, foreign companies seem to be increasingly willing to seek new forms of doing business: to engage in joint ventures; in some cases, to take their profit without an explicit equity involvement; to offer management contracts, and so on. Indeed it seems likely that the joint venture will be seen increasingly as a means of warding off the prospect of nationalization. The difficulty for the African country is likely to be that under such arrangements exploitation will certainly be less apparent but may well be no less real.

THE BALANCE OF PAYMENTS CONSTRAINT*

In macro-economic terms the need for external finance arises when the foreign earnings of African countries are not sufficient to cover the foreign costs of the desired investment programme. However, foreign private finance may occur even where foreign exchange is not scarce, when foreign capital is seeking to penetrate the economy in question. Also the persistence in cautious monetary policies by some of the African governments, even after the end of the currency board system, has on occasion meant that foreign finance has been sought to cover a purely domestic financial gap in conditions of external payments surplus.

The net effect of the provision of external finance should be the import of goods and services in excess of exports. It is interesting to note, however, that taking Africa as a whole (but excluding South Africa and Egypt) there is little evidence of significant net transfer of resources into the region. From 1964, despite considerable net inflows of official funds, African countries taken together have maintained a favourable balance of visible trade. The combination of this fact with the mediocre performance of the African countries in building up foreign exchange reserves indicates that there have been substantial private outflows, both in the form of repatriation of profits and the outflow of private capital.

Mining Export Economies

The overall positive visible trade balance on a continental basis of the latter part of the 1960s masks dramatic differences in performance from country to country. A few countries maintained very large visible trade surpluses in most years of this period—notably some of the mining economies. These are also the economies which have to finance large outflows of investment income. Nevertheless they have tended to be the economies with the most favourable balance of payments positions and with the least need for external finance.

Libya has built up the most considerable trade surpluses and foreign exchange reserves, as her oil exports have expanded. Indeed the trade surplus

---

* *See* tables 4, 5 and 6 (External Trade and Balance of Payments) pp. 55-58.

achieved as a result of the growth of the Libyan oil industry has been sufficient to explain the continent-wide surplus.

Zambia also found herself in the years immediately following independence with a large trade surplus and considerable reserves. However, an ambitious development programme, rising incomes and increasing costs of trade resulting from Rhodesia's U.D.I. resulted in the virtual elimination of the favourable current balance by 1967, although high copper prices restored the surplus position in the following year. It should be emphasized that the traditional vocabulary used here of "favourable" and "unfavourable" trade balance is misleading. It is appropriate for a government to expand its development to fully utilize available foreign exchange. The accumulation of reserves is of no virtue except in so far as it is necessary to maintain independence of action and desirable short-term flexibility in formulating economic policy.

Nigeria was a typical African agricultural-export economy which now finds its source of foreign earning shifting dramatically towards minerals. As the effects of the civil war are overcome and production expands to levels higher than those achieved prior to the war, oil promises to exceed the value of all other exports combined. Before the civil war (1966) oil exports had grown to the point where they accounted for one-third of Nigeria's export earnings. The oil deposits may have been an important contributory factor to the civil war; their exploitation will certainly make a major contribution to the solution of the balance-of-payments and fiscal problems resulting from the war.

The Nigerian government succeeded in minimizing the long-run financial impact of the war by avoiding the use of foreign loans. Instead the war was financed through domestic austerity and import controls, and a fast expanding, domestically held public debt. There was inflation, and foreign reserves were drastically reduced, but no great burden of external debt has been inherited from the war. Nigeria obviously faces great problems of economic reconstruction, and many questions can be raised about the underlying long-term economic strategy being pursued, but it seems likely that the purely financial consequences of the war should not provide any long-standing limitation on flexibility of economic policy.

Agricultural Export Economies

While the important mineral exporting nations have enjoyed a surplus payments position, the agricultural commodity exporters have been faced with a scarcity of external resources. In some cases this scarcity reached the point of actual crisis, which acted as a brake on overall development.

Ghana

Ghana was faced with a protracted condition of foreign exchange scarcity for much of the last decade. She had entered the 1960s still with very substantial reserves accumulated during the periods of high cocoa prices experienced throughout much of the 1950s. During the early 1960s a period of rising investment, particularly on projects with long gestation periods, and expanding government consumption was combined with an experience of extended depression in cocoa prices. In order to maintain the pace of investment and public spending, heavy debts were incurred, particularly of a short-term and supplier-credit nature. The point was reached where, with minimum foreign exchange reserves, short-term flexibility could only be achieved by further extensions in supplier credits. Following the change of régime in 1966 there was some hard bargaining with creditors and a modest rescheduling of debt. Additional respite was gained by the revival of cocoa prices and the resulting boost in exports in 1968. Prices fell again with an increase in the crop in 1969. The accumulated debt has meant that there will be a continuing need to commit foreign receipts to service the debt and therefore to continue to restrain imports.

Nkrumah has received a bad press for economic policies in the last years of his rule. There certainly was extravagance and mismanagement. However, the dilemma faced by the Ghanaians in managing their economy illustrates underlying structural problems which must be faced eventually by other African countries. Development, even when successful, can be a lengthy process. There are lags between the planning and construction of projects, and between construction and full operation. Plans made during periods of high export earnings may be implemented subsequently during periods of declining earnings, generating import demands at an unfortunate time. There may then be a further passage of time before the project produces a contribution to the balance of payments. In this situation governments will face the awkward choice of restraining development programmes to defend the payments situation, or taking risks with the reserve position in the hope of making an eventual development breakthrough. The danger of the latter course is that development has generally been a much lengthier process than was planned. The costs of protracted foreign exchange crises are high. In straight financial terms expensive forms of short-term external finance have to be resorted to. In addition, blows to domestic morale are suffered because of import scarcities, and eventually a loss of international freedom of manoeuvre results from the need to placate creditors and possible new lenders. This last point suggests that countries which wish to maintain political autonomy may well find it desirable to pursue cautious financial policies—strategic economic and political radicalism should be wedded to tactical fiscal conservatism.

Ghana became independent in March 1957, so that by the first half of the 1960s she was already involved in a very substantial post-independence development programme, including the large multi-purpose Volta river project. Most African colonies achieved independence during the 1960s, and only towards the end of the decade did patterns of post-independence development take shape.

East Africa

In the three east African countries, Kenya, Uganda and Tanzania, the financial situation at the beginning of the 1960s was dominated by the impact of independence as such. There had been an extended investment boom throughout a good part of the 1950s, partly financed by the high commodity prices of the first part of that decade, and partly a result of the public and commercial development of Kenya during and immediately after the Emergency. By the early 1960s the liquidity of the public sector had declined, whilst the announcement of impending independence, particularly for Kenya, led to a crisis of confidence by private investors. During the first part of the decade there was a decline in total investment and a flight of private capital. The flight of private capital was in part financed, in effect, by public borrowing overseas. In the case of land transfers in Kenya (the million-acre and associated schemes) the function of foreign lending was quite directly to buy out European farmers and allow them to transfer their capital overseas.

Following independence the three governments published development plans (Tanzania in 1964; Uganda in 1966; and Kenya in 1964, with a number of revisions in subsequent years) and began to take action to restore investment momentum.

Kenya was able to weather the period of capital outflow, partly as a result of the availability of considerable external finance, notably from the British. By the latter part of the 1960s Kenya had gained a new place as a centre for foreign investment. It was identified by official U.S. policy as one of the potential developers in Africa, received sustained United Kingdom financial support and was well favoured by other donors, including the World Bank. Private capital identified Nairobi as a base for regional penetration. Nairobi remains the commercial, tourist and industrial centre of the East African Common Market, despite the shift of the administrative centre to Arusha in Tanzania. There was, therefore, a revival of private investment in commercial development, hotel building and industry, and a widely expressed belief in the western countries that Kenya presented the soundest prospects for development in east and central Africa. As always with such choices, along with the attractiveness to international capital went an underlying nagging suspicion that the very pattern of capitalist, urban development may carry with it the seeds of future political instability.

Tanzania and Self-Reliance

The evolution of Tanzanian policy presents an interesting contrast. Problems arose in implementing the first five-year plan because of financial difficulties and implementation bottlenecks. The former in part resulted from the decline of sisal prices from 1965 on, and in part from the failure of aid to reach expected levels. (The United Kingdom froze new capital aid as a result of the break in diplomatic relations following the British failure to take effective action to deal with Rhodesia's U.D.I.) The Tanzanian response was to increasingly emphasize self-reliance and

domestic resource reliance, in which they achieved significant success. The emphasis on self-reliance was one of the themes of the Arusha Declaration of 1967, which resulted in nationalization of substantial parts of the foreign-owned sector. Self-reliant development required local control of the economy.

Indeed, the mood throughout Africa towards the task of financing development shifted during the 1960s towards a recognition that the primary basis for African development would have to be the mobilization by Africans of the resources available in their own continent, and the most eloquent spokesman for this point of view has been Tanzania's President Nyerere.

Some states after independence suffered from chronic financial problems inherent in their economic structure. Thus Senegal incorporated the old centre for the administration of French West Africa, Dakar, which became a city without a meaningful hinterland. Senegal remained heavily dependent upon France, both as a provider of financial support and as a customer for her peanuts. Dakar survives, with an over-elaborate superstructure including a substantial expatriate population.

Malawi was also heavily dependent upon external financial support when she became independent. In her case it was a lack of internal development rather than the existence of any particular inherited burden which was the problem. Previously one of the main economic functions of Malawi had been to supply labour to neighbouring economies. The inadequate tax base meant that the British exchequer had both to finance development spending and make a sizable contribution to the government recurrent budget, thus allowing a persistent deficit trade balance.

DEVELOPMENT AID

At the beginning of the 1960s the predominant sources of external public finance were the previous metropolitan powers, notably Britain and France, along with the U.S., which took a strong interest in Africa, particularly during the Kennedy period. Although these countries have remained important donors, there has been a diversification of financial sources which will be continued into the 1970s. While Britain, France and the U.S. have reduced their rate of net resource transfer, the contribution of other donors has expanded considerably. As a result of the reductions by the largest donors, net aid from western sources reached a plateau in the period 1962–65, from which there has since been a slight decline.

In exceptional cases the changing pattern came abruptly. This was so with Guinea. French support was abruptly withdrawn as part of the general break between the two countries. There was also a sharp, if less dramatic, change when Britain froze capital aid to Tanzania, as a result of the break in diplomatic relations in 1965. However, the more typical pattern has been for new bilateral donors to enter the aid field alongside the old metropolitan powers.

Table 2

TOTAL OFFICIAL BILATERAL AND MULTILATERAL NET FLOWS TO AFRICA, 1960–68

COUNTRIES AND AGENCIES SUPPLYING MORE THAN
$5 MILLION PER ANNUM

(U.S. $ million)

	ANNUAL AVERAGE	
	1960–66	1967–68
Belgium	75.78	64.82
Canada	5.85	24.52
Denmark	0.62	5.62
France	636.10	514.60
Germany	59.57	104.78
Italy	38.18	89.24
Netherlands	0.73	8.58
Norway	0.62	5.94
Portugal	38.06	46.40
Sweden	3.58	16.82
U.K.	193.84	169.26
U.S.A.	444.31	302.00
TOTAL BILATERAL	1,500.10	1,356.75
IBRD	52.10	35.10
IDA	0.57	34.14
EEC	59.18	101.52
UN	55.53	68.31
TOTAL	163.33	224.72
GRAND TOTAL	1,663.43	1,581.47

Totals include contributions by Australia, Austria' Japan, Switzerland, IFC and African Development Bank'

Source: Resources for the Developing World: the flow of financial resources to less-developed countries 1962–68, p. 267, OECD.

Multilateral Aid

On the multilateral front the most significant development during the late 1960s was the provision of finance through the World Bank's "soft-loan" affiliate, the IDA, which was able to provide finance both on better terms and for different types of project than the traditional World Bank loan. It is notable that the IDA was involved in provision of finance for agricultural and educational development, not areas in which the Bank had in the past played an active role. Despite a stated concern of the Bank to take an increasing interest in development in tropical Africa, in terms of total net flows, its role remains minor. Its influence, however, transcends that implied by the figures for financial transfers. The Bank has shown an increasing interest in creating consultative groups between donors to meet with recipients to discuss their aid problems, and has played an active role in providing services for project identification and evaluation. It has, for example, set up a field office in Nairobi to provide advisory services in east and central Africa. Teams from the World Bank are also active in assessing overall development programmes. From the African

point of view such activities may have their use in providing second opinions on development programmes and facilitating the flow of bilateral as well as multilateral aid, but they are also not without their dangerous aspects. The World Bank is an international institution, but not a truly multilateral one. It is dominated by western influences and has been, at the top, under American control throughout its history. Precisely because it is business-like and sophisticated, there is cause for concern that it could become the efficient conductor of a neo-colonial orchestra in Africa. On the other hand the UN agencies, while genuinely multilateral, have operated by and large at a fairly low level of operational effectiveness in Africa.

The increasing diversity of aid sources has been welcome not only because it has prevented a more severe decline in the total net flow of finance, but also because it has increased the room for manoeuvre of the African governments in negotiating with external economic interests, both public and private. Thus the availability of help from friendly powers who had come upon the aid scene during the 1960s made it much easier for Tanzania to implement her nationalization of the British banks than would have been possible at the beginning of the decade.

Scandinavian, German and Italian Aid

An especially useful role, realized to a small extent in practice and of greater potential importance, is to be played by the smaller western nations. The Scandinavian countries and Canada, for example, have expanded their role over the past decade, so that they now have programmes which, although small compared to the total, can nevertheless play a strategic role in particular instances. They are, for example, able to provide alternative sources of support not so loaded with cold-war implications or old colonial attachments, and unrelated to particular economic interests.

From the point of view of the western powers the role of the Scandinavians is satisfactory, in that broadly they represent the ideology of the west with their social democratic version of capitalism, and are seen to be preferable to the further involvement of the communist countries.

In terms of absolute financial impact, however, the emergence of Federal Germany and Italy as economic forces in Africa is the most obvious change in the pattern of finance available from the western countries. When the Federal German bilateral contribution is added to her share of the EEC development fund, it is clear that she is catching up with the U.K. as a source of public development funds in Africa. Italy has been particularly important in the few countries where her aid has been concentrated. In 1968 of $113.6 million made available in Africa, $48 million went to Egypt, $8.5 to Ethiopia, $10.8 to Somalia, $12.1 to Sudan and $13.2 to Zambia. In both the Italian and German cases the expanded aid programmes went along with increased commercial activity and private investment.

[continued on p. 59

Table 4

AFRICA'S EXTERNAL TRADE
IMPORTS C.I.F.
(U.S. $ million)

COUNTRY AND REGION	1948	1953	1958	1963	1965	1966	1967	1968	1969	1970	1971
SOUTH AFRICA[1,2]	1,424	1,194	1,555	1,698	2,459	2,304	2,687	2,632	2,988	3,556	4,039
DEVELOPING MARKET ECONOMIES											
Northern Africa:											
Algeria	482	579	1,139	683	671	639	639	815	1,009	1,257	n.a.
Egypt[3]	674	516	667	916	933	1,070	792	666	638	787	890[17]
Libya	22	31	97	239	320	405	476	645	676	554	n.a.
Morocco	389	489	393	442	445	476	517	549	560	684	691
Sudan	92	146	170	285	208	222	213	258	266	311	331
Tunisia	179	172	155	223	245	249	260	217	265	306	343
TOTAL NORTHERN AFRICA	1,890	1,970	2,640	2,790	2,820	3,060	2,900	3,150	3,410	3,900	4,240
Other Africa:											
Angola	49	85	130	147	195	207	275	303	322	369	422
Burundi	n.a.	n.a.	n.a.	31[14]	18	20	20	23	22	22	30
Cape Verde Islands	16	10	13	6	8	9	9	10	15	n.a.	n.a.
CEUCA (UDEAC):[6]											
Cameroon[7,16]	42	80	107	128	151	146	188	187	205	242	249
Central African Republic[7]		13	19	26	28	31	40	36	35	34	n.a.
Chad[7]	53	18	28	29	31	30	38	34	47	61	62
Congo (Brazzaville)[7]		40	58	62	65	70	82	84	78	57	n.a.
Gabon[7]		14	35	48	63	66	67	64	78	80	n.a.
Dahomey[5]	10	16	21	33	34	34	44	50	55	64	76
Ethiopia	45	56	75	111	150	162	143	173	155	172	189
French Terr. Afar, Issa	17	25	24	48	n.a.	n.a.	30	38	33	n.a.	n.a.
The Gambia	9	6	11	12	16	18	19	21	20	18	26
Ghana	127	207	237	365	445	352	310	308	347	411	n.a.
Guinea[5]	16	36	62	46	53	70	n.a.	n.a.	n.a.	n.a.	n.a.
Guinea (Bissau)	7	6	8	14	15	18	16	18	23	27	n.a.
Ivory Coast[5,8]	34	71	109	170	236	257	263	314	334	388	399
Kenya[9]	155	145	170	206	249	314	298	321	327	397	515
Uganda[9]		72	76	87	114	119	116	123	127	121	191
Liberia	9	19	38	108	105	112	125	107	114	150	157
Madagascar	78	129	126	127	138	142	145	170	183	170	213
Malawi[10,15]			n.a.	n.a.	57	76	70	70	74	86	109
Rhodesia[1,10]	240	328	n.a.	n.a.	335	237	262	290	279	329	395
Zambia[1,10]			n.a.	n.a.	295	345	429	455	437	502	555
Mali[5,11]	n.a.	n.a.	n.a.	34	43	36	34	37	39	47	55
Mauritania[5,11]	n.a.	n.a.	n.a.	30	24	22	37	35	45	48	n.a.
Mauritius	41	53	63	70	77	70	78	76	68	76	83
Mozambique	71	80	115	142	173	208	199	235	261	326	n.a.
Niger[5]	3	8	11	24	38	45	46	42	49	58	n.a.
Nigeria	169	303	466	581	770	718	626	541	696	1,059	1,510
Réunion	25	37	48	70	97	105	116	126	146	161	171
Rwanda	n.a.	n.a.	n.a.	n.a.	18	21	20	22	24	29	33
São Tomé and Príncipe	4	4	5	5	5	6	5	6	8	9	n.a.
Senegal[5,11]	115	176	208	156	160	155	158	180	200	193	218
Sierra Leone	20	31	67	84	108	100	90	91	112	117	113
Somalia	n.a.	n.a.	n.a.	45	50	42	40	48	52	45	63
Tanzania A[9,12]	81	80	94	113	140	178	182	214	199	272	338
Tanzania B[13]	11	16	15	15	12	13	8				
Togo	7	12	18	29	45	47	45	47	56	65	70
Upper Volta[5,8]	n.a.	8	9	38	37	38	36	41	48	47	50
Zaire[4]	191	363	362	254	321	343	256	310	410	533	n.a.
TOTAL OTHER AFRICA	1,710	2,640	3,380	3,940	5,110	5,180	5,220	5,520	5,990	7,110	8,290
TOTAL AFRICA (excl. South Africa)	3,600	4,620	6,020	6,730	7,930	8,240	8,120	8,670	9,400	11,010	12,520

[1] Imports f.o.b.

[2] Figures for all periods adjusted to approximate trade of present customs area.

[3] Includes trade with Syria for all periods.

[4] Prior to 1961, includes data for former Ruanda-Urundi.

[5] Trade with the countries of former French West Africa is excluded prior to 1962, by Senegal; prior to 1959, by Dahomey and Guinea; prior to 1960, by Niger; prior to 1961, by Ivory Coast, Mali, Mauritania and Upper Volta.

[6] Customs and Economic Union of Central Africa which, prior to 1966, was known as the Equatorial Customs Union, comprises Central African Republic, Chad (prior to 1969), Congo (Brazzaville), Gabon and, beginning 1966, Cameroon.

[7] Inter-trade between the countries of the Customs Union is excluded, except for Chad (beginning 1969).

[8] Data for Upper Volta are included with Ivory Coast in 1948.

Table 5

AFRICA'S EXTERNAL TRADE
EXPORTS F.O.B.
(U.S. $ million)

Country and Region	1948	1953	1958	1963	1965	1966	1967	1968	1969	1970	1971
SOUTH AFRICA[1,2]	557	830	1,096	1,400	1,483	1,689	1,910	2,109	2,143	2,159	2,186
DEVELOPING MARKET ECONOMIES											
Northern Africa:											
Algeria	420	397	488	759	637	621	724	830	934	1,009	n.a.
Egypt[3]	607	409	478	520	604	604	566	622	745	762	789
Libya	12	10	14	336	796	995	1,178	1,876	2,167	2,366	n.a.
Morocco	178	269	345	384	430	428	424	450	485	488	498
Sudan	99	128	125	226	195	203	214	233	248	293	328
Tunisia	61	111	153	126	120	140	149	158	166	181	216
TOTAL NORTHERN AFRICA	1,390	1,330	1,610	2,350	2,790	3,000	3,250	4,180	4,750	5,110	5,530
Other Africa:											
Angola	60	123	128	163	200	221	238	271	327	423	410
Burundi	n.a.	n.a.	n.a.	14[14]	9	10	14	14	12	24	19
Cape Verde Islands	10	10	11	12	11	10	12	10	10	n.a.	n.a.
CEUCA (UDEAC):[6]											
Cameroon[7,16]	36	75	115	135	139	145	158	189	226	226	206
Central African Republic[7]	50	14	16	22	26	31	29	36	36	31	n.a.
Chad[7]		14	25	23	27	24	27	28	32	30	28
Congo (Brazzaville)[7]		6	14	42	47	43	48	49	44	31	n.a.
Gabon[7]		22	39	72	96	100	120	124	141	121	n.a.
Dahomey[5]	12	15	18	13	14	11	15	22	27	33	42
Ethiopia	33	68	63	90	116	111	101	106	119	122	126
French Terr. Afar, Issa	9	13	16	22	n.a.	n.a.	5	4	1	n.a.	n.a.
The Gambia	9	8	12	9	14	16	18	13	12	17	13
Ghana	202	224	263	273	291	244	278	307	301	433	n.a.
Guinea[5]	10	23	23	55	54	58	n.a.	n.a.	n.a.	n.a.	n.a.
Guinea (Bissau)	5	6	7	6	4	3	3	3	4	3	n.a.
Ivory Coast[5,8]	42	109	150	230	277	311	325	425	453	469	456
Kenya[9]	105	64	93	142	145	174	166	175	191	217	219
Uganda[9]		94	130	153	179	188	184	186	198	246	235
Liberia	16	31	54	81	135	150	159	168	195	213	222
Madagascar	50	85	96	82	92	98	104	116	112	145	147
Malawi[10]			20	30	40	49	57	48	53	60	72
Rhodesia[1,10]	210	395	138	210	423	262	254	246	307	355	388
Zambia[1,10]			209	361	532	691	658	762	1,073	1,001	673
Mali[5,11]	n.a.	n.a.	n.a.	11	16	13	11	11	17	33	35
Mauritania[5,11]	n.a.	n.a.	n.a.	16	58	69	72	72	78	79	n.a.
Mauritius	44	58	61	90	66	71	64	64	66	69	65
Mozambique	40	56	71	101	108	112	122	154	142	156	n.a.
Niger[5]	6	10	18	22	25	35	33	29	24	32	n.a.
Nigeria	252	348	380	531	751	795	677	591	891	1,240	1,811
Réunion	20	31	32	38	34	39	36	46	45	51	44
Rwanda	n.a.	n.a.	n.a.	n.a.	14	12	14	15	14	25	22
São Tomé and Príncipe	9	9	8	6	5	6	8	9	9	8	n.a.
Senegal[5,11]	84	105	137	111	129	149	137	151	126	152	125
Sierra Leone	22	33	55	81	89	83	70	96	108	103	97
Somalia	n.a.	n.a.	n.a.	32	27	30	28	30	32	31	34
Tanzania A[9,12]	63	97	121	179	176	235	222	227	236	238	251
B[13]	8	22	14	14	11	14	16				
Togo	10	16	15	18	27	36	32	39	45	55	49
Upper Volta[5,8]	n.a.	5	5	11	14	16	18	21	21	18	16
Zaire[4]	245	398	406	318	336	465	436	504	644	735	n.a.
TOTAL OTHER AFRICA	1,640	2,630	3,030	3,880	4,840	5,200	5,100	5,510	6,520	7,420	7,660
TOTAL AFRICA (excl. South Africa)	3,030	3,960	4,650	6,230	7,630	8,200	8,360	9,680	11,270	12,520	13,190

[9] Inter-trade of local produce and locally manufactured goods between Kenya, Uganda and Tanzania (prior to 1968, Tanganyika) is excluded.

[10] Data for 1948 and 1953, general trade of the former Federation of Rhodesia and Nyasaland. Imports and national exports for 1958–63 exclude inter-trade between the members of the former federation.

[11] The trade of Mauritania and Mali is included under Senegal prior to 1960.
[12] Former Tanganyika.
[13] Former Zanzibar and Pemba.
[14] Includes data for Rwanda.
[15] Prior to 1971, imports f.o.b.
[16] Prior to 1963, East Cameroon only.
[17] Excluding crude petroleum.

Table 6

BALANCE OF PAYMENTS SUMMARY

(millions of U.S. dollars).

Country	Year	Goods, Freight and Insurance on Merchandise	Other Services and Private Unrequited Transfers	Central Government Unrequited Transfers	Non-monetary Sector Capital			Monetary Sector Capital and Gold		Net Errors and Omissions
					Direct Investment	Other Private Capital	Central Govt. Capital	Private Institutions	Central Institutions	
Algeria	1967	123[1]	− 37[1]	19	47	− 9	17	−21	−143	4
	1968	36[1]	− 79[1]	12	64	− 16	57	−22	− 62	10
	1969	−120[1]	−108[1]	22	41	− 11	43	−55	76	112
Chad	1968	− 16	− 1	16	n.a.	− 1	1	—	1	—
	1969	− 24	− 3	18	1	2	− 1	1	3	− 3
	1970	− 25	2	24	1	1	3	− 1	1	− 8
Dahomey	1966	− 21	− 2	17	1	—	− 1	− 2	1	7
	1967	− 35	− 1	20	—	8	− 1	2	1	6
	1968	− 22	− 4	20	2	—	1	—	− 4	5
Egypt	1966	−356[2]	177[2]	6	n.a.[3]	− 13[3]	128	60	− 3	1
	1967	−360[2]	74[2]	122	n.a.[3]	− 14[3]	108	−12	85	− 3
	1968	−185[2]	− 60[2]	251	n.a.[3]	− 17[3]	19	− 4	− 16	12
	1969	−227[2]	− 69[2]	288	n.a.[3]	− 15[3]	−66	34	59	− 4
	1970	−383[2]	− 76[2]	304	n.a.[3]	− 10[3]	15	32	111	−18
Ethiopia	1966	− 49	4	12	10	11	8	5	− 1	—
	1967	− 5	− 36	10	6	1	9	3	14	− 2
	1968	− 62	17	14	5	20	5	− 1	2	4
	1969	− 34	11	14	3	1	9	—	4	1
	1970	− 50	5	11	4	7	5	16	1	1
Gabon	1968	74	− 80	11	1	− 4	− 1	− 1	4	− 4
	1969	69	− 89	9	27	− 19	4	− 4	3	6
	1970	55	− 69	13	− 1	− 5	6	6	− 6	− 1
Ghana	1966	− 64	− 66	5	56	− 7	48	7	19	2
	1967	2	− 87	—	33	− 1	15	−16	46	8
	1968	32	− 88	—	17	3	21	− 3	8	10
	1969	33	− 83	1	10	− 1	36	16	3	−15
	1970	57	− 85	1	19	—	53	−11	− 55	9
Ivory Coast	1966	55	−101	19	− 2	14	3	−11	− 1	24
	1967	48	−106	14	6	6	20	34	− 8	6
	1968	113	−113	15	12	− 5	20	−30	− 5	− 7
	1969	126	−126	21	12	− 11	26	−26	3	−25
	1970	87	−130	22	12	6	21	− 3	− 31	13
Kenya	1966	− 49	21	9	n.a.[3]	5[3]	31	−10	− 20	13
	1967	− 78	13	5	n.a.[3]	21[3]	11	29	− 12	11
	1968	− 78	13	25	n.a.[3]	28[3]	19	−11	− 20	24
	1969	− 60	30	20	n.a.[3]	45[3]	17	− 2	− 63	13
	1970	−112	50	22	n.a.[3]	63[3]	25	− 3	− 50	—
Libya	1966	593	−485	—	−44	16	− 2	1	− 92	13
	1967	695	−574	− 77	19	6	− 1	6	− 46	−16
	1968	1,219	−883	− 84	−80	15	− 2	4	−155	−34
	1969	1,488	−1,040	−118	141	− 4	− 17	6	−377	−67
Malawi	1966	− 33	− 12	20	4	5	6	3	5	2
	1967	− 18	− 17	20	11	—	8	5	− 4	− 3
	1968	− 27	− 15	16	11	7	9	− 2	—	1
	1969	− 30	− 16	17	5	10	15	—	2	− 3
	1970	− 35	− 13	14	10	− 8	36	—	8	2
Mali	1966/67[4]	− 30	− 14	13	n.a.[3]	− 2[3]	22	− 1	6	6
	1967/68[4]	− 28	− 10	9	n.a.[3]	8[3]	17	5	12	3
	1968	− 22	− 10	8	n.a.[3]	− 13[3]	19	4	14	—
Mauritius	1966	—	− 4	9	—	1	2	− 1	3	− 3
	1967	− 16	− 1	3	—	1	4	4	10	− 3
	1968	− 8	2	5	—	1	3	3	− 6	2
	1969	—	5	2	1	2	4	− 3	− 12	1
	1970	− 2	7	2	2	1	1	4	− 17	—
Morocco	1966	− 37	− 32	18	n.a.[3]	− 3[3]	44	− 1	11	− 3
	1967	− 81	1	11	n.a.[3]	− 7[3]	59	− 2	22	2
	1968	− 84	7	19	n.a.[3]	− 15[3]	46	4	21	− 1
	1969	− 68	43	12	n.a.[3]	− 7[3]	39	− 6	− 12	− 4
	1970	−147	44	10	n.a.[3]	68[3]	47	− 2	− 31	
Nigeria	1966	102	−384	25	138	32	1	7	20	59
	1967	68	−335	34	111	39	21	6	93	−37
	1968	68	−342	38	130	89	4	−30	− 4	47
	1969	252	−428	24	140	− 30	5	− 5	− 13	55
	1970	207	−386	44	202	−105	12	5	− 90	94

Table 6 (continued)

BALANCE OF PAYMENTS SUMMARY
(millions of U.S. dollars)

Country and Currency Unit	Year	Goods, Freight and Insurance on Merchandise	Other Services and Private Unrequited Transfers	Central Government Unrequited Transfers	Non-monetary Sector Capital			Monetary Sector Capital and Gold		Net Errors and Omissions
					Direct Investment	Other Private Capital	Central Govt. Capital	Private Institutions	Central Institutions	
Sierra Leone	1966	− 18	− 10	3	7	3	5	—	2	8
	1967	− 19	− 11	3	6	6	9	− 1	6	1
	1968	4	− 9	2	7	2	7	− 2	− 12	1
	1969	− 3	− 10	3	16	—	2	− 2	− 9	3
	1970	− 12	− 9	3	12	6	2	− 1	− 2	− 1
Somalia	1966	− 15	− 6	10	n.a.[3]	2[3]	9	—	− 2	2
	1967	− 17	− 6	12	n.a.[3]	2[3]	7	− 1	2	1
	1968	− 18	− 4	19	n.a.[3]	2[3]	4	n.a.	− 3	
	1969	− 22	− 1	10	n.a.[3]	2[3]	16	n.a.	− 8	1
South Africa	1966	339	−363	23	117	94	−55	41	−209	13
	1967	48	−334	33	82	109	−81	−13	9	147
	1968	396	−340	49	256	205	1	− 8	−642	83
	1969	39	−448	42	244	− 28	− 6	39	48	70
	1970	−714	−520	54	353	229	149	−27	390	52
Sudan	1966	− 27	− 29	3	—	3	41	1	8	
	1967	− 22	− 26	2	2	2	26	− 1	25	− 4
	1968	− 30	− 22	− 1	—	− 1	23	13	16	2
	1969	− 1	− 27	− 1	—	1	36	−13	6	− 1
	1970	− 15	− 28	1	1	8	− 1	—	25	− 1
Tanzania	1966	12	− 16	− 2	n.a.[3]	17[3]	7	− 4	− 23	9
	1967	11	− 16	3	n.a.[3]	− 11[3]	22	−16	—	7
	1968	− 10	3	1	n.a.[3]	− 1[3,5]	22	—	15	n.a.[5]
	1969	19	6	1	n.a.[3]	− 2[3,5]	11	−15	− 1	n.a.[5]
	1970	− 55	2	2	n.a.	1	32	− 9	16	8
Tunisia	1966	−132	4	15	n.a.[3]	62[3]	41	—	11	− 1
	1967	−132	− 5	22	n.a.[3]	30[3]	76	—	− 6	15
	1968	− 79	14	30	n.a.[3]	10[3]	39	2	− 9	− 7
	1969	−109	29	32	6	17	39	− 8	− 1	− 5
	1970	−137	46	31	16	22	31	1	− 19	3
Uganda	1966	19	− 38	4	n.a.[3]	12[3]	26	− 7	− 14	− 2
	1967	25	− 38	3	n.a.[3]	8[3]	15	−11	1	− 3
	1968	23	− 31	4	n.a.[3]	− 3[3]	13	3	− 13	1
	1969	21	− 30	3	n.a.[3]	3[3,5]	19	− 8	7	n.a.[5]
Zaire	1966	110	−146	41	14	− 19	32	−27	—	− 5
	1967	156	−178	38	14	− 11	22	− 4	47	10
	1968	209	−199	35	11	− 23	18	22	− 70	− 3
	1969	212	−213	47	7	− 7	7	5	− 60	2
	1970	184	−250	52	43	− 56	8	− 9	13	—

[1] All transportation is included with "goods, freight and insurance on merchandise".

[2] All transportation and insurance are included with "other services and private unrequited transfers".

[3] "Direct investment" is included with "other private non-monetary sector capital".

[4] Years ending 30th June.

[5] "Net errors and omissions" are included with "other private non-monetary sector capital".

Source: United Nations, *Statistical Yearbook 1971*.

continued from p. 54]
Communist Aid

While such diversification can be seen as in part the result of the efforts of the traditional western donors to draw new contributors into the field, through activities in such arenas as the OECD Development Assistance Committee, other forms of diversification have been viewed with greater alarm in the west. There was concern first about the

Table 3
COMMUNIST COUNTRIES AID COMMITMENT
(1954–68—U.S. $ million)

	U.S.S.R.	EASTERN EUROPE	CHINA
Total Africa . .	858	348	296
of which:			
Algeria . .	232	22	50
Ghana . .	89	102	40

Source: Resources for the Developing World: the flow of financial aid to less-developed countries 1962–68, p. 304, OECD.

intrusion of the Soviet Union and the eastern European powers and, when western nerves had been calmed somewhat by familiarity (and recognition that the Soviet Union was not much more successful than the west in buying friends and influence), even greater alarm was engendered by the appearance of the Chinese on the scene. The U.S.S.R., in turn, has viewed China's involvement with little more enthusiasm than that shown by the U.S.

What is viewed by the cold-warriors of the west as potential subversion is, from the African point of view, a welcome alternative to dangerous over-dependence on the western powers, whose motives both in relation to white-dominated southern Africa and the stake of international capital throughout Africa are increasingly well understood. Although it would be a mistake for the African nations to encourage the great powers to compete in the aid field (as that can only too easily lead to less desirable forms of competition), the existence of the two communist blocs has provided a significant external element allowing for a degree of financial and political independence in Africa. During the late 1950s and 1960s this was most dramatically the case in relation to the Soviet Union's finance of the Aswan High Dam; currently the finance of the TanZam railway by the People's Republic of China is particularly noteworthy.

The Major Western Donors

Looking at the relative importance of the major donors, the size of the French commitment stands out because of both the relative emphasis on Africa in the overall French aid programme and the large size of that programme. In 1967, for example, it is reported that France disbursed U.S. $451.7 million in Africa out of a total net programme of U.S. $854.4 million. With the exception of Guinea, France has maintained a considerable commitment to her ex-colonies in Africa, not only in public aid and private investment, but also in maintaining an elaborate structure of technical assistance, particularly in the education system and the administrative services. The French aid commitment is thus a price the French pay for a continuing domination.

An important factor in the former French colonies, as well as in the ex-Belgian ones, is the association with the EEC under the second Yaoundé Convention, signed by 18 African states in 1969 (*see* chapter on EEC, p. 119). In addition to the trade arrangements the convention provides for financial and technical assistance. The members of the EEC subscribe to the European Development Fund, which has been set at a total of about U.S. $1 billion for the period 1969–75 and is available for the eighteen except for $82 million set aside for the territories still under the colonial rule of France and the Netherlands. France and Federal Germany are the two largest contributors to this fund, each contributing some 34.4 per cent of the total.

In contrast the U.K. commitment is modest. In 1968 she disbursed $177 million net in Africa out of a total aid programme of $460 million. One hundred million of this went to five recipients—Botswana ($14 million), Kenya ($26 million), Malawi ($19 million), Nigeria ($15 million) and Zambia ($26 million). The U.K. stabilized the size of her aid programme in the mid-1960s. It should be noted that although Africa does not claim such a large share of the total aid budget as in the French case, the British do provide a higher per capita commitment to the Commonwealth countries aided in Africa than to Asian Commonwealth recipients.

Belgium also concentrated her aid programme in Africa. In 1968 $63.8 out of $73.8 million aid went to Africa— mainly to Zaire (then Congo (Kinshasa)), Rwanda and Burundi.

The U.S. involvement in Africa has remained small in comparison with her dominance of southeast Asia and Latin America. Nevertheless a relatively modest programme in U.S. terms has been of considerable importance in Africa, particularly in those countries in which the U.S. has concentrated attention.

In 1968 the U.S. spent $275 million in Africa out of a total world programme of $3,355 million. This represented a severe decline from the level of activity maintained in the early 1960s. Although less than 10 per cent of total American aid flows to Africa, the U.S. remains the second largest bilateral donor after France.

In its reduced programme the USAID has attempted to maximize impact by concentrating on countries of "particular development promise". It must be admitted that the list chosen suggests political as much as economic criteria for assessing this. The countries chosen were Tunisia, Morocco, Ghana, Liberia, Ethiopia, Nigeria and the East African Community (of the last, in practice much more Kenya than Uganda and Tanzania). In addition

Zaire received special budget support and the Ivory Coast proved eligible for liberal assistance. Adjustments were made from time to time; thus Egypt presumably declined in development promise during 1967 when it was removed from the favoured list. In 1968 the recipients of the two largest donations were Morocco and Tunisia, receiving $54 million and $43 million respectively.

So far Japan's role in Africa has been mainly through trade, or through the medium of private investment. Towards the end of the decade it was becoming increasingly clear that it would be necessary for Japan to expand her aid commitment in Africa considerably if her growing position as trading partner and investor was to be maintained. During the 1970s it is likely that such an expansion will take place and the largely token programmes of the 1960s will give way to significant flows, particularly to those countries for whom Japan is already a leading trading partner.

Discussion about the total flow of aid is, in the last analysis, not very satisfactory, for it implies that increase in aid flows will usually finance greater development. The total pattern of aid may be seen to reflect the political and economic interests of the donors in maintaining either their own positions in Africa or their support of régimes which they feel to be suitable from one point of view or another. Where

the recipients are independent and aware, the availability of additional resources is no doubt desirable. But where the prerequisites to development include changes in the political régime, or the reduction of the influence of previous metropolitan powers, or an effective challenge to domination by foreign economic interests, funds may flow in order to maintain underdevelopment rather than to finance development.

Southern Africa

It is appropriate to end this article with a reference to South Africa, Rhodesia and the Portuguese colonies. British investors have a stake in the South African economy of the order of U.S. $3 billion. Portugal is increasingly having to encourage capital from more vigorous capitalist countries to develop her colonies—for example, the Cabora Bassa project involves, directly and indirectly, a wide international range of firms.

Handling the tensions involved in maintaining an active interest in the development of white-controlled southern Africa, alongside continuing exploitation of commercial possibilities in the rest of Africa, will be the primary challenge for western diplomacy in Africa in the coming decade. Western diplomats will need to be more than usually well endowed in the tricks of their trade to undertake that task.

SELECT BIBLIOGRAPHY

IMF. *Surveys of African Economies*. Vol. 1: Cameroon, Central African Republic, Chad, Congo (Brazzaville) and Gabon, 1968. Vol. 2: Kenya, Tanzania, Uganda and Somalia, 1969.

KAMARCK, A. M. *The Economics of African Development*. London, Pall Mall, New York, Praeger, 1967.

NEWLYN, W. T. *Money in an African Context*. Nairobi, O.U.P., 1967.

OECD. *Resources for the Developing World: the flow of financial resources to the less-developed countries 1962–68*.

ROBSON, P., and LURY, D. (Eds.). *The Economies of Africa*. London, George Allen and Unwin, 1969.

Africa and the European Economic Community

Timothy Curtin

INTRODUCTION

The year 1973 will be unusually important for the independent countries in Africa south of the Sahara. Early in January the African Commonwealth countries will be invited to attend the negotiations for the renewal of the Yaoundé Convention which are due to begin on August 1st, 1973. The countries taking part in these negotiations will be the nine members of the European Economic Community (EEC) on one hand, and on the other the existing eighteen countries associated with the EEC under the current Yaoundé Convention, together with as many of the thirteen African Commonwealth countries as wish to attend.* It is also possible that Ethiopia, Liberia, and Sudan might wish to take advantage of Article 60 of the Second Yaoundé Convention to apply for associate status and to join in the negotiations.

The August negotiations present, therefore, the possibility of a special association developing between most of Western Europe and almost the whole of sub-Saharan Africa. The North African countries are negotiating their own agreements with EEC. The new Yaoundé Convention will not be restricted to Africa, since developing countries of the Commonwealth in the Caribbean and the Pacific are also being invited to attend the negotiations. A list of the countries which will be invited to attend the negotiations appears in Annex B.

THE TREATY OF ROME

The genesis of the special relationship between European and African countries which is embodied in the Yaoundé Convention may perhaps be found in the first meeting of the Council of Europe in 1949. At that time the Western European countries were suffering from a severe shortage of convertible foreign exchange, namely dollars, and it was thought that trade which was based on the complementary resources of Africa and Europe and financed within European currency zones could overcome the dollar shortage. This concept was taken up in the Strasbourg Plan of 1952 which proposed that all the member states in the Council of Europe should participate in the trade and development aid relationship between the colonial powers and their colonies. The Plan contained many of the elements of the later Yaoundé Conventions. Subsequently, however, it was left to the French Government to insist during the negotiations for the establishment of the European Economic Community that provision should be made for a special relationship between the proposed Community and France's dependent territories. It was pointed out by the French that without such provision there

* Mauritius became an associate of the EEC under the Yaoundé Convention in 1972.

would be incompatibility between France's participation at the same time in both the European Economic Community and the economic system of the French Community. For if France was permitted to maintain its preferential trading relationships with its colonies, it would be difficult in practice to prevent the other members of the EEC from becoming involved in these preferences, since their importers and exporters would be able by routing consignments through France to obtain preferential access to the markets and products of the dependencies. The French Government was also no doubt anxious to share the burden of its overseas aid with the other members of the proposed EEC—at that time France's overseas aid exceeded the total aid (including private investment) of the other five countries.

These considerations led in due course to the inclusion in the Treaty of Rome of a special section (Part IV) on "The Association of the Overseas Countries and Territories", i.e. the non-European countries and territories which had special relations with Belgium, France, Italy and the Netherlands. The Association is based on the following main principles (Article 132):

1. All Members of the EEC would apply to their trade with the associated countries and territories the same treatment that they accorded each other under the Treaty.

2. For their part, the countries and territories would apply to Members of the EEC and to each other the same treatment as had been accorded to the "European State with which it had special relations."

3. All Members of the EEC would contribute to the investments required for the development of the associated countries and territories.

The Treaty of Rome included an "implementing convention" on the association of the overseas countries and territories with the Community which provided *inter alia* for the establishment of a Development Fund. This Convention, which may be regarded as the predecessor of the first Yaoundé Convention, was to have a duration of five years from 1958. By the time it expired most of the associated countries and territories had achieved independence, and of these all but Guinea requested that their association with the EEC should be maintained. A new agreement was therefore concluded and signed at Yaoundé in the Cameroon Republic in July 1963. This first Yaoundé Convention was renewed in July 1969 for a further period of five years (the first Yaoundé Convention having been allowed to run for an extra year).

The first Yaoundé Convention included a Declaration of Intent which set out three different possible forms of association with the EEC by third countries provided their level of development was comparable to that of the Associated States. Such countries could seek full associate status under the Yaoundé Convention itself, or a more limited association agreement, or a simple trade agreement.

There is an important distinction between association agreements and trade agreements which arises from Articles 1 and 24 of the General Agreement on Trade and Tariffs (GATT). This is that privileges contained in trade agreements which do not provide for "reciprocal rights and obligations, joint actions and special procedures" are supposed to be extended automatically to the rest of the world. This GATT requirement explains in part, and is often held to justify, the so-called reverse preferences granted by the Yaoundé associated states to the members of EEC. The EEC countries were also accorded preferences in the association agreements with Nigeria (1966) and Tanzania, Kenya, and Uganda (1968). Neither of these agreements came into force (because of incomplete ratification) but the second Arusha Agreement (1969) with Tanzania, Kenya, and Uganda retained the principle of reverse preferences; the EEC's trade agreements with some Mediterranean countries also provide for a measure of reciprocity in preferences.

THE YAOUNDÉ CONVENTION

The Yaoundé Convention (all references will be to the Second Yaoundé Convention signed on July 29th, 1969) contains four main sections or "Titles" covering Trade, Technical and Financial Co-operation, Rights of Establishment, and Institutions of the Association.

Trade

The Yaoundé Convention does not necessarily require the eighteen associated countries to grant tariff preferences to the six members of the EEC. Instead the Convention purports to establish eighteen free trade areas between the EEC on one hand and the eighteen individual associated states on the other. In practice, there are exceptions on both sides. Under Article 2, the EEC excludes products covered by its Common Agricultural Policy from the duty-free entry bestowed on other products of the associated states, while the associated states are able under Article 3 of the Convention to "retain or introduce . . . customs duties and charges having equivalent effect which are necessary to meet their development needs or which are intended to contribute to their budgets." Article 7 extends this exception to cover occasions of difficulty in the balance of payments of an associated state. In all cases the Convention requires the associated states not to discriminate *against* or *between* the members of the EEC (Article 3, para. 3 and Article 7, para. 3).

In the absence of these exceptions, the eighteen free trade areas which would then exist (eighteen, because the Convention does not provide for free trade between the associated states) would imply duty-free, i.e. preferential, treatment for products of the EEC in the associated states. The exceptions, however, limit the extent of free trade to particular commodities. But although the Articles of the Convention, which allow the associated states to retain

or introduce customs duties on products of the EEC, do not *require* such duties to be levied at preferential rates in favour of the EEC member states, most of the associated states have in fact granted such preferences. (Togo and Zaire have not done so, by virtue of Article 133 of the Treaty of Rome, which exempted certain countries—those bound by international obligations to maintain a non-discriminatory tariff—from the Treaty's requirement for the reduction and eventual abolition of tariffs on products of the members of the EEC).

The preferences granted by the associated states to the members of the EEC may be regarded either as a legacy of the colonial trading relationships or else as a first instalment in response to the Treaty of Rome's call for a progressive reduction in tariffs levied on EEC exports by the associated states (Article 133) and also to the requirement in Article 3 of the Yaoundé Convention: "Products originating in the Community shall be imported into each Associated State free of customs duties and charges having equivalent effect."

Preferences are granted by the Associated States in the following manner. Their external tariffs are split into fiscal duties, sometimes called "fiscal entries" which apply to all countries, and into customs duties, which apply to all countries other than the members of the EEC. The same procedure is followed in the Arusha Agreement in which, for example, there is a 26 per cent "fiscal entry" on imported typewriters, and also a 4 per cent "customs duty"; typewriters from EEC countries would attract only the first of these charges.

The impact of the present Yaoundé Convention and its predecessors on trade flows between the members of the EEC, and the associated states, and between these groups and the rest of the world may now be examined. It will be understood of course that the trade statistics show only what has happened, not what would have happened in the absence of the Conventions.

The first effect of the Conventions was as shown above to extend the scope of the colonial trading system of the French Community to the other members of the new European Economic Community. The figures in Table 1 suggest that this has led to a reduced dependence of the eighteen associated states on trade with France—and also with Belgium, the other main metropolitan country. (Italy's trade with Somalia should strictly be treated separately but this would be unlikely to alter the conclusion).

The statistics in Table 2 on imports by the EEC from the Yaoundé associates yield the surprising result that the share of the associates in the total imports of the EEC actually fell from 3.5 per cent in 1959 to 2.3 per cent in 1969. However, the share in the EEC's imports of all less developed countries also fell sharply, from 27.4 per cent to 19.6 per cent. The associates nevertheless experienced a slower rate of growth in the absolute level of their exports to the EEC than other less developed countries: over the ten years to 1969, associates' exports to the EEC increased by 101 per cent, while exports to the EEC of less developed countries as a whole increased by 122 per cent.

The very small share of the associates in the imports of the EEC in 1969 (just over 2 per cent) will have been noted. By contrast, as may be seen in Tables 3 and 4, the associates' exports to the EEC were 70.9 per cent of their total exports to all countries in 1968. The comparable figure for 1959 was 70.6 per cent, which implies that the extension of preferences to all the associates by West Germany, Netherlands, Italy,

Belgium and Luxembourg under the Treaty of Rome did not significantly increase the importance of the EEC countries as a market for the exports of the associates.

There is a similar surprising result in the case of the imports of the Yaoundé associates from the EEC. Here the share of the EEC fell from 67.2 per cent in 1959 to 65.4 per cent in 1968, while the share of the United States, Canada, and Japan increased from 8.3 per cent to 11.8 per cent (see Tables 3 and 4).

Table 1

EXPORTS BY ASSOCIATED STATES TO THE EEC
ANNUAL GROWTH RATES, 1958–69
(%)

EEC AS A WHOLE	FRANCE	BELGIUM-LUXEMBOURG	NETHERLANDS	FEDERAL GERMANY	ITALY
6.0	2.8	6.9	9.4	11.3	13.4

Source: G. Schiffler, "Enlargement of the EEC and Community Policies in the field of trade", in *Britain, the EEC and the Third World*, Overseas Development Institute, London, 1971.

Table 2

SHARE OF YAOUNDÉ ASSOCIATES IN EEC IMPORTS, 1959–69
(percentages of total imports)

	EEC AS A WHOLE	BELGIUM-LUXEMBOURG	NETHERLANDS	FEDERAL GERMANY	FRANCE	ITALY
Yaoundé Associates:						
1959	3.5	6.0	1.1	1.0	9.0	1.8
1969	2.3	4.8	1.1	1.0	3.9	1.6
All Developing Countries:						
1959	27.4	18.6	22.3	22.8	43.7	29.3
1969	19.6	15.6	15.6	18.3	21.4	26.0

Source: Britain, the EEC, and the Third World, Overseas Development Institute, London, 1971.

Table 3

EXPORTS AND IMPORTS OF LESS-DEVELOPED COUNTRIES TO AND FROM THE DEVELOPED COUNTRIES: 1959

		EXPORTS						IMPORTS					
		World	EEC	U.K.	Total Industrial Western Europe	U.S. and Canada	Japan	World	EEC	U.K.	Total Industrial Western Europe	U.S. and Canada	Japan
Total Less-Developed Countries	$ million	22,683.7	5,469.2	3,519.8	9,541.9	5,881.8	1,260.2	23,964.6	5,726.6	3,173.0	9,737.9	6,215.9	1,480.1
	%	100.0	24.1	15.5	42.1	25.9	5.6	100.0	23.9	13.2	40.6	25.9	6.2
Latin America	$ million	7,425.7	1,332.0	694.5	2,248.8	3,284.1	181.8	7,516.4	1,395.6	395.6	2,148.2	3,640.5	153.2
	%	100.0	17.9	9.3	30.3	44.2	2.4	100.0	18.6	5.3	28.6	48.4	2.0
Other Western Hemisphere	$ million	1,387.1	162.2	266.7	490.9	510.9	3.4	1,787.0	203.0	285.7	514.6	334.6	14.5
	%	100.0	11.7	19.2	35.4	36.8	0.2	100.0	11.4	16.0	28.8	18.7	0.8
Middle East	$ million	4,335.8	1,493.2	735.2	2,329.6	424.2	320.7	3,047.7	838.2	522.1	1,511.6	521.5	163.4
	%	100.0	34.4	17.0	53.7	9.8	7.4	100.0	27.5	17.1	49.6	17.1	5.4
Africa	$ million	3,869.3	1,753.8	931.3	2,765.3	370.6	61.2	4,608.1	2,135.9	880.2	3,135.6	281.2	144.8
	%	100.0	45.3	24.1	71.5	9.6	1.6	100.0	46.4	19.1	68.0	6.1	3.1
Asia	$ million	5,545.4	701.0	851.4	1,637.2	1,287.4	675.1	6,777.8	1,112.7	1,030.8	2,313.1	1,597.1	994.8
	%	100.0	12.6	15.4	29.5	23.2	12.2	100.0	16.4	15.2	34.1	23.6	14.7
Commonwealth Less-Developed Countries	$ million	5,617.1	913.2	1,670.2	2,707.5	996.2	352.4	6,508.7	1,014.5	1,771.8	2,952.6	1,122.2	504.3
	%	100.0	16.3	29.7	48.2	17.7	6.3	100.0	15.6	27.2	45.4	17.2	7.7
Yaoundé Associates	$ million	1,074.9	758.6	52.0	819.7	104.0	2.2	927.8	623.4	40.7	682.8	71.1	5.6
	%	100.0	70.6	4.8	76.3	9.7	0.2	100.0	67.2	4.4	73.6	7.7	0.6

Source: IMF/IBRD *Direction of International Trade.*

Table 4

EXPORTS AND IMPORTS OF LESS-DEVELOPED COUNTRIES TO AND FROM THE DEVELOPED COUNTRIES: 1968

		EXPORTS						IMPORTS					
		World	EEC	U.K.	Total Industrial Western Europe	U.S. and Canada	Japan	World	EEC	U.K.	Total Industrial Western Europe	U.S. and Canada	Japan
Total Less-Developed Countries	$ million	39,806.7	10,885.5	4,368.8	16,517.3	9,067.9	4,402.0	40,332.4	9,481.9	3,793.1	14,840.8	11,065.8	4,906.1
	%	100.0	27.3	11.0	41.5	22.8	11.1	100.0	23.5	9.4	36.8	27.4	12.2
Latin America	$ million	9,670.7	2,248.5	689.6	3,323.0	4,386.2	565.6	11,111.4	2,135.0	545.3	3,225.4	5,061.3	510.6
	%	100.0	23.2	7.1	34.3	45.4	5.8	100.0	19.2	4.9	29.0	45.6	4.6
Other Western Hemisphere	$ million	1,794.5	160.5	241.0	496.9	872.0	44.6	2,569.3	376.4	298.3	745.0	717.7	58.0
	%	100.0	8.9	13.4	27.7	48.6	2.5	100.0	14.7	11.6	29.0	45.4	2.3
Middle East	$ million	8,491.5	2,830.0	1,159.4	4,306.7	354.3	1,610.3	5,750.6	1,880.5	907.1	3,138.1	823.2	471.0
	%	100.0	33.3	13.4	50.7	4.2	19.0	100.0	32.7	15.8	54.6	14.3	8.2
Africa	$ million	8,589.3	4,532.9	1,333.4	4,942.1	772.9	335.5	7,159.1	3,282.8	965.6	4,474.3	823.3	318.5
	%	100.0	52.8	15.5	57.5	9.0	3.9	100.0	45.9	13.5	52.1	9.6	3.7
Asia	$ million	9,254.3	1,056.2	889.9	2,130.5	2,661.5	1,689.0	13,245.1	1,711.4	983.9	3,043.1	3,626.3	3,502.1
	%	100.0	11.4	9.6	23.0	28.8	18.2	100.0	12.9	7.4	23.0	27.4	26.4
Commonwealth Less-Developed Countries	$ million	8,771.6	1,276.1	1,591.9	3,156.0	2,121.3	973.7	10,108.0	1,454.1	1,644.1	3,401.2	2,656.0	1,254.7
	%	100.0	14.5	18.1	36.0	24.2	11.1	100.0	14.4	16.3	33.6	26.3	12.4
Yaoundé Associates	$ million	1,575.9	1,116.7	63.4	1,196.1	154.1	33.3	1,375.9	899.9	57.9	987.0	112.3	49.6
	%	100.0	70.9	4.0	75.9	9.8	2.1	100.0	65.4	4.2	71.7	8.2	3.6

Source: IMF/IBRD *Direction of International Trade.*

Table 5

IMPORTS BY EEC FROM YAOUNDÉ ASSOCIATES, DEVELOPING COUNTRIES AND REST OF WORLD*

($ million)

	1959	1969		1959	1969
Total Imports:			*Animal and Vegetable Oils and*		
Yaoundé Associates .	854.3	1,718.8	*Fats:*		
Other Developing Countries	4,850.1	11,255.3	Yaoundé Associates . .	87.3	77.1
All Countries . . .	24,294.7	75,577.7	Other Developing Countries	87.0	148.2
			All Countries . . .	403.6	622.3
Food and Live Animals: .			*Chemicals:*		
Yaoundé Associates .	254.9	488.5	Yaoundé Associates . .	2.9	6.4
Other Developing Countries	1,295.8	2,343.6	Other Developing Countries	38.6	105.9
All Countries . . .	4,531.5	10,511.3	All Countries . . .	1,266.5	5,526.5
Beverages and Tobacco:			*Manufactured Goods:*		
Yaoundé Associates .	7.8	5.7	Yaoundé Associates . .	185.3	559.5
Other Developing Countries	286.9	190.2	Other Developing Countries	242.2	1,366.4
All Countries . . .	566.9	978.3	All Countries . . .	4,695.8	17,435.0
Crude Materials, inedible:			*Machinery and Transport*		
Yaoundé Associates .	298.1	553.1	*Equipment:*		
Other Developing Countries	993.5	1,674.5	Yaoundé Associates . .	0.6	5.1
All Countries . . .	5,118.8	9,847.5	Other Developing Countries	16.8	75.8
			All Countries . . .	3,178.0	15,592.9
Mineral Fuels and Lubricants:			*Miscellaneous Manufactures*		
Yaoundé Associates .	15.1	21.1	*and Other Transactions:*		
Other Developing Countries	1,869.8	5,460.3	Yaoundé Association .	0.8	1.6
All Countries . . .	3,188.2	7,952.4	Other Developing Countries	10.2	178.8
			All Countries . . .	1,325.2	6,052.2

* Classified according to Standard International Trade Classification.

Source: Britain, the EEC, and the Third World, Overseas Development Institute, London, 1971.

Two conclusions may be drawn from these figures: firstly, that the Yaoundé Association has at best only preserved the previous pattern of trading relationships, and secondly, that the trade between the EEC and the associates is relatively more significant for the latter than for the former.

For an explanation of the trade statistics it is necessary to examine the commodity composition of both the tradeflows themselves and also of the system of tariff preferences.

The associated states are basically producers of primary products and raw materials, and since world trade has been growing more rapidly in manufactures than in other commodities, it is not surprising that they have not increased their share in the imports of the EEC. The associated states have been granted duty-free access to the EEC for manufactured goods but have not yet developed the capacity to produce and export such goods on a large scale. However, manufactured goods increased from 22 per cent of total exports to the EEC in 1959 to 33 per cent in 1969—and this category moved up from third to second most important category of imports in the same period. The less developed countries taken as a whole also increased the share of manufactures in their total exports to the EEC, i.e. 9 to 15 per cent. But while the associates' exports of manufactures increased by 200 per cent from 1959 to 1969, developing countries' manufactured exports increased by 300 per cent (see Table 5).

The Yaoundé Convention (as noted previously) exempts the members of the EEC from abolition of customs duties on products subject to the common agricultural policy (C.A.P.). However, Protocol 1 of the Convention provides that where associated countries "have an economic interest in exporting" the products covered by the C.A.P., the EEC will grant these products more favourable treatment than like products originating in third countries. There is an escape clause in respect of this provision, but the Community has in fact granted preferences on products like coffee and cocoa. However more "sensitive" products (i.e. those which are produced both in the EEC and in the associated states) may be affected by the escape clause; these products include grains, butter, beef, fruit and vegetables, oilseeds (including cakes and meals made from oilseeds), and sugar.

The EEC's common agricultural policy has undoubtedly been successful in increasing the Community's self-sufficiency in foodstuffs, and oils and fats, as may be seen in Table 6. The imports of foodstuffs by EEC members from each other rose from 32 per cent of total imports of foodstuffs in 1965 to 47 per cent in 1969; equivalent figures for oils and fats were 16 per cent (1965) and 29 per cent (1969). These figures help to explain the fall in the share of Yaoundé associates' exports to the EEC from 5.6 to 4.6 per cent of total EEC imports of foodstuffs between 1959 and 1969 (see Table 5).

3

Table 6

EEC IMPORTS OF FOODSTUFFS, OILS AND FATS, 1965 AND 1969*

Group/Commodity	Total Imports by EEC Members		Imports from non-EEC Area		Share of Imports from EEC Members in Total	
	1965 ($m.)	1969 ($m.)	1965 ($m.)	1969 ($m.)	1965 (%)	1969 (%)
Competing Foodstuffs† . . .	7,078	9,224	4,730	4,859	32.2	47.4
Live Animals . . .	448	707	335	383	25.2	45.8
Meat Preparations . . .	1,003	1,430	602	627	40.0	56.1
Dairy Products . . .	531	772	200	110	62.3	85.8
Fish	382	475	300	342	21.4	28.0
Cereals	1,617	1,808	1,230	979	24.0	45.8
Fruit and Vegetables . .	2,137	2,619	1,360	1,546	36.4	41.1
Sugar, etc.	206	252	145	112	29.6	55.5
Chocolate, etc. . . .	55	115	9	11	83.7	90.5
Fodder	643	947	533	728	17.1	23.1
Other Foodstuffs . . .	55	103	15	24	72.7	76.5
Animal, Vegetable Oils and Fats .	522	623	437	445	16.3	28.6

* Because wine is the only SITC Group 1 commodity covered by the C.A.P., and it appears only since November 1969, Group 1 is excluded from the table.

† Total foodstuffs minus "non-competing" tropical foodstuffs: coffee, cocoa, and tea.

Sources: P. Tulloch, "Developing Countries and the Enlargement of the EEC", *Review 5*, Overseas Development Institute, London; *Commodity Trade Statistics*, UN, various issues.

Financial and Technical Assistance

The Second Yaoundé Convention maintains the Development Fund originally established by the Treaty of Rome, with an increased subscription by the members of the EEC providing a total of $918 million for the period 1970–74 (compared with $730 million in 1964–69). Of this sum $748 million is in the form of grants, $80 million may be subscribed in the form of share-holdings, and $90 million will be provided in the form of loans from the European Investment Bank. The European Development Fund (EDF) contributes a small part of the total aid from EEC members to all developing countries—about 6 per cent in 1969.* EDF aid is also less than the bilateral aid of EEC members to the associated states. However EDF aid has certain specially attractive features for the recipients: 90 per cent of the aid is in the form of grants, and procurement (i.e. expenditure on supplies) may be made both in the members of the EEC and in the associated states. Bilateral aid by contrast is mostly in the form of loans tied to purchases from the donor countries. However, the ability of the associated states to supply all materials and equipment needed for an investment is limited, as also is the capacity of local contractors to compete successfully for EDF contracts (see Table 7).

The EDF has been the subject of some criticism on account of the elaborate and time-consuming procedures followed before projects are approved.

Certainly as Peter Tulloch has pointed out†, there is a considerable time-lag between the commitments and the disbursements of the EDF, although this may be largely attributable to implementation of projects being spread over a period of years, as for example in irrigation schemes.

The distribution of aid to the associated countries over a six-year period is shown in Table 8. EDF aid is probably the main component in "multi-lateral" aid to the associated countries. There is a rough correspondence between aid receipts and size of population, although it is questionable how far aid should bear a close relation to population size. National income per capita is an alternative criterion, used inversely so that proportionately more aid would be given to the countries with the lowest levels of income per head. The data reveal no clear pattern in this respect: Gabon has the highest per capita income, and ranked twelfth in EDF expenditures in 1964–70, but Senegal and Ivory Coast have relatively high per capita incomes (ranking 4th and 3rd amongst the associates) and received relatively large amounts of EDF aid in 1964–70 (ranking 3rd and 4th).

Rights of Establishment

This third section of the Yaoundé Convention is mainly intended to ensure that the associated states do not discriminate in the matters of right of establishment of companies, or provision of services, between the nationals or companies of the members of the EEC. However, the associated states are not required to grant privileges in this area to the nationals and

* Estimate by P. Tulloch, "Developing Countries and the Enlargement of the EEC", *Review 5*, Overseas Development Institute, London.

† loc. cit., p. 101.

Table 7

EEC MEMBER STATES' CONTRIBUTIONS TO EDF AND CONTRACTS GAINED FROM EDF,
BY END OF 1969

| | CONTRIBUTIONS | | CONTRACTS GAINED | | | |
| | First EDF | Second EDF | First EDF | | Second EDF | |
	%	%	$'000	%	$'000	%
Belgium	12.05	9.45	10,683	2.6	22,259	8.8
West Germany	34.4	33.75	19,686	4.9	58,049	22.9
France	34.4	33.75	185,767	45.7	98,781	39.0
Italy	6.9	13.7	52,590	12.9	25,218	10.0
Luxembourg	0.2	0.3	835	0.2	31	—
Netherlands	12.05	9.05	17,536	4.3	6,080	2.4
Associates*	—	—	118,791	29.2	43,109	17.0
Non-members	—	—	383	1.0	463	1.1
TOTAL . . .	100	100	406,266	100	253,080	100

* Including EEC-owned firms registered in associates.

Source: The European Development Fund: Access to Contracts, European Communities Commission, 1970.

companies of member countries beyond what they themselves receive in the member countries of the EEC. The section also contains guarantees by the associated states concerning repayment of capital and interest on loans of the EDF and the European Investment Bank.

Institutions of the Association

The Yaoundé Conventions established the following institutions:

the Association Council and the Association Committee,
the Parliamentary Conference of the Association,
the Court of Arbitration of the Association.

These institutions provide a framework for dealing with any problems of interpretation or implementation of the Convention. The institutions have therefore a limited range of functions which does not extend, for example, to problems of co-operation between the associated countries themselves.

Inter-African Co-operation

It was noted above that the Yaoundé Convention consists in effect of eighteen free trade areas between the EEC on one hand and the individual associated states on the other. This is not strictly correct since two groups of the former French colonies have attempted to maintain the pre-independence custom unions to which they belonged. Cameroon, Central African Republic, Congo and Gabon belong to the Central African Customs and Economic Union (UDEAC), and Dahomey, Ivory Coast, Mali, Mauritania, Niger, Senegal and Upper Volta belonged until recently to the West African Customs Union (UDEAO). In principle these organizations maintain a common external tariff and internal free trade, but in practice individual members of UDEAO were allowed to levy internal fiscal duties on goods originating in other member countries. The UDEAO has now been replaced by the West African Economic Community (CEAO).

The Yaoundé Convention does not—at least formally—exclude the possibility of establishment of customs unions or free trade areas between associated states and third countries in Africa, provided these are at "a comparable level of development" (Article 13). Such third countries would not qualify for privileged access to the EEC, unless, indeed, they applied for associate status under the Yaoundé Convention. Article 14 of the Convention allows the associated states to join in customs unions with other third countries than those specified in Article 13, but subject to application of the most favoured nation principle in Article 11. The omission of reference to Article 11 in Article 13 implies that associated countries are not obliged to extend to the members of EEC any privileges accorded *African* third countries at comparable levels of development. The Convention provides that the Association Council should be informed of any action taken under Articles 13 and 14.

The associated states have not as yet made use of Articles 13 and 14. These provisions, if they are retained in the next Yaoundé Convention, could have some bearing in the case of the East African Community—indeed at least two associated states (Somalia and Burundi) have already applied to join the East African Community, but these applications have probably not reached the point where the Association Council needs to be informed.

THE ARUSHA AGREEMENT

The three East African countries—Tanzania, Uganda and Kenya—established a special form of association with the EEC in 1969. The three governments were concerned to protect their export markets in the EEC from the effects of the special privileges accorded to the Yaoundé associates many of which produce a similar range of primary commodities. In

Table 8
ECONOMIC INDICATORS FOR THE YAOUNDÉ ASSOCIATES

Country	Area (sq. km.)	Population (millions) 1968	Projection 1985	Expenditure by EDF 1964-70 $ million	Gross domestic capital formation	Exports	Agriculture	Extracting industries	Manufacturing and building industries	Services and public administration	$ per head 1969
Mauritania	1,085,200	1.0	1.53	33.8	19.6	31.8	42.0	27.2	9.8	21.0	160
Senegal	196,800	3.6	5.20	99.7	10.8	15.8	32.6	0.3	17.3	49.8	225
Mali	1,203,800	4.8	7.42	75.3	10.5	6.2	48.2	—	12.6	39.2	85
Ivory Coast	322,500	4.0	6.20	98.0	15.0	27.5	37.2	0.3	18.1	44.4	304
Upper Volta	269,100	5.0	7.30	58.8	12.0	11.3	51.0	0.4	13.8	34.8	50
Dahomey	115,800	2.5	3.90	44.3	13.4	16.3	53.2	—	11.9	34.8	71
Niger	1,189,000	3.6	5.45	61.8	12.2	11.2	58.3	—	12.2	29.5	95
Togo	56,500	1.7	2.73	35.4	11.5	18.5	42.8	6.1	19.7	30.4	125
Cameroun	476,500	5.6	7.10	106.6	12.0	18.4	48.6	0.1	10.9	40.4	144
Chad	1,295,000	3.4	5.00	61.3	9.0	11.8	47.8	—	10.6	41.6	78
Central African Rep.	616,400	1.4	1.86	44.1	13.8	17.5	36.7	7.7	11.9	43.7	134
Gabon	267,000	0.5	0.55	38.2	15.4	37.6	25.5	23.6	14.6	36.3	550
Congo (Brazzaville)	342,000	0.9	1.20	45.2	—	26.6	35.3	1.8	13.1	50.3	201
Zaire	2,345,000	16.7	25.30	94.0	12.0	22.6	23.2	6.8	21.9	47.6	280
Rwanda	26,400	3.02	4.61	23.6	—	9.6	69.3	2.2	10.2	18.3	45
Burundi	27,700	2.4	3.60	25.4	4.8	9.7	71.7	—	6.6	21.7	53
Madagascar	591,000	7.0	10.60	116.3	8.8	12.5	37.8	0.7	10.6	50.9	120
Somalia	637,700	2.7	4.08	37.9	—	18.7	—	—	n.a.	n.a.	62
Total or Average	11,063,400	69.8	103.64	1,099.7	12.1	19.0	44.8	4.5	13.3	37.3	110

Source: Yearbook of Statistics, 1970, United Nations; Review of the Economic Situation in Africa 1970, UN Economic Commission for Africa; European Development Aid, EEC Commission, 1971.

Table 9
ECONOMIC INDICATORS FOR THE COMMONWEALTH "ASSOCIABLE" COUNTRIES IN AFRICA, IN 1968

Country	Area (sq. km.)	Population 1968	Projection 1985	U.K.	Total Bilateral	Bilateral and multilateral	Gross domestic capital formation	Exports	Agriculture	Extracting industries	Manufacturing and building industries	Services and public administration	$ per head 1968
The Gambia	10,400	0.4	0.5	2.8	2.9	3.1	11.9	25.4	59.0	—	5.1	35.9	151
Ghana	237,872	8.4	14.3	14.3	72.7	73.7	9.6	15.1	—	2.4	n.a.	n.a.	288
Kenya	582,700	10.0	16.0	23.6	40.3	57.8	15.3	21.3	34.8	0.5	18.8	45.9	127
Uganda	236,096	8.0	11.5	8.6	18.0	19.2	9.2	24.9	56.4	2.5	11.5	29.6	96
Tanzania	939,690	12.3	16.5	3.6	26.3	33.2	12.2	24.3	50.0	1.9	11.2	36.9	74
Malawi	126,337	4.3	7.0	18.1	22.6	25.5	11.5	16.2	58.3	0.1	12.8	28.8	69
Nigeria	923,850	61.0	107.0	12.3	69.2	101.9	8.9	13.0	54.9	2.6	12.7	29.8	66
Sierra Leone	72,300	2.5	4.5	1.1	9.6	10.3	8.8	23.7	32.4	19.1	10.6	37.9	177
Zambia	752,620	4.7	6.7	25.2	46.1	42.6	21.1	37.7	8.2	35.4	17.3	39.3	345
Botswana	575,000	0.6	1.5	13.7	15.2	16.4	18.9	15.8	44.2	—	13.1	42.7	108
Lesotho	30,300	1.0	2.0	10.3	11.8	14.7	7.8	8.7	66.7	1.4	2.8	29.1	75
Swaziland	17,400	0.3	0.8	7.1	7.2	8.3	12.9	42.4	28.9	14.5	19.7	36.9	201
Mauritius	1,865	0.8	1.4	9.1	9.2	8.6	10.2	32.0	26.1	—	23.6	50.3	217
Total or Average	4,506,430	114.2	189.7	149.8	351.1	415.1	12.2	23.5	43.3	8.0	13.3	36.9	109

Source: Development Assistance Report by Edwin M. Martin, Chairman of the Development Assistance Committee.

addition the East African countries have a substantial adverse balance of trade with the EEC—about EA £30 million in 1970.

The Arusha Agreement provides in principle for duty-free entry to the EEC for goods originating in the three Partner States of the East African Community. In addition the EEC members agree not to impose quantitative restrictions on imports from East Africa, but with certain exceptions: firstly, agricultural products subject to the EEC's common agricultural policy—these may enter duty-free, but will be liable to internal levies; and secondly, certain products of particular concern to the Yaoundé associates, namely, unroasted coffee, cloves, and tinned pineapples—for these products "duty-free quotas" are established, 56,000 metric tons for coffee, 860 metric tons for pineapples, and 120 metric tons for cloves. Exports to the EEC in excess of these quantities may become subject to duties. The East African countries for their part give the EEC tariff preferences on 59 items, at rates ranging from 2 to 9 per cent. These items included about 15 per cent of total East African imports from the EEC in 1968, and the implied cost of the preferences in terms of revenue foregone has been put at about EA £250,000.*

Some of the major East African exports to the EEC already enjoyed duty-free entry, such as sisal fibre, raw cotton, groundnuts, unwrought copper. Exports of such products to the EEC were worth about EA £11 million, whilst products receiving preferences were worth EA £19.5 million in 1970; however, some of the latter products are liable to duty-free quotas or internal levies which could nullify the nominal tariff preference. The exports to the EEC qualifying for tariff preferences represented about 8 per cent of total East African exports to all countries in 1970— but this proportion should rise as East African exports are directed from other markets to the EEC.

The Arusha Agreement is a trade agreement "embodying reciprocal rights and obligations"; there is also the common institution of the Association Council, and provision for arbitration of disputes where necessary. The Agreement contains provisions somewhat more limited than those of the Yaoundé Convention in respect of rights of establishment and payments arrangements. The major difference between the two types of association with EEC created at Yaoundé and Arusha is that the latter excludes financial and technical assistance; the East African countries do not therefore receive aid from the European Development Fund and the European Investment Bank, although they do of course receive aid bilaterally from the member countries of the EEC.

GREAT BRITAIN, THE EEC, AND AFRICA

Great Britain's third attempt at joining the European Economic Community achieved success with the conclusion of the Treaty of Brussels on January

* *See* N. N. Kitomari, "East Africa's Association with the EEC", *1971 Universities Social Sciences Council Conference*, Makerere, Uganda, p. 8.

22nd, 1972. The Treaty entered into force so far as Britain is concerned on January 1st, 1973. The Republic of Ireland and Denmark also joined the EEC on that date, but Norway did not ratify the Treaty of Brussels following an adverse referendum result on September 25th, 1972.

Protocol 22 of the Treaty of Brussels contains an offer to thirteen independent Commonwealth countries in Africa (and seven others in the Caribbean and the Pacific) to develop special relations with the EEC. Three alternative formulae are suggested (for the full text of the Protocol, see Annex A): firstly, participation in the next Yaoundé Convention; secondly, "conclusion of one or more special Conventions of Association . . . comprising reciprocal rights and obligations, particularly in the field of trade"; and thirdly, conclusion of trade agreements.

The Commonwealth countries which decide to take up this offer are invited to participate in negotiations on the option of their choice which will begin on August 1st, 1973. The countries which choose the first formula or option will participate "side by side" with the Associated African and Malagasy States in the negotiations for the next Yaoundé Convention (the present Convention expires by January 31st, 1975 at the latest).

There is special recognition in Protocol 22 of the problems arising from the membership of Botswana, Lesotho, and Swaziland in the South African Customs Union. South Africa is a "third country" from the point of view of the EEC and associated countries, and Protocol 22 repeats Article 11 of the Yaoundé Convention which requires associated states to apply not less than most favoured third country treatment to exports of the EEC. In other words, these three countries could have to grant the same access to the EEC in their markets as is enjoyed by South Africa. It would be difficult for South Africa to allow this because of the problems it would face in maintaining its own tariff on goods from the EEC when these enter the three countries duty-free.

A further specific problem referred to in Protocol 22 is that of the countries which rely heavily on exporting sugar. Sugar is a commodity in which the EEC could be self-sufficient, taken as a whole even in its enlarged form. However, the United Kingdom is a net importer of sugar, and the assurances in Protocol 22 imply no doubt that countries like Mauritius and the Caribbean Commonwealth countries will at the least be able to maintain their sugar exports to the new EEC at the current level of their exports to the former EEC and its recent new members. In the long run, though, the cane-sugar producers may well hope for a reduction in the EEC's protection of its beet-sugar producers.

The Commonwealth countries which opt for the first formula in Protocol 22 will qualify for aid from the European Development Fund. It seems unlikely that Britain and the other new members of the EEC will increase their total aid to developing countries as a result of their subscriptions to the EDF; increases in bilateral aid are therefore likely to be held back, but the net effect from the point of view of the associated countries is likely to be slight. Table 9 provides data on the present aid received by the thirteen "associable" African countries, and also on their population and levels of national income per capita.

CONCLUSION

The decisions of the "associable" countries as to which of the three formulae in Protocol 22 they should choose—and they are of course free to reject all three—will no doubt be based on the special circumstances of each country. There will be three basic factors in any assessment of how a particular associable country's external trade stands in relation to the new EEC: firstly, there must be an estimate of the value of the Commonwealth preferences hitherto enjoyed by associables which will in due course cease, following Britain's accession to the EEC; secondly, there must be an evaluation of the costs and benefits of the various types of association with the EEC; and thirdly—though this is largely the other side of the EEC coin—there are the costs and benefits

of not seeking an association with the EEC. One of the most difficult points to decide will be whether the General Scheme of Preferences (GSP), which is being offered to all developing countries by the EEC *without* reverse preferences being expected from them, is a satisfactory alternative to association. Much will depend on the structure of each country's exports, but there is also the constitutional point that the privileges of association are guaranteed by Treaty whereas the GSP may be unilaterally withdrawn.

Other factors which may be taken into account by the associable countries could include the possible greater scope for co-operation between the anglophone and francophone countries of West Africa in an enlarged Yaoundé Association. In addition there is the possibility that a negotiation with the EEC by all the 31 associated and associable countries—possibly supported also by Ethiopia, Sudan and Liberia—may achieve greater benefits for Africa than if the non-associated countries decide to go it alone or seek to make their own arrangements with the European Economic Community.

ANNEX A

PROTOCOL No. 22

ON RELATIONS BETWEEN
THE EUROPEAN ECONOMIC COMMUNITY
AND THE ASSOCIATED AFRICAN AND MALAGASY STATES
AND ALSO THE INDEPENDENT DEVELOPING COMMONWEALTH
COUNTRIES SITUATED IN AFRICA, THE INDIAN OCEAN,
THE PACIFIC OCEAN AND THE CARIBBEAN

I

1. The European Economic Community shall offer the independent Commonwealth countries listed in Annex VI to the Act of Accession the possibility of ordering their relations with the Community in the spirit of the Declaration of Intent adopted by the Council at its meeting held on 1/2 April 1963, according to one of the following formulae at their choice:

participation in the Convention of Association which, upon the expiry of the Convention of Association signed on 29 July 1969, will govern relations between the Community and the Associated African and Malagasy States which signed the latter Convention;

the conclusion of one or more special Conventions of Association on the basis of Article 238 of the EEC Treaty comprising reciprocal rights and obligations, particularly in the field of trade;

the conclusion of trade agreements with a view to facilitating and developing trade between the Community and those countries.

2. For practical reasons, the Community desires that the independent Commonwealth countries to which its offer is addressed, should take up a position with respect to this offer as soon as possible after accession.

The Community proposes to the independent Commonwealth countries listed in Annex VI to the Act of Accession that the negotiations envisaged for the conclusion of agreements based on one of the three formulae contained in the offer should begin as from 1 August 1973.

The Community accordingly invites the independent Commonwealth countries which choose to negotiate within the framework of the first formula to participate side by side with the Associated African and Malagasy States in negotiating the new Convention to follow the Convention signed on 29 July 1969.

3. In the event of Botswana, Lesotho or Swaziland choosing one of the first two formulae contained in the offer:

appropriate solutions must be found for the specific problems arising from the special circumstances of these countries, which are a customs union with a third country;

the Community must, in the territory of those States, enjoy tariff treatment not less favourable than that applied by those States to the most-favoured third country;

the provisions of the system applied, and particularly the rules of origin, must be such as to avoid any risk of trade deflection to the detriment of the Community resulting from the participation of those States in a customs union with a third country.

II

1. As regards the association arrangements to be made on the expiry of the Convention of Association signed on 29 July 1969, the Community is ready to pursue its policy of association both with regard to the Associated African and Malagasy States and with regard to the independent developing Commonwealth countries which become parties to the same association.

2. The accession of the new Member States to the Community and the possible extension of the policy of association should not be the source of any weakening in the Community's relations with the Associated African and Malagasy States which are parties to the Convention of Association signed on 29 July 1969.

The Community's relations with the Associated African and Malagasy States ensure for those States a range of advantages and are based on structures which give the Association its distinctive character in the fields of trade relations, financial and technical co-operation and joint institutions.

3. The Community's objective in its policy of association shall remain the safeguarding of what has been achieved and of the fundamental principles referred to above.

4. The provision of this association, which will be defined during the negotiations referred to in the third subparagraph in Part I (2) of this Protocol, must similarly take account of the special economic conditions common

to the independent developing Commonwealth countries situated in Africa, the Indian Ocean, the Pacific Ocean and the Caribbean, and the Associated African and Malagasy States, the experience acquired within the framework of association, the wishes of the Associated States and the consequences for those States of the introduction of the generalised preference scheme.

III

The Community will have as its firm purpose the safeguarding of the interests of all the countries referred to in this Protocol whose economies depend to a considerable extent on the export of primary products, and particularly of sugar.

The question of sugar will be settled within this framework, bearing in mind with regard to exports of sugar the importance of this product for the economies of several of these countries and of the Commonwealth countries in particular.

Source: Treaty of Accession, Cmd. 4862-I.

ANNEX B

(a) Countries referred to in Article 109 of the Act of Accession and Protocol No. 22

Barbados	Mauritius
Botswana	Nigeria
Fiji	Sierra Leone
The Gambia	Swaziland
Ghana	Tanzania
Guyana	Tonga
Jamaica	Trinidad and Tobago
Kenya	Uganda
Lesotho	Western Samoa
Malawi	Zambia

(b) Associated states of the EEC

Burundi	Mali
Cameroon	Mauritania
Central African Republic	Niger
Chad	Rwanda
Congo (Brazzaville)	Senegal
Dahomey	Somalia
Gabon	Togo
Ivory Coast	Upper Volta
Madagascar	Zaire

SELECT BIBLIOGRAPHY

KITOMARI, N. N. *"East Africa's Association with the EEC".* Universities Social Sciences Council Conference, Makerere, Uganda, 1971.

OKIGBO, P. N. C. *Africa and the Common Market.* London, Longmans, 1966.

OVERSEAS DEVELOPMENT INSTITUTE. *Britain, the EEC, and the Third World.* London, 1971.

UNCTAD. *Operational Guide to the Generalized System of Preferences.* Ref. TB/B/AC. 5/54, May 1972.

Problems of Educational Development*

Philip Foster

Educational progress in the new states of middle Africa over the quinquennium following the 1961 Addis Ababa conference gives cause for both satisfaction over past achievement and doubt as to the course that future educational strategies must take. The Addis Ababa target of a 1980 goal of universal, free and compulsory primary schooling now seems highly unrealistic. Moreover, it is unlikely that by 1980 African states will be able to provide secondary education for 30 per cent of all children completing primary courses or create university places for 20 per cent of students completing secondary schools, as was originally anticipated.

In the light of the more modest goals set for 1961–66, however, quantitative progress has been substantial if uneven. Over this period total primary enrolment has increased by 35 per cent (a shortfall of 10 per cent compared with target figures), while new entrants to first grade have increased by 20 per cent compared with a planned increase of 57 per cent. Notwithstanding these shortfalls total primary enrolments as a proportion of the relevant age group rose from 36 to 44 per cent over the quinquennium. Wastage rates, however, continued to increase and over a standard six-year system rose to 68 per cent, contrasted with an anticipated fall to 41 per cent.

It seems clear from existing data that the curve of primary expansion in middle Africa has now peaked. Clearly the least educationally advanced nations (e.g., Upper Volta, Mali, Niger, Ethiopia) may register impressive proportionate gains over the next decade, but more developed areas have already entered a period of rapid secondary expansion with a current increase of at least two to three times the rate prevailing at the primary level. Certainly observed growth in secondary schooling over 1960–65 was somewhat below estimates with a rise in total enrolments from 630,000 to 1,283,000 representing a gross increase of 104 per cent as against a planned expansion of 147 per cent. Since 1965, however, growth at the secondary level has quickened. Moreover, higher education is now entering a period of accelerated outputs: starting from a low base of 1 student per 500 in the relevant age group in 1960 university enrolments rose by 150 per cent to 68,000 in 1965 compared with a target rate of increase of 91 per cent. Quite strikingly expansion

at the secondary and higher levels has been disproportionately concentrated in the area of general and non-science subjects. Enrolments in vocational and technical schools rose by only 8 per cent as against a planned 12 per cent increase, while the proportion of university students pursuing scientific and technological subjects rather than rising to a projected 43 per cent actually fell by roughly 5 per cent to 36 per cent.

The general pattern of growth depicted here is, however, of extremely limited analytic utility and can, indeed, be misleading. First, for all its progress, middle Africa still remains the least educated of the continents. As already noted, enrolments at the primary level still fall far short of 50 per cent for the relevant age group while the comparable ratios for secondary and higher levels are less than 3 per cent and 0.26 per cent respectively. In comparison with most other developing areas middle Africa's educational pyramid remains narrow at the base and extraordinarily constricted at the summit and secondary level.

Second, such figures do not indicate the enormous educational diversity that exists in quantitative terms between African nations. It is a doubtful exercise, for example, to compare Ghana, which has some 60 per cent of its relevant age groups in primary school, 16 per cent in secondary or middle school and over 4,000 students in universities, with Mali which has a rudimentary system of higher education and proportionate enrolments of 14 per cent and 1 per cent respectively at the primary and secondary level. Ghana is, in some respects, quantitatively ahead of the educational position achieved by some western nations toward the end of the nineteenth century, while Mali exhibits an educational profile reached by Ghana a quarter of a century ago. Other African nations lie on a continuum between those extremes, and it is important to realize that this diversity predicates very different types of short-term educational planning and quite distinct long-term strategies to be pursued in individual states or regional development clusters.

Third, the study of educational development rates can lead us to indulge in the futile task of extrapolating growth curves. Past trends are *not* indicators of future expansion. Clearly numerical enrolments will continue to rise in future, while the rate of growth is almost certain to be slowest at the primary level, substantially greater at the secondary stage and extremely rapid in the higher sector. The shrewd observer will not move beyond this level of generality since two factors will conspire to make the educational scene in the 1970s and 1980s very different from that prevailing over the last two decades. The first of these is the accelerating rate of population growth (now as high as 3.5 per cent per annum in some areas). It follows that the relevant school age groups are growing at a higher rate than the increase in total population; the five–nine

---

* Discussion will focus on the states of middle Africa as defined in the Unesco publications included in the select bibliography appended to this article. Besides excluding the north African states of Algeria, Egypt, Libya, Morocco and Tunisia, this classification does not include Portuguese and Spanish colonial territories nor Rhodesia and the Republic of South Africa. Some of the issues raised here are relevant to the educational problems of colonial territories but South Africa exhibits such a radically different educational, social and economic profile from other African nations that it merits a distinct and extended treatment beyond the scope of this essay.

years age group alone is likely to have increased by 17 per cent over the period 1965–70. In other words enrolments must expand at a constantly accelerating rate if existing ratios are to be maintained. The second factor is rapidly increasing educational costs—in large measure attributable to substantial increases in primary teacher salaries. Between 1960 and 1965 the average proportion of national income spent on education in over 20 selected African nations rose from 3 to 4.2 per cent, and in several countries current expenditures already far exceed the recommended level of 5.78 per cent of G.D.P. envisaged by the Addis Ababa conference. The plain fact is that in the light of estimated population growth and current cost trends African states will be hard pressed to maintain present educational structures, let alone expand them. It is possible that the number of students at higher institutions could be increased with a parallel reduction in unit cost through more efficient utilization of existing physical and staff resources. Modest increases at lower per capita cost might also be achieved in the secondary sector, but at the primary level growing enrolments can only be achieved by allocating increasing proportions of G.D.P. to this type of schooling. Costs at this level cannot be slashed, and it is unlikely that increases in real G.D.P. will occur on such a scale as to finance massive primary expansion.

The prognosis is, therefore, gloomy, but it is especially so to those whose measures of educational development are cast in crude quantitative terms. Doubtless growing enrolments bolster the self-esteem of African leaders bent on catching up with the developed world. But the obsessive preoccupation with expanding student populations blinds them to the real educational issues in Africa: what are the actual economic, political and social consequences of educational growth, and how far are current outcomes in line with the educational objectives boasted? African planners would do well to avoid judging educational development on the basis of current approximations to planned target figures whose provenance is largely conventional and arbitrary. Indeed it is evident that the actual pattern of educational expansion in middle Africa between 1960 and 1970 has not been determined by the plans drawn up at Addis Ababa. The dynamics of educational growth are far more complex than educational statesmen believe; development is more often than not a reflection of the articulation (or lack of it) between educational structures and other societal sub-systems, and it is to these more substantive economic and social issues that we now turn.

EDUCATION AND ECONOMIC GROWTH

Behind most educational planning in Africa lies the explicit or implicit assumption that educational development can make a tangible, short- or long-term contribution to economic development, as measured by simple increases in real per capita income. Gross global correlations between the educational stock of nations and per capita income indicate a general relationship between education and economic growth,

but these are of little utility. Undoubtedly the greater diffusion of schooling makes some contribution to development (as well as reflecting current wealth), but the vital policy question in Africa is the extent to which the measured social returns to increased investment in education are greater than those accruing to alternative investments in road building, agricultural development, health, etc. With one or two notable exceptions the literature on African educational planning is silent on this question.

Indeed until now educational targets have either been based on entirely arbitrary assumptions (as at Addis Ababa), or they have been derived from an assessment of putative high-level and middle-level manpower needs. In the latter type of approach the estimate of such "needs" is extremely hazardous, and their conversion into educational equivalents is a suspect undertaking. Manpower planning cannot explicate the relation between education and economic growth and it does not indicate how varying types of educational input are transformed into economic outputs. Soon after independence manpower planners sometimes performed a useful function by providing data on replacement needs contingent on the "Africanization" of post-colonial bureaucracies. Since government has by this time been largely Africanized in many states, the usefulness of these exercises is now more limited, and it is ironic to note that experts who a few years ago stressed the inexhaustible "demand" for high and middle level manpower now bemoan the ominous signs of limited "absorptive capacity" in several nations of middle Africa.

More recently a modest beginning has been made in applying cost-benefit types of analysis to questions of educational planning in middle Africa. Here again there are distinct methodological problems connected with such an approach, but it is possible that it will enable planners in the future to make more rational economic decisions concerning the relative allocation of resources to education as opposed to alternative forms of investment. Moreover, cost benefit analyses may provide some guide as to the relative social and private returns accruing to investment in different types and levels of education. Conventional economic studies must, however, be supplemented by more specifically demographic investigations that cast light on the actual (rather than assumed) relationship between the educational systems and occupational structures of the new African states. None the less, although promising lines of investigation are now opening up, it is still true that we know little of the relationship of education with economic development, and the honest planner will be reluctant to provide global prescriptions for growth in middle Africa.

Inability to provide "master plans" does not preclude us from making pragmatic and limited judgments concerning the effectiveness of some current educational strategies designed to facilitate economic development. It is often asserted that a prerequisite of growth is the enlargement of the proportion of students studying technical, vocational and scientific subjects at all levels. In fact empirical evidence suggests that the correlation between the proportion of students following such curricula and the wealth of nations is extremely tenuous. Doubtless development requires skilled manpower, and, at higher levels, formal institutions must be created to meet this need. But it does not follow that schools are the most appropriate instrument for technical and vocational training for a wide range of occupations. On-the-job training is frequently a workable alternative to "vocationalizing" the schools, and the extremely high cost of adequate technical instruction makes rapid expansion of such facilities very unlikely. Indeed from a cost-benefit viewpoint it seems probable that some types of technical schooling generate rates of private and social return below those accruing to investment in general studies. Those who lament the lagging pace of development in technical and vocational education might well interpret the phenomenon in terms of cost-benefit constraints rather than attributing it to some mythical African disdain for manual work or technical studies. Whatever new evidence emerges concerning the role of technical schooling in economic development, present evidence would suggest that African states would be well advised not to allocate limited resources on a massive scale to this type of education in the belief that it constitutes the most rational form of investment.

A closely related issue concerns agricultural development. Quite obviously the well-being of African populations will be highly dependent on agriculture for the indefinite future, and education has now been dragged into discussion concerning agricultural development. Predictably many governments are attempting to inject a compulsory agricultural component into the curricula of the schools (especially at the primary level) in the hope that such an innovation will facilitate agricultural transformation. Current evidence would suggest that such policies will have limited effect. The major constraints on agricultural productivity are largely attributable to factors lying outside the purview of the schools, and primary institutions, in particular, are extremely clumsy instruments for the diffusion of new agricultural knowledge. A more reasonable approach would seem to be the diversion of resources to the education of *farmers* not schoolchildren. Flexible and intelligently planned extension services, diffusing the results of research and combined with attempts to transform land-tenure systems, might well do more to raise productivity than any forced integration of the schools into agricultural development plans.

The whole question of agricultural education is, of course, interconnected with discussion of the "school-leaver" problem in middle Africa. Increased outputs from the primary schools have led to the emergence of large numbers of youth involved in a search for employment in the modern sector of African economies; their concentration in urban centres has alarmed African governments, though it would seem that current preoccupation with the political consequences of unemployment is not always justified. More relevant to the economic problem connected with these "wasted" resources is the suggestion that the schools can improve the situation by curricular changes designed to stimulate a "return to the land".

Implicit in such curricular proposals is the assumption that "general" studies (whatever that term means at the primary level) produce disdain for agriculture and student demands for "white collar" employment. On the contrary, it must be asserted that the unemployment problem does not have a curricular source. It stems from quantitative disparities between rapidly expanding outputs of school-leavers and the sluggish generation of occupational opportunities (both manual and non-manual) in the "modern" sector of African economies. Curricular change will have little effect on the situation, and planners would do well to see the problem in terms of gross rates of population growth and the characteristics of emerging industry in Africa. So far as going "back to the land" is concerned, there is now evidence that many school-leavers of rural origin do return home if their search for urban employment proves fruitless. Are we to assume that such literate returnees are, in some way, more unfortunate or less productive than their illiterate peers who remained in the village?

It can be suggested that in raising some of the issues concerning education and economic development in Africa this paper has stressed what the schools cannot do rather than make more positive proposals. Scepticism is salutary, however, since African governments have so far expected too much of the schools. What we suggest is that in the context of economic objectives there should be less straining after gross quantitative goals and a more pragmatic evaluation of the possibilities of specific educational programmes. Although apparent "shortfalls" occur in primary education it is still not possible for us to assert that African nations have "under-invested" or "over-invested" in it relative to the alternative social rates of return accruing to expenditures in other educational or non-educational sectors. However, in view of their limited resources it seems likely that governments will have to devolve a higher proportion of primary school costs on to local communities rather than attempt further expansion that imposes crushing burdens on central revenues. Likewise, although it is often asserted that priority should be accorded to the development of secondary and higher education there is no sound evidence in terms of social (as opposed to private) rates of return that this is sound policy. Even given the present lack of data it is still plausible to suggest that per capita student cost in higher (and probably secondary) education could be reduced through the more effective utilization of plant and staff. Moreover, the social returns to these sectors could be raised by developing a greater proportion of costs to private individuals who can afford to pay fees. Only too frequently the indiscriminate award of public scholarships subsidizes students from wealthier homes at the expense of able students from humbler circumstances.

The case for heavier investment in technical training is not self-evident; at present the most viable policy would seem to be expansion only in so far as training costs cannot be devolved on to other agencies (both public and private). Finally, agricultural education should be predominantly focused on the active farming population and not concentrated in the primary schools whose major function must remain the diffusion of literacy and numeracy. It is in these latter areas that significant kinds of curricular reform and innovation have yet to be effected.

EDUCATION AND THE POLITICS OF EQUALITY

Unfortunately economic issues are not the only factors that force the hand of educational planners, for most African nations are also pledged to implement programmes designed to provide equality of educational opportunity for their citizens. In terms of strictly economic decision-making criteria it is plausible to suggest that imparities of educational access in geographical, social or ethnic terms do not necessarily impede growth. Indeed concentration of educational resources on certain areas or groups may be the most efficient way of generating short-term development. Yet few African governments command enough legitimacy to resist popular pressures to expand schooling way beyond the level suggested by purely economic considerations. Education in middle Africa remains the primary mode of access to occupational success and élite status, and, in this context, it is not surprising that in the competition for scarce resources education should become a major focus for inter-group conflict.

It is demonstrable that inequalities in educational access are substantial. Whatever their gross levels of enrolment, most African states exhibit great internal geographical inequalities in access to schooling. These imparities are compounded by substantial ethnic variations in rates of access, while at secondary and higher levels, differences in the "educational life chances" of various socio-economic groups are already apparent. Finally, in virtually every African nation the proportionate enrolment of women continues to lag at all levels.

Most governments have attempted to reduce imparities by building more schools and, in particular, diverting resources to backward areas. Yet one of the paradoxical results of expansionary programmes has often been that *short-run* regional inequalities often increase rather than diminish; a mere expansion in enrolments does not necessarily lead to greater "democratization" of educational opportunity in social, ethnic or regional terms, and patterns of inequality are extremely stable over long time spans.

Thus, in spite of the pressure of popular demand, current rates of population growth and economic constraints make attempts to create equality of educational opportunity largely futile, even if by "equality" we mean the existence of some form of crude ethnic and social "quota". Universal primary education seems an unattainable short-term goal, while the proportion of students proceeding to secondary and higher education must remain very small. In this context much current discussion concerning educational "élitism" is quite meaningless. In purely quantitative terms African educational systems will remain "élitist" whether governments wish it or not.

There is one other sense, however, in which the term "élitism" takes on significant meaning. So far, in spite of inequalities, the African schools have performed reasonably well in providing opportunities for able students from less favoured ethnic and social groups. Low levels of aggregate educational and social mobility have been associated with considerable fluidity in access to élite and middle level positions. Whether the schools will continue to perform this function is another matter. In a situation where proportionate (if not numerical) enrolments diminish and where the rate of economic development is sluggish it is possible to see the schools as contributing to the crystallization of more rigid status structures in African nations. In other words, far from maintaining a degree of "openness", they could function in such a manner as to perpetuate existing élites through the virtual monopolization of secondary and higher education by their offspring. The political consequences of such a situation would be manifold, and it is to this issue that President Nyerere has addressed himself in his *Education for Self-Reliance*. His strategies to combat such a development may not be workable but his perception of the problem is correct. The essential task confronting educational planners is not, therefore, the creation of equality of opportunity in a gross sense, but the attempt to combine modest increases in the size of educational systems with relative openness of access in order to facilitate continuing mobility.

PROBLEMS OF CURRICULUM

It has already been suggested that in the context of economic development African states have attached too much importance to curricular reform as an agent of change. But curricular controversies in Africa have a bearing on a much wider range of social and political issues. Schools are not only expected to contribute to national integration but also to diffuse "modern" knowledge while at the same time cultivating a reverence for and attachment to African traditions and culture. The observer is often struck by the Janus-like quality of the debate; curricular ideologues frequently seem unaware of the incompatibility of many of the objectives that they set for the schools. Yet it does not require great reflection to see that a curriculum whose principal goal is, for example, the maximization of the economic contribution of education might look very different from one whose primary task is the inculcation of "traditional values". Moreover, although schools everywhere can make measurable contributions to cognitive knowledge, their role in influencing attitudes, sentiments and dispositions is more equivocal. Thus, in the absence of hard data, curricular issues in Africa (as elsewhere) lend themselves to *ex cathedra* statements and inflated expectations.

One significant curricular theme over the years concerns the "Africanization" of the subject matter to be taught in the schools. The assertion that the colonial powers made no effort to tailor content to the African scene is, of course, an exaggeration; substantial efforts in this direction were made in several areas, though well-meaning efforts were often open to African accusations that they were attempts to provide inferior alternatives to metropolitan curricula. In recent years, however, many newly independent states have introduced a more substantial African content into the curriculum (particularly at lower levels). Clearly such efforts have been often most effective in the area of the social studies, but in science and arithmetic too examples drawn from the African scene have increasingly replaced those taken from the European environment. Although the cognitive, affective and behavioural outcomes of such curricular innovations are difficult to establish, most would concur that these developments are salutary and contribute in some measure to a sense of self-esteem and a greater appreciation of Africa's culture and history.

None the less, there is a measure of superficiality in viewing "Africanization" of the curriculum solely in terms of the replacement of European content by African materials; no magical outcomes can be expected from arithmetic texts, for example, that use yams rather than potatoes as units in problems. A more fundamental issue concerns the culturally determined cognitive apparatus that African children first bring to the school. Thus a course with a formal African content may yet be entirely unsuitable for pupils since it is based on inappropriate assumptions about the pattern of child development. As yet little work as been done on this theme in Africa, but what little exists suggests that children may acquire early culturally determined concepts of language and number that make the initial mastery of formal school materials extremely difficult.

It must be recognized, however, that the developmental needs of children rarely determine the curricula of the schools. More often than not, talk of "Africanization" or, more broadly, "cultural adaptation", is little more than rhetoric reflecting political exigencies and imperatives. This much is evident if we consider one of the potentially explosive curricular issues in Africa —that of language and the medium of instruction in the schools.

Up till now most African states have been content to adhere to precedents set by the former colonial power. Thus in most former French colonies the metropolitan language is used for official purposes and remains the sole medium of instruction in the schools. Typically in ex-British areas selected local languages are employed at lower levels, but these are progressively replaced by English at senior primary, secondary and higher institutions.

Currently, however, rather disparate language policies are beginning to appear in Africa, although everywhere political considerations seem paramount. A few former British territories are attempting to progressively replace local vernaculars by English as the medium of instruction in all schools. This policy proceeds from the assumption that since no local vernacular would be politically acceptable as a national language then English remains the only

workable alternative. Precisely the opposite phenomenon is occurring in certain Francophone areas, where increased experimentation with several local languages reflects a degree of "cultural" as opposed to "pragmatic" nationalism. A third variant is also apparent in some ex-British territories, where *one* African vernacular has been accepted both as the official national language and the medium of instruction in the schools. Such a course has been followed in Tanzania, where Swahili has been accorded national status, and a similar development now seems likely to occur in Kenya and possibly Uganda.

Although it has not assumed the dimensions that it has on the Indian sub-continent, the language issue in Africa is far from dead and might yet become the focus of substantial political controversy. The primacy of the political in the language context is very evident in so far as virtually no attention has been paid to potential economic consequences of alternative linguistic policies, nor do direct cost considerations seem to have been examined. Certainly cost issues are generally ignored in most curricular planning in Africa but in the context of the language issue they have particular salience.

The continued use of metropolitan languages in the schools and elsewhere enables materials to be available at relatively low cost. Even where texts, for example, are specially designed for African pupils they can often be used over a wide potential market. By contrast the production of materials for limited linguistic groupings leads to rapid escalation of unit costs. Moreover, the production of textbooks in African languages must be accompanied by the creation of a wide range of supplementary reading materials. There is little point in making children or adults literate in a language if there is nothing available to read. Unfortunately, with some exceptions, African languages are not so widely spoken as could lead to the development of a viable publishing industry. Hitherto governments have often subsidized vernacular presses but resources are too limited to do this on other than a limited scale. In other words the price of cultural nationalism can be very high.

This brings us to a far more general and concluding point. African states must face more seriously the problem of relative educational costs and benefits if the schools are to effectively contribute to development in the 1970s and 1980s. The pursuit of global educational targets has undoubtedly led to some dissipation of scarce resources. What is most needed at present is a sober evaluation of progress so far, rather than a renewed formulation of broad quantitative goals by yet another meeting of heads of state or ministers of education. Such an evaluation should not concern itself with whether quantitative targets have been met, but whether these targets in themselves have any substantive meaning in the context of development. In Africa, as elsewhere, the really vital questions concerning the role of education in development have hardly yet been asked, let alone answered.

SELECT BIBLIOGRAPHY

ABERNATHY, DAVID. *The Political Dilemma of Popular Education.* Stanford, Stanford University Press, 1969.

ADAMS, DON (Ed.). *Educational Planning.* Syracuse, Center for Educational Development, 1964.

BEEBY, C. E. *The Quality of Education in Developing Areas.* Cambridge, Harvard University Press, 1966.

BLAUG, MARK. *The Role of Education in Enlarging the Exchange Economy in Middle Africa.* Paris, Unesco, 1967.

CLIGNET, REMI and FOSTER, PHILIP. *The Fortunate Few: a Study of Secondary Schools and Students in the Ivory Coast.* Evanston, Northwestern University Press, 1966.

ERNY, PIERRE. *L'Enfant et son milieu en Afrique noire.* Paris, Payot, 1972.

FOSTER, PHILIP. *Education and Social Change in Ghana.* London, Routledge and Kegan Paul, 1965.

JOLLY, RICHARD (Ed.). *Education in Africa: Research and Action.* Nairobi, published for the African Studies Association of the United Kingdom by the East African Publishing House, 1969.

Planning Education for African Development. Nairobi, published for the Makerere Institute of Social Research by the East African Publishing House, 1969.

LLOYD, P. C. (Ed.). *The New Elites of Tropical Africa.* London, International African Institute, 1966.

NYERERE, JULIUS. *Education for Self-Reliance.* Dar es Salaam, Ministry of Information and Tourism, not dated.

SHEFFIELD, J. R. (Ed.). *Education, Employment and Rural Development.* Nairobi, East African Publishing House, 1967.

UNESCO. *Regional Educational Targets and Achievements 1960–65.* Paris, Unesco-OAU/CESTA/Ref. 2, April 1968.

Trends in the Financing of Education in Certain African Countries. Paris, Unesco-PAU/CESTA/Ref. 4, May, 1968.

Comparative Statistical Data on Education in Africa, Paris, Unesco-OAU/CESTA/Ref 1, April 1968.

The Religions of Africa

Geoffrey Parrinder

Like all other continents Africa has a mixed religious life, and there are both clear outward monuments to faith and also communal and personal attitudes which are much more difficult to assess and appreciate. The most obvious signs of religious life are the Christian churches and Islamic mosques, which are often some of the most distinctive buildings of towns and villages. The temples of "pagan" or traditional religions are much less evident, where they still exist, but the influence of the beliefs which they symbolize is considerable.

CHRISTIANITY

Christianity is the oldest of the great literary and universal religions which have been present in Africa for centuries. Although north Africa became largely Muslim from the seventh century A.D., Christianity survived in the Coptic (Egyptian) church in Egypt, which claims to have been founded by St. Mark. In Africa south or east of the Sahara it is only in Ethiopia that the Coptic church, an offshoot from Egypt, has flourished since its foundation in the fourth century. In Ethiopia alone Christianity is the established religion of an African state, and it has been called "an island of Christians in a sea of Muslims". It was long dependent upon Egypt, but since 1959 the head or *Abuna* of the Ethiopian church has been chosen from Ethiopian monks or bishops, and the emperor of the country has the title "Elect of God".

Nearly every village in Ethiopia has a church and school, and there are many fine ancient churches and monasteries. Church services follow the Orthodox pattern with perhaps some Jewish practices, such as the use of an ark and the observance of Saturday as well as Sunday as a holy day. Monks have a hard life, and work on the land as well as praying and meditating. Modern education has been prompted both by the state and by a dozen Protestant and Roman Catholic missions from abroad. The Coptic church rarely engaged in missions to neighbouring African lands until modern times, when there have been intensive efforts to evangelize pagan and Muslim areas of southern Ethiopia and Eritrea. Statistics for the population of Ethiopia vary considerably, but on any account Christians should form some two-thirds of the population of the whole country.

In modern times Christianity went to tropical and southern Africa over the sea and most ports and coastal towns have large churches. Inland they may be less numerous, if Islam dominates, but there are many large Christian communities in the interior of Nigeria, Ghana, Zaire, Uganda and South Africa. After the decline of Christianity in north Africa, due to the Muslim conquest, missions were virtually suspended until the fifteenth century when Portuguese travellers rounded Africa and entered Asia. Portuguese missions began then in Africa and flourished for nearly two centuries, but declined with Portuguese power. There were Protestant missions at the Cape among Hottentots from 1648, but large-scale Christian movements in Africa had to await the nineteenth century. Since then there has been a great influx of missions, and despite initial difficulties and resistance this century has seen the establishment of great Christian communities in Africa. Estimates of numbers vary, though churches keep rolls of members, adherents and scholars, and, while some claims may be optimistic, there is a large potential field for development. The largest numbers of Christians are to be found in South Africa (11 million), Zaire (9 million), Nigeria (6 million), and Uganda and Tanzania (each about 4 million). By denominations there are some 30 million Roman Catholics, 22 million Protestants, 8 million Independent Protestants, and 5 million Ethiopian Coptic. Churches are fewer in parts of Kenya, Swaziland and Dahomey, while Islamic areas of the eastern and western Sudan have been the most resistant to Christian missions.

Organization and Educational Role

The pattern of church life in Africa is similar to that of Europe and America, reproducing the variations of Protestantism and Roman Catholicism. Church buildings generally follow European models, in concrete Gothic and village chapel styles. Since there was little indigenous building in baked brick or stone before modern times, the few experiments in new styles of architecture that have been made use modern materials boldly, such as the concrete parabolas and granite tower of the Protestant chapel at Ibadan university in Nigeria. Forms of worship follow Mass or Matins or a free order, with only slight changes of music and costume, except in the Independent churches. Some experiments have been made, in Cameroon and Uganda, with African carving for church decoration and drums for church bells. Similarly the churches are organized into dioceses, parishes and circuits, as in the parent churches abroad.

After their early difficulties the churches came to concentrate more and more upon education, and many African schools remain under Christian management. In British colonial territories the Protestant missions in particular benefited from government subsidies for education, and in Portuguese and Spanish areas Roman Catholics enjoyed similar advantages. French governments were more reluctant to grant help to missions until after the Second World War. With independence such grants have continued, with even greater emphasis upon universal free education, though it is rarely compulsory. From primary and secondary schools there developed the new universities, generally government-sponsored but still indebted to the churches for many students and some staff. In addition to education the churches have been almost solely responsible for reducing African languages to writing, and translating books, especially the whole or parts of the Bible, into the vernaculars. The importance of such literary work in African languages cannot be overestimated, although the use of European tongues, particularly English and French by most educated Africans, tends to overshadow the role of vernacular literature. The churches have also engaged in medical work, with dispensaries and small hospitals, and while these cannot rival some of the great modern government hospitals, they were first in the field and still provide many services in villages and towns.

With such European dominance in church architecture, organization and education, it is tempting to regard the churches still as missions. But the mission period has largely passed, except in Portuguese and Spanish areas, and African churches are increasingly under African control. Most religious services are conducted by African priests and pastors, and the use of the vernaculars is probably increasing. There are still many foreign missionaries of all denominations, but the tendency is for them to engage in special tasks, generally teaching or administration, leaving local church life in African hands.

Independent Churches

In addition to churches which have been under mission control (and some still are), there are many Independent churches in Africa. These are sometimes called Ethiopians, Zionists, sects or revivalists, but they can be grouped more accurately under the historical title of Independents. Movements towards African self-government began in the churches from various causes: differences of opinion with missionaries, emotional revivalism, and the desire to evangelize by African means. Beginning towards the close of the nineteenth century, the Independents have grown in all tropical and southern African countries. It has been estimated that today there are about 3,000 such organizations in southern Africa, 300 in east Africa, and 500 each in central and west Africa.

The proliferation of Independency has been attributed to political deprivation, but that would not explain its growth outside southern Africa, and even there very few of the Independents have taken any part in politics. It has also been said that the Independents catered for polygamy, the plural marriage that is customary in African society. While it is true that some, but not all, do permit polygamy, this was only rarely the reason for their original secession from the parent church. The Independents are remarkably orthodox in most doctrines: they are strongly Biblical and generally retain the prayer and hymn books of their churches of origin. They like colourful ritual and prophecy and many of them were founded by prophetic figures, such as Shembe of Natal, Kimbangu of the Belgian Congo and Harris of the Ivory Coast. Some prophets were persecuted by colonial authorities. Kimbangu was imprisoned by the Belgian government for thirty years, yet remained steadfast in his faith. Many of the Independent churches stress healing by faith, reject both African and European medicines, and practise baptism by full immersion, which links up with purificatory rituals in earlier African religions. On Sundays in many African towns there are processions of Independent Christians, dressed in robes and beating drums, and baptisms are performed in rivers and the sea.

Christianity clearly has an important future in Africa, where it has been one of the most rapidly developing areas of church activity. The close association of missionaries with imperial governments limited as well as helped Christian work, but the transition to political independence has not yet greatly handicapped Christian progress. There is an even greater demand for education, literacy and hospitals, and here churches do special work. The development of African leadership, both among Independents and older churches, has been of great importance, and there are leaders in public life and politicians who testify to the help received from the church. Most dangerous to the church are racial policies and the divisions of warfare. In South Africa segregation of races has led to increasing strains upon those churches which have tried to include people of all colours, and the members of Independent African churches has continued to grow. In Angola, Zaire, Sudan and Nigeria the churches have suffered from guerrilla or open warfare, but they can also provide means of healing divisions.

ISLAM

The traveller arriving by air in the interior of Africa may be struck by the presence of the mosques and minarets of Islam, especially in countries bordering the eastern and western Sudan, though such buildings are also to be found in many coastal towns of east and west Africa. In contrast to Christian missionaries, the followers of the religion of the Prophet Muhammad generally went overland into tropical Africa.

Islam entered Egypt in A.D. 640 and by the end of that century had reached the Atlantic. Then it took centuries to consolidate its gains and only slowly turned to the south. The easiest trade routes were from Morocco down the western coast and up the River Senegal, and by the eleventh century Islam began to take root among the "negroes" of the western Sudan. The ancient empires of Ghana and Mali on the upper Niger came to have nominally Muslim rulers, though many traditional African religious customs still remain in these areas. Islam spread slowly, but not until the nineteenth century did its widest expansion in west Africa take place with the holy wars of the Fulani (Peul) tribes from Senegal to Nigeria. When British and French colonies were established, these recent Islamic conquests were recognized, with the result that many parts of west Africa were increasingly subjected to peaceful Islamic pressures and the application of Islamic laws. With its conquests, and the new colonial roads, Islam spread into the tropical forests and down to the coast, notably in Sierra Leone and western Nigeria, but much less so in Ghana, and hardly at all in eastern Nigeria.

East Africa is nearer to Arabia, the heartland of Islam, but progress down the Nile was checked by the Christian kingdom of Nubia, which fell to Islam only between the fourteenth and sixteenth centuries, and the remaining empire of Ethiopia. Arab traders established themselves on the west of the Red Sea and in the Horn of Africa, and Persian Muslim traders went farther south. Islamic centres grew up in places like Mogadishu, Mombasa, Zanzibar and Kilwa, and also in the north of Madagascar. By inter-marriage with Bantu women in east Africa a new people and language were founded, the Swahili or "coasters". But there were few Islamic ventures into the interior until increasing slave-trading in the nineteenth century sent Arab traders up to the great lakes. Hitherto the cohesion of African society in the hinterland had kept Islam at bay, and, when it began to penetrate, it was shortly followed by Christian missions.

Islam has not spread much into southern Africa because the Portuguese retained their hold on Mozambique. However, Indian and Malay labourers imported into Natal and the Cape were partly Muslim; and it is thought that not more than 5,000 Africans in South Africa are Muslims.

Belief and Practice

The faith and religious practices of Islam are much the same throughout Africa, from Morocco to Madagascar, though there are different styles of architecture. The name "Islam" means "submission" or "surrender" to God, and a "Muslim" or "Moslem", from the same root as Islam, is a "surrendered man". Muslims dislike the term Muhammadan or Mahometan to be applied to themselves or their religion since they worship God, Allah, and not Muhammad. The Prophet Muhammad, who lived in Mecca and Medina from A.D. 570 to 632, is regarded as having come in a succession of prophets, who include Moses and Jesus, but Muhammad is the last and "seal" of the prophets, the "apostle" (*rasūl*) par excellence.

The Koran (*Qur'ān*) is the "recitation" and infallible Word of God to Muslims, having been revealed through the angel Gabriel and dictated but not written by Muhammad, who is thought to have been illiterate. Although the Koran can be translated into other languages, all Muslims learn some of its verses in the original Arabic, and this language must be used in formal acts of public and private prayer, even if the African Muslims have no knowledge of any other Arabic words. Throughout Islamic Africa children can be heard in mosques and schools reciting Arabic verses from the Koran in sing-song fashion. Every chapter but one of the Koran opens with the *Bismillah*, "in the name of God", and this word is often inscribed, in Arabic or English, on lorries and houses as a protective text.

Mosques are "places of prostration" used for private or communal prayer. The faithful are called to prayer five times a day by a *Muezzin* or "caller", but the prayer may be said at home or in any public place. Muslims unroll their prayer mats and face towards Mecca and the holy shrine of the Ka'ba in that city. Especially in morning and evening there is the common sight of individuals or groups of Muslims bowing and prostrating themselves on their mats while muttering Arabic verses. Some great mosques are built of stone or brick, while many small ones are of mud. They consist of open courtyards or covered rooms, with a small sanctuary or niche indicating the direction of the Ka'ba. Mosques are open to visitors,

if they remove their shoes, and they often have fine tiled floors or carpets. There are no images, of course, and the only decorations are Arabic verses round the walls, but there is usually a pulpit and a reading desk for use in great communal prayers, the most important of which takes place about midday on Friday. Friday is not a day of rest, shops being open except during the midday prayer, and Sunday is often observed as a holiday.

There are special Islamic festivals, such as the birthday of the Prophet, anniversaries of local sheikhs or saints, and a sacrifice of sheep or other animals during the month of pilgrimage, the twelfth month of the Islamic lunar year. It is a religious duty to go on pilgrimage to Mecca at least once in a lifetime, and sacrifice forms part of the ritual there, but at the same time Muslims at home all over the Islamic world perform a similar sacrifice. Those who have been to Mecca assume the title *Hajji* ("pilgrim"). Most noticeable is the fast of *Ramadan*, the ninth month, during the whole of which no healthy adult Muslims should take any food or drink during the hours of daylight. Food may be eaten at night but this, added to the long daylight fasting, means that many Muslim workers are lethargic during *Ramadan*. Some modern reformers extend exceptions to fasting, from children and the sick, to students, soldiers and workers.

Orders

During *Ramadan* there are often visiting preachers or *Marabouts*, who come long distances and speak in mosques and streets about religious and social matters. They generally belong to those religious orders commonly called dervishes or "poor", which have more intensive religious practices than those which are required by the rather formal acts of daily prayer. A religious order is centred on a leader and follows his "path" (*tarīqa*). Of the numerous such orders in tropical Africa one of the oldest and most popular is the *Qadiriyya*. Founded by Abd al-Qadir in the twelfth century, it spread from Baghdad to Egypt and along much of northern Africa. It is powerful in west Africa; and in Senegal, under the name of *Muridiyya*, it has a great mosque at Touba which is a place of pilgrimage for a local saint, Ahmad Bamba of the Wolof tribe. In east Africa the *Qadiriyya* is the strongest order, but in Zanzibar and Kilwa the *Shadhiliyya*, founded by a leader of that name, is dominant. Very active in north and west Africa is the *Tijaniyya* order, founded by Ahmad al-Tijani in Algeria at the end of the eighteenth century. It is popular because of its liberalism and acceptance of worldly comforts, and it has spread into Senegal, the western Sudan and Nigeria.

Such orders are not sects, but they act as inner groups united by their leaders and their successors. A very different modern movement is the *Ahmadiyya* which came from India-Pakistan. Here in the nineteenth century Ghulam Ahmad founded a movement designed to attract Muslims, Hindus and Christians, though its aims have led to serious differences with orthodox Muslims and have not attracted many from the other religions. The *Ahmadiyya* became a strongly missionary movement, and it publishes a great deal of literature in English and other languages. *Ahmadiyya* missionaries visited west Africa from 1916 and east Africa from 1934. Their most important centres are in Ghana and Kenya, and there are others in Sierra Leone, Nigeria and Uganda. Despite intense efforts in propaganda and education, the numbers of *Ahmadiyya* are very small relative to the orthodox Muslim communities—about 30,000 in west Africa and less in east Africa.

The numbers of Muslims in Africa are difficult to calculate. In north Africa, apart from Egypt, they are usually taken to be practically identical with the whole population. In Ethiopia they form about a third of the population. By far the largest numbers of Muslims in tropical Africa are in Nigeria, mostly in the northern states but also in the west, numbering altogether over 14 million. It is remarkable that Islam has made little progress so far in the eastern regions of Nigeria, and the coastal areas of Dahomey, Togo, Ghana, the Ivory Coast and Liberia. In Guinea, Senegal and Niger there are about 2 million Muslims each. The Somalis are almost wholly Muslim, and so are many Eritreans. Islam is strong on the coastline of Kenya, Tanzania and northern Mozambique, but has much less influence in the interior.

Nearly all African Muslims are *Sunni*, following "custom", tradition and law as laid down by past schools of law. In Ethiopia, Somalia and much of east Africa the *Shafi'i* school rules; in west Africa, Sudan and Eritrea the *Maliki* school of law is followed. Apart from the above there are relatively small groups of *Shi'a* Muslims ("followers" of Ali), chiefly from India-Pakistan and found in east Africa, but their numbers are declining with stricter immigration policies. Some of these are *Khojas* who follow the Aga Khan. There are also Hindus, Sikhs and Parsis, whose numbers are diminishing, and in South Africa there are about a quarter of a million Hindus.

TRADITIONAL RELIGIONS

Christianity and Islam have been long in Africa, although only recently in tropical and southern regions, and they might claim to be traditional religions. But this term is coming to be used of the older and illiterate forms of African religious life which used to be known by the opprobrious names of "heathen" or "pagan". Other terms, such as "fetishism", "juju", and "witch-doctrine", have been common, but they are now abandoned in scholarly works as inaccurate and restrictive. If a "fetish" is defined as a fabricated object (from Latin *facticius*) which is worshipped, then such a practice is found in every continent and not just in Africa, and attention should be paid to more important African customs.

The visitor to Africa normally sees little evidence of the older traditional religions. There are no great stone temples, and the most outstanding religious buildings are churches and mosques. There are small temples, numerous in some countries like Dahomey where the old religion has remained strongly organized, but these are made of mud or sun-dried brick, although they may be decorated with wall paintings. Small wayside shrines, sometimes containing grotesque mud or wooden images, are to be seen in villages, but in modern towns they are crowded out or only found in corners of house courtyards.

There were no scriptures of old African religion, because literacy came only with Islam and Christianity, and, in the tropics, only in modern times. Old European travel books give occasional romantic accounts of festivals, but little of beliefs. In this century, however, much has been written on African religions, chiefly by missionaries and anthropologists. These works generally describe the beliefs and customs of limited tribal areas, though there are some composite volumes and comparative surveys available. The fact remains that there are very few accounts of African traditional belief from the inside, nor are more likely to appear, since literacy brings conversion to Christianity or secularism.

The clearest expressions of the traditional beliefs are in art, and the popularity of African wood carving in modern times has brought familiarity with some aspects of faith. Many African carvings are religious, a large number being associated with the dead and illustrating a profound belief in a future life. Wooden masks of many kinds are widely produced, especially in west and central Africa. Such masks are normally intended to be worn with a robe by a masquerader, acting the part of an ancestor on annual and special occasions. In many towns and villages processions of masked and robed figures appear at times, followed by assistants and interested crowds. There are also secret societies concerned with initiation rites and the suppression of witchcraft whose members appear robed from head to foot.

Wooden carvings are also found in small temples and household shrines, indicating a god or his attendants. Stone sculptures are more rare, but they occur from Sierra Leone to Nigeria, and in the ruins of stone buildings at Zimbabwe and neighbouring places in Rhodesia. Old rock paintings survive in many places, from the Sahara to southern Africa. Some of them were executed by Bushmen, but their descendants in South Africa no longer paint and the meaning of some of the old paintings is uncertain. Many of the rock paintings depict animals and hunting scenes and were probably connected with ritual magic.

Ancestral Cults

The ancestral cults are also connected with graves where ceremonies are occasionally held. In some places, notably in Ghana, stools are used by human beings and after their death the stools are regarded as shrines for the departed souls, at which libations and offerings are made at regular intervals. The presence of the ancestors is believed in; children are thought to re incarnate dead grandparents; and sterility or disease may be attributed to the anger of a ghost which needs to be appeased by a sacrifice. Dreams and visions of the dead play a large part in African thought, and they may account for a sudden disappearance or removal of a worker from an office or a shop.

Other spiritual beings which are believed in a re nature spirits—gods who are thought to dwell in hills and rivers, stones and trees. In west Africa there are many small temples for ceremonies in honour of the gods of thunder, water, earth and forest. Such shrines are less common in eastern and southern Africa, but many people there believe in nature spirits, though their chief ritual activities are concerned with the ancestors. Whereas ceremonies for the dead are generally performed by elders of the family or village, the gods may be served by part-time or full-time priests. A priest is a trained intermediary with a god, and he may be assisted by mediums, generally women, who go into trance and declare the will of the deity.

Above the gods and ancestors is the Supreme Being, who is properly named God. In many African languages he has his own name and titles and is regarded as being in a different class from the nature gods. This High God rarely receives any direct worship, but temples for his service are found in a few places: for example, among the Dogon of Upper Volta, the Ashanti of Ghana, and the Kikuyu of Kenya. However, if God has no temple, there is usually no priest or special day of worship for him, and some writers have regarded him as a remote and unimportant deity. Yet there is little doubt that most Africans have believed in a supreme God, father of gods and men, the creator of the universe about whom many stories are told in mythology. Although he may have no fixed worship, many people pray to him, without the help of a priest, when all else has failed. Some people make daily libations to God, or they think that the other gods pass the essence of their sacrifices on to the Supreme Being.

Magical Practices

African traditional religious beliefs have been represented as a pyramid, with the High God at the top, the great spiritual powers such as gods and ancestors at the sides, and the lower spiritual forces such as magic, divination and witchcraft at the base. Magical practices are very common. Most houses, shops and fields have little bundles of protective magic, and people wear lucky rings, bangles, necklaces, girdles and anklets. Students carry lucky charms for examinations and clerks hope for promotion by such means. Magic is generally protective, intended to keep away evil and bring fortune and fertility, and good magic is dispensed by a "medicine man", who is a public and respected figure. Muslim traders also sell magical remedies; and verses from both the Koran and the Bible are used for protection.

Very popular magical practices are those of divination and fortune-telling. There are elaborate systems in which a diviner seeks to uncover present secrets or future mysteries. These often involve passing a quantity of nuts from one hand to the other in order to obtain a propitious remainder, and lines or patterns are marked on a divining board covered with powder or sand. Complex figures are thus produced which are interpreted by the diviner according to traditional patterns and proverbs which he has learned during his long period of training. The Ifa oracle system of Nigeria is especially renowned and it has spread into neighbouring countries.

Harmful magic seeks to injure enemies, either by suggestion or by deliberate use of poison. The evil magician or sorcerer works at night and is a feared and anti-social being. Harmful or "black" magic should be distinguished from belief in witchcraft, which is widespread but often misrepresented. There are many African witch-doctors, who are not themselves witches, and their function is to cure those who are bewitched and seek out the supposed witches. It is believed that there are potentially evil people, especially women, who during the night change their forms or leave their bodies asleep at home, and fly off to high trees and wild places to join with their companions in cannibalistic feasts. There is no tangible evidence that such orgies take place, and, although confessions are made of these activities, they result from fear or from acceptance of the accusations of the witch-doctor. Since it is said that both the witch's and victim's bodies remain asleep in their huts, it is not the body that is eaten but "the soul of the flesh". Local witch-doctors hold regular inquisitions, since witchcraft power may be thought to be always latent in some people. Widescale witch-hunting movements also sweep across Africa from time to time, and these combine traditional ordeals with modern practices, using mirrors to detect witches and dispensing coloured medicines as cures. Belief in witchcraft survives because of the high rate of physical sickness and the existence of old and new kinds of personal and social misfortune. The high incidence of infant mortality, often over 20 per cent, causes people to look for a cause of unexplained death. They accuse grandmothers, mothers-in-law, co-wives and even mothers themselves of killing the babies. An improved standard of child health will undoubtedly do much to reduce accusations of witchcraft in Africa, as it did in Europe from the eighteenth century onwards.

Traditional Religion and Morality

Traditional religion is expressed in belief and in ritual word and action, on regular occasions and at intervals in the life cycle. At birth, adolescence, marriage and death ceremonies are held which involve all the family. Libations and offerings are given to various spirits and vows are made to observe the teachings of tradition. Thus morality is closely related to religion, which gives divine sanction for human laws. Traditional African societies were tightly knit and customs were strictly observed. Changes came about gradually, but in modern times the sudden and extensive influences of European ways in trade, education, politics and religion have brought about a decline in the older religion and morality. However, new religions bring new moralities and in many ways Islam or, in particular, the Independent churches make a synthesis of old and new which enables the transition to a new world to proceed more easily.

It is not possible to estimate precisely the numbers of those who practise the traditional religions in Africa, since they are little organized and produce no rolls of members. There are very few, if any, Africans who have had no contact at all with European government and trade, and most have come into some contact with Christian or Islamic religion. Older people often cling to tradition but allow their children to be educated and become Christian, with the consequent decline in traditional religious customs. Perhaps over fifty millions should be considered as adhering to the traditional religions, but many who are formally Christian and Muslim may observe some traditional practices or lapse into them in difficult times.

Future Development

Christianity and Islam are making great claims upon the religious allegiance of Africans, and these two religions have the great advantages of literacy, history and international links. There is little doubt that in time they will replace traditional religions in Africa, but many of the old beliefs and attitudes will survive for centuries because the cultural background, of which religion was an integral expression, is still powerful in determining the thoughts and actions even of educated men in modern African towns.

Modern Africa is a continent of mixed religion, in which different streams can be observed, but there is much inter-mingling and joining up of old and new worlds. Religion remains important for many people, and new religious movements often appear in a colourful guise. It is remarkable that among all this diversity of thought and behaviour there is considerable tolerance between religions in Africa. Persecution is rare south of the Sahara, and Christian, Muslim and traditionist often live together in harmony in the same family house, village or town.

SELECT BIBLIOGRAPHY

BARRETT, DAVID B. *Schism and Renewal in Africa: An Analysis of Six Thousand Contemporary Religious Movements*. Nairobi, Oxford University Press, 1969.

BEETHAM, T. A. *Christianity, the New Africa*. London, Pall Mall, 1967.

DAVIDSON, B. *The African Past*. Harmondsworth, Penguin Books, 1964.

FORTES, M., and DIETERLEN, G. (Eds.). *African Systems of Thought*. 1965.

GROVES, CHARLES PELHAM. *The Planting of Christianity in Africa*. 4 vols., Lutterworth Press, 1948–58.

HASTINGS, ADRIAN. *Church and Mission in Modern Africa*. London, Burns and Oates, 1967.

LEWIS, I. M. (Ed.). *Islam in Tropical Africa*. London, Oxford University Press, 1964.

MBITI, JOHN S. *African Religions and Philosophy*. New York, Praeger, 1970.
Concepts of God in Africa. London, S.P.C.K., 1970.

PARRINDER, E. G. *African Traditional Religion*. London, S.P.C.K., 1962.
Religion in Africa. Harmondsworth, Penguin Books, 1969.
Witchcraft, European and African. London, Faber, 1963.

SMITH, E. W. (Ed.). *African Ideas of God*. London, Edinburgh House, 1961.

TRIMINGHAM, J. S. *Islam in West Africa*. Oxford, Clarendon Press, 1959.
Islam in East Africa. Oxford, Clarendon Press, 1964.
The Influence of Islam upon Africa. London, Longmans, 1968.

PART TWO
Regional Organizations

REGIONAL ORGANIZATIONS

MEMBERSHIP OF AFRICAN REGIONAL ORGANIZATIONS

	OAU	AfDB	CEAO	CFA	Entente	EAC	EEC	OCAM	OMVS	UDEAC
Algeria . . .	x	x								
Botswana . . .	x	x								
Burundi . . .	x	x					x			
Cameroon . . .	x	x		x			x	x		x
Central African Republic	x	x		x			x	x		x
Chad	x	x		x			x	x		
Congo (Brazzaville) .	x	x		x			x	x		x
Dahomey . .	x	x	x	x	x		x	x		
Egypt . . .	x	x								
Equatorial Guinea .	x									
Ethiopia . . .	x	x								
Gabon . . .	x	x		x			x	x		x
The Gambia . .	x									
Ghana . . .	x	x								
Guinea . . .	x	x								
Ivory Coast . .	x	x	x	x	x		x	x		
Kenya . . .	x	x				x	x			
Lesotho . . .	x									
Liberia . . .	x									
Libya . . .	x	x								
Madagascar . .	x						x	x		
Malawi . . .	x	x								
Mali . . .	x	x	x				x		x	
Mauritania . .	x	x					x	x	x	
Mauritius . .	x							x		
Morocco . . .	x	x								
Niger . . .	x	x	x	x	x		x	x		
Nigeria . . .	x	x								
Rwanda . . .	x	x					x	x		
Senegal . . .	x	x	x	x			x	x	x	
Sierra Leone . .	x	x								
Somalia . . .	x	x					x			
South Africa . .										
Sudan . . .	x	x								
Swaziland . .	x	x								
Tanzania . . .	x	x				x	x			
Togo . . .	x	x		x			x			
Tunisia . . .	x	x								
Uganda . . .	x	x				x	x			
Upper Volta . .	x	x	x	x	x		x	x		
Zaire . . .	x	x					x	x		
Zambia . . .	x	x								

Key: OAU   Organization of African Unity
     AfDB   African Development Bank
     CEAO Communauté Économique de l'Afrique de l'Ouest
     CFA   Communauté Financière Africaine
  Entente Conseil de l'Entente
     EAC   East African Community
     EEC   European Economic Community (through association agreements)
     OCAM Organisation Commune Africaine, Malgache et Mauricienne
     OMVS Organisation pour la Mise en Valeur du Fleuve Sénégal
     UDEAC Union Douanière et Économique de l'Afrique Centrale

United Nations in Africa South of the Sahara

MEMBER STATES, WITH CONTRIBUTIONS AND YEAR OF ADMISSION

(% contribution to UN Budget for 1972)

Botswana	.	.	0.04	1966
Burundi	.	.	0.04	1962
Cameroon	.	.	0.04	1960
Central African Republic	.	.	0.04	1960
Chad	.	.	0.04	1960
Congo (Brazzaville)	.	.	0.04	1960
Dahomey	.	.	0.04	1960
Equatorial Guinea	.	.	0.04	1968
Ethiopia	.	.	0.04	1945
Gabon	.	.	0.04	1960
The Gambia	.	.	0.04	1965
Ghana	.	.	0.08	1957
Guinea	.	.	0.04	1958
Ivory Coast	.	.	0.04	1960
Kenya	.	.	0.04	1963
Lesotho	.	.	0.04	1966
Liberia	.	.	0.04	1945
Madagascar	.	.	0.04	1960
Malawi	.	.	0.04	1964
Mali	.	.	0.04	1960
Mauritania	.	.	0.04	1961
Mauritius	.	.	0.04	1968
Niger	.	.	0.04	1960
Nigeria	.	.	0.14	1960
Rwanda	.	.	0.04	1962
Senegal	.	.	0.04	1960
Sierra Leone	.	.	0.04	1961
Somalia	.	.	0.04	1960
South Africa	.	.	0.52	1945
Sudan	.	.	0.05	1956
Swaziland	.	.	0.04	1968
Tanzania	.	.	0.04	1961
Togo	.	.	0.04	1960
Uganda	.	.	0.04	1962
Upper Volta	.	.	0.04	1960
Zaire	.	.	0.05	1960
Zambia	.	.	0.04	1964

PERMANENT MISSIONS TO THE UNITED NATIONS
(with Permanent Representatives)

Botswana: 866 United Nations Plaza, Room 511, New York, N.Y. 10017; THEBE DAVID MOGAMI.

Burundi: 305 East 45th St., 21st Floor, New York, N.Y. 10017; NSANZÉ TÉRENCE.

Cameroon: 866 United Nations Plaza, Room 650, New York, N.Y. 10017; MICHEL NJINE.

Central African Republic: 386 Park Ave. South, Room 1614, New York, N.Y. 10016; MICHEL ADAMA-TAMBOUX.

Chad: 150 East 52nd St., Apartment 5C, New York, N.Y. 10022; (vacant).

Congo (Brazzaville): 801 2nd Ave., 42nd St., 4th Floor, New York, N.Y. 10017; NICOLAS MONDJO.

Dahomey: 4 East 73rd St., New York, N.Y. 10021; WILFRID DE SOUZA.

Equatorial Guinea: 440 East 62nd St., Apartment 6D, New York, N.Y. 10022; PRIMO JOSÉ ESONO MICA.

Ethiopia: 866 United Nations Plaza, Room 560, New York, N.Y. 10017; (vacant).

Gabon: 866 United Nations Plaza, Room 536, New York, N.Y. 10017; JEAN DAVIN.

The Gambia: (not yet established).

Ghana: 150 East 58th St., 27th Floor, New York, N.Y. 10022; (vacant).

Guinea: 295 Madison Ave., 24th Floor, New York, N.Y. 10017; Mme. JEANNE MARTIN CISSE.

Ivory Coast: 46 East 74th St., New York, N.Y. 10021; SIMÉON AKE.

Kenya: 866 United Nations Plaza, Room 486, New York, N.Y. 10017; JOSEPH ODERO-JOWI.

Lesotho: 866 United Nations Plaza, Suite 580, New York, N.Y. 10017; MOOKI V. MOLAPO.

Liberia: 866 Second Ave., New York, N.Y. 10017; NATHAN BARNES.

Madagascar: 301 East 47th St., Apartment 2H, New York, N.Y. 10017; BLAISE RABETAFIKA.

Malawi: 777 Third Ave., 24th Floor, New York, N.Y. 10017; NYEMBA WALES MBEKEANI.

Mali: 111 East 69th St., New York, N.Y. 10021; SEYDOU TRAORE.

Mauritania: 8 West 40th St., 18th Floor, New York, N.Y. 10018; MOULAYE EL HASSEN.

Mauritius: 301 East 47th St., Suite 3C, New York, N.Y. 10017; RADHA KRISHNA RAMPHUL.

Niger: 866 United Nations Plaza, Suite 570, New York, N.Y. 10017; (vacant).

Nigeria: 757 Third Ave., 20th Floor, New York, N.Y. 10017; EDWIN OGEBE OGBU.

Rwanda: 120 East 56th St., Room 630, New York, N.Y. 10022; FIDÈLE NKUNDABAGENZI.

Senegal: 51 East 42nd St., 17th Floor, New York, N.Y. 10017; MÉDOUNE FALL.

Sierra Leone: 919 Third Ave., 22nd Floor, New York, N.Y. 10022; ISMAEL BYNE TAYLOR-KAMARA.

Somalia: 236 East 46th St., 3rd Floor, New York, N.Y. 10017; ABDULRAHIM ABBY FARAH.

South Africa: 300 East 42nd St., 17th Floor, New York, N.Y. 10017; CARL F. G. VON HIRSCHBERG.

89

Sudan: 757 Third Ave., 12th Floor, New York, N.Y. 10017; RAHMATALLA ABDULLA.

Swaziland: 866 United Nations Plaza, Suite 420, New York, N.Y. 10017; N. M. MALINGA.

Tanzania: 800 Second Ave., 3rd Floor, New York, N.Y. 10017; SALIM AHMED SALIM.

Togo: 800 Second Ave., New York, N.Y. 10017; JACQUES D. TOGBE.

Uganda: 801 Second Ave., New York, N.Y. 10017; GRACE S. IBINGIRA.

Upper Volta: 866 Second Ave., 6th Floor, New York, N.Y. 10017; (vacant).

Zaire: 866 2nd Ave., 7th Floor, New York, N.Y. 10017; (vacant).

Zambia: 150 East 58th St., New York, N.Y. 10022; PAUL J. F. LUSAKA.

ECONOMIC COMMISSION FOR AFRICA—ECA

Africa Hall, Addis Ababa, Ethiopia

Telephone: 47200.

Initiates and takes part in measures for facilitating Africa's economic development. Member countries must be independent, be members of the UN and within the geographical scope of the African continent and the islands bordering it. ECA was founded in 1958 by a resolution of ECOSOC as the fourth UN regional economic commission.

MEMBERS

Algeria	Gabon	Malawi	Somalia
Botswana	The Gambia	Mali	South Africa*
Burundi	Ghana	Mauritania	Sudan
Cameroon	Guinea	Mauritius	Swaziland
Central African Republic	Ivory Coast	Morocco	Tanzania
Chad	Kenya	Niger	Togo
Congo (Brazzaville)	Lesotho	Nigeria	Tunisia
Dahomey	Liberia	Rwanda	Uganda
Egypt	Libya	Senegal	Upper Volta
Equatorial Guinea	Madagascar	Sierra Leone	Zaire
Ethiopia			Zambia

*Suspended by ECOSOC since 1963.

ASSOCIATE MEMBERS

(*a*) Non-Self-Governing Territories situated within the geographical scope of the Commission.

(*b*) Powers other than Portugal responsible for the international relations of those territories (France, Spain and the United Kingdom).

Associate Members may take part in the Commission's activities but may not vote.

ORGANIZATION

COMMISSION

Executive Secretary: ROBERT K. A. GARDINER (Ghana).

The Commission has held ten sessions since its inception:

1958	December	Addis Ababa
1960	January	Addis Ababa
1961	February	Tangier
1962	February	Addis Ababa
1963	February	Léopoldville
1964	February	Addis Ababa
1965	February	Nairobi
1967	February	Lagos
1969	February	Addis Ababa
1971	February	Tunis

Sub-Regional Offices: Lusaka, Niamey, Tangier, Kinshasa.

ACTIVITIES

Objectives. The work of the Commission is determined by decisions of its plenary sessions. The Commission is charged with the responsibility for promoting and facilitating concerted action for the economic and social development of Africa; for maintaining and strengthening the economic relations of African countries, both among themselves and with other countries of the world; for undertaking or sponsoring investigations, research and studies of economic and technological problems and developments; for collecting, evaluating and disseminating economic, technological and statistical information; and for assisting in the formulation and development of co-ordinated policies promoting economic and technological development in the region.

Areas of Activity. The ECA carries out its activities under the divisions of:

Trade, Fiscal and Monetary Affairs
Natural Resources and Transport
Industry and Housing
Statistics
Human Resources Development

ECA/FAO Joint Agriculture
Economic Research and Planning

There is also a *Technical Assistance and Programme Co-ordination Section*, a *Population Programme Centre*, dealing with population programmes and policies, together with general demography, a *Centre for Economic Co-operation*, and the *African Trade Centre*.

At the request of member states in the region the Commission also performs advisory services in various economic and social fields. Some of the main features of activities in these areas in 1971 are outlined below. Only a few of the many conferences, seminars and courses in all fields in which ECA participated with other organizations are mentioned.

Operations in 1971-72.

Trade, Fiscal and Monetary Affairs: During 1972 twelve trade promotion advisory missions went to nine African countries; six were follow-ups of earlier missions to the same countries—Ethiopia, Nigeria and Somalia, the other six were sent to Burundi, Egypt, Ghana, Liberia, Morocco and Sierra Leone. Two training courses on export promotion were conducted by ECA in co-operation with the UNCTAD/GATT International Trade Centre in Geneva, attended by 32 officials from eight countries. The Trade section of ECA also organized a pavilion at the All Africa Trade Fair (Nairobi, February-March 1972), which was visited by over 35,000 people. At the Fair a five-day *Symposium on Intra-African Trade* was held in collaboration with the OAU, at which it was decided to form an *Association of African Trade Promotions Organizations*, (originally recommended by the first ECA Conference of Ministers in Tunis in February 1971). A preparatory committee was established consisting of delegates from Chad, Kenya, Mali, Morocco, Sudan, Zaire and Zambia, and the matter was discussed again at the seventh meeting of the executive committee of ECA at Addis Ababa in April 1972.

Several ECA economic studies were submitted at various international conferences and meetings, including the *Regional Meeting on the Implications of the Use of Freight Containers in African Trade* (Addis Ababa, April 12th-21st), and the *Seventh Joint ECA/OAU Meeting on Trade and Development* (Geneva, August 10th-18th). At the third ministerial session of UNCTAD (Santiago, April 13th-May 21st), meetings of the African Group were serviced jointly by the ECA and OAU Secretariats, and a revised study on the *Restructuring of Africa's Trade* was issued with a view to assisting the African delegation. Among new ECA projects were missions undertaken in Lesotho, Nigeria and Zambia to assist with various fiscal and budgetary management schemes being conducted by their respective governments.

Natural Resources and Transport: The pre-feasibility study of the Trans-African Highway project, a continuous road running from Lagos to Mombasa, was completed, and the proposed route was adopted in April at the second meeting of the Co-ordinating Committee in charge of the scheme, which is made up of representatives from the six countries concerned—Cameroon, Central African Republic, Kenya, Nigeria, Uganda and Zaire. The meeting was attended by representatives from the OAU, AfDB,

EAC as well as ECA, and six donor countries—U.S.A., Japan, U.K., Federal Germany, Belgium, France. The next meeting of the Committee is scheduled for April 1973 in Kenya; meanwhile the Trans-African Highway Bureau will be carrying out a more detailed feasibility study.

Industry and Housing: In June 1972, the OAU's ninth Meeting of Heads of State approved Cairo as the venue for the Second Conference of the Ministers of Industry to be convened in October 1973.

Statistics: Two Regional advisers in demographic statistics assisted the Population Programme Centre in implementing feasibility missions on population censuses and surveys in Africa. Of 41 members of ECA only 15 have held a comprehensive population census since 1966. Twenty of the other 26 plan to carry out a census during the next three years under the African Census Programme (14 of these have never had a complete census).

Regular statistical publications are continuing (see list of publications), and many have been revised or published as new titles. A study on the *Terms of Trade of Developing Africa* has been published in the first issue of the revised *Statistical and Economic Information Bulletin*.

Social Development: Activity was concentrated on rural development and training. A new feature was the establishment of a regional programme for the advancement of women, which came about mainly as a result of *The Regional Conference on Vocational Training and Work Opportunities for Girls and Women*, (organized in co-operation with the German Foundation for Developing Countries), held at Rabat in May 1971. It was attended by 26 ECA countries, 8 international agencies, as well as UN specialized agencies. Subsequently a women's unit was established within the Social Development Section of the ECA, and a five-year Regional Programme (1972-76) was set up. Another meeting, *A Symposium on Rural Development in Africa in the 1970s*, held at Addis Ababa in August 1971, was attended by 28 international voluntary agencies and various UN bodies. As a follow-up to its recommendations a Voluntary Agencies Bureau (VAB) was established within the ECA Secretariat, in October 1971, to assist international voluntary agencies and member states, at their request, in pre-investment studies of selected projects, in developing co-operative savings and credit societies, and in the setting up of training centres in the region.

A Joint ECA/DANIDA (Danish International Development Assistance) *ad hoc* Study Group sent missions to Ethiopia, Ghana, Nigeria, Tanzania and Kenya which reported on the state of rural development training schemes. Other missions were sent to Burundi, Zaire and Rwanda to assist in reviewing government rural development projects, while advisory missions on public administration were sent by ECA to the following countries: Nigeria, Dahomey, Botswana, Mali, Gabon, Lesotho, Malawi, Kenya, Uganda, Tanzania, Zambia, Swaziland. The ECA Secretariat (with the ILO and FAO) also assisted the Government of Gabon in the appraisal of a regional development project in the N'Gounie region. The Association of Social Work Education in Africa (ANSEA) was set up early in 1972, with its headquarters in Addis Ababa, to promote teaching and research in the field of social work education in Africa, with the assistance of the Friedrich-Ebert-Stiftung in Bonn.

ECA/FAO Joint Agriculture: A modest initial project towards the implementation of Phase I of the *African Livestock Development Study—Southern/Central Africa* was launched, (the first venture of its kind to be undertaken by the ECA), covering seven countries: Botswana, Lesotho, Malawi, Swaziland, Tanzania, Zaire and Zambia. A study on Phase II of another project, *Intra-Regional Co-operation and Trade in the Field of Agriculture,* was completed by a consultant from the United States Bilateral Assistance Agency, entitled *Prospects for Production, Marketing and Trade in Livestock and Livestock Products in Eastern Africa to 1985.*

Economic Research and Planning: The Regional Institute for Population Studies, set up in Accra, started operations in February 1972. In April, African Governments were invited to nominate trainees for the second training course in October 1972. The second meeting of the Consultative Group on the African Census Programme (held at Addis Ababa, February 23rd-25th, 1972) was organized jointly by the ECA and UN secretariats, and was attended by representatives from Canada, U.K., U.S.A., and Yugoslavia in addition to those from African countries.

The Centre for Economic Co-operation directed most of its activities to carry out a special study commissioned by the fifth Meeting of the Executive Committee of ECA (May, 1971), entitled *African Economic Co-operation Efforts and Significance of the Enlarged European Economic Community for African Economies.* It was expected to have completed its report by the end of the year.

Institutional Machinery. As a result of recommendations made at ECA's ninth session the following institutional machinery was set up:

(a) *Conference of Ministers* which is vested with full powers to consider matters of general policy and the priorities to be assigned to the programme and other activities of the Commission. It reviews programme implementation and examines and approves the proposed programme of work, and considers reports submitted to it by the Executive Committee and the Technical Committee

of Experts. The Conference of Ministers holds its meetings every two years. The first meeting was held in Tunis in February 1971; the next will be held in Accra early in 1973.

(b) *Technical Committee of Experts* which meets once a year. It is composed of senior officials of member states concerned with economic affairs, and it examines studies prepared by the ECA Secretariat and assists in the formulation of the work programme aimed at ensuring co-operation between the Secretariat and member governments. It held its fourth meeting in Addis Ababa in September 1972.

(c) *Executive Committee* which is composed of representatives of 16 members states and which assists the Executive Secretary in the implementation of the resolutions and the work programme of the Commission, and provides links between the Secretariat, member states and the sub-regions. The Executive Committee meets at least twice a year. Its eighth meeting was held in November 1972.

Subsidiary Bodies. The Commission is empowered, under its terms of reference, to establish subsidiary bodies. Those now in existence and actively functioning are the *Conference of African Statisticians,* the *Conference of African Planners* and the *Conference of African Demographers,* each of which meets once every two years.

Relations with Other Organizations: WHO maintains a liaison office at ECA. In co-operation with ITU work has begun on a pan-African telecommunications system. ECA also runs a Joint Agricultural Division in conjunction with FAO.

Co-operation between ECA and the Organization of African Unity started with the signing of a UN/OAU agreement by the then Secretary-General of the United Nations, U Thant, and the then Secretary-General of the OAU, Diallo Telli, on November 15th, 1965. An ECA/OAU/UNESCO Inter-Secretariat Meeting was held in September 1972, and the seventh ECA/OAU Joint Meeting on Trade and Development was held in Geneva during the same month.

PUBLICATIONS

Economic Bulletin for Africa (twice yearly).
The Statistical Newsletter (quarterly).
Foreign Trade Newsletter (quarterly).
Agricultural Economic Bulletin (twice yearly).
Social Welfare Services in Africa (thrice yearly).
Natural Resources, Science and Technology Newsletter (quarterly).
Foreign Trade Statistics for Africa, Series A: Direction of Trade (quarterly).
Foreign Trade Statistics for Africa, Series B: Trade by Commodities (thrice yearly).

African Target (quarterly).
Planning Newsletter (bi-monthly).
Statistical Bulletin for Africa (quarterly).
Social Work Training Newsletter (quarterly).
Training Information Notice (quarterly).
Statistical Yearbook.
Survey of Economic Conditions (annual).
Statistical and Economic Information. Bulletin for Africa (quarterly).
Population Newsletter (quarterly).
Rural Development Newsletter (quarterly).

AFRICAN INSTITUTE FOR ECONOMIC DEVELOPMENT AND PLANNING
Dakar, Senegal

An autonomous organ of the ECA opened in 1963 with Special Fund assistance to train senior African officials in techniques of development planning and to serve as a

clearing house and documentation centre on all African development questions.
Director: SAMIR AMIN (Egypt).

UNITED NATIONS DEVELOPMENT PROGRAMME—UNDP

New York, N.Y. 10017, U.S.A.

Established in 1965 to aid the developing countries in increasing the wealth-producing capabilities of their natural and human resources by supporting economic and social projects, with pre-investment and technical assistance. The UNDP came into effect in January 1966, bringing together the previous activities of the Expanded Programme of Technical Assistance and the UN Special Fund. It functions under the authority of ECOSOC and of the General Assembly.

UNDP REPRESENTATIVES IN AFRICA SOUTH OF THE SAHARA

Botswana: Barclays Bank Building, Queens Rd., P.O.B. 54, Gaborone; *Rep.:* JOHN PHILLIPS. (Under overall aegis of UNDP Regional Rep. for South East Africa in Lusaka.)

Burundi: 3 rue du Marché, B.P. 1490, Bujumbura; *Resident Rep.:* MARCEL LATOUR.

Cameroon: Immeuble Kamden, rue Joseph Clère, B.P. 836, Yaoundé; *Resident Rep.:* BERTIN BORNA.

Central African Republic: rue Joseph Degrain, P.O.B. 872, Bangui; *Resident Rep.:* SALFO BALIMA.

Chad: Ave. du Général Brosset, B.P. 906, Fort-Lamy; *Resident Rep.:* FINN BONNEVIE.

Congo (Brazzaville): Ave. du Maréchal Foch, B.P. 465, Brazzaville; *Resident Rep.:* GIAN PENNACCHIO.

Dahomey: Ancienne Grande Chancellerie, Ave. Gouverneur Roume, B.P. 506, Cotonou; *Resident Rep.:* KARLFRITZ WOLFF.

Equatorial Guinea: 12 Paseo de la República, Aptdo 399, Santa Isabel; *Officer-in-Charge:* MARCEAU LOUIS.

Ethiopia: Regional Telecommunications Building (4th Floor), Churchill Rd., P.O. 5580, Addis Ababa; *Resident Rep.:* FRIEDRICH SEIB.

Gabon: Maison Papadopoulos, Quartier St. Benoît, B.P. 2183, Libreville; *Resident Rep.:* GUY TIROLIEN.

The Gambia: (covered by UNDP Regional Office for North West Africa in Dakar, Senegal).

Ghana: UN/FAO Building, Maxwell Rd., P.O.B. 1423, Accra; *Resident Rep.:* GORDON MENZIES.

Guinea: Ancienne Immeuble "Urbaine et Seine", Ave. de la République, B.P. 222, Conakry; *Resident Rep.:* ROGER POLGAR.

Ivory Coast: Angle rue Gourgas et Ave. Marchand, Abidjan-Plateau, B.P. 1747, Abidjan; *Resident Rep.:* KARL ENGLUND.

Kenya: Electricity House, Harambee Ave., P.O.B. 30218, Nairobi; *Resident Rep.:* BRUCE STEDMAN.

Lesotho: Oxfam House, Kingsway, P.O.B. 301, Maseru; *Rep.:* BRUCE TAYLOR. (Under overall aegis of UNDP Regional Rep. for South East Africa in Lusaka, Zambia.)

Liberia: Latco Building, Broad St., P.O.B. 274, Monrovia; *Resident Rep.:* CURTIS CAMPAIGNE.

Madagascar: 26 rue de Liège, P.O.B. 1348, Tananarive; *Resident Rep.:* JACQUELINE GRANGER. (Also covers Comoro Islands.)

Malawi: Adjacent to the Government Hostel, P.O.B. 46 Zomba; *Resident Rep.:* PETER LOWES.

Mali: Ministry of Planning Building No. 2, Koulouba, B.P. 120, Bamako; *Officer-in-Charge:* JACQUES GODFRIN.

Mauritania: Général de Gaulle St., B.P. 620, Nouakchott; *Officer-in-Charge:* REGINALD POLLARIS.

Mauritius: Anglo-Mauritius House, Intendance St., P.O.B. 253, Port Louis; *Resident Rep.:* JOHN BIRT.

Niger: Maison de l'Afrique, P.O.B. 256, Niamey; *Resident Rep.:* GILLES GRONDIN.

Nigeria: 11 Queen's Drive, Ikoyi, P.O.B. 2075, Lagos; *Resident Rep.:* STANLEY FRYER.

Rwanda: Ave. de l'Assemblée nationale, B.P. 445, Kigali; *Resident Rep.:* MALICK FALL.

Senegal: 2 Ave. Roume, B.P. 154 Dakar; *Regional Rep.* of UNDP in North West Africa: ALFRED JAEGER. (Also covers The Gambia.)

Sierra Leone: Bank of Sierra Leone Building, Siaka Stevens St., P.O.B. 1011, Freetown; *Resident Rep.:* ALFRED EDWARD.

Somalia: UN Compound, P.O.B. 24, Mogadishu; *Resident Rep.:* GAFOUR ABDOURASHIDOV.

Sudan: House No. 7, Block 5 R.F.E., Gama'a Ave., P.O.B. 913, Khartoum; *Resident Rep.:* LUCIANO CAPPELLETTI.

Swaziland: Embassy House, Morris St., P.O.B. 261, Mbabane; *Rep.:* HUGH GREENIDGE. (Under overall aegis of Regional Rep. of UNDP in South East Africa in Lusaka, Zambia.)

Tanzania: Matasalamat Mansions, 2nd Floor, Zanaki St., P.O.B. 9182, Dar es Salaam; *Resident Rep.:* LENNART MATTSSON.

Togo: 40 rue des Nations Unies, B.P. 911, Lomé; *Resident Rep.:* LÉONCE BLOCH.

Uganda: Embassy House, 2nd Floor, 9/11 Obote Ave., P.O.B. 7184, Kampala; *Resident Rep.:* WINSTON PRATTLEY.

Upper Volta: 210 ave. de la Gare, B.P. 575, Ouagadougou; *Resident Rep.:* DAVID CHARLES GANAO.

Zaire: Hotel Royal, Blvd. du 30 juin, B.P 7248, Kinshasa; *Resident Rep.:* JAIME RENART.

Zambia: Desai Building, Chiparamba Rd., P.O.B. 1966, Lusaka; *Regional Rep.* of UNDP in South East Africa: ANTONY C. GILPIN. (UNDP Offices in Botswana, Lesotho and Swaziland are under the overall aegis of the Regional Rep. in Lusaka.)

UNDP – ASSISTED PROJECTS IN AFRICA SOUTH OF THE SAHARA

As a result of recent structural changes individual countries now submit to the UNDP's Governing Council a "programme" outlining areas needing assistance. This programme lays down a general framework of overall national priorities and takes into account aid from other sources. This replaces the system whereby countries requested assistance from the UNDP for individual projects as the need arose. Each country is now alloted an Indicative Planning Figure (IPF) projecting the dollar value of UNDP assistance that can foreseeably be expected over a five-year period; this enables governments to plan their projects further in advance.

A more decentralized organization is now in operation. Four *Regional Bureaux*, headed by Assistant Administra-tors, share the responsibility for implementing the programme with the Administrator's office. A bureau for programme and policy co-ordination provides overall policy guidance and specialized technical expertise to the Regional Bureaux. Within certain limitations, larger-scale projects may now be approved and funding allocated by the Administrator, and smaller-scale projects by the Resident Representatives. The Resident Representative now co-ordinates all UN family technical assistance in his assigned country. He advises the government on formulating the country programme, monitors field activities, and acts as the leader of the UN team of experts working in the country.

UNDP EXPENDITURES AND INDICATIVE PLANNING FIGURES FOR PROJECTS IN AFRICA SOUTH OF THE SAHARA
($'000)

COUNTRY	EXPENDITURE 1959–71	IPF 1972–76
Botswana	3,395	5,800
Burundi	8,751	10,000
Cameroon	10,750	15,000
Central African Republic	5,487	7,500
Chad	3,779	7,500
Congo	8,935	7,500
Dahomey	6,195	7,500
Ethiopia	19,843	20,000
Gabon	10,188	7,500
Ghana	19,592	15,000
Guinea	11,757	15,000
Ivory Coast	12,205	15,000
Kenya	18,921	15,000
Lesotho	3,798	8,300
Liberia	8,987	10,000
Madagascar	14,739	10,000
Malawi	4,293	7,500
Mali	12,491	10,000
Mauritania	4,003	5,000
Mauritius	4,517	5,000
Niger	10,016	10,000
Nigeria	30,663	30,000
Rwanda	6,465	10,000
Senegal	14,064	10,000
Sierra Leone	6,430	7,500
Somalia	17,301	15,000
Sudan	20,761	20,000
Swaziland	2,701	5,700
Tanzania	16,363	15,000
Togo	10,008	10,000
Uganda	10,613	10,000
Upper Volta	8,248	10,700
Zaire	21,657	20,000
Zambia	9,961	15,000
TOTAL	377,877	393,000

UNDP-ASSISTED INDIVIDUAL COUNTRY PROJECTS APPROVED
DURING THE YEAR ENDED JUNE 30TH, 1972

COUNTRY	PROJECT	EXECUTING AGENCY	PROJECT DURATION (years)	TOTAL PROJECT COSTS (U.S. $)
Burundi	Secondary School Teacher Training Institute, Bujumbura (Phase II)	UNESCO	3	2,110,400
Cameroon . . .	Federal School for Posts and Telecommunications, Yaoundé	ITU	4	3,212,400
Central African Republic .	Accelerated Vocational Training Programme, Bangui	ILO	3	734,600
Congo	Forestry Training and Demonstration Centre, Mossendjo (Phase II)	FAO	3	1,238,400
Dahomey	Strengthening of the National Office for the Development of the Oueme Valley and Study for Extension on the Right Bank of the Oueme Valley	FAO	1	274,232
Equatorial Guinea .	Emergency Secondary Teacher Programme (OPAS)	UNESCO	1½	1,170,400
Ethiopia . . .	Rinderpest Control	FAO	3	1,558,400
Gabon . . .	Treatment, Drainage and Disposal of Solid and Liquid Wastes, Libreville	WHO	2½	733,400
	Supplementary Assistance in Forest Development	FAO	2	457,100
The Gambia . . .	Manpower Planning and Labour Statistics	ILO	1	118,319
Ghana	Training in Agricultural Mechanization, Tamale	FAO	2	234,200
Guinea	Supplementary Assistance to the Forestry Training and Development Centre	FAO	1	356,000
Ivory Coast . . .	Institute of Pedagogical Research, Abidjan (Phase II)	UNESCO	5	1,762,550
	Supplementary Assistance to the Development of Co-operative Enterprises	ILO	1	232,000
Kenya	National Industrial Vocational Training Programme (Phase II)	ILO	3½	2,070,988
	Exploration and Development of Geothermal Power	UN	3⅔	2,030,220
	Wildlife Management in Kenya	FAO	6	2,350,756
Lesotho	Supporting Administrative Services	UNDP	4	387,300
Liberia	Rural Basic Craft Training	ILO	3½	1,748,000
	Supplementary Assistance to the College of Agriculture and Forestry, Monrovia (Phase II)	FAO	2½	459,000
Madagascar . . .	Establishment of a Cyclone and Thunderstorm Forecasting, Detection and Warning System	WMO	3½	1,830,000
	Establishment of an Agrometeorological and Hydrometeorological Network for the Lake Alaotra Basin	WMO	3	592,000
Malawi	Economic Feasibility and Engineering Studies of Two Main Roads	IBRD	2	1,046,200
	Promotion of Integrated Fisheries Development in Malawi	FAO	4½	2,186,000
Mali	Productivity and Management Training Institute, Bamako	ILO	4	1,458,700
	Administrative Reform	UN	2	1,563,540
Mauritius	Trade Development and Services	UNCTAD	3½	303,332
Niger	National School of Public Health, Niamey (Phase II)	WHO	5	2,035,450
Nigeria	Supplementary Assistance to the Secondary School Teacher Training College, Owerri	UNESCO	1	1,050,000
Rwanda	Supplementary Assistance to the Pilot Plant for Industrialization and Pyrethrum Production	UNIDO	2	740,700
	Foundry Development Centre, Thies	UNIDO	4	1,153,200
Senegal	Mineral Exploration in Eastern Senegal	UN	2	447,980
	Development of the Casamance Forests	FAO	2	488,657

UNDP-ASSISTED INDIVIDUAL COUNTRY PROJECTS APPROVED
DURING THE YEAR ENDED JUNE 30TH, 1972—*continued*

COUNTRY	PROJECT	EXECUTING AGENCY	PROJECT DURATION (years)	TOTAL PROJECT COSTS (U.S. $)
Somalia	Technical Education and Vocational Training	UNESCO	4	1,859,950
	National Teacher Training Centre	UNESCO	4	4,528,300
	Mineral and Groundwater Survey (Phase III)	UN	2⅓	1,999,750
Swaziland	Industrial Advisory and Consultancy Services	UNIDO	2	225,800
Tanzania	Industrial Strategy	UNIDO	1½	239,467
	Industrial Studies and Development Centre (Phase II)	UNIDO	2	677,600
Uganda	Tick-Borne Cattle Diseases and Tick Control	FAO	4	1,086,963
Upper Volta	National Training Centre for Rural Handicrafts, Ouagadougou	ILO	4½	1,274,250
	Strengthening of Secondary Technical Education in the Technical High School of Ouagadougou	UNESCO	1	153,800
Zaire	Assistance to the Directorate of Investments	UNIDO	2	206,400
	Assistance to the Industrial Research Centre for Central Africa, Lubumbashi	UNIDO	4	1,902,000
Zambia	Assistance to the President's Citizenship College	ILO	3	3,925,900
	Training of Secondary School Teachers at the University of Zambia	UNESCO	4½	5,258,400
	Development of Basic Health Services	WHO	5	2,230,000

UNDP—ASSISTED REGIONAL PROJECTS APPROVED
DURING THE YEAR ENDED JUNE 30TH, 1972

PROJECT, WITH PARTICIPATING COUNTRIES	EXECUTING AGENCY	TOTAL (U.S. $)	UNDP (U.S. $)
Telecommunication Link between Bathurst (Gambia) and Kaolack (Senegal) . .	ITU	267,400	187,400
Programme of Educational Assistance to African Refugees in Bagamoyo (United Republic of Tanzania), Conakry (Guinea), and Nkumbi (Zambia) .	UNESCO	2,469,600	353,600

INTERNATIONAL BANK FOR RECONSTRUCTION AND DEVELOPMENT—IBRD (WORLD BANK)

1818 H St., N.W., Washington, D.C. 20433, U.S.A.

Aims to assist the economic development of member nations by making loans, in cases where private capital is not available on reasonable terms, to finance productive investments. Loans are made either direct to governments, or to private enterprise with the guarantee of their governments.

LOANS TO COUNTRIES IN AFRICA SOUTH OF THE SAHARA

TOTAL LOANS
(1947–June 1972)
($'000)

COUNTRY	NUMBER	AMOUNT
Botswana	1	32,000
Burundi	1	4,800
Cameroon	5	37,100
Congo	1	30,000
East African Common Services Authority* . . .	7	170,800
Ethiopia	12	108,600
Gabon†	4	54,800
Ghana	2	53,000
Guinea	3	75,200
Ivory Coast‡ . . .	8	93,900
Kenya	7	100,400
Liberia	6	20,950
Malagasy Republic . .	3	11,100
Mali‡	—	—
Mauritania . . .	1	66,000
Mauritius . . .	1	7,000
Nigeria . . .	16	458,400
Rhodesia§ . . .	5	86,950
Senegal‡ . . .	3	13,900
Sierra Leone . .	3	11,400
South Africa . .	11	241,800
Sudan . . .	6	134,000
Swaziland . . .	2	6,950
Tanzania . . .	3	42,200
Upper Volta‡ . .	—	—
Zaire . . .	5	120,000
Zambia . . .	10	171,550

APPROVED BANK LOANS 1971–72
(U.S. $ million)

COUNTRY	PURPOSE	AMOUNT
East African Community .	Development Finance Companies	8.0
Ethiopia .	Water Supply and Sewerage	10.8
Ivory Coast .	Roads	17.5
Kenya .	Airport	29.0
Liberia .	Development Finance Companies	1.0
Nigeria .	Education	17.3
	Roads	26.3
	Electric Power	76.0
Senegal .	Railways	6.4

* Jointly guaranteed by Kenya, Tanzania and Uganda.

† One of these loans, of $35 million, is jointly guaranteed by France, Gabon and the People's Republic of Congo.

‡ One loan for $7.5 million shown against Ivory Coast is shared with Mali, Senegal and Upper Volta.

§ Two of these loans, totalling $87.7 million, have been assigned in equal shares to Rhodesia and Zambia, but are shown against Rhodesia only.

Note: Joint Bank/IDA operations are only counted once, as Bank operations. When more than one loan is made for a single project, they are counted only once.

Source: World Bank/IDA 1972 **Annual Report**.

INTERNATIONAL DEVELOPMENT ASSOCIATION—IDA

1818 H St., N.W., Washington, D.C. 20433, U.S.A.

The International Development Association began operations in November 1960. Affiliated to the World Bank, the IDA advances capital on more flexible terms to developing countries.

DEVELOPMENT CREDITS TO COUNTRIES IN AFRICA SOUTH OF THE SAHARA

TOTAL CREDITS 1960–June 30th, 1972
(U.S. $'000)

COUNTRY	NUMBER	AMOUNT
Botswana	5	12,750
Burundi	3	3,280
Cameroon	5	43,250
Central African Republic	3	12,400
Chad	4	10,300
Congo	5	15,930
Dahomey	3	14,200
Ethiopia	9	83,200
The Gambia	1	2,100
Ghana	6	31,900
Kenya	12	83,300
Lesotho	1	4,100
Madagascar	4	44,400
Malawi	8	47,090
Mali	4	27,300
Mauritania	3	13,900
Niger	4	13,904
Nigeria	2	35,500
Rwanda	2	12,300
Senegal	6	35,350
Sierra Leone	2	10,800
Somalia	5	21,950
Sudan	2	32,800
Swaziland	1	2,800
Tanzania	11	78,000
Togo	1	3,700
Uganda	7	44,300
Upper Volta	4	12,000
Zaire	6	53,500

APPROVED IDA CREDITS 1971–72
(U.S. $ million)

COUNTRY	PURPOSE	AMOUNT
Botswana	Livestock	1.7
	Roads	2.0
Cameroon	Irrigation	3.7
	Education	9.0
Central African Republic	Education	3.9
Chad	Livestock	2.2
Congo	Roads	4.0
	Railways	6.3
Dahomey	Cotton and Food Crops	6.1
Ethiopia	Livestock	4.4
	Coffee Processing	6.3
	Development Finance Companies	11.0
	Roads	17.0
Kenya	Roads	22.0
Liberia	Rural Development	1.2
	Education	7.2
Madagascar	Irrigation	15.3
Malawi	Rural Development	6.6
Mali	Telecommunications	3.6
	Irrigation	6.9
Mauritania	Livestock	4.2
Rwanda	Roads	3.0
Senegal	Railways	3.2
	Urbanization	8.0
Sierra Leone	General Development	4.3
Somalia	Roads	9.6
Sudan	Food Crops	11.3
Tanzania	Tea Production	10.8
	Roads	6.5
Upper Volta	Rural Development	2.2
	Roads	2.8
Zaire	Development Finance Companies	10.0
	Education	6.5
	Roads	19.0

Source: World Bank/IDA 1972 Annual Report.

INTERNATIONAL FINANCE CORPORATION—IFC
1818 H St., N.W., Washington, D.C. 20433, U.S.A.

Founded in 1956 as an affiliate of the World Bank to encourage the growth of productive private enterprise in its member countries, particularly in the less-developed areas.

IFC INVESTMENTS IN COUNTRIES IN AFRICA SOUTH OF THE SAHARA AS AT JUNE 30TH 1972

	TYPE OF BUSINESS	FISCAL YEAR IN WHICH COMMITMENT WAS MADE	ORIGINAL COMMITMENT NET OF EXCHANGE ADJUSTMENTS (U.S. $)
Ethiopia:			
Cotton Company of Ethiopia, S.C.	Textiles	1965, 1970	3,126,826
Ethiopian Pulp and Paper, S.C.	Pulp and Paper	1966	1,908,501
H.V.A.-Metahara, S.C.	Sugar	1968	9,044,698
Ivory Coast:			
Banque Ivoirienne de Développement Industriel, S.A.	Development financing	1965	204,082
Kenya:			
Kenya Hotel Properties Ltd.	Tourism	1967, 1968	3,073,186
Panafrican Paper Mills (EA) Ltd.	Pulp and Paper	1970	14,651,799
Tourism Promotion Services (Kenya) Ltd. . .	Tourism	1972	2,420,000
Liberia:			
Liberian Bank for Industrial Development and Investment	Development financing	1966	250,000
Mauritania:			
Société Minière de Mauritanie	Copper mining and Treatment	1968	20,006,515
Mauritius:			
Dinarobin Inns and Motels Ltd.	Tourism	1971	610,250
Nigeria:			
Nigerian Industrial Development Bank Ltd. . .	Development financing	1964	1,400,000
Arewa Textiles Ltd.	Textiles	1964, 1967, 1970	1,574,910
Senegal:			
Société Industrielle d'Engrais au Sénégal . .	Fertilizer	1967	3,459,765
Bud Senegal, S.A.	Vegetable export	1972	51,467
Sudan:			
Khartoum Spinning and Weaving Company Ltd. .	Textiles	1964, 1972	2,211,795
Tanzania:			
Kilombero Sugar Company Ltd.	Sugar	1960, 1964	4,657,485
Uganda:			
Mulco Textiles Ltd.	Textiles	1965	3,508,436
Tourism Promotion Services (Uganda) Ltd. . .	Tourism	1972	1,110,000
Zaire:			
Société Financière de Développement . . .	Development financing	1970	2,000,000
Zambia:			
Zambia Bata Shoe Company Ltd.	Shoes	1972	1,077,642
Regional:			
SIFIDA—Société Internationale Financière pour les Investissements et le Développement en Afrique (SIFIDA Investment Co., S.A.)	Development financing	1971	500,000

UNITED NATIONS HIGH COMMISSIONER FOR REFUGEES—UNHCR

Palais des Nations, Geneva, Switzerland

The Office of the High Commissioner was established in 1950 to provide international protection for refugees and to seek permanent solutions to their problems. In 1967 the mandate of UNHCR was extended until the end of 1973.

ORGANIZATION

HIGH COMMISSIONER

High Commissioner (1966–73): Prince SADRUDDIN AGA KHAN.

Deputy High Commissioner: CHARLES H. MACE.

The High Commissioner is elected by the United Nations General Assembly on the nomination of the Secretary-General, and is responsible to the General Assembly and to ECOSOC.

EXECUTIVE COMMITTEE

The Executive Committee of the High Commissioner's Programme, established by ECOSOC, gives the High Commissioner policy directives, and advice at his request in the field of international protection. It meets once a year at Geneva, and special sessions may be called to consider urgent problems. Members: representatives of thirty-one states.

ADMINISTRATION

Headquarters includes the High Commissioner's Office, and the following divisions: External Affairs, Protection, Assistance, and Administration and Management. There are seven Regional or Area Offices, 22 Branch Offices, 11 Honorary Representatives, Correspondents or Consultants, and two Joint Offices located in 43 countries. Of the Regional and Branch Offices, 11 are located South of the Sahara.

REFUGEES IN AFRICA

FUNCTIONS

In Africa south of the Sahara, as in any other part of the world, the Office of the High Commissioner is concerned with refugees who have been determined on an individual basis to come within its mandate under the Statute, and with refugees whom it is called upon to assist under the terms of good offices resolutions adopted by the General Assembly of the UN. Such refugees are entitled to the protection of the Office irrespective of their geographical location. Refugees who are assisted by other United Nations agencies, or who have the same rights or obligations at nationals of their country of residence, are outside the mandate of UNHCR.

The main functions of the Office are to provide international protection, to seek permanent solutions to the problems of refugees, including voluntary repatriations resettlement in other countries and integration into the country of present residence, and to provide supplementary aid and emergency relief to refugees as may be necessary. All activities are carried out on a humanitarian and non-litical basis.

INTERNATIONAL PROTECTION

The main objective of international protection, which is the primary function of UNHCR, is to help refugees to cease to be refugees, and where voluntary repatriation is not applicable, to safeguard their rights and interests, seeking to ensure that they are granted a legal status as close as possible to that of nationals. UNHCR pursues these objectives by seeking to facilitate the acquisition by refugees of the nationality of their country of residence, through naturalization or otherwise, by promoting the conclusion of intergovernmental legal instruments in favour of refugees and by encouraging governments to adopt legal provisions for their benefit.

The main legal instruments concerning refugees are the 1951 Convention relating to the Status of Refugees, and the 1967 Protocol which extends provisions of the Convention to new groups of refugees. The application of these two instruments is supervised by UNHCR. In Africa the principal legal instrument is the Convention Governing the Specific Aspects of the Problems of Refugees in Africa, adopted under the auspices of the Organization of African Unity in September 1969. This Convention is complementary to the 1951 Convention and the 1967 Protocol and contains principles laid down in the United Nations Declaration on Territorial Asylum.

Among legal problems, the Office is called upon to devote special attention to the questions of asylum and *non-refoulement*, which are of crucial importance to refugees.

MATERIAL ASSISTANCE TO REFUGEES IN AFRICA

Emergency relief and supplementary aid: Emergency relief is provided in new refugee situations when food supplies and medical care are required on a large scale at short notice. This has frequently occurred in recent years in Africa where the World Food Program has provided considerable food supplies for the refugees' subsistence pending their first harvest.

Supplementary aid is provided for the neediest refugees and may include feeding, medical aid, or clothing.

Voluntary repatriation: The Office assists refugees wherever possible to overcome difficulties in the way of their repatriation. In cases where no funds are available for their transportation to their homeland, arrangements for payment of the cost involved may be made by UNHCR

Resettlement: Resettlement through migration is assuming more importance in Africa as a solution for the growing number of refugees of non-agricultural stock living in towns.

UNHCR co-operates closely with the Bureau for the Placement and Education of Refugees established by the OAU. The Bureau acts as a clearing house, and has appointed correspondents in a number of countries who submit dossiers of individual refugees who seek resettlement opportunities elsewhere for consideration by the governments to which they are accredited.

Local settlement: The great majority of refugees within the competence of UNHCR in Africa live on the land and receive UNHCR assistance under its annual assistance programmes. About two-thirds of the funds under these programmes (financial target in 1973: $7,839,400) are devoted to the rural settlement of refugees in Africa. As in other areas, UNHCR projects in that continent are implemented by governmental authorities or non-governmental organizations, or, in some cases, by organizations specialized in land settlement. Other agencies of the United Nations system co-operate closely with UNHCR.

In some cases, the refugees settle among the local population and require only marginal assistance from international sources, for example for the extension of schools or medical facilities to accommodate the increase in population represented by the refugees. In other cases, however, special rural communities have to be established on land made available for this purpose by the governments concerned.

In the initial stages of settlement the refugees are provided with food, clothing, shelter, simple medical care and education. UNHCR may pay the transportation costs of supplies made available by the World Food Program. In the settlement stage UNHCR supports such measures as the development of agriculture, and makes provision for a certain amount of infrastructure equipment including water supply, roads, vehicles and the provision of health and primary education facilities.

When the refugees have succeeded in growing their own food, as well as crops which can be sold for cash to meet their other necessities, the settlements can be said to be self-supporting.

The importance of education in the integration of refugees in Africa cannot be over-estimated. UNHCR assists through providing classrooms or contributing towards the expansion of existing primary schools. Care is taken to ensure that tuition fits into the national education system and financial responsibility for running the schools is passed to the governments as soon as possible. For secondary and higher education, UNHCR administers a special Education Account financed from trust funds and co-operates closely with the United Nations Training and Education Programme for Southern Africa.

ACTIVITIES IN 1971-72

The number of refugees who were the concern of UNHCR in more than twenty-five African countries was placed at the end of 1971 at about 1,000,000, virtually the same figure as in 1970. There were some 18,500 new arrivals in 1971, the great majority from territories under foreign administration. The influx of refugees from Portuguese Guinea into Senegal reached a high point during the summer of 1971 and increased the number of refugees in that country from 67,000 to 80,000. In contrast there were reductions through voluntary repatriation of some 9,000 Zambians from Zaire, some 8,000 Zairians (most of them from Burundi), and a number of Sudanese.

Refugees from territories under foreign administration continued to constitute an important proportion of the refugees in several African countries. By the end of 1971 there was an estimated total of about 415,000 refugees from Angola, 80,000 from Portuguese Guinea, 66,600 from Mozambique, and a few thousand others, including many from Namibia and South Africa, whose needs had been brought to the attention of UNHCR.

As further numbers of refugees were moved from reception centres near the border, the number of those established in UNHCR-assisted rural communities rose from some 200,000 at the end of 1970 to over 235,000 at the end of 1971.

Of the U.S.$4,080,675 committed under the 1971 programme for assistance to refugees in Africa, $3,966,984 were used for their settlement on the land. Programme funds were supplemented by $131,820 from the Emergency Fund and $945,056 from the trust funds earmarked mainly for the financing of post-primary educational assistance. Important supporting contributions, valued at about $1,700,000, were provided within the countries of residence of refugees, mainly in the form of arable land services. In addition, a number of refugees benefited from projects outstanding from previous years' programmes.

REGIONAL OFFICES OF UN SPECIALIZED AGENCIES AND OTHER BODIES

FOOD AND AGRICULTURE ORGANIZATION—FAO
Rome, Italy

Regional Office for Africa: P.O.B. 1628, Accra, Ghana; Regional Rep. MOÏSE MENSAH.

WORLD HEALTH ORGANIZATION—WHO
Geneva, Switzerland

Regional Office for Africa: P.O.B. 6, Brazzaville, Congo (Brazzaville); Dir. Dr. A. A. QUENUM.

UNITED NATIONS CHILDREN'S FUND—UNICEF
New York City, U.S.A.

Office of the Director for West Africa: B.P. 4443, Abidjan Plateau, Ivory Coast; Dir. CHEIKH H. KANE.

Office of the Director for East Africa: P.O.B. 7047, Kampala, Uganda; Dir. BRIAN JONES.

Office of the Director for Nigeria and Ghana: P.O.B. 1282, Lagos, Nigeria; Dir. (vacant).

INTERNATIONAL LABOUR ORGANISATION
Geneva, Switzerland

Regional Office for Africa: Chamber of Commerce Building, Mexico Square, P.O.B. 2788, Addis Ababa, Ethiopia; Regional Co-ordinator and Dir. M. A. O. NDISI.

Area Office in Dar es Salaam: Independence Ave. at corner of Mkwepu St., P.O.B. 9212, Dar es Salaam, Tanzania; Dir. D. LUSCOMBE.

Area Office in Lagos: 11 Okotie-Eboh St., P.O.B. 2331, Lagos, Nigeria; Dir. K. A. GHARTEY.

Area Office in Lusaka: P.O.B. 2181, Lusaka, Zambia; Deputy Dir. J. MPYISI.

Area Office in Yaoundé: B.P. 13, Yaoundé, Cameroon; Dir. TH. SIDIBÉ.

Area Office in Dakar: 22 rue Thiers, B.P. 414, Dakar, Senegal; Dir. A. M. HEL BONGO.

INTERNATIONAL CIVIL AVIATION ORGANIZATION—ICAO
Montreal, Canada

African Office: 15 blvd. de la République, P.O.B. 2356, Dakar, Senegal; ICAO Rep. B. BEDEL.

Middle East and Eastern Africa Office: 16 Hassan Sabri, Zamalek, Cairo, Egypt; ICAO Rep. G. KARLSSON.

UNITED NATIONS INFORMATION CENTRES

Burundi: ave. de la Poste et Place Jungers, Bujumbura; P.O.B. 2160; (also covers *Rwanda*.)

Cameroon: Yaoundé, P.O.B. 836.

Ethiopia: Africa Hall, Addis Ababa; P.O.B. 3001.

Ghana: Maxwell Rd. and Liberia Rd., Accra; P.O.B. 2339. (Also covers *Guinea* and *Sierra Leone*.)

Ivory Coast: Abidjan (*to be established*).

Liberia: 24 ULRC Building, Randall St., Monrovia; P.O.B. 274.

Madagascar: 267 rue de Liege, Tananarive; P.O.B. 1348.

Nigeria: 17 Kingsway Rd., Ikoyi, Lagos, P.O.B. 1068.

Senegal: 2 ave. Roume, Dakar; P.O.B. 154. (Also covers *The Gambia*.)

Sudan: House No. 9, Block 6.5.D.E., Nejumi St., Khartoum; P.O.B. 1992.

Tanzania: Matasalamat Building, Dar es Salaam; P.O.B. 9224. (Also covers *Kenya, Malawi, Uganda* and *Zambia*.)

Togo: rue Albert Sarrault, Coin Ave. de Gaulle, Lomé; P.O.B. 911.

Zaire: Building Deuxième République, blvd. du 30 Juin, Kinshasa; P.O.B. 7248.

African Development Bank—AfDB

B.P. 1387, Abidjan, Ivory Coast

Established September 1964 under the aegis of the UN Economic Commission for Africa, the Bank began operations in July 1966.

MEMBERS

Total Membership: 36 Independent African countries.

ORGANIZATION

BOARD OF GOVERNORS

Composed of one representative from each member state.

BOARD OF DIRECTORS

Consists of nine members; responsible for the general operations of the Bank.

President and Chairman of Board of Directors: ABDEL-WAHAB LABIDI (Tunisia).

Vice-Presidents: Sheikh M. A. ALAMOODY (Kenya), LOUIS NÈGRE (Mali), OLATUNDE VINCENT (Nigeria).

The Board of Directors meets annually, the eighth assembly having been held in Algiers in July 1972, the next to be held in Lusaka in 1973 and Rabat in 1974.

FINANCIAL STRUCTURE

The initial authorized capital stock of the Bank amounted to 250 million Units of Account (U.A.)*, comprising 25,000 shares of U.A. 10,000 each to be subscribed exclusively by the independent countries of Africa. Half of the capital stock is paid up, while the other half remains on call. Each member undertakes to subscribe in equal parts to the paid up stock and the callable stock. Initial subscribers to the capital stock were required to make payment in gold or convertible currency in six instalments over a five-year period ending in March 1969. At the Bank's last Annual Meeting in July 1972, the Board of Governors decided to raise the capital stock to U.A. 254.4 million, with a corresponding increase in the number of shares from 25,000 to 25,440.

At July 31st, 1972, the Bank's authorized capital had been fully subscribed and U.A. 85.9 million had actually been contributed to the paid-up half of the capital stock.

*One Unit of Account is equivalent to U.S. $1.08.

COUNTRY	SUBSCRIPTIONS (million U.S. $)
Algeria	24.5
Botswana	1.0
Burundi	1.2
Cameroon	4.0
Central African Republic	1.0
Chad	1.6
Congo (Brazzaville)	1.5
Dahomey	1.4
Egypt	30.0
Ethiopia	10.3
Gabon	30.0
Ghana	12.8
Guinea	2.5
Ivory Coast	6.0
Kenya	6.0
Liberia	2.6
Libya	30.0
Malawi	2.0
Mali	2.3
Mauritania	1.1
Morocco	15.1
Niger	1.6
Nigeria	24.1
Rwanda	1.2
Senegal	5.5
Sierra Leone	2.1
Somalia	2.2
Sudan	10.1
Swaziland	1.6
Tanzania	6.3
Togo	1.0
Tunisia	6.9
Uganda	4.6
Upper Volta	1.3
Zaire	13.0
Zambia	13.0
TOTAL	**281.4**

AIMS AND ACTIVITIES

The Bank seeks to contribute to the economic and social development of members either individually or jointly. To this end, it aims to promote investment of public and private capital in Africa, to use its normal capital resources to make or guarantee loans and investments, and to provide technical assistance in the preparation, financing and implementation of development projects. The Bank may grant direct or indirect credits; it may operate alone or in concert with other financial institutions.

A Pre-Investment Unit has been established within the Bank. Over a five-year period which ended in 1971, the UNDP provided U.S. $2.7 million, with the Bank contributing U.S. $2.2 million in counterpart funds, for the identification, evaluation and preparation of projects in member countries. A second five-year programme covering the period 1972-76 is now being envisaged. A co-ordinating committee for the identification of multinational projects in the field of power, transport and telecommunications has been established with ECA, IBRD and UNDP under the chairmanship of the African Development Bank. The Bank has also entered into co-operative agreements with FAO, UNESCO, ILO and OAU. The Bank is one of the executing agencies for UNDP projects in Africa.

In order to increase its capital resources and raise money for lending at concessionary terms, the Bank has promoted the establishment of an African Development Fund, which is open to contributions from the industrialized capital-exporting countries. Sixteen non-African countries have already pledged varying sums to the fund, whose charter was approved by the Bank's Board of Governors at its Eighth Annual Meeting in July 1972. The Fund is expected to commence operations early in 1973.

Together with a number of private banks, AfDB is promoting the International Financial Corporation for Investment and Development in Africa (Société internationale financière pour les investissements et le développement en Afrique—SIFIDA), registered in Luxembourg in July 1970, with a capital of $12.5 million.

The Bank is active in numerous other fields, including co-operation with African national development finance institutions, the joint financing of projects with other agencies, equity participation in national development banks and the granting of a wide variety of technical assistance facilities.

DISTRIBUTION OF AfDB LOANS AS AT JULY 31ST, 1972

AREA	SECTOR	No. OF PROJECTS	AMOUNT (U.A. '000)	TOTAL (by area)
NORTH	Agriculture	3	6,550	
	Power	1	2,800	
	Transport	3	6,700	16,050
WEST	Agriculture	1	1,600	
	Transport	2	6,400	
	Equity Participation	1	120	
	Line of Credit	3	3,850	
	Power	1	1,350	
	Industry	2	900	
	Telecommunications	1	1,400	
	Water Supply and Sewerage	1	1,500	17,120
EAST	Agriculture	2	2,200	
	Equity Participation	1	1,000	
	Line of Credit	1	2,000	
	Power	1	3,000	
	Industry	1	1,450	
	Transport	4	9,300	
	Water and Supply Sewerage	2	3,300	22,250
CENTRAL	Transport	1	2,300	
	Agriculture	1	431	
	Water Supply	1	1,210	
	Power	1	1,000	4,941
SIFIDA	Finance	1	500	500
WEST/CENTRAL	Transport (Air Afrique)	1	5,000	5,000
TOTAL AfDB COMMITMENTS		37		65,861

PRINCIPAL EVENTS

1961		Feasibility studies on the setting up of a regional development bank by multinational panel of experts.
1962		UN Economic Commission for Africa sets up Special Committee of nine member states to begin making arrangements to form Bank.
1963	Aug.	Conference of African Finance Ministers approves formation agreements.
1964	Sept.	Formation agreement comes into force; 65 per cent of authorized capital stock subscribed.
	Nov.	Inaugural meeting of Board of Governors, Lagos. Officials elected, Abidjan chosen as headquarters.
1966	July	Second annual meeting of Board of Governors.
1967	Aug.	Topographical and soil survey on section of proposed TanZam railway commissioned. Third annual meeting of Board of Governors, Abidjan.
	Oct.	Co-operative programme agreed with FAO.
1968	Aug.	Fourth annual meeting of Board of Governors, Nairobi.
1969	June	Co-operation agreed with UNESCO.
	Aug.	Fifth annual meeting of Board of Governors, Freetown.

1970	Aug.	Sixth annual meeting of Board of Governors, Fort-Lamy.
1971	March	Ratification by Board of Governors of co-operation agreement between AfDB and OAU.
	July	Seventh annual meeting of Board of Governors, Kampala.
	Sept.	Meeting of the Presidents of the Asian, Inter-American and African Development Banks at the IDB's Headquarters in Washington.
1972	April	Potential contributors to the African Development Fund met in Paris and approved the draft ADF Agreement.
	July	Eighth Annual Meeting of the Board of Governors, Algiers. The Board of Governors approved the draft Agreement Establishing the membership of the Gabonese Republic and set December 31st, 1972, as the date on which it will become a full member of the Bank. The Bank raised the authorized capital of the bank from U.A. 250 million to 254.4 million to enable Libya and Gabon to become members. The Board of Governors adopted a declaration calling for an African ministerial conference to define a common African position on monetary problems and development.

PUBLICATIONS

Annual Report.   **Quarterly Statements.**

Communauté Économique de l'Afrique de l'Ouest—CEAO

(West African Economic Community)

Ouagadougou, Upper Volta

An economic union between seven of the eight states of former French West Africa, created by a protocol of agreement signed in Bamako, Mali, in May 1970 by the Heads of State of the West African Customs Union (UDEAO), which it replaced.

MEMBERS

Dahomey	Mauritania	Senegal
Ivory Coast	Niger	Upper Volta
Mali		

ORGANIZATION

The Community was established by a treaty signed in Bamako on June 3rd, 1972 by the Heads of State of six of the member countries and the Foreign Minister of Dahomey.

CONFERENCE OF HEADS OF STATE

The Conference of Heads of State is the supreme organ of the Community. It is held at least once a year in each of the member states, in alphabetical order, and its President is the Head of State of the host country. Decisions of the Conference must be unanimous. It appoints the Secretary-General, accountant and financial controller of the Community.

COUNCIL OF MINISTERS

The Council of Ministers meets at least twice a year, and always at least one month before the Conference of Heads of State, usually at the seat of the Community. Each member state is represented by its Minister of Finance or a member of government, according to the subject under discussion. Decisions are taken unanimously.

GENERAL SECRETARIAT

This organization is responsible for liaison between member states and for the executive functions of the Community. It supervises the implementation of decisions of the Conference of Heads of State and the Council of Ministers. It also supervises the Community Development Fund. The Secretary-General is appointed for a four-year term.

Secretary-General: A. TAMBOURA (Upper Volta).

COURT OF ARBITRATION

A Court of Arbitration is to be set up; its composition, competence and procedure are to be determined in a protocol which will be approved by the Conference of Heads of State.

FUNCTIONS

The West African Economic Community, which replaces the West African Customs Union, aims not to be a true customs union but to provide an "organized zone of exchange" for agricultural products and a special preferential system for industrial goods. Economic co-operation, especially in industry and transport, is to be implemented by the Community's organs in order to improve communications and the distribution of goods and to harmonize industrial development.

Non-manufactured, crude products may be imported and exported within the Community without internal taxes.

Industrial products of member states, when exported to other member states, may benefit from the special preferential system based on the substitution of a *Regional Co-operation Tax*, which replaces all other import taxes. Certain products remain subject to special agreements. Compensation will be paid from the *Community Development Fund* to importing countries for any deficit resulting from this preferential system.

STATISTICS

TRADE WITH OTHER WEST AFRICAN COUNTRIES

(1970)

COUNTRY	EXPORTS TO WEST AFRICA		IMPORTS FROM WEST AFRICA	
	'ooo CFA francs	% of Total	'ooo CFA francs	% of Total
Dahomey . . .	1,575.0	17.5	1,707.2	9.7
Ivory Coast . . .	7,290.6	5.6	3,554.2	3.3
Mauritania . . .	738.0	3.0	1,348.5	8.7
Niger . . .	2,790.3	34.0	2,107.7	13.0
Senegal . . .	8,225.1	19.5	3,213.5	6.0
Upper Volta . . .	2,441.6	48.3	3,085.2	23.8

Table compiled from statistics published by the Central Bank of the West African States. Mali is not included since it is not a member of the West African Currency Union.

PUBLICATION

Journal Officiel

Conseil de l'Entente

A political and economic association of four states which were formerly part of French West Africa, and Togo, which joined in June 1966. The organization was founded in May 1959.

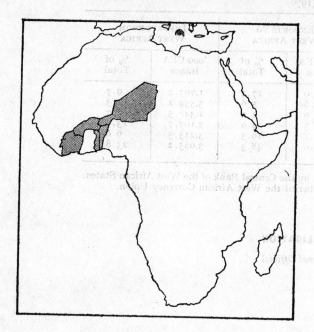

MEMBERS
Dahomey
Ivory Coast
Niger
Togo
Upper Volta

ORGANIZATION

THE COUNCIL

President: HAMANI DIORI (Niger).

The Council consists of the Heads of State and the President and Vice-President of the Legislative Assemblies of each member country, and the Ministers responsible for negotiations between the states. It is an executive body and members who fail to implement the decisions of the Council may be brought before a Court of Arbitration.

The Council meets twice a year, the place rotating annually between the capitals of the member states. The Head of State of the host country acts as President. Extraordinary meetings may be held at the request of two or more members.

COMMISSIONS

Commissions on Foreign Affairs, Justice, Labour, Public Administration, Public Works and Telecommunications, Posts and Telecommunications and on Epidemics and Epizootics have been set up.

Secretary-General: Mlle MAURICETTE LANDEROIN.
B.P. 1878, Abidjan, Ivory Coast.

TRADE AND DEVELOPMENT

There is complete freedom of trade and a unified system of external tariffs and fiscal schedules. A single system of administration for ports and harbours, railways and road traffic and a unified quarantine organization will be set up.

FONDS DE GARANTIE

Central Guarantee Fund originally conceived as the *Fonds de solidarité* to support development projects, transformed in June 1966 into a mutual aid and loan guaranty fund designed to encourage outside lenders to finance development projects in member countries. Total to be provided annually by member states equals 650 million francs CFA, of which 500 million will be contributed by Ivory Coast, 42 million each by Niger, Upper Volta and Dahomey, and 24 million by Togo.

FUNCTIONS

In August 1960 it was agreed that there should be:

1. An identical constitutional and electoral procedure in each State with elections to be held at the same time.
2. Identical organization of the Armed Forces of each State.
3. Identical administrative organization.
4. Identical taxation and tariff policies.
5. Common Bank of Amortization.
6. A common Diplomatic Corps.

Commissions were set up to study how these measures could be implemented, but little progress has been made.

AGREEMENTS WITH FRANCE

In April 1961 the member states signed agreements with France, covering defence, economic affairs, judicial matters, higher education, cultural relations, civil aviation and postal and telecommunications. Upper Volta did not sign the defence agreement.

East African Community

Established December 1967, the Community provides an institutional and legal framework to strengthen the Common Market between Kenya, Tanzania and Uganda and has absorbed the common services and research activities formerly controlled by the East African Common Services Organization.

MEMBERS

Kenya   Tanzania   Uganda

Zambia, Ethiopia, Somalia and Burundi have made formal application to join the Community.

HISTORY

The foundations of regional integration in east Africa were laid under British colonial rule. A customs union between Kenya and Uganda had been established in 1917, into which Tanganyika was drawn in successive stages. An East African Common Market was established in the 1920s, giving Kenya, Uganda and Tanganyika a common external tariff, designed to protect European-dominated highland agriculture in Kenya and the new industries in Nairobi and Mombasa. The East African Currency Board was established in 1917 and a common currency was in use in east Africa from that date until 1966, when the three countries set up their own central banks and issued national currencies.

In 1948 the East African High Commission, headed by the governors of the three territories, was set up to operate joint services in the fields of transport and communications, administration, research and education. In addition to the common external tariff, there were common monetary, banking and financial systems. These joint operations encouraged a sharp increase in trade within the region.

After independence the High Commission was replaced in 1961 by the East African Common Services Organization under the three Heads of State. Integrated activities were continued, and several joint ministerial committees were created.

There were no provisions for integrated economic planning or for harmonization of taxation and monetary policy, and the arrangements were increasingly threatened by the separate policies pursued by the three countries. The benefits derived from the union appeared to be largely in Kenya's favour, while Tanzania was the net loser. Industries, as well as the administrative headquarters of common services, tended to be concentrated in Kenya. Tanzania pressed for reforms of the economic institutions, and in 1964 the Kampala Agreement was signed, providing for the relocation of certain industries and joint measures to protect new industries in Uganda and Tanzania from Kenyan competition. However, the Agreement was badly implemented and led to bitter disputes between the member countries. In 1965 the EASCO was in danger of breaking up, and a Commission on East Africa was set up, composed of three senior ministers from each state, and chaired by a UN official, Professor Kjeld Philip. The Commission presented its report to the three governments in May 1966. On the basis of its recommendations, a Treaty for East African Economic Co-operation was drawn up and signed, coming into effect in December 1967.

The Treaty takes into account the need for planned development policies, a better framework for close co-ordination and more equitable allocation of gains and growth opportunities. Under the terms of the Treaty administrative offices have been relocated so that they are more equally divided between the member States, and the East African Development Bank has been established. The East African Common Market is given a legal basis as an integral part of the East African Community, established by the Treaty.

Accession of new members is provided for. In 1968 negotiations were opened between the East African Community and Zambia, Ethiopia, Somalia and Burundi, who had all applied to join the Community.

In October 1965 the UN Economic Commission for Africa sponsored a conference at Lusaka, at which the idea of an Economic Community of Eastern Africa was launched. This would embrace the East African Community, Zambia, Ethiopia and Burundi, and possibly Somalia, Malawi and Rwanda. A draft treaty was initialled at a conference of ministers in Addis Ababa in May 1966, and a Provisional Council created.

Negotiations between the European Economic Community and Kenya, Uganda and Tanzania were opened in 1965. In July 1968 an Association Agreement was signed at Arusha by the EEC and the members of the East African Community, but never came into force. A new Arusha Agreement was signed in September 1969 and will expire on January 31st 1975.

ORGANIZATION

EAST AFRICAN AUTHORITY

Responsible for the general direction and control over the executive functions of the Community. Composed of the Presidents of Kenya, Tanzania and Uganda. Three East African Ministers assist the Authority in the exercise of its executive functions and advise it generally on the affairs of the Community. The East African Ministers have no national responsibilities but are able to attend and speak at meetings of the Cabinet of the country by which they were nominated.

East African Ministers: AL NOOR KASSUM, WILLIAM RWETSIBA, Dr. ROBERT OUKO.

EAST AFRICAN LEGISLATIVE ASSEMBLY

Replaces the Central Legislative Assembly. Legislates on services provided by the Community.

Members: nine from each state, the three East African Ministers and Deputy Ministers, Secretary-General, Counsel to the Community, and a Chairman.

COMMON MARKET COUNCIL

Main organ for the supervision of the functioning and development of the Common Market; keeps its operation under review; settles problems and disputes arising from the implementation of the Treaty concerning the Common Market; considers methods of creating closer economic and commercial links with other States, associations of States and international organizations.

Members: the three East African Ministers, three National Ministers from each country.

OTHER COUNCILS

The following four Councils have also been established as consultative organs to advise Member States and the Community on planning and the co-ordination of policies; each is composed of the three East African Ministers and a varying number of national Ministers from each country:

Communications Council
Economic Consultative and Planning Council
Finance Council
Research and Social Council

COMMON MARKET TRIBUNAL

Composed of a Judicial Chairman, three members (one from each country) and a fourth chosen by the other three, plus the Chairman. Only member states are permitted to refer disputes to the Tribunal, although the Common Market Council may seek advisory opinions. Decisions, which are binding on member states, are reached by a majority vote.

Chairman: Prof. ELIHU LAUTERPACHT.
Members: Prof. PHILIP L. V. CROSS, JUSTICE SAMUEL W. NAMBUZI, ROBERT WILSON, (one place vacant).
Registrar: MAGANLAL D. DESAI.

CENTRAL SECRETARIAT

Arusha, Tanzania

Composed of the three Secretariats (Ministries): Finance and Administration (*Deputy Minister:* G. N. KALYA), Common Market and Economic Affairs (*Deputy Minister:* S. MUNABI), Communications, Research and Social Services (*Deputy Minister:* S. B. TAMBWE); Office of the Secretary-General, The Chambers of the Counsel to the Community and the Community Service Commission.

The Secretariat co-ordinates the work of the five Councils and is responsible for execution of the Councils' decisions. The Common Market and Economic Affairs Secretariat of the Central Secretariat is also charged with co-ordinating the implementation of the Association Agreement signed in September 1969 at Arusha, between the East African Community and the European Economic Community.

Secretary-General: CHARLES GATERE MAINA.
Counsel to the Community: PAULO SEBALU.

COURT OF APPEAL FOR EAST AFRICA

P.O.B. 30187, Nairobi

Permanent Members:

President: Mr. Justice W. A. H. DUFFUS.
Vice-President: Mr. Justice J. F. SPRY.
Justices of Appeal: E. J. E. LAW, B. C. W. LUTTA, A. MUSTAFA.
Registrar: T. T. M. ASWANI.

This Court, which was established in 1951, hears appeals from the Courts of Tanzania (except Zanzibar island, where it has no jurisdiction), Uganda and Kenya.

EAST AFRICAN DEVELOPMENT BANK
Kampala, Uganda

Established in 1967, the Bank's aims are as follows:

To provide financial and technical assistance to promote the industrial development of the member states; priority is given to industrial development in the relatively less developed countries and about 77 per cent of ordinary and special funds are to be invested in Tanzania and Uganda over consecutive five-year periods.

To further the aims of the East African Community by financing, wherever possible, projects designed to make the economies of the member states increasingly complementary in the industrial field.

To co-operate with national development agencies in the three countries in financing operations, and also with other institutions, both national and international, that are interested in the industrial development of member states.

The Bank's members are the three governments together with such other non-governmental bodies, enterprises and institutions whose membership is approved by the governments. Total initial subscriptions by the governments totals Sh. 120 million and the total authorized capital is Sh. 400 million. The Bank is administered by a Board of Directors appointed by the members.

Director-General and Chairman: IDDI SIMBA.
Directors: P. NDEGWA, S. K. MUKASA, E. P. MWALUKO.

COMMUNITY CORPORATIONS

The four Community Corporations are self-accounting, statutory bodies. The Railways, Harbours, and Posts and Telecommunications Corporations are each controlled by a Board of Directors consisting of a Chairman, three members (one from each member state) appointed by the East African Authority, and a Director-General. Board of Directors of the Airways Corporation is composed of a Chairman, Director-General, two members appointed by the Authority and two by each member state.

East African Railways Corporation: P.O.B. 30121, Nairobi; regional headquarters in each State; takes over the internal transport functions exercised by the *East African Railways and Harbours;* Director-General Dr. E. NJUGUNA GAKUO.

East African Harbours Corporation: Dar es Salaam, Tanzania; takes over the harbours functions formerly exercised by the *East African Railways and Harbours;* Director-General E. N. BISAMUNYU.

East African Posts and Telecommunications Corporation: P.O.B. 7106, Kampala; formerly the East African Posts and Telecommunications Administration. The service has been self-contained and self-financing since January 1949; there are regional headquarters in each partner state; Director-General J. KETO.

East African Airways Corporation: *Headquarters:* Embakasi Airport, P.O.B. 19002, Nairobi, Kenya; *Uganda Regional Office:* P.O.B. 523, Kampala; *Tanzania Regional Offices:* Airways Terminal, Tancot House, P.O.B. 543, Dar es Salaam, and P.O.B. 773, Zanzibar; operates extensive services throughout Kenya, Tanzania and Uganda; also regular scheduled services to Europe, the United Kingdom, Pakistan, India, Thailand, Hong Kong, Zambia, Rwanda, Zaire, Nigeria, Ghana, Ethiopia, Somalia and Egypt; Director-General J. A. OKOT.

COMMUNITY SERVICES

Community Service Commission: P.O.B. 1000, Arusha; f. 1957 as the Public Service Commission; establishment organization of the Community; no responsibilities in relation to the four Corporations.

East African Community Information Office: P.O.B. 1001, Arusha; news and information service for press, radio, magazines, and for the public. Arranges visits, exhibitions, and lectures, and produces literature.

The East African Directorate of Civil Aviation: P.O. Box 30163, Nairobi; established under the Air Transport Authority in 1948; to advise on all matters of major policy affecting Civil Aviation within the jurisdiction of the East African Community, on annual estimates and on Civil Aviation legislation; the Area Control Centre and an Area Communications Centre are at East African Community, Nairobi. Air traffic control is operated at Nairobi, Dar es Salaam, Entebbe and

Mombasa airports, at Wilson (Nairobi) Aerodrome and aerodromes at Arusha, Kisumu, Mwanza, Malindi, Moshi, Mtwara, Tabora, Tanga and Zanzibar; Dir.-Gen. Z. M. BALIDDAWA.

East African Industrial Council: P.O.B. 1003, Arusha; grants licences for the scheduled class of products included under the East African Industrial Licensing Act; Chair. E. D. U. SAWE.

East African Industrial Research Organization: P.O.B. 30650, Nairobi; f. 1942; research and advisory service in the technical problems of industrial development; Dir. C. L. TARIMU.

East African Literature Bureau: P.O.B. 30022, Nairobi; European Office: University Press of Africa, 1 West St., Tavistock, Devon, England; f. 1948; to encourage the publication and sale of books. Publishes, prints and distributes books, including adult education books; promotes African authorship; Dir. N. M. L. SEMPIRA.

East African Meteorological Department: P.O.B. 30259, Nairobi; Headquarters, Regional Meteorological Centre, Regional Telecommunications Hub and Central Services at Nairobi; Regional Headquarters and forecast offices at Dar es Salaam, Entebbe, Mombasa and Nairobi; Port Meteorological Offices at Mombasa and Dar es Salaam. Responsible for collection and study of meteorological and climatological data for East Africa, pure and applied meteorological research, provision of meteorological services to aviation, shipping, agriculture and the public; Dir.-Gen. S. TEWUNGWA; publs. *Annual Report, Memoirs, Technical Memoranda, Climatological Statistics.*

East African Natural Resources Research Council: P.O.B. 1002, Arusha; f. 1963; Sec. J. MIGUDA ALILA; responsible for the co-ordination of research relating to the Natural Resources of East Africa, especially as regards:

East African Fresh Water Fisheries Research Organization: Jinja, Uganda; f. 1946; exploitation of fisheries in Lake Victoria and all lakes and rivers in East Africa; Dir. Dr. J. OKEDI; publ. *Annual Report.*

East African Marine Fisheries Research Organization: Zanzibar; exploitation of marine fisheries in Indian Ocean; Dir. R. E. MORRIS (acting); publ. *Annual Report.*

The Tropical Pesticides Research Institute: Arusha, Tanzania; research in the application of insecticides, herbicides and fungicides, etc.; Dir. Dr. M. E. A. MATERU; publ. *Annual Report.*

East African Agriculture and Forestry Research Organization: P.O.B. 30148, Nairobi, Kenya; f. 1948; planning of research; soil science; plant genetics and breeding; forestry; systematic botany; animal industry; library of 20,000 vols.; Dir. Dr. B. N. MAJISU; publ. *Annual Report.*

The East African Veterinary Research Organization: Muguga, P.O. Kabete, Kenya; f. 1948; for research on diseases and conditions of importance to the East African territories and the production of vaccines against rinderpest and pleuropneumonia. Disease research includes virus infections of livestock with special emphasis on rinderpest and rinderpest-like diseases, tick-borne diseases, especially the Theilerias, Bovine pleuropneumonia and Helminthiasis. The physiology, metabolism and genetics of cattle, are aspects of animal production being studied; Dir. G. L. CORRY; publ. *Annual Report.*

East African Statistical Department: P.O. Box 30462, Nairobi; to provide statistical data on an East African basis; publ. *Economic and Statistical Review* (quarterly); Chief Statistician D. C. SINGH.

East African Tax Board: Includes representatives of the Customs and Excise and the Income Tax Departments (*see below*), the Community and the three Governments; tasks include correlation of the taxation systems of the three countries, keeping under review the work of the two taxation departments and ensuring their co-ordination, assisting in taxation planning. The Commissioners in each Member State under the authority of two Commissioners General are members.

East African Customs and Excise Department: P.O.B. 9061, Mombasa, Kenya; f. 1949; Commissioner-General G. M. WANDERA (Acting).

East African Income Tax Department: P.O.B. 30742, Nairobi; responsible for the assessment and collection of Income Tax in Kenya, Uganda and Tanzania, and for the assessment of Hospital Tax in Kenya. Offices in Nairobi, Mombasa, Nakuru, Kisumu, Kampala, Mbale, Mbarara, Dar es Salaam, Arusha, Tanga, Mwanza, Mbeya and Zanzibar Town; Commissioner-General H. NG'ANG'A (Acting).

Office of the East African Medical Research Council: P.O.B. 1002, Arusha, Tanzania; f. 1949; directs and co-ordinates the activities of the East African Institute for Medical Research, the East African Virus Research Institute, the East African Institute of Malaria and Vector-Borne Diseases, the East African Trypanosomiasis Research Organization, the East African Leprosy Research Centre and the East African Tuberculosis Investigation Centre; Sec. Dr. F. KAMUNVI; publs. *Annual Reports*, papers.

East African Institute of Malaria and Vector-Borne Diseases: P.O., Amani, Tanzania; f. 1949; work is divided between fundamental research, the application of knowledge to East African problems and the dissemination of knowledge among those concerned with antimalarial operations in East Africa and elsewhere; research concerns chiefly malaria and onchocerciasis and their vectors; Dir. P. WEGESA; publ. *Annual Report.*

East African Institute for Medical Research: P.O.B. 1462, Mwanza, Tanzania; formerly the East African Medical Survey and East African Filariasis Research Units; f. 1949; Dir. Dr. V. M. EYAKUZE; publ. *Annual Report*, scientific papers.

East African Leprosy Research Centre (The John Lowe Memorial), P.O.B. 44, Busia, Uganda; situated on the border of Kenya and Uganda, the Centre undertakes studies on problems of leprosy in East Africa and works out a method of satisfactory control of leprosy in the field without high costs. Scientists carry out study programmes by visits to rural areas and schools to find out how far the disease is spread and to set up small clinics for treatment and prevention of further infection. Research is undertaken into immunology and drug trials in leprosy. Dir. Dr. Y. OTSYULA; publ. *Annual Report.*

East African Trypanosomiasis Research Organization: P.O.B. 96, Tororo, Uganda; the laboratories study sleeping sickness in humans and nagana in animals; main lines of research: immunology, entomology, epidemiology, biochemistry, treatment and prevention of diseases; Dir. Dr. R. J. ONYANGO; publ. *Annual Report.*

East African Virus Research Institute: P.O.B. 49, Entebbe, Uganda; f. 1936 by the Rockefeller Foundation as the Yellow Fever Research Institute, it was taken over by the East African High Commission and by the East African Common Services Organization in 1950; in 1967 it became part of the East African Community. Work on yellow fever is now only one side of the general research on viruses, especially those carried by arthropods; Dir. Dr. G. W. KAFUKO; publ. *Annual Report.*

SUMMARY OF TREATY FOR EAST AFRICAN CO-OPERATION

Signed at Kampala, Uganda, on June 6th, 1967, by the Presidents of Kenya, Tanzania and Uganda.

PREAMBLE

Refers among other points to the fact that Tanzania, Uganda and Kenya have enjoyed close commercial, industrial and other ties for many years, and to the determination of the three Partner States to strengthen these ties and their common services, by the establishment of an East African Community, and a Common Market as an integral part of the Community.

CHAPTER 1
(Articles 1–4)
Aims and Institutions

General undertaking included that the three countries shall make every effort to plan and direct their policies with a view to creating conditions favourable for the development of the Common Market and the achievement of the aims of the Community.

CHAPTER 2
(Articles 5–8)
External Trade

Three countries to maintain a Common External Tariff.

Three countries will not enter into agreements whereby tariff concessions negotiated with any country outside the Community are not available to all three countries.

Three countries will take effective measures to counteract any deviation of trade, resulting from barter agreements, away from goods produced in East Africa to goods produced outside the Common Market.

CHAPTER 3
(Articles 9–16)
Inter-Territorial Trade

Guarantees freedom of transit across one State of goods destined for another country, subject to the normal customs and other rules.

Customs duty collected on goods imported into one of the three countries, but in transit to another, shall go to the second country.

Prohibits internal tariffs (except for the transfer tax; *see below*), and quantitative import restrictions upon goods produced in East Africa. Exceptions made in respect of goods covered by certain special obligations, certain agricultural goods, and for restrictions imposed for certain defined reasons (e.g. control of arms and munitions) or in defined circumstances (e.g. balance of payments difficulties).

One country must not engage in discriminatory practices against goods from either or both of the other countries.

CHAPTER 4
(Articles 17–18)
Excise Tariffs

Removal of present differences in the excise tariff which the Common Market Council determines to be undesirable in the interests of the Common Market, and establishment of a generally common excise tariff.

Excise duty collected on goods produced in one country, but transferred to another country, to be transferred to the second country.

CHAPTER 5
(Articles 19–21)
Measure to Promote Balanced Industrial Development

1. Harmonization of fiscal incentives offered by each country towards industrial development.

2. The Transfer Tax System:

The Transfer Tax: States which are in deficit in their total trade in manufactured goods with the other two States may impose transfer taxes upon such goods originating from the other two countries, up to a value of goods equivalent in each case to its deficit with that country. A transfer tax can only be imposed if goods of a similar description to those taxed are being manufactured, or are reasonably expected to be manufactured within three months, in the tax-imposing country. The industry to be protected by the tax must have a productive capacity equivalent to at least 15 per cent of the total domestic consumption of such products in the tax-imposing country or to a value of 2 million shillings E.A., whichever is the less.

Rate of Transfer Tax: limited to 50 per cent of the equivalent external customs tariff imposed on such goods coming from outside East Africa.

Collection: Customs and Excise Department of East Africa responsible for collection, administration and management of all transfer taxes; costs to be borne by the country or countries which imposed transfer taxes.

Limitations: No transfer tax can be imposed for longer than eight years, and all such taxes are to be revoked fifteen years after the Treaty comes into force. There will be an examination of the effectiveness of the system five years after the first tax is imposed. If a significant deviation of trade takes place to goods produced outside the Common Market, as a result of the imposition of transfer taxes, measures shall be taken to counteract such a deviation. If a tax-protected industry is able to export 30 per cent of its annual production to the other two countries, the transfer tax must be revoked, and if its exports to all countries reach 30 per cent, the situation can be considered by the Common Market Council. A country which comes into 80 per cent balance in its total trade in manufactured goods inside East Africa loses the right to impose new transfer taxes, although existing taxes will continue in force.

Anti-Dumping Provisions: Prohibit the transfer of manufactured goods at a price lower than their true value, in such a way as to prejudice the production of similar goods in each Partner State, and prohibit export subsidies for such goods (other than tax incentives and refunds of a general and non-discriminatory kind).

3. Establishment of the East African Development Bank (*see above*).

CHAPTER 6
(Article 23)
Industrial Licences

Present system of industrial licensing shall continue, in respect of articles now scheduled, until twenty years have expired since the commencement of the original legislation.

CHAPTER 7
(Articles 24–28)
Currency and Banking

Exchange of currency notes of the three countries (but not coin) at official par value without exchange commission and without undue delay (subject to exchange control laws and regulations not in conflict with the Treaty).

Bona Fide current account payments between the three countries permitted; all necessary permissions and authorities to be given without undue delay.

Controls may be exercised on capital payments and transfers under certain conditions. Monetary policies to be harmonized; meetings of the three Central Bank Governors to be held at least four times a year.

Reciprocal credits may be given by one Partner State to help another which is in need of balance of payments assistance, up to defined limits and for a period of not more than three years.

CHAPTER 8
(Article 29)
Other Fields of Co-operation

Harmonization of commercial laws in each State; co-ordination of surface transport policies.

CHAPTER 9
(Articles 30–31)
Common Market Council

(*See above:* Organization)

CHAPTER 10
(Articles 32–42)
Common Market Tribunal

(*See above:* Organization)

CHAPTER 11
(Articles 43–45)
Functions of the Community

The Community will operate the services formerly controlled by the East African Common Services Organization (EACSO); also to perform services on an agency basis, as agreed by the Authority, and pass laws on certain matters.

CHAPTER 12
(Articles 46–48)
East African Authority

(*See above:* Organization)

CHAPTER 13
(Articles 49–51)
East African Ministers

(*See above:* Organization)

CHAPTER 14
(Article 52)
Deputy East African Ministers

Allows the Authority, if at any time it considers it desirable, to appoint three Deputy East African Ministers to assist the Ministers.

CHAPTER 15
(Articles 53–55)
Five Councils

Establishes the following Councils: Common Market Council, Communications Council, Economic Consultative and Planning Council, Finance Council, Research and Social Council (*see above:* Organization).

CHAPTER 16
(Articles 56–60)
East African Legislative Assembly

(*See above:* Organization)

CHAPTER 17
(Articles 61–64)
Staff

Provides for the senior staff of the Community, including a Secretary General and a Counsel to the Community, and for the establishment of a Community Service Commission, which will have no responsibilities in relation to staff of the new Corporations.

CHAPTER 18
(Articles 65–70)
Finance

Creation of a General Fund and special funds, and the authorization of Community expenditure.

General Fund: to be financed by customs and excise revenue and the tax on gains or profits of companies engaged in manufacturing or finance.

Distributable Pool Fund: had been operated under the East African Common Services Organization (EACSO) to maintain those common services which are not self-supporting; the remainder of the Pool was distributed to Uganda and Tanzania. The Fund is to be retained, but to be distributed equally to the three countries. It is to cease altogether after the Partner States have paid the second instalment of their full initial subscriptions to the paid-in capital of the Development Bank.

CHAPTER 19
(Articles 71–79)
Four Corporations within the Community

(*See above:* Community Corporations)

CHAPTER 20
(Articles 80–81)
Court of Appeal for East Africa

Court of Appeal for Eastern Africa to continue as Court of Appeal for East Africa.

East African Community

CHAPTER 22
(Articles 83–86)
Decentralization

Location of headquarters and the new East African Tax Board.

CHAPTER 23
Auditor-General

Provides for audit and the functions of the Community Auditor-General.

CHAPTER 24
(Article 88)
Transitional Provisions

CHAPTER 25
(Articles 89–96)
General Provisions

Treaty to come into force on 1st December 1967; parts of Treaty dealing with Common Market to remain in force for fifteen years and then to be reviewed; other countries may negotiate for association with the Community or for participation in its activities; modification of the Treaty by common agreement; implementation measures by way of national legislation in the three countries; abrogation of the EACSO Agreements and past agreements on the Common Market.

STATISTICS

FINANCE

BUDGET*
(shillings)†

Revenue	1970–71 Estimates	Expenditure	1970–71 Estimates
General Fund Revenue	286,517,132	Court of Appeal for East Africa	1,355,575
Government of the United Kingdom	7,472,067	Capital Expenditure	74,479,407
Government of Kenya	588,923	Community Service Commission	793,100
Government of Tanzania	901,765	Office of the Secretary-General and East	
Government of Uganda	508,027	African Legislative Assembly	3,955,562
Nile Water Commission	48,000	Chambers of the Counsel to the Com-	
E.A. Airways	274,330	munity	1,666,105
E.A. Railways	1,474,704	Common Market and Economic Affairs	
E.A. Posts and Telecommunications	1,060,416	Secretariat	7,395,031
U.S. AID	205,702	Finance and Administration Secretariat	18,598,878
U.S. Department of Agriculture	180,000	Miscellaneous Services	20,575,165
Rockefeller Foundation	606,640	E.A. Customs and Excise Department	42,267,301
WHO	312,839	E.A. Income Tax Department	31,161,390
Kenya Hospital Authority	160,000	Communication and Research Secretariat	3,869,563
Desert Locust Control Organization	289,460	E.A. Industrial Research Organisation	1,689,514
UNSF	154,000	Natural Resources Research	23,147,375
		Medical Research	9,584,151
		E.A. Literature Bureau	2,490,382
		Higher Education	1,269,212
		E.A. Directorate of Civil Aviation	35,226,397
		E.A. Meteorological Department	17,958,652
		Audit Department	3,271,245
Total	300,754,005	Total	300,754,005

* Refers to East African Community (General Fund Services).
† 1972: 16.80 shillings = £1 sterling.

INTER-STATE TRADE
(£'000)

KENYA

COUNTRIES	IMPORTS				EXPORTS			
	1968	1969	1970	1971	1968	1969	1970	1971
Tanzania . .	3,692	4,018	5,938	7,932	13,069	12,848	14,752	14,743
Uganda . .	8,650	7,803	10,048	8,026	13,265	15,949	16,698	19,150
TOTAL . .	12,342	11,821	15,986	15,958	26,334	28,797	31,440	33,893

TANZANIA

COUNTRIES	IMPORTS				EXPORTS			
	1968	1969	1970	1971	1968	1969	1970	1971
Kenya . .	13,069	12,848	14,752	14,743	3,692	4,018	5,938	7,932
Uganda . .	2,029	1,713	1,995	816	855	1,177	1,438	1,898
TOTAL . .	15,098	14,561	16,747	15,559	4,547	5,195	7,376	9,830

UGANDA

COUNTRIES	IMPORTS				EXPORTS			
	1968	1969	1970	1971	1968	1969	1970	1971
Kenya . .	13,265	15,949	16,698	19,150	8,650	7,803	10,048	8,026
Tanzania . .	855	1,177	1,438	1,898	2,029	1,713	1,995	816
TOTAL . .	14,120	17,126	18,136	21,048	10,679	9,516	12,043	8,842

TRANSPORT

RAIL, ROAD, AND WATER TRANSPORT—PASSENGER, LIVESTOCK AND GOODS TRAFFIC

ITEM	UNIT	1968	1969	1970
PASSENGER TRAFFIC:				
Number of Passenger Journeys including Season Tickets .	'000	4,760	5,580	5,753
Total Passenger Receipts	£'000	1,737	1,915	2,144
Number of Passenger Train Miles . . .	'000	3,253	2,082	2,145
GOODS TRAFFIC:				
Public Tonnage Hauled	'000	5,247	5,368	5,884
Railway Tonnage Hauled	'000	1,015	811	707
Total Goods Traffic Hauled	'000	6,262	6,179	6,591
Total Goods Traffic Ton Miles	'000	2,539,782	2,560,317	—
Revenue from Public and Railway Paying Traffic .	£'000	22,732	22,650	28,946
LIVESTOCK CARRIED—Revenue . . .	£'000	420	493	484
PARCELS AND LUGGAGE CARRIED—Revenue . .	£'000 }	644	664	649
MAILS CARRIED—Revenue	£'000 }			

EAST AFRICAN RAILWAYS
TRACK MILEAGE

	MAIN LINES	PRINCIPAL LINES	MINOR AND BRANCH LINES	TOTAL SINGLE TRACK LINES	WORKED BUT NOT OWNED BY ADMINISTRATION	TOTAL
1965 . .	2,697	846	723	4,266	98	4,364
1966 . .	2,698	850	724	4,272	98	4,370
1967 . .	2,702	851	717	4,270	98	4,368
1968 . .	2,704	852	720	4,276	98	4,374
1969 . .	2,648	856	719	4 213	98	4 321
1970 . .	2,658	856	719	4,223	98	4,331

CIVIL AVIATION
EAST AFRICAN AIRWAYS CORPORATION

DETAIL	UNIT	1966	1967	1968	1969	1970
Aircraft Kilometres . . .	'000	14,162	13,772	15,375	18,024	n.a.
Passengers Carried . . .	number	284,001	343,707	422,050	451,085	510,293
Cargo Carried . . .	tons	4,276	6,157	8,185	8,907	9,700
Mail Carried . . .	,,	1,034	1,196	1,443	1,471	1,300
Capacity Ton Kilometres Offered .	'000	86,842	147,622	181,850	228,703	250,000
Load Ton Kilometres Carried .	,,	45,580	67,915	83,050	90,207	100,100
Weight Load Factor . . .	%	52.5	46	45.7	39.4	39.9
Gross Revenue . . .	£'000	10,412	13,060	14,891	17,720	16,600

EAST AFRICAN HARBOURS

DETAIL	UNIT	1966	1967	1968	1969	1970
Revenue	£ million	14.8	11.8	12.6	12.3	14.4
Ships Calling at E.A. Ports .	number	3,222	3,723	3,862	3,718	3,662
Cargo Handled . .	million d.w.t.	6.78	7.54	8.09	7.85	8.66
Passengers Embarked . .	number	45,633	42,478	39,567	40,632	38,259
Passengers Disembarked .	,,	45,413	42,047	36,184	31,899	29,631

European Economic Community

THE ASSOCIATED AFRICAN AND MALAGASY STATES

YAOUNDÉ CONVENTION

Burundi	Gabon	Rwanda
Cameroon	Ivory Coast	Senegal
Central African Republic	Madagascar	Somalia
Chad	Mali	Togo
Congo (Brazzaville)	Mauritania	Upper Volta
Dahomey	Niger	Zaire

ARUSHA AGREEMENT

Kenya	Uganda	Tanzania

INTRODUCTION

When, in March 1957, six European states—Belgium, France, Italy, the Netherlands, the Federal German Republic and Luxembourg—signed the Rome Treaty establishing the European Economic Community, the first four named controlled a number of overseas territories, some of them directly ruled colonies or territories with similar status, some protectorates and some United Nations Trust Territories. Largely on French insistence special provision for these territories was made under the Treaty and they were associated with the Community. The removal of tariffs between the six signatory states was the main provision which applied also to the dependencies, except that the latter could retain or reintroduce tariffs on their imports from the Six in the interests of protecting their own infant industries, their balances of payments and their revenues. In addition, the Six established a development fund of $581.25 million to provide grants to the associated territories in the period 1958–63.

The Convention of Association drawn up under the Rome Treaty had a duration of five years. Before this period had expired, nineteen of the associated territories had gained their independence. With the exception of Guinea they concluded a new convention with the Six which was signed in Yaoundé, Cameroon, on July 20th, 1963, and came into effect on June 1st, 1964, for another five-year period. This Convention incorporated the essential elements of the first convention, and a second European Development Fund was established with total resources of $730 million. Of this total $620 million was earmarked as grants and $46 million as special loans to the 18 Yaoundé Associates, with the remaining $60 million allocated as grants and $4 million in loans to the remaining dependencies of the Six.

The negotiation of the Yaoundé Convention took place in the closing months of the negotiations for British membership of the European Community which had resulted in the French veto of January 1963. In the course of the negotiations the Community had offered Africa and Caribbean members of the Commonwealth association with the Community, but the Commonwealth reaction had generally been cool. Subsequently the Six issued at the time of the signature of the Convention in July 1963 a declaration of intent offering trade concessions to other African countries with economies at a comparable stage of development to those of the 18 African and Malagasy signatory states, either through adhesion to the same convention, through separate association agreements, or through trade agreements. The response from Commonwealth states in Africa was warmer than on the previous occasion, the nature of the Yaoundé Convention being by then known. In November 1963 the Nigerian Government began talks with the Community about an association agreement and in February 1964 the members of the East African Community—Kenya, Uganda and Tanzania—made a joint approach with a similar aim. On July 16th, 1966, the Nigerian Government and the six Community countries signed an Association Agreement under the terms of which Nigerian exports would be admitted duty-free into the Community, with the exception of cocoa beans, groundnut oil, palm oil and plywood, which would be subject to quotas. Nigeria agreed to remove duties from imports from the Community except when duties served to help Nigerian development or to provide revenue. The subsequent *coup d'état* in Nigeria and later the civil war delayed and finally prevented ratification of the agreement by all seven signatory states before its proposed term expired on May 31st, 1969, the same date as the expiry of the Yaoundé Convention.

Negotiations with the three East African Commonwealth states advanced less rapidly and it was not until July 26th, 1968, that an agreement was signed in Arusha, Tanzania. It too was due to expire on May 31st, 1969, but again not all of the nine signatory states had completed ratification by that date. A new agreement, incorporating some modifications, was signed on September 24th, 1969. With the exception of coffee, cloves and tinned pineapple, for which quotas were agreed, the three African countries' exports to the Community will be admitted duty free, while these countries will remove duties on some sixty products imported from the Community, equivalent to tariff concessions varying from 2 to 9 per cent. Owing to ratification delays a provisional agreement in July 1970

119

implemented some provisions of the agreement pending its formal entry into force.

Meanwhile, negotiations between the Community and the 18 Yaoundé Associates for the renewal of the 1963–68 convention also ran into delays and it was not until July 29th, 1969, that a new convention ("Yaoundé II") was signed. The provisions of Yaoundé I had meanwhile remained in force. The new Convention followed the same lines as its predecessors, including the provision of development aid through a third European Development Fund. This fund comprises a total allotment for the Eighteen of $918 million, of which $748 million will be allotted in the form of grants, $80 million as special loans

the acquisition of shares and similar operations, and $90 million in loans on normal terms, subject to interest rebate, from the European Investment Bank. (Another $82 million is being provided in grants and loans to the Community countries' dependencies.) Owing to ratification delays among the 24 signatory states temporary provisions implementing the terms of the new Convention until December 31st, 1970, were introduced.

Prior to the opening in July 1970 of renewed negotiations for United Kingdom membership of the European Economic Community the Six agreed in principle that African member states of the Commonwealth would be offered association with the Community.

ORGANIZATION

YAOUNDÉ CONVENTION

Council of Association: 2 rue Ravenstein, Brussels 1, Belgium. Set up in 1963 under the Convention of Association with seventeen African States and Madagascar and is responsible for its broad working. Composed of the Council of Ministers and the Commission of the European Community, and one representative from each of the Associated Countries; the Chair is held in rotation; meets annually.

Association Committee: composed of one representative from each of the Community countries and the Associated States; carries out the everyday administration of the Convention.

Member of the European Commission with special responsibility for Overseas Countries and Territories: JEAN-FRANÇOIS DENIAU.

Parliamentary Conference of the Association: established under the Convention of Association with seventeen African States and Madagascar; composed of 54 members of EEC and 54 members of Associated States; meets annually.

Joint Committee: ensures continuing of Association's Parliamentary activity.

Court of Arbitration: composed of a President, appointed by Council of Association, and four independent judges. *President:* M. ROBERT LECOURT.

ARUSHA AGREEMENT

A *Parliamentary Committee* meets once a year and an *Administration Council* administers the Agreement.

ASSOCIATION AGREEMENTS

Treaty of Rome

Part IV of the Treaty of Rome, establishing the EEC, provides for the association with the EEC of non-European countries and territories that have special relations with Belgium, France, Italy and the Netherlands, in order to promote the economic and social development of these countries and territories and to establish close economic relations between them and the Community as a whole. The major provisions are as follows:

Members of the EEC, in their commercial exchanges with the countries and territories, to apply the same rules which they apply among themselves pursuant to the Treaty.

Each country or territory to apply, in its commercial exchanges with the Community States and with the other countries and territories, the same rules which it applied in respect of the European States with which it had special relations. EEC members to contribute to the investment required by the progressive development of the countries and territories.

Customs duties on trade between the Community and associated countries and territories to be progressively abolished according to the same timetables as for trade between member states themselves.

Associated countries and territories may, however, levy customs duties which correspond to the needs of their development and the requirements of their industrialization or which, being of a fiscal nature, have the object of contributing to their budgets.

First Convention of Association

A Convention implementing these provisions was signed in 1957 for a period of five years. This set up a Development Fund for Associated Overseas Countries and Territories for the purpose of promoting their social and economic development, in particular the development of health, educational, research and professional activities of their populations, and economic investments of general interest directly connected with the implementation of a programme including productive and specific development projects.

First and Second Yaoundé Conventions

Signed, July 1963, at Yaoundé, Cameroon, between the members of the EEC and the eighteen African and Malagasy States, the second Convention came into effect on June 1st, 1964, and expired on May 31st, 1969. Negotiations were completed in June 1969 for the renewal of the Convention. The new Convention will enter into force only after ratification by the parliaments of all 24 signatories but, regardless of the date of ratification, it will terminate on January 31st, 1975.

Some changes have been made to the terms of the Convention including the following: lowering of the common external tariff for a number of tropical products (coffee from 9.6 per cent to 7 per cent, cocoa from 5.4 per cent to 4 per cent, palm oil from 9 per cent to 6 per cent); the inclusion of a Protocol annexed to the Convention stipulating that Yaoundé II, and in particular Article 3 thereof, shall not prevent the Associated States from participating in a system of generalized preferences as recommended by UNCTAD; aid to production in the form of price support has been abandoned in favour of provisions for *ad hoc* intervention where a fall in world prices seriously jeopardizes the economy of an Associated State; the promotion of regional co-operation among the Associated States; undertaking by the Associated States to ensure proper maintenance for projects financed by the Community and to insert any request for financing into a development programme; strengthening of the right of Associated States to protect local industry, and in particular new industries.

SUMMARY OF THE SECOND YAOUNDE CONVENTION

Articles 1–16: *Trade.* The basic aim of the Association is free trade between the European Community and each of the associated states. In principle, free trade between the Community and the associated states was introduced on July 1st, 1968, when the Community's common external tariff came into force. However, the associated states retain the right to maintain, reimpose or increase customs duties on imports from the Community (in addition to fiscal duties) in the interests of their revenue, economic development, new industries and balance of payments. Conversely, the Community may impose a degree of protection for products subject to the common agricultural policy, though imports of these or similar products from the associated states are granted preference over imports from third countries.

Article 17–30: *Financial and Technical Co-operation.* Provide for continued operation of Development Fund and the spending over a five-year period of a total sum of $828 million on the same lines as before and also for promoting the diversification of the economies of the Associated States. The European Investment Bank will make loans of up to a total of $90 million, possibly at low interest rates.

Articles 31–40: *Right of Establishment, Services, Payment and Capital.*

Articles 41–55: *Institutions.*

Articles 56–66: *General and Final Provisions.*

SUMMARY OF THE ARUSHA AGREEMENT

Articles 2–15: *Trade.* Products originating in the East African Community are admitted to the EEC free of customs duties and charges with equivalent effect, without prejudice to the import rules for products subject to the European Community's common agricultural policy.

Annual quotas are established for unroasted coffee (56,000 metric tons), cloves (120 tons) and tinned pineapple (800 tons). In the event of imports of these products into the EEC exceeding these totals, the EEC is authorized to consult with the exporting countries about measures to avoid disturbing traditional trade flows. The EEC will grant preferential treatment, case by case, to EAC products subject to the common agricultural policy and to processed agricultural products after consultation with the East African countries.

Imports of about sixty products from the EEC into the EAC will be freed of customs duties and equivalent charges, and from quantitative restrictions, though in the interests of their development needs and budgetary revenues the East African states may retain or introduce duties or charges on these products, and retain or impose quotas.

The East African states are free to form customs unions or free-trade areas with African countries of comparable economic development, provided the provisions of this agreement concerning origin are not changed.

Articles 16–20: *Establishment.* The East African states agree that no discrimination shall be made between nationals or companies of the EEC states in matters of the right of establishment and the provision of services, and that more favourable treatment accorded to the nationals or companies of a third country shall be extended to EEC nationals or companies.

Articles 21–22: *Payments and capital.*

Articles 23–29: *Institutional provisions.* An Association Council comprising members of the EEC Council of Ministers and of the Commission and of the governments of the African states presides over the Association, and meets once annually. The Council may appoint a committee to provide continuity of co-operation. A Parliamentary Committee shall meet once a year to discuss matters concerning the Association; it shall consist of equal numbers of members of the European Community countries and the parliaments of the East African states.

Articles 30–38: *General and final provisions.*

EUROPEAN DEVELOPMENT FUND COMMITMENTS

(Situation at October 10th, 1972)

COUNTRIES AND TERRITORIES	FIRST EDF ($'000)	SECOND EDF ($'000)	THIRD EDF ('000 u/a)*
AASM (Associated African States and Madagascar):			
Burundi	4,926	20,858	15,789
Cameroon	52,798	54,253	29,790
Central African Republic	18,196	25,995	13,600
Chad	27,713	23,066	20,246
Congo (Brazzaville)	25,036	20,442	14,083
Dahomey	20,778	23,722	20,306
Gabon	17,761	20,490	17,680
Ivory Coast	39,644	58,596	21,534
Madagascar	56,265	69,927	31,648
Mali	42,023	33,583	28,259
Mauritania	15,377	18,562	4,158
Niger	31,291	30,340	33,852
Rwanda	4,942	19,105	20,933
Senegal	43,831	56,186	32,381
Somalia	10,089	28,100	22,351
Togo	15,936	19,663	14,304
Upper Volta	28,351	30,706	19,664
Zaire	19,593	75,231	24,880
TOTAL	474,550	638,825	385,458
OCT and OD (Overseas Countries, Territories and Departments of European Community Member States)	66,057	60,179	21,586
Algeria	25,320	—	—
New Guinea	4,490	—	—
Miscellaneous	10,833	21,032	—
Frozen Cred ts	—	—	4,038
Still to be Aillocated	—	10,000†	9,441
TOTAL	581,250	730,036	420,523

* Unit of account=U.S. $1.00 (First and Second EDFs)=U.S. $1.08 (Third EDF).
† As at January 1971.

TRADE BETWEEN THE EEC SIX AND THE ASSOCIATED STATES AND NIGERIA

	IMPORTS		EXPORTS	
	Total ($'000)	% from EEC	Total ($'000)	% to EEC
Burundi (1968)	22,790	48.0	16,207	16.6
Cameroon (1970)*	242,072	69.5	225,924	69.7
Central African Republic (1970)*	31,622	75.4	30,579	69.4
Chad (1970)	61,995	52.6	29,549	73.4
Congo (Brazzaville) (1970)*	57,233	75.2	30,830	54.5
Dahomey (1969)	55,000	59.0	27,000	60.0
Gabon (1970)*	79,831	73.8	121,184	56.7
Ivory Coast (1970)	387,837	68.7	468,815	62.0
Kenya (1970)†	397,668	20.2	216,861	17.1
Madagascar (1970)	170,497	75.4	144,843	41.0
Mali (1969)	39,000	47.0	17,000	17.0
Mauritania (1969)	44,000	47.0	79,000	62.0
Niger (1970)	58,368	61.5	31,623	64.1
Rwanda (1969)	24,000	34.0	14,000	32.0
Senegal (1970)	192,863	65.5	151,897	65.7
Somalia (1968)	47,572	40.5	29,683‡	30.9
Tanzania (1970)†	271,489	24.1	238,603	14.1
Togo (1970)	64,559	50.5	54,650	85.0
Uganda (1970)†	121,137	22.3	245,476	8.1
Upper Volta (1970)	46,677	58.6	18,202	24.1
Zaire (1969)	410,260	53.0	649,100	69.0
Nigeria (1969)	696,000	25.0	891,000	35.0

* Cameroon, the Central African Republic, Congo (Brazzaville) and Gabon form the Customs and Economic Union of Central Africa. Figures for these countries' imports and exports exclude inter-trade between members of the CEUCA (UDEAC).

† Excluding inter-trade between Kenya, Tanzania and Uganda in local produce and locally manufactured goods.

‡ Excluding re-exports.

The Franc Zone

The Franc Zone embraces all those countries and groups of countries whose currencies are linked with the French franc at a fixed rate of exchange and who agree to hold their reserves in the form of French francs and to effect their exchange on the Paris market. Each of these countries or groups of countries has its own central issuing Bank and its currency is freely convertible into French francs. This monetary union is based on individual agreements concluded between France and the various States who, after attaining independence, opted for independent sovereignty either within or outside the French Community.

The Maghreb members have much more independent monetary and economic policies than the thirteen sub-Saharan Franc Zone countries, due largely to the relatively more developed state of their economies, and the Tunisian and Moroccan currencies are no longer directly tied to the French franc. They hold part of their foreign reserves in French francs and the transaction of most of their international payments is made through the Paris exchange market; however, each country has created its own currency and their issuing banks are entirely autonomous.

Because of balance-of-payment stringencies, these countries restrict payments to other Franc Zone countries, in contrast with the free convertibility among the sub-Saharan members. The currencies of the Maghreb countries do not enjoy the unlimited backing of the French Treasury.

Mali withdrew from the Franc Zone in 1962, setting up her own currency, the Malian franc, and her own issuing Bank. However, in May 1967 she ratified a currency agreement with France covering her gradual return to the West African monetary zone, and France's guarantee of the convertibility of the Mali franc. Under the terms of the agreement, Mali was to reorganize her economy, and in May 1967 she devalued her franc by 50 per cent. The Mali franc returned to full convertibility with the French franc in March 1968, and agreement was reached on the establishment of a central issuing bank, to be jointly administered by France and Mali.

Guinea left the Franc Zone when she opted for independence outside the French Community in 1958. Togo joined in 1963.

MEMBERS

French Republic (Metropolitan France and the Overseas Departments and Territories, except French Territory of the Afar and Issa).

Cameroon, Central African Republic, Chad, Congo (Brazzaville), Dahomey, Gabon, Ivory Coast, Madagascar, Mali, Mauritania,* Niger, Senegal, Togo, Upper Volta (full members).

Algeria, Tunisia and Morocco retain national control over financial transfers.

* Mauritania announced on November 29th, 1972, its intention to leave the Franc Zone and create its own national currency.

CURRENCY

French franc: used in Metropolitan France and the Overseas Departments of Guadeloupe, French Guiana and Martinique.

1 CFP (*Communauté financière du Pacifique*) franc = 0.055 fr. Used in New Caledonia, French Polynesia, and Wallis and Futuna Islands.

1 CFA (*Communauté financière africaine*) franc = 0.02 fr. Used in the monetary areas of West Africa, Equatorial Africa and Cameroon, and also in the Overseas Department of Réunion and the Overseas Territories of the Comoro Islands and St. Pierre et Miquelon.

1 franc malgache = 0.02 fr. Used in Madagascar, where it replaced the CFA franc in 1963.

1 Mali franc = 0.01 fr. Used in Mali, where it replaced the CFA franc in 1962.

1 Algerian dinar = 1.125 fr. Replaced the Algerian franc in 1964.

The Tunisian dinar and the Moroccan dirham, created in 1958 and 1959 respectively, are not attached to the French franc but are negotiable on the basis of a fixed rate.

AFRICAN FINANCIAL COMMUNITY (COMMUNAUTÉ FINANCIÈRE AFRICAINE—CFA)

The CFA comprises all the states, except Guinea, which were part of French West and Equatorial Africa, and Cameroon, Togo and Madagascar. These full members of the Franc Zone are still grouped within the currency areas that existed before independence, each group having its own currency issued by a central Bank.

West African Monetary Union (*Union monétaire ouest-africaine*): Dahomey, Ivory Coast, Mauritania, Niger, Senegal, Upper Volta (all parts of former French West Africa) and Togo, which joined in 1963. Established by Treaty of May 1962; agreements on Co-operation were signed with France in 1963; two-thirds of the members of the Board of Directors of its central issuing Bank are provided by the member states and one-third by the French Government.

Monetary Union of Equatorial Africa and Cameroon (*Union monétaire de l'Afrique équatoriale et du Cameroun*): Central African Republic, Chad, Congo (Brazzaville), Gabon (the countries of former French Equatorial Africa) and Cameroon. Agreements on Co-operation were signed with France in 1960; the French Government provides half of the members of the Board of Directors of its central issuing Bank, the other half being provided by the member states.

Madagascar: Agreements on Co-operation were signed with France in 1960 and 1962; a national issuing Bank replaced the former Bank of Madagascar in 1962; the French Government provides half of the members of the issuing Bank's Board of Directors.

ORGANIZATION

The CFA and Malagasy francs are freely convertible into French francs at a fixed rate, through "Operations Accounts" established by agreements concluded between the French Treasury and the individual issuing Banks. The notes are backed fully by the resources of the French Treasury, which also provides the Banks with overdraft facilities.

The monetary reserves of the CFA countries are held in French francs in the French treasury. Exchange is effected on the Paris market and foreign assets earned by member countries are pooled in a Fonds de Stabilisation des changes (Exchange Stabilization Fund) which is managed by the Bank of France. Part of the reserves earned by richer members can be used to offset the deficits incurred by poorer countries. Member countries negotiate each

year their import programme with the French authorities.

New regulations drawn up in July 1967 provided for the free convertibility of currency with that of countries outside the Franc Zone. Restrictions are to be removed on the import and export of CFA and Malagasy banknotes, although some capital transfers will still be subject to approval by the governments concerned.

When the French Government instituted exchange control to protect the French franc following the May 1968 crisis, other Franc Zone countries were obliged to take similar action in order to maintain free convertibility within the Franc Zone. The CFA and Malagasy francs were devalued following devaluation of the French franc in August 1969.

CENTRAL ISSUING BANKS

Banque Centrale des États de l'Afrique Équatoriale et du Cameroun: 29 rue du Colisée, Paris 8e; f. 1955 under the title "Institut d'émission de l'AEF et du Cameroun"; re-created under present title in 1960; issuing house for the four equatorial African member countries and Cameroon; Pres. GEORGES GAUTIER; Dir.-Gen. CLAUDE BANOUILLOT.

Banque Centrale des États de l'Afrique de l'Ouest: 29 rue du Colisée, Paris 8e; f. 1955 under the title "Institut d'émission de l'AOF et du Togo" and re-created under present title by a treaty between the West African states and a convention with France in 1962; central issuing bank for the members of the West African Monetary Union; Pres. BABACAR BA; Dir.-Gen. ROBERT JULIENNE.

Banque Centrale du Mali: f. 1968; Chair. SEKOU SANGARE (Mali); Dir.-Gen. Mr. BUSSINE (France).

Banque de France: 1 rue de la Vrillière, Paris; f. 1800; issuing house for Metropolitan France; Governor OLIVIER WORMSER.

Institut d'Émission des Départements d'Outre-Mer: 233 blvd. Saint-Germain, Paris 7e; issuing house for the French Overseas Departments; Dir.-Gen. ANDRÉ POSTEL-VINAY.

Institut d'Émission d'Outre-Mer: 233 blvd. Saint-Germain, Paris 7e; issuing house for the French Pacific territories; Dir.-Gen. ANDRÉ POSTEL-VINAY.

Institut d'Émission Malgache: ave. Le Myre de Vilers, B.P. 550, Tananarive; f. 1962, replacing former Banque de Madagascar et des Comores, under the terms of the Co-operation Agreement signed with France in June 1960; issuing house for Madagascar; Dir.-Gen. JEAN KIENTZ.

ECONOMIC AID

France's ties with the African Franc Zone countries involve not only monetary arrangements, but also include comprehensive French assistance in the forms of budget support, foreign aid, technical assistance and subsidies on commodity exports.

Official French financial aid and technical assistance to developing countries is administered by the following agencies:

Fonds d'Aide et de Co-opération—FAC: 20 rue Monsieur, Paris 7e. In 1959 FAC took over from FIDES (Fonds d'Investissement pour le Développement Economique et Social) the administration of subsidies and loans from the French Government to the former French African States and Madagascar. FAC is administered by the Secretariat of State for Co-operation, which allocates budgetary funds to it.

Caisse Centrale de Co-opération Économique—CCCE: 233 Boulevard Saint-Germain, Paris 7e. Founded in 1941, and given present name in 1958. French Development Bank which executes the financial operations of FAC. Lends money to member States of the Franc Zone. Dir.-Gen. ANDRÉ POSTEL-VINAY.

Bureau de Liaison des Agents de Coopération Technique: 66 ter rue St.-Didier, Paris 16e.

FRENCH COMMUNITY

The Community was created by the 1958 Constitution, adopted by referendum by the countries of French West Africa (with the exception of Guinea, which opted for total and immediate independence), French Equatorial Africa and Madagascar, which all chose to become member states of the Community. The field of the Community's competence included foreign policy, defence, currency, economic and financial policy, strategic materials and higher education. Between October and December 1958 all the States of the Community were granted internal autonomy.

A Constitutional Act of June 1960 introduced the possibility of concluding agreements whereby a member state could become independent without ceasing to belong to the Community. Six states—Central African Republic, Chad, Congo (Brazzaville), Gabon, Madagascar and Senegal—decided to become independent within the Community which was then called the "renewed Community", while all the other states preferred total independence. France has concluded co-operation agreements in international law with all these states (including Togo and Cameroon which included territories entrusted to France by international mandate and therefore could not be members of the Community).

The Articles of the Constitution dealing with the Community have not been expressly abolished but are no longer applied today and the various organs of the Community have fallen into abeyance. The two main organizations now responsible for liaison between France and African and Madagascan states are:

Secretariat-General for the Community and African and Madagascan Affairs, 138 rue de Grenelle, Paris 7e; Sec.-Gen. JACQUES FOCCART.

Secretariat of State for Foreign Affairs in Charge of Co-operation, 20 rue Monsieur, Paris 7e; Sec. of State PIERRE BILLECOCQ.

CUSTOMS UNIONS

Under the terms of the first Yaoundé Convention, July 1963, all CFA countries and Madagascar became associate members of the European Economic Community. This Convention of Association stipulates the gradual abolition of tariff and quota restrictions for the whole Common Market, and therefore the guaranteed markets and prices for African produce in France are now being phased out.

The following regional common markets within the Franc Zone have been formed:

Communauté Économique de l'Afrique de l'Ouest (CEAO) (see chapter).

Union douanière et économique de l'Afrique centrale (UDEAC) (see chapter).

Organisation Commune Africaine, Malgache et Mauricienne (OCAM): a common market in sugar has been established (see chapter).

Organisation Commune Africaine, Malgache et Mauricienne—OCAM

B.P. 437, Yaoundé, Cameroon

Founded February 1965 in succession to the *Union africaine et malgache de coopération économique* (UAMCE), to accelerate the political, economic, social, technical and cultural development of member states within the framework of the OAU.

MEMBERS

Cameroon	Gabon	Rwanda
Central African Republic	Ivory Coast	Senegal
Chad	Madagascar	Togo
Congo (Brazzaville)*	Mauritius	Upper Volta
Dahomey	Niger	Zaire*

Mauritania left the organization in July 1965, but remains a member of the Technical Committees of OCAM.

* Under OCAM rules any country withdrawing from the organization must give one year's notice. Zaire and Congo (Brazzaville) announced their withdrawals in April and September 1972 respectively.

ORGANIZATION

CONFERENCE OF HEADS OF STATE AND OF GOVERNMENT

Chairman: LÉOPOLD SÉDAR SENGHOR (Senegal).

The supreme authority of OCAM meets once a year in ordinary session. The following meetings have been held:

Nouakchott, Mauritania	1965	February.
Abidjan, Ivory Coast	1965	May (Mauritania, Cameroon, Congo Republic absent).
Tananarive, Madagascar	1966	June.
Niamey, Niger	1968	January.
Kinshasa, Zaire	1969	January.
Yaoundé, Cameroon	1970	January.
Fort Lamy, Chad	1971	January.
Lomé, Togo	1972	April.

The next meeting is scheduled to be held in Port Louis, Mauritius in April 1973.

COUNCIL OF MINISTERS

Composed of Foreign Ministers of member states. Meets once a year in ordinary session. Responsible for implementing co-operation between OCAM countries as directed by the Conference of Heads of State.

TECHNICAL COMMITTEES

Committee on Sugar: implements provisions of the Common Sugar Market (*see below*, Accord africain et malgache du sucre), in particular the fixing of a guaranteed price for sugar in OCAM countries.

Scientific and Technical Research Committee: concerned with co-ordination of national research programmes.

Committee of PTT Experts.

Ad hoc *Committee for Insurance.*

Ad hoc *Meat Committee.*

Meeting of Statisticians.

Meeting of Film Makers

SECRETARIAT

Responsible for the administration of OCAM. Appointed by the Conference of Heads of State, upon the proposal of the Council of Ministers, for a minimum of two years.

Secretary-General: FALILOU KANE (Senegal).

Directeur de Cabinet: ALI B. TALL (Upper Volta).

DEPARTMENTS

Département des affaires économiques et financières: Dir. AMBROISE FOALEM (Cameroon).

Département des affaires culturelles et sociales, et santé: Dir. ALBERT EKUE (Dahomey).

OCAM is represented at the International Civil Aviation Organization (ICAO) in Montreal, Canada.

AIMS

Harmonization of Customs regulations.

Setting up an African Common Market.

Agreement on Double Taxation.

Regularization of insurance and other costs on trade exchanges.

Stabilization Funds in support of steady prices.

Harmonization of investment codes.

Suppression of subversion in African states.

AFRO—MALAGASY CO-OPERATION

Accord africain et malgache du sucre (*Common Sugar Market*): *Secretariat:* Fort-Lamy, Chad. An agreement, signed in June 1966, came into force in October 1966 and established a common market in sugar between members of OCAM. Both the sugar-producing countries (Congo-Brazzaville and Madagascar) and the consumer countries benefit from this agreement, which provides for the fixing each year of a guaranteed price for sugar in OCAM countries. A levy is imposed on sugar imported from non-member countries, though preference is given to European sugar (mainly from Belgium and France). This levy is placed in a common fund; Exec. Dir. ANTOINE ESSOMÉ.

Air Afrique: B.P. 21.017, Abidjan, Ivory Coast; provides international air services between member states and other countries (Cameroon withdrew from the airline in January 1971 and later set up her own national company); Pres. and Dir.-Gen. CHEIKH FAL (Senegal).

Comité des ministres des transports: Dakar, Senegal; f. 1962 to study transport problems within the former Union Africaine et Malgache (UAM); Sec.-Gen. CHEIKH FAL (Senegal).

Ecole Inter-Etat des Ingénieurs de l'Equipement Rural (EIER): Ouagadougou.

Institut Culturel Africain, Malagache et Mauricien (ICAM) (*Cultural Institute*): f. 1971; aims to align the activities of cultural centres in member countries, promote culture and co-operate with similar bodies in other areas.

Mouvement d'étudiants de l'organisation commune africaine, malgache et mauricienne (MEOCAM): f. 1967; student movement of the Afro-Malagasy Common Organization; Pres. KACK KACK (Cameroon).

Office africain et malgache de la propriété industrielle (OAMPI) (*Afro-Malagasy Industrial Property Office*): B.P. 887, Yaoundé, Cameroon; f. 1962 at Libreville on signature of an agreement by all OCAM states except Rwanda and Congo (Kinshasa), now Zaire; entered into force January 1964; administers the common national legislation on industrial designs, patents, and trade marks; Pres. KONAN BEDIÉ (Ivory Coast); Dir.-Gen. DENIS EKANI.

Organisation africaine et malgache du café (OAMCAF): Paris, France. The eight coffee producing countries of OCAM, including Togo, Dahomey and Ivory Coast, have formed themselves into the African and Malagasy Coffee Organization, which is treated as one unit for purposes of operation of the International Coffee Agreement. These countries receive a block quota under that Agreement and distribute it among themselves through their own consultative machinery.

Organisation pour le développement du tourisme en Afrique—ODTA: 6 rue Mesnil, Paris 8e, France; Pres. M. MAMOUDOU ABDOU; Sec.-Gen. JULIEN KONAN.

Union africaine et malgache des postes et télécommunications (UAMPT): B.P. 44, Brazzaville, Congo; f. 1961; the UAMPT is a Committee of Ministers of Posts and Telecommunications set up to study problems of common interest and to promote the co-ordination of postal and telecommunications services in member countries. Gen. Dir. JOACHIM BALIMA; publs. *Revue UAMPT, Compte rendu des conférences et des réunions.*

Other Ministerial Meetings: Education Ministers of OCAM countries meet annually, and other ministerial meetings are held irregularly.

Other Co-operation. There are plans to establish two multinational insurance companies, a joint shipping company, and to provide for mutual consultation on Planning. The Scientific, Technical Research Committee aims to co-ordinate national research programmes.

A Permanent African Committee on Higher Education has been established, with an office in each state. The African Computer Institute in Libreville, opened in October 1971, is run by OCAM, and trains computer specialists. In August 1972 France made a donation of 85.7 million CFA francs to the Institute, which will enable it to increase the maximum student intake from 20 to 75.

During a conference of the UAM at Tananarive in September 1961, the following agreements were drawn up, and remain in force between the members of OCAM:

Convention générale relative à la représentation diplomatique: foresees common diplomatic missions and meetings of heads of missions accredited to France and the United Nations to harmonise their policies.

Convention générale de coopération en matière de justice: the courts of each country are open to nationals of any other member country without discrimination. Aims to simplify and unify existing national judicial systems.

Convention générale relative à la situation des personnes et aux conditions d'établissement: provides for free movement of persons between member states.

PUBLICATIONS

Nations Nouvelles, quarterly review.   *Bulletin Statistique.*   *Chronique Mensuelle.*

CHARTER

(Signed June 1966 at Tananarive)

Article 1. Name of Organization: OCAM open to all independent and sovereign African States which request admission and accept the provisions of the Charter. New members to be unanimously elected.

Article 2. OCAM established in the spirit of the OAU to reinforce the co-operation and solidarity between Afro-Malagasy States and to accelerate their economic, social, technical and cultural development.

Article 3. Organization to promote co-operation by harmonizing the actions of members in the economic, social, technical and cultural fields, by co-ordinating their development programmes, and by facilitating consultations between them on external policies, due regard being given to the sovereignty and fundamental choice of each member.

Article 4. The Institutions of the Organization are:

The Conference of Heads of State and of Government.
The Council of Ministers.
The General Administrative Secretariat.

Articles 5–9. *Conference of Heads of State and of Government:* includes provision for convening extraordinary meetings on particular subjects; each member to have one vote.

Articles 10–14. *Council of Ministers:* includes provision for extraordinary meetings; each member to have one vote.

Articles 15–19. *General Administrative Secretariat:* responsible for the administrative functioning of the Organization, and for the supervision of common enterprises, notably Air Afrique and the UAMPT.

Article 20. *Budget:* to be prepared by the General Administrative Secretariat and to be approved by the Conference of Heads of State and of Government, on the recommendation of the Council of Ministers; to be made up of contributions from member states, in a proportion based on their national budgets; no one member may contribute more than 20 per cent of the total budget.

Article 21. *Signature and Ratification.*

Article 22. *Entry into force.*

Article 23. *Registration with the United Nations.*

Article 24. *Interpretation.*

Articles 25–26. *Miscellaneous Provisions.*

Article 27. *Resignation from the Organization.*

Article 28. *Amendment and Revision.*

Organisation pour la Mise en Valeur du Fleuve Sénégal—OMVS

(Organization for the Development of the Senegal River)

Dakar, Senegal

Founded in March 1972 to replace the Organisation des États Riverains du Sénégal. Its scope of activities is similar to that of the former Inter-States Committee for the Senegal River Basin, its prime object being the development of the Senegal River Basin.

MEMBERS

Mali   Mauritania   Senegal

ORGANIZATION

CONFERENCE OF HEADS OF STATE

The Conference of Heads of State meets whenever necessary to decide policy. The Chair is taken in alphabetical rotation for a two year term by each state.

Chairman: MOKTAR OULD DADDAH (Mauritania).

GENERAL SECRETARIAT

The General Secretariat is responsible to the Council of Ministers, and carries out its decisions. The Secretary-General is in charge of the administrative functions of the organization.

Secretary-General: MOHAMED OULD AMAR (Mauritania).

COUNCIL OF MINISTERS

The Council of Ministers is composed of one Minister from each member state and meets at least once a year, with extra-ordinary sessions if necessary. The Council formulates general policy, and approves development programmes concerning member states.

President: ROBERT N'DAW (Mali).

AIMS AND ACTIVITIES

The OMVS aims to implement the agreement of 11 March 1972 on the Statute of the Senegal River, to promote and co-ordinate the studies on and works for the development of the resources of the Senegal River Basin on the national territories of its member states. and to carry out all technical and economic missions entrusted to it by member states.

The Organization is continuing the studies of the Senegal River Basin as undertaken by the Inter-States Committee and afterwards by the OERS. Of the five pre-investment studies three have been completed, while two projects are still in progress—one on agricultural research and one on hydroagricultural development. A Documentation Centre has also been established to collate information on development.

Organization of African Unity—OAU

P.O. Box 3243, Addis Ababa, Ethiopia

Founded 1963 at Addis Ababa to promote unity and international co-operation among African states and to eradicate all forms of colonialism in Africa. Members: 41 African states.

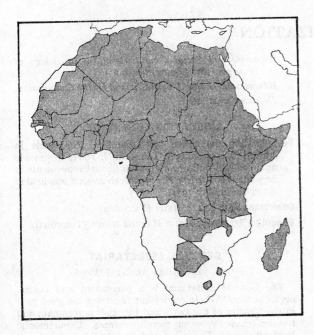

MEMBERS

Algeria	Malawi
Botswana	Mali
Burundi	Mauritania
Cameroon	Mauritius
Central African Republic	Morocco
Chad	Niger
Congo (Brazzaville)	Nigeria
Dahomey	Rwanda
Egypt	Senegal
Equatorial Guinea	Sierra Leone
Ethiopia	Somalia
Gabon	Sudan
The Gambia	Swaziland
Ghana	Tanzania
Guinea	Togo
Ivory Coast	Tunisia
Kenya	Uganda
Lesotho	Upper Volta
Liberia	Zaire
Libya	Zambia
Madagascar	

HISTORICAL INTRODUCTION

There were various attempts at establishing an inter-African organization before the OAU Charter was drawn up. In November 1958 Ghana and Guinea (later joined by Mali) drafted a Charter which was to form the basis of a Union of African States. In January 1961 a conference was held at Casablanca, attended by the heads of state of Ghana, Guinea, Mali, Morocco, and representatives of Libya and of the provisional government of the Algerian Republic (GPRA). Tunisia, Nigeria, Liberia and Togo declined the invitation to attend. An African Charter was adopted and it was decided to set up an African Military Command and an African Common Market.

Between October 1960 and March 1961 three conferences were held by French-speaking African countries, at Abidjan, Brazzaville and Yaoundé. None of the twelve countries which attended these meetings had been present at the Casablanca Conference. These conferences led eventually to the signing in September 1961, at Tananarive, of a charter establishing the *Union africaine et malgache*, which was succeeded in 1965 by the *Organisation commune africaine et malgache*.

In May 1961 a conference was held at Monrovia, attended by the heads of state or representatives of nineteen countries: Cameroon, Central African Republic, Chad, Congo Republic (ex-French) Dahomey, Ethiopia, Gabon, Ivory Coast, Liberia, Madagascar, Mauritania, Niger, Nigeria, Senegal, Sierra Leone, Somalia, Togo, Tunisia and Upper Volta. They met again (with the exception of Tunisia and with the addition of the ex-Belgian Congo Republic) in January 1962 at Lagos, and set up a permanent secretariat and a standing committee of Finance Ministers, and accepted a draft charter for an Organization of Inter-African and Malagasy States.

It was the Conference of Addis Ababa, held in 1963, which finally brought together African states despite the regional, political and linguistic differences which divided them. The Foreign Ministers of thirty African states attended the Preparatory Meeting held in May: Algeria, Burundi, Cameroon, Central African Republic, Congo (Brazzaville), Congo (Léopoldville), Dahomey, Ethiopia, Gabon, Ghana, Guinea, Ivory Coast, Liberia, Libya, Madagascar, Mali, Mauritania, Morocco, Niger, Nigeria, Rwanda, Senegal, Sierra Leone, Somalia, Sudan, Tanganyika, Tunisia, Uganda, United Arab Republic, Upper Volta.

The topics discussed by the meeting were: (1) creation of the Organization of African States; (2) co-operation among African states in the following fields: economic and social; education, culture and science; collective defence; (3) decolonization; (4) apartheid and racial discrimination;

(5) effects of economic groupings on the economic development of Africa; (6) disarmament; (7) creation of a Permanent Conciliation Commission; (8) Africa and the United Nations.

The Heads of State Conference which opened on May 23rd drew up the Charter of the Organization of African

Unity, which was then signed by the heads of thirty states on May 28th, 1963. The Charter was based essentially on the concept of a loose association of states favoured by the Monrovia Group, rather than the federal idea supported by the Casablanca Group, and in particular by Ghana.

ORGANIZATION

ASSEMBLY OF HEADS OF STATE

The Assembly of Heads of State and Government meets annually to co-ordinate policies of African States. Resolutions are passed by a two-thirds majority, procedural matters by a simple majority. Last meeting June 1972, Rabat (ninth).

Chairman (1972–73): King HASSAN of Morocco.

COUNCIL OF MINISTERS

Consists of Foreign and/or other Ministers and meets twice a year, with provision for extraordinary sessions. Each session elects its own Chairman. Prepares meetings of, and is responsible to, the Assembly of Heads of State. The eighteenth Session was held at Addis Ababa in February 1972.

ARBITRATION COMMISSION

Commission of Mediation, Conciliation and Arbitration: Addis Ababa; f. 1964; consists of 21 members elected by the Assembly of Heads of State for a five-year term; no state may have more than one member; has a Bureau consisting of a President and two Vice-Presidents, who shall not be eligible for re-election; to hear and settle disputes between member states by peaceful means; Pres. M. A. ODESANYA (Nigeria).

SPECIALIZED COMMISSIONS

The Assembly of Heads of State and Government at its third ordinary session at Addis Ababa in November 1966 ratified the recommendations for the regrouping of the Six Specialized Commissions into the following three:

Economic and Social Commission (also in charge of Transport and Communications).

Educational, Cultural, Scientific and Health Commission.

Defence Commission.

LIBERATION COMMITTEE

Co-ordinating Committee for Liberation Movements in Africa: Dar es Salaam, Tanzania; f. 1963; to provide financial and military aid to nationalist movements in dependent countries. The twentieth Session was held in Kampala in May 1972.

Chairman: SAIL ELINAWINGA (Tanzania).

Executive Secretary: Major HASHIM NBITA (Tanzania).

GENERAL SECRETARIAT

P.O.B. 3243, Addis Ababa, Ethiopia.

The General Secretariat is a permanent and central organ of the OAU. It carries out functions assigned to it in the Charter of the OAU and by other agreements and treaties made between member states. Departments: Political, Legal, Economic and Social, Educational and Cultural, Press and Information, Protocol, Administrative. The Secretary-General is elected for a four-year term by Assembly of Heads of State.

Secretary-General: NZO EKHAH NGHAKY (Cameroon).

Assistant Secretaries-General: H. B. MUSA (Nigeria), GRATIEN L. POGNON (Dahomey), MOHAMED SAHNOUN (Algeria), J. D. BULIRO (Kenya).

AIMS AND PURPOSES

To promote unity and solidarity among African States.

To co-ordinate and intensify their efforts to improve living standards in Africa.

To defend their sovereignty, territorial integrity, and independence.

To eradicate all forms of colonialism from Africa.

To promote international co-operation, having due regard to the Charter of the United Nations and the Universal Declaration of Human Rights.

BUDGET

Member states contribute in accordance with their United Nations' assessment. No member state shall be assessed for an amount exceeding 20 per cent of the yearly regular budget of the Organization.

PRINCIPAL EVENTS

1963

May Conference of Independent African States at Addis Ababa agreed to set up OAU. Co-ordinating Committee for Liberation Movements set up in Addis Ababa.

Aug. First meeting of Council of Ministers, Dakar. Recognition of the Angolan government-in-exile of Holden Roberto.

Nov. First extraordinary meeting of Council of Ministers, Addis Ababa, on the Algerian-Moroccan Border Dispute. *Ad hoc* Commission set up, to arbitrate in the dispute, consisting of Ethiopia, Ivory Coast, Mali, Nigeria, Senegal, Sudan and Tanganyika.

Dec. Meeting of the OAU *ad hoc* Commission in Abidjan. Idrissa Diarra (Mali) appointed President; Bamako designated headquarters of the Commission.

1964

Feb. Second extraordinary meeting of Council of Ministers, Dar es Salaam, to consider army mutinies in East Africa. Recommends replacement of British troops by detachments from other African states. Discussion of Ethiopian-Somalian border dispute.

Second regular meeting of Council of Ministers, Lagos. Resolution to refuse aircraft and ships going to and from South Africa overflight or transit facilities. Appeal to apply strict economic military, political and diplomatic sanctions against South Africa. The Council called on the British Government to prevent the threat of unilateral independence by the minority regime in Southern Rhodesia.

July First meeting of Assembly of Heads of State, Cairo. Permanent Secretariat and Headquarters established at Addis Ababa; Diallo Telli to be Secretary-General. Decision to incorporate the Commission for Technical Co-operation in Africa (CCTA) as an organ of OAU from January 1965.

Sept. Third extraordinary meeting of Council of Ministers, Addis Ababa, to discuss the Congolese situation. *Ad hoc* Commission set up, consisting of Cameroon, Ethiopia, Ghana, Guinea, Nigeria, Somalia, Tunisia, U.A.R. and Upper Volta, with Jomo Kenyatta as effective Chairman, to support the Congolese government in its policy of national reconciliation and seek to bring about normal relations between the Congolese government and its neighbours.

1965

Jan. CCTA incorporated as the Scientific, Technical and Research Commission of OAU.

Feb. Meeting of Council of Ministers at Nairobi proposes establishment of an African Defence Organization.

June Extraordinary session of Council of Ministers, Lagos. Five-member committee set up to examine allegations of subversion in Ghana. Five-member committee appointed to assist nationalist movements in Rhodesia.

Oct. Second Assembly of Heads of State, Accra. Chad, Dahomey, Gabon, Ivory Coast, Madagascar, Niger, Togo and Upper Volta were absent. Establishment of an African Defence Organization recommended. Committee of five on Rhodesia was set up.

Nov. First meeting of Committee of Five, Dar es Salaam.

Dec. Sixth extraordinary session of Council of Ministers convened at Addis Ababa to discuss Rhodesia's declaration of independence. Resolutions adopted to combat the illegal government in Rhodesia.

1966

Jan. Meeting of Committee of Five on Rhodesia in Accra.

Feb. Sixth Ordinary Session of Council of Ministers was held in Addis Ababa. Committee of solidarity with Zambia established.

Sept. Meeting of *ad hoc* Commission on Refugees in Addis Ababa. It was reported that there are about 480,000 African refugees from Angola, Congo (Democratic Republic), Mozambique, Portuguese Guinea, Rwanda and Sudan.

Nov. Seventh Ordinary Session of Council of Ministers met in Addis Ababa.

Meeting of Heads of State in Addis Ababa. Resolutions passed on Rhodesia and the border dispute between Ethiopia and Somalia.

1967

Jan. Meeting of the *ad hoc* Commission on the Algerian-Moroccan border dispute in Tangiers.

Meeting of the Consultative Committee on Budgetary and Financial matters.

Feb.–March Eighth Ordinary Session of the Council of Ministers held in Addis Ababa.

April Meeting of the Scientific Council for Africa in Addis Ababa.

Sept. Ninth Ordinary Session of the Council of Ministers met in Kinshasa.

Fourth meeting of the Assembly of Heads of State and Governments met in Kinshasa. Seventeen Heads of State attended. Appointment of Mission of Six Heads of State to find solution for Nigerian conflict. Agreement reached on border dispute between Somalia and Kenya.

Oct. Conference in Addis Ababa on the problems of the 750,000 refugees in Africa, jointly organized by OAU, Economic Commission for Africa, UN High Commissioner for Refugees and the Dag Hammarskjold Foundation. Recommendation made that each African country should absorb a number of refugees. A bureau for the education and placement of refugees is to be established within the framework of the OAU Secretariat.

1968

Feb.   Tenth ordinary session of the Council of Ministers held in Addis Ababa.

July   Meeting of Consultative Committee on Nigeria in Niamey. Discussions attended by both Nigerian and Biafran leaders.

Sept.   Fifth Meeting of Heads of State in Algiers. Twenty-two Heads of State attended. Resolution passed supporting Nigerian Federal Government's efforts to reunify the country. Resolution passed calling for withdrawal of foreign troops from Arab territory. Diallo Telli re-elected Secretary-General for a further four-year term.

Dec.   Conference of African nationalist organizations called by the OAU Liberation Committee was held at Morogoro, Tanzania. Recommendation made that in future, all guerrilla training should be carried out in Africa, and that military and technical instructors from countries outside Africa should not be allowed to lecture on politics or ideology. Seven leading nationalist organizations were represented.

1969

Feb.   14th Session of the OAU Liberation Committee. Stephen Mhando (Tanzania) elected Chairman.
Meeting of OAU Ministerial Council called on both sides in the Nigerian war to implement an immediate cease-fire and then negotiate.

March   Conference of African Ministers of Labour in Algiers. Ministers of 35 countries resolved to establish a single central trade union. Resolution passed calling for reform of the structure and programmes of the International Labour Organisation and for greater participation of African countries in its administration.

April   Meeting of OAU Consultative Committee on Nigeria in Monrovia, Liberia.

June   Agreement signed with UN High Commissioner for Refugees providing for close co-operation and regular consultations concerning refugee problems in Africa and measures to solve them.

July   OAU Conference on the peaceful use of atomic energy, Kinshasa.
Pan-African Cultural Festival held in Algiers.

Aug.–
Sept.   Thirteenth Ordinary Session of Council of Ministers held in Addis Ababa.

Sept.   Sixth Meeting of Heads of State held in Addis Ababa. Resolution passed appealing for a cease-fire and peace talks to end the Nigerian civil war, on the basis of a united Nigeria. Gabon, Ivory Coast, Sierra Leone, Tanzania and Zambia abstained.

Dec.   Ninth session of the Advisory Committee on Budgetary and Financial Matters held in Addis Ababa.

1970

Feb.   16th Session of the OAU Liberation Committee at Moshi, Tanzania. Efforts of the freedom fighters in the previous six months were commended and the setting up of a special fund to help liberation movements in Portuguese territories was recommended.

Feb.–
March   14th Session of Ministerial Council passed a resolution on decolonization which included an appeal to all nations not to collaborate on the Cabora Bassa dam project. It also condemned military and other co-operation by NATO countries with "the racist régimes of South Africa, Portugal and Rhodesia".

Aug.   Meeting of Council of Ministers. Resolution tabled by Kenya condemning western arms sales to South Africa. Decision made to reactivate the Defence Commission, with a new mandate, to concentrate on the "growing threat from southern Africa".

Sept.   Seventh Meeting of Heads of State, attended by 14 Heads of State and three Prime Ministers; other states sent delegations. Resolution passed demanding the withdrawal of Israeli forces from territories occupied in the June 1967 war. Resolution passed condemning arms sales to southern Africa particularly from Britain, France and Federal Germany. Eight countries did not support the resolution: Malawi, Ivory Coast, Dahomey, Rwanda, Niger, Gabon, Lesotho, Madagascar. The meeting decided to send a mission of Foreign Ministers to countries selling or intending to sell arms to South Africa, and also debated sanctions against countries with economic and trade relations with South Africa and Portugal. It also debated the request from liberation movements for increased aid.

Dec.   Extraordinary Session of Ministerial Council met in Lagos to discuss the events in Guinea in November. The Guinean Minister declared his country to be in favour of the stationing of an African military force in Guinea for its defence.

1971

Feb.   18th Session of the OAU Liberation Committee at Moshi, Tanzania. Efforts were made to reconcile differences between rival liberation movements in Rhodesia and in South Africa.

June   16th Session (postponed from March because of difficulties on Ugandan representation) and 17th Session of the Ministerial Council. Emperor Haile Selassie warned against a dialogue between black and white Africa.
Eighth meeting of Heads of State held in Addis Ababa, transferred from Kampala, Uganda. Resolution passed demanding the withdrawal of Israeli forces from territories occupied in the June 1967 war. Middle East Peace Committee, composed of 10 heads of state, set up. Resolution that there is no basis for meaningful dialogue with the "minority racist régime of South Africa". A committee was set up to mediate in a dispute between Guinea and Senegal.

Aug.   Middle East Peace Committee meeting in Kinshasa.

Nov.   Middle East Peace Mission visits Egypt and Israel.

1972

Feb. 18th Session of the OAU Council of Ministers, Addis Ababa. A resolution was adopted calling on the UN Security Council to strengthen sanctions against Rhodesia. It was decided to increase the special fund of the African Liberation Committee of the OAU by a substantial margin.

Feb.-March All Africa Trade Fair, Nairobi. The next Trade Fair is scheduled for 1976.

May 20th Session of the OAU Liberation Committee, Kampala. The Committee decided to assist African Nationalist guerrillas fighting in Rhodesia, and to increase aid to liberation movements in the Portuguese territories in Africa.

June 19th Session of OAU Council of Ministers, Rabat. Attended by all OAU countries except Malawi. Resolutions adopted included: a condemnation of all countries supplying arms to South Africa, and an appeal to EEC countries to abstain from trade relations with South Africa, owing to the latter's illegal occupation of Namibia (South West Africa); a call on Britain to convene a national constitutional conference to bring independence to Rhodesia under a democratic system based on majority rule; a decision to increase the number of members of the Liberation Committee from 11 to 15 (Congo, Libya, Mauritania, Morocco being the new members).

Ninth Assembly of OAU Heads of State and Government, Rabat. A record number of 40 Heads of State and Government attended, Malawi being the only absentee. King Hassan of Morocco was unanimously elected President of the OAU for the coming year. A resolution calling on Israel to withdraw from occupied Arab territory to the lines existing before June 5th, 1967 was unanimously adopted. The Assembly decided to increase by 50% the OAU Liberation Committee's annual budget.

The resolution on Rhodesia passed by the Council of Ministers (see above) was endorsed by the Assembly. Other resolutions included an appeal to EEC States to abstain from making trade agreements with Portugal, and a plea to OAU member countries to break off diplomatic relations with Portugal. Resolutions were also passed condemning countries who were continuing to sell arms to South Africa.

SUMMARY OF CHARTER

Article I. Establishment of the Organization of African Unity. The Organization to include continental African states, Madagascar, and other islands surrounding Africa.

Article II. Aims and purposes (see above). Fields of co-operation.

Article III. Member states adhere to the principles of sovereign equality, non-interference in internal affairs of member states, respect for territorial integrity, peaceful settlement of disputes, condemnation of political subversion, dedication to the emancipation of dependent African territories, and international non-alignment.

Article IV. Each independent sovereign African state shall be entitled to become a member of the Organization.

Article V. All member states shall have equal rights and duties.

Article VI. All member states shall observe scrupulously the principles laid down in Article III.

Article VII. Establishment of the Assembly of Heads of State and Government, the Council of Ministers, the General Secretariat, and the Commission of Mediation, Conciliation and Arbitration.

Articles VIII-XI. The Assembly of Heads of State and Government co-ordinates policies and reviews the structure of the Organization.

Articles XII-XV. The Council of Ministers shall prepare conferences of the Assembly, and co-ordinate inter-African co-operation. All resolutions shall be by simple majority.

Articles XVI-XVIII. The General Secretariat. The Administrative Secretary-General and his staff shall not seek or receive instructions from any government or other authority external to the Organization. They are international officials responsible only to the Organization.

Article XIX. Commission of Mediation, Conciliation and Arbitration. A separate protocol concerning the composition and nature of this Commission shall be regarded as an integral part of the Charter.

Articles XX-XXII. Specialized Commissions shall be established, composed of Ministers or other officials designated by Member Governments. Their regulations shall be laid down by the Council of Ministers.

Article XXIII. The Budget shall be prepared by the Secretary-General and approved by the Council of Ministers. Contributions shall be in accordance with the scale of assessment of the United Nations. No Member shall pay more than twenty per cent of the total yearly amount.

Article XXIV. Texts of the Charter in African Languages, English and French shall be equally authentic. Instruments of ratification shall be deposited with the Government of Ethiopia.

Article XXV. The Charter shall come into force on receipt by the Government of Ethiopia of the instruments of ratification of two thirds of the signatory states.

Article XXVI. The Charter shall be registered with the Secretariat of the United Nations.

Article XXVII. Questions of interpretation shall be settled by a two-thirds majority vote in the Assembly of Heads of State and Government.

Article XXVIII. Admission of new independent African states to the Organization shall be decided by a simple majority of the Member States.

Articles XXIX-XXXIII. The working languages of the Organization shall be African languages, English and French. The Secretary-General may accept gifts and bequests to the Organization, subject to the approval of the Council of Ministers. The Council of Ministers shall establish privileges and immunities to be accorded to the personnel of the Secretariat in the territories of Member States. A State wishing to withdraw from the Organization must give a year's written notice to the Secretariat. The Charter may only be amended after consideration by all Member States and by a two-thirds majority vote of the Assembly of Heads of State and Government. Such amendments will come into force one year after submission.

SCIENTIFIC, TECHNICAL AND RESEARCH COMMISSION—STRC

Nigerian Ports Authority Building, P.M.B. 2359, Marina, Lagos, Nigeria.

Formerly the Commission for Technical Co-operation in Africa (CCTA, set up in 1954), the STRC was established as one of the Commissions of the OAU in January 1965.

ORGANIZATION

GENERAL SECRETARIAT
Executive Secretary: A. O. ODELOLA.

BUREAUX

Inter-African Bureau for Soils (Bureau interafricain des sols)—BIS: B.P. 1352, Bangui, Central African Republic.

Inter-African Bureau for Animal Resources (Bureau interafricain pour resources animaux): P.O.B. 30786, Nairobi, Kenya.

Inter-African Phytosanitary Commission (Commission phytosanitaire interafricaine)—IAPSC: B.P. 4170 Niongkak, rue de l'Hypodrome, Yaoundé, Cameroon.

COMMITTEES AND CORRESPONDENTS

Inter-African Scientific Correspondent for Oceanography and Fisheries.

Inter-African Scientific Correspondent for the Conservation of Nature.

Inter-African Committee on Food Science and Food Technology.

Inter-African Committee on Mechanization of Agriculture

Inter-African Committee on Geology and Mineralogy.

Inter-African Committee on Biological Sciences.

Inter-African Committee on African Medicinal Plants.

International Council on Trypanosomiasis Research.

INTER-AFRICAN RESEARCH FUND

The object of the Fund, to which governments and official organizations may subscribe, is to promote joint scientific research and technical projects, in the following categories:

Broad surveys, including information and liaison work.

Research on problems by small highly specialized staffs operating over wide areas.

Research on problems which affect many countries but which should be investigated initially in one limited area.

JOINT PROJECTS

1. Climatological Atlas for Africa, University of the Witwatersrand, Johannesburg; published 1964.

2. Science and Development of Africa, c/o STRC Secretariat. Author Dr. E. B. WORTHINGTON.

3. Study of Migrations in West Africa. Director Dr. J. ROUCH, C.N.R.S.

4. Inventory of Economic Research, St. Anne's College, Oxford, Editor Miss P. ADY; published 1961.

5. Research into Absenteeism and Labour Turnover. Undertaken by the Governments of the six founder States of CCTA; published 1963.

6. Comparative Study on National Accounting Systems. Co-ordinator: MILTON GILBERT; published 1961.

7. Base Maps for Cartographical Work produced under the Auspices of the Commission. Professor S. P. JACKSON.

8. Mapping of Vector Diseases. Co-ordinator: Prof. VAN DEN BERGE.

9. Methodology of Family Budget Surveys. CCTA's Statistics Committee; published 1965.

10. Occupational Classification in Africa. In collaboration with ILO.

11. Pedological Map of Africa. Inter-African Pedological Service; published 1965.

12. Study of Methods of Promoting Private Investment.

13. Analyses of Sea Water. Inter-African Scientific Correspondent for Oceanography and Sea Fisheries.

14. Handbook on Harmful Aquatic Plants; publ. 1962.

15. Eradication of Rinderpest in Africa.

16. Bovine Pleuropneumonia Vaccine Research.

17. Tsetse Campaign in South-East Africa.

18. Psychometric Tests for use at end of Primary Education.

19. Gulf of Guinea Campaign (1968).

20. Map of the dangers of erosion in Africa; published 1962.

21. Regional Training Centre for French-speaking Customs Officers.

22. Regional Training Centre for English-speaking staff of National Parks.

23. Regional Training Centre for French-speaking Hydrological Assistants.

24. Regional Training Centre for French-speaking Hydrogeological Assistants.

25. International West African Atlas.

26. Improvement of major Cereal Crops.

PUBLICATIONS

Publications Bureau: Maison de l'Afrique, P.O.B. 878 Niamey, Niger.

African Soils: published by the Inter-African Bureau for Soils and Rural Economy—B.I.S.; (bi-lingual— English and French—3 issues).

Bulletin of Epizootic Diseases of Africa: published by the Inter-African Bureau for Animal Health—I.B.A.H. (English and French—4 issues).

Numerous publications on joint projects and scientific research on Africa, obtainable from the Lagos office.

L'Union Douanière et Économique de l'Afrique Centrale—UDEAC

(Central African Customs and Economic Union)

Bangui, Central African Republic

Came into operation in January 1966 and replaces the former *Union douanière équatoriale* (f. 1959).

MEMBERS*

Cameroon   Central African Republic   Congo (Brazzaville)   Gabon

* Central African Republic and Chad withdrew from the Union in April 1968 to form the Union des états de l'Afrique centrale (UEAC) together with Congo (Kinshasa) (now Zaire). Central African Republic subsequently rejoined UDEAC in December 1968.

ORGANIZATION

COUNCIL OF HEADS OF STATES

Meets at least once a year to determine general policy; the supreme organ of the Union. The presidency of the Council is by annual alphabetical rotation.

President (1972): Commandant MARIEN NGOUABI (Congo).

CONSULTATIVE COMMITTEE

Permanent deliberative body of the Union; comprises the Finance Ministers and Ministers concerned with economic development from each of the participating countries, and meets at least once a year.

GENERAL SECRETARIAT

In charge of the executive functions of the Union; composed of a Customs, Statistics and Fiscal division and a division of Development and Industrialization; associated with the Inter-State Accounts Agency; in January 1966 the Secretariat of the Conférence des chefs d'état de l'Afrique équatoriale was merged with that of UDEAC but became a separate institution again in December 1967. Sec.-Gen. PIERRE TCHANQUE (Cameroon).

FUNCTIONS

The main provisions of the Union, embodied in the Treaty of Brazzaville, aim to rationalize and harmonize the tariff and tax systems of the four member states, and include:

Customs Union: The group of four states constitutes a free trade area, in which the circulation of persons, merchandise, services and capital is free. A common external tariff, additional to previous duties and fiscal charges, is levied on all imports entering the region, except on goods from members of the European Economic Community and of the former Union africaine et malgache. A common investment code has been established.

Solidarity Fund: Compensates the land-locked Central African Republic for the loss of customs revenue on imports cleared in coastal member states but then re-exported inland. A total of 1,900 million frs. CFA have been donated to this fund.

Repartition of Industrial Projects and Harmonization of Development Plans and Transport Policies: The Union stimulates the rational development and diversification of the economies of member states, in order to multiply inter-state exchanges and to improve the standard of living of the population. The Executive Council decides on measures to harmonize development plans and transport policies. An oil refinery at Port Gentil, Gabon, is being constructed as a joint enterprise.

Uniform Tax System: The many internal revenue-raising taxes on industrial production have now been replaced by a single tax regime, fixed by the Executive Committee. The Council of Heads of State adopted an act regulating this matter in 1965.

Free Circulation of Persons and the Right of Establishment: Regulated by the convention signed in 1961 by UAM (*see* Chapter on *OCAM*).

La Banque centrale des états de l'Afrique équatoriale et du Cameroun: 29 rue de Colisée, Paris 8e, France; f. 1955; sole issuing bank for the four members of UDEAC; Pres. GEORGES GAUTIER.

PUBLICATIONS

Journal Officiel.
Bulletin d'Information de l'UDEAC (three a year).

Union des États de l'Afrique Centrale—UEAC

(Union of Central African States)

Kinshasa, Zaire

Founded at Fort-Lamy, Chad, on April 2nd, 1968.

MEMBERS*

Chad   Zaire

* The Central African Republic was one of the original members of UEAC but withdrew at the end of 1968.

ORGANIZATION

CONFERENCE OF HEADS OF STATE

This, the supreme organ of the Union meets at least once a year to fix the Union's budget and to orientate and harmonize policies in the fields of economy, trade, customs, transport, telecommunications, education, culture, health, science, technology, defence and security.

COUNCIL OF MINISTERS

Meets at least twice a year.

OFFICERS OF THE UNION

Executive Secretary-General: M. TRAOTOBAYE.
Chairman: General MOBUTU (Zaire).
Military Administrator: Colonel MOLANGIA (Zaire).

FUNCTIONS

Under its charter the Union has the following aims: the adoption of common tariffs for imports and the free movement of capital and persons between member states; cultural, scientific and technological co-operation between member states; solidarity and military assistance in the event of foreign aggression.

Membership of the Union is open to every independent African state.

Other Regional Organizations

These organizations are arranged under the following sub-headings:

Agriculture, Forestry and Fisheries
Aid and Development
Arts
Education
Government, Politics and Economics
Industrial and Professional Relations
Law
Medicine and Public Health

Press, Radio and Telecommunications
Religion
Science
Social Sciences and Humanistic Studies
Tourism
Trade and Industry
Transport

AGRICULTURE, FORESTRY AND FISHERIES

Food and Agricultural Organization (FAO): Viale delle Terme di Caracalla, 00100 Rome, Italy; f. 1945 as a specialized agency of the UN to help nations raise their standards of living by improving the efficiency of farming, forestry and fisheries (*see* chapter *United Nations in Africa South of the Sahara*, p.102).

REGIONAL COUNCILS AND COMMISSIONS

African Commission on Agricultural Statistics: c/o FAO Regional Office for Africa, P.O.B. 1628, Accra, Ghana; f. 1961 to advise member countries on the development and standardization of agricultural statistics. Mems.: 20 states.

African Forestry Commission: c/o FAO Regional Office for Africa, P.O.B. 1628, Accra, Ghana; f. 1959 to advise on the formulation of forest policy and to review and co-ordinate its implementation on a regional level; to exchange information and make recommendations. Mems.: 36 regional and 4 non-regional states. Sec. R. GUTZWILLER.

FAO/WHO Codex Alimentarius Commission: f. 1961 to make proposals for the co-ordination of all international food standards work and to publish a code of international food standards. Mems.: 74 states. Chair. J. A. V. DAVIES.

Joint FAO/WHO/OAU—(STRC) Regional Food and Nutrition Commission for Africa: c/o FAO Regional Office for Africa, P.O.B. 1628, Accra, Ghana; f. 1962 to provide liaison in matters pertaining to food and nutrition, and to review food and nutrition problems in Africa. Publs. *Bulletin, Special papers.*

OTHER ORGANIZATIONS

African Agricultural Credit Commission: Rabat, Morocco; f. 1966 to study agricultural finance problems. Mems.: Algeria, Ivory Coast, Libya, Morocco, Senegal, Tunisia, Upper Volta, Zaire.

Desert Locust Control Organization for Eastern Africa: P.O.B. 231, Asmara, Ethiopia; f. 1962 to promote most effective control of desert locust in the region by co-ordinating national efforts; maintains vehicles, insecticides, air surveys and conducts operational research and training programmes. Mems.: Ethiopia, France, Kenya, Somali Republic, Sudan, Tanzania and Uganda. Publs. *Desert Locust Situation Reports* (monthly, quarterly), *Annual Report, Technical Reports.*

Acting Dir. ADEFRIS BELLEHU (Ethiopia); Senior Scientist H. J. SAYER (U.K.).

East African Agricultural Economics Society: Department of Rural Economy and Extension, Makerere University, P.O.B. 7062 Kampala, Uganda; f. 1967 to promote the study and teaching of economics, statistics and related disciplines relevant to agriculture and rural development in Eastern Africa; holds meetings and publishes papers. Mems.: 125.

Pres. Dr. ISAIAH MUTUKU; Sec. Dr. PHILIP MBITHI. Publ. *East African Journal of Rural Development* (twice yearly).

Inter-African Bureau for Animal Resources (IBAR): P.O.B. 30786, Nairobi, Kenya; f. 1951 to ensure co-operation in matters of health, production and marketing of animals in all member states of the OAU.

Dir. P. G. ATANG, M.R.C.V.S. Publ. *Bulletin of Epizootic Diseases of Africa* (quarterly), *Annual Report.*

International African Migratory Locust Organization: Kara-Macina, Mali and B.P. 136, Bamako, Mali; f. 1955 to destroy the African migratory locust in its breeding areas and to conduct research on locust swarms. Mems.: governments of 21 countries.

Pres. (Admin. Council) Prof. T. AJIBOLA TAYLOR (Nigeria); Pres. (Exec.) P. EPOH ADYANG (Cameroon); Dir. G. DIAGNE. Publs. *Locusta, Bulletin mensuel d'information*, annual reports.

International Red Locust Control Organization for Central and Southern Africa: P.O.B. 37, Mbala, Zambia; f. 1971 as successor to *International Red Locust Control Service* to control Red Locust populations in recognized outbreak areas. Mems.: 11 countries.

Chair. D. H. LUZONGO (Zambia); Dir. K. W. KÜHNE (U.K.). Publs. *Annual Report*, and scientific reports.

West African Rice Development Association: Monrovia, Liberia; f. 1969 by FAO, UNDP and ECA to help West Africa become self-sufficient in rice; promotes co-operation in rice research, production and marketing; gives technical assistance and training.

AID AND DEVELOPMENT

Afro-Asian Rural Reconstruction Organization (AARRO): C/117-118, Defence Colony, New Delhi-3, India; f. 1962 to launch concrete and wherever possible co-ordinated action to reconstruct the economy of the rural peoples of Afro-Asian countries and to revitalize their social and cultural life. Mems.: governments of 11 African and 13 Asian countries.

Pres. Hon. A. A. MANUFIE (GHANA); Sec.-Gen. H. E. KRISHAN CHAND (India); Dir. and Co-ord. Programmes M. R. KAUSHAL. Publ. *Rural Reconstruction* (quarterly).

Joint Africa Board: 25 Victoria St., London, SW1H 0EX, England; f. 1923 to promote the agricultural, commercial and industrial development of the East

141

and Central African Territories; to educate public opinion; to promote good relations.

Chair. PATRICK WALL, M.P.; Sec. S. STANLEY-SMITH; Publs. *Annual Report, Report of Annual Meeting*, memoranda.

Lake Chad Basin Commission: Fort-Lamy, Chad; established May 1964. Mems.: Cameroon, Chad, Niger, Nigeria; composed of an Executive Secretary and two Commissioners from each Member State. Responsible for the co-ordination of the development of the Chad Basin, particularly the exploitation of the subterranean and surface water resources in relation to agricultural development, animal husbandry and fisheries. The UN Development Fund is contributing to a water resources survey costing $3 million, the USAID $275,000 for road transport and telecommunications feasibility studies, the French FAC $750,000 for a tsetse-fly eradication project. All three donors are also jointly financing a $2 million animal husbandry project.

Pres. Dr. BUKAR SHAYIB (Nigeria); Exec. Sec. MUHAMMADU A. CARPENTER (Nigeria).

Niger River Commission: Niamey, Niger; f. 1963 by the Act of Niamey, covering navigation and general economic development; budget of 20 million CFA francs; meets annually; first project to survey the navigability of the Niger River, with the Netherlands assistance. Mems.: Cameroon, Dahomey, Guinea, Ivory Coast, Mali, Niger, Upper Volta.

Admin. Sec. DÉSIRÉ VIEYRA.

West Africa Committee, The: 23 Lawrence Lane, London, E.C.2, England; f. 1956 to aid the economic development of Nigeria, Ghana, Ivory Coast, Sierra Leone and The Gambia. Mems.: 169.

Adviser Sir EVELYN HONE, G.C.M.G., C.V.O., O.B.E.; Sec. W. G. SYER, C.V.O., C.B.E.

ARTS

Afro-Asian Writers' Permanent Bureau: 104 Kasr El-Aini St., Cairo, Egypt; f. 1958 by Afro-Asians Peoples' Solidarity Organization; conferences of Asian and African writers have been held at Tashkent (1958), Cairo (1962), Beirut (1967), New Delhi (1970). Mems.: 78 writers' organizations.

Sec.-Gen. YOUSSEF EL-SEBAI (Egypt). Publ. *Lotus Magazine of Afro-Asian Writings* (quarterly in English French and Arabic).

Society of African Culture (*Société africaine de culture*): 42 rue Descartes, Paris 5e, France; f. 1956 to create unity and friendship among scholars in Africa for the encouragement of their own cultures and the development of a universal culture. Mems.: from 22 countries.

Pres. Dr. ERIC WILLIAMS; Sec.-Gen. ALIOUNE DIOP. Publ. *Présence Africaine* (quarterly).

EDUCATION

African and Malagasy Council on Higher Education (*Conseil africain et malgache de l'enseignement supérieure—CAMES*): c/o Ministère de l'éducation nationale, Ouagadougou, Upper Volta; f. 1968 to ensure co-ordination between member states in the fields of higher education and of research. Mems.: governments of French-speaking African countries and Malagasy.

Sec.-Gen. Prof. JOSEPH KI ZERBO (Upper Volta).

Agence de coopération culturelle et technique (*Agency for Cultural and Technical Co-operation*): 170 rue de Grenelle, 75007 Paris, France; f. 1970 in Niamey (Niger); aims to develop new forms of multilateral co-operation in the fields of education, culture, science and technology between partly or wholly French-speaking countries. Mems.: 23 member states (16 in Africa), one participating government and one associated state.

Sec.-Gen. JEAN-MARC LEGER (Canada). Publ. *Bulletin de Liaison* (quarterly).

Association of African Universities (*Association des universités africaines*): P.O.B. 5744, Accra North, Ghana; f. 1967 to encourage exchanges and co-operation between African university institutions and to collect and disseminate information on research and higher education in Africa. Mems.: 42 universities.

Pres. Mgr. T. TSHIBANGU (Zaire); Vice-Pres. Dr. HANDI EL NASHAR (Egypt).

Association universitaire pour le développement de l'enseignement et de la culture en Afrique et à Madagascar (**AUDECAM**) (*University Association for the Development of Education and Culture in Africa and Madagascar*): 54 ave. Victor Hugo, Paris 16e, France; provides technical assistance for education and educational research in developing countries with equipment, including audio-visual aids, documentation and information; organizes research studies.

Pres. JEAN THOMAS; Vice-Pres. PIERRE AUBA; Sec.-Gen. BERNARD CLERGERIE.

Institut fondamental d'Afrique noire (**IFAN**): B.P. 206, Dakar, Senegal; f. 1936, reconstituted 1959; scientific and humanistic studies of Black Africa; library of 51,710 vols.

Dir. Prof. AMAR SAMB. Publs. *Bulletin de l'IFAN*, *Série A—Sciences Naturelle* (4 a year), *Série B—Sciences Humaines* (4 a year), *Notes Africaines* (4 a year), *Mémoirs, Initiations et Etudes Africaines, Catalogues et Documents Instructions Sommaires.*

International Association for the Development of Libraries in Africa: B.P. 375, Dakar, Senegal; f. 1957 to promote the establishment in Africa of national libraries, public and school libraries and research libraries for universities, institutes and laboratories, and planning and organization of archives, documentation centres and museums.

Sec. EMMANUEL K. W. DADZIE (Togo).

West African Examinations Council: Headquarters Office, P.O.B. 125, Accra, Ghana; other offices in Lagos, Nigeria; Freetown, Sierra Leone; Bathurst, The Gambia; London, England; conducts School, Higher School Certificate and G.C.E. examinations in Ghana, The Gambia, Nigeria and Sierra Leone, at the request of the various Ministries of Education and also examinations for entry into the Public Services. Conducts examinations for teacher training colleges and other examinations for selection for secondary schools or for elementary school leavers at the request of the various Ministries of Education; holds examinations on behalf of the Universities of London and Cambridge, U.K. examining authorities and Educational Testing Service, Princeton, U.S.A.

Liberia is an associated member of the Council.

Registrar V. CHUKWUEMEKA IKE; Chair. (acting) Dr. S. T. MATTURI, C.M.G., PH.D.

GOVERNMENT, POLITICS, ECONOMICS

Africa Bureau, The: 48 Grafton Way, London, WIP 5LB; f. 1952. Aims: to inform about Africa; to help Africans in opposing unfair discrimination and to foster co-operation between races; to further economic, social and political development in Africa; to promote projects of education, development and racial co-operation; to administer funds for the foregoing.

Chair. Sir BERNARD DE BUNSEN; Sec. Miss E. M. BOND. Publ. *X-Ray on Southern African Affairs* (monthly).

African Centre for Administrative Training and Research for Development (*Centre africain de formation et de recherches administratives pour le développement—CAFRAD*), 19 rue Victor Hugo, B.P. 310, Tangier, Morocco; f. 1964 by agreement between Morocco and UNESCO; research into administrative problems in Africa, documentation of results, provision of a consultative service for governments and organizations; holds frequent seminars. Mems.: Algeria, Cameroon, Central African Republic, Egypt, Ghana, Ivory Coast, Kenya, Liberia, Libya, Mauritania, Morocco, Nigeria, Senegal, Somalia, Sudan, Togo, Tunisia, Zambia; aided by UNESCO; library of 7,000 vols. and 160 periodicals.

Pres. LOUAFI SKALLI; Dir. Gen. J. E. KARIUKI. Publs. *Cahiers Africains d'Administration Publique/African Administrative Studies* (twice a year), *CAFRAD News* (quarterly), *African Administrative Abstracts*.

Afro-Asian Organization for Economic Co-operation: AFRASEC Special P.O. Bag, Chamber of Commerce Building, Midan Al-Falaki, Cairo, Egypt; f. 1958 to speed up industrialization and implement exchanges in commercial, financial and technical fields. Mems.: Central Chambers of Commerce in 45 countries.

Pres. ZAKAREYA TEWFIK; Sec.-Gen. Dr. AMIN A. AWADALLA. Publ. *Afro-Asian Economic Review.*

Afro-Asian Peoples' Solidarity Organization (AAPSO): 89 Abdel Aziz Al Saoud Street, Manial, Cairo; f. 1957 as the Organization for Afro-Asian Peoples' Solidarity; acts as a permanent liaison body between the peoples of Africa and Asia and aims to ensure their economic, social and cultural development. Board of Secretaries is composed of 17 members from Algeria, Angola (liberation movements), China, Egypt, Guinea, India, Iraq, Japan, Morocco, Palestine, Somalia, South Africa (liberation movements), Provisional Revolutionary Government of the Republic of South Viet-Nam, Sudan, U.S.S.R., Tanzania, Zambia. Mems.: national committees and affiliated Organizations in 78 countries.

Sec.-Gen. YOUSSEF EL SEBAI (Egypt); Publs. *Afro-Asian Bulletin* (every 2 months), *Afro-Asian Women Bulletin* (irregular), etc.

Association of African Central Banks: Accra, Ghana; established in August 1968 under the auspices of ECA. Aims: to promote contacts in the monetary, banking and financial sphere in order to increase co-operation and trade among member states; to strengthen monetary and financial stability on the African continent. Articles of Association have been signed by Burundi, Ethiopia, Ghana, Kenya, Malawi, Mauritius, Sierra Leone, Somalia, Sudan, Tanzania and Zaire.

Chair. MENASSE LEMNA (Ethiopia).

Common Organization for Economic Co-operation in Central Africa (OCCEAC): Kinshasa, Zaire; f. 1969 at meeting of Foreign Ministers of Zaire, Rwanda and Burundi.

Conference of African Women: P.B. 310, Bamako, Mali; f. 1962 to accelerate the emancipation of African women and encourage them to participate in the social political and economic life of their country. Mems.: organizations in 28 countries.

Sec.Gen. Mrs. JEANNE MARTIN CISSÉ (Guinea).

International Centre for African Economic and Social Documentation (*Centre international de documentation économique et sociale africaine—CIDESA*): 7 Place Royale, 1000 Brussels, Belgium; f. 1961 to establish international co-ordination of economic and social documentation concerning Africa and to facilitate research; 89 member institutions.

Pres. Dr. G. JANTZEN; Vice-Pres. J. MEYRIAT; Sec. Gen. J. B. CUYVERS. Publs. *Bibliographical Index-*

cards (2,500 per year), *Bulletin of information on current research on human sciences concerning Africa* (twice a year), *Bibliographical Enquiries.*

Organization of Solidarity of the Peoples of Africa, Asia and Latin America (*Organización de Solidaridad de los Pueblos de Africa, Asia y América Latina—OSPAAAL*): Apdo. 4224, Havana, Cuba; f. January 1966 at the first Conference of Solidarity of the Peoples of Africa, Asia and Latin America. Permanent Body: Executive Secretariat composed of Secretary-General (Cuba) and four representatives from each continent. Objects: to unite, co-ordinate and encourage national liberation movements in the three continents and to oppose foreign intervention in the affairs of sovereign states, and to fight against racialism and all forms of racial discrimination.

Mems.: revolutionary organizations in 82 countries.

Sec.-Gen. OSMANY CIENFUEGOS GORRIARÁN (Cuba). Publs. *Tricontinental Bulletin* (monthly), *Tricontinental Magazine* (every two months).

INDUSTRIAL AND PROFESSIONAL RELATIONS

African Trade Union Confederation (ATUC): c/o AFRO-ICFTU Office, 231 Herbert Macaulay St., Yaba; P.M.B. 1038, Ebute-Metta, Lagos, Nigeria; f. 1962. Mems.: 41 national organizations grouping about 2 million workers in 30 countries.

Pres. LAWRENCE L. BORHA (Nigeria); Sec. DAVID SOUMAH (Senegal).

Afro-Asian Institute for Co-operative and Labour Studies: P.O.B. 16201, Tel-Aviv; f. 1960 by Histadrut. Aims: to train union workers, co-operators and government executives in the theory and practice of economic and social development problems, labour economics, trade unionism and co-operation; English-speaking, French-speaking and special courses.

Chair. Dr. ELIAHU ELATH; Dir. AKIVA EGER.

All African Trade Union Federation (AATUF): c/o 222 ave. des Forces Armées Royales, Casablanca, Morocco; f. 1961. Mems.: independent national trade union organizations.

Chair. MAHJOUB BEN SEDDIK (Morocco); Vice-Pres. KABA MAMADY (Guinea), Mouloud Oumeziane (Algeria), AHMED FAHIM (Egypt), MICHAEL KAMALIZA (Tanzania), PAUL BANTHOUD (Zaire), ZOUMANA TRADRE (Upper Volta), WAHAB GOODLUCK (Nigeria); Sec.-Gen. MAMADOU SISSOKO (Mali); Treas.-Gen. L. COULIBALY (Mali).

ICFTU African Information Service: 231 Herbert Macaulay Street, Yaba, Nigeria.

ICFTU African Research Service: P.O.B. 2317, Addis Ababa, Ethiopia.

Union générale des travailleurs d'Afrique noire (UGTAN): Dakar, Senegal; f. 1956. Mems.: national organizations in West African territories associated with the French Community.

Union pan-africaine des travailleurs croyants (*Pan-African Workers Congress—PAWC*): B.P. 8814, Kinshasa, Zaire; f. 1959 by amalgamation of *Confédération africaine des travailleurs croyants* and Christian organizations in the Congo.

Sec.-Gen. GILBERT PONGAULT (Zaire).

World Confederation of Labour Regional Office for Africa: P.O.B. 307, Bathurst, The Gambia.

Sec. G. PONGAULT.

LAW

Asian-African Legal Consultative Committee: 20 Ring Rd., Lajpat Nagar IV, New Delhi 24, India; f. 1956. Aims: to place the Committee's views on legal issues before the International Law Commission; to consider legal problems referred to it by member countries; to be a forum for Afro-Asian co-operation in legal matters. Reconstituted 1958 to enable participation by countries in the African continent.

Pres. Hon. T. S. FERNANDO (Ceylon); Sec.-Gen. B. SEN (India).

International African Law Association: 46 ave. de l'Arbalète, Brussels 17, Belgium; f. 1959 to unite those professionally concerned with law and legal problems in Africa, and to assist African governments, especially in the harmonization and unification of laws in Africa.

Pres. Mr. Justice KEBA M'BAYE; Sec.-Gen. Dr. J. VANDERLINDEN, Faculty of Law, Haile Selassie I University, Addis Ababa, Ethiopia. Publ. *Journal of African Law*.

MEDICINE AND PUBLIC HEALTH

International Scientific Committee for Trypanosomiasis Research (*Comité scientifique international de recherches sur la trypanosomiase*): Joint Secretariat, OAU/STRC, P.M. Box 2359, Lagos, Nigeria; f. 1949. Objects: To review the work on tsetse and trypanosomiasis problems carried out by the organizations and workers concerned in laboratories and in the field; to stimulate further research and discussion and to promote co-ordination between research workers and organizations in the different countries in Africa, and to provide a regular opportunity for the discussion of particular problems and for the exposition of new experiments and discoveries. Publ. Proceedings of ISCTR Conferences.

Organization for Co-operation and Co-ordination in the Fight against Endemic Diseases (*Organisation de co-opération et de coordination pour la lutte contre les grandes endémies—OCCGE*): Centre Muraz, B.P. 153, Bobo-Dioulasso, Upper Volta. Mems.: governments of Dahomey, France, Ivory Coast, Mali, Mauritania, Niger, Senegal, Togo, Upper Volta.

Pres. Dr. BÈNITIÉNI FOFANA; Sec.-Gen. Dr. CHEICK SOW; Dir. Centre Muraz Dr. J. H. RICOSSÉ. Other Centres of the OCCGE are:

Office de recherches pour l'alimentation et la nutrition africaine (ORANA): B.P. 2089, Dakar, Senegal.

Dir. Col. TOURY.

Institut d'opthalmologie tropicale de l'afrique (IOTA): B.P. 248, Bamako, Mali.

Dir. Dr. LOREAL.

Institut Marchoux: OCCGE, Bamako, Mali.

Dir.-Gen. LANGUILLON.

Organization for Co-ordination in the Fight against Endemic Diseases in Central Africa (*Organisation de coordination pour la lutte contre les endémies en l'Afrique centrale—OCEAC*): B.P. 288, Yaoundé, Cameroon; f. 1965. Mems.: Cameroon, Central African Republic, Chad, Congo People's Republic, Gabon. Aims: to standardize methods of fighting endemic diseases, to co-ordinate national action, and to negotiate programmes of assistance on a regional scale.

Pres. Dr. J. BAZOUM; Sec.-Gen. Dr. LABUSQUIÈRE. Publs. *Rapports Finals des Conférences Techniques* (annual), *Bulletins de Documentation*.

Permanent Inter-African Bureau for Tsetse and Trypanosomiasis: c/o Institut de Médecine Tropicale, Office National de la Recherche et du Développement, P.O.B. 1697, 33 ave. du Comité Urbain, Kinshasa, Zaire; f. 1949 to collect and publish documentary material and facilitate interchange of research workers and experts. Mems.: OAU countries (*see* chapter).

Dir. Prof. V. A. DEGROOTE.

Society of Haematology and Blood-Transfusion of African and Near Eastern Countries: Tunis, Tunisia; f. 1965 for the promotion and co-ordination of scientific research in the field of haematology.

Pres. Dr. SY BABA (Ivory Coast); Vice-Pres. Dr. BENABADJY (Algeria); Sec.-Gen. Dr. ALI BOUJNAH (Tunisia).

PRESS, RADIO AND TELECOMMUNICATIONS

African Committee for the Co-ordination of Information Media—CACMI (*Comité africain pour la coordination des moyens d'information*): Accra, Ghana; f. 1965 to harmonize the activities of the three major journalists' unions in Africa.

Sec. KOFI BATSA (Ghana).

Pan-African Union of Journalists—PAJU: Accra, Ghana; f. 1963 to promote the welfare and training of African journalists.

Sec.-Gen. KOFI BATSA (Ghana).

Union of African News Agencies (UANA): Algérie Presse Service, 7 bd. de la République, Algiers; f. 1963; meets annually; has proposed the creation of a Pan-African News Agency within aegis of OAU.

Pres. MOHAMED BOUZID (Algeria).

Union of National Radio and Television Organisations of Africa (*Union des organisations nationales de radio et télévision de l'Afrique*): 101 rue Carnot, B.P. 3237, Dakar, Senegal; f. 1962; co-ordinates radio and television services, including monitoring and frequency allocation, among African countries. Mems.: 24.

Pres. GARBA SIDIKOU (Niger); Sec.-Gen. MOHAMED EL BASSIOUNI (Senegal).

African Postal and Telecommunications Union: P.O.B. 593, Pretoria, Republic of South Africa; f. 1935. Aims: to improve postal and telecommunications services between member administrations. Mems.: 11 countries.

Dir. L. F. RIVE (Postmaster-General, South Africa).

African Postal Union—AfPU (*Union postale africaine*): 5 26th July St., Cairo, Egypt; f. 1961 to improve postal services between member states, to secure collaboration between them and to create other useful services. Mems.: governments of Algeria, Egypt, Ghana, Guinea, Mali, Morocco.

Dir. ABDEL AZIZ SHAKER (Egypt). Publ. *African Postal Union Review* (quarterly).

RELIGION

All Africa Conference of Churches: P.O.B. 20301, Nairobi, Kenya; f. 1958; an organ of co-operation and con tinuing friendship among Churches and Christian Councils in Africa. Mems.: include most major non-Catholic autonomous Churches in Africa.

Chair. Rev. RICHARD ANDRIAMANJATO (Madagascar); Gen. Sec. Canon BURGESS CARR (Liberia). Publs. *AACC Bulletin, Youth Newsletter*.

World Council of Churches Special Fund to Combat Racism: 150 route de Ferney, 1211 Geneva 20, Switzerland; f. 1969 as part of the Programme to Combat Racism. Aims: to use proceeds of the fund to support organizations combating racism but not eligible for the support of other units of the World Council; it represents a commitment to the struggle of these organizations for economic, political and social justice; special priority is to be given to the situation in South Africa and to areas where particular racial groups are in danger of physical or cultural extermination. Grants are made without control of the manner in which they are spent, to liberation or other groups whose work includes developing emergency economic, educational, health and social welfare programmes; research, documentation and information services and protest and pressure groups. The following table shows the first two allocations made of grants of special reference to Africa:

	1970 $	1971
Angola:		
Movimento Popular de Libertação de Angola (MPLA) . . .	20,000	25,000
Governo Revolucionário de Angola no Exil (GRAE)	20,000	7,500
União Nacional para a Independência Total de Angola (UNITA)	10,000	7,500
Guinea (Bissau):		
Partido Africano de Independência da Guiné e Cabo Verde (PAIGC)	20,000	25,000
Mozambique:		
Institute of the Frente de Libertação de Moçambique (FRELIMO) .	15,000	20,000
Netherlands:		
Angola Committee and Dr. Eduardo Mondlane Foundation (Foundation for the Promotion of Information about Racism and Colonialism)	5,000	—
Rhodesia:		
Zimbabwe African National Union	10,000	—
Zimbabwe African People's Union	10,000	—
Front for the Liberation of Zimbabwe (FROLIZI)	—	10,000
South Africa:		
African National Congress (ANC) .	10,000	5,000
South West Africa (Namibia):		
South West African People's Organization (SWAPO) . .	5,000	25,000
United Kingdom:		
The Africa Bureau . .	2,500	—
Anti-Apartheid Movement . .	5,000	—
International Defence and Aid Fund	3,000	—
Zambia:		
Africa 2000 Project . . .	15,000	5,000

SCIENCE

Association for the Taxonomic Study of Tropical African Flora (*Association pour l'étude taxonomique de la flore d'Afrique tropicale—AETFAT*): Conservatoire et Jardin Botaniques, 192 route de Lansanne, 1202 Geneva, Switzerland; f. 1950. Mems.: 620 individuals from 65 countries. Library in Brussels.

Sec.-Gen. Prof. Dr. J. MIÈGE. Publs. *AETFAT Index*, *AETFAT Bulletin* (annual).

Association of African Geological Surveys (*Association des services géologiques africains*): 74 rue de la Fédération, Paris 15e, France; f. 1929. Aims: synthesis of the geological knowledge of Africa and neighbouring countries; encouragement of research in geological and allied sciences for the benefit of Africa; dissemination

of scientific knowledge. Mems.: about 60 (Official Geological Surveys, public and private organizations).

Pres. J. E. CUDJOE (Ghana); Sec.-Gen. J. LOMBARD (France). Publs. maps and studies.

SOCIAL SCIENCES AND HUMANISTIC STUDIES

International African Institute (IAI) (*Institut international africain*): 210 High Holburn, London, WC1V 7BW, England; f. 1926; information centre on African ethnology, linguistics and social studies; holds seminars and conferences; library of 6,000 vols. Mems.: 2,700 in 97 countries.

Chair. Sir ARTHUR SMITH; Admin. Dir. Prof. DARYLL FORDE (U.K.); Sec. BASIL WHEELER. Publs. *Afria* and numerous monographs.

International Congress of Africanists (*Congrès international des Africanistes*): c/o *Présence Africaine*, 42, rue Descartes, Paris 5e, France; f. 1960 to organize and co-ordinate research in African Studies on an international basis, to promote co-operation with other organizations with similar objectives, and to encourage Africans to express themselves in all fields of human endeavour. Federated to the International Council for Philosophy and Humanistic Studies.

Pres. ALIOUNE DIOP (France); Exec. Sec. Prof. ALLASANE N'DAW, Faculté des Lettres, Université de Dakar, Senegal. Publ. *Proceedings of the First International Congress of Africanists* (in English and French).

TOURISM

Organisation pour le développement du tourisme en Afrique: 6 rue Mesnil, Paris 16e, France; f. 1961 to publicise member states; to help co-ordinate the work of tourist bodies to disseminate tourist information; to study legal, administrative and other measures to increase tourism; to help members acquire equipment for developing the industry; to represent members at international meetings. Mems.: 14 member nations.

Pres. KARIM DEMBELE; Dir. Gen. YOUSSOUPH GUEYE. Publs. *Rythmes*, brochures, etc.

TRADE AND INDUSTRY

African Groundnut Council: P.O.B. 3025, Lagos, Nigeria; f. 1965. Mems.: Gambia, Mali, Niger, Nigeria, Senegal, Sudan, Zaire. A promotion office has been established in Geneva, Switzerland.

Chair. USMAN ABDALLAH MADANI (Sudan); Exec. Sec. DIEUMB GUEYE (Senegal).

Cocoa Producers' Alliance: P.O.B. 1718, Western House, 8-10 Yakubu Gowon St., Lagos, Nigeria; f. 1962. Principal aims: to effect adjustment between production and consumption of cocoa, to prevent excessive price fluctuations; to protect the foreign exchange earnings of member countries; to expand and regulate consumption. Member states: Brazil, Cameroon, Ghana, Ivory Coast, Nigeria and Togo.

Chair. M. A. AKINTOMIDE (Nigeria).

Comité africain et malgache de la Zone Franc au sud du Sahara de la Chambre de Commerce Internationale (*African and Malagassy Committee of the Franc Zone south of the Sahara of the International Chamber of Commerce*): 5 rue Bellini, 92-Puteaux, France.

Pres. LUC DURAND-REVILLE; Sec.-Gen. J. NEVEU.

Institut d'administration des entreprises (*Institute of Business Management*): Centre Pédagogique, Université d'Aix-Marseille, 29 ave. R. Schuman, 13 Aix-en-Provence, France; provides business management training for small numbers of African and Malagasy personnel working in public or private enterprises in Africa and Madagascar.

Dir. MARCEL KESSLER.

Inter-African Coffee Organization: 45 ave. de Wagram, Paris 17e, France; f. 1960. Mems.: 16 coffee-producing countries in Africa.

Pres. SADOU AYATOU (Cameroon); Sec.-Gen. CHARLES KONAN BANNY (Ivory Coast).

TRANSPORT

African Aviation Federation: Nairobi, Kenya; f. 1969; to promote development of means of communication in Africa, co-operation among airline companies of member states, development of telecommunications between airports and the establishment of an aviation research centre. First Conference Cairo 1969.

Chair. R. AMPONSAH (Ghana).

Agence pour la sécurité de la navigation aérienne en Afrique et à Madagascar (ASECNA) (*Agency for the safety of aerial navigation in Africa and Madagascar*):

B.P. 3144, Dakar, Senegal and 75 rue La Boétie, Paris 8e, France; f. 1959. Mems.: 15.

Pres. LOUIS SANMARCO; Dir.-Gen. ROGER MACHENAUD.

Association of African Airways: c/o Air Afrique, 3 ave. Barthe, P.O.B. 21017, Abidjan, Ivory Coast; f. 1969 to give African air companies expert advice in technical, financial, juridicial and market matters. Mems.: 7 national African airlines and Air Afrique.

Trans-Sahara Liaison Committee: c/o UN Economic Commission for Africa, Addis Ababa, Ethiopia; f. 1965; this technical committee was formed to study the proposed trans-Saharan road route, the most favoured scheme being a road from Algiers to Tamanrasset branching towards Gao in Mali and Agades in Niger and joining existing routes to Tunisia. The estimated cost for a tarred road 7 metres wide, 2,800 km. long, is U.S. $85.1 million and it will take 10-12 years to complete. The committee reported to the UN Development Programme, which contributed $236,400 to an 8 month study of the scheme. Mems.: Algeria, Mali, Morocco, Niger and Tunisia.

PART THREE
Country Surveys

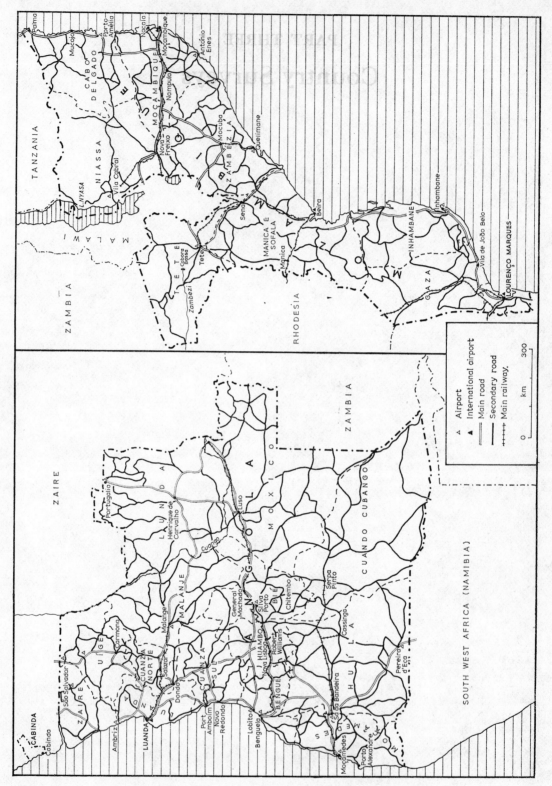

Angola and Mozambique.

Angola

PHYSICAL AND SOCIAL GEOGRAPHY

René Pélissier

PHYSICAL FEATURES

Angola has an area of 1,246,700 sq. km., which makes it Portugal's largest overseas province (about fourteen times the size of metropolitan Portugal). It is a massive country, the second in size, after Zaire, of the countries lying south of the Sahara. It is composed of fifteen districts, one of which, Cabinda, is physically separated from the fourteen others by the oceanic outlet of Zaire and the River Congo. On its landward side the enclave of Cabinda is surrounded by Congo (Brazzaville), as well as Zaire. Angola proper is bordered to the north and east by Zaire, to the east by Zambia and to the south by South West Africa (Namibia). Excluding Cabinda, it has the shape of a rough square, 1,277 km. from the northern to the southern border, and 1,236 km. from the mouth of the Cunene (Kunene) to the Zambian border.

Two-thirds of Angola is a plateau, the altitude of which is favourable to white settlement. The average height is 1,050–1,350 km., with higher ranges and massifs reaching above 2,000 km. The highest point of Angola is Mount Moco (2,620 m.) in the Huambo district; other peaks are Mount Mepo (2,583 m.) in the Benguela district and Mount Vavéle (2,479 m.) in the Cuanza Sul district. Through the central part of this inland plateau runs the watershed of Angola's rivers. The coastal plain on the Atlantic is separated from this plateau by a subplateau zone which varies in breadth from about 160 km. in the north to about 25–40 km. in the centre and south, where a thousand-metre escarpment provides grandiose views of the Serra da Chela. The Namib desert occupies the coastal plain well above Moçâmedes. Towards the Kwango basin in Zaire a sedimentary hollow forms the Cassange depression, in which cotton is grown. The north-western section of the Angolan plateau has jungle-covered mountains which are ideal for coffee-growing and which also provide easy shelter for African insurgents. The Cabinda enclave has the Mayombe range, which is covered by equatorial jungle.

Except for the Cuanza river, which is navigable up to Dondo (193 km. upstream) and which played a great historical role in opening up the interior of the Ngola kingdom, Angolan rivers do not provide easy access to the interior from the coast. On the other hand, they are harnessed for the production of electricity and for irrigation. Main rivers are, above the Cuanza, the Chiloango (Cabinda enclave), the Congo (Zaire in Portuguese), the M'bridge, the Loge, the Dande and the Bengo; the Cuanza, which is the main entirely Angolan river (960 km.); and the Longa, the Covo, the Catumbela, the Coporolo, and the Cunene, which forms the border with South West Africa. All these rivers have their mouths on the Angolan coast. Others such as the Cuando, Cubango and Zambezi rise in Angola, but their economic influence in the country is marginal because they cross the sparsely-populated eastern and southern zones. The Cassai (Kasai), Cuilo (Kwilu) and Cuango (Kwango) are known more for their importance to Zaire than for their upper reaches in Angola, although many tributaries of the Kasai cut into the Angolan plateau, exposing rich diamond fields in the Lunda district.

Angola has a tropical climate, locally tempered by altitude. The Benguela current along the coast influences and reduces rainfall in that part of the country which is arid or semi-arid. The interior uplands in the Bié, Huambo and Huila districts have a pleasant climate, in temperature not unlike the Portuguese climate, allowing permanent white settlement. On the other hand, along the Cuanza river, in the north-west and north-east and in the eastern and southern districts high temperatures (a parching heat along the South West African border) and heavy seasonal rainfall have tended to hinder white colonization wherever there are no exceptional incentives, such as coffee in the Congo districts of Zaire and Uige, and diamonds in Lunda.

POPULATION

Angola is an underpopulated country with only 5,673,046 people (according to the 1970 census). The population density was 4.55 persons per square kilometre. According to official estimates the population in 1968 was 5,458,500. It is overwhelmingly rural and tribal. In 1960 11 per cent was said to be living in urban centres of over 2,000 people. In 1960 the main ethnic divisions among the African population not legally considered as assimilated (i.e. *indigenas*) were: Ovimbundu (1,746,109); Mbundu (1,053,999); Kongo (621,787); Lunda-Chokwe (396,264); Nganguela (329,259); Nyaneka (138,191); Humbe (114,832); and Ovambo (115,442). All of them are of Bantu stock. Non-Bantu *indigenas* numbered less than 20,000. As well as the African *indigenas*, there were in 1960 37,873 Angolan-born black Africans who legally had the same status as whites and assimilated *mestiços*. They were called *assimilados*. Some Cape Verdians and São Tomenses were numbered among non-Angolan *mestiços* and blacks. Since September 1961 the distinction between *assimilados* and *indigenas* has been legally abolished, but former *indigenas* who have not asked for identity cards are still subjected to seeking administrative authorization to travel beyond their local area (*concelho or circunscrição*).

The African population on the whole is still predominantly engaged in food-crop farming and, in the south, in cattle-raising. Only in areas of coffee, cotton and maize growing does one see Africans engaged in commercial agriculture to any extent. Some 90 per cent of the active population is thought to be working in the farming and cattle-raising sectors, while mining (of diamonds, oil and iron ore) cannot seriously compete with this sector as far as the number of workers is concerned. Fishing is in a crisis, but the booming sector of industry should capture an ever-growing segment of the African population which is no longer in fishing.

URBAN CENTRES

The capital, Luanda, had 224,540 inhabitants in 1960. It had nearly 500,000 inhabitants in 1970, and has a large population now numbering more than 100,000. Skyscrapers, wide avenues and a general European appearance make the city centre look modern and aggressive. The poverty-stricken districts of the city, known locally as *muceques*, are predominantly black, but fairly large contingents of "poor whites" and *mestiços* modify their ghetto aspect. While social mobility is low and job-competition severe between races, this Angolan metropolis is the magnet which attracts many Mbundu in search of work or pleasure. Other Angolan races are much less interested in coming to this increasingly white city.

The Kongo have no large city of their own, since São Salvador, their traditional capital, is now a military outpost of no significance. Carmona in the coffee district of Uige has lost much of its appeal for the Kongo since the great massacres of 1961. It is now a booming Portuguese version of a frontier town, where more than 4,000 whites live. Malange is the second metropolis of the Mbundu and should become more important now that a tarred road links it with Luanda and the Lunda district. South of this chain of Mbundu centres on the Cuanza axis the Ovimbundu possess the twin complex of Lobito-Benguela, the population of which is certainly above 100,000. Here there is intense rivalry between the whites of historic Benguela and its competitor, booming Lobito, which is the outlet of the Benguela railway. On the plateau Nova Lisboa offers the image of a redeemed Portugal in the tropics. From here there is considerable rail traffic to the eastern regions, to Katanga and to Zambia, and easy road connexions with Luanda and South West Africa. The population of this new city is over 50,000. To the south, Moçâmedes is a fishing port and the outlet for the Cassinga iron ore. Still provincial by virtue of its remoteness, its importance has increased because of improved road connections with Sá da Bandeira, which is unique in having more white inhabitants than black. Other centres such as Silva Porto and Luso also suffer from remoteness. Cabinda city is experiencing a mild boom in petroleum, while pioneer towns like Serpa Pinto and Henrique de Carvalho have assumed new importance as centres of counter-revolutionary activity.

RECENT HISTORY OF PORTUGAL'S AFRICAN TERRITORIES

Basil Davidson

The colonial share-out of the late nineteenth century eventually confirmed Portugal in the possession of two large colonies in southern Africa, Angola in the west and Mozambique in the east; of a small colony in west Africa, often nowadays called Guinea (Bissau), after its capital city, in order to distinguish it from the neighbouring Republic of Guinea; and of two groups of islands, those of Cape Verde and, in the south Atlantic, of São Tomé and Príncipe. These territories are about twenty-two times the geographical size of Portugal; their total populations in 1970 amounted to between thirteen and fourteen million, of whom perhaps 350,000 were civilian Portuguese and other Europeans. Detailed population figures remain unknown.

In 1951, expecting admission to the United Nations —an ambition achieved in 1955—the government of Dr. Salazar introduced constitutional changes which abandoned the use of the word "colonies", and transformed these territories, at least in juridical terms, into "oversea provinces". That portion of their populations accepted as being of civilized status—in 1951 less than one per cent—was at the same time empowered to send elected deputies to Lisbon's single-party parliament. Disclaiming in this way to possess any non-self-governing territories, the Portuguese government afterwards refused to admit the right of any UN body to enquire into the condition of these African territories, now officially designated as integral parts of the motherland. For its part, the UN General Assembly refused to accept this exclusion on the grounds that these territories were still colonies in all but name, and has since continued, with growing emphasis and steadily enlarged majorities during the late 1960s, to pass resolutions condemning Portuguese imperial practice and theory, as well as to publish such relevant information as has come to hand. Unlike the nationalist movements to be noted later, this UN pressure has so far entirely failed to have any influence on Portugal, or to deprive Portugal of any significant support from its international friends and allies, especially those within the North Atlantic Treaty Organisation. It is arguable, however, that the mobilization of UN opinion against continued Portuguese rule in Africa may become more meaningful in the future.

EARLY VENTURES

National mythology has given the Portuguese the conviction of a colonial presence in Africa since the fifteenth century. With the partial exception of some of the Atlantic islands, this conviction is false. What is true is that the Portuguese maritime pioneers achieved a trading and raiding presence along the Guinea coast after the 1440s; in the Congo estuary and along the northern part of the coast of Angola after 1482; and at a few points on Africa's Indian Ocean seaboard in the wake of Vasco da Gama's great voyage of 1497–99. This faint early presence they were gradually able to transform into permanent emplacements and small trading settlements. In 1575 they founded Luanda on the Angolan coast and have held it ever since, but for a brief interlude of Dutch possession in the seventeenth century. Early in the sixteenth century they built forts on Mozambique Island and at Sofala on the Mozambique coast, and later established small settlements at Sena, Tete and elsewhere in the inland country.

While a few hundred soldiers and settlers became spasmodically involved in African affairs in Mozambique, and while much larger bodies of Portuguese were closely and sometimes continuously involved along the coast and in the near-coastal country of Angola, Portugal cannot be said to have wielded any real control over these territories until late in the nineteenth century, or even, for regions far from their main bases, until early in the twentieth. This weakness derived partly from the industrial and technological backwardness of Portugal itself, partly from the rivalry of other imperial powers, and partly from the strength of the African kingdoms and polities which faced and long resisted Portuguese invasion. In western Angola, for example, there was almost continuous warfare for nearly a hundred years after 1575.

THE "RIGHT OF OCCUPATION"

As a lightweight in the "scramble for Africa" Portugal was able to affirm its "colonial rights" only by dint of manoeuvring between stronger rivals, both at the Berlin conference of 1884–85 and afterwards. Thanks chiefly to British protection, the Portuguese were allowed to secure the "right of occupation" to most of the territory afterwards enclosed, but for this they paid what was to them a bitter price in being debarred from those central African lands which became Northern and Southern Rhodesia and Nyasaland, duly enclosed by Britain. Most of the present frontiers of Angola and Mozambique were fixed on the map by conventions of 1891 and soon after; the shape of Guinea (Bissau) emerged at much the same time after a number of conventions involving France or Britain. There was no serious threat to continued Portuguese occupation of the Cape Verde Islands, nor of São Tomé and Príncipe.

But the "right of occupation" was far from guaranteeing the fact itself. This was achieved after long years of military "pacification" only in the period immediately before and after the First World War, Portuguese claims to control continuing to be challenged by many armed uprisings in all three territories. Thus the story of Portuguese colonial rule cannot properly be said to begin, in any complete or systematic sense, until about 1910–20. It is a story which may be divided into three chief periods.

INSTALLING A COLONIAL SYSTEM

There was first of all a period of "primary installation" associated with several outstanding colonizers, notably Norton de Matos in Angola. A weak republican government in Lisbon, or rather a series of such governments, found it convenient—in fact they had little choice—to accept a considerable measure of decentralization; it was now that the basic frameworks of Portuguese administration, as well as their early infrastructure in terms of roads and a few railways, were laid down. Begun in 1903 by British interests, a railway from Lobito on the Atlantic coast finally reached the Zaire border in 1929. Diamond mining began in Angola. Nothing bloomed, whether for lack of money or enterprise, but the first slender shoots of a colonial harvest appeared above the soil of fragmentary effort. There took shape the "colonial pact" which was to bind these colonies to Portugal in characteristically rigid fashion. With the metropolitan country exercising a complete commercial monopoly, the colonies became protected markets for Portuguese exports, including wine, and, in return, began to supply Portugal with colonial produce at rates fixed in Lisbon. From the first, then, these colonies closely reflected the condition of the metropolitan country: if the latter should continue to stagnate, so would the former. What Antonio Enes has said of Mozambique in 1893 has remained generally true: "We have good land, and labour to work it; we lack only capital and initiative."

A second period opened with the overthrow of the Portuguese Republic in 1926 and the establishment of Dr. Salazar's authoritarian *Estado Novo* a few years later. The trend towards decentralization from Lisbon was stopped and to some extent reversed. The interests of the colonies were made more directly subject to the immediate interests of Portugal, as conceived by Dr. Salazar and his ideologues. The doctrine of Luso-African "unity" was affirmed in ways which made it clear that whatever might be thought good for Portugal would also be thought good for the colonies and their peoples. Along with this there came an abrupt end to all discussion of liberal or alternative policies and attitudes. A Colonial Act of 1933 duly embodied Salazarist imperial doctrine in constitutional measures which, with a few largely superficial changes of statute, remain substantially in force today. It can be said with little risk of exaggeration that the Portuguese territories are governed by assumptions and practices which have not altered since the overthrow of the Republic, or indeed, in their essence, since long before that.

Nothing that has happened in Africa south of the Sahara since the Gold Coast achieved internal self-rule in 1951, and independence as Ghana in 1957, appears in any way to have undermined official Portuguese pride in such long-enduring "stability". In this, of course, there has been more than doctrinal certitude or Lusitanian attachment to the great traditions of the fifteenth and sixteenth centuries. Portugal's spokesmen have repeatedly argued that Portugal is differently placed from other powers in Africa, in that Portugal is financially and industrially too weak to be able to withdraw politically without the fair probability that others, immediately, would take her economic place.

SEEDS OF DISCONTENT

A third large period opened with the great rebellion of 1961 in Angola, and with similar manifestations of African nationalism a little later in Mozambique and Guinea (Bissau.) These have brought the condition of Portuguese Africa into the centre of a world-wide debate. More than that, they have involved the Portuguese in the longest and in some respects the largest of any of the colonial wars of Africa except for Algeria in 1952–64. Not surprisingly these developments have had profound consequences for Portuguese colonial practice and even, to some extent, on Portuguese colonial theory. The doctrine of "no withdrawal" remains intact, but complacency about the condition of the African populations, or indifference to criticism, is less evident than before. To understand the origins and nature of this evolution, which still continues, it is necessary to consider, even if briefly, the reasons why African discontent took the form of insurrection.

Though for long apparently quiescent, a minority of Africans and mulattos who were conscious of their condition when compared with that of other African peoples, or of the Portuguese, were able to organize themselves in small clandestine groupings early in the 1950s. They were moved by traditions of past independence and of old anti-colonial wars to preserve it; by a desire to affirm their own cultural identities and to improve their peoples' condition; and, at any rate after 1953, by currents of African nationalism then crossing colonial frontiers from other and less rigidly controlled territories.

This early nationalism, little more at first than a muted form of protest against colonial rule, gained a hearing and was able gradually to enlarge its audience. The reasons why it could do this seem to have lain precisely in Lisbon's much-valued "stability". What this "stability" could actually mean, to Africans beginning to be aware of their real status in the world, is shown in the tables for education and other social services in the Statistical Surveys which follow: inadequate and approximate though they necessarily are, given the paucity of good information, they tell their own story. Yet they need a little further elucidation. This must bear especially on Portuguese claims to have exercised great tolerance in accepting Africans as equals. These claims rest on a certain Portuguese humanism, "anti-racialism", which undoubtedly exists. Unfortunately for African, it is a humanism which has had little or no application in Africa. According to census figures returned in 1950, a year before these colonies became "integral parts of the motherland", the proportion of the African population which had achieved "assimilated status"—and thus the right to education above a most elementary level, to exemption from forced labour, and to treatment that did not, at least in theory, discriminate against them as "uncivilized persons"—was about 0.75 per cent in Angola, and about 0.08 per cent in Mozam-

bique; in Guinea (Bissau) it was perhaps about 0.3 per cent, while in the islands it was theoretically total except for migrant labour brought from the mainland.

The vast majority, in other words, could benefit in no way from Portuguese racial tolerance. On the contrary, they were subject to the closest possible regulation as "natives" (being thus distinguished from *assimilados*). They were available for impressment to forced labour, or else to migrant labour under contractual conditions over which they had no control of any kind. They were deprived of all education or, at best, might achieve a year or two in a village school. They were further denied every right to organize in any mode of self-defence, whether social, economic, political or cultural. Over and beyond these restrictions many village people in all three mainland colonies were obliged to grow cash crops for sale on the Portuguese colonial market, but once again at prices which lay beyond their control. Among other things, this tended to reduce the quantity of food available to farmers to a point occasionally disastrous and always debilitating. In this respect it should be mentioned that the 1940s and 1950s heard many Portuguese voices raised in protest; some of these, such as that of the Bishop of Beira, were of considerable weight and authority. Yet the system was no longer in any way self-correcting, even within the necessarily narrow limits of colonial rule: such voices were ignored or repressed as merely mischievous or subversive.

In the wake of the Angolan rebellion of 1961, and the western attention that it drew, Lisbon felt it wise to introduce a number of constitutional reforms tending to the abolition of forced labour and the ending of the sharp distinction between "natives" and "civilized persons". But in one sense the damage was done and the reforms came too late, while in another sense they were too half-hearted to make any effective difference to an atmosphere that was now one of growing violence. At the same time it became evident that those foreign governments, notably of Britain and the United States, which were best placed to influence Portuguese policies in an evolutionary sense were, in fact, moved by larger considerations of strategy relating to Portugal's membership of the North Atlantic alliance and the value of the Azores as a major American military base.

Fatefully, then, the rebellions began—in 1961 in Angola, in 1963 in Guinea (Bissau), and in 1964 in Mozambique—and painfully they have continued.

A DECADE OF WARFARE

These rebellions overshadowed the Portuguese scene throughout most of the 1960s, not only in Africa but also at home. At the beginning of the decade Portugal's armed forces in the African colonies numbered only a few thousand men; by 1969 they included almost the whole Portuguese army, except for home-base establishments and one under-strength division attached to NATO, much of the Portuguese air force, and a significant part of the Portuguese navy, as well as large police and secret-police establishments. Generally estimated at a total of about

218,000 men—raised now by a conscription period lengthened to four years and extended to all able-bodied men between the ages of 18 and 45—the Portuguese army was said, at the end of 1971, to have around 142,000 men in Africa (perhaps 55,000 in Angola, 60,000 in Mozambique, and 27,000 in Guinea (Bissau)). Budget information since 1965 shows that

rather more than half of Portugal's actual annual national revenue has been absorbed by "defence and security" (*see* tables 1, 2, 3, 4), and spent, for the most part, on the African wars. Each year has brought "extraordinary budget allocations" for defence and security which have shown a steady annual increase (*see* table 4).

Table 1

AUTHORIZED PORTUGUESE GOVERNMENT EXPENDITURES 1965–67

(million escudos)

	1965	1966	1967
Public Debt	1,818.4	2,038.0	2,560.9
Higher organs of the State .	106.4	110.0	112.8
Defence and security . . .	7,705.3	8,441.6	10,233.4
Civil administration:			
(a) Government services . .	4,026.5	4,394.7	4,932.0
(b) Investments . . .	4,402.8	4,641.2	5,522.5
TOTAL AUTHORIZED EXPENDITURE . . .	18,059.4	19,625.6	23,361.6
TOTAL ORDINARY REVENUE (ACTUAL RECEIPTS)	15,173.4	16,942.5	19,896.6
Defence and security as a percentage of total authorized expenditure . .	43.0	43.8	44.0
Defence and security as a percentage of actual receipts . . .	51.0	49.8	51.5

Source: Lei de Meios para 1969. (Quoted in UN General Assembly document A/7623/ Add. 3, September 25th, 1969.)

Table 2*

GROWTH OF PORTUGUESE EXPENDITURE 1960–70

		PORTUGAL	ANGOLA	MOZAMBIQUE	GLOBAL
As a percentage of G.N.P. . .	1960	4	1	1	3
	1961	6	1	1	4
	1970	7	4	3	6
As a percentage of fixed capital .	1960	23	11	14	20
	1961	35	14	14	30
	1970	40	29	28	37
As a percentage of authorized budget expenditure . . .	1960	25	13	14	22
	1961	36	12	14	30
	1970	41	27	27	37

Source: UN General Assembly document A/8723 (Part IV), September 11th, 1972.

Table 3*
MILITARY BUDGETS OF PORTUGAL AND THE OVERSEAS TERRITORIES
(million escudos)

	PORTUGAL	OVERSEAS TERRITORIES	TOTAL	PERCENTAGE SHARE OF TERRITORIES
1967 . .	5,347.0	1,800.4	7,147.4	25.2
1968 . .	5,613.0	2,053.3	7,666.3	26.8
1969 . .	6,339.9	2,447.8	8,787.7	27.8
1970 . .	6,349.9	3,222.6	9,572.5	33.7
1971 . .	7,030.6	3,362.2	10,392.8	32.3

Source: UN General Assembly document A/8723/Add. 3, September 1st, 1972.

Table 4*
PORTUGAL'S BUDGETARY ESTIMATES FOR EXTRAORDINARY EXPENDITURE 1965–72
(million escudos)

	ESTIMATED ORDINARY EXPENDITURE	ESTIMATED EXTRAORDINARY EXPENDITURE			
		Defence and Security	Development Plan	Other	Total
1965 . .	10,712.1	3,527.0	2,389.2	111.0	6,027.2
1966 . .	11,026.5	4,011.0	2,203.3	169.5	6,383.8
1967 . .	12,605.4	5,347.0	2,145.4	106.5	7,598.9
1968 . .	13,663.6	5,613.0	2,920.9	137.4	8,671.3
1969 . .	15,286.9	6,339.9	3,521.3	177.1	10,038.3
1970 . .	17,846.6	6,349.9	4,372.3	255.5	10,147.7
1971 . .	19,617.9	7,030.6	4,947.2	453.9	12,431.7
1972 . .	22,065.8	7,583.4	6,192.2	1,033.7	14,809.3

Source: UN General Assembly document A/8723/Add. 3, September 1st, 1972.

* Tabular material revised by Editor.

At the beginning of the 1970s there was no sign that any of these wars were drawing to an end: if anything, they appeared on the whole to be still growing in size and violence. Of the actual military situation on the ground, whether in Angola, Guinea (Bissau), or Mozambique, the Portuguese official version said one thing, and the African nationalist version quite another. Striking a balance of much conflicting evidence, whether from Portuguese military *communiqués* and other Portuguese information, from nationalist claims, and from the reports of foreign observers on both sides, one could reach the following broad conclusions.

In Guinea (Bissau) the Portuguese army had lost control of about two-thirds of the territory, was now confined to fewer than fifty fortified posts and garrisons, mainly along the central north-south "spine" between Bissau and Bafata, and seemed incapable of regaining any general military initiative; this was in spite of a reinforcement of seven battalions sent to the territory in December 1968. It was reported on fairly good though unofficial evidence that Lisbon would now evacuate Guinea (Bissau), were it not for the fear

that withdrawal from the mainland must be followed by a far stronger nationalist pressure in the strategically valuable Cape Verde Islands.

In Angola the partial failure of the rebellion of 1961, coupled with severe repressive measures in that year and the next, said to have involved many thousands of African deaths, was followed by a lull in nationalist activity until 1966. There then occurred a new wave of guerrilla action, west of the Katangan borders of Congo (Kinshasa) and the borders of western Zambia. Nationalist guerrillas were able to establish military and political control in large parts of eastern Angola, and to press westward into the country's central and western districts. Since then there has been no sign of any slackening of Portugal's military effort here.

In Mozambique the main area of action after 1964 lay in the two northern provinces of Cabo Delgado and Niassa, where guerrillas have appeared justified in their claim to control large rural areas; in 1968, besides this, they were able to re-launch earlier operations against Portuguese garrisons in the Tete province, sporadic fighting being reported from there during

1969. As in Angola, there has been no sign of any reduction in the size of Portuguese effectives, or in the scope of their anti-guerrilla activity. Although the Portuguese have not yet lost so clearly the strategic initiative in Angola and Mozambique as in Guinea (Bissau), their own *communiqués* make it clear that their military situation in 1970 was in each case more difficult than before, and had now become extremely serious.

The nature and duration of these wars have posed interesting questions. Where has Portugal found the strength to continue waging them? Where, on their side, have the nationalist guerrillas? The first of these questions lies outside the scope of this article, yet it is relevant to the situation in the African territories to note that sophisticated armaments supplied under agreements with NATO powers have been regularly used in Africa. Published information shows that the Federal Republic of Germany seems to have played a key role, notably in air support. Thus in 1966 the Federal German government sold Portugal forty jet fighters for $10 million: Fiat G-91s, of the type R 4 originally designed for NATO use, which have an Italian airframe, a British engine, a French undercarriage and Dutch electronic equipment. These planes were sold by an agreement which stipulated, *inter alia*, that they were to be used exclusively in Portugal for defence purposes within the framework of the North Atlantic Pact. Their subsequent use for anti-guerrilla action in Africa, which has not been in question, was explained by a Lisbon foreign ministry spokesman (reported in *Flying Review International*, April 1966): "The transaction", he said, "was agreed within the spirit of the North Atlantic Pact. It was agreed that the planes would be used only for defensive purposes within Portuguese territory. Portuguese territory extends to Africa—Angola, Mozambique and Portuguese Guinea". The same official gloss has been used to cover the commitment of other types of imported aircraft, such as Nord 2502 Noratlas transports, small reconnaissance planes, several types of bombers, various types of helicopters, small naval craft for coastal patrols, napalm and other munitions.

The nationalist guerrillas, on their side, have received small-arms and ammunition, grenades, light automatics, and some mortars and recoilless cannon from the U.S.S.R., China, Czechoslovakia and one or two other communist countries, as well as a small amount of financial aid from French and other private or semi-official sources in the U.S.A. and from government sources in Sweden. They have also had material and financial aid from a number of African countries by way of the Liberation Committee of the Organization of African Unity, and, of course, they have captured a possibly significant quantity of war material from the Portuguese. But their principal source of strength has lain in their ability to mobilize the active support of growing numbers of village Africans: if in 1965 their effective guerrilla strength in all three territories may have totalled three or four thousand men under arms, or possibly fewer, reports in 1969 were generally agreed in placing their total strength at somewhere between ten and fourteen thousand men, or possibly more.

It is in respect of their capacity to mobilize and increase rural support—necessarily voluntary support in the conditions of guerrilla warfare—that their true importance will doubtless lie as these wars continue. Though in varying ways, according to their different circumstances, each of the main nationalist movements has shown itself capable of taking root in the loyalties and adherence of large rural populations who are pre-literate and pre-industrial: to the point by 1969, indeed, that the success of these movements might reasonably claim to be unique in the long history of guerrilla insurrection.

While acting separately and independently of each other, these movements in Angola, Guinea (Bissau), and Mozambique have followed much the same political strategy; and it is in this political strategy that the explanation of their repeated success may be chiefly found. It has been a strategy of clearing "liberated zones" within which, progressively as security improved, new social and political structures have been raised, so that, at least in minimal degree, the "promise of a better life" could be realized even in the midst of warfare. These structures have included a large number of elementary schools, some introduction of medical services, and widespread political participation by way of village committees.

Whether for reasons such as these, or by way of Portuguese reactions aimed at countering nationalist policies, it could be said that the general condition of the Portuguese African territories in 1970 was already markedly different from that of ten years earlier.

AFRICAN NATIONALIST ORGANIZATIONS
(Editorial Note)

The Portuguese authorities are at war with three separate African nationalist organizations, all of which have long been declared illegal. The only areas not affected by the war are the central districts of Cuanza Sul, Benguela and Huamba, which, together with Moçâmedes and Luanda, have the greatest concentration of Europeans. On December 13, 1972, an agreement was signed in Kinshasa uniting the MPLA and the FNLA (*see* below), following attempts at reconciliation by Presidents Ngouabi and Mobutu under the auspices of the OAU in June, and as a result some change might take place in the boundaries of the territory each side controls, which have been more or less static for the last year or so. The MPLA will greatly benefit from being able to use Zaire as a transit route for men and materials and can extend its area of operation.

Under its leader, Agostinho Neto, a doctor and poet, the Angola Popular Liberation Movement (MPLA) is easily the most effective of the three guerrilla organizations operating in Angola, a fact which the Portuguese themselves acknowledge. It was the first to begin an armed campaign against the Portuguese when it attacked police and government buildings in Luanda in February 1961 (the "cotton revolt" in Baixa de Cassange broke out at about the same time). Until 1963 the MPLA was hindered in its struggle by the Angola Popular Union (UPA), which also had its external base in Kinshasa but which, unlike the MPLA, had the backing of the Zaire Government. In 1963 the MPLA moved its base to Brazzaville, where the government was more sympathetic, and began to prepare for a switch in its main guerrilla activity to the east of the country, away from the UPA- and the Kongo-dominated areas. UPA actions against MPLA groups increased as the initiative passed to the latter organization from 1966 onwards, but were to little avail.

The MPLA's campaign in eastern Angola opened in 1967. Part of its staff in Brazzaville was moved to Lusaka, and in 1968 into Angola itself, with Lusaka becoming the main external base. The movement has expanded rapidly since then, helped by the proximity of Zambia and by the absence of settlers in Angola, and it now claims control of around one-third of Angola's territory. Political and guerrilla training centres have been set up in liberated areas and schools, clinics and a semblance of administration established. The centre of activity is in Moxico, Cuando-Cubango and part of Luanda, but fighting is in progress in twelve of the territory's fifteen administrative districts, including Moçâmedes and Huíla (bordering South West Africa), where operations began only in February 1972. Several foreign journalists and film crews have visited MPLA-controlled areas, staying for periods of up to several weeks. The Executive Committee of the MPLA meets inside Angola. The main strength of the MPLA is its appeal to Angolan nationalism, and not simply to an ethnically based nationalism. This was one of the reasons why the OAU in 1971 withdrew recognition of the GRAE/FNLA's seven-year old privilege of participating (but without voting) in OAU meetings and put Holden Roberto's organization on the same footing as the MPLA. An OAU military commission had already established, following an inspection of Angola in 1969, that the MPLA was the only effective fighting force there, and recognized the MPLA as the sole representative of the Angolan people. The major source of the MPLA's external aid is Eastern Europe and left-wing organizations in the West.

The National Union for the Complete Independence of Angola (UNITA) was formed in 1966 in Moxico. Its leader, Jonas Savimbi, was once Minister of Foreign Affairs in the GRAE, and also had connections with the MPLA. UNITA's main appeal is to the Ovimbundu, and its major guerrilla actions have been against the

Benguela railway. Following delays in transporting Zambia's copper exports, caused by UNITA sabotage to the railway, the Zambian Government expelled the organization from Lusaka in 1967. China has trained some of UNITA's fighters.

The UPA was the most active of the guerrilla movements until about 1965. It was responsible for the great Kongo uprising of March 1961, following which massacres by the government and settlers brought the total African dead to perhaps 50,000, as against probably less than 500 Portuguese fatalities. The movement's natural external base was Kinshasa, where many Baxikongo lived and where Holden Roberto, the UPA's leader was brought up. Following the suppression of the revolt later in 1961, dissensions began to appear in the movement, and an attempt was made to cover this up by forming, with the very small *Partido Democrático Angolano*, the *Frente Nacional de Libertação de Angola* (FNLA). The establishment of this "National Front" in March 1962 enabled Roberto to proceed with the formation in the following month of a "government-in-exile" (*Governo Revolucionário de Angola no Exílio—GRAE*), which by 1963 had won the recognition not only of its host, the Zaire Government, but also of the majority of African governments and the OAU. However, the GRAE, which has been aided by the U.S.A., has concentrated on diplomatic activity in Kinshasa and other capitals to the detriment of the war effort inside Angola, and the MPLA has replaced the UPA as the main guerrilla movement.

The GRAE/FNLA, despite its extravagant claims, has engaged only in occasional action over the last year or two, and its weakness is evident from the withdrawal by the OAU of its seat in the Organization in 1971, and a mutiny against Roberto in March 1972 in Kinkuzu training camp in Zaire, which had to be put down by Zairian troops. It was hardly suprising that in June 1972 Roberto was prepared to agree to co-operation with the MPLA, and in December to unification under the Angola Supreme Liberation Council (CSLA). This ended ten years of rivalry between the two movements, and will enable them to present the most effective resistance possible, the MPLA retaining responsibility for guerrilla activities while the FNLA continues to concentrate on diplomatic affairs and the administration of nationalist-controlled areas.

ECONOMY
René Pélissier

MAJOR CROPS

Only about 2 per cent of Angola's arable land is actively cultivated, and there is a wide degree of variation between the modern, Portuguese-owned or foreign-owned plantations and the subsistence farming of most Africans. The main crop exported is coffee, which is still the major commodity, with export earnings of 4,029,018,000 escudos in 1971. Angola is the second largest African producer and the United States is the best buyer of *robusta* coffee, grown mainly in Uige, Cuanza Norte, Cuanza Sul and Luanda. Production in 1970 was 204,000 metric tons. While production was seriously disturbed by the north-western rebellion of 1961, the tonnage has more than doubled since 1959. Coffee is grown in a variety of plantations (*fazendas*) ranging from the large *roça*-like companies employing thousands of *contratados* down to the family plantation with only a score of workers, where the owner combines agriculture with minor trade with local Africans. Africans in the north-western area have greatly benefited from this crop. They sell their coffee at fixed prices in official rural markets, where more than 70,000 tons were disposed of in 1968, with a revenue of over 360,000,000 escudos passing into African hands. It is estimated that over 200,000 people profit from coffee growing or marketing in Angola. While over-production, labour shortages and depressed prices are the main handicaps, one can safely say that coffee has been Angola's salvation since the terrible upheaval of 1961. It has been the best incentive to the resumption of peaceful relations in war-torn northern districts. However, certain political pressure groups favouring Angolan nationalism have pressed for a boycott of coffee purchases from Portugal. They have been relatively successful in the Netherlands during 1972.

Sisal exports reached 65,862 tons and were worth 237,640,000 escudos in 1970. Angola is Africa's second most important producer, but the crop has been adversely affected by a slump in world prices. The main producing regions are the Benguela plateau, Huíla, Cuanza Norte and Malange districts. Sisal production is a European preserve, and German entrepreneurs are prominent. About 95 per cent of Angolan maize, which ranks third or fourth among agricultural exports (171,683 tons worth 314,588,000 escudos in 1970), is grown by Africans, and Ovimbundu farmers around the Benguela railway have made it a cash crop and a staple of their diet. Portugal, Zaire and Mexico were the main buyers.

Cotton has slowly recovered from the slump which followed the abolition of forced cultivation in 1961. It is both a concessionary and an African cultivation. In 1970 cotton production was 81,555 tons unginned and 28,819 tons of fibre. Exports of raw cotton reached 23,653 tons which brought in a revenue of 421,711,000 escudos. The main areas of cultivation are the Baixa de Cassange in the Malange district,

famous for the anti-cotton revolt of 1961, and the region east of Luanda. Organized planters in the Cuanza Sul districts were responsible for a recent large increase in mechanized production (31,853 tons of unginned cotton in the district in 1970). An increasing part of production is processed in Angola by three textile mills, an achievement to which the Europeans have long aspired.

Sugar is controlled by three Portuguese companies operating on the plantation model. In 1970 11,357 tons were exported at a value of 42,158,000 escudos, while 67,000 tons were consumed locally in 1970.

On the whole, manioc is the main Angolan crop in terms of volume produced, and is the staple food of the majority of Africans. Production reaches 1,600,000 tons per year and most of it is consumed domestically with no transaction above the local market level. However, some of it is exported to Portugal and France. Declining exports of dried manioc amounted to 24,799 tons, worth 49,132,000 escudos, in 1970.

OTHER CROPS

Palm oil products have an open future since the crop is mainly restricted to a few large European plantations where it is grown in association with sugar-cane. Exports of oil totalled 11,309 tons in 1970, earning 62,491,000 escudos. Coconuts reached an export figure of 12,488 tons, worth 46,415,000 escudos in the same year, while beans sent abroad amounted to 12,049 tons (value 42,668,000 escudos). Other crops are important either as export or as local commodities. Tobacco grows well on the white-owned farms in the central and southern districts of Benguela, Huíla and Moçâmedes. 1,764 tons were exported in 1970 for a value of 53,864,000 escudos, leaving an ample supply for internal manufacture. Other commodities such as wheat (of low quality and insufficient for domestic consumption), rice, millet, sorghum, tropical and temperate fruit, cocoa, and peanuts are testimony to the agricultural future of Angola, provided investment capital and expertise can be deployed for this sector. Because of its large area and variety of climate, Angola is one of the most promising farming countries of southern Africa.

LIVESTOCK, FORESTRY AND FISHERIES

Livestock raising suffers from an absence of pastoralist tradition in northern Angola. The tsetse fly and the poor quality of the natural pastures are also adverse factors. In 1971 Angola had only about 3.7 million head of cattle, 878,000 goats, 342,000 pigs and 184,000 sheep. Only the southern and central districts, Huíla (which has 65 per cent of all Angola's cattle), Benguela, Huambo and Cuanza Sul, are important, either for African-owned herds, mainly of the Ovambo and Nyaneka-Humbe, or for Portuguese ranches. The dairy and meat industries are thriving, particularly as the white population is increasing. Some frozen meat is even exported to Portugal, but imports are still necessary. An interesting project aims at creating an export industry for Persian lamb skin (karakul) in the Moçâmedes district.

Forestry is important only in the Cabinda and Moxico districts, both of which are to some extent threatened by African insurgents. In 1970 Angola exported 129,380 tons of timber, valued at 198,679,000 escudos. Softwood plantations of eucalyptus and cypress are used for fuel and grow along the Benguela railway and near Benguela, where they are used for wood pulp and paper manufacture.

Fisheries are mainly in and off Moçâmedes, Porto Alexandre and Benguela. In recent years catches have declined dramatically, endangering the life of the fishmeal industry. In 1970 they totalled 377,770 tons. Most fishmeal and oil is sold in Europe, while dried fish is a staple food of the Africans. Some is exported to Zaire. In 1970, exports of fish derivatives reached 97,652 tons, worth 547,911,000 escudos.

SETTLEMENT SCHEMES

Of some note is the official scheme for settling metropolitan Portuguese peasants. These settlements (*colonatos*) have drawn much adverse comment from African nationalists and have raised somewhat unfounded hopes in Lisbon. The Cela scheme, which may have cost over 1,000 million escudos and has settled fewer than 500 families, is a typical example of over-optimistic planning. It has had limited success because of poor management, the low quality of the migrants and a general lack of administrative skill. The only tangible result has been the creation of a nucleus of 2,000 mildly prosperous Portuguese farmers between Luanda and Nova Lisboa.

A much more successful experiment has been the Matala scheme on the Cunene River, which settled approximately the same number of people by providing irrigated fields and richer crops. Official hopes are pinned on the harnessing, with South African assistance, of the Cunene River, but all the evidence suggests that village settlement of poor metropolitan peasants in the Angolan bush is motivated by political rather than by sound economic considerations. It is obvious that capital and modern techniques, rather than white farm-hands driving oxen, are essential to ensure the viability of this large-scale African agricultural scheme. In recent years, in an effort to insulate the African population from the guerrilla forces operating in the north-west and in the east, military and administrative authorities have launched a vast programme of re-grouping, arming, schooling and keeping close observation on the movements of rural people. More than one million people are affected. This has created huge problems, owing to poor administrative skills, authoritarian behaviour and, above all, to lack of preparation. Village life has been greatly disrupted in these areas. In the south, this programme has met with some resistance from the pastoralist tribes who see it as a means of evicting them from their traditional grazing lands.

MINERALS

Mining and manufacturing have long been lagging behind agriculture in the Angolan economy. This trend is being reversed as a result of new directions in investment policy in the 1960s. Three minerals are paramount, but some geologists hold the view that Angola is one of the richest countries of southern Africa. Diamonds are mined by the powerful Diamang company, which until recently had a near-monopoly. American and other investors have only recently been authorized to prospect outside the Diamang concession, which is active in the Lunda district at the Zairian border. About three-quarters of the production is gem stones, and Angola exports between four and five per cent of world diamond production. Diamang makes various contributions to the Angolan budget, among which is a 50 per cent share of the company profits. Angola exported more than two million carats in 1971, valued at 1,523,239,000 escudos, all of which went to Portugal where there is a diamond-cutting Diamang subsidiary in Lisbon.

A Belgian-owned company, Petrofina, struck oil in 1955 near Luanda. Subsequent financial transactions brought about the creation of Petrangol, which is jointly owned by the Province of Angola and Petrofina interests. Petrangol has constructed a 1,000,000-ton refinery in the suburbs of Luanda. The Angol and Texaco companies are also prospecting and drilling offshore near the Congo and Cuanza Rivers. Oil production, refining and distribution constitute the most important economic activity of Angola, and in 1970 exports were 5,065,000 tons, worth 1,736,000,000 escudos. But the greatest impetus to expansion came from the Cabinda Gulf Oil Company, which struck oil off-shore at Cabinda in 1966. Reserves of crude oil are estimated to be at least 300 million tons. Projected production is 150,000 barrels a day, twice the amount of Portugal's oil requirements. Further south, other French, Portuguese, American and South African interests are prospecting or investing in oil. It is certain that Angola has some of the most promising oil prospects in southern Africa, a factor which could reinforce a white south otherwise deficient in oil. In 1971, the value of oil production reached over 2,280 million escudos and a new Petrangol oilfield near the Congo mouth came into operation in 1972.

Iron mining started in 1956 and production averaged 700–800,000 tons annually in the 1960s from mines at Cuíma, Teixeira da Silva and Andulo in the Huambo and Bié districts. But the Cassinga mines in the Huíla district were the decisive factor in increasing production. The Cassinga mines, which belong to the Companhia Mineira do Lobito, have proven reserves of more than 1,000 million tons of high-grade haematite, and a railway spur has been built to link the mines with the Moçâmedes-Serpa Pinto railway. In 1971, 6,157,819 tons were exported, with a value of 1,292,986,000 escudos. The Krupp group of Essen and various German, Danish, Austrian and U.S. banks have participated in financing this development. The main buyers are Japan and West

Germany. A new harbour has been built north of Moçâmedes. Exports of seven million tons annually are envisaged through this modern harbour, where 50 tons of cargo can be loaded in one minute.

Other minerals abound. Copper-mining is to be resumed in the Uige district, and other deposits are known to exist in the Moçâmedes, Huíla and Moxico districts. Manganese ore is mined in the Malange district, 23,000 tons being exported in 1971. Work has begun on newly discovered gold-fields in southern Angola, where production was due to begin in 1972. Phosphate deposits exist in the Cabinda enclave; and salt is extracted along the coast. In short, Angola has a truly astonishing wealth of minerals which should ensure a viable economy, provided that the country can find investment and technical skill and recover its internal peace.

POWER

At the present time Angola's power potential exceeds its needs. In 1970 643,761,000 kWh. were produced and 548,859,000 consumed. Most of it is of hydroelectric origin, and there is an impressive dam on the Cuanza at Cambambe, which produced over 260,000,000 kWh. in 1970 and could easily double this figure. Aluminium smelting has been envisaged to take advantage of low-cost production. Luanda's industries are the main beneficiaries of Cambambe power. A formerly important dam at Mabubas on the Dande River was the first of Luanda's hydroelectric suppliers but is now largely disused. Further south, the Lobito-Benguela complex is provided with electricity by two privately owned dams, the Lomaum and the Biópio, both on the Catumbela River. Production was over 150,000,000 kWh. in 1970. Still further south, the Matala Dam serves the *colonato* Sá da Bandeira, Moçâmedes and Cassinga. However, this insufficiently productive project is only a minute part of the grandiose Portuguese-South African scheme for damming the Cunene River, thus providing South West Africa (Namibia), poor in power and water, with cheap electricity and a permanent water supply. The Gove dam in the Huambo course of the Cunene River is being completed with South African capital. A major power station at the Ruacaná Falls on the South West African border will regulate the river, irrigate Angola and Ovamboland in South West Africa, and provide cheap power for the Tsumeb mines and eventually for Walvis Bay. It is possible to accept a provisional figure for production of 1,000 million kWh. a year, but the prospect of settling Portuguese peasants in significant numbers seems less real. The Cunene scheme will be the Angolan counterpart of the Mozambican-South African Zambezi scheme.

INDUSTRY

Processing and manufacturing are assuming new importance as metropolitan manufacturers and authorities are loosening somewhat their traditional hold on the Angolan economy. The gross production value of manufacturing industries was 8,240 million escudos in 1970. Over 12 per cent of Angola's exports are now industrially processed products. Since 1962 the growth of industrial production has been 19 per cent per annum. Nevertheless, a great imbalance persists between bustling city ports, such as Luanda and Lobito, and stagnant inland cities. The food-processing industries are the most developed. In 1970 their production value was 2,622 million escudos. Beverages and tobacco manufactures are setting the pace, especially since the increase in the white population due to the introduction of more troops since 1961. Beverage production reached a value of 894 million escudos in 1970, and tobacco manufactures 385,636,000 escudos in 1970. Angolan beer is now a well-established beverage in this otherwise wine-importing country. Petroleum refineries processed 702,000 tons of crude oil in Luanda in 1970. Textiles have boomed since the ban on the creation of industries competing against metropolitan industries was lifted in 1966. Cotton is the chief staple and in 1970 textile industries occupied second place in Angola with 12.3 per cent of the manufacturing sector, worth 1,011 million escudos.

The low buying-power of the Africans is the main handicap to industry. Paper manufacturing, chemicals, glass, plastics, bicycles, car and truck assembly plants, and a project for the future mining of aluminium near the Cambambe Dam, in addition to cement and tyre production, are all evidence of a new spirit among Angolan, Portuguese and foreign investors. The results would be much more important if African consumers had more intensively entered the market economy.

The building trade is booming. In 1971, 1,580 houses and apartment blocks were completed. They were worth nearly 1,400 million escudos and half of them were in Luanda.

TRANSPORT AND TRADE

Angola has made a considerable effort to improve its communications network, the ultimate aim having been to link all fifteen district capitals by paved roads by the end of 1970. This goal was not reached, but the importance of all-weather roads is paramount to the development of the country and to its military operations. There were 5,317 kilometres of tarred roads in 1970, which hopefully should reach 8,500 kilometres by 1973 at a cost of over 500 million escudos. There are about 140,000 cars, trucks and motor cycles, and the road length was 45,817 kilometres in 1968.

Railways serve a dual purpose, to open the interior and to provide export channels for land-locked Shaba and Zambia, rich in minerals. Hence all railway lines run parallel and towards the coast. The Luanda and Moçâmedes railways are state-owned. The first is chiefly for local goods traffic and passengers, while the southern line is assuming a new importance as a carrier of iron ore from Cassinga. The central Benguela Railway (privately-owned) has international importance and is the strategic outlet for the Zairian and Zambian copper and zinc mines.

A stretch of new track, 150 kilometres long, is being laid in the Cubal area of the Benguela Railway. Most of the 1,934,000 passengers carried in 1970 were Ovimbundu. Other minor railways are of local importance. Total freight on Angolan railways was 8,791,015 tons in 1970.

Air transport is well developed, and 174,380 passengers were carried in 1971. A network of good airports or rural landing strips covers the province and would allow for prompt military reinforcements should the need arise. The main harbours are Lobito, Luanda and Moçâmedes, the latter outstripping the others in export tonnage, mostly iron ore. Another up-and-coming port is Cabinda.

External trade in 1970 saw an accentuation of the tendency evident in the previous year. Massive exports of iron and oil, coupled with record-breaking diamond exports, have reversed the 1967 and 1968 negative balance. Angola's trade balance is traditionally positive. In 1970 the country exported goods to the value of 12,172,187,000 escudos, and imported 10,594,665,000 escudos. Portugal is still by far the chief supplier of Angolan imports providing 35.12 per cent in 1970, followed by Federal Germany with 11.2 per cent and the United States with 10.9 per cent. Portugal is also the main buyer taking 34.3 per cent of total exports, followed by the United States with 15.6 per cent and the Netherlands with 10.8 per cent.

STATISTICAL SURVEY

AREA AND POPULATION

AREA (sq. km.)	POPULATION (1970 Census)	
	Total	Luanda (capital)
1,246,700	5,673,046*	475,328†

* In addition over 600,000 Angolan refugees live in exile, mostly in Zaire, and nationalist-held areas may contain over 100,000 people.

† Of which: 124,352 Whites, 36,431 Mestiços, 301,870 Blacks.

BIRTHS, MARRIAGES AND DEATHS
(1971)

CHURCH BAPTISMS	REGISTERED MARRIAGES	REGISTERED DEATHS
116,314	23,968	15,136

DISTRIBUTION OF POPULATION BY DISTRICT
(1970)

DISTRICT	AREA (sq. km.)	POPULATION	DENSITY (per sq. km.)
Cabinda	7,270	80,857	11.12
Zaire	40,130	41,766	1.04
Uíge	55,818	386,037	6.91
Luanda	33,789	560,589	16.59
Cuanza Norte	27,106	298,062	10.99
Cuanza Sul	59,269	458,592	7.73
Malanje	101,028	558,630	5.52
Lunda	167,786	302,538	1.80
Benguela	37,808	474,897	12.56
Huambo	30,667	837,627	27.31
Bié	71,870	650,337	9.04
Moxico	199,786	213,119	1.06
Cuando-Cubango	192,079	112,073	0.58
Moçâmedes	55,946	53,058	0.94
Huíla	166,348	644,864	3.87
TOTAL	1,246,700	5,673,046	4.55

OTHER MAIN TOWNS
POPULATION (1970 Census)

Nova Lisboa	61,885	Sa'da Bandeira	31,674
Lobito	59,528	Malange	31,599
Benguela	40,996	Cabinda	21,124

ECONOMICALLY ACTIVE POPULATION
(1960)

Agriculture, Forestry, Hunting, Fishing .	980,553
Mining and Quarrying	26,508
Manufacturing	86,012
Construction	56,990
Electricity, Gas, Water . . .	1,236
Commerce	63,737
Transport and Communications . .	30,273
Services	170,933
Others	5,724
TOTAL	1,421,966

AGRICULTURE

LAND USE*
('000 hectares)

Arable and Crops	900
Meadows and Pastures	29,000
Forests	43,200
Others	51,570
TOTAL	124,670

* As at 1953.

Source: FAO, *Production Yearbook 1971.*

PRINCIPAL CROPS

	AREA ('000 hectares)			PRODUCTION ('000 metric tons)			YIELD (100 kg. per hectare)		
	1969	1970	1971	1969	1970	1971	1969	1970	1971
Wheat . . .	20.0*	20.0*	20.0*	14.0	20.0	20.0*	7.0*	10.0*	10.0*
Maize . . .	600.0*	500.0*	530.0*	540.0	456.0	500.0*	9.0*	9.1*	9.4*
Millet and Sorghum .	91.0*	93.0*	93.0*	78.0	78.0	78.0	8.6*	8.4*	8.4*
Rice . . .	15.0*	25.0*	22.0*	16.0	39.0	34.0*	10.5*	15.5*	15.5*
Potatoes . .	5.0*	5.0*	5.0*	34.0	34.0	34.0*	63.0*	63.0*	63.0*
Sweet Potatoes, Yams .	17.0*	18.0*	n.a.	145.0	147.0	n.a.	85.0*	82.0*	n.a.
Cassava (Manioc) .	120.0*	120.0*	n.a.	1,590.0	1,600.0	n.a.	133.0*	133.0*	n.a.
Dry Beans . .	120.0*	120.0*	120.0*	64.0	66.0	65.0*	5.3*	5.5*	5.4*
Oranges, Tangerines .	n.a.	n.a.	n.a.	81.0	82.0	82.0*	n.a.	n.a.	n.a.
Palm Kernels .	n.a.	n.a.	n.a.	17.5	15.4	15.4*	n.a.	n.a.	n.a.
Palm Oil . .	n.a.	n.a.	n.a.	38.0	38.0	38.0*	n.a.	n.a.	n.a.
Groundnuts .	47.0*	47.0*	47.0*	32.0	32.0	32.0*	6.8*	6.8*	6.8*
Cottonseed . .	72.0	79.0	89.0	47.0	61.0	66.0	6.5	7.7	7.4
Sesame Seed .	6.0*	6.0*	6.0*	2.0	2.0*	2.0	3.3*	3.3*	3.3*
Castor Beans .	13.0*	13.0*	13.0*	5.0	5.0	5.0*	3.8*	3.8*	3.8*
Coffee . .	n.a.	n.a.	n.a.	215.0	204.0	210.0*	n.a.	n.a.	n.a.
Tobacco . .	5.0	6.0	6.0	4.1	5.0	5.5	7.8	7.7	8.5
Cotton (lint) .	72.0	79.0	89.0	23.0	30.0	33.0	3.3	3.8	3.7
Kenaf . .	2.0*	2.0*	2.0*	2.0*	2.0*	2.0*	10.0*	10.0*	10.0*
Sisal . .	70.0*	70.0*	n.a.	67.5	68.4	53.0	9.6*	9.8*	n.a.
Sugar Cane† . .	14.0*	14.0*	15.0*	685.0	683.0	764.0	489.0*	488.0*	499.0*

* FAO estimate.   † Crop year ending in year stated.

Source: FAO, *Production Yearbook 1971.*

COTTON PRODUCTION
(tons)

	UNGINNED COTTON	COTTON FIBRE
1961	13,099	4,323
1962	22,500	7,425
1963	13,700	4,521
1964	13,609	4,491
1965	19,506	6,437
1966	20,308	6,719
1967	27,361	9,032
1968	38,867	12,826
1969	60,057	19,820
1970	81,555	28,819
1971	86,013	35,478

COFFEE PRODUCTION
(tons)

VARIETIES	1969	1970	1971
Robusta:			
Ambriz . .	147,000	131,400	
Amboim . .	41,100	42,100	
Cazengo . .	17,000	21,300	n.a.
Cabinda . .	1,800	1,800	
Arábica . . .	8,100	7,400	
TOTAL . .	215,000	204,000	210,000*

* FAO estimate.

DAIRY PRODUCE

	1970	1971
Milk (litres) . . .	24,454,990	22,948,000
Butter (kg.) . . .	489,330	455,000
Cheese (kg.) . . .	857,505	1,443,000

LIVESTOCK

	1969	1970	1971
Cattle . .	2,171,144	2,727,000	2,994,000
Goats . .	759,276	821,000	878,000
Pigs . .	319,578	332,000	342,000
Sheep . .	161,197	171,000	184,000

FORESTRY
ROUNDWOOD PRODUCTION
('ooo cu. metres)

1968 . . .	6,349
1969 . . .	6,459
1970 . . .	6,500

FISHING
TOTAL CATCH
(metric tons)

1968 . . .	293,409
1969 . . .	417,450
1970 . . .	377,770

MINING
(metric tons)

	1968	1969	1970	1971
Haematite Iron Ore . . .	3,218,212	5,477,657	6,090,888	6,157,819
Manganese Ore . . .	9,150	29,070	23,000	23,000
Crude Petroleum . . .	749,514	2,457,512	5,065,105	5,721,331
Diamonds (carats) . . .	1,667,133	2,021,532	2,395,552	2,413,021
Asphalt Rock . . .	30,603	39,282	36,956	56,100
Sea Salt . . .	72,496	80,181	87,743	90,284
Gypsum . . .	10,160	n.a.	n.a.	n.a.

INDUSTRY
(metric tons)

	1969	1970	1971
Sugar	65,737	78,766	76,073
Beer ('ooo litres) .	60,811	70,794	81,907
Fishmeal .	98,921	74,151	72,488
Cement .	382,759	446,249	529,594
Cotton Blankets (number) .	640,000	579,000	679,000
Flour . .	60,956	68,439	72,023
Soap . . .	13,365	14,810	15,168
Tobacco . .	2,106	2,025	2,188
Butane . .	6,271	7,382	7,043
Fuel Oil .	389,265	391,679	388,847
Gas Oil .	98,389	98,377	100,807
Motor Spirit .	61,696	56,118	52,385
Paraffin . .	7,518	n.a.	n.a.
Asphalt . .	11,000	13,499	16,733

FINANCE

100 centavos = 1 Angolan escudo; 1,000 escudos = 1 conto.

Coins: 50 centavos; 1, 2.50, 10 and 20 escudos.

Notes: 20, 50, 100, 500 and 1,000 escudos.

Exchange rates: £1 sterling = 62.90 escudos (December 1972); 100 escudos = £1.59.

U.S. $1 = 27.02 escudos (August 1972); 100 escudos = $3.70.

ORDINARY BUDGET
('ooo escudos)

ORDINARY RECEIPTS	1971	1972	ORDINARY EXPENDITURE	1971	1972
Direct Taxes . . .	1,155,001	1,283,501	Provincial Debt . .	546,330	616,848
Indirect Taxes . .	1,833,000	2,163,000	Governments, etc. . .	38,840	45,394
Special Duties . .	1,140,201	1,766,399	Pensions, etc. . .	110,000	125,000
Dues, Service Returns .	538,006	641,666	Administration . .	2,363,249	2,941,054
State Enterprises, etc. .	401,120	371,940	Treasury . . .	215,272	242,586
Capital Returns, etc. .	84,760	74,670	Justice . . .	145,003	154,309
Repayments, etc. .	148,296	175,173	Development . .	3,097,620	3,517,854
Miscellaneous . .	3,390,534	3,756,359	Defence . . .	796,176	876,970
			Navy . . .	50,058	51,701
			Miscellaneous . .	1,317,370	1,648,016
			Other . . .	11,000	12,976
TOTAL . . .	8,690,918	10,238,708	TOTAL . . .	8,690,918	10,238,708

EXTRAORDINARY BUDGET
('ooo escudos)

EXTRAORDINARY RECEIPTS	1970	1971
Development Plans . .	895,000	1,174,000
Loan from Metropolitan Portugal	155,000	155,000
Overvaluation Tax . .	110,000	110,000
Receipts from Development Fund . . .	70,000	65,000
Share in the Income of Companhia de Diamantes de Angola . . .	230,000	—
Overseas Development Promissories . . .	80,000	120,000
Bonds	250,000	100,000
Balance of Accounts of Previous Periods . .	—	316,500
Loan from Banco de Angola	—	300,000
Coinage Profits . .	—	7,500
Other Extraordinary Receipts	658,653	733,444
Extraordinary Defence Tax	350,000	350,000
Balance of Accounts of Previous Periods . .	200,000	213,000
Receipts from Development Fund . . .	108,653	120,000
Tax on Increased Value .	—	50,444
TOTAL . . .	1,553,653	1,907,444

EXTRAORDINARY EXPENDITURE	1970	1971
Development Plan . .	895,000	1,174,000
Agriculture, Forestry and Stockbreeding . .	76,900	135,620
Fisheries . . .	35,130	8,300
Extractive and Manufacturing Industries . .	81,275	40,400
Rural Improvements . .	48,500	60,250
Electricity . . .	98,710	100,730
Distribution circuits .	2,100	500
Transports, Communications and Meteorology .	308,310	450,660
Tourism . . .	5,000	4,500
Education and Research .	141,555	240,790
Housing and Urbanization .	30,000	46,900
Health and Public Assistance	67,520	85,350
Other Extraordinary Expenditure	658,653	733,444
National Defence—Armed Forces . . .	425,000	450,000
Buildings and Monuments .	36,000	44,000
Subsidies for Local Improvements . . .	20,000	20,000
Expenditure on Works and Supplies for Transport of Ores in South Angola .	25,000	24,000
Expenditure Resulting from Supplies of Material by "General Trade" . .	24,000	36,780
Others . . .	128,653	158,664
TOTAL . . .	1,553,653	1,907,444

DEVELOPMENT EXPENDITURE
(1968–73—million escudos)

Agriculture, Forestry and Fishing . .	2,041
Mining	11,600
Transport and Communications . .	3,779
Manufacturing Industry . .	3,361
Education and Research . .	1,358
Power Supplies	1,238
Other Development . . .	2,007
	25,384

MILITARY EXPENDITURE 1971
(million escudos)

SOURCE OF FINANCING	
Territory's Ordinary Budget . . .	580.0
Autonomous Bodies . . .	249.2
Extraordinary Tax for Defence of Angola .	350.0
Special Credit to be Authorized During 1971	270.8
Overseas Military Defence Fund .	67.0
Contribution from Portugal's Extraordinary Budget	250.0
Other	151.0
TOTAL	1,918.0

In addition, territorial budget estimates for 1971 include 618.0 million escudos for other military and security expenditure.

Source: UN General Assembly document A/8723/Add. **3**, September 1st, 1972.

THIRD NATIONAL DEVELOPMENT PLAN 1968–73
Financing Programmes of the Overseas Territories
1968 and 1969
(million escudos)

SOURCES	1968	1969
National Sources . .	5,731.3	6,305.1
1. Government . .	3,060.8	3,014.0
Central . . .	1,079.7	679.5
Territorial . .	1,582.4	1,099.7
Autonomous Bodies .	16.4	801.8
Beira Railway .	97.0	82.5
Other . . .	285.3	350.4
2. Credit Institutions .	574.2	524.1
3. Private Companies .	2,096.3	2,767.1
External (Foreign) . .	2,768.7	4,170.0
1. Financing or for Purchase of Equipment	207.7	1,800.0
2. Direct Investments .	2,561.0	2,370.0
TOTAL . .	8,500.0	10,475.013

INTERNATIONAL BALANCE OF PAYMENTS OF THE ESCUDO ZONE
(million escudos)

	PORTUGAL		OVERSEAS TERRITORIES		ESCUDO ZONE	
	1969	1970	1969	1970	1969	1970
Trade	−16,926	−20,475	2,424	1,859	−14,502	−18,616
Invisibles	14,053	19,548	2,043	870	16,096	20,418
TOTAL CURRENT TRANSACTIONS .	− 2,873	− 927	4,467	2,729	1,594	1,802
Capital Movements . .	616	968	−849	−453	− 233	515
Errors, Omissions . . .	313	323	− 31	−109	282	214
TOTAL	− 1,944	364	3,587	2,167	1,643	2,531

BALANCE OF PAYMENTS OF PORTUGAL WITH OVERSEAS PROVINCES
(million escudos)

	1969			1970		
	Debit	Credit	Balance	Debit	Credit	Balance
CURRENT TRANSACTIONS	7,779	12,246	4,467	9,394	12,123	2,729
Merchandise	3,392	5,816	2,424	3,962	5,821	1,859
Current invisibles . . .	4,387	6,430	2,043	5,432	6,302	870
Tourism	12	494	482	24	552	528
Transport . . .	48	286	238	41	255	214
Insurance . . .	10	60	50	6	29	23
Capital revenue . .	107	1,170	1,063	46	945	899
State	3,728	2,992	−736	5,099	3,200	−1,899
Private transfers . .	115	815	700	79	771	692
Other services and payments .	367	613	246	137	550	413
CAPITAL OPERATIONS . . .			−849			− 453
Short term			66			6
Long term	1,590	675	−915	1,341	882	− 459
Private sector . . .	658	387	−271	307	268	− 39
Public sector . . .	932	288	−644	1,034	614	− 420
Errors and Omissions . . .			− 31			− 109
TOTAL			3,587			2,167

ANGOLA'S BALANCE OF PAYMENTS
(million escudos)

	1970			1971		
	Credit	Debit	Balance	Credit	Debit	Balance
Goods	9,196	10,271	−1,075	9,166	11,388	−2,222
Tourism	40	506	− 466	44	556	− 512
Transport	924	332	592	878	308	570
Insurance	17	21	− 4	20	23	− 3
Capital Earnings	43	671	− 628	13	210	− 197
Official Transfers	744	213	531	625	347	278
Private Transfers	12	342	− 330	14	324	− 310
Other Services	1,274	1,255	19	1,316	803	513
CURRENT ACCOUNT	12,250	13,611	−1,361	12,076	13,959	−1,883
Capital Account	1,058	457	601	877	807	70
COMBINED CURRENT AND CAPITAL ACCOUNT	13,308	14,068	− 760	12,953	14,766	−1,813

EXTERNAL TRADE
(excluding gold)
('000 escudos)

	1967	1968	1969	1970	1971
Imports	7,908,680	8,709,858	9,261,398	10,594,665	12,127,735
Exports	6,837,800	7,787,946	9,387,420	12,172,187	11,788,084

PRINCIPAL COMMODITIES

IMPORTS	1969	1970	1971
Vehicles and Accessories	933,573	1,017,683	1,392,909
Iron and Steel	781,253	849,372	996,453
Textiles	542,145	523,239	516,007
Wine	556,086	578,796	405,457
Tractors	201,095	223,820	290,492
Clothing	141,146	173,000	268,054
Wheat	110,882	139,690	160,220
Locomotives, etc.	164,353	72,117	57,768
Medicaments	296,232	363,698	n.a.
Petroleum Products	267,200	n.a.	n.a.
Excavating Machinery	185,770	n.a.	n.a.
Internal Combustion Engines	112,160	n.a.	n.a.
Edible Oil	103,040	n.a.	n.a.

EXPORTS	1969	1970	1971
Coffee	3,234,435	3,879,997	4,029,018
Crude Petroleum	485,110	1,397,378	1,811,551
Diamonds	1,843,173	2,340,087	1,523,239
Iron Ore	1,098,718	1,422,529	1,188,231
Raw Cotton	329,751	421,711	648,538
Sisal	196,821	237,640	221,192
Fish Meal for Cattle	347,210	288,716	209,340
Wood	224,104	198,679	189,273
Maize	305,129	314,588	171,809
Fuel Oil	99,083	117,639	155,465
Dried Fish	84,700	107,055	128,097
Wood Pulp	92,385	111,465	114,636
Palm Oil	48,345	62,491	63,849
Tobacco and Products	51,385	53,864	61,455
Coconut	42,558	46,415	26,544
Bananas	75,130	118,366	n.a.
Manioc	58,401	49,132	n.a.
Sugar	51,065	42,158	n.a.
Dried Beans	46,664	42,668	n.a.

TRADE BALANCE BY PRINCIPAL AREAS
(1961–68—million escudos)

	1964	1965	1966	1967	1968	1969	1970	1971
Foreign Countries	1,627.3	708.1	636.6	− 735.1	−399.0	−199.6	901.5	−380.2
Portugal	−552.8	−638.3	−278.1	− 518.1	497.8	75.8	444.8	−170.2
Other Portuguese Territories	− 12.9	− 28.9	− 49.5	36.5	− 14.4	73.5	20.9	− 58.2
Others*	91.7	105.3	102.8	145.8	189.3	176.8	210.3	269.6
NET TRADE BALANCE	1,153.3	146.2	411.8	−1,070.9	−921.9	126.0	1,577.5	−339.7

* Includes mainly supplies to navigation.

PRINCIPAL COUNTRIES

IMPORTS	1969	1970	1971
Portugal	3,421,746	3,728,308	3,832,307
Mozambique	170,479	187,321	}448,158
Macao	71,386	112,404	
Other Portuguese Territories	4,584	3,427	
Belgium-Luxembourg	343,289	305,248	393,944
Denmark	52,909	128,994	111,745
France	456,055	570,618	556,849
Federal Republic of Germany	965,301	1,185,282	1,378,987
Iran	188,159	145,691	n.a.
Italy	270,143	336,552	453,729
Japan	423,934	459,426	673,776
Netherlands	129,007	144,880	266,777
Norway	43,417	95,444	114,689
South Africa	294,064	419,761	443,460
Spain	91,317	84,387	167,175
Sweden	128,531	146,981	155,743
Switzerland	114,090	118,051	152,365
United Kingdom	837,074	992,597	1,092,233
U.S.A.	975,948	1,149,957	1,339,616

[continued on next page

PRINCIPAL COUNTRIES—*continued*]

EXPORTS	1969	1970	1971
Portugal	3,497,007	4,173,095	3,662,148
Mozambique	165,202	206,585	
Cape Verde Islands	89,687	52,581	
São Tomé and Príncipe . . .	51,356	50,337	390,001
Other Portuguese Territories . .	13,736	14,554	
Belgium-Luxembourg . . .	76,136	125,191	172,589
Canada	157,350	249,538	n.a.
Denmark	134,906	407,664	343,609
France	136,852	151,723	193,734
Federal Republic of Germany . .	753,812	771,648	319,521
Italy	78,070	79,760	93,112
Japan	437,958	797,606	1,192,663
Netherlands	1,076,319	1,318,157	863,134
South Africa	141,252	146,493	162,227
Spain	339,608	560,689	404,254
Sudan	107,576	—	n.a.
United Kingdom	171,361	431,783	178,353
U.S.A.	1,475,710	1,898,618	2,379,666
Zaire	54,990	143,507	144,155

TRANSPORT
RAILWAYS

	PASSENGERS CARRIED		FREIGHT (metric tons)	
	1970	1971	1970	1971
Luanda Railway . . .	526,634	693,285	406,232	400,686
Moçâmedes Railway . . .	238,980	272,128	6,455,201	6,405,607
Benguela Railway . . .	1,143,196	1,214,503	1,921,037	2,050,183

ROADS
(Motor Vehicles)

	1970	1971
Cars	87,001	102,604
Lorries	22,283	23,604
Motor Cycles . . .	17,383	18,386
Tractors . . .	7,113	8,108
TOTAL . . .	133,780	152,702

SHIPPING
('000 metric tons)

	LUANDA		LOBITO		MOÇÂMEDES		ANGOLA	
	1970	1971	1970	1971	1970	1971	1970	1971
Goods Loaded . . .	966.5	798.6	935.5	957.2	6,253.3	5,481.7	12,623.7	12,431.7
Goods Unloaded . .	704.4	712.7	738.7	962.1	154.1	183.3	1,720.3	2,033.5

Vessels handled: (1970) 5,359; (1971) 5,769.

CIVIL AVIATION
(Angola Airlines—DTA)

	1970	1971
Passengers Carried	146,765	174,380
Freight Transported (tons)	2,217	2,768
Mail Transported (tons)	1,102	892
Kilometres Flown	4,024,988	4,720,743

EDUCATION
(1970–71)

TYPE OF INSTITUTION	NUMBER OF SCHOOLS	NUMBER OF TEACHERS	NUMBER OF PUPILS
Primary	4,651	10,065	440,985
Secondary Academic	159	2,603	43,174
Secondary Technical	60	1,023	12,620
Ecclesiastic	9	96	937
University	1	225	2,088

Sources: Agência-Geral do Ultramar, Lisbon; Banco de Angola; Direcciás Provincial dos Servicos de Estatística, Luanda.

THE CONSTITUTION

In December 1970 the Portuguese Prime Minister, Dr. Caetano, announced changes in the status of Angola and Mozambique. They will have their own elected government with legislative powers, the right to negotiate their own contracts and raise taxes, and the right to refuse admission into their territories of Portuguese nationals and foreigners.

In September 1971 the Portuguese Government postponed legislative elections in the Overseas Provinces because of the impending changes in their constitutions. In January 1972 a proposed Organic Law was published, renaming Angola and Mozambique "States" and giving each a legislative assembly, as well as an advisory council which will have more autonomy in administering internal Provincial affairs. Legislative assemblies will meet twice a year, but not for more than four months at a time. The Governor-General of each Province will be equivalent in status to a Minister of State anywhere in the Metropole or Overseas Provinces, and can be present at Cabinet meetings. He will be assisted by a consultative council and will hold office for four years. The Portuguese National Assembly approved the Law on May 1st, 1972.

By special decrees of February 1955 and April and October 1961, the Province was divided into 15 districts as follows: Cabinda, Uige, Zaire, Luanda, Cuanza Norte, Cuanza Sul, Malange, Lunda, Benguela, Huambo, Bié, Cuando Cubango, Moxico, Moçâmedes and Huila. Each district is again divided into regions supervised by an administrator who acts as the resident magistrate.

THE GOVERNMENT

Governor-General: FERNANDO AUGUSTO SANTOS E CASTRO.

Commander-in-Chief of Portuguese Armed Forces in Angola: Gen. JOAQUIM LUZ CUNHA.

Commander of Portuguese Army in Angola: Gen. ERNESTO MACHADO DE OLIVEIRA DE SOUSA.

Legislative Council. Composed of 34 elected members (15 elected by direct popular vote) and two ex-officio members (the Procurator of the Republic and the Director of the Provincial Finance and Accounts Services).

Economic and Social Council. Composed of eight elected members, four government appointments and six permanent members (the Commanders-in-Chief of the Armed Forces, the Principal of the University and the Directors of the services of Civil Administration, Economy and Education).

POLITICAL PARTIES

Camissão de Província da Acçao Nacional Popular: Caixa Postal 1299, Rua Duarte Pacheco Pereira 16-2°, Apt. 52/55, Luanda; Portuguese government party; Pres. Dr. GUSTAVO NETO MIRANDA; Sec. FRANCISCO T. VENANCIO RODRIGUES; publ. *Boletim dos Filiados.*

The following organizations have all been declared illegal by the Portuguese Government:

Conferência das Organizações Nacionais das Colónias Portuguesas (CONCP): 18 rue Dirah, Hydra, Algiers, Algeria; f. 1961; central organization for MPLA, Angola, FRELIMO, Mozambique, PAIGC, Guinea, CLSTP, São Tomé.

Concelho Supremo de Libertação de Angola (CSLA) (*Angola Supreme Liberation Council*): Kinshasa, Zaire; f. 1972 by a union of the FNLA and the MPLA; meets at least twice a year; Pres. HOLDEN ROBERTO; Vice-Pres. AGOSTINHO NETO.

Frente Nacional de Libertação de Angola (FNLA) (*Angolan National Liberation Front*): Kinshasa, Zaire; f. 1962 by union of the *União dos Populações de Angola* and the *Partido Democrático Angolano*; have set up a Government-in-exile (GRAE); Leader HOLDEN ROBERTO.

Movimento Popular de Libertação de Angola (MPLA) (*Angola Popular Liberation Movement*): P.O.B. 1595, Lusaka, Zambia; f. 1956; Pres. AGOSTINHO NETO.

União Nacional para e Independência Total de Angola (UNITA) (*National Union for the Complete Independence of Angola*): Headquarters in Bié province; f. 1966; Leader Dr. JONAS SAVIMBI.

União dos Populações de Angola (UPA): Kinshasa, Zaire; f. 1954; formed the FNLA with *Partido Democrático Angolano* in 1962; Leader HOLDEN ROBERTO.

DEFENCE

Portugal has direct control of Angolan defence and has an army of 70,000 stationed in the country.

Commander-in-Chief of Portuguese Armed Forces in Angola: Gen. JOAQUIM LUZ CUNHA.

Commander of Portuguese Army in Angola: Gen. ERNESTO MACHADO DE OLIVEIRA DE SOUSA.

JUDICIAL SYSTEM

Courts of First Instance. These administer the Legal Code of Metropolitan Portugal. Cases may be finally referred to the Court of Second Instance and the Supreme Court in Lisbon.

RELIGION

Most of the population follow traditional beliefs.

ROMAN CATHOLIC CHURCH

Metropolitan See:

Archbishop of Luanda	Most Rev. MANUEL NUNES GABRIEL, Caixa Postal 1230, Luanda.
Auxiliary Bishop	Mgr. EDUARDO ANDRÉ MUACA.

Suffragan Sees:

Benguela	Rt. Rev. ARMAND AMARAL DOS SANTOS Caixa Postal 670, Benguela.
Carmona-São Salvador	Rt. Rev. JOSÉ FRANCISCO MOREIRA DOS SANTOS, Caixa Postal 239, Carmona.
Luso	Rt. Rev. FRANCISCO ESTEVES DIAS, Caixa Postal 88, Luso.
Melanje	Rt. Rev. POMPEU DE SÁ LEÃO Y SEABRA, Caixa Postal 192, Malanje.
Nova Lisboa	(vacant), Caixa Postal 10, Nova Lisboa.
Sá da Bandeira	Rt. Rev. ALTINO RIBEIRO DE SANTANA, Caixa Postal 231, Sá de Bandeira.
São Tomé e Príncipe	(vacant), Caixa Postal 146, São Tomé.
Silva Porto	Rt. Rev. MANUEL ANTÓNIO PIRES, Caixa Postal 16, Silva Porto.

There are 170 missions with a personnel of 1,388; Roman Catholics number about 2,236,959.

The Baptists have a number of missionary stations. There are about 796,695 Protestants.

THE PRESS

DAILIES

A Província de Angola: Caixa Postal 1312; f. 1923; owned by the Empresa Gráfica de Angola; Dir. RUY CORREIA DE FREITAS; circ. 41,000.

Diario de Luanda: Caixa Postal 1290; Rua Serpa Pinto, Luanda; f. 1930; owned by Gráfica Portugal, Editor BELMIRO DE OLIVEIRA VIEIRA; circ. 8,000.

O Comércio: Caixa Postal 1225; owned by the Nova Editorial Angolana; Dir. A. FERREIRA DA COSTA; circ. 10,000.

A.B.C.—Diario de Angola: Caixa Postal 1245; f. 1958; Dir. Col. BRAGA PAIXÃO; evening; circ. 3,000.

Boletim Oficial de Angola: Caixa Postal 1306, Luanda; f. 1845.

PERIODICALS

O Lobito: Caixa Postal 335, Lobito; Dir. CARLOS MIMOSO MOREIRA.

Intransigente: Caixa Postal 104, Benguela; twice weekly.

Jornal de Benguela: Caixa Postal 17, Benguela; Dir. HORÁCIO SILVA; twice weekly.

Jornal do Congo: Caixa Postal 329, Carmona; Dir. Dr. ANTÓNIO BORJA SANTOS; weekly; circ. 5,000.

O Apostolado: Caixa Postal 1230, Luanda; Dir. ALVES PEREIRA; published by the Catholic Missions of Portugal; twice weekly.

A Huila: Caixa Postal 539, Sá da Bandeira; weekly; Dir. Dr. RICARDO SIMÕES NUÑES.

Jornal da Huila: Caixa Postal 1322, Sá da Bandeira; Dir. VENÂNCIO GUIMÃRES SOBRINHO; weekly.

Noticia: Caixa Postal 6518, Luanda; circ. 35,000; weekly; Dir. Dr. JOÃO BATISTA DOS SANTOS.

A Voz do Bié: Caixa Postal 131, Silva Porto; f. 1961; weekly; Dir. Father JOSÉ DOS REIS RAMOS.

Angola Norte: Caixa Postal 339, Malange; weekly; Dir. Dr. ANTONIO MARGÃO ROBALO.

O Planalto: Caixa Postal 96, Nova Lisboa; twice weekly; Dr. ALTINO VAZ MONTEIRO.

O Namibe: Caixa Postal 328, Moçâmedes; twice weekly; Dir. MANUEL JOÃO TENREIRO CARNEIRO.

O Moxico: Caixa Postal 362, Luso; weekly; Dir. FERREIRA DA SILVA.

Angola Desportiva: Caixa Postal 6375, Luanda; weekly; Dir FERNANDO LAIMA.

Actualidade Economica: Caixa Postal 16462; weekly; Dir. ANTONIO PIRES.

Semana Ilustrada: Caixa Postal 2039, Luanda; weekly; Dir. Dr. FERNANDO DAVID LAIMA.

Revista de Angola: Caixa Postal 6446, Luanda; fortnightly; Dir. F. ARAUJO RODRIGUES.

Jornal Magazine: Caixa Postal 1098, Luanda; weekly; Dir. Dr. VICTOR HOMEN DE ALMEIDA.

PUBLISHERS

Imprensa Nacional de Angola: Caixa Postal 1306, Luanda; f. 1845; Gen. Man. Dr. ANTÓNIO DUARTE DE ALMEIDA E CARMO.

Empresa Gráfica de Angola: Caixa Postal 1312, Luanda; f. 1923, Dir. RUY CORREIA DE FREITAS, publ. *A Provincia de Angola* (daily).

Gráfica Portugal, Lda.: Caixa Postal 1290, Rua Serpa Pinto, Luanda; f. 1930; owners of *Diario de Luanda*.

NEA—Nova Editorial Angolana, S.A.R.L.: Caixa Postal 1225, Luanda; f. 1935; Man. M. POMBO FERNANDES; cap. 2om.; publ. *O Comercio*, 10,000 copies.

Gráfica de Benguela: Benguela.

Empresa Gráfica do Uige, Lda.: Caixa Postal 329, Carmona; f. 1958; Editor LUIZ M. RODRIGUES; circ. 4,500 publ. *Jornal do Congo* (weekly).

Gráfica de Planalto: Nova Lisboa.

Neográfica Lda.: Caixa Postal 6518, Luanda; publ. *Noticia Offset*; Caixa Postal 344, Luanda.

Industrias: A.B.C. Caixa Postal 1245, Luanda.

RADIO AND TELEVISION

RADIO

Emissora Oficial de Angola: Caixa Postal 1329, Luanda; f. 1953; government station; Dir. JOÃO ANTÓNIA DE OLIVEIRA PIRES.

Radio Clube de Angola: Caixa Postal 229, Luanda; commercial station; Pres. Com. M. DE ALBUQUERUQE E CASTRO.

Radio Comercial de Angola: C.P. 269, Sá de Bandeira; commercial station; Dir. M. F. DE ALMEIDA.

Radio Diamang: C.P. 1247, Dundo; private station owned by Companhia de Diamantes de Angola; Dir. Eng. JOÃO AUGUSTO BEXIGA.

Radio Eclesia: Caixa Postal 156, Luanda; religious station; Dir Padre J. M. PEREIRA.

There are 12 other commercial stations.

There are 100,000 radio receivers.

There is no television.

FINANCE

(cap.=capital; dep.=deposits; m.=million; amounts in escudos)

BANKING

Banco de Angola: 10 rua da Prata, Lisbon; Caixa Postal 1298, Luanda; central bank; f. 1926; cap. 300m.; dep. 19,488m. (Dec. 1971); Gov. Dr. MÁRIO ANGELO MORAIS DE OLIVEIRA.

Banco Comercial de Angola: Rua Visconde Pinheiro, Caixa Postal 1343, Luanda; f. 1956; cap. and res. 356m., dep. 4,709,504; Pres. A. CUPERTINO DE MIRANDA; Gen. Man. Dir. Dr. J. MANUEL NUNES DA GLORIA.

Banco de Crédito Comercial e Industrial: Av. dos Restauradores de Angola 79/83, Caixa Postal 1395, Luanda; f. 1965; cap. 200m., dep. 4,937m. (Dec. 1972); Chair. Dr. MIGUEL GENTIL QUINA; Man. Ing. ANIBAL TASSO DE FIGUEIREDO FARO VIANA; 61 brs. in Angola, 44 in Mozambique.

Banco de Fomento Nacional: P.O.B. 6191, Luanda.

Banco Interunidos: formed by Banco Espíritu Santo e Comercial de Lisboa and First National City Bank.

Banco Pinto e Sotto Mayor, S.A.R.L.: 28 Rua Áurea, Lisbon; Av. Paulo Dias de Novais 86, Luanda; f. 1914; Pres. EDUARDO FURTADO; cap. 500m., dep. 25,002m. (1970); 57 brs. in Angola, 45 brs. in Mozambique.

Banco Totta-Standard de Angola: Av. Paulo Dias de Novais No. 127, C.P. 5554, Luanda; f. 1966; associate of Totta and Açores and Standard and Charter Banking Group; cap. 150,000; dep. 1,506m.; Joint Man. Dirs. Dr. J. L. VAZ TECEDEIRO, J. J. H. VERMEULEN.

Caixa de Crédito Agro-Pecuário de Angola: Luanda, Caixa Postal 6080; f. 1961; cap. U.S. $8.5m.; agricultural loan bank; Gen. Man. Dr. PEDRO DE OLIVEIRA SIMÕES.

INSURANCE

Montepio Geral de Angola (*Mutual Aid Association*): Head Office: Largo D. João IV, No. 16, Luanda, Caixa Postal 402; f. 1933; Pres. RAFAEL GARCIA IBOLEON, Jr.; Sec. ALTINO AMADEU MAMEDE DE SOUSA E SILVA.

Cia. de Seguros Angola, S.A.R.L.: Av. Paulo Dias de Novais, 37, 1° Caixa Postal 721-C, Luanda; f. 1946; cap. 1om.; Chair. Compte V. LOPES ALVES; Sec. Dr. JOSÉ FRANCISCO RAMOS COSTA; Dir.-Gen. Dr. FERNANDO MOUZACO DIAS.

Confiança Mundial de Angola—Seguros: Av. Paulo Dias de Novais 93, Caixa Postal 500, Luanda.

Cia. de Seguros A Nacional de Angola, S.A.R.L.: Ave. Paulo Dias de Novais, 89-Luanda; P.O.B. 2921; f. 1957; cap. Esc. 27,500,000; Admin. A. LEITE DE MAGALHÃES; sub-directors: FRANCISCO A. RIBEIRO, A. RODRIGUES MOREIRA.

Cia. de Seguros Angolana, S.A.R.L.: Avenida Paulo Dias de Novais 84, Caixa Postal 738, Luanda; f. 1946; cap. $1om.; Dir. S. CARDOSO DE PINA.

Cia. Seguros Garantia Africa, S.A.R.L.: Caixa Postal 2726, Luanda; f. 195.; cap. and res. 73m.; Man. Dir. Dr. J. J. GOMES PEREIRA.

Cia. de Seguros Universal de Angola, S.A.R.L.: Caixa Postal 2987 and 12010/M, Luanda; f. 1957; cap. 15m.; Gen. Man. MANUEL MARIA DA FONSECA FREITAS; Dir. LUÍS JOSÉ PAIVA DE CARVALHO.

Cia. de Seguros Nauticos de Angola. S.A.R.L.: Rua Governador Eduardo Costa 69, Caixa Postal 5059, Luanda.

There are a number of Portuguese companies represented in Angola.

TRADE AND INDUSTRY

COMMISSIONS AND NATIONAL BOARDS

Direcção dos Serviços de Comércio (*Department of Trade*): Largo Diogo Cão, C.P. 1337, Luanda; f. 1970; Dir. ANTÓNIO AUGUSTO DE ALMEIDA; brs. throughout Angola.

Instituto dos Cereais de Angola (*Cereals Institute*): Caixa Postal 65, Luanda; Dir. M. DO VALE.

Instituto do Café de Angola (*Coffee Institute*): Caixa Postal 342, Luanda; Dir. E. DE A. NORONHA.

Instituto do Algodão de Angola (*Cotton Institute*): Caixa Postal 74, Luanda; f. 1938; Dir. M. A. CORRÊA DE PINHO.

Instituto das Industrias de Pesca (*Fishing Institute*): Caixa Postal 83, Luanda; Dir. Com. LUIS GONZAGA CLEMENTE DOS REIS.

CHAMBERS OF COMMERCE

Câmara Municipal de Carmona: Carmona; Pres. MANUEL JOAQUIM MONTANHA PINTO.

Câmara Municipal de Nova Lisboa: Nova Lisboa; budget for 1972 89,000 contos.

EMPLOYERS' AND LABOUR ORGANIZATIONS

Associação dos Agricultores de Angola (*Agriculturists' Association*): Luanda; Pres. Dr. ANTONIO MANUEL DA SILVA FERREIRA.

Associação dos Logistas de Luanda: Caixa Postal 1278.

Associação Industrial de Angola: Caixa Postal 1296, Luanda; f. 1930; publ. *Boletim da Associação Industrial de Angola* (weekly).

Associação Comercial de Luanda: Caixa Postal 1275, Luanda; f. 1864; Pres. J. F. VIEIRA; Sec. M. G. DELGADO.

Labour is organized in four national syndicates:

Sindicato Nacional dos Empregados do Comercio e da Industria da Provincia de Angola—SNECIPA (*National Syndicate of Workers of Commerce and Industry*): Caixa Postal 28, Luanda; f. 1897; mems. 45,991 (24,746 in central br.); 16 brs. (1970); Chair. Dr. FERNANDO DAVID LAIMA; Sec.-Gen. JOSÉ CELESTINO BRAVO-MARTINS.

Sindicato Nacional dos Motoriatas, Ferroviarios e Metalurgicos (*National Syndicate of Motor Transport, Railroad and Metal Workers*): Caixa Postal 272, Luanda; mems. 2,000 (1960); Pres. ANTONIO DE ALMEIDA CRUZ.

Sindicato Nacional dos Constructores Civis e Mestres de Obras (*National Syndicate of Civil Construction and Contractors*): Caixa Postal 5072, Luanda; mems. 1,750 (1960); Pres. ANTONIO MARTINS NOGUEIRA.

Sindicato Nacional dos Empregados Bancários de Angola: Largo João Fernandes Vieira No. 5/6, Luanda.

Liga Geral dos Trabalhadores de Angola (**LGTA**): Kinshasa, Congo; in exile.

TRADE FAIR

Feira Internacional de Luanda (*International Trade Fair of Luanda*): Caixa Postal 1296, Luanda; f. 1969; organized by the Industrial Association of Angola; annually in October.

MAJOR INDUSTRIAL COMPANIES

MINERAL

Cabinda Gulf Oil Company: 15a Rua Alfredo Trony, Luanda; mining of petroleum oil in Cabinda enclave; wholly owned subsidiary of U.S. Gulf Oil Corporation.

Companhia de Diamantes de Angola S.A.R.L. (DIAMANG): C.P. 1247, Luanda; Head Office Rua dos Fanqueiros 12, Lisbon 2, Portugal; f. 1917; cap. Esc. 294,100,000.

Prospecting for and mining of diamonds.

Chair. and Gen. Man. Dr. G. L. A. MOREIRA; 28,388 employees (1969).

Companhia do Manganês de Angola: 26-1, Rua João de Barros, Luanda; mining of high-grade iron ore.

Companhia Mineira do Lobito S.A.R.L.: C.P. 169, Luanda; f. 1929; cap. U.S. $200m.

Mining of high grade iron ore in the Cassinga mines and other ores in the area of its concessions.

Chair. M. P. DOS SANTOS; Vice-Chair. Dr. E. H. S. BRANDÃO.

Companhia de Petróleos de Angola (PETRANGOL): C.P. 1320, Luanda; f. 1957; cap. Esc. 900,000,000.

Holds concession rights for exploration and production over 28,596 sq. km.; owns the only Angolan oil refinery.

Pres. Gen. F. SANTOS COSTA; Gen. Man. H. B. VIEIRA; 1,400 employees.

Siderurgia Nacional: Rua Luis Motafio, Luanda; metal-plate manufacturing plant.

AGRICULTURAL

Companhia do Acucar de Angola: 77 Rua Direita, Luanda; production of sugar.

Companhia Geral dos Algodões de Angola (COTONANG): Avenida da Boavista, Luanda; production of cotton textiles.

Fabrica de Tabacos Ultramarina: Estrada de Cattete, Luanda; manufacture of tobacco products.

TRANSPORT

RAILWAYS

The total length of track operated is 3,110 km.

STATE-OWNED

Porto e Caminhos de Ferro de Luanda: Direcção de Exploração do Porto e Caminhos de Ferro de Luanda, Caixa Postal 1229, Luanda; f. 1886; serves an iron, cotton and sisal-producing region between Luanda and Malange; 608 km. of 1.067 m. gauge. Under the Development Plan it is proposed to continue the line 97 km. from Malange to Lui and eventually to the Zaire border; Dir. Eng. LUIS HENRIQUE ERVEDOSA ABREU.

Caminho de Ferro de Moçâmedes: Moçâmedes; 858 km. main line from Moçâmedes to Serpa Pinto via Sá da Bandeira, Matala and Entrocamento, with a 126-km. narrow gauge branch to Chiange; branches to Cassinga North (16 km.) and Cassinga South (94 km.), opened in 1967, carry 6 million tons of iron ore a year to Salazar Harbour, Moçâmedes.

PRIVATELY-OWNED

Companhia do Caminho de Ferro de Benguela (*Benguela Railway Company*): Head Office: Rua do Ataide 7, Lisbon, Portugal; African Management: Caixa Postal 32, Lobito, Angola; London Office: 6 John St., London, WC1N 2ES; f. 1902; runs from the port of Lobito across Angola via Nova Lisboa and Luso to the Zaire border where it connects with the K.D.L. system which in turn links with Zambia Railways thus providing the shortest West Coast route for Central African trade; 3 ft. 6 in. gauge; principal export freights carried: copper, cobalt, zinc, manganese ore and maize; principal import freights carried: general cargo, petrol and oils; length of track 1,348 km.; Pres. Dr. LUIS SUPICO PINTO; Man. Dir. Dr. MANUEL FERNANDES.

Companhia do Caminho de Ferro do Amboim: Porto Amboim; f. 1922; serves a coffee region between Amboim and Gabela; 123 km. of 0.60-metre gauge; Dir. FERNANDO M. TOURET.

ROADS

Tarred roads totalled in 1970, 5,317 km., and it is hoped this will increase to 8,500 km. by 1973 at a cost of over 500 million escudos. In the period 1965–68 10,000 km. of asphalt road were built; plans include a highway from Luanda to Cape Town, and another from Carmona to Quimbele, ultimately to be extended to the Zaire border, is under construction.

SHIPPING

Companhia Nacional de Navegação: Caixa Postal 20, Avenida Marginal, Luanda; Head Office: 85 Rua do Comercio, Lisbon; also brs. at Oporto and Beira; regular cargo and passenger services from Portugal to West and East Portuguese Africa; monthly cargo services from Hamburg, Bremen, Rotterdam, London, Liverpool to Portuguese East Africa.

Companhia de Serviços Marítimos—COSEMA: Caixa Postal 1360, Séde Largo de República, Luanda; f. 1950; brs. in Lobito, Porto Amboim, Moçâmedes, Sao Tomé; Dir. Commdt. MANUEL ALBUQUERQUE E CASTRO; Gen. Man. D. MADUREIRA E CASTRO.

FOREIGN SHIPPING AGENCIES

Robert Hudsons & Sons (Pty.) Ltd.: P.O.B. 6426, Luanda; suppliers of vehicles, agricultural, industrial and earthmoving equipment, aircraft and general goods; international forwarding agents at Luanda and Lobito; brs. and workshops in all main Angolan towns; agents in Angola for Clan Line, Texaco Overseas Tankship Ltd., etc.

Hull, Blyth (Angola) Ltd.: Caixa Postal 1214, Luanda; London Office: 1 Lloyds Avenue, E.C.3; agents in Angola for Cie. Maritime Belge, Elder Dempster Lines Ltd., B.P. Tanker Co. Ltd., Shell Tankers Ltd., Mobil Shipping Co. Ltd., and others; Chair. Viscount LEATHERS; Sec. G. B. WOODHOUSE, F.C.I.S.

CIVIL AVIATION
ANGOLA AIRLINE

Angola Airlines—D.T.A. (*Direcção da Exploração dos Transportes Aéreos*): Luanda, Caixa Postal 79; internal services, and services from Luanda to Windhoek (South-West Africa and São Tomé); fleet of five F-27 and six DC-3; Dir. J. S. MEDINA.

OTHER AIRLINES SERVING LUANDA

Transportes Aéreos Portugueses S.A.R.L. (T.A.P.): Lisbon; office in Luanda; Av. Paulo Dias Novais 79-80; P.O.B. 118; f. 1953; Principal Officials: Eng. ALFREDO QUEIROZ VAZ PINTO, Cte. JULIO SCHOLZ, Eng. EDUARDO MENDES BARBOSA, LUIS FORJAZ TRIGUEIROS; services to Portugal, Rhodesia, South Africa, Mozambique, U.S.A. and S. America.

South African Airways (S.A.A.): Head Office: S.A. Airways Centre, Johannesburg; Office in Luanda: Av. Paulo Dias de Novais 123; services between Luanda, Johannesburg and Windhoek.

VARIG (Brazil Airline): Edificio Sousa Machado, salas 113-5, Av. Paulo Dias de Novais 7 1 Luanda; weekly service from Rio de Janeiro to Luanda (through Johannesburg) and direct service Luanda Rio, started June 1970; Regional Man. SANTOS FERRO.

TOURISM

Centro de Informação e Turismo de Angola—CITA: Caixa Postal 1240, Luanda; Dir. Col. J. F. M. ILHARCO.

EDUCATION

The Transitional Development Plan, 1965–67, provided for investments in education in Angola of 540 million escudos, but only 107.8 million had actually been spent at the end of the period. In the Third Development Plan, 1968–73, 1,390 million escudos have been allocated, although the actual expenditure at the end of the first year was a quarter of the amount provided for. In 1968 6.5 per cent of total ordinary expenditure was devoted to primary and secondary education and 13 per cent to the University of Luanda.

There is a shortage of teachers, and textbooks are too costly for most families. Extra funds are available for education services run by Catholics, but Protestant missionaries have been discouraged from teaching and the numbers working in Angola dropped from 261 in 1961 to less than 50 in 1967.

Despite these difficulties total school enrolment at all levels rose by 20 per cent between 1965–66 and 1966–67. In the latter year about two-thirds of all children in primary schools were in the preparatory class (a pre-primary adaptation course for children who cannot speak Portuguese) or the first year; less than a fifth were in the second year; just over 10 per cent were in the third year; and only 7 per cent were in the the fourth year.

In 1970–71 there were 440,985 pupils in primary schools, 55,794 in secondary academic and technical schools, 937 at ecclesiastical institutions, and 2,088 students at university. At the end of 1967 a preparatory two-year course for secondary schools was extended from the Metropole to the African territories; this course provides for two years secondary education before a choice has to be made between an academic career (in a *liceu*) and a technical one.

LEARNED SOCIETIES
AND RESEARCH INSTITUTES

Centro de Estudos Humanísticos (*Centre for Humanist Studies*): Sá da Bandeira; history, literature and languages.

Centro de Investigação Científica Algodeira (*Cotton Scientific Research Centre*): Instituto do Algodão de Angola, Estação Experimental de Onga-Zanga, Catete; fibre technology laboratory, agricultural machinery station, crop irrigation station (Bombagem); library; Dir. Eng. Agr. JOAQUIM RODRIGUES PEREIRA.

Direcção Provincial dos Serviços de Geologia e Minas de Angola: C.P. 1260-C, Luanda; f. 1914; 506 mems.; Geology, Geological Mapping and Exploration of Mineral Deposits; library of 40,000 vols.; Dir. J. TRIGO MIRA; publs. *Boletim, Memória, Carta Geológica de Angola*.

Instituto de Angola: Caixa Postal 2767, Luanda; f. 1952; scientific, literary and artistic cultural institute; also seeks cultural relations with similar Portuguese and foreign institutions; 300 mems.; library of 3,500 vols.; Pres. Dr. WALDEMAR TEIXEIRA; publs. _Boletim do Instituto de Angola_ (quarterly), _Boletim Informativo, Boletim Analítico, Boletim Bibliográfico_ (monthly).

Instituto de Investigação Agronómica de Angola (_Agricultural Research Institute of Angola_): C.P. 406, Nova Lisboa; f. 1962; research is conducted in soils and chemistry, agronomy, forestry and agricultural biology; agrarian documentation centre; 46 scientific staff; publ. _Série Técnica, Série Científica._

Instituto de Investigação Científica de Angola (_Angola Scientific Research Institute_): Caixa Postal 3244, Luanda; f. 1955; departments of Biology, Geology-Geography, Humanities, Experimental Surgery; museums; documentation centre; Dir. Eng. Agr. VIRGILIO CANNAS MARTINS.

Instituto de Investigação Medica de Angola (_Angola Medical Research Institute_): Luanda; f. 1955.

Instituto de Investigação Vetinária: Nova Lisboa.

Missão Geográfica de Angola (M.G.A.) (_Angola Geographical Mission_): C.P. 432, Nova Lisboa, Angola; f. 1941; Dir. Eng. Geog. ALBERTO MANUEL HENRIQUES PEREIRA BASTOS.

Observatório Meteorológico e Magnético João Capelo (_João Capelo Meteorological and Magnetic Observatory_): Serviço Meteorológico de Angola, Rua Diogo Cão 20, Caixa Postal 1288-C, Luanda; f. 1879; library of 10,000 vols.; Dir. Eng. ALBERTO LEÃO DINIZ; publs. _Resultados das Observações Meteorológicas, Boletim geomagnético preliminar, Boletim sismológico_ (monthly), _Observações Meteorológicas de Superfície em Angola, Observações Meteorológicas de Altitude em Angola, Anuário Meteorológico, Tabelas Diversas_ (yearly).

LIBRARIES

Biblioteca Municipal: Caixa Postal 1227, Luanda; 14,600 vols.; Librarian ALBERTO SERRA JÚNIOR.

Biblioteca Nacional de Angola: Caixa Postal 2915, Luanda; 25,000 vols.; Dir. Dr. CARMO VAZ; (annexed to Museu de Angola, _see below_).

Arquivo Histórico de Angola: _see_ Museu de Angola.

MUSEUMS

Museu da Huila: Caixa Postal 445, Sá da Bandeira; f. 1956; Ethnography and Prehistory; Curator Dr. MACHADO CRUZ.

Museu de Angola: Caixa Postal 1267C, Luanda; f. 1938; National Archives, Art, History, Zoology, Botany, Geology, Ethnography; Dir. Eng. VIRGILIO CANNAS MARTINS; Curator Dr. MESQUITELA LIMA; publ. _Arquivos de Angola._

Museu de Congo: Caixa Postal 11, Carmona; f. 1965; Ethnography; Curator VIRGÍLIO PEREIRA.

Museu do Dundo: Dundo, Lunda; Ethnography, Anthropology, Zoology, Geology, Pre-history and History of Lunda; library of 8,000 vols.; Dir. of Biological Research Dr. A. DE BARROS MACHADO; publ. _Publicações Culturais da Companhia de Diamantes de Angola._

UNIVERSITY
UNIVERSIDADE DE LUANDA
CAIXAS POSTAIS 815 AND 1350, LUANDA

Telephone: Luanda 764

Founded 1963.

State control; Language of instruction: Portuguese; Academic year: October to July.

Rector: IVO SOARES.
Vice-Rector: MANUEL GOMES GUERREIRO.
Registrar: ALBERTO LUÍS GOMES.
Librarian: ANTÓNIO CERQUEIRA FERRAZ CORREIA.

Number of professors: 21.
Number of students: 2,385.

Publications: _Anuário do Universidade de Luanda, Boletim Informativo._

DEANS:

Faculty of Engineering: FERNANDO DE MELLO MENDES.
Faculty of Veterinary Sciences: VICTOR MANUEL PAIS CAEIRO.
Faculty of Medicine: NUNO RODRIGUES GRANDE.
Faculty of Agriculture and Forestry: VIRGÍLIO CANNAS MARTINS.
Faculty of Education: TORQUATO BROCHADO DE SOUSA.
Faculty of Sciences: FERNANDO NUÑES FERREIRA.

COLLEGES

Instituto de Educação e Serviço Social Pio XII (_Pius XII Institute of Education and Social Service_): Antigo Aeroporto Emilio de Carvalho, C.P. 18071, Luanda; f. 1962; 51 teachers, 245 students; library of 2,882 vols.; Dir. MARIA SUSANA DE ALMEIDA.

Centro de Estudos Humanisticos: Bandeira; courses in history, literature and languages.

SELECT BIBLIOGRAPHY

Portuguese Africa Generally

ABSHIRE, D. M., and SAMUELS, M. A. *Portuguese Africa, A Handbook*. London, Pall Mall, 1969.

CHILCOTE, RONALD H. *Portuguese Africa*. Prentice-Hall, Englewood, Cliffs, New Jersey, 1967.

DUFFY, J. *Portuguese Africa*. Harvard and Cambridge University Presses, 1959.
As *Portugal in Africa*. Harmondsworth, Penguin Books, 1962.

GALVÃO, HENRIQUE and SELVAGEM, CARLOS. *Império ultramarino português*. (4 vols.) Lisbon, 1950–53.

HAMMOND, RICHARD. *Portugal and Africa 1815-1910*. Stanford, 1966.

INSTITUTO SUPERIOR DE CIÊNCIAS SOCIAIS E POLÍTICA ULTRAMARINA (I.S.C.S.P.U.). *Cabo Verde, Guiné, São Tomé e Príncipe*. Lisbon, 196–.

KAY, HUGH. *Salazar and Modern Portugal*. London, 1970.

MOREIRA, A. *Portugal's Stand in Africa*. New York, University Publishers, 1962.

PATTEE, RICHARD. *Portugal and the Portuguese World*. Milwaukee, 1957.

UN. *Report of the Special Committee on Territories under Portuguese Administration*, A/7623/Add. 3, 25 September 1969. (General Assembly, 24th Session.)
Report of the Special Committee on the Situation with regard to the Implementation of the Declaration on the Granting of Independence to Colonial Countries and Peoples. Ch. VII: Territories under Portuguese Administration. A/8023/Add. 3, 5 October 1970. (General Assembly, 25th Session).

Angola

DAVIDSON, BASIL. *In the Eye of the Storm*. Longman, 1972.

ILÍDIO DO AMARAL. *Luanda*. Lisbon, 1968.

HEIMER, F. W. *Educacao e Sociedad nas Areas Rurais de Angola*. Missao de Inquéritos Agricolas de Angola, Luanda, 1972.

HERRICK, ALLISON BUTLER et al. *Area Handbook for Angola*. Washington, 1967.

FELGAS, HÉLIO. *Guerra em Angola*. Lisbon, 1962.

INSTITUTO SUPERIOR DE CIÊNCIAS SOCIAIS E POLÍTICA ULTRAMARINA (I.S.C.S.P.U.). *Angola*. Lisbon, 1964.

MARCUM, J. *The Angolan Revolution*, Vol. 1, 1954–62. Boston, M.I.T. Press, 1969.

MENDES, ALFONSO. *O Trabalcho Assalariado em Angola*. Lisbon, 1966.

WHEELER, D. L. "The Portuguese Army in Angola". *Journal of Modern African Studies*, 7/3, October 1969.

WHEELER, D. L., and PÉLISSIER, R. *Angola*. London, Pall Mall, 1971.

Botswana

PHYSICAL AND SOCIAL GEOGRAPHY*

John Amer

Botswana is situated in the heart of the sub-continent of southern Africa surrounded by South West Africa (Namibia) on the west, the latter's Caprivi Strip on the north, by Rhodesia on the north-east, and by South Africa on the south and south-east.

PHYSICAL FEATURES

Botswana occupies 231,805 sq. miles of the down-warped Kalahari Basin of the great southern African plateau which has here an average altitude of 3,000 ft. above sea-level. Gently undulating to flat surfaces, consisting of Kalahari sands overlying Archean rocks, are characteristic of most of the country but the east is more hilly and broken. Most of southern Botswana is without surface drainage and, apart from the bordering Limpopo and Chobe Rivers, the rest of the country's drainage is interior and does not reach the sea. Flowing into the north-west from the Angolan highlands the perennial Okavango River is Botswana's major system. Ninety miles after crossing the border the Okavango drains into a depression in the plateau to form the Okavango Swamps and the ephemeral Lake Ngami. From this enormous marsh covering 4,000 sq. miles there is a seasonal flow of water eastwards along the Botletle River 160 miles to Lake Dow and thence into the Makarikari Salt Pan. Most of the mean annual flow of over 6 million acre ft. brought into Botswana by the Okavango is lost through evaporation and transpiration in the swamps.

The Kalahari Desert, the home of the nomadic Bushmen and more accurately a semi-desert, dominates southern and western Botswana. From the near-desert conditions of the extreme south-west with an average annual rainfall around 5 in., there is a gradual increase in precipitation towards the north (25 in.) and east (15–20 in.). There is an associated transition in the natural vegetation from the sparse thornveld of the Kalahari Desert to the dry woodland savannah of the north and east and the infertile sands give way eastwards to better soils developed on granitic and sedimentary rocks.

RESOURCES AND POPULATION

Shortage of water is the biggest hindrance to the development of Botswana's natural resources. The country has an immense agricultural potential with an estimated 8 million acres suitable for cultivation, 5 per cent of which is actually farmed. This potential could be partly realized by using the vast water resources of the Okavango Basin for irrigation. Water from the Okavango could also help the further development of agriculture, mining, industry and power supplies in the east, with its substantial deposits of diamonds, copper, nickel, coal, manganese, asbestos and salt. The eastern strip as the best endowed and most developed region of Botswana possesses 80 per cent of the population of 630,000 (1971). Seven of the eight Batswana tribes and most of the 3,921 Europeans and 382 Asians are concentrated in the east, which has an average density of 6.6 persons per sq. mile compared with 0.7 per sq. mile over the rest of the country. An additional 35,000 males are usually temporarily absent, working mainly in Rhodesia and South Africa.

* *See* map on p. 832.

RECENT HISTORY

Jack Halpern

Three crucial factors have shaped the political history and life of Botswana: its geographical and economic position, poor and jutting into the heart of white-ruled South Africa and otherwise bordered by similarly white-ruled South West Africa and Southern Rhodesia, with only a minuscule river link with Zambia; the fact that it is almost unique in former British-ruled Africa in achieving independence without having spawned a significant African nationalist movement; and the strength of allegiances amongst its seven major tribal groups, which have been reinforced by the separation of some groups by vast distances, a low level of literacy and the absence, at least until very recently, of effective physical means, as well as mass media, of communications.

"Bechuanaland", said Cecil John Rhodes, "is the Suez Canal to the North." It was to secure this crucial road to the interior against German incursion from South West Africa that Britain reluctantly proclaimed Bechuanaland a Protectorate in 1885. The southern part was, for reasons largely of economy, incorporated into the then Cape Colony. For similar reasons, the rest of Bechuanaland was to be handed over to Rhodes' British South Africa Company. The local chiefs, led by Khama the Great of the Bamangwato (an ancestor of today's President, Sir Seretse Khama), successfully petitioned against this move; Rhodes got a strip for a railway; and the chiefs remained under British protection, with the explicit assurance that they would "continue to rule their own people much as at present".

BRITAIN AND THE KHAMAS

On the underlying assumption that Bechuanaland would sooner or later be incorporated into the Union of South Africa, which came into being in 1910, Britain did leave the country and its chiefs "much as at present" until after the National Party came to power in South Africa in 1948 and so systemized *apartheid* as to make incorporation unacceptable to British and world opinion, let alone to the Batswana people, who had been promised that they would be "consulted" before any such move took place. It is really only from this period onwards that one can meaningfully speak of political development in what is now Botswana.

True, a nominated Native and a separate, elected European Advisory Council were formed in 1920, and the former, renamed "African" in 1940, did serve as a largely chiefly forum in voicing African opposition to steadily maintained South African pressures for incorporation. These pressures were equally steadily reinforced by the European Advisory Council, most of whose members and electors were Afrikaner South Africans. But the only significant political crisis in the inter-war years centred on the remarkable Bamangwato royal house of Khama. The late Tshekedi Khama, uncle of the present President, was appointed regent in 1926 during Seretse Khama's minority. He successfully conducted a three-year legal and political battle with the administration through which the principle of tribal control of mineral rights and concessions was established. This he followed with a successful legal battle, carried in 1931 to the Privy Council, which reinforced chiefly powers.

World attention, however, was only twice focused on Bechuanaland. In 1933 the British administration tried to depose Tshekedi after a white youth who had consorted with a Mongwato girl and had assaulted a Mongwato youth was tried by the tribal court under Tshekedi and accepted a punishment of whipping. An enormous outcry followed. Naval forces were sent from Cape Town to Bechuanaland and a rough trial staged in front of howitzers, but the tribe refused to accept Tshekedi's deposition and, after an interval, he was reinstated as regent.

The better-known crisis came in 1948, when Seretse Khama, then studying in Britain before assuming his hereditary chieftainship of the important Bamangwato tribe, married a white woman, Ruth Williams. Tshekedi bitterly opposed the marriage, though the tribe came to accept it. More importantly, heavy pressures to bar Seretse from the chieftainship came from the Nationalist régime by then in power in South Africa and from the neighbouring white Rhodesian government. Mr. Patrick Gordon Walker, then Labour Commonwealth Secretary, persuaded Seretse to visit Britain and then, in what Sir Winston Churchill described as "a very disreputable transaction", barred him from returning home. When finally allowed to do so, it was on condition that he renounced the chieftainship.

This unjust suffering through racialist pressures has not made Seretse Khama racialist in turn, but rather has deeply committed him to non-racialism. Ironically, it was the forced condition that he return purely as an ordinary citizen which led him into the active politics, which began to develop a little later, and ultimately to the Presidency.

In 1950 the British administration finally agreed to the creation of a Joint Advisory Council, consisting of eight Africans and eight whites chosen by their respective Councils, plus four senior officials. But the demand for a Legislative Council was not conceded until 1958. The first elections were held in 1961, with Bechuanaland's then 3,200 whites electing 10 members and the 317,000 Africans being allowed 10 indirectly chosen members, plus two nominated from each group and 10 colonial officials.

PARTY POLITICS DEVELOP

So new is modern politics in Botswana that these first 1961 elections were not contested by today's major parties. The first political party was formed only in 1959, but this Bechuanaland Protectorate Federal Party, led by Mr. Leetile Disang Ratidladi, proved short-lived. The first really modern party, with a nationalist outlook that established Bechuanaland on the Pan-African map, was formed in December 1960. This was the Bechuanaland Peoples Party (BPP), founded by one of the Protectorate's handful of graduates, Mr. K. T. Motsete. Its Secretary-General, Mr. Motsamai Mpho, had been tried for treason as a member of the African National Congress in South Africa and maintained close links with that organization. A relatively rapid spread of political consciousness, and certainly of factionalism, was stimulated by an influx of politically experienced refugees from South Africa. Within a short time, the BPP split into two sections, which in many ways reflected the conflict in South Africa: the multi-racial (African National) Congress alliance, and the Pan-Africanist Congress. The former, led by Mr. Mpho, is now the small Botswana Independence Party (BIP). The latter, led by Mr. Philip Matante, is now the much more important Botswana Peoples Party (BPP).

Partly in reaction to the militant phraseology and connexions of the original BPP, Seretse Khama formed the more moderate Bechuanaland Democratic Party (BDP) in January 1962. In 1961 Seretse agreed to be a candidate for the indirect African elections to the Legislative Council, topped the final poll, and was appointed to the Executive Council. After the first elections, Mr. Khama recruited ten of the twelve African members of the Legco to the party, which at one stroke made the BDP a major force. Alarmed by the militancy of the rival BPP, a number of whites began also to support Mr. Khama's BDP as the lesser of available evils, and the British administration unofficially but efficiently groomed him as the first Prime Minister. This he duly became when the BDP, helped by his Bamangwato power base, his national reputation, and by some financial and organizational support from the liberal minority amongst the white settlers, swept the board at "one man—one vote" elections held in 1965 under a pre-independence Constitution granted by Britain.

INDEPENDENCE

Sir Seretse Khama, as he became on independence in September, 1966, has grown perceptibly in stature and political grasp in office. Whilst frequently subject to ill-health and with uncertain staying powers, he was fortunate in having as his deputy, and as Secretary-General of the BDP, Dr. Quet Masire, a former master-farmer, turned journalist, turned politician, of great shrewdness, intelligence, imagination and general ability.

The post-independence period, marred by years of dreadful drought and lack of finance (*see* Botswana Economy), has seen four significant party-political developments. The first is the firm establishment of the BDP as a national party and the acceptance of Sir Seretse as Botswana's leader. The second is the fading into relative insignificance of the Botswana Independence Party. The third is the apparent increased support in the "urban" centres since the October, 1969 general elections for Mr. Matante's Botswana People's Party. In the most recent local council elections in the commercial centre of Francistown, even the most energetic campaigning by Sir Seretse's BDP could not prevent Mr. Matante's BPP gaining a majority, and this was repeated in the local elections for the neighbouring North-Western District Council. (The BPP won both Francistown seats in the 1969 national parliamentary elections.) In both cases Sir Seretse's government vitiated Mr. Matante's success by increasing the number of nominated, as opposed to elected, members of the councils. This has increased Mr. Matante's pan-Africanist-phrased charge that the BDP is not only an undemocratic but also a "neo-colonialist" party, for he and the other two opposition parties are critical of the terms on which Sir Seretse's government is granting exploitation rights to the country's newly discovered mineral wealth (*see* Botswana Economy).

The fourth significant party-political development has been the emergence of a new party, the Botswana National Front. Founded by the marxist-orientated and able Dr. Kona, it somewhat changed its nature and gained greatly in stature and appeal when, a little incongruously, one of the country's most traditionalist and able chiefs, Chief Bathoen II, resigned his hereditary headship of the major Bangwaketse tribe after 40 years to stand as a private citizen for parliament on behalf of the National Front. In tribal terms, which continue to be of considerable importance in Botswana, Chief Bathoen II was only slightly less well known than his life-long friend and co-campaigner, the late Tshekedi Khama. Now the ex-Chief and two fellow-tribesmen have taken all three parliamentary seats in the Bangwaketse Reserve, unseating Vice-President Masire in the process. If an alliance were ever formed between the opposition parties, and in particular between the BNF, now led by Ex-Chief Bathoen, and Mr. Matante's BPP, Sir Seretse's BDP could face a serious

challenge. At present, however, this prospect seems remote.

Whilst still unable to dispense wholly with the support of the chieftainship, Sir Seretse's government has nevertheless significantly reduced the chiefs' powers, including the crucial one of land-allocation (land being held communally), and control of mineral concessions. How effectively these measures will be implemented remains to be seen. The four main points in the BDP programme are democracy, development, self-reliance and unity.

The past two years have seen a marked consolidation of Sir Seretse's leadership of his country and party, due to two factors: his health has greatly improved, and the Vice-President, Dr. Quet Masire, having lost his elected seat, holds office only as a presidential nominee. Increased functions have been taken over by the President's Office.

Whilst the President remains, in the normal sense of the term, at most a liberal conservative, some importance attaches to two key appointments which he has made. One is that as his Principal Private Secretary of Mr. John Syson, a leading young British Fabian. The other is that to the Ministry of Information of Mr. Joe Matthews, formerly in exile as the London representative of the South African ANC. Mr. Matthews, who is a lawyer and the son of Botswana's first Ambassador to the UN, the late Prof. S. K. Matthews, is considered by the South African authorities as one of the leading communists produced by their country, but Sir Seretse ignored considerable diplomatic pressure and stuck to his appointment.

The opposition parties have remained divided and, with the important exception of Francistown, largely ineffectual. Three developments have, however, signalled potential storm-centres. One is increasing discontent with what is seen as inadequate rural development. Notably, Mr. K. P. Morake, Assistant Minister for Development, has admitted that in this sphere communication between the government and the people had failed. Also, the continued existence of slums in Francistown (pop. 16,000), where some 3,000 destitute squatters provide a sharp contrast with the luxurious life of 940 whites, has continued to arouse resentment. Sir Seretse has had to face an eight-day debate in parliament on his major policy statement, in which the most telling criticisms came from back benchers of his own party, mainly on rural issues. Amongst the opposition parties, only Mr. Motsamai Mpho improved his standing. Bills have been introduced to give employment preference and obligatory training opportunities to Botswana citizens, and to close down racially exclusive clubs.

With the beginnings of development in the Selebi-Pikwe mining complex, which will bring an influx of South African white miners and technicians, Mr. Matante of the BPP has angrily reported to parliament that expatriate whites were insultingly calling Africans 'kaffirs'. In announcing the creation of a Parliamentary Standing Committee to keep this situation under review and ensure that the Penal Code's sanctions against racial insult were enforced, Sir Seretse specifically referred to Selebi-Pikwe. Sir Seretse has also said that he intends to prevent the emergence of a working class of Botswana miners who would be very highly paid in comparison with the income of the rural population. He has not, however, said what steps he intends to take. The present Trade Union Act requires 25 per cent membership in any industry for official recognition. At present there are four competing unions, all centered on the BPP stronghold of Francistown, with a total membership of some 1,400 members. At the same time, Sir Seretse has found it necessary to point out publicly that God, and not he, was responsible for the uneven location of Botswana's mineral wealth, most of which is concentrated in the area of the Bamangwato tribe, to which the President belongs. This points to more open tribal jealousies, and Sir Seretse has now accused the opposition parties of being tribally organized.

There has also been open friction between the government and the civil service, in which members of the landless Bakalaka tribe, who were once append-ages of the Bamangwato, are prominent. The President has found it necessary to tell civil servants publicly to stop using their positions for party-political ends or to resign. "Those whose principal object was to undermine the government's authority would not be permitted to subsidise their political activities from public funds."

It is now government policy to fill all senior jobs in the police with "citizens of the country by birth". This will, however, take place only as present officers retire or as their contracts lapse. Twelve local superinten-dents and 30 inspectors have been appointed since independence. Sir Seretse has taken full note of the crucial role of expatriates commanding the Lesotho police during and after Chief Jonathan's coup in that country. The Botswana government spent slightly more than R1 million between 1969 and 1970 on the 1,000 strong police, including its para-military units.

An official target-date for Botswana self-sufficiency in executive manpower has been fixed as 1990, but this no doubt realistic estimate has been poorly received in the urban areas which increasingly attract, but do not provide jobs for, those with some hard-won education. By 1970 there were 180 Botswana uni-versity students, 140 of them studying at UBLS. Between 1950 and 1970 the number of teachers training rose from 280 to 560, and the number of secondary school pupils from 1,300 to 3,900. The Development Plan calls for a decrease by 1975 of the doctor:population ratio from 1:24,000 to 1:14,000. In 1971 there were 30 doctors and 330 trained nurses in Botswana.

Relations with the White South and beyond

On the international stage, the Unilateral Declara-tion of Independence (U.D.I.) by Rhodesia has placed the Botswana Government in a difficult position. The railway on which Botswana itself depends, and which is presently the only rail link between South Africa and Rhodesia, is owned and operated by Rhodesia Railways. For simple reasons of economic survival, Botswana is in no position to take part in the economic sanctions against Rhodesia. Indeed, there is a growing pressure group in Rhodesia demanding the building of a 100-mile new rail line which would provide an alternative South African-Rhodesian connection which by-passes Botswana. Nevertheless, Sir Seretse has spoken out strongly against both the rebel Rhodesian regime and against *apartheid* and the sale of arms to South Africa, with whose economy Botswana continues to be intimately linked. He has continued to give conditional political asylum to anti-*apartheid* refugees, as well as having arranged for the settlement of some 3,000 refugees from Angola and two small groups from South West Africa (Namibia). At the same time, the inadequate Botswana police force—there is no army—has intercepted guerrilla fighters making their way to South West Africa and Rhodesia.

Sir Seretse's recent public declarations illustrate the delicate balancing postures into which history, geography and economics have forced Botswana. To the Lusaka Summit Meeting of Non-Aligned States in 1970 he stressed that: "If we appear reluctant to play an active and prominent part in the struggle for majority rule throughout southern Africa, it is not because we are unconcerned about the plight of our oppressed brothers in the white-ruled states of our region . . . We want to see majority rule established throughout southern Africa . . . and we are deter-mined to contribute towards the achievement of that noble goal. We are, however, aware that there is a limit beyond which our contribution cannot go without endangering our very independence". Subse-quently, to his own party conference in Botswana, he said: "Botswana cannot allow itself to be used as a springboard for violence against the minority regimes. Our task is to insulate ourselves from the instabilities their policies provoke".

Nevertheless, the Lusaka Summit speech led the South African Government to hold back from financial commitments sought by South African firms then negotiating with Botswana RST to develop the Selebi-Pikwe copper-nickel mining complex (*see* Economy), pending "clarification" of Sir Seretse's meaning.

There have been several other new points of tension between Botswana and South Africa during the past two years. When Rhodesian police handed over to the South African authorities an African whom they had arrested at a spot which Botswana claims is within her borders, Sir Seretse's government delivered a protest note to the South African govern-ment. They received no reply. Friction has also arisen over the arbitrary detention by the police of Botswana citizens visiting South Africa, and over the alleged abduction from Botswana of known opponents of *apartheid* to South Africa, which has been proved to have happened in the past. Here too the Botswana Government obtained no satisfaction. At the end of 1971 the Botswana Government lodged complaints with the both British Government and the Rhodesian régime about Rhodesians shooting at the Kazangula ferry on the Zambezi.

In December, 1971 South Africa's Foreign Minister, Dr. Muller, conferred with President Khama in Gaborone, the new Botswana capital. Subsequently the President, having once again refused South African governmental aid, said: "We are demonstrating that it is possible to co-exist with our powerful neighbour without sacrificing principle or national interest".

Botswana is a member both of the OAU and the UNO, and is now receiving American aid (*see* Botswana Economy) for the building of an all-weather highway and, reportedly, a bridge over the Zambezi which would link Francistown with Lusaka in Zambia. The South African Government claimed that Botswana has in fact no legal title to any common border with Zambia. This assertion was publicly rebutted by both the Botswana and the U.S.A. governments. If the dispute had gone to the International Court of Justice in The Hague it could have revived the whole question of the South African presence in South West Africa and its militarization of the Caprivi Strip (*see* South West Africa), thus underlining non-racial Botswana's difficult but crucial political importance in southern Africa.

This, however, was not wanted at that time by any of the parties, including, apparently, President Kaunda of Zambia, with whom Sir Seretse conferred. The South African Government accepted the situation when it became clear that no bridge was to be built, and that the river link was to be an improved ferry (*see* Economy). The South African motive in raising this potentially explosive issue was to pre-empt a bridge being built which would alter the effectiveness of the illegally militarized Caprivi Strip.

As South Africa was intimately interested in the success of Chief Jonathan's *coup d'état* in Lesotho

(*see* Lesotho p. 461), it seems unlikely that its government welcomed the secret negotiations through which Sir Seretse sought the support of other African countries in trying to persuade Chief Jonathan to accept fresh elections under the inspection of objective African observers. This initiative, however, failed for lack of support from Swaziland (*see* Swaziland).

Farther afield in Africa, Sir Seretse has made a point of strengthening friendly relations not only with Zambia but also with Tanzania, whose tenth anniversary celebrations he attended, and with Kenya, whose Vice-President, Mr. Daniel Moi, has paid an official visit to Botswana.

Internationally, Botswana has courageously demonstrated her "non-alignment" on two major issues. The first was her decision, despite the most intense pressure from South Africa, to establish full diplomatic relations not only with Czechoslovakia but also with the Soviet Union. South Africa dropped its discernible campaign against this now implemented move when it was announced that no ambassadors would take up residence in Botswana; instead, the Czech and Soviet ambassadors to Zambia are now also accredited to Botswana.

The more recent pressure against Botswana's "non-alignment" has come from the opposite side of the international spectrum: when it became known at the United Nations that Botswana intended to vote for the admission of the People's Republic of China, the U.S.A.'s Secretary of State, Mr. William Rogers, telephoned Sir Seretse in an attempt to persuade him to change his mind. Botswana, though heavily dependent on American financial aid (*see* Economy), voted for the admission of the People's Republic of China.

ECONOMY

Jack Halpern

In the decolonization of Africa there can seldom have been a more dramatic improvement in the post-independence economic position of a country than has occurred in Botswana.

At independence on September 30th, 1966, the former British Protectorate of Bechuanaland was unable to balance its current expenditure budget, let alone undertake desperately needed development work. Britain had ruled the country since 1896, but only provided budgetary grants-in-aid from 1955-56 onwards. In the eleven years preceding independence, the British Treasury provided Bechuanaland with only £23 million, of which £14 million went to balance the budget. An additional £550,000 per annum comes to the country from workers who have migrated to South Africa for lack of local employment opportunities.

THE ECONOMY AT INDEPENDENCE

The economy of this large but semi-arid country of 231,805 sq. miles still depended at independence almost wholly on the raising of cattle. By 1966, seven years of unprecedentedly severe drought had reduced Botswana's cattle herds by almost a third to a remaining total of some 900,000; food production, never large but, depending upon rainfall, usually consisting of subsistence crops such as sorghum, maize, millet, beans and some cash crops such as cotton, groundnuts and sunflowers, had dropped to practically zero. Over half of the African population depended upon relief feeding schemes, provided largely by the World Food Programme through the United Nations and its Food and Agricultural Organization (FAO). The cattle population has since increased, with the ending of the drought in the last months of 1966, to some 1,800,000, and emergency feeding schemes were discontinued at the request of the Botswana Government during 1967.

In 1966, there were only four significant known mineral resources: (i) two small, South African-owned manganese mines; (ii) one small, South African-controlled asbestos mine (since closed down); (iii) vast deposits of good though only medium-grade coal, which it seemed to the South African concessionaires uneconomic to exploit in the absence of local markets and in the face of competition from similar-grade but already efficiently exploited deposits in neighbouring South Africa and Southern Rhodesia (whose sole rail link runs through Botswana); and (iv) very large salt and soda-ash deposits in the Makarikari Salt Pan which Roan Selection Trust, the American-financed concessionaires, apparently hesitated to exploit because of the absence of adequate water supplies and electric power.

The only significant road in the country followed the already mentioned South African-Rhodesian rail link, which is operated by Rhodesia Railways. Communications in the rest of the country, apart from a very small internal light-aeroplane service, were as skeletal as its social services and its starving cattle. The only link which Botswana, which is also bordered by South West Africa and the Caprivi Strip, has with independent black-ruled Africa is a three to four hundred yard wide strip of the banks of the Zambezi River, where it meets with Zambia. Here, at this spot called Kazungula, a primitive ferry has long operated, but access to it is extremely difficult overland, though there is a bush landing-strip nearby. Whilst the Kazungula ferry had and has a general psychological effect on otherwise "white-encircled" Botswana and whilst it has a particularly important significance to South African anti-*apartheid* refugees, it has been of no commercial or economic importance whatever.

One other important obstacle which the country faced economically on independence was that under a Customs Union Agreement with South Africa, originally drafted when the Union of South Africa was formed in 1910, Botswana originally received 0.276 per cent, and since 1965, received 0.31 per cent of South Africa's customs and excise revenue. This deprived Botswana, which is also in a monetary union with South Africa, of one of the most important financial planning and control tools used by newly independent countries. In Africa, such countries raise on average over 40 per cent of revenue and control development, chiefly by tariff manipulation, protection of home industries, and by control of the flow of money.

On March 1st, 1970, however, the South African Government concluded a fresh Customs Agreement with the three former British High Commission Territories, now independent as Botswana, Lesotho and Swaziland. The new agreement not only promises to the three countries a larger share of South Africa's customs revenue. Under Article 6, Botswana (and each of its former sister-territories) may protect its infant industries from South African competition by levying additional duties on imports, whilst South Africa may not take such a step. Such protective duties will, however, only remain valid for eight years, unless all parties agree to an extension.

The limited capacity of the still largely subsistence-based economy to generate income is imposing serious constraints on government finances, obliging it to depend heavily on British aid. This, however, was promised only as £13 million over the three years 1966–69. Plans are afoot to improve the always problematical farming, and to increase the cattle population from 1.3 million head in 1967–68 to 2.5 million by 1975. A strict system of disease control has been established. Crop production is generally not favourable in Botswana.

MINERAL DEPOSITS

What has radically transformed the economic prospects of Botswana has been the post-independence finding of large and accessible deposits of minerals. Pre-eminent amongst these strikes has been the proving of some 37 million tons of nickel and copper at Pikwe, within a hundred miles of Francistown, the commercial centre. RST is an offshoot of American Metal Climax Inc. (AMAX), and has now formed Botswana RST in which Minerals Separation and Mond Nickel of Toronto also have interests. AMAX took up its 31 per cent entitlement. The mining operation could call for a £46 million expenditure, in which West German capital was also to be involved.

Simultaneously, the South African-based Anglo-American Corporation-De Beers group, headed by Mr. Harry Oppenheimer, has taken over the mining concessions originally obtained in the Tati area by Cecil John Rhodes, and has launched an 18 months crash programme to exploit similar nickel-copper deposits there. De Beers, through a locally registered subsidiary, is also poised to begin mining diamonds at Orapa, where one of the kimberlitic pipes discovered is believed to be among the largest in the world, likely to produce mainly industrial diamonds. A 150-mile road is being built to the Orapa area from Francistown is being financed by a loan from De Beers to the Botswana Government. Providing water remains one of the main difficulties, but there are now plans to pump water some 35 miles from the Botletle River, which is fed by the overflowing Okavango swamps in the north-west corner of Botswana. Both the copper-nickel and the diamond mine are expected to begin operations early in the 1970s, with 3.2 million carats production of diamonds by 1975.

Botswana RST, through its subsidiary Makarikari Soda Ltd., is now also expected to go ahead with the exploitation of the brine deposits. For a capital investment of some £3 million, exports valued at £1 to 2 million a year should be produced. Apart from selling salt to Southern Rhodesia, Zambia and Malawi, the Makarikari project should fill the 60,000 tons a year soda ash gap left in South Africa by Kenya's anti-*apartheid* decision not to continue supplying the Republic through I.C.I. There seems also to be a serious possibility of striking oil in Botswana; at present exploration is in the hands of Mobiloil. Other foreign companies are interested in gypsum and limestone, whilst antimony and sulphur are known to exist. A consortium of US Steel and two South African mining houses, Anglo Transvaal and Middle Wits., is now prospecting in western Botswana for minerals and gem stones. All this activity results from a preliminary survey which, in one expert's opinion, has "barely scratched the surface".

An agreement has been reached on royalties and taxes to be paid by Bamangwato Concessions in developing and exploiting mineral deposits in the Selebi-Pikwe complex. Binding for 50 years, the agreement stipulates 7½ per cent of profits to be paid as royalties. There will be a basic income tax of 40 per cent, increasing by 1 per cent for every 1 per cent rise in the profit-to-gross-revenue ratio above 48½ per cent, with a maximum of 65 per cent. Initial capital expenditure will be amortized over 5 years. Subsequent capital expenditure will be amortized immediately, with a proviso that Bamangwato Concessions' taxable profits in a given year will always be at least 25 per cent of its taxable profits before capital allowances have been credited. The Botswana Government is to receive its 15 per cent shareholding, free of charge, only when Bamangwato Concessions becomes a mining, as opposed to the present prospecting, company.

For the first ten years production, which is expected to begin in 1973-74, is planned to total 2 million metric tons of ore annually, yielding approximately 100,000 tons of sulphur, 16,000 tons of refined copper and 13,000 tons of refined nickel. Surface construction work at Selebi-Pikwe will be managed by the Texas firm of Brown Root, and licensing agreements have been made for using the Finnish Outokumpu flash smelting and sulphur reduction process once mining begins.

Now that large profits are in sight, the Botswana Government is finding it relatively easy to obtain international loan capital, often on very favourable terms, to develop the necessary infrastructure for mining and, perhaps subsequently, associated industrial development.

Then, too, the potential power needs of the mining enterprises have made the exploitation of the huge local medium-grade coal deposits a practical, almost a pressing, proposition. UNDP (United Nations Development Programme) has financed a pre-investment survey of the Selebi-Pikwe mining complex, and in December 1969, the IDA (International Development Association) approved a credit of $2.5 million to finance the costs of engineering design and preliminary works for infrastructure for the same copper-nickel area. Canada in June 1970 granted Botswana a £7 million interest-free loan for generating the requisite electricity through steam turbines utilizing local coal. Reserves of 150 million and over 400 million tons have been proved, and there may well be more. The cost of developing the infrastructure for Selebi-Pikwe is now estimated to be $60 million. The Botswana Government has applied to

the World Bank, which has completed a study of the country, for a $25 million loan for this project.

Nevertheless, the cost to the Botswana Government of providing the necessary infrastructure will be about £23 million, and here it comes up against the inability of its almost wholly pastoral people to generate sufficient development capital. On the concessions side, the Government has simplified matters by passing a law in 1967 which transferred all ownership rights to minerals from the tribe—there are seven major ones in the country—to the state. But with an estimated work force of 240,000, only 28,148 were wage-earners in Botswana in 1967-68. Ten per cent of Botswana's able-bodied men are at any given time forced to seek work in South African mines and, to a lesser extent, on farms, and even the mining developments are expected to create only 3,500 local jobs by 1974 and 5,300 by 1980. What is more, all the skilled and most of the semi-skilled new jobs will almost certainly be filled by South Africans, for Britain's educational neglect, despite gallant efforts by religious missions, was such that, at the last survey in 1964, only 21.8 per cent of the total population were found to be literate in Setswana and only 15 per cent were functionally literate in English.

FINANCE

Only rough "guestimates" exist on national income and output but it seems that the gross domestic product is between $50–55 million, giving a per capita income of less than $100. Nor, except for Botswana RST and Anglo-American at Orapa, in which the Botswana Government, thanks to the enlightened outlook of RST's Sir Ronald Prain, is to be given 15 per cent holdings, is it known to what extent, other than taxation, the government and people will share in the rich profits which will be made by outside capital through mineral development.

The terms of aid from the United Kingdom have now been renegotiated. The target date of Botswana becoming independent of this aid is 1972-73. Prior to this, Britain is committed to providing £5.1 million annually in budgetry grants for three years, together with development loans totalling £4.4 million. Annual Botswana budgets now reflect an increase of over 5 per cent in domestic revenue, brought about chiefly by an increase of slightly under R3 million received from South Africa under the revised Customs Agreement. Even so, British aid still constitutes an estimated 27 per cent of Botswana's annual revenue.

A 15 per cent annual growth rate is officially expected in the development plan for 1970-75, with the possibility that mining development could escalate this to 20 per cent. These figures must, however, be viewed against the country's present poverty, and against the question of how increased wealth will be distributed.

Economic inequality is a problem even today; Sir Seretse, himself one of the country's principal cattle owners, has recently expressed concern that 60 per cent of Botswana's cattle are owned by only 12 per cent of its farmers, that 60 per cent of those who do own cattle have less than 40 head each, and that 23 per cent of Botswana's farmers own no cattle at all.

For a time it looked as though the Swedish Government, unhappy that too much aid was going into mining infrastructure, might reduce its own contribution, but Sir Seretse appears to have satisfied them about his plans during a special visit to Stockholm at the end of 1970.

The South African Government has now stated that it has no intention of interfering with the recruitment of Batswana as migrant mineworkers. In 1971 over 30,000 of these remitted R1,061,600 to Botswana. The major centre of the far-flung operations of the South African mining companies' labour recruitment operations is in Francistown, whose airport is controlled by their organization.

Even if the planned growth rate is achieved, three out of five school leavers will be without jobs in Botswana by 1975. The country's adult labour force is increasing by an estimated 10,000 a year, whilst even on the most optimistic estimate only 2,000 jobs a year could open up.

Politically and economically, the government of Sir Seretse Khama has been alive to the danger that if, as at present is largely the case, South African—or even American or British—capital controls most important things in Botswana, independence could become a mere façade and the country could end up little better off than a liberalized *Bantustan*. Partly to avoid this danger, the government, whilst not limiting outside investment, has several times refused offers of grants-in-aid from the South African government. It did, however, find it necessary to float a £1 million bond issue on the Johannesburg Stock Exchange, which was readily taken up.

Hence a development of far-reaching importance has been the emergence of the Anglo-American Corporation of South Africa as the dominant mining group throughout Botswana. Sir Seretse's hopes of bringing in an international set of mineral developers collapsed when the West German government refused to guarantee the capital commitments into which Metallgesellschaft A.G. proposed to enter. This company had agreed to purchase two thirds of the nickel and all of the copper which Bamangwato Concessions, an offshoot of Botswana RST, would mine in the Selebi-Pikwe complex and which would be refined in the U.S.A. by American Metal Climax. However, in the reshuffle which followed the withdrawal of Metallgesellschaft's capital commitments, Anglo-American emerged as the dominant partner in Bamangwato Concessions, and hence in the country.

In its efforts to lessen its dependence on South Africa, the Botswana Government attached the greatest importance to a proposed all-weather highway linking Francistown with the Zambian capital of Lusaka, with a greatly improved, motorized ferry service capable of handling commercial cargo and replacing the present tenuous passenger transport across the Zambezi near Kazangula. In April 1970 the U.S.A. promised $6 million of aid for the building of this highway, and has publicly backed Botswana's rebuttal of South Africa's claim that no legal common border between Botswana and Zambia exists at all. On this point, Sir Seretse met to evolve a common strategy with Dr. Kenneth Kaunda, Zambia's President, and the South African Government accepted the situation on the basis that, as no bridge was to be built, the question of precise borders, which here are determined by the confluence of rivers, fell away.

But in all these things there are limits to how far Botswana can afford to irritate South Africa. Thus Botswana, totally dependent for communications and trade on South Africa and Rhodesia, has not been able to play any effective part in the UN-sponsored sanctions against Rhodesia. Officially, Sir Seretse Khama has forbidden the import of arms to Rhodesia via Botswana, but as Rhodesia Railways both own and operate the rail line through Botswana, he is in no position to enforce his decree. And if he goes too far, Rhodesian pressure for building a new and alternative direct rail link to South Africa, bypassing Botswana, will grow.

PROSPECTS FOR THE FUTURE

Leaving politics aside—which in southern Africa is hardly possible—the main problem for the Botswana Government is now to secure a fair share of the new mineral wealth for the Batswana people, how to spread this localized wealth over an overwhelmingly cattle-based economy, and how to guide changes in social institutions, such as land tenure, and especially through increased vocational and professional training and technical education, so as to enable the Batswana to meet the challenge and seize the opportunity of an increasingly varied and sophisticated economy.

And it will not be a quick or easy business. As an official Botswana publication puts it:

"The Government confidently expects that the development of mineral resources will result in financial independence for Botswana within the next ten years. But this local revenue, initially, will only in fact replace the British Government grant-in-aid to Botswana."

"It will be some time before the profits can be used to finance other developments in Botswana's economy."

Let me leave the last word with Botswana's President, Sir Seretse Khama, K.B.E.:

"We recognize that (mineral, associated industrial and commercial) economic growth will bring real benefits to all our people only if we continue to give first place to agricultural development. The vast majority of Batswana must in the forseeable future continue to earn their living on the land."

STATISTICAL SURVEY

AREA AND POPULATION

AREA (sq. km.)	POPULATION							
	Total (1971 Census)	Non-Citizens (1971 Census)	Tribes (1964 Census)					
			Bakgatla	Bakwena	Bamalete	Bamangwato	Bangwaketse	Batswana
600,372	620,000*	11,260	32,118	73,088	13,861	199,782	71,289	42,347

* In addition, there are estimated to be about 11,000 nomads.

ESTIMATED POPULATION BY DISTRICT (1971 Census)

Central	228,600	Kgatleng	35,800
Chobe	5,400	Kweneng	72,100
Francistown	19,900	Lobatse	12,900
Gaborone	18,400	Ngamiland	53,900
Ghanzi	17,400	Ngwaketse	79,200
Kgalagadi	17,300	North East	28,500
Barolong	12,200	Orapa	1,200
South East	22,700	Selebi-Pikwe	6,000

Principal Towns (1964 census): Serowe 34,182; Kanye 34,045; Molepolole 29,625; Gaborone (capital) 13,000 (1969 estimate).

EMPLOYMENT*

ECONOMICALLY ACTIVE POPULATION
(1964)

Agriculture, Forestry, Hunting and Fishing	227,649
Services	9,798
Construction	2,704
Commerce	2,468
Manufacturing	2,420
Transport, etc.	2,315
Mining	1,940
Electricity, Gas, Water	120

* The total of economically active persons in 1964 was 250,678 of which 125,477 were male and 125,201 female.

The number of Batswana recruited for South African mines in 1971 was 31,600. The income for Botswana in deferred payment and remittances was R1,061,600.

AGRICULTURE

LAND USE (1970)
('000 hectares)

Arable land	428
Permanent crops	1
Meadows and pastures	39,508
Forest land	958
Inland water	5,596
Other land	13,546
TOTAL	60,037

Source: FAO, *Production Yearbook 1971.*

PRINCIPAL CROPS

	Area ('000 hectares)			Production ('000 metric tons)			Yield (100 kg. per hectare)		
	1969	1970	1971	1969	1970	1971	1969	1970	1971
Maize . . .	47	30	38	18	5	17	3.8	1.5	4.3
Millet . . .	10	18	29	7	1	3	6.6	0.7	1.1
Sorghum . . .	104	122	161	30	8	73	2.9	0.7	4.6
Cow Peas . . .	20*	20*	25*	12*	12*	15*	6.0	6.0*	6.0*
Groundnuts . . .	4	4	6	5	4	6	10.5	8.6	10.5

* FAO estimate.

Source: FAO, *Production Yearbook 1971.*

LIVESTOCK

	1968	1969	1970/71
Cattle . .	1,250,209	1,441,197	1,832,000
Horses . .	11,092	11,840	11,143
Mules . .	544	559	1,068
Donkeys . .	30,785	36,035	64,000
Sheep . .	231,336	278,830	370,061
Goats . .	703,254	846,509	1,014,903
Pigs . .	2,457	2,708	15,472
Poultry . .	127,011	146,978	234,334

MEAT AND DAIRY PRODUCE
('000 metric tons)

	1969	1970	1971
Beef . . .	21	23	27*
Offal . . .	3*	3*	3*
Cows' Milk . . .	28*	29*	30*
Hens' Eggs . . .	0.2*	0.2*	0.3*

* FAO estimate.

HIDES AND SKINS
(metric tons)

	1968	1969	1970
Cattle Hides (raw) . . .	2,384	2,500*	2,700*
Cattle Hides (salted) . . .	312	320*	320*
Calf Skins (,,) . . .	68*	38	50*
Sheep Skins (,,) . . .	32*	41*	32*
Goat Skins (,,) . . .	80*	116*	104*

* FAO estimate.

FORESTRY
ROUNDWOOD PRODUCTION
('000 cubic metres)

1968 . . .	915
1969 . . .	922

MINING

	Unit	1969	1970	1971
Manganese	metric tons	22,200	48,300	35,600
Semi-precious Stones . . .	,, ,,	60.4	120.6	104.6
Diamonds	carats	31,453	463,595	871,800

FINANCE

South African currency: 100 cents = 1 Rand.
Coins: 1, 2, 5, 10, 20 and 50 cents; 1 Rand.
Notes: 1, 5, 10 and 20 Rand.
Exchange rates (December 1972): £1 sterling = 1.839 Rand; U.S. $1 = 78.29 S.A. cents;
100 Rand = £54.93 = $127.73.

BUDGET ESTIMATES
(R)

REVENUE	1970/71	1971/72	EXPENDITURE	1971/72	1972/73
Customs and Excise . .	4,585,000	8,287,000	Parliament . . .	89,517	93,809
Taxes and Duties . .	2,899,000	3,816,000	State President . . .	2,173,640	2,601,221
Licences	484,000	560,000	Ministry of Finance and Development Planning .	1,948,354	2,084,161
Receipts in respect of Departmental Services . .	693,000	980,000	Ministry of Health, Labour and Home Affairs .	1,831,418	1,984,425
Posts and Telegraphs .	977,000	1,275,000	Ministry of Agriculture . .	2,617,200	2,810,008
Revenue from Government Property . . .	1,131,000	1,286,000	Ministry of Education . .	1,675,443	2,145,617
Fines	59,000	64,000	Ministry of Commerce, Industry and Water Affairs .	1,550,923	2,225,538
Reimbursements . .	86,000	278,000	Ministry of Local Government and Lands .	1,321,945	1,650,350
Loan Repayments . .	315,000	346,000	Ministry of Works and Communications .	3,653,808	3,438,940
Interest . . .	231,000	200,000	Administration of Justice .	56,620	79,120
Miscellaneous . .	199,000	314,000	Attorney-General . . .	165,275	1,032,067
Sale of State Land .	50,000	—	Auditor-General . . .	56,031	69,801
TOTAL ORDINARY REVENUE	11,709,000	17,406,000	Recurrent Expenditure Arising from Development Expenditure .	—	100,000
			Public Debt Service Fund .	—	950,000
Grants and Loans from United Kingdom . .	715,000	571,000	Statutory Expenditure Public Debt . . .	1,198,496	1,297,823
Grant-in-Aid United Kingdom	496,000	1,918,000	Pensions, Gratuities and Compensation . .	718,725	666,600
Other Development Loans and Grants . .	592,000	—	Salaries and Allowances, Specified Officers .	28,231	27,000
TOTAL GRANTS AND LOANS	1,803,000	2,489,000	Overseas Services Aid Scheme	393,625	249,800
			Miscellaneous . . .	90,390	20,000
TOTAL REVENUE . .	13,512,000	19,895,000	TOTAL EXPENDITURE	19,569,641	23,526,280

NATIONAL DEVELOPMENT PLAN 1970–75 (R '000)

REVENUE (in sight)	TOTAL 1970–75	MAIN EXPENDITURE BY DEPARTMENTS	TOTAL 1970–75
U.K. Government	7,660	Agriculture	4,407
Netherlands Government . . .	88	Education	4,664
Danish Government . . .	340	Shashe Complex . . .	35,540
Swedish Government . . .	734	Interdepartmental Projects . .	1,323
IBRD and IDA	39,928	Public Works	22,366
Others	322	Water Branch	4,814
		Others (incl. unallocated expenditure) .	26,612
		TOTAL . . .	99,726
TOTAL . . .	49,072	Shortfall	50,654

NATIONAL ACCOUNTS
(R'ooo)

	1967/68	1968/69
GROSS DOMESTIC PRODUCT (at Factor Cost)	39,674	46,015
of which:		
Agriculture, hunting, forestry and fishing	18,329	21,566
Mining and quarrying	−1,082	−1,176
Manufacturing	3,569	2,845
Electricity, gas and water	306	308
Construction	2,040	1,864
Transport, storage and communication	2,402	3,412
Retail and wholesale trade, hotels and restaurants	2,464	2,968
Financing, insurance, real estate and business services	593	529
Community, social and personal services	981	1,259
Government services	7,737	9,469
Ownership of dwellings	2,335	2,971
Indirect Taxes *less* subsidies	2,535	2,098
GROSS DOMESTIC PRODUCT (at Market Prices)	42,209	48,113
Less consumption of fixed capital.	−2,711	−3,027
NET DOMESTIC PRODUCT	39,498	45,086
EXPENDITURE ON GROSS DOMESTIC PRODUCT	42,209	48,113
of which:		
Government final consumption	11,631	11,285
Private final consumption	41,688	47,497
Increase in stocks	−1,527	1,154
Gross fixed capital formation	9,862	9,933
Export of goods and services	8,355	10,276
Less Import of goods and services	−27,800	−32,032

EXTERNAL TRADE
(R'ooo)

	1966	1967	1968	1969	1970/71*	1971/72†
Imports	18,825	19,975	23,231	30,833	44,772	60,000
Exports	10,772	9,219	7,491	13,060	20,000	33,000
Balance	−8,053	−10,756	−15,740	−17,773	−24,772	−27,000

* From April 1st, 1970, the financial year is used, ending on March 31st.

† Preliminary figures.

PRINCIPAL COMMODITIES
(R'ooo)

IMPORTS	1967	1968
Food and Live Animals . .	5,549	5,800
Beverages and Tobacco . .	1,615	1,701
Crude Materials, Inedible, except Fuels . . .	—	349
Mineral Fuels, Lubrications and Related Materials	2,438	2,450
Animal and Vegetable Oils and Fats	—	13
Chemicals . . .	812	794
Manufactured Goods Classified Chiefly by Material . .	3,808	4,817
Machinery and Transport Equipment . . .	4,642	4,025
Miscellaneous Manufactured Articles . . .	2,300	2,375
Commodities and Transactions Not Classified According to Kind . . .	1,205	906
TOTAL. . .	22,370	23,231

EXPORTS	1967	1968
Live Cattle	414	5
Cattle Carcases . .	3,856	8,561
Sheep and Goats (live and carcases) . . .	78	168
Hides and Skins . . .	1,676	811
Wild Animal Skins . .	231	n.a.
Canned Meat . . .	269	9
Meat Extract . . .	1,320	n.a.
Abbatoir By-Products . .	681	81
Offals and Tallow . .	n.a.	124
Bonemeal . . .	n.a.	27
Carcasemeal . . .	n.a.	88
Butterfat . . .	n.a.	227
Other Animal Products . .	36	44
Beans and Cow Peas . .	203	121
Sorghum . . .	255	123
Manganese Ore . .	23	365
Semi-precious Stones . .	n.a.	3
Diamonds . . .	n.a.	211
Other Commodities . .	n.a.	2,803
TOTAL (incl. others) .	9,219	13,060

Of Botswana's exports of animal products in 1966 18 per cent in value (31.6 per cent in 1965) went to South Africa and 18.2 per cent to other African countries. Of the 1966 imports 65.4 per cent in value came from South Africa, and a substantial part of the remainder from Rhodesia.

TRANSPORT

RAILWAYS

Passengers carried (1969): 379,109; Total Mileage: 394.

Goods transported by rail (1969) (tons): To Botswana from Rhodesia, Zambia and Portuguese Territories 224,531; from South Africa 145,113; from stations in Botswana to other countries 738,828; internal 45,990.

ROAD TRAFFIC

	1968	1969	1970	1971
Vehicles registered* .	5,101	5,681	6,215	6,462

* Excludes government vehicles (1970: 1,337; 1971: 1,582).

CIVIL AIR TRAFFIC

	1964	1965	1966
Aircraft:			
Arrivals . . .	2,193	2,346	1,576
Departures . .	2,198	2,306	1,563
Passengers:			
Arrivals . . .	58,385	58,377	37,741
Departures . .	58,123	58,457	42,277
Goods, Mail:			
Arrivals (lb.) . .	1,493,251	2,583,337	2,192,296
Departures (lb.) .	2,043,907	2,582,337	4,391,017

COMMUNICATIONS MEDIA

	1968	1969	1970	1971
Telephones . .	2,966	3,536	3,680	4,032
Radio Licences . .	5,828	6,033	9,000	n.a.
Daily Newspapers .	1	1	1	1
Periodicals . . .	5	5	6	6

EDUCATION
(1971)

	INSTITUTIONS	STUDENTS
Primary . . .	288	78,442
Secondary . .	13	4,740
Teacher Training . .	3	302
Vocational Training .	16	1,177
Tertiary Institutions . .	—	254

THE CONSTITUTION

The new Constitution of Botswana came into operation on September 30th, 1966. The principal change from the 1965 Bechuanaland Constitution concerns the creation of the position of President, the holder of which took over the powers and responsibilities formerly exercised by the Prime Minister.

Executive power lies with the President of Botswana, who is also Commander-in-Chief of the armed forces. Election for the office of President is linked with the General Election of members of the National Assembly. Presidential candidates must receive at least 1,000 nominations. If there is more than one candidate for the Presidency, each candidate for office in the Assembly must declare which presidential candidate he supports. The candidate for President who commands the votes of more than half the elected members of the Assembly will be declared President. If the Presidency falls vacant the members of the National Assembly will themselves elect a new President. The President will hold office for the duration of Parliament.

There is also a Vice-President, whose office is Ministerial. The Vice-President is appointed by the President, and acts as his deputy in the absence of the President. The Cabinet consists of the President, the Vice-President, and eight other Ministers appointed by the President. Every member of the Cabinet accepts responsibility before the National Assembly for the policies of the Government.

The legislative power is vested in Parliament, consisting of the President and the National Assembly, acting after consultation in certain cases with the House of Chiefs. The President may withhold his assent to a Bill passed by the National Assembly, but if it is again presented to him after six months, he is required to assent to it unless he dissolves Parliament within 21 days.

The House of Chiefs has the Chiefs of the eight principal tribes of Botswana as *ex officio* members, 4 members elected by sub-chiefs from their own number, and 3 members elected by the other 12 members of the House. Bills and motions relating to chieftaincy matters and alterations of the Constitution must be referred to the House, which may also deliberate and make representations on any matter, including Bills affecting tribal interests.

The National Assembly consists of the Speaker, the Attorney-General, who does not have a vote, 31 elected members, and 4 specially elected members. There is universal adult suffrage. The life of the Assembly is five years.

The Constitution also contains a code of human rights, enforceable by the High Court.

THE GOVERNMENT

President: Dr. Sir SERETSE KHAMA, K.B.E.

CABINET
(*December* 1972)

President: Dr. Sir SERETSE KHAMA, K.B.E.

Vice-President and Minister of Finance and Development Planning: Dr. QUET K. J. MASIRE.

Minister of Agriculture: E. S. MASISI.

Minister of Education: B. C. THEMA, M.B.E.

Minister of Local Government and Lands: E. M. K. KGABO.

Minister of Commerce, Industry and Water Affairs: M. K. SEGOKGO.

Minister of Works and Communications: J. G. HASKINS.

Minister of Health, Labour and Home Affairs: M. P. K. NWAKO.

Minister of State: B. K. KGARI.

Assistant Minister in the Office of the President: D. KWELA-GOBE.

Assistant Minister for Finance and Development Planning: L. MAKGEKGEMENE.

Assistant Minister for Local Government and Lands: K. P. MORAKE.

DIPLOMATIC REPRESENTATION

HIGH COMMISSIONS AND EMBASSIES ACCREDITED TO BOTSWANA
(In Gaborone, unless otherwise stated)
(HC) High Commissioner; (E) Embassy.

Austria: Pretoria, South Africa (E).
Belgium: Pretoria, South Africa (E).
Canada: Pretoria, South Africa (HC).
China, Republic (Taiwan): (E); *Ambassador:* HSIN-YU LIU.
Czechoslovakia: Lusaka, Zambia (E).
Denmark: Lusaka, Zambia (E).
France: Lusaka, Zambia (E).
Germany, Federal Republic: Lusaka, Zambia (E).
Israel: Lusaka, Zambia (E).
Japan: Lusaka, Zambia (E).
Korea: Nairobi, Kenya (E).
Netherlands: Pretoria, South Africa (E).
Nigeria: (HC); *High Commissioner:* I. C. OLISEMEKA.
Romania: Lusaka, Zambia (E).
Sweden: Pretoria, South Africa (E).
Switzerland: Pretoria, South Africa (E).
Tanzania: Lusaka, Zambia (HC).
United Kingdom: P.M.B. 23 (HC); *High Commissioner:* G. D. ANDERSEN.
U.S.A.: (E); *Chargé d'Affaires:* CHARLES J. NELSON.
U.S.S.R.: Lusaka, Zambia (E).
Zambia: P.O.B. 362 (HC); *High Commissioner:* MALAMA SOKONI.

Botswana also has diplomatic relations with Japan, Kenya and Yugoslavia.

PARLIAMENT

NATIONAL ASSEMBLY
Speaker: Rev. ALBERT LOCK.
Attorney-General: M. D. MOKAMA.
Leader of the Opposition: PHILIP MATANTE.

(General Election of October 1969)

PARTY	VOTES	SEATS
Botswana Democratic Party .	52,859	24
Botswana People's Party .	9,239	3
Botswana National Front .	10,362	3
Botswana Independence Party .	4,601	1

HOUSE OF CHIEFS
Chairman: Chief SEEPAPITSO IV.

POLITICAL PARTIES

Botswana Democratic Party: P.O.B. 28, Gaborone; Pres. Sir SERETSE KHAMA; Vice-Pres. A. M. TSOEBEBE; Sec. Q. K. J. MASIRE; 24 seats in National Assembly.
Botswana People's Party: P.O. Francistown; Pres. P. L. MATANTE; 3 seats in National Assembly.
Botswana Independence Party: P.O. Box 37, Palapye; Pres. M. K. MPHO; Sec.-Gen. E. R. MOKOBI; Vice-Pres. J. G. GUGUSHE; one seat in National Assembly.
Botswana National Front: P.O.B. 11, Mahalapye; Parl. Leader Ex-Chief BATHOEN II; Vice-Pres. G. F. KGAKGE; Sec.-Gen. M. H. MHOIWA; 3 seats in National Assembly.

DEFENCE

Botswana has no army, but there is a police force of about 1,000.
Commissioner of Police: SIMON HIRSCHFIELD.

JUDICIAL SYSTEM

There is a High Court at Lobatse and Magistrates' Courts in each district. Appeals lie to the Court of Appeal for Botswana.
Chief Justice: Hon. T. AKINOLA AGUDA.
Registrar and Master of the High Court: F. X. ROONEY.
President of Court of Appeal: Hon. O. D. SCHREINER, M.C.
Senior Magistrate: P. T. W. POWELL.

RELIGION

Many people follow ancestral forms of worship. There are about 43,000 Christians including a large number of "Zionist" or Evangelical Christians.
Roman Catholic Bishop of Gaborone: Rt. Rev. U. C. J. MURPHY.
Anglican Bishop of Botswana: Rt. Rev. C. S. MALLORY.

THE PRESS

Daily News: Gaborone; Government-sponsored; circ. 8,500 in English, 4,500 in Setswana.
Kutlwano: Gaborone; monthly; Government-sponsored; in Setswana and English; circ. 10,000.
Mafeking Mail and Botswana Guardian: Mafeking; bilingual weekly; caters specially for the Mafeking district and Botswana.
Masa (*Dawn*): P.O. Francistown; a monthly publication of the Botswana People's Party.
Puo Pha (*Straight Talk*): P.O.B. 11, Mahalapye; a monthly publication of the Botswana National Front.
Therisanyo (*Consultation*): P.O.B. 28, Gaborone; monthly publication of the Botswana Democratic Party.

South African and Rhodesian papers also circulate.

RADIO

Radio Botswana: P.O.B. 52, Gaborone; broadcasts 119 hours a week in Setswana and English; f. 1965.

There were about 100,000 radio sets in 1972; Officer-in-Charge P. MOLEFHE.

FINANCE

Barclays Bank International Ltd.: Head Office: London; chief Botswana office: Gaborone, P.O.B. 478; brs. at Gaborone, Lobatse, Francistown, Mahalapye, Selebi-Pikwe and 17 agencies; Botswana Manager L. ATKINSON.
Standard Bank Ltd.: Head Office: London; brs. at Francistown, Lobatse, Mahalapye, Selebi-Pikwe, Orapa, Maun, Serowe and Gaborone. Botswana Manager: Gaborone.
National Development Bank: P.O.B. 225, Gaborone; f. 1964; priority given to agricultural credit for African farmers, and co-operative credit and loans for local business ventures.

TRADE AND INDUSTRY

Northern Botswana Chamber of Commerce: P.O.B. 2, Palapye; f. 1903; 28 mems.; Chair. C. W. FREEMAN; Sec. T. C. P. SHAW.

There are other Chambers of Commerce at Francistown, Serowe, Mahalapye and Selebi-Pikwe.

Botswana Meat Commission: Private Bag 4, Lobatse; f. 1966 by statute as Bechuanaland Meat Commission; cap. R1,588,325.

Slaughter of livestock, export of hides and carcases, boneless beef, production of by-products, canning. It is Botswana's chief industrial enterprise.

Chair. R. WHYTE; Gen. Man. A. J. ROBERTS, O.B.E.; 1,100 employees.

Botswana Game Industries (Pty.) Ltd.: Private Bag 30, Francistown; f. 1966; paid up cap. R368,000.

Tanners and dressers of game skins; taxidermists, ivory buyers, manufacturers of game skin products.

Man. Dir. PETER BECKER; Technical Dir. BODO MUCHE; 210 employees.

DEVELOPMENT ORGANIZATION

Botswana Development Corporation: Embassy Chambers, P.O.B. 438, Gaborone.

Botswana General Workers' Organization: Francistown.

Botswana Workers' Union: Francistown.

Botswana Trade Union Congress: Francistown.

Francistown African Employees' Union: P.O.B. 74, Francistown; f. 1949; Chair. P. M. TLHALERWA; Gen. Sec. G. M. K. MMUSI; 400 mems.

Department of Co-operative Development: P.O.B. 86, Gaborone; f. 1964; by December 1971, 78 co-operative societies were registered, of which 32 were marketing co-operatives, 13 consumer co-operatives, 29 thrift and loan societies, 1 co-operative union with membership of 13 marketing, 10 consumer societies and 2 others.

TRANSPORT

RAILWAYS

The main railway line from Cape Town to Rhodesia passes through the country entering at Ramatlabama and leaving at Ramaquabane (394 miles).

Rhodesia Railways: Bulawayo, Rhodesia; operate the railway system in Botswana.

ROADS

In 1970 there were 4,984 miles of gravelled or earth road: 1,565 miles of trunk roads, 1,478 miles of main roads and 1,941 miles of district roads. There are two short lengths of bitumen surface in Lobatse and Francistown. Work started in August 1970 on a 400-mile road linking Francistown (Botswana) with Livingstone (Zambia) across the Zambezi River.

CIVIL AVIATION

The principal airports are at Francistown and Gaborone.

Botswana Airways Corporation: P.O.B. 92, Gaborone; f. 1969; service to Lusaka from Francistown linking with London and daily services operated with South African Airways between Gaborone and Johannesburg; Gen. Man. C. G. KENYON.

TOURISM

Controller of Tourism, Department of Wildlife and National Parks: P.O.B. 4, Gaborone.

EDUCATION

Most Primary Schools are run by District and Town Councils and are financed from Local Government revenues (see the statistical table for numbers).

THE UNIVERSITY OF BOTSWANA, LESOTHO AND SWAZILAND

P.O. ROMA, LESOTHO, SOUTHERN AFRICA

Telephone: Roma 20.

Language of instruction: English; Academic year: July to April.

The University was established by Royal Charter on January 1st, 1964. It is the successor to Pius XII University College, which was established in 1945. In 1972 additional campuses were opened in Botswana and Swaziland although teaching is at present limited to Part I studies. In addition, the schools of Education and Adult Learning, whose headquarters are in Lesotho, have centres in Botswana and Swaziland, and Agriculture is taught at the Swaziland Agricultural College and University Centre (SACUC). The present student body is drawn from Botswana, Lesotho, Swaziland, the Republic of South Africa, Rhodesia, Malawi, Kenya, Britain, South West Africa, Canada and Eire.

Chancellor: His Majesty King MOSHOESHOE II of Lesotho.

Vice-Chancellor: C. A. ROGERS, M.A., PH.D.

Pro-Vice-Chancellors: H. O. H. VERNON-JACKSON, B.COMM., M.A., D.ED. (Botswana), J. A. NOONAN, C.B.E., M.A., D.PHIL. (Lesotho), S. M. GUMA, M.A., D.LITT.ET PHIL.

Registrar: M. SOUTHWOOD, M.A. (OXON.).

Librarian: J. HUTTON, B.A., LL.B.

Number of teachers: 90.
Number of students: 560.

The Botswana Agricultural College, the first of its kind in the country, was established in 1967. In Gaborone the Botswana Training Centre provides training in the fields of clerical, administrative and technical services. There is a veterinary school at Ramatlabama, and a third teachers training centre opened in 1968 in Francistown.

SELECT BIBLIOGRAPHY

BENSON, MARY. *Tshekedi Khama.* London, Faber & Faber, 1960.

HAILEY, Lord. *The Republic of South Africa and the High Commission Territories.* London, Oxford University Press, 1963.

HALPERN, JACK. *South Africa's Hostages. Basutoland, Bechuanaland and Swaziland.* Harmondsworth, Penguin Books, 1965.

KNIGHT, DAVID B. "Botswana", *Focus,* Vol. 20/3, November 1963. American Geographical Society.

RANDALL, DARRELL. *Factors of Economic Development in the Okavango Delta.* Chicago, University of Chicago, 1957.

SCHAPERA, I. *The Tswana.* London, International African Institute, 1953.

THOMAS, ELIZABETH MARSHALL. *The Harmless People.* London, Secker & Warburg, 1959.

Burundi

PHYSICAL AND SOCIAL GEOGRAPHY*

Burundi, like its neighbour, Rwanda, is exceptionally small in area (10,747 sq. miles) but has a relatively large population of 3,615,000 (1971 estimate). The result is a high density of about 330 per sq. mile. Burundi's political frontiers, apart from Rwanda's to the north, are shared with Zaire (formerly Congo (Kinshasa) to the west and Tanzania to the east. The natural divide between Burundi and Zaire is formed by Lake Tanganyika and the River Ruzizi on the floor on the western rift valley system. Eastwards from here the land rises sharply up to elevations of around 6,000 ft. in a range which stretches north into the much higher, and volcanic, mountains of Rwanda. Away from the edge of the rift valley elevations are lower, and most of Burundi consists of plateaux of between 4,500 and 6,000 ft. Here the average temperature is 68°F. and rainfall 47 in. In the valley the temperature averages 73°F., while rainfall is much lower at 30 in.

Population has concentrated on the fertile, volcanic soils at between 5,000 and 6,000 ft., away from the arid and hot floor and margins of the rift valley. The consequent pressure on the land has resulted in extensive migration, mainly to Tanzania and the Congo but also to Uganda. However, the measures in the East African countries to restrict employment to nationals, of which Uganda's measure of September 1970 is the latest to affect Burundians, are closing the outlets for such migrations. The ethnic composition of the population is much the same as Rwanda's: about 84 per cent Hutu, 15 per cent Tutsi, later arrivals in the country and until recently the unchallenged masters, and less than 1 per cent Twa, pygmoid hunters. However, historically the kingdoms of Ruanda and Urundi were almost invariably enemies, and traditional national feeling remains strong in both countries. Thus the assimilation of the two languages, Kirundi and Kinyaruanda, which correspond very closely, has yet to be achieved. The only towns of any note are Bujumbura (80,000), the capital and, as Usumbura, formerly the capital of the UN Trust Territory of Ruanda-Urundi; and Kitega (5,000), the ancient capital.

* See map on p. 896.

RECENT HISTORY†

René Lemarchand

The history of Burundi since independence may be reduced to a protracted sequence of factional struggles and intensifying ethnic claims and counterclaims, culminating in April and May 1972 with one of the most appalling ethnic slaughters ever recorded in the annals of independent Africa. Following the abortive Hutu-led *coup* of April 29th, 1972, an extraordinarily brutal and arbitrary repression got under way, resulting in an estimated 50,000 Hutu deaths. The systematic extermination of all literate Hutu elements has given the Tutsi minority unfettered control over civilian and military institutions, with the army acting as the pivotal element in the political system.

The anaemic apparatus built around the Uprona party (*Union et progrès national*), under the short-lived leadership of Prince Louis Rwagasore, proved thoroughly inadequate to contain the ethnic tensions that had been steadily building up since independence (1962). After Rwagasore's death, in 1961, the Crown emerged as the only source of legitimacy to which both Hutu and Tutsi could relate in any meaningful fashion. In order to accentuate the force of its own gravity in the political vacuum that followed independence, the Crown went to great lengths to ensure a proper balancing of ethnic interests in government.

Each of the five consecutive governments appointed by Mwami (King) Mwambutsa between 1963 and 1965 comprised an almost even proportion of Hutu and Tutsi; following the appointment of Pierre Ngendandumwe as Prime Minister, in 1963, each Prime Minister of Hutu origins was inevitably succeeded in office by a Tutsi.

With the abolition of the monarchy in 1966, following the seizure of power by a clique of civilian and military élites gravitating around Colonel Micombero, the most important stabilizing element in the political system disappeared as well. Repeated purges of Hutu officers and politicians have since further accentuated the all-Tutsi profile of the régime: by 1971 the distribution of ethnic affiliations within the *Conseil Suprême de la République* (CSR)—a junta-type organization set up by Micombero in October 1971—showed an overwhelming predominance of Tutsi elements (23 Tutsi, 2 Hutu, 2 Ganwa). The abrupt dismissal of all cabinet members by Micombero on April 29th, 1972, coinciding with an incipient Hutu uprising, gave the army and the *Jeunesses Révolutionnaires Rwagasore* (JRR) a free hand to repress the insurgents. Meanwhile the massacre of approximately 450 Hutu troops, in early

† For the history of Burundi before Independence, *see* the Recent History of Zaire (p. 990).

May, at the request of the army High Command, has since resulted in an all-Tutsi army.

The scale on which counter-revolutionary surgery has been performed has effectively neutralized the Hutu as an opposition force for the foreseeable future. By the same token it has created an unprecedented potential of ethnic hatred among the remainder of the Hutu community, and deprived the country of its ablest sons. In the name of slogans associated with the concept of "national revolution" what little potential there first existed to operate an economic and social revolution has been frittered away. Army rule in Burundi has thus brought a new caste to power whose contribution to nation-building is unlikely to go very far beyond the preservation of its own economic and social privileges.

ECONOMY

Burundi is one of the poorest states in the world. G.N.P. per capita stood at only just over £20 in 1970, and at UNCTAD III in Santiago in May 1972 the "Group of 77" (in fact comprising 96) developing countries classified Burundi as one of the least developed nations, needing special aid from the industrialized states. Burundi has never had a full census (one is due to be held in the next two years), but the population estimate for 1971 was 3,615,000. With an area of only 10,747 square miles, Burundi therefore has a population density of more than 330 per square mile, the second highest in mainland Africa. Most of its people are engaged in agriculture, mainly at subsistence level. The political upheavals and massacres of April-June 1972 seem likely to reduce still further the pitiful economic prospects of Burundi.

AGRICULTURE AND TRADE

The country's two main cash crops, coffee and cotton, provide almost all export earnings. The overwhelming dependence on coffee (about 80 per cent of total exports) has in the past led to balance of payments difficulties in times of falling world coffee prices. After the troubles of the first half of 1972 the marketing of Burundi's coffee faced fresh and far more serious difficulties, for most of the coffee is grown by Hutu peasant farmers and half a million Hutu were homeless at the time when the crop was ripening. But even if the bulk of the crop were eventually picked, disposing of it on the world markets would still have been a problem. Burundi's annual quota under the International Coffee Agreement is 17,000 tons (the year runs from October to September). In 1971 Burundi produced 24,500 tons, and the forecast for 1972, before the massacres, was a bumper 28,000 tons. Burundi will therefore have had to draw on its following year's quota, as in the past, or to have sold much more than it usually does to non-quota markets at about half the quota price. About 65 per cent of the coffee produced is *arabica* and most of this is sold to the U.S.A.

Cotton accounts for less than ten per cent of total exports. Mainly grown in the plain of Ruzizi, nearly all of it is sold to Belgium. Tea is the only other cash crop of importance. Cultivation began in 1963 with the assistance of the EDF and the first exports of the commodity were made five years later. The EDF in 1972 made further grants towards expanding and improving the Teza and Muramvya plantations. Foreign assistance has also been directed at the further development of other crops. On the Imbo plain land is being reclaimed for the cultivation of cotton and rice in an integrated rural development scheme aided by UNDP and FAO. Irrigated rice cultivation is also being encouraged in the Mosso region.

The development of livestock is hindered by the social system, which encourages the maintenance of cattle-herds that are far too large and far too little exploited. Some fishing is carried out in the waters of Lake Tanganyika, of whose resources UNDP is aiding the assessment.

MINERALS

Small amounts of bastnaesite, cassiterite and gold (some of which is sold illegally) are produced, and prospects for future discoveries are good, provided the necessary finance for exploration can be obtained. UNDP allotted over $900,000 in 1969 for prospecting which is expected to last about two and a half years. Oil has been detected in the Ruzizi valley, and preliminary investigations of its potential have begun.

INDUSTRY AND TRANSPORT

Industry is almost non-existent, what little there is mainly involving the processing of agricultural products—cotton, coffee, tea, etc. Industrial development is hampered by Burundi's distance from the sea (about 870 miles to Dar es Salaam and 1,250 miles to Matadi), which means that only manufactures capable of bearing the high costs of transport can be developed.

The network of roads is dense, but only about 50 of the 3,000 miles of routes are made up with asphalt, and these are the roads that connect Bujumbura with respectively the Zairian border, the airport and Muramvya. Improvements to the system have, however, been accorded priority by the government, and the road from Bujumbura to the Rwanda frontier is among those receiving attention. Lake Tanganyika plays a crucial role in Burundi's transport system, since most of her external trade is conducted along the lake between Bujumbura and Tanzania and Zaire. There is an international airport at Bujumbura.

AID AND FUTURE DEVELOPMENT

Burundi is likely to remain dependent on foreign assistance for some time, not only for capital projects but also for budgetary support. The multilateral agencies, such as the IDA and EDF, are involved in schemes to increase coffee production by training farmers, stabilizing prices, etc., but such aid can easily be vitiated by continued fluctuations in world prices which will mean further recourse to the IMF. The main bilateral donors of aid and technical assistance are Belgium, France and Federal Germany. China in 1972 granted Burundi a $20 million loan, payable from the beginning of 1972 until the end of 1976. Repayment will be made between 1982 and 1991 in the form of exports to China.

Burundi also receives aid (through the EDF) from the EEC, with which it has an association agreement under the Yaoundé Convention, Burundi is involved in the preliminary discussions on the enlargement of the EEC and its range of associates consequent upon Britain's accession to membership. Formal negotia-

tions begin during 1973 to hammer out new association terms by the beginning of 1975. An enlarged Yaoundé association, with the extension of existing trade preferences to all or most of the eligible Commonwealth countries, would not necessarily be to Burundi's advantage, but it might benefit from the vague promise made to Commonwealth sugar producers at the negotiations on British membership that countries very dependent on the export of one commodity alone will have their interests specially considered in the negotiations to come. Better prospects for real assistance in developing the economy are likely to emerge from eventual membership of the East African Community, which Burundi made formal application to join in 1968.

Burundi, Rwanda and Tanzania are at present co-operating in a two-year project, which began in June 1971, to explore and develop the water, power and mineral resources of the Kigela River. The project is supported by the UNDP, with a contribution of £325,000.

STATISTICAL SURVEY

AREA AND POPULATION

AREA (sq. miles)	Total (1971 est.)	POPULATION:				Refugees from Rwanda (1965 est.)	Bujumbura (capital) (1970 est.)	Kitega (1970 est.)
		Foreigners (1965 est.)						
		Africans	Europeans	Asians and Arabs				
10,747	3,615,000	24,730	4,190	2,913		160,000	80,000	5,000

EMPLOYMENT
(1965)

Traditional agriculture . . .	1,516,350
Fishing . . .	9,200
Craftsmen . . .	4,380
Shopkeepers . . .	11,250
Private sector (modern) . . .	58,130
Public sector . . .	13,980
Professional . . .	1,260
Total active population . . .	1,614,550

AGRICULTURE

PRINCIPAL CROPS
('000 metric tons)

	1969	1970	1971
Wheat	4	13	15*
Maize	237	182	200*
Millet	21	34	30*
Sorghum	51	96	105*
Rice	3	12	12*
Potatoes . . .	41	101	90*
Sweet Potatoes and Yams .	874	1,082	n.a.
Cassava (Manioc) . .	1,024	1,577	n.a.
Dry Beans . .	311	349	300*
Dry Peas . .	20	34	36*
Palm Kernels . . .	0.2*	0.2*	0.2*
Groundnuts . . .	22	21	21*
Cottonseed . . .	5	6	6*
Cotton (Lint) . .	3	3	3*
Coffee . . .	14.6	22.5	24
Tobacco . . .	1.5*	1.5*	1.5*

* FAO estimate.

Source: FAO, *Production Yearbook* 1971.

Bananas and Plantains: 1,310,800 metric tons in 1967.

LAND USE
(1970)

	Area (hectares)	Percentage distribution
Arable Land . .	1,038,000	37.30
Land under Permanent Crops	162,000	5.82
Meadows and Pastures . .	434,000	15.59
Forest . . .	70,000	2.52
All other Land . .	861,000	30.94
Inland Water . .	218,000	7.83
TOTAL AREA .	2,783,000	100.00

LIVESTOCK

	1969	1970
Cattle	685,000	683,000
Sheep	227,000	240,000
Goats	472,000	412,000
Pigs	17,000	20,000
Poultry	2,100,000	2,200,000

Source: FAO, *Production Yearbook 1971.*

FISHING
(metric tons)

	1965	1966	1967
Traditional Fishing .	8,728	10,101	6,634
Small-scale Fishing .	1,921	2,391	1,947
Industrial Fishing .	2,685	3,938	3,706
TOTAL .	13,334	16,430	12,287

Total Catch: (1968) 15,000; (1969) 15,600; (1970) 15,600.

INDUSTRY

	1966	1967	1968	1969	1970
Beer (hectolitres) . .	215,160	207,795	197,145	174,663	n.a.
Lemonade (hectolitres) . .	22,079	25,405	n.a.	n.a.	n.a.
Electricity* ('000 kWh.) . .	14,700	15,600	16,700	18,300	21,500

* Consumption, including purchases from Zaire.

FINANCE

100 centimes = 1 Burundi franc.

Coins: 1 franc.

Notes: 5, 10, 20, 50, 100, 500 and 1,000 francs.

Official exchange rates (December 1972): £1 sterling = 205.43 francs; U.S. $1 = 87.50 francs.

1,000 francs = £4.916 = $11.429.

BUDGET
(1968 estimates—million francs)

REVENUE		EXPENDITURE	
Direct Taxation	648.5	Defence	251.9
Customs	601.5	Other Administration . . .	355.0
Other Indirect Taxation. . . .	422.0	Education	422.3
Revenue from Services	130.0	Health and Social Services . .	186.6
Foreign Aid	2.7	Economic Services. . .	462.6
		Public Debt	113.2
TOTAL	1,382.7	TOTAL	1,791.6

1969 Budget: Revenue 1,694m. francs; Expenditure 1,754m. francs.

1970 Budget: Revenue 2,093m. francs; Expenditure 1,855m. francs.

BALANCE OF PAYMENTS
(million francs)

	1968		
	CREDIT	DEBIT	BALANCE
Merchandise	1,434.1	1,767.9	333.8
Freight and transport . . .	72.7	58.4	14.3
Travel and diplomatic expenditure . .	103.0	55.2	47.8
Investment income	—	238.3	−238.3
Government	42.1	232.4	−190.3
Other.	343.6	204.0	139.6
Foreign Aid:			
Aid from EEC (excluding Belgium) . .	83.9	—	83.9
Belgian Aid	227.5	—	227.5
Remittances from citizens abroad . .	121.0	—	121.0
Debt servicing	—	46.6	− 46.6
GLOBAL BALANCE	—	184.6	−184.6

EXTERNAL TRADE
PRINCIPAL COMMODITIES
(million francs)

IMPORTS	1967	1968	1970
Food	268.9	291.3	275
Energy	151.1	132.5	n.a.
Raw Materials and Semi-finished Products .	216.5	72.8	283
Industrial Mechanical and Electrical Products	451.4	446.6	350
Textiles and Leather	412.2	490.3	449
Other Industrial Products . . .	242.8	314.6	n.a.
TOTAL (incl. others) . . .	1,742.9	1,993.9	1,956

1969 Total: 1,905 million francs.
1971 Total: 2,613 million francs.

EXPORTS	1967	1968	1970
Coffee	1,216.0	1,054.1	1,800
Cotton	112.7	126.2	184
Skins	15.0	19.7	35
Tea	5.0	n.a.	8
Cotton Oilcakes	3.3	9.7	n.a.
Minerals	3.7	24.2	21
Other Products	52.9	62.9	n.a.
TOTAL	1,434.5	1,297.9	2,132

1969 Total: 1,039 million francs.
1971 Total: 1,622 million francs.

PRINCIPAL COUNTRIES
(million U.S. $)

IMPORTS	1968	1969	1970
Belgium	5.3	3.3	3.3
U.S.A.	2.3	2.1	3.0
Federal Germany . . .	2.6	2.1	2.0
Japan	2.3	1.8	3.1
Tanzania	2.2	2.8	2.5
France	1.5	1.3	2.0
Kenya	1.0	1.0	1.4
Netherlands	0.7	1.0	0.9
U.K.	0.9	0.6	0.8
Italy	0.6	0.2	0.9
Zaire	0.2	n.a.	n.a.
TOTAL IMPORTS . . .	22.9	21.6	22.3

EXPORTS	1968	1969	1970
U.S.A.	19.8	17.4	21.2
U.K.	4.4	2.1	4.5
Belgium	1.3	1.5	0.5
Zaire	0.9	n.a.	n.a.
France	0.6	0.3	0.4
Federal Germany . . .	0.4	0.7	2.0
Italy	0.1	0.5	1.4
Rwanda	0.7	0.5	0.3
Japan	—	0.1	0.9
Netherlands	—	—	0.1
TOTAL EXPORTS . . .	27.2	23.2	31.3

TRANSPORT

ROAD TRAFFIC

	1967	1968	1969
Passenger Cars .	2,900	3,200	3,200
Commercial Vehicles	1,200	1,400	1,400
TOTAL .	4,100	4,600	4,600

LAKE TRAFFIC
(Bujumbura—metric tons)

	1966	1967	1968
Goods:			
Arrivals . .	108,476	83,078	86,764
Departures . .	29,049	24,654	25,438

CIVIL AIR TRAFFIC
(Bujumbura Airport)

	1966	1967	1968
Passengers:			
Arrivals . .	17,346	13,034	13,094
Departures . .	20,173	15,824	13,694
Freight (metric tons):			
Arrivals . .	628.4	608.0	501.4
Departures . .	498.2	288.6	441.6

EDUCATION
(Number of pupils)

	1966–67	1967–68	1968–69	1969
Primary	153,451	171,870	181,530	182,444
Secondary	2,932	3,297	3,652	3,701
Vocational	1,617	1,878	1,746	2,264
Teacher Training	1,948	2,175	2,523	2,892
Ecole Normale Supérieure du Burundi . .	36	59	77	} 397
Université officielle de Bujumbura . .	251	235	286	

THE CONSTITUTION

Burundi obtained internal self-government as a kingdom in January 1962 and full independence in July 1962. On July 8th, 1966, the Mwami (King), Mwambutsa IV, was deposed by Prince Charles Ndizeye and the constitution, which provided for a legislative assembly of 33 members and a senate of 16, was suspended. On November 28th, 1966, Captain Micombero, who had been appointed Premier by Charles (as Mwami Ntare V), deposed the King and declared a republic with himself as President, heading a military National Committee of Revolution.

A republican constitution, providing for strong presidential powers and embodying changes in the administration of justice, is being drawn up. Each of the eight provinces is administered by a military governor.

President Micombero inaugurated a Supreme Council of the Republic on October 20th, 1971. The Council, which is composed of 27 army officers, has been set up to advise the President on all problems of national importance.

THE GOVERNMENT

President: Col. MICHEL MICOMBERO.

COUNCIL OF MINISTERS

(October 1972)

Prime Minister and Minister of the Interior: ALBIN NYAMOYA..

Minister of Foreign Affairs, Co-operation and Planning: ARTEMON SIMBANANIYE.

Minister of Communications and Aviation: MELCHIOR BWAKIRA.

Minister of Information: CAJETAN NOKOBAMYE.

Minister of the Economy: DAMIEN BARAKAMFITYIE.

Minister Delegate to the Presidency: ANTOINE NTAHOKAJA.

Minister of Justice: GABRIEL MPOZAGARA.

Minister of Civil Service: GREGOIRE BARAKAMFITYIE.

Minister of Finance: JOSEPH HICUBURUNDI.

Minister of Education and Culture: GILLES BIMAZUBUTE.

Minister of Agriculture and Livestock: PIERRE BIGAYIMPUNZI.

Minister of Public Health: Dr. CHARLES BITARIHO.

Minister of Social Affairs: BENOIT BIHORUBUSA.

Minister of Public Works, Transport and Equipment: LONGIN KANUMA.

DIPLOMATIC REPRESENTATION

EMBASSIES ACCREDITED TO BURUNDI

(In Bujumbura unless otherwise stated)

Austria: Nairobi, Kenya.

Belgium: 9 avenue de l'Industrie, B.P. 1920; *Ambassador:* P. VAN AHUTE.

Canada: Kinshasa, Zaire.

China, People's Republic: (E); *Ambassador:* CHEN FENG.

Czechoslovakia: Dar es Salaam, Tanzania.

Egypt: 31 ave. de la Liberté, B.P. 1520; *Ambassador:* SALAH EL NASHAR.

Ethiopia: Kinshasa, Zaire.

France: coin avenue de l'Uprona et avenue de l'Angola, B.P. 1740; *Ambassador:* HUBERT DE LA BRUCHOLLERIE.

German Federal Republic: 22 rue de la Résidence; *Ambassador:* FRANZ OBERMAIER.

Guinea: Dar es Salaam, Tanzania.

India: Kampala, Uganda.

Israel: Nairobi, Kenya.

Italy: Kampala, Uganda.

Japan: Kinshasa, Zaire.

Korea, Democratic People's Republic: Dar es Salaam, Tanzania.

Mali: Dar es Salaam, Tanzania.

Netherlands: Kinshasa, Zaire.

Romania: *Ambassador:* ALEXANDRU BUJOR.

Rwanda: *Ambassador:* CANISIUS KARAKE.

Somalia: Dar es Salaam, Tanzania.

Spain: Kinshasa, Zaire.

Switzerland: Nairobi, Kenya.

Syria: Dar es Salaam, Tanzania.

Tanzania: Kinshasa, Zaire.

United Kingdom: Kinshasa, Zaire.

U.S.S.R.: 9 ave. de l'Uprona, B.P. 1034; *Ambassador:* MICHEL KLEKOB.

U.S.A.: ave. Olsen, B.P. 1720; *Ambassador:* THOMAS MELADY.

Vatican: 1 chaussée de Kitega, B.P. 1068; *Chargé d'Affaires* WIILAM COREW.

Yugoslavia: Kampala, Uganda.

Zaire: 5 avenue Olsen, B.P. 872; *Ambassador:* Col. FERDINAND MALIBA.

PARLIAMENT

The Constitution was suspended on July 8th, 1966.

At the last election before the suspension, held on May 10th, 1965, *Uprona* won 21 seats, *Parti du Peuple* 10 and Independents 2 in the Legislative Assembly.

POLITICAL PARTY

Uprona (*Union et progrès national: Unity and National Progress*): declared sole party by royal decree of November 24th, 1966; decree confirmed by republican government; Party's charter accepted by the National Political Bureau on July 30th 1970; Pres. Col. MICHEL MICOMBERO; Sec.-Gen. ALBIN NYAMOYA.

Before November 24th, 1966, the main opposition party was the Hutu *Parti du Peuple.*

DEFENCE

The National Army and the police were combined by decree in 1967 and now form a force of 3,000.

Chief of Staff: Lt.-Col. THOMAS NDABEMEYE.

JUDICIAL SYSTEM

The judicial system is being reorganized and the changes will be incorporated in the new constitution.

Supreme Court: Bujumbura; Pres. JOSEPH BUKERA.

Court of Appeal: Bujumbura; Pres. GAÉTAN RUGAMBARARA.

Court of First Instance: Bujumbura; Pres. B. GAHUNGU.

RELIGION

AFRICAN RELIGIONS

Traditional belief is mainly in a God "Imana". Less than 40 per cent of the population are followers of traditional beliefs.

CHRISTIANITY

More than 60 per cent of the population are Christians, mostly Roman Catholics.

ROMAN CATHOLICS

Archbishop of Kitega: Most Rev. ANDRÉ MAKARAKIZA. Suffragan Sees: Bishop of Ngozi Rt. Rev. STANISLAS KABURUNGU, Bishop of Bujumbura Rt. Rev. MICHEL NTUYAHAGA, Bishop of Bururi Rt. Rev. JOSEPH MARTIN, Bishop of Muyinga Rt. Rev. NESTOR BIHONDA.

ANGLICANS

Anglicans number about 50,000 and form part of the Province of Uganda.

Archbishop of Uganda: Most Rev. E. SABITI.

Bishop of Burundi: Rt. Rev. Y. NKUNZUMWAMI, B.P. 58, Ibuye, Ngozi.

OTHER PROTESTANTS

There are about 200,000 other Protestants, some 160,000 of them Pentecostal.

ISLAM

About 1 per cent of the population is Muslim.

THE PRESS

All publications are strictly controlled by the government.

NEWSPAPERS

Tribune du Burundi: Bujumbura; weekly newspaper; French; circ. 1,500.

Unité et Révolution: Government Printing Office, B.P. 1400, Bujumbura; f. 1967 by UPRONA to replace former official publication *Infor-Burundi*; an international news service is supplied under special agreement by Tass; weekly.

Burundi Chrétien: Bujumbura; fortnightly newspaper; French; published by the Archbishopric of Kitega.

PERIODICALS

Bulletin Économique et Financier: monthly; Ministry of Economy and Finance, B.P. 482, Bujumbura.

Intumwa: Bujumbura; Catholic; Kirundi; monthly.

Kindugu: P.O.B. 232, Bujumbura; monthly; Swahili.

Ndongozi: P.O.B. 232, Bujumbura; Catholic; monthly; Kirundi.

RADIO

Voix de la Révolution: B.P. 1900, Bujumbura; Govt. station; broadcasts daily programme in Kirundi, Swahili and French; Dir. B. HUMUZA.

Radio Cordac: B.P. 1140, Bujumbura; f. 1963; missionary station; broadcasts daily programmes in Kirundi, Swahili, French and English; Dir. J. E. MORRIS.

There are an estimated 75,000 radio receivers.

FINANCE

(cap. = capital; p.u. = paid up; m. = million; amounts in Burundi francs).

BANKING

Burundi was one of the 19 founding members of the Association of African Central Banks.

CENTRAL BANK

Banque de la République du Burundi: B.P. 705, Bujumbura; f. 1964; cap. 30m.; Pres. BONAVENTURE KIDWINGIRA; Administrateurs PATRICE NSABABAGANWA, RAYMOND SETUKURU; Dir.-Gen. ANDRÉ ROBERT; publ. *Bulletin Trimestriel*.

Banque Nationale de Développement Economique (BNDE): Bujumbura, B.P. 1620.

Banque Belgo-Africaine Burundi: Blvd. de la Liberté, B.P. 585, Bujumbura; f. 1960; cap. 36m.; Chair. GEORGES LECLERQ.

Banque Commerciale du Burundi: B.P. 990, Bujumbura; f. 1960; Chair. DANIEL GILLET.

Banque de Crédit de Bujumbura: B.P. 300, Bujumbura; f. 1964; cap. and reserves 87m.; Pres. E. BONVOISIN; Man. Dir. TH. DE COSTER.

Caisse d'Epargne du Burundi: B.P. 615, Bujumbura; f. 1964; Man. L. NKUNDWA; Asst. Man. A. JABON.

FOREIGN BANKS

Banque du Zaïre: H.O.: 8 Ave. Paul Hanzeur, Kinshasa, Zaire.

Crédit Zaïrois, S.C.A.R.L.: H.O.: 191 Ave. Beernaert, Kinshasa, Zaire; branch in Bujumbura.

INSURANCE

Compagnie d'Assurances d'Outremer: Bujumbura.

TRADE AND INDUSTRY

CHAMBER OF COMMERCE

Chambre de Commerce et de l'Industrie du Rwanda et du Burundi: P.O.B. 313, Bujumbura; f. 1923; Pres. M. R. LECLERE; Hon. Sec. M. T. POJER; 130 mems.

TRADE UNION

Confédération générale du travail du Burundi (CGTB): Bujumbura; sole authorized union for Burundi workers; f. 1967 by amalgamation of all previous unions; closely allied with Uprona Party.

TRANSPORT

RAILWAYS

There are no railways.

ROADS

The road network is very dense and there are 545 km. of national routes (although only 80 km. are asphalt) and over 5,000 km. of other roads.

INLAND WATERWAYS

Bujumbura is the principal port on Lake Tanganyika and the greater part of Burundi's external trade is dependent on the shipping services between Bujumbura and Tanzania and Zaire.

CIVIL AVIATION

Air Zaire, East African Airways and Sabena operate services to Bujumbura, the airport of which is now being extended.

Burundi's national airline, inaugurated on April 6th, 1971, operates services to Kigali and Kinshasa.

EDUCATION

LEARNED SOCIETIES AND RESEARCH INSTITUTES

Alliance Française: B.P. 894, Bujumbura.

Département de Géologie et Mines du Burundi: Ministère de l'Economie, B.P. 745, Bujumbura; Dir. B. R. BANCIYEKO.

Institut des Sciences Agronomiques du Burundi (ISABU): B.P. 795, Bujumbura; f. 1962; applied agronomical research and farm management; Dir.-Gen. A. FOCAN.

Institut Murundi d'Information et de Documentation (IMIDOC): 7 ave. Malfeyt, B.P. 902, Bujumbura.

Laboratoire Médicale: Bujumbura; devoted to clinical analyses and physio-pathological research nutritional studies.

Service Météorologique de Bujumbura: Bujumbura; Dir. M. H. AREND.

LIBRARIES

Bibliothèque de l'Université Officielle: B.P. 1320, Bujumbura; f. 1961; 29,000 vols.; Librarian R. L. VRANCX.

Bibliothèque Publique: B.P. 960, Bujumbura; 26,000 vols.

U.S. Information Service Library: Bujumbura.

MUSEUM

Musée du Pays du Burundi: Kitega.

UNIVERSITY

UNIVERSITÉ OFFICIELLE DE BUJUMBURA

B.P. 1550, BUJUMBURA

Telephone: 3288.

Founded 1960, name changed from Centre Universitaire Rumuri 1964.

Chancellor: A. SIMBANANIYE.

Rector: M. KARIKUNZIRA.

Chief Administrative Officer: P. C. NUWINKWARE.

Librarian: R. VRANCX.

Number of teachers: 64.
Number of students: 365.

Publication: *Revue de l'Université Officielle de Bujumbura* (quarterly).

DEANS:

Faculty of Philosophy and Letters: H. BOON.

Faculty of Economic and Social Sciences: J. R. BONVIN.

Faculty of Sciences: A. DELVAUX.

Faculty of Law: A. VAN DE VYVER.

INSTITUTES

Lycée Technique: Bujumbura; f. 1949; training apprentices, craftsmen and professional workers; four workshops; mechanics, masonry, carpentry, electrical assembling; 450 students.

Centre Social et Éducatif—C.S.E.: Bujumbura; f. 1957; courses in crafts, photography, mechanics; 75 students.

SELECT BIBLIOGRAPHY

BLAKEY, K. A. *Economic Development of Burundi.* Cairo, Institute of National Planning, 1964.

BURUNDI. *Plan quinquennal de Développement Économique et Social du Burundi 1968–72* (édition provisoire), 2 vols. Bujumbura, 1968.

CART, HENRI PHILIPPE. "Study of Political Systems in Burundi", in *Etudes Congolaises.* Brussels, IX, March–April 1966, pp. 1–22.

CLIFFORD, ROBERT L. *Position Paper to support the Application of the Republic of Burundi for Association with the East African Community.* Bujumbura, Government Printing Office, 1968.

EUROPE FRANCE OUTREMER. *L'Afrique d'expression française et Madagascar,* 10e éd., pp. 37–43. Paris, June, 1970.

GOUROU, PIERRE. *Le Densité de la Population du Ruanda-Urundi: Esquisse d'une Etude Géographique.* Brussels, Institute Royal Colonial Belge, 1953.

HARROY, J. P., et al. *Le Ruanda-Urundi: Ressources Naturelles, ses Populations.* Brussels, Les Naturalistes Belges, 1956.

HAUSNER, KARL-HEINZ and JEZIC, BÉTRICE. *Rwanda Burundi.* Bonn, Kurt Schroeder, 1968.

LEMARCHAND, RENÉ. *Rwanda and Burundi.* London, Pall Mall, 1970.

LEMARCHAND, RENÉ. "Social Change and Political Modernisation in Burundi", *Journal of Modern African Studies,* IV, No. 4, 1966, pp. 417–32.

"LE MARCHÉ DU BURUNDI". *Marchés Tropicaux et Mediterranéens* (Paris), No. 1122, May 13th, 1967, pp. 1343–92.

LOUIS, WM. R. *Ruanda-Urundi, 1884–1919.* Oxford, Clarendon Press, 1963.

NSANZÉ, TÉRENCE. *Le Burundi au carrefour de l'Afrique.* Brussels, Remarques africaines, 1970.

L'Edification de la République du Burundi. Brussels, 1970.

RAWSON, DAVID P. *The Role of the United Nations in the Political Development of Ruanda-Urundi.* (Unpublished Ph.D. Dissertation, The American University, School of International Service, 1966.)

SOULIK, S. "Interview du Colonel Micombero", *Remarques Africaines,* No. 305, January 11th, 1968, pp. 6–9.

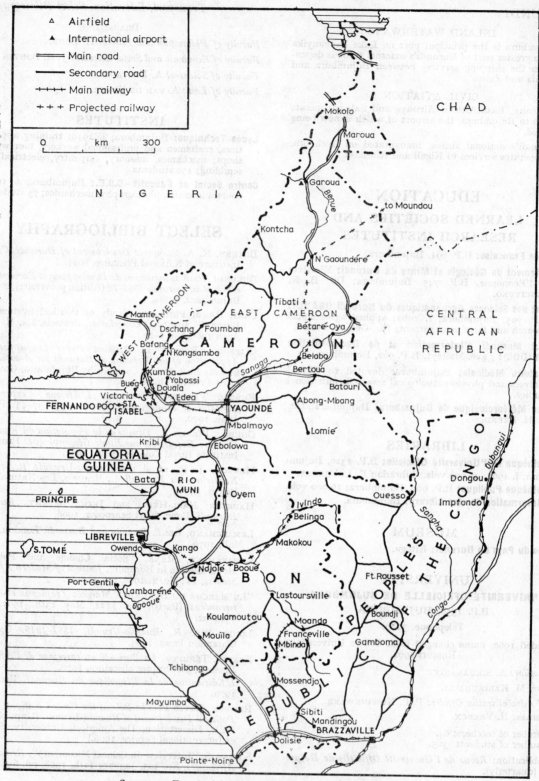

Cameroon, Equatorial Guinea, Gabon and Congo (Brazzaville).

Notes: Section of railway from Belabo to N'Gaoundéré under construction, Moanda-Mbinda link is cableway.

Cameroon

PHYSICAL AND SOCIAL GEOGRAPHY

John I. Clarke

PHYSICAL FEATURES

In the politically fragmented continent of Africa the United Republic of Cameroon may be classified among the middle-sized states. With 183,736 sq. miles and 5,836,000 inhabitants (est. 1970), it has half the area and about one-tenth of the population of neighbouring Nigeria, but twice the area and more than ten times as many people as another neighbour, Gabon. Smaller than twenty-two other African states, it is more comparable in size with European states like Sweden and Spain. The peculiarity of its triangular shape and its common boundaries with as many as six other countries—Nigeria, Chad, Central African Republic, Congo (Brazzaville), Gabon and Equatorial Guinea—are not unusual in Africa, being a common relic of the colonial "scramble"; but they can pose problems of neighbourliness and frontier control.

Located half-way between Algiers and Cape Town and half-way between Dakar and Dar es Salaam, Cameroon has a fairly central position within the African continent, with the additional advantage of a 124-mile coastline, a fact worth mentioning when fourteen African countries are landlocked. Cameroon also has a hinge-location between west and central Africa, and incorporates physical and human features of both. Consequently, it contains much regional diversity and can claim with some justice to synthesize much of the variety of tropical Africa.

PHYSICAL DIVERSITY

The diversity of physical environments in Cameroon arises from various factors including (a) its position astride the volcanic belt along the hinge between west and central Africa, (b) its intermediate location between the great basins of the Congo, the Niger and Lake Chad, (c) its latitudinal extent between 2° and 13° N., (d) its altitudinal range from sea level to over 13,000 ft., and (e) its spread from coastal mangrove swamp to remote continental interior.

In the south and centre is a large undulating and broken plateau surface of granites, schists and gneisses about 1,500–2,200 ft. above sea-level and rising northwards away from the Congo basin to the Adamawa plateau (3,000–5,000 ft.). North of the steep Adamawa escarpment, which effectively divides northern from southern Cameroon, lies the basin of the Benue River, a tributary of the Niger, floored by sedimentary rocks but strewn with inselbergs and buttes, and giving way in "the duck's beak" area of the far north to the alluvial plains of Lake Chad and the Logone River. In the west of the country is a long line of rounded volcanic mountains and hills stretching from cloud-enshrouded Mount Cameroon (13,352 ft.), the highest mountain in west and central Africa, north-eastwards along the former boundary between East and West Cameroon and then along the Nigerian border. Volcanic soils derived from these mountains are more fertile than most others in the country and have permitted much higher rural population densities than elsewhere.

Extending over 11 degrees of latitude, Cameroon has a marked south–north gradation of climates, from a seasonal equatorial climate in the south, with two rainy seasons and two moderately dry seasons of unequal length, through southern savannah and savannah climates with one dry and one wet season, to a hotter drier climate of the sahel type in the far north. Rainfall therefore ranges from over 200 in. in the southwest to less than 24 in. near Lake Chad.

Corresponding to this climatic zonation is a south–north gradation of vegetal landscapes: dense rain forest, Guinea savannah, Sudan savannah and thorn steppe. Man has certainly interfered with the regularity of this zonation, and so has relief, introducing on Mount Cameroon a remarkable vertical series of sharply divided vegetation zones. Associated with the latitudinal range of vegetation is a variation in wild life, from gorillas in the southern forests to elephants, giraffes and gazelles in the north.

HUMAN DIVERSITY

Although the total population of Cameroon is only 5,836,000, its composition and distribution is extremely diverse. Lying astride the so-called "Bantu line", the northern limit of Bantu peoples, Cameroon contains a bewildering array of ethnic groups and languages. In the southern forest regions Bantu peoples prevail, although in the more remote areas are pockets of Pygmies. North of the Bantu tribes live many semi-Bantu peoples of lesser known origin, including the ubiquitous Bamiléké. Further north the complexity increases with intricate patterns of Sudanese Negroes, Hamitic Fulani (or Foulbe) and Arab Choa.

The population has a very patchy distribution, with concentrations in the west, the south-central region and the Sudan savannah zone of the north, while the intervening areas are very sparsely inhabited, especially in the Guinea savannah zone, comparable with the Nigerian "Middle Belt", and the forested south-east.

A further element of human diversity is an important religious and social divide which lies across the country. While the cultivating peoples of the south and west have been profoundly influenced by Christianity and by the European introduction of an externally orientated colonial-type economy with plantations, commercial agriculture, forestry, railways, urbanization and some industrialization, the pastoral and sedentary peoples of the north are either

Muslim or pagan and have largely retained their traditional modes of life. Consequently, the south and west are much more developed, economically and socially, than the north, although the independent government has made efforts to reduce this regional disparity.

One aspect of this disparity is the southern location of the capital Yaoundé (178,000) and the main port of Douala (250,000) as well as most of the other towns. Much of their growth results from rural-urban migration, and many of the migrants come from overcrowded mountain massifs in the west; the Bamiléké constitute about 37 per cent of the inhabitants of Douala. Nevertheless, 84 per cent of all Cameroonians remain rural-dwellers, living in villages whose form

and house-types vary regionally, but whose humble character contrasts markedly with the cosmopolitan bustle of the two main cities.

One other major contrast in the social geography of Cameroon is between the former province of West Cameroon, with less than one-tenth of the area and just over one-fifth of the population, where English is the principal language, and the much larger more populous francophone area of East Cameroon. The contrasting impress of British and French rule is still evident in education, commerce, law, administration and in many other ways, although efforts at bilingualism and integration of transport networks and economies will help to reduce the disparities between the two provinces.

RECENT HISTORY

Victor T. Le Vine

EARLY HISTORY AND THE GERMAN PROTECTORATE (1884–1916)

Little is known about the Cameroon coast before the fifteenth century. The original inhabitants may have settled the bays, estuaries and inlets of the coast in a gradual migratory wave ending sometime during the thirteenth century; what is clear is that by the time the first Portuguese visitors appeared on the scene—possibly in 1472—they found a number of well established groups including the Bubi, Bakweri, and Douala. The first Portuguese explorations were of the island of Fernando Póo (named after one of the Portuguese captains), the coast below Mount Cameroon, and the estuary of the Wouri River. The Portuguese fished the river and caught a variety of seasonal crayfish, which they mistook for prawns (*camarões*). They named the river Rio dos Camarões, and the name, in various European permutations* came to designate the river, the coast, the territory, and the people of the area between Mount Cameroon and the Rio Muni (now the mainland part of the Republic of Equatorial Guinea).

For the next three hundred years, Portuguese, Spanish, English, French, German, and (toward the late 1800s) American traders and slavers operated along the Cameroon coast, until in the 1820s the appearance of a British anti-slavery squadron in the Bight of Biafra seemed to herald British hegemony over the coast. In 1858 the Rev. Alfred Saker founded an English Baptist mission community at Victoria, at the foot of Mt. Cameroon. However, contrary to general expectations, adroit German politicking and British footdragging resulted in the establishment of a German Kamerun Protectorate on July 12th, 1884. Credit for the German *coup* went to Gustav Nachtigal, the explorer and diplomat, who had sailed down the west African coast, first signing treaties with

Togolese chiefs, then arriving at Douala and convincing the Douala chiefs that the British could not be relied upon for protection. Edward H. Hewett, the British itinerant consul in the area, tried to head off Nachtigal, but arrived in Douala five days after the German flag had been hoisted and the protectorate established.†

The German protectorate lasted until 1916, when combined French-British-Belgian military operations drove the last German governor, Ebermaier, his officers and troops from the field and into Rio Muni and eventual internment. During the thirty years of Kamerun Protectorate, the Germans pursued policies —according to Prof. Harry Rudin's authoritative study—no worse or better than those of the other colonial powers. The Germans did lay the infra-structural foundation for the modern economy of the country: railways, roads, bridges, towns, hospitals and plantations. By 1912 they had extended the protectorate to Lake Chad, and delimited—in agreements with Britain and France—most of the eastern and western frontiers of the territory. Their administration was marred by the use of forced labour, some military excesses, and what were often harsh, if not cruel, methods of imposing their rule. Under the more enlightened colonial policies associated with the German colonial ministry under Ferdinand Dernburg (after 1906) many of these excesses were corrected, and numbers of southern Cameroonians were groomed for colonial positions, some, like the Douala prince, Douala Manga Bell, even matriculating from German universities with honours.

THE MANDATES (1922–46)

The wartime military occupation of the Kamerun Protectorate resulted in a *de facto* partition of the

---

* *Camarões*—Spanish; *Kamerun*—German; *Cameroun*—French; and *Cameroons*—English

---

† The miscue was not really "too late" Hewett's fault, but attributable to the British government's procrastination in the face of repeated requests for protection from the same Douala chiefs who later signed with Nachtigal.

territory into British and French spheres of influence. The division was recognized and crystallized by the creation of separate British and French mandates which allocated four-fifths of the territory to French administration, and the other fifth, comprising two long, non-contiguous areas along the eastern Nigerian border, to British administration. It was not until October 1st, 1961, when the Cameroon Federal Republic came into being, that the former British (Southern) Cameroons was reunited with the former French Cameroun.

The institutional arrangements that the French brought to their mandate differed only slightly from those already in operation in their Equatorial African territories. A civil Commissioner of the Republic, responsible directly to the Minister of Colonies, exercised the chief administrative powers. He was assisted by regional and district officers, and by an Administrative Council that, by 1927, began to include some indigenous *notables*. Local administration was vested in the French district officers (*Commandants de cercle*), whose work was to be "seconded" by compliant local chiefs and appointed Councils of Notables.

Between the wars, the French *mise en valeur* (development) programme was responsible for a fivefold increase in the value of the territory's trade, a development that went hand in hand with considerable growth in the cultivation of cocoa, palm oils, timber, and other export commodities. The French political record, however, is less creditable. The success of the *mise en valeur* owed much to a heavy tax burden and the use of conscript labour, the latter mostly during the 1920s. The extensive road network, which had been almost completed by 1933, the enlargement of the port of Douala, and the proliferation of European and native plantations usually seems to have been accomplished at the expense of the local populations. The administration, admittedly, developed the economy, but built up considerable ill-will because of the methods it used.

The *indigénat*, a system of administrative penalties applicable to all except *evolué* Africans and Frenchmen, the arbitrary deposition of traditional chiefs, as well as the seizure and forced alienation of communal lands, all also contributed to increasing discontent among articulate and educated Camerounians. The fact that the Permanent Mandates Commission of the League of Nations could admonish but otherwise do little about the worst French abuses further stimulated the frustration of prominent (particularly, Douala) Camerounians. Nevertheless, political discontent took few manifest, concerted, or organized forms: Garveyite agitators caused some stir, some religious feuds erupted briefly and violently, committees were formed to demand the return of lands "illegally" taken, and in the late 1930s, several groups were organized to provide low-keyed opportunity for educated Camerounians to articulate their dissent with administration policy.

Between the wars the British Cameroons, joined to Nigeria by an administrative union, was considered something of a backwater to the mainstream of Nigerian development. Though Britain posted some exceptionally able men to the territory, the British Cameroons lay relatively neglected, with only minimal funding and attention to stimulate its economic growth. Of the two parts of the British mandate, however, the Southern Cameroons was the more favoured; it already had a basic road, railway, port, and plantation structure left by the Germans, and its populations were relatively well educated in the mission and government schools distributed throughout the territory. The Northern Cameroons, joined to Northern Nigeria in another administrative union, was populated by Muslim Fulani, Islamized pagans, and various animist tribes. The former groups operated under Lugardian indirect rule, the latter remained aloof and fearful of contact with both their nominal Fulani overlords and the British administration. During the period of the mandate, what economic thrust was generated in the territory came from the German plantations on the Victoria plain and around the fringes of Mount Cameroon. Deprived of their plantations by the First World War, most German owners returned to repurchase them after 1924, and to resume their profitable cultivation of bananas, palm oil products, coffee, and tea. The plantations employed not only workers from the British Cameroons, but considerable numbers from the French Cameroun and southern and eastern Nigeria. (The presence of the latter would, in 1961, provide one of the more important arguments for rejecting affiliation with Nigeria.) Toward the end of the 1930s, many German settlers began working actively on behalf of the Nazi cause, and when the Second World War broke out in 1939, they were once again divested of their belongings and repatriated. The consolidation of a number of these former German plantations resulted in the post-war creation of the statutory Cameroon Development Corporation, the single most important industrial ornament of the British territory.

In the French Cameroun, the coming of the war forced the administration to seek to create a favourable atmosphere for patriotism, and when the territory "rallied" to General de Gaulle's cause in 1940, the move was applauded by most resident Frenchmen and virtually all members of the growing and increasingly articulate Camerounian intelligentsia.

TRUSTEESHIP AND THE RISE OF MODERN POLITICS

When the League of Nations, after several wartime years in limbo, extinguished itself in 1946, the Cameroon mandates were converted into United Nations trust territories, still under their respective French and British administrations. The trusteeship agreements, however, reflected new postwar international political realities: growing anti-colonial sentiment made it difficult and in the end, impossible for France or Britain to resist the United Nations Charter's promise of eventual self-determination for all inhabitants of trust territories, and to avoid the obligations of close international supervision of the administration, economy and politics of the two territories.

Moreover, the French constitutional reforms of 1946 radically changed the relations between France and its colonies. It is fair to suggest that between the opportunities for representation *before* the Visiting Missions and organs of the UN, and representation *in* Territorial Assemblies, the French National Assembly, the organs of the French Union and later those of the Community, extraordinary stimulus was generated for the creation of numerous political associations, groups, and parties. Some, to be sure, became the temporary handmaidens of prominent politicians such as Paul Soppo Priso, Jules Ninine, Louis Aujoulat, Charles Okala, and André-Marie Mbida. Other formations organized the communal interests of Douala, Bamiléké, Bassa, Fulani and other ethnic groups. Still others were the outgrowth of metropolitan French parties or trade unions. In all, between 1946 and 1960, over one hundred such groups were created, of which only a handful survived to 1960. These latter were parties that had developed superior organization, better leadership, or a broader electoral base than the rest.

Among this group was the *Union des populations du Cameroun* (UPC), organized in 1948 by trade unionists and probably the first Cameroun party to demand reunification of the two Cameroons and independence from France.

By May 1955, unable to gain power legally, the UPC tried to launch a revolt in the larger cities and towns of the French Cameroun. The attempt aborted, but at the cost of hundreds of lives and considerable destruction of property. The administration promptly banned the UPC, and its leaders fled to the British Cameroons and temporary sanctuary. Some, including Dr. Felix Moumié, found refuge and assistance in the capitals of ideologically compatible governments: Cairo, Khartoum, Algiers, Accra, Conakry and Bamako. The UPC's president, Um Nyobé, and several of his lieutenants returned to Cameroun to wage guerrilla war. Between 1957 and 1962 sporadic violence plagued the territory; it is estimated that between 10,000 and 20,000 people died as a result of guerrilla and counter-insurgency actions, and the economic cost to the affected areas (most of them in the west and south-west) was incalculable. Um Nyobé was killed by a government patrol in 1958, but it was not until 1963 that guerrilla activity had abated to the level of sporadic banditry. The internal (i.e. Cameroun-based) UPC was again given legal status in 1960 in return for a promise to co-operate with the government. The external UPC gradually lost its key leaders —Moumié was poisoned in 1962, Kingue died in 1968, Ouandié was executed in January 1971 after nine years in the *maquis*—and took on a marginal existence as one of the many so-called "liberation movements" subsidized by communist, radical marxist and socialist states.

The UPC galvanized Camerounian nationalism, and provided aims and programmes eventually adopted by all other parties. These included the Cameroun Democrats, whose leader, M. André-Marie Mbida, became the first Camerounian Prime Minister, and the Cameroun Union, founded in 1958, which eventually became the governing party under the leadership of M. Ahmadou Ahidjo.

Under the terms of the *loi cadre* of 1956, the first Cameroun government under M. Mbida was constituted in 1957; a year later a government crisis brought M. Ahidjo, Vice-Premier in Mbida's cabinet, to power. (Mbida himself fled to Conakry to join the exiled leadership of the UPC, but returned home in 1960 after making his peace with Ahidjo.) In the meantime, pressure in Cameroun and at the United Nations began to move the territory toward independence. The UPC tried to force the holding of a general election before the United Nations terminated the trusteeship, but failed, and on January 1st, 1960, the independent Cameroun Republic came into being. M. Ahidjo was elected the country's first President.

Political developments in the British Cameroons moved at a somewhat slower pace than was the case in the French trust territory. For one thing, politics in the two territories were at first linked with the rise and fortunes of Nigerian political parties and for another, though the UPC rebellion affected the Southern Cameroons, it did not have the same traumatic effects because few people were victimized by it. Between 1946 and 1954, when the Southern Cameroons assumed a quasi-federal status within Nigeria, most of the principal politicians were involved with the nascent political parties in Nigeria, and concerned themselves with acquiring regional autonomy for the trust territory. In October 1954 the Southern Cameroons House of Assembly met for the first time and Dr. Emmanuel L. M. Endeley, son of a prominent Bakweri chief, became Leader of Government Business. In 1955 the Kamerun National Democratic Party (KNDP) was formed by a Bamenda schoolteacher, John N. Foncha, with a programme of complete secession from Nigeria and unification with the French Cameroun. Also in 1955 the UPC directorate made its appearance in Kumba following the party's abortive revolt in Cameroun.

The KNDP and the UPC formed a loose alliance, but by the time the UPC was banned in the Southern Cameroons and its leaders deported (1957), Foncha and his party had become disenchanted with the UPC's extremism. The 1957 general elections resulted in a narrow win for the party led by Dr. Endeley, the Kamerun National Convention (KNC), but in January 1959 the KNDP won another election and Foncha became Premier. During the months following, discussions at the United Nations and a long-delayed compromise between Foncha and Endeley resulted in an agreement to hold a UN-supervised plebiscite in 1961 in both parts of the trust territory to decide their future attachments. Endeley campaigned for integration with Nigeria, while Foncha, playing on fears of Ibo domination in the Southern Cameroons, urged unification with the Cameroun Republic. On February 11th and 12th, 1961, voting in the Southern Cameroons resulted in a decision to join the Cameroun Republic in a federation, while Northern Cameroons voters elected to join the Northern Region of Nigeria.

On June 1st, 1961, the former Northern Cameroons became the Sardauna Province of Northern Nigeria, and on October 1st of that same year, the Southern Cameroons became the Western state of the new Cameroon Federal Republic. Shortly thereafter, Ahidjo and Foncha assumed the Presidency and Vice-Presidency of the federation, respectively.

Since federation and under the impulse of vigorous pressure from Ahidjo and East Cameroon, Cameroon moved to increasing political, economic, and social integration. During the 1961-71 period, Federal services in the two states took over progressively greater responsibilities, particularly in the areas of education, economic planning, finance, transportation, and agriculture. By 1966, most of the states' residual areas of jurisdiction—with the notable area of local administration, and in the West, chieftaincy affairs— had come under central control. Also in 1966, the dominant parties in the two states, the East's *Union Camerounaise* and the West's KNDP, along with several minor parties, merged into a single national party, *Union nationale camerounaise* (UNC). The "federalist"—as distinguished from the "regional" or separatist—point of view gained further ground in 1968, when Foncha, who had held the Prime Ministry of West Cameroon along with the Federal Vice-Presidency, was replaced in the former position by Solomon T. Muna, a strong supporter of President Ahidjo. In the 1970 Presidential elections Ahidjo was re-elected, with Muna becoming the Federation's Vice-President and later Western Prime Minister as well.

The régime received a further boost toward unity when, in 1970, it captured, tried and executed the last of the UPC *maquis* leaders, Ernest Ouandié. Also arrested and tried were the Catholic Bishop of N'kongsamba, Mgr. Ndongmo, who, along with several others, were charged with supplying arms to the guerillas and plotting the assassination of President Ahidjo. Ndongmo, Ouandié and two others were condemned to death, but Ndongmo's sentence was commuted to life imprisonment by President Ahidjo. The others were executed.

In 1971, the country's three major trade union confederations, two from the East and one from West, dissolved themselves and were reconstituted into the trade-union wing of the UNC. Finally, on May 20th, 1972, the régime proposed, and the voters over-whelmingly approved a new constitution creating a unitary state. Under the terms of the document, what was left of state autonomy and institutions came to an end: the states' legislatures (including the Western House of Chiefs and the Western Assembly), the state governments, as well as the office of Federal Vice-President, were abolished. In place of the old arrangements, the country would henceforth have a strong executive president, a national executive council of ministers responsible to the President, a unicameral National Assembly, and a completely centralized administrative system. In a subsequent Presidential Decree, the entire country was divided into regions, departments, sub-prefectures, and districts, each administered by civil servants operating in hierarchical order of responsibilty, and all ulti-mately responsible to the Minister of Territorial Administration.

President Ahidjo remained as President of the Cameroon, now renamed the United Republic of Cameroon. Also part of the new facts of Cameroonian political life was the undisputed, all-embracing supremacy of the UNC, which now comprised (with the exception of some religious bodies and a number of commercial organizations of a quasi-governmental nature) almost all cultural, professional, political, and social associations in the country.

ECONOMY

Reginald Herbold Green

AREA AND POPULATION

The total area of Cameroon is 476,000 sq. km. (183,736 sq. miles) and the 1970 population 5,836,000. Population growth is semi-officially estimated at 2 per cent but is probably about 2.5 per cent annually.

Major cities include Douala, the principal port and industrial centre (250,000), Yaoundé, the capital (178,000) and the tri-city of Tiko-Victoria-Buéa, former Western state capital and port (50,000). About one million people live in towns of 5,000 and above. One-eighth of the population lives in the coastal area, nearly a half in the forest zone, and two-fifths in the savannah-sahel regions. Population density varies widely from 260 per sq. mile in the coastal Wouri district to under 2 in some northern districts.

Migration from outside the Cameroon has in the recent past been significant only in respect of the European technical and economic élite and the largely Ibo trading and plantation group in the west. The latter have to a significant degree returned to Nigeria since 1961. Internal population flows from the west central highlands and, to a lesser extent, from the north to towns and to plantation/forestry wage employment have been significant. The Bamiléké people from the highlands have been particularly prominent in this flow with at least 100–125,000 now in Douala and Yaoundé and a high proportion of Bamiléké in bureaucratic, middle-level business, craft, small trading, and wage employment posts throughout southern and central Cameroon.

OVERALL PERSPECTIVE

Cameroon is among the more interesting African economies for four reasons. First, with a population approaching 6 million, a gross domestic product of more than $1,000 million, a moderately diversified production pattern, and a record of 4–5 per cent real annual growth of G.D.P. over the past decade it appears to possess a significant degree of economic viability and potential for development.

Second, the Cameroon is seeking to build regional links both through membership of the Central African Customs and Economic Union (UDEAC—Cameroon, Gabon, Congo (Brazzaville), Central African Republic) and through developing routes to the sea and sources of manufactures for its landlocked neighbours—Chad and the Central African Republic.

Third, the United Republic—until May 1972 a Federal Republic—is a merger of two territories with divergent colonial pasts. The problems of creating a customs union and handling subsequent price and wage increases in the West since the establishment of the Federal Republic in 1961 have been considerable, while those of ensuring that the stronger Eastern economy did not swamp the weaker and stagnant Western are not yet fully solved despite specific attention in the current development plan and policy. However, on balance the West probably has benefited economically by federation, and now full unification—before May 1972 its budget was 60 per cent financed from a Federal transfer and the 1951–61 decline in real per capita output appears to have been at last halted.

Fourth, under President Ahidjo the Cameroon has followed a relatively centrist political economic policy by comparison with other francophone African states. Compared with the Ivory Coast, Madagascar, and Senegal it has consistently sought to increase the diversity of its external economic contacts and to increase effective government involvement in and control over economic development while resting less confidence in unplanned and uncontrolled foreign private investment as the prime mover for development. On the other hand, it has adopted a far less radical stance than either Guinea or any Mali government and a moderately more cautious approach than Congo (Brazzaville). Government involvement in directly productive activity is limited and planning is more in support of private directly productive investment decisions than designed to influence or control them.

AGRICULTURE

About two-fifths of Cameroonian G.D.P. is derived from agriculture, fisheries, and forestry and about three-quarters of the population are engaged in this sector. Primary agricultural and forest products together with slightly processed forms made up 88 per cent of the 1970 export total of 66,210 million francs CFA, and 70 per cent of the 1971 total of 60,152 million francs CFA. Coffee, cocoa, bananas, logs and sawn timber, cotton, oilseeds and rubber are the principal products of the export sub-sector,

which makes up about 40 per cent of total sectoral output.

The 60 per cent consumed locally includes a relatively small local raw material share—particularly in timber, oilseeds, cotton, and tobacco—but consists primarily of foodstuffs consumed without substantial further processing. It is estimated that slightly over a fifth of food production is marketed and the balance consumed by the producers. This implies that overall the agriculture-fisheries-forestry output is 55–60 per cent monetized and 40–45 per cent producer consumed.

Export and Raw Material Sub-sector

Export production is mainly by small African farmers. Significant disparities in farm size exist but there does not appear to be a dominant African "planter class" analogous to that of the Ghanaian or Ivorian tree-crop areas. Estate production is distinctly secondary in importance with the partial exception of the former Western state, where the German estate system has survived, but not flourished, in the public-sector Cameroon Development Corporation. Timber production, however, is dominated by expatriate firms.

Coffee production (84,000 tons in 1970/71) is about 70 per cent *robusta* and 30 per cent *arabica* and has followed a fairly rapid, if erratic, upward trend since the early 1960s when it was around 50,000 tons. Cocoa output reached 130,000 tons in 1970/71 but has shown little growth over the past decade. While these two crops account for almost half of Cameroon exports, in neither is the Cameroon a major world source of supply. Banana exports, despite a big rise in production in 1970/71, are steadily declining, now standing at around 45,000 tons compared with 125,000 in the early 1960s. Loss of Commonwealth preference and a glut in EEC markets have sharply depressed prices.

Cotton lint production has trebled to 38,390 tons in just over a decade, with increasing quantities likely to be absorbed by the local textile industry, but tobacco output is now steadily outstripping the local market and exports are rising. Timber production has risen fairly rapidly—about half of it being exported as logs and another tenth as sawn timber, plywood and veneer, and the balance manufactured for local building material and furniture use.

Food Sub-sector

Food-crop output is probably rising at the same rate as population or slightly faster, i.e. from 2.5 to 3 per cent a year. Bananas, plantains, and starchy roots are important in the coastal and forest zones, groundnuts, millet, sorghum, lake fish, and livestock in the savannah and sahel zones, and maize and poultry in both. In value terms about 15 per cent of Cameroon food supply is imported but the quantitative significance is substantially lower and imported food consumption centred on the urban areas.

Daily per capita calorie availability probably averages 2,500–2,750, which is quantitatively satisfactory. However, with 80–85 per cent derived from starchy roots and cereals, protein and vitamin deficiencies are widespread. Further, certain areas face endemic malnutrition and perhaps half the population faces a pre-harvest "hungry season".

Farm productivity—in export as well as food crops—is low, albeit probably comparable in major crops to that of most other African countries. More serious is the little evidence of rapid improvement except for cotton and tobacco. Extension services and applied research capacity are limited, while experiments with quasi-monopoly companies providing extension services, input supplies, and marketing systems have had mixed and on the whole limited success.

INDUSTRY, POWER, MINING

Industry and power provide about a tenth of G.D.P. and local manufactures now meet perhaps 40 per cent of total demand for non-artisanal industrial products. Value added remains little over one-third of gross output of manufacturing, partly because of the large aluminium smelting plant based on imported alumina, but primarily because simple pre-export processing of raw materials and final-stage assembly and finishing of consumer goods are the typical industrial activities.

Except for the Edea dam and smelter complex, completed in 1958, the rapid growth of the industrial sector is a post-independence development. The Cameroon government has seen industry as critical for rapid growth and its main production centre of Douala as well suited to catering for UDEAC and Chad markets. It has also been willing to provide a variety of tax and financing incentives to induce foreign investment. Over the decade output has grown 15 per cent annually, largely from consumer goods import substitution and preliminary export processing. Limited progress toward more integrated industrial groupings may be in the process of achievement—e.g. aluminium smelting, rolling mill, household ware fabrication, and window frame and roofing sheet production—but by the middle or late 1970s the exhaustion of easy import substitution and export processing possibilities seems likely either to force more concerted attention to industrial strategy or to result in the stagnation of the sector.

Power

Edéa dam accounts for 98 per cent of Cameroon power generation of 1,100 million kWh. and the aluminium smelter for 88 per cent of total consumption. A number of other potentially attractive hydro-electric sites exist and one is likely to be developed when the north-central bauxite deposits are exploited.

Mining

Mining activity is not currently significant. Oil prospecting is in progress with traces and gas pockets giving grounds for cautious optimism as to final findings. A major bauxite deposit lies near the route of the Transcam Railway to N'Gaoundéré and will become accessible on completion of the railway's second stage in the mid-1970s. Smelting on site or transformation to alumina for smelting at Edea seem more likely options than transport of bauxite for over

1,000 km., especially as even at Edea the alumina plant would need to be constructed, since the present smelting operation is based on alumina, not bauxite, imports.

TRANSPORT

The Cameroon's road system totals 23,250 km. but of this only 1,050 km. are bitumenized while half are tracks. In the coastal and forest areas—with the exception of the south-east—the main road grids exist but at too low standards and with inadequate feeder networks. In the north even main links are often totally missing. Extensive upgradings and additions including better east–west and Cameroon–Chad links are scheduled for early construction. Total vehicles number about 35,000 including 13,000 lorries.

The rail system has expanded from 517 km. in 1965 to 843 in 1970 with the completion of a link line to the west and of the first phase (Yaoundé–Belabo) of the Transcam. The 328 km. second phase to N'Gaoundéré is under construction. Traffic, which rose from just under one million tons in 1969 to just over two million in 1970, is expected to continue to rise sharply in the next few years allowing significant rate cuts.

The first stage of the Transcam cost $25 million, and the cost of the second stage was estimated at $35-40 million, but this is now proving inadequate and EDF, FAC and US AID have all increased their aid. The Transcam is seen as a major developmental force making possible bauxite and forest exploitation, opening up central forest and savannah lands for agriculture and ranching, and creating a Douala–Chad/ C.A.R. axis furthering both transport and transit trade and exports of Camerounian manufactures.

Douala accounts for 90 per cent of Cameroonian port traffic and Tiko-Buéa for most of the rest. Douala's present throughput exceeds 1.5 million tons and by 1975 the 2 million ton capacity limit of the present port will be reached. At that stage a new port either near Douala or at Victoria will be required.

The national airline, Cameroon Airlines, was inaugurated in November 1971 after President Ahidjo had withdrawn his government's participation in Air Afrique, which is run under the auspices of OCAM. The Cameroon government has a 70 per cent holding in its national company, and Air France 30 per cent.

FOREIGN TRADE

Concentrated external trade dependence is a major characteristic of the economy. Exports plus imports total two-fifths of G.D.P. and over half of monetary G.D.P., while taxes levied on them exceed half of government revenue. The majority of manufactured goods are imported and the local industrial sector is critically dependent on imported raw materials and equipment.

Exports are concentrated in type with 90 per cent from a limited range of agricultural products and the bulk of the balance from aluminium (or more accurately hydroelectric power embodied in aluminium). Over a third are sold to France and as much to the other EEC members. Over half of imports come from France and a fifth from other EEC states. The import pattern is both historic and institutional—French firms, investors, advisers, and technical assistants have formed a very effective network of barriers to market erosion despite formal liberalization of imports from the other five EEC members in 1967.

Exports and imports have risen relatively rapidly from 33 and 29 thousand million francs CFA respectively in 1963 to 60 and 70 thousand million in 1971. In recent years there has been no steady pattern of surplus or deficit in the balance of trade. Official grant and loan receipts, rising to an average of $35 million annually over 1966–68, have preserved overall balance. The central bank held reserves of almost $50 million or three months' imports at the end of 1969.

Cameroon exports to Chad and UDEAC grew from quite negligible levels in the mid-1960s to 3.1 thousand million francs CFA in 1968, while imports had by then climbed to 2.2 thousand million. By 1971 exports to UDEAC countries had reached 3.3 thousand million francs CFA, while imports had climbed to a similar amount. Of exports 60 per cent and of imports 70 per cent were local manufacturers.

UDEAC has survived Chad's withdrawal and appears to be enjoying at least a certain measure of success in stimulating regional trade development. External duty harmonization and a special tax to transfer revenue from regional market exports to the consuming state are in full operation, as is a limited solidarity fund to transfer a share of coastal state customs revenue to landlocked states. The fund is partly to balance losses arising from reshipment of imports consigned to the coastal state but consumed inland and partly as a limited revenue transfer to the poorer states. Its limited success is demonstrated by Chad's withdrawal, as 65 per cent of the fund was formerly paid to Chad.

Industrial development harmonization is a UDEAC goal which has had some successes, e.g. the regional oil refinery at Port-Gentil; some failed agreements, e.g. in textiles; and relatively little overall impact to date. Given the foreign ownership of the industrial sector, the relatively *laissez faire* national policies, and the very weak secretariat position in UDEAC, the results are hardly surprising.

FINANCE AND INVESTMENT

The Cameroon franc is equivalent to one-fiftieth of the French franc. Currency and other traditional central banking functions are handled by the *Banque centrale des états de l'Afrique équatoriale et du Cameroun*, which is Franco-African in management and works very closely with the Bank of France.

Several foreign and local commercial banks operate in addition to a semi-public Cameroon Development Bank and a public National Investment Corporation. Domestic lending at the end of 1968

totalled about $140 million, deposits $85 million, and currency in circulation $55 million. Over the past five years currency in circulation has risen 50 per cent and demand deposits more than doubled.

Government current revenue totals 45,300 million francs CFA. Virtually all of the revenue is raised by indirect taxation. Recurrent expenditure absorbs 95 per cent of revenue with the remaining 5 per cent going to finance between a tenth and an eighth of public sector investment.

Other public development expenditure is covered by foreign grants and loans ($105 million of grants and $26 million of loans over 1966–68), and limited development bond and central bank finance channelled through investment institutions. Foreign public financial flows have been dominated by France (over 55 per cent) and the European Economic Community's institutions (25–30 per cent) but additional U.S.A., West German, and World Bank group funding is being sought with increasing success.

Total fixed investment is apparently running at approximately $120 million annually or rather under 15 per cent of G.D.P. Of this rather more than half is public, while, counting private foreign investment out of retained earnings, up to two-thirds is foreign. Following a sharp jump in 1964–65 investment growth appears to be now proceeding at about 10 per cent a year.

ECONOMIC DEVELOPMENT

Cameroon has achieved an average rate of annual real growth of Gross Domestic Product of between 4 and 5 per cent over the past twelve years. Per capita real G.D.P. has been growing at 1.5–2.5 per cent a year. Industry has maintained a high rate of expansion and food production has kept pace with population growth. Development planning has improved in concept and effectiveness with a number of key projects (e.g. the Transcam) already started. At the same time internal price, external payments and government revenue/expenditure stability have been maintained.

However, doubts must be expressed as to whether the present economic structure and strategy can generate growth for much longer. In fact the independent Cameroon has pursued the French colonial *mise en valeur* policy more rigorously and efficiently than did France, with clear short-term output gains but little reduction in external dependence.

The external and public finance balances are fragile—both rest on the continued and expanded flow of foreign grants and loans. The 1968–70 balance of payments results presented a more favourable position than will normally confront Cameroon because of windfall coffee and cocoa price levels, and the 1967 merchandise trade deficit reappeared, as expected, in 1971.

Cameroon planning has not yet had very much impact either on levels of domestic resource mobilization nor on their allocation. The absence of broad public ownership involvement or control in manufacturing has led to the absence of either a detailed industrial strategy or the instruments for implementing one. The multiplication of this last weakness across the member states of UDEAC goes far to explain the limits of that Community's ability to define and operate a common industrial strategy and/or plant allocation policy.

A more intense domestic tax effort, effective mobilization of domestic resources, active public sector financial participation in directly productive investment, and a reorientation of planning to set a framework within which private investment decisions are taken rather than a framework for supporting them once taken; these appear to be among the political economic changes likely to be needed to maintain Cameroon economic growth. If they are made by neighbouring states as well as by the Cameroon, the opportunities for planned regional development through an energetic UDEAC would be both broader and brighter.

STATISTICAL SURVEY

AREA AND POPULATION

AREA (sq. km.)			POPULATION (1970 estimates)		
Total	East Cameroon*	West Cameroon*	Total	East Cameroon	West Cameroon
476,000	432,000	44,000	5,836,000	4,393,500	1,442,500

*Division based on the Provinces of the Federal Republic (pre-1972).
Yaoundé (capital) 178,000; Douala 250,000.

EMPLOYMENT
(1971)

	MEN	WOMEN	TOTAL
Agriculture	30,440	1,617	32,057
Extractive Industries . . .	156	—	156
Manufactures	10,257	1,089	11,346
Chemical Industries . . .	4,895	421	5,316
Public Works	6,863	49	6,912
Electrical Industries . . .	1,950	133	2,083
Transport	12,260	171	12,431
Commerce	9,295	1,337	10,632
Public Service . . .	n.a.	n.a.	15,623
Others	2,208	292	2,500

AGRICULTURE
PRINCIPAL CROPS
(metric tons)

	1968	1969	1970
Cocoa*	65,620	73,820	130,000
Cocoa By-products* . . .	15,590	19,150	26,600
Coffee*	73,500	68,450	84,000
Bananas*	38,760	46,510	130,000
Cotton	18,840	22,590	38,390
Timber*	364,100	432,480	n.a.
Rubber	12,779	12,977	11,541
Palm Oil	21,588	16,532	23,434
Palm products	23,442	16,912	7,357
Groundnuts	6,122	14,965	23,500
Tea	1,072	980	1,184

* Exports.

LIVESTOCK
(1970—'000 head)

Cattle	3,800
Goats	1,500
Pigs	890
Poultry	5,190

Sea Fisheries: (1967) 11,830 tons, (1968) 14,963 tons, (1970) 21,200 tons.

MINING

	1968	1969	1970
Gold, refined (grammes)	16,370	7,300	15,000
Cassiterite ore, 66% (kg.)	51,000	41,600	40,000
Aluminium, refined (tons)	48,324	46,736	52,373

FINANCE

100 centimes = 1 franc de la **Communauté** Financière Africaine.

Coins: 1, 2, 10, 25, 50 and 100 francs CFA.

Notes: 50, 100, 500, 1,000, 5,000, and 10,000 francs CFA.

Exchange rates (December 1972): 1 franc CFA = 2 French centimes; £1 sterling = 593.625 francs CFA; U.S. $1 = 255.785 francs CFA.

1,000 francs CFA = £1.685 = $3.91.

BUDGETS
(million francs CFA)

	1969–70	1970–71	1971–72	1972–73
Revenue	36,983	38,500	45,300	52,700
Expenditure	33,034	38,500	45,300	52,700

THIRD FIVE-YEAR PLAN
(1971–76—million francs CFA)

Agriculture	20,720
Forestry	5,210
Stockbreeding	3,670
Industry and Mineral Prospecting	51,500
Power and Oil Refining	18,700
Roads and Bridges	26,400
Railways	15,900
Ports	6,500
Telecommunications	6,300
Civil Aeronautics and Meteorology	3,500
Education	21,500
Housing	15,000
Town Planning	11,400
Health	6,500
TOTAL (incl. others)	280,000*

* 149,000 million will be publicly financed and 131,000 million privately financed.

BALANCE OF PAYMENTS
('ooo francs CFA)

	1969			1970		
	Credit	Debit	Balance	Credit	Debit	Balance
Goods and Services:						
Merchandise .	50,654,006	46,237,181	4,416,825	60,743,000	55,238,000	5,505,000
Freight on Merchandise .	3,171,312	4,994,903	— 1,823,591	2,935,000	11,763,000	— 8,828,000
Transport . . .	942,954	2,884,718	— 1,941,764	2,651,000	3,365,000	— 714,000
Insurance . . .	1,544,920	2,733,466	— 1,188,546	1,760,000	3,205,000	— 1,445,000
Travel . . .	1,439,657	4,175,076	— 2,735,419	2,384,000	2,496,000	— 112,000
Revenue and Interest .	1,129,456	1,241,780	— 112,324	1,019,000	1,719,000	— 700,000
Salaries . . .	1,601,980	4,798,798	— 3,196,818	2,005,000	4,361,000	— 2,356,000
Other Services . .	6,381,915	7,868,822	— 1,486,907	5,079,000	9,736,000	— 4,657,000
Government Activities .	112,294	3,236,194	— 3,123,900	385,000	3,273,000	— 2,888,000
Gifts	1,234,466	189,248	— 1,045,218	2,518,000	163,000	— 2,355,000
Total . . .	68,212,960	78,360,186	—10,147,226	81,479,000	95,319,000	—13,840,000
Capital Sectors . .	5,403,095	1,204,415	4,199,480	7,584,000	2,008,000	5,576,000
GLOBAL TOTAL . .	73,616,055	79,564,601	— 5,947,746	89,063,000	97,327,000	— 8,264,000

EXTERNAL TRADE
(million francs CFA)

	1967	1968	1969	1970	1971
Imports . .	37,680	47,738	49,016	60,860	69,880
Exports . .	38,471	45,056	53,223	66,210	60,152

PRINCIPAL COMMODITIES

EXPORTS	1969	1970	1971*	EXPORTS	1969	1970	1971
Food, Drink, Tobacco .	5,507	5,771	3,540	Cocoa . . .	12,400	18,643	14,177
Energy, Lubricants .	2,761	2,761	1,827	Coffee (arabica) .	3,869	5,471	5,304
Primary Products .	2,424	2,990	1,197	Coffee (robusta) .	8,601	9,317	9,495
Vegetable or Animal				Bananas . .	1,324	1,683	763
Origin . .	1,037	1,291	230	Rubber . .	982	1,283	1,463
Mineral Origin . .	1,387	1,759	967	Groundnuts .	596	633	526
Semi-manufactured Pro-				Tobacco . .	1,135	n.a.	n.a.
ducts . .	5,987	7,000	3,512	Cotton Fibre .	2,877	3,172	4,216
Machinery Parts . .	10,677	16,274	n.a.	Palm and Palm-cabbage			
Transport Equipment .	5,278	6,505	3 309	Oil . . .	367	452	573
Other Equipment .	5,399	9,769	5,073	Tea . . .	79	136	161
Equipment for Agri-				Cocoa Pulp .	927	1,300	} 1,693
culture . .	322	332	182	Cocoa Butter .	3,324	4,745	
Equipment for Indus-				Logs . . .	3,454	4,316	} 4,147
try . .	5,077	9,437	4,891	Sawn and Rolled Wood .	1,174	1,253	
Consumer Products .	21,916	26,064	4,211	Aluminium Ore .	5,059	5,371	5,173
Domestic Salt . .	8,508	9,423	n.a.	Other Products .	7,055	7,504	n.a.

* Jan.-June

COUNTRIES

IMPORTS	1969	1970	1971
France . . .	26,187	28,992	34,950
Other EEC Countries .	11,198	12,098	13,350
Japan. . . .	1,285	1,569	1,122
UDEAC Countries .	2,719	3,508	3,370
United Kingdom . .	2,305	2,593	2,684
U.S.A. . . .	3,211	4,639	6,784

EXPORTS	1969	1970	1971
France . . .	19,153	20,603	17,162
Other EEC Countries .	24,174	28,109	24,133
Japan. . . .	793	1,172	1,708
UDEAC Countries .	2,846	3,016	3,348
United Kingdom . .	828	1,003	1,210
U.S.A. . . .	3,486	5,392	5,199

TRANSPORT

RAILWAYS
('000)

	1968	1969	1970
Passengers . .	1,459	1,590	3,822
Passengers-km. .	149,000	170,000	n.a.
Freight (tons) . .	1,035	985	2,008
Freight ton-km. .	208	215	n.a.

SHIPPING
(EAST CAMEROON)
(1966)

Freight (metric tons)		Passengers	
Entered	Cleared	Arrived	Departed
690,000	606,000	2,803	3,985

MOTOR VEHICLES
(New registrations)

	PRIVATE CARS	COMMERCIAL VEHICLES, LAND-ROVERS, ETC.	TOTAL (incl. others)
1965	1,880	1,718	3,792
1966	1,965	1,517	3,674
1967	2,427	1,993	4,765
1968	3,206	2,348	6,049
1969	3,620	2,372	6,685

CIVIL AVIATION
(1970)

Passengers		Freight (metric tons)	Mail (metric tons)
Arrived	Departed		
312,000	138,399	26,700	n.a.

EDUCATION

	1970–71		1971–72	
	Schools	Pupils	Schools	Pupils
Primary (East Cameroon):				
Public	1,888			
Catholic . . .	794			
Protestant . . .	621	n.a.	n.a.	n.a.
Other	75			
Secondary:				
Public	45	19,139	50	23,083
Private	124	36,892	141	42,222
Technical:				
Public	53	5,066	55	5,604
Private	66	14,060	78	15,843
Higher	11	2,690	11	3,559

Sources: Direction de la Statistique et de la Comptabilité Nationale, Yaoundé, Ministry of Education and Ministry of Mines and Energy.

THE CONSTITUTION

(Ratified by referendum May 20th, 1972)

The People of Cameroon

Declares that the human being, without distinction as to race, religion, sex or belief, possesses inalienable and sacred rights.

Affirms its attachment to the fundamental freedoms embodied in the Universal Declaration of Human Rights and the United Nations Charter and in particular to the following principles:

Everyone has equal rights and obligations. The State endeavours to assure for all its citizens the conditions necessary for their development.

Freedom and security are guaranteed to each individual subject to respect for the rights of others and the higher interests of the State.

No one may be compelled to do what the law does not prescribe.

Everyone has the right to settle in any place and to move about freely, subject to the statutory provisions concerning public order, security and tranquility.

The home is inviolate. No search may take place except by virtue of the law.

The privacy of all correspondence is inviolate. No interference shall be allowed except by virtue of decisions emanating from the judicial authorities.

No one shall be subjected to prosecution, arrest or detention except in the cases and according to the manner determined by the law.

The law may not have retrospective effect.

No one shall be judged or punished except by virtue of a law promulgated and published before the offence was committed.

The law ensures the right of everyone to a fair hearing before the courts.

No one shall be harassed because of his origin, opinions or beliefs in religious, philosophical or political matters, subject to respect for public order.

Freedom of religion and freedom to practise a religion are guaranteed.

The State is secular. The neutrality and independence of the State in respect of all religions are guaranteed.

The freedom of expression, the freedom of the press, the freedom of assembly, the freedom of association, and the freedom of trade unions are guaranteed under the conditions fixed by the law.

The Nation protects and promotes the family, the natural basis of human society.

The State ensures the child's right to education. The organization and control of education at all levels are bounden duties of the State.

Ownership is the right guaranteed to everyone by the law to use, enjoy, and dispose of property. No one shall be deprived thereof, save for public purposes and subject to the payment of compensation to be determined by the law.

The right of ownership may not be exercised in violation of the public interests or in such a way as to be prejudicial to the security, freedom, existence or property of other persons.

Everyone has the right and duty to work.

Everyone must share in the burden of public expenditure according to his means.

The State guarantees to all citizens of either sex the rights and freedoms set out in the preamble of the Constitution.

PART I

Sovereignty

1. (1) The Federal Republic of Cameroon, constituted from the State of East Cameroon and the State of West Cameroon, shall become a unitary State to be styled the United Republic of Cameroon with effect from the date of entry into force of this Constitution.

(2) The United Republic of Cameroon shall be one and indivisible.

(3) It shall be democratic, secular and dedicated to social service. It shall ensure the equality before the law of all its citizens.

(4) The official languages of the United Republic of Cameroon shall be French and English.

(5) The motto shall be: "Peace—Work—Fatherland".

(6) The flag shall be of three equal vertical stripes of green, red and yellow, charged with two gold stars on the green stripe.

(7) The national anthem shall be "O Cameroon, cradle of our forefathers".

(8) The seal of the United Republic of Cameroon shall be a circular medallion in bas-relief, forty-six millimetres in diameter, bearing on the reverse and in the centre the head of a girl in profile turned to the dexter towards a coffee branch and flanked on the sinister by five cocoa pods, encircled beneath the upper edge by the words "United Republic of Cameroon" and above the lower edge by the national motto "Peace—Work—Fatherland".

(9) The capital shall be Yaoundé.

2. (1) National sovereignty shall be vested in the people of Cameroon who shall exercise it either through the President of the Republic and the members returned by it to the National Assembly or by way of referendum; nor may any section of the people or any individual arrogate to itself or to himself the exercise thereof.

(2) The vote shall be equal and secret, and every citizen aged twenty-one or over shall be entitled to it.

(3) The authorities responsible for the direction of the State shall hold their powers of the people by way of election by universal suffrage, direct or indirect.

3. (1) Political parties and groups may take part in elections. They shall be formed and shall exercise their activities in accordance with the law.

(2) Such parties shall be bound to respect the principles of democracy and of national sovereignty and unity.

4. State authority shall be exercised by:
   The President of the Republic, and
   The National Assembly.

PART II

The President of the Republic

5. The President of the Republic, as Head of State and Head of the Government, shall ensure respect for the Constitution and the unity of the State, and shall be responsible for the conduct of the affairs of the Republic.

6. (1) The President of the Republic shall be elected by universal suffrage and direct and secret ballot.

(2) Candidates for the office of President of the Republic must be in possession of their civic and political rights and have attained the age of thirty-five years by the date of the election.

(3) The nomination of candidates, the supervision of elections and the proclamation of results shall be regulated by law.

(4) The office of President of the Republic may not be held together with any other elective public office or professional activity.

7. (1) The President of the Republic shall be elected for five years and may be re-elected. Election shall be by a majority of votes cast, and shall be held not less than twenty nor more than fifty days before the expiry of the term of the President in office.

(*a*) In case of temporary prevention, the President of the Republic may appoint a member of the Government to exercise his duties within the framework of a delegation of powers.

(*b*) In the event of vacancy of the Presidency as a result of death or permanent physical incapacity, duly ascertained by the Supreme Court, the powers of the President of the Republic shall immediately devolve upon the President of the National Assembly until election of a new President.

The interim President of the Republic may not amend the Constitution or modify the composition of the Government.

(*c*) In the event of vacancy of the Presidency as a result of resignation, such resignation shall only take effect as from the day on which the newly elected President shall take the oath.

(2) Voting to elect a new President shall take place not less than twenty nor more than fifty days after the vacancy.

(3) The President of the Republic shall take the oath in the manner aid down by the law.

8. (1) Ministers and Vice-Ministers shall be appointed by the President of the Republic. They shall be responsible to him and liable to be dismissed by him. He may delegate certain of his powers to them by Decree.

(2) The office of Minister or Vice-Minister may not be held together with parliamentary office, office as member of a body representing nationally any occupation or any public post or gainful activity.

9. The President of the Republic shall:

(1) Represent the State in all public activity and be head of the armed forces;

(2) Accredit ambassadors and envoys extraordinary to foreign powers;

(3) Receive letters of credence of ambassadors and envoys extraordinary from foreign powers;

(4) Negotiate and ratify agreements and treaties: Provided that treaties dealing with the sphere reserved by Article 20 to the legislature shall be submitted before ratification for approval in the form of law by the National Assembly;

(5) Exercise the prerogative of clemency after consultation with the Higher Judicial Council;

(6) Confer the decorations of the Republic;

(7) Promulgate laws as provided by Article 29;

(8) Be responsible for the enforcement of laws;

(9) Have the power to issue statutory rules and orders;

(10) Appoint to civil and military posts;

(11) Ensure the internal and external security of the Republic;

(12) Set up, regulate and direct all administrative services necessary for the fulfilment of his task.

10. The President of the Republic shall refer to the Supreme Court under the conditions prescribed by the law provided for in Article 32 any law which he considers to be contrary to this Constitution.

11. (1) The President of the Republic may where circumstances require proclaim by Decree a State of Emer-gency, which will confer upon him such special powers as may be provided by law.

(2) In the event of grave peril threatening the nation's territorial integrity or its existence, independence or institutions, the President of the Republic may proclaim by Decree a State of Siege and take all measures as he may deem necessary.

(3) He shall inform the nation by message of his decision.

PART III
The National Assembly

12. (*a*) The National Assembly shall be renewed every five years, and shall be composed of one hundred and twenty members elected by universal suffrage and direct and secret ballot.

(*b*) The National Assembly may, at the instance of the President of the Republic, decide by law to extend or shorten its term of office.

13. Laws shall be passed by a simple majority of the members present.

14. Before promulgating any bill, the President of the Republic may request a second reading. In this case, laws shall only be passed by the National Assembly by a majority of its membership.

15. (1) The National Assembly shall meet twice a year, the duration of each session being limited to thirty days.

(2) The opening date of each session shall be fixed by the Assembly's steering committee after consultation with the President of the Republic. In the course of one such session the Assembly shall approve the Budget: Provided that in the event of the budget not being approved before the end of the current financial year the President of the Republi shall have power to act according to the old budget at the rate of one-twelfth for each month until the new budget is approved.

(3) On request of the President of the Republic or of two-thirds of its membership the Assembly shall be recalled to an extraordinary session, limited to fifteen days, to consider a specific programme of business.

16. (1) The National Assembly shall adopt its own rules of organization and functioning in the form of a law to establish its standing orders.

(2) At the opening of the first session of each year it shall elect its President and steering committee.

(3) The sittings of the National Assembly shall be open to the public; provided that in exceptional circumstances and on the request of the Government or of a majority of its members strangers may be excluded.

17. Elections shall be regulated by law.

18. Parliamentary immunity, disqualification of candidates of sitting members and the allowances and privileges of members shall be governed by law.

PART IV
Relations between the Executive and the Legislature

19. Bills may be introduced either by the President of the Republic or by any member of the National Assembly.

20. The following shall be reserved to the legislature:

(1) The fundamental rights and duties of the citizen, including:
  protection of the liberty of the subject;
  human rights;
  labour and trade union law;
  the overriding duties and obligations of the citizen in respect of national defence.

(2) The law of persons and property, including:
  nationality and personal status;
  law of moveable and immoveable property;
  law of civil and commercial obligations.

(3) The political, administrative and judicial system in respect of:

elections to the National Assembly;

general regulation of national defence;

the definition of criminal offences not triable summarily and the authorization of penalties of any kind, criminal procedure, civil procedure, execution procedure, amnesty, the creation of new classes of Courts; the organization of the local authorities.

(4) The following matters of finance and public property:

currency;

budget;

imposition, assessment and rate of all dues and taxes; legislation on public property.

(5) Long-term commitments to economic and social policy, together with the general aims of such policy.

(6) The educational system.

21. (1) Provided that with regard to the subjects listed in Article 20, the National Assembly may empower the President of the Republic to legislate by way of Ordinance for a limited period and for given purposes.

(2) Such Ordinances shall enter into force on the date of their publication. They shall be tabled before the National Assembly for purposes of ratification within the time limit fixed by the enabling law.

(3) They shall remain in force as long as the Assembly has not refused to ratify them.

22. Matters not reserved for the legislature shall come under the jurisdiction of the authority empowered to issue statutory rules and orders.

23. Bills laid on the table of the National Assembly shall be considered in the appropriate committee before debate on the floor of the house.

24. The text before the Assembly shall be that proposed by the President of the Republic when the proposal comes from him, and otherwise the text as amended in committee, but in either case amendments may be moved in the course of the debate.

25. The President of the Republic may at his request address the Assembly in person, and may send messages to it; but no such address or message may be debated in his presence.

26. Ministers and Vice-Ministers shall have access to the Assembly and may take part in debates.

27. (1) The programme of business in the Assembly shall be appointed by the chairmen's conference, composed of party leaders, chairmen of committees and members of the steering committee of the National Assembly, together with a Minister or Vice-Minister.

(2) The programme of business may not include bills beyond the jurisdiction of the Assembly as defined by Article 20.

(3) Nor may any bill introduced by a member or any amendment be included which if passed would result in a burden on public funds or an increase in public charges without a corresponding reduction in other expenditure or the grant of equivalent new supply.

(4) Any doubt or dispute on the admissibility of a bill or amendment shall be referred for decision by the President of the Assembly or by the President of the Republic to the Supreme Court.

(5) The programme of business shall give priority and in the order decided by the Government, to bills introduced or accepted by it.

(6) Any business shall, on request by the Government, be treated as urgent.

28. (1) The National Assembly may inquire about governmental activity by means of oral or written questions and by setting up committees of inquiry with specific terms of reference.

(2) The Government, subject to the imperatives of national defence and the security of the State, shall furnish any explanation and information to the Assembly.

(3) The procedure of all committees of inquiry shall be laid down by law.

29. (1) The President of the Republic shall promulgate laws passed by the National Assembly within fifteen days of their being forwarded to him unless he requests a second reading or refers the matter to the Supreme Court.

(2) On his failure to do so within such period, the President of the National Assembly may record the fact and his promulgate.

(3) Laws shall be published in both official languages of the Republic.

30. (1) The President of the Republic, after consultation with the President of the National Assembly, may submit to a referendum any reform bill which, although normally reserved for the legislature, could have profound repercussions on the future of the Nation and the national institutions.

(2) This shall apply in particular to:

(a) Bills concerning the organization of the public authorities or the amendment of the Constitution;

(b) Bills to ratify international agreements or treaties having particularly important consequences;

(c) Certain reform bills relating to the law of persons and property, etc.

(3) The bill shall be adopted by a majority of valid votes cast.

(4) The referendum procedure shall be determined by law.

PART V

The Judiciary

31. (1) Justice shall be administered in the territory of the Republic in the name of the people of Cameroon.

(2) The President of the Republic shall ensure the independence of the judiciary, and shall appoint to the Bench and to the legal service.

(3) He shall be assisted in his task by the Higher Judicial Council, which shall give him its opinion on all proposed appointments to the Bench and on disciplinary sanctions concerning them.

(4) It shall be regulated as to procedure and otherwise by law.

PART VI

The Supreme Court

32. (1) The Supreme Court, in addition to the powers and duties provided for by Articles 7, 10 and 27 shall be responsible for the following matters:

(a) To give final judgment on such appeals as may be granted by law from the judgments of the Courts of Appeal wherever the application of the law is in issue;

(b) To decide complaints against administrative acts, whether claiming damages or on grounds of ultra vires.

(2) The composition of, the taking of cognizance by, and the procedure of the Supreme Court shall be laid down by law.

33. Where the Supreme Court is called upon to give an opinion in the cases contemplated by Articles 7, 10 and 27, its numbers shall be doubled by the addition of personalties nominated for one year by the President of the Republic in view of their special knowledge or experience.

PART VII

Impeachment

34. (1) There shall be a Court of Impeachment which shall be regulated as to organization and taking of cognizance and in other respects by the law.

(2) The Court of Impeachment shall have jurisdiction, in respect of acts performed in the exercise of their offices, to try the President of the Republic for high treason and the Ministers and Vice-Ministers for conspiracy against the security of the State.

PART VIII

The Economic and Social Council

35. There shall be an Economic and Social Council which shall be regulated as to powers and in other respects by the law.

PART IX

Amendment of the Constitution

36. (1) Bills to amend this Constitution may be introduced either by the President of the Republic or the National Assembly.

(2) Provided that any bill introduced by a member of the Assembly shall bear the signature of at least one-third of its membership.

(3) An amendment presented to the Assembly on the initiative of the members or of the President of the Republic shall be passed by a majority of the membership of the National Assembly.

(4) The President of the Republic may request a second reading, in which case the amendment shall be passed by a two-thirds majority of the membership of the National Assembly.

(5) The President of the Republic may decide to submit any amendment to the people by way of a referendum.

37. No procedure to amend the Constitution may be accepted if it tends to impair the republican character, unity or territorial integrity of the State, or the democratic principles by which the Republic is governed.

PART X

Transitional provisions

38. The President of the Federal Republic of Cameroon shall for the duration of his existing term be the President of the United Republic of Cameroon.

39. (1) The National Federal Assembly shall be recessed fifteen days after the entry into force of this Constitution and until new Parliamentary elections take place.

(2) Provided that the Steering Committee of this Assembly at present in office shall assume responsibility for current business.

40. The House of Assembly of East Cameroon and the House of Assembly and the House of Chiefs of West Cameroon shall cease to sit as from the entry into force of this Constitution. They shall be abolished within a maximum time-limit of six months.

41. The President of the Republic shall determine the terms and conditions for the transfer of powers from the former Federated States to the United Republic of Cameroon.

42. Within the twelve months running from the recessing of the National Federal Assembly, the fundamental laws provided for by this Constitution, as well as the legislative measures necessary for the setting up of constitutional organs, and, pending their setting up, for governmental procedure and the carrying on of the government shall be enacted by way of Ordinance having the force of law.

43. The Legislation resulting from the laws and regulations applicable in the Federal State of Cameroon and in the Federated States on the date of entry into force of this Constitution shall remain in force in all of their provisions which are not contrary to the stipulations of this Constitution, for as long as it is not amended by legislative or regulatory process.

44. This Constitution shall be registered and published in the *Official Gazette* of the State in French and English, the French text being authentic. It shall be implemented as the Constitution of the United Republic of Cameroon.

THE GOVERNMENT

HEAD OF STATE

President: AHMADOU AHIDJO.

(The President was elected on March 20th, 1970, by 97.5 per cent of the votes cast, for a period of 5 years.

CABINET

(December 1972)

Minister of State: SOLOMON TANDENG MUNA.

Minister of State, Secretary-General: PAUL BIYA.

Minister of State in charge of the Armed Forces: SADOU DAOUDOU.

Minister, Assistant Secretary-General: FRANÇOIS SENGAT-KOU.

Minister of Finance: CHARLES ONANA AWANA.

Minister of Foreign Affairs: VINCENT EFON.

Minister of Territorial Administration: VICTOR AYISSI MVODO.

Minister of Justice: SIMON ACHU ACHIDI.

Minister of Agriculture: JEAN KEUTCHA.

Minister of National Education: ZACHE MONGO-SOO.

Minister of Industrial and Commercial Development: SADJO ANGOKAY.

Minister of Health and Public Assistance: PAUL FOKAM KAMGA.

Minister of Labour and Social Welfare: ENOCH KWAYEB.

Minister of Public Service: FELIX SABAL LECCO.

Minister of Equipment and Housing: PAUL TESSA.

Minister of Territorial Planning: MAIKANO ABDOULAYE.

Minister of Posts and Telecommunications: EMMANUEL EGBE TABI.

Minister of Information and Cultural Affairs: VROUMSIA TCHINAYE.

Minister of Mines and Power: HENRY NAMATA ELANGWE.

Minister in charge of Missions at the Presidency: ABDOU-LAYE YADJI.

Minister of Livestock: YOUSSOUFA DAOUDA.

Minister of Youth and Sport: FELIX TONYE.

Minister of Transport: CHRISTIAN BONGWA.

Minister-Delegate at the Presidency, in charge of General State Inspection: GILBERT ANDZE JEROBER.

Deputy Minister of Health and Public Assistance: Mrs. DELPHINE TSANGA.

Deputy Minister of National Education: MARTIN NGEHA LUMA.

Deputy Minister of Equipment and Housing: KOUANDI ALIOU.

Deputy Minister of Agriculture: JOSEPH AWOUNTI CHONGWAIN.

Director of the Cabinet at the Presidency: PHILEMON BEB A DON.

PROVINCIAL GOVERNORS

Centre-South Province: GABRIEL MOUAFO.
Eastern Province: STANLAS BIAS.
Coastal Province: MARCEL MENGUEME.
Northern Province: OUSMANE MEY.
North-Western Province: GUILLAUME NSEKE.
Western Province: MARCEL MEDJO AKONO.
South-Western Province: TANDJONG ENOW.

DIPLOMATIC REPRESENTATION

EMBASSIES AND LEGATIONS ACCREDITED TO CAMEROON

(In Yaoundé unless otherwise indicated)

(E) Embassy; (L) Legation.

Algeria: Brazzaville, People's Republic of the Congo (E).

Austria: Lagos, Nigeria.

Belgium: B.P. 816 (E); *Ambassador:* JEAN BOUSSE.

Canada: B.P. 572 (E); *Ambassador:* PIERRE ASSELIN.

Central African Republic: B.P. 396 (E); *Ambassador:* EMMANUEL DINDY (also accred. to Gabon and Nigeria).

Chad: Bangui, Central African Republic.

China, People's Republic: (E); *Ambassador:* CHAO HSING CHIH.

Egypt: B.P. 809 (E); *Ambassador:* FATIH ABDEL HALIM KANDIL.

Equatorial Guinea: *Ambassador:* GUSTAVO WATSON BUEKO.

Finland: Lagos, Nigeria (E).

France: B.P. 102 Yaoundé (E); *Ambassador:* JACQUES DUPUY.

Gabon: B.P. 4130 (E); *Ambassador:* VINCENT MAVOUNGOU.

Germany, Federal Republic: B.P. 1160 (E); *Ambassador:* HANS-GERO VON HORTSMANN.

Guinea: Lagos, Nigeria (E).

India: Lagos, Nigeria (E).

Israel: B.P. 591 (E); *Ambassador:* HAINS YAARI.

Italy: B.P. 827 (E); *Ambassador:* ARMANDO MARCHETTI.

Japan: Kinshasa, Zaire (E).

Korea Republic: (E); *Ambassador:* MOON CHULSOON.

Lebanon: Dakar, Senegal (E).

Lesotho: Nairobi, Kenya (E).

Liberia: B.P. 1185 (E); *Ambassador:* PETER THOMSON.

Mali: Brazzaville, People's Republic of the Congo (E).

Mauritania: (E); Abidjan, Ivory Coast.

Morocco: Lagos, Nigeria (E).

Netherlands: Kinshasa, Zaire (E).

Nigeria: B.P. 448 (E); *Ambassador:* YUSUF SADA.

Norway: Lagos, Nigeria (E).

Pakistan: Lagos, Nigeria (E).

Philippines: Lagos, Nigeria (E).

Saudi Arabia: Lagos, Nigeria (E).

Spain: B.P. 877 (E); *Ambassador:* CARMELO MATESANZ.

Sudan: Lagos, Nigeria (E).

Sweden: Kinshasa, Zaire (E).

Switzerland: Lagos, Nigeria (E).

Tunisia: (E); *Ambassador:* MOHAMMED RIDHA BACH-BAOUAB.

Turkey: Lagos, Nigeria (E).

U.S.S.R.: B.P. 488 (E); *Ambassador:* IVAN MELNIK.

United Kingdom: Ave. Joseph Clerc, B.P. 547 (E); *Ambassador:* EDWARD FERGUSON.

U.S.A.: B.P. 817 (E); *Ambassador:* ROBERT MOORE.

Vatican: *Papal Nuncio:* Mgr. JEAN JADOT.

Yugoslavia: Brazzaville, People's Republic of the Congo (E).

Zaire: P.O.B. 639 (E); *Ambassador:* (vacant).

Cameroon also has diplomatic relations with Denmark, Ethiopia, Ghana, Greece, Libya, Monaco and Tanzania.

PARLIAMENT

NATIONAL ASSEMBLY

President: MARCEL MARIGOH MBOUA.
First Vice-President: NDELEY STEPHEN MOKOSSO.

Elections to the 120 seats in the newly formed National Assembly will be held at the beginning of 1973.

ECONOMIC AND SOCIAL COUNCIL

The Economic and Social Council is a national body set up under the unitary constitution to advise the Government on economic and social problems arising. It replaces the regional organizations which carried out similar functions on a smaller scale. The Council consists of 65 members, who meet several times a year, a permanent secretariat and a president appointed by Presidential decree. The members are nominated for a five-year term, whilst the secretariat is elected annually.

POLITICAL PARTY

Union nationale camerounaise (UNC): Yaoundé; f. 1966 by merger of the governing party of each state (*Union camerounaise* and the *Kamerun National Democratic Party*), two opposition parties in East Cameroon (the *Parti démocratique camerounais* and the *Cameroon Socialists*), and the two opposition parties in West Cameroon (the *Cameroon Union Congress* and the *Cameroon People's National Congress*, which had already agreed in August 1965 to co-operate with the ruling KNDP in West Cameroon); Pres. AHMADOU AHIDJO; publ. *l'Unité* (weekly).

The UNC Charter, outlining the party's internal and external policies, was published in April, 1969. It supports efforts towards the liberation and unification of Africa; it supports a democratic system of government within Cameroon; and it lays down that economic and social development should be achieved in Cameroon through encouraging private initiative while reserving for the state a determining and organizing rôle.

DEFENCE

Cameroon has an army, of 4,000, Gendarmerie of 3,000, National Guard of 2,000 and a civil police of 2,000. The navy numbers 150, and the air force 200. France has a bilateral defence agreement with Cameroon.

Commander-in-Chief of Army: Col. PIERRE SEMENGUE.

JUDICIAL SYSTEM

High Court: Yaoundé; can hear actions against the President, Vice-President, or Ministers; it can decide on the admissibility of any proposed law. When the Court sits to decide the admissibility of laws, it will have in addition to the Judges, an equal number of members chosen by the President. Nine titular Judges and nine substitute Judges preside. They are chosen by the National Assembly and are assisted by a Commission of Instruction, comprising a president and two magistrates of the Supreme Court.

The Legal System is closely modelled on that of France, with a Supreme Court, four Courts of Appeal and a number of Tribunaux de Première Instance, Labour Tribunes and Tribunes of Conciliation.

President of the Supreme Court: NGUINI MARCEL.
Procureur-Général: (vacant).

RELIGION

It is estimated that 45 per cent of the population follow traditional animist beliefs, 20 per cent are Muslims and 35 per cent Christians, Roman Catholics comprising 21 per cent of the total population.

Roman Catholic Missions: The total number of Roman Catholics is about 1,122,570 (including 26,368 catechumens). The Pères du Sacré-Coeur de Saint-Quentin, the Pères du Saint-Esprit, the Oblats de Marie-Immaculée, the Société de St. Joseph de Mill-Hill and the Petits Frères du Père de Foucauld are the most active missionary orders. There is a seminary for African priests at Nkol-Bisson and a Trappist monastery at Koutaba. The total number of priests (including Africans) is about 870.

Archbishop of Yaoundé: Mgr. JEAN ZOA; B.P. 207, Yaoundé.

BISHOPS

Bafia: ANDRÉ LOUCHEUR.

Bafoussam: DENIS NGANDE.

Bamenda: PAUL VERDZEKOV.

Buea: JULIUS PEETERS.

Douala: THOMAS MONGO.

Doumé: LAMBERT VAN HEYGEN.

Garoua: YVES PLUMEY.

Mbalmayo: PAUL ETOGA.

N'Kongsamba: ALBERT NDONGMO (sentenced to life imprisonment, January 1971).

Sangmélima: PIERRE-CELESTIN NKOU.

Protestant Churches: There are about 600,000 protestants, with about 3,000 Church and Mission workers, and four theological schools.

Fédération Évangélique du Cameroun et de l'Afrique Équatoriale: B.P. 491, Yaoundé; Sec.-Gen. Pastor E. MALLO; includes the following:

Église Presbytérienne Camerounaise: B.P. 579, Yaoundé; Sec.-Gen. Pastor NYEMB.

Église Évangélique du Cameroun: B.P. 89, Douala; Sec.-Gen. J. KOTTO.

Union des Églises Baptistes du Cameroun: B.P. 7, New-Bell, Douala; Pres. P. MBENDE.

Mission Protestante Norvégienne: B.P. 6, Ngaoundéré; Pres. M. FOLLESAY.

The Sudan Mission: B.P. 9, Meiganga; Pres. TH. NOSTBAKKEN.

Mission Fraternelle Luthérienne: Kaélé; Pres. M. STENNES.

Mission Unie du Sudan: Mokolo; Pres. E. EICHENBERGER.

Mission Baptiste Européenne: B.P. 82, Maroua; Pres. R. KASSÜLIKE.

Église Presbytérienne du Cameroun Occidental: Buea; Sec.-Gen. A. SU.

Église Protestante Africaine: Lolodorf; Pres. R. NGOUAH-BEAUD.

Église Évangélique Luthérienne du Cameroun: Meiganga; Pres. P. DARNIAN.

THE PRESS

DAILY

La Presse du Cameroun: B.P. 584, Douala; f. 1956; daily; French and English; circ. 12,000; Editor CHRISTIAN DE GASPERIS.

Cameroon Times: P.O.B. 200, Victoria; f. 1960; circ. 6,000; daily in English; Editor JEROME F. GWELLEM.

WEEKLIES

Abbia: Yaoundé; f. 1963; cultural; weekly.

L'Effort Camerounais: B.P. 807, Yaoundé; f. 1955; Roman Catholic weekly; Dir. J. PAUL BAYEMI; circ. 5,000.

Journal Officiel de la République du Cameroun: Imprimerie du Gouvernement, Yaoundé; weekly.

Le Peuple Camerounais: B.P. 144, Yaoundé; weekly; circ. 2,000.

La Semaine Camerounaise: B.P. 1068, Yaoundé; Protestant weekly; circ. 4,000.

L'Unité: Yaoundé; organ of *Union Nationale Camerounaise*; weekly.

La Voix des Jeunes: Imprimerie St.-Paul-Mvolyé, B.P. 550, Yaoundé; weekly; circ. 2,000.

PERIODICALS

Le Bamiléké: B.P. 94, Dschang; every two months.

Chambre de Commerce et d'Industrie: B.P. 97, Douala; monthly; circ. 1,500.

L'Informateur National: B.P. 392, Yaoundé; every two months.; circ. 2,000.

Mefoe: Elat, Ebolowa; monthly; circ. 3,200.

Miñañ: Elat, Ebolowa; monthly; circ. 1,000.

Le Monde Noir: B.P. 736, Yaoundé.

Mwendi Ma Baptiste: Mondoungue; monthly; circ. 1,000.

Nku-Tam-Tam: Imprimerie Coulouma et Cie., B.P. 134, Yaoundé; bi-monthly; circ. 4,000.

Les Nouvelles du Mongo: B.P. 1, N'Kongsamba; monthly circ. 3,000.

NEWS AGENCIES

Agence Camerounaise de Presse: B.P. 1170, Yaoundé; Dir. (vacant).

Agence France-Presse and Tass are also represented in Cameroon.

PUBLISHERS

Editions CLE: B.P. 4048, Yaoundé; f. 1963; Protestant-financed; specializes in original fiction and christian literature.

UNESCO Publishing Centre: B.P. 808, Yaoundé; f. 1961; official educational publications and printing training.

Librairie Saint Paul: B.P. 763, Yaoundé; education, medicine, philosophy, politics, religion and fiction.

RADIO

Radiodiffusion du Cameroun: B.P. 281, Yaoundé; Government service; Dir. DANIEL AMIOT-PRISO.

Radio Yaoundé: B.P. 281, Yaoundé; programmes in French, English and local languages; Dirs. E. M. MOUDJI, M. KAMDEM.

Radio Douala: B.P. 986, Douala; programmes in French, English, Douala, Bassa, Ewondo and Bamiléké; Dir. CÉLESTIN-LUCIEN SACK.

Radio Garoua: B.P. 103, Garoua; programmes in French, Hausa and Foulfoudé; Dir. BELLO MAL GANA.

Radio Buéa: Private Mail Bag, Buea; programmes in English, French, Bali, Douala and other local languages; Dir. F. WÉTÉ.

There are 214,000 radio receivers.

FINANCE

BANKING

Banque Centrale des Etats de l'Afrique Equatoriale et du Cameroun (BCEAEC): 29 rue du Colisée, Paris 8, France; B.P. 83, Yaoundé; bank of issue; Pres. G. GAUTIER; Gen. Man. C. PANOUILLOT; Cameroon Dir. ALFRED EKOKO.

Banque Camerounaise de Développement: B.P. 55, Yaoundé; f. 1951; Pres. OUSMANE MEY; Dir.-Gen. TITTI GOTTLIEB; cap. 1,500m. francs CFA.

Banque Internationale pour le Commerce et l'Industrie du Cameroun: ave. du 27 août, B.P. 5, Yaoundé; f. 1962; 9 brs.; several foreign banks have an interest in this bank, including Barclays Bank International Ltd.; Gen. Man. M. ROGER JOURDAN; cap. 500m. francs CFA.

Cameroons Bank Ltd.: Victoria; four brs.

Société Camerounaise de Banque: avenue Monseigneur Vogt, Yaoundé; f. 1961; cap. 400m. f. CFA; 7 agencies; Dir. ROBERT PLISSON.

Société Financière pour le Développement du Cameroun: B.P. 5493, Douala.

Société Générale de Banques au Cameroun: rue Mgr. Vogt, B.P. 244, Yaoundé; f. 1963; Pres. A. N. NJIMONKOUOP; Gen. Man. R. DUCHEMIN; cap. 600m. f. CFA; 4 brs.

FOREIGN BANKS

Banque Internationale pour l'Afrique Occidentale: 9 avenue de Messine, Paris; avenue de Gaulle, B.P. 4001, Douala.

Standard Bank of West Africa Ltd.: 37 Gracechurch St., London, E.C.3; B.P. 5348, rue Joffre, Douala; br. in Victoria.

DEVELOPMENT INSTITUTE

Société Nationale d'Investissement du Cameroun: B.P. 423, Yaoundé; f. 1964; Pres. M. NTAMAG; cap. 250m. francs CFA.

INSURANCE

Assurances Générales (Chanas et Privat): B.P. 109, Douala; cap. p.u. 3m. f. CFA; 3 agencies.

Les Assureurs-Conseils Camerounais (Faugère, Jutheau et Cie.): B.P. 544, Douala.

Agence Camerounaise d'Assurances: rue de l'Hippodrome, Yaoundé, B.P. 209; cap. p.u. 8m. f. CFA; Dir. CLAUDE GERMAIN.

Caisse Centrale de Co-opération Economique: Yaoundé, B.P. 46; Dir. JOSEPH PAOLINI.

Caisse Nationale de Réassurances: Yaoundé, B.P. 4180; Dir. TONYE BATCHAM.

SA E. Casalegno and Cie.: Douala, B.P. 443; Dir. ÉMILE CASALEGNO; cap. p.u. 5m. f. CFA.

TRADE AND INDUSTRY

CHAMBERS OF COMMERCE

Chambre de Commerce d'Industrie et des Mines du Cameroun: B.P. 4011, Douala; f. 1963; 138 mems., 100 in East Cameroon and 38 in West Cameroon; Pres. PAUL MONTHÉ; Sec.-Gen. JEAN MARIE TEDJONG; publ. *Bulletin Mensuel, Commerce Extérieur.*

Chambre d'Agriculture, de l'Elevage et des Forêts du Cameroun: B.P. 287 Parc Repiquet, Yaoundé; 44 mems.; Pres. EPHREM MBA; Sec. LOUIS WAMBO; publ. *Le Cameroun Agricole, Pastoral et Forestier* (monthly).

EMPLOYERS' ASSOCIATIONS

Groupement Interprofessionnel pour l'Etude et la Coordination des Intérêts Economiques au Cameroun: B.P. 829, Douala; f. 1957; 101 member associations; Pres. BERNARD CRETIN.

Syndicat des Commerçants Importateurs-Exportateurs du Cameroun: Douala, B.P. 97.

Syndicat des Industriels du Cameroun: B.P. 673, Douala,; f. 1953; Pres. M. NORGUIN.

Syndicats Professionnels Forestiers et Activitités connexes de Cameroun: B.P. 100, Douala.

Union des Syndicats Professionels du Cameroun: B.P. 829, Douala; Pres. LOUIS BEKOMBO.

West Cameroon Employers Association: Tiko.

TRADE UNION

National Union of Cameroon Workers (*Union nationale des travailleurs du Cameroun—UNTC*): Yaoundé; f. 1971; Pres. M. SATOUGLÉ.

DEVELOPMENT ORGANIZATIONS

Cameroons Development Corporation: Bota, Victoria; f. 1947; a statutory authority responsible for the development of 12 plantations of rubber, oil palms, bananas, tea, cocoa and pepper as a commercial enterprise on 28,343 hectares leased from the Government; negotiations with World Bank and Fonds Européen de Développement concluded in 1967 ensure tripled production by 1980 when total area planted should be about 33,000 hectares; Gen. Man. H. DE B. BROCK; Sec.-Gen. Dr. S. J. EGALE.

West Cameroon Development Agency: f. 1956; makes loans for economic development projects and training schemes; undertakes economic development projects; Gen. Man. T. F. S. KINGA; Chair. V. C. NEHAMI.

PRINCIPAL CO-OPERATIVE ORGANIZATIONS

Société Africaine de Prévoyance: Yaoundé, a provident society with branches in each region for each particular activity.

There are 83 co-operatives for the harvesting and sale of bananas and coffee and for providing mutual credit.

Co-operative Union of Western Cameroon Ltd.: policy-making and auditing body for all the societies in the Territory.

West Cameroon Co-operative Association Ltd.: P.O.B. 135, Kumba; founded as central financing body of the Co-operative movement; gives short-term credits to member societies and provides agricultural services for members; policy-making body for the Co-operative Movement in W. Cameroon; 143 member unions and societies with total membership of about 45,000; member of Internatoinal Co-operative Alliance; Pres. Chief T. E. NJEA.

Cameroon Co-operative Exporters Ltd.: P.O.B. 19, Kumba; f. 1953; mems. 8 societies; central agency for marketing of members' coffee, cocoa and palm kernels; Man. A. B. ENYONG; Sec. M. M. EYOH (acting).

Bakweri Co-operative Union of Farmers Ltd.: Dibanda, Tiko; produce marketing co-operative for bananas, cocoa and coffee; 14 societies, 2,000 mems.; Pres. Dr. E. M. L. ENDELEY.

MAJOR INDUSTRIAL COMPANIES

The following are some of the largest companies in terms either of capital investment or employment.

AGIP (Cameroun) S.A.: B.P. 4015, Douala; f. 1961; cap. 350m. francs CFA.
Distribution of petroleum products.
Dir. Gen. GERVASI MARIO; 108 employees.

ALUCAM—Compagnie Camerounaise de l'Aluminium Pechiney-Ugine: B.P. 54, Edéa; f. 1954; cap. 4,500m. francs CFA.
Aluminium smelter.
Dir. BERNARD CRETIN.

Société J. Bastos de l'Afrique Centrale: B.P. 94, Yaoundé; f. 1946; cap. 839 million francs CFA.
Manufacture of cigarettes.
Dir. J. BEAUGRAND; 170 employees.

Bata S.A. Camerounaise: B.P. 57, Douala; f. 1961; cap. 420 million francs CFA.
Shoe factory and retail.
Dir. GEORGES MAREINE.

S.A. des Brasseries du Cameroun: B.P. 4036, Douala; f. 1948; cap. 1,350 million francs CFA.
Production of beer and soft drinks, cold storage.
Dirs. PHILIPPE GRANDJEAN, MAURICE NORGUIN; 1,780 employees.

Complexe Chimique Camerounais: B.P. 4, Douala-Bassa; f. 1944; cap. 210 million francs CFA.
Manufacture of vegetable and palm oils and oilcake, soaps and detergents.

Société ELF de Recherches et d'Exploitation des Pétroles du Cameroun: B.P. 5396, Douala-Bassa; f. 1951; cap. 4,700 million francs CFA.
Off-shore prospecting and mining of petroleum.
Dir. MICHEL CLEMENT.

Guinness Cameroun S.A.: B.P. 1213, Douala; f. 1967; cap. 300 million francs CFA.
Production and marketing of "Guinness" Foreign Extra Stout and "Gold Harp" Lager.
Pres. E. CASALEGNO; Dir. Gen. J. H. CAWTHRA; 150 employees.

Société Industrielle des Cacaos: B.P. 570, Douala; f. 1949; cap. 500 million francs CFA.
Production of cocoa and cocoa butter.
Dirs. PIERRE FORCADE, ÉMILE TOS.

Société des Palmeraies de M'Bongo et d'Eséka: B.P. 691, Douala; f. 1969; cap. 810 million francs CFA.
Oil palm plantation.
Pres. of Administrative Council L. C. MPOUMA; Dir. Gen. P. MARCHAL; 736 employees.

SAFA-Cameroun: B.P. 399, Yaoundé; f. 1962; cap. 1,600 million francs CFA.

Plantation of para-rubber and production of rubber and latex.

Pres. M. BOURGES-MANOURY; Dir. ANDRÉ RAPASSE; 3,000 employees.

Société Shell du Cameroun: B.P. 4082, Douala; f. 1954; cap. 260 million francs CFA.

Import and distribution of petroleum and chemical products; manufacture of insecticide.

Man. R. L. W. SCOTT; 115 employees.

Société Sucrière du Cameroun: B.P. 857, Yaoundé; f. 1964; cap. 799 million francs CFA.

Sugar plantation.

Pres. Dir. Gen. JEAN VILGRAIN.

TRANSPORT

RAILWAYS

Régie des Chemins de Fer du Cameroun—REGIFERCAM (*Cameroon Railways Corporation*): B.P. 304, Douala; Dir. A. DESTOPPELEIRE.

Northern Line: Douala to N'Kongsamba 172 km.; metre gauge; link to West Cameroon from Mbanga to Kumba 29 km.; metre gauge.

Central Line: Douala to Yaoundé and Belabo 601 km.; metre gauge; link to Mbalmayo from Otele 37 km.; metre gauge.

Office de Chemin de Fer Transcamerounais (*Transcameroonian Railway Office*): B.P. 625, Yaoundé; supervises the building of the extension of the Central Line from Belabo to N'Gaoundéré (325 km., one metre gauge), scheduled for January 1974; Dir.-Gen. JEAN BAYON.

Besides the railway line from Mbanga to Kumba (29 km.) in the former West Cameroon there are 147 km. of narrow gauge railway running from the plantations to the ports.

ROADS

In 1971, there were 1,050 km. of bitumen-surfaced roads, 5,200 km. of unsurfaced secondary roads and 17,000 km. of unclassified roads. The unclassified roads are maintained by local authorities.

The road from Douala to Tiko (30 km.) was opened in 1969 and the road from Waza to Maltam in 1971. Direct routes between Waza and Mora, Kumba and Mamfé, Bolifamba and Banga have also been completed. Under the 1971–76 Plan emphasis has been laid on the development of the road network, particularly on the construction of a road linking the north and the south of the country.

SHIPPING

Ships of numerous lines call at Douala:

Barber West Africa Line: B.P. 4059.

Chargeurs Réunis: Boulevard Leclerc, B.P. 136.

Delta Line: c/o Chargeurs Réunis, B.P. 136.

Deutsche Afrika Linien: B.P. 263.

Elder Dempster: monthly service.

Mory et Cie.: rue Joffre, B.P. 572.

Palm Line: c/o SOCOPAO, B.P. 215.

SAMOA: Blvb. Leclerc, B.P. 1127; agents for Lloyd Triestino, Black Star Line, Seven Stars Line, Gold Star Line, Europa Africa Line.

Scandinavian West Africa Line: c/o B.P. 4057.

Société Africaine de Transit et d'Affrètement (SATA): Boulevard Leclerc, B.P. 546.

Société Navale Delmas-Vieljeux: rue Kitchener, B.P. 263.

SOCOPAO (Cameroun): B.P. 215; agents for Palm/Elder/Hoegh Lines, Bank Line, Dafra Line, Marasia S.A., Splosna Plovba, Greek West Africa Line, Veb Deutsche Seerederei, Polish Ocean Lines, Westwind Africa Line, Nautilus Keller Line, Morflot Moscow.

Société Navale de l'Ouest: c/o B.P. 4057.

Société Ouest-Africaine d'Entreprises Maritimes: rue du Roi Albert, B.P. 4057.

There are also ports at Victoria and Tiko, where Elder and Fyffes call weekly.

CIVIL AVIATION

There is an international airport at Douala, and a smaller one at Yaoundé. Work on a new airport at Douala was scheduled for completion by the end of 1972.

Cameroon Airlines: 44 Ave. Poincaré, Douala; f. 1971; services to Paris, Marseilles, Nice, Rome, London; also domestic flights and flights to other African states; fleet of one Boeing 707, two Boeing 737 and three DC-4; Pres. SAMUEL EBOUA.

Cameroon is also served by Air Afrique, Alitalia, Ethiopian Airlines, Pan Am, Sabena, Swissair and UTA.

POWER

The Edéa hydroelectric dam near Douala accounts for 98 per cent of Cameroon power generation, and aluminium smelting accounts for 88 per cent of total consumption.

Energie Electrique du Cameroun: B.P. 4029, Douala; f. 1948; cap. 1,500 million francs CFA; production of electricity; Dir. GEORGES DALMAIS; in 1969–70 produced 1,108 million kWh.

Electricité du Cameroun: B.P. 4077, Douala; f. 1963; cap. 500 million francs CFA; production of electricity; Dir. GEORGE DALMAIS; 1970–71 produced 176 million kWh.

TOURISM

Commissariat-Général au Tourisme: B.P. 266, Yaoundé; f. 1970; Commissaire-Général AMINOU OUMAROU.

CULTURAL ORGANIZATIONS

The four important centres for the creation, exhibition and sale of works of art are the handicraft centres of Maroua, Foumban, Bamenda and Douala.

L'Ensemble National: c/o le Ministère de la Jeunesse, de la Culture et de l'Education Nationale; the most famous representatives of Cameroonian traditional art.

EDUCATION

LEARNED SOCIETIES AND RESEARCH INSTITUTES

British Council: La Concorde, Avenue de l'Intendence, Yaoundé, (B.P. 818); Rep. K. WESTCOTT.

Bureau de Recherches Géologiques et Minières: B.P. 343, Yaoundé; f. 1959; 20 engineers and technicians; Dir. J. P. CARRIVE.

Centre Culturel d'Allemagne: rue de Narvik 4, B.P. 1067, Yaoundé; Dir. HOLGER HARTMANN.

Centre Culturel Français: avenue du 27 août, B.P. 513, Yaoundé; f. 1960; 3,500 mems.; 20,000 vols. in library; Dir. GEORGES LORENZO.

Centre Technique Forestier Tropical (CTFT): B.P. 832, Douala; f. 1964; forestry research; Dir. A. SCHIRLE; publ. *Bois et Forêts des Tropiques.*

Compagnie Française pour le Développement des Fibres Textiles (CFDT): B.P. 302, Garoua; brs. at Garoua, Maroua, Mora, Touboro and Kaele; textile research.

Institut de Recherches du Coton et des Textiles Exotiques— IRCT: Section Expérimentation Cotonnière du Cameroun; B.P. 22, Maroua; genetics, agronomy and phytosanitary defence; Dir. P. JACQUEMARD.

Institut de Recherches pour les Huiles Oléagineuses (IRHO): B.P. 243, Douala; f. 1949; Dir. J. N. REGAUD.

Institut de Recherches Tropicales Agronomiques et des Cultures Vivrières (IRAT): B.P. 2123, Yaoundé-Messa; stations at Guétalé par Mokolo, Dschang, Bambui, Yagoua; Dir. M. ROUANET.

Institut Français de Recherches Fruitières Outre-Mer: B.P. 13, Nyombé; research station; f. 1946; Dir. J. LECOR.

Institut Géographique National: Yaoundé, avenue Mgr.-Vogt. B.P. 157; f. 1945; survey office; Dir. J. LARIVÉ.

Institut Pasteur du Cameroun: B.P. 888, Yaoundé; f. 1959; 4 doctors and 1 biochemist; bio-medical research; Dir. Dr. P. RAVISSE.

Institut des Relations Internationales du Cameroun (IRIC): B.P. 1365, Yaoundé; f. 1971 by the Federal Government, the Carnegie Endowment for International Peace, the Swiss Division for Technical Co-operation and others; a bi-lingual establishment for training, research and documentation, and post-graduate studies; Dir. Dr. ADAMOU NDAM NJOYA.

Laboratoire Interdépartemental: B.P. 4046, Douala; attached to the Ministry of Health; research on hygiene and public health matters.

Office de la Recherche Scientifique et Technique Outre-Mer—Centre ORSTOM de Yaoundé: B.P. 193, Yaoundé; geology, pedology, hydrology, nutrition, agronomy, psycho-sociology, demography, economics, geography, archaeology, botany and vegetal biology, biology and amelioration of plants, and medical entomology; library; Dir. R. LEFÈVRE.

Service Météorologique (*Meteorological Service*): B.P. 186, Douala; f. 1934; departments of climatology, hydro-meteorology, agrometeorology, aeronautical meteorology; small library; Dir. W. MANDENGUE EPOY; publs. *Bulletin Agroclimatologique* (monthly), *Résumé du Temps* (monthly), *Bulletin Hydrométéorologique* (annually), *Annales Climatologiques du Cameroun.*

UNESCO Regional Centre for Producing Textbooks: Yaoundé; f. 1962; set up under the African Emergency Programme; provides printing equipment, printing supplies, expert editorial and technical staff; the textbooks cover all educational levels, publications in English and French.

U.S. Information Center: Yaoundé.

LIBRARIES AND ARCHIVES

Archives Fédérales: B.P. 1053, Yaoundé; f. 1952; conserves and classifies all documents relating to the Republic; library of 2,071 vols. and 20,000 cases of documents.

Bibliothèque du Centre IFAN du Cameroun: B.P. 339.

Douala; 3,500 medical books and scientific documentation.

Bibliothèque Nationale du Cameroun: B.P. 1053, Yaoundé; 10,000 vols.

UNIVERSITY

UNIVERSITÉ FÉDÉRALE DU CAMEROUN
(The Federal University of Cameroon)
B.P. 337, YAOUNDE
Telephone: 22-07-44.
Founded 1962.

Languages of instruction: English and French.

Chancellor: Z. MONGO-SOO.
Vice-Chancellor: JEAN IMBERT.
Secretary-General: P. MARCELLI.
Librarian: FRANÇOISE MAHIEU.

Library of 40,000 vols.
Number of teachers: 260
Number of students: 3,277.
Postgraduate courses began in 1972.

DEANS:
Faculty of Law and Economics: R. MENDEGRIS.
Faculty of Arts: J. MBOUI.
Faculty of Science: J. KAMSU KOM.

Centre Universitaire des Sciences de la Santé: B.P. 337, Yaoundé; f. 1969; 27 teachers, 132 students; Dir. G. L. MONEKOSSO.

AFFILIATED INSTITUTES:

Ecole Normale Supérieure: B.P. 47, Yaoundé; Dir. S. MBOM ABANE; 42 teachers, 414 students; library of 16,244 vols.; publ. *Revue Camerounaise de Pédagogie*.

Ecole Fédérale Supérieure d'Agriculture: B.P. 138, Yaoundé; f. 1960; Dir. A.-L. MATHIEU; 34 teachers, 60 students; library of 3,846 vols.

Ecole Fédérale Supérieure Polytechnique: B.P. 337 Yaoundé; f. 1971; three and five-year courses; Departments of Mechanical and Electrical Engineering; Civil Engineering, Public Works and Buildings; Electronics and Telecommunications; 7 teachers, 29 students; library being formed; Dir. C. BONTHOUX.

Ecole Supérieure Internationale de Journalisme de Yaoundé (ESIJY): B.P. 1328, Yaoundé; f. 1970; three-year courses open to students from Cameroon, Central African Republic, Gabon, Rwanda, Chad, Togo; library of 2,000 vols.; 28 teachers, 50 students; Dir. HERVÉ BOURGES; Gen. Sec. JOSEPH EVA.

Ecole Nationale d'Administration et de Magistrature: B.P. 1180, Yaoundé; f. 1960; library of 2,000 vols.; Dir. FRANÇOIS PERRET; 142 students.

SELECT BIBLIOGRAPHY

ANSPRENGER, FRANZ. *Politik im Schwarzen Afrika*. Cologne, deutscher Verlag, 1961.

ARDENER, E., ARDENER, S. and WARMINGTON, W. A. *Plantation and Village in the Cameroons: Some Economic and Social Studies*. London, Oxford University Press, 1960.

BEDERMAN, S. H. *The Cameroons Development Corporation: Partner in National Growth*. West Cameroon, Bota, 1968.

BILLARD, P. *Le Cameroun Fédérale*. 2 vols. Paris, 1968–69.

BOUCHAUD, JOSEPH. *La Côte du Cameroun dans l'histoire et la cartographie des origines à l'annexion allemande*. Yaoundé, Centre IFAN, 1952.

BUELL, RAYMOND LESLIE. *The Native Problem in Africa*. Vol. 2. New York, Macmillan, 1928.

GARDINIER, DAVID E. *Cameroons, United Nations Challenge to French Policy*. London, Oxford University Press, 1963.

HUGON, P. *Analyse du sous-développement en Afrique Noire: L'Example de l'Economie du Cameroun*. Paris, Presses Universitaires de France, 1968.

JOHNSON, WILLARD R. *The Cameroon Federation*. Princeton University Press, 1970.

LEMBEZAT, B. *Cameroun*. Paris, Nouvelles Editions Latines, 1964.

LE VINE, VICTOR T. *The Cameroons from Mandate to Independence*. Berkeley, University of California Press, 1964.
The Cameroon Federal Republic. Ithaca, Cornell University Press, 1971.

MORTIMER, EDWARD. *France and the Africans, 1944–1960*. London, Faber & Faber, 1969.

MVENG, ENGELBERT. *Histoire du Cameroun*. Paris, Présence Africaine, 1963.

RUBIN, NEVILLE NORDAU. *Cameroun*. London, Pall Mall, 1971.

RUDIN, HARRY R. *Germans in the Cameroons, 1884–1914*. London, Jonathan Cape, 1938.

SURET-CANALE, J. *Afrique noire occidentale et centrale*. Paris, Editions Sociales, Vol. I (3rd edn.) 1968, Vol. II 1964.

l'U.P.C. parle . . . Paris, François Maspero, 1971.

WELCH, CLAUDE E., JR. *Dream of Unity*. Ithaca, Cornell University Press, 1966.

Cape Verde Islands

PHYSICAL AND SOCIAL GEOGRAPHY*

René Pélissier

The Cape Verde Islands (Cabo Verde in Portuguese) lie about 250 miles west of Dakar (14° 48′ and 17° 12′ northern latitude; 22° 40′ and 25° 22′ western longitude). Consisting of ten islands and five islets, they constitute a Portuguese overseas province. The archipelago is divided into two groups according to the direction of the prevailing north-easterly wind:

(1) *Barlavento* (Windward) Islands, composed of Santo Antão (291 sq. miles), São Vicente (88 sq. miles), Santa Luzia (13 sq. miles), São Nicolau (132 sq. miles), Boavista (240 sq. miles), and Sal (83 sq. miles).

(2) *Sotavento* (Leeward) Islands, comprising the southern cluster of Maio (103 sq. miles), Santiago (383 sq. miles), Fogo (184 sq. miles) and Brava (25 sq. miles).

The total area is 1,517 sq. miles and the administrative capital is Praia (population 21,494 in 1970) on Santiago Island. The 1970 census figure was 272,071 inhabitants. An explosive birth rate forces a significant number of islanders to emigrate to Angola, Portuguese Guinea, São Tomé and formerly to other west African countries. The main centre of population is Mindelo (São Vicente), with 28,797 inhabitants in 1970, which is the foremost port and economic capital of the archipelago. Santiago is the most populous of the ten islands, with 129,358 inhabitants in 1970, followed by Santo Antão (44,916), Fogo (29,592), São Vicente (31,462).

Except for the low-lying islands of Sal, Boavista and Maio, the Cape Verde Islands are mountainous, craggy and deeply furrowed by erosion and volcanic activity. The highest point is on Fogo (8,572 ft.), which has an active volcano. Located in the semi-arid belt, the islands have an anaemic hydrography, and suffer from chronic shortages of rainfall, which, coupled with high temperatures (yearly average, 80°–72°F. at Praia), cause catastrophic droughts which have periodically devastated the islands. Famine (*fome* in Portuguese) is the haunting fear of the peasant population who, until recently, had no escape other than mass exodus to tropical plantations on São Tomé and Angola. Since 1968 a persistant drought has compelled Portugal to launch a massive relief programme to keep the population from starving. Over 40,000 workers paid by the government open tracks, and are hired by the Public Works Department. The number of dependents subsidized in this way is estimated to be 200,000, which means that four families out of five live on governmental charity. A desalination plant has recently been modernized in São Vicente to serve the needs of Mindelo which is otherwise deprived of drinkable water.

Ethnically, the archipelago boasts of being the "lusotropical laboratory" of Portuguese Africa, its main claim to this title coming from the miscegenation between Europeans of southern extraction (mostly Catholic and Jewish Portuguese), who came as settlers, and African slaves. About 60 per cent are of mixed descent, except on Santiago, where the majority is of pure African stock. Whites represent about 2 per cent and are Portuguese civil servants and military personnel. The vernacular is a creole Portuguese (*Crioulo*), archaic and influenced by African vocabulary, syntax and pronunciation. Illiteracy is still very prevalent.

* *See* map on p. 708.

RECENT HISTORY

See Recent History of Portugal's African Territories under Angola, p. 150.

ECONOMY

René Pélissier

Poverty is the dominant theme in this subsistence economy, which hinges on the vagaries of the rainfall and is threatened by local overpopulation in the wetter islands. The flat islands (Sal, Maio, Boavista), where the wind blows almost all the year round, have little farming, livestock-breeding being their main occupation. The other seven suffer from poor agricultural techniques, conservatism, lack of cash and incentives, erosion, and above all lack of rainfall. Food crops are maize, beans, cassava, sweet potatoes, supplemented wherever soils, terrain and rainfall permit, with bananas, vegetables, sugar-cane, fruits, etc. The main staples are beans and maize. Santiago is the main agricultural producer, followed by Santo Antão, Fogo and São Nicolau. Cash crops, such as bananas, *arabica* coffee, peanuts, castor beans and pineapples, are encouraged, but poor inter-island communications, general ignorance, paucity of government funds, and the lack of suitable available land militate against the development of a thriving agriculture. In 1970 Cape Verde exported potatoes, bananas, coffee, castor beans and tomatoes, but quantities are minimal owing to the prevailing climatic conditions. A rather exotic commodity, locally known as *purgueira* (*Jatropha curcas*), which grows wild, is also exported (for soap-making). A tourist complex is being built up on Boavista with Belgian capital. It includes three hotels with accomodation for 1,200 people.

In 1970, 4,207 cattle, 8,072 goats, 1,644 sheep, and 3,512 pigs were raised for food and milk. About 5,000 horses, donkeys and mules were the main form of transport in rural parts. Within two years, livestock has been reduced to a quarter or a tenth of its pre-drought levels. Fishing could be important, and is being slowly developed with modern appliances and boats, through German assistance and substantial government funds. The catch in 1970 was about 5,000 tons, with a value of 19,338,000 escudos (i.e. more than the total value of agricultural exports). About 1,500 local fishermen take part in this activity, which has ample opportunity for increase (mainly tuna-fish and lobsters). Mining is of little significance, puzzolana and salt being the main produce. In 1970, the main port of the islands, Mindelo on São Vicente, which still plays a transatlantic role, received 261 Portuguese ships (1,025,398 d.w.t.) and 1,179 foreign ships (12,540,913 d.w.t.).

FOREIGN TRADE

Traditionally, the country has a negative trade balance, which shows worsening trends. In 1970 imports were valued at 469,418,000 escudos and exports at 47,731,000 escudos. Portugal is the main trading partner, providing 57.5 per cent of Cape Verde's imports in 1970 and taking 71.3 per cent of its exports.

In brief, the Cape Verdian economy is underdeveloped and offers little prospect of future development; its main export is still the emigrants who tend to constitute a class of small civil servants in Portuguese Guinea and Angola, and field labourers in São Tomé, Angola and, more recently, Portugal itself.

STATISTICAL SURVEY

Area: 3,929 sq. km. (1,517 sq. miles).

Population: 272,071 (1970 census). Vital statistics (1970): births 9,379, deaths 2,883.

Agriculture: *Principal crops* are coffee, castor oil, maize, peanuts, sugar cane, vegetables (mainly potatoes, tomatoes, pimentoes, beans) and fruit (largely bananas). *Livestock* (1970): Horses, Mules and Asses 5,000, Cattle 4,207, Sheep 1,644, Goats 8,072, Pigs 3,512.

Fishing: 5,100 metric tons (1970).

Industry (1965—contos): Food Industries 21,076, Beverages 1,511, Tobacco 1,883, Frozen Goods 1,638.

Production (1970): Cement 17,000 metric tons, Quicklime 28,000 metric tons, Salt 18,000 metric tons, Frozen Fish 1,037 metric tons, Soft Drinks 115,000 hectolitres.

Finance: 100 centavos = 1 Cape Verde escudo; 1,000 escudos = 1 conto. Exchange rates: £1 sterling = 62.90 escudos (December 1972); 100 escudos = £1.59; U.S. $1 = 27.12 escudos (September 1972); 100 escudos = $3.69.

Currency in Circulation (1967—contos): Notes 94,373; Coins 4,834.

Balance of Payments (1970): Net balance with foreign countries: in credit 37,000 contos. Net balance with Portugal: in credit 26,000 contos.

Budget (1970—contos): Ordinary receipts 195,786, Extraordinary receipts 127,743, TOTAL 318,529; Ordinary expenditure 170,104, Extraordinary expenditure 122,743, TOTAL 292,847.

Military Budget (1972—contos): 37,700.

External Trade (1968—contos): Imports 281,926, Exports 40,772.

Commodities: *Imports:* Live Animals 4,640, Textiles 36,390, Food and Drink 39,694, Machinery 28,566. *Exports:* Live Animals 6,219, Textiles 115, Food and Drink 5,138, Machinery 203.

Countries: *Imports:* Portugal 177,261, Portuguese Overseas Provinces 31,406, Foreign Countries 73,134. *Exports:* Portugal 25,699, Portuguese Overseas Provinces 3,689, Foreign Countries 11,384.

Transport: *Roads* (1967): Cars 1,135, Lorries and Buses 315, Motor Cycles 351, Total 1,802.

International Shipping Freight (1969): 48,000 metric tons loaded, 536,000 metric tons unloaded.

Civil Aviation (1968): Planes landed 1,163, Passengers landed 4,445, Freight entered and cleared 133,239 kg.

Education (1968): *Primary:* Schools 257, Teachers 381, Pupils 19,680. *Secondary:* Schools 5, Teachers 85, Pupils 2,059. *Technical:* Schools 1, Teachers 28, Pupils 494.

THE GOVERNMENT

Governor: Comd. Leão Maria Tavares Rosado do Sacramento Monteiro.

POLITICAL PARTIES

Acção Nacional Popular: The Portuguese Government Party, formerly União Nacional.

The following organizations have been declared illegal by the Portuguese Government:

Conferência das Organizações Nacionais das Colónias Portuguesas (CONCP): 18 rue Dirah, Hydra, Algiers, Algeria; f. 1961; central organization for MPLA, Angola, FRELIMO, Mozambique, PAIGC, Guinea and Cape Verde, CLSTP, São Tomé; Pres. Samura Machel.

Partido Africano da Independencia da Guiné e Cabo Verde (PAIGC) (*African Party for Independence in Guinea and Cape Verde*): B.P. 298, Conakry, Guinea; Sec.-Gen. Amílcar Cabral. (For further details *see* Guinea (Bissau) chapter).

DEFENCE

There is an international airport on Sal island which is also an important airbase. This, and the naval base in the islands, are valuable elements in the NATO defence system, commanding as they do the air and sea routes between South America, Africa and Europe.

RELIGION

Roman Catholic

Suffragan See, Santiago de Cabo Verde (attached to the Metropolitan See of Lisbon): Rt. Rev. José Felipe do Carmo Colaço. There are about 206,000 Roman Catholics.

THE PRESS

Noticias de Cabo Verde: S. Vicente, Caixa Postal 15; f. 1932; weekly; independent; Dirs. Manuel Ribeiro de Almeida, Raul Ribeiro.

O Arquipélago: Caixa Postal 118, Praia, Santiago; weekly; publication of the official tourism department; Dir. Dr. Bento Levy.

Boletim Oficial: Caixa Postal 113, Praia-Santiago; official.

RADIO

Radio Clube de Cabo Verde: Caixa Postal 26, Praia, Santiago; private station; Pres. Manuel de Jesús Rodrigues.

Rádio Clube Mindelo: Caixa Postal 101, S. Vicente; private station; Dir.-Gen. F. J. Martins.

Rádio Barlavento: Caixa Postal 29, S. Vicente; government station; Pres. Francisco Lopes da Silva.

There are 15,000 radio receivers. There is no television service.

FINANCE

Issuing Bank

Banco Naiconal Ultramarino: 84 rua do Comercio, Lisbon; Praia; 3 brs. in Cape Verde Islands.

INSURANCE

Many leading Portuguese insurance companies have agents in the Cape Verde Islands.

TRADE AND INDUSTRY

INDUSTRIAL COMPANIES

Cable and Wireless Ltd.: Rua Infanta D. Henrique, Mindelo, S. Vicente.

Companhia de Pesca e Congelaçao de Cabo Verde S.A.R.L.: Mindelo, S. Vicente; fishing and canning.

Companhia Portuguesa Rádio Marconi: Achada de Santo António, Praia, Santiago.

Companhia da Pozolana de Cabo Verde: Porto Novo, Santo Antão.

Companhia Sao Vicente de Cabo Verde: Av. da Republica Mindello, S. Vincente.

Italcable: Mindelo, S. Vicente.

Salins du Cap Vert: Pedra de Lume, Sal.

Shell Portuguesa S.A.R.L.: Av. da Republica, Mindelo, S. Vicente; import and distribution of petroleum products.

TRANSPORT

ROADS

There were 1,500 km. of roads in 1965.

SHIPPING

Companhia Nacional de Navegação: agent at Praia-Santiago: A. C. de Souza (Sucrs.) Ltd.; (Head Office: Rua do Comércio 85, Lisbon).

Companhia Colonial de Navegação: agent at Santiago: Francisco José da Costa; Rua Sá da Bandeira 40-48, Praia; (Head Office: Rua Instituto Vergilio Machado, Lisbon).

Sociedade Geral do Comercio, Industria e Transportes: P.O.B. 56, Praia-Santiago; agent: João Benoliel de Carvalho, Ltda. (Head Office: Rua dos Douradores 11, Lisbon).

CIVIL AVIATION

Transportes Aéreos Cape Verde (T.A.C.V.): Praia; f. 1955; connects São Vincente, Praia, Sal, São Nicolau, Boavista, Fogo and Maio; Dir. Vasco de Oliveira e Melo.

South African Airways call at Sal on the Europe–South Africa route. T.A.P. services to Lisbon and Bissau, Guinea.

TOURISM

Centro de Informação e Turismo: Caixa Postal 118, Praia, Santiago; official tourism dept.

SELECT BIBLIOGRAPHY

(For general works on the Portuguese African territories *see* Angola Select Bibliography, p. 163).

A.G.U. *Cabo Verde.* Lisbon, 1966.

Ilídio do Amaral. *Santiago de Cabo Verde.* Lisbon, 1964.

Central African Republic

PHYSICAL AND SOCIAL GEOGRAPHY*

David Hilling

PHYSICAL FEATURES

Geographically the Central African Republic is a link between the Sudanese zone and the Congo basin, and the country consists mainly of plateau surfaces at 2–3,000 ft. which provide the watershed between drainage northwards to Lake Chad and southwards to the Oubangui/Congo system. In the Bongo Massif of the north-east heights of 4,500 ft. are obtained. There are numerous rivers, and during the main rain season (July–October) much of the south-east of the country becomes inaccessible as a result of extensive inundation. Only the Oubangui river is commercially navigable, and it provides the country's main outlet for external trade. Development is retarded by the land-locked location of the country and the great distance to the sea by way of the fluvial route from Bangui to Brazzaville and thence by the Congo-Ocean Railway to Pointe-Noire.

POPULATION

With an area of 240,000 sq. miles the country is marginally larger than France. However, it has a population of only 1.6 million and an overall population density of only 7 persons per square mile. The greatest concentration of population is in the western part of the country—large areas in the east are virtually uninhabited. There are numerous ethnic groups, but the Banda and Baya together make up roughly a half of the population, and Sango, a lingua franca, has been adopted as the national language. Although 90 per cent of the active population depend on agriculture, only 2 per cent of the country's area is under cultivation, and the tsetse fly restricts animal husbandry over most of the country.

NATURAL RESOURCES

Only in the extreme south-west of the country is the rainfall sufficient (50 in.) to give a forest vegetation. From the Lobaye region come coffee, cocoa, rubber, palm produce and timber. There is likely to be considerable development in this forest region when the proposed rail link with the Trans-Cameroon railway is constructed. Forest extends northwards along water courses beyond the main forest region, and in a belt beyond the forest cotton is the main cash crop.

Alluvial deposits of diamonds occur widely and in recent years have been increasingly exploited in both the east and west of the country. Likely to be of much greater economic importance after 1972 is uranium. Several uranium deposits have been identified and mining by dredging methods is shortly to start at M'Patou, north of Bangassou in the east of the country.

* See map on p. 246.

RECENT HISTORY

Robert Cornevin†

FRENCH EQUATORIAL AFRICA

The origins of the vast French Equatorial African possessions lie in a mediocre and unhealthy trading post on the Gabon coast. It had been established under a treaty signed in February 1839 by Bonêt-Willaumez and the local chief, Louis Dowé‡. The fort of Aumale was erected in 1843, and in 1849 Libreville was founded with 46 slaves, freed by the French from the negro brig *Elizia*. The town became the administrative centre of the Gulf of Guinea Settlements in 1860.

Early exploration of the interior was undertaken by French naval expeditions—particularly that led by Lieutenant-Commander Aymes in 1867—and by an American naturalist, Paul du Chaillu. Bouvier, Marche and the Marquis of Compiègne sailed up the Ogooué as far as the junction with the Ivindo and, forced to turn back, they met the first expedition of Savorgnan de Brazza in 1878.

During this first journey, between 1875 and 1878, Brazza went almost right across the Congo on foot. On his second expedition (1879–82) he hastily signed a treaty with Makoko, king of the Téké, to prevent Stanley extending his territorial acquisitions beyond the River Congo.

The accession of new territory to French rule necessitated administrative adjustments. In January 1881 the powers of the special commander in charge of Gabon were extended and an administrative service chief was assigned to him. Brazza was himself appointed the Commissioner for the Government in West Africa, and all land acquired was regrouped under his authority in 1883.

† For the 1973 edition, revisions have been made to this article by the Editor.

‡ Known to the English as King Denis and as "King William"; he controlled the southern bank of the Gabon estuary.

Briefly, between 1886 and the end of 1888, Gabon and Congo were re-divided and given financial autonomy. The whole area was renamed the French Congo by a decree of April 30th, 1891, but three years later the territory of Oubangui was parcelled out as a separate administrative area. The French Congo and Oubangui were each governed by Lieutenant-Governors from the end of 1897.

New expeditions were meanwhile launched as the European "scramble for Africa" continued. French claims were advanced as far as the Nile by the Marchand mission, and on March 21st, 1899, the boundaries of Franco-British interests were defined as the watershed between the Nile, Chad and Congo basins.

French sovereignty over Chad had been recognized in the Franco-German agreements of 1894, but the territory had yet to be conquered. In April 1900, therefore, three French columns converged on the Chari river; one from central Africa, via the Sudan, and by then commanded by Joalland and Meynier; the Foureau-Lamy contingent from the north; and Gentil's contingent from the Congo, which had already fought its way through the area of the future French Equatorial Africa. Their combined forces defeated the army of Rabah (an increasingly powerful leader from the eastern Sudan) at the battle of Kousseri on April 22nd. The "military territory of the land and protectorate of Chad" was proclaimed on September 5th by decrees which also abolished the Lieutenant-Governorship of Oubangui.

The wider significance of the Kousseri victory was that it enabled the English and the Germans to occupy territories over which they held nominal ownership, and it meant that the three blocks of French African territories—the Algerian Sahara, West Africa and Equatorial Africa—were geographically linked.

THE FORMATION OF THE A.E.F

The French Congo now constituted an immense territory, bordering on Spanish Guinea (formed on February 27th, 1900) and Portuguese Guinea (January 25th, 1901). Under the constitution decreed on July 5th, 1902, a Commissioner-General was to govern the whole French Congo from Libreville, assisted by a Lieutenant-Governor resident at Brazzaville, and a Chief Administrator for the district (no longer "military territory") of Chad. Decrees were issued in December 1903 and December 1906 on the organization of the general headquarters for the "possessions and dependent territories of the French Congo".

But the favourable example of the French West African federation (*Afrique orientale française*—A.O.F.) persuaded the French Government to decide on June 26th, 1908 on "the creation of the federal government of French Equatorial Africa (*Afrique équatoriale française*—A.E.F.) formed by the alignment of Gabon, the Middle Congo and Oubangui-Chari-Chad". At the federal level the Governor-General, assisted by a nominated Government Council, disposed of all civil and military power. Each of the constituent colonies enjoyed financial and administrative authority under a Lieutenant-Governor, assisted by a nominated Administrative Council.

The "pacification" of the indigenous tribes proved a lengthy and difficult process. Rabah's followers were overcome near Dikoa, but the Ouadaï region was penetrated only with difficulty. In January 1910 the Fiegenschuh column was massacred at Ouadaï Kadjer, and Colonel Moll was killed in the following November at the Doroté encounter. The credit for ending tribal resistance in Ouadaï and also in Borkou, which was under Sanusi attack, therefore fell to Colonel Largean in 1911–12. The capture of Ain Galaka in November 1913 completed a network of forts throughout the territory.

Economic development was modelled on the practice of Cecil Rhodes' British South Africa Company or that of the concessionaries in the Independent State of the Congo. Between 1898 and 1900 the French Congo was shared out among 40 concessionaries. These companies were granted (normally for 30 years) rights of tenure and exploitation, except of mineral resources, in exchange for a fixed annual payment and 15 per cent of profits.

The country faced enormous development problems, however. It is difficult of access and very sparsely populated; and the concessionaries' demands for labour—primarily for gathering ivory and rubber—imposed cruel hardships on the people. It was constantly necessary to requisition native porters because of the enormous size of the country and the difficulties of getting supplies and reinforcements through to the fighting in Chad, and this resulted in numerous abuses. A poll tax, imposed in 1902, aggravated the suffering of the indigenous population.

French public opinion was outraged by reports of conditions in the territory, and Brazza was sent to make an on-the-spot investigation (his secretary, Félicien Chellaye, has left a remarkable account of this period). Brazza fell seriously ill during the mission and on September 14th, 1905, on his way home he died at Dakar. This French "knight errant of African exploration", dying in Africa, assumed the proportions of a national hero.

In face of public denunciation, the colonial administration—which must have been party to the abuses—absolved itself of all responsibility. In 1910 it permitted the regrouping of companies showing a deficit and instituted a tighter regulation of the system of concessions.

The 1911 Franco-German agreement, made after the "Agadir affair", provided for major territorial adjustments. Germany renounced her rights to Morocco and to a small area of land, "the duck's beak", in the Logone area. But in return she received 272,000 sq. km. of French Equatorial Africa. The annexed area, designated New Cameroon, also encompassed Spanish Guinea in the south. French forces retook the land on the outbreak of war, which brought renewed suffering to the population. The requisitioning of porters was revived in the zones crossed by the colonial armies. Certain areas, moreover, experienced famine, made worse by the departure of administrative officers to the war front.

THE INTER-WAR YEARS

Chad ceased to come under the authority of Oubangui in April 1916 and was given the status of a colony in March 1920. Its borders with the colony of Niger (Tibesti was joined to Chad in 1930) and with Oubangui-Chari were delimited. The Sara tribes were included within Chad rather than in Oubangui-Chari.

Cotton cultivation was introduced into Chad in 1929. It was concentrated mainly in the area formerly known as *Dar el Abid*—the old hunting-ground and watering-place of Arab slave traders from the far north. The Administration sought the support of the traditional chiefs by granting them the right to cultivate an area of land, "the cord", for personal profit, but, regrettably, this system gave rise to abuses and did much to discredit the African chiefs.

The concessions scandal was largely responsible for a reorganization of the concessionaries. Their profitability was now guaranteed by vertical integration and conversion into trading companies. The *Société du Haut-Ogooué* (*SHO*), for example, extended its activities to "the negotiation of all agricultural business or undertaking . . . (whether) connected with finance, forestry, mining, import or export".

But public opinion in France was reawakened to scandals concerning the concessionaries by the award of the Prix Goncourt in 1921 to René Maran for *Batouala* and by the publication of André Gide's *Voyage au Congo* (1926). A widely-read press article and the campaign of the Socialist leader, Léon Blum, in the newspaper, *Le Populaire* also added to the publicity. The pressure of opinion was such that the Colonial Minister undertook before parliament not to renew or extend the leases of the companies.

Because the interior of the A.E.F. (except in Gabon) was accessible only by the Belgian railway from Matadi, it was decided to construct a railway across French territory from Brazzaville to Mayombé. Antonelli, the Governor-General appointed in 1924, refused to travel to Brazzaville by the Belgian line, but landed at Pointe-Noire and crossed the Mayombé massif on foot, following the projected French route. The Congo-Ocean railway was not finally completed, however, for ten years. Labour recruitment was the major problem. Workers had to be sent for from Chad and Oubangui-Chari, and manpower was constantly reduced by illness and desertion. The completion of the railway in 1934 opened the way for the remarkable development of the port of Pointe-Noire.

During the inter-war years the A.E.F. benefited also from public health measures, such as vaccination campaigns and measures against sleeping sickness. The other notable social advance was in education: the number of schools increased, particularly in Gabon and Middle Congo, and a college was founded at Brazzaville in 1935 to improve conditions for African officers in the A.E.F.

The economic crisis of the 1930s brought a fall in prices and budgetary receipts. In response administrative reforms, announced in June 1934, were designed to cut back the expense of maintaining one Governor-General and four Governors, which was considered excessive for a population of only 3 million. The federation was, therefore, transformed into a unitary colony of 20 departments, in turn grouped into regions (corresponding to the former federated colonies) administered by delegates of the Governor-General. However, the new arrangement was inadequate and fourteen new units were added in 1936. But no extra staff was provided, and the consequent dispersal of the administration proved so inefficient that the four federal territories were reconstituted in December 1937.

THE SECOND WORLD WAR AND DECOLONIZATION

After the Franco-German armistice of 1940 the A.E.F. and the Cameroons rallied to the support of Free France, and Brazzaville became the headquarters of General de Gaulle's Council for the Defence of the Empire and High Commission for Free French Africa. With indigenous troops from Chad and the A.E.F., Colonel Leclerc stormed the Oasis of Mouzouk and Kouffra before joining up in Tripoli with the allied pursuit of Rommel's forces from Tunisia.

The break with France, its almost exclusive customer and supplier, forced French Equatorial Africa to find new trade outlets, in particular in Great Britain and the Belgian Congo. The maintenance of the currency exchange rate at 176.625 francs to the pound was ensured by negotiations between the Defence Committee of the French Empire and the British Treasury. An efficient financial administration enabled savings to be deposited in a reserve fund, so that the A.E.F. never became a burden to the allies.

During this period, decisions were made without reference to the African élite, who loyally followed European rule. The Governor-General, Félix Eboué, a Negro from Guiana, was however concerned to promote African political involvement. On November 8th, 1941 he assembled a 50-man consultative commission of Governors, administrators, missionaries and traders which resulted in a memorandum where Eboué stated in particular that:

"We guarantee the stability of the native, by treating him as a person in his own right, that is to say, not as an isolated and interchangeable individual, but as a human being with his own traditions, a member of a family, a village and a tribe, capable of progressing within his own environment but very probably lost if he is taken out of it. We are particularly concerned with developing his feeling of personal dignity."

It was in this spirit that the rank of *notable evolué* and the institution of native districts came into being in 1942. The Brazzaville Conference, held between January 28th and February 8th, 1944, to discuss French colonial problems, was made up of Governors and high-ranking government officials, but it nevertheless played a far from negligible role in the process of decolonization. It is probable that nationalist pressure from north Africa had an impact on the meeting.

The French Union

The 1946 Constitution of the Fourth Republic and French Union created territorial assemblies in the A.E.F. and the A.O.F. where elected Africans could for the first time deliberate on financial and communal affairs. The ten-year (1946–56) experience in parliamentary practice under this constitution gave rise to the assertion of a degree of national consciousness, despite the provision of a federal assembly (*Grand conseil*) at Brazzaville with overall responsibility for the federation.

Under the constitution each of the four A.E.F. and the eight A.O.F. territorial assemblies consisted of two electoral colleges, one elected by French residents and the most educated Africans (*citoyens de statut français*) and a larger second college elected by enfranchised Africans (*citoyens de statut local*). The sizes of the first and second colleges in Chad were 15 and 30 respectively, in Oubangui-Chari 14 and 26, in Gabon and the Congo 13 and 24. But although smaller in absolute numbers, the first college was far larger relative to the number of voters in each college.

Political leadership took shape during these years, hand in hand with considerable strides in education: primary education was developed markedly, secondary schools were opened in each territory, and a growing number of students studied in Europe. Two former priests, Barthélémy Boganda and Fulbert Youlou, came to the fore in Oubangui-Chari and the Congo. A more complex situation arose in Chad, where the Muslim rulers of the north posed as defenders of the old colonial order in opposition to the newcomers, educated in the Catholic and Protestant missions.

After 1952 Gabriel Lisette, a West Indian who had originally come to the country as an administrator, dominated the Chadian political scene. He built up the *Parti progressiste tchadien* (PPT) as a section of the *Rassemblement démocratique africain* (RDA).* François Tombalbaye, his lieutenant in the PPT, succeeded him and has held power in the country ever since, with the support mainly of both the masses and the European-educated élite of the Sara people, but with little following in the Muslim north.

Meanwhile, the prosperity of the war-years had proved illusory. It was no longer possible to gather rubber. Cotton cultivation was promoted only by inhumane methods. The territories were undoubtedly creating wealth, but the Africans at the base of society remained in poverty. The economic activity stimulated by the war ceased after the Armistice. Bayardelle, who became Governor after Eboué's death in 1944, had faith in the A.E.F.'s economic future, however, and attempted to promote the harmonious development of all economic sectors.

*Founded by Felix Houphouët-Boigny in French West Africa in 1946, the RDA established sections in most of the territories of the A.O.F. and the A.E.F.

FIDES (*Fonds d'investissement et de développement économique et social*), established in 1946, injected new investment funds into the territories.

Federation versus National Identity

The 1956 Deferre *loi cadre* (enabling law) for overseas territories contained the germ of the later federations in West and Equatorial Africa, but a federal structure was not considered at a time when French aid supported each state individually. After an enthusiastic "yes" to the referendum of September 1958, the four former territories of the A.E.F. chose to become member states of the French Community. Oubangui-Chari became the Central African Republic, the Middle Congo the Congo Republic, Gabon the Republic of Gabon and Chad the Republic of Chad.

In place of the dual electoral college system, the *loi cadre* provided that the territorial assemblies be elected in a single electorate by universal suffrage. It gave a large measure of self-government to the A.O.F. and the A.E.F., placing emphasis upon the extension of responsible government at the territorial, rather than the federal, level. It has been variously condemned and praised for splitting the federations into separate states.

General de Gaulle's 1958 Constitution abandoned the principle that France and her overseas territories were indivisible. In place of the French Union was substituted the notion of the French Community. A semi-federal system with various common institutions—executive council, senate, court of arbitration etc.—the Community allowed member territories full internal self-government while retaining control over foreign affairs, defence, general economic policy and certain other matters.

All the French colonies, except Guinea, accepted the new Community Constitution in a referendum in September 1958—bearing testimony to the prestige and popularity that had attached to de Gaulle since the war. The following year, however, General de Gaulle agreed that African states could negotiate their independence and yet remain members of a modified Community.

Tension between the four territories had already been apparent at sessions of the *Grand conseil* in Brazzaville between 1946 and 1958. Representatives from Chad, Oubangui-Chari and Gabon complained on occasions, for example, that a disproportionate slice of the federal budget was allocated to the federal capital and the Middle Congo. Nevertheless, at meetings in Bangui and Paris in February and March 1960 the governments of the four autonomous republics decided to exercise their sovereignty jointly in the Union of Central African Republics (URAC), formed at Fort Lamy in the following May.

The Union did not become fully established, but the four states have retained some institutional bonds and have entered into various regional agreements, although these have operated only in the context of inter-African politics. The regional links have evolved heads of state conferences, technical organizations (for posts and telecommunications, and geology and mining) and, more recently, a joint central bank, a defence council, a foundation for higher education and a customs and economic union, UDEAC (which has proved unsuccessful in the case of Chad). However, despite these joint organizations and a common past, each of the states follows independent national policies.

THE CENTRAL AFRICAN REPUBLIC SINCE INDEPENDENCE*

The death of President Boganda in an air crash in March 1959 left a gap in the leadership of the former Oubangui-Chari, which David Dacko filled only with difficulty. Supported by Boganda's party, MESAN (*Mouvement pour l'évolution sociale de l'Afrique noire*), he managed nevertheless to impose a policy of austerity upon the country.

On December 31st, 1965, a military *coup d'état* brought Colonel Jean-Bédal Bokassa to power. Among the reasons advanced for the *coup* were profiteering and corruption (reportedly in the upper echelons of the civil service particularly) at a time of economic depression, allied to a suspicion of a pro-Chinese tendency in the government (culminating in the staging of a large Chinese exhibition in Bangui). Immediately after the *coup* all Chinese nationals were expelled from the country and diplomatic relations with China were broken.

Bokassa's Régime

An exceptional personality, faithful to General de Gaulle and Free France, Colonel Bokassa was promoted to the rank of General in 1967. He has declared his desire for national renovation and an end to corrupt politicians. At the same time he has declared himself to be, like David Dacko, the spiritual descend-

*For post-independence developments in the other former A.E.F. countries *see* under their respective chapters.

ant of Barthélémy Boganda, "the father of the nation".

In 1968 relations with France became strained. One effect was the formation, with Chad and Zaire of the UEAC (*Union des États de l'Afrique centrale*) in Bangui on February 1st. The refusal of the UEAC members to take part in that year's OCAM summit and the withdrawal of the C.A.R. and Chad from UDEAC at the end of March seemed to confirm the rupture with France. However, General Bokassa refused in November to attend the third anniversary celebrations of General Mobutu's accession to power and the Central African Republic soon rejoined UDEAC.

External problems were accompanied by domestic difficulties. In April 1969, Colonel Alexandre Banza, considered the second most important person in the country, was arrested and shot for an alleged attempt to instigate a plot against Bokassa.

Relations with France have typified the C.A.R.'s erratic conduct of foreign affairs. Although General Bokassa was given a respectful welcome in Paris in February 1969 by General de Gaulle, relations were once again strained in November by the expulsion of several French diamond mining companies. There was an improvement during 1970, and the détente was confirmed when Bokassa visited Paris for the funeral of General de Gaulle. In 1971, however, the two countries came into conflict once more over the C.A.R.'s desire to transfer the Central Bank's headquarters from Paris and to issue its own currency, and over its intention to break away from Air Afrique and extend the activities of its own Air Centrafrique.

Domestic affairs followed a similarly erratic pattern during the same period, characterized by numerous cabinet reshuffles. The future of General Bokassa's Government seemed to be confirmed in March 1972 when he was named Life President.

ECONOMY
Peter Robson†

INTRODUCTION

Of the active population of the Central African Republic about 85 per cent are engaged in agriculture, which generates nearly one-half of G.D.P. Much of agricultural production is for subsistence. Cotton and coffee are the main export crops. The service sector is fairly well developed, reflecting in part the country's transit trade. There is little industry. Mining, mainly of diamonds, is the major source of export earnings, amounting to around one-half for most of the past decade. Population estimates for the C.A.R. are not very reliable, but a partial census in 1971 produced an official estimate of 1,637,000 (excluding Sudanese refugees) for the whole country. This indicated a population density of nearly seven per square mile. The development of the economy since independence may be divided into two phases. Until 1965, under the

† For the 1973 edition, revisions have been made to this article by the Editor.

government of President Dacko, the economy stagnated. Gross domestic production increased from 29,600 million francs CFA in 1961 to 33,200 million francs CFA in 1965, when G.D.P. per head amounted to 24,000 francs CFA. Allowing for price increases, aggregate real product may have fallen over this period, and real product per head certainly did. This stagnation was associated with agricultural stagnation, marked in particular by a severe decline in the output of cotton. Government recurrent expenditures increased markedly, but gross investment did not rise significantly. With the end of French budget subsidies higher taxes and a forced loan were introduced, which generated widespread opposition. In January 1966 the army seized power. The new government under President Bokassa introduced measures to revive agriculture, and to encourage rural development. These measures have had some success, and G.D.P. in real terms is thought to have improved since 1966.

AGRICULTURE

Agriculture is concentrated in the tropical rain forest area in the south-west and the savannah lands in the central and north-west. The food crops, mainly cassava, millet, groundnuts and rice, are grown principally for domestic consumption. Cotton and coffee are the most important export crops and provide the principal source of cash income for the bulk of the population.

Regional development offices (*Offices régionaux de développement*—ORD) were created in 1964 and have been responsible for rural development at the regional level. National offices were also created afterwards to handle certain investment operations. The National Modernization Office (*Office national de modernisation* —ONM) was particularly concerned with fertilizer provision and mechanized agriculture. Other organizations were created for developing livestock and forests, and several special companies were set up in the field of rural development projects. Dissatisfaction with their progress led to the introduction of further measures of agricultural reorganization in 1970, and the operation of public agencies working in the field of agriculture was considerably affected. A single national organization to undertake the marketing of agricultural produce has also been established.

Cotton

Cotton output reached a record 43,600 tons in 1958-59 but declined to a level of 24,400 tons in 1965-66 which was admittedly a bad year. Not only yields but also acreage declined. Disposable incomes of planters were also reduced by tax and price increases, reducing the incentive to grow cotton. The new government of President Bokassa gave priority to expanding agriculture, in particular cotton, by a well conceived productivity programme involving extension, fertilizer and insecticide provision and some mechanization, all aided by the European Development Fund and FAC. This part of "operation Bokassa" has been remarkably successful, and by 1969-70 output had more than doubled by comparison with 1965-66, reaching aproximately 60,000 tons. The expansion has been due almost entirely to improvements in productivity, which new varieties have aided.

Until the changes of 1970 the purchase, transportation and sale of cotton were undertaken by the *Union cotonnière centrafricaine* (UCCA), a semi-public corporation created in 1964. This body has undertaken the modernization and regrouping of the cotton ginneries, and also of the oil mills. The formation of UCCA was followed by a reduction in marketing and processing costs.

A cotton stabilization fund commenced operations in 1964-65, and is responsible for the implementation of government policy on production and pricing. Before 1963/64 France provided financial support for Central African cotton production partly by meeting the losses of the previous stabilization fund. From 1963-64 to 1967-68 price support was provided by the EEC to the extent of 735 million francs CFA,

in addition to assistance to increase productivity. The new EDF no longer provides automatic price support, but there is an emergency fund of $65–80 million for price support not earmarked for particular products.

Coffee

Coffee is grown mainly on large European plantations but increasingly on small African farms, which by 1968-69 produced 30 per cent of the output on just over half the acreage. In recent years the acreage of plantations has diminished, whereas the acreage of family farms has increased. Output has fluctuated considerably during the decade. In 1968-69 it reached 9,566 tons then in 1969-70 it increased to a record output of 13,000 tons. Unlike cotton the purchase, processing and marketing of coffee was not entrusted to any public agency until the agricultural marketing changes of 1970. A coffee stabilization fund exists but it has intervened only once since the French price-support system was discontinued in 1964. Over the period 1964–65/1968–69 the European Development Fund provided through the stabilization fund assistance of 200 million francs CFA for improving production conditions in coffee, including treatment by insecticide, fungicides and fertilizers.

Groundnuts are an important food crop, usually grown in rotation with cotton. Output (shelled) for 1968-69 was 42,900 tons. The bulk of production is for domestic consumption though a small part (some 3,000 tons in 1968-69) is sold on local markets. None has been exported since 1965, although prior to that date one-third of the marketed crop was exported.

Livestock

The livestock industry, whose growth is handicapped by climate and by tsetse, is of recent development. Since 1950 efforts have been made to overcome its disadvantages, and the number of cattle increased fivefold to 463,000 head by 1968-69. Efforts are being made to extend the herds, to improve marketing, and to encourage the sedentary raising of cattle. Abattoirs and factories to utilize the products of the animal industries are also being promoted.

Forestry

The country's large forest resources are at present under-exploited, partly as a result of a lack of adequate roads and other low-cost means of transportation to the coast. Timber exploitation has nevertheless expanded considerably since it was begun in 1947, and particularly since 1968 following the formation of new companies geared to exportation. Between 1968 and 1969 fellings increased by 50 per cent.

MINING, MANUFACTURING, POWER AND TRANSPORTATION

Mining

Diamonds are virtually the only form of mineral production in the C.A.R. but uranium has been discovered near Bakouma, 480 km. east of Bangui. Reserves are estimated at 10,000 tons, and exploitation was expected to commence in 1972. However, the ore has been found to contain a high proportion of phosphate, and the cost of purifying the ore will be approximately double the current market price. The French Atomic Energy Commission, to whom the ore was to be sold, decided in May 1972 to renounce its mining rights.

Diamonds

Diamonds are found in alluvial deposits, mainly in the west of the country. Production has expanded rapidly in recent years from 69,662 carats in 1960 to 609,360 carats in 1968. Until 1960 diamond production was completely in company hands, but by 1968 nine-tenths of all diamonds were extracted by individual prospectors. In 1969 recorded production fell to 535,316 carats and by 1971 to 454,201 carats. The fall in production was much larger for the companies than for private prospectors, further reducing the share of companies to 5 per cent. The fall in output of the companies is explained in part by the closing of private mines as a result of difficulties with the government. Diamond smuggling to Congo (Brazzaville) also accounts for the failure of recorded production by artisans to increase significantly in recent years.

The marketing and sale abroad of diamonds produced by prospectors has since 1966 been in the hands of the National Diamond Office, which gave a mandate to a consortium to undertake this task. In March 1970 the National Diamond Office was dissolved and replaced by a government commissioner, who controls the operations of the purchasing offices. Central African diamonds are of high quality and have not met with the marketing difficulties encountered by lower quality diamonds in recent years.

Manufacturing and Power

Industrial production is little developed and is confined to the processing of primary products and some light manufactures. Industrial turnover excluding energy almost tripled over the period 1964–67, from 2,400 million to 6,900 million francs CFA in 1967, and increased substantially over the period 1967–69, principally as a result of the completion of two major undertakings—ICCA (*Industrie coton-nière centrafricaine*) and SICPED (*Societé centrafri-caine de produits alimentaires et dérivés*).

Industries processing primary products include oil mills (processing groundnuts, cottonseed, sesame, etc.), a flour mill, an abattoir and a brewery (*Motte cordon-nier Afrique*—MOCAF), which is the largest industry in this category.

The textile and leather industries constitute the chief industrial sector. Cotton ginning is carried out in 21 factories. A new textile complex, controlled by ICCA, has been completed and now forms C.A.R.'s largest single industrial enterprise, spinning, weaving and dyeing. Garments are made up in several factories, and shoes are also produced. Apart from these, a variety of smaller manufactures exist concerned with soap, paint, industrial gas, bricks, cycles and domestic utensils. Projects envisaged include a further textile complex, a variety of food processing industries and a cement factory.

Energy

Electricity is produced mainly in Boali by water power. Production nearly doubled over the period 1963–68 from 17 to 32 million kWh. In 1970, production rose to 45.7 million kWh, approximately an 11 per cent increase on the previous year.

A second hydro-electric power station upstream from Boali is scheduled for 1975.

Transport

There is an extensive system of roads but only a few are all-weather. The principal route for importation and exportation is the trans-equatorial route involving an 1,800 km. journey by river from Bangui to Brazzaville and rail from Brazzaville to Pointe-Noire. This route, which also serves traffic for Chad, has in the past been operated by a public corporation *Agence transéquatoriale des communications* (ATEC) servicing all UDEAC countries, but the port of Bangui was taken over from ATEC at the end of 1969, and the purchase of the river boats is to be negotiated. There is no rail service, and the principal river, the Oubangui, is navigable only below Bangui. Costs and difficulties of transportation are important obstacles to economic development. A programme of improvements to roads is being undertaken with external aid, and port facilities at Salo on the Sangha river are being improved. Agreement has been reached on the construction of a railway between Bangui and the Trans-Cameroon railway.

PUBLIC FINANCE

Current budgetary expenditure was 2,900 million francs CFA in 1960 and is estimated at 11,200 million for 1970, a fourfold rise. Ordinary revenue was 3,000 million francs CFA in 1960 and is estimated at 11,300 million for 1970. Capital expenditure in the main budget, 147 million francs CFA in 1960, is estimated at 859 million in 1970. French budgetary assistance was discontinued in 1966. Despite substantial increases in taxation, revenue has not kept pace with expenditure in the last few years. Substantial deficits have been incurred continuously since 1967, and the financial situation is precarious. Major increases in expenditure on personnel—already large—have contributed to this situation, as well as increased debt service expenditure. An austerity budget was introduced in 1970 involving sweeping tax increases and various measures to curb expenditure.

TRADE, AID AND THE BALANCE OF PAYMENTS

The foreign trade accounts of the C.A.R. have persistently shown a deficit in registered trade. It reached a peak of 3,700 million francs CFA in 1967 when both exports and imports were at record levels, but fell in 1968 to 1,000 million as a result of a reduction in imports and an increase in exports. Over the period 1960 to 1968 registered exports rose from 3,400 million francs CFA to 8,800 million. The principal Central African exports are diamonds, cotton and coffee, which represented respectively 53, 23 and 14 per cent of registered exports in 1968. Almost the whole of the growth in exports proceeds since 1960 has been due to diamonds.

Between 1968 and 1970 the share of exports taken by the EEC increased from 45 per cent to 69 per cent, with France as the main customer. In 1970 the EEC provided 75 per cent of imports, mainly from France. On trade with UDEAC countries, which mainly involves manufactures, the C.A.R. has also registered a deficit in recent years, which amounted in 1968 to 1,000 million francs CFA.

Since independence France has continued to be a major source of aid, but substantial aid funds have also been provided by the European Development Fund, including price support, aid to improve productivity and diversify the economy, and technical assistance.

The C.A.R.'s trade deficit is reinforced by a substantial net outflow for recurrent transfer payments and services. The resulting deficit is financed mainly by an inflow of aid and grants, and to some extent by an inflow of private long-term capital. In 1968–69, following measures to restrict credit, the overall payments position became slightly favourable in contrast to the deficitary position of the previous year, and external reserves increased.

DEVELOPMENT PLANNING

The first four-year development plan (1967–70) was introduced in 1967, providing for total expenditure estimated at 36,900 million francs CFA, of which 28,300 million was in the public sector. Nearly half of the resources required to finance the plan were expected to come from abroad. Particular attention was to be given to rural development and education. G.D.P. per head was expected to rise to 30,000 francs CFA by 1970. The plan was well conceived in structure, but ambitious in size. The cotton target was virtually attained by 1969, but coffee production fell considerably short of the target.

The second four-year development plan (1971–75) has been drawn up. Priority is again being given to the development of agriculture and stock-breeding, and also to the improvement in marketing agricultural products, to education and diversification of mineral prospecting.

PROBLEMS AND PROSPECTS

The Central African Republic is a poor country whose longer term prospects will be dependent in part upon improving transportation facilities. This should benefit economic development, in particular forestry. In the last few years the country has made determined efforts to come to grips with its economic problems, and in particular, the problem of rural development. The progress made in cotton demonstrates that rural producers are responsive to advice and incentives. Other action is aimed at stimulating the rural sector by encouraging the regrouping of villages to develop poles of development. In this way it is hoped to contain the rural exodus. Rural electrification should also help small industries. The budgetary situation is not strong, and it is clear that continued economic progress will demand sustained foreign assistance.

STATISTICAL SURVEY

Area: 622,984 sq. km. (240,535 sq. miles).

Population (1971 estimate): 1,637,000, excluding refugees from the Sudan, numbering 28,000 in 1966.

PRÉFECTURES

PRÉFECTURE*	CHIEF TOWN	POPULATION OF CHIEF TOWN (1968)
Ombella-M'Poko	Boali	238,000
Haute-Sangha	Berberati	38,000
Ouham	Bossangoa	35,000
Ouaka	Bambari	36,000
Nana-Mambere	Bouar	48,000
M'Bomou	Bangassou	28,000
Haute-Kotto	Bria	25,000
Lobaye	M'Baïki	18,000
Ouham-Pende	Bozoum	n.a.
Kemo-Gribingui	Sibut	n.a.
Basse-Kotto	Mobaye	n.a.
Bamingui-Bangoran	N'Délé	n.a.
Haut-M'Bomou	Obo	n.a.
Vakaga	Birao	n.a.

*Bangui (capital, an autonomous commune): population 1968, 298,579.

EMPLOYMENT
(Dec. 31st, 1962)

Working Population	Males	Females
480,000	230,000	250,000

AGRICULTURE

LAND USE, 1968
('ooo hectares)

Arable Land	5,840
Land under Permanent Crops . .	60
Permanent meadows and Pastures .	100
Forest Land . . .	7,400
Other areas (including rough grazing)	48,898
TOTAL . . .	62,298

PRINCIPAL CROPS

	AREA ('ooo hectares)			PRODUCTION ('ooo metric tons)			YIELD (kg. per hectare)		
	1969	1970	1971	1969	1970	1971	1969	1970	1971
Bananas . . .	20*	20	n.a.	170*	170*	n.a.	8,500*	8,500*	n.a.
Cassava (manioc) .	200*	200*	n.a.	1,000*	1,000*	n.a.	5,000*	5,000*	n.a.
Coffee . . .	n.a.	n.a.	n.a.	11	9	9.6	n.a.	n.a.	n.a.
Cottonseed . .	134	126	126*{	37	34	31	280	270	240*
Cotton (lint) . .				22	20	18	160	160	140*
Groundnuts (in shell) .	90*	105*	105*	75	85	85*	830*	810*	810*
Maize . . .	61	63	58*	47	48	45*	770	770	780*
Millet and Sorghum .	94	80*	80*	35	50*	50*	370	630*	630*
Oranges and Tangerines .	n.a.	n.a.	n.a.	11*	11*	11*	n.a.	n.a.	n.a.
Rice . . .	15	13	14	12	13	14	820	1,020	1,030
Sesame Seed . .	52*	52*	52*	16*	16*	16*	310*	310*	310*
Sweet Potatoes and Yams .	16*	16*	n.a.	47	47*	n.a.	2,900*	2,900*	n.a.

* FAO estimate.

LIVESTOCK NUMBERS

	1968–69	1969–70	1970–71
Cattle . .	463,000	470,000*	480,000*
Goats . .	515,000*	520,000*	530,000*
Sheep . .	63,000	64,000*	66,000*
Pigs . .	52,000*	54,000*	56,000*
Asses . .	1,000	1,000*	1,000*
Chickens .	1,050,000*	1,070,000*	1,100,000*
Ducks . .	5,000*	5,000*	5,000*

* FAO estimate.

OTHER AGRICULTURAL PRODUCTS
(metric tons)

	1969	1970	1971
Meat . . .	13,000*	13,000*	n.a.
Cows' milk . .	21,000*	21,000*	22,000*
Honey . .	4,500*	5,000*	5,000*
Raw Cattle Hides .	1,670*	1,690*	n.a.
Hen Eggs .	700*	700*	800*

* FAO estimate.

FORESTRY
ROUNDWOOD PRODUCTION
(cubic metres)

1968	1,991,000
1969	2,106,000

FISHING
(metric tons)

1968	3,000*
1969	3,000*
1970	3,000*

* FAO estimate

INDUSTRY AND MINING
COTTON MANUFACTURES

	1969	1970*
Loin-cloths (metres)	4,033,599	2,951,691
Cloth (metres)	811,362	885,992
Unfinished Cloth (metres) . . .	3,093,231	2,056,420
Gauze (sq. metres) .	749,849	298,228
Printed Cotton (metres) . . .	5,152,747	3,633,912
Blankets, Rugs, Covers, etc. (number) .	222,592	133,419
Cotton Wool and Carded Cotton (kg.) .	24,561	35,942

* January–August.

OTHER INDUSTRIAL AND MINERAL PRODUCTION

	Unit	1968	1969	1970
Beer .	hectolitres	90,768	97,089	102,000
Soft Drinks .	,,	n.a.	n.a.	31,000
Sawnwood .	cu. metres	52,000	55,000	55,000
Soap .	metric tons	n.a.	n.a.	2,134
Radio Sets .	number	n.a.	n.a.	9,000
Motor Cycles .	,,	n.a.	n.a.	6,000
Bicycles .	,,	n.a.	n.a.	9,000
Electric Energy .	'000 kWh.	34,500	41,200	45,700
Diamonds (carats) .	carats	609,360	535,317	494,000
Uranium .	tons	500*	500*	n.a.

Electric Energy (1971): 47.3 million kWh.
* Annual average.

FINANCE

100 centimes = 1 franc de la Communauté Financière Africaine.
Coins: 1, 2, 5, 10, 25 and 50 francs CFA.
Notes: 5, 10, 25, 50, 100, 500, 1,000, 5,000 and 10,000 francs CFA.
Exchange rates (December 1972): 1 franc CFA = 2 French centimes;
£1 sterling = 593.625 francs CFA; U.S. $1 = 255.785 francs CFA;
1,000 francs CFA = £1.685 = $3.91.

BUDGET
(million francs CFA)

REVENUE	1969	1970	1971	EXPENDITURE	1969	1970	1971
Income Taxes . .	1,030	990	1,288	Transfers to:			
Other Direct Taxes .	1,633	1,983	2,341	Households . .	344	386	337
Import Duties . .	2,511	2,380	2,230	National Bodies .	707	754	708
Export Duties . .	250	255	250	Foreign Bodies .	670	667	603
Taxes on Sales and Turn-				Gross Fixed Capital			
over . . .	1,260	1,380	1,321	Formation . .	669	860	1,292
Other Indirect Taxes .	1,892	2,030	2,156	Expenditure on:			
Income from Property .	347	313	403	Education . .	1,474	1,652	1,642
Contributions and Sub-				Public Health .	601	656	632
sidies . . .	400	415	550	Agriculture and			
Reimbursement of Loans				Cattle Rearing .	698	591	479
and Advances .	—	—	151	Interior . . .	615	741	838
Other Receipts . .	1,027	1,560	1,849	Defence . .	1,451	1,351	1,468
				Other Goods and Services	1,784	1,681	1,935
	10,350	11,306	12,539	Other Expenditures .	2,437	2,745	2,605
DEFICIT . .	1,100	778	—				
TOTAL . .	11,450	12,084	12,539	TOTAL . . .	11,450	12,084	12,539

EXTERNAL TRADE*
(million francs CFA)

	1967	1968	1969	1970	1971†
Imports . .	9,895	8,816	9,193	9,491	4,749
Exports . .	7,166	8,816	9,196	8,494	3,453

* Excluding trade with other countries in the Customs and Economic Union of Central Africa: Cameroon, Congo (Brazzaville), Gabon and, until 1969, Chad.

† January–June.

PRINCIPAL COMMODITIES

IMPORTS	1968	1969	1970*	EXPORTS	1968	1969	1970
Machinery . .	1,465	1,740	1,195	Diamonds . .	4,681	4,123	3,466
Cotton Textiles .	1,367	1,285	846	Coffee . . .	1,073	1,399	1,864
Motor Vehicles .	1,598	1,363	806	Cotton . . .	2,065	2,137	1,896
Petroleum Products .	589	691	21	Wood . . .	299	627	517
Shoes . .	86	122	63	Rubber . .	84	93	53*
Paper and Paper Products	277	257	161	Sesame . .	n.a.	4	—*
Clothing . . .	99	99	41	Palm Products .	26	6	5*
Tyres . . .	81	72	63				

* January–August.   * January–August.

PRINCIPAL COUNTRIES

IMPORTS	1968	1969	1970*
France	5,299	5,325	3,349
U.S.A. . .	458	466	345
Germany, Federal Republic	975	696	453
United Kingdom . .	390	409	198
Netherlands .	418	327	214

* January–August.

EXPORTS	1968	1969	1970*
Belgium/Luxembourg	27	497	n.a.
Chad .	n.a.	330	n.a.
France .	3,352	4,706	3,492
Germany, Federal Republic	148	176	n.a.
Israel . .	1,490	1,339	1,004
Italy . .	454	515	n.a.
Japan . .	62	152	n.a.
South Africa .	98	137	n.a.
United Kingdom .	242	248	106
U.S.A. .	2,783	814	19

* January–August.

TRANSPORT

ROAD TRAFFIC
Motor vehicles in use

	1968	1969
Passenger Cars .	4,300	5,000
Commercial Vehicles .	7,100	6,000
TOTAL . .	11,400	11,000

CIVIL AVIATION
Scheduled services*

	1968	1969	1970
Kilometres flown ('000)	1,511	1,688	1,719
Passenger-km. ('000) .	55,659	61,867	68,914
Cargo ton-km. ('000) .	4,665	5,539	5,811
Mail ton-km. ('oo) .	464	478	529

* Including one-twelfth of the traffic of Air Afrique, from which the Central African Republic withdrew in August 1971.

INLAND WATERWAYS TRAFFIC
(metric tons)

	1969	1970*
Freight loaded at Bangui	62,308	41,594
of which: freight from Chad	34,862	21,057
Freight unloaded at Bangui	154,225	109,396
of which: freight for Chad	18,592	16,604

* January–August.

EDUCATION
PUPILS, 1969.

	BOYS	GIRLS	TOTAL
Pre-primary . .	3,270	3,334	6,604
Primary . .	115,842	54,206	170,048
Secondary . .	6,068	1,163	7,231
Vocational . .	871	331	1,202
Teacher-training .	150	99	249
TOTAL .	126,201	59,133	185,334

Sources: Service de la Statistique et de la Conjoncture, B.P. 954, Bangui; FAO, *Production Yearbook 1971* (Rome, 1972).

THE CONSTITUTION

The Constitution of February 16th, 1959, was modified five times up until 1964, and was abrogated on January 4th, 1966, when a constitutional act was adopted giving the President full competence to act in all affairs of state.

THE GOVERNMENT

HEAD OF STATE

Life President of the Republic: Gen. JEAN-BÉDEL BOKASSA.

COUNCIL OF MINISTERS

(December 1972)

President of the Council of Ministers, Minister of National Defence, Minister of Information, Minister of Agriculture and Stockbreeding, Minister of Mining and Keeper of the Seals: Gen. JEAN-BÉDEL BOKASSA.

Minister of State in charge of Rural Development: ANGE PATASSÉ.

Minister of State in charge of Public Works, Housing and Transport: AUGUSTE M'BONGO.

Minister Delegate to the Presidency in charge of Territorial Administration: JEAN-LOUIS PSIMHIS.

Minister Delegate in charge of National Organizations: JEAN AMITY.

Minister Delegate in charge of the Government General Secretariat: HENRI PAUL BOUNDIO.

Minister Delegate in charge of Foreign Affairs: JOSEPH POTOLOT.

Minister of Finance, Industry and Commerce: ALPHONSE KOYAMBA.

Minister of Education, Youth, Sport and Arts: HENRY MAIDOU.

Minister of Health and Social Affairs: ANDRÉ DIEUDONNÉ MAGALÉ.

Minister of Posts and Telecommunications: ANTOINE GOALO.

Minister of Planning, International Co-operation and Statistics: ANDRÉ ZANIFFE TOUAMBONA.

Minister of Justice and Labour: FRANÇOIS GON.

Minister of Power: LOUIS PIERRE GAMBA.

Minister of Water Resources and Forests: CHRISTIAN SOMBODEY.

Minister Delegate in charge of War Veterans, National Pioneer Youth and Civil Service: ANTOINE FRANCK.

Deputy Minister for Rural Development: JOACHIM DA SILVA.

Secretary of State at the Presidency in charge of Missions: LOUIS ALAZOULA.

Secretary of State for Public Works: AUGUSTIN DALLOT BEFIO.

Secretary of State for Protocol and Welcome Services: EMMANUEL BONGOPASSI.

DIPLOMATIC REPRESENTATION

EMBASSIES AND LEGATIONS ACCREDITED TO
THE CENTRAL AFRICAN REPUBLIC

(E) Embassy; (L) Legation.

Belgium: Place de la République, Bangui (E); *Ambassador:* VICTOR ALLARD.

Cameroon: B.P. 935, Bangui (L); *Ambassador:* JEAN BIKANDA (also accred. to Gabon).

Canada: Yaoundé, Cameroon (E).

Chad: B.P. 461, Bangui (E); *Ambassador:* MUSTAPHA BATRANE.

China, Peoples Republic: *Ambassador:* LIAO TCHOUN KIN.

Congo, Peoples' Republic: B.P.1414, Bangui (E); *Ambassador:* ANTOINE MAKOUNAGO.

Egypt: Bangui (E); *Ambassador:* AHMED EL SAID KADEL HAK.

France: blvd. du Général-de-Gaulle, B.P. 784, Bangui (E); *Ambassador:* LAURENT GIOVANGRANDI.

Gabon: Yaoundé, Cameroon (E).

German Federal Republic: rue Lamothe, B.P. 901, Bangui (E); *Ambassador:* REINHARD HOLUBEK.

Ghana: Kinshasa, Zaire (E).

Israel: B.P. 569, Bangui (E); *Ambassador:* MICHAELI ITZAHAK.

Italy: (E); *Ambassador:* BENIAMINO DEL GIUDICE.

Japan: Kinshasa, Zaire (E).

Lebanon: *Ambassador:* SAID EL HIBRI.

Liberia: *Ambassador:* JENKINS COOPER.

Mali: Brazzaville, People's Republic of the Congo (E).

Netherlands: Yaoundé, Cameroon (E).

North Korea: *Ambassador:* RIM MYEUNG TCHEUL.

Spain: Yaoundé, Cameroon (E).

Sudan: Bangui; *Ambassador:* AMBROSE WOL.

Switzerland: Kinshasa, Zaire (E).

Tunisia: *Ambassador:* ABDEL HABIB AMMAR.

U.S.S.R.: B.P. 869, Bangui (E); *Ambassador:* DMITRI ZELENOV.

United Kingdom: Yaoundé, Cameroon (E).

U.S.A.: Place de la République, B.P. 924, Bangui (E); *Ambassador:* MERVIN MANFULL.

Vatican: *Nuncio:* Mgr. MARIO TAGLIAFERRI.

Zaire: B.P. 989, Bangui (E); *Ambassador:* FERDINAND MALILA.

The Central African Republic also has diplomatic relations with Albania, Czechoslovakia, Greece, Hungary, Libya and Romania.

PARLIAMENT

NATIONAL ASSEMBLY

The National Assembly was dissolved on January 4th, 1966.

POLITICAL PARTY

Mouvement d'évolution sociale de l'Afrique noire (MESAN): Leader Gen. JEAN-BÉDEL BOKASSA; Head of Secretariat GEORGES YAKITÉ.

A government decree passed in November 1968 banned all foreign political parties from the Republic.

DEFENCE

The total strength of the armed forces is approximately 3,000 men, comprising an army and several para-military forces. President Bokassa announced the disbandment of the small air force in July 1971.

Commander-in-Chief of the Armed Forces: Gen. BOKASSA.

Deputy Commander-in-Chief: Brig.-Gen. JEAN-CLAUDE MANDABA.

JUDICIAL SYSTEM

Supreme Court: Bangui; the highest juridical organ. Acts as a Court of Cassation in civil and penal cases and as Court of Appeal in administrative cases; President ANTOINE GUIMALI; Vice-Pres. M. LESCUYER.

There are a Criminal Court and 7 Civil Courts, with Justices of the Peace.

RELIGION

It is estimated that 60 per cent of the population follow traditional animist beliefs, 5 per cent are Muslims and 35 per cent Christian; Roman Catholics comprise 20 per cent of the total population.

Roman Catholic Missions: There are about 120 mission centres with a personnel of 2,689.

Archdiocese of Bangui: B.P. 798, Bangui; f. 1894; 24 missions, 55 priests; Archbishop Mgr. JOACHIM N'DAYEN.

Diocese of Berberati: B.P. 22, Berberati; f. 1923; 14 missions; 46 priests; Bishop Mgr. A.-C.-B. BAUD.

Diocese of Bangassou: B.P. 84, Bangassou; f. 1929; 21 missions, 39 priests; Bishop Mgr. ANTONIUS MAANICUS.

Diocese of Bossangoa: B.P. 7, Bossangoa; f. 1943; 11 missions, 33 priests; Bishop Mgr. L. T. CHAMBON.

Diocese of Bambari: B.P. 80, Bambari; f. 1920; 11 missions, 24 priests; Bishop (vacant); Apostolic Administrator Mgr. J. N'DAYEN.

Episcopal Conference: Secretariat B.P. 1518, Bangui.

Protestant Missions: In the Central African Republic, Chad, Gabon, and Congo (Brazzaville) there are nearly 1,000 mission centres with a total personnel of about 2,000.

Église Protestante de Bangui: Bangui.

PRESS

Bangui La So: Bangui; daily.

Journal officiel de la République Centrafricaine: twice-monthly.

Presse, La: B.P. 373, Bangui; daily.

FOREIGN PRESS BUREAUX

Agence France-Presse: B.P. 815, Bangui; Correspondent JEAN-NOËL GILLET.

Tass is also represented in Bangui.

RADIO

Radiodiffusion Nationale Centrafricaine: B.P. 940, Bangui; f. 1958; Government station; programmes in French, English and Sango languages; 44,000 listeners; Dir. V. TETEYA.

There were 46,000 radio receivers in 1970.

FINANCE

BANKS

CENTRAL BANK

Banque Centrale des Etats de l'Afrique Equatoriale et du Caméroun: 29 rue du Colisée, Paris; B.P. 851, Bangui; C.A.R. Dir. FRANÇOIS PEHOUA.

La Banque Nationale de Développement de la République Centrafricaine: B.P. 647, Bangui; f. 1961; cap. 420m. Francs CFA; Dir.-Gen. JOSEPH MOUTOU-MONDZIAOU.

Caisse Central de Coopération Economique: B.P. 817, Bangui; Dir. P. RAYNAUD.

Union Bancaire en Afrique Centrale: rue de Brazza, B.P. 59, Bangui; f. 1962; took over business of Crédit Lyonnais and Societe Générale; cap. 200m. Francs CFA; Pres. A. ALBESSART.

Banque Nationale Centrafricaine de Dépôts: Place de la République, B.P. 851, Bangui; f. 1971; cap. 150m. Francs CFA; Dir.-Gen. Mme BÉATRICE KONGBO.

INSURANCE

La Paternelle Africaine and Cie. Européenne d'Assurances des Marchandises et de Bagages: c/o S.A.F.C.I., B.P. 821, Bangui.

Société Jeandreau and Cie. S.A.R.L.: B.P. 140, Bangui; f. 1960; cap. p.u. 500,000 Fr. CFA; Dir. H. JEANDREAU.

Société de Représentation d'Assurances et de Réassurances Africaines (SORAREF): B.P. 852, Bangui; Dir. PIERRE DUROU.

Société Aéfienne d'Assurances: B.P. 512, Bangui.

TRADE AND INDUSTRY

Chambre National de Commerce: B.P. 813, Bangui; Pres. JEAN DE DIEU DESSAUDE. publ. *Bulletin Mensuel.*

Chambre des Industries et de l'Artisanat: B.P. 252, Bangui; Pres. JEAN SEBIRO.

Chambre des Mines: Bangui.

Chambre d'Agriculture, d'Élevage, des Eaux et Forêts et des Chasses: B.P. 850, Bangui; Pres. MAURICE OSCAR GAUDEVILLE.

EMPLOYERS' ORGANIZATIONS

Association Professionnelle des Banques: Bangui.

Groupement Interprofessionnel pour l'Etude et le Développement de l'Economie Centrafricaine (GIRCA): B.P. 627, Bangui; 100 mems.; planters, transporters, tradesmen and businessmen; Pres. M. PLANTEVIN; Vice-Pres. M. AZAIS; Sec. Gen. M. JAMAIS.

TRADE UNION

Union Générale des Travailleurs Centrafricains: B.P. 877, Bangui; became the sole recognized union in 1964; Pres. MAURICE GOUANDJA.

MAJOR INDUSTRIAL COMPANIES

The following are some of the largest companies in terms either of capital investment or employment.

Société Centrafricaine de Diamant Industriel: B.P. 78, Bangui; f. 1969.
Production of industrial diamonds.
Pres. Dir.-Gen. LOUIS ALAZOULA.

Société Commerciale du Kouilou Niari Centrafrique: B.P. 809, Bangui; cap. 100 million CFA.
Import-Export.
Dir.-Gen. CHRISTIAN REYNOUD; 480 employees.

Société d'Exploitations Forestières et Industrielles (SEFI): B.P. 3, Bangui; cap. 229 million Francs CFA.
Timber industry.
Dir. R. SAULNIER; 816 employees.

Société Franco-Centrafricaine des Tabacs: B.P. 1042, Bangui; f. 1966; cap. 140 million francs CFA.
Growing and curing of tobacco.
Pres. ANGE PATASSÉ; Dir.-Gen. JEAN DUPONT; 1,358 employees.

Industrie Cotonnière Centrafricaine (ICCA): ave. Jean-Bédel Bokassa, Bangui; f. 1966; cap. 586 million francs CFA.
Textile complex.
Pres. DERANT ENOCH LAKOUÉ; Vice-Pres. ANDRÉ ZANIFFE TOUAMBONA.

Société Industrielle Centrafricaine des Produits Alimentaires et Dérivés: B.P. 1356, Bangui; f. 1968; cap. 150 million francs CFA.
Manufacture of vegetable oils and soap.
Dir. M. CRITON.

Société Industrielle de République Centrafricaine: B.P. 1325, Bangui; f. 1967; cap. 100 million francs CFA.
Sawmill.
Dir. CHARLES SYLVAIN.

Compagnie des Mines d'Uranium de Bakouma: Bakouma; f. 1969; cap. 2,000 million francs CFA.
Preliminary operations for uranium mining.
Dir. CLAUDE LAURENT.

Motte Cordonnier Afrique (MOCAF): B.P. 806, Bangui; f. 1953; cap. 500 million francs CFA.
Production of beer and soft drinks.
Pres. BERTRAND MOTTE; Dir. HENRI DE CARNÉ; 155 employees.

Union Cotonnière Centrafricaine (UCCA): B.P. 997, Bangui; f. 1964; cap. 188 million francs CFA; state owns 42 per cent of shares.
Cotton ginning and production of textiles.
Pres. ANGE PATASSÉ; Dir.-Gen. F. JULLIEN DE POMMEROL.

TRANSPORT

TRANSPORT
RAILWAYS

There are no railways at present but a 1,100 km. line from Bangui to Fort-Lamy (Chad) is proposed. The total cost is estimated at 22,000,000 French Francs.

A railway is also due to be constructed from Sudan's Darfur province into the C.A.R.'s Vakaga province. An agreement between the two governments was signed in December 1971.

ROADS

Compagnie Nationale des Transports Routiers: Bangui; f. 1971; state-controlled.

There are about 19,000 km. of roads, 6,000 km. of which are passable at all seasons by heavy vehicles. Routes nationales 5,018 km., regional roads 3,789 km., rural roads 10,400 km. The main road from Bangui to Fort-Lamy (Chad) has been asphalted. The road from Damara to Sibut (57 km.) was completed in 1970, and a new road from Bangui to M'Baiki (100 km., 6 m. wide) crossing the Lobaye region was opened in July 1972.

INLAND WATERWAYS

Compagnie Nationale des Transports Riverains (CNTR): Bangui; f. 1971; state-controlled.

There are two navigable waterways. The first is open all the year and is formed by the Congo and Oubangui rivers; convoys of barges (of up to 800 tons load) ply between Bangui and Brazzaville. The second is the river Sangha, a tributary of the Oubangui, on which traffic is seasonal. There are two ports, at Bangui and Salo on the rivers Oubangui and Sangha respectively. Efforts are being made to develop the stretch of river upstream from Salo to increase the transportation of timber from this area.

CIVIL AVIATION

Air Centrafrique: B.P. 873, Rue du Président Boganda, Bangui; f. 1966 as Air Bangui, reorganized in 1971 when the Government planned to withdraw from Air Afrique; extensive internal services; fleet of one DC-3, one DC-8, one Caravelle and one Baron.

Air Afrique: B.P. 875, Bangui; the C.A.R. Government has a 7 per cent share in Air Afrique; *see* under Ivory Coast.

POWER

Energie Centrafricaine (ENERCA): B.P. 880, Bangui: f. 1963; state-owned company for the production and distribution of electricity; in 1971 47.3 million kWh. were produced; Dir. PAUL BAI.

TOURISM

Service du Tourisme: P.O.B. 655, Bangui; Dir. J. C. DALLA.

EDUCATION

LEARNED SOCIETIES AND RESEARCH INSTITUTES

Alliance Française: Bangui; 2 committees.

Centre d'Etudes sur la Trypanosomiase Animale: B.P. 39, Bouar; stations at Bewiti, Sarki; annexe at Bambari.

Office de la Recherche Scientifique et Technique Outre-Mer Centre ORSTOM de Bangui: B.P. 893, Bangui; f. 1948; pedology, hydrology, geophysics, geology, medical entomology; library of 1,700 vols.; 22 researchers and technicians; Dir. Y. CHATELIN.

Fondation Educationale Supérieure d'Afrique Centrale: B.P. 970, Bangui.

Institut d'Etudes Agronomiques d'Afrique Centrale: Wakombo, B.P. 7, M'Baiki; Dir. R. ELIARD.

Institut de Recherches Agronomiques Tropicales et de Cultures Vivrières (IRAT): f. 1964.

Institut Français du Café, du Cacao et Autres Plantes Stimulantes (IFCC): B.P. 44, M'Baiki, Boukoko; f. 1948; library shared with *Institut de Recherches Agronomiques*; Dir. A. SACCAS.

Centre de Recherches Agronomiques de Boukoko (*Agricultural Research Centre*): B.P. 44, M'Baiki, Boukoko; f. 1948; investigations into tropical agriculture and plant diseases, fertilization and entomology; library of 2,740 vols.; Dir. A. SACCAS.

Institut de Recherches du Coton et des Textiles Exotiques (IRCT): B.P. 188, Bangui; central research station at Bambari; Regional Dir. J. CADOU; Station Dir. J. CANQUIL.

Institut de Recherches pour les Huiles et Oléagineux (IRHO): B.P. 53, Grimari; Dir. B. LEDUC.

Institut Pasteur: B.P. 923, Bangui; f. 1961; research mainly on enterovirus and arbovirus; Dir. J. P. DIGOUTTE.

Station Expérimentale de la Maboké: par M'Baiki; f. 1963 under the direction of the Muséum National d'Histoire Naturelle, Paris; studies in the protection of materials in tropical regions, mycology, entomology, virology, zoology, botany, anthropology, parasitology, protection of natural resources; Dir. ROGER HEIM; publ. *Cahiers de la Maboké*.

MUSEUM

Musée Ethnologique: Bangassou; archaeological discoveries from Nzakara and Zandé districts; historical maps and documents.

UNIVERSITY

JEAN-BÉDEL BOKASSA UNIVERSITÉ
BANGUI

Founded 1970.

Faculties of law and economic sciences, letters and social sciences, medicine.

COLLEGES

Ecole Centrale d'Agriculture: Boukoko.

Ecole Territoriale d'Agriculture: Grimari.

SELECT BIBLIOGRAPHY

Works on the former A.E.F. countries generally

BALLARD, J. A. "Politics and Government in Former French West and Equatorial Africa: a Critical Bibliography". *Journal of Modern African Studies*, 3/4, pp. 589–605, 1965.

BANQUE CENTRALE DES ÉTATS DE L'AFRIQUE ÉQUATORIALE ET DU CAMEROUN. *Rapport d'Activité*, Exercise 1968–69. Paris, 1970.
Bulletin mensuel.
Études et Statistiques.

BRUEL, GEORGES. *La France Équatorial Africaine*, 1935.

BRUNSCHWIG, HENRI. *French Colonialism 1871–1914: Myths and Realities.* London, Pall Mall, 1966.

CARTER, G. M. (Ed.). *National Unity and Regionalism in Eight African States.* Ithaca, N.Y., Cornell University Press, 1966.

DREUX BREZÉ, JOACHIM DE. *Le Problème du regroupement en Afrique équatoriale.* Paris, Librairie Gale de Droit et de Jurisprudence, 1968.

HANCE, W. A. "Middle Africa from Chad to Congo (Brazzaville)", ch. XIV in *The Geography of Modern Africa.* New York and London, Columbia U.P., 1964.

IMF. *Surveys of African Economies*, Vol. 1. Washington, D.C., 1968.

ROBSON, PETER. "Economic Integration in Equatorial Africa", ch. 5 in *Economic Integration in Africa.* London, Allen and Unwin, 1968.

SAUTTER, GILLES. *De l'Atlantique au fleuve Congo.* Paris, Mouton, 1966.

SURET-CANALE, JEAN. *Afrique noire: occidentale et centrale.* Vol. I: *Géographie, civilisations, histoire.* Vol. II: *L'ère coloniale (1900–1945).* Paris, Editions Sociales, 1964 (Vol. II) and 1968 (Vol. I, 3rd ed.).

THOMPSON, VIRGINIA, and ADLOFF, RICHARD. *The Emerging States of French Equatorial Africa.* Stanford U.P., 1960.

TREZENEM, EDOUARD. *L'Afrique équatoriale française.* Paris, Ed. Maritimes et d'outre-mer, 1955.

UDEAC. *Bulletin des Statistiques Générales de l'UDEAC.* Brazzaville, Secrétariat-General de l'UDEAC.

ZIEGLÉ, HENRI. *L'A.E.F.* Paris, Berger-Levrault, 1952.

Central African Republic

DAMPIERRE, ERIC DE. *Les sultanats Zandé de l'Oubangui.* Paris, Plon, 1967.

GEORGES, M. "La vie rurale chez les Banda (C.A.R.)". *Cahiers d'Outre-Mer*, 16, pp. 321–59, 1963.

KALCK, PIERRE. *Central African Republic.* London, Pall Mall, 1971.
Réalités oubanguiennes. Paris, Berger Levrault, 1952.

SECRÉTARIAT GENERAL DU GOUVERNEMENT. *Notes et Études*, no. 2733. Paris, 1960.

TEULIERES, ANDRÉ. *L'Oubangui face à l'avenir.* Paris, Ed. de l'Union Française, 1953.

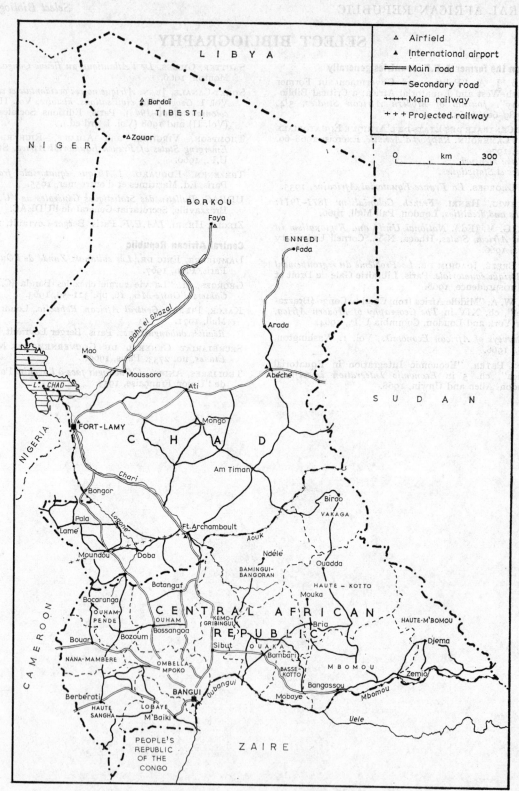

Chad and Central African Republic

Chad

PHYSICAL AND SOCIAL GEOGRAPHY

David Hilling

The Republic of Chad is the northernmost of the four independent states which emerged from French Equatorial Africa and is the largest in terms of size (495,800 sq. miles) and population (3.8 million). Traditionally a focal point for Saharan and equatorial African trade routes, the country's vast size, land-locked situation and great distance from the coast create problems for economic development.

RELIEF

The relief is relatively simple. From 800 ft. in the Lake Chad depression in the south-west the land rises northwards through the Guera Massif at 6,000 ft. to the mountainous Saharan region of Tibesti at 11,000 ft. Eastwards heights of 5,000 ft. are attained in the Quaddai Massif. In the south the watershed area between the Chari and Congo rivers is of subdued relief and only slight elevation. The only rivers of importance, both for irrigation and seasonal navigation, are the Chari and Logone, which flow across the south-west of the country and join at Fort-Lamy before flowing into Lake Chad.

CLIMATE AND VEGETATION

Stretching over 16° of latitude Chad has three well defined zones of climate, natural vegetation and associated economic activity. The southern third of the country has rainfall in excess of 20 in. a year, rising in the extreme south to 47 in. and has a savannah woodland vegetation. This is the country's richest agricultural zone, providing the two main cash crops, cotton and groundnuts, and a variety of local food crops (especially rice). Northwards, with rainfalls between 10 and 20 in. a year, there is a more open grassland, where there is emphasis on pastoral activity, limited cultivation of groundnuts and local grains, and some collection of gum arabic. Here also wildlife is plentiful and preserved in a number of reserves. The northern third of the country has negligible rainfall (e.g. Largeau with an annual average of 1 in.) and a sparse scrub vegetation which grades north into pure desert with little economic potential.

POPULATION

The total population is only 3.8 million and is markedly concentrated in the southern half of the country. Even there, however, population density is only 7 persons per sq. mile. In the better watered southern area are the one million Sara people, who comprise the main element in the population of sedentary cultivators and the largest single ethnic group among the Bantu. Further north the extensively Islamized negroid peoples of Sudanic type are mainly pastoralists of nomadic or semi-nomadic character. The northern three administrative regions (Borkou, Ennedi and Tibesti) have an area of 190,000 sq. miles but a population of only 82,000. Here the peoples are of Tuareg-Berber type and largely nomadic.

RECENT HISTORY*

R. Cornevin†

Chad's post-independence development has been a history of domination by the south over the north. The north is Muslim in religion, nomadic and pastoral in its mode of living, and still not free from the instabilities born of ancestral tribal divergencies. The south is wealthier and more populous, sedentary in its mode of life and largely Christian or animist. The European-educated Sara leaders from the former *Dar el Abid* ("land of the slaves") in the south have excluded the Muslim northerners from government and administration at all levels, and have to a certain extent exacted a revenge on the former Muslim slave traders. The latter have for too long shunned European education. Consequently they have experienced difficulties of assimiliation in a society which has been strongly influenced by the west and which has adopted French as the official language.

François Tombalbaye, a Protestant primary school teacher, has led the country since it became independent in August 1960. In January 1962 he moved against opposition by dissolving all political groups but his *Parti progressiste tchadien* (PPT). A year later a special PPT congress at Fort-Archambault formalized the one-party system. In January 1963 the government set up a National Planning Council and various banking institutions to implement a national credit policy. The creation of a single trade union in 1965 completed the transfer of the entire state organization into the hands of Tombalbaye.

The Saharan territories of Borkou, Ennedi and Tibesti were traditionally ungovernable and they therefore remained under French military administration until 1965. Then tension between senior Chad officials and the French army resulted in the recall of the troops at Chad's insistence. In their place, the Sara civil and military régime was autocratic, corrupt and (according to some reports) cruel, and aroused intense local bitterness.

BANDITRY AND REBELLION

In imposing his exclusive authority through the single-party system and by expelling his French advisers from the north, Tombalbaye stifled every form of legal opposition and drove opponents underground or into exile. Shortly after the institution of the PPT as the single authorized political party, Tombalbaye ordered the arrest of a number of prominent politicians on charges of plotting to raise the Muslim north against the Christian south. Riots in Fort-Lamy in September 1963 caused about twenty fatalities and led to the arrests of a former mayor of Fort-Lamy and a former Prime Minister. But dissidence continued, breaking out in October 1965 into rebellion with a tax riot at Mangalme, 500

km. east of Fort-Lamy, and in local clashes in the Ouadaï region, which caused serious border tension with Sudan. Terrorism and banditry were renewed in the Salamat region in 1967, and moved into the Saharan regions of the north in August 1968, when the rebels took the Aozou military post.

The considerable scale of fighting that developed after the tax riot at Mangalme in October 1965, was indicated by the casualty figures given by President Tombalbaye on August 11th, 1969: 1,126 rebels and 246 members of the armed forces killed. The Chad Press Agency later gave the figure for rebels killed as 2,791. There have also been reports of substantial pockets of rebellion near the borders with the Central African Republic and Cameroon, in addition to the known dissidents in the east and north.

Banditry, which has long been prevalent in eastern Chad even under the French, has clearly evolved into guerrilla warfare. Many of the dissidents are controlled by the Chad Liberation Front (FROLINAT), founded in 1966 by exiled politicians and now led by Dr. Abba Siddick, a former Minister of Education and a founder member of the PPT. FROLINAT has claimed that it opposes secession but insists on a specific identity for the north, the promotion of the teaching of Arabic and a bilingual educational system.

Anti-guerrilla operations were supported by a substantial French military force—1,600-strong, according to French official sources—between 1968 and 1971. A contingent of 1,000 men had been permanently stationed at Fort-Lamy, but in August 1968 Chad invoked the 1960 Franco-Chad Defence Pact in requesting additional French assistance to supress the serious outbreak of rebel activity at Aozou in the Tibesti region. The French sent two missions: a military relief contingent and a civil mission to reform the administration of the northern area. The garrison was withdrawn in June 1971, leaving an advisory mission of some 600 men.

President Tombalbaye has taken steps since early 1971 to reconcile dissident sections of the population. He has admitted that the original grievances of the rebels in the Eastern and Central provinces were genuine and should be redressed. The central government announced plans to release political prisoners, and to build schools, hospitals, roads and other infrastructural projects in these provinces. The reconciliation policy was confirmed by the seventh congress of the *Parti progressiste tchadien* at Fort-Archambault in the spring of 1971. A number of former political detainees were elected to the party's Political Bureau, and a resolution was adopted calling for the releases of some 150 political prisoners. Later in the year, during a visit to the Central African Republic, President Tombalbaye intervened to secure the release of six FROLINAT members detaines in Bangui.

*For the period before independence *see* Central African Republic Recent History, p. 213.

† For the 1973 edition, revisions have been made to this article by the Editor.

Some members of the Moubi tribe, which has provided the bulk of the eastern rebels since October, 1965, reportedly surrendered in response to the President's offers. Nonetheless, stubborn resistance continues in the north, where FROLINAT has greater influence. In May, 1971, President Tombalbaye visited the area and promised the release of former rebel leaders and the building of a new road linking Zorar with Kiouf in Libya.

Three months later, a projected *coup* attempt (the first ever against the Chad Government) was discovered and forestalled. The Chad Government accused the Libyan Government of complicity in the plot, alleging that the régime of Colonel Gaddafi planned to annex Chad so as to control the national economy and transform the country into an Arab State; diplomatic relations were temporarily broken.

The UEAC

Outbreaks of fighting continued throughout 1972, and in July and August a large number of arrests were made, including that of some prominent people, in connection with rebel activities.

Piqued at not being named President of OCAM, Tombalbaye in March 1968 left the Franc Zone's *Union douanière économique de l'Afrique centrale* (UDEAC), which gave little advantage to Chad, and joined with the Central African Republic and Congo —Kinshasa (now Zaire) in the *Union des Etats d'Afrique centrale* (UEAC), which Congo looked on with favour as an outlet to her industries. But the quarrel between President Bokassa of the Central African Republic and President Mobutu of Zaire has resulted in the union remaining purely formal.

ECONOMY

Peter Robson*

INTRODUCTION

Chad can be divided broadly into two socio-economic, political and geographical regions, with different religions, customs and languages. Most of the northern part of the country lies in the Sahara and is sparsely populated by at present disaffected nomadic and semi-nomadic Arab tribes. The southern part of the country, which is savannah, contains the bulk of the population and is inhabited mainly by a settled population of a variety of ethnic groups of Bantu stock. The largest of these, and effectively the ruling group, is the Sara.

The 1972 estimates put the population at 3.8 million giving a population density of 7 per sq. mile. Its rate of growth is estimated at 2.0 per cent per annum. Fort-Lamy with a population estimated in 1972 at 179,000 is the largest urban centre, followed by Sarh with a population of 43,700. There are two other towns, Moundou and Abéché, with populations of over 25,000.

Chad is one of the poorest and least developed countries of the African continent and its geographical isolation, climate and slender physical resources have resulted in an economy of very narrow range. Crop farming and nomadic cattle raising occupy most of the active population and account for most of the domestic product. Nearly half of the gross domestic product is accounted for by subsistence production. The industrial and commercial sectors are small. There are hardly any all-weather roads and no railways. The country is landlocked and its major economic centres are situated at distances varying between 900 and 1,800 miles from the sea. Its problems of economic development, which are in any case immense, are made still more acute by the difficulties between north and south. The government's approach to the country's economic development problems is determinedly liberal.

AGRICULTURE

About three quarters of the value of annual crop production is accounted for by subsistence farming. Cotton is the most important export crop and small amounts of gum arabic are also exported. The principal food crops are sorghum, millet and groundnuts. Cassava, rice, dates, maize and wheat are also grown for domestic consumption. Chad is practically self supporting in foodstuffs.

Cotton

Cotton is indigenous to Chad and its production has been widely promoted since the 1920s. Yields per hectare vary greatly from year to year according mainly to rainfall. Output of unginned cotton was a record 149,000 tons in the crop year 1968–69, and during the period 1966–67/1968–69 the average annual production was 125,000 tons, compared with 79,000 tons during the previous three-year period. In 1969–70 (the cotton is harvested in November/ December) output fell to 117,000 tons and in 1970–71 to 95,000 tons owing partly to unfavourable weather conditions.

Cotton production is promoted by a special service operated by the Ministry of Agriculture, which in recent years has devoted attention not only to increasing the area under cultivation but particularly to increasing the yield. The increase in production which has occurred in Chad of late (in the period 1957–58/1961–62 annual average production was about 67,000 tons a year) has been the result essentially of increases in yield, the area under cultivation having remained about the same since 1961–62. The ratio of ginned to unginned cotton has also increased as a result of the introduction of new varieties of cotton and as a result of improvements in planting

---

* For the 1973 edition, revisions have been made to this article by the Editor.

and ginning techniques. The programme initially envisaged for improving cotton producivity was substantially accelerated from 1968–69.

The purchase, ginning, transport and marketing of cotton in Chad are undertaken by a single company, *Société cotonnière du Tchad* (COTONCHAD), which purchases the entire output. A Cotton Stabilization Fund is operated which is an autonomous agency, charged with administering government policy with respect to cotton production and pricing and with supervising the activities of COTONCHAD. COTONCHAD purchases cotton from producers at a guaranteed price which is fixed by the Government each year at the beginning of the cotton season. If this guaranteed price exceeds the contractual purchase price, the Cotton Stabilization Fund reimburses the company for the difference. When the guaranteed price is lower than the contractual purchase price, the difference is paid by the company into the Stabilization Fund. The guaranteed price of 26 f. CFA per kilo of unginned cotton has not been changed since 1960–61, and it has in recent years been higher than the contractual price, necessitating support payments.

Prior to the 1963–64 cotton season France provided financial support for Chad's cotton production, principally by making up the losses incurred by the previous Stabilization Fund. In 1963–64 France discontinued such support but provided short term advances to the Stabilization Fund pending the implementation of EEC's agricultural support programme. Under the first Yaoundé Convention, EEC allocated to Chad 1,408 million f. CFA for the five-year period after association: 1,000 million f. CFA was to support the price of cotton and most of the balance was to promote diversification. Access to the production aid from EEC was made conditional upon the adoption of a productivity programme which, if successful, would have permitted the elimination of the price support scheme. The new Yaoundé Agreement does not provide for automatic price support, and the new EDF's Emergency Fund of $65–80 million is not earmarked for particular products or countries.

Other Crops

Gum arabic is tapped from traditional plantations, and modern plantations are being developed. The purchase and sale of gum arabic are the monopoly of the *Société nationale de commercialisation du Chad* (SONACOT). Production in 1969 was about 1,100 tons. A project to increase production to 2,000 tons in 1970 supported by the European Development Fund has so far failed, with production falling to 582 tons in 1971.

Among other food crops, groundnuts are produced. Production is of the order of 100,000 tons. Since 1966–67 total production has been consumed or processed into groundnut oil locally. Rice, a traditional crop, is being experimented with by modern methods, but the financial results have so far been unsatisfactory. In 1971 an estimated 20,000 tons of maize were produced, mainly in the polders of Lake Chad. Sugar-cane growing is at an experimental stage.

Animal Husbandry

Livestock plays an important role in the economy of Chad. It accounts for about one-fifth of the country's G.D.P. and it is the most important export after cotton. Cattle raising is concentrated mainly in the central part of the country; the herds, however, are moved long distances between the north and the south along traditional routes following a seasonal pattern. During the post-war period the number of livestock has expanded continually except for sheep. Livestock is chiefly exported on the hoof, for the most part clandestinely, without payment of taxes, and mainly to Nigeria where it is sold or bartered for consumer goods. In recent years refrigerated meat has been exported by air from Fort-Lamy and Sarh to Douala, Brazzaville and Kinshasa. There is a considerable potential for livestock, but to realize it will call for the upgrading of the herds and improvements in marketing arrangements.

MINING, MANUFACTURING AND POWER

Natron is at present the only mineral of importance in Chad and is found in pans on the northern edge of Lake Chad. It is used as salt, for human and animal consumption; in the preservation of meats and hides; and in soap production. Production in 1968–69 was about 5,000 tons.

Chad has the least developed industrial sector of any of the countries of equatorial Africa. Its main industry is cotton ginning, which is undertaken in some 20 cotton ginning mills and which accounts for nearly half of the turnover of the industrial sector. A sugar refinery, *Société sucrière du Tchad* (SOSU-TCHAD), based on sugar from Congo (Brazzaville), and a textile factory account for a substantial part of the remaining industrial output. Other important enterprises include slaughterhouses and refrigeration plants, a brewery, a flour mill, three rice mills, two brick factories, groundnut and cotton oil mills, a soft drink plant, radio and bicycle assembly plants, soap factories and construction enterprises.

Projects recently completed include a cigarette factory, based in the first place on imported tobacco, and a tyre retreading factory. Others under construction or shortly to commence include further oil mills and soap factories. Projects envisaged include a sugar refinery in Moyen Chari, to be based on locally grown sugar, a fish cannery, a meat extract factory, and factories for insecticides and detergents.

Electricity in Chad is generated by oil-powered plants operated by a public corporation *Société tchadienne d'énergie électrique* (STEE). The output of electricity tripled from 1962 to 1968, and in 1970 output at 41.9 million kWh. was 10 per cent up on that for the previous year.

Transportation within Chad is inadequate and expensive. Communications with the outside world are difficult, slow and costly because of the great distance from the sea, the character of the trade, and poor facilities in neighbouring countries. Transport limitations constitute a major obstacle to the country's economic development. Efforts are being made to improve the internal transport system, but these have lagged. Improvements in adjacent countries, especially in Cameroon, should also benefit Chad.

FOREIGN TRADE, AID AND PAYMENTS

Trade

Chad has a chronic trade deficit. For 1971 the recorded trade deficit (including trade with UDEAC countries) was 9,330 million francs CFA (exports 7,787 million francs CFA and imports 17,117 million francs CFA) and it has stood at approximately this level for several years. Cotton is by the far the most important export, accounting for about two-thirds of the recorded total, followed by meat and live animals (but clandestine trade in animals is estimated at six times the recorded figure).

The principal trading partner is France, which took 80 per cent of exports in 1969 and which supplied more than one third of imports, mainly manufactured goods and vehicles. Other EEC countries accounted for 10 per cent of total trade. Nigeria is the second most important source of imports followed by Congo (Brazzaville).

There was some diminution of Chad's imports from the other UDEAC countries in 1969 after Chad's withdrawal from UDEAC, but the decline had in fact been more marked in the previous year. Substantial declines in imports of manufactures from UDEAC in 1969 were, however, largely offset by a big increase in imports of petroleum products from the refinery at Port-Gentil in Gabon. Overall, Chad's recorded deficit with her former UDEAC partners was substantially unchanged at 2,000 million francs CFA in 1968 and 1969, but this was a reduction of about one-fifth from the previous year.

Aid

Since independence in 1960 Chad has remained heavily dependent upon foreign financial assistance. France has continued to be the principal supplier of foreign aid, but other sources, such as the European Development Fund, have also provided much aid.

The Balance of Payments

Chad's chronic deficit on its trade with its former partners in UDEAC and with the rest of the world has been financed in part by long term capital inflows, but mainly by external financial assistance. The remaining deficit has been financed by drawing upon the regional central bank. The overall effect has been a decline in Chad's external reserves, which are now negative. The deterioration of Chad's economic position since 1968 has meant that balance of payments difficulties could no longer be handled by this means, which meant in effect, recourse to the French Treasury. At the end of 1969 the IMF accorded drawing rights of U.S. $3,775,000 to help Chad to overcome its balance of payments difficulties.

PUBLIC FINANCE

Chad's ordinary budget revenue doubled from 1960 to 1965 and increased by a further 25 per cent in 1966. In the following three years revenue increased only modestly and was forecast at 11,800 million f. CFA in 1969. Despite a substantial rise of expenditure over the same period, this expansion sufficed to cover ordinary revenues until 1968.

In 1969 increased expenditure on the security forces to deal with the rebellion in the north caused a deterioration of the budgetary position and the actual outturn for 1969 was a substantial deficit.

For 1970 a very substantial deficit was for the first time in prospect, partly the result of further increased expenditure on security and the disappointing outturn in agriculture. The need to restore solvency necessitated widespread tax increases. Debt rearrangement is under discussion. Anticipated ordinary revenues for 1970 amount to 13,400 million f. CFA, an increase of 14 per cent over those estimated for 1969.

The development budget is expected to fall in 1970 to less than 4 per cent of total budgetary expenditure, though expenditures on developing productivity will be maintained.

DEVELOPMENT PLANNING

Chad's first five-year development plan (1966–70) provided for a total expenditure of 47,000 million f. CFA during the years 1966–70. Its main emphases were on (a) the diversification and increased productivity in agriculture; (b) the improvement of the transport system; (c) the development of human resources. The thrust of effort was to be on selective development. Thus industrial and educational development was to be concentrated upon Fort-Lamy, Fort-Archambault and Moundou. Similarly in agriculture efforts were to be focused on a few areas and a few crops, rather than dispersed more broadly.

G.D.P. stood roughly at £80 million (53,000 million f. CFA) in 1965 immediately prior to the commencement of the first five-year plan. It was expected to rise to about £105 million (71,000 million f. CFA) by 1970, a rise of more than 30 per cent. If achieved, income per head would have risen from about £24 (16,000 f. CFA) in 1965 to £29 (19,400 f. CFA) in 1970.

The second five-year plan (1971 – 75) gives priority to products which can be exported. Three major programmes involve cotton, livestock and sugar. The cotton target for 1975 is 200,000 tons. A substantial increase in beef production is envisaged. Major emphasis is to be given to sugar production, utilizing the waters of the Chari.

REGIONAL LINKS

Chad shares with Cameroon, Congo (Brazzaville), Gabon and the Central African Republic a common central bank (*Banque centrale des Etats de l'Afrique orientale et du Cameroun*) and a common currency (the CFA franc). Until recently its foreign exchange requirements were wholly met through the bank. Chad is also a member, together with Cameroon, Niger and Nigeria, of the Chad Basin Commission, and of OCAM.

Until the end of 1968 Chad was in addition a member of UDEAC, a customs union embracing the four members of the former A.E.F. together with Cameroon. At the end of 1968 Chad, together with the Central African Republic,* withdrew and joined the newly formed UEAC with Zaire. Chad had persistently complained of being affected adversely by the operation of UDEAC. Certainly the trade deficit with its partners was large, but fiscal redistribution payments from UDEAC's Solidarity Fund (1,200 million f. CFA in 1968) probably compensated Chad adequately for any cost it may have incurred in buying its partners' high-cost manufactures. Chad's withdrawal from UDEAC has left it with important economic and financial links with its former partners.

PROBLEMS AND PROSPECTS

The problems of accelerating economic development in Chad are immense. In the absence of mineral discoveries the prospects for a more satisfactory rate

* The Central African Republic returned to UDEAC before its departure became effective.

of economic progress will depend to a large extent on the possibilities of transforming traditional agriculture, in particular livestock production. Development has been slow, however, and further improvement will call for a considerable injection of capital and technical assistance. Transport improvements both within and without the country are also urgently needed.

The economic problems of the country have been exacerbated of late by unrest in the north and by declining cotton prices, which have given rise to severe budgetary problems. The maintenance of the vitally important agricultural improvement programme and the undertaking of further development projects particularly in the field of regional transport links must depend on the maintenance and expansion of foreign aid. Chad's financial position is such that only grants or very soft loans can be utilized.

The consolidation of regional links could conceivably help Chad's economic development in a modest way. Agreement was reached in December 1969 on the establishment of a Joint Commission between Cameroon and Chad. This may re-open the way to useful co-operation between the two countries. It is unlikely, however, that Chad's link with Zaire in the shape of UEAC will do any more for Chad than former membership of UDEAC.

STATISTICAL SURVEY

Area: 1,284,000 sq. km. (495,800 sq. miles).   **Population** (1972 estimate): 3,791,000.

PREFECTURES

	AREA (sq. km.)	POPULATION (1972)	DENSITY (per sq. km.)
Batha	88,800	335,000	3.8
Biltine	46,850	146,000	3.1
Borkou-Ennedi-Tibesti (B.E.T.)	600,350	82,000	0.1
Chari-Baguirmi	82,910	490,000	5.9
Guéra	58,950	181,000	3.1
Kanem	114,520	193,000	1.7
Lac	22,230	131,000	5.9
Logone Occidental	8,695	252,000	29.0
Logone Oriental	28,035	280,000	10.0
Mayo-Kebbi	30,105	555,000	18.4
Moyen-Chari	45,180	427,000	9.4
Ouadaï	76,240	352,000	5.6
Salamat	63,000	95,000	1.5
Tandjilé	18,045	272,000	15.1
TOTAL	1,284,000	3,791,000	2.95

CHIEF TOWNS
(Population—1972 estimate)

Fort-Lamy (capital)	179,000		Koumra	17,000
Sarh*	43,700		Bongor	14,300
Moundou	39,600		Doba	13,300
Abéché	28,100		Pala	13,200
Kélo	16,800			

* Fort-Archambault was renamed Sarh in July 1972.

EMPLOYMENT
(1964)

Cattle Raising	.	.	.	.	.	290,000
Other Agriculture	.	.	.	.	.	600,000
Fishing	.	.	.	.	.	10,000
Professions	.	.	.	.	.	4,600
Domestic Service	.	.	.	.	.	7,300
Industry	.	.	.	.	.	4,500

AGRICULTURE
LAND USE, 1968
('ooo hectares)

Arable and under Permanent Crops	.		.		7,000
Permanent Meadows and Pastures	.		.		45,000
Forest Land	.	.	.	.	16,500
Other Land	.	.	.	.	58,500
Inland Water	.	.	.	.	1,400
TOTAL AREA					128,400

PRINCIPAL CROPS

	AREA ('ooo hectares)			PRODUCTION ('ooo metric tons)			YIELD (kg. per hectare)		
	1969	1970	1971	1969	1970	1971	1969	1970	1971
Cassava (Manioc) . . .	17*	17*	n.a.	55*	55*	n.a.	3,200*	3,200*	n.a.
Cottonseed . . .	} 294	283	283*	{ 71	67	68	240	240	240*
Cotton (lint) . . .				{ 40	37	38	130	130	130*
Dates . . .	n.a.	n.a.	n.a.	22*	22*	22*	n.a.	n.a.	n.a.
Groundnuts (in shell) . .	162	160	160*	115	115	115*	710	720	720*
Maize . . .	6	12*	12*	12	20*	20*	1,920	1,670*	1,670*
Millet and Sorghum . .	921	1,050*	1,050*	651	715*	715*	710	680*	680*
Pulses . . .	185*	185*	185*	90*	90*	95*	490*	490*	510*
Rice . . .	36	33*	33*	37	33*	33*	1,010	1,000*	1,000*
Sesame Seed . . .	40*	40*	40*	12*	12*	12*	300*	300*	300*
Sweet Potatoes and Yams . .	12*	12*	n.a.	52*	52*	n.a.	4,300*	4,300*	n.a.
Wheat . . .	5	5*	5*	9	9*	9*	1,840	1,800*	1,800*

* FAO estimate.

LIVESTOCK

	1968–69	1969–70	1970–71
Cattle . .	4,500,000	4,550,000	4,500,000*
Goats . .	2,200,000	2,300,000*	2,400,000*
Sheep . .	1,800,000	1,800,000*	1,800,000*
Horses . .	15,000	150,000	150,000*
Asses . .	300,000	285,000	275,000*
Camels . .	355,000	370,000	370,000*
Chickens . .	2,800,000	2,900,000*	2,950,000*

* FAO estimate.

Source for Agriculture tables: FAO, *Production Yearbook 1971.*

OTHER AGRICULTURAL PRODUCTS
(metric tons)

	1969	1970	1971
Animal Meat† .	15,000	14,000	n.a.
Poultry Meat .	1,600*	1,600*	n.a.
Offal . .	9,000*	9,000*	n.a.
Tallow . .	1,400*	1,400*	n.a.
Cattle Hides .	5,500*	5,500*	n.a.
Sheep Skins .	1,290*	1,290*	n.a.
Goat Skins .	1,080*	1,100*	n.a.
Cows' Milk .	163,000*	165,000*	167,000*
Sheeps' Milk .	15,000*	16,000*	16,000*
Goats' Milk .	31,000*	31,000*	32,000*
Hen Eggs .	2,500*	2,500*	2,700*

* FAO estimate.

† Inspected production only, i.e. meat from animals slaughtered under government supervision.

FORESTRY
ROUNDWOOD PRODUCTION
(cubic metres)

1968	2,960,000
1969	2,970,000
1970	3,000,000

FISHING
FRESH-WATER CATCH
(metric tons)

1968	110,000
1969	110,000
1970	120,000

INDUSTRY
(1965–66)

	Metric Tons
Cotton Fibre	27,557
Groundnut Oil	4,000
Frozen Meat	2,664
Soda (Natron)	8,000

Salt production totalled 10,000 metric tons in 1970.

ELECTRIC ENERGY
Production for public use (kWh.)

1968	30,800,000
1969	38,000,000
1970	41,900,000

FINANCE
100 centimes = 1 franc de la Communauté Financière Africaine.
Coins: 1, 2, 5, 10 and 25 francs CFA.
Notes: 5, 10, 25, 50, 100, 500, 1,000, 5,000 and 10,000 francs CFA.
Exchange rates (December 1972): 1 franc CFA = 2 French centimes;
£1 sterling = 593.625 francs CFA; U.S. $1 = 255.785 francs CFA;
1,000 francs CFA = 1.685 = $3.91.

BUDGET
1969: Ordinary revenue 11,800 million francs CFA.
1970: Ordinary revenue 13,400 million francs CFA.
1971: Ordinary revenue 13,440 million francs CFA.
1972: Ordinary revenue 13,848 million francs CFA.

Both the current and development budgets are dependent on substantial French aid. In 1969 French aid amounted to some 1,200 million CFA francs, of which 300 million were granted to balance the current budget.

EXTERNAL TRADE*
(million francs CFA)

	1966	1967	1968	1969	1970	1971
Imports . . .	7,338	9,248	8,262	11,914	17,059	17,117
Exports . . .	5,848	6,635	6,824	8,020	8,205	7,787

* Prior to 1969, figures exclude trade with Cameroon, the Central African Republic, Congo (Brazzaville) and Gabon.

COMMODITIES

IMPORTS	1968	1969
Cereals	399	354
Sugar and Honey . .	8	950
Other food . .	447	648
Beverages and Tobacco .	179	484
Petroleum products . .	1,353	1,935
Chemicals . .	554	851
Textile yarn, fabrics, etc. .	791	952
Machinery (non-electric) . .	727	823
Electrical machinery . .	502	590
Road motor vehicles .	696	938

EXPORTS	1968	1969	1970
Live Cattle . .	94	120.3	159.6
Meat . . .	430	696	n.a.
Hides and Skins .	96	114.9	94.7
Raw Cotton . .	5,778	6,586.4	5,910.4
Natural Gums, Resins, etc. . .	107	80.3	34.8

Cotton (1971): 5,257.

COUNTRIES

IMPORTS	1967	1968	1969
Cameroon . . .	n.a.	n.a.	408
Congo (Brazzaville) .	n.a.	n.a.	1,269
France . . .	4,216	3,669	4,228
Germany, Federal Republic . .	571	567	420
Italy . . .	272	481	514
Netherlands Antilles .	389	153	28
Nigeria . . .	517	950	1,514
United Kingdom . .	275	226	439
U.S.A. . . .	954	804	625

EXPORTS	1967	1968	1969
Belgium/Luxembourg .	706.1	591	—
Cameroon . . .	n.a.	n.a.	82
Central African Republic	n.a.	n.a.	146
Congo (Brazzaville) .	n.a.	n.a.	203
France . . .	3,774.4	4,333	6,654
Gabon . . .	n.a.	n.a.	110
Germany, Federal Republic . .	186	114	26
Japan . . .	338.3	344	—
Morocco . . .	173	24	—
Nigeria . . .	528.5	192	265
United Kingdom . .	161.7	288	60
Yugoslavia . . .	229.3	178	—
Zaire . . .	233	362	291

TRANSPORT

ROAD TRAFFIC Motor vehicles in use		
	1968	1969
Passenger Cars . . .	3,700	3,200
Commercial Vehicles . . .	5,900	5,100
TOTAL . . .	9,600	8,300

CIVIL AVIATION Scheduled services*			
	1968	1969	1970
Kilometres flown ('000)	2,047	2,243	2,373
Passenger-km. ('000) .	65,324	73,435	78,953
Cargo ton-km. ('000) .	5,120	6,188	6,451
Mail ton-km. ('000) .	554	598	651

* Including one-twelfth of the traffic of Air Afrique.

Tourism: There are 118 tourist hotel bedrooms in the main towns, and simpler accommodation in outlying places. 3,000 tourists visited Chad in the 1967–68 tourist season (Dec.–July), half of them from France.

EDUCATION
(1970–71)

	SCHOOLS	PUPILS		
		Boys	Girls	Total
Primary	707	137,059	46,191	183,250
Public . . .	664	129,236	38,681	167,917
Private (Catholic and Protestant) .	43	7,823	7,510	15,333
Secondary	31	8,536	731	9,267
Public	26	8,157	429	8,586
Private	5	379	302	681
Technical	2	473	22	495
TOTAL . . .	740	146,068	46,944	193,012

Source: Service de la Statistique Générale, B.P. 453, Fort-Lamy.

THE CONSTITUTION

Principles: Defence of the rights of man and public liberties; building of a true democracy founded on the separation of powers. The Republic is indivisible, lay, democratic and social. Sovereignty resides in the people who exercise it by equal, universal and secret suffrage. Equality of race, origin and religion; freedom of belief and opinion, guarantee of education.

Head of State: The Head of State is Head of the Government and President of the Council of Ministers, which he appoints. He is elected by an electoral college consisting of the National Assembly, the Mayors and Councillors of the municipalities and rural communities, and the traditional tribal chiefs in the rural areas. His term of office is seven years.

Council of Ministers: Appointed by the President, Determines policy, law, and public office-holders.

National Assembly: Members are elected for five years. In case of a vote of no confidence the President may, after consultation with the President of the Assembly, dissolve Parliament.

Economic and Social Council: Advises the National Assembly on economic and social matters.

Political Party: Chad was officially declared to be a one-party state in November 1965.

THE GOVERNMENT

HEAD OF STATE

President: FRANÇOIS TOMBALBAYE.

COUNCIL OF MINISTERS

(November 1972)

President of the Council of Ministers and Minister of Defence, Planning and Veteran Affairs: FRANÇOIS TOMBALBAYE.

Minister of State at the Presidency: DJIBRINE KHERALLAH.

Minister of State in charge of Agriculture: MICHEL DJIDINGAR.

Minister of Foreign Affairs: BABA HASSANE.

Minister of Trade: ABDEL MOUTY TAHA.

Minister of Health and Social Affairs: Dr. JACQUES BAROUM.

Minister of Public Works, Mines and Geology: RAYMOND NAIMBAYE.

Minister of Stock-breeding and Animal Product Marketing, Production, Waters and Forests, Hunting and Fishing: MAHAMAT ABDELKERIM.

Minister of Tourism and Crafts: PIERRE-ALFRED DESSANDE.

Minister of National Education and Culture: BOHIADI BRUNO.

Minister of Territorial Improvement and Housing: ABDOULAYE DJONOUMA.

Guardian of the Seals, Minister of Justice: JOSEPH BRAHIM SEID.

Minister of the Interior: MAHAMAT DOUBA ALIFA.

Minister in charge of relations with Parliament: (vacant).

Minister of the Civil Service: MUSTAPHA BATRAN.

Minister of Finance: ELIE ADOLPHE ROMBA.

Minister of Transport and Telecommunications: ADOUM AGANAYE.

Minister Responsible for Party Organization: ADOUM TCHERE.

Secretary of State for Youth, Labour and Sports: MAHAMAT IDRISS.

Secretary of State for Stock-breeding, Animal Product Marketing, Waters and Forests, Hunting and Fishing: JEAN NICOLAS.

Secretary of State for Information, attached to the Presidency: AHMAT AMADIF.

Secretary of State for Agriculture and Rural Development: FRANÇOIS GOLO.

Secretary of State for National Education and Culture: ABDERAHIM DAHAB.

Secretary of State for Transport and Communications: ADOUM HAMID.

Secretaries of State in charge of Missions for the Presidency: OUMAR SEID, MAHAMAT ZEN ALI.

Head of the President's Office: BERNARD DIKOA GARANDI.

DIPLOMATIC REPRESENTATION

EMBASSIES AND LEGATIONS ACCREDITED TO CHAD

(In Fort-Lamy unless otherwise indicated)

(E) Embassy; (L) Legation

Belgium: Yaoundé, Cameroon (E).

Canada: Yaoundé, Cameroon (E).

Central African Republic: B.P. 115 (E); *Chargé d'Affaires:* PIERRE NGREGAÏ.

China, Republic (Taiwan): B.P. 104; *Ambassador:* FENG YU-TSENG.

Denmark: Kinshasa, Zaire (E).

Egypt: (E); *Chargé d'Affaires:* NAHIB A. EL DAIROUTY.

France: rue du Lieutenant Franjoux, B.P. 431 (E); *Ambassador:* FERNAND WIBAUX.

Gabon: Yaoundé, Cameroon (E).

German Democratic Republic: (E); *Ambassador:* Herr SCHUNKE.

Germany, Federal Republic: B.P. 893 (E); *Ambassador:* WERNER SELDIS.

Ghana: Kinshasa, Zaire (E).

Guinea: Brazzaville, Congo P.R. (E).

Italy: Yaoundé, Cameroon (E).

Japan: Kinshasa, Zaire (E).

Korea, Republic: Paris 16e, France (E).

Lebanon: Accra, Ghana (E).

Mali: Brazzaville, Congo P.R. (E).

Netherlands: Yaoundé, Cameroon (E).

Nigeria: B.P. 752; *Ambassador:* KABIR BAYERO.

Pakistan: Yaoundé, Cameroon (E).

Sudan: B.P. 45 (E); *Ambassador:* ABDEL AL SINADA.

Switzerland: Lagos, Nigeria (E).

Tunisia: Kinshasa, Zaire (E).

U.S.S.R.: B.P. 891 (E); *Ambassador:* EVGENY NERSESSOV.

United Kingdom: London England (E).

U.S.A.: ave. du Colonel d'Ornano, B.P. 413 (E); *Ambassador:* TERENCE ALPHONSO TODMAN.

Yugoslavia: Brazzaville, Congo P.R. (E).

Zaire: B.P. 910; *Ambassador:* NESTOR WATUM.

Chad also has diplomatic relations with the Democratic People's Republic of Korea and Turkey.

NATIONAL ASSEMBLY

President: ABBO NASSOUR.

Vice-Presidents: PAUL RARIKINGAR, ARABI EL GONI, LAMIDO SALEH, LEON MOGOUMBAYE.

ELECTION (*December* 1969)

Voting was on a single list of government candidates. There are 105 deputies, elected for a five-year term. A presidential referendum was held in June 1969. President Tombalbaye, the sole candidate, gained 93 per cent of the 1,479,000 votes.

POLITICAL PARTIES

Parti progressiste tchadien (PPT): Chad section of the *Rassemblement démocratique africaine* (RDA); has a Political Bureau of 36 members; Sec.-Gen. FRANÇOIS TOMBALBAYE.

There are several opposition groups, chiefly Muslim; all are banned and the leaders are in exile. One, FROLINAT (an acronym from National Liberation Front), claims to lead the revolt; its leaders are Dr. ABBA SIDDICK and HADJ ISSAKA.

DEFENCE

Chad's army numbers about 2,600 men. There are also some 4,000 men in the National Guard and other paramilitary forces. In 1971, some 2,200 French troops were stationed in the country. All were due to leave by the end of 1971, and French military intervention officially ended on September 1st, 1972. About 400 men attached to the medical and educational corps were to remain after this date.

Chief of Staff: Col. FÉLIX MALLOUM.

JUDICIAL SYSTEM

Supreme Court: Fort Lamy; f. 1962; the court for decisions on constitutional matters, it has a President, an Attorney-General and six counsellors in three chambers: judicial, administrative and financial; Pres. PIERRE DJIME.

High Court of Justice: Fort-Lamy; superior court, empowered to judge the President of the Republic and members of the Government in matters of complicity against the state. The members are elected by the National Assembly.

Court of Appeal: Fort-Lamy.

A criminal court sits at Fort-Lamy, Sarh, Moundou and Abéché, in addition to a tribunal in each of these towns.

RELIGION

It is estimated that 52 per cent of the population are Muslims, 43 per cent Animists and 5 per cent Christians, with Roman Catholics comprising 2 per cent of the total population.

Head of the Muslim Community: Iman MOUSSA.

Roman Catholic Missions: There are 43 mission centres and about 320 missionaries.

Archbishop of Fort-Lamy: Mgr. PAUL DALMAIS.
Bishop of Moundou: Mgr. LOUIS GAUMAIN.
Bishop of Sarh: Mgr. HENRI VENIAT.
Bishop of Pala: Mgr. HILAIRE DUPONT.

Protestant Missions: L'Entente Evangélique, B.P. 127, Fort-Lamy; a fellowship of churches and missions working in Chad: Eglise Baptiste, Eglise Evangélique au Tchad, Assemblées Chrétiennes, Eglise Fraternelle Luthérienne and Eglise Evangélique des Frères.

PRESS AND RADIO

Info-Tchad: B.P. 670, Fort-Lamy; daily news bulletin issued by Chad Press Agency, ATP.

Informations Economiques: B.P. 48, Fort-Lamy; weekly; edited by the Chambre de Commerce de la République du Tchad.

Journal Officiel de la République du Tchad: Fort-Lamy.

Cahiers de l'Unité: Fort-Lamy; monthly.

Bulletin Mensuel de Statistiques du Tchad: B.P. 453, Fort-Lamy; monthly.

Agence Tchadienne de Presse (ATP): B.P. 670, Fort-Lamy; daily in French; published by Ministry of Information; circ. 1,500.

Agence France Presse and Reuters are represented in Chad.

Radiodiffusion Nationale Tchadienne: Fort-Lamy, B.P. 892; government station; programmes in French, Arabic and Sara; a transmitter with a 100 kW circuit for short wave transmissions and a 20 kW circuit for medium wave were put into operation in June 1972; Dir. GRÉGOIRE BICQUET.

There are 60,000 radio licences.

FINANCE

BANKS

CENTRAL BANK

Banque Centrale des Etats de l'Afrique Equatoriale et du Cameroun: 29 rue du Colisée, Paris 8e; Fort-Lamy, B.P. 50; Dir. PIERRE GUICHETEAU.

Banque de Développement du Tchad: B.P. 19, Fort-Lamy; f. 1962; cap. 520m. francs CFA; Dir.-Gen. (vacant).

Banque Tchadienne de Crédit et de Dépôts: B.P. 461, 6 rue Robert-Lévy, Fort-Lamy; f. 1963; cap. 250m. francs CFA; Pres. A. MEAR.

Caisse Centrale de Co-opération Economique: B.P. 478, Fort-Lamy; Dir. M. LANGLOIS.

Banque Internationale pour l'Afrique Occidentale: 9 ave. de Messine, Paris; Fort-Lamy, P.O.B. 87; Sarh, P.O.B. 240; Dir. Fort-Lamy ANDRÉ BOULIÈRE.

Banque Nationale de Paris: 16 blvd. des Italiens, Paris; Fort-Lamy, B.P. 38; Dir. GUY ROMEO.

BANKERS' ORGANIZATIONS

Conseil National du Crédit: Fort-Lamy; f. 1965 to create a national credit policy and to organize the banking profession.

Association Professionelle des Banques au Tchad: Fort-Lamy.

INSURANCE

Twelve of the leading French insurance companies are represented in Fort-Lamy.

TRADE AND INDUSTRY

Chambre de Commerce, d'Agriculture et d'Industrie de la République du Tchad: Fort-Lamy, B.P. 458; Pres. GASTON PALLAI; Sec.-Gen. M. N'GANGBET; publ. *Bulletin des Informations Economiques.*

Chambre de Commerce de Sarh: Sarh.

TRADE UNIONS

Union Nationale des Travailleurs du Tchad (UNATRAT): B.P. 553, Fort-Lamy; f. 1968 as an amalgamation between two former unions; mems. 5,500; Pres. SEMOKO YAMARA; Sec.-Gen. ROBERT GORALLAH.

Union Interprofessionnelle du Tchad (UNITCHA): B.P. 94, Fort-Lamy; Dir. GILBERT MAILLARD.

Union Tchadienne de Transports: B.P. 39, Fort-Lamy; Agencies at Bangui, Moundou, Sarh; Dir. JEAN FABRY.

Union d'Entreprises de Constructions (UDEC): B.P. 229, Sarh.

DEVELOPMENT

Caisse Centrale de Coopération Economique: 110 rue de l'Université, Paris 7e; Fort-Lamy, B.P. 478.

Mission Permanente d'Aide et de Coopération: B.P. 898, Fort-Lamy; French technical mission; Head of Mission RENÉ GUILBAUD.

Société Hotelière du Tchad: c/o BDT B.P. 19, Fort-Lamy; Pres. BENOÎT PIRCOLOSSOU; Dir.-Gen. GEORGES DIGUIMBAYE.

MAJOR INDUSTRIAL COMPANIES

The following are some of the largest private and state-owned companies in terms of capital investment or employment.

Brasseries du Logone: B.P. 170, Moundou; f. 1962; cap. 300 million francs CFA.
Brewery.
Pres. Y. KERGALL; Dir.-Gen. C. BESCOS; 202 employees.

Société Cotonnière du Tchad (COTONTCHAD): B.P. 15, Fort-Lamy; f. 1971; fmrly. Société Cotonnière Franco-Tchadienne (COTONFRAN); 45 per cent government owned; cap. 595 million francs CFA.
Cotton ginning.
Dir. GABRIEL FULCHIRON.

Les Grands Moulins du Tchad: B.P. 173, Fort-Lamy; f. 1963; cap. 100 million francs CFA.
Flour-mill, manufacture of biscuits.
Dir. JEAN COLIN.

Manufacture de Cigarettes du Tchad: B.P. 572, Fort-Lamy; f. 1968; cap. 180 million francs CFA.
Manufacture of tobacco products.
Dir. Monsieur CIOFOLO.

Société Nationale de Commercialisation du Tchad (SONACOT): B.P. 630, Fort-Lamy; f. 1965; cap. 150 million francs CFA.
State monopoly for purchase and sale of gum arabic.
Pres. Dir.-Gen. ISSA RAMADAN.

Shell Tchad: B.P. 110, Fort-Lamy; f. 1954.
Distribution of petroleum products.
Dir. MICHEL BEDOUET; 73 employees.
(Subsidiary of Société Shell de l'Afrique Equatoriale).

Société Sucrière du Tchad (SOSUTCHAD): B.P. 37, Fort-Lamy; f. 1963; cap. 140 million francs CFA.
Sugar refinery.
Pres. Dir.-Gen. JEAN VILGRAIN; Dir. JEAN-CHARLES FLAMBERT.

Société Textile du Tchad: B.P. 238, Sarh; f. 1966; cap. 300 million francs CFA.
Textile mills.
Dir. AFRO BEVILACQUA.

TRANSPORT

Agence Transéquatoriale des Communications: B.P. 110, Sarh; f. 1959; develops common means of transport between the member states of the Scientific and Technical Research Committee of the OAU.

RAILWAYS

In 1962 Chad signed an agreement with Cameroon to extend the Trans-Cameroon railway from N'Gaoundéré to Sarh. The total cost will be about 2,700 million f. CFA, and survey work began in 1964. The railway has been constructed as far as Belabo, and the section from Belabo to N'Gaoundéré, the last major town in Cameroon before the Chad frontier, is now being built.

ROADS

There are about 30,000 km. of roads, of which 3,000 km. are classified. There are also some 20,000 km. of tracks suitable for motor traffic during the dry season from October to July. A 4,840-km. motor track from Rouiba, in Algeria, to Chad was opened in 1960. In 1968 the International Development Association granted Chad a U.S. $4 million loan for the improvement of its road system, notably in the provision of a direct link between Lake Chad and Fort-Lamy. Two stretches of road, from Fort-Lamy to Guelendeng and from Fort-Lamy to Massaquet, have been asphalted under this scheme. Studies were made in 1971 on a road from the north to the south of the country, linking three main regional centres of Fort-Lamy, Sarh and Aléché. The cost of the project is estimated at 12,000 million francs CFA.

INLAND WATERWAYS

There is a certain amount of traffic on the Chari and Logone rivers which meet just south of Fort-Lamy. The traffic is confined to the wet season, August-December.

CIVIL AVIATION

A new international airport at Fort-Lamy was inaugurated in January 1967.

Compagnie Nationale Air-Tchad: ave. Charles de Gaulle, Fort-Lamy; f. 1966; Government majority holding with 36 per cent UTA interest; regular passenger, freight and charter services within Chad; Pres. ADOUM AGANAYE; Gen. Man. MARCEL DUVERNOIS; fleet of one DC-4, two DC-3, one Beechcraft Baron and one Piper Cherokee.

Chad is also served by the following foreign airlines: Air Cameroon, Air Zaire, Sudan Airways and UTA.

POWER

Société Tchadienne d'Energie Electrique: B.P. 44, Fort-Lamy; f. 1968; cap. 238 million francs CFA; production and distribution of electricity and water; Dir. P. G. PINAULT; 250 employees. In 1970 42 million kWh. were produced, and in 1971 48 million kWh.

TOURISM

Ministère du Tourisme et de l'Artisanat: B.P. 748, Fort-Lamy; f. 1962; Dir. (vacant); also at B.P. 62, Sarh.

Agence Tchadienne de Voyages: Tchad-Tourisme, B.P. 894, Fort-Lamy; Pres. V. N'GAKOUTOU.

EDUCATION

Education in Chad follows the French pattern. In 1970-71 there were about 182,000 children in primary schools and 9,200 in secondary schools. There are 31 secondary schools including 15 general education colleges. For the country as a whole, literacy is just over 43 per cent.

A new scheme has been put into operation whereby those children about to leave primary school receive professional instruction and training in basic agricultural techniques. This is regarded as an effort to help the economy of the country.

Higher education is being developed as a co-operative matter between the member states of the Conférence des Chefs d'Etat de l'Afrique Équatoriale (Chad, Central African Republic, Congo Republic and Gabon) through the Fondation d'enseignement supérieur d'Afrique centrale (FESAC). In 1963 the National School of Administration was opened in Fort-Lamy, and the National School of Telecommunications at Sarh. A Veterinary School was opened in 1965 in Fort-Lamy. Subsequently schools for engineers, doctors and social assistants have opened in Fort-Lamy. A small number of students go on to University courses in France, mostly supported by the Fonds d'aide et de coopération.

RESEARCH INSTITUTES

Bardai Research Station: Bardai Oasis; f. 1965 by the Free University of Berlin; geographical station undertaking research in desert geomorphology; assisted by Berlin Research Association and the Berlin Senate; Dir. Dr. J. HÖVERMANN.

Bureau de Recherches Géologiques et Minières: B.P. 449, Fort-Lamy; Dir. M. ABADIE.

Bureau pour le Développement de la Production Agricole: B.P. 745, Fort-Lamy.

Centre de Documentation Pédagogique: B.P. 731, Fort-Lamy; f. 1962; publ. *L'Ecole Tchadienne.*

Office de la Recherche Scientifique et Technique Outre-Mer Centre ORSTOM de Fort-Lamy: B.P. 65, Fort-Lamy; geology, pedology, hydrology, hydrobiology, botany, archaeology, geophysics; library; Dir. P. AUDRY.

Institut de Recherches du Coton et des Textiles Exotiques (IRCT): B.P. 31, Moundou; f. 1939; cotton research (entomology, agronomy and genetics); Head of station at Bebedja Dr. BRADER; Regional Dir. C. MÉGIE.

Institut National Tchadien pour les Sciences Humaines: B.P. 503, Fort-Lamy; f. 1961; archaeological and ethnographical collections; library of 2,000 vols.; Dir. J.-P. LEBEUF.

Institut d'Élevage et de Médecine Vétérinaire des Pays Tropicaux: Laboratoire de Farcha, B.P. 433, Fort-Lamy; f. 1952; veterinary research and production of vaccine; 15 scientists; library of 1,100 vols.; Dir. Dr. A. PROVOST.

MUSEUM

Musée National: B.P. 503, Fort-Lamy; f. 1963; human palaeontology, prehistory and protohistory, ethnography, and scientific archives departments; Dirs. Prof. J. P. LEBEUF, J. CHAPELLE; publ. *Etudes et Documents tchadiens.*

UNIVERSITY

UNIVERSITÉ DU TCHAD

B.P. 1 117, FORT-LAMY

Founded 1971; consists of Institut Universitaire des Lettres, Langues et Sciences Humaines, Institut des Sciences Juridiques, Économiques et de Gestion, Institut des Sciences Exactes et Appliquées.

Rector: Prof. Dr. JEAN CABOT.

Secretary-General: HENRI HERNANDEZ.

Registrar: Mme LANGE.

Library of 3,000 vols.
Number of teachers: 25.
Number of students: 200.

COLLEGES

Collège Franco-Arabe: Abéché.

Ecole Nationale d'Administration: B.P. 768, Fort-Lamy; f. 1963; set up by the Government and controlled by an Administrative Council to train students as public servants; Dir. B. LANNE.

Ecole Nationale des Télécommunications: Sarh.

Institut d'Enseignement Zootechnique et Vétérinaire de l'Afrique Centrale: B.P. 683, Fort-Lamy; f. 1964; 12 teachers; Dir. J. THIBAUD.

SELECT BIBLIOGRAPHY

(For works on the former A.E.F. countries generally *see* Central African Republic Select Bibliography, p. 245.)

CHAPELLE, JEAN. *Nomades noirs du Sahara.* Paris, Plon, 1958.

DIGUIMNBAYE, GEORGES, and LANGUE, ROBERT. *L'Essor du Tchad.* Paris, Presses universitaires de France, 1969.

DIRECTION DE LA STATISTIQUE ET DES ETUDES. *Commerce extérieur du Tchad en 1969.* Fort-Lamy, 1970.

HUGOT, PIERRE. *Le Tchad.* Paris, Nouvelles Editions latines, 1965.

LEBEUF, ANNIE. *Les populations du Tchad.* Paris, 1959.

LE CORNEC, JACQUES. *Histoire politique du Tchad de 1900 a 1962.* Paris, Librairie générale de Droit et Jurisprudence, 1963.

LE ROUVREUR, ALBERT. *Sahariens et Sahéliens du Tchad.* Paris, Berger-Levrault, 1962.

LOUIS, P. *Contribution géophysique à la connaissance géologique du bassin du lac Tchad.* Bondy, France, ORSTOM, 1972.

SECRETARIAT GENERAL DU GOUVERNEMENT. *Notes et Etudes,* no. 2696. Paris, 1960.

Comoro Islands

PHYSICAL AND SOCIAL GEOGRAPHY

The Comoro Islands, an archipelago of four small islands, together with numerous islets and coral reefs, lie between the east African coast and Madagascar. Grande-Comore, on which the capital of the territory, Moroni, is situated, Mayotte, Anjouan and Mohéli, have between them a total area of only 838 sq. miles. The islands are volcanic in structure, and Mt. Kartala on Grande-Comore is still active. Climate, rainfall and vegetation all vary greatly from island to island. There are similar divergences in soil characteristics, though in this instance natural causes have been reinforced by human actions notably in deforestation and exhaustion of the soil.

The composition of the population of 280,000 is complex. Immigrants from the coast of Africa, Indonesia, Madagascar and Persia, as well as Arabs, had all arrived by about 1600. The Portuguese (in the early part of the sixteenth century), the Dutch and the French further complicated the ethnic pattern, the latter introducing into the islands Chinese (who have now left) and Indians. The different sections of the population are still not fully integrated. In Mayotte and Mohéli Arabic features are less evident, mainly because the two islands were settled by immigrants from the African coast and Madagascar. In fact, while Arab characteristics are strong in the islands generally, in particular in the coastal towns, the African is predominant in the territory as a whole. Historically, too, there was some unity between the islands, since members of the same noble family ruled each island. Swahili and Arabic were the main languages spoken before French colonization began in 1841.

Average density per sq. mile is 200, but this conceals great disparities between Mohéli, where it is about 50, and Anjouan, where it is nearly 400 and increasing rapidly in conjunction with growing pressure on the available land.

RECENT HISTORY

In 1841 the French landed on Mayotte and the king was persuaded to cede his island to France. The rulers of the other three islands followed his example one by one between 1886 and 1909, and in 1912 *Les Comores* was proclaimed a French colony. Two years later the islands became subject to the authority of the Governor-General of Madagascar. The Comoros thus became a minor appendage of a much larger, culturally very different and historically separate country. In these circumstances it was hardly surprising that the islands were neglected and remained virtually in their pre-colonial condition for most of the twentieth century.

With regular administration came improvements in health and mortality rates, but such economic and political development as was encouraged benefited only the foreign companies, the ruling nobility or the administrators themselves. While Comorians continued in their traditional subsistence activities, cash crops (vanilla, cocoa, etc.) were developed for export by French companies and landowners for profits in which few islanders shared. The traditional social structure remained almost untouched, the colonial régime being superimposed on it with members of the old ruling class being absorbed into the bureaucracy as minor officials. By the end of the Second World War there were still less than 500 pupils in French schools.

During the war the islands were occupied by the British following Madagascar's, and thus the Comoros', declaration for Pétain.

In 1946, when the Constitution of the Fourth Republic created the French Union, the Comoros were separated from Madagascar and became financially and administratively autonomous. The islands were also given, along with the other French colonies, representation in the French National Assembly (one member at first—Saïd Mohammed Cheikh, who sat from 1946 to 1962—and two after 1958) and in the Senate (one member). Following the *loi cadre* of 1956 and the creation of the Fifth French Republic in 1958, the Comoros remained a French overseas territory.

A law of December 22nd, 1961 (amended in January 1968), conferred complete internal autonomy on the territory, although the French High Commissioner still retains considerable powers. There is an elected Chamber of Deputies and a Council of Government, whose President is President of the whole territory. Saïd Mohammed Cheikh held this position until his death in March 1970 when Prince Saïd Ibrahim succeeded him.

In theory any Comorian can stand for election to the Chamber. However, opposition to the government is closely watched and soon suppressed if any real threat begins to appear (hence the main opposition is in exile); and, in any case, candidates effectively have to be proficient in French, a qualification which only about one per cent of the population possesses. Thus representation in the Chamber, as in the General Council (or local assembly) between 1946 and 1961, has remained in the hands of a small élite. Ministers, deputies and government officials are usually linked by family or business.

There have traditionally been two main political parties—the Comoros Democratic Union (UDC), or the "greens", and the Comorian People's Democratic Rally (RDPC), or the "whites"—but there is little to distinguish between them. Until recently they were both pledged to strengthening ties with France and securing more French aid, and it was normally disagreement only on the nature of this relationship which caused a break-up of the coalition of ministers, new elections and the formation of a new council with an almost identical programme. Early in 1972, however, the leader of the RDPC, Prince Saïd Mohammed Jaffar, publicly demanded independence from France, and in June he took over from Prince Saïd Ibrahim as President of the Council of Government. In September, the RDPC was joined in its demand for independence by the UCD, and one month later, in a deliberate move to precipitate elections, Prince Saïd Mohammed resigned and the Chamber of Deputies was dissolved. For the elections which followed on December 3rd, 1972, the RDPC, the UDC and the Comoros Progress Party (PEC) joined to form a "Union" standing for the principle of independence, and on the islands of Grande-Comore, Anjouan and Mohéli they soundly defeated the opposition of Prince Saïd Ibrahim's UMMA, which stood for independence only with the agreement of France. Only on Mayotte, which has traditionally supported the *status quo*, was the independence "Union" defeated, with an 80 per cent in favour of the Mayotte Movement.

It remains to be seen how the new Government will push forward with its demand for independence, and whether its new policy will either solve the acute economic problems, at the root of which is the semi-feudal land-tenure system, or reduce social tensions. The strategic importance to France of the islands, in particular Mayotte and Grande-Comore, where the French have military bases, will make France anxious to maintain the Comoros within its sphere of influence for as long as possible into the future.

Social tensions have been particularly evident among the largely African-derived peasant population. Young people have also been a source of unrest. In 1964 a youth club on Grande-Comore was suppressed as being marxist. In April 1968 there was a strike at Moroni High School and the violence which accompanied its termination resulted in the resignation of the entire Council of Government, excepting President Cheikh. On this occasion, and again in 1971, when there were demonstrations following the resignation of the Minister of Education, police and French *légionnaires* had to be brought in to maintain order.

The National Liberation Movement of the Comoros (MOLINACO), supported by the OAU, aims at complete independence and social revolution for the islands, and, although based in Dar es Salaam, it now has a political wing (the Comoros Progress Party—PEC) active in the islands. Following the change in policy of the main political parties, its rôle may be less significant in the future.

ECONOMY

The economy of the Comoros is in a disastrous state, and the poverty among the mass of the population is steadily worsening. Basic economic data for the Comoro Islands are still lacking, and an adequate long-term development plan has yet to be drawn up. Present short-term planning by the government accords greater priority to governmental institutions and tourism than to education and rural development.

There are no mineral resources, and any real development would have to begin with agriculture, which engages almost the whole population and provides all the territory's exports. But land hunger is acute. Some 35 per cent of the total area and most of the best land is owned by Europeans. In addition, land is let out to islanders in small plots, with no security of tenure, in return for services to the land-owners or foreign companies. The restraint on development of such feudalistic practices is not eased by peasant traditionalism in farming techniques. This conservatism is encouraged by aristocratic and religious leaders, reluctant to lessen their powers, and is reinforced by the lack of educational facilities.

The government has been encouraging the development of cash crops. However, such growth is unlikely to generate any real development because the chief beneficiaries are the foreign companies and landowners who transfer their profits to France, Madagascar, India, etc. and contribute little to local re-investment. There is thus a severe shortage of capital. Moreover, current expenditure, on which there is a large annual deficit, subsidized by France, accounts for nearly all the government revenues. A further difficulty arises from the fact that the Comoros' export crops—vanilla, jasmine, ylang-ylang and copra—compete directly with those of her closest neighbours in the Indian Ocean. Talks on co-operation have taken place between Madagascar, Mauritius, Réunion and the Comoros, but prospects for vanilla generally are darkened by growing competition, especially in the U.S.A., from a synthetic substitute.

Most of the Comoros' trade is with France, Madagascar, the U.S.A. and Federal Germany. The main imports are rice, most of which, together with sugar and sisal, is bought from Madagascar, and vehicles and petroleum products. Vanilla is the islands' main export, but in 1970 the amount sold abroad dropped from the previous year's total of 207 tons to 144 tons, with prospects for 1971 looking even worse. A further problem was the reduction of the U.S.A.'s annual quota for Comorian vanilla from 175 tons to 100 tons. Not surprisingly, there is a large trade deficit each year, and most of it is with France, which in 1969 supplied 48 per cent of the Comoros' imports, and with Madagascar, which supplied 40 per cent.

STATISTICS

Area: 2,171 sq. km. (838 sq. miles). **Population** (1970 estimates): 271,000 (including 1,500 Europeans); Moroni (capital) 15,000.

Agriculture (1971—metric tons): Cassava (manioc) 90,000, Rice 12,000, Sweet potatoes and yams 10,000, Copra 5,200, Maize 4,000, Vanilla 207, Cloves 268, Ylang-Ylang 64, Coffee 15; also sisal, perfumes, peppers and spices. In 1970 the coconut crop totalled 64 million nuts (FAO estimate).

Livestock (1970): Cattle 67,000, Goats 80,000, Sheep 6,000, Asses 3,000.

Fisheries: Annual catch: 2,000 metric tons approx.

Electric Energy (1968): 1.6 million kWh for public use.

Currency: 100 centimes=1 franc de la Communauté Financière Africaine. Exchange rates (December 1972): 1 franc CFA=2 French centimes; £1 sterling=593.625 francs CFA; U.S.$1=255.785 francs CFA; 1,000 francs CFA=£1.685=$3.91.

Budget (1971): 1,232,450,000 francs CFA; (1972): 1,498,436,000 francs CFA.

National Accounts (1968): Gross Domestic Product 7,100 million francs CFA (U.S. $111 per head).

Aid from France (local section of FIDES): (1971) 650m. francs CFA.

External Trade (1971): *Imports:* 2,834m. francs CFA (Rice, Petroleum products, Vehicles); *Exports:* 1,572m. francs CFA (Vanilla, Essences, Copra). Most trade is with France, the U.S.A., Federal Germany and Madagascar.

Roads (1971): 750 km. of officially classified roads, 1,970 motor vehicles.

International Shipping (1969): 132 vessels entered, 14,000 metric tons loaded, 45,000 metric tons unloaded.

Education (1969): Pre-primary 4 teachers, 51 pupils; Primary 235 teachers, 13,776 pupils; Secondary 60 teachers, 1,102 pupils.

THE GOVERNMENT

(October 1972)

High Commissioner: JACQUES MOURADIAN.

COUNCIL OF GOVERNMENT*

President and Minister of the Interior: Prince SAÏD MOHAMMED JAFFAR.

Minister of Health: Dr. M. HENRY.

Minister of Finances and the Economy: AHMED ABDOU.

Minister of Rural Development: MOHAMED TAKI.

Minister of Equipment: OMAR TAMOU.

Minister of Education: ALI MROUDJAE.

Minister of the Environment, Youth and Sport: MOHAMMED HASSANALY.

Minister of the Civil Service: ABDEREMANE SIDI.

* Resigned in October 1972. The subsequent elections were won by a "union" of parties led by Prince Saïd Mohammed Jaffar, but at the time this volume went to press, no new Council of Government had been appointed.

CHAMBER OF DEPUTIES

Following the dissolution of the Chamber of Deputies in October 1972, elections were held on December 3rd for which the RDPC, the UDC and the PEC (*see* Political Parties, below) joined to form a "union" standing for independence from France.

ELECTION DECEMBER 1972

	SEATS
"Union" parties in favour of independence from France	34
Parti du mouvement mahorais	5

POLITICAL PARTIES

Union démocratique des Comores (UDC) (*Comoros Democratic Union*): Moroni; supports independence from France.

Rassemblement démocratique du peuple comorien (RDPC) (*Comorian People's Democratic Rally*): Moroni; supports independence from France; Leader Prince SAÏD MOHAMMED JAFFAR.

Parti du mouvement mahorais (*Mayotte Movement Party*): Dzaoudzi; advocates the territory's becoming a French *département*.

Parti du Peuple (UMMA) (*People's Party*): Moroni; supports the *status quo*, with independence only with the agreement of France; Leader Prince SAÏD IBRAHIM.

Parti socialiste comorien (PASOCO) (*Comorian Socialist Party*): Moroni.

MOLINACO (*National Liberation Movement of the Comoros*): based in Dar es Salaam, with a political wing (PEC) active in the Comoros.

JUDICIAL SYSTEM

Superior Court of Appeal at Moroni; Courts of First Instance at Moroni, Mamoutzou and Mutsamudu; also 16 Qadi Courts (Muslim Law).

RELIGION

The majority of the population are Muslims.

RADIO

Comores-Inter: Office de Radiodiffusion-Télévision Française, B.P. 250, Moroni (Grande-Comore); Dir.-Gen. A. GERBI.

In 1970 there were 24,000 radio receivers.

FINANCE

Banque de Madagascar et des Comores: 23 ave. Matignon, Paris; Moroni (Grande-Comore).

TRADE

Chamber of Commerce: Moroni (Grande-Comore); Pres. M. FAVETTO.

TRANSPORT

There are approximately 750 km. of roads serviceable throughout the year; shipping services run to Madagascar from Moroni.

CIVIL AVIATION

Air Comores: B.P. 81, Moroni; services to Anjouan, Mayotte, Mohéli, and Dar es Salaam.

Foreign Airlines: Air France, Air Madagascar.

TOURISM

Alliance Touristique de l'Océan Indien: Moroni; Pres. MOHAMMED DAHALANI.

RESEARCH INSTITUTE

Institut de Recherches Agronomiques Tropicales et des Cultures Vivrières (IRAT): B.P. 146, Moroni, Grande-Comore; stations at Mutsamudu (Anjouan) and Coconi; Dir. M. LARCHER.

SELECT BIBLIOGRAPHY

BOURDE, ANDRÉ. "The Comoro Islands: problems of a microcosm", *Journal of Modern African Studies*, 3, 91–102, 1965.

Congo (Brazzaville)

PHYSICAL AND SOCIAL GEOGRAPHY*

David Hilling

POPULATION

Over 600 miles of the eastern boundary of the People's Republic of the Congo is provided by the Congo River, and the equator crosses the northern part of the country. The area of 132,000 sq. miles supports a population of 7 persons per sq. mile. Nearly 70 per cent of the population are dependent on agriculture, mainly of the bush-fallowing type, but this is supplemented where possible by fishing, hunting and gathering. The main ethnic groups are the Vili on the coast, the Kongo centred on Brazzaville, and the Téké, M'Bochi and Sanga of the plateaux in the centre and north of the country. Nearly 30 per cent of the total population are concentrated in the capital, Brazzaville (200,000), the main port of Point-Noire (100,000), and the railway towns of Jacob (15,000) and Dolisie (20,000).

PHYSICAL FEATURES AND RESOURCES

The immediate coastal zone is sandy in the north, more swampy south of Kouilou, and in the neighbourhood of Pointe-Indienne yields small amounts of petroleum. A narrow coastal plain does not rise above 300 ft., and the cool coastal waters modify the climate, giving low rainfall and a grassland vegetation. Rising abruptly from the coastal plain are the high-rainfall forested ridges of the Mayombé Range, parallel to the coast and rising to a height of 2,600 ft., in which gorges cut by rivers such as the Kouilou provide potential hydroelectric power sites. At Hollé, close to the Congo-Ocean Railway and at the western foot of the range, are considerable phosphate deposits, which are now being exploited. Mayombé also provides the important export commodity, timber, of which the main commercial species are *okoumé* and *limba*.

Eastwards the Niari valley has lower elevation, soils that are good by tropical African standards and a grassland vegetation which makes agricultural development easier. A variety of agricultural products such as groundnuts, maize, vegetables, palm oil, coffee, cocoa, sugar and tobacco, are obtained from large plantations, European farms, new colonies of African farmers and also peasant holdings. These products provide the support for a more concentrated rural population and the basis for some industrial development.

A further forested mountainous region, the Chaillu Massif, is the Congo basin's western watershed, and this gives way north-eastwards to a series of drier plateaux, the somewhat negative Batéké region and, east of the Likoula river, a zone of Congo riverine land. Here are numerous water courses, with seasonal inundation, and dense forest vegetation, which supports some production of forest products, although the full potential has yet to be realized.

* See map on p. 202.

RECENT HISTORY*

Robert Cornevin†

The country was governed under nine constitutional laws, passed between November 1958 and November 1959, until a new constitution conferring excessive presidential powers, was introduced in March 1961. Abbé Fulbert Youlou, the victor in the 1959 elections, became the country's first president.

Youlou's régime exacerbated tribal tensions. His markedly pro-western policies and support for Tshombe's secessionist régime in Katanga are also said to have been unpopular in the country.

THE "TROIS GLORIEUSES JOURNÉES"

Tension was increased in August 1963 with a draft scheme to merge opposition parties into a one-party system and to make the trade unions toe the line. During this month, when thousands of university and high school students were on vacation, mass demonstrations in Brazzaville, soon also involving large numbers of unemployed, were incited by the trade unions. The arrest of trade union leaders on August 13th provoked a general strike in Brazzaville, Pointe-Noire and Dolisie during which the arrested trade unionists were freed by force. The government proclaimed a state of emergency, but, after secret dealings, President Youlou resigned on the 15th, the army guaranteeing to maintain order while a provisional government was formed.

The 1963 Constitution, partly parliamentary and partly presidential, established a two-man executive, the President of the Republic and the Prime Minister. The new President, Alphonse Massamba-Débat, was a political figure, unlike the Prime Minister, Pascal Lissouba, a doctor of science and an agricultural expert. This government was evidence of the first major departure from colonial policy in central Africa and of an increasingly marked swing towards revolutionary paths. In 1964 the National Revolutionary Movement (MNR) was formed as the sole party declaring itself for Marxism-Leninism and the non-capitalist path of development. Its youth wing, the *Jeunesse du Mouvement National de la Révolution* (JMNR), developed into a para-military force and wielded growing power. State planning was introduced with the first five-year plan (1964–68) and a state sector was built up in industry, trade and agriculture.

On May 6th, 1966, Ambroise Noumazalay, the First Secretary of the MNR replaced Pascal Lissouba at the head of the government. After the failure of an attempted military *coup* in June 1966, the Congo experienced a long period of quiet. However, the growing influence of the JMNR and the closely-linked *Défense Civile* or "people's militia", led by

Cuban and Chinese instructors, resulted in a confrontation with the army in August-September 1968, in which the army triumphed. At the end of that year the army commander-in-chief, Marien Ngouabi, took over as head of state.

Successive Congolese governments since independence have had to face a variety of (often intertwined) forces: tribal tensions—between the Kouyou and M'bochi in the north, the southern towns, and the Lari and Kongo of the centre—political and idealogical dissension and rivalry between the army and the civil powers.

A power struggle between Massamba-Débat's moderates, unfavourable to radical change, and pro-communist extremists backed by the JMNR, had developed. In January 1968, Massamba-Débat dismissed Noumazalay and other conspicuously pro-communist ministers and took over the prime ministership himself in an apparent attempt to curb pro-communist elements. His action followed the revelation that Chinese in the country were training dissidents from neighbouring countries in guerrilla warfare.

THE RISE OF NGOUABI

In May the extreme left counter-attacked after announcing that an "imperialist plot", involving the landing of foreign mercenaries, had been foiled. On July 22nd the President offered his resignation if anyone more competent was prepared to assume the leadership. No volunteers were forthcoming, and on August 1st the President dissolved the National Assembly and the MNR Political Bureau, and ordered a number of arrests, including that of Ngouabi, allegedly to forestall a left-wing plot.

As in the 1966 *coup* attempt, tribal support for Ngouabi within the army (in 1966 his demotion had sparked the mutiny), and its growing conflict with the JMNR para-military groups, drew the army into the political battle. On this occasion, however, it successfully seized power (August 2nd). Although the President was recalled to office two days later, effective power rested with a supreme National Council of the Revolution. The President agreed that the JMNR be disarmed and the "people's militia" merged with the army. But clashes between the army and the JMNR continued and on September 4th President Massamba-Débat resigned.

The régime of President Ngouabi has continued the socialist policies of his predecessor. The political forms of a communist state have been adopted. A vanguard party, *Parti congolais du travail* (PCT), based on Marxist-Leninist theory and "democratic centralism" succeeded the MNR in December 1969. A new constitution was introduced, under which the party President, elected every five years, is also

---

* For the period before independence *see* Central African Republic Recent History, p. 213.

† For the 1973 edition, revisions have been made to this article by the Editor.

President of the State, newly designated the "People's Republic of the Congo". The party exercises the real power, through its Political Bureau and Central Committee.

On March 23rd 1970 an alleged invasion plot, supported by 30 members of the *gendarmerie*, was swiftly defeated. As a result an Extraordinary Congress of the PCT dissolved the *gendarmerie* and resurrected the "peoples' militia" as an adjunct to the army. The new militia was to be organized on Chinese lines as a security arm of the party, politically and ideologically trained "to ensure with fierce jealousy the fruits of the revolution". The youth movement was also revived at the congress and renamed the *Union de la Jeunesse Socialiste du Congo*. The aim of these changes was to bring the two organizations under effective party control.

Nonetheless, there were politically far-reaching student demonstrations against the government in 1971, culminating in a strike (young people comprise roughly half the population of Congo-Brazzaville and have traditionally been politically influential; President Ngouabi regarded their actions as constituting a hidden political opposition). In response the President promised extensive changes in party and government personnel. Several ministries were abolished and ministers dismissed, including Ange Diawara, Vice-President for the first few months of Ngouabi's régime, the Vice-President, Major Alfred Raoul, and Auxence Iekonga, the Foreign Minister. The Political Bureau of the PCT was cut from nine members to five (among the casualties was the First

Secretary, Claude-Ernest Ndalla) and about 50 members of the Central Committee were expelled.

Ndalla and Diawara had been closely identified with the JMNR and the associated *Défense Civile*, the Chinese trained people's militia, and their removal was regarded as a set-back for the extreme left. Both men were implicated in unsuccessful attempts to overthrow the Ngouabi government on February 22nd and May 17th 1972, and Diawara has been sentenced to death *in absentia*. Although the relatively moderate Major Raoul was among the accused plotters, the majority were extremist militant elements, who had been closely associated with overthrowing the Massamba-Débat régime in August.

The defeat of the two coup attempts and the consequent eclipse of the extreme left are unlikely to herald any fundamental deviation from Brazzaville's chosen course of political development. President Ngouabi has denied that Congo-Brazzaville has moved to the right and has re-affirmed his country's adherence to Marxist-Leninist principles.

State control has been extended over the economy. Externally, links with Cuba, China, the Soviet Union and other communist states have been maintained. The country remains, however, a member of the Franc Zone and an associate of the European Economic Community. It left the Afro-Malagasy Common Organization (OCAM) in 1972, but still relies on its economic links with France and with bodies such as the Central African Economic and Customs Union (UDEAC).

ECONOMY

Peter Robson*

INTRODUCTION

In recent years the socialist-oriented Congolese economy has undergone a difficult period of re-adjustment. Initially this was because of the dissolution of the federation of French Equatorial Africa, of which it had been the administrative centre. Later, after 1966, the entry of Cameroon into the area's customs union and related developments in the transport field to some extent altered the economic centre of gravity in the region. The still more recent loosening of the economic links among the member countries has also had the effect of rendering the Congo's position and prospects in the field of manufacture and commerce less favourable than in the past.

For several years the Goverment pursued a systematic policy of state participation in productive enterprise, but allowed the private sector continued activity especially in mining, forestry and transport. However, further moves to the left, notably following the 1969 assassination attempt on Ngouabi, have resulted in the present policy of "scientific socialism". All public services and transport systems have been nationalized and more government control introduced generally. Private investment is not encouraged except by large concerns such as oil companies. By state intervention an attempt is being made to control rising prices and to remedy the considerable yearly trade deficit. Since October 1971 all articles for sale whether of local or foreign origin, have been subject to official scrutiny, designed to keep prices in line with production costs, and to tax; since September 1972 all foreigners who wish to trade or do business must not only settle in the country, but must also pay for a special identity card.

Partly as a result of Brazzaville's former position as the capital of French Equatorial Africa, and partly because the Congo and Oubangui Rivers have long provided the main access to the Central African Republic and Chad, the Congo's economic structure is rather different from that of most countries of comparable levels of economic development. The service and administration sectors continue to be large but now account for approximately half the Gross Domestic Product, as opposed to nearly three-fifths in 1968. About 60 per cent of the population (estimated at nearly one million in 1971 and with a two per cent annual growth rate) is engaged in agriculture and forestry. The primary sector as a whole now accounts for over 35 per cent of G.D.P., compared to under 25 per cent in 1968, and although more than half of this is subsistence production, industrial agriculture is increasing. The manufacturing industry developed relatively well at an early stage, partly to serve the markets of the Central African Republic and

* For the 1973 edition, revisions have been made to this article by the Editor.

Chad. Industry continues to expand and accounts for some 15 per cent of G.D.P.

The country participates with Cameroon, the Central African Republic and Gabon in the Central African Customs and Economic Union (UDEAC). It shares with those countries a common central bank, the Central Bank of Equatorial African States and Cameroon (BCEAEC), and a common currency, the CFA franc issued by that bank. The CFA franc is freely convertible into French francs.

Economic growth during the past few years has been fairly satisfactory, though not spectacular, bearing in mind the extremely high rate of investment which has been undertaken. Over the last few years the rate of increase of the G.D.P. in current prices has been nearly 8 per cent. Allowing for the price increase which has taken place this probably means that the real rate of increase has been of the order of 3–4 per cent.

AGRICULTURE AND FORESTRY

With the exception of palm products, sugar and tobacco, which are grown on modern plantations, particularly in the Niari valley, most agricultural crops are grown by families on small farms. Government policy has aimed at increasing both productivity and acreage under cultivation, and to these ends it has embarked upon an ambitious agricultural extension programme. Despite an initial lack of success, due largely to the continued drift of labour from farms to urban areas, agricultural expansion has progressed considerably during the last three years. Nevertheless, in 1971 there were food shortages, which necessitated large rice imports and led to "operation manioc" by which it is hoped to make the country self-sufficient in manioc, its staple food crop; three farms of 7,500 acres were organized. Shortly afterwards the Congo's first State Farm (about 1,500 acres) was opened near Brazzaville by Chinese technicians.

The most important export crops are sugar cane and tobacco. Production of sugar cane tripled between 1965 and 1968 to over a million tons; it fell in 1970, when put under the control of the nationalized *Société Industriale et Agricole du Congo*, but reached a million tons again in 1971. With the largest capacity of the group, the Congo benefited from the OCAM sugar agreement of 1966, which afforded more than the world market price. Until recently both sugar and tobacco have been exported almost wholly to the other countries of UDEAC.

Other export crops grown include cocoa, coffee, groundnuts and palms. The quality of Congolese cocoa has recently been improved and production, which stood at 1,937 tons in 1971, will be further increased by an expected 3,000 to 4,000 tons per annum from a new project at Sangha. On the other hand coffee production has remained level at about 2,000 tons per annum for some time and half of this is too poor to be marketable. Groundnut production has also remained static (about 3,500 to 4,000 tons per annum), but palm groves are being extended to improve the already good production rate of palm oil. All agricultural products other than sugar are marketed by the *Office national de commercialisation des produits agricoles*, which processes, markets and transports them and has largely replaced long-standing European enterprises. The Rural Production Support Fund acts as a price stabilization board for export crops. Its deficits have been covered chiefly by grants from France.

Animal husbandry has developed slowly because of forest and tsetse fly, and the country is not self-sufficient in meat and dairy products, although numbers of livestock are increasing. Grants from EDF and PAM have enabled stock-rearing farms to be set up, and a project for the conversion of 80,000 hectares of the Niari Valley to pastureland is under consideration. Fishing is not well developed but is carried out commercially in a small way, especially for Tunny.

Forestry

Forests cover about half the country's total area and are a major natural resource. Exploitation began at the coast and has penetrated inland following the line of the Congo-Océan railway. There is further activity in the Congo basin from where rough timber is floated out. Other areas have not yet been opened up. Forestry is a major economic activity and timber by far the Congo's most important export. In 1970 the value of these exports fell, and it was decided to rationalize the industry, in particular by processing more wood before export and by improving transport facilities. In February 1971, 800 square kilometres of the main timber areas were nationalized and a new policy announced: concessions would be granted only to firms that promised capital investment, all exported timber would be taxed and this revenue used for reaforestation, forestry activities and the *Société nationale de transformation du bois* would be supervised directly by the Ministry of Forests and Waters; the nationalized *Office congolaise de l'okoumé* was set up with a monopoly over commerce in *okoumé* to replace the Gabon-Congo joint office. In addition the *Centre technique forestier tropical*, set up in 1970, was encouraged to undertake further research, and with UN help a training centre was set up at Mossendjo.

There were already 15 saw mills by 1971, and more are planned, together with processing plants for veneers and plywood, a paper mill, and in the long-term a cellulose factory. Three new complexes are under way, one to be financed by Romania. Forest resources in the north are being examined especially in the Sangha area and roads to open up the area are planned. The timber port opened at Pointe Noire in November 1971, and financed largely by French aid, allows a 40 per cent increase in timber exported, though some of this comes from the Central African Republic and south-east Cameroon. The most significant woods exploited are *okoumé* (which accounts for half the total timber exports) *limba* and mahogany.

After remaining stable at around 650,000 cubic metres since 1966, production rose in 1971 to a record 820,000 cubic metres.

MINING, MANUFACTURE, POWER AND TRANSPORTATION

Until the present time, mining has been of little significance in the Congo, and in 1969 mineral exports accounted for less than 5 per cent of total exports. Recently rich deposits of potassium chloride have been discovered at Holle, near Pointe-Noire. Facilities have been built to mine, refine, and transport the potassium to the Atlantic coast, and a pier to accommodate large bulk-carrying ships has been constructed near Pointe-Noire. The total cost of this project was 20,000 million francs CFA and it alone accounted for one-third of total investment over the period 1964–68. The project has been beset with difficulties but production for the first seven months of 1971, when the year's target was 430,000 tons, reached 225,000 tons. Export has now begun and reserves are thought to be of about three million tons.

Deposits of crude petroleum at Pointe Indienne have now been almost exhausted, but in 1969 Elf-Congo discovered a large off-shore oil field near Pointe Noire, "Emeraude Marine". Exploitation began in 1970 and by the end of 1972 production should have reached two million tons a year. While in the past petroleum has been exported in its crude state, the vastly increased rate of production (from about 70,000 tons in 1969 to 430,000 tons in 1971) has led to plans for the building of a refinery. Natural gas deposits are exploited at Pointe Indienne and produced 14,800,000 cubic metres in 1971. Lead, zinc, tin and copper are produced in small quantities and deposits of high-grade iron ore, phosphate and bauxite are known. Prospecting continues with foreign technical assistance. All mines are state-owned and the state must have at least a 20 per cent share in all mining concerns.

Manufacturing and Power

Manufacturing is relatively well developed in the Congo; among French-speaking African countries its relative contribution to the G.D.P. is higher only in Senegal, Ivory Coast and Cameroon. Production is concerned mainly with the processing of agricultural and forest products. Most of the industry is in Brazzaville, Pointe-Noire and the Niari valley. There are two breweries, three soft drink bottling works, oil and flour mills, two sugar factories, two fish-curing plants and a cigarette factory. Other enterprises include a shoe factory (BATA), soap, perfumes, glass, matches, gramophone records, metal processing and construction, sandbricks, furniture and paints.

Recent developments include the establishment of a state-owned cement factory, which was completed in 1968 and has a production capacity of 80,000 tons a year, and the state-owned textile complex at Kinsouli. The latter, established with Chinese technical assistance, involves an investment of 1,500 million francs CFA, and has a production capacity of nearly four million yards a year. It is to be enlarged to include a clothing section and, in the longer term, a synthetic textiles unit will be integrated into the complex. A shipyard (CHACONA), set up at a cost of 312 million francs CFA and financed mainly by China, launched its first ship in 1972.

Production and distribution of electricity has been in the hands of a state-owned corporation since 1967. Its total capacity is 29,620 kWh, and in 1970 production was 68 million kWh. Most output comes from the hydro-electric plant at Djoué and the diesel power station at Pointe Noire, and there are other, smaller diesel power stations. The projected Kouilou Dam is intended to provide hydro-electric power for a large industrial complex to be built nearby, and a further hydro-electric plant is planned on the Bouenza, south of Brazzaville, to be funded by China and with an initial capacity of 70,000 to 80,000 kWh.

Transportation

Congo plays an important role in the transequatorial transport system (until recently operated on an interstate basis) which links Chad and the Central African Republic with the Atlantic coast; all of the rail and much of the river portion of the system is located in the Congo. Other transport facilities and especially the internal road network are little developed owing to great distances and dense equatorial forest. The *Agence transcongolaise des communications* plans to increase the capacity of the Congo-Océan railway by 40 per cent, relying mainly on French aid, and to construct a river port at Ouessa on the Sangha. In addition a major project is under consideration to open up the north by a "dorsal spine", from Ouesso to Fort Rousset and Brazzaville, crossed by another route between Belinga (Gabon) and Bangui (Central African Republic). In general, poor communications constitute a major obstacle to economic development.

DEVELOPMENT PLANNING

The Congo's first development plan (*Plan intérimaire congolais*) covered the five-year period 1964–68. It envisaged a total expenditure of 50,700 million francs CFA (excluding the agro-industrial complex of SOSUNIARI*) and an annual investment rate equivalent to about 30 per cent of the G.N.P. Of this, the largest share, 40 per cent, was to be allocated to industrial production, some 15 per cent to primary production, about one-fifth to economic infrastructure and nearly a quarter to social infrastructure. It was anticipated that the aggregate G.D.P. would rise from 25,500 million francs CFA at the commencement of the plan period, to 38,700 million francs CFA at its termination, a rate of growth of 8½ per cent. The G.D.P. per head was estimated to increase from 32,000 francs CFA (£48) to 45,000 francs CFA (£67).

Of the public investment, which accounted for 60 per cent of planned expenditure, about a quarter was to be financed from domestic sources, mainly the

budget, and the balance was to be sought from foreign sources, particularly FAC, EDF, the World Bank and the CCCE. Private sector investment was also expected to come mainly from foreign sources.

An important aim of the plan was to reduce the economic and social inequalities existing between the urban centres and the rest of the country in the hope of discouraging urbanization, which of late has become a major problem. As to production goals, a substantial increase in output was projected for the modern and traditional parts of the agricultural sector, including a 60 per cent increase in the output of groundnuts, rice and palm kernels, an 80 per cent increase in the production of cocoa and a 130 per cent increase in the production of meat. A large expansion was envisaged also for the industrial sector. In the field of infrastructure, feeder roads were to be improved and more hospitals, technical and agricultural schools were to be set up.

Mainly because of shortfalls in funds but partly because of delays in project preparation and execution, the first plan period was extended until 1970. At the same time, planned expenditures for certain industrial projects were increased. In its agricultural aspects the plan has proved a failure and few of the targets have been attained. A substantial growth rate for agriculture is also projected in the 1970–75 development plan, but even if this is attained, the value of marketed agricultural output will remain low.

TRADE, AID AND THE BALANCE OF PAYMENTS

In recent years total registered exports† have expanded considerably, although provisional figures show a drop in 1970. Over the period 1960 to 1968 they increased from 4,400 million francs CFA to 8,400 million francs CFA. The main source of this growth has been timber exports, which accounted for 75 per cent of registered exports in 1968. Another major contribution to export growth in the early sixties was export of manufactures to other countries of the customs union, but these exports have not increased since 1964 while imports almost doubled between 1967 and 1969 to 1,329 million francs CFA. Federal Germany, Netherlands and the United Kingdom have become the Congo's most important trade partners owing partly to the growth of diamond re-exports. France continues to be a significant market and also by far the largest supplier of imports, accounting for over 50 per cent of total imports in 1969.

The Congo has a chronic visible trade deficit with countries outside UDEAC. To an extent this is offset by a favourable visible balance in trade with other members of the customs union and by invisible earnings with the same countries for transport and distributive services. In 1968 the registered trade

---

* This involves sugar plantations, a sugar factory, a paper factory utilizing *bagasse*, an animal feed factory, a distillery for industrial alcohol, and sisal plantations.

---

† These figures exclude diamond exports (3,800 million in 1968) which are re-exports of stones imported clandestinely, and which do not figure in the import statistics. Official statistics also take no account of bilateral barter deals with communist countries.

deficit (excluding diamonds) was 12,200 million francs CFA. About 2,800 million francs worth of goods, mainly manufactures, was sold to other members of the customs union in 1968, partly offset by imports from the same source amounting to 700 million francs CFA. The overall deficit is thus large, and indeed, it has regularly exceeded total exports.

Congo's huge trade deficits are added to by substantial net private transfer payments. The aggregate deficit has been financed partly by an inflow of grants and official loans and there has also been a sizeable net inflow of private long-term capital in recent years, to finance mining and other projects. The remaining deficit has been offset by Congo's favourable balance on services, derived in particular from earnings in respect of transport services provided to inland African countries. For the year 1968–69 the overall balance of payments registered a surplus, larger than in the previous year, and external reserves improved.

In recent years the Congo has received much aid. In the first place, communist countries have provided aid, frequently in the form of goods for sale. Aid from the west to the Congo has been the highest relative to the G.D.P. of any country in francophone Africa— over 16 per cent of G.D.P. for 1966–68—and amongst the highest in absolute terms. In the light of this, any major expansion of aid from the west in the foreseeable future seems improbable. Links with China are particularly close and China continues to give important technical and financial assistance, as does the U.S.S.R. and also France, despite the nationalization of French private interests.

PROBLEMS AND PROSPECTS

Despite its adjustment problems and chequered political history, and the uneasy balance between revolutionary fervour and private enterprise, the recent economic growth of the Congo has not been unsatisfactory, mainly because of the favourable impact of a few large-scale projects upon the economy. However, future prospects within the planned socialist framework now seem good, so long as political stability can be maintained.

An attempt is being made to reduce the high level of expenditure, particularly upon administrative services, which renders any contribution to development finance difficult despite high tax burdens. The management of institutions in the expanded public sector gives rise to much concern—many companies are running at a loss and control mechanisms are recognized to be ineffective—both in respect of state farms and in respect of industrial projects.

Export earnings should continue to improve, partly as a result of potash sales, and help to alleviate the foreign exchange shortage. Urbanization is likely to continue to be a problem, even if agricultural improvement plans are effective—if present trends continue, one-half of the population will live in urban areas by 1980.

Plans have been drawn up for many new industrial projects, but in many instances the outlook is not promising, since the domestic market itself is far too small to support much industry except at high cost, and within UDEAC there is strong competition for industries, in particular from Cameroon. This competition will be enhanced by changes in progress in the region's system of inland transportation.

If industrialization cannot support the required expansion, renewed efforts will be called for in other directions. With the improvement in the overseas market for tropical woods a further development of forest products may afford some opportunities. Apart from this, there is evidently a need to improve agriculture, and to develop justifiable agriculturally based industries. With large-scale foreign aid, progress in these fields should be possible.

STATISTICAL SURVEY

Area: 342,000 sq. km. (132,000 sq. miles).

Population (1971 UN estimate): 958,000. Principal towns (1971): Brazzaville 200,000; Pointe-Noire 100,000, Dolisie 20,000, Jacob 15,000. Main ethnic groups: Kongo 350,000, Téké 150,000, M'Bochi 95,000.

AGRICULTURE

COMMERCIAL PRODUCE
(metric tons)

	1968	1969	1970	1971
Shelled Groundnuts . .	n.a.	3,024.0	1,873.2	1,608.4
Unshelled Groundnuts . .	3,900	2,290.8	1,362.0	1,065.9
Cocoa	1,285	1,491.6	723.6	1,937.5
Coffee	1,755	1,380.0	2,217.7	896.3
Maize	n.a.	61.2	574.8	903.2
Paddy	1,108	2,586.0	3,147.6	745.4
Palm Fruits . . .	2,893	1,881.6	2,434.8	2,521.3
Tobacco . . .	740	314.4	456.0	351.9
Palm Nuts . . .	n.a.	2,218.8	3,301.2	1,681.0

Sugar Cane (1969/70—total harvest): 1,054,000 metric tons.

Livestock (1971): Cattle 42,000; Sheep and Goats 116,000; Pigs 28,000.

OTHER PRODUCTION
(metric tons)

	1968	1969	1970	1971
Fisheries:				
Various Fish . . .	10,000	1,720	3,418	6,891
Tunny	21,600	9,109	11,521	13,351
Forestry:				
Okoumé	n.a.	200,970	193,070	n.a.
Mining:				
Gold (kg.)	157	121	83	95
Lead and Zinc . . .	4,100	12,380	n.a.	n.a.
Copper	2,610	198	n.a.	2,070
Crude Oil . . .	43,000	24,215	18,943	14,433
Potassium . . .	n.a.	70,000	200,000	430,000
Industry:				
Palm Oil . . .	2,765	308	406	n.a.
Cane Sugar . . .	102,000	51,800	53,362	16,252
Beer ('000 hectolitres) .	n.a.	76	66	96
Soap	n.a.	4,184	4,522	4,746
Tobacco	n.a.	974	989	904

FINANCE

100 centimes = 1 franc de la Communauté Financière Africaine.
Coins: 1, 2, 5, 10 and 25 francs CFA.
Notes: 5, 10, 50, 100, 500, 1,000, 5,000 and 10,000 francs CFA.
Exchange rates (December 1972): 1 franc CFA = 2 French centimes;
£1 sterling = 593.625 francs CFA; U.S. $1 = 255.785 francs CFA;
1,000 francs CFA = £1.685 = $3.91.

BUDGET

1970: Balanced at 18,000m. francs CFA.
1971: Balanced at 19,555m. francs CFA.
1972: Balanced at 21,853m. francs CFA.

EXTERNAL TRADE*

(million francs CFA)

	1967	1968	1969	1970
Imports	20,231	20,605	20,291	15,910
Exports†	11,730	12,189	11,384	8,564

* Excluding trade with other countries in UDEAC and, prior to 1969, Chad.

† Including re-exports of industrial diamonds (worth 810 million francs CFA in 1970) originating in Zaire, but not included under imports.

COMMODITIES

IMPORTS	1967	1968	1969	EXPORTS	1967	1968	1969
Fish	662	740	849	Raw Sugar	804	91	209
Cereals	584	645	752	Refined Sugar	498	189	648
Other Food	802	843	943	Molasses	171	54	66
Alcoholic Beverages	511	503	603	Coffee	138	143	165
Petroleum Products	1,187	595	636	Cocoa Beans	133	205	240
Chemicals	1,358	1,440	1,647	Beverages and Tobacco	50	40	180
Paper and Paperboard	456	529	463	Palm Nuts and Kernels	159	151	93
Woven Cotton Fabrics	1,007	863	968	Saw and Veneer Logs	4,082	4,960	5,651
Iron and Steel	1,273	1,093	800	Timber	86	170	257
Metal Structures and Parts	625	1,017	49	Industrial Diamonds*	3,944	3,834	1,682
Machinery (non-electric)	2,728	3,529	2,732	Crude Petroleum	89	152	99
Electrical Machinery	1,300	1,581	1,257	Chemicals	2	6	282
Railway Vehicles	540	293	1,457	Veneer Sheets	786	1,157	1,286
Road Motor Vehicles	1,501	1,685	1,837	Non-electric Machinery	30	234	70
Ships and Boats	525	87	214				
Clothing	530	580	610				

* Re-exports of stones imported clandestinely and not included in import statistics.

PRINCIPAL COUNTRIES

IMPORTS	1967	1968	1969	EXPORTS	1967	1968	1969
Belgium and Luxembourg	395	521	437	Belgium and Luxembourg	466	1,452	960
China (People's Republic)	622	422	393	France	1,731	1,286	1,576
France	10,927	11,946	11,573	Federal Germany	2,163	2,641	1,981
Federal Germany	2,533	1,987	1,701	Israel	601	588	611
Italy	683	459	621	Italy	246	372	555
Japan	243	357	434	Ivory Coast	46	180	262
Mauritania	455	507	524	Netherlands	2,410	1,997	1,646
Netherlands	714	727	765	South Africa	379	592	698
Netherlands Antilles	242	64	61	Spain	46	64	381
United Kingdom	417	632	433	United Kingdom	1,926	1,507	684
U.S.S.R.	551	306	90	U.S.A.	208	294	213
U.S.A.	830	1,073	1,375	Zaire	577	171	28

TRANSPORT

(freight in metric tons)

	1969	1970	1971
Railways:			
Passengers	1,221,600	1,256,400	1,007,300
Freight	1,483,200	1,608,000	1,507,200
Sea Transport:			
Ships (arrived and departed)	2,256	2,052	2,139
Passengers arrived	1,610	239	311
Freight loaded	1,323,200	2,354,400	2,757,200
Freight unloaded	506,400	518,400	581,500
River Transport:			
Freight loaded	177,737	223,034	217,103
Freight unloaded	185,639	214,480	224,444
Air Transport:			
Planes (arrived and departed)	7,400	8,955	n.a.
Passengers (arrived and departed)	99,880	131,008	110,537
Freight loaded	3,246	3,407 ⎫	10,693
Freight unloaded	5,887	6,825 ⎭	
Road Traffic:			
Private Vehicles	1,983	1,677	1,293
Trade Vehicles	514	398	461

EDUCATION

(1971–72)

	NUMBER OF SCHOOLS	NUMBER OF PUPILS	NUMBER OF TEACHERS
Primary	920	260,534	3,800
Secondary	60	37,430	672
Technical	32	4,086	n.a.

A National University was opened in 1971 with 1,436 students.
85.5 per cent of the population receives or has received schooling.

Source: Direction du Service National de la Statistique, B.P. 2031, Brazzaville.

THE CONSTITUTION

(Promulgated on January 3rd, 1970.)

PROMULGATION OF THE CONSTITUTION

The Chairman of the Central Committee of the Congolese Workers' Party (PCT), President of the Republic, Chief of State, Chairman of the Council of State.

Whereas, the Act of August 14th, 1968, establishing the National Council of the Revolution;

Whereas, the Fundamental Act of August 14th, 1968, amending the Constitution of December 8th, 1963, of the Republic of the Congo;

Whereas, the Act No. 13 of the National Council of the Revolution, dated December 28th, 1969, summoning the party congress;

Whereas, Act No. 14 of the National Council of the Revolution, dated December 30th, 1969, establishing the closing of this congress;

Whereas, the work of the constituent congress of the Congolese Workers' Party held at Brazzaville, December 28th–30th, 1969;

Whereas, the statutes of the Congolese Workers' Party and the Constitution of the Republic of the Congo, adopted December 30th, 1969, by the above-mentioned constituent congress;

Whereas, the powers conferred by said statutes upon the Chairman of the Congolese Workers' Party and the powers conferred by the Constitution of December 30th, 1969, upon the President of the Republic, Chief of State, and President of the Council of State;

Hereby orders:

Article 1. The Constitution of the People's Republic of the Congo adopted on December 30th, 1969, by the constituent congress of the Congolese Workers' Party, is hereby promulgated.

Article 2. The Constitution of the People's Republic of the Congo, attached to this ordinance, shall be published in the *Journal officiel de la République.*

Constitution of the People's Republic of the Congo

The ultimate purpose of the class struggle is the seizure of power. When the proletariat confronts the bourgeoisie, it must have the heart to seize power so as to establish the dictatorship of the proletariat. It is through this power that it will be able to organize the new society; it is through the dictatorship of the proletariat that the proletariat will be able to crush the other classes and stop the exploitation of man by man.

The birth of a vanguard party, a party of the proletariat, could not possibly fit in with the archaic structures of the colonial state.

Since the PCT represents a victory of the Congolese proletariat, it was quite normal that a new state should be born, along with the popular institutions which will tend to put an end to the long night of domination.

FIRST PART. FUNDAMENTAL PRINCIPLES

Title I. The People's Republic of the Congo

1. The Congo, a sovereign and independent state, is a people's republic, one, indivisible, and secular, in which all power springs from the people and belongs to the people.

2. Sovereignty resides in the people and all public powers spring from the people through a single people's party, the PCT, whose organization is spelled out in its statutes.

3. Outside the party the popular masses exert power by means of the representative organs of state power, consisting of the people's councils. These bodies are freely elected by the people and range from the people's councils of the communes, via the people's councils of the districts, all the way to the people's councils of the regions.

4. All representative agencies of state power are elected by the citizens through direct, equal, secret universal suffrage. In all agencies of the state power the representatives of the people are responsible to the party agencies. All acts of government agencies, of the administration, and of the courts must be based on the law.

5. The slogan of the People's Republic of Congo is: WORK—DEMOCRACY—PEACE. Its basic principle is the government of the people, by the people, and for the people. Its flag has a rectangular shape, it is a lively red, and at the top, to the left of the flag pole, it has an insignia representing two green palms crossed along their bottom, in whose middle there are represented a crossed sickle and hammer in golden yellow, all of this surrounded by a golden yellow, five-pointed star. National anthem: *Les Trois Glorieuses.* The seal of state and the arms of the Republic are spelled out by law.

Title II. Public Liberties and the Freedoms of the Human Personality

6. The human person is sacred. The state has the obligation to respect and protect it. Everyone has the right to free development of his personality, amid respect for the rights of others and for public order. The liberty of the human person is inviolable. No one can be charged, arrested, or detained except in cases determined by the law promulgated here prior to the infraction which this law is concerned with.

7. Domicile is inviolable. Requisitions may be ordered only in the forms and under the conditions provided for by law.

8. Secrecy of letters and all other forms of correspondence may not be violated, except in case of criminal investigation, mobilization, and state of war.

9–14. (*Not available.*)

15. The People's Republic of Congo grants the right of asylum on its territory, to foreign nationals who are persecuted because of their activities in support of democracy, the national liberation struggle, freedom of scientific and cultural work, and for the defence of the rights of the working people.

16. Defence of the fatherland is the sacred duty of all citizens of the People's Republic of the Congo. Treason against the people is the greatest crime.

19. All nationals are guaranteed freedom of conscience and religion. Religious communities are free in questions having to do with their faith and its outward exercise. It is forbidden to abuse religion and the Church for political purposes. Political organizations based on religion are banned.

20. Marriage and the family are under the protection of the state. The state determines the legal conditions for marriage and for the family. A legal marriage may be

contracted only before the competent agencies of the state. Parents whose children were born out of wedlock have the same obligations and duties toward these children as they have toward their legitimate children.

Title III. Social and Economic System

30. In the People's Republic of the Congo, the means of production consist of the common property of the people which is in the hands of the state, property belonging to the people's co-operative organizations, as well as property of private persons or corporations.

31. The land is the property of the people. No real estate or traditional law shall validly oppose any initiative taken by the state or the local communities in an effort to improve the land. Everyone shall freely dispose of the product of the land, the fruit of his own work. In the name of the people, the state shall regulate the individual or collective use of the land, as required.

32. In order to protect the vital interests of the people, to raise their standard of living, and to make use of all possibilities and all economic forces, the state directs the economic life and development of the country according to a general plan. Basing itself on the economic sector of the state and on the sector of the co-operatives, it exercises general control over the sector of the private economy.

With a view to the implementation of its general plan, the state will base itself on the labour union organizations of workers and employees, on the peasant co-operatives, and possibly on other organizations of the working masses.

33. Private property as well as the right to inheritance of private property are guaranteed. No one may use his private property rights to the detriment of the community. Limitations on private property may be ordered by government regulation when this is in the general interest. Expropriation may take place only on the basis of a law.

SECOND PART. ORGANIZATION OF STATE

Title IV. President of the Republic and Council of State

36. The Chairman of the Central Committee of the PCT is the President of the Republic and the Head of State. He is responsible for national unity, for the implementation of the constitution, and for the regular operation of the government. He guarantees the continuity of the state. He is the guarantor of national independence, of the integrity of the territory, and of the compliance with the provisions of international agreements.

37. The President of the Republic is elected for a five-year term by the party congress in accordance with the party statutes.

Presidential elections are mandatory every fifth year in the term of the President of the Republic and must be held at a date determined by the party Central Committee.

38. The President of the People's Republic of Congo will appoint the Vice-Chairman of the Council of State, upon nomination by the party Central Committee. He will terminate his functions after notice from the Central Committee. He presides over the meetings of the Council of State. He causes the preparation and maintenance of the minutes of Council of State meetings. His deputy is the Vice-Chairman of the Council of State, as required.

39. On the basis of a proposal from the vice-chairman of the Council of State, following an opinion from the members of the Politburo, the President of the Republic will appoint the other members of the Council of State and terminate their functions.

40. When a vacancy in the office of the President of the Republic, for any reason whatever, or the disability of the President is established by the Central Committee, summoned for this purpose and decreeing with an absolute majority of its members, the functions of the President of the Republic—with the exception of the powers enumerated in Articles 38, 39, 45, and 47—shall be temporarily carried out by a member of the Politburo appointed by the Central Committee of the Congolese Workers' Party. The party congress shall be convened within three months after the establishment of this vacancy for the purpose of electing the new President of the Republic.

41. At the time of his inauguration the President of the People's Republic shall take the following solemn oath before the Central Committee of the Congolese Workers' Party:

"I swear loyalty to the Congolese people, to the Revolution, and to the Congolese Workers' Party. Guided by Marxist-Leninist principles, I pledge to defend the party statutes and the Constitution, to devote all my strength to the triumph of the proletarian ideals of the Congolese party through work, democracy, and peace."

42. The President of the party shall legislate by ordinance-law in enlarged session of the Politburo and the Council of State.

43. The President shall control the exercise of regulating authorities by the Council of State under the conditions spelled out by law. He shall sign ordinances and decrees. The acts of the President of the Republic shall be countersigned by the Vice-Chairman of the Council of State and the ministers involved, with the exception of those provided for in Articles 44–47.

44 and 45. (*Not contained in original text.*)

46. The Chairman of the Party Central Committee, President of the People's Republic, and Head of State may—when circumstances so require and after an opinion has been obtained from the Politburo and the Council of State—by decree proclaim a state of siege or a state of emergency which shall confer upon him special powers under the conditions determined by law.

47 and 48. (*Not contained in original text.*)

49. The Council of State is the highest executive and administrative agency of the People's Republic of Congo. It includes the following:

The Chairman of the Central Committee of the Congolese Workers' Party, President of the Republic, Chief of State, who shall preside over the Council, the Vice-Chairman of the Council of State; and the ministers and secretaries of state.

50. The Council is responsible to the President of the People's Republic, the Head of State.

51. The Vice-Chairman of the Council of State shall direct the action of the Council of State. He shall see to the implementation of laws and ordinances. He shall exercise regulatory power under the control of the Head of State.

52. The acts of the Vice-Chairman of the Council of State shall be countersigned by the ministers responsible for their execution.

53. Apart from cases expressly provided for in the articles of the Constitution, the Council of State shall mandatorily be informed of the following:

Decisions concerning the general policy of the Republic; agreements with foreign powers; bills and drafts of laws; ordinances, decrees, and regulations; proclamation of a state of siege and a state of alert.

54. The Council of State of the People's Republic of the Congo:

(*a*) will co-ordinate the activities of the ministers, the commissions, the government agencies and other institutions under their direct control;

(*b*) will prepare the economic plan of the state and the budget and will submit them to the Central Committee for approval; it will also supervise their execution;

(*c*) will take all measures necessary to assure and defend the constitutional system and protect the rights of citizens;

(*d*) will create commissions and institutions for the application of the directives of the Council of State;

(*e*) will determine the internal organization of ministries and institutions within its area of competence.

Title V. International Treaties and Agreements

55. The President of the Republic is in charge of the overall direction of international negotiations. He shall sign and ratify international treaties and agreements.

56. Peace treaties, trade treaties, treaties pertaining to international organizations, treaties committing government finances, treaties modifying dispositions of a legislative nature, treaties pertaining to the status of persons or involving the cession, exchange, or addition of territory may be ratified only on the basis of a law. They shall take effect only after they have been properly ratified.

No cession, exchange, or addition of territory is valid without the agreement of the Congolese people who shall be called upon to express themselves through a referendum, after consultation of the population groups involved.

57. (*Not contained in original text.*)

58. Regularly ratified treaties and agreements have higher authority, as of their publication, than laws, with the reservation that each agreement or treaty is properly implemented by the other party.

Title VII. The Agencies of Administrative and Local Government Units

59. (*Not contained in original text.*)

60. The organization and operation of the public services of the state shall be determined by law.

61. The people's councils are agencies of state power in the localities, the communities, the districts, and the regions.

62. Special laws shall determine the juridical status, power, attributes, and operation of these agencies.

Title VIII. Revision

63. The initiative for the revision of the Constitution is held by the PCT Central Committee. Revision is final after it has been approved by the Central Committee.

64. No revision proceedings may be started or pursued if they infringe upon territorial integrity. The popular form of the state cannot be the subject of a revision.

THE GOVERNMENT

(*November* 1972)

POLITICAL BUREAU OF THE CONGOLESE WORKERS' PARTY (PARTI CONGOLAIS DU TRAVAIL—PCT)

President: Commandant MARIEN NGOUABI.
Vice-President: ANGE-EDOUARD POUNGUI.
Commissioner for Planning: (vacant).
Commissioner for Propaganda and Organization: PIERRE NZÉ.
Commissioner for the National People's Army: (vacant).

Commissioner for Finance and Equipment: ANGE-EDOUARD PONGUI.

CENTRAL COMMITTEE OF THE PCT

President: Commandant MARIEN NGOUABI.
Members: 40 others, including the other five members of the Political Bureau.

COUNCIL OF STATE

Chairman and Minister of Defence: Commandant MARIEN NGOUABI.
Minister of Labour and Minister of Justice: M. ALEXANDRE.
Minister of Foreign Affairs: HENRI LOPES.
Minister of Health and Social Affairs: DIEUDONNE ITOUA.
Minister of Transport and Civil Aviation: LOUIS-SYLVAIN GOMA.

Minister of Trade: DIEUDONNE MANOU MAHUNGU.
Minister of Posts and Housing: VICTOR TAMBA TAMBA.
Minister of Industry, Mines and Tourism: JUSTIN LEKOUNDZOU.
Minister of Primary and Secondary Education: CHRISTOPHE MOUKEKE.
Minister of Technical and University Education: TSHISTER TCHIKAYA.

DIPLOMATIC REPRESENTATION

EMBASSIES AND LEGATIONS ACCREDITED TO CONGO PEOPLE'S REPUBLIC

(In Brazzaville unless otherwise indicated)

(E) Embassy; (L) Legation.

Algeria: B.P. 2100 (E); *Ambassador:* AHMED SALEM.

Belgium: B.P. 225 (E); *Ambassador:* FERNAND EDMOND.

Cameroon: Bangui, Central African Republic (E).

Canada: Kinshasa, Zaire (E).

Central African Republic: B.P. 10; *Ambassador:* AUGUSTE MBOYE.

Chad: B.P. 461 (E); *Ambassador:* THOMAS KEIRO.

China, People's Republic: Conakry, Guinea (E).

Cuba: (E); *Ambassador:* MANUEL AGRAMONTE.

Czechoslovakia: (E); *Chargé d'Affaires:* VLADIMIR ZIAK.

Egypt: (E); *Ambassador:* AHMED FAWZI HASSAN.

Equatorial Guinea: (E); *Ambassador:* CLEMENTE ATEBA.

Ethiopia: (E); *Ambassador:* JACOB GUEBRE LIOULL.

France: rue Alfassa, B.P. 2089 (E); *Ambassador:* PIERRE HUNT.

Gabon: *Ambassador:* FÉLICIEN-GASTON OULUNA.

Germany, Federal Republic: place de la Mairie, B.P. 2022 (E); *Ambassador:* MANFRED RICHTER.

Guinea: (E); *Ambassador:* SADAM MOUSSA TRAORÉ.

India: Kinshasa, Zaire.

Israel: B.P. 2023 (E); *Ambassador:* NAHUM GUERSHOME.

Italy: Yaoundé, Cameroon (E).

Korea, D.P.R.: *Ambassador:* YOUN HI JOU.

Lebanon: Dakar, Senegal (E).

Mali: (E); *Ambassador:* HALIDOU TOURÉ.

Mauritania: *Ambassador:* AHMED OULD DIE.

Netherlands: Kinshasa, Zaire (E).

Romania: (E); *Ambassador:* GEORGHE STOIAN.

Rwanda: Kinshasa, Zaire (E).

Senegal: Kinshasa, Zaire (E).

Sudan: Kinshasa, Zaire (E).

Sweden: Kinshasa, Zaire (E).

Switzerland: Kinshasa, Zaire (E).

Tunisia: Kinshasa, Zaire (E).

U.S.S.R.: *Ambassador:* AFANASSEKO EUGENIE IVANOVITCH.

Viet-Nam, Democratic Republic: *Chargé d'Affaires:* LONG THUAN PHUOC (E).

Viet-Nam, Provisional Revolutionary Government of the Republic of South: PHAN VAN QUANG.

Yugoslavia: (E); *Ambassador:* NIKOLA STEFANOVSKI.

Zaire: B.P. 2457 (E).

The People's Republic of Congo also has diplomatic relations with the German Democratic Republic, Hungary and the United Kingdom.

POLITICAL PARTY

Parti congolais du travail—PCT (*Congolese Workers' Party*): in December 1969 replaced the *Mouvement national de la révolution*, which was formed after the overthrow of the Youlou government in August 1963 and which had been the sole party since 1965.

JUDICIAL SYSTEM

Revolutionary Court of Justice: created January 1969; competent in cases involving the security of the state; has nine judges selected from list of 50 by Central Committee of PCT; Pres. (vacant).

Supreme Court: Pres. CHARLES ASSEMEKANG.

There is also a court of appeal, a criminal court, *tribunaux de grande instance* (County courts), *tribunaux d'instance* (Magistrate's courts), labour courts, and *tribunaux coutumiers* (courts of common law), the latter to be replaced by *tribunaux d'instance*.

DEFENCE

There is an army of 2,000 men, a gendarmerie of 1,500 and a police force of 850. There are also small naval and air forces.

Commander-in-Chief: Commandant MARIEN NGOUABI.

Chief of Staff: Commandant YHOMBI-OPANGO.

Commander of the People's Militia: Senior Adjutant ALEXANDRE MOLITON.

RELIGION

It is estimated that just over half of the population follow traditional Animist beliefs. Just under half are Christians (Roman Catholics 271,997, Protestants 134,650). Muslims number about 4,540. Church activities are limited by the state and church schools no longer exist.

Roman Catholic Church: One Archdiocese, two dioceses.
Archdiocese of Brazzaville: P.B. 2301, Brazzaville; f. 1883; 157,650 mems.; 227 religious staff; 19 missions; Archbishop H.E. Mgr. EMILE BIAYENDA; publ. *La Semaine Africaine*.
Diocese of Pointe-Noire: B.P. 659, Pointe-Noire; f. 1883; 142,000 mems.; Bishop H.E. Mgr. JEAN-BAPTISTE FAURET.
Diocese of Fort-Rousset: Fort-Rousset; f. 1950; 76,000 mems.; 82 religious staff; 16 missions; Bishop (vacant).

Protestant Missions: In all four Equatorial states (the Congo and Central African Republics, Chad and Gabon) there are nearly 1,000 mission centres with a total personnel of about 2,000.

Eglise Evangélique du Congo: B.P. 3205, Brazzaville; Pres. Rev. R. BUANA KIBONGI.

PRESS

A press censorship committee has been in operation since November 1968.

DAILIES
(Brazzaville unless stated)

Congo Matin: B.P. 495; f. 1965; circ. 500; Publisher F. BOUDZANGA.
Journal Officiel de la République du Congo: B.P. 58.
Le Courrier d'Afrique: B.P. 2027; daily; circ. 45,000.
L'Eveil de Pointe-Noire: B.P. 660, Pointe-Noire; daily; circ. 500; Editor S. B. PACI.
Le Journal de Brazzaville: B.P. 132; Publisher M. J. DEVOUE.
Le Petit Journal de Brazzaville: B.P. 2027; f. 1958; daily; Dir. M. ADAM.

PERIODICALS
(Brazzaville)

Bulletin Mensuel de la Chambre de Commerce de Brazzaville: monthly.
Bulletin Mensuel de Statistique: B.P. 2031; monthly.
Etumba: B.P. 23; weekly journal of PCT.
Information-Jeunesse: B.P. 2066.
Nouvelle Congolaise: weekly newspaper.
La Semaine: B.P. 2080; f. 1952; published by Archdiocese of Brazzaville; weekly; circulates in Congo, Gabon, Chad and the Central African Republic; Dir. A. DUCRY; circ. 7,000.
L'Envoi: B.P. 601; monthly.

PRESS AGENCIES

Agence Congolaise d'Information (A.C.I.): B.P. 2144, Brazzaville; f. 1961; autonomous, but associated with A.F.P. and D.P.A.; Dir. A. B. SAMBA; daily bulletin.

FOREIGN BUREAUX

Novosti (A.P.N.): B.P. 170, Brazzaville; Bureau Chief G. KUSHCHIN.

Tass is also represented in Brazzaville. The Government closed down offices of Agence France Presse in June 1971.

RADIO AND TELEVISION

Television began transmission in 1963 and now transmits for 25 hours a week, of which 8 hours are educational programmes.

Radiodiffusion-Télévision Nationale Congolaise: B.P. 2241, Brazzaville; Dir. FRANÇOIS ITOUA.
La Voix de la Révolution Congolaise: B.P. 2241, Brazzaville; national broadcasting station; programmes in French and vernacular languages; Dir. M. MALONGA.
Radio Brazzaville: B.P. 108, Brazzaville; f. 1940, as of Free France; O.R.T.F. programmes in French, English and Portuguese until taken over by Congo Government August 1972.

In 1972 there were 16,800 radios and 75,000 televisions.

FINANCE

(cap. = capital; m. = million)

BANKS
CENTRAL BANK

Banque Centrale des Etats de l'Afrique Equatoriale et du Cameroun: Brazzaville, B.P. 126; Dir. J. E. SATHOUD.

COMMERCIAL BANKS

Banque Commerciale Congolaise: Ave. du 28 Août, B.P. 79, Brazzaville; Ave. du Général de Gaulle, B.P. 760, Pointe-Noire; rue de la Mairie, B.P. 149, Dolisie; f. 1963; cap. 180m. francs CFA; Pres. JUSTIN LEKOUNDZOU.

Banque Nationale de Développement du Congo (BNDC): B.P. 2085, Brazzaville; f. 1961; cap. 462m. francs CFA; 58.4 per cent State owned; gives financial and technical help to all development projects; Dir.-Gen. BERNARD BOUTI.

Caisse Centrale de Coopération Economique: B.P. 96, Brazzaville; Dir. MICHEL LANGLOIS.

Crédit Foncier de l'Ouest Africain: B.P. 116, Brazzaville.

FOREIGN BANKS

Bank of America N.T. and S.A.: Brazzaville.

Banque Internationale pour l'Afrique Occidentale: 9 ave. de Messine, Paris; B.P. 33, Brazzaville, Dir. ROLAND BOITELLE; Pointe-Noire, B.P. 695, Dir. YVES DURAND.

Banque Belge d'Afrique S.C.A.R.L.: Head Office: 19 ave. Ministre Rubbens, Kinshasa, Zaire; branches at Brazzaville, B.P.25 and Pointe-Noire, B.P. 86.

Banque Internationale pour le Commerce et l'Industrie du Congo: Avenue du 28 Août 1940, Brazzaville, B.P. 147; Pointe-Noire, B.P. 661; Dolisie, B.P. 20; f. 1963; affiliated to Banque Nationale de Paris and Société Financière pour les Pays d'Outre Mer; cap. 150m. francs CFA; Pres. and Gen. Man. E. MOUTERDE; Man. G. BEROT; publ. *Rapport annuel*.

Société Générale de Banques au Congo: Brazzaville, place de la Poste, B.P. 122; Pointe-Noire, Ave. du Général de Gaulle, B.P. 55; Paris representation: 50 blvd. Haussmann, Paris 9e; f. 1963; cap. 200m. francs CFA; deposits 1,443m. francs CFA (Dec. 1970); Pres. Dir.-Gen. ROGER DUCHEMIN.

INSURANCE

Agence Congolaise d'Assurances S.A.R.L.: B.P. 790, ave. Col.-Genin, Pointe-Noire; f. 1959; cap. 1m. francs CFA; Dir. M. LIBERMAN.

Les Assureurs Conseils Congolais Faugère et Jutheau et Cie.: B.P. 25, ave. Colonna-d'Ornano, Brazzaville; cap. 9,750,000 francs CFA; Dir. MICHEL BABINET.

Société Equatoriale d'Assurances: B.P. 56, ave. Lumumba, Brazzaville; cap. 1m. francs CFA.

TRADE AND INDUSTRY

CHAMBERS OF COMMERCE

Chambre de Commerce, d'Agriculture et d'Industrie de Brazzaville: B.P. 92, Brazzaville; Pres. CHRISTIAN DIALLO-DRAMEY.

Chambre de Commerce, d'Agriculture et d'Industrie du Kouilou-Niari: B.P. 665, Pointe-Noire; branch in Dolisie; Pres. E. EBOUKA-BABACKAS.

Chambre des Mines de l'Afrique Equatoriale: B.P. 26, Brazzaville; Pres. M. DE LAVALEYE.

TRADE ORGANIZATIONS

Délégation de la Fédération des Industries Mécaniques et Transformatrices des Métaux: B.P. 20-56; Pres. M. CHAUVET.

Office National de Commercialisation des Produits Agricoles (ONCPA): Brazzaville; Chair. BONIFACE MATINGOU.

Syndicat des Commerçants, Importateurs et Exportateurs de l'Afrique Equatoriale (SYCOMIMPEX): B.P. 84, Brazzaville; Pres. M. AGOSTINI; Sec.-Gen. M. FULCHIRON.

Syndicat des Industries de l'Afrique Equatoriale (SYNDUSTREF): B.P. 84, Brazzaville; Pres. M. JEANBRAU; Sec.-Gen. M. FULCHIRON.

PROFESSIONAL ORGANIZATION

Union Patronale et Inter-professionnelle du Congo (UNI-CONGO): B.P. 42, Brazzaville.

TRADE UNION

Confédération Syndicale Congolaise: Brazzaville; f. 1964; Gen.-Sec. ANATOLE KONDO.

DEVELOPMENT

Société de Développement Régional de la Vallée de Niari et de Jacob: Jacob; f. 1966; Dir. JEAN-MICHEL MOUMBOUNOU.

Société pour le Développement de l'Afrique Equatoriale: B.P. 909, Pointe-Noire; B.P. 56, Brazzaville.

MAJOR INDUSTRIAL COMPANIES

The following are some of the largest private and state-owned companies in terms of capital investment or employment.

AGIP (Brazzaville) S.A.: B.P. 2076, Brazzaville; f. 1962; cap. 280m. francs CFA.
Import and distribution of petroleum products.
Pres. MASSINO DEL BO; Dir. FONTANA ROMANO; 75 employees.

BATA-Pointe-Noire S.A.: B.P. 32, Pointe-Noire; f. 1965; cap. 100m. francs CFA.
Manufacture of shoes.
Dir. JEAN MESSY.

Brasserie de Brazzaville: B.P. 105, Avenue du Nouveau Port, Brazzaville; f. 1968; cap. 150m. francs CFA.
Production of beer.
Pres. Dir.-Gen. J.-M. PLOUVIER; 180 employees.

Cimenterie Domaniale de Loutété: B.P. 12, Loutété; f. 1968; state-owned; cap. 900m. francs CFA.
Production of cement.
Dir.-Gen. JEAN-MICHEL MOUMBOUNOU.

Société Congolaise des Bois: Pointe-Noire; f. 1964; cap. 120m. francs CFA.
Timber mill.
Dir. R. BRESSER.

Société Congolaise des Brasseries Kronenbourg: B.P. 1147, Pointe-Noire; f. 1963; cap. 300m. francs CFA.
Production and sale of beer and soft drinks, ice and carbon dioxide.
Dir. JACQUES PERNIN; 230 employees.

Société Forestière du Niari S.A.: B.P. 205, Pointe-Noire; f. 1936; cap. 290m. francs CFA.
Timber (especially *okoumé* wood).
Dir. M. JAUD.

Société Industrielle et Agricole du Congo (SIACONGO): Amalgamation of Société Industrielle et Agricole du Niari (SIAN) and Société Sucrière du Niari S.A. (SOSUNIARI); nationalized 1970; largest industrial concern.
Plantation of sugar cane, sugar refining, milling of wheat, manufacture of cattle food, refining of groundnut oil.

Compagnie des Potasses du Congo: B.P. 1175, Pointe-Noire; f. 1964; cap. 2,500m. francs CFA.
Prospecting for and mining of potassium salts.
Pres. Dir.-Gen. M. CHEYSSON; Dir.-Gen. M. LAFONT; 1,100 employees.

Société Shell Congo-Brazzaville: B.P. 2008, Brazzaville; f. 1954; cap. 230m. francs CFA.
Import and distribution of petroleum and chemical products, manufacture of insecticide.
Dir.-Gen. LOUIS WESSELING; 400 employees.

Société Textile du Congo (SOTEXCO): B.P. 211, Brazzaville; state-owned.
Textile complex: spinning, weaving, bleaching, dying, printing, knitting.
Dir. PASCAL OCKYEMBA-MORLENDE.

TRANSPORT

RAILWAY

Chemin de Fer Congo-Océan: Pointe-Noire, B.P. 651; 515 km. of track from Brazzaville to Pointe-Noire. Only diesel trains are used. A 286 km. section of line linking the manganese mines at Moanda (in Gabon), via a cableway to the Congo border with the main line to Pointe-Noire was opened in 1962. A programme of modernization of both track and rolling stock is under way, helped by $6.3m. loan from the IDA in April 1972.

ROADS

There are 11,000 km. of roads usable throughout the year, of which 310 km. are bitumened. The network consists of 3,768 km. main roads and 7,232 km. secondary roads, with the principal routes linking Pointe-Noire with Brazzaville and also Ouesso, and Dolisie with Cameroon, via Gabon.

INLAND WATERWAYS

Brazzaville

Agence Transcongolaise des communications (ATC): B.P. 670, Pointe-Noire; f. 1969 to control nationalization of transport; financed the newly opened port of Ouesso; most important state enterprise with an annual budget of 6,400m. francs CFA; Dir. M. EBOUCKA-BABACKAS.

Cie. Générale de Transports en Afrique Equatoriale: B.P. 76; f. 1962; cap. 800m. francs CFA; Dir. M. GAULTIER.

Société Ouest-Africaine d'Entreprises Maritimes: B.P. 674 Pointe-Noire; f. 1959; cap. 115m. francs CFA; Dir. JEAN ROZIE.

Société Equatoriale de Navigation: B.P. 35, Brazzaville; f. 1963; cap. 20m. francs CFA; Dir. JEAN ANSLERT.

Transit Congo Oubangui Tchad: B.P. 2052, Brazzaville; f. 1963; cap. 5m. francs CFA; Dir. M. LANCOMBE.

SHIPPING
Pointe-Noire

Cie. Maritime des Chargeurs Réunis: B.P. 656; agents for Cie. Fabre S.G.T.M., Congona, Elder Dempster Lines, Palm Lines, Cie. Maritime Belge, Nautilus, Shell International Marine Ltd., Gaz Ocean, Nigerian Lines, Delta Lines, Navigen Co., Unicorn; Dir. GUY JAQUEMIN.

Société Navale Delmas-Vieljeux: B.P. 679.

SOAEM (Congo): B.P. 674; agents for Société Navale de l'Ouest, Lloyd Triestino, Lloyd Brasileiro, Dafra Line, Scandinavian West Africa Line, East Asiatic Co., General Steam Navigation Co., Compagnie Navale des Pétroles, Texaco Inc., Compania Colonial de Navigacao, Compania National de Navigacao, Sociedade Geral de Comercio Industria e Transportes, Société Agret, Cobrecaf, Cie. française d'armement maritime, Gold Star Line, A. Halcoussis, Denis Frères, Purfina, Somara, Société Navale Caennaise, Scandinavian East Africa Line, Zim Cargo Line, Saga.

UMARCO: B.P. 723; agents for Farrell Line, Holland West Africa Line, Royal Interocean Lines, Scindia Line, Mobil Shipping Co., Sabline, Panatrans.

CIVIL AVIATION

The important, international airports are at Brazzaville—Maya-Maya, which has the longest runway of French-speaking Africa (3,300 metres), and Pointe-Noire; a third is to be built at Impfondo. There are also 22 smaller aerodromes.

Air Afrique: Head Office in Abidjan, Ivory Coast (*q.v.*); People's Republic of the Congo has a 7 per cent share.

Lina Congo (Lignes Nationales Aériennes Congolaises) (*Congolese National Airline Co.*): avenue du Colonel Colonna d'Ornano, B.P. 2203, Brazzaville; f. 1966; two-thirds government-owned; controls all domestic flights; fleet of two AN-24, one F27, one DC-6B, two DC-3; Pres./Dir. Gen. A. MAKANGOU; Gen. Man. M. A. MACKOUBIL.

The following lines also serve Brazzaville: Aeroflot, Air France, Air Mali, Iberia, K.L.M., Sabena and U.T.A.

POWER

Société Nationale d'Energie: B.P. 95, Brazzaville; f. 1967; state-owned corporation for the production and distribution of electricity; total capacity: 29,620 kW; 1970 production 68 million kWh. Dir. Gen. ANDRÉ BATANGA.

TOURISM

Office National Congolaise du Tourisme: B.P. 456, Brazzaville; Dir. FÉLIX MALEKAT.

EDUCATION
LEARNED SOCIETIES AND RESEARCH INSTITUTES

Bureau de Recherches Géologiques et Minières: B.P. 431, Brazzaville; attached to B.R.G.M. centre at Libreville, Gabon; Dir. M. NICAULT.

Bureau pour le Développement de la Production Agricole (BDPA): B.P. 2222, Brazzaville.

Centre Culturel Français: B.P. 2141, Brazzaville; f. 1962; library of 5,000 vols.; Dir. C. HURLOT.

Centre Technique Forestier Tropical: B.P. 764, Pointe-Noire; f. 1958; forestry research; Dir. B. MARTIN.

Conseil National de la Recherche Scientifique et Technique: Brazzaville; f. 1966; special commissions for medical science, agronomic and pastoral sciences, forestry research, marine science and fisheries, hydrology, geology, botany, anthropology, educational and industrial research; Pres. THE COMMISSIONER FOR PLANNING.

Institut Africain: Mouyondzi; living African languages.

Institut d'Etudes Congolaises: Brazzaville; Dir. M. MALONGA.

Institut de Recherches du Coton et des Textiles Exotiques: B.P. 13, Madingou.

Institut de Recherches pour les Huiles et Oléagineux: Sibiti; Dir. A. MALLA.

Office de la Recherche Scientifique et Technique Outre-Mer Centre O.R.S.T.O.M. de Brazzaville: B.P. 181, Brazzaville; pedology, hydrology, botany, medical entomology, sociology and psychosociology, ethnology, archaeology, linguistics, geography, geology, phytopathology and applied zoology; library; Dir. A. BOUQUET.

Office de la Recherche Scientifique et Technique Outre-Mer Centre Océanographique O.R.S.T.O.M. de Pointe-Noire: B.P. 1286, Pointe-Noire; f. 1950; biological and physical oceanography; Dir. J. C. LE GUEN; publ. *Documents Scientifiques du Centre de Pointe-Noire.*

Station Fruitière du Congo: B.P. 27, Loudima; f. 1963; Dir. C. MAKAY.

U.S. Information Center: Brazzaville.

LIBRARY

Bibliothèque de l'Université Nationale du Congo: B.P. 2025, Brazzaville; f. 1959; 33,000 vols.; Chief Librarian M. SCHAACK.

UNIVERSITY AND COLLEGES
UNIVERSITÉ NATIONALE DU CONGO
B.P. 69, BRAZZAVILLE

Founded 1961 as Centre d'Enseignement Supérieure; opened as University 1971.

Rector: H. MASSON.

Number of books in library: 33,000.

Number of students: 1,436.

CONSTITUENT INSTITUTES:

Ecole Normale Supérieure d'Afrique Centrale: P.O.B. 237, Brazzaville; f. 1962 under UN Special Fund; students are admitted from the Central African Republic, Chad and Gabon.

Ecole Supérieure des Sciences: B.P. 69, Brazzaville; f. 1960; Dir. A. GRJEBINE.

Ecole Supérieure de Lettres.

Ecole de Droit.

———————

Centre d'Etudes Administratives et Techniques Supérieures: administrative and judicial centre, school of arts.

Collège Technique, Commercial et Industriel de Brazzaville (et centre d'Apprentissage): Brazzaville; f. 1959; for African students; Dir. HUBERT COUPPEY.

Ecole Nationale d'Administration: Brazzaville; 56 students.

Lycée Technique d'Etat (*Technical College*): Brazzaville; commercial, general and industrial sections; Principal H. COUPPEY.

Centre de Formation Professionnelle Agricole: Sibiti.

SELECT BIBLIOGRAPHY

(For works on the former A.E.F. countries generally *see* Central African Republic Select Bibliography, p. 227.)

AMIN, S., and COQUERY-VIDROVITCH, C. *Histoire économique du Congo 1880–1968*. Paris, Anthropos, 1969.

GIDE, ANDRÉ. *Voyage au Congo*. 1926.

SORET, MARCEL. *Les Kongo nord occidentaux*. Paris, Presses universitaires de France, 1959.

VENNETIER, P. *Géographie du Congo-Brazzaville*. Paris, Gauthier Villars, 1966.

"Population et économie du Congo-Brazzaville." *Cahiers d'Outre Mer* (Bordeaux), pp. 360–81, 1962.

"Problems of Port Development in Gabon and Congo", ch. II in HOYLE, B. S., and HILLING, D. (Eds.), *Seaports and Development in Tropical Africa*. London, 1970.

WAGRET, JEAN-MICHEL. *Histoire et sociologie politiques du Congo*. Paris, Librairie générale de droit et de jurisprudence, 1963.

Dahomey

PHYSICAL AND SOCIAL GEOGRAPHY *

R. J. Harrison Church

The Republic of Dahomey, a small west African state, west of Nigeria, has an area of 43,480 sq. miles. From a coastline of some 60 miles on the Gulf of Guinea the republic extends inland about 410 miles to the Niger river. The population was estimated at 2,792,000 in 1971.

The Fon and Yoruba of the south for long supplied each other's captives to European slave traders. In colonial days they enjoyed educational advantages and, like the Senegalese, were prominent in administration throughout French West Africa. After independence many were expelled to Dahomey, where there is great unemployment or underemployment of literates. The northern peoples, such as the Somba and Bariba, are less westernized.

The coast is a straight sand-bar, pounded by heavy surf on the seaward side and backed by one or more lagoons and former shorelines on the landward side. Rivers flow into these lagoons, Lakes Anémé and Nokoué being estuaries of two rivers whose seaward exits are obstructed by the sandbar. A lagoon waterway is navigable for barges to Lagos (Nigeria).

North of Lake Nokoué the Ouémé River has a wide marshy delta, with considerable agricultural potential. Elsewhere the lagoons are backed northward by the Terre de Barre, a fertile and intensively farmed region of clay soils. North again is the seasonally flooded Lama swamp, whose peaty soils are difficult to reclaim. Beyond are areas comparable with the Terre de Barre, and the realm of the pre-colonial Dahomey kingdom, with its capital at Abomey.

Most of the rest of the country is underlain by Precambrian rocks, with occasional bare domes, lateritic cappings on level surfaces, and poor soils. In the north-west are the Atacora Mountains whose soils, though less poor, are much eroded. On the northern borders are Primary and other sandstones, extremely infertile and short of water.

Although iron, chrome, rutile and phosphates occur, none can currently be worked economically. There are good possibilities of locating oil in the south.

Southern Dahomey has an equatorial climate, most typical along the coast, though with a low rainfall of some 50 in. Away from the coast the dry months increase until a tropical climate prevails over the northern half of the country. There a dry season alternates with a wet one, the latter being of seven months in the centre and four months in the north; the rainfall still averages 50 in.

* *See* map on p. 364.

RECENT HISTORY

Michael Crowder and Donal Cruise O'Brien

(Revised for this edition by KAYE WHITEMAN)

THE ORIGINS OF FRENCH INTEREST IN WEST AFRICA

France had long-standing connexions with only one part of the vast but poor West African Empire she established at the end of the nineteenth century. As early as 1659 a French trader, Cavallier, established the town of St. Louis on an island at the mouth of the River Senegal, which gave access to gum arabic and slaves from the interior. France had also been from time to time owner of the small island of Gorée off Çape Verde, which was prized and fought for by other European powers with west African interests as an entrepôt for the export of slaves to the New World and as a staging post on the voyage round Africa to the Indian Ocean.

In St. Louis France began the remarkable experiment of personal assimilation of Africans into French culture which was to become an important theme in her colonial philosophy. By the time of the capture of St. Louis by the British during the Napoleonic Wars, the town had a mixed Franco-African population of 7,000. Of these a sizable number were of mixed blood and had adopted the French way of life as their own—a mulatto had even become mayor of St. Louis. In 1789 the *habitants* of St. Louis had sent their *cahier* of grievances to the States-General.

In 1817 St. Louis was handed back to the French, who conducted agricultural experiments in the immediate hinterland of St. Louis with the object of finding out whether the area would lend itself to agricultural settlement. The failure of these experiments meant that Senegal ceased to be looked on as a possible area for settlement by Europeans.

Till the 1850s interest in Senegal was limited to the trade in gum arabic along the river, where a series of French trading posts had been established.

Trade was made precarious by the exactions of the Moors inhabiting the north bank of the river. In 1850 an official commission visited Senegal and recommended that France expand her interests in the region; their justification was the groundnut, which grew freely in the arid Senegalese hinterland and was to become the basis of the colony's future prosperity.

In 1854, under the Second Empire, General Louis Faidherbe was appointed Governor of Senegal. He was to be the real founder of France's West African Empire. He secured the gum arabic trade in Senegal by subduing the Moors and he established a French Protectorate over much of the hinterland, warding off, in the process, the imperial ambitions of El Hajj Omar, the founder of the great Toucouleur Empire of Ségou. In St. Louis itself he streamlined the administration, founded a bank, and organized the famous *Tirailleurs sénégalais*, the African troops who, under European officers, were to be the main instrument for the conquest of the rest of France's huge West African Empire.

Elsewhere in west Africa French trading interests at this time were marginal. Trading posts had been established at Assinie and Grand Bassam on the Ivory Coast, and the old French trading post at Ouidah in Dahomey had been reopened. The French occupation of west Africa was to begin, not from these footholds, but from the Senegalese base.

WEST AFRICA ON THE EVE OF THE FRENCH CONQUEST

France's huge West African Empire contained a wide variety of people, speaking many different languages and living under widely differing political systems. It is therefore difficult to give anything but the most superficial characterization of the area in pre-colonial times, except to point to those features that were significant for the future of French colonial rule. West Africa, geographically, can be broadly divided into three zones: desert, savannah and forest. Vast stretches of the future French West Africa consisted of desert. Two colonies, Mauritania and Niger, were essentially desert territories, while much of Soudan (Mali) consisted of Sahara lands. Only Ivory Coast and Guinea were in the forest, and their northern areas, like Senegal, Upper Volta, Dahomey and Togo were savannah.

During the nineteenth century a series of *jihads*, or wars of Islamic reform, had swept across the west African savannah. At the time of the French expansion along the River Senegal, El Hajj Omar, the *Tijaniyya* reformer, was trying to extend his newly founded empire to the Senegalese coast. Thwarted by Faidherbe, he turned his attentions eastwards and left to his successors an empire that covered most of modern Mali. In Guinea and the hinterland of the Ivory Coast Almamy Samory founded his great Mandingo Empire on the very eve of the French conquest. In Niger many areas had been inspired by the *jihad* led by Usman dan Fodio of Sokoto. In fact, France's conquest of the savannah

lands can be seen as the conflict of two imperialisms: Africano-Mohammedan and Euro-Christian. The dominant groups in Senegal, Mauritania, Guinea, Soudan (Mali) and Niger were all Muslim, and were deeply opposed to occupation by the infidel. Under these Muslim rulers, and alongside them, lived large numbers of Africans who adhered to their traditional religions, and who often collaborated with the French to obtain their independence from the Muslims.

In the non-Muslim areas of Upper Volta, Ivory Coast and Dahomey the French were to meet with resistance as fierce as any they met in the Muslim areas. In Dahomey the kingdom of that name, which controlled much of the area comprising the present independent state of Dahomey, violently opposed French occupation, as did the Mogho Naba, or Emperor of the Mossi, in Upper Volta. In the Ivory Coast opposition in the southern areas was often sustained village by village and was not finally put down till the time of the First World War.

THE FRENCH CONQUEST

The reason for the success of the French conquest must be attributed primarily to their superior weapons. The African armies, even when they were as sophisticated as that of Samory, could never obtain adequate supplies of European arms, and, more important, never procured the Gatling or Maxim guns. These "machine" guns enabled the Europeans, with comparatively small forces, to stand up to African armies often ten times their size.

The French conquest followed the direction established by Faidherbe—eastwards along the Senegal River to the Niger. Soldiers rather than civilians dictated the course of the conquest, with the result that France occupied large tracts of commercially useless land, whereas Britain, whose military expeditions were largely dictated by trade considerations, obtained much smaller but commercially more valuable areas.

Broadly all opposition to French rule in the future French-speaking colonies had been put down by the end of the First World War. Effectively each colony had been occupied by the following dates:

Senegal, 1890; Upper Volta, 1892; Soudan (Mali), 1893; Dahomey, 1893; Guinea, 1898; Niger, 1906; Mauritania, 1910; Ivory Coast, 1914.

THE ESTABLISHMENT OF FRENCH ADMINISTRATION IN WEST AFRICA

It was not until 1895 that the various colonies established in west Africa by the French were brought under a Governor-General of French West Africa based in Senegal. Even then Dahomey was excluded. Between 1895 and 1904, whilst the conquest was still proceeding, there were numerous changes in the constitution of the federation. By 1904 it had taken its eventual shape, though Upper Volta was not created until 1920 when it was excised from parts of

Niger, Ivory Coast and Soudan. It was dismembered in 1932 but re-created in 1947.

At first the Governor-General was substantive Governor of Senegal and administered the federation from the Senegalese capital of St. Louis. In 1904 the office of Governor-General was separately constituted and the capital of the French West African federation established at Dakar. The Governor-General alone had the right to correspond with the Minister of Colonies in Paris, who was responsible to the Cabinet rather than to the Chamber of Deputies, since the colonies were for the most part ruled by decree rather than legislation. The Governor-General controlled all senior appointments other than those of the Lieutenant-Governors of the constituent colonies, and certain other specified senior posts. He controlled the defence forces, posts and telegraphs, public works, and sanitary services, including medicine and agriculture. Most important of all he controlled customs and had an independent budget, one of whose principal objectives was the rational development of the federation as a whole. With such powers the Governor-General could oblige the Lieutenant-Governors to refer to him in all important matters of local policy.

The Governor-General and his Lieutenant-Governors were not subject to local legislative councils as in British West Africa. Indeed neither the Governor-General nor the Lieutenant-Governors had legislative powers as such: they could only propose legislation to the Minister of Colonies in Paris, who would issue the necessary decree.

There was a Federal Advisory Council called the *Conseil de gouvernement*, but the Governor-General was not obliged to take its advice. The Lieutenant-Governors had *conseils administratifs*, by whose advice they were similarly not bound. In Senegal, however, as a result of the early experiments in assimilation in that colony, a *Conseil-Général* had been established for the *quatre communes* of Saint Louis, Gorée, Dakar and Rufisque. The members of this council were elected by popular votes of the inhabitants, who were French citizens. The *Conseil-Général* had the key legislative function of controlling the budget for the whole of Senegal, not just the *quatre communes*. Each of these had their own mayors and municipal budgets.

In 1920 the French administration, on the pretext of broadening the base of representation, tried to weaken the position of the Senegalese *Conseil-Général*, now redesignated the *Conseil colonial*, by nominating a number of chiefs from the Protectorate equal to the number of citizen members. In 1924, however, the citizen-councillors managed to block the budget and only consented to pass it when they were given a majority of seats over the Protectorate members.

The other "democratic" check to the administration was the deputy for Senegal. Since 1848 Senegal had sent a deputy to Paris, except for the period of the Second Empire. The deputy could, if so inclined, directly criticize the Minister of Colonies in the Chamber of Deputies. In 1914 the citizens of the *quatre communes*, to whom the franchise was limited, elected Blaise Diagne as their first African deputy.

Two of his predecessors had been *métis* (mulatto) Senegalese.

Though Diagne was elected on a radical platform, he was effectively bought off by the administration and in 1918 acted as High Commissioner for the recruitment of troops from French black Africa for the European front. In 1931 he actually became French Under-Secretary of State for the Colonies.

Until the reforms introduced by the Constitution of the Fourth Republic, the administration of French West Africa was largely unhampered by criticism or effective checks from its African population.

LOCAL ADMINISTRATION

While the Governors-General had overriding authority in the federation, its very size and the difficulties of communication meant that a great deal had to be decided not only by the Lieutenant-Governors but by the *Commandants de cercle* (district commissioners) on the spot. Indeed, in the early years of administration perhaps the key figures were the local French administrators (*Chefs de subdivision*) and the African chiefs. While assimilation had been pursued as a policy in the nineteenth century in Senegal, by the twentieth century it was realised that the task of implementing a full-scale policy of turning Africans into French citizens with the same rights and duties would not work. Financially, given the resources of French West Africa, it was out of the question. At a practical level it seemed impossible to assimilate people as fiercely attached to their traditional culture as the majority of Africans were. The French therefore decided to administer West Africa at the local level through chiefs.

However, these chiefs had no formally recognized powers of their own, only those specifically accorded them by the French administration. Large chieftaincies were broken up, small chieftaincies were grouped together under a single chief and peoples without chiefs were given them for the sake of administrative uniformity. The chiefs became very much the sergeants and corporals of the Empire. Where traditional chiefs were incompetent they were replaced by French nominees: literate old soldiers, or ex-clerks were often preferred to illiterate legitimate heirs.

The chiefs did the "dirty-work" of the administration—collecting taxes, rounding up forced labour, recruiting for the army, and supervising compulsory crop cultivation. The administration backed up their authority with para-military *gardes de cercle*. A key role was played by the administrators' interpreters, since administrators moved so frequently from post to post that they rarely if ever learnt the local language. The interpreter, controlling negotiations between the impermanent administrator and permanent chief could thus gain much power.

The ordinary people had no real recourse to justice. Their chiefs were stripped of all their criminal and most of their civil jurisdiction. The judicial régime for the *sujets*, as distinct from the *assimilés* who outside the *quatre communes* numbered fewer than 2,000 as late as 1939, was the notorious and much hated *indigénat*. Under this the French administration could summarily imprison *sujets*, including chiefs, for up to 14 days. The administration thus had on paper all the means of exercising very firm control over the local population. However, clever chiefs could, within the apparently rigid administrative framework, exercise considerable powers. Many of them even held their own courts in secret.

THE ECONOMIC REGIME

One of the principal preoccupations of the administration in French West Africa during the colonial period was to exploit the resources of the colony. While the import and export trade was in the hands of a few large French companies like SCOA (*Société commerciale de l'ouest africain*) and CFAO (*Compagnie française de l'Afrique occidentale*), the administration stimulated economic activity in several ways, the principal one being of course taxation. This encouraged the production of the so-called cash crops for export, such as groundnuts, cocoa, coffee, cotton, and palm products in those areas where they would grow, and forced peasants in those areas which grew no cash crops to migrate into areas which did. This accounts for the large-scale migrations of labour from Upper Volta, Soudan and Niger into Senegal, Guinea, Ivory Coast and Ghana.

Apart from taxation, the administration resorted to compulsory crop cultivation, particularly of cotton in Upper Volta, as a means to increasing production. Another technique employed was forced labour, not only for public projects like roads and railways, but also for European plantation owners in Ivory Coast and Guinea.

While the administration did interfere with the economic process in these ways, the French commercial companies had effectively free rein during the colonial period, profiting from the activities of the administration, since they handled the export of the increased quantities of crops that resulted from its policies. While at first sight the large companies like SCOA, CFAO, Maurel et Prom, NOSOCO, etc., seemed to constitute an oligopoly whose intense competition could have benefited the African producer and purchaser, in fact they produced a monopolistic situation. Cross-representation on boards, price-rings and local area monopolies deprived the African peasant of the benefits of competition.

While in the pre-colonial period the Africans had controlled the middleman trade between European exporter and African peasant producer, during the colonial period this position was wrested from them by the Lebanese. Content with lower profit margins, the Lebanese forced African middlemen and petty European traders out of business within a short time of their moving into areas formerly controlled by African or European middlemen. By the outbreak of the Second World War there were almost no African entrepreneurs of any significance in French West Africa.

THE SECOND WORLD WAR AND REFORMS

The Second World War was a turning point in French West Africa's history. After two years under a pro-Vichy régime, which isolated it from the main currents of the war, it became, with French Equatorial Africa, de Gaulle's first base, a vital link in the allied strategy.

In January 1944 de Gaulle called the famous Brazzaville Conference at which political, social and economic reforms were outlined for France's colonies. These reforms were in large measure a recognition of the major role French black Africa, in particular French Equatorial Africa, had played in keeping the Free French Movement alive. From the beginning of 1943 to the end of the war French West Africa became a major source of supply of men and materials on a compulsory basis for the Free French.

The reforms proposed at Brazzaville and partially enacted in the new Constitution of the Fourth Republic provided for African representation in the National Assembly, the Senate and the Assembly of the French Union. It also provided for the establishment of local councils, such as Senegal had had, for all the constituent colonies of the French West Africa. However, while the Senegalese council was elected on a single roll, the others were elected by dual roll, one for former *sujets*, one for citizens, who were mostly Metropolitan French who would otherwise not have been able to secure representation. In the social field forced labour and the hated *indigénat* were abolished, while economically provision was made for the development of the infrastructure of the federation. During the period 1946–60 over £400 million was spent on roads, railways, ports. airfields, schools, hospitals, water supplies, agricultural development, etc. under FIDES—*Fonds d'investissement et développement économique et social*,

In the political sphere, despite the existence of the new local councils, the focus of attention was Paris. African politicians were primarily concerned with securing the deputyships in the National Assembly, for real power lay there, not in the local councils. Indeed, the slender margins by which the unstable post-war governments of France held power meant that the votes of the African deputies could often be vital. The African deputies allied with or formally joined metropolitan parties, while building up their own parties at home, not only to ensure re-election to the deputyship, but to control the local councils and the *Grand Conseil*, or federal council in Dakar. While in real terms neither the local or federal councils had much power, and were certainly not intended, as Brazzaville made clear and the new constitution confirmed, as the basis of self-government, they did exercise control over the budget.

The principal parties which arose in response to the new constitutional situation were Houphouët-Boigny's *Rassemblement démocratique africain* (RDA), Senghor's *Convention africaine* and Lamine Gueye's *SFIO*. The only party with a wide appeal throughout the federation was the RDA, though until 1951 it was persecuted by the French administration because of its Communist connexions.

THE LOI CADRE, THE REFERENDUM AND INDEPENDENCE

The period 1946–56 saw rapid political developments in the neighbouring British west African territories culminating in self-government and independence for Ghana. By contrast the burden of French policy had been the closer association of the African colonies with the metropolitan political process in a Franco-African Community. Togo, which France had taken over from the Germans under League of Nations mandate and now administered as a UN trust territory, proved something of a problem. Administered as a separate country, it had a political life of its own and its inhabitants had the right of appeal to the United Nations. To head off potential independence movements in that territory, France accorded it a considerable degree of autonomy, which she felt obliged to give to the French West African territories in case they were inspired by the Ghanaian example or became envious of the concessions made to Togo.

In 1956 therefore the famous *loi cadre* was passed establishing local government for the constituent colonies but significantly not one for the federation as a whole. This reflected the desires of Houphouët-Boigny who did not want his rich Ivory Coast to subsidize a federal executive at Dakar. The majority of African politicians of all parties, in particular Houphouët-Boigny's own RDA, advocated the creation of a strong federal executive council and accused France of trying to balkanize French West Africa in order to dominate it.

Against this background de Gaulle came to power in May 1958 and proposed his new constitution whose main provision for Africa was a Franco-African Community in which the constituent territories of French West Africa would have a certain amount of local autonomy but would deliberate on matters such as defence, higher education, and monetary system in a Community composed of France and the constituent territories *not* the federations of West and Equatorial Africa. Acceptance of the Constitution implied rejection of the federations. Rejection of the Constitution, de Gaulle made clear, would mean independence "with all its consequences".

All the black African territories, with the exception of Guinea, voted for the Constitution, their leaders largely sharing President Tsiranana of Madagascar's dilemma: "When I let my heart talk, I am a partisan of total and immediate independence; when I make my reason speak, I realize that it is impossible". Guinea soon learnt what de Gaulle meant by "consequences". All French aid and personnel were withdrawn and Guinea had to go it alone.

Nevertheless within less than two years the rest of French West Africa had become independent. The main drama of these two years was the fight by the federalists to salvage as much as they could of the old French West African federation. While Senegal, Soudan, Upper Volta and Mauritania actually met in December 1958 to plan a new Mali Federation, pressures by France and Houphouët-Boigny reduced the eventual participants in the Federation to Senegal and Soudan, which linked up in January 1959. The marriage was an unhappy one from the start, and was not recognized by the French until finally France conceded independence to her French West African territories in the summer of 1960, as she had to Togo on April 1960. The Mali Federation broke up in August and the only inter-state grouping to survive independence was, bizarrely, the *Conseil de l'Entente*, comprising Ivory Coast, Upper Volta, Dahomey and Niger, and based on the leadership of Houphouët-Boigny, the arch anti-federalist. The *Conseil de l'Entente*, however, was primarily an economic union. With the exception of Guinea, the states of French West Africa achieved independence on good terms with, and strong economic and political dependence on, France. However, after the break-up of the Mali Federation, Soudan, which took over the name of Mali, took an increasingly hostile stand towards France, because she felt French interests had been a major factor in the break-up of the Federation.

DAHOMEY SINCE INDEPENDENCE*

Since independence in 1960, Dahomey has experienced no less than six (bloodless) *coups d'état*. Economic difficulties, reflected in a chronic inability to balance the budget, largely explain this extraordinary instability. Dahomey has a highly developed educational system, and under colonial rule had exported trained manpower throughout French Africa. Following independence many French-speaking states took measures to exclude foreign Africans, and Dahomey was faced with a reflux of highly qualified personnel. The local educational system, in the meantime, produces more than enough candidates for the skilled jobs available. The result has been unemployment, disguised unemployment, and a civil service expansion out of all proportion to the country's resources.

The President at independence was Hubert Maga, a politician with support in the north of Dahomey, who ruled in alliance with Sourou Migan Apithy. This régime fell in 1963 after trade union and student riots, when army intervention brought to power the ex-opposition leader Justin Ahomadegbe in coalition with Apithy. This unstable coalition lasted till November 1965, when the army intervened once more and Colonel Soglo formed a government of soldiers and technicians. This régime in turn was overthrown late in 1967 by a group of younger army officers who installed Lt.-Col. Alley as head of state in preparation for a return to civilian rule. A strong presidential constitution was approved by referendum in March 1968, and presidential elections followed in May. These were annulled after heavy abstentions, as

---

* For post-independence development in the other former A.O.F. countries *see* under their respective chapters.

the three principal candidates (Apithy, Maga, Ahomadegbe) had previously been disqualified. In August, Dr. Zinsou was nominated as President, but his régime was overthrown by army officers who installed Lieutenant-Colonel de Souza as head of government in 1969. After abortive elections in 1970, in which Maga, Ahomadegbe and Apithy stood as Presidential candidates, and which brought the country to the verge of strife between north and south, a Presidential Commission was formed, consisting of the three candidates.

This became the Presidential Council, in which each of the members in rotation was to serve a two-year term as President. The first President was Maga, and to the surprise of everybody, including the council members, his term lasted its allotted time. The new constitutional set-up met its first major test in the transfer of power, which many predicted could not be successful, and the tension of the months immediately preceeding it was heightened by mysterious events in February 1972, which proved to be a *coup* attempt instigated by Colonel Kouandété, the main architect of the *coups* of 1967 and 1969. Friction resulted between the President-designate, Ahomadegbe, and Maga, whom Ahomadegbe suspected of wanting to prevent his accession. Colonel Kouandété was put on trial only after Ahomadegbe had come to power, when he was condemned to death, though the sentence was not carried out.

[On October 26th, 1972, the army, led by Major Kerekou, who had taken part in the 1967 *coup*, overthrew the Presidential Council and within 24 hours established a new military Government. Soldiers entered the Presidential Palace and interrupted a cabinet meeting; shots were heard, but there seems to have been little resistance and no casualties. Ahomadegbe and Maga were immediately put under house arrest, as was Apithy on his return from Paris, and their release depends on the findings of a special commission which Kerekou has set up to examine the Presidential Council's administration. Kerekou justifies the army's intervention on the grounds that the Presidential Council was essentially divisive, with each of the three members supported only by his own region, and also corrupt and economically unsound, allowing nepotism and misappropriation of public funds. His new Government consists of twelve young army officers drawn equally from the three main regions of Cotonou, Porto Novo and the north. His stated aims are national unity and a fair economic policy. In place of the Consultative Assembly a 100-member Advisory Committee, said to be representative of all Dahomeyans, is to help define government

policy through three sub-committees dealing with general policy, finance and the economy, social and cultural affairs. There seems to be no likelihood in the near future of power being returned to a civilian administration, as has been the case in the past after a military takeover, as Kerekou appears to be adamant that health must first be restored to the economy and political wounds healed. *Editor*.]

The Presidential Council resolved nothing and there is nothing to suggest that Dahomey's basic economic problems were being seriously confronted. If the chronic budget deficits seemed to have been reduced for the moment, this was due not so much to the Presidential Council as to troubles in Nigeria, which began during the civil war, when Nigeria imposed tight controls. This led to a great increase in the smuggling of imported goods into Nigeria and of cocoa from Nigeria (calculated to have been worth over £2 million in the 1971–72 cocoa season). It is true that the council was relatively free from labour disruptions, partly because it lifted the crippling "twenty per cent" deduction (a kind of poll tax, which had led to general strikes in 1965 and 1967). It is also true that it was able to compensate for this loss of government revenue by fiscal means, although many observers have been puzzled by exactly how this has been done. However, Dahomey's economy is still basically unpromising. Even the oil deposits on which some hopes have been placed have proved for the moment to be uncommercial, although there is prospect of exploitation in a few years' time.

Thus Dahomey still has to look outside for assistance. The principle source of aid has undoubtedly been France, who is for example, contributing substantially to the cost of the new University of Dahomey at Abomey Calavi (the decision not to locate this in the intellectual capital, Porto Novo, was the cause of one of the biggest rifts in the Council's first two years. But there are signs that Dahomey is looking to oil-rich Nigeria as a possible alternative, should for any reason the French prove ungenerous in the future. Nigeria has already provided a £1 million long-term loan to be used mainly for improving the international highway from Dahomey to Nigeria. [The military government has sent goodwill missions to Nigeria, Ghana, Ivory Coast, Upper Volta, Niger and Togo with messages to the head of state from Kerekou, who is particularly keen to cultivate good relations with Nigeria. He would like to see economic co-operation between the two countries and has advocated a Benin Union between Dahomey, Nigeria and Togo. His government is pledged to honour all the country's existing international agreements. *Editor*.]

ECONOMY

Samir Amin*

HISTORICAL BACKGROUND

If any country has been truly ruined by the balkanization of west Africa, that country is Dahomey. Densely populated and possessing considerable resources, this region, where the savannah extends as far as the sea, saw the creation, in the pre-colonial period, of a series of states whose civilization ranks among the most brilliant of the continent. In the middle of the nineteenth century the coast of Dahomey was already exporting as many palm products (palmetto and oil) as on the eve of independence after seventy years of colonial rule. Colonization endowed the country, like others, with an infra-structure and institutions which were "modern", or, more correctly, European, but it certainly did not bring about development from the economic point of view—that had already taken place. Indeed, what colonization caused was an economic decline, because the profits from trade which had previously gone to merchants and local states were now appropriated by colonial trading companies.

The great misfortune of Dahomey arises from the development of the A.O.F. and the *loi cadre*, which led to the independence as separate states of all the constituent parts of the federation. Dahomey never recovered from this serious balkanization. For not only were the years which followed to show the impossibility both of improving agriculture and of industrializing this little state, but also the return of the Dahomeyans who had been expelled from other territories was to make impossible any attempt at the proper management of public finance. The first state of the group with the sad distinction of having unemployed intellectuals and middle classes, Dahomey was also the first to suffer a "brain drain" to Europe. Thus Dahomey's resources became handicaps.

This explains the extraordinarily disturbed political life of Dahomey. The continual deterioration of public finances and a very serious decline in the standard of living have resulted in permanent instability and repeated strikes, demonstrations and *coups d'état*.

It is fashionable, when speaking of Dahomey, to talk of "tribal quarrels". It is true that the ethnic groups of the south of the country have a very high awareness of their distinctiveness, but it would be more appropriate to speak of regional problems than of tribal differences. For colonialism created a colony extending about 660 km. from north to south, with a poor and neglected hinterland behind the narrow coastal zone of Cotonou-Porto Novo.

POPULATION

Between 1961 and 1971 the population of Dahomey rose from 2.1 to 2.8 million inhabitants (annual

* For the 1973 edition revisions have been made to this article by the Editor.

growth rate approximately 2.8 per cent). The southern regions have more than 70 per cent of the population, and this, together with southern Nigeria, is the heaviest rural density in western Africa: 120 inhabitants per sq. km. But the urbanization of the country is still rudimentary. The townships of Cotonou–Porto-Novo (230,000 inhabitants), of Ouidah and Abomey (80,000 inhabitants) in the south and of Parakou and Djongou (33,000 inhabitants) in the north make up barely 12 per cent of the country's population. The urban growth rate is still relatively low (less than 5 per cent per annum). Some 46 per cent of Dahomey's people are under 15 years of age.

DAHOMEY'S TRADITIONAL ECONOMY

More than a million hectares of this small state are cultivated; in the south 50–60 per cent of workable land is in fact cultivated, so that the former long fallow periods are no longer possible. Agriculture is based on maize (216,000 metric tons in 1970), manioc (736,000 tons) and yams (605,000 tons), and, to a lesser extent, millet and sorghum (60,000 tons) in the north. Of the 720,000 hectares cultivated 400,000 are devoted to maize, 130,000 to manioc, 60,000 to yams and 130,000 to millet. The yield per hectare remains stationary and supply per capita is definitely declining, although it is impossible to put a figure on it. Fishing, which is a valuable source of protein, suffered difficulties because of the increase of salt in the lagoon following the creation of the port of Cotonou, but its yield is recovering and rose from 1,600 tons in 1965 to 4,220 in 1970. In the same period the number of trawlers in operation doubled to 120.

Livestock farming, practised in its widespread traditional form in the north, is based on a herd of 590,000 cattle and 1,200,000 sheep and goats; in the south 345,000 pigs are kept. Meat production is insufficient, hence the necessity of importing animals from Niger.

The country's principal exports come from the so-called "natural" palm plantations which cover 400,000 hectares. This crop was in fact considerably extended by the work of village communities and slaves in the nineteenth century before colonization. More intensive cultivation by selected industrial palm plantations was started in 1962, financed by external aid from France and the EEC, and carried on by the *Société national pour le développement rural* (SONADER), but this has so far involved only 25,000 hectares and production is not yet significant. In these circumstances it is obvious why the export of palm products was relatively stationary between 1960 and 1970. Dahomey's principal industries are based on this production: five palm oil factories, and one palmetto oil factory with a capacity of 60,000 metric tons, all managed by the *Société nationale des huileries du Dahomey* (SNAHDA).

The other export products are insignificant. Groundnuts provide less than 10,000 metric tons ready shelled for export. Nevertheless, an oil factory with a capacity of 45,000 tons in the shell is being built. The production of Allen cotton, under the aegis of CFDT, has been started in the north, and now supplies over 30,000 tons of fibre. *Karité* almond nuts and cashew nuts are also produced. Between 1961 and 1968, at constant prices, exports showed an average annual growth rate of only one per cent.

Considering also the deterioration in market prices, the situation is tragic. Groundnuts and cotton have to be subsidized by the EEC (under the "price support" subsidies) and by the Export Price Stabilization Fund, while the traditional palm products cannot stand up to competition from industrial plantations unless given support (the subsidies in this case are referred to as "structural improvement").

DAHOMEY'S MODERN ECONOMY

Despite her relative lack of urbanization Dahomey has a high standard of education and, furthermore, has had it for much longer than other countries. In 1971–72 30 per cent of the eligible age-group attended primary schools, which had 186,000 pupils. In addition there were already 27,000 secondary school pupils and about 2,500 students in higher education. These numbers are increasing rapidly. By virtue of its large middle class Dahomey only receives a limited number of technical experts from Europe (250 since 1961). Moreover, the number of Europeans living in the country is small—about 2,000.

In spite of these advantages Dahomey's "modern" economy remains rudimentary, although the country is certainly not lacking in mineral potential. In 1968 Union Oil of California discovered oil off-shore, which will doubtless be developed in a few years. The search for phosphates and uranium continues. Local limestone is used by a cement factory of 100,000 tons capacity. The iron ore in the north of the country, is of poor quality (30–40 per cent grade) and could only be exploited for a local steelworks, but there are no plans for one. The country may have significant reserves of chrome. Certainly the production of electrical energy is still quite insufficient for any serious industry. This production, supplied by power stations, which rose from 6.1 million kWh. in 1959 to 20.2 in 1967 and 33.4 in 1970, is chiefly absorbed by domestic and city use. But the agreement signed in 1968 with Togo and Ghana for the utilization of the energy from Akosombo has enabled imports of electricity to rise to 50 million kWh. since 1971; prices will be maintained and the profits used for the extension of electrical plant in the three countries.

For long possessing only a wharf, Cotonou has since 1964 had a port which handled 284,000 metric tons of merchandise in that year and 544,000 in 1969. But a very large part of the traffic is still bound for Niger. This is emphasized by the flow of traffic on the Dahomey-Niger Joint Organization (OCDN) railway, 580 km. long. In 1963 consignments to and from Niger amounted to 95,000 tons, as against 45,000 tons of internal traffic. In 1967 the two figures were respectively 150,900 and 34,200 tons. The *Opération Hirondelle*, and the subsidies it requires, are financed at the expense of a railway deficit of the order of 120 million francs CFA a year. Most internal transportation uses roads (of which there are about 7,600 km.)

It is difficult to speak of "industries" when the main ones are palm oil factories, the palmetto oil factory and groundnut oil and shelling factories of 10,000 tons capacity, and when the greatest industrial project carried out in the first ten years of independence was the kenaf factory of the *Société dahoméenne du Kénaf*, a joint Italian-Dahomeyan company. Inaugurated in 1968, the factory, with a capacity of 16,000 tons of fibre and 5,000 tons of sackcloth, has been functioning very badly owing to the delay in the implementation of the kenaf cultivation project, but the opening of a new plantation will enable the factory to supply local needs, leaving 60 per cent of its output for export. The country also has a small soft-drink factory, transistor assembly workshops, factories assembling cycles and Citroën vehicles, factories producing frozen shrimps, a pasta factory, a paint factory, a factory turning out 600,000 pairs of plastic sandals, and a small textile industry with a 600 ton capacity (ICODA—*Industrie cotonnière du Dahomey*).

It is hardly surprising therefore that there were only 28,500 Dahomeyan wage- and salary-earners in 1967, 19,000 of them in the public sector (and 13,900 in the central government alone). Industry employs barely 2,150, building 1,100, business and banking 2,500 and transport and communications 3,250.

MASSIVE FOREIGN AID AND ECONOMIC STAGNATION

Few countries are as dependent as Dahomey on foreign aid. In the nine years from 1960 to 1968 the country received an annual average of 3,900 million francs CFA, representing about 8.7 per cent of the G.D.P. About 2.300 million francs CFA per annum of this official aid, used for capital goods and projects, permitted the financing of the greater part of real investments. The rest went to financing current public expenditure and to price support.

However, production stood still during the entire decade and the standard of living continued to drop. For the four years from 1963 to 1966, for which more precise details are available, it will be noted that the volume of public investment rose to a yearly average of 3,900 million francs CFA, of which 3,000 million were financed by foreign aid and used for capital projects. But if the 1,700 million francs CFA of official aid not used for capital projects (1963–66 annual average) are taken into account, it appears that public savings were in fact negative and that the whole of public investment—and more besides—was in reality financed from abroad. Of private investment, which the accounts show to be of the order of 3,000 million francs CFA a year, less than 1,000 million go to the modern sector.

The amount of official aid devoted to investment is well known. In particular France, through the FAC and loans from the CCCE, financed the building of the port of Cotonou, which alone absorbed 8,000 million francs CFA between 1959 and 1965. This explains among other things the high level of investments made in 1963. The EDF gave priority to the gradual restoration of the palm plantations, and a loan from the *Kreditanstalt* financed the palmetto oil works. The rest went on infrastructure (roads), social capital (education and health), town planning, and government needs (radio, government buildings, telephones, etc.).

In the modern private sector the only significant investments—other than in oil prospecting—are those affecting the factory at Kénaf and a few small industries: a yearly average of the order of 1,200 million francs CFA and very unevenly distributed from year to year.

The real per capita G.N.P. declined considerably from 21,000 francs CFA (at 1968 CFA exchange rates) in 1959 to 18,000 francs CFA in 1968, or a drop of 17 per cent. This seems quite probable when one takes into account the very feeble rate of growth of agricultural exports: average rural income fell from 11,000 francs CFA at 1968 rates in 1959 to 10,000 in 1968, with about half this accounted for by farming families consuming their own produce. Revenue from non-agricultural activities, higher than that of agriculture (for a population 6.7 times smaller, which amounts to a per capita income about seven times higher), is also roughly constant and does not prevent growing unemployment, estimated by the authorities at 10,000 in 1967 (a very optimistic estimate). The deterioration in wage- and salary-earners' buying power explains the permanent series of wage claims, and the *Salaire minimum interprofessionel garanti* (SMIG), fixed since 1966 at 26–38 francs CFA according to area, had to be increased by 4 per cent in 1969 under collective agreement in the private sector, after an outbreak of strikes.

PERMANENT CRISIS IN PUBLIC FINANCE AND BALANCE OF PAYMENTS

In 1959 public expenditure was of the order of 5,500 million francs. Current budgetary expenditure rose to 7,300 million francs CFA in 1966 and 11,829

million francs CFA in 1972. Added to that is the expenditure by the provinces and urban districts, which is about 13 per cent of that of the central government. Never in the country's tragic circumstances has this budget been in balance, in spite of the rise of tax revenue from 12 to 15 per cent of the G.D.P. The treasury's deficit between 1960 and 1968 was of the order of 1,500 million francs CFA a year, an average of 20 per cent of expenditure. In the same period the accumulated public deficit rose to 13,400 million francs CFA, financed to the sum of 23,000 million by French budgetary subsidies, 500 million from BCEAO advances and the liquidation of the treasury's assets and 5,600 million from a short-term loan by private creditors. In these circumstances there has never been any question of development financed by the state.

At the end of 1967 the public foreign debt rose to 10,100 million francs CFA, 7,600 million debts to other governments and 2,400 million debts to private sources abroad (chiefly commercial credits). In total, then, the external and internal debt reached 15,700 million francs CFA (more than 30 per cent of the G.D.P.). The institution of a tax-farming system with payment by results for the tax collected was decided on in 1969.

The tragedy of Dahomey's public finance is not, as one is too easily led to believe, the result of political instability. On the contrary, it is the cause of this instability. And it is in the folly of balkanization, coming after 70 years of colonial stagnation, not to say repression, that the root cause is to be found.

Dahomey's balance of payments is still obscure. The economic accounts between 1963 and 1969 show that the average percentage of imports covered by exports was only 49 per cent. Added to returns from exports are various current earnings for transporting products to and from Niger, pensions paid by France, expenditure in Dahomey by foreign embassies and tourists, etc. which amount to a yearly average of 2,000 million francs CFA. Miscellaneous current expenses in the other direction (Dahomeyan embassies abroad, travel, students, etc.) do not exceed a yearly average of 500 million francs CFA.

Official external aid having amounted to a yearly average of 3,900 million francs CFA, and the inflow of private capital 1,200 million, the balance of payments is struck—as in 1959—by a number of private transfers amounting to a yearly average of 2,700 million francs CFA.

STATISTICAL SURVEY

AREA (sq. km.)	TOTAL POPULATION (1971 est.)	POPULATION OF TRIBES (1969 estimates)								
		Fon	Adja	Bariba	Yoruba	Aizo	Somba	Fulani	Coto-Coli	Dendi
113,048*	2,792,000	850,000	220,000	175,000	160,000	92,000	90,000	68,000	45,000	30,000

* 43,480 sq. miles.

DÉPARTEMENT	CHIEF TOWN	POPULATION OF CHIEF TOWN (1969 est.)
Ouémé	Porto-Novo (capital)	74,000
Atlantique	Cotonou	120,000
Borgou	Parakou	16,000
Zou	Abomey	29,000
Atacora	Natitingou	n.a.
Mono	Lakossa	n.a.

Employment: Small farmers 750,000; Commerce 3,600; Public Works 6,000; Railways 2,850.

Agriculture (1970—metric tons): Cassava (manioc) 736,000, Sweet potatoes and yams 605,000, Maize 216,000, Palm kernels 94,300, Millet, sorghum and fonio 60,000, Groundnuts (in shell) 57,000, Dry beans 25,000, Cottonseed 18,000, Cotton (lint) 14,000, Bananas 10,000*.

Livestock (1971): Cattle 590,000, Sheep 555,000, Goats 650,000, Pigs 345,000.

Fishing (1970): 4,220 metric tons.

Industry (1971): Palm oil 77,000 metric tons, Palmetto oil 28,000 metric tons; (1970–71): Beer 104,000 hl., Carbonated soft drinks 43,000 hl.

Currency: 100 centimes = 1 franc de la Communauté Financière Africaine.
Coins: 1, 2, 5, 10 and 25 francs CFA.

(* FAO estimate).

Notes: 50, 100, 500, 1,000, 5,000 and 10,000 francs CFA. Exchange rates (December 1972): 1 franc CFA = 2 French centimes; £1 sterling = 593.625 francs CFA; U.S. $1 = 255.785 francs CFA; 1,000 francs CFA = £1.685 = $3.91.

Budget (1971): Revenue 9,316m., Expenditure 10,603m. francs CFA; (1972) Revenue 10,429.4m., Expenditure 11,829.4m. francs CFA.

Five-Year Plan (1966–70—m. francs CFA): Total investment 35,128 (Foreign Public Aid 20,500); Rural Development 12,065; Communications and Power 10,250; Industrial and Commercial Development 9,934; Social and Administrative Development 2,870.

An interim plan covers the years 1971–72, to complete projects not fully executed by the end of the 1966–70 plan. A new plan will be drawn up for the period 1973–76.

EXTERNAL TRADE
(million francs CFA)

	1965	1966	1967	1968	1969	1970	1971
Imports	8,491	8,264	10,745	12,208	14,129	17,825	21,201
Exports	3,367	2,585	3,750	5,508	6,937	9,070	11,649

COMMODITIES

IMPORTS	1967	1968	1969
Food and live animals	1,686.3	1,626.5	1,744.1
Tobacco and products	391.3	679.3	613.8
Petroleum products	453.2	559.4	480.6
Chemicals . .	776.1	1,012.3	1,352.5
Woven cotton fabrics	1,658.1	1,930.1	2,427.3
Iron and Steel .	404.1	311.0	492.2
Machinery (non-electric . .	1,222.0	1,118.5	1,145.5
Electrical machinery	412.0	545.6	561.9
Road Motor Vehicles	728.2	1.002.0	887.6
TOTAL (incl. others)	10,704.5	12,202.9	14,124.4

EXPORTS	1967	1968	1969
Coffee (green and roasted) . .	142.0	66.1	334.7
Other food . .	425.8	603.4	1,500.0
Tobacco and products	118.4	184.9	315.2
Groundnuts (green) .	229.6	274.2	264.3
Palm nuts and kernels . .	140.0	331.0	273.3
Other oilseeds, nuts and kernels .	267.0	353.8	418.2
Raw cotton (excluding linters) . .	331.5	680.3	807.1
Palm oil . .	263.6	431.7	431.3
Palm kernel oil .	895.3	1,778.3	1,500.7
Machinery and transport equipment .	136.0	282.9	94.2
* TOTAL (incl.others)	3,751.7	5,504.1	6,937.3

COUNTRIES

IMPORTS	1967	1968	1969
Belgium/Luxembourg .	371	404	538
China, People's Republic	243	317	332
France . . .	5,327	5,114	5,475
Germany, Federal Republic . . .	493	505	700
Italy	1,014	1,051	568
Ivory Coast . .	192	224	415
Japan . . .	72	219	313
Netherlands . .	301	962	1,039
Nigeria . . .	178	249	302
Senegal . . .	364	415	429
Togo . . .	247	316	452
United Kingdom . .	251	471	610
U.S.A. . . .	460	479	802
* TOTAL (incl. others) .	10,705	12,203	14,124

EXPORTS	1967	1968	1969
Belgium/Luxembourg .	171	156	83
France . . .	1,300	2,014	2,491
Germany, Federal Republic . . .	243	439	557
Italy . . .	53	33	145
Japan . . .	155	206	375
Netherlands . .	558	332	900
Nigeria . . .	169	304	913
Senegal . . .	45	101	188
Togo	205	327	135
United Kingdom .	6	157	93
U.S.A. . . .	529	1,192	669
*TOTAL (incl. others)	3,752	5,504	6,937

1970: France 7,455, United Kingdom 952, U.S.A. 948.

1970: France 3,574, Nigeria 847, United Kingdom 381, U.S.A. 444.

* In some cases, totals differ slightly from the figures given in the summary table for trade, which are those published by the national statistical authority.

Source: Mainly *Overseas Associates, Foreign Trade* (Statistical Office of the European Communities, Luxembourg).

TRANSPORT

Railways (1969): Passengers 1,044,000, Freight 225,000 tons; receipts totalled 993m. francs CFA.

Roads (1970): 20,000 vehicles of which about one half were private cars.

Shipping (1971): Vessels entered 755, total tonnage 2,076,000; Goods loaded 195,000 tons, unloaded 413,000 tons; Passengers embarked 179, disembarked 173.

Civil Aviation (1970): Passenger arrivals 18,594; Freight unloaded 941 tons, loaded 687 tons; mail loaded and unloaded 160 tons.

EDUCATION
(1971–72)

	SCHOOLS	PUPILS
Primary . . .	852	186,000
Secondary . . .	60*	27,000
Technical . . .	7*	2,000
Teacher Training, etc. .	4	2,553
University . . .	1	600

* 1970 figures.

THE CONSTITUTION*

A Charter of "fundamental law" was introduced in May 1970 after the Military Directory had established a three-man Presidential Commission. The Charter is to regulate the political life of the state until general elections have been held and constitutional government restored. The Charter was signed by the three members of the Presidential Commission, and its operation is guaranteed by the army.

The Charter provides for a Presidential Commission, a Cabinet, a Consultative Assembly, Departmental and Urban Consultative Assemblies, and a Supreme Court. The "supreme organ of state" is the Presidential Commission. This meets when summoned by two of the members, and has to reach unanimous decisions, except when one

member withholds his assent to a decision three times, in which case a majority decision suffices.

Members of the Presidential Commission attend Cabinet meetings. The Consultative Assembly, according to the draft decree issued by the Cabinet in February 1971, would have 30 members (it was inaugurated in June 1972 with 36 members), divided into economic, social and general policy sections, and advises the Presidential Commission and the Cabinet.

The chairmanship of the Presidential Commission rotates every two years. The Chairman exercises the functions of head of state, leader of the government and chief of the armed forces. For the first period until May 1972, Hubert Maga was Chairman. Justin Ahomadegbé took over after him, and in 1974 he in turn will be succeeded by Sourou Apithy.

* The Constitution was invalidated by the military *coup d'état* of October 26th, 1972.

THE GOVERNMENT

(*December* 1972)

HEAD OF STATE
President: Major MATHIEU KEREKOU.

CABINET
President and Minister of Defence: Major MATHIEU KEREKOU.
Minister of Foreign Affairs: Major MICHEL ALADAYE.
Minister of Finance: Deputy Quartermaster THOMAS LAHAMI.
Minister for Justice and Legislation: Major BARTHELEMY OHOUENS.
Minister of Information and Tourism: Major PIERRE KOFFI.

Minister of Rural Development and Co-operation: Captain MAMA DJOUGOU.
Minister for the Civil Service: Captain JANVIER ASSOGBA.
Minister of Transport and Mines: Captain ANDRE ACHADE.
Minister of Health and Social Affairs: Captain DJIBRIL MORIBA.
Minister of Public Works, Posts and Telecommunications: Captain NESTOR BEHETON.
Minister of the Interior and of Security: Captain MICHEL AIKPE.
Minister of National Education, Youth and Sports: Captain HILAIRE MADJEGOUME.

DIPLOMATIC REPRESENTATION

EMBASSIES AND LEGATIONS ACCREDITED TO DAHOMEY

(E) Embassy; (L) Legation.

Algeria: Accra, Ghana (E).
Belgium: Abidjan, Ivory Coast (E).
Bulgaria: Lagos, Nigeria (E).
Canada: Accra, Ghana. (E).
China, Republic (Taiwan): Cotonou (E); *Ambassador:* TCHEN HOU-JOU.
Czechoslovakia: Accra, Ghana (E).
Ethiopia: Lagos, Nigeria (E).
France: B.P. 766, Cotonou (E); *Ambassador:* MICHEL VAN GREVENYNGHE.
Gabon: Abidjan, Ivory Coast (E).
Germany, Federal Republic: blvd. de France, B.P. 504, Cotonou (E); *Ambassador:* Dr. KARL WAND.
Ghana: B.P. 488, Cotonou (E); *Ambassador* (vacant).
Guinea: (E); *Ambassador:* LAYE KOUROUMA.
Haiti: rue Bellamy, Porto-Novo (E); *Ambassador:* (vacant).

Hungary: Accra, Ghana (E).
India: Lagos, Nigeria (E).
Israel: B.P. 55, Cotonou (E); *Ambassador:* MORDEKHAI DRORY.
Italy: Abidjan, Ivory Coast (E).
Japan: Abidjan, Ivory Coast (E).
Korea, Republic: Abidjan, Ivory Coast (E).
Lebanon: Abidjan, Ivory Coast (E).
Mali: Accra, Ghana (E).
Mauritania: Dakar, Senegal (E).
Netherlands: Abidjan, Ivory Coast (E).
Niger: Cotonou (L); *Chargé d'Affaires:* DODO BOUKARY.
Nigeria: Cotonou (E); *Chargé d'Affaires:* O. O. SIHOYAN.
Norway: Lagos, Nigeria (E).
Pakistan: Lagos, Nigeria (E).

Poland: Accra, Ghana (E).

Spain: Abidjan, Ivory Coast (E).

Sudan: Lagos, Nigeria (E).

Sweden: Lagos, Nigeria (E).

Switzerland: Abidjan, Ivory Coast (E).

Tunisia: Abidjan, Ivory Coast (E).

U.S.S.R: B.P. 881, Cotonou (E); *Ambassador:* IGOR SOUKOUSKY.

United Kingdom: Lomé, Togo (E).

U.S.A.: B.P. 119, Cotonou (E); *Ambassador:* ROBERT ANDERSON.

Vatican: *Apostolic Pro-Nuncio:* Mgr. GIOVANNI MARIANI (also accredited to Senegal and Niger).

Viet-Nam, Republic: Abidjan, Ivory Coast (E).

Yugoslavia: Accra, Ghana (E).

Dahomey also has diplomatic relations with Central African Republic, Romania and Zaire.

NATIONAL ADVISORY COMMITTEE

Created to replace the former National Consultative Assembly, the Advisory Committee was inaugurated in October 1972.

It consists of 100 members chosen to represent the whole country and, working through three sub-committees, to define government policy in all fields. The sub-committees are concerned with general policy, finance and the economy, and social and cultural affairs.

POLITICAL PARTY

The Presidential Council had hoped to establish national unity by the creation of a single party, but as yet no such party has been set up.

DEFENCE

Dahomey has an army of 3,000 men, and an air force of 150; in addition a parachute command and a squadron of 120 commandos are on constant stand-by.

Chief of Staff: Major MATHIEU KEREKOU.

Director of State Security: Lieut. FRANÇOIS FOULIN.

JUDICIAL SYSTEM

THE SUPREME COURT: Cotonou

President of the Supreme Court: IGNACIO PINTO.

The work of the Supreme Court is divided into Constitutional, Administrative, Judicial and Accountancy Chambers and has been carried out since 1970.

There is a *tribunal de conciliation* in each of the 31 sub-prefectures and in main centres and a *tribunal de première instance de deuxième classe* (Magistrate's Court) at Porto-Novo, Cotonou, Ouidah, Abomey, Parakou, Natitingou and Kandi. The Court of Appeal, which has jurisdiction over the Assize Court, sits at Cotonou.

RELIGION

According to the 1961 census 65 per cent of the population hold animist beliefs, 15 per cent are Christians (12 per cent Catholics, 3 per cent Protestants) and 13 per cent Muslims. There are 257 Protestant mission centres with a personnel of about 120. In the Roman Catholic archdiocese of Cotonou, which extends over Dahomey and Niger, there are 470 mission centres with a total personnel of some 2,500.

Archbishop of Cotonou: Mgr. BERNARDIN GANTIN (resident in Rome).

PRESS AND PUBLISHERS

Etablissement National d'Edition et de Presse (E.N.E.P.): Cotonou.

L'Action Populaire: rue de Ouidah, Carré 405, B.P. 650, Cotonou; f. 1964; supported Mr. Ahomadegbe; daily; Dir. JULIEN AZA.

L'Aube Nouvelle: B.P. 80, Porto Novo; daily.

La Croix du Dahomey: B.P. 32, Cotonou; fortnightly.

Daho-Express: B.P. 1210, Cotonou; government daily; circ. 1,000.

Daho Matin: Carré 96, Cotonou; political; quarterly.

Le Démocrat: Dahomey Press Agency, B.P. 72, Cotonou; daily.

L'Etendard: Pavilion 29, Akpapa, Cotonou; quarterly.

Journal Officiel de la République du Dahomey: Porto-Novo; published by the Government Information Service; fortnightly.

La Patrie Dahoméenne: Porto-Novo; fortnightly; supported M. Apithy.

La Voix du Peuple: Dahomey Press Agency, B.P. 72, Cotonou; daily.

Walloguede (Journal du Parti): Dahomey Press Agency, B.P. 72, Cotonou; fortnightly.

Agence Dahoméenne de Presse: B.P. 72, Cotonou; f. 1961; national news agency; section of the Ministry of Information; Dir. M. DAMALA.

Deutsche Presse-Agentur and Tass also have offices in Dahomey.

RADIO AND TELEVISION

Voix de la Révolution Dahoméenne: Cotonou, B.P. 366; Government station broadcasting in French, Fon, Yoruba, Bariba, Mina, Peuhl and Dendi; Dir.-Gen. (vacant).

There were 85,000 receivers in use at December 31st, 1970.

Following an agreement signed with France in May 1972 television was to be introduced before the end of the year.

FINANCE

BANKS

CENTRAL BANK

Banque Centrale des Etats de l'Afrique de l'Ouest: 29 rue du Colisée, Paris; Cotonou, B.P. 325; Man. M. B. N'DIAYE.

Banque Dahoméenne de Développement: rue des Cheminots, Cotonou, B.P. 300; f. 1961; cap. 300m. francs CFA; Pres. FLORENT YEHOUESSI; publ. *Rapports d'activité* (annual).

Caisse Centrale de Coopération Economique: ave. Giram, B.P. 38, Cotonou; Dir. PIERRE CANOT.

Société Dahoméenne de Banque: rue de Révérend Père Colineau, B.P. 85, Cotonou and B.P. 262, Porto Novo; f. 1962; cap. 250m. francs CFA; associated with Crédit Lyonnais; Dir. ZDELPHENSE LEMON.

Agricultural Credit Bank: Cotonou; Govt. Commr. Col. PAUL EMILE DE SOUZA.

FOREIGN BANKS

Banque Internationale pour l'Afrique Occidentale: 9 ave. de Messine, Paris; Cotonou, B.P. 47; f. 1961.

Banque Nationale de Paris: 16 blvd. des Italiens, Paris; Cotonou, Avenue du Gouverneur-Général Clozel, B.P. 75; br. at Porto-Novo; Dir. Cotonou: PAUL GILLOUX.

INSURANCE

Cotonou

L'Union: B.P. 739.

L'Union-Vie: B.P. 80.

TRADE AND INDUSTRY

CHAMBER OF COMMERCE

Chambre de Commerce, d'Agriculture, et d'Industrie du Dahomey: ave. Général de Gaulle, Cotonou, B.P. 31; Pres. PIERRE FOURN; Sec. MICHEL LABELLE.

PROFESSIONAL ORGANIZATIONS

Association des Syndicats du Dahomey (Asynda): Cotonou; Pres. PIERRE FOURN.

Groupement Interprofessionnel des Entreprises du Dahomey (GIDA): B.P. 6, Cotonou; Pres. M. BASTIAN.

Jeune Chambre Economique: Pres. JEAN-BONIFACE AKANNI.

Syndicat des Commerçants Africains du Dahomey (Syncad): Cotonou.

Syndicat des Commercants Importateurs et Exportateurs: B.P. 6, Cotonou; Pres. M. THOMAS.

Syndicat Interprofessionel des Entreprises Industrielles du Dahomey: Cotonou; Pres. M. DOUCET.

Syndicat des Transporteurs Routiers du Dahomey: Cotonou; Pres. PASCAL ZENON.

TRADE UNIONS

Confédération Dahoméenne des Travailleurs Croyants (CDTC): Bourse du Travail, Cotonou; f. 1952; affiliated to IFCTU; 1,000 mems.; Gen. Sec. GABRIEL AHOUE.

Confédération Nationale des Syndicats Libres (CNSL): Bourse du Travail, Cotonou; f. 1964; 2,250 mems.; Gen. Sec. ETIENNE AHOUANGBE.

Union Générale des Syndicats du Dahomey (UGSD): Bourse du Travail, Cotonou; f. 1964; 8,000 mems.; Sec.-Gen. HONORAT OGOUBIYI-AKILOTAN.

Union Générale des Travailleurs du Dahomey (UGTD): B.P. 69, Cotonou; f. 1961; 10,000 mems.; Sec.-Gen. JACOB PADONOU; publ. *Le Patriote.*

MAJOR INDUSTRIAL COMPANIES

The following are some of the largest private or state-owned companies in terms either of capital investment or employment.

S.A. Aluminium Alcan du Dahomey: B.P. 304, Cotonou; company in process of incorporation; subsidiary of Aluminium Limited of Canada (ALCAN); manufacture of sheet-metal and aluminium products.

Société des Brasseries du Dahomey (SOBRADO): B.P. 135, route de Porto-Novo, Cotonou; f. 1957; cap. 550m. francs CFA, of which 94 per cent owned by French holding company SOGEPAL.

Production of beer, soft drinks and ice.

Pres. HENRI FAIVRE; Dir.-Gen. ROBERT BAILLY.

Société Dahoméenne Agricole et Industrielle du Kénaf (SODAK): B.P. 955, ave. Clozel, Cotonou; f. 1963; cap. 343m. francs CFA.

Cultivation of kenaf and export of kenaf fibre, manufacture of twine, pack-cloth and sacks.

Pres. Dir.-Gen. EMILE PARAISO; Dir.-Gen. ANTOINE BOMA; 464 employees (including head office).

Société Dahoméénne de Textiles: B.P. 34, Cotonou; cap. 600m. francs CFA; state participation; textile production.

Industrie Cotonnière du Dahomey (ICODA): B.P. 208, Cotonou; f. 1968; cap. 150m. francs CFA.

Bleaching, printing and dyeing of imported fabrics.

Pres. Dir.-Gen. M. MARCHAL.

Mobil Oil Afrique Occidentale: B.P. 251, Cotonou; cap. 900m. francs CFA.

Import of Petrol.

Inspecteur Résident A. HOMBERT; 48 employees.

Société Nationale des Huileries du Dahomey (SNAHDA): B.P. 312, Cotonou; f. 1962; cap. 600m. francs CFA, state-owned company.

Production of palm oil, palmetto and oil cake.

Dir.-Gen. LEONARD MABUDU.

Société Shell de l'Afrique Occidentale: B.P. 285, route de l'aviation, Cotonou; f. 1952.

Distribution of petroleum and chemical products, fertilizers.

Dir. J. A. BURTIN; 50 employees. (Subsidiary of Société Shell de l'Afrique Occidentale Abidjan, *see* Ivory Coast.)

TRANSPORT AND TOURISM

TRANSPORT

RAILWAYS

Organisation Commune Dahomey-Niger des Chemins de Fer et des Transports (OCDN): P.O.B. 16, Cotonou; f. 1959; Dahomey has a 63 per cent share, Niger 37 per cent. The main line runs for 438 km. from Cotonou to Parakou in the interior; a branch runs westwards via Ouidah to Segboroué (37 km.). There is also a line of 107 km. from Cotonou via Porto-Novo to Pobé near the Nigerian border. Total length of railways: 579 km. There are 12 diesel locomotives, 11 shunting locomotives, 9 rail cars, 21 carriages, 368 wagons. Dir. M. BOITTIAUX.

The planned extension of the line from Parakou to Dosso (Niger) will be 520 km. long, cost 9,329m. francs CFA and should be completed by 1975.

ROADS

The system is well developed. There are a total of 6,400 km. of classified roads and a further 1,200 km. of tracks suitable for motor traffic in the dry season. The roads along the coast and those from Cotonou to Allada and from Parakou to Malanville, a total of 700 km., are bitumen-surfaced.

SHIPPING

An extensive programme of expansion, at Cotonou, involving a deep water port with one jetty 1,700 metres long and another 800 metres long was completed in 1964 and officially inaugurated in 1965. Further expansion is in progress.

SHIPPING LINES CALLING AT COTONOU

Acomar: c/o Socopao-Dahomey, B.P. 253

Barber West African Line.

Cie. Maritime des Chargeurs Réunis: c/o Société Navale Delmas et Vieljeux, B.P. 213.

Compagnie Fabre: c/o Société Navale Delmas et Vieljeux, B.P. 213.

Deutsche Afrika Linien and Woermann Linie: c/o Société Navale Delmas-Vieljeux, B.P. 213.

Elder Dempster: c/o Socopao-Dahomey, B.P. 253.

Farrell Lines.

Holland West Afrika Lijn: c/o Union Maritime et Commerciale, B.P. 128.

Hugo Stinnes Transozean Schiffahrt G.m.b.H.: c/o S.A.M.O.A., B.P. 694.

Lloyd Triestino, S.p.A., di Navigazione: c/o S.O.A.E.M., B.P. 74.

Nouvelle Cie. des Paquebots (N.C.P.): c/o Société Navale Delmas et Vieljeux, B.P. 213.

Palm Line Ltd.: c/o Socopao, B.P. 253.

Royal Interocean Lines.

Scandinavian West Africa Line.

Société Navale de L'Ouest: c/o S.O.A.E.M., B.P. 74.

Société Navale Delmas et Vieljeux: ave. Mgr.-Steinmetz, B.P. 213.

Splošna Plovba: c/o Socopao, B.P. 253.

United West Africa Service: c/o Socopao, B.P. 253.

CIVIL AVIATION

The main airport at Cotonou has a 2.4 km. runway and there are secondary airports at Parakou, Natitingou, Kandi and Abomey.

Air Afrique: Cotonou, avenue du Gouverneur Ballot, B.P. 200; the Dahomey government has a 7 per cent share in Air Afrique (*see* under Ivory Coast).

Union de Transports Aériens (U.T.A.): Cotonou, ave. du Gouverneur Ballot, B.P. 200.

TOURISM

Direction Générale du Tourisme: Ministry of Labour and Tourism. B.P. 89, Cotonou; Dir. PIERRE. COMPLAN

POWER

Compagnie Centrale de Distribution d'Energie Electrique: B.P. 123, Cotonou; f. 1948; cap. F.14,400,000.

Production and distribution of electricity.

Pres. Dir.Gen. FRANÇOIS MUNICH; 130 employees.

There are 4 diesel power stations with a total capacity of 11,660 kW., and potential output of 50 million kWh.; output increased from 23,145,000 kWh. in 1966 to 33,433,000 kWh. in 1970, of which almost all was supplied by the stations at Cotonou and Porto-Novo.

Communauté Electrique du Bénin: established between Dahomey and Togo; office at Lomé; *see* under Togo.

EDUCATION

RESEARCH INSTITUTES

Institut de Recherches du Coton et des Textiles Exotiques (IRCT): B.P. 715, Cotonou; f. 1942; brs. at Allada, Parakou, Save; Regional Dir. PH.-J. P. RICHARD; library of 200 vols.; publ. *Coton et Plantes à Fibres Jutières, Coton et Fibres.*

Institut de Recherches Agronomiques Tropicales et des Cultures Vivrières (IRAT): B.P. 422, Cotonou; f. 1961; stations at Niaouli and Ina; Dir. R. WERT.

Institut de Recherches Appliquées du Dahomey (IRAD): Porto-Novo; f. 1942; library of 8,000 vols.; Dir. S. S. ADOTEVI; publ. *Etudes Dahoméennes.*

Institut de Recherches pour les Huiles et Oléagineux (IRHO): Pobé; Oil Palm Station; f. 1946; Dir. M. DUNAIS; Semé-Podji; Coconut Station; Dir. M. TCHIBOZO.

Institut Français de Recherches Fruitières Outre-Mer (IFAC): B.P. 89, Abomey; f. 1965; Dir. G. MONTAGUT.

Office de la Recherche Scientifique et Technique Outre-Mer Centre O.R.S.T.O.M. de Cotonou: B.P. 390, Cotonou; pedology, hydrology; library; Dir. P. VIENNOT (*see* main entry under France.)

Direction des Mines, de la Géologie et des Hydrocarbures: B.P. 249, Cotonou; f. 1971; formerly *Service des Mines et de la Géologie;* 52 mems.; branch of Ministry of Transport and Mines; library; Dir. J. LALEYE.

ARCHIVES, LIBRARY AND MUSEUMS

Archives Nationales de la République du Dahomey: B.P. No. 3, Porto Novo; f. 1914; conserves and classifies official state documents; Dir. ABDOU SERPOS TIDJANI.

Bibliothèque Nationale: Porto Novo; 7,500 vols.

Musée d'Abomey: Abomey.

Musée de Cotonou: Cotonou.

UNIVERSITY

UNIVERSITÉ DU DAHOMEY

ABOMEY-CALAVY, B.P. 526, COTONOU
Founded 1970

State-supported; independent; language of instruction: French.

Rector: EDOUARD ADJANOHOUN.

Secretary-General: MICHEL ASSOGBA.

Library of 12,000 vols.

Number of teachers: 52.

Number of students: 600.

Publications: *Annuaire* and students' guide.

DIRECTORS:

Department of Scientific and Technical Studies: GEORGES BOUIX.

Department of Literary and Linguistic Studies: Mme MIREILLE MASSUE.

Department of Medical and Para-Medical Studies: EDOUARD GOUDOTE.

Institute of Public and Business Administration: MANASSÉ AYAYI.

SELECT BIBLIOGRAPHY

Works on the former A.O.F. Countries generally

AJAYI, J. F. ADE and CROWDER, MICHAEL (Eds.). *The History of West Africa*, Volume One.

BALLARD, J. A. "Politics and Government in Former French West and Equatorial Africa: a Critical Bibliography." *Journal of Modern African Studies*, 3/4, pp. 589–605, 1965.

BRUNSCHWIG, HENRI. *French Colonialism 1871–1914: Myths and Realities*. London, Pall Mall, 1966.

COLEMAN, J. S., and ROSBERG, C. G. (Eds.). *Political Parties and National Integration in Tropical Africa*. Berkeley, University of California Press, 1964.

CROWDER, MICHAEL. *West Africa under Colonial Rule*. London, Hutchinson, 1968.

FOLTZ, W. J. *From French West Africa to Mali Federation*. New Haven, Yale U.P., 1965.

HARGREAVES, J. D. *West Africa: The Former French States*. Englewood Cliffs, N.J., Prentice-Hall, 1967.

HARRISON CHURCH, R. J. *West Africa* (6th edn.). London, Longmans, 1968.

LUSIGNAN, GUY DE. *French-Speaking Africa since Independence*. London, Pall Mall, 1969.

MORGAN, W. B., and PUGH, J. C. *West Africa*. London, Methuen, 1969.

SCHACHTER-MORGENTHAU, RUTH. *Political Parties in French-Speaking West Africa*. London, O.U.P., 1964.

SURET-CANALE, JEAN. *Afrique noire: occidentale et centrale*. Vol. I: *Géographie, civilisations, histoire*. Vol. II: *L'ère coloniale (1900–1945)*. Paris, Editions Sociales, 1964 (Vol. II) and 1968 (Vol. I, 3rd edn.).

SURET-CANALE, JEAN, and NIAN, DJIBRIL TAMSIR. *Histoire de l'Afrique occidentale*. Paris, Présence Africaine, 1961.

THOMPSON, VIRGINIA. *West Africa's Council of the Entente*. Ithaca and London, Cornell University Press, 1972.

THOMPSON, VIRGINIA, and ADLOFF, RICHARD. *French West Africa*. London, O.U.P., 1958.

Dahomey

CORNEVIN, ROBERT. *Le Dahomey*. Paris, Presses universitaires de France, 1965.
Histoire du Dahomey. Paris, Berger-Levrault, 1962.

HARRISON CHURCH, R. J. *West Africa* (6th edn., Chapter 25). London, Longmans, 1968.

JOURNAUX, A., PÉLISSIER, P., and PARISSE, R. *Géographie du Dahomey*. Caen, Imprimerie Ozanne, 1962.

Equatorial Guinea

PHYSICAL AND SOCIAL GEOGRAPHY*

René Pélissier

PHYSICAL FEATURES

This Republic (known as Guinea Ecuatorial in Spanish) has an area of 28,051 sq. km. with 245,989 inhabitants (1960 census). For administrative purposes the territory is divided into two provinces, Fernando Póo: 2,034 sq. km., including Annobón Island (17 sq. km.) and Río Muni: 26,017.5 sq. km., including three coastal islets, Corisco (15 sq. km.), and the Great and Little Elobeys (2.5 sq. km.). Fernando Póo is a parallelogram-shaped island, 72 km. by 35 km., made of three extinct volcanoes. To the north lies the Pico de Santa Isabel (3,007 m.) with an easy access. In the centre of the island is the Pico de Moca (Moka) of alpine height, where cattle and horses can be raised. Further south, the Gran Caldera constitutes the remotest and least developed part of the island. Mountain lakes exist at 1,790 m. (Moka). The coast is steep to the south. Santa Isabel, which is on the rim of a sunken volcano, is the only natural harbour. There are open roadsteads at San Carlos and Concepción. Fertility is high due to the existence of volcanic soils. At the bottom of the Guinean archipelago lies the remote island of Annobón, which is in the southern hemisphere, south of the Portuguese island of São Tomé.

Continental Río Muni is a jungle enclave bordered to the north by Cameroon and in the east and south by Gabon. A coastal plain rises steeply toward the Gabonese frontier. Main orographic complexes are the spurs of the Monts de Cristal of Gabon. Highest peaks are Monte Chocolate (1,110 m.), Piedra de Nzas (1,200 m.), Monte Mitra (1,200 m.) and Monte Chime (1,200 m.). The main river is the Río Benito (called the Woleu in Gabon), non-navigable except for a 20-km. stretch, which divides Río Muni in two. On the Cameroon border is the Río Campo. Its tributary, the Kye, is the *de facto* eastern border with Gabon. The Río Muni is not a river but the mouth of several Gabon and Río Munian rivers, among which the Utamboni is notable. The coast is a long beach with low cliffs towards Puerto Iradier. There is no natural harbour.

POPULATION

The country has an equatorial climate with heavy rainfall, especially in Fernando Póo. The average temperature of Santa Isabel is 77°F. and the average rainfall is in excess of 2,000 mm. Moisture is prevalent everywhere in the island except on the Moka heights. Río Muni has less debilitating conditions, Bata being somewhat drier and cooler than Santa Isabel, which has one of the most inhospitable climates of the Bight of Biafra.

Of a population of 245,989 in 1960, 7,086 were Europeans. While no reliable later statistics exist, it is safe to assume that the 2,864 Europeans of Río Muni (1960) have dwindled to a few hundred at most since the crisis of March 1969, and the 4,222 Europeans on Fernando Póo may have declined to about 1,000. In 1960 Fernando Póo had 62,612 inhabitants, including 1,415 on Annobon. Río Muni had 183,377. The racial composition is unusually complex for such a small political unit. Main ethnic groups are, in Río Muni, the Fang (*Pamues* in Spanish). They are the dominant and driving people of Río Muni. They may represent 80–90 per cent of the population of Río Muni. North of the Benito river are the Ntumu Fang, and to the south of it the Okak Fang. Coastal tribes—the Kombe, Balengue, Bujeba, etc.—have been pushed towards the sea by Fang pressure. Both Fang and coastal peoples are Bantu and Equato-Guinean citizens. African foreigners are Hausa traders, Ibo, Ibibio and Efik contract workers from Nigeria, who work on the lumbering sites. In Fernando Póo live the Bubi who are the original inhabitants of the island. There may be about 15,000 of them now, under the political sway of their Fang compatriots. The Fernandino (a few thousand) are the descendants of former slaves liberated by the British, mingled with long-settled immigrants from Sierra Leone, Ghana, Nigeria and Cameroon. Formerly a black bourgeoisie, they have lost much of their status. Continental Río Munians (mostly Fang) have flocked to the island in recent years to join the civil and military services. Annobónians are fishermen and sailors. All these are citizens of the new Republic, but altogether they may still be a minority on the island, compared with the mass of Nigerian contract workers (mostly Ibo, Efik and Ibibio) employed on the cocoa plantations. Recently these numbered over 30,000, but economic conditions since 1969 and since the Biafran war may have modified their numbers.

The main city is Santa Isabel (perhaps 25,000 inhabitants in 1970), the capital of Fernando Póo and of the Republic, as well as the main economic, educational and religious centre. The other town of some note is San Carlos. Bubi villages are scattered in the eastern and western parts of the island. The plantations also have significant groups of Nigerian migrants sometimes living in compounds. On the mainland the only city is Bata. Other ports are Río Benito and Puerto Iradier. Inland, Micomeseng, Niefang, Ebebiyin and Evinayong are small market and administrative centres.

---

* *See* map on p. 202.

RECENT HISTORY

René Pélissier

While nominally Spanish since the end of the eighteenth century, Fernando Póo was not entirely explored before 1900, while the coast of Río Muni was held by France except for a small Spanish enclave around Cabo San Juan. The Treaty of Paris (1900) delimited the frontiers of Río Muni, but except for coastal settlements, no Spanish authority was recognized by the Fang of the enclave. Effective inland occupation was ended in the late 1920's. Meanwhile cocoa production on Fernando Póo was following the São Tomé pattern; namely the concentration of arable land in Spanish hands, the importation of foreign workers (notably Liberians), and intensive cultivation. The Spanish Civil War was marginal in equatorial waters, after the quick conquest of Republican Río Muni by a Nationalist expedition from Ifni and the Canary Islands. The dreams nurtured during the Second World War by Spanish expansionists of an empire taken from Britain in Nigeria and France in Equatorial Africa came to nothing. The real development of the colony dates from the post-war period when Spain subsidized cocoa and coffee exports, opened up new tribal lands for Spanish companies in Fernando Póo, started to educate and look after the welfare of her wards, and developed the Río Muni hinterland by making roads and opening new Catholic missions. Africans were legally minors (*indigenas*) except for a tiny minority of *emancipados*. On July 30th, 1959, the colony, which was then governed by an Admiral, was made an integral part of Spain as the Equatorial Region of Spain, divided into two provinces on the metropolitan pattern. Once the *indigenato* system was abolished, all Africans became technically full citizens of Spain and as such returned six representatives to the *Cortes* in Madrid. The first elections ever held in Spanish Africa took place in 1960. In December 1960, three Hispano-Guineans sat in the *Cortes*, the first black men ever to do so.

THE MOVE TOWARDS INDEPENDENCE

While this policy of administrative assimilation was going on, African nationalists refused to be made black Spaniards against their own wishes. They took refuge in Gabon and in Cameroon. Main groups were the *Movimiento Nacional de Liberación de la Guinea Ecuatorial* (MNLGE, subsequently MONALIGE), led by Atanasio Ndong, and the *Idea Popular de la Guinea Ecuatorial* (IPGE) of pseudo-Marxist leanings. Both were Fang-oriented. Denounced as a colonialist country by the Nationalists, Spain discreetly veered to less troubled waters by granting in September 1963 a measure of autonomy to her Region, with a joint legislative body for the two provinces and a cabinet consisting of eight African councillors and a president, to be elected by the assembly. A Spanish High Commissioner was to replace the Governor-General. These paper reforms were approved by the referendum of December 15th, 1963, and early in 1964 a new regrouping of moderate nationalists took place around Bonifacio Ondó Edu. This was the *Movimiento de Unión Nacional de la Guinea Ecuatorial* (MUNGE). From summer 1964 to October 12th, 1968, MUNGE was in power, but its autonomous government was severely attacked by IPGE and MONALIGE as an ineffective puppet body. After protracted negotiations between the nationalists and Spain, which was anxious to parry United Nations criticism, and if possible, to rescue Fernando Póo's riches from Fang ambitions, a constitution was finalized and approved in the summer of 1968. Independence was granted on October 12th, 1968. Bonifacio Ondó Edu was defeated, and after much contention between Atanasio Ndong and Francisco Macías Nguema, the latter became the first President of the new Republic. But Spain, who had made considerable investments, was wearying of incessant calls for assistance from the new President. Relations with Spain became strained in February and March 1969, after an abortive *coup d'état* by Foreign Minister Atanasio Ndong, who was killed as a result, along with some of President Macías' political opponents. Anti-white incidents in Río Muni led to a mass departure of Spanish residents, followed by the near collapse of Río Muni's economy, and serious threats to the prosperity of Fernando Póo. While new agreements in the fields of economy and education were concluded with Spain in 1969, and subsequently renewed, notably in 1972, the future of the Republic still depends upon the goodwill of Madrid. On February 2nd, 1970, all political parties were fused into the *Partido Unico Nacional* (PUN).

Firmly held in the grip of the authoritarian President Macías Nguema, Equatorial Guinea is surviving on the verge of bankruptcy. Access of foreigners to the Republic is severely controlled by the President, who has complete power and was appointed Life President on July 14th, 1972. Whatever economic life is worth mentioning is concentrated in the cocoa plantations of Fernando Póo where a shortage of labourers has been felt since the departure of large contingents to Nigeria after the close of the Biafran conflict. Agreements of co-operation have been signed with Cameroon and Nigeria. Twenty thousand Nigerian workers left the island after completing their contract, and in 1972 Equatorial Guinea negotiated new agreements to recruit 15,000 Nigerian field-workers under improved conditions. Help from China has been slow in materializing. In September 1972 tension with Gabon was acute due to armed incidents off Corisco Island, said to be a training camp for political refugees from Cameroon, Gabon and the Central African Republic. Following an offer of mediation from Congo (Brazzaville) and Zaire, the two Governments agreed that an OAU special commission should be set up to fix their maritime border.

ECONOMY

René Pélissier

Equatorial Guinea has a three-commodity economy which thrives only thanks to Spain's policy of subsidizing cocoa and coffee export prices. Cocoa is the *raison d'être* of Fernando Póo, which has the right soil and climate for intensive, model cultivation in factory-like plantations (*fincas*). More than 41,000 hectares with over 1,000 plantations on the island are under cocoa. Over 800 plantations belong to Africans, mostly Bubi and Fernandinos, but most of the acreage and production is European. About 90 per cent of Equato-Guinean cocoa is grown on Fernando Póo, only 10,200 hectares growing in Río Muni. Production in 1966–67 was 38,207 tons, but with the expulsion or departure of Portuguese and Spanish plantation owners and technicians in 1970, both quality and quantity have deteriorated; in 1971–72, production reached only 32,000 tons. Most of the cocoa crop is bought up at preferential rates by Spain.

Coffee is grown chiefly by Río Munian Fang along the Cameroon border. The general quality is mediocre and production has been dropping or stagnating since independence. Production in 1968 was 8,450 tons, but more recently has dropped to little over 7,000 tons.

The third mainstay of the economy is timber. Lumbering sites are in Río Muni, mainly along the coast and the lower reaches of the Río Benito, but pushing inland as exhaustion forces the exploration of new areas. Heavily mechanized, this industry requires considerable investment, and as a result is entirely held by Europeans. Friction with lumbering companies was one cause of the 1969 crises. In 1967 production reached 337,438 tons, mostly exported to Spain and Germany.

Other crops are bananas from Fernando Póo, palm oil from Río Muni and cassava from African planters. The unsettled state of Río Muni has done much to reduce exports. Fishing had been developing off the coast of Fernando Póo, where a Spanish concern had a fishing fleet.

Industry is minimal in this predominantly agricultural country. Some cocoa- and coffee-processing is done locally. Sawn timber from Río Muni was acquiring new importance in the pre-independence days. No mineral is exploited, but oil-prospecting off Fernando Póo and Río Muni was recently carried out. Electricity production in 1967 was 9,470,000 kWh. in Fernando Póo, and 5,700,000 in Río Muni in 1967.

The transport system is good in Fernando Póo where about 160 km. of tarred roads allow easy exportation of cocoa through Santa Isabel and bananas through San Carlos. A road runs round most of the northern part of the island; Río Muni has a tarred road from Bata down to Río Benito along the coastal plain. Other tarred sections of the Bata-Ebebeyin northern road link with the Gabonese network. Disrepair and general lack of purpose have done much to deteriorate a formerly excellent network of earth roads linking all administrative posts. There are no railways.

The main harbour is Santa Isabel which has regular services to Spain and the rest of Europe. Internal traffic between Bata and Santa Isabel is irregular. With Annobón, services seem to be more erratic still. Communications with Nigeria and Douala are maintained to bring in and repatriate contract workers.

Civil aviation is the main mode of transport between the island and Río Muni. A new subsidiary company of Iberia, LAGE, flies the Santa Isabel-Bata run and between Santa Isabel and Douala, Cameroon. Otherwise, international flights are provided by Iberia and Air Cameroun. Tourism is not encouraged.

While Equatorial Guinea had formerly the highest export trade per capita of any African country, with $135 per head in 1960, the present political situation and the lack of reliable current statistics lead one to suppose that this position may have been lost to more stable countries with small populations and equally sought-after commodities.

STATISTICAL SURVEY

Area: 28,051 sq. km. (Río Muni 26,000 sq. km.).

Population: (1960) Río Muni 183,377 (2,864 Europeans), Fernando Póo 61,557 (4,170 Europeans), Annobón 1,403, Santa Isabel (capital, on Fernando Póo) 37,185, Bata (in Río Muni) 27,024. (1968) Total estimated population 250,000.

The European population has decreased considerably since the March 1969 crisis, and there are now probably less than 100 Spaniards left in Río Muni and about 1,000 on Fernando Póo.

Agriculture (1970—metric tons): Cassava (manioc) 42,000*, Sweet potatoes and Yams 27,000*, Bananas 12,000*, Coffee 7,200, Palm oil 4,000*, Palm Kernels (export only) 2,000, Abaca 100*; (1970–71): Cocoa beans 30,000. (* F.A.O. estimates).

Livestock (1964): 3,000 cattle, 24,100 sheep, 28,150 goats.

Fishing (1966): over 1,000 tons.

Forestry (1967): 337,438 tons of timber.

Electricity Production(1967): Fernando Póo 9,470,000 kWh, Río Muni 5,700,000 kWh.

Currency: 100 céntimos=1 Guinea peseta.
Coins: 5, 10 and 50 céntimos.
Notes: 1, 5, 25, 50, 100, 500 and 1,000 pesetas.
Exchange rates: 1 Guinea peseta=1 Spanish peseta.
£1 Sterling=149.025 pesetas (December 1972); 1,000 pesetas=£6.71. U.S. $1=63.59 pesetas (Sept. 1972); 1,000 pesetas=$15.73.

Budget (1969–70): Revenue 712,470,000 pesetas, Expenditure 1,139,045,701 pesetas.

External Trade (1971, first half): (million pesetas) Imports from Spain 454.8; Exports to Spain 867.2.

Transport (1967): *Shipping:* ships entering 663, ships leaving 663; *Civil Aviation:* passengers arriving Santa Isabel 13,863, passengers leaving Santa Isabel 14,166; passengers arriving Bata 7,350, passengers leaving Bata 7,681.

Education: (1966) 147 elementary schools with 21,421 pupils, 32 primary schools with 1,565 pupils, and 271 teachers; (1966–67) 2,095 (310 white) secondary students; about 100 students study abroad, mostly in Spain.

THE CONSTITUTION

The constitution of Equatorial Guinea was approved by referendum on August 15th, 1968, and came into force on October 12th, 1968.

The constitution recognizes the United Nations Declaration of Human Rights, and proclaims the democratic nature of the Republic. The system of government is presidential, and all governing bodies are elected by universal adult suffrage.

The executive body is a Council of Ministers, appointed by the President and responsible to him. The legislative arm is an elected Assembly of 35 deputies, who also exercise some control over the actions of Ministers. A Council of the Republic, with three members each from Fernando Póo and Río Muni elected by the respective Province Councils, has the function of mediating in any dispute between the executive and legislature, and of resolving any conflict of authority between the central government and the Province Councils.

The two Province Councils have specified responsibilities under the constitution; the Councils are elected by universal adult suffrage.

The administration of justice is guaranteed by the Constitution according to principles of independence, security of office and responsibility. The Supreme Tribunal, situated in Santa Isabel, is the highest judicial authority.

Guinean nationals are defined for the purposes of elections as all persons of African origin born in Equatorial Guinea, and their children, provided in both cases that they possessed Spanish nationality before October 12th, 1968. There are four electoral districts: Río Muni (19 deputies), Fernando Póo (12 deputies), Annobón (2 deputies) and the islands of Corisco, Elobey Grande and Elobey Chico (2 deputies). In the first two, representation is proportional, based on party lists; in the two smaller districts, there is a simple majority list system.

Representation in the Council of Ministers is also proportional; at least one third of the members must be drawn from Fernando Póo.

On July 14th, 1972 President Macías Nguema was appointed Life President by the Assembly and the Council of the Republic.

THE GOVERNMENT

HEAD OF STATE

Life President: FRANCISCO MACÍAS NGUEMA.

(*Elected September 29th, 1968; proclaimed Life President July 14th, 1972.*)

CABINET

(*November 1972*)

President, Minister of Defence and Minister of Foreign Affairs: FRANCISCO MACÍAS NGUEMA (Río Muni).

Vice-President, Minister of Trade: EDMUNDO BOSIO DIOCO (Fernando Póo).

Minister of Labour: ROMAN TOICHOA (Fernando Póo).

Minister of Industry and Mines: RICARDO MARTINES PELANO ERIMOLA-YEMA (Río Muni).

Minister of Agriculture: JOSÉ NSUE EANGUE OSA (Río Muni).

Minister of Education: AGUSTÍN DANIEL GRANGE MOLAY (Río Muni).

Minister of Health: Dr. PEDRO ECONG ANDEME (Fernando Póo).

Minister of the Interior: ANGEL MASIE NATUTUMDE (Río Muni).

Minister of Public Works: JESÚS ALFONSO OYONO (Río Muni).

Minister of Finance: ANDRÉS NKO IVASA (Río Muni).

Minister of Justice: JESÚS OWORO NDONGO (Fernando Póo).

DIPLOMATIC REPRESENTATION

EMBASSIES ACCREDITED TO EQUATORIAL GUINEA

The following countries have established diplomatic relations with Equatorial Guinea: Cameroon, Czechoslovakia, France (*Ambassador:* HENRI BERNARD), Gabon,* Ghana, D.P.R. Korea, Nigeria (*Ambassador:* Brig. W. BASSEY), Romania, Spain, U.S.S.R., United Kingdom,* U.S.A., Yugoslavia.

* Ambassador resident in Cameroon.

NATIONAL ASSEMBLY

ELECTIONS, SEPTEMBER 22ND, 1968

PARTY	SEATS
Monalige . . .	10
Munge . . .	10
IPGE . . .	8
Unión Bubi . . .	7
TOTAL .	35

POLITICAL PARTIES

The following pre-independence parties were reportedly merged in October 1968:

IPGE (Popular Idea of Equatorial Guinea), Movimiento de Unión Nacional de la Guinea Ecuatorial—MUNGE (National Union Movement), Movimiento Nacional de Liberación de la Guinea Ecuatorial—MONALIGE (National Liberation Movement), Bubi Union.

Following the abortive coup of March 1969, led by the Minister of Foreign Affairs, ATANASIO NDONG, who was killed, all parties were merged in February 1970 into a Partido Unico Nacional under the President of the Republic, who has assumed most of the powers of the former rival leaders.

JUDICIAL SYSTEM

An independent and secure judiciary is guaranteed by the constitution. The Supreme Tribunal at Santa Isabel is the highest court of appeal.

RELIGION

Some Africans retain traditional forms of worship. There are Spanish Catholic and American Presbyterian and English Methodist missions. Europeans are nearly all Catholics.

Bishop of Sta. Isabel: Mgr. FRANCISCO GÓMEZ MARIJUAN.

Bishop of Bata: RAPHAEL NZE ABUY.

THE PRESS

Boletín Oficial: Santa Isabel; fortnightly legal review; circ. 1,300.

Ebano: Santa Isabel; daily; Spanish; circ. 1,000.

La Guinea Española: Catholic Mission, Santa Isabel; f. 1903; Spanish monthly; literary and scientific; circ. 1,050.

Hoja Parroquial: Santa Isabel; weekly news; circ. 1,500.

Potopoto: Bata; weekly; Spanish; general news; circ. 550.

RADIO AND TELEVISION

There are two radio stations, both operated by the Government.

Radio Ecuatorial: Apdo. 57, Bata, Provincia de Río Muni; commercial station; Dir. E. E. NAVARRO MAÑEZ.

Emisora de Radiodifusión Santa Isabel: Apdo. de Correos 195, Santa Isabel, Fernando Póo; services in Spanish, Fang, Pamue, Bubi, Annobonés, Combe and English; Dir.-Gen. JIMÉNEZ MARHUENDA.

There are 71,500 radio receivers in the country. In 1968 the Spanish Government inaugurated a television transmitter above Santa Isabel in Fernando Póo.

FINANCE

BANKING

Banco Central de Guinea Equatorial: Santa Isabel; f. 1969; central bank.

Banco Español de Credito: Santa Isabel.

Banco Exterior de España: Léon 1, Apdo. 39, Santa Isabel; branch in San Carlos.

TRADE AND INDUSTRY

Comité Sindical del Cacao: Fernando Póo; grouping of cocoa planters (mainly Spanish owners or leasers and some Portuguese) which buys, stocks and sells the product; used to have paramount role on Fernando Póo.

Cámaras Oficiales Agrícolas de Guinea: Fernando Póo and Río Muni; buys cocoa and coffee from African planters, who are partially grouped in co-operatives.

TRANSPORT AND TOURISM

ROADS

Fernando Póo: a semi-circular tarred road serves the northern part of the island from Santa Isabel down to Batete in the west and from Santa Isabel to Bacake Grande in the east, with a feeder road from San Carlos to Moka and Bahía de la Concepción; total length about 160 km.

Río Muni: a tarred road links Bata with Río Benito in the west; another road partly tarred, links Bata with the frontier post of Ebebiyin in the east and then continues into Gabon; other earth roads join Acurenam, Mongomo de Guadalupe and Nsork; total road network about 1,015 km.

SHIPPING

The main ports are Santa Isabel (general cargo), San Carlos (bananas), Bata (general cargo), Río Benito and Puerto Iradier (timber).

Compañía Transmediterránea: serves Barcelona–Cadiz–Santa Isabel–San Carlos–Bata route and the Bilbao–Cadiz–Equatorial Guinea route, sailing alternately from Barcelona and Bilbao, usually once a month; in 1968 there were six ships for the transatlantic service and two more for internal traffic between Fernando Póo, Río Muni and Annobón (via São Tomé).

Arrivals and repatriation of Nigerian workers takes place through the Santa Isabel–Calabar service.

Of the 663 ships entering and leaving Guinea in 1967 534 were Spanish, 31 German (of the Woermann Linie), 27 British and 10 Norwegian.

CIVIL AVIATION

There are international airports at Bata and Santa Isabel.

Lineas Aéreas Guinea Ecuatorial (LAGE): Bata Airport; f. 1970 as a subsidiary of Iberia (the Spanish airline); scheduled services from Santa Isabel to Bata and Douala (Cameroon), formerly flown by Iberia; fleet of two Convair CV-440.

Air Cameroun also links Bata with Douala, and Iberia also serves Equatorial Guinea.

SELECT BIBLIOGRAPHY

Spanish Africa generally

AREILZA, J. MA. DE, and CASTIELLA, F. MA. *Reivindicaciones de España.* Madrid, 1941.

PÉLISSIER, RENÉ. *Los Territorios Españoles de Africa.* Madrid, 1964.

Guinea

BAGUENA CORELLA, LUIS. *Guinea.* Madrid, 1950.

BERMAN, SANFORD. *Spanish Guinea: an annotated bibliography.* Washington, D.C., Catholic University of America Libraries, 1961.

PÉLISSIER, RENÉ. *Études hispano-guinéennes.* Paris, 1969

SERVICIO INFORMATIVO ESPAÑOL. *España y Guinea Ecuatorial.* Madrid, 1968.

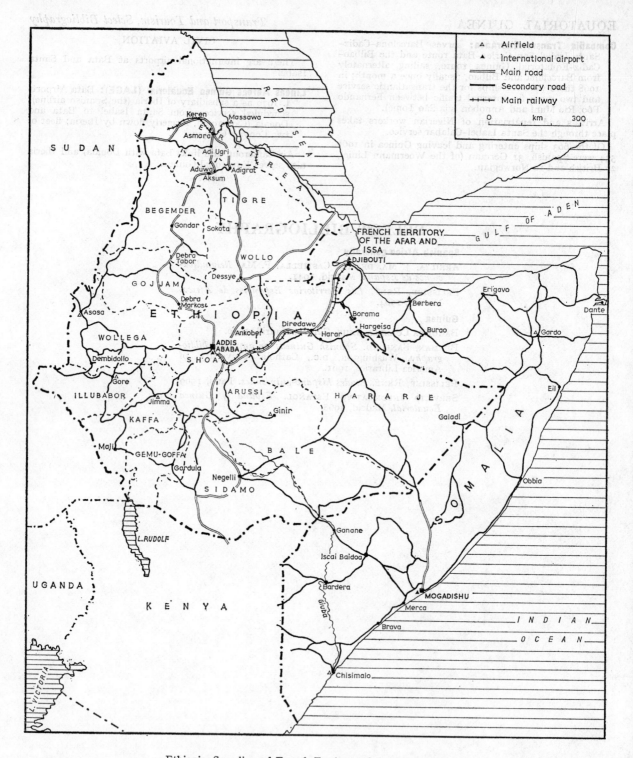

Ethiopia, Somalia and French Territory of the Afar and Issa

Ethiopia

PHYSICAL AND SOCIAL GEOGRAPHY

G. C. Last

The Empire of Ethiopia, which stretches south and west from the Red Sea coast to form the hinterland of the Horn of Africa, has a compact shape. It extends from latitude 3°N. to 18°N. and from longitude 33°E. to 48°E. and its east-west north-south dimensions are therefore approximately equal, enclosing an area of about 1,220,000 sq. km. Ethiopia's western neighbour is Sudan; to the south it shares a border with Kenya; and to the east and south-east lie the small Territory of the Afar and Issa, and Somalia. To the north-east, Ethiopia has nearly 1,000 km. of coastline along the Red Sea and offshore from Massawa, the northern port, are the Dahlak Islands, a low-lying coral group, part of Ethiopian territory.

The country is divided into 14 administrative provinces including the province of Eritrea which, until September 1962, had federal status. The capital, Addis Ababa, is located in Shoa province not far from the geographical centre of the country.

PHYSICAL FEATURES

Elevations range from around 100 m. below sea-level in the Dallol Depression (Kobar Sink) to the south of Massawa to a number of mountain peaks over 4,000 m., which dominate the plateaux and of which the highest is Ras Dashen, rising to 4,620 m., in the Semien Mountain massif, north-east of Lake Tana. The major relief regions have been created by the forces responsible for the East African rift system and, as recently understood, by the continental drift movement, in which Africa is gradually pivoting away from the block of South Arabia. The southern half of Ethiopia is bisected by the rift valley, which ranges from 40 to 60 km. in width and whose floor is occupied by a number of lakes (Zwai, Langano, Abiata, Shala, Awasa, Abaya or Margherita and Chamo). In the latitude of Addis Ababa, the western wall of the rift turns north and runs parallel to the west coast of Arabia, leaving a wide plain between the escarpment and the Red Sea coast, which gradually narrows until, north of Massawa, the foothills of the escarpment are almost on the coastline. The eastern wall of the rift turns to the east in the latitude of Addis Ababa, forming an escarpment looking north over the Afar Plains. These escarpments are nearly always abrupt, commanding extensive views over the lowlands some 1,000 m. below, and are broken at only one point near Addis Ababa where the Awash River descends from the rim of the plateau. It is at this point that the railway from Djibouti reaches the highlands.

The plateaux to the west of the rift system dip gently towards the west and are drained by right bank tributaries of the Nile system, which have carved deep and spectacular gorges. The Eritrean Plateau is drained by the Mareb (Gash) and the Barka Rivers, whose seasonal flood water is lost in the desert to the west and north. The plateaux to the north of Lake Tana are drained by the Tekeze and Angareb Rivers, headwaters of the Atbara. The central plateaux are drained by the Abbai (Blue Nile) River and its tributaries. The Abbai rises in Lake Tana and is known as the Blue Nile in Sudan. Much of the flood water in the Blue Nile system comes from the left bank tributaries (e.g. Didessa and Dabus), which rise in the high rainfall region of south-west Ethiopia. This southern region is also drained by the Akobo, Gilo and Baro Rivers which form the headwaters of the Sobat River. The only river of significance to the west of the rift valley which is not part of the Nile system is the Omo, which drains southwards into Lake Rudolph and is known in its upper course as the Gibe. The rift valley itself contains a number of closed river basins, including the largest, the Awash, which flows north from the rift valley proper into the Afar Plain and terminates in Lake Abe. The highlands to the east of the rift are drained south-eastwards by the head-streams of the Webi Shebelli and Juba river systems.

As a result of earth movements, associated volcanic activity and subsequent erosion, the plateau surfaces are generally covered by thick deposits of Tertiary lavas, but the deep gorges, protected from widening by the hard lava cap have often cut down through Cretaceous, Jurassic and Triassic sedimentaries to the Precambrian basement. However, in the north, in Tigre province, the Tertiary lavas have been removed over wide areas, exposing limestones and sandstones and in the extreme north, in Eritrea, basement rocks from the surface. In the rift valley and Afar Plains, Quaternary volcanics cover much of the surface and overlie the Quaternary basalts. In the area to the south of the Dallol Depression, there are a number of active cones and vents. To the south-east of the rift valley the plateaux are less extensive but high mountain areas capped by plateau basalts overlook the wide plains of the Ogaden, where sandstones and limestones predominate.

SOILS AND NATURAL RESOURCES

Over most of the high plateaux, the decomposition of volcanic rocks has produced reddish brown clay soils and black cotton soils. Although they are generally deficient in phosphorus, good crops can be obtained from these soils. However, over wide areas on slopes and in the more densely populated rural areas, soil erosion has been severe. The extreme is reached in Tigre and Eritrea provinces. The prevalence of soil erosion is partly due to high rural population densities in the malaria-free highlands but it is also the natural consequence of heavy seasonal rainfall and a highly dissected landscape which has long since been denuded of its natural forest cover over much of the country.

Although the exploitation of gold and copper ores dates from prehistoric times on the Eritrean Plateau, the mineral resources of Ethiopia are largely unknown and are the subject of an extensive exploration programme in the current Five-Year Development Plan. There are alluvial gold workings in the Adola (Kebre Mengist) region of Sidamo province and platinum workings which are now being reopened near Yubdo in Wollega province. There is a small output of iron ore from Eritrea. It is likely that the Eritrean plateau region will yield more extensive copper and iron deposits, but probably the area with the highest mineral potential lies in the west and south-west in Wollega, Illubabor and Kaffa provinces, where Precambrian rocks are also found on the surface. However, this region is at the moment the least accessible and much of it is covered by rain-forest.

Extensive potash deposits have been proven in the Dallol Depression and it is hoped that successful exploitation will generate exports rising towards 1 million tons a year. Potash would then dominate the mineral scene in Ethiopia.

Exploration for oil has been carried on for some years in the Ogaden region without success but there have been recent strikes of natural gas with oil traces in the Red Sea offshore from Massawa. Finally, estimates are now being made of the geothermal power potential of extensive sources in the Afar Plain region. If these prove economic, it will be possible to harness this source of power for the development of the chemical industry based on the Dallol potash deposits.

With its high rainfall and precipitous relief, Ethiopia is well-endowed with hydroelectric power potential. Four plants are already in operation along the course of the Awash River, south of Addis Ababa, and a fifth project begins shortly. The Blue Nile River basin has been extensively studied and a large number of sites identified at which power production could be coupled with irrigation schemes. One plant is now under construction at Finchaa, west of Addis Ababa, and among the projects which offer a high future potential is the control of the Beles river, a right-bank tributary of the Abai in Gojjam province. A French team of experts is currently surveying the Webe Shebeli River basin to determine its power and irrigation potential.

CLIMATE AND VEGETATION

Ethiopia lies within the tropics but the wide range of altitude produces considerable variations in temperature conditions which are reflected in the traditional zones of the *dega* (the temperate plateaux), the *kolla* (hot lowlands) and the intermediate frost-free zone of the *woina dega*. The boundaries between these three zones lie at approximately 2,400 m. and 1,700 m. above sea-level. Average annual temperature in the *dega* is about 61°F., in the *woina dega* about 72°F. and in the *kolla* at least 79°F.

The seasonal oscillation of the inter-tropical convergence zone over Ethiopia causes a main rainy season over most of the country during June, July and August, when moist equatorial air is drawn in from the south and west.

Bearing in mind that there are significant variations in local climates and in the duration and intensity of rainfall, the climatic conditions can be described generally in terms of well-watered highlands and uplands, mostly receiving at least 1,000 mm. of rain a year with the exception of the Eritrean and Tigrean Plateaux, and dry lowlands, generally having less than 500 mm. of rain, with the significant exception of the Baro and Akobo River plains in the south-west, which lie in the path of summer rain-bearing winds.

The natural vegetation of the plateaux and highlands above 1,800 m. is coniferous forest (notably *zigba* and *tid*), but these forests have now largely disappeared and are found today only in the more inaccessible regions, e.g. in the Bale highlands and on the slopes of Mt. Jiba, to the west of Addis Ababa. In the south-west higher rainfall with lower elevations and higher temperatures has produced extensive broad-leafed rain-forests with a variety of species including abundant *karraro*. Although there has been a steady encroachment by shifting cultivators, these forested areas in Illubabor and Kaffa provinces are relatively remote and have not yet been subjected to extensive commercial exploitation. Their main significance is the presence of the coffee bush which grows wild as part of the natural undergrowth and supplies a significant proportion of Ethiopia's exports. Above the tree line on the plateaux are wide expanses of mountain grassland. In the lowlands, dependent on rainfall conditions, there is a range of dry-zone vegetation, from limited areas of desert through thorn scrub to acacia savannah. An important natural resource in Ethiopia is the extensive natural rangelands, particularly in the Borena and Ogaden plains in the south, a fact which is responsible for Ethiopia's estimated cattle population of 26 million head.

POPULATION AND CULTURES

Present knowledge of population is derived from the sample rural studies and the major towns survey conducted by the Central Statistical Office of the government. There has never been a population census in Ethiopia and the only full censuses have been carried out in Addis Ababa and Asmara. Knowledge of population size, distribution and structure is therefore based on estimates.

Total population in 1971 was estimated at 25.2 million. The overall growth rate accepted for the Third Five-Year Development Plan (1968–73) is just over 2.1 per cent per annum with an urban growth rate of just over 5 per cent per annum. Since over 50 per cent of the population is aged 19 years or below and nearly 70 per cent 29 years or below, this, coupled with the early age of marriage in Ethiopia, implies a rapidly increasing population growth rate.

The urban population is in 248 towns of various sizes, ranging from Addis Ababa with around 700,000 to 34 settlements with less than 1,000 population. More than 50 per cent of the towns surveyed have less than 3,000 population and over 50 per cent of the urban population is located in three towns— Addis Ababa, Asmara and Dire Dawa. Total urban population is now just over two million.

Overall density of population is 21 per sq. km. However, this figure hides a very wide variation between provinces and sub-districts, as might be expected from the variety of natural environments.

Generally speaking, the distribution of population reflects the pattern of relief. The highlands, having a plentiful rainfall, are the home of settled agriculture. Land over 2,000 m. is free of the malarial mosquito, a factor contributing to the non-occupation of lowlands which are suitable for farming. It would not be unreasonable to assume that 10 per cent of the population lives below the 1,000 m. contour, 20 per cent between 1,000 and 1,800 m. and 70 per cent above the 1,800 m. contour line. Nearly all the major settlements are in the highlands. The notable exceptions are special cases such as the two ports (Massawa and Aseb), border posts (e.g. Tessenei and Moyale), the river port of Gambela and the railway creations, Dire Dawa and Nazareth. All the provincial capitals were located in the highlands but, with the gradual eradication of malaria and the improvement of medical services, there is some movement towards lower elevations. Thus, in Illubabor, the capital has moved from Gore to Matu, in Sidamo it has moved from Yirgalem to Awasa, and in Gemu-Goffa from Chencha to Arba Minch.

Many factors in recent and less recent history have combined to produce a strong sense of nationhood in Ethiopia. But this is a nation which, in almost every aspect of the study of its human geography, reveals a fascinating variety. There is a multitude of languages and a variety of cultural patterns, including for example the plough culture of the northern plateaux and the hoe culture of the south; there are settled cultivators and nomadic pastoralists. In the broadest analysis, two factors are responsible for this variety. First, the very location of Ethiopia on the crossroads between south-west Asia and Africa, and between the Nile Valley and the Mediterranean region and the rest of Africa to the south have made the Ethiopian region the scene of successive human migrations and settlement. Very early inhabitants of the Ethiopian highlands were Cushitic people, of whom in the north small groups like the Agau remain, whereas in the south the Cushitic people are represented by a number of linguistic and cultural groups, such as the Galla, the Sidama and the Konso. The migration of people from south-west Arabia brought significant linguistic and cultural developments to the Ethiopian region in the shape of Semitic languages, plough cultivation and construction in stone and, with marginal influences from the Nilotic people along the western borders and the presence of some Bantu groups in the south, present-day Ethiopia has a rich and complex human pattern which includes, for example, well over 100 languages.

The second basic factor in both the distribution of the people and the existence of cultural variety is the range of physical environs. These environs have not only determined to a large extent the patterns of occupation and the nature of human activities but they have also contributed to more subtle variations in cultural patterns. For example, the highly dissected landscape, inhabited by groups of people living in comparative isolation from each other, has contributed to the development of a large number of dialects on the already complex language base.

RECENT HISTORY

R. Pankhurst

THE REIGN OF TEWODROS

Ethiopian history dawns in the bright yet shadowy glory of the Aksumite Empire (established perhaps half a millennium before the birth of Christ), which gave way in the early Middle Ages to the Ethiopian medieval state, known in Europe as the Land of Prester John, and regarded with much interest as the only Christian Kingdom in Africa or Asia. By the nineteenth century, however, the powers of the monarch had been usurped by the nobles, and the empire had largely disintegrated into several semi-independent provinces, whose rulers often fought among themselves. Memories of a great and glorious past were none the less not forgotten, and cultural contacts, largely through the Church, were preserved. Indeed, recognition of the country's former greatness and unity provide the background for the rise of Emperor Tewodros II (1855–68), the protagonist of modern Ethiopia.

Tewodros, originally known as Kassa, was the son of a minor chief on the western frontier, and, becoming a freelance soldier, soon made himself a power in the land. Ras Ali, the then ruler of Gondar, the capital, sent an army against him, but, on its defeat, arranged for him to marry his daughter. Kassa proceeded to strengthen his position. Having made himself master of Gondar and Amhara province, he defeated Wube, the ruler of Tigre, in 1855 and proclaimed himself Emperor, adopting the name of Tewodros. This was a significant appellation, for legend, then widely believed, prophesied that a king of this name would one day appear who would rule justly, wipe out Islam and capture Jerusalem. Tewodros did much to justify this name. Determined to reunify the country and to rebuild its old-time splendour he reorganized the army, attempting in particular to abolish the old practice whereby the soldiers looted the countryside, and succeeded in bringing much of the empire under his control. Opposition from the provincial nobles, and, apparently, also from the Church, was, however, his undoing, and by the 1860s his power was visibly on the wane. Determined to obtain gunsmiths and other craftsmen from abroad, he wrote for help to Queen Victoria, but, his letter not being answered, he angrily imprisoned her envoy and other foreigners. In 1867 the British Government despatched an expedition against his mountain fortress of Magdala. Tewodros was defeated, and, to avoid capture, he committed suicide on April 13th, 1868.

THE RISE OF MENELIK

Tewodros' death left the empire once more in a state of disunity. Two important personalities nevertheless soon afterwards emerged: Menelik, already by this time king of the southerly province of Shoa, and Kassa, a chieftain of Tigre, who in 1871 was crowned Emperor Yohannes IV. The latter, a major figure of nineteenth-century Ethiopia, was more conservative

than Tewodros, but proved himself more successful. Bringing under his control the greater part of the northern provinces, he decisively defeated Egyptian encroachments in 1875-76, and in the following decade held his own against both the Sudanese Dervishes and the Italians, whose seizure of the Red Sea port of Massawa in 1885 effectively opened the era of the European "scramble for Africa" in this part of the continent. In 1889, however, Yohannes met his death fighting against the Dervishes, and was succeeded as Emperor by Menelik, until then king of Shoa.

Menelik, for practical purposes the founder of modern Ethiopia, continued the work of reunification, above all by taking over the provinces of the south. His greatest preoccupation was, however, with the expansion of the Italians, who claimed a Protectorate over Ethiopia (on the basis of the treaty of Uccialli, which they had signed with him in 1889). Menelik rejected this claim, devoted his energies to strengthening his army, and finally defeated the invaders on March 1st, 1896, at the battle of Adowa. This victory, the most remarkable of an African over a European army since the time of Hannibal, may justly be said to mark the beginning of modern Ethiopian history.

ETHIOPIA AFTER THE BATTLE OF ADOWA

The personality of Menelik, who reigned from 1865 to 1913, first as King of Shoa, and, after 1889, as Emperor of Ethiopia, was a decisive factor in the development of the country. Much influenced by Tewodros, at whose court he had been brought up, he was well aware of the importance of unifying the ancient realm and beginning its modernization. The battle of Adowa, in which he captured all the Italians' cannon and over five-sevenths of their rifles, had given him enormous local and international prestige. This enabled him to settle speedily his problems with the Italians, who had by then withdrawn to their Red Sea colony of Eritrea. On October 26th, 1896, they signed the peace treaty of Addis Ababa, wherein they agreed to the annulment of the earlier treaty of Ucciali, and recognized the absolute and complete independence of Ethiopia. Menelik, on the other hand, did not consider himself in a position to insist on an Italian withdrawal from Eritrea. His enhanced position was, however, evident from the fact that the British and French governments sent diplomatic missions to Ethiopia in the next few months, agreements with the two countries being signed on March 14th and March 20th, 1897, respectively. Other missions arrived from the Sudanese Mahdists, the Ottoman Sultan and the Russian Tsar, while the French, British, Russians and Italians opened permanent legations in Addis Ababa. A year or so later the Emperor embarked on a major military and diplomatic venture when he sent one of his commanders, Ras Tesemma, as far as the White

Nile with instructions to make contact with a French force under Captain Marchand, which was due to arrive from the west African coast. Marchand, however, failed to appear when expected, and Tesemma was obliged to withdraw because of sickness in his ranks. Hopes of close Franco-Ethiopian co-operation were greatly weakened after the Fashoda crisis in Anglo-French relations.

Menelik meanwhile had become increasingly involved in the work of modernizing his country. He was temperamentally most interested in new inventions of all kinds, and displayed an almost childlike fascination with new equipment, an Italian observer, De Castro, humorously declaring that if a builder of castles in the air arrived with a plan to construct an escalator from the earth to the moon the Emperor would have made him build it "if only to see whether it could be done". In the later 1880s Menelik had moved his capital to Addis Ababa, which was officially named by the Empress Taytu in 1887, and in 1892 he reorganized the system of taxes in Shoa, instituting a tithe for the upkeep of the soldiers and putting an end to the old system whereby they looted from the peasantry. In 1894 he introduced the country's first national currency and postage stamps, and granted to his Swiss adviser Ilg a concession for the construction of a railway and telegraph from Djibouti in the French Somali Protectorate. In the same year he despatched the first three students abroad for study at government expense: they went to Switzerland, later students to Russia. The eucalyptus tree was introduced from Australia at about the same time, in all probability by a Frenchman, Mondon-Vidailhet. Construction of the railway line had been delayed until after the battle of Adowa, but started in earnest in 1897. Train services from the coast to Dire Dawa began in 1902, though a serious dispute that year resulting from the French government's involvement in the railway company's finances led to six years delay in further construction, and the line did not reach Akaki, 15 miles from Addis Ababa, until 1915. A Russian Red Cross hospital opened its doors in 1898, and continued to operate until 1906. Telegraph lines to Djibouti, Eritrea, and several provincial centres were laid by French and Italian engineers in the next few years. A mint was set up in 1902, and work on the first modern road, from Addis Ababa to Addis Alem, was begun in the same year, later road building being greatly assisted by the coming of the first steam roller in 1904. The Bank of Abyssinia, the first such institution in the country, was founded in 1905 as an affiliate of the National Bank of Egypt. The Emperor's failing health and the increasing complexity of government led to the establishment in 1907 of the country's first cabinet. In the same year the first modern hotel, the "Etege", was opened. The first modern educational establishment, the Menelik II School, came into existence in 1908, the first government hospital, the Menelik II Hospital, in 1910, and the first state printing press in 1911. In the last years of the nineteenth and the first decade of the twentieth century Ethiopia thus acquired its first modern institutions. This was achieved largely through the help of the French, British and Italians, the Emperor being most careful not to fall unduly under the influence of any one European power.

EUROPEAN INTERFERENCE

Though various foreign powers had assisted significantly in Menelik's modernizing work, the latter years of the reign witnessed deteriorating relations between the Emperor and the three colonial powers, Britain, Italy and France, whose territories bordered Ethiopia on every side and cut her off from access to the sea. Expectation of his imminent death caused them to draw together in 1906 when, on December 13th, they signed a tripartite convention for mutual co-operation. It stated that the three Powers had a common interest in maintaining the integrity of Ethiopia, but that, in the event of the *status quo* being disturbed, they agreed to safeguard their own interests. These were stated to consist of a British interest in the Nile Valley, and hence in the area of the Blue Nile; an Italian interest in Eritrea and Somaliland, and hence in the area of the Blue Nile; an Italian interest in Eritrea and Somaliland, and hence in adjacent areas of Ethiopia; and a French interest in the French Somali Protectorate, and hence in its hinterland. The three Powers thus divided the country into spheres of influences, their object being, as Harrington said, to avoid competing against each other for the Emperor's favour, as they had done in the past, and instead to "follow out a policy in the interests of whites as against blacks". The Emperor, as might be expected, was not pleased by this turn of events. When the agreement was in due course presented to him he proudly replied: "The Convention of the three Powers has reached me. I thank them for having acquainted me with their desire to consolidate and maintain the independence of our Realm. But this actual Convention . . . is subordinate to our authority . . . and cannot in any way bind our decision."

Menelik's subsequent death in December 1913 withdrew from the stage the sovereign who had preserved his country's independence throughout the period of the scramble for Africa, brought under his firm control the so long disunited provinces, and laid the foundations of a modern state. His demise was the more serious in that a struggle for succession soon developed: his grandson and heir, Lij Iyasu, took over the government, but soon alienated important sections of the population, including much of the nobility of Shoa. Apparently in the hope of winning support among the Muslims, as well as possibly obtaining access to the sea, then denied him by the Italians, French and British at the coast, the young ruler leant heavily on their enemies, the Germans, Austrians and Turks, thereby earning for himself the hostility of the allied powers. A rebellion soon broke out in Shoa, and Iyasu was defeated in 1916, whereupon it was decided that Menelik's daughter, Zawditu, should become Empress, and that Ras Makonnen's son, Tafari, should be Regent and Heir to the Throne.

THE ADVENT OF HAILE SELLASSIE

The advent of Tafari Makonnen, the future Emperor Haile Sellassie, was important in providing the country with a determined and energetic leader able to resume the policy of modernization which Menelik had initiated. Conservative opposition to change was none the less strongly felt during the next few years, when authority was often precariously balanced between the Empress and the Regent, each with their separate palaces and followers.

Among the Regent's first reforming acts were the establishment in 1922 of a ministry of commerce and a public works department. He took a keen interest in the improvement of roads, particularly in and around the capital, and personally surveyed the work day by day. Several concessions for the construction of roads were granted in the next few years.

The Regent was also much concerned with questions of foreign affairs, and on September 28th, 1923, succeeded in gaining Ethiopia's admission into the League of Nations. In the following year he issued his first decree for the gradual eradication of slavery, and undertook a European tour, which helped to awaken the country to the need to take the outside world seriously into account, as well as to accelerate the speed of modernization. The Regent protested vigorously in November 1925 when the British foreign secretary agreed with the Italian dictator, Mussolini, in Rome that Britain and Italy considered Ethiopia still partitioned on the basis of the tripartite agreement of 1906, and relations with the two European powers reached a critical stage.

The subsequent coming to Ethiopia in 1929 of the first aeroplanes, which until then had been excluded by the conservative attitude of some of the nobles, was a portent of things to come.

Significant developments took place in these years in the fields of education and health. The Regent had despatched 25 students abroad to Europe and America by 1924. In the same year he established a new hospital, the Bet Sayda, and, one year later, opened a new government school, the Tafari Makonnen School. In the following year he engaged a Belgian military mission to train his bodyguard.

On the death of the Empress Zawditu in 1930 Tafari Makonnen assumed the throne as Emperor Haile Sellassie, and was crowned on November 2nd, a memorable occasion attended by many foreign representatives. The tempo of development seems now to have increased. An important law was proclaimed in 1930 for the more efficient survey and registration of land, and the same year a ministry of education came into existence. In 1931 the Emperor introduced the country's first written constitution, with a parliament of two houses. In the same year the old Bank of Abyssinia, which had been a private company, was replaced by a national bank, the Bank of Ethiopia, and steps were taken to reorganize the currency. The year 1931 also witnessed the enactment of a second anti-slavery decree designed to accelerate the pace of emancipation, and an anti-slavery bureau was created in the following year. In 1932 a ministry of public works was set up to assist with the building of roads and bridges which was then going on. A temporary radio station was put into operation in 1933, to be replaced by a more powerful station, erected by an Italian company, in 1935. Several new schools and hospitals were also opened in these years, including the first girls' school, the Empress Manan School, which was established in 1931. Increasing numbers of students were also sent abroad for study and, on their return, began to enter government service, constituting the Emperor's main weapon of reform. In 1934 a military college was set up with the aid of Swedish officers at Holeta, and a decree was enacted to curtail the labour services exacted from the peasants, while in 1935 legislation appeared for the reform of the land tax. The reforms of this period were, however, by now increasingly overshadowed by the threat of Italian invasion.

THE ITALIAN INVASION AND OCCUPATION

In the early 1930s Mussolini began to turn his attention towards Ethiopia. In the spring of 1932 he despatched General De Bono, his minister for the colonies, to Eritrea on a tour of inspection, and on the latter's return the fascist leaders agreed, as De Bono later explained, that Italy's "colonial future must be sought in East Africa". The Duce accordingly ordered him "to go full speed ahead", and be "ready as soon as possible". The pretext for invasion came at the end of the year when a mixed Anglo-Ethiopian boundary commission, which had been surveying the borders of British Somaliland, was confronted by Italian troops at Wal Wal, a post 100 km. on the Ethiopian side of the Italian Somaliland frontier. Ethiopian and Italian soldiers clashed there on December 5th, whereupon the Italians demanded that the Ethiopian Government should apologize and pay heavy compensation. Ethiopia rejected these demands, proposing instead that the dispute be referred to arbitration in accordance with the Italo-Ethiopian treaty of friendship of 1928. Mussolini refused this suggestion, whereupon the Emperor appealed to the League of Nations. Then followed eleven months of fruitless negotiations at Geneva, while Mussolini frantically pushed forward his war preparations, turning the Italian colonies on Ethiopia's seaboard, north and south, into bases for the coming war.

The Italians began their invasion, without any declaration of war, on October 3rd, 1935. The League of Nations found Italy guilty of aggression, but failed to take any effective action to halt the invading armies. These enjoyed overwhelming superiority of arms and virtually complete control of the air, from which they showered poison gas as well as high-explosive and incendiary bombs on the defending forces. On March 31st, 1936, the Emperor Haile Sellassie engaged the enemy at May Chew, north of Lake Ashangi, but was obliged to retire. On May 2nd he set forth from his capital to lay the case of Ethiopia before the League of Nations in person. The invading army of Marshal Badoglio entered Addis Ababa on May 5th; and on June 30th the Emperor delivered his famous address at Geneva to the delegates to the League, asking them, "What answer am I to take back to my people?"

The fascist occupation of Ethiopia, which for the first time brought the greater part of the Horn of Africa under one administration, was accompanied by large-scale Italian expenditure. Immediate strategic interests, as well as long-term economic considerations, caused the invaders to devote the greater part of their efforts to road-building, on which for a time as many as 60,000 Italian workmen were employed, though this figure had fallen by 1939 to 12,000 Italians assisted by 52,000 "native" labourers. The basis of a national road network was thus established, but at the price of gravely restricting other economic activity. The settlement of Italian farmers in the highlands was also initiated, the first such settlers being established at Bishoftu and Holeta on the outskirts of the capital. To cater for the growing Italian population, which by 1939 exceeded 130,000 in Italian East Africa as a whole, a large number of European-type houses were constructed in the principal towns on the basis of a rigid separation of European and non-European, while in the capital some 20,000 Ethiopian citizens were transferred to the projected "native city". Inter-marriage or even cohabitation between the two races was strictly punished. A number of new hospitals were constructed, mainly for Europeans, and several of the old Ethiopian schools were reopened for the instruction of Italian children, education of the "native population" being rigidly controlled. Several national monuments were removed, including one of the ancient obelisks of Aksum, which was taken to Rome, where it stands to this day.

Ethiopian Resistance

Though the invaders easily captured Ethiopia's towns, they encountered vigorous resistance in the interior. Patriot leaders such as Abebe Aragay, Geresu Duke, Belay Zeleke and the Kassa brothers, in some cases operating only twenty or so kilometres from the capital, organized bands of soldiers to resist the Italians in most provinces. The patriots, many of whom were self-made men not directly drawn from the summit of the old feudal nobility, were strongest in Gojam, Amhara and Shoa. An attempt on the life of the Italian Viceroy General Graziani, made in Addis Ababa by two Eritreans in February 1937, was followed by swift and ferocious retaliation in which several thousand Ethiopians, including a good proportion of the educated population, were deliberately massacred. Graziani was later replaced as Viceroy by the Duke of Aosta, who attempted a somewhat more liberal policy in the hope of placating popular opposition. The patriots, however, continued their resistance, thereby immobilizing large Italian armies and preventing the realization of all but a few of Mussolini's dreams of empire.

THE SECOND WORLD WAR

Mussolini's declaration of war on Britain and France on June 10th, 1940 brought immediate comfort to the Ethiopian patriots who, after four lone years of struggle, at last found themselves with allies. The massive Italian armies in east Africa, on the other hand, were now isolated. They succeeded without much difficulty in occupying British Somaliland and also made probes into Sudan and Kenya, but were soon to be paralyzed by increasing allied strength in the area.

The Emperor Haile Sellassie, who had spent the greater part of his exile in Britain, meanwhile was struggling to gain official status as an ally. On the outbreak of the European war he had written to the British government offering his services, but the government, anxious to avoid offending Mussolini, had vouchsafed no reply. Even after the Duce's entry into the European conflict Britain adopted a cautious policy. There was reluctance to treat an African state on terms of equality or to give support to what many regarded as a "native insurrection" against a colonial regime, as well as scepticism as to the Emperor's ability to rally the people of Ethiopia around him, or, if rallied, as to their capacity to render any satisfactory contributions to the war. The Emperor's personality and the failure of Britain to support him in 1935–36 had, however, left a poignant impact on British public opinion, and in the latter part of July 1940 the government agreed that he should be allowed to assist in the common struggle. He accordingly left Britain for Sudan on July 25th. Once in Khartoum he was again confronted with procrastination by the British, though Ethiopian refugees flocked to meet him.

Pressure of events now led to increasing Anglo-Ethiopian co-operation. On August 12th the British government despatched into Gojam a small mission, mission 101, commanded by a British officer, Brigadier Sandford. Then at a British ministerial conference held in Khartoum in October it was decided that the Emperor would be afforded a small amount of weapons and that Ethiopians fighting against the Italians should be accorded the title of patriots, and no longer be referred to as merely rebels against Italian rule. On November 20th another British officer, Colonel Orde Wingate, was flown into Gojam with promises of speedy, though limited, aid.

THE LIBERATION OF ETHIOPIA

The liberation campaign opened on January 19th, 1941, when the northern allied army crossed the frontier from Sudan into Eritrea. On the following day the Emperor, with Wingate as his principal adviser, entered Ethiopian territory at Om Idla. Four days later the southern allied army struck from Kenya. The stage was thus set for an allied offensive which in a matter of months was to sweep the Italians out of east Africa.

The Emperor, who had by then advanced across most of Gojam, wished to enter Addis Ababa immediately after its capture by South African forces on April 6th, but this was strongly opposed in British military circles on the grounds that any immediate resumption of Ethiopian rule might endanger the lives of the many Italians in the city. Eventually, however, he decided to advance on the capital without his ally's consent, and accordingly returned to the capital in triumph on May 5th, five years after the Italian seizure of the city in 1936. In a speech delivered that day he declared the inauguration of a "new era".

The collapse of Italian rule created a host of problems. Massive Italian investment during the occupation and the magnitude of the subsequent fighting had disrupted the economy, and trade was at a standstill. The pre-war government, on the other hand, had been disbanded, and many educated personnel had been killed. Moreover, large sections of the population, by no means necessarily loyal, were in possession of large quantities of Italian arms. The presence of 40,000 Italian civilians, still enemy nationals, who had to be provided with food and medical attention, was a further embarrassment. Still another problem arose from the emergence of the patriots, whose leaders naturally claimed appointment in the new administration as a reward for past services, even though they might have few other qualifications.

ANGLO-ETHIOPIAN RELATIONS

One of the first questions facing the restored Ethiopian government was its relations with the British, who, though in large measure liberators of the country had now become its occupying power. Anglo-Ethiopian relations were at the outset almost inevitably ambiguous, for the liberation had been effected with a speed which precluded much consideration of the future, the only British policy statement being one by Foreign Secretary Eden on February 4th, 1941, that the government "would welcome the reappearance of an independent Ethiopian State and recognize the claim of Emperor Haile Sellassie to the throne".

Official British views were further clarified in high-level talks held in Cairo in February and March, which, according to an official report, resulted in "the rejection of any idea of a protectorate or the provision of a strong western administration of the country". After the Emperor's return, however, there was often tension between the Ethiopians and the British, whose ideas on the future government of the country differed radically. The Ethiopians expected to assume full national sovereignty without delay. The Emperor accordingly appointed his first cabinet on May 11th, whereupon the British representative, Brigadier Lush, complained that this could not be effected "until a peace treaty has been signed with Italy". The British eventually accepted the ministers' appointment, but "chose to regard them as merely advisers" to the British administration. Tension was further increased by the presence in the Ethiopian capital of South African troops, who attempted to continue the colour bar earlier established by the Italians. Sir Philip Mitchell, chief British political officer in the Middle East, urged the British government to adopt a hard line with the Ethiopians, but was only partially successful, as there was a feeling in London that Great Britain should demonstrate to the world that she could liberate a country without imposing political strings. Sir Philip nevertheless pressed the Emperor to agree to abide by British advice "in all matters touching the Government of Ethiopia"; to levy taxes and allocate expenditure only with "prior approval of His Majesty's Government"; to grant British courts jurisdiction over foreigners; "to raise no objection" if the British commander-in-chief "found it necessary to resume military control of any part of Ethiopia"; and not to raise armed force or undertake military opera-

tions "except as agreed by His Majesty's Government representative". Haile Sellassie considered these proposals intolerable, and telegraphed to London to ask Winston Churchill why a treaty between the two countries was so long delayed. The British Prime Minister replied that this had been due to a desire to ensure that nothing remained in the draft agreement "which could be interpreted as interfering with your sovereign rights or the independence of Ethiopia". Steps were then taken to formalize relations between the two states. An Anglo-Ethiopian agreement, signed in Addis Ababa on January 31st, 1942, recognized Ethiopia as an independent sovereign state, and laid down that the Emperor was free to form a government. Britain agreed to provide the Ethiopian government with £3,250,000 over the next four years, control of expenditure being entirely in the hands of the Emperor, and undertook to make British advisers subject to his authority. The Emperor in return reluctantly agreed that the reserved area, a stretch of Ethiopian territory adjacent to the French Somali Protectorate, then in Vichy hands, should be retained under British military administration, as well as a strip of land along the Addis Ababa-Djibouti railway, and the Ogaden, the Somali-inhabited province which had been part of Ethiopia until 1936 when the Italians had annexed it to their colony of Somalia. Perhaps the most positive result of the agreement was the coming of a British military mission, which organized the Ethiopian army on modern lines. The Ethiopian police force likewise came into existence through British help.

The British occupation of eastern Ethiopia was modified by a second Anglo-Ethiopian agreement signed on December 9th, 1944, after three months of protracted negotiations. It provided for the British evacuation of the area of the railway. However, the Ethiopian Government agreed to allow the British continued occupation of the other areas, though it did so "without prejudice to their underlying sovereignty". The continued British occupation was, however, bitterly resented by the Ethiopians, particularly after 1946 when the British Foreign Secretary, Bevin, proposed that the area be permanently severed from Ethiopia. On July 24th, 1948, however, the British government at last agreed to withdraw from the Ogaden, though the British withdrawal from the reserved area, including the Haud, did not take place until after the later Anglo-Ethiopian agreement of November 29th, 1954, when Ethiopia thus finally reassumed full sovereignty within her pre-war domains.

POST-WAR RECONSTRUCTION

The late 1940s and early 1950s also constituted an important period of reconstruction, which witnessed the establishment of a new bank, the State Bank of Ethiopia, a new currency, in 1942, and first national air services, by Ethiopian Air Lines, in 1946. Other promising developments included the reopening of the pre-war schools, as well as the establishment of several new ones, among them the Haile Sellassie Secondary School, founded in the capital in 1943. Prior to the war there had been opposition to education in many circles but by now there was a great thirst for it among the young. All the schools had waiting lists, and the Emperor declared that wherever he went children hailed his car, crying, "School! School!". The first institution of higher learning, the University College of Addis Ababa, came into existence in 1950, the nucleus of the later Haile Sellassie I University.

The Problem of Eritrea

The post-war years also witnessed protracted discussions over the future of Eritrea, and the former Italian colonies generally. During the liberation campaign the people of Eritrea had been promised freedom from Italian rule, and in October 1944 the British Foreign Secretary had made it clear in the House of Commons that the Italian empire in Africa was "irrevocably lost". In the peace treaty of February 10th, 1947, Italy was accordingly made to agree to the surrender of its colonies, the disposal of which was left to the four powers, Britain, the U.S.A., the U.S.S.R. and China. The four foreign ministers, however, failed to agree, and a joint commission of investigation sent to Eritrea in 1947 also produced divided recommendations. Further inconclusive discussions followed at several ensuing sessions of the

United Nations, which eventually despatched another enquiry commission whose members again differed on the proposals. At the end of the year the international organization none the less at last decided that Eritrea should be federated with Ethiopia under the Ethiopian Crown. The federation came into official existence on September 11th, 1952, but the Eritrea Assembly later voted on November 14th, 1962, for the territory's outright union with Ethiopia, so that Eritrea became an integral part of the empire on the following day.

Economic and political developments of these years included the country's first general election on the basis of adult universal suffrage, the formulation of the first five-year plan, both in 1957, and an abortive *coup d'état* by the Imperial Bodyguard in December 1960. With the emergence of the independent African states in the late 1950s and early 1960s Ethiopia became increasingly involved in African diplomacy, Addis Ababa being chosen as headquarters of the United Nations' Economic Commission for Africa in 1958 and of the Organization of African Unity in 1963.

[*Editorial note:* Since 1963 the Eritrean liberation movement has been in conflict, so far unresolved, with Government forces in the province (*see* Political Parties).]

ECONOMY
Detlev Karsten

NATURAL RESOURCES

Agricultural land is Ethiopia's main natural asset. Of the total area, 841,000 sq. km.—69 per cent—are classified as agricultural land, but only 15 per cent of this is actually cultivated. One can find vast areas of unutilized or underutilized land in practically all climatic zones. In most regions there is also sufficient rainfall, although it is unevenly distributed over the year. There is considerable soil erosion, due to the use of methods of cultivation that are inimical to soil conservation and due to deforestation and overgrazing. Larger forests now exist only in remote parts of the country and are not exploited on a substantial scale.

Mineral deposits that would justify large-scale exploitation have not yet been discovered. There is some gold and platinum, and also a major potassium deposit south of Massawa. Neither oil nor coal has been found, but exploration is continuing. As far as energy is concerned, Ethiopia has a high potential for hydro-electricity, the exploitation of which has barely started. In future there may also be a good chance of generating electricity from geothermal energy.

OVERALL VIEW OF THE ECONOMY*

Ethiopia is, judged by the G.D.P. per capita, one of the least developed countries in Africa. A population of about 24 million had in 1970 a G.D.P. of about E$4,000 million, or about E$165 per capita (E$1.00 = U.S. $0.40). The origin of the G.D.P. by sectors reveals

the importance of primary production, a characteristic typical of an early stage of economic development.

About 45 per cent of the total production is assumed to take place at subsistence level; a sizable proportion of the subsistence farmers are nomads.

A remarkable feature of the Ethiopian economy is the prevailing dualism, that is the existence of almost completely separate traditional and modern sectors. There is a wide discrepancy between the two with hardly any contact between them and consequently little prospect for an evolutionary change of the traditional sector. The dualism partly coincides with the imbalance in regional development—some towns and a few cash-crop areas are developing relatively quickly, while the remainder of the country remains in stagnation. This backwardness can partly be explained by the fact that the very idea of development is relatively new to Ethiopia—not until the end of the Italian occupation did Ethiopia embark on a programme of real modernization. It is also true that Ethiopia —when compared with other African countries—had little exposure to modern ideas due to its century-long seclusion and to the short duration of its colonial period (1936–42).

---

* Not only are the statistical services in Ethiopia still in their infancy, but also statistics are reported sometimes for the Ethiopian calendar year and sometimes for the Ethiopian fiscal year, both of which differ from the Gregorian Calendar. Figures for the subsistence sector are even more unreliable.

Table 1
GROSS DOMESTIC PRODUCT AT FACTOR COST BY INDUSTRIAL ORIGIN
(1969)*

	E$ MILLION	%
Agriculture . . .	2,108.7	54.8
Agriculture . . .	2,011.8	52.3
Forestry . . .	92.7	2.4
Hunting . . .	1.2	—
Fishing . . .	3.0	0.1
Industries . . .	633.8	16.5
Mining and Quarrying . .	9.1	0.2
Manufacturing . .	211.5	5.5
Handicrafts and Small-Scale Industry . .	177.2	4.6
Building and Construction .	214.3	5.6
Electricity and Water .	21.7	0.6
Wholesale and Retail Trade .	319.8	8.3
Transport and Communication .	142.8	3.7
Other Services . . .	644.8	16.7
Banking, Insurance and Real Estate . .	49.5	1.3
Public Administration and Defence . . .	203.9	5.3
Ownership of Dwellings .	147.4	3.8
Educational Services .	70.0	1.8
Medical and Health Services.	24.8	0.6
Domestic Services .	58.6	1.5
Other . . .	90.6	2.4
TOTAL . .	3,849.9	100.0

Source: Central Statistical Office.

*For previous years *see* Statistical Survey, p. 323.

INFRASTRUCTURE

Personal Infrastructure

There is a very low level of general education—about 95 per cent of the people are illiterate, and only 11 per cent of primary school age children were enrolled in schools in 1967. This situation is aggravated by the adherence to traditional prejudices that are detrimental in so many ways to modernization. This is particularly true of the widespread prejudice against manual labour and of ideas about cattle known as the "east African cattle complex". The traditional outlook is reinforced by the teachings of the extremely conservative Ethiopian Orthodox Church.

Government schools provide six years of primary education, followed by three years of junior secondary education and another three years of senior secondary education. These schools give a general academic education, and, so far, the curriculum has not been adjusted to the specific needs of the country. Instruction is for six years in Amharic; even this for a large number of students is not their mother-tongue. Beginning with grade seven the medium of instruction is English; this is the consequence of the shortage of qualified Ethiopian teachers and the unavailability of advanced Amharic textbooks. In 1968–69 total enrolment in all government schools was 470,000 (the population estimate for the same year was 23.7 million). The drop-out rates are extremely high with many students remaining in school for one year only, and very few students obtaining the Ethiopian School Leaving Certificate after 12 years of education.

In addition to the government schools education is provided by private schools (total enrolment in 1968–69; 68,000), mission schools (enrolment 59,000), and schools of the Ethiopian Orthodox Church (no enrolment figures are available).

The few schools are mainly in towns and are regionally concentrated. For example, the 20 per cent of Ethiopia's population living in the central province of Shoa (which includes the capital, Addis Ababa) account for 32 per cent of the total enrolment in government schools. Not more than 30 per cent of the students are girls.

There is a shortage of skilled workers of all kinds, particularly in technical fields. This is linked with an abundance of low-level clerical manpower and of unskilled labour, most of which is disguised agricultural unemployment. A serious problem with all kinds of skilled operatives is that they have to be bilingual. This requirement applies both to their education, which is mostly in English, and to their work. People who can satisfy these requirements are reluctant to accept subordinate positions.

There are a number of governmental and private schools for professional training; the total annual output of medium-level technicians is about 400. The problem with such technicians is that they are often not willing to work manually and feel entitled to supervisory jobs. These graduates often encounter difficulties in securing a job, partly because of exaggerated salary demands. For instance, a technician expects after graduation from the Bahar Dar Polytechnic Institute a starting salary of E$350 (compared with an unskilled worker's typical salary of E$30–40 per month). The starting salary of a technician is clearly out of proportion to his competence.

The most important source of high-level manpower is the Haile Sellassie I University in Addis Ababa with a total number of graduates (with first degrees) of 390 in 1970, among them 44 engineers. There are also a number of Ethiopian students abroad—about 1,800 in 1968–69. But there is a shortage of very competent and experienced people in practically all fields, especially in engineering and medicine.

Another problem is the scarcity of Ethiopian entrepreneurs. This is partly attributable to cultural traditions which result in lack of initiative, and a reluctance to take risks and to assume responsibilities. The majority of the larger firms are in the hands of expatriates; particularly important are Armenians, Italians, Greeks, Arabs and Indians. To close this gap, an ILO-run Centre for Ethiopian Management gives courses in pertinent subjects.

Education contributes in two ways to an undesirable migration to urban centres: first, people are attracted to the towns because of the better facilities for education, and second, even people with minimum education flock to towns hoping to find a white-collar job. On the other hand educated people are very reluctant to go to the countryside.

Institutional Infrastructure

Ethiopia recognized the need for development planning late in the 1950s, and the first development plan ran from 1958–63. Ethiopia is now in its third five-year plan (1968–73). So far as the public sector of the economy is concerned, the development plans are intended to be directive, imposing commitments and restrictions as to capital expenditure and projects which should be implemented. So far as the private sector is concerned, the plans can only be indicative of desired objectives. Government measures can be, and are, of course, utilized to stimulate and encourage those investments and projects which would further the implementation of the plan, while discouraging those which would not. The private sector comprises in particular the fields of agriculture, manufacturing industries and handicrafts, building and construction, domestic and foreign trade, and transportation. The development plans are, however, in many ways unrealistic, mainly because they were established with little participation from "below", that is from the institutions that have to execute the plan, and because the plans were not based on sound project studies. It is also true that the system of public administration and the abilities and attitudes of most civil servants are not conducive to economic progress.

The civil service structure of Ethiopia is weak. Characteristic of the Ethiopian bureaucracy is the widespread fragmentation of functions and duties between numerous institutions, the duplication of work, a reluctance to assume responsibility, and the concentration of multiple jobs in the hands of a few individuals. All this results in a lack of cohesion and co-ordination in the formulation and execution of policy. This lack of co-ordination is obvious in the central governmental structure, where there are 18 ministries and a confusing number of autonomous institutions. It is even worse in the provincial and local administration. The country is divided into 14 provinces, 87 sub-provinces and 391 districts. The shortage of trained manpower and of financial resources at all levels limits the speedy execution of decisions as well as the communication between the central government and the lower levels. A very serious problem for private enterprise is that all government decisions take much time, and are largely unpredictable owing to the discretionary powers of each civil servant.

Physical Infrastructure

Because of the mountainous nature of the country, communication links are expensive to establish, and the costs of operation are high.

Ethiopia has a total of about 8,190 km. of all-weather roads (1969–70). That means that, if we take a strip of 10 km. on either side of the road as within easy reach of the highway, less than 12 per cent of the area of the country has access to a road. In rural areas, therefore, pack animals and human porterage play a dominant role. Very often the existing roads are in poor condition, thus contributing to the high costs of transportation. There are so far no all-weather road connexions to neighbouring countries. The highway system is under rapid expansion, mainly financed by foreign loans.

The country has two narrow-gauge railways. One connects Addis Ababa to the Red Sea port, Djibouti, and has a total length of 880 km., of which 782 km. are on Ethiopian territory. The other runs 306 km. from the Red Sea port of Massawa to Asmara and Agordat. Both railways charge very high rates.

Inland waterways do not play a role in modern transport—only one river is navigable. Ethiopia has two Red Sea ports, Assab and Massawa, but also depends heavily on the port of Djibouti. Since 1965 Ethiopia has also had a national shipping line, which runs five vessels.

Air transport is very important for access to remote areas. Ethiopian Air Lines has an extensive domestic network with about 30 airports served regularly. In 1969 it transported 117,000 passengers on domestic flights with an average distance of 180 miles per passenger, and the domestic freight volume was 500,000 ton miles in the same year. Ethiopian Air Lines also runs an impressive international service.

The telecommunications network more or less follows the road system. Most towns along the roads can be reached for a few hours per day by telephone. The most important towns off the main road can be contacted by radio transmitters. Only four towns have telex connexion. International calls are possible by radio telephone. Less widespread are the postal services. There were in 1970 altogether 100 towns and villages (out of 248 settlements listed as towns) that are served by permanent post offices; a few more are served by mobile offices.

Most larger towns have a public electricity supply. There are two large interconnected systems; one in the Addis Ababa–Nazareth–Dire Dawa area, which is mainly supplied with hydroelectricity, and the other around Asmara. Towns outside these areas have self-contained systems supplied with small diesel power plants. Total electricity production in 1968–69 was 341 million kWh., 70 per cent of which was hydro-electricity.

SECTORAL DEVELOPMENT

Agriculture

Agriculture is the mainstay of the Ethiopian economy. More than 80 per cent of the population relies for its livelihood on agriculture and the large majority of peasants is engaged in subsistence activities. The modern sector of agriculture—mainly commercial farms—has a share of only 7 per cent in agricultural production.

In spite of the large number of people in agriculture Ethiopia is barely self-sufficient in food production. This is attributable to the extremely low productivity in the traditional sector of agriculture. The most pressing problems of this sector are methods of cultivation which are archaic and at a very low level of technology, the often incentive-killing land tenure situation, the difficulties in domestic trade, unsuitable methods of storage, etc. Commercial farms face difficulties in marketing their products due to high costs of production and the often prohibitive costs of transportation. These high costs make exports of many farm products virtually impossible. The most important crops of Ethiopia and their relative significance can be seen in table 2.

Table 2
PRODUCTION OF MAJOR CROPS
(1969–70 est.—'ooo tons)*

Cereals:	
Barley	1,495.6
Maize	909.0
Sorghum	1,036.8
Teff	1,342.6
Wheat	808.0
Other	159.9
Ensete	476.5
Industrial Plants:	
Cotton	13.7
Ensete Fibre	13.1
Sisal	3.1
Sugar Cane	1,129.5
Tobacco	2.1
Oil Seeds	492.2
Pulses	634.6
Fruits and Stimulants:	
Fruits	80.9
Gesho	93.2
Chat	6.2
Coffee	170.0
Vegetables	769.6

Source: Central Statistical Office.

* For more detailed data *see* Statistical Survey, p.319.

NOTES:

TEFF (*Eragrostis abyssinica*) is an indigenous grain of Ethiopia and is an important element of the Amhara diet.

ENSETE (*Ensete edulis horan*), the so-called false banana, is the staple food of a large number of Ethiopian people, living mainly in the south-west of the country; a by-product of the food production is a strong fibre which is used in the modern sector for sack-production.

The leaves of the GESHO plant (*Rhamnus prinoides*) are used as a sort of hops in the preparation of local beer.

The leaves of the CHAT plant (*Catha edulis*) are chewed as a stimulant mainly by the Muslim population.

Ethiopia has also a very high livestock population, as can be seen from table 3.

Table 3
LIVESTOCK POPULATION
(1969–70 est.—million)

Cattle	26.2
Sheep	12.7
Goats	11.3
Horses	1.4
Mules	1.4
Donkeys	3.9
Camels	1.0
Poultry	48.1

Source: Central Statistical Office.

Much of the livestock cannot be regarded as a productive asset because of its very poor condition and the owners' reluctance to sell it.

To break the deadlock in agricultural development Ethiopia is now embarking on regional development projects which follow the example set by the Chilalo Agricultural Development Unit, a joint project of the Ethiopian and the Swedish Government. This is so far the only successful approach to the development of subsistence farming.

Manufacturing Industry

Manufacturing industry contributes only 5.5 per cent to the G.D.P. of Ethiopia, and the total employment in this sector is less than 50,000 (figures for 1968–69). Table 4 reflects the structure of manufacturing industry.

The insignificant role of manufacturing industries results from the failure so far to discover minerals which could become the basis of industrial development, and also from the smallness of the domestic market for manufactures due to the low purchasing power of the rural population. Ethiopia has comparative advantages that would allow the building up of an export-oriented industry but both natural as well as institutional factors have resulted in a very high cost level of the existing industry. Manufacturing industry is exclusively import-substituting, and only viable under heavy protection. This early phase of industrialization, the setting up of import-substituting industries, has come to an end because there are no further projects where the demand is above the domestic production threshold of modern plants. Further development, therefore, will follow the expansion of the domestic market.

The dualism characteristic of the low stage of development can also be observed in industry. There are, on the one hand, relatively modern factories working with imported machinery and methods, and, on the other, the traditional handicrafts, which in rural areas are often only supplementary to the main occupation of farming. There is also regional disequilibrium: more than 90 per cent of all industrial establishments are concentrated in less than 1 per cent of the area of the country, that is the Addis Ababa–Nazareth region, the Dire Dawa–Harar region and the Asmara–Massawa region.

FOREIGN TRADE AND
BALANCE OF PAYMENTS

Since 1958 Ethiopia has had a persistent trade deficit. The figures for the last five years are given in table 5.

About 30 per cent of imports are current industrial inputs, 20 per cent machinery and about 50 per cent consumer goods; a sizable proportion of the latter (about 8 per cent of total imports) are private cars.

The dominant position in exports is occupied by coffee, which in 1969 accounted for almost 60 per cent of total exports. This dangerous position of relying heavily on one commodity is aggravated by the fact that the bulk of this coffee (70 per cent in 1969) is

Table 4

NUMBER OF ESTABLISHMENTS, EMPLOYMENT AND SALES VALUE BY INDUSTRIAL BRANCHES

(1968–69)

	NUMBER OF ESTABLISHMENTS		NUMBER OF EMPLOYEES		SALES VALUE	
	Absolute	%	Absolute	%	E$ million	%
Food	125	28.3	8,538	17.5	113.9	24.4
Beverages . . .	37	8.4	3,155	6.5	50.4	10.8
Tobacco	2	0.5	562	1.2	13.7	2.9
Textile	50	11.3	21,656	44.5	157.3	33.7
Leather and Shoe . .	24	5.4	2,001	4.1	18.1	3.9
Wood	72	16.3	3,111	6.4	13.2	2.8
Non-Metallic . . .	39	8.8	3,822	7.9	23.0	4.9
Printing	27	6.1	1,579	3.3	8.9	1.9
Chemical	37	8.4	2,563	5.3	39.8	8.5
Steel, Metal and Electrical . .	29	6.5	1,620	3.3	28.7	6.2
TOTAL . . .	442	100.0	48,652	100.0	467.0	100.0

Source: Central Statistical Office.

Table 5

ETHIOPIA'S FOREIGN TRADE*

(E$ million)

	IMPORTS	EXPORTS AND RE-EXPORTS	TRADE GAP
1965 . .	375.7	289.8	85.9
1966 . .	404.3	277.0	127.3
1967 . .	357.4	252.7	104.7
1968 . .	432.5	266.0	166.5
1969 . .	388.3	298.1	90.2

Source: Central Statistical Office.

* For full trade figures *see* Statistical Survey, p. 323-4.

sold in one market, that is the U.S.A. In the order of importance, the other main export items of Ethiopia are hides and skins (10 per cent of total exports in 1969), vegetables and fruits (9 per cent) and oilseeds (9 per cent). The share of manufactures in exports is below 5 per cent.

Ethiopia has had deficits on the current account of balance of payments since 1958, and in 1969 this deficit amounted to E$22.5 million. So far these deficits have been balanced by a considerable capital inflow, where long-term loans (mainly development aid) to the government have been more important than foreign private investment. Technical assistance also accounted for a considerable inflow of foreign exchange, and the total value of this assistance, together with grants, received by Ethiopia in 1968–69, amounted to E$60 million.

PUBLIC FINANCE

Total government revenue (without technical assistance and foreign loans) accounts for about 12 per cent of the G.D.P. A summary of the budgetary revenue is given in table 6. Table 7 gives the breakdown of expenditure.

About 24 per cent of the budgetary revenue derives from technical assistance and foreign loans. Within the domestic revenue direct taxes have a share of about 23 per cent, whereas indirect taxes of all kinds accounts for 62 per cent. The most important individual source of revenue is the taxation of foreign trade.

It is interesting to note that "national defence" and the "maintenance of internal order" together claim more than 35 per cent of current expenditure, while agriculture is allocated not even 3 per cent of total expenditure. Education, with close on 13 per cent, seems also not to be given sufficient emphasis. Altogether the budget does not give enough attention to types of expenditure that will encourage growth in the future. In addition budgets have not so far been related to the annual programmes of implementation of the development plans.

Table 6

SUMMARY OF GOVERNMENTAL REVENUE

(1969–70—E$ million)

Direct Taxes	102.3
Domestic Indirect Taxes . .	121.8
Taxes on Foreign Trade . .	152.7
External Assistance . . .	88.0
Proceeds from External Loans .	48.6
Other	66.3
TOTAL	579.7

Source: Central Statistical Office.

Table 7

SUMMARY OF GOVERNMENT EXPENDITURE
(1969–70—E$ million)

Current Expenditure	473.6
General Services	213.8
National Defence	85.3
Internal Order and Justice . .	81.8
Foreign Relations	9.4
Finance and Planning . . .	16.0
Other General Administration . .	21.3
Economic Services. . . .	44.1
Agriculture	10.4
Industry and Commerce . .	4.7
Public Works and Communications	29.0
Social Services . . .	94.2
Education and Culture . . .	69.0
Public Health	20.6
Social Affairs	4.6
Contribution to Pension Fund . .	13.8
Unallocated Expenditure . .	107.7
Capital Expenditure . . .	106.1
Social Development . . .	28.0
National Community Development .	1.7
Education	10.1
Public Health	16.2
Economic Development . .	77.3
Road Construction . . .	32.8
Other Infrastructure . . .	3.1
Mining	1.1
Manufacturing Industry . . .	7.5
Agriculture	4.3
Other Projects	14.6
Projects covered by External Assistance	14.1
Public Buildings	0.8
TOTAL GOVERNMENT EXPENDITURE	579.7

Source: Central Statistical Office.

The National Bank of Ethiopia as the central bank is responsible for monetary policy and exchange control. The most important commercial banks are the government-owned Commercial Bank of Ethiopia and the privately-owned Addis Ababa Bank, Banco di Roma and Banco di Napoli. Until 1970, there were also two development banks, the Development Bank of Ethiopia and the Ethiopian Investment Corporation; they were merged in 1970 to become the "Agricultural and Industrial Development Bank S.G."

The bulk of the Ethiopian population is not aware of the advantages the banking system can offer and, especially in the rural areas, people prefer to keep their money hidden, turning, if in need of a loan, to private money-lenders, who charge exorbitant rates of interest.

The total amount of money in circulation at June 30th, 1972, was E$415.5 million, of which $306.0 million consisted of coins and banknotes and the rest of demand deposits. Ethiopia is a member of the IMF but has foreign exchange control. One can safely say that the Ethiopian dollar is overvalued in terms of hard currencies, but this has not so far resulted in a serious decline in foreign exchange reserves because artificially high coffee prices, due to the International Coffee Agreement, and also substantial development aid have resulted in an inflow of foreign exchange. On the whole Ethiopia is following a conservative monetary policy, and inflationary pressure is slight. On the other hand, it may also be true that monetary policy has not helped the economy to break out of its nearly stagnant condition.

FUTURE OUTLOOK

The increase of agricultural productivity is absolutely essential for Ethiopian development. Indeed, it is also a precondition of development in other sectors. The most fruitful approach towards increasing agricultural productivity seems to be to concentrate efforts on promising regions. This concentration is necessary because it is impossible with Ethiopia's limited resources to provide the needed infrastructure for the whole country at once. This piecemeal approach may also facilitate certain institutional changes, such as land reform and a reform of domestic trade.

The other field where a determined effort is required is education. More consideration should be given to a type of education that acknowledges the fact that Ethiopia will remain a predominantly agricultural country for many generations. The breaking down of traditional irrationalities may call for a more comprehensive learning process than can be expected from the customary student-teacher relationship, under which prejudices of the teacher are passed on to the student, and radical change is made unlikely within less than a few generations.

Since Ethiopia has financed most of her progress—mainly in infrastructure—with foreign loans, she has to ensure growth in exports, without which servicing and repayment of the loans will be difficult. Again the only sector that can produce a surplus is agriculture. Unless Ethiopia takes resolute action in both these fields, agriculture and education—and this seems to be possible only in the face of political resistance from the beneficiaries of the present system—she will remain in the quasi-stagnation that characterizes the economy now.

STATISTICAL SURVEY

AREA AND POPULATION

Area: 1,221,900 sq. km. (471,778 sq. miles), including Eritrea (117,600 sq. km.).

Population (1971 estimate): 25,248,000. Average annual birth rate 45.6 per 1,000, death rate 25.0 per 1,000 (UN estimates for 1965–70).

GOVERNORATES
(1967 estimates)

PROVINCE	POPULATION ('000)	CAPITAL	PROVINCE	POPULATION ('000)	CAPITAL
Arussi	1,110.8	Asella	Illubabor	663.2	Matu
Bale	1,348.4	Goba	Kaffa	688.4	Jimma
Begemder	1,588.4	Gondar	Shoa	3,747.0	Addis Ababa
Eritrea	1,589.4	Asmara	Sidamo	1,521.4	Awasa
Gemu-Goffa	840.0	Arba Minch	Tigre	2,307.3	Makale
Gojjam	1,576.1	Debra Markos	Wollega	1,429.9	Lekemti
Hararje	3,341.7	Harar	Wollo	3,119.7	Dessye

Chief Towns (1968 population): Addis Ababa (capital) 684,100, Asmara 190,500.

Employment (1970 estimates): Total economically active population 11,428,000, including 9,668,000 in agriculture.

AGRICULTURE

LAND USE, 1968
('000 hectares)

Arable and under Permanent Crops .	12,900
Permanent Meadows and Pastures . .	66,000
Forest Land	8,800
Other Land	22,390
Inland Water	12,100
TOTAL	122,190

PRINCIPAL CROPS

	AREA ('000 hectares)			PRODUCTION ('000 metric tons)			YIELD (kg. per hectare)		
	1969	1970	1971	1969	1970	1971	1969	1970	1971
Bananas . . .	2.2*	2.2*	n.a.	50*	50*	n.a.	22,700*	22,700*	n.a.
Barley	1,735	1,755*	1,770*	1,496	1,525*	1,550*	860	870*	880*
Chick-peas . . .	290	294	298*	181	185	189*	620	630	630*
Coffee (green beans) .	618	n.a.	n.a.	170	205	215	275	n.a.	n.a.
Dry Beans . . .	94	95*	96*	72	72*	74*	770	760*	770*
Dry Broad Beans . .	144	148*	152*	138	138*	143*	960	930*	940*
Dry Peas . . .	135	137*	139*	126	127*	130*	940	930*	940*
Flax for Seed . .	120	122*	125*	62	60	66*	520	490*	530*
Lentils . . .	174	178*	180*	106	107*	109*	610	600*	610*
Maize	847	860*	870*	909	950*	960*	1,070	1,100*	1,100*
Millet, Sorghum and Teff .	3,703	4,420*	4,450*	2,539	2,700*	2,750*	690	610*	620*
Potatoes . . .	30	30*	31*	161	162*	163*	5,300	5,400*	5,300*
Sesame Seed . . .	141	150*	150*	69.4	70*	70*	490	470*	470*
Sweet Potatoes and Yams .	58	59	59*	248	253	254*	4,300	4,300	4,300*
Wheat	1,070	1,090*	1,100*	808	840*	860*	760	770*	780*
Other Pulses . .	96*	97*	98*	58*	59*	60*	600*	610*	610*

* FAO estimate.

319

LIVESTOCK

	1968–69	1969–70	1970–71
Cattle	26,108,000	26,232,000	26,330,000*
Sheep	12,509,000	12,679,000	12,800,000*
Goats	11,207,000	11,263,000	11,320,000*
Asses	3,837,000	3,853,000	3,900,000*
Horses	1,393,000	1,404,000	1,415,000*
Mules	1,400,000	1,412,000	1,440,000*
Camels . . .	981,000	987,000	990,000*
Pigs . . .	15,000	15,000	17,000*
Poultry . . .	47,200,000	48,100,000	46,800,000*

* FAO estimate.

LIVESTOCK PRODUCE
(metric tons)

	1968	1969	1970
Beef and Veal . . .	248,000	248,000*	248,000*
Mutton and Lamb . .	91,000	92,000*	94,000*
Poultry Meat . .	50,000*	51,000*	52,000*
Offal . . .	74,000*	76,000*	76,000*
Other Meat . .	14,000*	14,000*	14,000*
Tallow . . .	9,000*	10,000*	10,000*
Cows' Milk . .	488,000	502,000	516,000
Goats' Milk . .	90,000*	92,000*	94,000*
Sheep's Milk . .	5,000*	5,000*	5,000*
Butter . . .	37,000	38,000*	39,000*
Hen Eggs . .	61,300*	61,400*	61,500*
Cattle Hides . .	63,546*	64,701*	95,025*
Sheep Skins . .	8,730*	6,973*	8,795*
Goat Skins . .	7,556*	7,819*	5,680*
Camel Hides .	2,520*	2,520*	2,600*

* FAO estimate.

Source for Agriculture tables: FAO, *Production Yearbook 1971.*

FORESTRY

ROUNDWOOD PRODUCTION
(cubic metres)

1966 . .	21,000,000
1967 . .	21,537,000
1968 . .	22,038,000

Source: FAO, *Yearbook of Forest Products.*

SAWNWOOD
(cubic metres)

1967 . . .	58,000
1968 . . .	59,000
1969 . . .	60,000
1970 . . .	63,000

Source: United Nations *Statistical Yearbook 1971.*

FISHING
(metric tons)

1967 . . .	10,800
1968 . . .	6,900*
1969 . . .	5,800*
1970 . . .	7,000*

* FAO estimate.

Source: FAO, *Yearbook of Fishery Statistics 1970.*

MINING

Gold (kg.)				Salt (metric tons)			
1967	.	.	734	1967	.	.	212,000
1968	.	.	1,208	1968	.	.	215,000
1969	.	.	1,319	1969	.	.	234,000
				1970	.	.	260,000

PETROLEUM PRODUCTS
('000 metric tons)

	1967*	1968*	1969*	1970*
Liquefied Petroleum Gas . . .	—	2	2	2
Motor Spirit	26	78	69	69
Kerosene	—	1	2	—
Jet Fuels	—	14	26	31
Distillate Fuel Oils . . .	59	146	140	165
Residual Fuel Oils . . .	43	91	272	311
Bitumen (asphalt) . . .	2	12	7	16

* 12 months ending September 10th of year stated.

OTHER INDUSTRY

CHIEF PRODUCTS	UNIT	1965*	1966*	1967*
Wheat flour . . .	metric tons	40,358	42,030	58,952
Macaroni	,,	4,893	4,076	4,523
Vegetable oils . . .	,,	5,633	5,343	8,146
Refined sugar . . .	,,	61,698	68,861	76,868
Meat	,,	10,543	13,378	7,955
Cotton yarn . . .	,,	5,620	7,459	9,221
Blankets	number	40,000	95,000	84,000
Cement	metric tons	72,899	88,930	137,649
Hydrated lime . . .	,,	7,355	10,732	11,051
Cigarettes	'000	440,991	527,849	587,971
Leather shoes . . .	pairs	627,828	648,000	609,000
Beer	hectolitres	157,395	184,600	215,500
Timber	cubic metres	13,000	14,506	15,700
Glass bottles . . .	'000	15,721	18,000	15,100
Round iron bars . .	metric tons	n.a.	8,800	12,000
Corrugated iron sheet . .	,,	n.a.	5,567	14,259
Electric energy . . .	million kWh.	246	277	320

1968*: Refined sugar 71,000 metric tons, Cotton yarn 4,700 metric tons, Cement 174,000 metric tons, Cigarettes 715 million, Electric energy 361 million kWh.

1969*: Wheat flour 42,000 metric tons, Refined sugar 70,000 metric tons, Cotton yarn 5,000 metric tons, Cement 166,000 metric tons, Cigarettes 750 million.

1970*: Refined sugar 85,000 metric tons.

* Year ending September 10th.

FINANCE

100 cents = 1 Ethiopian dollar.
Coins: 1, 5, 10, 25 and 50 cents.
Notes: 1, 5, 10, 20, 50, 100 and 500 dollars.
Exchange rates (December 1972): £1 sterling = E$5.406; U.S. $1 = E$2.303;
E$100 = £18.50 = U.S. $43.43.

BUDGET
(E$ million)

Revenue	1967–68*	1968–69*	1969–70*
Taxes on Income	76.59	103.82	105.65
Import Duties	103.28	115.45	123.12
Export Duties	25.82	26.95	28.20
Sales and Turnover Taxes . . .	103.75	136.53	114.50
Other Indirect Taxes . . .	9.11	9.50	10.49
Sales and Charges . . .	12.68	15.32	17.52
Current Transfers from Households .	12.33	13.35	5.86
Current Transfers from Abroad .	95.46	90.83	90.02
Net Surplus from Government Enterprises	7.14	11.65	29.15
Other Receipts	16.15	18.81	18.27
	462.31	542.21	542.78
Deficit	51.95	82.66	66.98
Total	514.26	624.87	609.76

Expenditure	1967–68*	1968–69*	1969–70*
Interest on Public Debt . . .	13.82	17.86	16.16
Subsidies	2.26	1.29	5.47
Current Transfers to:			
Households	22.45	20.09	20.12
Local Governments . . .	—	0.30	—
Abroad	2.93	3.67	3.81
Current Expenditure on Goods and Services .	374.90	422.65	434.53
Gross Capital Formation . . .	97.90	159.01	129.67
Total	514.26	624.87	609.76

* Twelve months ending July 7th.

Note: Transactions represent a consolidation of the current and capital accounts. Figures for 1968–69 and 1969–70 are estimates. Expenditures include (in E$ million) 1967–68: Defence 86.79, Education 56.84, Public health 23.88, Agriculture 19.66; 1968–69: Defence 86.79, Education 67.42, Public health 27.76, Agriculture 15.98.

Source: United Nations, *Statistical Yearbook 1971.*

Currency in Circulation (June 30th, 1972): E$306 million

GROSS DOMESTIC PRODUCT AT PURCHASERS' VALUES
(E$ million)

ECONOMIC ACTIVITIES	1967	1968	1969
Agriculture, Hunting, Forestry and Fishing .	1,902.6	2,004.9	2,119.5
Mining and Quarrying	12.1	11.2	9.1
Manufacturing	298.1	333.9	388.7
Electricity, Gas and Water	17.9	20.5	21.7
Construction	217.6	208.5	214.3
Wholesale and Retail Trade, Restaurants and Hotels	246.2	286.0	319.8
Transport, Storage and Communication . .	125.7	139.8	142.8
Other Producers and Services* . . .	628.2	667.3	821.7
TOTAL	3,448.4	3,672.1	4,037.6

* Including a statistical discrepancy.

BALANCE OF PAYMENTS
(E$ million)

	1969		1970		1971*	
	Credit	Debit	Credit	Debit	Credit	Debit
Goods and Services	455.25	505.75	467.00	566.00	500.25	623.75
Merchandise f.o.b.	297.50	326.25	305.75	360.75	314.00	396.75
Non-monetary gold	3.25	—	1.50	—	1.00	—
Freight and insurance	3.00	62.00	3.75	68.50	4.00	75.25
Other transportation . . .	50.75	14.50	55.50	19.75	62.25	23.00
Travel	14.75	17.00	15.75	18.75	19.75	18.25
Investment income	12.75	33.00	16.25	35.50	11.75	41.00
Other government	39.50	25.00	37.50	21.00	42.75	18.75
Other private	33.75	28.00	31.00	41.75	44.75	50.75
Unrequited Transfers	61.50	33.50	52.00	32.00	55.00	32.50
Private	24.00	31.50	23.50	30.00	26.75	31.25
Government	37.50	2.00	28.50	2.00	28.25	1.25
Capital (excluding reserves and related items)	31.25	—	82.50	—	77.25	—
Non-monetary sectors (net) . . .	32.00	—	42.50	—	77.50	—
Direct investment . . .	6.75	—	9.75	—	14.25	—
Other private long-term (net) . .	6.00	—	8.00	—	5.50	—
Other private short-term (net) . .	—	15.25	14.75	—	25.25	—
Local government	11.50	—	5.00	—	—	—
Central government (net) . . .	23.00	—	5.00	—	32.50	—
Monetary sectors (net) . . .	—	0.75	40.00	—	—	0.25
Deposit money banks (net) . .	—	0.75	40.00	—	—	0.25
Reserves and Related Items (net) . .	—	10.50	2.00	—	17.00	—
Liabilities	3.00	—	0.50	—	3.00	—
Assets	—	13.50	1.50	—	14.00	—
Net Errors and Omissions . . .	1.75	—	—	5.50	6.75	—

* Provisional.

Source: International Monetary Fund, *Balance of Payments Yearbook.*

EXTERNAL TRADE
(E$ million)

	1965	1966	1967	1968	1969	1970	1971
Imports . .	375.7	404.3	357.4	432.5	388.3	429.1	472.0
Exports . .	289.8	277.0	252.7	266.0	298.1	305.8	314.0

PRINCIPAL COMMODITIES

IMPORTS
(E$'000)

	1967	1968	1969*
Food and Live Animals	22,950	19,129	19,687
Textile Fibres and Waste . . .	14,057	19,157	14,765
Crude Petroleum	6,466	14,572	16,241
Petroleum Products	24,592	12,121	11,454
Chemicals	34,503	40,957	43,506
Rubber Tyres and Tubes . . .	12,476	11,874	11,303
Textile Yarn and Thread . . .	12,855	11,466	11,382
Textile Fabrics, etc.	15,089	11,100	11,440
Iron and Steel	17,288	20,753	17,289
Machinery (non-electric) . . .	42,356	59,805	55,216
Electrical Equipment	24,702	22,684	25,524
Road Motor Vehicles	40,469	39,686	38,528
Aircraft	5,575	46,378	11,404
Clothing (except furs) . . .	14,406	14,365	12,843
TOTAL (incl. others) . . .	357,369	432,522	388,227

* Unrevised.

EXPORTS, EXCLUDING RE-EXPORTS
(E$'000)

	1967	1968	1969
Dry Pulses	19,666	21,364	22,242
Other Fruit and Vegetables . .	8,534	7,260	6,726
Coffee (green or roasted) . . .	139,182	152,957	173,946
Other Food	17,158	15,349	15,026
Goat and Kid Skins	9,890	8,695	8,422
Sheep and Lamb Skins . . .	13,356	13,066	14,924
Other Hides and Skins . . .	7,590	3,154	5,813
Sesame Seed	11,385	14,040	15,607
Other Oilseeds, Nuts and Kernels .	11,315	7,399	7,579
TOTAL (incl. others) . . .	249,976	258,047	291,999

1970: Coffee E$181,300,000; Hides and skins E$24,500,000.
1971: Coffee E$175,200,000; Hides and skins E$25,700,000.

PRINCIPAL COUNTRIES
(E$ million)

IMPORTS	1967	1968	1969*	EXPORTS	1967	1968*	1969†
France . . .	11.89	21.41	19.82	France . . .	9.17	8.09	8.92
Germany, Federal				French Terr. Afars			
Republic . .	50.02	48.70	55.63	and Issas	7.72	7.82	18.98
India . . .	5.25	6.39	8.27	Germany, Federal			
Iran . . .	15.02	13.39	19.67	Republic . .	13.64	21.06	28.79
Israel . . .	6.03	9.82	11.07	Italy . . .	20.95	16.28	21.18
Italy . . .	67.69	77.18	59.83	Japan . . .	10.88	11.44	14.19
Japan . . .	48.76	40.74	42.14	Saudi Arabia . .	13.92	17.40	17.21
Netherlands . .	12.38	12.49	10.53	Sri Lanka (Ceylon) .	3.92	7.61	5.29
United Kingdom .	27.58	40.70	39.03	U.S.S.R. . .	7.59	7.68	4.19
U.S.A. . .	33.62	80.09	39.98	United Kingdom .	10.60	9.41	9.57
				U.S.A. . .	108.96	112.65	125.60
TOTAL (incl. others)	357.37	435.52	388.23	TOTAL (incl. others)	252.70	258.05	298.42

* Unrevised.

* Excluding re-exports.
† Unrevised.

COFFEE EXPORTS, 1967
(metric tons)

China (People's Republic) . . .	739
France	1,707
Germany, Federal Republic . .	2,063
Italy	2,095
Japan	2,036
Norway	855
Saudi Arabia	940
Spain	1,005
Sweden	913
U.S.S.R.	1,307
U.S.A.	56,106
TOTAL (incl. others) . . .	73,594

TRANSPORT

RAILWAYS*

	1967	1968	1969
ADDIS ABABA—DJIBOUTI:			
Passenger-km. ('ooo) .	82,000	83,000	92,000
Freight ('ooo net ton-km.) .	216,000	190,000	220,000

* Excluding Eritrea but including traffic on that portion of the Djibouti–Addis Ababa line which runs through the French Territory of the Afar and Issa.

ROADS
(Number of vehicles in use)

	1968	1969	1970
Passenger Cars . . .	29,500	33,000	47,200
Commercial Vehicles . .	9,700	10,800	12,300

SHIPPING

INTERNATIONAL SEA-BORNE TRAFFIC

	1967	1968	1969
Vessels Entered ('ooo net reg. tons)	3,350	n.a.	n.a.
Goods Loaded ('ooo metric tons) .	475	685	610
Goods Unloaded ('ooo metric tons)	569	813	880

CIVIL AVIATION

			1968	1969	1970
Kilometres flown ('000)	.	.	10,305	10,396	10,738
Passenger-km. ('000)	.	.	298,678	300,380	314,325
Cargo ton-km. ('000)	.	.	16,939	15,751	15,143
Mail ton-km. ('000)	.	.	1,735	1,621	1,612

Tourist arrivals: (1969) 46,521 (incl. 10,272 from the U.S.A.); (1970) 53,187 (incl. 11,289 from the U.S.A.).

EDUCATION
(Number of pupils)

TYPE OF SCHOOL				1968–69	1969–70	1970–71
Primary	.	.	.	514,000	590,500	655,500
Junior Secondary	.	.	.	56,900	63,200	72,300
Senior Secondary	.	.	.	32,000	42,500	63,000
Teacher Training	.	.	.	2,400	2,500	2,800
Vocational and Technical	.	.	.	7,200	6,200	6,200
University	.	.	.	3,900	4,600	4,500
TOTAL	.	.	.	616,400	709,500	794,300

Source: Central Statistical Office, Addis Ababa.

THE CONSTITUTION

The present constitution came into force in 1955 and under its terms divides political power between the Emperor and a bicameral parliament.

THE EMPEROR

The Emperor appoints Ministers, determines the powers of Ministries and controls officials. With the advice and consent of Parliament he may declare war. As Commander-in-Chief he appoints officers and may determine the size of the armed forces. He may declare a state of siege, martial law or national emergency. The Emperor directs Foreign Affairs. He alone has the right to settle disputes with foreign powers and to ratify treaties and other international agreements. All treaties requiring territorial adjustment or financial expenditure require the approval of both Houses of Parliament. The Emperor has the right to originate legislation and other resolutions in Parliament and to proclaim laws when they have been passed by Parliament. He convenes annual and extraordinary sessions of Parliament and has the right to dissolve the same by an order providing at the same time for the appointment of a new Senate and/or election of a new Chamber of Deputies, within four months from the date of the order. He appoints the members of the Senate but the members of the Chamber of Deputies are elected.

In April 1966 a Cabinet of Ministers selected by the Prime Minister was approved by the Emperor. This was the first occasion on which such a procedure was adopted.

MINISTERS

The Prime Minister is appointed by the Emperor to whom he submits the proposed Cabinet Ministers. The Cabinet is responsible to the Prime Minister. The Prime Minister and Cabinet are collectively responsible for legislative proposals to the Emperor and to Parliament. The Prime Minister presents to Parliament proposals of legislation made by the Council of Ministers and approved by the Emperor and presents to the Emperor the proposals of legislation approved by Parliament and decrees proposed by the Council of Ministers. All Ministers have the right to attend any meeting of either Chamber of Parliament and to speak there. They may be obliged to attend, either in person or by deputy, in either Chamber on the request of a majority vote and to answer verbally or in writing questions concerning their office.

PARLIAMENT

Parliament is composed of the Chamber of Deputies and the Senate. The Chamber has 210 members elected by universal adult suffrage every four years. The Senate is composed of a maximum of 105 members appointed by the Emperor for a term of six years with one-third of its members reaching the end of their term every two years. Senators may be reappointed for more than one term. The Chambers may meet in joint session or separately. The date of their regular sessions is fixed by the Constitution. Laws may be proposed to either or both Chambers either by the Emperor or by ten members of either Chamber. Proposals for legislation approved by both Chambers are sent to the Emperor who may return them for further consideration. In case of emergency during a Parliamentary recess decrees may be promulgated by the Emperor having the force of law but such decrees must subsequently be ratified by Parliament. No taxation may be imposed except by law and all financial legislation must originate in the Chamber of Deputies.

ERITREA

In 1950 a UN resolution provided for the federation of Ethiopia and Eritrea. The new constitution came into force in September 1952.

Late in 1962 Eritrea was incorporated as a Governorate of Ethiopia and the separate Assembly was dissolved. (There are now fourteen Governorates in Ethiopia.)

THE GOVERNMENT

HEAD OF STATE

Emperor of Ethiopia: His Imperial Majesty HAILE SELLASSIE I.

CABINET

(November 1972)

Prime Minister and Minister of the Pen: H.E. Tsahafi Teezaz AKLILOU ABTE WOLD.

Minister of the Imperial Court: H.E. TSEHAFE TAEZAZ TEFERRA WORK.

Minister of Commerce. Industry and Tourism: H.E. Ato KETEMA YIFRU.

Minister of Agriculture: H.E. Ato ABEBE RETTA.

Minister of Finance: H.E. Ato MAMO TADDESSE.

Minister of Education and Fine Arts: H.E. Ato SEIFU MAHTEME-SELASSIE.

Minister of Community Development and Social Affairs: H.E. Ato MULATU DEBBEBE.

Minister of Posts and Communications: H.E. LIDJ ENDAL-KACHEW MAKONNEN.

Minister of Public Health: H.E. KETEMA ABEBE.

Minister of Interior: H.E. Ato GETAHUN TESSEMA.

Minister of Justice: H.E. Ato AKALE WORK HABTEWOLD.

Minister of Foreign Affairs: H.E. Dr. MINASSIE HAILE.

Minister of National Defence: Lt.-Gen. KEBEDE GABRE.

Minister of Mines: H.E. Ato AMANUEL ABRAHAM.

Minister of Information: H.E. Dr. TESFAYE GABRE-EGZY.

Minister of Public Works: H.E. SALAH HINIT.

Minister of Land Reform: H.E. Ato BELAI ABAI.

Minister, Commissioner for Civil Service and Pensions: H.E. Ato TADESE YACOB.

Minister in the Office of the Prime Minister: H.E. Ato SEYOUM HAREGOT.

Permanent Delegate to the United Nations: H.E. DEJAZMACH ZAWDE GABRE-SELLASSIE.

GOVERNORATE OF ERITREA

Deputy-Governor: H.E. Lt.-Gen. DEBEBE MARIAM.

DIPLOMATIC REPRESENTATION

EMBASSIES AND LEGATIONS ACCREDITED TO ETHIOPIA

(In Addis Ababa unless otherwise stated)

(E) Embassy; (L) Legation.

Algeria: (E); *Ambassador:* ABDEL-AZIZ HASSINE.

Austria: Churchill Rd., P.O.B. 137 (E); *Ambassador:* Herr LIBSCH.

Belgium: Fikre Mariam St., P.O.B. 1239 (E); *Ambassador:* RICHARD HUYBRECHT.

Botswana: (E); *Ambassador:* E. M. ONTAMMENTSE.

Bulgaria: P.O.B. 987, near Guenet Hotel (E); *Ambassador:* KRAYON VLADOV.

Burundi: Maj.-Gen. Abebe Damtew Ave. (E); *Ambassador:* JOSEPH NDABANIWE.

Cameroon: (E); *Ambassador:* MOHAMMED HAMAN DIKO.

Canada: Ethiopia Hotel, Box 1130 (E); *Ambassador:* CHARLES J. WOODWORTH.

Chad: (E); *Ambassador:* ABDURAHMAN MUSA.

Chile: Ras Desta Damtew Avenue, P.O.B. 1904 (E); *Chargé d'Affaires:* HERNÁN SÁNCHEZ.

China, P.R.: (E); *Ambassador:* YU PEI WEN.

Colombia: (E); *Ambassador:* GUILLERMO NANNETTI.

Czechoslovakia: Churchill Rd., P.O.B. 3108 (E); *Ambassador:* ZEDNEK HAJEK.

Denmark: (E); *Ambassador:* KJELD MORTENSEN.

Ecuador: (E); *Ambassador:* (vacant).

Egypt: Filwoha Meda, P.O.B. 1611 (E); *Ambassador:* HASSAN SIRI ESMAT.

Equatorial Guinea: (E); *Ambassador:* SAMUEL EBUKA.

Finland: near Princess Tsahai Memorial Hospital, P.O.B. 1017 (E); *Ambassador:* VEIKKO HEITANEN (also accred. to Kenya).

France: (Kabanna District) Omedla Rd., P.O.B. 1464 (E); *Ambassador:* ALBERT TRECA.

Germany, Federal Republic: P.O.B. 660 (E); *Ambassador:* Dr. KURT MUELLER.

Ghana: near Princess Tsahai Memorial Hospital, P.O.B. 3173 (E); *Ambassador:* Y. B. TURKSON.

Greece: Asfaw Wossen St., P.O.B. 1168 (E); *Ambassador:* NICOLAS COLUMBOS.

Guinea: (E); *Ambassador:* TOURE HADY.

Haiti: Jimma Rd., P.O.B. 1443 (E).

Hungary: Sudan St., near Police Station No. 5, P.O.B. 1213 (E); *Ambassador:* Dr. JANOS PATAKI.

India: Dejazmatch Beyene Merid Ave., P.O.B. 528 (E); *Ambassador:* K. C. SENGUPTA.

Indonesia: Dejazmatch Beyene Merid Ave., P.O.B. 1004 (E); *Ambassador:* H. M. AMIN AZEHARI.

Iran: Ras Desta Damtew Ave., P.O.B. 1144 (E); *Ambassador:* MOHAMMED GHAVAN.

Israel: Near Tafari Makonnen School, P.O.B. 1075 (E); *Ambassador:* URI LUBRANI.

Italy: Kembebit District, P.O.B. 1105 (E); *Ambassador:* LUIGI SABETTA.

Ivory Coast: P.O.B. 3668 (E); *Ambassador:* GERVAIS ATTOUNGBRE (also accred. to Kenya and Tanzania).

Jamaica: (E); *Ambassador:* ASTON FOREMAN (also accred. as High Commissioner to Ghana, Nigeria, Tanzania and Zambia).

Japan: Dejazmatch Beyene Merid Ave., P.O.B. 1499 (E); *Ambassador:* TAISAKU KOJIMA.

Kenya: (E); *Ambassador:* P. ECHARIA.

Korea, Republic: P.O.B. 2047 (E); *Ambassador:* CHANG CHI RYONG.

Liberia: near Mexico Square, P.O.B. 3116 (E); *Ambassador:* EARNEST EASTMAN.

Malawi: Ras Desta Damtew Ave., P.O.B. 2316 (E); *Ambassador:* C. M. MOKONA.

Malaysia: off Dejazmatch Beyene Merid Ave., P.O.B. 3656 (E); *Chargé d'Affaires:* ABDULLAH BIN ALI.

Mali: (E); *Ambassador:* BOUBACAR DIALLO.

Mexico: Kera Sefer, P.O.B. 2962 (E); *Ambassador:* R. M. PASQUEL (also accred. to Senegal).

Mongolia: Cairo, Egypt (E).

Morocco: (E); *Ambassador:* HARKETT ADRAHIM (also accred. to Kenya, Tanzania and Uganda).

Netherlands: near Old Airport, P.O.B. 1241 (E); *Ambassador:* W. P. L. DE BOER.

Nigeria: (E); *Ambassador:* E. O. SANU.

Pakistan: (E); *Ambassador:* S. A. H. SAHNI.

Peru: (E); *Ambassador:* O. B. CONTI.

Poland: Ketchene District, P.O.B. 1123 (E); *Ambassador:* JAN KRZYWICKI.

Romania: (E); *Ambassador:* TITUS SINU.

Rwanda: (E); *Ambassador:* NIZEYIMANA JOSEPH.

Saudi Arabia: Mesfin Harar St., P.O.B. 1104 (E); *Chargé d'Affaires:* ALI ALGUFAIDY.

Senegal: Africa Ave. (E); *Ambassador:* M. LAPYR.

Somalia: Abuare River's Quarter, P.O.B. 1006 (E); *Ambassador:* ABDULRAHMAN AHMED ALI.

Spain: Asfaw Wossen St., P.O.B. 2312 (E); *Ambassador:* Dr. SALVADOR PRUNEDA.

Sudan: near Mexico Square, P.O.B. 1110 (E); *Ambassador:* OSMAN ABDULLAH HAMID.

Swaziland: (E); *Ambassador:* B. G. SIMELAND.

Sweden: Ras Tesemma Sefer, P.O.B. 1029 (E); *Ambassador:* ERLAND KLEEN.

Switzerland: Jimma Rd. near Old Airport (E); *Ambassador:* ROGER DURR.

Tanzania: Dejazmatch Beyene Merid Ave., P.O.B. 1077 (E); *Ambassador:* GEORGE MAGOMBE.

Thailand: Chamber of Commerce Building, 4th Floor, P.O.B. 2764 (E); *Ambassador:* C. KIATTINAT.

Trinidad and Tobago: Ras Tessema Sefer, P.O.B. 330 (E); *Ambassador:* ISABEL U. TESHEA (also accred. to Senegal).

Tunisia: (E); *Ambassador:* TOUFIK SMIDA.

Turkey: Jimma Rd., (near Old Airport), P.O.B. 1506 (E); *Ambassador:* ZIYA TEPEDELEN (also accred. to Tanzania).

Uganda: (E); *Ambassador:* K. L. LUBEGA.

U.S.S.R.: Fikre Mariam St., P.O.B. 1500 (E); *Ambassador:* LEONID F. TEPLOV.

United Kingdom: Fikre Mariam St., P.O.B. 858 (E); *Ambassador:* WILLIAM MORRIS.

U.S.A.: Asfaw Wossen St. (E); *Ambassador:* ROSS ADAIR.

Vatican: P.O.B. 588; *Apostolic Nunciate:* Rev. MAURICE PERRIN.

Yemen Arab Republic: Patriot St. (behind Garden Hotel), P.O.B. 664 (A); *Ambassador:* ABDU OTHMAN MUHAMMAD.

Yugoslavia: Oureal Quarter, P.O.B. 1341 (E); *Ambassador:* JOZE INGOLIA.

Zaire: near Old Airport (E); *Ambassador:* BAGBENI AGEITO.

Zambia: Old Airport (E); *Ambassador:* P. M. NGONDA.

Ethiopia also has diplomatic relations with Albania, Argentina, Brazil, Cameroon, Congo (Brazzaville), Gambia, Iraq, Jamaica, Kuwait, Lebanon, Madagascar, Mauritania, Nepal, Norway, Panama, Singapore and Venezuela.

PARLIAMENT

SENATE

President: Lt.-Gen. ABBY ABEBE.

105 members appointed by H.I.M. The Emperor for a term of six years.

CHAMBER OF DEPUTIES
(General Election, June-July 1969)

President: The Hon. ATO SEIFE TADEFFE.

250 members elected by universal adult suffrage every four years.

POLITICAL PARTIES

No political parties are allowed, but there are two opposition groups with separatist aims which operate clandestinely:

Eritrean Liberation Front (ELF): Damascus, Syria; f. 1963; Leader OSMAN SALEH SABBE.

ELF has perhaps 1,000–2,000 men under arms and even more supporters in Eritrea. Mainly Muslim, its aim is the separation of Eritrea from Ethiopia, which incorporated the region as its most northern province in 1963. ELF causes widespread disruption to communications, destroying trains and attacking planes of

Ethiopian Air Lines. Actual battles with government forces are less frequent, though the commander of the security forces was killed by the ELF in November 1971. The Front's control is most effective in the less populated parts of the province in the north. ELF announced in November 1971 that the first "Congress of the Eritrean Revolution" was being held in the liberated areas of Eritrea.

West Somalia Front: f. 1970; based in the east of Ethiopia and representing the Somali of Ogaden; allied with the ELF.

DEFENCE

The army numbers about 41,000, the air force 2,500 and the navy 1,400. There is also an equivalent total of men in a para-military force.

Commander of the Ground Forces: Lt.-Gen. DIRAFFE DUBALE.

Deputy-Governor of Eritrea: H.E. Lt.-Gen. DEBEBE MARIAM.

JUDICIAL SYSTEM

The Supreme Imperial Court: Addis Ababa.

President: Afe Negus TESHOME HAILE MARIAM.

The President sits with two other judges. The Court has eight divisions each presided over by a Vice Afe Negus. The Supreme Court has jurisdiction only to hear appeals from the High Court. Appeals can go from the Supreme Imperial Court to the Emperor sitting in Chilot (*Court*) in accordance with Ethiopian custom.

The High Court: Addis Ababa; sits in 12 Divisions each of 3 Judges: 1. Appeals; 2. Criminal; 3. Civil; 4. Land; 5. Government.

Taqlai Ghizat High Courts (*General Governorate High Courts*): each Court has a presiding judge and two other judges. There are no foreign judges. The Governor-General of a province may sit as the presiding judge, criminal and civil.

Awraja Ghizat Courts (*Provincial Courts*): composed of three judges, criminal and civil.

Warada Ghizat Courts (*Regional Courts*): criminal cases and limited civil actions.

Meketel Warada Courts (*Sub-Regional Courts*): one judge sits alone with very limited jurisdiction, criminal only.

RELIGION

CHRISTIANS

Imperial Ethiopian Orthodox Union Church: official Church of the Emperor and State; founded in the fourth century A.D. There are about 19 million members.

His Holiness the Patriarch ABUNA TEWOFLOS, P.O.B. 1283, Patriarchate, King George IV St., Addis Ababa. Archbishop THEOPHILOS, Parliament Square, Addis Ababa.

Roman Catholic Church

Alexandrine-Ethiopian Rite:

Metropolitan See: Addis Ababa; Archbishop Mgr. ASRATE MARIAM YEMMERU, Archbishop's House, P.O. Box 1903, Addis Ababa; Eparchy of Adigrat, Adigrat; Eparchy of Asmara, Asmara.

Latin Rite:

Vicar Apostolic of Asmara: (vacant), P.O.B. 224, Asmara; there are also Vicarates Apostolic at Harar and Jimma.

Greek Orthodox Church

Archbishop of Aksum: Most Rev. Dr. METHODIOS FOUYAS, P.O.B. 571, Addis Ababa.

Armenian Orthodox Church

Father ZAVEN ARMOUNIAN; St. George's Armenian Church, Addis Ababa.

Anglican Church

The Rev. PHILIP J. COUSINS; P.O.B. 109, Queen Elizabeth St., Addis Ababa; f. 1926; 175 mems; publ. *Roar* (fortnightly).

American Presbyterian Church: P.O.B. 3507, Addis Ababa.

A number of Protestant, Anglican and Roman Catholic missions work in Ethiopia. The Lutheran Church is found in both urban and rural areas.

MUSLIMS

Approximately 35 per cent of the population are Muslims.

TRADITIONAL BELIEFS

It is estimated that between 5 and 15 per cent of the population follow traditional African rites and ceremonies.

THE PRESS

DAILIES

Addis Soir: Addis Ababa; French; circ. 3,000; Editor Ato MESEIN BERHANE.

Addis Zemen: Ministry of Information, Addis Ababa; Amharic; circ. 10,000; Editor NEGASH GEBREMARIAM.

Ethiopian Herald: Ministry of Information, Addis Ababa; English; circ. 8,000; Editor Ato TEGEGNE YETESHA-WORK.

L'Ethiopie Aujourd'hui: Addis Ababa; French.

Hebret: Asmara; official journal; circ. 2,800; Tigrigna and Arabic.

Quotidiano dell' Eritrea: Asmara; Italian; circ. 4,500.

Sandek Anamachin: Addis Ababa; Amharic.

Voice of Ethiopia: National Patriotic Association, P.O.B. 1244, Addis Ababa; Amharic and English; Editor PERCY O. RICHARDS; circ. 4,000.

Ye Ethiopia Dimts: Addis Ababa; Amharic; circ. 10,000; Editor Ato FIKRE SELASSIE WOLDE HANNA.

PERIODICALS

Andnet: Weekly; Tigrigna, Amharic and Arabic; circ. 1,000.

Addis Reporter: Addis Ababa; monthly; English.

Bollettino: Ave. Ras Makonnen, Asmara; English, Arabic, Italian and Tigrigna; publ. bi-monthly by the Chamber of Commerce; circ. 700; Dir. E. DE PAOLI.

Elete Sembet: Weekly; Amharic; official journal; circ. 1,000.

Ethiopia Observer: f. 1936; quarterly; publ. in Ethiopia and Britain; P.O.B. 1896, Addis Ababa and 57 Carter Lane, London, E.C.4; English; RICHARD and RITA PANK-HURST.

Ethiopia Zartu: Weekly; Amharic.

Ethiopian Mirror: Quarterly; P.O.B. 1364, Addis Ababa; English; general interest.

Ethiopian Trade Journal: Quarterly; P.O.B. 517, Addis Ababa; published by Addis Ababa Chamber of Commerce; Editor GHION HAGOS; circ. 2,500.

Lunedi del Medio Oriente: Weekly; Asmara; Italian; circ. 2,200; Editor Signor ALBERTO FARINO DI SANTA CROCE.

Mattino del Lunedi: P.O.B. 500, Asmara; f. 1953; Italian; weekly; Editor ANGELO GRANARA; circ. 2,500.

Menen: Monthly; National Patriotic Association, P.O.B. 1364, Addis Ababa; English and Amharic; illustrated; Editor HOMER SMITH.

Monthly Bulletin: P.O.B. 517, Addis Ababa; published by Addis Ababa Chamber of Commerce; monthly; English; review of economic affairs; Editor GHION HAGOS; circ. 3,000.

Negarit Gazeta: Ministry of the Pen, Addis Ababa; Official Gazette giving notice of laws and orders; English and Amharic.

Wotaderna Alamoaus: Weekly; Military Journal; Amharic; Editor Lt. ASEFFA GEBRE MARYAM.

Wotaderna Guiziou: Weekly; Military Journal; Amharic Editor Ato DAMTE ASEMAHEIGN.

PRESS AGENCIES

FOREIGN BUREAUX

Agenzia Nazionale Stampa Associata (A.N.S.A.): P.O.B. 1001; Chief LUIGI LINO.

Tass and Agence France Presse also have bureaux in Ethiopia.

PUBLISHER

Oxford University Press: P.O.B. 1024, Addis Ababa; f. in Ethiopia 1965; educational and academic publishing in English and Amharic; Man. Ato TESFAYE DABA.

RADIO AND TELEVISION

RADIO

Radio Ethiopia: P.O.B. 1020, Addis Ababa; f. 1941; Amharic, English, French, Arabic, Afar and Somali; listeners 5 million including listeners to public address systems in major towns; advertising is accepted; Gen. Man. A. N. HAPTEWOLD; Dir.-Gen. for Radio NEGASH GEBRE-MARIAM.

Radio Voice of the Gospel: P.O.B. 654, Addis Ababa; f. 1961; Lutheran World Federation Broadcasting Service; medium-wave local services; short-wave services in thirteen languages to Asia, the Middle East and Africa and Madagascar; Gen. Dir. Rev. Dr. SIGURD ASKE; Station Dir. Rev. ERNST BAUEROCHSE; publ. *RVOG News.*

There are 163,000 radio receivers in the country.

TELEVISION

Ethiopian Television Service: P.O.B. 1020, Addis Ababa; Television services were inaugurated in 1964, under the management of Thomson Television International and operated by the government; advertising is accepted; Dir. A. N. HAPTEWOLD; Dir.-Gen. for TV SAMUEL FERENJI.

There are about 8,500 sets in Ethiopia. In Asmara, Eritrea, there is a closed circuit service for the American Armed Forces with about 1,000 receivers.

FINANCE

(cap. = capital; p.u. = paid up; E$ = Ethiopian Dollar; dep. = deposits; m. = million)

BANKING

STATE BANKS

In December 1963 the State Bank of Ethiopia was divided into the National Bank of Ethiopia and the Commercial Bank of Ethiopia (S.C.):

National Bank of Ethiopia: Haile Sellassie I Square, P.O.B. 5550 Addis Ababa; f. 1964; total assets (April 1971) E$491m.; issuing bank; Gov. H.E. Ato MENASSE LEMMA; Vice-Gov. Ato YAWAND WOSSEN MANGASHA; publ. *Quarterly Bulletin.*

Commercial Bank of Ethiopia (S.C.): Haile Sellassie I Square, P.O.B. 255, Addis Ababa; f. 1964; cap. p.u. E$30m., dep. E$369m. (1970); state-owned bank for commercial business; 80 brs.; Chair. TADESSE YACOB; Gen. Man. TAFFAR DAGUEFE; publ. *Annual Report.*

OTHER BANKS

Addis Ababa Bank: P.O.B. 751, Addis Ababa; f. 1963; 40 per cent owned by National and Grindlays Bank; brs. in Addis Ababa, Agaro, Asmara and Jimma (18 in all); cap. E$5m., dep. E$44.6m. (1970); Chair. Ato ABEBE KEBEDE; Man. Dir. Ato DEBEBE H. YOHANNES; Man. H. M. T. HOLROYD.

Agricultural and Industrial Development Bank S.C.: P.O.B. 1900, Addis Ababa; f. 1970 from a merger of the Development Bank of Ethiopia and the Ethiopian Investment Corporation; provides finance for development of industry and agriculture; cap. p.u. E$53m.; Chair. H.E. Ato MAMO TADDESSE (Minister of Finance); Man. Dir. H.E. Ato ASAFA DEMISSIE; publs. *Newsletter, Annual Report, Policy Papers.*

Banco di Napoli (Ethiopia) S.C.: P.O.B. 228, Ave. Empress Mennen 40, Asmara; f. 1970 to take over the Asmara branch of the Banco di Napoli; cap. E$ 2m., dep. E$8.6m. (1970); Gen. Man. DONATO SINISCALCO.

Banco di Roma, Ethiopia S.C.: Zerai, Derres Square, Asmara; f. 1967: brs. in Addis Ababa, Assab, Modjo and Massawa; cap. E$4m.; Pres. Bitwoded ASFAHA WOLDE MIKAEL; Gen. Man. GIORGIO GIORGETTIO.

INSURANCE

(Addis Ababa, unless otherwise stated)

African Solidarity Insurance Co. S.C.: Afsol House, Haile Sellassie I Square, P.O.B. 1890; f. 1963; Gen. Man. D. G. SGOLOMBIS; Man. D. L. FLACK.

Blue Nile Insurance Corporation S.C.: P.O.B. 2192, Papassinos Bldg., Ras Desta Dampten Ave., Addis Ababa.

Imperial Insurance Co. of Ethiopia Ltd.: Velissariou Bldg., Cunningham Street, P.O. Box 380, Addis Ababa f. 1951; p.u. cap. E$500,000; Gen. Man. A. ZOGRAPHOS.

TRADE AND INDUSTRY

CHAMBERS OF COMMERCE

Ethiopian Chamber of Commerce: P.O.B. 517, Addis Ababa; f. 1947; 564 mems.; Pres. TAFFARA DEGUEFE; publs. *Ethiopian Trade Journal, Monthly Trade Bulletin,* and various books and papers dealing with Ethiopian business, commerce and investment.

Camera di Commercio, Industria e Agricoltura dell' Eritrea: Ave. Ras Makonnen, Asmara, P.O.B. 856; f. 1947; Pres. E. DE PAOLI.

TRADE ORGANIZATION

Ethiopian Coffee Exporters Association: P.O.B. 1982, Addis Ababa; 28 mems.; Exec. Sec. Ato ASSRATE H. DEFERESU.

EMPLOYERS ORGANIZATION

Federation of Employers of Ethiopia (FEE): Addis Ababa; f. 1964; 40 mems.

TRADE UNIONS

Confederation of Ethiopian Labour Unions (CELU): CELU Bldg., P.O.B. 3653, Addis Ababa; f. 1962; 82,000 mems.; 149 affiliates; affiliated to ICFTU; Sec.-Gen. FISSEHA TSION TEKIE; publ. *Voice of Labour* (fortnightly).

Ethiopian Railway Workers' Syndicate: Dire Dawa.

OIL

Four companies are at present prospecting for oil along the Red Sea coast. One, Mobil Esso Ethiopia Inc., has found natural gas offshore north of Massawa. Oil and natural gas is also thought to exist in the province of Bale in southern Ethiopia.

TRANSPORT

RAILWAYS

Franco-Ethiopian Railway: P.O.B. 1051, Addis Ababa; f. 1908; 782 km.; runs from Addis Ababa to Djibouti; Pres. H.E. LIDJ ENDALKACHEW MAKONNEN; Dir.-Gen. B. PETIT.

Northern Ethiopian Railways Share Company: Massawa, Eritrea; 306 km.; runs from Massawa on the Red Sea through Asmara to Agordat; Gen. Man. GHETATCHEW MEDHANE.

ROADS

Imperial Highway Authority: P.O.B. 1770, Addis Ababa; constructs and maintains roads and bridges throughout Ethiopia. Out of a total system of 23,400 km. of primary, secondary, feeder roads and trails, there are 8,190 km. of all-weather gravel and asphalt roads. A further 1,000 km. are to be built during the Third Five-Year Plan, i.e. by September 1973.

General Ethiopian Transport Share Company: P.O.B. 472, Addis Ababa; runs urban services in Addis Ababa; long distance services connecting all important provincial towns, and limited tourist services.

SHIPPING

Irregular services by foreign vessels to Massawa and Assab (port for Addis Ababa). Since 1960 Assab's facilities have been greatly extended and the port can now handle over a million tons of merchandise annually. It has a new refinery with an annual capacity of 500,000 tons. Much trade goes through Djibouti (French Territory of the Afar and Issa).

Aden Coasters Ltd.: P.O.B. 723, Addis Ababa.

A. Besse and Co. (Ethiopia) S.C.: P.O.B. 1897, Addis Ababa.

Filli Biga and Co. S.C.: Head Office: P.O.B. 1108, Asmara; f. 1965 as a subsidiary of SCAC/SOCOPAO (France); branches at Addis Ababa, Assab, Massawa and Djibouti.

Cie. Maritime Auxiliaire d'Outre-Mer: P.O.B. 1230, Addis Ababa.

Ethiopian Shipping Lines (The): P.O.B. 2572, Addis Ababa; f. 1966; cargo, tanker services Red Sea-Europe; Chair. H.E. LIDJ ENDALKACHEW MAKONNEN; 6 vessels.

Ethiopian Trans-Atlantic Line—(ETIOMAR): Addis Ababa; f. 1966; to trade between Assab and N. American ports.

Gellatly, Hankey and Co. (Ethiopia) S.C.: P.O.B. 906, Asmara; brs. at Addis Ababa, Massawa, Assab and Dire Dawa.

Mitchell Cotts and Co. (Ethiopia) Ltd.: P.O. Box 527, Addis Ababa; f. 1960; branches at Asmara, Massawa, etc.; Chair. J. K. DICK, F.C.A.; Man. L. T. CARLINE.

Savon and Riès (Ethiopian Shipping) Co.: P.O.B. 215, Asmara; one cargo vessel.

Matteo De Marzo: P.O. Box 536, Asmara.

Flli. de Nadai: P.O. Box 731, Asmara.

S.A. Navigatana: P.O. Box 1161, Asmara.

CIVIL AVIATION

Ethiopian Airlines: Haile Sellassie I Airport, P.O.B. 1755, Addis Ababa; f. 1945; operates regular domestic and international services; fleet of 9 DC-3, 2 Boeing 720B, 2 Boeing 707, 3 DC-6B, 3 Cessna 180, 4 Piper Cub, 1 Bell 47J Helicopter; Chair. H.E. LIDJ ENDALKACHEW MAKONNEN; Gen. Man. Lt.-Col. SEMRET MEDHANE.

Air Djibouti, Air India, Alitalia, EAAC, EgyptAir, Lufthansa, MEA, Saudi Arabian Airlines, Sudan Airways and Yemen Arab Airlines also serve Addis Ababa.

TOURISM

The two names by which Ethiopia is known—Land of the Queen of Sheba and Land of the Lion of Judah—indicate some of the richness of her historical and cultural background. The Land of Sheba was one of the wealthiest and most powerful kingdoms of ancient times and extended farther than the present boundaries of Ethiopia into what is now the Yemen. It was a centre of international trade. Axum was the original capital of the Queen of Sheba and still provides a relic of its former glory in the form of two obelisks carved from solid granite. A seventeenth-century cathedral, built on the site of a chapel of A.D. 340, is a shrine where the Emperors were crowned for many years; the Treasury contains a collection of ancient crowns and vestments. Other early monuments of Ethiopia's civilization are the rock-hewn churches at Lalibela, with intricate carvings and many paintings, which are in part of Axumite origin.

Christianity was introduced into Ethiopia early in the fourth century A.D. and the country soon became a stronghold of the Coptic branch. The strength of early Christian faith can be seen today in the monasteries on islands in Lake Tana and the fortress monastery at Debre Damo, which was never taken by force; it could only be reached by climbing a 60-ft. rope and is now the site for the Festival of Timkat. During the Middle Ages Ethiopia became isolated from the rest of the world (from this period there remains the walled city of Harar, at the top of a mountain pass), and was weakened by frequent Muslim incursions and internal problems, but it remained independent and in the mid-nineteenth century reunification took place and the building of modern Ethiopia was begun. Although the sixteenth and seventeenth centuries were a period when

Ethiopia was isolated and threatened by internal strife, they were also a time of flourishing building, particularly of a religious nature; of especial note are the churches and castles of Gondar, the capital of Ethiopia for more than 200 years.

Because of the rugged nature of its landscape and the moral strength of its inhabitants Ethiopia has remained relatively little influenced by outside forces, and traditions are very strong—the present monarch, Haile Selassie I, is the 225th in the Solomonic dynasty, established by Solomon and the Queen of Sheba. Apart from many places of historical interest to be visited, Ethiopia also offers many different types of scenery and climate, including the source of the Blue Nile and the falls at Tiss Abbai, and a great variety of wild life and big game. Modern cities such as Addis Ababa and Asmara also contain much of historical interest.

Tourism has grown rapidly in recent years, rising from 9,340 tourists in 1962 to 53,187 in 1970. Income from visitors amounted to about E$16 million in 1967. All the main tourist centres are served by good hotels.

Ethiopian Tourist Organisation: P.O.B. 2183, Addis Ababa; f. 1961; Administrator H.E. Ato HAPTE SELLASSIE TAFFESSA.

Creative Arts Centre: Addis Ababa; f. 1963.

THEATRE

Haile Sellassie I University: P.O.B. 1176, Addis Ababa; TSEGAYE GABRE-MEDHIN.

EDUCATION

Education in Ethiopia has begun to expand considerably in recent years. In the academic year 1970–71 there were approximately 790,000 pupils enrolled in primary and secondary schools, contrasting with a figure ten years previously of 200,000. The Division of Adult Education announced that over 900,000 people had completed its literacy courses in the 1964–69 period. Even so the literacy rate was still estimated at less than 10 per cent in 1969. The virtual absence of a colonial period is thought to be a serious disadvantage in reforming and expanding the educational system. The established Church still exercises a very conservative influence over much of the system, which is even more inadequate outside Christian Amharic speaking areas.

There are a number of organizations and private bodies providing educational facilities in Ethiopia, the largest being the government, but still assisted very substantially by the churches and missions. About a quarter of all those undergoing education at all levels are taught in non-government establishments.

Primary education accounts for by far the highest proportion of all students: 655,500 out of 794,300 in 1970–71. Within this group two tendencies are strongly marked; one the growing proportion of girls in the youngest grades; the other the marked fall in numbers through the grades, sometimes as much as forty per cent from one year to the next. However, it is reported that the holding capacity of classes is rapidly improving. Mission schools have the best teacher/pupil ratios of around 1:25, compared to the average of 1:40 in other groups.

Senior secondary education is supplemented by vocational and technical schools. There is a serious lack of secondary teachers; half of them (in the senior sector) being foreigners. There has been, however, a steady improvement in teachers' qualifications.

Higher education is divided between the national university, Haile Sellassie I University in Addis Ababa with about 5,000 students in 1971–72, and the new University of Asmara, a Catholic foundation set up in 1967. There is also a Polytechnic Institute at Bahir-Dar, and in addition about 2,000 Ethiopian students receive higher education abroad, often with financial assistance from the host country.

LEARNED SOCIETIES AND RESEARCH INSTITUTES

British Council: P.O.B. 1043, Artistic Building, Haile Sellassie I Ave., Addis Ababa; f. in Ethiopia 1959; library: *see* Libraries; Rep. J. G. MILLS.

Desert Locust Control Organization for Eastern Africa: P.O.B. 4255, Addis Ababa; f. 1962 by Ethiopia, France, Somalia, Kenya, Uganda and Tanzania to survey and control desert locusts; Sudan joined in 1968; Dir. ADEFRIS BELLEHU.

Ethiopian Medical Association: P.O.B. 2179, Addis Ababa; f. 1961; Pres. Dr. TAYE MEKURIA; publ. *Ethiopian Medical Journal* (quarterly).

Forestry Research Institute: Haile Sellassie I University, P.O.B. 1176, Addis Ababa; f. 1962; Dir. (vacant); publ. *Timbers of Ethiopia* (irregular).

Geological Survey of Ethiopia: P.O.B. 486, Addis Ababa; f. 1968; department of Ministry of Mines; Dir. D. B. Dow.

Geophysical Observatory: Haile Sellassie I University, P.O.B. 1176, Addis Ababa; f. 1958; located on the magnetic equator, for study of geomagnetic transients and the equatorial electrojet; also for study of the seismicity, geotectonics and gravity anomalies of the Ethiopian Rift System; Dir. P. GOUIN, M.SC., F.R.A.S.; publs. *Bulletin of the Geophysical Observatory* and *Contributions from the Geophysical Observatory* (irregular).

Goethe-Institut (*German Cultural Institute*): P.O.B. 1193, Addis Ababa; f. 1962; Dir. F. D. VOLLPRECHT.

Government Mapping and Geography Institute: P.O.B. 597, Addis Ababa; f. 1955; conducts geodetic and cadastral surveying, mapping and geographical research; 250 mems.; library of 1,000 vols.; Dir of Research D. ASSAYE; publ. *Ethiopian Geographical Journal* (twice yearly).

Institut de Recherches Agronomiques Tropicales et des Cultures Vivrières (IRAT): P.O.B. 6, Awassa (Sidamo); Dir. M. CHEVREAU.

Institut Ethiopien d'Archéologie: P.O.B. 1907, Addis Ababa; conducts archæological excavations at Axum, Yeha, Matara, Adulis and is compiling a notebook of historical geography; Minister in Charge H.E. ATO TEKLE TSADEK MEKOURIA; Archæologist FRANCIS ANFRAY; Philologist ROGER SCHNEIDER; Prehistorians GERARD BAILLOUD and JEAN CHAVAILLON; publs. *Annales d'Ethiopie* (twice-yearly review), *Tarik* (review), *Cahier de l'Institut Ethiopien d'Archéologie*.

Institute of Agricultural Research: P.O.B. 2003, Addis Ababa; division of the Ministry of Agriculture; Dir. Dr. DANGNATCHEW YIRGOU.

Institute of Ethiopian Studies: Haile Sellassie I University, P.O.B. 1176, Addis Ababa; f. 1963; advanced study and documentation centre; library and ethnological-historical museum; Dir. Dr. RICHARD PANKHURST; Librarian and Curator STANISŁAW CHOJNACKI; publs. include *Journal of Ethiopian Studies* (bi-annually), *Register of Research on Ethiopia and the Horn of Africa* (annual), *List of Periodical Publications in Ethiopia* (every two years), *Publications in Ethiopia* (annual).

Istituto Italiano di Cultura: P.O.B. 1635, Addis Ababa; f. 1960; Dir. Prof. ALBERTO DEL PIZZO.

Mission Française O.R.S.T.O.M. d'Etudes au Wabi-Sheballi: P.O.B. 3267, Addis Ababa; pedology, hydrology. (*See* main entry under France.)

U.S. Information Center: Patriots' Street, P.O. Box 1014, Addis Ababa; Avenue Ras Alula 44, Asmara.

LIBRARIES

American Library: P.O.B. 1014, Addis Ababa; f. 1950; 8,000 vols.; 7 branches; Librarian MICHAEL GABRE EGZIABLIER.

Asmara Public Library: 20 Haile Sellassie I Ave., Asmara; f. 1955; 5,200 vols.

British Council Library: P.O.B. 977, Asmara; 4,000 vols.

National Library: P.O. Box 717, Addis Ababa; f. 1944; 63,000 vols.; Dir. KANAZMATCH ZAWDE TADESSE; Librarians: H. W. LOCKOT, YEMANEHE WALELEGNE.

University Library: P.O.B. 1176, Addis Ababa; f. 1950; 247,020 vols.; collection includes rare books, pamphlets and maps on Ethiopia published abroad; special attention is paid to the collection of books in the Amharic language; specialist branch libraries in Addis Ababa, Alemaya and Gondar; Librarian RITA PANKHURST.

MUSEUMS

Musée Archéologique: c/o Institut Ethiopien d'Archéologie, P.O.B. 1907, Addis Ababa; Minister-in-Charge H.E. ATO KEBBÉDÉ MIHAEL.

Museum of the Institute of Ethiopian Studies: Haile Sellassie I University, P.O.B. 1176, Addis Ababa; f. 1952; ethnological collections, including Ethiopian implements, clothes, weapons and pottery. A complete set of coins of Harar is of special historical value; collection of traditional Ethiopian paintings (14th-20th cent.); Ethiopian stamps; Curator STANISŁAW CHOJNACKI.

UNIVERSITIES

HAILE SELLASSIE I UNIVERSITY

P.O. BOX 1176, ADDIS ABABA

Telephone: 10844

University College founded 1950, University 1961. The University has Extension Centres in Asmara, Harar, Dire Dawa and Debre Zeit.

Chancellor: His Imperial Majesty HAILE SELLASSIE I, Emperor of Ethiopia.

President: Dr. AKLILU HABTE.

Academic Vice-President: Dr. MULUGETA WODAJO.

Vice-President for Business and Development: Dr. FASSIL GEBRE KIROS.

Registrar: Ato ALEMU BEGASHAW.

Librarian: Mrs. R. PANKHURST.

Number of teachers: 650.

Number of students: 4,978.

Publications: *Journal of Ethiopian Studies, Bulletin of Ethnological Society, Bulletin of the Geophysical Observatory,* etc.

DEANS:

College of Agriculture: Dr. MELAKE HAILE MENGESHA.

Faculty of Arts: Dr. TAYE GULILAT.

College of Technology: Ato KASSA HAILE (Assoc. Dean).

College of Business Administration: Dr. W. PERKETT.

Faculty of Education: Ato LAKEW MULAT.

Engineering College: Prof. R. J. BISANZ.

Faculty of Law: Prof. CLIFF THOMPSON.

Faculty of Medicine: Sir IAN HILL.

Public Health College, Gondar: Dr. ZELEKE BEKELE.

Faculty of Science Dr. DAWIT DEGEFU.

School of Social Work: Ato SEYOUM G. SELASSIE.

Theological College: Dr. V. C. SAMUEL.

University Extension: Dr. SOLOMON INQUAI.

UNIVERSITY OF ASMARA

P.O.B. 1220, ASMARA

Telephone: 11513

Founded 1958 by the Pie Madri della Nigrizia; University status 1967.

Chancellor: His Imperial Majesty HAILE SELLASSIE I.

President: Dr. MARIANORA ONNIS.
Registrar: Sister ANNA RONCALLI.
Librarian: Dr. CONCETTA VALLARTA.
  The library contains 32,000 volumes.
  Number of teachers: 100.
  Number of students: 1,195.
  Faculties of Arts, Law, Commerce, and Science.

National School of Music: c/o Ministry of Education and Fine Arts, Addis Ababa.

Polytechnic Institute: Bahar-Dar; f. 1963; agricultural mechanics, industrial chemistry, electrical technology, wood-working and processing technology, textile technology; 517 students.

SELECT BIBLIOGRAPHY

BARKER, A. J. *The Civilizing Mission: The Italo-Ethiopian War*. London, Cassell, 1968.

BEQUELE, ASSEFA, and CHOLE, ESHETU. *A Profile of the Ethiopian Economy*. Addis Ababa, Oxford University Press, 1969.

BERKELEY, G. F. H. *The Campaign of Adowa and the Rise of Menelik II*. London, 1935.

CLAPHAM, C. *Haile-Sellassie's Government*. London, 1969.

FARAGO, L. *Abyssinia on the Eve*. London, 1935.

GINZBERG, ELI, and SMITH, HERBERT A. *A Manpower Strategy for Ethiopia*. Addis Ababa, 1966.

GRAHAM, A. M. S. "Northeast Africa" in HODDER, B. W., and HARRIS, D. R. (Eds.), *Africa in Transition, Geographical Essays*, pp. 97–158, London, 1967.

GREENFIELD, R. *Ethiopia, A New Political History*. New York, Praeger, 1955.

GRYZIEWICZ, S., et al. "An Outline of the Fiscal System of Ethiopia", *Ethiopia Observer*, Vol. VIII, No. 4, p. 293, 1965.

HALLPIKE, C. R. *The Konso of Ethiopia. A Study of the Values of a Cushitic People*. Oxford University Press, 1972.

HESS, ROBERT L. *The Modernization of Autocracy*. Ithaca and London, Cornell University Press, 1972.

HUFFNAGEL, H. P. *Agriculture in Ethiopia*. FAO, Rome, 1961.

IMPERIAL ETHIOPIAN GOVERNMENT, CENTRAL STATISTICAL OFFICE. *Statistical Abstract of Ethiopia*. Published annually since 1963.

IMPERIAL ETHIOPIAN GOVERNMENT. *Third Five Year Development Plan* (1968–73). Addis Ababa, 1968.

IMPERIAL ETHIOPIAN GOVERNMENT. *Second Five Year Development Plan* (1963–67). Addis Ababa, 1962.

LAST, G. C. "Introductory Notes on the Geography of Ethiopia", *Ethiopia Observer*, Vol. VI, No. 2, pp. 82–134, 1962.
  A Geography of Ethiopia. Ministry of Education, Addis Ababa, 1965.

LEVINE, DONALD N. *Wax and Gold: Tradition and Innovation in Ethiopian Culture*. Chicago, Chicago University Press, 1965.

MILLER, CLARENCE J., et al. *Development in Agriculture and Agro-Industry in Ethiopia*. Addis Ababa, Stanford Research Institute, 1969.

MOSLEY, L. O. *Haile Selassie*. London, Weidenfeld and Nicolson, 1964.

PANKHURST, R. *Economic History of Ethiopia, 1880–1935*. Addis Ababa, 1968.

PERHAM, M. *Government of Ethiopia*. London, 1948.

QUARANTA, F. *Ethiopia, an Empire in the Making*. London, 1939.

SALVEMINI, G. *Prelude to World War II*. London, 1953.

SCHWARZ, WILLIAM C. K., et al. *Industrial Investment Climate in Ethiopia*. Addis Ababa, Stanford Research Institute, 1968.

SOMMER, J. W. "Ethiopia", *Focus*, Vol. XV, No. 8. American Geographical Society, April 1965.

STEER, G. L. *Caesar in Abyssinia*. London, 1936.
  Sealed and Delivered. London, 1942.

WOLDE, MARIAM MESFIN. *A Preliminary Atlas of Ethiopia*. Addis Ababa, 1962.

WYLDE, A. B. *Modern Abyssinia*. London, 1901.

French Territory of the Afar and Issa*

I. M. Lewis

(Revised for this edition by Virginia Luling)

The French Territory of the Afar and Issa (known formerly as French Somaliland) is France's last oversea African territory and one of the most arid and inhospitable terrains in the continent. Its area is only 21,783, sq. km. and its population is about 100,000. The population is almost evenly divided between Somali (Issa and other clans) and Afar, both of whom are Muslims and speak related Cushitic languages. Most of them live as pastoral nomads herding their camels and flocks over the volcanic rock-strewn desert, in which patches of arable land are a rare occurrence.

France's involvement, dating from 1859, centres on the port, Djibouti (Jibuti), the French rival to Aden and the main outlet and point of entry for Ethiopia's trade, which is carried on the Franco-Ethiopian railway—the only line of rail in the Horn of Africa—up into the Ethiopian highlands to Addis Ababa and Dire Dawa. Ethiopian interest in the territory, which follows from her economic dependence on Djibouti, is strengthened by the fact that many of the Afar and Issa spill over into Ethiopia and move as nomads back and forth across the frontiers, which have little relevance to the social geography of the region. The engagement of the Somali Democratic Republic, which is the other interested party, follows directly from the strong Somali element in the indigenous population, and the fact that Djibouti has long attracted Somali immigrants from the adjacent northern regions of the republic in search of work. Thus, recent political developments in the territory have inevitably been affected by the competing interests of these neighbouring states, whose relations are already strained because of the conflict over their mutual frontier (see Recent History of Somalia).

Through their greater numbers in Djibouti, in which most of the territory's population is concentrated, the Somali initially dominated local political develop-ments. However, the less urbanized and more neglected Afar population, with French support, gained political ascendancy in the referendum held in March 1967 to decide the future status of the territory. A majority of the voting population, mainly Afar, opted for the continuation of the French connection, while most of those Somali who were permitted to vote sought independence, and presumably, eventual union with the Somali Democratic Republic. The bitterness occasioned by this result and the change in the territory's name led to a series of incidents, but some degree of harmony was apparently restored between the two communities and at the 1968 elections for a new Chamber of Deputies in the territory the Afar leader Ali Arif and his progress party (*Regroupement démocratique Afar*) gained 26 of the available 32 seats. Although the remaining seats were won by a Somali party, Ali Arif also enjoyed some Somali support and the Government formed by him contained three Somali ministers as well as eight Afar. An election in 3 districts in 1971 produced no changes. Against repeated demands by Somalia that France should grant the people their right of self determination (implying that this was not done in 1967), the French Government has reasserted that the Territory is and will remain French.

France retains control of foreign affairs and defence, as well as several other responsibilities, and is represented by a High Commissioner.

In spite of the recession following the closure of the Suez Canal, some port activity has been maintained at Djibouti, and important harbour works have been carried out, with aid from France and the EEC. The 1971 budget balanced at 64.5 million French francs. Imports in 1970 amounted to 61,406 tons. Exports are negligible.

* See map on p. 304.

STATISTICAL SURVEY

Area: 21,783 sq. km. **Population** (UN estimate, 1972): 99,000. Djibouti *cercle* 62,000 (1970). Other main towns Tadjoura, Dikhil, Ali Sabieh, Obock.

Agriculture: There is little cultivated land. *Livestock* (estimates): 10,000 Cattle, 80,000 Sheep, 600,000 Goats, 6,000 Asses, 2,000 Camels.

Fishing: About 700 tons of sea fish annually.

Currency: The Djibouti franc. Exchange rates (December 1972): 1 Djibouti franc=2.591 French centimes; £1 sterling=443 Djibouti francs; U.S.$1=197.47 Djibouti francs; 1,000 Djibouti francs=£2.257=$5.064. The Djibouti franc did not follow the French devaluation of August 1969.

Budget (1969): 2,227 million francs; (1970) 2,414 million francs.

French Aid: This amounted to 28.8 million French francs in the 1961–68 period.

External Trade: (1967—million Djibouti francs): Exports 706 (593 to France); Imports 6,713 (France 2,830, other EEC countries 712, U.K. 523).

Shipping: Traffic has fallen heavily since the closing of the Suez Canal in June 1967. 3,074 ships called in 1965, less than 900 in 1969.

Education (1968): Primary—6,932 pupils in 19 public schools and 7 private schools; Secondary—604 pupils in 3 schools; Technical—203 students in 2 colleges.

THE CONSTITUTION

The Territory is administered by a Governmental Council of from six to twelve Ministers, presided over by a President who acts as the Head of State. These Ministers are elected by the Territorial Assembly and have the right to pass legislation affecting the administration of the Territory. The Territorial Assembly consists of 32 members, elected by direct universal suffrage. One Deputy and one Senator are elected to the National Assembly and the Senate in Paris. The French High Commissioner has responsibility for foreign policy, defence, currency, credit, citizenship and law other than traditional civil law. The Territory is divided into four administrative areas: Djibouti, Dikhil, Ali-Sabieh and Tadjoura (including the sub-district of Obock).

THE GOVERNMENT

High Commissioner: GEORGES THIERCY.
Deputy High Commissioner and Financial Administrator: ANDRÉ MARTIN DELAHAYE.

COUNCIL OF GOVERNMENT
(*November* 1972)

President, Minister of Public Works and the Port: ALI ARIF BOURHAN.
Minister of Home Affairs: AHMED DINI AHMED.
Minister of Finance and Planning: LUCIEN VETILLARD.
Minister of Labour: ABDI DEMBIL EGUAL.
Minister of Public Offices: OMAR FARAH ILTIREH.
Minister of Education, Sport and Youth: OMAR MUHAMMAD KAMIL.
Minister of Economic Affairs: HASSAN MUHAMMAD MOYALE.
Minister of Public Health and Social Affairs: CHELEM DAOUD CHEHEM.
Minister of Information and Tourism: DJIBRIL HASSAN REALEH.

CHAMBER OF DEPUTIES

(*Elections November* 1968)

Regroupement démocratique Afar . . .	26 seats
Union des peuples africaines . . .	6 seats
	32 seats

Partial elections were held in three districts in March 1971. Voting was for candidates on an official list, and the results confirmed those of 1968.

Representative to the National Assembly: ABDUL KADER MOUSSA ALI.
Representative to the Senate: HAMADOU BARKAT GOURAT.

POLITICAL PARTIES

Regroupement démocratique Afar: Djibouti; ruling party; Pres. ALI ARIF BOURHAN.
Union des peuples africaines: Djibouti; Pres. HASSAN GOULED.
Democratic Union Party: Addis Ababa, Ethiopia; exiled Afar Party.
Djibouti Liberation Movement: Dire Dawa, Ethiopia; Afar party.

JUDICIAL SYSTEM

There is a Tribunal Supérieur d'Appel, a Tribunal de Première Instance and a Justice de Paix. Criminal cases come under the jurisdiction of the Tribunal Supérieur d'Appel, which is the only criminal court. Civil matters come under the jurisdiction of the Tribunal de Première Instance and the Tribunal Supérieur d'Appel in cases affecting Europeans and other French citizens. Cases involving native customary law are heard by a Qadi, who has conciliatory functions, and by Tribunals of the 1st and 2nd degree.

President of the Tribunal Supérieur d'Appel: M. GESLIN.
President of the Tribunal de Première Instance: G. JAMBON.
General Attorney: L. BOCLE.

RELIGION

Islam: almost the entire native population are Muslims; Qadi of Djibouti SAYED ALI ABOUBAKER ASSAKAF.
Roman Catholics: Secretariat of the Bishopric, B.P. 94, Djibouti; there are about 7,500 Roman Catholics; Bishop of Djibouti Mgr. BERNARDIN HENRI HOFFMANN.
Protestants: Église Évangelique Française à l'Extérieure: ave de la République, B.P. 416, Djibouti; f. 1957; 400 mems.; Pasteur ROGER MULLER; publ. *Echos Protestants de la Mer Rouge* (quarterly).
Orthodox: there are about 350 Greek Orthodox; Archimandrite STAVROS GEORGANAS.

PRESS AND RADIO

Carrefour Africain: Djibouti, B.P. 393; twice a month; published by the Roman Catholic mission; circ. 500.
Journal Officiel: Imprimerie Administrative, B.P. 268, Djibouti; twice a month.
Le Réveil de Djibouti: Djibouti, B.P. 268; weekly; published by the Information Service, Ministry of the Interior; circ. 1,850–2,000; Dir. J. MAHAUT.

ORTF-Djibouti: B.P. 97, Djibouti; administered by Office de la Radiodiffusion-Télévision Française; daily programmes in French, Afar and Arabic; 23 hours radio, and 3 hours television per day, except on Monday; Dir. A. DAUMAS. There were 8,000 radio sets in 1971, and 2,500 television sets.

FINANCE

CENTRAL BANK

Trésorerie du Territoire Française des Issas: B.P. 19, place Albert Bernard, Djibouti.

Banque de l'Indochine: 96 boulevard Haussmann, Paris; Djibouti, place Lagarde, B.P. 88.
Banque Nationale pour le Commerce et l'Industrie (Océan Indien): Head Office, 7 place Vendôme, Paris; Djibouti, place Lagarde, B.P. 99.
Commercial Bank of Ethiopia, S.C.: Addis Ababa; P.O. Box No. 187, Djibouti.

INSURANCE

Some ten European insurance companies maintain agencies in Djibouti.

TRADE AND INDUSTRY

Chambre de Commerce et d'Industrie: B.P. 84, Djibouti; f. 1912; 14 mems.; Pres. SAID ALI COUBÈCHE; Sec. MOHAMMED DJAMA ELABE; publ. *Bulletin Mensuel de la Chambre de Commerce et d'Industrie de Djibouti.*

Union Syndicale Interprofessionelle des Entreprises de TFAI: Pres. M. V DELL'AQUILA.

Association Professionelle des Banques: Banque de l'Indochine, Djibouti; Pres. M. JACQUES RININO.

Union des Syndicats Indépendants Autochtones: Sec. ABDULLAHI AMIR.

Syndicat Autochtone des Cheminots: Sec. M. CASSIM.

TRANSPORT

RAILWAY

Compagnie du Chemin de Fer Franco-Ethiopien: Addis Ababa, P.O.B. 1051; f. 1908; 781 km. of track, linking Djibouti with Addis Ababa; metre gauge; Pres. Lidj ENDALKACHEW MAKONNEN.

ROADS

There are approximately 1,875 km. of roads, of which 75 km. are bitumen-surfaced, including the 40-km. road from Djibouti to Arta. Of the remaining 1,800 km., 800 km. are serviceable throughout the year, the rest only during the dry season.

SHIPPING

Djibouti

Aden Coasters Ltd.: rue Marchand, B.P. 125; Gen. Man. I. FERMON.

Air Djibouti: place Lagarde, B.P. 505; agents for Cie des Messageries Maritimes, Cie Maritime Belge, Société Navale Caennaise, Cie Auxiliaire de Navigation, Cie Africaine d'Armement, Cie Générale Translantique, Mitsui OSK Lines; also Agents for Air France and Air Madagascar; Man. Dir. J. DESCOUSIS.

Compagnie Maritime de l'Afrique Orientale: rue du Port, B.P. 89; agents for Achille Onorato, Cie. Maritime des Chargeurs Réunis, Ellerman Lines, Kerk Line, Netherlands Lloyd Line, Nouvelle Cie. Havraise Péninsulaire, Rotterdamsche Lloyd, Scandinavian East Africa Line, Stoomvaart Maatschappij Nederland, Svenska Ostasiatiska Kt., Worms et Cie. and Zim Israel Navigation Co.; Gen. Agent M. POUPEAU.

Cie. Maritime (Est Africaine) Ltd.: Agents for Hellenic Lines Ltd., A. Halcoussis & Co., International Navigation, Heinrich C. Horn; Dir. G. EFTHIMIATOS.

French Somaliland Shipping Co.: blvd. de la République, B.P. 15; agents for Deutsche Ostafrika Linie, Hamburg-Amerika Linie, Immediate Transport Co. (Aden), Norddeutscher Lloyd and Società d'Armamento Gestioni Navali; Dir. M. COUNINIS.

Gellatly Hankey et Cie. (Djibouti) S.A.: rue de Genève, B.P. 81; agents for American President Line, Blue Funnel Line, Bibby Line, Hoegh Line, Nippon Yusen Kaisha, P. Henderson, Peninsular and Orient, Yugoslav Line, B.I. Steam Navigation, Maersk Lines, Waterman Lines, National Shipping Corpn.; Dir. G. W. JOHN.

J. J. Kothari & Co. Ltd.: P.O.B. No. 171, place Lagarde; agents for Fratelli d'Amico, Shipping Corporation of India, Mogul Line, United Arab Maritime, Sudan Shipping Line, Onofrio Palmieri, Massawa and others; Dir. R. J. KOTHARI, S. J. KOTHARI, J. J. KOTHARI.

Mitchell Cotts and Co. (Ethiopia) Ltd.: blvd. de la République, B.P. 85; agents for Clan Line, Fearnley and Eger, Harrison Line, Iraqi Maritime Transport Co., Maldivian National Trading Corp., and other shipping and trading companies; Dir. FAHMY S. CASSIM.

Société d'Armement et de Manutention de la Mer Rouge (SAMER): B.P. 10; agents for Pacific International Line, Cunard Brocklebank, Glen Line, Wilhelm Wilhelmsen Co., Pakistan Shipping Co., Aktiebolaget Svenska Östasiatiska Kompaniet, Texaco, Chevron Shipping Co., Kie Hock Shipping Co.; Chair. A. E. BESSE; Man. Dir. VINCENT DELL AQUILA.

Société Maritime L. Savon et Riès: ave. St. Laurent du Var, B.P. 125; agents for Blue Star Line, Port Line, Svedel Line, Concordia Line, Lloyd Triestino, Louis Dreyfus, Polish Ocean Lines, Isthmian Lines and D.D.G. Hansa; Dir. H. A. JONES.

CIVIL AVIATION

Djibouti

Air Djibouti: B.P. 505; f. 1962; internal flights and services to Aden, Ethiopia, Somalia and Yemen; agents for Basco (Aden), Somali Airlines and Yemen Airlines; airtaxi and charter services; fleet of two DC-3 and one Bell JetRanger; Chair. F. LEGREZ; Man. Dir. J. DESCOUSIS; Dirs. J. C. CARRAUD, H. DE FOURNOUX, J. BONNEAU.

Air France, Air Madagascar, Democratic Yemen Airlines, Ethiopian Airlines, Somali Airlines, and Yemen Arab Airlines also serve Djibouti.

SELECT BIBLIOGRAPHY

LEWIS, I. M. *The Modern History of Somaliland.* London, Methuen, 1965.

LULING, VIRGINIA. *A South Somali Community.* To be published in 1973.

THOMPSON, VIRGINIA, and ADLOFF, RICHARD. *Djibouti and the Horn of Africa.* London, O.U.P., 1968.

Gabon

PHYSICAL AND SOCIAL GEOGRAPHY*

David Hilling

PHYSICAL FEATURES AND RESOURCES

Located astride the equator, the Republic of Gabon has an area of 103,000 sq. miles and comprises the entire drainage basin of the westward-flowing Ogooué River, together with the basins of several smaller coastal rivers such as the Nyanga and Como.

The low-lying coastal zone is narrow in the north and south but broader in the estuary regions of the Ogooué and Gabon. South of the Ogooué numerous lagoons, such as the N'Dogo, M'Goze, and M'Komi, back the coast, and the whole area is floored with Cretaceous sedimentary rocks, which at shallow depth yield oil. The main producing oil fields are in a narrow zone stretching southwards from Port-Gentil. The interior consists of Precambrian rocks, eroded into a series of plateau surfaces at heights from 1,500 to 2,000 ft. and dissected by the river system into a number of distinct blocks, such as the Crystal Mountains, the Moabi Uplands and the Chaillu Massif. This area is one of Africa's most mineralized zones, and traditional small-scale mining of gold and diamonds has now been replaced in importance by large-scale exploitation of manganese at Moanda since 1962 and uranium at Mounana since 1961. There are numerous deposits of high-grade iron ore, and mining will commence at the Belinga deposit (660 million tons) in the mid-1970s, following completion of a railway running 350 miles to the coast near Libreville.

CLIMATE AND VEGETATION

Gabon has a truly equatorial climate with uniformly high temperatures, high relative humidities and mean annual rainfalls from 60 to 120 in. Some 74 per cent of the country's surface is forest-covered, and okoumé (*Aucoumea Klaineana*) provided the basis for the country's economy until superseded by minerals in the 1960s. Grassland vegetation is restricted to the coastal sand zone south of Port-Gentil and parts of the valleys of the Nyanga, upper N'Gounié and upper Ogooué.

POPULATION

Agricultural development in the potentially rich forest zone has been limited by the small size of the country's population. This has now grown to nearly a million, thus average population density is ten persons per sq. mile. Greater rural confederations are found in Woleu N'Tem, where coffee and cocoa are the main cash crops, and around Lambaréné, where palm oil and coffee are important. The three main urban concentrations now account for 20 per cent of the total population—Libreville (the capital), Port-Gentil (centre of the petroleum industry) and Franceville/Moanda (the mining centre).

*See map on p. 202.

RECENT HISTORY†

Robert Cornevin‡

The first President of the Republic, Léon M'Ba, had been closely associated with the political development of Gabon after 1946. He had endured thirteen years under house arrest at Bambari (today in the Central African Republic) imposed by the colonial administration. Formerly militant in the League for the Rights of Man, in 1946 he founded the joint Franco-Gabonese Committee. Despite two defeats in legislative elections (1951 and 1956) he was elected Mayor of Libreville in November 1956, and in the same year was nominated Vice-President of the Government Council (the President of which, by the terms of the *loi cadre*, was *ex officio* the Governor).

Undisputed leader of the *Bloc démocratique gabonais*, the territorial branch of Houphouët-Boigny's *Rassemblement démocratique africain* (RDA), he was elected President of the Republic on February 12th, 1961, receiving 99.6 per cent of the votes cast. In his Government of National Union, he brought forward his long-standing rival, Jean Hilaire Aubame, to the post of Foreign Minister. Aubame headed the Gabonese branch of the *Parti de Regroupement africain* (PRA), the inter-territorial movement led by Léopold Senghor of Senegal. A major difference between PRA and the RDA was that the former supported the formation of federal groupings in Africa whereas the latter was strongly opposed to such groupings (underlying the attitude of M'ba and Houphouët-Boigny was the consideration that Gabon and the Ivory Coast were economically the best endowed of the former French States of West and Central Africa and would be in a position of supporting poor neigh-

† For the period before independence *see* Central African Republic Recent History, p. 213.

‡ For the 1973 edition revisions have been made to this article by the Editor.

339

bours in any federal system). Both were members of the Fang tribe but Aubame drew much of his support from northern Gabon and being more radical in outlook, appealed more to youth. M'ba's support, however, was more widely-based.

Friction between the two men quickly revived after the 1961 election. Aubame was deprived of his foreign affairs portfolio in 1963 and appointed President of the Supreme Court. M'ba considered applying a law prohibiting a member of parliament from holding the post of Supreme Court President, but calculated that his small parliamentary majority precluded this action. He therefore dissolved the National Assembly in January 1964 and later announced that new elections would be held on February 23rd.

FRENCH INTERVENTION

A military *coup d'état* on February 18th deposed M'Ba and set up a Revolutionary Committee under the leadership of Aubame. M'Ba appealed to France for help under defence agreements signed between France and Gabon in 1960, and as a result of French military intervention he was reinstated as President. Aubame, then aged 52, was sentenced to 10 years' imprisonment for treason.

Elections in April of that year gave President M'Ba's *Bloc démocratique gabonaise* (BDG) 31 of the 47 seats in the National Assembly. Aubame's party, re-organized and re-named, won the other 16 seats. Over the next two years almost all the opposition members joined the BDG, leaving Gabon virtually a one-party state. No opposition candidates presented themselves in the elections held in March 1967 and the BDG was returned for a 5-year term.

Despite his authoritarian practices, M'Ba created the office of Vice-President of the Republic in February 1967, which facilitated a peaceful transfer of power at his death (on November 28th) to his 32-year old deputy, Albert-Bernard Bongo. As a result of a government reshuffle in January 1968 a number of younger men, including close associates of President Bongo and former opposition members, came to power. On March 12th, 1968, President Bongo announced the formal institution of one-party government in Gabon and the creation of a single new party, the *Parti démocratique gabonaise* (PDG). The new party, whose motto is "Dialogue-Tolerance-Peace", was declared to guarantee national unity and the abolition of ethnic discrimination, and to adhere to the principles of the *Rassemblement démocratique africain*.

INTERNATIONAL RELATIONS

Gabon has diplomatic relations with all its immediate neighbours and, together with Cameroon, the Central African Republic and Congo (Brazzaville), is a member of the *Union douanière et économique de l'Afrique centrale* (UDEAC). Despite a lack of political sympathy with its left-wing government, Gabon is sedulous in maintaining good relations with Congo (Brazzaville) because of its transport difficulties in the south-east.

Relations with Equatorial Guinea, however, were extremely strained for a time during September 1972. Gabon extended her territorial waters to 170 miles on August 23rd, and was accused by the government of Equatorial Guinea of invading all its islands. Agreement was reached in November between President Bongo and President Macías of Equatorial Guinea on the formation of an OAU special commission to fix the maritime frontier between the two countries.

Gabon is an associate member of the EEC, but nonetheless continues to rely heavily on French investment and aid. France supplies 60 per cent of Gabon's imports and is the customer for over 40 per cent of Gabonese exports, showing particular interest in the country's uranium and other mineral wealth. President Bongo has aimed at economic independence through diversification of trade and aid and investment sources, without jeopardizing French backing and support. Because of its economic dependence on France, Gabon's foreign policy tends to be identified with that of France. In the Nigerian civil war Gabon recognized Biafra and supported the secessionists against the Federal Government. Gabon is interested in the concept of "francophonie" and belongs to the *Agence de Coopération Culturelle et Technique*, which groups over 20 French-speaking countries, including Canada. Diplomatic relations with Canada were suspended between 1968 and 1970 after Gabon had issued a direct invitation to Quebec to take part in a Conference of Ministers of Education of francophone countries.

Gabon is among the few sub-Saharan African countries not having diplomatic relations with Communist States. A few bilateral trade agreements have been signed, however; for example, Romania is buying Gabonese timber and Czechoslovakia is importing manganese.

ECONOMY

Peter Robson*

INTRODUCTION

Although over half of Gabon's population is engaged in agriculture, the economy rests primarily on the exploitation of timber and mineral resources. Agricultural production is mainly for subsistence. Commercial agriculture is little developed, due to transport difficulties, generally poor soils and better opportunities to earn money incomes in other branches of the economy. The market economy is largely dominated by foreign enterprises in forestry, mining, and trade which generate and remit a high proportion of G.D.P.

Recent estimates of the population have been proved completely inaccurate by the 1972 census, which shows that it has more than doubled during the last ten years and is now 950,000, with an average density of 10 to the square mile. Despite this growth urban unemployment is virtually non-existent.

In recent years the rapid exploitation of the country's natural resources has produced an impressive rate of economic growth. Over the decade 1957 to 1967 there was nearly a fourfold increase in G.D.P. in current prices. For 1967 G.D.P. was estimated at about 51,300 million francs CFA giving a product per head of 110,000 francs CFA (£165), the highest in Africa south of the Sahara, excepting South Africa. Investment has remained high during this period, although there was some falling off towards the end of the decade. Private investment has been dominant, but public investment in infrastructure has risen substantially in recent years. Growth has been accompanied by important structural changes. With the depletion of coastal forests the share of forest products in G.D.P. began to decline, but after stagnating until 1967 the value of output recovered in 1968 and has continued to rise. The share of agriculture has been dwindling and its output in absolute terms has stagnated. The main source of growth has been the development of the mineral industries, especially uranium, manganese and petroleum.

AGRICULTURE

Agriculture is of diminishing importance in Gabon; its development is hampered by limited land, an inadequate transport system and declining prices for export crops. Government economic policy has been directed mainly towards encouraging development in other sectors of the economy, although of late rather more attention has been given to agriculture.

The principal export crops are cocoa, coffee and palm oil, but in 1968 these contributed less than 2 per cent of export earnings and production is increasing only slowly under the second development plan. Food crop production is insufficient to meet domestic demand and large quantities of agricultural and dairy products are imported.

Animal husbandry is hardly practised at all in Gabon. The prevalence of tsetse is one major obstacle to its development. There are plans to expand the fishing industry which at present cannot provide for the home market, as the annual total catch is only between 3,000 and 4,000 tons.

FORESTRY

Gabon possesses vast forests and, until the commencement of mineral exploitation in the early 1960s, the economy was virtually dependent upon the timber industry. *Okoumé*, a soft wood employed in the manufacture of plywood, is the most important timber in Gabon, and Gabon is the world's largest producer. Timber exploitation is carried out by large mechanized European firms, and by Gabonese enterprises, including family concessions on a non-mechanized basis (*coupes familiales*) and mechanized enterprises of various sizes. With the depletion of forests in the accessible "first zone", exploitation has been expanded in the "second zone", but in this region rapids preclude river transportation, and exploitation is dependent upon the construction of a road network. This is already under way, in part financed by the European Development Fund and the World Bank. In addition two million hectares of concessions in the "third zone" along the route of the projected Owendo-Booué railway, have recently been sold.

Output of *okoumé*, which had been stagnant or declining since 1964, revived in 1968 and 1969 with the favourable development of the market for tropical woods. The increase in output in 1968 was to an important extent due to a substantial increase in African production (by 25 per cent), encouraged by the government policy of reserving licences in the first zone to Gabonese, by favourable cutting conditions and by improved prices. Output of *okoumé* attained a record level in 1971 of 1,024,000 tons. Re-afforestation has been proceeding for some years and accelerated towards the end of the last decade. The programme is designed to enable *okoumé* production to be maintained.

Numerous other woods are exploited, including mahogany, ebony and walnut. Production has accelerated recently and in 1971 reached 133,000 cubic metres.

MINING

The main source of Gabon's considerable economic growth in the last decade has been the exploitation of her rich mineral resources. Most of the mineral output is exported except for the natural gas, considerable quantities of which are utilized domestically mainly

---

* For the 1973 edition revisions have been made to this article by the Editor.

for electricity generation, and part of the petroleum output. In 1971 over 30 million cubic metres of natural gas were extracted. The exploitation of petroleum began in 1957 and production reached nearly six million tons in 1971. Exports, amounting to four-fifths of total production, were valued at 10,400 million francs CFA in 1968. Petroleum for consumption in Gabon and the other UDEAC contries is refined at Port-Gentil, which has a capacity of 1 million tons a year. Petroleum reserves amounting to several years' output at current rates are known, and prospecting for further supplies continues.

The exploitation of uranium began in 1961. The ore is extracted at Mounana and concentrated before exportation. It is sold exclusively to the French Atomic Energy Commission. Production was 1,200 tons in 1971 and reserves amount to about ten years' output. Manganese exploitation started in 1962 and Gabon has become the third largest producer of manganese in the non-communist world. Output totalled 1,831,000 tons in 1971 and the huge reserves should last 150 years at the present rate of exploitation.

One of the largest iron ore deposits in the world exists around Belinga in the north-east of Gabon, and its exploitation is planned when a necessary rail link to the coast (at Owendo) has been completed. Lead, zinc and phosphate are known to exist and further prospecting is under way.

MANUFACTURING, POWER AND TRANSPORTATION

Gabon's manufacturing sector is relatively small, but has been growing steadily since 1967. In 1966 it accounted for only 6 per cent of G.D.P., and half of this contribution was represented by timber processing. The main weight of Gabon's development effort during the early years of independence was placed on the expansion of the export-oriented industries of mining and forestry. This fostered the development of an economy characterized by an extreme form of economic dualism in which a highly capital-intensive export sector operates beside an agricultural sector producing mainly for subsistence.

More recently Gabon has sought to develop industries based on natural resources. By 1967 small industries existed for processing coffee and rice and for manufacturing soap, oxygen and acetylene, prefabricated concrete, and confectionery. The oil refinery came into operation in 1967 and has now reached full capacity; 976,000 tons of crude petroleum were treated in 1971, and the second development plan envisages expansion. There is a thriving brewery and soft drink plant which is to build a second factory in Franceville, and another major plant produces flour, animal feed, eggs and, since 1972, cigarettes. Further industries include cement, textile-printing (five million metres in 1971), metal forestry equipment and plastic household goods. The wood processing industry continues to be of prime importance with 17 saw mills, three veneer factories, several furniture workshops, and a plywood factory

which exports to 50 countries; less wood is being exported as sawn timber, and production of plywood has risen from 72,000 cubic metres in 1970 to 80,000 cubic metres in 1972. Current plans for expansion include factories for nails, electric batteries, lump sugar, marble slabs, cellulose, fertilizer, shoes and paints. The President continues to exhort his people to increased initiative in setting up and expanding industrial concerns and has created *Promogabon* to give technical help and loans.

Electricity is produced and distributed in eight urban centres by a semi-public company, the *Société d'énergie et d'eau du Gabon* (SEEG), mainly on the basis of thermal plants using oil or natural gas. There is considerable potential for hydro-electric power in Gabon and the first hydro-electric plant at Kinguélé was completed in 1972. It will provide inexpensive power for industry in the Como estuary and for Libreville. Over the period 1960–71 annual consumption of electricity increased from 17 million kWh. to 114 million kWh.

Gabon's surface transportation system is inadequate. There are no railroads but for the link between Pointe-Noire and the Moana manganese mine, and the main rivers are navigable only for the last 50–100 miles or so of their course to the Atlantic Ocean. The road network is poorly developed and much of it is unusable during the rainy seasons. The opening up of the second forest zone has necessitated giving more attention to road transportation since the rivers in the second zone are not navigable. In order to overcome the obstacles which the poor transport system presents to economic development, a substantial investment in transport has been undertaken in the last eight years. A 560 km. railway, "le Trans-gabonais", is planned. Work on the first section, from Owendo to Booué (330 km.), should begin in 1973 and be completed by 1977. A second section will continue from Booué to Belinga. The railway will be government-owned and operated and financed largely by overseas grants and loans. Operating costs will be shared by the *Société des mines de fer de Mekambo*, as transportation of iron ore will be its principle use. Port improvements at Port-Gentil have been undertaken and a deep-water port at Owendo is under construction.

FOREIGN TRADE, AID AND THE BALANCE OF PAYMENTS

Registered exports to countries outside the customs union increased by over 200 per cent during the period 1960–71, from 11,826 million francs CFA to 38,607 million francs CFA. Over the same period recorded imports rose from 7,800 million francs CFA to 22,232 million francs CFA, and Gabon's sustained surplus on registered trade increased steadily to a level of 16,375 million francs CFA. This surplus is offset to a small extent by a deficit on trade with other members of the customs union, which in 1970 amounted to 1,155 million francs CFA. The structure of exports underwent a substantial change during the 1960s as the mining industry developed.

During the previous decade timber and its products accounted for nearly three-quarters of export earnings; by 1971 they accounted for only one third. Petroleum also accounted for a third and manganese and uranium for 16 per cent and five per cent respectively.

France is the principal export market (33 per cent in 1968), though its share has fallen substantially from 51 per cent in 1960. It is followed by the United States, which purchases a substantial part of the output of manganese, and Federal Germany.

Since independence Gabon has been the recipient of considerable foreign aid from the west. At the outset aid came mainly from France; although this increased subsequently, France's relative contribution to grants has fallen. Grants from the European Development Fund account for much of the other aid, with most of the remainder coming from Federal Germany, U.S.A. and IBRD (World Bank). Over the period 1960–67 aid was received from the *Fonds d'aide et de coopération* (FAC) to the extent of 6,800 million francs CFA; while 4,300 million francs CFA were received from the first EDF.

Gabon's favourable trade balance is normally reinforced by an inflow of grants and, from time to time, by substantial inflows of private long-term capital, mainly for mining. However, there is normally a substantial deficit on account of recurrent transfer payments and services, the latter reflecting large transfers of dividends and interest by foreign enterprises operating in Gabon. In the year 1968–69 the overall payments position showed a favourable balance in contrast to the deficitary position of the previous year, and external reserves improved.

Tourism is greatly encouraged and has expanded in recent years. Receipts totalled 276 million francs CFA in 1971.

PUBLIC FINANCE

Each year since 1962 Gabon has realized a substantial surplus on its ordinary budget, enabling a considerable contribution to be made to the financing of the development budget. Development expenditure has, however, usually been larger than the realized ordinary surplus, resulting in an overall budgetary deficit.

In 1961 revenue totalled 4,600 million francs CFA and over the period 1962–72 the size of revenue quadrupled to 31,300 million francs CFA, of which 38 per cent was used for development.

DEVELOPMENT PLANNING

Gabon has steadily pursued a policy of encouraging the private sector. In the first five-year development plan 1966–70 private investment represented about 60 per cent of the total investment of 90,000 million francs CFA. Of the public sector investment, 1 per cent was for agriculture, 75 per cent was for infrastructure and 8 per cent for social services. The plan was designed to organize the economy and consolidate Gabonese independence in conjunction with a policy of "Gabonization".

The second development plan (1971–75) is intended to unite the country politically, administratively, economically and socially and to pursue a liberal, outward-looking economic policy. Investment totals 149,000 million francs CFA, a 66 per cent increase on the first plan. Of this private investment accounts for 56 per cent, while 24 per cent will come from foreign grants and loans. Sixty per cent is being used for production, 35 per cent for infrastructure, notably transport, and 3 per cent for social services. Twenty-one per cent will be devoted to industrialization, 20 per cent to mining, 9 per cent to forestry, 6 per cent to power and 1 per cent to rural development. It is hoped that G.D.P. will increase by 7 per cent each year.

PROBLEMS AND PROSPECTS

With the help of a stable government favourably disposed towards free enterprise, and rich natural resources, Gabon has achieved a creditable rate of growth in the past decade, and its level of G.D.P. is high. Given continued foreign assistance, its development programmes should be capable of achievement. The economic situation however is not without its difficulties. Gabon is an arch-example of an enclave economy, and much of its recent development has made little difference to the majority of its inhabitants. Moreover, some of the sources on which recent economic growth has rested cannot be depended on in the later 1970s; in particular the output of manganese and uranium is not expected to expand significantly. Unless further mineral deposits are discovered, growth in the near future must depend on the exploitation of the immense iron ore reserves in the Mékambo region. Secondary sources of growth have been found in the further development of processing industries and of manufacturing.

STATISTICAL SURVEY

AREA AND POPULATION

AREA (sq. km.)	POPULATION (1972 census)
267,000	950,000

PRINCIPAL TOWNS

POPULATION (1972)

Libreville (capital)	75,000
Port-Gentil	30,000
Lambaréné	7,000

EMPLOYMENT

(1972)

Agriculture	267,000
Forestry, Mining and Construction . .	60,000
Commerce and Industry . . .	8,200
Civil Service	8,000
Other (incl. Military, Clergy, Students) .	38,200

AGRICULTURE

PRINCIPAL CROPS

('000 metric tons)

	1969	1970	1971
Cereals .	3*	3*	3*
Cassava (Manioc) .	167*	167*	n.a.
Bananas .	10*	10*	n.a.
Palm Oil .	2	2*	2*
Coffee .	1.2	0.9	0.9

	1969/70	1970/71	1971/72
Cocoa Beans (October to September) . .	4.7	5.0	5.0

* FAO estimates.

Source: FAO, *Production Yearbook 1971.*

Livestock (1970): Horses 3,382, Goats 86,682, Pigs 6,032.

FORESTRY

('000 metric tons)

	1967	1968	1969	1970	1971
Okoumé . .	750	842	928	924	1,024
Other Woods . .	113	159	195	189	n.a.

FISHING

('000 metric tons)

	1967	1968	1969	1970
Total Catch . .	3.2	3.0*	3.8	4.0*

* FAO estimates.

Source: FAO, *Yearbook of Fishing Statistics 1970.*

MINING

	UNIT	1967	1968	1969	1970	1971
Petroleum . . .	'000 metric tons	2,240	n.a.	5,030	5,364	5,785
Manganese . . .	,, ,, ,,	1,124	1,227	1,377	1,451	1,831
Uranium . . .	metric tons	1,452	1,371	1,388	1,077	1,200
Gold . . .	kg.	514	443	501	n.a.	n.a.

INDUSTRY

	Unit	1970
Beer	hectolitres	50,000
Soft Drinks . . .	,,	25,000
Flour	metric tons	7,968
Bran	,, ,,	1,501
Cattle Feed . . .	,, ,,	1,050
Printed Textiles . .	'ooo metres	5,000
Cement . . .	metric tons	23,000
Electricity . . .	'ooo kWh	110,156

FINANCE

100 centimes = 1 franc de la Communauté Financière Africaine.

Coins: 1, 2, 5, 10 and 25 francs CFA.

Notes: 50, 100, 500, 1,000, 5,000 and 10,000 francs CFA.

Exchange rates (December 1972): 1 franc CFA = 2 French centimes.

£1 sterling = 593.625 francs CFA; U.S. $1 = 255.785 francs CFA;

1,000 francs CFA = £1.685 = $3.91.

Budget: (1971) 24,523 million francs CFA, of which Development Budget 7,862 million francs CFA

Budget: (1972) 31,300 million francs CFA, including Investment Budget 11,776 million francs CFA, of which Development Budget 6,300 million francs CFA.

SECOND DEVELOPMENT PLAN 1971–75
(million francs CFA)

INVESTMENT		RESOURCES	
Production	92,114	*Internal Public Funds* . . .	28,749
Forestry and Wood Industries . .	13,776	State Budget . . .	26,018
Mining	29,182	Public Organizations . .	2,731
Power and Water . . .	11,948	*External Public Funds* . . .	36,723
Industry	31,913	*Private Funds*	84,428
Commerce, Transport and Services .	3,500		
Rural Development . . .	1,795		
Infrastructure	53,375		
Railway	16,500		
Roads	11,030		
Airways	4,375		
Ports	2,686		
Posts and Telecommunications . .	1,265		
Radio and Television . .	819		
Tourism	4,510		
Urbanization and Administration .	12,190		
Social Services	4,411		
Health	2,430		
Education . . .	1,833		
Social Action . . .	148		
TOTAL	149,900	TOTAL	149,900

EXTERNAL TRADE
(million francs CFA)

	1964	1965	1966	1967	1968	1969	1970	1971
Imports* . . .	13,742	15,425	16,209	16,585	15,875	20,127	22,139	22,232
Exports* . . .	22,253	23,686	24,669	29,516	30,714	36,663	33,610	38,607

* Excluding trade in gold and trade with other UDEAC countries: Cameroon (from 1966), the Central African Republic, Congo (Brazzaville) and, prior to 1969, Chad.

Source: UDEAC.

COMMODITIES
(million francs CFA)

IMPORTS	1967	1968	1969	EXPORTS	1967	1968	1969
Food and Live Animals	1,438	1,594	1,741	Cocoa Beans . .	377	406	482
Alcoholic Beverages .	927	812	782	Saw and Veneer Logs .	7,274	8,440	11,029
Petroleum Products .	173	267	294	Railway Sleepers . .	341	401	280
Chemicals . .	1,030	1,076	1,403	Manganese Ores and			
Textile Yarn, Fabrics				Concentrates .	8,034	6,455	7,429
etc. . .	610	804	801	Uranium and Thorium			
Iron and Steel .	938	1,111	1,537	Ores and Concentrates	1,971	1,793	1,788
Machinery (non-electric)	2,942	2,658	3,766	Crude Petroleum . .	8,882	10,392	12,552
Electrical Equipment .	1,096	936	1,281	Veneer Sheets . .	411	123	38
Road Motor Vehicles .	1,771	1,711	2,105	Plywood . .	1,489	1,808	2,083
Aircraft . .	228	265	572				
Clothing (except furs) .	398	424	525				
TOTAL (incl. others)	16,585	15,875	20,109	TOTAL (incl. others)	29,516	30,714	36,663

Source: Mainly *Overseas Associates, Foreign Trade* (Statistical Office of the European Communities, Luxembourg).

COUNTRIES
(million francs CFA)

IMPORTS	1967	1968	1969	EXPORTS	1967	1968	1969
Belgium/Luxembourg .	300	418	495	France . . .	10,500	10,280	12,923
France . . .	9,918	8,974	11,735	Federal Germany .	3,298	2,818	3,146
Federal Germany .	1,222	1,338	1,691	Netherlands . .	1,754	1,328	1,892
Italy . . .	504	371	467	Netherlands Antilles .	1,310	3,651	4,292
Netherlands .	511	701	771	Senegal . .	774	1,134	1,258
United Kingdom .	556	668	697	United Kingdom . .	1,166	1,112	1,190
U.S.A. . .	1,521	1,521	2,157	U.S.A. . .	5,757	3,773	4,015
TOTAL (incl. others)	16,585	15,875	20,109	TOTAL (incl. others)	29,516	30,714	36,663

Source: mainly *Overseas Associates, Foreign Trade* (Statistical Office of the European Communities, Luxembourg). The total of 1969 imports differs slightly from that given in the summary total of trade, which includes the latest figures supplied by the UDEAC.

TRANSPORT

ROAD TRAFFIC
(Number of vechiles in use)

	1968	1969	1970
Cars .	5,230	5,921	7,100
Buses .	134	168	188
Goods Vehicles .	4,490	4,936	5,800

SHIPPING

	LIBREVILLE			PORT-GENTIL		
	1968	1969	1970	1968	1969	1970
Ships Entered .	770	792	n.a.	920	885	961
Passenger Arrivals and Departures .	3,338	2,868*	n.a.	2,434	n.a.	n.a.
Freight Loaded ('ooo metric tons) .	343	1,215	n.a.	3,827	4,546	3,551
Freight Unloaded ('ooo metric tons)	159	370	n.a.	82	89	73

* Ferry services were withdrawn from November 1st, 1969.

CIVIL AVIATION
(Libreville and Port-Gentil)

	1969	1970
Aircraft Arrivals and Departures	19,485	21,374
Passenger Arrivals and Departures .	149,690	149,770
Freight Loaded (metric tons) .	3,030	3,764
Freight Unloaded (metric tons) .	6,723	8,454

EDUCATION
(1971–72)

	SCHOOLS	STUDENTS
Primary .	678	105,600
Secondary .	41	9,387
Technical .	12	1,733
Teacher Training .	6	231
University .	1	172*

* There were 618 students at universities abroad.

THE CONSTITUTION

(Revised, February 1967)

Preamble: Upholds the Rights of Man, liberty of conscience and of the person, religious freedom and freedom of education. Sovereignty is vested in the people, who exercise it through their representatives or by means of referenda. There is direct, universal and secret suffrage.

Head of State: The President is elected by direct suffrage for a seven-year term and is eligible for re-election. He is Head of State, of the administration and of the Armed Forces. The President may, after consultation with his Ministers and the leaders of the National Assembly, order a referendum to be held. There is a Vice-President elected by direct suffrage. He will replace the President in case of his disability for any reason.

Executive Power: Executive power is vested in the President and the Council of Ministers, who are appointed by the President and are responsible to him. The President presides over the Council.

Legislative Power: The National Assembly is elected by direct suffrage for a seven-year term and normally holds two sessions a year. It may be dissolved or prorogued for up to 18 months by the President, after consultation with the Council of Ministers and the President of the Assembly. The President may return a Bill to the Assembly for a second reading when it must be passed by a majority of two-thirds of the members. If the President dissolves the Assembly, elections must take place within 40 days.

Judicial Power: The President guarantees the independence of the Judiciary and presides over the Conseil Supérieur de la Magistrature. There is a Supreme Court and a High Court of Justice. The High Court, which is composed of deputies of the National Assembly elected from among themselves, has power to try the President or members of the government.

THE GOVERNMENT

HEAD OF THE STATE

President: ALBERT-BERNARD BONGO.

Vice-President: LÉON MEBIAME.

COUNCIL OF MINISTERS

(December 1972)

President of the Republic, Prime Minister, Minister of Defence, Information, Development, Planning and Territorial Organization: ALBERT-BERNARD BONGO.

Vice-President, Minister of Co-ordination: LÉON MEBIAME.

Ministers of State:

Deputy Vice-President, Labour, Social Security, Relations with the Assemblies: JEAN STANISLAS MIGOLET.

Foreign Affairs and Co-operation: GEORGES RAWIRI.

Environment and Forestry: FRANÇOIS NGUEMA-NDONG.

Public Works, Housing and Town Planning: PAUL MALEKOU.

At the Presidency in Charge of Planning, Development and Territorial Organization: AUGUSTIN BOUMAH.

Ministers:

Interior: Lt.-Col. RAPHAEL MAMIAKA.

Justice: VALENTIN OBAME.

Agriculture, Stock-Breeding and Rural Economy: JEAN-BAPTISTE OBIANG-EKOMIE.

Economy and Finance: PAUL MOUKAMBI.

Health and Population: SIMON ESSIMENGANE.

Education and Scientific Research: JEROME OKINDA.

Civil Service and Administrative Reform: Dr. BENJAMIN NGOUBOU.

Mines, Industry, Energy and Water Resources: EDOUARD-ALEXIS MBOUY-BOUTZIT.

Posts and Telecommunications and Ex-Servicemen: ÉMILE BIBALOU-ABIBOUKA.

Forestry and Water Resources: RIGOBERT LANDJI.

Transport and Civil Aviation: BONJEAN-FRANCOIS ONDO.

Secretary General at the Presidency (ranking as Minister): RENÉ RADEMBINO-CONIQUET.

Minister Delegate at the Presidency in Charge of External and Social Affairs: MICHEL ESSONGE.

Youth and Sport: EMMANUEL MEFANE.

Secretaries of State:

Tourism: Major JACQUES IGOHO.

At the Presidency and Head of State's Personal Representative: MARTIN BONGO.

Public Works, Housing and Town Planning: JEAN MBOUDY.

DIPLOMATIC REPRESENTATION
EMBASSIES ACCREDITED TO GABON
(In Libreville unless otherwise stated)

Belgium: Brazzaville, People's Republic of the Congo (E).

Cameroon: Bangui, Central African Republic (E).

Canada: Yaoundé, Cameroon (E).

Central African Republic: Libreville (E); *Ambassador:* ANTOINE M'BARY-DABA.

Chad: Bangui, Central African Republic.

China, Republic: B.P. 625, Libreville; *Ambassador:* TIMOTHY T. H. HUANG.

Congo, People's Republic: *Ambassador:* FRANÇOIS-XAVIER OLASSA.

Equatorial Guinea: *Ambassador:* CLEMENTE ATEBE NSOH.

France: B.P. 25, Libreville; *Ambassador:* JEAN RIBO.

Germany, Federal Republic: B.P. 299, Libreville; *Ambassador:* (vacant).

India: Kinshasa, Zaire (E).

Israel: B.P. 1201, Libreville; *Ambassador:* MAIR SHAMIR.

Italy: B.P. 2251, Libreville (E); *Ambassador:* FURIO ZAMPETTI.

Japan: B.P. 1785, Libreville (E); *Ambassador:* T. KIKKAWA.

Korea, Republic: Paris (E).

Lebanon: *Ambassador:* B. NEZIH BULIND.

Malta: B.P. 3048, Libreville (E); *Ambassador:* GUY LE GOUVELLO.

Netherlands: Yaoundé, Cameroon.

Spain: B.P. 1157, Libreville; *Ambassador:* R. G. JORDANA Y PRATS.

Sudan: Kinshasa, Zaire, (E).

Sweden: Kinshasa, Zaire, (E).

Switzerland: Kinshasa, Zaire (E).

Tunisia: Libreville (E); *Ambassador:* ABDEL HAMID ANMAR.

Turkey: Lagos, Nigeria (E).

United Kingdom: Yaoundé, Cameroon (E).

U.S.A.: B.P. 185, Libreville; *Ambassador:* JOHN McKESSON.

Vatican: Yaoundé, Cameroon.

Zaire: Libreville (E); *Ambassador:* MWANE KIKANGALA EBULAYA YA BWANA.

Gabon also has diplomatic relations with Central African Republic, Mali and Viet-Nam (Republic).

NATIONAL ASSEMBLY
President: GEORGES DAMAS ALEKA.

ELECTION
(February 1969)

PARTY	SEATS
Bloc Démocratique Gabonais . . .	47

POLITICAL PARTY
Parti démocratique gabonais (PDG): Libreville; f. 1968 in succession to the *Bloc démocratique gabonais* (*BDG*); made sole political party by presidential decree of March 12th, 1968, which stated that the Party would be the guarantee of national unity and of the abolition of ethnic discrimination; Sec.-Gen. and Founder ALBERT BONGO; publ. newspaper, *Dialogue*.

DEFENCE
The army consists of one batallion, the air force of one squadron and there is a small navy.

Chief of Staff of the Armed Forces: Brig. Gen. NAZAIRE BOULINGUI.

JUDICIAL SYSTEM
Supreme Court: Libreville; has four chambers: constitutional, judicial, administrative, and accounts; Pres. PAUL MARIE GONDJOUT.

High Court of Justice: Libreville; members appointed by and from the deputies of the National Assembly.

Court of Appeal: Libreville.

Cour de Sureté de l'Etat: Libreville; 12 members; Pres. ALBERT-BERNARD BONGO.

Conseil Supérieure de la Justice: Libreville; Pres. ALBERT-BERNARD BONGO; Vice-Pres. Minister of Justice *ex officio.*

RELIGION
Gabon is the most Christianized of the states of the French Community in Africa. Sixty-five per cent of the population are Christians, Roman Catholics comprising 42 per cent of the total population. Forty-two per cent are Animists and less than 1 per cent Muslims.

Roman Catholic Missions: Ste. Marie, Libreville, B.P. 1146.

There are 250,000 Roman Catholics with 36 Missions, 100 Priests, 57 Brothers, 130 Sisters and 251 schools with 37,494 pupils.

Archbishop of Libreville: Mgr. ANDRÉ FERNAND ANGUILÉ.

Bishop of Mouila: Mgr. KWAOU; B.P. 95 Mouila.

Bishop of Oyem: Mgr. FRANÇOIS NDONG.

Protestant Missions:

Eglise Evangélique du Gabon: B.P. 80, Libreville; f. 1842; the Church has 20 Pastors, 180 African teachers, 4 colleges, 66 primary schools and 2 hospitals making a Christian community of about 60,000; Pres. Pastor BASIL NDONG AMVAME.

Christian and Missionary Alliance: The Alliance devotes its activities to the south of the country. There is a total Christian community of 16,000, 7 Pastors, 29 Missionaries, 1 college and several primary schools with 20 teachers.

PRESS

Libreville

Actualités gabonaises: Gabon Embassy, Paris, France; monthly review.

Bulletin quotidien d'Information: daily; issued by Agence Gabonaise d'Information; circ. 500.

Gabon d'Aujourd'hui: B.P. 750, Libreville; weekly; published by the Ministry of Information.

Gabon Matin: L'Agence gabonaise de presse, B.P. 168, Libreville; daily.

Bulletin Evangélique d'Information et de Presse (BEIP): B.P. 80; monthly; religious.

Patrie gabonaise: B.P. 168, Libreville; monthly.

Le Patriote: B.P. 469.

Bulletin Mensuel de la Chambre de Commerce d'Agriculture, d'Industrie et des Mines du Gabon: B.P. 2234; f. 1937.

Bulletin mensuel statistique de la République gabonaise: B.P. 179, Libreville; monthly bulletin of the National Service of Statistics.

Journal du Lycée de Libreville.

PRESS AGENCY

Agence Gabonaise d'Information: Libreville, B.P. 168.

RADIO AND TELEVISION

Radiodiffusion Télévision Gabonaise: Libreville, B.P. 150; started transmission 1959; Government station; programmes in French and local languages; 65,000 receivers; Dir. KOUNDA KIKI.

Radio-Gabon: Libreville; national service.

Radio-Moanda-Franceville: regional service.

Télévision Gabonaise: Libreville, B.P. 1029; started transmission 1963. There are about 65,000 receivers.

Director of Radio and Television PAUL OKUMBA D'OKWATSEGUE.

FINANCE

BANKS

(cap.=capital; amounts in francs CFA)

CENTRAL BANK

Banque Centrale des Etats de l'Afrique Equatoriale et du Cameroun: 29 Rue du Colisée, Paris; Libreville, B.P. 112; cap. 250m.; Dir. M. OYÉ MBA.

Banque Gabonaise de Développement: B.P. 5, Libreville; f. 1959; cap. 110m.; Pres. of Admin. Council MICHEL ANCHOUEY; Dir.-Gen. JEAN FÉLIX MAMALEPOT.

Banque Internationale pour l'Afrique Occidentale: Paris; B.P. 106, Libreville; f. 1965; Dir. RENÉ LACLABERE.

Banque Nationale de Paris: 16 blvd. des Italiens, Paris; Libreville, rue Schoelcher, B.P. 41; Dir. JEAN CHAPUT.

Union Gabonaise de Banque: Libreville, avenue Colonel-Parant, B.P. 315; f. 1962; cap. 450m.

INSURANCE

There are no national insurance companies, but some twenty foreign firms, notably the major French insurers, operate agencies in Gabon.

TRADE AND INDUSTRY

CHAMBER OF COMMERCE

Chambre de Commerce, d'Agriculture et d'Industrie et des Mines du Gabon: Libreville, B.P. 2234; f. 1937; regional offices at Port-Gentil, Oyem, Ndjoté, Mouila and Moanda; Pres. JEAN RÉMY AYOUNE.

EMPLOYERS' FEDERATIONS

Union Interprofessionnelle, Economique et Sociale du Gabon (UNIGABON): Libreville, B.P. 84; f. 1959; groups together the principal industrial, mining, public works, forestry and shipping concerns; Pres. M. VIALLET; Sec. Gen. M. J. KIEFFER.

Office National des Bois du Gabon (ONBG): B.P. 67, Libreville; Dir. PIERRE BARRAUD.

Syndicat Forestier du Gabon: B.P. 84, Libreville; Pres. M. DESVIGNE; Gen. Sec. J. KIEFFER.

Syndicat des Entreprises Minières du Gabon: Libreville, B.P. 578; f. 1960; Pres. M. JEANTET; Sec.-Gen. C. L. DURAND.

Syndicat Professionel des Usines de Sciages et Placages du Gabon: Pres. M. POUZIN.

Syndicat des Commerçants Importateurs et Exportateurs (SCIMPEX—Gabon): Pres. M. JEAN.

TRADE UNIONS

Confédération Gabonaise des Travailleurs Croyants: B.P. 361, Libreville; f. 1956; 8,000 mems.; 19 affiliates; affiliated with the International Federation of Christian Trade Unions and the Pan-African Union of Christian Workers; Sec.-Gen. WALKER ANGUILET.

Fédération Générale des Travailleurs du Gabon: B.P. 1046, Libreville; f. 1962; 6,800 mems.; 4 affiliates; affiliated to ICFTU; Sec.-Gen. LAURENT ESSONE-NDONG.

MAJOR INDUSTRIAL COMPANIES

The following are some of the largest companies in terms either of capital investment or employment.

Société des Brasseries du Gabon (SOBRAGA): B.P. 20, Libreville; f. 1966; cap. 375m. francs CFA.

Manufacture of beer and soft drinks.

Pres. Dir.-Gen. PIERRE CASTEL; Dir. A. BERTON.

ELF-SPAFE: B.P. 525, Port-Gentil; f. 1934; name changed to Société des pétroles d'Afrique équatoriale (SPAFE) 1960, and now associated with ELF/ERAP, Shell, Gulf and Chevron; cap. 15,000m. francs CFA.

Prospecting for and mining of petroleum.

Pres. Dir.-Gen. M. LUGOL; Dir. M. JEANTET; 860 employees.

Société Equatoriale de Raffinage: B.P. 530, Port-Gentil; f. 1965 by governments of Cameroon, Congo, Gabon, Tchad and Central African Republic; cap. 1,200m. francs CFA.

Refines locally mined crude oil.

860 employees.

Société pour l'Expansion des Boissons Hygiéniques au Gabon (SEBOGA): Libreville; cap. 200m. francs CFA.

Import and distribution of beer and soft drinks; since 1972 manufacture of soft drinks.

Société d'Exploitations Gabonaises: B.P. 66, Port-Gentil; f. 1934; cap. 254m. francs CFA.

Timber industry and sawmills.

Pres. Dir.-Gen. ROLAND BRU.

Société Gabonaise de Grands Magasins (GABOMA): B.P. 2104, Libreville; f. 1967; cap. 200m. francs CFA.

General retail trade.

Pres. Dir.-Gen. J. JOIGNY; Dir.-Gen. J. CARRIERE; 200 employees.

Société Gabonaise des Oleágineux: B.P. 633, Libreville; f. 1962; two-thirds state participation; cap. 30m. francs CFA.

Palm oil plantations.

Pres. Dir.-Gen. DANIEL ASSOUMOU.

Société de Gestion de la Compagnie Française du Gabon: B.P. 521, Port-Gentil; head office 46 rue Boissière, Paris 16e; f. 1953; cap. 371m. francs CFA.

Manufacture of timber and plywood.

Pres. Dir.-Gen. ANDRÉ CHARRON; Dir.-Gen. ROBERT AUZANNEAU; 1,500 employees.

Société Industrielle Textile du Gabon: B.P. 1171, Libreville; f. 1968; cap. 130m. francs CFA.

Textile printing.

Dir. ROGER GAILLARD.

Société des Mines de Fer de Mekambo: B.P. 4, Makokou; f. 1960; cap. 200m. francs CFA.

Mineral prospecting and future iron ore mining.

Pres. GERARD DE L'EPINE.

Compagnie des Mines d'Uranium de Franceville: B.P. 578, Libreville; f. 1958; cap. 1,000m. francs CFA.

Pres. JACQUES LUCIUS.

Société meunière et avicole du Gabon (SMAG): f. 1969; cap. 140m. francs CFA, of which 28 per cent is state-owned.

Production of eggs, cattle-food, flour for bread-making.

Compagnie Minière de l'Ogooué (COMILOG): B.P. 578, Libreville; f. 1953; cap. 4,000m. francs CFA.

Manganese mining.

Pres. ANDRE LAURAINT; Dir.-Gen. HENRI SYLVOZ.

Palmiers et Hévéas du Gabon (PALMEVEA): B.P. 326, Libreville; f. 1956; cap. 145m. francs CFA; 49 per cent of shares owned by the Government, 51 per cent by subsidiary of U.A.C.

Production of palm oil from the produce of 80 hectares.

Dir. Dr. KAUFMANN.

Shell Gabon: B.P. 146, Port-Gentil; f. 1960; cap. 1,000m francs CFA.

Prospecting for and mining of petroleum oil in Gabon.

Pres. M. LACOUR-GAYET; Dir.-Gen. M. CREPET; 410 employees.

TRANSPORT AND TOURISM

TRANSPORT

RAILWAYS

Chemin de Fer de Gabon: Ministère chargé de Mission, Libreville; Sec. PAUL MOUKAMBI.

The manganese mine at Moanda is connected with Pointe-Noire by a 76-km. cableway and a 296-km. railway. Work will begin in 1973 on a 330km. railway from Owenda to Booué, which will eventually be extended to Belinga, a total of 560 km.

ROADS

The total network of 6,031 km. (1971) includes 2,722 km. main roads, of which 103 km. are tarred, and 2,212 km. secondary roads, of which 48 km. are tarred; 350 km. of new road is under construction.

SHIPPING

The two principal ports are Port-Gentil (mainly for timber exports) and Libreville. A deep-water commercial port is under construction at Owendo.

Société Navale Chargeurs Delmas Vieljeux: Libreville, B.P. 77 and 2121, and Port-Gentil, B.P. 522; merged with Compagnie Maritime de Chargeurs Réunis in 1971.

SOAEM: B.P. 72, Libreville and B.P. 518 Port-Gentil; shipping freight.

CIVIL AVIATION

International airports at Libreville and Port-Gentil. Twenty-six other public aerodromes and 55 private ones linked mostly with forestry and oil industries.

Air Gabon: Port-Gentil, B.P. 240; f. 1956; the fleet comprises two Beechcraft 18, one Cessna 310, two Britten-Norman Islanders, one B.-N. Trislander, one Piper Aztec, one Piper Seneca, one Piper Cherokee, one Navajo, two Twin Comanches and seven helicopters. Gen. Man. PIERRE NICAISE, Man. CHARLES GUILLOTEAU; 73 employees.

Transgabon (Société Nationale Transgabon): Libreville, B.P. 2206, and Port-Gentil, B.P. 199; f. 1951; internal cargo and passenger services; fleet comprises one DC-4, three DC-3, one Britten-Norman Islander, one Bonanza. Pres. PAUL OKUMBA; Dir.-Gen. J. C. BROUILLET; 175 employees.

Air Afrique: Gabon has a seven per cent share in Air Afrique; *see* Ivory Coast.

Air Zaire and UTA also operate services to Libreville.

TOURISM

Office National Gabonais du Tourisme: B.P. 403, Libreville; Commissioner General ATHANASE BOUANGA.

POWER

Société d'Energie et d'Eau du Gabon: B.P. 1187, Libreville; f. 1950; semi-public company; cap. 550m. francs CFA.

Production and distribution of electricity and drinking water

Dir.-Gen. JEAN VIOLAS; 600 employees.

In 1971 production reached 114 million kWh.

EDUCATION

In line with the policy of "Gabonization" of management, education is a high priority and currently receives 18.7 per cent of the budget. Almost all the population (97 per cent) has attended or is attending school, and there is a literacy campaign for adults. Since 1960 several institutions of higher education have been opened: *École gabonaise d'administration* (1962), *Institut polytechnique* (1964), which will form a future faculty of sciences, *Institut de technologie universitaire* (1970), which trains engineers, and the National University (1970).

LEARNED SOCIETY AND RESEARCH INSTITUTES

Alliance Française: Franceville.

Bureau de Recherches Géologiques et Minières: B.P. 175, Libreville; f. 1960; Dir. M. ARNOULD.

Centre Technique Forestier Tropical: Section Gabon; B.P. 149, Libreville.

CNRS Mission Biologique du Gabon: B.P. 18, Libreville-Makokon; Dir. A. BROSSET.

Institut de Recherches Agronomiques Tropicales et des Cultures Vivrières (IRAT): B.P. 43, Libreville; Dir. G. COURS D'ARNE.

Office de la Recherche Scientifique et Technique Outre-Mer Centre ORSTOM de Libreville: B.P. 3115, Libreville (Gros-Bouquet):f. 1960; hydrology, pedology, sociology, psychosociology, ethnology, ethnomusicology; Dir. D. MARTIN.

LIBRARY

Bibliothèque du Centre d'Information: Libreville; f. 1960; 6,000 vols.; 80 current periodicals.

UNIVERSITY AND COLLEGES

UNIVERSITÉ NATIONALE DU GABON

BOULEVARD LÉON M'BA, LIBREVILLE

Founded 1970

Number of teachers: 50 full-time, 25 part-time.
Number of students: c. 550.

Ecole Gabonaise d'Administration: Libreville.

Ecole Territoriale d'Agriculture: Oyem.

Institut Gabonais d'Etudes Juridiques: P.O.B. 46, Libreville.

Institut Polytechnique de l'Afrique Centrale: B.P. 1158, Libreville; f. 1964; Dir. P. LAFITTE.

SELECT BIBLIOGRAPHY

For works on the former A.E.F. countries generally *see* Central African Republic Select Bibliography, p. 227.)

BOUQUEREL, JACQUELINE. *Le Gabon*. Paris, Presses universitaires de France, 1970.

CHARBONNIER, FRANÇOIS. *Gabon: Terre d'avenir*. Paris, Ed. Maritimes et Coloniales, 1957.

COMMISSARIAT AU PLAN. *Comptes économiques du Gabon*. Libreville, 1968.

DESCHAMPS, HUBERT. *Traditions orales et archives du Gabon*. Paris, Berger-Levrault, 1962.

HANCE, W. A., and VAN DONGEN, I. S. "Gabon and its main gateways", *Tijdschrift v. Econ. en Soc. Geog.* II, pp. 286–95, 1961.

HILLING, D. "The Changing Economy of Gabon", *Geography*, 1963, 155–65.

INTERNATIONAL MONETARY FUND. *Surveys of African Economies*, Vol. I. Washington, D.C., 1968.

McKAY, J. "West Central Africa" in MANSELL PROTHERO R. (Ed.), *A Geography of Africa*, London, 1969.

NEUHOFF, H. O. *Gabun*. Berlin, Springer-Verlag, 1967.

RAPONDA-WALKER, ANDRÉ. *Notes d'histoire du Gabon*. Montpellier, imprimerie Charité, 1960.

VENNETIER, P. "Problems of port development in Gabon and Congo", Ch. II in HOYLE, B. S. and HILLING, D. (Eds.), *Seaports and Development in Tropical Africa*, London, 1970.

The Gambia

PHYSICAL AND SOCIAL GEOGRAPHY*

R. J. Harrison Church

The Republic of The Gambia is Africa's smallest state, for its area is but 4,261 sq. miles. Its population, estimated in 1971 at 380,000, is the smallest excepting only Equatorial Guinea. Apart from a very short coastline The Gambia is an enclave in Senegal. The two countries have common physical and social phenomena, but differ in history, colonial experience and economic affiliations.

The Gambia is essentially the valley of the navigable Gambia River, Africa's only good waterway. Around the estuary (2 miles wide at its narrowest point) and the lower river the state is 30 miles wide, and extends eastward either side of the navigable river for 292 miles. In most places the country is only 15 miles wide with but one or two villages within it on either bank, away from mangrove or marsh. The former extends a hundred miles upstream, the limit of the tide in the rainy season, although in the dry season the tide penetrates another 37 miles upstream.

Some mangrove on the landward sides has been removed for swamp rice cultivation. Behind are seasonally flooded marshes with fresh water grasses, and then on the upper slopes of Tertiary sandstone there is woodland with fallow bush and areas cultivated mainly with groundnuts and millet, the important cash and food crops. Annual rainfall in The Gambia averages 30–45 in. Ocean vessels of draughts of up to 19 ft. can always reach Kuntaur, 150 miles upstream, and those of lesser draught Georgetown, 176 miles upstream. River vessels regularly call at Fatoto, 288 miles upstream, the last of 33 wharf towns served by schooners or river boats. Unfortunately, this fine waterway is underutilized because it is largely cut off from its natural hinterland by the nearby boundary.

* See map on p. 708.

RECENT HISTORY

A. G. Hopkins†

A recent book on The Gambia's achievement of independence is sub-titled *The Birth of an Improbable Nation*, and it is undoubtedly true that in the eyes of foreign observers the country has a somewhat quixotic image. The oddity lies not simply in the granting of independence to such a tiny and financially dependent territory, but in the country's very existence. For Gambians themselves, however, the quixotic is reality, and the improbabilities are hard facts which lie at the centre of their modern history and future prospects.

The modern history of The Gambia dates from 1888–89. In 1888 the country was made into a separate colony, having previously been administered in association with other British possessions in west Africa. This event, however, was not an expression of Britain's desire to extend her rule in that part of the world. On the contrary, in the 1860s and 1870s The Gambia was used as a pawn in negotiations with France with the aim of exchanging it for more desirable territory elsewhere. The fact that the colony remained in British hands was the result of pressure from British merchants trading there, together with the failure of the government to strike a satisfactory bargain with the French. In 1889 a boundary settlement was reached with France which drew the frontiers tightly round the new colony, leaving it as a small spike in the side of the large and still growing colony of Senegal. This development, which was the result of a combination of French enterprise and British lassitude cut across the economic and cultural unity of the region as a whole, and posed problems of viability which The Gambia has had to face ever since.

In the years between 1888 and 1945 (that is the greater part of the colonial period) The Gambia acquired many of the classic features of British imperial rule. The customary machinery of colonial government was established at Bathurst, consisting of a Governor, a handful of expatriate assistants, and Executive and Legislative Councils. The Gambian administration was too small to be either despotic or effectively enlightened. Down to 1945 it concerned itself mainly with keeping the peace and collecting taxes. Admittedly, the government had to spend

† For the 1973 edition, revisions have been made to this article by the Editor.

money as well as gather it, but since over two-thirds of the budget was automatically accounted for by the salaries and pensions of officials, the problem of what to do with the remainder was scarcely a major issue. The two dominant principles of self-sufficiency and minimum government made indirect rule inevitable from the outset. Outside a small area around Bathurst, the country was divided into administrative regions in which the chiefs, though supervised by Travelling Commissioners, were allowed to continue ruling their people. Groundnuts, the mainstay of the export economy, were already the staple item of overseas trade before 1888, and their subsequent development owed little or nothing to government action. Thus the impact of British rule was very limited, and its principal effect was to consolidate the *status quo* rather than to begin a process of cumulative economic, political and social change.

After 1945 The Gambia was affected by a number of changes which eventually led to independence in 1965. These were partly initiated by the British of their own accord, and were partly the result of pressures exerted by political organizations in The Gambia. The dialogue between the two was on the whole orderly and constructive: the British had no real desire to retain The Gambia, which had become a financial liability in the 1950s, while the Gambians, though anxious to run their own affairs, realized that it was important for them to maintain good relations with Britain. Otherwise, they might be driven, for economic reasons, into a disadvantageous association with Senegal.

After the Second World War the British began to modify their ideas of colonial government, and more money was spent on The Gambia. Bathurst harbour was improved and a start was made on modernizing the colony's roads. The years 1948–51 saw a major attempt to diversify exports, with the launching (and sinking) of a project for the large-scale production of eggs. The fiasco of the Yundum egg scheme, which lost nearly £1 million, left the colony as dependent on groundnuts as it had been a hundred years before. Less erratic, but slow progress was made in improving social services. In 1940 there were only six primary schools in the whole of the large protectorate area. By 1960 the number had risen to thirty-seven, and in the 1950s some Gambians were also being trained for senior posts in the civil service. Medical services had long been neglected: the infant mortality rate was high, and malaria and malnutrition were (and still are) common. By the early 1960s a number of dispensaries had been established outside Bathurst, which contained the colony's only hospital. All the same, the advance was scarcely revolutionary. In 1961 there were still only five doctors serving the whole country.

INDEPENDENCE

Political developments tended to lag behind, and take their cue from, progress made elsewhere, notably in Ghana and Nigeria. Modern political parties did not develop until the 1950s. The first three major parties (the Democratic Party, the Muslim Congress Party and the United Party) based their support mainly on the Wolaf inhabitants of Bathurst. Sir Dawda Jawara's People's Progressive Party, which was formed in 1960, was the first to draw its strength from the hinterland by appealing successfully to the numerically dominant Mandingo people, and by emphasizing the neglect which the interior had suffered. The chief aim of all parties at this time was to secure increased representation for the Gambian people. In 1960 elections to a House of Representatives were held under a new constitution. The results were indecisive, but they did demonstrate that universal suffrage had deprived the chiefs of much of their support. The Colonial Office then decided to press ahead and grant full internal self-government. A new constitution was drawn up in 1962, and The Gambia became self-governing in the following year. The government which brought The Gambia to independence in 1965 was a coalition led by Sir Dawda and P. S. N'Jie, a former Chief Minister and founder of the United Party.

The years since independence have been remarkable mainly for their stability: of the four former British territories in west Africa, The Gambia is the only one not to have experienced a military *coup*. The People's Progressive Party, still led by Sir Dawda, has remained in power, though P. S. N'Jie has been in opposition since 1966. In 1970 The Gambia became a Republic; Sir Dawda, its first President, was re-elected in the March 1972 general elections, when his People's Progressive Party won 28 of the 32 elected seats. The two major pre-occupations of the government have been economic development and relations with Senegal. These are large problems which will take many years to solve, but a start was made in 1967. A five year-plan covering agriculture, transport and education was launched, and the same priorities were laid down in the succeeding 1971–74 plan. Also in 1967 a treaty of association was concluded with Senegal, though this did not prevent underlying Gambian fears of absorbtion by her larger neighbour occasionally coming to the surface. One such instance was in January, 1971 when a drive by the Senegalese against smuggling led to minor border incidents between the two countries. Relations were soon patched up, however. In March a joint defence and security agreement was concluded and later President Jawara paid visits to Dakar and Paris.

ECONOMY

Douglas Rimmer

Note on the Currency Unit

The West African Currency Board pound was replaced by The Gambian pound in 1965, without change in the one-for-one parity with sterling. The Gambian pound was devalued along with sterling in November 1967 to maintain the local value of Currency Board and Marketing Board reserves, and of British aid. In March 1971 the Central Bank of The Gambia was inaugurated, and in July 1971 a new, decimalized currency was adopted, replacing the old at the rate of five dalasis to the pound. The parity with sterling was maintained following the floating of the pound in June 1972.

GROUNDNUTS

Even by tropical African standards The Gambia is minute as a national economy, with a population of perhaps 380,000 (315,000 at the census of April 1963) contained in an area of 4,000 sq. miles along the banks of The Gambia river, and a gross domestic product put at £17.1 million in 1970/71. Groundnuts (including, in recent years, 40–60 per cent of the crop processed as oil) have for long constituted all but a few per cent of exports of domestic produce, but there is also a substantial re-export trade, partly illicit, with the surrounding territory of Senegal. The state of trade in The Gambia therefore depends partly on movements of purchasing power in Senegal. The main influence on The Gambian prosperity is, however, the value of groundnut exports. This depends on the size of harvests and on movements of world prices, which are unaffected by The Gambia's own output. The government's recurrent budget is financed very largely by import duties and taxation of groundnut exports, and consequently is vulnerable to changes in the value of external trade.

Poor groundnut harvests at the beginning of the 1960s led to dependence on a British grant-in-aid for the balancing of the recurrent budget, and agreement was reached that this assistance might continue to be provided after independence. But, as a result of an increase in the value of external trade, the grant-in-aid was dispensed with from 1967/68 onward. Purchases for export by The Gambia Produce Marketing Board, the statutory monopoly, have risen from an average of about 70,000 long tons p.a. of undecorticated nuts in the early 1960s to 120,000 tons p.a. in the last seven crop-years (1965/66–1971/72). This result is attributed to the continuing influx of non-Gambian farmers, and to government extension work and the increasing use of fertilizers. It has also owed something to a growth of illicit exports of Senegalese groundnuts to The Gambia; relative producer prices have moved in favour of The Gambia since 1967. Expectations that Gambian purchases would drop to 100,000 tons p.a. in the early 1970s, with improvements in Senegalese purchasing arrangements, have not yet been fulfilled. As it happens, world groundnut prices have been at unusually high levels in 1970–72.

FINANCE AND DEVELOPMENT

Financial dependence on the U.K. for development expenditure continues. Of the £3.32 million spent under the 1967–71 development programme, £2.86 million was provided as interest-free loans by the U.K., which has also promised at least £2 million towards the 1971–74 programme of £4.2 million. The Gambia also receives U.K. technical assistance valued at £250,000 p.a. Recurrent expenditure is presently running at about £4.0 million p.a. and development expenditure at under one million pounds. Recorded exports averaged £6.4 million p.a. during 1968–72 and imports nearly £8.4 million. The recorded trade deficit and net invisible payments are covered partly by external aid and partly by surplus on the contraband account with Senegal.

The development programmes have been concentrated on transport and communications and the raising of yields of groundnuts and of rice (the staple food), with some attempt to diversify production. Rice imports have been running at 10–14,000 tons p.a., but swamp rice cultivation is being developed with technical assistance from Taiwan and a loan from the International Development Association, and there are hopes of achieving self-sufficiency in the crop. Pilot schemes of production of cotton and limes are under way. Tourism (mainly from Sweden) has caught on, though there are doubts as to its value to The Gambia. The river serves as a major artery of trade and transport, and all-weather road mileage has more than doubled since 1960. The 1971–74 development programme includes major improvements of the airport at Yundum and modernization and enlargement of the port of Bathurst (an interest-free loan of £875,000 for the first phase of the latter project has been obtained from the International Development Association). The UN Development Programme has undertaken a new survey of the river at the joint request of The Gambia and Senegal.

RELATIONS WITH SENEGAL

Some form of integration with Senegal has often been suggested to be the natural destiny of The Gambia, as an enclave within a country of twenty times its own area. From the official Senegalese standpoint The Gambia is an inconvenience, both because it divides Senegal physically and because it is a smuggling base. Smuggling of manufactured imports into Senegal goes on because the Gambians have freer access than the Senegalese to world sources of supply; and because the over-valuation of the CFA franc makes imported manufactures cheap relative to Senegalese manufactures, provided they can be got free of duty or at Gambian rates of duty, which are generally lower than Senegalese rates. Smuggling of Senegalese groundnuts into The Gambia is probably mainly a matter of physical convenience for Senegalese farmers in the vicinity of the river, and the "loss" of, say, 20,000 tons in a Senegalese crop of up to a million would not appear to be critical. There are, of course, interests in Senegal which favour a continuation of the smuggling trade, and, even from the official standpoint, the activity serves a useful role as a scapegoat. A customs union of the two territories has been under fitful discussion since 1964. It is difficult, however, to see any advantage to Gambian residents in an alignment of The Gambia's tariffs with those of Senegal, or in preferential treatment of Senegalese manufactures in Gambian markets. Some forms of economic co-operation between the countries, notably in the development of the River Gambia, might be worthwhile, but a customs union would not appear to be essential for this purpose, except perhaps as a price exacted by the Senegalese.

Despite The Gambia's size, its economic record in the last decade compares favourably with that of most other West African countries. Service of external debt represented only 1 per cent of the value of exports in 1970. External reserves stood at nearly £8.7 million in April 1972, over a year's worth of imports.

The Marketing Board has been able to subsidize groundnut producer prices (as in 1967/68), whilst in recent years its stabilization reserve has grown despite increases of the producer price from £27 in 1967 to £36 in 1972. Smallness has been advantageous in discouraging wilder ambitions, and the economy has not had to support such encumbrances as air and shipping lines, a university, subsidized manufacturing industries, or armed forces. By African standards, the human and livestock population densities are high, and, in the light of estimated rates of increase, the government recognizes a need for more intensive agricultural practices. The dependence of the government's development expenditure on external aid is likely to persist, and the country's dependence on a single cash crop leaves it exceptionally exposed to fluctuations in its harvests and in world prices for oilseeds. Consequent on the United Kingdom's entry to the European Economic Community, The Gambia will seek associated status on the basis of the Yaoundé Convention, since otherwise its groundnut oil exports —which earn about two-fifths of its foreign exchange —would face a 10 per cent tariff in the U.K.

STATISTICAL SURVEY

Area: 4,261 square miles.

Population (mid-1971 est.): 378,730; Bathurst 36,570. Nearly half the inhabitants belong to the Mandingo tribe.

Employment: (Sept. 1970) Central and Local Government 6,278, Commercial and others 2,224.

AGRICULTURE

PRINCIPAL CROPS
(Production—'000 metric tons)

	1969	1970	1971
Millet and Sorghum . .	45*	30*	45*
Rice (Paddy) . . .	66	50	60*
Cassava (Manioc) . .	6*	6*	n.a.
Bananas . . .	80	85	n.a.
Palm Kernels (exports only)	2	2	2*
Groundnuts (unshelled) ..	114	117	117

* FAO estimate.

Source: FAO, *Production Yearbook 1971.*

Livestock (mid-1971): Cattle 260,000, Goats 107,586, Sheep 100,000, Pigs 3,000, Poultry 300,000.

FINANCE

100 butut = 1 dalasi.

Coins: 1, 5, 25 and 50 butut.

Notes: 1, 5 and 25 dalasi.

Exchange rates (December 1972): £1 sterling = 5.00 dalasi; U.S. $1 = 2.13 dalasi.

100 dalasi = £20 = $46.96.

(*Note:* The dalasi was introduced on July 1st, 1971, replacing the Gambia pound at the rate of G£1 = 5.00 dalasi. Some of the figures below are given in G£.)

BUDGET

RECURRENT REVENUE AND EXPENDITURE
(£)

	REVISED ESTIMATES			ESTIMATES
	1969–70	1970–71	1971–72	1972–73
Revenue	3,276,258	5,086,635	4,087,762	3,930,326
Expenditure	3,656,460	4,661,273	4,349,844	3,997,004
Deficit or Surplus . . .	−380,202	425,362	−262,082	−66,678

Four Year Plan (1971-74): 21,000,000 dalasi; Communications 10,197,000; Agriculture 4,135,375; Education 1,195,000.

GROSS DOMESTIC PRODUCT
(£'000)

	1968–69	1969–70	1970–71
Agriculture, Forestry and Fishing . . .	8,688.9	8,751.1	9,526.8
Quarrying	62.7	59.0	62.5
Manufacturing	352.3	392.3	375.8
Construction	62.5	73.4	63.0
Electricity and Water	50.3	50.7	51.6
Wholesale and Retail Trade . . .	2,683.6	2,795.3	3,218.9
Transport and Communications . .	833.6	639.8	1,019.1
Financial Services	163.3	177.0	148.4
Public Administration	1,075.1	1,040.0	1,154.1
Miscellaneous Services	1,083.1	1,317.9	1,502.7
GROSS DOMESTIC PRODUCT AT CURRENT FACTOR COSTS	15,055.4	15,296.5	17,122.9
Import Duties	2,151.4	1,695.3	2,000.0
GROSS DOMESTIC PRODUCT AT CURRENT PRICES	17,206.8	16,991.8	19,122.9

BALANCE OF PAYMENTS
(£ million)

	1968–69	1969–70	1970–71
Current Account:			
Visible Trade:			
Exports (f.o.b.)	7.4	6.6	8.0
Imports (f.o.b.)	−8.7	−6.7	−8.8
Trade Balance	−1.3	−0.1	−0.8
Invisible Balance	−0.7	−0.4	−0.8
BALANCE ON CURRENT ACCOUNT . .	−2.0	−0.5	−1.6
Capital Account:			
Marketing Board	−0.5	−0.1	−0.1
Government Capital	0.9	0.5	0.7
Private Capital	—	—	0.5
BALANCE ON CAPITAL ACCOUNT .	0.4	0.4	1.1
Overall Surplus or Deficit . . .	−1.6	−0.1	−0.5
Monetary Institutions:			
Commercial Banks	−0.1	—	−0.2
Official Institutions	0.1	−1.0	−1.2
TOTAL MONETARY INSTITUTIONS .	—	−1.0	−1.4
Net Unrecorded Items	1.6	1.1	1.9

EXTERNAL TRADE
(£'000)

Imports: (1966–67) 7,083, (1967–68) 7,520, (1968–69) 9,329, (1969–70) 7,123.1.
Exports: (1966–67) 6,133, (1967–68) 5,366, (1968–69) 7,377, (1969–70) 6,557.4.

PRINCIPAL COMMODITIES

IMPORTS	1968–69		1969–70	
	Quantity (tons)	Value (£'000)	Quantity (tons)	Value (£'000)
Rice	12,309	813	13,994	690,394
Wheat Flour	2,453	117	2,610	130,931
Kola Nuts	458	62	5,109	63,777
Sugar and Confectionery . .	7,845	298	6,570	331,998
Tobacco and Cigarettes . .	400	435	316	677,637
Other Food and Drink . .	—	627	—	361,676
Petroleum Products . . .	—	281	—	254,590
Fabrics, Cotton and Synthetic .	—	2,527	—	1,255,381
Clothing	—	240	—	146,304
Footwear	—	147	—	96,493
Bags and Sacks . . .	—	108	—	156,443
Medicines and Drugs . .	—	199	—	144,186
Cement	17,380	140	7,543	94,114
Metal Sheets . . .	503	54	—	256,995
Machinery (except Electrical) .	—	325	—	257,688
Radio Sets	—	279	—	139,402
Motor Cars and Lorries . .	—	400	—	253,686
All Other Goods . . .	—	2,279	—	1,881,451

EXPORTS	1968–69		1969–70	
	Quantity (tons)	Value (£'000)	Quantity (tons)	Value (£'000)
Groundnuts, Shelled . . .	52,170	4,065	37,521	3,065
Groundnut Meal . . .	27,507	1,156	29,543	894
Groundnut Oil . . .	10,506	1,721	5,745	2,293
Palm Kernels . . .	2,448	165	1,556	101
Dried Fish . . .	667	27	864	45
All Other Goods . . .	—	35	—	159

PRINCIPAL COUNTRIES
(G£'000)

IMPORTS	1966/67	1967/68	1968/69	EXPORTS	1966/67	1967/68	1968/69
Burma . . .	338	314	135	Belgium . . .	146	121	138
China (People's Republic) .	374	473	1,223	Czechoslovakia . .	—	251	176
France . . .	186	165	233	France . . .	18	133	1,095
Federal Germany .	168	217	303	Federal Germany .	38	140	84
Hong Kong . .	197	167	266	Italy . . .	466	126	154
Japan . . .	1,344	1,128	1,734	Netherlands . .	35	485	803
Netherlands . .	226	277	285	Portugal . . .	1,333	280	1,007
United Kingdom .	2,553	3,041	2,851	Senegal . . .	1	8	475
				Switzerland . .	385	79	407
				United Kingdom .	3,670	3,698	2,817
TOTAL . . .	7,083	7,520	9,329	TOTAL . . .	6,133	5,366	7,377

Source: UN *Yearbook of International Trade Statistics 1969.*

TRANSPORT

Roads (1970): Cars and Commercial Vehicles 2,730 (licences issued).

Shipping (1970–71): Principal port Bathurst; Ships entered 303, Tonnage entered 623,661.

Civil Aviation (1968): 1,948 planes landed.

EDUCATION
(Dec. 1970)

	SCHOOLS	TEACHERS	PUPILS
Primary . . .	95	690	16,867
Secondary . .	21	328	5,178
Vocational . .	2	18	181
Teacher Training .	1	12	149

Sources (unless stated): President's Office, Bathurst; Standard Bank *Annual Economic Review: Sierra Leone & The Gambia*, August 1971.

THE CONSTITUTION

The present Constitution came into effect on April 24th, 1970, when The Gambia became a Republic.

The President is Head of State and Commander-in-Chief of the armed forces. There is a Vice-President who is leader of government business in the House.

The House of Representatives consist of a Speaker and a Deputy Speaker (elected by the House) and 32 Members (elected by universal adult suffrage), 4 Chiefs (elected by the Chiefs in Assembly), 3 nominated Members, and the Attorney-General. Parliaments have a five-year term.

THE GOVERNMENT

PRESIDENT AND CABINET

(*November* 1972)

President: Sir Dawda Jawara.

Vice-President and Minister of External Affairs: A. D. Camara.

Minister of Finance: J. M. Garba Jahumpa.

Minister of Education: Alhaji M. C. Cham.

Minister of Health and Labour: Alhaji K. Singateh.

Minister of State, President's Office: B. L. Sanyang.

Minister of Agriculture: A. B. N'Jie.

Minister of Local Government: Alhaji Yaya Ceasay.

Minister of Works and Communications: Alhaji A. S. Jack.

Attorney-General: Alhaji M. L. Saho.

DIPLOMATIC REPRESENTATION

HIGH COMMISSIONS AND EMBASSIES
ACCREDITED TO THE GAMBIA
(In Bathurst unless otherwise stated)
(HC) High Commission; (E) Embassy.

Algeria: (E); *Ambassador:* Aziz Haceme.

China, Republic of (Taiwan): (E); *Ambassador:* Dr. Mei-Sheng Shu.

France: (E); Dakar, Senegal.

Germany, Federal Republic: Dakar, Senegal (E).

Guinea: (E); *Ambassador:* Kassory B. Bangoura.

India: Dakar, Senegal (HC).

Italy: Dakar, Senegal (E).

Mali: Dakar, Senegal (E).

Mauritania: Dakar, Senegal (E).

Nigeria: (HC); *High Commissioner:* M. Sani (acting).

Senegal: (E); *Ambassador:* Saher Gaye.

Sierra Leone (HC); *High Commissioer:* Alieu Badra Mansaray.

United Kingdom: 78 Wellington St.; *High Commissioner:* J. R. W. Parker.

U.S.A.: (E); *Chargé d'Affaires:* C. C. Strong.

The Gambia also has diplomatic relations with Austria, Belgium, Canada, Czechoslovakia, Egypt, Ghana, Hungary, Israel. Japan. Korean Republic, Lebanon. Libya, Morocco, Netherlands, Pakistan, Spain. Sweden, Switzerland, Tunisia, Turkey, U.S.S.R., Republic of Viet-Nam and Zambia.

NATIONAL ASSEMBLY

(Election March 1972)

	Seats
People's Progressive Party . .	28
United Party . . .	3
Independent . . .	1

Speaker: (vacant).

Nominated Members (without vote): Alhaji Sir Alieu Suleyman Jack, M. B. N'Jie, Jallow Sanneh, The Attorney-General.

POLITICAL PARTIES

People's Progressive Party (PPP): f. 1958; Leader Sir Dawda Jawara; advocates economic and cultural links with Senegal; merged with Gambia Congress Party 1968.

United Party (UP): P.O.B. 63, Buckle St., Bathurst; f. 1952; approx. 131,000 mems.; Leader P. S. N'Jie; Gen. Sec. Coun. K. W. Foon.

People's Progressive Alliance (PPA): Bathurst; f. 1968; formed by four former ministers expelled from PPP in September 1968; Leader Sherif Sisay.

DEFENCE

There is no army, but the 560-strong civil police includes a field force of 150 men.

JUDICIAL SYSTEM

The judicial system of the Gambia is based on English Common Law but includes subsidiary legislative instruments enacted locally, and a Muslim Law Recognition Ordinance by which a Muslim Court exercises jurisdiction in certain cases between, or exclusively affecting, Muslims.

The Supreme Court: Consists of the Chief Justice and the Puisne Judge; has unlimited jurisdiction; appeal lies to the Court of Appeal.

Chief Justice: P. R. Bridges, Q.C., C.M.G.

Puisne Judge: A. Nithianandan.

Master and Registrar: R. R. C. Joiner (acting).

The Gambia Court of Appeal: Established in 1961 to succeed the Sierra Leone and the Gambia Court of Appeal. It is the Superior Court of Record and consists of a President, Justices of Appeal and other Judges of the Supreme Court *ex officio*.

President: C. F. Dove Edwin (acting).

Justice of Appeal: J. B. Marcus Jones.

The Bathurst Magistrates Court, the Kanifing Magistrates Court and the **Divisional Courts:** the subordinate courts are all courts of summary jurisdiction presided over by a Magistrate or in his absence by two or more lay Justices of the Peace. They have limited civil and criminal jurisdiction, and appeal lies from these courts to the Supreme Court.

The Muslim Courts have jurisdiction in matters between, or exclusively affecting, Muslim Gambians and relating to civil status, marriage, succession, donations, testaments and guardianship. The Courts administer Muslim Law. A Cadi, or a Cadi and two assessors, preside over and constitute a Muslim Court. Assessors of the Muslim Courts are Justices of the Peace of Muslim faith.

Group Tribunals are established by the Government under the Group Tribunals Ordinance, 1933. Group Tribunals may try criminal cases which can be adequately punished by 12 months' imprisonment or a fine of £25 or both, and civil cases up to a £50 suit value. Their jurisdiction in land matters is unlimited.

RELIGION

ISLAM

Imam of Bathurst: Alhaji MOMODU LAMIN BAH.

The vast majority of the people are Muslims.

AFRICAN RELIGIONS

There are a few animists, mostly of the Jola tribe.

ANGLICAN

PROVINCE OF WEST AFRICA

Archbishop of the Province of West Africa and Bishop of Sierra Leone: Most. Rev. M. N. C. O. SCOTT, D.D., DIP.TH., Bishopscourt, P.O.B. 128, Freetown, Sierra Leone.

Bishop of the Gambia and the Rio Pongas: Rt. Rev. JEAN RIGAL ELISEE, M.A., Bishop's House, P.O.B. 51, Bathurst.

(For other sees in the Province of West Africa *see* under Nigeria, Religion.)

ROMAN CATHOLIC

Bishop of Bathurst: Most Rev. MICHAEL MOLONEY, C.B.E., C.S.SP., D.D.

OTHER CHURCHES

Methodist Church: Rev. E. S. C. CLARKE, P.O.B. 288, Bathurst.

THE PRESS

Gambia Echo: 2 Russell St., Bathurst; weekly; circ. 400. Editor J. R. FORSTER.

Gambia News Bulletin: Bathurst; Government newspaper issued 3 times weekly; Editor the Dir. of Information and Broadcasting Services, Bathurst; circ. 2,000.

Gambia Onward: Bathurst; thrice weekly; duplicated; Editor R. ALLEN.

Progressive: Bathurst; thrice weekly; duplicated; Editor M'BAKE N'JIE.

The Nation: People's Press Printers, Bathurst, P.O.B. 334; fortnightly; Editor W. DIXON-COLLEY.

The New Gambia: twice weekly; Editor B. M. TARA-WALLEY.

RADIO

Radio Gambia: Bathurst; f. 1962; non-commercial government service of information, education and entertainment; English and local languages; 50,000 receivers.

Radio Syd: P.O.B. 280, Bathurst; commercial station; broadcasts in English, French and local languages; tourist information in Swedish; Dir. Mrs. B. WADNER.

FINANCE

BANKING

Commercial and Development Bank of The Gambia: Bathurst; f. 1972; Gen. Man. OUSAINOU N'JIE.

Standard Bank of West Africa Ltd.: P.O.B. 259–260, Bathurst; f. 1916; Bank of Issue; Head Office: 37 Gracechurch St., London, E.C.3.

INSURANCE

Bathurst

Commercial Union Assurance Co. Ltd.: London; Rep. Maurel Frères S.A., P.O. Box 269.

Compagnie Française de L'Afrique Occidentale—C.F.A.O., S.A.: Marseille; Rep. P.O. Box 297.

Eagle Star Insurance Co. Ltd.: London; Rep. R. S. Madi Ltd., 11 Russell Street.

Motor Union Insurance Co. Ltd.: London; Rep. Maurel et Prom.

Northern Assurance Co. Ltd.: London; Rep. United Africa Co. of Gambia Ltd.

White Cross Insurance Co. Ltd.: London; Rep. Compagnie Française de l'Afrique Occidentale, P.O.B. 297.

TRADE AND INDUSTRY

CHAMBER OF COMMERCE

Gambia Chamber of Commerce: P.O.B. 333, Bathurst; f. 1961; affiliated to Commonwealth Chamber of Commerce, London; Pres. R. MADI; Sec. P. W. F. N'JIE.

MARKETING ORGANIZATIONS

Gambia Produce Marketing Board: Marina Foreshore, Bathurst; Chair. S. G. BRUCE-OLIVER; Gen. Man. A. DRAPER.

Gambia Co-operative Banking and Marketing Union: 4 MacCarthy Square, Bathurst; Sec.-Man. M. M. JALLOW.

EMPLOYERS' ASSOCIATION

Gambia Employers' Association: P.O.B. 333, Bathurst; f. 1961; affiliated to the Overseas Employers' Federation, London; Chair. J. MADI; Sec. P. W. F. N'JIE.

TRADE UNIONS

Gambia Labour Union: 21 Clarkson St., P.O.B. 508, Bathurst; f. 1928; 6,000 mems.; affiliated to the World Confederation of Labour (formerly IFCTU); Pres. B. B. KEBBEH; Gen. Sec. M. S. CEESAY.

Gambia Workers' Union: 68 Hagan St., Bathurst; f. 1958; Sec. M. E. JALLOW.

Gambia Trades and Dealers' Union: f. 1960.

CO-OPERATIVE UNION

Gambia Co-operative Union Ltd.: P.O.B. 505, Bathurst; Sec.-Man. D. E. K. SANNEH.

MAJOR COMPANIES

All those listed below, excepting *S. Madi Ltd.*, are branches of overseas companies.

Adonis Enterprises Ltd.: Bathurst.
General merchants and hotel managers.
Man. K. MILKY; 300 employees.

C.F.A.O.: Bathurst.
General merchants.
Man. H. BERGE; 100 employees.

K. Chellarams and Sons: Bathurst.
General merchants.
Man. G. VASNANI; 200 employees.

Elder Dempster Agencies Ltd.: Bathurst.
Shipping.
Man. C. Booth; 90 employees.

Gambia Milling and Trading Co Ltd.: Bathurst.
Oil milling.
Mans. R. Madi, J. Madi; 400 employees.

G.R.T. and Co.: Bathurst.
River transport—groundnuts and general cargo.
Man. V. King; 200 employees.

S. Madi Ltd.: Bathurst.
Groundnut buying agents.
Mans. R. Madi, J. Madi; 50 employees.

Swiss Cold Stores (Gambia) Ltd.
Fishing.
Man. D. Tsuzuki; 360 employees.

TRANSPORT

ROADS

At the beginning of 1965 there were 322 miles of all-season roads in Gambia, about 129 bitumenized and over 180 all-season laterite surface. There are about 470 miles of local roads available in the dry season (December–July) but closed during the rains. The South Bank trunk road, linking Bathurst with the Trans-Gambia highway, was completed during 1963 and is being extended to Basse. Improvements to the Trans-Gambian Ferry were discussed at the Senegalese-Gambian Inter-Ministerial Committee meeting in February 1969.

SHIPPING

Regular shipping services to Bathurst are maintained by **Elder Dempster Lines** and **Palm Lines**. Other British and Scandinavian lines run occasional services.

A river service is maintained between Bathurst and Basse at ten-day intervals.

CIVIL AVIATION

Gambia Airways: P.O.B. 268, Bathurst; handling agency only; owns no aircraft; Gen. Man. A. G. Batchily. 1,948 aircraft landed in 1968. The only airport is at Yundum, 7 miles from Bathurst.

FOREIGN AIRLINES

Air Senegal: Bathurst.

British Caledonian Airways: P.O.B. 268, Bathurst.

Nigeria Airways: WAAC (Nigeria) Ltd., 11–12 Buckle St., P.O.B. 272, Bathurst; Rep. Shafi'i A. Usuf.

SELECT BIBLIOGRAPHY

Burton, Benedict (Ed.). *Problems of Smaller Territories.* London, Athlone Press, 1967.

Deschamps, H. *Le Sénégal et la Gambie.* Paris, Presses Universitaires de France, 1967.

Gailey, Harry A. *A History of The Gambia.* London, Routledge and Kegan Paul, 1964.

The Gambia Oilseeds Marketing Board. *Annual Reports.*

The Gambia Currency Board. *Annual Reports.*

Harrison Church, R. J. *West Africa* (6th edn.). London, Longmans, 1968.

Morgan, W. B., and Pugh, J. C. *West Africa.* London, Methuen, 1969.

Rice, Berkeley. *Enter Gambia: the Birth of an Improbable Nation.* London, Angus and Robertson, 1968.

Robson, Peter. "Problems of Integration between Senegal and Gambia", in Hazlewood, Arthur (Ed.), *African Integration and Disintegration,* pp. 115–28. London, O.U.P., 1967.

Southorn, Lady Bella. *The Gambia.* London, 1952.

Third Development Programme 1971–72 to 1973–74. Bathurst, The Government Printer, 1971.

West Africa. Weekly. London.

Ghana, Ivory Coast, Upper Volta, Togo and Dahomey.

Ghana

PHYSICAL AND SOCIAL GEOGRAPHY

E. A. Boateng

PHYSICAL FEATURES

Structurally and geologically Ghana exhibits many of the characteristics of sub-Saharan Africa, with its ancient rocks and extensive plateau surfaces marked by prolonged sub-aerial erosion. About half the surface area is composed of Precambrian metamorphic and igneous rocks, most of the remainder consisting of a platform of Palaeozoic sediments believed to be resting on the older rocks. The Palaeozoic sediments, which are composed mostly of little disturbed beds of clay and sandstone, occupy a vast area in the north-central part of the country and form the Voltaian basin, whose uplifted edges along the north and south give rise to high plateaux of between 1,000 and 2,000 ft., bordered by impressive outward-facing scarps. Surrounding this basin on all sides, except along the east, is a highly dissected peneplain of Precambrian rocks averaging between 500 and 1,000 ft. above sea level but containing several distinct ranges of up to 2,000 ft. Along the eastern edge of the Voltaian basin and extending right down to the sea near Accra is a narrow zone of highly folded Precambrian rocks with a north-east/south-west trend, composed mainly of quartzites, sandstones, and phyllites and forming the Akwapim-Togo ranges. These ranges vary in height between 1,000 and 3,000 ft. and contain the highest points in Ghana. Not only are they the most conspicuous mountain feature in Ghana, but they continue northward across Togo and Dahomey to form one of west Africa's major relief features known as the Togo-Atakora range. The south-east corner of the country, below the Akwapim-Togo ranges, is occupied by the gently rolling Accra plains, which are underlain by the oldest of the Precambrian series known as the Dahomeyan and containing extensive areas of gneiss. Only in the broad delta of the Volta in the eastern part of the Accra plains, and in the extreme south-west corner of the country along the Axim coast are there to be found extensive areas of young rocks of from Tertiary to Recent age; while in the intervening littoral zone scattered patches of Devonian sediments combine with the rocks of the Precambrian peneplain to produce a picturesque coastline of sandy bays and rocky promontories.

The drainage is dominated by the Volta system which occupies the Voltaian basin and includes the vast artificial lake of over 3,000 sq. miles formed behind the hydroelectric dam at Akosombo. Most of the other rivers, such as the Pra, Ankobra, Tano and a number of smaller ones, flow between the southern Voltaian plateau and the sea. South of Kumasi is Lake Bosomtwi, believed to be of caldera origin, while along the coast are numerous lagoons, formed mostly at the mouths of the smaller streams.

CLIMATE AND VEGETATION

Like other parts of the Guinea coast, Ghana's climate is mainly the result of the interplay between two principal airstreams: the hot, dry, tropical, continental air mass or harmattan from the north-east, and the moist, relatively cool, maritime air mass or monsoon from the south-west across the Atlantic. The Inter-Tropical Convergence Zone, along which these two air masses meet, oscillates north and south in accordance with the movements of the overhead sun and mainly determines the incidence of rainfall. In the southern part of the country, where the highest rainfall of between 50 and 86 in. occurs, there are two rainy seasons (April–July and September–November), while in the northern part, with totals of between 45 and 50 in., rainfall occurs in only a single season between April and September, followed by a long dry season dominated by the harmattan. In this area and also in the Accra plains, which have an anomalously low annual rainfall of around 30 in., the predominant vegetation is savannah and scrub, in contrast with the rich tropical forest vegetation found in the heavy rainfall zone of the south. There is much greater uniformity as regards mean temperatures, which average between 77.9°F. and 84.2°F. These temperatures, coupled with the equally high relative humidities, which drop significantly only during the harmattan, tend to produce oppressive conditions, relieved only by the relative drop in temperature at night, especially in the north, and the local incidence of land and sea breezes near the coast.

THE SOCIAL ENVIRONMENT

Ghana's present population is estimated at 8.5 million and the annual rate of growth at approximately 2.4 per cent. Considering that the country has an area of only 92,100 sq. miles, of which by no means all is agriculturally useful, a number of serious social and economic problems are likely to arise unless the basis of the economy, which is at present mainly of the subsistence agricultural type, can be greatly broadened and the high rate of population growth brought under control. Another striking and potentially disturbing feature of the population is its youthfulness (over 61 per cent were under 25 years of age in 1960). The highest population densities are found in the urban and cocoa farming areas in the southern part of the country, and also in the extreme north-eastern corner, where intensive compound farming is practised. Altogether there are no less than 75 different languages and dialects, each more or less associated with a distinct tribal group. The largest of these groups are the Akan, Mole-Dagbani, Ewe, and the Ga-Adangbe, which form respectively 44.1, 15.9, 13 and

8.3 per cent of the population. Fortunately the divisive tendencies which might be expected to arise from this situation have been kept under control, largely as a result of imaginative governmental policies over many decades, and it is possible to speak of a single national consciousness embracing all the diverse elements with their varied traditions and cultures. Even so, a distinction can be made between the southern peoples on the one hand, who have come most directly and longest under the influence of modern European life and the Christian religion, and the northern peoples on the other hand, whose tradi-

tional modes of life and religion have undergone relatively little change, thanks largely to their remoteness from the coast where the European impact first began some five centuries ago. Even among the southern peoples there are significant disparities, the Akan group dominating all the rest in size and extent. There is little doubt that one of the most potent unifying forces has been the adoption of English as the official national language, although, in keeping with the characteristic Ghanaian genius for compromise, it is supplemented officially by some five local languages covering the entire country.

RECENT HISTORY

Dennis Austin

Two themes, intertwined, explain a great deal of the recent history of the country which was once called the Gold Coast and which became the independent state of Ghana on March 6th, 1957. The ancient, mediaeval empire of Ghana in the northern savannah area of west Africa (*florebat* A.D. 800) had only a romantic tenuous connexion with the present republic, the name being borrowed from history to promote a moral and adorn a country. There are scholars who have argued that there may be a continuing connexion through migration between the 8 million people of Ghana and those of the former empire, which lay some hundreds of miles to the north-west of the present frontiers of Ghana; but the evidence is not at all certain, and the prime object of the renaming in 1957 was to assert that the glories of the African past (undefined) had reappeared in the new dawn of nationalist independence.

BRITISH RULE

Of the two intertwined themes one is familiar enough: the opposition to (British) colonial rule on the part of local political groups, culminating in the United Gold Coast Convention in 1947 under J. B. Danquah and the Convention People's Party in 1949 under Kwame Nkrumah. Agitation for reform had a relatively long history in the country, amply described by standard political histories of these years (*q.v.* D. B. Kimble, *Political History of Ghana*, 1963). It was preceded by armed resistance to British rule by the central Ashanti kingdom under the *assantehene* who, exiled from his capital in Kumasi in 1896, was allowed to return in 1925. The establishment of colonial rule from 1900 onwards, including its extension under a League of Nations mandate to part of the former German colony of Togoland in 1919, was peacefully carried through. There was no European settlement, the climate being unattractive and unsuitable for European agriculture, and no major alienation of land from a country of peasant proprietors. These continued to live out their lives under the local authority of chiefs and elders in the little kingdoms and states which rested on the legitimacy

of a traditional past, reinforced by colonial power and a network of clan groups owing allegiance to a Stool or Skin as symbols of a pre-colonial past.

The early proto-nationalist parties were based mainly on the southern coastal towns—Accra, Cape Coast, Sekondi-Takoradi. They were able to press for reform of the colonial administration through the Legislative Council of official and unofficial members among whom were not only the chiefs but representatives (elected on a narrow franchise) of the "intelligentsia"—that distinctive social class of Christian-educated lawyers, doctors, newspaper proprietors and businessmen who competed as best they could with the powerful expatriate trading companies like the United Africa Company, cocoa firms like Cadbury and Fry, mining companies like the Ashanti Gold Fields, and timber firms. In the inter-war years, therefore, the country was governed by a triple élite of colonial officials, chiefs, and the intelligentsia. Its economy was dominated by the export of cocoa, gold, timber and manganese, and the import of manufactures from the west, principally from Britain. Inter-African trade with its neighbours was minimal; but the country was relatively wealthy— with a good infrastructure of roads, ports, railways, schools and elementary social services—and it attracted a large number of migrants from beyond its borders. There was a remarkable period of economic expansion in the 1920s, probably the greatest leap forward in the country's history, when cocoa growing, and the wealth which flowed from it, spread through the southern and central regions of the country— an economic renaissance which was cut back cruelly (with lamentable social consequences) by the world economic slump of the 1930s. It was then that the movement for reform began to gather momentum, a movement accelerated by the particular hardships imposed by the Second World War in which west African, including Gold Coast, troops saw active service in east Africa and Burma.

By 1947 discontent had been brought together at a national level through the United Gold Coast Convention. The most active figures were Danquah and Nkrumah, the latter being brought back from desultory academic pursuits in the United Kingdom to become secretary of the new party. By 1949 a more radical movement had emerged, which carried Nkrumah with it, to form the Convention People's Party. It appealed in general terms to the "common man", and more specifically to a new social class of discontented school leavers seeking employment and an expansion of their own petty trading activities. Its slogan was admirably succinct: "Self-Government Now". With this it challenged the more cautious, lawyer-like demand of the UGCC: self-government in the shortest possible time. The colonial administration, and the British government, hesitated; detained the UGCC leaders in 1948; locked up Nkrumah in 1950; and then yielded. A nation-wide constitution granted a qualified form of ministerial government and elections were allowed in 1951 on a wide suffrage, the main exception being the northern region where a cash economy and the spread of education were still in their infancy.

CPP IN POWER

So there began the period of CPP rule under Nkrumah which lasted until the intervention of the army and the police in February 1966. It began well as a broad based-party régime which commanded the affections as well as the interests of a large section of the population. If, to some observers, it was a large "patron-client association" by which those in pursuit of jobs attached themselves to those who were in positions to offer employment by their control of the government, it was also a movement which carried along with it a nationalist emotion eager to put an end to colonial rule. The combination proved irresistible. Successful in the first elections of 1951, the CPP went on to win the elections of 1954 and 1956. With 72 seats in a national assembly of 104, the party was able to persuade the British that it was a legitimate instrument to which power could be transferred. And so it happened: independence was granted on March 6th, 1957, amidst mutual protestations of goodwill from the CPP, the colonial government, the British, and the international community.

There the story might rest, success (if not virtue) reaping its due reward. But we must turn now to the second theme. Who were the Ghanaian nation? And who were the leaders who formed the government of the new nation state? The movement against colonial rule followed a familiar path along which the British withdrew in very good order and with good grace as the nationalists advanced. But there was conflict too within Ghanaian society—a conflict in particular over where power should lie. Part of the quarrel was "territorial", a more accurate label than "tribal" since the quarrel often developed between rival groups of the same "ethnic origin".

A list of the main opposition parties to Nkrumah's Convention People's Party is a good indication of the spread of dissent—dissent from, and within, the main nationalist movement of which the CPP claimed to be the exclusive voice. In 1954 a Northern People's Party was formed to protect and advance the interests of the savannah peoples who lacked cocoa or

mining or forest resources. But it, too, was divided by rivalries between local chiefdoms, with the result that the CPP was able to latch on to these local disputes and gain adherents from one side or the other. There was also a small Muslim Party, centred mainly on the Muslim quarters of the large towns. And in September 1954 the Ashanti produced their own protest party—the National Liberation Movement, although once again the CPP was able to combat the party's regional appeal by its own nationalist stance and by exploiting local divisions within the Ashanti-Brong-Ahafo regions. In 1957 the Ga people of the capital, Accra, formed a protest group (*Ga Shifimo Kpee*) which resented and tried to reverse its dwindling position (under 50 per cent) in the town which they had founded.

These different opposition parties came together at the end of 1957 as a United Party under Dr. K. A. Busia, a former Professor of Sociology at the University of Ghana. They were united primarily by a dislike of the centralizing tendencies of the CPP. Their original programme had included the demand for a loosening of the structure of central government in the direction of "federalism", a demand transmuted after independence into a catalogue of grievances against the monopoly of power exercised by Nkrumah and his party. They were not fundamentally opposed to the boundaries or definition of the new Ghana state, only to the distribution of power within it. But there was a further category of dissent of a somewhat different order: the Togoland Congress, formed in 1954—with much earlier origins—among the Ewe of the south-east of the pre-1919 Gold Coast and the southern Ewe-speaking people of the former Trust Territory of Togoland. The eastern part of the Territory under French rule was now moving towards independence as a separate state under M. Sylvanus Olympio, and the Ewe people of Ghana were unsure of their allegiance. Hence the demand for "reunification" of all the Ewe peoples across the international frontier between Ghana and Togo.

Such was the array of forces which tried to challenge the main nationalist party, the CPP. And in the 1956 election, on the eve of independence, the balance was clearly on the side of the CPP: 72 seats against 32 for the mixed group of opposition parties (including 4 seats for the Togoland Congress).

CENTRALIZING POLITICS

We must introduce into this picture a different dimension of conflict—not between "territorial groups" but between social categories. The opposition United Party drew the greater part of its strength from its regional bases of support. But it was also a party whose leaders tended to reflect the views of the rather better-educated, professional members of the "intelligentsia". When the CPP entered office in 1951 a shift of power occurred not simply from British colonial to African nationalist hands, but from one section of local Ghanaian society to another. The CPP was a nationalist party dominated by those who had been excluded from power by the old triple élite of the colonial officials, the chiefs, and the intelligentsia. They came out of the large number of elementary schools, and by weight of numbers and their nationalist appeal they pushed aside the more conservative leadership of the United Gold Coast Convention. But these "displaced nationalists"—as indeed they were—bided their time, and seized the opportunity of the local regional movements of dissent to challenge Nkrumah and the CPP. They failed, but continued in existence, gaining some adherents from rivalries within the CPP, losing many more of their members as the CPP began to use the authority and rewards of the state to reinforce its own power as a party.

By 1960 the CPP appeared almost to have crushed its opponents. A referendum for a Republic, with Nkrumah as President, claimed to be supported by 90 per cent of the electorate in a popular vote. And by 1964 Ghana was a legalized single-party state. In place of its earlier nationalist platform, an ideology of a sort was put together which attempted to weave together pan-African programmes and "African socialist" beliefs. It was called "Nkrumahism", and included a growing veneration of the leader under a new style and title—*Osagyefo* ("Successful in War"). The pan-African programme was developed from a series of conferences between the growing number of independent African states, the first on African soil being held in Accra in April 1958. The socialist ideology was partly a response to a nationalist belief that the powers of the state needed to be used to "Africanize" the economy—state industries, state farms, a state-sponsored work force (the Builders' Brigade)—and partly the outcome of Nkrumah's own belief in the efficacy of what might loosely be called "left-wing philosophies". One must remember, too, that the African scene outside Ghana was increasingly troubled, above all by the misfortunes which overtook the newly independent Congo in 1960, and also by a growing belief among African leaders, particularly Nkrumah, in the reality of neo-colonialist pressures. True, these beliefs did not prevent the amassing of a great deal of private wealth by CPP leaders; nor did they prevent large-scale investment by the Americans and the British in the one great economic act of the Nkrumah régime, the Volta River Project, whereby the Volta river was dammed and the hydro-electric power generated by its flow turned to the manufacture of alumina from bauxite. None the less, between 1964 and the *coup* in 1966, Ghana became a "socialist-single-party-state" (dominated by Nkrumah) which was beginning to look as much to the U.S.S.R. and eastern Europe as to Britain and America for its political structure of control, and for new outlets of trade and sources of aid.

Within the country itself politics became clandestine and violent. There were two attempts to assassinate Nkrumah: in August 1962 at the small northern village of Kulungugu, where a hand grenade wounded the president and killed a number of his entourage; and in January 1964 when a police constable failed to shoot Nkrumah, at close range, within the presidential headquarters at Flagstaff House. The ruling party turned increasingly to severe measures of control, through the 1958 Preven-

tive Detention Act under which its opponents were detained for periods of five years without trial; through press censorship; through the promotion and demotion of chiefs friendly or hostile to the régime; and through the manipulation of the electoral system, culminating in the June 1965 election when the number of M.P.s was increased to 189—all the candidates being nominated by the central committee of the party and declared "elected" unopposed on polling day—when nobody voted. A web of power was spun over the country through different "apparat" groups: a restructured and controlled TUC, a Farmers' Council, a Young Pioneers' movement, a Women's League, and the like. At the end of 1964 the party clashed with the judiciary when the High Court delivered a verdict with which Nkrumah disagreed in a treason trial involving former members of Nkrumah's own party and government: the Chief Justice, Sir Arku Korsah, was dismissed by the President under powers granted him by the single-party parliament. There were quarrels also between the army and the party: Nkrumah dismissed his British G.O.C., General Alexander, in 1961, and in 1965 compulsorily retired his two senior Ghanaian officers, General Otu and General Ankrah. A new Presidential Guard Regiment was recruited to rival the regular army, but at this point conspiracy turned to rebellion. The police, under Inspector-General John Harlley, and the army, under Colonel Kotoka and Major Afrifa, seized the advantage of Nkrumah's absence from the country in Peking to take control of the country after a brief, though not entirely bloodless, *coup*.

MILITARY RULE

Why did they intervene? Probably for two reasons—personal and national, plus the reasonable assumption that the armed forces would be well received if they did act. The personal reasons are clear. The army and police much disliked interference by Nkrumah and the CPP with their own structure of command, particularly after the formation of the Presidential Guard Regiment, trained and advised by Russian officers. But there were more general causes: the move by Nkrumah towards the U.S.S.R. and eastern Europe, the growing scarcity of goods and a worsening balance of payments, the attack by the party on the civil service and the judiciary, the use of the Preventive Detention Act, and the withering of the popular base of the party which, deprived of a formal opposition to combat, had turned in on itself in a series of internal squabbles to the neglect of its once popular support. Of these causes the deterioration of the economy was probably beyond the control of any government at a time when the world cocoa price fell catastrophically from its abnormally high price of over £400 a ton in the mid-1950s to under £100 a ton by 1965–66; but these national hardships were made a great deal worse by a public and conspicuous corruption among the party's leaders. There was thus a general (though by no means universal) rejoicing on the evening of February 24th, 1966, when the army proclaimed the end of the

CPP and the establishment of a National Liberation Council of four army and four police officers under the chairmanship of General Ankrah.

There followed three and a half years of military rule during which two trends could be discerned. One was the appearance of divisions within the ruling junta, partly factional, partly the consequence of civilian, political pressures upon the military and police. The other feature of their rule was its clearly temporary nature since, almost from the first months of office, the NLC began to put into motion the machinery of constitutional reform whereby they could be replaced by civilian rulers. These two characteristics were of course interrelated: politics began to enter the army and the army was thereby quickened in its resolve to have done with the burdens of government.

NLC DIVISIONS

The misfortunes which befell the NLC can be quickly listed, but one must remember that they occurred against a very difficult background of foreign indebtedness and domestic inflation. In May 1967 there was an attempt at a second *coup* by a small group of officers and men led by Lt. Arthur who drove 99 miles from Ho in the Transvolta region to Accra, killed Col. Kotoka, seized the radio station and forced General Ankrah to flee from Christianborg Castle (the NLC seat of government). They were later overpowered, brought before a court martial, found guilty and shot in public before a large crowd in Black Star Square. The attempt was almost certainly personal, not tribal or ideological, based on discontent with rates of promotion and a vainglorious desire to seize power. Nothing as serious happened again, but there were numerous indications of a division between the army and police and between individual members of the NLC. Ankrah was obliged to resign from the Council; charges were brought (and later dropped) against General Otu, chief of the defence staff; and differences began to appear of a political nature based on regional and/or ethnic loyalties. It was commonly supposed, for example, that the members of the NLC—Afrifa and Ocran—who were from the Akan regions of Ashanti and the south—were sympathetic to the political ambitions of Dr. Busia—an Akan; and that the Inspector-General of Police, John Harlley, and Inspector Deku, from the Ewe-speaking areas of Transvolta, were more inclined to K. A. Gbedemah, an Ewe and a CPP minister until he fled the country in 1961. (General Ankrah, on the other hand, was a Ga; Yakubu, another member of the NLC, was a northerner.) Such differences were not of paramount important at first: Kotoka was an Ewe who became a national hero. But as politics began to restart, and Busia and Gbedemah emerged as the two most powerful contestants, each with a large following, so the rivalry between them spread from civilian society into the armed forces.

Despite (and perhaps because of) these difficulties, the NLC hardly hesitated in its intention to transfer power back to civilian rulers. The work of "demilitar-

ization" went steadily forward by means of commissions of inquiry into the misdeeds of the past; a constitutional commission; constitutional proposals; a Constituent Assembly (partly elected, partly nominated); and, on August 29th, 1969, a general election. Certain limits were placed on those who could stand. All leading members of the former régime were debarred, as well as those found by a Commission of Inquiry to be unable to account satisfactorily for private funds accumulated during the Nkrumah period, an impediment which eventually unseated Gbedemah (through a complicated process of tribunals and court cases) after the election. Limits were also imposed by the Constituent Assembly, and written into the new constitution of the Second Republic, on the future civilian régime. It cannot, for example, establish single-party rule; it must respect a bill of rights; it must divide its power between a parliament, prime minister, president, and a council of state; and it must bow to interpretations of the constitution by the supreme court.

CIVILIAN GOVERNMENT RETURNS

The election itself was most scrupulously conducted and freely contested. In all, five parties took part, of which only two contested all but one of the 140 single member constituencies—the Progress Party led by Dr. Busia, and the National Alliance of Liberals led by K. A. Gbedemah. The result was a sweeping victory for Progress:

	VOTES	%	SEATS	%
Progress . .	876,378	59	105	75
NAL . .	454,646	30.4	29	21
Others . .	162,347	10.9	6	4
TOTAL .	1,493,371	100	140	100

Expressed in regional terms the picture was as follows:

REGION	SEATS	PROGRESS	NAL	OTHERS
Ashanti . .	22	22	—	—
Brong Ahafo .	13	13	—	—
Central Region .	15	15	—	—
Western Region .	13	10	—	—
Eastern Region .	22	18	4	—
Volta Region .	16	2	14	—
Upper Volta .	16	13	3	—
North . . .	14	9	5	—
Accra . . .	9	3	3	3

Dr. Busia's victory ought to have been predictable, since he had many advantages over his main opponent. Busia is an Akan, who form the majority of the population. He was known to be in close touch with the dominant (Akan) group on the NLC; and he had been prominent since 1966–67 in national affairs through bodies like the Centre for Civic Education, so that by the time that the ban on party politics was lifted in May 1969 he had already begun to put together a party following. Above all, he represented a new start in national life, having consistently opposed the Nkrumah régime at home and from exile. Those who disliked the corruption and bullying of the previous government turned naturally therefore to Busia and Progress. Gbedemah, on the other hand, lacked these advantages. He was an Ewe, in difficulties with the NLC over whether he could stand for election; and he stood too close still—despite his exile—to the misdeeds of the past: he had, after all, been one of the founders of the CPP and one of the authors of the Preventive Detention Act.

BUSIA TAKES OFFICE

So Progress took office on October 1st, 1969, first with a triumvirate-presidency of Afrifa, Ocran and Harlley, then in 1970 with E. Akufo Addo, an elderly lawyer (who had been chairman of the Constitutional Commission) as President. The new government has not been free from worries. The economy is still in difficulties, unemployment in the towns running as high as 17 per cent. There is the continuing problem of foreign indebtedness, low cocoa prices, rising imports, and the need to retrench at a time when expectations of a new start in public life are high. Partly in an attempt to deal with some of these problems, the new government turned against the large number of aliens in the country—(about 800,000)—in December 1969 and expelled a large proportion of them, hoping thereby to provide jobs for Ghanaians, to lower the high rate of urban crime, and reduce the outflow of remittances. Early in 1970, it was the turn of the civil service; 568 senior and junior members being arbitrarily dismissed. And when one of those dismissed—E. K. Sallah—sought redress in the courts for wrongful dismissal, the prime minister clashed with the judiciary, threatening in April 1970 that "if the Judges want to play politics, I am quite ready to take them on".

These were unhappy, sometimes mystifying, events, made worse at the end of 1971 by blanket legislation against any attempt to promote the (very unlikely) return of Nkrumah, and by the government's attack on the T.U.C. and its Secretary-General, Benjamin Bentum. But it is still possible to remain reasonably optimistic that the new government will provide a more rational, more responsive, less arbitrary and less corrupt form of rule than that given by the former CPP government. The opposition has drawn together to form a new Justice Party under Eric Majiditey; and there is a lively though small opposition press still, notably *The Spokesman* and the *Legon Observer*. The intellectual ability of the present government's leaders is certainly higher, although it is reasonable to assume that the rank and file support for Progress is not essentially different from that given to the CPP in its early years. There has been change at the top, but even after the measure of social revolution carried through in 1950, continuity at the bottom is very unlikely to have been broken. The question mark of course is the familiar uncertainty about "responsiveness" since what the generality of people want is not simply "good government" but one capable of distributing the material benefits of good govern-ment. The budget of July 26th, 1971, was very austere, imposing cuts and excess duties on a wide range of imports. And the labyrinthine problem of the country's debts of over £100 million, on which repayment is to resume in 1972, still remains as a major burden.

THE SECOND COUP

On January 10th, 1972 Dr. Busia left the country to consult an eye specialist in London. Three days later a section of the army under Lt.-Col. Ignatius Kutu Acheampong staged a second *coup*, resulting in the overthrow of the Second Republic, including the constitution, parliament, and the Progress Party. Busia flew back to West Africa on the 14th, to Abidjan in the neighbouring Ivory Coast, and stayed there for five days, but to no avail. Guns were unanswerable, particularly when there was already a growing discontent with the party leaders.

From June 1971 to this new intervention by the army, basic foodstuffs such as rice, sugar, yams, sardines and plantains, were in short supply, cocoa prices fell sharply, and the cost of imported goods went up: the result was an overall deficit at the end of the year of C63 million. To try to meet the problem, the Progress Government (on IMF advice) devalued the cedi (*see* Economy, below). Despite the increase in wages and salaries, the effect was calamitous: the price of both local and imported goods rocketed. Public discontent had already been voiced through the T.U.C. over the government's Development Levy (a 5 per cent tax on wages) and other aspects of the July budget; and the government had passed, under emergency legislation, a new Industrial Relations Act on September 10th (by 86 votes to 28) which abolished the T.U.C. Dr. Busia's government had clashed earlier with the civil service and the judiciary, and the year had closed amidst uneasy forebodings of what the future might bring.

There were more direct causes of the *coup*, including familiar complaints by army officers over the curtailing of their allowances and privileges. Colonel Acheampong, who had been Administrator of the Western Region under the NLC, admitted that he had begun to plan his *coup* as early as 1970. Now he is in full charge, ruling by decree through a National Redemption Council of army, naval, and air force officers, and police. The *coup* was indifferently received but not opposed. On January 15th, Major-General Afrifa, part author of the first *coup* in 1966, was placed under arrest, accused of having tried to stage a counter-*coup* with Maxwell Owusu, Administrator of the Ashanti region, and Lt.-Colonel Osei Owusu, on behalf of Dr. Busia. But the T.U.C. came out in support of the new Council, and so did Mr. Eric Madjitey the former Leader of the Parliamentary Opposition Justice Party. The NRC then began to lock up the Progress members of parliament and party officials prior to bringing them before a Commission of Inquiry to judge whether their "assets" had been unlawfully acquired during their brief period of power. The NRC also enlisted the help of Mr.

Gerald Moore as Attorney General, and appointed a number of their own members as ministers in charge of departments. The leading figures are Major Selormey, Air Marshal Ashley-Larsen, J. H. Cobbina (Inspector-General of Police), Major-Gen. Addo, and Major-Gen. Nathan Aferi. The Council also drew together an advisory Economic Committee under Mr. Amon Nikoe of the Ministry of Finance.

Its first steps were bold, including a revaluation of 42 per cent, bringing the cedi to an equivalent of 78 US cents. The Development Levy was abolished, the T.U.C. reconstituted, and (on February 5th) the NRC repudiated a number of medium-term debts, consisting mainly of suppliers' credits contracted during the Nkrumah period, on the grounds that they had been "tainted and vitiated with corruption". An austerity programme banned the import of luxuries and the system of open licensing; and the former programme of rural development was given great emphasis under an Operation Feed Yourself campaign.

The main lines of economic policy were laid down on June 15th, 1972.

On April 27th, 1972 the former President Kwame Nkrumah died in exile in Conakry at the age of 62. After an unseemly wrangle, his body was flown back (after the intercession of the Nigerian government) on July 7th and buried at his birthplace, Nkroful, in the Western Region. The 20,000 mourners were led by Col. Acheampong and speculation grew on the likelihood of a revival of the former president's policies. It was encouraged by the NRC's reinstatement in favour of former Nkrumah men (such as John Tettegah and Kofi Badu) and its repudiation of any "dialogue with apartheid". Yet it would probably be wrong to stress such signs. A new régime is always likely to look approvingly on the enemies of its own opponents. The NRC leaders are soldiers struggling with a difficult economy and begining to talk of plots against them. Such are the compulsions of most African régimes uneasily placed in office.

ECONOMY

Douglas Rimmer

Note on the Currency Unit

At independence the West African Currency Board pound was replaced by a Ghanaian pound but without change in the one-for-one parity with sterling. In July 1965 the Ghanaian pound was replaced by a decimalized currency unit, the cedi, at the rate of C2.40 to the pound. In February 1967 a new cedi was introduced, replacing the old currency at the rate NC2.00 to C2.40. The official exchange rate became NC1.00 = 10s. sterling = U.S. $1.40. In July 1967 the new cedi was devalued by 30 per cent, and , following the devaluation of sterling in November 1967, the official exchange rate became NC1.00 = 8s. 2d. sterling = U.S. $0.98. In November 1971 the external value of the cedi was pegged to the dollar instead of gold, and at the end of the year, the cedi was devalued by 44 per cent in terms of the dollar. This devaluation was partially rescinded in February 1972, when the official rate was fixed at C1.00 = U.S. $0.78 (= 30p. sterling). The net result of the devaluation of December 1971 and the subsequent revaluation was a devaluation of the cedi by about 20 per cent in terms of the dollar and 27 per cent in terms of sterling. For convenience, money values in this article are expressed in pounds sterling at contemporaneous rates of exchange.

INTRODUCTION

Like other tropical African economies, the Ghanaian economy has grown mainly by the activation of under-employed labour and unutilized natural resources to supply overseas demand. In mining and in timber extraction, an admixture of foreign enterprise and capital was required, but the growing of cocoa, which continues to provide the export staple of the country, has been entirely an indigenous activity. Commercialized home-market activities have developed—in food farming and distribution, in building and urban services, and in manufacturing—but export earnings continue to dominate the prospects of growth of cash-incomes. Subsistence activity (in providing food, shelter, and fuel) was estimated to constitute, around 1962, about 20 per cent of household expenditures—a low proportion by tropical African standards.

The annual figures of gross domestic product are compiled from expenditure categories, and the only published estimates of the industrial composition of G.D.P. relate to the year 1960. At that time, agriculture (including logging and fishing) and services (including transport, distribution, personal services and traditional crafts) were estimated to account together for nearly 75 per cent of the total. Construction was put at 10 per cent, public administration at 6 per cent, mining at 5 per cent, and manufacturing and public utilities at 4 per cent. Since 1960 the shares in total output of manufacturing, public administration and (especially before 1966) construction must have grown. In general, the urban economy has been growing relatively to the rural economy; but this was happening also before 1960, and a marked and rapid transformation of the structure of the economy, which was attempted in the early 1960s, cannot be said to have been achieved.

The terms of trade were on a favourable trend in the early post-war period, and export proceeds doubled between 1948 and 1959. Private consumption and government expenditure were rising, and official institutions and the commercial banks accumulated foreign-exchange assets which reached a peak of £208 million at the end of 1955. When export proceeds levelled off after 1959, imports and government expenditure continued to rise, and the external reserves were run down rapidly within a few years. In face of the deteriorating external situation import restrictions and exchange control were introduced in 1961, and from the same date the government resorted to borrowing from the banking system and to medium-term commercial borrowing from abroad to obtain the resources which could not be secured from tax increases. The attempted diversification of the economy through the establishment of numerous state enterprises was a major field of public spending, while infrastructural investments, which had already been important in the 1950s, continued with diminishing care given to the pay-offs which they might yield. In the period 1960–65 £100 million was raised by deficit financing, and foreign suppliers' credits estimated at £160 million were taken up. The expansion of domestic purchasing power, coupled with import controls, produced inflation, especially in 1964–65 when the Accra retail price index rose by some 70 per cent.

After the *coup* of February 1966, the first military government sought to stabilize prices by holding down government expenditure and some forms of money-incomes, and to relieve the pressure of the medium-term debt on the balance of payments by making rescheduling agreements with creditor countries in 1966–68. Moratorium interest on the deferred debt payments increased the medium-term debt total by about 20 per cent, but the average annual servicing charge for the period 1966–71 was reduced by means of the agreements by about 70 per cent. An inflow of aid in the form of long-term concessional loans occurred after 1966, and an attempt at fundamental resolution of the balance of payments problem was made by the devaluation of 1967. Finally, the commodity terms of trade, which had been depressed by the expansion of Ghana's cocoa exports in the 1960s, again moved favourably from 1967.

The civilian government which took office in October 1969 took the view that a politically acceptable rate of expansion of the economy demanded the conversion of the medium-term external debt into long-term low-interest loans by the governments of the creditor countries. Policies of expansion were launched in anticipation of agreement of this highly contentious matter. The government also took major steps, in its budgets of 1970 and 1971, toward liberalization of the foreign exchange régime, substituting import surcharges, some export bounties and taxes on invisibles —a kind of disguised devaluation—for the administrative controls on imports. These policies prevented accumulation of foreign exchange reserves despite substantial growth of export proceeds in 1968–70. In 1971 cocoa prices broke, and export earnings fell off while import spending continued to rise with the further removal of licensing control. The result was short-term indebtedness—i.e. arrears of payments on import bills—totalling £35 million by the end of the year. The risk that Ghana would be denied further imports drove the government to make its clean devaluation in December 1971, and the second *coup* swiftly followed.

The new government (the National Redemption Council) retained as much of the devaluation of December 1971 as was necessary to make good the removal of the import surcharges. On the medium-term debt, it endorsed the thinking of its predecessor to the extent of repudiating entirely debts of some £13 millions due to four British companies; abrogating also £27 million of moratorium interest due to be paid between 1972 and 1982 under the rescheduling agreements; and announcing that payments on the remaining medium-term debt would be made only on the basis of the terms currently applicable to credits granted by the International Development Association, the "soft-loan" affiliate of the World Bank. Credit for imports thereupon ceased to be forthcoming, and the government was obliged to espouse a policy of stern self-sufficiency, with an import budget for 1972 of only half the value of 1971 imports.

POPULATION

The census of March 1960, which is believed to have been fairly accurate, enumerated a total population of 6,727,000, with a median age of only 18 years. The economically active population was recorded at 2,561,000, with 61 per cent engaged in agricultural pursuits and 31 per cent in services. The population density was 73 per sq. mile, with the heaviest concentration found in southern Ghana west of the Volta river, where about three-fifths of the total population lived in less than a quarter of the country's land area. Urban population (living in towns of more than 5,000 inhabitants) was 23 per cent of the whole. The populations of the largest towns were: Accra, 338,000; Kumasi, 181,000; and Sekondi-Takoradi, 75,000.

Crude birth and death rates have been estimated in the range of 50–54 and 21–24 per thousand respectively. The average number of births per woman has been estimated at about seven. Expectation of life at birth is put at about 45 years. The total population at the census of March 1970 is put provisionally at 8,546,000, which gives an annual rate of increase of 2.4 per cent since 1960; but there may have been undercounting in 1970. It is thought that about half the annual increase is being absorbed by the towns. The rapid rate of increase, the rate of urbanization, and the youthfulness of the population are important factors underlying the growth of "social overhead" expenditures, especially on education (primary education became free in 1952 and nominally compulsory in 1961).

The population has been geographically mobile in response to economic opportunities. The 1960 census enumerated 16 per cent of the economically active native population as long-distance migrants (persons counted outside the regions in which they had been born) and another 24 per cent as short-distance migrants (persons counted outside the localities, but within the regions, of their birth). In addition, 537,000 foreign-born persons were enumerated—nearly all foreign-born west Africans, with the largest contingents from Togo, Upper Volta, and Nigeria. These figures relate mainly to permanent settlers. There is also considerable temporary migration (mainly to employment in commercialized agriculture), which to a large extent escaped the census. In the past the annual flow of temporary migrants may have reached 300,000 across Ghana's boundaries and another 200,000 between northern and southern Ghana; but these flows may have diminished after 1961. Making allowance for temporary migrants, and including Ghanaian-born dependants of persons of foreign origin, the foreign element in the population of 1960 at the peak of the seasonal immigration must have been in excess of one million, say about 15 per cent of the whole. At the end of 1969, in an effort to relieve unemployment and other urban pressures, the government decided to enforce legal requirements relating to residence permits against foreign Africans. As a result there occurred an exodus of aliens, and estimates of the number driven out range up to half a million.

EXTERNAL TRADE AND PAYMENTS

On the average of the years 1968–70 cocoa beans and products accounted for 67 per cent of total exports of domestic produce, minerals for 13 per cent, timber for 9 per cent, and aluminium for 9 per cent. In recent years there has been a tendency for timber and minerals to diminish in relative importance. There has also been some growth in the processed cocoa element in the cocoa total, and aluminium exports have appeared since 1967 with the setting up of the VALCO smelter at Tema. About 30 per cent of imports consist of consumers' goods, 40 per cent raw and semi-finished materials, 25 per cent capital equipment, and 5 per cent fuel and lubricants. After 1966 there was some shifting away from capital equipment and building materials and toward food and manufacturing materials. Food imports, running in 1970 at 14.5 per cent of the total, reflected the inability of domestic agriculture to meet the more refined dietary wants of consumers. Ghana's main trading partners are the U.K. (24 per cent of total external trade in 1970), the EEC countries (23 per cent), the U.S.A. (18 per cent), the U.S.S.R. and eastern Europe (9 per cent), and Japan (6 per cent). The share of the U.S.S.R. and eastern Europe rose rapidly in the early 1960s, but has fallen from a peak of 24 per cent in 1965. Trade with African countries is relatively small (2.3 per cent in 1970), but doubtless some trade with neighbouring countries escapes record.

Total export proceeds, after the levelling off in 1960, remained stable at about £113 million until 1966–67, when there was a fall to about £100 million p.a., followed by a rise to £138 million in 1968, £161 million in 1969, and £200 million in 1970. In 1971 export proceeds fell back to about £158 million. A main explanation of the movement of export proceeds is fluctuations in the Ghanaian cocoa crop and, since the country supplies nearly one-third of world output, the consequential fluctuations in world cocoa prices. The experience of recent years has been that decreases in the Ghanaian crop are more likely than increases to raise export earnings. Until 1972, import totals were governed not only by current export earnings but

also, in the early 1960s, by the spending of reserves and the acceptance of medium-term commercial credits; in the later 1960s by the receipt of foreign aid; and in 1971 by the accumulation of short-term external debt.

The balance of visible trade was in deficit between 1960 and 1967 by about £20 million p.a. on average. The deficit on invisibles probably averaged about £25 million p.a. in that period. The overall current deficit reached a peak of almost £80 million in 1965. In 1968 and 1970 surpluses, averaging about £20 million p.a., were earned for the first time since 1958, though the deficits on invisibles—increased by the rising level of imports—were sufficient still to leave overall current deficits of around £20 million p.a. In 1971 the trade account returned to deficit, and the overall current deficit may have reached £70 million.

DOMESTIC COMMERCE

A small number of large and long-established foreign companies continue to be important in the import trade, though they have now largely withdrawn from retail transactions, save in department stores in the major towns and for certain "technical" goods. Since 1962 the publicly-owned Ghana National Trading Corporation (created by purchase of A. G. Leventis & Co.) has existed alongside the expatriate companies, and until 1966 it enjoyed preferential treatment with respect to import licensing. At the retail levels independent Ghanaian and other African traders compete with the GNTC and with Lebanese and a few Indian businesses. The complex and highly fragmented trade in locally produced foodstuffs, the other major distributive sector, is almost wholly in African hands.

In 1968 the government announced that small-scale retail and wholesale trade and the representation of overseas manufacturers (together with taxi services and small-scale manufacturing) would henceforth be reserved for Ghanaian enterprise. Most of these restrictions were enforced through legislation from August 1st, 1970.

TRANSPORT

The country's major ports are both artificial: Takoradi, built in the 1920s, and Tema, which was opened in 1961 to replace the Accra roadstead, and which has become an industrial centre. The tonnages of cargo handled in 1969 were 2,559,000 at Tema and 2,952,000 at Takoradi. There are 592 miles of railway, making a triangle between Takoradi, Kumasi, and Accra-Tema. Exports of manganese, bauxite, logs and cocoa make up about 80 per cent of total railway freight tonnage. There are about 20,000 miles of roads. The road system is good by tropical African standards, but was allowed to deteriorate in the 1960s, feeder roads in particular being neglected. New vehicle registrations dropped from an annual average of about 10,000 in 1958–63 to 7,700 in 1964–69, because of import restrictions and increases in vehicle taxation. Vehicle spare parts have also been scarce in recent years, and the internal distributive system has deteriorated physically. The creation of the Volta Lake, stretching some 250 miles inland from the

Akosombo Dam, opens up new possibilities for internal transportation, but as yet the lake has acted as a further impediment. There is an international airport at Accra and other airports at Kumasi, Takoradi, and Tamale. Ghana Airways—financially one of the least successful of the generally unsuccessful state corporations—provides the domestic services and participates in international services.

AGRICULTURE

It is estimated that arable land and land under tree crops make up about 22 per cent of the total area, and that one-third of this is under cocoa. Annual cocoa output, which averaged 240,000 tons in the 1950s, rose sharply to 420,000 tons in 1960–64, and to 570,000 tons in the crop-year 1964–65. Since then annual output has averaged just under 400,000 tons, but with a very low crop (334,000 tons) in 1968–69, and a high crop in 1971–72.(These figures exclude cocoa exported illegally, which in some years is believed to have reached 30,000 tons.) Cocoa output depends in the long run on planting and re-planting, and in the short run it is strongly affected by weather conditions, the incidence and control of diseases and pests, and the relationship of producer prices to harvesting costs. The Cocoa Marketing Board has a statutory monopoly of export, buying through agents at a producer price fixed by the government for each season. Mainly because of the fiscal charges placed on the Board, the producer price has almost invariably been pitched far below the price being realized in world markets. Producer prices were reduced from a range of 70–80s. (per headload of 60lb.) in the 1950s to 40–60s. in the 1960s (the reduction being even greater in real terms), and the fall in CMB purchases since 1965 is partly attributed to this decline in the rate of renumeration. One motive for the devaluation of 1967 was the desire to raise the producer price in cedi terms without loss of official revenue from cocoa, and on five other occasions since the *coup* of 1966 the producer price has been raised in an effort to encourage production—though the effect of additional cocoa exports on Ghana's external earnings is questionable. Other export crops are coffee, palm kernels, copra, bananas, sheanuts and (for West African markets) kolanuts, but these are of very minor importance.

Staple crops are cassava, yams, cocoyams, and plantains, and, in the north, maize, Guinea corn and millet. Some rice is also grown. Market shortages of locally produced foodstuffs in recent years are perhaps mainly attributable to shortcomings of the distributive system. The effect on food production of the large-scale and mechanized state farms, which were set up in the early 1960s, appears to have been negligible (though some of these have been retained for the production of industrial raw materials), and food farming remains, like cocoa farming, a "peasant" activity. Cattle farming is restricted to northern Ghana and the Accra plains. Livestock imports from adjacent territories have been considerable, though declining since 1960 because of shortage of foreign exchange. Domestic fisheries (marine and Volta Lake)

currently supply 70–80 per cent (by value) of the total consumption of fish and fish products.

Timber production increased very rapidly in the post-war period until 1960, but exports were checked by experimentation with a Timber Marketing Board in 1960–63, and the increase of output has not since resumed. In recent years annual log production has been about 50 million cu. ft. of which 35–45 per cent is exported as logs. Sawn timber output has dropped from 16 to 13 million cu. ft. between 1965 and 1969, and the sawmills have been operating below capacity. Over half of the sawn timber output is exported. About one-fifth of the forest zone is reserved, constituting the permanent resource base of the timber industry. At present over 60 per cent of total log output is from unreserved forest. Only a small proportion of the many species of trees in the forest is at present commercially exploited.

POWER

Until 1966 electricity production was from diesel generating plants run by the State Electricity Corporation and the mines. Generation of hydroelectricity at the Volta Dam began in 1966, and by 1969 the Volta River Authority supplied 98.0 per cent of a total national electricity consumption of 2,772 million kWh. Over 70 per cent of total consumption in 1969 was purchased by a single customer, the American-owned VALCO alumina smelter, which with the dam constitutes the Volta River Project, executed after many years of study and negotiation during 1961–66. VALCO provides a guaranteed basic market for Volta electricity, thus ensuring the servicing of the foreign loans raised for the dam; in return it receives its power at virtually cost price and enjoys long-term fiscal concessions and guarantees. The return on the government's equity in the dam depends on the growth of non-smelter demand for power, especially other industrial demand, and this has so far disappointed expectations. However, agreement was reached in 1969 for the sale of Volta power to Togo and Dahomey, and transmission lines to Lomé and Cotonou are being built. The power plant at Akosombo is being enlarged from 4 units of 512 megawatts capacity to 6 units of 768 megawatts.

MINING

On the average of the years 1965–69 gold accounted for 48 per cent of the gross value of mineral production, diamonds for 29 per cent, manganese for 20 per cent, and bauxite for 3 per cent. The volume index of mineral production has been falling since 1961. Six gold mines are operated, five with the support of a government subsidy by the State Mining Corporation, which operates marginal workings purchased by the government in 1961 and 1965. The sixth is the rich Ashanti Goldfields mine at Obuasi, which was taken over in 1968 by Lonrho Ltd. Gold production has declined from 921,000 fine ounces in 1963 to 704,000 in 1970. Diamonds, which are mainly industrial stones, are mined both by the Consolidated African Selection Trust and two smaller foreign companies, and by African diggers. Because of an apparent decline in diggers' output, total recorded production has fallen from 3,273,000 carats in 1960 to 2,550,000 in 1970. The African diggers were contributing over half of total output at the beginning of the decade, but recorded output in this sector of the industry fell steeply after the introduction of exchange control in 1961 and the establishment of a Diamond Marketing Board as monopoly purchaser of Ghanian output in 1963. With the suspension of licensing of diggers in 1965–66 it was reduced to a few per cent of total output. No doubt the physical capacity of the digging sector is also diminishing, but there is probably much unrecorded diggers' production which is smuggled out of the country. Manganese comes from a single mine at Nsuta operated by the African Manganese Company. Annual output has fallen from nearly 600,000 tons in 1965 to 392,000 tons in 1970. Bauxite is mined at Awaso in the Western Region by the British Aluminium Company and annual output is around 300,000 tons.

In July 1972 the government was reported to have told foreign-owned mining and timber enterprises of its intention to acquire a participating interest in their operations.

Ghana's extensive bauxite deposits figured prominently in the early discussion of the Volta River Project, but in the project as finally implemented the smelter at Tema is supplied by imported alumina. The capital costs were thus avoided of developing new mines in proximity to Tema (Kibi in the Eastern Region was the likely site), of building a new railway, and of constructing an alumina plant. However, it now seems likely that the Kibi deposits will be developed and an alumina plant built by the Kaiser Corporation (the major shareholder in VALCO) in conjunction with a Japanese consortium. There are also deposits of low-grade iron ore in northern Ghana, and the creation of the Volta Lake might some day make possible the commercial exploitation of these. During 1970 licences for mineral oil exploration were issued, and off-shore drilling has begun.

MANUFACTURING

Manufacturing industry is made up of many small establishments and a small number of medium-sized and large establishments. The latter, making use of modern forms of organization and capital-intensive technologies, is often regarded as the manufacturing sector proper. It includes the VALCO aluminium smelter, the annual capacity of which was expected to reach 145,000 tons in 1972; sawmills and plywood and veneer plants, which supply export as well as home markets; and cocoa processing (in 1969 about 11 per cent of total value of cocoa exports was in the form of cocoa butter and paste). Relatively long-established home market industries include brewing and distilling, vehicle assembly, and the manufacture of soft drinks, biscuits, cigarettes, and cement. Petroleum products have been refined from imported crude since 1963.

Textiles and footwear have been rapidly growing industries. Many other industries were established in the 1960s, often with governmental control or participation, including steelmaking (from scrap), meat processing, pharmaceuticals, sugar refining, flour-milling and glassmaking. Manufacturing output has grown rapidly on a small base, but most plants have been underutilized, and many unprofitable, because of poor initial planning and shortages of imported raw materials and spare parts.

PUBLIC FINANCE

A budgetary deficit first appeared in 1959–60. Successful efforts to increase tax revenue were made. Increases in import duties, changes in income tax rates and assessments, the introduction of a sales tax and other measures produced an annual average increase of 14 per cent in tax revenue between 1960 and 1965. But government spending rose even faster: over the same period it almost doubled, from £93 to £181 million. By 1963 the deficit was running at an annual rate of £50 million and was being met mainly by *ad hoc* expedients. After the *coup* of 1966 government policy was to hold expenditure down to the level that could be met by ordinary revenue and assured capital receipts, with development expenditure being cut back, if necessary, as the financial year proceeded. In the period of civilian government from 1969 to 1971, deficit financing continued to be avoided, but the government's commitment to economic growth prevented its using the budget to restrain the increase of import demand resulting from its liberalization of external transactions. Government spending therefore grew as rapidly as the growth of revenue, emanating from rising export values, would allow it. Hence foreign exchange reserves were not built up, and the falling back of export proceeds in 1971 led to short-term indebtedness and the devaluation at the end of that year.

The second military government, with its external credit lines extinguished, reintroduced administrative controls in 1972 to bring import values into line with current external earnings. As a counterpart of this action, Ghanaian self-sufficiency was stressed in official pronouncements. But the central feature of the Ghanaian economy since 1961 has been the failure of self-sufficiency to develop; that is the relative inability to alter the structures of production and demand so as to meet the requirements of a partially closed economy. In face of relatively inflexible productive structures and tastes, neither the devaluation of 1967 nor the import surcharges of 1970–71 were effective in displacing imports by home production. It seems unlikely that military exhortations will succeed where these measures failed. Administrative controls therefore seem likely to persist, but past experience has shown that the economy is not easily controlled—partly because of Ghana's porous frontiers, partly because of the frailty of the controllers.

STATISTICAL SURVEY

AREA AND POPULATION

PROVISIONAL CENSUS RESULTS 1970

AREA (sq. miles)	TOTAL POPULATION	WESTERN	CENTRAL	ACCRA C.D.	EASTERN	VOLTA	ASHANTI	BRONG-AHAFO	NORTHERN	UPPER
92,100	8,545,561	768,312	892,593	848,825	1,262,882	947,012	1,477,397	762,673	728,572	857,295

Chief Tribal Groups (1960 census) (per cent): Akan 44, Mole-Dagbani 15.9, Ewe 13, Ga-Adangbe 8.3, Guan 3.7, Gurma 3. 5

CHIEF TOWNS

POPULATION ('000)

(1968 estimate)

Accra (capital) .	633.9*	Cape Coast†	.	41.2
Kumasi .	343.0*	Tamala†	.	40.4
Sekondi-Takoradi .	128.2	Tema†	.	14.9

*1970 estimate.   †1960 census.

EMPLOYMENT

PERSONS ENGAGED IN WAGE-EARNING EMPLOYMENT

	1966	1967	1968	1969
Agriculture, Forestry and Fishing . .	49,243	43,659	47,536	46,516
Mining and Quarrying . . .	25,548	26,299	26,236	25,955
Manufacturing	35,820	41,155	44,849	52,874
Construction	46,475	47,790	54,783	57,467
Electricity, Water and Sanitary Services	15,030	14,381	16,023	17,642
Commerce.	35,482	35,628	36,913	35,930
Transport, Storage and Communications	31,537	29,962	36,374	29,571
Services	122,367	122,477	128,547	134,859
	361,502	361,351	391,261	400,814

AGRICULTURE

PRINCIPAL CROPS

('000 metric tons)

	1969	1970	1971
Sugar Cane†	284	522	374
Maize	304	442	430*
Millet	88	93	100*
Sorghum	83	86	110*
Rice (paddy)	61	69	70*
Sweet Potatoes and Yams . .	1,305	1,617	n.a.
Cassava (Manioc) . . .	1,320	1,596	n.a.
Onions	17*	17*	n.a.
Tomatoes	35	37	n.a.
Oranges and Tangerines . .	63	71	60*
Other Citrus Fruits . . .	26	26	26*
Pineapples	26	30	n.a.
Palm Kernels	34	37	37
Palm Oil	55	60	60
Groundnuts (unshelled) . .	61	60	70*
Coconuts (million nuts) . .	168	201	n.a.
Copra and Coconut Oil (exports only) .	3	3	3*
Coffee	5.7	4.5	5.1
Cocoa Beans (purchases for export)‡ .	414.3	396.2	411.5

* FAO estimates.   † Figures relate to crop year ending in year stated.
‡ Figures relate to 12-month period ending September 30th of year stated.

Source: FAO, *Production Yearbook 1971.*

COCOA EXPORTS

	Total		United Kingdom		Rest of Sterling Area		United States	
	Tons	Value £'000	Tons	Value £'000	Tons	Value £'000	Tons	Value £'000
1967	329,640	65,335	38,988	7,928	13,775	2,728	73,225	14,482
1968	329,984	92,800	40,630	11,127	11,635	3,180	72,225	10,994
1969	121,335	79,145	40,050	26,225	17,725	12,008	63,560	40,912
1970	154,527	122,219	30,435	26,279	21,580	19,005	102,512	76,935

LIVESTOCK

	1968/69	1969/70	1970/71
Horses	4,000*	4,000*	4,000*
Asses	22,000*	23,000*	24,000*
Cattle	580,000	606,000	599,000
Pigs	320,000*	330,000*	340,000*
Sheep	640,000	681,000	1,177,000
Goats	760,000*	770,000*	775,000*
Poultry	9,700,000*	9,900,000*	10,000,000*

* FAO estimate.

Source: FAO, *Production Yearbook 1971.*

FISHING
('ooo tons)

	1967	1968	1969
Herring . . .	42.7	12.2	30.4
Trawl Fish . .	31.2	23.2	38.4
Line Fish . .	2.4	5.3	1.8
Unsorted . .	8.7	25.2	40.8
Tuna . .	11.2	24.6	23.6
Total . .	96.2	90.5	135.0

FORESTRY
(million cu. ft.)

	1966	1967	1968	1969
Logs . .	49	47	49	56
Sawn . .	14	12	12	13

MINING

	1966	1967	1968	1969	1970
Gold ('ooo fine oz. troy) . . .	684	763	740	707	704
Diamonds ('ooo carat) Total . .	2,819	2,538	2,447	2,391	2,550
African diggers	47	19	16	7	8
Companies . . .	2,772	2,519	2,431	2,384	2,542
Manganese ('ooo tons) . .	568	491	407	328	392
Bauxite ('ooo tons) . .	347	345	280	242	337

INDUSTRY
(1969—over 10 employees)

	No. of Works	Employees
Food (except Milling and Bakery) . .	19	6,231
Bakery	28	650
Beverages, Tobacco . . .	19	3,492
Textiles, Clothes	11	6,278
Wood (except furniture) . . .	46	2,259
Furniture, Fixtures . . .	22	1,213
Printing, Publishing . . .	26	3,196
Leather	4	236
Chemicals	14	1,310
Non-metallic products . . .	3	267
Metals, Machinery . . .	11	1,606
Body Making, Car and Cycle repairs .	48	4,625
Miscellaneous	14	874

FINANCE

100 pesewas = 1 new cedi.

Coins: $\frac{1}{2}$, 1, $2\frac{1}{2}$, 5, 10 and 20 pesewas.

Notes: 1, 5 and 10 cedis.

Exchange rates (December 1972): £1 sterling = 3.015 cedis; U.S. $1 = 1.282 cedis;

100 cedis = £33.17 = $78.00.

(*Note:* Between November 1967 and August 1971 the central exchange rates were £1 = 2.449 cedis = $2.40.)

BUDGET
(1971–72 estimates— cedis '000)

REVENUE	
Export Duty on Cocoa . . .	73,800
Taxes, etc.	296,840
Other Items	49,690
TOTAL . . .	420,330

EXPENDITURE	RECURRENT	DEVELOPMENT
Agriculture . . .	26,771	6,429
Mining and Forestry .	4,479	2,992
Trade, Industry and Tourism . . .	1,079	547
Construction . . .	15,458	46,870
Transport and Communications . . .	11,014	11,464
Education . . .	69,124	12,501
Health . . .	27,163	9,236
Youth and Rural Development . .	4,141	15,558
Internal Administration .	27,238	7,263
General Administration .	58,381	25,604
Development Administration and Financing .	17,795	3,377
Defence . . .	31,400	8,150
TOTAL . .	430,382	151,403

1972-73 Budget (million cedis): Current revenue 386.4, Current expenditure 329.0; Capital revenue 84.5, Capital expenditure 97.8.

NATIONAL ACCOUNTS
(million cedis)

	1966	1967	1968	1969
AVAILABLE RESOURCES:				
Private consumption expenditure .	1,337	1,286	1,467	1,626
General government consumption expenditure	261	308	363	412
Gross domestic fixed capital formation, including stocks	261	219	234	259
Exports	219	265	368	425
	2,078	2,078	2,432	2,722
USES OF RESOURCES:				
Gross domestic product . .	1,793	1,778	2,074	2,328
Imports	285	300	358	394
	2,078	2,078	2,432	2,722

CURRENCY AND RESERVES

	1967	1968	1969	1970
Currency in Circulation (cedis '000) . .	130,684	141,667	163,846	167,047
Gold Reserve Holdings (U.S. $'000) . .	5,592	5,592	5,592	5,595

BALANCE OF PAYMENTS
(million cedis)

	1968	1969	1970
Current Account:			
Visible trade:			
Exports	281.5	326.2	409.8
Imports (f.o.b.)	−266.9	−296.0	−387.0
Trade balance . . .	14.6	30.2	22.8
Invisible balance . . .	− 52.6	− 69.7	− 89.8
Transfer payments . . .	− 13.5	− 12.6	− 9.6
BALANCE ON CURRENT ACCOUNT .	− 51.5	− 52.1	− 76.6
Capital Account:			
BALANCE ON CAPITAL ACCOUNT . .	48.5	61.5	75.5
Overall Surplus or Deficit . .	− 3.0	9.4	− 1.1
Monetary Institutions:			
IMF account . . .	11.2	− 5.5	− 23.7
Special Drawing Rights . .	—	—	11.8
Central Bank . . .	− 3.4	− 13.2	1.5
Commercial Banks . . .	− 2.6	16.2	− 11.3
TOTAL MONETARY INSTITUTIONS . .	5.2	− 2.5	− 21.7
Net Unrecorded Items . . .	− 2.2	− 6.9	22.8

Source: Standard Bank Review, March 1972.

FOREIGN AID*
(million U.S. $)

Source	Total up to 1964	Total up to 1967	1967	1968	1969	1970
United States Grants	16.0	22.3	3.6†	2.0	2.7	2.7
United States Credits	14.3	44.4	32.5	18.3	26.9	30.1
IBRD Loans	26.0	46.5	—	0.2	—	—
Other International Agency Aid .	9.0	86.0	25.0	9.9	10.8	—
Other Western Aid	10.0	25.3	20.3	15.9	22.1	18.5
Soviet Aid	104.2	129.4	10.4	—	15.6	—
Chinese People's Republic . .	42.0	43.1	—	—	—	—
Czechoslovakia	14.0	34.6	4.2	—	—	—
Other Communist Aid	59.7	69.8	3.9	1.1	0.3	—

* Figures are Provisional.   † Financial Year Basis.

EXTERNAL TRADE

	1965	1966	1967	1968	1969	1970	1971
	('ooo cedis)						
Imports	320,051	251,209	261,523	314,032	354,391	419,047	450,600
Exports, incl. re-exports	226,882	191,394	245,122	338,782	333,264	467,378	387,900

COMMODITIES
('ooo cedis)

Imports	1968	1969	1970	1971*
Food	51,013	55,178	79,474	46,347
Beverages and Tobacco . . .	5,035	1,611	3,924	2,395
Crude Materials	6,277	5,393	9,420	9,251
Mineral Fuels	21,488	22,871	24,358	19,770
Oils and Fats	3,952	5,862	3,835	3,887
Chemicals	48,349	55,093	66,874	52,713
Manufactures	76,265	97,438	100,847	69,450
Machinery	85,968	94,518	100,848	96,083
Miscellaneous Items . . .	13,950	14,601	16,377	14,164
Other Transactions . . .	1,734	1,827	5,805	7,142

Exports	1968	1969	1970	1971*
Cocoa	185,600	219,700	300,399	181,263
Logs	16,258	} 39,100	19,875	13,594
Sawn Timber	12,296		17,096	8,162
Bauxite	1,493	1,393	1,276	1,504
Manganese Ore	10,546	7,000	7,209	4,446
Diamonds	17,430	13,867	14,467	6,468
Gold	25,792	25 668	25,697	18,009
Re-exports and Other Items . .	69,367	n.a.	81,359	58,768

* Provisional figures for January–August.

COUNTRIES
('ooo cedis)

IMPORTS	1968	1969	1970	1971*
United Kingdom	86,610	95,033	99,068	80,504
Canada	7,100	6,592	4,637	2,405
Hong Kong	2,586	4,505	6,284	3,441
Nigeria	1,495	4,025	2,598	4,924
Other Commonwealth . .	9,845	11,090	12,075	7,372
Federal Republic of Germany .	36,034	37,769	44,691	41,495
Italy	7,210	8,892	9,944	8,663
France	6,312	8,450	15,290	12,482
Belgium/Luxembourg . .	883	2,478	4,969	4,289
Netherlands	13,455	16,758	16,604	10,589
U.S.A.	59,981	65,210	75,718	48,562
Japan	17,332	20,772	25,772	30,070
Communist Countries . .	24,148	31,209	34,598	20,763
Other Countries . . .	39,491	39,888	64,664	43,022
Parcel Post	1,549	1,721	2,135	2,621
TOTAL	314,032	354,391	419,047	321,202

EXPORTS	1968	1969	1970	1971*
United Kingdom	91,927	106,292	109,430	61,772
Canada	10,465	4,073	5,306	4,397
Hong Kong	838	714	624	312
Nigeria	1,461	834	1,192	1,382
Other Commonwealth . .	9,386	10,076	21,249	8,967
Federal Republic of Germany .	33,717	33,480	45,610	32,360
Italy	9,944	10,880	14,704	9,334
France	1,956	4,143	2,336	1,401
Belgium/Luxembourg . .	5,026	7,912	5,976	2,650
Netherlands	37,622	33,699	43,710	28,214
U.S.A.	59,896	48,236	83,963	69,074
Japan	23,108	26,185	30,325	25,936
Communist Countries . .	31,650	20,292	74,297	28,524
Other Countries . . .	21,764	26,380	28,652	12,565
Parcel Post	22	68	103	67
TOTAL	338,782	333,264	467,377	286,955

* Provisional figures for January–August.

TRANSPORT

RAILWAYS

YEAR	PASSENGERS CARRIED	FREIGHT TONS CARRIED	PASSENGER-KILOMETRES	NET TON-KILOMETRES
1967 . . .	7,079,369	1,704,848	404,414,574	286,245,898
1968 . . .	7,357,605	1,576,882	425,111,184	276,280,622
1969 . . .	7,930,999	1,624,788	474,165,098	302,195,361
1970 . . .	7,956,135	1,645,398	542,635,604	310,724,148

ROAD TRANSPORT
(licences current)

Year	Total	Cars (incl. Taxis)	Motor Cycles	Public Conveyances	Goods Vehicles	Trailers and Caravans	Special Service Vehicles	Public Service Vehicles	Tractors and Mechanized Equipment
1966 .	46,771	26,250	2,902	2,761	11,873	353	1,938	116	578
1967 .	52,155	27,551	2,846	3,460	14,872	567	2,048	79	732
1968 .	53,601	29,450	3,079	4,942	12,464	466	2,347	177	676

SHIPPING

Year	Vessels Entered (number)	Vessels Cleared (number)	Tonnage Entered (net reg. tons)	Tonnage Cleared (net reg. tons)	Cargo Loaded (tons)	Cargo Unloaded (tons)
1967 . .	1,593	1,604	5,248,820	5,251,927	1,960,856	2,210,637
1968 . .	1,538	1,595	5,282,917	5,311,602	1,143,521	2,361,207
1969 . .	1,538	1,546	5,497,667	5,470,969	2,204,622	2,944,863
1970 . .	1,565	1,553	5,464,632	5,464,445	2,154,759	4,164,329

CIVIL AVIATION

	1967	1968	1969
Arrivals . . .	110,859	137,223	137,935
Departures . .	114,492	141,212	142,126
Freight set down (kg.) .	1,361,992	1,680,330	2,145,310
Freight picked up (kg.) .	1,312,704	1,677,145	1,340,642

EDUCATION
(1967–68)

	Number of Pupils	Number of Teachers
Primary Schools . .	1,389,804	46,960
Secondary Schools . .	52,852	2,899
Technical and Trade Establishments . .	12,149	578
Teacher Training Colleges .	18,814	1,247
Higher Education Institutes	5,426	902

Source (except where stated): Central Bureau of Statistics, Accra.

THE CONSTITUTION

The Constitution promulgated in August 1969 was abolished in January 1972 following the army *coup d'état*.

THE GOVERNMENT

NATIONAL REDEMPTION COUNCIL

(*December* 1972)

Chairman of the Council and Commissioner for Defence, Finance, Information and Economic Affairs: Col. I. K. ACHEAMPONG.

Commissioner for Agriculture: Maj.-Gen. D. K. ADDO.

Commissioner for Education, Culture and Sports: Lt.-Col. P. K. NGEGBE.

Commissioner for Foreign Affairs: Maj. KWAME BAAH.

Commissioner for Health: Col. J. C. ADJEITEY.

Commissioner for Internal Affairs: J. H. COBBINA.

Attorney-General and Commissioner for Justice: E. N. MOORE.

Commissioner for Labour, Social Welfare and Co-operatives: Maj. KWAME ASANTE.

Commissioner for Lands and Mineral Resources: Maj.-Gen. D. C. K. AMENU.

Commissioner for Local Government: Maj.-Gen. N. A. AFERI.

Commissioner for Trade and Tourism: Maj. J. FELLI.

Commissioner for Transport and Communications: Maj. A. H. SELORMEY.

Commissioner for Industries: Maj. K. B. AGBO.

Commissioner for Works and Housing: Col. VICTOR COKER-APPIAH.

DIPLOMATIC REPRESENTATION

EMBASSIES AND LEGATIONS IN ACCRA

(E) Embassy; (L) Legation; (HC) High Commission.

Afghanistan: Cairo, Egypt.

Algeria: House No. F.606/1, Off Cantonments Rd., X'borg, P.O.B. 2747 (E); *Ambassador:* BOUFELDJA AIDI.

Argentina: Lagos, Nigeria.

Austria: Lagos, Nigeria.

Australia: No. 6/26 Milne Ave., Off McCulloch Ave., Airport Residential Area, P.O.B. 2445 (HC); *High Commissioner:* J. M. McMILLAN.

Belgium: Plot 56 Cantonments, Off Rangoon Ave., P.O.B. 5060, Accra-North (E); *Ambassador:* JULES MARCHAL.

Brazil: No. 6 Kanda Estate, P.O.B. 2918 (E); *Ambassador:* LYLE AMAURY TARRISSE.

Bulgaria: House No. C.744/3, Farrar Ave., Asylum Down, Third Crescent Rd., S.4, P.O.B. 3193 (E); *Ambassador:* D. TCHORBADJIEV.

Canada: E.115/3, Independence Ave., P.O.B. 1639 (HC); *High Commissioner:* NOBLE E. C. POWER (also accred. as Ambassador to Dahomey and Togo).

China, People's Republic: (E); *Ambassador:* KO HUA.

Czechoslovakia: C.260/5, Kanda High Rd. No. 2, P.O.B. 5226, Accra North (E); *Ambassador:* Dr. JOSEF ZABOKRTSKY.

Denmark: Plot No. 67, Dr. Isert's Rd., North Ridge (West) Residential Area, P.O.B. 3328 (E); *Ambassador:* Mrs. NONNY WRIGHT.

Egypt: House No. F.805/1, Off Cantonments Rd., P.O.B. 2508 (E); *Ambassador:* A. A. EL-MOURSI.

Ethiopia: 13 Morocco Rd., Independence Ave., P.O.B. 1646 (E); *Ambassador:* GOYTOM PETROS.

France: 12th Rd., Off Liberation Ave., P.O.B. 187 (E); *Ambassador:* PIERRE ANTHONIOZ.

Federal Republic of Germany: Valdemasa Lodge, 7th Ave. Extension, North Ridge, P.O.B. 1757 (E); *Ambassador:* HELMUT MULLER.

Hungary: H/No. F.582 A/1, Salem Rd., Christiansborg, P.O.B. 3027 (E); *Ambassador:* JANOS LORINCZ-NAGY.

India: House No. Z-21, Off Dempster Rd., Airport Residential Area, P.O.B. 3040, (HC); *High Commissioner:* S. BIKRAM SHAH.

Indonesia: Lagos, Nigeria (E).

Iraq: Lagos, Nigeria.

Israel: New Town Rd., Accra New Town, P.O.B. 3275 (E); *Ambassador:* AVRAHAM COHEN.

Italy: Switchback Rd., P.O.B. 140 (E); *Ambassador:* Dr. GUGLIELMO FOLCHI.

Ivory Coast: House No. C.1037/3, Off 7th Ave. Extension, North Ridge Area, P.O.B. 3445 (E); *Ambassador:* DENIS COFFI BILE.

Jamaica: Addis Ababa, Ethiopia.

Japan: Rangoon Ave, Off Switchback Rd., P.O.B. 1637 (E); *Ambassador:* YO KAMIKAWA.

Lebanon: 43 Rangoon Ave., P.O.B. 562 (E); *Chargé d'Affaires:* JEAN HAZOU.

Lesotho: Nairobi, Kenya.

Liberia: House No. F.675/1, Off Cantonments Rd., Christiansborg, P.O.B. 895 (E); *Ambassador:* THEOPHILUS THOMAS.

Libya: Lagos, Nigeria.

Malaysia: Lagos, Nigeria.

Mali: Crescent Rd., Block 1, P.O.B. 1121 (E); *Ambassador:* GUORDO SOW.

Mexico: Off Dempster Rd., Plot Z.26, Airport Residential Area, P.O.B. 1984 (E); *Ambassador:* ERNESTO MADERO.

Netherlands: 89 Liberation Rd., Independence Circle, P.O.B. 3248 (E); *Ambassador:* CHRISTIAAN BENJAMIN ARRIËNS.

Niger: E.104/3, Independence Ave., P.O.B. 2685 (E); *Ambassador:* TIECOURA ALZOUMA.

Nigeria: Nigeria House, 65 Farrar Ave., Asylum Down, P.O.B. 1548 (HC); *Chargé d'Affaires:* PETER U. ONU.

Norway: Lagos, Nigeria.

Pakistan: Plot 11, Ring Rd. East (E); *Ambassador:* S. A. MOID.

Philippines: Lagos, Nigeria.

Poland: House No. F.820/1, Off Cantonments Rd., X'borg, P.O.B. 2552 (E); *Chargé d'Affaires:* ZYGMUNT KROLAK.

Romania: 49 Farrar Ave., Adabraka, P.O.B. M.112 (E); *Ambassador:* GHEORGE IASON.

Saudi Arabia: House No. F.868/1, Off Cantonments Rd., P.O.B. 670 (E); *Chargé d'Affaires:* FOUAD IBRAHIM EL-ALFY.

Senegal: Fifth Ave. Extension (Behind Police Headquarters), P.O.B. 3208 (E); *Ambassador:* LOUIS LAURENT KANDE.

Sierra Leone: C.135/3, Asylum Down, P.O.B. 6706 (HC); *Acting High Commissioner:* H. M. LYNCH-SHYLLON.

Spain: Airport Residential Area, Off Dempster Rd., P.O.B. 1218 (E); *Ambassador:* JUAN JOSÉ CANO Y ABASCAL.

Sweden: Lagos, Nigeria.

Switzerland: Off 7th Ave. Extension, P.O.B. 359 (E); *Ambassador:* FRIEDRICH SCHNYDER.

Togo: Leventis House near Cantonments Roundabout, P.O.B. 4308 (E); *Ambassador:* SYLVAIN T. BABELEME.

Tunisia: Abidjan, Ivory Coast.

Turkey: Plot No. Z/25, Off Dempster Rd., Airport Residential Area, P.O.B. 3104 (E); *Chargé d'Affaires:* ERKUT ONART.

Uganda: House No. A.72, North Labone, P.O.B. 4260 (HC); *High Commissioner:* Brig. SHABAN OKUNI OPOLOT (also accred. to Nigeria).

U.S.S.R.: F.856/1, Ring Rd. East, P.O.B. 1634 (E); *Ambassador:* V. I. CHEREDNIK.

United Kingdom: Barclays Bank Bldg., High St., P.O.B. 296 (HC); *High Commissioner:* HENRY S. H. STANLEY.

United States of America: Intersection of Rowe Rd. and Liberia Rd., P.O.B. 194 (E); *Ambassador:* FRED L. HADSEL.

Upper Volta: House No. 772/3, Asylum Down, Off Farrar Ave., P.O.B. 651 (E); *Ambassador:* PAUL TENSORE ROUMBA.

Venezuela: Lagos, Nigeria.

Yugoslavia: Plot No. B.79, Ring Rd. North Extension, P.O.B. 1629; *Ambassador:* TRIFUN NIKOLIC.

Zaire: 58 Rangoon Ave., Off Switchback Rd., P.O.B. 5448 Accra North (E); *Ambassador:* GREGOIRE M. LUNTUMBUE.

Ghana also has diplomatic relations with Dahomey, Guinea and the German Democratic Republic.

NATIONAL ASSEMBLY

The Assembly was dissolved in January 1972, following the army *coup d'état*.

POLITICAL PARTIES

The ban imposed on political parties in February 1966 was lifted on May 1st, 1969, but reimposed in January 1972 after the *coup d'état*. Before that time, the following parties existed:

Progress Party: Accra; f. 1969; Leader Dr. KOFI A. BUSIA.

Justice Party: Accra; f. 1970 after a merger of the National Alliance of Liberals, United Nationalist Party and the All Peoples' Republican Party; Leader E. MADJITEY.

People's Action Party: Accra; f. 1969; Leader IMORU AYARNA.

People's Popular Party: Accra; banned until 1970 as being Nkrumahist.

DEFENCE

The total armed force of 18,600 comprises an army of 16,500, a navy of 1,000, and an air force of 1,100. In addition there is a workers' brigade of 3,000 with basic military training.

Commander-in-Chief of the Ghana Armed Forces: Col. I. K. ACHEAMPONG.

Chief of the Defence Staff: Brig. N. Y. R. ASHLEY-LARSEN.

Commander of the Army: Col. E. O. ERSKINE.

Commander of the Navy: Commodore P. F. QUAYE.

Commander of the Air Force: Brig. C. BEAUSOLEIL.

JUDICIAL SYSTEM

The civil law in force in Ghana is based on the Common Law, doctrines of equity and general statutes which were in force in England in 1874, as modified by subsequent Ordinances. Ghanaian customary law is, however, the basis of most personal, domestic and contractual relationships and the Supreme Court has power to enforce it. Criminal law is based on the Criminal Code, enacted at the end of the nineteenth century and dependent on English Criminal Law, and since amended at intervals. In September 1972 the National Redemption Council abolished the Supreme Court, previously the premier court in Ghana. It said that the court had only sat twice since its establishment, and claimed that its continued existence could no longer be justified after the suspension of the 1969 Constitution which set it up. The supreme tribunal in Ghana is now the Court of Appeal.

The Court of Appeal: The Court of Appeal consists of the Chief Justice and not less than five Judges of the Court of Appeal. It has jurisdiction to hear and determine appeals from any judgement, decree or order of the High Court.

The High Court: The High Court of Ghana consists of the Chief Justice and not less than twelve Puisne Judges and has an original jurisdiction in all matters, civil and criminal. Trial by jury is practised in criminal cases in Ghana and the Criminal Procedure Code, 1960, provides that all trials on indictment shall be by a jury or with the aid of Assessors.

The Circuit Court: Circuit Courts were created in 1960, and the jurisdiction of a Circuit Court consists of an original jurisdiction in civil matters where the amount involved does not exceed NC4,000. It has also jurisdiction with regard to the guardianship and custody of infants, and original jurisdiction in criminal matters in case of offences other than those where the maximum punishment is death or life imprisonment. Finally it has appellate jurisdiction from decisions of any District Court situated within its circuit.

District Courts: District Magistrates exercise summary jurisdiction throughout the country. In criminal cases Magistrates have jurisdiction to impose sentences of imprisonment up to one year and fines not exceeding NC500. They also hear civil suits in which the amount involved does not exceed NC1,000.

Juvenile Courts have been set up in Accra, Kumasi, Koforidua, Sekondi, Tamale, Sunyani and Ho. They consist either of three citizens selected from a panel of Juvenile Court Magistrates or of a Stipendiary Magistrate sitting with two of the panel. The public is excluded from proceedings of Juvenile Courts which are empowered to place a child in the care of a relative, Probation Officer or other suitable person, to negotiate with parents to secure the good behaviour of a child.

Local Courts: Local Courts now replace the former Native Courts. They have both civil and criminal jurisdiction. In civil cases they enjoy exclusive jurisdiction in cases where customary law is involved and in personal suits up to £100. They have limited criminal jurisdiction and cannot impose a fine exceeding £25 or a sentence of three months imprisonment. However, they have unlimited jurisdiction as to persons of all races living within their areas of jurisdiction. Control is exercised by the Judges of the Circuit and High Court by way of appeals and reviews in accordance with the Courts Act, 1960. Appeals lie either to the Circuit or High Court, depending on the nature of the suit. Whilst in land causes a person aggrieved by any decision may appeal to the High Court, in succession causes he may appeal to the Circuit Court.

Chief Justice: Mr. Justice CRABBE.

High Court Judges: Mrs. ANNIE JIAGGE, J. KINGSLEY-NYINAH, E. N. P. SOWAH, P. E. N. K. ARCHER, R. J. HAYFRON-BENJAMIN, G. KORANTENG-ADDOW, SAMPSON BAIDOO, J. S. A. ANTERKYI, D. F. ANNAN, ENOCH EDUSEI, R. H. FRANCOIS, S. M. BOISON, E. K. WIREDU.

RELIGION

According to the 1960 census, the distribution of religious groups was:

	per cent
Christians	42.8
Traditional Religions	38.2
Muslims	12.0
No Religion	7.0

CHRISTIANITY

The Christian community in Ghana is divided principally into Anglicans, Roman Catholics, Methodists and Presbyterians.

ANGLICAN COMMUNITY
PROVINCE OF WEST AFRICA

Archbishop of the Province of West Africa and Bishop of Sierra Leone: Most Rev. M. N. C. O. SCOTT, C.B.E., D.D., DIP.TH., Bishopscourt, P.O.B. 128, Freetown, Sierra Leone.

Bishop of Accra: Right Rev. ISHMAEL SAMUEL MILLS LEMAIRE, P.O.B. 8, Accra.

(For details of other sees in the Province of West Africa *see* under Nigeria, Religion.)

ROMAN CATHOLIC CHURCH

Archbishop: Most Rev. JOHN KODWO AMISSAH, P.O.B. 112, Cape Coast.

Bishops: Rt. Rev. GABRIEL CHAMPAGNE, P.O.B. 42, Tamale; Rt. Rev. ANTHONY KONINGS, P.O.B. 150, Kpandu; Rt. Rev. Dr. DOMINIC KODWO ANDOH, P.O.B. 247, Accra; Rt. Rev. JOSEPH ESSUAH, P.O.B. 236, Takoradi; Rt. Rev. PETER K. SARPONG, P.O.B. 99, Kumasi; Rt. Rev. PETER DERY, P.O.B. 63, Wa; Rt. Rev. GERARD BERTRAND, P.O.B. 4, Navrongo.

METHODIST CHURCH

President: Rev. T. WALLACE KOOMSON.

Secretary: Rev. I. K. A. THOMPSON, B.D.

Methodist Church of Ghana: Liberia Rd., P.O. Box 403, Accra; became fully autonomous July 1961; 238,538 mems.

PRESBYTERIAN CHURCH

Presbyterian Church of Ghana: P.O.B. 1800, Accra; 244,405 mems.; Moderator Rt. Rev. G. K. SINTIM MISA.

OTHER CHURCHES

A.M.E. Zion Church: P.O.B. 239, Sekondi.

A.M.E. Zion Church (East): P.O.B. 2820, Accra.

A.M.E. Zion Church (West): A.M.E. Zion Church Educational Unit, P.M.B., Osu-Accra.

Christian Council of Ghana: Rev. W. F. BRANDFUL, P.O.B. 919, Accra.

Christian Methodist Episcopal Church: P.O.B. 3906, Accra.

Evangelical-Lutheran Church: P.O.B. 197, Kaneshie; 123 mems.

Evangelical-Presbyterian Church: P.O.B. 18, Ho.

Ghana Baptist Convention: P.O.B. 1, Abuakwa, Ashanti.

Mennonite Church: West Africa Office, P.O.B. 6484, Accra; Co-ordinator Pastor W. E. ROTH; Ghana Office, P.O.B. 5484, Accra; Moderator EBENEZER K. NIMO; 475 mems.

Salvation Army: P.O.B. 320, Accra.

AFRICAN RELIGIONS

A large proportion of people practise various traditiona beliefs.

ISLAM

There are a considerable number of Muslims in the Northern Region.

THE PRESS

NEWSPAPERS

DAILY

Daily Graphic: Brewery Rd., P.O.B. 742, Accra; f. 1950; circ. 125,000; Editor J. W. K. DUMOGA.

Ghanaian Times, The: P.O.B. 2638, Accra; f. 1958; circ. 100,000; Editor A. KUNTI N. MENSAH.

Pioneer: Box 325, Kumasi, Ashanti; f. 1939, suppressed 1962–66; Exec. Editor S. ARTHUR; Editor A. D. APPEA; suspended by N.R.C. decree 1972.

Spectator: P.O.B. 2638, Accra.

WEEKLIES

Business Weekly: P.O.B. 2351, Accra; f. 1966; Editor MARK BOTSIO; circ. 5,000.

Cape Coast Standard: P.O.B. 60, Cape Coast; official Roman Catholic paper; circ. 4,000.

Echo: Echo Publications Ltd., P.O.B. 3460, Accra; Editor S. KISSI-AFARE; circ. 30,000; suspended by N.R.C. decree 1972.

Herald, The: Accra; f. 1969.

Northern Review: P.O.B. 55, Tamale.

Radio Review & TV Times: Ghana Broadcasting Corporation, P.O.B. 1633, Accra; Editor JOHN E. EDU; circ. 20,000.

Standard, The: P.O.B. 60, Cape Coast; f. 1938; National Catholic paper; Editor Rev. Father MARTIN T. PETERS; circ. 8,200 (weekly).

Sunday Mirror: Brewery Rd., P.O.B. 742, Accra; f. 1953; publ. Ghana Graphic Co. Ltd.; circ. 69,827; Editor NICHOLAS ALANDO.

Sunday Star: P.O.B. X16, James Town, Accra; f. 1966; Editor FRANCIS AWUKU.

Weekly Spectator: P.O.B. 2638, Guinea Press Ltd., Accra; f. 1963; Suns.; Editor AUGUSTUS BRUCE; circ. 45,000.

MAGAZINES AND REVIEWS

FORTNIGHTLY

The Ghana Information Services, P.O.B. 745, Accra, publishes the following works:

Akwansosem (Akuapem Twi): Editor K. S. ODAME.

Kakyevole (Nzema): Editor F. K. ERWVAH; circ. 10,500.

Mansralo (Ga): Editor N. A. NIMOI.

Motabiala (Ewe): Editor K. S. A. GWOPONE.

Nkwantabisa (Fante): Editor A. E. F. MENDS; (Asante-Twi): Editor D. Y. KYEI.

Ghana World: P.O. Box 2208, Accra; Publ. Ghana World Publications.

Legon Observer: c/o L.S.N.A., Legon; f. 1966; Editor YAW TWUMASI; circ. 11,000.

MONTHLY

African Woman: P.O.B. 1496, B135/1 Ring Road West, Accra; f. 1961; Editor SOPHIA ORGLE.

Catholic Voice: P.O.B. 60, Cape Coast; publ. Archdiocese of Cape Coast; Editor Father MARTIN T. PETERS; circ. 4,000 (monthly).

Christian Messenger: P.O.B. 3075, Accra; f. 1859; English, Twi, Fante and Ga editions; circ. 20,000; Editor E. OFORI ADDO.

Drum: Drum Publications (Ghana) Ltd., P.O.B. 1197, Accra; circ. 45,000; Editor JOSEPH MENSAH.

Flamingo Magazine: P.O.B. 242, Accra; f. 1960; general family magazine; Editor GERALD MALMED; circ. 100,000.

Ghana Farmer: Ministry of Agriculture, Accra; publ. Publicity and Information Section.

Ghana Journal of Education: Ministry of Education, P.O.B. M.45, Accra; f. 1969; quarterly; circ. 12,000.

Ghana Trade Journal: P.O.B. 2351, Accra; f. 1959; Editor MARK BOTSIO; circ. 5,000.

Kasem Labaare: P.O.B. 55, Tamale; f. 1951; Kasem language; Editor A. C. AZIIBA.

Lahabale Tsusu: P.O.B. 55, Tamale; f. 1951; Dagbani language; Editor T. T. SULEMANA.

New Ghana: Department of Information Services, P.O.B. 745, Accra.

What's on in Ghana: P.O.B. 2643, Accra; Editor A. ADUMUA-BOSSMAN.

OTHER PERIODICALS

Economic Bulletin of Ghana: Economic Society of Ghana, P.O.B. 22, Legon; Editor Prof. JOHN COLEMAN DE GRAFT-JOHNSON.

Ghana Journal of Science: Ghana Science Association, P.O. Box 7, Legon.

Ghana Teacher: Ghana Union of Teachers, P.O.B. 209.

Ghana Review: Information Services Department, P.O.B. 745, Accra; f. 1961; review of economic, social and cultural affairs; twice a month; circ. 24,000; Editor SIMON IKOI-KWAKU.

West African Pharmacist: Faculty of Pharmacy, University of Science and Technology, Kumasi; f. 1959; six a year.

NEWS AGENCIES

Ghana News Agency: P.O.B. 2118, Accra; f. 1957; Chair. KWAMINA ATTA KAKRA ERSKINE; Gen. Man. KOW BONDZIE BROWN.

Agence France-Presse: P.O.B. 3055; Chief EDWARD ANKRAH.

Associated Press: P.O.B. 2017, Accra; Chief A. A. PATERSON.

Czechoslovak News Agency: P.O.B. 4209, Accra.

Reuters: P.O.B. 2860, Accra; Chief ALLAN REDITT.

The following agencies are also represented: Deutsche Presse-Agentur and Tass.

PUBLISHERS

Anowuo Educational Publications: P.O.B. 3918, Accra; f. 1966; educational books, novels and poetry in English and the nine main Ghanaian languages; about 30 titles annually; Publisher SAMUEL ASARE KONADU.

Bureau of Ghana Languages: P.O.B. 1851, Accra.

Business Publications: P.O.B. 2351, Accra; publishers of *Business Weekly, Ghana Trade Journal, Ghana Business Guide.*

Ghana Universities Press: P.O.B. 4219, Accra; f. 1962; publishes academic works for all the universities and institutions of higher education in Ghana; Dir. N. K. ADZAKEY, B.A., DIP.ED., M.ED.

Methodist Book Depot Ltd.: P.O.B. 100, Cape Coast; brs. in Accra, Kumasi, Takoradi, etc.; publishers, booksellers, manufacturing stationers; Man. Dir. RICHARD MATHIESON.

Moxon Paperbacks Ltd.: P.O.B. M160, Accra; f. 1967; publishers of travel and guide books, handbooks, Africana, modern novels and poetry; quarterly catalogue of Ghana books and periodicals in print; Proprietor R. J. MOXON, O.B.E.

State Publishing Corporation (Publishing Division): P.O.B. 4348, Accra; f. 1965; 30 titles annually, chiefly primary school.

Waterwille Publishing House: P.O.B. 195, Accra.

RADIO AND TELEVISION

Ghana Broadcasting Corporation: Broadcasting House, P.O.B. 1633, Accra; f. 1935; Dir.-Gen. S. B. MFODWO, B.A.; Dirs. S. AMARTEIFIO, A. A. OPOKU, J. L. MILLS.

RADIO

There is a national service with services in English and six Ghana languages; also an external service in English, French, Portuguese, Hausa, Swahili and Arabic. There are 40 relay stations and approximately 750,000 radio receivers.

TELEVISION

The television service came into operation in 1965; stations at Accra, Kumasi and Sekondi-Takoradi, with a relay station at Tamale.

In 1971 there were an estimated 20,000 television receivers in the country.

FINANCE

BANKING

(cap.=capital; p.u.=paid up)

CENTRAL BANK

Bank of Ghana: P.O.B. 2674, Accra; f. 1957; cap. NC4m. Gov. J. H. FRIMPONG-ANSAH.

COMMERCIAL BANKS

Agricultural Development Bank: P.O.B. 4191, Accra; f. 1965; cap. NC30m.; 51 per cent state-owned; credit facilities for agriculturists; Chair. and Man. Dir. E. N. AFFUL.

Ghana Commercial Bank: P.O.B. 134, Accra; f. 1953; state-owned; cap. p.u. NC5m., dep. NC152,522,231 (June 1968); Man. Dir. K. GYASI-TWUM; over 100 branches.

National Investment Bank: Liberty Avenue, P.O.B. 3726, Accra; f. 1963; p.u. cap. NC10.8m.; Chair. and Man. Dir. E. P. L. GYAMPOH.

Ghana Savings Bank: General Post Office, Accra.

FOREIGN BANKS

Barclays Bank of Ghana Ltd.: Head Office, 54 Lombard St., London, E.C.3; Head Office in Ghana: High St., Accra P.O.B. 2949; Ghana Dirs. G. D. HOLDER, AMISHADAI LARSON ADU, A. E. AMBROSE, R. G. DYSON, N. E. IRELAND, E. N. OMABOE, R. MENSAH.

Standard Bank Ghana Ltd.: High St., P.O.B. 768, Accra; cap. NC4.3m.; dep. and a/c. NC100,593,101; Chair. GEOFFREY WILLIAM SMITH.

INSURANCE

GHANAIAN COMPANIES

The State Insurance Corporation of Ghana: Accra; f. 1962 to undertake general insurance for the public.

There are 8 foreign insurance companies in Ghana, 6 British and 2 Indian.

TRADE AND INDUSTRY

PUBLIC BOARDS AND CORPORATIONS

Ghana Industrial Holding Corporation: P.O.B. 2784, Accra f. 1968; took over the management of the 19 state enterprises, including the steel, paper, bricks, paint, sugar, textile and boat-building factories; aims to run these on a commercial basis; foreign investment in some of these interests is being encouraged; Man. Dir. I. ACKOM MENSAH.

Capital Investments Board: P.O.B. M193, Accra; central investment promotion agency of the Government; Chair. KWAME D. FORDWOR; Acting Sec. ENOCH A. AGBOZO.

Cocoa Marketing Company (Ghana) Ltd.: P.O.B. M108, Accra; London Office: 64–66 Oxford St., London, W.1; New York Office: 565 Fifth Ave., New York, N.Y. 10017; f. 1961; markets Ghana's cocoa beans, as well as cocoa butter and cocoa cake produced by West African Mills, Takoradi; before establishment Ghana's cocoa was marketed in London by Ghana Cocoa Marketing Company, London, which went into liquidation in September 1961; wholly-owned subsidiary of State Cocoa Marketing Board (*see* below).

Ghana Cocoa Marketing Board: P.O.B. 933, Accra; f. 1947; incorporated 1961 into Ghana Agricultural Produce Marketing Board, reconstituted 1963, reconstituted 1965; responsible for purchase and export of cocoa, coffee, palm kernels and palm kernel oil, copra, coconut, shea nuts, shea butter, groundnuts, bananas, kola nuts and other produce; Chief Exec. J. G. AMOAFO.

Ghana Food Marketing Corporation: P.O.B. 4245, Accra; f. 1965, to replace Food Marketing Board, which before May, 1963 was division of Ghana Agricultural Produce Board; buys, stores, preserves, distributes and sells foodstuffs throughout the country, and organizes exports of foodstuffs for which no local market is available; thus ensures increased production by provision of assured markets and guaranteed prices as well as an even flow of foodstuffs throughout the year; 8 regional centres for preservation, storage, distribution and sales: Accra, Kumasi, Sekondi-Takoradi, Cape Coast, Ho, Sunyani, Tamale, Wa.

Ghana National Trading Corporation: P.O.B. 67, Accra; f. 1961; engages in trade in same way as other trade and commercial organizations and organizes exports and imports of commodities determined by the Corporation.

Ghana Shipping Corporation: Accra.

Ghana Timber Marketing Board: P.O.B. 515, Takoradi; f. 1960, incorporated 1961 into Ghana Agricultural Produce Marketing Board, reconstituted 1963; assists general development and controls exports of timber; 10 mems.; Chair. K. A. ADUFO, K. SEKYI-CANN.

Ghana Water and Sewerage Corporation: P.O.B. M194, Accra.

Ghana Workers' Brigade: P.O.B. 1853, Accra; f. 1957; agricultural wing 7,284 mems.; voluntary organization to organize youth otherwise unemployed for large-scale agricultural and food production enterprises and other development projects of public value; under Ministries of Agriculture and Youth and Rural Development; national organizer J. E. S. DE GRAFT-HAYFORD.

Graphic Corporation: Brewery Rd., P.O.B. 742, Accra; f. 1950 to publish the *Daily Graphic* and *Sunday Mirror*; also publishes *Ghana Year Book*; Chair. J. B. ODUNTON; Man. Dir. (vacant).

National Standards Board: c/o P.O.B. M245, Accra; f. 1967; establishes and promulgates standards to ensure high quality of goods produced in Ghana; promotes standardization, industrial efficiency and development and industrial welfare, health and safety; Certification and Mark Scheme (introduced January 1971).

State Diamond Marketing Corporation: P.O.B. M108, Accra; f. 1965 as successor to Diamond Marketing Board incorporated in 1962 to take over functions of Accra Diamond Market; charged with securing the most favourable terms for sale of diamonds produced in Ghana; controls and fixes prices paid to winners and producers; Chair. J. H. FRIMPONG-ANSAH; Man. Dir. E. K. NANTWI.

State Farms Corporation: Accra.

State Fishing Corporation: P.O.B. 211, Tema; f. 1961; Government sponsored deep-sea fishing, distribution and marketing (including exporting) organization; owns about 12 deep-sea fishing trawlers; about 1,000 staff employed; Chief Exec. Dr. K. E. ADJEI.

State Gold Mining Corporation: P.O.B. 109, Tarkwa; Accra Office, P.O.B. 3634; London Office, Bush House, North-East Wing, Aldwych, London, W.C.2; f. 1961; manages five gold mines bought by the Ghana Government in 1961: Tarkwa Goldfields (Amalgamated Banket Areas), Prestea Goldfields (Ariston), Bibiani Goldfields, Konongo Goldfields, Dunkwa Goldfields; Chair. J. S. ADDO; Man. Dir. J. BENTUM-WILLIAMS.

State Hotels Corporation: P.O.B. 7542, Accra North; f. 1965; responsible for all state-owned hotels, restaurants, etc.; charged with providing such establishments of a reasonable standard in all main cities and towns; 13 brs.; Gen. Man. NORMAN G. LAWRENCE.

State Housing Corporation: P.O.B. 2753, Accra; f. 1955 to increase housing in Ghana; manages over 19,000 properties; Chair. Lt.-Col. G. Y. BOAKYE; Man. Dir. ANDREWS N. NARTEY.

Tema Development Corporation: P.O.B. 46, Tema; f. 1952; responsible for administration, planning and development of Tema township; Man. Dir. O. S. ADAMS; publ. *The Tedeco Annual Report* (circ. 6,000).

CHAMBERS OF COMMERCE

Ghana National Chamber of Commerce, The: P.O.B. 2325, Accra; f. 1961; 584 mems.; Pres. PAUL YEBOA; Sec. ISAAC K. ATIOGBE.

Member Chambers:

Accra District Chamber: 352 mems.

Ho District Chamber: 5 mems.

Keta District Chamber: 7 mems.

Koforidua District Chamber: P.O.B. 266, Koforidua; 34 mems.

Kumasi District Chamber: P.O.B. 528, Kumasi; 80 mems.

Sekondi/Takoradi District Chamber: P.O.B. 45, Takoradi; 56 mems.

Sunyani District Chamber: 5 mems.

Tamale District Chamber: 8 mems.

Tarkwa District Chamber: 10 mems.

COMMERCIAL AND INDUSTRIAL ORGANIZATIONS

Export Promotion Council: Ministry of Trade, P.O.B. 47, Accra; f. 1969; chair. and representatives appointed by Ghana Manufacturers' Association, Ghana National Chamber of Commerce, Ghana Timber Federation, Ghana Timber Producers' Association, Ghana Timber Marketing Board, Bank of Ghana, National Investment Bank, Agricultural Development Bank, Cocoa Marketing Company, Ghana Cocoa Marketing Board and the National Standards Board.

Indian Merchants' Association: P.O.B. 2891, Accra; f. 1939; Sec. SADHWANI JAYDEE.

Institute of Chartered Accountants (Ghana), The: P.O.B. 4268, Accra; f. 1963; 177 mems.; Pres. S. I. K. BOAKYE-AGYEMAN; Hon. Sec. J. K. FORSON.

Lebanese and Syrian Traders' Association: P.O.B. 1080, Accra; f. 1956; 38 mems.; Principal Officers E. S. NASSAR, A. F. NASSAR.

EMPLOYERS' ASSOCIATION

Ghana Employers' Association: Kojo Thompson Rd., P.O.B. 2616, Accra; f. 1959; 277 mems.; Chair. ALFRED GAISIE; Vice-Chair. CHRISTOPHER RICHARDS; Chief Exec. F. BANNERMAN-MENSON; publ. *Newsletter* (monthly).

AFFILIATED BODIES

Ghana Booksellers' Association: P.O.B. 899, Accra.

Ghana Chamber of Mines, The: P.O.B. 991, Accra; f. 1928; promotes mining interests in Ghana; Dir. and Sec. J. E. AMPAH, F.R.ECON.S.

Ghana Electrical Contractors' Association: P.O.B. 1858, Accra.

Ghana National Contractors' Association: c/o J. T. Osei and Co., P.O.B. M11, Accra.

Ghana Port Employers' Association, The: P.O.B. 2241, Accra.

Ghana Timber Federation, The: P.O.B. 246, Takoradi; f. 1952; aims to promote, protect and develop Timber Industry of Ghana; Chair. H. WALTERS.

TRADE UNIONS

Ghana Trades Union Congress: Hall of Trade Unions, P.O.B. 701, Accra; f. 1945; governed by an Executive Board comprising the Chairmen and Secretaries of each of the 17 national unions, the Secretary-General and the Chairman of the Executive Board; 7 specialized departments; total membership 342,480 (1970); Chair. DAVID EYGIR; Sec.-Gen. B. A. BENTUM, publs. *Ghana Workers' Bulletin* (fortnightly).

The following unions are affiliated to the Congress:

Teachers' and Educational Workers' Union: 14,000 mems.

Public Services Workers' Union: 24,000 mems.

Ghana Private Road Transport Union: 20,000 mems.

Local Government Workers' Union: 38,000 mems.

Construction and Building Trades Union: 39,103 mems.

Maritime and Dockworkers' Union: 10,000 mems.

Posts and Telecommunications Workers' Union: 5,000 mems.

Timber and Woodworkers' Union: 14,000 mems.

General Transport and Petroleum Workers' Union: 7,600 mems.

Industrial and Commercial Workers' Union: 80,000 mems.

General Agricultural Workers' Union: 35,000 mems.

Mine Workers' Union: 23,000 mems.

Health Services Workers' Union: 9,000 mems.

Railway Enginemens' Union: 900 mems.

National Union of Seamen: 3,000 mems.

Railway and Ports Workers' Union: 7,388 mems.

Public Utility Workers' Union: 12,518 mems.

CO-OPERATIVES

Alliance of Ghana Co-ops Ltd.: P.O.B. 2068, Accra; f. 1951; co-ordinates activities of all co-operative societies; Pres. F. K. ABOAGYE; Sec. E. F. K. ATIEMO; Registrar E. F. ASIEDU.

The co-operative movement began in Ghana in 1928 among cocoa farmers, and grew into the largest farmers' organization in the country. It was dissolved by the government in 1960, but re-established in 1966 after the *coup d'état* of February 24th. There are now 2,050 societies with a total membership of 65,400, capital of over £2.9m. and annual trade of £9.8m. The Alliance has 7 Apex affiliates:

The Ghana Co-operative Marketing Association: P.O.B. 832, Accra.

The Ghana Co-operative Transport Association Ltd.: P.O.B. 2068, Accra.

The Ghana Co-operative Distillers Association: P.O.B. 3640, Accra.

The Ghana Co-operative Fishing and Fish Marketing Association Ltd.: P.O.B. 149, Tema.

The Ghana Co-operative Poultry Farmers Association Ltd.: Box 6604, Accra.

Sekondi Takoradi Co-op Tailors Society Ltd.: Box 0338, Takoradi.

Assin-Abura Co-op Forest Produce Marketing Society: Box 75, Assin-Foso.

TRADE FAIR

Ghana International Trade Fair: Accra; Second Ghana International Trade Fair, February 1st–11th, 1971; theme: "Africa Progresses"; object: to help open up new markets for products of developing countries, and for goods of industrially-developed countries in Africa; and also to enable foreign companies to investigate establishing new industries in Ghana and other emergent countries; Principal Commercial Officer J. A. SITTIE.

MAJOR INDUSTRIAL COMPANIES

The following are some of the largest companies in terms either of capital investment or employment.

African Manganese Co.: P.O.B. 2, Nsuta; mining of manganese.

Ashanti Gold Fields Corporation Ltd.: P.O.B. 10, Obuasi; f. 1897; cap £3,745,674.

Gold mining. The Corporation leases mining and timber concessions from the Government of Ghana who are joint owners with Lonrho Ltd.

Chair. A. H. BALL; Gen. Man. (Ghana) I. D. B. CORNER; 7,500 employees.

BP Ghana Ltd.: P.O.B. 553, 95 Kojo Thompson Rd., Accra; f. 1965; wholly owned subsidiary of BP (West Africa) Ltd., a member of the international BP group.

Import and distribution of petroleum products, fuelling marine vessels at Tema and Takoradi, and aircraft at Kotoka International Airport.

Man. Dir. D. R. JOHNSTON; 250 employees.

British Aluminium Co. Ltd.: P.O.B. 1, Awaso; head office London; mining of bauxite; Gen. Man. J. V. PUCKNEY.

The Cocoa Products Factory (G.C.M.B.): P.O.B. 218, Effia Junction Industrial Estate, P.O.B. 218, Takoradi; f. 1964; cap. NC 2,000,000.

The factory is operated under the control of the State Cocoa Marketing Board to process high-grade cocoa products for export to the world market.

Gen. Man. F. A. MENSAH, A.C.A.; 460 employees.

Lever Bros. (Ghana) Ltd.: P.O.B. 1648, Accra; production of soaps, toilet preparations; Man. Dir. M. C. HAGAN.

Total Ghana Ltd.: P.O.B. 2537, Liberty Ave., Castle Rd. Junction, Accra; f. 1960; cap. NC 1,200,000; subsidiary of Compagnie Française des Pétroles, ave. Michel Ange, Paris.

Distribution of petroleum products.

Gen. Man. D. BOUSCATIE; 140 employees.

The United Africa Co. of Ghana Ltd.: P.O.B. 64, Liberty Ave., Accra; f. 1955; gross cap. employed NC 85,000,000; group composed of sixteen units; subsidiary of the United Africa Co. Ltd., London.

The group is engaged in timber and plywood production, food processing, department store trading, vehicle assembly and bus manufacture, toiletries and cosmetics manufacture, merchant trading, pharmaceuticals, brewing, textile weaving and printing.

Chair. CHRISTOPHER RICHARDS; Deputy Chair. DAVID ANDOH; 11,000 employees of which 500 in management.

VALCO (Volta Aluminium Co. Ltd.): P.O.B. 1117, Accra; aluminium smelter, subsidiary of Kaiser Aluminium Inc., at Tema.

TRANSPORT

RAILWAY AND PORTS DEVELOPMENT

Ghana Railway and Ports Authority: Box 251, Takoradi; is responsible for the operation of 592 miles of railway and the deep-water harbour at Takoradi and for the maintenance of 8 lighthouses and the new deep-water harbour at Tema, opened in January 1962; Gen. Man. P. O. AGGREY.

ROADS

There are 19,236 miles of roads, of which 4,420 miles (1,912 miles bitumen) are maintained by the Division of Public Construction. Regional Organizations maintain 3,896 miles, Local and Municipal Councils 5,920, and there are about 5,000 miles of private and Chiefs' roads.

Automobile Association of Ghana: Fanum Place, Boundary Road, P.O. Box 1985, Accra; f. 1961; mems. 3,000; Chair. E. A. METTLE-NUNOO; Exec. Dir. DELA SESHIE.

Ghana-Upper Volta Road Transport Commission: Ouagadougou, Upper Volta; f. 1968.

SHIPPING

Black Star Line Ltd.: P.O.B. 2760, Accra; f. 1957; Government owned line to provide Ghana with her own merchant marine. Operates passenger and cargo services to northern Europe, the United Kingdom, Canada and the eastern United States, the Gulf of Mexico, the Mediterranean and West Africa. Agents for Gold Star Line Ltd., Zim West Africa Lines Ltd., Seven Stars Africa Line and Nigerian National Shipping Line; fleet of 16 freighters; Man. Dir. G. K. B. DE GRAFT-JOHNSON.

Barber Line: P.O.B. 210, Takoradi; 3-weekly cargo service to U.S.A., limited passenger service.

Compagnie Fabre Marseille: Liner Agencies (Ghana) Ltd., P.O.B. 214, Tema; and P.O.B. 210, Takoradi; once monthly sailings to Mediterranean ports.

Compagnie de Navigation Fraissinet et Cyprien Fabre: Palm Line (Agencies) Ltd., P.O. Box 212, Takoradi; coastal services, services to North Africa and Europe.

Guinea Gulf Line, The: Liner Agencies (Ghana) Ltd., P.O.B. 214, Tema; P.O.B. 210, Takoradi; services to United Kingdom and Europe.

Holland West-Afrika Lijn N.V.: P.O.B. 269, Accra; P.O.B. 216, Tema; and P.O.B. 18, Takoradi. *See* Royal Interocean Lines.

Kawasaki Kisen Kaisha Ltd.: Liner Agencies (Ghana) Ltd., P.O.B. 214, Tema; and P.O.B. 210, Takoradi; monthly sailings to Japan, Hong Kong and Singapore via South Africa.

Liner Agencies (Ghana) Ltd.: P.O.B. 66, Accra; P.O.B. 210, Takoradi; P.O.B. 214, Tema; freight services to and from United Kingdom, Europe, U.S.A., Canada, Japan and Italy; intermediate services between West African ports; freight services from India and Pakistan; Gen. Man. J. R. G. IRVINE.

Mitsui O.S.K. Lines Ltd.: formerly **Osaka Shosen Kaisha** Liner Agencies (Ghana) Ltd., P.O.B. 214, Tema; and P.O.B. 210, Takoradi; twice-monthly services to Japan, Hong Kong and Singapore via South Africa.

Nautilus Line S.A.: Union Maritime et Commerciale, P.O.B. 2013, Accra; services to Mediterranean ports, Portugal, Spain and West Africa.

Royal Interocean Lines: Agents Holland West-Afrika Lijn N.V., P.O.B. 269, Accra; and P.O.B. 18, Takoradi; cargo express service Japan, China, Hong Kong, Malaysia, South and East Africa, South America, Australia and New Zealand.

Woermann-Line: P.O.B. 3317, Accra; services to Europe.

CIVIL AVIATION

The main international airport is at Accra.

Ghana Airways Corporation: Ghana House, P.O.B. 1636, Accra; f. 1958; Government-owned company operates international, regional and domestic services; Chair. R. R. AMPONSAH; Man. Dir. E. H. BOOHENE; fleet of three DC-3, two Viscounts, one VC-10, one HS 748.

Accra is also served by the following foreign airlines Air Afrique, Alitalia, Air Mali, BOAC, British Caledonian Airways, EgyptAir, Ethiopian, KLM, Lufthansa, MEA, Nigeria Airways, PAA, Swissair, UTA.

POWER

Electricity Corporation of Ghana: f. 1966 as successor to Government Electricity Department; total maximum demand in 1969 was about 109,300 kW., with output of 523m. units by 92,340 consumers.

The Volta River Authority: P.O.B. M77, Accra; operates the Volta hydro-electric power station at Akosombo; with four units installed, has an initial capacity of 512 MW; total capacity is 792 MW plus 15 per cent overload; electricity used for mining and the industries, smelting aluminium and domestic consumption; main contract awarded in April 1961; formal completion of the dam wall in February, 1965; formal inauguration of Project, January 1966; financing arrangements for 5th and 6th units finalized and tenders called on November 17th, 1969; agreement for the sale of power to neighbouring Togo and Dahomey signed August 22nd, 1969; Chief Exec. E. L. QUARTEY.

ATOMIC ENERGY

Atomic Energy Commission: P.O.B. 80, Legon/Accra; construction of a nuclear reactor at Kwabenya, near Accra, which was begun in 1964, was halted early in 1966 as an economy measure. The Commission's present field of activity is mainly in connection with the applications of radioisotopes in agriculture and medicine; publ. *Annual Reports.*

TOURISM

Ghana Tourist Corporation: P.O.B. 3106, Accra; Man. Dir. Maj. W. A. ODJIDJA.

Ghana Tourist Company Ltd.: Fiase Lodge, Ring Road Central, P.O.B. 2923, Accra; affiliated to I.A.T.A. and International Union of Official Travel Organizations, Geneva; Chair. E. K. DADSON; Man, Dir. V. K. AKAKPO.

State Hotels Corporation: P.O.B. 7542, Accra North. (*See* Trade and Industry, Public Boards and Corporations.)

EDUCATION

Primary, secondary and technical education are free, and compulsory for children aged six to twelve in the primary schools and twelve to sixteen in the middle schools. The number of schools has greatly increased during the past decade. There are two universities with over 3,000 students and a new university college has been set up at Cape Coast.

At present, because of Ghana's financial crisis, the education programme is unlikely to be expanded. In his budget speech for 1972–73, Col. Acheampong announced cuts in state aid to schools and universities.

ACADEMY

GHANA ACADEMY OF ARTS AND SCIENCES

(formerly Ghana Academy of Sciences)

P.O. BOX M.32, ACCRA

Founded 1959.

Aims to promote the study, extension and dissemination of knowledge of the arts and sciences.

Patron: H.R.H. The Prince PHILIP, Duke of EDINBURGH, K.G., P.C., G.B.E., F.R.S.

President of the Council: Justice N. A. OLLENNU, G.M.

Vice-President and Chairman of the Humanities Section: Prof. E. A. BOATENG, G.M.

Vice-President and Chairman of the Sciences Section: Prof. F. T. SAI.

Secretary: Prof. J. C. DE GRAFT-JOHNSON, G.C.O.M.

Treasurer: Dr. (Mrs.) S. B. G. DE GRAFT-JOHNSON, G.M.

Members of the Council: Assoc. Rev. Prof. C. G. BAETA, O.B.E., G.M., Prof. A. A. BOAHEN, Prof. S. R. A. DODU, Prof. J. YANNEY-EWUSIE, Prof. J. H. NKETIA, G.M., Prof. K. BENTSI-ENCHILL.

Publications: *Proceedings* (annual).

AFFILIATED BODY:

Encyclopaedia Africana Secretariat: P.O.B. 2797, Accra; f. 1962 to organize the production of an encyclopaedia of African life and history; works through national co-operating committees in various parts of Africa; Dir. Prof. L. H. OFOSU-APPIAH.

Council for Scientific and Industrial Research: P.O.B. M.32, Accra; incorporated 1968; created to exercise control over the research institutes and units previously maintained by the Ghana Academy of Sciences and to encourage scientific and industrial research relevant to national development; Chair. M. DOWUONA; Sec. K. M. SAPE (acting); central library of 3,000 vols., 1,000 periodicals; Librarian J. A. VILLARS; publs. *CSIR Recorder, Ghana Journal of Science, Ghana Journal of Agricultural Science, Annual Report.*

ATTACHED RESEARCH INSTITUTES:

Animal Research Institute: P.O.B. 20, Achimota; Officer-in-Charge Dr. A. J. E. BUCKNOR.

Building and Road Research Institute: Univ. P.O.B. 40, Kumasi; f. 1952; library of 8,000 vols.; Dir. Assoc. Prof. J. W. S. DE GRAFT-JOHNSON.

Cocoa Research Institute: P.O.B. 8, Tafo; Dir. Dr. E. J. A. ASOMANING.

Crops Research Institute: P.O.B. 3785, Kumasi; Dir. Dr. W. K. AGBLE.

Food Research Institute: P.O.B. M20, Accra; f. 1964; food processing, preservation, storage, analysis marketing, etc.; Acting Dir. W. F. K. CHRISTIAN; publ. *Food Research Institute Bulletin.*

Forest Products Research Institute: Univ. P.O.B. 63, Kumasi; f. 1963; library of 500 vols.; Dir. F. W. ADDO-ASHONG; publ. *Quarterly Newsletter.*

Institute of Aquatic Biology: P.O.B. 38, Achimota; Dir. Dr. LETITIA E. OBENG.

Institute of Standards and Industrial Research: P.O.B. M.32, Accra; Dir. E. LARTEY.

Soil Research Institute: P.O.B. 1433, Kumasi; Dir. K. A. QUAGRAINE.

Water Resources Research Unit: P.O.B. M.32, Accra; Officer-in-Charge E. LARTEY.

LEARNED SOCIETIES AND RESEARCH INSTITUTES

(*see* also under Universities)

Alliance Française: P.O.B. 1573, Accra; f. 1958; library of 3,000 vols.; 300 mems.; Pres. Mme A. CHRISTIAN; Dir. J.-P. TECOURT.

Arts Council of Ghana: P.O.B. 2738, Accra; f. 1958; to promote and develop the arts and preserve traditional arts; Chair. Dr. OKU AMPOFO; Exec. Sec. K. DOUSE-MAWU.

British Council, The: P.O.B. 771, Accra; Rep. H. C. BURROW, O.B.E.; Regional Offices: P.O.B. 1996, Kumasi; library: *see* Libraries.

Central Clinical Laboratory: P.O. Box 300, Accra; f. 1920; laboratory services and training of personnel; research on tropical medicine and allied subjects; library of 7,500 vols.; Senior Officer W. N. LAING, M.B., CH.B., D.T.M. & H., D.C.P.

Classical Association of Ghana: University of Ghana; f. 1952; 17 mems.; Chair. Dr. J. H. O. MACQUEEN; Treas. and Sec. DAPHNE HEREWARD.

Economic Society of Ghana: P.O.B. 22, Legon; f. 1954; Pres. E. N. AFFUL; publ. *Economic Bulletin of Ghana*.

Geological Survey of Ghana: P.O.B. M.80, Accra; f. 1913; geological mapping and geophysical surveying of the country, research and evaluation of mineral sources; library of 22,112 vols.; Dir. J. E. CUDJOE, M.SC., M.I.M.M., F.G.A.A.SC.; publs. *Annual Report*, memoirs and bulletins.

Ghana Bar Association: Legon; Pres. B. J. DA ROCHA.

Ghana Geographical Association: University of Ghana; f. 1955; Pres. Prof. E. A. BOATENG; Hon. Sec. P. A. NORTEY, Jr.

Ghana Library Association: P.O.B. 4105, Accra; f. 1962; Pres. A. N. DE HEER, F.L.A.; Sec. F. K. DZOKOTO, A.L.A.

Ghana Meteorological Services Department: P.O.B. 87, Legon; f. 1937; serves civil and military aviation, agriculture, forestry, engineering and medical research; 380 mems.; Dir. F. A. A. ACQUAAH; Deputy Dir. N. A. GBECKOR-KOVE; Senior Meteorologist S. E. TANDOH; publs. numerous regular and irregular reports.

Ghana Science Association: University of Ghana, P.O.B. 7, Legon; f. 1959; Pres. Dr. A. J. E. BUCKNOR; Sec. W. Z. COKER.

Goethe Institute: P.O.B. 3196, Accra; Dir. Dr. H. SCHWABE-DISSEN.

Historical Society of Ghana: University of Ghana; f. 1952; formerly Gold Coast and Togoland Historical Soc.; Pres. Prof. A. A. BOAHEN; Sec. Dr. K. DARKWAH; publs. *Transactions, Ghana Notes and Queries*.

Pharmaceutical Society of Ghana: D.431/3, Knutsford Ave., P.O.B. 2133, Accra; f. 1935; aims to advance chemistry and pharmacy and maintain standards of the profession; library of 250 vols.; 418 mems.; Pres. V. K. AIDOO, M.P.S.G.; Hon. Gen. Sec. K. A. OHENE-MANU, M.P.S.G.

West African Examinations Council: Headquarters Office, Accra, Ghana; other offices in Lagos, Nigeria; Freetown, Sierra Leone; London, England; f. 1952 by the four West African Commonwealth countries; Liberia admitted in 1969 on associate membership status; conducts School Certificate/GCE, Higher School Certificate Examinations in Nigeria; School Certificate/GCE and Advanced Level Examinations in The Gambia, Ghana and Sierra Leone; also selection examinations for entry into secondary schools and similar institutions, the Public Services, final examinations for teacher training colleges at the request of the various Ministries of Education; holds examinations on behalf of the University of London and U.K. examining authorities and the Educational Testing Service, Princeton, New Jersey, U.S.A.; Registrar V. C. IKE; publs. *Annual Report, Bulletin* (bi-annual).

West African Science Association: c/o Geology Dept., P.O.B. 7, University of Ghana, Legon, Ghana; f. 1953; originally covered Ghana, Nigeria and Sierra Leone, now includes Ivory Coast and Senegal; Pres. Prof. V. A. DYENUGA; Sec. L. A. K. QUASHIE; publs. *The West African Journal of Science* (annually).

LIBRARIES

Accra Central Library: Thorpe Road, P.O. Box 663, Accra; central reference library; union catalogues.

Achimota School Library: Achimota; f. 1927; number of vols. 14,500; Librarian D. J. HOLT.

African Bureau of Educational Documentation: Accra; f. 1961; deals with curricula and methods, school health, textbooks, extra-curricular activities; UNESCO-assisted.

Ashanti Regional Library: Bantama Rd., P.O.B. 824, Kumasi.

British Council Library: P.O.B. 771, Accra; 28,000 vols.; br. at Kumasi, 15,100 vols.

Central Reference and Research Library (C.S.I.R.): P.O.B. M.32, Accra; f. 1964; 3,000 vols., 1,200 current periodicals; Librarian J. A. VILLARS, F.L.A.; publs. *Literature Summary* (monthly), *Union List of Titles of Scientific Journals in Ghana Libraries, C.S.I.R. Recorder*.

Ghana Library Board: P.O.B. 663, Accra; f. 1950; comprises Accra Central Library (1956), regional libraries at Kumasi (1954), Sekondi (1955), Ho (1960), Tamale (1959), Research Library, Accra (1961), Bolgatanga (1969); branches at Cape Coast, Dunkwa, Hohoe, Obuasi, Takoradi, Tarkwa, Koforidua, Jasikan, Keta, Konongo, Oda, Kpandu, Sunyani, Nkawkaw and Tema; mobile libraries, children's libraries; 800,000 vols.; Dir. of Library Services ADOLFUS OFORI.

Library of the Building and Road Research Institute (C.S.I.R.): Univ. P.O.B. 40, Kumasi; 10,486 books and pamphlets; Asst. Librarian R. J. T. NETTEY, A.L.A.

Library of the Cocoa Research Institute (C.S.I.R.): P.O.B. 8, Tafo; 6,508 vols., 1,090 pamphlets and reprints, and 464 periodicals; Librarian E. K. TETTEH, A.L.A.

Library of the Medical Research Institute: Medical Research Centre, Accra; f. 1920; 7,000 vols.; 175 current periodicals.

National Archives of Ghana: P.O.B. 3056, Accra; f. 1946, legal recognition 1955; charged with the collection, custody, rehabilitation and reproduction of all Public Archives, including valuable private papers; regional offices, which serve as record centres and cater for local history, in Kumasi, Cape Coast, Sekondi, Tamale, Sunyani, Koforidua and Ho; library of 1,500 vols.; Chief Archivist J. M. AKITA; publs. *Annual Report*, exhibition catalogues, etc.

Research Library on African Affairs: P.O.B. 2970, Accra; f. 1961; collection, processing and dissemination of recorded literature, history and culture of all Africa; 10,986 vols., 510 periodicals; Librarian A. N. DE HEER, F.L.A.; publs. *Bi-monthly Current Bibliography*, *Annual Ghana National Bibliography*, Special Subject Bibliographies.

Sekondi Regional Library: Old Axim Rd., P.O.B. 174, Sekondi.

University of Ghana Library (Balme Library): P.O.B. 24, Legon; f. 1948; 247,000 vols., 4,500 current periodicals; Librarian E. Y. AMEDEKEY, B.A., F.L.A.

University of Science and Technology Library: Kumasi; 68,777 vols.; 1,620 periodicals; Librarian G. M. PITCHER, F.L.A.

MUSEUMS

Ghana National Museum: Barnes Road, P.O. Box 3343, Accra; f. 1957; controlled by the Ghana Museum and Monuments Board; archaeological and ethnological finds from all over Ghana and West Africa; modern works by Ghanaian artists; the preservation and conservation of ancient forts and castles and traditional buildings; the achievement of man in Africa; Chairman of the Board NENE ANNORKWEI II; Dir. R. B. NUNOO.

Ghana Museum of Science and Technology: P.O.B. 3343, Accra; f. 1965; construction of the main buildings has just begun; a temporary exhibition hall with an open-air cinema is used for the display of working models, charts, films and other exhibits on science and technology; collection of exhibits for permanent galleries has begun; Officer-in-Charge E. A. ASANTE.

West African Historical Museum: P.O.B. 502, Cape Coast; f. 1971; sponsored by the Ghana Museums and Monuments Board and the University of Cape Coast; it is intended that the museum will play a fundamental role in a new education system for Ghana in which "participation" techniques are of increasing importance in schools; research facilities will be developed; library in course of construction; Research Officer DOIG SIMMONDS, M.S.I.A., F.R.A.I.

UNIVERSITIES

UNIVERSITY OF GHANA

P.O. BOX 25, LEGON, NR. ACCRA

Telephone: Accra 75381.

Founded 1948 as the University College of Ghana (then Gold Coast); raised to University status 1961.

Language of instruction: English; Academic year: October to June; State control.

Vice-Chancellor: A. A. KWAPONG, PH.D.
Pro-Vice-Chancellor: Prof. S. LA-ANYANE, PH.D.
Registrar: E. A. K. EDZII, B.A.
Librarian: E. Y. AMEDEKEY, B.A., F.L.A.

Number of teachers: 456.
Number of students: 2,525.
Publications: Annual Reports, *University of Ghana Reporter, Calendar.*

DEANS:

Faculty of Agriculture: S. LA-ANYANE, PH.D.
Faculty of Arts: J. O. DE GRAFT-HANSON, M.A.
Faculty of Law: Justice A. N. E. AMISSAH, M.A.
Faculty of Science: F. G. T. O'B. TORTO, PH.D.
Faculty of Social Studies: K. B. DICKSON, PH.D.
Faculty of Medicine: S. R. A. DODU, M.D., D.T.M. & H., F.R.C.P.

ATTACHED INSTITUTES:

School of Administration: P.O.B. 78, Legon; Dir. Dr. K. E. ADJEI, M.B.A., PH.D.

Institute of Adult Education: P.O.B. 31, Legon; Dir. Prof. K. A. B. JONES-QUARTEY, M.A.

Institute of African Studies: P.O.B. 73, Legon; Dir. Prof. J. H. NKETIA, B.A.

Institute of Statistical, Social and Economic Research: P.O.B. 74, Legon; Dir. C. O'LOUGHLIN, M.SC., PH.D.

Medical School: P.O.B. 4236, Accra; Dean Prof. S. DODU, M.D., D.T.M. & H., F.R.C.P.

AGRICULTURAL RESEARCH STATIONS:

Agricultural Research Station: P.O.B. 43, Kade.
Officer-in-Charge: Dr. A. A. OPOKU, M.SC., PH.D.

Agricultural Research Station: P.O.B. 9, Kpong.
Officer-in-Charge: E. J. A. KHAN, M.SC.

Agricultural Research Station (Nungua): P.O.B. 38, Legon.
Officer-in-Charge: M. BAFI-YEBOAH, M.V.S., DR.MED., V.E.T.

UNIVERSITY OF SCIENCE AND TECHNOLOGY
KUMASI

Telephone: 3201-3210.

Founded 1951 as College of Technology, raised to University status 1961.

Language of instruction: English; State control; Academic year: October to June (three terms).

Chancellor: (vacant).
Vice-Chancellor: Dr. EMMANUEL EVANS-ANFOM, M.B., CH.B., D.T.M.H., F.R.C.S., F.I.C.S.
Registrar: A. S. Y. ANDOH, M.A.
Librarian: G. M. PITCHER, F.L.A.

Number of teachers: 250.
Number of students: 1,394.
Publications: *The Kumasitech, University Calendar, Annual Report.*

DEANS:

Faculty of Agriculture: Prof. S. SEY.
Faculty of Architecture: Prof. R. L. BARCLAY.
Faculty of Art: Prof. E. V. ASIHENE.
Faculty of Engineering: B. KWAKYE (acting).
Faculty of Pharmacy: Prof. A. N. TACKIE.
Faculty of Science: Prof. F. A. KUFUOR.

UNIVERSITY OF CAPE COAST
CAPE COAST

Telephone: Cape Coast 2440-2449.

Founded 1962.

Language of Instruction: English; State control; Academic year: September/October to June/July (3 terms).

Vice-Chancellor: Prof. E. A. BOATENG, M.A., B.LITT.
Registrar: E. V. D. MANTE, B.SC.(ECON.).
Librarian: E. K. KORANTENG, F.L.A.

Number of teachers: 170.
Number of students: 1,005.

Publications: *Journal of the University of Cape Coast, Calendar, Information Brochure, Annual Report by the Vice-Chancellor, University Gazette.*

DEANS:

Faculty of Science: Assoc. Prof. J. YANNEY EWUSIE, PH.D., M.I.(BIO.), F.G.A.
Faculty of Arts: Prof. P. MORTON-WILLIAMS, PH.D.
Faculty of Education: Rev. Dr. N. K. DZOBO, M.A., PH.D.

COLLEGES

Accra Polytechnic: P.O.B. 561, Accra.

Accra Technical Training Centre: P.O.B. M-177, Accra; f. 1966, attached to Ministry of Education; to train tradesmen for industry and civil service; number of students: 260; library of 2,942 vols.
Principal: E. L. BREESE.

Government Technical Institute: P.O.B. 206, Sunyani; f. 1967; 20 teachers; 300 students; library of 1,405 vols.; Librarian G. E. A. YEBOAH; Pres. E. B. KUMA-MINTAH.

Ho Technical Institute: 217 Ho, Volta Region; telephone Ho 456; f. 1968.

Principal: F. M. K. DZRADOSI.

Librarian: Mr. AGRA.

Library: 1,500 vols.

Number of teachers: 29.

Number of students: 524.

HEADS OF DEPARTMENTS

Automotive: A. S. K. KPODO, F.T.C., G.I.M.I.

Business Studies: S. R. K. BATCHAR.

Catering: Mrs. RANDALL-BULL.

Building: K. K. BREW.

Takoradi Polytechnic: P.O.B. 256, Takoradi.

Tamale Technical Institute: P.O.B. 67, Tamale.

Tarkwa School of Mines: Ministry of Education, P.O.B. 237, Tarkwa; f. 1953; training of technicians for the mining industry, and other trade training; library of 2,500 vols.

Principal: J. E. PHILPOTT.

Koforidua Technical Institute: P.O.B. 323, Koforidua; telephone Koforidua 2405; f. 1960.

Principal: P. C. NOI.

Library: 2,000 vols.

Number of teachers: 9.

Number of students: 206.

Kpandu Technical Institute: Technical Division, Ministry of Education, P.O.B. 76, Kpandu, Volta Region; telephone Kpandu 22; f. 1956.

Principal: W. J. MERRY.

Registrar: G. A. EKUADZI.

Librarian: H. F. DJENTUH.

Library: 1,000 vols.

Number of teachers: 32.

Number of students: 465.

DEANS:

Automotive: S. E. YOYOWAH.

Science and Mathematics: B. P. KHANOURIE.

General Subjects: H. F. DJENTUH.

Mechanical Engineering: S. Y. KOKOR.

Carpentry: E. A. ESSILFIE.

Business Studies: G. M. BAWI.

SELECT BIBLIOGRAPHY

AFRIFA, A. A. *Ghana Coup d'Etat.* London, Frank Cass, 1967.

AMIN, SAMIR. *Trois expériences africaines de développement: le Mali, la Guinée et le Ghana.* Paris, Presses universitaires de France, 1965.

AUSTIN, DENNIS. *Politics in Ghana 1946–60.* London, Oxford University Press, 1964.

BING, G. *Reap the Whirlwind.* London, McGibbon and Kee, 1968.

BIRMINGHAM, WALTER, NEUSTADT, I., and OMABOE, E. N. *A Study of Contemporary Ghana,* Vol. I "The Economy of Ghana", Vol. II "Some Aspects of Social Structure". London, George Allen and Unwin, 1966, 1967.

BOATENG, E. A. *A Geography of Ghana.* London, Cambridge University Press, 2nd edn., 1970.

BRETTON, H. L. *Rise and Fall of Kwame Nkrumah.* London, Pall Mall, 1967.

BUSIA, K. A. *Africa in Search of Democracy.* London, Routledge and Kegan Paul, 1967.

CENTRAL BUREAU OF STATISTICS. *Annual Economic Survey.* Accra.

DICKSON, K. B. *A Historical Geography of Ghana.* Cambridge University Press, 1969.

ECONOMIC SOCIETY OF GHANA. *Economic Bulletin of Ghana.* Quarterly. Legon.

Ghana 1960 Population Census Report. Accra.

FITCH, BOB, and OPPENHEIMER, MARY. *Ghana: End of an Illusion.* New York and London, Monthly Review Press, 1966.

FOSTER, P., and ZOLBERG, A. R. (Eds.). *Ghana and the Ivory Coast. Perspectives and Modernization.* University of Chicago Press, 1972.

GENOUD, R. *Nationalism and Economic Development in Ghana.* New York, Praeger in co-operation with the Centre for Developing-Area Studies, McGill University, London, 1969.

HARRISON CHURCH, R. J. *West Africa.* London, Longmans, 6th edn., 1968.

HILL, POLLY. *The Migrant Cocoa-Farmers of Southern Ghana.* Cambridge, Cambridge University Press, 1963.

KAY, GEOFFREY (Ed.). *The Political Economy of Colonialism in Ghana.* A Collection of Documents and Statistics 1900–60. Cambridge University Press, 1972.

KILLICK, A., and SZERESZEWSKI. "The Economy of Ghana", in ROBSON, P., and LURY, D. A. (Eds.), *The Economies of Africa,* pp. 79–126. London, George Allen and Unwin, 1969.

KIMBLE, DAVID. *Political History of Ghana.* London, Oxford University Press, 1963.

MABOGUNJE, AKIN L. *Regional Mobility and Resource Development in West Africa.* London African University Publishers Group Ltd., 1972.

NKRUMAH, KWAME. *Autobiography.* London, Nelson, 1958. *Dark Days in Ghana.* London, Lawrence and Wishart, 1968.

OFFICE OF THE PLANNING COMMISSION. *Seven-Year Plan for National Reconstruction and Development, Financial Years 1963/1964–1969/1970.* Accra, 1964.

Two-Year Development Plan, A Plan for the Period mid-1968 to mid-1970. Accra, 1968.

PINKNEY, R. *Ghana under Military Rule 1966–1969.* London, Methuen, 1972.

RIMMER, DOUGLAS. "The Crisis in the Ghana Economy", *Journal of Modern African Studies,* 4/1, 17–32, May 1966.

Guinea

PHYSICAL AND SOCIAL GEOGRAPHY*

R. J. Harrison Church

The Republic of Guinea, formerly French Guinea, has exceptionally varied landscapes, peoples and economic conditions. The republic has an area of 94,926 sq. miles, and a population estimated at just over 4,000,000 in 1971.

Guinea's coast is part of the extremely wet south-western sector of west Africa, which has a monsoonal climate. Thus Conakry, the capital, has five to six months with almost no rain, whilst 170 in. fall in the remaining months, July and August usually receiving 93 in. The ria coastline has shallow drowned rivers and estuaries with much mangrove growing on alluvium eroded from the nearby Fouta Djallon mountains. The Baga people have removed much of the mangrove and bunded the land for rice cultivation. Only at two places, Cape Verga and Conakry, do ancient hard rocks reach the sea. At the latter they have facilitated the development of the port, capital and routes inland, whilst the weathering of these rocks produced bauxite which has been quarried on the offshore Los Islands.

Behind the swamps a gravelly coastal plain, some 40 miles wide, is backed by the steep, often sheer, edges of the Fouta Djallon, which occupies the west-centre of the country. Much is over 3,000 ft. high, and consists of level Primary sandstones (possibly of Devonian age) which cover Precambrian rocks to a depth of 2,500 ft. The level plateaux, with many bare lateritic surfaces, are the realm of Fulani herders, who here alone in west Africa keep dwarf Ndama cattle. Rivers are deeply incised in the sandstone. These more fertile valleys were earlier cultivated with food crops by slaves of the Fulani, and then with banana, coffee, citrus and pineapple on plantations

under the French. Falls and gorges of the incised rivers have great hydroelectric power potential. This is the more significant in view of large deposits of bauxite, e.g. those quarried and converted into alumina at Fria, and others being developed at Boké for aluminium manufacture. The climate is still monsoonal but, although the total rainfall is lower—about 70 in. annually—it is more evenly distributed than on the coasts as the rainy season is longer. In such a mountainous area there are sharp variations in climatic conditions over a short distance, and from year to year.

Precambrian rocks reappear in the Guinea Highlands and the Niger Plains, south-east and east respectively of the Fouta Djallon. Unfortunately, there are many lateritic exposures in the Niger Plains, so that the seasonally flooded valleys are more fertile, and are cultivated for rice by Malinké people. The Milo and Niger are navigable into Mali for small boats.

On the Liberian border the Guinea Highlands rise to 5,800 ft. at Mt. Nimba where haematite iron ore, mined on the Liberian flank since 1963, occurs. These rounded mountains contrast greatly with the level plateaux and deep narrow valleys of the Fouta Djallon. Rainfall is heavier than in the latter, but is again more evenly distributed, so that only two or three months are without significant rain. However, relative humidity is high, and mists are common. Coffee, kola and other crops are grown in the forest of this area, unfortunately remote from Conakry but accessible by road from Monrovia or by mineral railway from Buchanan, Liberia. Diamonds are washed from gravels in the foothills north of Macenta and west of Beyla.

* See map on p. 708.

395

RECENT HISTORY*

Michael Crowder and Donal Cruise O'Brien

(Revised for this edition by KAYE WHITEMAN)

The Republic of Guinea achieved independence in 1958 as a result of an overwhelming popular vote in the constitutional referendum of that year. Guinea was the only French African territory to vote against continued association with France and for immediate independence, and was the object of a series of punitive reprisals on the part of the outgoing French authorities. Files and equipment were destroyed, while personnel, technical assistance, and financial aid were abruptly withdrawn.

The new government, led by President Sekou Touré and the *Parti démocratique de Guinée*, was thus forced to construct a wholly new administrative framework. This was done on the basis of the machinery of the ruling party, one of the best organized in Africa, and political mobilization for the tasks of economic development was at the outset very successful. Economic difficulties none the less accumulated, as the new (1960) national currency became subject to rapid inflation and as the nationalized import/export system failed to function effectively. Aid from the Soviet Union was cut short following the expulsion of the Russian ambassador in 1961, since which time the United States has been the principal source of aid and investment. Relations with France have improved little since independence.

Opposition to the government, although denied formal expression, has persisted in the face of continued economic difficulties: many Guineans (estimated at half a million) are forced to seek work abroad. The government has attacked popular apathy and hostility through its campaign for a "cultural revolution" on the Chinese model, launched in 1967 and continuing to the present. The campaign has included extensive educational reform, a mass literacy project, and the creation of revolutionary councils down to the village level.

Since independence Guinea's foreign policy has fluctuated between extreme isolationism, usually at times of internal political crisis, and a conciliatory outward-looking policy at times of relative stability at home. The former predominated in the years 1965–66. Poor relations with France and several African countries continued throughout this period, and diplomatic ties with the U.K. were severed in December 1965 over the Rhodesian issue. In 1966 a plot to overthrow Sekou Touré led to a serious deterioration in relations with Senegal and the American Peace Corps was expelled, while Nkrumah's presence in Guinea, following the coup in Ghana which ousted him, made the prospect of renewed relations with Ghana even more remote.

There was a change of attitude in 1967, however, following the PDG Party Congress at which a resumption of relations with the U.K. and France was approved. The U.K. signed an agreement to this effect in February 1968, but De Gaulle declined to make a similar move. New backing was given by Guinea to the Organization of Senegal River States (OERS) in 1967, and in April 1968 the government made efforts to start a West African Economic Grouping (Guinea had withdrawn from the Franc Zone in 1958), but these received a setback with the fall of Modibo Keita in Mali in November 1968, and the army plot in Guinea the following spring. Nevertheless, by the end of 1969 the outward looking approach seemed to be on its feet again. A World Bank loan for bauxite production, made in the autumn of 1969, was one stimulus to a more liberal approach, while relations with France (broken off in in 1965) improved after De Gaulle's fall from power—there were even signs that some agreement might be reached on outstanding problems such as the settlement of mutual debts. Relations with Ivory Coast also improved, and close ties with Sierra Leone, Guinea's staunchest friend in West Africa, were maintained.

Guinea's whole outlook was again reversed, following the most disastrous setback of recent years—the invasion of Guinea on November 21st, 1970, by an external force which, apart from killing some Guineans and foreign residents, destroyed the local PAIGC offices and Sekou Touré's summer palace, and released from prison opponents of Touré and Portuguese soldiers captured in Guinea (Bissau) by PAIGC. The force was repelled the next day. A UN fact-finding mission was sent to Guinea in response to Sekou Touré's request for immediate military assistance, and concluded that the invaders numbered between 350 and 400, mostly either Guinean dissidents or Africans of the Portuguese army, and commanded by white Portuguese officers. Lisbon denied any part in the invasion, and it is probable that the action was planned by Portuguese in Guinea (Bissau) under the direction of the Governor-General and Commander-in-Chief there, Gen. Spinola.

Waves of arrests followed in Guinea. Among those accused of involvement in the invasion were seven former ministers and the Archbishop of Conakry. Since Western powers other than Portugal were also believed in Guinea to have been implicated, many Europeans were also arrested, and 100 West Germans expelled. In January 1971 91 people were sentenced to death and 66 to life imprisonment. It is not clear how many executions were actually carried out, but at least eight people are known to have been executed, including three senior civil servants and a former commissioner of police. Most neighbouring countries were accused of aiding and abetting Guinea's enemies, but the worst casualty was Senegal, with whom relations had been fairly good in the four years prior to the invasion; disagreements between the two

---

* For the period before independence *see* Recent History of Dahomey, p. 282.

countries culminated in Guinea's withdrawal from the OERS, which was disbanded and later replaced by the OMVS excluding Guinea. Close ties with Sierra Leone were reinforced after Siaka Stevens's assumption of power in 1968; a defence agreement was signed in March 1971, following the attempt to overthrow Stevens, and about 300 Guinean troops were sent to Freetown to help restore order.

Arrests and trials had been continuing in Guinea throughout 1971, but by early 1972 a number of alleged conspirators had been released (it is not clear how many); cabinet changes were made in February, and elections were held in March to all party committees. General Gowan's visit to Guinea in the same month marked the beginning of a new phase of outwardness in Guinea's foreign policy, and paved the way for renewed contacts with other African states. A reconciliation with Senegal took place at a meeting

in Monrovia under the auspices of the OAU—Sekou Touré's first visit to another country for four years. Dr. Nkrumah's funeral in May was the occasion of visits to Guinea by a number of Heads of State, including the Presidents of Liberia and Mauritania. But Sekou Touré's refusal to return Nkrumah's body to Ghana caused a setback in relations with that country, although he later reversed this decision and the body was flown back to Ghana in June 1972. President Ahidjo of Cameroon also paid a visit to Guinea during the year, as did President Mobutu of Zaire who signed an agreement to import bauxite to Zaire for processing into alumina. Fidel Castro of Cuba made a five-day visit in May, and in July Sekou Touré had a friendly meeting with Félix Houphouët-Boigny, President of the Ivory Coast; he also attended ceremonies celebrating the 125th anniversary of Liberian independence, on July 26th.

ECONOMY

Samir Amin*

AGRICULTURE

Guinea can be divided into four very different natural regions, and within these traditional subsistence cultivation is relatively varied.

Traditional stock-raising is carried out by the Fulani in the Fouta Djallon, where in addition savannah cereals, millet and, in particular, fonio, used to be cultivated by the Fulani's slaves, the Rimaibé. Millet is grown in the upper Malinké region, manioc in the low Soussou coastal region and rice in Forest Guinea. In 1959 principal crop production figures were estimated at 270,000 metric tons of paddy, 270,000 tons of millet, sorghum, fonio and maize, and 750,000 tons of manioc and potatoes, which represented a daily ration of 2,500 calories and a value of 10,700 million current francs CFA. The growth rate of crop production was very small, barely keeping pace—as in other African countries—with the growth of the rural population. Food shortages have led to rationing and the necessity for food aid from the U.S.A. Livestock figures for 1971 were estimated at 1,830,000 head of cattle, 500,000 goats and 480,000 sheep.

Agricultural exports, extremely low at the time of independence, have made little progress (*see* table 1). The banana plantations, which had reached their maximum production level of 100,000 tons in 1955, saw a slump in output between 1955 and 1958 following the outbreak of banana disease. After 1958 the withdrawal of European planters and the end of French protection led to more difficulties. Exports in 1970–71 reached only 7,000 tons. Production of other plantation crops is also small: 10,500 tons of coffee, of which more than half is smuggled into Liberia, and 26,000 tons of palm-cabbage. Only pineapple production has shown a net increase in the last few years (up to 25,000 tons). Exports of ground-

nuts to Europe, despite a net increase, are stagnating at about 4,000 million Guinea francs (FG). To these figures can be added about 1,000 million francs worth of agricultural exports to neighbouring African countries, in the form of livestock and citrus fruits.

Agricultural exports are the monopoly of *Guinexport*. A Stabilization Fund partially compensates the deficit arising from the high prices paid to producers. Losses accumulated by *Guinexport* from 1960 to 1968 reached a total of 3,700 million FG.

MINERAL PRODUCTION

Guinea's principal exports are its mineral products. Guinea possesses the world's third largest bauxite deposits. Those on the island of Kassa have been almost exhausted and were abandoned in 1967. The island of Tamarra has now taken its place and the American company Halco has been granted the concession to exploit the deposits, against various royalties and taxes amounting to one million dollars per annum. The processing of bauxite into aluminium is carried out by *Compagnie internationale pour la production de l'alumine Fria* (Olin Mathieson Chemical Corp., U.S.A. and Péchiney), which invested 35,000 million FG between 1957 and 1960. The plant began operating in 1960 and reached its full capacity of 480,000 tons in 1963. Since 1966 production has been raised to 535,000 tons. A total of 19,000 people live in the new Fria complex.

In October 1969 Guinea and the Halco company concluded an agreement which provides for the setting up of the *Compagnie mixte des bauxites de Guinée*, to work the bauxite deposits at Boké. The agreement envisages investments totalling 190 million dollars, of which 85 million are to be provided by the

---

* For the 1973 edition, revisions have been made to this article by the Editor.

Table 1

NATIONAL ACCOUNTS 1959–69*

('ooo million FG)

	Start of Ten-Year Period	End of Ten-Year Period	Annual Growth Rate (%)
Gross Domestic Product at Factor Cost and Constant 1959 Prices:			
Traditional Economy	23.0	28.8	2.5
Agricultural Exports	4.0	4.0	—
Mining	1.4	3.0	7.5
Manufacturing Industry	0.3	2.5	20.0
Construction and Public Works	1.4	3.0	7.5
Transport, Commerce and Services	9.4	15.0	4.8
Administration	4.0	11.0	10.0
Total G.D.P.	43.5	67.3	4.5
Population ('ooo):			
Rural	2,720	3,440	2.5
Urban	180	360	7.0
Total	2,900	3,800	2.6
Public Finances (current 'ooo million):			
Administration Expenditure	7.0	16.0	8.5
Fiscal and Parafiscal Revenue	7.7	15.0	7.0
Investments:			
Gross Investments†	8.0	12.0	4.2
Foreign Finance	4.6	8.2	6.0
Balance of Payments:			
Exports	12.0	14.0	1.6
Imports:			
Fria	2.0	2.0	—
Plan	4.0	6.0	4.2
Current	6.0	9.0	4.2
Foreign Capital:			
Allocated to Development Projects	4.6	8.2	6.0
Current	1.0	3.0	12.0

* All the figures are calculated on the basis of the relative rates shown in the last column.
† Excluding mining companies.

Guinean government for infrastructural works, including 135 km. of railway and a port at Kamsar. For this purpose the government of Guinea will receive a World Bank loan of $65 million which was granted at the time when the agreement was signed. In July 1971 the World Bank granted an additional loan of $9 million to increase the annual production target from 6.6 million tons to 9.2 million. Guinea is to receive 65 per cent of net profits derived from the working of the deposits, and holds 49 per cent of the capital of the company, while the Halco group holds 51 per cent. Exporting is due to begin in 1973. Simultaneously with the conclusion of the agreement, the IMF, having paid little attention to Guinea up to that time, came to the aid of the Guinea franc, granting a line of credit of $3.8 million. When operational the mine is expected to provide Guinea with sufficient profits to be able to make the Guinea sily convertible currency.

A similar agreement was signed in November 1969 by Guinea and the U.S.S.R. for the working of

bauxite deposits at Kindia. Production will be exported to Russia at the rate of 3 million tons per year.

Agreements have also been signed with Yugoslav and Swiss companies respectively for the exploitation of the Dabola and Tougue bauxite deposits.

The iron ore on the Kaloum peninsula (near Conakry), worked since 1953 by an Anglo-French group, provided a stable output of about 700,000 tons from 1960 onwards. The deposits, 170 million tons of 50 to 55 per cent grade ore, were very inferior to those of Mount Nimba, which has 300–600 million tons of 65 to 67 per cent grade ore, and working of the Kaloum deposits was abandoned in 1967. A preliminary agreement is still being negotiated with various foreign groups for the working of the Mount Nimba deposits, the main hindrance to agreement being the provision of the necessary transport network.

Diamond mining was controlled before independence by foreign companies (*Soguinex* and *Société Minière de Beyla*), which were nationalized in 1961. Production has since fallen to a quarter of what it was.

INDUSTRY, INFRASTRUCTURE AND SERVICES

Since independence no industry worthy of the name has been set up in Guinea. During the course of the first three-year plan (1960–63) and of the first five years of the seven-year plan (1964–70), about ten small industrial projects came into being, all in the sphere of light industry. These included a textile factory, which is to supply 75 per cent of the local market (24 million metres), an assembly plant for American lorries, a cigarette and matches factory (financed by China), a sawmill (financed by the Soviet Union), a furniture-making factory and a brickworks (both financed by Yugoslavia), a canning factory with an envisaged output of 3,000 tons of tomatoes, 900 tons of fruit and 800 tons of meat (financed by the Soviet Union), a glassworks, a small oil-mill and soap-works. In February 1971 work started on a ceramics factory in co-operation with North Korea; and a cement factory is being built by a Spanish company.

Production of electricity grew from 100 million kWh. in 1960 to 200 million kWh. in 1968 (of which 65 per cent was consumed by Fria).

The inadequacy of the transport infrastructure severely hampers Guinea's development. The road network, already inadequate in 1958, has not been given the benefit of foreign aid that has been granted to other countries which were formerly French possessions. The surfacing of the middle section of the road from Conakry to N'Zérékoré, near the Mount Nimba iron-ore deposits, was finished in 1971. In March 1972 Sierra Leone and Guinea agreed to link their capitals by road and phone as soon as possible. Major stretches of the Conakry-Kankan railway, which crosses the Fouta mountains, need rebuilding.

DEVELOPMENT PLANS AND ECONOMIC POLICY

The first three-year plan in fact took four years to be implemented (July 1960–April 1964): 40,000 million FG were invested, of which 4,500 were in the agricultural sector, 7,300 in industry and 13,000 in transport. The seven-year plan which followed, beginning in May 1964, envisaged investments of 130,000 million FG, of which 16,000 was for agriculture, 29,000 for industry and 61,000 for transport. From 1964 to 1969, nearly 50 per cent of projected investments had been made (*see* tables for Agriculture, Mining and Electricity in Statistical Survey, p. 401–2).

In spite of the fact that a great number of projects have been realized, planning has not led to the projected results. It is clear that real growth has been small. The traditional sector supplied in 1959 a product valued at about 23,000 million FG; this amount increased, like the rural population, by 25 per cent in ten years. Agricultural output for export, on the other hand, has stagnated at around 4,000 million FG, at constant prices. Mining output, estimated to be worth 1,400 million FG in 1959, grew to 3,000 million at constant prices in ten years (about 5 per cent of G.D.P.), that of manufacturing from 300 million to 2,500 million and that of construction and public works from 1,400 million to 3,000 million. Transport, commerce and services have grown from 9,400 million to 15,000 million and administration from 4,000 million to 11,000 million. This gives an overall annual growth of about 4.5 per cent, i.e. a per capita figure of 2 per cent.

On January 1st, 1959, the population of Guinea was estimated at 2.9 million inhabitants, with only 180,000 "urbanized" (in built-up areas of more than 2,500 inhabitants) of which 90,000 were in Conakry. In 1969 the population was 3.8 million, that of Conakry being 172,500. However, even now there are only seven towns of more than 10,000 inhabitants outside the capital: Kankan, Kindia, Labé, Fria, Macenta, Mamou and N'Zérékoré. Although the rate of urbanization has been relatively high (10 per cent per annum for Conakry, 4 per cent for the other towns, and 7 per cent for all urban centres), Guinea's urban population remains small (9.5 per cent of the total population in 1969 as against 6.2 per cent in 1959).

In 1968 25,000 people were employed by the administration, 3,400 in the mines, 5,800 in industry, 4,500 in power and water services, 4,200 in construction, 6,500 in transport, 17,900 in services and commerce, 3,500 in hotels and domestic service; this makes a total of about 71,000 urban workers, to which can be added 29,200 wage-earning workers in agriculture, fishing and mining. In 1963 there were about 50,000 non-agricultural wage-earners, of which 21,000 were civil servants. The labour force was growing much faster than production, representing a potential unemployment problem, but it was largely absorbed by the overstaffing of administrative offices and state enterprises.

However, Guinea's economic policy was based on other factors. The year 1959 was certainly not a "normal" year: the abrupt withdrawal of French officials and the discontinuance of all forms of aid, following Guinea's accession to independence, led to various difficulties. Aid from eastern countries— which took the form of goods supplied to State Trading Boards created for this purpose—allowed the country to overcome its immediate financial difficulties. However, Guinea's membership of the West African monetary zone and the consequent absence of control of capital outflow from the country, facilitated a serious flight of capital from Guinea. In these conditions, Guinea could hardly have avoided the necessity of creating, as it did on March 1st, 1960, its own national currency.

It was against this background that the first three-year plan was drawn up and submitted to the Congress of the PDG which met at Kankan in the spring of 1960. The broad guidelines of this rapidly drafted plan refer to reforms to be carried out to the main structures: decolonization and the setting up of socialist structures. Altogether the management of some seventy state enterprises with a turnover of 35,000 million FG in 1967 (which represents the largest part of the turnover of the modernized sector, excluding mining), has shown poor, though not catastrophic, results: 3,000 million FG of gross profits per annum, which only just covers the necessary depreciation.

PUBLIC FINANCE AND THE MECHANISM OF INFLATION IN GUINEA

Guinea's ordinary budget (*see* Statistical Survey, p. 403) has almost always been balanced and has frequently shown even relatively large surpluses. Expenditure rose from 8,000 million FG in 1960 to over 19,000 million in 1967–68. The surpluses were in the region of 1–2,000 million FG per annum up to 1964, but they have dwindled in recent years. The growth of current expenditure (8.5 per cent per annum) has certainly been more rapid than that of the economy as a whole. The principal causes of this increase have been defence expenditure and the accelerated development of education (table 2).

Table 2
EDUCATION: NUMBER OF PUPILS

	1960	1963	1968
Primary . .	80,000	160,000	300,000
Secondary . .	5,300	n.a.	25,000

Taxation has had to be proportionately higher to compensate for the smaller royalties paid by the mining companies, which amount to less than 6 per cent of total fiscal and other revenue. The growth rate of total fiscal and other revenue, including mining royalties, has been less than 7 per cent per annum at current prices.

The cost of executing the plan has varied sharply from one year to the next. On average from 1960 to 1968 the expenditure under this head has been about 10,000 million FG annually, progressing from 8,000 to 12,000 million FG during the course of the ten-year period. Some 62 per cent of this budget is financed by foreign loans, which increased yearly from 4,600 million FG during the first half of the ten-year period to 8,200 million during the last half. Foreign aid for the first plan came almost entirely from countries of the eastern bloc, but for the second plan more assistance was given by western countries, principally the U.S.A. Local savings—budget surpluses earmarked for the plan, state trading profits, investments in voluntary labour—has supplied another 20 per cent of the required finance. The remainder (an annual average of 2,000 million FG) is met by inflationary means.

The precise division of responsibility for inflation among each of three possible sources—current administrative deficit, the financing of investments and deficits incurred by state enterprises—is difficult to evaluate, and such an estimate might be artificial (insofar as "profit-earning capacity" is determined on the basis of artificial prices). But one figure is certain: the total inflationary gap, which is in the region of 50,000 million FG over 8 years (more than 6,000 million FG per annum). Compared with Guinea's G.D.P. at the beginning of this period (approximately

60,000 million FG), this gap is considerable: it represents 10 per cent of G.D.P.

Inflation has led to a disorderly rise in prices, in spite of a price-freeze, official since 1959, and a considerable development in black market activities, including a market in foreign exchange, fed by illicit exporters.

BALANCE OF PAYMENTS AND EXTERNAL DEBT

Exports rose sharply from 5,000 million FG in 1958 to more than 12,000 million by 1960 and they stood at around 14,000 million in 1968–69. Mining accounted for more than 60 per cent of total sales. When the iron ore of Mount Nimba and the bauxite deposits of Boké are developed, a new jump in export figures should occur, and iron ore will represent 90 per cent of total exports.

Imports other than those of Fria and those of capital goods financed by foreign aid under the terms of the plan stood at around 7,500 million FG on average during the ten-year period. In spite of restrictive measures they have tended to grow faster than exports. While the growth rate of exports remains at 1.6 per cent per annum, that of imports is currently 4.2 per cent. However, an important part of these imports—basic foodstuffs—has for several years been supplied by American aid.

Between 1945 and 1958 Guinea had received from FIDES about 25,000 million FG (of which almost 60 per cent was in the form of grants). From 1960 to 1965 it received more than 45,000 million FG of foreign aid, of which 20,000 million were in long-term loans from eastern countries and 19,000 million were American aid (half in food products), the remainder being supplied by various western countries (Federal Germany, U.K., etc.) and the IBRD. Between 1965 and 1968 it received 18,000 million from the U.S.A. and 12,000 million from eastern countries.

This massive aid however has not enabled Guinea to attain a satisfactory equilibrium in its balance of payments. In fact, to the total trade deficit must be added the transfers of income by the mining companies (3,000 million FG) and by foreign technicians (2–3,000 million). Moreover, massive repayments of external debt have begun in the last few years. Guinea in 1960 had only a very small external debt, of about 3,400 million FG, less than its net foreign assets, which amounted to 5,500 million. By the end of 1965, Guinea's external debt had risen to 43,000 million FG and by the end of 1968 to more than 65,000 million. Two-thirds of this debt are made up of long-term capital equipment loans, but the proportion of private suppliers of medium-term credit tends to increase. On the other hand, short-term debts (for the supply of consumer goods) to the eastern countries with which Guinea has clearing agreements are very considerable: more than 15,000 million FG. One-third of this debt has been converted into long-term debt. The annual cost of the debt service (interest and repayments) has risen since 1968–69 to more than 4,000 million and absorbs one-third of export earnings.

STATISTICAL SURVEY

AREA AND POPULATION

(1963)

Region	Area (sq. km.)	Population ('000)	Region	Area (sq. km.)	Population ('000)
Beyla	17,452	170	Kindia	8,828	152
Boffa	6,003	90	Kissidougou	8,872	133
Boké	11,053	105	Kouroussa	16,405	93
Conakry	308	172	Labé	7,616	283
Dabola	6,000	54	Macenta	8,710	123
Dalaba	5,750	105	Mali	8,800	152
Dinguiraye	11,000	67	Mamou	6,159	162
Dubréka	5,676	86	N'Zérékoré	10,183	195
Faranah	12,397	94	Pita	4,000	154
Forécariah	4,265	98	Siguiri	23,377	179
Fria	n.a.	27	Télimelé	8,155	147
Gaoual	11,503	81	Tougue	6,200	75
Gueckédou	4,157	130	Youkounkoun	5,500	55
Kankan	27,488	176	**Total**	**245,857**	**3,360**

Mid-1971 Population (UN estimate): 4,013,000.

Births and Deaths: Annual average birth rate 47.2 per 1,000, death rate 25.1 per 1,000 (UN estimates for 1965–70).

Principal Towns: Conakry (capital) 172,500 (1969 estimate), Kankan 76,000 (1964), Kindia 55,000 (1964).

Employment (1970): Total economically active population 1,904,000, including 1,589,000 in agriculture (ILO and FAO estimates).

AGRICULTURE

PRINCIPAL CROPS

('000 metric tons)

	1969	1970	1971
Maize	68*	68*	68*
Millet and Sorghum	150*	150*	150*
Rice (Paddy)	368	400	400*
Yams and Sweet Potatoes	82*	82*	n.a.
Cassava (Manioc)	470	480	n.a.
Citrus Fruits	80*	80*	80*
Bananas	80	85	n.a.
Pineapples	13	13	n.a.
Palm Kernels (exports only)	15	15	15*
Groundnuts (in shell)	25	25	25*
Coffee	12	10.5	10.5
Tobacco	1.3*	1.3*	1.3*

* FAO estimates.

Source: FAO, *Production Yearbook 1971* (Rome, 1972).

LIVESTOCK

(FAO estimates—'000)

	1968–69	1969–70	1970–71
Cattle	1,780	1,800	1,830
Sheep	460	470	480
Goats	490	500	500
Pigs	23	24	25
Asses	3	3	3
Chickens	3,900	4,000	4,200

LIVESTOCK PRODUCTS

(FAO estimates, metric tons)

	Cows' Milk	Hen Eggs
1969	41,000	4,100
1970	42,000	4,200
1971	43,000	4,400

FORESTRY
ROUNDWOOD PRODUCTION
(cu. metres)

1967	.	.	2,188,000
1968	.	.	2,213,000
1969	.	.	2,238,000
1970	.	.	2,200,000

Source: FAO, *Yearbook of Forest Products.*

Sea fishing (1969–71): Total catch 5,000 metric tons each year (FAO estimate).

MINING

	1960–63*	1964	1965	1966	1967	1968	1969
Bauxite ('000 tons)† . .	340	184	241	251	250	1,000	1,000
Alumina ('000 tons) . .	330	484	520	525	530	535	535
Iron Ore ('000 tons)‡ .	740	427	553	705	264	—	—
Diamonds ('000 carats) .	45	52	42	49	29	n.a.	n.a.

* Annual averages.

† Excluding bauxite processed into aluminium by Fria.

‡ Kaloum iron ore worked-out; target for iron ore production of Mount Nimba mine is not yet known.

ELECTRICITY
(million kWh.)

CONSUMERS	1960	1961	1962	1963	1964	1965	1966	1967	1968
Fria	77	109	115	119	125	130	126	128	129
Others . . .	24	25	32	37	43	47	60	70	73

1971 targets: Fria and Boké 300 million kWh.; Public Sector 100 million kWh.

FINANCE

100 centimes = 1 Guinea franc (FG).
Coins: 5, 10 and 25 FG.
Notes: 50, 100, 500, 1,000, 5,000 and 10,000 FG.
Exchange rates (December 1972): £1 = 533.81 FG; U.S. $1 = 227.36 FG;
1,000 FG = £1.873 = $4.398.

Note: It was announced in October 1972 that a new currency unit, the sily
(divided into 100 corilles), is to be introduced. The sily is equivalent to 10FG.

BUDGET
('000 million FG)

	1960	1961	1962	1963	1963–64	1964–65	1965–66	1966–67	1967–68	1968–69
Outturn:										
Revenue . . .	7.6	8.7	9.1	10.4	12.2	13.2	16.2	14.4	15.6	n.a.
Expenditure .	8.0	7.6	7.2	11.1	10.5	11.7	16.2	16.1	19.1	n.a.
Estimates:										
Fiscal, Parafiscal .	7.7	8.3	9.5	10.0	10.5	9.8	11.8	11.0	14.5	13.3
Other Revenue*	0.5	0.4	0.2	1.2	1.2	6.4	6.2	9.6	7.7	10.0
Expenditure:										
Salaries and Wages .	0.5	5.1	4.7	5.0	4.9	8.2	9.5	11.3	11.9	11.7
Goods and Services .	0.5	3.0	3.1	2.5	1.8	3.1	3.9	4.2	4.6	5.2
Public Debt .	0.5	0.1	0.1	0.8	1.0	3.7	3.3	3.8	4.4	5.6
Other Expenditure .	0.5	0.5	1.8	2.9	4.0	1.2	1.3	1.3	1.3	1.0

* Since 1964 this figure includes payments into the Equalization Fund, and the depreciation funds of the state enterprises
in 1966–67 it also includes the revenue of the National Railways Board.

1970-71 Budget (revised estimates): 23,300 million FG.
1971-72 Budget (ordinary estimates): 27,800 million FG.

EXTERNAL TRADE

BALANCE OF TRADE
('000 million current FG)

	1964–65	1965–66	1966–67	1967–68	1968–69
Exports:					
Agricultural Products .	3.5	4.0	4.1	4.6	5.1
Minerals . .	9.3	8.8	8.5	8.5	9.0
Imports:					
Fria . . .	2.9	2.4	1.6	1.8	1.8
Plan . . .	3.2	3.3	2.4	4.7	3.0
Other . . .	9.8	9.3	9.2	5.8	11.3
Balance. . .	−3.1	−2.2	−0.6	0.8	−2.1

PRINCIPAL COMMODITIES
(million FG–1962)

IMPORTS		EXPORTS	
Motor Cars and Parts . . .	1,705	Fresh Bananas	1,120
Cotton Textiles . . .	2,050	Raw Coffee	712
Machinery	1,195	Fresh Pineapple	167
Petroleum Products . .	1,188	Groundnuts	315
Iron and Steel . . .	887	Palmetto	735
Metal Products . . .	705	Iron Ore	665
Electrical Equipment . .	604	Aluminium Ore	23
Rice	1,546	Aluminium	6,663
Cement	420	Diamonds	498

PRINCIPAL COUNTRIES
(million FG—1962)

IMPORTS		EXPORTS	
France	2,381	France	2,036
Other Franc Zone	653	Other Franc Zone	1,680
German Federal Republic .	1,252	Eastern Bloc	2,914
U.S.S.R.	3,269	Dollar Zone	1,462
United States	1,814	Netherlands	469

PRINCIPAL COUNTRIES
(million U.S. $—1968)

IMPORTS		EXPORTS	
France	9.2	Norway	9.9
U.S.A.	6.3	Spain	6.0
Federal Germany	3.4	U.S.A.	4.5
United Kingdom	1.7	Cameroon	4.5
Switzerland	1.1	Federal Germany . . .	4.1
Spain	0.1	Switzerland	3.7
Cameroon	0.1	Austria	3.4
TOTAL (incl. others) . .	70.0	TOTAL (incl. others) . .	55.0

TRANSPORT
(1962)

Railways: Passengers 591,000, Passenger-km. 43m., Freight 123,000 metric tons, Freight ton-km. 42m.

Roads: Cars 7,600, Lorries and Commercial Vehicles 11,500 (1968), Tractors 125, Other 133.

Shipping: Vessels entered 709, Freight entered 614,163 metric tons, Freight cleared 1,314,154 metric tons, Passengers 8,008.

Civil Aviation (scheduled services, 1969): 720,000 km. flown; 15,920,000 passenger-km.; 100,000 cargo ton-km.

EDUCATION

Education (1966–67): Primary: 1,605 schools, 149,527 pupils; Secondary: 252 schools, 36,379 pupils; Tertiary: 660 students. Pupils (1968): Primary 167,340, Secondary (general) 33,448, Vocational 5,334, Teacher-training 2,954, Tertiary 942.

Source: Direction de la Statistique Générale et de la Mécanographie, Conakry; IMF, *International Financial Statistics.*

THE CONSTITUTION

(promulgated November 1958; amended October 1963)

The Constitution was altered and enlarged according to Law No. 1 on October 31st, 1963. The principle of the Republic is "Government of the people by the people for the people".

1. The State is a Democratic Republic.

3. Sovereignty rests in the people, and is exercised by their representatives in the National Assembly.

The National Assembly

4–8. Equal and secret elections for the National Assembly on a national list are held every five years.

10. Representatives enjoy the usual parliamentary immunity.

11. A permanent Commission elected from the National Assembly manages the business of the Assembly between sittings (two per year).

9. The first duty of the Assembly is to pass laws.

14. The President and the Representatives are responsible for the initiation and formulation of laws.

17. The Representatives are in control of the Budget and expenditure; limited only in that any proposal for an increase in expenditure must be accompanied by a corresponding increase in revenue.

The President

20. The President is Commander-in-Chief of the Armed Forces.

21. Executive power is practised solely by the President; the Cabinet is nominated by him and subordinate to him.

22. The President is elected for a period of seven years and can stand for re-election as often as he wishes.

24. The President is responsible to the Assembly, but there are no definite curbs upon the executive.

28. If the Presidency is vacant the Cabinet continues to govern until a new President is elected.

The Judiciary

35. The President guarantees the independence of the judiciary; he also has the power to pardon. The Judges are responsible only to the law.

36. The accused has a right to defence.

The Basic Rights and Duties of the Citizen

39. All the inhabitants of the Republic of Guinea have the right to vote.

40–46. The Constitution confers the right of freedom of speech, assembly, coalition, demonstration and conscience upon all citizens; the Press is free, the post is secret, property is inviolable; all citizens have the right to work, go on holiday, to receive social support and education, and to go on strike.

42. It is the duty of all citizens to uphold the Constitution, to defend their country, and to fulfil social responsibilities.

45. Racial discrimination, or regional propaganda is punishable by law.

THE GOVERNMENT

HEAD OF STATE

President: AHMED SEKOU TOURÉ (re-elected January 1968 for a seven-year term by 99.7 per cent of electorate; sole candidate).

CABINET

(December 1972)

President: AHMED SEKOU TOURÉ.

President's Private Domain:

    Minister Delegate to the Presidency: SAIFOULAY DIALLO.

    Minister of Information and Ideology: LOUIS BEHAZIM.

Prime Minister: Dr. LOUIS LANSANA BEAVOGUI.

    Minister of the People's Army: TOUMANI SANGARE.

    Minister of Foreign Affairs: FILY CISSOKO.

    Minister of Planning: ALIOUME DRAME.

    Minister of Financial Control: FODÉ MAMADOU TOURÉ.

Interior and Security Domain: MOUSSA DIAKITÉ.

    Minister of Justice: DIALLO TELLI.

    Minister of the Interior and Security: DAMANTANG CAMARA.

    Minister of Local Development for Middle Guinea: SEKOU CHERIF.

    Minister of Local Development for the Forest Region: MAMADOU BOUMBOYA BELLA.

Minister of Local Development for Maritime Guinea: KARAMOKO KAUYATÉ.

Minister of Local Development for Upper Guinea: CHERIF MABANOU.

Culture and Education Domain: MAMADI KEITA.

    Minister of Scientific Research and Documentation: SIKÉ CAMARA.

    Minister of Pre-University Education and Literacy: MOKTAR DIALLO.

    Minister of Higher and Television Education: LOUIS OLIMÉ.

    Minister of Youth, Arts and Sport: ABDOULAYE DIALLO (BALDENG).

Social Domain: ALPHA BOCAS BARRY.

    Minister of Health: Dr. KEKOURA CAMARA.

    Minister of Social Affairs: MAFOURY BAMFOURA.

    Minister of the Civil Service and Labour: ABDOULAYE DIALLO.

Trade and Communications Domain: N'Famara Keita.

Minister of Internal Commerce: Abdoulaye Sory.

Minister of External Commerce: Mamad Kaba.

Minister of Posts and Telecommunications: Salifou Touré.

Economy and Finance Domain: Ismaël Touré.

Minister of Industry and Energy: Laminé Condé.

Minister of Finance: Mamadou Boumboura Bella.

Minister of Mines and Geology: Mohamed Alminé Touré.

Minister of Public Works, Urban Affairs and the Environment: Diomba Mara.

Minister of Rural Development: Alpha Bacar Barry.

Governor of Banks: N'Faly Sangare.

PARTI DEMOCRATIQUE DE GUINEE (PDG)

The Party is the ultimate source of authority in the country, possessing "sovereign and exclusive control of all sections of national life".

Secretary-General: President Sekou Touré (*re-elected October 2nd, 1967, and designated "Supreme Head of the Revolution" and "Supreme Servant of the People"*).

Bureau Politique National: 25 members, including the Secretary-General and the six Ministers.

DIPLOMATIC REPRESENTATION

EMBASSIES AND LEGATIONS ACCREDITED TO GUINEA

(In Conakry unless otherwise stated)

(E) Embassy; (L) Legation.

Algeria: B.P. 1004 (E); *Ambassador:* Messaoudi Zitouni (also accred. to Liberia and Sierra Leone).

Belgium: B.P. 871 (L); *Chargé d'Affaires:* Marcel de Moudt.

Bulgaria: B.P. 629 (E); *Ambassador:* Boris Milev (also accred. to Congo Republic (Brazzaville)).

Canada: (E); Dakar, Senegal.

China, People's Republic: B.P. 714 (E); *Ambassador:* Chai Tse-min.

Cuba: B.P. 71 (E); *Ambassador:* Oscar Oramas.

Czechoslovakia: rue d l'Aviation, B.P. 1009 *bis* (E); *Ambassador:* Milos Vojta.

Egypt: B.P. 389 (E); *Ambassador:* Osman Aly Assal.

German Democratic Republic: *Ambassador:* Guenther Fritsch.

Ghana: (E); *Ambassador:* to be appointed.

Hungary: B.P. 1008 *bis* (E); *Ambassador:* Gusztav Gogolyak (also accred. to Mali and Mauritania).

India: B.P. 186 *bis* (E); *Ambassador:* R. R. Sinha (also accred. to Mali).

Indonesia: B.P. 722 (E); *Ambassador:* Mohamed Ali Moersid.

Italy: B.P. 84 (E); *Ambassador:* Mario Ungaro.

Japan: (E); *Ambassador:* Tatsuo Hirose.

Korea, Democratic Republic: B.P. 723 (E); *Ambassador:* Kim Kwan Seup.

Liberia: B.P. 18 (E); *Ambassador:* Christie W. Doe.

Mauritania: (E); Dakar, Senegal.

Mongolia: (E); *Ambassador:* Toumbachin Pourevjal (also accred. to Mali).

Morocco: (E); *Ambassador:* Mahfoud El Khatib.

Nigeria: B.P. 54 (E); *Ambassador:* L. J. Dosunmu.

Pakistan: (E); Accra, Ghana.

Poland: B.P. 1063 (E); *Ambassador:* Wlodimierz Migon.

Romania: B.P. 348 (E); *Ambassador:* Niculai Iaan Vancea (also accred. to Mali).

Saudi Arabia: (E); *Ambassador:* Nasser Gouth.

Senegal: *Ambassador:* (vacant).

Sierra Leone: B.P. 625 (E); *Ambassador:* Kojo Randall.

Spain: (E); *Ambassador:* Nicolas Martin.

Syria: (E); *Ambassador:* Naim Kadah.

Turkey: (E); Accra, Ghana.

U.S.S.R.: B.P. 329 (E); *Ambassador:* Alexander Startsev.

United Kingdom: (E); *Ambassador:* John Curle.

U.S.A.: B.P. 503 (E); *Ambassador:* James Loeb.

Venezuela: (E); Lagos, Nigeria.

Viet-Nam, Democratic Republic: B.P. 1551 (E); *Ambassador:* Nguyen-Thuong (also accred. to Congo Republic (Brazzaville)).

Yugoslavia: B.P. 1554 (E); *Ambassador:* Vrlje Cedomil.

Guinea also has diplomatic relations with Albania, Cameroon, Congo (People's Republic), Ethiopia, Finland, The Gambia, Jordan, Lebanon, Mali, Netherlands, Norway, Sweden, Switzerland, Tanzania, Togo, Tunisia, Turkey and Upper Volta.

DEFENCE

Guinea has an army of 5,000, a navy of 300 and an air force of 800. There is also a People's Militia of about 30,000, in addition to the para-military gendarmerie, Republican Guard and civil police, who together number about 1,700. The air force is well equipped with MiGs provided by the U.S.S.R.

Chief of Staff of Armed Forces: (vacant).

NATIONAL ASSEMBLY

President: LÉON MAKA.

Composition: All 75 Deputies are members of the Parti Démocratique de Guinée.

Elections: January 1968; the term is for five years.

POLITICAL PARTY

Parti démocratique de Guinée (PDG): Conakry; *Congrès national* meets every four years; in the intervals the plenary body of the Party is the *Conseil national de la révolution* (*CNR*); the chief executive body is the *Bureau politique national* of 25, including the President and the six Ministers, and the other executive bodies are the *Comité central* of 45 (15 elected by the *Congrès national*, plus the 30 secretaries of the local federal parties) and the *Comité exécutif de la révolution*, which corresponds to the local party organizations and which comprises the Secretary-General and six political commissars.

Other Party organizations: *Comité national des femmes; Confédération nationale des travailleurs guinéens (CNTG)*.

JUDICIAL SYSTEM

There is a High Court whose jurisdiction covers political cases. The Cour d'Appel, the Chambre des Mises en Accusation and the Tribunal Supérieur de Cassation are at Conakry.

Tribunaux du Ier Degré exist at Conakry and Kankan and have jurisdiction over civil and criminal cases and also act as Industrial Courts. A Justice of the Peace sits at N'Zérékoré.

Procurator-General: SIKÉ CAMARA.

Président, Cour d'Appel: FODÉ MAMADOU TOURÉ.

RELIGION

It is estimated that 62 per cent of the population are Muslims, about 35 per cent animists and 1.5 per cent Christians, mostly Roman Catholics.

In May 1967, the President ordered that all priests should be Guinea nationals.

Roman Catholic Missions: L'Archevêché, B.P. 1006 *bis*; in the archdiocese of Conakry there are about 32 mission centres, with a personnel of 41; Archbishop of Conakry Mgr. RAYMOND TCHIDIMBO (*condemned to hard labour for life January 1971 for plotting against state*).

Protestant Missions: There are six mission centres, four run by British and two by American societies.

PRESS AND RADIO

Horoya (*Dignity*): Guinea Press Service, Conakry, B.P. 191; twice weekly; organ of the Parti démocratique de Guinée.

Horoya Hebdomadaire: B.P. 191, Conakry; f. 1969; weekly.

Journal officiel de Guinée: Conakry, B.P. 156; fortnightly government publication.

Travailleur de Guinée: Conakry; organ of the Confédération National des Travailleurs Guinéens.

NEWS AGENCIES

Agence Guinéen de Presse: B.P. 191, Conakry; f. 1960; Dir. ALPHA DIALLO.

FOREIGN BUREAUX

APN—Novosti Press Agency: c/o U.S.S.R. Embassy, Conakry.

Tass is also represented.

RADIO

Radiodiffusion Nationale de Guinée: B.P. 617, Conakry; programmes in French, English, Créole-English, Portuguese, Arabic and local languages; Dir. E. TOMPARA.

In 1969 there were about 90,000 receiving sets.

FINANCE

(cap. = capital; FG = Guinea franc.)

BANKING

CENTRAL BANK

Banque Centrale de la République de Guinée: Boulevard du Commerce, B.P. 692, Conakry; f. 1960; cap. 500m. FG; Gov. BALLA CAMARA.

Banque Guinéenne du Commerce Extérieur: Conakry; cap. 150m. FG.

Banque Nationale de Développement Agricole: Conakry; Dir. GNAN FELIX MATHOS.

Crédit National pour le Commerce, l'Industrie et l'Habitat: B.P. 137 Conakry; f. 1961; in 1962 it took over the Banque de l'Afrique Occidentale.

INSURANCE

Conakry

National Insurance Co.: B.P. 719; f. 1961; State company.

Société Guinéenne d'Assurances: B.P. 500.

Ten of the main French insurance companies maintain agencies in Conakry.

TRADE AND INDUSTRY

CHAMBER OF COMMERCE

Chambre Economique de Guinée: B.P. 609, Conakry; f. 1960; replaces the former Chamber of Commerce and Chamber of Agriculture and Industry; Pres. BAIDI GUEYGE.

TRADE UNION

Confédération National des Travailleurs Guinéens (CNTG): P.O.B. 237, Bourse du Travail, Conakry; Pres. MAMADI KABA; 100,000 mems.; 19 federations and national unions, 32 local administrative offices; integrated with PDG (*see* Political Party); publ. *Le Travailleur de Guinée*.

MAJOR INDUSTRIAL COMPANIES

The following are some of the largest companies in terms either of capital investment or employment.

Compagnie des Bauxites de Guinée: Coléah Mafanco, Corniche, Conakry; f. 1964; cap. $2m.; state owns 49 per cent of shares.
Bauxite mining at Boké to begin shortly.
Pres. Dir.-Gen. LAWRENCE HARVEY.

Brasseries de Guinée: B.P. 345, Conakry; f. 1958; cap. 350m. FG.
Manufacture of beer and soft drinks.
Dir.-Gen. JEAN MEURET; Dir. HENRI FAIVRE; 130 employees.

Compagnie Internationale pour la Production de l'Alumine Fria: B.P. 334, Conakry; f. 1957; cap. 8,400m. FG.
Aluminium smelter at Fria.
Dir. RAYMOND BAGNOL.

Société Minière de Beyla: Beyla; state-owned diamond mining company.

Entreprise Nationale de Briqueterie et de Céramique: Kobaya; state-owned; manufacture of bricks and ceramics.

Entreprise Nationale de Tabacs et de Cigarettes: Kissoko; state-owned manufacture of tobacco products.

Total Guinée: B.P. 306, Immeuble Lesage, Conakry; f. 1961; cap. 220m. FG.
Import of petroleum products under state control; the Government of Guinea has responsibility for sales and distribution.
Pres. C. BRICKA; Dir. A. M. LEBRUN; 40 employees.

TRANSPORT

RAILWAY

Chemins de Fer de Guinée: B.P. 581, Conakry; Dir. PIERRE DIANÉ; 662 km. of 1 metre gauge track from Conakry to Kankan in the east of the country, crossing the Niger at Kouroussa. A second line, 104 km. long, links Conakry and the aluminium works at Fria. A new line from Kankan to Bamako in Mali is being financed by China.

ROADS

There are some 18,000 km. of classified roads (325 km. tarred in 1968), and 2,500 km. of seasonal tracks. The main roads are those running along the coast from Sierra Leone to Portuguese Guinea (via Conakry) and from Conakry into the interior, with branches to the frontiers of Senegal, Sudan and the Ivory Coast.

SHIPPING

Conakry's 2,450 metres of quays provide 9 alongside berths for ocean-going vessels.

E.N.T.R.A.T.: P.O.B. 315, Conakry; state stevedoring and forwarding firm; Dir.-Gen. A. AMADOU BA.

Société Navale Guinéenne: P.O.B. 522, Conakry; f. 1968; state shipping firm; agents for Cie. Maritime des Chargeurs Réunis, Cie. de Navigation Fraissinet et Cyprien Fabre, Delta Steamship Lines Inc., Elder Dempster Line, Hanseatic Africa Line, Leif Hoëgh and Co. A/S, Lloyd Triestino, Nouvelle Compagnie de Paquebots (N.C.P.), Palm Line Ltd., Scandinavian West Africa Line, Société Navale de l'Ouest, United West Africa Service; Dir.-Gen. YAYA KEITA.

CIVIL AVIATION

Air Guinée: Conakry, B.P. 12; f. 1960; internal and regional services.

Aeroflot, Air Afrique, Air Mali, Č.S.A. (Czechoslovakia), Interflug, Sabena and U.T.A. also serve Conakry.

POWER

Société Nationale d'Electricité: B.P. 322, Conakry; state-owned company for the production of electricity; Dir. MAMADOU LAMINE TOURÉ.

EDUCATION

Education is free. There were over 300,000 children at school in 1968. There are three grades of school—Primary, Upper Primary and Secondary—and there are also vocational training institutes. In 1966 about 1,000 Guinean students were studying abroad. The eight national languages have been taught since 1968, although French remains in use for the time being, and since August 1968 "councils of the cultural revolution" have been established in the villages to assist this programme.

LEARNED SOCIETIES AND RESEARCH INSTITUTES

Centre de Recherches Rizicoles: Kankan.

Institut de Recherches Fruitières: B.P. 36, Kindia; f. 1961; Dir. C. KEITA.

Institut National de Recherches et Documentation: B.P. 561, Conakry; Dir. S. BOUNAMA SY.

Institut de Recherches et de Biologie Appliquée Pastoria: B.P. 146, Kindia; former **Institut Pasteur**, nationalized 1965; research on anthropoid apes; production of various vaccines; Dir. Dr. T. CAMARA.

Secrétariat d'Etat à la Recherche Scientifique: B.P. 561, Conakry; f. 1969; formerly the Guinea branch of the Institut Français d'Afrique Noire; administers the National Archives, the National Library and Museum, l'Institut des Traditions Populaires, la Section des Sciences Sociales, la Section des Sciences Exactes, l'Institut de Recherche Fruitière de Foulaya, l'Institut de Recherches et de Biologie Appliquée, le Secrétariat d'UNESCO; Sec. of State SIKÉ CAMARA; publs. *Recherches Africaines* (quarterly), *Cahiers, No. 1 Inventaires des Archives*.

U.S. Information Center: c/o American Embassy, Cultural Dept., B.P. 711, Conakry.

LIBRARIES

Bibliothèque Nationale: Conakry; f. 1960; 10,000 vols., also special collection on slavery (about 500 books, pamphlets and MSS.); 300 current periodicals; courses in librarianship; Librarian Mrs. LALANDE ISNARD, M.A., DIP.LIB.

Archives Nationales: B.P. 561 Bis, Conakry; f. 1960; Dir. KEÏTA SIDIKI KOBÉLÉ.

MUSEUMS

Musée National: Conakry; f. 1960; Curator MAMADOU SAMPIL.

Mount Nimba National Reserve: nature reserve for wild animals.

There are regional museums at Youkounkoun, Kissidougou and N'Zérékoré.

COLLEGES

Institut Polytechnique de Conakry: B.P. 1147, Conakry; f. 1963; est. by the Soviet Union, with teaching staff drawn principally from Russia, France and Belgium; to train engineers and teachers; the library will hold 15,000 vols.

Faculties of Science, Civil Engineering, Geology and Mining, Letters, Agriculture, Medicine and Pharmacy, Chemistry, Electrical Engineering.

Director of Studies: A. BOISRAYON.

Number of students: 120.

Ecole Nationale des Arts et Métiers: Conakry; f. 1966.

Ecole Supérieure d'Administration: Conakry; f. 1964.

SELECT BIBLIOGRAPHY

For works on the former A.O.F. states generally *see* Dahomey Select Bibliography, p. 297.)

AMEILLON, B. *La Guinée, bilan d'une indépendance*. Paris, Maspero, 1964.

AMIN, SAMIR. *Trois expériences africaines de développement: Le Mali, la Guinée et le Ghana*. Paris, Presses universitaires de France, 1965.

DUMONT, RENÉ. *Afrique noire: développement agricole: reconversion de l'économie agricole: Guinée, Côte d'Ivoire, Mali*. Paris, Presses universitaires de France, 1962.

HARRISON CHURCH, R. J. *West Africa* (6th edn., ch. 25). London, Longmans, 1968.

MABILEAU, A., and MEYRIAT, I. (Eds.). *Décolonisation et régimes politiques en Afrique noire*. pp. 159 ff. Paris, 1967.

SY, M. S. *Recherches sur l'exercise du pouvoir politique en Afrique noire (Côte d'Ivoire, Guinée, Mali)*. Paris, 1965.

TOURÉ, SEKOU. *L'action politique du parti démocratique en Guinée*. Conakry, 1962.

L'expérience guinéenne et l'unité africaine. Paris Présence Africaine, 1959.

Guinea (Bissau)

PHYSICAL AND SOCIAL GEOGRAPHY*

René Pélissier

Guinea (Bissau), properly known as the Portuguese overseas province of Guinea, is a territory wedged between Senegal to the north and the Republic of Guinea to the east and south, with various coastal islands such as Caió, Pecixe, Bissau, Arcas, Bolama, Como, and Melo, and an offshore archipelago, the Bissagos or Bijagós Islands. This archipelago comprises eighteen main islands, among which are Caravela, Caraxe, Formosa, Uno, Orango, Orangozinho, Bubaque and Roxa. The whole province is administered as a unit from the capital and main port of Bissau, which has replaced the former capital Bolama. The territory has an area of 36,125 sq. km., including some low-lying ground which is periodically submerged at high tide. Except for some higher terrain close to the Guinea border (about 300 metres), the relief consists of a coastal plain deeply indented by rias which play a useful role in internal communications, and a transition plateau, forming the *planalto de Bafatá* in the centre, and the *planalto de Gabu*, which abuts on the Fouta Djallon. The main physical characteristics of Guinea are its meandering rivers and wide estuaries, where it is difficult to distinguish mud, mangrove and water from solid land. The main rivers are the Cacheu, the Mansôa, the Geba and Corubal complex, the Rio Grande, and, close to the Guinean southern border, the Cacine. Ocean-going vessels of shallow draught can reach most of the main population centres, and flat-bottomed tugs and barges can penetrate to nearly all significant outposts except in the north-east sector. Administratively, Guinea consists of 10 *concelhos* and 3 *circunscrições*.

The climate is tropical, hot and wet with two seasons. Maritime and Sahelian influences are felt. The average temperature is about 68°F. May and April are the hottest months (about 84°F.), January and December the coldest (about 73°F.). Rainfall is abundant (1,000–2,000 mm. in the north), and excessive on the coast. The interior is a savannah or light savannah woodland, while coastal reaches are covered with mangrove, swamps, rain forest and tangled forest. In 1970 the population in Portuguese-held areas was 487,448, with a rather high density of 17.5 persons per sq. km., which is above the African average. The main population centre is Bissau, which had over 65,000 residents in 1971, following the evacuation of people from some inland areas caught in the cross-fire of the Portuguese and the nationalists. Bafatá, Bolama, Farim, Teixeira Pinto, Mansôa, Nova Lamego, Catió and Bissorã are the other important towns, and their significance has increased since the beginning of the war. The *concelho* at Bissau had 118,572 inhabitants in 1970. No reliable figures for the present total population are available, but it is safe to say that it is well under the 800,000 mark claimed by the nationalists. At least 90,000 refugees live outside the country. The war has caused havoc among the rural communities, which in the Portuguese-controlled areas tend to be concentrated in fortified and garrisoned villages, or in the areas liberated and controlled by the nationalists are liable to be bombed by the Portuguese air force.

Before the war the main ethnic divisions among the Africans were as follows: a colony of Cape Verdeans, *mestiços*, some *assimilados* of Guinean stock, and the *indígenas*, whose main tribes were the Balante (about 30 per cent), the Fulani or Fula (20 per cent), the Mandyako (14 per cent), the Malinké or Mandingo (12.5 per cent), and the Pepel (7 per cent). The non-Africans are mainly Portuguese civil servants and traders, and Syrian and Lebanese traders. Guinea has never been a settler colony.

A Guinean *crioulo* is the lingua franca, but both the Portuguese and the PAIGC nationalists have stepped up their campaign for literacy in Portuguese. Contrary to the position in the Cape Verde Islands, Catholicism is still of marginal importance. The Portuguese have found their staunchest allies among the semi-feudal Muslim Fulani and Malinké, while PAIGC activists draw their strength from their Balante followers and various de-tribalized or former *assimilados*.

* *See* map on p. 708.

RECENT HISTORY

See Recent History of Portugal's African Territories under Angola, p. 150.

ECONOMY
René Pélissier

The chaotic state of the economy is the consequence of the war, but, even before it started, Guinea (Bissau) was not much of an economic proposition. Agriculture is the mainstay of such economic life as persists. It is entirely an African activity, since there are no European settlers. Among foodcrops rice is the staple food of the population. Swamp rice and upland rice amount to about 170,000 tons, and in record years some of it is exported. The PAIGC has devoted much attention to intensifying this culture in the areas it controls since Amilcar Cabral, its leader, is an agronomist. So have the Portuguese. Maize, beans, cassava, and sweet potatoes play a relevant part at the village level. Traditional exports are groundnuts, grown in the interior as an extension of the Senegalese cultivation, and palm-oil products in the islands and on the coast. In 1968 51,302,000 escudos' worth of groundnuts, and 25,375,000 escudos' worth of coconuts were exported, accounting for about 60 per cent and 30 per cent respectively of the value of exports. In 1970, 13,937 tons of groundnuts, 1,191 tons of cashew nuts and 6,787 tons of coconuts were exported.

Cattle-breeding is a very important activity among Balante and Muslim tribes of the interior. In 1971 270,000 head of cattle, 175,000 goats, 150,000 pigs and 65,000 sheep were registered. Meat consumption is significant, and some hides and skins are exported. Fishing is developing and 1,451 tons were landed in 1970.

Industry is negligible, except for food-processing and building. In fact, Guinea has a war economy superimposed upon a typically backward, peasant economy where most products are bought and sold by a Portuguese firm, the Companhia União Fabril (CUF), its subsidiaries and one or two local merchants. Some bauxite, oil and other minerals have been found or are prospected for, but the unsettled political and military conditions are not conducive to their exploitation. A large deposit of 200 million tons of bauxite was reported in the Boé area in 1972.

STATISTICS

Area: 36,125 sq. km.

Population (1970 Portuguese census): 487,448. In addition to this figure, there are about 20,000 Metropolitan Portuguese troops in Guinea. Close to 90,000 refugees live in Senegal, and nationalist-held areas may contain anything between 40,000 and the 400,000 claimed by PAIGC, the actual figure being closer to the lower estimate.

Agriculture: *Principal Crops* (1971—metric tons): Groundnuts 65,000, Cassava 37,000 (1970), Rice 35,000, Palm Kernels 12,000 (exports only), Palm Oil 8,000, Rubber 100 (exports only). *Livestock* (1970–71): Cattle 270,000, Goats 175,000, Pigs 150,000, Sheep 65,000, Asses 3,000.

Industry: (1970—metric tons): Rice 4,607, Groundnuts 14,621, Vegetable Oils 2,558.

Finance: 100 centavos = 1 Guinea escudo; 1,000 escudos = 1 conto. Exchange rates: £1 sterling = 62.90 escudos (December 1972), 100 escudos = £1.590; U.S. $1 = 27.12 escudos (September 1972), 100 escudos = $3.687.

Budget (1970—contos): Ordinary receipts 333,207, extraordinary receipts 210,621, Total 543,828; Ordinary expenditure 308,103, extraordinary expenditure 210,621, Total 518,724.

Currency in Circulation (1971): Notes 223,106 contos, Coins 34,805 contos, Total 257,911 contos.

External Trade (1970—contos): Imports 786,035; Exports 89,814.

Commodities: *Imports* (1970): Vegetable Products 79,875; Food, Beverages and Tobacco 124,496; Mineral Products 65,877; Textiles and Products 125,271. *Exports* (1970): Vegetable Products 80,333; Food, Beverages and Tobacco 2,110.

Countries: *Imports* (1970): Portugal 434,884; Portuguese Overseas Provinces 47,419; Foreign Countries 303,732. *Exports* (1970): Portugal 78,913; Portuguese Overseas Provinces 3,008; Foreign Countries 7,893.

Transport: *Roads* (1971): Cars 2,986, Lorries and Buses 1,006, Motor Cycles 661, Total 4,653. *Shipping* (1971): Vessels entered 106, Freight unloaded 50,579 metric tons. *Civil Aviation* (1971): Passengers landed 12,886, Freight entered and cleared 22,640 kg.

Education (1971–72): *Primary:* Schools 199,* Teachers 803, Pupils 34,125; *Pre-secondary:* Pupils 1,900; *Secondary:* School 1, Pupils 757; *Technical:* School 1, Pupils 500; *Secondary and Technical:* Teachers 158. The PAIGC is reported to have about 20,000 pupils in its schools.

* 1967 figure.

THE GOVERNMENT

Governor: Gen. ANTÓNIO SEBASTIÃO RIBEIRO DE SPÍNOLA.

POLITICAL PARTIES

Acção Nacional Popular: The Portuguese Government party, formerly União Nacional.

Partido Africano da Independencia da Guiné e Cabo Verde (PAIGC) (*African Party for Independence in Guinea and Cape Verde*): B.P. 298, Conakry, Guinea (*illegal in Guinea Bissau*); Sec.-Gen. AMÍLCAR CABRAL.

The PAIGC is the most successful of the liberation movements in Portuguese-controlled Africa. It was formed in 1956 by Amílcar Cabral and Raphael Barbosa (who was arrested by the Portuguese in 1962 and later forced to disown the PAIGC). After Portuguese police had killed about 50 striking dockers at Pidgiguiti in August 1959, the PAIGC decided to engage in all-out struggle to achieve their aim of winning freedom for Guinea and Cape Verde as a single independent state. In 1960 Cabral established himself in Conakry and the party started training in the Republic. The party machinery was slowly built up until in mid-1962 a campaign of sabotage against the Portuguese could begin. In 1963 full-scale attacks began on Portuguese army installations and on towns. By 1972, despite the presence of up to 30,000 Portuguese and African troops, the PAIGC claimed control of some two-thirds of the territory, with the Portuguese and their supporters confined mainly to fortified garrisons and villages. The PAIGC have placed great emphasis on improving the quality of life of the people, and schools and hospitals have been set up in the liberated areas, as well as citizens' committees.

In November 1970 a force directed by Portuguese invaded Conakry in the neighbouring Republic of Guinea and destroyed the PAIGC offices there.

Frente para a Libertação e Indepêndencia da Guiné (FLING) (*National Independence Front*): Consists of *Mouvement de libération de la Guinée dite portuguaise* (*MLG*) led by FRANÇOISE MENDY, and *Union des populations de Guinée dite portuguaise* (*UPG*), leader BENJAMIN PINTO-BULL; based in Dakar, Senegal (*illegal in Guinea Bissau*).

DEFENCE

Portugal has direct control of the defence of Guinea (Bissau). The total Portuguese armed forces in the colony may number as many as 50,000, including those enlisted locally.

Commander-in-Chief of Armed Forces: Gen. ANTÓNIO DE SPÍNOLA.

RELIGION

ROMAN CATHOLIC

Apostolic Prefecture Bissau: C.P. 20, Bissau; f. 1955; Apostolic Prefect Mgr. AMÂNDIO NETO.

THE PRESS

A Voz de Guiné: Editor Father CRUZ DE AMARAL.

Government Gazette: Bissau; weekly; official announcements.

Boletim Cultural de Guiné Portuguesa: Bissau; quarterly.

Boletim da Associação Comercial, Industrial e Agricola da Guiné: Bissau.

Boletim da União International de Bissau: Bissau.

RADIO

Emissora Oficial da Guiné Portuguesa: Av. da Republica, Caixa Postal 191, Bissau; Government Station; Pres. C. RUIVO.

There are 8,317 radio receivers. There is no television service.

FINANCE

ISSUING BANK

Banco Nacional Ultramarino: 84 rua do Comercio, Lisbon; C.P. 38, Bissau; f. 1917; Man. ALBERTO DE ALMEIDA COELHO.

DEVELOPMENT ORGANIZATION

Fundo de Crédito do Guiné: f. 1966 under Investment Plan; 1965–67 to finance development.

INSURANCE

The following Portuguese insurance companies have agents in Portuguese Guinea:

Comércio e Industria, S.A.R.L.: Bissau; Sociedade Comercial Ultramarina, Caixa Postal 23; (Head Office: Rua Arco do Bandeira 22, Lisbon 2).

Tagus, S.A.R.L.: Head Office: Rua do Comercio 40–64, Lisbon; agent in Portuguese Guinea: JOSÉ LOPES ABREU, Caixa Postal 86, Bissau.

Império: Casa Gouvêa, Caixa Postal 44; (Head Office: Rua Garrett 56, Lisbon 2).

Ultramarina, S.A.R.L.: Av. Gov. Carvalho Viegas, Caixa Postal 257; Bissau; (Head Office: Rua da Prata 108, Lisbon).

TRANSPORT

ROADS

There were 3,184 km. of roads in 1972, of which 350 km. were tarred.

SHIPPING COMPANIES

Companhia Nacional de Navegação: agents at Bissau: EMPRESA ANTONIO DA SILVA GOUVEIA, S.A.R.L. (Head Office: Rua do Comércio 85, Lisbon).

Companhia Colonial de Navegação: Rua de S. Julião, 63 Lisbon-2, C.P. 2747; agents at Bissau: SOCIEDADE COMERCIAL ULTRAMARINA, C.P. 23, Bissau.

Sociedade Geral de Comércio, Industria e Transportes: agents at Bissau: EMPRESA ANTONIO SILVA GOUVÊA, S.A.R.L. (Head Office: Rua dos Douradores 11, Lisbon).

CIVIL AVIATION

There is an aerodrome at Bissau and a weekly service is provided by T.A.P. from Cape Verde, and a service four times weekly to Lisbon.

Transportes Aereos da Guiné Portuguesa: Aeropuerto Craveiro Lopes, Bissau; fleet of one Dornier Skyservant, two Dornier 27, three Cessna U206 and one Cessna F172; Dir. JOSÉ LEMOS FERREIRA.

EDUCATION

Museu da Guiné Portuguesa: Caixa Postal 37, Bissau; departments of History, Ethnography, Natural Sciences and Economics; library of 14,000 vols.; Keeper JOAQUIM AUGUSTO AREAL.

Centro de Estudos da Guiné Portuguesa: Caixa Postal 37, Bissau; f. 1945; library of 9,623 vols.; Pres. Dr. CARLOS LEHMAN DE ALMEIDA; Sec. JOAQUIM AUGUSTO AREAL; publs. *Boletim Cultural da Guiné Portuguesa* (quarterly), *Memórias*.

SELECT BIBLIOGRAPHY

(For works on the Portuguese African Territories generally see Angola Select Bibliography, p. 175.)

CABRAL, AMÍLCAR. *Revolution in Guinea: an African People's Struggle. Selected Texts.* London, Stage 1, 1969.

CHALIAND, GÉRARD. *La lutte armée en Afrique.* Paris, Maspero, 1967. As *Armed Struggle in Africa.* New York and London, Monthly Review Press, 1969.

Guinée "portugaise" et Cape Vert en Lutte pour leur Indépendance. Paris, Maspero, 1964.

CHILCOTE, RONALD H. "The Political Thought of Amílcar Cabral", *Journal of Modern African Studies,* 4/3, 101–22, 1967.

DAVIDSON, BASIL. *The Liberation of Guiné.* Harmondsworth, Penguin Books, 1969.

TEIXEIRA DA MOTA, A. *Guiné Portuguesa* (2 vols.). Lisbon. 1964.

Ivory Coast

PHYSICAL AND SOCIAL GEOGRAPHY*

R. J. Harrison Church

The Republic of the Ivory Coast is Ghana's western neighbour, and is economically the most important of the successor states of French West Africa. The republic has an area of 124,504 sq. miles, and a population estimated at 4,416,000 in 1971. There is a diversity of peoples, the Agni and Baoulé having cultural and other affinities with the Ashanti of Ghana. The Senoufo of the north are famous for their wooden masks.

From the border with Liberia eastwards to Fresco the coast has cliffs, rocky promontories and sandy bays. East of Fresco the rest of the coast is a straight sandbar, backed, as in Dahomey, by lagoons. None of the seaward river exits are navigable, and a canal was finally opened from the sea into the Ebrié lagoon at Abidjan only in 1950, after half a century's battle with Nature.

Although Tertiary sands and clays fringe the northern edge of the lagoons, they give place almost immediately to Archaean and Precambrian rocks, which underlie the rest of the country. Manganese is

quarried from such weathered rocks north of the lagoon at Grand Lahou, whilst diamonds are obtained from gravels south of Korhogo, and north and south-east of Séguéla. Granites are dominant in the west, where, apart from occasional domes, the Man Mountains and the Guinea Highlands on the border with Liberia and Guinea are the only areas of vigorous relief in the country.

Except for the north-western fifth of the Ivory Coast, the country has an equatorial climate. This occurs most typically in the south, which receives 50–95 in. of rain p.a., with two maxima, and where the relative humidity is high. Much valuable rain forest survives in the south-west, but elsewhere it has been extensively planted with coffee, cocoa, bananas, pineapple, rubber and oil palm. Tropical climatic conditions prevail in the north-west, with a single rainy season of five to seven months, and 50–60 in. of rain annually. Guinea savannah occurs here, as well as in the centre of the country, and projects southwards around Bouaké.

* *See* map on p. 364.

RECENT HISTORY†

Michael Crowder and Donal Cruise O'Brien

(Revised for this edition by KAYE WHITEMAN)

Independence was achieved in 1960, although it was rumoured that the Ivorian leader, Felix Houphouët-Boigny, was reluctant to abandon the security of the colonial status of that territory in favour of the dubious benefits of independence. Houphouët-Boigny as President, and his *Parti démocratique de la Côte d'Ivoire* as ruling party, have remained in power since that time without formal opposition. The relative security of the régime has been assured by massive French technical assistance, and also by an economic growth rate without parallel in west Africa (8 per cent per annum in G.N.P. since independence).

Political unrest was manifest in the early years after independence, especially among radical students (several of whom were arrested in 1961) and trade unionists. Two plots against the régime were uncovered in 1963, apparently representing a coalition of hostile forces: left-wing youth, discontented politicians, and northerners who resented southern domination in the government. Party purges followed the discovery of these plots, and the army was reduced in size. By the end of 1964 the government felt secure

enough to introduce a set of far-reaching social reforms, abolishing polygamy, the bride price, and inheritance in the female line. The main plotters of 1963 were released within four years.

The events of May 1968 in France were followed by student disturbances in the Ivory Coast, and a new outbreak came in May 1969 with an educational strike, which was broken by the arrest of the principal leaders. A riot against resident African foreigners occurred in Abidjan in September 1969. Among educated Ivorians there is much resentment at the slow pace of Africanization since independence, which leaves French nationals a decade later still occupying jobs at the level of clerk and shop-assistant. These and many other grievances were openly expresssed by participants in a series of "public dialogues" held by the leading government figures following the 1969 riots. In 1970 a law restricting immigration from neighbouring African countries was introduced.

---

† For the period before independence *see* Recent History of Dahomey, p. 282.

In general, however, the internal position in the Ivory Coast has remained calm. Attempts have been made, as in Senegal, to lessen the generation gap between the old guard of the party and the restless youth of schools and the university by introducing a younger generation of "technocratic" ministers into the government. Elements from other countries, notably those of the Council of the Entente, who have been seen as disruptive influences at the university have been sent home, with the result that more and more Abidjan University is for Ivorians alone. This is in line with the nationalist trend in university education throughout francophone Africa.

There have been minor disturbances, such as those among the Sanwi in the south-east in late 1969 and those in Gagnoa in November 1970, both because of regional grievances, but on the whole the policy of reconciliation has been effective. In April 1971 the President released the last of the men who had been jailed eight years before in the period of the "plots" and virtually admitted that the charges had been baseless. Others had already been amnestied, and the remainder no longer presented any political threat. President Houphouët-Boigny is now very much an elder statesman, and his power is quite unchallenged, although there is speculation about his succession, in view of his occasional periods of poor health. There are a number of contenders but no obvious successor in sight.

FOREIGN POLICY

In foreign policy the years since independence have been marked by a number of initiatives, not all of them successful. Although a founder member of the OAU, President Houphouët-Boigny has been sceptical about its effectiveness and even more doubtful that he could exercise any influence in its councils. For these reasons he has not been to an OAU summit since 1963 and has preferred to concentrate on the regional grouping of francophone states, OCAM, which he helped to form in 1965, and the Council of the Entente.

The operation of bringing Moïshe Tshombe's government in Congo (Kinshasa), now Zaire, into OCAM to give it African respectability, and the Ivory Coast's recognition of Biafra, the secessionist state of Eastern Nigeria, were both due to the President's personal initiative. Both schemes proved fruitless. In addition attempts by the President to give more substance to the Council of the Entente, notably the "double nationality" plan of 1965, met with disappointment, because of opposition from the Ivorian middle classes.

President Houphouët-Boigny's most recent foreign policy initiative has probably been his most controversial. This was the proposal for a dialogue between black African states and South Africa, which was launched in April 1971 at a press conference in Abidjan, to which journalists from all over the world were invited. The matter had initially been mentioned the previous November, but had not been pursued, and when the Ivory Coast tried to follow it up after the press conference, few countries gave their support. Madagascar, Malawi and Gabon were in favour, and the countries of the Entente did not oppose it, because of their sentimental ties with the Ivory Coast. Ghana, however, changed its attitude at the OAU summit. The President had tried to put the proposal in the context of "neutrality in Africa", which is a policy linked with his almost fanatical anti-communism, but it was felt that the scheme had originated in France, which has close commercial ties with South Africa. Many African states said that the first dialogue should be between white and black in South Africa, and suspected that the Ivory Coast was more interested in trade with and investment from South Africa. The Ivorian President also claimed that "dialogue" was in accord with the Lusaka Declaration, which had been approved by the OAU in 1969, but other African states felt that this had made abandonment of *apartheid* and minority rule a pre-condition. In 1972 "dialogue" with South Africa was not discussed at the OAU summit, so completely had it been defeated the year before. Houphouët-Boigny's fear of communism was proved to outweigh any subservience to French dictates, when, at the same time as the People's Republic of China was admitted to the UN, the Ivory Coast strengthened its already good relations with Taiwan.

ECONOMY

Samir Amin*

The Ivory Coast's economic growth rate, which had been given a stimulus in 1950 with the opening of the Vridi canal and the Abidjan deep-water harbour, speeded up during the period 1950–60, increasing from 7 per cent to 8 per cent per annum, and further during the period 1960–70, when the annual increase grew to 11 per cent. The faster pace after independence was associated with a move into sectors characteristic of foreign development, and with the development of import-substitution industries: in 1960–65 the annual rates of increase included 7 per cent for agriculture, of which 3 per cent was subsistence agriculture, 9–10 per cent for agricultural exports, and almost 20 per cent for forestry, 13–14 per cent for industry, handicrafts and building, 10 per cent for transport, commerce and services, and 12–13 per cent for public administration.

The main subsistence crops are roots and tubers, and cereals. Production of the former (yams, plantains and manioc) rose from 853,000 tons of yam equivalent in 1950 to 1,504,000 tons in 1965, while production of the latter (rice, maize and millet) increased during the same period from 193,000 tons to 300,000 tons of rice equivalent. The Ivory Coast's development has been based mainly on exports of coffee, cocoa, bananas, pineapples and timber (table 1):

Table 1
EXPORTS ('ooo tons)

	1950	1965
Coffee	55	250
Cocoa	50	120
Bananas	20	15
Pineapples	—	40
Timber	90	1,250

Total exports in this period increased over four times.

After 1960 another growth factor was the foundation of light industry (e.g. flour mills, an oil mill, canning, brewing, cigarettes, textiles and plastic product factories, sawmills, vehicle assembly plants). These were to substitute for imports which had previously come largely from Dakar, up to that time the industrial centre for the whole of French West Africa. The estimated turnover of industry and handicrafts, at 1965 prices, increased from 4,900 million francs CFA in 1950 to 51,100 million francs CFA in 1965.

Table 2
POPULATION ('ooo)

	TOTAL POPULATION	URBAN POPULATION
1920	1,540	25
1950	2,170	160
1965	3,835	684
1970	4,310	915

Economic growth has been accompanied by an equally fast population growth rate and increased urbanization (table 2).

The influx of immigrants, chiefly from the Mossi district of Upper Volta, increased from 100,000 in 1950 to 950,000 in 1965. These immigrants have provided vital manpower for the plantations and newer urban activities. In 1965 the foreign African population comprised a quarter of the total population, 35–40 per cent of active male workers, half of all urban workers, more than 60 per cent of urban workers outside the civil service, and half to two-thirds of plantation labour.

THE STRUCTURE OF DEVELOPMENT EXPENDITURE

The investment requirements for such rapid growth were naturally large, rising progressively from 15 per cent of the G.D.P. at the beginning of the period to 19 per cent at the end of it. During the ten-year period 1950–59, the chief impetus came from public investment in infrastructure, which made up 50 per cent of the total; whereas during the following five years, the lead was taken by industrial investment, the proportion of which rose from 12 per cent to 25 per cent.

At the same time the growth of public revenue and expenditure made it possible to devote a larger surplus to capital equipment. Whereas taxation rose progressively from 15 per cent of G.D.P. around 1950 to 20 per cent at the end of the period, current administrative expenditure did not exceed 16 per cent of G.D.P. in 1965, compared with 12 per cent in 1950.

THE BALANCE OF PAYMENTS

Despite its very rapid growth during the period 1950–65, the Ivory Coast's economy has experienced no external payments problems. This is due to having based development policy on the export of primary commodities. While in these fifteen years the value of exports multiplied 4.4 times, G.D.P. increased only 3.5 times. Even though the net flow of capital transfers and interest and dividend payments has increased considerably—in 1950 the Ivory Coast received 4,600 million francs CFA of public and private capital at 1965 value and paid out 7,000 million francs CFA; in 1965 she received only 15,400 million francs CFA and paid out 25,200 million francs CFA—the remarkable growth of exports has maintained the balance of payments.

The achievement of such a rapid and balanced growth is not at all mysterious. The history of the colonial era has many comparable examples. The only difference between other recent instances of colonial exploitation (e.g. Senegal, south-east Nigeria and Katanga) and that of the Ivory Coast is that the other countries were exploited earlier and their

* For the 1973 edition, revisions have been made to this article by the Editor.

development took place over a longer period, whereas in 1950 the Ivory Coast still had the status of a colonial "reserve" and was wholly undeveloped. The result was naturally a more extreme growth rate than elsewhere.

Economic and social change has not yet affected all the rural areas, although it is true that the traditionally isolated and backward areas now contain only a third of the rural population, compared with 60 per cent in 1950. In the plantation areas, deep social divisions have appeared. In 1965 about 20,000 wealthy planters owned about a quarter of the land, employed two-thirds of the wage-earning force, and had an average annual income of about 400,000 francs CFA.

FUTURE PROBLEMS OF GROWTH

After 1965, the Ivory Coast's economic growth began showing a clear tendency to slow down. In the years 1964–68 G.D.P. was respectively 240,000 million, 239,600 million, 258,000 million, 275,700 million and 326,500 million francs CFA, giving an annual average growth rate at current prices of 7.6 per cent. Since the annual rise of the price index was 3.8 per cent, the annual average growth rate at fixed prices was about 4 per cent. The index of volume of exports for each year between 1962 and 1968 rose from 84 to 100, 120, 117, 115, 107 and 137 respectively. The very bad harvest of 1967 was compensated by a very good one the following year, and the average annual growth rate of exports (volume) was between 7 per cent and 8 per cent, that is, higher than the growth rate of G.D.P., showing the export-orientated nature of the country's economic development. As exports steadily increased, G.D.P. reached 365,600 million francs CFA in 1969 and 409,500 million francs CFA in 1970.

Furthermore, the establishment of a range of light industries for import substitution, which was another incentive for investment and growth from 1960 to 1965, also seems likely to slow down in future, according to official estimates of private capital imports into the Ivory Coast. The official balance of payments, established in 1963, shows the following figures for private capital investment over the period since 1963 (table 3):

Table 3
PRIVATE CAPITAL INVESTMENT
(million francs CFA at current exchange rates)

1963	.	.	.	4,700
1964	.	.	.	4,900
1965	.	.	.	3,000
1966	.	.	.	3,000
1967	.	.	.	3,000
1968	.	.	.	1,800

In the urban sector of the economy, change has been less marked as urban society has been extended rather than transformed. Personal income has in fact kept much the same proportions, although the volume of it has increased vastly. The proportion of all income of foreign enterprise in the economy has remained much the same—about 50 per cent of the gross non-agricultural product. The increasing dominance of foreign capital is nevertheless shown by the increase in the profits of large companies, which have risen from 28 per cent to 40 per cent of foreign non-agricultural income. It is also shown by the high level of European salaries, still about 40 per cent of total salaries in the productive sector, compared with 60 per cent in 1950. Europeans still hold all key positions and alone provide technical, administrative and economic expertise.

Imports for the years 1962–68 are shown in table 4:

Table 4
IMPORTS
(million francs CFA at current exchange rates)

1962	.	.	.	39,000
1963	.	.	.	42,000
1964	.	.	.	59,000
1965	.	.	.	58,000
1966	.	.	.	64,000
1967	.	.	.	65,000
1968	.	.	.	76,000

The average annual growth rate was therefore 13 per cent at current prices, or 10 per cent at constant prices. The official balance of payments shows total transfers of profit increasing from 14,000 million francs CFA in 1963 to 18,000 million in 1965 and 26,000 million in 1968. The annual growth rate of transfers is thus about 13–14 per cent a year, almost three times as high as the rate of increase in production.

However, despite such negative indications, the Ivory Coast's balance of payments is not unhealthy; external assets increased from 5,800 million francs CFA at the end of 1952 to 15,700 million at the end of 1962 and then to 22,400 million at the end of 1968. These reserves represented 14 per cent of the value of imports in 1962 and 29 per cent in 1968. There are two main reasons for this. In the first place prices for coffee and cocoa improved markedly after 1965. Secondly, foreign official aid did not decrease as had been predicted. Foreign governmental transfers to the Ivory Coast (both current and capital), according to the official balance of payments, are shown in table 5:

Table 5
FOREIGN GOVERNMENTAL
TRANSFERS TO IVORY COAST
(million francs CFA at current value)

1963	.	.	.	5,600
1964	.	.	.	5,300
1965	.	.	.	8,800
1966	.	.	.	5,500
1967	.	.	.	3,700
1968	.	.	.	8,600

The favourable development of the financial structure which took place between 1960 and 1965 (that is, resulting in a reduction of foreign capital) did not last long. Private domestic savings failed to overtake foreign investment; local public savings, although they did increase, also failed to do so.

Like the balance of payments, internal public finances also have a healthy outlook. Net bank assets of the Treasury increased from 3,100 million francs CFA at the end of 1962 to 9,300 million at the end of 1965 and 10,300 million at the end of 1968. It must be borne in mind, however, that since 1965 the growth of public current expenditure has kept pace with the basic real growth of the economy. According to the national accounts the index of G.D.P. and that of current expenditure in 1968 were the same (133 on a base of 100 in 1965). On the other hand, between 1965 and 1968 tax and other forms of revenue increased by only 17 per cent.

Thus public capacity to finance development seems to be diminishing. In fact, a very large part of the development budget (*budget spécial d'investissement et d'équipment*) is really current expenditure in disguise. The Treasury has been able to finance its deficit easily enough by resorting to foreign loans. The public debt increased from 8,700 million francs CFA at the end of 1960 to 20,500 million at the end of 1965, and its annual rate of growth, about 20 per cent, is accelerating.

The development of the Ivory Coast has led to obvious contradictions in the social field. Urbanization is speeding up; Abidjan now has an estimated population of over 450,000. Unemployment in this wealthy country has reached a massive level over the last five years, and is beginning to present serious problems.

According to the Ministry of Labour a growth of 10 per cent in the gross domestic product has been accompanied by an increase of only 5 per cent in the number of wage-earners. From 1960 to 1967, the number of non-agricultural jobs increased by 57 per cent, but the urban population increased faster, by 115 per cent in Abidjan.

STATISTICAL SURVEY

AREA AND POPULATION

Area (sq. km.)	Population (1969 est.)				
	Total	Foreign	Abidjan (capital)	Bouaké	Gagnoa
322,463	4,200,000	1,000,000	500,000	100,000	45,000

Mid-1971 population (UN estimate): 4,416,000.

Births and Deaths: Annual average birth rate 46.0 per 1,000; death rate 22.7 per 1,000 (UN estimates for 1965–70).

EMPLOYMENT
(January 1st, 1964)

Total population: 3,708,000 (male 1,867,000; female 1,841,000).

Economically active: 1,850,000 (male 979,000; female 871,000).

Agriculture, Forestry, Hunting and Fishing	1,600,000
Mining	3,070
Manufacturing	15,550
Construction	16,590
Electricity, Gas and Water . .	6,810
Commerce	125,300
Transport and Communication . .	41,870
Services	40,810
TOTAL	1,850,000

Source: Direction de la statistique, Abidjan, *Bulletin mensuel de statistiques.*

AGRICULTURE

LAND USE, 1968
('ooo hectares)

Arable Land .	7,809
Under permanent crops .	1,050
Permanent Meadows and Pastures .	8,000
Forest .	12,000
Other Land .	2,941
	31,800
Inland Water	446
TOTAL AREA .	32,246

PRINCIPAL CROPS
('ooo metric tons)

	1969	1970	1971
Maize .	260	231	280
Millet and Fonio .	41	37	42*
Sorghum .	14	13	13*
Rice (paddy) .	303	316	310*
Sweet Potatoes and Yams .	1,541	1,572	n.a.
Cassava (Manioc) .	532	540	n.a.
Bananas .	172	179	n.a.
Pineapples .	90	111	n.a.
Palm Kernels .	23	26	30
Palm Oil .	36.5	52.4	69.0
Groundnuts (unshelled) .	43	43	43*
Cottonseed .	20	18	20
Copra .	5.3	6.9	7.7
Coffee .	279.6	240	249
Cocoa Beans (year ending September) .	144.5	180.7	179.6
Cotton (lint) .	14	13	15
Natural Rubber (dry weight) .	7.1	10.9	10.5*
Coconuts (million) .	50	64	n.a.

* FAO estimates.

Source: FAO, *Production Yearbook 1971.*

LIVESTOCK
('ooo)

	1968/69	1969/70	1970/71
Cattle.	392	396	400*
Pigs .	169	167	168*
Sheep.	799	829	850*
Goats .	800	778	770*
Poultry .	7,700*	7,900*	8,000*

* FAO estimates.
Source: FAO, *Production Yearbook 1971.*

LIVESTOCK PRODUCTS
(metric tons)

	1969	1970	1971
Cows' Milk .	9,000*	10,000*	10,000*
Beef and Veal .	29,000	28,000*	28,000*
Mutton and Lamb .	9,000	9,000*	9,000*
Pork .	4,000	4,000*	4,000*
Hen Eggs .	5,100*	5,200*	5,400*

* FAO estimate.
Source: FAO, *Production Yearbook 1971.*

FORESTRY
ROUNDWOOD PRODUCTION
(cu. metres)

1967	.	.	8,397,000
1968	.	.	8,939,000
1969	.	.	8,989,000

Source: FAO, *Yearbook of Forest Products.*

FISHING
(metric tons)

	1967	1968	1969
Sea	62,900	65,800	67,000
Inland Water . .	4,000	4,000	4,000
TOTAL CATCH .	66,900	69,800	71,000
Value of Fish Landed (million francs CFA) .	2,612	3,130	3,038

Source: FAO, *Yearbook of Fishery Statistics 1970.*

MINING

	1967	1968	1969	1970
Manganese (metric tons) . . .	64,168	51,543	57,690	10,377
Diamonds ('ooo metric carats) . .	176	187	202*	213*

* *Source:* U.S. Bureau of Mines.

INDUSTRY

	TURNOVER ('ooo million francs CFA)		NUMBER OF ENTERPRISES IN 1968	TOTAL INVESTMENTS UNTIL JAN. 1ST, 1968 ('ooo million francs CFA)	NUMBER OF EMPLOYEES 1968	WAGES 1968 ('ooo million francs CFA)
	1962	1968				
Food Industries . . .	5.9	20.4	97	11.3	6,483	1.5
Mining	1.4	1.3	4	3.6	1,362	0.5
Metals	1.9	6.2	30	2.1	1,863	0.8
Chemicals, Fats, Rubber . .	3.0	8.9	33	5.0	2,198	0.7
Wood	2.6	9.1	73	5.3	7,500	2.5
Textiles	2.2	10.2	24	6.4	5,412	1.4
Building	1.0	2.6	10	1.6	626	0.2
Miscellaneous Industries . .	—	3.6	34	2.1	1,960	0.7
TOTAL MANUFACTURING INDUSTRIES . .	17.9	62.5	305	37.3	21,404	8.2
Power and Water . . .	1.9	9.7	4	19.7	1,705	1.3
GRAND TOTAL . .	19.8	72.2	309	57.0	23,109	9.5

Source: "Principales industries ivoiriennes", Chambre d'Industrie de Côte d'Ivoire (1969).

PRODUCTION

		1967	1968	1969	1970
Sawnwood	'ooo cu. metres	271	n.a.	110	125
Liquefied Petroleum Gas . .	'ooo metric tons	9	11	10	10
Motor Spirit	,, ,, ,,	147	155	159	169
Kerosene	,, ,, ,,	40	53*	39*	48*
Jet Fuels	,, ,, ,,	44	27*	41*	41*
Distillate Fuel Oils . . .	,, ,, ,,	181	199	218	199
Residual Fuel Oils . . .	,, ,, ,,	227	233	267	229
Electric Energy . . .	million kWh.	314	372	440	517
Thermal	,, ,,	121	115	186	257
Hydro	,, ,,	193	257	254	260
Cigarettes†	million	1,360	1,500	1,978	2,000

Source: UN, *Statistical Yearbook 1971*, except:

* *Source:* U.S. Bureau of Mines.

† *Source:* U.S. Department of Agriculture.

FINANCE

100 centimes = 1 franc de la Communauté Financière Africaine.

Coins: 1, 2, 5, 10, 25 and 100 francs CFA.

Notes: 100, 500, 1,000 and 5,000 francs CFA.

Exchange rates (December 1972): 1 franc CFA = 2 French centimes.

£1 sterling = 593.625 francs CFA; U.S. $1 = 255.785 francs CFA.

1,000 francs CFA = 1.685 = $3.91.

RECURRENT BUDGET
(million francs CFA)

REVENUE	1967	1968	EXPENDITURE	1967	1968
Direct Taxes . . .	6,700	7,235	Education . . .	7,109	8,327
Indirect Taxes . . .	29,320	32,100	Defence	3,619	3,789
Licence Fees . . .	1,500	1,100	Public Health . . .	4,194	3,789
Others	2,280	2,765	Local Government Grants .	5,929	6,018
			Public Works and Housing .	4,977	5,219
			Public Administration .	7,159	7,552
			Agriculture . . .	1,430	1,822
			Foreign Affairs . .	955	1,085
TOTAL . . .	39,800	43,200	TOTAL (incl. others) .	39,800	43,200

CAPITAL BUDGET 1965–68
('ooo million francs CFA)

REVENUE	1965	1966	1967	1968
Revenue from Taxes . . .	7.2	9.6	7.8	8.6
Contribution from Stabilization Funds .	—	1.3	3.0	2.1
Loans	5.5	4.3	6.8	9.3
TOTAL	12.7	15.2	17.6	20.0

EXPENDITURE	1965	1966	1967	1968
Agriculture and Industry . . .	4.4	5.2	6.5	9.1
Transport and Infrastructure . . .	4.3	3.5	5.3	5.4
Administration	2.4	2.5	2.8	2.8
Education and Health . . .	0.3	2.7	1.7	1.5
Research	1.3	1.3	1.3	1.2

1971 Budget: 62,700 million francs CFA.

1972 Budget: 68,200 million francs CFA. The investment
and equipment budget amounts to a further 34,900m.
francs CFA.

FIVE-YEAR PLAN (1971–75)

Public investment will be 252,000m. francs CFA. Half
of this is allocated to infrastructure and 20 per cent to
agriculture. The growth rate envisaged is 4.1 per cent per
annum for agriculture and 12 per cent p.a. for industry.

BALANCE OF PAYMENTS 1963–68
('000 million francs CFA)

REVENUE	1963	1964	1965	1966	1967	1968
Exports	57.4	73.2	68.4	76.7	80.3	104.9
Public Transfers	4.4	4.2	5.4	4.8	3.6	3.8
Capital: Private Sector . .	4.7	4.9	3.0	3.0	3.0	1.8
Public Sector . .	1.2	1.1	3.4	0.7	0.1	4.8

EXPENDITURE	1963	1964	1965	1966	1967	1968
Imports	41.9	58.1	58.3	63.6	65.1	77.6
Investment Income . . .	5.1	7.0	6.6	8.4	8.9	9.5
Miscellaneous Private Transfers .	3.6	5.0	3.7	5.8	6.2	7.5
Savings Transfers	5.4	7.3	7.5	8.7	8.9	9.2

Source: IMF.

NATIONAL ACCOUNTS 1960–68
('000 million francs CFA)

	1960	1964	1965	1966	1967	1968
Gross Domestic Production . .	130.5	216.8	214.0	232.7	247.3	289.1
Gross Domestic Product . .	142.6	239.7	239.6	258.0	275.7	320.4
Agriculture: Local Consumption .	28.0	—	36.5	35.4	36.5	} 99.1
Marketed Production .	33.0	—	47.8	52.7	49.6	
Industry	13.8	—	29.8	38.2	40.7	} 63.5
Handicrafts	6.1	—	10.8	12.1	14.5	
Transport and Services . .	16.2	—	33.4	33.7	38.4	} 126.5
Commerce	33.4	—	55.6	58.5	67.6	
F.B.C.F.	19.1	—	43.6	47.1	49.8	58.9
Administrative Expenditure . .	5.7	—	9.6	10.6	11.5	12.8
Exports	44.4	—	70.9	78.3	82.5	108.4
Imports	34.1	—	63.7	67.8	72.2	85.5

Revised totals of Gross Domestic Product ('000 million francs CFA): 326.5 in 1968; 365.6 in 1969; 409.5 in 1970.

EXTERNAL TRADE*
(million francs CFA)

	1964	1965	1966	1967	1968	1969	1970	1971
Imports	58,834	58,301	63,533	64,872	75,676	86,235	107,704	110,838
Exports	74,501	68,418	76,657	80,262	104,890	118,223	130,190	126,558

* Excluding trade in gold.

PRINCIPAL COMMODITIES

IMPORTS	1969	1970
Food, Drink, Tobacco . . .	12,344	16,425
Fuels	4,499	5,123
Raw Materials	2,272	2,960
Semi-manufactures . . .	14,430	20,626
Agricultural and Industrial Equipment	24,556	30,932
Consumer Goods . . .	27,183	31,638

EXPORTS	1969	1970
Green Coffee	30,169	43,172
Cocoa Beans	26,350	26,742
Cocoa Pulp	1,927	2,304
Cocoa Butter	3,820	2,915
Timber	35,119	29,335
Raw and Unprocessed Cotton	2,114	2,066
Cotton Print	1,587	1,832
Bananas	3,005	3,208
Rubber	903	1,192
Tinned Pineapples . . .	1,666	2,379
Fresh Pineapples . . .	596	782
Pineapple Juice . . .	450	648
Diamonds	518	412
Manganese Ore . . .	167	258

PRINCIPAL COUNTRIES

IMPORTS	1969	1970
France	39,966	49,788
Other Franc Zone . . .	8,806	10,375
United Kingdom . . .	2,221	2,684
U.S.A.	7,135	8,527
German Federal Republic .	7,463	9,285
Italy	4,557	6,945
Netherlands	3,994	5,161
Belgium and Luxembourg .	2,179	2,794
Japan	1,389	2,699
Sino-Soviet Bloc . . .	990	1,590
Formosa	1,212	1,140
Norway	394	669
Sweden	280	534
Switzerland	409	552
Hong Kong	694	630

EXPORTS	1969	1970
France	37,112	42,526
Other Franc Zone . . .	8,662	9,062
United Kingdom . . .	4,786	4,373
U.S.A.	16,465	24,323
German Federal Republic .	11,372	12,506
Italy	12,826	11,204
Netherlands	10,927	11,792
Belgium and Luxembourg .	2,667	11,792
Japan	2,316	2,191
Sino-Soviet Bloc . . .	1,478	1,006
Spain	2,643	2,564

TOURISM
Tourist arrivals at hotels: (1970) 44,826; (1971) 48,722.

TRANSPORT

RAILWAYS
(including Upper Volta traffic)

	1969	1970	1971
Passengers ('000) . .	2,478	2,565	2,631
Passenger/km. ('000) . .	522,000	626,000	701,000
Freight ('000 metric tons) .	774	756	801
Freight (million net ton/km.) .	394	424	448

ROADS
(Motor vehicles in use—'000)

	1968	1969	1970
Passenger Cars . . .	40.6	47.0	56.4
Commercial Vehicles . .	30.0	33.0	40.1

SHIPPING

	ABIDJAN			SASSANDRA		
	1969	1970	1971	1969	1970	1971
Vessels entered (number) . . .	2,847	2,544	2,880	689	523	625
Vessels entered ('000 net reg. tons) . .	9,388	9,716	10,886	2,389	2,021	2,259
Passenger arrivals (number) . . .	3,556	412	281	—	—	—
Passenger departures (number) . .	5,190	953	853	—	—	—
Freight unloaded ('000 tons) . . .	2,002	2,335	2,616	4.91	1.70	1.40
Freight loaded ('000 tons) . . .	3,149	2,733	2,726	437	628	n.a.

Source: INSEE, *Données Statistiques* (Paris, 1972).

CIVIL AVIATION
(Scheduled services*)

	1968	1969	1970
Kilometres flown ('000) . . .	1,546	1,708	1,770
Passenger-km. ('000) . . .	58,953	65,820	70,670
Freight ('000 ton-km.) . . .	4,760	5,628	5,876
Mail ('000 ton-km.) . . .	479	492	540

* Including one-twelfth of the traffic of Air Afrique.

COMMUNICATIONS MEDIA

	1968	1969	1970
Telephones	24,390	27,220	31,000
Daily Newspapers . . .	n.a.	3	3
Radio Sets ('000) . . .	67	70	75
Television Sets ('000) . . .	6.7	10	11

Source: UN, *Statistical Yearbook 1971.*

EDUCATION
(1969)

	NUMBER OF TEACHERS	NUMBER OF PUPILS
Pre-primary . . .	n.a.	3,567
Primary . . .	10,094	464,817
General Secondary . .	1,910	53,267
Vocational . .	402	4,794
Teacher Training . .	95	1,615
University . .	126	2,042

Source: UN, *Statistical Yearbook 1971.*

Source (unless otherwise stated): Ministère des Finances, des Affaires Economiques et du Plan, Abidjan.

THE CONSTITUTION

(*October 31st, 1960*)

Preamble: The Republic of the Ivory Coast is one and indivisible. It is secular, democratic and social. Sovereignty belongs to the people who exercise it through their representatives or through referenda. There is universal, equal and secret suffrage. French is the official language.

Head of State: The President is elected for a 5-year term by direct universal suffrage and is eligible for re-election. He is Head of the Administration and the Armed Forces and has power to ask the National Assembly to reconsider a Bill, which must then be passed by two-thirds of the members of the Assembly; he may also have a Bill submitted to a referendum. In case of the death or incapacitation of the President his functions are carried out by a deputy chosen by the National Assembly.

Executive Power: Executive power is vested in the President who appoints a Council of Ministers.

Legislative Power: Legislative power is vested in a National Assembly of 100 members, elected for a 5-year term of office at the same time as the Presidential elections. Legislation may be introduced by either the President or by a member of the National Assembly.

Judicial Power: The independence of the judiciary is guaranteed by the President, assisted by a High Council of Judiciary.

Economic and Social Council: An advisory commission representing employers, unions and Government.

THE GOVERNMENT

HEAD OF STATE

President: Félix Houphouët-Boigny.

(re-elected November 29th, 1970)

COUNCIL OF MINISTERS

(*November* 1972)

President of the Council of Ministers and Minister of Defence: Félix Houphouët-Boigny.

Ministers of State: Auguste Denise, Dr. Blaise N'dia Koffi, Germain Coffi Gadeau.

Minister of State for Tourism: Matthieu Ekra.

Minister of State in charge of relations with the National Assembly: Loua Dimoande.

Minister of Justice and Keeper of the Seals: Camille Alliali.

Minister of the Interior: Nanlo Bamba.

Minister of Foreign Affairs: Arsène Assouan Usher.

Minister of the Armed Forces and Civic Services: Kouadio M'Bahia Blé.

Minister of Economic and Financial Affairs: Henri Konan Bedia.

Minister of Construction and Town Planning: Alexis Thierry-Lebbe.

Minister of Planning: Mohamed Diawara.

Minister of Posts and Telecommunications: Souleymane Cissoko.

Minister of Agriculture: Abdoulaye Sawadogo.

Minister of Scientific Research: Jean Lorougnon Guede.

Minister of Technical Education and Professional Training: Ange Barry-Battesti.

Minister of Health and Population: Hippolyte Aye.

Minister of the Civil Service: Joseph Tadjo Ehue.

Minister of Public Works and Transport: Grah Kadji.

Minister of Animal Production: Dico Garbah.

Minister of Labour and Social Affairs: Vanie Bi Tra.

Minister of Youth, People's Education and Sports: Etienne Ahin.

Minister of Information: Edmon Zegbehi Bouazo.

Minister of National Education: Paul Akoto Yao.

Secretary of State for Primary Education and Educational Television Broadcasting: N'Guessan Dikibié.

Secretary of State for the Budget: Abdouleh Kone.

Secretary of State for Mines: Gui Dibo.

Secretary of State for Posts: Mamadou Doukoure.

Secretary of State for National Parks: Koffi Attobra.

Secretary of State for Reafforestation: Jacques Toro.

Secretary of State for Culture: Hié Nea Jules.

DIPLOMATIC REPRESENTATION

EMBASSIES ACCREDITED TO IVORY COAST

(In Abidjan unless otherwise stated)

Algeria: 53 blvd. Clozel, B.P. 1015; *Chargé d'Affaires:* MOHAMED KHOURI.

Argentina: Dakar, Senegal (E).

Belgium: 21 ave. Chardy, B.P. 1800; *Ambassador:* (vacant).

Brazil: Immeuble Delafosse, B.P. 20.910; *Ambassador:* FERNANDO C. DE BITTENCOURT BERENGUER.

Canada: Immeuble "Le Général", B.P. 21.194; *Ambassador:* GILLES MATHIEU.

China, Republic (Taiwan): Résidence Crosson-Duplessis, ave. Crosson-Duplessis; *Ambassador:* TCHENG KOA JOEI.

Denmark: Accra, Ghana (E).

Egypt: 40 rue de la Canebière, Coccody, B.P. 2104; *Chargé d'Affaires:* IHSAN TALAAT.

Ethiopia: B.P. 20.802; *Ambassador:* ATO HAÏLE MECHECHA.

Finland: Lagos, Nigeria (E).

France: 3 blvd. Angoulvant, B.P. 1393; *Ambassador:* JACQUES RAPHAEL-LEYGUES.

Germany, Federal Republic: 11 ave. Barthe, B.P. 1900; *Ambassador:* JACOB HASSLANCHER.

Gabon: Immeuble Shell, ave. Lamblin, B.P. 20.855; *Ambassador:* JOSÉ J. AMIAR.

Ghana: Résidence de la Corruche, blvd. du Général de Gaulle, B.P. 1871; *Ambassador:* Col. M. K. GBAGONAH.

Haiti: Porto-Novo, Dahomey (E).

India: Dakar, Senegal (E).

Israel: 43 blvd. de la République, B.P. 1877; *Ambassador:* NISSIM YOSMA.

Italy: 16 rue de la Canebière, Coccody, B.P. 1905; *Ambassador:* FULVIO RIZZETTO.

Japan: ave. Chardy, B.P. 1329; *Ambassador:* OSAMU KATAOKA.

Korea, Republic: Immeuble "Le Général", B.P. 21.040; *Ambassador:* CHULL NAM.

Lebanon: 22 ave. Delafosse, B.P. 2227; *Ambassador:* MOHAMED TOUFIC.

Lesotho: Nairobi, Kenya (E).

Liberia: Immeuble "Le Général", B.P. 2541; *Ambassador:* (vacant).

Mali: blvd. Lagunaire, B.P. 2746; *Ambassador:* (vacant).

Malta: *Ambassador:* EDOUARD LOBKOWICZ.

Mauritania: 37 blvd. du Général de Gaulle; *Ambassador:* SIDNA OULD CHEIKH TALEB BOUYA.

Morocco: 10 blvd. Roume, B.P. 146; *Ambassador:* BOUDEKER BOUMEHDI.

Netherlands: Immeuble Shell, 48 ave. Lamblin, B.P. 1086; *Ambassador:* M. VAN DER MAADE.

Niger: 23 blvd. Angoulvant, B.P. 2743; *Ambassador:* EL HADJ ALLEDE.

Nigeria: 53 blvd. de la République, B.P. 1906; *Ambassador:* JOHN O. OMOLODUN.

Norway: Immeuble Shell, 48 ave. Lamblin, B.P. 607; *Ambassador:* PER THEE NAEVDAL.

Pakistan: Accra, Ghana (E).

Sierra Leone: Monrovia, Liberia (E).

Spain: B.P. 2589; *Ambassador:* TEODOMIRO DE A. COLOMER.

Sweden: Monrovia, Liberia (E).

Switzerland: Immeuble Franchet d'Espéray, Angle ave. Franchet d'Espéray et rue Lecoeur, B.P. 1914; *Ambassador:* ETIENNE SUTER.

Thailand: Lagos, Nigeria (E).

Tunisia: Immeuble Shell, 48 ave. Lamblin, B.P. 2099; *Ambassador:* R. B. BAOUAB.

United Kingdom: Immeuble Shell, 48 ave. Lamblin, B.P. 2581; *Ambassador:* (vacant).

United States: 5 rue Jesse Owens, B.P. 1712; *Ambassador:* JOHN F. ROOT.

Upper Volta: 2 ave. Terrason de Fougères, B.P. 908; *Ambassador:* MICHEL KOMPAORE.

Viet-Nam: Immeuble Nour-al-Hayat, ave. Chardy, B.P. 531; *Ambassador:* NGUYEN VAN LOC.

Yugoslavia: Bamako, Mali (E).

Zaire: 29 blvd. Clozel, B.P. 20151; *Ambassador:* ANTOINE NGWENZA MBENGANA.

Zambia: Immeuble "Le Général", B.P. 21.199; *Ambassador:* MWALE SITEKA GIBSON.

NATIONAL ASSEMBLY

President: PHILIPPE YACÉ.

Vice-Presidents: MARIE-BERNARD KOISSY, CLÉMENT ANET BILÉ, GON COULIBALY, MAURICE OULATÉ, BENOÎT TOUSSAGNON.

ELECTION, NOVEMBER 29TH, 1970

All 100 seats were won by the *Parti démocratique de la Côte d'Ivoire.*

POLITICAL PARTY

Parti démocratique de la Côte d'Ivoire: the national part of the West African *Rassemblement démocratique africain;* headed by a political bureau of 25 mems. and a guiding committee of 85; Pres. FÉLIX HOUPHOUËT-BOIGNY; Sec.-Gen. PHILIPPE YACÉ.

DEFENCE

The army numbers 4,000, the navy 100 and the air force 300. There is also a gendarmerie of 2,000.

Chief of Staff of the Army: Gen. PAUL THOMAS D'AQUIN OUATTARA.

JUDICIAL SYSTEM

Since 1964 all civil, criminal, commercial and administrative cases have come under the jurisdiction of the *tribunaux de première instance* (Magistrates' courts), the assize courts and the Court of Appeal, with the Supreme Court as supreme court of appeal.

Courts of First Instance: Abidjan, Pres. LAZENI COULIBALY; Bouaké, Pres. FADIKA MAMADOU; Daba, Pres. TAHAR CHÉRIF HAMZA; there are a further 25 courts in the principal centres.

Court of Appeal: Abidjan; hears appeals from the Courts of 1st instance; Pres. M. BELFER.

The Supreme Court: B.P. 1534, Abidjan; has four chambers: constitutional, judicial, administrative and auditing; Pres. ALPHONSE BONI.

The High Court of Justice: composed of Deputies elected from and by the National Assembly. It is competent to impeach the President or other members of the Government. Pres. PHILIPPE YACÉ; Vice-Pres. MARCEL LAUBOUET; mems. FRANÇOIS OUÉGNIN, AMOAKON DIHYE, DRAMANE COULIBALY, AMBROISE SAMBA KONÉ, CHÉRIF MAMÉRY.

State Security Court: composed of a President and six regular judges, all appointed for five years; deals with all offences against the security of the State; Pres. A. BONI.

RELIGION

It is estimated that 65 per cent of the population follow traditional animist beliefs, 23 per cent are Muslims and 12 per cent are Christian, of whom Roman Catholics account for 8.5 per cent of the total population.

ROMAN CATHOLICS

There are about 495,000 Roman Catholics. The Church operates 111 mission stations.

Archbishop of Abidjan: Mgr. BERNARD YAGO; B.P. 1287, Abidjan.

Bishop of Katiola: Mgr. EMILE DURRHEIMER, B.P. 110, Katiola.

Bishop of Gagnoa: Mgr. NOEL TEKRY, B.P. 527, Gagnoa.

Bishop of Bouaké: Mgr. ANDRÉ DUIRAT, B.P. 591, Bouaké.

Bishop of Daloa: Mgr. PIERRE ROUANET, B.P. 686, Daloa.

Bishop of Abengourou: Mgr. EUGÈNE KWAKU, B.P. 92, Abengourou.

Bishop of Man: Mgr. BERNARD AGRÉ, B.P. 447, Man.

OTHER CHRISTIAN COMMUNITIES

Mission Biblique: B.P. 8020, Abidjan; f. 1927; 8 missions; publ. *L'Appel de la Côte d'Ivoire.*

Christian and Missionary Alliance: B.P. 585, Bouaké; f. 1929; 7 mission stations; Superintendent FRED POLDING; publ. *Ivory Coast Today.*

Conservative Baptist Foreign Mission Society: Ferkessedougou, B.P. 111; f. 1947; active in the northern area in evangelism, teaching and medical work.

Eglise Protestante Méthodiste: 41 blvd. de la République, B.P. 1282, Abidjan; *c.* 86,000 mems.; Pres. Pastor SAMSON NANDJUI.

The Bible Society in Francophone West Africa: Abidjan, B.P. 1529; Sec. Rev. JOSUÉ DANHO; circ. of Scriptures 228,662 (1971).

Gospel Missionary Union: Man; 5 missions.

Mission Evangélique: B.P. 5, Zuénoula; established 1939; 11 mission stations; Field Dir. J. REIDER; Eglise Protestante du Centre de la Côte d'Ivoire: M. TEHI EMMANUEL, same address.

PRESS

Bulletin mensuel de la Chambre d'agriculture: Abidjan, B.P. 1291.

Bulletin mensuel de la Chambre d'industrie: Abidjan, B.P. 1758.

Bulletin mensuel de statistiques: Direction de la statistique, Abidjan, B.P. 222.

Bulletin Quotidien d'Information: Abidjan; published by Ivory Coast News Agency (*Agence Ivoirienne de Presse*), B.P. 4312, 11 ave. Bir-Hakein; f. 1961; evenings; Dir. BLAISE AGUI MIEZZAN; circ. 800.

Champion: c/o Centre de Publications Evangéliques, Abidjan, B.P. 8900; f. 1964; religious; quarterly; Editor D. GENTIL; circ. 15,000.

Eburnea: Ministry of Information, Abidjan; monthly.

Entente Africaine: P.O.B. 20991, Abidjan; Editor JUSTIN VIEYRA; Publishers Inter Afrique Presse; quarterly review.

Fraternité: Treichville, B.P. 1212; organ of the Parti Démocratique de la Côte d'Ivoire; weekly; Political Dir. FÉLIX HOUPHOUËT-BOIGNY.

Fraternité-Matin: blvd. du Général de Gaulle, Abidjan, B.P. 1807; f. 1964; official Party daily; Dir.-Gen. MAMADOU COULIBALY; Asst. Dir.-Gen. LAURENT DONA FOLOGO; circ. 33,000.

l'Industriel de la Côte d'Ivoire: Syndicat des industriels, Abidjan, B.P. 1340.

Le Journal des Amis du Progrès de l'Afrique Noire: B.P. 694; f. 1957; five issues a week; left-wing political; Editor DOUTE GILBERG; circ. 10,000.

Journal officiel de la Côte d'Ivoire: Ministry of the Interior, Abidjan; weekly.

Sports Abidjan: B.P. 932, Abidjan; weekly.

NEWS AGENCIES

Agence Ivoirienne de Presse (AIP) (*Ivory Coast News Agency*): 11 ave. Bir-Hakeim, B.P. 4312; f. 1961; Dir. TAO ISSIAKA; publs. *Bulletin Quotidien* (daily), *Ivory Coast* (English fortnightly bulletin).

FOREIGN BUREAUX

Agence France-Presse: 8 rue Paris-Village, B.P. 726, Abidjan; Chief JEAN AGEORGES.

Société d'Information et de Diffusion Abidjanaise: Abidjan; f. 1963; Man. Dir. MAMADOU COULIBALY.

RADIO AND TELEVISION

Radiodiffusion Télévision Ivoirienne: Abidjan, B.P. 2261; government station broadcasting in French and local languages; regional station at Bouaké; Dir. L. DIALLO.

In 1970 there were 75,000 receivers.

Télévision Ivoirienne: Abidjan, B.P. 8883; f. 1963; stations at Abidjan, Bouaké, Man and Koun; Man. G. TANOH.

In 1970 there were 10,550 television receivers.

FINANCE

BANKS

CENTRAL BANK

Banque Centrale des Etats de l'Afrique de l'Ouest: 29 rue du Colisée, Paris; Abidjan: ave. Terrasson de Fougères, B.P. 1769; Manager M. ELIARD.

African Development Bank: B.P. 1387, Abidjan; f. 1964; cap. authorized $U.S. 250m.; Pres. ABDELWAHAB LABIDI.

Banque Nationale pour le Développement Agricole (BNDA): 11 avenue Barthe, B.P. 2508, Abidjan; f. 1968; Dir.-Gen. AUGUSTE DAUBREY.

Banque Internationale pour l'Afrique Occidentale: Paris; f. 1965; Abidjan, B.P. 1274; Dir. ANDRÉ CHARDON.

Banque Internationale pour le Commerce et l'Industrie de la Côte d'Ivoire S.A.: B.P. 1298, 16 ave. Barthe, Abidjan; f. 1962; affiliated to Banque Nationale de Paris, Société Financierè, Barclays Bank International Ltd.; cap. 500m. francs CFA; 3 brs.; Pres. L. KONAN; Man. Dir. EMMANUEL MOUTERDE; Gen. Man. JEAN VITTORI.

Banque Ivoirienne de Développement Industriel: B.P. 4470, Abidjan; f. 1965; cap. 700m. CFA; Gov. M. DIAWARA; Dir.-Gen. ALPHONSE DIBY.

Caisse Autonome d'Amortissement: Immeuble SMGL, avenue Barthe, B.P. 670, Abidjan; Dir. ANDRÉ HOVINE.

Caisse Centrale de Coopération Economique: 13 boulevard Roume, B.P. 1814; Dir. FRANÇOIS TERRACOL.

Caisse Nationale des Marchés de l'Etat (CNME): Abidjan.

Crédit de la Côte d'Ivoire: 22 avenue Barthe, B.P. 1720, Abidjan; f. 1955; development bank; cap. 800m. CFA; dep. 14,663m.; Dir.-Gen. RENÉ AMICHIA.

Fonds National d'Investissement (FNI): Abidjan.

Société Générale de Banques en Côte d'Ivoire: 5 ave. Barthe, B.P. 1355, Abidjan; f. 1962 to take over branches of Société Général; cap. 1,500m. francs CFA; 10 brs., 12 sub-brs.; Man. Dir. P. DUCHEMIN; Man. GÉRARD MADELIN.

Société Ivoirienne de Banque: 34 blvd. de la République, B.P. 1300, Abidjan; f. 1962 to take over branches of Crédit Lyonnais; cap. 625m. francs CFA; 7 brs.; Pres. A. BAROU; Gen. Man. G. BOCHATON.

Société Nationale de Financement (SONAFI): 19 ave. Delafosse, B.P. 1591, Abidjan; f. 1962; cap. 300m. francs CFA; Dir.-Gen. CAMILLE KONAN.

Association Professionelle des Banques et Etablissements Financiers: B.P. 20 900, Abidjan; Pres. JEAN VITTORI.

DEVELOPMENT ORGANIZATIONS

Société pour le Développement et l'Exploitation du Palmier à Huile (SODEPALM): B.P. 2049, Abidjan; f. 1963; national development organization for palm oil; Dir. ANDRÉ FRAISSE.

Société pour le Développement minier de la Côte d'Ivoire (SODEMI): B.P. 2816, Abidjan; f. 1962; national organization for mineral research; Pres. EDOUARD EBAGNITCHIE.

INSURANCE

Abidjan

Assureurs Conseils de Côte d'Ivoire: Faugère and Jutheau et Cie., 2 ave. Lamblin, B.P. 1554.

Comité des Assureurs de la Côte d'Ivoire: B.P. 20.963, Abidjan; Pres. G. LECLERC.

Crédit Foncier de l'Ouest-Africain: ave. Lamblin, B.P. 3.

SACRA (Société Africaine de Courtage et de Représentation d'Assurances): B.P. 20995, Abidjan; p.u. cap. 25m. francs CFA; Dir. GÉRARD GAILLARD.

TRADE AND INDUSTRY

CHAMBERS OF COMMERCE

Chambre de Commerce de la Côte d'Ivoire: Abidjan, B.P. 1399; Pres. F. MASSIEYE; publ. daily and monthly bulletins.

Chambre d'Agriculture de la Côte d'Ivoire: Abidjan, B.P. 1291; Pres. OKA NIANGOIN; Sec.-Gen. DOGOH PIERRE; publ. monthly bulletin.

Chambre d'Industrie de la Côte d'Ivoire: Abidjan, B.P. 1758; Pres. ANDRÉ BLOHORN; publ. monthly bulletin.

PRINCIPAL EMPLOYERS' ASSOCIATIONS

Abidjan

Association Interprofessionelle de la Côte d'Ivoire: B.P. 1340, Abidjan; Pres. A. BLOHORN; Sec.-Gen. P. MEYER.

Syndicat des Commercants Importateurs et Exportateurs de la Côte d'Ivoire (SCIMPEX): Annexe de la Chambre de Commerce, B.P. 20,882; Pres. M. KELLER.

Syndicat des Entrepreneurs et des Industriels de la Côte d'Ivoire: B.P. 464; Pres. PIERRE CHICHET.

Syndicat des Industriels de Côte d'Ivoire: 11 bis avenue Lamblin, B.P. 1340; Pres. ANDRÉ BLOHORN; Sec.-Gen. PH. MEYER; publ. *l'Industriel de la Côte d'Ivoire* (monthly).

Syndicat des Négociants Importateurs et Agents de Marques de Matériel Automobile ou Agricole de la Côte d'Ivoire: B.P. 1399; f. 1953; 18 mems.; Pres. M. BROSSET.

Syndicat des Producteurs Forestiers: B.P. 318, Abidjan; Pres. A. LEGRAS.

Union des Employeurs Agricoles et Forestiers: B.P. 2300, Abidjan; f. 1952; Pres. HUGUES DE QUATREBARBES.

Syndicat pour la Défense des Intérêts Généraux des Planteurs et Cultivateurs de la Côte d'Ivoire: Treichville, B.P. 6085; Pres. ALEXANDER DJABIA.

Syndicat Agricole Africain: B.P. 24, Treichville; Pres. JOSEPH ANOMA.

CO-OPERATIVE

Coopérative Agricole de Production Bananière et Fruitière de Côte d'Ivoire (COFRUCI): B.P. 1550, Abidjan; f. 1968; Pres. EDOUARD EBAGNITCHIE.

TRADE UNION

Union Générale des Travailleurs de Côte d'Ivoire: B.P. 1749; Abidjan; f. 1962; 200,000 mems.; Sec.-Gen. JOSEPH COFFIE.

MAJOR INDUSTRIAL COMPANIES

The following are some of the largest companies in terms either of capital investment or employment.

BATA S.A. Ivoirienne: B.P. 1762, Abidjan; f. 1963; cap. 317m. francs CFA.
Manufacture and sale of footwear and plastic products. Dirs. MM. KANKA and RIGAL; 649 employees.

Blohorn S.A.: Vridi industrial zone, Abidjan; f. 1971; cap. 361m. francs CFA.
Production of palm oil including cooking oil, soap, margarine.

BP Centre Ouest Afrique S.A.: B.P. 555, Résidence Franchet d'Espérey, Abidjan; f. 1966; cap. 455m. francs CFA.
Import and distribution of petroleum products.
Dir.-Gen. B. T. BOUGERET; Commercial Dir. P. DUPONT; 211 employees.

Compagnie Africaine de Produits Alimentaires (CAPRAL): Abidjan; f. 1962; cap. 350m. francs CFA.
Production of soluble coffee in association with Nestlé.

Entreprise Forestière des Bois Africains S.A.: B.P. 958, Abidjan; f. 1956; cap. 344,280,000 francs CFA.
Lumber industry and sawmills.
Administrator VICTOR BALET; Dir. M. KUNG; 900 employees.

Esso Standard Afrique S.A.: B.P. 1598, Immeuble Nour al Hayat, Abidjan; f. 1965; cap. 300m. francs CFA.
Distribution of petroleum products.
Pres. Dir.-Gen. A. C. PORTOLANO; Vice-Pres. R. F. LACOURT; 30 employees.

Ets. R. Gonfreville: B.P. 584, Bouaké; f. 1922; cap. 990m. francs CFA.
Spinning, weaving, dyeing and printing of textiles and cotton, manufacture of clothing.
Pres. LUC DURAND-REVILLE; Asst. Dirs.-Gen. JEAN DELACOUR, NICOLAS STAUFFER; 2,800 employees.

Grands Moulins d'Abidjan (GMA): Abidjan; f. 1963; cap. 2,000m. francs CFA.
Flour milling and production of animal feed.

Peyrissac-Côte d'Ivoire: B.P. 1272, 23 ave. du Général-de-Gaulle, Abidjan; f. 1963; cap. 400m. francs CFA.
Sale of hardware, industrial materials, vehicles and telephonic equipment.
Dir. JACQUES ROSSIGNOL; 360 employees.

Société Africaine de Cacao: B.P. 1045, Abidjan; f. 1964; cap. 1,155m. francs CFA of which 35 per cent state owned.
Manufacture of cocoa butter and oil-cake.
Dirs. MM. LACARRE and SCHMUCK; 260 employees.

Société Africaine de Plantations d'Hévéas: B.P. 1322, 13 blvd. Roume, Abidjan; f. 1956; cap. 3,000m. francs CFA.
Production of para-rubber.
Chair. GUEDE LOROUGNON; Man. Dir. R. DE PONTON D'AMECOURT; 3,000 employees.

Société des Ananas de Côte d'Ivoire: Abidjan; f. 1951; cap. 471m. francs CFA of which 24 per cent state owned.
Pineapple canning.

Société d'Etude et de Développement de la Culture Bananière: B.P. 1260, Abidjan; f. 1959; cap. 239m. francs CFA.
Cultivation of bananas.
Pres. Comte DE BEAUMONT; 1,416 employees.

Société Industrielle Textile de Côte d'Ivoire (SOTEXI): B.P. 20981, Abidjan; f. 1967; cap. 350m. francs CFA.
Textile bleaching, dyeing and printing.
Dirs. MM. MATSUKAKA and LAGARDE; 600 employees.

Société Ivoirienne de Raffinage (S.I.R.): B.P. 1269, Abidjan; f. 1962; cap. 1,000m. francs CFA.
Oil refinery.
Dir. JEAN-CLAUDE LARTIGAU.

Société Ivoirienne de Textiles (IVOTEX): B.P. 34, Abidjan; in process of incorporation; cap. 2,700m. francs CFA; textile complex.

Société Ivoirienne d'Engrais: B.P. 7061, Abidjan; f. 1965; cap. 550m. francs CFA.
Fertilizer factory.
Dirs. ROLAND BELE and HERMANN MUHLFELD; 150 employees.

Société Ivoirienne des Tabacs (SITAB): Abidjan; cap. 760m. francs CFA of which 40 per cent Ivorian owned.
Production of cigarettes.

Société Ivoirienne d'Oxygène et d'Acétylène: B.P. 1753, blvd. de Marseille, Abidjan; f. 1962; cap. 423m. francs CFA.
Manufacture and sale of industrial and medical gases and soldering equipment.
Pres. Dir.-Gen. P. BRUNEL; Dir.-Gen. J. QUARTERO; 100 employees.

Société Shell de l'Afrique Occidentale: B.P. 1248, 46 ave. Lamblin, Abidjan; f. 1928; cap. 605m. francs CFA.
Distribution of petroleum and chemical products.
Dirs. J. ORSATELLI and I. BAHBOUT; 530 employees.

Sodepalm-Palmivoire-Palmindustrie: Abidjan; consists of: state-owned Sodepalm (f. 1963, cap. 400m. francs CFA), Palmivoire (f. 1969, part state owned, cap. 50m. francs CFA) and Palmindustrie (f. 1969, part state owned, cap. 2,500m. francs CFA).
Production of palm oil and palmettos by Sodepalm and Palmivoire in five factories owned by Palmindustrie.

TRANSPORT AND TOURISM

TRANSPORT

RAILWAYS

Régie du Chemin de Fer Abidjan-Niger: Abidjan, B.P. 1394; f. 1904; 1,196 km. of track open of which the main line is 1,145 km. of track linking Abidjan with Ouagadougou, the capital of Upper Volta; 625 km. are in the Ivory Coast; Dir. LANCINA KONATE.

ROADS

There are 6,850 km. of bitumen-surfaced roads; 18,000 km. of all weather earth roads and 14,000 km. of tracks.

Société Ivoirienne de Transports Publics: B.P. 1822, Abidjan; f. 1964; cap. 17,500m. francs CFA; road transport.

SHIPPING

Abidjan

Compagnie Maritime de l'Afrique Noire (COMARAN): B.P. 640, Abidjan.

Cie. Maritime des Chargeurs Réunis: 25 avenue Général de Gaulle, B.P. 1285.

Delta Line: B.P. 894.

Gold Star Line: c/o SAMOA, B.P. 1611.

Holland-West Afrika Lijn NV: c/o Union Maritime et Commerciale, B.P. 1559.

Italian West Africa Line: c/o SOCOPAO, B.P. 1297.

Jugolinija: Cie. Foncière et Commerciale de Distribution, km. 1, rue du Port Bouet, B.P. 4308.

K Line: c/o SOCOPAO, B.P. 1297.

Lloyd Triestino: c/o SAMOA, rond-point du Nouveau Port, B.P. 1611.

Mitsui OSK Lines Ltd.: Transcap-Shipping, B.P. 358.

Palm Line: c/o SOCOPAO, B.P. 1297.

Royal Interocean Lines: c/o Union Maritime et Commerciale, B.P. 1559.

Scandinavian West Africa Line: c/o SOAEM, B.P. 1727.

Seven Star Line: c/o SAMOA, B.P. 1611.

Société Ivoirienne de Transport Maritime (SITRAM): 4 ave. Général de Gaulle, B.P. 1546; f. 1967; 5 ships.

Société Navale de l'Ouest: c/o SOAEM, rond-point du Nouveau Port, B.P. 1727.

Société Navale Chargeurs Delmas et Vieljeux: 17 ave. Lousi-Barthe, B.P. 1281; Dir. J.-M. BOILEDIEU.

Splošna Plovba: c/o SOCOPAO, Km. 1, blvd. de Marseille, P.O.B. 1297, Abidjan.

Transcap-Shipping: B.P. 358; Agents for Elder Dempster Lines, Barber Line, Guinea Gulf Line, Marine Chartering Co., Svea Line, Mitsui-OSK Line, Palm Line, Nordana Line, Nautilus Line (Keller), Hoegh Line; Dir. P. GODOC.

Union West Africa Line: c/o SOAEM, B.P. 1727.

United West Africa Service: c/o SOMICOA, B.P. 640.

CIVIL AVIATION
Abidjan

Air Afrique (Société Aérienne Africaine Multinationale): ave. L. Barthe, B.P. 21017, Abidjan; f. 1961; fleet of five DC-8, two Caravelles, two YS-11A, three DC-4, one DC-3 (three DC-10 on order); Pres. CHEIKH FAL; Dir.-Gen. J. CADEAC D'ARBAUD; Sec.-Gen. GUIBRIL N'DIAYE; Gen. Rep. for Europe JEAN-CLAUDE DELAFOSSE, 53 rue Ampère, Paris 17e.

Air Afrique was established by an agreement between Sodetraf (Société pour le Développement du Transport Aérien en Afrique) and 11 states, formerly French colonies, who each had a 6 per cent share; Cameroon withdrew in 1971, Chad in 1972; Sodetraf now has a 30 per cent share and the following have 7 per cent: Central African Republic, Congo, Dahomey, Gabon, Ivory Coast, Mauritania, Niger, Senegal, Togo, Upper Volta.

Ivoire: B.P. 1027; f. 1963; owned by Government (60 per cent), Sodetraf (20 per cent) and Air Afrique (20 per cent); internal services; fleet of two DC-3, one Aztec, one Baron; Chair. V. NIACIDIE; Man. L. GIROUX.

The following air lines also serve the Ivory Coast: Air Zaire, Air Mali, Alitalia, Ghana Airways, KLM, MEA, Nigeria Airways, PAA, Sabena, Swissair and UTA.

TOURISM

ICTA (Ivory Coast Travel Agency): P.O.B. 2636, Abidjan.

POWER

Energie Electrique de la Côte d'Ivoire: B.P. 1345, Abidjan; f. 1952; cap. 1,400m. francs CFA.
Distribution of electricity and water.
Dir.-Gen. LAMBERT KONAN.

EDUCATION

The Government provides education at nominal rates and attendance at primary school is compulsory, although the attendance rate is only 50 per cent. For the year 1971–72 there were 515,000 pupils in state primary schools, 100,000 in private primary schools, and 75,000 in secondary schools. An extension of television education programmes is underway, in order to reach all primary schools by 1980,

when it is envisaged that there will be 720,000 pupils. The Government's education policy aims to accelerate the evolution of society, to assure that each individual is equipped to participate in this evolution, and to develop technical instruction. Two new technical *lycées* are under construction. The University has 3,092 students, of whom 2,055 are Ivorians, and in addition a number of students study abroad especially at French universities.

RESEARCH INSTITUTES

(*see* also under University)

Centre des Sciences de la Nature: B.P. 398, Abidjan; research in earth and natural sciences; f. 1944 as part of the former centre of the Institut Français d'Afrique Noire in the Ivory Coast; Dir. J. L. TOURNIER.

Centre des Sciences Humaines: B.P. 1600, Abidjan; f. 1960; ethnological and sociological research, especially in the cultural and religious field; museology, conservation, exhibitions; Dir. Dr. B. HOLAS; *see also* Musée de la Côte d'Ivoire.

Centre de Recherches Zootechniques: B.P. 449, Bouaké; Dir. M. BOUVIER.

Centre Technique Forestier Tropical: B.P. 8033, Abidjan; f. 1962; research in silviculture and pisciculture; library of 1,800 vols.; Dir. GUY DE LA MENSBRUGE.

Direction de la Géologie et de la Prospection Minière: B.P. 1368, Abidjan; Dir. M. BARDET.

Direction de la Recherche Scientifique: Abidjan; controls Centre des Sciences de la Nature, Musée Ethnographique, Laboratoire d'Hydrobiologie, Laboratoire d'Ecologie Tropicale and the Station Géophysique de Lamto; conducts research in Human and Natural Sciences; Dir. J. L. TOURNIER.

Institut d'Elevage et de Médecine Vétérinaire des Pays Tropicaux: B.P. 449, Bouaké; Dir. M. COULOMB.

Institut d'Hygiene: Abidjan.

Institut de Recherches Agronomiques Tropicales et des Cultures Vivrières (IRAT): B.P. 635, Bouaké; stations at Bouaké, Ferkessedougou, Gagnoa, Man and Tombokro; Dir. M. DUMONT.

Institut de Recherches du Coton et des Textiles Exotiques (IRCT) (*Research Institute on Cotton and Tropical Textiles*): B.P. 604, Bouaké; f. 1946; 12 mems.; Dir. A. ANGELINI; publ. *Bulletin* (3 times a year).

Institut de Recherches pour les Huiles et Oléagineux (IRHO) (*Research Institute for Oils and Oily Substances*): La Mé, B.P. 13, Bingerville; f. 1923; oil palm research (Breeding, Agronomy, Pathology).

Institut de Recherches sur le Caoutchouc (IRCA) (*Institute of Rubber Research*): B.P. 1536, Abidjan; f. 1956; library of 800 vols.; Dir. P. COMPAGNON; publ. *Revue Générale du Caoutchouc.*

Institut des Fruits et Agrumes Coloniaux (FAC) (*Institute of Tropical and Citrus Fruits*): B.P. 606, Abidjan.

Institut Français de Recherches Fruitières Outre-Mer (IFAC): B.P. 1470, Abidjan; brs. at Azaguié and Anguededou.

Institut Français du Café et du Cacao (IFCC) (*Cocoa and Coffee Research Station*): B.P. 1827, Abidjan; f. 1958; Dir. M. BELIN.
Station Centrale: Divo.
Bureaux et Laboratoires: Bingerville.
Station Régionale: Abengourou.
Station Régionale: Guiglo.
Centres d'essais multilocaux: San Pedro, Tomboko, Zagne, Tiassale.

Office de la Recherche Scientifique et Technique Outre-Mer (ORSTOM):

Centre d'Adiopodoumé: B.P. 20, Abidjan; f. 1946; geology, pedology, hydrology, botany and vegetal biology, biology and amelioration of plants, soil, biology, applied zoology, agronomy, phytopathology, geology; laboratory for utilization of radio isotopes; experimental biological station; library; Dir. J. P. TONNIER.

Centre de Recherches Océanographiques d'Abidjan: B.P. V 18, Abidjan; physical, chemical and biographical oceanography; library; Dir. F. POINSARD; publs. *Scientific Documents* (quarterly).

Centre de Petit Bassam: B.P. 4293, Abidjan; psychosociology, economics, demography, geography, sociology; Dir. J. P. TROUCHAUD.

Société pour le Développement Minier de la Côte d'Ivoire—SODEMI: B.P. 2816, Abidjan; f. 1962; carries out a programme of geological exploration and mineral prospecting; library of 2,100 vols., 100 current periodicals; Dir.-Gen. G. BERTHOUMIEUX; publs. *Rapport annuel*, and *c.* 250 geological or prospecting reports.

Station Géophysique de Lamto: B.P. 398, Abidjan; seismological and climatological studies; Dir. J. L. TOURNIER.

LIBRARIES

Bibliothèque Centrale de la Côte d'Ivoire: Abidjan-Treichville, B.P. 6243; f. 1963; a service of the Ministry of National Education; public lecture service; library; 14,000 volumes; founded with the help of UNESCO; Librarian P. ZELLI ANY-GRAH.

Bibliothèque de l'Université d'Abidjan: B.P. 8859, Abidjan; f. 1963; 30,000 vols. and 980 periodicals; Librarian Mme M. DOSDAT.

Bibliothèque du Centre Cultural Américain: B.P. 1866; Abidjan.

Bibliothèque du Centre Culturel Français: ave. Nogues, Abidjan; 1,000 vols.

Bibliothèque du Service d'Information: B.P. 1879, Abidjan.

Bibliothèque Municipale: Platena, Abidjan; 50,000 vols.

Bibliothèque Nationale: B.P. 20915, Abidjan; scientific library of 6,000 vols. and 700 current periodicals; part of the former centre of the Institut Français d'Afrique Noire in the Ivory Coast; Dir. Mme LIGUER-LAUBHOUET KETTY-LINA; publ. *La Bibliographie de la Côte d'Ivoire* (annual).

MUSEUMS

Musée de la Côte d'Ivoire: B.P. 1600, Abidjan; exhibits of ethnographical, sociological, artistic and scientific nature; attached to the Centre des Sciences Humaines; Dir. Dr. B. HOLAS.

UNIVERSITY

UNIVERSITÉ D'ABIDJAN
B.P. 1880, ABIDJAN

Telephone: 492-95, 492-99.

Founded as the Centre d'Enseignement Supérieur d'Abidjan 1958; University 1964.

Language of instruction: French.

Rector: Prof. J. GARAGNON.
General Secretary: Mlle SANGARET.

Librarian: Mme M. DOSDAT.

Number of teachers: 189.
Number of students: 3,092.

Publications: *Annales de l'Université d'Abidjan, Bulletin des Instituts de Recherche de l'Université d'Abidjan.*

DEANS:

School of Law: J. GARAGNON.
School of Letters: Mme C. VALETTE.
School of Medicine: Dr. P. PENE.
Faculty of Sciences: J. BAUDET.

ATTACHED RESEARCH INSTITUTES:

Centre Universitaire de Recherche et de Développement: groups the following:

Ethnosociology Institute: Dir. C. PAIRAULT.
Tropical Geography Institute: Dir. F. DOUMENGE.
Tropical Ecology Institute: Dir. J. SOULIE.
Applied Linguistics Institute: Dir. G. CANU.
African History and Archaeology Institute: Dr. A. BONY.

UNIVERSITY TECHNOLOGICAL INSTITUTES:

Institute of Commerce: Dir. Mme VEAUX.
Institute of Applied Psychology: Dir. Mlle SARROLA.
Institute of Medical Laboratory Techniques: Dir. M. DOUCET.

COLLEGES

Ecole de Statistique d'Abidjan: B.P. 8003, Abidjan, Cocody; f. 1961; 115 students; library of 820 books; Dir. FRANÇOIS YATTIEN-AMIGUET.

Ecole Nationale d'Administration: B.P. 2551, Abidjan; f. 1960; 157 students; library of 3,760 vols.; Dir. MICHEL BERNARD.

Ecole Nationale des Postes et Télécommunications: Abidjan.

Ecole Nationale Supérieure Agronomique: B.P. 8035, Abidjan.

Ecole Nationale Supérieure des Travaux Publics: B.P. 2279, Abidjan; f. 1962; comprises l'Ecole d'Ingénieurs and l'Ecole de Techniciens; library of 3,000 vols.; 67 teachers, 115 students; Dir. J. MOUY.

SELECT BIBLIOGRAPHY

(For works on the former A.O.F. states generally *see* Dahomey Select Bibliography, p. 297.)

AMIN, SAMIR. *Le développement du capitalisme en Côte d'Ivoire.* Paris, 1966.

AVENARD, J.-M. *Le milieu naturel de la Côte d'Ivoire.* Bondy, France, ORSTOM, 1972.

DIAWARA, MOHAMED TIEKOURA. "The Ivory Coast—Birth of a Modern State. *Progress*, pp. 66–70, 1967.

DUMONT, RENÉ. *Afrique Noire: développement agricole: reconversion de l'économie agricole: Guinée, Côte d'Ivoire, Mali.* Paris, Presses universitaires de France, 1962.

FOSTER, P., and ZOLBERG, A. R. (Eds.). *Ghana and the Ivory Coast. Perspectives and Modernization.* University of Chicago Press, 1972.

HARRISON CHURCH, R. J. *West Africa* (6th edn., ch. 22). London, Longmans, 1968.

ROUGERIE, G. *La Côte d'Ivoire.* Paris, Presses universitaires de France, 1964.

SY, M. S. *Recherches sur l'exercise du pouvoir politique en Afrique noire (Côte d'Ivoire, Guinée, Mali).* Paris, 1965.

WILDE, JOHN DE, et al. *Agricultural Development in Tropical Africa.* Johns Hopkins Press, 1967.

ZOLBERG, ARISTIDE R. *One-Party Government in the Ivory Coast.* Princeton, Princeton University Press, 1964, 2nd edn. 1969.

Kenya

PHYSICAL AND SOCIAL GEOGRAPHY*

W. T. W. Morgan

The present boundaries of the Republic of Kenya have their origin in the spread of British influence from the coast, centred on Zanzibar and Mombasa, which resulted in the establishment of the East Africa Protectorate in 1895. Boundary adjustments, however, resulted in a westward shift of the country, with the inclusion of the former Eastern Province of Uganda, bordering Lake Victoria, in 1902 and of northern Turkana in 1926, and with the transfer of Jubaland in the east to Italian Somalia in 1924. Boundaries with Ethiopia and the Sudan (the 'Ilemi Triangle') have only recently been regularized. Kenya was proclaimed a Crown Colony in 1920 and independent in 1963, when the rights of the Sultan of Zanzibar to a strip of coastal land were also ceded. A Republic was proclaimed in 1964.

The total area of Kenya is 224,961 sq. miles or 219,788 sq. miles excluding inland waters (mostly Lake Rudolf and part of Lake Victoria). It is bisected by the equator and extends from approximately 4°N. to 4°S. and 34°E. to 41°E. It is three hours ahead of Greenwich time.

PHYSICAL FEATURES

The physical basis of the country is of extensive erosional plains, cut across ancient crystalline rocks of Precambrian age. These are very gently warped—giving an imperceptible rise from sea-level towards the highlands of the interior which have their base at about 5,000 ft.

The height of the Kenya Highlands has been greatly augmented by outpourings of Tertiary lavas, giving plateaux at 8–10,000 ft. and with isolated extinct volcanoes yet higher: Mt. Kenya (17,058 ft.) and Mt. Elgon (14,178 ft.). The Great Rift Valley bisects the country from north to south and is at its most spectacular in the highlands, where it is some 40 miles across and bounded by escarpments 2–3,000 ft. high. The trough is dotted with lakes and volcanoes which are inactive but generally associated with steam vents and hot springs. Westward the plains incline beneath the waters of Lake Victoria, and eastwards they have been down-warped beneath a sediment-filled basin, which is attracting exploration for oil.

CLIMATE

Although Kenya is on the equator, its range of altitude results in temperate conditions in the highlands above 5,000 ft., with temperatures which become limiting to cultivation at about 9,000 ft., while Mt. Kenya supports small glaciers. Average temperatures may be roughly calculated by taking a sea-level mean

of 80°F. and deducting 3°F. for each thousand feet of altitude. For most of the country, however, rainfall is more critical than temperature. In the west of the country, near Lake Victoria and in the highlands west of the Rift Valley, rainfall is generally adequate for cultivation and falls in one long rainy season. East of the Rift Valley there are two distinct seasons: the long rains (March–May) and the short rains (September–October). Rainfall is greatest at the coast and in the highlands, but the extensive plains below 4,000 ft. are arid or semi-arid. In the highlands rain is greatest on the easterly or southerly aspects.

NATURAL RESOURCES

Only 15 per cent of the area of Kenya can be expected to receive a reliable rainfall adequate for cultivation (30 in. in four years out of five). These high rainfall areas by the Lake, in the highlands and at the coast, tend to be intensively cultivated on a small-scale subsistence basis with varying amounts of cash cropping. Subsistence crops are in great variety but most important and widespread are maize, sorghum, cassava and bananas. The principal cash crops, which provide the majority of exports, are coffee (*arabica*), tea, pyrethrum and sisal. The first three are particularly suited to the highlands and their introduction was associated with the large-scale farming on the alienated lands of the former "White Highlands". The herds of cattle, goats, sheep and camels of the dry plains are as yet of little commercial value and support a low density of largely subsistence pastoralists.

Forests are largely restricted to the rainy upper levels of the highlands, where the limited output possible from the natural forests led to the introduction of plantations of conifers and of wattle.

Fisheries are of local importance around Lake Victoria and are of great potential at Lake Rudolf. Sea fishing includes large game species (marlin, swordfish, etc.) attractive to tourists.

The very important and rapidly expanding tourist industry benefits from the presence of sandy beaches behind coral reefs and without sharks, the wild game which still roams over the semi-arid plains and the pleasant climate and attractive scenery of the highlands.

POPULATION AND CULTURE

The final results of the 1969 census give a total population of 10,942,705. The density of nearly 50 per sq. mile is near the average for Africa, but, since the nation is so dependent upon the land and only a small proportion of it is cultivable, very high densities

* See map on p. 896.

431

(reaching to over a thousand per square mile) have resulted in the favoured areas. Approximately 75 per cent of the population is contained on only 10 per cent of the area. With such pressure on cultivable land the high rate of population increase (4.0 per cent p.a.) is causing concern. By rough regional groupings, 8.5 million people may be said to live in the south-west corner of the country (Lake, 3.5 million; Eastern Highlands, 3.5 million; Central and Western Highlands, 1.5 million) with another million concentrated along the coast. Less than ten per cent of the population live in cities or towns with a population exceeding 2,000, and most of these are in Nairobi (478,000) and Mombasa (246,000).

Kenya has been a meeting place of major population movements in the past and on a linguistic and cultural basis the people have been divided into Bantu, Nilotic, Nilo-Hamitic (Paranilotic) and Cushitic groups. Persian and Arab influence at the coast is seen in the Islamic culture and the Swahili language, which has become a lingua franca, although English is widely used. Land holding and social habits and attitudes are largely conditioned by tribal traditions, which are, however, at their weakest in the areas of the former "White Highlands" and in the growing towns. The towns also contain the majority of the non-African minorities of some 139,000 Asians, 40,000 Europeans and 28,000 Arabs.

RECENT HISTORY
John Lonsdale

Kenya's modern history has hinged upon the south-western quadrant of the country. This area, which is high, much of it above the 4,000 ft. level and with a relatively reliable rainfall, supports now, as it probably did in 1900, three-quarters of the population. In 1969 Kenya's peoples numbered just under 11 million, in 1900 perhaps two million. Its twentieth century history has been conditioned by white settlement; its previous history was one of African colonization. As frontier societies, the African communities were small in scale and lightly governed. Trade was local; it consisted, in the main, of exchanges between the cattle-herder and the cultivator. But there was change afoot as the nineteenth century progressed. From mid-century, coastal caravans took over routes pioneered by the Kamba people. As traffic increased, so political authorities among the Luo and Luyia peoples of the Lake Victoria basin were consolidated, and among the Kikuyu to the east. On the central highlands the pastoral Masai, never as strong as their reputation, suffered the disasters of civil war, smallpox and rinderpest and pleuro-pneumonia among their cattle. To the north, outside this highland zone, lay barely peopled deserts penetrated at times by Ethiopian traders and increasingly by Somali nomads; at the coast the Arab communities declined as economic activity shifted perceptibly to Zanzibar.

THE COLONIAL PERIOD, 1895–1963

A British protectorate was declared in 1895, primarily to secure the route to Uganda. The low priority of the East Africa Protectorate itself—it was not annexed as a Colony, under its present name, until 1920—meant that the area was administered by the British Consul-General in Zanzibar until 1902. Meanwhile, over a period of six years from 1895 and at a cost to the British taxpayer of over £5 million, a railway had been built from Mombasa to the Lake by imported Indian labour. It had to be made to pay. By 1902 the government accepted white settlement in the cool highlands as the obvious answer. But by 1914 there were barely one thousand European landholders. Few of them were as yet making any money, and African peasant production was greater in volume and value. The idea of creating a "white man's country" appeared to be fantasy. Few government officials shared this dream; they hoped that European and African could coexist. But the seeds of future conflict had already been sown. The extension of administration barely preceded that of settlement; it had occasioned a myriad of armed African resistances. Much of Masailand and smaller but more contentious areas of Kikuyuland were alienated to Europeans. Taxation and pressure on officially appointed chiefs forced out African labourers whose material wants were few and leisure preference high. Tenuous control from London and settler demands led by Lord Delamere resulted in the creation of a Legislative Council in 1907. On this the much larger Indian community, whose trading skills were essential to opening up the country, was barely represented and the Africans not at all.

Settler Interests

The First World War gave opportunity for the settlers to consolidate their unofficial hold on government. They secured elective representation on the War Council which co-ordinated civil support for the campaign in German East Africa. Elections to the Legislative Council followed in 1919, with settlers also on the Governor's Executive Council. Four years of political crisis ensued, on the issue of Indian representation. It was resolved in 1923 with the British declaration that "the interests of the African natives must be paramount"; the settler goal of responsible government was also out of the question for the time being. The Southern Rhodesians had achieved just this status in the same year—but they had had no Indian opposition. Meanwhile African political organization was stirring, especially among the Kikuyu in Nairobi but also among the Luo. It had been galvanized by the harsh experience of war, by the influenza epidemic thereafter, fresh land alienations, intensified tax and labour demands and by the spread of missionary education. Missionary statesmen in London had put forward the "native paramountcy" formulation; but in Nairobi over twenty Africans had been killed while protesting against the arrest of Harry Thuku, the Kikuyu leader. The chiefs and mission teachers who then led African opinion were mollified somewhat by the introduction of Local Native Councils in 1925. For twenty years thereafter African organizations concentrated largely on attempts to entrench these local governments in defence against the settlers at the centre. These latter, meanwhile, worked successfully to bend the infrastructure of communications and government services to support their economic sector against the African and, fruitlessly, to create a closer union of British territories in eastern Africa in which they would predominate. A succession of commissions from Britain examined this proposal and the clash of two principles which made Kenya the pivot of Empire—native trusteeship and settler responsibility. By the time the world depression descended it was clear that the settlers would never get their way. But the future was just as uncertain for the Africans and Indians.

In the Second World War Kenya was again in the front line, this time against the Italians in Ethiopia and Somalia. Settler farmers at last attained prosperity; their leaders managed the official production boards. White confidence revived in keeping with the grandiose schemes for the colonies' role in the post-war reconstruction of Britain. One of their number achieved quasi-ministerial responsibility as the Member for Agriculture. Meanwhile the government was aghast at the ecological ruin which was impending in the tribal reserves; an unreformed African agriculture could barely sustain the growing population. As white farmers prospered, black peasants were subjected to increasing government controls. Soaring price inflation hit those who flocked to the towns in an often vain search for work. An explosion could not be long delayed.

The Struggle for Independence—"Mau Mau"

It came in 1952. The state of emergency declared then was not completely lifted until early 1960. The first real African nationalist organization, the Kenya African Union, had been formed in 1944 in support of the first African nominated to the Legislative Council, Eliud Mathu. KAU's programme was politically moderate but economically revolutionary in demanding African access to the "White Highlands". For a government preoccupied with economic development and reliant upon settler initiative this was out of the question. Denied any real victories, KAU's pan-tribal coalition among the educated élite never mustered much popular support, save among the Kikuyu. This exception was not surprising. The Kikuyu now had the best access to education; they predominated among the urban labourers and had tasted strike action. One-quarter of them lived as tenant "squatters" on European farms; as the landowners adopted more capital-intensive methods so they restricted these squatters' rights and numbers. Above all the Kikuyu had a long tradition of political militancy, brooding upon their lost lands; and in a strong cultural nationalism originating in the 1920s they had been the

first among the Africans to think of themselves as one people. But they had also been the first to lift African politics from its local mould and, in 1929, to send a representative to England. Jomo Kenyatta was to remain there, on and off, until 1946. As, therefore, the more impatient leaders of KAU began to organize for mass civil disobedience in the late 1940s it was natural that they should both seek and find their support among the Kikuyu. But if "Mau Mau's" violence against Europeans is totally explicable, this was insignificant compared with that wreaked upon fellow Kikuyu. For by 1950 Kikuyu rules of land tenure, overwhelmed by population explosion, were in total disarray; what could not be secured in the courts might be won with the gun. While government reacted against a militant form of African nationalism, the Kikuyu themselves were sucked into an internal civil war. At both these levels "Mau Mau" has left an enduring mark on Kenya's subsequent history.

In 1953 Kenyatta, president of KAU since 1947, was found guilty of managing "Mau Mau", a verdict surprising in that his moderation had earned him assassination threats from the militants. British troops assisted the local forces in containing the rebellion, an object largely achieved by 1955. At a time when race relations were embittered by the twin barbarities of revolt and repression some Europeans, led by Michael Blundell, saw that their future survival depended on acceding to some measure of the multi-racial partnership in government which now represented British policy throughout east and central Africa. London seized this opportunity to force reform. By 1955 there was an African minister; in 1957 direct African elections to the Legislative Council on a restricted franchise. Meanwhile, 13,000 Africans, almost all of them Kikuyu, and 32 European civilians had been killed; nearly 80,000 Kikuyu were in detention camps. As part of the counter-revolution, the government pressed a vigorous programme of land reform, first in Kikuyuland, then in the African agricultural areas elsewhere; African farm incomes doubled between 1955 and 1962 in a period of falling prices. But Kikuyuland lay under siege, and other peoples, the Luo especially, filled the political and economic vacuum.

KANU and KADU

With African political organizations at the national level banned until 1960 the mantle of urban leadership fell upon the young Luo trade unionist, Tom Mboya, whose chief rival was a fellow Luo, Oginga Odinga. Like all other politicians Odinga was obliged, both by social custom and government regulation, to build a rural and so tribal base. The Africans' only unity lay in their legislative councillors' demand for majority rule, and this façade cracked in 1960 when a transitional constitution foreshadowed this goal, but raised the further issue of the distribution of power. The major economic prize was the Highlands, to which African access had been accepted in principle in 1959. The small pastoral peoples in the area, anxious to defend their historical claims, made common cause with the coastal peoples, who resented the Kikuyu and Luo penetration of Mombasa. Together they formed the Kenya African Democratic Union under Ronald Ngala.

The Kikuyu and Luo led most of the agriculturalists—and their urban brethren—into the Kenya African National Union.

Independence was delayed for a further three years. KANU, the majority party in two elections, was rent by faction, and it also owed allegiance to the absent Kenyatta, whom most whites regarded as a leader "to darkness and death". The government thus worked for a time with KADU, while safeguards were sought for the immigrant minorities. Kenyatta was at last released in August 1961, and his KANU entered a coalition government with KADU. Kenyatta's moderation and KANU's electoral strength together persuaded the British to concede independence in December 1963, by which time many white settlers had been bought out and landless Africans were being installed in their place.

INDEPENDENCE

The fragility of the new state was soon exposed. In January 1964 elements of Kenya's army mutinied, in common with those of its neighbours. The mutiny was quickly suppressed with British aid, and thereafter the army was fully employed in combating Somali irregulars within the north-eastern frontier, until in late 1967 a Somali-Kenyan agreement deprived the *shifta* of external support. Meanwhile, at the declaration of a republic on the first anniversary of independence the KANU government dismantled the KADU-inspired regional constitution and strong central powers, never greatly weakened, were restored. Kenya also became a *de facto* one-party state, as KADU merged itself with the ruling party. The process of consolidation continued as President Kenyatta raised the now Africanized provincial administrative service to the same high prestige it had enjoyed in colonial days. In 1965 legislation was introduced to secure greater government control over trade union affairs.

This last move reflected growing factionalism in party and government, the dominant grouping fearing that the unions might provide an organized popular base for opposition. KANU itself had lost almost all semblance of organization. Not only, as in other African states, had much of the available talent been absorbed by government, but no one faction could afford to risk a strong party organization falling into the hands of another. In 1964 internal dissension reflected district or tribal competition for development funds; the Kikuyu in particular were felt to be unduly favoured. By 1965 the debate was increasingly ideological in tone, with the old rivals Odinga and Mboya leading the radical and conservative groupings. The radicals attacked class differentiation among Africans and called for more nationalizations; the conservatives believed Kenya's highly developed export sector to be too fragile to survive such treatment, a caution stigmatized by their critics as deference to neo-colonialism. Odinga received much support from the poorer Kikuyu, some of them ex-"Mau Mau" guerrillas, who were championed by Bildad Kaggia;

Mboya won the tacit support of Kenyatta and other Kikuyu leaders. An open breach occurred early in 1966. Odinga, under suspicion of receiving cash and arms from communist sources, lost his deputy leadership of KANU. He resigned the vice-presidency of the country and joined a new opposition, the Kenya People's Union, with Kaggia as his deputy. His thirty parliamentary supporters were deprived of their seats by a constitutional amendment, and in the subsequent "little general election" the KPU won overwhelming support in Odinga's Luo homeland, but little elsewhere.

Nevertheless pressures increased upon government, caused mainly by the disparity between a 3.3 per cent annual population growth and the slow expansion of opportunity. KPU activity was restricted and some of its leaders detained. The latent problem of the 180,000 Asians was then faced with the passing in mid-1967 of the Trade Licensing Act, which reserved some areas and commodities exclusively to citizens. Only about 40 per cent of the Asians had either qualified automatically for local citizenship or taken it out in the two-year grace period after independence. There was a flood of non-citizens to Britain which was only stemmed by the 1968 Commonwealth Immigration Act. Then, against a background of rumoured Kikuyu manoeuvre against him, Tom Mboya was assassinated in July 1969. Kenya had lost her most able minister and one of her few non-tribal men, a tragedy underlined by the spate of Kikuyu oathing which followed. After Luo deaths during a Presidential visit to Luoland the KPU was banned; its leader, Odinga, was held in detention for fifteen months. Nevertheless, in the all-KANU general election of late 1969, two-thirds of the former M.P.s lost their seats to younger and better-educated men. This mobility among the political élite, which is much assisted by the continuing Africanization of the agricultural and business sectors, has for the time being secured a political stability which was left unshaken by the disclosure early in 1971 of a plot to overthrow the government. The dozen convicted conspirators, all of them Luo or Kamba, had apparently made little or no impression upon the army, despite the subsequent resignation of the Kamba chief of staff. Tensions remain below the surface. They are fuelled by the high rate of unemployment and are focussed both upon the degree of advantage secured by the Kikuyu in most spheres of life and, more generally, on the occasionally publicised corruption of men in public office. These tensions have not been made any the easier to resolve by the growing foreign exchange shortage in Kenya, as earlier experienced by her partners in the East African community; and any recession in Uganda's commercial sector, consequent upon the expulsion of much of her Asian community, will have an adverse effect on Kenya's own industry and trade. Yet political stability has acquired a still greater premium with the recent emergence of tourism as Kenya's single largest industry, and there is good reason to believe that Kenya, now well versed in crisis management, will survive the always looming crisis of Kenyatta's succession.

ECONOMY

Peter Robson*

INTRODUCTION

The population of Kenya at the 1969 census was 10,942,705, giving an average density of population of 48 per sq. mile, much of it concentrated in the south-western highlands, the coastal strip and the lake area. The rate of growth of population is estimated at 4.0 per cent per annum.

Agriculture is the main occupation and source of income of the bulk of the people but marketed agricultural produce, though important, generates a share of G.D.P. which is relatively low for a country of Kenya's income level. On the other hand, the service and manufacturing sectors are substantially more important than would normally be expected. The development of manufacturing and services has been bound up with the presence in Kenya of a substantial number of non-African settlers, whose high incomes have generated a high demand for manufactures and services. Consequently the economy was early able to develop service and processing and manufacturing facilities, which provided not only for its own needs, but also for those of Uganda and Tanzania. All three countries participate in a customs union, and, until recently, a common-product market, and there continue to be close trading and other links.

The character and to some extent the pace of economic development since independence have been profoundly influenced by this legacy, and by measures taken, both by Kenya and by its neighbours, in response to them. At independence, the export-oriented agriculture in Kenya was based upon large-scale commercial agriculture of the "White Highlands" and on European- and Asian-owned plantations. Much of the government's agricultural effort immediately after independence, and indeed until recently, was devoted to a land reform programme designed to transfer land from the European settlers and to resettle Africans upon it. More recently, with the Trade Licensing Act, which came into effect in 1968, the government has turned its attention to commerce, a marked feature of which has been the preponderance of non-African and frequently non-citizen businesses. In these and other spheres the need to Kenyanize the economy has had, and is continuing to have, important economic effects.

In addition to this, the desire of Kenya's partners in the common market to develop manufacturing and service industries to serve their own and their partners' markets has had a considerable influence on Kenya's development and policies in manufacturing in the last few years.

In spite of the cost and difficulties necessarily involved initially in these measures, Kenya's record since independence entitles it to be placed, in terms of the growth of output, among the most successful of the less developed countries. Over the five years 1964–69, the economy progressed at a cumulative annual rate of growth of 7.6 per cent in current prices, or 6.3. per cent in real terms. In 1971 it grew by 5.7 per cent, the slower rate being largely due to drought. Allowing for its rate of population growth, which is exceptionally high by African standards, an increase of real product per head of about 3 per cent per annum has been achieved. For 1970 G.D.P. per head was estimated at K£50. Expansion has been greatly aided by an adequate supply of capital from domestic sources and from overseas.

AGRICULTURE

Agriculture continues to dominate Kenya's economy, although its share of G.D.P. has declined slightly in recent years. In 1969 it accounted for 34 per cent of total G.D.P. compared with 38 per cent in 1964. More than half of the agricultural output is subsistence production.

Unlike many less developed countries in Africa, Kenya produces a variety of cash crops which helps to make its economy less vulnerable to fluctuations in export prices. Agricultural output, however, is greatly dependent upon the weather: there is little irrigated production, and during 1971, for example, production was greatly affected by drought. In the market sector a distinction is made between output from large and small farms. The large farms correspond mainly to what is left of European farming and the plantations and estates, and the small farms correspond to African smallholdings. In the early 1960s, with land reform and the growth of coffee production on African farms, the share of small farms in marketed output increased rapidly. Over the period 1967–69, however, the share of smallholders stagnated and in 1969 it fell slightly to 49.6 per cent. This was associated with the growth of coffee berry disease (CBD) and the end of large transfers of land from large to small farms.

The value of marketed agricultural output increased from K£57.4 million in 1965 to K£70.2 million in 1968 and to K£75.2 million in 1969. Of the 7 per cent increase in output in 1969 the largest contribution came from coffee and tea, whose outputs were 35 and 20 per cent higher respectively than in 1968. The principal crops are coffee, tea, wheat, maize and sugar, which together accounted for four-fifths of the K£58.5 million output of crops in 1972. Other important crops are sisal and pyrethrum. Except for maize and some wheat, marketed crops are mainly for export. Livestock and dairy production are important activities, both for domestic consumption and export: in 1969 the value of output of livestock products was K£20 million of which 60 per cent was accounted for by meat and 30 per cent by dairy products. In 1970 the total value increased to K£23.3 million and in 1971 to K£25.5 million.

*For the 1973 edition, revisions have been made to this article by the Editor.

Kenya's leading export crop is coffee. Most of the output is high grade *arabica*. A Coffee Marketing Board controls coffee production and handles much of the marketing. Kenya is a member of the International Coffee Agreement and ships the bulk of its crop to quota markets. Kenya's quota for 1969–70 has been cut by 5,000 tons to 47,555 metric tons following her inability in the last three years to meet her exports to quota markets, due mainly to coffee berry disease.

After reaching a peak in 1966, which represented more than a doubling of output since 1960, coffee production fell off badly in 1967 and 1968 due to CBD. The expansion in 1969 to 53,600 metric tons was due to recovery from CBD. Although smallholder coffee production exceeded output from estates, it has not shown the same recovery from disease, for few small farmers have been able to apply the necessary treatments. In 1971 the total production of coffee was 59,459 metric tons. The output from smaller co-operatives declined, owing to smaller yields, but estate production rose and the final production figures showed a small increase on those for 1970.

Tea has been a rapidly expanding crop in the past decade. Production reached a peak of 41,077 metric tons in 1970, as past plantings reached the production stage, but dropped back the following year. Most tea is still produced on large estates but the share of small farms (25 per cent in 1971) is expanding rapidly under the new high density settlement schemes of the Tea Development Authority, created in 1964. Tea exports declined to 30,072 metric tons, and the prices received were lower, the average producer price falling from K£335 per metric ton in 1970 to K£296 per metric ton in 1971.

Sisal production which reached a peak of 70,200 tons in 1963, subsequently declined and in 1971 was about 45,000 metric tons. Most of the output comes from large estates. At prevailing low prices due to the development of substitutes and competition from other countries, most estates are barely able to cover costs and their number is falling.

The output of pyrethrum, of which Kenya is a major producer, suffered a serious decline in 1969 but has since recovered and in 1971 production reached 143 metric tons, almost its previous level. Pyrethrum is a major cash crop in the land settlement programme. The Pyrethrum Board of Kenya allocates quotas and attempts to improve production and its quality.

Kenya's principal food crop is maize. The bulk of the output is for subsistence. Most of the marketed output is delivered to the Maize and Produce Board for sale in towns, and more recently for export. In recent years the price of maize has been supported in order to maintain farm income and to encourage production. Kenya plans to export increasing quantities of maize in the future. In 1970 output fell for the second year running, owing partly to adverse weather conditions, and deliveries to the Maize Board fell by 27 per cent to 205,662 metric tons. A loss of K£1.3 million was made in 1969 on exporting maize but such subsidies are expected to disappear as production becomes more efficient. The drought caused a considerable increase

in domestic demand during 1971, and, although production recovered a little, it was necessary to import maize. The producer price increase in September 1971 is likely to have raised the yield in 1972. Wheat production exceeds domestic requirements, and is being curtailed in order to equate to domestic demand.

Since 1964, livestock and dairy products have increased their share slightly of the value of marketed production. During 1969 the value of livestock output grew but dairy production stagnated, though during 1971 there was a marked increase because of higher producer prices. At independence the bulk of marketed milk production came from European farms. Production from African farms subsequently increased substantially, partly under the impetus of settlement and rural dairy development schemes for smallholders. The bulk (90 per cent) of marketed production is handled by Kenya Co-operative Creameries.

Large resources are being devoted to range development with a view to increasing the development of the livestock industry.

LAND REFORM

Until 1960 about three million hectares of land, mainly in the so-called "White Highlands", were reserved for the exclusive use of Europeans. About half of this land was in the mixed farming areas and the remainder was used mostly for plantations producing coffee, tea, sisal, or for ranching.

Up to the present, Africans have not acquired a substantial interest in either the ranches or the plantations, partly because of the size of the capital investment involved. By 1970, however, a high proportion of the land formerly used for European large-scale mixed farms had been transferred to Africans, usually after extensive subdivision, under a variety of settlement schemes. Of these schemes, the "Million Acre Settlement Scheme", started in 1961 and now virtually completed, is the most important. Loan finance and grants were provided for these purposes by the British government. The Million Acre Scheme involved settling over 34,000 families on 135 settlement schemes, comprising Low Density Schemes with an average farm size of 15 hectares and target cash incomes of K£100 per annum, High Density Schemes with an average farm size of 11 hectares and target incomes of between K£25 and K£70 per farm and several large-scale co-operative farms and ranches. The average cost of establishing each small scale farm under the Million Acre Scheme was in excess of K£700.

Problems have been experienced with these schemes in relation to the level of production and loan repayments. Only a small proportion of farms have reached the target income levels, although some targets may have been too ambitious. There are heavy arrears on loan repayments. Less than 5 per cent of the settlers are paid up in full and, at the beginning of 1970, 45 per cent of the total amount billed was in arrears. During 1968–69 the value of recorded marketed production in settlement areas also declined sharply from K£2.4 million in the previous year to K£1.9

million. Measures are under way to improve the productivity and performance of the schemes.

Apart from land transfer, an important aspect of land reform in Kenya is concerned with changing the tenure system in the traditional African areas in order to provide farmers with title deeds and, where necessary, to consolidate scattered fragments of land into one holding. Such reforms act as a powerful stimulant to agricultural development and ease the problem of the provision of agricultural credit. The programme commenced in the Central Province in 1956. By 1968–69 1,618,000 hectares had been dealt with, mainly in the agricultural, rather than the pastoral areas, where progress lags.

MANUFACTURING, MINING AND CONSTRUCTION, POWER AND TRANSPORT

Over the period 1964–68 the manufacturing sector grew at about 5.7 per cent per annum but its share of total G.D.P. has remained constant at about 10 per cent since 1964. Gross product in 1967 was K£42.4 million. The food, drink and tobacco sector was the largest, accounting for 27 per cent of the total product, followed by vehicle assembly and repair (18 per cent), chemicals and petroleum (13½ per cent) and textiles, footwear and clothing (9 per cent). Other important industries include machinery, non-metallic minerals, metal products and publishing and printing. A wide range of projects is in hand or shortly to commence, including the K£12.5 million pulp and paper mill at Broderick Falls, textile mills, synthetic resins and a vehicle tyre plant.

Mining activity in Kenya is so far limited, but the value of the country's mineral output is expected to increase considerably since the discovery of at least two million tons of lead and silver at Kinangoni, north of Mombasa, and the exploitation of a fluorspar ore deposit in the Kerio valley by the Fluorspar Company of Kenya. In 1971 the production of soda ash was valued at nearly K£1.9 million out of a total mineral production of K£2.8 million. The other principal products are salt, gold and limestone. Prospecting for oil and other minerals continues.

After stagnation in the early years of the decade the building and in particular the construction industry revived and experienced a high rate of growth during 1964–68. At present there are major plans both for government buildings, and numerous other building projects in various parts of the country. The government is currently undertaking 1,300 projects and in this sector is ahead of Development Plan target rates.

Electricity is supplied inland by hydroelectric plants in the Tana River basin and at the coast by an oil-fired plant. This supply is supplemented by a bulk supply from Owen Falls in Uganda. Over the period 1959–69 demand for electricity has grown by about 6.7 per cent per annum. Plans are under way to increase the capacity of the system and its flexibility; when the Kamburu project on the Tana River is completed in 1974 it will more than double the country's electric power capacity.

Kenya has an extensive transport system, including road, rail, coastal and inland water and air. A project to construct more water berths at Mombasa has already begun, and the Port Reitz airport is to be modernized. The road network consists of 43,973 kilometres of roads. A railway runs from the coast at Mombasa through Nairobi to Western Kenya, and to points in Uganda and Tanzania. An extensive internal airways system exists. A national road transport undertaking (Kenatco), mainly concerned with road haulage, operates in competition with private hauliers.

TOURISM

The expected expansion of tourism in Kenya has been confirmed. In 1971 the total foreign exchange receipts from tourism were estimated to be K£24 million which represents a 30 per cent increase on the 1970 figure of K£18.5 million. There was a 26 per cent increase in days spent by visitors in Kenya, as well as a slight increase in their average expenditure. Two thousand new hotel beds were installed during 1971, and there were over 13,000 beds available in early 1972. The earnings target for 1974 is K£37 million, which requires an annual increase of 15 per cent.

Considerable planning in the development of accomodation, transport and entertainment facilities is being undertaken by the government and by private enterprise. The government-owned Kenya Tourist Development Corporation had loan investments and shareholding totalling K£1.85 million at the end of 1971. It has an interest in several new projects including the construction of game lodges and hotels. In 1971–72 the budget for publicity which is handled by the Ministry of Tourism and Wildlife was increased to K£300,000 and tourist offices have been set up around the world.

UNEMPLOYMENT

Urban unemployment and rural underemployment are found in most less developed countries but they present particularly difficult problems for Kenya, with its high rate of population growth. Their solution will call for a variety of policies affecting rural development and the urban-rural wage differential, and even then a solution within the framework of the present social and economic order is by no means assured.

After a period of stagnation for some years, wage employment has increased somewhat in the last two or three years, to reach just over one million. Over the period 1967–69 wage employment rose by just under 46,000 and the labour force grew by 220,000. Thus the number of new jobs in the last two years has been only one-fifth of actual additions to the labour force. Not all of the difference would be unemployed, but there can be no doubt that a substantial proportion actively seek wage employment and that many of those who choose or are forced to join the ranks of the self-employed will, because of shortage of land and other factors, be underemployed. The potential threat this disparity represents to stable economic growth, both directly and indirectly, is disturbing.

In the past the government has taken a number of steps to reduce unemployment directly. These include the establishment of a National Youth Service, and road construction. A further device was the Tripartite Agreement of 1964, which invoked a moratorium on wage increases by trade unions and in return the provision of 34,000 new jobs by employers. A new Tripartite Agreement was announced to take effect in July 1970, which will once more require all employers, including the government, to take on an additional 10 per cent of workers. During the first twelve months of this agreement 35,200 jobs were created which was less than the hoped-for target of 40–45,000, but the rate of growth in employment during 1971 at 5.5 per cent was the highest for years. The Uganda government's decision to terminate the employment of African non-citizens added to Kenya's immediate difficulties, since many of these mainly unskilled workers were Kenyans.

FOREIGN TRADE, AID AND THE BALANCE OF PAYMENTS

Kenya's economy is heavily dependent upon foreign trade. In 1970 total exports amounted to 27 per cent of monetary G.D.P. Kenya typically has a substantial deficit in visible trade with countries outside East Africa, which is partly offset by a surplus in trade with the other two countries of the East African Community. In 1971 the deficit with countries outside East Africa was K£105.8 million, partly offset by the surplus with Uganda and Tanzania giving an overall deficit of K£87.8 million. The visible trade deficit has remained a fairly constant proportion of total trade over the past decade but in 1971 it worsened considerably.

Over the period 1961 to 1971 exports to countries outside East Africa increased from K£35.3 million to K£73.2 million.

Coffee, Kenya's leading export, amounted to K£19.5 million in 1971 (compared with K£10.6 million in 1961) or about 27 per cent of the total. Tea, which has increased from K£4 million in 1961 to K£12.7 million in 1970 though it dropped to K£11.9 million in 1971, has become the country's second most important export, having displaced sisal in 1964. Exports of petroleum products (based on imported crude) which commenced in 1963 have grown (with exports to Zambia) to occupy third place. In 1970 they amounted to K£8.2 million. Unlike many less developed countries, Kenya has a well diversified export trade.

Kenya's exports to the other East African countries expanded by 85 per cent between 1961 and 1965 to reach a peak of K£29.9 million. Partly as a result of restrictions imposed by the other two countries, exports declined in 1967 and 1968 but they have since recovered and reached a new record of K£33.9 million in 1971. Leading exports include food products, and a range of miscellaneous manufactured goods.

Pattern of Trade

Sterling area countries provide the major outlet for Kenya's exports and took 38 per cent of the total in 1969. Britain was the largest single importer, taking 22.6 per cent, and Zambia, to whom exports have been growing rapidly since 1964, has moved into second place among the sterling importers, accounting in 1969 for 6.3 per cent. The European Economic Community took 19 per cent of exports, Germany alone accounting for 11.5 per cent. The U.S.A. was the third largest outlet, accounting in 1969 for 7.6 per cent of exports. In 1970 Britain took 21 per cent, the EEC 18.6 per cent, and North and South America 11.9 per cent of exports.

Sterling area countries accounted for nearly 40 per cent of total imports in 1969. Britain is the largest source of imports (31 per cent of the total). EEC countries supplied just over 20 per cent, with Germany figuring as the principal EEC supplier, and the second most important supplier. Japan overtook Iran in 1969 to become the third most important supplier, accounting for 8 per cent of total imports—not far short of Germany's share. In 1970 Britain supplied 29 per cent, the EEC 20.2 per cent, Japan 10.7 per cent and North and South America 9 per cent of imports.

Aid

Since independence Kenya has received substantial but declining amounts of aid. Over the five-year period 1964–65 to 1968–69 total official aid and grants amounted to nearly K£64 million, falling from K£20 million at the commencement of the period to K£8 million at the end. About one-third was made up of grants and the rest by loans. The United Kingdom provided nine-tenths of the loans and seven-tenths of total assistance. About 11 per cent of the total came from IDA and 4 per cent from Federal Germany. Aid for 1969–70 was estimated to be slightly higher than for the previous year at about K£11 million.

Balance of Payments

Kenya's balance of payments position, having previously been strong, was considerably weaker in 1971. The small surplus in the balance on current and long-term capital account recorded in 1968 was greatly exceeded in 1969. But in 1971 there was a decline in the net inflow from long-term capital movements, particularly in the net capital receipts of private enterprises. The balance of payments surplus of K£12.6 million in 1970 is estimated to have become a deficit of some K£32 million in 1971. The net outflow of monetary and short-term capital movements was some K£28 million, and the foreign exchange reserves of the banking system fell by K£21.2 million, being affected by the increase in imports, stagnant export earnings and lower capital receipts. The government adopted various measures to stop the fall, and by early 1972 the outflow had been halted and there had been a recovery to K£67 million in March 1972 from the October 1971 figure of K£62.4 million. During 1971 Kenya was affected by international monetary changes that caused the devaluation of the Kenya shilling, which remained pegged to the U.S. dollar.

The introduction of exchange control in 1965 undoubtedly contributed to the consolidation of Kenya's payments position in recent years by checking the outflow of private capital. Another factor was the effect of the Banking Act which required foreign banks to bring in capital. Government borrowing has also increased. Side by side with this surplus there was a substantial increase in the liquidity of the commercial banking system together with the rise in reserves, and this liquidity became excessive.

PUBLIC FINANCE

Over the fiscal years 1960–61 to 1971–72 central government expenditure as a whole increased by 140 per cent from K£50.9 million to K£127 million and development expenditures have represented a growing proportion of the total. Over the past five years British aid to the recurrent budget has dropped from about 13 per cent in 1964–65 to less than 1 per cent in 1969–70. The buoyant growth of revenue from domestic sources has been sufficient to allow the elimination of recurrent budgetary assistance and also to generate a surplus over expenditure for transfer to the development budget, thus reducing the dependence on external sources in this area. Although the share of external grants and loans in the development budget has declined from about 80 per cent in 1964–65, it still accounted for about 38 per cent of total development revenue in 1969–70. The growing proportion of development revenue represented by domestic sources reflects local institutional developments which have permitted domestic savings to be mobilized more effectively. The principal domestic source of government borrowings is the National Social Security Fund which was set up in 1966. In the last ten years public debt has grown by 126 per cent.

During 1971–72 government recurrent expenditure was estimated at K£127 million of which development spending was K£56 million. Gross expenditure for 1972–73 is budgeted at K£201 million and recurrent expenditure at K£132 million. The estimates for development expenditure for 1972–73 are K£69 million. Estimated aid for the development account is K£27 million and this aid together with other external receipts totals K£34.5 million. The government needs the remainder from local sources and is to borrow K£10 million from the Central Bank, and raise the remaining amount from the expected surplus on the recurrent budget, long-term bond issues on the local market and new taxes.

DEVELOPMENT PLANNING

Development policy in Kenya emphasizes the role of private enterprise in industry and commerce. Finance is provided through specially established finance companies, in part with the object of facilitating African participation, but direct participation by the state in productive enterprises is limited.

Kenya's First Development Plan, revised in 1966, covers the period 1964–70. Important objectives of the plan were to raise national income and to facilitate the Kenyanization of the economy, until then largely in expatriate hands; for the latter purpose a major expansion of education was envisaged to provide the necessary skills, and a land transfer programme was established.

Over the period 1964–69 the real rate of growth of the economy has been equal to the target set out in the Development Plan, though actual performance fluctuated greatly from year to year. The service industries, including government, exceeded their projected growth targets, whereas the productive industries notably agriculture, manufacturing, building construction and electricity fell short of theirs. The short-fall in manufacturing was in part due to the restrictions imposed by Tanzania and Uganda and partly to the failure of several key projects to get under way during the period. Nevertheless, capital formation in the private sector nearly achieved the levels set. Public capital formation, however, fell far short of the targets, due to delays in project formulation, loan negotiations and difficulties of obtaining skilled manpower.

Kenya's Second Development Plan covers the projected growth of the economy over the calendar years 1970–74 and the investment programme of the government for 1969–70 to 1973–74. A basic object of the plan is to accelerate rural development in the interests of economic balance and to rectify the imbalance between rural and urban incomes—an important factor in urban migration. A variety of measures are to be taken to improve the planning machinery with particular reference to implementation. A higher growth target has been set than in the previous plan—an average of 6.7 per cent. The contribution to growth in the monetary sector by the various sectors is projected as follows: agriculture 13 per cent, manufacturing 18 per cent, trade and transport 26 per cent, general government 19 per cent, other 24 per cent. Central government development expenditures over the period will amount to approximately K£180 million. Of this, the domestic contribution, partly from surpluses on the recurrent budget but mainly from local borrowing, will be rather less than half, and foreign grants and loans rather more than half (K£95 million). The total capital inflow required to cover the deficit in the balance of payments and debt amortization is K£270 million. Allowing for the K£95 million for the central government and other public sector borrowing, K£140 million will have to be found by the private sector. Foreign exchange may clearly turn out to be a major constraint if steps are not taken to improve the foreign balance.

REGIONAL ARRANGEMENTS AND PROBLEMS

Kenya enjoys close economic links with the other two East African countries who are its partners in the East African Economic Community. This Community, which came into existence on December 1st, 1967, was designed to continue on a more equitable basis the established customs union and the arrangements for common services which had long existed among the three countries. The main characteristics of existing arrangements are as follows: there is a common external tariff and a qualified common market for products; a range of public services, including the East African Development Bank, railways, airways, posts and telegraphs, income tax and customs and excise departments are operated on an East African basis. The monetary union which operated until 1966 no longer exists, each country having its own currency and Central Bank, but monetary links are close and normally funds move freely and bank notes are interchangeable. Negotiations for the accession of new members have been going on for some time.

An important innovation of the Treaty was the institution of a transfer tax. Effectively this permits Tanzania and Uganda under certain conditions to tax imports of manufactures from Kenya for the purpose of protecting their own infant industries. The provisions of the Treaty have now been in force for two years and transfer taxes have been imposed on a range of Kenya's manufactures. Although these taxes must hamper Kenyan exports they may provide a more favourable context for trade than the previous restrictions.

There can be no doubt that the restrictions imposed by Tanzania and Uganda on Kenyan manufactures prior to the Treaty slowed down its rate of growth of manufacturing industry. In 1969, however, Kenya's trade with the rest of East Africa rose, more than recovering the ground lost in 1968, and the overall trade gap widened in Kenya's favour to about K£17.9 million in 1971.

PROBLEMS AND PROSPECTS

The present position of the Kenyan economy with lower foreign reserves and rising imports, is weaker than it was in 1969. In the long term, much will depend on whether the present political stability

continues. However, industrial production, which rose by 13.2 per cent in 1971, is expected to remain high and growth in tourism will undoubtedly continue. Prices for coffee and tea are still low, though agricultural output as a whole is expected to recover during 1972, and the level of rainfall has been satisfactory since the drought of 1971.

The continued high rate of population growth puts a major strain on the economy, not only in terms of expenditure but also in terms of the economic, social and political strains which result from imbalance between the growth of the labour force and employment opportunities. This has prompted short-term expedients which may be detrimental to growth. Wholly satisfactory means have not yet been found to reconcile the proper emphasis on Kenyanization with the satisfactory initiation and implementation of projects—either in the public or in the private sector. The underlent position of the banks and their high liquidity is associated with the relatively slow rate of development of the private sector recently. If the Kenyan economy is to continue to grow as rapidly as it has in the past, means will have to be found to improve the capacity of the government to initiate and implement projects. In the private sector, means will have to be found for reconciling the justified desire for Africanization in commerce and industry with the supply of qualified experienced and creditworthy African entrepreneurs. This is not just a question of the provision of finance. A judgement on recent fiscal policies must turn largely on whether there are idle resources in the Kenyan economy which can be activated to accelerate growth by financial means or whether the Kenyan economy is for the time being at the limit of feasible growth, given the scarcities of skilled factors and access to natural resources. Of course these scarcities can be overcome, by education, experience, and by further agricultural reforms, probably as much in the traditional sector as elsewhere. But all this will take time.

STATISTICAL SURVEY

AREA
(sq. km.)

TOTAL	LAND	WATER	LAKES		NATIONAL PARKS		
			Victoria (in Kenya)	Rudolf	Tsavo	Aberdare	Mount Kenya
582,646*	569,250	13,396	3,831	6,405	20,899	572	464

* 224,961 sq. miles.

LAND CLASSIFICATION, 1968
(sq. km.)

TYPE OF LAND	AREA
Trust land and private freehold land which was formerly Trust land. . . .	464,259
National Forests	9,753
Urban Area	954
Government reserves (agricultural, veterinary, railway, etc.) . . .	1,160
Alienated government land . . .	26,698
Private freehold land which was not formerly Trust land (incl. settlement schemes) .	6,703
National Parks	22,071
Unalienated government land . .	46,512
Open water	4,603
	582,646

POPULATION
(1969 Census—provisional figures)
PROVINCES

TOTAL	CENTRAL	COAST	EASTERN	NORTH-EASTERN	NYANZA	RIFT VALLEY	WESTERN
10,942,705*	1,663,100	936,000	1,899,200	244,200	2,115,800	2,219,400	1,335,200

* Final figure.

The estimated total population for 1970 is **11,247,000** and for 1971 **11,694,000**

CHIEF TOWNS

Nairobi (capital)	.	477,600	Eldoret	.	.	.	16,900
Mombasa .	.	245,700	Kitale	.	.	.	11,500
Nakuru	.	47,800	Nanyuki	.	.	.	11,200
Kisumu	.	30,700	Kericho	.	.	.	10,900
Thika	.	18,100	Nyeri	.	.	.	9,900

1970 estimates: Nairobi **535,200**, Mombasa **255,400**.

MAIN TRIBES OF KENYA
(1962 Census)

	MALE	FEMALE	TOTAL
Kikuyu . . .	810,856	831,209	1,642,065
Luo . . .	561,721	586,614	1,148,335
Luhya . . .	533,180	553,229	1,086,409
Kamba . . .	455,215	478,004	933,219
Kisii . . .	266,978	271,365	538,343
Meru . . .	214,991	224,930	439,921
Mijikenda . .	199,587	215,300	414,887
Kipsigis . .	170,447	171,324	341,771
Turkana . .	89,973	91,414	181,387
Nandi . . .	83,535	86,550	170,085
Masai . . .	75,002	79,077	154,079
Ogaden . .	66,507	55,138	121,645
Tugen . . .	54,934	54,757	109,691
Elgeyo . . .	51,310	49,561	100,871
All others . .	500,398	482,836	983,234
TOTAL . .	4,134,634	4,231,308	8,365,942

In addition, non-Africans numbered 270,321 in 1962 and only 209,000 in 1969.

Births and Deaths:

Annual average birth rate 47.8 per 1,000, death rate 17.5 per 1,000 (UN estimate for 1965–70).

MIGRATION

	IMMIGRANT ARRIVALS	LONG-TERM EMIGRANTS
1968	16,973	11,497
1969	19,082	13,526
1970	19,879	14,020
1971	1,643	n.a.

EMPLOYMENT

Total labour force (1970): 4,319,000 economically active, including 3,472,000 in agriculture (ILO and FAO estimates).

TOTAL REPORTED EMPLOYEES*
(1969—'000)

	ALL RACES	AFRICAN	ASIAN	EUROPEAN
Agriculture and Forestry . . .	178.7	177.0	0.6	1.1
Private Industry and Commerce . .	211.4	179.0	23.4	8.5
Public Services	237.2	226.0	7.4	4.2
All Employees	627.3	582.0	31.4	13.8

1970 figures: Agriculture and Forestry 183.7, Private Industry and Commerce 213.3, **Public Service** 247.5, Total 644.5.

* This table refers only to employment in urban areas and on large farms. Employment in other areas is estimated to be between 300,000 and 500,000.

AGRICULTURE

PRINCIPAL CROPS
('ooo metric tons)

	1969	1970	1971
Wheat	210	205	210*
Maize	1,425	1,500	1,400*
Millet and Sorghum	330*	330*	330*
Sugar Cane†	1,301	1,451	1,750
Potatoes	200*	200*	210*
Sweet Potatoes and Yams	463*	463*	n.a.
Cassava (Manioc)	620*	620*	n.a.
Pulses	280*	280*	280*

* FAO estimate. † Crop year ending in year stated.

Fruit and Nuts (FAO estimates): Pineapples: 27,000 metric tons in 1969, 40,000 metric tons in 1970; Coconuts: 65 million per year (annual average, 1961–65).

Source: FAO, *Production Yearbook 1971* and *Monthly Bulletin of Agricultural Economics and Statistics.*

CROP DELIVERIES
(metric tons)

	1969	1970	1971
Sugar Cane .	1,375,657	1,551,200	1,528,002
Wheat . .	241,558	221,486	205,869
Maize* .	280,330	205,662	256,590
Rice .	22,744	28,547	29,983
Tea .	36,060	41,077	36,290
Coffee .	52,384	58,337	59,459
Sisal .	49,834	43,930	44,827
Seed Cotton	17,111	14,017	16,764
Pyrethrum Extract .	81.0	95.2	142.8

*Deliveries to the Marketing Board only.

LIVESTOCK
('ooo)

	1968–69	1969–70	1970–71
Cattle . . .	7,908	8,600	8,500
Sheep . . .	4,056	3,700	3,700
Goats . . .	4,334	4,000	4,000
Pigs . . .	70	72	75
Camels . . .	312	315	320
Poultry . . .	10,300	10,600	11,900

*FAO estimate.

DAIRY PRODUCE
('ooo metric tons)

	1969	1970	1971
Cow's milk . . .	803*	820	840*
Sheep's milk . . .	16*	15*	15*
Goat's milk . . .	43*	40*	40*

*FAO estimate.

('ooo kg.)

	1968	1969
Butter . . .	4,188	3,426
Ghee . . .	813	813

('ooo litres)*

	1969	1970	1971
Whole milk (sales) .	101,982	103,011	105,777
Milk for Butter .	88,918	105,395	79,163
Milk for Ghee .	21,107	18,905	13,397
Milk for Cheese .	4,474	4,606	4,716

*Factory production only.

MEAT PRODUCTION†
('ooo metric tons)

	1969	1970	1971
Beef and Veal‡ . .	28	30*	32*
Pork . . .	4*	5	5*

*FAO estimate.

† Meat from indigenous animals, including the meat equivalent of exported live animals.

‡ Commercial production only.

OTHER AGRICULTURAL PRODUCTS
(metric tons)

	1969	1970	1971
Hen Eggs . . .	14,700*	15,100	16,200*
Wool: Greasy . .	2,100	2,200	2,200*
Clean . .	1,000	1,100	1,100*

* FAO estimate.

FORESTRY
ROUNDWOOD PRODUCTION
('ooo cubic metres)

1967	.	.	8,153
1968	.	.	8,174
1969	.	.	8,400

Source: FAO, *Yearbook of Forest Products.*

FISHING
(metric tons)

	1968	1969	1970
Inland water . .	22,100	25,200	25,800
Sea . . .	6,000	6,700	7,900
Total Catch .	28,100	31,900	33,700
Value of fish landed (K£'ooo)	1,223	1,391	1,517

Source: FAO, *Yearbook of Fishery Statistics 1970.*

MINING

	1967	1968	1969
Gold (kg.) . .	1,038	994	557
Salt (metric tons) .	27,000	29,000	42,000

INDUSTRY

	Unit	1968	1969	1970	1971
Wheat Flour	'ooo metric tons	75.0	90.2	127.9	70.6*
Soda Ash	,, ,, ,,	117.4	102.7	160.1	161.2
Cement	,, ,, ,,	543.2	642.4	792.1	794.0
Sugar	metric tons	81,438	115,052	125,291	93,405†
Soap	,, ,,	20,403	24,003	23,421	21,932†
Cigarettes . . .	,, ,,	1,764	1,814	2,081	1,656†
Beer	'ooo hectolitres	600.0	647.6	795.3	673.5†
Mineral Waters . . .	,, ,,	227.5	278.8	314.3	260.0†
Oil Refined . . .	million litres	2,254.6	2,510.0	2,508.3	2,966.2
Electricity . . .	million kWh.	380.3	459.4	508.6	406.5†

* January–June.   † January–September.

FINANCE

100 cents=1 Kenya shilling (Ks.).
Coins: 5, 10, 25 and 50 cents; 1 and 2 Ks.
Notes: 5, 10, 20, 50 and 100 Ks.
Exchange rates (December 1972): £1 sterling=16.81 Ks.; U.S. $1=7.143 Ks.;
100 Ks.=£5.949=$14.00.

(*Note:* In this survey the symbol "K£" is used to denote amounts of 20 Ks., equivalent to £1.19 sterling.)

RECURRENT BUDGET
(K£'000—1968–69)

REVENUE		EXPENDITURE	
Income Tax	23,611	General Services	22,720
Export Duties	351	Roads	2,420
Customs and Excise . . .	33,623	Education	8,969
Stamp Duties	911	Health	4,741
Other Licences, Duties and Taxes .	6,702	Agriculture	7,647
Provision of Goods and Services .	7,737	Public Debt	8,954
Miscellaneous	4,125	Pensions and Gratuities . . .	3,757
TOTAL (incl. others) . .	85,743	TOTAL (incl. others) .	80,515

Budget (1969–70): Revenue K£96.21m.; Expenditure K£89.74m.

Budget (1970–71): Revenue K£109.16m.; Expenditure K£104.32m.

Budget (1971–72): Revenue K£119m.; Expenditure K£120.51m.

Budget (1972–73): Revenue K£136m.; Expenditure K£132m.*

DEVELOPMENT
(K£'000)

EXPENDITURE	1967–68	1968–69	1969–70*
Land Settlement	1,173	1,903	2,101
Commerce and Industry . . .	732	1,111	1,180
Roads	4,569	6,024	8,005
Education	1,974	2,921	2,176
Health	872	1,172	2,056
Agriculture and Forestry . . .	4,387	4,373	4,079
Armed Forces	333	275	344
Tourism and National Parks .	703	410	435
TOTAL (incl. others) .	19,575	24,465	28,471

Development Expenditure: (1971–72) K£51.5m.; (1972–73) K£69m.*

* Estimates.

Five-Year Development Plan (1970–74): Total Investment K£683m. (Public Sector K£244m., Private Sector K£439m.); Principal fields of Central Government Development Expenditure: Transport 26 per cent, Agriculture (including Land Settlement) 21 per cent, Social Services (including Education) 27 per cent; Development Expenditure is expected to have increased from K£29m. in 1969–70 to K£42.5m. in 1973–74 or at the rate of 10 per cent per annum.

GROSS DOMESTIC PRODUCT
(million K£)

INDUSTRY	1968	1969	1970*
GROSS PRODUCT AT FACTOR COST:			
Outside Monetary Economy:			
Agriculture	84.96	88.98	91.88
Forestry	3.11	3.26	3.39
Fishing	0.14	0.14	0.15
Building and Construction	8.65	8.97	9.55
Water	3.11	4.15	4.42
Ownership of Dwellings	8.98	9.58	10.38
Total Product Outside Monetary Economy	108.95	115.08	119.77
Monetary Economy:			
Enterprises and Non-Profit Institutions:			
Agriculture	57.73	62.05	66.34
Forestry	2.95	3.20	3.61
Fishing	1.13	1.14	1.25
Mining and Quarrying	2.31	2.72	3.07
Manufacturing and Repairing	50.06	57.19	64.84
Building and Construction	14.79	19.76	21.58
Electricity and Water	6.44	6.93	7.83
Transport, Storage, Communications	36.19	37.81	41.57
Wholesale and Retail Trade	44.20	46.87	53.13
Banking, Insurance, Real Estate	15.51	17.58	19.55
Ownership of Dwellings	15.13	16.25	17.06
Other Services	16.51	17.32	18.88
Total Enterprises	262.95	288.82	318.71
Private Household (Domestic Services)	3.56	3.56	3.68
General Government:			
Public Administration	20.32	21.86	22.63
Defence	4.08	4.10	4.33
Education	18.46	23.13	23.91
Health	7.94	9.21	9.16
Agricultural Services	5.79	6.13	6.46
Other Services	7.28	8.09	8.20
Total General Government	63.85	72.54	74.69
Total Product—Monetary Economy	330.36	364.92	397.08
TOTAL GROSS PRODUCT AT FACTOR COST (Monetary and Non-Monetary)	439.32	480.00	516.85
Indirect Taxes	38.08	42.17	46.07
Less Subsidies	2.64	2.10	1.23
TOTAL GROSS PRODUCT AT MARKET PRICES	474.76	520.07	561.69

* Provisional.

EXTERNAL TRADE*
(K£'000)

	1966	1967	1968	1969	1970	1971†
Imports	112,396	106,596	114,765	116,950	142,026	184,100
Exports	58,073	59,589	62,941	68,510	77,451	78,400

* Excluding inter-trade of local produce and locally manufactured goods between Kenya, Uganda, Tanganyika and, beginning 1968, Zanzibar.   † Provisional figures.

COMMODITIES
(K£'000)

IMPORTS	1968	1969	1970	1971*
Crude Petroleum	9,656	10,168	11,023	9,599
Motor Vehicles and Chassis . . .	8,072	9,894	11,473	12,893
Agricultural Machinery and Tractors .	2,295	1,911	2,420	2,324
Industrial Machinery (including electrical) .	14,690	15,427	22,413	22,135
Iron and Steel	6,147	6,473	9,004	8,635
Fabrics of Cotton . . .	2,752	1,923	1,022	928
Fabrics of Synthetic Fibres . . .	3,183	2,354	3,849	2,782
Paper and Paper Products . . .	4,798	5,697	6,648	6,374
Pharmaceutical Products . . .	2,194	2,459	2,712	2,633
Fertilizers	1,875	2,272	3,041	2,444

(K£'000)

DOMESTIC EXPORTS†	1968	1969	1970	1971*
Coffee (not roasted)	12,808	16,837	22,259	14,635
Sisal (fibre and tow) . . .	2,020	1,717	1,865	1,077
Tea	10,041	11,271	12,704	8,234
Pyrethrum (extract and flowers) . .	3,040	2,795	2,163	1,927
Meat and Meat Products . .	3,026	2,595	2,853	2,187
Hides and Skins (undressed) . .	1,671	1,871	1,653	1,695
Manufactured Goods:				
Soda Ash	1,132	904	1,673	1,548
Wattle Extract . . .	1,134	1,144	1,141	977
Petroleum Products . . .	6,111	7,623	8,176	6,406
Cement	1,174	1,434	1,644	1,212
Other	3,397	4,014	4,467	4,391

* January–September.   † Excluding re-exports.

COUNTRIES
(K£'ooo)

	IMPORTS				DOMESTIC EXPORTS*			
	1968	1969	1970	1971†	1968	1969	1970	1971†
Western Europe:								
United Kingdom .	36,110	36,453	41,459	42,236	14,894	14,787	14,847	10,110
EEC . . .	23,627	24,283	28,651	28,580	11,583	12,894	13,295	9,966
Other . .	4,713	5,799	7,048	7,714	3,695	4,640	6,823	3,785
Eastern Europe . .	2,554	2,605	3,476	3,935	1,386	1,278	1,953	1,980
North and South America	8,756	9,595	12,805	12,891	5,406	6,496	8,299	4,272
Africa . . .	1,247	1,279	1,833	2,148	6,883	8,235	9,158	8,745
Asia:								
Japan . .	7,968	9,344	15,196	14,834	1,702	1,287	1,225	1,762
Other . .	22,827	21,545	23,697	21,876	5,743	5,392	7,372	5,538
All Other Countries .	6,961	6,046	7,859	3,320	6,503	8,324	8,634	6,614
TOTAL . .	114,764	116,951	142,026	137,534	57,795	63,332	71,606	52,772

* Excluding re-exports.   † January–September.

INTER-COMMUNITY TRADE

	TANZANIA		UGANDA	
	Imports	Exports	Imports	Exports
1968 . .	3,742	13,486	9,137	13,756
1969 . .	4,018	12,845	7,803	15,949
1970 . .	5,938	14,752	10,048	16,698
1971* . .	5,883	10,624	6,222	14,941

* January–September.

TOURISM
ARRIVALS OF VISITORS AND PERSONS IN TRANSIT

NATIONALITY	1969	1970	1971
British . . .	99,113	100,339	99,025
Federal German .	15,712	23,067	37,781
Other European .	44,700	52,485	67,420
American and Canadian .	45,656	51,511	63,605
Indian and Pakistani .	15,819	17,483	17,946
Ugandan and Tanzanian .	50,890	60,471	69,427
Other African . .	9,168	10,638	16,513
All Others . .	12,256	22,780	22,910
TOTAL . .	293,314	338,773	394,627

TRANSPORT

EAST AFRICAN RAILWAYS

Total track mileage (1972) 5,897 km., in Kenya, Uganda and Tanzania, combined.

ROADS
(New registrations of vehicles)

	MOTOR CARS	LIGHT VANS ETC.	LORRIES ETC.	BUSES AND COACHES	MOTOR CYCLES	OTHER NEW VEHICLES	SECOND-HAND VEHICLES	TOTAL
1967 . .	6,014	4,212	1,621	339	978	1,186	1,601	15,951
1968 . .	5,631	3,465	1,483	271	1,016	1,186	1,146	14,198
1969 . .	6,389	4,232	1,760	311	1,244	1,045	1,111	16,092
1970 . .	7,680	4,959	2,469	435	1,317	1,427	1,317	19,604
1971* . .	6,174	4,091	1,559	396	1,005	873	1,256	15,354

* Provisional.

SHIPPING
ENTERED*

	NUMBER OF VESSELS	NET TONNAGE	NUMBER OF PASSENGERS	CARGO '000 tons
1968 . . .	1,882	7,656,000	36,634	5,487
1969 . . .	1,813	7,446,000	41,869	5,092
1970 . . .	1,762	7,214,700	36,948	5,795
1971 . . .	1,859	7,510,000	23,311	5,570

* Mombasa only.

CIVIL AVIATION
EXTERNAL AIR TRAFFIC*

	NUMBER OF PASSENGERS		FREIGHT KG.	
	Arrivals	Departures	Unloaded	Loaded
1968 . .	248,100	266,800	5,124,000	7,915,000
1969 . .	285,600	295,700	5,457,000	9,570,000
1970† . .	320,100	328,100	5,970,900	11,008,400

* Nairobi Airport only.   † Estimates.

EDUCATION

	NUMBER OF ESTABLISHMENTS		NUMBER OF TEACHERS	NUMBER OF PUPILS	
	1969	1970	1969	1969	1970
Primary and Intermediate Schools . .	6,111	6,123	38,312	1,282,297	1,427,589
Secondary Schools and Secondary Technical Schools	694	783	5,267	115,246	126,855
Vocational Schools	10	10	145	2,344	} 10,443
Teacher Training Colleges	27	27	522	7,194	

In 1970 there were 10,443 students at university.

Sources (*unless otherwise stated*): East African Statistical Department, Nairobi; Ministry of Economic Planning and Development, Nairobi; Ministry of Information, Broadcasting and Tourism, Nairobi; *Kenya Statistical Digest*, Ministry of Finance and Planning, Nairobi; *Annual Economic Review*, Standard Bank.

THE CONSTITUTION

The Independence Constitution for Kenya came into force in June, 1963, with the introduction of full internal self-government.

Amendments were made in November, 1964, by which Kenya became a Republic within the Commonwealth. Under the terms of the Constitution, individual rights and liberties are protected, including freedom of expression and assembly, privacy of the home, the right not to be detained without cause, and the right of compensation for compulsory purchase of property.

By a voluntary evolution the Republic of Kenya is now a One-Party State governed by a united Central Government. For administrative purposes, the country is divided into seven Provinces, each of which has a Provincial Council playing a purely advisory role, especially in respect of rural development. The Provincial Councils and County Councils are maintained by grants from the Central Government, but raising of all other taxes and of foreign investment capital is the sole responsibility of Central Government.

The central legislative authority is the National Assembly consisting of a single elected assembly. There are 158 Representatives elected for four years, and 12 Members nominated by the President.

Executive power is in the hands of the President, Vice-President and Cabinet. The Cabinet shall be formed by the President, who, following constitutional amendments adopted in June 1968, is to be directly elected by popular vote at general elections. In the event of his death or resignation the Vice-President will assume the Presidency, with limited powers, for a maximum period of three months. The Presidency becomes vacant on the dissolution of Parliament.

In October, 1963, certain amendments to the Constitution were introduced. The Police and Public Services are to be centrally controlled. Changes in the Constitution about Human Rights, structure of Regions, Land, the Senate, and amendment procedure can only be made by a 75 per cent majority vote of the National Assembly. Changes concerning other clauses, including those affecting Regional powers, may be made by a 75 per cent vote of the Assembly or failing this by a two-thirds majority in a national referendum.

THE GOVERNMENT

HEAD OF STATE

President of the Republic: Mzee Jomo Kenyatta.

Vice-President: Daniel Arap Moi.

CABINET

(December 1972)

President and Commander-in-Chief: Mzee Jomo Kenyatta.

Vice-President and Minister of Home Affairs: Daniel Arap Moi.

Minister of State at the President's Office: Mbiyu Koinange.

Minister of Foreign Affairs: Dr. Njoroge Mungai.

Minister of Finance and Economic Planning: Mwai Kibaki.

Minister of Defence: James S. Gichuru.

Minister of Agriculture and Animal Husbandry: Jeremiah J. M. Nyagah.

Minister of Health: Isaak Omolo Okero.

Minister of Local Government: Dr. Julius G. Kiano.

Minister of Works: James Nyamweya.

Minister of Power and Communications: Ronald G. Ngala.

Minister of Labour: Eliud N. Mwendwa.

Minister of Tourism and Wildlife: Juxon L. M. Shako.

Minister of Lands and Settlement: Jackson H. Angaine.

Minister of Housing: Paul J. Ngei.

Attorney-General: Charles Njonjo.

Minister of Information and Broadcasting: Dr. Zachary Onyonka.

Minister of Natural Resources: William O. Omamo.

Minister of Co-operatives and Social Services: Masinde Muliro.

Minister of Commerce and Industry: James C. N. Osogo.

Minister of Education: Taita A. Towett.

DIPLOMATIC REPRESENTATION

EMBASSIES AND HIGH COMMISSIONS ACCREDITED TO KENYA

(Nairobi, unless otherwise indicated)

(E) Embassy; (HC) High Commission.

Algeria: Dar es Salaam, Tanzania (E).

Australia: Jeevan Bharati Bldg., Harambee Ave., P.O.B. 30360 (HC); *High Commissioner:* K. H. ROGERS.

Austria: Hughes Bldg., Kenyatta Ave., P.O.B. 30560 (E); *Ambassador:* Dr. FRIEDRICH KUDERNATSCH.

Belgium: Silopark House, Queensway, P.O.B. 30461 (E); *Ambassador:* M. ARNOLD J. E. DE COEYER.

Botswana: *Ambassador:* EMMANUEL ONLUMETSE.

Brazil: Harambee Ave., P.O.B. 30754; (E); *Ambassador:* F. T. DE MESQUITA.

Bulgaria: P.O.B. 30058 (E); *Ambassador:* KRAYO VLADOR.

Burundi: Dar es Salaam, Tanzania.

Canada: Kimathi St., IPS Building, P.O.B. 30481 (HC); *High Commissioner:* W. M. OLIVIER (also accred. to Uganda).

Ceylon: *Ambassador:* M. FONSECA.

China, People's Republic: Woodlands Rd., (off Hurlingham Rd.), P.O.B. 30508 (E); *Ambassador:* WANG HUI-MIN.

Colombia: P.O.B. 30661; *Consul:* CESAR ALVARADO.

Cyprus: Koinang St., P.O.B. 30515; *Ambassador:* M. GRAMMANOPOULOS.

Czechoslovakia: Crauford Rd., P.O.B. 30204 (E); *Ambassador:* J. UHER.

Denmark: Hughes Bldg., Kenyatta Ave., P.O.B. 412 (E); *Ambassador:* HANS KUHNE.

Egypt: Total Bldg., Koinange St., P.O.B. 30285 (E); *Ambassador:* MOHAMED TAWFIK.

Ethiopia: State House Ave., P.O.B. 5198 (E); *Ambassador:* ABATE AGHIDE.

Finland: P.O.B. 1017, Addis Ababa, Ethiopia (E).

France: Embassy House, Harambee Ave., P.O.B. 1748 (E); *Ambassador:* RENÉ MILLET.

Germany, Federal Republic: Embassy House, Harambee Ave., P.O.B. 30180 (E); *Ambassador:* Dr. RUHFUS.

Ghana: Coronation Bldg., Government Rd., P.O.B. 8534 (HC); *High Commissioner:* E. K. OTOO.

Greece: Kimathi St. (E); *Ambassador:* MICHAEL MOUZAS.

Guinea: P.O.B. 2969, Dar es Salaam, Tanzania (E).

Hungary: Arboretum Rd., P.O.B. 30275 (E); *Ambassador:* JOSEF BAJNOK.

India: Jeevan Bharati Bldg., Harambee Ave., P.O.B. 30074 (HC); *High Commissioner:* K. CHANDRASEKHARAN NAIR.

Iraq: (E); *Ambassador:* HASSAN KITTANY.

Israel: Bishops Rd., P.O.B. 30354 (E); *Ambassador:* REUVAN DAFNI.

Italy: Prudential Assurance Bldg., Wabera St., P.O.B. 30107 (E); *Ambassador:* Marquis GIOVANNI REVEDIN DI SAN MARTINO.

Ivory Coast: *Ambassador:* GUIRANDOU N'DIAYE.

Japan: Bank of India Bldg., Kenyatta Ave., P.O.B. 20202 (E); *Ambassador:* RYUICHI ANDO.

Korea, Republic: Kimathi St., P.O.B. 30455 (E); *Ambassador:* IN HAN PAIK.

Kuwait: Kimathi St., P.O.B. 2353 (E); *Ambassador:* SAEED Y. SHAMMAS.

Lesotho: P.O.B. 4096 (HC); *High Commissioner:* M. B. MDINISO.

Liberia: P.O.B. 30546 (E); *Ambassador:* R. FRANCIS OKAI.

Madagascar: Sclaters Rd., P.O.B. 30793; *Ambassador:* ANDRE RAMANKOTO.

Malawi: Ottoman Bank Bldg., P.O.B. 30453 (HC); *High Commissioner:* E. D. PHAKAMEA.

Malaysia: Government Rd., P.O.B. 8916; *Ambassador:* H. LEONARD.

Mali: Dar es Salaam, Tanzania (E).

Morocco: Addis Ababa, Ethiopia (E).

Netherlands: Baring Arcade, Kenyatta Ave., P.O.B. 1537 (E); *Ambassador:* J. C. VAN BEUSEKOM.

Nigeria: Agip House, Haile Selassie Ave., P.O.B. 30516 (HC); *High Commissioner:* I. C. OLISEMEKA.

Norway: Silopark House, Queensway, P.O.B. 6363 (E); *Ambassador:* S. GJELLUM.

Pakistan: Government Rd., P.O.B. 30045 (HC); *High Commissioner:* KHYBER KHAN.

Poland: Archer Rd., P.O.B. 30086 (E); *Ambassador:* Dr. EMIL HACHULSKI.

Romania: Dar es Salaam, Tanzania.

Rwanda: Kampala, Uganda (E).

Senegal: *Ambassador:* YOUSSOUF SYLIA.

Somalia: Sclaters Rd., Rockwell Close, Westlands, P.O.B. 30769 (E); *Ambassador:* ABDULLAH FARAK.

Spain: P.O.B. 5503 (E); *Ambassador:* MIGUEL VELARDE.

Sudan: Shankardass House, Government Rd., P.O.B. 8784 (E); *Ambassador:* MOHAMMED ELAMIN.

Swaziland: *High Commissioner:* B. J. SIMELANE.

Sweden: Silopark House, P.O.B. 432 (E); *Ambassador:* CARL-GEORGE CRAFOORD.

Switzerland: Cargen House, Harambee Ave., P.O.B. 20008 (E); *Ambassador:* Dr. D. R. PESTALOZZI.

Tunisia: Addis Ababa, Ethiopia (E).

Turkey: Silopark House, Queensway, P.O.B. 30785 (E); *Ambassador:* SADUN TEREM.

U.S.S.R.: Lenana Rd., P.O.B. 30049 (E); *Ambassador:* DMITRY GORYUNOV.

United Kingdom: Shell-BP Bldg., Harambee Ave., P.O.B. 30465 (HC); *High Commissioner:* Sir ERIC NORRIS.

U.S.A.: Cotts House, Wabera St., P.O.B. 30137 (E); *Ambassador:* ROBINSON McILVAINE.

Vatican: Churchill Ave., P.O.B. 14326 (Apostolic Nunciature); *Apostolic Nuncio:* Most Rev. Archbishop PEIRLUIGI SARTORELLI.

Yemen Arab Republic: (E); *Ambassador:* M. ABDULLA FASAYIL.

Yugoslavia: State House Ave., P.O.B. 30504 (E); *Ambassador:* IVO PELICON.

Zaire: P.O.B. 8106; *Ambassador:* JACQUES MASSA.

Zambia: Koinange St., Uniafric House, P.O.B. 8741 (HC); *High Commissioner:* A. M. KALYATI.

Kenya also has diplomatic relations with Ireland.

NATIONAL ASSEMBLY

The Senate and House of Representatives were merged in February 1967 to form a single Assembly of 158 elected members, and 12 co-opted members.

Speaker: F. M. G. MATI.

Deputy Speaker: Dr. M. WAIYAKI.

ELECTIONS, DECEMBER 1969

Only KANU was represented in the primary elections to the National Assembly, in which 108 new members were elected.

POLITICAL PARTY

Kenya African National Union (KANU): P.O. Box 12394, Nairobi; f. 1960; a nation-wide African party which led the country to self-government and independence; Pres. JOMO KENYATTA; 8 provincial Vice-Pres.

DEFENCE

Of a total armed force of 7,170, the army numbers 6,300, the navy 250 and the air force 620. The civil police numbers 11,500 and includes some para-military units. Military service is voluntary.

Commander-in-Chief of the Armed Forces: Mzee JOMO KENYATTA.

Deputy Chief of Defence Staff: Brig. KAKENYI.

JUDICIAL SYSTEM

The Court of Appeal for East Africa: P.O.B. 30187, Nairobi.

The High Court of Kenya: Nairobi; has unlimited criminal and civil jurisdiction at first instance, and sits as a court of appeal from subordinate courts in both criminal and civil cases. The High Court is a court of admiralty. There is a resident Puisne Judge at Mombasa, Nakuru and Kisumu. Regular sessions in Kisii, Nyeri and Meru.

Chief Justice: Hon. JAMES WICKS.

Puisne Judges: Hons. C. B. MADAN, E. TREVELYAN, CHANAN SINGH, C. H. E. MILLER, L. G. E. HARRIS, L. P. MOSDELL, A. H. SIMPSON, K. C. BENNETT, A. A. KNELLER, J. M. WAIYAKI, M. G. MULI, Sir D. J. SHERIDAN.

Registrar: J. O. NYARANGI.

SUBORDINATE COURTS

Resident Magistrates' Courts: have country-wide jurisdiction, with powers of punishment by imprisonment up to five years or by fine up to K£500.

District Magistrates' Courts: of First, Second and Third Class; these have jurisdiction within Districts and powers of punishment by imprisonment up to five years, one year and six months respectively, or by fine up to K£500, K£100 and K£50 respectively.

Kadhi's Courts: have jurisdiction within Districts, to determine questions of Muslim law.

RELIGION

African religions, beliefs and forms of worship show great variety both between races and tribes and from one district to another. The Arab community is Moslem, the Indians are partly Moslem and partly Hindu, and the Europeans and Goans are almost entirely Christian.

Moslems are found mainly along the coastline but the Moslem faith has also established itself among Africans around Nairobi and other towns up-country and among some tribes of the Northern Frontier Province.

Christian missions are active and about 25 per cent of Africans are Christian and East Africa is also an important centre for the Baha'i faith.

CHRISTIANS

National Christian Council of Kenya: Gen. Sec. J. KAMAU, P.O.B. 5009, Nairobi.

ANGLICAN PROVINCE OF KENYA

Archbishop (*and Bishop of Nairobi*): Most Rev. F. H. OLANG', P.O.B. 40502, Nairobi.

Bishops:

Maseno North: Rt. Rev. J. I. MUNDIA, P.O.B. 1, Maseno.

Maseno South: Rt. Rev. EVAN AGOLA, P.O.B. 114, Kisumu.

Mombasa: Rt. Rev. P. MWANG'OMBE, P.O.B. 72, Mombasa.

Mount Kenya: Rt. Rev. OBADIAH KARIUKI, P.O.B. 121, Fort Hall.

Nakuru: Rt. Rev. N. LANGFORD-SMITH, M.A., P.O.B. 56, Nakuru.

ROMAN CATHOLIC CHURCH

Archbishop: Most Rev. MAURICE OTUNGA, P.O.B. 14231, Westlands, Nairobi.

Bishops:

Eldoret: Most Rev. JOHN NJENGA, P.O.B. 842, Eldoret.

Kisii: Most Rev. TIBERIUS MUGENDI, P.O.B. 140, Kisii.

Kisumu: Most Rev. J. DE REEPER, P.O.B. 150, Kakamega, Kisumu.

Kitui: Most Rev. W. DUNNE, P.O.B. 119, Kitui.

Machakos: Most Rev. RAPHAEL NDINGI, P.O.B. 344, Machakos.

Marsabit: Most Rev. C. H. CAVALLERA, P.O. Maralal.

Meru: Most Rev. L. BESSONE, P.O.B. 16, Meru.

Mombasa: Most Rev. EUGENE BUTLER, P.O.B. 83131, Mombasa.

Nakuru: Apostolic Administrator Father DENIS NEWMAN.

Ngong: Mgr. C. DAVIES, P.O.B. 24801, Karen, Nairobi.

Nyeri: Most Rev. C. GATIMU, P.O.B. 288, Nyeri.

Prefecture Apostolic of Lodwar: Mgr. JOHN MAHON, P.O. Lodwar, via Kitale.

There are some 1,150,000 Roman Catholics in Kenya.

PRESBYTERIAN CHURCH OF EAST AFRICA

Moderator: Rt. Rev. CHARLES MUHORO KARERI, P.O.B. 8286, Nairobi.

Other Protestant denominations are also represented in Kenya.

PRESBYTERIAN CHURCH OF KENYA

Moderator: Rev. CRISPUS KIONGO, P.O.B. 8268, Nairobi.

METHODIST CHURCH OF KENYA

President: Rev. LAWI IMATHIU, P.O.B. 7633, Nairobi.

BAHA'I

There are 118 centres of Baha'i worship in Kenya. Chief African house of worship Kikaya Hill, Kampala, Uganda.

THE PRESS

DAILIES

Daily Nation: P.O.B. 49010, Nairobi; f. 1960; Man. Editor J. RODRIGUES; circ. 69,990.

East African Standard: P.O.B. 30080, Nairobi; f. 1902; Editor KENNETH BOLTON; circ. 37,000.

Taifa Leo: P.O.B. 9010, Nairobi; Swahili; f. 1960; daily and weekly edition; Editor A. G. MBUGUA; circ. 27,087.

SELECTED PERIODICALS

WEEKLIES

Africa Samachar: P.O.B. 41237, Nairobi; f. 1954; Gujarati; Editor C. N. BHATT; circ. 18,000.

Baraza: P.O.B. 30080, Nairobi; f. 1939; Swahili; Editor FRANCIS JOSEPH KHAMISI; circ. 55,000.

Kenya Gazette: P.O.B. 30128, Nairobi; f. 1898; government notices of non-commercial nature and amendments to laws; every Friday, edited for Government of Republic of Kenya; circ. 5,000.

Kitale Weekly: P.O.B. 179, Kitale; every Wednesday.

New Era: P.O.B. 46854, Nairobi; f. 1966; for young people; Editor KUL BHUSHAN; circ. 5,000.

Sunday Nation: P.O.B. 9010, Nairobi; English; Editor P. D. DARLING; circ. 47,500.

Sunday Post: P.O.B. 30127, Nairobi; f. 1936; English; Editor H. L. THORNTON; circ. 16,000.

Taifa Weekly: P.O.B. 9010, Nairobi; f. 1958; Editor A. G. MBUGUA; circ. 14,500.

Trans Nzoia Post.: P.O.B. 34, Kitale; f. 1930; local news, every Wednesday; Editor N. G. LAKHANI.

FORTNIGHTLY

Sikio: P.O.B. 30121, Nairobi; English/Swahili; organ of East African Railways; Editor the Public Relations Officer; circ. 18,000.

MONTHLIES

Afrika Nyota: P.O.B. 9010, Nairobi; Swahili; Editor ANTHONY GEORGE MBUGUA; circ. 33,498.

Africa ya Kesho: P.O. Kijabe; Swahili; Editor J. N. SOMBA; circ. 10,000.

Arrow: P.O.B. 4959, Nairobi; English; f. 1956; children's newspaper; Editor BARBARA PHILLIPS; circ. 25,000.

Drum: P.O.B. 3372, Nairobi; f. 1956; East African edition; Editor TABAN-LO-LLYONG.

East Africa Journal: P.O.B. 30571, Nairobi; Editor Dr. B. A. OGOT; political, economic, social and cultural; circ. 3,000.

E. A. Medical Journal: P.O.B. 41632, Nairobi; f. 1924; Editor HILLARY P. OJIAMBO, M.D.; circ. approx. 1,000.

Flamingo: P.O.B. 20223, Nairobi; f. 1961; Kenya edition of African family magazine; non-political; Editor GERALD MALMED.

Kenya Coffee: P.O.B. 30566, Nairobi; f. 1935; English; publ. by Coffee Board of Kenya; Editor S. N. KINYUA.

Kenya Dairy Farmer: University Press of Africa, Bank House, P.O.B. 43981, Nairobi; f. 1956; English and Swahili; Editor Mrs. J. McALLEN; circ. 4,000.

Kenya Farmer (Journal of the Agricultural Society of Kenya): c/o English Press, P.O.B. 30127, Nairobi; f. 1954; English and Swahili editions; Editor Mrs. I. BAKER; circ. 18,000.

Lengo: P.O.B. 2839, Nairobi; f. 1964; Swahili; Editor ODHIAMBO W. OKITE; circ. 20,000.

Sauti ya Vita: P.O.B. 575, Nairobi; f. 1928; Swahili/English; Salvation Army; Editor Major LAWRENCE COLEMAN; circ. 9,100.

Target: P.O.B. 2839, Nairobi; f. 1964; English; Editor ODHIAMBO W. OKITE; circ. 15,000.

Today in Africa: P.O. Kijabe; English; Editor E. H. ARENSEN; circ. 10,000.

Twi ba Meru: P.O.B. 16, Meru; Kimeru; Roman Catholic; Editor Fr. J. BONZANINO; circ. 5,000.

Uchumi wa Kahawa: P.O.B. 2768, Nairobi; f. 1962; Swahili; Editor E. N. KURIA; African coffee growers; circ. 5,000.

Ukulima wa Kisasa: P.O.B. 9010, Nairobi; f. 1961; Swahili; Editor MOHAMED KOOR; circ. 20,000.

OTHER PERIODICALS

Africana: P.O.B. 49010, Nairobi; f. 1962; incorporating the East African Wild Life Society's Review; Editor JOHN EAMES; circ. 16,000; quarterly.

African Scientist: P.O.B. 30197, Nairobi; Editor Dr. T. ODHIAMBO; circ. 2,000; three times a year.

Busara: P.O.B. 30197, Nairobi; Editor Prof. GURR; circ. 2,000; three times a year.

East African Directory: P.O.B. 41237, Nairobi; f. 1960; commercial directory of seven East African countries; Editor G. C. KIMANI; annual.

E.A. Pharmaceutical Journal: Journal of the Pharmaceutical Society, University Press of Africa, Bank House, P.O.B. 43981, Nairobi; f. 1970; English; Editors Mrs. S. NANJI JUMA and P. PATEL; circ. 4,700; quarterly.

Education in Eastern Africa: P.O.B. 45869, Nairobi; Editor JOHN C. B. BIGALA; circ. 2,000; twice yearly.

Inside Kenya Today: P.O.B. 30025, Nairobi; English; Editor-in-Chief P. J. GACHATHI; circ. 20,000; quarterly.

Kenya Education Journal: P.O.B. 2768, Nairobi; f. 1958; English; Editor W. G. BOWMAN; circ. 5,500; quarterly.

Plan (Architectural Association of Kenya Journal): University Press of Africa, Bank House, P.O.B. 43981, Nairobi; f. 1971; Editor Mrs. E. MANN; circ. 3,000; twice monthly.

Proceedings of the East African Academy: P.O.B. 30756, Nairobi; f. 1963; quarterly.

Spear: P.O.B. 30121, Nairobi; f. 1952; English; published by East African Railways; circ. 6,000; quarterly.

The Journal of the Language Association of Eastern Africa: P.O.B. 30571, Nairobi; Editor T. P. GORMAN; circ. 2,000; twice yearly.

Transafrican Journal of History: P.O.B. 30571, Nairobi; Editor J. A. KIERAN; circ. 2,000; twice yearly.

Women in Kenya: P.O.B. 308, Nairobi; English; quarterly.

NEWS AGENCIES

Kenya News Agency: Information House, Nairobi; f. 1964; teleprinter service based on Reuter, A.F.P., U.P.I., Tass and Home Service.

FOREIGN BUREAUX

Agence France-Presse: P.O.B. 8406, Nairobi.

AP: P.O.B. 47590, Nairobi; Correspondent ANDREW TORCHIA.

Ceteka: P.O.B. 8727, Nairobi.

Ghana News Agency: P.O.B. 6977, Nairobi.

Novosti Press Agency: P.O.B. 30383, Nairobi; Chief. V SAVELYEV.

Reuters: P.O.B. 9331, Nairobi.
Tass also has a bureau in Nairobi.

PUBLISHERS

African Life Publications: P.O.B. 49010, Nairobi; f. 1954; *Africana magazine.*

East African Literature Bureau: P.O.B. 30022, Nairobi; f. 1948; part of East African Community; encourages publication and sale of books; publishes, prints and distributes books, including adult education books; promotes African authorship; Dir. N. M. L. SEMPIRA.

East African Publishing House: P.O.B. 30571, Nairobi; educational, academic and general; also publishes *East Africa Journal* and other periodicals; Dirs. Dr. B. A. OGOT, Dr. I. N. KIMAMBO, Prof. W. B. BANAGE, Dr. D. S. NKUNIKA, H. KALBITZER, J. C. NOTTINGHAM.

Oxford University Press, Eastern Africa Branch: P.O.B. 12532, Nairobi; educational and general books; Gen. Man. R. G. HOUGHTON.

University Press of Africa: Bank House, Government Rd., P.O.B. 3981, Nairobi.

RADIO AND TELEVISION

RADIO

Ministry of Information and Broadcasting: P.O.B. 30025, Nairobi; responsible for Voice of Kenya, the national broadcasting service.

Voice of Kenya: P.O.B. 30456, Nairobi; Kenya Broadcasting Service f. 1959, changed to Kenya Broadcasting Corporation in 1962, changed to State Institution with present name 1964; Dir. J. R. KANGWANA.

Voice of Kenya operates three services: *National:* Kiswahili; *General:* English; *Vernacular:* Hindustani, Kikuyu, Kikamba, Kimeru, Kimasai, Somali, Borana, Luluyia, Kalenjin, Kisii, Kuria, Rendile, Teso, Turkana, Luo; 341 hours' broadcasting a week in 17 languages.

Number of radio receivers: 800,000.

TELEVISION

Voice of Kenya Television: Nairobi; television started in October 1962; revenue from licence fees and commercial advertisements; the first installation was at Nairobi in Band 1 on the 625-line system, and there is a second station at Kisumu. A station is planned at Mazeras and a repeater at Nakuru. A television service started in Mombasa on June 1st, 1970.

Number of TV receivers: 26,850.

FINANCE

BANKING

Central Bank of Kenya: P.O.B. 30081, Nairobi; f. 1966; cap. 45m. Ks.; bank of issue, has assumed the Kenyan responsibilities of the former East African Currency Board; 82 branches; Gov. DUNCAN NDEGWA; Chair. J. N. MICHUKI; Gen. Man. P. B. NOBLE.

Agricultural Finance Corporation: P.O.B. 30367, Nairobi; provides loans to farmers for agricultural purposes including purchase.

COMMERCIAL BANKS

Algemene Bank Nederland N.V.: Head Office: 32 Vijzelstraat, Amsterdam, Netherlands; f. 1824; branches at Nairobi (Man. A. TH. HEERENS) and Mombasa (Man. J. J. TER BURG).

Bank of Baroda: Mandvi, Baroda, India; f. 1908; Kenya Head Office: Nairobi; branches at Mombasa, Kisumu and Thika; cap. Ind. Rs. 250m.; dep. Ind. Rs. 4,210m.

Bank of India: Head Office: Express Towers, Nariman Point, Bombay, India; f. 1906; branches at Nairobi (Man. N. C. PARIKH), Kisumu, and Mombasa (Man. P. R. MEHTA).

Commercial Bank of Africa Ltd.: P.O.B. 30437, Commercial Bank Building, Standard St., Nairobi; f. 1967 to take over branches in Kenya and Uganda of Commercial Bank of Africa Ltd., incorporated in Kenya; affiliated to Société Financiére pour les Pays d'Outre-Mer, Geneva; Man. Dir. P. HUIZER; Gen. Man. R. M. STANLEY.

Grindlays Bank International (Kenya) Ltd.: P.O.B. 30113, Nairobi; f. 1970; res. K£520,000; merchant and international bankers; 40 per cent government holding; 81 offices in Kenya including 8 in Nairobi and 4 in Mombasa; Gen. Man. R. PLANT.

Habib Bank (Overseas) Ltd.: Nkrumah Rd., Fort Mansion, P.O.B. 83055, Mombasa; f. 1952; cap. p.u. Pak. Rs. 5m.; dep. Pak. Rs. 903,589,780 (June 1972).

Kenya Commercial Bank: Nairobi; f. 1970; 60 per cent government holding.

National Bank of Kenya Ltd.: P.O.B. 12497, Nairobi; f. 1968; cap. p.u. Ks. 15,000,000, dep. Ks. 170,318,440 (June 1971); Chair. P. NDEGWA; Gen. Man. R. S. ATTWOOD.

Standard and Barclays Bank of Kenya Ltd.: Kenyatta Ave., Nairobi; f. 1971; 50 per cent government holding.

STOCK EXCHANGE

Nairobi Stock Exchange: Queensway House, York St., P.O.B. 43633, Nairobi; f. 1954; Chair. F. M. THUO.

INSURANCE

NATIONAL COMPANIES

Jubilee Insurance Co. Ltd.: P.O.B. 30376, Nairobi; f. 1937; Chair. Sir EBOO PIRBHAI, O.B.E.; Man. Dir. P. I. W. VOLKERS, A.C.I.I.

Kenya National Assurance Co.: Nairobi; f. 1965; cap. Ks. 6,015,000; Government holding 67 per cent.

Pan Africa Insurance Co. Ltd.: Pan Africa Insurance Bldg., Kilindini Rd., P.O.B. 90383, Mombasa; f. 1946; cap. p.u. K. sh. 8,000,000; Chair. CHIMANLAL AMBALAL PATEL; Man. A. A. PATEL; Exec. Dir. M. D. NAVARE.

Pioneer General Assurance Society Ltd.: P.O.B. 20333, Nairobi; f. 1930; Chair. OSMAN ALLU; Man. Dir. NIMJI JAVER KASSAM.

FOREIGN COMPANIES

Some twenty of the main British firms, eight Indian companies, and several other insurance organizations are represented in Kenya.

TRADE AND INDUSTRY

East African Industrial Council: P.O.B. 1003, Arusha, Tanzania; grants licences for the scheduled class of products included under the East African Industrial Licensing Ordinance; Chair. D. MWIRARIA.

CHAMBERS OF COMMERCE

Kenya National Chamber of Commerce and Industry: Embassy House, Harambee Ave., P.O.B. 47024, Nairobi; f. 1965; Pres. Z. K. GAKUNJU; Chief Exec. A. M. MATHU.

Constituent Branches:

Mombasa Branch: P.O.B. 90271, Mombasa.

Nakuru Branch: P.O.B. 178, Nakuru.

Kisumu Branch: P.O.B. 771, Kisumu.

Kericho Branch: P.O.B. 407, Kericho.

Meru Branch: P.O.B. 136, Meru.

Kakamega Branch: P.O.B. 420, Kakamega.

Thika Branch: P.O.B. 147, Thika.

Eldoret Branch: P.O.B. 313, Eldoret.

Machakos Branch: P.O.B. 243, Machakos.

Nyeri Branch: P.O.B. 207, Nyeri.

Busia Branch: P.O.B. 86, Busia.

Bungoma Branch: P.O.B. 186, Bungoma.

Embu Branch: P.O.B. 172, Embu.

TRADE ASSOCIATIONS

East African Hides & Skins Exporters' Association: P.O.B. 2384, Mombasa; Secs. Tombooth Ltd.

East African Tea Trade Association: Box 42281, Nairobi; f. 1956; 167 mems.

East African Tanners' Association: c/o Post Office, Limuru.

Hard Coffee Trade Association of Eastern Africa: Box 288, Mombasa; 170 mems.; Pres. H. G. FABIAN.

Kenya Wattle Manufacturers' Association: P.O. Box 190, Eldoret.

Mild Coffee Trade Association of Eastern Africa: P.O.B. 2732, Nairobi; f. 1945; 80 mems.

STATUTORY BOARDS

Central Province Marketing Board: P.O.B. 189, Nyeri.

Coffee Board of Kenya: P.O.B. 30566, Nairobi; f. 1947; Chair. E. N. KURIA; Gen. Man. J. MURENGA.

Kenya Dairy Board: P.O. Box 30406, Nairobi.

Kenya Sisal Board: Mutual Building, Kimathi St., P.O.B. 1179, Nairobi; Exec. Officer R. WILSON-SMITH.

Maize and Produce Board: P.O.B. 30586, Nairobi; f. 1966; Chair. L. G. SAGINI; Gen. Man. J. E. OPEMBE.

Nyanza Province Marketing Board: P.O. Box 217, Kisumu.

Pyrethrum Board of Kenya: P.O.B. 420, Nakuru; f. 1935; 21 mems.; Chair. I. KURIA.

Pyrethrum Marketing Board: P.O.B. 420, Nakuru; f. 1964; Chair. I. N. KURIA; publ. *Pyrethrum Post* (twice-yearly).

Tea Board of Kenya: P.O.B. 20064, Nairobi; f. 1951; 13 mems.; Chair. Sir P. S. T. MIRIE; Sec. B. C. A. SCOTT.

DEVELOPMENT CORPORATIONS

Agricultural Development Corporation: Nairobi; f. 1965 to promote and execute schemes for agricultural development and reconstruction.

Commonwealth Development Corporation: P.O.B. 43233, Nairobi; the C.D.C. had 46 projects in the East Africa Region in December 1969.

Development Finance Co. of Kenya Ltd.: P.O.B. 30483, Nairobi; f. 1963; private limited company with government participation; cap. £3m.

East African Industrial Research Organization: P.O.B. 30650, Nairobi; f. 1942; research and advisory service in the technical problems of industrial development; Dir. C. L. TARIMU.

Industrial and Commercial Development Corporation: P.O.B. 5519, Nairobi; f. 1954; financed by the Government; facilitates the industrial and commercial development of Kenya; Chair. J. KERAGORI; Exec. Dir. J. E. MATU WAMAE.

Kenya Tea Development Authority: P.O.B. 30213, Nairobi; f. 1960 to develop tea growing among African smallholders, supported by the Kenya Government, C.D.C., the World Bank and German Federal Republic; 50,000 registered growers (1969–70); Chair. JACKSON KAMAU; Gen. Man. C. K. KARANJA. On its formation the Kenya Tea Development Authority took over the duties of the Special Crops Development Authority which had been founded in 1960.

Settlement Fund Trustees: c/o Ministry of Lands and Settlements, P.O.B. 30450, Nairobi; administers one of the most ambitious land purchase programmes involving over one million acres for resettlement of African farmers. Over 34,000 plots were allocated to 34,000 families between June 1963 and May 1971.

EMPLOYERS' ASSOCIATIONS

Federation of Kenya Employers: Consular House, Coronation Avenue, P.O.B. 9311, Nairobi; f. 1956; 3,720 mems., 10 affiliated associations; Pres. D. C. ALLEN, M.B.E.; Exec. Officer DAVID RICHMOND.

AFFILIATES

Kenya National Farmers' Union: P.O. Box 3148, Nairobi; f. 1947; 2,500 mems.; non-racial; amalgamated with Kenya African National Traders' and Farmers' Union 1961; Pres. The Rt. Hon. Lord DELAMERE; Exec. Officer ALEC WARD.

Kenya Tea Growers' Association: P.O. Box 320, Kericho; f. 1931; 54 mems.; Exec. Officer J. BARKER.

Kenya Sisal Growers' Association.

Kenya Coffee Growers' Association: P.O. Box 12832, Nairobi; f. 1960; Chair. Maj. V. E. KIRKLAND.

Kenya Sugar Employers' Union.

Distributive and Allied Trades Association.

Motor Trades Association.

Engineering Employers' Association.

Tobacco, Brewing and Bottling Employers' Association.

Grain Milling and Food Processing Employers' Association.

Kenya Farmers' Association (Co-operative) Ltd.: P.O. Box 35, Nakuru.

TRADE UNIONS

Central Organization for Trade Unions: Solidarity House, P.O.B. 13000, Nairobi; f. 1965 as the only federal body of Trade Unionism in Kenya; Pres. S. NJOKA; Sec.-Gen. J. D. AKUMU.

PRINCIPAL AFFILIATED UNIONS

Building and Construction Workers' Union: P.O.B. 9628, Nairobi; Gen. Sec. J. MURUGU.

Chemical Workers' Union: P.O.B. 13026, Nairobi; Gen. Sec. WERE D. OGUTU.

Common Services African Civil Servants' Union: P.O.B. 4065, Nairobi; Gen. Sec. M. KIMEU.

Dockworkers' Union: P.O.B. 8207, Mombasa; 7,600 mems.; Gen. Sec. JUMA BOY.

Domestic and Hotel Workers' Union: P.O.B. 7326, Nairobi; 34,700 mems.; Gen. Sec. D. MUGO.

Electrical Trades Workers' Union: P.O.B. 20226, Nairobi; Gen. Sec. MORRIS JAMES OKUMO.

External Telecommunication Workers' Union: P.O.B. 30488, Nairobi; Gen. Sec. S. M. MURIU.

Game and Hunting Workers' Union: P.O.B. 7509, Nairobi; Gen. Sec. M. NDOLO.

Kenya African Custom Workers' Union: P.O.B. 9178, Mombasa; Gen. Sec. S. N. SEIF.

Kenya Commercial, Food and Allied Workers' Union: Kundi Bldg., P.O.B. 6818, Nairobi; multiracial; 12,900 mems.; Gen. Sec. G. S. MUHANJI.

Motor Engineering Workers' Union: P.O.B. 6025, Likoni, Mombasa; 5,900 mems.; Gen. Sec. J. AKAMA.

Kenya Timber and Furniture Workers' Union: P.O.B. 13172, Nairobi; 12,200 mems.; Gen. Sec. E. OSOTSI.

Kenya Union of Sugar Plantation Workers: P.O.B. 766, Kisumu; Gen. Sec. J. D. AKUMU.

Local Government Workers' Union: P.O.B. 10828, Nairobi; Gen. Sec. J. KAREBE.

Motor Engineering and Allied Workers' Union: P.O.B. 4926, Nairobi; Gen. Sec. F. OMIDO.

Kenya Plantation and Agricultural Workers' Union: P.O.B. 1161, Nakuru; 43,400 mems.; Gen. Sec. P. MWANGI.

National Union of Seamen: P.O.B. 1123, Mombasa; Gen. Sec. I. S. ABDALLAH.

Petroleum and Oil Workers' Union: P.O.B. 10376, Nairobi; Gen. Sec. OMEGA OSENA.

Printing and Kindred Trade Workers' Union: P.O.B. 12358, Nairobi; Gen. Sec. WILSON E. C. MUKUNA.

Quarry and Mine Workers' Union: P.O.B. 8125, Nairobi; Gen. Sec. F. ODIYO.

Railway African Union: P.O.B. 12029, Nairobi; 16,100 mems.; Pres. I. OWUOR MANGO; Gen. Sec. JOHNSON MWANDAWIRO; African.

Shoe and Leather Workers' Union: P.O.B. 9629, Nairobi; Gen. Sec. J. A. AWICHI.

Tailors and Textile Union: P.O.B. 12076, Nairobi; f. 1948; Pres. S. OSORE; Gen. Sec. W. K. MUGERWA; African.

Transport and Allied Workers' Union: P.O.B. 5171, Nairobi; f. 1946; African; Pres. WALTER OSADHO; Gen. Sec. JAMES CHEGGE; 6,200 mems.

Union of Postal and Telecommunication Workers: P.O.B. 8155, Nairobi; Gen. Sec. C. ADONGO.

PRINCIPAL INDEPENDENT UNIONS

Senior Civil Servants' Association of Kenya: P.O.B. 40107, Nairobi; f. 1959; 2,000 mems.; Pres. F. B. MAIKO; Gen. Sec. B. A. OHANGA; publ. *The Senior Civil Servants' Magazine.*

East African Railways and Harbours Asian Union (Kenya): P.O.B. 1270, Mombasa; f. 1947; 1,017 mems.; Pres. L. V. THAKAR; Gen. Sec. M. S. JASWAL.

Kenya National Union of Teachers: P.O.B. 30407, Nairobi; f. 1957; Sec.-Gen. S. J. KIONI.

MAJOR INDUSTRIAL COMPANIES

The following are a few of the largest companies in terms either of capital investment or employment.

A. Baumann and Company Ltd.: P.O.B. 538, Mansion House, Nairobi; f. 1926, incorporated 1948; cap. K£1,063,089.

The company's branches in Kenya, Tanzania and Uganda carry on business as steamship agents, warehousemen, provender millers, exporters of tea; it owns its own coffee plantations and has substantial investments in a large number of local companies and industries.

Chair. E. BAUMANN; Man. J. M. SMITH; 500 employees.

Kenya Breweries Ltd.: P.O.B. 30161, Nairobi; manufacture of lager beers, Guinness stout and malting barley.

East African Portland Cement Co. Ltd.: P.O.B. 101, Nairobi; production of cement and allied products.

Consolidated Holdings Ltd.: P.O.B. 30080, Nairobi; f. 1919; cap. K£2,140,410.

Holding company with interests in all three East African countries in printing, carton making, packaging, distribution of office equipment and drawing office supplies, road transport contractors, shipping and travel agencies, tour operators, paper mills and newspaper publication.

Chair. M. W. HARLEY; Man. Dir. R. J. SHARPLES, F.C.A.; 2,600 employees.

Hughes Limited: P.O.B. 30060, Nairobi; f. 1949; cap. K£796,563.

Ford agents; sale and maintenance of a range of their products and other agricultural equipment.

Man. Dir. W. DUNLOP; Company Sec. J. P. T. FOSTER; 990 employees.

Kenya Co-operative Creameries Ltd.: P.O.B. 30131, Nairobi; markets the bulk of dairy produce.

TRANSPORT

TRANSPORT

RAILWAYS

East African Railways Corporation: P.O.B. 30121, Nairobi; self-contained and self-financing organization within the East African Community; Chair. D. WADADA; Dir.-Gen. Dr. E. NJUGUNA GAKUO, B.COM., M.A., DR.RER.POL.

There are 3,663 route miles of metre-gauge line in East Africa. The main lines are from Mombasa to Nairobi (Kenya) and Kampala (Uganda) and from Dar es Salaam (Tanzania) to Mwanza (Tanzania).

ROADS

East African Road Services Ltd.: P.O.B. 30475, Nairobi; provide bus services within East Africa from Nairobi to Dar es Salaam, Moshi, Kampala, Mombasa and to all major towns in Kenya.

There are approximately 43,973 km. of roads of varying quality. A total of £11.9m. was spent on road improvement under the 1966–70 development plan. In August 1968 a 309-mile trunk road from Nairobi to Mombasa was opened to traffic. Road development is continuing and the Kenya section of the Nairobi–Dar es Salaam road was tarmacadamized in 1972. Reconstruction to make an all-weather road joining Nairobi to Addis Ababa is well under way in both Kenya and Ethiopia.

SHIPPING

East African Harbours Corporation: P.O.B. 9184, Dar es Salaam, Tanzania; responsible for the harbours functions formerly exercised by the *East African Railways and Harbours*; Chair. P. K. KINYANJUI.

Eastern Africa National Shipping Line: Kilindini; f. 1966 by the co-operation of East and Central African governments and Southern Line Ltd.

Southern Line Ltd.: P.O.B. 90102, Mombasa; managing agents for Eastern Africa National Shipping Line, operating liner services between East Africa and Europe and the Far East.

***

Barber Lines: Mombasa; monthly service to U.S.A. Gulf Ports.

Bay of Bengal African Line: Agents: The African Mercantile Co. (Overseas) Ltd., P.O.B. 90110, Mombasa; cargo services between E. African ports and Bangladesh, Burma, India and Sri Lanka.

British India Line: Agents: Mackenzie Dalgety (Kenya) Ltd., P.O.B. 90120, Mombasa; joint service with Union Castle Line to United Kingdom and continental ports.

Christensen Canadian African Lines: P.O.B. 80149, Mombasa; direct service to and from Canada via South and East African ports.

Clan Line: Agents: The African Mercantile Co. (Overseas) Ltd., P.O.B. 90110, Mombasa; cargo services between the United Kingdom and East African ports.

D.O.A.L. (Deutsche Ost Afrika Linie): P.O.B. 90171, Mombasa; services to Europe.

Farrell Lines: Mombasa; monthly services to North Atlantic and U.S.A. East Coast Ports.

Harrison Line: Agents: The African Mercantile Co. (Overseas) Ltd., P.O.B. 90110, Mombasa; services between U.K. and East African ports.

Jadranska Slobodna Plovidba: P.O.B. 84831, Mombasa; services to and from Adriatic and Red Sea ports.

Lloyd Triestino Line: c/o Mitchell Cotts & Co. (East Africa) Ltd., Kilindini Rd., P.O.B. 90141, Mombasa; monthly passenger and cargo services to Italy.

Lykes Lines: P.O.B. 90150, Mombasa; services to U.S.A. Gulf ports via South African ports.

Mitsui O.S.K. Lines Ltd.: P.O.B. 49952, Nairobi; services to Japan, Hong Kong and Malaysia.

NedLloyd (EA) Ltd.: P.O.B. 80149, Mombasa; Africa/Europe services to and from Mediterranean and N.W. Continental ports; Africa/Pacific to U.S.A., Pacific ports and Vancouver.

Oriental African Line: Agents: The African Mercantile Co. (Overseas) Ltd., P.O.B. 90110, Mombasa; cargo services between E. African ports and Malaysia, Singapore, Thailand, Indonesia, Hong Kong and Japan.

Robin Line (*Moore McCormack Lines Inc., Robin Line Service*): c/o Mitchell Cotts and Co. (East Africa) Ltd., Kilindini Rd., P.O.B. 90141, Mombasa; services to U.S.A. Atlantic ports from Kenya and Tanzania, and South and Portuguese East Africa.

Royal Interocean Lines: P.O.B. 90342, Mombasa; services to Singapore/Malaysia, Hong Kong and Japan, Australia, New Zealand and Persian Gulf, with connections to other Far East, Pacific and South American and West African ports.

Scandinavian East Africa Line: Agents: The African Mercantile Co. (Overseas) Ltd., P.O.B. 90110, Mombasa; services between E. African and Scandinavian and Baltic ports.

The Shipping Corporation of India Ltd.: Head Office: Steelcrete House, Dinshaw Wacha Rd., Bombay; Branches: P.O.B. 2653, Calcutta, P.O.B. 82364, Mombasa; services include regular and fast cargo services from India to East Africa.

Southern Line Ltd.: P.O.B. 90102, Mombasa; managing agents for Eastern Africa National Shipping Line, operating liner services between East Africa and Europe and the Far East.

Svedel Line: P.O.B. 84831, Mombasa; freight services between East Africa and Red Sea/Continental ports.

Swedish East Africa Line: Mombasa; services via Suez to Scandinavian, Baltic and North French ports.

Union-Castle Line: Agents: Mackenzie Dalgety (Kenya) Ltd., P.O.B. 90120, Mombasa; joint service with British India Line offers regular sailings to United Kingdom.

Zim Lines: P.O.B. 150, Mombasa; services to Eilat via Red Sea ports.

CIVIL AVIATION

Caspair Limited: Head Office: P.O.B. 42890, Nairobi; Entebbe (Uganda) Office: P.O.B. 59, Entebbe; Man. Capt. STRETTON; f. 1947; Man. Dir. H. R. PARKER; aircraft charter, sales and maintenance.

East African Airways Corporation: *Headquarters:* Sadler House, Koinange St., P.O.B. 41010, Nairobi, Kenya; f. 1945; owned by the East African States; operates extensive services throughout Kenya, Tanzania and Uganda; also regular scheduled services to Europe, the United Kingdom, Pakistan, India, Zambia, Ethiopia, Somalia, Mauritius and Malawi; passenger and cargo charters are operated by Simbair, a subsidiary of EAA; fleet of four VC 10, three DC-9, four Fokker F-27, four Twin Otter and six DC-3; Chair. Chief A. S. FUNDIKIRA; Dir.-Gen. JUSTIN OYERE OLWENDO OKOT (Uganda).

The East African Directorate of Civil Aviation: P.O.B. 30163, Nairobi; established under the Air Transport Authority in 1948; to advise on all matters of major policy affecting Civil Aviation within the jurisdiction of the East African Community, on annual estimates and on Civil Aviation legislation; the Area Control Centre and an Area Communications Centre are at East African Community, Nairobi. Air traffic control is operated at Nairobi, Dar es Salaam, Entebbe and Mombasa airports, at Wilson (Nairobi) Aerodrome and aerodromes at Arusha, Kisumu, Mwanza, Malindi, Moshi, Mtwara, Tabora, Tanga and Zanzibar; Dir.-Gen. Z. M. BALIDDAWA.

Safari Air Services Tours Ltd.: Head Office: P.O.B. 41951, Nairobi; f. 1969; Man. Dir. JUDY HOURY; tour operators.

The following international airlines run regular services to and from Kenya: Air Zaire, Air France, Air India, Air Madagascar, Alitalia, BOAC, EgyptAir, El Al, Ethiopian Air Lines, KLM, Lufthansa, Olympic, PAA, Sabena, SAS, Somali Airlines, Sudan Airways, Swissair, TWA and Zambia Airways.

POWER

The Kenya Power Co. Ltd.: P.O.B. 7936, Shell BP House, Nairobi; f. 1954; financed by a debenture issue of K£7,500,000.
Bulk generation and importation of electrical energy. Has two hydro-stations on the Tana River, and imports 30 mW. from the Uganda Electricity Board. The bulk is sold to the East African Power and Lighting Co. Ltd.
Chair. V. A. MADDISON; Sec. A. N. NGUGI.

The East African Power and Lighting Co. Ltd.: P.O.B. 30099, Nairobi; f. 1922; cap. K£9,741,504.
The only distributor of electrical power to the public in Kenya.

Chair./Chief Exec. J. K. GECAU; Gen. Man. ISAAC LUGONZO; 2,700 employees.

TOURISM

Ministry of Tourism and Wild Life: P.O. Box 30027, Nairobi; the national tourist body for Kenya.

Kenya Tourist Development Corporation: P.O.B. 42013, Nairobi; f. 1965; Gen. Man. R. M. MAINA; Deputy Gen. Man. W. A. O. MUTSUNE; Finance Man. A. S. BASSAN.

OVERSEAS OFFICE

United Kingdom: Kenya Tourist Office, 318 Grand Buildings, Trafalgar Square, London, W.C.2.

EDUCATION

Education is not compulsory and less than half of the population is literate. The government provides or assists in the provision of schools. Education is multi-racial at all levels. The University College in Nairobi was elevated to the status of National University in July 1970 when the University of East Africa, of which it was formerly a part, dissolved. About 5,000 students a year study overseas.

LEARNED SOCIETIES

Agricultural Society of Kenya: P.O.B. 30176, Nairobi; f. 1901; encourages and assists agriculture in Kenya; holds ten shows per year; Chair. Hon. J. M. WANJIGI, M.P.

British Council, The: Kenya Cultural Centre, P.O.B. 751, College Rd., Nairobi; Rep. R. A. HACK; Regional Offices: Box 90590, City House, Nyerere Ave., Mombasa; Old Barclays Bank Building, Oginga Odinga Rd., P.O.B. 454, Kisumu.

East Africa Natural History Society: P.O.B. 44486, Nairobi; f. 1909; 500 mems.; Pres. J. S. KARMALI; publ. *Journal of the East African Natural History Society and the National Museum.*

East African Library Association: P.O.B. 46031, Nairobi; f. 1956 to promote, establish and improve libraries and book production; approx. 200 mems.; Sec. J. M. NGANGA, A.L.A.

East African Wild Life Society: P.O.B. 20110, Nairobi; maintains interest in wild life and its conservation; 14,000 mems.; publs. *Africana* (quarterly), *East African Wild Life Journal* (annually).

Goethe Institut: P.O.B. 9468, Nairobi; Dir. F. NAGEL.

Kenya History Society: Hon. Sec., P.O. Box 14474, Westlands, Nairobi; f. 1955; objects are the collection of documents and antiquities, archaeological research, and the publication of historical and antiquarian papers; Chair. Col. R. D. CROFT WILCOCK.

Mines and Geological Department: Cathedral Rd., P.O.B. 30009, Nairobi; f. 1933; administers laws governing mining and prospecting; provides information on the geology and minerals of Kenya; produces geological maps of the country; 97 mems.; library of 22,000 vols.; Commissioner L. D. SANDERS, B.SC., PH.D., A.M.I.M., C.ENG., F.G.S.; Chief Geologist J. WALSH, B.SC., PH.D.; publ. *Annual Report.*

Mombasa Law Society: P.O.B. 1386, Mombasa; f. 1922; 56 mems.; Pres. SADIQ GHALIA; Sec. AHMEDALI Y. A. JIWAJI.

RESEARCH INSTITUTES

(*See* also under University)

British Institute in Eastern Africa: P.O.B. 47680, Nairobi; f. 1960; library of 1,400 vols.; research into the history and archaeology of Eastern Africa, for which a number of studentships are offered; Pres. L. P. KIRWAN, G.M.C.; Dir. NEVILLE CHITTICK; publ. *Azania* (annually).

Coffee Research Station: P.O.B. 4, Ruiru; f. 1949; Dir. C. BOULD, M.SC., PH.D.; coffee berry disease research and new systems of coffee culture; publ. *Annual Report.*

Cotton Research Station: P.O. Kibos, Nyanza Province; Dir. J. H. BRETTELL.

Desert Locust Control Organization for Eastern Africa: P.O.B. 30023, Nairobi; f. 1962; headquarters in Asmara, Ethiopia.

East African Community: P.O.B. 1001, Arusha, Tanzania; Sec.-Gen. C. G. MAINA; the East African Community administers 12 research groups, the following in Kenya (for others *see* chapters on Tanzania and Uganda):

East African Agriculture and Forestry Research Organization: P.O.B. 30148, Nairobi; f. 1948; planning of research; soil science; plant physiology; plant genetics and breeding; forestry and forest entomology; systematic botany; animal industry; library of 20,000 vols.; Dir. Dr. B. N. HAJISU, PH.D.; publ. *Annual Report*, and edits *East Africa Agriculture Journal.*

East African Industrial Research Organization: P.O. Box 1587, Nairobi; f. 1948; provides advice for established local industrial concerns and gives assistance in the establishment of new industries on the utilization of local materials; Dir. C. TARIMO; publ. *Annual Report.*

East African Leprosy Research Centre (*The John Lowe Memorial*): P.O.B. 44, Busia, Uganda (situated on Kenya side of Uganda/Kenya border); Dir. Y. OTSYULA; publ. *Annual Report.*

East African Veterinary Research Organisation: P.O. Box 32, Kikuyu; f. 1948; preparation and issue of biological products and research into animal health and animal diseases; Dir. A. RASHID; publ. *Annual Report.*

Grassland Research Station: P.O.B. 144, Molo; f. 1952; sub-station of the National Agricultural Research Station, Kitale; Officer-in-Charge I. J. PARTRIDGE.

Institute for Medical Research and Training: c/o Medical Research Laboratory, P.O. Box 30141, Nairobi; f. 1964 for research and doctor training; *see* also Medical Training Centre, Medical School, under Colleges.

Interafrican Bureau for Animal Resources: P.O.B. 30786, Nairobi; Dir. Dr. P. G. ATANG.

Kenya Sisal Board Research Unit: P.O.B. 7, Thika; f. 1939; Research Officer W. A. BURGWIN. Research into the agronomy of sisal, end uses and allied matters.

Medical Research Laboratory (Medical Department, Kenya): P.O.B. 30141, Nairobi; all branches of medicine; library; Dir. M. G. ROGOFF.

National Agricultural Laboratories: Ministry of Agriculture; P.O.B. 30028, Nairobi; Dir. and Senior Soil Chemist S. N. MUTURI, M.SC.; Senior Plant Pathologist J. J. ONDIEKI, M.SC.; Senior Entomologist J. B. MUTMAMIA, M.SC.; Senior Cotton Officer K. J. BROWN, PH.D.; Heads of Potato Unit S. K. NJUGUNA, M.SC. and W. BLACK, PH.D.; Official Seed Tester D. N. MARIRA.

Plant Breeding Station: Ministry of Agriculture, P.O. Njoro; f. 1927; 20 professional staff; Officer-in-Charge Dr. M. W. CORMACK; improvement of wheat, barley and oats.

Pyrethrum Bureau, The: P.O.B. 420, Nakuru; P.O.B. K-2383, Hong Kong; f. 1960; Technical information on pyrethrum as an insecticide; publ. *Pyrethrum Post* (twice yearly); Technical Dir. D. R. MACIVER.

Tea Research Institute of East Africa: P.O.B. 91, Kericho; studies on the production of tea, with special emphasis on agronomic, botanical and chemical aspects; substations in Tanzania and Uganda; library; Dir. E. HAINSWORTH.

Ministry of Agriculture Division of Veterinary Services: P.O. Kabete; f. 1903; library of 15,100 vols.; Dir. I. E. MURIITHI, B.V.M.S., M.R.C.V.S.; publ. *Annual Report*.

LIBRARIES

British Council Library: P.O.B. 40751, College Rd., Nairobi; f. 1948; 11,000 vols.; brs. at Mombasa (15,000 vols.) and Kisumu (16,000 vols.); Librarian G. A. R. DAVIS, A.L.A.

Central Government Archives: P.O.B. 30050, Nairobi.

Desai Memorial Library: P.O. Box 1253, Nairobi; f. 1942; public library and reading room; 31,800 vols.; books in Swahili, Gujarati, Hindi, Urdu, Gurumukhi and English; reference, newspaper and periodical sections; 1,151 mems.; Pres. A. M. SADARUDDIN; Sec. HARSHAD JOSHI.

East African Agriculture and Forestry Research Organization Library: P.O.B. 30148, Nairobi; approx. 30,000 vols.; joint library with the East African Veterinary Research Organization; Research Librarian L. D. ROGERSON, A.L.A.

Ismail Rahimtulla Trust Library: P.O.B. 333, Nairobi; 5,250 vols.; Librarian C. M. PATEL.

Kenya National Archives: P.O.B. 30520, Nairobi.

Kenya National Library Service: P.O.B. 30573, Nairobi; f. 1967; 50,000 vols., 200 periodicals; br. at Kisumu; Chief Librarian FRANCIS OTIENO PALA, M.A., B.LS.

McMillan Memorial Library: P.O.B. 791, Nairobi; f. 1931; 110,000 vols. in Lending Library, 10,000 vols. in Reference Library; Chief Librarian RALPH OPONDO, A.L.A.

Seif Bin Salim Public Library: P.O.B. 90283, Mombasa; f. 1903; 18,399 vols., general subjects, mainly in English and Gujarati; Librarian Mrs. M. D. KARKARIA.

United States Information Service Library: P.O.B. 30143, Nairobi; arts, history, science; 5,000 vols., 100 periodicals; Librarian P. E. BOCK.

University of Nairobi Library: P.O.B. 30197, Nairobi; f. 1956; 95,000 vols., 1,300 periodicals; includes collections of various professional institutions; Librarian J. NDEGWA, F.L.A.

MUSEUMS

Fort Jesus Museum: P.O.B. 82412, Mombasa; f. 1960; inside 16th-century Portuguese fortress overlooking Mombasa harbour; finds from various Arab-African sites and from Fort Jesus show the history of the Kenya coast; library of 280 vols. and numerous offprints; Curator N. A. MUDOGA.

National Museum: P.O.B. 40658, Nairobi; f. 1911; all branches of natural history, pre-history, and geology; controlled by Museum Trustees of Kenya; joint library with East Africa Natural History Society, 10,000 vols.; Dir. R. E. LEAKEY; publ. *Journal of The East Africa Natural History Society and National Museum.*

Stoneham Museum and Research Centre: P.O. Kitale; collection of Africana, anthropology, art, botany, geology, zoology; library of 6,000 vols., and scientific publications; Dir. Lt.-Col. H. F. STONEHAM, O.B.E.

UNIVERSITY

UNIVERSITY OF NAIROBI

P.O.B. 30197, NAIROBI, KENYA

Telephone: Nairobi 27441.

Telegraphic Address: Varsity, Nairobi.

Founded in 1956 as Royal Technical College of East Africa, new name, with university college status, in 1961.

Principal: Dr. JOSEPH N. KARANJA, M.A.
Registrar: S. KARANJA, M.A.
Librarian: J. NDEGWA, M.A., F.L.A.

Number of teachers: 340.
Number of students: 3,857.

DEANS:

Faculty of Agriculture: Prof. R. B. CONTANT.
Faculty of Architecture, Design and Development: R. H. NELMS.
Faculty of Arts: Dr. J. J. OKUMU.
Faculty of Commerce: Prof. J. D. MUIR.
Faculty of Education: Dr. F. F. INDIRE.
Faculty of Engineering: P. M. GITHINJI.
Faculty of Law: G. G. S. MUNORU.
Faculty of Medicine: Prof. J. M. MUNGAI.
Faculty of Science: Dr. D. ODHIAMBO.
Faculty of Veterinary Medicine: Prof. G. M. MUGERA.

CONSTITUENT COLLEGE:

Kenyatta College: P.O.B. 43844, Nairobi; concentrates on producing graduate teachers for secondary schools and teacher training colleges.

Number of students: 280.

ATTACHED INSTITUTES:

Institute of Adult Studies: f. 1961; offering short courses and a one-year course to mature students.
Director: P. G. H. HOPKINS.

Institute for Development Studies: f. 1965; engaging in research into economic, social and African cultural affairs.

Director of Social Science Division: J. S. COLEMAN.
Director of Institute of African Studies: B. A. OGOT.

School of Journalism: P.O.B. 30179, Nairobi; f. 1970.
Director: W. H. McATEER (acting).

Number of teachers: 6.
Number of students: 23.

COLLEGES

East Africa Conservatoire of Music: P.O. Box 1343, Nairobi, Kenya; f. 1944; Dir. NAT KOFSKY, HON.R.C.M.

Egerton College: P.O. Njoro; Diplomas in Agriculture, Farm Management, Animal Husbandry, Range Management, Dairy Technology, Agricultural Engineering, Vocational Agriculture; Principal Dr. P. T. OBWAKA, PH.D.

Institute for Medical Research and Training:

Medical Training Centre: c/o the Senior Medical Officer in Charge, P.O.B. 30195, Nairobi; for training all para-medical personnel in Kenya.

Medical School: Kenyatta National Hospital, c/o the Dean of the Faculty of Medicine, P.O.B. 30588, Nairobi; for training doctors.

Kenya Institute of Administration: P.O. Lower Kabete; f. 1961; Residential training for the Kenya Public Service in Public Administration, Local Government, Community Development, Co-operative Development, Social Work, Management, Probation, Lay Magistrates and allied fields; library of 40,000 vols. and a fully equipped Audio-visual Aids Centre and Language Laboratory; Principal H. J. NYAMU; 65 teachers, 550 students; publs. *Journal, Administration in Kenya, K.I.A. Occasional Papers.*

Kenya Polytechnic: P.O.B. 20318, Nairobi; f. 1961; Depts. of Engineering, Science, Building, Business Studies, Printing, Catering and Hotel Training, Technical Teacher Training.

Principal: H. F. MTULA, B.A.

Number of teachers: 133.

Kenya School of Law: P.O.B. 30369, Nairobi; f. 1963.

Principal: T. JACKSON.

Registrar: J. V. ANDERSON.

Librarian: A. WETINDI.

Library of 2,500 volumes.

Number of students: 110.

Mombasa Polytechnic: P.O.B. 90420, Mombasa; f. 1948; number of students 1,000; C. & G. Craft and U.L.C.I.; full-time, part-time and evening technical courses; Business studies and Science evening classes.

Principal: P. C. KING'ORI.

Number of teachers: 42.

Number of students: 600 (full time).

Strathmore College of Arts and Sciences: P.O.B. 25095, Nairobi, Kenya; f. 1960; residential college for 225 students, offering courses in Science and Accountancy.

SELECT BIBLIOGRAPHY

Works on Kenya, Tanzania and Uganda generally

GREGORY, ROBERT G. *India and East Africa. A History of Race Relations within the British Empire 1890–1939.* Oxford University Press, 1972.

MANGAT, J. S. *A History of the Asians in East Africa c. 1895–1912.* Oxford, Clarendon Press, 1969.

MORGAN, W. T. W. (Ed.). *East Africa: its Peoples and Resources.* Nairobi, Oxford University Press, 1970.

NICHOLLS, C. S. *The Swahili Coast.* London, Allen and Unwin, 1972.

PEARSON, D. S. *Industrial Development in East Africa.* Nairobi, Oxford University Press, 1969.

Report of the East African Royal Commission 1953–1955, Cmd. 9475. London, H.M.S.O., 1955.

Surveys of African Economics, Vol. 2: Kenya, Tanzania, Uganda and Somalia, Washington, D.C., International Monetary Fund, 1969.

Treaty for East African Co-operation. Nairobi, Government Printer, 1967.

VAN ARKADIE, BRIAN, and GHAI, D. "The East African Economies", in ROBSON, P., and LURY, D. (Eds.), *The Economies of Africa.* London, Allen and Unwin, 1969.

Kenya

African Socialism and its Application to Planning in Kenya. Sessional Paper No. 10, Nairobi, Government Printer, 1965.

BENNETT, G. *Kenya, A Political History; the Colonial Period.* London, Oxford University Press, 1963.

BLUNDELL, SIR MICHAEL. *So Rough a Wind.* London, Weidenfeld and Nicolson, 1964.

DALE, I. R., and GREENWAY, P. J. *Kenya Trees and Shrubs.* Nairobi, Buchanan's Kenya Estates Ltd. in association with Hatchards, 1961.

EDWARDS, E. O. "Development Planning in Kenya since Independence", *East African Economic Review, 4/2,* 1968.

GERZEL, C. *The Politics of Independent Kenya.* London, Heinemann; Nairobi, East Africa Publishing House, 1970.

HUXLEY, E. *White Man's Country,* 2 vols. London, Chatto and Windus, 1935, reprinted 1956.

MBOYA, TOM. *The Challenge of Nationhood.* London, André Deutsch, 1970.

MORGAN, W. T. W. *Nairobi: City and Region.* Nairobi, Oxford University Press, 1967.

MORGAN, W. T. W., and SHAFFER, N. MANFRED. *Population of Kenya: distribution and density.* Nairobi, Oxford University Press, 1966.

MUNGEAM, G. H. *British Rule in Kenya, 1898–1912.* London, Clarendon Press, 1966.

MURRAY-BROWN, JEREMY. *Kenyatta.* London, Allen and Unwin, 1972.

ODINGA, OGINGA. *Not Yet Uhuru.* London, Heinemann, 1967.

OMINDE, S. H. *Land and Population Movements in Kenya.* London, Heinemann, 1968.

PULFREY, W. *Geology and Mineral Resources of Kenya.* Nairobi, Government Printer, 1960.

Republic of Kenya, *Development Plan 1970–74.* Nairobi, Government Printer.

ROSBERG, C. G., and NOTTINGHAM, J. *The Myth of "Mau Mau".* New York, Praeger; London, Pall Mall; Nairobi, East Africa Publishing House; 1966.

SHEFFIELD, J. R. (Ed.). *Education, Employment and Rural Development.* Nairobi, East Africa Publishing House, 1967.

Treaty for East African Co-operation. Nairobi, Government Printer, 1967.

Lesotho

PHYSICAL AND SOCIAL GEOGRAPHY*

John Amer

PHYSICAL FEATURES

This small country of 11,716 sq. miles is completely surrounded by South Africa. It is situated at the highest part of the Drakensberg escarpment on the eastern rim of the South African plateau. About two-thirds of Lesotho is very mountainous. Elevations in the eastern half of the country are mostly above 8,000 ft. and in the north-east and along the eastern border exceed 11,000 feet. This is a region of very rugged relief, bleak climate and a heavy annual rainfall of 75 in., where the headstreams of the Orange River have cut deep valleys. Westwards the land descends through a foothill zone of rolling country between 6,000 and 7,000 ft. to Lesotho's main lowland area. This strip of land along the western border, part of the high veld, averages 25 miles in width and lies at around 5,000 ft. Yearly rainfall averages here are between 25 and 30 in. and climatic conditions are generally more pleasant. However, frost may occur throughout the country in winter and hail is a summer hazard everywhere. The light, sandy soils developed on the Karoo sedimentaries of the western lowland compare unfavourably with the fertile black soils of the Stormberg basalt in the uplands. The temperate grasslands of the west also tend to be poorer than the montane grasslands of the east.

POPULATION AND NATURAL RESOURCES

The marked physical contrasts between east and west are reflected in the distribution and density of population, which numbered 935,000 (excluding absentee workers) in 1971. Apart from some 2,000 Europeans and a few hundred Asians, the population is entirely Basotho. No land can be alienated to non-Basotho and the Europeans are mainly engaged in administration, missions and commerce. Approximately two-thirds of the population are concentrated in the western lowland and dense settlement is also found in the valleys of the upland zone. Lesotho suffers from severe overpopulation, partly because of the unsuitability of much of the east for human settlement. Population pressure has resulted (i) in permanent settlement up to 8,000 ft. in the higher areas, formerly used for summer grazing; (ii) in very serious soil erosion, particularly in the west; and (iii) in the country's inability to support all its population, necessitating migration of labour to South Africa, on which some 200,000 males are dependent for paid employment. Unfortunately, Lesotho's prospects for future development are not very great. Only about one-eighth of its area is cultivable and the country is not well endowed with natural resources apart from water. Plans for the export of a regulated water supply and hydroelectric power to South Africa are presently under study. Their implementation would involve the construction of a dam at Oxbow on the Malibamatso River, together with other dams. Mineral resources are disappointing; at present mineral production is limited to small diamond operations in the Mokhotlong area of the north-east.

* See map on p. 758.

RECENT HISTORY

Jack Halpern

The Basotho (Basuto), who owe the formation of their nation in the early nineteenth century to the consummate political skills of their founder Moshesh, are a remarkable people. They are noted for having the highest literacy rate in southern Africa, a strong sense of proud, corporate identity symbolized by their Paramount Chief (who was recognized as King shortly before formal independence on October 4th, 1966), and a high degree of political awareness and sophistication. The latter qualities have been fostered by the constant threat to their independent survival posed by the total encirclement of their poor and eroded mountain kingdom by the Republic of South Africa.

Moshesh, who was probably the most outstanding early leader produced by southern Africa, welded the Basotho together from the remnants of tribes which had been made refugees through the inter-African "wars of calamity" launched by the Zulu kings Chaka and Dingaan, only to be caught up in the wider British-Boer conflict. At the cost of losing large areas of Basutoland to the expansionist Boers, Moshesh finally persuaded Britain to assume direct responsibility for Basutoland in 1884, and the Basotho became British subjects. One explicit proviso was that no white should be allowed to acquire land in Basutoland, and this has been observed to the present day.

Except for heeding, at times reluctantly, the unwavering opposition of all the Basotho to incorporation into South Africa, for which provision had been made in the Act of Union of 1910, British policy was characterized for over half a century by indifference and parsimony.

Britain, in effect, let a proliferating chieftainship govern until the 1930s. This entrenchment of chiefs had as its political effect a strong conservative resistance to belated British attempts to centralize and modernize the administration of the country and, subsequently, to hostility on the part of influential chiefs to the pace-setting Basutoland Congress Party which, *inter alia*, demanded changes in the chiefs' crucial allocations of land-use (*see* Lesotho Economy, page 465) and judicial functions. With some notable exceptions, the Basotho chiefs have been and are a politically conservative element.

The Basotho have a long but latterly atrophying tradition of practising democracy through the local or national *pitso* or general assembly. With the consent of a national *pitso* in 1903 the Basutoland National Council was established to advise on domestic affairs. Ninety-four of its 100 members were nominated by the Paramount Chief, and it was naturally highly conservative, with a long and ultimately successful struggle necessary to transform it into a largely elected body.

After the Second World War, however, the British administration, whilst still hamstrung by lack of funds from London and cheaply recruited and therefore largely low-calibre administrators from South Africa, began to build up a centralized administration which, though lacking any clear policy or plan, sometimes approved of and helped the pressures for democratization that the Basotho themselves generated. The administration, however, steadfastly refused to discuss the need for an elected Legislative Council, though even so eminent an authority as Lord Hailey urged its immediate establishment in a report commissioned by the Secretary of State for Commonwealth Relations, published in 1953. But Lord Hailey's report did lead to the appointment of an Administrative Reforms Committee under Sir Henry Moore, which reported in 1954. Moore's terms of reference excluded the question of a Legislative Council, but the determined attempt by every shade of Basotho opinion to force consideration by Moore of the Legislative Council issue proved a turning point in Basotho political life and the effective beginning of its modern form.

With the Nationalist Party in surrounding South Africa energetically engaged since 1948 in its policy of *apartheid*, physical incorporation had become a dead letter, but South African influence had not. What now emerged in Basutoland were the parties, groupings and issues which are the important factors in the political life of independent Lesotho, and which have led to its present crisis.

The Moore Report was rejected by the Basutoland National Council; 66 of its members wrote to London and demanded the replacement of the Resident Commissioner (in effect the Governor); and the British Government dropped the Report. The Council, in 1955, then formally requested internal self-government; Britain agreed to consider proposals, which the Basotho unanimously submitted in 1958. These in effect formed the basis of a constitution granted by Britain, and the first elections were held in 1960. The new Basutoland Council's powers were severely limited, the electoral procedures indirect and tortuous, but, for the first time, in the heart of South Africa, a predominantly black electorate had its substantially democratic say in affecting its government.

Political developments in Lesotho are lent a wider significance by the otherwise crippling fact of its encirclement by South Africa. This encirclement offers the opportunity to compare Lesotho's international connections, such as membership of the UN, the Commonwealth and the OAU, as well as its genuinely self-determined internal politics, with the adjacent South African Bantustans.

Conversely, political life in Lesotho has been heavily influenced by that of South Africa. Prominent Lesotho leaders cut their political milk-teeth in the Republic's now-banned African National Congress, and other parties. Added to this of course, is the heavy political influence which the South African whites, and especially the government and its supporters, have exerted in Basutoland-Lesotho, mainly through economic measures but also through privately channelled financial party support. This has far exceeded the limited political and financial aid selectively given through the OAU and, it seems from the pre-independence elections of 1965, the funds allegedly originating from Moscow and from Peking.

The Basutoland Congress Party, founded in 1952 by Mr. Ntsu Mokhehle and led by him ever since, marked the beginning of modern party politics in Lesotho. Mokhehle built his Congress Party on modern lines, influenced by South Africa's ANC, his attendance at the 1958 All-African Peoples' Conference and by Kwame Nkrumah's Pan-Africanism and charisma. The Basutoland Congress Party handsomely won the 1960 elections, and was instrumental in pushing for the pre-independence constitution of 1964. Ntsu Mokhehle has, however, suffered a series of defections of leading Congress members. His attitude towards the chieftainship changed, too, from one of nationalistic support in the 1950s to hostility. Whilst always conceding, as any Lesotho leader must, the necessity of a *modus vivendi* with South Africa, Ntsu Mokhehle has been and remains the most outspoken opponent of *apartheid*, and today describes himself as a socialist wanting to integrate Lesotho as far as possible with the independent African world. Politically experienced refugees, many still linked with their banned South African parties, have become prominent in Lesotho politics. Since 1962 Mokhehle, alleging ANC plots to oust him, has worked with the rival PAC.

Second in the 1960 elections was the Marema Tlou Party, formed in 1957 by Chief Matete. He was instrumental in helping Bereng Seeiso, who had been studying at Oxford, to force his step-mother, who had been Regent since his childhood, to surrender to him his hereditary place as Paramount Chief. Under the constitution this gave Prince Bereng important powers of nomination to the legislature. The antagonism between him and Leabua Jonathan, who is a minor chief, stems from the latter's support in this "placing" struggle for the conservative old female Regent. Bereng, subsequently King Moshoeshoe II, has conducted a long but unsuccessful campaign for direct executive power.

In 1961 Mr. Bennet Khaketla, a BCP co-founder, was forced into a break by Mr. Mokhehle, and formed the Basutoland Freedom Party, which attracted Congress Party members who had fallen out with Mokhehle. Also formed in 1961 was the Communist Party of Lesotho, but this has played no discernible part in politics.

INDEPENDENCE

Before the 1965 elections the radically-orientated Freedom Party merged with the royalist Marema Tlou—a strange alliance—the new name being the Marema Tlou Freedom Party (MTFP). In 1964 a leadership struggle saw Chief Matete replaced as leader by Dr. Seth Makotoko who, as a medical student in Johannesburg, had also been a member of the ANC Youth League. Despite Dr. Makotoko's abilities and the tacit support of the King, not to speak of alleged financial support from, of all places for a still royalist party, Moscow—the MTFP only came third in the 1965 elections.

These elections were narrowly won by the Basutoland National Party, which had been formed by Chief Leabua Jonathan in 1958. Despite strong support from the hierarchy of the Roman Catholic Church, which is obsessed by an alleged communist danger and is an extremely influential body in Lesotho, the inexperienced Jonathan (himself a convert) did extremely poorly in 1958. By 1965, however, with financial and organizational support from South Africa, Jonathan's BNP came out on top. Whilst declaring his dislike of *apartheid*, Jonathan has successfully presented himself as the man who could achieve the best possible "deal" and closest but still independent relations with South Africa. He alone was permitted into South Africa to campaign amongst the thousands of Basuto migrant workers there, and it would seem that his concentration on bread and butter issues, expressed in the exhortation to "think of your stomachs", appealed particularly to Basotho women who, voting for the first time, comprise a majority of the electorate.

In office, Chief Jonathan has shown increasing toughness, shrewdness and determination, though his opponents naturally question his wisdom.

The British Labour Government helped him at the final constitutional conference, in London in June 1966, by refusing a demand for pre-independence elections made, in an alliance of convenience, by the BCP and MTFP (who in 1960 had between them gained 151,663 votes against the BNP's 108,162). It also rejected the King's demands, now moderated to the power to refer fundamental legislation affecting the future of the country to a national referendum, which would clearly include the fields of defence, external affairs and internal security.

When, shortly after independence, the King continued to demand such power, and scattered unrest occured, Prime Minister Jonathan acted with great toughness. The King was confined to his modest palace, deportation orders issued against four of his advisers, and both Mr. Mokhehle and Dr. Makotoko arrested on charges which were subsequently dropped. The King was forced to sign an undertaking to abdicate if he again interfered in political affairs, though the House of Chiefs, who alone have the power to deal with the kingship and succession, refused to ratify this.

Chief Jonathan broke new ground by making two visits to Dr. Verwoerd, then South Africa's Prime Minister, and was received as an independent Prime Minister. He obtained South African agreement to proceed with the Mailbamatso River Project (formerly the Oxbow Scheme, *see* Economy, p. 465); appointed Mr. Anton Rupert, the Afrikaner who built the Peter Stuyvesant cigarette group, as his industrial adviser; placed seconded South African officials in key positions such as Attorney-General, and Chief Electoral Officer; and simultaneously armed the police—there is no army—more heavily and "purged" it politically.

Thus, when it became clear that he was losing the general election in January 1970, he was in a position to take the most drastic measures to hold on to power.

The Constitution has been suspended; government by decree established; opposition leaders arbitrarily imprisoned; their parties and publications banned; and the courts, in effect, temporarily abolished by the decision of the Chief Justice appointed by Jonathan to suspend his court and return for a time to South Africa. The King was effectively forced to abdicate and go into exile in Holland, leaving his young and inexperienced wife as Regent and his brother under arrest, but he returned in December 1970, accepting a proclamation which prohibits him from taking part in politics. A countrywide campaign of intimidation against critics or opponents of Chief Jonathan has taken place; the civil service, already stretched, has been purged; and a number of attempts at armed opposition in various parts of Lesotho have been bloodily crushed by the élite Police Mobile Unit.

In these operations, Chief Jonathan relied heavily on the loyalty of an English expatriate named Roach, who commanded the police para-military unit, and, reportedly, on arms, ammunition, light aircraft and helicopters emanating from South Africa. It would seem that more than 1,000 men took up arms against Chief Jonathan, and that the police killed about 500 people, some not involved in the fighting.

The stand taken by different churches is significant. The Anglican church took no stand. The hard-liners swung the important Roman Catholic church behind Jonathan because of his avowed anti-communism. The Evangelical church, however, supported the opposition. Its publication, *Leselinyana*, was banned after reporting allegations that opposition followers were being tortured by the police.

In May 1970 Mr. Mokhehle, the arbitrarily imprisoned BCP leader, was moved into "protective custody" whence he reportedly offered to serve in Chief Jonathan's cabinet if fresh and free elections were held at the end of one year. His demands for bringing in British troops and for a Commonwealth Commission of Inquiry into the general elections were apparently dropped.

Towards the end of 1970, Chief Jonathan decreed a five-year "holiday from politics", promising in the meantime to meet "attempts to foster indecision" with force. Mr. Mokhehle had previously warned that once Chief Jonathan's government obtained resumed British aid all serious attempts to work out internally an agreed solution would cease. By the end of 1971, Mr. Mokhehle had been released from custody but placed under house arrest, and over 150 of Chief Jonathan's opponents were believed to be still in gaol. The government announced that Mr. Mokhehle had "signed an agreement to refrain from interfering in certain things".

On Lesotho's fifth anniversary of independence, on October 4th, 1971, Chief Jonathan announced that all political detainees would be released in January 1972, in order "to create a better climate conducive to normalization and reconciliation". Subsequent developments seemed to indicate that Chief Jonathan was preparing for the long-discussed coalition with both the BCP and the MFP. If this was so, however, it seems that he was forced to bow to the ultra-intransigents in his cabinet, notably the Minister to the Prime Minister, Chief Peete Peete, and the Minister of Agriculture, Chief Sekhonyana 'Maseribane. Despite prayers offered up by all churches for political unity at this time, the situation remained unchanged. In a twelve-man cabinet, Chief Jonathan retains the portfolios of Internal Security, Defence and Chief Electoral Officer.

The King's 1972 resumption, on a two months per year basis, of his interrupted Oxford studies would seem to indicate a further diminution of his role, even as a constitutional monarch, in Lesotho's political life.

FOREIGN RELATIONS

Chief Jonathan reacted strongly to African criticism of his *coup d'état*. He resented outside attempts at diplomatic conciliation, including one made by Botswana's President, Sir Seretse Khama (*see* Botswana—Recent History, page 176). Taking the offensive, he sent an assistant minister to Nigeria to affirm Lesotho's staunch independence. Rejecting an OAU appeal not to to proceed with his reported intention to expel—and therefore hand over to South Africa—political refugees in Lesotho, Chief Jonathan riposted by saying: "They want to Cubanize us at our expense. This I will not allow". This was followed by an attack on OAU member-countries for being

unwilling to accept refugees from Lesotho. A letter from 27 South African refugees had been smuggled out to the OAU, and received wide publicity in London.

To explain Lesotho's position, a mission visited Botswana, Ethiopia, Zaire, Kenya, Malawi, Nigeria, Tanzania and Zambia. This led to the establishment of diplomatic relations with Zambia and, according to Chief Jonathan, several offers of scholarships and training courses.

Chief Jonathan attended the Addis Ababa summit meeting of the OAU, where Lesotho and Malawi were the only countries to abstain on a resolution calling on Western powers not to continue supplying arms to South Africa. On his way home, Chief Jonathan discussed this matter in London with the British Prime Minister, Edward Heath.

Chief Jonathan also attended the October 1970 session of the UN, and had talks on investment and aid with the U.S. Secretary of State. On this and other more recent occasions, Chief Jonathan publicly proclaimed his adherence to his interpretation of the Lusaka Manifesto regarding the possibility of "dialogue" with South Africa: force could never change South Africa's policies, but Lesotho could be the bridge for dialogue.

Possibly to illustrate his independence of view, Chief Jonathan has recently made what is for him a sharp public criticism of *apartheid*, which for the first time caused the South African Prime Minister, Mr. Vorster, to attack him publicly. This aside, the relations between the South African and Lesotho governments have remained close and harmonious.

Initial South African reactions to Chief Jonathan's *coup d'état* were cautious, but once he showed that he was firmly in control and retrospectively justified his actions as nipping "a Communist take-over" in the bud, official South African-Lesotho relations returned to normal. Britain and the U.S.A. suspended aid and withheld recognition for some months, but aid was resumed after Chief Jonathan had appealed on humanitarian grounds for famine relief. Diplomatic relations were subsequently restored.

Chief Jonathan has promised a new Constitution, and is clearly thinking of creating a one-party state. It remains to be seen whether the tremendous pressures to which he has subjected the traditional Basotho sense of nationhood survives with sufficient strength to make Lesotho something more than a political as well as an economic South African satellite, and under black dictatorship at that.

ECONOMY
B. D. Giles

AGRICULTURE

Agriculture employs 48 per cent of the male labour force and accounts for about two-thirds of the Gross Domestic Product, subsistence agriculture for about one-quarter. This probably underestimates the subsistence sector because maize (mealies), the principal crop, is often sold by farmers and re-purchased later for home consumption. Substantial amounts of sorghum and wheat are grown, plus some peas, beans and barley. Despite the higher nutritional and market value of alternative crops, most farmers persist with maize. Yields are very low; the only firm figures available come from the 1960 agricultural census which estimated between 700 lb. and 800 lb. per acre for all the crops mentioned above with the exception of beans (320 lb.). There is about one acre of arable land per head of the resident population. This, together with the low yields, would not produce the widespread poverty that exists if there were alternative sources of income that were adequately exploited. Unfortunately, until very recently, there was none.

The principal livestock products marketed are wool and mohair. Here again yields are low. The quality is good and, in the case of wool, it has been improved by substantial imports of merino sheep. Marketing arrangements leave a good deal to be desired, although the Ministry of Agriculture is trying to improve them. In the past the products have not been adequately cleaned and sorted, and traders are alleged to have paid uniform prices without regard to quality. They are sold at the regular auctions at the coast in South Africa.

The large number of cattle seems to be of little commercial value. Neither meat nor milk appear to form an appreciable part of the ordinary diet. Cattle are bartered for younger animals or sold to cattle speculators in South Africa. The Ministry of Agriculture has made some successful interventions in recent years, but the whole of the trade is by no means covered. An abattoir is sometimes proposed, but the uneven flow of stock and the absence of ancillary services probably rule out a successful operation in this field at present.

The system of land tenure is a major obstacle to development. Law and custom in this field is incredibly complex and any brief statement runs the risk of being misleading in some respects. All land is held by the King in trust for the Basotho nation, and it is allocated on his behalf by chiefs. There are no property rights in land, and no land taxes. Land as such cannot be sold, and the sale of a building can only be effected if the appropriate chief re-allocates the land to the purchaser—which he invariably seems to do. This slight element of doubt about the transferability of land has been known to deter potential investors and it has severely limited the acceptability of real estate as collateral for loans. In urban areas recent legislation enables allocations of land to be properly registered and certificates are now issued which appear to be acceptable to the banks as security for mortgages. In rural areas there is no right to compensation for improvements on giving up a holding, and a peasant may lose part of his land if it is more than sufficient to support his family. Dispossession for this reason is rare, but the belief that it could happen may help to account for the low yields that are found. The Basotho are greatly attached to their land tenure system, regarding even leasehold with great suspicion. It has conferred one great benefit on the country: there is not a significant white settler problem.

LINKS WITH SOUTH AFRICA

Poverty and lack of opportunity at home impel many people to seek employment in South Africa. Estimates of the number depend on definitions. The 1966 census enumerated 116,000 Africans who had been absent from the country for not more than five years. Of these, 98,000 were males, 83,000 of them between the ages of 15 and 50. In 1969 it is estimated that 45 per cent of the male labour force was employed in South Africa, a fact which helps to account for the backwardness of agriculture and for the difficulty of obtaining labour for public works that sometimes arises; only 7 per cent of males are in paid employment in Lesotho, and these largely in Government service. New long-term settlement in South Africa is practically impossible for non-whites, and most of the absentees are on short-term contracts with gold mines and collieries. Recruiting agencies for mining companies maintain offices throughout the country. It is arguable that the long-term effects of this short-term migration partly explain the country's economic backwardness, but there would be formidable problems if this source of employment suddenly disappeared. Apart from its direct effects on the standard of living of the migrants and their families, remittances make a substantial contribution to financing the enormous trade gap. In recent years imports have been in the region of R23 million per annum and exports about R4 million. In 1967 migrants' remittances contributed R4.5 million towards the R20 million deficit; budgetary and capital aid (mainly from the United Kingdom) plus customs and excise revenue from South Africa covered most of the remainder.

Mine employment is but one of the links between Lesotho and South Africa. Together with Botswana and Swaziland they form a customs union which dates formally from 1910, being part of the settlement made in the aftermath of the Boer War. A new agreement was signed in December 1969 which takes some account of changes in southern Africa in the last sixty years and of recent thinking on the effects of customs unions. The South African tariff of customs and excise is applied, with few exceptions, to the whole area and the revenue is shared on a basis that goes some way to recognizing the costs to the smaller countries of trade diversion. There is some provision for consultation, and some concessions are made to the special needs of the smaller countries, for example, by allowing some limited protection for infant industries. The outcome of the negotiations suggests that all three former High Commission Territories may obtain better terms from the Republic than the United Kingdom even tried to obtain during the colonial era. Revenue received under the Agreement rose from R1.9 million in 1968–69 to an estimated R6.7 million in 1972–73; part of the increase is attributable to the introduction of sales tax in the area, and the fact that liquor duties are no longer hived off. As a result, the British grant-in-aid of the Budget fell from R5 million to Ro.7 million. Although total revenue has been fairly stable its quality has improved in that most of it is now received as of right under long-term international agreement, and very little on what may be regarded as *ex gratia* terms.

There is a *de facto* monetary union covering the same area as the customs union. All four countries plus South West Africa (Namibia) use the South African rand. There is no formal monetary agreement and the Lesotho government, like the governments of Botswana and Swaziland, has no influence over monetary policy, no share in the profits of the currency issue and no automatic borrowing facilities at the South African Reserve Bank. The Standard Bank and Barclays Bank International were formerly the only banks operating in the country, the former being the government's banker, but the Bank for Economic Development for Equatorial and Southern Africa, registered in Luxembourg and whose head office is with the Union Bank of Switzerland in Zurich, planned to open its first southern Africa office in Maseru in 1972. There are no official exchange reserves in the usually accepted sense, but South African exchange controls have not hitherto obstructed the legitimate business of residents, and care is taken to ensure that Lesotho does not constitute a gap in the Republic's own system of controls.

Of necessity the tax structure closely resembles that of Lesotho's surrounding neighbour. With free movement of goods and fairly free movement of capital, Lesotho cannot impose higher rates for fear of diverting activity to South Africa, and the desperate need for revenue to finance essential government services precludes the feasibility of lower rates.

Other links with South Africa are found in the marketing of some agricultural products, the purchase of a bulk supply of electricity and, in the future, the possible sale of water and hydroelectric power to the Witwatersrand and Orange Free State from the Malibamatso River Project, which is being investigated in the mountains in the north and in which the South African government has agreed in principle to co-operate.

INDUSTRIAL DEVELOPMENT

Lesotho claims the highest literacy rate in Africa, and there is a general impression that in white collar jobs the Basotho are probably of above average ability for southern Africa. This, together with the fact that there is no colour bar, may perhaps provide a basis for some industrial development.

Manufacturing accounted for only 0.7 per cent of G.D.P. in 1966–67. The Lesotho National Development Corporation was established in 1967 to try to stimulate this sector. It has acted vigorously, under excellent management, and has pioneered, or participated in setting up, numerous small enterprises in such fields as tyre-retreading, tapestry weaving, candle-making, fertilizer blending, diamond cutting and polishing, and other activities are projected; it has helped to bring quite a large hotel to Maseru and another is planned for Leribe, as well as a 3,300 square metre shopping centre in Maseru to be financed largely by a South African insurance group. Tax incentives are offered to new enterprises. Diamond mining is being developed in the mountains where large expatriate firms are replacing the primitive diggings with modern mining operations. No other significant minerals are known to exist, but exploration has been far from exhaustive.

The recently published First Five-Year Development Plan (1970/71—1974/75) anticipates expenditure of R29 million in the public sector, nearly one half going to roads and agriculture. Industrial development, which is obviously needed to provide employment for school leavers, is left mainly to foreign enterprise, with some participation by the LNDC, and tax incentives. Of the R29 million less than R20 million is in sight, and only Ro.5 million is expected to be raised internally, the rest being sought in loans and grants from abroad. The plan does not cover the Malibamatso River Project, the future of which is not yet settled.

Even before the political events of January 1970 the country faced formidable economic problems. The acute shortage of fertile land, the problem of soil erosion and the primitive approach to farming make it highly unlikely that the 2.5 per cent per annum increase in population can be absorbed into agriculture. Mining development—especially diamond mining—is unlikely to be labour intensive, although it may make a substantial contribution to government revenue and reduce the dependence on external aid. The pull of Johannesburg, Durban and the western Cape creates problems for industrial development in the rest of the customs area, not only in Lesotho, and the assistance given by the Republic to "border" industries on the fringes of the "Bantu homelands" may divert firms that might otherwise consider establishing themselves in the mountainous kingdom. The attraction of what is, by African standards, a well-educated indigenous labour force without the limitations caused by job reservation and a colour bar, has not so far compensated for the absence of many basic facilities. For an economist it is often more illuminating to think of Lesotho as a very depressed area in South Africa rather than as a separate country.

STATISTICAL SURVEY

AREA

11,716 square miles.

POPULATION
(1966 Census)

			Men	Women	Total
African	.	.	367,087	482,926	850,013
European	.	.	801	781	1,582
Asian	.	.	367	399	766
Total	.	.	368,255	484,106	852,361
Absentee*	.	.	97,529	19,744	117,273
Grand Total	.		465,784	503,850	969,634

* Citizens working in South Africa.

Mid-1971 estimate: 935,000, excluding absentee workers.

Births and Deaths: Average annual birth rate 38.8 per 1,000, death rate 21.0 per 1,000 (UN estimates for 1965–70).

DISTRICTS
(1968 est.)
Each District has the same name as its chief town.

						POPULATION
Maseru	.	.	.	.	.	182,000
Berea	.	.	.	.	.	100,000
Butha-Buthe	.	.	.	.	.	55,000
Leribe	.	.	.	.	.	139,000
Mafeteng	.	.	.	.	.	103,000
Mohale's Hoek	.	.	.	.	.	97,000
Mokhotlong	.	.	.	.	.	55,000
Quacha's Nek	.	.	.	.	.	57,000
Quthing	.	.	.	.	.	65,000

Capital: Maseru, population 14,000 in 1966.

EMPLOYMENT

There are about 15,000 paid jobs in Lesotho. During 1967 77,414 Basotho were employed in coal and gold mines in the Republic of South Africa. Of the resident 1966 population of 852,361, there were 436,696 economically active (163,529 males and 273,167 females), mainly in agriculture. Of the African population of 850,013, an estimated 743,082 were dependent on agriculture.

RECRUITMENT AND REMITTANCES OF BASOTHO IN SOUTH AFRICA

	1968	1969
Numbers Recruited	80,712	86,420
Voluntary Deferred Pay .	R1,041,098	R1,327,188
Remittance Payments .	R1,100,787	R1,376,189

AGRICULTURE

LAND USE, 1962
('ooo hectares)

Arable Land	353
Permanent Meadows and Pastures . .	2,495
Other Areas	188
TOTAL	3,036

LIVESTOCK
('ooo)

	1968–69	1969–70	1970–71
Sheep	1,842*	2,000	2,100*
Goats	920*	930*	940*
Cattle	390*	400*	410*
Pigs	66*	67*	68*
Horses	64*	63*	62*
Asses	43*	45*	48*
Mules	3*	3*	4*

* FAO estimate.

Source: FAO, *Production Yearbook 1971* (Rome, 1972).

PRINCIPAL CROPS
('ooo metric tons)

	1969	1970	1971
Wheat	59	60*	70*
Barley	3*	2	3*
Maize	95	40*	80*
Sorghum	42	30	60*
Dry Peas	15*	15*	16*

* FAO estimate.

Source: FAO, *Production Yearbook 1971* (Rome, 1972).

LIVESTOCK PRODUCTS
(metric tons)

	1969	1970	1971
Cows' Milk . . .	28,000*	29,000*	30,000*
Beef and Veal† .	12,000*	13,000*	13,000*
Mutton and Lamb†	10,000*	11,000*	11,000*
Wool: Greasy . .	4,500	4,500	4,500*
Clean . .	2,200	2,200	2,200*

* FAO estimate.

† Meat from indigenous animals only, including the meat equivalent of exported live animals.

AGRICULTURAL EXPORTS
(1968)

Wool (1968–69) . . .	lb.	10,215,824
Wheat (1969) . . .	200-lb. bags	55,000
Sorghum . . .	,,	n.a.
Peas . . .	,,	15,000
Beans (1969) . . .	,,	11,000
Mohair . . .	lb.	2,519,243
Hides . . .	number	15,165
Skins . . .	,,	74,137

Maize Imports (bags): (1967–68) 176,200; (1968–69) 370,000; (1969–70) 360,000.

MINING
DIAMONDS
(carats)

1968 . . .	12,000
1969 . . .	30,000
1970 . . .	18,000

FINANCE

South African currency = 100 cents = 1 rand.

Coins: 1, 2, 5, 10, 20 and 50 cents; 1 rand.

Notes: 1, 5, 10 and 20 rand.

Exchange rates (December 1972): £1 sterling = 1.839 rand; U.S. $ = 78.29 S.A. cents.

100 rand = £54.93 = $127.73.

BUDGET
(Rand)

REVENUE	1967–68	1968–69	EXPENDITURE	1967–68	1968–69
Taxes	1,288,000	1,314,100	Education	2,235,744	2,164,630
Customs and Excise*	1,775,000	1,845,000	Agriculture, Co-operatives		
Posts and Telegraphs	391,881	413,260	and Marketing	1,005,813	981,412
Licences and Duties	358,700	421,200	Health and Social Welfare	1,076,768	988,257
Fees of Court or Office	71,000	102,200	Police	951,347	1,372,208
Judicial Fines	60,000	70,000	Public Works	814,334	882,818
Earnings of Departments	578,625	675,925	Interior	547,333	585,382
Interest	10,200	10,000	Justice	471,529	365,057
Rents from Government			Finance	579,601	714,138
Property	143,000	155,000	Prisons	312,590	331,920
Miscellaneous	125,740	210,860	Posts and Telecommunica-		
Reimbursements	112,600	6,600	tions	324,506	354,953
			Prime Minister's Office	n.a.	581,490
TOTAL	4,914,746	5,223,945	Foreign Affairs	n.a.	309,476
Overseas Service Aid Scheme	175,326	173,207	All Other Items	2,881,286	1,416,697
British Loans†	110,779	95,162			
British Grant in Aid	—	5,131,959			
Other Grants in Aid	6,000,000	424,065			
TOTAL REVENUE	11,200,851	11,048,338	TOTAL EXPENDITURE	11,200,851	11,048,338

* Lesotho is a member of the South African Customs Union, and receives a percentage of the total revenue collected.

† 1968–69 = Exchequer Loans

ESTIMATED REVENUE	1969–70
Taxes	1,588,000
Customs, Excise and Sales Duty	1,970,000*
Posts and Telegraphs	448,000
Department Earnings	783,000
Miscellaneous	1,075,000
TOTAL	5,864,000
British Loans	91,000
British Grants in Aid	4,971,000†
South African Grants in Aid	397,000
TOTAL REVENUE	11,323,000

* This figure may be more than doubled by the new Customs Agreement. The estimate for 1971–72 is R5,900,000.

† This figure is still uncertain owing to Britain's refusal until June 1970 to recognize Chief Jonathan's government after his seizure of power in January. Britain later agreed to give budgetary aid of up to £1,175,000 and development aid of £850,000 during 1970–71. Other countries have been asked for aid because of the famine of May–June.

Estimated Expenditure (1969-70): R11,323,000.

Estimated Revenue and Expenditure (1970-71): R11,705,000.

Estimated Revenue (1971-72) R10,300,000.

Estimated Expenditure (1971-72): R11,300,000.

NATIONAL ACCOUNTS, 1966–67
(Rand '000)

FACTOR INCOMES		VALUE ADDED BY INDUSTRY	
Wages and Salaries	12,008	Agriculture	32,485
Gross Operating Profits . . .	2,144	Mining and Quarrying . . .	978
Gross Income of Rural Households and		Manufacture	317
Unincorporated Enterprises .	31,121	Construction	805
Government Income from Property .	186	Retail and Wholesale Trade . .	2,033
Personal Income from Property .	2,146	Transport and Communications . .	430
		Electricity, Gas and Water . .	273
GROSS DOMESTIC PRODUCT .	47,605	Welfare Services . . .	3,055
(at factor cost)		Financial and Professional Services .	450
Migrant Workers Remittances .	4,484	Government Administration . .	4,059
Net Income Paid Abroad . .	−198	Domestic, Catering and Other Services .	387
		Property Incomes	2,332
GROSS NATIONAL PRODUCT .	51,891	GROSS DOMESTIC PRODUCT .	47,605
(at factor cost)		(at factor cost)	

G.D.P. at purchasers' values (12 months ending March 31st): 49,520,000 rand in 1966–67; 48,720,000 rand in 1967–68.

BALANCE OF PAYMENTS—GLOBAL SUMMARY
(Rand '000)

	1965–66			1966–67		
	Credit	Debit	Balance	Credit	Debit	Balance
Goods and Services . .	10,588	19,986	−9,398	11,769	24,354	−12,585
Transfer Payments . .	11,556	1,172	10,384	12,553	909	11,644
Capital and Monetary Gold .	98	132	−34	1,097	137	942

EXTERNAL TRADE
(Rand '000)

IMPORTS	1969	1970	EXPORTS	1969	1970
Foodstuffs and Livestock .	5,500	5,982	Livestock and Foodstuffs:		
Beverages and Tobacco . .	1,243	1,116	Cattle	579	684
Crude Materials . . .	337	314	Sheep	68	104
Mineral Fuels and Lubricants .	1,399	1,476	Other Live Animals . .	—	33
Animal and Vegetable Oils .	89	198	Wheat . . .	426	927
Chemicals	1,541	1,273	Peas and Beans . .	219	127
Manufactured Goods . .	3,896	3,983	Other Foodstuffs . .	19	11
Machinery and Transport					
Equipment . . .	2,839	3,058	TOTAL . .	1,311	1,888
Miscellaneous Manufactured			Crude Materials:		
Goods . . .	5,984	4,816	Wool	874	547
Commodities n.e.s. . .	1,079	590	Mohair . . .	470	416
			Hides and Skins . .	46	24
			Diamonds . . .	1,174	652
			Other	—	11
			TOTAL . .	3,875	3,536
			TOTAL OTHER EXPORTS .	194	180
TOTAL	23,907	22,876	TOTAL EXPORTS . .	4,069	3,716

Most trade is with the Republic of South Africa; detailed figures for trade by countries are not available.

TRANSPORT

MOTOR VEHICLE REGISTRATION
(1969)

Total 4,905; Private Cars 2,111, Combies 60, Vans 731, Landrovers 552, Trucks 564, Buses 120, Tractors 497, Motor Cycles 71, Trailers 199.

EDUCATION
(1968)

	NUMBER OF SCHOOLS	ENROLMENT
Primary	1,124	179,386
Secondary . . .	27	4,141
Teachers Training Colleges .	7	675
Technical and Vocational Schools . . .	5	511
Universities . . .	1	159*

* Basotho students only.

Sources: Kingdom of Lesotho *Annual Statistical Bulletin* 1969; Standard Bank *Annual Economic Review: Botswana, Lesotho, Swaziland*, November 1971.

THE CONSTITUTION

(The Constitution was suspended in January 1970 and a new one is being drawn up.)

The King, Motlotlehi Moshoeshoe II, is Head of State and constitutional monarch. The executive body is the Cabinet consisting of the Prime Minister and not fewer than 7 other Ministers. There are two houses in the Parliament. The Senate contains the 22 principal chiefs and 11 other persons nominated by the King.

The National Assembly has 60 members elected by universal adult suffrage in 60 single member constituencies. The Prime Minister must be able to command majority support in the National Assembly. If challenged, the government must establish in the courts, that where there are several ways of achieving its objective, the means least restrictive of civil liberties has been chosen.

THE GOVERNMENT

Head of State: His Majesty King MOSHOESHOE II (christened Constantine Bereng Seeiso).

COUNCIL OF MINISTERS
(*December* 1972)

Prime Minister, Defence and Internal Security, Chief of Electoral Affairs: Chief J. LEABUA JONATHAN.

Deputy Prime Minister and Minister of Agriculture, Co-operatives and Community Development: Chief SEKHON-YANA N. 'MASERIBANE.

Minister of Foreign Affairs: Chief PEETE N. PEETE.

Minister of the Interior: GABRIEL C. MANYELI.

Minister of Finance, Commerce and Industry, Economic Planning and Statistics: RETS'ILISITSOE SEKHONYANA.

Minister of Works, Posts and Communications: PHILEMON SETLOKOANE MATETE.

Minister of Justice and Aliens Control: A. MONALELI.

Minister of Health, Education and Social Welfare: C. D. MOLAPO.

Minister to the Prime Minister: Chief MATETE P. MAJARA.

Ministers of State: Chief SELBOURNE R. LETSIE, Chief TLOHANG LEROTHOLI.

Minister of State Attached to Minister of Health: J. MOTHEPU.

DIPLOMATIC REPRESENTATION

EMBASSIES AND HIGH COMMISSIONS
ACCREDITED TO LESOTHO
(E) Embassy; (HC) High Commission.

China, Republic (Taiwan): Maseru (E); *Ambassador:* T. J. LIU.

France: Gaborone, Botswana (E).

India: Blantyre, Malawi (HC); *High Commissioner:* SAURA KUMAR CHOWDHRY.

United Kingdom: Maseru (HC); *High Commissioner:* H. G. M. BASS.

U.S.A.: Maseru (E); *Chargé d'Affaires:* NORMAN BARTH.

Lesotho also has diplomatic relations with Austria, Belgium, Canada, Federal Republic of Germany, Ghana, Iran, Israel, Italy, Japan, Kenya, Republic of Korea, Netherlands, Nigeria, Sweden, Switzerland and Vatican City.

PARLIAMENT

NATIONAL ASSEMBLY

ELECTION, JANUARY 27TH, 1970

Only 46 seats had been declared before a state of emergency was declared and the election results invalidated. At that time the National Party had reportedly won half the 46 seats and the Congress Party the other half.

SENATE

President: (vacant).

There is also a College of Chiefs which has the power under traditional law to depose the king by a vote of the majority.

POLITICAL PARTIES

(*All opposition parties were banned in January 1970.*)

Basotho National Party: P.O.B. 124, Maseru; f. 1959; 80,500 mems.; Leader Chief LEABUA JONATHAN; Gen. Sec. Dr. K. T. MAPATHE; publ. *Mareng-A-Meso.*

Congress Party: P.O.B. 111, Maseru; f. 1952; 75,000 mems.; Leader NTSU MOKHEHLE; Sec.-Gen. K. CHAKELA; Treas.-Gen. S. R. MOKHEHLE; Nat. Chair. G. KHASU; publs. *Makatolle, The Range, Commentator.*

Marema Tlou Freedom Party: P.O.B. 475, Maseru; f. 1962; 50,000 mems.; Pres. Dr. T. G. MOHALEROE; Vice-Pres. EDWIN LEANYA; Sec.-Gen. B. M. KHAKETLA.

Lesotho United Democratic Party: Nqechane, P.O. Leribe; Leader CHARLES MOFELI.

Communist Party: P.O.B. 330, Maseru; f. 1961; inaugural conference May 5th, 1962; about 500 mems.; Sec. JOHN MOTLOHELOA; publ. *Tokoloho*.

DEFENCE

Lesotho has no armed forces, but the police force of 1,500 includes some para-military units.

JUDICIAL SYSTEM

The Judicial department of the territory is the responsibility of the Minister of Justice.

Chief Justice of Lesotho: Hon. H. R. JACOBS.

Court of Appeal. A Lesotho Court of Appeal was established after independence in 1966 to replace the previous court of appeal which served all three former High Commission Territories. Members of the Court of Appeal are: Justice O. D. SCHREINER (President), Justice I. A. MAISELS and Justice A. MILNE.

The High Court. This is a Superior Court of Record, and in addition to any other jurisdiction conferred by local law, possesses and exercises all the jurisdiction, power and authorities vested in a Divisional Court of the Supreme Court of South Africa. Appeals may be made to the Court of Appeal.

District Courts. Each of the nine districts possesses the following subordinate courts: Resident Magistrate Courts, or First Class, Second Class and Third Class.

Judicial Commissioners' Courts. These deal with civil and criminal appeals from Central and Local Courts. Further appeal may be made to the High Court.

Central and Local Courts. There are 71 of these courts, of which 58 are Local Courts and 13 are Central Courts which also serve as courts of appeal from the Local Courts. They have limited jurisdiction on civil and criminal cases.

RELIGION

About 75 per cent of the people are Christians.

Christian Council of Lesotho: Gen. Sec. P.O.B. 260, Maseru.

ANGLICAN

CHURCH OF THE PROVINCE OF SOUTH AFRICA

Bishop of Lesotho: P.O.B. 87, Maseru; Rt. Rev. J. A. ARROWSMITH MAUND, M.C., B.A.

ROMAN CATHOLIC

Archbishop of Maseru: P.O.B. 267, Maseru; about 259,268 adherents; His Grace ALPHONSUS LIGUORI MORAPELI.

Bishop of Leribe: Rt. Rev. PAUL KHOARAI.

LESOTHO EVANGELICAL

President: Rev. J. M. DIAHO, P.O.B. 27, Mafeteng.

THE PRESS

Koena News: P.O.B. 358, Maseru; publ. by Dept. of Information.

Leselinyana la Lesotho: P.O.B. 7, Morija; f. 1863; Lesotho Evangelical Church; fortnightly; Sesotho, with occasional articles in English; Editor E. M. MOTUBA; circ. 6,457 (banned by the Government).

Lesotho News: P.O.B. 111, Ficksburg, Orange Free State, South Africa; f. 1927; weekly; English; Editor G. BOSCH; circ. 800.

Moeletsi oa Basotho (*The Counsellor of Basotho*): P.O. Mazenod; f. 1933; Catholic weekly; Sesotho and English; Editor Rev. Father F. MAIROT, O.M.I.; circ. 12,000.

Mohlabani (*The Warrior*): Mohlabani Printers and Publishers, P.O.B. 65, Maseru; f. 1954; fortnightly; Sesotho and English; Editor B. M. KHAKETLA; circ. 10,000.

Mareng-A-Meso: P.O.B. 557, Maseru; f. 1965; organ of the Basotho National Party; weekly; Sesotho and English; Editor Chief N. J. MOLAPO.

Molia: P.O.B. 353, Maseru; publ. by Dept. of Information; thrice weekly; circ. 15,000 (banned Jan. 1970).

PUBLISHERS

Mazenod Institute: P.O.B. 18, Mazenod, Lesotho; f. 1931; educational and religious books; Sotho literature and dictionary; *Moeletsi oa Basotho*; Man. Father M. GAREAU, O.M.I.

Morija Sesuto Book Depot: P.O.B. 4, Morija; f. 1861; run by the Lesotho Evangelical Church; publishers and booksellers of religious works, school books, linguistic and historical books and novels mainly in Southern Sotho and English.

Morija Printing Works: P.O.B. 5, Morija; printers and bookbinders.

RADIO

Radio Lesotho: P.O.B. 552, Maseru; programmes in Sesotho and English; two medium wave transmitters and one short wave transmitter; Dir. of Information G. J. J. GELDENHUYS; Head of Broadcasting J. J. NIEMANDT.

Radio Station 7PA22: Catholic School Secretariat, P.O.B. 80, Maseru; one short-wave station; educational programmes in Sesotho, English and French; Dir.-Gen. M. GAREAU, O.M.I.; Mgr. F. MARIOT; Dir. Tec. B. CHABOT.

Number of radio receivers: 10,100.

FINANCE

BANKING

Barclays Bank International Ltd.: P.O.B. 115, Maseru; Man. J. A. BAMBER, Maseru; 1 sub-branch and 2 agencies; Leribe Branch, P.O.B. 121, Leribe; Man. J. R. PHELPS.

Standard Bank Ltd.: P.O.B. 4 and 22, Maseru; Man. A. R. CHILTON-JONES; branch at Mohale's Hoek, sub-branch at Leribe and 12 agencies.

Post Office Savings Bank: Maseru; f. 1966; dep. R2,000,000.

Bank for Economic Development for Equatorial and Southern Africa: was to open in Maseru during 1972.

TRADE AND INDUSTRY

DEVELOPMENT ORGANIZATION

Lesotho National Development Corporation: P.O.B. 666, Maseru; f. 1967; first national factory, Kolonyama candle factory, opened under its auspices in September 1968; carpet and tyre-retreading factories opened early 1969; other operations include a furniture factory, potteries, two diamond prospecting operations, a fertilizer factory, a clothing factory, a diamond cutting and polishing works, a jewellery factory, a housing company, an international hotel with a gambling casino, Lesotho Airways Corporation and a training centre for motor mechanics; Chair. Prime Minister Chief LEABUA JONATHAN; Man. Dir. WYNAND VAN GRAAN.

MARKETING ORGANIZATION

Lesotho Farmers' Produce Marketing Corporation: P.O.B. 800, Maseru; f. 1971; sole organization for marketing livestock from Lesotho; agents appointed by it give farmers advance payments of up to one-half the estimated slaughter value of their stock and pay out the balance later after the animals have been resold in South Africa; the agents operate under the rules of the South African Meat Control Board; Man. Dir. THOMAS T. MAKASE.

TRADE UNIONS

Lesotho General Workers Union: P.O.B. 322, Maseru; f. 1954; Chair. L. RAMATSOSO; Sec. A. MOFA' MERE.

Lesotho Industrial Commercial and Allied Workers Union: P.O.B. 144, Maseru; f. 1952; Chair. R. MONESE; Sec. T. MOKHEHLE.

Lesotho Labour Organization: P.O.B. 26, Mohale's Hoek; f. 1962; Chair. J. MOHAPI; Sec. A. MOTSEKO.

Lesotho Transport and Telecommunication Workers Union: P.O.B. 266, Maseru; f. 1959 as Basutoland Federation of Labour; Pres. S. RAFUTO; Sec. S. MOREKE.

Lesotho Union of Printing, Bookbinding and Allied Workers: P.O. Mazenot, Maseru; f. 1963; Pres. G. MOTEBANG; Sec. P. K. MONESE.

National Union of Construction and Allied Workers: P.O.B. 327, Maseru; f. 1967; Pres. L. PUTSOANE; Sec. T. TLALE.

Union of Employers in Lesotho: P.O.B. 79, Maseru; f. 1961; Chair. E. R. CLIFFORD; Sec. P. S. HOGGE.

Union of Shop Distributive and Allied Workers: P.O.B. 327, Maseru; f. 1966; Pres. P. BERENG; Sec. J. MOLAPO.

CO-OPERATIVE SOCIETIES

Registrar of Co-operatives: MACDONALD MABOTE, P.O.B. 89, Maseru.

By the end of 1960, there were 193 co-operative societies with a total membership of about 21,000 and a turnover of roughly R204,700. The development of these societies is a Government responsibility, and the first Registrar of Co-operative Societies was appointed in 1968.

Finance and Marketing Co-operative Union of Lesotho; Maseru.

Lesotho Co-operative Savings Society: P.O.B. 167, Maseru; Sec. J. NKBELE.

TRANSPORT

RAILWAYS

The territory is linked with the railway system of the Republic of South Africa by a short line from Maseru to Marseilles on the Bloemfontein/Natal main line.

ROADS

The main road system, 560 miles, is principally confined to the western lowlands. A 90-mile stretch of the main lowland road, from Leribe in the north to Tsoaing, past Maseru, has been bitumenized and is now all-weather. Other parts of this road are being improved to an all-weather gravel surface. Many other new roads, principally in the mountains, are being constructed under self-help campaigns, and the government has given top priority to road construction. There are 367 miles of minor roads serving trading stations and Basotho villages; these are maintained by the traders and subsidized by the government. There are about 1,600 miles of bridle paths which are constructed and maintained by the Basotho Administration.

CIVIL AVIATION

Lesotho Airways Corporation: P.O.B. 861, Maseru; fleet of one Cessna 337, one Aermacchi AL60, one Cessna 205 and two Cessna 180; Chair. H. M. NTS'ABA; Gen. Man. M. S. PIKE.

There are 32 air strips in Lesotho, with scheduled charter, tourist, government communications and mail services between Maseru and all the main centres. There is also a scheduled passenger service (thrice weekly), using HS 748 pressurized aircraft, between Maseru and Jan Smuts Airport, near Johannesburg, operated jointly by Lesotho National Airways and South African Airways.

POWER

Lesotho Electricity Corporation: P.O.B. 423, Maseru; f. 1969; supplies Maseru, Mohale's Hoek, Quthing, Leribe, Ficksburg Bridge, Mapoteng, Roma, Mazenod, Morija and the surrounding areas; supplies to Mafeteng and Butha-Buthe will be available during 1973; Man. Dir. W. P. FORD.

EDUCATION

All primary education is free, and is largely in the hands of the three main missions (French Evangelical, Roman Catholic and Church of England) under the direction of the Ministry of Education. There are 1,116 schools and institutions in the territory. Post-secondary education is provided by the University of Botswana, Lesotho and Swaziland at Roma. Nearly R1.5 million of the R4 million devoted to education in the First Five-Year Development Plan (1970/71–1974/75) is to be spent on the National Teacher Training College, and R662,750 on the improvement and extension of the facilities in secondary schools.

LEARNED SOCIETY AND RESEARCH INSTITUTES

British Council, The: P.O.B. 429, Hobson's Square, Maseru; library (*see* below); Rep. C. THOMAS.

Ministry of Agriculture, Co-operatives and Marketing: P.O.B. 24, Maseru; research station at Maseru and field experimental stations.

Geological Survey Department: Dept. of Mines and Geology, P.O.B. 750, Maseru; Commr. W. C. FAIRBAIN.

LIBRARIES AND ARCHIVES

British Council Library: P.O.B. 429, Maseru; f. 1965; 19,300 vols.

Lesotho Government Archives: P.O.B. 47, Maseru; f. 1958; undertakes research; records date from 1869; Archivist M. L. MANYELI.

University of Botswana, Lesotho and Swaziland Library: P.O. Roma, via Maseru; f. 1945 as Pius XII University College Library; 77,000 vols.; Librarian J. HUTTON, B.A., LL.B.

UNIVERSITY AND COLLEGE

THE UNIVERSITY OF BOTSWANA, LESOTHO AND SWAZILAND

P.O. ROMA, LESOTHO, SOUTHERN AFRICA

Telephone: Roma 20.

Language of instruction: English; Academic year: July to April.

Established by Royal Charter 1964. The University is successor to Pius XII University College, which was established in 1945. In 1972 additional campuses were opened in Botswana and Swaziland, where at present teaching is limited to Part I studies. The University does not exclude anyone on the grounds of race, religion, sex or country of origin.

Chancellor: H.M. King MOSHOESHOE II of Lesotho.

Vice-Chancellor: C. A. ROGERS, M.A., PH.D.

Pro-Vice-Chancellors: H. O. H. VERNON-JACKSON, B.COMM., M.A., D.ED. (Botswana), J. A. NOONAN, C.B.E., M.A., D.PHIL. (Lesotho), S. M. GUMA, M.A., D.LITT.ET PHIL.

Registrar: M. SOUTHWOOD, M.A. (OXON.).

Librarian: J. HUTTON, B.A., LL.B.

Number of teachers: 90.
Number of students: 560.

Faculties of Agriculture (Swaziland only), Arts, Education, Economics, and Social Studies; Division of Extra-Mural Studies.

LESOTHO AGRICULTURAL COLLEGE

P.O.B. 829, MASERU

Telephone: 2372.

Founded 1955.

Language of instruction: English; State control; Academic year: September to July (three semesters).

Principal: J. P. PARMITER, D.SC., B.SC.(AGRIC.).

Registrar: M. NYOKOLE.

SELECT BIBLIOGRAPHY

ASHTON, H. *The Basuto.* London, O.U.P., 1952.

BUREAU OF STATISTICS. *Annual Statistical Bulletin.* Maseru.

HAILEY, Lord. *South Africa and the High Commission Territories.* London, O.U.P., 1965.

HALPERN, JACK. *South Africa's Hostages: Bechuanaland, Basutoland and Swaziland.* Harmondsworth, Penguin Books, 1965.

H.M.S.O. *Basutoland, Bechuanaland Protectorate and Swaziland. Report of an Economic Survey Mission.* London, 1960.

LEISTNER, G. M. E. *Lesotho: Economic Structure and Growth.* Pretoria, Africa Institute, 1966.

SPENCE, J. E. *Lesotho: the Politics of Dependence.* London, O.U.P. for the Institute of Race Relations, 1967.

STANDARD BANK. *Annual Economic Review: Botswana, Lesotho, Swaziland.* London, October 1971.

STEVENS, RICHARD P. *Lesotho, Botswana and Swaziland.* London, Pall Mall, 1967.

Liberia

Willi Schulze

PHYSICAL AND SOCIAL GEOGRAPHY*

The Republic of Liberia was founded in 1847 by freed American negro slaves who settled along the western Guinea coast between Cape Mount (11° 20′ W.) and Cape Palmas (7° 40′ W.) from 1821 onwards. Liberia extends from 4° 20′ N. to 8° 30′ N. with a maximum depth of 175 miles between Buchanan and Nimba. It occupies an area of 43,000 sq. miles between Sierra Leone to the west, the Republic of Guinea to the north, and the Ivory Coast to the east.

PHYSICAL FEATURES

An even coastline of 355 miles with a powerful surf, rocky cliffs and bar-enclosed lagoons makes access from the Atlantic Ocean difficult except at the modern ports. The flat coastal plain, 10 to 35 miles wide, carries a man-made forest-savannah mosaic. The interior hills and mountain ranges, with altitudes from 600 to 1,200 ft., are part of an extended peneplain, covered by evergreen (in the south) or semi-deciduous (in the north) rain-forests. Liberia's greatest elevations are located in the northern highlands, e.g. the Nimba mountains (4,540 ft. above sea level) and the Wologisi Range (4,530 ft.). Here the Guinea savannah with its elephant grass is expanding. Rapids and waterfalls mark the descent from the higher to the lower belts. The spectacular St. John's Falls and some others may become major touristic attractions and important sources of electric energy in the future.

Liberia has two rainy seasons near Harper and one rainy season from May to October in the rest of the country. From Monrovia, with an average of 183 in. a year, rainfall decreases towards the south-east and the hinterland, reaching 88 in. at Ganta. Average temperatures are more extreme in the interior than at the coast. Monrovia has an annual average of 79°F., with absolute limits at 92°F. and 58°F. respectively. At Tappita temperatures may rise to 111°F. in March and fall to 48°F. during cool harmattan nights in December or January. Mean water temperature on the coast is 80°F. Short heavy line squalls in spring and autumn mark the shift of north-east trade wind and south-west monsoon.

POPULATION: ETHNIC STRUCTURE AND SOCIAL PROBLEMS

The majority of the Liberian population belong to 16 autochthonic African tribes, subdivided into 124 paramount chiefdoms with 372 clan chiefdoms. Most numerous are the Kpelle (211,000) and the Bassa (166,000). Other well-known groups are the seafaring Kru and the Vai, who invented the Vai script about A.D. 1815. Less numerous but of great political significance are the descendants of the 22,120 settlers who immigrated into Liberia between 1822 and 1892. Together with some 5,000 Fanti fishermen, 3,000 Lebanese traders and other foreign groups Liberia's total population at the first census in 1962 was 1,016,443. In 1971 it was estimated at 1,571,477. With an average density of 40 to the sq. mile the country is underpopulated, though recent estimates suggest a growth rate of more than 3 per cent each year. Social problems result from internal migration to the capital, which grew from 41,590 to 81,000 between 1956 and 1962 (reaching approximately 180,000 in 1971), and to the mines. Tropical diseases and illiteracy (at a rate of 91.1 per cent of the population of 10 years of age and over) are other social problems.

* See map on p. 708.

475

RECENT HISTORY

THE FOUNDATION OF LIBERIA

Between 1822 and 1892 some 16,400 freed negro slaves from the southern U.S.A.—formerly known as "Americo-Liberians"—settled at different places along the "Malagueta" or "Grain Coast" under the auspices of the American Colonization Society and six other philanthropic organizations. About 5,700 Africans freed from slaving vessels by the British and the American navies—formerly known as "Congoes" —also established themselves there.

The immigrants had to struggle against a most unfavourable geographical environment and against internal and external difficulties, most of which were the consequence of the isolation of the small colonies.

The geographical environment—the strong surf, the poor sandy soil on the edge of the coastal plain, then covered by tropical rain-forests, the hot humid climate, and a host of tropical diseases—made the Guinea coast one of the most difficult places in Africa for unprepared people, whose only connexion with Africa was their race. Out of 4,472 immigrants who settled between Monrovia and Greenville from 1822 to 1843 only 2,275 were enumerated during the 1843 census. This means that 50 per cent had either returned to the U.S. or died.

The problems arising from the various forms of isolation were no easier to overcome. Until 1967–68 there was no road connexion from Monrovia to Robertsport, Greenville and Harper—three of the five county headquarters along the coast—and until 1945 no car could travel from the capital to any of the three neighbouring countries.

Even more serious were the consequences of the ambitions of the various colonization societies to establish their own independent territories, such as "Mississippi in Africa" at Greenville or "Maryland in Liberia" around Harper. This resulted in internal political isolation until the independence of Liberia was declared in 1847. Even then Maryland joined the republic only in 1857. It also led to external political isolation, because Liberia never was a legal colony of the U.S.A., whose assistance from 1847 up to the First World War was mainly of a theoretical or moral kind and did not even prevent a number of boundary encroachments between 1882 and 1910.

The establishment of political units like "Mississippi in Africa" on the model of the southern U.S.A. made many settlers consider themselves the civilized vanguard of the race who had the task of dominating the "natives" or "aborigines" and spreading Christianity.

THE BEGINNINGS OF UNIFICATION

One necessity at the beginning of the twentieth century was to abolish "the old attitude of indifference toward the native population" and encourage their "gradual inclusion into the citizenship of the country". These proposals by A. Barclay, President of Liberia from 1904 to 1912, were the beginning of social changes.

In 1905, a new law introduced in the hinterland a dual system of administration based on native chiefs and district commissioners of the Liberian government. In 1923 supplementary and revising regulations were issued which were modelled on Lord Lugard's system of indirect rule, with paramount chiefs, clan chiefs and town chiefs, of whom over five hundred took part in the famous Suenh conference on the invitation of President King. In 1925 he became the first Liberian president to visit the interior and meet the native chiefs. Through his unification policy President W. V. S. Tubman intensified the integration process, so that the social and political isolation of the descendants of the settlers has been practically eradicated. Through intermarriage and the adoption by settlers of tribal children, who took the names of their foster fathers and often hold important positions now, ethnic isolation has largely been removed.

When the U.S.A. more and more neglected her protégé after 1847, Liberia could expect assistance with her economic and political problems only from the European states. This period ended with the advent of Firestone in 1926.

THE EUROPEAN PERIOD

From the diverse American colonization societies Liberia had received an annual amount of U.S. $102,171; on an average, including transport to Africa, etc., the country's own revenues were only U.S. $8,853 in 1845. After independence this discrepancy became a vital problem, when not only American assistance decreased but also Liberia's principal export commodities—coffee, palm oil and cane sugar—were no longer attractive on the world market. In order to prevent financial breakdown, a British loan was taken up in 1871. This year marked the beginning of the "European period", which reached its climax before the First World War but continued until 1925, when 90 per cent of Liberia's imports and 87 per cent of her exports came from or went to European countries; only 26 of 904 ships calling at Liberian ports, in that year, flew the American flag.

Great Britain was the first nation to recognize the Republic of Liberia in 1848 and to open a regular steamship line in 1853. After 1901 the British-owned West African Gold Concession Ltd.—after 1903 a section of The Liberian Development Chartered Corporation—prospected for minerals. Most important was the foundation of the Mount Barclay Rubber Plantation Company in 1906 by Sir Harry Johnston, on whose behalf the German Humpelmayer planted the first *Hevea* trees in the country. The high yield and the excellent growth of the 135,000 trees of the plantation may have influenced H. S. Firestone's decisions on rubber production in Liberia.

The Liberian government had "to choose between economic prosperity and political dangers" (R. L. Buell) and negative political consequences were bound to result from these economic developments. They consisted of boundary disputes with Britain (finally settled in 1911) and France (not settled until 1928) and in foreign influence within the country. This was exerted mainly through the "Liberian" Frontier Force, whose British Commander also took over the police in 1908, and through an international customs receivership imposed on Liberia for the servicing of foreign debts in connexion with additional loans received in 1906 and 1912.

Germany has had old trade connexions with Liberia since 1849, when C. Woermann & Co. began to establish "factories" at all ports of entry and in the interior. There were about 20 dependencies of Hamburg houses in the country before 1914. Already in 1910 Germany had built a cable station in Monrovia and maintained the German-Liberian Bank, and she was the principal trade partner until Liberia had to interrupt all relations in 1917. Soon after the First World War Germany and the Netherlands, through the old traditions of the Dutch East Africa Company, again became the principal customers of Liberia, while Britain remained the main supplier for some time. Of the total trade in 1922 (imports and exports), Germany held 36.5 per cent, Britain 36.2, the Netherlands 13.5 and the U.S.A. 5.2 per cent. With the coming of Firestone in 1926 the "European period" ended. In 1930 the British bank in Monrovia was withdrawn and replaced by a Firestone subsidiary, and in 1943 the British currency was replaced by the American dollar.

THE FIRESTONE PERIOD

The Firestone Plantations Company started operations with the tapping of the former British Mt. Barclay plantation in 1926; with clearing and planting at Harbel (from *Harv*ey and Anna*bel* Firestone), 30 miles east of Monrovia; and at Gedetarbo on the Cavalla River in 1927. With some 80,000 acres under rubber the Harbel estate is the largest continuous *Hevea* plantation in the world and Firestone has been the country's principal employer for forty-five years. Because of her smallness, poverty and isolation, the establishment of the powerful, rich and well-organized "firestone state" was "a decisive event in the modern history of Liberia" (W. C. Taylor).

It was not only decisive because it made rubber the principal cash crop, but also because it brought fundamental changes in the financial, social and political spheres. Through the much criticized loan agreement of 1927 Firestone put the country under American financial supervision. But the company also provided regular income to 5–10 per cent of the population and to the Liberian government. Firestone's system of labour recruitment—approved by the government—was also criticized, but it contributed to the formation of a trained, healthy and better educated labour force, familiar with the principles of the modern money economy. The political interest of the U.S.A. government in the Firestone operations made the company a stabilizing factor in Liberia and in west Africa. Its presence, however, did not prevent internal conflict, nor an investigation by the League of Nations Committee on Forced Labour sent to the Spanish plantations on Fernando Póo who reported in 1930. The Christy report caused political changes in the Liberian executive, and caused the U.S.A. and Britain to sever diplomatic relations with Liberia for five years.

However, the presence of Firestone and its technical facilities, in combination with the strategic location of the country, were decisive factors leading up to the defence area agreement of 1942. This authorized the U.S.A. to build the Robertsfield air base, which Firestone had in any case begun in 1941. The visits of the U.S. President, F. D. Roosevelt, to Liberia in 1943 and of President E. Barclay, together with President-elect W. V. S. Tubman, to the U.S.A., and Liberia's reluctant declaration of war on Germany and Japan in 1944 were indications that by the Second World War the U.S.A. had become the dominating political factor for Liberia. Moreover, Firestone continued to maintain its economic dominance for some years.

THE TUBMAN PERIOD

In his inauguration address on January 1st, 1944, President William Vacanarat Shadrach Tubman emphasized two principles of his government's future policy, "to encourage the investment of foreign capital in the development of the country", and "to strive at the assimilation and unification of our various populations". Both the principles—later known as the "open door policy" and "unification policy"—sharply contrast with the political ideas of the seventeen previous Liberian presidents, who tried to close the interior to foreign traders and/or regarded the coastal settlers as the leading group. The Tubman reforms meant revolutionary changes to the country, attained by evolutionary means.

The starting point of the unification policy was the seventh amendment to the Liberian constitution of July 26th, 1847. This amendment of 1945 gave representation in parliament to the hinterland provinces. The eighth amendment of 1947 gave the right of suffrage to all Liberian citizens, including women, provided they held real estate or other property, or they owned a hut and paid taxes on it. Other measures were the revision of the "regulations for governing the hinterland" in 1949 and their inclusion in the Liberian code of laws of 1956. "National Execution Councils", as were held at Harper in 1954 and at Kolahun in 1963, and "Unification Councils" enabled the president to meet the tribal population, to decide law suits, and to promulgate the idea of unity. Unification was further advanced by a law signed in 1963 converting the three hinterland provinces into four counties in 1964, and by the creation of a "cultural centre" near Monrovia with tribal huts, etc.

The "open door policy" made slow progress in the beginning; up until 1950, only two major concessions were added to Firestone: the Liberia Mining Company and the Liberia Company, founded by Stettinius for the production of cocoa and for other economic activities. Total trade in that year amounted to U.S. $38.2 million, and 90 per cent of Liberian exports went to the U.S.A., which also provided 70 per cent of the imports. Since 1950 Liberia has attracted over 50 foreign companies with total investments of some

U.S. $800 million, including the nearly U.S. $300 million of the Swedish-Liberian-American Minerals Company (LAMCO). Total trade in 1968 reached U.S. $277.5 million, of which the U.S.A.'s share of Liberian exports had dropped to 43.9 per cent and of imports to 43.4 per cent. Some diversification of Liberia's trading patterns had therefore taken place. In addition, the contribution of Firestone to the Liberian budget decreased from 35.9 per cent in 1955 to less than 6 per cent in 1968.

In the social field President Tubman improved the conditions of the "Workman's Compensation and Protection Act" of 1943 by raising minimum wages to 8c per hour in agricultural and 15c per hour in industrial occupations. Furthermore, the right to a pension (40 per cent of last net income after 25 years of work or after reaching 60 years) was introduced in 1961 and a modern labour code in 1963.

In the field of international relations the wind of change was particularly strong. Before 1920 Liberian diplomats represented their country only in London and Paris; in that year the U.S.A. was added. Now, Liberia is represented in more than 30 countries, and over 20 countries are represented in Liberia. Perhaps even more important is the role Liberia has played at many international conferences, especially as a founding member of the United Nations in 1945 or at Bandung in 1955. The political influence Liberia has on African affairs through its president is shown by the WHO conference at Monrovia in 1957, the Sanniquellie conference of three independent African states in 1959 and the Monrovia conference of twenty African statesmen. Here in 1961 the "Monrovia group" of non-socialist African states was formed in opposition to the socialist "Casablanca group". Both groups united in the Organization of African Unity (OAU) at Addis Ababa, to whose formation Liberia contributed in a decisive degree.

In summary it may be said that social and ethnic problems within the country have not been completely rooted out, but that Liberia is no longer isolated. The policies of President Tubman have led Liberia from a "century of survival" (R. L. Buell) into a century of national and international co-operation resulting in political stability, social transformation and economic growth.

President Tubman died in July 1971, but the succession of his Vice-President, W. R. Tolbert, to the Provisional Presidency seems unlikely to produce any major changes of policy.

ECONOMY

Although in the world market Liberia appears as mainly a mineral producer, 73.2 per cent of her total exports in 1970 being accounted for by iron ore and diamonds, the country remains basically agricultural, with some 75 per cent of the working population employed on the land and only about 2 per cent (12 per cent in the cash economy) in mining.

AGRICULTURE, FORESTRY AND FISHING

The staple crops are rice and cassava (manioc); with palm oil and some fish or meat they are the basis of the national diet. Other crops like yams, eddoes, sweet potatoes, ocra and groundnuts, and fruit like plantains, oranges, mangoes, avocados or grapefruits are of secondary or local importance. Some of the main problems of Liberian subsistence agriculture are the low yields of rice of only 500 to 700 lb. per acre on an average, the low total production of about 100,000 tons per year, and the destruction on some 50,000 acres per year of valuable timber worth about U.S. $1,500 per acre by the method of land rotation with bush fallowing. The Liberian government has made several efforts to increase production and protect the forests. In 1962 specialists from Taiwan started testing vegetables, fibre plants and 20 varieties of paddy rice at Gbedin (near Ganta), which yielded over 4,000 lb per acre. They are also advising local farm co-operatives and training Liberian advisers of the agricultural extension service.

In order to increase total production and reduce rice imports, which increased from 3,800 tons in 1953 to 23,300 tons in 1960 and to 48,236 tons in 1970, the government started the "operation production" campaign in 1963. Its results have not been too encouraging, mainly because of the strong internal migration of young, male manpower to the iron ore mines, towns and rubber plantations. President Tolbert hopes to close the gap between rice production (about 100,000 tons per year) and consumption (about 150,000 tons) within 10 years. Since 1972 the Liberian Agricultural Development Corporation (LADCO), which is in charge of rice imports, has made great efforts to intensify production near Foya and Monrovia. In September 1970 the West African Rice Development Association (WARDA) with headquarters at Monrovia was established by seven West African states. For the protection of the timber resources a forest conservation law was passed in 1953 which declared a number of areas as "national forests", of which twelve with a total size of 3.8 million acres (15,500 sq. km.) existed in 1970.

Liberia's principal cash crops are rubber, coffee and cocoa. Although the Firestone Plantations Company has remained the principal rubber producer of the country, with a share of 56.6 per cent in the dry rubber content produced in 1969, it has lost its leading position in terms of acreage and number of employees. The two Firestone estates represented 30.4 per cent of the total area under rubber in 1970, while the other six foreign companies held 17.1 per cent and some 4,200 Liberian farmers possessed 52.5 per cent. Some 16,000 employees including 8,400 tappers work at the two Firestone plantations as against 19,000 workers on the other plantations. Altogether some 45,000 persons, that is about 45 per cent of all paid workers, are occupied in the rubber industry. The shortage of tappers is most acute at the small Liberian farms, of which 2,850 have a size of less than ten acres. Other problems are low yields (600 lb. dry rubber content per acre, as compared with 1,300 lb. at Firestone/Harbel), poor management and high transport charges. About one-third of the mature *Hevea* trees at the private farms have not been tapped for several years because they are not able to produce economically at the minimum price at the Liberian buying stations. In spite of the decreasing world market price for natural rubber, production has shown an average increase of 10 per cent per annum since 1965. While in that year output was 50,984 metric tons, the volume rose to 61,687 tons in 1967, to 69,669 in 1969 and to 80,267 in 1971.

Coffee production has shifted to northern Liberia with a centre between Voinjama and Kolahun, where mainly *Coffea robusta* is cultivated. Production figures show heavy changes according to the annual prices on the world market and the quantities smuggled into Liberia from the neighbouring countries. Since 1967 coffee exports have remained at a level between 4,000 and 5,000 tons. In 1969 4,364 metric tons were sold, and in 1970 the figure was 4,944 tons. Cocoa has been introduced into Maryland County from Fernando Póo. An attempt by the Liberia Company to repeat "the phenomenal growth of the cocoa industry in the Gold Coast" (R. E. Anderson) at the Cocopa plantation near Ganta was a failure, and rubber is now grown. Cocoa exports have decreased from 2,286 metric tons in 1968 to 1,633 tons in 1970 when the export price was only 28 cents per pound as compared with 36 cents in 1969. A banana plantation near Greenville also turned to rubber growing when "Panama-disease" broke out in 1955. Recent experiments with tobacco in Nimba County and with oil palms near Buchanan show promising results.

Most promising, apart from the further development of ocean fisheries, is the future exploitation of the great forest reserves. A national forest inventory made from 1960 to 1967 showed that there is an average timber potential of 10,000–15,000 cu. m. per sq. km. on a closed forest area of six million acres (25,000 sq. km.), and that a mean total number of 15,000–20,000 trees grow on 1 sq. km., including the recently discovered and very versatile saw, peel and pulp species, *Tetraberlinia tubmaniana*, which differs from most tropical trees by growing in single dominant stands. Since 1967 there has been a great increase in timber production; the shipment of logs rose from 496,300 cubic feet in 1967 (valued at U.S. $ 534,100) to 5,061,600 cubic feet (valued at $5,819,700) in 1970. Another important forest product is palm nuts, from which about 6,000–8,000 tons of palm oil are produced per year and 12,000–15,000 tons of kernels are exported. As palm-products could become important for the diversification of Liberian agriculture, the government has encouraged the development of two plantations, one at New Cess near Buchanan and the other near the Mafa river in Grand Cape Mount

County, with a total of 8,500 acres planted. The total concession area totals 44,000 acres. Synthetic fibres reduced exports of piassava, once an important product, from 3,800 tons to only 155 tons in the period 1960–68. Piassava shipping has practically ceased since 1969 when only 48 tons, worth U.S. $5,280, were sold.

Livestock consists mainly of cattle, sheep, goats and poultry; there are few pigs and no horses or donkeys. In Bong County, there were 2,552 heads of cattle in 1967, from which a total of 15–20,000 is estimated for Liberia as a whole. There were about 100,000 laying hens with a production of about 15 million eggs in 1970. Fish production (mainly by the Mesurado Fishing Co.) rose from 1,180 tons in 1960, and 3,993 tons in 1963 to 11,625 tons (including 706 tons of shrimps) in 1969–70.

MINING

Minerals and mining have become more and more important to the Liberian economy, beginning with the opening of the Bomi Hills iron ore mine by the Liberia Mining Company (LMC) in June 1951. In 1957 diamond findings in the lower Lofa River area resulted in a rush of thousands of plantation workers to Weasua and other places in the Gola forest. The value of diamond exports ($1.4 million in 1965) reached a record level of $9.1 million in 1968. The value of production fell to $5.7 million in 1970, while the volume of 800,000 carats remained roughly constant during the intervening period. Several other minerals were discovered later, e.g. bauxite, copper, columbite-tantalite, corundum, lead, manganese, tin and zinc. Of economic interest are the deposits of barite in the Gibi Range near Kakata, where in 1966 reserves of some two million tons were discovered, and of kyanite at Mount Montro near Harbel, where deposits of 10 million tons were located during exploration between 1958 and 1967. In 1968 three American companies obtained permission to conduct seismic exploration for petroleum off the Liberian coast. Exploratory drillings by the three concessionaires (Union Carbide, Frontier Oil, Chevron Oil), each holding areas of 3,000 to 4,100 square metres, were not successful until 1972.

Iron ore mining has been the principal industry of Liberia since 1961, when the value of ore exports for the first time replaced rubber at the top of the export list. This development was due to the fall in rubber prices of 30.5 per cent between 1960 and 1963, and also to the establishment of three more mines. With the assistance of the Liberia Mining Company, in which the Republic Steel Corporation holds a 60 per cent interest, the National Iron Ore Company (NIOC) mine, which is 85 per cent Liberian-owned, was opened on the Mano River in 1961. The biggest iron ore deposits—probably over 1,000 million tons, including at least 235 million tons of high-grade ore of 65 to 70 per cent iron content—have been exploited by the Liberian-American-Swedish Minerals Company (LAMCO) since 1963. With investments of nearly U.S. $300 million, covering the construction of Africa's first pelletizing plant at Buchanan, opened in 1968, a new port and a 170-mile railway, the Nimba project is probably the biggest private enterprise in the whole of Africa. Its main shareholders are the Swedish Grängesberg Company, together with five other Swedish firms, and the U.S. Bethlehem Steel Corporation (25 per cent). The fourth of Liberia's open-cast mines in the Bong Range north of Kakata was opened in 1965 by the Bong Mining Company (70 per cent German, 25 per cent Italian) on behalf of the German-Liberian Mining Company (DELIMCO), of which the Liberian Government, in accordance with the so-called "Tubman formula", holds a 50 per cent interest, the same as in LAMCO. With 23.3 million long tons, of which LAMCO produced 46.6 per cent in 1970, Liberia ranked among the world's ten principal producers and among the five main exporters of iron ore. Its position will become even stronger when the exploitation of the Bie Mountains deposits, halfway between the Bomi Hills and the Mano River mines, begun in 1968, is intensified, and when the iron ore reserves of the Wologisi Range in Lofa County are mined by the Liberian Iron and Steel Corporation (LISCO), which was granted a concession in 1967. If plans for the participation of Japanese firms (which are also interested in the Bie Mountains deposits) are realized, iron ore production in Lofa County could start in 1976 with an output of 10 million tons. Prospecting in the Tokadeh area near Nimba has provided encouraging results, and extraction will commence in 1973 at a rate of 1.5 million tons a year.

INDUSTRY

These concessions have helped to improve Liberia's technical and social infrastructure through the construction of roads, ports, airfields, schools and hospitals. Their contribution to economic development in general is nevertheless limited, as no secondary industries based on iron ore or rubber have been established. There are mainly small enterprises in the manufacturing sector, mainly construction firms, saw mills, repair shops, and tailors' shops; over 80 per cent have less than ten employees. The few larger plants with over 50 employees include the rubber factories at the concession sites and the beverage industry, represented by a Coca-Cola and other bottling plants and by a brewery built in 1961. A chemical and explosives factory was established near Robertsfield in 1964. In the same year the Industrial Park near Paynesville was established by the Liberian Development Company on behalf of the Liberian Government, starting with a shoe factory with Swedish interests in 1964 and with a metalo-plastics firm under Lebanese direction in 1965. In 1968 a petroleum refinery with an annual capacity of 650,000 tons was built in the same area by the Liberia Refinery Company (LRC).

Smaller than this 12-million-dollar project is a cement factory, built in 1968 in Monrovia by the Lebanese "Liberian Cement Corporation" (LCC) at U.S. $2.5 million. Its capacity is 125,000 tons of clinker cement per year. Several smaller projects were started under the Investment Incentives Code of April, 1966, e.g. a rum distillery, an umbrella factory and a package plant for salt, rice, etc. In 1969–70 the Liberian Produce Marketing Corporation (LPMC), jointly owned by the government and the Danish East Asiatic Company, constructed an oil mill at Buchanan (costing $1.2 million). New private enterprises include a rice mill ($1.0 million), a factory for aluminium parts ($0.5 million) and a confectionery plant ($0.2 million). In 1969 the petroleum refinery produced 79.5 million gallons of fuels, worth $7.9 million, and started the sale of asphalt in 1970. The main problem of most industries is the small market, and other problems are the concentration in the Monrovia region and the small number of Liberian entrepreneurs—of 1,703 enterprises registered in Monrovia in 1967 (industry and trade), 63.4 per cent were owned by Lebanese and only 16.6 per cent by Liberians. Prospects for industrial development could improve by such measures as the protocol setting up the West African Economic Grouping, which was signed by nine of the fourteen countries that met in Monrovia in 1968, or the agreement on the construction of a hydro-electric power plant on the Cavalla River signed by Liberia and the Ivory Coast in 1970.

TRANSPORT AND POWER

The length of Liberia's road network nearly doubled between 1958 and 1970, when it reached 4,100 miles, of which about 230 miles were tarred. Nearly one-third of these roads were built by private concessions. The number of motor vehicles was about 23,000 in 1970. The railways from Monrovia to Mano River via Bomi Hills (92 miles), from Monrovia to the Bong Mine (50 miles) and from Buchanan to Nimba (168 miles) have all been built for the transport of iron ore. According to agreements of 1967–68 the LAMCO railway will also be utilized for the transport of logs and rubber and for the Guinea transit trade. The principal ports are Monrovia with 13.2 million tons landed and loaded in 1970 (including 12 million tons iron ore shipped), Buchanan with 11.9 million tons (including 11.6 million tons of iron ore), Greenville with 126,045 tons (including 97,099 tons of logs), Harper (59,626 tons) and Robertsport. In 1970, with a registered tonnage of over 33 million tons, the Liberian flag ranked first on the seas. The Liberian National Airways, with two DC-3, and six air-taxi companies serve internal transport needs. International air traffic through Roberts International Airport reached 44,165 passengers landed and loaded in 1970.

The public electric power generating capacity has more than trebled from 15,140 kW. in 1964 to 51,000 kW. in 1966, when the Mt. Coffee Hydroelectric Station was put into service. In the same year total energy production was 339 million kWh., of which 221 million kWh. were generated by some 325 big or small diesel plants at the concessions, missions or factories. In 1970, with an installed capacity of 224,000 kW. (of which 82,000 kW. was public) over 570 million kWh. were produced.

PUBLIC FINANCE

In the sector of public finance, the Liberian revenues rose from U.S. $40 million in 1964 to $65.2 million in 1970. External development assistance varied from U.S. $19.5 million in 1964 to 29.7 million in 1966 and 20.8 million in 1970, excluding IMF drawings. Debt service payments were rescheduled in 1963 and amounted to U.S. $11.3 million in 1964 and $20.6 million in 1970. During the same period, per capita income increased from an average of U.S. $138.6 to $184. The United States accounted for about two-thirds of the loans and grants, followed by Federal Germany and the United Nations.

Liberia's economic growth after World War II is reflected in the increase of overseas trade from U.S. $38.2 million in 1950 (imports and exports) to $151.8 million in 1960 and to $363.4 million in 1970. One major problem is the danger of replacing the rubber mono-culture (88.1 per cent of total export value in 1951) by another mono-structure, iron ore (77 per cent of national exports in 1970). In both cases prices have declined considerably. Another serious question is co-operation between the members of the projected West African Free Trade Area; only 1 per cent of Liberia's exports is sent to Sierra Leone, Guinea and the Ivory Coast. Future development in trade or industry depends not only on Liberia's good prospects for agricultural and minerals production but also on a large market which allows full use of present and future industrial capacities, e.g. as in the possible integrated West African steel plant at Buchanan.

STATISTICAL SURVEY

AREA AND POPULATION

AREA	POPULATION (1971 est.)	
sq. miles	Total	MONROVIA (capital)
43,000	1,571,477	180,000

Foreign Population (1964): 30,818.

Births and Deaths (1969–70): Annual birth rate 51 per 1,000, death rate 16 per 1,000.

EMPLOYMENT
ECONOMICALLY ACTIVE POPULATION (1962 census)*

	MALE	FEMALE	TOTAL
Agriculture, Forestry, Hunting and Fishing .	194,581	138,536	333,117
Mining	14,071	370	14,441
Manufacturing	7,730	742	8,472
Construction	11,852	180	12,032
Electricity, Gas and Water . . .	366	9	375
Commerce	7,604	3,936	11,540
Transport and Communications . .	3,683	94	3,777
Services	21,230	3,708	24,938
Others	2,443	659	3,102
TOTAL	263,560	148,234	411,794

* Excluding armed forces.

Source: Bureau of Statistics, National Planning Agency, *Statistical Newsletter.*

EMPLOYMENT AND EARNINGS BY INDUSTRY
(Earnings in U.S. $'000)

INDUSTRY	1970 (November)				1971 (November)			
	Employment		Earnings		Employment		Earnings	
	Number	Per cent	Amount	Per cent	Number	Per cent	Amount	Per cent
Agriculture . . .	24,696	54.1	1,265	25.6	24,746	53.0	1,500	30.4
Mining . . .	11,232	24.6	1,976	40.0	11,165	24.0	2,014	40.9
Manufacturing . .	2,049	4.5	410	8.3	2,354	5.1	342	6.9
Construction . .	1,361	3.0	185	3.7	1,344	2.9	168	3.4
Electricity . .	679	1.5	206	4.2	781	1.7	93	1.9
Commerce . .	2,041	4.5	462	9.4	2,352	5.0	408	8.3
Transport . .	2,622	5.7	193	3.9	2,773	5.9	184	3.7
Services . .	954	2.1	244	4.9	1,097	2.4	221	4.5
TOTAL . .	45,634	100.0	4,941	100.0	46,612	100.0	4,930	100.0

AGRICULTURE
LAND USE, 1964
('000 hectares)

Arable and Under Permanent Crops .	3,850
Permanent Meadows and Pastures .	240
Forest	3,622
Other Land	1,919
Inland Water	1,506
TOTAL . . .	11,137

PRINCIPAL CROPS
(metric tons)

	1969	1970	1971
Cassava (Manioc) . . .	370,000*	370,000*	n.a.
Rice (Paddy) . . .	153,000	138,000	91,000
Maize	33,000*	33,000*	33,000*
Natural Rubber (dry weight)† .	66,900	75,600	67,100
Palm Kernels† . . .	11,700	14,100	16,600
Coffee . . .	4,500	5,100	4,500
Cocoa Beans‡ . . .	1,700	1,800	1,800

Palm oil production (1963): 41,200 metric tons.

* FAO estimate.   † Exports only.   ‡ Twelve months ending September.

ACREAGE AND PRODUCTION OF RUBBER CONCESSIONS AND PRIVATE RUBBER FARMS
(lb. dry rubber content—1971)

ENTERPRISE	LOCATION	ACREAGE UNDER RUBBER	ACREAGE IN PRODUCTION	PRODUCTION
Firestone Plantations Company . . .	Harbel and Cavalla	88,895	63,940	95,700,000
The Liberia Company	Cocopa	5,398	3,586	4,188,522
B. F. Goodrich Liberia Inc. . . .	Clay (Kle)	14,013	11,639	14,809,400
African Fruit Company Laeisz & Co. .	Greenville	5,376	4,215	4,188,750
Uniroyal Liberian Agricultural Company .	Buchanan	18,201	11,560	7,489,004
Salala Rubber Corporation . . .	Salala	5,133	4,276	3,600,000
Other Companies	Liberia	86,000	63,349	53,411,008
GRAND TOTAL . . .	Liberia	223,016	162,565	183,386,684

LIVESTOCK
('ooo—FAO estimates)

	1968–69	1969–70	1970–71
Sheep	147	150	156
Goats	137	139	140
Pigs	80	82	83
Cattle	27	28	30
Chickens . . .	1,600	1,650	1,750
Ducks	140	145	150

Production of hen eggs (FAO estimates, metric tons):
1,500 in 1969; 1,600 in 1970; 1,700 in 1971.
Source: FAO, *Production Yearbook 1971.*

FORESTRY
ROUNDWOOD PRODUCTION
('ooo cubic metres)

1967 . . .	1,146
1968 . . .	1,303
1969 . . .	1,500
1970 . . .	1,600

Source: FAO, *Yearbook of Forest Products.*

FISHING
(metric tons)

	1967	1968	1969
Sea	13,500	15,600	18,500
Inland Water . .	4,000*	4,000*	4,000*
TOTAL CATCH .	17,500	19,600	22,500*
Value of Fish Landed (U.S. $'ooo) . .	4,463	5,157	6,116

* FAO estimate.
Source: FAO, *Yearbook of Fishery Statistics 1970.*

MINING

	1967	1968	1969
Iron Ore ('ooo metric tons)* . . .	12,575	13,292	14,786
Gold (kg.) . . .	159	100	n.a.
Diamonds ('ooo carats)†	569	730	836

* Metal content.   † Exports only.

PRODUCTION OF IRON ORE CONCESSIONS
(gross weight, million long tons—1971)

CONCESSION	LOCATION	PRODUCTION
Liberian American Swedish Minerals Company (LAMCO)	Nimba Mountains	10.88
The Liberia Mining Company (LMC) . .	Bomi Hills	2.71
The National Iron Ore Company (NIOC) .	Mano River	4.13
German-Liberian Mining Company (DELIMCO)	Bong Range	4.01
TOTAL	Liberia	21.73

Source: Information from the iron ore concessions.

INDUSTRY

	UNIT	1968	1969
Cement	'ooo metric tons	59	73
Motor Spirit*	,, ,, ,,	2	44
Kerosene*	,, ,, ,,	—	23
Distillate Fuel Oils* . . .	,, ,, ,,	6	91
Residual Fuel Oils* . . .	,, ,, ,,	17	105
Electricity Energy . . .	million kWh.	573	632

Source: U.S. Bureau of Mines.

FINANCE
100 cents=1 Liberian dollar.
Coins: 1, 2, 5, 10, 25 and 50 cents; 1 dollar (U.S. coins are also legal tender).
Notes: 1, 5, 10 and 20 dollars.
Exchange rates (December 1972): £1 sterling=L$2.348; U.S. $1=L$1.00.
L$100=£42.59=U.S. $100.00.

BUDGET
(million U.S.$)

REVENUE	1970	1971
Income Tax . . .	11,000	7,600
Iron Ore Profit Sharing . .	9,850	14,000
Other Direct Taxes . . .	6,600	8,100
Import Duties . . .	17,100	19,000
Export Duties . . .	1,300	825
Consular Fees, etc. . . .	1,200	1,500
Vessel Registration and Tonnage Tax . . .	n.a.	6,200
Other Revenues . . .	14,255	11,520
IMF Drawings (net) . . .	2,000	2,100
TOTAL . . .	63,305	70,845

EXPENDITURE	1970	1971
Recurrent Expenditure . .	38,669	42,034
Debt Servicing . . .	21,539	20,479
Development Expenditures .	4,990	8,686
TOTAL . . .	65,200	71,200
Development Financed from Abroad	7,300	n.a.

GROSS NATIONAL PRODUCT
AT FACTOR COST 1966–70
(million $)

YEAR	GNP
1966 . .	231.5
1967 . .	243.5
1968 . .	259.5
1969 . .	284.0
1970 . .	297.7

FOREIGN ASSISTANCE TO LIBERIA 1968–70
(million $)

DONOR	1968			1970			1971		
	Type		Total	Type		Total	Type		Total
	Loans	Grants		Loans	Grants		Loans	Grant	
United States . . .	6.47	9.77	16.24	2.5	4.9	7.4	3.8	7.9	11.7
World Bank . . .	0.25	—	0.25	1.7	—	1.7	5.1	—	5.1
African Development Bank .	—	—	—	1.4	—	1.4	—	—	—
United Nations . . .	—	1.10	1.10	—	3.2	3.2	—	2.9	2.9
Federal Germany . .	0.55	0.08	0.63	0.1	1.6	1.7	—	1.3	1.3
Republic of China . .	—	0.22	0.22	—	0.4	0.4	—	0.4	0.4
Sweden . . .	—	0.20	0.20	—	0.2	0.2	—	0.3	0.3
Great Britain . . .	—	0.10	0.10	—	0.2	0.2	—	0.3	0.3
Other . . .	—	0.21	0.21	—	0.3	0.3	—	0.3	0.3
TOTAL . .	7.27	11.68	18.95	5.7	10.8	16.5	8.9	13.4	22.3

EXTERNAL TRADE

Imports: (1968) $108.5 million; (1969) $114.6 million; (1970) $149.0 million; (1971) $159.7 million.

Exports: (1968) $169.0 million; (1969) $195.9 million; (1970) $213.7 million; (1971) $224.0 million.

COMMODITIES
($'000)

IMPORTS	1970	1971	EXPORTS	1970	1971
Food	20,744	24,376	Rubber	36,181	32,498
Beverages and Tobacco .	3,222	4,522	Iron Ore	150,689	160,617
Raw Materials . . .	1,767	1,657	Palm Kernels . . .	1,992	2,168
Mineral Fuels and Lubricants .	9,527	11,841	Cocoa	1,015	1,255
Oils and Fats . . .	665	889	Coffee	3,339	4,013
Chemicals . . .	9,663	11,549	Diamonds . . .	5,470	5,650
Manufactured Goods (classified) .	37,872	35,231	Other Commodities . .	14,770	17,797
Machinery and Transport Equipment	50,082	54,174			
Miscellaneous . . .	15,524	15,415			
TOTAL . . .	149,066	159,654	TOTAL . . .	213,456	223,998

COUNTRIES
($'000)

IMPORTS	1970	1971		EXPORTS	1970	1971
United States	46,387	51,918		United States	49,452	49,830
Federal Germany . . .	21,691	15,622		Federal Germany . . .	38,107	41,367
United Kingdom . . .	11,063	14,512		United Kingdom . . .	14,004	7,583
Netherlands	16,202	13,013		Netherlands	32,571	33,635
France	3,730	4,212		France	14,256	12,208
Belgium	1,844	2,315		Belgium	14,707	11,737
Japan	12,212	13,143		Japan	16,045	24,681
Italy	3,663	3,419		Italy	22,111	28,675
Sweden	5,351	5,203		Sweden	1,190	242
Others	27,553	39,063		Others	11,290	14,040
TOTAL . . .	149,696	162,420		TOTAL . . .	213,733	223,998

TRANSPORT
SEA TRAFFIC: MONROVIA
(long tons)

	1970	1971
General Cargo Landed and Loaded . .	539,946	533,771
Iron Ore Loaded . .	12,092,455	10,658,376
Petroleum Landed . .	436,697	510,497
TOTAL CARGO HANDLED	13,069,078	11,702,644

* Jan.-June

ROADS
(Number of registered vehicles)

1962	. .	9,898	1968	. .	19,681
1964	. .	10,137	1969	. .	21,156
1966	. .	11,732	1970	. .	23,210

EDUCATION

	No. OF SCHOOLS	No. OF STUDENTS	No. OF TEACHERS
1968 . .	990	130,871	3,880
1969 . .	n.a.	147,187	4,200
1970 . .	1,087	138,125	4,265
1971 . .	1,121	146,571	4,316

Source: Ministry of Planning and Economic Affairs, Monrovia.

THE CONSTITUTION

Liberia was founded by the American Colonisation Society in 1821, and constituted a free and independent Republic on July 26th, 1847. The Constitution of the Republic is modelled on that of the United States of America. Authority is divided into the Legislative, the Executive, and the Judicial.

Legislative authority is vested in a Legislature consisting of two Houses: the Senate, with 18 members, elected for a six-year term; and the House of Representatives elected for four years, consisting of 52 members.

Electors must either pay a hut tax, or own property in fee simple, or own land. They must be citizens of Liberia.

The Executive power rests with the President, who, with the Vice-President, is elected for an eight-year term. They may be re-elected for periods of four years.

THE GOVERNMENT

President: WILLIAM R. TOLBERT, Jnr.

THE CABINET
(December 1972)

Minister of State: Dr. ROCHEFORT L. WEEKS.

Minister of the Treasury: Hon. STEVEN TOLBERT.

Attorney-General: CLARENCE SIMPSON, Jnr.

Postmaster-General: McKINLEY A. DASHIELD.

Minister of National Defence: ALLEN H. WILLIAMS.

Minister of Local Government, Rural Development and Urban Reconstruction: E. JONATHAN GOODRIDGE.

Minister of Education: GEORGE F. SHERMAN.

Minister of Public Works: GABRIEL TUCKER.

Minister of Agriculture: JAMES T. PHILIPS, Jnr.

Minister of Commerce, Industry and Transportation: W. DENNIS, Jnr.

Minister of National Planning and Economic Affairs: D. FRANKLIN NEAL.

Minister of Information, Cultural Affairs and Tourism: EDWARD B. KESSELLY.

Minister of Health and Welfare: Mrs. MAI BADMORE.

Minister of State for Presidential Affairs: Hon. E. REGINALD TOWNSEND.

Minister of Public Utilities Authority: TAYLOR E. MAJOR.

Minister of Lands and Mines: (vacant).

Minister of Youth and Labour: J. JENKINS PEAL.

DIPLOMATIC REPRESENTATION

EMBASSIES ACCREDITED TO LIBERIA
(In Monrovia unless otherwise indicated)

Belgium: Camp Johnson Hill.

Cameroon: P.O.B. 616, Corner of Newport St., and U.N. Drive.

Canada: Accra, Ghana.

China, Republic of (Taiwan): P.O.B. 27, Sinkor.

Dahomey: Mamba Point.

Denmark: P.O.B. 209.

Egypt: P.O. Box 462, Mamba Point.

Ethiopia: P.O. Box 460, Sinkor.

France: P.O.B. 279, Mamba Point; *Ambassador:* ROGER VINCENOT.

Germany, Federal Republic: P.O.B. 34, Sinkor.

Ghana: P.O.B. 614, Mamba Point; *Ambassador:* Mrs. O. LAMPTE.

Guinea: P.O. Box 461, Front Street.

Haiti: P.O. Box 41, Mamba Point.

India: Accra, Ghana.

Israel: P.O. Box 407, Sinkor.

Italy: P.O. Box 255, Mamba Point.

Ivory Coast: P.O. Box 126, Sinkor.

Japan: Accra, Ghana.

Korea, Republic of: Rabat, Morocco.

Lebanon: P.O. Box 134, Mamba Point.

Mali: P.O. Box 611, Sinkor.

Netherlands: P.O. Box 284, Capitol Hill.

Niger: Mamba Point.

Nigeria: Conakry, Guinea.

Sierra Leone: 152 Benson St.; *Ambassador:* Dr. R. E. KELFA-CAULKER.

Spain: P.O. Box 275, Sinkor.

Sweden: C. D. B. King Bldg., Broad St.

Switzerland: Accra, Ghana.

U.S.S.R.: Monrovia.

United Kingdom: P.O.B. 120, Mamba Point; *Ambassador:* M. J. MOYNIHAN, M.C.

U.S.A.: P.O.B. 98, Mamba Point; *Ambassador:* SAMUEL Z. WESTERFIELD.

Upper Volta: Mamba Point.

Vatican: Mamba Point (Apostolic Nunciature).

Yugoslavia: Accra, Ghana.

Zambia: (E); Abidjan, Ivory Coast.

Liberia also has diplomatic relations with the following states: Austria, Greece, Indonesia, Mauritania, Norway, Panama, the Philippines, Senegal and Zaire.

CONGRESS

SENATE
Eighteen members.

President: F. TOLBERT (Acting)

HOUSE OF REPRESENTATIVES
Fifty-two members.

Speaker: R.A. HENRIES.

POLITICAL PARTY

True Whig Party: in power for more than fifty years; progressive democratic.

DEFENCE

The National Guard numbers 4,000, the navy and coast-guard service 150, the para-military force 6,000 and the civil police 750. Liberia has a bilateral military assistance agreement with the U.S.A.

JUDICIAL SYSTEM

The judicial authority in the Republic of Liberia is vested in the Supreme Court, the Circuit Courts, and the Lower Courts. There are ten Circuit Courts, two established at Monrovia and the others throughout the country. One Territorial Court is established in the Marshall Territory, and one in River Cess Territory. Lower Courts function in the Districts and Settlements.

Chief Justice: JAMES A. A. PIERRE.

Associate Justices: A. H. ROBERTS, W. E. WORDSWORTH, LAWRENCE MITCHELL, C. L. SIMPSON, Jnr.

RELIGION

Liberia is officially a Christian state though complete religious freedom is guaranteed throughout the Republic. Christianity and Islam are the two main religions. Most Liberians hold traditional beliefs.

Christian Churches represented in Liberia include the following:

Providence Baptist Church: Corner of Broad and Center Streets, Monrovia; f. 1822 by the Rev. Lott Carey of Richmond, Virginia, U.S.A., and others; oldest church and oldest building in Liberia; its history is closely bound up with the history of Liberia; Pastor Rev. Dr. JOHN B. FALCONER; Chair. of Board of Trustees Deacon WILLIAM E. DENNIS; Sec. DEACON SAMUEL HILL. Associated with: **The Liberia Baptist Missionary and Educational Convention, Inc.:** f. 1880; Pres. Rev. Dr. WILLIAM R. TOLBERT, Jnr.; National Vice-Pres. Rev. T. I. B. FINDLEY; Gen. Sec. NATHANIEL R. RICHARDSON.

Methodist Church in Liberia: P.O.B. 1010, Monrovia; f. 1833; approx. 20,000 adherents, 220 congregations, 218 ministers, 18 schools; Resident Bishop, Bishop STEPHEN TROWEN NAGBE, Sr.; Sec. Rev. ISAAC M. DAVIS; Educational Sec. Rev. ARTHUR F. KULAH.

Roman Catholic Church: Catholic Mission, P.O.B. 297, Monrovia; f. 1907; approx. 20,000 mems., 7,000 pupils in elementary schools, 5,000 in high schools and colleges.

Vicar-Apostolic of Monrovia: His Grace, Archbishop P. FRANCIS CARROLL, S.M.A., Apostolic Nunciature, Monrovia.

Vicar-Apostolic of Cape Palmas: Most Rev. PATRICK KRA JUWLE, Cape Palmas.

Education Secretary: F. VAN VYFEYKEN, S.M.A.

Assemblies of God in Liberia: P.O.B. 40, Monrovia; 235 churches; approx. 9,000 adherents.

American Protestant Episcopal Church: Monrovia; f. 1836; approx. 12,612 mems.; 40 elementary schools, 5 high schools and 1 college; approx. 12,600 mems.; Bishop: Rt. Rev. GEORGE D. BROWNE.

Other denominations are: African Methodist Episcopal Church, African Methodist Episcopal Zion Church, Evangelical Lutheran Church, National Baptist Mission, Presbyterian Church in Liberia.

Islam: divided into two denominations, Ahmadyya and Mohammedanism. The total community is about 200,000.

THE PRESS

NEWSPAPERS

Daily Listener, The: P.O.B. 35, Monrovia; f. 1950; Editor-in-Chief and Publisher CHARLES C. DENNIS; circ. 3,500.

Diplomatist & News Digest, The: Johnson St., Monrovia; f. 1961; weekly; Editor and Publisher KINGSPRIDE UGBOMA; circ. 500.

Liberian Age, The: P.O.B. 286, Monrovia; f. 1946; twice weekly; circ. 10,000.

Liberian Star, The: P.O.B. 691, United Nations Drive, Monrovia; f. 1964; five times a week; independent; Publisher Republic Press of Liberia Inc.; Editor H. B. COLE.

PERIODICALS

Kpelle Messenger, The: Kpelle; Kpelle-English monthly newspaper; Kpelle Literary Center, Lutheran Church, P.O.B. 1046, Monrovia.

Liberia Journal of Commerce and Industry: Palm Publications Co., Bank of Liberia Bldg., Monrovia; quarterly; Man. Editor JAMES C. DENNIS.

Liberian Churchman, The: Robertsport Cape, Mount Country, Liberia; journal of the Protestant Episcopal Church; every two months; Editor Rt. Rev. D. H. BROWN; circ. 1,000.

Liberian Review, The: P.O.B. 268, Monrovia; illustrated quarterly; Editor HENRY B. COLE; circ. 5,000.

Liberian Year Book, The: P.O.B. 268, Monrovia; f. 1956 Editor HENRY B. COLE; circ. 15,000.

Liberian Trade and Industry Handbook: P.O.B. 286, Monrovia; annual; Editors HENRY B. COLE and ARTHUR B. CASSELL, Sr.; circ. 10,000.

Loma Weekly Paper, The: P.O.B. 1046, Monrovia; bilingual weekly in Loma and English.

New Day: Fundamental & Mass Education Department of Public Instruction, Monrovia: illustrated monthly for new literates; Editor Mrs. MARGARET TRAUB; circ. 500.

Palm: Monrovia; news magazine; monthly.

Saturday Chronicle: P.O.B. 35, Monrovia; f. 1969; weekly; Publisher and Editor-in-Chief CHARLES C. DENNIS, Sr., circ. 8,000.

Sunday Digest: P.O.B. 35, Monrovia; f. 1967; weekly; Publisher and Editor-in-Chief CHARLES C. DENNIS, Sr., circ. 3,500.

PRESS AGENCIES

Ministry of Information, Cultural Affairs and Tourism: Monrovia; receives world news from centres, UPI, AP, AFP, and Tass.

FOREIGN BUREAUX

Reuters and UPI have offices in Monrovia; Tass has a correspondent.

RADIO AND TELEVISION

Liberian Broadcasting Corporation: P.O.B. 594, Monrovia; controls all forms of broadcasting, Gen. Man. G. HENRY ANDREWS.

RADIO

E.L.B.C.: P.O.B. 594, Monrovia; f. 1959; commercial station jointly sponsored by Liberian Government and Overseas Rediffusion Ltd.; also operates a relay station for the BBC World Service; Gen. Man. G. H. ANDREWS.

ELWA: P.O.B. 192, Monrovia; Station of the Sudan Interior Mission; religious, cultural and educational broadcasts in English, French, Arabic and 35 West African languages; Gen. Man. Rev. WILLIAM THOMPSON.

Lamco Broadcasting Station (ELNR): Nimba; owned by Lamco J. V. (*see* Transport); relays BBC World News, E.L.B.C. programmes and broadcasts its own programmes in English and African languages for Lamco workers; Gen. Man. R. MORRIS.

Voice of America: Washington, D.C. 20547, U.S.A.; Monrovia; a short-wave relay station, the biggest in Africa, came into operation in 1964; broadcasts in English, French and Swahili.

Number of radio receivers: 155,000 (1972).

TELEVISION

ELTV: Liberian Broadcasting Corporation, P.O.B. 594, Monrovia; f. 1964; commercial station.

Number of TV receivers: 7,000 (1972).

FINANCE

BANKING

Bank of Liberia Inc.: P.O.B. 131, Carey and Warren Streets, Monrovia; f. 1955; affiliate of Chemical Bank, New York; full service commercial bank; Man. TOM DUFFY.

Bank of Monrovia: P.O.B. 280, Ashmun St., Monrovia; f. 1955 as an affiliate of the First National City, New York; 7 brs.; Pres. ELLIS BRADFORD.

Chase Manhattan Bank N.A.: Corner of Randall and Ashmun Streets, P.O.B. 181, Monrovia; f. 1961; one sub-branch; f. 1970; Gen. Man. PETER G. BATES.

International Trust Co. of Liberia: P.O.B. 292, 80 Broad St., Monrovia; f. 1948; br. at Nimba; Pres. HENRY N. CONWAY, Jnr.

Liberian Bank for Industrial Development and Investment (LBIDI): 100 Broad St., Monrovia; f. 1965 by IFC, Liberian, European and U.S. investors; development bank, cap. $1m.

Liberian Trading and Development Bank Ltd. (TRADEVCO): P.O.B. 293, 80 Ashmun St., Monrovia; f. 1955; cap. $200,000, dep. (1970) $4,055,957; Chair. MASSIMO SPADA; Man. F. BERNANDINI.

Union National Bank (Liberia) Inc.: Water-Randall Streets, P.O.B. 655, Monrovia; f. 1962; Lebanon-owned with a 20 per cent holding by Liberians; cap. $1m.

INSURANCE

International Trust Co. of Liberia: 80 Broad St., P.O.B. 292, Monrovia; Pres. HENRY N. CONWAY, Jnr.

TRADE AND INDUSTRY

LIBERIA-U.S. COMMISSION

Joint Liberia-U.S. Commission for Economic Development: Ashmun St., P.O.B. 141, Monrovia; f. 1950; Exec. Sec. EMMETT HARMON.

CHAMBER OF COMMERCE

Liberia Chamber of Commerce: P.O.B. 92, Monrovia; f. 1951; Pres. Hon. P. CLARENCE PARKER; Sec.-Gen. DAVID N. HOWELL.

DEVELOPMENT ORGANIZATION

Liberian Development Corporation: Department of Commerce and Industry Bldg., Monrovia; f. 1961; independent agency of the Government; to stimulate industrial development and foster existing industries; Gen. Man. Mrs. LOUISE SUMMERVILLE; Exec. Sec. E. MOMOLOU FREEMAN; pubis. *Feasibility and prefeasibility studies*, other technical documents (reports).

EMPLOYERS' ASSOCIATION

Liberian Businessmen's Association: Monrovia; Pres. EMMANUEL SHAW.

TRADE UNIONS

Congress of Industrial Organizations: 29 Ashmun St., P.O.B. 415, Monrovia; Pres. W. V. S. TUBMAN, Jnr.; Sec. TOM SAWYER; 5 affiliated unions.

Labour Congress of Liberia: 71 Gurley St., Monrovia; Sec.-Gen. P. C. T. SONPON; 8 affiliated unions.

MAJOR INDUSTRIAL COMPANIES

The following are some of the largest companies in terms either of capital investment or employment.

Bong Mining Company: P.O.B. 538, Monrovia; f. 1961; cap. U.S. $16.5m.
Operating Company for DELIMCO (German Liberian Mining Company), P.O.B. 538, Monrovia. Carries out iron ore mining, upgrading of crude ore and transportation of concentrate to Port of Monrovia for shipment abroad. Present capacity: 4m. tons of concentrate and 2m. tons of pellets annually.
Pres. Dr. EUGEN PLOTZKI; Gen. Man. K. A. HEDDERICH; 2,500 employees.

Firestone Plantations Company: P.O.B. 140, Harbel; f. 1926.
Operates two rubber plantations totalling approximately 103,000 acres; purchases rubber from private farmers; processes rubber for shipment to the world market; carries out research and development.
Vice-Pres. and Man. Dir. JOHN P. CARMICHAEL, 16,290 employees.

Liberia American Swedish Minerals Company (LAMCO): P.O.B. 69, Monrovia; mining of iron ore; Liberian Government holds 50 per cent of shares.

Liberian Cement Corporation: Freeway, Monrovia; manufacture of cement.

The Liberia Company: P.O.B. 45, Broadstreet, Monrovia; f. 1947; cap. U.S. $1m.
Travel and shipping agents; business agents for HALCO mining and COCOPA rubber plantations.
Pres. J. T. TRIPPE (New York); Asst. Vice-Pres. and Resident Man. L. DE VROOM; 828 employees.

Liberian Iron and Steel Corporation: P.O.B. 876, Monrovia; f. 1967; mining of iron ore.

Liberian Mining Company: P.O.B. 251-2, Monrovia; mining of iron ore.

Liberia Refinery Co.: Mamba Point, Monrovia.

National Iron Ore Company: P.O.B. 548, Monrovia; state-owned company for the mining of iron ore.

Texaco Africa Ltd.: P.O.B. 360, Bank of Liberia Building, Monrovia; f. 1920; paid-up capital incorporated in Canada.
Distributors of petroleum products. Man. C. PEEL; 40 employees.

United States Trading Company: P.O.B. 140, Monrovia; f. 1949; subsidiary of Firestone Tyre and Rubber Company, Akron, Ohio, U.S.A.
Distribution of Firestone products; Ford U.S.A. and U.K. vehicle sales and service, wholesalers and retailers of foodstuffs and beverages.

TRANSPORT AND TOURISM

TRANSPORT
RAILWAYS

Bong Mining Co. Ltd.: P.O.B. 538, Monrovia; 50 miles of track to transport iron ore from Bong Town to Monrovia; Gen. Man. K. A. HEDDERICH.

Liberian Mining Co.: P.O.B. 251-2, Monrovia; 92 miles of track, Bomi to Monrovia, for transport of iron ore; Vice-Pres. and Gen. Man. W. K. SCHEIBE.

National Iron Ore Company: track carries ore to Bomi, linking with the Liberian Mining Co.'s line to Monrovia; Gen. Man. CH. RULE.

Lamco J.V. Operating Co.: Roberts International Airport; 168 miles of standard track extending from Buchanan to the iron ore mine at Nimba; opened 1963; Gen. Man. O. WIJKSTROEM; Man. Operation Buchanan OLLE GORANSSON; Man. Operation Nimba JOHN BERGE.

There are no passenger railways.

ROADS

The mileage of public and private roads is estimated at 4,100. The main trunk road is the Monrovia–Sanniquellie Motor Road extending north-east from the capital to the border of French West Africa, near Ganta, and eastward through the hinterland. A trunk road has been completed to Tappita, headquarters of District 3, Central Province, and has been extended through Eastern Province. The entire route from Monrovia to Cape Palmas was finished in 1963. In 1969 the U.S. Agency for International Development granted Liberia a 10-year interest-free loan of $975,000 for road construction.

SHIPPING

In 1967 the National Port Authority was created to develop and manage all Liberian ports (Exec. Officer Board of Dirs. GEORGE E. TUBMAN). The Free Port, largest of Monrovia's nine ports, is directed by the Monrovia Port Management Company Ltd., comprising the Republic of Liberia and seven American firms: Farrell Lines Inc., Firestone Plantations Co., Liberia Co., Liberia Mining Co. Ltd., Mississippi Shipping Co. (Delta Line), Socony-Vacuum Oil Co. and Texas Co.; Pres. of the Board Admiral WAVEHOPE.

There are about 150 shipping companies registered at Monrovia.

The principal lines calling at Monrovia are: Chargeurs Réunis, Delta Lines, Elder Dempster Lines, Farrell Lines, Hanseatischer Afrika-Dienst, Holland-West Africa Line, Jugolinija, Lloyd Triestino, Palm Line, Royal Interocean Lines, Scandinavian West Africa Line, United West Africa Service.

CIVIL AVIATION

Liberia's chief airport is at Robertsfield Airport, 50 miles east of Monrovia. A five-year development plan for this airport is being financed by a $4,000,000 loan agreement between the U.S. and Liberian Governments. Spriggs Payne Airfield, Sinkor, Monrovia, handles chiefly internal traffic. There are numerous other airfields and airstrips, some linking Spriggs Payne Airfield with Robertsfield.

NATIONAL LINES

Liberian National Airlines Inc.: Robertsfield International Airport; f. 1949; services from Robertsfield and Monrovia to Buchanan, Cape Palmas and Sinoe; fleet of two DC-3; Pres. A. ROMEO HORTON; Gen. Man. Capt. F. H. SYPHERT.

Air Taxi Company of Liberia: P.O.B. 183, Monrovia; operates internal services; Pres. Hon. SAMUEL D. GEORGE; Bus. Man. J. CAESAR GREENE.

Ducor Air Transport Company (DATCO): Spriggs Payne Airfield; internal services.

FOREIGN AIRLINES

Monrovia is also served by the following foreign airlines: Air Afrique (Ivory Coast), Air Guinée, Air Mali, Ghana Airways, KLM, MEA, Nigeria Airways, PAA, Sabena, SAS, Swissair, UTA.

TOURISM

Bureau of Tourism: Office in the Ministry of Information, Cultural Affairs and Tourism; Minister Hon. G. HENRY ANDREWS; Deputy Minister for Tourism Hon. T. NELSON WILLIAMS.

EDUCATION

Education is provided by the state and by religious organizations. The Four-Year Development Programme launched in 1967 aimed to increase the number of primary pupils from 64,000 to 80,000 in 1970, and to increase secondary education from 8,400 to 13,500. There is one university.

LEARNED SOCIETIES AND RESEARCH INSTITUTES

Central Agriculture Experimental Station: Suakoko; f. 1946; under Ministry of Agriculture; research on crops, animal husbandry, horticulture, soil, and inland fisheries; rice research under UNDP Project; service centre for supply of improved seeds, plant material and animals; Dir. Dr. A. RATHORE.

Geological, Mining and Metallurgical Society of Liberia: P.O.B. 9024, Monrovia; f. 1964; Pres. JOSEPH G. RICHARDS; Sec. M. W. GODA BAKER; publ. *Bulletin*.

The Liberian Institute of the American Foundation for Tropical Medicine, Inc.: P.O.B. 64, Harbel; f. 1952; research into the tropical diseases of man; the diseases of domestic animals which can be a source of food in tropical countries; and the improvement and development of crops which can be grown in the tropics as food for man and domestic animals; Dir. E. W. REBER.

Nimba Research Laboratory: c/o Lamco J. V. Operating Co., Grassland, Nimba, Robertsfield; f. 1962; under supervision of Nimba Research Committee of International Union for Conservation of Nature and Natural Resources in co-operation with UNESCO; biological and ecological exploration and field work in the Mount Nimba region and conservation; library of 100 vols. and access to LAMCO library, Yekepa; Chair. KAI CURRY-LINDAHL, Bruce House, Standard St., Nairobi.

LIBRARIES

Government Public Library: Ashmun St., Monrovia; f. 1959; 15,000 vols.

Liberian Information Service Library: Monrovia; reference.

United States Information Service Library: Broad St., Monrovia; operated jointly by the Liberian Government and the United States Government; 6,000 vols., 121 periodicals.

UNESCO Mission Library: Monrovia.

University of Liberia Libraries: University of Liberia, Monrovia; f. 1862; 50,000 vols., 900 periodicals; 8 professional librarians; Dir. C. WESLEY ARMSTRONG.

UNIVERSITY AND COLLEGES

UNIVERSITY OF LIBERIA
MONROVIA
Telephone: 22537.

Founded as Liberia College 1862; University 1951.

Language of instruction: English; Academic year: February to December (two semesters).

By the amended Charter of 1961 the University incorporates the following colleges: College of Liberal and Fine Arts (Liberia College), The Louis Arthur Grimes School of Law, The William V. S. Tubman Teachers' College, The College of Agriculture and Forestry.

Visitor and Chairman Ex-officio of the Board of Trustees: Dr. WILLIAM TOLBERT, Jr., President, Republic of Liberia.

Dean of Administration: Dr. ADVERTUS A. HOFF.

Registrar: Mr. JAMES J. COOPER.

Controller: L. E. GBEYON.

Librarian: C. W. ARMSTRONG.

Library of 50,000 volumes.
Number of teachers: *c.* 140.
Number of students: 1,000.

Publications: *The University of Liberia Catalogue and Announcements, The University of Liberia Journal, This Week on Campus, A Short History of Liberia College and the University of Liberia, University of Liberia Register of Graduates, The University of Liberia Law Journal, The William V. S. Tubman Teachers' College Bulletin.*

DEANS:

College of Liberal and Fine Arts: Dr. JOHN BERNARD BLAMO.

William V. S. Tubman College of Teachers' Training: Dr. MARY A. BROWN.

Louis Arthur Grimes School of Law: Prof. J. W. GARBER.

College of Agriculture and Forestry: PATRICK D. BROPLEH (acting).

Division of Science, College of Liberal and Fine Arts: Mrs. AGNES COOPER DENNIS (Chairman).

Institute of African Studies: Mrs. FATIMA M. FAHNBULLEH (Director).

Extramural Studies: R. D. GIFFORD (Director).

BOOKER WASHINGTON AGRICULTURAL AND INDUSTRIAL INSTITUTE
KAKATA

Owned and operated by the Government of Liberia through the Department of Education, and a Board of Managers.

Principal: M. KRON YANH WEEFUR.

CUTTINGTON COLLEGE AND DIVINITY SCHOOL
c/o EPISCOPAL CHURCH OFFICE BUILDING,
P.O.B. 277, MONROVIA
Telephone: Monrovia 21065.

Founded 1889 (closed 1929 and reopened 1949).

Cuttington College is maintained by the Protestant Episcopal Church of America, in co-operation with the Methodist Board of Foreign Missions and the United Lutheran Church. It maintains a working relationship with the United States Associated Colleges of the Midwest and is a member of the Association of Episcopal Colleges (U.S.A.).

Language of instruction: English; Academic year: March to November.

Chairman of the Board of Trustees: A. B. CUMMINGS.

President: CHRISTIAN E. BAKER, B.S.A., B.S., D.V.M.

Business Manager: ADDO DAVIES.

Registrar: MAYME L. BRUMSKIN.

Librarian: H. MINNIE KING.

The library contains approx. 48,000 vols., 200 periodicals.

Number of teachers: 29.
Number of students: 195.

Publications: *Cuttington Review, Echoes of Cuttington, Cuttington College and Divinity School Catalogue, Phebe Nursing Brochure.*

DEANS:

Dean of Instruction: MELVIN J. MASON, M.A., ED.D.

Dean of Men: HARRY ODODA, M.A.

Dean of Women: IRENE McINTOSH, B.S.

Dean of Student Services: J. LAURORE, B.A., DIP.TH.

HEADS OF DIVISIONS:

Education: C. TEMPLIN, M.A.

Social Science: R. BRADFORD, PH.D.

Humanities: J. LAFONTANT, B.SC.

Science: K. C. JOHN, PH.D.

Nursing: H. KOHLER, B.SC., M.A.

SELECT BIBLIOGRAPHY

AZIKIWE, N. *Liberia in World Politics.* London, 1934.

BROWN, G. W. *The Economic History of Liberia.* Washington, 1941.

BROWN ENGINEERS. *Transportation Survey of Liberia.* New York, 1963.

BUELL, R. L. *Liberia: A Century of Survival, 1847–1947* (African Handbooks, 7). Philadelphia, University of Pennsylvania Press, 1947.

CLOWER, R. W., DALTON, G., HARWITZ, M., and WALTERS, A. A. *Growth Without Development: An Economic Survey of Liberia.* Evanston, 1966.

HIMMELHEBER, H., and U. *Die Dan.* Stuttgart, 1958.

HUBERICH, C. H. *The Political and Legislative History of Liberia,* 2 vols. New York, 1947.

JOHNSTON, Sir HARRY. *Liberia,* 2 vols. London, 1906.

LIEBENOW, J. G. *Liberia, the Evolution of Privilege.* Ithaca and London, Cornell University Press, 1969.

McLAUGHLIN, R. U. *Foreign Investment and Development in Liberia.* New York, Washington, London, 1966.

PORTER, P. W. "Liberia", *Focus,* 12/1, September, 1961. *Population Distribution and Land Use in Liberia.* Ph.D. Thesis (unpublished). London, 1956.

REPUBLIC OF LIBERIA. *Reports of the 1962 Census of Population.* Monrovia, 1964. *Annual Reports* of Government Departments.

RICHARDSON, N. R. *Liberia's Past and Present.* London, 1959.

SCHULZE, W. *Economic Development and the Growth of Transportation in Liberia.* Occasional Paper No. 1 of the Sierra Leone Geographical Association. Freetown, 1965.
"Liberia. Bevölkerungsstruktur und Bevölkerungsverteilung", *Geograph. Taschenbuch 1966/9,* pp. 147–159, 1968.
"The Ports of Liberia: Economic Significance and Development Problems", in HOYLE, B. S., and HILLING, D. (Eds.), *Seaports and Development in Tropical Africa.* London, 1969.

SCHWAB, G. *Tribes of the Liberian Hinterland.* Papers of the Peabody Museum, vol. 31. Cambridge, Mass., 1947.

TAYLOR, W. CH. *The Firestone Operations in Liberia.* (5th Case Study on U.S. Business Performance Abroad.) New York, National Planning Association, 1956.

TIXIER, G. *La République du Liberia.* Paris, Berger-Levrault, 1970.

WESTERMANN, D. *Die Gola.* Hamburg, 1921. *Die Kpelle.* Göttingen, 1921.

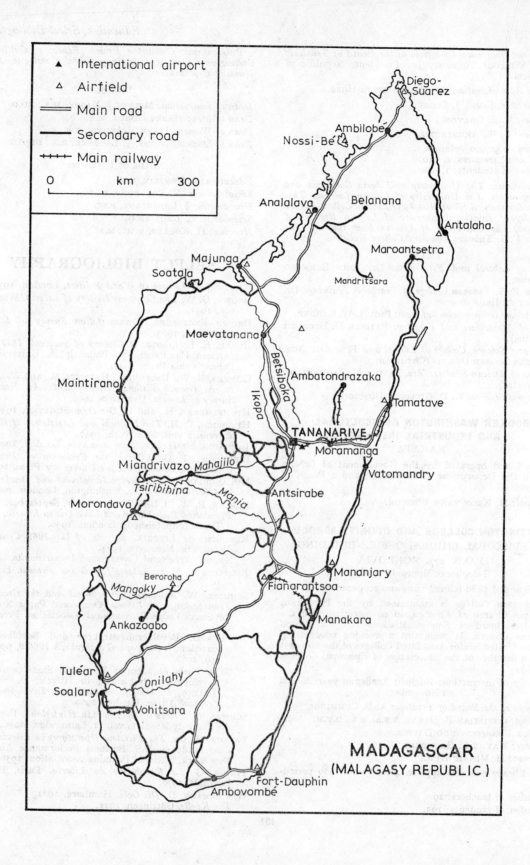

International airport ▲
Airfield △
Main road ══════
Secondary road ─────
Main railway ┼┼┼┼┼

0   km   300

Diego-Suarez

Ambilobe

Nossi-Bé

Belanana

Analalava

Antalaha

Maroantsetra

Majunga

Soatala

Mandritsara

Maevatanana

Ambatondrazaka

Maintirano

Betsiboka

Ikopa

Tamatave

TANANARIVE

Moramanga

Miandrivazo

Mahajilo

Vatomandry

Tsiribihina

Mania

Antsirabe

Morondava

Mananjary

Beroroha

Fianarantsoa

Mangoky

Manakara

Ankazoabo

Tuléar

Soalary

Onilahy

Vohitsara

MADAGASCAR
(MALAGASY REPUBLIC)

Fort-Dauphin

Ambovombé

Madagascar

Virginia Thompson

PHYSICAL AND SOCIAL GEOGRAPHY

PHYSICAL ENVIRONMENT

Madagascar, now called the Malagasy Republic, is the fourth largest island in the world, and is separated from the African mainland by the Mozambique channel. It is 994 miles (1,600 km.) long from north to south, its width varies between 279 and 354 miles (450–570 km.), and it covers an area of 226,658 sq. miles (587,041 sq. km.). Geologically the island is composed basically of crystalline rock. That rock structure forms the central highlands which rise abruptly from the narrow eastern coastal strip but descend gradually to the wide plains of the west coast. Topographically Madagascar can be divided into six fairly distinct regions.

Diégo-Suarez province in the north is virtually isolated by the island's highest peak, Mt. Tsaratanana, 9,000 ft.(2,800 metres). Tropical crops can be grown in its fertile valleys, and its great natural harbour is still an important French naval base. Another rich agricultural region lies in the north-west, where a series of valleys converge on the port of Majunga. To the south-west along the coastal plains lies a well-watered region where there are large animal herds and crops of rice, cotton, tobacco, and manioc. The southernmost province, Tuléar, contains most of Madagascar's known mineral deposits, as well as extensive cattle herds, despite the almost total lack of rainfall. In contrast, the hot and humid climate of the east coast favours the cultivation of the island's most valuable tropical crops—coffee, vanilla, cloves, and sugar-cane. Although this coast lacks sheltered anchorages, it is the site of Madagascar's most important commercial port, Tamatave. Behind its coral beaches a continuous chain of lagoons, some of which are connected by the Pangalanes Canal, provides a partially navigable internal waterway. The island's mountainous hinterland is a densely populated region of extensive rice culture and stock raising. Despite its relative inaccessibility, this region is Madagascar's administrative and cultural centre, the focal point being the capital city of Tananarive.

Climatic conditions are as divergent as the island is geographically compartmentalized. They vary from tropical conditions on the east and north-west coasts to the hotness and dryness of the west coast, the extreme aridity of the south, and the temperate zone in the central highlands. Forests have survived only in some areas of abundant rainfall, and elsewhere the land has been eroded by over-grazing and slash-and-burn farming methods. Most of the island is savannah-steppe, and much of the interior is covered with laterite. Except in the drought-ridden south, rivers are numerous and flow generally westward, but many are cut by rapids and waterfalls, and few are navigable except for short distances. Madagascar's isolation is undoubtedly responsible for the survival there of its unusual flora and fauna.

POPULATION

Geography and history account for the diversity and distribution of the island's population. Its 18 "tribes" are the descendants of successive waves of immigrants from such diverse areas as south-east Asia, continental Africa, and Arab countries. The largest and most distinctive cultural group are the Merina and Betsileo (totalling some 2.5 million), who live mainly in the central highlands, while the so-called côtiers, of whom the most numerous are the Betsimisaraka (997,000), inhabit the peripheral areas. The figure of an overall density of 11 persons to the square kilometre means little, for parts of the south and west are almost uninhabited, whereas the central provinces of Fianarantsoa and Tananarive, which account for only 4 per cent of the total area, contain 27 per cent of the island's total population. Madagascar, as a whole, is still underpopulated, although the Malagasys are increasing at the rate of 2.2 per cent per annum. By 1970 the population totalled 6,750,000 (compared with about four million before the Second World War), of whom nearly half are under 15 years of age. Their diverse origins and uneven distribution have created a strong sense of regionalism and in some cases have perpetuated tribal antagonisms. These have been only slightly attenuated by a marked degree of cultural unity and continuous internal migrations, of which the sharp increase in the urban population is the outstanding recent manifestation.

Despite the current exodus from rural areas, the urban component accounts as yet for only 14 per cent of the total population. Although Tananarive, with 335,000 residents in 1968, has been growing at a slower rate than in the early 1960s (now about 4,000 persons a year), Tamatave, the next largest city, has but 55,000, and the population of each of the other five provincial capitals does not exceed 50,000. The towns, however, contain almost all the European element, the most numerous being French nationals (33,100 metropolitan Frenchmen, and about 47,000 others from the nearby islands of Réunion and the Comoros). The number of metropolitan French has markedly declined since 1960, whereas that of the Asians, the next most important alien economic minority, is steadily increasing, even though their immigration and economic activities have been severely restricted since the late 1930s. The Indians, who total more than 17,000, are concentrated on the west coast, where they control the trade in textiles and jewellery. The Chinese, numbering about 8,900, live scattered throughout the east coast region, where they specialize in selling foodstuffs, in small-scale banking operations, and in collecting rural produce.

Administratively the Asians are everywhere organized into *congrégations*, each under a chief chosen by them but appointed by and responsible to the government. Although foreigners form less than 1 per cent of the total population and play no overt political role in Madagascar, the Asians' rapid natural growth, their cultural unassimilability, their ties with the world's two most populous nations and, above all, their economic power give rise to concern on the part of the Malagasy government.

RECENT HISTORY

FRENCH RULE

Great Britain's recognition in 1890 of France's dominant position in Madagascar enabled France to annex the island six years later and to retain it in the French political and economic orbit for the next 70 years. The conquest did not, however, resolve the basic ethnic and religious conflicts which remained, despite Madagascar's comparatively high degree of political development, and for which the rivalry between the two European powers had been to some degree responsible during much of the nineteenth century.

By 1828 the rulers of the Merina tribe, who were probably of Malayo-Polynesian origin, had asserted their sovereignty and imposed their language throughout most of Madagascar. Their subsequent conversion by British Protestant missionaries had important collateral consequences. Emissaries of the London Missionary Society not only gave the Malagasy language a written form, but also influenced the islanders' political evolution by reinforcing the existing divisions between the Merina and Betsileo peoples of the central highlands and the predominantly Negroid coastal tribes (*côtiers*), who were largely converted to Catholicism by French Jesuits.

Malagasy Resistance

Open, though sporadic, resistance to these alien political and cultural influences persisted until the early twentieth century. In 1904 General Gallieni, governor of Madagascar from 1896 to 1905, completed the French conquest of the island, gave it an administrative framework, and installed state schools and medical facilities to supplement those that had been started by the missionaries. Gallieni also encouraged study of the Malagasy language and culture, introduced new crops, and integrated the island with France's economy.

The discovery of a nationalist "plot" in 1915, followed by growing Malagasy demands for French citizenship, led to the establishment in 1924 of an advisory council called the *Délégations Financières*. This concession, however, failed to satisfy Malagasy aspirations for more self-government because the members of the council were nominated, Europeans outnumbered native councillors, and the two groups neither met nor voted together. Nor was the far more liberal régime instituted in 1946 regarded as satisfactory, although Madagascar now elected representatives to the French parliament and also to a territorial assembly, which had some control over the budget. By then all the Malagasys had become French citizens, but the franchise was restricted to the small Gallicized élite, territorial assemblymen were indirectly elected by provincial councils, French—not Malagasy—was the sole official language, and no change was made in the dual-electoral-college system.

The 1947 Revolt

Resentment at their subordinate status was felt especially by the educated Merina, who still regarded themselves as Madagascar's legitimate rulers. It was the Merina who inspired the bloody revolt of 1947, but the *côtiers* who mainly bore its brunt. The number of victims who died during the revolt and its harsh repression has been estimated by different authorities at 11,000 and 80,000, and the repercussions of this holocaust are felt to this day. Inevitably that episode reinforced the antagonism between the island's two main ethnic groups, as well as the authoritarian nature of the colonial régime. It was not until 1956 that the French parliament passed the *loi cadre*, which instituted universal adult suffrage and gave Malagasy a significant share in the executive power.

INDEPENDENCE

The *loi cadre* paved the way for a resumption of Malagasy political activities that had been in abeyance since the repression of the 1947 revolt. To fill the void and weight the political balance against the more nationalistic and educated Merina, the colonial administration encouraged the development of a party composed of *côtiers*. Thus, in 1957, was formed the *Parti social démocrate* (PSD) under the leadership of Philibert Tsiranana, a schoolteacher of the Tsimihety tribe, who had acquired political experience as Madagascar's deputy in the French national assembly, where he had joined the socialist party. His diploma from Montpellier University won him the respect of the *côtier* élite, and his genial personality, boundless energy, and practical commonsense endeared him to the Malagasy masses. The PSD expanded rapidly throughout the island, and in 1960 Tsiranana was easily elected the first president of independent Madagascar. The granting of independence by France in 1960 without an armed struggle was a decisive factor in establishing the close collaboration that subsequently characterized Franco-Malagasy relations.

PSD DOMINANCE

The 1959 Malagasy constitution was of the presidential type, and Tsiranana increasingly utilized his executive authority to consolidate his own power and centralize the government. His civil-servant appointees augmented the administration's powers over Madagascar's local-government institutions, which comprised six elected provincial councils, 26 urban communes and 739 rural communes. In the bi-cameral legislature all but three deputies out of 107, and two senators out of 54, were members of the PSD. Progressively the PSD absorbed all but two of its many early rivals, and the only organized opposition of any significance was the left-wing AKFM, or Party of the Congress of Independence, founded in 1958. The AKFM's able and cultured leader is a Merina Protestant minister, Richard Andrianamanjato, who has been re-elected seven times mayor of Tananarive, which is his party's stronghold. Thus the age-old conflict between *côtiers* and Merina acquired an organized, modern political form, and despite some inroads made by the PSD throughout the 1960s, their respective geographical and ethnic bastions remained almost unchanged. The PSD by its numerical preponderance, its control of government jobs, and the skill of its leaders enjoyed almost unchallenged power throughout the decade following independence. The only significant elements that escaped its control were the hierarchies of the two principal Christian churches, the press, and a growing number of radical young intellectuals.

Economic Policy

Developments since 1969 brought to an end the long period of political peace and governmental stability that Madagascar enjoyed under PSD rule. Faced with the marked deterioration of the island's economy that followed closure of the Suez Canal in 1967, the strikes in France during 1968, and the franc's devaluation in 1969, the government has felt constrained to develop policies that not only revitalized the radical opposition but caused a rift inside the PSD. The government's efforts to induce the legislature to confirm a 1964 agreement granting certain monopolies to the French firm of *Grands Moulins de Dakar* in return for huge investments encountered such hostility that it had to be rescinded. Then the authorities' cultivation of closer economic ties with the Republic of South Africa, initiated in 1967, met with such opposition that a formal pledge had to be given that they would not lead to diplomatic relations with Pretoria. In both cases the AKFM's stand was supported by PSD dissidents who, without subscribing to the ideology of the AKFM's communist element and while acknowledging Madagascar's need to expand its foreign trade and sources of investment, were alarmed by the increasingly conservative and authoritarian trend of the government.

FOREIGN POLICY

Madagascar's diplomatic relations have been confined to countries of the western bloc, although it has trade agreements with the U.S.S.R. and its east European satellites. From mainland Africa the Malagasys have traditionally held themselves aloof, because they feel either superior or indifferent to the black Africans. After independence, however, Tsiranana realized the danger of Madagascar's isolation in an area he believed to be increasingly threatened by Chinese communist inroads. So he joined the successive organizations created by the moderate francophone Africans, and became one of the most loyal supporters of the *Organisation commune africaine, malgache et mauricienne* (OCAM). More recently Tsiranana cultivated the friendship of President Banda of Malawi, whose even closer ties with South Africa have won him the opprobium of the rest of black Africa. Pragmatic and realistic, both men reacted to generally analogous pressures by pursuing an economic policy that alienated the most nationalistic of their compatriots.

TSIRANANA'S ILLNESS AND PSD DISSENSIONS

Disagreement over the PSD's economic policies probably would not have become so intense in 1969 had Tsiranana's serious illness not necessitated his absence from Madagascar until May 1970. Inevitably the question of his succession brought to the fore a long-simmering rivalry between the PSD's two other main leaders. André Resampa was Tsiranana's oldest and strongest collaborator and the principal organizer of the PSD, as well as the founder of its co-operative societies (*syndicats de communes*). As secretary-general of the PSD and Minister of Interior, Resampa controlled the party and administrative machinery, and also the 2,400-man security forces, but his authoritarian character and tactlessness had created serious animosities. His main rival in the PSD was Jacques Rabemananjara, the Foreign Minister. As one of the three exiled leaders of the 1947 revolt and as a poet of international renown, the latter had the respect of both Malagasy nationalists and intellectuals. Rabemananjara, however, was also regarded as a weak and spendthrift administrator prone to favour foreign big business, and he had no popular following. The third member of the triumvirate which governed Madagascar in Tsiranana's absence was Vice-President Calvin Tsiebo, whose conciliatory talents, loyalty to the president, and lack of personal ambition enabled him to prevent either of his more brilliant colleagues from gaining the ascendancy. Nevertheless, Tsiranana's prolonged absence and the Resampa-Rabemananjara rivalry widened the rifts in the party, whose huge membership, tenuous ideology, long tenure of office, and dependence on one charismatic leader had weakened its ability to withstand the forces eroding it.

The Opposition Forces

Madagascar's multiparty system was a showpiece in which the PSD could afford to take pride because that party was able indirectly to obstruct the political activities of its opponents, who in any case were few in number and even more disunited. The influence of the press, of which the most important publications were pro-PSD, was largely confined to the Tananarive area, and the radio broadcasts, which had a wider impact, were government-controlled. Although the ecclesiastical authorities were often critical of PSD policies, the Malagasy Christians were about equally divided between Protestants and Catholics and together they comprised not even half the total population. Potentially the strongest opposition to the government was that of the educated Malagasy youth, whose growing number and lack of employment were becoming economically dangerous but whose sole organization among the students of Tananarive University was apparently apolitical. The only organized opposition forces were those of four political parties, whose following was small and localized and whose only common denominator was hostility to the PSD and a strongly nationalistic orientation. Dr. Raseta's *Mouvement d'Union Nationale* disappeared after its crushing defeat in the September 1970 elections; the MONIMA of Monja Jaona had roots only in the Tuléar region; Alexis Bezaka's Christian-Democrat Party, restricted to the Tamatave area, split asunder in April 1970; and Andriamananjato's AKFM was basically a party of Tananarive's Merina bourgeoisie.

The surprisingly strong showing made by the AKFM in the December 1969 senatorial elections was less a reflection of growing support for its policies than of discontent with those of the PSD. Yet it alarmed Resampa into reorganizing his party in the areas where the AKFM had made inroads, to such effect that the legislative elections of September 1970 confirmed the PSD's dominant position throughout the island and the limitation of the AKFM's constituency to the urban Merina. Then and later it became clear that the AKFM was too narrowly based ever to win a national election, and that it had neither the strength nor the inclination to overthrow the government by force—the only means apparently now left to oust the PSD from power. It was the impoverished peasantry of the arid Tuléar region, exasperated by excessive taxation and the abuses committed by local officials, who, in April 1971, were the first to take up arms under Jaona's leadership against the government. Tsiranana attributed this revolt to a "Maoist plot," and in the course of his swift and harsh repression there were many deaths (variously estimated at 46 and 2,000), some 500 alleged ringleaders were arrested, and, more significantly, the MONIMA—albeit legally banned—was transformed from a left-wing regional group into an opposition movement with a following among Malagasy students and urban radicals.

Since returning to Madagascar, Tsiranana had become increasingly intolerant of opposition, and determined to carry out single-handed his self-imposed mission to save Madagascar from communist subversion. Despite opposition from inside and outside the PSD, he persisted in strengthening the links he had forged with South Africa, and he made only minor concessions to the demands of student strikers for a loosening of Madagascar's economic and cultural ties with France. Resampa, as first in line to succeed him in the presidency and as the PSD's outstanding champion of a more nationalistic and socialistic policy, was demoted in February 1971 to a minor cabinet post. On June 1, he was arrested on unsubstantiated charges of plotting with the American ambassador, whose recall was requested by Tsiranana.

The latter half of 1971 was marked by reports of two more "communist plots" and the arrest, dismissal, or transfer of Resampa's partisans in the PSD and the civil service. Despite the resultant weakening of the PSD machinery, support from influential segments of the Malagasy élite, and his impaired health, Tsiranana presented himself as the sole candidate in the presidential elections of January 30th, 1972. According to the official tally, he won 99.9 per cent of the votes cast by 86 per cent of the registered electorate, and he interpreted this "victory" as an overwhelming popular endorsement of this person and his policies. Yet on May 13th, 1972, two weeks after his third inauguration as president, riots broke out in Tananarive between the security forces and a coalition of students, teachers, labourers, and urban unemployed (*zoam*) which became the nucleus of the KIM, or Federation of the May 13th Movement. After 3 days of violence in which 34 persons were killed, Tsiranana gave full powers to General Gabriel Ramanantsoa, the apolitical Merina aristocrat, who was chief of staff of Madagascar's 10,000-man armed forces.

THE MILITARY GOVERNMENT

General Ramanantsoa's determination to restore law and order inspired confidence even among the opposition groups, none of which was prepared to take over the government and whose members feared a revival of tribal antagonism between Merina and *côtiers*. He soon separated the labourers from the student dissidents by granting the former a wage increase and strike pay. Then, by annulling the head and cattle taxes, prosecuting corrupt officials, and introducing austerity measures and price and currency controls, he won widespread popular support. By naming military officers to key posts in his government and as provincial governors he ensured obedience to his orders. General Ramanantsoa's background as a commissioned officer in the French army reassured France (whose troops stationed in Madagascar had not intervened to bolster Tsiranana), as did the general's insistence on retaining Tsiranana as a figurehead president despite the student's demands for his resignation.

To a large extent, the KIM was appeased by Ramanantsoa's steps to renegotiate the co-operation agreements with France, "malagasize" the school system, disavow the South African agreements, liberate all political prisoners, and lower the voting age from 21 to 18. Moreover, he allowed the KIM freedom to organize study groups throughout the island, whose purpose was to prepare for a national congress that would lay down the guidelines for Madagascar's second republic. In September 1972, the KIM congress was held at Tananarive and was attended by some 10,000 delegates, who had been chosen not for their tribal affiliations but as representatives of all "the living forces" in Malagasy society. After 2 weeks of free debates, the sense of this congress was summed up in a series of resolutions designed to ensure Madagascar's political, economic, and cultural independence. This was to be done largely by eliminating foreign monopolies, foreign military bases, and foreign control of the school system, and by reorienting Madagascar's external relations to exclude imperialistic régimes and include more "progressive" ones.

Even before the KIM congress met, General Ramanantsoa assumed the authority to declare martial law and, without committing himself to any precise policy, proposed that the form of Madagascar's government for the next 5 years be determined by a referendum to take place on October 8. If the vote was affirmative, all the elective institutions created under the 1959 constitution would be eliminated and replaced by two councils, whose members would be appointed by the military administration. Should the vote be negative, the armed forces would withdraw from the political scene. Since the reaction of all the political parties and religious organizations to his proposal was generally favourable, and the only

advocates of a negative vote were KIM extremists and Tsiranana himself, the result of the referendum was a foregone conclusion. Although about a quarter of the registered electorate, notably in the coastal provinces of Diégo-Suarez, Majunga and Tamatave abstained from voting, some 96 per cent of those who cast their ballots on October 8, 1972 gave General Ramanantsoa a mandate to govern Madagascar for the next five years.

[*Editorial Note*: General Ramanantsoa's early attempt at reform through "Malagization" of education met immediate opposition from the *côtiers* in Tamatave, who feared domination by the Merina. *Lycée* students went on strike, and serious general disturbances followed in early December between the two racial groups, resulting in the imposition of martial law on December 14th. Hundreds of Merina fled to Tananarive or to a military camp.]

ECONOMY

Madagascar's perennial handicaps of geographical isolation, dependence on world markets, poor internal communications, shortage of labour, and frequently adverse climatic conditions have been compounded by the local repercussions of two world wars and a major world economic depression, the closure of the Suez Canal in 1967, and the rapid growth of the population. Two-thirds of the 300,000 wage-earners are unskilled, and urban unemployment has been increasing with the rural exodus to the towns. In general agricultural production is stagnant, the trade deficit has been mounting, and only in the industrial domain is progress being made.

AGRICULTURE

Farming and herding are almost the only occupations of the Malagasys, 85 per cent of whom live in rural areas. Agriculture provides 90 per cent of the island's exports, but most of the agricultural output is consumed by the producers. Rice is the basic Malagasy food (135 kg. per capita annually), and it is the main crop grown by more than two-thirds of the peasantry. Paddy output increased from 1.2 million tons in 1960 to 1.9 million by 1971, and some 50,000 tons of the best quality are annually exported, but an even larger amount of rice has to be imported each year to feed Madagascar's fast-growing population. Coffee is Madagascar's major export (51,900 tons in 1971), accounting for 26 per cent of the total in terms of value. Its output, however, is generally stationary, because most plantations are over-age, there are frequent cyclones, and competition in world markets is severe. The two latter handicaps also hamper the production and sale abroad of Madagascar's increasing crops of sugar and bananas. The production of vanilla, cloves, and pepper has generally increased in recent years, but the markets for them are very limited and subject to sharp price fluctuations. On the west coast, the expanding production of cotton and peanuts has not offset the current decline in sales of its traditional exports of sisal, tobacco and Cape peas. In general Madagascar's agricultural output for export did not meet the goals of the first five-

year development plan (1964–69), nor has it kept pace with the population's growth as regards foodstuffs.

As to the other produce of the rural economy, fishing on an industrial scale under Japanese tutelage shows promise, despite the coastal tribes' indifference to the commercialization of this traditional occupation. Forests are a minor resource at best, and the work of reforestation has been too costly and too belatedly undertaken to check the soil erosion caused mainly by the Malagasys' practice of starting bush fires to fertilize their land. Despite the existence of large cattle herds (some 10 million head), animal husbandry is neither a source of proportionate cash income nor of meat, consumption of which declined from 53.6 lb. (24.3 kg.) per capita a year in 1964 to 44.8 lb. (20.3 kg.) in 1968. Cattle are hoarded by the Malagasys as a latent form of capital, a mark of prestige, and a source of sacrificial animals indispensable for the ancestral religious cult. Here, as in agriculture, the Malagasys' resistance to change and indifference to producing beyond their immediate needs hinder the government's efforts to increase yields and sales. Attempts to popularize modern techniques and promote commercialization through the establishment of state farms and of various cooperative societies have met with little success. In 1969 the average annual cash income per Malagasy was estimated at 40,000 FMG (Malagasy francs, of which one is worth 0.02 French franc, to which Madagascar's currency is pegged).

The Malagasy Republic's first development plan (1964–69) allotted 51 per cent of its funds to improving the means of communication and 23 per cent to agricultural production. Largely because only 91 of the anticipated 151 billion FMG francs were invested, many of the plan's goals were not reached except in the industrial domain. The second plan (1972–74) has been given a more socialistic orientation, with priority to increased agricultural output through agrarian reform, higher prices and greater credit facilities for producers, and more technical training to farmers and herders. In industry and trade, state enterprises and organizations are to have a larger share. Execution of this plan requires investments of 123 billion FMG, equal parts of which are to be supplied by national revenues, subsidies from foreign sources, and a loan raised in France.

INDUSTRY

Between 1962 and 1968 investments in industry totalled 14,950 million FMG, yet industrial output accounts for but 15 per cent of the national wealth, and industry provides employment for only 25,000 persons of an active population estimated at over three million. Electric-power production has grown steadily to reach 200 million kWh. a year, but its distribution is restricted largely to the central provinces. The great majority of Madagascar's industries are those processing agricultural produce, and the most important of those recently established have been financed by foreign capital. These include a cement plant, a paper-pulp factory, a cotton-spinning and weaving combine, two automobile assembly plants, and an oil refinery. As for minerals, of Madagascar's 67 known ores only mica and graphite (as well as semi-precious stones) have been regularly mined for export. Since 1967, however, about a dozen foreign companies have been actively prospecting for nickel, bauxite, and above all petroleum; and chromite shipments began in 1969. In view of the scarcity of local or foreign capital, Madagascar's only hope of emerging from its present economic stagnation seems to lie in its mineral potential. The outlook for further developing Madagascar's mining potential is relatively good, but recently official hopes have been concentrated on the Narinda project. This involves building a deep-water port and ship-repair facilities for tankers plying the Mozambique Channel, as well as related industries nearby. With the eclipse of Tsiranana, its realization seems unlikely, considering its dependence on South Africa's collaboration.

FINANCE

The island has indeed received substantial grants and loans from an ever wider range of sources, mainly from France (580,000 million FMG between 1960 and 1969) and other EEC countries, but also from the United Nations, the United States and Israel. Increasingly, however, foreign aid is taking the form of technical rather than financial assistance, and it is made available more for political than for economic reasons. Madagascar's production and transport costs are high, and it produces little that cannot be found more cheaply, of better quality, and—with the exception of vanilla—in greater quantity in less remote sources. Furthermore, Madagascar's trade is subject to factors almost all of which are beyond its government's control—generally declining world prices for its exports, rising costs for its imports, and a local commercial structure almost wholly in foreign hands. The island's foreign trade is controlled by long-established French firms and its domestic commerce mainly by Indians and Chinese; and the profits made by foreign capitalists are usually repatriated rather than invested locally.

The volume of Madagascar's budget has been growing far more rapidly than its foreign trade, on which the national revenues are mainly dependent, and between 1971 and 1972 it rose by 21 per cent. Of the 52.4 billion FMG of anticipated revenue in 1972, Madagascar was to provide 46.1 billion from its own resources, 82 per cent of which derive from indirect taxes, mainly on imported goods. Operating costs for 1972 have been estimated at 36.5 billion FMG, of which 20.4 billion are slated to pay government personnel and 2.6 billion to the servicing of the public debt. Madagascar has certainly been living beyond its means and can balance its budgets only thanks to foreign aid, but it should be noted that an increasing share of its revenues has been earmarked for the economic services and that generous allocations have also been made to those of health and education.

Currently, half of Madagascar's school-age children attend school, and in 1971 more than 7,000 students were enrolled at Tananarive University. Furthermore, the island has 11 principal and 490 secondary hospitals and medical centres, which are staffed by 550 doctors, 45 pharmacists, 20 dentists and 600 midwives, not to mention more than 2,000 nurses and social workers. On the other hand, the 30 per cent growth in the civil service between 1963 and 1968 has saddled Madagascar with 34,198 functionaries, whose number and pay are disproportionate to its needs and resources, and this proliferation can be explained only in terms of party politics. Moreover, also in 1968, Madagascar imported 14,000 million FMG worth of consumer goods compared with 11.2 billion for equipment materials. The year 1969 ended with a record deficit of over 17,000 million FMG.

By 1969 Madagascar's financial plight had become sufficiently alarming for the government to draw up its first "austerity" budget, which reduced the deficit to a mere 2,000 million FMG. This was done not only by somewhat compressing administrative expenditures but also by raising the 3 per cent tax on business transactions to 12 per cent. As a result the already rising living costs soared to such heights that the tax had to be reduced on essential merchandise, and the minimum wage and family allowances for wage-earners, frozen respectively since 1963 and 1960, slightly increased. Unemployment grew apace among the educated Malagasy youth, many of whom were already alienated by the government's determinedly pro-western policy, refusal to nationalize public utilities, and failure to carry out its proclaimed socialist precepts. Anti-government tracts appeared in the streets of Tananarive, and even a French technical assistant circulated a pamphlet strongly criticizing the official development plan and some highly placed politicians and administrators charged with its application. In May 1972 the spreading economic malaise surfaced at the political level and brought about the downfall of Tsiranana's government. The orientation of Madagascar's next administration can only be surmised, but it will probably be far less dependent on France in every domain and more nationalistic and socialistic in its foreign and domestic policies.

STATISTICAL SURVEY

AREA AND POPULATION

AREA (sq. km.)	POPULATION (1970)	FOREIGNERS (1968)				
		French	Comorians	Indians	Chinese	Others
587,041	6,750,000	48,835	37,200	17,180	8,900	3,600

PRINCIPAL ETHNIC GROUPS
(1967)

Hova (Merina)	.	1,744,700	Antaisaka	.	.	455,000
Betsimisaraka		997,600	Sakalava	.	.	381,800
Betsileo	.	806,200	Antandroy	.	.	370,500
Tsimihety	. .	477,300				

CHIEF TOWNS
(1968—estimates)

Tananarive (capital)	.	335,000	Diégo-Suarez	.	.	41,000
Tamatave .	.	55,000	Tuléar	.	.	34,000
Majunga .	. .	50,000	Antsirabé	.	.	28,000
Fianarantsoa	. .	47,000				

REGISTERED BIRTHS AND DEATHS, 1970

BIRTHS	BIRTH RATE	DEATHS	DEATH RATE
263,217	39.0 per 1,000	95,045	14.1 per 1,000

Birth registration is estimated to be 70 per cent complete and death registration 50 per cent complete. Rates for 1966 (based on a sample survey) were: Births 46 per 1,000, deaths 25 per 1,000.

SALARIED EMPLOYMENT
(1965)

AGRICULTURE	MINING	INDUSTRY	CONSTRUCTION AND PUBLIC WORKS	COMMERCE AND PROFESSIONS	TRANSPORT	DOMESTIC SERVICE	PUBLIC SERVICE
50,434	9,249	22,158	27,436	24,623	13,237	29,506	14,146

In 1970 the active population was estimated to be 3,516,000, of whom 3,040,000 were engaged in agriculture.

AGRICULTURE

LAND USE
('ooo hectares)

Arable and Under Permanent Crops . . .	2,856
Permanent Meadows and Pastures . .	34,000
Forest	12,470
Other Land	8,828
Inland Water	550
TOTAL	58,704

PRINCIPAL CROPS
('ooo metric tons)

	1969	1970	1971
Maize	143	109	118
Rice (Paddy)	1,858	1,865	1,873
Sugar Cane*	949	1,113	1,239
Potatoes	97	94	108
Sweet Potatoes and Yams . .	367	350	n.a.
Cassava (Manioc) . . .	1,253	1,218	n.a.
Dry Beans	56	49	52†
Oranges and Tangerines . .	47	57	62
Bananas	257	262	n.a.
Pineapples	35	35	n.a.
Groundnuts (in shell) . .	44	41	40
Cottonseed	17	7	23
Cotton (Lint)	6	7	9
Tung Nuts	5	5†	n.a.
Coffee	63.9	66.6	65.5
Cocoa Beans‡ . . .	0.8	0.9	1.1
Tobacco	5.6	4.9	5.7
Sisal	29.5	26.3	25

Cloves (1968): 2,800 metric tons.

* Crop year ending in year stated. † FAO estimate.

‡ Twelve months ending in September of year stated.

Source: FAO, Production Yearbook 1971.

LIVESTOCK
('ooo)

	1968–69	1969–70	1970–71
Cattle	10,422	9,881	10,000*
Pigs	522	525	530*
Sheep† . . .	605	492	500*
Goats	773	876	900*
Chickens . . .	10,900*	11,000	11,200
Ducks	1,900*	2,000	2,050*
Geese	1,900*	2,000	2,100*
Turkeys . . .	900*	1,000*	1,050*

* FAO estimate.

† Figures relate to animals registered for taxation.

Source: FAO, Production Yearbook 1971.

LIVESTOCK PRODUCTS
(metric tons)

	1969	1970	1971
Cows' Milk . . .	37,000*	38,000*	40,000*
Beef	114,000*	118,000*	112,000*
Hen Eggs . . .	9,200	9,200	9,500*
Honey	13,000	13,500*	14,000*

* FAO estimate.

Source: FAO, Production Yearbook 1971.

FORESTRY
ROUNDWOOD PRODUCTION
('000 cubic metres)

1967	.	.	4,500
1968	.	.	4,781
1969	.	.	4,862
1970	.	.	5,000

Source: FAO, *Yearbook of Forest Products.*

FISHING
(metric tons)

	1967	1968	1969
Inland Water . .	41,000	45,800	51,000
Sea . . .	16,900	17,200	18,000
TOTAL CATCH . .	57,900	63,000	69,000

Source: FAO, *Yearbook of Fishery Statistics 1970.*

MINING

	UNITS	1967	1968
Graphite	(metric tons)	16,405	16,430
Salt	,,	14,000	17,000
Mica	,,	741	906
Industrial Beryls	,,	30	65.10
Industrial Garnets	,,	5	1.35
Quartz	,,	40	1.35
Gold	kg.	24	15
Precious Stones	,,	112	—

1969: Salt 22,000 metric tons; Chromium ore 18,582 metric tons; Gold 20 kg.

1970: Chromium ore 43,444 metric tons; Gold 17 kg.

INDUSTRY

	Unit	1967	1968	1969	1970
Raw Sugar	metric tons	108,000	105,000	99,000	108,000
Tapioca	,, ,,	6,477	5,300	n.a.	n.a.
Vegetable Oils	,, ,,	5,000	6,000	n.a.	n.a.
Cereal Flour	,, ,,	2,000	2,000	n.a.	n.a.
Condensed Milk	,, ,,	1,396	1,032	n.a.	n.a.
Beer	hectolitres	53,000	68,000	n.a.	n.a.
Wine	,,	8,000	7,000	n.a.	n.a.
Soft Drinks	,,	97,000	114,000	n.a.	n.a.
Cigarettes	million	765	780	790	951*
Tobacco	metric tons	1,021	1,241	n.a.	n.a.
Sawnwood	cubic metres	87,000	n.a.	n.a.	n.a.
Cotton Yarn	metric tons	4,107	4,791	4,600	4,900
Woven Cotton Fabrics . .	,, ,,	3,600	4,200	3,700	4,700
Cement	,, ,,	60,000	68,000	76,000	76,000
Liquefied Petroleum Gas . .	,, ,,	n.a.	6,000	6,000	8,000
Motor Spirit . . .	,, ,,	56,000†	101,000	95,000	125,000
Kerosene	,, ,,	24,000†	40,000	49,000	n.a.
Jet Fuels	,, ,,	11,000†	13,000†	12,000†	n.a.
Distillate Fuel Oils . . .	,, ,,	71,000†	112,000	126,000	157,000
Residual Fuel Oils . . .	,, ,,	126,000†	152,000	158,000	210,000
Lubricating Oils . . .	,, ,,	n.a.	n.a.	7,000†	n.a.
Bitumen (Asphalt) . . .	,, ,,	n.a.	n.a.	7,000†	n.a.
Paints	,, ,,	1,472	1,907	n.a.	n.a.
Soap	,, ,,	1,304	1,836	n.a.	n.a.
Nails, Screws, Nuts, etc. . .	,, ,,	1,080	1,392	n.a.	n.a.
Electric Energy	million kWh.	180	195	209‡	246‡

Sources: United Nations, *Statistical Yearbook 1971* and *The Growth of World Industry,* except:

    * *Source:* U.S. Department of Agriculture.

    † *Source:* U.S. Bureau of Mines.

    ‡ *Source:* Agency for International Development, U.S. Department of State.

FINANCE

100 centimes = 1 franc Malgache.

Coins: 1, 2, 5, 10 and 20 francs MG.

Notes: 50, 100, 500, 1,000 and 5,000 francs MG.

Exchange rates (December 1972): £1 sterling = 593.625 francs MG; U.S. $1 = 255.785 francs MG.
1,000 francs MG = £1.685 = $3.91.

Budget (1970): balanced at 43,205m. FMG.

Budget (1971): balanced at 43,289m. FMG.

Five-Year Plan (1970–74): Minimum sum for investment 120,000m. FMG; the main emphasis of the plan will be on agricultural development.

Currency in Circulation: (May 1972): 22,950 million francs MG.

NATIONAL ACCOUNTS

GROSS DOMESTIC PRODUCT AT PURCHASERS' VALUES
(million francs MG)

1966 . . .	181,600
1967 . . .	192,900
1968 . . .	208,200
1969 . . .	224,200
1970 . . .	247,700

GROSS DOMESTIC PRODUCT BY ECONOMIC ACTIVITY
('000 million francs MG)

	1968	1969	1970
Agriculture, Hunting, Forestry and Fishing	60.9	61.8	74.6
Mining and Quarrying	3.1	3.9	4.8
Manufacturing	23.3	25.8	28.6
Construction	8.1	8.5	8.8
Wholesale and Retail Trade, Restaurants and Hotels	29.6	33.6	35.3
Transport, Storage and Communication .	14.5	16.1	17.4
Other Producers and Services* . .	68.8	74.5	78.2
TOTAL . . .	208.2	224.2	247.7

* Including import duties.

EXTERNAL TRADE
(million FMG)*

	1964	1965	1966	1967	1968	1969	1970	1971
Imports . . .	33,429	34,089	35,004	35,847	41,937	46,153	47,346	59,262
Exports . . .	22,654	22,632	24,132	25,711	28,608	29,154	40,222	40,807

* Excluding trade in gold and military goods.

PRINCIPAL COMMODITIES
(million FMG)

IMPORTS	1968	1969	1970	EXPORTS	1968	1969	1970
Petroleum Products . .	2,492	3,138	2,406	Coffee	8,803	8,170	10,935
Cotton Textiles .	2,501	1,445	3,021	Rice	3,047	2,438	3,072
Metal Products .	1,895	2,510	6,343	Vanilla . . .	2,530	3,013	3,610
Machinery . .	3,860	5,825	5,534	Sugar . . .	1,575	1,656	1,547
Electrical Equipment .	2,326	2,900	2,965	Tobacco . . .	383	542	n.a.
Vehicles and Parts .	3,902	3,907	5,637	Cloves and Clove Oil .	1,958	407	4,697
				Raffia . . .	698	516	n.a.
				Groundnuts . .	298	241	n.a.

PRINCIPAL COUNTRIES
(million FMG)

IMPORTS	1968	1969	1970
France . . .	26,423	23,949	25,982
Iran . . .	240	243	n.a.
U.S.A. . . .	2,111	2,969	2,688
German Federal Republic .	2,587	4,323	4,287
India . . .	63	87	n.a.
United Kingdom . .	759	851	839
Netherlands . .	902	1,307	1,171
Italy . . .	1,474	1,859	2,800

EXPORTS	1968	1969	1970
France . . .	9,601	10,584	13,756
Other Franc Zone Countries	6,026	6,329	n.a.
U.S.A. . . .	6,430	6,910	9,117
United Kingdom . .	898	714	777
German Federal Republic .	1,038	1,112	1,651
Italy . . .	449	603	n.a.
Netherlands . .	331	277	n.a.
Japan . . .	464	678	1,267

TRANSPORT

RAILWAYS

	1970	1971
Passengers ('000) . .	2,365	2,585
Passenger/km. (millions) .	182	200
Freight ('000 metric tons) .	703	755
Ton/km. (millions) . .	233	246

ROADS

	1966	1967
Cars	34,992	37,610
Lorries	24,824	25,800
Buses	1,626	2,030
Other Commercial Vehicles .	2,123	2,140

1968: 40,500 Cars, 32,400 Commercial vehicles.
1969: 43,100 Cars, 34,800 Commercial vehicles.
1970: 45,500 Cars, 42,300 Commercial vehicles.

SHIPPING

	MAJUNGA		TAMATAVE	
	1970	1971	1970	1971
Vessels Entered . . .	1,584	1,620	933	945
Passengers Arrived . .	3,522	2,530	1,125	2,227
Passengers Departed .	3,761	3,248	1,729	2,511
Freight Entered ('000 tons) .	178	222	341	365
Freight Cleared ('000 tons) .	134	120	319	287

CIVIL AVIATION

	PASSENGERS		FREIGHT (metric tons)	
	Arrived	Departed	Unloaded	Loaded
1969 . .	80,425	77,231	1,863	3,679
1970 . .	83,284	84,929	2,033	4,672
1971 . .	92,359	93,456	2,154	5,031

Source (for Railways, Shipping and Civil Aviation): I.N.S.E.E., *Données Statistiques*, Paris, 1972.

COMMUNICATIONS
TELEPHONES IN USE

1967 . . .	22,701
1968 . . .	23,993
1969 . . .	25,258
1970 . . .	27,000

EDUCATION
(1968–69)

	SCHOOLS	PUPILS
Primary	4,111	815,000
Secondary . . .	246	67,030
Technical	83	8,285
Higher	n.a.	4,000

Source (unless otherwise stated): Secrétariat d'Etat à l'Information et au Tourisme, Tananarive.

THE CONSTITUTION*
(*Promulgated April 1959, Revised June 1960 and June 1962*)

Principles: The Rights of Man; equality for all, without distinction of origin, race or religion, liberty of expression and of association, guaranteed protection of the family, property and education. The republic is one, indivisible, democratic and social. Sovereignty resides in the people who exercise it by universal suffrage.

Head of State: The Head of State is the President of the Republic.

Executive Power: The Government consists of the President of the Republic, elected for a seven-year renewable term by universal suffrage, a Vice-President and ministers appointed by the President. The President of the Republic is thus also head of the government. He has power to dissolve the National Assembly on the advice of the Senate and after consultation with the President of the National Assembly.

Legislative Power: The *National Assembly* is elected by universal suffrage for five years and meets in ordinary session twice a year. The *Senate* examines all proposed legislation and meets during the ordinary sessions of the Assembly. Two-thirds of the Senators are elected by provincial, municipal and rural authorities, the remainder are nominated by the government. The carrying of a motion of censure by the Assembly entails the resignation of the government and the President must form a new government. If the programme of the new government is not approved by the Assembly, the latter must be dissolved and new elections held. If the new Assembly fails to approve the programme of the new government, the President must resign and cannot stand again.

Local Government: Madagascar is divided into six provinces, each province having a Chef de Province at its head appointed by the President and a General Council consisting of councillors elected for five years and the deputies and senators of the province.

Revision of the Constitution may be proposed by the President and the members of the Assembly and Senate. The proposal must be adopted in identical terms by both Assembly and Senate and the republican form of government must not be prejudiced.

*Gen. Ramanantsoa's government is pledged to draw up a new Constitution.

THE GOVERNMENT

HEAD OF GOVERNMENT

Maj.-Gen. GABRIEL RAMANANTSOA (*appointment ratified by referendum October* 1972).

CABINET

(*December* 1972)

Head of Government, Chief of the Armed Forces, in charge of the Ministry of Defence: Maj.-Gen. GABRIEL RAMANANTSOA.

Minister of Territorial Planning: Brig. GILLES ANDRIAMAHAZO.

Minister of Justice: JACQUES ANDRIANADA.

Minister of Cultural Affairs and National Education: Dr. JUSTIN MANAMBELONA.

Minister of Economy and Finance: ALBERT-MARIE RAMAROSON.

Minister of Social Affairs: Dr. ALBERT ZAFY.

Minister of Home Affairs and Commander of the National Gendarmerie: Lt.-Col. RICHARD RATSIMANDRAVA.

Minister of Information: Maj. JOËL RAKOTOMALALA.

Minister of Foreign Affairs: Capt. DIDIER RATSIRAKA.

Minister of Rural Development: Dr. EMMANUEL RAKOTOVAHINY.

Minister of Civil Service and Labour: DANIEL RAJAKOBA.

Head of the Province of Tuléar: Capt. SOJA.

Head of the Province of Majunga: Cmdr. MAMPILA.

Head of the Province of Tananarive: Cmdr. RAYMOND RAZAFINTSALAMA.

Head of the Province of Tamatave: Capt. RAVELOSON MAHASAMPO.

Head of the Province of Fianarantsoa: Lt.-Col. LUCIEN RAKOTONIRAINY.

Head of the Province of Diégo-Suarez: Capt. GUY ALBERT SIBON.

DIPLOMATIC REPRESENTATION

EMBASSIES ACCREDITED TO MADAGASCAR

(In Tananarive unless otherwise stated)

Austria: Addis Ababa, Ethiopia.

Belgium: Nairobi, Kenya.

China, People's Republic: (E); *Ambassador:* to be appointed.

France: Maison de France, Antaninarenina; *Ambassador:* MAURICE DELAUNEY.

German Federal Republic: 101 route circulaire, Ambodirotra; *Ambassador:* ALFRED B. VESTRING.

Ghana: Kinshassa, Zaire.

Greece: Addis Ababa, Ethiopia.

India: 77 ave. Maréchal Foch; *Ambassador:* NUGAHALLI KESAVAN.

Israel: 32 rue Guillain; *Ambassador:* MAÏM RAPHAEL.

Italy: 22 rue Docteur Besson; *Ambassador:* LIONELLO COZZI.

Japan: rue Etienne-Planton; *Ambassador:* SHIRO SHIMIZI.

Netherlands: Addis Ababa, Ethiopia.

Norway: Nairobi, Kenya.

Pakistan: Dar es Salaam, Tanzania.

Spain: Nairobi, Kenya.

Sweden: Addis Ababa, Ethiopia.

Switzerland: ave. de Lattre de Tassigny; *Ambassador:* HEINZ LANGENBACHER.

United Kingdom: rue Choiseul, Parc d'Ambohijatovo; *Ambassador:* TIMOTHY CROSTHWAIT.

U.S.A.: 14 rue Rainitovo, Antsahavola; *Ambassador:* JOSEPH A. MENDENHALL.

Vatican: (Apostolic Nunciature); *Apostolic Nuncio:* MICHEL CECCHINI.

Madagascar also has diplomatic relations with Algeria, Argentina, Austria, Canada, Finland, Philippines, Tunisia, Turkey, Romania, U.S.S.R. and Yugoslavia.

PARLIAMENT*

SENATE

President: SIMÉON JAPHET.

ELECTIONS JULY, 1969

PARTY	SEATS
Parti social démocrate	48
Nominated Members	6

NATIONAL ASSEMBLY

President: ALFRED NANY.

ELECTIONS SEPTEMBER 1970

PARTY	SEATS
Parti social démocrate . . .	104
Parti du congrès de l'indépendance . .	3

Out of 2,612,856 votes cast, PSD 2,413,421, PCIM 186,626.

* To be replaced by a People's National Development Council for the five-year term of General Ramanantsoa's Government.

POLITICAL PARTIES

Parti social démocrate (PSD): rue Carayon, Tananarive; f. 1957 by PHILIBERT TSIRANANA; majority party throughout the country; Sec. Gen. ABDOU LAMBERT LODA.

Parti du congrès de l'indépendance de Madagascar (PCIM or AKFM): 43 ave. Maréchal Foch, Tananarive; f. 1958; 420 member sections; official opposition party; left wing; Pres. RICHARD ANDRIAMANJATO; Sec.-Gen. GISÈLE RABESAHALA.

Parti démocratique chrétien malagasy: Lot II, 120 Andravoahangy, Tananarive; formerly *Rassemblement national malgache*; re-formed 1962, merged with Manjakavahoaka 1968; Leader ALEXIS BEZAKA.

Mouvement National pour l'Indépendance de Madagascar (MONIMA): left wing, nationalist party; Leader MONJA JAONA.

No party is represented in the Government.

DEFENCE

Madagascar has compulsory military or civic service of two years and the total armed forces number 10,000. Of these the army is the major force with a small navy and air force and there is a para-military gendarmerie of 4,000.

Chief of Armed Forces: Maj.-Gen. GABRIEL RAMANANTSOA.

Commander of the Gendarmerie: Lt.-Col. RICHARD RATSIMANDRAVA.

JUDICIAL SYSTEM*

Supreme Court: 8 Anosy, Tananarive; Pres. EDILBERT RAZAFINDRALAMBO.

Attorney-General: RAFAMANTANANTSOA.

Chamber Presidents: RAHARINAIVO, RAKOTOBE, MARMOT.

Advocates-General: RATSISALOTAFY, ROUSSEAU.

Counsellors: MAMELOMANA, THIERRY, MANIELONANANA, RANDRIANARIVELO, RANDRIANASOLO, Mme RADAODY, ANDRIANTAHINA, MARSON, RAJAONARIVELO, RANJEVA, MANJAKAVELO.

Court of Appeal: Tananarive; Pres. ARMAND RAFALIHERY.
Attorney-General: VICTOR RAMANITRA.
Chamber Presidents: RABEMALANTO, KEROMES.
Counsellors: COSTECALDE, Mme RAKOTOARISOA, RANDRIANARISOA, Mlle RAZAFIMANDIMBY, Mme RAJAONAH, Mme RABENORO, HERBELQ.

Courts of First Instance: at Tananarive, Tamative, Majunga, Fianarantsoa, Diégo-Suarez and Tuléar; for civil and commercial matters; also Courts of Petty Sessions.

Criminal Courts: at the Court of Appeal; presided over by a Counsellor. Justices of the Peace sit in the main centres.

* Reforms were to take place in 1972 and changes may have occurred in the system.

RELIGION

It is estimated that 57 per cent of the population follow traditional animist beliefs, 38 per cent are Christians (with Roman Catholics comprising 20 per cent of the total population) and 5 per cent are Muslims.

Roman Catholic Church: Three archdioceses:

Archbishop of Tananarive: Cardinal JÉRÔME RAKOTOMALALA; there are six dioceses and about 541 mission centres with a total personnel of 1,800.

Archbishop of Diego Suarez: Mgr. ALBERT JOSEPH TSIAMOANA; two dioceses.

Archbishop of Fianarantsoa: Mgr. GILBERT RAMANANTOANINA; B.P. 1170; seven dioceses.

Eglise Episcopale de Madagascar: 24 rue Jean Laborde, Tananarive; f. 1874; about 35,000 mems.; Anglican; Bishop in Madagascar Mgr. JEAN MARCEL.

Eglise de Jésus-Christ à Madagascar: 19 rue Fourcadier, B.P. 623, Tananarive; f. 1968; Pres. Rev. JOSEPH RAMAMBASOA; Gen. Sec. Rev. RICHARD RAKOTONDRAIBE; publ. *Vaovao F.J.K.M.* (French information bulletin).

Christian Council of Madagascar: Theological College, Fianarantsoa; f. 1963; Pres. Prof. Dr. RAKOTO ANDRIANARIJAONA.

Church of Jesus Christ in Madagascar: 6 rue George V, Tananarive.

Lutheran Church: Fianarantsoa; Pres. Dr. R. ANDRIANARIJAONA.

Church of the Lord's Disciples: Soatanana; Pres. BENJAMIN RANDRIANAIVO.

Adventist Church: Mandrosoa, Tananarive; Pres. M. RAJOELISON.

Independent Church of Antranobiriky: rue Admiral Peter, Tananarive; Pres. M. Z. RANDRIANAIVO.

THE PRESS

PRINCIPAL DAILIES

Le Courrier de Madagascar: 2 rue Amiral de Hell, Tananarive; in French and Malagasy; Editor PIERRE VILLEZ; circ. 26,800.

Imongo Vaovao: 11-K 4 bis Andravoahangy, Tananarive; opposition paper; Dir. RAMAMONJISOA CLEMENT; circ. 1,000.

Madagasikara Mahaleotena: Imprimerie Centrale, Analakely, Tananarive; official; Editor E. RABARISON; circ. 5,000.

Madagascar-Matin: 1 ave de Lattre de Tassigny, Tananarive; in French and Malagasy; Editor ROBERT HANTZBERG; circ. 26,800.

Maresaka: 12 ave. Rigault-Isotry, Tananarive; f. 1954; independent; Editors S. RAKOTOARIMAH, M. RALAIARIJAONA; Malagasy circ. 5,500.

Ny Gazetintsika: Imprimerie Masoandro, Ampasanisadoda, Tananarive; Dir. EDOUARD RATSIMANDISA.

Vaovao: B.P. 271, Tananarive; f. 1894; Government paper; Editor XAVIER RANAIVO; circ. 17,000.

PRINCIPAL PERIODICALS

L'Aurore: Majunga; French weekly; circ. 5,000.

Bulletin Bimestriel de la Chambre de Commerce de Tananarive: Tananarive; every two months.

Bulletin de la Société du Corps Médical Malgache: Imprimerie Volamahitsy, Tananarive; monthly; Dir. Dr. RAKOTOMALALALA.

Bulletin de Madagascar: Direction de la Presse (Ministère d l'Information), Place de l'Indépendance, B.P. 271, Tananarive; f. 1950; economics, society, culture, linguistics, education; monthly; Editor M. RANDRIAMAROZAKA; circ. 1,400

L'Ecole Publique de Madagascar: Direction des Services Académiques de la République Malgache; f. 1951; teaching administration; monthly.

Fanasina (*Salt*): B.P. 1574, Analakely-Tananarive; f. 1957; independent; politics, economics, literature; weekly; Dir. PAUL RAKOTOVOLOLONA; circ. 10,000.

Fanilo: Imprimerie Catholique Fianarantsoa; weekly; Dir. J. RAJAOBELINA.

Hehy: B.P. 1648, Tananarive; f. 1949; fortnightly; humorous; Editor C. ANDRIAMANANTENA; circ. 15,000.

Info-Madagascar: Service de la Presse, Direction de l'Information, B.P. 271, Tananarive; f. 1966; weekly; Editor G. RAMAMONJISOA; circ. 1,000.

L'Information Economique Juridique de Madagascar: Tananarive; every two months.

Journal Officiel de la République Malgache: B.P. 38, Tananarive; f. 1883; official publication; French; weekly; Editor M. BOARLAZA.

Lakroan'i Madagasikara: Imprimerie Catholique Ambatomena, Fianarantsoa; weekly; Editors F. RÉMY RALIBERA, F. XAVIER TABAO; circ. 8,000.

Lumière: Fianarantsoa; French Catholic weekly; Dir. CHARLES R. RAKOTONIRINA; circ. 10,500.

La République: Tananarive; organ of the Parti Social Démocrate; Dir. VINCENT RABOTOVAVY; Editor A. ANDRIATSIAFAJATO; circ. 8,000.

Revue de Madagascar: Service de Presse du Ministère de l'Information, B.P. 271, Tananarive; f. 1933; annual; Dir. DÉSIRÉ RAZANAMAHOLY; circ. 1,600.

Revue Médicale de Madagascar: B.P. 1655, Tananarive; monthly; Dir. Dr. GOULESQUE.

There are numerous other Malagasy publications appearing in Tananarive and provincial capitals.

PRESS AGENCY

Agence Madagascar-Presse: 3 rue du R. P. Callet, Behoririka, B.P. 386, Tananarive; f. 1962; Dir. EMILE RAKOTONIRAINY; publ. *Bulletin Quotidien d'Information.*

PUBLISHERS

Fanontam-Boky Malagasy: Tananarive.

Imprimerie des Arts Graphiques: B.P. 194, rue Dupré, Tananarive; f. 1931.

Imprimerie Centrale: P.O.B. 1414, Tananarive; f. 1959; university and school books; Man. M. HANTZBERG.

Imprimerie Industrielle Catholique: Fianarantsoa.

Imprimerie Nationale: B.P. 38, Tananarive; all official publications; Dir. PARFAIT RAVALOSON.

Librairie-Imprimerie Protestante: Imarivolanitra, Tananarive; f. 1865; religious and school books; Man. GEORGES ANDRIAMANANTENA.

Société Malgache d'Edition: Ankorondrano, B.P. 659, Tananarive; f. 1943; Gen. Man. ANDRÉ IZOUARD.

Trano Printy Loterana: B.P. 538 ave. Grandidier, Antsahamanitra, Tananarive; f. 1968, formerly *Imprimerie Luthérenne*, f. 1877; religious, educational and fiction; Man. Rev. LAUREL O. JOHNSON.

RADIO AND TELEVISION

Radiodiffusion Nationale Malgache: Tananarive, B.P. 442; Government station; fourteen transmitters; programmes in French and Malagasy; foreign service in French and English; Dir. ROGER RABESAHALA.

There is also a Rediffusion station at Fenoarivo, with eight transmitters.

Number of radio receivers: 540,000 in 1970.

Télévision Malagasy: Tananarive B.P. 3964; f. 1967 by Government decree to install and operate a national television service; started operations in Tananarive district 1967; programmes in French and Malagasy; Dir. JOCELYN RAFIDINARIVO.

Number of television receivers: 3,200 in 1970.

FINANCE

(cap. = capital; p.u. = paid up; dep. = deposits)

BANKS

NATIONAL BANKS

Institut d'Emission Malgache: ave. Le-Myre-de-Vilers, BP 550, Tananarive; f. 1962; administrative council of eight; Pres. VICTOR MIADANA; Dir. Gen. JEAN KIENTZ.

Banque Malgache d'Escompte et de Crédit (BAMES): B.P. 183, Tananarive; f. 1964; cap. FMG 750m.; Pres. D. RAKOTOPARE; Gen. Man. JEAN MARIE SÉGUR.

Banque Nationale Malgache de Développement (BNP): ave. Le-Myre-de-Vilers, B.P. 365, Tananarive; f. 1961; administrative council of twelve; cap. FMG 2,000m.; Pres. EMILE RAMAROSAONA; Dir. Gen. CHRISTOPHE ANDRIANARIVO.

FOREIGN BANKS

Banque Française Commerciale S.A.: 74 rue St. Lazare, Paris, France; Tananarive, rue de Liège, B.P. 440.

Banque de Madagascar et des Comores: 23 ave. Matignon, Paris 8e, France; Tananarive, B.P. 196, 14 ave. Etienne Fumaroli; cap. French francs 14.4m.; dep. 230m.; Pres. and Man. Dir. MAURICE GONON.

Banque Nationale pour le Commerce et l'Industrie (Océan Indien): 7 place Vendôme, Paris, France; Tananarive, 74 ave. du 18 Juin, B.P. 174.

INSURANCE

Syndicat Professionnel des Agents Généraux d'Assurances: Tananarive, 3 rue Benyowski, B.P. 487; f. 1949; Pres. RICHARD MAYER; Sec. YVES DENIER.

The principal French insurance companies, and a few British and Swiss companies, have offices in Tananarive.

TRADE AND INDUSTRY

CHAMBER OF COMMERCE

Fédération des Chambres de Commerce, d'Industrie et d'Agriculture de Madagascar: B.P. 166, Tananarive, 20 rue Colbert; Pres. JEAN RAMAROMISA; Sec.-Gen. H. RATSIANDAVANA.

There are Chambers of Commerce, Agriculture and Industry at Antalaha (Pres. C. TSIHOMANKARY), Antsirabé (Pres. RAJAOFERSON), Diégo-Suarez (Pres. BLAISE RANTOANINA), Fianarantsoa (Pres. vacant), Fort-Dauphin (Pres. E. J. DIBOKA), Majunga (Pres. J. RAZAFINDRABE), Mananjary (Pres. PAUL BALLISTE), Morondava (Pres. vacant), Nossi-Bé (Pres. M. BLEUSEZ), Tamatave (Pres. J. RAMORASATA), Tananarive (Pres. H. RAZANATSEHENO) and Tuléar (Pres. J. ETONO).

DEVELOPMENT ORGANIZATIONS

Bureau de Développement et de Promotion Industriels (BDPI): 43 SIAG, ave. Marcel Olivier, B.P. 31, Tananarive.

Société Nationale d'Investissement (SNI): P.O.B. 222, Tananarive; f. 1962; by the end of 1972 SNI had nearly 2,000m. FMG invested in 50 industrial projects; Dir. Gen. DAVID RAKOTOPARE.

PRINCIPAL EMPLOYERS' ORGANIZATIONS

Union des Syndicats d'Intérêt Economique de Madagascar (USIEM): Place Roland Garros, B.P. 1338, Tananarive; f. 1946; 41 syndicates; 2,700 firms; Pres. E. ALLAIN; Sec. MARULLAZ PIERRE DUCHENE; publ. *l'Union Economique*.

Syndicat des Entrepreneurs: Tananarive, 407 route Circulaire, B.P. 522.

Syndicat des Exploitants Forestiers et Agriculteurs Malgaches: Tananarive; Pres. BERNARD RABEFANIRAKA.

Syndicat des Exportateurs de Vanille de Madagascar: Antalaha; 23 mems.; Pres. Monsieur BOURDILLON.

Syndicat des Importateurs et Exportateurs de Madagascar: 2 rue Georges Mandel, B.P. 188, Tananarive; Pres. Monsieur FONTANA.

Syndicat des Industries de Madagascar: 41 rue de Choiseul, B.P. 1695, Tananarive; Pres. DANIEL CARRÉ.

Syndicat des Industries Mécaniques: 22 rue Béréni, Tananarive.

Syndicat des Planteurs de Café: Tananarive, rue de Liège, B.P. 173.

Syndicat des Riziers et Producteurs de Riz de Madagascar: 2 rue Georges Mandel, B.P. 1329, Tananarive.

TRADE UNIONS

Confédération Chrétienne des Syndicats Malgaches (CCSM) (*Fivondronam-Ben'ny Sendika Kristianina Malagasy—SEKRIMA*): Soarano, route de Majunga,

B.P. 1035, Tananarive; f. 1937; Pres. JÉRÔME ELOI RAKOTO; Gen. Sec. HUBERT BLAISE ROBEL; 151 affiliated unions, 41,230 mems.

Confédération des Travailleurs Malgaches (*Fivomdronam-Ben'ny Mpiasa Malagasy—FMM*): 3 ave. Maréchal Joffre, Ambatomitsanga, B.P. 1558, Tananarive; f. 1957; Sec.-Gen. C. RANDRIANATORO; 30,000 mems.

Fédération de l'Education Nationale (FEN): Tananarive; Sec.-Gen. JEAN FAUGEROLLE.

Confédération Malgache des Syndicats Libres (Force Ouvrière): Tananarive.

Union des Syndicats Autonomes de Madagascar (USAM): Ampasadratsarahoby, Lot II-H-67, Faravohitra, B.P. 1038, Tananarive; Pres. NORBERT RAKOTOMANANA; Sec.-Gen. VICTOR RAHAGA; 46 affiliated unions; 29,445 mems.

Union des Syndicats Patronaux de Madagascar (USPM): Tananarive.

Union des Syndicats des Travailleurs de Madagascar (*Firaisan'ny Sendika eran'i Madagaskara—FISEMA*): f. 1956; Cimelta, Tananarive; 30,000 mems.

MAJOR INDUSTRIAL COMPANIES

The following are some of the largest companies in terms either of capital investment or employment.

AGIP: 13 rue Amiral-Pierre, Tananarive; cap. m. FMG;40 oil prospecting; Dir. PIER F. BARNABA.

AGIP (Madagascar) S.A.: B.P. 1159, Place Soarano, Tananarive; f. 1962; cap. 500m. FMG.

Sale of petroleum products, management of MOTEL-AGIP.

Dir.-Gen. VINCENZIO MARUCCI: 129 employees.

Compagnie des Ciments Malgaches: B.P. 302, Majunga; cap. 625m. FMG; cement works; Dir. J. SCHNEEBERGER.

Compagnie Malgache des Pétroles CALTEX: B.P. 883, 41 rue Choiseul, Tananarive; f. 1961; cap. 160,040,000 FMG.

Sale of petroleum products, including aviation fuel.

Dir.-Gen. J. F. HARDY; 121 employees.

Compagnie Minière d'Andriamena (COMINA): B.P. 936, Tananarive; f. 1966; cap. 550m. FMG; 20 per cent state owned.

Chrome mining.

Pres. Dir.-Gen. HENRY DE BRIE; Dir. PAUL MASCLANIS.

La Cotonnière d'Antsirabe: B.P. 45, route d'Ambositra, Antsirabe; f. 1952; cap. 1,953m. FMG.

Spinning, weaving, printing and dyeing of textiles.

Pres. Dir.-Gen. MAMAD ISMAIL; Dir.-Gen. AZIZ HASSAM ISMAIL; 2,500 employees.

Société Américaine, Grecque et Malgache "Industrie de la Viande": B.P. 3172, 1 ave. de Lattre de Tassigny, Antsahavola, Tananarive; cap. 300m. FMG.

Abattoir, meat-canning, manufacture of meat products.

Pres. Dir.-Gen. G. S. REPPAS; Dir.-Gen. T. C. BACOPOLOUS; 500 employees.

Société des Cigarettes Melia de Madagascar: B.P. 128, Antsirabe; f. 1956; cap. 400m. FMG.

Manufacture of cigarettes.

Dir. Monsieur CASSEL; 297 employees.

Société Malgache de Raffinage: B.P. 433, Tamatave; f. 1964; cap. 750m. FMG.

Refinery for hydrocarbons imported from the Middle

East, chiefly Iran; production from the concessionary companies prospecting for off-shore oil in Madagascar has not yet commenced.

Dir.-Gen. JACQUES GLANTENET; 230 employees.

Société Malgache d'Exploitations Minières: B.P. 266, Tananarive; f. 1926; cap. 130m. FMG.

Mining of graphite and mica.

Pres. Dir.-Gen. JEAN SCHNEIDER; Dir.-Gen. LUCIEN DUMAS.

Société Sucrière de la Mahavavy: B.P. 173, Tananarive; f. 1949; cap. 1,450m. FMG.

Sugar refinery at St. Louis.

Pres. Dir.-Gen. GABRIEL DAHER; Dir.-Gen. JEAN NANTES.

TRANSPORT

RAILWAYS

Réseau National des Chemins de Fer: B.P. 259, Tananarive; f. 1909; 550 miles of track linking Tamatave on the east coast with Antsirabé in the interior via Moramanga and Tananarive, a branch line from Moramanga to Lake Alaotra and Morarano (chrome traffic) and a line from Manakara on the south-east coast to Fianarantsoa; Dir.-Gen. JEAN RALAIVAO.

ROADS

There are nearly 40,000 km. of roads and tracks in Madagascar. Of these, approximately 2,000 km. are bitumen-surfaced roads and 23,000 km. are roads and tracks serviceable throughout the year.

Automobile Club de Madagascar: B.P. 571, Tananarive; f. 1949; Pres. CHARLES RAZAFINDRATANDRA; publ. *Guide Routier et Touristique.*

INLAND WATERWAYS

The Pangalanes Canal runs for 700 km. near the east coast from Tamatave to Farafangana. The west coast rivers are also navigable. A new port is planned in the Bay of Narinda, 140 km. north of Majunga.

SHIPPING

Société Malgache des Transports Maritimes: 29 rue de la Batterie, B.P. 107, Tamatave, f. 1963, services to Europe; Pres. LAMBERT LODA ABDOU, Dir. HUBERT RAJAOBELINA.

Compagnie Malgache de Navigation: rue Rabearivelo, B.P. 1021, Antsahavola, Tananarive.

Cie. Maritime des Chargeurs Réunis: Tamatave, rue du Commerce.

Royal Inter-Ocean Lines: Tamatave, c/o S. A. M. Darrieux & Co., rue du Commerce.

Bank Line, India Natal Line and **Oriental African Line:** Tamatave, c/o F. W. Ducommun, B.P. 89.

B.P. Tanker Co. and **Shell International Marine Ltd.:** Tamatave, c/o Société Industrielle et Commerciale de l'Emyrne, B.P. 61, rue Sylvain Roux.

Svedel Line and **Cie. des Transports et Remorquages:** Diégo-Suarez, c/o Ets. A. Stéfani, B.P. 25.

Scandinavian-East Africa Line: c/o La Ligne Scandinave Agence Maritime, 1 *bis* rue Clémenceau, B.P. 679, Tananarive.

CIVIL AVIATION

Société Nationale Malgache des Transports Aériens (*Air Madagascar*): 31 ave. de l'Indépendance, Tananarive; f. 1962; internal service and weekly external services;

51 per cent owned by the state, 40 per cent by Air France; fleet comprises one Boeing 707, two Boeing 737, five DC-4, one Nord, ten Pipers, five Twin Otter; Pres. D. ANDRIANTSITOHAINA; Dir.-Gen. JACQUES ALEXANDRE.

Madagascar is also served by Air France, Alitalia and South African Airways.

POWER

Electricité et Eaux de Madagascar: B.P. 200, Tananarive; f. 1928; cap. F25m.; production of electricity and water; Dir. PIERRE BRUCHET.

Société d'Energie de Madagascar: B.P. 495, Tananarive-Antsahavola; f. 1953; cap. 250m. FMG; production of electricity; Dir. Gen. EDMOND OLIVIER RAZAFIMBELO.

TOURISM

Commissariat au Tourisme et aux Arts Traditionnels: 8 rue Fumarolli, B.P. 610, Tananarive; Commissioner JAOZAFY BERNARD; publ. *Revue de Madagascar* (biennial).

CULTURAL ORGANIZATIONS

Ministère de l'Information, du Tourisme et des Arts traditionnels: Ave. de France, Tananarive.

Département des Arts du Ministère des Affaires Culturelles: Place Goulette, Tananarive; concerned in promoting all the arts.

Imadefolk—Institut Malgache des Arts dramatiques et folk-loriques: Centre Culturel Albert Camus, ave. de l'Indépendance, Tananarive; f. 1964; theatre tours at home and abroad; traditional songs and dances; Dir. ODÉAM RAKOTO.

Ny Antsaly: Anatihazo-Isotry, Tananarive; f. 1960; traditional music and dancing; Dir. SYLVESTRE RANDAFISON.

EDUCATION

Education in Madagascar is both public and private. Efforts are being made to increase the number of schools and the primary schools can now accommodate over half the children. There is one university which is closely linked to France and where 200 of the 260 teachers are French, but a new policy of "Malagization and Democratization" has been introduced.

LEARNED SOCIETIES AND RESEARCH INSTITUTES

Académie Malgache: Tsimbazaza, Tananarive; f. 1902; studies in human and natural sciences; monthly meetings; Pres. Dr. P. RADAODY RALAROSY.

Alliance Française: Tananarive.

Bureau de Recherches Géologiques et Minières: B.P. 458, Tananarive; Dir. L. FOURNIE.

Centre Technique Forestier Tropical: B.P. 904, Tananarive; a branch of the central organization in France; f. 1961; Dir. R. ROUANET.

Fondation Nationale de l'Enseignement Supérieur: Campus Universitaire d'Ambohitsaina, B.P. 566, Tananarive; f. 1960; co-ordinates all higher education.

Goethe Institut: B.P. 1200, Tananarive; f. 1961; 200 mems.; Dir. Dr. C. VON SCHOELER.

Institut de Recherches Agronomiques de la République Malgache: B.P. 1444, Tananarive; stations at Alaotra, Antalaha, Betioky-sud, Ivoloina, Diégo-Suarez, Majunga, Fianarantsoa and Tuléar; Dir. J. VELLY.

Institut Géographique National de Madagascar: 3 rue Jean Laborde, B.P. 456, Andohalo, Tananarive; f. 1945; Dir. M. PERREAU-SAUSSINE.

Institut Pasteur: B.P. 1274, Tananarive; f. 1898; biological research; library of 3,000 vols.; Dir. E. R. BRYGOO; publ. *Archives de l'Institut Pasteur de Madagascar* (2 a year).

Institut d'Hygiène Sociale: Tananarive.

Observatoire de Tananarive: Université de Madagascar, Faculté des Sciences, B.P. 3843, Tananarive; f. 1889; affiliated to the University 1967; study of climatology, terrestrial magnetism, seismology, VLF Waves propogation and the ionosphere; Dir. J. M. DE COMARMOND; publs. *Mesures Magnétiques* (annual), Bulletins.

Office de la Recherche Scientifique et Technique Outre-Mer, Centre Océanographique (ORSTOM) de Nossi- Bé: B.P. 68, Nossi-Bé; geology, oceanography, nutrition; library; Dir. A. CROSNIER.

Centre ORSTOM de Tananarive: B.P. 434, Tananarive; geophysics, geology, pedology, hydrology, botany and plant biology, phytopathology and applied zoology, agronomy, medical entomology, sociology, economy, ethnology, history, geography; library; Dir. P. DE BOISSEZON.

Région de Recherches Vétérinaires et Zootechniques de Madagascar: directed by Institut d'Elevage et de Médecine Vétérinaire des Pays Tropicaux.
Laboratoire Central de l'Elevage.
Centre de Recherches Zootechniques: Kianjasoa.
Centre de Recherches Zootechniques: Miadana.

Service des Archives et de la Documentation de la République Malgache: 23 rue general Aubé, Tsaralalana-Tananarive; f. 1959; library of 3,100 vols.; Head of Department Mme RAZOHARINORO.

Service Géologique: B.P. 280, Tananarive; f. 1926; library of 42,919 vols.; Dir. A. RAZAFINI PARANY; publs. *Rapport annuel, Travaux du Bureau Géologique, Annales géologiques, Documentation du Service Géologique, Atlas des fossiles caractéristiques de Madagascar.*

LIBRARIES

Archives de Madagascar: B.P. 3384, Tananarive; f. 1958; *c.* 2,000 vols.; Dir. J. VALETTE.

Bibliothèque du Centre Culturel "Albert Camus": 11 avenue Grandidier, Isoraka, Tananarive; f. 1962; 13,630 vols.

Bibliothèque Municipale: Antsirabé; Librarian JEANNE RABODOMALALA.

Bibliothèque Municipale: avenue du 18 juin, Tananarive; f. 1961; 4,350 vols.

Bibliothèque Nationale: Antaninarenina, B.P. 257, Tananarive; f. 1961; 123,000 vols.; special collections: History, Literature, the Arts, Applied Sciences, Information on Madagascar; Dir. J. RATSIMANDRAVA; publs. *Bibliographie de Madagascar* (annually), *Dingana* (bi- annual revue).

Bibliothèque Universitaire: Campus Universitaire, Ambohitsaina, B.P. 908, Tananarive; f. 1960; 85,000 vols.; Dir. Mlle. DE NUCÉ; publ. *Bibliographie Annuelle de Madagascar.*

U.S. Information Center Library: 26, rue Colbert, Tananarive; f. 1961; 4,000 vols.; Dir. Miss PATRICIA CONNOR.

MUSEUMS

Musée d'Art et d'Archéologie: 18 rue Docteur Villette, Tananarive; affiliated to the University; Dir. P. VERIN.

Musée Historique: Palais de la Reine, Tananarive.

UNIVERSITY

FONDATION CHARLES-DE-GAULLE
(UNIVERSITÉ DE MADAGASCAR)
CAMPUS UNIVERSITAIRE AMBOHITSAINA
B.P. 566, TANANARIVE
Telephone: 260-00.

Founded 1961.

Rector: THOMAS RAHANDRAHA.

Library: *see* Libraries.

Number of teachers: 260.
Number of students: 7,000.

Faculté de Droit et des Sciences Economiques: Campus Universitaire, Ambohitsaina, Tananarive.
Dean: C. CADOUX.
Number of teachers: 30.
Number of students: 2,031.

Faculté des Sciences: Campus Universitaire, Ampasampito, Tananarive.
Dean: T. RAHANDRAHA.
Number of teachers: 62.
Number of students: 976.

Faculté des Lettres et Sciences Humaines: Campus Universitaire, Ambohitsaina, Tananarive.
Dean: S. RAJAONA.
Number of teachers: 52.
Number of students: 1,018.

Ecole Nationale d'Administration Malgasy: Campus Universitaire, Ambohitsaina, Tananarive; f. 1960.
Director: A. RAMANGAHARIVONY.
Director of Studies: G. INDRIANJAFY.
Administrative Secretary: A. RAZAFIMAHEFA.

Ecole Nationale de Médecine et Pharmacie: Campus Universitaire, Ambohitsaina, Tananarive.
Director of Studies: P. RANDRIANARIVO.
Number of students: 399.

Ecole Nationale de Promotion Sociale: route du Fort Voyron, Befelatanana, Tananarive.
Director: J. C. MAESTRE.
Number of students: 87.

Ecole Nationale des Travaux Publics: Campus Universitaire, Ambohitsaina, Tananarive.
Director: R. REISS.
Number of students: 31.

Ecole Nationale Supérieure Agronomique: Campus Universitaire, Ambohitsaina, Tananarive.
Director: A. GUICHON.
Number of students: 107.

Institut d'Etudes Judiciaires: Campus Universitaire, Ambohitsaina, Tananarive.
Director: H. VIDAL.

Ecole Nationale des Cadres des Entreprises: Campus Universitaire, Ambohitsaina (B.P. 905), Tananarive.
Director: J. OBRECHT.

Institut Universitaire de Technologie Industrielle
Ampasampito, Tananarive.
Director: B. DOLPHIN.

Institut Universitaire de Technologie Agricole: Campus
Universitaire, Tananarive.
Director: A. GUICHON.

Institut Universitaire de Gestion: Ampasampito,
Tananarive.
Director: J. OBRECHT.

Institut de Recherches pour l'Enseignement des Mathématiques: Campus Universitaire, Tananarive.
Director: B. BA.

Institut de Linguistique Appliquée: Campus Universitaire, Tananarive.
Director: C. FOUCHE.
Museum: *see* Museums.

Instituts de Préparation aux Enseignements du Second Degré:
Director: J. RAZAFINTSAIAMA (Sciences).
Director: Y. DAUGE (Letters).

Station Marine de Tuléar: B.P. 141, Tuléar.
Administrative Director: P. MARS.
Scientific Director: Prof. PERES.

COLLEGE
Collège Rural d'Ambatobe: B.P. 1629, Tananarive; Dir.
M. ROGER RAJOELISOLO.

SELECT BIBLIOGRAPHY

CADOUX, CHARLES. *La République Malgache.* Paris, Berger-Levrault, 1970.

DECARY, R. *Moeurs et coutumes malgaches.* Paris, 1951.

DESCHAMPS, H. *Histoire de Madagascar.* Paris, 1960.

GENDARME, R. *L'Economie de Madagascar.* Paris, 1960.

HESELTINE, NIGEL. *Madagascar.* London, Pall Mall, 1971.

JANICOT, C., and RANAIVO, F. *Madagascar.* Paris, 1968.

KENT, R. *From Madagascar to the Malagasy Republic.* New York, 1962.

MANONI, O. *Psychologie de la colonisation.* Paris, 1950.

RABEMANANJARA, J. *Nationalisme et problèmes malgaches.* Paris, 1958.

RALAIMIHOATRA, E. *Histoire de Madagascar,* 2 vols. Tananarive, 1966–67.

THOMPSON, V., and ADLOFF, R. *The Malagasy Republic* Stanford University Press, 1965.

Malawi

PHYSICAL AND SOCIAL GEOGRAPHY*

John Amer

The landlocked Republic of Malawi is a long, narrow country some 520 miles from north to south varying in width from 50 to 100 miles, which is aligned along the southern continuation of the east African rift valley system. Essentially Malawi is a plateau country of varying height bordering the deep rift valley trench which averages 50 miles in width. The northern two-thirds of the rift valley floor are almost entirely occupied by Lake Malawi with a mean surface of 1,550 ft. above sea-level, whilst the southern third of the rift valley is traversed by the River Shire draining Lake Malawi, via the Shallow Lake Malombe, to the River Zambezi. The plateau surfaces on either side of the rift valley lie mainly between 2,500 and 4,500 ft., but very much higher elevations are attained, particularly in the north (between 5,000 and 8,000 ft.) and in the south (between 6,000 and almost 10,000 ft.).

The great variation in altitude and the country's latitudinal extent are responsible for a wide range of climatic, soil and vegetational conditions within Malawi's comparatively small land area of 36,325 sq. miles. There are three climatic seasons. During the cool season, from May to August, there is very little cloud and mean temperatures on the plateau areas are 60°F. to 65°F. and in the rift valley between 68°F. and 76°F. Light rain may fall occasionally on the higher south-eastward facing slopes. In September and October, prior to the rains, a short hot season occurs when humidity is increasing and mean temperatures of 80°F. to 86°F. are experienced in the rift valley, and of 72°F. to 76°F. on the plateaux. Between November and April, the rainy season, over 90 per cent of the rain falls. Most of Malawi receives between 30 and 40 in. annual rainfall, but some areas in the higher plateaux experience over 60 in. The broad climatic contrasts are thus between the somewhat cooler, wetter upland areas and the lower-lying rift valley, which tends to receive less rainfall and which in places is excessively hot.

Malawi is fortunate in possessing some of the most fertile soils in south-central Africa. Of particular importance are those derived from Recent sediments—alluvial, lacustrine and aeolian—in the lake-shore plains, the Lake Chilwa-Palombe plain and the upper and lower Shire valley. Good plateau soils occur in the Lilongwe-Kasungu high plains and in the tea-producing areas of Cholo, Mlanje and Nkhata Bay Districts. Although just over half the land area of Malawi is considered suitable for cultivation, only approximately one-third of this area is cultivated at present; this is an indication of the agricultural potential yet to be realized. The lakes and the River Shire represent considerable water resources and an irrigation potential scarcely utilized as yet. It is fortunate that these resources occur in proximity to some of the most fertile areas. The middle Shire, a 50-mile stretch of rapids and waterfalls, has a high hydroelectric potential, the initial exploitation of which began in 1966.

Malawi is one of the more densely peopled countries of Africa, with an average of 111 persons per sq. mile and a "de facto" population of 4,039,583 in 1966. This number includes 11,464 Asians and 7,395 Europeans, but not an estimated 270,000 Malawians—about one-quarter of the male labour force—who work in Rhodesia, Tanzania, South Africa and Zambia owing to the limited opportunities for paid employment within Malawi. As the result of physical, historical and economic factors Malawi's population is very unevenly distributed. The Southern Region, the most developed of the three regions, possesses 52 per cent of the population, whilst the Northern Region has only 12 per cent. The movement of the capital from Zomba to Lilongwe in the Central Region is intended to help redress Malawi's regional imbalance in economic development and population distribution.

See map on p. 650.

RECENT HISTORY

John McCracken

THE COLONIAL SETTLEMENT

The declaration in 1891 of a protectorate over what was to be known as Nyasaland marked the culmination of several years of increasing British involvement in the Malawi regions. Following the arrival of Scottish missionaries in the mid-1870s, the Glasgow-based African Lakes Company was founded in 1878 and a British Consul was appointed to the area in 1883. Portuguese claims of sovereignty over the Shire Highlands alarmed missionaries in the 1880s who appealed without success for Foreign Office protection. In 1889, however, Cecil Rhodes offered to pay for the administration of the territories north of the Zambezi as well as those south, in the hope that eventually he would obtain control of both. Freed from the need to finance the extension of British rule, the Foreign Office in 1890 sent Portugal an ultimatum which forced her to withdraw. A year later the arrival of Harry Johnston as the first commissioner signalled the opening stages in the campaign to transform the paper partition into the reality of formal rule.

The process by which the British gained control over Malawi was a slow and arduous one. Skilfully taking advantage of the rivalry between the settled agricultural peoples—Chewa, Manganja, Tonga, Tumbuka—and such new predatory raiders as the Ngoni and the Yao, Johnston followed a policy of "divide and rule" at least partly imposed on him by the paucity of his resources. A series of campaigns against Yao chieftaincies south of Lake Malawi was followed in 1895 by an attack on the Arab trader Mlozi near Karonga in which Yao and Tonga mercenaries were both involved. In 1896 Gomani's Maseko Ngoni were defeated, and two years later Mpezeni's Ngoni in north-eastern Zambia were finally crushed. By that time several of the Yao states had been so weakened that the colonial government could make only limited use of them in its new administrative system.

The imposition of colonial rule was paralleled by the creation of a new economic order. Because a number of European coffee plantations had been established in the Shire Highlands from the 1880s it was natural that government policy in the 1890s should be designed to further their activities rather than those of African peasant farmers. Johnston's land policy enabled European settlers to obtain large areas of land at a nominal price. His taxation programme, introduced in some districts as early as 1892, was designed to force Africans to work for several months of the year on European estates. His schemes and those of his successors for capital investment were centred on the region of European settlement. The first stretch of railway to be opened, in 1908, ran from Blantyre to Port Herald on the lower Shire river, a route that made it of primary value only to those farmers situated in the Shire Highlands.

Two main consequences can be traced from these developments. Firstly, the concentration of markets and of communication facilities south of the lake ensured that African cash-crop production would take place principally in the southern and later in the central region. Most northern people concentrated on subsistence farming and were forced to meet their growing needs through employment either in the labour centres of southern Malawi or, increasingly, in the mines and on the farms of Rhodesia and South Africa. In 1903 some 6,000 migrants crossed the ferry at Feira to go south in search of work. By 1958 it was estimated that 170,000 men were in employment outside Malawi.

Secondly, the creation of a small settler economy in the Shire Highlands had profound consequences for later political developments. Land alienation was extensive there; many Africans were made tenants-at-will with little or no legal right to the land they cultivated; all were subjected to the insults and tensions inherent in the growth of a colonial culture. The disruption of traditional political authorities by Johnston prevented any rebellion equivalent to the Rhodesian risings of 1896. But by 1915 new mission-educated men had emerged capable of articulating African grievances in dynamic form. In that year a bloody and futile rising was set in motion by the Rev. John Chilembwe.

AFRICAN POLITICS

John Chilembwe is one of the most remarkable figures of central African history. A Yao from Chiradzulu, he was influenced as a young man by the radical British evangelist, Joseph Booth, and accompanied him to America in 1897. Three years later he returned to Chiradzulu anxious to bring improvements to his homeland. During the next decade he built up the Providence Industrial Mission, opened a chain of independent schools and introduced cash-crops like tea and coffee.

By 1914 Chilembwe had abandoned his desire to work within the colonial framework. Existing economic grievances were deepened by the famine of 1913 and by the obstacles placed in his path by certain settlers. The recruitment of porters and askaris following the outbreak of the First World War was the deciding factor. In November 1914 Chilembwe sent an eloquent letter to the local newspaper complaining of the injustices involved in forced African participation. Two months later, on January 23rd, 1915, the rising began. Only three Europeans were killed and at no time was its success in prospect. Chilembwe himself was shot while trying to escape and his lieutenants were imprisoned or hanged. Chilembwe's movement in military terms was thus a fiasco of no importance. Its deeper significance lies in the fact that it demonstrated to Africans the possibility of accepting the attributes of European society while rejecting European control.

The evident failure of violence as a political tactic was followed by what John Iliffe has termed "an age of improvement". Frustrated by the lack of colonial development in the inter-war years, African teachers and clerks pursued policies of educational and economic betterment designed to improve their own position in relation to that of their European rulers. The native associations and independent churches which they founded in no way threatened the sovereignty of the colonial régime. Nevertheless, by linking small groups of Malawians to each other on a non-tribal basis, the associations did provide a network of political contacts out of which the Nyasaland African Congress could emerge in the 1940s. The first president of Congress, Levi Mumba, was also founder of the earliest North Nyasa native association in 1912 and architect of several others in the 1920s. Similarly, by providing areas of African control in a European-dominated society, bodies like the African National Church, founded in 1929, could offer valid solutions to problems of Christian acceptance and social unity. Some independent church leaders like Y. Z. Mwase and Hanoc Phiri attempted to organize improvements in education through African initiative. Their failure to generate significant change was one reason for the drive towards new political activities in the 1950s.

FROM NYASALAND TO MALAWI

Three factors help to account for the rise of mass nationalism in Malawi. The first of these was evident in the period of transition in the 1940s when the frustration felt by members of native associations at their inability to force concessions from the government was paralleled by the increasing tendency of the government to tackle problems at a territorial rather than a local level. The result in 1944 was the foundation of the Nyasaland African Congress, a feeble reformist body in its early years, but one which did provide the framework for nationwide political action.

The formation of the Federation of Rhodesia and Nyasaland undoubtedly contributed to popular involvement in Congress. From the 1890s when Scottish missionaries successfully thwarted Rhodes' attempt to bring Nyasaland under the control of the British South Africa Company, schemes for close association of the country with territories to the south were almost invariably opposed by Africans and their white liberal supporters. In the 1920s and 1930s plans put forward for amalgamation were fiercely attacked, and when in 1949 the settlers changed their aim from amalgamation to federation the resistance remained as strong as ever. It grew in 1951 when the British government accepted the desirability of the scheme, and came to a climax in 1953 when Federation was formally launched. Opposed by new leaders on the grounds that its implementation would destroy hopes of achieving

ndependence for Malawi, Federation was regarded with suspicion by many chiefs who feared that the introduction of direct rule policies would hit at the basis of their power. Thousands of ordinary Malawians also regarded its advent with hostility. Many had first-hand experience as migrant labourers of Southern Rhodesian conditions. They were anxious to prevent such conditions being extended to their homeland.

Independent of the Federation issue was the growth of peasant discontent from the late 1940s. Attempts to stimulate cash-crop production in Malawi in the years after 1945 created problems of soil erosion which the government countered by introducing a series of Natural Resources Ordinances dealing with the usage of land and the limitation of stock. Regulations such as these were often clumsily imposed and sometimes detrimental in their economic effects. Disliked by many farmers, they were resisted by some and often came to be regarded as practical manifestations of Federation. Some Congress leaders involved themselves in resistance. Others dissociated themselves from it. But whether or not Congress was intimately concerned the effects were the same. The groundswell of rural discontent gave a marked impetus to nationalist politics.

Although widespread discontent existed by the early 1950s, tne leadership of Congress was too weak to articulate it in an effective manner. No attempt was made to capitalize on the riots which broke out in the Cholo district of the Shire Highlands in August 1953, and consequently the disturbances were isolated and sporadic, and eventually petered out. A couple of years later, however, changes in the character of Congress could be noted in the growing influence of a group of young radicals headed by H. B. M. Chipembere and Kanyama Chiume, and in the increasingly militant demands for self-government and universal suffrage. As the movement gathered strength in the rural areas, so it developed the techniques and symbols of the mass political party—the slogans of *kwaca* (the dawn), the national flag and the monthly, later weekly, news-sheet.

All that was lacking, Chipembere wrote, was a charismatic leader to pull the movement together. He, Chiume and the other radicals were too young and inexperienced to take on the role. Instead they turned to Dr. Hastings Kamuzu Banda, who, though he had spent nearly forty years in the United States and Britain, had retained close links with Congress. In July 1958 Banda arrived back in Malawi to take over the leadership of the party. His vigorous denunciations of the Federation, combined with the forceful campaigning of his lieutenants, provoked a series of clashes between his followers and colonial officials leading to the declaration of a state of emergency in March 1959, the banning of the party and the arrest of its leaders.

The fact that mass nationalism does not inevitably achieve independence can be seen from the situation in Southern Rhodesia, where the National Democratic Party was destroyed by settler action. In Malawi, however, the British government was still directly responsible. Its political plans for Central Africa had been jeopardized by opposition to Federation. Its economic plans for the production of increased food-stuffs had been hindered by resistance to opposition measures. Now with the rise of the new Malawi Congress Party from September 1959 its coercive measures were seen to be equally ineffective. Faced with the dilemma of maintaining control through the continued use of armed force (52 Africans had been killed during the emergency) or of getting out altogether, the British Colonial Secretary, Ian Macleod, decided on the latter alternative. Dr. Banda was released in April 1960 and invited to talks in London. The elections of August 1961 brought the Malawi Congress Party sweeping victory, and these were followed in January 1963 by the attainment of responsible self-government. On July 6th, 1964, six years to the day from Dr. Banda's return to the country, the protectorate of Nyasaland became the independent state of Malawi.

INDEPENDENCE AND AFTER

The emergence of one of the most conservative political régimes in Africa in the 1960s from a country with one of the most militant nationalist movements took place partly because of Malawi's economic dependence on the south. A small poor country whose only access to the sea was by rail through Portuguese colonial territory, Malawi, by the time of independence, was so securely part of the southern African economic complex that even the most radical politician might have baulked at challenging white supremacy too hard. Not only did thousands of Malawi migrants still work in South Africa and Rhodesia, these two countries were Malawi's main trading partners on the African continent.

Radical politicians, moreover, were largely absent from Malawi in the years after independence. Because the main aim of the Congress Party had been to break the Federation rather than to bring about revolutionary change, internal divisions among Africans played little part in the nationalist struggle, and radical new elements were forced to share power with older conservative forces.

These elements suffered a major reverse in September 1964 when six senior ministers were dismissed or resigned from the Cabinet following their failure to persuade Dr. Banda to speed up Africanization or to pursue stronger anti-colonial policies. Opposed by a major segment of the Malawi intelligentsia, Banda reacted by giving greater responsibilities to white expatriates and by drawing for popular support upon less well-educated sections of the population, particularly from among his own Chewa people. As the dispute degenerated into open warfare, Chipembere, the government's most formidable opponent, took refuge in the Mangoche hills to the east of Lake Malawi, and from there in February 1965 launched a successful raid on Fort Johnston which ended with his rebuff at Liwonde ferry and subsequent withdrawal from Malawi. With the opposition crushed, Banda reasserted his control and in July 1966 was elected President of the new Republic. Briefly challenged in October 1967 by a small armed band of

exiles led by the former Minister of Home Affairs, Yatuta Chisiza, he emerged from the crisis stronger than ever when Chisiza and 14 other members of the band were killed. Since then rumours of plots have occasionally circulated in Malawi but the only tangible threat to the Government has come from the FRELIMO guerrillas in neighbouring Mozambique whose activities in the Tete province have periodically threatened Malawi's communications with the south. Inside the country Dr. Banda's position has appeared unassailable. Sworn in as Life President in July 1971, he had closely supervised four months earlier the first parliamentary elections to be held since independence. The candidates, recommended in the first instance by local committees, were all unopposed, and national voting, therefore, did not take place.

Freed from the need to consult colleagues, Dr. Banda since 1964 has followed policies which strikingly contrast with the socialist and anti-colonial postures taken by some of his African neighbours. Like the "improvers" of the 1930s he has tended to equate the success of an individual Malawian with the progress of the Malawi nation as a whole, and for this reason has vigorously encouraged cabinet ministers and civil servants to follow his own example in buying farms, employing labour and investing in commercial concerns. He has also welcomed private and government investment from the West, though this has not prevented him taking steps to "localize" the Malawi economy, partly by restricting the areas in which Asians can trade, partly by establishing African-controlled corporations to compete with the European firms that operate in the country.

In foreign affairs Dr. Banda's active promotion of friendly relations with Portugal and South Africa has alienated him from most other African leaders. The opening of diplomatic ties with South Africa in 1967 was followed in the next year by the acceptance of a loan from the Republic of £4.7 million to finance the first stage of the new capital to be built at Lilongwe. Mr. Vorster's visit to Malawi in May 1970 marked a further stage in the new alliance. It was followed by the raising to ambassadorial level of diplomatic contacts between the two countries, and by the Malawi President's colourful State visit to South Africa in August 1971. To Dr. Banda such contacts were not only economically and militarily advantageous but could help to break down the system of *apartheid*. An advocate of "conversion through kindness", he drew on his own personal experience to argue that significant progress had been made when the student who had been snubbed by whites in a cafeteria in Chicago in the early 1930s could dine with the Prime Minister of South Africa forty years later.

The friendship which Malawi has shown to South Africa has not always been extended to her two African neighbours—Zambia and Tanzania. Relations with Tanzania were clouded in 1965 when Dr. Banda accused the government of assisting several of his former ministers to organize subversive activities against him. Two years later a boundary dispute erupted over Malawi's claim to ownership of the whole of the northern half of Lake Malawi, including the shores directly bordering on Tanzania. And this claim was enlarged in September 1968 by Dr. Banda's suggestion that Malawi's natural boundaries extended at least 100 miles north of the Songwe river as well as east and west into Zambia and Mozambique. Relations with Zambia have since improved—the opening of a Zambian High Commission in July 1971 was followed by an increase in the number of visits from Zambian

ministers and officials to Malawi. But Tanzanian attitudes have tended to harden. One of the East and Central African states that produced the Mogadishu Declaration of October 1971 criticising the visits of African leaders to South Africa, Tanzania has waged a campaign to have Malawi expelled from the Organization of African Unity—a campaign that up to now has not met with success.

ECONOMY

Douglas Lamb

ECONOMIC STRUCTURE

On the attainment of independence Malawi faced economic problems characteristic of many low-income tropical countries, several in acute form. Chief among impediments to accelerated development were: an extensive, low-productivity, subsistence agricultural sector; an absence of commercially exploitable mineral deposits; a Gross Domestic Income per capita of only K39.5 p.a. constricting savings and local markets; excessive concentration of a limited modern sector around Blantyre much of it controlled from Southern Rhodesia; a still embryonic educational system, particularly at secondary and vocational levels; an inadequate transport network, especially for a landlocked country; and, finally, an annual budgetary deficit of nearly K12 million due mainly to the inability of an independent Malawi to sustain a level of recurrent expenditures on the public services previously supported by Federal finance.

The effective mobilization of the country's population and agricultural, livestock, fishing, forestry and potential hydroelectric power resources therefore mainly presupposed a massive foreign-aided government programme of infrastructural development allied with those institutional reforms necessary for its implementation. The resultant transformation of Malawi's economic structure and performance of its developing economy since independence provide a focus for this survey.

Monetization of the economy has increased steadily since 1964. Nevertheless, subsistence activities still accounted for 40 per cent of the gross domestic product in 1971. Marketed agricultural, fishing and forestry production provided 17 per cent of domestic output, while the spectacular expansion of secondary industry, including manufacturing, building and construction, whose contribution to the G.D.P. rose from 8 to 15 per cent between 1964 and 1969, slowed down in 1971 reducing the share of monetary secondary activities to 14 per cent. Within the tertiary sector, commercial services, like distribution, transport and banking, comprised 18 per cent of the domestic product, with a further 10 per cent in the form of public administration, security, health and education services. The growing role of modern, higher-productivity activities, in manufacturing, particularly from 1964 to 1969, and now increasingly

in agriculture, has enabled Malawi to achieve a creditable overall economic performance. In the first seven years since independence total G.D.P. at market prices rose from K151.4 million to K319.2 million. In real terms this constitutes an increase of 5.9 per cent per annum and compares favourably with average growth rates for both developed countries and those of the third world. Moreover, trading gains from steadily improving terms of trade during the post-independence period have secured a still higher average annual rate of 6.5 per cent for the country's real domestic income. This aggregate rate of growth must, however, be viewed against an estimated average rate of population increase of some 2.5 per cent per annum, to indicate an annual rate of advance of domestic real income per capita of 4 per cent between 1964 and 1971. The "de facto" population in mid-1971 is about 4.6 million, making Malawi heavily populated by African, though not Asian, standards. Other population features of economic interest include its youthfulness, the median age being only 17.5 years in 1966 when 44 per cent were under 15; its homogeneity, non-Africans forming only 0.5 per cent of the total; and the large number of Malawians, approximately 250,000, mostly males, in wage employment abroad, mainly in South Africa, Rhodesia and Zambia, labour migration being a long-standing characteristic of the Malawi economy.

Total gross fixed capital formation, at a record K52 million, accounted for over 16 per cent of the domestic product in 1971, compared with less than 9 per cent in 1964. Significantly, after five years during which private and public sector consumption had exceeded the country's gross national product, in 1970 national savings became positive at a level of 5 per cent of GNP and contributed to over one quarter of national investment demands. With fixed investment averaging 15 per cent of GDP over the seven years since independence, Malawi's GDP per person in 1971 rose to K70.

AGRICULTURE

Agriculture, the most important sector of the economy supports 90 per cent of the population. Probably 70 per cent of active males are engaged in producing subsistence needs, surpluses of food crops for commercial sale and export cash crops. Malawi's crops can be divided into two groups. The first is those grown by indigenous smallholders on land held under customary tenure, about 85 per cent of total land, and cultivated on an estimated 3.36 million acres during the 1968–69 growing season, 90 per cent of them concentrated in the Central and Southern Regions and a substantial proportion being under mixed cropping. Maize, the chief food crop, was grown on 2.6 million acres, pulses on 2.1 million, millet and sorghum on 1.2 million, groundnuts on 1.1 million, cassava on 0.7 million, and sweet and Irish potatoes on 0.4 million acres. Rice, cotton and fire-cured, sun/air-cured and Oriental tobaccos also enjoyed substantial acreages. Secondly, export crops, principally tea, flue-cured and Burley tobaccos, and tung, are grown on specialized estates, until recently mostly by European companies or 'third-generation' settlers, as is sugar, mainly for home consumption.

The size and pattern of Malawi's agricultural production vary however not only with the extent of annual plantings, themselves subject to influences like producer prices, incomes and quotas, but also with very unpredictable weather conditions and incidence of pests and disease. Customary land cash crops and surpluses for commercial sale, in particular dark-fired tobacco, groundnuts, cotton, rice and maize, are normally purchased by the Agricultural Development and Marketing Corporation, formerly the Farmers' Marketing Board. The F.M.B. in controlling farmer prices has been seeking to increase agricultural production on non-private land through the maintenance of price stability and the provision of improved inputs, at cost or subsidized prices, and processing, research, marketing and export promotion functions. This policy has been maintained by the new ADMARC whose overall operation appears subject to normal commercial criteria. ADMARC payments to growers reached a record K14.2 million in 1971 for purchases totalling 157,000 tons.

Major Exports

Smallholder and estate crops together achieved record export earnings of K45.9 million in 1971. With the continuance of economic sanctions against Rhodesia, increasing world demand and prices for flue-cured and Burley varieties during the late 1960's enhanced export prospects for tobacco, Malawi's leading foreign currency earner, and induced heavy estate investment and rapid development of indigenous tobacco growers' schemes. As a result, greatly increased quantities combined with improved average prices for all types of tobacco except Burley produced sales worth K20.1 millions. 40 per cent higher than in 1970, from a total production of 57.9 million lb., double that for 1969. The outlook for Malawi's plain teas, her second most important export with 1971 sales of 41.0 million lb. realizing K11.7 million, has been encouraging, steady expansions in acreage, production and export quantities having been partly discounted in 1969 by an abrupt fall of 30 per cent in the average London price. Continuing international consultations and export quotas were expected to correct the growing imbalance between world exports and consumption. Neverthe-

less the 1970 recovery of the Malawi tea price to above the 1968 level and subsequent firmness in 1971, owed more to labour unrest in plantations and docks in India, and drought conditions in East Africa, followed by production losses suffered by Pakistan in the East Bengal conflict, than to international marketing measures. Growing markets for Malawi's third ranking export, the large hand-shelled confectionery-grade groundnut, accounting for over 50 per cent of world sales, will not be fully exploited until production levels, depressed periodically by adverse weather conditions and rosette disease, recover their 1967 peak. Maize exports, which are dependent on the size of annual surpluses, and were running at over K2 million a year between 1967 and 1969, fell to zero in 1970 following a difficult growing season with very irregular rainfall, which necessitated imports of 100,000 tons from southern Africa to meet shortages. Exports began a recovery to K0.4 million in 1971. Medium staple cotton, cassava, and to an increasing extent rice and sunflower seed are also important foreign exchange earners. Since 1969 Malawi has been a net exporter of both fish and sugar. The raising of export cash crop receipts depends chiefly at this stage on improving quality and the reliability of production levels, as well as on increasing the volume of output.

Malawi's agricultural development programme, centred on three major schemes covering over one million acres and costing over K10 million, is designed to raise yields per acre by encouraging simple improvements in farming technique with greater use of fertilizer, pest control, irrigation and equipment. Enlarged extension and credit services, training courses, research and the raising of marketing efficiency are important elements in this strategy. The reorganization and consolidation of holdings, with registration of title to land, will make more economic-sized plots available for smallholder settlement and stimulate farm investment.

Finally, mention should be made of progress in the development of livestock, fisheries and pulpwood plantations to supply a projected pulp and paper industry. In addition, Malawi has been allocated an annual sugar quota of 15,000 tons in the United States market. Beginning in 1973, this should add K1.5 million to the country's export earnings and require an expansion of domestic production from 36,000 to 60,000 tons if growing local demands and the quota are to be met.

INDUSTRY

Rapid expansion of a very limited industrial base, accorded high priority at independence, had boosted estimated manufacturing output to K28.4 million, nearly four times its 1964 level, a rate of growth far in excess of that for the economy as a whole. Government encouragement of private enterprise has led initially to the attraction of foreign private direct investment and management expertise, especially in collaboration with the K2.35 million, wholly government-owned Malawi Development Corporation, established in 1964 to promote new enterprises through participation in their equity and loan finance. Total M.D.C. investments in subsidiary and associated companies, covering manufacturing, distribution, hotels and tourism, commercial fishing and agricultural estates, finance and property, amounted to over five million kwacha at the end of 1971. Inaugurated as a statutory corporation, the M.D.C. became a limited liability company at the beginning of 1970 and continued in 1971 to generate a surplus for reinvestment in the group's activities. A favourable investment climate has been created through a good record of political and monetary stability and infrastructural development. Direct inducements have been offered in the form of low-cost estate sites, tariff protection, exclusive licensing where justified, generous investment allowances, and unrestricted repatriation of capital, profits and dividends. Consequently Malawi's industry now covers a growing variety of fields. Apart from the traditional export industries of tea and tobacco manufacture, important categories include: milling; manufactured sugar and other foods; beer, spirits and soft drinks; clothing and footwear; meat, fish, fruit and vegetable canning; oils and soaps; radios and batteries; cement and bricks; saw-milling; matches; metal products; tyre retreading and vehicle assembly; repairs. Significantly, the share of traditional export industries in manufacturing output was halved between 1964 and 1969 by spectacular growth in consumer and intermediate goods industries. In 1971, while intermediate goods production was depressed by difficulties in cement supply, strong rises in personal consumption spending continued to expand the turnover of consumer goods firms and increasing activity was assured for agro-based processing industries, as export crops like tobacco and cotton recorded very high volumes. However, because of their much higher capital-labour ratios (K2,600 on average, for new enterprises in 1971,) newer industries have made much less impact on manufacturing employment which rose from 11,050 to 22,000, well under half the rate of increase for output. As the experience of establishing two canning factories in 1969–70 indicates, absorption of growing numbers of school and college leavers will require more labour-intensive manufacturing activities, especially in the agricultural sector. The first, and easiest, phase of industrial development, based on more obvious cases of import-replacement, is now, however, almost complete. Future growth will depend on a widening of the local market and imaginative export promotion to provide a viable scale of production for further import-substituting firms and new export-oriented industries utilizing domestic agricultural produce. Efforts to widen the domestic market took concrete form in 1971 when the newly established Import and Export Company of Malawi, a wholly owned subsidiary of the Malawi Development Corporation, commenced operations intended to improve the distribution network for the benefit of rural communities throughout the country. Wholesale and retail outlets were acquired from Bookers (Malawi) Ltd., until then predominant in this sphere, with the objective of eventual Malawianization of rural retail trading.

Power

The Electricity Supply Commission of Malawi operates both thermal and hydroelectric power stations, having a total installed capacity of 38.71 mW., located mainly in the Southern Region. 24 mW. of hydroelectric power capacity were established at Nkula Falls in 1966-67, but additional demand anticipated from industrial development and the new capital at Lilongwe led to successful negotiation of a project for a second hydroelectric power station financed jointly by IDA and the African Development Bank. First-stage construction of this second power station at Tedzani Falls is scheduled for completion in 1973 while a 66Kv. transmission line between Nkula Falls and Lilongwe will be brought into operation in 1972. Estimated growth of demand in the 1970s while below the spectacular 22 per cent annual rate of increase in consumption between 1965 and 1970, indicates a likely need for still further generating facilities about the middle of the decade.

Transport

Malawi Railways operates 289 miles of the 515 mile single-line rail link from Salima, on the central lake-shore, to the Mozambique port of Beira, Malawi's traditional trade outlet on the Indian Ocean. Her new rail link to provide access to the port of Nacala, north of Beira, was completed in July 1970. Freight traffic, boosted by heavy Zambian transit consignments to a 1968 peak of 126.4 million net ton miles, fell by a third after the opening of the TanZam oil pipeline. However, a major recovery occurred in 1970 and the 1971 estimate is little short of the 1968 record. Rail passenger traffic, depressed by increasing road and airline competition from 1967 to 1969, more than regained its 1966 level in both 1970 and 1971. Malawi Railways gross operating surplus in 1971 was more than 80 per cent higher than in 1969 but still fell nearly a third short of the record gross profits of 1967. Despite increasing freight and passenger loads, Malawi Railways lake service vessels continue to incur a large operating deficit.

Malawi's 1,818 miles of main road are being upgraded and feeder and crop-extraction roads extended. Road transport, especially goods vehicles and motor cycles in the last two years, has shown a steady rate of growth.

With Blantyre becoming a focal point for regional air services in southern Africa since U.D.I., there has been a rapid development in air traffic, with passenger traffic soaring from 79,614 to 195,256 and freight from 418,900 Kg. to 1,528,000 Kg. between 1964 and 1971. Seven foreign national airlines operate services into Blantyre's Chileka airport, apart from Air Malawi which now has scheduled flights to Nairobi, Beira, Lusaka, Ndola, Salisbury and Johannesburg, as well as extensive internal services.

Growing investment in communications and hotel facilities also forms part of the programme to boost tourism.

EXTERNAL TRADE AND PAYMENTS

Malawi's prospects for sustained development depend primarily on improved export performance. The primary producer's typical dependence on international commodity trade is heightened in Malawi's case by an absence, so far, of exportable minerals, although the variety of her agricultural exports affords some degree of protection from fluctuations both in the domestic production of individual crops and in world commodity prices. Nevertheless in 1971 agricultural products still accounted for 94 per cent of domestic export receipts of K49.0 million. The three leading commodities (tobacco, a record K21.8 million, 32 per cent higher than in 1970, tea K11.7 million and groundnuts K5.9 million) earned 80 per cent, with raw cotton and rice together contributing about 7 per cent, and manufactured exports, mainly clothing, footwear and cattlecake under 3 per cent. Although exports of most agricultural products increased and a record export tonnage of 127,000 tons was achieved, with tobacco now providing 45 per cent of domestic export receipts the trend to greater relative diversification of export crops has been reversed. With re-exports at between K7 million and K10 million since the Rhodesian U.D.I., total merchandise exports rose from K25 million in 1964 to K58.6 million in 1971. The United Kingdom, the traditional market for Malawi's exports, took 43 per cent in 1971. Rhodesia, the U.S.A., Ireland, the Netherlands, South Africa, Zambia and the Federal Republic of Germany followed in order of importance.

Total merchandise imports soared from K28.6 million in 1964 to a record K89.9 million in 1971, the principal categories being manufactured are consumer goods, machinery and transport equipment, building and industrial materials, piece goods and petroleum products. The composition of imports is increasingly influenced by the heavy demands for capital equipment, industrial inputs and building materials created by public sector development programmes and the growth of import-substituting industries. Final consumer goods feature correspondingly less strongly in the import bill. Malawi's leading suppliers in their 1971 order were the United Kingdom, Rhodesia, South Africa, Japan, the Federal Republic of Germany, the U.S.A., Zambia and Australia. Malawi's traditional trading pattern was affected by the Rhodesian U.D.I. in 1965 and devaluation of the Malawi pound in 1967. Termination of the Trade Agreement with Rhodesia, exposing the latter's exports to higher Malawian tariffs, and devaluation both made Rhodesia a higher-cost source of supply. The leading position she enjoyed in 1965 was, as a result, swiftly eroded and ceded to the U.K., now pre-eminent in Malawi's trade. South African loan finance for the Nacala rail link and new capital city has contributed to a sharp rise in her exports to Malawi since 1969.

With regard to international payments, consistently adverse balances on merchandise trade and on factor and non-factor services have been only partially offset by a favourable balance on transfers, itself progressively weakened by the annual reduction in the British budgetary grant-in-aid. In consequence since 1965 Malawi has run a large overall current account deficit which has been met increasingly by long-term government borrowing. with additional support provided by inflows of private capital investment funds. At the close of 1971 the foreign exchange reserves stood at K22.8 million, equivalent to three months imports and K9.1 million higher than the level five years previously, although non-recurrent proceeds from the sale of the Zambezi Bridge have contributed to their buoyancy, which has been further strengthened by instalments of Special Drawing Rights at the beginning of 1970 and 1971.

BANKING AND FINANCE

The Reserve Bank of Malawi began its own note issue in 1964, the basic currency unit being the Malawi pound which stood at par with the British pound until February, 1971, when a decimal currency was introduced. The major unit is now the kwacha, equal to 100 tambala, the minor unit, and equal to 50p (sterling). Until 1969 commercial banking business was conducted by two foreign banks, Barclays Bank D.C.O. and the Standard Bank. Early in 1970 the Commercial Bank of Malawi, jointly owned by a major Portuguese bank and the Malawi Development Corporation, commenced operations with the aim of encouraging greater indigenous participation in business. Local involvement in banking increased again significantly in July, 1971, when Barclays Bank D.C.O. and the Standard Bank amalgamated their Malawi businesses and joined with local capital to form the National Bank of Malawi, with Government nominees holding 49 per cent of the ownership and the remainder shared equally between the two banks. Banking developments of economic interest include growing use of demand deposits, whose ratio to the total money supply increased to 61 per cent at the end of 1971, impressive growth of business and personal urban and rural savings, and rapid increases in the level of domestic credit to the private sector and government. Outstanding Government Treasury Bills, first introduced in 1965, amounted to K6.0 million at the end of 1971, still K2.0 million below the legal maximum. Longer-term industrial and consumer finance is provided on a small scale by two finance houses.

Government management of the country's public finances since independence has been cautious and orthodox. Total recurrent and development expenditure nevertheless swelled from K37.4 million in 1964 to an estimated K84.6 million in the 1971–72 financial year. The principal heads of revenue-account expenditure of K50.9 million were education (16.8 per cent), public debt charges (16.5 per cent, and in absolute amount 70 per cent higher than in 1969), administration (13.2 per cent), defence and security (11.5 per cent), natural resources (7 per cent) and health (6.4 per cent). The emphasis of planned development spending of K33.7 million in 1971/72 changed from that in the previous year when over one half was devoted to transport and communications, 28.7 per cent was scheduled for natural resources, 24.2 per cent for transport and communications, 9.5 per cent for power and 9.3 per cent for the new capital city, and 6.7 per cent for education.

Over the same period from 1964, domestic receipts increased from K17 million to nearly K43 million. Chief sources of revenue in 1971–72 were import duties (K10.6 million), income taxes on companies and self-employed (K7.6 million), personal income taxes (K6.3 million), income from government entrepreneurship (K2.7 million), excise duties (K2.7 million), and licences (K1.4 million). A new, and powerful contributor to revenue is the surtax, introduced in 1970, whose rate was doubled to ten per cent for the 1971/72 financial year. This sales tax at the retail level is estimated to have collected over K7 million in 1971/72. The ratio of total tax revenue, at K35.8 million, to the gross national product rose from 10.2 per cent in 1969 to 11.2 per cent in 1971/72. With the quickening pace of import-substituting industrialization, receipts from income taxes and excise duties are rising strongly, while the relative yield from import duties, the traditional source of revenue, declines.

Clearly, the increasing magnitude of central government expenditure since independence could not have been achieved without the help of external financial resources. By 1972 these amounted to the considerable figure of K185 million, to which the U.K. budgetary grant-in-aid had contributed K55 million and other grants and loans on recurrent account a further K26 million. The remainder consisted of "direct" development aid which will be analysed later. Nevertheless, increased domestic revenue has permitted U.K. budgetary aid to be reduced from K12 million in 1965 to K0.8 million in 1971/72 and to be scheduled for elimination in 1973. Similarly, a rising proportion of development spending is being financed from local resources. This improvement in the country's public financial position is impressive.

Public Sector Debt.

As a result of this post-1966 surge in foreign long-term borrowing, externally held government debt exceeded K102 million by the end of 1971, although average effective terms continued to soften to 2.6 per cent interest p.a. with repayment over 23.6 years. The foreign indebtedness of public enterprises, principally electricity, water, railways, airways, housing, flue-cured tobacco and Smallholder Tea Authorities, had reached K11.8 million making a total public sector servicing requirement of K6.6 million pre-empting 13 per cent of 1971's estimated domestic export earnings.

Domestic counterpart funds to foreign financial aid have been acquired through medium- and long-term government borrowing in the local "capital" market managed by the Reserve Bank, which deals in local post-independence and old Nyasaland stock. Since independence over K2.0 million a year, net of refunding, has been raised. Reserve Bank holdings of outstanding issues amounting to K32.8 million at the end of 1971 were commendably modest at K2.8 million or 8.5 per cent of the total. Total public debt

including that of public enterprises now stands at over K150 million.

FOREIGN AID AND ECONOMIC DEVELOPMENT

Between 1964 and 1971/72 development account expenditures amounted to over K138 million. Transport and agriculture have been priority sectors throughout this period. From 1964 to 1969 27 per cent of development spending was allocated to transportation, 21 per cent to agriculture, forestry and fishing, and 10 per cent to education. Commercial and industrial development, administrative buildings, and water, sanitation and housing projects also received substantial capital funds. Initial development strategy has therefore laid heavy stress on remedying basic infrastructural deficiencies, especially in communications. Leading emphasis in 1971/72 has begun to shift to agriculture which was planned to receive an equal 22 per cent share with transportation, with the new capital city, power and education allocated 14, 10 and 7 per cent respectively. As mentioned earlier, development expenditures of this order have depended largely on foreign bilateral and multilateral financial assistance, now received almost entirely in the form of loans, in sharp contrast to pre-1966 practice. In the post independence period grants of over K100 million have been made available principally by the United Kingdom, with the International Development Association, South Africa, West Germany, the United States, Denmark and the African Development Bank also important donors. Substantial "non-monetary" aid in the form of technical assistance, equipment and training has also been supplied with the U.S.A. the leading contributor. The Malawi Government's three year rolling public sector investment programme is revised annually to provide for changes in development policy, in expected availability of resources, and in planned rates of project completion. Implementation of most of the programme continues to require successful negotiation of external development resources.

Yet Malawi's development prospects over this decade depend not merely on a continued high level of foreign assistance but also on its effective utilization. Two major preconditions for the latter are the maintenance of monetary and fiscal stability, which implies a restricting of public sector development expenditures within the limits of available aid and the generation of additional domestic savings to provide local counterpart funds for development projects; and also the identification of, and direction of external resources into, relatively quick pay-back investments, earning foreign currency, especially in agriculture. Development should not then be inhibited by acute pressures on the foreign exchange reserves which have been experienced by other African countries, particularly in the middle of the 1970s when loan servicing requirements will become heavier and the budgetary grant-in-aid will have been phased out.

STATISTICAL SURVEY

AREA AND POPULATION

AREA (sq. miles)	POPULATION 1966	AFRICANS	EUROPEANS	ASIANS AND OTHERS
45,747*	4,039,583	4,020,724	7,395	11,464

1971: Estimated total population; 4,549,000.
* Includes 9,422 sq. miles of inland water.

REGIONS

REGIONS	POPULATION	CHIEF TOWNS	POPULATION
Southern	2,067,140	Zomba (capital)	19,666
		Blantyre	104,461
Central	1,474,952	Lilongwe	19,425
Northern	497,491	Mzuzu	8,490

LAND DISTRIBUTION
(1968—'000 acres)

Unalienated African Trustland	.	.	.	19,500
Unalienated Government Land	.	.	.	3,200
Freehold .	.	.	.	400
Leasehold	.	.	.	200
TOTAL	.	.	.	23,300

EMPLOYMENT

SECTOR	1969 Number Employed	1969 Percentage of Total Employment	1970 Number Employed	1970 Percentage of Total Employment	1971* Number Employed	1971* Percentage of Total Employment
Agriculture, Forestry and Fishing .	48,281	32.9	53,695	33.7	57,629	33.3
Mining and Quarrying . . .	996	0.7	676	0.4	747	0.4
Manufacturing . . .	17,691	12.1	19,462	12.2	21,982	12.7
Electricity and Water . . .	1,530	1.0	1,737	1.1	2,138	1.2
Construction . . .	17,193	11.7	18,355	11.5	17,713	10.2
Wholesale, Retail, Hotels and Restaurants .	10,975	7.5	12,250	7.7	13,823	8.0
Transport, Storage and Communications . . .	8,367	5.7	8,490	5.3	9,120	5.3
Financing, Insurance and Business Services . . .	1,116	0.8	1,228	0.8	1,397	0.8
Community, Social and Personal Services . . .	40,351	27.5	43,448	27.3	48,753	28.1
TOTAL . . .	146,500	100.0	159,342	100.0	173,302	100.0
of which:						
Private . . .	99,893	68.2	110,092	69.1	120,375	69.5
Government . . .	46,607	31.8	49,250	30.9	52,927	30.5

* Estimate.

AGRICULTURE

MARKETED PRODUCTION OF MAIN CROPS

CROP	1966	1967	1968	1969	1970*	1971
Tea (production of made tea— million lb.) . . .	33.8	37.1	34.8	37.3	41.3	41.0
Tobacco (million lb.) . .	40.8	35.6	33.5	28.8	48.9	57.9
Flue Cured (auction sales) . .	2.7	4.0	6.1	6.1	10.3	14.1
Burley (auction sales) . .	5.3	5.9	6.7	7.6	12.5	12.5
Fire Cured (auction sales) . .	26.7	23.2	18.4	13.0	22.0	26.3
Sun/Air (auction sales) . .	6.1	2.5	2.3	2.1	4.1	5.1
Groundnuts (ADMARC's purchases —'ooo short tons) . . .	46.5	47.3	25.1	40.9	29.8	41.9
Seed Cotton (ADMARC's purchases —'ooo short tons) . . .	14.6	13.2	12.8	20.2	23.5	24.4
Maize (ADMARC's purchases—'ooo short tons)	62.5	100.0	92.2	58.1	9.1	37.3
Pulses (ADMARC's purchases—'ooo short tons)	20.3	23.3	3.8	18.1	8.9	19.0
Raw Sugar (production—'ooo short tons	3.7	18.1	21.9	29.6	36.1	38.0
Paddy (ADMARC's purchases—'ooo short tons) . . .	4.5	5.1	2.3	9.3	9.9	20.0

TEA PRODUCTION AND EXPORTS 1968–71

	1968	1969	1970	1971
Tea Acreage ('ooo acres) . . .	35.7	37.1	37.6*	n.a.
Production (million lb.) . . .	34.8	37.3	41.3*	n.a.
Exports (million lb.) . . .	34.8	38.0	39.0	40.0
Exports f.o.b. (K million) . . .	9.6	9.5	11.0	11.7
Average Price c.i.f. (d/lb.)† . .	40.58	28.1	43.4*	n.a.

* Estimate.   † Weighted average London auction price.

LIVESTOCK
('ooo)

				1967	1968	1969
Cattle	.	.	.	464	480	491
Sheep	.	.	.	81	90	81
Goats	.	.	.	668	617	599
Pigs .	.	.	.	149	180	150

FOREST INDUSTRY DIVISION SALES BY CATEGORIES

	1968	1969	1970	1971
Sawn Timber (K) . . .	280,400	318,000	388,300	485,000
Volume (cu. ft.) . . .	213,665	244,647	277,360	346,400
Creosoted Products (K) . . .	94,900	112,700	83,496	105,000
Other Products (K) . . .	61,000	95,100	156,274	160,000*

* Estimate.

FISH IMPORTS, EXPORTS AND ESTIMATED LANDINGS

	1969	1970	1971
Estimated Landings (short tons) . . .	26,000	37,000	40,000
Imports:	140,974	217,800	169,932
Fresh/Frozen (lb.)	50,791	25,000	10,784
(K)	20,100	13,100	10,445
Salt/Dried (lb.) . . .	288,237	915,000	183,000
(K)	56,664	105,700	66,000
Preserved (lb.)	300,290	460,000	437,409
(K)	64,210	99,000	93,487
Exports:	142,480	272,565	283,523
Fresh/Frozen (lb.) . . .	471,495	306,528	370,901
(K) . . .	43,710	36,969	59,857
Salt/Dried/Smoked (lb.) . . .	598,527	1,382,073	1,188,276
(K) . . .	98,780	235,596	223,666
Aquarium Fish Exports (K)* . . .	27,206	38,000	57,400

* Value on c.i.f. basis.

FINANCE

100 tambala = 1 kwacha.

Coins: 5 and 10 tambala.

Notes: 50 tambala; 1, 2 and 10 kwacha.

Exchange rates (December 1972): £1 sterling = 2.009 kwacha; U.S. $1 = 85.57 tambala.

100 kwacha = £49.78 = $116.86.

BUDGET
(K'000)

Year	Total Receipts	Total Expenditure
1968	53,946	54,300
1969	59,926	60,504
1970–71 . . .	85,498	82,115
1971–72 . . .	83,774	84,634

GOVERNMENT REVENUE* INCLUDING PUBLIC ENTERPRISE SURPLUSES
(K '000)

REVENUE	1968	1969 (Revised Estimate)	1970–71 (Revised Estimate)
Import Duties	8,940	9,622	9,650
Income Tax on Persons	4,790	5,636	6,228
Income Taxes on Companies and Self-Employed	5,180	5,750	6,100
Excise Duties	980	1,786	2,350
Surtax	—	—	2,980
Other Tax Revenue	1,204	1,574	1,846
TOTAL TAX REVENUE . .	21,094	24,368	29,154
Profits/Losses of Public Enterprises .	1,074	5,194	1,034
Income from Entrepreneurship and Property .	1,970	2,590	2,906
Other Non-Tax Revenue . . .	2,370	2,352	4,027
Interest and Loan Redemption . .	1,604	1,664	2,486
Other Revenue Account Revenue .	598	588	1,329
Other Development Account Revenue .	168	100	212
TOTAL NON-TAX REVENUE . .	5,414	10,136	7,967
TOTAL REVENUE . . .	26,508	34,504	37,121
Add: Fees, Sales and Recoveries, Borrowing and Grants	28,512	31,068	50,385
Less: All Public Enterprise Profits/Losses .	1,074	5,194	1,034
TOTAL RECEIPTS ON REVENUE AND DEVELOPMENT ACCOUNTS . .	53,946	60,378	86,472

* Revenue defined to exclude grants and loans from any source. Detailed definition of the categories are given in Public Sector Financial Statistics, 1970.

In 1971–72 the revised estimate of the total receipts on the Revenue and Development Accounts is K83,774,000 of which Tax Revenue is K35,830,000.

GOVERNMENT EXPENDITURE ON REVENUE AND DEVELOPMENT ACCOUNTS
(K'000)

FUNCTION	1964	1965	1966	1967	1968	1969*	1970–71 (Revised Estimate)
General Services	7,882	10,124	11,124	10,602	10,338	11,206	11,646
Natural Resources	2,834	3,428	4,492	5,362	6,508	8,416	10,308
Education	4,914	5,494	6,318	7,206	7,972	9,228	11,647
Health	1,810	2,236	2,690	2,862	2,930	3,106	3,284‡
Transport				3,494	5,644	7,464	19,414‡
Works†	19,934	20,400	23,608	4,092	3,886	4,620	5,816
Other				15,370	17,022	16,464	24,095
TOTAL (GROSS) . .	37,374	41,682	48,232	48,988	54,300	60,504	86,210

***1969 Revised Estimate:** No allowance has been made for the underexpenditure of some K2 million on Development Account as no functional analysis of this underexpenditure is available.
† Comparable figures not available before 1967.
‡ Includes K10 million for Nacala.

(Continued overleaf)

GOVERNMENT EXPENDITURE ON REVENUE AND DEVELOPMENT ACCOUNTS—(*Continued*)

(Proportion of total—%)

FUNCTION	1964	1965	1966	1967	1968	1969‡	1970–71 (Revised Estimate)
General Services	21.1	24.3	23.0	21.6	19.0	18.5	13.5
Natural Resources . . .	7.6	8.2	9.3	11.0	12.0	13.9	12.0
Education	13.2	13.2	13.1	14.8	14.7	15.3	13.5
Health	4.8	5.4	5.6	5.8	5.4	5.1	3.8
Transport†				7.1	10.4	12.4	22.5
Works*	53.3	48.9	49.0	8.4	7.1	7.6	6.7
Other				31.3	31.4	27.2	28.0
TOTAL (GROSS) .	100.0	100.0	100.0	100.0	100.0	100.0	100.0

* Revised estimate for calendar 1969; no allowance has been made for the underexpenditure of some K2 million on Development Account as no functional analysis of this underexpenditure is available.
† Comparable figures not available before 1967.   ‡ Includes K10 million for Nacala (11.6 per cent).

MONEY SUPPLY
(K'ooo)

1968 (Dec.)	1969 (Dec.)	1970 (Dec.)	1971 (Dec.)
15,113	28,481	32,681	38,810

SUMMARY OF DEVELOPMENT PROGRAMME
1972/73–74/75

HEAD	(K'ooo)	%
Community and Social Development	120	0.1
Education	4,909	5.2
Finance, Commerce and Industry	4,430	4.7
Government Buildings . .	3,765	4.0
Health	4,994	5.3
Housing	1,649	1.8
Miscellaneous Services . .	1,077	1.1
Agriculture	27,886	30.9
Fisheries	730	0.8
Forestry and Game . .	2,515	2.7
Surveys and Lands . .	889	0.9
Veterinary Services . .	3,000	3.2
New Capital . . .	15,217	16.1
Posts and Telecommunications .	3,193	3.4
Power	2,171	2.3
Transportation . . .	14,473	15.3
Water Supplies and Sanitation .	1,866	2.0
Works Organization . . .	224	0.2
TOTAL . .	93,108	100.0

MALAWI DEVELOPMENT CORPORATION INVESTMENT
(K'ooo)

	TOTAL MDC INVESTMENT		
	End of 1970*	End of 1971†	End of 1972‡
Milling, Food, Beverages	1,696	1,725	1,964
Tourism, Hotels, Catering .	948	953	945
Wholesaling, Retailing .	436	774	906
Finance, Property .	205	366	412
Agriculture, Fisheries .	548	548	330
Textiles, Clothing .	382	382	382
Construction Materials .	102	103	103
Metal Products . .	88	84	80
Chemicals, Paper, Electronics . .	46	165	165
TOTAL .	4,451	5,100	5,287

* Audited.   † Provisional.   ‡ Estimated.

FOREIGN EXCHANGE RESERVES
(K'ooo—at December 31st)

RESERVES	1966	1967	1968	1969	1970	1971
Reserve Bank . . .	13,594	15,054	14,410	14,146	21,050	22,276
Commercial Banks . . .	−1,612	−5,112	−3,494	−2,542	−2,536	−1,745
Banking System . . .	11,982	9,942	10,916	11,604	18,514	20,531
Other Official* . . .	1,715	3,701	4,350	3,357	3,285	2,226
TOTAL . . .	13,697	13,643	15,266	14,961	21,799	22,757

* Other official reserves consist of the Reserve position with IMF, Treasury balances with the Crown Agents' and a balance account of the proceeds from the sale of the Zambezi Bridge.

BALANCE OF PAYMENTS: NET FLOWS
(K million)

ITEM	1966	1967	1968	1969	1970	1971*
Current Account:						
Imports f.o.b./f.o.r. . . .	−54.1	−50.2	−57.0	−61.0	−68.4	−75.6
Exports f.o.b./f.o.r. . . .	34.6	40.4	40.0	43.2	47.5	58.0
Merchandise Balance .	−19.5	− 9.8	−17.0	−17.8	−20.9	−17.6
Non-Factor Services . .	− 9.7	−11.1	−14.5	−16.5	−15.6	−17.5
Factor Income . . .	− 5.6	− 7.8	− 7.0	− 5.7	− 4.9	− 6.6
Balance on Goods and Services .	−34.8	−28.6	−38.5	−40.0	−41.4	−41.7
Private Transfers . .	0.7	1.3	1.6	1.7	1.7	1.7
Government Transfers . .	16.2	16.4	14.9	13.8	11.4	9.4
Balance on Transfers .	16.9	17.7	16.5	15.5	13.1	11.1
BALANCE ON CURRENT ACCOUNT .	−17.9	−10.9	−22.0	−24.5	−28.3	−30.6
Capital Movements:						
Private Long-Term Capital .	3.2	3.5	7.6	8.5	− 3.5	6.5
Public Long-Term Capital .	5.2	9.2	11.7	15.2	29.0	16.6
Other, and Errors and Omissions .	5.0	− 2.2	4.2	0.4	8.0	8.5
TOTAL CAPITAL MOVEMENTS .	11.3	10.5	22.7	24.1	33.5	31.6
Allocation of SDRs (Special Drawing Rights)	—	—	—	—	1.6	—
Change in Foreign Exchange Reserves	4.5	0.5	− 1.6	0.3	− 6.8	− 1.0

* Estimate.

EXTERNAL TRADE
(K million)

	1968	1969	1970	1971
Imports	58.2	61.5	71.4	89.9
Exports	33.8	36.6	40.3	49.0

COMMODITIES
(K'000)

IMPORTS	1969	1970	1971
Goods Mainly for Final Consumption:			
Motor Cars and Bicycles . . .	2,056	2,408	2,805
Piece Goods . .	3,770	3,506	3,872
Motor Spirit . .	942	1,893	2,282
Other . . .	12,002	14,545	15,564
TOTAL	18,770 (31%)	22,352 (27%)	24,523 (27%)
Capital Equipment:			
Transport Equipment n.i.e. . . .	7,384	9,569	9,708
Other . . .	7,978	9,807	10,454
TOTAL	15,362 (25%)	19,376 (23%)	20,162 (22%)
Materials for Building Construction . .	5,994 (10%)	6,128 (7%)	7,437 (8%)
Goods Mainly for Intermediate Consumption:			
Petroleum Products n.i.e. . . .	2,332	4,479	5,324
Parts, Tools and Miscellaneous appliances . . .	1,840	3,365	4,029
Other . . .	15,782	25,316	27,008
TOTAL	19,954 (32%)	33,160 (40%)	36,361 (40%)
Other . . .	1,398 (2%)	1,464 (3%)	1,370 (3%)
TOTAL	61,478 (100%)	82,480 (100%)	89,853 (100%)

EXPORTS	1969	1970	1971
Smallholder Crops:			
Tobacco* . . .	6,372	8,272	11,419
Groundnuts . .	5,590	4,241	5,877
Cotton . .	1,730	2,777	2,544
Beans, Peas, etc. .	1,022	1,038	1,243
Maize . . .	2,132	—	400
Cassava . .	638	724	546
Sunflower Seed .	172	46	317
Rice . . .	274	556	958
Coffee . .	100	102	161
TOTAL .	18,030	17,756	23,465
Estate Crops:			
Tobacco† . . .	6,223	8,178	10,385
Tea . . .	9,526	10,916	11,743
Tung Oil . .	306	411	247
Sisal . .	2	—	—
Sugar . . .	92	30	40
TOTAL .	16,149	19,535	22,415
Main Manufactures:			
Cattle Cake . .	359	343	360
Cement . .	—	—	—
Wooden Boxes .	53	84	82
Clothing and Footwear . .	467	524	388
Other‡ . .	186	260	273
TOTAL .	1,065	1,211	1,103
TOTAL DOMESTIC EXPORTS (incl. other)§ .	36,570	40,340	49,003

* Dark-fired, fire-cured, sun/air-cured and oriental tobacco.

† Flue-cured and burley tobacco.

‡ Glycerol, paper products, holloware, fishing nets.

§ Mainly: fish, hides and skins, precious stones and migrants' effects.

COUNTRIES
(K'000)

IMPORTS	1969	1970	1971
United Kingdom . .	18,236	18,998	25,210
Rhodesia . .	10,446	15,505	13,277
South Africa .	8,820	8,968	9,476
Japan . .	3,212	3,752	6,511
U.S.A. . .	2,356	3,719	3,643
West Germany .	2,166	2,697	3,733
Zambia . .	2,636	2,498	3,198
Australia . .	1,056	1,321	2,573
All Other Countries	12,550	13,909	22,232
TOTAL .	61,478	71,367	89,853

EXPORTS	1969	1970	1971
United Kingdom . .	16,816	19,536	21,122
Rhodesia . .	2,364	3,130	3,445
South Africa .	1,210	1,708	2,147
U.S.A. . .	2,292	1,197	2,315
Netherlands .	1,428	1,847	2,260
Ireland . .	972	1,136	2,262
West Germany .	1,043	1,242	917
Zambia . .	3,054	1,305	1,987
All Other Countries .	7,409	9,239	12,548
TOTAL .	36,588	40,340	49,003

TOURISM

	1970	1971
Arrivals	9,814	10,220
Total Expenditure (K'ooo)	478	576

TRANSPORT

RAILWAYS

	1969	1970	1971
Passengers (number)	737,500	840,600	837,000
Freight (short ton miles)	90,400	117,700	124,000

ROADS
(Number of licensed motor vehicles)

	1970	1971
Cars	9,771	9,862
Goods vehicles	7,747	8,367
Tractors	749	1,124
Motor cycles	1,658	2,693

TRAFFIC AT CHILEKA AIRPORT (BLANTYRE)

YEAR	PASSENGERS	FREIGHT ('ooo kg.)	MAIL ('ooo kg.)
1967	96,050	820.3	128.9
1968	104,117	970.9	159.1
1969	131,423	1,094.1	161.7
1970	161,866	1,133.9	188.2
1971	195,256	1,528.0	171.0

EDUCATION

AFRICAN EDUCATION
GOVERNMENT, LOCAL AUTHORITY, AIDED AND UNAIDED SCHOOLS

	NUMBER OF PUPILS			NUMBER OF TEACHERS		
	1966	1967	1968	1966	1967	1968
Primary	286,056	297,456	333,876	8,744	8,104	8,564
Secondary	6,539	7,970	9,283	404	424	508
Teacher Training	1,226	1,160	1,037	140	120	119
Technical and Vocational	900	551	536	119	65	53

The University of Malawi at Blantyre had 980 full-time students in 1969.

Source: National Statistical Office, Zomba; *Budget Document No. 4,* Malawi Government.

THE CONSTITUTION

A new Constitution was introduced in 1966. Malawi is a one-party state with a Presidential form of government. There is a unicameral parliament of 73 members.

Fundamental Rights

The following rights are guaranteed by the Constitution: life, personal liberty, protection from slavery and forced labour, from inhuman treatment, from deprivation of property, privacy of the home, security under the law, freedom of conscience, of expression, of assembly and association, of movement, protection from racial discrimination.

The President

Malawi is a Republic with a President. By an amendment of November 1970, provision was made for a Life President. Dr. Banda accepted the position in 1971.

Parliament

There is a Parliament, consisting of the President and the National Assembly. The National Assembly has 73 members, 60 elected and 13 nominated. A Speaker is elected from among the ordinary members of the Assembly.

The Assembly may change the Constitution by a two-thirds majority on the second and third readings. All members must belong to the Malawi Congress Party. The Parliamentary term is normally five years. The President has power to prorogue or dissolve Parliament.

Executive Powers

Executive power is exercised by the President acting as Prime Minister. Ministers are responsible to the President.

Judicature

The Judicature is a separate organ of the Government. There is a High Court, consisting of the Chief Justice and not less than two Puisne Judges, a Supreme Court of Appeal, and subordinate courts. The Local Courts were renamed Traditional Courts and given greater powers in November 1969. There is also a Judicial Service Commission with power to appoint judicial officers. During 1970, three new Traditional Courts were set up having jurisdiction in each of Malawi's three regions, and a National Traditional Court of Appeal was set up for the whole of Malawi.

THE GOVERNMENT

Life President: Ngwazi Dr. H. KAMUZU BANDA, LL.D., PH.B., M.D., L.R.C.P., L.R.C.S., L.R.F.P.S., Minister of Justice, Defence, External Affairs, Works and Supplies, Agriculture and Natural Resources.

CABINET

(*December* 1972)

Minister of Trade, Industry and Tourism, Transport and Communications: ALEKE BANDA.

Minister of Finance: D. MATENJE.

Minister of Health: P. L. MAKHUMULA NKHOMA.

Minister of Education: J. D. MSONTHI.

Minister of Local Government and Community Development and Social Welfare: M. M. LUNGU.

Minister of Labour: J. W. DELEZA.

Minister of State in the President's Office: A. MUWALO NQUMAYO.

Minister of Information and Broadcasting: R. T. C. MUNYENYEMBE.

Regional Ministers:
  Northern Region: M. Q. Y. CHIBAMBO.
  Central Region: J. R. KUMBWEZA BANDA.
  Southern Region: G. C. CHAKUMBA PHIRI.

Minister without Portfolio: R. B. CHIDZANJA NKHOMA.

Minister without Portfolio: A. GADAMA.

DIPLOMATIC REPRESENTATION

EMBASSIES AND HIGH COMMISSIONS ACCREDITED TO MALAWI

(E) Embassy; (HC) High Commission; (L) Legation.

Austria: Nairobi, Kenya (E).

Belgium: Bujumbura, Burundi (E).

Botswana: Lusaka, Zambia (HC).

China, Republic (Taiwan): Glyn Jones Rd., Blantyre, P.O.B. 929 (E); *Ambassador:* Dr. CHIN-YUNG CHAO.

Denmark: Nairobi, Kenya (E).

France: Kamuzu Highway, Blantyre, P.O.B. 90 and 920 (E); *Ambassador:* J. NOUVEL.

Federal Republic of Germany: Kamuzu Highway, Limbe, P.O.B. 5695 (E); *Ambassador:* Herr VON WARTENBURG.

India: 1st Floor, Shree Satyanaraya Bldg., Glyn Jones Rd., Blantyre, P.O.B. 398 (HC); *High Commissioner:* S. K. CHOWDRY.

Iran: Addis Ababa, Ethiopia (E).

Israel: 3rd Floor, Development House, Rooms 307–312, Henderson St., Blantyre, P.O.B. 689 (E); *Ambassador:* YAACOV MONBAZ.

Italy: Lusaka, Zambia (E).

Japan: Nairobi, Kenya (E).

Korea, Republic: Nairobi, Kenya (E).

Netherlands: Lusaka, Zambia (E).

Nigeria: Kampala, Uganda (E).

Norway: Nairobi, Kenya (E).

Portugal: Martins and Noronha Bldg., Kamuzu Highway, Limbe, P.O.B. 5596 (E); *Ambassador:* Dr. V. F. PEREIRA.

South Africa: 6th Floor, Delamere House, Victoria Ave., Blantyre, P.O.B. 1072 (E); *Ambassador:* JAN FRANÇOIS WENTZEL.

Sweden: Lusaka, Zambia (E).

Switzerland: Nairobi, Kenya (E).

United Kingdom: Mkulichi Rd., Zomba (HC); *High Commissioner:* R. HAYDON.

U.S.A.: 5th Floor, Nyrho House, Victoria Ave., Blantyre, P.O.B. 380 (E); *Ambassador:* WILLIAM C. BURDETT.

Vatican: Lusaka, Zambia.

Zambia: Blantyre (HC); *High Commissioner:* R. K. CHINAMBU.

NATIONAL ASSEMBLY

Speaker: ALEC NUYASULU.

The Malawi Congress Party holds all seats. The last election was held in April 1971.

POLITICAL PARTY

Malawi Congress Party: P.O.B. 5250, Limbe; f. 1959; succeeded the Nyasaland African Congress; Life Pres. Dr. HASTINGS KAMUZU BANDA; Sec.-Gen. ALEKE BANDA.

DEFENCE

The armed forces comprise one full infantry battalion of 1,150 and 3,000 civil police. A second battalion is now being formed.

Army Commander: Col. MATEWERE.

Police Commissioner: M. C. KAWAWA.

JUDICIAL SYSTEM

The Courts administering justice are the Supreme Court of Appeal, High Court, Magistrates' Courts and Traditional Courts.

THE HIGH COURT consists of the Chief Justice and three Puisne Judges. The High Court has unlimited jurisdiction in civil and criminal matters. It hears appeals from the Magistrates' Courts. The Minister of Justice has the power to restrict appeals from Traditional Courts where the majority of civil cases are heard and determined to Traditional Appeals Courts. Appeals from the High Court go to the Supreme Court of Appeal in Blantyre.

Chief Justice: The Hon. Sir J. SKINNER.

Registrar: M. R. TRUWA, P.O.B. 954, Blantyre.

RELIGION

AFRICAN RELIGIONS

Most of the Africans follow their traditional religions.

CHRISTIANS

Anglican Community: Bishop of Lake Malawi: Rt. Rev. JOSIAH MTEKATEKA, P.O.B. 24, Nkhotakota; f. 1882; 50,000 mems.; Bishop of Southern Malawi: Most Rev. DONALD S. ARDEN (Archbishop of Central Africa), P.O. Kasupe; f. 1888; 30,000 mems.; publ. *Ecclesia* (monthly); circ. 2,250.

Roman Catholic Church: Archbishop of Blantyre: Most Rev. JAMES CHIONA, Archbishop's House, P.O.B. 385, Blantyre; Bishops: Rt. Rev. PATRICK AUGUSTINE KALILOMBE, W.F., Bishop's House, P.O.B. 33, Lilongwe; Rt. Rev. MATHIAS CHIMOLE, Bishop's House, Zomba, P.O.B. 115; Rt. Rev. CORNELIUS CHITSULO, Bishop's House, P.O.B. 80, Dedza; Rt. Rev. JEAN JOBIDON, W.F., Bishop's House, P.O.B. 2, Mzuzu; Rt. Rev. E. J. F. VROEMEN, S.M.M., Bishops' House, P.O.B. 14, Chiromo; Rt. Rev. A. ASSOLARI, S.M.M., Prefect of Mangochi, P.O.B. 38, Mangochi; Catholic Secretariat, P.O.B. 5368, Limbe; Major Seminary, P.O.B. 23, Mchinji; the Roman Catholic Church has 821,738 baptized members and 117,068 catechumens, and runs 624 schools in Malawi.

Church of Central Africa (Presbyterian): Blantyre Synod; P.O.B. 413, Blantyre; Gen. Sec. Rev. J. D. SANGAYA; Livingstonia Synod: P.O. Livingstonia; Gen. Sec. Rev. P. C. MZEMBE; Mkhoma Synod: Gen. Sec. Rev. K. MGAWI; Total membership 711,000.

The Catholic Secretariat: P.O.B. 5368, Limbe; Sec. Gen. Rev. Fr. G. v.d. ASDONK, S.M.M.

Christian Council of Malawi: P.O.B. 5368, Blantyre; Chair. Rev. K. J. MGAWI; Sec. Rev. S. P. KAMANGA.

Evangelical Association: Chair. W. S. SAUKILA, P.O.B. 13, Chola; Sec. Pastor G. W. BANDA, P.O.B. 2, Salima.

OTHER RELIGIONS

Of the Asians in Malawi over 50 per cent are Muslims and about 25 per cent are Hindus. There are also a small number of African Muslims.

THE PRESS

African (The): P.O.B. 133, Lilongwe; f. 1950; fortnightly, Catholic periodical; English, Chichewa; Editor A. MBEDE; circ. 14,000.

Kuunika: Presbyterian Church of Central Africa, P.O. Mkhoma; f. 1909; Chichewa; Editor J. J. MBUKA BANDA.

Malawi Government Gazette: Government Printer, Box 53, Zomba; f. 1894; weekly.

Malawi Government Gazette: Government Printer, Box 53, Zomba; f. 1894; weekly.

Malawi News: P.O.B. 5699, Limbe; f. 1959; organ of Malawi Congress Party; twice a week; Editor HARVEY MLANGA; circ. 15,000.

Moni: P.O.B. 5592, Limbe; f. 1964; Chichewa, English; monthly; Editors Montfort Press; circ. 13,500.

The Times: P.O.B. 458, Ginnery Corner, Blantyre; f. 1895; English; twice weekly; Editor AL. S. OSMAK.

Vision of Malawi: Published by the Ministry of Information and Broadcasting, P.O.B. 494, Blantyre; f. 1964; quarterly; Government publication in English, This is Malawi, monthly; Malawi Mwezi Uno, monthly, in Chichewa.

The Daily Times: Blantyre; from January 1st, 1973.

PUBLISHERS

Blantyre Printing and Publishing Co. Ltd.: P.O.B. 6, Blantyre; f. 1895; Man. Dir. D. BURNETT; Gen. Man. G. BARRETTA.

Malawi Printing and Publishing Co.: P.O.B. 6, Blantyre.

The White Fathers: Likuni Parish, P.O.B. 133, Lilongwe; Treas. Gen. H. ROSARY PARISH.

RADIO

Malawi Broadcasting Corporation: P.O.B. 30133, Chichiri, Blantyre 3; f. 1964; Dir.-Gen. B. D. KALIYOMA; Dir. of Programmes P. T. KANDIERO; statutory body; semi-commercial, semi-state financed; domestic services in English and Chichewa, 0300-2115 (G.M.T.) daily, incl. *"International Service"* 1600-1800 hrs. (G.M.T.) in the 90 metre band.

There are approximately 107,000 radio sets in use in Malawi.

FINANCE

BANKING

Reserve Bank of Malawi: P.O.B. 565, Blantyre; f. 1964; Bank of Issue; Gov. J. Z. U. TEMBO.

Commercial Bank of Malawi: P.O.B. 1255, Blantyre; P.O.B. 5091, Limbe; f. 1970; jointly owned by Malawi Development Corporation and Portuguese interests; encourages greater Malawian participation in business; Chair. J. P. JARQIM; Deputy Chair. J. POMBEIRO DE SOUSA; Gen. Man. M. RIBEIRO DA SILVA; cap. K1,150,000; dep. K9,500,000.

National Bank of Malawi: Head Office, P.O.B. 945' Henderson St., Blantyre; cap. K1m.; Chair. J. G. KAMWENDO; Man. Dir. O. A. STEVENSON; brs. at Blantyre (3), Lilongwe (2), Limbe (2), Mzuzu, Zomba; agency representation throughout Malawi.

INSURANCE

The National Insurance Co. Ltd.: P.O.B. 501, Blantyre; f. 1971; cap. K200,000; Agencies throughout Malawi.

TRADE AND INDUSTRY

Malawi Buying and Trade Agents: Abbey House, 6 Victoria St., London, S.W.1; official buying agents to the Malawi Government, the Malawi Railways and all Statutory Corporations in Malawi; promotion of Trade, Tourism and Investment in Malawi; recruitment of Professional and Technical staff for service in Malawi; registered office Malawi Railways Ltd.

CHAMBER OF COMMERCE

The Chamber of Commerce and Industry of Malawi: P.O.B. 258, Blantyre; f. 1892; 350 mems.; Chair. A. M. HORNBY; Sec./Man. M. C. SALIMA.

INDUSTRIAL AND COMMERCIAL ORGANIZATIONS

Tea Association (Central Africa) Ltd.: P.O.B. 950, Blantyre; f. 1936; 29 mems.; Chair. J. S. STREET; Sec. Business Services Ltd.

Tobacco Association: P.O.B. 15, Blantyre; f. 1928; 159 mems., Chair. J. A. A. HENDERSON, M.P.; Sec. G. D. M. HENDERSON.

Tobacco Exporters' Association of Malawi: P.O.B. 5653, Limbe; f. 1931; 16 mems.; Chair. J. E. BISHOP.

Agricultural Development and Marketing Corporation (ADMARC): P.O.B. 5052, Limbe; purchases and exports groundnuts, cotton, tobacco, maize, coffee, beans, peas, oilseed, etc.; assists generally in the development and improvement of agriculture; Exec. Chair. L. W. MASIKU.

GOVERNMENT DEVELOPMENT CORPORATION

Malawi Development Corporation: P.O.B. 566, Blantyre; f. 1964; to assist agriculture, commerce and industry by way of equity, loans and management advice; Chair. S. B. SOMANJE; Gen. Man. A. S. BRASS.

EMPLOYERS' ASSOCIATIONS

Employers' Consultative Association of Malawi: P.O.B. 950, Blantyre; f. 1963; 31 mems.; Chair. J. BROOKFIELD; Sec. Business Services Ltd.

Agricultural Employers' Association: P.O.B. 950, Blantyre; f. 1960; 46 mems.; Chair. A. SCHWARZ; Sec. Business Services Ltd.

Master Builders', Civil Engineering Contractors' and Allied Trades' Association: P.O.B. 5099, Limbe; registered 1955; paid up membership 56; Sec. D. TURQUAND-YOUNG.

Master Printers' Association: P.O.B. 6, Blantyre; f. 1962; 9 mems.; Chair. G. P. BARRETTA; Sec. D. BURNETT.

Motor Traders' Association of Malawi: P.O.B. 311, Blantyre; registered 1954; paid-up membership 35; Chair. F. E. LACEY; Sec. Business Services Ltd.

Road Transport Operators' Association: P.O.B. 950, Blantyre; registered 1956; paid-up membership 9; Chair. J. BROOKFIELD; Sec. Business Services Ltd.

TRADE UNIONS

Trades Union Congress of Malawi: P.O.B. 355, Blantyre; f. 1964; 6,500 mems.; Chair. J. D. LIABUNYA; Gen. Sec. L. Y. MVULA; Treas. A. NANCUELE.

PRINCIPAL AFFILIATED UNIONS

Building Construction, Civil Engineering and Allied Workers' Union: P.O.B. 110, Limbe; f. 1961; 1,300 mems.; Pres. D. J. CHANACHE; Gen. Sec. G. SITIMA.

Malawi Railway Workers' Union: P.O.B. 393, Limbe; f. 1954; 2,100 mems.; Pres. F. L. MATENJE.

Organizations not affiliated to T.U.C.M.:

Malawi National Teachers' Association: P.O.B. 252, Limbe; f. 1964; 3,000 mems.; Pres. M. M. MKANDAWIRE; Sec.-Gen. R. J. MEHTA.

Malawi Government Employees' Association, The: P.O.B. 64, Blantyre; 300 mems.; Pres. M. MUGHOGHO; Gen. Sec. G. M. NAMATE.

Overseas Officers' Association: P.O.B. 207, Zomba; 224 mems.; Sec. Mrs. B. M. EVANS.

MAJOR INDUSTRIAL COMPANIES

The following are some of the largest companies in terms of capital investment or employment.

Imperial Tobacco Group Ltd.: P.O.B. 5050, Limbe; f. 1907; subsidiary of Imperial Tobacco Group Ltd., 1 Grosvenor Place, London, SW1X 7HB; assets in Malawi approx. £2,000,000.

Supplies the manufacturing units of the Imperial Tobacco Group in the United Kingdom and other buyers; manufactures packing cases and barrels from own forests and sawmill in Limbe; manufactures plywood, blockboard, tea chest shooks and flush panel doors.

Dirs. J. F. RHODES, O.B.E. (Man.), J. E. BISHOP, R. A. S. STURGESS, J. A. WHITELOCK; 2,700 employees during season, 900 during off-season.

Lonrho (Malawi) Ltd.: P.O.B. 5498, Churchill Rd., Limbe; f. 1963; cap. £200,000; total issued cap. of Lonrho group companies in Malawi is approximately £4,900,000, composed of the following industries:

The Sugar Corporation of Malawi Ltd.: Sugar.

The Central Africa Co. Ltd.: Tea and tobacco.

General Construction Co. Ltd.: Construction.

Chibuku Products Ltd.: Brewing.

The Brick and Tile Co. Ltd.: Brick making.

Alumina Corporation of Malawi Ltd., Corundum Mining Corporation Ltd.: Mining.

David Whitehead and Sons (Malawi) Ltd.: Textiles.

Leopard Developments Ltd.: Petroleum products.

The Central African Transport Co.: Motor trading.

Farming and Electrical Services Ltd.: Agricultural equipment.

Halls' Garage Ltd.: Motor trading.
Chair. A. H. Ball; Man. Dir. L. G. Blackwell; 12,000 employees throughout the group.

Malawi Distilleries Ltd.: P.O.B. 924, McLeod Rd., Heavy Industrial Site, Blantyre; f. 1967; cap. £150,000.
Sole producer of potable spirits for local consumption and export.
Gen. Man. D. W. Eaton; 25 employees.

The Portland Cement Co. (Malawi) Ltd.: P.O.B. 523, Heavy Industrial Area, Blantyre; f. 1957; cap. £1,000,000; manufacture and distribution of cement, projected capacity 225,000 short tons p.a.
Man. Dir. J. L. Henderson; Dir./Sec. F. R. Wilks; 900 employees.

TRANSPORT

RAILWAYS

Malawi Railways Ltd.: Regd. Offices: Abbey House, 6 Victoria St., London, S.W.1; P.O.B. 5144, Limbe; Chair. G. N. Dunlop; Exec. Chair. D. R. Katengeza; Gen. Man. A. Baker.

The 822 route kilometres of railway between the port of Beira in Mozambique and the railhead at Salima are operated by three separate companies, Malawi Railways Ltd., Central Africa Railway Co. Ltd. (which is a wholly owned subsidiary of Malawi Railways Ltd.) and the Trans-Zambesia Railway Company. The most spectacular engineering feature is the Lower Zambezi Bridge across the River Zambezi at Sena, with its thirty-three main spans and a length of 12,064 ft. It was opened on January 14th, 1935, and is the largest single track railway bridge in the world.

The line has a rail/lake interchange station at Chipoka on Lake Malawi whence steamer services are operated by the railways to other lake ports in Malawi.

A new line of 101 kilometres has been constructed from a point ten miles south of Balaka eastwards to the Mozambique border to link up with Nova Freixo on the Nacala Line. This provides Malawi, as well as countries to the west, with a direct railway route to the deep-water port of Nacala, some 550 miles north of Beira. The line was completed and opened in July 1970 by the President of the Republic of Malawi.

ROADS

The total road mileage in the country is approximately 10,721 kilometres, of which 2,929 kilometres are main roads. The spinal column of the road system runs from the Salisbury-Blantyre road east and then north through Blantyre, Lilongwe and Mzimba to join Tanzania and Zambia at Tunduma. Other important roads link this north-south route with the railway and Lake Malawi in the east, and Zambia and Portuguese East Africa in the west. A 300-mile highway along the edge of Lake Malawi, the "Kamuzu Highway", is under construction. All main, and most secondary roads, are all-weather roads. A further 140 miles from Liwonde to the new capital at Lilongwe will be bitumenized.

CIVIL AVIATION

The country's main airport is at Chileka, 11 miles from Blantyre.

Air Malawi Ltd.: P.O.B. 84, Blantyre, also in Johannesburg, Salisbury and Nairobi; f. 1967; national airline replacing the local service of Central African Airways Corpn.; services to Salisbury, Zomba, Beira, Johannesburg, Lusaka, Ndola, Nairobi, Seychelles, Lilongwe, Mzuzu, Chilumba, Karonga, Salima and Mangoche; Chair. P. Howard; Gen. Man. John Bryne; fleet of one BAC 1-11, two HS 748, two Viscount, two Britten-Norman Islander.

Leopard Air Ltd.: P.O.B. 70, Thyolo, Blantyre Airport; private air charter company; Cessna Dealer, P.O. Chileka.

Capital Air Services Ltd.: P.O.B. 236, Lilongwe.

Malawi is also served by the following foreign airlines: BOAC, DETA, EAA, SAA, Air Rhodesia and Zambia Airways.

TOURISM

Department of Tourism: Ministry of Information and Tourism, P.O.B. 402, Blantyre; responsible for Malawi tourist policy, administers Government rest houses, sponsors training of hotel staff; publs. Tourist literature; in 1971 foreign exchange receipts from tourism totalled K610,000.

POWER

Electricity Supply Commission of Malawi: P.O.B. 30224, Chichiri, Blantyre; production and distribution of electricity; Gen. Man. D. J. Dalton.

EDUCATION

Malawi has high literacy and there are over 350,000 African children receiving primary education and 13,276 receiving secondary in 1971. Secondary education is provided in government-aided schools. The University of Malawi opened in October 1965. Many students go to Great Britain and the U.S.A. and the numbers of qualified graduates are increasing.

LEARNED SOCIETY AND RESEARCH INSTITUTES

British Council, The: Lalji Kurji Bldg., Glyn Jones Rd., P.O.B. 456, Blantyre; library (*see* below); Rep. E. H. Semmens.

Geological Survey of Malawi: P.O.B. 27, Liwonde Rd., Zomba; f. 1921; geological mapping and survey; library of 5,000 vols.; Dir. F. Habgood; publs. *Bulletins, Reports, Memoirs*.

Ministry of Agriculture and Natural Resources: P.O.B. 303, Zomba; controls the following stations directly:

Chitedze Agricultural Research Station: P.O.B. 158, Lilongwe; f. 1948; conducts applied research into general agronomy of the Central Region and into livestock improvement, especially of local Zebu cattle; attached to the station is the Certificate training college of the Department of Agriculture, Colby College; f. 1956.

Bvumbwe Agricultural Research Station: P.O.B. 5748,
Limbe; f. 1950 to conduct applied research into tree and horticultural crops, especially tung and coffee, and the general agronomy of the Southern uplands.

Makanga Agricultural Research Station: P.O. Chiromo;
f. 1953 to conduct applied research into the general agronomy of the Lower Shire Valley, specializing in cotton and irrigated crops.

Lunyangwa Agricultural Research Station: P.O. Mzuzu;
f. 1968 to conduct applied research into the general agronomy of the Northern Region, specialising in rice, coffee and pasture work.

Fisheries Research Unit: P.O.B. 27, Monkey Bay;
f. 1954; researches into fisheries of Lake Malawi.

Mikolongwe Livestock Improvement Centre: P.O.B. 5193,
Limbe; f. 1955 to improve productive capacity of local Zebu cattle and fat tailed sheep; the station also contains the Poultry Improvement Unit and the Veterinary staff training school.

Tea Research Foundation of Central Africa: P.O.B. 51,
Mulanje; f. 1966 to promote research into tea production in Central and Southern Africa, and other tea producing regions; Dir. R. T. ELLIS.

Veterinary Research Laboratory: P.O.B. 55, Blantyre;
researches into endemic diseases of Malawi.

The Ministry of Agriculture is also indirectly responsible for research work at the following stations:

Agricultural Research Council of Malawi: Makoka
Research Station, Private Bag 3, Ntondwe; f. 1967; research units at Makoka (cotton development, biometry), Chitedze (grain legumes); Chair. Dr. H. C. PEREIRA, D.SC.; Dir. J. P. TUNSTALL, O.B.E.

Forest Research Institute: Private Bag 6, Dedza; tree
breeding and research into wood products.

LIBRARIES AND ARCHIVES

British Council Library, The: P.O.B. 456, Blantyre; f. 1951; 18,000 vols.; Librarian W. E. NAGANGWA; Zomba Branch: 7,000 vols.; Lilongwe Branch: 6,600 vols.; Librarian M. J. MIDGLEY.

Malawi National Library Service: Ginnery Corner, Blantyre; f. 1968; fiction and reference works, supplies books to library centres and to individuals; 70,000 vols.

National Archives of Malawi: P.O. Box 62, Zomba; f. 1947; as branch of Central African Archives; became National Archives of Malawi 1964; Public Archives, records management, historical manuscripts, national library (legal deposit library for all material published in Malawi), films, microfilms, gramophone records, postage stamps, coins, tape recordings, photographs and maps; 11,000 vols., 450 periodicals; Dir. J. D. C. DREW, M.A.; publ. *Malawi National Bibliography* (annual).

University of Malawi Library: P.O.B. 5200, Limbe; f. 1965; 130,000 vols.; Librarian W. J. PLUMBE.

U.S. Information Service Library: St. Andrew's St., Blantyre; 2,500 vols.

MUSEUM

Museum of Malawi, The: P.O.B. 512, Blantyre; f. 1964. Curator T. N. SEENO.

UNIVERSITY

UNIVERSITY OF MALAWI
P.O.B. 5097, LIMBE

Founded 1964.

Language of instruction: English; Private control; Academic year: September to July.

Chancellor: H.E. Dr. H. KAMUZU BANDA.
Vice-Chancellor: Dr. IAN MICHAEL, C.B.E., PH.D.
Provost: A. B. CHILIVUMBO, M.A., PH.D.
Registrar: JOHN BANDA, B.A.

Number of teachers: 140.
Number of students: 1,087.

CONSTITUENT INSTITUTES:

Bunda College of Agriculture: P.O.B. 219, Lilongwe.
Principal: T. C. PINNEY, PH.D.
The library contains: 7,000 vols.
Number of students: 183.
Professor of Agriculture: T. C. PINNEY.

Chancellor College of Arts and Science: P.O.B. 5200, Limbe.
Principal: (vacant).
Registrar: S. M. H. NYIRENDA.
The library contains: 73,000 vols.
Number of students: 359.

Institute of Public Administration: P.O.B. 600, Blantyre.
Principal: V. G. DAVIDSON.
The library contains: 13,000 vols.
Number of students: 85.
Professor of Law: V. G. DAVIDSON.

Malawi Polytechnic: Private Bag 3, Chichiri, Blantyre 3.
Principal: G. J. WILLIAMS.
Registrar: J. E. CHIPETA.
The library contains 22,000 vols.
Number of students: 650, of which 275 are in diploma courses.
Head of Business Studies Department: J. BARRACLOUGH.
Head of Mathematics and Science Department: G. F. WILLIAMSON.
Head of Engineering Department: A. B. LEE.

Soche Hill College: P.O.B. 5496, Limbe; f. 1962; three-year diploma courses, five-year degree courses, one-year certificate courses in teacher-training.
Principal: B. H. KAWONGA.
Number of students: 137.

SELECT BIBLIOGRAPHY

AGNEW, Lady S. (Ed.). *Malawi in Maps*. London, University of London Press (forthcoming).

BANDA, H. K., and NKUMBULA, H. M. *Federation in Central Africa*. London, 1951.

HANNA, A. J. *The Beginnings of Nyasaland and North-Eastern Rhodesia* 1859–95. Oxford, Clarendon Press, 1956.

McCRACKEN, JOHN. "The Nineteenth Century in Malawi" and "African Politics in Twentieth Century Malawi", in RANGER, T. O. (Ed.) *Aspects of Central African History*. London, Heinemann, 1968.

NATIONAL STATISTICAL OFFICE. *Malawi Population Census: Final Report*. Zomba, Government Printer, 1968.

OLIVER, ROLAND. *Sir Harry Johnston and the Scramble for Africa*. London, Macmillan, 1957.

PEARSON, D. S., and TAYLOR, W. L. *Break Up—Some Economic Consequences for the Rhodesias and Nyasaland*. Salisbury, Phoenix Group, 1962.

PIKE, J. G. *Malawi: a Political and Economic History*. London, Pall Mall, 1968.

PIKE, J. G., and RIMMINGTON, G. T. *Malawi: a Geographical Study*. London, O.U.P., 1965.

PRESIDENT'S OFFICE, ECONOMIC PLANNING DIVISION. *Economic Report*. Annually. Zomba.

Report of the Nyasaland Commission of Enquiry (Devlin Report). Cmd. 814, 1959.

RESERVE BANK OF MALAWI. *Economic and Financial Review*. Quarterly.

ROTBERG, ROBERT I. *The Rise of Nationalism in Central Africa*. London, O.U.P., 1966.

SHEPPERSON, G., and PRICE, T. *Independent African*. Edinburgh, Edinburgh U P., 1958.

STOKES, E. T., and BROWN, R. (Eds.). *The Zambesian Past*. Manchester, Manchester U.P., 1966.

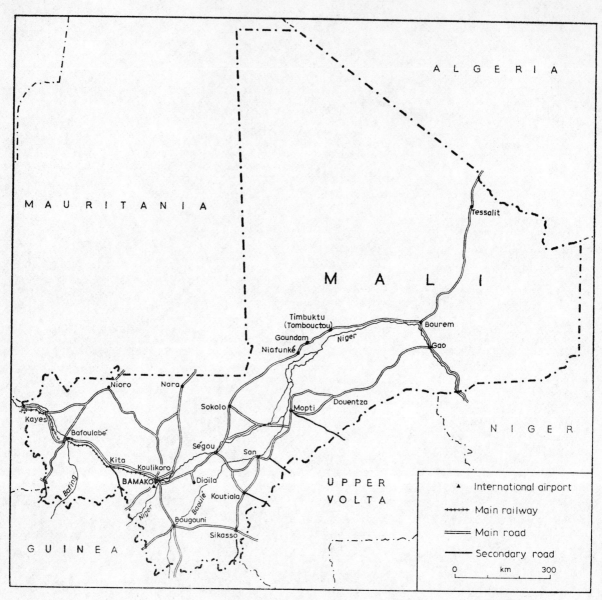

Mali.

Mali

PHYSICAL AND SOCIAL GEOGRAPHY

R. J. Harrison Church

With an area of 478,767 sq. miles, the Republic of Mali is only slightly smaller than Niger, west Africa's largest state. Like Niger and Upper Volta, Mali is landlocked. It is some five times the size of the United Kingdom, and extends about a thousand miles from north to south and from east to west, with a narrowing at the centre. Its population was estimated to be 5,143,000 in 1971.

The ancient Basement Complex rocks of Africa have been uplifted in the mountainous Adrar des Iforas of the north-east, whose dry valleys bear witness to formerly wetter conditions. Otherwise the Precambrian rocks are often covered by Primary sandstones, which have bold erosion escarpments at, for example, Bamako and east of Bendiagara. At the base of the latter live the Dogon people, made famous by Marcel Griaule's study. Where the Niger River crosses a sandstone outcrop below Bamako, rapids obstruct river navigation, giving an upper navigable reach above Bamako, and another one below it from Koulikoro to Ansongo, near the border with the Niger Republic.

Loose sands cover most of the rest of the country and, as in Senegal and Niger, are a relic of drier climatic conditions. They are very extensive on the long border with Mauritania and Algeria.

Across the heart of the country flows the Niger River, a vital waterway and source of fish. As the seasonal floods retreat, they leave pasture for thousands of livestock desperate for food and water after a dry season of at least eight months. The retreating floods also leave damp areas for man, equally desperate for cultivable land in an arid environment. Flood water is sometimes retained for swamp rice cultivation, and has been made available for irrigation, particularly in the "dead" south-western section of the Inland Niger Delta.

The delta is the remnant of an inland lake, in which the upper Niger once terminated. In a more rainy era this overflowed to join the then mighty Tilemsi River, once the drainage focus of the now arid Adrar des Iforas. The middle and lower courses of the Tilemsi now comprise the Niger below Bourem, at the eastern end of the consequential elbow turn of the Niger. The eastern part of the delta, which was formed in the earlier lake, is criss-crossed by "live" flood-water branches of the river; whilst the relic channels of the very slightly higher western part of the delta are never occupied naturally by flood water and so are "dead". However, these are used in part for irrigation water retained by the Sansanding barrage, which has raised the Niger by an average of 14 ft.

Mali is mainly dry everywhere, with a rainy season of four to five months and a total rainfall of 44 in. at Bamako, and of only about seven weeks and an average fall of 9.3 in. at Gao. North of this there is no rain-fed cultivation, but only semi-desert or true desert, which occupies nearly one-half of Mali. There the main hope is of finding oil.

Distances to the nearest foreign port from most places in Mali are at least 800 miles, and, not surprisingly, there is much seasonal and permanent emigration.

RECENT HISTORY*

Michael Crowder and Donal Cruise O'Brien

(Revised for this edition by KAYE WHITEMAN)

The present republic of Mali, the ex-colonial territory of French Soudan, achieved its independence in 1960. For a brief period (1959–60) it had formed a federation with Senegal, under the common name of Mali, and on the break-up of the federation (June 1960) it kept the latter name.

The governing party at the time of independence, the *Union soudanaise*, controlled all eighty seats in the National Assembly, and the party's leader, Modibo Keita, became President of the Republic. The two principal opposition party leaders were arrested in 1962 (subsequently dying in custody), and in the 1964 elections opposition candidates were not allowed to present themselves.

Opposition to the régime none the less persisted, especially as a consequence of economic failures. The government in 1962 created an independent currency, effectively leaving the franc zone, and rapid inflation followed. Increased taxes and cuts in government salaries aroused resentment, and the many petty traders were antagonized by the government's efforts to bring trade under the control of the state bureaucracy. The government's efforts to develop a socialist economic policy were hampered by continuing financial difficulties, and in 1967 negotiations with

* For the period before independence *see* Recent History of Dahomey, p. 282.

France secured a re-entry to the franc zone in return for a devaluation of 50 per cent and extensive French supervision of the economy. This in turn provoked opposition from militant youths, who saw the régime as having succumbed to colonialist pressures.

Austerity measures designed to redress the financial situation aroused further opposition, but the decisive factor leading to the downfall of the Keita régime in 1968 was the arrest of several army officers by the newly formed and increasingly vocal People's Militia. The officers felt collectively threatened after the arrests, and feared a drastic reduction in the size of the army. On November 19th, in a bloodless *coup*, the Military overthrew Keita and his government, and a new government in the form of a 14-member Military Committee of National Liberation assumed power, with Lt. Moussa Traoré as President and Capt. Yoro Diakité as head of government.

In principle a return to civilian rule was being considered by the new régime, but the likelihood of this being achieved became ever more remote. Economic recovery was the government's first priority, but it made little significant progress in this field. Its position was further weakened by internal divisions, notably the rift between Lt. Traoré, chief man of action in the *coup*, and Capt. Diakité, reputedly the brains behind it. Although Lt. Traoré had been less in the limelight than the Prime Minister, he had greater support, and managed to remove Diakité as head of the government in September 1969. Diakité's fall from grace was accelerated after the discovery of the plot led by Capt. Silas Diaby in August 1969. In the autumn of 1970 there were rumours that Diakité had been under house arrest, but he returned to the government for three months with increased power before being dropped altogether early in 1971. In March 1971 he was arrested, and in August 1972 sentenced to life imprisonment. There were reports in July of a further split in the government between Traoré, now a Colonel, and Capt. Kissima Doukara, the powerful Minister of Defence and the Interior, but they appear to have settled their differences.

The government's foreign policy has not differed much from that of the preceding régime. Despite Col. Traoré's official visit to France in April 1972, and the increase in the number of French advisers in Bamako, Mali has refrained from rejoining the Central Bank of West African States and from adopting the CFA franc—even though it is identical to all intents and purposes to the Mali franc. Relations with the U.S.S.R. and the People's Republic of China have remained very cordial.

ECONOMY

Samir Amin

Mali, the second largest country in west Africa, has no outlet to the sea, and the viable part of the country lies entirely in the Sahelian-Sudanese areas, irrigated by the River Niger. At the time of independence Mali had a population of 4.1 million. Colonial rule left it undeveloped, so that there is now scarcely any urban development; its exports are worth very little and derive mainly from cotton, traditional stock-raising and fishing; and its infrastructure and administration are extremely limited.

1960-70: STAGNATION OF PRODUCTION AND CREATION OF A PUBLIC SECTOR

The five-year plan, 1960–65, set out some very ambitious development objectives. It provided for an annual growth rate of 8 per cent which required the efficient involvement of 2–3 million peasants, the development of 22,000 hectares of land in the area under the control of the *Office du Niger* and 67,000 hectares elsewhere, a vigorous programme aimed at improving the semi-nomadic type of stock-raising, and also the setting up of the country's first industries. Investments amounting to about 78,000 million francs CFA were envisaged—in other words, ten times more than in the four years in which FIDES had been operating. Since it had been decided that foreign capital should meet no more than 60 per cent of the country's requirements, it was necessary to impose a policy of great austerity: from 1962 onwards public current expenditure had to be brought practically to a halt.

After only the first years of independence the plan had fallen short of expectations. Difficulties had begun to appear and showed no signs of diminishing: stagnation of agricultural production; the inefficiency of the bureaucratic system involved in winning the support of the peasants and setting up co-operatives; the tendency to choose "prestige" projects to the detriment of productive projects; and the increase in administrative costs, which in three years (1959–62) rose by 72 per cent.

The dominant position of foreign capital was to be gradually eliminated by the creation of state companies in the main sectors of the economy, particularly in the fields of foreign trade (the *Société malienne d'importation et d'exportation* had the monopoly of groundnut exports and of the imports of primary products), transport (*Air Mali* and the *Régie des transports du Mali*), mineral and oil exploration (a Mines Bureau with a monopoly right over all exploration), and public works.

At the same time rural co-operatives were established with the object of gradually leading Mali peasants towards socialist systems of organization. The series of reform measures was completed by the gradual creation of institutions for independent monetary administration: a treasury and exchange control (September 1960), and a national currency and issuing bank, the *Banque de la République du Mali* (July 1962).

In such a poor country and in such difficult conditions policies of this type entailed obvious dangers. Success or failure depended on the political relations existing between the small ruling class coming from the *Union soudanaise* and the rural and urban masses. The absence of any effective organization of these masses and the fact that they had no control over the state machinery meant that Malian "socialism" was little more than an idea and consisted mainly in the development of an inefficient state bureaucracy.

The huge gap between the plan's objectives and the results actually attained may be measured. Production during the 1960s rose by no more than a mediocre 1.8 per cent per annum at constant prices, while the population grew by 2.2 per cent.

In agriculture the annual growth rate was only about 1.5 per cent. Groundnut exports fell continuously from about 50,000 tons (shelled) at the beginning of the period to about 20,000 tons at the end. Millet production stagnated: the country had to resort to importing wheat and rice (and even millet) to provide food for its capital, small though it was. (Bamako, which is the only real town in the country, grew from 130,000 inhabitants in 1960 to 200,000 in 1970.) Enormous investments were swallowed up by the *Office du Niger* without any results to show for them, and these represented the greater part of agricultural investments. Mechanization was put into practice without previous thought or planning, and incessant changes of plans both in the types and form of cultivation and in the social organization of the peasants only served to perpetuate the astonishing inefficiency of the colonial *Office du Niger*. Traditional stock raising and fishing, however, did continue to grow at the same rate as in previous years, and the increasing surpluses of these activities were exported to the Ivory Coast and Ghana. But the bad management of monetary affairs deprived the Malian state of the benefit of this growth, since the proportion of illicit exports continued to increase, thus allowing on the one hand the financing of illicit imports (which avoided the steadily rising import taxes) and on the other hand the illicit export of capital (thus facilitating the free exchange of the Mali franc abroad). Total exports stagnated—7,800 million current francs CFA in 1959; 9,500 million Mali francs in 1968—while illicit exports accounted for about 50 per cent of total exports.

In non-agricultural sectors of the economy (excluding transport and commerce) total results seem rather better on a quantitative basis. Growth in these sectors was 5–6 per cent per annum at constant prices. Mineral exploration during this period (up to the fall of the régime) absorbed more than 3,500 million francs CFA, yet no important finds were made. In 1966 a small hydroelectric plant, SOTUBA, began operating and brought a short-term solution to the problem of Bamako's electricity supply. In the manufacturing sector several projects got off the ground. Six of these were in the agricultural foodstuffs field (groundnut oil at Koulikoro, the *Office du Niger* sugar refinery, cotton mills, refrigerated abbatoirs, mills and fruit preserving plants at Baguineda), three in other light industries (textiles, tobacco and matches, and footwear) and two in basic industry (cement and metalworking). Industry absorbed 13 per cent of total investments, which were financed up to 92 per cent by foreign aid. The state companies, which in 1967 supplied 90 per cent of industrial production, were on the whole ill-conceived and badly managed, with the exception of those projects financed by China, particularly the textile factory at Ségou, the cigarette and match factory and the sugar refinery, which are almost the only valid industrial enterprises in the country. On the other hand development of infrastructure works during the ten-year period has been considerable. In seven years 15,000 million francs CFA were invested in the construction of roads, 5,000 million in the construction of airports, in river transport and communications and 14,000 million in public and private building programmes (of which 20 per cent was financed by private savings—in the housing sector). The state sector was responsible in 1967 for about 40 per cent of this expenditure.

Commerce and transport are extensively nationalized, the state sector in 1967 accounting for 90 per cent of trade in products other than petroleum products and for 65 per cent of transport, but they have been resounding failures. The state commercial sector achieved only 10 per cent of the profits envisaged, in spite of enjoying a monopoly position.

Growth in the whole agricultural sector is reflected in an increase of 80 per cent in turnover between 1961 and 1966, the state share of the sector increasing from 20 to 66 per cent, while private commerce diminished from 45 to 8 per cent.

Even in the social field, to which the régime had paid particular attention, results were poor. The school attendance rate is said to have increased from 8 per cent in 1959 to 23 per cent in 1968, and the number of hospital beds in that period to have multiplied $2\frac{1}{2}$ times. However, the significance of these and other achievements in the social sector is diminished by their low quality, their concentration in urban areas and their administrative costs.

INFLATION 1960–1970

The permanent inflationary process which has dogged Mali since independence is not really difficult to understand. Faced with stagnating production, the state resorted to creating monetary income in steadily increasing quantities in order to meet its current administrative expenditure and to finance investments over and above those financed by foreign aid, while public enterprises, running heavy deficits, added their debts to the public debt. The total amount of monetary support to the public sector (the state and public enterprises), leaving aside the amount of the revalued external debt following the 1967 devaluation (105,000 million francs CFA), rose by an annual average of 6,200 million from 1961 to 1968. Compared with the national income—which was about 60,000 million francs CFA at the beginning of the ten-year period and which remained stagnant in real terms during the course of that period—this represents an enormous inflationary gap equal to about 10 per cent of the total domestic product and to about 20 per cent of the country's production in monetary terms. Local savings of liquid resources could not absorb such a large volume of surplus money, which is why the currency in circulation, which fills a part of the inflationary gap, has increased by only 1,600 million francs per annum. The total volume of currency in circulation, which doubled in eight years from 1960 to 1968, finds a perceptible parallel in price increases, which have also doubled during the same period.

It is not easy to pinpoint the causes of this public deficit, since there is so much confusion in the handling of state finances: "disguised" state subsidies to public enterprises confuse all public accounts. Moreover the artificial nature of many prices renders fairly meaningless any attempt to locate the causes of the deficit. It seems nevertheless that the volume of administrative expenditure expressed in current francs has risen at an average annual rate of about 11–12 per cent, from 9,000 million francs CFA in 1959 (i.e. 15 per cent of G.D.P. which was in the region of 60,000 million francs at current prices) to 24,000 million francs CFA in 1968 (i.e. 20 per cent of G.D.P. which was in the region of 110 to 120,000 million francs at real current prices). Taxing this proved impossible, and the deficit in current public expenditure was of the order of 2,300 million francs per annum from 1959–68.

Execution of the plan—expenditure on administrative investments (infrastructure) and the equipment of state enterprises—and the deficit incurred by public enterprises were therefore responsible for an average of 3,400 million francs per annum of the inflationary gap, i.e. approximately 55 per cent of the total gap. In ten years (1959–69) the total volume of investments was in the region of 90,000 million francs at current prices (of which 75,000 million were made under the terms of the plan), divided between infrastructure and administration (amounting to approximately 60 per cent) and state enterprises (about 30 per cent). Foreign aid allocated for these investment operations (grants and loans net of repayments) covered only 78 per cent of these investments (70,000 million francs) and domestic private savings (self-financing of businesses, financing of housing, etc.) barely 11 per cent. The state therefore financed about 10,000 million francs of investments (i.e. an annual average of about 1,000 million) by monetary means. The deficit incurred by public enterprises was, therefore, in the region of 2,400 million francs per annum. For while the textiles factory at Ségou and the tobacco and matches industry showed a profit of 2,000 million francs during the last three years of the period (1965–68) and the state commercial sector an annual average of 1,000 million, all the other enterprises showed huge losses, particularly Air Mali, the RTM, the railways, the *Office du Niger*, the abattoirs and SONETRA.

The inflationary gap led inevitably to an external debt. Official and illicit exports stagnated during the ten-year period at around 10,000 million francs at current prices, while imports grew from 10–12,000 million to annual average totals of 16–17,000 million during the second half of the period (1965–69). These import figures show very irregular trends, corresponding to those of investments. The annual growth rate of imports was about 7 per cent until 1965, after which date, due to lack of funds, imports stabilized and an accelerated rise in prices resulted. Total current operations from 1964–68 incurred an average annual deficit of 9,300 million francs. To this deficit must be added that of the legal transfer of private capital, i.e. 1,700 million francs, and that of illicit transfers (illicit exports less illicit imports), i.e. 2,800 million francs. This deficit could not be covered by foreign development aid, which averaged about 6,300 million francs per annum but with a marked tendency to diminish (8,200 million francs in 1964; 4,600 million in 1968), and there has been a resulting real balance of payments deficit of about 7,400 million francs per annum (of which only 4,600 million are recorded in the official balance).

FALL OF THE RÉGIME AND DIFFICULTIES FACED BY ITS SUCCESSORS

Although it was not until November 19th, 1968 that a military *coup d'état* brought his régime to an end, Modibo Keita had already admitted failure in May 1967, when he agreed to Mali's return to the franc zone.

In practice, all socialism had meant to this régime was developing the public sector. It was based on the urban world of public administration. The number of civil servants rose from 13,300 in 1961 to 23,900 in 1968, and there were also about 9,000 employees in state enterprises and several thousand soldiers. The proportion of national income claimed by this very small section of the population continued to increase: that part represented by salaries doubled in ten years, reaching 26 per cent in 1969. Since efficient taxing of the rural masses was impossible, because they remained almost entirely outside the market economy, the state had to survive on foreign aid. Until June 1962 it covered its deficits by makeshift means which were made possible by Mali's membership of the franc zone. Between 1962 and 1967 the countries of the eastern bloc took over the role of aid donor. At the domestic level public deficit was covered by various monetary means, masked in part by fortuitous circumstances.

The external debt was covered from a variety of sources. Foreign aid consisted of an IMF standby credit of 2,000 million Mali francs in 1964; long-term credits for equipment of 32,000 million francs from the U.S.S.R., 7,500 million from China, 7,000 million from the U.A.R., etc.; and currency loans including 15,700 million francs from China and 1,600 million from the U.S.S.R. Recourse was also made to temporary devices like a moratorium on transfers made by large foreign companies—oil companies, forwarding agents, etc.—which brought in a total of about 1,500 million francs; and the blocking of public transfers and suspension of external debt servicing, which had reached 5,000 million Mali francs when the régime admitted failure in spring 1967.

In May 1967 the régime capitulated and signed with France an agreement on Mali's return to the franc zone. On May 5th the Mali franc was devalued by half and on April 1st, 1968 convertibility with the franc was re-established. The *Banque de la République du Mali* was wound up and a new *Banque Centrale du Mali* (BCM) set up, managed "jointly" by Mali and France. Devaluation, accompanied by a wages freeze, was to lead to the restoration of equilibrium in internal finances and in the external balance of payments. However, these measures failed. The public debt persisted; exports did not rise; imports did not diminish; and capital was not repatriated. In November 1968 a military *coup* defeated the régime.

The social basis on which the new régime is founded does not differ from that of its predecessor. On the "recommendation" of French technicians, who have returned to the important posts, a "recovery programme" (1970–73) has been drawn up. This envisages "priority" for agriculture, doubling cotton production from 40,000 to 85,000 tons; dismantling the co-operatives, and the intervention of French companies entrusted with rural development (*Cie. française pour le développement des fibres textiles—CFDT* for cotton, *Sté. d'aide technique et de coopération—SATEC* for groundnuts); the return to private control of viable industries and the winding up of the others; the re-establishment of private commerce; the abandoning of mineral exploration; cutting down investments in infrastructural and social spheres, particularly in education; and the re-direction of foreign trade towards France. None of these measures has restored internal and external financial equilibrium. The proportion of imports from the west increased from 19 per cent in 1965 to 70 per cent in 1969 and that of exports from 21 to 68 per cent. At the same time the proportion of foreign trade represented by the private sector increased from 5 per cent to 22 per cent. However, the external debt has not decreased, France replacing the eastern bloc countries in its financing through the channel of an operations account. Mali's debt has risen by 4,000 million francs CFA per annum since 1968. In order to restore equilibrium in external finances, public finances inside the country must be put right—but this cannot be done without affecting the interests of the civil service on which the new régime, like its predecessor, is based.

STATISTICAL SURVEY

AREA AND POPULATION

AREA sq. km.	POPULATION (1971)
1,240,000*	5,143,000

* 478,767 sq. miles.

MAIN TRIBES
(1963 estimates)

BAMBARA	FULANI	MARKA	SONGHAI	MALINKÉ	TOUAREG	SÉNOUFO	DOGON
1,000,000	450,000	280,000	230,000	200,000	240,000	375,000	130,000

Chief Towns: Bamako (capital) 182,000 (1968), Kayes, Ségou, Sikasso, Mopti, San, Tombouctou (Timbuktu).

Births and Deaths: Average annual birth rate 49.8 per 1,000, death rate 26.6 per 1,000 (UN estimates for 1965–70).

Employment (1970): Total economically active population 2,756,000, including 2,511,000 in agriculture (ILO and FAO estimates).

AGRICULTURE

PRINCIPAL CROPS
('ooo metric tons)

	1969	1970	1971
Millet, Sorghum and Fonio . . .	913	600	900
Rice (Paddy) . .	119	138	150
Maize . . .	126	80*	80*
Sugar Cane† . .	50	55	61
Sweet Potatoes and Yams . .	67*	67*	n.a.
Cassava (Manioc) . .	150	155	n.a.
Pulses . . .	9*	9*	9*
Groundnuts (in shell) .	122	158	170
Cottonseed . .	23	37	42*
Cotton (Lint) . .	18	22	25*

* FAO estimate.

† Crop year ending in year stated.

Source: FAO, *Production Yearbook 1971.*

LAND USE, 1970
('ooo hectares)

Arable and Under Permanent Crops . .	11,600
Permanent Meadows and Pastures . .	30,000
Forest	4,457
Other Land	75,943
Inland Water	2,000
TOTAL	124,000

LIVESTOCK
('ooo)

	1968–69	1969–70	1970–71
Cattle . . .	5,350	5,350	5,500*
Sheep . . .	5,750	5,750	5,900*
Goats . . .	5,500	5,500	5,650*
Pigs . . .	32	32	33
Horses . . .	170	170	174*
Asses . . .	476	476	460*
Camels . . .	218	218	215*
Poultry . . .	13,400*	13,500*	14,000*

* FAO estimate.

Source: FAO, *Production Yearbook 1971.*

LIVESTOCK PRODUCTS
(metric tons)

	1969	1970	1971
Cows' Milk . .	102,000*	103,000*	104,000*
Sheep's Milk . .	32,000*	32,000*	33,000*
Goats' Milk . .	63,000*	62,000*	61,000*
Butter . . .	2,000	2,000	n.a.
Beef and Veal† .	48,000*	50,000*	50,000*
Mutton and Lamb† .	32,000*	33,000*	34,000*
Hen Eggs . .	7,000*	7,000*	7,100*
Cattle Hides . .	6,800*	7,000*	6,600*
Sheep Skins . .	3,335*	3,480*	3,625*
Goat Skins . .	2,450*	2,500*	2,520*

* FAO estimate.

† Meat from indigenous animals only, including the meat equivalent of exported live animals.

Source: FAO, *Production Yearbook 1971.*

FORESTRY
ROUNDWOOD PRODUCTION
('ooo cubic metres)

1967 . . .	2,515
1968 . . .	2,560
1969 . . .	2,590
1970 . . .	2,600

Source: FAO, *Yearbook of Forest Products.*

Fishing (1967–70): Total catch 90,000 metric tons of freshwater fish each year (FAO estimate). In 1966 about 30 per cent of the catch was dried and smoked.

Mining (1967–70): About 4,000 metric tons of unrefined salt produced each year.

INDUSTRY

	UNIT	1968	1969	1970
Vegetable Oils	metric tons	3,000	4,000	n.a.
Refined Sugar	,, ,,	5,000	5,000	5,000
Sugar Confectionery . . .	,, ,,	280	480	980
Beer	'ooo hectolitres	n.a.	n.a.	960
Soft Drinks	,, ,,	44	46	50
Cement	metric tons	n.a.	n.a.	40,000
Soap	,, ,,	6,220	2,641	2,645
Electric Energy . . .	million kWh.	35	37	40

Source: United Nations, *The Growth of World Industry.*

Other industries include cotton ginning, hardware and brickmaking.

FINANCE

100 centimes = 1 Mali franc.

Exchange rates (December 1972): 1 Mali franc = 1 French centime = 50 centimes CFA.

£1 sterling = 1,187.25 Mali francs; U.S. $1 = 511.57 Mali francs.

10,000 Mali francs = £8.42 = $19.55.

Note: In recent years the central exchange rates for the Mali franc have fluctuated as follows:
Sterling: July 1962 to May 1967, £1 = 691.19 Mali francs; May to November 1967, £1 = 1,382.38 Mali francs; November 1967 to August 1969, £1 = 1,184.89 Mali francs; August 1969 to June 1972, £1 = 1,333.01 Mali francs.

Dollars: July 1962 to May 1967, $1 = 246.853 Mali francs; May 1967 to August 1969, $1 = 493.706 Mali francs; August 1969 to August 1971, $1 = 555.419 Mali francs; present rate fixed in December 1971.

Budget (1969): 23,000m. Mali francs, partly financed through French budgetary assistance.

1970 estimates: Expenditure 22,651 million Mali francs.

1971: Expenditure 24,709 million Mali francs; Revenue 22,994 million Mali francs.

Three-Year Plan (1970–1973): Organized by the Council of Planning to replace the first five-year plan which failed to reach its target. The Plan lays more emphasis upon the development of industry, and the total sum needed amounts to 77,500 million Mali francs of which 66,000 million will be provided by foreign aid.

Currency in Circulation (April 1972): 21,560 million Mali francs.

National Accounts (1964): Gross Domestic Product 84,500 million Mali francs at purchasers' values.

FOREIGN PUBLIC DEBT, 1968
('ooo million Mali francs)

U.S.S.R.	.	32.6
France	.	26.9
China, People's Republic . .	.	23.5
Egypt	.	7.3
Ghana	.	6.5
Other Countries . .	.	5.2
IMF and IBRD . .	.	9.0
TOTAL . .	.	110.0

EXTERNAL TRADE
(million Mali francs)

	1968	1969	1970	1971
Imports . . .	16,937	20,100	26,200	30,500
Exports . . .	5,300	8,760	18,240	19,630

PRINCIPAL COMMODITIES

IMPORTS	1968	1969	EXPORTS	1968	1969
Sugar and Honey . . .	1,903	1,143	Live Cattle . . .	664	3,624
Other Food	1,157	1,715	Live Sheep, Lambs and Goats .	40	625
Petroleum Products . . .	1,301	1,759	Fish (salted, dried or smoked) .	691	1,259
Animal and Vegetable Oils and			Oil-Seed Cake and Meal, etc. .	82	237
Fats	544	29	Other Food . . .	170	245
Chemicals	1,459	2,044	Groundnuts (green) . . .	562	253
Woven Cotton Fabrics . .	1,307	1,374	Other Oil-Seeds, Nuts and		
Other Textile Fabrics, Yarn, etc.	930	843	Kernels	382	547
Lime, Cement, etc. . . .	561	368	Raw Cotton (excl. linters) .	2,099	895
Iron and Steel	954	501	Fixed Vegetable Oils . .	163	603
Machinery (non-electric) . .	787	1,281			
Electrical Equipment . .	660	1,036	TOTAL (incl. others) . .	5,300	8,941
Road Motor Vehicles. . .	1,271	1,934			
Other Transport Equipment .	210	1,903			
TOTAL (incl. others) . .	16,937	20,099			

Source: mainly *Overseas Associates, Foreign Trade* (Statistical Office of the European Communities, Luxembourg). Totals for 1969 differ slightly from the figures given in the summary table for trade, which are those of the national statistical authority.

PRINCIPAL COUNTRIES

IMPORTS	1968	1969	EXPORTS	1968	1969
Belgium/Luxembourg . .	128	339	China, People's Republic . .	280	0
China, People's Republic . .	2,236	1,706	France	866	1,434
Egypt	347	610	Germany, Federal Republic .	147	10
France	5,345	7,790	Ghana	507	1,877
Germany, Federal Republic .	422	572	Ivory Coast	1,337	3,509
Italy	38	486	Japan	327	411
Ivory Coast	1,498	1,725	Netherlands	446	1
Japan	315	131	Senegal	816	425
Netherlands	309	303	U.S.S.R..	0	212
Poland	282	14	Upper Volta	106	230
Senegal	1,218	1,685			
Switzerland	54	674	TOTAL (incl. others) . .	5,300	8,941
U.S.S.R..	3,116	1,976			
United Kingdom . . .	267	240			
U.S.A.	163	530			
TOTAL (incl. others) . .	16,937	20,099			

Source: mainly *Overseas Associates, Foreign Trade* (Statistical Office of the European Communities, Luxembourg). Totals for 1969 differ slightly from the figures given in the summary table for trade, which are those of the national statistical authority.

TRANSPORT

Railways (1967–68): Passengers 702,700, Passenger/km. 77.6m.; Freight 225,633 tons, Freight ton/km. 103.6m.

Roads (1969): 4,500 passenger cars; 5,700 commercial vehicles.

River Traffic (1967–68): Passengers 71,939; Freight 62,001 metric tons; Passenger/km. 22m.; Freight ton/km. 36.3m.

Civil Aviation (1971): Aircraft (arrivals and departures) 2,025; Passenger arrivals 29,486; Passenger departures 26,036; Freight unloaded 986 metric tons; Freight loaded 501 metric tons.

COMMUNICATIONS

Radio sets: 60,000 in 1970.

Telephones: 5,000 in 1970.

EDUCATION
(1969)

	TEACHERS	PUPILS		
		Male	Female	Total
Pre-primary	135	2,390	2,345	4,735
Primary	6,265	155,744	62,672	218,416
Secondary: General . .	233	2,429	394	2,823
Vocational . .	281	2,322	567	2,889
Teacher-Training . .	93	1,263	206	1,469
Tertiary	92	357	35	392
Special	5	50	—	50
TOTAL . . .	7,104	164,555	66,219	230,774

Source (unless otherwise stated): Direction Générale de la Statistique, Bamako.

THE CONSTITUTION
(September 1960)

The 1960 Constitution was abrogated by the Military Committee for National Liberation (CMLN), which in November 1968 replaced it by a "Fundamental Law". Under this, the CMLN and the Supreme Court rule by decree until a constitutional referendum has been held. The President of the CMLN acts as Head of State, and is Commander-in-Chief of the Armed Forces.

THE GOVERNMENT

HEAD OF STATE

President: Col. MOUSSA TRAORÉ.

MILITARY COMMITTEE FOR NATIONAL LIBERATION

President: Col. MOUSSA TRAORÉ.

Vice-President: Capt. BABA DIARRA.

Commissioner: Capt. YOUSSOUF TRAORÉ.

Permanent Secretary: Capt. FILIFING SISSOKO.

Members: Captains J. MARA, K. DOUKARA, T. BAGAYOKO, M. SANOGO, C. S. SISSOKO, M. KONÉ and K. DEMBÉLÉ.

PROVISIONAL GOVERNMENT

(*November* 1972)

Prime Minister: Col. MOUSSA TRAORÉ.

Minister of Foreign Affairs and Co-operation: Capt. CHARLES SISSOKO.

Minister of Defence, Interior and Security: Capt. KISSIMA DOUKARA.

Minister of Information: Capt. YOUSSOUF TRAORÉ.

Minister of Finance and Trade: Capt. BABA DIARRA.

Minister of Justice: Capt. JOSEPH MARA.

Minister of Health and Social Affairs: BÉNITIÉNI FOFANA.

Minister of Industrial Development and Public Works: ROBERT N'DAW.

Minister of Production: SIDI COULIBALY.

Minister of Public Service and Labour: SORI COULIBALY.

Minister of Education, Youth and Sport: Prof. YAYA BAGAYOKO.

Minister of Transport, Public Works, Tourism and Tele-communications: Capt. KARIM DEMBÉLÉ.

Secretary of State for Social Affairs: Mme. INNA SISSOKO.

Chairman of the Development Bank: TIÉOULÉ KONATÉ.

DIPLOMATIC REPRESENTATION

EMBASSIES AND LEGATIONS ACCREDITED TO MALI

(In Bamako unless otherwise stated)

(E) Embassy; (L) Legation.

Albania: (E); *Ambassador:* GAGO PAZA.

Algeria: (E); *Ambassador:* HOCINE BENYELLES.

Argentina: (E); *Ambassador:* MARIO RAUL PICO.

Belgium: Abidjan, Ivory Coast (E).

Brazil: Dakar, Senegal (E).

China, People's Republic: B.P. 112 (E); *Ambassador:* MENG YUEH.

Czechoslovakia: (E); *Ambassador:* VÁCLAV HRADEC.

Egypt: (E); *Ambassador:* ANWAR FARID NASSER.

France: B.P. 17 (E); *Ambassador:* LOUIS DALLIER.

Germany, Federal Republic: (E); *Ambassador:* JOACHIM VON STÜLPNAGEL.

Ghana: *Ambassador:* AWOSU DARKO.

Guinea: (E); *Ambassador:* KAMONO ANSOU.

Hungary: Conakry, Guinea (E).

India: *Ambassador:* R. R. SINHA.

Indonesia: Conakry, Guinea (E).

Israel: B.P. 351 (E); *Ambassador:* ASHER HAKENY.

Italy: Conakry, Guinea (E).

Japan: Dakar, Senegal (E).

Korea, Democratic People's Republic: (E); *Ambassador:* KIM DJOUNG KEUL.

Lebanon: Dakar, Senegal (E).

Liberia: Dakar, Senegal (E).

Mauritania: Dakar, Senegal (E).

Mongolia: Conakry, Guinea (E).

Morocco: B.P. 78 (E); *Chargé d'Affaires:* (vacant).

Netherlands: Dakar, Senegal (E).

Pakistan: Dakar, Senegal (E).

Poland: (E); *Ambassador:* EUGENIUSZ KULAGA.

Senegal: (E); *Ambassador:* MOUSTAFA CISSÉ.

Sierra Leone: (E); *Ambassador:* SORSON IBRAHIM CONTEN.

Spain: Dakar, Senegal (E).

Sweden: Abidjan, Ivory Coast (E).

Switzerland: Dakar, Senegal (E).

Tunisia: Dakar, Senegal (E).

Turkey: Dakar, Senegal (E).

United Kingdom: Dakar, Senegal (E).

U.S.A.: B.P. 34 (E); *Ambassador:* M. G. E. CLARK.

U.S.S.R.: (E); *Ambassador:* LEONID MOUSSATOV.

Upper Volta: (L); *Representative:* HENRI OUATTARA.

Viet-Nam, Democratic Republic: B.P. 48 (E); *Ambassador:* VU HAC BONG.

Yugoslavia: B.P. 207 (E); *Ambassador:* ZDRAVKO PECAR.

In June 1969 Mali granted recognition to the Provisional Revolutionary Government of the Republic of South Viet-Nam. Mali also has diplomatic relations at ambassadorial level with Canada, The Gambia and Haiti.

PARLIAMENT

The National Assembly was abolished in January 1968. The President and, since November 1968, the Military Committee for National Liberation rule by decree.

POLITICAL PARTIES

The "Fundamental Law" proclaimed in November 1968 guaranteed freedom of political activity within the law. By late 1972 no details of any active political parties were available.

DEFENCE

Of a total armed force of 3,650, 3,500 are in the army and 150 in the air force. There is a gendarmerie of 1,500 and a civil police of 1,000. A national police college was opened in April 1971.

Chief of Staff of the Army: Chef de Bataillon BENEM POUDIOUGOU.

JUDICIAL SYSTEM

Supreme Court: Bamako; established September 1969; 19 members; judicial section comprising three civil chambers and one criminal chamber; administrative section dealing with appeals and fundamental rulings; members are nominated for five years and may not be members of the Government nor practice law privately during that time; Pres. ASSANE SEYE.

Court of Appeal: Bamako.
There are two Tribunaux de Première Instance (Magistrate's Courts).

RELIGION

It is estimated that 65 per cent of the population are Muslims, about 30 per cent Animists and 5 per cent Christians, with Roman Catholics comprising 1 per cent of the total population.

Chief Mosque: Bagadadji, Place de la République.

Roman Catholic Church: Run by the Missionaries of Africa (White Fathers); six areas: Archdiocese of Bamako, dioceses of Segou, Sikasso, Kayes, San and Mopti-Gao; 38 parishes; 287 religious staff (43 Africans); 59,200 lay mems.; also maintains 55 schools with 13,800 pupils, and several medical centres; Archbishop of Bamako Mgr. LUC SANGARÉ.

Protestant Missions: There are many mission centres with a total personnel of about 370, run by American societies.

PRESS

Barakela (*Worker*): mimeographed daily bulletin.

Bulletin d'information: Bamako; published daily by the Agence Nationale d'Information.

Journal Officiel de la République du Mali: B.P. 1463, Bamako; published by the Government printers at Koulouba.

L'Essor (*Progress*): B.P. 1463, Bamako; organ of the Military Committee for National Liberation; mimeographed daily and weekly editions; Dir. (vacant).

Bulletin de Statistiques: Ministry of Planning, Bamako; monthly.

Bulletin de Liaison: Office du Niger, Ségou.

Le Mali: Ministry of Information and Tourism, Bamako; f. 1965; monthly.

NEWS AGENCIES

FOREIGN BUREAUX

Agence France-Presse: B.P. 778, Bamako; Correspondent LAURENT CHENARD.

Četeka, Novosti and Tass maintain bureaux in Mali.

PUBLISHER

Editions Populaires: Bamako; school books, historys sociology, folk-tales.

RADIO

Radio Mali: B.P. 171, Bamako; f. 1957; government station; programmes in French, English, Bambara, Peulh, Sarakolé, Tamachek, Sonrai, Moorish, Ouolof; Dir-Gen. MOUSSA KEITA.

In 1970 there were 60,000 receiving sets.

FINANCE

BANKS

CENTRAL BANK

Banque Centrale du Mali: B.P. 206, Bamako; f. 1968; cap. 1,000m. Mali francs; Pres. SEKOU SANGARE, Dir.-Gen. GEORGES DUSSINE.

NATIONAL BANKS

Banque de Développement du Mali: B.P. 94, Bamako; f. 1968; cap. 1,000m. Mali francs; Pres. Dir.-Gen. TIÉOULÉ KONATÉ; Joint Dir.-Gen. MAMADOU HAÏDARA; regional brs. at Gao, Mopti, Ségou, Sikasso and Kayes.

Banque Malienne de Crédit et Dépôts: ave. Modibo Keita, B.P. 45, Bamako; f. 1961; formerly Crédit Lyonnais; cap. 150m. Mali francs; Pres. and Gen. Man. D. DIAKITE.

FRENCH BANKS

Banque Internationale pour l'Afrique Occidentale: 9 ave. de Messine, Paris; ave. Mohammed 5, B.P. 15, Bamako; 49 per cent owned by First National City Bank of New York.

Caisse Centrale de Coopération Economique: B.P. 32, rue Festard, Bamako.

INSURANCE

Several French companies maintain agencies in Bamako.

TRADE AND INDUSTRY

Chambre de Commerce, d'Agriculture et d'Industrie de Bamako: B.P. 46, Bamako; telegraph CHAMBCOM; f. 1908; 46 mems.; Pres. El Haj DOSSOLO TRAORE; Sec.-Gen. BONOTA TOURÉ; publs. *Bulletin quotidien, Circulaire mensuelle d'information.*

Chambre de Commerce, d'Agriculture et d'Industrie du Mali Occidental: B.P. 81, Kayes; Act. Pres. DEMBA SISSOKO; Sec. Gen. BAKARY DIAWARA.

Chambre de Commerce de Kayes: B.P. 81, Kayes; Pres. DEMBA SISSOKO; Sec. Gen. BACARY DIAWARA.

Société de Constructions Radioéléctriques du Mali (SOCORAM): Bamako; f. 1965 by the Government as a part of the Five Year Plan to develop the electronic industry in Mali; cap 40m. Mali francs.

Société Malienne d'Importation et d'Exportation (SOMIEX): B.P. 182, Bamako; state-owned company for the export of groundnuts and the import of primary products; Dir. OUMAR COULIBALY.

SOMIEY: Bamako; employers' federation.

Syndicat des Transporteurs Soudanais: Bamako.

DEVELOPMENT ORGANIZATIONS

Mission permanente d'aide et de coopération: B.P. 84, Bamako; French Government body for the administration of technical assistance schemes; Chief of Mission M. EDOUARD FOBBES LEPRUN.

Office du Niger: Ségou; f. 1932; taken over from the French Government in 1958; the French project involved a major dam, begun in 1935, 45 miles above Ségou, to direct water into extensive irrigation networks covering one million hectares to be devoted to rice and cotton on the left bank of the Niger. By 1958 a mere 48,000 hectares had been irrigated. Since independence the irrigated area has been extended by 4,000 hectares per year. The office also operates a number of research stations.

TRADE UNIONS

All trade unions were dissolved in November 1968. They were allowed to resume activities in December 1969, but in October 1970 the CMLN dissolved the provisional consultative committee of the *Union nationale des travailleurs du Mali* (UNTM) and in January 1971 most of the members of the committee were arrested.

MAJOR INDUSTRIAL COMPANIES

Société des Conserves du Mali: B.P. 146, Bamako; f. 1962; state-owned company for canning, preserving and jam-making; Dir.-Gen. AMADOU HAKO.

Société d'Exploitation des Briqueteries: B.P. 1963, Bamako; f. 1963; state-owned company for the production of bricks and for quarrying; Dir.-Gen. MAMADOU M'BO.

DSBI Ingenieurberatung: B.P. 148, Bamako; head office Neumarkt 49, Köln, German Federal Republic; f. 1955; cap. approx. 250,000 DM.

Independent firm of consulting engineers; industrial building, civil engineering, surveying, road building. Dirs. Dipl.-Ing. BRANDT; Dr.-Ing. H. WALTER; 250 employees.

Compagnie Malienne des Textiles (COMATEX): B.P. 52, Ségou; textile complex; Dir.-Gen. SAMBALA SISSOKO.

Société Nationale des Tabacs et Allumettes du Mali: B.P. 59, Bamako; state-owned company for the production of cigarettes and matches; Dirs. BAMBA KADARI, BAKARY CAMARA.

TRANSPORT

RAILWAY

Chemin de Fer Dakar-Niger: Bamako; Dir. D. DIALLO. 1,287 km. of track linking Dakar (Senegal) with Bamako and Koulikoro, of which some 640 km. are in Mali; metric guage. Passenger services twice weekly Bamako–Dakar, freight services daily, and one petrol train weekly.

Plans have been drawn up, with Soviet help, for a new line via Siguiri and Kouroussa, linking Bamako with the existing Guinean railway which runs to Conakry. This line would give Mali a second outlet to the Atlantic.

ROADS

There are about 12,000 km. of classified roads, of which only about 5,500 km. are practical for motor traffic throughout the year.

The roads between Bamako and Bougouni (160 km.) and between Bamako and Ségou (240 km.) are asphalted. The length of asphalt roads totalled 1,600 km. in 1972.

INLAND WATERWAYS

Société Malienne de Navigation: Bamako, B.P. 150.

The Niger is navigable throughout its course through Mali (1,782 km.) from July to March. The *Ateliers et Chantiers du Mali* (A.C.M.) has a monopoly of the river traffic over the major part of the course, from Koulikoro to Gao.

CIVIL AVIATION

The principal airport is at Bamako, but the facilities there are not suitable for large jet aircraft. A new airport is being built at Senou, 14 km. outside Bamako, with French aid and should be ready for use in 1973.

Air Mali: B.P. 27, Bamako; state airline; cap. 50m. Mali francs; daily services to West Africa, weekly services to Paris; local services; fleet: one Boeing 727, three DC-3, two Ilyushin 18, two Antonov 24B, one AN 2; administrative council: seven mems.; Dir. M. TRAORÉ.

Mail is also served by the following foreign airlines: Air Afrique, Air Guinée, Aeroflot, Interflug and UTA.

TOURISM

Office Malien de Tourisme: B.P. 222, Place de la République, Bamako; f. 1966; Dir. MAMADOU SY.

Touring-Club: B.P. 104, Grand Hotel, Bamako; Delegate A. CHAZAL.

POWER

Energie du Mali: B.P. 69, ave. Lyautey, Bamako; f. 1961; cap. 100 million Mali francs.

Production and distribution of electricity and water. Dir.-Gen. BOCAR THIAM; 681 employees.

EDUCATION

Since 1962 education has been organized in two cycles of four to five years each, replacing the traditional French division into Primary and Secondary levels.

In 1968–69 there were 218,416 primary students, 7,181 students in secondary and technical schools and 392 students undergoing higher education.

In 1966–67, 1,249 Mali students held grants for study abroad, including about 300 in France.

A national adult literacy campaign is being vigorously promoted. There were 740 centres of instruction with an estimated 42,235 pupils in 1966–67.

RESEARCH INSTITUTES

Centre National de Recherches Fruitières: B.P. 30, Bamako; f. 1962; Mission in Mali of the Institut Français de Recherches Fruitières Outre-Mer (IFAC); controls experimental plantations, phytopathological laboratory, technological laboratory and pilot schemes; Dir. P. JEANTEUR.

Centre National de Recherches Zootechniques: B.P. 262, Bamako; f. 1927; experimental farm with Animal Husbandry section, Swine section, Poultry section, Pasture section and Biochemistry section; library of 1,000 vols.; Dir. Dr. ZANGA COULIBALY.

Centres de Recherche Rizicole: Two rice research centres, at Kankan and at Ibetemi.

Institut de Recherches Agronomiques Tropicales et des Cultures Vivrières (I.R.A.T.): B.P. 438, Bamako; f. 1962; controls stations at Bamako, Koulikoro, Kogoni par Nioro, Ibetemi (Mopti), and sub-stations at Kita and Koporokenie-Pe; General agronomy, Land amelioration, Cultural techniques, Fertilization needs, Plant breeding (sorghum, pennisetum, short and floating rices, maize, wheat, groundnuts and formerly sugar cane); Dir. M. CATHERINET.

Institut de Recherche Scientifique du Mali: Bamako; Koulouba; Dir. ABDOULAYE FINIGARÉ.

Institut de Recherches du Coton et des Textiles exotiques (I.R.C.T.): one cotton research centre, at M'Pesoba.

Institut d'Ophthalmologie Tropicale (I.O.T.A.): B.P. 248, Bamako; specializes in trachoma research; Dir. Dr. N. TOUFIC.

Institut de Recherches sur la Lèpre: Bamako; f. 1935; medical research, teaching, treatment and epidemiology, specializing in leprosy; Dir. J. LANGUILLON.

Service Metéorologique: B.P. 237, Bamako; Dir. N. KEITA.

SONAREM (Service de Documentation): B.P. 2, Kati; 1961; geology, mining, technology; Dir. V. KANÉ.

Stations de Recherches de l'Office du Niger: Bougomi and Sahel (cotton), Kayo (rice), Soninkoura (fruit).

LIBRARIES AND ARCHIVES

Archives Nationales du Mali, Institut des Sciences Humaines: Koulouba, Bamako; f. 1913; Archivist ABDOULAYE GAMBY N'DIAYE.

Bibliothèque Nationale, Institut des Sciences Humaines: Koulouba, Bamako; f. 1913; 5,000 vols., 200 current periodicals; Librarian ABDOULAYE GAMBY N'DIAYE.

Bibliothèque de l'Institut Interafricain du Travail: B.P. 152, Bamako; 2,900 vols.

Bibliothèque Municipale: Bamako.

Centre de Documentation Arabe: Timbuktu; in course of being founded; to assemble, conserve, and microfilm more than 5,000 Arabic MSS. which have been discovered in numerous private libraries in and around Timbuktu.

Centre Français de Documentation: Ambassade de France, B.P. 17, Bamako; f. 1962; 10,000 vols.; public library.

Library of the Office du Niger: Ségou; 1,800 vols., 4,000 brochures, 90 periodicals; agriculture, irrigation, general science.

COLLEGES

Ecole Nationale d'Administration: Bamako.

Ecole Nationale d'Ingénieurs: B.P. 242, Bamako.

Ecole de Médecine: Bamako; f. 1968.

SELECT BIBLIOGRAPHY

(For works on the former A.O.F. countries generally *see* Dahomey Select Bibliography, p.297).

AMIN, S. *Trois expériences africaines de développement: le Mali, la Guinée et le Ghana.* Paris, Presses universitaires de France, 1965.

BRASSEUR, PAULE. *Bibliographie Générale du Mali (Anciens Soudan Français et Haut-Senegal-Niger).* Institut Français d'Afrique Noire, Dakar, 1964.

DE WILDE, JOHN et al. *Agricultural Development in Tropical Africa.* Baltimore, Johns Hopkins Press, 1967.

DUMONT, RENÉ. *Afrique Noire: développement agricole: reconversion de l'économie agricole: Guinée, Côte d'Ivoire, Mali.* Paris, Presses universitaires de France, 1962.

FOLTZ, W. J. *From French West Africa to Mali Federation.* Yale University Press, 1965.

HARRISON CHURCH, R. J. *West Africa*, Chapter 15 (6th edition). London, Longmans, 1968.

SY, M. S. *Recherches sur l'exercise du pouvoir politique en Afrique noire (Côte d'Ivoire, Guinée, Mali).* Paris, 1965.

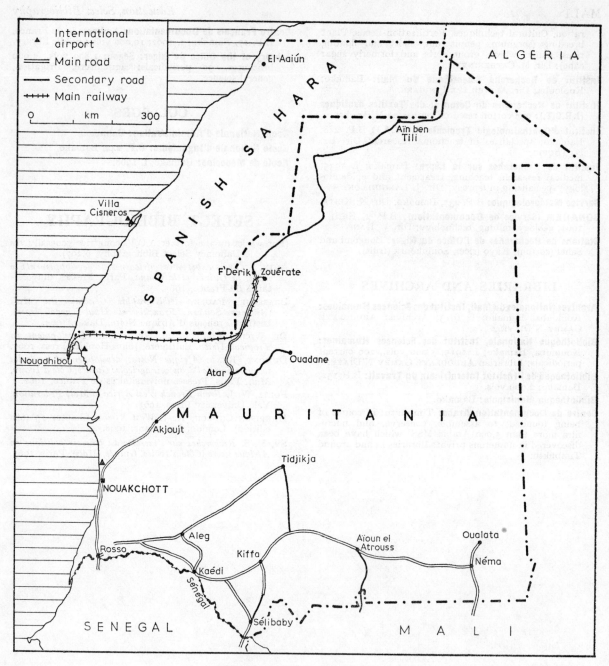

Mauritania and Spanish Sahara

Mauritania

PHYSICAL AND SOCIAL GEOGRAPHY

David Hilling

POPULATION

The Islamic Republic of Mauritania, with an area of 397,950 sq. miles (1,030,700 sq. km.), is approximately the size of France and Spain together. Geographically the country acts as a link between the Arabic Maghreb and Negro west Africa. Moors, heterogeneous groups of Arab/Berber stock, speaking dialects of Hassaniyya, make up three-quarters of the one million population. The Moors are divided on social and descent criteria rather than skin colour into a superior group, the Bidan or "white" Moors, and a group, probably of servile origin, known as the Harattin or "black" Moors. All are essentially nomadic pastoralists. The country's Negro population (the Toucouleur, Soninké, Bambara and Wolof) are mainly sedentary cultivators and are concentrated in a narrow zone in the south, especially along the Senegal River.

PHYSICAL FEATURES

Geologically Mauritania is a part of the vast western Saharan "shield" of crystalline rocks, but these are overlain in parts with sedimentary rocks, and some 40 per cent of the country has a superficial cover of unconsolidated sand. Relief has a general north-east/south-west trend, and a series of westward-facing scarps separate monotonous plateaux, which only in western Adrar rise above 1,600 ft. Locally these plateaux have been eroded, so that only isolated peaks remain, the larger of these being known as *kedia* and the smaller as *guelb*. These are often minerally enriched, the most famous being the *djbel le-hadid* ("iron mountains") of the Kedia d'Idjil, where 7–9 million tons of high-grade iron ore are now mined annually. Copper is mined at Guelb-el-Moghrein, near Akjoujt.

CLIMATE AND VEGETATION

Two-thirds of the country may be classed as "Saharan", with rainfall absent or negligible in most years and always less than 4 in. In parts vegetation is inadequate to graze even the camel, which is the main support of the nomadic peoples of the northern and central area. Traditionally this harsh area has produced some salt, and dates and millet are cultivated at oases such as Atar. Southwards rainfall increases to about 24 in. a year. Here vegetation will support sheep, goats and cattle, and cultivation, based mainly on the seasonally flooded alluvial zone (*chemama*) along the Senegal and its tributaries, supports the country's most densely settled sedentary population.

RECENT HISTORY

Michael Crowder and Donal Cruise O'Brien*

Independence was accorded in 1960 to a government headed by President Moktar Ould Daddah, whose political power had previously been built by the French colonial administration. France has continued to give active support to the President and his party, the *Parti du peuple mauritanien*. Opposition has come principally from two sources: from those in the north of the country who favour union with Morocco, a movement which has been contained by a French military presence; and from those in the south of the country who fear Arab domination. The introduction of Arabic as a compulsory language in secondary schools provoked a series of demonstrations by black pupils who feared that they would be under a disadvantage in relation to Moors who already spoke Arabic at home. These fears were compounded by a government decision in early 1968 to make Arabic an official language together with French, and by a slow reorientation of foreign policy towards the Arab world and away from black Africa. The organized expression of political opposition has however been stifled since independence. The PPM has controlled all seats in the National Assembly, and opposition parties have been banned where necessary. Periodic elections serve only to ratify the nomination made in the party caucus.

Since 1969 the linguistic-racial divisions have been less significant than agitation on the political left of the ruling party. This has been strongly influenced by trends both in France and in the Arab states, and seen in both student and trade union circles. There had been some agitation prior to the visit by France's President Pompidou in January 1971, which led to the closing of several schools and eventually to the replacement of the Education Minister. At the same

---

* Revised for this edition by KAYE WHITEMAN and the Editor.

time a number of trade union personalities were jailed, which led to demonstrations in May, put down by riot police. The trade union question has been complicated by a split in the movement, caused by the Government's attempt to integrate the movement with the PPM. This was first suggested in 1969 and met opposition, especially from the teachers' union, as a result of which the Government and the PPM set up a National Commission of Trade Union Reconciliation and denied any union or group the right to express political ideas contrary to those of the PPM. A series of strikes in the autumn of 1971 ncluded one at the MIFERMA iron ore mine, which completely interrupted production for two months. In June 1972 the PPM published a communiqué once again decrying the schism and confusion in the trade union movement. It reiterated that all unions must integrate with the party, and in July it announced

that this integration must be complete within six months.

President Ould Daddah's foreign policy has become substantially more radical, particularly in its support of the radical Arab states, with whom he has developed increasingly good relations. The Moroccan Government, which claimed all Mauritania as "Greater Morocco" in 1960, has accepted its neighbour's separate existence, and President Ould Daddah was formally reconciled with King Hassan II at the Islamic summit in Rabat in 1970. In 1972 Mauritania joined with both Morocco and Algeria in denouncing foreign occupation of the Sahara, and with the latter in supporting anti-colonialist liberation groups against the Portuguese and South Africa. A significant Chinese presence has now been established at Nouakchott, but the ties with France remain of primary importance.

ECONOMY

Samir Amin [*]

The urbanization and modernization of Mauritania are very recent phenomena. The capital, Nouakchott, an artificial city founded after independence, has a population of 48,000, Nouadhibou (formerly Port Etienne) 20,000, Kaédi, the Toucouleur capital, 12,000, Atar, traditional chief town of the north, about 10,000; the population of Zouérate has grown to 10,000 since iron ore began to be mined there.

There are about 30,000 wage- and salary-earners, 11,000 in government and 19,000 in the mines and in private business. Total incomes throughout the productive economy amount to some 3,700 million francs CFA, of which more than 60 per cent is earned by the senior grades, almost entirely European and numbering about 1,000. In this society, which was until so recently sunk in lethargy, sudden social transformations were precipitated by the establishment of Nouakchott and later the opening up of the iron mine (involving the railway to the town of Zouérate and the port of Nouadhibou, etc.) A growing contingent of labourers is emigrating to France from the river area, the exact number of which is unfortunately not known but amounts to several tens of thousands.

THE TRADITIONAL ECONOMY

The river region is said to produce about 100,000 tons of millet each year, and the oases 15,000 tons of dates. Livestock numbers about 2,700,000 cattle, 2,900,000 sheep, 2,450,000 goats and 700,000 camels. Little more can be said about the "traditional" economy, which today contributes something in the region of 12-14,000 million francs CFA to the annual gross domestic product.

Although virtually unknown, this traditional economy is not uniformly "stagnant", as is often believed, although it is true of agriculture in the river region, and the oases, where practically no improvements have been made. The redevelopment of the Senegal river is still in its early planning stages. The Organization of Senegal River States (OERS) finally broke up in 1971, following long disputes between Guinea and Senegal. A new organization, the Organization for the Development of the Senegal River (OMVS), was later formed by Mauritania, Mali and Senegal. Gum arabic, which sustained the flourishing trade of Saint Louis in the nineteenth century, now plays only an insignificant part in the country's economy (exports: 7,000 tons a year).

Stock rearing, on the other hand, has profited both from the growing demand for meat in the towns of Senegal and from favourable prices. With an excellent commercial network at their disposal, which is entirely under state control, the stock breeders exploit their herds to far greater advantage than previously. The few measures taken to boost the livestock industry (vaccinations and improved watering) have shown a considerable yield. Mauritania exports cattle worth more than 2,000 million francs CFA a year, most of the trade unrecorded.

THE STATE WITHIN THE STATE: MIFERMA

The discovery in the 1950s of a rich deposit of iron ore in the north of the country, where reserves are estimated at over 100 million tons and the grade at 66 per cent, was to transform, in the new Islamic Republic of Mauritania of the 1960s, the terms of its integration into the international capitalist system.

---

[*] For the 1973 edition, revisions have been made to this article by the Editor.

The Iron Mining Company of Mauritania (*Société anonyme des Mines de fer de Mauritanie*—MIFERMA), established in 1959, is controlled by the French Department of Mining Research (*Bureau de recherches géologiques et minières*—BRGM), which holds 24 per cent of the capital, and French steel interests (32 per cent) in association with British (19 per cent), Italian (15 per cent) and German (5 per cent) concerns. A share of 5 per cent of the capital was granted to the state of Mauritania in 1964. From 1960 to 1963 about 45,000 million francs worth of industrial works were completed in the region, including a 635 km. railway and the development of a mining port. The export of ore, which began in 1963, now stands at eight million tons per year, and its annual value of about 17,000 million francs represents more than 80 per cent of the country's total export earnings.

MIFERMA's activity is the chief cause of the very rapid economic growth between 1960 and 1966: multiplied by 2.4 in seven years, gross domestic product shows at current prices a growth rate of about 13 per cent a year. The part played by "secondary" activities in this product, still negligible in 1959 at only 4 per cent, is now predominant at over 45 per cent.

It would, however, be wrong to conclude that this sort of growth could cause the country's economy to "take off". The growth of the economy is entirely confined to the mining sector and its immediate dependencies—especially rail transport. As in the other petroleum and mining countries, there has been practically no perceptible effect on economic life as a whole. Moreover, a slackening in the growth of mining is reflected immediately in a strictly parallel slackening in the growth of the G.D.P. This made the strike that closed MIFERMA during October and November 1971 all the more serious. The cause of the strike seemed to be resentment at the control by foreign personnel of all the key posts in what is the state's most influential economic organization.

The fact remains that, however meagre the payments made by the company to the state—since 1965 the different duties, taxes and levies collected previously have been replaced by a uniform levy of 9 per cent of exports earning—they have facilitated the liquidation of the budgetary deficit traditional to this country, which is lacking in taxable resources. But even if these payments have eased the position in this respect, they scarcely permit any improvement in the local capacity to provide public finance, particularly in view of the burden of the infrastructure works, and the recurrent expenses they involve— which can be considered as directly subordinated to the needs of the mining economy.

THE EXTENSION OF THE MODERN SECTOR

The conditions for the establishment of MIFERMA were settled during the colonial era. For the mining of its copper the state of Mauritania has for some years been trying to obtain more favourable conditions. Established in 1967 for the mining of ore in Akjoujt, *Société minière de Mauritanie* (SOMIMA) receives 22 per cent of its capital from the state, against 44.6 per cent from Charter Consolidated (the Anglo-American group), 15 per cent from the *Société financière* (SFI), 6.13 per cent from BRGM and 12.27 per cent from private French interests (Pennaroya, the *Banque de Paris et des Pays Bas* and the *Cie. financière d'outre mer*). Anticipated investments are of the order of 14,000 million francs CFA, which will enable about 50,000 tons of copper concentrate to be exported between 1970 and 1988, using the Nouakchott road and redeveloped port. After 1977 the budget will be supplemented by 1-2,000 million francs CFA a year from duties and taxes, which should amount to 15,500 million.

The coast of Mauritania—particularly the Arguin banks—is famous for its great wealth of fish. But until now Mauritania has obtained only a marginal profit from this wealth. Indeed only a tenth of all catches are handled locally: 15,000 tons are brought in by Senegalese fishermen, 5,000 by Canary Islanders and 6,000 by modern industrial fisheries established in Mauritania, while 300,000 tons of the fish caught never see Mauritanian soil. Two recently founded semi-public companies will constitute the nucleus of a partially "Mauritanized" fishing industry.

One can hardly use the word "industry" in talking about Mauritania. MIFERMA alone was responsible for 28.5 million of a total electrical power consumption of 36.5 million kWh. in 1967, the remainder being supplied by the private company SAFELEC and used almost entirely for domestic usage and public lighting in the capital. There is also a water shortage, so serious that the setting up of a desalination plant is being considered at Nouakchott.

Only a few small light industries are planned for the future: the manufacture of loaf sugar from imported crystals, a flour-mill, an abattoir and a small textile complex. The founding of the port of Nouakchott established modern warehouses, especially for petroleum products, managed by the *Société mauritanienne d'entreposage des produits pétroliers* (SOMEPP) and approved in 1966. The building of Nouakchott and Zouérate has justified the work of the *Société d'urbanisme et de construction immobilière de Nouakchott* (SUCIN) which erected housing worth a total of 3,000 million francs CFA between 1959 and 1964.

INVESTMENT, PUBLIC FINANCE AND THE BALANCE OF PAYMENTS

Throughout the colonial period Mauritania, a "colony of little interest", was entitled to only very few investments by the mother country. From 1946 to 1959 Mauritania received about 3,800 million current francs CFA, through the colonial plans of FIDES. At the time of independence only 3 per cent of children in Mauritania attended school and there were no hospitals.

The first "plan" of 1960-62 raised the level of investments to a very high point: probably 25 per cent of the G.D.P. But this figure is misleading, resulting from the massive investments made by MIFERMA.

The second "plan" of 1963-67 maintained the volume of gross investments at an average of 22 per cent of the G.D.P., the average yearly investments having been of the order of 6,700 million francs, for an average product of 30,000 million. But here again, out of a total of 18,400 million francs of private investment, the mining sector accounted for 11,300. Public investment of the order of 8,300 million francs CFA (or 2,100 million a year) must be taken into account, representing seven per cent of the G.D.P. and a third of total public expenditure. The foreign debt, still very slight (6.5 per cent of the G.D.P. at the end of 1967), has not been substantially increased by the financing of public investment, 92 per cent of which has been provided by foreign aid, because aid has been chiefly in the form of grants from France (through the FAC) and Europe (through the EDF).

The 1970–73 plan gives priority to improving livestock quality, though considerable improvements to the fishing industry are also envisaged.

Although Mauritania's national accounts are extremely rudimentary, everything points to the fact that the proportion of the G.D.P. represented by government consumption has decreased very considerably over the past decade. In 1959 government consumption, 4,300 million francs, represented about 30 per cent of the G.D.P. (2,500 million on salaries, local and French, in all departments, and 1,800 million on current consumption of goods and services). Mauritania did not then seem "viable" without regular financial assistance. In 1968 the cost of services rose to 6,300 million francs, technical aid included, or 17 per cent of the G.D.P. The growth of public expenditure has in fact been curbed—4.2 per cent a year at current prices—whereas the growth of the G.D.P. has been of the order of 11 per cent (again at current prices) due to the working of the mines. Taxation revenue, increased by mining dues, has permitted not only the elimination of foreign "budgetary aid" but also the provision at certain times of surpluses that it has been possible to allot to the capital budget.

The country's national savings still amount to practically nothing. Public savings are almost nil:

an average of 160 million francs CFA a year from 1963 to 1967—barely 0.5 per cent of the G.D.P. Local private savings, supplying 2,400 million francs in the four years from 1963 to 1967, represent only 2 per cent of G.D.P. Foreign private capital and public aid alone continue to finance a growth still wholly supported from abroad.

The dependence of this growth on external factors is reflected in the increasing importance of exports in G.D.P. In 1959 total exports, reduced to the traditional products of cattle and gum, represented 22 per cent of G.D.P. Exports now usually represent 55–60 per cent of G.D.P., iron ore alone providing around 80 per cent of the total. This enormous growth in exports has so far warded off any balance of payments difficulties. For between 1959 and 1968 exports increased at an average yearly rate of 22 per cent, while imports increased at a far more modest 10 per cent, including MIFERMA imports, or 4 per cent excluding them. In 1959 the trade balance was very considerably in the red, imports being around 7,000 million francs and exports 3,200 million. The deficit was covered by current governmental aid and largely organized moreover within the federal framework of the A.O.F. Today the trade balance has an ample surplus (8,000 million francs) which is largely used to repay foreign capital invested in the country. Mauritania, once an undeveloped colonial reserve, is today more of an underdeveloped country. So import growth has moved parallel with export growth since 1965, that is, when the work of MIFERMA reached its operational levels. This explains why this rich mining country has only ludicrously few foreign assets (in 1968 Mauritania's reserves represented only 10 per cent of imports), which have moreover been halved since 1962.

The balance of payments does in fact show that the burden of the payments made to service the foreign capital is responsible for this disjointed and uneven growth and is far from negligible. Official foreign aid totalling some 2.3 thousand million francs is not nearly enough to offset transferred profits. It follows that if the trade surplus were to be reduced, the natural balance of payments deficit would be in danger of reaching alarming proportions. The development of copper in Akjoujt will most probably postpone this prospect, which none the less is inherent in the logic of "developing the underdeveloped".

STATISTICAL SURVEY

AREA AND POPULATION

The eight regions are known only by a number; the capital comprises a separate District.

REGIONS	CHIEF TOWN	AREA (sq. km.)	POPULATION (July 1972 estimate)
I	Néma . .	166,000	190,000
II	Aïoun El Alrouss	57,000	99,000
III	Kiffa . .	46,800	190,000
IV	Kaédi . .	14,100	95,000
V	Aleg . .	131,200	210,000
VI	Rosso . .	112,400	220,000
VII	Atar . .	471,200	89,000
VIII	Nouadhibou .	31,000	29,000
District	Nouakchott .	1,000	48,000
	TOTAL .	1,030,700	1,180,000

PRINCIPAL TOWNS
POPULATION (July 1972 estimates)

Nouakchott (capital) .	48,000	Kaédi	13,000
Nouadhibou (Port-Etienne)	20,000	Rosso	13,000
F'Derick (Fort-Gouraud) .	18,000	Atar	10,000

Births and Deaths: Average annual birth rate 44.4 per 1,000, death rate 22.7 per 1,000 (UN estimate for 1965–70).

EMPLOYMENT
(1972)

Agriculture	360,000
Wage and Salary Earners:	
Public Sector	11,000
Private Sector . . .	19,000

AGRICULTURE
LAND USE, 1964
('ooo hectares)

Arable Land	258
Land Under Permanent Crops . .	5
Permanent Meadows and Pastures .	39,250
Forest	15,134
Other Areas	48,423
TOTAL . . .	103,070

Source: FAO, Production Yearbook 1971.

PRINCIPAL CROPS
(metric tons)

	1969	1970	1971
Millet and Sorghum . . .	110,000	81,000	80,000*
Maize	4,000	4,000	3,000*
Rice	650	1,365	n.a.
Wheat	400	240	n.a.
Sweet Potatoes and Yams . .	3,000*	3,000*	n.a.
Cow Peas	10,000*	10,000	10,000*
Dates	13,000	15,000	15,000*
Groundnuts	1,000	3,000	n.a.

* FAO estimate.

Source: mainly FAO, *Production Yearbook 1971.*

LIVESTOCK
('000)

	1968–69	1969–70	1970–71
Cattle . . .	2,600*	2,660*	2,700*
Sheep . . .	2,700*	2,800*	2,900*
Goats . . .	2,300*	2,400*	2,450*
Asses . . .	220*	225*	230*
Horses . . .	21*	23*	24*
Camels . . .	685*	690*	700
Poultry . . .	2,400*	2,500	2,600

* FAO estimate.

Source: FAO, *Production Yearbook 1971.*

LIVESTOCK PRODUCTS
(FAO estimates, metric tons)

	1969	1970	1971
Cows' Milk . .	84,000	85,000	86,000
Sheep's Milk .	41,000	42,000	43,000
Goats' Milk . .	81,000	82,000	84,000
Hen Eggs . .	2,100	2,200	2,300

Source: FAO, *Production Yearbook 1971.*

FORESTRY
ROUNDWOOD PRODUCTION
(cubic metres)

1967 . . .	511,000
1968 . . .	521,000
1969 . . .	531,000

Source: FAO. *Yearbook of Forest Products.*

MINING
IRON ORE PRODUCTION
(gross weight, metric tons)*

1967 . . .	7,452,000
1968 . . .	7,704,000
1969 . . .	8,457,000
1970 . . .	9,118,000
1971 . . .	8,600,000

* The metal content is approximately 66 per cent.

Copper ore (1971): 5,340 metric tons; Salt (1969): 500 metric tons.

There are also plans for exploiting gypsum and titanium deposits.

Fishing: Total catch in 1967 was 30,700 metric tons (sea 17,700, inland water 13,000). Exports of fish: 31,500 metric tons in 1970; 22,600 metric tons in 1971.

Industry: Date packing, frozen meat, dried and frozen fish, matches, carpets, a national printing office and other light industrial enterprises.

FINANCE

100 centimes = 1 franc de la Communauté Financière Africaine.
Coins: 1, 2, 5, 10 and 25 francs CFA.
Notes: 50, 100, 500, 1,000 and 5,000 francs CFA.
Exchange rates (December 1972): 1 franc CFA = 2 French centimes.
£1 sterling = 593.625 francs CFA; U.S. $1 = 255.785 francs CFA.
1,000 francs CFA = £1.685 = $3.91.

Budget (1970 estimates): Balanced at 8,257 million francs CFA.
(1971 estimates): Balanced at 9,000 million francs CFA.
(1972 estimates): Balanced at 10,413.5 million francs CFA.

Development Budget (1972 estimate): 1,400 million francs CFA.

Currency in Circulation (March 1972): 2,143 million francs CFA.

NATIONAL ACCOUNTS

('000 million francs CFA at current prices)

	1959	1960	1961	1962	1966
Primary Production . .	10.3	10.6	11.2	11.0	11.8
Secondary Production . .	0.6	4.1	6.2	7.9	15.7
Tertiary Production . .	1.1	1.5	2.0	2.1	3.3
Administrative Salaries . .	2.5	3.2	3.4	3.4	3.8
GROSS DOMESTIC PRODUCT	14.5	19.4	22.8	24.4	34.6

1968: Gross Domestic Product 47,100 million francs CFA.

EXTERNAL TRADE*

(million francs CFA)

	1964	1965	1966	1967	1968	1969	1970
Imports . . .	3,879	5,864	5,523	9,105	8,713	11,764	13,138
Exports . . .	11,307	14,219	17,089	17,779	17,714	20,015	21,998

* Recorded transactions only. Trade crossing land frontiers is understated.

COMMODITIES

IMPORTS	1967	1968	1969
Food and Live Animals	1,457	2,137	n.a.
Cereals and preparations	416	557	669
Rice	384	489	n.a.
Sugar, sugar preparations and honey	454	807	819
Sugar and honey	452	804	n.a.
Tea and maté	420	604	n.a.
Mineral Fuels, Lubricants, etc.	333	646	658
Petroleum products	304	610	n.a.
Chemicals	424	338	n.a.
Basic Manufactures	1,761	1,783	n.a.
Articles of rubber	306	308	n.a.
Textile yarn, fabrics, etc.	285	196	n.a.
Iron and steel	392	580	1,008
Machinery and Transport Equipment	4,796	3,397	n.a.
Machinery (non-electric)	2,897	1,501	2,808
Electrical equipment	567	513	552
Railway vehicles	593	482	282
Road vehicles	710	591	1,029
Road motor vehicles	698	572	n.a.
TOTAL (incl. others)	9,105	8,713	11,764

EXPORTS	1967	1968	1969
Food and Live Animals	1,032	985	n.a.
Fish, fresh and simply preserved	1,023	971	1,158
Fish, salted, dried or smoked	513	574	685
Iron Ore and Concentrates	15,820	15,816	17,417
Natural Gums, Resins, etc.	411	427	n.a.
Machinery and Transport Equipment	399	283	n.a.
Machinery (non-electric)	142	126	n.a.
Aircraft	172	50	n.a.
TOTAL (incl. others)	17,779	17,714	20,015

Note: In addition, unrecorded exports of cattle had an estimated value of 2,070 million francs CFA in 1967.

1970: Recorded exports 21,998 million francs CFA, including: Iron ore 20,924 million. Estimated value of all exports (including trade with Mali and Senegal from February 1st) was 24,680 million francs CFA, of which: Iron ore 21,400 million; fish 2,030 million.

1971: Recorded exports of Iron ore 20,400 million francs CFA. Estimated value of all exports 25,129 million francs CFA, including: Iron ore 20,850 million; fish 2,140 million.

COUNTRIES

IMPORTS	1967	1968	1969
Belgium/Luxembourg	176	409	462
China, People's Republic	593	743	1,040
Congo (Brazzaville)	1	141	324
France	4,142	4,146	4,435
Germany, Federal Republic	357	367	568
Italy	296	149	98
Spain	133	124	377
United Kingdom	185	422	1,160
U.S.A.	2,173	1,218	1,686
TOTAL (incl. others)	9,105	8,713	11,764

EXPORTS	1967	1968	1969
Belgium/Luxembourg	2,153	2,572	2,424
Congo (Brazzaville)	459	490	566
France	3,669	3,300	3,935
Germany, Federal Republic	2,996	2,699	2,829
Italy	2,572	2,124	2,654
Japan	466	1,074	495
Netherlands	161	2	559
Senegal	6	47	470
Spain	828	521	766
United Kingdom	3,555	4,255	4,720
TOTAL (incl. others)	17,779	17,714	20,015

1971: Principal suppliers were France (40.7 per cent of total imports), the U.S.A. (18.0 per cent), the United Kingdom (7.2 per cent), Senegal (5.8 per cent) and Federal Germany (5.3 per cent).

1971: Principal clients were France (21.3 per cent of total exports), the United Kingdom (16.4 per cent), Belgium and Luxembourg (13.1 per cent), Federal Germany (11.6 per cent), Italy (11.5 per cent), Spain (8.6 per cent) and Japan (7.7 per cent).

Source (for commodity and country tables): UN, *Yearbook of International Trade Statistics 1969.*

TRANSPORT

Road Traffic (January 1st, 1972): 10,993 motor vehicles in use, including: 4,862 passenger cars; 5,768 vans and trucks.

Shipping (1971): 8,600,600 metric tons of iron ore and 7,393 metric tons of copper ore were exported through Point-Central and Nouakchott; 67,272 metric tons of other merchandise were exported through Nouadhibou; 63,800 metric tons of merchandise were imported through Nouakchott, while a further 15,500 metric tons entered through Point-Central and Nouadhibou.

Civil Aviation (1971): 96,030 passenger arrivals and departures; 3,031 tons of freight received and dispatched.

Tourist Accommodation: Nouakchott had 97 tourist hotel bedrooms in August 1972.

Education (1971–72): Primary Education 31,945 pupils; Secondary Education 3,745; Technical Education 234; 489 university students at institutes abroad.

Source (unless otherwise stated): Ministère de l'Information et de la Fonction Publique, Nouakchott.

SUMMARY OF THE CONSTITUTION

(Promulgated May 20th, 1961. Revised February 12th, 1965, July 12th, 1966, and February 1968.)

Sovereignty: The State is republican, indivisible, democratic and social. Islam is the religion, and there is freedom of conscience and of religious practice. Government resides in the Mauritanian people who exercise it through representatives and by referenda. Suffrage is universal, equal and secret. It is open to all Mauritanian citizens of both sexes who are over age, and who hold civil and political rights.

Government: The President decides and conducts the policy of the country. The sole candidate for the Presidency is appointed by the *Parti du peuple mauritanien* (*PPM*) and the President is elected by direct and universal suffrage for five years. The President orders the administration and the internal security forces, exercises power according to law, executes the laws, appoints state officials, and negotiates and concludes settlements with the Community and its member states. He nominates and dismisses the members of the government. The members of the government take the oath in front of the bureau of the National Assembly.

National Assembly: Legislative power belongs to the Assembly, which is elected for five years. All citizens of the Republic over 25 years of age, holding civil and political rights, are eligible for seats. The PPM is the only official party and institutionalized as such. The Assembly holds two ordinary sessions a year. The Assembly can hold a special session at the request of the President or of the majority of members.

The Supreme Court: Its organization and functions are determined by the Constitution.

Justice: The judiciary is independent of any other authorities. Judges may under certain circumstances be removed from office. Justice is administered in the name of the people of Mauritania. The President of the Republic is guarantor of the independence of the magistrature.

Local Government: The organs of local government are the region and the commune, administered by the local councils.

Revision: The power to revise the Constitution is in the hands of the Prime Minister and the members of the Assembly.

THE GOVERNMENT

HEAD OF STATE

President: MOKTAR OULD DADDAH (re-elected August 1966 and 1971).

CABINET
(*November 1972*)

President: MOKTAR OULD DADDAH.

Minister of Foreign Affairs: HAMDI OULD MOUKNASS.

Minister of National Defence: SIDI MOHAMED DIAGANA.

Guardian of the Seals and Minister of Justice: MOULOUM OULD BRAHAM.

Minister of the Interior: AHMED BEN AMAR.

Minister of Planning and Research: MOHAMED OULD CHEIKH SIDYA.

Minister of Finance: DIARAMOUNA SOUMARÈ.

Minister of Rural Development: DIOP MAMADOU AMADOU.

Minister of Industrialization and Mines: SIDI OULD CHEIKH ABDELLAHI.

Minister of Trade and Transport: AHEMDOU OULD ABDALLAH.

Minister of Equipment: ABDALLAH OULD DADDAH.

Minister of Culture and Information: AHMED OULD SIDI BABA.

Minister of Technical Education, Professional Training and Further Education: MOHAMEDEN BABAH.

Minister of Secondary Education, Youth and Sports: BA MAMADOU ALASSANE.

Minister of Religious Education and Religious Affairs: ABDALLAHI OULD BOYÉ.

Minister of Civil Service and Labour: BARO ABDOULAYE.

Minister of Health and Social Affairs: ABDALLAH OULD BAH.

DIPLOMATIC REPRESENTATION

EMBASSIES ACCREDITED TO MAURITANIA

(In Nouakchott unless otherwise stated)

Albania: Algiers, Algeria.
Algeria: Dakar, Senegal.
Austria: Dakar, Senegal.
Belgium: Dakar, Senegal.
Bulgaria: Bamako, Mali.
Canada: Dakar, Senegal.
China, People's Republic: B.P. 196; *Ambassador:* FENG YU-CHIU.
Czechoslovakia: Bamako, Mali.
Egypt: B.P. 176; *Ambassador:* AHMED MOHAMED TOHAMY.
France: B.P. 189; *Ambassador:* ADRIEN DUFOUR.
Gabon: *Ambassador:* JOSÉ AMIAR.
Germany, Federal Republic: *Ambassador:* WOLF VON ARNIM.
Ghana: Dakar, Senegal.
Guinea: *Ambassador:* EL HADJ M'BEMBA DIAKHABY.
Hungary: Conakry, Guinea.
India: Dakar, Senegal.
Italy: Dakar, Senegal.

Japan: Dakar, Senegal.
Khmer Republic: Dakar, Senegal.
Korea, Democratic People's Republic: Bamako, Mali.
Kuwait: *Ambassador:* NOURI ABDESSALAM CHOUAÏB.
Libya: *Ambassador:* MOHAMED AHMED ALMAGRAHI.
Mali: Dakar, Senegal.
Mongolia: Algiers, Algeria.
Morocco: *Ambassador:* MOHAMED MESFIOUI.
Netherlands: Dakar, Senegal.
Senegal: B.P. 611; *Ambassador:* ALIOUNE CISSE.
Spain: B.P. 232; *Ambassador:* DON JUAN ITURRALDE.
Switzerland: Dakar, Senegal.
Syria: *Ambassador:* (vacant).
Tunisia: Dakar, Senegal.
U.S.S.R.: B.P. 258; *Ambassador:* MIKHAILOVITCH LAVROJ.
United Kingdom: Dakar, Senegal.
United States: *Ambassador:* ROBERT STEIN.
Viet-Nam, Democratic Republic: Bamako, Mali.
Yugoslavia: Dakar, Senegal.

Mauritania also has diplomatic relations with Cameroon, Ivory Coast, Jordan, Lebanon, Romania, Saudi Arabia, Sudan and the Provisional Revolutionary Government of the Republic of South Viet-Nam.

PARLIAMENT

NATIONAL ASSEMBLY

(*General Election of August* 1971)

President: DA OULD SIDI HAÏBA.
Composition: all 50 members belong to the *Parti du peuple mauritanien.*

POLITICAL PARTY

Parti du peuple mauritanien (PPM): B.P. 61, Nouakchott; f. 1961 by coalition of the *Parti du regroupement mauritanien, Union nationale mauritanienne, Nahda* and *Union des socialistes musulmans mauritaniens;* the only recognized party; National Political Bureau of 15 mems.; Sec.-Gen. MOKTAR OULD DADDAH; Perm. Sec. ABDOUL AZIZ SALL.

DEFENCE

The total armed forces number 1,530 of which the Army numbers 1,400, the Navy 30 and the air force 100. There is a gendarmerie of 500 and a civil police of 1,000. Compulsory military service was introduced in 1962.

Chief of Staff of the Army: Capt. MAUSTAPHA OULD MOHAMED SALECK.

JUDICIAL SYSTEM

Supreme Court: Nouakchott; f. 1961; intended to ensure the independence of the judiciary; the Supreme Court is competent in electoral matters; Pres. AHMED OULD MOHAMED SALAH; Vice-Pres. ABDULLAH OULD BOYÉ.

High Court of Justice: consists of a President, who is a stipendiary magistrate, and eleven other judges, six of whom are elected by the National Assembly from amongst its members, and five of whom are elected by the Assembly from a list of Islamic lawyers.

The Code of Law was founded in 1961 and subsequently modified to integrate modern law with Muslim institutions and practices. Seventy-five per cent of the Magistrature and all clerks of the court are now Mauritanian nationals. The main courts are: a *tribunal de premier instance* (Magistrate's court) with six regional sections, 42 *tribunaux de cadis* (departmental civil courts), labour courts, military courts and the Court of State Security.

RELIGION

The population is almost entirely Muslim of the Malekite sect, less than 1 per cent being Christian. The most important of the religious groups is that of the Qadiriya (Leader M. OULD SHEIKH SIDYA). Chinguetti, in the district of Adrar, is the seventh Holy Place in Islam. The very few Roman Catholics, who are mainly aliens, come under the jurisdiction of the Archbishop of Nouakchott, MICHEL BERNARD.

PRESS

Journal Officiel: Ministry of Justice, Nouakchott; twice monthly.

Nouakchott Information: Direction de l'Information, Nouakchott; daily.

Le Peuple: P.P.M., Nouakchott; bi-monthly in French and Arabic.

NEWS AGENCY

Agence France-Presse: B.P. 217, Nouakchott; Correspondent JEAN-MARIE BLIN.

RADIO

Radiodiffusion Nationale de Mauritanie: B.P. 200, Nouakchott; four transmitters, two of 30 kW.; broadcasts in French, Arabic, Wolof, Toucouleur and Sarakolé; advertising is accepted; Dir. MOHAMED OULD WEDADY; Sec.-Gen. YAHYA OULD ABDI.

Number of radio receivers: 75,000.

There is no television.

FINANCE

BANKING

CENTRAL BANK

Banque Centrale des Etats de l'Afrique de l'Ouest: 29 rue du Colisée, Paris 8e, France; B.P. 227, Nouakchott; f. 1955; Man. for Mauritania P. BRAEMER.

Banque Internationale pour l'Afrique Occidentale: 9 ave de Messine, Paris 8e, France; Nouakchott; offices also at Nouadhibou, Rosso, Zouérate and Akjoujt.

Banque Mauritanienne de Développement: B.P. 219, Nouakchott; f. 1962; cap. francs CFA 200m. of which 58 per cent state-owned.

Société Mauritanienne de Banque: B.P. 614, ave. Gamal Abdel Nasser, Nouakchott; f. 1967; owned by the state and several foreign banks; cap. 50m. francs CFA; Pres. ROGER DUCHEMIN; Dir. MARCEL VIELLET.

DEVELOPMENT

Société d'équipement de la Mauritanie: B.P. 28, Nouakchott; f. 1964; the state holds a majority interest; Pres. and Dir.-Gen. MAMADOU CISSOKO.

INSURANCE

Cie. d'Assurances Générales: Nouadhibou.

Société Africaine d'Assurances: c/o Société Commerciale de Transports Transatlantiques, Nouadhibou.

TRADE AND INDUSTRY

CHAMBER OF COMMERCE

Chambre de Commerce, d'Agriculture, d'Elevage, d'Industrie et de Mines de la Mauritanie: Nouakchott, B.P. 215; f. 1954; Pres. SIDI EL MOKTAR N'DIAYE; Sec.-Gen. ELIMANE ABOU KANE; publ. *Bulletin* (twice monthly).

INDUSTRIAL ORGANIZATIONS

Société Mixte d'Importation et d'Exportation (SONIMEX): B.P. 290, Nouakchott; f. 1966; holds a monopoly of imports of consumer goods such as rice, tea, sugar and exports of gum-arabic; cap. 500m. francs CFA; Dir.-Gen. AHMED OULD DADDAH.

Union Nationale des Industriels, Commercants et Entrepreneurs de Mauritanie (UNICEMA): B.P. 383, Nouakchott; f. 1958; Pres. G. ESQUILAT, Sec.-Gen. J. MALVAES.

TRADE UNIONS

A National Commission of Trade Union Reconciliation was set up at the end of 1970 to resolve the split in the *Union des Travailleurs de Mauritanie* caused by the opposition of some unions to affiliation to the ruling PPM.

Union des Travailleurs de Mauritanie: B.P. 63, Bourse du Travail, Nouakchott; f. 1961 by merger of *Union Nationale des Travailleurs de Mauritanie;* and *Union Générale des Travailleurs de Mauritanie;* 10,000 mems.; affiliated to ICFTU; Sec.-Gen. MALIK FALL.

Unions affiliated to the Union des Travailleurs de Mauritanie:

Fédération du Commerce et de l'Alimentation: f. 1963.

Fédération de la Construction: f. 1963.

Fédération de l'Education Nationale: f. 1963.

Fédération de la Santé: f. 1963.

Fédération des Mines et des Industries Extractives: f. 1963.

Fédération de l'Administration Intérieure: f. 1963.

Fédération des Activités Rurales: f. 1963.

Fédération des Transports et Télécommunications: f. 1963.

MAJOR INDUSTRIAL COMPANIES

Frigorifique Survif: B.P. 87, Nouadhibou; f. 1963; cap. 350m. francs CFA.
Canning of fish; 150 employees.

Industries Mauritaniennes de Pêche S.A.: B.P. 100, Nouadhibou; f. 1966; cap. 2,000m. francs CFA.
Industrial fishing, fishmeal canning, freezing and drying fish.
Pres. J. MORALES SANCHEZ; Dir. J. M. PORTO ROMERO; 1,100 employees.

Société Mauritanienne d'Entreposage de Produits Pétroliers (MEPP): B.P. 340, Nouakchott; f. 1966; cap. 86m. francs CFA.
Petroleum stockage.
Pres. P. AMEYE; Dir. MARTIN CRISTIANI.

Société Mauritanienne des Gaz Industriels: B.P. 39, Nouadhibou; f. 1966; cap. 40m. francs CFA.
Manufacture of industrial gases.
Pres. PAUL LALAGUE; Dir. DANIEL BENDER.

MINERALS

DEVELOPMENT

Société Nationale Industrielle et Minière: Nouakchott; f. 1972; national company for State intervention in research, exploitation and transformation of minerals.

IRON ORE

Société Anonyme des Mines de fer de Mauritanie (MIFERMA): 87 rue la Boétie, Paris 8e; B.P. 42, Nouadhibou; F'Dérik; 200 millions tons of iron ore are known to be available for immediate exploitation, of comparable quality to Swedish ores, yielding 66 per cent pure iron; capital 13,300m. francs CFA; Hon. Pres. LEROY BEAULIEU; Pres. Delegate JEAN AUDIBERT.

Ownership:		Per cent
Mauritanian Government .	.	5.00
French Bureau of Geological and Mining Research	.	23.89
French Steel Concerns	.	9.49
French Financial Concerns .	.	22.42
British Steel Corporation	.	19.00
Italian FINSIDER Group .	.	15.20
German THYSSEN Group .	.	5.00

COPPER ORE

Société Minière de Mauritanie (SOMIMA): B.P. 275, Nouakchott; f. 1967; exploitable reserves are estimated at 7.7m. tons; a total investment of U.S.$6om. is anticipated; cap. 2,000m. francs CFA; initial production was expected to be at an annual rate of 28,000 tons of copper-in-concentrates; Pres. MOHAMED BA.

Ownership:		Per cent
Mauritanian Government .	.	22.00
Charter Consolidated Ltd.	.	44.60
S.F.I.	.	15.00
Société Min. et Mét. de Penarroya	.	6.57
B.R.G.M.	.	6.13
Cie. Fin de Paris et des Pays-Bays	.	3.77
Cofimer .	.	1.93

OIL

Prospecting is being undertaken by the Planet Oil and Mineral Corpn., Texas, U.S.A.

TITANIUM

Syndicat de Recherches d'Ilménite: Paris; Nouakchott; joint venture of the French Bureau of Geological and Mining Research and Etablissements Kuhlmann; proved deposits of 4m. tons of mineral sands.

TRANSPORT

RAILWAYS

A railway connecting Nouadhibou with Tazadit and the new iron ore fields at F'Dérik was opened in 1963 and is 650 km. long. Known as the Miferma railway, it is used primarily for transporting iron ore to the coast.

S.A. des Mines de Fer de Mauritanie: 87 rue de la Boétie, Paris 8e, France; owns the railway.

ROADS

There are about 6,200 km. of roads and tracks including 560 km. of tarred road. Two important routes have recently been completed (Nouakchott–Rosso, Nouakchott–Akjoujt) and another is under construction (Kaédi–Kiffa).

Etablissements Lacombe et Cie.: B.P. 204, Nouakchott; road transport.

INLAND WATERWAYS

Messageries du Sénégal: Saint Louis (Senegal); the river Senegal is navigable by small coastal vessels as far as Kayes (Mali) and by river vessels as far as Kaédi in the wet season; in the dry season as far as Rosso and Boghe, respectively.

SHIPPING

Nouadhibou (Port Etienne)

Compagnie Pacquet, Société Navale Delmas et Vieljeux and S.N.I.E

Several shipping companies serve Nouadhibou and Nouakchott, the most important being La Compagnie Paquet and La Compagnie Maurel-Prom.

The Nouadhibou development programme, which will make the port one of the most important in Africa, is estimated to cost £50 million. The port of Nouakchott is also being developed, to handle the copper from Akjoujt.

CIVIL AVIATION

There are two airfields, at Nouadhibou and Nouakchott, and a number of smaller airstrips.

Air Mauritanie: B.P. 41, Nouakchott; f. 1963; scheduled domestic services from Nouakchott and Nouadhibou and international services to Dakar, Las Palmas and Casablanca; 170 employees; fleet of one IL-18, one DC-4, three DC-3 and one Navajo; Dir.-Gen. AHMED OULD BAH.

Air Afrique: Mauritania has a seven per cent share in Air Afrique; *see* under Ivory Coast.

Mauritania is also served by the following airlines: Iberia and Union des Transports Aériens (UTA).

TOURISM

The Secretariat General of Traditional Crafts and Tourism at the Presidency of the Republic is responsible for the development of tourism in Mauritania.

Secrétariat Général à l'Artisanat et au Tourism: B.P. 246, Nouakchott; f. 1962; Sec.-Gen. ABEIDY OULD GOURIABY.

POWER

Société Mauritanienne d'Electricité: B.P. 355, Nouakchott; f. 1968; cap. 88m. francs CFA.
Production of electricity and water.
Pres. MOHAMED LEMINE OULD LIMAN; Dir. J. J. LAPARRE.

EDUCATION

Education in Mauritania has expanded rapidly since 1960. In that year there were 156 primary schools and 7,500 pupils, in 1964 250 schools with 19,105 pupils, and by 1970 690 classes with 31,925 pupils. The number of secondary school students has risen from 1,306 in 1963 to 3,650 in 1972. There are nine secondary schools and three technical schools. Classes are given chiefly in French, to meet the requirements of modern industrial and economic development but Arabic has also been an official language since 1967 and is an essential subject for the Baccalauréat. It is intended that all schools use both languages. The traditional Arab culture of the *marabout* priests is encouraged, and there are over 100 such teachers, as well as a number of others giving instruction in Arabic in government schools in the south of the country, where the population is dominantly negro.

A bilingual teacher-training college has been opened at Nouakchott and an Ecole normale supérieure took its first students in 1971. The Institute of Islamic Studies at Boutilimit, founded in 1961, is attended by 200–300 students, including some from Senegal, Mali and Nigeria. Plans are in hand to expand the capacity to 1,000. About 200 students attend foreign universities especially in France, Senegal and the U.S.S.R.

In spite of the big expansion of education, only about 12 per cent of the population of Mauritania is literate.

Successful experiments have been carried out in setting up nomadic schools which travel with the tribes who make up the great majority of the population, and it may be expected that this will lead to increased expansion of educational facilities.

RESEARCH INSTITUTES

Direction des Mines et de l'Industrie: B.P. 199, Nouakchott; Dir. Y. BARBIER.

Station du Palmier-Dattier de Kankossa: Kankossa, via Kiffa; attached to the Institut Français de Recherches Fruitières Outre-Mer; Dir. P. MUNIER.

Stations de recherche agronomique: Aïoun el Atrouss (agriculture), Akjoujt, Kaédi (pedology), Kankossa (dates; run by the French Institute for Overseas Fruit Research), M'Baika (research is devoted chiefly to three fields: soil improvement, livestock diseases, and fruit and arable seed selection).

LIBRARIES

Arab Library: Boutilimit; library of the late Grand Marabout, Abd Allah Ould Cheikh Sidya.

Arab Library: Chinguetti; several private religious libraries, totalling 3,229 vols., including pre-Islamic MSS.; Librarian MOHAMED ABDALLAHI OULD FALL.

Arab Library: Kaédi; ancient religious texts.

Arab Library: Mederdra; Librarian MOHAMED ABDARRAHMANE OULD SALEK.

Arab Library: Oualata.

Arab Library: Tidjikja; Librarian AHMEDOU OULD MOHAMED MAHMOUD.

Bibliothèque Nationale: B.P. 20 Nouakchott; dependent on Ministry of Cultural Affairs; f. 1965; depository for all the country's publications; documentation centre for western Africa; 10,000 vols., collection of over 4,000 old MSS.; 8 mems.; Head Librarian OUMAR DIOUWARA; Historian Prof. MOKTAR OULD HAMIDOU.

Bibliothèque Publique Centrale: B.P. 77, Nouakchott.

Centre de Documentation Pédagogique: B.P. 171, Nouakchott; f. 1962; 1,000 vols., 58 periodicals; educational and general works; Librarian MOHAMMED SAID.

Mauritanian Library of IFAN: Pointe Sud, Saint-Louis, Senegal; f. 1943; 4,025 vols., 180 periodicals; covers the early history and natural resources of the country.

National Administrative and Historical Library: B.P. 77, Nouakchott; f. 1955; 1,000 vols., 50 periodicals; Librarian LIRVANE N'GAM.

COLLEGE

Institut national des hautes études islamiques: Boutilimit; f. 1961; 300 students. An expansion programme is in hand to bring the capacity to 1,000 students.

SELECT BIBLIOGRAPHY

(For works on the former A.O.F. countries generally *see* Dahomey Select Bibliography, p. 297.)

DESIRÉ-VUILLEMIN, GENEVIÈVE. *Contribution à l'histoire de la Mauritanie de 1900 à 1934*. Dakar, Clairafrique, 1962.

EAGLETON, WILLIAM. "The Islamic Republic of Mauritania". *Middle East Journal*, 19/1, 1965.

GARNIER, CHRISTINE, and ERMONT, PHILIPPE. *Désert fertile: une nouvelle état, la Mauritanie*. Paris, Hachette, 1960.

GERTEINY, A. G. *Mauritania*. London, Pall Mall, New York, Praeger, 1967.

HARRISON CHURCH, R. J. "Port Etienne—A Mauritanian Pioneer Town". *Geographical Journal*, pp. 498–504. London, December, 1962.

HILLING, D. "Saharan Iron Ore Oasis", *Geographical Magazine*, pp. 908–917, September, 1969.

TOUPET, C. "Les grands straits de la République Islamique de Mauritanie". *L'Information Géographique*. Paris, 1962.

TOUPET, C. "Nouadhibou (Port Etienne) and the Economic Development of Mauritania", in Hoyle, B. S., and Hilling, D. (Eds.) *Ports and Development in Tropical Africa*, Chapter 3. London, 1970.

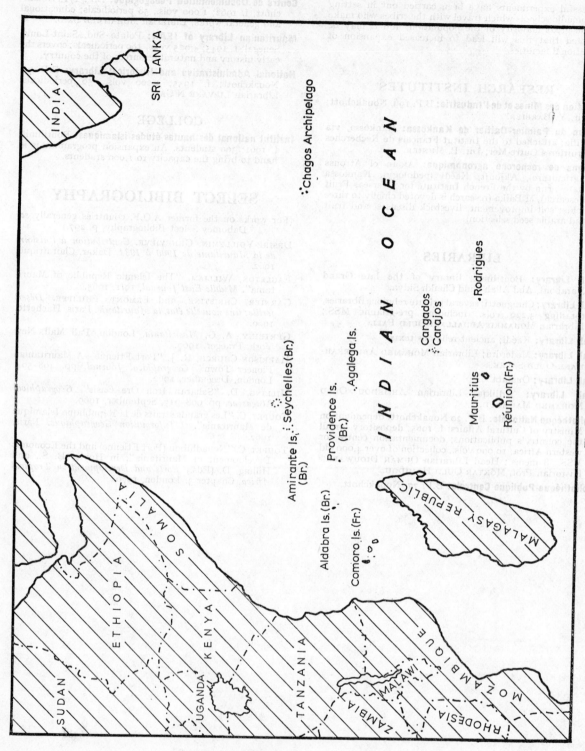

The Indian Ocean islands

Mauritius

PHYSICAL AND SOCIAL GEOGRAPHY

E. C. Dommen*

The island of Mauritius lies in the Indian Ocean 500 miles east of Madagascar (20° S., 57° E.), 720 sq. miles in area. It is volcanic, consisting of a plain rising from the north-east to the Piton de la Petite Rivière Noire (2,711 ft.) in the south-west, broken by abrupt volcanic peaks and gorges, and is almost completely surrounded by a coral reef. Including other islands, mainly Rodrigues, the whole country has an area of 789 square miles.

The climate is sub-tropical maritime, but with two distinct seasons; furthermore, the warm dry coastal areas contrast with the cool rainy centre. Mauritius, like Rodrigues, is liable to cyclones, particularly between December and March.

The island's population (whose composition is detailed in the Statistical Survey, p. 570) is 830,606 (December 1971), giving a density of 1,154 per sq. mile. The annual rate of growth of population fell steadily from over 3 per cent in 1963 to 1.62 per cent in 1968, partly through increasing emigration (4,585 net in 1968 compared to 252 in 1963) and partly through a birth-rate declining from 39.9 per thousand in 1963 to 25 per thousand in 1971. Over 44 per cent of the population inhabit the urban area extending from

Port Louis—the capital and business centre—on the north-east coast to Curepipe in the centre.

1,143 ships visited Port Louis in 1971 compared to about 700 per annum in the years immediately before the closing of the Suez Canal, although the volume of freight unloaded has remained constant. 1,196 airplanes landed in 1971, depositing 58,348 passengers.

Mauritius is linked to the rest of the world by cable, radio and radio telephone, operated and maintained by Cable & Wireless Ltd. The company has installations in Port Louis and Rodrigues.

Rodrigues, a volcanic island of 42 sq. miles surrounded by coral reef, 350 miles east of Mauritius (19° S., 63° E.), is an integral part of the state of Mauritius. Its population (estimate, June 1970) is about 22,000.

Mauritius has two dependencies: *Agalega*, two islands with a total area of 27 sq. miles and some 400 inhabitants, 700 miles north of Mauritius (10° S., 56° E.); and *St. Brandon* (or Cargados Carajos), 22 islets without permanent inhabitants but used as a fishing station, 250 miles north-north-east of Mauritius (16° S., 59° E.).

* Although the author is on the Commonwealth Secretariat, the views he expresses here are entirely his own.

RECENT HISTORY

Adele Simmons

EARLY HISTORY

Arab and Portuguese traders used Mauritius as a fuelling place, and the Dutch tried twice in the seventeenth century to begin settlements on the island, but the first permanent inhabitants of Mauritius were settlers from France. These settlers brought with them slaves from east Africa and Madagascar, whose descendents comprise 28 per cent of the Mauritian population.

In 1810, the British captured Mauritius from France, and when slavery was abolished in the colonies in 1831, the Franco-Mauritian planters turned to India for labour. By 1861, 192,000 Indians accounted for nearly two-thirds of the island's population. Nearly three-quarters of the Indian population was Hindu. Muslim indentured labourers and Muslim traders formed a minority within the Indian population.

The history of the indenture system was long and unhappy. Laws to protect the immigrants were few, poorly defined, and rarely enforced. In spite of occasional efforts to reform the labour laws, the injustices continued until immigration was officially ended in 1913.

CONSTITUTIONAL HISTORY

Prior to 1848, Mauritius' constitutional history was far from complex. The first Council of Government, established in 1825, included five official members of the government. In 1831, responding to petitions from the sugar planters, the Secretary of State for the Colonies expanded the council to include seven official members and seven unofficial members, who were to represent the most prominent planters and merchants of the island. A constitutional reform in 1885, introduced under the governorship of John Pope-Hennessy, only strengthened the planter élite by limiting the franchise to those who met rigid property and income requirements.

Political alliances in Mauritius prior to 1935 were based on friendship rather than issues, and were confined primarily to the Franco-Mauritian and Creole élite. With few exceptions, the Indians were excluded from politics.

BEGINNINGS OF NATIONALISM

In 1936, an articulate Creole medical doctor, Maurice Curé, founded the Mauritius Labour Party, the island's first political party. Basing his programme on that of the British Labour Party, Curé told the labourers that they were entitled to higher wages, better housing, improved hospital care and the right to form trade unions. Curé presented petitions to the governor asking that the labourers be represented in the Council of Government, that the franchise be extended to include the working classes, and that labour laws be changed to conform to International Labour Organisation conventions. While the government dismissed Curé as a "haphazard demagogue"* and a "windbag",† Curé built a constituency among the labourers and the small planters on the estates. The labourers' grievances were ignored, and rioting broke out in August 1937. Six people were killed as labourers refused to report to work, sabotaged factories, and burned cane fields.

The 1937 riots pointed to the need for strong and representative labour organizations and mechanisms for including the Indian community in Mauritian politics. But it was not until 1945 that leading representatives of all interested groups and communities met with the govenor to make recommendations for constitutional revision. As promulgated in 1947, the new constitution provided for a Legislative Council of 34: 19 elected members, 12 nominated members, and 3 official members. Men and women over 21 who could prove they could write simple sentences in any language could vote.

The constitution forced a complete realignment in Mauritian politics. The wide franchise ensured that the Franco-Mauritians would lose their control of elective politics, and promised a new role for the Indians. Of the elected members, only one was Franco-Mauritian, while seven were Creole, and ten were Indians of Hindu religion, and mostly men with professional training.

Between 1948 and 1959, the Indian community consolidated its political strength. Seewoosagur Ramgoolam, an Indian doctor who had been an early supporter of the Labour Party, assumed leadership of the party in the Legislative Council. And in the 1955 election, the Labour Party, still an alliance of the Creole working class and the Indian intellectuals and labourers, won 13 of the 19 seats.

Following the 1955 elections, the Labour Party demanded constitutional change that would guarantee universal adult suffrage, the introduction of the ministerial system, and a clear limitation of the government's powers. Two London conferences, the visit of an electoral commission, and intense political debate between the Labour Party and the party of the Franco-Mauritian and Creole élite, the *Ralliement mauricien* (later the *Parti mauricien*), over the nature of the electoral system, preceded the publication of a new constitution in 1959. At the same time, two new special interest parties were formed: the Independent Forward Bloc, a rural based Hindu party which felt the Labour Party was too élitist,

and the Muslim Committee of Action, which sought to forward the interests of the Muslim community. The Muslim Committee of Action allied with the Labour Party in the 1959 elections to win 23 of the 40 elected seats.

Between 1960 and 1965, Mauritius progressed steadily towards independence. The principle of full internal self-government was approved by the Secretary of State at a conference in London in 1961, and in spite of internal division and economic crises, Ramgoolam's Labour Party remained the strongest single party in the Legislative Assembly following the 1963 elections.

But opposition to the Labour Party, and to independence in particular, was crystallizing. By 1963 the *Parti mauricien*, led by a young and charismatic barrister, Gaeton Duval, was expanding to include the Creole lower class. Duval appealed directly to all Creoles to support him and oppose independence, which, he feared, would lead to Hindu domination. Duval's own communalism was but one source of new tension in Mauritius. Uncertainty and fear led to violence in the south in May 1965, as well as a breakdown of co-operation between the *Parti mauricien* and the Labour Party in the all-party government.

The political question that obsessed Mauritian politicians was the future status of the island. It was to settle this issue that the Secretary of State called a constitutional conference in London in September 1965. While the Labour Party, supported somewhat ambivalently by the Muslim Committee of Action and the Independent Forward Bloc, favoured independence, the *Parti mauricien* put forward a complicated economic argument in favour of "association" with Great Britain. After three weeks of debate, the Secretary of State cleared the way for independence. If, following a general election, the majority of the Assembly asked for independence, independence would be granted. Although the *Parti mauricien* waged an impressive campaign, the election was decisive. With solid Hindu backing, considerable Muslim support, and some Creole votes, Ramgoolam's newly formed Independence Party‡ won 39 seats. In March 1968 Ramgoolam became the country's first Prime Minister.

INDEPENDENCE

Independence, which started off ominously in 1968, has brought changes. The economy has been helped by the closing of the Suez Canal and by agreements permitting the Russians to use the port. In 1970 Mauritius became a member of the *Organisation commune africaine et malgache* (OCAM). In addition, Ramgoolam brought the *Parti mauricien* into the government, creating a coalition of all communal groups. Duval and his ministers became responsible for the areas in which they had been most critical of the government: foreign affairs and development. Following a split within the *Parti mauricien*,

---

* C.O. 167/890, file 57004, Minute by C. Carstairs, Assistant Principal, Colonial Office, April 18th, 1936.

† C.O. 167/897, file 57227, Minute by Dawe, Principal, Colonial Office, October 26th, 1937.

‡ The Independence Party was an alliance of the Labour Party, the Muslim Committee of Action, and the Independent Forward Bloc.

Duval resigned as Foreign Minister in November 1970, but has maintained his position of political influence in Port Louis.

Recently, the strongest opposition to the government has come from a new political organization, the Movement Militant Mauricienne (MMM), organized by Paul Beranger, a young Franco-Mauritian who had participated in the student strikes in Paris in 1968. Returning to Mauritius, Beranger criticized the government for its failure to distribute incomes more equitably in Mauritius and for the extravagances of the Mauritian ministers. He commented harshly on the close relationship between the government and the unions. Beranger's support came from Mauritian youth of all groups: Hindu, Creole and Muslim. The MMM followers were bright and energetic; they edited a provocative newspaper, *Le Militant*, which was the only newspaper to actively criticize the government.

The potential influence of the MMM was not recognized until September 1970. At that time a by-election was held in Triolet—Ramgoolam's constituency—for one of the three electoral seats from that district. The government candidate, an older man who owned a bus company, was soundly defeated by Der Veraswamy, a young, energetic MMM member. The victory in Triolet led Beranger to call for national elections. The government response, however, was to uphold its earlier agreement with Duval and maintain that elections had legally been postponed until 1976.

Elections were unlikely, and Beranger began to organize the trade unions. By December 1971, the peak of MMM power, the MMM claimed control of three of the major unions in the sugar industry, the bus unions, the teachers' and the hospital workers,

unions. But it was the relationship between the MMM and the dockers that led to the greatest dispute.

In August 1971, the dockers went on strike. Most of the strikers were MMM supporters but, once the strike began, Beranger lost control. While Beranger saw the danger of a dock strike that was "too effective", he could not persuade the dockers to return to work.

Eventually, Ramgoolam declared a State of Emergency, sealed off the docks and brought in strike breakers, but not before the inconveniences and hardships caused by the 40-day strike became acute. The shortages of milk, eggs, meat and other supplies were soon blamed on the MMM.

The government arrested Beranger and the other MMM leaders and held them for 20 days. MMM supporters lost their jobs on the docks; public meetings were banned; a State of Emergency continued into 1972. In March 1972, 120 key leaders in the MMM were arrested in an effort to ensure that the MMM would not disrupt a scheduled visit by the Queen. At the end of 1972, 27 MMM leaders remained in jail. In the face of the strong government crack down, sharp differences within the MMM leadership appeared.

By the close of 1972 the MMM was severely weakened. Ramgoolam remains in control of the political machinery of the island, and his position has been strengthened by a 700,000-ton sugar crop and rising sugar prices. Even so, many fear that the government is held together largely through the strength of Ramgoolam's personality and will not, therefore, survive him. A smooth transition following Ramgoolam's departure from politics will be essential to political stability in Mauritius. For in Mauritius, as in other plural societies, political tensions can and do elicit primary, in this case ethnic or religious, loyalties that can divide the country.

ECONOMY*

E. C. Dommen†

The Gross National Product of Mauritius in 1968 was Rs. 840 million (Rs. 1,086 per head), entirely generated in the cash economy—there is no subsistence sector. Income per head has been roughly stagnant in money terms (it was Rs. 1,062 in 1953) but it fluctuates widely according to the weather and sugar prices. It was, for instance, Rs. 1,283 in 1963—exceptionally good weather and high world sugar prices—and Rs. 827 in 1960—two exceptionally damaging cyclones.

Gross investment amounts to about 20 per cent of G.N.P. The total amount fell from a peak of Rs. 177 million in 1964 (following the 1963 sugar boom) to

* Although Rodrigues is an integral part of the state of Mauritius, most economic data refer to the island of Mauritius only. The figures in this section therefore refer to the island only, unless stated otherwise.

† For the 1973 edition, revisions have been made to this article by the Editor.

Rs. 141 million in 1968. Construction of dwellings has remained around one-quarter of the total but the proportion of directly productive investment has fallen.

The economy is very open; visible exports have amounted typically to around 40 per cent of G.N.P. and visible imports to 45 per cent. The deficit has been met mainly by aid, in particular from Britain, though, owing to the buoyancy of the sugar market, a 1972 balance of payments surplus of about Rs. 100 million was expected. In 1968 Mauritius imported Rs. 421 million worth of goods. Of these, manufactures amounted to Rs. 119.6 million, and revenue to Rs. million. Rice, the staple food, is almost entirely imported; this cost Rs. 56 million. In 1971 rice imports fell to Rs. 31 million out of total imports to the value of Rs. 462 million.

A four-year Development Plan (1971–75) was

drawn up for the public sector, allowing for expenditure of Rs. 660 million over the total period. Current expenditure for the year ending December 1971 amounted to Rs. 119.6 million, and revenue to Rs. 135.6 million. Capital expenditure of Rs. 34.8 million represented only 23 per cent of the sum projected for the year as a whole. The slow performance in the first year of the plan is accounted for by Mauritius' low capacity for absorption rather than by inadequate financial resources. Of the planned capital expenditure for the first year of the Plan, Rs. 17 million was to be devoted to a scheme for relieving the massive unemployment problem, and the rest, in large part, to water supply and port development and to agricultural and fisheries projects.

Exports are dominated by sugar and molasses. Of visible exports in 1968 of Rs. 354 million, sugar and molasses were Rs. 333 million (93.9 per cent). Tea has been growing in importance, rising from Rs. 5.5 million in 1963 to Rs. 9.6 million in 1968. "Other" exports, a useful indicator of the success of Mauritius' diversification efforts since it includes the newer agricultural and industrial exports, has grown erratically but rapidly from Rs. 1.8 million in 1963 to Rs. 4 million in 1968.

The sugar industry directly generates about one-third of both G.N.P. and employment. 621,087 tons of sugar were produced in 1971, while production was expected to total 675,000 tons in 1972. Sugar cultivators can be divided into millers and planters. The millers control the 22 estates with factories; these factories also process the cane grown by the 29,000 planters who cultivate almost half the area under sugar. Some 70,000 workers are employed during the crop season. Of the total tonnage of sugar exported—530–600,000 tons per year—about two-thirds is sold to Britain under the Commonwealth Sugar Agreement; a further 17,000 tons is sold to the U.S.A. at a similar price and the remainder is sold as far as possible at preferential prices to the U.K., Canada or elsewhere. Unusually heavy rains in August indicated a drop in the production of the processed crop for 1972.

Aloe fibre, from wild plants for the most part, is used in the manufacture of sacks at the Government Sack Factory for the transport of sugar from the sugar mills to the docks and for the import of rice and flour. Given the changing methods of handling sugar the future of the industry is precarious. It produces some 1,400 tons per year and is estimated to provide employment for some 2,500 families.

The sugar industry was for a long time able to provide employment and a reasonable average income per head (compared to other less developed countries) for the people, but the industry is reaching the limits of possible expansion and can no longer keep pace with the growth in population. Unemployment is therefore growing; it may now exceed 26,000 out of a working population of some 210,000. The overriding need is therefore to diversify into activities providing employment and—given the density of population—a high yield in value added per acre. Mauritius' application for association with the EEC is relevant in this context.

Tea grows in the humid highlands, which are unsuitable for sugar. It has been cultivated since the eighteenth century on a limited scale, but since 1959 the government has been expanding the area and distributing it to smallholders grouped into co-operatives. The area under tea has grown from 4,000 acres in 1959 to 10,800 in 1968, producing 2,288 tons of manufactured tea, of which 1,700 tons worth Rs. 9.6 million were exported. The government appointed a Tea Development Authority in 1971, whose work is partly financed by World Bank investment.

The cultivation of food crops is becoming more widespread, usually in intercrop or interline with sugar. In particular, there have been increases in the production of tomatoes (from 5,456 tons in 1964 to 8,780 tons in 1968) and maize (25 to 376 tons). There has also been some increase in export crops although these are on a very small scale (e.g. ginger, from 469 to 882 tons). The production of potatoes rose from 5,930 tons in 1964 to 9,578 in 1968, but fell again to 5,200 tons in 1969. An agricultural marketing board was established in 1964; its impact on the development of foodcrop cultivation has been considerable. Research, which although of a high standard had until recently been entirely concentrated on sugar, is now being conducted into food crops as well. Pilot rice schemes are under way and experiments are being conducted into oilseeds to feed a projected mill (there is already an edible oil refinery).

Tobacco, a long-established crop, has expanded to the point where the local output of cigarettes is composed entirely of local tobacco, apart from certain luxury grades. Output in 1971 was 562 tons.

Some 2,000 fishermen are engaged in inshore fishing, but of these only one-quarter can be regarded as full-time professionals. Over-population and unemployment has led to over-fishing, and the total catch is declining. Oysters are being developed for export.

Deep sea fishing to supply white fish to the local market is expanding rapidly. Japanese and Chinese firms use Mauritius as a tuna fishing base. Their contribution to the local economy has hitherto been small.

Manufacturing (excluding the processing of sugar cane) accounts for about 7 per cent of G.N.P. The engineering industry, created in the eighteenth century for military purposes, has for nearly two centuries primarily served the sugar industry, but it is now striving to diversify. A number of import-substituting industries have been established, some for many years (cigarettes, matches) but most during the 1960s (beer, soap, margarine, etc.).

The scope for further import-substituting industries is limited; potential export industries are therefore being actively sought by both government and the private sector; legislation to create export processing zones with a number of fiscal and other incentives has been put into effect. The development plan provides for a yearly growth rate of 11.4 per cent for industrial employment. The most remarkable existing export industry is the partial processing of watch jewels. Bus bodies, furniture, clothing, footwear, etc.

are also exported but on a small and erratic scale. Development of Mauritian external trade should be favoured by the island's membership of OCAM and associate membership of the EEC through the Yaoundé Convention, as well as by the export processing zones.

Given the abundant rainfall and precipitous water courses, most electricity is generated from hydro sources. The sugar factories produce their own heat and power from sugar waste; they sell surplus electricity to the Central Electricity Board—typically some 15 per cent of the total available to it. The remainder is produced in oil-powered thermal stations; its importance relative to hydro power varies widely with rainfall. In Rodrigues a small generator supplies the hospital and one or two public buildings in Port Mathurin.

Five commercial banks operate, of which one—the Mauritius Commercial Bank, established in 1838—is local. A Development Bank, incorporating the business of the earlier Mauritius Agricultural Bank, was established in 1964.

The tourist industry has been growing rapidly; in 1968 some Rs. 17 million were spent by 15,000 holidaymakers, of whom a half came from Réunion, and the remainder (in declining order of importance) from Madagascar, South Africa, Britain and elsewhere.

In 1971 tourist arrivals numbered 37,000; by 1975 hotel projects should provide expanded facilities to cope with an expected total of 75,000 visitors. Further expansion of the industry is being actively pursued. Mauritius is a member of the _Alliance touristique de l'Ocean Indien_.

Although education is not yet compulsory, Mauritius enjoys a high rate of scholarity; in 1971 there were, including Rodrigues, 152,331 pupils in primary schools (about 90 per cent of the relevant age group) and 45,198 in secondary schools. There is a growing emphasis on technical and vocational education, as indicated by the recent establishment of a technical secondary school, a vocational training centre and a university which concentrates on technical and vocational subjects. There is a long tradition among the middle classes of sending their children to university abroad, in particular to Britain, France and India.

Rodrigues is an agricultural and fishing community producing mainly for subsistence. An integrated scheme of agricultural education, land improvement and re-settlement has been under way for several years. The island provides Mauritius with animals for food, onions and garlic, to a total value of Rs. 1.3 million in 1968.

STATISTICAL SURVEY

Area (sq. miles): Mauritius 720; Rodrigues 42; Agalega 27.

Population: Island of Mauritius (Dec. 1971) 830,606; *Towns* (1971): Port Louis (capital) 142,000, Beau Bassin/Rose-Hill 73,000, Curepipe 53,000; *Ethnic groups* (1971 estimates): 575,123 Indo-Mauritians (437,365 Hindus, 137,758 Muslims), 230,487 general population (including Creole and Franco-Mauritian communities) and 24,996 Chinese.

Employment (Sept. 1971): Agriculture, etc. 59,700, Services 35,400, Manufacturing 9,400, Construction 2,200, Commerce 4,300, Total 140,100.

Agriculture (1971): Sugar cane 5,255,570 metric tons, Tea 19,837 metric tons, Tobacco 562 metric tons.

Forestry (1970): Timber 370,000 cu. ft., Firewood 2,261,000 cu. ft.

Industry (1971): Sugar 621,087 metric tons, Molasses 140,158 metric tons, Tea (manufactured) 4,089 metric tons, Aloe Fibre 1,976 metric tons, Alcohol 13,478 hectolitres, Rum 14,916 hectolitres.

FINANCE

100 cents = 1 Mauritian rupee.

Exchange rates (December 1972): £1 sterling = 13.33 rupees; U.S. $1 = 5.679 rupees.

100 rupees = £7.50 = $17.61.

BUDGET 1970–71
(Rupees)

REVENUE		EXPENDITURE	
Direct Taxes	63,486,091	Administration, Police, etc. . . .	28,241,489
Indirect Taxes	142,406,449	Financial Services	73,649,395
Receipts from Public Utilities . .	22,556,911	Agricultural Services . . .	8,261,158
Receipts from Public Services . .	9,166,294	Public Works	19,705,751
Rent of Government Property . .	2,032,099	Commerce and Industry . . .	1,216,006
Interest and Royalties . . .	12,546,217	Education and Cultural Affairs .	35,989,085
U.K. Reimbursements . . .	659,637	Health	26,983,042
Admiralty Reimbursements . .	147,825	Labour	1,180,016
Other Reimbursements . .	6,667,250	Local Government and Co-operative Development	8,461,154
Redemption of Loans	—	Housing, Lands and Town and Country Planning . . .	2,377,577
		Information and Broadcasting .	1,517,359
		Social Security . . .	30,887,177
		Communications . . .	10,548,706
		External Affairs, Tourism and Emigration . . .	5,486,466
TOTAL . . .	259,668,773	TOTAL . . .	254,504,384

BALANCE OF PAYMENTS
(Rupees million)

	1969			1971		
	Credit	Debit	Balance	Credit	Debit	Balance
Goods and Services:						
Merchandise and non-monetary gold .	365	327	38	352	406	−54
Transport, travel, freight and insurance	70	92	−22	129	156	−27
Investment income . . .	13	14	− 1	19	15	4
Government n.e.s. . . .	11	6	5	17	17	10
Other services	23	16	7	22	18	4
Transfer payments . . .	21	10	11	35	11	24
Capital and Monetary Gold:						
Non-Monetary Sector:						
Private transactions . . .	15	2	13	26	—	26
Government transactions . .	23	—	23	—	5	− 5
Allocation of special drawing rights .	—	—	—	13	—	13
Monetary Sectors:						
Commercial bank transactions . .	—	20	−20	23	—	23
Central institutions transactions .	21	86	−65	—	9	− 9
Net Errors and Omissions . .	11		11	—	9	− 9

EXTERNAL TRADE
(1971)

Imports (Rs.): 461.6m. (Rice 31.3m., Electrical goods and Machinery 59.8m., Fertilisers 16.8m., Petroleum products 28.9m.).

Countries: United Kingdom Rs. 100.9m., Burma Rs. 17.3m., Australia Rs. 30.2m., South Africa Rs. 36.0m.

Exports (Rs.): 360.6m. (Sugar 313.3m.).

Countries: United Kingdom Rs. 198.4m., Canada Rs. 101.1m., U.S.A. Rs. 21.9m., South Africa Rs. 15.8m.

TRANSPORT

Roads (Dec. 1971): Private Cars 11,657, Taxis 1,357, Buses 770, Commercial Vehicles 4,388, Government Vehicles 1,050, Motor Cycles 3,115, Auto Cycles 2,691.

Shipping (1971): Entered: Ships 1,143, Passengers 3,268, Freight 669,885 tons; Cleared: Ships 1,097, Passengers 3,525, Freight 635,801 tons.

Civil Aviation (1971): Landed: Planes 1,196, Passengers 58,348, Freight 504,483 kg.; Departed: Planes 1,197, Passengers 61,036, Freight 697,611.

EDUCATION
(1971)

	SCHOOLS	PUPILS
Pre-Primary . . .	344	9,860
Primary	354	152,331
Secondary . . .	139	45,198
Teacher Training . .	1	668
Vocational and Technical .	10	549
University . .	1	2,191

Students Overseas (1971): 1,964 (excluding nursing students).

Source: Central Statistical Office, Rose Hill.

THE CONSTITUTION

The Mauritius Independence Order, 1968, as amended by the Constitution of Mauritius (Amendment) Act No. 39 of 1969, provides for a Cabinet consisting of the Prime Minister and not more than twenty other Ministers. The Prime Minister, appointed by the Governor-General, is the member of the Legislative Assembly who appears to the Governor-General best able to command the support of the majority of members of the Assembly. Other Ministers are appointed by the Governor-General acting in accordance with the advice of the Prime Minister.

The Legislative Assembly consists of the following:

(i) The Speaker.
(ii) Sixty-two elected members.
(iii) Eight additional members.

(iv) The Attorney-General, who may not be an elected member, as is the case at present.

For the purpose of electing members of the Legislative Assembly, the island of Mauritius is divided into twenty three-member constituencies. Rodrigues returns two members. The official language of the Legislative Assembly is English but any member may address the Chair in French.

The State of Emergency, which has been in force since just before independence in 1968, was revoked at the end of 1970. At the same time a Public Order Act, giving the Government wide-ranging powers in certain situations, came into force. A State of Emergency was reimposed in December 1971.

THE GOVERNMENT

Governor-General: (Vacant)

COUNCIL OF MINISTERS
(December 1972)

Premier and Minister of Defence, Internal Security and Information and Broadcasting: The Rt. Hon. Sir SEEWOOSAGUR RAMGOOLAM, Kt.

Minister of Finance: The Hon. V. RINGADOO.

Minister of Health: Sir HAROLD H. WALTER, Kt.

Minister of Education and Cultural Affairs: The Hon. R. JOMADER.

Minister of Labour and Social Security: The Hon. Dr. B. GHURBURRUN.

Minister of Agriculture and Natural Resources: The Hon. S. BOOLELL.

Minister of Works: The Hon. A. H. M. OSMAN.

Minister of External Affairs, Tourism and Emigration: The Hon. GAËTAN DUVAL.

Minister of Industry and Commerce: The Hon. J. G. MARCHAND.

Minister of Local Government: The Hon. J. E. M. L. AH CHUEN.

Minister of Justice: The Hon. J. P. HEIN.

Minister of Communications: The Hon. R. RAULT.

Minister of Economic Planning and Development: K. JAGAT-SINGH.

Minister of Housing, Lands and Town and Country Planning The Hon. Sir A. R. MOHAMED.

Minister of Youth and Sports: The Hon. BASANT RAI.

Minister of Employment: The Hon. CYRIL LECKNING.

Minister of State for External Affairs, Tourism and Immigration: S. A. PATTEN.

Minister of Co-operatives and Co-operative Development: (vacant).

DIPLOMATIC REPRESENTATION

EMBASSIES AND HIGH COMMISSIONS ACCREDITED TO MAURITIUS
(In Port Louis unless otherwise stated)
(E) Embassy; (HC) High Commission.

Australia: Dar es Salaam, Tanzania (HC).

Belgium: Nairobi, Kenya (E).

Canada: Dar es Salaam, Tanzania (HC).

China, People's Republic: Sunray Hotel (E); *Ambassador:* WANG TSE.

Egypt: Dar es Salaam, Tanzania (E).

France: rue St. Georges (E); *Ambassador:* RAPHÄEL TOUZE.

German Federal Republic: Tananarive, Madagascar (E).

India: Fifth floor, Bank of Baroda Bldg., Sir William Newton Street (HC); *High Commissioner:* KRISHNA DAYAL SHARMA.

Israel: Tananarive, Madagascar (E).

Italy: Tananarive, Madagascar (E).

Japan: Tananarive, Madagascar (E).

Madagascar: Sir William Newton Street (E); *Chargé d'Affaires:* J. RAZAFIARISON.

Netherlands: Nairobi, Kenya (E).

Pakistan: Anglo-Mauritius House, Indendance Street (E); *Ambassador:* ANWAR KHAN.

Switzerland: Addis Ababa, Ethiopia (E).

U.S.S.R.: Floreal (E); *Ambassador:* V. A. ROSLAVTSEV.

United Kingdom: Cerné House, La Chaussée (HC); *High Commissioner:* PETER A. CARTER, C.M.G.

U.S.A.: Anglo-Mauritius Building (E); *Ambassador:* WILLIAM BREWER.

Vatican: Tananarive, Madagascar.

Mauritius also has diplomatic relations with China (People's Republic), Denmark, Finland, Norway, Portugal, Sweden and Yugoslavia.

LEGISLATIVE ASSEMBLY

Speaker: The Hon. Sir H. R. VAGHJEE.

Deputy Speaker: The Hon. R. GUJADHUR.

The results of the election of August, 1967, were as follows:

PARTY	SEATS*
Independence Party	43
P.M.S.D.	27

* Includes the eight additional members (the most successful losing candidates of each community).

The membership of the various parties in the Assembly by summer 1972 was as follows:

PARTY	SEATS*
Labour Party	33
P.M.S.D.	19
C.A.M.	4
I.F.B.	6
Independents	6
Vacant.	3

POLITICAL PARTIES

Parti mauricien social démocrate: Port Louis; national party representing all communities; campaigned against independence in the 1967 election; Pres. Hon. J. H. YTHIER, M.L.A.; Parl. Leader Hon. GAËTAN DUVAL, M.L.A.

Parti travailliste (Labour Party): Port Louis; Pres. Hon. Dr. R. CHAPERON, M.L.A.; Parl. Leader Hon. Sir SEEWOOSAGUR RAMGOOLAN, M.L.A.

Independent Forward Bloc: 14 Vallonville St., Port Louis; f. 1958; democratic party; 6 seats; Pres. Hon. G. GANGARAM, M.L.A.;

Comité d'action musulman: Port Louis; supports the interests of the Indo-Mauritian Muslims; Pres. Hon.

A. M. OSMAN, M.L.A.; Parl. Leader Hon. A. R. MOHAMED, M.L.A.

Mauritius People's Progressive Party: 38 Sir William Newton St., Port Louis; affiliated member of Afro-Asian Peoples Solidarity Organization since 1963; Sec. Gen. T. SIBSURUN.

Le Mouvement du Peuple: Port Louis; f. Nov. 1971; aims to eradicate capitalist exploitation; Founder M. K. SOOBRAYEN.

Mauritian Militant Movement (MMM): Port Louis; Leaders PAUL BERANGER, DER VERASWAMY, FAREED MUTTUR (all arrested Aug. 1971); publ. *Le Militant*.

JUDICIAL SYSTEM

The laws of Mauritius are derived partly from the old French Codes suitably amended and partly from English Law. The Judicial Department consists of the Supreme Court, presided over by the Chief Justice and four other Judges who are also Judges of the Court of Criminal Appeal, the Intermediate Court, the Court of Civil Appeal, the Industrial Court and 10 District Courts. The Master and Registrar is the executive officer of the Judicial Department and is also Judge in Bankruptcy.

Supreme Court: Superior Court of Record.

Court of Criminal Appeal.

Court of Civil Appeal.

Intermediate Court.

District Courts: presided over by Magistrates.

Industrial Court: jurisdiction over labour disputes.

Chief Justice: Hon. Sir M. LATOUR-ADRIEN.

Senior Puisne Judge: Hon. H. GARRIOCH.

Puisne Judges: Hon. C. MOOLLAN, Hon. D. RAMPHUL and Hon. M. RAULT.

RELIGION

Hindus 54 per cent, Christians 30 per cent, Muslims 14 per cent, Buddhists 2 per cent.

The main religion of those of European and African descent is Roman Catholic (approximately 265,000 adherents); Bishop JEAN MARGEOT, Port Louis. In 1962 there were 6,700 members of the Church of England and 3,980 other Protestants. The Anglican Bishop of Mauritius is the Rt. Rev. ERNEST EDWARD CURTIS, M.A., Phoenix, whose diocese includes the Seychelles. The Minister for the Presbyterian Church of Scotland is the Rev. T. ROBERTSON, H.C.F.

PRESS AND PUBLISHERS

DAILIES

Action: 20 Lord Kitchener St., Port Louis; f. 1957; English and French; Editor S. RAMEN; circ. 10,000.

Advance: 5 Dumat St., Port Louis; f. 1939; English and French; Editor JEHAN ZUEL; circ. 13,000.

Central Daily News: 38 Royal Rd., Port Louis; f. 1960; Chinese; Editor KWOO SUNG YEUN; circ. 1,600.

Le Cernéen: 8 St. Georges St., Port Louis; f. 1832; English and French; circ. 13,500; Editor REYNALD OLIVIER.

China Times: Joseph Rivière St., Port Louis; f. 1953; Chinese; Editor L. S. AH-KENG; circ. 2,000.

Chinese Daily News: 32 Remy Ollier St., Port Louis; f. 1932; Chinese; Editor TU WAI MAN; circ. 1,500.

Le Citoyen: Lord Kitchener St., Port Louis; f. 1963; English and French; Editor JIMMY NORTON.

Congress: Brabant St., Port Louis; f. 1964, published daily since 1966; English and French; Editor D. VARMA.

L'Express: 3 Brown Sequard St., Port Louis; f. 1963; English and French; circ. 15,000; Editor Dr. P. FORGET.

Le Mauricien: 8 St. Georges St., Port Louis; f. 1908; English and French; circ. 9,000; Editor YVES RAVAT.

New Chinese Commercial Paper: 19 Joseph Rivière St., Port Louis; f. 1956; Chinese; circ. 1,200; Editor YEUNG LAM KO.

The Nation: Port Louis; circ. 6,200; Publisher Independent Publications.

L'Orage: 4 Barracks St., Port Louis; f. 1968; English and French; Editor MAXIME CELESTE.

Star: 3 President John Kennedy St., Port Louis; f. 1963; English and French; circ. 7,000; Editor Dr. H. FAKIM.

WEEKLIES

Aryoday: 16 Frère Felix de Valois Street, Port Louis; f. 1949; English and Hindi; Editor M. Mohit (Hindu), D. N. Beegun (English); circ. 2,000.

Blitz: 27 Edith Cavell St., Port Louis; f. 1967; French and English; Editor E. Edoo.

Le Bouclier: Editions Nassau, Rue Barclay, Rose-Hill; circ. 20,000.

Carrefour: 1 Barracks St., Port Louis; f. 1959; French and English; circ. 10,000; Editors Marie Thérèse Mortelé.

Le Dimanche: 3 Vieux Conseil St., Port Louis; f. 1961; English and French; Editor Regis Nauvel.

Eclaireur: 8 Barracks Street, Port Louis; f. 1963; French, English and Tamil; Editor T. Narrainen.

L'Ecole: 46 Dupont Street, Beau-Bassin; f. 1964; English and French; Editor Mrs. M. R. Goder.

Hebdo-Jeunesse: 3 Vieux Conseil St., Port Louis; f. 1965; French; Editor A. Legallant.

Hit News: 5 Barracks St., Port Louis; f. 1968; French and English; Editor D. Guddoye.

Janata: 5 Dumat St., Port Louis; f. 1947; Hindi; twice weekly; Editor L. Badry.

Juniorama: Editions Nassau, Rue Barclay, Rose-Hill; f. 1971; circ. 20,000.

Magazine Littéraire Nassau: Editions Nassau, Rue Barclay, Rose-Hill; f. 1971; circ. 10,000.

Mauritius Times: 23 Bourbon St., Port Louis; f. 1954; weekly; English and French; circ. 5,500; Editor D. Bheenuck.

Notre Semaine: Editions Nassau, Rue Barclay, Rose-Hill; f. 1971; weekly; circ. 20,000.

Les Nouvelles: 5 Casernes St., Port Louis; f. 1969; French and English; Editor J. C. M. Chuttoo.

Rallye Press: 3 Thomy Pitot St., Port Louis; f. 1967; English and French; Editor J. de L'Estrac.

Le Travailleur: 38 Sir William Newton St., Port Louis; f. 1968; French and English; Organ of the Mauritius People's Progressive Party; Editor T. Sibsurun.

Tribune Ouvrière: 42 Pope Henessy Street, Port Louis; f. 1952; French; circ. 1,600; Editor Philippe Gonee.

La Vie Catholique: 42 Pope Henessy St., Port Louis; f. 1930; French; circ. 10,000; Editor Levis Espitalier-Noël.

Week-End: St. Georges St., Port Louis; f. 1966; French and English; Editor J. Rivet.

FORTNIGHTLIES

L'Etincelle: 29 Corderie Street, Port Louis; f. 1964; Editor A. A. H. Ghanty.

Le Message: Dar-es-Salaam; P.O.B. 6, Rose Hill; f. 1961; English and French; Editor M. A. Qureshi; circ. 1,000.

Nav Jeevan: 23 Bourbon Street, Port Louis; f. 1960; Hindi; Editor S. M. Bhagat; circ. 3,000.

Tamil Voice: 12 Farquhar St., Port Louis; f. 1964; English, French and Tamil; Editor C. Narayanan.

La Voix de L'Islam: Mesnil, Phoenix; f. 1951; English and French; Editor A. A. Peeroo; circ. 2,000.

Zamana: 14 Vallonville St., Port Louis; f. 1948; Hindi, French, English and Sanskrit; Editor B. Bucktowar-singh.

MONTHLIES, QUARTERLIES, ETC.

Le Figaro: 42 Corderie St., Port-Louis; f. 1965; French; Editor I. Dossa.

The Guardian: 11 Lislet Geoffrey St., Port Louis; English and French.

Indian Cultural Review: Port Louis; f. 1936; English and French; Editor Sir Seewoosagur Ramgoolam.

International Opportunites Advertiser: (A) 113 Boundary, Rose-Hill; f. 1969; magazine for trade, friendship, exchange, tourism and industrial promotion; English and French; every two months; Editor J. C. Dinan; circ. 3,000.

International Trade Opportunities Directory: 113 Boundary, Rose-Hill; f. 1973; for importers/exporters, manufacturers, travel, trade, etc.; annual; Editor J. C. Dinan.

Le Progrès Islamique: 51 Solferino St., Rose Hill; f. 1948; English and French; monthly; Editor Mrs. A. N. Sookia; circ. 1,000.

Revue Agricole et Sucrière de l'Ile Maurice: University of Mauritius, Reduit; French and English; Editor Prof. E. Limfat.

La Revue Artistique: Cité Gabriel Martial, Port Louis; f. 1935; English and French; twice monthly; Editor Joseph Tranquille; circ. 3,000.

Revue de Marie: 20 Sir Celicourt Antelme St., Rose Hill; French; monthly; Editor Claude Peril.

Trait d'Union: P.O. Box 278, Port Louis; f. 1959; English and French; monthly; Editor Edwin de Robillard, M.B.E.

Youth Mirror: Port Louis; f. 1968; Editor Azad Dhomun.

PUBLISHERS

Editions Croix du Sud: 1 Barracks St., Port Louis; general; Dir. Maria Thérèse Mortelé.

Editions Nassau: Rue Barclay, Rose-Hill; f. 1970; publishes magazines; Pres. Dir.-Gen. R. A. Y. Vilmont; Sec.-Gen. E. H. Dennemont.

RADIO AND TELEVISION

Mauritius Broadcasting Corporation: Forest Side; f. 1964; national radio and television station; has a monopoly over broadcasting in the island; Dir.-Gen. J. R. Delaître; Sales Man. Jacques Cantin.

There are 121,591 radio sets in use.

Television services started in February 1965. There are 19,600 licences.

FINANCE

BANKS

Bank of Mauritius: P.O.B. 29, Port Louis; f. 1967 as central bank; cap. p.u. Rs. 10m.; Gov. A. BEEJADHUR; Man. Dir. G. BUNWAREE.

Development Bank of Mauritius: f. 1936 as *Mauritius Agricultural Bank*; reorganized 1964; cap. Rs. 10m.

Mauritius Co-operative Central Bank: Port Louis; f. 1948; 211 mem. societies; Chair. P. R. MADIAH; Gen. Man. M. SIDAMBARAM, F.C.C.S., F.B.S.C.

Barclays Bank International Ltd.: Sir William Newton St., Port Louis; 6 brs., 2 sub-brs. and 6 agencies in Mauritius; Manager J. M. LAWSON.

Bank of Baroda: Head Office: Baroda, India; Sir William Newton St., Port Louis; cap. Rs. 80m.; Man. C. J. SHAH.

Habib Bank Overseas Ltd.: Port Louis; f. 1952; Pakistani Bank; cap. Rs. 10m.; Man. Sh. EHSANUDDIN.

Mauritius Commercial Bank Ltd.: 11 Sir William Newton St., Port Louis; f. 1838; cap. Rs. 7m.; 12 brs.; Gen. Man. P. L. EYNAUD.

Mercantile Bank Ltd.: Head Office: Hong Kong; Place d'Armes, Port Louis; 7 brs.; Man. J. C. WRIGHT.

INSURANCE

Anglo-Mauritius Assurance Society Ltd.: Anglo-Mauritius House, Intendance St., Port Louis; incorp. 1951; Chair. RAYMOND LAMUSSE, O.B.E.; Gen. Man. G. LA HAUSSE DE LALOUVIERE.

Birger & Co. (Insurance) Ltd.: 18 Jules Koenig St., Port Louis; incorp. 1954; Man. ISIA BIRGER.

Dynamic Insurance Co. Ltd.: 3 Desforges St., Port Louis; incorp. 1955; Chair. J. H. CONSTANTIN.

Mauritius Livestock Insurance Co. Ltd.: 14 Bourbon St., Port Louis; incorp. 1957; Chair. PHILIPPE GOUPILLE.

Mauritius Union Assurance Society Ltd.: 13 Sir William Newton St., Port Louis; incorp. 1948; Man. Dir. A. NOEL COIGNET.

Ramdharry Insurance Co. Ltd.: 15 Bourbon St., Port Louis; incorp. 1957; Dirs. DEOKEENANUN RAMDHARRY, TALAWONSING RAMDHARRY, DOOMROWSING RAMDHARRY.

Swan Insurance Co. Ltd.: 6–10 Intendance St., Port Louis; incorp. 1955; Chair. RAYMOND HEIN, Q.C.

Forty-eight British companies and 33 other companies have branches in Mauritius.

TRADE AND INDUSTRY

CHAMBERS OF COMMERCE

Mauritius Chamber of Commerce and Industry: Anglo-Mauritius House, Port Louis; f. 1850, inc. 1892; 120 mems.; Pres. C. CURRIMJEE; Vice-Pres. P. HUGNIN.

Chinese Chamber of Commerce: 5 Joseph Rivière St., Port Louis; f. 1908, inc. 1914; to protect the interests of Chinese traders and to see to the welfare of Chinese immigrants; Pres. LEUNG LIOONG PHEOW; Sec. MARCEL LAI FAK YU.

TRADE UNIONS

Mauritius Federation of Labour: Port Louis; affiliated to WFTU; Pres. L. BADRY; Gen. Sec. L. LUBIDINEUSE.

Mauritius Trade Union Congress: 7 Guy Rozemont Square, Port Louis; 12,562 mems.; 17 affiliated unions; Gen. Sec. SERGE CLAVERIE.

PRINCIPAL UNIONS

Agricultural and Other Workers' Union: 6 Edith Cavell St., Port Louis; 12,000 mems.; Pres. L. BADRY; Sec. P. I. K. BHATOO.

Government and Other Manual Workers' Union: 6 Edith Cavell St., Port Louis; 1,163 mems.; Pres. I. ALLYBOKUS; Sec. L. LUBIDINEUSE.

Government Servants and Other Employees' Association: 194 Royal Rd., Beau-Bassin; f. 1945; 4,342 mems.; Pres. A. H. MALLECK H. AMODE; Sec. R. SUMPUTH.

Government Labour Power Union: 7 Guy Rozemont Square, Port Louis; 950 mems.; Pres. L. L'AIMABLE; Sec. P. KERPAL.

Government Teachers' Union: 10 Canal Street, Beau-Bassin; 848 mems.; Pres. B. DABEE; Sec. H. ERNEST.

Plantation Workers' Union (Amalgamated Labourers' Association): 8 Little Pump St., Port Louis; 19,896 mems.; Pres. H. RANARAIN, M.L.C.; Sec. M. C. BHAGIRUTTY.

CO-OPERATIVE SOCIETIES

There are 335 Co-operative Societies in Mauritius and Rodrigues.

The Mauritius Co-operative Union Ltd.: Co-operation House, Dumat St., Port Louis; f. 1952; 211 member societies; Sec. P. MAUREEMOOTOO.

The Mauritius Co-operative Agricultural Federation: Port Louis; f. 1950; 153 mems. Societies; Chair. P. KISTNAH; Sec. J. CHUNDUNSING.

Mauritius Co-operative Wholesale Ltd.: Port Louis; f. 1949; 53 mem. societies; 32 brs.; Sec. P. T. BAROSEE.

TRANSPORT AND TOURISM

TRANSPORT

ROADS

Mauritius has approximately 16 km. of motorway, 1,593 km. of main roads, 517 km. of secondary roads and 177 km. of other roads. 85 per cent of the roads have been asphalted.

SHIPPING

Regular services to Europe are provided by the Clan Line, Union Castle Line, Scandinavian East Africa Line, Messageries Maritimes Ltd. and Nouvelle Cie. Havraise Péninsulaire. Royal Interocean Lines provides a Far East-South Africa, South America, Australia, Africa service.

Other services are provided by Bank Line, Zim Israel, Compagnie Malgache de Navigation, Société Mauritienne de Navigation and Colonial Steamships Co. Ltd.

Director of Marine: Capt. V. C. NICOLIN.

CIVIL AVIATION

Director of Civil Aviation: (Vacant).

Air Mauritius: 1 Sir William Newton St., Port Louis; services to Réunion and to South Africa in partnership with South African Airways; Man. P. BOULLE.

Mauritius is linked by air with Europe, Africa, India and Australia by the following airlines: Air France, Air India, B.O.A.C., East African Airways, Lufthansa, Qantas, S.A.A. and Zambia Airways. In 1972 a thrice-weekly air service to Rodrigues was inaugurated, using initially one Piper Navajo. A regular air cargo service between France and Mauritius was also begun.

TOURISM

Mauritius Government Tourist Office: Cerné House, La Chaussée, Port Louis; Gen. Man. RÉGIS FANCHETTE.

EDUCATION

Standards are high, most of the population being literate. Over 150,000 children attend primary schools, and in addition there are about 140 secondary schools, 10 vocational and technical colleges, a teaching training college and a small university.

LEARNED SOCIETIES AND RESEARCH INSTITUTES

Académie Mauricienne de Langue et de Littérature: Curepipe; 16 life members; Sec. C. DE RAUVILLE; publ. *Oeuvres et Chroniques de l'Océan Indien.*

British Council, The: Royal Road, Rose Hill, Port Louis; Rep. P. J. C. DART, M.A.; library (*see* Libraries).

Mauritius Institute: P.O.B. 54, Port Louis; f. 1880; a branch of the Ministry of Education; research centre for the study of the local fauna and flora; a public library and two museums are also attached to the Institute; Director C. MICHEL, A.M.A.; publs. *Annual Reports, Bulletin.*

Royal Society of Arts and Sciences of Mauritius: Mauritius Institute, Port Louis; f. 1829; Royal title 1847; 5 honorary, 107 ordinary mems.; Pres. C. ROUILLARD; Hon. Sec. C. RICAUD; publ. *Proceedings.*

Société de l'Histoire de l'Ile Maurice: 13 Sir W. Newton St., Port Louis; f. 1938; 350 ordinary mems.; Pres. MAURICE PATURAU; Hon. Sec. G. RAMET; publs. *Bulletin, Dictionary of Mauritian Biography.*

Société de Technologie Agricole et Sucrière de l'Ile Maurice: Mauritius Sugar Industry Research Institute, Réduit; f. 1910; 320 mems.; Pres. JACQUES DUPONT DE RIVALTZ DE SAINT ANTOINE; Hon. Sec. C. FIGON; publ. *La Revue Agricole et Sucrière de Maurice.*

Sugar Industry Research Institute: Réduit; f. 1953; research on cane breeding, agriculture, soils, diseases, pests, weeds, botany and sugar manufacture, as well as on food crops cultivated between rows of sugar-cane and between cane cycles; Dir. R. ANTOINE, B.SC., A.R.C.S., DIP.AG.SCI.; 20 senior research workers; publs. *Annual Report, Weed Flora, Occasional Papers.*

LIBRARIES

British Council Library: Rose Hill; f. 1949; 14,800 vols.

Carnegie Library: Queen Elizabeth II Avenue, Curepipe; 25,000 vols.; Librarian C. DE RAUVILLE.

City Library: P.O.B. 422, Port Louis; f. 1851; 42,000 vols.; Librarian J. G. THÉLÉMAQUE.

Mauritius Archives: Sir William Newton Street, Port Louis; f. 1815; contains records of the French Administration (1721–1815) and the British Administration (1810 onwards); comprises Divisions of Manuscript Records, Printed Records, Notarial Registry, Land Registry and

Maps and Plans, and a Photographic Service; Chief Archivist Dr. H. ADOLPHE; publs. *Annual Reports, Memorandum of Books Printed in Mauritius* (quarterly), *Bulletin.*

Mauritius Institute Public Library: P.O.B. 54, Port Louis; f. 1902; 41,900 vols., including an extensive collection of books, articles and reports on Mauritius; Librarian S. JEAN-FRANÇOIS, A.L.A.

MUSEUMS

Historical Museum: Mahebourg; f. 1950; a branch of the Mauritius Institute; comprises collection of old maps, engravings, water-colours and naval relics of local interest, exhibited in an 18th-century French house.

Mauritius Herbarium, The: Sugar Industry Research Institute, Réduit; f. 1960; public herbarium for education and research; specialises in flora of Mascarene Islands.

Port Louis Museum: Mauritius Institute, Port Louis; comprises a Natural History Museum; f. 1885; collections of fauna, flora and geology of Mauritius and of the other islands of the Mascarene region; Dir. C. MICHEL, A.M.A.

UNIVERSITY

UNIVERSITY OF MAURITIUS
REDUIT

Telephone: 4-1041.

Founded 1965.

Language of instruction: English; Academic year: September to June.

The primary aim of the University is the greater development of the Island. Teaching programmes and research projects concentrate particularly on those areas where the country can expect relatively short-term returns, i.e. on Economics and Public Administration, Engineering Technology, Agriculture and Natural Resources and Education.

Pro-Chancellor and Chairman of the Council: The Hon. Sir HARILAL VAGHJEE.

Vice-Chancellor: P. O. WIEHE, C.B.E., D.SC.

Registrar: R. LAMY, B.A.

Number of teachers: 49.

Number of students: 923 full-time, 1,268 part-time.

HEADS OF SCHOOLS:

School of Administration: W. F. COOPER, M.A., M.SC.
School of Agriculture: A. S. MACDONALD, B.SC.
School of Industrial Technology: M. E. L. M. LIM FAT, M.SC., M.CHEM.E., M.I.AGR.E.

DEPENDENCIES OF MAURITIUS

RODRIGUES

Area 42 square miles. Population (1968) 22,400. Administered by a Magistrate and Civil Commissioner who is advised by a committee composed of the Agricultural Officer, the Senior Medical Officer, the Roman Catholic and Anglican parish priests, the Manager of Cable and Wireless Station and 11 Rodriguans appointed by the Governor.

THE LESSER DEPENDENCIES

The Lesser Dependencies are the islands of Agalega, lying about 700 miles north of Mauritius and Cargados Carajos, about 250 miles to the north-east. (In 1965 the Chagos Archipelago, formerly administered by Mauritius, became part of the new British Indian Ocean Territory—*see* under Seychelles.)

SELECT BIBLIOGRAPHY

BALOGH, T., and BENNETT, C. J. M. *Commission of Enquiry into the Sugar Industry*. Port Louis, Government Printer, 1963.

BENEDICT, BURTON. *Mauritius, A Plural Society*. London, 1965.
Indians in a Plural Society: A Report on Mauritius. London, H.M.S.O., 1961.

FAVOREU, LOUIS. *L'île Maurice*. Paris, Berger-Levrault, 1970.

HOPKIN, W. A. B. *Policy for Economic Development in Mauritius*. Port Louis, Sessional Paper No. 6 of 1966.

MEADE, J. E. et al. *The Economic and Social Structure of Mauritius*. London, Sessional Paper No. 7 of 1960, Methuen, reprinted by Frank Cass and Co., 1968.

TITMUSS, R. M., and ABEL-SMITH, B. *Social Policies and Population Growth in Mauritius*. London, Sessional Paper No. 6 of 1960, Methuen, reprinted by Frank Cass and Co., 1968.

TOUSSAINT, AUGUSTE. *Bibliography of Mauritius 1501–1954*. Port Louis, 1956.
Port Louis, deux siècles d'histoire (1735–1935). Port Louis, 1946.
Histoire des îles Mascareignes. Paris, Berger-Levrault, 1972.

Mozambique

PHYSICAL AND SOCIAL GEOGRAPHY*

René Pélissier

PHYSICAL FEATURES

Mozambique is the second largest Portuguese African territory with an area of 783,030 sq. km. (including 9,652 sq. km. for the Portuguese share of Lake Nyasa). It is an elongated territory indented by Malawi. The largest measurements are 1,965 km. from the Natal border to the Tanzanian border at the Rovuma mouth, and 1,130 km. in width from the Tete salient to the ocean. Its neighbours are, to the north, Tanzania, to the east Malawi, Zambia and Rhodesia, and to the south South Africa and Swaziland. It consists of ten administrative districts subdivided into *concelhos* and *circunscrições*. With some exceptions towards the Zambian, Malawian and Rhodesian border, it is generally a low-lying plateau of moderate height descending through a sub-plateau zone to the Indian Ocean. Main reliefs are Monte Binga (2,436 m.), the highest point of Mozambique on the Rhodesian border in the Manica e Sofala district, Monte Namúli (2,419 m.) in the Zambézia district, the Serra Zuira (2,227 m. in the Manica e Sofala district), and several massifs which are a continuation of the Malawi Shire Highlands into northern Mozambique. The coastal lowland is narrower in the north but widens considerably as it goes south, so that terrain less than 1,000 m. high makes up about 45 per cent of the total Mozambican area. The shoreline is 2,470 km. long and generally sandy and bordered by lagoons, shoals and strings of coastal islets in the north. Mozambique is sectioned by at least 25 main rivers which all flow to the Indian Ocean. The largest and most historically significant is the Zambezi whose 820 km. Mozambican section is navigable for 460 km. This great river which flows from Eastern Angola has provided the Portuguese with easy access to the interior of Africa from the eastern coast. Other rivers of main hydroelectric or irrigational interest are the Incomáti, the Limpopo, the Save, the Buzi, the Punguè, the Licungo, the Ligonha, the Molocuè, the Mocubúri, the Lúrio, the Molúli, the Montepuez, the Messalo and finally the frontier Rovuma and its main tributary the Lugenga.

Two main seasons, wet and dry, divide the climatic year. The wet season has monthly averages between 80° and 85°F. with cooler temperatures in the interior uplands. The dry cooler season has June and July temperatures of 65°–68°F. at Lourenço Marques.

POPULATION

Mozambique is much more densely populated than Angola. In 1960, the total population was 6,603,653 persons of whom 2,098 were orientals, 97,245 whites, 17,241 Indians and Pakistanis, 6,455,614 blacks and 31,455 *mestiços*. 2,545 non-Portuguese Europeans, mostly British and South African, lived in the country.

Provisional figures from the 1970 census put the total population at 8,233,834. Several hundred thousand migrant workers live in South Africa. Rhodesia and Zambia. In addition tens of thousands of refugees live in Tanzania, Zambia and Malawi. The population of nationalist held-areas may amount to 100,000 (1972). Main cities are the capital, Lourenço Marques, a modern and bustling sea-port which in 1960 had more than one-third of the European and Asian population. Its population was 178,000 in 1960 (over 40,000 whites) and had grown to 383,775 by 1970. The second sea-port of the country is Beira (58,970 persons in 1960, of whom 13,498 were whites) which is the sea-port for landlocked Rhodesia. Nampula, on the railway-line to the Niassa district and Malawi, had 103,985 (3,500 whites). The population of Quelimane was 66,301 (3,000 whites). Other towns of some importance are João Belo, Inhambane, Tete, Vila Cabral and Porto Amélia with administrative, transport or economic functions. Estimated white population is now probably over 200,000 including soldiers. A significant part of the white population emigrates clandestinely to South Africa where conditions are better. North of the Zambezi, the main ethnic groupings among the African population, which belongs to the cultural division of Central Bantu, are the Makua-Lomwe groups, who form the chief ethnolinguistic subdivision of all Mozambicans. Although there are no statistics for 1970, they may represent about 40 per cent of the population (2,293,000 in 1950). They live in the Zambézia, Moçambique, Niassa and Cabo Delgado districts, and are Islamized. The Yao (or Ajaua) live in the Niassa district and also in Malawi. They are Islamized and keen tradesmen. The fiercest opponents of the Portuguese are the Makonde, a warlike, xenophobic, animist people who live on either side of the Rovuma border. There were 136,000 in 1950 but only a few tens of thousands now live in Mozambique. Other northern groups are the Nyanja and Chewa around lake Nyasa and in the Tete district (166,000 in 1950); the Swahili-speaking people of the coast of Cabo Delgado and Mozambique districts; and clusters of little-studied tribes in the Zambezi valley. South of the great dividing river, the main group is the Thonga (1,460,000 in 1950) who figure prominently as Mozambican mine labourers in South Africa. The Chopi and the Tonga (240,400 in 1950) are coastal people of the Inhambane district who have had opportunities for education. North of the Tonga area lies the Shona group of more than a million. It is also strong in Rhodesia. Lesser groups make Mozambique a gigantic ethnic puzzle where education and modernization seem to give the Tonga a relative advantage. This ethnic diversity is one of the main trump-cards of the Portuguese in keeping control of this largely artificial juxtaposition of sometime rival groups.

* *See* map on p. 148.

RECENT HISTORY

See Recent History of Portugal's African Territories under Angola, p. 150.

ECONOMY

René Pélissier

AGRICULTURE

About 88 per cent of the population is engaged in agriculture, while about 80 per cent of exports in the late 1960s were of agricultural origin. Although only 5 per cent of arable lands are cultivated, agriculture accounts for 27 per cent of the G.D.P. As a rule, climatic and physical conditions are somewhat better than in Angola, and African farmers more progressive. Large-scale modern agriculture is mainly Portuguese. About 3,000 farms and plantations are known to exist, employing more than 130,000 people on over four million acres, while African plots cover some seven million acres.

Cashew nuts are of relatively recent exploitation. Unshelled nuts were first exported to India from the coastal belt of northern Mozambique. Now a sizable proportion of nuts are mechanically decorticated locally before export. In 1970, 184,000 metric tons were produced. India and the U.S. are important markets. In 1970 63,941 tons were exported worth 855,158 contos.

The cotton crop was 138,142 metric tons in 1970. Forced cultivation by African farmers working for the great concessionary companies was open to abuse until it was abolished in 1961, because of the low prices paid to farmers and the coercive measures employed. Cotton is the main cash crop of northern Mozambique, with more than 500,000 African growers in the Cabo Delgado, Niassa, Moçambique and Zambézia districts. After local processing and consumption 44,291 metric tons of raw cotton worth 738,597 contos were exported in 1970.

Sugar is produced by large cane-growing companies such as the Sena Sugar Estates Ltd. on a tributary of the Zambezi, the Companhia Colonial do Buzi, south of Beira, and the Sociedade Agrícola de Incomati, north of Lourenço Marques. This formerly monopolistic system produced about 215,000 tons of sugar in 1968, and in 1970 exports, mainly to Portugal, reached 178,628 tons worth 555,203 contos. Heavy investments in the sugar industry have been made by the five major companies.

Mozambique ranks third after Kenya and Malawi among African producers of tea. The Zambézia hills and mountains close to the Malawi border are the main producing area. 16,576 tons worth 234,071 contos were exported in 1970. These exports went mainly to the U.K., Portugal and the U.S. About 40,000 Africans are employed on tea plantations.

Copra is chiefly grown on immense plantations on the coastal belt of the Zambézia and Moçambique districts. It is also a popular crop among Africans who use the oil and other copra products in daily life. The main company is the Companhia do Boror, north of Quelimane. In 1970 some 46,000 tons of copra were exported with a value of 238,841 escudos.

As in Angola, sisal was introduced by German planters. In 1970 28,193 tons were produced. On account of low world prices, this crop has fallen into a period of crisis. It is a typical plantation crop, concentrated on about twenty estates west of the ports of Moçambique, Nacala and Porto Amélia. In 1970 21,338 tons of sisal were exported, mainly to Portugal.

Maize (410,000 tons in 1969) is grown both on African farms and European plantations, along the Beira railway as well as in the Limpopo plain and Lourenço Marques district. About 102,000 tons of rice were produced in 1970 in the irrigated lowlands. Some rice is exported. Wheat is insufficient (about 10,000 tons in 1968). Oil seeds such as sesame and sunflower seeds and above all peanuts (118,000 tons in 1968) allow for some exports to Portugal. Oil processing amounts to over 25,000 tons annually. Bananas and citrus fruits are exported, as well as potatoes, tobacco and kenaf.

Livestock is still of secondary importance, due to the existence of the tsetse fly over about two-thirds of the country. Most of the cattle is raised south of the Save River, particularly in the Gaza district which has about 500,000 head. In 1970 figures were: 1,338,238 cattle; 150,104 sheep; 670,419 goats and 200,693 pigs. The Limpopo *colonato* and the area surrounding Lourenço Marques have European cattle ranches to provide the capital with meat and dairy products. Mozambique has to import fresh and prepared meat to meet the European demand.

Mozambique, like Angola, occupies a special place in the plans for settling Portuguese farmers in Africa. On the whole, the Portuguese immigrants are of a higher standing than those going to Angola and therefore tend to avoid living in the bush. An important settlement project for Europeans is the Limpopo Valley Scheme which started in the 1950s. About 1,000 Portuguese and 500 African families live on partially irrigated land and grow wheat, rice and cotton which is marketed through co-operatives. In the Revué basin, west of Beira, small *colonatos* have been started by Portuguese and Mozambican families. Madeiran settlers are being established in the Niasa and Zambézia districts. Other schemes include the drainage of marshes and the damming of local rivers. As in Angola, these efforts have to be seen in their political context, which is the aim of "whitening" the Mozambican bush. Costs are out of proportion to the settling of a few thousand families from Portugal, and the gigantic plans envisaged for the Zambezi Valley (establishing 1,000,000 Portuguese farmers) are simply utopian, given the reluctance of Portuguese farmers to settle in the heart of Africa as opposed to its more pleasant city-ports, and the irresistible attraction of closer industrialized Europe for the migrants. It is to be noted that in contrast to Angola, a large part of the bush trade is in the hands of orientals.

Forestry has developed chiefly along the Beira railway and in the wetter Zambézia District. Most of the exports are sawn timber, construction timber, etc., with a ready market in South Africa. Fishing is a relatively recent development on this extensive coast. 7,634 tons of fish were landed in 1970, and a bright future seems guaranteed to industrial fishing.

MINERALS

While mineral riches have been known to outsiders from antiquity, their real working is still limited to rare minerals and coal at Moatize near Tete. Coal production is about 350,000 tons. Two companies sell their production to the local railways and some is exported. Small quantities of columbo-tantalite are exported, and reserves have been found in northern Mozambique. Ilmenite exists in the area north of the mouth of the Zambezi River. An extremely important iron-ore deposit of 360 million tons estimated reserves has been discovered near Namapa in the Moçambique district. This could prove to be the equivalent of Cassinga for Mozambique. A Japanese corporation plans to invest $50 million in its exploitation. A rail link to the port of Nacala is also envisaged. New deposits of manganese, radioactive minerals (e.g. uranium), asbestos, iron, diamonds and natural gas have been found and await investors.

At present Mozambique must import all the oil it requires. The Lourenço refinery can handle 800,000 tons of crude oil annually but production was under 700,000 tons in 1970. Oil-prospecting is actively pursued by American, French, German and South African companies, both off-shore near Beira and on the mainland.

POWER

In 1970 Mozambique had an installed capacity of 354,914 Kws. Power will be the great mainstay of Mozambique's economy when the Cabora Bassa Dam becomes operational. A consortium, ZAMCO, composed of South African, German, and French firms has been granted a contract for the construction of the dam. The cost of the first stage has been estimated at $315 million. Over 18,000 million kWh. per year are planned, making Cabora Bassa the foremost hydroelectric project in Africa. (Aswan was only 10,000 million). A 150-mile lake will reach the Zambian border and grandiose plans have been made to irrigate 3.7 million acres in this otherwise economically backward salient of Mozambique. Tete could be developed as an iron and steel industrial centre, and the Zambezi made navigable from Tete to the sea. Plainly, the importance of the project exceeds the frontiers of Mozambique, and the main customer will be South

Africa, by means of an 800-mile high-tension line. The political implications of having their main source of cheap electric power abroad seem to forecast the direct participation by South Africa against FRELIMO guerrillas who have pledged themselves to destroying the Cabora Bassa Dam before its first stage is completed in 1974. So far construction work has progressed according to schedule in spite of the intensification of guerrilla activities on the roads linking the site to Tete, Rhodesia and Malawi as well as on the Tete railway.

At present, main hydroelectric plants are on the Revué River, west of Beira at Chicamba Real and Mavuzi. Further south, on the Limpopo, is the dam which helps to irrigate the *colonato*. Projects are being studied on the Sabié and Incomatí rivers, where investment of about 1,500 million escudos is planned. Another dam at Massinguir (Elephant River) is due to increase the irrigation potential of the Limpopo. Work started on this project in 1972.

INDUSTRY

Industries are mainly devoted to the processing of primary materials. Mozambique is still heavily dependent on South African industrial products, but investment is slowly changing the picture. Food-processing is still the main sector of industrial production. Sugar-refining (285,786 tons in 1970 worth 1,015,682 contos) industries related to the cashew-nut (445,251 contos in 1970), and wheat-processing are of some importance. Heavy investments from Portugal, South Africa, Italy and Great Britain have established export-oriented industries. On the other hand, the beverage industry (450,000 contos in 1970) is still lagging behind its Angolan counterpart but tobacco manufacture is on the increase (379,836 contos in 1970). Cotton spinning and weaving (250,000 contos in 1970) are done at Vila Pery and in the Moçambique district. 385,000 tons of cement were manufactured in 1970 and work on the Cabora Bassa dam has provoked new investment in this industry. A fertilizer plant is in production at Matola. A steel plant is being erected by Rhodesian and Mozambique interests at Beira, iron ore will be supplied mainly from the Tete region, and electric power from the Chicamba dam. Other secondary industries produce glass, ceramics, paper, tyres and railway carriages. By 1969 industrial output had trebled since 1961.

TRANSPORT

Mozambique derives much of its income from charges on goods carried between Rhodesia, Zambia, Malawi and South Africa and its ports. Railways play a dominant part in this middleman economy. In 1970, 3,703 km. of track existed, and carried 5,381,000 passengers and 16,874,000 tons of freight. Main lines are the Lourenço Marques—Ressano Garcia line to the South African border, the Lourenço Marques—Goba line, to the Swaziland border, and the Lourenço Marques—Malvérnia line to the Rhodesian border in the south. These lines are state-owned. From Beira run the Beira Railway to the Rhodesian border, a state-owned line, the Trans-Zambézia Railway (private) to the Malawi border, and the Tete line (state-owned). In the north, the Mozambique network is mainly represented by the Nacala-Malawi line with a branch-line to Vila Cabral, completed in 1970 and state-owned. All these lines are intended primarily to export the products of land-locked countries, and secondarily to transport Mozambican goods. Most of the international lines are controlled by international conventions, since their effective functioning is vital to Mozambique's neighbours. The operation of the Beira and Lourenço Marques lines is highly profitable to the Mozambican treasury.

This railway-dominated country is lacking in good roads but there are plans to build 10,000 km. of paved roads by 1980. In 1970 there were only 37,106 km. of roads and tracks. Unfortunately, the main roads are penetration lines toward the border and are grossly insufficient for Mozambique's purposes. A north-south paved road from the Malawi border to the south is under construction. Most of the northern districts are lacking in roads, and this has adversely effected Portuguese anti-guerrilla operations. A new bridge across the Zambezi river has been completed in Teté on the Rhodesia-Malawi route (1972).

The main ports are Lourenço Marques, Beira, Nacala and Quelimane. Lourenço Marques has an excellent, multi-purpose harbour which in 1969 recorded 2,837,000 tons of merchandise unloaded, and 7,451,000 loaded. Beira had 971,000 tons unloaded and 1,136,000 loaded. Nacala had 160,000 tons unloaded and 115,000 tons loaded. The two first-mentioned exist chiefly as outlets for South Africa, Swaziland, Rhodesia, Zambia, Malawi and Zaire. Worthy of mention is the strategic oil pipeline from Beira to Umtali in Rhodesia, embargoed since 1966. In 1970 10,138,513 metric tons of freight were loaded and 4,642,141 tons unloaded in Mozambique ports.

Air transport is operated by the state-owned DETA. There are sixteen airports, of which three are of the international type. There were 126,270 passengers carried on internal services in 1969.

TOURISM

A very important activity, it hinges on the influx of Rhodesians and South Africans who drive to Beira and the southern beaches. Gorongosa Park, half-way between Rhodesia and Beira is also a great attraction. American and European big-game hunters are also catered for. In 1970 Mozambique had 266 hotels, motels and boarding houses containing 4,131 beds and received 296,112 guests. Receipts from tourism in 1969 amounted to 403,000 contos, which represented an increase of 13.3 per cent over 1968.

TRADE

Traditionally, Mozambique's balance of trade has a heavy deficit due to the fact that trade with third countries is grossly negative. Portugal is the main buyer of Mozambique's exports (taking about 45 per cent in 1970), mainly raw sugar and cotton. Imports from Portugal are low (27.6 per cent in 1970). In 1970 imports had a total value of 9,302,188 contos and amounted to 1,869,069 metric tons in weight. Exports totalled 4,496,866 contos in value and weighed 1,979,724 metric tons. The chief imports for domestic use in 1970 were as follows: wheat (145,907 contos), bottled wine (221,193 contos), petroleum (377,571 contos), medicines 171,769 contos; dyes (223,193 contos); tubes (115,323 contos); tractors (180,158 contos); motorcars 576,087 contos. The transit functions of the country are revealed by the latest available figures (1968); indirect transit: 12,237,469 contos; direct transit; 21,613,365 contos. Mozambique's annual growth rate in the years 1964 to 1968 was in the order of 9 per cent. About 45 per cent of the gross domestic product came from the primary sector, 14 per cent from the manufacturing sector and the balance was made up by tourism and transport.

In spite of important contributions to the invisible income from the transit trade, tourism from Rhodesia and South Africa, and remittances from Mozambican workers in South Africa, the balance of payments showed a deficit of 1,633,000 contos in 1970 and a further deterioration was forecast in 1971.

In short, as regards trade Mozambique is much less internationally-oriented than Angola, and its transit functions have tended to mask its potentialities, which as yet have hardly been tapped. It seems that the Cabora Bassa Dam, if completed as planned, will provide the great stimulus to Mozambique's economy. It is also quite certain that this project will link Mozambique's fate more and more to that of English-speaking Africa. Its satellite position in the southern African galaxy seems to be reinforced by the project, and the political implications are self-evident.

STATISTICAL SURVEY

AREA AND POPULATION

AREA (sq. km.)	POPULATION (1970)*		BIRTHS (1969)	MARRIAGES (1969)	DEATHS (1969)
	Total	Lourenço Marques (cap.)			
783,030	8,233,834	383,775	26,103	8,599	11,008

* Provisional figures.

Agriculture (principal crops—'ooo metric tons) (1970): Tea 5,045; (1968): Sugar 214 (estimated production 1970 350), Cashew 102, Sisal 29, Rice 184, Maize 410 (1969); (1968–69): Cotton 138.

Livestock (1970): Cattle 1,338,238, Sheep 150,104, Goats 670,419, Pigs 200,693, Asses, horses, mules and donkeys 20,872.

Forestry (1968): Wood and logs 169,472 cu. m., Charcoal 6,470,420 metric tons.

Fishing (1970): 7,634 metric tons.

INDUSTRY AND MINING

	1968	1969	1970
Beer ('ooo litres) . .	26,905	35,259	43,735
Cement (tons) . . .	288,243	309,514	385,002
Cigarettes (tons) . .	2,046	2,303	2,551
Cotton, Raw (tons) . .	41,725	43,348	39,320
Maize Flour (tons) . .	84,833	110,673	n.a.
Sisal (tons) . . .	31,799	26,927	28,193

	1968	1969	1970
Sugar (tons) . . .	214,452	228,317	285,786
Vegetable Oils (tons) .	32,593	36,120	46,378
Bauxite (tons) . . .	3,275	4,393	7,146
Coal (tons) . . .	314,408	276,788	351,016
Salt (tons) . . .	30,629	27,459	28,742

FINANCE

100 centavos = 1 Mozambique escudo; 1,000 escudos = 1 conto.

Coins: 10, 20 and 50 centavos; 1, 2.50, 5, 10 and 20 escudos.

Notes: 50, 100, 500 and 1,000 escudos.

Exchange rates: £1 sterling = 62.90 escudos (December 1972); 100 escudos = £1.590.
U.S. $1 = 27.12 escudos (September 30th, 1972); 100 escudos = $3.687.

Budget (1970): *Revenue* 6,452m., *Expenditure* 6,451m. escudos.
(1972): *Estimated expenditure:* 8,893,102,000 escudos; 1,076,317,650 escudos are to be spent on the armed forces.

1968 DEVELOPMENT ALLOCATION

('ooo escudos)

Agriculture, Forestry and Fishing . .	357,580
Extractive and Manufacturing Industries .	688,000
Construction, Public Works and Rural Development	24,700
Power	128,000
Commerce	15,028
Transport and Communications . .	831,562
Education and Research . . .	170,460
Tourism	4,000
Health and Welfare	30,200
TOTAL	2,249,530

Under its Third Development Plan 1968–73 Portugal has provided 15,555.7 million escudos.

CURRENCY IN CIRCULATION
(contos)

	1968	1969	1970
Notes	1,755,809	1,851,329	2,025,729
Coin	246,639	268,063	268,524
TOTAL . . .	2,002,448	2,119,392	2,294,253

BALANCE OF PAYMENTS
(1970 contos)

	CREDIT	DEBIT	BALANCE
Goods and Services:			
Merchandise	4,230,090	8,190,466	−3,960,376
Tourism	459,455	287,721	171,734
Transport	2,179,782	189,688	1,990,094
Insurance	34,467	56,834	− 22,367
Capital returns . . .	1,786	289,187	− 287,401
Government	222,152	31,153	190,999
Other services . . .	1,309,958	510,961	798,997
Total	8,437,690	9,556,010	−1,118,320
Transfer Payments . . .	50,995	251,517	− 200,522
CURRENT BALANCE . .			−1,318,842
Capital Operations:			
Private capital operations . .	519,338	729,765	− 210,427
Public capital operations . .	2,917	43,606	− 40,689
Total	522,255	773,371	− 251,116
Deficit			−1,569,958

(For the balance of payments of all the Overseas Provinces with Portugal *see* Angola Statistical Survey, p. 160.)

EXTERNAL TRADE*
(contos)

	1968	1969	1970
Imports.	6,740,137	7,490,993	9,302,188
Exports.	4,420,172	4,081,035	4,449,866

PRINCIPAL COMMODITIES*
(contos)

IMPORTS	1968	1969	1970	EXPORTS	1968	1969	1970
Wines . . .	306,084	270,006	261,577	Raw Cotton .	635,570	794,535	738,597
Petroleum (crude) .	379,497	377,791	377,571	Sisal .	91,414	89,119	75,020
Cotton Textiles .	341,203	339,825	310,772	Timber .	183,794	207,245	197,241
Crude and Semi-refined Iron .	255,382	261,631	383,617	Vegetable Oils .	237,126	208,194	264,427
				Cashew Nuts .	1,057,906	779,988	855,158
Machinery excl. Electrical . .	736,609	895,605	1,406,062	Copra .	277,126	198,071	238,841
Electrical Machinery	325,801	314,051	415,461	Raw Sugar .	411,327	547,687	555,203
Vehicles . .	787,391	1,063,803	1,443,871	Tea . .	295,848	234,036	234,071

* Provisional figures.

PRINCIPAL COUNTRIES
(contos)

	IMPORTS			EXPORTS		
	1968	1969	1970	1968	1969	1970
Portugal	2,223,502	2,337,543	2,568,807	1,595,895	1,679,148	1,723,630
Portuguese Overseas Territories . .	231,996	236,634	328,058	213,149	215,081	246,155
Australia	—	17,591	167,042	—	4,259	13,585
Belgium-Luxembourg . . .	151,683	117,190	170,773	—	22,567	30,269
France	224,307	259,768	315,883	—	79,583	60,840
German Federal Republic . .	510,547	635,787	713,019	95,120	127,963	118,823
Iraq	—	377,975	363,599	—	—	65
Japan	—	396,305	561,380	—	34,227	42,127
Italy	135,006	148,703	281,582	—	63,948	81,196
Netherlands	143,506	111,259	141,250	95,625	58,932	94,974
South Africa	793,330	1,127,222	1,368,015	456,473	419,563	464,944
United Kingdom	651,064	607,950	759,507	268,535	196,742	220,666
U.S.A.	337,506	488,918	910,887	461,689	400,884	461,689

* Provisional figures.

TRANSPORT

Railways (1970): Passengers carried 5,381,000, Freight carried 16,874,000 metric tons.

Roads (1968): Cars 64,222, Lorries and Buses 14,876, Motor Cycles 3,614.

Inland Waterways (1969): Passengers carried 192,607; Freight carried 161,740 metric tons.

Shipping (1969): Lourenço Marques and Beira: vessels entered 2,979; freight unloaded 3,807,935, freight loaded 8,587,174 metric tons.

Civil Aviation (1969): Planes arrived 29,467; Passenger arrivals 162,764, Freight 3,481 metric tons.

Pipeline: A pipeline 311 km. long links Beira with the Rhodesian oil refineries. It has not been used since December 1965, as a result of the international embargo on oil exports to Rhodesia, imposed in November 1965.

EDUCATION
(1968)

TYPE	NUMBER OF SCHOOLS	NUMBER OF TEACHERS	NUMBER OF PUPILS
Primary .	3,691	6,274	485,045
Secondary			
Technical .	29	770	14,233
Teacher			
Training .	12	104	1,061
Universities .	1	157	813

Source: Instituto Nacional de Estatística, Lisbon.

THE CONSTITUTION

In January 1972 a proposed Organic Law was published, renaming Angola and Mozambique "States" and giving each a legislative assembly and an advisory council. These will exercise more autonomy in the administration of Provincial affairs. The legislative assemblies will meet twice a year but not for more than four months at a time.

The Governor-Generals of each Province will have the status of a metropolitan Minister of State and will be assisted by a consultative council. He can attend cabinet meetings. The Law was approved by the Portuguese National Assembly on May 1st, 1972.

THE GOVERNMENT

Governor-General: Ing. MANUEL PIMENTEL DOS SANTOS.

Commander-in-Chief of Portuguese Armed Forces in Mozambique: Gen. KAULZA DE ARRIAGA.

Legislative Council. Composed of 27 elected members and two ex-officio members (The Procurator of the Republic and The Director of the Provincial Finance and Accounts Services).

Economic and Social Council. Set up in 1964 in place of the Government Council to assist the Governor-General in his executive and legislative functions.

POLITICAL PARTIES

Acção Nacional Popular: Lourenço Marques; Portuguese government party, formerly União Nacional.

The following organizations are illegal:

Frente de Libertação de Moçambique (FRELIMO) (*Mozambique Liberation Front*): P.O.B. 15274, Dar es Salaam, Tanzania; Pres. SAMORA MACHEL; Vice-Pres. MARCELINO DOS SANTOS.

FRELIMO was formed in 1962 by the merger of three existing nationalist parties. One was the earliest party to be formed among Mozambicans, the *União Democrática Nacional de Moçambique* (UDENAMO), founded in 1960. Another was the Mozambique African Nationalist Union (MANU), formed in 1961. Both these groups, like the third, the *União Africana de Moçambique Independente* (UNAMI), arose among migrant Mozambican workers in the neighbouring British colonies. The first President and Vice-President of FRELIMO were Dr. Eduardo Mondlane and Uria Simango. Dr. Mondlane had previously been on the UN Secretariat and a professor at Syracuse University.

FRELIMO launched its military campaign in September 1964, when small groups of guerrillas infiltrated into Mozambique from the north. Activity was confined at first mainly to Cabo Delgado and Niassa provinces, where it later claimed control of two-thirds of the territory. FRELIMO's second party congress was held in Niassa province in July 1968 and was attended by foreign observers. During 1969 FRELIMO devoted more attention to Tete province, where preparations for the building of the Cabora Bassa dam had begun. By 1971 the situation in the province had deteriorated so far that the Portuguese had imposed strict military rule and ordered all travellers to move only with military convoys.

During 1969 FRELIMO suffered internal troubles. In February Dr. Mondlane was killed by a parcel bomb in his office. In April a former Provincial Secretary in Cabo Delgado, Lazaro Kavandame, defected to the Portuguese, and seven other guerrillas followed. Then in November Uria Simango, one of the new three-man Presidential Council along with Marcelino dos Santos and Samora Machel, was expelled from the party. The Portuguese predicted a big breakthrough in their struggle against the freedom fighters. But, if anything, guerrilla activity increased in the summer and autumn of that year, and by the end of it even the Portuguese admitted to twice as many fatalities (134) as in the previous year and a drop in the number of guerrillas killed from 657 to 524.

The Portuguese now have at least 60,000 troops in Mozambique, with possibly another 40,000 trained and armed Africans. FRELIMO claims control of a fifth of the territory, where it has set up clinics, primary schools and agricultural production units.

Comissão Revolucionário de Moçambique (COREMO) (*Mozambique Revolutionary Commission*): Lusaka, Zambia; f. 1965 as fusion of three nationalist parties; Pres. Sec. PAULO GUMANE.

Mozambique Liberation Movement (MOLIMO): Dar es Salaam; f. 1970; splinter group of FRELIMO; Sec. Gen. HENRIQUES NYANKALE.

DEFENCE

There is an estimated Portuguese armed force of 60,000 in the country plus those enlisted locally.

Commander-in-Chief: Gen. KAULZA DE ARRIAGA.

JUDICIAL SYSTEM

Courts of First Instance. These administer the Legal Code of Metropolitan Portugal. Cases may be finally referred to the Court of Second Instance and the Supreme Court in Lisbon.

RELIGION

The population is mainly animist, but there are about 815,000 Moslems and 960,000 Christians (660,000 Roman Catholics).

ROMAN CATHOLIC CHURCH

Metropolitan See:

Lourenço Marques	Rt. Rev. D. CUSTÓDIO ALVIM PEREIRA, Caixa Postal 258, Lourenço Marques; publ. *Diario*.

Suffragan Sees:

Beira . . .	(vacant), Caixa Postal 544, Beira.
Inhambane	Rt. Rev. D. ERNESTO GONÇALVES DA COSTA, Caixa Postal 178, Inhambane.
João Belo . .	(vacant).
Nampula .	Rt. Rev. D. MANUEL VIEIRA PINTO, Caixa Postal 84, Nampula.
Porto Amélia	Rt. Rev. D. JOSÉ DOS SANTOS GARCIA, Caixa Postal 12, Porto Amélia.
Quelimane .	Rt. Rev. D. FRANCISCO NUNES TEIXEIRA, Caixa Postal 292, Quelimane.
Tete . . .	Rt. Rev. D. FELIX NIZA RIBEIRO, Caixa Postal 218, Tete.
Vila Cabral	Rt. Rev. D. ENRICO DIAS NOGUEIRA, Caixa Postal 111, Villa Cabral.

Missions 245, Schools 3,978, Mission Personnel 6,930 Catholics 1,158,250.

There are some 288,000 Protestants.

THE PRESS

DAILIES

Diario: Caixa Postal 536, Lourenço Marques; f. 1905; circ. 12,000; Dir. Dr. JOAQUIM LUIS DOS SANTOS, O.P.

Diario de Moçambique: Caixa Postal 643, Beira; f. 1950; Portuguese; circ. 12,000; Editor J. D. HENRIQUES COIMBRA.

Notícias: Caixa Postal 327, Lourenço Marques; f. 1926; morning; circ. 27,000; Dir. Dr. DOMINGOS JOAQUIM MASCARENHAS E SILVA.

Noticias de Beira: Caixa Postal 81, Beira; f. 1915; morning; circ. 10,000; Editor VICTOR GOMES.

A Tribuna: C.P. 1822, Lourenço Marques; f. 1962; Dir. Dr. FERNANDO AMARO MONTEIRO; circ. 15,000.

PERIODICALS AND MAGAZINES

LOURENÇO MARQUES

Boletim Oficial da Provincia de Moçambique: Caixa Postal 275; f. 1854; three times weekly; Government and official announcements.

Boletim da Sociedade de Estudos: Caixa Postal 1138; f. 1930; six times a year, Pres. ANTÓNIO SILVA DE SOUSA; circ. 1,000.

Brado Africano: Avda. 24 de Julho, No. 315, Caixa Postal 461; f. 1918; weekly; published by Associação Africana de P. de Moçambique, circ. 1,500.

EM—Economia de Moçambique: Caixa Postal 1607, Beira; Dir. Dr. ANTONIO DE ALMEIDA; monthly; economics and finance.

Renovação: Caixa Postal 1016; f. 1961; weekly; Dir. Dr. COUTO JÚNIOR.

Voz de Moçambique: Caixa Postal 888; f. 1960; fortnightly; Dir. Eng. HOMERO DA COSTA BRANCO.

BEIRA

Voz Africana: Rua D. João de Mascarenhas; Dir. JOSÉ ANTÓNIO DE TRINDADE; Editor P. COSTA.

PUBLISHERS

LOURENÇO MARQUES

Imprensa Nacional da Provincia de Moçambique: Caixa Postal 275; f. 1854; Dir. MÁRIO CAMPOS LOBO DA FONSECA; publs. *Boletim Oficial, Anuário Estatístico, Comércio Externo, Estatística Agrícola, Censo da População, Estatística Industrial, Revista de Entomologia*, and other statistical information and reports.

Empresa Moderna Lda.: Avenida da Republica 13, Caixa Postal 473, f. 1937, Dirs. LOUIS GALLOTI, EURICO BENTO, A. R. FERREIRA.

Papeleria e Tipografia Colonial, Lda.: Rua Salazar 41, Caixa Postal 1077.

Editora Minerva Central: 66 Rua Consiglieri Pedroso 84, Caixa Postal 212, f. 1908, stationers and printers, educational, technical and medical text-books, Propr. J. A. CARVALHO & Co. LTD.

A. W. Bayly & Ca. Lda.: Av. da Republica 195–197, Caixa Postal 185.

RADIO

Radio Clube de Moçambique: Caixa Postal 594, Lourenço Marques; non-profit organization; programmes in Portuguese, English, Afrikaans and local dialects; Dir.-Gen. AUGUSTO DAS NEVES GONÇALVES.

Emissôra do Aero Clube da Beira: Caixa Postal 3, Beira; private commercial station; f. 1936; programmes in Portuguese and local languages; Dir. F. J. SILVÉRIO MOITEIRA.

Radio Pax: Caixa Postal 594, Beira; f. 1954; religious station administered by Franciscans; programmes in Portuguese and local languages; Dir. Rev. ANTONIO GONSALVES.

Radio Mocidade: C.P. 219, Lourenço Marques, programmes in Portuguese, Man. Dr. J. A. ALMEIDA NOGUEIRA.

There are 100,000 radio receivers.

A study group is examining the possibility of television broadcasts from stations in Lourenço Marques, Beira, Quelimane and Nampula.

FINANCE

(cap.=capital; dep.=deposits; m.=million; amounts in escudos)

BANKING

ISSUING BANK

Banco Nacional Ultramarino: 84 rua do Comércio, Lisbon; Caixa Postal 423, Lourenço Marques; f. 1864; cap. 500m., dep. 16,683m. (Dec. 1971); Gov. (vacant); Vice-Govs. Dr. A. J. de CASTRO FERNANDES, Dr. L. PEREIRA COUTINHO.

Banco Comercial de Angola: Head Office Av. Fontes Pereira de Melo 39–1°, Aptdo. 2257, Lisbon; R. Consiglieri Pedroso 99, C.P. 4002, Lourenço Marques; Man. R. R. DE BRITO.

Banco de Crédito Comercial e Industrial: Head Office: Av. dos Restauradores de Angola 79/83, Caixa Postal 1395, Luanda, Angola; Praça 7 de Março 45, Lourenço Marques; f. 1965; cap. 200m., dep. 4,937m. (Dec. 1971); Man. Dir. TEIXEIRA ABREU; 47 brs. in Mozambique.

Banco de Fomento Nacional: Head Office: 26 Rua Monzinho da Silveira, Lisbon 2; Mozambique Branches: 988 and 1008 Ave. da República, P.O.B. 2077, Lourenço Marques; 66 Ave. Paiva de Andrada, P.O.B. 1648, Beira; Telex 6-253; 2 brs. in Angola.

Banco Pinto e Sotto Mayor S.A.R.L.: 28 rua Áurea, Lisbon; f. 1914; Pres. EDUARDO FURTADO; cap. 900m., dep. 19,008m. (Dec. 1970); 45 brs. in Mozambique.

Banco Standard Totta de Moçambique S.A.R.L.: Praça 7 de Março No. 1, C.P. 1119, Lourenço Marques; f. 1966; associate of Banco Totta Açores and the Standard Bank Ltd.; 31 brs.; cap. 112,500m.; dep. 1,475,346m.; Man. Dir. N. E. PARKIN.

Casa Bancaria de Moçambique: Av. Pêro de Anaia, Hotel Moçambique, Beira; f. 1972; Dir. A. A. Magalhães de Mendonça.

INVESTMENT ASSOCIATION

Sociedade Moçambicana de Administração e Gestão de Bens, S.A.R.L.: Av. da República 1675, P.O.B. 2732; Lourenço Marques; f. 1967; minimum cap. 20m. contos; aims to administer and negotiate the total goods and real estate which make up the *Fundo de Investimentos Ultramarino* (Overseas Investment Fund), as well as issuing certificates; Chair. Dr. V. J. DA COSTA.

INSURANCE

Inspecção de Credito e Seguros da Provincia de Moçambique.

MOZAMBIQUE COMPANIES

Companhia de Seguros "Lusitania", S.A.R.L.: Caixa Postal 1165, Lourenço Marques; f. 1947; cap. 30m.; Chair. ANSELMO DE SOUSA PINTO; Gen. Man. Dr. R. DA SILVA RAMOS.

Companhia de Seguros A Mundial de Moçambique S.A.R.L.: Caixa Postal 514, Beira; f. 1857; cap. 10m.; Dir. Dr. ARMINDO DOS SANTOS PINHO.

Companhia de Seguros Tranquilidade de Moçambique: Avda. de República 1203, Caixa Postal 9, Lourenço Marques; cap. 20m.; Chair. Dr. J. PEREIRA MARTINHO.

Companhia de Seguros Náuticus: Edifício Náuticus, Avda. da República 1383, Caixa Postal 696, Lourenço Marques; f. 1943; cap. 6m.; general; Chair. Dr. ANTÓNIO M. MASCARENHAS GAIVÃO.

There are a large number of Portuguese companies represented in the Province.

TRADE AND INDUSTRY

REGULATING COMMISSIONS

Junta de Comércio Externo (*Board of External Trade Economic Co-ordination*): Praça 7 de Março, Lourenço Marques, Caixa Postal 654; f. 1956; Man Dr. FERNANDO CATALÃO DIONISIO.

Instituto dos Cereais de Moçambique (*Mozambique Cereals Inst.*): Avda. da República No. 882-6°, Lourenço Marques.

Instituto do Algodão de Moçambique (*Cotton Institute of Mozambique*): Head Office: Caixa Postal 806, Lourenço Marques; f. 1938; Chair. RAUL WAHNON CORREIA PINTO.

LABOUR ORGANIZATIONS

Sindicato Nacional dos Empregados Bancarios da Provincia de Moçambique (*National Syndicate of Bank Employees of Mozambique*): Avenida de República 49, 6° Lourenço Marques; f. 1946; 1,020 mems.; Pres. JOSÉ JOAQUIM COUTO DE OLIVIERA; Sec. OLÍVIO MALHEIRO VAZ.

Sindicato Nacional dos Empregados do Comercio e da Industria da Provincia de Moçambique: (*National Syndicate of Commercial and Industrial Employees of Mozambique*): Avenida Pinheiro Chagas 1267, Lourenço Marques, Caixa Postal 394; f. 1898; about 13,500 mems.; Pres. JOSÉ PEREIRA LOPES; Sec. Dr. SECUNDINO ALONSO.

Sindicato Nacional dos Operarios da Construção Civil e Oficios Correlativos (*National Syndicate of Civil Construction and Related Services*): Avda. Luciano Cordeiro Nos. 937–945, Lourenço Marques; f. 1949; about 19,417 mems.; Pres. ALFREDO DA COSTA LEMOS; Sec. CRISPIM DA SILVA TEIXEIRA.

Sindicato Nacional dos Ferroviários de Manica e Sofala e do Pessoal do Porto da Beira (*National Syndicate of Railways of Manica and Sofala and of Personnel of the Port of Beira*): P.O.B. 387, Beira; f. 1945; about 819 mems.; Pres. DOMINGOS VIEIRA MARTINS; Sec. RUI HENRIQUE FERREIRA.

Sindicato Nacional dos Motoristas e Oficios Correlativos (*National Syndicate of Motor Transport Operators and Related Services*): Avenida 24 de Julho 133, Lourenço Marques; f. 1948; about 3,500 mems.; Pres. JOSÉ ZEFERINO; Sec. ARMANDO LUÍS DA COSTA.

TRANSPORT

RAILWAYS

The total length of track operated in 1970 was 3,703 km. excluding the Sena Sugar Estates Railway (90 km. of 0.92 m. gauge), which serves only the company's properties. The railways are now all State-owned, with the exception of the Trans-Zambesia Railway Company. A link is being built between Nova Freixo and Mpimbe in Malawi to give Malawi direct rail access to the port of Nacala.

STATE-OWNED RAILWAYS

Direcção dos Portos, Caminhos de Ferro e Transportes de Moçambique: Caixa Postal 276, Lourenço Marques; government department administering the following railways:

The Lourenço Marques System: consisting of the following main lines: (1) Lourenço Marques-Ressano Garcia; connects with the South African Railway system at the Transvaal border, and provides with that system through-railway transport to Johannesburg, the Rand area and Botswana; (2) Lourenço Marques-Goba; a new rail link with the Swaziland iron mines of Bomvu Ridge was opened in November 1964; (3) Lourenço Marques-Malvérnia (on the Rhodesian border) providing through transport to Rhodesia, Zambia and the South-East Congo, total track 783 km., 1.067 m. gauge.

Mozambique System: Caixa Postal 16, Nampula; Nacala to Inova Guarda; br. from Lumbo to Rio Monapo; the extension to Malawi through Nova Freixo was opened in August 1970.

Beira System: Caixa Postal 472, Beira; the main line runs from Beira to the Rhodesian town of Umtali via Vila de Manica and Vila Pery providing through transport to Rhodesia and Zambia, total track 318 km., 1.067 m. gauge. The system also includes:

Tete Railway: Dona Ana to the Moatize coal mines, 254 km. of 1.067 metre gauge, the railway is to be continued northwards to Furancungo.

Dondo-Malawi Line: From Dondo through Sena to Malawi frontier, connecting with Blantyre and including branch line from Inhamitanga to Marromeu; total track 423 km.

Inhambane and Gaza System: Caixa Postal 5, Inhambane; from Inhambane to Inharrime 91 km., 1.067 metre gauge; from João Belo to Chicomo, and a branch from Manjacazo to Marão totalling 141 km., 0.75 metre gauge.

Quelimane System: Caixa Postal 73, Quelimane, from Quelimane to Mocuba 145 km., 1.067 metre gauge.

PRIVATE RAILWAY

Trans-Zambesia Railway Co. Ltd.: Head Office: Avenida da Liberdade, 227, 7°, Lisbon 2, Portugal; Registered Office: 40-42 Cannon St., London, E.C.4, England; Executive Office: Predio Tamega, P.O.B. 61, Beira, Mozambique; runs from Dondo to Sena on the South bank of the Zambesi; 181 miles, 1.067 metre gauge, Chair. and Man. Dir. VIVIAN L. OURY (London); Man. Dir. in Lisbon J. B. CORREA DA SILVA (Paço d'Arcos),

Man. Dir. Resident in Mozambique Eng. FERNANDO SEIXAS, P.O.B. 276, Lourenço Marques; Executive Man. ILIDIO TAVARES, P.O.B. 61, Beira, Mozambique.

ROADS

There were, in 1970, 37,106 km. of roads in Mozambique, of which 4,050 km. were classified as first-class roads Work was due to begin in 1972 on a 116-mile, R2m. tarred road to link Lourenço Marques with the Natal border.

SHIPPING

Much development work is being carried out on the ports and three new canals were completed in 1964. New quays for handling minerals from the interior of Africa have been built at Lourenço Marques and a port expansion scheme estimated at £12m. will include extension of quays, increasing warehouse space and building cold storage facilities, intended to double the port's capacity in three years; the port of Beira is being expanded. A large new harbour to accommodate mining activities is planned between Bilene and Ponto do Ouro at an estimated cost of 1,000 escudos.

Companhia Moçambicana de Navegação: f. 1969; Caixa Postal 786, Lourenço Marques; agents: Navetur-Soc. de Agencias de Turismo e Transportes de Moçambique; Dir. Dr. B. DE ALMEIDA.

Companhia Nacional de Navegação: General agents: Navetur—Soc. de Agenc as de Turismo e Transportes de Mocambique, C.P. 2694, Lourenco Marques.

Empresa do Limpopo: Rua Araujo, Caixa Postal 145, Lourenço Marques; f. 1905; coastal service along Portuguese East African coast from Lourenço Marques to Mocimboa da Praia, cargo and passenger service; Man. Dr. JOÃO SÁ NOGUEIRA.

CIVIL AVIATION
MOZAMBIQUE AIR LINE

Direcção de Exploração dos Transportes Aéreos (DETA): Aeroporto, Caixa Postal 2060, Lourenço Marques; f. 1936; operates domestic services and on the following international routes: Lourenço Marques–Johannesburg Lourenço Marques–Durban; Lourenço Marques–Manzini, Swaziland; Beira–Salisbury; and Beira–Blantyre; fleet: five Douglas DC-3, one Douglas C-47, three Fokker F27, two Boeing 737-200; Dir. ABEL NEVES DE AZEVEDO.

Mozambique is also served by the following airlines: Air Madagascar, Air Malawi, S.A.A. and T.A.P.

TOURISM

Centro de Informação e Turismo: Caixa Postal 614, Lourenço Marques. Tourist revenue 1965: 190,000 contos; 1966: 235,000 contos.

EDUCATION

LEARNED SOCIETIES AND RESEARCH INSTITUTES

Arquivo Histórico de Moçambique (*Mozambique Historical Archives*): C.P. 2033, Lourenço Marques; library of 4,160 vols.; Dir. ALEXANDRE LOBATO.

Direcção dos Serviços de Geologia e Minas: Caixa Postal 217, Lourenço Marques; f. 1930; 157 mems.; Geological studies and Mining research; 15,000 books in library; Dir. J. R. F. REBOLO; publs. *Boletim dos Serviços de Geologia e Minas de Moçambique, Carta Geológica de Moçambique.*

Instituto do Algodão de Moçambique (*Cotton Research Institute*): Caixa Postal 806, Lourenço Marques; f. 1962; departments of agronomy, botany, soils, economics, genetical cytology, entomology and phytopathology; 4 experimental stations; library of 2,500 vols., 210 journals and reviews; Dir. Eng. Agr. MARIO DE CARVALHO; publ. *Memórias e Trabalhos.*

Instituto de Investigação Científica de Moçambique (*Mozambique Institute of Scientific Research*): Caixa Postal 1780, Lourenço Marques; f. 1955; departments of Biology, Geography, Geology, Social Sciences; library and scientific documentation centre, Museu Dr. Alvaro de Castro incorporated since 1959, see below; Dir. Prof. Dr. A. XAVIER DA CUNHA; publs. *Revista de Entomologia de Moçambique, Novos Taxa Entomológicos, Boletim do Centro de Documentação Científica, Memórias do Instituto de Investigação Científica de Moçambique, Trabalhos do Instituto de Investigação Científica de Moçambique, Bibliografia Florestal de Interesse Africano, Publicações de Informação e Divulgação.*

Instituto Provincial de Saúde Pública de Moçambique (*Mozambique Public Health Institute*): Avenida Fernandes Tomáz 179, Caixa Postal 1572, Lourenço Marques; f. 1955; departments of Epidemiology (Malacology, Demography and Statistics), Microbiology (Protozoology, Helminthology, Bacteriology), Clinical Pathology (Therapeutics, Biochemistry, Haematology, Pathology), Documentation and Scientific Information; Dir. L. T. DE ALMEIDA FRANCO.

Missão Geográfica de Moçambique—MGM (*Mozambique Geographical Mission*): Caixa Postal 288, Lourenço Marques; f. 1932.

Observatório Astronómico e Meteorológico Campos Rodrigues (*Campos Rodrigues Astronomical and Meteorological Observatory*): Serviço Meteorológico de Moçambique, Caixa Postal 256, Lourenço Marques; f. 1907; Dir. Eng. FERNANDO AUGUSTO LEAL; publs. *Anuário de Observações* (3 vols.), I *Observações Meteorológicas de Superficie,* II *Observações Meteorólogicas de Altitude, Boletim Séismique, Informações de Caracter Astronómico, Boletim Geomagnetico Preliminar, Boletim Meteorológico para a Agricultura, Publicações Eventuais.*

Sociedade de Estudos da Província de Moçambique (*Society for the Advancement of Science in Mozambique*): P.O. Box 1138 (Lourenço Marques); f. 1930; 680 mems., library of 25,000 vols.; the Society is divided into 13 sections: Overseas Administration, Social Sciences, Economy and Finance, Agriculture, Brazilian Studies, French Studies, Humanities, Jurisprudence and Legislation, Mathematics and Engineering, Biology and Medicine, Soil Protection, Physico-Chemical Sciences; Pres. Dr. VICTOR HUGO VELEZ GRILO; publ. *Boletim* (bi-monthly).

LIBRARIES

Arquivo Histórico de Moçambique: C.P. 2033, Lourenço Marques; 2,872 vols.; Dir. ANTONIO DE ANDRADE REBELO.

Biblioteca Municipal: Lourenço Marques; 7,951 vols.

Biblioteca da Sociedade de Estudos da Província de Moçambique: Lourenço Marques; 25,000 vols.

Biblioteca Nacional de Moçambique (*National Library of Mozambique*): Lourenço Marques; f. 1961; 95,000 vols.; Dir. Dr. JORGE GOUVEIA CRÓ.

MUSEUMS

Museu Dr. Alvaro de Castro: Caixa Postal 1780, Lourenço Marques; f. 1911; Natural History Museum and Ethnographic Gallery; Dir. Prof. Dr. A. XAVIER DA CUNHA.

Museu Freire de Andrade: Department of Geology and Mines, Lourenço Marques; f. 1940; Dir. Eng. JOSÉ DOS REIS FERNANDES REBOLO.

UNIVERSITY

UNIVERSIDADE DE LOURENÇO MARQUES

C.P. 257, LOURENÇO MARQUES

Telephone: 26426, 27851-2.

Founded 1962.

State control; Language of instruction: Portuguese; Academic year: October to July.

Rector: Prof. Dr. JOSÉ ALBERTO DA GAMA FERNANDES DE CARVALHO.

Administration Officer: Dr. MARIA CAMARATE DE CAMPOS.

Librarian: JORGE MANUEL DE MORAIS GOMES BARBOSA.

Number of teachers: 260.
Number of students: 1,180 men, 930 women, total 2,110.

Publications: *Revista Ciências* (eight sections), *Revista dos Estudantes, Boletim da Universidade.*

DEANS:

Faculty of Arts: Dr. J. M. M. GOMES BARBOSA.
Faculty of Medicine: Prof. Dr. M. RIBEIRO A.
Faculty of Engineering: Prof. Dr. J. BARREIROS MARTINS.
Faculty of Agriculture: Prof. Dr. J. M. BASTOS DE MACEDO.
Faculty of Veterinary Sciences: Prof. Dr. J. DA SILVA TENDEIRO.
Faculty of Sciences: Prof. Dr. A. X. CUNHA MARQUES.

SELECT BIBLIOGRAPHY

(For works on the Portuguese African territories generally *see* Angola Select Bibliography, p. 175.)

BOLEO, OLIVEIRA. *Moçambique.* Lisbon, 1961.

ISCSPU. *Moçambique.* Lisbon, 1965.

MONDLANE, E., *The Struggle for Mozambique.* London and Baltimore, Penguin Books, 1969.

SPENCE, C. F. *Moçambique.* Cape Town, 1963.

LIBYA

ALGERIA

MALI

NIGER

CHAD

L. CHAD

NIGERIA

UPPER VOLTA

DAHOMEY

Nguigmi
Diffa
Termet
Gouré
Zinder
Tanout
Agadez
Tessaoua
Maradi
Madaoua
Tahoua
Birni-n-Konni
Dogondoutchi
Filingué
Dosso
Niger
Tillabéri
NIAMEY

▲ International airport
═══ Main road
─── Secondary road

km
0   300

Niger

Niger

PHYSICAL AND SOCIAL GEOGRAPHY

R. J. Harrison Church

The Republic of Niger is the largest state in west Africa, and one of its three landlocked ones. With an area of 489,190 sq. miles (1,267,000 sq. km.) it is larger than Nigeria, its immensely richer southern neighbour, which is Africa's most peopled country. The low population of Niger, estimated at 4,239,000 in 1972, is largely explained by Niger's aridity and remoteness. Two-thirds of the country is desert, most of the north-east being uninhabitable.

In the north-centre is the partly volcanic Aïr massif, with many dry watercourses remaining from earlier wetter conditions. Agadez in Aïr receives, on average, no more than about 7 in. (180 mm.) of annual rainfall, and that in only two months. Yet the Tuareg keep considerable numbers of livestock by moving them seasonally to areas farther south, where underground water is available from wells sunk into the Intercalary rocks of Jurassic to Cretaceous age.

South again, along the Niger-Nigerian border, are sandy areas where the annual rainfall of some 22 in. (560 mm.) just permits the cultivation of groundnuts and millet by Hausa farmers, as in adjacent northern Nigeria. Cotton is cultivated in small, seasonally flooded valleys and depressions.

In the south-west is the far larger, seasonally flooded Niger valley, the pastures of which nourish livestock that have to contend with nine months of drought for the rest of the year. Rice and other crops are grown by the Djerma and Songhai peoples as the Niger flood declines.

Niger thus has three very disparate physical and cultural foci, with no dominant ethnic group like the Mossi of the Upper Volta, or the Bambara of Mali. Unity has been encouraged by French aid and economic advance but the attraction of richer Nigeria is considerable. Distances to the nearest ports of Cotonou in Dahomey and Lagos in Nigeria are at least 850 miles (1,370 km.), both routes requiring breaks of bulk, and the latter foreign exchange.

RECENT HISTORY*

Michael Crowder and Donal Cruise O'Brien

(Revised for this edition by KAYE WHITEMAN)

At independence in 1960 the government of President Hamani Diori had only recently consolidated its political dominance, with considerable help from the French colonial administration. Diori's principal opponent, Bakary Djibo, had incurred the wrath of the French by campaigning (unsuccessfully) for complete independence in the French constitutional referendum of 1958. Djibo's party, the Sawaba, was then banned in 1959, and Djibo himself went into exile. Since independence the illegal Sawaba has been sporadically active. In December 1963 eighty people were arrested for plotting against the régime, and in 1964, following guerrilla incidents along the Nigerian border, seven "terrorists" were court-martialled and publicly shot in the capital. Very harsh government repression was followed by an unsuccessful attempt on Diori's life in 1965.

Despite such opposition Diori has remained in power throughout the decade following independence. His pro-French posture has made it possible for him to ensure considerable financial, technical and even military assistance from the ex-colonial power. These links are made yet more secure by the discovery of a large deposit of uranium in Niger, exploited by the

French Atomic Energy Commission since 1971. There have been tensions within the governing group, notably between activists of the ruling party (the *Parti progressiste nigérien*) and civil service personnel. Following charges of corruption in the civil service the party was reorganized in 1968 and given a much more important role in the national administration.

The opposition of the early sixties, however, seemed to have died down by the end of the decade. This was partly due to the opportunities offered to some of the more talented younger men in the administration, and partly to Diori's success in building an image as a statesman on the African scene; he mediated successfully between Chad and Sudan in 1967, and more recently between Chad and Libya.

More interesting have been his attempts to take a certain distance from the French, although he had come to power with French assistance in the first place and had been the beneficiary of considerable financial, technical, and even military assistance from the ex-colonial power. It was thought that the

---

* For the period before independence *see* Recent History of Dahomey, p. 282.

discovery of uranium deposits would tie him even more securely to the French, as the exploitation of these (the largest in black Africa so far discovered) has been mainly in the hands of the French Atomic Energy Commission. The present world glut of uranium, however, caused the French to have second thoughts about expanding the mine (the first phase of which was inaugurated late in 1971), to the disquiet of the Niger Government, which has seen in revenues from uranium a way out of the country's extreme poverty.

Tension in relations with the French developed in 1972, apparently because of government suspicions

that French technical assistants were contributing to the ferment in Niger's schools. In the summer Niger asked for a renegotiation of her co-operation agreements with France.

There have also been French suspicions of Niger's growing relations with Nigeria. Niger supported the federal side in the Nigerian civil war, and has become very close in the post-war period, which has meant a certain estrangement from President Diori's old colleague of the RDA, President Houphouët-Boigny of Ivory Coast. Niger has also developed relations with Libya to the north, and has received aid from both Nigeria and Libya.

ECONOMY

Samir Amin*

Niger more than any other country of former French West Africa is the outcome of the absurd boundaries drawn up during the colonial partition and later administrative subdividing. The population has expanded from 3.1 million in 1960 to 4.2 million in 1972, a growth rate of 2.6 per cent per year, and four-fifths are farmers, the remainder being Fulani or Tuareg stockbreeders. With a few towns and poorly educated population Niger seems scarcely viable.

THE TRADITIONAL ECONOMY

Traditional farming and stockrearing generates two-thirds of G.D.P. The main food production—millet and sorghum—is of the order of 1 million metric tons a year, and its growth corresponds roughly to that of the rural population. This food production occupies most of the cultivated land, which represents only 3 per cent of the state's area. Livestock, estimated in 1971 at 4.4 million cattle and 9 million sheep and goats, is still the main export, in spite of the rapid progress made by groundnuts during the past decade. As all over the region, this extensive stockrearing is making appreciable progress, stimulated by demand from the highly-populated coastal region, southern Nigeria and Dahomey. Livestock production is growing at an estimated 3 per cent a year, as are exports. River fishing (8,000 tons) provides similarly expanding exports.

Groundnut production grew at a rate of 7 per cent over the period 1960–70, and, despite a drop in output since then, was largely responsible for Niger's overall economic growth. Groundnut production is at its most successful in the Hausa border strip around Maradi and Zinder. Sociological studies have shown here that a phenomenon of "micro-kulakization", originating with Hausa traders, encourages a differentiation between the classes which is favourable to this kind of development, whereas in the Djerma-Songhai district,

traditionally warrior rather than trading or peasant communities, the economic balance is sought in the emigration of young men, especially to Ghana. This emigration, which has been studied in depth, affects about 50,000 men.

Cotton, its development stimulated by the CFDT, has been less successful. Production, which started in 1956, reached 11,000 tons in 1971.

"International specialization" thus forces Niger to supply raw materials which can only pay for peasant labour at very low rates, and consequently the rural economy cannot generate any savings to finance its own development. An aggravating circumstance is Niger's refusal to make use of Nigeria's railway network and the extravagant detour made by road from Maradi to Niamey towards Parakou, before taking the Dahomey railway in order to enable the port of Cotonou to operate on a profitable basis.

THE MODERN ECONOMY

Niger is poorly urbanized. In 1972 only four towns had more than 20,000 inhabitants, Niamey, Zinder, Maradi and Tahoua. Their total population rose from 87,000 inhabitants in 1960 to 209,083 in 1972, or by about 6 per cent a year, and in 1972 the total represents barely 5 per cent of the country's population. On the basis of the urban population non-agricultural production (24,000 million francs CFA in 1964) gives a per capita yield of the order of 150,000 francs CFA compared with less than 12,000 francs for the rural population.

Niger's industrial achievements in these circumstances are very modest. The groundnut oil factory (24,000 tons capacity) and cotton "ginneries" (8,500 tons capacity), provide direct outlets for agricultural production, and make up a unit which is in any case protected by the high cost of transport (of rival goods). A local textile industry of 2,000 tons capacity is planned on a scale suitable for the limited Niger market. The Malbaza cement works (35,000 tons capacity), inaugurated in 1966, is also justified by the

---

* For the 1973 edition revisions have been made to this article by the Editor.

high cost of transporting imported goods although its capacity—exceeding that of the small local market—does make necessary financial sacrifices. Some light industries already in production or at the planning stage give Niger the "classic" pattern of "industrial" enterprises in contemporary Africa. These are flour milling (4,000 metric tons), rice milling (5,500 tons), a soap factory, a brewery and a soft drinks factory, plastics products (sandals and utensils), metal products and agricultural equipment), abattoirs and a tannery, a tomato canning factory, a printing press, a tile and brick factory, and the assembly of radio sets. The whole of industry employs barely a thousand workers.

The mineral resources developed so far have been insignificant: cassiterite mined at Aïr by a joint company, Say's iron ore (a low grade of 40 per cent) and Tahoua's gypsum and phosphates would only be of importance if they were to establish a locally-centered industrial growth that is not envisaged. The uranium mine discovered at Arlit by the French Atomic Energy Commission and the associated processing plant began production in 1971, producing 400 tons in the first year, worth almost 2,000 million francs CFA, with a target of 15,000 tons in 1974. The mine will supply the state with revenue (64 per cent of the profits earned), but will not by any means provide the basis of local industrial expansion. The mining company, SOMAIR, is under French control (40 per cent of the capital is held by the Commissariat of Atomic Energy, 40 per cent by French private interests and 20 per cent by the state of Niger), after several attempts at negotiations with Great Britain, Federal Germany and Japan had been abruptly terminated. In short, investments of the order of 13,000 million francs CFA give a short-lived stimulus to economic activity, disguising the falling-off of business in the other sectors.

Power is very expensive and the high growth in electricity consumption (13 per cent a year) is still very largely governed by domestic consumption and public town use. In the future cheaper power will come from the hydro-electric plant at Kaindra, Nigeria.

The whole transport policy is in need of review. The road network (6,998 km. at the time of writing) and the number of vehicles (2,073 lorries) have been planned with a view to making the country independent of Nigeria. Created in 1959 to support the "Operation Hirondelle", the Dahomey-Niger Joint Organization of Railways and Transport (*Organisation commune Dahomey-Niger des chemins et du transport*—OCDN) shows for that reason operational losses of more than 200 million francs CFA a year on average, mainly met until 1964 by subsidies (7.60 francs per km./ton) from the governments of Niger and Dahomey. Moreover, the Organization is regularly reviewed as a result of the disputes between the two countries.

The meagre force of wage and salary-earners—about 23,000, of whom almost half are employed by the government and only a thousand by industry—and the very slow increase in this force create unemployment problems, in spite of the country's low degree of urbanization. The replacement of Dahomey citizens by Niger nationals, particularly in 1964–65, probably alleviated for a time the burden of unemployment among people with limited educational qualifications. For, in spite of everything, education is expanding at the exceptionally rapid rate of 15 per cent a year in primary schools, whose numbers rose from 35,000 pupils in 1962 to 71,000 in 1966 and to more than 88,000 in 1970–71, while the attendance rate rose from 5 per cent to 13 per cent of the population of school age. More than one-third of wage-earners are paid on the guaranteed minimum occupational salary scale (SMIG) of 27 francs an hour, which has been frozen at that level since 1962.

Here, as in other countries, it was the inadequacy of commercial enterprise, more than ideological reasons, which led the state to intervene for the promotion of state commerce. The *Société nigérienne de commercialisation de l'arachide* (SONARA), established in 1962 (in the form of a joint company, the state owning 50 per cent of the capital), and the *Société nationale de commerce et de production* (COPRO-NIGER), which provisions on a monopoly basis zones deprived of basic necessities, show a trade figure of over 6,000 million francs CFA. Here, as elsewhere, if these bodies make practically no profits which could contribute towards financing the development of the economy, it is not so much because they are badly managed as because they are placed in an almost impossible position.

INVESTMENTS AND PUBLIC FINANCES

A relatively serious attempt at planning has been made in Niger. The first four-year plan (1961–64) anticipated investments of 30,100 million francs CFA, of which 25,200 million were in fact made. The second plan (1965–68) envisaged investments of 43,200 million francs CFA, of which apparently more than 30,000 million were made, and some 47,800 million were provided for the third plan (1969–72). The actual rise in investments, which seems to be around 5 per cent a year, would in fact be parallel to that of G.D.P.

Nearly all public investment is financed by foreign aid. Local private capital finances a fraction of the building of homes and various transport needs (e.g. lorries). In spite of Niger's investment code which was adopted in 1961 and which, although very liberal, was rather more complex than in other countries, foreign capital has not been forthcoming, except for the mining of uranium, owing to the unprofitability of industrial ventures in the country's basic conditions. So in almost every sphere what has been achieved has been the work of joint companies. The infrastructure (roads and power supplies, education and especially town planning) has absorbed about 60 per cent of investments undertaken during the decade. In the "immediately productive" sectors themselves agriculture and livestock have received more than half the money and industry only 15 per cent of all investments, concentrated on the several projects listed above.

Official external aid received by Niger in 1960–68 totalled 29,000 million francs CFA, increasing from 2,600 million to 4,800 million (a yearly average of about 3,700 million). Of this 16,700 million francs CFA was spent on capital projects (a yearly average of 2,100 million) rising from 1,200 to 3,400 million between 1960 and 1968). The rest, i.e. 12,600 million (a relatively stable yearly average of 1,500 million), represents the different forms of current public aid: budget subsidies from France and the *Conseil de l'Entente;* technical assistance (minus the costs provided by Niger) and miscellaneous current aid (scholarships, training courses, etc.); and finally the price support measures for groundnuts and cotton introduced by the EDF to aid crop diversification. But part of this current aid—budget subsidies from France—is used for the local capital budget, whose total has risen progressively from 500 million francs CFA in 1960 to 900 million in 1969–70. It can thus be concluded that all public investments are financed by official external aid. The third plan (1969–72) was, like its predecessors, a collection of projects submitted for the approval of the providers of aid: out of 47,810 million francs CFA anticipated investments, 38,300 million had to be financed from abroad.

Almost all foreign aid having been, until recent years, supplied in the form of grants, the public foreign debt remains slight. At the end of 1966 it amounted to 4,600 million francs CFA (less than 6 per cent of G.D.P.), with the interest on it running at 300–400 million francs CFA (3.5 per cent of exports). But the tendency in the last few years has been to make use of relatively costly public and private loans (commercial credits already represented a debt of 900 million francs CFA at the end of 1966).

If the income from uranium is delayed, difficulties in public finance are likely. The operational budget in fact rose progressively from 5,000 million francs CFA in 1960 to 11,886 million in 1972. Added to this since 1963 is the local authorities' expenditure, now 1,000 million francs CFA and showing a growth rate at current prices of around 9 per cent per annum, undoubtedly much higher than the basic economic growth rate. As for local tax and other returns, these rose from 3,800 million francs CFA in 1960 to 8,900 million in 1966–67, showing a growth rate of 14 per cent per year. The level of taxation seems to have risen considerably. The improvement of customs control at the frontiers has played an essential part in this increase. Since 1966, however, the growth of revenue has slowed down considerably, as is revealed by the stagnation of duties collected by the customs service (between 3,800 and 3,900 million francs CFA from 1966 to 1969). Thus the budget has never been without a deficit.

The Treasury's deficit, as we have seen, has been defrayed by current external aid, given chiefly in the form of budget subsidies, which is why the fall in public reserves has remained small.

FOREIGN TRADE AND THE BALANCE OF PAYMENTS

As in the case of the Upper Volta, Niger's foreign trade is only partially recorded by the authorities. The export of groundnuts and related products (oil-cake and oil) which make up the bulk of the recorded exports (cotton still being negligible) has clearly expanded as has groundnut production at a rate of 7 per cent, rising from 3,000 to 6,000 million francs CFA between 1960 and 1970, with large fluctuations according to the climatic conditions. Cattle exports, far less recorded, were estimated in 1960 at 180,000 cattle and 520,000 sheep and goats, which, at a price of 12,000 francs CFA a head for the former and 2,000 francs for the latter, totals 3,200 million francs CFA. The growth of these exports during the 1960s was estimated at 3 per cent a year, and the rise in prices 10 per cent, so that exports should amount to 4,600 million current francs in 1970. The civil war in Nigeria greatly disorganized exports bound chiefly for the southern regions of that country, but since the end of the war Niger's exports have returned to normal. In all, exports rising from 6,200 to 10,600 million current francs CFA increased during the decade at the rate of 5.5 per cent per year.

There is scarcely any doubt that the growth rate of imports has been higher. Real total imports have risen from 6,900 to 14,200 million current francs CFA between 1960 and 1970, at an increase of 7.5 per cent per year. The growing trade deficit has been met by increasing foreign contributions.

The balance of payments thus reconstituted shows a balance of private transfers of around 5,000 million francs CFA, which is relatively stable (*see* table 1).

Table 1

BALANCE OF PAYMENTS 1960–70

	EXTREMES 1960–70	ANNUAL AVERAGE 1960–70
Revenue:		
Exports . . .	6.2–10.6	8.4
Official Foreign Development Aid .	1.2–3.4	2.1
Official Current Aid .	1.6	1.6
Miscellaneous Current Returns . .	1.6–2.4	2.0
Private capital . .	2.0	2.0
Foreign Assets . .	0.4	0.4
Expenditure:		
Imports . . .	6.9–14.2	10.5
Miscellaneous Current Transfers .	0.9–1.5	1.2
Private Transfers . .	approx. 5.0	4.8

The balance of transfers of private savings and company profits is altogether comparable to that obtained for the other countries of west Africa, taking into account the number of Europeans (6,000) and the volume of production of the non-agricultural economy (about 20,000 million francs CFA).

STATISTICAL SURVEY

AREA AND POPULATION

AREA sq. km.	POPULATION—1972 estimates					
	Total	Hausa	Djerma-Songhai	Fulani (Peulh)	Tuareg, etc.	Beriberi-Manga
1,267,000*	4,239,000	2,276,343	1,000,404	449,334	127,170	385,749

*489,190 sq. miles

CHIEF TOWNS
(1972 est.)

Niamey (capital)	.	102,000	Maradi . . .	37,079
Zinder . . .		39,427	Tahoua . . .	30,577

AGRICULTURE
PRINCIPAL CROPS
('000 metric tons)

	1969	1970	1971
Maize	2	2	2*
Millet	1,095	901	800
Sorghum	289	337	300
Rice	39	37	40
Sugar Cane (crop year ending in year stated)	25	25	25*
Sweet Potatoes and Yams .	9	10*	n.a.
Cassava (Manioc) . . .	199	200*	n.a.
Onions	27	30*	n.a.
Cow Peas	160	150*	150*
Dates	5*	5*	5*
Groundnuts (unshelled) . .	207	235	240
Cottonseed	8	6	7*
Cotton Lint	4	3	4*

* FAO estimates.

Source: FAO, *Production Yearbook 1971.*

LIVESTOCK
('000—FAO estimates)

	1968/69	1969/70	1970/71
Horses . . .	170	180	180
Donkeys . . .	340	360	370
Cattle . . .	4,200	4,300	4,400
Pigs . . .	22	23	26
Sheep . . .	2,700	2,750	2,800
Goats . . .	5,900	6,000	6,200
Camels . . .	390	400	410
Poultry . . .	6,500	6,750	7,000

Source: FAO, *Production Yearbook 1971.*

LIVESTOCK PRODUCTS
(FAO estimates)

	1969	1970	1971
Hides and Skins ('000) .			
Cattle . . .	180	233	n.a.
Sheep . . .	408	233	n.a.
Goat . . .	1,046	1,316	n.a.
Milk ('000 metric tons) .			
Cow . . .	105	108	110
Sheep . . .	14	14	15
Goat . . .	118	119	120
Hen Eggs (metric tons) .	4,400	4,500	4,500

Source: FAO, *Production Yearbook 1971.*

MINING

	1967	1968	1969	1970
Tin Ore (metric tons) . . .	32	75	76	37

INDUSTRY

	1969	1970	1971
Beer and Soft Drinks ('000 hl.) . . .	n.a.	n.a.	47
Electricity (million kWh.) .	33	39	42

FINANCE

100 centimes = 1 franc de la Communauté Financière Africaine.
Coins: 1, 2, 5, 10 and 25 francs CFA.
Notes: 50, 100, 500, 1,000 and 5,000 francs CFA.
Exchange rates (December 1972): 1 franc CFA = 2 French centimes.
£1 sterling = 593.625 francs CFA; U.S. $1 = 255.785 francs CFA.
1,000 francs CFA = £1.685 = $3.91.

BUDGET
(1969–70—million francs CFA)

REVENUE		EXPENDITURE	
Customs	4,107	Public Services and Works . . .	120
Indirect Taxes	1,717	Interior	1,182
Direct Taxes.	3,994	Education	1,400
		Health	875
		Rural Economy	782
TOTAL (inc. others) . . .	10,806	TOTAL (inc. others) . . .	10,806

1970-71 Budget: balanced at 10,903m. francs CFA.

1971-72 Budget: current expenditure 11,886m. francs CFA; investment budget 1,914m. francs CFA.

Development Plan: The three-year plan (1970–73) is a part of the overall ten-year plan (1965–74), and is based on an investment of 44,731m. francs CFA.

The principle investors are the IBRD, providing 29.2 per cent, the European Development Fund, providing 24 per cent, and the Fonds d'Aide et Coopération, providing 23.3 per cent. The greatest expenditure will be on the improvement of industrial production, and the expansion of communications.

EXTERNAL TRADE
(million francs CFA)

The figures below are taken from the records of the Customs Posts at the frontiers. These records are not fully representative of external trade for much smuggling occurs, particularly between Niger and Nigeria.

	1965	1966	1967	1968	1969	1970	1971
Imports .	9,297	11,115	11,352	10,237	12,570	16,213	14,975
Exports .	6,250	8,574	8,226	7,125	6,250	8,795	10,670

PRINCIPAL COMMODITIES

IMPORTS	1969	1970	1971*	EXPORTS	1969	1970	1971
Cotton Textiles . .	2,268	3,077	1,220	Live Animals . . .	891	1,390	1,322*
Electrical Equipment .	575	797	152	Groundnuts, Shelled . .	3,721	4,934	2,958*
Machinery . . .	2,163	1,434	1,098	Oil-cake, Cattle Feed, etc. .	63	193	133
Metal Products . .	678	1,194	n.a.	Tin Ore	16	—	n.a.
Motor Vehicles and Parts .	524	624	1,281	Hides and Skins . .	216	232	197
Petroleum Products . .	n.a.	1,208	573*	Groundnut Oil . . .	249	566	567
Sugar	422	515	260	Gum Arabic . . .	13	93	n.a.
Beverages . . .	249	175	n.a.	Kidney Beans . . .	116	n.a.	n.a.

* Nine months.

PRINCIPAL COUNTRIES

IMPORTS	1969	1970	1971	EXPORTS	1969	1970	1971
France	6,122	7,428	4,315*	France	3,921	4,110	3,799*
Other Franc Zone . .	1,570	2,012	909*	Other Franc Zone . .	627	1,056	755
Netherlands . . .	541	785	494	Nigeria	1,009	1,738	1,750
U.S.A.	639	863	738	Italy	246	1,312	257
German Federal Republic .	802	1,260	684	United Kingdom . .	22	39	89*
United Kingdom . .	230	366	307	Ghana	152	233	87

* Nine months.

TRANSPORT
ROADS

	CARS	BUSES AND COACHES	GOODS VEHICLES	TRACTORS	MOTORCYCLES AND SCOOTERS
1967 . .	2,859	73	1,549	228	469
1968 . .	3,303	68	1,660	301	513
1969 . .	4,742	107	1,811	351	544
1970 . .	5,427	140	1,965	420	582
1971 . .	6,118	167	2,073	457	n.a.

CIVIL AVIATION

	1968	1969	1970
Aircraft Arrivals and Departures . . .	2,370	2,955	2,930
Passenger Arrivals and Departures . .	34,932	36,849	37,554
Freight Loaded (metric tons) . . .	1,421	1,620	1,709
Freight Unloaded (metric tons) . . .	1,704	2,394	2,238
Mail Handled (metric tons) . . .	198	168	165

Source: Institut Nationale de la Statistique et des Etudes Economiques, *Données Statistiques.*

EDUCATION
(1970–71)

TYPE	NUMBER OF SCHOOLS	NUMBER OF PUPILS
Primary . . .	698	88,594
Secondary . . .	28	6,531
Technical . . .	1	188
Teacher Training . .	5	494

Source (unless otherwise stated): Service de la Statistique et de la Mécanographie.

THE CONSTITUTION

(*November* 1960)

Preamble: Affirms principles of democracy, human rights and civil liberties. The Republic is a secular state and sovereignty belongs to the people who exercise it through their representatives or by means of referenda. There is universal adult suffrage. French is the official language.

Head of State: The Head of State is the President, who is elected for a term of five years by direct universal suffrage and is eligible for re-election. He appoints the ministers, who are not members of the National Assembly. He is President of the Council of Ministers, head of the administration and armed forces. He may put legislation to a referendum.

Executive Power: Executive power is vested in the President and the Council of Ministers.

Legislative Power: Legislative power rests with the National Assembly, which is elected at the same time as the President. It normally holds two sessions annually. Legislation may be introduced either by the members or by the President, who may demand a second reading of a Bill.

Judicial Power: The Supreme Court has four Chambers, a constitutional chamber, a civil section, the audit section and the High Court of Justice. The High Court of Justice is composed of deputies elected by and from the National Assembly and has power to impeach the President or Ministers.

Economic and Social Council: An advisory body.

Conseil de l'Entente: In May 1959 Niger joined with the Ivory Coast, Dahomey and Upper Volta to form the Conseil de l'Entente.

THE GOVERNMENT

HEAD OF STATE

President: HAMANI DIORI (re-elected October 1970).

COUNCIL OF MINISTERS

(November 1972)

President of the Council: HAMANI DIORI.

Minister of State for the Interior: DIAMBALLA Y. MAIGA.

Minister of State for National Defence: LÉOPOLD KAZIENDE.

Minister of Finance and of Saharan and Nomadic Affairs: MOUDDOUR ZAKARA.

Minister of Public Works, Transport and Town Planning: HAROU KOUKA.

Minister of Mines, Geology and Water Resources: NOMA KAKA.

Minister of Foreign Affairs: BOUKARY SABO.

Minister of Rural Economics: MAHAMANE DANDOBI.

Minister of Economic Affairs, Trade and Industry: AMADOU ISSAKA.

Minister of Justice: BARKIRE ALIDOU.

Minister of Posts and Telecommunications: ISSA IBRAHIM.

Minister of Public Health: MOSSI AMADOU.

Minister of the Civil Service and Labour: GARBA KATAMBE.

Minister of Development and Co-operation: HAROUNA BEMBELLO.

Minister Delegate at the Presidency, for Information: MAIDAH MAMOUDOU.

Minister Delegate at the Presidency, for Social Affairs: MAI MAIGANA.

Minister of National Education, Youth and Sport: DAN DICKO DAN KOULODO.

Secretary of State for the Interior: BOUBAKAR MOUSSA.

Secretary of State for Rural Economics: SOUNA ADAMOU.

DIPLOMATIC REPRESENTATION

EMBASSIES ACCREDITED TO NIGER

(In Niamey unless otherwise stated)

Algeria: *Ambassador:* ABDERAHBMAYE NEKLI.

Belgium: Abidjan, Ivory Coast.

Canada: Abidjan, Ivory Coast.

China, Republic: B.P. 732, Niamey; *Ambassador:* LEE HAW-HSING.

Egypt: *Chargé d'Affaires:* T. A. OYOUN.

Ethiopia: Lagos, Nigeria.

France: B.P. 240; *Ambassador:* PAUL GASCHIGNARD.

German Federal Republic: B.P. 629, Niamey; *Ambassador:* ALEXANDER ARNOT.

Israel: B.P. 624, Niamey; *Ambassador:* YEHOSHUA RASH.

Italy: Abidjan, Ivory Coast.

Japan: Abidjan, Ivory Coast.

Korea, Republic: Abidjan, Ivory Coast.

Lebanon: Abidjan, Ivory Coast.

Libya: B.P. 683, Niamey; *Ambassador:* SENOUSSI MAAREF.

Mauritania: *Ambassador:* AHMED OULD DIÉ.

Morocco: *Ambassador:* BOUBEKER BOUMEHDI.

Netherlands: Abidjan, Ivory Coast.

Nigeria: B.P. 617, Niamey; *Ambassador:* SANI KONTAGORA.

Norway: Abidjan, Ivory Coast.

Pakistan: Lagos, Nigeria.

Romania: *Ambassador:* GHEORGE IATON.

Spain: Monrovia, Liberia.

Sudan: Lagos, Nigeria.

Sweden: Lagos, Nigeria.

Switzerland: Abidjan, Ivory Coast.

U.S.S.R.: *Ambassador:* G. D. SOMOLOV.

United Kingdom: Abidjan, Ivory Coast.

U.S.A.: B.P. 201; *Ambassador:* R. McCLELLAND.

Viet-Nam, Republic: Abidjan, Ivory Coast.

Niger also has diplomatic relations with Dahomey, Ivory Coast, Kuwait, Liberia, Luxembourg, Morocco, Peru, Poland, Saudi Arabia, Sierra Leone, Tunisia and Yugoslavia.

PARLIAMENT

NATIONAL ASSEMBLY

President: BOUBOU HAMA.

Vice-Presidents: T. MAIARY, AMADOU HASSANE, GADO SABO.

Election October 1970. All 50 members belong to the *Parti progressiste nigérien.*

POLITICAL PARTIES

Parti progressiste nigérien (PPN): Niamey; Niger section of the *Rassemblement démocratique africain* (RDA); Pres. BOUBOU HAMA; Sec.-Gen. HAMANI DIORI.

The Sawaba Party, which opposed De Gaulle's 1958 constitutional proposals, is illegal, and its leader Djibo Bakary lives in exile in Conakry, Guinea.

DEFENCE

The army numbers 2,000 men and the air force 100. There is also a gendarmerie of 400, a national guard of 1,000 and a civil police of 500.

Chief of Staff: Major BALLA ARABE.

JUDICIAL SYSTEM

Supreme Court: consists of three chambers: Constitutional, Judicial and Administrative; Pres. EL HADJ DIALLO OUSMAN BASSAROU; Attorney Gen. GEORGES SALLES.

Court of Appeal: Niamey: Pres. VIAUD-MURAT.

Tribuneaux de première instance (*District Magistrate's Courts*): at Niamey, Maradi and Zinder; with sections at Tahoua, Birni-N'Konni, Agadez, Diffa and Dosso.

Justices of Peace: at Tillabéri, Ouallam, Dosso, Madaoua, Tessaoua, Gouré, N'Guigmi, Bilma and Birni-N'Gaoure.

Labour Courts: are set up at Niamey, Zinder, Maradi, Tahoua, Birni-N'Konni, Agadez, Dosso and Diffa.

Court of State Security: Martial court for criminal offences.

RELIGION

It is estimated that 85 per cent of the population are Muslims, 14.5 per cent Animists and 0.5 per cent Christians. The most influential Muslim groups are the Tijaniyya, the Senoussi and the Hamallists.

Roman Catholic Missions: Diocese of Niamey, B.P. 208, Niamey; f. 1961; 12 mission centres, 22 priests, 12,000 Catholics; Bishop of Niamey Mgr. HIPPOLYTE BERLIER.

Protestant Missions: 13 mission centres are maintained, with a personnel of 90.

PRESS AND RADIO

Le Niger: B.P. 368, Niamey; f. 1961; edited by the Service de l'Information; weekly; circ. 800.

Le Temps du Niger: B.P. 368, Niamey; f. 1960; mimeographed daily news bulletin of the Service de l'Information; circ. 1,300; Dir. SIDIKOU GARBA.

Journal Officiel de la République du Niger: B.P. 211, Niamey; monthly.

Office de Radiodiffusion-Télévision du Niger (ORTN): Niamey, B.P. 361; Government station; programmes in French, Hausa, Zerma, Tamachek, Kanuri, Fulfuldé, English (twice a week) and Arabic; Dir.-Gen. GANI ISSAKA; 100,000 radio receiving sets (1972).

FINANCE

(cap. = capital; m = million; amounts in francs CFA)

BANKS
CENTRAL BANK

Banque Centrale des Etats de l'Afrique de l'Ouest: 29, rue du Colisée, Paris; Niamey, Rond-Point de la Poste, B.P. 487; f. 1955; cap. 3m.; br. at Zinder; Pres. J. COLLIN; Gen Man. R. JULIENNE.

COMMERCIAL BANKS

Banque de Développement de la République du Niger: Niamey, B.P. 227; f. 1961; cap. 450m. CFA of which 57.7 per cent state-owned; Pres. BOUBOU HAMA.

Banque de l'Afrique Occidentale: B.P. 203, Niamey.

Caisse Centrale de Coopération Economique: B.P. 212, Niamey.

Crédit du Niger: P.O.B. 213, Niamey; f. 1958; cap. 220m. of which 50 per cent state-owned; Pres. Dir.-Gen. BOUBOU HAMA; Dir. OUMAROU MOUSSA.

Union Nigérienne de Crédit et de Co-opération: B.P. 296, Niamey; f. 1962; cap. 245m.; Government owned; Pres. BOUBOU HAMA; Dir. AHMED MOUDDOUR.

Caisse Nationale de Crédit Agricole (CNCA): B.P. 295, Niamey; f. 1967; cap. 67m.; Pres. BOUBOU HAMA; Dir. MARIKO KELETIGUI.

Banque Internationale pour l'Afrique Occidentale: 9 ave. de Messine, Paris; Niger Office: P.O.B. 628, Niamey; branches: P.O.B. 164, Zinder and P.O.B. 2, Maradi.

United Bank for Africa Ltd. (USA): Niamey.

INSURANCE

Several French insurance companies are represented in Niger.

TRADE AND INDUSTRY

CHAMBERS OF COMMERCE

Chambre de Commerce, d'Agriculture et d'Industrie du Niger: B.P. 209, Niamey; f. 1954; 40 elected mems., 20 official mems.; Pres. J. NIGNON; Sec.-Gen. OUSMANE BEN MAMADOU; publ. *Weekly Bulletin*.

Chambre de Commerce et d'Agriculture de Maradi: B.P. 79, Maradi.

Chambre de Commerce et d'Agriculture de Zinder: B.P. 83, Zinder.

DEVELOPMENT

Centre Technique Forestier Tropical (CTFT): P.O.B. 225, Niamey.

Commissariat Général au Développement: Niamey; f. 1965; under the direct supervision of the President.

Compagnie Française pour le Développement des Fibres Textiles: B.P. 717, Niamey.

Fonds National d'investissement (FNI): Niamey; f. 1969 by the Government; finances development projects with revenues from tax on uranium and French aid.

Fonds National pour le Développement Economique et Social: Niamey.

Société Nationale de Commerce et de Production (COPRO-NIGER): B.P. 615, Niamey; state-owned company for supply of commodities to rural areas; cap. 150m. francs CFA; Dir.-Gen. J. NIGNON.

EMPLOYERS' ORGANIZATIONS

Syndicat des Entreprises et Industries du Niger: Niamey, B.P. 95.

Syndicat des Transportateurs et Routiers du Niger: Niamey.

Syndicat des Commerçants Importateurs et Exportateurs du Niger: Niamey, B.P. 137; Pres. M. LAMBERT; Sec. M. VIRMONT.

Syndicat Patronal des Entreprises et Industries du Niger: Niamey, B.P. 95.

Syndicat des Ingénieurs, Cadres, Agents de Maîtrise, Techniciens et Assimilés du Niger: Niamey.

TRADE UNIONS

Union Nationale des Travailleurs du Niger—U.N.T.N.: Niamey; f. 1960; divided into three sections for Maradi, Niamey and Zinder; affiliated to the African Trade Union Confederation; 27 affiliates; 15,000 mems.; Sec.-Gen. RENÉ DELANNE.

MAJOR INDUSTRIAL COMPANIES

The following are among the largest companies engaged in industrial production.

Société des Brasseries du Niger (BRANIGER): B.P. 890 route du Dosso, Niamey; f. 1968; cap. 300m. francs C.F.A.

Manufacture of beer and soft drinks.

Vice-Pres. HENRI FAIVRE; Dir.-Gen. ROBERT BAILLY; 73 employees.

Société des Mines de l'Aïr: B.P. 892, Niamey; f. 1968; cap. 2,700m. francs CFA.

Uranium mining at Arlit.

Pres. JACQUES LUCIUS; Dir. MICHEL BOLLOT.

Société Nigérienne de Cimenterie: B.P. 355, Niamey; f. 1963; state-owned company for the production of cement; cap. 650m. francs CFA; Pres. Dir.-Gen. ARY TANIMOUNE; Dir. CHARLES BUFFEVANT.

Société Nigérienne de Commercialisation de l'Arachide (SONARA): B.P. 473, Niamey; f. 1962; cap. 300m. francs CFA, of which state owns 50 per cent.

Marketing of groundnut and its products.

Pres. Dir.-Gen. AMADOU GAOH; Dir.-Gen. MAITOURARE GADJO; 410 employees.

Société Nigérienne de Produits Céramiques: B.P. 536, Niamey; f. 1966; cap. 62m. francs CFA.

Manufacture of bricks and ceramics.

Dirs. A. ALKALY, MAITOURARE GADJO; 55 employees.

Société de Transformation des Mils et Sorghos (SOTRA-MIL): Zinder; f. 1967; cap. 74m. francs CFA, of which 56 per cent state-owned. Milling of millet and sorghum and manufacture of pasta, semolina and biscuits from this flour.

TRANSPORT AND TOURISM

TRANSPORT

ROADS

There are 6,905 km. of national roads and 93 km. of regional roads, of which 602 km. are bitumenized, and 5,200 km. of local roads and tracks.

RAILWAYS

Organisation Commune Dahomey-Niger des Chemins de Fer et du Transport (OCDN): Niamey; P.O.B. 16, Cotonou, Dahomey; f. 1959; manages the Benin-Niger railway.

A railway is proposed between Niamey and Tillabéri.

INLAND WATERWAYS

Cie. Bénin-Niger: maintains a service on the River Niger from Niamey to Gaya-Malanville from October to March.

CIVIL AVIATION

Air Afrique: Niger Delegation, B.P. 84, Imm. Petrocokino, Niamey; Niger has a 7 per cent share in Air Afrique; *see* under Ivory Coast.

Air Niger: Immeuble Sempastous (B.P. 205), Niamey; services from Niamey to Tahoua, Maradi, Zinder and Agadez; fleet of one DC-4, two DC-3; Dir.-Gen. P. GABRIELLI.

Niamey is also served by the following airlines: Air Mali, Sabena and UTA.

TOURISM

Office du Tourisme du Niger: B.P. 612, Niamey; Dir. ISSOUFOU SEYFOU.

POWER

Société Nigérienne d'Électricité: B.P. 202, Niamey; f. 1968; cap. 214m. francs CFA.

Production of electricity and water.

Dir. BOUKARI KANÉ.

EDUCATION

Niger has a literacy rate of about 11 per cent, but the government is taking steps to expand educational services with French and UNESCO assistance. At least half the population is under 20 years old. In the academic year 1970–71 there were 88,600 primary school pupils in 698 schools, most of which are public. Only some 10 to 15 per cent of children of school age actually attend a school. There were also 7,337 secondary and technical students. The mixed Lycée at Niamey has no commercial classes, but there are a technical college and a technical lycée at Maradi. A National School of Administration was set up in 1963, and in 1971 a Centre d'Enseignement Supérieur was opened, which is intended to become the nucleus of a future university. So far it offers only scientific and technical subjects. In addition there are five teacher-training colleges in Niger (with 494 students in 1970–71) and about 200 students attend foreign universities.

RESEARCH INSTITUTES

Bureau de Recherches Géologiques et Minières: B.P. 458, Niamey; Dir. M. GREIGERT.

Centre Nigérien de Recherches en Sciences Humaines—CNRSH—IFAN: B.P. 318, Niamey; f. 1960; library of 4,737 vols.; Dir. DIOULDÉ LAYA; Sec. I. GARBA; publs. *Etudes Nigériennes*, *Mu kaara Sani* (three times yearly).

Centre Régional de Recherche et de Documentation pour la Tradition Orale: B.P. 369, Niamey; f. 1968 by agreement with UNESCO; 23 mems.; library of 5,000 tape recordings of songs, tales, fables and historical records in the following languages: Fulfuldé, Hausa, Zerma, Songhay, Tamasheq, Kanuri; aims to collect, transcribe, translate and publish all works of the oral tradition from

West Africa, Cameroon and Chad; Pres. HAMA BOUBOU; Exec. Sec. ISSAKA DANKOUSSOU; publ. *Bulletin périodique de liaison et d'information.*

Centre Technique Forestier Tropical—CTFT: B.P. 225, Niamey; f. 1963; silviculture and soil conservation; Dir. J. C. DELWAULLE.

Compagnie Française pour le Développement des Fibres Textiles—CFDT: B.P. 52, Maradi.

Institut de recherches agronomiques tropicales et des cultures vivrières—IRAT: B.P. 150, Niamey; soil science; stations at Tarna and Kolo; Dir. J. NABOS.

Laboratoire vétérinaire de Niamey: Niamey.

Office de la Recherche Scientifique et Technique Outre-Mer-Mission O.R.S.T.O.M. à Niamey: B.P. 223, Niamey; hydrology; Dir. (vacant).

Station Avicole et Centre d'Elevage Caprin: Maradi; f. 1961; Dir. HASSANE BAZA; publ. *Report* (annual).

Station Sahélienne Expérimentale de Toukounous: Service d'Elevage du Niger, Toukounous/Filingué; f. 1931; selection and breeding of Zebu Azaouak cattle and distribution of selected bulls to improve the local heterogeneous breed; Dir. Dr. Dr. MANFRED LINDAU; publs. *Berlin Münchner Tierärztliche Wochenschrift,* Annual Report.

LIBRARY AND ARCHIVES

Archives de la République du Niger: Niamey; f. 1913; documents to the end of the 19th century.

Centre de Documentation: Commissariat Général au Développement, Présidence de la République, Niamey; f. 1965; Librarian ALOU MOUMOUNI.

MUSEUM

Musée National du Niger: B.P. 248, Niamey; f. 1959; representative collection of tribal costumes, crafts, tribal houses, park, zoo; Curator PABLO TOUCET.

COLLEGES

Centre d'Enseignement Supérieur de Niamey: B.P. 237, Niamey; f. 1971 with a view to establishing a Faculty of Sciences in the future; 27 teachers, 100 students; Dir. Prof. BOUBAKARBA; Sec.-Gen. JEAN PIRON.

Ecole Nationale d'Administration du Niger: B.P. 542, Niamey; f. 1963 to train civil servants and other officials; library of 11,000 vols.; number of teachers: 28 full-time, 24 part-time; number of students: 354 pre-service, 418 in-service; Dir. E. F. HENTGEN.

SELECT BIBLIOGRAPHY

(For works on the former A.O.F. countries generally *see* Dahomey Select Bibliography, p. 297.)

BONARDI, PIERRE. *La République du Niger.* Paris, 1960.

CLAIR, ANDRÉ. *Le Niger, Pays à Découvrir.* Paris, Hachette, 1965.
  Le Niger indépendant. Paris, ATEOS, 1966.

LA DOCUMENTATION FRANÇAISE. *Bibliographie sommaire de la République du Niger.* Paris, 1969.

HALLETT, ROBIN (Ed.). *The Niger Journal of Richard and John Lander.* London, Routledge, 1965.

HARRISON CHURCH, R. J. *West Africa* (6th edn., ch. 17) London, Longmans, 1968.

SERVICE DE L'INFORMATION. *Le Niger.* Niamey, December 1969.

SÉRÉ DE RIVIÈRES, EDMOND. *Histoire du Niger.* Berger-Levrault, Paris, 1966.

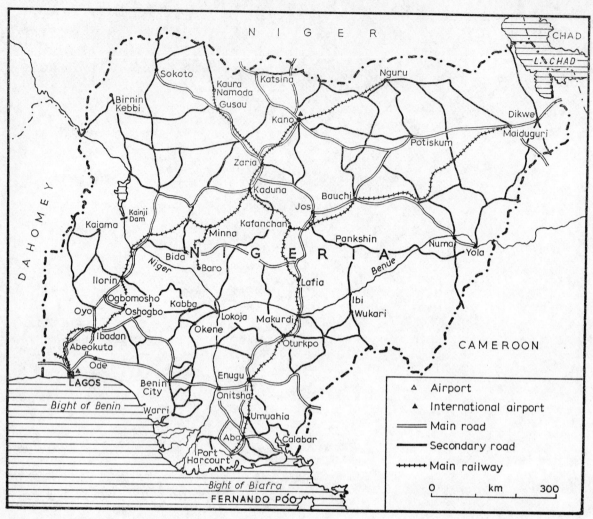

Nigeria

Nigeria

PHYSICAL AND SOCIAL GEOGRAPHY

Akin L. Mabogunje

The Federal Republic of Nigeria lies almost at the eastern end of the broad sweep of the west African coastline and is demarcated by latitudes 4° and 14° N. parallel and longitudes 3° and 15° E. meridian. The country is bounded on the west, north and east by the French-speaking republics of Dahomey, Niger and Cameroon respectively and on the south by the Atlantic Ocean. It has an area of 356,669 sq. miles which, although more than three times the area of the United Kingdom, puts it fourteenth among African countries.

In spite of its relatively small area Nigeria is the most populous country on the continent, having more than 50 million people. It came into being on January 1st, 1900, having been given its name by Lady Shaw, wife of Lord Lugard, the first Governor-General of the new country. It passed through a series of constitutional changes culminating in the creation of a federation of three regions in 1952 and the granting of independence on October 1st, 1960. After a series of political crises the country was in 1967 given a new federal structure comprising twelve states, the smallest of which has a population of 1.4 million—greater than that of a number of African countries.

PHYSICAL FEATURES

Compared to east, central and southern Africa the physical features of Nigeria are of modest dimensions. The highest lands are along the eastern border of the country and rise to a maximum of 6,700 ft. at Vogel Peak, south of the Benue River. Much of the highland is greatly dissected, providing quite spectacular scenery, unfortunately too far away from the more traditional routes of tourist travels.

The Jos Plateau does not suffer this disability. Located close to the centre of the country, the plateau is everywhere over 4,000 ft., rising to 5,841 at Share Hill and 5,572 ft. at Wadi Hill. Its short-grass, open scenery, as well as its scarp face to the south, east and west, are some of the most impressive sights in the country. The Jos Plateau is also a veritable watershed, from which rise virtually all streams flowing from the northern half of Nigeria to Lake Chad and to the Rivers Niger and Benue.

Away from the plateau the land drops steadily northwards, although nowhere getting below 1,000 ft. except in river valleys. This area is described as the High Plains of Hausaland and is characterized by a broad expanse of level sandy plains, broken here and there by rocky dome outcrops. To the south-west across the Niger River similar relief is represented in the Yoruba Highlands, where the rocky outcrops are surrounded by forests or tall grass and form the major watershed for rivers flowing northwards to the Niger and southwards to the sea.

Elsewhere in the country, lowlands of less than 1,000 ft. predominate. Such lands are found stretching inland from the coast for over 150 miles and continuing farther in the trough-like basins of the Niger and Benue Rivers. Lowland areas also exist in the Rima and Chad basins at the extreme north-west and north-east of the country respectively. Everywhere the lowlands are gently undulating, being dissected by innumerable streams and rivers flowing in broad sandy valleys.

The most important river in Nigeria is the Niger, the third longest river of Africa. Taking its course in the Fouta Djallon mountains to the north-east of Sierra Leone, the Niger enters Nigeria for the last one-third of its 2,600-mile course. It flows first south-easterly, then due south and again south-easterly to Lokoja, where it receives the waters of its principal tributary, the Benue. From here the river flows due south until Aboh, where it loses itself in the innumerable interlacing distributaries of its delta. The Benue for its part rises in the Republic of Cameroon, flows in a south-westerly direction to its junction with the Niger, and receives on its course the waters of the Katsina Ala and Gongola rivers. The other main tributaries of the Niger within Nigeria are the Sokoto, Kaduna and Anambra rivers. Other important rivers in the country include the Ogun, the Oshun, the Imo and the Cross. Many of these flow into the sea through a system of lagoons, the most impressive of which runs west from Okitipupa through Lagos to beyond the western borders of Nigeria.

Beyond the lagoon is the Nigerian coastline characterized by being relatively straight and with few natural indentations. Everywhere along the surf-beaten coast a strong longshore drift gives rise to the formation of sand bars, blocking entrances to harbours and necessitating constant dredging and sand-removing operations.

CLIMATE

With its generally low relief and its situation well within the tropics Nigeria has a climate which is characterized by relatively high temperatures throughout the year. The average annual maximum varies from 95°F. in the north to 87°F. in the south; the average annual minimum from 73°F. in the south to 65°F. in the north. On the Jos Plateau and the eastern highlands altitude makes for relatively lower temperatures, with the maximum no more than 82°F. and the minimum sometimes as low as 57°F. There is, however, considerable variation in daily and seasonal rhythm. In general both the mornings and evenings are cooler than the noon period, when the sun is virtually overhead. Similarly the cloudiness keeps out much solar radiation and tends to reduce day-time temperature during the rainy season.

The annual rainfall total decreases from over 150 in. at Forcados on the coast to under 25 in. at Maiduguri in the north-east of the country. The length of the rainy season also shows a similar decrease from nearly twelve months in the south to under five months in the north. Rain starts in January in the south and progresses gradually across country. June, July, August and September are the rainiest months throughout the country. In many parts of the south, however, there is a slight break in the rains for some two to three weeks in late July and early August, giving rise to the well-known phenomenon of the little dry season. No such break occurs in the northern part of the country, and the rainy season continues uninterrupted for three to six months. Incessant thunder and lightning accompany the beginning and end of the rainy season.

SOILS AND VEGETATION

The broad pattern of soil distribution in the country reflects both the climatic conditions and the geological structure. In general we distinguish between heavily leached, reddish-brown, sandy soils in the south and light or moderately leached, yellowish-brown, sandy soils in the northern parts. The difference in colour relates to the extent of leaching the soil has undergone.

The nutrient content of the soil is, however, related to the geological structure. Over a large part of the northern and south-western areas of the country geological structure is that of old crystalline Basement complex rocks. These are highly mineralized and give rise to soils of high nutrient status, although variable from place to place. On the sedimentary rocks found in the south-east, north-east and north-west of the country the soils are sandy and less variable but are deficient in plant nutrient. They are also very susceptible to erosion.

The vegetation of the country shows clear east-west zonation. In general mangrove and rain forests are found in the south, occupying about 20 per cent of the area of the country, whilst grassland of various types occupies the rest. Four belts of grassland are identified. Close to the forest zone is a derived savannah belt, which is believed to have resulted from the frequent firing of previously forested areas. This belt is succeeded by the Guinea, the Sudan and the Sahel Savannah in that order northward. The height of grass and density of wood vegetation decrease with each succeeding savannah belt.

RESOURCES

Although nearly 70,000 sq. miles of Nigeria is in the forest belt, only 9,000 sq. miles account for most of the timber resources of the country. These forests are mainly in the Western, Mid-Western and South-Eastern States of the country. Nigeria exports a wide variety of tropical hardwoods, and internal consumption has been growing rapidly.

Cattle, goats and, to a lesser extent, sheep constitute important animal resources. Most of the cattle, numbering nearly 12 million, are found in the Sudan grassland belt in the far north, which is free of the tsetse. Poultry is growing in importance, and so is the number of pigs.

Coastal waters are becoming important fishing grounds. Traditionally, however, major sources of fish have been Lake Chad in the extreme north-east, the lagoons along the coast, the creeks and distributaries of the Niger delta and the various rivers in the country.

Mineral resources are varied, although exploration of many has only just begun. Tin is found in alluvial deposits on the Jos Plateau and has been exported from Nigeria for over fifty years. Annual production is around 10,000 tons. Associated with tin is columbite, of which the country is the world's largest producer. Extensive medium-grade iron ore exists and plans are afoot to start iron and steel production in the country.

Fuel resources include sub-bituminous coal, worked at Enugu for over fifty years. Total reserves are small, estimated at no more than 250 million tons. More impressive are the petroleum reserves, estimates of which are constantly being altered with each new discovery in the offshore area. Daily production is now well over a million barrels. Nigerian oil has special value on the world market in being sulphur-free. Natural gas is also found in abundance, but at present much of this is simply put to the flame.

POPULATION

Although racially negroid the Nigerian population exhibits extreme ethnic diversity. Well over 250 ethnic groups are identified, some numbering less than 10,000 people. Ten groups, notably Hausa-Fulani, Yoruba, Ibo, Kanuri, Tiv, Edo, Nupe, Ibibio and Ijaw, account for nearly 80 per cent of the total population. Total population increased from 16 million in 1911 to over 50 million in 1970. Much of the population is concentrated in the southern part of the country, as well as in the area of dense settlement around Kano in the north. Between these two areas is the sparsely populated Middle Belt.

Urban life has a long history in Nigeria with centres like Kano (1963 population 295,432), Zaria (166,170), Ife (130,050) and Benin (100,694) dating from the Middle Ages. Recent economic development, however, has stimulated considerable rural-urban migration and led to the phenomenal growth of such cities as Lagos (665,246), Port Harcourt (179,563) and Kaduna (149,910). All in all nearly 16 per cent of the Nigerian population live in urban areas, making the country perhaps the most urbanized in black Africa.

RECENT HISTORY

J. F. Ade Ajayi*

CONQUEST

Britain acquired the territory of Nigeria in several stages. The Delta of the Niger had been a major centre of British trade. Her ambition in the nineteenth century was to penetrate through the Delta or through the Yoruba country to the famous markets of the Sokoto Caliphate and Bornu. While encouraging traders and missionaries to pioneer up the Niger, she took more active steps to secure the Yoruba route by conquering Lagos in 1851 and formally annexing it in 1861. As the pressure of international rivalry increased in the 1880s, Britain claimed three spheres of influence in Nigeria: Lagos and the Yoruba hinterland, the Oil Rivers of the Niger Delta, and the vast territories of the Muslim emirates in the north. It was easy enough to convince other European powers of claims in the first two areas; the third was established largely through the activities of Sir George Goldie who united British trading firms on the Niger and bought out two competing French firms. He then persuaded the British government to recognize his company's commercial monopoly and to delegate to it political administration of the area. Through negotiation with the French and the Germans, these claims were accepted in Europe and the boundaries of Nigeria began to emerge on the map. Besides the colony of Lagos ruled by the Colonial Office, there were the Lagos Protectorate and the Oil Rivers Protectorate under the Foreign Office, and the Niger Territories under the Royal Niger Company. It was quite another matter to get the Nigerian peoples to accept effective British rule.

In the Lagos Protectorate the long-standing Yoruba wars provided an opportunity for British intervention. But even after both camps agreed to break up in 1886, the war continued to simmer over issues like the position of Offa claimed by both Ilorin and Ibadan. The British then decided in 1892 to conquer as an example to others the Ijebu, who could be more easily reached along the coast, and to send the Lagos Governor into the interior offering treaties and reconciliation. Thereafter, British Residents were accepted but it required several military exercises in Oyo, Ibadan and other places to get the people to realize that the Resident was no longer an ally that could be argued with or repudiated, but a conqueror who had come to stay and whose word was law. In the Oil Rivers, Jaja of Opopo (1888) and Nana of Itshekiriland (1894) were deported for trying to impose their own regulations on trade. Benin was conquered (1897) and the Oba made to acknowledge the overlordship of the British by prostrating. The Royal Niger Company burnt down Onitsha more than once and in 1897 mounted a major war against Bida and Ilorin. When it became obvious that the Company was not able to bring the emirates under effective rule, Britain abrogated its charter and assumed direct rule. Lugard was appointed to establish the West African Frontier Force and under-take the conquest of Northern Nigeria beyween 1901 and 1906.

AMALGAMATION

It was in the process of trying to establish effective rule over the different peoples of Nigeria that the artificial nature of the initial demarcations of territory became obvious. Boundaries had to be more clearly defined and rationalized. The boundaries of the Oil Rivers Protectorate were adjusted to include the Igbo- and Edo-speaking peoples of the interior, from whose territories the palm oil came. Its name was changed to the Niger Coast Protectorate. In 1900, the Colonial Office assumed control of all the territories. In 1906, as no rational boundary existed between the Lagos Protectorate and the Niger Coast Protectorate—the intervening Benin empire had close links with both—the two were merged into the Protectorate of Southern Nigeria. By 1914, it was recognized that the economies of Southern and Northern Nigeria were complementary, and that the railway system and the ports had to be developed together and the customs duties shared. To minimize rivalry, boundary disputes and other causes of friction between the two, it was decided to amalgamate them. Nigeria thus emerged as a single country.

This act of amalgamation has been one of the most crucial events in Nigeria's history. It was undertaken essentially for the convenience of the British administrators, and the Nigerian peoples were not even consulted about it. But the British themselves were led to it by the pre-existing historical, cultural and economic factors that made the establishment of international boundaries as lines of human divide anywhere within Nigeria difficult to sustain. These factors included the age-long traffic along caravan routes from Hausaland to Yorubaland, Hausaland to Bornu, Bornu to Adamawa and down the Benue; close cultural and economic links between Yorubaland and Benin, Benin and Onitsha and the Delta; traffic along the lagoons and creeks and the Niger, and so on. This interlocking chain of connexions did not make Nigeria a united country, but, even at the beginning of the colonial period, it was powerful enough to persuade the British to see the wisdom of establishing a joint administrative system and of pursuing unified economic development.

The union established by the British was a limited union. Lord Lugard was appointed Governor-General to give policy direction and to co-ordinate railway development, customs duties, currency, telegraphs, surveys and such technical departments. However, day to day administration in the Protectorates, including local government, taxation, education, health and agriculture, was delegated to two Lieutenant-Governors who remained very powerful officials.

---

* For the 1973 edition, revisions have been made to this article by the Editor.

pattern of the Indirect Rule he had pioneered in the north, but because of differences in the traditional political systems, the results were very different, especially in eastern Nigeria. Other developments also tended to go along different lines. Hausa was almost as important as English as the language of administration in the north, while in the south English was predominant to the almost total exclusion of the local languages. While missionaries dominated education in the south and made rapid advances, they were restricted in large parts of the north where age-old Islamic education remained dominant and the local administrations severely controlled the introduction of Western education. The Nigerian Council created to bring some of the traditional rulers of the country together in an advisory capacity was given so little power that few people thought it worthwhile to attend and it fizzled out. When in 1922 a Legislative Council was created, African representation was limited to the colony and southern Nigeria. There was, therefore, no political forum where Nigerians could meet together. Thus, although administratively there was a unified system, the predominant policy was to try and keep the Nigerian peoples themselves apart.

Nevertheless, the central administration became more and more powerful and the powers of the Lieutenant-Governors declined gradually. The importance of the technical departments increased as economic development became more important and purely political administration for the maintenance of law and order ceased to be the sole end of the colonial government. The central secretariat in Lagos expanded, until in 1939 the two Lieutenant-Governors were replaced by three less powerful Chief Commissioners.

THE COLONIAL IMPACT

The basic idea of Indirect Rule was to preserve as much of the traditional institutions as possible and to use them as agents of colonial rule, to maintain stability by discouraging social change and yet encourage just enough economic development to produce revenue to run the administration. It was a policy of expediency full of contradictions and difficult to maintain in practice. It was calculated to satisfy the basic yearnings of the mass of the people and the traditional rulers who feared that subjection to an alien people with foreign and often incomprehensible ways would disrupt their own way of life and the customs of their fathers. However, without allaying the fears of the traditionalists, it dissatisfied the most likely supporters of colonial rule, who welcomed the foreigners because they wanted change from the old ways. Britain assumed sovereignty and the initiative to decide the pace and direction of change. The customs and institutions she chose to support and preserve were often not the ones most desired by the people. In the name of natural justice and humanity, and in support of Christian missionaries, many religious practices and social customs were challenged. Consequently, many traditional sanctions which held society together were under-

mined. While the growth of Islam as a personal and communal religion was encouraged, its threat as an alternative world system to the Christian Europeans' was challenged. The Sokoto Caliphate as a religio-political system was virtually broken up in favour of the autonomy of each emirate and contacts with the main stream of world Islamic movements in the Middle East were discouraged.

The Nigerian peoples themselves did not expect the preservation of traditional ways of life *per se* to give them security in the changing circumstances of the colonial era. They tended to see in the colonial régime new opportunities that, if not exploited to improve one's own position, would be exploited by others to one's disadvantage. For in the constitution of Native Authorities, approval of title-holders, the siting of administrative headquarters, courts, treasuries, railways and railway stations, roads, schools, markets and dispensaries, the British officials were making decisions that greatly affected the historical and future relationships of various peoples, towns, villages and clans. Many individuals and communities found ways of exploiting the new opportunities and politics centred around efforts to manipulate the new forces as much as possible to one's advantage.

Thus, in spite of every effort of the officials to shield the northern emirates from intercourse with southerners, the completion of the railways and the expansion of roads encouraged large-scale migration and accelerated the pace of cultural and economic contacts among Nigerian peoples. The cultivation of cash crops encouraged the migration of labour and the expansion of the internal market for foodstuffs. Northern traders followed their cattle southwards and sent kolanuts back in return. To supervise this exchange, Hausa-Fulani settlements developed in several southern towns. On an even larger scale, colonies of southern traders, mechanics, railway and postal officials, teachers and other products of mission schools emerged outside the walls of practically every northern city. New urban centres developed like Port Harcourt at the port and terminus of the Eastern Railway, Jos and Bukuru on the Bauchi tin mines, or Kaduna and Enugu as administrative centres. While some famous nineteenth-century trading cities like Bonny, Opopo and Calabar to some extent lay apart from the main stream of the new developments, others like Lagos, Ibadan, Kano and Onitsha grew rapidly in size and complexity, absorbing new immigrants from different parts of the country.

THE RISE OF NATIONALIST POLITICS

It was within these urban centres that by the 1930s a growing number of people were expressing discontent at subjection to foreign rule. This discontent had never fully died down since various peoples took up arms in the 1890s and early part of this century to oppose the establishment of the colonial régime. When the armies were defeated, several Muslims emigrated from Sokoto towards the Sudan, away from the rule of the unbelievers. Many adherents of African traditional religions persecuted Christians and boycotted schools. Others revolted against the payment of taxes or the imposition of unfamiliar courts and laws. The memories of these acts of resistance lingered on in the rural areas, but the hopelessness of armed revolt and the severity of the repressions left the initiative to the educated classes to try other approaches. To start with, they thought in terms of organizing themselves on a Pan-African, Negro, or West African basis. After 1922, with a Legislative Council providing for the election of three representatives from Lagos and one from Calabar, Nigeria gradually became the focus of their attention.

Herbert Macaulay had succeeded in dominating the politics of Lagos. He was a surveyor by profession, trained at government expense, but discriminated against in the civil service. An accomplished musician, a loyal subject of Queen Victoria and in many ways a typical Victorian gentleman, he became more and more the spokesman for the anti-colonial discontent. His interest in land valuation and ownership brought him in close contact with the traditional rulers who were the custodians of the land. This led him to see the importance of the educated professional élite working closely with the rulers who continued to enjoy the support of the masses. Macaulay became the champion of the land and political rights of the Lagos traditional élite. He also tried to make himself the tribune to whom Nigerians with grievances in other towns could appeal for help. His reputation as an indomitable fighter with powerful friends in England and with uncanny powers of ferreting out information to embarrass the colonial government became legendary. The more he was persecuted by the Lagos administration the more he became a hero. His Nigerian National Democratic Party won all elections to the Legislative Council from Lagos until 1939.

Meanwhile, other factors were extending the scope of nationalist politics to other urban areas. The growing numbers of Western-educated Nigerians were pressing for participation in local government through democratization of the Native Authorities. Ethnic unions established by the new immigrants into the urban areas to provide mutual aid and comfort took interest in pressing for such participation. The experimentation in local government reforms in Eastern Nigeria precipitated by the Aba Women's Riot of 1929 encouraged this development particularly among Ibibio and Ibo unions. The ethnic unions thus became more and more political. From local government reforms, they were soon demanding better educational facilities and other amenities, less discrimination in civil service appointments and more participation of Nigerians in the government of the country.

The world depression sharpened this growing discontent with economic grievances. The fall in the prices of cash crops keenly affected African produce buyers and transport owners. European firms frustrated their attempt to participate in the export/import trade or to share credit facilities through the banks. The agreement of these firms to combine to fix low producer prices and high prices for their imports outside the operation of the world market further underlined the exploitative nature of the colonial economy. The African produce buyers and transport owners replied by organizing a boycott and trying to get farmers' co-operative unions to support them in withholding their produce. Branches of the Lagos, later Nigerian, Youth Movement were being formed in different towns to debate and formulate ideas of political action to redress these economic grievances.

THE MAKING OF
NIGERIA'S CONSTITUTION

The British played down the importance of these manifestations of discontent but proceeded even before the outbreak of the Second World War to consider proposals for a suitable constitution under which Nigerians could participate more in the discussion and, in a somewhat distant future, even in the management of their own affairs. The idea was to create such institutions as would enable Nigerians to become involved in the responsibilities of government while they continued to learn from the British the arts of parliamentary government. The answer of British officials in 1947 was the Richards Constitution, which was promulgated without any consultation with Nigerians. It proposed that representatives of the various Native Authorities, meeting in Regional Councils of northern, eastern and western Nigeria, should delegate some of their members to a central Legislative Council to discuss common Nigerian problems. Its chief merit was that it offered, for the first time, a common political forum for the whole of Nigeria. However, to use the Native Authorities as the basis of representation was unacceptable to the Western-educated élite who, especially in the south, had been excluded from those councils and who viewed them as unprogressive agents of colonial rule. The educated élite would have preferred direct elections, though with a franchise limited to the "enlightened" educated minority.

The British agreed in 1949 to abrogate the Richards Constitution but insisted on involving not just the educated élite but also the mass of the people and the traditional rulers in an extensive exercise of constitution-making at village, district and provincial levels. The result of this widespread involvement was to bring into the open the problem of translating the limited cultural and economic contacts in Nigeria into concerted political action and eventual common nationhood. Although the pace of advancement towards autonomy and sovereignty continued to be discussed heatedly, it soon ceased to be the major issue. It became overshadowed by the question by whom and in what manner the powers being given up by the British were to be shared, how self-government would mean adequate participation of all groups in Nigeria and not the domination of all by a few. Various constitutional conferences in Lagos and London throughout the period 1949–60 sought the right and acceptable constitution. Political parties became divided along regional lines. They became forums for resolving intra-regional disputes and for safeguarding regional interests. The National Council for Nigeria and the Cameroons (N.C.N.C.) which, under the leadership of Dr. Nnamdi Azikiwe and Herbert Macaulay, had evolved as a national front to fight the Richards Constitution, became more and more an eastern, and particularly Ibo, party. The Northern Peoples Congress (N.P.C.) was northern by definition and dominated by the traditional élite of the Hausa-Fulani, led by Ahmadu Bello, the Sardauna of Sokoto, premier of the northern region. The Action Group which had roots in the Nigerian Youth Movement was essentially a western and Yoruba-dominated party. Minority groups within each region who felt their interests neglected started to organize splinter parties.

The policy of the N.P.C. was to ensure that the north did not become dominated by southerners who had had better facilities to acquire Western education. They therefore opted for strong regional autonomy as well as a united north dominating the central government on account of its size. They demanded at least 50 per cent representation, and would tolerate nothing that might endanger this position, like the demand for the creation of more regions or the adjustment of boundaries to allow Ilorin and Kabba to join the Yoruba west. On the issues they maintained skilful flexibility, taking their stand in a way to win support for northern interests or at least to keep their southern opponents divided. The Action Group, led by Obafemi Awolowo, the premier of the west, also stood for strong regional autonomy, at least to limit the extent to which the west, in the days of the post-war boom in cocoa prices, was subsidizing the rest of the country. It pressed for a rapid advance to self-government and the adjustment of boundaries to enable Lagos, Ilbrin and Kabba to be integrated with the west. In return, they were willing to agree to the creation of more regions to allow the non-Yoruba parts of the west to have a region of their own and to break up the preponderance of the north. The N.C.N.C., under pressure from eastern migrants in different parts of the country, favoured a centralized constitution with rights of easy access to land, jobs and trading opportunities for all Nigerians in all parts of the country. Eventually, they accepted the strength of the demand for a federal constitution, but they continued to press for as strong a central government as possible and the sharing of revenue according to need rather than derivation.

The constitution as it gradually emerged moved from the 1949 idea of a centralized government devolving power to newly created regions to the 1954 position of autonomous regions delegating specific powers to a federal government, sharing others like education, agriculture, health and economic development on a concurrent list, leaving reserved powers with the regions. Even then, the federal government remained powerful. It was in charge of defence and in control of the army. Attempts to regionalize the police were contained. What is more, the financial powers of the federal government over customs and excise, currency, banking and international trade,

the most important and most elastic sources of revenue, ensured that these powers would grow. Various formulas were worked out for the allocation of revenue from the central government to the regions, combining the principle of derivation with that of national interest in the general overall level of development in the country. It was also decided that Lagos should remain a federal territory, separate from the west, but that no new regions should be created until pressure from the area ascertained through a plebiscite should indicate the need for it. The eastern and western regions became internally self-governing in 1956, the northern in 1959, and the federation prepared for independence on October 1st, 1960.

TOWARD NATIONHOOD

The federal constitution represented the substantial measure of agreement that, in spite of conflicting interests and divisive forces, Nigerians were able to achieve by balancing the interests of the dominant groups in the north, east and west. In the hard political bargaining that went on, many interests could not be satisfied and many people faced independence with some misgiving. In the hard-fought election of 1959, no party emerged with a majority, but, because of the preponderant size of the north, the N.P.C. was the largest party. Its parliamentary leader, Sir Abubakar Tafawa Balewa was asked to form a government. His party chose to ally with the N.C.N.C., and the Action Group went into opposition. Sir Abubakar was a trained schoolmaster from Bauchi. Since 1949, he had emerged as a leading spokesman of the north, moderate and well-spoken. He had first been appointed Prime Minister under the 1954 constitution and now he led the country to independence. Dr. Azikiwe, the N.C.N.C. leaders, was appointed Governor-General, and, when a Republic was declared in 1963, he became the President. Awolowo, the Action Group leader, became the leader of the opposition, and his deputy replaced him as premier of the west.

The test of the country's unity and constitution was not long in coming. The prospect of a bleak future in opposition split up the Action Group between supporters of the leader who strove to maintain the federal opposition as the alternative government and those of the deputy leader, S. L. Akintola, who wished to join the government. The N.P.C./N.C.N.C. alliance succumbed to the temptation of helping the divided opposition party to destroy itself. In a test of strength, the federal government took over the administration of the western government for six months, at the end of which the Akintola minority faction of the Action Group was installed in power and the mid-west region was created out of the west. Charges of treasonable felony were brought against Awolowo and other leaders of the majority Action Group. They were convicted and jailed. With the Action Group thus incapacitated, the N.P.C. and N.C.N.C. soon found themselves in open confrontation and the tripartite balance envisaged in the constitution was dangerously upset.

There was fierce controversy over the census which should have provided the basis for constituency delimitation. The conduct and the result of the 1964 elections were similarly disputed. Open violations of electoral procedures were common and the N.C.N.C. and their allies tried to boycott the election. The Prime Minister became estranged from the President and some elements suggested the army should take over power. A compromise was worked out but no one expected it to last. The balance of power in the country was being further complicated. Oil had been discovered in the minority areas of the east and, from the poorest region seeking a centralized constitution under which natural resources could be jointly shared, the east became potentially the richest region and its leaders were less willing to tolerate a subordinate political position. The open rigging of the election in the west led to a breakdown of law and order in the region and brought to the open the N.P.C./N.C.N.C. confrontation. A group of mainly Ibo army majors tried to resolve the political impasse in January 1966 by staging a *coup*. They killed the Prime Minister, the premiers and senior army officers from the north and west. The surviving leaders of the army stepped in to establish a military régime under Major-General Johnson Aguiyi-Ironsi.

The country welcomed the Ironsi régime as a way out of the recurrent political crises. Military governors were appointed to run the government of each region, carry out sweeping reforms and find a new basis for Nigerian unity. However, as it became known in the army how one-sided were the killings of army officers and politicians in the January *coup*, there was growing disaffection particularly among troops of northern origin who formed the bulk of the infantrymen. The Ironsi régime also came increasingly under the control of Ibo civil servants and professionals who wished to take advantage of the *coup* to establish the more centralized constitution which the N.C.N.C. sought but failed to achieve in the 1950s. A decree of May 1966 abolishing the federation and establishing a unitary government provoked anti-Ibo riots in many parts of the north. Two months later, fighting broke out between Ibo and northern troops at the Abeokuta garrison and it spread to other locations. Ironsi and the military governor of the west with whom he was staying were taken away and killed. Several Ibo army officers were also killed and the northern troops threatened to secede and break up the country. The army chief of staff, Lt.-Col. Yakubu Gowon, assumed control and gradually began to restore order, but the military governor of the east refused to recognize him as commander-in-chief and head of state on the grounds that he was not the most senior surviving army officer. Gowon restored the federal structure and convened a meeting of regional representatives in Lagos to discuss the future of the country. Various proposals came forward in favour of a confederal arrangement. However, while they were meeting, more fighting broke out in the north and thousands of Ibo civilians were killed and their property looted and destroyed. The military governor of the east summoned all easterners to return home and all non-easterners except mid-western Ibos to leave the east. Efforts to find a compromise, including a meeting of military governors in Ghana, proved unsuccessful. The dispute escalated and the east, led by Lt.-Col. Ojukwu, decided on secession. However, two days before this was announced, Gowon proclaimed a state of emergency, assumed full powers and divided the country into twelve states. This was to find a fresh basis for Nigerian unity. In the short run, it was calculated to ensure support for the federal cause from minority groups, especially in the east, from whose territories most of the oil came and who had been seeking states of their own. In the long run, it was intended to remove the fear of domination of the federation by the north on account of its preponderant size. The east used this as a final reason for declaring themselves the independent state of Biafra. Civil war broke out in July 1967 and lasted till January 1970 before the secessionist leaders surrendered.

As well as gravely affecting Nigeria's development, the war caused serious though not lasting damage to African unity and to Nigeria's relations with non-African countries who lent at least tacit, and in some cases material, support to the secessionists. The conflict polarized the attitudes of African countries; Nigeria broke off relations with the countries who recognized Biafra, though relations in these cases were restored after the surrender of the secessionist forces. Attempts at mediation came from several sources, including the OAU, which supported the Federal cause, the Commonwealth Secretariat, Ghana and the Vatican. But the respective attitudes of the two sides became more entrenched as the military conflict dragged on, and the solution finally lay in Federal military victory.

The scope and the long duration of the conflict caused great hardship, particularly to civilian Ibos through starvation caused by the blockade of the Biafran enclave, which was only partially broken by charitable organizations. Fighting did not stop until the whole of the territory controlled by the secessionists was occupied by the Federal army. Fears from some quarters that revenge would be exacted by the Federal authorities upon the Ibo people in general were unfounded, however, and a remarkable feature of the post-war period was the degree of re-absorption of important Ibo personnel into Federal employment. As an arena for foreign countries interested in the oil resources of the east, the struggle became a cause of some diplomatic embarrassment to those who backed either side, since both were liable to accusations of acting against the interests of the civilian Ibo population. Accusations that Britain, notably, was lending support to a policy of genocide against the Ibos led to a British commission being sent to report on the situation. The Federal cause was much helped by military supplies from Britain and the Soviet Union; in the early stages of the conflict the Federation had been further endangered by a movement for independence in the Mid-Western region, necessitating military occupation of the area in September 1967.

In 1970, after the cessation of hostilities, General Gowon issued a nine-point plan providing for various reforms whose central purpose was the restoration of civilian rule by 1976. Meanwhile, under military rule the federation of twelve states has not, since the war of secession, shown the potential for political or tribal disequilibrium of the constitutional system is replaced.

The eastern leaders were not the first group of people in Nigeria to threaten secession and ignore the strength of the historical and economic bonds that held the country together. The north had threatened secession in 1953 and again in July 1966. The west threatened to secede in 1954 over the question of the position of Lagos. In each case as the full implications of secession were considered the leaders moved back from the brink. The eastern

leaders were alienated by the killings of May–October 1966 and, lured by the vision of oil revenues, they were the first to attempt to carry out the threat of secession. Faced with that, other groups in Nigeria sank their differences and rallied to defend the existence of the federation. In the conflict, Nigeria acquired a new self-confidence and a new maturity. It became obvious that the problems that would arise from the break-up of Nigeria were more serious than the problems of keeping the country together. The links that bind the country seem frail and fragile enough, but each time there is any danger of ignoring them, their significance suddenly becomes obvious.

ECONOMY
Ojetunji Aboyade

POPULATION

The estimated total population of Nigeria was 31.5 million according to the 1952–53 census. This implies an overall annual growth rate of 2.1 per cent over the preceding two decades. However, the 1963 census put the total population at 55.7 million, with an implied growth rate of 5.6 per cent per annum over the decade. Reactions to this census result have varied from outright rejection to qualified acceptance. It is clear that such growth rate between censuses is unusually high when compared with the situation in other countries with similar socio-cultural characteristics but with better demographic data. Officially, the country's estimated total population was put at 69,524,000 in 1972, but the UN estimate for the same year was 58 million.

Informed opinion making independent estimates put the population of Nigeria in 1963 at somewhere between 41.5 and 45 million. If we take the upper limit of 45 million, this would still give a high annual growth rate of about 4 per cent. On the other hand, if we take the lower limit of 42 million, it would yield an annual growth rate of 2.5 per cent, which is roughly comparable with the 2.25 per cent rate between the 1931 and 1952–53 censuses. It would also be more in line with the experience of other developing countries in a similar stage of demographic transition as Nigeria. However, in the light of recent indirect evidence (e.g. statistical field returns of the mass vaccination campaign), the current official figure of total population may well be nearest the truth, thus indicating gross undercounting in the 1931 and 1952–53 censuses.

The population of Nigeria is unevenly distributed on the land. The south is, in general, more densely populated than the north. The south-west also has the greatest concentration of urban population. According to the 1952–53 census the population in centres of 20,000 persons or more amounted to 11 per cent of the total population of the country. By 1963, the proportion had risen to 16 per cent. This means that, if the

annual growth rate of the whole population was 2.5 per cent, the average annual growth rate of urban population must have been about 6 per cent. All indications are that the rate of rural-urban migration is increasing.

The young dependants (children below 15 years of age) comprise over 40 per cent of the population. Persons over 50 years of age form about 8 per cent of the population, while the intermediate or the productive age group (15–49 years) constitute under 50 per cent. The dependency ratio is thus very high in Nigeria.

Since the Second World War there have been significant improvements in environmental sanitation, and modern medical aids have been increasingly introduced in Nigeria. These have had effects on both the death rate and the birth rate, and hence on the population growth rate. Estimates of death rate (about 25 per 1,000) and birth rate (about 50 per 1,000) give an approximate population growth rate of 2.5 per cent each year.

Nigeria is an African country *par excellence*. It is estimated that only about 0.05 per cent of the country's population are non-Africans in origin.

AGRICULTURE

Agriculture has been the most important sector of the Nigerian economy. But its dominance today in the determination of the country's economic progress is valid more in an accounting sense than as the dynamic engine of growth. It is true that agriculture is still playing a vital role in the economic development of Nigeria. It provides the food to meet the needs of an increasing population, raw materials for industries, export earnings to finance imports and provide needed foreign exchange, and a surplus for generating urban income and employment. But over the last decade, the central stimulus of growth in the Nigerian economy has been shifting imperceptibly from agriculture.

Agriculture (together with livestock, forestry and fishing) contributed about 61.2 per cent of the gross domestic product at current factor cost in 1962 (£804.8 million out of £1,315.4 million). By 1967 its contribution had declined to 55.6 per cent (£892.2 million out of £1,605 million). Although the proportional contribution of agriculture has thus declined and will continue to diminish, there is no doubt that its dominance as the single most important sector in the economy will remain for another two decades.

The G.D.P. of Nigeria at 1962 prices rose from £1,023.9 million in 1958 to £1,583.1 million in 1966. There was thus an average annual growth rate of 5.6 per cent. Agricultural production, on the other hand, rose from £869.5 million over the same period. This average annual growth rate of 3.3 per cent for agriculture was the slowest among all the major sectors of the economy.

Although only about one-fifth of agricultural output was exported in 1960, this constituted about four-fifths of total value of exports for that year. By 1969, however, the share of the principal agricultural products (cocoa, palm kernels, groundnuts and groundnut oil, rubber and raw cotton) in the total export earnings had fallen heavily to about 38 per cent. Apart from the civil war, the real explanation is to be found in the spectacular growth of crude petroleum exports.

About 70 per cent of the working population is engaged in agricultural and allied activities. It is not easy to demarcate between farmers wholly engaged in production for domestic and export markets and production for markets and subsistence. In most cases both export crops and domestic food crops are cultivated side by side in the same area and on the same farm unit. There is also scarcely an area of the country producing completely for barter or subsistence.

The major agricultural export commodities are groundnuts, groundnut oil, cocoa, palm kernels, palm oil, raw cotton, cotton seed and rubber. In 1970 groundnuts and groundnut oil accounted for 7.7 per cent of total export earnings (yielding £33.4 million), cocoa 15.0 per cent (£66.5 million), raw cotton 1.5 per cent (£6.6 million), and palm oil and palm kernels 2.6 per cent (£11.4 million). The low level of palm produce exports was due to the heavy decline in activity in the war-affected areas. In 1967, Nigeria supplied 22.9 per cent of the total world exports of cocoa beans, 22.3 per cent of cotton seed and 34.7 per cent of groundnuts.

Besides the peasant farm units there are new forms of farm organization which increasingly constitute the growing points of the sector. These include the plantation system and the farm settlement scheme sponsored by public authorities. The Nigerian Produce Marketing Company and the State marketing boards dominate the marketing of export produce. Among other things the boards are responsible for stabilizing producer prices by fixing legal minimum prices for a whole season at a time. Less successfully, the Boards also attempt to minimize price variation between one

season and another through the appropriate use of stabilization funds, which they may be able to build up from their trading profits.

As has been pointed out, only in a national accounts sense can one talk of the share of subsistence or non-market component of output in Nigerian conditions. Even then no one really knows the magnitude of subsistence output for certain. The peasant mode of production, characterized by smallholdings, simple techniques of production and bush-fallow system of cultivation, is the basis of the Nigerian agricultural system for both export and domestic commodities.

The principal food crops are maize, guinea corn, yams, cassava, rice and millet. Despite the much-vaunted criticism of the peasant system and the need for a "modernized" system of farming to replace the traditional methods of production, it is recognized that the peasant system has so far performed fairly well in both the domestic and export markets. It has undoubtedly been efficient and responsive to market incentive.

MINING

Nigeria is endowed with many material resources. The share of mining in the gross domestic product has been rising rapidly over the last decade. The mineral commodities vary from the alluvial gold deposits in the west and the tin mines in the north to the coal, lead-zinc and petroleum in the east, mid-west and the continental shelf.

The production of crude petroleum has greatly increased in recent years, rising from 13.3 million tons in 1965 to over 74 million tons in 1971. Early in 1970 the production of crude oil reached one million barrels a day. With this increase crude petroleum has shot itself into a position of dominance as the country's principal earner of foreign exchange. The oil exports which formed about 25.9 per cent of total export earnings in 1965 had risen to 70 per cent by 1971, reaching a record of over £400 million in receivable foreign exchange. This was a phenomenal growth when compared with the export level of £36 million in 1968, during the war, constituting then about 17 per cent of the total export earnings. In 1958 oil formed only 0.8 per cent of total receivable Nigerian export earnings. Up till 1964 the entire output of Nigeria's crude oil was exported. With the completion and operation of the oil refinery at Port Harcourt in 1965 a small proportion of the crude oil production started to be refined in the country. In 1972, Nigeria became a member of the Organization of Petroleum Exporting Countries (OPEC).

Coal was the first commercial energy source to be exploited in Nigeria. It has been produced in the Enugu area of eastern Nigeria since 1915. From then until 1959 production increased gradually to a peak of 900,000 tons. In the following years, however, coal output reduced considerably due to a reduction in demand. Domestic consumption, for instance, decreased from a peak of 828,000 tons in 1958 to 628,000 tons in 1966. In 1967 the civil war caused a complete shut-down of all coal-mining at the Enugu collieries.

Coal exporting has generally not been very important. On average 85 per cent of the domestic coal consumption has been purchased by only three main consumers—the Electricity Corporation of Nigeria, the Nigerian Railway Corporation, and the Nigerian Cement Company at Nkalagu. The role of the coal industry in the Nigerian economy has not been a very significant one. In 1959, when coal production reached its maximum, its contribution to the gross domestic product at current factor cost was £1.7 million, or 0.18 per cent. This contribution declined to £0.9 million or 0.06 per cent in 1966. On the whole the future of the Nigerian coal industry cannot be regarded as bright.

Other minerals include tin ore, columbite, lead, gold, zinc, wolfram, limestone and cassiterite. Until the discovery of oil the tin industry on the Jos Plateau formed the backbone of the country's mining industry. Almost all the tin ore is smelted locally by the Makeri Smelting Company Limited at Jos, which started operation in 1962. Exports of refined tin in 1967 totalled 10,800 i.t., valued at £13.1 million. The yearly production of columbite for the period 1958–68 averaged 2,000 tons, worth about £1.2 million.

Nigeria is the sixth largest producer of tin among the countries belonging to the International Tin Council, and by far the most important producer of columbite, supplying approximately 95 per cent of the world's industrial requirements. From 1958 to 1964 cassiterite production increased continuously from 8,400 i.t. to 11,800 i.t. Since 1965, however, the yearly output has oscillated around 12,700 i.t.

POWER

Nigeria has both thermal and hydroelectric power plants. Formerly emphasis was more on the thermal units, but with the completion in 1968 of the multi-purpose Kainji Dam, which has planned hydroelectric capacity of 880 MW, the position is now changing. The Kainji hydroelectric plant is operated by the Niger Dams Authority, but the main producer of thermal electricity and distributor of all electricity is the Electricity Corporation of Nigeria. A little hydro-electricity is, however, produced on the Jos Plateau by the independent Nigerian Electricity Supply Corporation, mainly to run the tin industry. Total electricity generation in Nigeria in 1970 amounted to 1,550 million kWh., of which 1,365 million kWh. came from hydroelectric plants.

INDUSTRY

Both manufacturing and building industries have grown rapidly since the 1950s. While the gross domestic product has been growing at about 5 per cent per annum, manufacturing has been increasing by about 10 per cent over the last two decades. However, industrial output still constitutes only about 7 per cent of the gross domestic product.

Building and construction have more than doubled their production since the achievement of independence in 1960, growing at an average annual growth rate of about 11 per cent. Despite this phenomenal growth rate the share of the building and construction sector in the total gross domestic product is still only about 5 per cent.

Nigeria's manufacturing is still dominated by first-generation light industries of the import-substitution type, although there are signs of new structural breaks towards intermediate products and semi-heavy industries. The average size of industrial establishment is still only about 140 people. The real importance of manufacturing in Nigeria derives from its potential contribution to the process of economic growth through its impact on the character and quality of capital formation and the promotion of high-level manpower skill. It constitutes one of the dynamic growing points of the economy. Public policy in Nigeria is thus designed to accelerate the process of rational industrial development. Part of the government's active interest in industrial promotion is reflected by the increasing direct and indirect participation by the public sector in manufacturing ownership, control and management.

Indigenous private capital and management has not in the past played a very significant role in the development of medium-scale or large-scale manufacturing industries. But with the recent development of a domestic capital market, coupled with the government's active encouragement of indigenous enterprises, there are now signs of increasing private financial participation in industry by Nigerians. Nevertheless, private-venture capital by Nigerians is to be found substantially in small-scale industries or in investment outlets with a short gestation period and less complex managerial structure. Probably by far the most important way in which the government has influenced industrial development is through fiscal incentives in the form of protective tariffs, capital allowances, tax holidays, pioneer status, approved status and similar schemes. At least before the civil war reassuring declarations were made to foreign private interests about the unlikelihood of nationalization or expropriation, and in favour of free international capital movement and profit repatriation. However, following the experiences of the civil war, the wisdom of this open-door policy, deriving from a *laissez faire* ideological posture adopted by the government, has been questioned in relation to the long-term requirements of national development. In consequence many policy reforms are being undertaken in the aftermath of the war.

COMMERCE

Aside from the disruptions caused by the civil war Nigeria's foreign trade has continued the upward trend begun after the Second World War.

The value of merchandized exports rose from £135.8 million in 1959 to £646.7 million in 1971. The increase in value has been almost entirely the result of increased export volume, export prices contributing little or nothing to this increase. Merchandized imports also rose (though at a slower rate than merchandized exports) from £179.4 million in 1959 to £539.5 million in 1971.

The growth of petroleum exports has contributed significantly to the change in the structure of exports. In 1959 four traditional commodities—cocoa, palm oil, palm kernels and groundnuts (including groundnut oil and cake) contributed about 70 per cent of total exports, while petroleum contributed only 1.7 per cent. However, by 1965, the share of these commodities has declined to 51.6 per cent, and further still, by 1971, to 18 per cent. The share of crude petroleum rose to 25.9 per cent in 1965 and reached a level of 70 per cent in 1971.

There have also been important changes in the structure of imports. The share of consumer goods (both durable and non-durable) fell from 51 per cent of the total import bill in 1959 to 30.6 per cent in 1969. Over the same period the value of capital goods imported rose from 46 per cent to 68.2 per cent.

These changes reflect the rapid expansion of manufacturing industries (some of them based on imported raw materials) and the increased demand for heavy equipment generated by capital projects under the First National Development Plan, 1962–68, as well as by the growing oil industry. The higher duties on imported consumer goods and the general restriction on non-essential imports, which have been two important aspects of commercial policy since the early 1960s, have also contributed to this trend.

The significant changes in the direction of international trade over the period have been the decreasing share of the United Kingdom in both the import and export trades of Nigeria and the corresponding increase in the share of the EEC countries. The share of the United Kingdom in Nigerian exports declined from 50.5 per cent in 1959 to about 27 per cent in 1969, while she supplied only 30 per cent of Nigeria's imports in 1969 as compared with 45.3 per cent in 1959. On the other hand the share of the EEC in Nigeria's exports increased from 34 to 41 per cent over the same period, while its share in Nigeria's imports increased from 18 to 26 per cent. These trends reflect a move away from the close dependence on the United Kingdom which had been the established pattern of commercial relations before independence. It is, however, significant that trade between Nigeria and the United States was increasing over the same period.

Nigeria had a consistent deficit on balance of visible trade in the decade 1955 to 1965. In 1966, however, the balance of trade showed a surplus of £31 million. Smaller surpluses were realized in 1967 and 1968. In 1969 a record trade surplus of £69.5 million was attained. However, the balance of payments has still not caught up with the surpluses of the first decade after the Second World War.

Nigeria has a large and dynamic market for domestic commerce. It has had a long tradition of domestic trade; and inter-state commerce has become over the last two decades one of the important engines of economic growth. Apart from the large distribution network for the export and import trades, Nigeria has for long had an intricate system of domestically produced and traded commodities in the sectors of agriculture, livestock, fishing and crafts.

Given a fairly free mobility of products and of factors of production, the size of the national market has become a major force in the growth of industry. It has also promoted a higher degree of regional specialization than would be found in many other African countries smaller in size and less endowed in natural resources. The crucial importance of preserving the national market for the country's development process was, in fact, one vital point of principle in the civil war of 1967–70.

TRANSPORT

Nigeria's main rail lines run from south to north, bringing produce from the hinterland to the ports for export and for hauling imports to the hinterland for distribution. Despite active competition from road transport the railway still plays a vital role in the commerce of the country. In 1966 the number of passengers carried by the railway was 11.6 million, and the tonnage of goods hauled was 2.9 million.

For land transportation, however, roads have become increasingly important over the last three decades. Nigeria has a network of roads running from south to north, as well as in the east–west direction. Road transport, in fact, dominates inter-state commerce; and the greatest expansion in land transportation is taking place in the road sector.

Nigeria's principal ports are now Lagos, Warri, Port Harcourt and Calabar. These ports influence the north–south design of the road system. At the two major ports of Lagos and Port Harcourt before the civil war the foreign-bound cargoes loaded in 1960 amounted to 19 million tons, while coastal cargo loaded was 1.1 million tons. The amount of foreign cargo unloaded in the same year was about 2.5 million tons, while coastal cargo unloaded was 795,300 tons.

Air transport is relatively young in Nigeria, but for a country so large and with such great economic potential there is undoubtedly a good future for the development of civil aviation. In 1966 the number of passengers carried by the Nigerian Airways was 118,170. For the same period freight traffic recorded was 465 tons for mail, while commercial freight stood at 1,226 tons.

PUBLIC FINANCE

The total current revenue of the Federal and the Regional (now State) governments increased from £96.3 million in 1959 to £318.6 million in 1970. Total recurrent expenditure increased from £98.9 million to £284.5 million. During 1967–69 the revenue and expenditures were lower than those of 1966 because of the exclusion of the accounts of those states most directly affected by the civil war. As a proportion of the gross domestic product total revenue rose from 9.8 per cent in 1959 to 11.8 per cent in 1966, while the proportion of total expenditure increased from 10.1 per cent to 10.9 per cent.

The main heads of revenue are tax revenue (including import and export duties, excise duties, company tax and personal income tax), mining and royalties, and interests and payments. The main heads of expenditure are administration, social and community services (including education and health), economic services and transfers.

In the structure of government revenue there has been a shift from import duties to excise duties. Although revenue from export duties fell in the decade after independence, due mainly to the decline in duties on cocoa and palm produce, there were increased receipts from company taxation and mining royalties.

Despite the understandably high expenditure on defence in the period 1968–70, expenditure on administration increased steadily both absolutely and in proportion to total expenditure, and there has also been a rise in outlay on education and health within the total expenditure for social and community services. Within the economic services the rise in expenditure was most spectacular in construction and least so in agriculture. Total capital expenditure rose substantially from £56.5 million in 1959 to an estimated £190 million in 1970.

For the economic sector the increase was much greater, rising from £25.2 million in 1959 to an estimated £144 million in 1970.

Current surpluses were invariably not sufficient to cover capital expenditures. The resulting deficit was financed mainly through raising internal short-term and long-term loans, and through drawing on foreign cash balances.

The importance of domestic finance in relation to foreign aid in the execution of capital projects was demonstrated in the First National Development Plan of 1962–68. Of the £793 million budgeted for the public sector in the plan about one-half (£390 million) was to be raised internally. Experience during the execution of the plan showed that foreign aid fell short of expectation. As a result of the shortfall in external receipts the government had to resort more to internal sources (including borrowing) for financing projects.

The Nigerian currency is the Nigerian pound issued by the Central Bank of Nigeria. There are many commercial banks in the country which play a very active part in the economic life of the country, particularly in the process of monetary expansion.

EDUCATION

Probably not more than 10 per cent of Nigeria's total population can be regarded as literate in any admissible sense. But formal education has greatly expanded in the country since the end of the Second World War. Alongside this expansion has been the realization of the need to structure the educational system to meet the nation's effective manpower requirement. On the higher level of formal education efforts are geared towards producing graduates possessing high professional, technical and administrative qualifications, with an increasing bias towards the pure and applied sciences.

The manpower and educational needs of the country have been surveyed and projections made about future enrolment and output at various stages of the educational ladder.

It was estimated that by 1970 the enrolment in primary schools would be over four million. By 1966 it was three million, having risen from 2.8 million in 1962. The expansion of primary education has fallen far short of the projected target in the north. It had been planned to have at least 50 per cent of the children in school by 1970, but it seems unlikely that enrolment in 1970 was much above 25 per cent.

The expansion of secondary grammar school education has maintained the pace set by the projections in the whole Federation. Here the primary objective was to achieve an annual intake of not less than 45,000 in 1970. Total enrolment in such schools rose from 195,000 in 1962 to 215,000 in 1968.

In respect of sixth form work (which is the main controlling factor in the number of students proceeding to university institutions) the goal was to bring the number of students preparing for the Higher School Certificate or the Advanced-Level General Certificate of Education to over 10,000 by 1970. By 1966 6,000 students were already in sixth form classes leading to Higher School Certificate alone.

The projection for teachers was 5,000 diploma awards annually from teacher-training institutions. By 1965 the output was already over 4,000.

One area which seems to have fallen well behind schedule is technical education. As against a projected annual output of 5,000 technicians, the total student population in all such institutions was only about 18,000 by 1968.

A target enrolment of 10,000 students in all the five universities in the country was set for 1970. By 1966, 9,150 students, of whom 7,252 were pursuing degree courses, were already enrolled in all the Nigerian universities. But for the closure of one of the universities in 1967–69, as a result of the civil war, the target total enrolment would probably have been surpassed by 1970.

However, there has been a gap between goal and reality in the proportion of university students taking courses in the pure and applied sciences. Only 46 per cent of the university student population were in such fields in 1966, as against the projection that by 1970 75 per cent of all university students would be enrolled for the pure and applied sciences.

The general level of adult literacy is being gradually raised through various adult education programmes. For the country as a whole a substantial amount of money (some £60 million) is spent on various educational programmes each year. Public authorities are responsible for about 75 per cent of that expenditure, representing almost 20 per cent of their consolidated budget expenditures.

DEVELOPMENT AND PLANNING

There is little doubt that the Nigerian economy has performed fairly well over the last two decades. Before independence the gross domestic product at constant prices grew at about 4 to 5 per cent per annum. Parallel structural key indicators over the same period include a steady increase in the gross investment ratio; a remarkable export surplus resulting in accumulated foreign exchange reserves; modest shifts in the composition of production away from agricultural activities towards manufacturing, public utilities, building and construction, transport, communications and banking; and acceleration of the rate of urbanization.

While the economy grew steadily over the whole pre-independence decade, there is reason to believe that Nigeria experienced some deceleration in economic growth in the second half of the 1950s.

There is no doubt that the first quinquennium of the decade after independence (1960–65) witnessed a steady expansion in general economic activity. The growth rate of the gross domestic product at constant prices picked up again, reached and surpassed the 4 to 5 per cent level which was averaged in the preceding decade.

Apart from the growing balance of payments difficulties the striking features of the Nigerian economy in this period include the steady decline in the relative contribution of agriculture, forestry and fishing to the gross domestic product; the upsurge in the production of crude oil; the intensification of import-substitution industries by the establishment of medium-scale and large-scale manufacturing plants; a sustained building boom; and the expansion of social services, especially in the field of high-level education.

During this period also capital formation as a proportion of gross national product rose from about 12.2 per cent to about 15.14 per cent. But even more remarkable was the growth in domestic saving, which as a proportion of the gross national product rose from about 8 per cent to about 12 per cent. The proportion of capital formation attributable to current domestic saving increased from about 60 per cent to about 74 per cent during the period.

Foreign private investment shifted on a massive scale from its traditional areas of trading business, plantation and transport to the new growing points of manufacturing and processing. This, however, does not indicate that all was well with the Nigerian economy during this period. There were structural weaknesses, especially in the area of policy formation and social mobilization.

The second half of the post-independence decade (1966–70) coincided with the national crisis which resulted in the civil war. By 1965 the peak of growth in the post-independence Nigerian economy had passed. The impetus had weakened. The political crisis of 1966 only served to aggravate an already deteriorating situation. The growth rate of the gross domestic product slumped to under 3 per cent even before the outbreak of the civil war in the middle of 1967. Preliminary indications show that the major explanation for the decline in growth rate is to be sought on the domestic front; and especially in the fact that government spending as well as private investment had started to weaken by 1965.

The first serious attempt at planning was the National Development Plan for the period 1962–68, although there was not a total absence of development guidelines in the country before 1962—there were various programmes of development and welfare under the colonial régime. But even with the first national plan, the implementation process was very defective, whatever the shortcomings in conception and design. Generally speaking, the approach to development planning in Nigeria has been half-hearted. It has been characterized by a great deal of underspending and weak administrative control, resulting in considerable underfulfilment and structural distortion.

FUTURE PROSPECTS

Nigeria's main assets are human talents and the abundant supply of natural resources.

The high incidence of underemployment and unemployment, notably among school leavers, is widely regarded as one of the most serious social and political, as well as economic, problems facing the country. Related to the potentially abundant natural resources is also the problem of their full utilization, in the face of weaknesses in innovation and the application of science and technology to production processes.

Another problem facing the Nigerian economy arises out of its "mixed" nature. Some strategic means of production, distribution and exchange are under private (often foreign) ownership and control. Nationalistic, progressive policies are not easy in such a setting. Dynamic comprehensive planning is also especially difficult. Added to these drawbacks are the perennial problems of efficient management of public enterprises and of effective leadership by the public sector generally.

These are some of the problems to which the post-war National Reconstruction and Development Plan, 1970–74, is addressed. If the basic social, organizational and national economic management issues can be successfully resolved, there is no doubt that Nigeria will become a major economic power in Africa within the next generation. It possesses all the ingredients for revolutionary economic development and social change.

STATISTICAL SURVEY

AREA AND POPULATION

(Census, November 1963)

STATE	AREA (sq. miles)	POPULATION	PERSONS PER SQ. MILE	STATE CAPITAL (with population)
North-Western . . .	65,143	5,733,296	88	Sokoto (89,817)
North-Central .	27,108	4,098,305	151	Kaduna (149,910)
Kano . . .	16,630	5,774,842	347	Kano (295,432)
North-Eastern .	103,639	7,793,443	75	Maiduguri (139,965)
Benue-Plateau .	40,590	4,009,408	99	Jos (90,402)
Kwara . . .	28,672	2,399,365	84	Ilorin (208,546)
Lagos . . .	1,381	1,443,567	1,045	Lagos (665,246)
Western . . .	29,100	9,487,525	326	Ibadan (627,379)
Mid-Western .	14,922	2,535,839	170	Benin City (100,694)
East-Central .	11,310	7,227,559	639	Enugu (138,457)
South-Eastern .	11,166	3,622,589	324	Calabar (76,418)
Rivers . . .	7,008	1,544,314	220	Port Harcourt (179,563)
TOTAL . .	356,669	55,670,052	156	

It is generally believed that the 1963 enumeration overstated the number of inhabitants, but the reported total provided the basis for subsequent official estimates of the country's population. Listed below are two sets of mid-year estimates, one official and the other prepared by the Population Division of the United Nations:

YEAR	TOTAL POPULATION ('000)	
	Official Estimates	UN Estimates
1963 . . .	n.a.	46,324
1964 . . .	57,062	47,491
1965 . . .	58,489	48,676
1966 . . .	59,951	49,882
1967 . . .	61,449	51,116
1968 . . .	62,986	52,386
1969 . . .	64,560	53,702
1970 . . .	66,174	55,074
1971 . . .	n.a.	56,511
1972 . . .	69,524	58,020

Note: Both sets of estimates assume a steady growth of population and take no account of the military activities and economic blockade which followed the attempted secession of the former Eastern Region ("Biafra") in 1967-70.

CHIEF TOWNS

POPULATION (1970 estimates)

Lagos (Federal capital)	875,417	Ado-Ekiti . .	187,239
Ibadan . . .	745,756	Kaduna . . .	178,208
Ogbomosho . .	380,239	Mushin . . .	173,520
Kano . . .	351,175	Maiduguri . .	166,374
Oshogbo . .	248,394	Enugu . . .	164,582
Ilorin . . .	247,896	Ede . . .	159,938
Abeokuta . .	222,630	Aba . . .	155,720
Port Harcourt .	213,443	Ife . . .	154,589
Zaria . . .	197,524	Ila . . .	136,328
Ilesha . . .	197,111	Oyo . . .	133,548
Onitsha . .	193,793	Ikere-Ekiti . .	127,447
Iwo . . .	188,506	Benin City . .	119,692

Births and Deaths: Average annual birth rate 49.6 per 1,000; death rate 24.9 per 1,000 (UN estimates for 1965-70).

EMPLOYMENT
ECONOMICALLY ACTIVE POPULATION
(1963 Census)

Agriculture, Fishing, etc.	10,201,328
Sales	2,806,071
Crafts, Production Process, Labouring	2,190,073
Services, Sports, Recreation	870,884
Professional, Technical, etc.	440,613
Transport, Communications	279,255
Clerical	228,018
Mining, Quarrying, etc.	13,856
Unspecified	891,415
Unemployed	344,921

AGRICULTURE
LAND USE, 1961
('000 hectares)

Arable and Under Permanent Crops	21,795
Permanent Meadows and Pastures	25,800
Forest Land	31,592*
Other Areas	13,190
TOTAL	92,377

* Data from the world forest inventory carried out by the FAO in 1963.

PRINCIPAL CROPS
('000 metric tons)

	1969	1970	1971
Maize	1,219*	1,220*	1,220*
Millet	2,800*	2,800*	2,800*
Sorghum (Guinea Corn)	3,500*	3,500*	3,500*
Rice	563	550	550*
Sugar Cane[1]	240*	240*	240*
Sweet Potatoes and Yams	12,500*	13,500*	n.a.
Cassava (Manioc)	6,800*	7,300*	n.a.
Cow Peas and Other Pulses	700*	710*	700*
Palm Kernels[2]	177.2	305	310
Soybeans[2]	34	25	33*
Groundnuts (in shell)	1,365	780	1,100
Cottonseed	110	180	80
Cotton (Lint)	55	91	40
Sesame Seed[3]	25	20	20*
Copra[4]	2.1	2.1*	2.1*
Coffee	3.0	5.4	3.9
Cocoa Beans [2, 5]	191.8	222.9	300.0
Tobacco	10.3	12.0	17.5
Natural Rubber[6]	56.8	59.3	65.0

* FAO estimate.
[1] Crop year ending in year stated.
[2] Purchases for export.
[3] Commercial production only.
[4] Exports of copra and coconut oil in copra equivalent.
[5] Twelve months ending in September of year stated. 1971–72: 284,500 metric tons.
[6] Exports only.
Coconuts (1968–70): 200 million nuts each year (FAO estimate).
Palm oil ('000 metric tons): 425 in 1969; 488 in 1970; 500 in *1971*.

Source: FAO, *Production Yearbook 1971.*

LIVESTOCK
('000—FAO estimates)

	1968–69	1969–70	1970–71
Cattle	11,500	11,550	11,600
Sheep . . .	7,900	8,000	8,100
Goats . . .	23,300	23,400	23,500
Pigs . . .	800	820	840
Horses* . .	340	335	300
Asses* . . .	860	840	820
Camels . .	18	19	20
Poultry . .	80,000	82,000	83,000

* Figures relate to the former Northern Region only.
Source: FAO, *Production Yearbook 1971.*

LIVESTOCK PRODUCTS
(FAO estimates, metric tons)

	1969	1970	1971
Cows' Milk . .	403,000	405,000	407,000
Beef and Veal .	173,000	174,000	175,000
Mutton and Lamb .	108,000	111,000	112,000
Hen Eggs . .	78,400	80,400	82,500
Cattle Hides .	21,800	21,800	21,900

Source: FAO, *Production Yearbook 1971.*

Butter production (official estimates): 23 metric tons in 1967; 112 metric tons in 1968.

FORESTRY
ROUNDWOOD PRODUCTION
(cubic metres)

1966 . .	50,841,000
1967 . .	52,244,000
1968 . .	53,492,000
1969 . .	55,235,000

Source: FAO, *Yearbook of Forest Products.*

EXPORTS
('000 cu. ft.)

	1968	1969	1970*
Logs . . .	8,687	9,062	3,266
Sawn Timber . .	2,101	2,348	822

* Jan.–June.

EXPORTS OF LOGS AND SAWN TIMBER
BY MAIN SPECIES
(cu. ft.)

	1968	1969
Obeche . . .	4,096,654	4,069,955
Abura . . .	1,681,528	1,520,528
Agba . . .	1,452,494	708,087
Masonia . .	424,796	451,132
African Mahogany .	453,616	298,723

FISHING
(metric tons)

	1967	1969
Sea . . .	66,800	60,900
Inland water .	52,500	54,800
TOTAL .	119,300	115,700

Source: FAO, *Yearbook of Fishery Statistics 1970.*

MINING

		1967	1968	1969	1970	1971
Coal	'ooo metric tons	203*	—	16	58	75
Gold	kilogrammes	1	7	9	n.a.	n.a.
Lead Ore . . .	metric tons	553	—	—	—	n.a.
Tin Concentrates . .	,, ,,	9,490	9,804	8,741	7,959	7,320
Columbite . . .	,, ,,	1,914	1,129	1,491	n.a.	n.a.
Kaolin . . .	,, ,,	330	n.a.	n.a.	n.a.	n.a.
Natural Gas . . .	million cubic metres	181	147	64	81	n.a.
Crude Petroleum . .	'ooo metric tons	16,817	7,127	27,001	54,203	74,640

*Source: U.S. Bureau of Mines.

INDUSTRY

OUTPUT AND EMPLOYMENT, 1968*

(Establishments with 10 or more employees)

	NUMBER OF ESTABLISH-MENTS	PERSONS ENGAGED†	GROSS OUTPUT IN PRODUCERS' VALUES (£'ooo)
Food Products	89	10,296	45,392
Beverages	11	2,820	20,696
Tobacco	4	2,427	11,143
Textiles	47	21,149	41,664
Clothing (except footwear) . . .	12	683	1,017
Leather Products	11	1,004	2,473
Footwear	7	989	2,408
Wood Products (except furniture) . .	57	7,073	3,879
Furniture and fixtures (non-metal) . .	33	2,575	1,495
Paper and Paper Products . . .	10	1,195	3,361
Printing and Publishing	54	5,419	4,876
Industrial Chemicals	5	413	1,172
Other Chemical Products . . .	33	4,701	16,540
Miscellaneous Petroleum Products . .	4	103	3,960
Rubber Products	25	3,376	8,959
Other Plastic Products	16	1,362	2,805
Pottery and Glass	6	835	794
Other Non-metallic Mineral Products . .	15	2,348	7,389
Metals and Metal Products . . .	58	9,189	30,329
Machinery (non-electric)	5	450	398
Electrical Machinery, Apparatus, etc. . .	13	822	2,298
Transport Equipment	9	1,779	11,016
Scientific Equipment	3	67	71
Other Manufactured Products‡ . .	98	6,625	27,380
TOTAL MANUFACTURING INDUSTRIES‡ .	625	87,700	251,520
Metal Ore Mining	73	45,310	11,100
Electric Light and Power . . .	41	6,190	12,130

* Excluding the former Eastern Region.   † Including homeworkers.
‡ Including sales and repair of vehicles and transport equipment.

Source: Annual Industrial Survey.

PRODUCTION

	Unit	1967	1968	1969	1970
Tinned Meat	metric tons	1,385	1,104	1,151	n.a.
Margarine and Other Prepared Fats .	,, ,,	2,695	2,290	2,809	3,712
Vegetable Oils	,, ,,	130,000	174,000	174,000	n.a.
Wheat Flour	,, ,,	99,111	91,572	126,567	191,000
Biscuits	,, ,,	8,774	4,569	6,722	11,855
Raw Sugar	,, ,,	21,000	8,000	12,000	12,000
Sugar Confectionery . . .	,, ,,	7,021	7,136	11,110	14,142
Prepared Animal Feeds . . .	,, ,,	3,000	10,000	n.a.	n.a.
Beer	hectolitres	606,357	709,053	878,122	1,065,000
Soft Drinks	,,	200,000	194,000	248,000	336,000
Cigarettes	million	5,142	5,668	6,269	8,502
Cotton Yarn, Pure	metric tons	1,600	2,604	3,005	4,033
Woven Cotton Fabrics . . .	million sq. metres	195	183	236	224
Knitted Fabrics	metric tons	553	497	2,053	1,686
Women's Leather Footwear . .	'ooo pairs	1,545	2,584	3,576	n.a.
Other Non-rubber Footwear . .	,, ,,	7,160	5,351	7,529	n.a.
Sawnwood	cubic metres	340,000	425,000	494,000	n.a.
Plywood	,, ,,	20,000	24,000	28,000	n.a.
Paints	metric tons	5,568	5,007	8,006	12,000
Soap	,, ,,	38,579	27,591	28,073	29,558
Motor Spirit	,, ,,	108,000	—	—	184,000
Kerosene	,, ,,	83,000	—	—	123,000
Distillate Fuel Oils . . .	,, ,,	250,000	—	—	201,000
Residual Fuel Oils . . .	,, ,,	158,000	—	—	292,000
Liquefied Petroleum Gas . .	,, ,,	n.a.	2,000	19,000	n.a.
Bicycle and Motor Cycle Tyres .	'ooo	777	955	1,123	n.a.
Other Road Vehicle Tyres . .	,,	141	201	240	n.a.
Rubber Footwear	'ooo pairs	1,744	3,098	3,270	4,312
Cement*	metric tons	750,000	573,600	566,400	596,000
Tin Metal, Unwrought . . .	,, ,,	9,278	10,001	8,981	8,069
Nails, Screws, Nuts, Bolts, etc. .	,, ,,	7,166	4,049	5,939	n.a.
Radio Receivers	number	111,089	118,818	133,495	207,000
Television Receivers . . .	,,	571	234	2,714	6,000
Lorries Assembled	,,	4,643	4,128	6,213	7,502
Electric Energy	million kWh.	1,112	1,105	1,248	1,550

1971: Cement 665,000 metric tons; Tin metal 7,350 metric tons.

* Incomplete coverage, beginning July 1967.

Source: mainly United Nations, *The Growth of World Industry.*

FINANCE

240 pence (d.) = 20 shillings (s.) = 1 Nigerian pound.

Coins: ½d., 1d., 3d., 6d., 1s., 2s.

Notes: 5s., 10s., £N1, £N5.

Exchange rates (December 1972): £1 sterling = 15 Nigerian s. 7¾d.; U.S. $1 = 6s. 6.95d.

£N100 = £127.83 sterling = $304.00.

Note: It has been announced that a new decimal currency unit, the naira (equivalent to 10 Nigerian shillings), is to be introduced in January 1973. The naira will be divided into 100 kobo.

FEDERAL BUDGET

(Twelve months ending March 31st—£N'000)

Revenue	1966–67	1967–68	Expenditure	1966–67	1967–68
Customs and Excise . . .	108,667	93,334	Communications . . .	77	179
Direct Taxes . . .	16,041	22,060	Works and Survey . . .	7,429	6,947
Mining	18,372	16,955	Police and Prisons . . .	9,787	7,617
Post and Telegraph . .	1,329	1,215	Army	7,827	20,249
Reimbursements . .	1,291	1,298	Education and Health . .	8,517	9,048
Licences and Internal Revenue .	23,897	26,252	Contribution to the Development Fund	6,629	28
			For Regional Governments .	68,584	61,387
Total	169,597	161,114	**Total** (incl. others) .	169,075	153,747

1968–69 Budget: Revenue £N150m.; Expenditure n.a.

(£N million)

	1969–70	1970–71		1971–72
	Revised Estimates	Original Estimates	Revised Estimates	Estimates
Recurrent Revenue . . .	191.7	279.2	326	475
Less: Statutory Appropriation to State Governments	92.0	115.3	109	126
Revenue Retained by Federal Government	99.7	163.9	217	349
Recurrent Expenditure . . .	109.9	142.6	186	219
Contribution to Development Fund .	—	10.0	10	120
Overall Surplus/Deficit . . .	−10.2	11.3	21	10

STATE BUDGETS
(£N million)

	1970–71	1971–72
Benue-Plateau . . .	13.5	18.8
East-Central . . .	29.0	25.9
Kano . . .	12.2	22.5
Kwara . . .	11.3	16.0
Lagos . . .	13.2	16.1
Mid-Western . . .	22.0	29.3
North-Central . . .	19.2	23.0
North-Eastern . . .	20.5	27.0
North-Western . . .	18.3	26.9
Rivers . . .	24.6	29.2
South-Eastern . . .	10.2	13.6
Western . . .	27.7	38.9

SECOND NATIONAL DEVELOPMENT PLAN 1970–74
INVESTMENT AND FINANCING
(£N million)

Public Sector Capital Investment:		*Public Sector Financing:*	
Economic	580.8	Federal and State Budget Surpluses .	450.2
Social	286.4	Public Corporation and Marketing Board Surpluses	106.5
Administration	148.7	Central Bank and Other Domestic Borrowing	72.3
Financial Obligations . . .	9.5	External Finance . . .	151.0
Nominal Total . . .	1,025.4		
Less: Transfers . . .	37.2		
Gross Public Investment . .	988.2		
Less: Probable Spill-over . .	208.2		
Net Public Investment . . .	780.0		780.0
Private Sector Investment:		*Private Sector Financing:*	
Incorporated Business: Oil . .	267.5	Capital Inflow	412.5
Incorporated Business: Non-Oil . .	425.3	Net Corporate Capital Reserves .	307.5
Households	123.0	Personal Saving . . .	95.8
	815.8		815.8
TOTAL INVESTMENT . .	1,595.8	TOTAL FINANCE . . .	1,595.8

PUBLIC SECTOR CAPITAL INVESTMENT BY STATE
(£N million)

	ECONOMIC				SOCIAL		ADMINIS-TRATION	TOTAL
	Agriculture	Industry	Transport	Sector Total	Education	Sector Total		
Benue-Plateau . .	2.9	1.9	7.0	12.9	5.2	11.4	2.2	26.5
East-Central . .	10.4	5.6	5.0	24.9	8.0	21.7	4.2	50.8
Kano	16.7	3.5	5.5	28.6	8.1	20.2	3.3	52.1
Kwara . . .	2.4	2.2	3.3	10.2	2.6	10.8	1.8	22.8
Lagos . . .	3.0	2.5	4.0	12.4	3.8	12.2	2.5	27.1
Mid-Western . .	4.1	5.4	8.9	21.2	6.8	16.2	1.1	38.5
North-Central .	3.2	2.6	6.3	13.2	9.1	22.9	1.5	37.6
North-Eastern .	4.1	4.0	10.0	20.6	4.4	12.5	2.7	35.8
North-Western .	4.0	2.5	3.3	11.9	7.4	15.1	3.1	30.1
Rivers . . .	4.3	4.0	7.5	18.1	5.6	13.3	2.6	34.0
South-Eastern .	7.7	3.0	6.2	17.8	4.2	10.9	0.9	29.6
Western . .	14.0	8.0	8.4	35.5	24.5	46.9	3.0	85.4
All States . .	76.8	45.2	75.4	227.3	89.7	214.1	28.9	470.3
Federal Government .	30.8	40.8	167.1	353.5	49.1	72.3	119.8	555.1
TOTAL . .	107.6	86.0	242.5	580.8	138.8	286.4	148.7	1,025.4

GROSS DOMESTIC PRODUCT
(£N million—at 1962–63 factor cost)

	1969–70*	1970–71	1971–72
Agriculture, Livestock, etc. . .	767.3	894.4	935.0
Mining and Quarrying . .	150.5	296.2	412.4
Manufacturing and Crafts . .	142.5	164.5	189.1
Electricity and Water . .	10.0	11.3	13.4
Building and Construction .	61.0	96.0	110.0
Distribution . . .	198.0	235.0	256.0
Transport and Communications .	63.0	74.5	83.8
General Government . .	111.4	114.4	117.5
Education	51.0	54.0	57.0
Health	11.1	13.6	14.7
Other Services . . .	39.0	42.0	46.0
TOTAL . .	1,604.8	1,995.9	2,234.9

* Excluding the three States of the former Eastern Region.

PROJECTED GROSS DOMESTIC PRODUCT
(£N million—at factor cost and constant 1962 prices)

	1968–69	1969–70	1970–71	1971–72	1972–73	1973–74
Agriculture, Livestock, Forestry and Fishing	805.8	801.8	809.8	826.0	850.0	880.6
Mining	55.6	68.4	95.8	134.1	187.7	266.5
Manufacturing and Crafts . .	126.3	142.7	162.0	184.7	212.4	246.4
Electricity and Water Supply . .	10.5	11.2	12.2	13.2	14.4	15.8
Building and Construction . .	73.4	76.3	80.1	85.3	92.1	99.9
Distribution	191.0	190.0	193.8	199.7	206.1	212.9
Transport	49.8	50.4	51.7	53.2	55.3	57.8
Communication . . .	7.8	8.1	8.9	9.9	11.1	12.6
General Government . . .	49.1	52.0	52.8	54.4	56.0	58.0
Education	47.3	49.2	51.4	54.5	58.6	63.3
Health	9.1	9.7	10.4	11.1	12.5	13.7
Other Services . . .	50.5	54.0	56.8	59.8	62.7	65.8
TOTAL	1,475.2	1,513.8	1,585.6	1,685.9	1,819.7	1,993.3

Gross fixed investment is expected to rise from £340 million in 1970–71 to some £412 million in 1973–74.

MONEY SUPPLY*
(£N million)

	1967	1968	1969	1970
Currency with Non-Bank Public .	103.7	91.5	136.6	185.2
Demand Deposits	53.0	72.5	92.8	144.8
TOTAL MONEY SUPPLY .	156.7	164.0	229.4	329.7
Savings and Time Deposits . .	65.6	91.8	107.7	168.4

* December of each year.

Currency in Circulation (June 30th, 1972): £N167 million.

BALANCE OF PAYMENTS
(£N million)

	1967		1968†		1969‡		1970§	
	Oil	Non-Oil*	Oil	Non-Oil	Oil	Non-Oil	Oil	Non-Oil
Current Account:								
Visible Trade:								
Exports (f.o.b.) .	72.0	166.8	37.0	171.4	131.0	182.3	263.0	180.0
Imports (c.i.f.) .	−17.5	−200.9	− 9.9	−181.2	−11.1	−217.8	10.0	349.0
Trade Balance . .	54.5	− 34.1	27.1	− 9.8	119.9	− 35.5	253.0	−169.0
Transport, Freight and Insurance . .	—	0.8	—	2.2	—	4.2		
Investment Income .	−19.8	− 20.6	—	− 53.9		− 55.0		
Other Services . .	−31.5	− 40.0	−28.2	− 38.7	−44.8	− 49.2		
Transfer Payments:								
Private . . .	—	− 4.5	—	3.5	—	2.0		
Official . . .	—	12.2	—	13.7	—	8.4		
BALANCE ON CURRENT ACCOUNT . .	3.2	− 86.2	− 1.1	− 83.0	75.1	−125.1		
Capital Account:								
Private Capital .	45.5	6.0	29.9	49.3	−19.2	55.6	n.a.	n.a.
Government Capital .	—	9.9	—	0.8	—	1.4		
BALANCE ON CAPITAL ACCOUNT . .	45.5	15.9	29.9	50.1	−19.2	57.0		
Overall Surplus or Deficit	48.7	− 70.3	28.8	− 32.9	55.9	− 68.1		
Monetary Sectors:								
Commercial Banks .	—	2.6	—	2.0	—	− 1.9		
Federal Institutions .	—	31.1	—	5.0	—	− 5.7		
TOTAL MONETARY SECTORS . .	—	33.7	—	− 3.0	—	− 7.6		
Net Unrecorded Items .	−12.1		7.1		19.8			

* All sectors except for oil prospecting and mining companies.   † Revised.   ‡ Provisional.   § Estimate.

EXTERNAL TRADE
(£N million)

	1964	1965	1966	1967	1968	1969	1970	1971
Imports . .	253.9	275.1	256.4	223.6	193.2	248.7	378.2	539.5
Exports . .	214.7	268.3	284.1	241.8	211.1	318.2	442.7	646.7

COMMODITY GROUPS
(£N'000)

	IMPORTS			EXPORTS		
	1968	1969	1970*	1968	1969†	1970*
Food and Live Animals	14,196	20,866	13,098	65,730	69,782	51,359
Beverages and Tobacco	1,173	798	704	11	5	1
Crude Materials, inedible, except fuels .	5,267	5,739	3,494	71,108	73,146	33,559
Mineral Fuels, Lubricants and Related Materials	14,551	15,630	7,939	37,539	136,087	105,248
Animal and Vegetable Oils and Fats .	289	192	176	12,935	15,276	7,629
Chemicals	22,448	30,392	19,167	28	107	48
Basic Manufactured Goods . . .	54,687	71,988	46,251	16,358	17,147	10,979
Machinery and Transport Equipment .	60,473	73,238	59,544	—	—	—
Miscellaneous Manufactured Articles .	14,005	13,413	9,009	105	192	70
Commodities and Transactions not classified according to kind	6,095	16,434	4,329	2,691	7,948	1,024
TOTAL	193,184	248,691	163,711	211,085	323,175	211,573

* Jan.–June.   † Unrevised figures. Revised total (£N'000): 318,200.

PRINCIPAL COMMODITIES

IMPORTS	VALUE (£N'000)		
	1967	1968	1969
Cereals and Preparations . . .	6,348	4,889	8,611
Petroleum Products . . .	8,175	14,392	15,323
Medicaments	4,298	5,359	6,878
Paper and Paperboard . . .	5,734	5,542	6,469
Textile Yarn, Fabrics, etc. . .	33,046	20,030	23,770
Iron and Steel . . .	15,297	14,262	20,574
Machinery (non-electric) . . .	29,315	27,602	30,535
Electrical Equipment . . .	16,329	13,278	14,190
Road Motor Vehicles . . .	20,009	15,472	22,051

EXPORTS	QUANTITIES ('000 tons)			VALUES (£N'000)		
	1968	1969	1970*	1968	1969†	1970*
Cocoa	205.5	170.8	108.0	51,741	52,596	41,926
Groundnut Cake .	170.7	167.9	79.8	4,894	5,007	2,546
Benniseed (Sesame Seed)	14.9	16.1	7.7	1,167	1,371	697
Raw Cotton . .	14.0	14.0	11.0	3,267	3,356	2,491
Cotton Seed .	28.5	41.6	37.7	884	1,005	812
Groundnuts .	638.0	517.0	190.0	37,953	35,811	14,227
Hides and Skins .	7.2	7.2	2.8	3,913	3,985	1,648
Palm Kernels .	159.0	176.1	80.9	10,173	9,756	4,896
Rubber . .	52.0	56.4	31.1	6,311	9,644	5,011
Timber—Logs ('000 cu. ft.)	8,687.0	9,062.0	3,266.0	2,531	2,979	1,112
Timber—Sawn ('000 cu. ft.)	2,101.0	2,348.0	822.0	1,027	1,241	495
Crude Petroleum .	6,899.5	26,866.5	20,840.7	36,999	136,011	105,187
Groundnut Oil .	109.1	99.4	43.0	9,454	10,897	5,393
Palm Kernel Oil .	26.9	36.7	n.a.	3,326	3,888	n.a.
Leather . .	2.0	1.7	n.a.	1,639	2,170	n.a.
Tin Metal (unwrought) .	11.3	10.1	6.1	13,714	13,925	9,503

* Jan.–June.   † Unrevised figures.

COUNTRIES
(£N'000)

IMPORTS	1968	1969	1970*
Sterling Area:			
Hong Kong . .	2,325	2,363	2,455
India . .	1,785	1,766	1,292
Pakistan .	1,958	3,344	n.a.
United Kingdom .	59,882	86,346	53,785
TOTAL STERLING AREA	71,497	99,189	60,062
Non-Sterling Area:			
Belgium-Luxembourg .	3,284	3,215	2,890
China, People's Rep.	3,720	5,475	n.a.
Czechoslovakia	3,410	2,874	1,589
Denmark . .	1,182	1,989	1,329
Egypt . .	971	2,287	n.a.
France . .	7,183	8,012	4,741
Federal Germany .	21,231	26,393	20,137
Italy . .	13,782	13,535	8,615
Japan . .	7,164	9,435	10,720
Netherlands . .	7,830	11,624	6,182
Netherlands Possessions .	2,684	2,528	1,032
Norway . .	2,105	1,428	1,076
Poland . .	2,007	2,044	n.a.
Spain . .	949	1,981	n.a.
Sweden . .	1,832	1,945	n.a.
Switzerland .	1,805	2,913	n.a.
U.S.S.R. .	897	1,628	n.a.
U.S.A. . .	22,289	29,292	22,833
TOTAL NON-STERLING AREA . . .	119,742	145,540	102,698

EXPORTS†	1968	1969	1970*
Sterling Area:			
Ghana . .	463	1,344	210
Hong Kong . .	288	485	105
Ireland . .	1,096	1,301	857
United Kingdom .	61,939	87,709	64,347
TOTAL STERLING AREA	64,838	95,186	75,968
Non-Sterling Area:			
Belgium-Luxembourg .	5,881	5,009	1,810
Brazil . .	5,498	8,530	n.a.
Canada . .	5,543	7,364	5,140
Denmark . .	3,793	5,800	879
France . .	11,540	31,946	12,653
Federal Germany .	17,863	19,313	13,139
Italy . .	13,118	14,493	9,977
Japan . .	3,664	3,315	1,834
Netherlands . .	27,036	42,797	33,745
Norway . .	954	2,353	1,836
Portugal . .	4,092	4,825	n.a.
Spain . .	5,883	5,449	n.a.
Sweden . .	1,657	8,371	n.a.
Switzerland .	3,153	1,803	n.a.
U.S.S.R. . .	5,484	8,219	n.a.
U.S.A. . .	16,039	40,001	22,768
TOTAL NON-STERLING AREA . . .	141,659	224,490	133,948

* Jan.–June.   † Excluding re-exports.

TOURISM
ARRIVALS BY COUNTRY OF ORIGIN

	1966	1967	1968	1969	1970
United Kingdom . . .	2,939	5,869	5,828	4,338	3,113
U.S.A.	3,106	4,069	3,654	1,556	1,480
Others and Unspecified* .	10,833	11,891	13,891	7,873	8,501
TOTAL* . . .	16,878	21,829	23,373	13,767	13,094

* Including arrivals of Nigerian nationals resident abroad: 2,695 in 1966; 1,383 in 1967; 1,775 in 1968; an unspecified number in 1969; and 2,263 in 1970.

Source: United Nations, *Statistical Yearbook.*

TRANSPORT
RAILWAYS
(Twelve months ending March 31st)

	1967–68	1968–69	1969–70	1970–71
Passenger-km. (million) . . .	397	586	728	987
Net ton-km. (million)* . . .	1,613	1,788	1,615	1,595

* Including the railways' own service traffic.

ROADS
MOTOR VEHICLES IN USE

	1967	1968	1969
Passenger Cars . . .	70,300	42,800	39,300
Commercial Vehicles . .	31,900	22,500	23,700
TOTAL . . .	102,200	65,300	63,000

Source: United Nations, *Statistical Yearbook 1971.*

ROAD MILEAGE

	1964	1965	1966
Tarred	8,865	9,338	9,476
Gravel or Earth	44,676	46,198	45,780
TOTAL . .	53,541	55,536	55,256

MERCHANT SHIPPING FLEET
(registered at June 30th each year)

	DISPLACEMENT (gross tons)
1968 . .	71,000
1969 . .	98,000
1970 . .	99,000
1971 . .	96,000

INTERNATIONAL SEA-BORNE SHIPPING

	1967	1968	1969	1970
Vessels Entered ('000 net tons) . .	5,636	4,794	1,945	5,343
Goods Loaded ('000 metric tons) . .	16,765	9,181	28,903	53,551
Goods Unloaded ('000 metric tons) .	2,223	2,832	3,279	3,693

CIVIL AVIATION
Scheduled Services

	1967	1968	1969	1970
Kilometres Flown ('000) . . .	4,584	3,905	5,524	5,381
Passenger-km. ('000) . . .	152,921	154,336	190,542	213,623
Cargo ton-km. ('000) . . .	4,717	4,671	5,396	5,835
Mail ton-km. ('000) . . .	1,148	1,010	1,060	1,098

COMMUNICATIONS

RADIO AND TELEVISION
(Receivers in use at December 31st)

Year	Radio	Television
1963 . .	400,000	10,000
1964 . .	600,000	15,000
1965 . .	n.a.	30,000
1966 . .	n.a.	40,000
1967 . .	n.a.	42,000*
1968 . .	1,260,000	n.a.
1969 . .	1,265,000	53,000
1970 . .	1,275,000	75,000

* September.

TELEPHONES
(Number in use at January 1st)

1967 . .	73,000
1968 . .	77,883
1969 . .	75,900
1970 . .	81,440
1971 . .	80,000

Source: American Telephone and Telegraph Company.

Newspapers: 24 dailies in 1966, including 20 with a combined average circulation of 417,000 copies per issue.

EDUCATION
(1966)

	Number of Establishments	Number of Teachers	Number of Students
Primary Schools	14,907	91,049	3,025,981
Secondary Schools	1,350	11,644	211,305
Technical Schools . . .	73	789	15,059
Teacher Training Colleges .	193	1,837	30,493
Universities (1971) . . .	6	2,628	17,495

Sources (except where otherwise stated): Federal Office of Statistics, Lagos; *Nigeria Trade Journal*; Standard Bank *Annual Economic Review: Nigeria,* June 1972; *Barclays Overseas Survey 1971; Nigeria Year Book 1971; Nigeria Handbook 1970;* United Nations, *Statistical Yearbook 1971.*

THE CONSTITUTION

A new Constitutional Decree was published in Lagos on March 17th, 1967, to replace all earlier Decrees. The following are its principal provisions:

1. Legislative and executive power is vested in the Supreme Military Council. The Chairman of the Council is the head of the Military Government. The Supreme Military Council is composed of the Regional Military Governors and the Military Administrator of the Federal Territory; the Heads of the Nigerian Army, Navy and Air Force, the Chief of Staff of the Armed Forces and the Inspector-General of Police or his Deputy.

2. The Supreme Military Council can delegate powers to a Federal Executive Council, which is predominantly composed of civilian Commissioners drawn from all the States of the Federation, with Gen. Gowon, Rear-Admiral Wey and Alhaji Kam Selem representing the armed forces. The Federal Attorney-General and the Secretaries to Federal and State Governors, as well as other appropriate officials, may attend the meetings of either Council in an advisory capacity.

3. On certain matters of legislation, the concurrence of all the Military Governors is required. These matters in-

clude any decrees affecting or relating to the territorial integrity of a State, or altering entrenched clauses of the 1963 Constitution, or affecting the Federation in respect of trade, commerce, transport, industry, communications, labour, the public service or public finance (including approval of new capital projects in Federal estimates), or affecting external or security affairs, or affecting the professions and higher education.

4. Special powers are given to the Supreme Military Council to override State legislation, with the concurrence of a majority of Military Governors, if that legislation impedes the exercise of Federal authority or constitutes a danger to the continuance of Federal Government in Nigeria.

5. The creation of new States will be treated as an entrenched clause of the Constitution.

6. Certain additional matters covered by the Decree include: the revived power to appoint local authority police; one Federal Supreme Court judge will be appointed by each State; decrees made since January 1966 may be repealed or amended by individual Military Governors; the new Decree cannot be challenged in a court of law; power of appointment to higher Civil Service posts is in the hands of the Supreme Military Council, acting on the advice of the Public Service Commission.

On May 27th, 1967 the Supreme Military Council issued a decree creating 12 states out of the four existing Regions.

Northern Region was divided into six States and Eastern Region into three. Lagos State was created by the merger of the Colony Province of Western Region with the Federal Territory of Lagos. The rest of Western Region became Western State. The Mid-Western Region retained the same boundaries as Mid-Western State.

FEDERAL GOVERNMENT

SUPREME MILITARY COUNCIL

Chairman: Gen. YAKUBU GOWON.
Members: Vice-Admiral JOSEPH E. A. WEY (Head of the Nigerian Navy), Brig. IKWE (Commandant of the Nigeria Air Force), Maj.-Gen. DAVID EJOOR (Chief of Staff (Armed Forces)), Maj.-Gen. EKPO (Chief of Staff (Supreme Headquarters)), Col. BISSALA (Chief of Staff (Army)), Alhaji KAM SELEM (Inspector-General of Police). The Military Governors of the twelve states in the Federation are *ex-officio* members of the committee.

FEDERAL EXECUTIVE COUNCIL
(*December* 1972)

Chairman and Commander-in-Chief of Armed Forces: Gen. YAKUBU GOWON.
Commissioner for Finance: Alhaji SHEHU SHAGARI.
Commissioner for Establishments: Vice-Admiral J. E. A. WEY.
Commissioner for External Affairs: Dr. OKOI ARIKPO.
Commissioner for Communications: JOSEPH S. TARKA.

Commissioner for Agriculture and Natural Resources: Dr. J. O. J. OKEZIE.
Commissioner for Education: Chief A. Y. EKE.
Commissioner for Health: Alhaji AMINU KANO.
Commissioner for Economic Development and Reconstruction: Dr. A. ADEDEJI.
Commissioner for Labour and Information: Chief ANTHONY ENAHORO.
Commissioner for Internal Affairs and Inspector-General of Police: Alhaji KAM SELEM.
Commissioner for Justice and Attorney-General: Dr. W. GRAHAM-DOUGLAS.
Commissioner for Mines and Power: SHETTIMA ALI MONGUNO.
Commissioner for Industries: Dr. J. E. ADETORO.
Commissioner for Transport: Dr. R. A. B. DIKKO.
Commissioner for Works and Housing: L. O. OKUNNO.
Commissioner for Trade: W. BRIGGS.

STATE GOVERNMENTS

There are between eight and twelve Ministries in each State, each headed by a Commissioner and together presided over by the Governor.

NAME	CAPITAL	GOVERNOR
North-Western	Sokoto	M. FARUK
North-Central	Kaduna	Lt.-Col. ABBA KYARI
Kano State	Kano	ABDU BAKO
North-Eastern	Maiduguri	Col. MUSA USMAN
Benue-Plateau	Jos	J. D. GOMWALK
Kwara	Ilorin	Col. D. L. BAMIGBOYE
Lagos State	Lagos	Col. M. O. JOHNSON
South-Eastern	Calabar	Brig. U. J. ESUENE
Rivers State	Port Harcourt	Lt.-Cmdr. DIETE-SPIFF
East-Central	Enugu	UKBABI ASIKA
Mid-Western	Benin	Col. S. O. OGBEMUDIA
Western	Ibadan	Brig. W. ROTIMI

DIPLOMATIC REPRESENTATION

HIGH COMMISSIONS AND EMBASSIES IN LAGOS

(HC) High Commission; (E) Embassy.

Argentina: 93 Awolowo Rd., Ikoyi (E); *Ambassador:* FRANCISCO BENGOLEA.

Australia: 21-25 Yakubu Gowon St., P.O.B. 2427 (HC); *High Commissioner:* P. N. HUTTON.

Austria: 8-10 Yakubu Gowon St., P.O.B. 1914 (E); *Ambassador:* Dr. ALEXANDER K. OTTO.

Belgium: 8-10 Yakubu Gowon St., P.O.B. 149 (E); *Ambassador:* M. DE BRUYNE.

Brazil: 21-25 Yakubu Gowon St. (E); *Ambassador:* PAULO RIO BRANCO NABULO DE GOUVEA.

Bulgaria: 25 Norman Williams St., S.W. Ikoyi (E); *Ambassador:* ILIA IGNATOV.

Cameroon: 26 Moloney St. (E); *Ambassador:* EL HADJI HAMMADOU ALIM.

Canada: Tinubu St., P.O.B. 851 (HC); *High Commissioner:* ALAN S. McGILL.

Chad: 2 Goriola St., Victoria Island, P.M.B. 2801 (E); *Chargé d'Affaires:* ABAKAR ABOUA ABDELKERIM.

China, People's Republic: 19A Taslim Elias Close, Victoria Island, P.O.B. 5653 (E); *Ambassador:* YANG CHI-LIANG.

Czechoslovakia: 2 Alhaji Masha Close, Ikoyi, P.O.B. 1009 (E); *Ambassador:* JAROMÍR VRLA.

Dahomey: 36 Breadfruit St., P.O.B. 5705 (E); *Ambassador:* LUIZ VICTOR ANGELO.

Denmark: 12 Eleke Crescent, Victoria Island, P.O.B. 2390 (E); *Ambassador:* TROELS MUNK.

Egypt: 81 Awolowo Rd., Ikoyi, P.O.B. 538 (E); *Ambassador:* KANAL MOHAMED ABDUL-KHEIR.

Equatorial Guinea: 6 Alhaji Bashorun St., S.W. Ikoyi (E); *Ambassador:* JOSE W. OKORI-DOUGAN.

Ethiopia: Ademola St., Ikoyi, P.M.B. 2488 (E); *Ambassador:* ATO ARAYA OGBAZY.

Finland: 8–10 Yakubu Gowon St., P.O.B. 4433 (E); *Ambassador:* K. ENSIO ILMARI HELANIEMI.

France: 161 Taslim Elias Close, Victoria Island, P.O.B. 567 (E); *Ambassador:* M. A. ROGER.

German Federal Republic: 15 Eleke Crescent, Victoria Island, P.O.B. 728 (E); *Ambassador:* Dr. ERNST JUNG.

Greece: 150 Yakubu Gowon St., P.O.B. 1199 (E); *Chargé d'Affaires:* EFTHIMIOS TZAFERIS.

Guinea: 8 Abudu Smith St., Victoria Island, P.O.B. 2826 (E); *Ambassador:* LAYE KOUROUMA.

Hungary: 9 Louis Solomon Close, Victoria Island, P.O.B. 3168 (E); *Chargé d'Affaires:* ENDRE GALAMBOS.

Iceland: 388B Herbert Macauley St., P.O.B. 2498, Yaba (E); *Ambassador:* N. P. SIGURDSSON.

India: 40 Marina, P.M.B. 2322 (HC); *High Commissioner:* A. N. MEHTA.

Indonesia: 5 Anifowoshe St., P.O.B. 3473 (E); *Ambassador:* Maj.-Gen. ALIBASJAH SATARI.

Iraq: 7 Keffi St., Ikoyi, P.O.B. 2859 (E); *Chargé d'Affaires:* ABDUL-RAZZAK M. SALIH.

Ireland: 31 Marina, P.O.B. 2421 (E); *Ambassador:* TADHG O'SULLIVAN.

Israel: 7-9 Alhaji Kanike Close, Ikoyi, P.M.B. 2284 (E); *Ambassador:* YISSAKHAR BEN-YAACOV.

Italy: 72 Campbell St., P.O.B. 2161 (E); *Ambassador:* Dr. LUIGI GASBARRI.

Japan: 24-25 Apese St., Victoria Island, P.M.B. 2111 (E); *Ambassador:* AKIRA SHIGENITSU.

Kenya: Room 601, Federal Palace Hotel, Victoria Island (HC); *High Commissioner:* J. K. KIMANI (acting).

Lebanon: 57 Raymond Njoku Rd., S.W. Ikoyi (E); *Ambassador:* BULIND BEYDEUN.

Liberia: 23 Ademola St., P.O.B. 3007 (E); *Ambassador:* J. DUDLEY LAWRENCE.

Libya: 46 Raymond Njoku Rd., Ikoyi, P.O.B. 2860 (E); *Ambassador:* RAMADAN GREIBIL.

Malaysia: Kofo Abayomi/Anifowoshe St., Victoria Island, P.O.B. 3729 (HC); *High Commissioner:* ABDUL MANAF MOHAMED (acting).

Netherlands: 24 Ozumba Mbadiwe Ave., Victoria Island (E); *Chargé d'Affaires:* G. W. BENDIEN.

Niger: 15 Adeola Odeku St., Victoria Island, P.M.B. 2736 (E); *Ambassador:* IBRAHIM LOUTOU.

Norway: 8-10 Yakubu Gowon St., P.M.B. 2431 (E); *Ambassador:* P. M. MOTZFELDT.

Pakistan: P.O.B. 2450 (E); *Ambassador:* G. SAMUNDOIN KHAN.

Philippines: 8 Mekunwen Rd., Ikoyi, P.O.B. 2948 (E); *Chargé d'Affaires:* (vacant).

Poland: 32 Gerrard Rd., Old Ikoyi, P.O.B. 410 (E); *Ambassador:* JOSEF FILIPOWICZ.

Romania: 30 Raymond Njoku Rd., Ikoyi, P.O.B. 595 (E); *Ambassador:* GHEORGHE IASON.

Saudi Arabia: 182 Awolowo Rd., Ikoyi, P.O.B. 2836 (E); *Ambassador:* MANSOUR AREF.

Senegal: 4-6 Oil Mill St., P.M.B. 2197 (E); *Ambassador:* LAMINE DIAKHATE.

Sierra Leone: 192 Awolowo Rd., Ikoyi, P.O.B. 2821 (HC); *High Commissioner:* WILLIAM FITZJOHN.

Spain: 9 Queen's Drive, P.M.B. 2738 (E); *Ambassador:* EDUARDO S. DE ERICE.

Sudan: 40 Awolowo Rd., Okoyi, P.O.B. 2428 (E); *Ambassador:* Maj.-Gen. MUBARAK OSNAN RAHAMA.

Sweden: 8-10 Yakubu Gowon St., P.O.B. 1097 (E); *Ambassador:* L. B. T. ARVIDSON.

Switzerland: 11 Anifowoshe St., Victoria Island, P.O.B. 536 (E); *Ambassador:* FRIEDER H. ANDRES.

Syria: 4 Raymond Njoku Rd., Ikoyi, P.O.B. 3088 (E); *Ambassador:* Dr. ZAKARIA SIBAHI.

Tanzania: 45 Ademola St., Ikoyi (HC); *High Commissioner:* PHILEMON P. MURO.

Thailand: 1 Ruxton Rd., Old Ikoyi, P.O.B. 3095 (E); *Ambassador:* ARI BUPHAVESA.

Togo: 96 Awolowo Rd., Ikoyi, P.O.B. 1435 (E); *Chargé d'Affaires:* NICHOLAS M. AKOU.

Turkey: 3 Okunola Martins Close, Ikoyi, P.O.B. 1758 (E); *Ambassador:* TALAT BENLER.

U.S.S.R.: 5 Eleke Crescent, Victoria Island (E); *Ambassador:* B. S. VOROBYOVA.

United Kingdom: 62-64 Campbell St., P.M.B. 12136 (HC); *High Commissioner:* Sir CYRIL PICKARD.

U.S.A.: 1 King's College Rd. (E); *Ambassador:* JOHN REINHARDT.

Venezuela: 10 Ikoyi Crescent, Ikoyi, P.O.B. 3727 (E); *Ambassador:* LUIS ALBERTO OLAVARRIA.

Yugoslavia: 7 Maitama Sule St., Ikoyi, P.M.B. 978 (E); *Ambassador:* M. Božović.

Zaire: 23A Kofo Abayomi Rd., Victoria Island (E); *Ambassador:* A. TSHILUMBA-KABISHI BENDELEMUABO.

Zambia: 11 Keffi St., S.W. Ikoyi (HC); *High Commissioner:* A. S. MASIYE.

Nigeria also has diplomatic relations with Algeria, Central African Republic, Chile, Jordan, Malawi, Mali, Mauritania, Trinidad and Tobago, Uganda, Upper Volta and Uruguay.

POLITICAL PARTIES

All political parties were banned in May 1966 after the military coup d'état.

DEFENCE

Of a total armed force of 274,000, the army numbers 262,000 men, the navy 5,000 and the air force 7,000. There is also a civil police of 31,000. Military service is voluntary.

JUDICIAL SYSTEM

The High Courts of Justice are superior Courts of Record and have unlimited jurisdiction in the first instance except in certain cases which are reserved to the Federal Supreme Court, for example, disputes between any of the component parts of the Federation involving any question as to the existence or extent of any legal right, and matters arising under any Treaty or affecting Consular Officers or any international organization outside Nigeria. The High Courts also have jurisdiction to hear appeals from Magistrates' and Native Courts.

The Magistrates' Courts have original jurisdiction in a large variety of civil and criminal cases, some also have jurisdiction to hear appeals from Native Courts. The offices of Chief Magistrate have been retained in all areas.

Customary Courts have been retained throughout the Federation. The law administered in those Courts is, generally speaking, the Native Law and Custom prevailing in the area of their jurisdiction.

The Federal Supreme Court is the final Court of Appeal in Nigeria, consisting of the Chief Justice and eight Justices of the Supreme Court.

The Judges of the Federal Supreme Court and of the High Courts of Justice are appointed by the President. Judges of the High Courts of the States are appointed by the Governor of each State.

FEDERAL SUPREME COURT

Chief Justice of the Federation: Dr. TASLIM O. ELIAS.

Federal Justices: Mr. Justice G. B. A. COKER, Sir IAN LEWIS, Sir UDO UDOMA, Mr. Justice C. O. MADARIKAN, Mr. Justice A. FATAYI-WILLIAMS, Mr. Justice G. S. SOWEMIMO.

RELIGION

AFRICAN RELIGIONS

The beliefs, rites and practices of the people of Nigeria are very diverse, varying from tribe to tribe and family to family. Approximately 10,000,000 persons profess local beliefs.

MUSLIMS

There are large numbers of Muslims in Northern and Western Nigeria, and over 26 million were enumerated in the whole of Nigeria in the 1963 Census.

Spiritual Head: The Sardauna of Sokoto.

CHRISTIANS

The 1963 Census recorded over 19 million Christians in Nigeria.

ANGLICAN
PROVINCE OF WEST AFRICA

Archbishop of the Province of West Africa and Bishop of Sierra Leone: Most Rev. M. N. C. O. SCOTT, C.B.E., D.D., DIP.TH., Bishopscourt, P.O.B. 128, Freetown, Sierra Leone.

BISHOPS

Aba: Rt. Rev. H. A. I. AFONYA, P.O.B. 212, Aba.

Accra: Rt. Rev. I. S. M. LeMAIRE, Bishopscourt, P.O.B. 8, Accra.

Benin: Rt. Rev. AGORI IWE, M.B.E., J.P., Bishopscourt, P.O.B. 82, Benin.

Ekiti: Very Rev. J. A. ADETILOYE, B.D.A.K.C., Bishopscourt, Ekiti.

Enugu: Rt. Rev. G. N. OTUBELU, Uwani, P.O.B. 418, Enugu.

Gambia and the Rio Pongas: Rt. Rev. JEAN RIGAL ELISÉE, P.O.B. 51, Bathurst, The Gambia.

Ibadan: Rt. Rev. T. O. OLUFOSOYE, P.O.B. 3075, Bishopscourt, Ibadan.

Lagos: Rt. Rev. S. I. KALE, M.B.E., M.A., DIP.TH., 29 Marina, P.O.B. 13, Lagos.

The Niger: Rt. Rev. L. M. UZODIKE, P.O.B. 42, Onitsha.

The Niger Delta: Rt. Rev. YIBO ALILABO FUBARA.

Northern Nigeria: Rt. Rev. F. O. SEGUN, Kaduna.

Ondo: Rt. Rev. EMANUEL OLAWALE IDOWU.

Owerri: Rt. Rev. B. C. NWANKITI, DIP.TH., Bishop's House, Egbu, P.O.B. 31, Owerri.

ROMAN CATHOLIC

National Episcopal Conference of Nigeria: *Secretariat:* P.O.B. 951, Lagos; Chair. Most Rev. Dr. F. A. ARINZE, Archbishop of Onitsha; Sec. Rt. Rev. Dr. A. SANUSI, Bishop of Ijebu-Ode.

Archbishop of Kaduna: Most Rev. JOHN MACCARTHY, Archbishop's House, P.O.B. 14, Kaduna.

BISHOPS

Idah: Rt. Rev. Mgr. L. GRIMARD, P.O.B. 3, Idah.

Ilorin: Rt. Rev. WILLIAM MAHONY, P.O.B. 169, Ilorin.

Jos: Rt. Rev. JOHN REDDINGTON, P.O.B. 494, Jos.

Lokoja: Rt. Rev. Dr. A. MAKOZI, P.O.B. 31, Lokoja.

Maiduguri: Rt. Rev. TIMOTHY COTTER, P.O.B. 58, Maiduguri.

Makurdi: Rt. Rev. D. MURRAY, P.O.B. 21, Makurdi.

Minna: Rt. Rev. Mgr. E. FITZGIBBON, P.O.B. 58, Minna.

Sokoto: Rt. Rev. MICHAEL DEMPSEY, P.O.B. 51, Sokoto.

Yola: Rt. Rev. PATRICK SHEEHAN, P.O.B. 57, Yola.

Archdiocese of Lagos: the Vicar Capitular, P.O.B. 8, Lagos.

BISHOPS

Benin City: Rt. Rev. PATRICK J. KELLY, D.D., P.O.B. 35, Benin City.

Ekiti: Rt. Rev. Dr. M. FAGUN, P.O.B. 10, Ado-Ekiti.

Ibadan: Rt. Rev. RICHARD FINN, D.D., P.M.B. 5057, Ibadan.

Ijebu-Ode: Rt. Rev. ANTHONY SANUSI, P.O.B. 32, Ijebu-Ode.

Ondo: Rt. Rev. WILLIAM R. FIELD, S.M.A., D.D., P.O.B. 46, Akure.

Oyo: Rt. Rev. OWEN McCOY, P.O.B. 78, Oshogbo.

Warri: Rt. Rev. LUCAS NWAEZEAPU, P.O.B. 303, Warri.

Archbishop of Onitsha: Most Rev. FRANCIS ARINZE, Archbishop's House, P.O.B. 411, Onitsha.

BISHOPS

Calabar: Rt. Rev. BRIAN DAVIS USANGA, P.O.B. 1044, Calabar.

Enugu: Rt. Rev. GODFREY OKOYE, P.O.B. 302, Enugu.

Ikot Ekpene: Rt. Rev. DOMINIC EKANDEM, O.B.E., P.O.B. 70, Ikot Ekpene.

Ogoja: Rt. Rev. THOMAS McGETTRICK, Bishop's House, St. Benedict's, P.O.B. 27, Ogoja.

Owerri: Rt. Rev. MARK UNEGBU, Villa Assumpta, P.O.B. 85, Owerri.

Port Harcourt: (vacant), P.O.B. 1113, Port Harcourt.

Umuahia: Rt. Rev. ANTHONY NWEDO, P.O.B. 99, Umuahia.

THE PRESS

In English unless otherwise specified.

DAILIES

Daily Express: Commercial Amalgamated Printers, 5-11 Apongbon St., P.O.B. 163, Lagos; Editor REMI ILORI.

Daily Sketch: Sketch Bldgs., Ijebu By-Pass, P.M.B. 5067, Ibadan; f. 1964; Western State of Nigeria Government-owned company; Gen. Man. THEOPHILUS ADETOLA AWOBOKUN; Chair. Alhaji BUSARI O. OBISESAN; Editor J. AYO ADEDUN; circ. 19,140.

Daily Times: The Daily Times of Nigeria Ltd., 3-5 Kakawa St., P.O.B. 139, Lagos; f. 1925; Editor HENRY OLUKAYODE ODUKOMAIYA; circ. 205,000.

Midwest Echo: P.O.B. 1114, Benin City; f. 1958; Editor EMMANUEL EWEKA; circ. 25,000.

Morning Post: Nigerian National Press, Malu Rd., Apapa, P.M.B. 2099, Lagos; f. 1961; Editor MAGNUS BARA-HART; circ. 56,000.

New Nigerian: New Nigerian Newspapers Ltd., Ahmadu Bello Way, Kaduna; f. 1966; Editor MAMMAN DAURA; circ. 45,000.

Nigerian Observer: The Mid-West Newspapers Corporation, 18 Airport Rd., Benin City; f. 1968; Editor PIUS AGUN; circ. 40.000,

Nigerian Tribune: 98 Shittu St., P.O.B. 78, Ibadan; f. 1949; Action Group of Nigeria; circ. 30,000; Editor AYO OJEWUNMI.

West African Pilot: 34 Commercial Ave., Yaba; Main organ of Zik Enterprises Ltd.; circ. 47,323; Editor SAMPLE DIMA OPUIYO.

SUNDAY PAPERS

Sunday Observer: Midwest Newspapers Corporation, 18 Airport Rd., Benin City; f. 1968; Editor NEVILLE M. UKOLI; circ. 60,000.

Sunday Post: Nigerian National Press Ltd., P.M.B. 1154, Malu Rd., Apapa, Lagos; f. 1961; Editor A. SOGUNLE; circ. 70,000.

Sunday Sketch: Sketch Bldgs., Ijebu By-Pass, P.M.B. 5067, Ibadan; f. 1964; Western State of Nigeria Government-owned company, Editor OLAJIDE ADELEYE; circ. 22,900.

Sunday Star: People's Star Press, Yemetu Aladorin, Ibadan; f. 1966.

Sunday Times: The Daily Times of Nigeria Ltd., 3-7 Kakawa St., P.O.B. 139, Lagos; f. 1953; Editor SAM AMUKA; circ. 240,000.

WEEKLIES

Eleti-Ofe: 28 Kosoko Street, Lagos, P.O. Box 467; f. 1923; English and Yoruba; Editor OLA ONATADE; circ. 30,000.

Gaskiya ta fi Kwabo: New Nigerian Newspapers Ltd., Kaduna; f. 1939; Hausa; Editor Alhaji UTHMAN MAIRIGA; (twice weekly).

Imole Owuro: People's Star Press, Yemetu Aladorin, Ibadan; f. 1962.

Independent (The): P.M.B. 5109, Ibadan; f. 1960; English; Editor Rev. F. B. CRONIN-COLTSMAN; circ. 13,000; national Catholic weekly.

Irohin Imole: 15 Bamgbose St., Lagos; f. 1957; Yoruba; Editor: TUNJI ADEOSUN.

Irohin Yoruba: 212 Yakubu Gowon St., P.M.B. 2416, Lagos; f. 1945; Yoruba, Editor S. A. AIIBADE; circ. 70,000.

Lagos This Week: 5 Williams St., Lagos; Editor YEMI MARTINS.

Lagos Weekend: 3-5-7 Kakawa St., P.O.B. 139, Lagos; f. 1965; news and pictures; Fri.; published by Daily Times group; Editor SEGUN OSOBA; circ. 90,000.

Nigerian Catholic Herald: Ondo St., P.O.B. 19, Lagos; English; St. Paul's Press Catholic Mission.

Nigerian Radio-T.V. Times: Broadcasting House, Lagos; Editor A. Y. S. TINUBU.

Nigerian Statesman: 7 Kester Lane, Lagos; f. 1947; Socialist; circ. 14,165; Editor O. DAVIES.

Sporting Record: 3 Kakawa St., P.O.B. 139, Lagos; f. 1961; Editor CYRIL KAPPO; circ. 50,000.

Truth (The Weekly Muslim): 45 Idumagbo Ave., P.O.B. 418, Lagos; f. 1951; Editor M. A. SHAHID.

West Africa: Daily Times of Nigeria Ltd., P.O.B. 139, 3-7 Kakawa St., Lagos; f. 1917; Editor DAVID WILLIAMS.

ENGLISH PERIODICALS

Africa Magazine: Lagos; monthly.

African Challenge: P.M.B. 12067, Lagos; f. 1951; 10 times a year; religious and educational; English; also "Yoruba Challenge" (6 issues yearly); Editor T. O. ONAJOBI; circ. 102,000.

African Journal of Pharmacy: Development House, 21 Wharf Rd., P.O.B. 399, Apapa; f. 1970; incorporating "West African Pharmacist"; monthly; circ. 5,000; Editor BODE LADEJOBI.

Amber: 122 Investment House, P.O.B. 2592, Lagos; monthly.

Construction in Nigeria: P.O.B. 282, Lagos; journal of the Federation of Building and Civil Engineering Contractors in Nigeria; monthly, Editor M. M. NORTON; circ. 3,500.

Drum: P.M.B. 2128, Lagos; f. 1954; picture monthly; circ. 172,000; Editor OLU ADETULE.

Film: Drum Publications Nig. Ltd., P.M.B. 2128, Lagos; f. 1967; photo weekly; circ. 55,000; Editor OLU ADETULE.

Flamingo: P.O.B. 237, Lagos; f. 1960; monthly; Editor GERALD MALMED; circ. 100,000.

Home Studies: P.O.B. 139, Lagos; f. 1964; monthly; Editor Mrs. YETUNDE MAKANJU; circ. 18,000.

Ibadan: University of Ibadan, f. 1956; two a year; Editor Prof. T. ADESANYA I. GRILLO, Dept. of Anatomy, University of Ibadan.

Insight: P.O.B. 139, 3 Kakawa St., Lagos; features about contemporary problems in Nigeria, Africa and the world; quarterly; Editor SAM AMUKA; circ. 5,000.

Management in Nigeria: P.O.B. 139, Lagos; bi-monthly; journal of Nigerian Institute of Management.

Modern Woman: P.O.B. 2583, Lagos; f. 1969; Editor TOYIN ONIBUWE-JOHNSON.

Nigeria: Exhibition Centre, Marina, Lagos; f. 1932; travel, cultural, historical and general; quarterly.

Nigeria Magazine: P.O.B. 2099, Lagos; f. 1932; travel, cultural, historical and general; quarterly; circ. 14,000; Editor T. O. A. ADEBANJO.

Nigeria Trade Journal: Federal Ministry of Information, Commercial Publications Section, Lagos; quarterly; London Agents: Africa and Overseas Press Agency Ltd.; 122 Shaftesbury Ave., London, W.1.

Nigerian Businessman's Magazine: 39 Mabo St., Surv-Lere-Lagos; monthly; Nigerian and overseas commerce.

Nigerian Engineer: P.O.B. 5624, Lagos; quarterly; published for the Nigerian Society of Engineers; Editor A. O. MADEDOR; circ. 750.

Nigerian Grower and Producer: P.M.B. 12002, Lagos; quarterly.

Nigerian Journal of Economic and Social Studies: published March, July and November by the Nigerian Economic Society, University of Ibadan; Editor Dr. O. TERIBA.

Nigerian Journal of Science: publication of the Science Association of Nigeria; f. 1966; bi-annual; Editor Prof. T. ADESANYA I. GRILLO.

Nigerian Opinion: Nigerian Current Affairs Society, Faculty of the Social Sciences, University of Ibadan; f. 1965; monthly; economic and political commentary; Chief Editor BILLY DUDLEY.

The Nigerian Sportsman: P.O.B. 5624, Lagos; quarterly; published for the National Sports Commission; Editor J. A. ELUEZE; circ. 10,000.

Nigerian Teacher: 3 Kakawa St., P.O.B. 139, Lagos; quarterly.

Nigerian Worker: United Labour Congress, 97 H. Macaulay St., Lagos; Editor LAWRENCE BORHA.

Radio-Vision Times: Western Nigerian Radio Vision Service, Television House, P.O.B. 1460, Ibadan; monthly; Editor ALTON A. ADEDEJI.

Sadness and Joy: Drum Publications Nig. Ltd., P.M.B. 2128, Lagos; f. 1968; photo weekly; circ. 55,000; Editor OLU ADETULE.

Spear: 3-5 Kakawa St., P.O.B. 139, Lagos; f. 1962; family magazine; Editor TONY MOMOH; circ. 110,000.

Teacher's Monthly: General Publications Section, Ministry of Education, P.M.B. 5052, Ibadan.

Trust: Drum Publications Nig. Ltd., P.M.B. 2128, Lagos; f. 1971; mid-month pictorial; circ. 90,000; Editor OLU ADETULE.

West African Chartered Engineer: Lagos; twice yearly.

West Africa Link: Mainland Press, Block 2, Unit 8; Industrial Estate, Yaba, P.O.B. 2965, Lagos; f. 1964; monthly; bi-lingual French and English; Editor ALEXANDER CHIA.

West African Builder and Architect: P.M.B. 12002, Lagos; six a year.

West African Journal of Biological and Applied Chemistry: University of Ibadan; f. 1957; quarterly; Editor O. BASSIR.

West African Journal of Education: Institute of Education, University of Ibadan; f. 1957; three a year; circ. 1,600; Editors Prof. J. A. MAJASAN, Dr. E. A. YOLOYE.

West African Medical Journal: P.M.B. 12002, Lagos; six a year; Editor Prof. H. ORISMEJOLOMI THOMAS, C.B.E.

Western Nigerian Illustrated: Ministry of Information, Western Nigerian Government, Ibadan; quarterly.

Women's World: P.O.B. 139, Lagos; Acting Editor AGBEKE OGUNSANWO; circ. 20,000.

VERNACULAR PERIODICALS

Jakadiya: Ministry of Information, Kaduna; Hausa; monthly.

Yoruba Challenge: P.M.B. 12067, Lagos; f. 1954; six a year; religious and educational; Yoruba; published by Sudan Interior Mission; Editor-in-Chief J. K. BOLARIN; circ. 60,000.

PRESS AGENCIES

FOREIGN BUREAUX

A.P.: 29 Maloney St., Lagos; Correspondent ARNOLD ZEITLIN.

Ghana News Agency: P.O.B. 2844, Lagos.

Novosti: 6 Akanbi Damola St., South-West Ikoli, Lpgos; Chief E. KORSHUNOV.

Reuters: Kajola House (5th floor), 62/64 Campbell St., Lagos.

D.P.A., The Jiji Press and Tass also have offices in Lagos.

PUBLISHERS

African Universities Press: P.O.B. 3560, Lagos; educational and general; 10–15 titles annually.

Commercial Amalgamated Printers Ltd.: P.O.B. 163, 5/11 Apongbon St., Lagos.

Daily Times of Nigeria Ltd.: 3-5 Kakawa St., P.O.B. 139, Lagos; publishers of *Daily Times, Sunday Times, Lagos Weekend, Sporting Record, Spear Magazine, Woman's World, Home Studies, Insight and Nigerian Year Book*; Chair. and Man. Dir. Alhaji BABATUNDE JOSE.

Ethiope Publishing Corporation: Benin; f. 1970; books and periodicals; Chair. J. P. CLARK.

Gaskiya Corporation: Zaria; printing and publishing corporation wholly owned by the six states of Northern Nigeria; Gen. Man. CLAUDE SCOTT.

Government Press: Federal Ministry of Information, Printing Division, Lagos.

Longmans (Nigeria) Ltd.: P.M.B. 1036, 52 Oba Akran Ave., Ikeja.

Mbari: P.M.B. 5162, Ibadan; occasional fiction, plays, poetry, *Black Orpheus*.

Macmillan and Co. (Nigeria) Ltd.: P.O.B. 1463, Ibadan; Warehouse: P.O.B. 264, Yaba; Man. Dir. OLU ANULOPO.

Nigeria Technical Publications Ltd.: 34 McCarthy St., P.O.B. 5624, Lagos; branches in Kaduna and Enugu; publs. *Construction in Nigeria, Nigerian Sportsman, Nigerian Engineer*.

Nigerian National Press: P.M.B. 1154, Apapa; f. 1961; publishers of *Nigerian Sunday Post* and *Nigerian Morning Post*; Chair. Alhaji EATARI ALI.

Onibonoje Press and Book Industries (Nigeria) Ltd.: P.O.B. 3109, Ibadan; educational and general publishers and printers.

Oxford University Press Nigerian Branch: P.M.B. 5095, Oxford House, Iddo Gate, Ibadan; Warehouse at Jericho, Ibadan; Chair. T. T. SOLARU; Man. M. O. AKINLEYE.

Pilgrim Books Ltd.: African Universities Press; P.O.B. 3560, Lagos; f. 1966; educational books for Africa; merged with African Universities Press; Gen. Man. W. T. SHAW.

RADIO AND TELEVISION

RADIO

Nigerian Broadcasting Corporation: Broadcasting House, Lagos; f. 1957. The Corporation was set up as a public independent and impartial broadcasting system controlled by a board of Governors. The Federal Parliament gave the Minister responsible for broadcasting control over the Corporation's policy and board appointments in August 1961. Services are operated from Lagos (National Programme), Kaduna, Ibadan, Benin, Enugu, Ilorin, Katsina, Kano, Sokoto, Zaria, Jos, Maiduguri, Calabar, Port Harcourt, Onitsha, Warri, Abeokuta, Ijebu-Ode. Chair. of Central Board Alhaji ABUBAKAR TATARI-ALI; Dir.-Gen. E. V. BADEJO; Dir. of Programmes CHRISTOPHER KOLADE; Sec. O. FASHINA.

Programmes are broadcast in English and the following Nigerian languages:

Hausa	Tiv	Urhobo
Yoruba	Nupe	Edo
Ibo	Idoma	Ijaw
Fulani	Igalla	Itsekiri
Kanuri	Igbirra	Efik
	Birom	

Northern States Broadcasting Area: Broadcasting House, Kaduna; State Controller Mallan J. H. CINDO.

Western Broadcasting Area: Broadcasting House, Ibadan; State Controller OLAOLU OMIDEYI.

Mid-Western Broadcasting Area: services formally launched December 1966; State Controller EMMANUEL OMO-BELO FADAKA.

Eastern States Broadcasting Area: Broadcasting House, Enugu; State Controller SAMUEL NWANERI.

External Service of NBC ("Voice of Nigeria"): International services in English, French, Arabic, Hausa; f. 1962.

Radio-Television Kaduna: P.O.B. 250, Kaduna; f. 1961; operated by 6 Northern States of Nigeria with Nigeria Radio Corporation, EMI Electronics Ltd. and Granada Group Ltd. for sound and television; has one of the biggest transmitters in Africa; Chair. Alhaji IDRIS GANA; Gen. Man. A. ZORU.

Rediffusion (Nigeria) Ltd.: P.O.B. 3156, Ibadan, and Rediffusion House, Lagos; f. 1952; subsidiary of Rediffusion Ltd., London; wired broadcasting service in Ibadan, Lagos and 90 other towns and villages; distributes the programmes of the Nigerian Broadcasting Corporation; 52,000 subscribers (1969); Dir. and Gen. Manager E. A. D. SAUL.

Western Nigeria Radiovision Service Ltd. (WNTV-WNBS): P.O.B. 1460, Ibadan; f. 1959; commercial radio and television service; educational, public service and commercial broadcasts received in Lagos, Western States, and parts of Republic of Dahomey; Gen. Man. TEJU OYELEYE; Public Relations Officer ALTON A. ADEDEJI.

There were 1,275,000 radio receivers at the end of 1970.

TELEVISION

Nigerian Broadcasting Corporation (Television): P.M.B. 12005, Lagos; f. 1962; part of Nigerian Broadcasting Corporation; Dir.-Gen. E. V. BADEJO; Dir. of Television M. A. OLUMIDE; Controller of Programmes O. OLUSOLA; Sales Man. B. OVBIAGELE; Head of Programme Planning AYO OKESAWYA; Controller of News EMMANUEL BIOTER OTERSOPE.

Radio-Television Kaduna Northern Nigeria: *see* under Radio, above.

Western Nigeria Radiovision Service: *see* under Radio, above.

There were 75,000 television receivers at the end of 1970.

FINANCE

BANKING

(cap. =capital; p.u.=paid up; dep.=deposits; m.=million; £N=Nigerian pounds)

Central Bank of Nigeria: Tinubu Square, P.M.B. 12194, Lagos. f. 1958; issuing bank; cap. p.u. £N1.25m.; dep. £N19.78m. (Dec. 1971); general reserves £N1.92m. (Dec. 1970); Gov. Dr. C. N. ISONG.

Post Office Savings Bank: operates services like commercial banks.

African Continental Bank Ltd.: 148 Yakubu Gowon St., P.M.B. 2466, Lagos; f. 1948; cap. p.u. £6m.; Chair. Dr. P. N. C. OKIGBO; Gen. Man. C. K. N. OBIH.

Bank of Lagos Ltd.: 5–7 Balogun St., P.M.B. 2337, Lagos; f. 1958; cap. p.u. £N250,000; Chair. Rt. Hon. A. LAWSON; Man. JOHN H. SCHMID.

Bank of the North Ltd.: P.O.B. 219. Kano; f. 1959; cap. p.u. £N1.35m., dep. £N16.44m. (Dec. 1970).

Berini Bank: 38 Balogun Square, P.M.B. 2371, Lagos; f. 1959; cap. p.u. £N400,000; Chair. H. E. PIERRE BEY EDDE, Gen. Man. ERNEST CASSIS.

Co-operative Bank of Eastern Nigeria Ltd.: Milton Ave., Aba; f. 1961.

Co-operative Bank of Western Nigeria Ltd.: Co-operative Bldgs., New Court Rd., P.M.B. 5137, Ibadan; f. 1953; res. £N1.1m.; cap. p.u. £605,005; 13 brs.; Pres. Pastor E. T. LATUNDE, O.B.E.; Gen. Man. G. ADELOYE ONAGORUWA, LL.B., A.I.B., B.L.

Muslim Bank (West Africa) Ltd.: 16 Williams St., Lagos; br. at Ibadan.

National Bank of Nigeria Ltd.: 82-86 Yakubu Gowon St., Lagos; f. 1933; nationalized by the Western State of Nigeria Govt. in 1961; cap. p.u. £N3.24m., dep. £N28.36m. (June 1970); Pres. M. A. RANGOONWALA; Man. Dir. ANWAR QADIR.

Nigerian Acceptances Ltd.: 47 Marina, P.O.B. 2432, Lagos; merchant bankers.

Nigerian Industrial Development Bank Ltd.: P.M.B. 2357, Mandilas House, 96-102 Yakubu Gowon St., Lagos; f. 1964 to finance industry, mining, hotels and tourism generally, to attract foreign capital and personnel, and to encourage investment; cap. p.u. £N3.0m.: Chair. Mallam AHMADU COOMASSIE; Gen. Man. S. B. DANIYAN.

N. Nigeria Development Bank: Kaduna; f. 1963; cap. £2m.

United Bank for Africa Ltd.: P.O.B. 2406, 47 Marina, Lagos; f. 1961; 24 brs.; cap. p.u. £N2.25m.; Chair. Sir PATRICK REILLY, G.C.M.G., O.B.E.; Gen. Man. G. J. L. SCHNEIDER.

Wema Bank Ltd.: 52–54 Deuton St., Ebute-Metta, P.M.B. 1033; 8 brs.

FOREIGN BANKS

Arab Bank (Nigeria) Ltd.: 36 Balogun Square, P.O.B. 1114, Lagos; f. 1969; cap. £N750,000; res. £N48,108; Chair A. M. SHOMAN; Man. Dir. H. A. DARWISH; 3 brs.

Bank of America (Nigeria) Ltd.: 138–146 Yakubu Gowon St., P.O.B. 2317, Lagos; br. at Port Harcourt.

Bank of India Ltd.: P.O.B. 1252, 47-48 Breadfruit St., Lagos; f. 1962; cap. £N750,000; dep. £N950,993; Man. R. M. BOSE.

Barclays Bank of Nigeria Ltd.: P.M.B. 2027, 40 Marina, Lagos; f. 1969; cap. 5.5m., dep. 128,032,905 (Sept. 1970); Chair. and Gen. Man. G. A. O. THOMSON; 87 brs. and agencies.

International Bank for West Africa Ltd.: 94 Yakubu Gowon St., Lagos; brs. at Apapa, Kano and Port Harcourt.

Standard Bank Nigeria Ltd.: Head Office, 35 Marina, P.O.B. 5216, Lagos; cap. £N3,880,000; 68 brs. throughout Nigeria; Chair. C. P. JOHNSTON.

STOCK EXCHANGE

Lagos Stock Exchange: P.O.B. 2457, 114 Yakubu Gowon St., Lagos; f. 1960; three Dealing Members; Chair. S. B. DANIYAN; Sec. M. A. ODEDINA, F.C.I.S., A.A.I.A.; publ. *Lagos Stock Exchange Daily List.*

INSURANCE

African Alliance Insurance Co. Ltd.: 112 Yakubu Gowon St., Lagos; Man. Dir. T. A. BRAITHWAITE.

African Insurance Co. Ltd.: 134 Nnamdi Azikewe Street, P.O.B. 274, Lagos.

Eastern Insurance Co.: Head Office, Lagos; f. 1961.

Great Nigeria Insurance Co. Ltd.: 39–41 Martins St., Lagos; f. 1960; life and property insurance; cap. p.u. £N90,000; Man. Dir. F. O. OGUNLANA.

Guinea Insurance Co. Ltd.: P.O.B. 1136, Lagos, f. 1958, fire, accident, marine, cap. p.u. £N76,000, Man. A. T. CAIN, F.C.I.I.

Lion of Africa Insurance Co. Ltd.: (Incorporated in Nigeria) P.O.B. 2055, Ebani House, 149/153 Yakubu Gowon St., Lagos, all classes, cap. p.u. £N135,000, Gen. Man B. LAND, F.INST.D.

NEM Insurance Company (Nigeria) Ltd.: 12–14 Yakubu Gowon St., P.O.B. 654, Lagos.

New Africa Insurance Co. Ltd.: Head Office: 31 Marina, Lagos; incorporated 1955; life, fire, accident, marine; cap. p.u. £N200,000; Chair. Alhaji SHEHU AHMED, O.O.N., O.B.E.

Nigerian General Insurance Co. Ltd.: 1 Nnamdi Azikewe St., P.O.B. 2210, Lagos; f. 1951; 15 brs.; Gen. Man. J. A. AWOYINKA.

Royal Exchange Assurance: 31 Marina, P.O.B. 112, Lagos.

United Nigeria Insurance Co. Ltd.: 53 Marina, Lagos; bra. throughout Nigeria; Gen. Man. J. H. DAY.

West African Provincial Insurance Co.: Head Office: Wesley House, 21 Marina, P.O.B. 2103, Lagos.

TRADE AND INDUSTRY

CHAMBERS OF COMMERCE

Association of Chambers of Commerce, Industry & Mines of Nigeria: P.O.B. 109, Lagos; mems. Chambers of Commerce of Lagos, Calabar, Ibadan, Kano, Jos, Warri, Benin, Sapele and Enugu; Pres. Chief S. L. EDU.

African Chamber of Commerce: 73 Oluwole St., P.O.B. 478, Lagos.

Benin Chamber of Commerce: P.O.B. 487, Benin City.

Calabar Chamber of Commerce: P.O.B. 76, Calabar; 16 mems. (trading and shipping companies).

Enugu Chamber of Commerce: P.O.B. 734, Enugu.

Ibadan Chamber of Commerce: P.M.B. 5213, Ibadan.

Kano Chamber of Commerce and Industry: P.O.B. 10, Kano; 104 mems.; Pres. A. J. AKLE.

Lagos Chamber of Commerce and Industry: 131 Yakubu Gowon St., P.O.B. 109, Lagos; f. 1888; 380 mems.; Pres. J. ADE TUYO; Sec. Mrs. J. ADUKE MOORE, B.L.

Nigerian National Chamber of Commerce: f. 1960; Pres. M. A. AJAO.

Ondo Chamber of Commerce: P.O.B. 3, Ondo.

Onitsha Chamber of Commerce: 50 Old Market Rd., P.O.B. 181, Onitsha; f. 1953; Chair. C. T. ONYEKWELY, Sec. ALEXANDER IBEKWE AGWUNA.

Port Harcourt Chamber of Commerce: P.O.B. 71, Port Harcourt.

Sapele Chamber of Commerce: P.O.B. 109, Sapele.

Warri Chamber of Commerce: P.O.B. 302.

TRADE ASSOCIATIONS

Abeokuta Importers and Exporters Association: c/o Akeweje Bros., Lafenwa, Abeokuta.

Ijebu Importers and Exporters Association: 16 Ishado St., Ijebu-Ode.

Nigerian Association of African Importers and Exporters: 35 Kosoko St., Lagos.

Nigerian Association of Native Cloth Dealers and Exporters: 45 Koesch St., Lagos.

Nigerian Association of Stockfish Importers: 10 Egerton Rd., Lagos.

Union of Importers and Exporters: P.O.B. 115, Ibadan; f. 1949; Chair. E. A. SANDA; Sec. C. A. ADEGBESAN.

OTHER ORGANIZATIONS

Nigeria Employers Consultative Association: P.O.B. 2231, 31 Marina, Lagos; f. 1957; 450 mems.; Dir. W. G. TRACY; publ. *NECA News*.

The Institute of Chartered Accountants of Nigeria: 60 Marina, P.O.B. 1580, Lagos.

Association of African Miners: 32 Lonsdale St., Jos.

Association of Master Bakers, Confectioners and Caterers of Nigeria: 13-15 Custom St., Lagos, P.O.B. 4; f. 1951; 250 mems.; Acting Pres. J. ADE TUYO; Sec. M. A. OKI, F.INST.B.B.

Federation of Building and Civil Engineering Contractors in Nigeria: 34 McCarthy St., P.O.B. 282, Lagos; publ. *Construction in Nigeria* (monthly); circ. 3,500.

Indian Merchants Association: Inlaks House, 19 Martins St., P.O.B. 2112, Lagos.

Institute of Chartered Accountants of Nigeria: 60 Marina, P.O.B. 1580, Lagos.

Lagos Association of Benin Carvers: 16 Tinubu St., Lagos.

Nigerian Chamber of Mines: P.O.B. 454, Jos; f. 1950; Pres. G. GRIFFIN; Sec. Lt.-Col. H. E. BARLOW.

Nigerian Livestock Dealers Association: P.O.B. 115, Sapele.

Nigerian Recording Association: 9 Breadfruit St., P.O.B. 950, Lagos.

Nigerian Rubber Dealers Association: Sapele.

Nigerian Society of Engineers: Lagos.

Nigeria Timber Association: 19 Shopeju St., Shogunle, P.M.B. 1185, Ikeja; f. 1957; Pres. S. A. PITAN; Sec. J. H. BEELEY.

Pharmaceutical Society of Nigeria: 4 Tinubu Square, P.O.B. 546, Lagos.

Union of Niger African Traders: 18 Notteridge St., Onitsha.

PUBLIC CORPORATIONS AND DEVELOPMENT ORGANIZATIONS

Development Corporation (West Africa) Ltd.: Akuro House, 5 Custom Street, Lagos; subsidiary of the Commonwealth Development Corporation; provides finance and personnel for viable commercial projects; commonly operates through locally registered companies in partnership either with Government or with commercial firms.

Eastern Nigeria Development Corporation: P.M.B. 1024, Enugu; f. 1954; main duties are to improve the quantity and quality of oil-palm produce and of other food casn crops; administers a number of industrial and agricultural projects, improves methods of transport; cap. (1963) £N9m.; publ. *Eastern Nigeria Development Magazine* (quarterly).

Federal Institute of Industrial Research: P.M.B. 1023, Ikeja; f. 1955; plans and directs industrial research and provides technical assistance to Nigerian industry; specializes in foods, minerals, textiles, natural products, industrial intermediates and others; Dir. I. A. AKINRELE.

Gaskiya Corporation: Zaria; f. 1938; owned by Northern State Government; undertakes printing.

Lagos Executive Development Board: P.O.B. 907, Lagos; f. 1928; planning and development of Lagos; 9 mems.; Chair. Dr. G. A. WILLIAMS, Medical Officer of Health, Lagos; Chief Executive Officer S. O. FADAHUNSI.

New Nigeria Development Company Ltd.: 18/19 Ahmadu Bello Way, Kaduna; f. 1968; development/investment agency owned by the six state governments of Northern Nigeria; Chair. Mallam AHMED TALIB; Sec. Mallam HALILU USMAN BIDA.

New Nigeria Development Company (Properties) Ltd.: P.M.B. 2040, Kaduna; helps to create better living conditions throughout the six Northern States of Nigeria.

Niger Delta Development Board: P.M.B. 5067, Port Harcourt; Chair. and 7 mems.

Nigerian Industrial Development Bank: P.M.B. 2357, M. & K. House, 96-102 Yakubu Gowon St., Lagos; f. 1964; to finance industry and mining, to attract foreign capital and personnel and to further the growth of investment; cap. p.u. £N6.5m.; Chair. Mallam AHMADU COOMASSIE; Gen. Man. S. B. DANIYAN.

Northern Nigeria Development Corporation: 18-19 Ahmadu Bello Way, Kaduna; f. 1968; government sponsored finance agency responsible for schemes of economic benefit to the six states of Northern Nigeria.

Northern Nigeria Investments Ltd.: P.O.B. 138, Kaduna; f. 1959 jointly by the Commonwealth Development Corporation and the New Nigeria Development Co. Ltd. to investigate and promote commercial projects, both industrial and agricultural in the six Northern States of Nigeria; present share capital £N4.4m.; Man. P. D. PARTRIDGE, B.COM., F.C.A.; Sec. JAMES PARRISH, F.C.A.

Price Control Board: f. 1970; under Federal Ministry of Trade; 23 mems.; fixes basic price for controlled commodities.

Western Nigeria Agricultural Credit Corporation: Lebanon St., P.M.B. 5200, Ibadan; f. 1964; controlled by Military Governor; grants loans to farmers; promotes agricultural development by encouraging modern methods of farming; participates in establishment of rubber plantations; Chair. S. A. YEROKUN, Gen. Man. E. O. OTITOJU.

Western Nigeria Development Corporation: P.M.B. 5085, Ibadan; f. 1959 in succession to Western Region Production Development Board (f. 1949); responsible for initiating industrial and agricultural schemes; now has 10 agricultural projects covering cocoa, rubber, palm products, coffee, pineapple and cashew; industrial projects now number 31, 5 of which are wholly owned and managed by the Corporation; the remaining 26 industries are partly owned with foreign and indigenous investors; also owns 2 modern hotels.

Western Nigeria Housing Corporation: Ibadan; f. 1958 to develop house building and industrial estates in the Region; grants mortgages and loans for house purchase and operates a savings scheme; Chair. F. A. O. SHOGA; Gen. Man. A. ADESIDA.

Western Nigeria Printing Corporation: Ibadan; f. 1956 to produce school exercise books; also prints a wide range of literature and vernacular publications for adult education.

Western Nigeria Finance Corporation: P.M.B. 5119, Ibadan; f. 1955; finances projects which further the economic development of Western Nigeria, particularly industrial enterprises; Chair. Chief TAJUDEEN OKI; Exec. Dir. Chief A. A. AKISANYA; Acting Sec. E. O. AKISANYA; Acting Sec. E. O. OTITOJU.

MARKETING BOARDS

The competence of the State Marketing Boards includes: fixing the legal minimum buying price of primary produce for the whole season and minimising price alterations from season to season; maintaining and improving the quality of export produce; aiding economic development and research by grants, loans, investments; supplying produce to industries processing local primary produce.

Nigerian Produce Marketing Company Ltd.: 72 Campbell St., Lagos; f. 1958; markets all produce purchased for export by State Marketing Boards; Chair. Alhaji ALAMANU.

Northern States Marketing Board: Yakubu Gowon Way, P.M.B. 2124, Kaduna; f. 1954; serves all six Northern States; Chair. Alhaji YAHAYA GUSAU, O.F.R., O.B.E.

Western State Marketing Board: P.M.B. 5032, Ibadan; Chair. M. A. AKINTOMIDE.

Eastern Nigeria Marketing Board: Produce House, Work Rd., Port Harcourt; Chair. N. U. AKPAN.

TRADE UNIONS

FEDERATIONS

Labour Unity Front: 16A Bishop St., Lagos; f. 1963; Sec.-Gen. GOGO NZERIBE.

Nigerian Trade Union Congress (NTUC): 16 Bishop St., Lagos; Pres. ABDUL WAHAB GOODLUCK; Sec.-Gen. S. U. BASSEY.

Nigerian Workers' Council (NWC): 7 Montgomery Rd., Yaba, Lagos; f. 1962; Sec.-Gen. CHUKWURA NNEMEKA.

United Labour Congress of Nigeria: 97 H. Macaulay St., Ebute-Metta, Lagos; affiliated to I.C.F.T.U.; officially recognized by Govt.; 600,000 mems.; Pres. Alhaji YUNUSA KALTUNGO; Gen. Sec. Chief AYOOLA ADELEKE.

PRINCIPAL UNIONS

Amalgamated Union of Building and Woodworkers of Nigeria: 46 Osholake St., Ebute-Metta, Lagos; f. 1963; 70,000 mems.; Pres. E. EKAHARTTA; Sec.-Gen. R. O. GBADAMOSI.

C.F.A.O. and Associated Companies' African Workers' Union: 365 Herbert Macaulay St., Yaba, Lagos; f. 1957; 5,000 mems.; Gen. Sec. O. ESHIETT.

Consolidated Petroleum, Chemical and General Workers' Union of Nigeria: 231 Herbert Macaulay St., P.M.B. 1065, Yaba; Gen. Sec. A. E. OTU, publ. *The News*.

Nigeria Civil Service Union: 23 Tokunboh St., P.O.B. 862, Lagos; f. 1912; 11,520 mems.; Sec. ALABA KALEJAIYE.

Nigerian Coal Miners' Union: 17-19 Udi Ave., Udi Siding, Enugu; f. 1951; 32,300 mems.; Gen. Pres. E. A. BASSEY; Gen. Sec. J. J. MADU.

Nigerian Dockers' Transport and General Workers' Union: 9 Rosamond St., Suru-Lere, Yaba; f. 1950; 3,500 mems.; Gen. Sec. A. E. OKON.

Holts African Workers' Union: 31 Bola St., Ebute-Metta, Lagos; 8,000 mems.; Pres. O. O. ODUYE; Gen. Sec. E. A. OMODARA.

Nigerian Union of Local Authority Staff: P.O.B. 3050, Mapo Hill, Ibadan; f. 1942; 15,000 mems.; Pres. J. A. WOYE, Sec. Chief A. A. ADEGBAMIGBE, Treas. S. I. AMOLE.

Association of Locomotive Drivers, Firemen, Yard Staff and Allied Workers of Nigeria: 231 Herbert Macauly St., Yaba; f. 1940; 3,500 mems.; Gen. Sec. DEJI OYEYEMI.

Medical and Health Department Workers' Union: 9 Aje St., Yaba; f. 1941; 5,000 mems.; Gen. Sec. H. I. S. UCHE.

Nigerian Mines Workers' Union: P.O.B. 40, Bukuru; f. 1948; 15,000 mems.; Gen. Sec. Mr. LANIYAN.

Municipal and Local Authorities Workers' Union: 28, Clifford St., Ebute-Metta, Lagos; f. 1951; 5,000 mems.; Gen. Sec. S. U. BASSEY.

Union of Post and Telecommunications Workers of Nigeria: 16 Bishop St., P.O.B. 1020, Lagos; f. 1942; 3,500 mems.; Pres. S. A. ADESUGBA; Gen. Sec. G. C. NZERIBE.

Public Utility Technical and General Workers' Union of Nigeria and Cameroons: 48 Coates St., Ebute-Metta; f. 1941; 16,793 mems.; Sec. N. O. ESHIETT.

Railway and Port Transport Staff Union: 97 Herbert Macaulay St., Ebute-Metta, Lagos; f. 1937; 4,600 mems.; Gen. Sec. H. P. ADEBOLA.

Nigeria Union of Teachers: 29 Commercial Ave., P.M.B. 1044, Yaba, Lagos; f. 1931; 58,000 mems.; Gen. Sec. A. F. ADE AWOLANA; Pres. Rev. J. A. AKINYEMI; Vice-Pres. O. OMOZ OARHES; publ. *Nigerian Schoolmaster*.

U.A.C. and Associated Companies' African Workers' Union of Nigeria: 83A Simpson St., Yaba; f. 1955; 10,510 mems.; Pres. D. O. EHIOGHAE; Gen. Sec. F. N. KANU.

CO-OPERATIVES

There are over 4,500 Co-operative Societies in Nigeria.

Co-operative Federation of Nigeria: c/o Co-operative Div., Ministry of Labour, P.M.B. 12505, Lagos.

Association of Nigerian Co-operative Exporters Ltd.: New Court Rd., P.O.B. 477, Ibadan; f. 1945; producers/exporters of cocoa and other cash crops.

Co-operative Supply Association Ltd.: 349 Herbert Macaulay St., Yaba, Lagos; importers and dealers in agricultural chemicals and equipment, fertilizers, building materials, general hardware, grocery and provisions.

Co-operative Union of Western Nigeria Ltd.: P.M.B. 5101, New Court Rd., Ibadan; education, publicity.

East Central State Co-operative Produce Marketing Association Ltd.: Ministry of trade, Enugu; f. 1970; cap. £2,258; Pres. J. U. AGWU; Vice-Pres. S. O. IHEANACHO.

Kabba Co-operative Credit and Marketing Union Ltd.: P.O.B. 25, Kabba; f. 1953; producers of food and cash crops and dealers in consumer goods; Pres. A. B. PHILLIPS; Man. H. A. SHEM.

Lagos Co-operative Union Ltd.: c/o Co-operative Div., Ministry of Labour, Lagos; co-operative publicity.

MAJOR INDUSTRIAL COMPANIES

The following are some of the largest companies in terms either of capital investment or employment.

African Timber and Plywood (Nigeria) Ltd.: P.M.B. 4001, Sapele; f. 1925; subsidiary of United Africa Co. Ltd., London.
Extraction of hardwood logs, processing and export of timber.
Chair. G. V. H. GARDNER; 3,250 employees.

Amalgamated Tin Mines of Nigeria Ltd.: managed by A.O. Nigeria Ltd., P.O. Jos, Benue-Plateau State; wholly-owned subsidiary of Amalgamated Tin Mines of Nigeria (Holdings) Ltd., London; f. 1969; cap. £N1,500,000; production of tin concentrate from ore and separation of columbite; Chair. D. M. DENT-YOUNG.

Gulf Oil Co. (Nigeria) Ltd.: P.M.B. 2469, Lagos; off-shore petroleum mining.

I.C.I. (Nigeria) Ltd.: P.O.B. 1004, 24 Commercial Rd., Apapa; distribution of chemicals, dyestuffs, fertilizers and man-made fibres.

Lever Brothers (Nigeria) Ltd.: P.O.B. 15, 15 Dockyard Rd., Apapa; f. 1924; £N1,200,000.
Manufacture of detergents, edible fats and toilet preparations.
Chair. and Man. Dir. W. C. S. CARRUTHERS; 1,400 employees.

Mobil Producing Nigeria: P.M.B. 12054, Lagos; off-shore petroleum mining.

Nigerian Breweries Ltd.: 1 Abebe Village Rd., Iganmu, Apapa; production of beer and soft drinks.

Nigerian Oil Mills Ltd.: P.O.B. 342, Kano; production of vegetable oil products.

Nigerian Petroleum Refining Co.: Alese Eleme, Port Harcourt; petroleum refinery.

Nigerian Sugar Co. Ltd.: P.M.B. 65, Bacita Estate, Jebba, Kwara State; f. 1961; cap. £N2,980,000.
Growing of sugar cane and manufacture of cane sugar and allied products, e.g. bagasses, molasses.
Chair. P. C. ASIODU; Gen. Man. E. J. MOL; 3,500 employees.

Nigerian Textile Mills Ltd.: P.M.B. 1051, Ikeja, Lagos State; f. 1960; £N1,500,000.
Spinners, weavers and finishers.
Dir. S. O. ABIDOGUN; 3,000 employees.

Nigerian Tobacco Co. Ltd.: P.O.B. 137, 8-10 Yakubu Gowon St., Lagos; f. 1951; cap. £N7,500,000.
Manufacture of tobacco products.
Chair. H. P. MACDONALD; Sec. C. ADE ATOKI; 3,516 employees.

Phillips Petroleum Oil Co. (Nigeria) Ltd.: P.M.B. 12612, Lagos; petroleum oil mining in conjunction with AGIP.

Shell-B.P. Petroleum Development Co. of Nigeria Ltd.: Freeman House, 21–22 Marina, B.M.B. 2418, Lagos; the largest of the oil companies in Nigeria; responsible for on-shore and off-shore mining.

Shell Nigeria Ltd.: 38-39 Marina, Lagos, Nigeria; f. 1970; cap. £N7 million.
Import and distribution of petroleum products.
Man. Dir. R. P. REID; 800 employees.

Texaco Nigeria Ltd.: P.O.B. 166, 241 Igbosere Rd., Lagos; petroleum marketing.

Texaco Overseas (Nigeria) Petroleum Co.: 12th Floor, Western House, 8-10 Yakubu Gowon St., P.O.B. 1986, Lagos; offshore petroleum mining.

The West African Portland Cement Co. Ltd.: P.O.B. 1001, 40 Marina, Lagos; production of cement.

TRANSPORT

RAILWAYS

Nigerian Railway Corporation: Ebute Metta, Lagos; f. 1955; has wide powers to enable it to operate as a commercial undertaking and is responsible for the management and operation of Nigerian railways, including the fixing of rates and fares, subject to an upper limit fixed by the Federal Minister of Transport, who may also intervene on important matters of policy, Chair. Alhaji IBRAHIM DASUKI; Acting Gen. Man. T. I. O. NZEGWU; Acting Sec. J. T. D. DUNCAN, publs. *Nigerail* (House Journal), *Nigerian Railway Annual*.

Length of Railways: 2,178 miles.

ROADS

There are about 49,500 miles of motor road, of which over 7,500 miles are bitumen surfaced.

On April 2nd, 1972, Nigeria changed from left-hand to right-hand drive.

INLAND WATERWAYS

Inland Waterways Department: Federal Ministry of Transport, Lagos; responsible for all navigable waterways; publ. *Navigational Bulletin*.

Niger River Transport: Burutu; Gen. Man. G. M. DUNCAN.

SHIPPING

The principal ports are Lagos (Apapa) and Port Harcourt. In 1966 the World Bank granted Nigeria £3.5m. for expansion of Port Harcourt, which will enable ships of 33,000 tons to come alongside the main wharf.

Nigeria Shipping Federation: P.O.B. 107, N.P.A. Commercial Offices Block "A", Wharf Rd., Apapa; f. 1960; Chair. D. SYKES; Gen. Man. D. B. ADEKOYA.

Nigerian Ports Authority: Private Mail Bag No. 12588, 26/28 Marina, Lagos; f. 1955; is responsible for the general cargo quays in Lagos and Port Harcourt, and harbour facilities in the 11 Nigerian ports; dredging, lighting, survey work and lighthouses; Chair. A. I. WILSON; Gen. Man. J. O. M. BOLANLE; publs. *NPA News* (quarterly), *NPA Annual Report, NPA Brochure, The History of the Ports of Nigeria.*

Nigerian National Shipping Line Ltd.: Development House, 21 Wharf Rd., P.O.B. 326, Apapa; f. 1959; government-owned; operates cargo and limited passenger fast services between West Africa, the United Kingdom and the Continent; Chair. Chief I. O. DINA; Gen. Man. Dr. H. DEHMEL; Sec. J. O. ITODO.

The following shipping companies run cargo and passenger services to Nigeria:

Acomar: c/o Scanship (Nigeria) Ltd., P.O.B. 2269, Lagos.

Barber Steamship Lines Inc.: 17 Battery Place, New York, N.Y. 10004, U.S.A.

Black Star Line: (*see* State Shipping Corporation).

Chargeurs Line (Compagnie Maritime des Chargeurs Réunis): UMARCO, P.O.B. 94, Apapa.

Delta Line (Delta Steamship Lines Inc.): Union Maritime et Commerciale, P.O.B. 217, Lagos.

Deutsch-Afrika Linie: Woermann Agency (Nigeria) Ltd., 21 Warehouse Rd., Apapa. P.O.B. 593, Lagos.

Elder Dempster Lines Ltd., Guinea Gulf Line: P.O.B. 167, Lagos.

Fabre Line (Compagnie Fabre & S.G.T.M.): UMARCO (Nigeria) Ltd., P.O.B. 94, Apapa.

Farrell Lines Inc.: P.M.B. 1151, Apapa; bi-monthly services to North America; Man. (West Africa) Capt. R. H. BALLARD.

Gold Star Line: Lagos and Niger Shipping Agencies Ltd., P.M.B. 192. Apapa.

Greek West Africa Line: c/o Scanship (Nigeria) Ltd., P.O.B. 2269, Lagos.

Guinea Gulf Line Ltd.: c/o Elder Dempster Agencies Ltd., P.O.B. 167, Lagos.

Holland West Afrika Lijn N.V.: P.O.B. 20, Lagos; North-west Europe to West Africa.

John Holt Ltd.: P.O.B. 157, Ebani House, 149–153 Yakubu Gowon St., Lagos.

Hugo Stinnes Transozean Schiffahrt G.m.b.H.: Transocean Nigeria Ltd., Development House, 21 Wharf Rd., P.O.B. 1101, Lagos.

Kawasaki Kisen Kaisha Ltd.: Palm Line Agencies of Nigeria Ltd., P.O.B. 531, Lagos; monthly direct service to Japan via Hong Kong.

Leif Hoegh & Co.: c/o Scanship (Nigeria) Ltd., P.O.B. 2269, Lagos.

Lloyd Triestino, S.p.A.: UMARCO, P.O.B. 94, Apapa.

Marasia: c/o Scanship (Nigeria) Ltd., P.O.B. 2269, Lagos.

Marconi International Marine Co. Ltd.: 4 Creek Rd., P.O.B. 211, Apapa.

Mitsui Line: Palm Line Agencies of Nigeria Ltd., P.O.B. 531, Lagos.

Nedlloyd: P.O.B. 20, Lagos; Europe to West Africa services.

Nigerline (U.K.) Ltd.: Oriel Chambers, Water St., Liverpool, L2 8TG, England; f. 1972; subsidiary of the Nigerian National Shipping Line Ltd.; Man. Dir. D. A. OKWURAIWE.

Palm Line Ltd.: c/o Palm Line Agencies of Nigeria Ltd., P.O.B. 531, Lagos.

Polish Ocean Line: c/o Scanshid (Nigeria) Ltd., P.O.B. 2269, Lagos.

Royal Interocean Lines: Holland West-Afrika Lijn, N.V.. P.O.B. 20, Lagos.

Scandinavian West Africa Line: Union Maritime et Commerciale, P.O.B. 94, Apapa.

Seven Stars (Africa) Line (Zim Israel Navigation Co. Ltd.): Lagos and Niger Shipping Agencies Ltd., P.O.B. 192, Apapa.

Splosna Plovba: c/o Scanship (Nigeria) Ltd., P.O.B. 2269, Lagos.

State Shipping Corporation (Black Star Line): 21-23 King George V Rd., P.O.B. 1488, Lagos.

Veb Deutsche Seereederei: c/o Scanship (Nigeria) Ltd., P.O.B. 2269, Lagos.

Woermann Line: c/o Scanship (Nigeria) Ltd., P.O.B. 2269, Lagos.

CIVIL AVIATION
INTERNAL

Nigeria Airways: W.A.A.C. (Nigeria) Ltd., Airways House, Lagos Airport (P.O.B. 136); f. 1958 as successor to West African Airways Corpn.; operates internal services and links Nigeria with Ghana, Sierra Leone, Gambia, Cameroon; VC1 service to the United Kingdom via European airports; pool service with Pan-American Airways to New York; Chair. OYELEYE ADEIGBO; Gen. Man. BIRGER GROENLUND.

Aero Contractors Company of Nigeria: P.O.B. 2519, 8–10 Yakubu Gowon St., Western House, Lagos; f. 1959; Man.-Dir. C. MEIJERINK; air charter company.

Pan African Airlines (Nigeria): P.M.B. 1054, Ikeja; charter air company.

INTERNATIONAL

The following international airlines also serve Nigeria: Aeroflot, Air Afrique, Air Zaire, Air Togo, Alitalia, BOAC, British Caledonian, EAAC, EgyptAir, Ethiopian Airlines, Ghana Airways, KLM, Lufthansa, MEA, PAA, Sabena, Swissair and UTA.

POWER

Electricity Corporation of Nigeria: 24-25 Marina, P.M.B. 2030, Lagos; f. 1950; chief authority for the generation and supply of electricity in Nigeria; Chair. Sir MILES CLIFFORD.

Niger Dams Authority: P.M.B. 12605, Lagos; f. 1962; operating and maintaining Kainji hydroelectric plant and 330 kV. transmission lines and sub-stations in Nigeria; Chair. Alhaji AHMADU DANBABA.

Nigerian Coal Corporation: Enugu; f. 1950; generally controls the coal industry including mining development and the distribution of coal; operates one colliery near Enugu.

TOURISM

Nigeria Tourist Association: P.O.B. 2944, 47 Marina, Lagos; f. 1963; Sec.-Gen. I. A. ATIGBI, B.A.; publs. *Nigeria Tourist Guide, Hotels and Catering in Nigeria,* and a wide range of other information material for tourists.

EDUCATION

LEARNED SOCIETIES

Association for Teacher Education in Africa: University of Ife, Ile-Ife; Chair. Prof. A. BABS FAFUNWA.

British Council, The: P.O.B. 3702, Western House, Yakubu Gowon St., Lagos; Rep. P. G. LLOYD; Regional offices in Benin City, Ibadan, Enugu, Yaba, Kaduna and Kano City; libraries (*see* Libraries).

Geological Survey of Nigeria: P.O.B. 2007, Kaduna South; f. 1930; evaluation of Nigeria's economic resources and consultation on geological problems; library of 10,000 vols.; publs. *Annual Report, Bulletins, Occasional Papers, Records of the Geological Survey, G.S.N. Reports,* geological maps and explanatory notes.

German Cultural Institute (Goethe-Institut): 174 Yakubu Gowon St., P.O.B. 957, Lagos; f. 1961; teaching of German language; cultural activities; library of 3,000 vols.; Dir. Dr. R. KLATT.

Historical Society of Nigeria: c/o Dept. of History, University of Ife, Ile-Ife; f. 1955 to encourage interest and work in connection with the study of history, especially Nigerian history; Pres. Prof. J. F. A. AJAYI; Sec. Prof. I. A. AKINJOGBIN; publs. *Journal* and *Tarikh* (twice-yearly), *Bulletin of News* (quarterly).

Istituto Italiano di Cultura: 77 Brickfield Road, Lagos; Dir. Prof. UMBERTO COMI.

Nigerian Bar Association: Ibadan; f. 1962; Pres. Chief ROTIMI WILLIAMS.

Nigerian Economic Society: c/o Faculty of Social Sciences, University of Ibadan, Ibadan; f. 1958; to advance social and economic knowledge particularly about Nigeria; 147 mems.; Pres. Dr. S. U. UGOH; Sec. Dr. I. I. U. EKE; publ. *Nigerian Journal of Economic and Social Studies* (3 a year, Editor Prof. O. ABOYADE).

Nigerian Geographical Association: c/o Dept. of Geography, University of Ibadan, Ibadan; f. 1955; to further interest in geography and its methods of teaching with special reference to Nigeria; 500 mems.; Pres. Prof. G. J. A. OJO; Sec. Dr. P. O. SADA; publ. *Nigerian Geographical Journal.*

Nigerian Institute of International Affairs: Kofo Abayomi Rd., Victoria Island, G.P.O. Box 1727, Lagos; f. 1963 to provide a non-political forum for the study of international affairs; library of 18,700 vols.; Dir.-Gen. (vacant); Librarian BANJI OLORUNTEGBE, B.SC., DIP. LIB.

Nigerian Institute of Management: 145 Yakubu Gowon St., P.O.B. 2557, Lagos; f. 1961; a professional body for managers and administrators from both private and public sectors; 1,200 mems.; Dir. O. I. A. AKINYEMI; library of 1,000 vols.; publ. *Management in Nigeria.*

Nigerian Library Association: c/o Ibadan University Library, Ibadan; f. 1952; Pres. Mrs. F. A. OGUNSHEYE, M.A., M.L.S.; Vice-Pres. S. B. AJE, M.A., F.L.A.; Hon. Sec. S. O. ODERINDE; Treas. N. O. ITA, F.L.A.; 325 mems.; publs. *N.L.A. Newsletter* (quarterly), *Nigerian Libraries* (3 times yearly).

Lagos State Division: publs. *Lagos Librarian, Occasional Papers.*

Western State Division: publs. *Newsletter, Proceedings of Annual Conferences.*

Science Association of Nigeria: P.O.B. 4039, Ibadan; f. 1958; Pres. Dr. F. M. A. UKOLI; Hon. Sec. Dr. A. C. ADEBONA, Dept. of Biological Sciences, University of Ife; 450 mems.; publ. *Nigerian Journal of Science.*

U.S. Information Centers: Cocoa House, P.M.B. 5089, Ibadan; No. 5 Prince Edward's Way, Kaduna; P.M.B. 3059, Kano; 41 Broad St., Lagos.

RESEARCH INSTITUTES

(*see* also under Universities)

Federal

Agricultural Research Station: Umudike. Eastern Nigeria.

Cocoa Research Institute: Ibadan; f. 1962.

Federal Department of Agricultural Research: Moor Plantation, P.M.B. 5042, Ibadan; f. 1910; research on soils and crop nutrition, improvement of food crops and control of plant diseases and pests; library of 4,000 vols., 300 current periodicals; Dir. B. O. E. AMON; publs. *Annual Report, Memoranda, Index of Agricultural Research.*

Federal Department of Forest Research: P.M.B. 5054, Ibadan; Dir. D. E. IYAMABO, B.SC., M.F.; publs. *Information Bulletin, Technical Notes, Research Papers, Bulletin, Index of Research, Annual Report* (irregular).

Federal Department of Veterinary Research: Vom-Jos; f. 1924; intensive research into animal health; service to West African countries in respect of vaccine and other biological products and of training livestock superintendents and laboratory technicians; advisory duties to Federal Government on animal health and industry; library of 6,800 vols., 115 current periodicals and 80 annual reports; Dir. Dr. M. GONI; Librarian D. O. OBORO; publs. *Index of Veterinary Research* (annual), *Annual Report, Research Papers* (irregular), *Current Contents* (monthly).

Federal Fisheries Service: P.M.B. 12529. Lagos.

Federal Institute of Industrial Research: P.M.B. 1023, Ikeja; f. 1955; plans and executes inter-governmental research, provides technical assistance to industry and serves as testing unit for Nigerian Standards Organization; Dir. Dr. I. A. AKINRELE.

Institute for Agricultural Research, Ahmadu Bello University: P.M.B. 1044, Samaru, Zaria; f. 1924. Dir. Dr. M. DAGG; research staff of 101 covering agronomy, plant-breeding, plant pathology, cotton, entomology, crop physiology, animal nutrition, pastures, soil science, soil survey and agricultural engineering and economics; library of 10,353 vols., 10,950 pamphlets, 738 current periodicals; publs. *Samaru Research Bulletins, Samaru Agricultural Newsletter* (bi-monthly), *Samaru Miscellaneous Papers, Soil Survey Bulletins, Soil Survey Reports,* Annual Reports.

Nigeria Educational Research Council: c/o Federal Ministry of Education, Lagos; f. 1965; curriculum development and general educational research; Chair. Chief B. SOMADE; Sec. GANI A. BELO; publs. *Report of the National Conference on Education: Philosophy of Education 1969, Report of National Workshop on Primary School Curriculum.*

Nigerian Institute for Oil Palm Research: P.M.B. 1030, Benin City; f. 1939; responsible for research in oil palm production and for recommending improved methods; library of 6.000 vols., 300 periodicals; Dir. E. OGOR, B.A.; publs. *Journal, Annual Report.*

Nigerian Institute for Trypanosomiasis Research: P.M.B. 2077, Kaduna; f. 1951 to undertake research into human and animal trypanosomiasis; Acting Dir. Dr. A. A. AMODU.

West African Cocoa Research Institute: P.M.B. 5244, Moor Plantation, Ibadan; Dir. Dr. L. K. OPEKE.

LIBRARIES

British Council Libraries: Lagos, f. 1951, 19,500 vols.; Ibadan, f. 1947, 15,100 vols.; Kano, f. 1950, 14,400 vols.; Benin, f. 1965, 12,000 vols.; Kaduna, f. 1960, 14,000 vols.

Central Medical Library: Federal Laboratory Service, Yaba, Lagos; f. 1945; serves the entire country; 12,000 vols.; Librarian S. O. FALAYI.

Eastern Nigeria Library Board: Private Mail Bag, Enugu; the Board was established in 1955 to establish, equip, manage and maintain libraries in the Eastern Region; Dir. of Library Services K. C. OKORIE, O.O.N., M.B.E., F.L.A.

  Regional Central Library: Ogui Road, Enugu; f. 1956; permanent premises opened in 1959; lending and reference library activities; legal deposit and regional centre for bibliographical information and research; the book-stock consists of 134,000 volumes, Nigeriana collection, and a mobile library unit; the library was part of a UNESCO pilot project. The Board now has four divisional libraries in operation at Port Harcourt, Ikot Ekpene, Umuahia-Ibeku and Onitsha; a fifth divisional library is being planned at Abakaliki; the Board, in association with local authorities, now operates three branch libraries at Calabar, Owerri and Aba; publ. *Annual Report.*

Lagos City Libraries: Lagos; 69,061 vols.; Librarian Mrs. E. E. OKU.

National Archives: Chapel Rd., University of Ibadan, P.M.B. 4, University of Ibadan Post Office, Ibadan; f. 1951, legally recognized 1957; charged with collection and preservation of all public records including private papers; library of 4,000 vols.; branch offices at Enugu and Kaduna; Controller S. O. SOWOOLU; publs. *Annual Report, Special Lists,* etc.

National Library of Nigeria: 4 Wesley St., P.M.B. 12626, Lagos; f. 1962; 600,000 vols., 1,675 current periodicals; Dir. S. B. AJE, M.A., F.L.A.; Chair. Dr. R. A. ADELEYE, PH.D.; Sec. A. O. ODELEYE, M.SC.; publs. *Special Libraries in Nigeria, The Arts in Nigeria: A Selective Bibliography, 18th and 19th Century Africana in the National Library of Nigeria, The National Library of Nigeria: A Guide to its Use, Index to Selected Nigerian Periodicals 1965, Bibliography of Nigerian Arts, Bibliography of Biographies and Memoirs on Nigeria, Nigerian Languages: a Bibliography, Index to selected Nigeriana in Serials 1966, Lagos Past and Present: a Historical Bibliography, Nigerian Books in Print 1968.*

North Central State Library: P.M.B. 2061, Kaduna; f. 1953 but partly depleted with creation of states in 1968; 40,000 vols.; Senior Librarian SAIYID ABDUL MOID; publs. *Annual Report, School Book Lists, West African List of Holdings, List of Items received under the Copyright Law.*

University of Lagos Library: University of Lagos, Yaba, Lagos; f. 1962; 100,000 vols., 3,000 periodicals; Librarian E. B. BANKOLE, A.B., M.S., A.L.A.; publs. *Annual Report, Unilag: Quarterly News Bulletin, Reader's Guide, Library Notes.*

Ibadan University Library: Ibadan; f. 1948; 265,000 vols., 4,500 periodicals; Librarian T. OLABISI ODEINDE, B.SC., A.L.A.; publs. *Annual Report, Library Record, Ibadan University Library Bibliographical series.*

University of Nigeria Libraries: Nsukka, East Central State; f. 1960; total of 68,400 vols. at Nsukka, Enugu and the Economic Development Institute; Librarian S. C. NWOYE, A.L.A.

Western State Library: P.M.B. 5082, Ibadan; f. 1954; 78,000 vols.; Librarian R. A. AREJE.

Western State Ministry of Agriculture and Natural Resources Library: P.O.B. 5013, Ibadan; f. 1958; 20,000 vols. and 1,000 periodicals on agriculture; branches at Akure, Odeda, Ilesha, Mokola; Librarian S. A. WINJOBI, A.L.A.; publs. *Annual Report, Reader's Guide.*

MUSEUMS

The museums controlled by the Federal Department of Antiquities (headquarters at Jos) are as follows:

Benin Museum: Benin; Benin antiquities, bronzes.

Jos Museum: Jos, Benue-Plateau State; f. 1952; ethnography and archaeology of Nigeria; terracotta Nok figurines, modern and traditional Nigerian pottery; zoological and botanical gardens; museum of traditional architecture; transport museum; UNESCO School for Museum Technicians; pottery workshop; national monuments section; library of 6,000 vols. and 1,600 Arabic MSS.; Curator ANNA CRAVEN; Superintendent of monuments M. BABA GALADIMA.

National Museum: Onikan Rd., Lagos; f. 1957; ethnography, archaeology and traditional art; Dir. EKPO EYO.

Ife Museum: Ife; f. 1954; bronze, terracotta and stone antiquities of Ife.

Oron Museum: Oron; f. 1959; ancestral carvings of the Oron area.

Gidan Makama Museum: Kano; f. 1959; local art work.

UNIVERSITIES

AHMADU BELLO UNIVERSITY

ZARIA

Telephone: Zaria 2581, 2585.

Founded 1962.

Language of instruction: English.

Chancellor: The Hon. Sir UDO UDOMA, LL.B., M.S., PH.D.

Vice-Chancellor: I. S. AUDU, M.B., B.S., M.R.C.P., D.T.M. & H., D.C.H., HON. L.H.D.

Registrar: K. LUPTON, O.B.E., M.A.

Librarian: B. ARMITAGE, F.L.A.

  Number of teachers: 650, including 66 professors.

  Number of students: 3,835, including 77 foreign students.

  Publications: *University Calendar, University Prospectus, Vice-Chancellor's Annual Report, University Bulletin, University Research Report, University Public Lectures, Student Handbook, University Gazette,* Annual Reports of Directors of attached Institutes.

DEANS:

Faculty of Administration: Prof. D. H. BRENNECKE, M.S., M.B.A., D.B.A.

Faculty of Agriculture: Prof. J. A. FEWSTER, PH.D., A.R.I.C.

Faculty of Arts and Islamic Studies: Prof. K. RAYAN, M.A., L.T.

Faculty of Arts and Social Sciences: Prof. G. WALTON, M.A., M.LITT.

Faculty of Education: Prof. D. A. BAIKIE, D.F.A., M.SC., ED.D.

Faculty of Engineering: Prof. J. W. BROOKS, M.SC., D.ENG., M.E.I.C.

Faculty of Environmental Design: G. W. BURDEN, DIP.ARCH., A.R.I.B.A.

Faculty of Law: Prof. Z. Mustafa, LL.M., PH.D.

Faculty of Medicine: Prof. H. Scarborough, M.B., CH.B., PH.D., F.R.C.P., F.R.S., F.R.C.P.

Faculty of Science: Prof. Mary Hallaway, M.A., D.PHIL., A.R.I.C.

Faculty of Veterinary Medicine: Prof. E. H. Coles, D.U.M. PH.D.

Attached Institutes:

Institute of Administration: P.M.B. 1013, Zaria; f. 1954 and attached to the University in 1962.
Director: M. M. Tukur, B.A., M.I.P.A.
Secretary: A. S. Maiyaki, B.A.

Institute for Agricultural Research and Special Services: P.M.B. 1044, Samaru, Zaria; f. 1962.
Director: Dr. M. Dagg, PH.D.
Secretary A. A. Jarma, B.SC., B.AGRIC.

Institute of Education: Main Campus, Samaru, Zaria; f. 1965.
Director: A. F. Ogunshola, M.ED., PH.D.
Secretary: Y. Aliyu, B.A.

Institute of Health: Main Campus, Samaru, Zaria; f. 1967.
Director: U. Shehu, M.B.B.S., L.R.C.P., M.R.C.S., D.P.H., F.M.C.P.H.
Secretary: W. J. C. Rositter, M.A., F.H.A.

Child Development Research Institute: Main Campus, Samaru, Zaria.

Attached College:

Abdullahi Bayero College (*Faculty of Arts and Islamic Studies*): P.M.B. 3011, Kano; f. 1960 and attached to the University in 1962.
Provost: S. A. S. Galadanci, B.A., DIP.ED.

Other Attached Units:

Division of Agricultural and Livestock Services Training: P.M.B. 1044, Zaria; f. 1971; Dir. W. L. Prawl, M.SC., ED.D.

School of Basic Studies: Main Campus, Samaru, Zaria; f. 1970; Principal U. S. H. Maigida, M.A. (acting).

UNIVERSITY OF BENIN
P.M.B. 1154, BENIN CITY
Telephone: 343.
Founded 1970.

Vice-Chancellor: Prof. Kenneth R. Hill, M.D., F.R.C.P., F.R.I.C., F.R.C.PATH.
Registrar: Chief D. R. Oduaran, J.P., LL.B., A.H.A., BAR.-AT-LAW.
Librarian: Dr. W. J. Harris, B.A., F.N.Z.L.A.

Library of 6,264 vols.
Number of teachers: 43.
Number of students: 250.

Deans:

Faculty of Engineering: Prof. D. E. Turnbull, PH.D., C.ENG., F.I.MECH.E., M.I.P.E.
Faculty of Medicine and Pharmacy: Prof. T. Belo-Osagie, B.SC., M.D., M.R.C.O.G.
Faculty of Science: Prof. R. W. H. Wright, PH.D.

UNIVERSITY OF IBADAN
IBADAN
Telephone: Ibadan 62550.

(London Office: 3 Gower St., London, W.C.1; Telephone: 01-636-9766/7.)

Founded 1962. Previously established as University College, Ibadan, 1948.

Visitor: Gen. Yakubu Gowon.
Chancellor: Sir Kashim Ibrahim, K.C.M.G., M.B.E.
Pro-Chancellor and Chairman of Council: Chief Sir Samuel Manuwa, C.M.G., O.B.E., M.D., F.R.C.S., F.R.C.P., F.A.C.S., F.A.C.P., F.R.S. (EDIN.), F.R.S.A.
Vice-Chancellor: Prof. H. Oritsejolomi Thomas, C.B.E., M.B., F.R.C.S.
Registrar: S. J. Okudu, B.A.
Librarian: T. Olabisi Odeinde, B.SC., A.L.A.

Library: *see* Libraries.
Number of teaching staff: 615.
Number of students: 3,768.
Publications: *Calendar, Annual Report, Research Bulletin of the Centre for Arabic Documentation* (bi-annual), *The Gazette* (bi-monthly), *Vice-Chancellor's Bulletin.*

Deans:

Faculty of Arts: T. A. Bamgbose, PH.D.
Faculty of Science: O. Awe, PH.D.
Faculty of Medicine: O. O. Akinkugbe, M.D., D.PHIL., F.R.C.P.
Faculty of Agriculture, Forestry and Veterinary Science: A. Fayemi, M.SC., PH.D.
Faculty of Social Sciences: O. Aboyade, PH.D.
Faculty of Education: S. H. O. Tomori, M.A., PH.D., DIP.ED.

Institute of Education: Dir. J. A. Majasan.

Institute of Child Health: Dir. A. U. Antia.

Nigerian Institute of Social and Economic Research: f. 1957; conducts and assists social and economic research; library of 8,000 vols.; Dir. H. M. A. Onitiri, PH.D., M.A.; Admin. Sec. A. Ijose, M.A.; publs. *Annual Report, Information Bulletin.*

UNIVERSITY OF IFE
ILE-IFE
(Ibadan Branch, Ibadan)
Founded 1961.

State control; Language of instruction: English; Academic year: September to June.

Chancellor: Chief Obafemi Awolowo, B.COM., LL.B., HON. L.L.D., D.SC.(ECON.), BAR-AT-LAW.
Vice-Chancellor: Dr. H. A. Oluwasanmi, M.A., PH.D.
Pro-Chancellor: Chief T. T. Solaru, M.A., B.D.
Registrar: H. J. Balmond, B.A.
Librarian: J. O. Dipeolu, B.A., A.L.A.
Bursar: K. J. Hamilton-Smith, F.C.A., A.C.W.A.

Number of teachers: 370.
Number of students: 2,879.
Publications: *Calendar, Odu* (A Journal of West African Studies), *Journal of Administration* (quarterly), *Monthly Newsletter.*

Deans:

Faculty of Agriculture: A. A. Adegbola.
Faculty of Arts: I. A. Akinjogbin.
Faculty of Social Sciences: G. J. A. Ojo.
Faculty of Law: O. I. Odumodu, LL.M., PH.D.

Faculty of Science: B. L. SHARMA.
Faculty of Education: L. J. BHATT.
Faculty of Pharmacy: E. RAMSTAD.
Faculty of Technology: C. P. HOWAT.
Faculty of Health Science: T. A. I. GRILLO.

AFFILIATED INSTITUTES:

Institute of Administration: University of Ife, P.M.B. 5246, Ibadan; f. 1963; quasi-autonomous institution within the University; provides graduate and specialist courses and consultancy services, and conducts basic and applied research.

> *Director:* A. ADEDEJI, B.SC.(ECON.), M.P.A., PH.D.
> *Librarian:* D. AGIDEE, F.L.A.

> Library of 20,000 vols. and 560 serials.
> Publications: *Quarterly Journal of Administration, Annual Report.*

Institute of African Studies: f. 1962 purely as a research institute; organized in four sections: African Languages with Arabic, Archaeology, Art and Art History, Performing Arts (Drama, Choreography, Musicology and Cinematography); Dir. Prof. H. U. BEIER, B.A.; publs. *Odu, Journal of West African Studies, Annual Report, Handbook.*

Institute of Agricultural Research and Training: P.M.B. 5027, Moor Plantation, Ibadan; f. 1970; trains agriculturalists and provides research facilities in Tropical Agriculture for postgraduate students; Dir. C. S. HOLTON, M.S., PH.D.; Sec. I. A. ADEBANJO, LL.B.

Institute of Education: f. 196 ; sponsored by the University, the West State Ministry of Education and the Association of Principals of Teacher Training Colleges and Secondary Schools in the State; a mobile library equipped with books, audiovisual aids and film aids demonstration among colleges and secondary schools; Dir. A. B. FAFUNWA, M.A., PH.D.; Sec. M. O. OLASEINDE, M.ED.; publ. *News Bulletin* (quarterly).

Institute of Physical Education: f. 1970; Dir. I. A. AKIOYE, M.E.D. (acting).

UNIVERSITY OF LAGOS
LAGOS
Telephone: 41360-9.

Founded 1962.

Language of instruction: English; Academic year: September to June.

Visitor: Gen. YAKUBU GOWON.
Chancellor: Rt. Hon. NNAMDI AZIKIWE.
Pro-Chancellor: MALLAM NUHU BAYERO.
Vice-Chancellor: Prof. J. F. ADE AJAYI.
Registrar: S. ADE OSINULU.
Librarian: E. B. BANKOLE.

> Library: *see* Libraries.
> Number of teachers: *c.* 350.
> Number of students: *c.* 2,400.

> Publications: *Gazette* (3 times yearly), *Calendar, Annual Report, Newsletter* (weekly).

DEANS:

Faculty of Social Studies: Prof. T. M. YESUFU.
Faculty of Law: Prof. T. O. ELIAS.
Faculty of Engineering: Prof. I. O. OLADAPO.
School of Humanities: Prof. R. A. AKINOLA.
School of Mathematical and Physical Sciences: Prof. CHIKE OBI.
School of Biological Sciences: Prof. S. H. Z. NAQVI.

School of African and Asian Studies: Prof. ADEBOYE BABALOLA.
School of Administration: Prof. M. A. ADEYEMO.

College of Medicine
IDI-ARABA, SURULERE, P.M.B. 12003, LAGOS
Language of instruction: English; State control.

Chairman of the Court of Governors: A. AKILU.
Provost: F. O. DOSEKIN, M.A., M.D., F.L.S.
Secretary: Z. A. ALABI, D.P.A.

> Number of teachers: 57.
> Number of students: 306.
> Publications: *Gazette, Prospectus.*

College of Education
AKOKA, YABA, LAGOS
Chairman of the Court of Governors: The Hon. Mr. Justice J. A. ADEFARASIN.
Provost: C. O. TAIWO, O.O.N., O.B.E., M.A., M.SC., DIP.ED.
Secretary: S. A. DAWODU, M.A., DIP.ED.

> Number of teachers: 52.
> Number of students: 542.

ATTACHED INSTITUTES:

Comparative Education Study and Adaptation Centre.
> *Director:* Chief H. M. B. SOMADE.

Continuing Education Centre.
> *Director:* E. A. TUGBIYELE.

Institute of Child Health.
> *Director:* Dr. O. RANSOME-KUTI.

Institute of Computer Sciences.
> *Director:* Dr. O. J. FAGBEMI.

Institute of Mass Communication.
> *Director:* Prof. J. F. SCOTTON.

UNIVERSITY OF NIGERIA
NSUKKA, EAST CENTRAL STATE
Telephone: Nsukka 48, 49, 50, 51, 52, 53.

Founded 1960.

State control; Language of instruction: English; Academic year: September to June.

Chancellor: Alhaji ADO BAYERO, Emir of Kano.
Vice-Chancellor: Prof. H. C. KODILINYE, M.B., CH.B., D.O., D.O.M.S.
Registrar: JOHN MANGOLD, M.A.
Librarian: S. C. NWOYE, B.A., DIP.LIB., A.L.A.

> Library: *see* Libraries.

> Number of teachers: *c.* 600.
> Number of students: 3,363.

> Publications: *University of Nigeria Calendar* (annual), *Information Handbook for Prospective Students* (annual), *University Gazette* (bi-monthly).

DEANS:

Faculty of Agriculture: Prof. A. N. A. MODEBE.
Faculty of Arts: Dr. C. C. IFEMESIA.
Faculty of Business Administration: Dr. W. O. UZOAGA (acting).
Faculty of Education: Dr. B. O. UKEJE.
Faculty of Engineering: Dr. M. O. CHIJIOKE.
Faculty of Law: Dr. C. OGWURIKE.
Faculty of Medicine: Prof. C. NWOKOLO.
Faculty of Science: Prof. A. N. U. NJOKU-OBI.
Faculty of Social Studies: Prof. C. OKONJO.
Faculty of Environmental Studies: to be appointed.

ATTACHED INSTITUTES:

Economic Development Institute: University of Nigeria, Enugu Campus, Enugu, East Central State.

Institute of African Studies: University of Nigeria, Nsukka, East Central State.

COLLEGES

COLLEGE OF TECHNOLOGY
P.M.B. 1108, ENUGU

Telephone: 3346, 3647.

Founded 1965.

President: S. L. EKEOCHA.
Registrar: A. B. C. MADUBOKO (acting).
Librarian: Mrs. M. A. NWAKOBY.

Library of 2,500 vols.

Number of teachers: 34.

Number of students: 650 full-time, 600 part-time.

HEADS OF DEPARTMENTS:

Science: C. O. ODUNUKWE.
Business Studies: M. C. OKOYE.
Mechanical Engineering: D. O. OGBONNA.
Electronics and Electrical Engineering: H. O. D. OKEAHIA-LAM.
Building and Civil Engineering: B. C. UZOECHINA.
Fine Art: D. I. OZOIGBO.

THE POLYTECHNIC
P.M.B. 5063, IBADAN

Telephone: 21771.

Founded 1961, Polytechnic status 1970.

President: Prof. AYO OGUNSHEYE, B.SC., M.A.
Registrar: E. O. ADETUNJI, B.A.

Library of 3,500 vols.

Number of teachers: 50.

Number of students: 500.

KADUNA POLYTECHNIC
P.M.B. 2021, KADUNA

Telephone: 22541.

Founded 1968.

Principal: MALLAM MOHAMMED DIKKO, B.SC.
Secretary: MALLAM S. M. KANGIWA.
Librarians: M. A. BELLO, A.L.A., A. SAMBO.

Library of 4,000 vols.

Number of teachers: 170.

Number of students: 2,700.

DIRECTORS:

College of Science and Technology: J. P. W. WARD, O.B.E., B.A., A.R.I.C.S. (acting).
Staff Development Centre: D. R. OMOKORE, B.SC.
Survey Unit: J. P. W. WARD, O.B.E., B.A., A.R.I.C.S.

COLLEGE OF SCIENCE AND TECHNOLOGY
P.M.B. 5080, PORT HARCOURT, RIVERS STATE

Founded 1971.

Chairman of Council: K. DIETE-SPIFF, PH.D., L.R.C.P. M.R.C.S.
Rector: S. J. UNA, PH.D. (acting).
Registrar: F. J. ELLAH, B.A.

Library of 5,000 vols.

Number of teachers: 30.

Number of students: 220.

Publication: *Calendar* (annual).

DIRECTORS:

School of Basic Sciences: T. M. ADENIRAN, PH.D. (acting).
School of Engineering: J. G. CHINWAH, PH.D. (acting).
School of Preliminary Studies: H. H. HATHERLY, M.B.E., B.A.

COLLEGE OF TECHNOLOGY
YABA, LAGOS

Founded 1948.

Principal: Dr. E. A. AKINLEYE, PH.D., C.ENG., M.I.E.E., M.N.S.E.
Registrar: T. O. SHOTUNDE, B.SC.(ECON.).
Librarian: S. O. ISHOLA, A.L.A.

The library contains 21,000 vols.

Number of teaching staff: 95 full-time.

Number of students: 663 full-time, 476 part-time, 630 residential places.

___

School of Agriculture: P.M.B. 623, Akure, Western State; f. 1957; about 550 students; library of 2,100 vols.; Principal J. S. A. OLAYEMI; publs. *The Tractor, The Thorn, The Dam.*

School of Agriculture: Moor Plantation, Ibadan; f. 1921; Principal F. A. TERIBA; 122 students.

School of Africulture: Kabba, Kwara State, Nigeria; f. 1963; 92 students; 1,340 vols.; Principal D. A. PETU.

School of Agriculture: Samaru, P.O.B. 164, Zaria; f. 1924; 266 students; 9,000 vols.; Principal H. E. GOERTZ.

School of Agriculture: Umudike, Umuahia, East Central State; f. 1955; technical agricultural training with certificate and diploma courses; library of over 2,000 vols.; 160 students; Principal JOHN C. OBI, M.SC., D.T.A.

School of Forestry: Federal Department of Forestry, P.M.B. 5011, Ibadan; f. 1941; technical forestry training with certificate and diploma courses; library of over 2,000 vols.; Principal I. I. EVO, B.SC.; Officer in Charge of Training D. M. WARD; 6 teachers, 140 students.

School of Dental Hygiene: 1 Broad St., P.M.B. 12562, Lagos; f. 1957; Principal J. R. I. ANA, F.D.S.

Federal School of Dispensing Assistants: P.O.B. 456, Lagos.

SELECT BIBLIOGRAPHY

ABOYADE, O. *Foundations of an African Economy: A Study of Investment and Growth in Nigeria.* New York, Praeger, 1966.
"The Nigerian Economy" in *The Economics of Africa,* Robson, P., and Lury, D. A. (Eds.). London, Allen and Unwin, 1969.

ADEDEJI, A. *Nigeria Federal Finance: its Development, Problems and Prospects.* London, Hutchinson Educational, 1969.

AJAYI, J. F. A., and SMITH, R. *Yoruba Warfare in the Nineteenth Century.* Cambridge, 1964.

AKPAN, NTIEYONG U. *The Struggle for Secession 1966–1970.* London, Cass, 1972.

AWOLOWO, CHIEF OBAFEMI. *Awo.* Cambridge, Cambridge University Press, 1960.

AYANDELE, E. A. *The Missionary Impact on Modern Nigeria, 1842–1914.* Ibadan, 1966.

AZIKIWE, NNAMDI. *Zik: A Selection from the Speeches of Nnamdi Azikiwe.* Cambridge, Cambridge University Press, 1961.

BIOBAKU, SABURI O. *The Egba and their Neighbours.* Oxford, 1957.

BUCHANAN, K. M., and PUGH, J. C. *Land and People of Nigeria.* London, 1955.

CRONJE, SUZANNE. *The World and Nigeria.* London, Sidgwick and Jackson, 1972.

CROWDER, MICHAEL. *The Story of Nigeria.* London, 1962.

DIKE, K. ONWUKA. *Trade and Politics in the Niger Delta 1830–1885.* Oxford, 1959.

EICHER, C. K., and LIEDHOLM, C. (Eds.). *Growth and Development of the Nigerian Economy.* Michigan, Michigan State University Press, 1970.

EZERA, KALU. *Constitutional Developments in Nigeria.* Cambridge, 1964.

FORDE, DARYLL (Ed.). *Efik Traders of Old Calabar.* Oxford, 1956.

GAILEY, HARRY A. *The Road to Aba: A Study of British Administrative Policy in Eastern Nigeria.* University of London Press, 1971.

HATCH, JOHN. *Nigeria: A History.* London, Secker and Warburg, 1971.

HAY, A., and SMITH, R. *Interregional Trade and Monetary Flows in Nigeria, 1964.* Oxford, Oxford University Press, 1970.

HELLEINER, G. K. *Peasant Agriculture, Government and Economic Growth in Nigeria.* Irwin, Illinois, Homewood, 1966.

HODGKIN, THOMAS. *Nigerian Perspectives, an Historical Anthology.* London, 1960.

HOGBEN, S. J., and KIRK-GREENE, A. H. M. *The Emirates of Northern Nigeria.* London, 1966.

ITA, NDUNTUEI O. *Bibliography of Nigeria.* London, Cass, 1972.

JONES, G. I. *Trading States of Oil Rivers.* Oxford, 1963.

KEAY, R. W. J. *An Outline of Nigerian Vegetation.* Lagos, 1949.

KILBY, P. *Industrialization in an Open Economy: Nigeria, 1945–1966.* London, Cambridge University Press, 1969.

KIRK-GREENE, A. H. M. *Crisis and Conflict in Nigeria. A Documentary Sourcebook 1066–1970.* 2 vols. London, Oxford University Press, 1971.

MACKINTOSH, JOHN P. *Nigerian Government and Politics.* London, 1966.

MINERS, N. J. *The Nigerian Army 1956–66.* London, Methuen, 1971.

FEDERAL MINISTRY OF ECONOMIC DEVELOPMENT. *National Development Plan, 1962–68.* Lagos, 1962.

FEDERAL MINISTRY OF ECONOMIC DEVELOPMENT AND RECONSTRUCTION. *National Plan for Reconstruction and Development, 1970–74.* Lagos, 1970.

NIGERIAN ECONOMIC SOCIETY, UNIVERSITY OF IBADAN. *Nigerian Journal of Economic and Social Studies,* Vols. I–XI. Ibadan, 1958–1969.

ODUMOSU, OLUWOLE IDOWU. *The Nigerian Constitution, History and Development.* London and Lagos, 1963.

OKIGBO, P. N. C. *Nigerian National Accounts, 1950–57.* Enugu, Federal Ministry of Economic Development, 1962.

OKPAKU, JOSEPH (Ed.). *Nigeria: Dilemma of Nationhood.* Westport, Conn., Greenwood, 1972.

OLUWASANMI, H. A. *Agriculture and Nigerian Economic Development.* Ibadan, Oxford University Press, 1966.

ONYEMELUKWE, C. *Problems of Industrial Planning and Management in Nigeria.* Longmans, 1966.

OYINBO, JOHN. *Nigeria: Crisis and Beyond.* London, Charles Knight, 1972.

POST, K. W. J. *The Nigerian Federal Election of 1959.* Oxford, 1963.
New States of West Africa. London, 1964.

REYMENT, R. A. *Aspects of the Geology of Nigeria.* Ibadan, 1965.

ST. JORRE, JOHN DE. *The Nigerian Civil War.* London, Hodder and Stoughton, 1972.

SCHATZL, L. H. *Petroleum in Africa.* Ibadan, Oxford University Press, 1969.

SKLAR, RICHARD L. *Nigerian Political Parties, Power in Emergent African Nation.* Princeton, 1963.

SMOCK, AUDREY C. *Ibo Politics: The Role of Ethnic Unions in Eastern Nigeria.* Cambridge, Harvard University Press, 1971.

SOKOTO, SARDAUNA OF. *My Life.*

STOLPER, W. F. *Planning Without Facts; Lessons in Resource Allocation from Nigeria's Development.* Cambridge, Mass., Harvard University Press, 1966.

UDO, R. K. *Geographical Regions of Nigeria.* London, 1970

WHITAKER, C. S. *The Politics of Tradition: Continuity and Change in Northern Nigeria 1946–66.* London, Oxford University Press, 1970.

YESUFU, T. M. (Ed.). *Manpower Problems and Economic Development in Nigeria.* Ibadan, Oxford University Press, 1969.

Réunion*

Réunion is a volcanic island lying at the southern extremity of the Mascarene Plateau, which extends northwards through Mauritius to the Seychelles. Mauritius lies some 120 miles to the north-east, Madagascar about 400 miles to the west. The island is roughly oval in shape, being about forty miles long and up to thirty miles wide; the total area is 980 sq. miles (2,510 sq. km.). The population was estimated at 457,900 in 1971, giving a very high population density of nearly 500 to the sq. mile. Volcanoes have developed along a north-west to south-east angled fault; all but one are now extinct, though their cones still rise to 10,000 ft. and dominate the island. Dense forests covered most of the island before human settlements existed, but these have now been almost entirely destroyed. The heights and the frequent summer cyclones help to create abundant rainfall, especially on the north-eastern (windward) side. Temperatures vary greatly according to altitude, being tropical at sea-level but with winter frosts occuring frequently in the uplands.

Réunion was uninhabited by man until its occupation by French settlers in 1642. The French East India Company then established victualling bases, and slaves were brought in from Africa to provide farm labour. Many more slaves followed when coffee became an important export crop in the eighteenth century. However, trade suffered when the island was cut off from France by the British blockade during the Napoleonic wars—Britain occupied Réunion from 1810 to 1814. When returned to France, the colony proved unable to export coffee competitively in nineteenth century conditions, and first spices then sugar cane became the dominant crop. France abolished slavery in 1848, but the flourishing sugar plantations continued to bring in indentured labour from Indo-China, India and several East African territories. This immigration formed the basis of to-day's exceptional racial mixture. Whilst nearly all the island's leaders are white, there has been considerable racial interbreeding; large numbers of "poor whites" still exist, and hence no colour-bar system has grown up. France ruled Réunion as a colony until 1946 when, in common with certain Caribbean territories, it received full departmental status. Thus it is today regarded as an integral part of the French Republic, with an administration similar to those in the metropolitan departments. Three representatives are sent to the National Assembly in Paris, and two to the Senate.

Sugar has been the principal crop and the basis of the whole economy for over a century—indeed Réunion is second only to Mauritius as an example of a one-crop economy. The cane is grown on nearly all the good cultivable land up to 2,600 ft. on the leeward side of the island except in the relatively dry north-west, and up to 1,600 on the windward side. Although the volcanic soil is fertile and most cultivation has now been organized into large estates, the quality and yield are not as good as in Mauritius, and further progress is hindered by out-dated land laws and restrictions. Total sugar production amounted to 186,000 tons in 1971–72. Some vanilla is produced for export in the south-east. A variety of vegetables and fruits are grown, and the island is self-sufficient in cattle and pigs. Overall, however, substantial food imports are necessary to supply the dense population.

No mineral resources have been discovered, and the only industry of consequence is the processing of sugar. Sugar accounts for about 80 per cent of exports, most of the remainder being the by-products of rum and molasses. Over 70 per cent of total trade is with France, nearly all the rest being with the franc zone, the EEC countries excluding France, southern Africa and Madagascar. There is a very large trade deficit; in 1971 receipts for exports only covered about 27 per cent of the import bill. The gap is partly covered by French financial assistance and receipts from expatriates in France.

Réunion's economic future would seem to be essentially dependent upon France's willingness to continue both the direct subsidies and the hidden subsidy implicit in the island's status as a fully fledged *département*, despite the low tax yield from its generally poor citizens. Such willingness was expressed by Pierre Messmer (then French Minister for Overseas Departments and Territories) when he visited Réunion in 1971 and promised moves to promote more effective economic and social assimilation of the Department to Metropolitan France. These included transferring greater local responsibility to the Prefecture than is allowed in France, as well as increased investment for the development of employment, agriculture and communications. Such moves, while welcomed by the political establishment adhering to the French parliamentary majority, were criticized by the Réunion Communist Party, which remains hostile to the island's Departmental status. Réunion, however, has too few resources and is too distant from major centres of population to have much prospect of developing industry or tourism on a large scale. Potential agricultural development is limited, although the ambitious Bras de la Plaine irrigation scheme was completed in the south-west early in 1969. However, such schemes can be little more than palliatives in the face of a 3 per cent per annum population growth rate. Substantial emigration to France will no doubt continue, but considerable unemployment already exists, and unrest directed against the present inflexible social structure is likely to increase. Thus the outlook remains unsettled.

* *See* map on p. 564.

STATISTICS

Area: 2,510 sq. km. **Population** (1971): 457,900, Saint-Denis (capital) 87,000 (1968).

Employment (1969): Agriculture 32,000, Industry 20,000, Commerce 14,700, Administration and services 22,800, Domestic Service 10,500.

Agriculture (1971–72): Sugar 186,180 metric tons, Vanilla 143 metric tons, Tea 281 metric tons, Maize 10,000 metric tons, Onions 3,000 metric tons.

Livestock (1971): Cattle 45,000, Pigs 75,000, Goats 15,000, Sheep 2,500.

Currency: 100 centimes = 1 franc de la Communauté Financière Africaine. Coins: 5, 10, 20, 50 and 100 francs CFA. Notes: 500, 1,000 and 5,000 francs CFA. Exchange rates (December 1972): 1 franc CFA = 2 French centimes. £1 sterling = 593.625 francs CFA; U.S. $1 = 255.785 francs CFA. 1,000 francs CFA = £1.685 = $3.91.

Budget (1971): Revenue 67,250 million francs CFA (local origin 24,600, French origin 42,650); Expenditure 67,250 million francs CFA (Ministries 47,000, Social Security 17,500, other 2,750).

External Trade (1971): *Imports:* 63,904 million francs CFA (Foodstuffs, Machinery, Fertilizers, Vehicles); *Exports:* 14,132 million francs CFA (Sugar, Rum, Molasses, Essences, Vanilla, Fruit). Three-quarters of trade is with France.

Shipping (1971): Vessels entered 449, Freight entered 606,970 metric tons, Freight cleared 230,985 metric tons.

Civil Aviation (1971): Passengers entered 57,248, Passengers cleared 59,708; Freight entered 3,440 metric tons, Freight cleared 737 metric tons; Mail handled 523 metric tons.

Education (1971–72): *Primary:* Teachers 4,507, Pupils 107,754; *Secondary:* Teachers 1,422, Pupils 32,271. There is a teacher training college (500 students) and a university college (625 students).

THE GOVERNMENT

(*November* 1972)

Prefect: PAUL COUSSERAN.

President of the General Council: Dr. PIERRE LAGOURGUE.

Representatives to the National Assembly: HENRI SERS, JEAN FONTAINE, MARCEL CERNEAU.

Representatives to the Senate: GEORGES REPIQUET, ALFRED ISAUTIER.

Political Parties: Almost all the French parties are represented and in October 1972 the formation was reported of "Le Groupe du progrès", a socialist party distinct from the French Socialist Party. An important group, the "Association Réunion département français", owes allegiance to the French U.D.R. and is anti-autonomist. It is opposed notably by the Communists.

Judicial System: Cour d'Appel at Saint-Denis (Pres. M. DUPERTUYS); two Tribunaux de Grande Instance, five Tribunaux d'Instance.

Religion: 420,000 of the population are Roman Catholics; Bishop of Saint-Denis S.E. Mgr. GEORGES GUIBERT, 42 rue de Paris, Saint Denis, B.P. 55.

PRESS AND RADIO

Saint-Denis

Croix-Sud: B.P. 382, Saint-Denis; f. 1924; weekly; Editor R. P. PAYET.

Journal de l'Ile de la Réunion: 42 rue A.-de-Villeneuve, B.P. 98; daily; Dir. HENRI CAZAL.

La Démocratie: 143 rue Maréchal-Leclerc; twice weekly; Dir. L. SALEZ.

La Gazette de l'Ile de la Réunion: weekly.

Le Cri du Peuple: daily.

Tribune: weekly.

Trident: weekly.

Témoignages: 76 rue Maréchal-Leclerc, B.P. 192; f. 1944; daily; Communist; Editor BRUNY PAYET; circ. 5,000.

Hebdo-Bourbon: weekly.

Saint-Pierre

Le Sudiste: rue Lislet Geoffrey; political; weekly.

Radio Réunion: place du Barachois, B.P. 309; Government station administered by Radiodiffusion-Télévision Française; Dir. M. I. COLONNE; daily services; in 1972 there were 86,000 radio and 26,140 television sets.

FINANCE

cap. = capital; dep. = deposits; m. = million

BANKS

CENTRAL BANK

Caisse Centrale de Coopération Economique: 233 Boulevard Saint-Germain, Paris 7e; Saint-Denis.

Banque de la Réunion: Saint-Denis, 15 rue Jean-Chatel; cap. 200m. fr. C.F.A.; Pres. R. DE LA FORTELLE; Dir.-Gen. A. GOY.

Banque Nationale pour le Commerce et l'Industrie (Océan Indien): 7 place Vendôme, Paris; Saint-Denis, rue Juliette Dodu.

Caisse d'Epargne et de Prévoyance: 77 rue de Paris, Saint-Denis.

Caisse Régionale de Crédit Agricole Mutuel de la Réunion: Cité des Lauriers "les Camélias", B.P. 84; f. 1949; Pres. HENRY ISAUTIER; Dir. JEAN DE CAMBIAIRE.

INSURANCE

More than twenty major European insurance companies are represented in Saint-Denis.

TRADE AND INDUSTRY

Saint-Denis

Bureau de Promotion Industrielle: rue de Nice.

Chambre de Commerce et d'Industrie de la Réunion: B.P. 120; Pres. JACQUES CAILLE.

Jeune Chambre Economique: B.P. 120; f. 1963; 43 mems.; Pres. M. J. M. DUPUIS.

Société de Développement Economique: 22 rue de Paris.

Syndicat des Commerçants: 13 rue Edouard.

Syndicat des Fabricants de Sucre de l'Ile de la Réunion: 46 rue Labourdonnais.

Syndicat des Producteurs de Rhum de l'Ile de la Réunion 46 rue Labourdonnais.

Syndicat des Industries, des Travaux Publics et du Bâtiment: B.P. 108.

TRANSPORT

RAILWAYS

There are no railways on Réunion.

ROADS

A Route Nationale runs all round the island, generally following the coast and linking all the main towns. Another Route Nationale crosses the island from south-west to north-east linking Saint-Pierre and Saint-Benoit. Routes Nationales 322 km., Departmental roads 657 km., other roads 961 km.

SHIPPING

Cie. des Messageries Maritimes: B.P. 10, 10 rue Alexandre de Lasserve, La Pointe des Galets, St.-Denis.

Navale et Commerciale Havraise Péninsulaire: Résidence du Barachois, P.O.B. 62, St.-Denis.

Scandinavian East Africa Line, Bank Line, Clan Line, Union Castle Mail Steamship Co., and States Marine Lines: Société de Manutention et de Consignation Maritime (S.O.M.A.C.O.M.), B.P. 7, Le Port.

CIVIL AVIATION

The following airlines serve Réunion: Air France, Air Madagascar, Air Mauritius.

TOURISM

Syndicat d'Initiative Office du Tourisme: rue Rontauny, Saint-Denis; Pres. M. VAUTHIER.

Alliance Touristique de l'Ocean Indien: Préfecture, Saint-Denis.

Six thousand tourists visited Réunion in 1971.

EDUCATION

SOCIETIES AND RESEARCH INSTITUTES

Académie de la Réunion: 107 rue Jules Auber, Saint-Denis; f. 1913; 25 mems.; Pres. H. FOUCQUE; Sec.-Treas. Y. DROUHET; publ. *Bulletin.*

Association Historique Internationale de l'Océan Indien: B.P. 349, Saint-Denis.

Institut de Recherches Agronomiques Tropicales et des Cultures Vivrières (IRAT): B.P. 116, Saint-Denis; Dir. M. DADANT.

Société des Sciences et Arts: 22 rue Labourdonnais, Saint-Denis; Pres. Mme MAS.

Société Médicale de la Réunion: 4 rue Méziaire Guignard, Saint-Pierre; f. 1965; Pres. Dr. ROLE; Sec. Dr. M. TURQUET; publ. *Bourbon Médical* (quarterly).

LIBRARIES AND MUSEUMS

Archives Départementales: B.P. 289, Saint-Denis; Dir. ANNIE LAFFORGUE.

Bibliothèque Centrale de Prêt: place Joffre, Saint-Denis; f. 1956; 60,000 vols.; Dir. YVES DROUHET.

Bibliothèque Départementale: rue Roland Garros, Saint-Denis; f. 1856; 35,000 vols.; Dir. YVES DROUHET.

Bibliothèque Municipale: rue Rodier, Saint-Pierre; f. 1970; 15,000 vols.; Dir. JULES VOLIA.

Muséum d'Histoire Naturelle: Jardin de l'Etat, Saint-Denis; f. 1854; library of 1,800 vols.; zoology collection; Dir. H. GRUCHET.

Musée des Beaux Arts Léon-Dierx: Saint-Denis; f. 1912; Curator H. WACQUIEZ.

COLLEGE

Institut d'Etudes Juridiques, Economiques et Politiques: 12 ave. de la Victoire, B.P. 847, 97-4 Saint-Denis; f. 1950; library of 5,000 vols.; attached to the University of Aix-Marseille II.

SELECT BIBLIOGRAPHY

DEFOS DU RAU, JEAN. *L'Ile de la Réunion. Étude de géographie humaine.* Institut de Géographie, Bordeaux, 1960.

LELOUTRE, J.-C. *La Réunion, département français.* Paris Maspero.

TOUSSAINT, AUGUSTE. *Histoire des Iles Mascareignes.* Paris, Berger-Levrault, 1972.

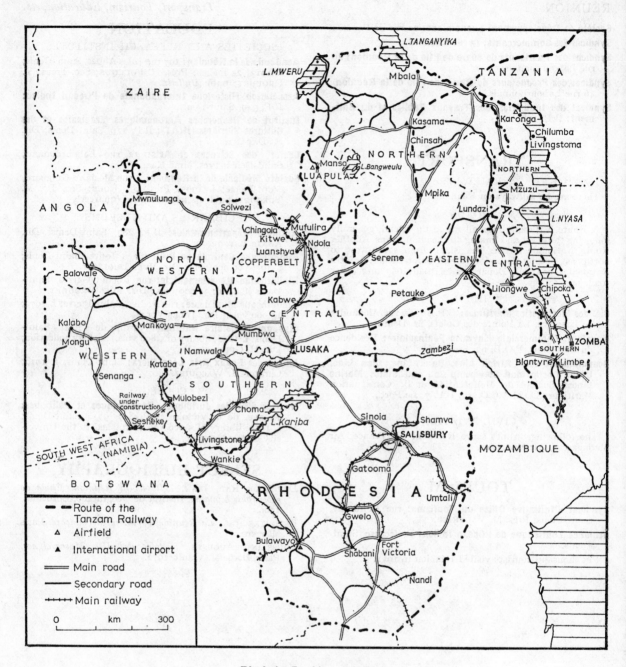

Rhodesia, Zambia and Malawi

Rhodesia

PHYSICAL AND SOCIAL GEOGRAPHY

G. Kay

Rhodesia extends from 15° 30′ to 22° 30′ S. and from 25° to 33° E. and has an area of 150,820 sq. miles (389,000 sq. km.). It is landlocked and has four neighbours: Botswana, Zambia, Mozambique and South Africa. It depends largely for its overseas trade on rail routes to Beira and Lourenço Marques in Mozambique, and to Cape Town, Durban and other ports in South Africa. The 1969 census showed Rhodesia's population to be 5,071,000; it is estimated that the rate of increase is about 3.5 per cent per annum. In 1972 it is estimated to be 5,690,000. Rhodesia unilaterally assumed independence of the United Kingdom on November 11th, 1965.

PHYSICAL FEATURES

Rhodesia lies astride the high plateaux between the Zambezi and Limpopo. It consists of four relief regions. The highveld is comprised of land above 4,000 ft. (1,220 m.) and extends across the country from south-west to north-east; it is most extensive in the north-east. The middleveld, land between 3,000 and 4,000 ft. (915–1,220 m.), flanks the highveld; it is most extensive in the north-west. The lowveld, land below 3,000 ft. (915 m.), occupies the Zambezi basin in the north and the more extensive Limpopo and Sabi-Lundi basins in the south and south-east. These three regions consist predominantly of gently undulating plateaux, except for the narrow belt of rugged, escarpment hills associated with faults along the Zambezi trough. Also the surfaces are broken locally where particularly resistant rocks provide upstanding features. For example, the Great Dyke, a remarkable intrusive feature over 300 miles (480 km.) in length and up to 6 miles (10 km.) wide, gives rise to prominent ranges of hills. The fourth physical region, the eastern highlands, is distinctive because of its mountainous character. Inyangani rises to 8,503 ft. (2,594 m.) and many hills exceed 6,000 ft. (1,800 m.). This narrow mountainous belt along the border with Mozambique marks the uplifted edge of the great tableland of south-central Africa.

CLIMATE

Temperatures are moderated by altitude. Mean monthly temperatures range from 22°C. in October and 13°C. in July on the highveld to 30°C. and 20°C. in the low-lying Zambezi valley. Winter months are noted for a wide diurnal range; night frosts are not uncommon on the high plateaux and can occasionally be very destructive.

Rainfall is largely restricted to the period November–March and, except on the eastern highlands, is very variable. Also, in view of high rates of evapotranspiration, in many parts of the country it is low for commercial crop production. Mean annual rainfall ranges from 55 in. (1,400 mm.) on the eastern highlands, to 30 in. (800 mm.) on the north-eastern highveld and to less than 15 in. (400 mm.) in the Limpopo valley. Development of Rhodesia's mediocre water resources for industrial, agricultural and domestic uses is a continually pressing need which, to date, has been met by a major dam-building programme. Underground water resources are limited.

AGRICULTURAL POTENTIAL, MINERALS AND POWER

Soils vary greatly. Granite occurs over more than half of the country and mostly gives rise to infertile sandy soils; these are, however, amenable to improvement. Kalahari Sands are also extensive and provide poor soils. Soil forming processes are limited in the lowveld and, except on basalt, soils there are generally immature. Rich, red clays and loams occur on the limited outcrops of Basement Schists, which are also amongst the most highly mineralized areas of Rhodesia.

However, climatic factors are the chief determinants of agricultural potential and six broad categories of land have been defined largely on bio-climatic conditions. They are as follows:

Region I (1.6 per cent of the country) with good, reliable rainfall; suitable for specialized and diversified farming, including tree crops.
Region II (18.7 per cent) with moderately high rainfall; suitable for intensive commercial crop production with subsidiary livestock farming.
Region III (17.4 per cent) with mediocre rainfall conditions; suitable for semi-extensive commercial livestock farming with supplementary production of drought-resistant crops.
Region IV (33 per cent) with low and unreliable rainfall; suitable for semi-extensive livestock production.
Region V (26.2 per cent) semi-arid country; suitable for only extensive ranching.
Region VI (3.1 per cent—probably underestimated) because of steep slopes, skeletal soils, swamps, etc., is unsuitable for any agricultural use.

Recently large-scale irrigation works in the south-eastern lowveld have overcome climatic limitations, and the area around Chiredzi, once suitable only for ranching, is now a major developing region under the auspices of the Sabi-Limpopo Development Authority.

Rhodesia is endowed with a wide variety of workable mineral deposits, which include gold, asbestos, copper, chrome, nickel and tin. Iron ore, limestone, iron pyrites, phosphates and other minerals also contribute significantly to local industrial development. Most mineral deposits occur on the highveld and adjacent parts of the middleveld. The Wankie coalfield (in the remote north-west) is a plentiful source of cheap coal, coke and coal by-products. The 700 MW. generators at Kariba provide ample electricity for present needs, but most thermal power-stations are dormant. Rhodesia lacks oil.

SOCIAL STRUCTURE

The population of Rhodesia is diverse. In 1972 it was estimated to consist of 5,400,000 Africans, 262,000 Europeans (mostly of Rhodesian, South African or British origins) and 27,300 Asians and Coloureds. The African population may be divided into two broad tribal or linguistic groups, the Ndebele and the Shona, popularly known as the Matabele and the Mashona. There are, in addition, several minor tribal groups, such as the Tonga, Sena, Hlengwe, Venda and Sotho.

Salisbury, the capital city, in 1969 had a population of 385,000 including 105,420 non-Africans (i.e. 42 per cent of all non-Africans); and Bulawayo, the second city, had a population of 245,600 including 58,000 non-Africans (23 per cent). Less than 15 per cent of the non-Africans live in rural areas, and the extensive European farmland is in the hands of about 6,000 armers or farming companies. The predominantly urban, affluent experience (average annual earnings of non-Africans in 1968—R$2,828) is in marked contrast to African life.

In the period 1965–68 African employees averaged 617,000 and their average annual earnings in 1968 were R$288. Less than half of the African labour force in paid employment lived in urban townships. Forty-two per cent worked on European farms; and domestic servants (15 per cent) constituted the second largest category of employees. African workers are drawn not only from Rhodesia's tribal lands but also from Malawi, Mozambique and, to a much lesser extent, Zambia. Foreign labour probably constitutes about one-third of the labour force. Migrations into the employment centres are predominantly male. Consequently there are more than 200 men per 100 women in the African urban population and about 150 men per women in African society on European farms.

The majority of Africans (over 60 per cent) live in tribal areas, most of which are overpopulated and overstocked, and they depend upon subsistence production, supplemented by small and irregular sales of surplus crops and livestock, by occasional casual employment, and by remittances from migrant labourers. Rural African society is enfeebled by labour migration; for example, there are less than 70 men per 100 women, and most men in their prime and with education are absent. In both urban and rural society, however, children constitute approximately half of the total population.

Since 1930 the land of Rhodesia has been divided into social categories by the Land Apportionment Act. In 1969 the division was as follows:

	per cent
Tribal Trust Land (occupied by Africans according to tribal custom) . .	41.6
African Purchase Area (individual holdings occupied by African farmers) . .	4.4
European Area (European farmland plus all urban areas). . . .	37.0
National Land (Forest Reserves, National Parks, etc.)	10.9

The Land Apportionment Act has been replaced by the Land Tenure Act which provides a more equal allocation of land in terms of area between the races, i.e. it has increased the European Area largely at the expense of Unreserved and National Lands to give near-parity with the extent of the African areas.

RECENT HISTORY

Richard Brown

COMPANY RULE AND THE GROWTH OF SETTLER POWER

By 1900 the political uncertainties surrounding the gamble in private colonization by Cecil Rhodes's British South Africa Company, which had occupied Mashonaland in 1890 and conquered Matabeleland in 1893, were over. Widespread religious organizations, whose functions and extent were unknown to the whites, had enabled the two main African societies, the Shona and the Ndebele (or Matabele), to overcome their historic enmity and co-operate in mounting the substantial uprisings of 1896–97; but neither their resistance, nor the earlier raid on the Transvaal by the Company's Administrator, L. S. Jameson, persuaded Britain to assume direct responsibility for the new territory. Instead the B.S.A.C. was left in administrative control on the basis of the Royal Charter granted to it in 1889.

The risings did, however, lead to increased imperial supervision. More significantly, Britain also sought to limit the Company's freedom of action by giving substantial representation to the white settlers in the newly-established Legislative Council. The political influence of the settlers increased still further when the Company began to foster white farming following the realization that Rhodesia's gold resources, the original lure for the Company, were not nearly as extensive as had been supposed. In 1907 the settlers were granted a majority in the legislature, and by 1914, on the renewal of the Charter, their right to succeed to the Company's powers was conceded in principle.

Since Rhodesia was an off-shoot of English-speaking South Africa, to which Afrikaners were none the less welcome, its laws and customs were modelled on those of Natal and the Cape, and the unusually swift political advance of the settlers owed a good deal to the expectation that Rhodesia would eventually become part of South Africa. Yet in the 1922 referendum which preceded the end of Company rule, a substantial majority (8,774 to 5,989) voted against incorporation in the Union and in favour of separate status as a largely self-governing colony. Under the constitution which came into force on October 1st, 1923, Britain retained a right of veto on discriminatory and constitutional matters. This, it has been shown, acted as an important negative restraint on Rhodesian governments and, in particular, prevented the removal from Africans of their largely theoretical right to the franchise; but in most respects Britain did little to prevent the consolidation of a racially stratified and segregated society in the 1920s and 1930s.

LAND APPORTIONMENT AND SEGREGATION

The foundation of what was known as "parallel development" or the "two pyramids" policy was the Land Apportionment Act of 1930, which severely restricted the access of Africans to land by dividing the country very unequally in relation to population into two racially exclusive parts. Measures were taken to prevent Africans from competing in the markets for agricultural produce, while the strong bargaining power of the white skilled workers protected them too from competition through the operation of the Industrial Conciliation Act of 1934. Taxation, the pass laws, land pressures, and the development of new wants ensured that the main role of Africans in the economy was as labour migrants to the European towns, farms, and mines. Little attention was paid to the development of African commercial farming in the Native Purchase Areas which had been set aside, in addition to the Reserves, under the Land Apportionment Act.

It was the structure built up in the inter-war period, and owing much to the experiences of the depression, which stood at the centre of the conflicts of the 1950s and 1960s, and which came under strain not only because of the rise of substantial African challenges, but also because the beginnings of industrialization profoundly altered the basis on which it had been established.

INDUSTRIALIZATION AND FEDERATION

Until the Second World War the economy of Rhodesia was a struggling one in which the export of primary products from small-scale mining and European farming remained dominant. The war brought about favourable opportunities for economic development, and these were effectively taken by the government, led since 1933 by Godfrey Huggins (later Lord Malvern). Inflation was controlled, and iron and steel and textile industries successfully fostered with government assistance. War conditions brought artificial protection to the infant manufacturing industry, which soon became the leading growth sector. The demand for strategic minerals and for agricultural produce, particularly tobacco, helped to contribute to a rate of growth estimated at 9 per cent per annum for the period 1938–58. In the post-war era the boom continued, and immigration, mainly from Britain and South Africa, caused a steep rise in the white population (from 80,500 in 1945 to 205,000 in 1958).

These developments helped to bring the long-debated question of closer political association with Northern Rhodesia (Zambia) and Nyasaland (Malawi) to a conclusion. Although Southern Rhodesia (Rhodesia) would have preferred amalgamation and the elimination of direct British control in the two northern territories, when this was ruled out by Britain, a majority of the electorate (25,570 to 14,729) agreed to the alternative of federation, after a campaign in which the economic advantages—the

copper revenues of Northern Rhodesia, the labour
supplies of Nyasaland, and the market for manufactures of both—were particularly stressed. The
Federation came into being with Huggins as its
first Prime Minister on October 1st, 1953, Sir Roy
Welensky succeeding him in 1956. It proved of
particular economic benefit to Rhodesia, but the
African nationalist movements in Nyasaland and
Northern Rhodesia frustrated Welensky's hopes of
obtaining Dominion status for the Federation while
it was still white-controlled. When Britain conceded
constitutions which brought African governments to
power in Nyasaland (1961) and Northern Rhodesia
(1962), the pressure to permit secession could no
longer be resisted. These developments led to the
dissolution of the Federation on December 31st,
1963; in the south they were interpreted by many
Europeans as having resulted from British appeasement and thus helped to harden white opinion
against the post-war trend towards African advancement.

HUGGINS AND REFORM

Even before the controversies surrounding the
Federation brought African questions into the fore-
front of political life, Huggins had come to believe
that the far-reaching implications of industrialization
would require an end to segregation and a deliberate
attempt to foster the growth of an African middle
class. From the early 1940s he began to point to the
need for a fuller use of the country's human resources:
manufacturers needed a more reliable and skilled
African labour force than prevailed with migratory
labour, and they would also benefit from increased
African purchasing power if wages rose and if productivity expanded in the rural areas. Yet policies
of this kind would adversely affect the interests of
the majority of Europeans, and since the political
system gave virtually all whites but only a handful
of Africans the vote, power ultimately rested with
those who were most vulnerable to any programme
of African advancement.

Nevertheless, while the "establishment" party of
Huggins, in which urban and business interests had
a strong voice, remained in power, its policies, based
on the slogan of racial partnership, moved away
from those of the pre-war period. Urban wages were
increased and steps taken to improve accommodation
in the fast-growing African townships surrounding,
but not part of, the European towns. Increased
expenditure and attention was given to African
commercial agriculture. African education greatly
expanded: the first government secondary school for
Africans opened in 1946, and in 1957, after the
necessary amendments to the Land Apportionment
Act, a non-racial university was opened. Following
prolonged controversy a new Industrial Conciliation
Act in 1959 for the first time extended officially
recognized rights of trade unionism to some categories of African worker. The formal barriers preventing African entry to apprenticeship and to the
civil service were removed in 1959 and 1960, and
discrimination in the use of some public and private
amenities was lessened. In the political field a franchise act in 1957 increased the number of African
voters by means of a special roll, and in 1961 provision
for limited African membership of Parliament was
introduced.

These changes had little immediate impact on the
everyday life of the vast mass of Africans and did
not significantly reduce inequalities: the gap in
average wages and the amount spent on each white
child and on each black child in school remained
stubbornly separated by a factor of ten. Moreover,
liberal policies aroused white opposition, both within
and outside the governing party. Thus Garfield Todd,
who had succeeded Huggins as Prime Minister in
1953, was removed from office and replaced by Sir
Edgar Whitehead early in 1958 by the action of his
own party when his advocacy of liberal measures
was considered to be an electoral risk; and in the
ensuing general election (June 1958) only the existence
of a preferential voting system kept the United
Federal Party in power. The eclipse of Todd, who
alone of white politicians appeared capable of retaining significant African support; the slow-down
in economic growth from 1958; and the increasing
African challenge to all aspects of white domination
began a period of increasingly bitter political conflict.

THE AFRICAN CHALLENGE

Although as a mass movement African nationalism
developed with great speed only in the second half
of the 1950s, the pre-war period had seen the tentative
appearance of many of its diverse strands. Modern
political activities were first employed in the campaign
mounted during and after the First World War for
the restoration of the Ndebele kingship. More terri-
torially focused pressure groups appeared in the
1920s and 1930s when small élite associations like the
Rhodesia Bantu Voters Association (1923) and the
Southern Rhodesian African National Congress
(1934) attempted to make themselves heard on
grievances such as land, education, the franchise,
and the economic and social colour-bars. Elements
of protest on a wider scale were to be found in the
popular, but loosely organized and poorly led Industrial and Commercial Workers' Union (1927), and
in many of the independent and millenarian churches
which appeared in increasing numbers from the late
1920s.

By 1945 the changing economic tempo had begun
to give African protest more vigour and a wider
outlook. The rapid growth of the towns and of the
number of Africans in wage employment (from
376,900 in 1946 to 610,000 in 1956) was reflected in
an effective strike by African railway workers in
1945 and by a more general strike in 1948. In the
rural areas land shortage and overcrowding, compulsory destocking, and the forcible removal of
Africans in terms of the Land Apportionment Act
from land required for post-war immigrants led to
much discontent. Above all, the Land Husbandry
Act of 1951, which struck at the roots of both rural
and urban life, acted as a catalyst for mass nationalism. The act involved the substitution of semi-
individualized for communal tenure, partly in an

effort to conserve the land and improve farming methods; but in African eyes the measure was only necessary because of the grossly unequal distribution of land. Underestimates of the numbers entitled to holdings and the often coercive and hasty methods of implementation stiffened opposition when the act began to be applied on a wide scale from 1955. Worst affected were many young labour migrants who lost their right to land and security without any prospect of wage and welfare facilities sufficient to support a permanent existence outside the reserves. It was young men in this position who did most to bring a revived African National Congress into existence in 1957. The ANC campaigned strongly for the redress of rural and urban grievances, and built up wide support at a time when many of the more established African leaders continued to explore the possibilities of working within the parliamentary parties. However, the fall of Todd, the quickening pace of political change elsewhere in Africa, and Whitehead's ban on the ANC in February 1959 and the detention or restriction without trial of several hundred of its activists, drew more of the wealthier and educated Africans into the National Democratic Party formed in January 1960.

The NDP's aim was "one man, one vote", which it sought to achieve by a combination of moral pressure, civil disobedience, and propaganda abroad. But tactics which succeeded in countries directly ruled by Britain did little to shift the deadlock inside Rhodesia. Whitehead, aided by even more stringent security laws passed in 1960, continued to deal toughly with the nationalists: the NDP was banned in December 1961 and its successor, the Zimbabwe African People's Union, in September 1962.

THE 1961 CONSTITUTION AND THE FALL OF WHITEHEAD

Meanwhile, Whitehead sought to retain white support by pressure to rid Rhodesia of the remaining elements of British control and made strenuous efforts to create a body of African support detached from the nationalists. Both these aims found expression in the 1961 Constitution, negotiated at a conference which, on British insistence, included an NDP delegation. The Constitution increased the size of the legislature to 65 seats, 15 of which an estimated 50,000 African voters, on a roll with lower property and educational qualifications, could expect to control. In place of most of Britain's remaining powers the Constitution provided for a Declaration of Rights and a Constitutional Council with limited powers intended to prevent further discriminatory legislation, but unable to influence laws already in force. The Constitution implied eventual majority rule at a rate which would be determined by the white minority's existing control over African advancement.

The NDP delegation at first hesitantly supported the proposals, but they were later rejected by an NDP Congress and in an unofficial referendum organized by the party. In place of participation the nationalists pressed for a further constitutional conference. The electorate, however, accepted the new Constitution by a majority of two to one in the official referendum in July 1961, a verdict which later events suggested owed more to the emphasis in the campaign on the elimination of British powers and to the massive show of strength against a threatened African strike shortly before the poll, than to a willingness to accept eventual African majority rule.

Whitehead had little success in enrolling African voters against the nationalist boycott, and his promises to repeal the Land Apportionment Act and outlaw racial discrimination during the 1962 election campaign alarmed the majority of European voters without convincing African potential voters of his ability to satisfy both white and black aspirations. The fall of Whitehead in the election ended rule by a party which, under a variety of names, had held power with a single brief exception since the end of Company rule. Its successor, the Rhodesian Front, first halted and then reversed the reformist trend initiated by Huggins twenty years before.

THE RHODESIAN FRONT AND INDEPENDENCE

The RF had been formed earlier in election year by an amalgamation of white opposition groups under the leadership of Winston Field. It was well organized, wealthy, and had enthusiastic grass roots support, particularly from white farmers and artisans, who were attracted by the party's demand for the retention of the Land Apportionment Act and by its hostility to racial integration and the 1961 Constitution. In office its campaign for independence, paradoxically on the basis of the 1961 Constitution, consolidated its hold on white opinion, though not before the party itself had replaced Field as Prime Minister in April 1964 because of his apparent unwillingness to risk unilateral action. Under Smith by-elections confirmed the continuing swing in favour of the RF, and in the general election of May 1965 the party completely vanquished its white opponents by winning all 50 "A" roll seats.

The government's ability to contemplate a unilateral declaration of independence was also strengthened by its increasing control over broadcasting and by its success in curtailing the activities of the African nationalists. It was able to override the Constitutional Council and introduce mandatory sentences, including the death penalty, for a wide range of offences, as well as obtain rights of detention and restriction extended for up to five years. In August 1964 the *African Daily News* was suppressed and both wings of the nationalist movement proscribed. Unity had been lost exactly a year before with the formation of the Zimbabwe African National Union by a breakaway group led by the Rev. N. Sithole and bitterly opposed to Joshua Nkomo's continued leadership of ZAPU (which, after the ban in 1962, had remained in existence, but without a public organization). Following the split an outbreak of inter-party violence weakened the movement and largely replaced the attempts to force a constitutional change by isolated acts of sabotage and attacks on European property. During 1964 and 1965 imprisonment, preventive detention, and restriction removed virtually all levels of African nationalist leadership from public life. Leaders in exile, however, began to infiltrate armed guerrillas into the country on a limited scale, and by 1967 their activities were sufficiently serious to lead to the presence of armed South African police in Rhodesia. Guerrilla incursions have continued intermittently and are a significant feature of the Rhodesian situation, but the unfavourable terrain in the more populous areas and the effectiveness of the security forces seem likely to prevent any quick success. The guerrilla effort has probably been hampered by the failure, despite repeated efforts, to heal the split in the nationalist movement.

Meanwhile, in the prolonged negotiations which preceded the unilateral declaration of independence on November 11th, 1965, Britain was induced to consider granting independence on the basis of five— later six—general principles (*see* The Constitution, page 676), to which successive British governments adhered. Critics of the British position maintained that the history of South Africa showed that once independence was granted safeguards were worthless. Nevertheless, the Rhodesian government was unwilling to accept any proposals which could not be seen to slow down the rate of African political advancement implied by the 1961 Constitution or to submit its own proposals to a test of opinion sufficiently representative to be acceptable to Britain.

SINCE U.D.I.

After U.D.I. the basic position of the two sides remained unchanged. Britain had publicly ruled out the use of force to quell the rebellion even before U.D.I., and relied on progressively increased economic sanctions to produce a negotiated settlement and a realignment of political forces among the whites. Of these forces there was little sign in subsequent years. While sanctions brought Smith to the abortive negotiations with the Labour Prime Minister on board H.M.S. *Tiger* (December 2nd–4th, 1966) and H.M.S. *Fearless* (October 9th–13th, 1968), it was the British who were twice seen to offer concessions. In 1969 the Rhodesian Government provocatively emphasized its confidence by enacting a new Constitution which came into force and also made Rhodesia a Republic on March 2nd, 1970.

The new Constitution, while allowing a theoretical eventual parity of representation between Africans and Europeans, permanently excludes majority rule and—for the first time in Rhodesian history— completely separates the franchise on a racial basis by eliminating the common roll. The Constitution also reduces the proportion of directly elected African members of Parliament and substitutes representation through tribally constituted electoral colleges. This provision is in line with the régime's reliance on the African chiefs for support. Under the direct rule system practised in Rhodesia since the rebellions, the autonomy of the chiefs was severely curtailed, and it is only since the rise of African nationalism that they

have increasingly been drawn into the central political arena as supporters of the government, on whom the chiefs now rely for office and emoluments.

The first general election held under the provisions of the 1969 Constitution in April 1970 confirmed the RF's hold on power when the party won all 50 seats reserved for Europeans. The election was also characterised by the poor support given to the multi-racial and moderate Centre Party's European candidates and by the even worse showing of the "ultras" (of the Republican Alliance), spokesmen for an even more complete racial separation than has yet been proposed under the RF's policy of "separate development" and which is so far embodied mainly in the Constitution and in the Land Tenure Act (*see* page 676).

The implementation of the 1969 Constitution did not prevent the new Conservative government in Britain from moving cautiously in 1970 and 1971 towards keeping its pledge of making a fresh attempt at settling the independence dispute. This policy culminated in the agreement on a proposed settlement reached in Salisbury in November 1971. Although the terms for independence were based only on modifications to the 1969 Constitution and were thought in many quarters to make no more than a gesture towards the spirit of the first four principles, the proposals did contain, in conformity with the fifth principle, provisions for a test of the agreement's acceptability "to the people of Rhodesia as a whole". The appointment of a commission under Lord Pearce to canvass all sections of opinion, and also the clause in the agreement by which the Rhodesian Government had to allow a more open expression of African opinion, provided for the first time for many years a focus for African political activity. After a period of sporadic disorder much of the strong African feeling became channelled by the newly-formed African National Council led by Bishop Abel Muzorewa, the first substantial African political association to operate effectively since the banning of the nationalist parties in 1964. In place of the apparent passivity of the previous years, the commission found both the urban and rural areas "alive with political activity at the grass-roots" and had little hesitation in reporting that the Salisbury agreement did not meet the fifth principle since the majority of Africans opposed the settlement proposals. The commission noted that Africans particularly distrusted the motives and intentions of the Rhodesian Government; that they were dissatisfied with the indefiniteness and delay surrounding majority rule; and that they were highly critical of the total absence of African involvement in the settlement negotiations.

The British Government accepted the Pearce Report when it was finally published in May 1972, and the dispute over independence remained unchanged: sanctions continued in force and Rhodesia continued to operate the 1969 Constitution unamended. However, in the months that followed it appeared that both governments might in the end seek ways to overcome the stumbling-block of the Pearce report. It was thought that some such hopes lay behind Smith's resistance to well-publicized pressure from within the

RF to bring in yet more measures of racial segregation. This pressure was a reminder that the consolidation of U.D.I. owed much to diplomatic, economic, and military support from South Africa. By 1972 it was clear that Rhodesia, still not free from sanctions and without the formal recognition of a single country, had greatly increased its dependence on its powerful southern neighbour, on whom, moreover, Rhodesia's social system was now more closely modelled than at any time since the Second World War.

ECONOMY

Timothy Curtin

Seven years after the illegal declaration of independence the Rhodesian economy continues to disappoint expectations of collapse or stagnation, despite continued sanctions. The maintenance of the nominal gold par value of the Rhodesian dollar in December 1971 when both Zambia and South Africa devalued their currencies was perhaps no more than a gesture of defiance—the Rhodesian currency has no international status—but reflected nevertheless the underlying strength of the economy. Sanctions however continue to prevent full realization of the growth potential of the economy. The United States' resumption of chrome imports from Rhodesia remains the only avowed reversal of sanctions by any country. The breakdown of the projected Anglo-Rhodesian Settlement means that Rhodesia's economic development must continue to be based on internally generated sources of growth. An additional if indirect reinforcement of sanctions arises from Rhodesia's exclusion from both the General Scheme of Preferences offered to developing countries by the advanced industrial countries and also, and more importantly, from the offer of association with the EEC made to African Commonwealth countries (*see* "Africa and the EEC"). Almost all African countries will in future enjoy duty-free access to the enlarged EEC market for both their primary products and their manufactures. Rhodesia's loss is the greater for its larger capacity to have taken advantage of these preferences in normal circumstances.

GROSS NATIONAL PRODUCT

Rhodesia's gross national product was R$1,163 million in 1971; the hypothetical exchange rate with the U.S.$ is R$1.0 = U.S. $1.52. National income per head is U.S. $318.

The steady reduction in the importance of agriculture and mining in the Rhodesian economy may be seen in table 1; the associated growth in the importance of manufacturing and the tertiary sectors indicates Rhodesia's transition from underdeveloped to semi-developed status. Thus the Rhodesian economy is structurally more akin to the South African than the Zambian economy, as may be seen in table 2.

The composition of gross domestic expenditure is shown in table 3. For most of the period that Rhodesia—then known as Southern Rhodesia—formed part of the Federation of the Rhodesias and Nyasaland (1953-63), gross fixed capital formation was as high as a quarter of domestic expenditure, but from 1960 to 1966 investment declined both absolutely and relative to G.D.P. until it was as low as R£40 million. Since 1966 the trend has been reversed, and at 16 per cent of G.D.P. in 1970 fixed investment was comfortably above the minimum of 10 per cent suggested by Rostow as a necessary condition for take-off into self-sustained growth.

Analysis of the distribution of the national income in Rhodesia requires additional categories to those which apply to more advanced or more homogeneous

Table 1

INDUSTRIAL ORIGIN OF THE GROSS DOMESTIC PRODUCT
(percentage distribution)

	1955	1960	1965	1970	1971
Agriculture	21	19	19	17	17
Mining	8	7	7	6	6
Manufacturing . . .	14	16	19	22	23
Construction	8	7	4	6	6
Electricity and Water . .	2	3	4	4	3
Transport and Communications .	8	9	9	6	7
Wholesale and Retail Trade . .	15	15	14	13	13
Banking, Insurance, Real Estate .	5	6	6	6	5
Public Administration, Defence, Health and Education . . .	7	8	9	10	10
Services	10	10	9	10	10
Gross Domestic Product (i) % .	100	100	100	100	100
(factor cost) (ii) R$ million .	373	562	707	958	1,088

Table 2

INDUSTRIAL ORIGIN OF GROSS DOMESTIC PRODUCT IN
SOUTH AFRICA, RHODESIA AND ZAMBIA

(percentages)

	SOUTH AFRICA (1967)	RHODESIA (1968)	ZAMBIA (1967)
Agriculture	12	16	9
Mining	12	6	34
Total Primary Sectors	*24*	*22*	*43*
Manufacturing	21	19	10
Construction	6	6	7
Electricity and Water	3	5	1
Transport and Communications	10	8	6
Wholesale and Retail Trade	13	13	13
Banking, Insurance and Real Estate	4	7	5
Public Administration and Services	10	10	10
Other Services	9	10	5
Total Secondary and Tertiary Sectors	*76*	*78*	*57*
Gross Domestic Product (i) %	100	100	100
(ii) R$ million	9,032	780	751

Table 3

COMPOSITION OF GROSS DOMESTIC EXPENDITURE 1970

	R$ MILLION	%
Private Consumption (Money Economy)	632.5	61
African Rural Household Consumption	63.8	6
Government Current Expenditure	121.7	12
Gross Fixed Capital Formation	169.6	16
of which:		
Land Improvement	4.5	
Mine Development	3.8	
Building and Works	97.5	
Plant, Machinery, etc.	63.8	
Net Increase in Stocks	44.5	4
Gross Domestic Expenditure	1,032.0	100
Net Exports of Goods and Services	6.7	
Gross Domestic Product at market prices	1,038.7	

Note: "African rural household consumption" is an estimate of the market value of production for own consumption in the subsistence economy.

countries. The classic tripartite division into land, labour, and capital will not do because European and African workers are in effect different factors of production in Rhodesian conditions. At the same time it is necessary to distinguish between incomes generated in the money economy, where almost all land is owned by Europeans, and the subsistence economy, which is coterminous with the African tribal trust lands reserved for African ownership.

Wages and salaries received by both sections of the labour force (African and non-African) amounted to R$461 million in 1968, which was 57 per cent of the gross national product and somewhat lower than the comparable figure for developed countries. African employees numbered 663,000 or 87 per cent of the total working force, but their share of total wages remained as for many years only 40 per cent. Average earnings of African workers were R$288; average earnings of the 95,600 non-African employees were R$2,828.

The share of Africans in the national income includes, in addition to earnings of employees (R$190 million), the estimated money value of production for own consumption (R$59 million gross), sales of agricultural output (R$6 million), and the income of unincorporated business enterprises (R$9 million). These items add up to R$264 million or R$53 per capita. The residual share of non-Africans in the national income, including rents and profits of government enterprises, public corporations and companies, is R$549 million, or R$2,196 per capita.

RHODESIA

The rate of increase of the gross national product has averaged 4 per cent since 1960, but inflation and population growth have meant that real income per head has at best remained constant. It is important to realize that the national income statistics in Rhodesia, as in other countries with large subsistence sectors, do not attempt to provide an accurate index of economic welfare in the subsistence economy. The estimate of the value of "production for own consumption by rural households" (table 3) is based on the assumed consumption of the "average" family, valued at urban prices, and multiplied by the number of families residing in the subsistence economy. Thus rural per capita incomes are by definition constant (except in so far as urban prices vary), even as population grows.

AGRICULTURE

The Land Apportionment Act of 1930 was the basis of land ownership and hence of systems of agriculture in Rhodesia until November 1969, when the Land Tenure Act, introduced by the Smith régime, replaced it. This new Act increased the area allotted to Europeans, assigning 44.95 million acres to them and 44.95 million to Africans. The 40 million acres comprising the African reserves retain traditional forms of land tenure, but in some 3.7 million acres Africans are able to buy land on freehold tenure. Maize is the staple crop in the African reserves, but millet and groundnuts are also important. According to a 1960 estimate Africans owned over two million cattle, traditionally the main form of wealth in African societies. Surplus cattle and crops are sold; together with the sales of the 7,000 or so farmers in the Native Purchase Areas, total sales amounted to R$7 million in 1968, or 5 per cent of gross sales from European agriculture. Cash sales from African agriculture in Rhodesia may also be compared with the level of exports of agricultural crops from, say, Malawi of R$20 million (excluding tea grown on European-owned estates).

European agriculture in Rhodesia is very highly developed and until 1965 produced a third of the country's total exports. In that year (the last for which data is available) 7,790 Europeans owned or leased farms, employing 2,696 non-Africans and 244,508 Africans. Total output was R$129 million (valued at producer prices) of which tobacco accounted for 50 per cent and livestock for 20 per cent. As a result of sanctions tobacco production has been cut back by a half from its former level of about 250 million pounds a year. Tobacco farmers have sought to diversify into cotton and cattle with varying success. After the declaration of independence Rhodesia also lost its quota in the Commonwealth Sugar Agreement; the sugar estates partially diversified into wheat but have also latterly regained some export markets, notably in Botswana.

African employment in European agriculture as a whole (including company-owned estates) fell from 274,000 in 1965 to 256,000 in 1968 but showed signs of strong recovery in 1969, reaching as high as 300,000 in June.

European and African agriculture do not by and large compete with each other. Africans are not permitted to grow flue-cured tobacco and they tend to be discouraged from offering their maize to the statutory Grain Marketing Board, which deducts a levy (used to finance public works in African areas) from its purchase price to African but not to European growers. Although the African-owned cattle herd is almost double the size of the European-owned herd, sales at R$4 million in 1965 are substantially less than European sales at R$15.4 million. Differences in quality are an important factor, and the social significance of cattle to Africans may also be relevant. However, exports of African-owned cattle from Botswana, which had a herd of 1.3 million in 1964 (compare the African herd in Rhodesia of two million) amounted to R$5.4 million in that year.

There are signs that agriculture is regaining its position as the economy's leading sector. The total value of output (including African sales) went up by R$35.4 million in 1971 or 15 per cent. The volume of deliveries of maize, cotton, and wheat increased by 82, 46, and 39 per cent respectively. The resulting maize surplus earned valuable foreign exchange from exports to Zambia (£4 million) and Malawi (£2.4 million) which had poor crops in 1970–71. The value of cattle slaughterings, dairy produce, and even tobacco sales also increased (by 23, 10 and 23 per cent), though the tobacco figure is artificial, the result of an increase in the support price paid by the Government. The 1972–73 budget again includes a very substantial provision (about R$20 million) for buying in the tobacco crop.

MINING

A wide variety of minerals is mined in Rhodesia, and mining exports in 1965 were worth R$65 million or about 20 per cent of total exports, though they were not, of course, very large in relation to the mining exports of South Africa and Zambia. In 1965 the most important mineral was asbestos, with exports worth R$21.6 million, followed by chrome (R$7.6 million), coal and coke (R$4.8 million), pig-iron (R$5 million), ferro-chrome (R$3.4 million), other iron and steel exports (R$4 million), copper (R$13 million) and gold (R$14.4 million in 1964, but stockpiled by the central bank in 1965). Lithium, limestone, and tin were also important, but total production of many other minerals known to be present in Rhodesia did not exceed R$2 million. The most important new development since 1965 has been the opening up by the Anglo-American Corporation of South Africa of nickel mining at Bindura, which could, it has been suggested, double the total value of Rhodesian mining exports. Anglo-American are expanding their phosphate operations at Dorowa, though here total production is absorbed by the domestic market.

Mineral exports have been less affected by sanctions than agricultural exports, though patterns of trade have certainly been altered. For example, chrome exports to the United States which were running at R$3.4 million in 1965 had to be redirected, allegedly to China! It has been claimed that mineral exports set new records in 1968–69, but detailed statistics have not been issued. However, both African and non-African employment in mining has increased since 1965 from 46,600 (all races) to 57,600 in 1972. The volume of mineral production is said to have increased by 9 per cent in 1971, but weak world metal prices during the year restricted the increase in value to only 3 per cent, giving a total value of R$101 million. The total value of output in 1972 is likely to be reduced as a result of the Wankie colliery disaster in June.

INDUSTRY

Rhodesia's wide range of mineral resources satisfies most domestic requirements of basic raw materials, with the exception of crude oil. However, the substantial coal reserves at Wankie could be used, as in South Africa, to produce oil, given the necessary investment. Despite sanctions this expedient has not had to be resorted to, since oil supplies have not been seriously impeded by the British blockade of Beira.

The resilience of the Rhodesian economy in the face of sanctions must be largely ascribed to the success of the country's manufacturers in turning their attention from exporting to Zambia, which has made strenuous efforts to reduce its imports from Rhodesia, to production for the domestic market. The import controls which were introduced shortly before the declaration of independence in order to protect the balance of payments also had the effect of providing protection to manufacturers seeking to alter the quality and the range of their output. The effects of sanctions on the pattern of manufacturing production are quite strikingly apparent in the data shown in the volume index of manufacturing production (table 4). The

industries adversely affected by sanctions were those which lost export markets without finding substitutes at home or abroad, like tobacco grading and packing, or which lost basic imports, like the oil refinery at Umtali, which was obliged to close down when the blockade of Beira prevented the landing of crude oil—hence output of chemical and petroleum products was no higher in 1969 than in 1965. Transport equipment and workshops, which includes vehicle assembly, is another industry which was directly affected by sanctions, in this case the British government's embargo on motor car assembly components, which forced the Ford and British Leyland plants to close down. By contrast foodstuffs, textiles and clothing, paper and printing, and wood and furniture, all added about twice as much to output in the five years 1964–69 as in the previous five years 1959–64.

The rapid growth in manufacturing output in the early years after UDI has been sustained, with an increase of 15 per cent in 1971. This is particularly impressive in that the more easily substitutable imports will long have been replaced by domestic production. The main increases came in textiles and non-metallic mineral products (fertilizers etc.). Manufactured exports are increasing again, especially to South Africa but also to Malawi. South Africa's 14 per cent devaluation at the end of 1971 may make it difficult for Rhodesia to repeat the 14 per cent increase in manufactured exports to the Republic in 1971—and this possibly explains the decision to let the Rhodesian dollar follow the Rand when the latter floated with sterling in June 1972.

More Europeans were employed in manufacturing than in any other sector in 1971, but manufacturing is third to agriculture and domestic service as a source of employment for Africans (*see* table 5). The relatively

[*continued p.* 664]

VOLUME INDEX OF MANUFACTURING PRODUCTION
(Average 1964 = 100)

Table 4

Period	Food-stuffs	Drink and Tobacco	Textiles	Clothing and Foot-wear	Wood and Furni-ture	Paper and Print-ing	Chemical and Petro-leum Products	Non-Metallic Mineral Products	Metals and Metal Products	Trans-port Equip-ment and Work-shops	Other Manu-factur-ing Groups	All Manu-factur-ing Groups
1961	86.9	79.6	95.3	95.7	72.3	89.8	77.7	120.1	73.3	78.2	110.0	84.0
1962	94.3	84.4	93.7	90.7	74.2	95.1	81.9	98.3	72.8	79.7	100.5	84.9
1963	95.6	85.0	94.5	106.5	82.7	93.4	91.6	95.4	85.1	98.0	96.4	84.9
1964	100.0	100.0	100.0	100.0	100.0	100.0	100.0	100.0	100.0	100.0	100.0	92.0
1965	110.1	95.2	114.1	105.4	111.8	112.8	118.9	103.2	109.1	111.1	82.5	100.0
1966	113.3	90.7	115.1	104.8	118.2	97.6	93.1	97.1	100.1	75.9	82.5	108.7
1967	116.2	90.6	142.0	122.9	121.7	103.5	98.1	110.6	117.8	75.9	78.9	98.6
1968	124.1	91.1	155.2	122.9	124.0	108.8	112.5	155.9	132.1	71.3	82.2	107.2
1969	133.4	97.1	227.8	131.1	133.0	119.1	125.8	165.2	151.0	83.8	90.4	117.8
1970	157.3	108.3	215.3	133.1	151.1	144.2	153.9	201.2	180.8	97.6	90.3	133.5
1971	175.3	114.7	254.5	144.9	161.3	155.3	166.1	238.2	203.1	99.4	111.4	150.2

Table 5

ANNUAL AVERAGE NUMBER OF EMPLOYEES BY INDUSTRIAL SECTOR

(A) AFRICANS

('000)

Period	Agriculture and Forestry	Mining and Quarrying	Manufacturing	Construction	Electricity and Water	Distribution, Restaurants and Hotels	Finance, Insurance and Real Estate	Transport and Communications	Services					Total Less Agriculture	Grand Total
									Public Administration	Education	Health	Private Domestic	Other		
Annual Average															
1958	253.0	57.1	70.6	65.2	5.2	42.1	1.4	14.3	18.6	15.5	4.3	90.9	13.8	399.0	652.0
1959	259.0	52.5	72.3	60.1	5.3	43.7	1.7	14.7	19.0	15.8	4.9	92.7	15.8	397.7	657.0
1960	270.0	52.3	73.1	58.1	5.6	44.3	1.6	15.2	19.3	16.3	5.5	94.6	15.8	401.2	671.0
1961	272.0	48.5	71.6	45.9	5.0	43.0	1.8	15.9	20.0	18.0	6.2	94.7	16.4	387.7	658.0
1962	272.0	44.1	64.2	37.5	4.7	42.5	1.8	15.7	20.4	18.9	6.0	94.7	15.6	373.7	646.0
1963	282.0	40.9	65.4	30.7	3.7	40.8	1.9	15.1	20.5	20.3	6.2	94.7	14.5	353.3	635.0
1964	293.0	41.6	69.2	29.5	3.7	41.5	2.1	14.6	17.7	21.2	6.0	93.7	16.1	353.3	646.0
1965	289.0	43.6	68.8	30.6	3.7	40.9	2.3	15.4	20.1	22.3	6.4	94.7	16.1	365.4	654.0
1966	272.0	45.7	75.0	31.8	3.8	38.3	2.5	15.2	21.0	22.2	6.6	95.7	18.0	370.4	642.0
1967	271.0	47.3	82.3	33.0	4.1	40.1	2.5	15.4	23.0	21.5	6.9	97.8	18.5	385.5	657.0
1968	282.0	48.4	90.6	38.5	4.1	42.9	2.6	15.5	24.3	22.2	7.2	102.0	18.5	407.7	690.0
1969	300.0	50.4	99.9	42.0	4.0	46.2	2.6	15.5	25.9	20.3	7.2	105.8	19.7	430.1	731.0
1970	290.0	55.0	102.0	44.4	4.2	45.7	2.8	16.6	27.1	19.9	7.5	108.4	22.8	454.1	743.0
1971	301.0	53.9	105.8	49.2	4.2	50.2	2.8	18.2	26.9	20.4	7.9	114.2	23.8	478.0	779.0

Table 5 (continued)

ANNUAL AVERAGE NUMBER OF EMPLOYEES BY INDUSTRIAL SECTOR

(B) NON-AFRICANS

Period	Agriculture and Forestry	Mining and Quarrying	Manufacturing	Construction	Electricity and Water	Distribution, Restaurants and Hotels	Finance, Insurance and Real Estate	Transport and Communications	Services				Total Less Agriculture	Grand Total
									Public Administration	Education	Health	Other		
Annual Average														
1958	3,700	2,920	13,910	10,140	1,440	19,370	5,650	8,100	7,890	3,890	2,270	6,280	81,860	85,600
1959	4,040	2,830	14,300	9,530	1,590	20,200	5,800	8,370	8,000	4,390	2,300	6,470	83,780	87,800
1960	4,250	2,790	14,490	9,390	1,480	20,000	5,630	8,650	8,070	4,700	2,310	6,690	85,100	89,400
1961	4,270	2,660	14,890	7,440	1,470	20,200	5,460	8,960	8,960	4,900	2,430	6,730	84,130	88,400
1962	4,360	2,670	15,020	6,850	1,230	19,740	5,410	9,380	9,070	5,180	2,400	7,330	84,280	88,600
1963	4,440	2,630	14,340	6,070	1,210	20,520	5,630	9,150	9,410	5,400	2,610	6,950	83,920	88,400
1964	4,390	2,740	14,290	5,680	1,200	20,050	5,690	8,900	8,980	5,480	2,660	7,090	82,700	87,100
1965	4,360	2,950	15,320	5,980	1,220	19,630	5,740	9,440	9,600	5,630	2,800	7,170	85,140	89,500
1966	4,370	3,140	15,880	6,210	1,310	17,680	5,780	9,780	10,380	5,740	2,860	7,570	85,720	90,100
1967	4,090	3,230	17,070	6,370	1,380	18,670	5,930	9,950	10,760	5,790	2,920	8,000	87,630	91,700
1968	4,060	3,340	17,680	6,980	1,410	19,340	6,380	9,790	11,010	5,930	3,010	8,340	91,490	95,600
1969	4,540	3,450	18,690	7,480	1,440	19,670	6,550	9,820	11,330	6,120	3,040	8,870	94,920	99,500
1970	4,700	3,740	19,340	7,880	1,440	20,180	6,780	10,040	11,530	6,580	3,180	9,660	99,000	103,700
1971	4,490	3,670	20,190	8,310	1,590	20,680	7,070	10,320	12,170	6,600	3,480	9,850	103,620	108,100

Table 6
BALANCE OF PAYMENTS: CURRENT TRANSACTIONS
(R$ million)

Item	1970			1971		
	Receipts	Payments	Net Receipts	Receipts	Payments	Net Receipts
Goods	282.3	249.6	32.7	299.7	298.3	1.4
Imports/Exports . . .	256.3	234.9	21.4	270.8	282.4	−11.6
Re-Exports	6.1	—	6.1	6.5	—	6.5
Non-Monetary Gold, net . .	11.7	—	11.7	12.8	—	12.8
Internal Freight to Border . .	8.6	15.1	− 6.5	8.0	16 5	− 8.5
Timing and Coverage Adjustments .	−0.4	0.4	−	1.6	− 0 6	2.2
Services	49.3	62.2	−12.9	56.4	76 6	−20.3
External Freight and Insurance . .	—	17.6	−17.6	—	24 1	−24.1
Fares	6.0	6.2	− 0.2	6.2	6.8	− 0.6
Transit Freight . . .	14.2	—	14.2	16.1	—	16.1
Other Transportation . . .	6.4	2.2	4.3	7.9	4.3	3.6
Foreign Travel . . .	17.4	23.9	− 6.6	20.3	23 9	− 3.6
Government, n.e.s. . . .	0.3	0.7	− 0.4	0.3	0 8	− 0.4
Other	5.1	11.7	− 6.6	5.5	16.8	−11.3
Investment Income . . .	11.9	35.6	−23.7	18.4	38 5	−20.1
Government	—	1.0	− 1.0	—	1.5	− 1.5
Public Authorities . . .	3.4	5.9	− 2.5	3.9	2.1	1.8
Corporate Bodies . . .	6.1	28.7	−22.6	11.6	35.0	−23.4
Personal Sector . . .	2.4	—	2.4	2.9	—	2.9
Transfers	11.7	15.5	− 3.8	13.9	17.8	− 4.0
Migrants' Funds . . .	3.2	1.9	1.3	3.0	2.4	0.6
Personal Remittances . . .	2.8	3.1	− 0.4	2.7	3.9	− 1.2
Government	—	0.1	− 0.1	—	—	—
Grants and Donations to Institutions .	1.4	—	1.4	2.7	0.4	2.3
Remittances of Migrant Workers . .	—	0.5	− 0.5	—	0 5	− 0.5
Pensions	2.0	4.1	− 2.1	2.8	3.1	− 0.4
Other	2.3	5.7	− 3.4	2.7	7.6	− 4.8
Total Current Transactions . .	355.2	362.9	− 7.7	388.4	431.3	−42.9

Table 7
BALANCE OF PAYMENTS: CAPITAL ACCOUNT
(R$ million)

Item	1970			1971		
	Net Increase in Liabilities	Net Increase in Assets	Net Inflow of Capital	Net Increase in Liabilities	Net Increase in Assets	Net Inflow of Capital
Net Balance on Current Account . .	355.2	362.9	−7.7	388.4	431.3	−42.9
Capital Transactions . . .	9.0	0.5	8.5	24.7	0.3	24.3
Government	1.7	0.2	1.5	− 4.8	0.2	− 5.0
Public Authorities . . .	5.1	0.3	4.8	− 2.4	0.4	− 2.8
Corporate Bodies . . .	3.4	—	3.4	25.4	—	25.4
Other Private Capital Transactions .	−1.3	—	−1.3	− 1.6	—	− 1.6
Open Market Investments . .	0.1	−0.1	0.1	8.0	− 0.3	8.3
Total Current and Capital Transactions	364.2	363.4	0.8	413.0	431.6	−18.6

Table 8

ANNUAL AVERAGE EARNINGS

(A) AFRICAN EMPLOYEES

(R$)

| PERIOD | AGRICULTURE AND FORESTRY* | MINING AND QUARRYING | MANUFACTURING | CONSTRUCTION | ELECTRICITY AND WATER SERVICES | WHOLESALE AND RETAIL TRADE | BANKING, INSURANCE AND FINANCE | TRANSPORT AND COMMUNICATIONS | GOVERNMENT ADMINISTRATION | SERVICES | | | | TOTAL* |
										Education	Health	Private Domestic	Other	
1958	104	212	216	218	184	216	244	296	232	258	220	176	192	169
1959	104	222	230	218	234	228	258	318	240	292	212	182	208	175
1960	106	230	250	212	242	238	278	332	248	294	220	188	224	179
1961	108	244	284	236	294	256	304	386	274	424	248	196	260	195
1962	111	248	328	244	312	316	368	418	312	438	300	204	270	210
1963	122	264	366	298	336	324	430	518	324	462	352	212	274	224
1964	123	288	396	328	360	352	486	574	338	468	362	220	276	235
1965	123	298	416	352	368	376	524	618	344	486	438	224	284	246
1966	124	300	424	348	386	388	580	624	360	502	486	226	286	255
1967	122	308	432	348	396	412	590	638	364	516	496	234	316	262
1968	122	322	444	380	408	432	620	636	376	542	532	242	340	272
1969	122	334	476	371	408	436	656	638	408	544	564	244	390	280
1970	126	334	478	428	448	454	714	626	409	590	579	256	430	298
1971	124	353	485	478	486	480	744	717	476	659	619	260	452	314

* Amended.

Table 8 (continued)

ANNUAL AVERAGE EARNINGS

(B) EUROPEAN, ASIAN AND COLOURED EMPLOYEES

(R$)

| PERIOD | AGRICULTURE AND FORESTRY | MINING AND QUARRYING | MANUFACTURING | CONSTRUCTION | ELECTRICITY AND WATER SERVICES | WHOLESALE AND RETAIL TRADE | BANKING, INSURANCE AND FINANCE | TRANSPORT AND COMMUNICATIONS | GOVERNMENT ADMINISTRATION | SERVICES | | | TOTAL |
										Education	Health	Other	
1958	1,950	2,822	2,352	2,542	2,434	1,834	2,224	2,450	2,236	2,130	1,578	1,818	2,182
1959	2,250	2,988	2,354	2,466	2,420	1,868	2,278	2,490	2,270	2,102	1,544	1,840	2,206
1960	2,312	3,052	2,424	2,582	2,588	1,890	2,338	2,498	2,434	2,204	1,624	1,888	2,268
1961	2,300	3,106	2,528	2,572	2,708	1,986	2,342	2,466	2,458	2,226	1,640	1,894	2,308
1962	2,332	3,194	2,594	2,578	2,782	2,026	2,430	2,604	2,512	2,274	1,650	1,930	2,372
1963	2,512	3,254	2,714	2,722	3,012	2,032	2,452	2,726	2,618	2,292	1,908	1,952	2,438
1964	2,634	3,324	2,788	2,772	3,174	2,112	2,584	2,844	2,574	2,210	1,862	1,918	2,488
1965	2,760	3,438	2,872	2,902	3,220	2,208	2,584	2,912	2,684	2,258	1,904	1,922	2,576
1966	2,548	3,486	2,956	2,988	3,322	2,314	2,654	3,136	2,770	2,314	2,048	1,912	2,664
1967	2,602	3,490	3,040	2,918	3,390	2,380	2,790	3,210	2,780	2,384	2,038	1,952	2,722
1968	2,570	3,640	3,164	3,106	3,584	2,500	2,958	3,212	2,920	2,546	2,166	2,084	2,836
1969	2,666	4,224	3,332	3,193	3,672	2,534	3,110	3,394	3,082	2,700	2,314	2,180	2,971
1970	2,535	4,456	3,606	3,273	3,840	2,654	3,280	3,600	3,129	2,709	2,388	2,442	3,108
1971	2,736	4,810	3,780	3,720	4,368	2,955	3,326	3,886	3,386	3,114	2,660	2,650	3,375

continued from p. 660]
low ratio of African to European employees in manufacturing (5 to 1, compared with 64 to 1 in agriculture) sums up a good deal of Rhodesian political economy. Africans are mainly engaged in unskilled labour, and there are neither training facilities nor apprenticeship opportunities to enable them to aspire to jobs which are in any case reserved for Europeans. Nevertheless, African employment in manufacturing expanded sufficiently after 1965 to offset most of the fall in employment in agriculture.

The most important new development in Rhodesian industry is the construction of a nitrogenous fertilizer plant at Que Que (centre of the iron and steel industry and half-way between the main industrial centres of Salisbury and Bulawayo). When completed, the plant will be useful both in saving foreign exchange and in providing cheaply an input which has become particularly important with the need for Rhodesian agriculture to diversify out of tobacco into crops less suited to the sandy soils on which tobacco did so well.

BALANCE OF PAYMENTS

Rhodesia's balance of payments in 1970 and 1971 South Africa amounted to only R$55 million, so it seems on current account of R$30 million in 1965 to a deficit of R$43 million in 1971 would have been cause for alarm to the authorities in Rhodesia had it not been for the substantial inflow of private capital denoted by the increase of R$25 million in corporate bodies' liabilities in 1971.

The import controls which were imposed in 1965 remain in force and have attracted adverse comment from some South African manufacturers who find themselves facing competition from Rhodesian concerns in their own domestic market. Rhodesian traders also find the controls irksome, which is not surprising in the context of the decline in the total value of exports and imports from R$525 million in 1965 to R$382 million in 1968, a fall of 27 per cent. But the controls are unlikely to be lifted in the near future whilst the adverse balance of trade persists, and although exports were at much the same level in 1967 and 1968 as in 1966, the first year of sanctions, imports were allowed to rise from R$169 in 1966 to R$207 in 1968 to permit the expansion of industries using imported capital equipment.

The destination and origin of Rhodesian exports and imports are not published, but it is obvious that South Africa has become the clearing house for Rhodesia's foreign trade. South African statistics show a substantial increase in that country's exports to the rest of Africa after 1965. Allowing for South Africa's known exports and re-exports to Zambia, Malawi, Angola and Mozambique (the only countries which admit to trading with South Africa), there remain R$166 million worth of exports to Rhodesia and other shy importers. In 1965 Rhodesia's imports from South Africa amounted to only R$55 million, so it seems clear that South Africa exports herself or re-exports up to R$100 million or so of goods which up to 1965 were consigned direct to Rhodesia by other countries.

Rhodesia's balance of payments showed the biggest overall deficit since UDI in 1971, no less than R$18.6 million, but this was in the compass of reserves which had risen by almost the same amount over the previous two years. Nevertheless a deficit of this size increases surprise at Rhodesia's decision not to devalue in December 1971. Notionally the Rhodesian dollar was revalued by 8.57 per cent against the U.S.$ and by 14 per cent against the Rand. This apparent foolhardiness after so many years of sanctions is readily explained by the very fact of sanctions, which constitute the main constraint on Rhodesian exports rather than the exchange value of the currency. Even more than for most developing countries the prices of Rhodesia's main exports are beyond its control. Equally devaluation would be irrelevant as a device to control imports when these are already subject to stringent direct controls. One side-effect of the decision not to devalue is a fall in the real income of residents living off income derived from South Africa or England.

The deficit on the current account of the balance of payments of R$42.9 million in 1971 arose from the continued faster growth of imports than of exports and from the deficit on invisibles. It has been estimated (by Robin Adams in *The Banker*, July 1972) that payments to the sanctions-breaking middle-men may be as much as £25 million a year and this could partly explain the rising deficit on invisibles.

(*See* tables 6 and 7.)

SANCTIONS AND THE STANDARD OF LIVING

It is often suggested that sanctions have been counter-productive, making white Rhodesians more intransigent, whilst causing hardship among the African population whose interests the United Nations has been attempting to defend. It is impossible to say what would have happened if sanctions had not been imposed, but the data—admittedly aggregative—in tables 5 and 8 suggests that Africans are certainly not worse off than they were in 1965, since employment and average earnings (allowing for price increases) have if anything risen faster since sanctions were imposed in 1966 than in the first half of the decade. Similarly, white Rhodesians have also been able to maintain their real standard of living since 1965, average earnings actually rising by 35 per cent between 1965 and 1971 while the consumer price index went up by only 18 per cent. In each case an ending of sanctions would probably bring about faster increases in average real incomes than the present annual rate of about 2 per cent. It is of course true that the consumer price index does not adequately reflect changes in the quality or the range of goods available. However visitors to Rhodesia always return with tales of shops well stocked with imported luxury goods. These goods are the result of the so-called NCI (no currency involved) or barter deals which are exempt from import controls. But although living standards have been maintained in the face of sanctions, the real economic issue facing Rhodesia is the aspiration of the African population for the opportunity to attain a quite different life style from the best they can hope for under white rule.

STATISTICAL SURVEY

AREA AND POPULATION

AREA (sq. miles)	POPULATION (June 1972) (est.)			
	TOTAL	AFRICANS	EUROPEANS	OTHERS
150,820	5,690,000	5,400,000	262,000	27,300

CHIEF TOWNS (Dec. 1971 est.)

Salisbury (capital) .	463,000		Gatooma . . .	24,000
Bulawayo . .	284,000		Shabani . . .	17,000
Umtali . . .	51,000		Sinoia . . .	15,000
Gwelo . . .	52,000		Marandellas . .	11,000
Que Que . . .	38,000		Fort Victoria . .	13,000
Wankie . . .	22,000		Redcliff . . .	10,000

LAND DISTRIBUTION
(1971 —'000 acres)

European Area:	
Forest Land	1,823
Parks and Wild Life Land . . .	4,431
General Land	38,671
Specially Designated Land . .	23
Total European Area . . .	44,948
African Area:	
Forest Land	439
Parks and Wild Life Land . . .	631
Purchase Land	3,669
Tribal Trust Land	39,910
Specially Designated Land . .	300
Total African Area . . .	44,949
National Area	6,618
TOTAL	96,515

MIGRATION

	EUROPEANS*		ASIANS AND COLOUREDS*		NON-INDIGENOUS AFRICAN ADULT MALES†	
	Immigrants	Emigrants	Immigrants	Emigrants	Immigrants	Emigrants
1962 . . .	6,062	9,940	134	n.a.	53,820	65,200
1963 . . .	5,093	14,320	206	110	45,220	51,300
1964 . . .	7,000	15,410	130	228	40,370	48,600
1965 . . .	11,128	7,670	178	172	26,920	30,300
1966 . . .	6,418	8,510	131	160	17,430	33,630
1967 . . .	9,618	6,300	201	118	16,280	20,960
1968 . . .	11,864	5,650	149	149	19,350	21,910
1969 . . .	10,929	5,890	146	113	15,880	18,020
1970 . . .	12,227	5,890	118	128	13,000	22,270
1971 . . .	14,743	5,340	138	81	10,500	20,250

* Exclusive of migration with Malawi and Zambia during the years 1961–63.

† Figures for years prior to 1965 include some juvenile males.

EMPLOYMENT

	1969		1970		1971	
	Africans	Others	Africans	Others	Africans	Others
Agriculture, Forestry and Fishing . .	300,500	4,540	290,500	4,590	303,400	4,490
Mining and Quarrying . . .	50,400	3,450	53,300	3,740	53,900	3,670
Manufacturing . . .	90,600	17,660	99,900	18,690	105,800	20,190
Building and Construction . .	42,000	7,480	44,400	7,880	49,200	8,310
Electricity and Water . .	4,000	1,410	4,200	1,440	4,200	1,590
Distribution, Restaurants and Hotels	46,200	19,340	45,700	19,670	50,200	20,680
Finance, Insurance and Real Estate	2,600	6,380	2,800	6,550	2,800	7,070
Transport and Communications .	15,500	9,820	16,600	10,040	18,200	10,020
Public Administration . . .	25,900	11,330	27,100	11,530	26,900	12,170
Education	20,300	6,120	19,900	6,580	20,400	6,600
Health	7,200	3,040	7,500	3,180	7,900	3,480
Private Domestic Service . .	105,800	} 8,870	108,400	} 9,660	114,200	} 9,850
Other Services	19,700		22,800		23,800	
TOTAL (rounded) . .	731,000	99,500	743,000	103,600	781,000	108,100

AGRICULTURE

SALES OF PRINCIPAL CROPS AND LIVESTOCK
(R$ million)

	1968	1969	1970	1971
European Production . .	93.5	122.9	117.9	148.2
African Production . .	5.5	11.1	8.3	13.1
TOTAL . .	98.9	134.0	126.3	161.3

AGRICULTURAL OUTPUT
(R$ million)

EUROPEAN PRODUCTION

	1967	1968	1969	1970	1971
Gross Sales	127.9	109.4	140.4	140.1	173.3
Farm Retentions . . .	17.8	24.0	26.8	24.4	24.7
TOTAL VALUE . .	145.7	133.4	167.2	164.5	198.0

AFRICAN PRODUCTION

	1967	1968	1969	1970	1971
Sales to Marketing Authorities .	11.9	6.7	13.5	10.8	16.0
Approximate Consumption by Rural Households . . .	49.3	48.3	50.1	56.7	55.5
TOTAL . . .	61.2	55.0	63.6	67.5	71.5

EUROPEAN-OWNED LIVESTOCK

	1968	1969	1970	1971
Cattle	2,034,746	2,268,877	2,514,173	2,708,997
Sheep	315,377	362,876	356,139	327,013
Pigs	82,800	80,635	91,519	79,842
Equines	8,219	8,117	8,193	8,151
Goats	32,285	35,467	38,976	35,027

ELECTRICITY CONSUMPTION
(million kWh.)

	1968	1969	1970	1971
Agriculture and Forestry . .	183.2	182.1	233.7	256.3
Mining and Quarrying .	503.1	602.0	704.6	769.9
Manufacturing Industries . .	1,059.6	1,219.0	1,440.5	1,544.1
Domestic Consumers .	531.0	550.7	599.5	636.2
Others	318.8	341.4	388.4	420.1
TOTAL . . .	2,595.7	2,895.2	3,366.7	3,626.6

MINERAL PRODUCTION
(R$ '000)

	1963	1964	1965
Gold . . .	14,202	14,456	13,790
Asbestos . .	11,994	13,696	17,050
Chrome Ore . .	3,790	4,438	5,248
Coal . . .	6,156	6,864	7,744
Copper . . .	6,468	8,312	12,566
TOTAL (incl. others) .	47,470	53,508	64,000

1966 total: 65,200; 1967 total: 66,800; 1968 total: 67,400;
1969 total: 87,000; 1970 total: 98,700; 1971 total: 101,200.

(tons)

	1963	1964	1965
Gold ('000 fine oz,) .	566	574	550
Asbestos . .	142,255	153,451	176,151
Chrome Ore . .	412,394	493,371	645,500
Coal . . .	3,020,889	3,351,000	3,868,385
Copper . . .	18,488	18,341	19,819

INDUSTRY
(R$'000)

	1968*	1969*	1970*
Mining and Quarrying	84,728	105,730	122,888
Meat Industry	32,470	34,365	39,790
Grain Mill Products	35,081	35,618	46,062
Bakery Products	14,249	15,552	17,483
Dairy and Other Food Products	36,154	38,193	41,736
Alcoholic Beverages	15,398	17,455	20,115
Soft Drinks	6,059	6,384	7,340
Tobacco Manufacturing	13,620	16,621	16,816
Clothing and Footwear	34,897	38,537	45,330
Other Textiles	42,723	57,924	57,544
Wood Industries, except Furniture	9,442	11,097	13,583
Furniture, except Metal	7,186	8,326	10,562
Pulp, Paper and Board	11,713	13,366	15,564
Printing and Publishing	13,509	15,793	18,523
Fertilizers and Pesticides	25,887	32,826	37,559
Soap Preparations and Pharmaceuticals	15,665	16,317	19,180
Other Chemical Products, including Plastic and Rubber	24,143	27,048	31,432
Cement, Bricks and other Non-Metal Products	17,380	20,003	24,592
Metal Industries, except Machinery	58,943	75,164	102,814
Machinery, including Electrical	23,945	28,933	37,332
Transport and Equipment	28,085	35,757	38,675
Other Industries	4,445	5,481	6,272
TOTAL MANUFACTURING INDUSTRIES	470,996	550,760	648,304
Electricity Generation and Distribution	45,059	48,813	54,530
Water Supply	6,943	6,412	7,270
TOTAL ALL INDUSTRIES	607,726	711,715	832,992

* Year ending June 30th.

FINANCE
100 cents = 1 Rhodesian dollar.

Coins: bronze ½c., 1c.; cupronickel 2½c., 5c., 10c., 20c., 25c.

Notes: R$1, R$2, R$10.

Unofficial exchange rates (December 1972): £1 sterling = R$1.677; U.S. $1 = 71.43 Rhodesian c.

R$100 = £59.63 = U.S. $140.00.

BUDGET
(R$'000)

	1967–68	1968–69	1969–70	1970–71	1971–72 (estimates)
Revenue	165,212	184,065	203,952	213,440	229,060
Expenditure	168,106	187,972	201,895	213,832	236,495
Surplus or Deficit	−2,894	−3,907	2,057	−392	−7,435

BUDGET ESTIMATES
(1970–71—R$'000)

REVENUE		EXPENDITURE	
Basic Tax on Income or Profits . . .	98,250	Agriculture (incl. Research and Specialist Services)	24,234
Customs and Excise	42,120	Public Works	7,515
Sales Tax	32,250	Treasury (Supply Services) . . .	4,079
Betting Tax	450	Pensions (mainly Civil and Defence) . .	8,807
Stamp Duties and Fees	4,100	British S.A. Police	16,886
Business Licences	1,450	Conservation and Extension . . .	2,068
Education Fees	3,715	Internal Affairs	9,628
Health Services	2,050	Labour and Social Welfare . . .	2,435
Aviation and Landing Fees . . .	585	Health	18,475
Agricultural Services	470	Roads and Road Traffic . . .	7,959
Interest, etc.	24,800	Civil Aviation	1,731
Pension Contributions of Government Employees	6,400	Education (European, Coloured and Asian) .	18,732
Rent of Government property . . .	1,750	Mines and Lands, National Parks, etc. .	5,631
Estate Duties	1,350	Water Development	2,107
Share of Profits: Reserve Bank of Rhodesia .	1,300	African Education	21,400
Mining Fees and Royalties . . .	1,300	Service of Debt	32,424
Other Revenue	6,720	Veterinary Services	2,828
		Army, Air Force	19,738
		Local Government and Housing . .	1,197
		Other Expenditure	28,621
TOTAL	229,060	TOTAL	236,495

NATIONAL ACCOUNTS
(million R$)

	1969	1970	1971*
GROSS DOMESTIC PRODUCT (factor cost) . .	892.6	957.7	1,088.3
of which:			
Wages and salaries	500.6	542.8	609.0
Income from unincorporated enterprise .	141.5	144.7	159.0
Gross operating profits . . .	229.9	246.2	294.3
Income from property . . .	20.6	23.9	26.1
Income from abroad	−16.9	−18.8	n.a.
GROSS NATIONAL INCOME . . .	851.1	886.6	n.a.
Indirect taxes *less* subsidies . .	65.1	81.0	94.8
GROSS NATIONAL PRODUCT (market prices) .	940.8	1,019.2	1,163.0
Balance of imports and exports of goods and services	24.8	6.7	n.a.
Private consumption	566.9	632.5	n.a.
African rural household consumption .	60.2	63.8	n.a.
Government current expenditure . .	114.3	121.7	n.a.
Gross fixed capital formation . .	154.3	169.6	n.a.
Increase in stocks	37.2	44.5	n.a.

* Provisional.

INDUSTRIAL ORIGIN OF THE GROSS DOMESTIC PRODUCT
(percentage distribution)

	1965	1969	1970	1971*
Agriculture	18.6	18.2	16.9	16.7
Mining	7.0	7.0	6.6	5.9
Manufacturing	20.0	20.3	22.6	23.2
Construction	4.7	6.5	6.5	6.6
Electricity and Water . . .	3.1	3.7	3.6	3.3
Transport and Communications .	8.6	7.7	6.8	7.0
Wholesale and Retail Trade . .	14.6	11.9	11.9	12.7
Banking, Insurance, Real Estate .	3.6	4.7	5.0	4.8
Public Administration, Defence, Health and Education	10.6	10.8	10.8	10.9
Services	9.2	9.2	9.3	8.9
Gross Domestic Product (i) %	100.0	100.0	100.0	100.0
(factor cost) (ii) R$ million .	687.0	893.0	958.0	1,088.0

* Provisional.

COMPOSITION OF GROSS DOMESTIC EXPENDITURE 1970

	R$ MILLION	%
Private Consumption (Money Economy) .	632.5	61.3
African Rural Household Consumption . .	63.8	6.2
Government Current Expenditure . . .	121.7	11.8
Gross Fixed Capital Formation . .	169.6	16.4
of which:		
Land Improvement	4.5	
Mine Development	3.8	
Building and Works . . .	97.5	
Plant, Machinery, etc. . . .	63.8	
Net Increase in Stocks	44.5	4.3
Gross Domestic Expenditure . .	1,032.0	100.0
Net Exports of Goods and Services .	6.7	
Gross Domestic Product at market prices .	1,038.7	

Note: "African rural household consumption" is an estimate of the market value of production for own consumption in the subsistence economy.

BALANCE OF PAYMENTS: CURRENT TRANSACTIONS
(R$ million)

Item	1970			1971*		
	Receipts	Payments	Net Receipts	Receipts	Payments	Net Receipts
Goods	273.3	249.6	23.7	299.7	298.3	1.4
Imports/Exports . . .	247.5	234.9	12.6	270.8	282.4	−11.6
Re-Exports	6.1	—	6.1	6.5	—	6.5
Non-Monetary Gold, net . .	11.7	—	11.7	12.8	—	12.8
Internal Freight to Border . .	8.6	15.1	− 6.5	8.0	16.5	− 8.5
Timing and Coverage Adjustments .	−0.6	−0.4	− 0.2	1.6	− 0.6	2.2
Services	50.2	67.2	−17.0	56.4	76.6	−20.3
External Freight and Insurance .	—	19.1	−19.1	—	24.1	−24.1
Fares	6.0	6.2	− 0.2	6.2	6.8	− 0.6
Transit Freight	14.2	—	14.2	16.1	—	16.1
Other Transportation . . .	6.9	2.2	4.7	7.9	4.3	3.6
Foreign Travel	17.4	23.9	− 6.6	20.3	23.9	− 3.6
Government, n.e.s. . . .	0.3	0.7	− 0.4	0.3	0.8	− 0.4
Other	5.5	15.1	− 9.6	5.5	16.8	−11.3
Investment Income . . .	16.6	35.4	−18.8	18.4	38.5	−20.1
Government	—	0.6	− 0.6	—	1.5	− 1.5
Public Enterprises . . .	3.3	1.8	1.6	3.9	2.1	1.8
Companies	10.5	33.0	−22.5	11.6	35.0	−23.4
Personal Sector . . .	2.7	—	2.7	2.9	—	2.9
Transfers	13.0	15.6	− 2.6	13.9	17.8	− 4.0
Migrants' Funds . . .	3.2	1.9	1.3	3.0	2.4	0.6
Personal Remittances . . .	2.8	3.1	− 0.4	2.7	3.9	− 1.2
Government	—	0.1	− 0.1	—	—	—
Grants and Donations to Institutions .	2.7	0.2	2.6	2.7	0.4	2.3
Remittances of Migrants Workers .	—	0.5	− 0.5	—	0.5	− 0.5
Pensions	2.0	4.1	− 2.1	2.8	3.1	− 0.4
Other	2.3	5.7	− 3.4	2.7	7.6	− 4.8
Total Current Transactions . .	353.0	367.8	−14.8	388.4	431.3	−42.9

* Provisional.

BALANCE OF PAYMENTS: CAPITAL ACCOUNT
(R$ million)

Item	1970			1971*		
	Net Increase in Liabilities	Net Increase in Assets	Net Inflow of Capital	Net Increase in Liabilities	Net Increase in Assets	Net Inflow of Capital
Net Balance on Current Account . .	353.0	367.8	−14.8	388.4	431.3	−42.9
Capital Transactions . . .	18.7	1.0	17.7	24.7	0.3	24.3
Government	1.5	0.2	1.3	− 4.8	0.2	− 5.0
Public Enterprises . . .	−2.3	0.3	− 2.7	− 2.4	0.4	− 2.8
Companies	15.0	1.5	13.5	25.4	—	25.4
Other Private Capital Transactions .	−1.3	—	− 1.3	− 1.6	—	− 1.6
Open Market Investments . .	5.8	−1.0	6.9	8.0	− 0.3	8.3
Total Current and Capital Transactions	371.7	368.8	2.9	413.0	431.6	−18.6

* Provisional.

GOLD RESERVES OF
RESERVE BANK OF RHODESIA
(R$'ooo—Nov. 1965)*

Gold	7,280	
Foreign Assets	36,738	
TOTAL	44,018	

*Latest available figure.

CURRENCY IN CIRCULATION
(million R$—June 1970)

	NOTES	COIN	TOTAL
In Public Circulation . .	29.7	3.7	33.4

December 1971 total: R$ 37.9m.

EXTERNAL TRADE
(million R$)

	1968	1969	1970	1971
Imports	207.0	199.4	234.9	282.4
Exports and Re-exports, excl. gold .	175.9	219.0	253.6	277.2

No detailed official trade figures have been published since 1965.

COMMODITIES
(R$'ooo)

IMPORTS	1964	1965	EXPORTS	1964	1965
Food	19,400	18,688	Food	23,930	29,308
Beverages and Tobacco .	7,470	6,960	Fresh and Frozen Meat .	5,984	8,456
Tobacco . . .	5,548	5,270	Canned Meat and Meat **Pre-**		
Crude Materials, inedible . .	10,934	9,780	parations . . .	4,100	5,046
Mineral Fuels and Lubricants .	12,374	11,822	Sugar	6,970	6,964
Petroleum Products .	11,538	11,056	Beverages and Tobacco .	83,958	99,610
Animal and Vegetable Oils .	1,112	2,606	Tobacco . . .	78,444	93,936
Chemicals . . .	23,032	26,900	Crude Materials, inedible . .	33,626	38,784
Fertilizer . .	6,300	8,698	Asbestos Fibre . .	20,030	21,522
Machinery and Transport .	62,478	76,020	Chrome Ore . .	5,000	7,620
Machinery, except Electrical .	28,034	31,864	Mineral Fuels and Lubricants .	12,872	18,978
Railway Engines and Vehicles.	3,224	4,676	Coal . . .	3,314	4,446
Motor Vehicles and Spares .	17,466	24,288	Animal and Vegetable Oils .	700	632
Miscellaneous Items . .	79,674	86,802	Chemicals . . .	9,086	9,152
Paper and Board . .	5,144	5,492	Machinery and Transport .	12,686	17,168
Textiles . . .	16,612	19,916	Miscellaneous Items . .	59,784	71,278
Iron and Steel . .	10,490	10,302	Clothing . . .	10,614	10,834
			Refined Copper . .	7,104	12,112
			Pig Iron . . .	5,100	4,946

COUNTRIES (R$'ooo)

COMMONWEALTH COUNTRY		1964		1965	
		IMPORTS	DOMESTIC EXPORTS	IMPORTS	DOMESTIC EXPORTS
Australia		4,762	3,174	5,230	2,312
Botswana		658	2,108	144	3,182
Canada		3,130	2,926	3,936	1,644
Hong Kong		1,048	1,042	1,086	2,294
India		1,780	2,034	2,646	1,676
Malawi		3,258	11,040	2,794	15,476
Malaya		1,110	2,118	1,008	3,128
United Kingdom		65,610	60,880	72,710	62,302
Zambia		10,376	60,468	8,640	72,180
Other Commonwealth		3,678	5,496	3,842	6,276
TOTAL COMMONWEALTH		95,410	151,286	102,036	170,470

FOREIGN COUNTRY		1964		1965	
		IMPORTS	DOMESTIC EXPORTS	IMPORTS	DOMESTIC EXPORTS
Belgium		1,826	5,148	4,560	3,190
France		3,308	1,466	4,008	1,584
German Federal Republic		8,308	15,820	9,730	25,616
Iran		6,462	382	7,568	102
Italy		4,034	2,610	5,062	4,502
Japan		8,774	11,120	13,212	14,800
Mozambique		2,750	1,374	2,742	1,898
Netherlands		4,804	4,536	5,912	7,450
South Africa		52,726	17,064	54,922	25,590
Sweden		2,162	1,126	3,046	1,256
Switzerland		1,238	2,756	1,432	3,598
United States of America		14,712	7,934	16,394	6,988
Zaire		52	2,984	82	3,468
Other Foreign		9,048	11,006	8,026	14,346
TOTAL FOREIGN		120,204	85,326	136,696	114,388
Parcel Post		860	30	846	52
TOTAL ALL COUNTRIES . . . . . (including Commonwealth)		216,474	236,642	239,578	284,910
Gold Bullion, Concentrates, etc.		56	14,228	62	13,648

TOURISM

TOTAL NUMBER OF TOURIST ARRIVALS

1966	.	.	286,995
1967	.	.	297,292
1968	.	.	319,224
1969	.	.	355,490
1970	.	.	364,070
1971	.	.	393,910

TRANSPORT

RAIL TRAFFIC

RHODESIA RAILWAYS (including operations in Botswana)

	1969–70*	1970–71*	1971–72†
Total Number of Passengers ('000) .	2,814	2,782	2,517
Net Metric Tons ('000) .	11,719	11,686	10,309
Gross Ton-Kilometres (million) .	14,411	14,283	12,667
Net Ton-Kilometres (million) .	6,500	6,293	5,637
Financial Statistics:			
Gross Revenue (R$'000) .	65,512	65,295	57,464
Operating Expenditure (R$'000) .	58,113	60,916	53,005
Net Operating Revenue (R$'000) .	7,399	4,379	4,459

* Year ending June 30th.   † Year ending April 30th.

ROAD TRAFFIC
(est.)

	1966*
Passenger .	113,123
Commercial .	28,979
Motor Cycles and Scooters .	8,363
Others (excluding Caravans and Trailers).	9,252

* May.

AIR TRAFFIC

AIR RHODESIA

	KILOMETRES FLOWN		LOAD TON-KILOMETRES FLOWN		PASSENGERS CARRIED '000
	Aircraft '000	Passenger '000	Passenger '000	Cargo and Mail '000	
Year ending June 30th, 1969 .	4,727	134,744	11,278	970.1	228.9
Year ending June 30th, 1970 .	5,151	155,836	12,988	983.1	263.4
Year ending June 30th, 1971 .	5,668	175,528	14,597	959.7	300.3
Year ending June 30th, 1972 .	6,073	196,320	16,288	973.4	344.3

COMMUNICATIONS MEDIA

	1970*	1971†	1972†
Telephones .	131,572	136,165	146,281
Radio Licences .	30,795	31,282	32,025
Concessionary Radio Licences .	127,519	130,071	139,470
Combined Radio and Television Licences .	48,072	51,075	57,947
Daily Newspapers .	2	2	2

* December.   † June.

EDUCATION

AFRICAN EDUCATION

	Number of Schools		Number of Pupils		Number of Teachers	
	1971	1972	1971	1972	1971	1972
Primary	3,518	3,516	655,629	715,835	16,728	17,230
Secondary	131	140	28,146	29,170	1,297	1,418
Vocational/Technical/Teacher-Training	31	34	2,909	3,106	139	173
Agricultural College . .	1	1	80	80	13	14
Evening and Part-time Schools .	47	33	2,652	1,732	n.a.	n.a.
Special (Physically Handicapped) .	7	8	541	583	n.a.	65

EUROPEAN, ASIAN AND COLOURED

	Number of Schools		Number of Pupils		Number of Teachers	
	1971	1972	1971	1972	1971	1972
Primary	186	187	39,808	40,654	1,636	1,670
Secondary	49	48	27,170	28,153	1,526	1,608
Technical/Teacher-Training . .	3	3	3,696	3,963	193	214
Agricultural College . . .	1	1	83	85	18	18
University*	1	1	993	978	195	195

* Multi-racial.

Source: Central Statistical Office, Salisbury.

THE CONSTITUTION

CONSTITUTIONAL DEVELOPMENT

THE Shona and Ndebele peoples of the area which is now Rhodesia first had to contend with European encroachment on their land in the late 1880s. The British South Africa Company was granted a Royal Charter in 1889 for the purpose of promoting trade, commerce, civilization and good government in the region occupied by the Shona and Ndebele. However, following the founding of Salisbury in 1890 by a group of white settlers organized by Cecil Rhodes, resentment at the instrusion of Europeans increased among Africans and open resistance began in 1893. Only after the great uprisings of 1896–97 was this resistance finally broken. The British South Africa Company continued to administer the colony until 1923, when the colony became self-governing under the United Kingdom after the settlers had decided against entering the Union of South Africa.

The 1923 Constitution

The 1923 Constitution granted the Colony full self-government, except that legislation affecting African interests, the Rhodesia railways and certain other matters were reserved to the British Secretary of State. These reservations fell away in time so far as internal affairs were concerned, excepting those which concerned differential legislation affecting the African population. Formal international relations were conducted for Southern Rhodesia by the British government. Other external relations were the responsibility of the colonial government.

Federation

In September 1953 the Federation of Rhodesia and Nyasaland, linking Northern and Southern Rhodesia with Nyasaland, came into existence. Under the Federal Constitution, approved by the minority electorate in Southern Rhodesia and by the Legislative Councils in the other two territories, responsibility for defence, the regulation of commerce and industry, immigration, health, European education and European agriculture was transferred from the Government of Southern Rhodesia to the Federal Government. African affairs, internal security, industrial relations and certain other matters remained in the hands of the Southern Rhodesian Government.

The 1961 Constitution

In 1959 the Southern Rhodesian Government proposed that the Constitution of Southern Rhodesia should be revised, with a view to transferring to Southern Rhodesia the exercise of the powers vested in the British Government. Following consultations between the two Governments an Order in Council embodying a new constitution was made on December 6th, 1961. This eliminated all the reserved powers save for certain matters of a somewhat formal nature, to which reference is made under the next heading. It also conferred on Southern Rhodesia wide powers for the amendment of her own Constitution and contained a number of important additional features such as a Declaration of Rights and the creation of a Constitutional Council designed to give confidence to all the peoples of Southern Rhodesia that their legitimate interest would be safeguarded.

Dissolution of the Federation

Following the dissolution of the Federation of Rhodesia and Nyasaland in December 1963 the Southern Rhodesian Government resumed the powers which had been transferred to the Federal Government in 1953.

In 1964, it was agreed between the British and Southern Rhodesian Governments that the term "Colony" should be dropped and that henceforward the country should be referred to as "Southern Rhodesia". In October 1964, following the independence of Zambia (Northern Rhodesia), the Southern Rhodesia Government dropped the prefix "Southern". Rhodesia is fully self-governing in respect of its internal affairs, but because it does not yet enjoy sole responsibility for its international relations it cannot be regarded as an independent sovereign state.

Unilateral Declaration of Independence (U.D.I.)

On November 11th, 1965, the Smith Government, elected by the almost exclusively white electorate, unilaterally declared Rhodesia independent of the British Crown and with the assumption of independence, the Constitution of Rhodesia 1965 was issued by the new régime to replace that of 1961, and provisions under the Southern Rhodesian Order in Council, 1961, were held to be of no effect. The Queen, acting through her representative the Governor, dismissed the Government of Rhodesia, and the British Parliament passed the Southern Rhodesia Act, which declares that Southern Rhodesia (the legal name of the country now, although "Rhodesia" remains in common usage) continues to be part of Her Majesty's dominions and that the Government and Parliament of the United Kingdom continue to have responsibility and jurisdiction for and in respect of it. The Southern Rhodesia Constitution Order 1965 which was made under this Act declares that any constitution which the régime in Rhodesia may purport to promulgate is void and of no effect. The Order also prohibits the Legislative Assembly from making laws or transacting any other business and declares any proceedings in defiance of this prohibition void and of no effect. It also suspends the ministerial system, empowers the Governor to exercise his functions without seeking ministerial advice and empowers a Secretary of State as well as the Governor to exercise the executive authority of Rhodesia on Her Majesty's behalf.

The Five (Six) Principles

Successive British Tory Governments have been guided in their approach towards the problem of granting Rhodesia independence by five principles (the 1964–70 Labour Government also recognized a sixth):

1. The principle and intention of unimpeded progress to majority rule, already enshrined in the 1961 Constitution, would have to be maintained and guaranteed.
2. There would also have to be guarantees against retrogressive amendment of the Constitution.
3. There would have to be immediate improvement in the political status of the African population.
4. There would have to be progress towards ending racial discrimination.
5. The British Government would need to be satisfied that any basis proposed for independence was acceptable to the people of Rhodesia as a whole.
6. It would be necessary to ensure that, regardless of race, there was no oppression of majority by minority or of minority by majority.

PROVISIONS OF 1961 CONSTITUTION

The Cabinet and Legislative Assembly

The Cabinet consists of twelve ministers including the Prime Minister. In addition there are a number of parliamentary secretaries.

The Legislature consists of 65 members, 15 of whom are elected on a lower roll, from 15 electoral districts. Fifty are elected on an upper roll from constituencies. Members are all elected for a period of five years.

There will be no power of disallowance by the Sovereign of an Act passed by the Legislative Assembly except in the case of an Act which:

(a) is inconsistent with any international obligations imposed on the Sovereign in relation to Southern Rhodesia; or

(b) alters to the injury of the stockholders or departs from the original contract in respect of any stock issued under the Colonial Stock Acts by the Southern Rhodesia Government on the London market.

Such laws may be disallowed within six months of their being passed.

Constitutional Safeguards

With the introduction of the new constitution in November, 1962, the right of the British Government to veto changes in the constitution has been replaced by safeguards entrenched in the new constitution. The British Government will retain power for amendments affecting the position of the Sovereign and the Governor, international obligations and undertakings by the Southern Rhodesia Government affecting loans. The Legislature has power to alter the constitution by two thirds majority of the total members of Parliament. The specially entrenched sections of the constitution can only be amended by a two thirds majority of the legislature's total membership in addition to a majority vote cast in a referendum of each of the four principal racial groups (namely European, African, Asian and Coloured), or after the Queen has assented to the amendment.

The specially entrenched sections are those relating to the Declaration of Rights, Appeals to the Privy Council, the Constitutional Council, the Judiciary, increasing franchise qualifications, securing Civil Service pensions and the Boards of Trustees of Tribal Trust Land, their powers and terms of trust. In addition, if any racial limitation on the ownership or occupation of land is more restrictive than that existing on the day prior to the introduction of the new constitution, it will be treated as an entrenched section.

The Constitutional Council

Composition

The Constitutional Council consists of a Chairman and eleven members, which must include two Europeans, two Africans, one Asian, one Coloured, and two persons who are either advocates or attorneys of not less than 10 years' standing. The chairman is appointed by the Governor on the advice of the Chief Justice. The members are appointed by an electoral college which includes the Chief Justice and puisne judges of the High Court and the President of the Council of Chiefs.

Qualifications

Members must be, _inter alia_, over thirty-five years of age, Southern Rhodesian citizens and resident in the country for ten of the previous fifteen years.

Functions

The Constitutional Council reports to the Governor and the Speaker of the Legislature on all Bills (except money Bills) passed by the Legislature and informs them whether the Bill conflicts with the provisions of the Declaration of Rights. This is done within 30 days after the passing of the Bill, unless an extension of time is granted. In the event of there being a conflict with the Declaration of Rights the Bill may only be presented to the Governor for assent after a two thirds majority vote in the legislature, or after a simple majority vote together with a delay of six months.

The Declaration of Rights

An entrenched section of the Constitution, this sets out the fundamental rights and freedoms to be enjoyed by the people of Southern Rhodesia. Such rights apply without distinction to race, colour or creed. They afford protection from infringement by the Legislature, Executive, corporate bodies or private persons. The courts will enforce the rights and there is an ultimate appeal to the Judicial Committee of the Privy Council.

The Franchise

Voters must be citizens of Southern Rhodesia, over twenty-one years of age, with two years continuous residence in the country and three months residence in the constituency or electoral district immediately preceding application for enrolment. Voters must be able to complete the application for a voter's form, unassisted and in English. Additional qualifications are:

"A" Roll

(a) Income of £792 during each of two years preceding date of claim for enrolment _or_ ownership of immovable property of value £1,650 or (b) (i) Income of £528 during each of two years preceding date of claim for enrolment, _or_ ownership of immovable property of value of £1,100; _and_ (ii) completion of a course of primary education of prescribed standard or (c) (i) Income of £330 during each of two years preceding date of claim for enrolment, _or_ ownership of immovable property of value of £550; _and_ (ii) four years secondary education of prescribed standard or (d) Appointment to the office of Chief or Headman.

"B" Roll

(a) Income at the rate of £264 per annum during the six months preceding date of claim for enrolment _or_ ownership of immovable property of value £495 or (b) (i) Income at the rate of £132 per annum during the six months preceding date of claim for enrolment, _or_ ownership of immovable property of value of £275; _and_ (ii) two years secondary education, or (c) Persons over thirty years of age with: (i) Income at the rate of £132 per annum during the six months preceding date of claim for enrolment _or_ ownership of immovable property of value of £275; _and_ (ii) completion of a course of primary education of a prescribed standard or (d) Persons over thirty years of age with income at the rate of £198 per annum during the six months preceding the date of claim for enrolment; _or_ ownership of immovable property of value £385 or (e) All kraal heads with a following of 20 or more heads of families or (f) Ministers of Religion.

There is no limit to the number of persons who can register but in elections in constituencies "B" Roll votes will not count for more than 25 per cent of the "A" Roll votes cast, and vice versa in electoral districts.

Where there are three or more candidates standing for election in any constituency or electoral district, a voter may use a preference vote for the candidate of his second choice. In the event of the candidate polling the most number of votes but not getting an overall majority, the bottom candidate drops out and the preference votes on his ballot papers are added to the remaining candidates.

Tribal Trust Land

The Native Reserves and the Special Native Area, which existed prior to the bringing into operation of the new Constitution have now been placed in one category described as "Tribal Trust Land". This land, which is reserved in the Constitution for occupation by tribes on a basis of communal tenure, comprises some 40 million acres out of a total land area of 96 million acres. The land is vested in a Board of Trustees, which is a corporate body with perpetual succession and power to sue and to be sued. The Board cannot be abolished nor can its powers be diminished, nor can the terms of its Trust be varied unless the Bill designed to accomplish any of these objectives obtains a two thirds majority in Parliament, and is agreed to by each of the four principal racial communities.

INDEPENDENCE CONSTITUTION

WITH the assumption of independence, the Constitution of Rhodesia, 1965, was issued to replace that of 1961, and provisions under the Southern Rhodesia Order in Council, 1961, are held to be of no effect.

The Colonial Laws Validity Act, 1965, and the Powers of Disallowance and the Reservation of Bills have been repudiated under the new Constitution. Orders in Council and royal instructions through the Governor are likewise repudiated.

The form of Government remains a constitutional monarchy, with Her Majesty the Queen represented as Head of State by the Officer Administering the Government. Executive powers vested in him include the appointment and accreditation of Diplomatic Representatives, the ratification of international treaties, the proclamation of martial law or state of emergency, the declaration of war and peace and the conferment of honours and precedence. Temporary provisions gave the Officer Administering the Government complete freedom of constitutional amendment for the first six months of the independence period.

The Legislature is made the Sovereign legislative power in and over Rhodesia, and no Act of Parliament of the United Kingdom is held to extend to Rhodesia unless extended thereto by Act of the Legislature of Rhodesia. The Legislature has power to amend the Constitution by a two-thirds majority of the total membership of Parliament, without the need of referenda among the four racial groups or approval by the Queen on British Ministerial advice, as stipulated in the 1961 Constitution.

In respect of the Delimitation of Constituencies and Electoral Districts the 1965 Constitution follows closely the 1961 Constitution. The new Constitution has removed some of the safeguards on judicial independence, however, and appeals to the Judicial Committee of the Privy Council are no longer provided for. Ultimate appeal under the Declaration of Rights is to the Appellate Division of the High Court of Rhodesia, not to the Judicial Committee of the Privy Council as before. In the Constitutional Council it is no longer provided that two of the members shall be African. In regard to the Tribal Trust Land Board, agreement by the four principal racial communities to changes in the powers and terms of trust is no longer needed, such changes being subject to a two-thirds vote of Parliament, the Speaker's certificate, and the assent of the Officer Administering the Government.

The following Emergency Regulations are in force: Maintenance of Law and Order; Censorship of Publications; Postal and Radio Communications; Dissemination of Information; Control of Goods and Services; African Affairs; Control of Government Employees. These give the Government powers of intervention in a wide range of private and public affairs. The state of emergency declared prior to Rhodesia's declaration of independence in November 1965 has been periodically renewed ever since that time.

Subsequent Amendments: In September 1966 the Constitutional Amendment Act became law, having passed all the parliamentary stages by two-thirds majorities. Under its terms the Rhodesian government is given power to detain or restrict individuals in the interests of defence, public safety or public order, without recourse to proclamation of a state of emergency. These powers are held not to contravene the human rights explicitly protected under the 1961 Constitution. Persons detained in special centres may be obliged to perform tasks of forced labour. Other powers granted under the Act include the enablement to control and regulate publication of information about restricted persons and detention camps, the ability to detain individuals without a special order, pending consideration of the issue of such an order, and the ability to acquire property in satisfaction of any tax, rate or due. The widening of the powers of the tribal courts is a further feature of the new Act. Customary law is made applicable to all Africans in Rhodesia, whether or not indigenous to the country, while the tribal courts are held to be non-discriminatory even when members of the court are interested parties. Finally, a number of regulations increase the government's control over tribal trust land.

In October 1966 another Act, the African Affairs Amendment Act, became law. This widened the authority of Rhodesian chiefs by giving them administrative powers in tribal areas.

In February 1967 a five-man Commission was set up by the government to advise on "the constitutional framework which is best suited to the sovereign independent status of Rhodesia and which is guaranteed to protect and guarantee the rights and freedoms of all persons and communities in Rhodesia and ensure the harmonious development of Rhodesia's plural society, having regard to the social and cultural differences amongst the people of Rhodesia, to the different systems of land tenure, and to the problems of economic development."

REPUBLICAN CONSTITUTION

(*November* 1969)

In a referendum held on June 20th, 1969, the constitutional proposals of the Rhodesian Front were approved by 54,724 votes to 20,776. At the same time the predominantly white electorate also approved the proposal to declare Rhodesia a republic by 61,130 to 14,327 votes. The relevant constitutional legislation giving effect to these proposals received the necessary two-thirds majority in the Legislative Assembly in November 1969: this legislation consisted of the Constitution of Rhodesia Bill, the Electoral Bill, the Land Tenure Bill and the High Courts (Amendments) Bill. The Constitutional Bill was signed by the Officer Administering the Government on November 29th, 1969, but did not come into operation until after the first general election under the new constitutional and electoral arrangements in April 1970.

PROVISIONS OF THE REPUBLICAN CONSTITUTION

There is a President in and over Rhodesia, who is Commander-in-Chief of the Armed Forces of Rhodesia. The term of office is five years, and a second term is permissible but not a third.

Legislative power is vested in a legislature consisting of the President and Parliament, and Parliament consists of a Senate and a House of Assembly.

The Senate comprises 23 members, ten Europeans elected by the European members of the House of Assembly, and ten African chiefs, elected by an electoral college consisting of members of the Council of Chiefs. Five of these African Senators shall be chiefs in Matabeleland and five chiefs in Mashonaland.

The remaining three Senators are appointed by the President.

The House of Assembly initially consists of 66 members, 50 Europeans, elected by voters on the European roll, and 16 African members. Half of these, four from Mashonaland and four from Matabeleland, are elected by Africans on an African voters roll, the other half, again drawn equally from Matabeleland and Mashonaland are elected by electoral colleges made up from African chiefs, headmen and councillors from African councils.

When the aggregate of income tax assessed on the income of Africans exceeds sixteen sixty-sixths of that assessed on the income of Europeans and Africans then the number of African members in the House of Assembly will increase in proportion but only until the number of African members equals that of the European members.

To advise the President there is an Executive Council, consisting of the Prime Minister and other such persons, being Ministers as the President, on the advice of the Prime Minister may appoint.

The President appoints as Prime Minister the person, who, in his opinion, is best able to command the support of a majority of the members of the House of Assembly and acting on the advice of the Prime Minister, he appoints other Ministers.

OTHER PROVISIONS

Under the terms of the Constitutional Amendment Act of 1966, whose main provisions still remain in force, the Rhodesian Government is given power to detain or restrict individuals in the interests of defence, public safety or public order, without recourse to proclamation of a state of emergency. These powers are held not to contravene the human rights explicitly protected under the 1961 Constitution. Persons detained in special centres may be obliged to perform tasks of forced labour. Other powers granted under the Act include the enablement to control and regulate publication of information about restricted persons and detention camps, the ability to detain individuals without a special order, pending consideration of the issue of such an order, and the ability to acquire property in satisfaction of any tax, rate or due. The widening of the powers of the tribal courts is a further feature of the new Act. Customary law is made applicable to all Africans in Rhodesia, whether or not indigenous to the country, while the tribal courts are held to be non-discriminatory even when members of the court are interested parties.

LAND TENURE ACT

The Land Tenure Bill was passed by the Legislative Assembly in November 1969, and received the signature of the Officer Administering the Government on November 29th.

The Act, which repeals the Land Apportionment Act, regulates the ownership, leasing and occupation of land in all areas on racial grounds and preserves the special status of the Tribal Trust Land within the African area.

The total extent of Rhodesia is approximately 96.5 million acres which was divided by the Land Apportionment Act as follows: European Area 35.6 million acres, Tribal Trust Land 40.1 million acres, Native Purchase Area 4.3 million acres, National Land 105 million acres, Unreserved Land 6.0 million acres.

Previously only Tribal Trust Lands were specially protected under the Constitution. The Native Purchase Area and European Area enjoyed no such protection.

Under the new Act all areas are similarly protected, but there are now only three areas which are: European Area 44.95 million acres, African Area 44.95 million acres, National Area—reserved for the purpose of Wild Life Conservation and National Parks—6.6 million acres.

Exchange of land between one area and the other are controlled by two Boards of Trustees, one of which watches over the interests of Europeans and the other the interests of Africans.

ANGLO-RHODESIAN CONSTITUTIONAL PROPOSALS

(November 1971)

In November 1971 the British Foreign Secretary (Sir Alec Douglas Home) and Lord Goodman met Mr. Ian Smith and agreed on a settlement. The settlement was subject to it being acceptable to Rhodesians as a whole in the opinion of the Pearce Commission, which tested opinion in Rhodesia between January and March 1972.

The settlement proposed that the number of African seats (now 16) will increase as more Africans meet voting qualifications, until they equal the Europeans' present 50 seats. The creation of new African seats will depend on the growth of a new higher African electoral roll, the qualifications being the same as those for Europeans. Two seats will be added for each 6 per cent rise in the higher African roll, but half the new seats will be filled by indirect election by the College of Chiefs. When the 50-50 parity has been achieved, an independent commission will recommend whether or not 10 Common Roll seats should be added, to be voted for by all on the European and higher African rolls. By this time both rolls should have about the same numbers. As more Africans qualified, they could out-vote the Europeans and produce an African majority in the Assembly. An agreed blocking mechanism will prevent retrogressive legislation. An independent commission will examine racial discrimination. Britain and Rhodesia will join in a £100 million development and educational programme and Africans will get more land. Once the British Government is satisfied by Rhodesian action on the franchise, discrimination and detainees, Parliament will be asked to grant Rhodesia independence and to end sanctions.

On May 23rd, 1972 the report of the Pearce Commission was presented to the House of Commons by the Foreign Secretary. The conclusion of the Commission was that "the people of Rhodesia as a whole did not regard the proposals as acceptable as a basis for independence". Whilst expressing the hope that a solution within the five principles could be found in the future, the Foreign Secretary said that the British Government accepted the verdict of the Commission and that sanctions would continue.

THE GOVERNMENT

(Not recognized by United Kingdom or UN.)

President: CLIFFORD WALTER DUPONT.

THE CABINET

(December 1972)

Prime Minister: IAN DOUGLAS SMITH.

Deputy Prime Minister and Minister of Finance and Posts: JOHN JAMES WRATHALL.

Minister of Roads and Traffic, Transport and Power: ROGER TANCRED ROBERT HAWKINS.

Minister of Foreign Affairs, Defence and Public Service: JOHN HARTLEY HOWMAN.

Minister of Internal Affairs: LANCE BALES SMITH.

Minister of Information, Immigration and Tourism: PIETER KENYON FLEMING VOLTELYN VAN DER BYL.

Minister of Justice, Law and Order: DESMOND WILLIAM LARDNER-BURKE.

Minister of Health, Labour and Social Welfare: IAN FINLAY MCLEAN.

Minister of Commerce and Industry: BERNARD HORACE MUSSETT.

Minister of Local Government and Housing: MARK HENRY HEATHCOTE PARTRIDGE.

Minister of Agriculture: DAVID COLLVILLE SMITH.

Minister of Education: ARTHUR PHILIP SMITH.

Minister of Lands and Water Development: PHILIP VAN HEERDEN.

Minister of Mines: IAN BIRT DILLON.

DIPLOMATIC REPRESENTATION

No country has yet recognized Rhodesia. South Africa has an accredited Diplomatic Mission in Salisbury and Portugal has a Consul-General.

PARLIAMENT

LEGISLATIVE ASSEMBLY

Speaker: A. R. W. STUMBLES.
Clerk of the House: L. J. HOWE-ELY.

GENERAL ELECTIONS (April 1970)

AFRICAN ROLL	VOTES	SEATS	EUROPEAN ROLL	VOTES	SEATS
Centre Party	2,147	7	Rhodesian Front	39,028	50*
National People's Union . .	1,000	1	Centre Party	5,629	—
Rhodesia African Party . .	301	—	Republican Alliance . . .	1,633	—
United National Progressive Party .	70	—	Independents . . .	4,538	—
All African People's Party . .	63	—			
Independents	747	—			
TOTAL . . .	4,328	8	TOTAL . . .	50,828	50

* 13 of these seats were uncontested.

Note: Another 8 African members are elected by electoral colleges of chiefs, headmen and councillors.

COUNCIL OF CHIEFS

Twenty-six elected members.
President: Chief ZWIMBA of Sinoia District.

POLITICAL PARTIES

Rhodesian Front: P.O.B. 242, Salisbury; governing party with 50 seats (1970); aims to maintain Rhodesia's independence; Pres. IAN D. SMITH; Chair. D. FROST.

African National Council (ANC): Salisbury; f. March 1972, after originally having been formed in December 1971 as an *ad hoc* organization to campaign for the rejection of the Anglo-Rhodesian settlement proposals; 3 M.P.s are associated with the party; Chair. Bishop ABEL MUZOREWA.

Centre Party: 22 Jameson Ave., Salisbury; f. August 1968; merged with Rhodesian Constitutional Association (f. 1965 as successor to white section of Rhodesia Party); stands for united, independent Rhodesia, with one parliament for all Rhodesians, advancement by merit, and the eradication of racial discrimination (though without forced integration in residential areas); multi-racial; Pres. PAT BASHFORD; Vice-Pres. (vacant); publ. *Centre Point*.

National Association of Coloured People: Chair. GERRY RAFTOPOULOS.

National People's Union: Salisbury; f. 1969; one seat in Assembly; Leader CHAD CHIPUNZA; Pres. G. CHAVUNDUKA.

Rhodesia Party: f. 1972; Interim Committee Head; ROY ASHBURNER.

Rhodesia African Party: P.O.B. 1552, Bulawayo; f. 1970; Pres. R. C. MAKAYA; Vice-Pres. E. J. MHLANGA.

United Front Against Surrender: Salisbury; f. February 1972 by union of Republican Alliance, Rhodesia National Party and Conservative Association; supports "overriding principle that the white man's position must be supreme for all time".

Zimbabwe African People's Union (ZAPU): P.O.B. 20128, Dar es Salaam, Tanzania; f. 1961; African nationalist party advocating universal adult suffrage; Leader JOSHUA NKOMO (held without trial); Gen. Sec. EDWARD NDHLOVU: banned September 1962 now operating from Lusaka, Zambia.

Zimbabwe African National Union (ZANU): f. 1963 after split in ZAPU; African nationalist; Leader Rev. N. SITHOLE (imprisoned); *(banned)*.

DEFENCE

Of a total armed force of 4,700, the army numbers 3,500 men and the air force 1,200. Military service of twelve months duration is compulsory for white Rhodesians, and there is a military reserve of 10,000 men who have completed three years part-time training. Para-military forces number 8,000 active and 35,000 reservist, and there is a civil police of 5,000.

JUDICIAL SYSTEM

The legal system is Roman-Dutch, based on the system which was in force in the Cape at the time of the occupation. Cape Ordinances form the basis of much of the early legislation.

The High Court has two Divisions, General and Appellate. The Appellate Division is the superior court of record, and the supreme Court of Appeal under the terms of the 1965 Constitution. It consists of the Chief Justice, the Judge President, and a number of judges of appeal.

The General Division of the High Court comprises the Chief Justice, the Judge President and appointed puisne judges. Regular and periodical courts are presided over by Magistrates and Assistant Magistrates.

Chief Justice: Rt. Hon. Sir HUGH BEADLE, P.C., C.M.G., O.B.E.

Judge President: Mr. Justice H. N. MacDONALD.

Judge of Appeal: Mr. Justice J. V. R. LEWIS.

Judges: Mr. Justice E. W. G. JARVIS, C.M.G., Mr. Justice H. E. DAVIES, Mr. Justice B. GOLDIN, Mr. Justice J. GREENFIELD, Mr. Justice J. B. MACAULAY, Mr. Justice C. E. L. BECK.

RELIGION

AFRICAN RELIGIONS
Most Africans follow traditional beliefs.

CHRISTIANS
ANGLICANS
PROVINCE OF CENTRAL AFRICA
Archbishop of Central Africa: Most Rev. DONALD S. ARDEN (Kasupe, Malawi).

BISHOPS IN RHODESIA
Mashonaland: Rt. Rev. J. P. BURROUGH (Salisbury).
Matebeleland: Rt. Rev. S. M. WOOD (Bulawayo).

CATHOLICS
There are 475,540 Roman Catholics in Rhodesia.
Archbishop of Salisbury: Most Rev. FRANCIS MARKALL, S.J.

BISHOPS
Bulawayo: Rt. Rev. ADOLPH G. SCHMITT, C.M.M.
Gwelo: Rt. Rev. ALOIS HAENE, S.M.B.
Umtali: Rt. Rev. DONAL R. LAMONT, O. CARM.
Wankie: Rt. Rev. IGNATIUS PRIETO VEGA, S.M.I.
Catholic Secretariat: P.O.B. 2591, Salisbury.

OTHER DENOMINATIONS
Dutch Reformed Church: P.O.B. 967, 35 Jameson Ave., Salisbury; est. in Rhodesia 1891; the Central African Synod comprises Rhodesia and Malawi; 17 parishes, 14,000 adherents; Gen. Sec. Rev. J. T. H. DE JAGER.

Evangelical Lutheran Church: P.O. Mnene, via Belingwe; est. in Rhodesia 1963 (mission since 1903), Sec. Bishop S. B. STRANDVIK; 22,000 mems.; publ. *Chiedza Chirepo*, monthly.

Methodist Church: First Church est. in Salisbury in 1891; Chair. and Gen. Supt. Rhodesia District, Rev. ANDREW M. NDHLELA, P.O.B. 8298, Salisbury; membership 45,571 (1971); Methodist Community approx. 113,000 (1971).

Presbyterian Church: f. 1904; Salisbury City; Ministers Rev. A. C. MILNE, B.A., Rev. W. H. WATSON, D.D.; Session Clerk G. COOPER; Sec. Miss M. W. ROBINSON, M.A.; P.O.B. 50; membership 17,000.

Salvation Army (Rhodesia Territory): f. 1891; Territorial Commander Commissioner F. J. ADLAM; P.O.B. 14, Salisbury; Staff: 1,200 officers and employees, 40,000 (approx.) members.

United Congregational Church of Southern Africa: P.O.B. 31083, Braamfontein, Transvaal; Sec. for Rhodesia Rev. G. O. LLOYD.

United Methodist Church: f. 1890; P.O.B. 8293, Causeway, Salisbury; Bishop of Rhodesia ABEL MUZOREWA; membership 45,000.

JEWS
Central African Jewish Board of Deputies: P.O.B. 1456, Bulawayo; Pres. Hon. A. E. ABRAHAMSON; approx. 6,000 adherents; publs. *The Board, Central African Zionist Digest*.

THE PRESS

DAILIES
Chronicle, The: P.O.B. 585, Bulawayo; f. 1894; Bulawayo and throughout Matabeleland; English; Editor R. J. FOTHERGILL; circ. 26,773.
Rhodesia Herald, The: P.O.B. 396, Salisbury; f. 1891; Salisbury and elsewhere in Central Africa; English; Editor R. MEIER; circ. 64,496.

Umtali Post: P.O.B. 96, Umtali; f. 1893; Mondays, Wednesdays and Fridays; Editor ERIC RICHMOND.

WEEKLIES AND PERIODICALS
African Times: fortnightly; Editor J. WATSON.
Avondale Observer: P.O.B. 1160, Salisbury; monthly; circ. 5,000.

Central African Journal of Medicine: P.O.B. 2073, Salisbury; f. 1955; monthly; Editor Dr. M. GELFAND.
Chamber of Mines Journal: Thomson Newspapers Rhodesia (Pvt.) Ltd., P.O.B. 1683, Salisbury; f. 1960; monthly.
Citizen, The: P.O.B. 1160, Beatrice Rd., Salisbury; f. 1953; weekly; English; Editor C. THEO.
Country Times: Country Times Press (Pvt.) Ltd., 208 Birmingham Rd., Marandellas; twice-monthly.
Development Magazine: P.O.B. 1622, Salisbury; f. 1948; monthly; English; Man. Editor E. ROY WRIGHT; circ. 3,000.
Die Rhodesier: P.O.B. M.P. 88, Mount Pleasant, Salisbury; monthly.
Enterprise: P.O.B. 638, Salisbury; monthly.

Fort Victoria Advertiser: P.O.B. 138, Fort Victoria; f. 1959; independent; general; weekly; Editor STUART ROGERS; circ. 1,100.

Gatooma Mail: P.O.B. 126, Gatooma; f. 1921; Thursdays; Editor D. BURKE.

Greendale News: P.O.B. 1160, Salisbury; monthly; circ. 4,000.

Gwelo Times: P.O.B. 66, 51 Fifth St., Gwelo; f. 1897; Thursdays; Editor B. K. CHARLESWORTH; circ. 2,900.

Hatfield Record: P.O.B. 1160, Salisbury; monthly; circ. 2,200.

Highlands Times: P.O.B. 1160, Salisbury; monthly; circ. 4,400.

Homecraft: P.O.B. 8263, Causeway, Salisbury; published by the National Federation of Womens' Institutes of Rhodesia in English, Shona and Ndebele; f. 1962; monthly; Editor MARY LEDINGHAM; circ. 7,000.

Look and Listen: P.O.B. H.G. 200, Highlands, Salisbury; weekly; Editor BARBARA MILLER.

M. & M. Gazette: P.O.B. 1160, Salisbury; monthly; circ. 4,000.

Makoni Clarion: P.O.B. 17, Rusape; monthly.

Mashoko é Que Que: P.O.B. 186, Que Que; f. 1965; monthly; African; Editor O. R. ASHTON; circ. 2,000.

Midlands Observer: P.O.B. 186, Que Que; f. 1953; Fridays; English; Man. Editor O. R. ASHTON; circ. 1,550.

Mining in Rhodesia: Thomson Newspapers Rhod. (Pvt.) Ltd., P.O.B. 1683, Salisbury.

Modern Farming: P.O.B. 1622, Salisbury; f. 1964; Man. Editor PETER SMYTH; circ. 7,500.

Moto (*Fire*): P.O.B. 779, Gwelo; f. 1958; monthly; Shona and English; political, cultural, religious; Editors PAUL CHIDYAUSIKU, JOHN ZACHARY, MENARD MASVINGISE; circ. 35,000.

Motor Trader and Fleet Operator: Thomson Newspapers Rhod. (Pvt.) Ltd., P.O.B. 1683, Salisbury; official organ of the Rhodesian Motor Trade Association.

Mt. Pleasant Courier: P.O.B. 1160, Salisbury; monthly; circ. 4,000.

Murimi: P.O.B. 1622, Salisbury; monthly; Editor CORNELIUS WOTYORKA.

National Observer: P.O.B. 2473, Bulawayo; monthly; Editor ELIZA MAHAJA.

News of Hartley: Citizen Press, P.O.B. 1160, Salisbury; weekly; circ. 750.

Outpost: P.O.B. H.G. 106, Highlands, Salisbury; f. 1911; monthly; English; Editor A. P. STOCK; circ. 5,000.

Parade and Foto-Action: P.O.B. 3798, Salisbury; f. 1953; monthly; English; Editor LEONIS M. LAMBIRIS.

Qua: P.O.B. 2377, Salisbury; monthly.

Rhodesia Agricultural Journal: P.O.B. 8108, Causeway, Salisbury; f. 1903; six per year; Editor W. B. CLEGHORN; circ. 2,000.

Rhodesian Bottle Store and Hotel Review (B.H.R.): Thomson Newspapers Rhod. (Pvt.) Ltd., P.O.B. 1683, Salisbury; f. 1951; official organ of Liquor Trade Associations; monthly.

Rhodesian Builders' and Architects' Year Book and Buyers' Guide: Thomson Newspapers Rhod. (Pvt.) Ltd., P.O.B. 1683, Salisbury.

Rhodesia Calls: P.O.B. 8045, Causeway, Salisbury; f. 1960; every two months; Editor A. GERRARD ABERMAN; travel; circ. 18,000.

Rhodesian Caravaner: P.O.B. 8045, Causeway, Salisbury; f. 1969; every two months; Publisher A. GERRARD ABERMAN; Editor CLIVE WILSON; circ. 2,500.

Rhodesian Farmer: P.O.B. 1622, Salisbury; f. 1928; weekly journal of the Rhodesia National Farmers' Union and Rhodesia Tobacco Association and affiliated bodies; English; circ. 7,500; Editor D. H. B. DICKIN.

Rhodesian Financial Gazette: Baker Ave., P.O.B. 2023, Salisbury; weekly; broadly pro-government; Editor R. HAYNES; circ. 5,000.

Rhodesian Insurance Review: Thomson Newspapers Rhod. (Pvt.) Ltd., P.O.B. 1683, Salisbury; f. 1955; monthly.

Rhodesian Property & Finance: P.O.B. 2266, Salisbury; f. 1956; monthly; Editor WILFRED BROOKS; circ. 6,200.

Rhodesia Railways Magazine: P.O.B. 596, Bulawayo; f. 1952; monthly; Editor J. BRYANT; circ. 8,800.

Rhodesian Tobacco Journal: Thomson Newspapers Rhod. (Pvt.) Ltd., P.O.B. 1683, Salisbury; f. 1949; monthly.

Rhodesian Woman: P.O.B. U.A. 439, Salisbury; f. 1950; monthly; English; Editor JOANMARIE FOBBS.

Shield: P.O.B. 3194, Salisbury; monthly; English; Editor F. MEALING.

Sitima: P.O.B. 596, Bulawayo; official organ for African staff of the Rhodesia Railways in Rhodesia and Botswana; monthly; Editor J. BRYANT; circ. 10,000.

Sunday Mail: P.O.B. 396, Salisbury; f. 1935; English; Editor J. A. ROBERTSON; circ. 79,469.

Sunday News: P.O.B. 585, Bulawayo; f. 1930; English; Editor P. H. C. J. TUDOR-OWEN; circ. 22,820.

Teacher in New Africa: 107 Moffat St., P.O.B. 3513, Salisbury; f. 1964; monthly; English; Man. V. R. COHEN.

Umbowo: P.O.B. P. 7024, Umtali; United Methodist Church newspaper.

Waterfalls Sentinel: P.O.B. 1160, Salisbury; monthly; circ. 2,000.

Weekly Express: P.O.B. 1160; circ. 17,500 (African readership).

You: P.O.B. 3793, Salisbury; f. 1950; monthly; English; for women; Editor ROBERT DUNCAN.

NEWS AGENCIES

Inter-African News Agency (Pvt.) Ltd.: P.O.B. 785, Salisbury; f. 1964; subsidiary of the South African Press Association; Chair. L. K. S. WILSON; Editor CLAUDE COOK, M.B.E.

FOREIGN BUREAUX

Agence France—Presse: 604 Robinson House, Union Ave., Salisbury (P.O.B. 2023); Rep. PETER NIESEWAND.

UPI: 604 Robinson House, Union Ave., Salisbury (P.O.B. 2023); Rep. PETER NIESEWAND.

Reuters also have a bureau in Salisbury.

PUBLISHERS

A. C. Braby (Rhod.) (Pvt.) Ltd.: P.O.B. 1027, Bulawayo; telephone directory publishers.

Associated Publications (Pvt.) Ltd.: P.O.B. 3798, Salisbury; f. 1946.

B. & T. Directories (Rhodesia) (Private) Ltd.: P.O.B. 2119, Bulawayo.

Burke Enterprises (Pvt.) Ltd.: P.O.B. 550, Gatooma.

The Citizen Press (Pvt.) Ltd.: P.O.B. 1160, Salisbury.

Dominion Press (Pvt.) Ltd.: P.O.B. 1160, Salisbury.

Independent Newspapers (Pvt.) Ltd.: P.O.B. 1160, Salisbury.

Kingstons Limited: P.O.B. 2374, Salisbury; brs. in Bulawayo, Gwelo, Que Que and Umtali.

Longman Rhodesia (Pvt.) Ltd.: P.O.B. S.T. 125, Southerton, Salisbury; f. 1964; member of the Longman group; representing Oliver and Boyd, Livingstone, Churchill, Penguin Books Ltd.

Mambo Press: P.O.B. 779, Gwelo; f. 1958; religion, education and fiction in English and African languages; Dir. ALBERT PLANGGER; Man. JAMES AMREIN.

Mercantile Publishing House (Pvt.) Ltd.: P.O.B. 1561, Salisbury.

Moore Printing and Publishing: P.O. Box 110, Sinoia.

Morris Publishing Co. (Pvt.) Ltd.: P.O. Box 1435, Salisbury.

Oxford University Press: Roslin House, Baker Ave., Salisbury; br. of London firm.

Publications (C.A.) (Pvt.) Ltd.: P.O.B. 1027, Bulawayo.

Rhodesian Farmer Publications: P.O.B. 1622, Salisbury; farming books for Southern Africa.

The Rhodesian Printing and Publishing Co. Ltd.: P.O.B. 396, Salisbury; P.O.B. 96, Umtali; P.O.B. 585, Bulawayo.

Rhodesian Publications (1969) (Pvt.) Ltd.: P.O.B. 3745, Salisbury.

Thomson Newspapers Rhod. (Pvt.) Ltd.: P.O.B. 1683, Salisbury; trade journals.

Unitas Press Ltd.: P.O.B. 3230, Salisbury.

Vision Publications: P.O.B. 1532, Salisbury; f. 1954.

RADIO AND TELEVISION

Rhodesia Broadcasting Corpn.: P.O.B. 444, Highlands, Salisbury; f. 1964; Chair. J. M. HELLIWELL; Dir.-Gen. J. C. NEILL.

RADIO

GENERAL AND COMMERCIAL SERVICES: news, information and entertainment; the main centre is in Salisbury, but there are studios in Bulawayo and Umtali. The Corporation broadcasts 20 news services daily.

AFRICAN SERVICE: broadcasts in three vernacular languages and English; studios in Salisbury and Bulawayo.

In June 1972 there were 171,495 radio licences.

TELEVISION

Rhodesia Broadcasting Corpn.: Stations at Salisbury, Gwelo and Bulawayo.

Rhodesia Television Ltd.: P.O.B. H.G. 200, Highlands, Salisbury; programme contractors; commercial organization; studios in Salisbury and Bulawayo.

Ministry of Education: The Secretary for African Education, P.O.B. 8022, Causeway, Salisbury; and The Secretary for Education, P.O.B. 8024, Causeway, Salisbury.

There are 212,350 radio receivers and 51,000 television receivers.

FINANCE

BANKING

(cap.=capital, p.u.=paid up, dep.=deposits, m.=million)

Reserve Bank of Rhodesia (*Central Bank*): P.O.B. 1283, Salisbury; f. May 1964 to take over the functions of the Bank of Rhodesia and Nyasaland in Rhodesia from June 1965; the bank has sole right of issue; cap. R$2m.; Gov. N. H. B. BRUCE. Britain has appointed Sir HENRY HARDMAN as Governor and Trustee to R.B.R.

British and Rhodesian Discount House Ltd.: P.O.B. 3321, Southampton House, Union Avenue, Salisbury; f. 1959; cap. p.u. R$300,000, dep. R$21,423,000 (Aug. 1972); Chair. D. G. NICHOLSON; Man. M. G. GISBORNE.

Discount Co. of Rhodesia Ltd.: P.O.B. 3424, Fanum House, Jameson Ave. Central, Salisbury; f. 1959; cap. p.u. R$450,000, dep. R$33,430,000 (Feb. 1972); Chair. G. ELLMAN-BROWN, C.M.G.; Man. Dir. G. WILDE.

Rhodesian Banking Corporation Ltd.: P.O.B. 3198, Salisbury; f. 1967 to take over the Rhodesian branches of the Netherlands Bank of South Africa; cap. R$2,761,200; Chair. R. S. WALKER, M.B.E.; Gen. Man. G. H. M. BEAK.

Rhodesian Acceptances Ltd.: Rhodesian Acceptances House, 67 Jameson Ave., Salisbury; f. 1956; cap. p.u. R$1,000,007, dep. R$14.3m. (1971); Chair. Sir KEITH ACUTT, K.B.E.; Man. Dir. L. P. NORMAND.

MERCHANT BANKS

Accepting House of Rhodesia: Salisbury; f. 1971; all shares held by Bank of Lisbon and South Africa.

Merchant Bank of Central Africa Ltd.: P.O.B. 3200, Century House West, Baker Avenue, Salisbury; f. 1956; cap. p.u. R$2m.; Chair. G. C. V. COPPEN; Man. Dir. K. DEWAR.

OTHER BANKS

Barclays Bank Limited: London; Local Head Office: Manica Rd., Salisbury, P.O.B. 1279; Gen. Man. D. M. ELLIS COLE; 32 brs., 67 agencies.

National and Grindlays Bank Ltd.: London; Salisbury: 64 Baker Ave. and 11 other brs., 16 sub-offices; Man. Dir. J. G. D. GORDON.

Standard Bank Ltd., The: London; P.O.B. 373, Salisbury; branches in all important towns; Gen. Man. A. G. CALDER.

INSURANCE

Insurance Corpn. of Rhodesia Ltd.: I.C.R. House, Cnr. Manica Rd./Angwa St., P.O.B. 2417, Salisbury; Man. ERIC WILDER.

Old Mutual Fire and General Insurance Company of Rhodesia (Pvt.) Ltd.: Mutual House, Speke Ave., P.O.B. 2101, Salisbury; f. 1958; cap. R$2,186,952, assets R$1,726,179; Chair. R. F. HALSTEAD, I.C.D., C.B.E.; Gen. Man. W. H. EDWARDS.

TRADE AND INDUSTRY

CHAMBERS OF COMMERCE

Associated Chambers of Commerce of Rhodesia: 5th Floor, Electricity Centre, Jameson Ave., P.O.B. 1934, Salisbury; f. 1919; 2,100 mems.; 17 constituent chambers of commerce throughout Rhodesia; Gen. Sec. M. BRITTEN; publ. *Commerce* (monthly). Constituent Chambers in: Bindura, Bulawayo, Chipinga, Gwanda, Gwelo, Gatooma, Kariba, Karoi, Lowveld, Que Que, Marandellas, Victoria, Hartley, Salisbury, Sinoia, Umtali and Victoria Falls.

Salisbury Chamber of Commerce: 5th Floor, Electricity Centre, Jameson Ave., P.O.B. 1934, Salisbury; f. 1894; 1,000 mems.; Pres. W. HARRIS; Sec. C. C. CLARKE.

INDUSTRIAL AND EMPLOYERS' ASSOCIATIONS

Confederation of Employers: Salisbury.

African Turkish Tobacco Growers' Association: Salisbury; f. 1960; membership open to growers in all territories.

Agricultural Marketing Authority: P.O.B. 8094, Causeway, Salisbury; f. 1967.

Association of Rhodesian Industries: Friern House, 7 Speke Ave., Salisbury; f. 1957; represents the interests of industry in Rhodesia; Pres. B. BLAKE; Dir. J. C. GRAYLIN, I.C.D., C.M.G.

Bulawayo Agricultural Society: P.O. Famona, Bulawayo; sponsors of Trade Fair Rhodesia; Pres. Sir FREDERICK CRAWFORD, G.C.M.G., O.B.E.; Gen. Man. P. ST. A. ROACH, F.I.E., A.I.V.(S.A.).

Bulawayo Chamber of Industries: P.O.B. 2317; f. 1951; 328 mems.; Pres. Clr. J. GOLDWASSER.

Bulawayo Landowners' and Farmers' Association: P.O.B. 9003, Hillside, Bulawayo.

Bulawayo Master Builders' and Allied Trades' Association: P.O.B. 1970, Bulawayo; f. 1919; 136 mems.; Pres. A. P. GLENDINNING; Sec. E. FRIEND.

Chamber of Mines of Rhodesia, The: P.O.B. 712, Salisbury; f. 1939; Pres. I. M. COWAN; Gen. Man. K. A. VANDERPLANK; publs. *Annual Report*, *Chamber of Mines Journal* (monthly).

Gatooma Farmers' and Stockowners' Association: P.O.B. 100, Gatooma; 108 mems.; Chair. C. D. P. RAYNOR; Sec. P. L. JAMES, F.C.I.S., F.C.C.S.

Industrial Council of the Meat Trade (Bulawayo Area): P.O.B. 1149; Bulawayo; Sec. QUICK & JOHNS (PVT.) LTD.

Industrial Council of the Motor Industry of Matabeleland: P.O.B. 1149; Bulawayo; Sec. QUICK & JOHNS (PVT.) LTD.

Industrial Development Corporation of Rhodesia Ltd.: P.O.B. 8531, Causeway, Salisbury; f. 1963; Chair. N. CAMBITZIS.

Manicaland Chamber of Industries: P.O.B. 78, Umtali; f. 1945; 55 mems.; Sec. T. W. STEPHENSON.

Midlands Chamber of Industries: P.O.B. 142, Gwelo; 67 mems.; Sec. C. RAMPF.

National Industrial Council of the Building Industry of Rhodesia: St. Barbara House, Baker Ave./Moffat St., Salisbury; Sec. R. D. W. DUTTON.

National Industrial Council of the Engineering and Iron and Steel Industry: 5th Floor, Chancellor House, Jameson Ave., P.O.B. 1922, Salisbury; f. 1943; Chair. C. W. LANDER, C.B.E.; Gen. Sec. A. G. MAYCOCK, F.I.ARB.(LOND.).

Que Que Farmers' Association: P.O.B. 240, Que Que; f. 1928; 80 mems.; Sec. B. KAULBACK.

Rhodesia National Farmers' Union: P.O.B. 1241, Salisbury; f. 1942; 6,200 mems.; Gen. Man. J. R. MELLOR; publ. *The Rhodesian Farmer* (weekly).

Rhodesian Smallworkers' and Tributors' Association: P.O.B. 100, Gatooma; f. 1906; 34 mems.; Chair. P. M. MAY; Hon. Sec. P. L. JAMES, F.C.I.S., F.C.C.S.

Rhodesia Tobacco Association: P.O.B. 1781, Salisbury; 1,700 mems.; Pres. V. HURLEY; Chief Exec. Officer J. M. MORTEN; publ. *The Rhodesian Farmer* (weekly, with Rhodesian National Farmers' Union).

Rhodesian Tobacco Corporation: Salisbury; f. 1966 to market the tobacco crop; total received from sales (1966) £11.5m. approx., government subsidy £5m. approx.; about 40 per cent of the 1966 crop has been sold.

Rhodesian Tobacco Marketing Board: P.O.B. 1781, Salisbury; Chair. R. A. GRIFFITH, M.B.E.; Gen. Man. H. G. STONHILL.

Salisbury Chamber of Industries: Salisbury; Pres. C. W. DEWHURST.

Salisbury Master Builders' and Allied Trades' Association: P.O.B. 1502, Salisbury; f. 1921; 200 mems.; Chair. R. P. SCHWARER; Sec. JAS. Y. GILCHRIST.

Tobacco Export Promotion Council of Rhodesia: R.T.A. House, Baker Ave., P.O.B. 8334, Causeway, Salisbury.

Umtali District Farmers' Association: P.O.B. 29, Umtali; 97 mems.; Chair. J. WOOD; Sec. Mrs. J. FROGGATT.

TRADE UNIONS

African Trade Union Congress: 65 Sinoia St., Salisbury; f. 1957; Gen. Sec. E. V. WATUNGWA; there are 9 affiliated unions with a total membership of 29,198.

Main affiliates:

Commercial and Allied Workers' Union: Kingsway, Salisbury; 4,000 mems.; Pres. J. ZENDAH.

Engineering and Metal Workers' Union: 12 Kilmarnock Bldg., Fife St., Bulawayo; 732 mems.; Pres. A. F. TSOKA.

Railway Associated Workers' Union: P.O.B. 2276, Bulawayo; 11,000 mems.; Pres. S. T. MASHINGAIDZE; Gen. Sec. A. J. MHUNGU.

Trade Union Congress of Rhodesia: P.O.B. 556, Bulawayo; f. 1954; name changed 1964; 16,359 mems.; Pres. H. B. BLOOMFIELD; Gen. Sec. P. LENNON.

Main affiliates:

Associated Mine Workers of Rhodesia: P.O.B. 228, 34 Sixth St., Gwelo; 5,400 mems.; Pres. H. B. BLOOMFIELD.

Rhodesian Railway Workers' Union: P.O.B. 556, Bulawayo; mems. 5,600; Pres. J. KINLEY; Gen. Sec. P. LENNON.

Typographical Union of Rhodesia: P.O.B. 27, Bulawayo; and P.O.B. 494, Salisbury; 1,500 mems.; Sec. (Bulawayo) J. TAYLOR; Sec. (Salisbury) A. C. CAIN.

United Steelworkers' Union of Central Africa (USUCA): Schattil's Bldg., Musgrave Rd., Redcliffe; 1,100 mems.; Pres. D. JOUBERT; Sec. J. EVANS.

National African Federation of Unions: Salisbury; f. 1965; 14,669 mems; Pres. S. S. NKOMO; Gen. Sec. MATHIAS KAVIYA.

Main affiliates:

Agricultural and Plantation Workers' Union: P.O.B. 1806, Bulawayo; 9,000 mems.; Pres. F. NGWENYA.

Building and Woodworkers' Union: Kingsway, Salisbury; 1,700 mems.; Pres. N. L. KARAMBWA; Gen. Sec. MORRIS CHIRONDA.

Municipal Workers' Union: 1676 4th St., 9th Rd., Makokoba, Bulawayo; 1,800 mems.; Pres. D. C. GAMBI; Gen. Sec. C. D. CHIKWANA.

Principal non-affiliated unions:

Air Transport Workers' Association: P.O.B. 1, Salisbury Airport, Salisbury; 450 mems.; Pres. R. A. WINZER; Sec. E. C. MAKAYI.

Amalgamated Engineering Union: 506-509 Kirrie Bldgs., Abercorn St., Bulawayo (P.O.B. 472); 3,000 mems.; Gen. Sec. D. V. MULLER.

National Association of Local Government Officers and Employees: P.O.B. 2956, Salisbury; Pres. P. E. COLE; Sec. Mrs. W. W. BEATON.

Salisbury Municipal Employees' Association: P.O.B. 448, Salisbury; 1,700 mems.; Chair. P. E. COLE; Sec. Mrs. M. W. BEATON.

Tailors' and Garment Workers' Union: P.O.B. 9019, Harare, Salisbury; 2,241 mems.; Pres. P. B. MOYO; Gen. Sec. G. ELIA.

Transport Workers' Union: P.O.B. 1936, Bulawayo; Chair. S. P. BHEBHE.

TRADE FAIR

Trade Fair Rhodesia: P.O. Famona, Bulawayo; f. 1960; Pres. Sir FREDERICK CRAWFORD G.C.M.G., O.B.E.; Gen. Man. P. ST. A. ROACH, F.E.I., A.I.V.(S.A.).

MAJOR INDUSTRIAL COMPANIES

The following are nine of the ten top companies (*source:* supplement to *Financial Mail*, March 26th, 1970).

B.A.T. Central Africa Ltd.: P.O.B. 687, Paisley Rd., Salisbury; f. 1920; cap. R$3m.

Manufacture of tobacco products; operations in Rhodesia are conducted in many distribution centres through B.A.T. Rhodesia Ltd., a wholly owned subsidiary.

Chair. W. BASSON; 586 employees.

Hippo Valley Estates Ltd.: P.O.B. 1, Chiredzi.

Johnson and Fletcher Ltd.: P.O.B. 588, 21 Sinoia St., Salisbury; f. 1897; cap. R$3m.

Import and distribution of building materials, hardware, etc., operates a separate thermal engineering division for air conditioning and commercial refrigeration.

Chair. G. R. A. JOHNSON; Dirs. J. C. FLETCHER, K. B. CROOKES; 720 employees.

Plate Glass Bevelling and Silvering Co. Ltd.: Mafeking Rd., Bulawayo.

Rhodesian Breweries Ltd.: P.O.B. 327, Netherlands House, Speke Ave., Salisbury; f. 1946; cap. R$10m.

Brewing, food processing, tourist hotels management.

Chair. J. V. SAMUELS; Man. Dir. J. D. CARTER; 1,000 employees.

Rhodesia Cement Ltd.: Cement House, Selborne Ave., Bulawayo.

Rhodesia Sugar Refineries Ltd.: P.O.B. 8203, Club Chambers, Baker Ave., Salisbury.

Rhodesia Tea Estates Ltd.: P.O.B. 335, Umtali.

Salisbury Portland Cement Co. Ltd.: P.O.B. 3898, Club Chambers, Baker Ave., Salisbury; f. 1954; cap. R$2,500,000.

Production of cement and cement-based paints.

Man. Dir. C. W. DEWHURST; Sec. G. A. HENDRY; 510 employees.

TRANSPORT AND POWER

RAILWAYS

Rhodesia Railways: P.O.B. 596, Bulawayo; originally f. 1899 and reconstituted 1967 when joint operation by Rhodesia and Zambia ceased and each became responsible for its own system; Chair. W. N. WELLS; Gen. Man. T. A. WRIGHT.

Trunk lines run from Bulawayo south through Botswana to the border with the Republic of South Africa, connecting with the South African Railways; north-west to the Victoria Falls, where there is a connection with Zambia Railways; and north-east to Salisbury and Umtali connecting with the Mozambique Railways' line from Beira. From a point near Gwelo, a line runs to the south-east, making a connection with the Mozambique Railways' Limpopo line and with the port of Lourenço Marques. The present lines total 3,239 kilometres.

ROADS

The road system in Rhodesia totals 78,470 kilometres of which 8,470 kilometres are designated main roads.

MOTORISTS' ORGANIZATION

Automobile Association of Rhodesia: Fanum House, 57 Jameson Ave. Central, P.O.B. 585, Salisbury; f. 1923; 51,000 mems.; Pres. Mrs. W. J. CHAMPION, M.B.E.; Gen. Man. J. R. SORRIE.

CIVIL AVIATION

Air Rhodesia Corporation: Salisbury Airport; f. 1967; successor to Central African Airways Corporation; services to Johannesburg, Beira, Durban, Lourenço Marques, Vilanculos, Blantyre and Mauritius; Gen. Man. Capt. P. A. TRAVERS; fleet of 7 Viscount; 3 DC-3.

Rhodesian Air Services (Pvt.) Ltd.: P.O.B. 735, Salisbury; associate of Protea Airways (Pty.) Ltd., Johannesburg, South Africa.

Rhodesia United Air Carriers (Pvt.) Ltd.: Salisbury Airport; f. 1960; aircraft charter; branches at Bulawayo and Victoria Falls; Man. Dir. C. MYERS.

The following international airlines also serve Salisbury: Air Malawi, D.E.T.A., S.A.A., T.A.P.

POWER

Sabi-Limpopo Authority: P.O.B. 8113, Causeway, Salisbury; f. by Statute 1965; to exploit, conserve and utilize water resources in the low veld of south-east Rhodesia, the Melsetter Highlands and the area around Fort Victoria; Chair. N. CAMBITZIS.

TOURISM

Rhodesia National Tourist Board: 95 Stanley Ave., P.O.B. 8052, Causeway, Salisbury; f. 1963; Dir. M. V. GARDNER (acting); publ. *Rhodesia Calls*.

OVERSEAS OFFICES

Mozambique: Predio Santos Gil, 5° Andar, Avenida da Republica, P.O.B. 2229, Lourenço Marques.

South Africa: Carlton Centre, Commissioner St., P.O.B. 9398, Johannesburg; 2219 Trust Bank Centre, Corner Adderley and Riebeeck Streets, P.O.B. 2465, Cape Town; 315 Smith St., Durban Club Place; P.O.B. 1689, Durban.

Switzerland: P.O.B. 561, 4001 Basle.

U.S.A.: 535 Fifth Ave., New York, N.Y. 10017.

EDUCATION

Estimated expenditure for African education in 1971–72 was R$22.4m., for non-African education R$20.1m. There were 759,534 African pupils in 1972 and 67,500 non-Africans. The University of Rhodesia provides multi-racial higher education, and in 1972 the total enrolment of students was 978, including 400 Africans.

LEARNED SOCIETIES

Botanical Society of Rhodesia: Salisbury; f. 1934; Hon. Sec. J. R. JAMES, P.O.B. 461, Salisbury.

Herpetological Association of Africa: Umtali Museum, Umtali, Rhodesia; Sec. D. G. BROADLEY.

Institution of Mining and Metallurgy (Rhodesian Section): P.O.B. 405, Salisbury; f. 1931; Hon. Sec. I. A. TAYLOR.

National Association for the Arts: 22 Bradfield Rd., Hillside, Salisbury; f. 1968; Chair. H. FINN; Sec. Mrs. C. HEPWORTH.

Rhodesian Agricultural and Horticultural Society: P.O.B. 442, Salisbury; Sec. G. E. GILBERT-GREEN.

Rhodesia Scientific Association: P.O.B. 978, Salisbury; f. 1899; 250 mems.; Pres. P. A. DONOVAN; Vice-Pres. M. A. RAATH; Hon. Sec. J. H. WILSON; publ. *Proceedings and Transactions*.

Rhodesian Society of Arts: P.O.B. 927, Salisbury.

U.S. Information Service: 42 Angwa Street, Salisbury.

RESEARCH INSTITUTES

(*see also under University*)

Agricultural Research Council of Central Africa: P.O.B. 3397, Salisbury; f. 1964; succeeded Agricultural Research Council of Rhodesia and Nyasaland; operates research teams in Southern Rhodesia, Malawi and Zambia; Chairman F. BAWDEN, F.R.S.; Dir. H. C. PEREIRA, D.SC.; Sec. R. W. CLEEVE-EDWARDS, C.A.

Blair Research Laboratory: P.O.B. 8105, Causeway, Salisbury; Dir. Dr. V. DE V. CLARKE.

Cancer Association (Rhodesia) The: P.O. Box 3388, Bulawayo; f. 1959; 423 mems.

Central Statistical Office: P.O.B. 8063, Causeway, Salisbury; f. 1927; co-ordinated statistical service for the Government of Rhodesia; staff of 147; Dir. C. A. L. MYBURGH, M.COMM., PH.D., F.S.S., A.S.A.

Department of Metallurgy, Ministry of Mines: P.O.B. 8340, Causeway, Salisbury; investigations on methods of economic extraction from precious, base-metal and non-metallic ores.

Department of Veterinary Services; Tsetse and Trypanosomiasis Control Branch: P.O. Box 8283, Causeway, Salisbury; under the Ministry of Agriculture; f. 1961; for the control of trypanosomiasis and tsetse fly and the investigation of methods of control; laboratory at Salisbury and two research stations in Zambezi Valley.

Gatooma Research Station: P.O.B. 396, Gatooma; f. 1925; maintained by the Ministry of Agriculture; cotton agronomy, breeding and pest research, and sorghum breeding; Officer-in-Charge J. A. GLEDHILL, M.A. (CANTAB.) (acting); publs. *Rhodesia Agricultural Journal, Rhodesian Journal of Agricultural Research.*

Geological Survey of Rhodesia: P.O.B. 8039, Causeway, Salisbury; f. 1910; geological mapping and survey of mineral resources; library of 1,341 vols., 6,500 reprints, 7,000 periodicals; Dir. J. W. WILES; publs. *Annual Reports, Bulletins, Mineral Resources Series,* short reports, and maps.

Grasslands Research Station: Private Bag 701, Marandellas; f. 1929; research on pasture, animal and crop production for the high-rainfall sandveld area, selection and testing of *Rhizobium* strains and commercial production of legume inoculants; Dir. T. C. D. KENNAN.

Henderson Research Station, Fisheries Centre: Ministry of Agriculture, Private Bag 222A, Salisbury; research on fish resources and hydrobiology and development of fishing industries in Rhodesia.

Matopos Research Station: Private Bag K. 5137, Bulawayo; f. 1903; Agricultural research, substations at Tjolotjo and Nyamandhlovu; Officer-in-Charge, H. K. WARD; publ. *Annual Report.*

Meteorological Service: P.O. Box 8066, Causeway, Salisbury; f. 1897; Dir. J. E. STEVENS; publs. *Monthly Meteorological Summaries, Rainfall Handbook Supplements, Climate Handbook Supplements,* daily weather reports and forecasts, weekly rainfall maps during rainy season Nov.-Mar.

Affiliated Institute:

Goetz Observatory: P.O. Box 562, Bulawayo; also seismology.

Public Health Laboratory: P.O. Box 8079, Causeway, Salisbury; f. 1921; Dir. Dr. K. G. GADD; Pathologists Dr. R. F. LOWE, Dr. C. M. D. ROSS; Chief Medical Technologist V. CARLISLE.

Standards Association of Central Africa: Coventry Rd., Salisbury; f. 1957; sponsored by the Governments of Rhodesia and Malawi; 260 mems.; Chair. F. E. BUCH.

Tobacco Research Board of Rhodesia: P.O. Box 1909, Salisbury; a statutory body est. 1950 by Tobacco Research Act; board represents growers, buyers, and Ministry of Agriculture; operates four research stations; library of 8,000 vols., 560 periodicals; Chair. J. W. FIELD; Dir. I. McDONALD, B.SC., M.A., PH.D., A.R.I.C.; publs. *Bulletins* and *Interim Reports*.

Veterinary Research Laboratory: P.O.B. 8101, Causeway, Salisbury; f. 1909; research in the animal diseases and the production of vaccines; Dir. G. J. CHRISTIE.

LIBRARIES AND ARCHIVES

Library of Parliament: P.O.B. 8055, Causeway, Salisbury; f. 1899; 70,000 vols.; Librarian G. DELLAR, A.L.A.

National Archives of Rhodesia: Private Bag 729, Causeway, Salisbury; f. 1935 as the Government Archives of Southern Rhodesia; incorp. archives of Northern Rhodesia and Nyasaland and designated the Central African Archives 1947; became National Archives of Rhodesia and Nyasaland 1958–63; reverted January 1964 to Rhodesian Government, and responsibility for Northern Rhodesia and Nyasaland archives ceased; also serves Rhodesian municipalities and holds archives of late Federation of Rhodesia and Nyasaland; comprises divisions of Public Archives, Records Management, Historical Manuscripts, Oral History, National Library (legal deposit library) including Pictorial and Map Collections; photo-copying service available; Dir. E. E. BURKE, F.L.A.; Deputy Dir. R. W. S. TURNER; publs. *Oppenheimer Series, Reports, Bibliographical Series, Occasional Papers, Rhodesia National Bibliography* (annual), *Guide to the Public Archives of Rhodesia, Vol., 1, 1890–1923, Guide to the Historical Manuscripts in the National Archives of Rhodesia.*

National Free Library of Rhodesia: P.O. Box 1773, Bulawayo; f. 1943 as national lending library for educational, scientific and technical books and national centre for inter-library loans; 40,000 vols.; Librarian N. JOHNSON, A.L.A.

Public Library: P.O.B. 586, Bulawayo; f. 1896; reference, lending, junior library; postal service to rural readers; Africana/Rhodesian collection; legal deposit library for Rhodesia; 50,000 vols.; librarian R. W. STACEY, F.L.A.

Queen Victoria Memorial Library: P.O.B. 1087, Salisbury; f. 1902; 49,000 vols.; Librarian and Sec. Mrs. M. ROSS-SMITH, F.L.A.

Turner Memorial Library: Umtali; f. 1902; 19,900 vols.; Librarian Mrs. R. S. HAMMET.

University of Rhodesia Library: P.O.B. M.P.45, Mount Pleasant, Salisbury; f. 1956; 190,000 vols.; 3,500 periodicals; Medical library; Law library; Education library; Map library; Africana collection; photo-copying facilities; Catalogue of Courtauld Collection of Roman coins; Librarian A. HARRISON, B.A., A.L.A.; publs. *Periodicals in Rhodesian Libraries*, and occasional papers.

MUSEUMS AND ART GALLERIES

The National Museums of Rhodesia: P.O.B. 8540, Causeway, Salisbury; administered by a Board of Trustees appointed by the Minister of Internal Affairs; Dir. of Museums REAY H. N. SMITHERS, O.B.E., D.SC., F.Z.S.; Sec. Mrs. R. HANLEY; publs. occasional papers, *Arnoldia* (Rhodesia), monographs, pamphlets.

National Museum: Selborne Ave., P.O.B. 240, Bulawayo; f. 1901; geological, entomological and zoological exhibits; study collections covering Ethiopian region, with special reference to southern Africa; historical, ethnographical and prehistoric exhibits and study collections appertaining to Rhodesia and adjacent regions; Curator and Keeper of Invertebrate Zoology E. C. G. PINHEY, D.SC., F.L.S., F.R.E.S.; Keeper of Vertebrate Zoology M. P. S. IRWIN, F.Z.S.; Keeper of Mammalogy V. J. WILSON, F.Z.S.; Keeper of Geology C. C. SMITH, B.SC.; Keeper of Antiquities C. W. D. PAGDEN, B.A.

Queen Victoria Museum: P.O.B. 8006, Causeway, Salisbury; f. 1902; zoological, ethnographical, archaeological and historical exhibits and study collections appertaining to Rhodesia and adjacent areas, with special reference to Mashonaland; Curator M. A. RAATH, B.SC.

Umtali Museum: Victory Ave., Umtali; f. 1954; geological, zoological, ethnographical, archaeological and historical exhibits and study collections, appertaining to Rhodesia and its Eastern Districts in particular; Curator and Keeper of Herpetology D. G. BROADLEY, PH.D.; Keeper of Zoology H. D. JACKSON.

National Gallery of Rhodesia: P.O.B. 8155, Causeway, Salisbury; f. 1957; permanent collection includes works by Reynolds, Gainsborough, Morland, Murillo, Ribera, Bellini, Pannini, Mantegna, Caracciolo, Rodin, and traditional and contemporary African art; art library and reading room; Dir. F. McEWEN, O.B.E.

UNIVERSITY

THE UNIVERSITY OF RHODESIA

P.O.B. M.P. 167, MOUNT PLEASANT, SALISBURY

Telephone: Salisbury 36635, 35674

Telegraphic Address: University, Salisbury

Academic year: March to December.

In February 1955 a Royal Charter was granted to the University College of Rhodesia and Nyasaland. The College became the University of Rhodesia under revised statutes adopted in 1970, but the Charter was preserved as the basic constitutional instrument of the University.

Principal and Vice-Chancellor: Rev. Prof. R. CRAIG, M.A., PH.D., HON.D.D., S.T.M.

Vice-Principal and Deputy Vice-Chancellor: Prof. G. BOND, PH.D., A.R.C.S., C.ENG., M.I.M.M., F.G.S.

Registrar: K. V. MACQUIRE, O.B.E., M.A.

Librarian: A. HARRISON, B.A., A.L.A.

Number of teachers: 190.

Number of students: 1,342.

Publications: *Calendar, Prospectus.*

DEANS:

Faculty of Arts: Prof. R. S. ROBERTS, PH.D.

Faculty of Education: P. G. S. GILBERT, B.SC., DIP.ED.

Faculty of Medicine: Prof. W. F. ROSS, B.SC., M.B., CH.B., D.P.H.

Faculty of Science: Dr. G. D. SCOTT, PH.D.

Faculty of Social Studies: A. J. DIXON, M.A., B.LITT.

ATTACHED INSTITUTES:

Centre for Inter-Racial Studies.
Director: M. W. MURPHREE, M.A., PH.D.

Institute of Adult Education.
Director: J. McHARG, M.A., L.R.A.M.

Institute of Education.
Director: R. C. BONE, M.A.

Institute of Mining Research.
Director: K. A. VIEWING, B.SC., PH.D., D.I.C., A.I.M.M., F.G.S.

Science Education Centre.
Director: P. G. S. GILBERT, B.SC., DIP.ED.

COLLEGES

Chibero College of Agriculture: Private Bag 901, Norton; f. 1961; Three-year Diploma in Agriculture for Africans.
Principal: D. P. HANHAM.
Library of 976 vols.
Number of teachers: 16.
Number of students: 80.
Publication: *Agricultural Education.*

Gwebi College of Agriculture: Private Bag 376B, Salisbury; f. 1950.
Principal: F. B. RHODES.
The college provides a two-year course, leading to the Diploma in Agriculture.
Library of 2,000 vols.
Number of teachers: 23.
Number of students: 84.

Nyatsime College: Seke; f. 1960; African secondary and technical college, giving four-year course in Cambridge O Level, five-year course in Business Education and five-year courses leading to City and Guilds of London Institute examination.
Principal: D. M. K. SAGONDA, B.A.

Rhodesian College of Music: Civic Centre, Rotten Row, Salisbury C.3; f. 1948.
Chairman: B. W. S. O'CONNELL.
Director: W. D. CALDWELL.
Registrar: Mrs. E. M. WAY.

Salisbury School of Art: Corner Rhodes Avenue/Eighth-Street, Salisbury.

Salisbury Polytechnic: P.O.B. 8074, Causeway, Salisbury; number of students: approx. 5,000. Full-time and sandwich courses for Technicians and Craftsmen; courses in Printing and Adult Education; full-time and part-time courses in Commercial subjects to B.Com. level; library of 10,000 vols.; Principal D. J. CLOSE.

SELECT BIBLIOGRAPHY

ARRIGHI, G. *The Political Economy of Rhodesia.* The Hague, 1967.

BARBER, J. *Rhodesia: The Road to Rebellion.* London, 1967.

BARBER, W. J. *The Economy of British Central Africa.* Oxford, 1961.

BULL, T. (Ed.). *Rhodesian Perspective.* London, 1967.

CURTIN, T., and MURRAY, D. *Economic Sanctions and Rhodesia.* London, 1967.

GANN, L. *A History of Southern Rhodesia.* London, 1965.

GANN, L., and GELFAND, M. *Huggins of Rhodesia.* London, 1964.

GRAY, R. *The Two Nations.* London, 1960.

LEYS, C. *European Politics in Southern Rhodesia.* Oxford, 1959.

MASON, P. *Birth of a Dilemma.* London, 1958.

MLAMBO, E. *Rhodesia: Struggle for a Birthright.* London, 1972.

PALLEY, C. *The Constitutional History and Law of Southern Rhodesia, 1888–1965.* Oxford, 1966.

RANGER, T. *Revolt in Southern Rhodesia 1896–7.* London, 1967.

RANGER, T. (Ed.). *Aspects of Central African History.* London, 1968.

SHAMUYARIRA, N. *Crisis in Rhodesia.* London, 1965.

VAMBE, LAWRENCE. *An Ill-Fated People: Zimbabwe Before and After Rhodes.* London, Heineman, 1972.

WEINRICH, A. K. H. *Chiefs and Councils of Rhodesia.* London, Heinemann Educational, 1971.

YUDELMAN, M. *Africans on the Land.* Oxford, 1964.

See also: a symposium on Rhodesia in the *Journal of Commonwealth Political Studies* (July, 1969).

The course of the negotiations on independence between the British and Rhodesian governments can be studied in the following Command Papers:

Cmnd. 2073 (1963); Cmnd. 2807 (1965); Cmnd. 3171 (1966); Cmnd. 3793 (1968); Cmnd. 4065 (1969); Cmnd. 4835 (1971); Cmnd. 4964 (1972)—Pearce Commission Report.

Rwanda

PHYSICAL AND SOCIAL GEOGRAPHY*

Pierre Gourou

Rwanda, like Burundi, stands out among the independent states of black Africa for both the smallness of its territory (10,169 sq. miles) and the density of its population (a 1970 total of 3,724,000). The population, again as in Burundi, is composed of Hutu (about 84 per cent), Tutsi (about 15 per cent) and Twa (1 per cent), and the language is Kinyarwanda, a Bantu language which is similar enough to Kirundi to be assimilated with it.

It seems at first sight strange that Rwanda has not been absorbed into a wider political entity. Admittedly the Rwandan nation has long been united by language and custom and was part of a state that won the respect of the east African slave-traders. However, other ethnic groups, such as the Kongo, Luba, Luo and Zande, which were well established and organized in small territorial areas, have not been able to develop into national states. That Rwanda has been able to achieve this is partly the result of developments during the colonial period. While part of German East Africa, Rwanda (or Ruanda-Urundi as it then was with Burundi) was treated as a peripheral state of little economic value. After the 1914–18 war it was entrusted to Belgium as a mandate by the League of Nations and, although administered jointly with the Belgian Congo, was not absorbed into the larger state. Moreover, the historic separateness and national traditions of both Rwanda and Burundi have prevented their amalgamation.

PHYSICAL CONDITIONS

Although the land supports a high population density, physical conditions are not very favourable. Rwanda's land-mass is very rugged and broken up. Basically it is part of a Precambrian shelf from which, through erosion, the harder rocks have obtruded, leaving the softer ones submerged. Thus very ancient folds have been raised and a relief surface carved out with steep gradients covered with a soil poor in quality because of its fineness and fragility. Rwanda's physiognomy therefore consists of a series of sharply defined hills, with steep slopes and flat ridges, which are intersected by deep valleys, the bottoms of which are often formed by marshy plains. The north is dominated by the lofty and powerful chain of volcanoes, the Virunga, whose highest peak is Karisimbi (14,826 ft.) and whose lava, having scarcely cooled down, has not yet produced cultivable soil.

The climate is far from favourable for economic activity, with a daily temperature range of as much as 25°F. Kigali, the capital (25,000 inhabitants), has an average temperature of 66°F. and 40 inches of rain. Altitude is a factor which modifies the temperature (and prevents sleeping sickness above about 3,000 ft.), but such a factor is of debatable value for agriculture. Average rainfall is only barely sufficient for agricultural purposes, but two wet and two relatively dry seasons are experienced, making two harvests possible.

* See map on p. 896.

RECENT HISTORY*

René Lemarchand

In sharp contrast with the recent history of its neighbour to the south (Burundi), the political evolution of Rwanda has been characterized by a gradual consolidation of the gains made by the Hutu in the years immediately preceding independence. Owing to the greater rigidity of ethnic cleavages, in Rwanda the prospects of independence not only failed to enhance the legitimacy of the Crown but in fact raised those very issues around which anti-monarchical sentiments crystallized. Having ceased to be a referee, the Crown became a political football long before it could alter the rules of the game. A year and half before the country's scheduled accession to independence Rwanda was a kingdom without a king;

moreover, following the so-called "*coup* of Gitarama*"*, in January 1961, the Hutu élites were able to exercise substantial control over the institutions of government both at the national and provincial levels.

The comparatively early juncture at which Hutu elements launched their revolution, together with the support they received from the Belgian authorities on the spot and Catholic missionaries, made the success of the revolution almost a foregone conclusion. Under the leadership of Grégoire Kayibanda, the *Parti de l'Émancipation du Peuple Hutu* (*Parmehutu*) emerged as a fairly cohesive political organization, extending its ramifications to each of the country's seven prefectures. Although civilian and military élites are,

* For the period before independence *see* Recent History of Zaire, p. 990.

as in Burundi, drawn from the same ethnic stratum, the army in Rwanda remains under civilian control. Owing to the circumstances of its birth the army has been from the very outset animated by sentiments which sustained and reinforced the revolutionary aspirations of the civilian élites. Its ethos is that of the nation-in-arms. Defending the state against its domestic and foreign enemies is part of the fundamental reconstruction of society envisaged by President Kayibanda.

Cultural and regional discontinuities within the Hutu stratum nonetheless persist, as between northerners and southerners, Kiga and non-Kiga, *bakonde* (patrons) and *bagererwa* (clients), all of which tend to reflect social and economic differentiations inherent in the Hutu subculture. The vested interests of northern politicians in maintaining a form of clientage (*ubukonde*) that some might regard as "feudal" is certainly one major reason why Kayibanda has consistently avoided all initiatives implying a

redistribution of wealth and social status in the north. Through regional and ethnic arithmetic an attempt is made to incorporate within the party and the government a wide variety of regional and economic interests. Meanwhile, however, many of the characteristics of the *ancien régime* have reappeared in a new guise, with President Kayibanda casting himself in the role of a presidential monarch.

As in Burundi, power in Rwanda is the monopoly of a specific ethnic segment. Yet Hutu rule in Rwanda means the rule of politicians claiming to represent 95 per cent of the population, whereas army rule in Burundi is not only equated with Tutsi rule, but, for the Hutu masses, with minority rule of the worst kind. With each society moving ever more firmly in the direction of ethnic homogeneity at the élite level, chances of a violent confrontation between them are likely to increase correspondingly, with the Zairian army perhaps adding yet another dimension to the conflict.

ECONOMY

Like Burundi, Rwanda's two main physical handicaps to economic development are the extreme population density, and the distance from the sea. The population problem is aggravated by the current rate of growth, which is estimated to be 2.8 per cent per annum. Such a growth will necessitate a doubling of food production in the next thirty years simply to maintain the people of Rwanda at subsistence level. Since population pressure has aggravated the soil erosion caused by leaching and other natural causes, land unexploited at present in the east of the country and in the marshy plains must be utilized.

The agricultural sector accounts for almost the total economic activity of Rwanda, and within that sector about 95 per cent of the total value of agricultural production is subsistence crops.

The main food crops are sweet potatoes, millet, beans, peas, rice and maize. Bananas are also grown both for food and for making beer. The Tutsi subsist mainly on the milk, meat and blood of their cattle.

The major cash crop is coffee, exports of which were worth 656 million Rwanda francs in 1969, compared with the earnings of the other major primary exports, pyrethrum (36.0 million francs), hides and skins (25.6 million) and tea 69.3 million). The government is attempting to diversify the crops grown for export through the *Office des cultures industrielles du Rwanda* (OCIR), set up in 1964. This is concentrating its efforts on tobacco, cotton, pyrethrum, forestry and, above all, tea. The programme will take ten years to fulfil and is being aided by the EEC. In addition the EDF, together with FAO and the World Bank, is involved in aiding the setting up of local farming communes (*paysannats*).

The industrial sector follows the usual pattern for

the less developed African states, and food-based industries, such as the processing of coffee and tea, a sugar factory, brewery, etc., predominate. Otherwise there are two small textile concerns, small chemical and engineering works, and various other enterprises based on transistors, sandals and plastics, and printing.

Cassiterite is the most important mineral produced, and is second only to coffee in exports, earning 439 million Rwanda francs in 1969. Wolframite is also important as an export. The mining sector as a whole is controlled by four Belgian companies, and most exports are destined for the EEC and the U.S.A. The only other mineral worthy of note is the natural gas which is being exploited in Lake Kivu.

Rwanda's relief is ideal for power generation, and in addition to the Mururu station on the Ruzizi, which has a maximum capacity of 20,400 kW., there are installations at Ntaruka and Gisenyi. A new hydroelectric project at Mukungwa is being studied with the aid of the EDF. Rwanda, Burundi and Tanzania are co-operating at the same time in a two-year project to determine the water, power and mineral resources of the Kigera River Basin. The project is supported financially by the UNDP.

Apart from Rwanda's relatively well-developed road system, communications in the country are poor. Rwanda's trade is dependent on the ports of Mombasa, Dar es Salaam and Matadi. There are no railways.

Most of Rwanda's trade is with Belgium, with a significant proportion going to other EEC countries and the U.S.A. Belgium and the EEC are also the main suppliers of aid.

STATISTICAL SURVEY

AREA AND POPULATION

AREA (sq. km.)	POPULATION (1967 estimates)				
	Total (1970)	Tribes			Capital
		Hutu	Tutsi	Twa	Kigali
26,338*	3,724,000	2,520,000	500,000	20,000	25,000

* 10,169 sq. miles.

Births and Deaths (1970): Registered births totalled 120,000 (birth rate 35.5 per 1,000) and registered deaths 25,000 (death rate 7.0 per 1,000). Registration is not, however, complete. UN estimates for 1965–70 put the average annual birth rate at 51.8 per 1,000 and the death rate at 23.3 per 1,000.

EMPLOYMENT
(1968)

Agriculture	18,097
Mining	11,135
Manufacturing . . .	11,077
Building	3,538
Water, Electricity, Sanitation .	2,614
Commerce	3,815
Transport	1,322
Services	12,981
Civil Service	1,751
Technical Assistance . .	490
Education	6,781
Domestic Work* . . .	10,000
TOTAL	83,600

* Estimate.

Total Labour Force (1970): In an estimated population of 3,609,000 (probably an under-estimate), the economically active numbered 1,955,000, including 1,775,000 engaged in agriculture (ILO and FAO estimates).

LAND USE, 1970
('000 hectares)

Arable Land	522
Under Permanent Crops . .	182
Permanent Meadows and Pastures .	817
Forest Land	328
Other Land	675
Inland Water	110
TOTAL AREA	2,634

AGRICULTURE

PRINCIPAL CROPS
(metric tons)

	1969	1970	1971
Maize	41,000	64,000	60,000
Sorghum	126,000	156,000	140,000*
Potatoes	129,000	126,000	126,000*
Sweet Potatoes and Yams .	324,225	417,000	n.a.
Cassava (Manioc) . .	282,500	345,000	n.a.
Dry Beans . . .	146,124	144,000	140,000*
Dry Peas	60,948	65,000	63,000*
Bananas and Plantains .	1,638,000	n.a.	n.a.
Groundnuts (in shell) . .	7,000	6,000*	6,000*
Coffee	14,200	14,100	12,000
Tea	800	1,245	2,000
Tobacco	900	800*	800*

* FAO estimate.
Source: mainly FAO, *Production Yearbook 1971.*

LIVESTOCK
('000)

	1968–69	1969–70	1970–71
Cattle . .	680	710	740*
Sheep . .	227	228*	230*
Goats . .	620*	600*	600*
Pigs . . .	47	54	60*
Chickens . .	600	510	550*

* FAO estimate.

Source: FAO, *Production Yearbook 1971.*

LIVESTOCK PRODUCTS
(metric tons)

	1968	1969	1970	1971
Cows' Milk	35,000	37,000	39,000*	40,000*
Goats' Milk	7,000*	6,000*	6,000*	6,000*
Beef and Veal	8,000*	8,000*	8,000*	n.a.
Mutton and Lamb	3,000*	3,000*	3,000*	n.a.
Hen Eggs	300*	300*	300*	300*
Cattle Hides (dry) . . .	540	480	579	n.a.
Sheep Skins	174*	179*	168	n.a.
Goat Skins	500*	470*	450*	n.a.

* FAO estimate.

Source: FAO, *Production Yearbook 1971.*

Forestry (1967–70): An estimated 4.5 million cubic metres of roundwood removed for fuel each year. In addition, 6,000 cubic metres of logs for industrial wood were taken in 1967. Other forest products (1967): 30 metric tons of bamboo.

FISHING
(metric tons)

1967 . . .	1,000
1968 . . .	900
1969 . . .	1,000
1970 . . .	1,300

MINING
(metric tons)

	1967	1968	1969
Cassiterite* . .	2,006	1,797	1,784
Wolframite† . .	536	624	486
Beryl . .	109	149	267
Colombo-tantalite .	31	28	30

Natural gas: about one million cubic metres per year.

* Tin metal content (metric tons): 1,343 in 1967; 1,340 in 1968; 1,340 in 1969; 1,320 in 1970; 1,320 in 1971.

† Tungsten trioxide content (metric tons): 350 in 1967; 407 in 1968; 319 in 1969; and 2,152 in 1970.

INDUSTRY

	1967	1968	1969
Beer ('000 hectolitres) .	117	176	129
Radio Receivers (number) .	6,000	6,000	4,000

In 1966 there were 14 manufacturing enterprises, with a total of 3,000 employees.

Electric energy production (million kWh.): 10.8 in 1963 (including 10.3 from hydroelectricity); 48.1 in 1966 (hydroelectricity 46.8).

FINANCE
100 centimes = 1 Rwanda franc.
Coins: 1, 5 and 10 francs.
Notes: 20, 50, 100, 500 and 1,000 francs.
Exchange rates (December 1972): £1 sterling = 216.245 Rwanda francs;
U.S. $1 = 92.105 Rwanda francs.
1,000 Rwanda francs = £4.624 = $10.857.
(*Note:* Between April 1966 and December 1971 the Rwanda franc was valued at 1 U.S. cent.)

BUDGET
('000 R.F.)

	1966	1967	1968	1969
Revenue	1,266,555	1,501,178	1,375,335	1,636,618
Expenditure	1,130,904	1,499,415	1,382,580	1,664,000

Currency in Circulation (June 30th, 1972): 1,499 million Rwanda francs.
Gross Domestic Product (1963): U.S. $97 million (unofficial estimate).

EXTERNAL TRADE
(million R.F.)

	1967	1968	1969	1970	1971
Imports	2,022.2	2,245.8	2,362.4	2,909.9	3,298.3
Exports	1,399.9	1,472.4	1,410.0	2,461.3	2,233.3

PRINCIPAL COMMODITIES
('000 R.F.)

IMPORTS	1967	1968	1969
Food and Live Animals	153,190	198,400	260,560
Cereals and preparations	79,590	72,970	133,240
Beverages and Tobacco	24,100	83,310	140,300
Tobacco and manufactures	5,690	47,870	105,920
Petroleum Products	122,160	141,020	150,190
Chemicals	100,130	137,830	155,960
Basic Manufactures	802,310	933,880	807,830
Textile yarn, fabrics, etc.	360,190	443,400	335,340
Cotton yarn and fabrics	115,020	174,700	125,650
Synthetic and regenerated yarn, fabrics	183,160	233,620	158,170
Iron and steel	137,790	147,610	141,570
Machinery and Transport Equipment	456,100	418,720	464,870
Machinery (non-electric)	125.200	108,790	106,370
Electrical equipment	60,070	94,350	93,060
Transport equipment	270,830	215,570	265,438
Road vehicles	216,910	202,720	257,080
Miscellaneous Manufactured Articles	182,460	118,220	186,380
TOTAL (incl. others)	2,022,150	2,245,770	2,362,370

EXPORTS	1967	1968	1969
Food and Live Animals	805,270	914,370	728,510
Barley	3,230	17,560	1,860
Coffee (green and roasted)	774,350	846,790	656,069
Tea	23,600	46,900	69,331
Hides and Skins (undressed)	24,700	13,250	25,630
Tin Ores and Concentrates	416,460	343,900	438,570
Tungsten Ores and Concentrates	100,710	159,350	154,110
Pyrethrum	29,480	17,420	36,004
Cinchona Bark	4,440	9,540	11,640
TOTAL (incl. others)	1,399,920	1,472,410	1,409,990

Source: mainly United Nations, *Yearbook of International Trade Statistics 1969.*

1970: Coffee 57.0% of total export earnings; tin 19.0%.
1971: Coffee 50.3%; tin 20.5%.

PRINCIPAL COUNTRIES
('ooo R.F.)

IMPORTS	1967	1968	1969
Belgium/Luxembourg	561,470	407,700	362,442
Burundi	77,650	50,940	37,630
France	117,490	89,450	121,340
Germany, Federal Republic	186,740	265,090	257,723
Hong Kong	34,750	37,690	45,560
Italy	22,540	31,190	39,665
Japan	248,090	305,050	328,719
Kenya	55,660	123,590	176,216
Netherlands	33,420	37,050	32,699
Uganda	272,540	309,270	275,051
United Kingdom	71,250	102,130	133,590
U.S.A.	138,990	153,050	156,258
Zaire	18,170	67,080	70,300
TOTAL (incl. others)	2,022,150	2,245,770	2,362,370

Source: mainly United Nations, *Yearbook of International Trade Statistics 1969.*

EXPORTS*	1967	1968	1969
Belgium/Luxembourg	435,530	347,590	417,450
Burundi	33,100	25,480	26,320
France	7,590	35,170	8,510
Japan	21,590	22,560	15,950
Kenya	7,270	33,600	91,100
Netherlands	11,040	16,230	21,290
Uganda	62,110	104,340	107,030
United Kingdom	11,300	39,570	34,020
U.S.A.†	n.a.	n.a.	n.a.
Zaire	11,650	21,320	2,850
TOTAL (incl. others)	1,399,920	1,472,410	1,409,990

* Including certain goods consigned at Mombasa, in Kenya, for which the distribution by country is not known. The value of these exports (in 'ooo Rwanda francs) was: 591,850 in 1967; 818,720 in 1968; and 664,150 in 1969.

† The United States received more than 49 per cent (by value) of Rwanda's exports in 1965, but figures for subsequent years are not available.

Source: United Nations, *Yearbook of International Trade Statistics 1969.*

TRANSPORT

Roads (1969): Passenger Cars 3,400, Commercial vehicles 1,900.

Shipping (1962): Lake Kivu freights 70,000 metric tons.

Civil Aviation (1964): Passenger arrivals 18,928, departures 19,800; Freight entered 737 tons, cleared 693 tons; Mail 108 tons.

COMMUNICATIONS

Telephones (at January 1st): 1,389 in 1969; 1,433 in 1970.

Radio: 30,000 receivers in use at December 31st, 1970.

EDUCATION
(1968–69)

	PUPILS
Elementary Schools	394,099
Secondary Schools (subsidised) . .	9,332
Higher Education	470

Scholarships at universities abroad: 207.

THE CONSTITUTION

(promulgated November, 1962)

The Republic of Rwanda was proclaimed in January 1961, following the abolition by public referendum of the Monarchy.

The Republic. Rwanda is a democratic, social and sovereign State. There is equality among citizens, who exercise national rights through their representatives.

Civil Rights. Fundamental liberties as defined in the Declaration of Human rights are guaranteed.

The Executive. Executive power is exercised by the President and his Ministers. The President is elected for four years by direct universal suffrage and may be re-elected. The President, who nominates and dismisses Ministers, presides over the Council of Ministers; negotiates and terminates all treaties; promulgates laws; may suspend but not dissolve the National Assembly; exercises the prerogative of mercy; and is the Commander-in-Chief of the Armed Forces.

Legislative power. Exercised jointly by the National Assembly and the President. The National Assembly, which is elected by universal direct suffrage, votes laws and the budget.

The Judiciary. The Supreme Court is the guardian of the Constitution. It has sole jurisdiction over penal matters affecting the President, Ministers or Deputies if indicted by a three-quarter majority of the National Assembly.

Revision of the Constitution. Both the President and the National Assembly may initiate Constitutional reforms.

THE GOVERNMENT

Head of State: President GRÉGOIRE KAYIBANDA.

COUNCIL OF MINISTERS
(December 1972)

Premier: President GRÉGOIRE KAYIBANDA.

Minister of Interior and Justice: ANDRÉ SEBATWARE.

Minister of the National Guard and Police: Lt.-Col. JUVÉNAL HABYALIMANA.

Minister of National Education: GASPARD HARELIMANA.

Minister of Posts, Telecommunications and Transport: AUGUSTIN KAMOSO.

Minister of Agriculture and Livestock: DAMIEN NKEZABERA.

Minister of Co-ordination of Economical, Technical and Financial Affairs: M. D. GASHONGA.

Minister of Finance: FIDÈLE NZANANA.

Minister of International Co-operation: AUGUSTIN MUNYANEZA.

Minister of Family and Community Development: ATHANASE SHIRAMAKA.

Minister of Commerce, Mines and Industry: ANASTASE MAKUZA.

Minister of Information and Tourism: FRODUALD MINANI.

Minister of Health: THEODORE SINDIKUBWABO.

Minister of Co-operation and Political and Administrative Affairs: Capt. BAPTISTE SEYANGA.

Minister of Public Works: FRANÇOIS NHUNGUYINKA.

Secretary of State for Planning: EMMANUEL HITAYEZU.

Secretary of State for Civil Service: GODEFROID NYILIBAKWE.

Secretary of State for Sports and Youth: Capt. ANDRÉ BIZIMANA.

DIPLOMATIC REPRESENTATION

EMBASSIES ACCREDITED TO RWANDA

Belgium: B.P. 81, Kigali; *Ambassador:* FRANS BAEKE-LANDT.

Burundi: *Ambassador:* GABRIEL NDICUNGUYE.

France: B.P. 53, Kigali; *Ambassador:* ROBERT PICQUET.

Germany, Federal Republic: B.P. 335, Kigali; *Ambassador:* M. W. FROEWIS.

India: Kampala, Uganda.

Israel: B.P. 313, Kigali; *Chargé d'Affaires a.i.:* HAIM HARARI.

Italy: Kampala, Uganda.

Japan: Kinshasa, Zaire.

Netherlands: Kinshasa, Zaire.

Switzerland: Ave. de l'Assemblée, Kigali; *Chargé d'Affaires a.i.:* ROBERT SUTER.

Tanzania: Kinshasa, Zaire.

U.S.S.R.: B.P. 40, Kigali; *Ambassador:* G. JILIAKOV.

United Kingdom: Kampala, Uganda.

U.S.A.: B.P. 28, Kigali; *Ambassador:* ROBERT F. CORRIGAN.

Vatican: B.P. 261, Kigali; *Apostolic Nuncio:* Mgr. CAREW

Yugoslavia: Kampala, Uganda.

Zaire: Kigali; *Ambassador:* NGYESE MI SOMA.

Rwanda also has diplomatic relations with Austria, Canada, Chad, China (People's Republic), Czechoslovakia, Denmark, Egypt, Ethiopia, Ghana, Guinea, Korea (Republic of), Luxembourg, Nigeria, Romania, Senegal and Spain.

LEGISLATIVE ASSEMBLY

President: THADDÉE BAGARAGAZA.
Vice-President: JOSEPH NDWANIYE.

ELECTIONS, OCTOBER 1969

The governing party, MDR—Parmehutu, won all 47 seats. Opposition parties refused to present any candidates at the 1965 elections, and have since gone out of existence.

POLITICAL PARTIES

Mouvement démocratique républicain—Parmehutu (*Republican Democratic Movement Parmehutu*): P.O.B. 19, Gitarama, supported by the Hutu people. Aims: to overthrow the feudal regime of Tutsi minority; Pres. G. KAYIBANDA, Sec. ATHANASE MBARUBUKEYE.

DEFENCE

The military forces consist of a national guard of 2,750, a gendarmerie of 400 and a civil police of 800.

Chief of Staff: Lt.-Col. JUVÉNAL HABYALIMANA.

JUDICIAL SYSTEM

The judiciary is independent of the Executive. Codified law is administered by the Courts of First Instance and the Court of Appeal. Traditional law is administered by the Supreme Court.

CODIFIED LAW

Court of Appeal: Kigali.

Courts of First Instance: there are ten Courts of First Instance.

TRADITIONAL LAW

Supreme Court of Rwanda: Nyabisindu; five sections for administration of Lower Courts, Constitutional Law, Council of State, Cassation, and Public Accounts; Pres. FULGENCE SEMINEGA.

RELIGION

AFRICAN RELIGIONS

Traditional belief is mainly in a God "Imana". About half the population are followers of traditional beliefs.

CHRISTIANITY

ROMAN CATHOLIC

Archdiocese of Kabgayi: B.P. 715, Kigali; f. 1900; Archbishop Most Rev. ANDRÉ PERRAUDIN; Suffragan Sees: Bishop of Nyundo Rt. Rev. ALOYS BIGIRUMWAMI, Bishop of Kibungo Rt. Rev. JOSEPH SIBOMANA, Bishop of Butare Rt. Rev. JEAN BAPTISTE GAHAMANYL, Bishop of Ruhengeri Rt. Rev. PHOCAS NIKWIGIZE.

There are 1,824,505 adherents and 387 priests in Rwanda.

ANGLICANS

Under the Province of Uganda:

Archbishop of Uganda: Most Rev. ERICA SABITI, D.D.

Bishop of Rwanda: Rt. Rev. A. SEBUNUNGURI, B.P. 61, Kigali.

There are about 120,000 adherents in Rwanda.

OTHER PROTESTANTS

About 250,000; there is a substantial Seventh Day Adventist minority.

ISLAM

There are a few Muslims.

PRESS AND RADIO

PERIODICALS

Co-operative Trafipro: B.P. 302, Kigali; importation/exportation.

Imhavo: B.P. 63, Kigali; twice monthly; Kinya-rwanda; circ. 40,000.

Kinya Mateka: Archevêché de Kabgayi, B.P. 761, Kigali; twice a month; Dir. S. M. L. MOULART.

Hobe: B.P. 761, Kigali; monthly; Dir. S. M. L. MOULART.

Rwanda-Carrefour d'Afrique: B.P. 83, Kigali; publ. by Ministry of Foreign Affairs; monthly; French.

RWANDA

BROADCASTING

Radiodiffusion de la République Rwandaise: B.P. 83, Kigali; broadcasts daily programme in Kinya-rwanda, Swahili, French and English; Dir. of Information NOEL BUREGEYA; Chief Editor PIERRE CLAVER KARANGWA.

Deutsche Welle Relay Station Africa: Kigali; broadcasts daily in German, English, French, Hausa, Kiswahili and Amharic.

There were 30,000 radio receivers in 1970.

FINANCE

(cap.=capital; p.u.=paid up; m.=million; amounts in Rwanda Francs)

BANKING

CENTRAL BANK

Banque Nationale du Rwanda: B.P. 531, Kigali; f. 1964; Gov. M. HATTORI; Vice-Gov. J. BIRARA.

SAVINGS BANK

Caisse d'Épargne du Rwanda: Kigali; f. 1964.

COMMERCIAL BANKS

Banque Commerciale du Rwanda S.A.R.L.: Kigali; f. 1963; brs. in Butare, Byumba, Cyangugu and Gisenyi; cap. 50m.; Res. 13m.; Man. for Rwanda L. ROEGIERS.

Banque de Kigali: B.P. 175, Kigali; f. 1966; cap. 50m.; dep. 368m.; Pres. I. HAKIZIMANA; Man. L. DEGROOT.

DEVELOPMENT BANK

Banque Rwandaise de Développement: Kigali; f. 1967; cap. p.u. 50m.

TRADE AND TRANSPORT

TRADE UNIONS

Confédération générale du travail du Rwanda (CGTR): Kigali; union for Banya-Rwanda workers.

Union des Travailleurs du Rwanda (UTR): Kigali; affiliated to IFCTU.

RAILWAYS

There are no railways.

ROADS

There are 1,465 km. of highways and 3,945 km. of minor roads. Rwanda's first asphalt road, now under construction, will link Kigali with Kabale in S.W. Uganda.

INLAND WATERWAYS

There are services on Lake Kivu from Kibuye to Zaire.

CIVIL AVIATION

There are airfields at Butare, Gisenyi and Gabiro; the international airport is at Kigali. Rwanda is served by the following foreign airlines: Air Zaire, EAAC and Sabena.

MAJOR INDUSTRIAL COMPANIES

BRALIRWA: P.O.B. 180, Gisenyi; manufacture of beer and soft drinks.

COREM: P.O.B. 19, Kigali; tin-mining.

Georwanda: B.P. 19, Kigali; f. 1945; cap. 150m. RF. Mining of tin and other metals.
Dir. G. SAUVENIER; 1,100 employees.

Hatton and Cookson: Kigali; retail of food, hardware, electrical equipment, building materials and general merchandise.

Minétain-Rwanda: B.P. 266, Kigali; f. 1929; cap. 100m. RF. Mining of cassiterite, colombo-tantalite, wolfram, beryl amblygonite.
Dir. HERIN JOSEPH, 2,770 employees.

Murri Frères: B.P. 110, Chantier de Kigali, Kigali; f. 1963; private company.
Heavy engineering and construction.
Proprietor PIETRO MURRI; Dir. MARINO CALLIGARIS; 350 employees.

SOMUKI: Rutongo-Kigali; tin-mining.

TOURISM

Ministère de l'Information et du Tourisme: B.P. 83, Kigali; Minister FRODUALD MINANI.

EDUCATION

Schools are run by the State and by missions but cannot yet provide education for all children. A few students go to Zaire or Belgium for higher education. According to the law of August 1966 primary school is free and obligatory for children of seven to eleven years, and parents may choose where their children are educated.

RESEARCH INSTITUTES

Institut des Sciences Agronomiques du Rwanda—I.S.A.R: B.P. 138, Butare; f. 1932; 950 personnel; four centres:
Rubona: living plants, economic plants (coffee, tobacco, etc.), zootechnics and agronomy.
Songa: zootechnics.
Rwerere: high-altitude cultures (tea, wheat), zootechnics.
Karama: zootechnics, agricultural planning, hydro-climatology.

Service Géologique du Rwanda: Ministère du Commerce, des Mines et de l'Industrie, B.P. 15, Ruhengeri; f. 1962; geological services to the Government and private industry; to prepare a geological map of Rwanda; prospecting; library of 3,610 vols.; Dir. P. CORMINBOEUF; publ. *Bulletin du Service Géologique* (annual).

UNIVERSITY

UNIVERSITÉ NATIONALE DU RWANDA

B.P. 117, BUTARE

Telephone: 11-12-16.

Founded 1963.

Language of instruction: French; State control; Academic year: September to July (three terms).

Honorary President: The President of Rwanda, H.E. GRÉGOIRE KAYIBANDA.
Rector: SYLVESTRE NSANZIMANA.
Vice-Rector: JOHN MACFARLANE.
Registrar: GERARD SLEDSENS.
Librarian: PAULETTE TRUDEAU.

Library of 38,000 volumes.
Number of teachers: 47.
Number of students: 410.
Publication: *L'Informateur.*

Deans:

Faculty of Letters: R. M. Cattin, o.p.
Faculty of Medicine: L. Van Dendriessche.
Faculty of Sciences: M. Lefrançois.
Faculty of Social and Economic Sciences: N. Ruhashyan-
kiko.

Affiliated Institute:

Institut National de Recherche Scientifique: P.O.B. 80,
Butare; f. 1947 as the Institut pour la Recherche
Scientifique en Afrique Centrale; undertakes basic
research in anthropology, economics, geophysics, and
in animal, vegetable and mineral resources; library of
3,000 vols.; 2 stations at Uinka and Mimuli; Dir. and
Prof. of Botany Paul Deuse; Prof. of Linguistics
André Coupez; Prof. of Social Anthropology Marcel
D'Hertefelt; Prof. of Nutrition H. Vis; publ. *Publi-
cations de l'Institut.*

TECHNICAL COLLEGE

École Technique Officielle Don Bosco: B.P. 80, Kigali;
f. 1956.

SELECT BIBLIOGRAPHY

Gourou, Pierre. *La densité de la population au Ruanda-
Urundi.* Brussels, 1953.

Lemarchand, René. *Rwanda and Burundi.* London, Pall
Mall, 1970.

Louis, Wm. R. *Ruanda-Urundi, 1884–1919.* Oxford,
Clarendon Press, 1963.

'Le Marché du Rwanda", *Marchés tropicaux et Méditer-
ranéens,* 1145, October 1967.

Vanderlinden, J. "La République rwandaise" in
Encyclopédie politique et constitutionelle. Paris, Berger-
Levrault, 1970.

St. Helena

(WITH ASCENSION AND TRISTAN DA CUNHA)

PHYSICAL AND SOCIAL GEOGRAPHY

St. Helena lies in the South Atlantic Ocean, latitude 16° S., longitude 50° 45′ W., 700 miles south-east of Ascension and about 1,200 miles from the south-west coast of Africa. It is 10.5 miles long and 6.5 miles broad, covering an area of 47 sq. miles.

St. Helena is rugged and mountainous and of volcanic origin. The highest peak, Mount Actaeon, rises to 2,685 ft. The only inland waters are small streams, few of them now perennial, fed by springs in the central hills. These streams and rain-water are sufficient for domestic water supplies and a few small irrigation schemes.

The cool South Atlantic trade winds blow throughout the year. The climate is mild and varies little, the temperature in Jamestown, on the sea-coast, ranging in summer between 70°F. and 85°F., and in winter between 65°F. and 75°F. Inland it is some 10°F. cooler.

Rainfall figures (in inches) over three years show a similar variation between Jamestown (10–12 in.) and the eastern district (34–37 in.)

The last census was on July 24th, 1966, when the total population was 4,649. The estimated population at December 31st, 1970, was 4,952.

According to the last census the division of the population was as follows:

St. Helenians	4,470
U.K. citizens	116
Other Commonwealth citizens	16
Others	47

The language of the island is English and the majority of the population belong to the Church of England.

St. Helena has one of the mildest climates in the world. There are no endemic diseases of note but the population is unusually susceptible to epidemic afflictions and minor ailments, both of which may be attributable to the island's isolation.

Jamestown, the capital, is the only town and has a population of some 1,600.

HISTORY

The then uninhabited island of St. Helena was discovered on May 21st, 1502, by the Portuguese navigator João da Nova Castella, on his homeward voyage from India. He named it in honour of Saint Helena, mother of the Emperor Constantine the Great, whose festival falls on that day. The existence of the island appears to have remained unknown to other European nations until 1588 when it was visited by Captain Cavendish on his return from a voyage round the world. A charter to occupy and govern St. Helena was issued by Charles II to the East India Company in December 1673 and it remained under that company until April 1834 when it was brought under the direct government of the British Crown by an Act of Parliament of 1833. Napoleon Bonaparte was exiled in St. Helena from 1815 until his death in 1821. Longwood House, in

which he lived, is an important Napoleonic museum; it is in the custody of the French Republic.

During the nineteenth century St. Helena was an important port of call on the route from Europe to India, but after the opening of the Suez Canal its importance declined.

The UN Committee on Decolonization has called for measures to transfer power to elected representatives, to lessen economic inequality and to safeguard against foreign, particularly South African, settlement and economic infiltration. In 1968 a South African concern, the South Atlantic Trading and Investment Company, bought up the local trading company; fears of foreign control over trade and the possible introduction of South African racial practices were voiced in the House of Commons at the time, but without significant issue.

ECONOMY

The pattern of employment according to the 1966 census was as follows:

	MALES	FEMALES	TOTAL
Professional, Technical and Related Workers .	41	89	130
Managerial, Administrative and Clerical Workers	88	40	128
Sales Workers	23	63	86
Farmers, Fishermen, etc.	128	—	128
Workers in Transport and Communications Operations	97	5	102
Craftsmen, Production Process Workers, etc. .	241	58	299
Service Workers	12	138	150
Security Forces	14	1	15
Not Classified	524	—	524
TOTAL	1,168	394	1,562

The main crops are common and sweet potatoes and vegetables. In the past the islanders grew formio (New Zealand flax), used in the manufacture of flax fibre (hemp). At the end of 1965 the market price of hemp dropped considerably and production ceased in 1966.

Individuals hold land either in fee simple or by lease. Immigrants require a license to hold land. Crown land may be leased on conditions approved by the Governor. The Government farms approximately half the arable area and either farms or controls some four-fifths of the grazing areas. Commonage grazing areas are made available by Government to private stock owners on a *per capita per mensem* basis. There is at present no scheme for land re-settlement and no pressure of demand for additional land. The grazing areas have not sufficient watering points to allow their sub-division into viable smallholdings and the economic nature of arable agriculture is such as not to be attractive to smallholders. It is, therefore, difficult to envisage any change in the present system of land holding.

Fish of many kinds are plentiful in the waters around St. Helena but the catch is usually insufficient to meet the demand. Towards the end of 1965 a licence was granted to a fishing concern in South Africa to develop the island's fish resources, but the company has obtained very poor results.

There is no industry.

The timber resources of the island are so small that all timber for construction purposes has to be imported. There are no minerals of any kind.

There were no exports in 1970.

The main imports are motor vehicles, fuel oils and motor spirit, flour, meat (salted including hams and bacon), and beer and stout. Total imports for 1969 were valued at £460,960.

The St. Helena Growers' Co-operative Society is the only one on the island. It is both a consumers and a marketing society and provides consumer goods such as seeds, implements, and feeding stuffs to its members, and markets their produce, mainly vegetables, locally, to visiting ships and to Ascension Island. The local market is limited and is soon over-

supplied, and this together with the decrease in the number of ships calling over recent years has inhibited the growth of this enterprise.

The only port in St. Helena is Jamestown, which is an open roadstead with a good anchorage for ships of any size.

There is no airport or airstrip in St. Helena and no railway. The total all-weather road mileage is 46.6. Of this 37.5 miles are bitumen sealed. In addition there are about 18 miles of earth roads used mainly by animal transport and only usable in dry weather by motor vehicles. All roads have steep gradients and sharp curves.

The Union Castle Mail Steamship Company is the only company providing a shipping service to the island. In 1970 there were 14 calls northbound from Cape Town to Southampton and 15 southbound from Britain, by two ships carrying 12 passengers each. No cargo (except a small tonnage of frozen food) is carried by these vessels to or from Ascension or St. Helena, but four cargo ships northbound and four southbound call each year.

A further allocation of funds was provided for an extension of the development programme for the period up to March 1971, bringing the total allocation, since the inception of Colonial Development and Welfare assistance in 1947, to £1,226,000,

While a considerable proportion of the funds are being devoted to road improvement and to development in agriculture, other phases of the programme include housing, extension of the electricity distribution system, teacher training, medical services, etc. A survey of water resources has been undertaken and implementation of the recommendations began in early 1970.

Revenue and expenditure for the four years 1967–70 were as follows:

	REVENUE (£)	EXPENDITURE (£)
1967	490,545	450,173
1968	514,285	485,497
1969	511,580	563,515
1970	471,537	519,392

STATISTICS

Area: 47.3 square miles.

Population (1970): 4,952; Jamestown (capital) 1,600; Births 167; Deaths 49.

Livestock (1970): Cattle 982, Sheep 1,260, Goats 1,200, Horses 19, Donkeys 686, Pigs 370, Poultry 10,856.

Forestry (1969): 3 sq. miles.

Currency: 100 pence=£1 (United Kingdom currency).

Budget (1970 estimate): *Revenue* £471,537; *Expenditure* £519,392.

External Trade (1969): *Imports* £460,960 (fuel oils and motor spirit £57,317, meat £25,715, motor vehicles £16,113, beer and stout £18,600, flour £18,902); *Exports* (1968): £14,710. Trade is mainly with the United Kingdom and South Africa.

There were no exports in 1969 or 1970.

Transport (1969): *Roads:* 672 vehicles; *Shipping:* Tonnage entered and cleared 171,901; ships 102.

Education (1969): Primary Schools 8, Pupils 753; Senior Secondary Schools 4, Pupils 350. There are 60 full-time teachers.

THE CONSTITUTION

An Order in Council and Royal Instructions of November 1966, which came into force on January 1st, 1967, provided for a Legislative Council, consisting of the Governor, 2 *ex officio* members (the Government Secretary and the Treasurer) and 12 elected members; and an Executive Council, consisting of the Government Secretary and the Treasurer as *ex officio* members and the Chairmen of the Council Committees (all of whom must be members of the Legislative Council). The Governor presides at meetings of the Executive Council.

Council Committees, a majority of whose members are members of the Legislative Council, have been appointed by the Governor and charged with executive powers and general oversight of departments of government.

THE GOVERNMENT

Governor: THOMAS OATES, C.M.G., O.B.E.

EXECUTIVE COUNCIL

President: The GOVERNOR.

Ex-Officio Members: The GOVERNMENT SECRETARY, The TREASURER.

Members: THE CHAIRMEN OF THE COUNCIL COMMITTEES.

LEGISLATIVE COUNCIL

President: The GOVERNOR.

Ex-Officio Members: The GOVERNMENT SECRETARY, The TREASURER.

Elected Members: 12.

JUDICIAL SYSTEM

There are four Courts on St. Helena. The Supreme Court, the Magistrate's Court, the Small Debts Court and the Juvenile Court. Provision exists for a St. Helena Court of Appeal which can sit in Jamestown or London.

The Chief Justice: The Hon. W. E. WINDHAM.

Magistrate: Major E. J. MOSS, C.B.E., M.C., J.P.

RELIGION

The majority of the population belong to the Anglican Communion of the Christian Church.

ANGLICAN

Diocese of St. Helena: The Right Reverend EDMUND CAPPER, O.B.E.; Bishopsholme, St. Helena; the See is in the Church of the Province of South Africa.

ROMAN CATHOLIC

Priest-in-Charge: The Reverend J. KELLY, O.F.M.CAP.; Sacred Heart Church, Jamestown; total members 30.

THE PRESS

News Review: Jamestown; f. 1941; Government-sponsored weekly; Editor E. M. GEORGE; circ. 950.

RADIO

Government Broadcasting Station: Information Office, The Castle, Jamestown; 16 hours weekly; Information Officer E. M. GEORGE.

There were 600 radio receivers in 1970.

FINANCE
BANKS

Government Savings Bank: Jamestown; total estimated deposits December 31st, 1970, £363,336.

INSURANCE

Alliance Assurance Co. Ltd.: Agents: Solomon & Co. (St. Helena) Ltd., Jamestown.

TRADE AND INDUSTRY
CHAMBER OF COMMERCE

St. Helena Chamber of Commerce: Jamestown.

TRADE UNION

St. Helena General Workers' Union: Market St., Jamestown; 1,050 mems. (1970); Sec. Gen. E. BENJAMIN.

CO-OPERATIVE

St. Helena Growers' Co-operative Society: for vegetable marketing; 43 mems.; total sales 1969 £4,320.

TRANSPORT
ROADS

There are 46.6 miles of all-weather motorable roads in the island, 37.5 bitumen sealed, and a further 18 miles of earth roads, which can only be used by motor vehicles in dry weather. All roads have steep gradients and sharp curves. There are no railways or airfields.

SHIPPING

Union Castle and **Clan Lines:** to and from the United Kingdom and South Africa; the only service.

EDUCATION

Education is compulsory and free for all children between the ages of five and fifteen but power to exempt after the age of fourteen rests with the Education Officer. The standard of work at the Secondary Selective School is increasingly being geared to "O" Level requirements of the London University General Certificate of Education. The literacy rate is 100 per cent.

There is a free public library in Jamestown financed by the Government and managed by a committee and a branch library in each country district.

ASCENSION

(WIDEAWAKE ISLAND)

The small island of Ascension lies in the South Atlantic (7° 56' S., 14° 22' W.) 700 miles north-west of St. Helena. Its area is 34 sq. miles and the population at December 31st, 1970 was 1,232, of whom 750 were St. Helenians. The majority of the remainder were expatriate personnel of Cable and Wireless Ltd. and the United States base. The population varies from time to time as it is largely determined by the employment offered by these two stations. The island was discovered by the Portuguese on Ascension Day 1501. It was uninhabited until the arrival of Napoleon in St. Helena in 1815, when a small British naval garrison was placed there. The island remained under the supervision of the British Admiralty until it was made a dependency of St. Helena by Letters Patent in 1922 and came under the control of the Secretary of State for the Colonies.

Ascension is a barren, rocky peak of purely volcanic origin, destitute of vegetation except for about ten acres around the top of the peak (2,870 ft.), where Cable and Wireless Ltd. run a farm producing vegetables and fruit and permitting the maintenance of about 2,000 sheep and 185 cattle and pigs. The island is famous for turtles, which land there from December to May to lay their eggs in the sand. It is also a breeding ground of the sooty tern, or wideawake, vast numbers of which settle on the island every eight months to lay and hatch their eggs. All wildlife except rabbits and cats is protected by law. Shark, barracuda, tuna, bonito and other fish are plentiful in the surrounding ocean.

Cable and Wireless Ltd. own and operate an important cable station which connects the Dependency with St. Helena, Sierra Leone, St. Vincent, Rio de Janeiro and Buenos Aires, and through these places, over the Company's system, with all parts of the world.

In 1942 the Government of the United States of America, by arrangement with the British Government, established an air base which became of considerable importance during the period of hostilities. The United States Government subsequently re-occupied Wideawake Airfield under an agreement with the British Government in connection with the extension of the Long Range Proving Ground for guided missiles centred in Florida.

A British Broadcasting Corporation relay station on the island was opened in 1966.

Area (square miles): 34.

Population (1970): 1,232 (St. Helenians 750); Births 19, Deaths 2 (1969).

Agriculture (1969): Vegetables 46,341 lb., Milk 18,494 gals.; Sheep 2,000, Pigs 144.

Budget (1968 est.): Revenue £16,000, Expenditure £90,000.

Government: The Government of St. Helena is represented by an Administrator.

Administrator: Brig. H. W. D. McDONALD, D.S.O.

Transport: Roads (1968): 745 vehicles; Shipping (1968): tonnage entered and cleared 435,183, ships 82; calls are made by Union Castle or Clan Line ships from St. Helena. Calls are also made by H.M. ships and occasional private yachts.

TRISTAN DA CUNHA

Tristan da Cunha is a small island in the South Atlantic Ocean, lying about midway between South America and South Africa. It is volcanic in origin and nearly circular in shape, covering an area of 38 sq. miles and rising in a cone to 6,760 ft. The climate is typically oceanic and temperate. Rainfall averages 66 in. per annum.

Possession was taken of the island in 1816 during Napoleon's residence in St. Helena, and a garrison was stationed there. When the garrison was withdrawn, three men, headed by Corporal William Glass, elected to remain and become the founders of the present settlement. Because of its position on a main sailing route the colony thrived until the 1880s, but with the replacement of sail by steam, the island ceased to occupy a position on a main shipping route and a period of decline set in. No regular shipping called and the islanders suffered at times from a shortage of food. Nevertheless, attempts to move the inhabitants to South Africa were unsuccessful. The islanders were engaged chiefly in fishing and agricultural pursuits.

The United Society for the Propagation of the Gospel has maintained a missionary teacher on the island since 1922; a number of missionaries had also served on the island prior to this. In 1932 the missionary was officially recognized as Honorary Commissioner and Magistrate.

By Letters Patent dated January 12th, 1938, Tristan da Cunha and the neighbouring unsettled islands of Nightingale, Inaccessible and Gough were made dependencies of St. Helena, though as a matter of practical convenience the administration of the group continued to be directly supervised by the Colonial Office.

In 1942 a meteorological and wireless station was built on the island by a detachment of the South African Defence Force and was manned by the Royal Navy for the remainder of the war. The coming of the Navy reintroduced the islanders to the outside world, for it was a naval chaplain who recognized the possibilities of a crawfish industry on Tristan da Cunha. In 1948 a Cape Town based fishing company was granted a concession to fish the Tristan da Cunha waters. Many of the islanders found employment with the fishing company. In 1950 the office of the Administrator was created. The Administrator is also the magistrate.

On October 10th, 1961, a volcanic cone erupted close to the settlement of Edinburgh and it was necessary to evacuate the island. The majority of the Islanders returned to Tristan da Cunha in 1963. The Administration has been fully re-established and the Island Council re-formed. The population at the end of 1970 was 280.

The island is isolated and communications are restricted to a few calls a year by vessels from Cape Town and an occasional call by a passing ship. There is, however, a wireless station on the island which is in daily contact with Cape Town. A local broadcasting service was introduced in August 1966. A radio-telephone service was established in 1969.

The island community depend upon fishing for their livelihood. The company holding the fishing concession has built a new fish-freezing factory and the shore-based fishing industry is being developed following the construction of a harbour funded from an £80,000 grant from the British Government. The industry employs almost all of the working population.

The 1969–70 budget as expected showed a small deficit which was met from reserves. Colonial Development and Welfare assistance are providing funds for a new hospital and a new school.

Area (square miles): Tristan da Cunha 38, Inaccessible Island 4, Nightingale Island ¾, Gough Island 35.

Population (1970): 280 on Tristan; there is a small weather station on Gough manned by a team of South Africans.

Constitution: The Administrator, representing the British Government, is aided by a Council of 8 elected and 3 nominated members which has advisory powers in legislative and executive functions. The Council's advisory functions in executive matters are performed through small committees of the Council dealing with the separate branches of administration.

Government: The Administrator: Maj. J. I. H. FLEMING.

Legal System: The Administrator is Magistrate. There is one Justice of the Peace.

Religion: All the islanders are Christian. Their padre is Rev. A. A. WELSH.

SELECT BIBLIOGRAPHY

BLAKESTON, OSWELL. *Isle of Helena.* London, Sidgwick and Jackson, 1957.

BOOY, D. M. *Rock of Exile: a narrative of Tristan da Cunha.* London, Dent, 1957.

CHRISTOPHERSON, ERLING, and others. *Tristan da Cunha* (translated by R. L. Benham). London, Cassell, 1940.

CHRISTOPHERSON, ERLING (Ed.). *Results of the Norwegian Scientific Expedition to Tristan da Cunha, 1937–1938,* 16 parts. Oslo, Oslo University Press, 1940–62.

GOSSE, PHILIP. *St. Helena, 1502–1938.* London, Cassell, 1938.

HUGHES, CLEDWYN. *Report of an enquiry into conditions on the Island of St. Helena . . . (and) observations by the St. Helena Government on Mr. Hughes' report.* 1958, 2 parts.

KORNGOLD, RALPH. *The Last Years of Napoleon: his captivity on St. Helena.* London, Gollancz, 1960.

MARTINEAU, GILBERT. *Napoleon's St. Helena.* London, John Murray, 1968.

STONEHOUSE, BERNARD. *Wideawake Island: the story of the British Ornithologists Union Centenary Expedition to Ascension.* London, Hutchinson, 1960.

THOMPSON, J. A. K. *Report on a visit to Ascension Island.* St. Helena Government Printer, 1947.

São Tomé and Príncipe

René Pélissier

PHYSICAL AND SOCIAL GEOGRAPHY*

The archipelago of São Tomé and Príncipe is the smallest overseas province of Portugal in Africa. Both islands are in the Gulf of Guinea on a south-west/north-east alignment of formerly active volcanoes. They comprise two main islands, the rocky islets of the Pedras Tinhosas, and, south of São Tomé, the Rolas islet which is bisected by the line of the equator. Their total area is 964 sq. km. of which São Tomé occupies an area of 854 sq. km. Before 1961 the fort of São João Baptista de Ajuda, an enclave in the Dahomean town of Ouidah, was administered as part of the province by a resident administrator. This historical relic of the slave-trade era was annexed by the Republic of Dahomey in August 1961, but it is still sentimentally looked on by the Portuguese as part of São Tomé and Príncipe.

São Tomé is a plantation island where the eastern slopes and coastal flatlands are covered by huge cocoa and coffee estates (roças) belonging to Portuguese companies, alongside a large number of small native farmers. All these are carved out of an extremely dense mountainous jungle which dominates this equatorial island. The highest peak is the Pico de São Tomé (2,024 m.), surrounded by a dozen lesser cones above 1,000 m. in height. Craggy and densely forested terrain is intersected by numerous streams.

The island of Príncipe is extremely jagged and indented by numerous bays. The highest point is the Pico de Príncipe (948 m.).

Both islands have a warm and moist climate, with an average yearly temperature of about 80°F. There is a climatic station on the slopes of Pico de São Tomé for Europeans. Due to the abundant rainfall and high temperatures the climate is like that of a hothouse.

The total population in 1970 was 73,811, of which São Tomé had 69,149 inhabitants and Príncipe 4,662. The capital city is São Tomé, with about 7,000–8,000 people. It is the main export centre of the island. Inland villages on São Tomé are mere clusters of houses of native São Tomenses. Príncipe has only one small town of about 1,000 people, Santo António. In fact, most people live not in villages or towns but in plantation compounds. The population is predominantly migrant labour, contract workers from Cape Verde who stay for a three-year period, but tend to settle around the roça complex. The native-born people (filhos da terra), are the descendants of imported slaves and southern Europeans who settled in the sixteenth and seventeenth centuries. Miscegenation has been common, but the massive influx of Angolan and Mozambican contract workers until about 20 years ago has re-Africanized the filhos de terra. Both on account of the economic crisis which has reduced the power of absentee plantation owners (roceiros), and as an aftermath of the Batepá troubles of 1953, working conditions on the roças are much improved. About 1,500 Portuguese plantation administrators and employees, civil servants, traders and soldiers live in the islands. Descendants of former castaway slaves who escaped from a sinking slaver in the seventeenth century and who formed a formidable maroon republic in the mountains of São Tomé are now peaceful fishermen, and are known as the Angolares.

*See map on p. 202

RECENT HISTORY

(See Recent History of Portugal's African Territories under Angola, page 150).

ECONOMY

Commercial agriculture is the mainstay of the islands, which are basically two large export-orientated plantations. There are about 110 plantations on São Tomé. The land belongs mainly to Portuguese companies and individuals, except for a negligible slice around the capital which is still native-held. The *filhos da terra* either rent or till their own patches. About 29 per cent of G.D.P. derives from the primary sector and 30 per cent from the tertiary sector. Cocoa production reached a peak at the beginning of the century when São Tomé and Príncipe together ranked as one of the main world producers. Now production is about 10,000 tons yearly (11,034 metric tons in 1971). Exhaustion of soil fertility, archaic techniques and antiquated plants, disease, the difficulties of recruiting labour and a slump in world prices have done much to lessen the cultivation of cocoa. As a rule, the *filhos da terra* do not like working for the *roceiros*, whose attitudes and record of bad labour practices are still clearly remembered. Cape Verdians and some willing creoles are encouraged by the authorities to settle on the land by technical assistance and the purchase of dilapidated *roças* which are then partitioned and sold to farmers.

Coffee, formerly grown in association with cocoa, is now a token amount (70 metric tons in 1971). Palm oil (697 metric tons in 1971), copra (5,111 metric tons in 1971) and coconuts (871 metric tons in 1971) are slowly being developed to bolster the sagging export trade. Bananas are a relatively new export commodity (41,848 metric tons in 1970). Fishing is embryonic, as is industry. Tourism is growing slowly as the islands have become a port of call for some cruise liners, but, apart from roads, the infrastructure is deficient.

Because of the overwhelming importance of the plantations, the islands' economic life is entirely dependent on external markets. The trade balance is usually positive due to the small value of imports. In 1970 the islands imported 38,856 metric tons (value 260,522 contos), and exported 18,787 metric tons (value 237,440 contos), leaving a trading deficit of 23,082 contos. Main trading partners are Portugal, the Netherlands, Germany and Angola. In 1970 cocoa exports were worth 189,291 contos.

The islands' main problems are the reluctance of the *filhos da terra* to enter the market economy on a large scale, the failure of the *roças* to adapt to modern techniques and marketing, and the over-reliance of the economy on two or three export commodities. As regards the labour market, the bad name that the islands have earned through former practices is the main handicap which must be overcome in order to attract new sources of manpower from continental Africa. On the whole, São Tomé is chiefly a provider of exotic commodities and some civil servants of intermediate ranks to Angola and other Portuguese territories.

STATISTICS

Area: 964 sq. km.

Population (1971): 76,218. Births 3,275, Marriages 118, Deaths 859.

Agriculture: *Principal crops* (metric tons—1971): Copra 5,111, Coconuts 871, Cocoa 11,034, Coffee 70. *Livestock* (1971): Horses, Mules and Asses 266, Cattle 2,366, Sheep 1,543, Goats 651, and Pigs 2,662.

Fishing (1971): 856 metric tons.

Industry (1971—metric tons): Maize Flour 88, Lime 804, Palm Oil 679, Soap 658, Meat Preparations 28, Dried Fish 31.

Finance: 100 centavos = 1 Guinea escudo; 1,000 escudos = 1 conto. Exchange rates: £1 sterling = 63.05 escudos (December 1972); 100 escudos = £1.590; U.S. $1 = 27.12 escudos (September 1972); 100 escudos = $3.687.

Budget (1971): Receipts 173,394 contos, Expenses 184,897 contos.

Development Plan (1971): Investment 81,904 contos.

Currency in Circulation (1971): Notes 33,316 contos, Coins 9,454 contos.

External Trade (1971—contos): Imports 221,164; Exports 197,860.

Commodities (1971): *Imports:* Vegetable Products 31,546, Food, Beverages and Tobacco 43,233, Mineral Products 17,817, Chemicals and Products 22,413, Textiles and Products 24,766. *Exports:* Vegetable Products 34,236, Food, Beverages and Tobacco 147,949.

Countries (1971): *Imports:* Portugal 102,128, Portuguese Overseas Provinces 58,015, Foreign Countries 61,021. *Exports:* Portugal 73,629, Portuguese Overseas Provinces 4,996, Foreign Countries 109,235.

Transport: *Roads* (1971): Cars 1,486, Lorries and Buses 265, Motor Cycles 309. *Shipping* (1971): Vessels entered 132, Freight entered 18,354 metric tons, Freight cleared 39,553 metric tons. *Civil Aviation* (1971): Passengers landed 5,912, Freight entered and cleared 82 metric tons.

Education (1971): *Primary:* Schools 44, Teachers 271, Pupils 9,018; *Secondary:* Schools 2, Teachers 73, Pupils 1,463; *Technical:* Schools 4, Teachers 34, Pupils 112.

THE GOVERNMENT

Governor: Col. João Cecílio Gonçalves.

POLITICAL PARTIES

Acção Nacional Popular: The Portuguese Government party, formerly União Nacional.

Comité de Libertação de São Tomé e Príncipe (*Committee for the Liberation of São Tomé*): (*illegal*) Sec.-Gen. Tomás Medeiros.

RELIGION

ROMAN CATHOLIC

S. Tomé and Príncipe: Suffragan See, S. Tomé (Metropolitan See of Luanda)—*see* under Angola); Bishop (vacant), Caixa Postal 146, São Tomé.

THE PRESS

Imprensa Nacional: Caixa Postal 28, S. Tomé; f. 1836; weekly; Dir. MANUEL LOPES DE SÁ.

A Voz de São Tomé: P.O.B. 93; weekly; Dir. Dr. RICARDO JORGE RIBEIRO BRAVO.

RADIO

Emissora Regional de São Tomé e Príncipe da Emissora Nacional de Radiodifusão: Av. Infante D. Henrique, Caixa Postal 44, S. Tomé; f. 1958; official station; Pres. CARLOS ALBERTO FERREIRA DIAS.

There are 7,000 radio receivers. There is a closed circuit television service.

FINANCE

ISSUING BANK

Banco Nacional Ultramarino: 84 rua do Comercio, Lisbon; São Tomé· sub-agency at Príncipe.

DEVELOPMENT ORGANIZATION

Caixa de Crédito de São Tomé e Príncipe: P.O.B. 168; f. 1965 to finance the development of agriculture and industry; cap. $54,545, dep. $83,636; Man. Dir. Dr. JOSÉ FREDERICO FERREIRA EPIFANIO DA FRANCA; publ. *Annual Report.*

INSURANCE

The following Portuguese insurance companies have agents in S. Tomé and Príncipe:

A Mundial, S.A.R.L.: Ilha de S. Tomé, agents: AUSPÍCIO DE MENESES, LDA.; (Head Office: Largo do Chiado 8, Lisbon).

Tagus, S.A.R.L.: Ilha de S. Tomé; Head Office: Rua do Comércio 40-64, Lisbon; agents: SILVA & GOUVEIA, LDA.

Tranquilidade, S.A.R.L.: S. Tomé; Head Office: Rua Cândido dos Reis 105, Oporto.

Fidelidade: S. Tomé; Head Office: Largo do Corpo Santo 13, Lisbon.

INDUSTRIAL COMPANIES

Companhia Agrícola Angolares: C.P. 14, São Tomé.

Companhia Agrícola Bela Vista: Príncipe.

Companhia Agrícola das Neves: C.P. 62, São Tomé.

Companhia Agrícola Ultramarina: C.P. 24, São Tomé.

Companhia Colonial Agrícola: C.P. 21, São Tomé.

Companhia da Ilha do Príncipe: C.P. 60, São Tomé.

Companhia Ilhéu das Rolas: C.P. 20, São Tomé.

Companhia Roças Plateau e Milagrosa: C.P. 163, São Tomé.

TRANSPORT

ROADS

There were 288 km. of roads in 1970.

SHIPPING

Companhia Nacional de Navegação: agent in S. Tomé: LIMA & GAMA LTD., (Head Office: Rua do Comércio 85, Lisbon).

Companhia de Serviços Marítimos (COSEMA): Agency in S. Tomé.

Companhia Nacional de Navegação: agents in S. Tomé (Head Office: Rua Instituto Vergilio Machado, Lisbon).

Sociedade Geral do Comércio Indústria e Transportes S.A.R.L.: agent in S. Tomé: SILVA & GOUVÊA S.A.R.L., (Head Office: Rua dos Douradores 11, Lisbon).

CIVIL AVIATION

Serviço de Transportes Aéreos: São Tomé, a government airline with services to Príncipe, Porto Alegre and Cabinda, Angola; freight services to Luanda, Fernando Pó; Dir. A. A. GROMICHO.

Also D.T.A. services to Ambrizete and Luanda, Angola.

EDUCATION

Primary education is compulsory for children over six years of age. After this they may proceed to the government secondary school (liceu) in São Tomé or to the technical school.

Biblioteca Municipal Dr. Henriques da Silva: Caixa Postal 46, São Tomé; 4,280 vols.; Librarian ARISTIDES DE OLIVEIRA.

SELECT BIBLIOGRAPHY

(For works on the Portuguese African territories generally *see* Angola Select Bibliography, p. 175.)

A.G.U. *São Tomé e Príncipe.* Lisbon, 1964.

TENREIRO, FRANCISCO. *A Ilha de São Tomé.* Lisbon, 1961.

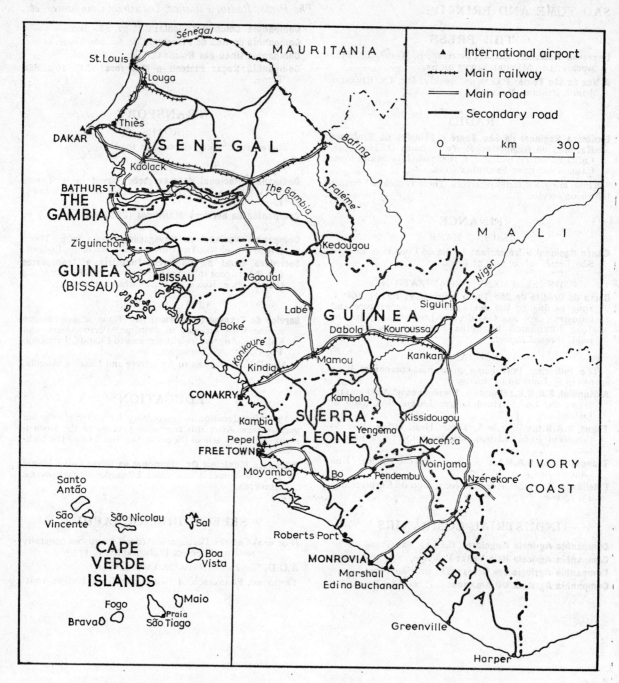

Senegal, The Gambia, Guinea (Bissau), Guinea, Sierra Leone, Liberia and Cape Verde Islands.

Senegal

PHYSICAL AND SOCIAL GEOGRAPHY

R. J. Harrison Church

Senegal, the most westerly state of Africa, has an area of 75,750 sq. miles (196,192 sq. km.) and a population estimated at 3,822,000 in 1970. The southern border is first with Guinea (Bissau) and then with the Republic of Guinea on the northern edge of the Primary sandstone Fouta Djallon. In the east the border is with Mali, in the only other area of bold relief in Senegal, where there are Precambrian rocks in the Bambouk mountains. The northern border with Mauritania lies along the Senegal River, navigable for small boats all the year to Podor and for two months to Kayes (Mali), but little used. The river has a wide flood plain, annually cultivated as the waters retreat. The delta soils are saline, but irrigation is being developed.

The Gambia is a semi-enclave which has resulted in its magnificent river playing no positive role in Senegal's development, and which isolated the Casamance from the rest of Senegal before the Trans-Gambian Highway was opened in 1958.

Apart from the high eastern and south-eastern borderlands most of the country has monotonous plains, which in an earlier wetter period were drained by large rivers in the centre of the country. Relic valleys, now devoid of superficial water, occur in the Ferlo desert, and these built up the Sine-Saloum delta north of The Gambia. In a later dry period north-east to south-west trending sand dunes were formed, giving Senegal's plains their undulating and ribbed surfaces. These plains of Cayor, Baol, and Nioro du Rip are inhabited by Wolof and Serer cultivators of groundnuts and millet. The coast between St. Louis and Dakar has a broad belt of live dunes. Behind them, near Thiès, both calcium and aluminium phosphates are quarried and phosphatic fertilizer is produced.

The Cape Verde peninsula results from Tertiary volcanic activity which created offshore islands, later joined to the mainland by coastal currents and back swirl. Cape Verde is formed by one of the two extinct volcanoes—*les Mamelles*. Exposure to south-westerly winds is responsible for Cape Verde's verdant appearance and rich colouring, in contrast to the yellow dunes to the north. South of the peninsula, particularly in Casamance, the coast is a drowned one of shallow estuaries.

Senegal's climate is very varied, and the coast is remarkably cool for the latitude (Dakar 14° 49′ N.). The Cape Verde peninsula is particularly breezy, because it projects into the path of northerly marine trade winds. Average temperatures lie between 18° and 31°C., and the rainy season is little more than three months in length. Inland both temperatures and rainfall are higher, and the rainy season in comparable latitudes is somewhat longer. Casamance lies on the northern fringe of the monsoonal climate. Thus Ziguinchor (12° 35′ N.) has four to five months rainy season with 64 in. (1,626 mm.) annual rainfall, nearly three times that received by Dakar. The natural vegetation ranges from Sahel savannah north of about 15°N., through Sudan savannah in south-central Senegal, to Guinea savannah in Casamance, where the oil palm is common.

RECENT HISTORY*

Michael Crowder and Donal Cruise O'Brien

(Revised for this edition by KAYE WHITEMAN)

The colonial territory of Senegal, with French Soudan, formed the federation of Mali in 1959. The break-up of the federation brought the separate independence of Senegal in 1960. Léopold Senghor became President of the new republic and has held this post to the present time. Mamadou Dia became Prime Minister, with broad executive power, and the governing party (the *Union progressiste sénégalaise*—UPS) embarked on a comprehensive programme of economic development oriented to the rural sector. The fall of Dia in 1962, after an alleged attempt at a *coup d'état*, was followed by a partial relaxation of government effort in the field of development. A revised constitution was introduced to strengthen presidential powers, and approved in a popular referendum of 1963. Elections later in the same year saw a decisive victory of the governing party over the opposition (led by the *Bloc des masses sénégalaises* of Cheikh Anta Diop), but rioters in Dakar protested against electoral fraud: these riots were quelled by troops with several deaths.

Organized political opposition declined following these incidents, as rival parties saw little hope of victory in elections controlled by the governing party. The government declared certain parties illegal, while others sought the best conditions to amalgamate with

---

* For the period before independence *see* Recent History of Dahomey, p. 282.

the ruling UPS. In 1966 the last legal opposition party, the *Parti du régroupement african—Sénégal*, joined the UPS, while three of its leaders received ministerial posts. Opposition none the less persists within the governing party, deeply divided into competing factions, although elections with a single list provide a formal impression of national unanimity —as in 1968, when the UPS won 99 per cent of the votes cast in a general election. Opposition also persists among those sectors of the population most affected by the country's worsening economic situation. Economic decline is caused basically by falling world prices for the country's export monocrop, groundnuts. The withdrawal of French subsidies in 1967 brought a particularly sharp fall in the groundnut price, and poor harvests in the past three years have nullified a programme to compensate for price falls by increased production. Economic difficulties brought wage freezes, and consequent trade union unrest. This unrest exploded in 1968 with a student strike at Dakar University, in the wake of the French protests of May. A student strike which led to a military occupation of the University was followed by a general strike called by the National Union of Senegalese Workers (UNTS). A potentially revolutionary situation was averted by a show of force, and the President only survived through the loyalty of the armed forces, which are heavily reinforced at upper levels with French advisers. Massive concessions to the workers brought about a settlement (as in France), and the students were promised educational reforms.

The "new deal" for the unions was imperfectly applied and their power was reduced the following year by a government manoeuvre when they tried to repeat the direct action of the previous year. The official trade union organization is now the National Confederation of Senegalese Workers (CNTS), affiliated to the ruling party, and although some powerful unions such as the teachers have remained outside it, their effectiveness has been curbed. Reforms in the University, such as the introduction of "equivalence" for Dakar degrees, replacing degrees which had the full legality of French degrees, and the speeding up

of Africanization of senior posts (there is now a Senegalese Rector in Dakar University), have not changed the basic situation in higher education, which still depends on France for three-quarters of its finance. The University, although more quiescent in the 1972 academic year than for some time, must still be counted one of the focal points of potential opposition to the government.

Following the 1968 crisis President Senghor set about modifying the country's political structure and in 1970 a constitutional amendment was approved by referendum. This recreated the post of Prime Minister, but in a much more clearly subordinate position than in the 1960 constitution. The new Prime Minister, Abdou Diouf, was formerly a civil servant whose speciality was economics. Since his appointment his main concern has been to solve the country's economic problems. This has left the President with more time to concentrate on foreign affairs, such as the OAU's Middle East Peace Mission. The Diouf appointment has also been seen as the grooming of a successor; at the time the President spoke hopefully of an eventual "poetic retirement" by the end of the 1970s.

However, Senegal's underlying economic problems have continued. The cumulative effect of bad harvests and bad management created what was called *le malaise paysan* (peasant malaise), which was apparent in a return to subsistence crops instead of groundnuts, and in some cases a refusal to pay taxes. Disaster aid from the EEC enabled the government to write off the peasant debts, and the plentiful rainfall brought about an improved harvest in 1971–72.

The uncertainties inherent in a monoculture economy remain, and the country's financial situation is worsened by a proliferating and very expensive administration, partly the inheritance of Senegal's previous dominance in the French West African Federation. The tendency to date for government expenditure to outrun revenue has been compensated for by an extensive programme of French aid, which of course implies continued dependence on the ex-colonial power.

ECONOMY

Samir Amin

The economic development of Senegal under colonial rule had a lead of several decades over that of the other parts of French West Africa. This progress was based on the remarkable development of groundnut production, which began on a large scale in 1885. The growth curve shows an annual increase of 8.8 per cent from 1885 to 1914 and 2.7 per cent from 1918 to 1940. It remained stagnant up to 1950, then during the 1950s quickly recovered to a rate of 7.7 per cent per annum, dropping to 4 per cent during the 1960s. This growth seems not only to have come to a halt in the last years of the 1960s, but was even reversed, due to the reduction in culti-

vated area for the first time in the history of the country, apart from wartime periods. Increased production was only possible as long as the land available did not impose a limit. This has been overcome with new land settlements. Predictions for the 1971–72 groundnut crop were around 750,000 tons.

The increasing importance of millet has also helped rural productivity. Once maximum population density had been reached, higher yields were necessary. Up to 1950, methods of cultivation had remained practically unchanged. Since then there have been efforts to cut down the work-force by using draught animals and to increase the yield per hectare by wider use of selected seeds and of fertilizers. Because of the decrease in the marginal productivity of labour which occurs when extensive methods are abandoned in favour of the relatively intensive methods of modernized cultivation, the real return for a day's work falls when expansion of agricultural activity is impossible (because of rural density); and it remains practically unchanged, even if expansion is possible, as in the northern zone. In the central and southern zones modernization even at best brings an increase of only 20 to 25 per cent in the return for a day's work.

In fact the decisive factor in the expansion of the groundnut economy has been the development and improvement of transport systems. All things considered, expressed as a percentage of the value of the product exported (c.i.f.) to European ports, the real costs of internal transport have been reduced by 60–80 per cent, according to the production zones, between 1890 and 1965.

As there has been no possibility of capitalist-type development, it is not surprising that the new forms of social organization which grew up with the expansion of groundnut cultivation were of a feudal nature. Although it is very difficult to obtain quantitative information about this "kulakization" of the land, certain facts are absolutely clear: e.g. the strong links between concentration of groundnut cultivation (especially on new land) and of equipment and livestock as monetary means, the appearance of "wage-earning" manpower (25 per cent of labour on holdings of over 15 hectares—covering about 14 per cent of all cultivated land). Even within the co-operative movement disparities have grown considerably, for these co-operatives have as their object the promotion of individual enterprise among the peasants. At the same time as the establishment of the co-operatives the state began nationalizing trade in 1960.

PROBLEMS OF INDUSTRIALIZATION
1959–69

Senegal's lead over the other territories of former French West Africa lies not only in the sphere of agricultural development. On the basis of the domestic market created by this agricultural development, light industry has been set up, thus obviating the need for certain imports. Today Senegal is easily first among west African countries in this sector, leading even Nigeria.

The industrial growth rate at current prices from 1959 to 1969 was of the order of 7.3 per cent and 6.3 per cent at constant prices. The average annual growth indices relating to production from 1959 to 1968 show a rate of 8.9 per cent for power, 28 per cent for mining, 3.3 per cent for food industry, 10 per cent for textiles and 8.7 per cent for other industries. An examination of volume indices for the principal commodities shows that for a large number of the traditional industries of Cape Verde progress has been very poor. Production of cement, tobacco, matches, accumulator batteries, beer and soft drinks, textiles, footwear, chemicals, corn and flour, etc., has stagnated.

The main industrial achievements of the decade were recorded by industries orientated towards foreign markets such as mining, and production of phosphates rose from 407,000 tons in 1961 to 1,600,000 in 1971. Expansion within the important oilseed milling industry increased the production of refined oil from 36,000 tons in 1961 to 56,200 tons in 1967, and that of crude oil from 116,700 to 120,800 tons. Grinding capacity has reached one million tons. A certain number of industrial projects, particularly in the conserving industry (tunny), as well as the establishment by SIES of a fertilizer factory, have helped to improve some indices. The expansion of electrical power production at the rate of 10 per cent per annum and the SAR oil refinery have also helped. Together these largely export-orientated industries do not form an integrated group and, for this reason, have had only a very limited influence on total growth.

During the 1960s growth rates at current prices were 3.2 per cent for agriculture, stock-raising and fishing; 7.3 per cent for industry and 3.2 per cent for G.D.P. The latter rate is tending to fall, having been 4 per cent during the period 1959–64 and only 1.9 per cent for 1965–69. At constant prices, these rates are as follows: 3.0 per cent for agriculture, 6.3 per cent for industry and 2.5 per cent for G.D.P. The result is that per capita production at current prices has increased only by 1.1 per cent per annum.

The urban population growth rate is 6 per cent per annum, the number of people living in the towns having grown from 700,000 in 1959 (22 per cent of total population which was then 3,150,000), to 1,250,000 in 1969 (32 per cent of the population of 3,800,000). The potential work-force rose by 115,000. This led to a massive increase in visible and disguised unemployment from 11 to 38 per cent of the work-force.

FINANCING OF INVESTMENTS

The volume of gross investments has been considerable. From 1961 to 1968 gross capital formation grew steadily from 9.3 per cent of G.D.P. to 13.3 per cent, the average annual volume of investments being of the order of 20,000 million francs CFA during the ten-year period.

These investments may be broken down by sector, giving the following average annual figures for 1959–68: infrastructure and administration 44 per cent, agriculture 21 per cent, power and mining 14 per cent (main investments here being in phosphates and the oil refinery), industry 14 per cent (of which 42 per cent was for agricultural industry, chiefly the oil mills, 20 per cent for fertilizers and 38 per cent for all other light industry, textiles, etc.), construction 4 per cent, transport, services and commerce 22 per cent.

Almost all investment in the productive economy comes from the foreign sector.

Table 1
PATTERN OF INVESTMENT FINANCING
(1961–68—'000 million francs CFA)

	ANNUAL AVERAGE	TENDENCY
Gross Investments:		
Administrative . .	8.8	Stable
Private . . .	11.2	Increasing
TOTAL . .	20.0	
Financing:		
Domestic Savings:		
Public . . .	4.6	Diminishing rapidly
Private Senegalese .	2.2	Stable
Private foreign (repayments) . .	4.5	Stable
Foreign Contribution:		
Public (net) . .	4.0	Stable
Private (new capital) .	4.5	Increasing
Reduction in foreign Assets . .	0.2	Increasing

Public investment—an annual average total of 8,800 million francs CFA—has been financed less and less by public savings (the surplus of tax revenue over administrative expenses). Public savings declined steadily, falling from 5,500 million francs CFA in 1961 to 2,200 million in 1968 (the annual average amount being 4,600 million). Net foreign contributions allocated for development financing, with an annual average amount of about 4,000 million, tended to remain stable, and recourse to monetary measures became increasingly necessary, resulting finally in an accelerated fall in foreign-currency reserves.

The pattern of investment financing may be seen in table 1.

PROBLEMS OF PUBLIC FINANCE

Senegal's public finances have been in difficulties not so much because of the growth in expenditure, as because of the very inadequate income whose relative stagnation is linked with that of the economy as a whole. The proportion of G.D.P. represented by public consumption rose steadily from 17.1 per cent in 1961 to 21.2 per cent in 1968. In 1964–65 Senegal employed about 100 civil servants for every 10,000 inhabitants, compared with, for the same period, 67 in the Ivory Coast, 57 in Dahomey, 27 in Mali and 24 in Niger. During the 1950s the number of primary school pupils doubled, but during the period 1959–69, it increased two and a half times, the proportion of school-age children attending school having risen from 24 to 35 per cent, while the number of secondary and technical school pupils

increased five times (the proportion having risen in this field from 5 to 14 per cent).

Economic stagnation had an adverse effect on tax and other revenue, which increased from 34,500 million francs CFA in 1962–63 to 36,200 million in 1968–69, showing an annual average increase since 1961 of 2.8 per cent, and of practically nil since 1965. The surplus allocated for capital equipment was therefore steadily reduced from 5,800 million in 1961–62 to nil in 1968–69, while the combined current and capital budgets showed a growing deficit, varying considerably from one year to the next between 1,000 and 3,000 million, with an annual average of 2,100 million during the decade, i.e. a cumulative average of 12,000 million from 1960 to 1969. It was only possible to cover about 37 per cent of this deficit with long- and medium-term loans, mostly foreign. The remainder was covered by monetary measures. The Groundnut Stabilization Fund supplied the basis for these monetary measures—6,500 million was drawn on for the three-year period between 1966–67 and 1968–69.

BALANCE OF PAYMENTS IN CONTINUING DEFICIT

Increases in exports during the decade were very slight (1.9 per cent per annum), and the same applied to imports. On average, for the four-year period 1965–68, exports amounted to about 43,800 million francs CFA, including earnings from the transport of goods to Mali.

The total current balance is more or less in equilibrium. There was a net contribution of foreign public capital, an average of 10,300 million francs CFA per annum, and, taking into account the reduction in Senegal's foreign assets, the net inflow of private capital was 12,600 million per annum.

No more than 37 per cent of total foreign public capital goes to development; 6,500 million francs CFA represent in part current French technical assistance (after the deduction of local costs borne by Senegal, and amounting to approximately 5,000 million francs for some 2,700 personnel) and in part various current aid projects. These consist in particular of the commodity price supports provisionally supplied by the EEC (averaging 1,200 million francs from 1965 to 1968), and loans from the French Treasury. Of the capital really allocated to development projects—4,700 million francs gross per annum—a decreasing proportion consists of grants (80 per cent in 1964 to 57 per cent in 1968), while loans increasingly make up the remainder. As a result Senegal has a generally increasing foreign debt. However, up till now this debt has remained very slight, of the order of 1,700 million francs CFA at June 30th, 1969.

STATISTICAL SURVEY

AREA AND POPULATION

AREA (sq. km.)	POPULATION (1970)			
	Total	African	French and others	Dakar (capital and Commune du Grand Dakar)
196,192	3,822,000	3,777,000	45,000	693,000

Principal Ethnic groups (1960 census): Wolof 709,000, Fulani 324,000, Serer 306,000, Toucouleur 248,000, Diola 115,000.

Chief Towns (1970): Dakar 436,000, Kaolack 96,000, Thiès 91,000, Saint-Louis 81,000, Ziguinchor 46,000.

Births and Deaths: Average annual birth rate 46.3 per 1,000; death rate 22.8 per 1,000 (UN estimates for 1965–70).

EMPLOYMENT
(1964)

Agriculture, Fishing	4,045
Mining, Industry	18,804
Transport	15,496
Public Works, Building . . .	14,176
Commerce, Banks	15,786
Services	14,664
TOTAL	82,971

Total Labour Force (1970): Economically active population 1,705,000, including 1,288,000 in agriculture (ILO and FAO estimates).

AGRICULTURE

PRODUCTION
(metric tons)

	1969–70	1970–71	1971–72*
Millet and Sorghum . .	634,833	400,876	601,735
Cow Peas . .	22,584	17,777	21,875
Rice . . .	155,989	90,545	101,700
Maize . . .	48,840	38,746	n.a.
Cassava (Manioc) .	176,773	133,100	n.a.
Potatoes . .	16,255	9,718	n.a.
Cotton . . .	11,500	11,610	18,318

* Provisional.

Livestock (1971—'000 head): Cattle 2,674, Sheep and Goats 2,804, Asses 186, Horses 205, Pigs 175.

Fishing (1971): total catch 221,828 tons.

GROUNDNUTS
('000 tons)

	1967/68	1968/69	1969/70
Total Production . .	1,005	830	789
Production not Marketed (incl. Seeds) . .	163	232	194
Deliveries to Oil Mills .	558	461	509
Deliveries to Shelling Plants . .	284	137	85
Exports (shelled) . .	197	95	58

Total Production: (1970/71) 583,000 tons; (1971/72—provisional) 917,500 tons.

Source: Bulletin de la B.C.E.A.O.

MINING
(metric tons)

	1970	1971
Aluminium Phosphate . .	130,380	146,632
Lime Phosphate . .	998,000	1,454,167

INDUSTRY
(metric tons)

	1970	1971
Groundnut Oil . . .	177,000	117,000
Sugar	21,000	30,000
Cement . . .	241,186	240,778
Beer ('000 hectolitres) .	106	114
Cotton Fabric ('000 metres) .	7,002	7,693
Electricity (million kWh.) .	287	303

FINANCE

100 centimes = 1 franc de la Communauté Financière Africaine.
Coins: 1, 2, 5, 10 and 25 francs CFA.
Notes: 50, 100, 500, 1,000 and 5,000 francs CFA.
Exchange rates (December 1972): 1 franc CFA = 2 French centimes.
£1 sterling = 593.625 francs CFA; U.S. $1 = 255.785 francs CFA.
1,000 francs CFA = £1.685 = $3.91.

PUBLIC FINANCE
('000 million francs CFA)

	1966–67	1967–68	1968–69
Tax and Other Revenue .	37.1	37.4	37.6
Current Expenditure*	33.9	35.4	37.1
of which:			
Personnel† .	19.2	20.0	21.2
Equipment .	9.7	10.0	10.2
Capital Expenditure‡ .	8.8	5.8	7.9

* Excluding debt repayments.
† Including Senegal's contribution to technical assistance costs.
‡ Including investments financed by foreign aid.

Budget (1971–72) (million francs CFA): Balanced in revenue and expenditure at 51,940; of which 1,015 is extraordinary revenue. Main items of expenditure were personnel (51.6 per cent) and capital expenditure (18.25 per cent). Education received about 12.7 per cent; the Armed Forces 9.4 per cent; Health and Social Affairs 7.1 per cent; and the Ministry of Tourism 1.2 per cent.

FOREIGN OFFICIAL PUBLIC AID
('000 million francs CFA)

	1966	1967	1968
Transfers . . .	8.0	7.5	7.7
of which:			
French Technical Assistance .	6.1	6.3	6.2
Grants . . .	3.6	4.0	2.7
Loans . . .	1.0	0.7	2.1
Total . .	12.5	12.2	12.5

EXTERNAL AID 1970
(million francs CFA)

France (EDF)	76,170
U.S.A. (1965) . . .	1,786
German Federal Republic . .	3,660
U.S.S.R.	1,650
UN (dollars) . . .	240,000

FOUR-YEAR PLAN 1969–73
(million francs CFA)

	Total	%
Agriculture	21,685.50	18.5
Livestock	1,559.10	1.3
Fishing	5,167.80	4.4
Forests	875.50	0.8
Total for the Rural Section . . .	29,287.90	25.0
Industry	21,905.00	18.7
Crafts	220.30	0.2
Tourism	7,090.50	6.1
Commerce . . .	} 1,442.00	1.2
Transport (commercial) . .		
Total for the Industrial Section . . .	30,657.80	26.2
Roads	7,506.65	6.4
Railways	2,693.00	2.3
Ports and Inland Waterways .	1,645.00	1.4
Airports	1,308.00	1.1
Posts and Telecommunications .	1,811.96	1.6
Total for Infrastructure . . .	14,964.61	12.8
Town Planning . . .	12,110.00	10.4
Water Resources . . .	7,837.50	6.7
Health	2,239.24	1.9
General Education . . .	6,669.00	5.7
Technical Education . .	1,196.00	1.0
Information, Culture, Youth, Sports	1,077.60	0.9
Total for Education and Welfare . . .	31,129.34	26.6
Administrative Equipment . .	473.00	0.4
Research	8,559.60	7.3
Local Expenditure . . .	1,927.24	1.7
Total . . .	10,959.84	9.4
General Total . . .	116,999.49	100.0

EXTERNAL TRADE
(million francs CFA)

Imports: (1966) 38,300; (1967) 40,401; (1968) 44,680; (1969) 51,299; (1970) 53,558; (1971) 60,561.
Exports: (1966) 36,800; (1967) 33,890; (1968) 37,358; (1969) 31,906; (1970) 42,180; (1971) 34,707.

PRINCIPAL COMMODITIES

IMPORTS	1969	1970	1971
Milk Products .	1,712	1,585	2,130
Rice . . .	4,674	3,335	4,639
Sugar . . .	1,720	2,518	2,907
Petroleum Products	3,825	2,723	3,763
Wood . . .	721	742	748
Paper . . .	1,384	1,745	1,765
Textiles . .	2,324	3,273	4,125
Metal Goods .	4,278	2,937	1,936
Machinery . .	4,862	4,829	4,493
Electrical Apparatus	2,013	2,270	2,583
Vehicles and Spares .	2,234	3,345	4,442

EXPORTS	1969	1970	1971
Groundnuts . .	4,044	2,691	1,785
Groundnut Oil .	9,176	12,971	7,409
Oilcake . .	3,868	4,594	3,138
Calcium Phosphate .	2,714	3,300	3,785
Hides and Skins .	339	343	249
Wheat Flour . .	615	736	186

PRINCIPAL COUNTRIES

	IMPORTS			EXPORTS		
	1969	1970	1971	1969	1970	1971
France	20,800	27,499	28,697	19,230	22,962	17,971
German Federal Republic .	5,800	3,464	3,540	633	928	528
Italy	1,624	1,727	1,906	935	1,079	1,509
Netherlands . . .	1,345	1,267	1,636	1,638	2,945	2,358
Nigeria	1	4	657	33	238	259
United Kingdom . .	498	751	990	645	847	1,122
U.S.A.	3,246	2,555	3,631	87	173	180

TRANSPORT

Railways (1971): Number of Passengers 2,842,000; length of permanent track: 1,034 km.

Roads (1971): Cars 40,380, Lorries 18,078, Buses 3,485.

Shipping (1971): Vessels entered and cleared 11,118; Passengers: arrivals 10,290, departures 10,265; Freight entered 1,991,000 tons, Freight cleared 1,858,000 tons.

Civil Aviation (1971—Dakar airport): Passenger arrivals and departures 206,253, in transit 137,650.

EDUCATION
(1970–71)

	STUDENTS		TEACHERS	MATRICULATION EXAM PASSES
	MALE	FEMALE		
Primary . . .	164,932	101,451	6,500*	21,030
Secondary . . .	35,529	13,376	n.a.	5,766
Teacher Training . .	424	197	n.a.	n.a.
Dakar University . .	3,804*	886*	n.a.	1,962†

* 1971–72.   † Passes in all university examinations.

Sources: Direction de la Statistique, Ministère des Finances et des Affaires Économiques, Dakar; and *Spotlight on Senegal*, Ministry of Information, Dakar, 1972.

THE CONSTITUTION

(Promulgated March 7th, 1963, revised June 20th, 1967)

Preamble: Affirms the Rights of Man, liberty of the person and religious freedom. National sovereignty belongs to the people who exercise it through their representatives or by means of referenda. There is universal, equal and secret suffrage. French is the official language.

The President: The President of the Republic is elected by direct universal suffrage for a five-year term and is eligible for re-election. He holds executive power and conducts national policy with the assistance of ministers chosen and nominated by himself. He is Commander of the Armed Forces and responsible for national defence. He may, after consultation with the President of the National Assembly and with the Supreme Court, submit any draft law to referendum. In circumstances where the security of the State is in grave and immediate danger, he can assume emergency powers and rule by decree. The President of the Republic can be impeached only on a charge of high treason or by a secret ballot of the National Assembly carrying a three-fifths majority.

The National Assembly: Legislative power is vested in the National Assembly which is elected by universal direct suffrage for a five-year term at the same time as the Presidential election. The Assembly discusses and votes legislation and submits it to the President of the Republic for promulgation. The President can direct the Assembly to give a second reading to the bill, in which case it may be made law only by a three-fifths majority. The President of the Republic can also call upon the Supreme Court to declare whether any draft law is constitutional and acceptable. Legislation may be initiated by either the President of the Republic or the National Assembly.

Amendments: The President of the Republic and Deputies to the National Assembly may propose amendments to the Constitution. Draft amendments are adopted by a three-fifths majority vote of the National Assembly. Failing this they are submitted to referendum.

Judicial Power: The President appoints the members of the Supreme Court of Justice, on the advice of the Superior Court of Magistrates, which determines the constitutionality of laws. A High Court of Justice, appointed by the National Assembly from among its members, is competent to impeach the President or members of the Government.

Local Government: Senegal is divided into seven regions, each having a Governor and an elected Local Assembly.

On February 26th, 1970, the Constitution was amended. The President can no longer stand for a third term of office, and the office of Prime Minister is recreated to apply policies determined by the President. The President retains control of foreign affairs, the army and certain judicial matters.

French Community: In June 1960 Senegal signed Agreements with France to become an independent member of the French Community.

Gambia-Senegal Treaty of Association: Signed April 1967 to promote co-operation between the two countries; provisions include annual meetings of heads of governments, an Inter-State Ministerial Committee (already existing since 1961) and a permanent secretariat; committees, under the supervision of the Inter-State Ministerial Committee, deal with existing agreements covering foreign affairs and security, and the joint development of the Gambia River Basin.

THE GOVERNMENT

HEAD OF STATE

President: LÉOPOLD-SÉDAR SENGHOR.

COUNCIL OF MINISTERS

(January 1973)

Prime Minister and Minister of Tourism and of Defence: ABDOU DIOUF.

Minister of Foreign Affairs: COUMBA N'DOFFENE DIOUF.

Minister of Justice: AMADOU CLÉDORH SALL.

Minister of the Interior: JEAN COLLIN.

Minister of Finance: BABACAR BA.

Minister of Rural Economy: HABIB THIAM.

Minister of Information: OUSMANE CAMARA.

Minister of Technical Instruction and the Formation of Cadres: DOUDOU N'GOM.

Minister of National Education: ASSANE SECK.

Minister of Industrial Development: LOUIS ALEXANDRENNE.

Minister of Civil Service and Labour: AMADOU LY.

Minister of Co-operation: (vacant).

Minister of Public Health and Social Welfare: Dr. DAUOUDA SOW.

Minister of Culture: ALIONUE SÈNE.

Secretary of State to the Prime Minister: ADAMA DIALLO.

Secretary of State to the Prime Minister in charge of Youth and Sports: LAMINE DIACK.

Secretary of State for Foreign Affairs: ADAME N'DIAYE.

Secretary of State in charge of the National Plan: OUSMANE SECK.

Secretary-General of the Government: ALIOUNE DIAGNE.

Secretary-General for the Presidency of the Republic: M. DIOP.

Director of the Cabinet of the President: MOUSTAFA NIASSE.

Director of the Cabinet of the Prime Minister: DIAKHA DIENG.

DIPLOMATIC REPRESENTATION

EMBASSIES AND LEGATIONS ACCREDITED TO SENEGAL

(In Dakar unless otherwise stated)

(E) Embassy; (L) Legation.

Algeria: 5 rue Mermoz (E); *Ambassador:* AZIZ HACENE.

Argentina: Imm. B.I.A.O. 1er étage, Place de l'Indépendance (E); *Ambassador:* OSWALDO GUILLERMO G. PINEIRO.

Austria: 36 blvd. Pinet-Laprade, B.P. 3247 (E); *Ambassador:* AUGUST TARTER.

Bangladesh: 22 rue Carnot (E); *Ambassador:* MOHAMED ANWARUL HAQ.

Belgium: route de la Corniche, B.P. 524 (E); *Ambassador:* RENÉ THIMSTER.

Brazil: Imm. B.I.A.O., 2e. étage, Place de l'Indépendance, B.P. 136 (E); *Ambassador:* JOÃO CABRAL DE MELO NETO.

Bulgaria: (E); *Ambassador:* IANLHO CHRISTOV IVANOV.

Canada: Imm. Daniel Sorano, blvd. de la République (E); *Ambassador:* RAOUL JEAN GRENIER (also accred. to Mauritania).

China, People's Republic: (E); *Ambassador:* WANG CHIN-CHUAN.

Denmark: Rabat, Morocco (E); *Ambassador:* HANS BERTELSEN.

Egypt: Imm. Daniel Sorano, B.P. 474 (E); *Ambassador:* NEGUIB KADRI.

Ethiopia: 36 blvd. Pinet-Laprade, 2e étage, B.P. 379 (E.); *Ambassador:* ZENEBE HAILE.

Finland: Lagos, Nigeria (E).

France: 1 rue Thiers, B.P. 4035 (E); *Ambassador:* HUBERT ARGOD.

Gabon: Abidjan, Ivory Coast.

Gambia: 5 ter. rue de Thiong/rue de Dr. Thèze, B.P. 3248 (E); *Ambassador:* SAMUEL JONATHAN OKIKI SARR.

German Federal Republic: 43 ave. A. Saurraut, B.P. 2100 (E); *Ambassador:* ULRICH SCHESKE.

Ghana: 23 ave. Maginot, 1er étage (E); *Ambassador:* Col. JOSHUA MAHAMADU HAMIDU.

Guinea: rue Marsat, B.P. 7010 (E); *Ambassador:* MAMADOU TOUNKARA.

Haiti: 55 ave. Albert-Sarraut, B.P. 1552 (E); *Ambassador:* MARTIN CELESTIN DELENOIS.

India: 15 allées Canard, B.P. 398 (E); *Ambassador:* HARI KRISHAN SINGH.

Iran: (E); *Ambassador:* MONTEZA ADLE TABATABAI.

Israel: 57 ave. Albert Sarraut, 3e. étage, B.P. 2907 (E); *Ambassador:* MOSHÉ LIBA.

Italy: Imm. Daniel Sorano, B.P. 348 (E); *Ambassador:* LUDOVICI ARTENISIO.

Japan: Imm. B.I.A.O., Place de l'Indépendance, B.P. 3140 (E); *Ambassador:* KIYOSHI SUGANUMA.

Khmer Republic: 140 rue Blanchot, B.P. 3326; *Ambassador:* CHAN YOURAN.

Korea, Republic: Paris 16e., France (E).

Lebanon: 18 blvd. de la République, B.P. 234 (E); *Ambassador:* Dr. ISSAM HAIDAK.

Liberia: 21 ave. Faidherbe, B.P. 2110 (E).

Mali: 48 ave. Maginot, B.P. 478 (E); *Ambassador:* ZANGUÉ DIARRA.

Mauritania: 37 blvd. du Général de Gaulle, B.P. 1119; *Ambassador:* DEY OULD BRAHIM.

Mexico: Addis Ababa, Ethiopia (E).

Morocco: Imm. Daniel Sorano, B.P. 490 (E); *Ambassador:* FADEL BENNANI.

Netherlands: 5 ave. Carde (E); *Ambassador:* J. P. ENGELS.

Nigeria: 9 ave. Roume, B.P. 3129 (E); *Ambassador:* TAFAWA BALEWA.

Norway: Abidjan, Ivory Coast (E).

Pakistan: 22 rue Carnot, rez de chaussée/1er étage (E); *Ambassador:* ANWARUL HAQ.

Poland: Point-E, Canal IV, Route de Ouakam (E); *Ambassador:* TADEUSZ MATYSIAK.

Romania: (E); *Ambassador:* NICOLAE IOAN DANCEA.

Saudi Arabia: rues Béranger Féraud et Masclary (E); *Ambassador:* FARID YOUSSEF BASRAWI.

Spain: Imm. Daniel Sorano, B.P. 2091 (E); *Ambassador:* JOSÉ LUIS OCHOA Y OCHOA.

Sierra Leone: Bathurst, The Gambia (E).

Sweden: 43 ave. Albert-Sarraut, B.P. 2052 (E); *Ambassador:* L. VON CELSING.

Switzerland: 1 rue Victor Hugo, B.P. 1772 (E); *Ambassador:* JEAN RICHARD.

Trinidad and Tobago: Addis Ababa, Ethiopia (E); *Ambassador:* Mme ISABEL TESHA.

Tunisia: rue El-Hadj Seydou Nourou Tall, B.P. 3127 (E); *Ambassador:* ALI HEDDA.

Turkey: Imm. B.I.A.O., Appt. Fls. 1er étage, Place de l'Indépendance, B.P. 6060, Etoile (E); *Ambassador:* ORHAN CONKER.

U.S.S.R.: ave. Jean-Jaurès, B.P. 3180 (E); *Ambassador:* DIMITRI NIKIFOROV.

United Kingdom: 20 rue du Dr. Guillet, B.P. 6025 (E); *Ambassador:* IVOR FORSYTH PORTER (also accred. to Dahomey and Mauritania).

U.S.A.: Imm. B.I.A.O., place de l'Indépendance, B.P. 49 (E); *Ambassador:* E. G. CLARK.

Vatican: rue I, Cité Fann (Apostolic Internunciature); *Apostolic Delegate for West Africa:* Mgr. GIOVANNI MARIANI.

Viet-Nam, Democratic Republic of: *Ambassador:* NGUYEN DUC THIENG.

Viet-Nam, Republic of: 72 blvd. de la République (E); *Ambassador:* (vacant).

Yugoslavia: Rocade Fann-Bel-Air, route de Ouakam (E); *Ambassador:* ACO SOPOV.

Zaire: Imm. Daniel Sorano, 2e. étage, B.P. 2251 (E); *Ambassador:* FERDINAND KAYAKWA KIMOTO.

Zambia: (E); *Ambassador:* SITEKE G. MWALE.

Senegal also has diplomatic relations with Greece, Ivory Coast, Democratic People's Republic of Korea, Kuwait, Monaco Panama and Uruguay.

NATIONAL ASSEMBLY

President: AMADOU CISSÉ DIA.

ELECTION, FEBRUARY 1968

All 80 seats were won by the Union progressiste sénégalaise.

POLITICAL PARTY

Union progressiste sénégalaise (UPS): national section of the *Parti fédéraliste africaine* (PEA); government party; Sec.-Gen. LÉOPOLD-SÉDAR SENGHOR. In 1966, by agreement, the former opposition party *Parti du regroupement africain* was incorporated into the U.P.S.

DEFENCE

There is a total armed force of 5,900 of which the standing army numbers 2,700 men in units of parachutists, engineers, signals, motorized infantry and gendarmerie. All males between the ages of 20 and 60 are liable to national service. The army is closely involved in government development projects. The air force is equipped with light reconnaissance aircraft and helicopters. The navy is composed of two coastal patrol-boats.

Army Chief-of-Staff: Lt.-Col. IDRISSA FALL.

JUDICIAL SYSTEM

Supreme Court: f. 1960; Pres. KÉBA M'BAYE; Sectional Pres. MENOUMBÉ SAR, LAÏTY NIANG BRUNO CHERAMY.

High Court of Justice: f. 1962; composed of members of the National Assembly.

High Council of the Magistrature: f. 1960; Pres. LÉOPOLD-SÉDAR SENGHOR (*President of the Republic*); Vice-Pres. AMADOU CLÉDOR SALL.

Court of Appeal: Dakar; Pres. ABDOULAYE DIOP.

Public Prosecutor's Office: Attorney General OUSMANE GOUNDIAM; Advocate General CHARLES HENRY DUPUY-DOURREAU; Public Prosecutor OUMAR N'DIAYE.

RELIGION

MUSLIM

About 76 per cent of the population are Muslims. The three principal brotherhoods are the *Tijaniyya*, the *Qadiriyya* and the *Mouride*.

Grand Imam: Alhaji AMADOU LAMINE DIENE.

NATIVE BELIEFS

About 14 per cent of the population follow traditional beliefs, mainly animist.

CHRISTIANITY

About ten per cent of the population are Christian, mainly Roman Catholics.

Roman Catholic: Archbishop of Dakar: Mgr. HYACINTHE THIANDOUM, B.P. 1908, Dakar.

Suffragan Bishops:
Kaolack: Mgr. THÉOPHILE ALBERT CADOUX.
St. Louis de Sénégal: Mgr. PROSPER DODDS.
Thiès: Mgr. FRANCESCO SAVERIO DIONE.
Ziguinchor: Mgr. AUGUSTIN SAGNA.

Protestant Church: 49 rue Thiers, Dakar, B.P. 847; 42 rue Carnot, Dakar.

THE PRESS

DAKAR

Le Soleil: B.P. 92; f. May 1970; National daily sponsored by the Union progressiste sénégalaise; circ. 20,000.

L'Information Africaine: 38 ave. W.-Ponty, B.P. 338; f. 1950; daily; Editors E. LALANNE, J. PEILLON; circ. 15,000.

Journal officiel de La République du Sénégal: Dakar; government paper.

Africa: 30 Bol Pinet Lapade, B.P. 1826; f. 1957; economic review of West Africa.

Afrique Médicale: 8 rue Jules-Ferry; f. 1960; medical review; circulates throughout Francophone tropical Africa.

Afrique, Mon Pays: 24 ave. Gambetta.

Awa: Imprimerie Diop, rue de Reims, angle rue Dial Diop.

Bafila: 26 ave. Gambetta, B.P. 1845.

Bingo: 17 rue Huart, B.P. 176; f. 1952; illustrated monthly; Editor JOACHIM PAULIN; circ. 100,000.

La Semaine à Dakar: weekly.

Médecine d'Afrique Noire: 38 ave. William-Ponty; Dakar; f. 1952; monthly; Dir. EMILE LALANNE; circ. 10,000.

Le Moniteur Africain du Commerce et de l'Industrie: Société Africaine d'Edition, B.P. 1877; f. 1961; weekly; Editor-in-Chief JEAN THIBAULT; circ. 10,000; the only French economics weekly produced in black Africa.

L'Observateur Africain: 29 rue Paul Holle.

Revue Française d'Etudes Politiques Africaines: Société Africaine d'Edition, B.P. 1877; f. 1966; monthly; Dir. P. BIARNES; Editor-in-Chief PH. DECRAENE.

Sénégal d'Aujourd'hui: 58 blvd. de la République, B.P. 546; monthly.

Terre Sénégalaise: B.P. 269; monthly; Dir. J. B. GRAULLE.

L'Unité Africaine: 72 blvd. de la République, B.P. 1077; weekly; organ of the U.P.S.; Editor OUSMANE N'GOM.

La Voix des Combattants: Ecole El Hadj-Malick Sy.

PRESS AGENCIES

Agence de Presse Sénégalaise: Imm. Maginot, Dakar; f. 1959; Dir. BARRA DIOFF.

FOREIGN BUREAUX

Agence France-Presse: B.P. 363, Dakar; Dir. E. MAKEDONSKY.

Novosti: B.P. 3180, Corner Jean-Jaurès Ave. and Carnot St., Dakar.

DPA, Reuters and Tass also have bureaux in Dakar.

PUBLISHERS

Clairafrique: B.P. 2005, rue Sandiniery 2, Dakar; politics, law, sociology.

Grande Imprimerie Africaine: 9 rue Thiers, B.P. 51, Dakar; f. 1917; law, administration; Dir. HENRY O'QUINN.

Institut Fondamental d'Afrique Noire (IFAN): B.P. 206, Dakar; scientific and humanistic studies of Black Africa.

Maison du Livre, La: B.P. 2060, Dakar; fiction and belles-lettres.

Société Africaine d'Editions et de Publication: rue de Reims, Dakar.

Société d'Edition et de Presse Africaine: 17 rue Huart, Dakar.

RADIO AND TELEVISION

Radiodiffusion du Sénégal: B.P. 1765, Dakar; broadcasts in French and four vernacular languages; international service in Arabic, English and Portuguese; Dir.-Gen. ALIOUNE FALL.

There are 275,000 radio sets.

Télévision du Sénégal: B.P. 2375, Dakar; f. 1964; Government-sponsored educational service; pilot project with one 50-kW. transmitter.

There are 1,500 television sets.

FINANCE

(cap.=capital; m.=million; all amounts in francs CFA, unless otherwise stated.)

BANKS

CENTRAL BANK

Banque Centrale des Etats de l'Afrique de l'Ouest: 29 rue de Colisée, Paris 8e; Dakar, ave. W.-Ponty, B.P. 3159; cap. and reserves 3,547m.; Chair. B. A. BABACAR; Man. ROBERT JULIENNE.

Banque Internationale pour le Commerce et l'Industrie du Sénégal: B.P. 392, 2 ave. Roume, Dakar; f. 1962; cap. 500m.; Pres. DJIME GUIBRIL N'DIAYE; Gen. Man. P. ESCOUBEYRON.

Banque Nationale de Développement du Sénégal: B.P. 319, Dakar; f. 1964; cap. 1,360m.; Dir.-Gen. HAMET DIOP.

Banque Sénégalaise de Développement (B.S.D.): Dakar, 2 *bis* rue Béranger Féraud; f. 1960; cap. 1,000m.; Dir. LOUIS KANDÉ.

Crédit Populaire Sénégalais: Dakar, 35 rue Carnot; cap. 360m.

Union Sénégalaise de Banques pour le Commerce et l'Industrie (U.S.B.): blvd. Pinet-Laprade, B.P. 56, Dakar; f. 1961; cap. 690m.; Pres. TANOR THIENDELLA FALL.

FOREIGN BANKS

Banque Centrale des Etats de l'Afrique de l'Ouest: B.P. 3159, Dakar; Dir. FRANÇOIS ELIARD.

Banque Internationale pour l'Afrique Occidentale: 9 ave. de Messine, Paris; Dakar, place de l'Indépendance, B.P. 129.

Société Générale de Banques au Sénégal: Dakar, B.P. 323, 19 ave. Roume; f. 1962; cap. 500m.; Admin. Délégué ROGER DUCHEMIN.

INSURANCE

Comité des Sociétés d'Assurances de Sénégal: 43 ave. A. Sarraut, B.P. 1766, Dakar; Pres. PIERRE HENRI DELMAS; Sec. JEAN-PIERRE CAIRO.

Societe Africaine d' Assurances: B.P. 508, Dakar; f. 1945; cap. 9 million; Dir. PIERRE VERNET.

TRADE AND INDUSTRY

CHAMBERS OF COMMERCE

Chambre de Commerce, d'Industrie et d'Artisanat de la Région du Fleuve: rue Bisson, Saint-Louis-du-Sénégal, B.P. 19; f. 1869; Pres. El Hadji MOMAR SOURANG; publ. *Weekly Bulletin.*

Chambre de Commerce d'Industrie et d'Artisanat de la Région du Sine Saloum: Kaolack, B.P. 203; Pres. PIERRE FOURNIER.

Chambre de Commerce d'Industrie et d'Artisanat de la Casamance: B.P. 26, Ziguinchor; f. 1908; Pres. YOUS-SOUPH SEYDI.

Chambre de Commerce, d'Industrie et d'Artisanat de la Région de Thiès: ave. Foch, Thiès, B.P. 20; f. 1883; 32 mems.; Pres. El Hadji DIAGNE; Sec.-Gen. RENÉ BARBÈRES.

Chambre de Commerce, d'Industrie et d'Artisanat de la Région du Cap Vert: B.P. 118, Dakar; Sec.-Gen. AMADOU SOW.

Chambre de Commerce, d'Industrie et d'Artisanat de la Région de Diourbel: Diourbel; Pres. CHEIKH DIONGUE.

Chambre de Commerce, d'Industrie et d'Artisanat de la Région du Sénégal Oriental: Tambacounda; Pres. AMADOU GAYE.

PRINCIPAL EMPLOYERS' ASSOCIATIONS

Dakar

Délégation de la Fédération des Industries Mécaniques et Transformatrices des Métaux: 43 ave. Maginot, B.P. 1858; Pres. M. BARRAQUÉ.

Syndicat des Commerçants Importateurs et Exportateurs de l'Ouest Africain: 14 ave. Albert-Sarraut, B.P. 806.

Syndicat des Agents Maritimes de la Côte Occidentale de l'Afrique: 8-10 allées Canard, B.P. 167 and 138.

Syndicat des Entrepreneurs de Bâtiment et de Travaux Publics de l'Ouest Africain: 12 ave. Albert-Sarraut, B.P. 593; f. 1930; 46 mems.; Pres. PIERRE MEYNENG.

Syndicat des Entrepreneurs de Transports et Transitaires de l'Afrique Occidentale: 47 ave. Albert Sarraut, B.P. 233; Pres. J. NÈGRE.

Syndicat des Entreprises de Manutention des Ports d'Afrique Occidentale (SEMPAO): 8 allées Canard, B.P. 164.

Syndicat des Fabricants d'Huile et de Tourteaux du Sénégal: 11 allées Canard, B.P. 131; Pres. ROGER LAUNAY.

Syndicat Patronal des Industries de Dakar et du Sénégal: 12 ave. Albert-Sarraut, B.P. 593; f. 1944; 101 mems.; Pres. MARC DELHAYE.

Union Fédérale des Syndicats Industriels et Commerciaux et Artisanaux: 2 ave. Gambetta, B.P. 221.

Union Intersyndicale d'Entreprises et d'Industries de l'Ouest Africain: 12 ave. A. Sarraut, B.P. 593; Pres· MARC DELHAYE.

TRADE UNIONS

Confédération Nationale des Travailleurs Croyants: B.P. 1474, Dakar; 3,000 mems.; Pres. DAVID SOUNAH; Sec.-Gen. CHARLES MENDY.

Union Nationale des Travailleurs du Sénégal (UNTS): B.P. 840, Dakar; affiliated to Union Générale des Travailleurs d'Afrique Noire; 100,000 mems.; merged with Confédération Sénégalaise du Travail 1966; Gen.-Sec. MAGATTE THIAW.

Confédération Nationale des Travailleurs Sénégalais (CNTS): f. 1969; affiliated to Union progressiste sénégalaise; Pres. DOUDOU N'GOM.

MAJOR INDUSTRIAL COMPANIES

The following are some of the largest companies in terms either of capital investment or employment.

Compagnie Africaine de Produits Alimentaires: B.P. 127, route du Service Géographique, Dakar; f. 1952; cap. 480m. francs CFA.

Sugar refinery.

Pres. M. D'ESPIES; Dir. M. GODY; 280 employees.

Compagnie Sénégalaise des Phosphates de Taïba: B.P. 1713, 47 ave. de la République, Dakar; f. 1957; cap. F81,403,700.
Extraction of high-grade calcium phosphate.
Pres. MAX ROBERT; Dir.-Gen. CLAUDE GABRIEL; 915 employees.

Ets. V. Q. Petersen et Cie.: B.P. 125, Dakar; f. 1938; cap. 1,500m. francs CFA.
Groundnut oil factory.
Pres. ROBERT LEMAIGNEN; Dir.-Gen. ROGER LAUNAY.

Peyrissac-Sénégal: B.P. 193, 9 rue Parchappe, Dakar; f. 1963; cap. 531m. francs CFA.
Import and retail of general merchandise, particularly hardware and vehicles.
Dir. GILBERT BONNEMAISON; 370 employees.

Société Africaine de Raffinage: B.P. 203, Dakar; f. 1961; cap. 1,000m. francs CFA.
Oil refinery at M'Bao.
Dir.-Gen. ANDRÉ JOIN.

Société Africaine des Pétroles: B.P. 203, Dakar; f. 1955; cap. 5,250,000m. francs CFA.
Petroleum prospecting.
Pres. Dir.-Gen. GILBERT LUGOL.

Société Dakaroise de Grands Magasins: B.P. 2070, 31 ave. Albert-Sarraut, Dakar; f. 1953; cap. 194m. francs CFA.
Import of general merchandise.
Dir. PIERRE JONETTE; 136 employees.

Société Industrielle d'Engrais au Sénégal (SIES): B.P. 3377, 3 ave. Carde, Dakar; f. 1968; cap. 1,100m. francs CFA.
Manufacture of fertilizers.
Dir.-Gen. A. BERNOS; Dir. of Mines M. GOUILLART; 250 employees.

Société Ouest-Africaine des Ciments: B.P. 29, 9 rue Zola, Dakar; f. 1942; cap. 600m. francs CFA.
Manufacture of Portland cement.
Pres. ANDRÉ LINDENMEYER; Dir.-Gen. PIERRE CREMIEUX; 260 employees.

Société de Teinture, Blanchiment, Apprêts et d'Impressions Africaine: B.P. 527, Dakar; f. 1957; cap. 1,998m. francs CFA.
Bleaching, dyeing and printing of textiles.
Pres. Dir.-Gen. JOSEPH RIEBEL; Dir.-Gen. MOHAMED MEKOUAR.

TRANSPORT

RAILWAYS

Régie des Chemins de Fer du Sénégal: Thiès; total length of line 1,034 km. One line runs from Dakar north to St. Louis (262 km.) with a branch to Linguera (129 km.); the main line runs to Bamako and the Niger (643 km. in Senegal); Dir. FALY BA.

ROADS

In 1971 there were 15,422 km. of roads, of which 2,294 km. were bitumenized and 689 km. were earth roads.

MOTORISTS' ORGANIZATION

Automobile-Club du Sénégal: B.P. 295, Dakar.

INLAND WATERWAYS

Dakar

Société des Messageries du Sénégal: 35 blvd. Pinet-Laprade, B.P. 209; river traffic on the Senegal from Saint-Louis to Kayes (Mali); also coastal services.

Paquet et Cie. Général Transatlantique: c/o Union Sénégalaise d'Industries Maritimes, 8 and 10 allées Canard, B.P. 164.

SHIPPING

Dakar

Cabotage Intercolonial: 55 rue de Grammont.

Chargeurs Réunis: 8 and 10 allées Canard, B.P. 138–167; agents for Messageries Maritimes, Cie. Fabre SGTM, Nigerian National Lines, Delta Line, Nouvelle Cie. Havraise Péninsulaire de Navigation, Elder Dempster Lines.

Compagnie Fabre—SGTre: 8 and 10 allées Canard.

Compagnie Générale Transatlantique: 8 and 10 allées Canard, B.P. 164.

Compagnie de Navigation Paquet: 8 and 10 allées Canard.

Companhia Colonial de Navigação: c/o R. Alcantara et Fils, 1 rue Parent, Dakar; f. 1925.

Delmas-Vieljeux: 8 and 10 allées Canard, B.P. 164.

Elder Dempster Lines: c/o Compagnie Maritime des Chargeurs Réunis, 8 and 10 allées Canard, B.P. 138.

Farrell Lines, Scindia Steam Navigation Co., Henry Abram Ltd., Van Nievelt, Goudriaan and Co.: c/o Umarco, 53 blvd. Pinet-Laprade; Man. GEORGE GUIMONT.

Royal Interocean Lines: Peyrissac-Sénégal, rue Parchappe 9, Dakar, B.P. 193.

Scandinavian East Africa Line: c/o Ets. Buhan et Teisseire, place Kermel.

CIVIL AVIATION

Air Sénégal: place de l'Indépendance, B.P. 3132, Dakar; Aéroport de Yoff, B.P. 8010, Dakar; f. 1971; extensive internal services linking Dakar with all parts of Senegal; fleet of one DC-3 and three deHavilland Doves; Dir. FERNAND BRIGAUD.

Air Afrique: Senegal has a 7 per cent share in Air Afrique; *see* under Ivory Coast.

Senegal is also served by the following foreign airlines: Aerolíneas Argentinas, Aeroflot, Air Zaire, Air France, Air Guinée, Air Mali, Air Mauritanie, Alitalia, ČSA, Ghana Airways, Lufthansa, Nigeria Airways, PAA, Royal Air Maroc, Swissair.

TOURISM

Secrétaire d'Etat du Tourisme: 1 bis place de la République, B.P. 2018, Dakar; Dir. YOUSSOU TH. DIOP.

ARTS FESTIVAL

World Festival of Negro Art: ave. du Barachois, B.P. 3201, Dakar; f. 1965; bi-annual; Bureau Pres. ALIOUNE DIOP; Sec.-Gen. DJIBRIL DIONE.

POWER

Compagnie des Eaux et Electricité de l'Ouest Africain: B.P. 93, Dakar; f. 1929; cap. 4,000m. francs CFA.
Production and distribution of electricity and water.
Dir. I. DIOP; production in 1971 was 344m. kWh.

ATOMIC ENERGY

Ministère du Plan, du Développement et de la Coopération Technique: Dakar; the government body responsible for nuclear affairs.

EDUCATION

There is compulsory education for all children between the ages of six and fourteen years. Nearly 50 per cent of school-age children are provided for. Four new secondary schools, each with places for 400 pupils, were due to open in 1971. There is one university.

LEARNED SOCIETIES

Alliance Française: B.P. 1777, Dakar.

American Cultural Center: 38 avenue de la République, Dakar; f. 1958; library of 4,700 vols.

Centre d'Etudes et de Documentation Législatives Africaines (CEDLA): Dakar.

Institut Géographique National (Centre en Afrique de l'Ouest): Route du Front de Terre, B.P. 4016, Hann Dakar; f. 1945; relations with the governments of Senegal, Mauritania, Mali, Upper Volta, Togo, Dahomey, Niger and the Ivory Coast; cartography of the eight States; Dir. M. TRAIZET.

RESEARCH INSTITUTES

Bureau de Recherches Géologiques et Minières: B.P. 268, Dakar; Dir. M. DELAFOSSE.

Centre de Géophysique ORSTOM (Office de la Recherche Scientifique et Technique Outre-Mer) de M'Bour: B.P. 50, M'Bour; f. 1951; magnetism, seismology, meteorology, magnetotelluric and geomagnetic prospecting; Dir. C. BLOT.

Centre de Recherches et de Documentation du Sénégal (C.R.D.S.): B.P. 382, Saint-Louis; f. 1943 as Centre IFAN-Senegal; 15 mems.; library of 13,000 vols.; Dir. FÉLIX BRIGAUD; Librarian IBRAHIMA SOUMARE.

Centre de Recherches Zootechniques de Dahra-Djoloff: Dahra-Djoloff; f. 1950 as Centre d'Elevage du Djoloff.

Centre National de Recherches Agronomiques de Bambey: Bambey; f. 1921; under direction of Institut de Recherches Agronomiques et Tropicales (IRAT); fundamental and applied agricultural research; 24 research mems.; library of 4,000 vols.; Dir. L. SAUGER; Research Co-ordinator D. SENE; publ. *Rapport de synthèse*; *Annuaire analytique des travaux de l'IRAT au Sénégal et en Mauritanie* (each annually).

Secteur de Recherches agronomiques de Casamance (Ziguinchor).

Station de Recherches agronomiques de Sera.

Station de Recherches Agronomiques de Richard-Toll.

Station IRAT de Saint-Louis.

Centre Océanographique de Dakar-Thiaroye: B.P. 2241, Dakar; African centre administered by ORSTOM; oceanography; library; Dir. C. CHAMPAGNAT.

Centre Technique Forestier Tropical: Division des Recherches Piscicoles, Résidence Faidherbe; B.P.28, Richard-Toll; f. 1966; fishery research; Dir. C. REIZER.

Compagnie Française pour le Développement des Fibres Textiles (CFDT): B.P. 3216, Dakar.

Institut d'Hygiène Sociale: ave. Blaise-Diagne, Dakar.

Institut Fondamental d'Afrique Noire: Université de Dakar, B.P. 206, Dakar; f. 1936, re-constituted 1959; scientific and humanistic studies of Black Africa; library and museums (*see below*); Dir. Prof. AMAR SAMB; publs. *Bulletin de l'I.F.A.N.*, Série A—Sciences Naturelles (trimestriel), Série B—Sciences Humaines (semestriel), *Notes Africaines* (tri-mestriel), *Mémoires de l'I.F.A.N.*, *Initiations et Etudes Africaines, Instructions Sommaires*, Catalogue, Documents, etc.

Institut de Recherches pour les Huiles Oléagineuses: brs. at Louga, Tivaouane, M'Bambey.

Institut Pasteur: B.P. 220, Dakar; f. 1906; medical research; library of 1,126 vols., 54 periodicals; Dir. Dr. Y. ROBIN; publ. *Annual Report*.

Laboratoire National de L'Élevage et de Recherches Vétérinaires: B.P. 2057, Dakar; f. 1935; six departments; library of 10,800 vols; Dir. J. ORUE.

Office de la Recherche Scientifique et Technique Outre-Mer Centre ORSTOM de Dakar-Hann: B.P. 1386, Dakar; soil biology, pedology, medical entomology, hydrology, geology, nematology, demography, economics, zoology, botany; library; Dir. A. PERRAUD.

Office de la Recherche Scientifique et Technique Outre-Mer (ORSTOM) Station Ecologique de Richard-Toll: B.P. 20, Richard-Toll; ecology, ornithology; Dir. Dr. G. MOREL.

Organisme de Recherches sur l'Alimentation et la Nutrition Africaines (ORANA): 39 Avenue Pasteur, B.P. 2089, Dakar; research on African foods and nutritional values, investigations, documentation, teaching; Dir. Dr. J. TOURY.

LIBRARIES

Archives de Sénégal: Immeuble administratif, ave. Roume, Dakar; f. 1913; 13,500 vols., 850 periodicals; Dir. J. F. MAUREL; publ. *Bulletin Bibliographique* (quarterly).

Bibliothèque de l'Institut Fondamental d'Afrique Noire: B.P. 206, Dakar; 51,710 vols.; 6,800 brochures; 3,950 collections of periodicals; 1,535 microfilms; 2,560 maps; 30,000 photographs; 2,000 slides; 12,100 files of documents.

Bibliothèque de l'Alliance Française: 10 rue Colbert, B.P. 1777, Dakar; f. 1948; 10,000 vols.; Librarian M. CAUSSADE.

Bibliothèque de l'Université de Dakar: B.P. 2006, Dakar; f. 1952; Law, Humanities, Medicine, Pharmacy, Veterinary Science, Sciences; 184,841 vols., 11,700 pamphlets, 4,800 periodicals; Dir. JEAN DONATI.

MUSEUMS

Musées de l'Institut Fondamental d'Afrique Noire:

Musée d'Art Africain de Dakar: B.P. 206, Dakar; f. 1936; ethnography and African art; Curator A. DIOP; Administrator B. THIAM.

Musée Historique: Gorée; Curator S. M. CISSOKO.

Musée de la Mer: Gorée; Curator R. ROY.

UNIVERSITY

UNIVERSITÉ DE DAKAR
(University of Dakar)
DAKAR-FANN

Telephone: 329-76.

Founded 1949, University 1957.

State control; Language of instruction: French;
Academic year: October to July.

Rector and President: SEYDOU MADANI SY.

Vice-President: PAUL MORAL.

Secretary-General: GEORGES DORION.

Librarian: JEAN DONATI.

Library: see Libraries.

Number of teachers: 237.

Number of students: 4,580.

Publications (periodical): *Annales Africaines* (annual),
Annales de la Faculté des Sciences (annual), *Bulletin et
Mémoires de la Faculté mixte de Médecine et de Pharmacie*
(annual).

DEANS:

Faculty of Law and Economics: A. BOCKEL.

Faculty of Medicine and Pharmacy: M. SANKALE.

Faculty of Sciences: S. NIANG.

Faculty of Arts and Humanities: P. MORAL.

ATTACHED INSTITUTES:

Centre de Linguistique Appliquée de Dakar (CLAD): Dir.
M. CALVET.

**Centre de Recherches, d'Etudes et de Documentation sur
les Institutions et la Législation Africaines (CREDILA):**
Dir. P. BOUREL.

Centre de Recherches Economiques appliquées (CREA):
Dir. (vacant).

Centre de Recherches psychopathologiques: Dir. HENRI
COLLOMB.

Centre d'Etude des Sciences et Techniques de l'Information:
f. 1965; offers Diploma courses in journalism; Dir.
GEORGES GALIPEAU.

Centre des Hautes Etudes Afro-Ibéro-Américaines: con-
cerned with all matters interesting Africa and Latin
America in the fields of Law, Science and the Arts; Dir.
RENÉ DURAND.

Cours de Langue et Civilisation françaises: Dir. MICHEL
WORONOFF.

Ecole de Bibliothécaires, Archivistes et Documentalistes:
Faculty of Arts and Social Sciences, B.P. 3252, Dakar;
f. 1963, attained present status as university institute
1967; provides a two-year librarianship course, giving
priority to students from French-speaking countries in
Africa; Dir. A. BOUSSO.

Ecole normale supérieure: Dir. AMADOU TRAWARE.

Institut de Médecine Tropicale Appliquée: Dir. MARC
SANKALE.

Institut de Pédiatrie Sociale: Dir. M. V. DAN.

Institut de Physique Météorologique: Dir. (vacant).

**Institut de Recherches pour l'Enseignement de la Mathé-
matique (IREM):** Dir. (vacant).

Institut des Sciences et Médecine Vétérinaires: f. 1969;
instruction at doctorate level; Dir. J. FERNEY.

Institut d'Odontologie et de Stomatologie: Dir. GUY
GRAPPIN.

Institut Fondamental d'Afrique Noire (*see under* Research
Institutes).

Institut Universitaire de Technologie: B.P. 3266, Dakar;
Dir. MICHEL GUILLOU.

COLLEGES

Ecole Nationale d'Administration du Sénégal: B.P. 5209,
Dakar; f. 1959; Dir. A. N'DENE N'DIAYE.

**Institut Africain de Développement Economique et de
Planification:** rue 18 Juin, Dakar; administered by the
UN; the longest courses last three months in Dakar for
each part of the nine-month course, but there are
shorter courses arranged in various parts of Africa on a
regional, sub-regional or national basis; Dir. SAMIR
AMIN.

SELECT BIBLIOGRAPHY

(For works on the former A.O.F. states generally *see*
Dahomey Select Bibliography, p. 297.)

CROWDER, MICHAEL. *Senegal: A Study in French Assimilation Policy.* London, 1967 (Revised Edn.).

DESCHAMPS, H. *Le Sénégal et la Gambie.* Paris, Presses
universitaires de France, 1964.

DIARASSOUBA, VALY CHARLES. *L'Evolution des structures
agricoles du Sénégal.* Paris, Editions Cujas, 1968.

HARRISON CHURCH, R. J. *West Africa.* Sixth Edn., Chapter
12. London, Longmans, 1968.

HYMANS, JACQUES LOUIS. *Léopold Sédar Senghor.* Edinburgh University Press, 1972.

MILCENT, ERNEST, and SORDET, MONIQUE. *Léopold Sédar
Senghor et la naissance de l'Afrique moderne.* Paris,
Editions Seghers, 1969.

O'BRIEN, RITA CRUISE. *White Society in Black Africa: The
French of Senegal.* London, Faber and Faber, 1972.

PELISSIER, P. *Les Paysans du Sénégal.* 1966.

Seychelles

PHYSICAL AND SOCIAL GEOGRAPHY*

The Seychelles archipelago consists of a scattered group of 40 granitic and 45 coralline islands in the Western Indian Ocean. The islands take their name from the Vicomte Moreau de Séchelles, Controller General of Finance in the reign of Louis XV. The group also includes numerous rocks and small cays. Its land area is 107 sq. miles.

The largest of the islands is Mahé, named after a former French Governor of Mauritius, which has an area of about 57 sq. miles and is approximately 17 miles long from north to south. Mahé lies 940 miles due east of Mombasa, 1,750 miles south-west of Bombay, and rather more than 600 miles north of Madagascar. Victoria, the capital of Seychelles and the only port of the archipelago, is on Mahé. It is the only town in Seychelles of any size and has a population of about 14,000.

The granitic islands, which are all of great scenic beauty, rise fairly steeply from the sea and Mahé has a long central ridge which at its highest point, Morne Seychellois, reaches 3,000 ft. Praslin, second largest island in the group, is 27 miles from Mahé and the

other granitic islands are within a radius of 35 miles. The coral islands are reefs in different stages of formation, rising only a few feet above sea-level.

For islands so close to the Equator, the climate is surprisingly pleasant. Maximum shade temperature at sea level averages 29°C. (85°F.) but during the coolest months, the temperature may drop to 24°C. (75°F.) At higher levels temperatures are rather lower and the air fresher. There are two seasons, hot from December to May, and cooler from June to November while the south-east monsoon is blowing. Rainfall varies over the group; the greater part falls in the hot months during the north-west monsoon and the climate then tends to be humid and somewhat enervating. The mean annual rainfall in Victoria taken over the past 67 years is 93 in. and the mean average temperature 25°C. (76°F.). All the granitic group lie outside the cyclone belt. High winds and thunderstorms are rare.

The total population of Seychelles in 1971 was 52,650. In 1971 there were 1,832 births and 462 deaths.

*See map on page 564.

HISTORY

There is some evidence to suggest that the Seychelles Islands were known and visited in the Middle Ages by traders from Arabia and the Persian Gulf sailing to and from ports in East Africa with the monsoons; they are clearly associated with the great Portuguese voyages in the Indian Ocean. The Amirantes group was sighted by Vasco da Gama on his second voyage to India in 1502.

The French first explored the islands in 1742 (at the instigation of the French Governor of Mauritius, the Vicomte Mahé de Labourdonnais), and they claimed possession of them in 1756, although still leaving them uninhabited. In 1794 the French garrison surrendered to Captain Newcome of the H.M.S. *Orpheus*, but the Commandant, M. de Quincy, continued his administration on behalf of the French Republic until 1810. The Treaty of Paris (1814) finally confirmed British possession of the Seychelles and of the Ile de France, now known as Mauritius. The two colonies continued to be administered as a single unit, and de Quincy continued in office until his death in 1827, having served the French for twenty years and the British for eighteen.

The Seychelles were administered by a series of Commissioners appointed from Mauritius until 1872, when the first steps towards separation were taken with the appointment of a Board of Civil Commissioners with financial autonomy. The powers of this

Board were extended in 1874, and in 1888 an Order-in-Council was passed giving the Seychelles an administrator with a nominated Executive and Legislative Council. In 1897 the Administrator was given full powers of Governor and six years later, by the Letters Patent of 1903, the separation of Mauritius and the Seychelles was completed and Seychelles became a Crown Colony with its own Governor and Executive and Legislative Councils.

At the London Constitutional Conference in March 1970 there was full agreement on the plan to establish a ministerial system in the Seychelles, but Lord Shepherd, Minister of State at the Foreign Office, who presided at the Conference, rejected a plan for integration with Britain, on the precedent of Hawaii or the Isle of Man, which was put forward by Mr. James Mancham, leader of the main Seychelles political party.

The UN Committee on Decolonization has called for steps to transfer power to freely elected representatives of the people, to eliminate the gap between rich and poor, and to prevent the infiltration of foreign economic interests and settlers into the territories, particularly those from South Africa. However, both Mr. Mancham's party, the Seychelles Democratic Party, and the Seychelles People's United Party (led by Mr. F. A. René) stand for the closest association with the United Kingdom.

ECONOMY

The main diet in the islands is rice, fish and lentils. Meat is eaten occasionally and vegetables are usually available.

The Seychelles fishing industry is for the most part undeveloped, the local fishermen relying solely on traditional methods and equipment for their livelihood. Fish being a staple food of the islanders, virtually the entire catch goes for local consumption, although a few tons of salted fish are exported every year, mostly to Tanzania.

Recently local fishermen have received help in various ways—including the acquisition of deep-freezers for keeping bait—from grants provided by the United Kingdom Committee of the Freedom From Hunger Campaign. The Seychelles Government has adopted a project originally sponsored by the *Union Chrétienne Seychelloise* with probable financial assistance from Oxfam to provide a cold store for freezing and keeping fish during periods of glut, thus ensuring a balanced supply throughout the year. This scheme, when it is realised, should revolutionize the Seychelles fishing industry.

The main export crops are coconuts, cinnamon, patchouli and vanilla, but tea is now being produced. The Seychelles Tea Company has some 375 acres of tea planted and will be extending this to 400 acres. Of these, 200 acres are being planted on behalf of the Seychelles Government for allocation in five-acre plots to small settlers. The first nine settlers were installed on their plots in 1970. A factory has been built and production of tea on a small scale began in August 1966. It is hoped that small holdings and private estates will also be encouraged to plant tea.

Total exports in 1971 were valued at Rs. 8,026,272 and imports in 1970 at Rs. 55,393,000. Britain is the main customer and supplier. Copra and cinnamon bark are the two leading exports, each valued at about Rs. 3.5 million.

The main classes of imports in 1968 by quantity and value were flour, rice, sugar and other foodstuffs; kerosine, petrol and diesoline; cotton piece goods and other articles.

The principal form of direct taxation is income tax. This is chargeable on all earned or investment income arising in or derived from the territory. In addition tax is payable by residents on investment income arising in Seychelles or on earned income remitted thereto, the basis of assessment being income arising in the calendar year preceding year of assessment.

The principal sources of indirect taxation are customs duties at varying rates. Licensing exists for most trades and professions. There is also a succession duty at a graduated scale.

The territory's revenue for 1971 was estimated at £1,858,202 which included £464,650 in Budgetary Aid from the U.K. Total expenditure for the year 1971 is estimated at £2,338,894.

The Port of Victoria has about one square mile of deep water roadstead for ships of all sizes and an inner harbour of about half that area for small craft. The whole harbour area is protected by a chain of small islands and a reclamation scheme to establish a separate and new port area began in 1970. The new harbour, due to be completed by 1974, will take vessels up to 12,000 tons and of a draught of not more than 32 feet. The number of vessels entered and cleared from Victoria in 1972 was 311. Tonnage handled in 1972 was 14,510 loaded and 83,789 unloaded. An international airport on Mahé was opened in July 1971. Mahé has an extensive road system of which 55 miles are now surfaced. On the island of Praslin the trans-island road from Grand'Anse to Baie Ste Anne is also surfaced.

Radio Seychelles, a government-owned and equipped broadcasting station opened in July 1965 and broadcasts in the medium wave band (225.4 metres, 1,331 kilocycles) for eight hours daily.

STATISTICS

Area: 107 square miles (Mahé 57, Praslin 16, Silhouette 6, La Digue 4).

Population (1971): 52,650, Port Victoria (capital) 13,622; Births 1,832; Deaths 462; *Employment:* Agriculture and Fishing 4,680, Domestic Service 1,740, Building 4,130, Manufacturing 940, Trade and Transport 1,680, Education 740, Public Administration 590.

Agriculture (1971): Copra (excluding copra from British Indian Ocean Territory) 3,490 tons, Cinnamon Bark 1,297 tons, Cinnamon Oil 17 tons.

Livestock (1971): Cattle 1,976, Pigs 7,356, Poultry 63,428.

Fishing (1971 exports): 544 kg. Salted Fish.

Finance: 1 Rupee=100 cents, £1 sterling=13.33 Rs.; Budget (1972): Est. Revenue Rs. 36,070,443, Expenditure Rs. 57,536,436.

External Trade: Imports (1970): Rs. 55,393,000; Exports (1971): Rs. 8,026,272 (Copra Rs. 3,574,021, Cinnamon Bark Rs. 3,322,405, Cinnamon Oil Rs. 403,993, Guano Rs. 331,532.

Transport (1971): Roads: 2,978 vehicles. Shipping: Cargo landed 83,789 tons; Cargo shipped 14,510 tons; total net registered tonnage of all vessels (excluding warships) entered and cleared with cargo 932,390 tons; number of calls by vessels 311.

Education (1972): Primary: 35 schools, 10,074 pupils; Junior Secondary: 11 schools, 1,859 pupils; 2 Secondary Grammar schools, 655 pupils; 1 Teacher Training College; 1 Vocational School.

THE CONSTITUTION

Under the new Constitution introduced during 1970 there is a Council of Ministers, consisting of a Chief Minister, up to 4 other Ministers and 3 *ex officio* members, and presided over by the Governor or his Deputy. All the Ministers are elected members of the Legislative Assembly, which comprises 15 elected members and 3 *ex officio* members. Elections are held every five years.

THE GOVERNMENT

Governor: Sir BRUCE GREATBATCH, C.M.G., C.V.O., M.B.E.

Deputy Governor: The Hon. J. R. TODD, M.L.C.

Chief Minister: The Hon. JAMES R. M. MANCHAM, F.R.S.A., M.L.C. (elected).

In the 1970 elections the Seychelles Democratic Party won ten seats and the Seychelles People's United Party won five seats.

POLITICAL PARTIES

Seychelles Democratic Party: Victoria; f. 1963, advocating a policy of integration with the United Kingdom, or as close an association as possible; ten seats in Legislative Assembly; Leader J. R. M. MANCHAM, M.L.C.; publ. *Seychelles Weekly.*

Seychelles People's United Party: Victoria; left-wing party urging independence for Seychelles; five seats in Legislative Assembly; Pres. Hon. F. A. RENE; Vice-Pres. Hon. G. SINON, M.L.C.; publ. *The People* (weekly).

JUDICIAL SYSTEM

There are two Courts, the Supreme Court and the Magistrates' Courts. The Supreme Court is also a Court of Appeal from the Magistrates' Courts. Appeals from the Supreme Court in respect of criminal matters go to the Seychelles Court of Appeal in London and thence to the Judicial Department of the Privy Council. Appeals from the Supreme Court in respect of civil matters go to the Supreme Court of Mauritius and thence to the Judicial Department of the Privy Council.

Chief Justice: The Hon. Sir GEORGE SOUYAVE.

Attorney-General: The Hon. J. A. O'BRIEN QUINN, M.L.A.

RELIGION

Almost all the inhabitants are Christian, 90 per cent of them Roman Catholics and about 9 per cent Anglicans.

ROMAN CATHOLIC

Bishop of Seychelles: The Right Reverend OLIVIER MARADAN, C.B.E., P.O.B. 43, Port Victoria.

ANGLICAN

Bishop of Mauritius: The Right Reverend E. E. CURTIS; Bishop's House, Phoenix, Mauritius.

THE PRESS

Le Seychellois: P.O.B. 32, Victoria; daily except Sunday f. 1898 under title of *Reveil*; publ. in English and French Conservative; Editor SADEC RASSOOL; Man. GUSTAVE DE COMARMOND, M.B.E.; publishers: Le Seychellois Press Ltd., Harrison St., Victoria, Mahé; circ. 1,500.

L'Echo des Iles: P.O. Box 12, Victoria; fortnightly; Roman Catholic mission; circ. 2,200.

Le Nouveau Seychellois: Victoria; organ of Le Parti Seychellois; Editor VICTOR WESTERGREEN; circ. 500.

The People: P.O.B. 154, Victoria; organ of the Seychelles People's United Party; weekly; Editor R. JUMEAU; circ. 750.

Seychelles Bulletin: Dept. of Information and Broadcasting, Victoria; daily; Editor ANTONIO BEAUDOIN; circ. 1,100.

Seychelles Weekly: P.O.B. 131, Victoria; organ of the Seychelles Democratic Party; Editor F. A. GRANDCOURT; circ. 2,000.

RADIO

Radio Seychelles: Victoria, Mahé; power 10 kW. on 1331 kHz.; transmissions 8 hours daily; Man. and Chief Engineer Group Captain E. C. PASSMORE, C.B.E.; approx. 10,000 receivers and 40,000 listeners; programmes in English, French and Creole.

FINANCE

BANKS

Government Savings Bank: Port Victoria, Mahé; Grand Anse, Praslin; for deposit accounts.

The Seychelles Agricultural Loans Board: P.O.B. 54, Victoria; f. 1937, reconstituted 1968; agricultural loans; Chair. The Financial Secretary; Man. The Director of Agriculture.

SEYCHELLES

Barclays Bank International Ltd.: P.O.B. 167, Victoria, Mahé.

The Standard Bank: P.O.B. 241, Victoria. Mahé.

Post Office Savings Bank: Victoria, Mahé; Grand Anse, Praslin.

INSURANCE

There are 7 insurance companies with agencies on the Islands.

TRADE AND INDUSTRY

TRADE UNIONS

There are 9 trade unions: Teachers' Union; Cable and Wireless Limited Staff Union; Christian Workers' Union; Licensed Bakers' Union; Stevedores', Winchmen and Dock Workers' Union; Transport and General Workers' Union; Civil Servants' Union; Seychelles Building, Construction and Civil Engineering Workers' Union; Artisans', Engineers', Constructors' and Builders' Union.

MARKETING ORGANIZATION

Seychelles Copra Association: P.O.B. 32, Victoria, Mahé, Seychelles; f. 1953; an association of planters, producers and dealers who control the export of copra in bulk on behalf of its members; Pres. SULEMAN ADAM; Vice-Pres. SADEC RASSOOL; Sec. GUSTAVE DE COMARMOND, M.B.E.

TRANSPORT AND TOURISM

ROADS

There are 55 miles of tarmac road and 21 miles of motorable earth roads on Mahé. Praslin has 4 miles of tarmac road and 20 miles of earth roads. La Digue has 8 miles of earth road.

SHIPPING

The Shipping Corporation of India Ltd.: two-monthly service; agents Jivan Jetha and Co., P.O.B. 16, Mahé.

Trade and Industry, Transport and Tourism, etc.

The Union Lighterage Shipping Company Ltd.: P.O.B. 38, Mahé; f. 1926; agents for P. and O., Royal Interocean, Union Castle, Shaw Savill and Farrell Lines, which run occasional services.

A ferry four times a week between Victoria and the Islands of Praslin and La Digue is operated by the Port and Marine Dept.; capacity 100 persons.

CIVIL AVIATION

The airport at Mahé, financed by the British Government, was completed in 1971. The 9,800 ft. airstrip was constructed on reclaimed land on Mahé's east coast. BOAC began flights in February 1972 with a service of four flights a week. British Caledonian Airways run weekly services from London (Gatwick) and Air Mahé run domestic flights. The U.S.A.F. satellite racking unit operates an amphibious aircraft between Mombasa and Port Victoria, for their own use, and also carry mail and urgent supplies.

TOURISM

Department of Tourism, Information and Broadcasting: Kingsgate House, Victoria; Government P.O.B. 92, Victoria; Government department financed under the Development Plan; Dir. J. A. ROBINSON.

Tourists (1971): 3,175; estimated expenditure £500,000.

EDUCATION

The official language is English and state education at primary and secondary levels is in English. The family language is Creole, a *patois* of French. In all there are 35 primary schools with an enrolment figure for 1972 of 10,071. In addition there are over 20 pre-primary infant and organized kindergarten schools. There are 11 junior secondary and two secondary grammar schools, with a total enrolment of 2,514 pupils. There is one vocational training centre and one teacher training college.

BRITISH INDIAN OCEAN TERRITORY

The Colony consists of the Chagos Archipelago, about 1,200 miles north-east of Mauritius and the islands of Aldabra, Farquhar and Desroches in the western Indian Ocean. It was set up in 1965 to provide defence facilities for the British and United States Governments. The Chagos Archipelago, which includes the coral atoll Diego Garcia, was formerly administered by the Government of Mauritius. The other three groups were administered by that of the Seychelles.

It is possible that Diego Garcia could play a key role in Western defence strategy in the Indian Ocean, especially as the alternative policy for Britain, at least, involves closer military co-operation with South Africa. According

to the British Ministry of Defence all the islands of the Territory are available for both British and U.S. bases, and the question of their use for these purposes is under review.

Area: 175 sq. miles approx.

Population (June 1968): 1,019 (Chagos Archipelago 803, Farquhar 50, Desroches 120, Aldabra 42).

Commissioner: THE GOVERNOR OF THE SEYCHELLES.

Administrator: J. R. TODD, Queen's Bldg., Victoria, Mahé, Seychelles.

SELECT BIBLIOGRAPHY

BENEDICT, B. *People of the Seychelles.* H.M.S.O., 1966.

ROWE, J. W. F. *Report on the economy of the Seychelles and its future development.* Government Printer, Mahé, 1959.

THOMAS, A. *Forgotten Eden.* Longmans, Green. 1968.

TOUSSAINT, A. *History of the Indian Ocean.* Routledge and Kegan Paul, 1966.

WEBB, A. W. T. *Story of Seychelles.* Seychelles, 1964.

Sierra Leone

PHYSICAL AND SOCIAL GEOGRAPHY*

Peter K. Mitchell

PHYSICAL ENVIRONMENT

From the surf beaches of the south-west the land rises in a flight of irregular steps to the broad plateaux of the ill-defined Atlantic/Niger watershed at the north-eastern frontier. Despite the ruggedness suggested by the country's name, what impresses is the horizontal aspect of Sierra Leone landscapes, developed over millenia upon largely Precambrian structures. But there is little monotony. Ascents, occasionally abrupt, to older uplifted erosion surfaces divert the eye—most impressively along sections of a major escarpment, 80 miles inland, separating a western lowland zone (c. 400 ft.) from the country's more elevated interior half (c. 1,600 ft.). Incised valleys— floors punctuated by rapids and minor falls—carry drainage south-westward; only locally or along a coastal sedimentary strip do rivers flow through open terrain.

A geologically recent submergence of major flood-plains, particularly north of Cape St. Ann, has brought tide-water into contact with the rocky margins of the ancient shield, barring the way to up-river navigation. Water-borne trade has found compensation in sheltered deep-water anchorages, notably off Freetown, principal port and capital, where a line of coastal summits almost 3,000 ft. high make for an easy landfall. The Portuguese navigator's metaphor for this peninsular range has been extended to apply to the whole of this populous country (about 2.6 million people in 27,925 sq. miles).

Intrusive gabbros form this *Serra Lyoa*; elsewhere, isolated blocks or hill groups emerging from age-smoothed expanses are rock-bare granites or the metamorphic roots of long-vanished mountain chains. Scenically attractive and often capped with forest remnants, the latter were zones of mineralization: iron, chromite, gold, rutile and bauxite. Kimberlite, a late and localized intrusion in the southern high plateaux, weathered and sorted, yields extensive diamond-rich alluvials.

Differences in seasonal and regional incidence of humidity and rainfall are important. Prolonged rains (mid-June to mid-September) are bracketed by showery weather with many squally thunderstorms, such spells beginning earlier in the south-east. Consequently, the growing season is longest here (although total rainfall—over 200 in. locally—is greater along the coast) and the "natural" vegetation is tropical evergreen forest; cash crops such as cocoa, coffee, kola and oil-palm do well in this area. The savannah-woodlands of the north-east have less rain (75 to 100 in.), a shorter period for plant growth and a dry season made harsh by desiccating harmattan winds, with cattle-rearing, groundnuts and tobacco as potential commercial resources. Semi-deciduous forest occupies most intervening areas, but long peasant occupation has created a mosaic of short-term crop-land, fallow re-growth plots and occasional tracts of secondary forest.

A partly autochthonous colonization is creating permanent rice-lands from mangrove swamp in the north-west and other floodlands elsewhere. Such innovation contrasts with a widespread bush-fallowing technique, giving low yields of rain-fed staples, normally rice, but cassava (specially on degraded sandy soils) and millets in the north. Extensive farming still provides most of the nation's food, employing three-quarters of the labour force.

SOCIAL FACTORS

Traditional *mores* still dominate, in spite of the westernizing influences of employment in mining, of education and of growing urbanization. Extended family, exogamous kin-groups and the paramount chieftaincies form, with the binding force of initiation societies, a social nexus closely mirrored by a hierarchy of hamlet, village and rural centre: 29,000 non-urban settlements, including the rare isolated impermanent homestead. Islam more readily finds common ground with a pervasive animism than does Christianity, though each has many adherents.

Self-identity is linked closely with membership of an ethno-linguistic group. The Creoles, concentrated but no longer dominant about the metropolis, possess a unique society reminiscent of Victorian Britain. Inland, the material culture and non-negroid genetic admixture of the Fula, cattle-keepers encroaching from Futa Djallon, are most distinctive. A 'Westminster' style parliament, with universal suffrage, has recently caused a polarization of the remaining dozen groups into camps: 'northern' with a Temne focus, 'southern' about a Mende nucleus, while the eastern Kono stand a little aside. Whether these tendencies have been temporarily created by political activity or reflect fundamental long-term regional affiliations and divisions is problematic.

See map on p. 708.

RECENT HISTORY

Christopher Fyfe

SIERRA LEONE UNDER BRITISH COLONIAL RULE

In 1896 a British Protectorate was proclaimed over the hinterland of the coastal Colony of Sierra Leone, which had been British since the late eighteenth century. It covered an area about the size of Scotland, divided into small independent chiefdoms. Some, but not all, of the ruling chiefs had previously been persuaded to make what they supposed were treaties of friendship with the British. Not until 1898, when their new government imposed a hut tax, did they realize that they had lost their sovereignty. In the north an outstanding military leader, Bai Bureh, rose in protest in the Hut Tax War. In the south too there was violent resistance, organized through the dominant secret society, the Poro Society. But they could not withstand the overwhelming mastery of European arms and were defeated. After 1898 there was no further large-scale armed resistance against the government.

The Protectorate was administered under the principles of "indirect rule", which guided much of British policy in west Africa. Chiefs went on ruling much as before, advised by British administrative officials. Together they preserved law and order, with the aid of the Court Messenger Force, a semi-military police. Movements of protest in the chiefdoms were easily, and usually unobtrusively, suppressed. Traditional ways were deliberately preserved by European officials and African chiefs alike. As in the period before British rule, the economy was predominantly subsistence, with surplus produce (chiefly palm oil, palm kernels and groundnuts) exported to Europe in return for manufactured imports. A railway was built which was specially designed to carry freight at low speed, to increase the volume of exports. Otherwise there was little economic change. Land remained in communal ownership. The government spent little on education. A few missionary societies opened schools, but only a tiny minority of the Protectorate peoples learnt even to read or write.

The Sierra Leone Colony with the capital, Freetown, was administered separately from the Protectorate. Its inhabitants, known as "Creoles", were descendants of freed slaves who had been captured in transit across the Atlantic by the British navy, and then liberated and settled in the Colony. They had the status of British subjects and a strongly anglicized culture which they had acquired through several generations of missionary education. There were several secondary schools in Freetown and a higher institution, Fourah Bay College, founded in 1827 by the Church Missionary Society. From 1876 its students could qualify for a degree awarded by Durham University. So there was a large well-educated élite, including doctors, lawyers and ministers of religion. In the late nineteenth century some Creoles also occupied senior posts in government service.

But in the twentieth century the British Empire became increasingly stratified on racial lines. Creoles were squeezed out of office and confined to subordinate posts. Despite their British citizenship, they were treated as inferiors in their own homes. Hence they grew embittered. They were allowed some political representation in the legislature, but their representatives were heavily outnumbered by European officials. In the Colony, as in the Protectorate, policy decisions were made by the governor and his executive council, subject to the approval of the Secretary of State for the Colonies in London, and were carried out by an administrative hierarchy of white officials.

PRELUDE TO INDEPENDENCE

In Sierra Leone, as elsewhere in British West Africa, the second world war brought a change of policy. For the first time British government money was made available for development. The colour bar was removed from government service. After the war successive British governments declared explicitly that the colonies should move towards self-government.

A new constitution had therefore to be drawn up. Although the Creoles were a small minority in the population of Colony and Protectorate combined, many of them felt that their educational achievements entitled them to demand a constitution that would give them a special entrenched status. But in 1951 a unitary constitution was introduced which gave political power to those who won a majority of votes. The dominant political party, the Sierra Leone People's Party (SLPP), which won office in 1951, was therefore a Protectorate-based party. It was led by Dr. (later Sir) Milton Margai, a Mende from the south and the first Protectorate man to have qualified in Britain as a medical practitioner.

During the next decade British rule was gradually phased out and Margai's government took over. There was little conflict between the departing government and its African successor. British officials moved out of the executive council which became a cabinet, responsible to a parliamentary majority. The legislature was reconstituted to make it into a national parliament. Opposition parties formed to fight the SLPP, but it retained its majority at each election.

ECONOMIC DEVELOPMENT

The 1950s also brought economic transformation. The country's mineral resources, high-grade iron ore and diamonds, which had been exploited on a small scale by British companies since the 1930s, were now exploited on a large scale. Diamond mining was controlled by the Sierra Leone Selection Trust, a subsidiary of an international corporation. During the early 1950s it became common knowledge that diamonds did not necessarily need to be mined by machinery—they could be picked up from river beds by hand. From all over the country people rushed to the diamond-producing areas to look for wealth. Attempts were made to enforce the S.L.S.T. monopoly but it proved impossible. After long negotiations with the government, the company agreed to give up some of its concessionary rights, and eventually private diamond-diggers were allowed to prospect under government licence. The control of diamond mining and smuggling nevertheless remained a serious problem for successive governments.

Whatever problems the diamond rush may have caused, it spread wealth throughout the country as never before. Revenue rose steadily from mineral royalties, and from customs duties on the consumer goods imported by the newly rich. Money was now available (supplemented by grants from the British Colonial Development and Welfare Fund) to provide the infrastructure of a developing economy. The road system was developed to fit it for large-scale motor transport; bridges were built to replace ferries across the many rivers which intersect the country. Internal air transport was introduced. The railway however— a wasting asset built for a different era—was run down.

The government could also spend money on medical services, hitherto much neglected, and on education. Secondary education was greatly expanded. Fourah Bay College was enlarged and its academic standards raised.

These sudden changes brought social upheavals too. Villagers who had grown up under the paternal rule of district Commissioner and chief, had their eyes opened to new possibilities. Many left home to dig for diamonds or to work on the new public works programmes. Yet the paternal system of government went on, for the SLPP, like the colonial government from which it was taking over, supported the authority of the chiefs. All through the 1950s there was disturbances in the Provinces (as the Protectorate was renamed), culminating in widespread riots in 1955–56 in the north. Nevertheless as independence approached the country as a whole was peaceful.

THE MARGAI GOVERNMENTS

On April 27th, 1961, Sierra Leone became an independent state within the Commonwealth. The British governor was replaced, as Queen's representative, by a Sierra Leonean governor-general, Sir Henry Lightfoot-Boston, formerly speaker of the parliament. Sir Milton Margai was the first prime minister. When he died in 1964 his brother, Sir Albert, succeeded him.

Economic expansion continued during the early 1960s with large-scale expenditure on government projects. New educational institutions were opened, including another university college at Njala with a technological emphasis. In 1969 Njala University College and Fourah Bay College amalgamated as constituent colleges of the University of Sierra Leone.

The SLPP, despite appeals to national unity, still drew its main support from the chiefs. The opposition groups, which coalesced round Siaka Stevens, leader of the All Peoples Congress (APC), resented the government's attachment to what they felt were reactionary sectional interests. It was also believed that Sir Albert Margai, under cover of introducing a new republican constitution, was going to set up a one-party state which would give him a permanent monopoly of power. Hence the SLPP lost its initial popularity.

In March 1967 there was a general election and the APC gained a majority. As the results came in, the head of the army, Brigadier David Lansana, a Margai supporter, seized power, to prevent Stevens from taking over. Two days later his own officers repudiated him and took power themselves.

THE N.R.C. AND THE RETURN TO CIVILIAN RULE

Seven officers, five military and two police, formed a National Reformation Council under the chairmanship of Colonel A. T. Juxon-Smith. Their declared aims were to restore the economy, which had been allowed to run down, to end corruption, which had become blatantly widespread, and then return the country to civilian rule. At first the people seemed ready to accept them. But as the months passed and they showed no signs of relinquishing office popular feeling turned against them, particularly within the ranks of the army.

In April 1968 a group of private soldiers mutinied. Aided by some of their N.C.O.s they arrested the officers and restored civilian rule. The APC took power on the strength of the majority it had won at the election the year before, with Stevens as prime minister. Parliamentary government was restored with the SLPP as opposition party.

Political instability continued, and in November 1968 a state of emergency was imposed, lasting four months. In September 1970 two leading ministers, Dr. Mohammed Forna and Mohammed Bash-Taqi, resigned and joined Dr. John Karefa-Smart and other dissidents in a new opposition party, the United Democratic Party. Again a state of emergency was proclaimed. The UDP was banned and most of its leaders were arrested. Subsequently they were released, except for the two former ministers who remain in prison indefinitely. Three army officers were then detained and charged with plotting a *coup*. Meanwhile, in the hope of lessening the expatriate hold on the country's economy, the Government negotiated agreements to take a 51 per cent share in the mining companies operating in Sierra Leone. Government security measures were, however, still unable to prevent continued diamond smuggling.

In March 1971 the army commander, Brigadier John Bangura, was involved in another attempted military *coup*. Two attempts were made to assassinate Stevens, but enough of the army remained loyal to him to suppress the mutiny. He immediately signed a defence agreement with President Sekou Touré of Guinea, who had already been concerned to extend his own defence commitments since the abortive Portuguese-engineered attack on Guinea of 1970. Guinean troops were flown in to support the Government. Bangura and three other officers were executed. In April a constitutional bill was finally passed through Parliament declaring Sierra Leone a republic, and Stevens became executive president. Guinean soldiers remained stationed in Sierra Leone, giving reinforcement to the Government.

ECONOMY
Douglas Rimmer

Note on the Currency Unit

The West African Currency Board pound was replaced in 1965 by a national currency unit, the leone, at the rate of 2 leones to the pound. The leone was devalued along with sterling in November 1967, and the exchange rate has been maintained at Le.2 = £1.

INTRODUCTION

Until the 1930s, when diamond and iron-ore mining began, the exports of Sierra Leone were entirely agricultural. Minerals assumed the larger share of the total value of exports in the mid-1950s, and today mining activities dominate the external trade, therefore powerfully affecting the public finances and the whole money-economy of the country.

Favourable agricultural export prices in the early post-war period and the subsequent diamond boom produced rapid increases in imports, living standards, and government expenditure. So far as this economic progress depended on illicit diamond digging and dealing, it occurred in the teeth of governmental resistance and as a result of the breakdown of law and order over part of the country. Between about 1960 and 1967 the growth of exports (legal and illegal) slowed down, and possibly ceased. Government expenditure and imports continued to rise, and external debt was accumulated as the budgetary situation deteriorated and the foreign exchange reserves were run down. In 1966 support from the IMF had to be sought, and public spending and the taking up of foreign suppliers' credits were checked. In 1968-69 the fortunes of the economy rather unexpectedly revived with rises in the prices and volumes of diamonds and other exports, but the revival was checked by a recession in the diamond market in 1970.

A population of 2,180,000 was enumerated by the census of April 1963. The economically active population was put at 908,000, of whom 77 per cent were attributed to the agricultural sector. Official projections of population since 1963 have been based on rates of increase of 1.3 and 1.5 per cent p.a., which appear to be low rates by west African standards. Taking the 1.5 per cent rate and assuming undercounting by 5 per cent in 1963, the 1972 population would be about 2.6 million. Estimates of the gross domestic product have been made for the years since 1963-64. On the average of 1963-67 agriculture is believed to account for 33 per cent of G.D.P., mining for 18 per cent, transport, trade, public administration and other services for 38 per cent and manufacturing, building and public utilities for the remaining 11 per cent. Over one fifth of the G.D.P. estimate represents the imputed value of subsistence output, almost wholly in agriculture. The 1971 G.D.P. figure is put at Le.340 million at current prices.

EXTERNAL TRADE AND PAYMENTS

Starting from only some Le.14 million in 1950, exports had probably doubled in value by 1954 and reached a level of around Le.60 million by the end of the decade (with allowance made for diamond smuggling, which is believed to have been at a level of Le.20-30 million p.a. in the late 1950s). The volume of diamond smuggling probably fell in the early 1960s, and in 1963-67 total recorded or legal exports averaged Le.60 million p.a.

The balance of trade, with allowance made for smuggled diamonds, seems to have become adverse in 1961 and to have continued so until 1968. Recorded exports and imports show a deficit of around Le.7 million p.a. in 1965-67, and the deficit in the current balance of payments has been estimated at Le.20 million p.a. in the same period. By the end of 1966 the official foreign exchange reserves had been reduced to about Le.11 million (from Le.30 million in 1964), while external debt totalling over Le.50 million, with a large medium-term element, had been accumulated. In the late 1960s charges on the external debt were running at around Le.8 million p.a.

Between 1967 and 1968 the value of recorded diamond exports rose (in leone terms) by over 50 per cent, and there were also substantial increases in the values of exports of agricultural produce, iron ore and rutile. A favourable trade balance was recorded in 1968 and reserves recovered to a peak of Le.32 million in April 1970. In 1970 and 1971, however, total recorded exports declined slightly from the record Le.87.8 million of 1969, while imports continued in excess of Le.90 million. At the end of 1971 the reserves stood at Le.25.8 million.

Of the average annual value of Le.85.6 million in recorded exports in 1969-71 78 per cent was in minerals (including diamonds 63 per cent, iron ore 12 per cent), 20 per cent in domestic agricultural produce (including palm kernels 7 per cent, and coffee, cocoa, piassava, kolanuts), and 2 per cent in re-exports. In recent years, food has accounted for about 20 per cent of total imports, machinery and transport equipment for slightly more, and fuel for about 8 per cent; the residue has consisted mainly of manufactured consumers' goods, particularly textiles, clothing and footwear. In 1971 63 per cent of recorded domestic exports went to the U.K. and 16 per cent to the EEC countries. The main sources of imports were the U.K. (29 per cent), the EEC countries (19 per cent), Japan and the U.S.A.

AGRICULTURE

According to the G.D.P. estimates field and tree crops account for about 85 per cent of the total value of agricultural output (including animal husbandry, forestry, and fishing). Rice is the major crop, and the other staple foods, grains and cassava, are of relatively minor importance. Export crops, though important as a source of cash-income for farmers, account for only about 10 per cent of the total notional value of agricultural output. About three-fifths of the value put on agricultural output in 1966–67 was estimated to consist in subsistence production. It appears that the ex-farm value of locally marketed food supply would be around Le.20 million a year, about the same level as food imports. The biggest sector of the economy is largely uncommercialized.

For the most part, export crops have been handled by the Sierra Leone Produce Marketing Board, which has a statutory buying monopoly. The Board kept its producer prices sufficiently low in relation to world market prices to amass reserves totalling about Le.7 million in 1964. At about this time the Board embarked on a development programme, which included the establishment of numerous oil palm and other plantations, and of several processing ventures (palm kernel oil, instant coffee, groundnut oil, etc.). By the end of 1966 both the reserves and the working capital of the Board were wholly committed in this way; the Board was heavily indebted to its buying agents; and produce buying was stopping for want of finance. Most of the plantations and the uncompleted processing establishments were subsequently abandoned as unlikely ever to be profitable. The Board was rehabilitated in 1967 with the help of a sterling loan from the Standard Bank, and agricultural exports have revived from the very low levels attained in that year.

MINING

Poaching on the preserves of the diamond mining company, the Sierra Leone Selection Trust, became widespread in the early 1950s, and smuggled diamonds became the country's principal export. The government attempted to bring the situation under control by its Alluvial Diamond Mining Scheme of 1956, reducing SLST's concession to an area of 284 sq. miles around Koidu, legalizing alluvial mining by licensed diggers outside the SLST areas, and setting up an official buying organization to purchase the diggers' output. This became the Government Diamond Office, managed by a subsidiary of the Diamond Corporation, and the sole legal exporter of diamonds mined under the ADMS. Illicit digging on the company's concession has nevertheless continued, possibly growing in scale again in the late 1960s. Further, sales to the GDO (which may be of legally or illegally mined diamonds) have been highly responsive to taxation, output being easily diverted to the contraband trade. The government has therefore not found it practicable to impose more than a modest tax charge (currently an export duty of $7\frac{1}{2}$ per cent) on the independent diamond dealers. Recorded or legal exports of diamonds are highly variable from year to year, but on the annual average of 1963–67 they amounted to 1.48 million carats, valued at Le.34 million, SLST being credited with about one-third of the totals. In 1968 and 1969 both sectors of the industry increased their recorded output markedly, and, with a favourable trend in prices, the export value reached Le. 58.5million in the latter year. The company has continued to

expand output (to nearly 1 million carats in 1970), but with a drop in recorded diggers' output and the downturn in prices in 1970, export value declined to Le.49.9 million in 1971.

Iron ore is mined by the Sierra Leone Development Company (DELCO) at Marampa, from where the concentrates are carried by a company railway to Pepel for shipment. Exports averaged 2.12 million tons, valued at Le.10 million, in 1963–67, when the mine was working below capacity. Long-term contracts with Japanese steel mills, signed in 1968, have revitalized the industry and led to heavy investment in improving port facilities at Pepel. Output in 1971 was 2.51 million tons.

Exports of bauxite by the Sierra Leone Ore & Metal Company (SIEROMCO) began in 1964 and had risen by 1971 from 127,000 to 552,000 tons, the latter figure realizing a value of Le.2.5 million. Rutile exporting from Sherbro Minerals' mine began in 1967, but in April 1971 the company suspended operations. Subsequently the mine has been reactivated by American interests operating through Sierre Rutile Ltd.

Mineral exploration continues in Sierra Leone. Iron ore deposits are known to exist in the Tonkolili Valley, but their relative inaccessibility and the quality of the ore makes their exploitation unlikely. The opening by German interests of a second rutile mine appears possible.

In December 1969 the government announced its intention of acquiring compulsorily a 51 per cent holding in the share-capital of each of the four mining companies. Agreement with SLST was reached in September 1970, and negotiations with DELCO began in 1972, but it appears possible that the decision will not be implemented with SIEROMCO and the rutile miners. The agreement with SLST provides for the setting up of a jointly owned company —the National Diamond Mining Company (DIMINCO)—and the compensating of SLST by £2.55 million of negotiable government bonds, redeemable over eight years in bi-annual instalments. Hopes that the government's participation in diamond mining would improve the policing of the concession area have been disappointed, and, indeed, the situation appears rather to have deteriorated further. The Minister of Lands and Mines was reported in June 1972 to have put the value of illegally exported diamonds at Le.24–40 million p.a.

MANUFACTURING TRADE AND TRANSPORT

Within the very limited market provided by Sierra Leone the more obvious kinds of import substitution (e.g. brewing, cigarettes, flour-milling) have been made. Before the military coup of March 1967 both the government and (as already mentioned) the SLPMB were actively promoting further industrial ventures, the former in, for example, oil refining, hotel services and the manufacture of cement, shoes and metal windows. The cement works was closed down early in 1970, the Cape Sierra Hotel stood empty until

1971, and many other recent ventures require heavy public subsidization. The oil refinery came on stream at the end of 1968, and prices of petroleum products in the country have consequently risen. Recent policy statements on industralization have stressed agro-based industries and export possibilities, as opposed to the earlier emphasis on import substitution.

At the wholesale level the trade in import goods is very largely in the hands of a small number of European firms, with substantial participation by Lebanese and Indian merchants. The Lebanese are also prominent in retail trading from fixed premises. Market and itinerant trade is carried on by Africans. Between 1963 and 1969 a series of legislative measures was passed (though not always enforced and sometimes repealed) to curtail foreign participation in retail trade, and also in specified services and small-scale manufacturing activities. At the end of 1968 Ghanaian fishermen were expelled from Sierra Leone.

New government ventures include a National Trading Company in the import trade, a National Insurance Company and a National Shipping Company; the establishment of an indigenous commercial bank is being encouraged.

About 5,000 miles of road exist, though less than one-tenth of the mileage is hard-surfaced. Improvement of the road system is a major part of the current development programme. A 292-km. narrow-gauge railway connects Freetown with its hinterland; it has been making a loss of about Le.1 million a year, and the government has now accepted that it should be phased out. There is an international airport at Lungi, recently modernized, and domestic air services are provided by a national airline. A major quay extension at Freetown harbour was opened early in 1970.

PUBLIC FINANCE

Government recurrent expenditure rose from about Le.25 million in 1961–62 to Le.40 million p.a. in the years 1966–67 to 1969–70 and Le.55 million in 1971–72. Development expenditure has been steadier at around Le.10 million p.a. However, the capacity to cover capital expenditure out of tax revenue was almost extinguished. In 1968–69 to 1970–71 a combination of restraint in spending and increase in tax revenue (resulting mainly from the revival in exports, but also from some aspects of the DIMINCO agreement) produced current account surpluses averaging Le.6.7 million. After 1971 the resumed growth of recurrent spending again threatened to run down the current account surplus, though the Government is committed to the policy that domestic fiscal resources should provide for a substantial proportion of the development budget. In 1971/72 current revenue was slightly below recurrent spending. In the estimates for 1972/73 current revenue is put at Le.59.1 million and expenditure at Le.58.2 million. It is hoped to raise development spending in the year to Le.14.8 million (as compared with Le.11 million in 1971–72), and over half this total is looked for as foreign loans and grants. Current revenues are strongly affected by external trade, about 45 per cent of the estimated total for 1972–73 coming from import and export duties, and 15 per cent from company and mining taxation.

The precarious economic balance of Sierra Leone was lost as a result of the adventurous "development" policies of the government and the Marketing Board in the years immediately after independence—policies which the present government regards as having been actuated by desires for personal enrichment. In 1965–68 the government was living from hand to mouth, depending on IMF support in its external payments, and on budgetary assistance from the foreign-owned banks and mining enterprises. The prospect had brightened by 1969, partly through the more sober policies adopted by the government and the Marketing Board. The economic fortunes of the country continue, however, to hinge on the volume and value of its exports. Falling diamond prices in 1970 produced a setback to the fiscal recovery of the recent past, and the partial nationalization of mining introduced new imponderables. Economic changes that would diminish the relative importance of mining in the country's economy are not yet conspicuous.

STATISTICAL SURVEY

AREA AND POPULATION

AREA (square miles)			POPULATION (1963 Census)		
TOTAL	FREETOWN AND RURAL AREAS	PROVINCES	TOTAL	FREETOWN AND RURAL AREAS	PROVINCES
27,925	215	27,484	2,180,355	195,023	1,985,332

1971 Total Population (est.): 2,600,000.

Main Tribes: Mende 673,000, Temne 550,000.

Chief Towns: Freetown (capital) 170,000, Bo 26,000, Kenema 13,000, Makeni 12,000.

EMPLOYMENT
PERSONS IN PAID EMPLOYMENT*
(1963)

Agriculture	3,500
Commerce	4,400
Mining	8,100
Transport	7,100
Construction	11,000
Services	17,000

* These figures take no account of the high proportion of the population active in the subsistence sector.

AGRICULTURE
PRODUCTION
('ooo metric tons)

CROP	1967	1968	1969	1970
Rice (Paddy)	468.0	426.0	407.0	425.0
Cocoa (Beans)	4.1	2.2	4.0	5.0
Coffee	4.8	5.7	5.4	7.5
Groundnuts (in shell)	9.0*	9.0*	9.0*	9.0*
Palm Kernels (exports)	21.8	65.3	60.0	59.2
Palm Oil	41.0	42.0	45.0	47.0
Maize	10.0	11.0	12.0	14.0

* FAO estimate.

Source: United Nations, *Statistical Yearbook 1971.*

Livestock (1961): Cattle 175,000, Sheep and Goats 55,000.

FORESTRY
PRODUCTION

	1967	1968	1969	1970
Sawn Timber (cu. m.)	10,000	11,000	12,000	13,000

Fisheries (1965): 6,000 tons.

MINING

	1968	1969	1970	1971
Diamonds ('ooo carats) . .	1,683	2,020	1,955	1,934
Bauxite ('ooo tons) . .	463	434	389	552
Iron Ore ('ooo tons) . .	2,516	2,335	2,389	2,569
Rutile ('ooo tons) . .	6	28	29	16

DIAMOND PURCHASES BY GOVERNMENT DIAMOND OFFICE

	1967	1968	1969	1970	1971
Carats ('ooo) . . .	759	863	1,102	1,048	1,031
Export Value (Le. million) . .	21.8	25.4	33.7	26 2	25.2

Source: Government Diamond Office.

INDUSTRY*

	UNIT	1970	1971
Cigarettes	million sticks	492	731
Acetylene	'ooo cu. ft.	972	829
Oxygen	,, ,, ,,	2,517	2,089
Carbon Dioxide . . .	'ooo lb.	246	195
Paint	'ooo imp. gal.	92	92
Spirit	,, ,, ,,	44	22
Beer and Stout . . .	,, ,, ,,	1,260	1,304
Confectionary . . .	'ooo lb.	2,252	2,339
Salt	,, ,,	—	11,272
Matches	gross boxes	50,750	51,750
Plastic footwear . . .	'ooo pairs	549	522
Nails	cwt.	12,055	11,484
Motor Spirit . . .	m. imp. gal.	13 1	11 9
Gas, Diesel and Fuel Oils .	,, ,, ,,	47 0	49 0
Kerosene	,, ,, ,,	8 9	9 3

* Cleared through excise authorities.
Source: Bank of Sierra Leone.

FINANCE

100 cents = 1 leone.

Coins: 1, 5, 10 and 20 cents; 50 leone (gold).

Notes: 1, 2 and 5 leone.

Exchange rates (December 1972): £1 sterling = 2.00 leone; U.S. $1 = 85.19 Sierra Leone cents.

100 leones = £50 = $117.39.

BUDGET 1971–72
(Le. million)

CURRENT BUDGET		DEVELOPMENT BUDGET	
Current Revenues:			
Indirect Taxes:		Revenues:	
Import Duties	19.7	Balance on Current Account . . .	1.1
Export Duties	3.9	Foreign Loans and Grants . . .	4.6
Excise Duties	9.7	Other Development Revenues. . .	0.8
Direct Taxes:			
Company Taxes	7.1		
Mining Taxes	0.7		
Income Taxes	2.7		
Miscellaneous Revenues . . .	7.9		
Total Recurrent Revenues . . .	51.7	Total Receipts	6.5
Current Expenditures . . .	50.6	Total Development Expenditure . .	10.1
Surplus on Current Account . . .	1.1	Overall Deficit	3.6

MONEY SUPPLY
(Le. million)

	1968	1969	1970	1971
Currency Outside Banks . . .	17.8	20.2	18.8	20.9
Demand Deposits	8.7	10.2	9.4	9.6
MONEY SUPPLY . . .	26.5	30.4	28.2	30.5

BALANCE OF PAYMENTS
(Le. million)

	1967	1968	1969	1970
Current Account:				
Visible Trade:				
Exports	49.0	77.2	87.6	84.3
Imports	−56.9	−66.5	−82.1	−85.9
Trade Balance . . .	− 7.9	10.7	5.5	− 1.6
Invisible Trade:				
Freight, Insurance and Travel .	− 1.2	− 0.7	− 2.6	− 1.6
Investment Income . .	− 8.2	− 8.1	− 6.2	− 6.6
Other Services . . .	− 4.6	− 6.5	− 8.6	− 9.5
Balance on Goods and Services .	−21.9	4.6	−11.9	−19.2
Transfer Payments . .	1.5	3.0	3.6	4.3
BALANCE ON CURRENT ACCOUNT	−20.4	− 1.6	− 8.3	−14.9
Capital Account:				
Private Capital . . .	8.9	7.2	13.6	14.4
Government Capital . .	6.4	5.5	1.9	1.9
BALANCE ON CAPITAL ACCOUNT	15.3	12.7	15.5	16.3
Overall Surplus or deficit . .	− 5.1	11.5	7.2	1.4
Monetary Institutions:				
Central:				
IMF Account . . .	3.8	− 0.3	− 1.3	− 6.2
Marketable Assets . .	− 0.3	− 8.3	12.6	0.6
Deposits	0.2	− 1.3	−19.2	4.2
Other (including WACB notes and coin) . .	—	—	—	—
Other Monetary Institutions:				
Marketable Assets . .	—	—	—	—
Deposits	− 0.7	− 1.6	− 1.3	− 0.5
TOTAL MONETARY INSTITUTIONS	3.0	−11.5	− 9.2	− 1.9
Net Unrecorded Items . . .	2.1	0.4	2.0	0.5

EXTERNAL TRADE
(Le. '000)

	1967	1968	1969	1970	1971
Imports . .	65,288	75,474	93,134	97,263	94,268
Exports* . .	45,492	79,720	87,754	85,540	83,384

* Including re-exports.

PRINCIPAL COMMODITIES

IMPORTS	1969	1970	1971
Food . . .	15,373	20,464	18,184
Beverages and Tobacco .	2,761	2,841	3,548
Crude Materials . .	1,188	1,107	986
Mineral Fuels . .	5,670	4,554	6,934
Oils and Fats . .	762	1,087	855
Chemicals . . .	5,645	6,161	6,780
Manufactures . .	27,449	25,981	24,029
Machinery . . .	22,202	24,970	22,751
Miscellaneous Goods .	10,977	8,781	8,713
Other Items . .	1,107	1,317	1,488
Re-exports . .			
TOTAL . . .	93,134	97,263	94,268

EXPORTS	1969	1970	1971
Kola Nuts . . .	170	120	197
Coffee . . .	3,018	4,215	3,457
Cocoa Beans . .	2,791	3,321	2,683
Ginger . . .	469	352	339
Palm Kernels . .	4,641	6,999	5,915
Iron Ore . . .	10,262	10,169	11,430
Bauxite . . .	1,391	1,130	2,516
Piassava . . .	354	462	532
Diamonds . . .	58,540	52,803	49,978
Other Items . .	3,872	4,903	5,021
	2,246	1,066	1,316
TOTAL (incl. re-exports) .	87,754	85,540	83,384

PRINCIPAL COUNTRIES

IMPORTS	1969	1970	1971
United Kingdom . .	28,869	28,717	27,170
Other Commonwealth Countries . .	7,378	11,119	12,601
Japan . . .	9,502	9,009	9,619
Netherlands . .	3,230	3,255	4,281
Federal Germany . .	4,494	6,780	5,742
U.S.A. . . .	7,760	8,421	6,710
France . . .	3,584	3,950	4,901
Italy . . .	2,014	1,497	1,427
Other Countries . .	26,303	24,515	21,816
TOTAL . . .	93,134	97,263	94,268

EXPORTS	1969	1970	1971
United Kingdom . .	62,340	54,570	51,529
Other Commonwealth Countries . .	346	191	
	7,078	8,301	641
Netherlands . .	3,618	2,802	7,754
Federal Germany . .	12,126	18,610	4,512
Other Countries . .			17,632
TOTAL (excl. re-exports)	85,508	84,474	82,068

Source: mainly *Standard Bank Review.*

TRANSPORT

Roads (1965): Motor cars 11,104; Lorries and Buses 5,800.

Shipping (1963): Vessels 1,972; Goods Handled 443,700 metric tons; Petroleum Handled 227,800 metric tons.

Civil Aviation (1964): Passenger-miles 17 million; Freight ton-miles 103,000.

EDUCATION

(1969–70)

	NUMBER OF ESTABLISHMENTS	NUMBER OF STUDENTS
Primary Schools	1,023	154,898
Secondary Schools . . .	81	29,058
Technical Colleges . . .	4	860
Teacher Training Colleges . .	9	879
Higher Education . . .	2	1,116

Source (unless otherwise stated): Government Information Services, Freetown.

THE CONSTITUTION

(April 1971)

Sierra Leone became an independent sovereign nation on April 27th, 1961, and a republic on April 19th, 1971; it is a member of the British Commonwealth.

The Constitution provides for an Executive President, elected for five years, with a maximum of two terms, and a Cabinet headed by a Prime Minister, who is also Vice-President. Not more than three Ministers may be appointed from outside the House of Representatives. The House of Representatives consists of a Speaker and Deputy Speaker, and a total of 85 elected members, and 12 Paramount Chiefs who do not stand for office under party auspices. Constitutional provisions are designed to safeguard certain fundamental democratic liberties, concerning the House of Representatives, elections, appointments, the Supreme Court, the office of Paramount Chief and the independence of the judiciary.

Under the 1961 Constitution a general election was required for approval of any fundamental constitutional change. However, since the new Constitution is basically the same as the republican constitution approved by the House of Representatives during Sir Albert Margai's term of office, the Government considered the March 1967 general election to have provided the necessary approval for the changeover to a republic which took place in April 1971. Certain clauses of the Margai Constitution which the present Government does not agree with and which could not be altered under the 1961 procedure for constitutional amendments are to be changed as the need arises.

THE GOVERNMENT

President: Dr. Siaka Probyn Stevens.

CABINET

(January 1973)

Vice-President, Prime Minister and Minister of the Interior: Sorie Ibrahim Koroma.

Minister of Finance: Christian Kamara-Taylor.

Minister of Agriculture and National Resources: A. G. Sembu Forna.

Minister of External Affairs: Solomon Pratt.

Attorney-General: L. A. M. Brewa.

Minister of Lands and Mines: S. B. Kawusu Konteh.

Minister of Trade and Industry: S. A. Fofana.

Minister of Works: D. F. Shears.

Minister of Information and Broadcasting: J. Barthes-Wilson (acting).

Minister of Development: Sahr Gandi-Capio.

Minister of Transport and Communications: Edward Kargbo.

Minister of Education: J. Barthes-Wilson.

Minister of Social Welfare: S. A. T. Koroma.

Minister of Housing and Country Planning: N. A. P. Buck.

Minister of Labour: F. B. Turay.

Minister of Health: J. C. O. Hadson-Taylor.

Resident Minister, Northern Province: Bangali Mansaray

Resident Minister, Southern Province: G. Gobio Lamin.

Resident Minister, Eastern Province: F. S. Anthony.

Minister of State: Paramount Chief Bai Koblo Pathbana II.

Minister of State: Paramount Chief A. J. Jaia Kai Kai.

DIPLOMATIC REPRESENTATION

HIGH COMMISSIONS AND EMBASSIES
ACCREDITED TO SIERRA LEONE

(In Freetown unless otherwise stated)

(HC) High Commission; (E) Embassy; (L) Legation.

Algeria: Conakry, Guinea (E).

Canada: Lagos, Nigeria (HC).

China, People's Republic: 29 Wilberforce Loop (E); *Ambassador:* Chao Cheng-Yi.

Egypt: 20 Pultney St. (E); *Chargé d'Affaires:* Salah El-Din Mourad.

France: 2 Pademba Rd. (E); *Ambassador:* Andre Mahoudeau-Campoyer.

The Gambia: 3 George St. (HC); *High Commissioner:* M. B. Wadda (acting).

German Federal Republic: 18 Siaka Stevens St. (E).

Ghana: 21 Charlotte St. (HC); *High Commissioner:* The Tolon Na.

Guinea: Liverpool St. (E); *Ambassador:* Alpha Camara.

Israel: Percival St. (E); *Ambassador:* Ben Yehuda.

Italy: The Maze, Congo Cross (E); *Chargé d'Affaires a.i.:* Dr. M. F. Catalano.

Ivory Coast: 1 Wesley St. (L); *Chancellor:* Tuan Yao Mathieu.

Lebanon: Leone House, Siaka Stevens St. (E); *Chargé d'Affaires:* Gilbert Ghazi.

Liberia: Brookfields Rd. (E); *Ambassador:* George T. Brewer.

Nigeria: Cathedral House (Third Floor), Gloucester St. (HC); *High Commissioner:* J. Tanko Yusuf.

Spain: Accra, Ghana (E).

U.S.S.R.: 13 Walpole St. (E); *Ambassador:* I. F. Filippov.

United Kingdom: Standard Bank Building, Wallace Johnson St. (HC); *High Commissioner:* I. B. Watt, c.m.g.

U.S.A.: Walpole St. (E); *Ambassador:* Clinton L. Olson.

Zambia: Abidjan, Ivory Coast (HC).

Sierra Leone also has diplomatic relations with Belgium, Bulgaria, Czechoslovakia, Dahomey, Ethiopia, Hungary, India, Republic of Korea, Democratic Republic of Korea, Lesotho, Madagascar, Netherlands, Niger, Pakistan, Philippines, Poland, Senegal, Sweden, Switzerland, Tanzania, Tunisia, Upper Volta and Yugoslavia.

HOUSE OF REPRESENTATIVES

Speaker: Sir Emile Fashole-Luke, K.B.E.

Elections, March 1967

Party	Seats
All-People's Congress	32
Sierra Leone People's Party . . .	32
Independents	2

The number of ordinary members in the House of Representatives is to be increased to 85 when the next general election is held in 1973.

POLITICAL PARTIES

All People's Congress (APC): won a small majority in the 1967 election, but prevented from taking power by the military coup; the United People's Party merged with this party in 1966; Leader SIAKA PROBYN STEVENS.

Sierra Leone People's Party (SLPP): Freetown; f. 1951; formed the government party (in alliance with United Progressive and People's National Parties) until 1967; Leader SALIA JUSU-SHERRIFF.

United Democratic Party: f. Sept. 1970; merged with four-month old National Democratic Party; leader Dr. JOHN KAREFA-SMART. (*Banned October* 1970).

DEFENCE

There is an army of 1,500 and a navy of 100. There is a para-military force of 300 and a civil police of 2,100.

Commander-in-Chief of the Armed Forces: President SIAKA STEVENS.

JUDICIAL SYSTEM

The Common Law of England and the doctrines of equity and Statutory Law which were applicable in 1880 are in force in Sierra Leone; and certain English Statutes after 1880 have from time to time been brought into force by Ordinance.

The Court of Appeal: Consists of a President, Justice of Appeal and the Judges of the superior courts of the Territories. Appeals lie to the Judicial Committee of the Privy Council.

President: C. O. COLE (acting).

Justices of Appeal: G. DOVE EDWIN, J. B. MARCUS-JONES, Dr. HENRY WIJAKONE TAMBIAH.

The Supreme Court has the same jurisdiction as the High Court of Justice in the United Kingdom, except in certain minor cases arising exclusively between natives, where native law or custom is decisive. It is the Court of Appeal for all subordinate courts and appeal against its own decisions may be made to the Sierra Leone Court of Appeal.

Magistrates' Courts have jurisdiction in civil cases:

(*a*) in the Freetown District "on any cause or matter which may lawfully be brought before them", and

(*b*) in the Provinces, in any matter (except libel or slander) between or involving non-natives or between a native and the holder of a trading licence (whether a native or not).

In criminal cases the jurisdiction of the Magistrates' Courts is limited to summary cases and to preliminary investigations to determine whether a person charged with an offence triable by the Supreme Court shall be committed for trial.

Native Courts have jurisdiction, according to native law and custom, in all matters between natives which are outside the jurisdiction of other courts (*see* above).

In some cases, e.g. in trading cases which involve more than £50 or in land disputes involving two or more Chiefdoms, or cases which are of particular importance, the District Commissioner has the right to inquire and to decide whether the case shall go before the Supreme Court.

Chief Justice: C. O. E. COLE, C.M.G.

Puisne Judges: R. B. MARKE, C.B.E., S. C. W. BETTS, C. A. HARDING, A. J. MASSALAY, P. R. DAVIES, S. J. FORSTER.

Attorney-General: L. A. M. BREWAH.

Master and Registrar, Supreme Court: O. M. GOLLEY (a.i.)

RELIGION

AFRICAN RELIGIONS

Beliefs, rites and practices are very diverse, varying from tribe to tribe and family to family.

ISLAM

Islam is widespread in parts of Sierra Leone.

CHRISTIANITY

ANGLICANS

Archbishop of the Province of West Africa and Bishop of Sierra Leone: Most Rev. M. N. C. O. SCOTT, C.B.E., D.D., DIP.TH., Bishopscourt, P.O.B. 128, Freetown. (For details of other sees in the Province of West Africa *see* under Nigeria, Religion.)

ROMAN CATHOLICS

Archbishop of Freetown and Bo: Most Rev. THOMAS JOSEPH BROSNAHAN, P.O.B. 98, Freetown.

Bishop of Makeni: Rt. Rev. Mgr. F. AUGUSTO AZZOLINI, P.O.B. 1, Makeni.

Bishop of Kenema: Rt. Rev. Mgr. JOSEPH GANDA, Bishop's House, Kenema.

THE PRESS

DAILIES

Daily Mail: 29–31 Rawdon St., P.O.B. 53, Freetown; f. 1931; Government-owned; Editor CLARENCE E. LABOR; circ. 15,000.

Nation: Town Hall Building, Lightfoot Boston St., Freetown; f. 1971, replacing *Unity Independent*, which was earlier closed by the Government; Government-owned; Editor SAM SHORT.

PERIODICALS

Advance: Endrina Sq., 72 Dambara Rd., Bo; f. 1948; twice weekly; Editor S. E. LABOR JONES.

African Crescent: P.O.B. 11, Bo; f. 1955; monthly; English; Editor M. A. BASHIR; circ. 600.

African Standard: 7 Trelawney St., Freetown; weekly.

African Vanguard: 5 Wellington St., Freetown; twice weekly; circ. 4,000.

Akera Ka Kathemne: Provincial Literature Bureau, P.O.B. 28, Bo; f. 1962; monthly; Themne; Editor Rev. R. A. JOHNSON.

Freeman: P.O.B. 250, Freetown; English language monthly; published by the Catholic Mission; Editor Fr. B. McMAHON.

Gospel Bells: 5 Frederick St., P.O.B. 868, Freetown; weekly; English; religious.

Konomanda: Koidu; f. 1969; All-People's Congress-sponsored news-sheet.

Kono Spark, The: The Spark Publications, Sina Town Rd., P.O.B. 81, Koidu Town; f. 1967; African Nationalist with strong Pan-African leanings; twice weekly, Mon. and Thurs.; Editor KAI ABDUL FORDAY; circ. 1,500.

Madora: Walpole St., Freetown; weekly; English.

People: 12 Free St., Freetown; supports Sierra Leone People's Party.

Renascent African: 30 Lumley St., Freetown; weekly.

Seme Loko: Provincial Literature Bureau, P.O.B. 28, Bo; f. 1938; monthly; Mende; Editor Rev. R. A. JOHNSON.

Shekpendeh: 31 Oxford St., Freetown; twice weekly; English; circ. 9,000.

Sierra Leone Observer: 3 Hospital Road, Bo; weekly; circ. 4,000.

Sierra Leone Outlook: P.O.B. 1169, Freetown; six a year; English; Editor Rev. S. A. WARRATIE.

Sierra Leone Trade Journal: Ministry of Information and Broadcasting, Water St., Freetown; f. 1961; quarterly; circ. 5,000.

Sunday Flash: 29–31 Rawdon St., Freetown; Government-owned; Editor Mrs. DAISY BONA.

West African Star: Freetown; f. 1962; religious and general; weekly; Ed. RIGSBY TOM DAVIES; circ. 3,000.

We Yone: Fort St., Freetown; twice weekly, in English; APC party newspaper; Editor ARIKA AWUTE-COKER.

NEWS AGENCY

FOREIGN BUREAU

Tass and Agence France—Presse are the only foreign bureaux in Freetown.

PUBLISHER

The Government Printer: Government Printing Dept., George St., Freetown.

RADIO AND TELEVISION

RADIO

Sierra Leone Broadcasting Service: New England, Freetown; f. 1934 and since 1958 has been operated by the Department of Broadcasting of the Sierra Leone Government. There are two short-wave transmitters and receiving stations in Freetown. Broadcasts are made in English and four Sierra Leonean languages, Mende, Limba, Temne and Krio. There is also a weekly broadcast in French. Dir. of Broadcasting JOSEPH W. O. FINLAY, Jr.

There are about 50,000 radio sets.

TELEVISION

Sierra Leone Broadcasting Service: The television service was established in 1963 and is now an integral part of the Broadcasting Service. Transmissions are limited to a radius of 15 miles around Freetown; 4 hours of programmes daily.

There are about 2,000 television sets.

FINANCE

BANKING

Bank of Sierra Leone: P.O.B. 30, Freetown; f. 1963; central bank; cap. Le.1.5m.; Governor S. L. BANGURA; Gen. Man. C. J. SMITH.

Barclays Bank of Sierra Leone Ltd.: Head Office: P.O.B. 969, Freetown; Chair. and Gen. Man. D. E. HUGHES; 10 brs., 2 agencies.

Intra Bank S.A.L.: Private Mail Bag, 28 Walpole St., Freetown; f. 1963; branches at Bo, Koidu, Kenema; Man. EDWARD G. ABBOUD.

National Development Bank Ltd.: Leone House, 21-23 Siaka Stevens St., P.M.B., Freetown; f. 1968; provides medium- and long-term finance and technical assistance to enterprises which are owned and managed predominantly by private interests and which appear on careful investigation to be economically viable and likely to make significant contributions to the economic development of Sierra Leone; major shareholders include the African Development Bank, Bank of Sierra Leone, other commercial banks, and insurance, trading and mining companies operating in Sierra Leone; auth. cap. Le. 1m., subordinated interest free loan of Le. 1m. from Government of Sierra Leone; Man. Dir. ABAYOMI TEJAN.

Standard Bank of Sierra Leone Ltd.: Oxford St., London; P.O.B. 69, Freetown; 11 other branches throughout the country; cap. 4m.

INSURANCE

The principal British companies are represented, and a Sierra Leonian company is being established by the Government.

TRADE AND INDUSTRY

CHAMBER OF COMMERCE

Chamber of Commerce of Sierra Leone: P.O.B. 502, Freetown; f. 1961; Pres. H. E. B. JOHN.

GOVERNMENT ORGANIZATIONS

Government Diamond Office: P.O.B. 421, Freetown; f. 1959; all diamonds are exported through this office; Chair. Executive Board G. L. V. WILLIAMS, C.B.E.

National Trading Co. Ltd.: has import monopoly for sugar, tinned milk, corned beef, sardines, baked beans, cooking oil, onions, tomato paste, tea and coffee; Man. Dir. J. C. D. SOLOMON.

Sierra Leone Investments Ltd.: A. Momodu Allie House, P.O.B. 263, Freetown; f. 1961 to stimulate economic activity.

Sierra Leone Produce Marketing Board: Queen Elizabeth II Quay, Freetown; f. 1949 to secure the most favourable arrangements for the marketing of Sierra Leone produce and to stimulate agricultural development; Chair. Paramount Chief KENEWA GAMANGA, M.B.E., J.P.; Man. Dir. DENIS NICHOLS.

Sierra Leone Rice Corpn.: Freetown; f. 1965 to assist farmers with rice cultivation; mills and markets locally grown rice; also imports to augment local product of rice; Sec. E. J. SILLAH.

EMPLOYERS' ASSOCIATIONS

Sierra Leone Employers' Federation: P.O.B. 562, Freetown; Chair. A. D. WURIE, C.B.E.; Exec. Officer A. E. BENJAMIN.

Association of Builders and Building Contractors: 18 mems.

Sierra Leone Chamber of Mines: P.O.B. 456, Freetown; comprises the four principal mining concerns.

TRADE UNIONS

Sierra Leone Labour Congress: 4 Pultney St., Freetown; f. 1966 by the merger of the Sierra Leone Federation of Labour and the Sierra Leone Council of Labour; approx. 18,000 mems. (20 per cent of all wage and salary earners) in 12 affiliated unions; Pres. G. A. CARAMBA-COKER; Vice-Pres. A. W. HASSAN; Sec.-Gen. E. T. KAMARA.

Principal affiliated unions:

Clerical, Mercantile and General Workers' Union: 19 Pultney St., Freetown; f. 1945; 3,600 mems.; Gen. Sec. M. S. LAHAI.

Railway Workers' Union: The Technical Institute, 11 Dan St., Freetown; f. 1919; 1,780 mems.; Gen. Sec. T. S. MAMMAH.

Sierra Leone Artisans' and Allied Workers' Union: 4 Pultney St., Freetown; f. 1946; 7,600 mems.; Gen. Sec. Aluseni B. CONTEH.

Sierra Leone Dockworkers' Union: 182 Fourah Bay Rd., Freetown; f. 1962; 2,650 mems.; Sec.-Gen. J. I. SANDI.

Sierra Leone Maritime and Waterfront Workers' Union 4 Pultney St., Freetown; f. 1946; 5,600 mems.

Sierra Leone Motor Drivers' Union: 17 Charlotte St., Freetown; f. 1960; 1,900 mems.

Sierra Leone Transport and General Workers' Union: 4 Pultney St., Freetown; f. 1946; 1,600 mems.; Gen. Sec. H. N. GEORGESTONE.

United Mineworkers' Union: 4 Pultney St., Freetown; f. 1944; 5,500 mems.; Gen. Sec. E. T. KAMARA.

Also affiliated to the Sierra Leone Labour Congress: General Union of Construction Workers, Sherbro Amalgamated Workers' Union, Sierra Leone Articled Seamen's Union, Sierra Leone Seamen's Union.

The following unions are not affiliated to the Sierra Leone Labour Congress: Sierra Leone Plantation Workers' Union, The Southern and Eastern Provincial General Workers' Union, Sierra Leone Teachers' Union (1,600 mems.).

CO-OPERATIVES AND MARKETING BOARDS

Very rapid progress has been made in the field of Co-operation. By the end of 1966 there were 797 primary societies with a total membership of 41,629. In addition, by mid-1966, there were 524 thrift and credit societies, grouped into ten Thrift and Credit Unions to facilitate undertaking large-scale operations.

The Registrar of Co-operative Societies, who is attached to the Ministry of Trade and Industry, is based in Freetown, with eight area offices spread through the provinces.

MAJOR INDUSTRIAL COMPANIES

Aureol Tobacco Co. Ltd.: P.O.B. 109, Wellington Industrial Estate, Freetown; f. 1959; cap. Le.1.5m.
Production of cigarettes.
Gen Man. R. G. I. LEONARD; 300 employees.

Bata Shoe Co. Sierra Leone Ltd.: P.O.B. 111, Wallace Johnson St., Freetown; footwear manufacturers and distributors.

J. T. Chanrai and Co. (S.L.) Ltd.: P.O.B. 57, 11 Rawdon St., Freetown; f. 1893; cap. £300,000.
Importation of motor spares, air-conditioners, refrigerators, building materials, textiles and provisions.
Dirs. P. P. MAGNANI and H. N. MANSUKHANI; 200 employees.

Compagnie Française de l'Afrique Occidentale: P.O.B. 70, Howe St., Freetown.

The Diamond Corporation (Sierra Leone) Ltd.: 25-27 Siaka Stevens St., Freetown; mining of diamonds.

National Diamond Mining Co. (Sierra Leone) Ltd.: P.O.B. 11, Spiritus House, Howe St., Freetown (head office); f. 1970; incorporates Sierra Leone Selection Trust Ltd., which was nationalized; cap. Le.10 million.
Diamond mining.
Chair. Dr. B. M. SANDY; Man. Dir. G. M. SMITH; 5,000 employees.

Plastic Manufacturing Sierra Leone Ltd.: P.O.B. 96, Wilkinson Rd., Freetown; footwear manufacturers.

Sierra Leone Brewery Ltd.: P.O.B. 721, Freetown; f. 1961; cap. Le.1 m.
Brewing and marketing of stout and lagers.
Gen. Mans. T. J. DAVIES and C. ALLPORT; 320 employees.

Sierra Leone Development Co.: DELCO House, Oxford St., Freetown; iron ore mining at Marampa.

Sierra Leone Diamonds Ltd.: 25 Pultney St., Freetown; mining of diamonds.

Sierra Leone Ore and Metal Co.: 1 Old Railway Line, Wilberforce, Freetown; mining of bauxite.

Sierra Leone Petroleum Refinery Co. Ltd.: Clinetown, Freetown; 50 per cent government owned; operates a refinery.

TRANSPORT

RAILWAY

Sierra Leone Government Railway: Clinetown; f. 1899; two sections of the railway have already been closed, and the Government intends to phase out the whole system; 292 km. of narrow gauge track remain in use; Gen. Man. A. E. GRIFFIN.

There are also 93 km. of track owned by the Sierra Leone Development Company, used for carrying iron ore from Marampa to Pepel.

ROADS

All Government and most other roads are motorable throughout the year although occasionally ferries may be closed for a few days by abnormal flooding. There are 1,985 miles of first-class roads maintained by the Public Works Dept., 2,175 miles of roads maintained by local authorities, and 180 miles owned and maintained by private companies. Construction of a new road between Bo and Kenema, 32 miles long, including a 700 ft. bridge, started in November 1970; and a new 200-mile road linking Liberia and Sierra Leone will be built with aid from the World Bank, the British Government, the Federal German Government and the UNDP.

Director of Road Transport: E. B. M. SAVAGE.

Sierra Leone Road Transport Corporation: Blackhall Rd., P.O.B. 1008, Freetown; f. 1965; operates transport services throughout the country. A road haulage service was inaugurated in 1971 which will eventually replace the railway network; by 1972 a fleet of 21 vehicles covered the whole country. Chair. Dr. N. A. COX-GEORGE.

INLAND WATERWAYS

Recognised launch routes, including the coastwise routes from Freetown northward to the Great and Little Scarcies rivers and southward to Bonthe, total almost 500 miles. Some of the upper reaches of the rivers are only navigable for three months of the year (January to March). Nevertheless a considerable volume of traffic uses the rivers.

SHIPPING

Sierra Leone Ports Authority: Freetown; operates the Port of Freetown, which has full facilities for ocean-going vessels; Gen. Man. Capt. A. R. MACAULAY.

Sierra Leone Shipping Agencies Ltd.: P.O.B. 74, Freetown; shipping, clearing and forwarding agency; agents for some 60 foreign shipping companies of which about 20 call regularly at Freetown; Gen. Man. J. E. HUGHES. Foreign shipping lines with offices in Freetown:

Chargeurs Line: rep. Transcap (Sierra Leone) Ltd., P.O.B. 704.

Delta Line: rep. Union Maritime et Commerciale (UMARCO), P.O.B. 417.

Deutsche Afrika Linien and Woermann Linie: rep. African and Overseas Agencies (S.L.) Ltd., P.O.B. 70.

Gold Star Line: rep. Union Maritime et Commerciale (UMARCO), P.O.B. 417.

Guinea Gulf Line Ltd.: rep. Staveley and Co. Ltd., P.O. Box 96.

Hanseatic Africa Line: rep. Transcap (Sierra Leone) Ltd., P.O.B. 704.

Hoegh Lines: rep. Scanship (Sierra Leone) Ltd., 1 College Rd., P.O.B. 130.

Jugolinija: rep. Scanship (Sierra Leone) Ltd., 1 College Rd. P.O.B. 130.

Kon. Nedlloyd N.V.: rep. Union Maritime et Commerciale (UMARCO), P.O.B. 417; Europe/West Africa service.

Lloyd Triestino S.p.A.: rep. Union Maritime et Commerciale (UMARCO), P.O.B. 417.

Royal Interocean Lines: rep. Union Maritime et Commerciale (UMARCO), P.O.B. 417.

Scandinavian West Africa Line: rep. Scanship (Sierra Leone) Ltd., 1 College Rd., P.O.B. 130.

United West Africa Service: rep. Scanship (Sierra Leone) Ltd., 1 College Rd., P.O.B. 130.

CIVIL AVIATION

Director of Civil Aviation: R. R. WRIGHT, A.R.AE.S.

Sierra Leone Airways: Leone House, Siaka Stevens St., Freetown (Head Office); Freetown International Airport, Lungi; operates daily services from Hastings Aerodrome, Freetown, to principal points in the country, by four-engined Heron aircraft (H.S. 114); handles all types of aircraft at international airport; operates once weekly V.C. 10 flights to London and Robertsfield, and twice weekly BAC 1-11 service Freetown/Robertsfield/Accra/Lagos; all operated by British Caledonian; Chair. T. C. LUKE; Gen. Man. Capt. E. H. CHAMBERS.

FOREIGN AIRLINES

The following foreign airlines provide services to Freetown: Air Afrique, Air Guinée, Air Mali, British Caledonian, C.S.A., EgyptAir, Ghana Airways, Interflug, K.L.M., M.E.A., Nigeria Airways and U.T.A.

TOURISM

Tourist and Hotels Board: 28 Siaka Stevens St., Freetown.

POWER

Guma Valley Water Co.: f. 1961; responsible for all existing water supplies in Freetown and surrounding villages, including the Guma Dam and associated works. Second phase to double the capacity of the Treatment Works and Trunk Main now nearing completion.

Sierra Leone Electricity Corpn.: Freetown; supplies all electricity in Sierra Leone.

EDUCATION

LEARNED SOCIETIES AND RESEARCH INSTITUTES

British Council, The: Tower Hill, P.O.B. 124, Freetown.

Geological Survey Division: Ministry of Mines, Lands and Labour, New England, Freetown; f. 1918; to locate mineral deposits and to advise on all matters relating to the earth; library of 16,000 vols. including periodicals; Dir. A. H. GABIRI; publs. *Annual Report, Bulletin, Short Papers* (all annually).

Institute of Marine Biology and Oceanography: Fourah Bay College, University of Sierra Leone, Freetown; f. 1966: undertakes research in oceanography, marine algae and plankton, fishery biology; Dir. Dr. IVAN W. O. FINDLAY (acting).

Sierra Leone Society: c/o Department of Modern History, University of Sierra Leone, Freetown; f. 1918; literature, arts, music; publ. *Sierra Leone Studies* (twice yearly).

Sierra Leone Science Association: c/o Institute of Marine Biology and Oceanography, Fourah Bay College, University of Sierra Leone, Freetown; Pres. E. T. COLE; Hon. Sec. Dr. I. W. O. FINDLAY.

U.S. Information Center: Walpole St., Freetown.

LIBRARIES AND MUSEUM

Fourah Bay College Library: University of Sierra Leone, Freetown; 80,000 vols., 973 current periodicals; Librarian Mrs. G. M. SHERIFF, B.A., M.S., F.L.A. (acting).

J. J. Thomas Library: Water St., Freetown; 19,000 vols.

Public Archives of Sierra Leone: c/o Fourah Bay College Library, P.O.B. 87, Freetown; Hon. Archivist Mrs. G. M. SHERIFF.

Sierra Leone Library Board: P.O.B. 326, Freetown; f. 1961; aims to provide a national library service; 380,000 vols.; libraries at Freetown, Bo, Magburaka, Makeni, Port Loko, Kambia, Pujehun, Kailahun, Kenema, Kono, Bonthe, Mattru; Chief Librarian M. B. JONES.

Sierra Leone National Museum: Cotton Tree Building, P.O.B. 908, Freetown; historical, ethnographical and archaeological collection; Curator DOROTHY A. VAN AMSTERDAM-CUMMINGS.

UNIVERSITY AND COLLEGES
UNIVERSITY OF SIERRA LEONE
FREETOWN

Established 1967 and incorporating Fourah Bay College and Njala University College; Inaugurated February 1969.

Chancellor: Sir SAMUEL BANKOLE JONES, Kt., M.A., D.C.L.

Vice-Chancellor: Dr. S. T. MATTURI.

FOURAH BAY COLLEGE

P.O.B. 87, FREETOWN

Telephone: Freetown 7631.

Language of Instruction: English; Academic year: October to June (three terms).

Founded by the Church Missionary Society in 1827, it was affiliated to the University of Durham in 1876 and became a constituent college of the University of Sierra Leone in 1966.

Visitor: H.E. Dr. SIAKA STEVENS.
President: Most Rev. and Rt. Hon. Dr. A. M. RAMSEY, P.C.
Principal: Prof. Rev. Canon H. A. E. SAWYERR, C.B.E.
Vice-Principal: Prof. M. E. K. THOMAS.
Registrar: I. S. A. COLE, M.A. (acting).
Bursar: M. A. SERAY-WURIE, A.A.C.C.A.
Librarian: GLADYS M. D. SHERIFF, B.A., M.S. (acting).

The library contains 80,000 vols.
Number of teachers: 115.
Number of students: 889.

NJALA UNIVERSITY COLLEGE

PRIVATE MAIL BAG, FREETOWN

Founded 1963.

Language of Instruction: English; Private control; Academic year: October to June (three terms).

Council Chairman: Paramount Chief M. K. JIGBA II.
Principal: S. T. MATTURI, C.M.G., B.SC., PH.D.
Registrar: P. M. DIMOH, B.A.
Deputy Librarian: O. O. OGUNDIPEH, M.A., F.L.A.

Number of teachers: 114.
Number of students: 321.

ATTACHED INSTITUTES:

Rice Research Station, Njala University College: Rokupr; Research programme includes breeding, screening introduced varieties, agronomic practices, mechanization of rice farming, economic and social analysis of rice production problems; Basic studies concerned with soils, physiology, disease and pest control; Training Dir. H. WILL, PH.D.

Milton Margai Training College: Goderich, nr. Freetown; f. 1960; trains secondary teachers.

Number of teachers: 40, including Unesco staff.
Number of students: 390.

Library of 10,000 vols.
Principal: S. A. SOLADE ADAMS, M.A., DIP.ED.

S. B. Thomas Agricultural College: Mabang; first agricultural college in West Africa.

National College of Music: Freetown.

Technical Institute: Congo Cross, Freetown; City and Guilds Craft and Technician Courses and Commercial Education; Acting Principal A. S. K. HARDING.

Technical Institute: Kenema; vocational courses.

SELECT BIBLIOGRAPHY

BANK OF SIERRA LEONE. *Economic Review* (quarterly). Freetown.

BANTON, MICHAEL. *West African City*. London, 1957.

BHATIA, RATTAN J., SZAPARY, GYORGY, and QUINN, BRIAN. "Stabilization Program in Sierra Leone", *IMF Staff Papers*, 16/3, pp. 504–28, November 1969.

CENTRAL STATISTICS OFFICE. *National Accounts of Sierra Leone 1963–64 to 1966–67*. Freetown, 1969.

CLARKE, J. I. *Sierra Leone in Maps*. London, 1966.

FYFE, CHRISTOPHER. *A History of Sierra Leone*. London, 1962.
Sierra Leone Inheritance. London, 1964.

FYFE, CHRISTOPHER, and JONES, ELDRED. *Freetown—A Symposium*. Freetown, 1968.

KILSON, MARTIN. *Political Change in a West African State— A Study of the Modernization Process in Sierra Leone*. Cambridge, Mass., 1966.

PORTER, ARTHUR. *Creoledom*. London, 1963.

REES, HOWARD. "The Economic Development of Sierra Leone", in BIRMINGHAM, W. B., and FORD, A. G. (Eds.), *Planning and Growth in Rich and Poor Countries*, pp. 195–227. London, Allen and Unwin, 1966.

SAYLOR, RALPH GERALD. *The Economic System of Sierra Leone*. Durham, N.C., Duke University Press, 1967.

Sierra Leone Studies. Freetown, 1919–38 and 53-.

VAN DER LAAN, H. L. *The Sierra Leone Diamonds*. London, Oxford University Press, 1965.

WELLESLEY-COLE, A. *Kossoh Town Boy*. London, 1960.

Somalia

I. M. Lewis

PHYSICAL AND SOCIAL GEOGRAPHY*

The Somali Democratic Republic lies in the extreme north-eastern corner or "Horn" of Africa, jutting out into the Indian Ocean and facing Arabia, with which it has had centuries of contact through trade and Arab settlement. To the north-west it is bounded by the tiny French enclave round Jibuti (Djibouti), now known as the French Territory of the Afar and Issa; and its western and southern neighbours are Ethiopia and Kenya. The country takes its name from its population, the Somali, a Muslim Cushitic-speaking people who stretch far beyond its present frontiers into these neighbouring states. Out of the total of some four million, an estimated 2,864,000 Somalis live sparsely distributed and mainly as pastoral nomads in the 246,201 sq. miles (637,657 sq. km.) of the republic itself.

Most of their terrain consists of dry savannah plains, with a high mountain escarpment in the north, facing the coast. The climate is hot, though pleasant on high ground and along the coast during June–September, with a poor rainfall which rarely exceeds 20 in. in the most favourable regions. Only two permanent rivers—the Juba and Shebelle—water this dry land. Both rise in the Ethiopian highlands, but only the Juba regularly flows into the sea. The very large expanse of territory between these two rivers is the richest agriculturally and constitutes a zone of mixed cultivation and pastoralism. Here sorghum millet and maize are grown, and along the rivers, on irrigated plantations, the banana export crop and citrus fruits.

This potentially rich zone contains remnants of Bantu groups—partly of ex-slave origin—and is also the home of the Digil and Rahanwin, who speak a distinctive dialect and are the least nomadic element in the population. Of the other Somali clans—the Dir, Isaq, Hawiye and Darod, primarily pastoral nomads who occupy the rest of the country—the Hawiye along the Shebelle valley are the most extensively engaged in cultivation, although a small subsidiary pocket of cultivation (involving Dir and Isaq) also occurs in the north-west highlands.

In this overwhelmingly pastoral country permanent settlements are small and widely scattered, except in the agricultural regions, and for the most part are tiny trading centres built round wells. There are few large towns. Mogadishu, the capital, which dates from at least the tenth century as an Islamic trading post, has a population of 179,000; and the other main centres are: Hargeisa (population 60,000), capital of the northern regions, and Berbera (population 50,000) and Kismayu, the principal northern and southern ports respectively.

See map on p. 304.

RECENT HISTORY

(Revised for this edition by Virginia Luling)

The Somalis have a long history, beginning with their role as suppliers of myrrh and frankincense in antiquity. They played a significant part as bellicose warriors in the religious wars between Muslim and Christian in the sixteenth century—when Ethiopia was almost won for Islam. This tradition of religious conflict is still a significant factor today. The proud sense of independence, which the most forceful of Somali religious leaders have always championed, found its most dramatic recent expression in the twenty-years war waged by the so-called "Mad Mullah" (Sayyid Muhammad Abdille Hasan) between 1900 and 1920 against the British, Ethiopian and Italian colonizers of Somali territory. Inspired by this tradition of independence, though in an entirely peaceful manner, the present republic was formed on July 1st, 1960, by the merger of the former British Somaliland Protectorate (the "northern regions") with the UN Trust territory and ex-Italian colony of Somalia (the "southern regions").

BRITISH AND ITALIAN RULE

Having drawn up with the clans of the area a series of bilateral treaties (which she was later to interpret in a singularly unilateral fashion), Britain assumed control of the northern regions in 1886. The British objective was principally to safeguard the trade links with her colony in Aden, particularly to ensure its supply of Somali mutton, and to keep other interested powers out (especially France). With the latter object in mind Italy was encouraged to establish a colony in the southern regions in the same period. Later, having failed to supply the desired answer to the metropolitan population problem, Italian Somalia became, with Eritrea, a strategic base for the eventual Italian conquest of Ethiopia in 1936. Following the defeat of the Italians in east Africa in the Second World War, however, both territories were placed under British military administration and, for the first time in the south, educational and other progressive policies were pursued which encouraged the development of modern

Somali nationalism. The Somali Youth League, which was to become the most influential and long-lived nationalist party, was founded as a youth club in 1943. In the Four-Power and later UN debates concerning the disposal of Italy's former colonies the British foreign secretary, Ernest Bevin, suggested that the two Somali territories, as well as the Somali area of Ethiopia also under British administration at this time, should be joined together in a single Somali state. In the event, partly as a result of Russian opposition, this proposal had to be abandoned, and in 1950 Italy returned to Somalia as trusteeship authority for the United Nations with the task of preparing Somalia for self-rule by 1960. The British Protectorate had meanwhile reverted to civilian rule, while most of the Somali areas in Ethiopia had been returned to Ethiopian control.

INDEPENDENCE

In the decade ending in 1960 the Italians did much to prepare their former colony for independence, greatly expanding education and other social services, and progressively devolving political and administrative authority. In short, almost everything was achieved except the most difficult task of making Somalia viable economically. Spurred on by these events and with less and less reason for staying on in the north, Britain similarly prepared its "cinderella of empire", as it has been well-named, for the same destiny. British rule was relinquished in the north four days before Somalia was due to attain self-government. Thus on July 1st, 1960, following previous negotiations between the politicians of the two regions, the two ex-colonies joined together as the Somali Republic. The President of the southern legislative assembly was proclaimed provisional head of state, a position largely inspired by the Italian model, and the two legislatures joined together at Mogadishu (now the national capital) to form a single national assembly with 123 seats (33 for the north, and 90 for the more populous south). The two dominant political parties in the north merged with the S.Y.L., the ruling party in the south, to form a tripartite coalition government; and Dr. Abdirashid Ali Shirmarke, a leading S.Y.L. politician who had recently returned from studying political science in Italy, was chosen as the first prime minister. He belonged to the Darod clan, while the provisional President—confirmed in office a year later—was Hawiye. As the executive leader the new premier soon formed a government, which was to set the pattern for all others since, consisting of a judicious balance of northern and southern members representative of all the main Somali clans.

PROBLEMS OF UNIFICATION

This smooth political transition left many problems unsolved. The northern British and southern Italian administrative, legal, and fiscal systems differed materially, and the separate colonial legacies—symbolized in their subjects' attachment to the two foreign languages—at first exerted a powerful divisive effect. Such discord was offset, at least to some extent, by the traditional Somali culture which both regions shared, and by the presence of clans straddling the old colonial boundaries. The short decade of British rule in the south, before the return of the Italians, also facilitated integration and paved the way for the gradual eclipse of Italian by English as the main foreign language (triumphing even over Arabic). Internal harmony was further encouraged, at the price of external conflict, by the strong commitment of all political leaders to the nationalist struggle which aimed at extending the boundaries of the new state to include the missing Somali communities in Ethiopia, French Somaliland, and northern Kenya. While most of the new African states lacked any viable cultural homogeneity which could serve as a basis for strong national sentiments, the republic possessed this in abundance. Its problem, almost unique in relation to its neighbours, was to complete the process not of nation-building but of state-formation which rested on the principle of self-determination for Somalis. Since this involved the surrender of territory to Somalia, the republic's powerful neighbours were as reluctant to concede Somali demands as the Somalis were anxious to press them.

This conflict over the right to separate self-determination for the Somali communities outside the republic cast a long shadow over politics within the state. The republic's first government, formed in 1960, had thus to pursue this issue externally as forcefully as it dared, while also attending to all its manifold internal problems. In these circumstances the internal political divisions were reduced to a viable accommodation during the first three years of independence. By 1963 the north—which had lost most, because of its small size and because the capital was in the south—had come to accept the republic as an inescapable, if sometimes regrettable, fact of life. The two northern political parties, based on rival northern clans, had fallen apart with the creation of a new national opposition party, leaving the S.Y.L. still in power and with a new access of support. In the 1964 elections, while the S.Y.L.—now with strong northern as well as southern support—comfortably secured the majority of seats in the assembly, the new opposition party won most of the remainder.

CONFLICT WITH ETHIOPIA AND KENYA

These party political developments took place at a time of strong national feeling. Having failed to induce Britain to grant separate independence to the Somalis of northern Kenya, and having consequently broken off diplomatic relations with London, the republic had switched the immediate focus of its campaign to the Somali regions of Ethiopia. The severely strained relations between the two neighbouring states had now degenerated into outright military conflict. The formation of a new government after the elections provided the occasion for a return to the uneasy truce, but the tide of Somali nationalist fervour was still running high.

The 1964 government confirmed the tacit principle that the president and premier should belong to different clans. A fierce struggle within the Darod leadership of the S.Y.L. led to the appointment of a new Darod prime minister, Abdirazaq Haji Husseyn, whose selection by the Hawiye president left the party seriously split between those who supported the new premier and those who sided with his predecessor. The new government continued most of the policies of the previous regime. The republic continued to receive aid from both the western and eastern blocs, its increasing reliance on Russian equipment for the army (and American aid for the police) becoming more significant as the main emphasis in the Somali unification campaign swung back to northern Kenya. Here, shortly after that state's independence, Somali nationalists began their struggle which developed into the bitter *shifta* war.

POLITICAL FRAGMENTATION

Within the republic itself the emphasis was still on economic and social development. However, the full impact of the considerable volume of foreign aid received was steadily diminished by spreading nepotism and corruption and by the unstable situation produced by division within the Darod ranks of the S.Y.L. which came to a head with the election of a new president in 1967. The national assembly (which elects the president) chose the defeated premier, Dr. Abdirashid Ali Shirmarke, who, having thus satisfactorily turned the tables on his successor, formed a new government with Muhammad Haji Ibrahim Egal (a northerner of the Isaq clan) as prime minister.

It was now evident that the campaign for Somali unification pursued by previous governments had proved a dismal failure. In the March 1967 referendum in French Somaliland, expertly manoeuvred by the French authorities, a majority of voters had rejected independence which the Somali section of the electorate had sought as a step towards union with the republic. The Somalis in Ethiopia were as firmly held in check as before, and in northern Kenya the nationalist cause had degenerated into a savage guerrilla war which had brought only suffering and repression to the civilian Somali population. The new premier accordingly reversed previous policy and, with the mediation of President Kaunda, succeeded in achieving a détente with Kenya and Ethiopia. The *shifta* war gradually ceased, and the three countries undertook to engage in serious negotiations towards a lasting settlement. Now that the external pressure on the republic had diminished, the smaller constituent units of the traditional political structure came to the fore again with an upsurge of divisive tribalism which found no effective outlet in the existing national political parties.

In conformity with these trends, despite new regulations inhibiting the formation of one-man tribal parties, over a thousand candidates contested the 123 seats available in the elections of March 1969. With the resources of the state at its disposal, and with considerable gerrymandering the S.Y.L. again secured victory, and Muhammad Haji Ibrahim Egal was re-appointed as premier. The usual clan coalition government was formed; and at the first meeting of the new assembly, with a single exception, all the other members of the house crossed the floor to join the govern-

ment, hoping thus to participate in the spoils of office. The republic had now become a one-party state in fact, if not in name, and the government's position seemed impregnable. Because of the prevailing political atomization, however, the government and the assembly were in reality no longer effectively representative of the public at large. Public discontent was aggravated by the complaints, often fully justified, of the hundreds of disappointed candidates, and by the increasingly autocratic style of rule assumed by both the president and premier.

THE 1969 COUP

The inevitable climax occurred strangely fortuitously. In pursuance of a factional quarrel the president was assassinated on October 15th while the premier was out of the country. At this news, Muhammad Haji Ibrahim Egal hurried back to Mogadishu to secure the election of a new president favourable to his interests. When it became obvious that the assembly would elect his candidate, on the eve of the election on October 21st the army, with the compliance of the police, stepped in and seized control in a bloodless coup. Members of the government and other leading politicians were placed in detention, parliament was closed, and a Supreme Revolutionary Council constituted from army and police officers. The Council announced that it had acted to preserve democracy and justice, and to eliminate corruption and tribalism. To symbolize these aims the country was renamed the Somali Democratic Republic. The President of the S.R.C., Major-General Muhammad Siad Barre has become titular Head of State. Under his leadership, and aided by a civilian council of secretaries with quasi-ministerial functions, the S.R.C. has since replaced all civilian provincial and district administrators by army officers. Army officers have also been placed in all the ministries to oversee routine work and to check the misappropriation of funds. Some officials have been brought to trial on charges of corruption, but the political leaders, who have not been formally charged, and a former commander of the police displaced from office by the previous civilian government precisely because of his integrity remain in detention. President Barre has stated that his aim is eventually to convene a National Congress to decide on the political institutions of the future; in the meanwhile he remains to a large extent in personal control. A three-man advisory board has been set up to assist him in his functions. Under his guidance Somalia is to develop along broadly socialist lines. Local banks have been nationalized. Ordinances have been passed controlling prices, limiting salaries, and forbidding any government employee from owning more than one house. Censorship boards have been set up to cover the news and entertainment media. In 1971 a campaign against "tribalism" was launched by radio and press, and the public urged to fight against it. In spite of this, the S.R.C. has not escaped the political necessity of balancing its own composition on clan lines.

In May 1971, the then vice-president of the S.R.C., Mohamed Ainanshe Guleid, was arrested with several associates on charges of conspiring against the state and plotting to reinstate capitalism. In May of the next year he and two others were sentenced to death, and executed by firing squad in July. Others accused received prison sentences varying between life and one year.

In external relations, although there has been a move towards alliances with the eastern block, ties with Italy have been maintained as well as with the Arab countries. The détente with Kenya and Ethiopia continues, and President Barre has repeatedly said that Somalia is determined to settle her disputes with her neighbours in a spirit of "African brotherhood". Under his leadership, Somalia has taken an increasingly active part in international African politics.

ECONOMY
(Revised for this edition by Virginia Luling)

AGRICULTURE

The economy is based principally on the herding of camels, cattle, sheep and goats which both provide for the subsistence needs of most of the population and furnish a substantial export trade in livestock on the hoof, skins, and clarified butter. Exports of these have risen dramatically since independence, reaching a peak in 1964 when they were valued at almost £13 million, and outstripped the other main export product, bananas. These are grown on plantations, originally pioneered by Italian settlers, along the Juba and Shebelle rivers. In the first five years of independence banana production increased by over 70 per cent, 184,000 metric tons being produced in 1967, although only half that crop was then exported owing to the closure of the Suez canal. The recent introduction of newer, faster and better-equipped ships has enabled the trade to recover from the effects of the Suez closure. The main market is Italy where Somali bananas have long enjoyed preferential treatment; the EEC, of which the republic is an associate member, also applies a 20 per cent common external tariff. Other fruits, as yet chiefly for local consumption, are grown on plantations in the same area, and the production of cane sugar, grown and processed by a company in which the government holds half shares, has now expanded to about 50,000 metric tons, which roughly corresponds to domestic requirements.

The area between the rivers, of which at present only some 37,000 acres (15,000 hectares) out of an estimated potential of 18.5 million acres (7.5 million hectares) are under cultivation, also provides the subsistence maize and sorghum crops of the southern Somali. The full utilization of this fertile belt, envisaged in development plans, should meet the grain needs of the domestic market and provide a subsidiary export crop. Chinese-aided experiments in rice-growing may eventually enable the republic to dispense with its costly imports of this food. Work on a large Russian-aided state farm along the Juba, interrupted through lack of local Somali funds after the ground was cleared, is now to be resumed on a more modest scale. Work on a similarly precipitate, though initially promising wheat-growing project in the north-west, abandoned after poor rains some years ago, is again being resumed gradually.

MINERALS AND INDUSTRIAL PROJECTS

Oil exploration has so far proved disappointing, although there are geological indications that deposits should be found. However, a promising new resource is offered in the recent discovery of large uranium ore deposits to the west of Mogadishu: exclusive prospecting rights have been granted to a subsidiary of the Italian company, E.N.I. There are as yet no other major industries, although a Soviet-aided meat processing plant, which is expected to produce 20 million tins of meat annually, was opened at Kismayu in 1969. A similarly Soviet-aided fish factory at Las Koreh in the north will process 5,000 tons of tuna fish annually. It will be some time before any of these and other new industries make any appreciable change in the republic's economic position, which remains heavily indebted to foreign countries.

PUBLIC FINANCE

Despite the rise in exports (mainly to Italy and Aden) since independence, imports (mainly from Italy and Aden) have also increased. In 1967 when a decrease in the reserve position of the Somali National Bank followed the closure of the Suez Canal, imports cost over £15 million and receipts from exports yielded little over £10 million. Service payments to foreign countries amounted to £6.3 million and receipts to only £3.4 million. By June 1968 the nation's external debt had risen to £18.5 million and the Somali National Bank also owed £2 million to the IMF.

Budgetary expenditure has risen sharply since independence, and receipts which derive principally from indirect taxation (especially customs and excise dues) have failed to take up the slack. Since 1969, the revolutionary government has made vigorous attempts at increasing the country's self-sufficiency. The 26 million Somali shillings allocated to the development budget for 1973 were stated to have been raised without foreign contributions. However, the ordinary budget for the same year relies heavily on foreign aid and loans, and there does not seem to be any immediate prospect for Somalia of dispensing with them.

FOREIGN AID AND DEVELOPMENT PROJECTS

If the republic has had to rely extensively on foreign sources simply to meet recurrent expenditure, its dependence on external finance for development is almost complete. A substantial amount of aid, much of it in long-term low-interest loans, has in fact been received but has yet to produce any proportionate return. By 1966 Italy had contributed some £30 million (inclusive of budget aid), the U.S.S.R. about £20 million, and the U.S.A. only slightly less: the total received in grants and loans amounted at this time to over £73 million. Between 1963 and 1970 a series of plans were launched by the Government for improving the resources of the country. Though these overall schemes proved too ambitious, a good deal was accomplished during those years.

In addition to the projects mentioned earlier, the U.S.S.R. provided a new port at Berbera, which, by enabling larger modern vessels to berth at the port, has greatly stimulated the livestock export trade, and which should also make possible the exploitation of the abundant gypsum deposits near the port. The republic's main port at Kismayu, built with American aid, is now also in operation, and a new port for Mogadishu is also planned. Communications linking Kismayu to the banana growing areas of the Juba, and eventually to those of the Shebelle also, have greatly benefited from the construction of new tarmac roads along the coast and to the grain-growing area of Baidoa in the southern hinterland. New airports are now in use at both Hargeisa and Mogadishu, and Somali Airlines operate regular internal services, with connexions to Nairobi and Aden, using Viscounts. Alitalia fly the only direct jet service from Europe. China which has provided the new national theatre has now also contributed an interest-free loan of eight million Swiss francs. Federal Germany, as well as contributing to road construction, and other projects, has opened a textile factory to process local cotton.

In social services there have been similar improvements with a great expansion of education, a number of new secondary schools having been opened, and continued prospective developments at the republic's University College, which is linked to Italy. Health services also expanded with the creation of a large EEC-financed general hospital at Mogadishu, which, however, although well-equipped, has experienced serious difficulties in doctor and nurse staffing. Radio services have similarly been extended and improved. Both agricultural and livestock development agencies are engaged in increasing levels of production in these two sectors of the economy; and water supplies, both in the interior and in the main towns, are still being extended.

The revolutionary régime has been particularly concerned to encourage the sort of self-help rural development projects in school building or sell digging, for instance, which had already before 1969 produced good results. Their policy is to develop the Somali economy along basically socialist lines, though private enterprise on a small scale is encouraged as having its part to play, and to aim for self sufficiency particularly in food-production. In 1971 a 3-year Development Programme was published; this envisaged government expenditure of nearly 1,000 million Somali shillings, mainly on communications, water resources, agriculture, industry, health and livestock. Almost 80 per cent of the funds were to be found from foreign sources. Projects under way include more road-building in the north of the country, a new airport at Kismayu, and a new 300-bed hospital in Mogadishu. It remains true, however, that the standard of living of the greater part of the Somali population is low and precarious.

STATISTICAL SURVEY

Area: 246,201 square miles (637,657 square kilometres).

Population: Total (1971 est.): 2,864,000; Mogadishu (1966) 172,000; Hargeisa (1966) 60,000; Kismayu (1966) 60,000; Merca (1965) 56,000; Berbera (1966) 50,000; Giamama (1964) 22,000.

Births and Deaths: Average annual birth rate 45.9 per 1,000; death rate 24.0 per 1,000 (UN estimates for 1965–70).

Employment (1970): Total economically active population 1,085,000, including 893,000 in agriculture (ILO and FAO estimates).

AGRICULTURE

PRINCIPAL CROPS
(FAO estimates, metric tons)

	1968	1969	1970	1971
Maize	42,000	40,000	35,000	35,000
Millet and Sorghum . .	67,000	63,000	50,000	50,000
Sugar Cane*	277,000†	393,000†	450,000	450,000
Sweet Potatoes and Yams . .	2,000	3,000	3,000	n.a.
Cassava (Manioc) . . .	23,000	23,000	25,000	n.a.
Dry Beans . . .	2,000	2,000	2,000	2,000
Citrus Fruit . . .	4,000	4,000	4,000	4,000
Bananas	140,000†	150,000	150,000	n.a.
Groundnuts (in shell) . .	2,000	2,000	2,000	2,000
Cottonseed . . .	2,000	2,000	2,000	2,000
Cotton (Lint)	1,000	1,000	1,000	1,000
Sesame Seed . . .	6,000	6,000	6,000	6,000
Tobacco	100	100	100	100

* Crop year ending in year stated. † Official estimate.

Source: FAO, *Production Yearbook 1971.*

LIVESTOCK
('ooo—FAO estimates)

	1968–69	1969–70	1970–71
Cattle . .	2,800*	2,800*	2,850
Sheep . .	3,900	3,900	3,950
Goats . .	4,800	4,900	5,000
Pigs† . .	6	7	7
Asses . .	24	23	22
Mules . .	20	20	21
Camels . .	3,000	3,000	3,000*
Chickens . .	1,900	2,000	2,100

* Official estimate.
† In former Italian Somaliland only.

Source: FAO, *Production Yearbook 1971.*

LIVESTOCK PRODUCTS
(FAO estimates, metric tons)

	1968	1969	1970
Cows' Milk . .	88,000	89,000	91,000
Goats' Milk . .	65,000	64,000	63,000
Beef and Veal . .	15,000	15,000	15,000
Mutton and Lamb .	15,000	15,000	15,000
Edible Offal . .	11,000	11,000	11,000
Other Meat . .	25,000	25,000	25,000
Hen Eggs . .	1,400	1,500	1,600
Cattle Hides . .	2,420	2,420	2,500
Sheep Skins . .	1,980	1,875	2,175
Goat Skins . .	4,450	4,538	4,625

1971: Cows' milk 92,000; goats' milk 63,000; hen eggs 1,700.

Dairy Produce (official estimates, 1970): Butter 45 metric tons; Cheese 2 metric tons.

Sources: FAO, *Production Yearbook 1971*; United Nations, *The Growth of World Industry.*

Forestry (1967–69): 560,000 cubic metres of roundwood removed each year.

Sea Fishing (1968–70): Total catch 5,000 metric tons each year (FAO estimate).

INDUSTRY

RAW SUGAR
(metric tons)

1967	.	.	32,000
1968	.	.	36,000
1969	.	.	51,000
1970	.	.	50,000

ELECTRIC ENERGY
(million kWh.)

1967	.	.	19.0
1968	.	.	22.0
1969	.	.	26.0
1970	.	.	20.2

Note: Figures refer to production for public use in Mogadishu, Merca, Giohar and Hargeisa.

OTHER PRODUCTS, 1970

Tinned Meat	.	metric tons	1,973
Condensed Milk and Cream	.	metric tons	227
Ethyl Alcohol	.	hectolitres	41,000
Soft Drinks	.	hectolitres	3,000
Leather Footwear	.	pairs	27,000
Soap	.	metric tons	197
Concrete Products	.	cubic metres	14,000

Source: United Nations, *The Growth of World Industry.*

In 1969 there were 127 manufacturing establishments with five or more persons engaged. Their combined staff was 4,300 and the gross output for the year was 108,800,000 Somali shillings.

FINANCE

100 centesimi = 1 Somali shilling.
Coins: 1, 5, 10 and 50 centesimi; 1 shilling.
Notes: 5, 10, 20 and 100 shillings.
Exchange rates (December 1972): £1 sterling = 16.268 Somali shillings; U.S. $1 = 6.925 Somali shillings.
100 Somali shillings = £6.151 = $14.44.

BUDGET
('000 Somali Shillings)

EXPENDITURE					1970	1971	1972
Defence	.	.	.	.	80,153	81,253	92,000
Interior	.	.	.	.	54,435	6,869*	7,268*
Finance	.	.	.	.	18,450	19,409	17,181
Public Works	.	.	.	.	94,499	18,114	17,186
Health and Labour	.	.	.	27,939	23,551	21,694
Education	.	.	.	.	23,787	20,970	20,216
TOTAL (including others)	.				409,495	407,664	507,000†

* Does not include police; in 1971 43,750,000 shillings were apportioned to police expenditure, in 1972 42,494,100 shillings.

† Includes 163,278,000 shillings for development programmes.

THREE-YEAR PLAN 1971–73

Total outlay: 402,284,600 shillings; transport and communications 128,574,600 shillings; agriculture 40,000,000 shillings; water resources 40,000,000 shillings; industry 48,000,000 shillings.

Currency in Circulation (December 31st, 1970): 150 million Somali shillings.

Gross Domestic Product (1963): U.S. $154 million.

BALANCE OF PAYMENTS
(million Somali Shillings)

	1968	1969	1970	1971
Current Account:				
Trade Balance	−115	−125	− 98	−127
Travel	20	2	− 7	− 16
Central Government (n.i.e.) . .	1	9	5	23
Other Services	—	7	− 34	− 11
Private Transfers . . .	4	10	6	15
Central Government Transfers .	137	74	87	122
CURRENT BALANCE . . .	6	− 23	− 41	6
Capital Account:				
Private	17	7	32	21
Central Government . . .	27	73	52	24
CAPITAL BALANCE . . .	44	80	84	45
Net Errors and Omissions . . .	1	7	− 4	− 9
Net Surplus or Deficit . . .	50	57	39	42
Allocation of Special Drawing Rights .	—	—	{ 18 −57	14 − 56

EXTERNAL TRADE
('ooo Somali Shillings)

	1965	1966	1967	1968	1969	1970	1971
Imports .	353,700	300,300	286,400	339,800	369,798	322,170	447,563
Exports .	192,000	213,900	198,500	212,000	231,910	224,346	246,441

PRINCIPAL COMMODITIES
('ooo Somali Shillings)

IMPORTS	1967	1968	1969	1970	1971
General manufactured goods . .	77,902	103,293	82,565	76,085	111,524
Yarn, fabrics and clothing* . .	34,453	43,413	24,615	25,525	36,406
Cereals and cereal products . .	35,264	34,962	48,828	55,006	104,777
Transport equipment . . .	48,769	64,829	46,591	32,925	28,727
Non-electrical machinery . . .	20,338	23,096	31,484	14,027	19,003
Mineral fuels	15,217	14,339	19,149	20,266	18,949
Sugar	810	7,953	1,011	933	1,048

EXPORTS	1967	1968	1969	1970	1971
Bananas	68,370	59,684	55,723	62,813	63,827
Livestock	97,876	124,395	132,014	119,268	123,376
Hides and Skins . . .	8,904	11,742	17,080	14,835	18,061
Wood and Charcoal . . .	11,405	4,980	5,791	15	6
Fish Products	491	239	2,964	1,511	2,638
Meat and Meat products . .	2,393	2,976	2,965	6,670	21,408

* Also included in General manufactured goods.

PRINCIPAL COUNTRIES
('ooo Somali Shillings)

IMPORTS	1969	1970	1971	EXPORTS	1969	1970	1971
Italy	114,409	94,955	121,191	Italy	61,827	58,555	55,148
Arabian Peninsula	12,319	16,708	11,584	Arabian Peninsula	154,852	143,341	147,869
U.S.S.R.	13,052	21,428	21,428	U.S.A.	4,833	1,537	291
U.S.A.	39,894	25,502	25,502	Egypt	614	1,527	5,569
U.K.	33,358	20,076	20,076	U.K.	1,534	607	612
Iran	4,870	7,568	7,568	Kenya	1,098	4,760	4,737
India	4,430	4,568	4,134				
Japan	30,455	23,914	23,974				
German Federal Rep.	31,134	29,434	29,434				
Ethiopia	12,047	8,880	8,880				
Kenya	16,941	16,946	16,946				

TRANSPORT

ROADS

In 1968 there were 13,223 licensed vehicles.

SHIPPING

MERCHANT FLEET
(Registered at June 30th each year)

	DISPLACEMENT (gross tons)
1968	59,000
1969	295,000
1970	369,000
1971	593,000

INTERNATIONAL SEA-BORNE SHIPPING	1969	1970	1971
Number of Vessels	626	n.a.	n.a.
Goods Loaded ('ooo metric tons)	318	264	294
Goods Unloaded ('ooo metric tons)	261	251	398

Shipping statistics are for the major harbours of Berbera, Mogadishu, Kismayu and Merca.

CIVIL AVIATION
SCHEDULED SERVICES

	1967	1968	1969	1970
Kilometres Flown ('ooo)	565	710	860	730
Passenger-km. ('ooo)	7,240	8,440	12,750	9,890
Cargo ton-km. ('ooo)	95	90	100	90

Communications (1970): 50,000 radio receivers; 5,000 telephones.

EDUCATION

(Student numbers 1971–72)

	GOVERNMENT SCHOOLS	PRIVATE SCHOOLS	TOTAL
Elementary . . .	31,364	8,858	40,222
Intermediate . . .	16,594	3,921	20,515
Secondary . . .	5,810	2,019	7,829
TOTAL . .	53,768	14,798	68,566

Source (unless otherwise stated): Central Statistical Department, Ministry of Planning and Co-ordination, Mogadishu.

THE CONSTITUTION

A new Constitution is being drawn up following the 1969 coup. In the meantime the Revolutionary Council is the supreme authority in the country.

THE GOVERNMENT

HEAD OF STATE

President of the Supreme Revolutionary Council: Maj.-Gen. MUHAMMAD SIAD BARRE.

SUPREME REVOLUTIONARY COUNCIL

(*January* 1973)

President: Maj.-Gen. MUHAMMAD SIAD BARRE.

MEMBERS

Brig.-Gen. HUSSEIN KULMIE.
Col. ABDALLA MUHAMMAD FADIL.
Col. ALI MATTAN HASCI.
Col. MAHAMOUD MIREE MUSA.
Col. MUHAMMAD SH. OSMAN.
Col. ISMAIL ALI ABUCAR.
Col. MUHAMMAD ALI SHIRREH.
Col. AHMED SULEIMAN ABDULLE.
Lt.-Col. MOHAMOUD GHELLE YUSUF.
Lt.-Col. FARAH WAIS DULLEH.

Lt.-Col. MUSA RABILLE GOD.
Lt.-Col. AHMED MUHAMMAD FARAH.
Maj. AHMED HASSAN MUSA.
Maj. MUHAMMAD OMER GES.
Maj. OSMAN MUHAMMAD GELLE.
Maj. MUHAMMAD YUSUF ELMI.
Maj. ABDI WARSAMA ISAAK.
Maj. ABDIRAZZAK MUHAMMAD ABUCAR.
Maj. ABDULKADIR HAJI MUHAMMAD.

GOVERNMENT RESPONSIBILITY

(*January* 1973)

Vice-President, Secretary of State for Defence and Commander-in-Chief of the Armed Forces: MUHAMMAD ALI SAMATUR.

Vice-President and Secretary of State for the Interior: HUSSEIN KULMIE.

Vice-President and Secretary of State for Information and National Guidance: ISMAIL ALI ABOKOR.

Secretary of State for Education: Maj. ABDIR AZZAK M. ABUCAR.

Secretary of State for Health: Dr. MUHAMMAD ADAN.

Secretary of State for Agriculture: B. MOHAMED HASSAN.

Secretary of State for Minerals: MUHAMMAD BURRALEH.

Secretary of State for Planning: AHMED MUHAMMAD MOHAMOUD.

Secretary of State for Finance: MUHAMMAD YUSUF WEYRAH.

Secretary of State for Foreign Affairs: OMAR ARTEH GHALIB.

Secretary of State for Public Works: Col. MUHAMMAD SH. OSMAN.

Secretary of State for Rural Development and Livestock SAID IBRAHIM HAJI SAID.

Secretary of Justice and Religion: SHAYKH ABDULGHANI SHAYKH AHMAD.

Secretary of Labour and Sport: Lt. Col. MUSA RABILLEH.

Secretary of Industry: Dr. IBRAHIM MEGAG SAMATUR.

Secretary of Commerce: Dr. MUHAMMED WARSAME.

Secretary of Posts, Telegraphs and Telephones: Lt. Col. AHMAD MAHAMUD FARAH.

Secretary of Transport: Dr. ABDULAZIZ NUR HERSI.

DIPLOMATIC REPRESENTATION

EMBASSIES AND LEGATIONS IN MOGADISHU

(E) Embassy; (L) Legation.

China, People's Republic: Via Scire Uarsama (E); *Ambassador:* FAN TSO-KAI.

Czechoslovakia: Via Londra (E); *Ambassador:* MIROSLAV NOVOTNY.

Egypt: Via Agostino Franzoi (E); *Ambassador:* ABDUL AZIZ GAMIL.

Ethiopia: Via Benedetti (E); *Ambassador:* AYALEW MANDEFRO.

France: Corso Primo Luglio (E); *Ambassador:* ROBERT DUVAUCHELLE.

German Democratic Republic: (E); *Ambassador:* WERNER HERKLOTZ.

Germany, Federal Republic: Via Muhammad Habi (E); *Ambassador:* JOSEPH HOLICK.

India: Via Balad (E); *Ambassador:* (vacant).

Iraq: (E); *Ambassador:* (vacant).

Italy: Via Trevis (E); *Ambassador:* GIULIO TERRUZZI.

Kenya: (E); *Ambassador:* J. K. ILAKO.

Korea, Democratic Peoples Republic: (E); *Ambassador:* KWAK CHOL SU.

Netherlands: (E); *Ambassador:* (vacant).

Pakistan: (E); *Ambassador:* COM. ABDUL HAMEED.

Saudi Arabia: Vardiglei Burhindi (E); *Ambassador:* ALI AWAD.

Southern Yemen: (E); *Ambassador:* SALIM RABI ALI.

Sudan: Via Cavour (E); *Ambassador:* MUAWIYA IBRAHIM SOURIG.

Syria: Via Washington (E); *Ambassador:* BAHA-ADDIN NAQQAR.

Tunisia: (E); *Ambassador:* TOUFIK.

U.S.S.R.: Corso Italia (E); *Ambassador:* ALEXEI S. PASIUTIN.

United Kingdom: Via Londra (E); *Ambassador:* JAMES BOURN.

U.S.A.: Corso Primo Luglio (E); *Ambassador:* MATTHEW LOORAM.

Viet-Nam, Democratic Republic of: (E); *Ambassador:* LUU QUY TAN.

Yemen Arab Republic: Corso Primo Luglio (E); *Ambassador:* MUHAMMAD ABDULLA ALFUSAYIL.

Yemen, People's Democratic Republic: (E); *Ambassador:* ABDUL BARRI KASSIM.

Yugoslavia: (E); *Ambassador:* SINIASA KOSUTIC.

Somalia also has diplomatic relations with Austria, Belgium, Bulgaria, Hungary, Indonesia, Japan, Jordan, Kuwait, Lebanon, Libya, Malta, Nigeria, Poland, Sweden and Turkey.

NATIONAL ASSEMBLY

The National Assembly was dissolved when the Government was overthrown on October 21st, 1969.

POLITICAL PARTIES

All political parties were banned after October 21st, 1969.

DEFENCE

Of a total armed force of 15,000, the army numbers 13,000 men, the navy 250 and the air force 1,750. In addition there are 500 para-military border guards. Military service is voluntary.

JUDICIAL SYSTEM

The Judiciary is independent of the executive and legislative powers.

Laws and acts having the force of law must conform to the provisions of the Constitution and to the general principles of Islam.

Supreme Revolutionary Court: Mogadishu; as the highest judicial organ, has jurisdiction over the whole territory of the State in civil, penal, administrative and accounting matters.

National Security Court: Mogadishu; established following the 1969 coup to try members of the former government and their officials; Pres. MUHAMMAD SHEIKH OSMAN.

Military Supreme Court: established 1970 to try members of the armed forces; Pres. MUHAMMAD ALI SHERMAN.

Courts of Appeal: There are Courts of Appeal in Mogadishu and Hargeisa, with two Sections: General and Assize.

Regional Courts: There are eight Regional Courts, with two Sections: General and Assize.

District Courts: There are 48 District Courts, with two Sections: Civil and Criminal. The Civil Section has jurisdiction over all controversies where the cause of action has arisen under Sharia Law (Muslim Law) or Customary Law and any other Civil controversies where the value of the subject matter does not exceed 3,000 Shillings. The Criminal Section has jurisdiction with respect to offences punishable with imprisonment not exceeding three years, or fine not exceeding 3,000 Shillings, or both.

Qadis: Civil matters such as marriage and divorce are handled by District Qadis under the Sharia (Islamic) law and other traditional laws.

The National Security Court was set up by the Supreme Revolutionary Council in April 1970; it is open to the public and is presided by three military judges led by Col. MOHAMED SHEIKH OSMAN. Appeal lies only to the Supreme Council.

RELIGION

ISLAM

Islam is the State religion. Most Somalis are Sunni Muslims.

ROMAN CATHOLICS

Vicar Apostolic: ANTONIO SILVIO ZOCCHETTA, P.O. Box 273, Mogadishu.

The Apostolic Vicariate was established in 1928. There are about 1,500 Catholics in Somalia, mostly of Italian origin.

PRESS

Bollettino Mensile della Camera di Commercio, Industria ed Agricultura della Somalia: P.O.B. 27, Mogadishu; f. 1944; monthly; Italian; published by Chamber of Commerce of Somalia; Dir. Dr. ATHOS BARTOLUCCI, circ. 2,000.

Corriere della Somalia: Palazzo del Governo, P.O.B. 315, Mogadishu; daily; Arabic and Italian; Government Information Department.

'Dawn': Mogadishu; weekly; English; government owned; circ. over 2,000; Editor YUSUF HASSAN ADAM.

Najmat-October: Mogadishu; daily; Arabic.

New Era: every three months; English, Italian, Arabic.

People's Union: P.O.B. 98, Hargeisa; weekly; published in Arabic by private concern; aligned to the Somali Democratic Union; circ. 1,200.

Stella d'Ottobre: Mogadishu; daily; circ. 3,000.

NEWS AGENCIES
FOREIGN BUREAUX

ANSA: Ambasciata d'Italia, Mogadishu; Chief MARIA LUISA BOHANNI.

Novosti: P.O.B. 963 Mogadishu; Chief V. BULIMOV.

Tass also has a bureau in Mogadishu.

RADIO

National Broadcasting Service: Radio Mogadishu, Voice of the Somali Democratic Republic, Mogadishu; main government service; broadcasts in Somali, English, Italian, Arabic, Swahili, Amharic and Qoti; Dir. of Broadcasting M. ABSHIR.

Radio Somali: P.O.B. 14, Hargeisa; Northern Region Government station; broadcasts in Somali, and relays Somali and Amharic transmission from Radio Mogadishu; Dir. of Broadcasting H. ABDI DUALEH.

Number of radio receivers: 50,000, some of which are used for public address purposes in small towns and villages.

There is no television service.

FINANCE

BANKING

cap.=capital; dep.=deposits; m.=million; (funds in Somali Shillings)

On May 7th, 1970, all banks were nationalized.

CENTRAL BANK

Banca Nazionale Somala: P.O.B. 11, Mogadishu; f. 1960; Central Bank and currency issuing authority; brs. in Baidoa Belet Uen, Berbera, Bosaso, Burao, Galcaio, Gardo, Giamama, Hargeisa, Kismayu and Merca; cap. 1m., reserves 15m. (1969); Gov. Dr. ABDWAHMAN NUR HERSI; Man. Dir. Dr. OMAR AHMED OMAR.

COMMERCIAL BANK

Somali Commercial Bank: P.O.B. 26, Mogadishu; f. 1971 to take over nationalized branches of National and Grindlays Bank Ltd., Banco di Roma, and Banco di Napoli; cap. 52.5m.; Gen. Man. SAID MOHAMED ALI.

FOREIGN BANKS

All foreign banks in Somalia were nationalized under an order of the Supreme Revolutionary Council on May 7th, 1970. They now become agencies of the Somali National Bank. The banks then operating in Somalia were the Banco di Napoli, Banco di Roma, Banque de Port Said and National and Grindlays Bank.

DEVELOPMENT BANK

Somali Development Bank: P.O.B. 1079, Mogadishu.

INSURANCE

Cassa per le Assicurazioni Sociali della Somalia: P.O.B. 123, Mogadishu; f. 1950; workmen's compensation; Pres. HAJI OSMAN MOHAMMED; Dir.-Gen. Dr. MOHAMMED AHMED MOHAMMED.

A number of Italian companies operate in Somalia, but will cease when the government-established National Insurance Co. is opened.

TRADE AND INDUSTRY

CHAMBER OF COMMERCE

Chamber of Commerce, Industry and Agriculture: P.O.B. 27, Mogadishu. In January 1961, 320 European, 156 Somali, 23 Arab, 24 Indian and Pakistani and 3 North American enterprises were registered as members; Dir. Dr. ATHOS BARTOLUCCI.

TRADE ORGANIZATION

National Agency of Foreign Trade: P.O.B. 602, Mogadishu; principal foreign trade agency; state owned; branch in Berbera.

DEVELOPMENT CORPORATION

Agricultural Development Corporation: Mogadishu; f. 1971; by amalgamation of previous agricultural and machinery agencies and grain marketing board; supplies farmers with equipment and materials at reasonable prices.

TRADE UNIONS

Confederazione Generale dei Lavoratori della Somalia (C.G.L.S.): c/o Somali Democratic Union, Mogadishu; f. 1961; three affiliated unions; affiliated to W.F.T.U.; Pres. MOHAMMED FARAH ABDI; Sec.-Gen. ABDULLAHI ADEN.

Confederazione Somala dei Lavoratori (C.S.L.) (*Somali Confederation of Workers*): P.O.B. 642, Mogadishu; f. 1949; membership 62,520 in 22 unions; affiliated to ICFTU and ATUC; the Somali Federation of Labour merged with C.S.L. in 1965, making this the national union; Pres. SAID YUSUF ALI "Bos"; Gen. Sec. OMAR NUR ABDI; publ. *Okdi Hagsatada* (The Voice of the Working Class) (monthly).

TRANSPORT

RAILWAYS

There are no railways in Somalia.

ROADS

17,750 km., about 600 km. asphalted, the rest mainly gravel. Many roads were destroyed in the heavy floods of 1961. An ambitious road building and maintenance project was launched in 1965. The International Development Association is helping to finance a 125-mile road project linking Afgoi (near Mogadishu) with Baidoa. There were 13,900 licensed vehicles in 1969.

SHIPPING

Merca, Berbera, Mogadishu and Kismayu are the chief ports. New deep-water extensions to Berbera harbour, constructed by the Soviet Union, were opened early in 1969, and the facilities at Kismayu have been extended with American assistance.

Brocklebank Line: monthly service Oct. to April from United Kingdom to Berbera; agents A. Besse and Co. (Somalia) Ltd., P.O.B. 121, Berbera.

Clan Line: regular calls at Berbera Oct. to April; agents A. Besse and Co. (Somalia) Ltd., P.O.B. 121, Berbera.

Lloyd Triestino: regular passenger and cargo service to Italy; agents Agenzia Marittima, P.O.B. 126, Mogadishu.

Other lines call irregularly at Somali ports.

Somali "Dhows" sail between East Africa, Aden and Arabia.

CIVIL AVIATION

Mogadishu has an international airport with landing facilities for aircraft up to DC-8 class. A new international airport is under construction at Kisimayu with similar facilities. Hargeisa airport can accommodate aircraft up to Viscount class.

Somali Airlines: Piazza della Solidarieta Africana, P.O.B. 726, Mogadishu; 51 per cent government-owned and 49 per cent owned by Alitalia; operates internal passenger and cargo services and international services to Aden and Nairobi; fleet of two Viscount, 3 DC-3, 2 Cessna; Pres. Dr. MOHAMED SHARIF MOHAMUD; Vice-Pres. Capt. GUIDO FARACCI; Dir.-Gen. Lt.-Col. OSMAN ABDUL-KADIR.

FOREIGN AIRLINES

The following foreign airlines serve Somalia: Aeroflot, Alitalia, Democratic Yemen Airlines, EAA., EgyptAir.

EDUCATION

Somalia is developing a national education system from two different systems inherited from 80 years of partition under colonial rule. Before independence, Arabic and English were the languages of instruction in schools in the North, and Italian in the South. Now, however, Italian teachers are being trained to teach in English, which has been adopted as the language of instruction in secondary schools, while Arabic is the main language in primary schools. UNESCO is helping with the organization of courses, the training of under-qualified teachers and, jointly with the U.S.S.R., the publication of selected textbooks.

The number of children attending school is rising rapidly; in 1971–72 the total approached 70,000 pupils, over three times the figure in 1961.

LEARNED SOCIETIES

British Council: P.O.B. 989, Jirdeh Hussein Bldg., Corso Somala, Mogadishu; Rep. D. A. LATTER.

L'Institut Culturel et Social: Mogadishu.

Casa degli Italiani: Mogadishu; organizes meetings, art exhibitions, etc.

RESEARCH INSTITUTES

Geological Survey Department: Ministry of Mining, P.O.B. 744, Mogadishu; library of 500 vols.; Dir. V. N. KOZERENKO.

Institute for the Preparation of Serums and Vaccines: Mogadishu.

Laboratory of Hygiene and Prophylaxy: Mogadishu; sections in medicine and chemistry.

Society of Medicine and Tropical Hygiene: Mogadishu.

Survey and Mapping Department: P.O.B. 24, Mogadishu; f. 1966; the official surveying and mapping department; Dir. MUSA ADAN WADADID.

LIBRARIES

Biblioteca del l'Istituto Universitario della Somalia: Mogadishu; Librarian ELIAS M. MOHAMUD.

British Council Library: Mogadishu; f. 1970.

Hargeisa Local Government Council Library: Hargeisa; f. 1958; public library.

National Library: Mogadishu; f. 1934; 8,000 vols.; Librarian A. H. ABDURAHMAN.

Secretariat Library: Hargeisa: predominantly non-fiction.

Société Dante Alighieri: Mogadishu; library of books on Italian culture.

MUSEUM

Museé National de la Garesa: Mogadishu; ethnographical, historical and natural science collections.

UNIVERSITY

UNIVERSITÁ NAZIONALE DELLA SOMALIA
(National University of Somalia)

P.O.B. 15, MOGADISHU.

Telephone: 2535.

Founded 1954; University status 1959; National University 1971.

Language of Instruction: Italian.

President: (vacant).
Administrator: MICHELE PIRONE.
Librarian: ELIAS M. MOHAMUD.

Number of teachers: *c.* 20.
Number of students: *c.* 790.

Faculties of Law, Economics, Natural Sciences, Science, Agriculture, Teacher Training.

COLLEGES

School of Islamic Disciplines: Mogadishu; includes a faculty of law; 299 students.

École Industrielle: Mogadishu; departments of radio, carpentry, mechanics, electricity, building construction.

School of Public Health: 25 students.

School of Seamanship and Fishing: 18 students.

Technical College: Burgo; f. 1965; 4-year courses.

Veterinary College: Mogadishu; 30 students; 10 teachers; Project Dir. Dr. J. NEILSEN (acting).

SELECT BIBLIOGRAPHY

ABRAHAM, R. C. *Somali-English Dictionary.* London, 1964.

ANDRZEJEWSKI, B. W., and LEWIS, I. M. *Somali Poetry, an Introduction.* 1964.

BELL, C. R. V. *The Somali Language.* 1953.

BURTON, R. F. *First Footsteps in East Africa.* London, Everyman, 1943.

CONTINI, P. *The Somali Republic: an experiment in legal integration.* 1969.

DRYSDALE, J. *The Somali Dispute.* 1964.

HESS, R. L. *Italian Colonialism in Somalia.* 1966.

KARP, M. *The Economics of Trusteeship in Somalia.* 1960.

LEWIS, I. M. *A Pastoral Democracy.* 1961.
   The Modern History of Somaliland: from Nation to State. 1965.
   Peoples of the Horn of Africa. 1969 (reprint).

TOUVAL, S. *Somali Nationalism.* 1963.

Republic of South Africa

South Africa

PHYSICAL AND SOCIAL GEOGRAPHY

John Amer

The Republic of South Africa occupies the southern extremity of the African continent and except for a relatively small area in the northern Transvaal lies poleward of the Tropic of Capricorn, extending as far as latitude 34° 51′ south. The Republic has an area of 471,445 sq. miles and has common borders on the north-west with South West Africa (Namibia), which it administers, with Botswana on the north, and with Rhodesia, Mozambique and Swaziland on the north-east. Lesotho occurs as an enclave within the eastern part of the Republic.

PHYSICAL FEATURES

Most of South Africa consists of a vast plateau with upwarped rims, bounded by an escarpment. Framing the plateau is a narrow coastal belt. The surface of the plateau varies in altitude from 2,000 to 6,500 ft. above sea-level, but is mostly above 3,000 ft. It is highest on the east and south-east and dips fairly gently towards the Kalahari Basin on the north-west. The relief is generally monotonous, consisting of undulating to flat landscapes over wide areas. Variation is provided occasionally by low ridges and *inselberge* (or *kopjes*) made up of rock more resistant to erosion. There are three major sub-regions:

(i) the High Veld between 4,000 and 6,000 ft. forming a triangular area which occupies the southern Transvaal and most of the Orange Free State;

(ii) a swell over 5,000 ft. high aligned WNW.–ESE., part of which is known as the Witwatersrand, rising gently from the plateau surface to the north of the High Veld and forming a major drainage divide;

(iii) the Middle Veld, generally between 2,000 and 4,000 ft., comprising the remaining part of the plateau.

The edges of the plateau, upwarped during the Tertiary, are almost everywhere above 5,000 ft. Maximum elevations of over 11,000 ft. occur on the south-east in Lesotho. From the crests the surface descends coastwards by means of the Great Escarpment which gives the appearance of a mountain range when viewed from below, and which is known by distinctive names in its different sections. An erosional feature, dissected by seaward-flowing rivers, the nature of the escarpment varies according to the type of rock which forms it. Along its eastern length it is known as the Drakensberg; in the section north of the Olifants River fairly soft granite gives rise to gentle slopes, but south of that river resistant quartzites are responsible for a more striking appearance. Further south again, along the Natal-Lesotho border, basalts cause the Drakensberg to be at its most striking, rising up a sheer 6,000 ft. or more in places. Turning

westwards the Great Escarpment is known successively as the Stormberg, Bamboes, Suurberg, Sneeuberg, Nieuwveld, and Komsberg, where gentle slopes affording access to the interior alternate with a more wall-like appearance. The Great Escarpment then turns sharply northwards through the Roggeveld Mountains, following which it is usually in the form of a simple step until the Kamiesberg are reached; owing to aridity and fewer rivers the dissection of this western part of the escarpment is much less advanced than in the eastern (Drakensberg) section.

The Lowland margin which surrounds the South African plateau may be divided into four zones:

(i) The undulating to flat Transvaal Low Veld, between 500 and 2,000 ft. above sea-level, separated from the Mozambique coastal plain by the Lebombo Mountains on the east, and including part of the Limpopo valley in the north.

(ii) The South Eastern Coastal Belt, a very broken region descending to the coast in a series of steps, into which the rivers have cut deep valleys. In northern Natal the Republic possesses its only true coastal plain, some 40 miles at its widest.

(iii) The Cape Ranges, consisting of the remnants of mountains folded during the Carboniferous, and flanking the plateau on the south and south-west. On the south the folds trend E.–W. and on the south-west they trend N.–S., the two trends crossing in the south-western corner of the Cape Province to produce a rugged knot of mountains and the Ranges' highest elevations (over 7,000 ft.). Otherwise the Cape Ranges are comparatively simple in structure, consisting of parallel anti-clinal ridges and synclinal valleys. Narrow low-lands separate the mountains from the coast. Between the ridges and partially enclosed by them, e.g., the Little Karoo, is a series of steps rising to the foot of the Great Escarpment. The Great Karoo, the last of these steps, separates the escarpment from the Cape Ranges.

(iv) The Western Coastal belt is also characterized by a series of steps, but the slope from the foot of the Great Escarpment to the coast is more gentle and more uniform than in the south-eastern zone.

The greater part of the plateau is drained by the Orange River system. Rising in the Drakensberg within a short distance of the escarpment, as do its two main perennial tributaries the Vaal and the Caledon, the Orange flows westward for 1,200 miles before entering the Atlantic Ocean. However, the western part of its basin is so dry and its tributaries there consequently seasonal, that it is not unknown for the Orange to fail to reach its mouth during the dry season. The large-scale Orange River Project, a comprehensive scheme for water supply, irrigation and hydro-electric generation, will aid water conservation in this western area and lead to its development. The only other single major system is that of the Limpopo, which rises on the northern slopes of the Witwatersrand and drains most of central and northern Transvaal to the Indian Ocean. Apart from some interior drainage to a number of small basins in the north and north-west, the rest of the Republic's drainage is peripheral. Relatively short streams rise in the Great Escarpment, although some rise on the plateau itself, having cut through the escarpment, and drain directly to the coast. With the exception of riparian strips along perennial rivers most of the country relies for water supplies on underground sources supplemented by dams. None of the Republic's rivers are navigable.

CLIMATE AND NATURAL VEGETATION

Except for a small part of northern Transvaal the climate of South Africa is subtropical, although there are important regional variations within this general classification. Altitude and relief forms have an important influence on temperature and on both the amount and distribution of rainfall, and there is a strong correlation between the major physical and the major climatic regions. The altitude of the plateau modifies temperatures and because there is a general rise in elevation towards the equator there is a corresponding decrease in temperature, resulting in a remarkable uniformity of temperature throughout the Republic from south to north (cf. mean annual temperatures: Cape Town, 62°F; and Pretoria, 63°F.). The greatest contrasts in temperature are, in fact, between the east coast, warmed by the Mozambique Current, and the west coast, cooled by the Benguela Current (cf. respectively, mean monthly temperatures: Durban, January, 76°F., July, 64°F.; and Port Nolloth: January, 60°F., July, 54°F.). Daily and annual ranges in temperature increase with distance from the coast, being much greater on the plateau (cf. mean annual temperature range: Cape Town, 14°F.; Pretoria, 20°F.).

The areas of highest annual rainfall largely coincide with the outstanding relief features, over 25 in. being received only in the eastern third of South Africa and relatively small areas in southern Cape Province. Parts of the Drakensberg and the seaward slopes of the Cape Ranges experience over 60 in. West of the Drakensberg and to the north of the Cape Ranges there is a marked rain-shadow, and annual rainfall decreases progressively westwards (cf. Durban 45 in., Bloemfontein 21 in., Kimberley 16 in., Upington 7 in., Port Nolloth 2 in.). Virtually all the western half of the country, apart from southern Cape Province, receives less than 10 in. and the western coastal belt's northern section forms a continuation of the Namib Desert. Most of the rain falls during the summer months (November to April) when evaporation losses are greatest, brought by tropical marine air masses moving in from the Indian Ocean on the east. However, S.W. Cape Province has a winter maximum of rainfall with dry summers. Only the narrow southern

coastal belt between Cape Agulhas and East London has rainfall distributed uniformly throughout the year. Snow may fall occasionally over the higher parts of the plateau and the Cape Ranges during winter, but frost occurs on an average for 120 days each year over most of the interior plateau, and for shorter periods in the coastal lowlands with the exception of Natal where it is rare.

Variations in climate and particularly in annual rainfall are reflected in changes of vegetation, sometimes strikingly as between the S.W. Cape's Mediterranean shrub type, designed to withstand summer drought and of which the protea—the national plant—is characteristic, and the drought-resistant low Karoo bush immediately north of the Cape Ranges and covering much of the semi-arid western half of the country. The only true areas of forest are found along the wetter south and east coasts—the temperate evergreen forests of the Knysna district and the largely evergreen subtropical bush, including palms and wild bananas, of the eastern Cape and Natal, respectively. Grassland covers the rest of the Republic, merging into thorn veld in N.W. Cape Province and into bush veld in northern Transvaal.

MINERAL RESOURCES

South Africa's mineral resources, outstanding in their variety, quality and quantity, overshadow all the country's other natural resources. They are mainly found in the ancient Precambrian foundation and associated intrusions and occur in a wide curving zone which stretches from the northern Transvaal through the Orange Free State and northern Cape Province to the west coast. To the south of this mineralized zone, possibly the richest in the world, the Precambrian rocks are covered by Karoo sedimentaries which generally do not contain minerals with the exception of the Republic's extensive deposits of bituminous coal. The latter occur mainly in the eastern Transvaal High Veld, the northern Orange Free State and northern Natal, mostly in thick, easily worked seams fairly near to the surface. Total reserves are estimated at approximately 225,000 million tons. However, the quality of much of the coal is relatively poor and only some 350 million tons of coking coal have been proved.

The most important mineral regions in the Precambrian zone are the Witwatersrand and northern Orange Free State producing gold, silver and uranium; the diamond areas centred on Kimberley, Pretoria, Jagersfontein and Koffiefontein; and the Transvaal bushveld complex containing multiple occurrences of a large number of minerals, including asbestos, chrome, copper, iron, magnesium, nickel, platinum, tin, uranium and vanadium. Important manganese and iron ore deposits occur in northern Cape Province in the Postmasburg-Kuruman and Sishen areas, respectively. This list of occurrences and minerals is by no means exhaustive. The country's first economic deposit of natural gas was discovered off the southern coast of Cape Province in early 1969; prospecting for petroleum continues.

ETHNIC GROUPS AND POPULATION

Five major ethnic groups make up South Africa's multi-racial society. The "Khoisan" peoples—Bushmen, Hottentots and Bergdamara—are survivors of the country's earliest inhabitants. The negroid Bantu-speaking peoples fall into a number of tribal groupings. The major groups are formed by the Nguni comprising Zulu, Swazi, Ndebele, Pondo, Tembu and Xhosa on the one hand, and by the Sotho and Tswana on the other. Together all the above groups numbered 15.2 million in 1970. The 3.8 million European or "white" peoples, who dominate the political, economic and social organization of the Republic, are descended from the original seventeenth-century Dutch settlers in the Cape, refugee French Huguenots, British settlers from 1820 onwards, Germans, and more recent immigrants from Europe and ex-colonial African territories. The major language groups are Afrikaans (65 per cent) and English (35 per cent). The rest of the total population of 21.4 million (1970 census) is made up of 2.0 million "Cape

Coloureds", people of mixed race, and 0.6 million Asians, largely of Indian origin.

The general distribution of the population is related to agricultural resources, more than two-thirds living in the wetter eastern third of the Republic and in southern Cape Province. Heaviest concentrations are found in the Witwatersrand mining area—the Johannesburg Metropolitan Area has 1.4 million people—and in and around the chief ports of Cape Town, Port Elizabeth and Durban. Europeans have a widespread geographical distribution, but over 80 per cent live in towns. Relatively few Africans are resident in Western Cape Province and whilst an increasing number are becoming town dwellers over 60 per cent still reside in the tribal reserves which extend in a great horseshoe along the south-eastern coastal belt and up to northern Transvaal and then south-westwards through western Transvaal to N.E. Cape Province. Members of the "Cape Coloured" group are mainly found in the Cape Province and the Asians are largely confined to Natal and the Witwatersrand.

HISTORY

J. D. Omer-Cooper

EARLY POPULATIONS

In South Africa, peoples practising a late stone-age technology and an economy restricted to hunting and gathering survived into historical times. As late as the 17th century, San (Bushman) hunting bands still occupied much of the hinterland of the Cape as far north as the Orange River as well as the dry lands of South West Africa (Namibia). They shared occupation of these areas with a closely related people the Khoi-Khoi (Hottentots) who in addition to hunting and gathering kept sheep and cattle. Ancestors of the present Bantu-speaking peoples of South Africa may have begun settling south of the Limpopo as early as the third century A.D. They brought with them the art of extracting and working iron and other minerals and practised agriculture as well as cattle keeping. Their chiefdoms constituted relatively complex political societies with many of the characteristics of states in the modern sense. By the latter part of the eighteenth century, they had occupied most of South Africa north of the Orange River and east of the Kalahari. On the east coast, they had advanced still further and were beginning to settle the area immediately to the south-west of the great Fish River.

ESTABLISHMENT AND EXPANSION OF THE WHITE SETTLEMENT

In 1652, the Dutch East India Company established a refreshment station on the site of present-day Cape Town. A nucleus of permanent settlers was created by allowing a number of the Company's servants to leave its service and establish themselves as free

burghers growing crops on their own account for sale to the Company. The original small nucleus was expanded by further assisted immigration including that of a number of Huguenot refugees from the religious persecution of Louis XIV. Thereafter it continued to expand by natural increase. Importation of slaves and the absorption of Khoi-Khoi as farm workers allowed a pattern of farming depending on the exploitation of non-white labour by white land-owners to develop. This in turn enabled individual whites to exploit much larger holdings than those originally envisaged. The difficulties of making a living as a wheat or wine farmer at the Cape where the market was severely restricted, encouraged many whites to move into the hinterland and establish themselves as cattle ranchers. In the climatic and economic circumstances, however, large areas of land were needed to maintain the number of cattle required to make ranching viable. An area of 6,000 acres came to be accepted as the minimum size for a cattle farm. Thus, as the white population grew it sought constantly to expand the area under its control at a very rapid rate. With each generation the white settlers took more and more land from the indigenous peoples, and either absorbed them as farm workers or drove them further into the interior.

CLASS AND COLOUR: THE CONSOLIDATION OF RACE PREJUDICE

The stratification of society along lines of colour soon began to be reflected in the realm of ideas in the development of a pattern of racial attitudes, beliefs and prejudices which rationalized and served to maintain that stratification. These attitudes were further strengthened by the fears and hatreds born of bitter struggles against San and Khoi-Khoi resistance which slowed down and occasionally temporarily halted but could not reverse the expansion of the white colony. By the late 18th century, distinctions of colour had come by many whites to be regarded as a divinely ordained social absolute and any suggestions of equality between the races a threat to the white way of life.

By the end of the 18th century, white settlers pushing up the east coast had encountered the advance guard of the Bantu-speaking peoples in the vicinity of the Great Fish River, white expansionism now met formidable resistance and a long series of border wars began.

FRONTIERSMEN VERSUS THE METROPOLITAN GOVERNMENT

In the last years of the Dutch East India Company's rule, border conflict and the oppression of non-white servants by their white employers brought the Company's government into conflict with the white frontiersman. The attempts of an energetic magistrate to impose the rule of law on the frontier area led to rebellion by the farmers and the proclamation of two short-lived white republics at Swellendam and Graaf Reinet. This basic pattern of white expansion and reduction of the indigenous peoples to a strongly subordinated working class, African resistance, governmental attempts to limit border conflict and ameliorate the lot of African servants and resulting tension between frontier farmers and the government persisted through the temporary British occupation of the Cape from 1795–1803. It remained implicit in the situation though veiled by a temporary calm during the brief period of rule by the Batavian Republic from 1803–1806. In that year the British occupied the Cape once again, this time to stay, and it was not to be long before the underlying tensions came once more to the fore.

THE MISSIONARY FACTOR

By this time, missionaries representing the new evangelical and philanthropic enthusiasm that was conquering the middle classes in Europe had begun to establish themselves in growing numbers in South Africa. The missionary ideal of Christianizing and "civilizing" African society along western lines, implying the development of Africans as independent producers and consumers and an African middle class of preachers, teachers, traders and professional men, was in conflict with the ethos of settler society, which required that they be restricted to labouring rôles on white owned farms and enterprises.

The coming of the missionaries, backed as they were by politically powerful groups in the home country, exacerbated tensions between the settler community and the Government and fostered contradictions within South African society which have subsequently grown ever more pronounced. Missionary and philanthropic pressures resulted in the removal of discriminatory regulations governing the Khoi-Khoi within the colony which kept them in virtual serfdom to their white masters. Ordinance No. 50 of 1828 placed free colonial persons in the colony on a basis of legal equality with whites. In 1834 the emancipation of slaves was undertaken. The white frontier farmers found their control over their labour force gravely weakened and felt moves towards legal equality between persons of different race a threat to their white way of life and system of values. They were also acutely frustrated by their failure to overcome the resistance of the Xhosa branch of the Bantu-speaking peoples on the eastern frontier. Indeed it was not until 1811–12 with the assistance of British troops that the frontier of white settlement was advanced in this area even as far as the Great Fish River. Thereafter, in subsequent wars further minor advances were made but not nearly enough to satisfy the settlers' need for farms. Indeed in 1820 the land hunger of the white settlers was made worse by the introduction of substantial numbers of English settlers to the eastern frontier area.

THE MFECANE

While tensions within the Cape colony were mounting in this way African society beyond its borders was undergoing a profound upheaval. In Zululand, Shaka, building on the achievement of the Mtethwa chief Dingiswayo, welded a large number of chiefdoms into a centralized militarist kingdom with a large standing army of young men organized in age-regiments, stationed in special military towns under commoner officers appointed for their military ability. His troops were drilled to fight in close formation wielding short-handled stabbing spears and protecting themselves behind an ordered line of body-length shields. The rise of the Zulu kingdom set in motion a chain of migrations and upheavals which affected most of South Africa beyond the colonial borders and vast areas of Central and East Africa. It led to the rise of a series of large-scale kingdoms including the Swazi kingdom, Lesotho, the Pedi kingdom of the eastern Transvaal and the Ndebele kingdom established in the western Transvaal and subsequently in Rhodesia. As a result of the upheaval, peoples gathered in heavy concentrations in defensible areas temporarily leaving wide areas in Natal, the Orange Free State and the Transvaal apparently empty. As news of this situation reached the Cape through the reports of travellers, traders and missionaries, the possibility of mass secession and settlement in these desirable empty areas opened up to the land hungry and discontented Afrikaner farmers.

THE BOER GREAT TREK

When after yet another frontier war in 1834–35, the strength of Xhosa resistance and philanthropic pressures on the British Government combined to deny the frontier farmers the prospect of abundant new land on the well-watered east coast, they began moving out of the colony in large numbers on a great trek to the north aimed at establishing an independent polity where "proper relations" could be maintained between masters and servants.

Military success against the Zulu and Ndebele ensured the permanence of white settlement in Natal, the Orange Free State and the Transvaal. Each of these areas then became a growth point for further white expansion at the expense of the Bantu-speaking peoples. The situation of endemic frontier conflict on the eastern border of the Cape was thus extended to the whole of South Africa. Through many bitter wars the area of white occupation was steadily expanded but the whites were by no means always victorious. The persistence of areas of African landownership in the independent states of Botswana, Lesotho and Swaziland and in the areas now designated as Bantustans is a testimony to successful African resistance rather than white forbearance.

BRITAIN FAILS TO CONTROL POST-TREK DEVELOPMENTS

In the aftermath of the great trek, British policy vacillated between the alternatives of annexing the new areas of white settlement in the interests of protecting the indigenous peoples and maintaining peace in the sub-continent and leaving whites and Africans to fight it out on their own in the interests of economy. An initial forward policy leading to the annexation of Natal and the Orange River sovereignty (comprising the area of the modern Orange Free State and Lesotho) was followed by a policy of withdrawal embodied in the Sand River Convention guaranteeing freedom from British interference to the Transvaal whites in 1850, the abandonment of the Orange River sovereignty and the signing of the Bloemfontein Convention with the Orange Free State in 1852. Simultaneously, the Cape was launched on the first step towards self-government by the establishment of the Cape Parliament based on a non-racial economic franchise which, while providing some limited political opportunities for non-whites, nevertheless ensured white political supremacy and increased the settlers' power in the colony.

In spite of the general move towards withdrawal of responsibility in South Africa the annexation of Natal was not undone, and as ex-trekkers left the colony in protest at British rule they were replaced by English settlers. Subsequently the development of sugar plantations and shortage of labour led to the importation of Indian workers who settled down to form a further element in South Africa's complex racial pattern.

In 1868, the dangers of conflict between the Orange Free State and Lesotho spilling over into the Cape led to the extension of British authority over the Sotho kingdom of Moshoeshoe and the beginning of a new forward policy.

DIAMONDS

The discovery of diamonds in West Griqualand and the beginnings of their exploitation which took place at this time marked the start of an economic revolution in South Africa. It began the transition from an almost wholly agricultural economy to a predominantly industrial and urban one. It required the employment of large numbers of Africans who were largely drawn from the still remaining areas of exclusive African settlement as migrant workers. It thus went with and accelerated a new tendency, already clearly seen in the annexation of the Lesotho kingdom, towards the establishment of white rule over Africans on the land and the utilization of such areas of African settlement as labour reservoirs for the white controlled areas in place of the longer established process of progressive expropriation of African farmers by expanding white settlers. This new process of bringing African areas of settlement under white political control accelerated in the latter part of the 19th century in spite of fierce resistance. By the end of the century it had been effectively completed.

THE FAILURE OF THE BRITISH CONFEDERATIVE POLICY

The discovery of diamonds came at a time when British policymakers were becoming convinced of the desirability of going back on the policy of abandonment and fostering a federation of white states in South Africa under the leadership of the Cape. To make this possible the Diamond Fields area was annexed in 1872 and the idea of federation was subsequently actively pushed. Resistance to the idea from the Cape, which had been granted responsible government in 1872, resulted in frustration which prompted the British authorities to attempt to break the deadlock by annexing the Transvaal Republic which was bankrupt and had recently been defeated in a war with the Pedi chief Sekukuni. This dramatic move however merely hardened opposition in South Africa to a British inspired move to Federation. To mitigate opposition to Federation in South Africa and to win the support of the Transvalers war was forced on the most powerful independent African polity in South Africa, the Zulu kingdom. It began with a major disaster for British arms at Isandhlwana. Though this was subsequently retrieved and the Zulu kingdom defeated, the British Government's confidence in its South African policy had been shaken and the military prestige of British troops gravely undermined.

Thus, when the Transvaal farmers rose in rebellion and defeated British forces in a number of engagements culminating in the disaster of Majuba Hill, Britain reverted to a policy of withdrawal and restored the Transvaal to effective internal independence in the Pretoria Convention. The annexation of the Transvaal and the subsequent successful freedom struggle of the Transvalers inspired strong sympathy amongst Afrikaans-speaking whites all over South Africa and marked the beginning of a South Africa-wide Afrikaner nationalist movement.

AFRIKANER NATIONALISM: INTERNATIONAL COMPETITION: GOLD IN THE TRANSVAAL

Britain had thus abandoned the attempt to establish control over the Afrikaner republics of the Transvaal and Orange Free State and aroused an anti-British Afrikaner nationalism in the Cape colony itself at the very time that her paramountcy in the sub-continent was to be challenged by international competition which made itself forcibly apparent in the German annexation of South West Africa in 1884. This situation forced British policy back to a new forward policy marked by the extension of British rule over modern Botswana, and by the extension of the authority of the Cape and Natal colonies over the remaining independent African polities along the eastern seaboard. The tensions inherent in the political situation in South Africa were gravely worsened by the consequences of the discovery of gold in the Transvaal which now replaced the Cape as economically the most powerful state in the sub-continent. To preserve British paramountcy in a situation of international competition it now seemed essential to extend a measure of British control over the Transvaal lest it drew the other South African states into its orbit. To achieve this Cecil Rhodes was given support to enable his British South Africa Company to occupy Rhodesia and create a new dominant British possession to the north of the Transvaal.

ORIGINS OF THE SOUTH AFRICAN WAR

When it became apparent that Rhodesia was not going to outclass the Transvaal as a gold producer but was relatively poor, Rhodes was given government support for his schemes to promote a rebellion among the foreign white mineworkers (Uitlanders) in Johannesburg and to lead a column of British South Africa Company forces to crush the rebels. This plot ended disastrously in the fiasco of the Jameson Raid, and the conflict between the principle of British paramountcy and the Afrikaner Republics' insistence on independence was further sharpened. Thereafter the British Government, egged on by the ultra-imperialist High Commissioner Milner, brought increasing pressures to bear on the Transvaal to make concessions which would effectively destroy the Republics' independence. Realizing that the British Government would be satisfied with nothing less than this, the Boer Republics in desperation declared war and invaded the British colonies on October 12th, 1899.

Though the pattern of race relations was the fundamental issue which would determine the whole nature of South African society, it was not the most prominent in the minds of the British authorities as the South African War drew to a close. The most urgent problem seemed to them to ensure that South Africa should remain firmly within the British Empire. In the Peace of Vereeniging in 1902 the British negotiators agreed that the issue of non-European voting rights in the ex-Republics would not be raised until these had been restored to responsible government.

With the war over, the High Commissioner Milner, aided by a team of able young university graduates (the Milner "kindergarten"), energetically set about the task of reconstruction. Milner's plan was to establish British influence firmly in the ex-Republics by anglicizing the Afrikaans-speaking population. This was to be achieved by a programme of public education in which English would form the medium of instruction. He also planned to settle substantial numbers of English-speaking settlers on the land in the Transvaal. Milner's anglicization policy, however, roused intense fears among the Afrikaans-speaking population. The Boers who had been demoralized and deeply divided in the aftermath of the war drew together in a movement to found a rival system of Christian National Education to preserve their cultural and linguistic heritage. The Afrikaner nationalist current soon began to flow in political channels.

The second part of Milner's plan depended on revitalizing the economy of South Africa generally and the Transvaal in particular. This meant that the Witwatersrand gold mines must be brought into full operation as quickly as possible. Faced with a shortage of African labour, Milner imported Chinese workers to restart the mines. This roused intense opposition from whites in South Africa and an outcry in Britain against the discriminatory conditions to which the Chinese were subject. The slogan of "Chinese slavery" helped the Liberal Party to oust the Conservatives from office in Britain in 1906. The victory of the Liberal Party brought radical changes in policy towards South Africa. The Liberals sought to reconcile the Boers to membership of the British Empire by generous political concessions. Responsible government was introduced in the Transvaal and Orange River colonies. Two Boer parties appeared on the tide of Afrikaner nationalism: the Hetvolk Party in the Transvaal under Botha and Smuts and the Oranjie Unie Party under Fischer and Hertzog in the Orange Free State. These parties captured the administration of the two colonies. In 1907 the pro-British Progressive Party administration of Dr. Jameson gave way to the South Africa Party headed by an Englishman, Merriman, but drawing its main support from the Afrikaner Bond.

FORMATION OF THE UNION

So long as power remained in British hands the Boers had held back from the idea of unification, but once their political victory was complete in most of South Africa they speedily took the initiative. In 1908 a National Convention met to work out the terms of unification.

Faced with the alternatives of a federal or a unitary system the National Convention accepted the more radical solution. The previously separate states were to be reduced to provinces with very limited local powers within a South African union. The issue of the union franchise thus became the crucial issue that would determine the distribution of political power within the South African community. In the final compromise non-whites were denied the right to sit in the Union Parliament, but existing non-European voting rights were preserved in the Cape and protected by the provision that any measure reducing these rights would require a two-thirds majority of both Houses sitting together.

African nationalism was nurtured by the historical experience of struggle against white encroachment and conquest. It is rooted in the whole history of South Africa, which is not the story of white initiative alone but of a complex interaction of the activities of whites and those of other races in South Africa. As European rule consolidated itself, African rejection of white claims to inborn superiority and rights of leadership expressed themselves in secessions from white-controlled mission churches and the formation of independent churches under African leadership.

The formation of breakaway churches was only a symptom of general attitudes towards white domination and claims to superiority which were often held just as strongly by those who remained within the mission churches as by those who left them. Simultaneously with the growth of the "Ethiopian" movement which got under way in the late 1880s, members of the African western-educated élite were taking the first steps towards the formation of political movements of the modern type. This began most naturally in the Cape where in the 1880s the Cape Native Voters' Association was founded. In 1884 J. T. Jabavu launched the first African newspaper *Imvo Zabantsundu*, and in 1902 the Rev. John Dube launched the *Ilanga lase Natal* at Durban. A first step towards the formation of a political movement on the part of the Coloured people was taken in 1902 when Dr. Abdullah Abdurahman founded the African Peoples Organisation (APO).

The franchise arrangements in the proposed Union constitution posed an obvious threat to the political rights of the non-white peoples of South Africa, and the fact that the constitution had to be accepted by the British Parliament afforded an opportunity for organized protest. A South African Native National Conference, the first African political organization on a national scale, sent two delegates to London. The African Peoples Organisation also sent a protest delegation, as did liberal whites. These attempts to influence the British Parliament proved of no avail, and in 1910 South Africa began its life as a united and virtually independent state under a constitution which gave the white minority an almost complete monopoly of political authority.

THE WHITE PARTIES

With the formation of the Union the Hetvolk Party in the Transvaal, the Oranjie Unie Party of the Orange Free State and the South Africa Party in the Cape amalgamated under the name of the South Africa Party and obtained an overall majority in the Union Parliament. The dominant spirit in the party was that of two Boer War leaders, Louis Botha and Jan Smuts. They were both men of broad views who had reconciled themselves to South Africa remaining clearly associated with Britain, provided that white

South Africans were free to control their own affairs. Their aim, like that of Rhodes and Onze Jan Hofmeyer before them, was to bring English-speaking and Afrikaans-speaking South Africans together as a united ruling caste. They saw white South African society as part of the mainstream of European culture and had no deep suspicions of English language and culture or the development of capitalist commerce and industry in South Africa. Within the same party, however, there were others with more parochial views, more specifically Afrikaner nationalists, who saw the Afrikaans-speaking group as a nation in itself with a language and culture in danger of being swamped by English. They resented South Africa's continuing association with Britain and looked back with nostalgia to the Boer Republics. The most powerful representative of this group was Hertzog, who remained undisputed leader of the South Africa Party in the Orange Free State. Tensions within the South Africa Party led to a split in 1912. After a speech in which Hertzog had maintained that the two white groups should develop separately and that power in South Africa should be exclusively in the hands of true Afrikaners, he was turned out of the Cabinet. The following year Hertzog and his supporters formed the National Party.

THE ANC

The year 1912 which saw the split within the South Africa Party's ranks also saw the foundation of the first continuing national African political organization. In that year the South African Native National Congress, later renamed the African National Congress (ANC), was born. The ANC has the longest record of continuous political activity of any African nationalist movement in South Africa. Its membership was at first very restricted, including mainly educated professional men and chiefs, and it initially made very limited demands, aiming mainly at gaining social and political acceptance for the African élite within the structure of white-dominated society. It sought to follow the road of moderate constitutional action, and its first meeting was marked by fervent singing of "God save the King". The year after its foundation, however, the African National Congress was faced with a major issue.

One of the most important steps taken by the Union government before the First World War was the Natives Land Act of 1913. It aimed to consolidate white possession of land in South Africa outside the areas delimited as African Reserves. Under the Act Africans were denied the right to purchase land in white areas and the system under which Africans in many areas had been allowed to continue living on white-owned lands as share-croppers or rent-paying tenants was outlawed. Africans were evicted on a massive scale from white-owned lands, especially in the Orange Free State. Loss of their homes frequently involved loss of stock as they wandered helplessly in search of somewhere to pasture them. Many families were reduced to destitution. The African National Congress protested at the Act and its consequences, and sent a deputation to petition the King. In spite of a most eloquent appeal to the conscience made in Solomon Plaatje's *Native Life in South Africa*, its effects were in vain.

The years 1913–14 also saw an important and partially successful struggle by the Indian population of South Africa against the discriminatory conditions to which they were subjected. A young Indian lawyer, Gandhi, took the lead in organizing a passive resistance campaign. It was in this connexion that he developed his doctrine of passive resistance, *Satyaghra*, later to be employed on a much larger scale in India itself. The movement succeeded in winning some concessions from the South African authorities, though not a fundamental change of the position. The example of the Indian passive resistance idea was, however, to serve as an inspiration for later protest movements in South Africa.

THE FIRST WORLD WAR AND THE DEPRESSION

The outbreak of the First World War and South Africa's active participation on the side of Britain and against Germany placed a heavy strain on the loyalties of many Afrikaners. A half-hearted and ill-organized rebellion in 1914 was swiftly stamped out and South African troops captured German South West Africa, participated in the conquest of German East Africa (Tanganyika), and served in Europe itself. In spite of the collapse of the rebellion the spirit which lay behind it was very much alive and tended to grow stronger as the war went on. The Nationalist Party, however, increased its strength in the rural areas of the Orange Free State and Transvaal, and in some parts of the Cape. It clung to its narrow concept of the Afrikaner nation, persisting in opposition to South Africa's participation in the war and when it was over petitioning the League of Nations for the re-establishment of the Boer Republics.

More important than the world war in determining the development of South African society was the economic depression which followed the immediate post-war boom. As prices fell, large numbers of weaker and less efficient farmers became insolvent and were forced to leave the land for the towns just as opportunities for employment there were contracting. For a section of the white population the slump greatly exacerbated the consequences of the ending of the frontier period in South African history. With the establishment of fixed frontiers the process of expanding the area of white settlement by trekking to new lands as population increased was brought virtually to an end. The only alternative was either a decrease in the size of farms, which tended to reduce them below the margin of economic viability, or a move to the towns. The Afrikaans-speaking section of the white population, who formed the great bulk of the white rural population, and whose educational and cultural background left them less well equipped to cope with the complexities of the modern world, were the most severely affected by the depression. As they moved into the towns they entered a sphere dominated by English language and culture, where jobs were few and where their rural skills, *mores* and values were largely irrelevant. The situation generated a bitter nationalist spirit and a determination on the part of the Afrikaner to use political power to save himself from his economic difficulties and to force the dominant groups in the urban centres to respect his language and culture.

The onset of the depression brought into the open a new form of racial conflict which had been temporarily masked in the period of prosperity. In the early days of industrial (predominantly mining) development in South Africa there existed no African labour force with modern industrial skills. Skilled work in the mines was thus performed by whites, most of whom came from outside South Africa. Because of their scarcity and their monopoly of industrial skills they were able to demand higher rates of pay than were paid for comparable jobs in most other industrial countries. Unskilled work on the other hand was performed by non-whites at wages lower than in most other countries. The labour hierarchy in the mines with its highly paid, exclusively white, upper segment, separated by a large economic gap from the mass of lowly paid, black, unskilled workers, mirrored the general pattern of race relations in society at large.

When Chinese workers temporarily supplemented Africans after the Anglo-Boer War, white skilled workers were able to entrench their position by securing legislation prohibiting the employment of non-Europeans in certain categories of work. Other categories were protected for whites by convention. Shortly after the end of the world war white workers succeeded in getting the mine owners to agree to a standstill arrangement under which whites would retain a monopoly of all the jobs which were reserved to them at the time. As prices fell, however, mine owners were no longer prepared to continue this arrangement. The Chamber of Mines preferred to do away with the standstill agreement and the white workers, caught between the aspirations of the African workers and the interests of the mine owners, reacted desperately. A series of strikes culminated in open rebellion in 1922, during which the white workers seized control of the Rand for a few days. Smuts, however, rushed troops to the scene and after some fighting the Rand rebellion was suppressed. Defeated militarily, the white workers turned to political action through the Labour Party. An alliance was now forged between the Labour Party and the Nationalist Party representing the more conservative farmers. It was a natural alliance of interest. The white workers wished to preserve the racial stratification within the industrial labour hierarchy, while the farmers wanted to keep cheap labour on the land and to preserve the system of racial stratification of society in general, on which the maintenance of their increasingly archaic, semi-feudal farming system depended. Both groups disliked and feared English and Jewish big business, which dominated the towns and seemed to threaten their economic interests, social status and culture. As the constitution excluded the great majority of Africans from the vote, this "populist" alliance was able to gain a parliamentary majority in the 1924 election.

NATIONALIST-LABOUR GOVERNMENT

The pact-government, led by Hertzog, was faced with the problem of checking the pauperization of a substantial section of the white population. Two lines of action were followed simultaneously: to increase the total urban employment available and to preserve a greater proportion of this total for whites only. South Africa was launched on a path which would lead it away from exclusive dependence on mining and farming to become a major centre of manufacturing industry. At the same time a policy of protecting white employment from African competition by reserving categories of employment for whites only was vigorously pursued. Africans were even removed from employment in some areas and replaced by whites. This was particularly marked in the state-owned railway system. This line of action went with a general policy of increased segregation, intended to preserve South Africa as a white man's country. The African population was to be restricted as far as possible to the reserves. The towns were to be preserved for the white man. White political control over South Africa's destiny was to be strengthened by abolishing the right of Africans to vote at the Cape.

Thus the pact-government laid the foundations and sketched the outlines of the policy which has later come to be known as *apartheid*. The pact-government failed, however, to secure the necessary two-thirds majority needed to remove African voters from the Cape voters roll. In 1929 it went to the country on an openly racialist platform, and the "black peril" election of 1929 returned the alliance to power. By this time, however, some leaders of the Labour Party under the influence of socialist ideas were changing their attitudes on racial matters. They began to see African workers as part of the working class rather than simply as a threat to the living standards and status of white workers. This change in attitude was not shared to any great extent by Labour voters and, as the Party moved to the left, so the white workers, whose composition was becoming increasingly Afrikaans-speaking, tended to transfer their votes to the Nationalist Party. After 1929 the Labour Party ceased to be a major political force.

Soon after the "black peril" election South Africa was hit by the consequences of the slump which followed the Wall Street crash of 1930. The government's attempt to cling to the gold standard made matters worse. The Nationalist Party, which still found itself unable to alter the entrenched clause protecting African voting rights at the Cape, saw its popularity dwindle. The idea of a coalition with the South Africa Party gained ground. In March 1933 the coalition was brought about, and after a resounding victorious election later in the year the two parties fused in 1934 to found the United Party. Hertzog, who remained Prime Minister, was then able with the aid of Smuts to alter the entrenched clause protecting non-white voting rights. Africans were now denied the right to register as voters in the Cape and given a much less valuable form of separate representation. The rights of Euro-African (Coloured) voters were not, however, removed from the roll at this time.

ACTIVITIES OF THE ANC AND ICU

The economic circumstances which afflicted the poorer sections of the white community in the period between the world wars weighed much more heavily still on the mass of the African population. Apart from the inevitable sufferings of the poorest section of the community in a period of depression, they were faced with increasing discrimination in favour of the poor white. The African response, like that of the whites, was to attempt through organization and political and economic action to bring pressure on the authorities to alleviate their plight. The African Nationalist Congress reached an early high point in 1919–20 when it launched a campaign against the regulations requiring African males to carry passes. These documents, which served both as means of identification and as permits authorizing an African to live in a particular place, were (and still are) a major means by which the movement of Africans could be (and are) controlled in the interest of the whites. Of all the regulations to which Africans have been subject in South Africa, those associated with the pass system involve the greatest degree of personal humiliation and suffering. In response to the ANC campaign hundreds of Africans took part in a peaceful campaign of protest, publicly burning their passes as an expression of their rejection of the hated system. The movement, however, was met by severe repressive measures and fairly speedily crushed.

Another organization, the Industrial and Commercial Union (ICU), founded by a Malawian, Clements Kadalie, in 1919 then became for a time the most powerful mouthpiece of African opinion. The ICU grew to really massive proportions in the period of the first pact-government administration and reached its high point in 1928. Though normally a form of trade union organization and conducting much of its activity on the economic front, the ICU looked beyond the mere improvement of the economic lot of its members within the existing social system. It was the first African political organization to acquire the dimensions of a true mass movement and it extended its influence outside South Africa to Southern Rhodesia. The mass nature of the organization, which made its plans and activities public knowledge, and the overwhelming power of the white-controlled state apparatus made full revolutionary activity impossible. The lack of any lever in the political system which could be used to extort concessions meant that constitutional action could yield no major advances. Frustration led to a series of splits, and the ICU collapsed even more rapidly than it had risen, leaving the ANC once more the main vehicle of African aspirations.

THE UNITED PARTY AND THE "PURIFIED" NATIONALISTS

The fusion of the Nationalist and South Africa Parties to form the United Party was not acceptable to a small group of extreme nationalists led by Daniel Malan. In July 1934 they broke away to form the "Purified" Nationalist Party, now known simply as the Nationalist Party. The group was tiny in Parliament but had considerable support in the country at large, as it expressed the bitter nationalist feeling born of the Afrikaner sense of disinheritance in the new industrial society.

Malan was a member of the *Broderbond*, an extremist secret society formed in 1918 to fight for the Afrikaner language and culture and for political power for true Afrikaners. His extreme nationalist group was strengthened by the strains resulting from the rise of Nazi Germany and the growing tensions which preceded the outbreak of the Second World War. The Nazi idea of a master race and the concern with racial purity appealed to some white South Africans. In 1938 the celebrations marking the opening of the Voortrekker memorial in Pretoria raised nationalist emotion to a new pitch. Two new Afrikaner organizations were formed. The *Reddingdaadsbond* was an economic organization formed with the object of securing Afrikaner participation in the ownership and control of industry. The *Ossewa brandwag* was a semi-secret organization, influenced by Nazi ideas and organized on para-military lines, to preserve the spirit of the great trek and win political power for the Afrikaners.

The outbreak of war in 1939 found white South Africans deeply divided. These divisions were reflected in Parliament, where a large section of the United Party headed by Hertzog wanted a policy of neutrality, while Smuts and another section of the Party favoured going into the war on the British side. Smuts won a narrow majority for his view, and South Africa entered the war, but the United Party split. Hertzog went into opposition alongside the purified nationalists. One of his colleagues, Oswald Pirow, who had been Minister of Defence before the war, went further and formed the New Order to fight for an Afrikaner Republic on Nazi lines.

During the Second World War South Africans of all races served on many fronts, notably in the campaign to liberate Ethiopia in the north African desert campaigns and Italy. Non-white South Africans were denied the right to bear arms and restricted to non-combatant though often equally dangerous roles. During the war pressure on manpower resources necessitated a more efficient use of labour, and the industrial colour bar was modified to allow non-whites into some categories of employment previously reserved for whites. Under the impact of war the interdependence of South Africa's different racial groups could not be ignored and rather more liberal attitudes to racial matters began to be expressed in the ruling circles of the United Party.

The opposition, on the other hand, became even more extreme in its attitudes, and the nationalists, having emerged as the main leaders of extreme Afrikaner nationalism, began to systematize their attitude to racial matters in terms of *apartheid*.

APARTHEID

Apartheid is an amalgam of traditional South African practice, racial superiority, Calvinist theology and a certain amount of paternalist philanthropy. The word itself means "separateness". Every race, according to the doctrine, has a unique destiny of its own and a unique cultural contribution to make to the world. Different races must therefore be kept separate and allowed to develop along their own lines. Contact between different races which might have the result of contaminating the purity of racial culture must be reduced to the absolute minimum. Though primarily concerned with maintaining the segregation of the main racial groups, *apartheid* thinkers carry the principle of segregation considerably further than this. Thus they argue not merely that Africans as a racial group should be kept separate from whites, but that different African ethnic groups each have their own unique culture and should as far as possible be kept separate from one another. Within the white group the idea of an exclusive community of true Afrikaners which should be preserved from contamination by English language and culture remains significant.

The theory requires that each racial group should have part of South Africa as a homeland in which it can develop its own culture along its own lines. In the case of the African population the development of the existing reserves with some enlargement as national homelands for the different African ethnic groups has always been projected. Among supporters of *apartheid* there has always been a difference of opinion between those who regard the doctrine merely as a way of systematizing policies aimed at the preservation of white supremacy (*baaskap*) and those more theoretically and idealistically inclined who have a genuine belief in positive *apartheid*. The latter group believes in the ultimate ideal of territorial separation and the development of African homelands into African states, which might eventually even be given full independence. In reality the differences between these points of view, though significant, are not of fundamental importance. The areas contemplated as homelands for the great majority of the total population of South Africa amount to about 12 per cent of the total land area. They do not include any of the major known deposits of mineral wealth or any major industrial centres. They do not have any major port. Apart from the Transkeian areas, which form a consolidated block with closely neighbouring Lesotho, most of the projected homelands are scattered isolated enclaves within white South Africa. They can never support the whole African population. Even if granted full independence, they can be no more than labour reserve areas for the white-dominated parts of the country.

As South Africa approached the general election of 1948, the United Party appeared to be in an unassailable position. The election was fought by the Nationalist Party on the issue of race relations, but the United Party failed to produce any coherent alternative to the apparently clear and definite concept of *apartheid*. To everyone's surprise, not least their own, the Nationalists won a small majority and Daniel Malan was able to form a government. In the 1948 election the Nationalists gained a parliamentary majority on the basis of a minority of the votes. They were helped to power by the weighting in favour of rural constituencies provided for in the Union constitution, and even then they probably owed their majority as much to the promise of white bread as to the attractions of their *apartheid* doctrines. It might have seemed reasonable at the time to expect that their victory would be ephemeral. It has not proved to be so. The Nationalists have remained in power ever since, steadily increasing their majority in each election held between 1948 until 1970. They achieved the culmination of their nationalist aspirations when, after winning a referendum in 1960, they made South Africa a Republic.

The maintenance and consolidation of Nationalist power has been no accident but arises from the logic of the South African situation. That society had developed a system of social and economic stratification along lines of colour in its agrarian period. The white segment of society, which occupied a privileged position, inevitably struggled to preserve that system of stratification as it came to be increasingly threatened by the consequences of industrial growth. The doctrine of *apartheid* systematizes a programme for the preservation of the traditional order in an extreme and clear-cut form which appeals directly to those sections of the white population who feel themselves threatened by any change, however gradual. *Apartheid* is the systematic expression of the interests of that "populist" alliance of back-veld farmers and white workers which first emerged at the time of the Nationalist-Labour pact. Once the Nationalists were in power the implementation of *apartheid* policies exacerbated tensions within society, increasing fear of the African majority on the part of the whites and strengthening their preference for a tough government with an apparent solution to the racial problem. The increasing strength of the governing party between 1948 and 1970 was paralleled by the decline of opposition within the white community. The United Party, the main opposition group in Parliament, was unable to advance any real alternative to *apartheid*. Its electoral support depended on the English-speaking voters and some sections of the Afrikaans-speaking population who for a variety of historical and other reasons preserved their loyalty to it. They shared with Nationalist Party voters a determination to preserve white political supremacy and the traditional pattern of social segregation. In so far as capitalist influence has been stronger in the United Party, however, it has favoured a modification of racial stratification on the economic front to allow more efficient use of labour. So far as the United Party has had a policy on racial matters, therefore, it has been one of economic integration within the existing system of white political control and social segregation. It is a policy which appears to threaten the vital interests of white workers in favour of more thorough-going and efficient capitalist exploitation of labour resources.

THE IMPLEMENTATION OF APARTHEID

The implementation of *apartheid* after 1948 has followed the main lines implicit in the policy itself. Action to increase segregation in public places and on

trains, buses and other forms of transport was one of the first to be taken up and has been constantly pursued ever since, together with other measures aimed at reducing and ideally abolishing social, cultural and even religious association of persons of different races.

Residential segregation in urban areas has been systematically pursued through the implementation of the Group Areas Act, which provides for the designation of residential areas for occupation by a particular racial group only. Members of other racial groups who live there then have to sell their property and move to other areas designated for them.

Control over non-white migration to the towns has been progressively tightened up by measures which subject non-whites to great hardships and indignities, contributing to the break up of families and other social evils. Radical changes in non-white education were initiated by the Bantu Education Act (1953), which ended the older unified system of education, placed African education under strict governmental control and aimed to ensure that Africans would not be educated for positions in society that they were not to be allowed to hold. This development was followed in 1959 by the Separate Universities Act, which denied non-whites the right of access to those universities that had previously admitted them along with whites. It decreed the establishment of a series of separate racial universities and tribal colleges, all under strict government supervision and control.

As measures aimed at increasing and strengthening segregation within the white occupied areas of South Africa have been completed and reinforced, and as South Africa has been increasingly criticized by world opinion for its policies, the emphasis has shifted slightly in favour of the so-called "positive" aspects of *apartheid*. This is an attempt both to justify South African policies to humanitarian world opinion and to provide a safety valve for African political aspirations in a form which will not threaten white political and economic supremacy in South Africa as a whole. The development has coincided with the complete suppression of African political activity in the white-occupied areas of the country. Positive *apartheid* has been carried furthest in the Transkei, which in 1963 was given internal self-government. Its constitution, however, allotted 64 of the 109 seats in the legislature to chiefs, who are appointed by the South African President. In the 1963 election 38 of the 45 elected members supported Victor Poto, who stood for multi-racial development in the Transkei, but Kaizer Matanzima, whom the Republican government supported, became Prime Minister. Moreover, because of its economic weakness, the Transkei is dependent on the Republican government for the financing of the greater part of its budget.

As late as January 1971 only the Transkei had a Legislative Assembly. Since then however Legislative Assemblies have been authorized in the Ciskei, Bophuthatswana, Lebowa (North Sotho), Gazankulu (Machangana), Venda, Basotho Quaqwa and KwaZulu (Zululand) homelands.

The fact that behind the rhetoric the primary

purpose of *apartheid* is to maintain the traditional economic and social system of white South Africa, rather than as the theory implies to divide up the country into a number of economically and politically independent states, is clearly revealed by the Nationalist government's reaction to the recommendations of its own Commission. The Commission on the Socio-Economic Development of the Bantu areas set up in 1950 under the chairmanship of Professor F. Tomlinson worked on the assumption that the intention of *apartheid* was indeed the ultimate territorial separation of the races in economically autonomous societies. Its most optimistic estimate was that by the end of the century the homelands might accommodate about 70 per cent of the African population. This was however based on figures for the growth of African population which the Commission itself felt to be improbably conservative. If alternative figures regarded as more probable by the Commission were accepted the homelands would accommodate less than 60 per cent of the African population by the year 2,000 and the number remaining in the white areas would still be greater than that of all other racial groups in those areas. Even to achieve this degree of territorial segregation however the Commission stressed the need for substantial industrialization of the homelands. It recommended that they be opened to European capital investment and estimated that in the first 10 years the Government would have to spend over £104 million on development. In actual fact government expenditure between 1956 and 1961 amounted to only £7.9 million. The recommendation that European capital be allowed into the homelands was not accepted. Instead a Bantu Investment Corporation was set up with an initial capital of £500,000, a truly derisory figure in view of the massive industrial investment required. In more recent years with the swing in favour of "positive *apartheid*" in Nationalist thinking, expenditure on the Bantustans has been very heavily increased. For example the estimates of the Department of Bantu Administration for 1970/71 included R 39.8 million for development works by the South African Bantu Trust and in mid-1970 the Bantu Investment Corporation announced a plan to invest R 86 million over 5 years. Closer examination however shows that a very large proportion of the development expenditure on the Bantustans is on housing and the development of townships rather than on creating a potentially autonomous industrial system. It is thus hardly surprising that only a tiny fraction of the 50,000 jobs outside the agricultural sector which the Tomlinson Commission recommended should be created annually has in fact been created. Instead of a programme of full-scale industrialization of the homelands including the development of heavy industry as suggested by the Tomlinson Commission the Government has laid its main emphasis on the development of Border industries. The idea of Border industries indeed expresses in the clearest possible form the underlying meaning of *apartheid*. The idea is to build industries in white areas near the borders of the homelands and use African labour which resides in the homelands but comes into the white areas to work. The white eco-nomy will thus continue to exploit African labour, but be relieved of much of the social cost and of the need to grant social or political rights to the workers whose aspirations in these regards must be fulfilled within the economically powerless homelands.

Though *apartheid* is a conservative doctrine aimed at preventing South African society evolving away from the traditional pattern of stratification based on race, its dogmatic application as a systematic theory to a situation which had grown up piecemeal and subject to many local variations has involved very extensive and severe disruptions of established patterns of life, as well as the hardships arising from the attempt to freeze society in an archaic mould at a time of rapid economic transformation. The implementation of *apartheid* has thus created grave tensions in society and aroused bitter opposition from both non-European peoples and whites.

In addition, the government has been faced in some cases with the reluctance of local councils and its own officials to implement measures which involve great hardship and disruption. To enforce its measures, therefore, the South African government has greatly extended its control over all sections of the population and ruthlessly stamped on all forms of opposition. Starting with the Suppression of Communism Act in 1950, subsequently strengthened by amendments aimed at excluding the right of the courts to protect individual rights, the government has created the legal basis for the exercise of police-state control over its citizens. The provision for the detention of suspects for periods of 90 days without trial, with the possibility of indefinite prolongation by further 90-day periods is simply the logical development of this trend. Security controls are now centralized under the recently created Bureau of State Security (BOSS).

OPPOSITION TO APARTHEID

The adoption and implementation of *apartheid* by the South African government naturally brought strong opposition from African nationalism, and from both white and non-white world opinion. After the collapse of the ICU, the ANC in the 1930s greatly broadened its membership and evolved away from a narrow élite organization towards a truly mass movement. In the 1940s a more radical Youth Wing was formed which ultimately gained control of the ANC organization and pressed it in the direction of radical mass action. In April 1952 the African National Congress and the South African Indian Congress launched a massive campaign of passive resistance to unjust laws which proved one of the most significant public demonstrations ever conducted by non-whites in South Africa. Africans, Indians, Eurafricans and some whites, including the son of a previous Governor-General, openly broke *apartheid* laws and allowed themselves to be arrested.

The government responded by imprisoning over 8,000 people, and sentences of whipping were widely imposed. In October 1952 long-repressed racial feeling broke out in Port Elizabeth and East London in violent riots. The government blamed them on the passive resistance campaign. The ANC asked for an enquiry but the government refused. Emergency legislation was rushed through and the defiance campaign was effectively crushed.

The co-operation in opposition to *apartheid* by different racial groups in the defiance campaign was taken a stage further when in 1955 the African National Congress, South African Indian Congress, the Coloured Peoples Political Organisation and the White Congress of Democrats met in Kliptown near Johannesburg and drew up the Freedom Charter laying down the basic principles for a non-racial, democratic South Africa. In December 1956 the government arrested 156 members of the movement belonging to all racial groups. They were charged with plotting the violent overthrow of the state. The Treason Trial dragged on till 1961, when it finally ended with the acquittal of all the accused. In the meantime the ANC was deprived of most of its leadership, and in 1958 a number of its supporters who felt that the policy of co-operating with the Congresses representing other racial groups was weakening the resistance struggle broke away to form the Pan-Africanist Congress (PAC). Under the leadership of Robert Sobukwe, however, the PAC developed a policy on racial matters little different from that of the ANC.

African resistance to aspects of *apartheid* was not confined to nation-wide protests organized by the nationalist movements. In 1950 violence broke out in the African reserve of Witzieshoek in protest at a Government cattle culling drive. In 1957 in the Morice district an upheaval provoked by the attempt to force women (previously immune from this regulation) to carry pass books was savagely repressed. In 1958 riots in villages in Sekhukhuneland were equally severely put down. On the economic front one of the most significant examples of African mass action took place in 1957 when a boycott of municipal buses took place on the Rand in protest at a rise in prices. Thousands of Africans walked to work over long distances. In spite of attempts by the authorities to break the boycott it was ultimately successful. The price was restored to its previous level. In 1960 violent riots broke out at Cato Manor in Durban and nine policemen were killed.

The most important local resistance movement since the Bambata Rebellion of 1906 broke out in East Pondoland in 1960. It was aimed against the imposition of Bantu authorities, a stage in the government's plans for implementing positive *apartheid*. This move, which would greatly strengthen the hands of pro-government chiefs, was deeply resented. A popular movement headed by a Mountain Committee (so named on account of the mass meetings held in the mountains) began in East Pondoland and spread to the rest of the Pondo country. Using the sanction of hut burning against African opponents and government collaborators and the weapon of boycott against white traders who gave information about its activities, the movement established a considerable measure of control over most of Pondoland. The government sealed off the area from the rest of the country and brought in troops, armoured cars and spotter planes. A state of emergency was proclaimed, and the revolt was eventually stamped out.

In March 1960 police opened fire on an unarmed crowd which had gathered around the police station at Sharpeville in response to a PAC anti-pass campaign. Sixty-seven Africans were killed, many shot in the back as they fled. Demonstrations against the killings took place in many parts of South Africa and in other parts of the world. The government response was to arrest Sobukwe, who subsequently served a long term of imprisonment, and to ban the African National Congress and the Pan-Africanist Congress. All the legal means of political activity open to Africans were thus removed.

The Sharpeville shootings and the banning of African political organizations constitute a crucial turning point in South African history. They finally convinced non-white political leaders and their sympathizers that peaceful methods offered no hope of progress, and that political and social change can only be brought about by violence. In 1961 and 1962 two secret organizations "Umkhonto we Sizwe" and "Poqo" came into existence with the object of achieving political change through the sabotage of white property. With the banning of African political parties some of their leaders went underground, the best known being Nelson Mandela. Arrested at last, he was tried with a number of others at Rivonia in 1963. Mandela, who used the trial to pronounce a formidable indictment of the South African government and its repressive policies, was sentenced to life imprisonment. African leaders like Mandela accepted the necessity for violence with great reluctance and have persisted in attempting to avoid actions involving attacks or danger to persons. The fact remains, however, that after Sharpeville conflict between the races has begun to move in the direction of organized violence, and unless some substantial change takes place within the South African system for other reasons, violence is bound to escalate, however gradually. Since Sharpeville, indeed, increasing numbers of young men have left the country for training in the tactics of guerrilla warfare and subversion. They have made repeated attempts to fight their way back into the country and raise insurrection, but the control of the South African authorities appears to be nearly perfect. It can be anticipated, however, that the nationalist groups will in return adopt increasingly sophisticated methods of infiltration and subversion. The simultaneous explosion of devices which showered African nationalist leaflets into the air in a number of South African cities in September 1970 indicates that the surface calm may belie the underlying reality.

SOUTH AFRICA AND THE WORLD

The development and implementation of *apartheid* has provoked the indignation of public opinion all over the world. Pressure on South Africa from the international community has increased as the new nations, largely non-white in population and previously subject to colonialism, have gained independence and have begun to establish a significant position for themselves in the world community. The decolonization of Africa, the emergence of independent African states on the world scene and the achievement of a measure of African unity, however limited, through the Organization of African Unity (OAU) have greatly increased these pressures. In 1961, largely through the opposition of new leaders like Julius Nyerere of Tanganyika to her racist policies, South Africa was forced to withdraw her application to remain in the Commonwealth after she had become a republic. (The white electorate had approved the change of status in a referendum in October 1960). It has found itself increasingly ostracized, notably in the realm of sport, and excluded from many international organizations. International pressure has been brought to bear on South Africa through the United Nations, which has provided the international forum for the new nations. Much of this pressure has been concentrated on South Africa's legal Achilles heel, its right to continue the administration of the former German colony of South West Africa (Namibia), placed under South African administration as a mandated territory by the League of Nations after the First World War.

In response South Africa has been able to rely on the fact that the large financial investment by western powers in her economy and the important market she provides for their manufactures prevents moral disapproval from expressing itself in any seriously damaging action. She has also benefited from her strategic position in the geopolitical struggle between east and west (hence the U.K.'s presence in the Simonstown naval base); and the western powers have thus blocked effective enforcement of UN decisions on Namibia. The development of the war in Angola and Mozambique, Rhodesia's U.D.I. and the intrusions of African nationalist guerrillas have drawn South Africa into increasing involvement economically and militarily in the areas which form part of her economic hinterland and valuable buffer-zones of front-line defence. Increasingly, southern Africa is becoming one economic, social and military complex with South Africa as its nucleus.

ECONOMIC DEVELOPMENTS

The implementation of *apartheid* in conditions of continuing rapid economic change and industrial expansion gives rise to many contradictions. Sheer scarcity of skilled manpower has led to non-whites making considerable advances in the labour hierarchy in spite of official opposition. This has even happened on the South African Railways, the traditional citadel of white-protected labour. Non-white purchasing power has become an increasingly important element in the economy. The spread of mechanization to the agricultural economy and the increasing urbanization of the rural Afrikaner has been eroding one of the main bases of *apartheid*. The expansion of the economy has gone a long way towards resolving the problem of white pauperization. The interests of white labour no longer consist simply in protecting categories of employment from non-white competition.

In some areas at least white workers, in common with management, could gain from a more liberal policy which would ease manpower bottlenecks and make possible increased production, which in turn would allow for wage increases. Increasingly the stratification which *apartheid* seeks to defend is ceasing to correspond with the economic facts. There are contradictions within the aims of *apartheid* itself. The development of the African homelands as self-governing Bantustans, however limited their real autonomy may be, involves allowing Africans in these areas to hold positions of responsibility carrying financial reward and status higher than that of many whites, a development which directly contradicts the basic aim of maintaining the horizontal stratification of society in racial status groups. South Africa's involvement in world trade, essential to the development of its industrial economy, poses further problems in a world where non-white nations are becoming increasingly important in the economic sphere.

These problems reveal themselves most forcibly in South Africa's developing relations with independent African nations. The independence of the enclave states of Lesotho, Botswana and Swaziland has raised difficult issues. South African industry needs labour from these areas and markets in them for manufactured goods. Co-operation in projects of economic development with these states is highly desirable in other ways, as notably in the case of Lesotho over control of the Orange River. Political co-operation and goodwill between South Africa and these states is important, if they are to be prevented from becoming centres of freedom-fighting activity. Maintenance of such relations, however, requires that the political leaders of these states must be received as important dignitaries and given the status, facilities and treatment normally reserved in South Africa for whites only.

"VERLIGTE" POLICIES

South Africa's industrial expansion and her increasing dependence on the export of manufactured goods rather than primary products creates an imperative need to expand markets for her produce outside her frontiers. The developing nations of Africa constitute the most hopeful area for such expansion, as well as a tempting field for the investment of South African capital. South Africa, moreover, has always relied on importing labour from beyond her frontiers. Without this, internal labour costs would have to rise very much more rapidly than they do at present and the resulting change in the economic position of Africans would shake the whole structure of *apartheid*. These are the reasons behind the so-called "outwardgoing" policy increasingly adopted in the latter years of Verwoerd (who was assassinated in 1966) and greatly expanded under Vorster. This policy of expanding economic relations with other nations and with African nations in particular has so far revealed itself most spectacularly in South Africa's relationships with Malawi. In return South Africa has had to accord Malawian delegations a status which amounts virtually to that of honorary whites.

Tensions amongst the advocates of *apartheid* produced by these contradictions led to the split between the *Verkrampte* and *Verligte* sections of the Nationalist Party in anticipation of the 1970 general election. In these elections the *Verkrampte* group, who denounced all modifications of *apartheid* in the interest of an outward-looking policy in Africa and the world, were electorally wiped out. For the first time also the United Party was able to make gains at the Nationalist Party's expense. The South African white electorate thus appears to be convinced that it can most successfully maintain the reality of *apartheid* at home by outward economic expansion, even at the cost of token modifications of the system for a few non-whites from outside the national boundaries.

In the last two years however contradictions and tensions within the policy of *apartheid* have become increasingly apparent. A racially exclusivist Black Power movement, the natural response to *apartheid*, has emerged amongst African, Asian and Coloured students and resulted in clashes with the authorities. This in turn sparked off massive demonstrations of sympathy by white students at English-speaking universities in face of severe police repression, revealing the deep uneasiness of conscience especially among some younger whites which lies beneath the political surface. African leaders in the Bantustans have begun to find their feet and express themselves in increasingly trenchant terms. From the Transkei has come the demand for the incorporation of enclaves of white settlement and for the expansion of frontiers to link up with the Ciskei and to incorporate the port of East London. Bantustan leaders have travelled

outside South Africa to Malawi and to Western Europe. Led most vocally by Chief Buthelezi of KwaZulu they have been demanding not only accelerated progress towards full political independence but the ending of social and economic discrimination in South Africa as a whole. Far from providing a harmless safety value for African political aspirations, and thus helping to preserve the traditional stratification of society in the rest of South Africa, the Bantustans are beginning to emerge as increasingly important sources of pressure for a radical transformation of the white South African system. Caught up in the dilemmas of its own policies and fearing the erosion of its political support in favour of the United Party on the one hand and the *Verkramptes* on the other, government actions have become increasingly erratic and inconsistent. On the one hand a definite promise has been made to grant full political independence as sovereign states to the Bantustans within a decade. On the other Bantustan leaders have been warned to limit their travels and curb their criticisms of South African society. Student protests have been put down with great severity and in a recent by-election at Oudtshoorn the Nationalist Party reverted to a narrowly reactionary and anti-English Afrikaner nationalism. Yet at the same time there is no indication that the outward-looking policy with its inevitable implications for the traditional pattern of white South African life is being abandoned or seriously revised. South Africa thus appears to be drifting aimlessly as structural changes, hastened by the very policy which aimed to prevent them, erode the bases on which white society and its political and social value systems have rested.

ECONOMY

Leo Katzen

NATURAL RESOURCES

The Republic of South Africa covers an area of 471,445 square miles lying between latitudes 22° and 35° south. Its climate varies from "mediterranean" in the south-west to sub-tropical in the north-east but most of the country enjoys a temperate climate with summer rainfall. The diversity of the climate enables the production of a wide range of crops but largely because of inadequate and erratic rainfall only about 15 per cent of the land surface is suitable for arable farming. Topographic difficulty is the main factor limiting the extent of irrigation to less than 3,000 square miles. But the ambitious R 450 million Orange River Project, which is in the process of construction, is expected eventually to increase the total irrigated area by about 40 per cent. A much larger area of the country is suitable for animal husbandry but even here the carrying capacity of the land is fairly low by international standards. In spite of improvements in farming methods and conservation techniques in recent years, South Africa remains

a relatively poor crop-raising country which also imposes limits on animal husbandry, for which it is better suited. Nevertheless, because of a high degree of specialization, experience, advanced methods and considerable capital investment, certain branches of farming such as fruit and wool continue to make a substantial contribution to the economy and exports in particular.

South Africa's long coastline has few natural harbours, but close to her shores are some of the richest fishing areas in the world. In 1969 1,850,852 short tons of inshore pelagic fish were landed in the closely linked South African and South West African industry. The combined catch was the eighth largest in the world, and the industry is the world's second largest producer of fish meal after Peru. The products of the industry, fish meal and oil, canned fish, frozen rock lobster tails, fresh, smoked and frozen trawler fish, were valued at over R 100 million in 1970, 90 per cent of which was exported.

It is in mineral deposits, though, that South Africa's

greatest wealth lies. The discovery of first diamonds and then more importantly gold in the latter part of the nineteenth century was the basis of the country's modern economic development. A huge complex of heavy and light industry has grown up in the interior based initially upon the gold mining industry. South Africa has long been the world's largest gold producer (75 per cent of world output excluding U.S.S.R.) and reserves are such that she will continue to hold this position for the foreseeable future. But although gold still dominates mineral production, there are abundant deposits of nearly every important mineral in the country. The production of minerals other than gold has been steadily increasing in relative importance, accounting for 47 per cent of the total value of mining production of R 1,563 million in 1970. There are huge reserves of iron ore and coal (with a pit head price which is probably the lowest in the world). She is the largest producer in the western world of platinum and antimony; the world's second largest producer of asbestos, vermiculite and sillimanite; and a significant producer of uranium with the world's largest known deposits. The country's reserves of manganese, chrome, vermalite and fluorspar are also estimated to be the largest in the western world. In addition she is a large producer of copper, lead and zinc. Only two major mineral products—oil and bauxite—have not been found in economic quantities. Currently a large-scale search, encouraged by the government, is being conducted for oil with limited results to date.

POPULATION

According to the results of the May 1970 census the total population of South Africa was about 21.4 million. Its chief characteristic and one that dominates South African society is the great racial, linguistic and cultural heterogeneity of its people. The four broad groups making up the population are: (i) Africans (officially referred to as Bantu) who are members of the Bantu-speaking group of African tribes (15.2 million in 1970 and 70.1 per cent of the population); (ii) whites who are of European descent (3.8 million—17.8 per cent of the population); (iii) Coloureds who are of mixed racial origin (2 million—9.3 per cent of the population); (iv) Asians (mainly Indians) in the Natal province (0.6 million—2.8 per cent of the population). Within these four groups there is, however, further diversity. The Africans are made up of several tribes speaking a number of different Bantu languages. The most important are the Xhosa and Zulu of the Nguni language group and Tswana, Pedi and Southern Sotho of the Sotho group. The Whites are divided into an Afrikaans- and English-speaking group roughly in the ratio of 3 to 2. Although the vast majority of Coloureds speak Afrikaans there is considerable diversity of culture and religion among them. For instance a small sub-group of Malay descent are Moslems while the rest are mostly Christians. The Asians, mostly from India, are also divided between Moslems and Hindus speaking a variety of Indian languages.

Although the population has increased by more than three and a half times since 1911 (the year of the first full census—5,973,000 total population), the racial composition of the population has not altered very much. The percentage of whites has declined from 21.4 in 1911 to 17.8 in 1970 while that of each of the three non-white groups has risen. There are currently, however, considerable differences in the rates of natural increase of the different groups. In 1970 the natural increase in the white group was only 1.5 per cent compared with 2.3 per cent and 2.7 per cent in the Coloured and Asian groups respectively. On the other hand a fairly high rate of net immigration on the part of whites in recent years (35,845 in 1971) has boosted the overall increase of this group to an average annual rate of 2 per cent in the census period 1960–70 compared with 2.9 per cent for Coloureds and 2.6 per cent for Asians. The African population recorded the highest rate of increase averaging 3.2 per cent per annum compared with 1.9 per cent in the previous census period. In the absence of statistics of births and deaths for Africans, however, it is difficult to determine how much of this rise is due to a change in the rate of natural increase, because better census coverage and immigration (in the 1960 census 583,000 Africans were recorded as having been born outside South Africa) may also be factors of some importance. The overall growth rate of the total population was 3 per cent per annum, which is 0.5 per cent above the previous census period and the highest ever recorded in South Africa.

South Africa had a density of only 45 persons per square mile in 1970. This low figure is misleading because of unevenness in the distribution of population. Besides normal high densities in urban areas (52.1 per cent of the population in 1970), rural density is also high in the African reserves (only 13 per cent of the total area of South Africa with a density of 63 per square mile compared with 27 per square mile for the country as a whole in 1951). This is because of restrictions on their mobility and right to own land in other parts of the country. Density is below average in white rural areas and particularly low in large arid areas in the west.

The occupational distribution of the economically active population in 1960 was as follows: out of a total economically active population of 5,691,000 (36 per cent of the total population of 16,003,000), 1,698,000 were engaged in agriculture, forestry and fishing, (30 per cent of the economically active), 605,000 in mining (11 per cent), 679,000 in manufacturing (12 per cent), 279,000 in construction (5 per cent), 38,000 in electricity, gas and water (1 per cent), 458,000 in commerce (8 per cent), 215,000 in transport (4 per cent), 1,228,000 in services (21 per cent) and 493,000 unemployed or unspecified (9 per cent). Although the proportion of the population engaged in agriculture has steadily declined over the years, it still remains the largest sector of employment in the economy because of the large number of African peasants in the reserves, contrasting sharply with the relatively small contribution that it makes to the national income (11.1 per cent in 1960/61). This is the most important vestige of dualism in the economy, and it lingers because of the persistence of the migratory labour system and restrictions on the permanent entry of Africans into the modern economy.

NATIONAL INCOME

In the fifty years 1911/12 to 1961/62 net domestic product at current prices grew from R 266 million to R 5,036 million. Allowing for price increases and population growth real income per head more than doubled in this period averaging 1.8 per cent growth per annum. Growth in the 1960s was exceptionally high, rivalling that of Japan. Gross domestic product at current market prices more than doubled between 1960 and 1970 growing at an average rate of 8.9 per cent per annum. In real terms the rate of increase was 5.9 per cent and 2.9 per cent per capita per annum. In 1971 gross domestic product at market prices was R 13,607 million and gross national product R 13,127 million. This represented an increase in real terms of only 3.6 per cent over the previous year, however, because of a recession in the economy. Gross domestic product per capita in 1970 was R 576 (£296), which puts South Africa well ahead of other African countries (except Libya) in income per head, and in the ranks of the medium-developed countries in the world. Income is, however, very unevenly distributed in South Africa, as witnessed by the differential between skilled and unskilled wage rates which broadly reflect the income differences between whites and non-whites—mostly Africans. In manufacturing the wage differential is 6 to 1 rising to as much as 18 to 1 in mining (compared with the differential in North America and Western Europe ranging from 5 to 3 or 4).

The contribution to national income of the three main productive sectors—manufacturing, mining and agriculture—has changed markedly over the years. In 1911/12 mining was in the lead contributing 27.1 per cent of net domestic product, agriculture second with 17.4 per cent and manufacturing only 6.7 per cent. Manufacturing steadily increased its relative position overtaking mining as the leading sector during the Second World War. By 1963/64 (the latest year for which comparable statistics are available) manufacturing was well in the lead with 27.8 per cent of net domestic product, mining second with 12.6 per cent and agriculture only 9.2 per cent. The expansion of manufacturing from relative insignificance at the time of the formation of the Union of South Africa in 1910 to the largest sector is undoubtedly the most important structural change in the economy over the last 60 years.

INVESTMENT AND SAVING

From the discovery of diamonds and gold in the nineteenth century foreign investment played a vital role in developing these industries and the economy in general. By 1936 it was estimated that R 1,046 million had been invested in South Africa representing 43 per cent of total foreign investment in Africa. Another large wave of foreign investment associated with the Orange Free State goldfields took place after the Second World War but there was a slowing down after that with an actual outflow in the years 1959–64. Since 1965 foreign investment has again been positive. In 1970 total foreign liabilities of South Africa stood at R 5,818 million (of which R 3,371 million to the Sterling Area—mainly the United Kingdom). Foreign assets in that year (including gold reserves) were R 2,400 million—mainly in Rhodesia, Zambia and Malawi. Although the foreign stake in South Africa is still very considerable, ownership of South African assets has steadily passed to South African nationals. Whereas in 1917 over 85 per cent of gold mining dividends was paid out to foreigners, this had fallen to 27 per cent in 1963.

In 1971 gross domestic investment was R 4,008 million amounting to 29.5 per cent of gross domestic product at market prices. Three quarters of this unusually high level of capital formation was financed by gross domestic saving (R 3,032 million or 22.3 per cent of gross domestic product), R 737 million net capital inflow from abroad (a post-war record), and R 239 million from gold and other foreign reserves.

MANUFACTURING INDUSTRY

Unlike its counterparts in other parts of Africa, manufacturing industry is by far the largest sector of the South African economy measured in terms of contribution to G.D.P. It is also the fastest growing sector. In 1970 it contributed R 2,657 million to G.D.P. at factor cost, employing 1,189,000 (January 1970) people of all races (three-quarters of the work force non-white).

The mining industry, except for a limited number of industries servicing it, did not at first stimulate local manufacturing to any extent. The mining industry favoured cheap imports, so little protection was offered to local manufacturers. It was only in 1925 that an active policy of protecting local industry was first adopted. As a consequence industry grew significantly in the latter half of the 1920s, particularly in consumer goods production. But it also saw the foundation of heavy industry under state auspices with the establishment of the Iron and Steel Corporation of South Africa (ISCOR) in 1928. By 1939 net industrial output was double the 1929 level and during the Second World War industry overtook mining as the largest single sector with continued expansion in the post-war period. Industrial progress in the 1960s has been particularly rapid. Its contribution to G.D.P. at factor cost grew at an average annual rate of 10.2 per cent between 1961 and 1970. The physical volume of production grew at 8.5 per cent per annum from 1961 to 1970, while employment grew at 6.1 per cent per annum, indicating increases in productivity over the same period.

Industry is heavily concentrated in four industrial areas—southern Transvaal, western Cape, Durban-Pinetown, Port Elizabeth-Uitenhage—accounting for over 80 per cent of industrial net output and employment. Over half the country's industry is now located in the southern Transvaal alone (the area comprising Pretoria, Johannesburg, Reef towns and Vereeniging) and the tendency has been for this concentration to increase at the expense of the ports and rural areas. Largely to stem the flow of Africans to "white" industrial areas, the state has been attempting in recent years to decentralize industrial location by attracting industries to proclaimed border areas near African reserves. Financial assistance in the form of tax concessions, loans, reduced railway rates, exemptions from wage regulation, etc., have been granted to industrialists in these areas. Between 1960 and 1968, R314 million was directly invested in new secondary industry in border areas, involving the setting up of 135 new industrial concerns and expanding 74 existing ones. Employment in this period rose from 76,000 to 145,000, of whom 109,000 were Africans. But as yet this development has been largely confined to three areas all close to existing industrial areas: Rosslyn (north-west of Pretoria), Hammarsdale (near Durban-Pinetown) and Pietermaritzburg. On the other hand industrial development in the African reserves has been negligible to date. To remedy this situation the government decided in 1968 to permit white entrepreneurs and capital, hitherto prevented from investing in the reserves, limited rights of entry. In 1969 it was also decided to extend border area concessions to the reserves.

Brief mention can only be made of developments in some of the main classes of industry.

Metal Products and Engineering

This is the largest sector of industry, including basic metals, metal products, machinery and transport equipment, employing 396,000 workers with gross output valued at R 2,539 million in 1970. The steel industry is the most important branch of this sector with output of ingot steel exceeding 5 million tons in 1970, having grown at an average annual rate of 8 per cent in the last decade. The industry is dominated by the state-owned South African Iron and Steel Corporation (ISCOR) which supplied 65 per cent of the local market in 1970–71, and with its new steel-works at Newcastle in addition to older plants at Pretoria and Vanderbijl Park, plans to bring its annual capacity up to 10.5 million ingot tons by 1981–82. Because of favourable location, raw material and labour costs, and efficient scale of production, South African steel is among the cheapest in the world. Not only does it not need the protection it received before the war but it is now well placed to enter export markets. To this end ISCOR recently linked with Voest of Austria to convert ore from the Sishen area to steel semis for export to Europe.

The motor industry is another important branch of this sector which has grown rapidly since the first Ford assembly plant was established at Port Elizabeth in 1924 with an output of 13,000 vehicles. In 1970 the industry produced 298,000 vehicles (202,000 cars and 96,000 commercial vehicles) contributing about 7 per cent to G.D.P. The vast majority of cars now sold in South Africa contain at least 52 per cent local content by weight, thereby qualifying for special tariff rates as "locally manufactured" models. By 1976, to qualify for these rates,

local content has to reach 66 per cent, which will mean that engine blocks and body shells will have to be produced locally. But in common with this industry in other developing countries it faces the problem of rising costs with increasing local content because of the lack of economies of scale enjoyed in the major producing countries. This is further aggravated by an overproliferation of models (43 basic models and 146 variants in the next phase of local manufacture).

Food, Beverages and Tobacco

Industries processing local farm produce were among the first to develop in South Africa. While this sector has expanded over the years and contributes importantly to exports, its relative position has declined from 32 per cent of the net value of manufacturing output in 1925 to 17 per cent in 1963.

Clothing and Textiles

The clothing industry, already well established before the war, now supplies 90 per cent of local demand. In 1970, 115,000 clothing, knitwear and hosiery workers and 34,000 footwear workers produced a gross output of R 442 million. The textile industry is essentially a post-war development which now meets 60 per cent of the country's textile needs. A labour force of 83,000 produced a gross annual output of about R 388 million in 1970.

Chemicals

This industry had an early beginning with the manufacture of explosives for the gold mines. The Modderfontein factory near Johannesburg is now probably the world's largest privately owned explosives factory. Fertilizer production is a key branch of this industry. But the most important development in recent years was the establishment of Sasol, the state-owned oil-from-coal plant in the northern Orange Free State which began production in 1955. Based on cheap coal, it is the largest plant of its kind in the world producing 10 per cent of the country's petrol requirements. It has generated a large and growing chemical complex whose products to date include ammonium sulphate, tars, waxes, solvents, plastics, synthetic rubber and gas.

FARMING

Reference has already been made to the declining role of farming as a source of income in the South African economy. The vagaries of climate and unstable world prices are largely responsible for this. The effect of recurrent drought can be dramatically seen in the fluctuations in maize production—the staple food of the African population and most important single item in South African farming—from an output of 99.7 million bags in the 1967–68 season to 55 million bags in 1968–69 and 67.6 million bags in 1969–70 to a record expected crop of 112.5 million bags in 1971–72. Wool exports, which are second in importance after gold, fell by 30 per cent in 1970 to R 74.3 million compared with the previous year because of a fall in world prices. The low overall productivity of farming relative to other sectors is also reflected in the fact already referred to that, although employing about 30 per cent of the economically active population, it contributed only 8.4 per cent to G.D.P. in 1970. Very low yields on the part of large numbers of inefficient African subsistence farmers in the reserves is the main reason for this. But even white farmers, who are relatively efficient, have comparatively low yields by international standards. In maize farming, for example, yields per acre are only a quarter of those in the U.S.A.

Despite these problems agricultural products still figure prominently in South African exports. Depending on the size of crop a large percentage of the local production of wool, maize, sugar, groundnuts, tobacco, citrus and deciduous fruits is normally exported. In processed as well as unprocessed form, agricultural products account for about a third of total export earnings (excluding gold), with Britain as the main market.

MINING

Although having given way to manufacturing as the leading sector, mining is still of great importance in the economy, as it has been for the last hundred years. It is still expanding rapidly with an average annual increase of 5.8 per cent in the value of output and 4.6 per cent in physical volume in the 1960s, employing a total work force of 651,000 (587,000 Africans) in 1970. Gold mining still dominates the scene with a record output of 976.3 kilograms of gold in 1971 valued at R 893 million, employing 419,000 workers in 1968. Since the Second World War new gold mines in the Orange Free State, Far West Rand, Klerksdorp and Evander areas have not only replaced output from the worked out mines on the old Rand but have greatly increased total output. It is predicted, however, that barring new discoveries, gold output will begin to decline in the 1970s. Unless tonnage milled increases substantially, recent increases in the price of gold will not offset this decline because of the policy of the industry of lowering the grade of ore mined as the price rises. As mentioned before though, the production of other minerals has rapidly gained in importance since the war. Whereas in 1946 gold accounted for 80 per cent of mineral output, it had fallen to 56 per cent in 1969. There has been a great expansion in the output of uranium, platinum, nickel, copper, coal, antimony, diamonds, vanadium, asbestos, iron ore, fluorspar, chrome, manganese and limestone to name only the most important. These minerals also figure large in South Africa's exports amounting to R 347 million in 1971 excluding gold and diamonds. Together with gold and diamonds minerals account for over half of the country's exports. Increased iron ore exports to Japan, in particular, look promising for the future with the recent decision to build a new railway line from the high-grade ore Sishen area in the northern Cape to Saldanha Bay. By 1980 it is expected that 30 million tons per annum will be exported at a value of R 220 million.

TRANSPORT AND COMMUNICATIONS

With no navigable rivers the transport system is entirely dependent on its rail and road network, with air transport playing a small but increasing role. The state-owned railways covered 22,116 kilometres in 1971 (approximately a third of all the railway mileage in sub-Saharan Africa). 42,065 million ton miles of traffic and 552 million passenger journeys were carried in 1971. 21,241 vessels called at South African and South West African ports in 1971 and South African harbours handled 47 million tons of cargo in that year—76.5 per cent of it at the principal ports of Durban and Cape Town. Airways carried 656.6 million passenger miles internally in 1970 and 1094 million abroad. South African Railways and Harbours, which also controls South African Airways and the country's system of oil pipelines, is the largest commercial undertaking in the country, employing 250,000 people and a total expenditure of R 959 million in 1971.

An extensive road network of 653,700 kilometres of national, provincial and rural roads cover the country. Road transport has grown rapidly since the war. The number of motor cars rose from 471,000 in 1950 to 1,563,000 in 1970, commercial vehicles from 124,000 to 428,000 and buses from 4,400 to 34,000. Private long distance road haulage is restricted, however, by the operation of the Motor Carriers Transportation Act designed to protect the railways.

Telecommunications are fairly extensively developed with 1.5 million telephones in use in 1970 (about half the total in Africa) of which 77 per cent are automatic. A national subscriber trunk dialling network is being installed with automatic dialling already available between major cities.

POWER AND WATER
Electricity

In 1969 South Africa generated 36,000 million kWh. of electricity, amounting to 57 per cent of Africa's electrical power and a per capita consumption equal to that of Western Europe. The bulk of this supply is generated by the state-controlled Electricity Supply Commission (ESCOM) via a regional grid system. By 1972 a national grid system was expected to be in operation. At an average cost of .56 cents per unit in 1969, South Africa's electricity is among the cheapest in the world. This is largely due to the low cost of coal, which is the main source of fuel for power generation. Nearly half of the country's coal production (22 million tons of the 59 million tons produced in 1971) goes to electricity production. Additional power in the future will also be generated by hydro-electric stations in the Orange River Project, the Cabora Bassa dam in Mozambique and nuclear power stations in the Cape.

Water

Water supply is increasingly becoming a problem for the future location of industry. The Vaal river, which is the main source of water supply for the large concentration of manufacturing industry and mining in the southern Transvaal and northern Orange Free State, is nearing the limit of its capacity. Even with planned increases in supply to the Vaal from the Tugela basin in Natal, it is unlikely that this river will meet future requirements by the end of the century. It is likely, therefore, that Natal with its much greater water supply will have a higher rate of growth of industry than the Transvaal in the future.

FOREIGN TRADE

South Africa is highly dependent on international trade. In 1971 imports were R 2,885 million, equal to 26.5 per cent of net national income at factor cost. In spite of rapid industrialization, with the encouragement of import-replacement industries by protective tariffs and comprehensive direct import control machinery in operation since 1948, imports are no smaller a proportion of national income than their average of 24 per cent in the 1930s. The composition of imports, however, has changed considerably over the years. Whereas in 1910 food, drink, clothing and textiles constituted 46 per cent of total imports, these consumer goods are only a small fraction today with intermediate and capital goods making up the bulk of imports. 92 per cent of imports in 1968 were manufactured whereas only 38 per cent of exports were in this category and even here a large proportion of exports classified as manufactured are lightly processed agricultural and mineral products. The country remains heavily dependent, therefore, on agriculture and mining (gold in particular) to pay for imports. South Africa is, however, less subject than most primary producing countries to the adverse effects of fluctuations in the prices of primary products because of the stabilizing effect of large gold exports (37 per cent of total exports in 1971).

Total merchandise exports (excluding gold) were R 1,561 million in 1971. Britain still is and always has been South Africa's main trading partner taking 27 per cent of her exports and supplying 23 per cent of her imports in 1971. Japan is the second largest customer taking 12 per cent of her exports. Exports to the rest of Africa were 19 per cent, but most of this trade is concentrated on Rhodesia and Zambia. Exports to countries north of Zambia were only R 20 million in 1970 compared with R 24 million in 1961 as most of these countries boycott trade with South Africa.

With the imposition of strict exchange control regulations in 1961 after the massive outflow of foreign capital following the political disturbances of 1960, South Africa has been able to protect herself against disturbances to the balance of payments on capital account. Together with a renewed inflow of foreign capital in recent years and carefully managed import controls, reserves of gold and foreign exchange were in excess of R 1,000 million at the beginning of 1970 from the low point of R 196 million in 1960. The reserve position deteriorated again in the recession of 1970/71. But with the devaluation of the rand in December 1971, a sharp rise in the free market price of gold, the resumption of large-scale capital inflows and the decision to float the rand with sterling in June 1972, the reserve position improved markedly in 1972.

FINANCE

The South African currency is the rand issued by the South African Reserve Bank. Following a 12.28 per cent devaluation in December 1971 and a further devaluation of 4.2 per cent in October 1972 it is equal to $1.27732 or R29.75 equals one fine ounce of gold. Although a member of the Sterling Area it has not been the practice of the commercial banks since 1942 and more stringently since 1961 to keep reserves in London. Banking follows the British tradition with a few large branch banks dominating the scene. The two largest banks, Barclays Bank International and Standard, have their head offices in London but the third largest, Volkskas, has its head office in South Africa. In addition to commercial banks, a whole range of financial institutions have developed since the war including merchant banks, discount houses and a fairly well developed short-term money market.

Public finance is conducted along orthodox lines. In 1969 government current revenue was R 2,377 million (20.4 per cent of G.D.P. at market prices). The main sources of revenue were R 1,182 million and R 964 million in direct and indirect taxes respectively. Government current expenditure including subsidies and transfers in 1969 was R 1,838 million (15.8 per cent of G.D.P. at market prices). The surplus on current account, which is a normal feature of government budgeting in South Africa, is used to finance public fixed investment which together with public corporations accounted for as much as 47.3 per cent of total gross fixed investment. Although still officially committed to a basically private enterprise economic system, the state has over the years become increasingly involved via the Industrial Development Corporation in a whole new range of commercial activities in addition to traditional infrastructure and public utility enterprises.

ECONOMIC DEVELOPMENT

South Africa has undoubtedly achieved remarkable economic development in recent years with one of the highest growth rates in the world in the last decade. Yet there are several reservations about this development and some disturbing questions occur about the future. In the first instance a reservation arises about the *distribution* of the fruits of recent development. After several years of "separate development" the African reserves remain as wretched and over-populated as ever. But even in the modern sector, although there has been a considerable increase in African employment, the real income of Africans has hardly increased at all and still remains low. The gap in income between whites and Africans, reflected in the differential between skilled and unskilled earnings already referred to, has in fact widened. Besides the serious social consequences of low incomes on the part of the vast majority of Africans, it will have a restricting effect on the future growth of manufacturing industry which requires an expanding local market as export markets are still limited. Low incomes are closely linked with the web of legislative restrictions on the geographic mobility, employment and acquisition of skills on the part of Africans which has resulted in low productivity and a serious underutilization of the potential labour resources of the country. A by-product of these restrictions is a shortage of skilled labour which has already reached serious proportions in some industries and services, notably gold mining, construction and the railways, and threatens to slow down growth in the future. Even at a growth rate of 5½ per cent per annum, the target rate of the Economic Development Programme accepted by the government, which is below that achieved in the 1960s, a bottleneck in skilled labour is expected to arise under present arrangements. The conflict between economic development on the one hand and restrictions on the integration of Africans into the modern sector of the economy on the other is likely to intensify in the future. If economic growth is sacrificed for the almost certainly unattainable goal of complete social, political and economic separateness of the different races in South Africa, the consequences for all the people and not just the Africans will be grave.

STATISTICAL SURVEY

AREA AND POPULATION

	TOTAL* (1970)	CAPE PROVINCE	NATAL	TRANSVAAL	ORANGE FREE STATE
AREA (sq. miles) . .	471,445	278,380	33,578	109,621	49,866
POPULATION ('000) .	21,448	4,236	2,140	6,389	1,649
Whites . . .	3,751	1,102	442	1,890	296
Bantu . . .	15,058	1,360	1,116	4,267	1,317
Asiatics . . .	620	22	515	81	—
Coloureds . . .	2,019	1,752	67	151	36

* Excludes Walvis Bay, which has an area of 434 sq. miles and a population of 12,648 (1960), which is administered as part of South West Africa (Namibia).

CHIEF TOWNS

POPULATION (1970)

Cape Town (capital) .	825,752	Bloemfontein . .	180,179
Pretoria (capital) .	571,541	Benoni . .	162,794
Johannesburg .	1,407,963	Springs . .	104,090
Durban . .	874,003	East London . .	125,195
Port Elizabeth .	386,577	Pietermaritzburg .	160,315
Germiston .	139,472	Welkom . .	131,767

Transkei (Bantu Homeland) in the south-east of the Republic: Area: 15,831 square miles; Population (1970) 1,751,142 (Bantu 1,733,931, White 9,556, Coloureds 7,645, Asian 10); Capital Umtata.

POPULATION GROUPS

(1970—'000)

Zulu	4,026
Xhosa .	3,930
Tswana .	1,719
Sepedi (North Sotho)	1,604
Seshoeshoe (South Sotho)	1,452
Swazi .	499
Shangaan .	737
Venda .	358
South Ndebele	233
North Ndebele	182
Other Bantu	318
Whites	3,751
Coloureds	2,019
Asians	620
TOTAL	21,448

CENSUS RETURNS

Year	All Races Total	Whites		
		Total	Male	Female
1936	9,619,000	2,009,000	1,021,000	988,000
1946	11,449,000	2,380,000	1,198,000	1,182,000
1951	12,716,000	2,647,000	1,325,000	1,322,000
1960	16,002,797	3,088,492	1,539,103	1,539,000
1970	21,448,169	3,751,328	1,867,850	1,883,478

Year	Total Non-Whites			Bantu		Asiatics		Coloureds and Malays	
	Total	Male	Female	Male	Female	Male	Female	Male	Female
1936	7,610,000	3,832,000	3,778,000	3,324,000	3,293,000	120,000	101,000	389,000	383,000
1946	9,068,000	4,623,000	4,445,000	4,007,000	3,844,000	149,000	137,000	467,000	464,000
1951	10,068,000	5,128,000	4,940,000	4,386,000	4,208,000	190,000	178,000	553,000	555,000
1960	12,914,305	6,504,390	6,409,915	5,488,000	5,392,000	241,637	235,488	553,000	555,000
1970	17,696,841	8,693,295	9,003,546	7,390,246	7,667,706	309,433	311,003	993,616	1,024,837

BIRTHS

				Number			Rate (per 1,000)		
				Whites	Asiatics	Coloureds	Whites	Asiatics	Coloureds
1964	.	.	.	79,901	17,330	79,359	24.0	33.3	46.6
1965				81,488	17,140	77,416	24.0	32.2	44.2
1966				82,548	17,429	78,644	23.7	31.9	43.6
1967				81,635	16,833	80,410	22.9	30.0	43.3
1968				81,525	17,866	80,396	22.4	31.0	42.0
1969				87,613	21,435	78,604	23.5	36.3	40.1
1970				90,186	21,394	76,462	24.0	34.3	37.8

DEATHS

				Number			Rate (per 1,000)		
				Whites	Asiatics	Coloureds	Whites	Asiatics	Coloureds
1965	.	.	.	30,487	4,121	26,561	9.0	7.7	15.2
1966				29,962	3,999	26,948	8.6	7.3	14.9
1967				32,015	4,251	29,276	9.0	7.6	15.7
1968				32,664	4,331	28,450	9.0	7.5	14.9
1969				32,040	4,192	28,032	8.6	7.2	14.2
1970				34,060	4,398	29,338	9.1	7.0	14.5

IMMIGRATION AND EMIGRATION
(Whites only)

COUNTRY OF BIRTH OR DESTINATION	IMMIGRANTS			EMIGRANTS		
	1969	1970	1971*	1969	1970	1971†
United Kingdom . . .	16,954	21,323	6,575	2,842	3,041	1,371
German Federal Republic . .	3,374	2,980	1,460	672	609	366
The Netherlands . . .	1,453	1,364	521	263	346	189
Italy	1,370	956	368	170	63	66
Rhodesia	3,441	2,964	1,850	2,639	2,343	2,011
Zambia	2,916	1,635	640	109	56	17
Malawi	103	101	55	67	25	13
Tanzania	109	64	21	1	—	—
Kenya	552	369	109	4	12	4
Mozambique . . .	455	186	111	21	23	5
North America . . .	642	730	359	446	278	142
Australasia . . .	1,099	1,025	944	871	1,311	582
TOTAL (incl. others) . .	41,446	41,523	17,181	9,018	9,154	5,238

Total immigrants (1971): 35,845; Total emigrants (1971): 8,291.

* January–June.　　　　† January–August.

EMPLOYMENT

	WHITES		NON-WHITES		TOTAL	
	1969	1970	1969	1970	1969	1970
Mining . . .	62,791	62,638	565,072	594,177	627,863	656,815
Manufacturing . .	268,500	276,900	827,000	887,200	1,095,500	1,164,100
Construction . .	54,600	59,500	258,100	296,200	312,700	355,700
Transport . .	113,437	110,000	109,606	112,000	223,043	222,000
Communications .	35,881	38,505	15,923	27,150	51,804	55,655
Public Authorities .	238,879	273,135	405,459	403,884	644,338	641,019

In 1969 about 1,700,000 of the population were engaged in agriculture, of which 1,455,000 Bantu, 118,000 Whites.

AGRICULTURE

CROP	UNIT	1967	1968	1969	1970
Maize	'ooo metric tons	9,762	5,316	5,339	6,133
Sorghum . . .	,, ,, ,,	844	207	232	n.a.
Rye	,, ,, ,,	7.7	12.7	7.3	n.a.
Wheat	,, ,, ,,	1,089	1,270	1,328	1,358
Barley	,, ,, ,,	41	34	18	30
Oats	,, ,, ,,	170	143	110	117
Dry Beans . . .	,, ,, ,,	n.a.	n.a.	50	n.a.
Cotton	,, ,, ,,	11	15	23	19
Sugar	'ooo lb.	15,547	n.a.	n.a.	n.a.
Tobacco . . .	1,000 metric tons	27.8	38.2	38.3	33.9*
Potatoes . . .	,, ,, ,,	499	458	776	n.a.

* FAO estimate.

Source: UN *Statistical Yearbook 1971.*

FRUIT

DECIDUOUS FRUIT (metric tons)					CITRUS FRUIT (Exports—units of 35 lb.)		
	1970	1971	1972*			1969	1970
Apples . . .	123,589	132,174	179,632	Oranges . . .		16,030,074	15,428,000
Grapes . . .	27,695	33,760	33,334	Grapefruit . . .		3,794,391	3,711,000
Peaches . . .	1,184	1,262	1,413	Lemons . . .		421,297	305,000
Pears . . .	26,286	30,246	36,501	Naartjies . . .		2,155	2,347

* Estimates.

LIVESTOCK
('ooo head)

	1966/67	1967/68	1968/69	1969/70
Cattle . . .	12,260*	12,145	11,780	12,251
Pigs . . .	1,400*	1,290	1,240	1,230*
Sheep . . .	35,251	35,978	36,059	39,136
Horses . . .	460*	460*	450*	440*

* FAO estimate.

Source: UN *Statistical Yearbook 1971.*

VALUE OF LIVESTOCK PRODUCTS
(Rand 'ooo)

	1967	1968	1969
Cattle for slaughter* .	134,200	147,200	139,200
Sheep for slaughter .	62,600	64,400	74,900
Pigs for slaughter* .	21,700	21,300	24,000
Fresh Milk . . .	68,100	77,500	79,000
Poultry Products . .	57,300	59,700	63,600
Dairy Products . .	58,700	66,200	69,500

* Including the value of hides and skins.

FISHERIES

PELAGIC FISH CATCH IN SOUTH AFRICAN WATERS
(metric tons)

Type	1969	1970
Pilchards	58,472	63,119
Maasbanker	31,867	10,001
Mackerel	97,188	82,428
Anchovy	170,399	214,944
Total	357,926	370,502

TRAWL CATCH
('ooo lb.)

Type	1969	1970
Stockfish.	152,552	138,540
Kingklip	4,500	4,639
Sole	2,112	2,207
Kabeljou	4,371	3,675
Maasbanker . . .	13,022	15,820
Offal	33,837	32,411
Other	24,399	23,544
	234,794	220,838
Natal Rock Lobster . .	314	165
Other Crustaceans . .	820	929
Total	235,927	221,931

MINING*
(Rand 'ooo)

	1967	1968	1969	1970	1971
Gold	763,327	777,532	779,417	805,412	892,831
Uranium	n.a.	n.a.	n.a.	n.a.	n.a.
Silver	3,506	5,000	4,346	4,343	n.a.
Iron Ore	23,110	29,536	27,610	28,654	23,469
Copper	97,723	99,427	114,746	137,657	75,345
Manganese Ore . .	23,868	23,559	25,374	26,100	30,888
Chrome Ore . . .	7,682	8,913	9,706	10,546	11,800
Tin (metal concentrates) . .	3,921	4,078	4,293	3,418	3,230
Coal	85,908	97,283	106,082	115,998	n.a.
Asbestos	26,469	31,714	30,881	33,567	34,849
Diamonds	158,400	193,600	221,300	175,600	166,000
Lime and Limestone . .	12,767	13,610	15,295	17,165	19,578

* Exports.

MINERAL PRODUCTION
('ooo metric tons)

	1969	1970	1971
Antimony . . .	29.6	28.8	23.9
Asbestos . . .	258.1	287.4	319.4
Chrome . . .	1,197.4	1,427.3	1,644.0
Coal . . .	52,741.5	56,611.7	58,866.0
Copper . . .	126.2	149.2	157.4
Fluorspar . . .	150.2	173.0	238.9
Iron Ore . . .	8,785.9	9,272.0	10,946.3
Manganese . . .	2,642.7	3,053.5	3,155.7
Phosphates, Crude . .	1,678.2	1,684.9	1,729.5
Vanadium . . .	4.6	4.3	4.0
Diamonds (metric carats) .	7,862.8	8,111.5	7,031.2
Gold (kg.) . . .	973.0	1,000.4	976.3

INDUSTRY
GROSS SALES
(Rand '000)

	1967	1968	1969
Processed Foodstuffs	930,899	990,791	994,417
Beverages and Tobacco	348,252	373,381	392,084
Textiles	298,727	297,596	357,964
Clothing and Knitted Products . . .	226,044	229,852	236,997
Footwear	84,770	87,272	84,658
Wood and Wood Products . . .	88,792	96,961	118,281
Furniture	104,505	117,959	125,282
Paper and Paper Products . . .	204,350	218,904	234,232
Printing, Publishing and Allied Industries .	117,521	130,822	168,584
Leather and Leather Products . . .	28,308	28,058	36,286
Rubber Products	102,015	107,362	134,576
Chemicals and Chemical Products . .	469,559	500,540	498,211
Non-metallic Mineral Products . . .	227,595	240,992	307,662
Basic Iron and Steel Products . . .	312,622	322,371	416,930
Basic Non-ferrous Metals	100,324	108,695	152,444
Metal Products	546,787	639,506	506,159
Machinery (except Electrical Machinery) .	292,701	308,539	312,697
Electrical Machinery and Equipment .	337,510	377,708	265,181
Railroad Equipment	81,704	70,977	43,679
Motor Vehicles	275,792	289,025	338,791

FINANCE

100 cents = 1 rand.

Coins: 1, 2, 5, 10, 20 and 50 cents; 1 rand.

Notes: 1, 5, 10 and 20 rand.

Exchange rates (December 1972): £1 sterling = 1.839 rand; U.S. $1 = 78.29 S.A. cents.

100 rand = £54.39 = $127.73.

BUDGET (estimate) 1972–73
(Rand million)

REVENUE		EXPENDITURE	
Income Tax	1,556.0	General Government Expenditure (incl. Community, Social and Economic Services)	3,184.4
Departmental and Miscellaneous Receipts .	101.9		
Interest and Dividends	142.9		
Total Inland Revenue . . .	1,800.9	Government Enterprises and Public Corporations	382.8
Customs and Excise (net) . . .	760.7	Auxiliary Services supplied against Compensation	26.2
TOTAL (incl. net result of budget proposals)	2,802.9	TOTAL	3,603.4

Expenditure on Revenue account is R 2,800.2 million out of R 3,603.4 million.

NATIONAL ACCOUNTS
(Rand million)
South Africa and South West Africa (Namibia)

	1967	1968*	1969*	1970*
INCOME/SUPPLY:				
Wages and salaries	4,887	5,393	5,907	6,657
Income from property by households . .	1,931	1,802	1,910	1,979
Corporate saving . . .	301	333	462	382
Direct taxes on corporations . .	545	591	704	797
Income from property by general government	216	186	198	201
Less Interest on public debt . .	97	122	178	168
Residual item	—85	18	65	65
Net national income at factor cost .	7,698	8,201	9,068	9,913
Provision for depreciation . . .	870	945	1,027	1,134
Indirect taxes	644	714	916	1,017
Less Subsidies	102	102	117	145
GROSS NATIONAL PRODUCT AT MARKET PRICES	9,110	9,758	10,894	11,919
Net factor payments to the rest of the world	349	394	445	485
GROSS DOMESTIC PRODUCT AT MARKET PRICES	9,459	10,152	11,339	12,404
Import of goods and non-factor services .	2,307	2,270	2,591	3,107
TOTAL SUPPLY OF GOODS AND SERVICES .	11,766	12,422	13,930	15,511
EXPENDITURE/DEMAND:				
Private consumption expenditure . .	5,685	6,252	6,889	7,649
Current expenditure by general government.	1,041	1,146	1,301	1,455
Gross domestic fixed investment . .	2,219	2,316	2,620	3,061
Change in inventories . . .	472	23	325	581
Residual item	—85	18	65	65
GROSS DOMESTIC EXPENDITURE . .	9,332	9,755	11,200	12,811
Export of goods and non-factor services .	2,434	2,667	2,730	2,700
TOTAL DEMAND FOR GOODS AND SERVICES .	11,766	12,422	13,930	15,511
PERSONAL INCOME AND EXPENDITURE:				
Wages and salaries	4,887	5,393	5,907	6,657
Income from property by households . .	1,931	1,802	1,910	1,979
Current transfers received from general government	211	230	273	330
Transfers from the rest of the world . .	60	84	81	71
Current income	7,089	7,509	6,171	9,037
Less Direct taxes	482	534	539	578
Personal disposable income . . .	6,607	6,975	7,632	8,459
Less Private consumption expenditure .	5,685	6,252	6,889	7,649
Less Transfers to the rest of the world .	32	35	39	46
Less Current transfers to general government	25	27	30	35
PERSONAL SAVING	865	661	674	729

* Preliminary.

GROSS DOMESTIC PRODUCT BY KIND OF ECONOMIC ACTIVITY
(Rand million)

	1967	1968	1969*	1970*
BUSINESS ENTERPRISES:				
Agriculture, forestry and fishing	1,047	963	1,005	1,036
Mining and quarrying	1,050	1,114	1,202	1,203
Manufacturing	2,010	2,143	2,391	2,657
Electricity, gas and water	228	253	277	306
Construction (contractors)	353	395	457	547
Wholesale and retail trade, catering and accommodation	1,241	1,378	1,503	1,623
Transport, storage and communication	861	910	992	1,072
Finance, insurance, real estate and business services	827	946	1,093	1,247
Community, social and personal services	165	183	211	240
Sub-Total	7,781	8,285	9,131	9,931
General Government	793	883	965	1,100
Other Producers (non-profit institutions and domestic servants)	344	373	412	458
GROSS DOMESTIC PRODUCT AT FACTOR COST	8,917	9,540	10,507	11,490

* Provisional.

GOLD RESERVES AND CURRENCY IN CIRCULATION
(At year's end—Rand million)

	1967	1968	1969	1970	1971
S.A. Reserve Bank—Gold Reserves	413	881	790	472	331.6
S.A. Reserve Bank—Foreign Exchanges	72	104	91	209	132.3
TOTAL GOLD RESERVES AND FOREIGN EXCHANGES	485	985	881	681	463.9
Coin and Banknotes in Circulation	382.3	404.2	455.6	510.3	607.1
Demand Deposits	1,334.2	1,656.8	1,780.5	1,738.3	1,798.5
Other Short- and Medium-Term Deposits	1,140.0	1,387.7	1,569.3	1,784.7	1,770.4
TOTAL MONEY AND NEAR-MONEY	2,856.5	3,448.6	3,805.5	4,033.3	4,276.0

BALANCE OF PAYMENTS
(including South West Africa)
(Rand million)

	1969*	1970*	1971*
Current Account:			
Merchandise:			
Imports f.o.b.	−2,148	−2,579	−2,888
Exports f.o.b.	1,486	1,420	1,481
Trade Balance	− 662	−1,159	−1,407
Net Gold Output	847	837	918
Service Payments (net)	− 491	− 570	− 567
Total Goods and Services (net receipts)	− 306	− 892	−1,056
Transfers (net receipts)	61	49	51
BALANCE ON CURRENT ACCOUNT	− 245	− 843	−1,005
Capital Movements:			
Private Sector	186	453	564
Long Term	161	326	383
Short Term	− 7	89	70
Errors and Unrecorded Transactions	32	38	111
Central Government and Banking Sector	− 6	104	199
Long Term	17	103	106
Short Term	− 23	1	93
TOTAL CAPITAL MOVEMENTS (net flow)	180	557	763
Change in Gold and Foreign Exchange Reserves	− 65	− 286	− 242
SDR Allocations and Valuation Adjustments	7	24	86
Total Change in Gold and Foreign Exchange Reserves	− 58	− 262	− 156

* Provisional.

EXTERNAL TRADE
(excluding gold)
(Rand '000)

	1966	1967	1968	1969	1970	1971
Imports f.o.b.	1,645,540	1,919,320	1,880,100	2,134,600	2,547,200	2,884,700
Exports f.o.b.	1,206,300	1,364,100	1,506,300	1,531,000	1,542,100	1,561,300

COMMODITIES
(Rand million)

IMPORTS	1969	1970	1971
Vegetable Products	56.4	61.0	54.6
Minerals and Products	138.7	144.4	208.0
Chemicals and Products	132.8	160.0	187.0
Plastic and Rubber Products	79.5	99.2	102.8
Paper and Products	71.8	87.1	85.6
Textiles and Articles	227.9	240.4	257.5
Base Metals and Articles	136.7	200.1	235.7
Machinery and Electrical Equipment	556.7	706.0	785.4
Transport Equipment	407.0	466.4	579.8
Optical and Measuring Instruments	81.6	97.8	98.1
Others	245.7	284.8	290.2
TOTAL	2,134.8	2,547.2	2,884.7

COMMODITIES—*Continued*].

EXPORTS	1969	1970	1971
Vegetable Products	126.7	148.0	170.7
Prepared Foodstuffs	153.3	152.3	163.8
Minerals and Products	204.4	232.9	244.2
Chemicals and Products . . .	65.9	70.6	76.2
Hides and Skins	40.7	39.5	36.6
Paper and Products	39.2	37.0	37.1
Textiles and Articles	130.5	96.1	72.6
Precious Stones	269.4	215.3	227.0
Base Metals and Articles . . .	250.9	261.3	222.3
Machinery and Electrical Equipment .	74.5	81.2	97.5
Others	178.6	207.9	213.3
TOTAL	1,534.1	1,542.1	1,561.3

Source: Department of Customs and Excise.

COUNTRIES
(Including data for South West Africa (Namibia), Botswana, Lesotho and Swaziland)
(Rand '000)

IMPORTS	1968	1969	1970	1971
Australia	30,000	39,251	60,437	62,141
Belgium	20,500	23,953	33,990	37,969
Canada	44,600	53,063	70,495	47,305
France	67,000	61,196	88,097	104,718
German Federal Republic . . .	253,700	292,913	373,993	408,869
Italy	78,000	84,856	104,342	105,221
Japan	124,000	188,425	220,759	292,118
Netherlands	42,200	41,408	58,414	58,379
Sweden	30,500	37,865	45,096	43,932
Switzerland	37,200	40,803	49,584	56,050
United Kingdom	449,500	499,562	561,221	670,574
U.S.A.	332,900	370,487	423,379	469,767

(Rand '000)

EXPORTS	1968	1969	1970	1971
Australia	13,100	13,211	12,774	14,285
Belgium	52,000	63,088	55,788	56,928
Canada	24,300	28,280	28,175	38,897
France	37,500	42,992	37,822	38,338
German Federal Republic . . .	101,300	102,829	109,521	110,167
Hong Kong	15,436	22,435	23,968	26,363
Italy	43,000	44,536	43,176	37,144
Japan	204,500	151,240	181,152	182,170
Netherlands	31,500	32,369	34,939	36,381
Spain	14,624	15,952	13,920	14,728
United Kingdom	476,000	510,722	446,589	417,939
U.S.A.	104,200	108,243	128,917	118,516

TOURISM

VISITORS FROM	1968	1969	1970	1971*
Africa	192,070	199,165	225,221	159,145
Europe	79,135	93,515	116,813	91,879
Asia	2,096	2,322	3,098	2,868
America	18,537	22,115	30,235	28,829
Australasia . . .	7,934	11,124	14,327	10,624
TOTAL . . .	299,772	328,241	389,694	291,345

* Jan.–Aug. Final total for 1971: 458,059.

TRANSPORT
RAILWAYS

	1969	1970	1971
Freight traffic ('000 tons) . .	120,856	126,851	128,800
Passenger journeys ('000) . .	493,110	521,529	552,032

ROADS
VEHICLES LICENSED 1970 (estimate)

CARS	BUSES	COMMERCIAL VEHICLES	MOTOR CYCLES
1,653,000	34,000	428,000	132,000

SHIPPING*
(Year ended 31st March)

CARGO HANDLED ('000 tons)

	LANDED	SHIPPED	TOTAL (including cargo transhipped)
1969 . .	18,227	19,118	37,796
1970 . .	21,556	18,005	39,957
1971 . .	27,979	18,881	47,218
1972 . .	28,353	22,343	51,049

VESSELS HANDLED

	NUMBER	REGISTERED TONNAGE ('000 cubic metres)	
		NET	GROSS
1969 . .	21,652	198,291	342,405
1970 . .	20,044	205,146	350,757
1971 . .	21,241	225,563	380,735
1972 . .	19,134	227,735	379,998

* Includes South West Africa.

CIVIL AVIATION

	MILES FLOWN	PASSENGERS CARRIED	PASSENGER MILES ('000)	AIR FREIGHT (lb.)	AIR FREIGHT TON-MILES	AIR MAIL (lb.)	AIR MAIL TON-MILES
Internal Services							
1968	8,277,548	887,136	470,072	19,233,831	5,491,739	4,892,341	1,470,346
1969	9,284,089	1,066,969	568,155	24,044,579	6,944,894	5,347,428	1,608,279
1970	11,303,225	1,244,780	656,618	29,545,575	8,451,213	5,656,736	1,704,202
International Regional Services							
1968	583,795	53,540	24,230	1,170,090	285,586	273,006	63,302
1969	747,197	61,607	29,789	1,120,004	280,329	264,256	63,210
1970	1,133,036	75,613	43,425	1,408,785	434,471	238,318	59,963
International Overseas Services							
1968	8,669,373	113,705	647,616	6,544,078	20,060,384	1,498,898	4,697,346
1969	10,497,686	134,353	749,042	8,667,198	24,791,450	1,601,202	5,226,348
1970	13,202,736	178,437	1,050,725	9,431,316	29,534,618	1,409,677	4,522,173

COMMUNICATIONS MEDIA

	DAILY NEWSPAPERS	CIRCULATION	TELEPHONES	LICENSED RADIOS
1969 .	22	n.a.	1,311,864	1,770,486
1970 .	20	1,382,609	1,572,709	2,014,311

EDUCATION
(1968)

CATEGORIES	NUMBER OF INSTITUTIONS		NUMBER OF TEACHERS		NUMBER OF STUDENTS	
	White	Non-White	White Institutions	Non-White Institutions	White	Non-White
Primary and Secondary . .	2,624	9,885	38,472	52,604	820,626	2,509,422
Teacher-Training	19	39	849	651	10,276	7,380
Residential Universities and University Colleges . . .	10	5	5,019	496	48,726	6,477
University of South Africa (correspondence)	1		386		17,161	3,575

Sources (except where otherwise stated): South African Reserve Bank, *Quarterly Bulletin*; South Africa House, London; Standard Bank *Annual Economic Review: South and South West Africa*, July 1971.

THE CONSTITUTION

The Union of South Africa, embracing the Cape Colony, Natal, the Transvaal and the Orange River Colony in a dominion under the British Crown, was established May 31st, 1910. Following the Statute of Westminster of 1931 the South African Parliament in 1934 passed the Status of the Union Act, which defined the Union as a 'sovereign independent state' with eventual right of secession from the Commonwealth. Since then the representation of non-Whites in Parliament has gradually been reduced with the implementation of the policy of 'separate development' (*see* Bantu Homelands below). In 1936 Cape Africans were removed from the common voters' roll. In 1948 the Indians' right to elect three White representatives under an Act of 1946 was abolished; and a year later the Whites in the mandated territory of South West Africa were given 6 seats in the South African Assembly and 4 in the Senate. In 1956, after the failure of the measure in 1950, a bill to remove the Cape Coloureds from the common voters' roll was passed by a joint sitting of the Assembly and a newly enlarged and reorganized Senate. Africans lost their limited representation in Parliament in 1959. On May 31st, 1961, the Republic of South Africa was established after a majority (849,176) of the 1,633,772 White voters registered their approval in a referendum held in October 1960, and at the same time South Africa left the Commonwealth. The only major change the Republican Constitution made was to substitute a State President for the Queen. English and Afrikaans retained their equal status as the official languages. In 1968 the elimination of the remaining non-White representatives from Parliament, the members elected for the Coloured people, was provided for.

Executive Power

Executive power is vested in a State President, acting on the advice of Ministers of State or the Cabinet, composed of a Prime Minister and 17 other Ministers. The President is elected by an electoral college of members of the Senate and House of Assembly, presided over by the Chief Justice or a Judge of Appeal. He holds office for a seven-year term and is not eligible for re-election unless "it is otherwise decided" by the electoral college. He is Head of State and Commander-in-Chief of the Armed Forces. The Ministers are members of the Executive Council and they are appointed to administer such departments of State as are established by the State President-in-Council. Deputy Ministers, not exceeding eight in number, may be appointed by the State President to assist Ministers in the administration of departments of State. Deputy Ministers are not members of the Executive Council.

Parliament

The Parliament of the Republic consists of the State President, a Senate and a House of Assembly. The State President has power to summon, prorogue and dissolve Parliament, either both Houses simultaneously or the House of Assembly alone. There must be a session of Parliament at least every twelve months.

The Senate

Senators must be nationals of European descent, at least 30 years of age, qualified as voters, and resident at least five years within the Republic.

The Senate, as constituted in December 1965, consists of 54 white members: 41 elected by the electoral colleges of the four provinces (14 for the Transvaal, 11 for the Cape Province, 8 each for the Orange Free State and Natal) and two similarly elected for South West Africa. Eleven members are nominated by the State President, two for each of the four provinces and South West Africa (of whom half are chosen for their thorough knowledge of the reasonable wants and wishes of the non-White people) and one special representative of the interests of the Cape Coloured people.

The House of Assembly

Members of the House of Assembly must be nationals of European descent, must be registered voters and resident for at least five years in the Republic. The House of Assembly continues for five years unless previously dissolved.

All White persons over the age of 18 are entitled to vote, except those who have been convicted of treason. murder, or any other offence punishable by a term of imprisonment without option of a fine.

The House consists of 166 White members; 160 directly elected by White citizens, aged 18 years or over, to represent the electoral divisions of the Republic, and 6 similarly elected to represent the electoral divisions of South West Africa.

Representation of Coloureds

The Coloured Persons Representative Council Act of 1964 established a Council for Coloured Affairs whose function is to advise the Government in regard to matters affecting the interests of the Coloured people of the Republic. This Council has become a self-governing body for the Coloured people with extensive legislative and administrative powers and consists of 40 members elected by Coloured voters and 20 nominated members. It is called the Coloured Person's Representative Council. First elections took place in September 1969. All Coloured men and women over 21 are able to vote.

Representation of Bantu

Five of eleven nominated Senators are selected for their thorough acquaintance with the reasonable wants and wishes of the African peoples.

The Native Affairs Act, 1920, made provisions for the establishment in African areas of local and general councils with minor powers of local self-government somewhat on the lines of the Glen Grey District Council (established in 1894) and the district and general councils then functioning in the Transkeian Territories.

The Representation of Natives Act, 1936, transferred Cape Africans from the same voters' lists as Whites to the Cape Native Voters' Roll and, as a *quid pro quo* for their rights to participate in ordinary elections, empowered them to elect three members of the House of Assembly and two members of the Cape Provincial Council. Special representation for the African population of the Republic as a whole was provided for in that, through electoral colleges Africans could elect four Senators to represent their interests in Parliament, and could also elect some members of the Natives Representative Council, established by the Act.

(For development of the Bantustans and present representation of Africans *see* section at end of chapter.)

Procedure

Money Bills must originate in the House of Assembly, which may not pass a Bill for taxation or appropriation unless it has been recommended by message from the State President during the session. The amendment of money

Bills by the Senate is restricted and such Bills, when passed by the House of Assembly in any session, may become law even if the Senate in the same session fails to pass them or passes them with amendments to which the House of Assembly cannot agree. Other Bills, with the exception of those which alter or repeal the provisions of sections 108 and 118 of the Republic of South Africa Constitution Act, may in the event of disagreement between the two Houses, become law after rejection by the Senate in two successive sessions. The provisions of sections 108 and 118 of the Republic of South Africa Constitution Act, relating to the equality of the two official languages of the Republic and the amendment of that Act, may not be altered or repealed unless the Bill embodying the alteration or repeal is passed by both Houses of Parliament sitting together, and at the third reading is agreed to by not less than two-thirds of the total number of members of both Houses.

The State President may assent to, or withhold assent from, a Bill. Two copies of every law, one in English and one in Afrikaans, are to be enrolled on record in the office of the Registrar of the Appellate Division of the Supreme Court of South Africa. In case of conflict between the two copies, that signed by the State President shall prevail.

Each member of each House must make an Oath or Affirmation of Allegiance. A member of one House cannot be elected to the other, but a Minister and a Deputy-Minister may sit and speak, but not vote, in the House of which he is not a member.

Provincial Government

Provision is made for the appointment of an administrator in each province, who holds office for a term of five years. In each province there is also a provincial council consisting of the same number of members as are elected in the province for the House of Assembly, but in no case is the membership to be less than 25. A member of a provincial council ceases to be a member on being elected to either House of the Central Parliament. The powers of the provinces, which relate chiefly to the administration of local affairs (mainly roads, hospitals and education) are subordinate to the powers of the Central Parliament and all provincial ordinances require the consent of the State President-in-Council.

An executive committee of four persons, not necessarily members of the council, together with the administrator as chairman, is elected by the provincial council at its first meeting after each general election. This committee carries on the administration of affairs on behalf of the provincial council. The administrator may, and when required to do so must, act on behalf of the State President-in-Council in regard to all matters in respect of which no powers are reserved or delegated to the provincial council.

THE GOVERNMENT

State President: Rt. Hon. J. J. FOUCHÉ.

CABINET

(*January* 1973)

Prime Minister: Rt. Hon. B. J. VORSTER.

Minister of Transport: Hon. B. J. SCHOEMAN.

Minister of National Education: Hon. J. P. VAN DER SPUY.

Minister of Finance: Dr. the Hon. N. D. DIEDERICHS.

Minister of Agriculture: Hon. H. SCHOEMAN.

Minister of Defence: Hon. P. W. BOTHA.

Minister of Tourism and Indian Affairs: Sen. O. P. F. HORWOOD.

Minister of Foreign Affairs: Dr. the Hon. H. MULLER.

Minister of Health, Coloured and Rehoboth Affairs: Dr. the Hon. S. W. VAN DER MERWE.

Minister of Labour, Posts and Telegraphs: Hon. M. VILJOEN.

Minister of Bantu Administration and Development and Bantu Education: Hon. M. C. BOTHA.

Minister of Justice and of Prisons: Hon. P. C. PELSER.

Minister of Mines, Immigration, Sports and Recreation: Dr. the Hon. P. G. J. KOORNHOF.

Minister of the Interior, Information, Social Welfare and Pensions: Dr. the Hon. C. P. MULDER.

Minister of Community Development and of Public Works: Hon. A. H. DU PLESSIS.

Minister of Planning and Statistics: Hon. J. J. LOOTS.

Minister of Police and Economic Affairs: Hon. S. L. MULLER.

Minister of Water Affairs and Forestry: Hon. S. P. BOTHA.

DEPUTY MINISTERS

Deputy Minister of Transport: J. W. RALL.

Deputy Minister of Finance and of Economic Affairs: J. C. HEUNIS.

Deputy Minister of Bantu Administration and Education: T. N. H. JANSON.

Deputy Minister of Agriculture: J. J. MALAN.

Deputy Minister of the Interior, Social Welfare, Pensions, Police, and Coloured and Rehoboth Affairs: J. T. KRUGER.

Deputy Minister of Bantu Development: A. J. RAUBENHEIMER.

DIPLOMATIC REPRESENTATION

EMBASSIES AND LEGATIONS IN PRETORIA

(E) Embassy; (L) Legation.

Argentina: 1059 Church St., Hatfield (E); *Ambassador:* F. DEL SOLAR DORREGO.

Australia: 302 Standard Bank Buildings, Church Square (E); *Ambassador:* T. W. CUTTS.

Austria: 6th Floor, 611 Centenary Building, Bureau Lane (E); *Ambassador:* Dr. P. ZEDTWITZ.

Belgium: 275 Pomona St., Muckleneuk (E); *Ambassador:* M. W. J. SWINNEN.

Brazil: 22nd Floor, Poynton Centre, Church St. West (L); *Minister:* D. S. DA MOTA.

Canada: Netherlands Bank Centre, Cnr. Church and Beatrix Sts. (E); *Ambassador:* A. G. CAMPBELL (also accred. as HC to Botswana, Lesotho and Swaziland).

Finland: 310 Sunnyside Galleries, Sunnyside (L); *Chargé d'Affaires:* K. UGGELDAHL.

France: 807 George Ave., Arcadia (E); *Ambassador:* Baron PHILIPPE DE LUZE.

Germany, Federal Republic: 180 Blackwood St., Arcadia (E); *Ambassador:* E. STRÄTLING.

Greece: 995 Pretorius St. (E); *Ambassador:* M. C. ECONO-MIDES.

Israel: 496 Lanham St. (L); *Minister:* (vacant).

Italy: 796 George Ave. (E); *Ambassador:* Dr. A. PIERAN-TONI.

Malawi: 99 Burns St., Colbyn (E); *Ambassador:* JOE KACHINGWE.

Netherlands: 1st Floor, Netherlands Bank Building, Church St. (E); *Ambassador:* A. H. HASSELMAN.

Portugal: 261 Devenish St. (E); *Ambassador:* Dr. J. E. DE MENESES ROSA.

Spain: 286 Bosman St. (E); *Ambassador:* Count PEÑAR-RUBIAS.

Sweden: 521 Pretorius St., P.O.B. 1664 (L); *Minister:* Baron C. J. M. RAPPE.

Switzerland: 818 George Ave., P.O.B. 2289 (E); *Ambassador:* T. CURCHOD.

United Kingdom: Greystoke, 6 Hill St. (E); *Ambassador:* Sir J. BOTTOMLEY, K.C.M.G.

U.S.A.: Thibault House, Pretorius St. (E); *Ambassador:* JOHN G. HURD.

South Africa also has relations with the Republic of China, Denmark, Iran, Japan, Lebanon, Norway and Uruguay.

PARLIAMENT

(Cape Town)

THE SENATE

President: Senator the Hon. J. DE KLERK.

ELECTION NOVEMBER 1970

	NATIONAL PARTY	UNITED PARTY
Transvaal . .	12	3
Cape Province . .	8	3
Orange Free State .	8	—
Natal . . .	1	7
South West Africa .	2	—

There are 10 nominated members.

THE HOUSE OF ASSEMBLY

Speaker: The Hon. H. J. KLOPPER, M.P.

ELECTION APRIL 1970

	SEATS
National Party	118
United Party	47
Herstigte Nasionale Party . . .	—
Progressive Party	1

Of the 2,028,487 white voters on the electoral roll in the 154 seats which were contested 1,508,284 went to the polls. Votes and percentages for each main party were: National Party 820,968 (54.43 per cent), United Party 561,647 (37.23 per cent), Progressive Party 51,760 (3.43 per cent), Herstigte Nasionale Party 53,763 (3.56 per cent).

COLOURED PEOPLE'S REPRESENTATIVE COUNCIL
Chairman: TOM SWARTZ.

ELECTION JULY 1972

	SEATS
Labour Party	22
Federal Coloured Peoples' Party . .	31*
National Coloured Peoples' Party . .	1
Republican Coloured Party . .	1
Independent	4
Conservative Coloured Peoples' Party . .	—
TOTAL . . .	59

* Elected membership of the Council is 40. The remaining 20 seats were filled by the Government with supporters of the Federal Party, which is pro-Government. The Federal Party therefore secured a majority in the Council over the Labour Party, which opposes *apartheid*, and Tom Swartz, leader of the Federal Party, was appointed Chairman.

THE BANTU HOMELANDS
See separate section at end of chapter.

POLITICAL PARTIES

National Party: P.O.B. 245, Pretoria; f. 1912; aims: (1) to safeguard the White nation in their South African homelands: (2) to lead the Bantu nations to effective self-government in their homelands; (3) to give all nations equal opportunity to develop the social and political organizations best suited to their own particular characteristics and aspirations; (4) to raise living standards in White and Bantu homelands alike. Leader B. J. VORSTER.

United Party: National Mutual Building, Church Square, Cape Town; f. 1934; seeks a solution of racial problems through the creation of a Federation of Races governed by a Central Parliament in which all racial groups will be represented. The United Party believes in the necessity to maintain overall white political control. Leader Sir DE VILLIERS GRAAFF.

Herstigte Nasionale Party: Pretoria; f. Oct. 1969 by M.P.s expelled from National Party; believes in word of God as defined by Calvinism, that *apartheid* must be more strictly applied, that external relations must not affect South Africa's sovereignty and that immigration must be controlled to preserve Christian national civilization, favours Afrikaans becoming the National language; Leader Dr. ALBERT HERTZOG; Deputy Leader JAAP MARAIS.

Progressive Party: 6th Floor, Garmor House, Plein St., Cape Town; f. 1959 by breakaway from United Party; aim: a new Constitution based on the principles of maintenance of western civilization and protection of fundamental human rights, irrespective of race, colour, or creed; one representative in Parliament; Leader C. W. EGLIN; Nat. Chair. H. G. LAWRENCE; Chair. Nat. Exec. R. A. F. SWART.

African National Congress of South Africa: f. 1912; aims to establish a non-racial society in co-operation with left-wing and liberal organizations of other races; banned April 1960 after Sharpeville shootings; Acting Pres. OLIVER TAMBO; Sec.-Gen. ALFRED NZO.

Pan-Africanist Congress of Azania: f. 1959; splinter group from the African National Congress; believes that a democratic society can only come through African and not multiracial organizations; banned April 1960 after Sharpeville shootings; Pres. ROBERT SOBUKWE.

Indian National Congress of South Africa: Indian organization working with African National Congress in exile; Leaders Dr. DAIDOO, Y. CACHALIA.

DEFENCE

Out of total armed forces of 17,300 regulars, the army has 10,000, the navy 2,300 and the air force 5,000. Military training is compulsory for all white citizens. A Coloured Cadet Corps has been established. The Citizen Force reserve totals 92,000 of which the army has 80,000, the navy 9,000 and the air force 3,000. Para-military forces number 75,000 Kommandos, organized and trained as a home guard. The strength of non-commissioned members of the South African Police Force at December 31st, 1971, was 30,397, of which 15,330 were non-white.

Head of South African Defence Forces: Admiral H. H. BIERMANN.

JUDICIAL SYSTEM

The common law of the Republic of South Africa is the Roman-Dutch law, the uncodified law of Holland as it was at the time of the cecession of the Cape in 1806. The law of England is not recognized as authoritative, though the principles of English law have been introduced in relation to civil and criminal procedure, evidence and mercantile matters. In all other matters, however, Roman Dutch law prevails.

The Supreme Court consists of an Appellate Division; three Provisional Divisions in the Cape Province, one Provincial and one Local Division in each of the provinces of the Transvaal and Natal and one Provincial Division in the Orange Free State and South West Africa. Except for the fact that the local divisions in the Transvaal and Natal have no jurisdiction to hear appeals, they exercise within limited areas the same jurisdiction as Provincial Divisions.

The provinces are further divided into districts and regions with Magistrates' Courts, whose criminal and civil jurisdiction is clearly defined. From these courts appeals may be taken to the Provincial and Local Divisions of the Supreme Court, and thence to the Appellate Division.

THE SUPREME COURT

APPELLATE DIVISION

Chief Justice: Hon. N. OGILVIE-THOMPSON.

Judges of Appeal: Hon. F. L. H. RUMPFF, Hon. D. H. BOTHA, Hon. P. J. VAN BLERK, Hon. E. L. JANSEN, Hon. G. N. HOLMES, Hon. P. J. WESSELS, Hon. H. J. POTGIETER, Hon. W. G. TROLLIP, Hon. P. J. RABIE, Hon. G. VAN R. MULLER.

PROVINCIAL AND LOCAL DIVISIONS

Judge President (*Cape of Good Hope*): Hon. A. B. BEYERS.

Judge President (*Transvaal*): Hon. P. M. CILLIÉ.

Judge President (*Natal*): Hon. N. JAMES.

Judge President (*Orange Free State*): Hon. J. N. C. DE VILLIERS.

Judge President (*Eastern Cape*): Hon. A G. JENNETT.

Judge President (*South West Africa*): Hon. F. H. BADEN-HORST.

Judge (*North-West Cape*): Hon. G. F. DE VOS HUGO.

RELIGION

THE DUTCH REFORMED CHURCH
(Nederduitse Gereformeerde Kerk)

The churches in the four provinces are governed by a synod in each province, united in 1962 under a General Synod which will meet every four years. There are 953 Dutch Reformed Churches in the Union with a membership of 1,695,951 (1960).

CAPE PROVINCE

Moderator: Dr. J. S. GERICKE.

Secretary of Synod and Director of Information Bureau: Rev. W. A. LANDMAN, P.O.B. 930, Cape Town.

NATAL

Moderator: Rev. C. COLYN, Private Bag 9030, Pietermaritzburg.

Commissioner: Rev. S. J. DU TOIT, Gus Brown Ave., Warner Beach.

ORANGE FREE STATE

Moderator: Rev. Dr. A. VAN DER MERWE, P.O.B. 263, Kroonstad.

Scriba Synodi: Rev. Dr. A. J. MINAAR, 110 Andries Pretorius St., Bloemfontein.

NORTHERN TRANSVAAL

Moderator: Dr. S. J. O'BRIEN GELDENHUYS, 325 Hay St., Brooklyn, Pretoria.

Commissioner: Rev. J. E. POTGIETER, P.O.B. 433, Pretoria.

SOUTHERN TRANSVAAL

Moderator: Rev. D. P. M. BEUKES, 18 Central Rd., Lynden East, Johannesburg.

Commissioner: Rev. S. J. ELOFF, 55 President St., Potchefstroom.

THE CHURCH OF THE PROVINCE OF SOUTH AFRICA

The Church of the Province of South Africa is one of the many autonomous branches of the Anglican Communion constituted outside England. It is (like the Church of Ireland, the Protestant Episcopal Church of the U.S.A., and the Church of England in Australia) in full communion with the Church of England. Approx. 1,500,000 mems.

Church of the Province of South Africa: Church House, 1 Queen Victoria St., P.O.B. 1932, Cape Town; Sec. and Treas. G. D. ABERNETHY, B.COM., C.A. (S.A.).

Archbishop of Cape Town and Metropolitan of the Province: Most Rev. ROBERT SELBY TAYLOR, D.D., Bishopscourt, Claremont, Cape.

Bishops

Bloemfontein .	Rt. Rev. FREDERICK A. AMOORE, B.A., Bishop's Lodge, 16 York Rd., Bloemfontein.
Damaraland .	Rt. Rev. COLIN O'BRIEN WINTER, M.A., Bishop's House, Windhoek, South West Africa (Namibia). (*Expelled by South African Government, March 1972*).
George .	Rt. Rev. PATRICK H. F. BARRON, Bishop's Lea, George, C.P.
Grahamstown .	Rt. Rev. BILL B. BURNETT, M.A., L.TH., Bishopsbourne, Grahamstown, C.P.
Johannesburg .	Rt. Rev. LESLIE STRADLING, D.D., Bishop's House, Westcliff, Johannesburg.
Kimberley and Kuruman	Rt. Rev. PHILIP W. WHEELDON, O.B.E., M.A., Bishopsgarth, Kimberley.
Lebombo .	Rt. Rev. DANIEL CABRAL, Caixa Postal 120, Lourenço Marques, Mozambique.
Lesotho .	Rt. Rev. JOHN A. ARROWSMITH MAUND, M.C., B.A., Bishop's House, P.O.B. 87, Maseru, Lesotho.

Natal	.	Rt. Rev. Thomas George Vernon Inman, D.D., P.O.B. 726, Durban.
Port Elizabeth	.	Rt. Rev. Philip W. R. Russell, M.B.E., B.A., L.TH., Bishop's House, 14 Buckingham Rd., Port Elizabeth.
Pretoria	.	Rt. Rev. E. G. Knapp-Fisher, M.A., Bishop's House, Celliers Street, Pretoria.
St. Helena	.	Rt. Rev. Edmund M. H. Capper, O.B.E., L.TH., Island of St. Helena.
St. John's	.	Rt. Rev. James Leo Schuster, M.A., Bishopsmead, Umtata.
Swaziland	.	Rt. Rev. A. G. W. Hunter, B.A., Bishop's House, P.O.B. 118, Mbabane, Swaziland.
Zululand	.	Rt. Rev. A. H. Zulu, B.A., L.TH., P.O.B. 147, Eshowe, Zululand.

THE ROMAN CATHOLIC CHURCH

In 1960 there were 684,414 members of the Roman Catholic Church in South Africa.

Southern Africa Catholic Bishops' Conference (S.A.C.B.C.): P.O.B. 941, Standard Bank Buildings, Church Square, Pretoria.

PROVINCE OF CAPE TOWN

Archbishop of Cape Town: H.E. Cardinal Owen McCann, D.D., D.PH., B.COM., D.LITT.; 12 Bouquet Street, Cape Town.

Bishops

Aliwal: Rt. Rev. Bishop John Lueck, S.C.J., P.O.B. 27, Aliwal North.

Oudtshoorn: Rt. Rev. Bishop Manfred Gottschalk, S.A.C., P.O.B. 97, Oudtshoorn.

Queenstown: Rt. Rev. Bishop J. Rosner, S.A.C., P.O.B. 182, Queenstown.

Port Elizabeth: Rt. Rev. Bishop J. P. Murphy, P.O.B. 425, Port Elizabeth.

De Aar: Rt. Rev. Bishop Joseph De Palma, S.C.J., P.O.B. 73, De Aar.

PROVINCE OF DURBAN

Archbishop of Durban: Most Rev. Archbishop Denis E. Hurley, O.M.I., D.D.; 408 Innes Rd., Durban.

Bishops

Marianhill: Rt. Rev. Bishop Elmar Schmid, C.M.M., Bishop's House, P.O. Marianhill.

Eshowe: Rt. Rev. Bishop Aurelian Bilgeri, O.S.B., D.D., P.O.B. 53, Eshowe.

Umtata: Rt. Rev. Bishop Henry Karlen, C.M.M., P.O.B. 85, Umtata.

Kokstad: Rt. Rev. Bishop J. E. McBride, O.F.M., D.PH., D.D., F O.B. 65, Kokstad.

Zululand: Rt. Rev. Mgr. A. M. Dennehy, O.S.M., St. Lucia Catholic Mission, P.O. St. Lucia Estuary.

PROVINCE OF PRETORIA

Archbishop of Pretoria: Most Rev. Archbishop John C. Garner, D.D., D.PH.; 125 Main St., Waterkloof, Pretoria.

Bishops

Johannesburg: Rt. Rev. Bishop H. Boyle, D.D., P.O.B. 17054, Hillbrow; Rt. Rev. Bishop P. Butelezi, O.M.I. (Auxiliary Bishop).

Lydenburg-Witbank: Rt. Rev. Bishop Anthony Reiterer, M.F.S.C., P.O.B. 561, Witbank.

Pietersburg: Rt. Rev. Bishop D. C. Van Hoek, O.S.B., P.O.B. 166, Pietersburg.

Rustenburg: Rt. Rev. Mgr. H. L. Hallett, C.S.S.R., P.O.B. 107, Rustenburg.

Volksrust: Rt. Rev. Mgr. M. Banks, O.F.M., P.O.B. 275, Volksrust.

Klerksdorp: Rt. Rev. Mgr. D. Verstraete, O.M.I., P.O.B. 532, Klerksdorp.

Louis Trichardt: Rt. Rev. Mgr. J. Durkin, M.S.C., P.O.B. 127, Louis Trichardt.

Manzini (Swaziland): Rt. Rev. Bishop R. J. Casalini, O.S.M.

PROVINCE OF ORANGE FREE STATE

Archbishop of Bloemfontein: Most Rev. Archbishop Joseph P. Fitzgerald, O.M.I., D.D., P.O.B. 362, Bloemfontein.

Bishops

Kimberley: Rt. Rev. Bishop J. Bokenfohr, O.M.I., D.D., P.O.B. 309, Kimberley.

Keimoes: Rt. Rev. Bishop J. B. Minder, O.S.F.S., P.O.B. 146, Springbok.

Kroonstad: Rt. Rev. Bishop Gerard van Velsen, O.P.A., P.O.B. 129, Kroonstad.

Bethlehem: Rt. Rev. Bishop Peter Kelleter, C.S.S.P.

Gaborone (Botswana): Rt. Rev. Bishop C. J. Murphy, P.O.B. 267, Gaborone.

THE EVANGELICAL LUTHERAN CHURCH

The Federation of Evangelical Lutheran Churches in Southern Africa (FELCSA), formed in 1966 and meeting every three years, is a general synod embracing 13 European and non-European Lutheran churches, including three in South West Africa and one in Rhodesia. Each church has its own leader, who is either a bishop or a president (präses). In 1960 there were 499,246 Lutherans in South and South West Africa.

Non-White Churches

Cape-Orange Region: Bishop G. Zittlau, 12 Haberfeld St., Klisserville, Kimberley.

Tswana Region: Bishop D. P. Rapoo, Box 536, Rustenburg, Transvaal.

South-Eastern Region: Bishop Paulus Ben Mhlungu, P.O.B. 204, Mapumulo, Natal.

Transvaal Region: Bishop P. G. Pakendorf, Box 15196, Lynn East, Pretoria.

Eastern Province (Moravian Church): Superintendent and Bishop Rt. Rev. Dr. S. Nielsen, Mvenyane, P.O. Cedarville, East Griqualand; Africans only.

Western Cape Province (Moravian Church): Bishop Dr. B. Krüger, 32 Ranelagh Rd., Newlands, Cape Province; Chair. of Provincial Board Rev. A. W. Habelgaarn; Coloureds only; publ. *Die Huisvriend* (twice-weekly); circ. 3,000.

White Churches

Transvaal: Präses J. Wernecke, P.O.B. 17098, Hillbrow, Johannesburg. (The German Lutheran Congregations in Rhodesia are incorporated in this church.)

Hermannsburg: Präses H. Hahne, P.O.B. 1067, Pietermaritzburg, Natal.

Cape: Präses H. von Delft, 26 Hofmeyr St., Stellenbosch, Cape Province.

The German mission societies (the Berliner, Hermannsburger, Rheinische and Herrnhuter) are also important. The German Lutheran congregations in Southern Africa are united in various Evangelical-Lutheran churches which together with other Lutheran congregations of European background form the United Evangelical Lutheran Church in Southern Africa.

OTHER CHURCHES

Bantu Presbyterian Church of South Africa: P.O. Mpolweni, Natal; Gen. Sec. Rev. A. V. NZIMANDE.

Baptist Union of South Africa: 210 Transafrica Building, Wolmarans St., Johannesburg; f. 1877; Pres. Rev. R. J. VOKE; Gen. Sec. C. W. PARNELL; 46,511 mems.; publ. *South African Baptist;* circ. 4,000.

Church of England in South Africa: P.O.B. 1530, Cape Town; began with the British occupation of the Cape at the beginning of the nineteenth century, and continued to exist after the secession of the Church of the Province of South Africa in 1870; 19 European Churches (including 2 in Rhodesia), 2 Coloured and over 150 African; Bishops: Rt. Rev. S. C. BRADLEY, L.TH.; Rt. Rev. P. P. CHAMANE; Rt. Rev. W. D. DOUGLAS; Registrar H. HAMMOND, M.A.; publ. *Church News;* circ. 3,000.

Methodist Church of South Africa, The: Methodist Connectional Office, P.O.B. 2256, Durban, Natal; f. 1883; Pres. Rev. S. G. PITTS; Sec. Rev. CYRIL WATKINS; 382,898 mems.; publ. *Dimension.*

Nederduitsch Hervormde Kerk Van Afrika: P.O. Box 2368, Pretoria; governed according to Presbyterian Church regulation by a General Church Assembly; Administrator A. B. VAN N. HERBST, 210 Jacob Maré Street, Pretoria; total membership 190,342.

Presbyterian Church of Southern Africa: Head Office: Saambou Building, 112 Commissioner St., P.O.B. 11347, Johannesburg; f. 1897; Gen. Sec. and Clerk of the Assembly: Rev. E. S. PONS, M.A.; 63,000 mems.; publ. *The Christian Leader* (circ. 20,000), Proceedings of General Assembly.

Reformed Church in South Africa (Die Gereformeerde Kerk): P.O.B. 20004, Northbridge, Potchefstroom; f. 1859; publishes ecclesiastical and missionary periodicals; Principal Officer I. J. LESSING, P.O.B. 20004, North Bridge; total membership 139,744, all races.

United Congregational Church of Southern Africa: P.O.B. 31083, Braamfontein, Transvaal; f. 1799; Chair. Rev. D. R. BRIGGS; Secs. Rev. JOSEPH WING, Rev. J. F. THORNE; Regional Secs. Rev. J. K. MAIN (Botswana), Rev. B. SPONG (Central), Rev. J. T. PARSONS (Eastern Cape), Rev. W. G. M. ABBOTT (Natal), Rev. G. O. LLOYD (Rhodesia), Rev. J. F. THORNE (Western Cape); 120,000 mems.; publ. *The Christian Leader.*

JEWISH COMMUNITY

The Jews have been associated with South Africa since its earliest days. There was a party of Jews among the 1820 settlers. An organized Jewish community was founded at Cape Town in 1841 and there are now about 200 congregations in the country, most of them having their own synagogues. The official representative of the World Zionist Organization (and of its various funds and institutions in South Africa) is the South African Zionist Federation. In 1960 there were 108,497 Jews in South Africa.

South African Jewish Board of Deputies: P.O.B. 1180, Johannesburg; f. 1912; is the representative institution of South African Jewry; is composed of all the important congregational and Jewish institutions in South Africa; there are about 116,000 Jews in South Africa; Pres. MAURICE PORTER; Chair. D. K. MANN.

THE PRESS

DAILIES

CAPE PROVINCE

Argus, The: 122 St. George's St., P.O.B. 56, Cape Town; f. 1857; evening; English; Independent; circ. 115,654; Editor W. W. MACKENZIE.

Burger, Die: 30 Keerom St., P.O.B. 692, Cape Town; f. 1915; morning; Afrikaans; supports National Party; circ. 64,263; Editor P. J. CILLIÉ.

Cape Times: 77 Burg Street, Cape Town; f. 1876; morning; English; Independent; circulation 75,407; Editor A. H. HEARD.

Daily Dispatch: 33 Caxton Street, P.O. Box 131, East London; f. 1872; morning; English; Independent; circ. 26,833; Editor D. J. WOODS.

Daily Representative: 64 Cathcart Rd., Queenstown; f. 1859; evening; English; circ. 1,723; Man. Dir. F. L. GREEN; Editor M. ARNOT.

Diamond Fields Advertiser: P.O.B. 610, Kimberley; f. 1878; morning; English; Editor M. B. LLOYD.

Eastern Province Herald: Newspaper House, 19 Baakens St., P.O.B. 1117, Port Elizabeth; f. 1845; morning; English; Independent; circ. 29,729; Editor H. E. O'CONNOR.

Evening Post: 19 Baakens St., P.O.B. 1121, Port Elizabeth; f. 1947; afternoon; Independent; English; circ. 24,000 daily edition, 51,000 weekend edition; Editor J. G. SUTHERLAND.

Grocott's Mail: 40 High St., P.O.B. 179, Grahamstown; English; Independent; Editor A. TEMPLE.

Oosterlig, Die: P.O.B. 525, Port Elizabeth; f. 1937; pro-Government; Editor D. J. VAN ZYL; readership approx. 50,000.

NATAL

Daily News, The: 85 Field St., Durban; f. 1878; evening; English; Editor J. M. W. O'MALLEY.

Natal Mercury: 12 Devonshire Place, P.O.B. 950, Durban; f. 1852; morning; English; circ. 72,056; Editor-in-Chief JOHN D. ROBINSON.

Natal Witness: 244 Longmarket St., P.O.B. 362, Pietermaritzburg; f. 1846; morning; English; Editor S. R. ELDRIDGE.

ORANGE FREE STATE

Friend, The and Goldfields Friend: 21 Charles St., P.O.B. 245, Bloemfontein; f. 1850; morning; English; Independent; Editor P. MULLER.

Volksblad, Die: P.O.B. 267, Bloemfontein; f. 1904; evening; Afrikaans; pro-government; circ. daily edition 36,194, weekend edition 31,532; Editor S. F. ZAAIMAN.

TRANSVAAL

Hoofstad: Hoofstad Pers Bpk., P.O.B. 442, Pretoria; Afrikaans; supports Nationalist Party; Man. W. P. M. SCHOOMBEE.

Pretoria News: 216 Vermeulen St., P.O.B. 439, Pretoria; f. 1898; evening; English; Independent; Editor A. T. MYBURGH; Man. R. J. R. GITTINS.

Rand Daily Mail: P.O.B. 1138, 171 Main St., Johannesburg; f. 1902; morning; English; Independent; circ. 139,324; Editor RAYMOND LOUW; Man. J. N. McCLURG.

Star, The: 47 Sauer St., P.O.B. 1014, Johannesburg; f. 1887; evening; English; Independent; Editor J. P. JORDI.

Transvaler, Die: 8 Empire Rd. Extension, Auckland Park, P.O.B. 5474, Johannesburg; f. 1937; morning; Afrikaans; supports National Party; circ. 43,000; Editor C. F. NÖFFKE.

Vaderland, Die: 8 Empire Rd. Extension, Auckland Park, Johannesburg; f. 1914; Afrikaans; supports National Party; circ. 51,532; Editor A. M. VAN SCHOOR; Man. Dir. M. V. JOOSTE.

World, The: P.O.B. 6663, Johannesburg; f. 1932 as a weekly; daily in 1962; English language newspaper catering exclusively for the African people; circ. approx. 108,359; Editorial Dir. C. E. STILL.

WEEKLIES AND FORTNIGHTLIES

CAPE PROVINCE

Argus Week-end Edition, The: P.O.B. 56, Cape Town; f. 1857; Saturday; English; circ. 156,072; Editor W. W. MACKENZIE.

Cape Herald, The: P.O.B. 56, Cape Town; weekly; Editor D. WIGHTMAN; circ. 63,121.

Courier: Bank St., P.O.B. 64, Beaufort West; f. 1869; Friday; Editor RUFUS DERCKSEN.

District Mail, The: P.O.B. 58, Somerset West; f. 1928; Friday morning; local news; Editor NORMAN McLEOD.

Eikestadnuus: P.O.B. 28, Stellenbosch; Friday; English and Afrikaans; Editor Mrs. TINKA BOTHA.

Graaff-Reinet Advertiser: P.O.B. 31, Graaff-Reinet; f. 1864; rural; twice weekly; Independent; Editor A. R. KNOTT-CRAIG.

Huisgenoot: P.O.B. 1802, Cape Town; f. 1916; weekly; Editor P. A. JOUBERT.

Imvo Zabantsundu (*Bantu Opinion*): P.O.B. 190, Kingwilliamstown; f. 1884; Editor J. G. GEURTSE.

Jongspan, Die: P.O.B. 1802, Cape Town; f. 1935; only Afrikaans juvenile weekly in South Africa; Editor C. MOSTERT.

Kerkbode, Die: P.O.B. 4539, Cape Town; f. 1849; official organ of the Dutch Reformed Church of South Africa; Editor Dr. W. J. G. LUBBE.

Mafeking Mail and Botswana Guardian: P.O.B. 64, Mafeking; f. 1899; English and Afrikaans; Fri., Editor J. PODBREY; circ. 1,600.

Mercury, The: P.O.B. 122, King-williamstown; f. 1875; Thursday; general; English; Editor D. J. WOODS.

Midland News and Karroo Farmer: P.O. Box 101, Cradock; f. 1891; English; weekly; Editor J. B. FINLAISON.

Paarl Post: Upper New St., P.O.B. 248, Paarl; f. 1875; Tuesdays and Fridays; Afrikaans and English; Independent; Editor M. HENDLER.

South African Medical Journal: P.O.B. 643, Cape Town; weekly; organ of the Medical Association of South Africa; Editor P. J. VAN BILJON, M.D., CH.B., M.D.

South Western Herald: 119 York St., George; f. 1881; twice weekly; Man. S. R. BELL.

Uitenhage Chronicle: P.O.B. 44, 122 Caledon St., Uitenhage; f. 1880; weekly; general; English and Afrikaans; Editor E. M. HARPER.

Uitenhage Times, The: P.O.B. 46, Uitenhage; f. 1864; bilingual; Prop. and Editor J. S. HULTZER.

Umthunywa: Owen St., P.O.B. 129, Umtata; f. 1937; English and Xhosa; Editor J. D'OLIVEIRA.

Uniondale and Langkloof Medium: P.O.B. 31, Graaff Reinet; f. 1937; general news; Editor R. C. KNOTT-CRAIG.

NATAL

Farmers' Weekly: P.O.B. 83, Mobeni, Natal; f. 1911; Wednesday; agriculture; Editor W. C. HYMAN.

The Graphic: P.O.B. 2339, Durban; English; f. 1950; weekly; Editor M. S. ACHARY.

Ilanga: 128 Umgeni Rd., Durban; f. 1903; weekly; Zulu; Ed. Dir. A. F. RETIEF.

Indian Opinion: Private Bag, Durban; f. 1903; English and Gujerati; Editor Mrs. SUSHILA M. GANDHI.

Ladysmith Gazette: P.O.B. 500, Ladysmith; f. 1902; Thursday; circ. 2,800; Editor and Advt. Man. R. M. ROBINSON.

Leader, The: P.O.B. 2471, Durban; f. 1940; Ind.; English; weekly; Indian newspaper; Editor S. S. R. BRAMDAW.

Personality: 1322 South Coast Rd., Mobeni, Durban; f. 1957; Friday; national fortnightly magazine, incorporating *The Outspan*; Editor LEON BENNETT.

Newcastle Advertiser: P.O.B. 144, Newcastle; f. 1901; weekly; English and Afrikaans; Editor Mrs. K. F. KOBRIN.

Scope: 1322 South Coast Rd., Mobeni, Durban; f. 1966; Friday; national weekly news magazine; Group Editor JACK SHEPHERD-SMITH, Editor LEON BENNETT.

Sunday Tribune: P.O.B. 1491, Durban; f. 1947; English; Independent; Editor J. E. C. SCOTT.

Umafrika: P.O. Marianhill, Natal; Zulu weekly; f. 1911; circ. 11,000; Editor CRISPIN GRAHAM, C.M.M.

ORANGE FREE STATE

Bethlehem Express: 10 Muller St., P.O.B. 555, Bethlehem; f. 1905; bilingual; farming and commercial; circ. 2,075; Editor T. C. ROFFE, M.C.

Noordeltke Stem, Die/The Northern Times: Murray St., P.O.B. 309, Kroonstad; English and Afrikaans; Friday; Editor E. J. DE LANGE.

People's Weekly: P.O.B. 286, Bloemfontein; f. 1911; English; Independent; circ. 6,500.

TRANSVAAL

African Jewish Newspaper: 25 Davies Street, Doornfontein, Johannesburg; f. 1931; Friday; Yiddish; Editor LEVI SHALIT.

Boksburg Advertiser and Boksburg Volksblad: P.O. Box 136, Boksburg; English and Afrikaans; Friday; Editor S. GILL.

Brandwag, Die: 8 Empire Road Extension, Auckland Park; P.O.B. 845, Johannesburg; f. 1937; weekly; Afrikaans; circ. 113,500; Editor I. D. VAN DER WALT.

Darling: P.O.B. 83, Mobeni, Durban; f. 1952; weekly; Editor W. C. HYMAN.

Germiston Advocate and Germiston Koerant: P.O.B. 7, Germiston; f. 1923; weekly; English and Afrikaans; Editor and Man. S. GILL.

Middelburg Observer: P.O.B. 36, Middelburg; f. 1903; weekly; coal mining, farming and educational.

Northern Review: P.O.B. 45, Pietersburg; English and Afrikaans; Friday.

Post: Drum House, 62 Eloff St. Extension, P.O.B. 3413, Johannesburg; Editor P. S. SMITH.

Potchefstroom Herald: 3B Olën Lane, Potchefstroom; f. 1908; weekly; English and Afrikaans; Editor R. W. INGRAM.

Rapport: 102 Jorrissen St., Braamfontein; P.O.B. 8422, Johannesburg; f. 1971; Afrikaans Sunday newspaper; Editor W. J. WEPENER.

Rustenburg Herald: P.O.B. 170, Rustenburg; f. 1924; weekly; English and Afrikaans; Prop. Rustenburg Herald (Pty.) Ltd.; Managing Editor H. M. WULFSE.

S.A. Mining and Engineering Journal: Balgownie House, 66 Commissioner St., Johannesburg; f. 1891; technical journal; Gen. Manager P. H. CLARK; Editor G. M. THAIN.

The South African Financial Gazette: P.O.B. 8161, Johannesburg; f. 1964; weekly; English; Editor MARTIN SPRING.

South African Jewish Times (incorp. the **Rhodesian Jewish Journal**): P.O.B. 2878, Johannesburg; f. 1936; English-Jewish weekly; circ. 13,000; Editor ARTHUR MARKO-WITZ.

Stage and Cinema: P.O.B. 1574, Johannesburg; f. 1946; cinema, entertainment, fashion; fortnightly; Man. Editor R. L. FINLAYSON; circ. 40,000.

Sunday Express: 171 Main St., P.O.B. 1067, Johannesburg; f. 1934; English; Independent; circ. 203,870; Editor M. A. JOHNSON.

Sunday Times: 171 Main St., P.O.B. 1090, Johannesburg; f. 1906; English; Independent; circ. 470,000; Editor JOEL MERVIS.

Vereeniging and Vanderbijlpark News: P.O.B. 122, Vereeniging; f. 1915; Thursday; circ. 8,000; Editor B. BYRNE-DALY.

Weekend World: P.O.B. 6663, Johannesburg; f. 1968; general weekly; Editor C. E. STILL; circ. 177,396.

West Rand Review-Koerant: P.O.B. 171, Krugersdorp; f. 1898; Editor P. V. J. WALT.

West Rand Times and Westrander: Grand Chambers, Ockerse Street, P.O. Box 93, Krugersdorp; f. 1934; bilingual; Editor S. GILL.

Westelike Stem, Die: 110 King Edward Street, Potchefstroom; f. 1915; Afrikaans newspaper; circulation 3,000.

Zionist Record: P.O.B. 150, Johannesburg; f. 1908; weekly; bilingual; circ. 10,000; Editor S. GILL.

MONTHLIES
CAPE PROVINCE

Commercial Opinion (_Journal of the Association of Chambers of Commerce of South Africa_): P.O.B. 566, Cape Town; f. 1923; circ. 15,060; Editor W. B. WEST, B.COM.

Education: 24 Grove Bldg., Grove Ave., Claremont, Cape Town; f. 1890; organ of the South African Teachers' Association; circ. 2,750; Editors W. T. and I. FERGUSON.

New African, The: P.O.B. 2068, Cape Town; politics and the arts.

South African Banker, The: P.O.B. 61510, Marshalltown, Transvaal; published by The Institute of Bankers in South Africa; f. 1904; circ. 14,500; Editor PETER KRAAK.

South African Outlook: Outlook Publications (Pty.) Ltd., P.O.B. 245, Rondebosch; f. 1870; ecumenical and racial affairs; Editor FRANCIS WILSON.

South African Shipping News and Fishing Industry Review: P.O.B. 80, Cape Town; f. 1946; Editor MICHAEL STUTTAFORD.

Unie, Die: P.O. Box 196, Cape Town; f. 1905; educational; organ of the South African Teachers' Union; Editor L. C. BRUWER.

Wamba: 1 Leeuwen St., Cape Town; educational; publ. in seven Bantu languages; Editor C. P. SENYATSI.

Wynboer, Die: Kaapag Trust (Pty.) Ltd., P.O.B. 115, Stellenbosch; f. 1931; devoted to the interest of viticulture and the wine and spirit industry of South Africa; Editor G. R. F. MEYER.

NATAL

Home Front: c/o Mercury Building, Devonshire Place, P.O. Box 950, Durban; f. 1928; ex-Service magazine; Editor Mrs. M. DAWKINS.

Natal Review: 413 Paynes Buildings, West Street, P.O. Box 2434, Durban; English; trade review.

Reality: P.O.B. 1104, Pietermaritzburg; f. 1969; general political; Liberal; every two months.

ORANGE FREE STATE

Merino: P.O. Box 402, Bloemfontein; f. 1941; circ. 23,000; Editor S. H. J. VAN VUUREN.

Patriot: P.O. Box 286, Bloemfontein; f. 1916; official organ of the Sons of England Society of Southern Africa; circ. 2,000; Editor A. W. G. SCOTT.

TRANSVAAL

Commercial Transport: P.O.B. 8308, Johannesburg; f. 1946; monthly; Editor S. BUTCHER.

Ditaba: P.O.B. 164, Potgietersrus; f. 1959; English and Sotho; Editor DANIEL TSEBE.

Drum: 62 Eloff St. Extension, Johannesburg; f. 1951; twice monthly; circ. 80,000 in southern Africa, 400,000 throughout the continent; Editor P. SELWYN-SMITH.

Financial Times and Industrial Press: P.O.B. 6620, Johannesburg; monthly; Editor D. TOMMEY.

Food Industries of South Africa: P.O.B. 8308, Johannesburg, R.S.A.; f. 1948; Editor I. PHILIP.

Forum, The: P.O.B. 7108, Johannesburg; Editor N. A. G. CALEY.

Journal of the South African Institute of Mining and Metallurgy: P.O.B. 61019, Marshalltown, Transvaal; f. 1894; circ. 2,300; Hon. Editor H. P. CARLISLE.

Mining and Industrial Review: P.O.B. 9259, Johannesburg; f. 1907; Editor LEO LAVOO.

Ons Jeug: P.O. Box 2406, Pretoria; f. 1951; religious; Editor G. VAN DER WESTHUIZEN; circ. 12,000.

Photography and Travel: P.O.B. 8620, Johannesburg; f. 1963; monthly; Editor CECIL HOLMES; circ. 8,000.

Postal and Telegraph Herald: P.O.B. 9186, Johannesburg; f. 1904; English and Afrikaans; circ. 12,000; Editor L. J. VAN DER LINDE.

Railway Engineering: P.O.B. 8308, Johannesburg; f. 1957; twice monthly; Editor KEN MILWARD.

S.A. Engineer and Electrical Review: P.O.B. 8308, Johannesburg; f. 1918; trade and technical; Joint Editors C. WALLER, A. WATERS.

South African Architectural Record: 75 Howard House, Loveday Street, Johannesburg; f. 1915; journal of the Institute of South African Architects; Editor W. DUNCAN HOWIE, A.R.I.B.A., M.I.A.

South African Builder: Federated Insurance House, cnr. Harrison St. and De Villiers St., P.O.B. 11359. Johannesburg; f. 1923; official journal of Building Industries Federation (South Africa); circ. 4,745; Editor G. DE C. MALHERBE.

South African Garden and Home: P.O.B. 83, Mobeni, Durban; f. 1947; monthly; Editor W. M. HYMAN.

South African Mechanical Engineer, The: P.O.B. 61019, Marshalltown, Johannesburg; f. 1892; journal of the South African Institution of Mechanical Engineers; Hon. Tech. Editor E. A. BUNT; Prod. Editor Mrs. L. KRAFT.

S.A. Mining and Engineering Journal: P.O.B. 8308, Johannesburg; f. 1891; trade and technical; Editor P. HOLZ.

South African Mining Review: 709-711 Union House, Main St., Johannesburg; f. 1907; Editor D. I. HADDON.

South African Nursing Journal: P.O.B. 1280, Pretoria; f. 1935; official organ of the South African Nursing Association; circ. 33.450; Editor BARBARA L. ALFORD.

South African Philatelist: P.O.B. 375, Johannesburg; published by the Philatelic Federation of Southern Africa; Hon. Editor J. M. WEINSTEIN.

Southern African Financial Mail: P.O.B. 9959, Carlton Centre, Commissioner St., Johannesburg; f. 1959; circ. 21,000; Editor GEORGE PALMER.

SASSAR (South African Railways Magazine): P.O.B. 1111, Johannesburg; f. 1910; Man. Editor P. LE F. STRYDOM.

Utlwang: P.O. Box 170, Rustenburg; Tswana (Bantu); Prop. Utlwang Tswana Publications (Pty.) Ltd.; Managing Editor H. M. WULFSE.

Wings over Africa: P.O.B. 68585, Bryanston, Transvaal; f. 1941; the aviation news magazine of Africa; Editor and Man. Dir. J. K. CHILWELL.

QUARTERLIES

CAPE PROVINCE

South African Law Journal: P.O.B. 30, Cape Town; f. 1884; Editor ELLISON KAHN, B.COM., LL.M.

TRANSVAAL

Lantern: P.O. Box 1758, Pretoria; organ of the Foundation for Education, Science and Technology (formerly S.A. Assoc. for Advancement of Knowledge and Culture); Managing Editor V. C. WOOD.

Motorist, The: P.O.B. 7068, Johannesburg; f. 1902; official journal of the Automobile Association of S.A.; twice per month; Editor A. BEZUIDENHOUT; circ. 450,000.

South African Journal of Economics: P.O.B. 31213, Braamfontein; English and Afrikaans; Man. Editor Prof. D. J. J. BOTHA.

South African Journal of Medical Sciences: Witwatersrand University Press, Jan Smuts Ave., Johannesburg; f. 1935; Editor Prof. H. B. STEIN.

South African Journal of Physiotherapy: P.O.B. 11151, Johannesburg; official journal of South African Society of Physiotherapy; Editor Miss E. M. BOTTING.

NEWS AGENCIES

South African Press Association: P.O.B. 7766, Mutual Buildings, Harrison St., Johannesburg; f. 1938; 28 mems.; Chair. D. P. DE VILLIERS; Man. R. A. WILSON; Editor E. H. LININGTON.

FOREIGN BUREAUX

Agence France-Presse: P.O.B. 3462, Lydney House, 99 Goud St., Johannesburg; Bureau Man. EDMOND MARCO.

AP: 701-3 Union Centre, 31 Pritchard St., Johannesburg; Chief KENNETH L. WHITING.

Jewish Telegraphic Agency: de Villiers and Banket Sts., Johannesburg.

Reuters General News Division: P.O.B. 2662, Mutual Building, Harrison St., Johannesburg; also has offices in Cape Town, Durban and Port Elizabeth.

Reuters Economic Services: P.O.B. 2662, Glencairn, Market St., Johannesburg.

UPI: P.O.B. 2385, Standard Bank Chambers, 1st Floor, 33 Troye St., Johannesburg.

DPA also has an office in South Africa.

PRESS ASSOCIATION

Newspaper Press Union of South Africa: P.O.B. 10537, 914 9th Floor, B.P. Centre, 36 Kerk St., Johannesburg; f. 1882; 168 mems.; Pres. L. E. A. SLATER; Sec. G. G. A. UYS.

PUBLISHERS

Argus Printing and Publishing Co. Ltd.: P.O.B. 1014, 47 Sauer St., Johannesburg; f. 1889; newspapers; Chair. and Man. Dir. L. E. A. SLATER; Gen. Mans. J. D. ST. C. HENNESSY and C. L. C. HEWITT.

Balkema, A. A.: 93 Keerom St., Cape Town; science, literature, history, architecture, fine arts.

Buren Publishers: P.O.B. 673, Cape Town; general fiction and non-fiction.

Butterworth and Co. (South Africa) (Pty.) Ltd.: P.O.B. 792, Durban.

Cape and Transvaal Printing and Publishing Co. Ltd.: P.O.B. 81, 77 Burg St., Cape Town; Chair. C. S. CORDER; Man. Dir. G. M. C. CRONWRIGHT.

Central News Agency Ltd.: P.O.B. 1033, Johannesburg.

Christian Publishing Co.: P.O.B. 132, Roodepoort, Transvaal; f. 1939; religious books and children's books in colour; Principal Officers TIMO CROUS, LEON WATSON, MAURICE SPIES, Mrs. M. M. CROUS.

Combined Publishers (Pty.) Ltd.: subsidiary of the Argus Printing and Publishing Co., 5th Floor, Star Building, 47 Sauer St., P.O.B. 8620, Johannesburg; reference books.

Constantia Publishers: P.O.B. 5, Cape Town; general fiction and non-fiction.

Da Gama Publishers (Pty.) Ltd.: 311 Locarno House, Loveday St., Johannesburg; prestige, industrial and travel books and journals; Man. Dir. FRANK DE FREITAS.

David Philip Publishers: Arderne Cottage, Scott Rd., Claremont, Cape Town; general.

Die Kinderpers: P.O.B. 2652, Cape Town; juvenile and educational.

Goeie Hoop-Uitgewers (Bpk.): P.O.B. 972, Johannesburg.

Government Printer: Bosman St., Pretoria.

H.A.U.M.: 58 Long St., P.O.B. 1371, Cape Town; general educational and juvenile.

Hugh Keartland Publishers Ltd.: P.O.B. 9221, Johannesburg; general fiction and non-fiction.

Human and Rousseau (Pty.) Ltd.: P.O.B. 5050, Cape Town; English and Afrikaans books; Dirs. J. J. HUMAN, L. ROUSSEAU, D. J. OPPERMAN, F. J. DAVIN.

Janda (Pty.) Ltd.: P.O.B. 2177, Cape Town; limited editions, art and flowers; Dirs. DAVID SCHRIRE, J. P. SCHRIRE, R. B. DEVITT.

Juta and Co. Ltd.: P.O.B. 30, Cape Town; f. 1853; Dirs. J. A. B. COOPER, T. G. DUNCAN, Q.C., J. D. DUNCAN, G. F. LAURENCE, J. E. CALDER, B. W. PARIS, J. E. DUNCAN, legal, technical, educational, general.

J. P. Van Der Walt and Seun (Edms.) Bpk.: P.O.B. 123, Pretoria; f. 1947; general; Man. Dir. J. P. VAN DER WALT.

Longman Southern Africa (Pty.) Ltd.: Vrystaat St., Paarden Eiland, Cape Town; education and general; representing Longman Group, Penguin Books, Oliver and Boyd, Churchill/Livingstone and Wills and Hepworth.

Lovedale Press: Lovedale, C.P.

McGraw-Hill Book Co.: P.O.B. 23423, Joubert Park, Johannesburg; educational and general.

Macmillan S.A. (Publishers) Ltd.: P.O.B. 23134, Joubert Park, Johannesburg; educational and general.

Maskew Miller Ltd.: 7-11 Burg St., P.O.B. 396, Cape Town; f. 1893; educational, scientific, general and fiction; Chair. B. W. MASKEW MILLER.

Nasionale Boekhandel: P.O.B. 119, Parow, Cape Province; fiction, general (English and Afrikaans).

Nasou Ltd.: P.O.B. 105, Parow; educational.

Oxford University Press: P.O.B. 1141, Cape Town; Gen. Man. N. C. GRACIE.

Perskor Publishers: P.O.B. 845, Johannesburg; f. 1971 as a result of a merger between Afrikaanse Pers-Boekhandel and Voortrekkerpers; general and educational; Gen. Man. D. S. VAN DER MERWE.

President Publishers: P.O.B. 1774, Johannesburg; Afrikaans fiction.

Pro Rege Press: P.O.B. 343, Potchefstroom; educational, religious and general.

Reijger Publishers: P.O.B. 2153, Cape Town; general fiction and non-fiction.

Romantica Press: P.O.B. 799, Cape Town; general fiction and non-fiction.

Shuter and Shuter (Pty.) Ltd.: P.O.B. 109, Pietermaritzburg; f. 1921; educational in English and Zulu, general; Chair. F. B. OSCROFT.

C. Struik Publishers (Pty.) Ltd.: P.O.B. 1144, Cape Town; specialists in all books dealing with Africa; Dirs. G. STRUIK, Mrs. J. W. STRUIK VAN HARTINGSVELDT, P. STRUIK.

Tafelberg Uitgewers: P.O.B. 879, Cape Town; children's books, fiction and non-fiction, historical books, etc.

Thomson Publications, South Africa (Pty.) Ltd.: P.O.B. 8308, Johannesburg; trade and technical; Chair. B. PAVER.

Timmins, Howard: P.O. Box 94, Cape Town; f. 1937.

University Publishers and Booksellers (Pty.) Ltd.: P.O.B. 29, Stellenbosch, C.P.; text and children's books.

Van Schaik, J. L., Ltd.: P.O.B. 724, Pretoria; fiction, general, educational; English, Afrikaans and vernacular.

Via Afrika Ltd.: P.O.B. 1097, Bloemfontein; Bantu educational.

White, A. C., Printing and Publishing Co. (Pty.) Ltd.: P.O.B. 286, Bloemfontein.

William Heinemann (South Africa) (Pty.) Ltd.: P.O.B. 11190, Johannesburg; fiction and general.

Witwatersrand University Press: Jan Smuts Avenue, Johannesburg; f. 1938; academic; Publ. Officer N. H. WILSON.

World Printing and Publishing Co. (Pty.) Ltd.: P.O.B. 6663, Johannesburg; f. 1932; publishers of *The World*, *Weekend World*, *Ilanga*, newspapers serving the African market; Chair. L. E. A. SLATER; Man. Dir. J. D. ST. C. HENNESSY; Editorial Dirs. C. E. STILL, E. RETIEF.

South African Publishers' Association: P.O.B. 122, Parow; founded in 1946 the Association affords book publishers the means of dealing collectively with many problems. It represents publishers in dealing with government departments, local authorities and other institutions. Chair. H. G. JAEKEL; Sec. P. G. VAN ROOYEN.

PUBLICATIONS BOARD

South African Publications Control Board: P.O.B. 9069, Cape Town; f. 1963; controls all entertainments and reading matter except daily and weekly newspapers; Chair. J. J. KRUGER.

RADIO AND TELEVISION

RADIO

South African Broadcasting Corporation: P.O. Box 8606, Johannesburg; Chairman of Control Board Dr. P. J. MEYER; Dir. Gens. J. N. SWANEPOEL, C. D. FUCHS.

Broadcasting in South Africa is carried on exclusively by the South African Broadcasting Corporation, a public utility organization established on 1 August 1936 in terms of the Broadcasting Act No. 22. In 1949 the Act was amended to empower the SABC to broadcast to South-West Africa and to foreign countries. The SABC derives its revenue from two sources: listeners' licences and the sale of time on its advertising services.

Licences (1972): approx. 2,350,000 licence holders.

DOMESTIC SERVICES

English Service; Afrikaans Service; Springbok Radio (the three national services); Radio Highveld; Radio Port Natal; Radio Good Hope (the three regional advertising services.

Radio South Africa: all-night service from 12.00 midnight to 5.00 a.m.

Radio Bantu: broadcasts in Zulu, Xhosa, Southern Sotho, Northern Sotho, Tswana, Tsonga, Venda, Ndonga, Kuanyama, Nama/Damara and Herero.

Lourenco Marques Radio: This station is owned by the Radio Club of Mozambique but the youth oriented programmes and advertising service are managed by the SABC. It broadcasts nationwide on shortwave and medium wave for 168 hours per week.

EXTERNAL SERVICE

Voice of South Africa: Bloemendal, near Johannesburg; short-wave station: broadcasting in English, Afrikaans, French, Portuguese, Dutch, German, Tsonga, Swahili and Chichewa.

Orlando Rediffusion Service (Pty.) Ltd.: 110-112 Denhil, Corner Bertha and Jorissen Sts., Braamfontein, Johannesburg; subsidiary of Rediffusion Ltd., London; f. 1952; wired broadcasting system distributing special "Bantu" programmes of the South African Broadcasting Corporation in the native township of Orlando; programmes 16 hours daily; Man. R. D. RAMSAY, 10,400 subscribers (1962).

TELEVISION

In April 1971 the Government accepted the essentials of the report of the Commission of Inquiry into Television, set up in December 1969. The Government approved in principle the introduction of a statutorily controlled television service, which would respect the Christian values of South Africa and the social structure of its various communities.

Services will begin in 1976, and will be run by the South African Broadcasting Corporation. Initially there will be a service of about 37 hours a week on one channel only, in English and Afrikaans. Later a decision will be taken on separate services in English, Afrikaans and the main Bantu languages.

FINANCE

BANKING

(cap. = capital; p.u. = paid up; dep. = deposits; m. = million;
R. = Rand)

CENTRAL BANK

South African Reserve Bank: Church Square, Pretoria;
f. 1920; cap. p.u. R.2m.; dep. R.412m. (March 1972);
Gov. Dr. T. W. DE JONGH; Sen. Deputy Gov. Dr.
D. G. FRANZSEN; publs. *Quarterly Bulletin, Annual
Economic Report.*

COMMERCIAL BANKS

Bank of Lisbon and South Africa Ltd.: 286 Bosman St.,
Pretoria, and four branches; f. 1965; cap. 80m. escudos.

Barclays National Bank Ltd.: P.O.B. 1153, Johannesburg;
Chief Gen. Man. H. S. MORONY, O.B.E.; cap. and res.
R.83m.; publ. *Barclays National Review.*

The First National City Bank (South Africa) Ltd.: 60
Market St., Johannesburg; a subsidiary of First
National City Bank of New York (U.S.A.); eight
branches; Man. Dir. G. L. BENNETT.

French Bank of Southern Africa Ltd.: 50 Marshall St.,
Johannesburg, and ten branches; f. 1949; subsidiary of
Banque de l'Indochine, Paris; cap. p.u. R.2.3m.; dep.
R.83.01m. (Dec. 1971); Man. Dir. R. M. B. AGIER;
Asst. Gen. Mans. F. M. MANGAN, P. CAVARD.

Nedbank Ltd.: Nedbank Central, 81 Main St., Johannes-
burg; f. 1888; formerly Netherlands Bank of South
Africa Ltd.; fully South African owned; cap. R.12.5m.;
dep. R.577m. (Sept. 1971); Man. Dir. G. S. MULLER;
Sen. Gen. Mans. D. T. NICHOLSON, R. J. N. ABRAHAM-
SEN.

South African Bank of Athens Ltd., The: 103 Fox St.,
Johannesburg; f. 1947; cap. R.1m.; dep. R.10.6m.;
Man. Dir. JOHN ZOUNGOS.

Standard Bank of South Africa Ltd., The: 78 Fox St.,
Johannesburg; f. 1962; cap. p.u. R.38,180,200 (1970);
Chief Gen. Man. G. M. F. OXFORD; publ. *Standard
Bank Review* (monthly).

The Stellenbosch District Bank Ltd.: Bird St., Stellenbosch;
f. 1882; cap. p.u. R.97,700; dep. R.12m. (1971); Chair.
P. K. MORKEL.

Volkskas Ltd.: P.O.B. 578, 229 Van Der Walt St., Pretoria;
f. 1935; cap. R.14m.; dep. R.699m. (March 1971);
Chair. Dr. J. A. HURTER; Man. Dir. D. P. S. VAN
HUYSSTEEN; 502 offices.

GENERAL BANKS

Nefic Ltd.: Cnr. Church and Andries Sts., Pretoria; a
wholly owned subsidiary of the Netherlands Bank of
S.A. Ltd.; cap. p.u. R.2.5m.; provides medium- and
long-term finance; Chair. F. J. C. CRONJE.

Rand Bank Ltd.: 57 Commissioner St., Johannesburg;
f. 1966; cap. p.u. and res. R.4.6m.; dep. R.71.6m.;
specializes in shipping and confirming, the financing
of the movement of goods and leasing and hire purchase financing; Man. Dir. PIET BOTHA.

Santam Bank Ltd.: Cnr. Burg and Castle Sts., P.O.B.
653, Cape Town; cap. p.u. R.3.5m.; dep. R.111m.
(1972); Chair. C. H. J. VAN ASWEGEN; Man. Dir.
T. J. STEYN.

FINANCE HOUSES

Central Finance Corporation of South Africa Ltd.: Commissioner St., Johannesburg; f. 1956; merchant
bankers; Chair. M. S. LOUW; Gen. Man. and Sec.
J. A. VENTER.

Credit Corporation of South Africa Ltd.: Hollard Place,
71 Fox St., Johannesburg; f. 1946; a registered
banking institution; 12 brs. throughout South Africa;
provides medium-term instalment finance for the purchase or leasing of machinery, office equipment,
commercial vehicles, automobiles, etc.; Letters of
Credit established for direct imports by instalment
buyers; Chair. Dr. B. H. HOLSBOER.

Industrial Development Corporation of South Africa Ltd.:
P.O. Box 6905, Johannesburg; f. 1940; a Statutory
Body; Chair. J. J. KITSHOFF.

Industrial Finance Corporation of South Africa Ltd.: P.O.
Box 8575, Johannesburg; f. 1957; provides capital for
development of industry in South Africa; mems. include
principal mining groups, commercial banks and life
assurance companies operating in the Republic, the
South African Reserve Bank and the Industrial
Development Corporation of South Africa Ltd.; Sec.
K. L. KINGMA.

Land and Agricultural Bank of South Africa: Cnr. of
Paul Kruger and Visagie Sts., P.O.B. 375, Pretoria.

National Industrial Credit Corporation Ltd.: 12 New St.
South, Johannesburg; finance and discounting
business; cap. p.u. R.2.2m.; Chair. C. F. TODD.

Sentrale Aksepbank Bpk. (Central Merchant Bank Ltd.):
18 Fox St., Johannesburg; cap. p.u. R.10m.; dep.
R.136m.; Chair. (vacant); Man. Dir. H. P. DE VILLIERS.

South African Scottish Finance Corp. Ltd.: P.O.B. 7482,
Johannesburg; subsidiary of Credcor Bank Ltd.;
cap. p.u. R.600,000; dep. R.6m. (1971); 12 branches
throughout South Africa; provides medium-term
instalment finance for the purchase or leasing of
machinery, office equipment, commercial vehicles,
automobiles, etc.; Letters of Credit established for
direct imports by instalment buyers; Chair. Dr. B. H.
HOLSBOER.

Trade & Industry Acceptance Corporation Ltd.: 13th Floor,
Cape Towers, MacLaren St., P.O.B. 61992, Marshalltown, Johannesburg; finance for business to acquire
machinery and equipment on deferred payment or
lease.

Trust Bank of Africa Ltd.: The Trust Bank Centre, P.O.B.
2116, Cape Town; f. 1954; banking investment and
insurance services, including international finance and
trade; cap. p.u. and reserves R.39m.; dep. R.600m.
(1971); Man. Dir. J. S. MARAIS; Gen. Man. A. P. J.
BURGER.

Union Acceptances Ltd.: Union Acceptances House, 66
Marshall St., P.O.B. 61845, Marshalltown, Johannesburg; brs. at Cape Town, Durban, Port Elizabeth;
f. 1955; total group assets R.170.2m. (Dec. 1971);
registered merchant bank providing banking facilities,
investment advice, economic research, and handling
new issues, mergers, amalgamations, take-over bids,
investment management of portfolios, closed-end
trusts and mutual fund, company and financial
analysis, economic research, shipping, export finance,
deposits and foreign exchange and insurance broking;
Chair. M. W. RUSH; Deputy Chair. H. A. WILLIAMS;
Man. Dir. C. CARRINGTON.

UDC Bank Ltd.: 10th Floor, Unicorn House, cnr. Marshall
& Sauer Sts., Johannesburg; f. 1937; money accepted
on deposit; finance for hire-purchase or leasing of
plant, machinery, private and commercial vehicles;
cap. R.2,500,000; dep. R.49,109,782; Chair. C. W.
DACE; Man. Dir. I. R. SUMMERS.

Western Bank Ltd.: Schlesinger Centre, Braamfontein, Johannesburg; f. 1968 through merger of Colonial Bank Ltd. and Western Credit Bank Ltd.; cap. p.u. R.1.8m.; dep. R.116m. (June 1971); Chair. JOHN S. SCHLESINGER; Man. Dir. D. B. SANGER.

MERCHANT BANKS

The Hill Samuel Group (S.A.) Ltd.: 70 Fox St., Johannesburg; a subsidiary of Hill Samuel & Co. Ltd., London; specialize in full range of merchant banking facilities, general insurance broking and pension fund consulting; cap. R.7.2m.; dep. R.20.6m.; Chair. G. V. RICHDALE; Chief Exec. F. J. LEISHMAN.

SAVINGS BANK

Post Office Savings Bank: Dept. of Posts and Telegraphs, Union Bldgs., Pretoria.

DISCOUNT HOUSES

The Discount House of South Africa Ltd.: 60 Market St., Johannesburg; cap. p.u. R.2m.; Chair. G. C. FLETCHER, M.C.; Man. Dir. C. J. H. DUNN.

The National Discount House of South Africa Ltd.: Loveday St., Johannesburg; cap. p.u. R.2.41om.; dep. R.198m. (1971); Chair. D. L. KEYS; Man. Dir. K. J. B. SINCLAIR; total assets R.206m. (1971).

National Finance Corporation: Reserve Bank Bldg., P.O.B. 427, Pretoria.

DEVELOPMENT ORGANIZATIONS

Standard Bank Development Corporation of S.A. Ltd.: 78 Fox St., Johannesburg; cap. p.u. R.12,000,000 (1970); Man. Dir. J. A. ROGAN.

Standard Bank Investment Corporation Ltd.: 78 Fox St., Johannesburg; f. 1969; cap. p.u. R.38,181,000 (1970); Man. Dir. W. T. PASSMORE; publ. *Standard Bank Review* (monthly).

BANKING ORGANIZATION

Institute of Bankers in South Africa: P.O.B. 61510, Marshalltown, Johannesburg; f. 1904; 14,400 mems.; Sec. Gen. PETER KRAAK; publ. *The South African Banker.*

STOCK EXCHANGES

Johannesburg Stock Exchange: P.O.B. 1174, Johannesburg; f. 1887; market value of listed shares in 1,089 companies: R.26,324,643,000 (June 1972); Pres. RICHARD LURIE.

INSURANCE

A.A. Mutual Life Assurance Association Ltd.: Automutual House, 20 Wanderers St., P.O.B. 1653, Johannesburg; Chair. PHILIP SCEALES; Gen. Man. W. H. PLUMMER.

African Life Assurance Society Ltd.: African Life Centre, 117 Commissioner St., P.O.B. 1114, Johannesburg; f. 1904; Chair. M. D. MOROSS; Chief Gen. Man. R. A. L. CUTHBERT.

African Mutual Trust & Assurance Co. Ltd.: 34 Church St., P.O.B. 27, Malmesbury; f. 1900; Chief Gen. Man. R. A. L. CUTHBERT.

Atlantic & Continental Assurance Co. of South Africa Ltd.: A.C.A. Building, 102 Commissioner St., P.O.B. 5813, Johannesburg; f. 1948; Chair. and Man. Dir. S. R. HELLIG.

Aviation Insurance Co. of Africa Ltd.: 9th Floor, St. Andrew's Bldg., 39 Rissik St., Johannesburg; Gen. Man. D. TILLEY.

Bastion Insurance Co. Ltd.: Netherlands Insurance Centre, Smit, Eloff and Wolmarans St., Braamfontein, Johannesburg; Gen. Man. N. ROSS.

Central Board for Co-operative Insurance Ltd.: 7th Floor, Siemens Bldg., cnr. Biccard and Wolmarans Sts.,

P.O.B. 31275, Braamfontein; Gen. Man. P. A. C. CLOETE.

Commercial Union Assurance Co. of South Africa Ltd.: Commercial Union House, cnr. Rissik and Main Sts., P.O.B. 222, Johannesburg; Gen. Man. J. W. BIRKINSHAW.

Credit Guarantee Insurance Corpn. of Africa Ltd.: Avril Malan Building, 57/59 Commissioner St., P.O.B. 9244, Johannesburg; f. 1956; Gen. Man. M. DE KLERK.

Federated Employers' Insurance Co. Ltd.: Federated Insurance House, 1 de Villiers St., P.O.B. 666, Johannesburg; f. 1944; Chair. J. A. BARROW; Man. Dir. H. J. S. EVERETT.

General Accident Insurance Co. South Africa Ltd.: General Assurance Building, 86 St. George's St., P.O.B. 558, Cape Town; Gen. Man. D. A. BLACK.

Guarantee Life Insurance Co. Ltd.: Schlesinger Centre, 222 Smit St.; Chair. M. D. MOROSS; Man. Dir. Dr. S. PEER.

Guardian Assurance Company South Africa Ltd.: Allied Building, corner Bree and Rissik Sts., P.O.B. 8777, Johannesburg; Gen. Man. G. H. WATSON.

Hollandia Reinsurance Company of South Africa Ltd.: 404 Pearl Assurance House, Foreshore, P.O.B. 3238, Cape Town; f. 1953; Chair. R. J. RUMBELOW; Deputy Chair. E. J. SLAGER; Man. T. P. J. M. PLATTENBURG.

Incorporated General Insurances Ltd.: Auckland House, 18 Biccard St., Braamfontein, Johannesburg; Gen. Man. I. M. A. LEWIS.

Liberty Life Association of Africa Ltd.: Guardian Liberty Centre, 39 Wolmarans St., Braamfontein, P.O.B. 10499, Johannesburg; f. 1958; mem. of the world-wide Guardian Royal Exchange Assurance Group.

Malmesbury Board of Executors and Trust and Fire Assurance Company: Hill St., Malmesbury.

Marine and Trade Insurance Company Ltd.: Harmain House, 26 Harrison St., P.O.B. 10509, Johannesburg; f. 1953; Chair. E. MELAMED; Gen. Man. L. D. GODDARD.

Maritime and General Insurance Co. Ltd.: 3rd Floor, Howard House, 23 Loveday St., Johannesburg; Gen. Man. D. P. GALLIMORE.

Metlife: Metropolitan Life Building, Central Square, Pinelands, Cape Province.

Monument Assurance Corporation Ltd.: De Korie Bldg., 46 De Korie St., Braamfontein, Johannesburg.

Mutual and Federal Insurance Co. Ltd.: Standard Bank Centre, Fox St., P.O.B. 1120, Johannesburg; Man. Dir. J. A. VAN RYNEVELD.

National Employers' General Insurance Co. Ltd.: Amcor House, Marshall St. (between Harrison and Simmonds Sts.), Johannesburg, and P.O.B. 61286, Marshalltown, Transvaal; Man. Dir. R. H. HYDE, F.C.I.I.

National Employers' Life Assurance Co. of South Africa Ltd.: Amcor House, Marshall St. (between Harrison and Simmonds Sts.), P.O.B. 61286, Marshalltown, Transvaal; Gen. Man. R. H. HYDE.

Netherlands Insurance Co. of South Africa Ltd.: Netherlands Insurance Centre, Smit, Eloff and Wolmarans St., Braamfontein; Gen. Man. A. J. HUNINK; Asst. Gen. Man. N. ROSS.

Norwich Union Insurance Society of South Africa Ltd.: 4th Floor, Norwich Union House, 91 Commissioner St., Johannesburg; Gen. Man. K. G. PALMER.

Old Mutual (South African Mutual Life Assurance Soc.): Mutualpark, Jan Smuts Drive, P.O.B. 66, Cape Town; f. 1845; Chair. Brig. G. C. G. WERDMULLER, C.B.E., E.D., J.P.; Man. Dir. J. G. VAN DER HORST; Gen. Man. J. C. PIJPER.

President Insurance Co. Ltd.: 6th Floor, Rentmeester Building, 52 Commissioner St., Johannesburg; Gen. Man. Dr. H. BRINK.

Protea Assurance Co. Ltd.: Protea Assurance Building, Greenmarket Sq., P.O.B. 646, Cape Town; Deputy Chair. and Man. Dir. JOHN FISHER, F.C.I.S., F.C.I.I.

Provincial Insurance Co. of Southern Africa Ltd.: 1201 Parkade, Strand St., P.O.B. 1335; Cape Town, Gen. Man. J. H. HARRIES, F.C.I.I.

The Rand Mutual Assurance Co. Ltd.: Chamber of Mines Buildings, Main and Hollard Sts., P.O.B. 61413, Marshalltown, Johannesburg; f. 1894; Chair. R. J. C. GOEDE; Man. R. W. S. MOLYNEUX.

Reinsurance Union of South Africa Ltd.: 1 de Villiers St., P.O.B. 6325, Johannesburg; f. 1950; Chair. H. J. S. EVERETT; Gen. Man. T. N. PEACE; Sec. W. H. GREENWOOD.

Rondalia Assurance Corporation of South Africa Ltd.: Rondalia Bldg., Visagie St., P.O.B. 2290, Pretoria; f. 1943.

Royal Insurance Co. of South Africa Ltd.: Standard Bank Centre, 78 Fox St., P.O.B. 1120, Johannesburg; Man. Dir. J. A. VAN RYNEVELD.

Santam Insurance Co. Ltd.: Burg St., P.O.B. 653, Cape Town; f. 1918; Chair. C. H. J. VAN ASWEGEN; Man. Dir. I. J. STEYN.

Shield Insurance Co. Ltd.: Shield Insurance House, Main Rd., Rosebank, P.O.B. 1520, Cape Town; Gen. Man. S. WINBERG.

Shield Life Insurance Ltd.: 183 Sir Lowry Rd., P.O.B. 115, Cape Town; Man. Dir. JULIEN C. KARNEY.

South African Eagle Insurance Co. Ltd.: Eagle Star House, 70 Fox St., P.O.B. 61489, Marshalltown, Transvaal; Chair. Sir BRIAN MOUNTAIN; Chief Gen. Man. F. N. HASLETT, F.C.I.I.

South African Mutual Fire and General Insurance Co. Ltd.: Standard Bank Centre, Fox St., P.O.B. 1120, Johannesburg; f. 1921; Man. Dir. J. A. VAN RYNEVELD.

South African Trade Union Assurance Society Ltd.: Traduna House, 58 Frederick Street, P.O. Box 8791, Johannesburg; f. 1941; Chair. C. H. CROMPTON; Gen. Man. A. SUMNER.

The Southern Life Association: Great Westerford, Rondebosch, Cape Town; f. 1891; Chair. C. S. CORDER; Man. Dir. A. J. BURFORD.

Southern Insurance Association Ltd.: Allied Bldg., 46 St. George's St., P.O.B. 297, Cape Town; Gen Man. S. H. H. BRADBURN.

Standard General Insurance Co. Ltd.: Standard General House, 12 Harrison St., P.O.B. 4352, Johannesburg; f. 1943; Chair. LEIF EGELAND; Man. Dir. C. G. CAVALIERI.

Stenhouse (Pty.) Ltd.: 6th Floor Norwich Union House, Durban; f. 1964.

Suid-Afrikaanse Nasionale Lewensassuransie-Maatskappy (*South African National Life Assurance Co.*): P.O. Box 1, Sanlamhof, C.P.; f. 1918; Chair. A. D. WASSENAAR; Man. Dir. P. J. F. SCHOLTZ.

Suid-Afrikaanse Phoenix Assuransie Maatskappy Beperk: Phoenix House, 42 Burg St., P.O.B. 1827, Cape Town, Gen. Man. P. W. HOLT.

Swiss South African Reinsurance Co. Ltd.: 10th Floor, Swiss House, 86 Main St., P.O.B. 7049, Johannesburg; f. 1950; Chair. H. BYLAND; Gen. Man. W. STRICKER.

U.B.S. Insurance Co. Ltd.: 6th Floor, United Buildings, cnr. Fox and Eloff Sts;. Chair. P. W. SCEALES; Gen. Man. J. L. S. HEFER.

Union and National Insurance Co. Ltd.: 107 Commissioner St., P.O.B. 5277, Johannesburg; Chair. R. M. FORMBY; Man. Dir. D. A. McDONALD; Gen. Man. and Sec. K. NILSSON.

Union and South-West Africa Insurance Co. Ltd.: United Buildings, Kaiser St., Windhoek, S.W.A.; P.O.B. 908, Cape Town; Gen. Man. A. J. ASSITER.

Westchester Insurance Co. (Pty.) Ltd.: Suite D, 8th Floor, 41 Hans Strijdon Ave., Cape Town.

Woltemade Insurers Ltd.: Constantia Buildings, Andries Street, Pretoria; Man. Dir. A. J. MARAIS.

TRADE AND INDUSTRY

CHAMBERS OF COMMERCE

Association of Chambers of Commerce: P.O.B. 566, Cape Town and P.O.B. 694, Johannesburg; f. 1892; 119 principal chambers of commerce and local chambers are members; Pres. N. D. SEMPILL; Exec. Dir. H. S. MABIN; publ. *Commercial Opinion*.

PRINCIPAL MEMBERS

Chamber of Commerce: P.O.B. 87, Bloemfontein; f. 1883; Exec. Sec. Mrs. R. KIBUR; 675 mems.

Chamber of Commerce: P.O.B. 204, Cape Town; 1,429 mems.

Chamber of Commerce: P.O.B. 1506, Durban; 3,000 mems.

Chamber of Commerce: P.O.B. 93, East London; 346 mems.

Chamber of Commerce: P.O.B. 687, Johannesburg; 2,417 mems.

Chamber of Commerce: P.O.B. 65, Pietermaritzburg; 474 mems.

Chamber of Commerce: P.O.B. 48, Port Elizabeth; 870 mems.

Chamber of Commerce: P.O.B. 72, Pretoria; 315 mems.

Chamber of Commerce and Industry: P.O.B. 201, Springs; 240 mems.

Zululand Chamber of Commerce: P.O.B. 99, Empangeni; 234 mems.

INDUSTRIAL ORGANIZATIONS

South African Federated Chamber of Industries: P.O.B. 4516, 4th Floor, Nedbank Centre, cnr. Kerk and Beatrix Sts., Pretoria; f. 1917; Pres. S. R. BACK; Dir. Dr. D. C. KROGH; Alt. Dir. J. M. BURGER; Deputy Dir. P. F. THERON; publ. *F.C.I. Viewpoint*; mems. affiliated to the Federated Chamber of Industries.

Border Chamber of Industries: P.O.B. 27, East London; f. 1919; Sec. C. G. POTGIETER; 50 mems.

Cape Chamber of Industries: P.O.B. 1536, 5th Floor, Broadway Industries Centre, Heerengracht, Cape Town; f. 1904; Dir. R. M. LEE, B.A., LL.B.; 868 mems.

Chamber of Mines of South Africa: 5 Hollard St., P.O.B. 809, Johannesburg; f. 1889; Pres. R. C. J. GOODE; 136 mems.

Federation of Master Printers of South Africa: P.O.B. 1200, Johannesburg; f. 1916; Sec. C. R. THOMPSON; 858 mems.

Footwear Manufacturers' Federation of South Africa: P.O.B. 2228, Port Elizabeth; f. 1944; Dir. A. G. EVERINGHAM; 40 mems.

Industrial Development Corporation of South Africa Ltd.: P.O.B. 6905, Johannesburg; f. 1940; issued cap. R.295m.; Chair. J. J. KITSHOFF.

Leather Industry Suppliers' Association: Secs. Midland Chamber of Industries, P.O.B. 2221, Port Elizabeth; f. 1949; 19 mems.; Chair. H. GERSTEL.

Midland Chamber of Industries: P.O.B. 2221, S.A. Wool Board Bldg., Grahamstown Rd., Port Elizabeth; f. 1917; Dir. I. L. KRIGE; 350 mems.

Natal Chamber of Industries: P.O.B. 1300, Durban; f. 1904; Sec. P. H. THOMAS, B.A.; 926 mems.

National Association of Automobile Manufacturers of South Africa: P.O.B. 2221, Port Elizabeth; f. 1935; Dir. F. N. LOCK.

National Association of Woolwashers and Carbonizers of South Africa: Secs. Midland Chamber of Industries, P.O.B. 2221, Port Elizabeth; f. 1952.

National Chamber of Milling, Inc.: Head Office: 801 Siemens House, Biccard St., Braamfontein (P.O.B. 8609), Johannesburg; f. 1936; Man. and Sec. J. BARENDSE; the Chamber comprises all principal commercial wheat millers in South Africa, with wheat-milling plants in all the parts of the Republic, and is representative of practically the whole of commercial wheat milling in South Africa.

National Clothing Federation of South Africa: P.O.B. 8107, Johannesburg; f. 1945; handles all matters of economic importance to the industry; Dir. F. H. WHITAKER.

National Textile Manufacturers' Association: P.O.B. 1300, Durban; f. 1947; Sec. P. H. THOMAS, B.A.; 16 mems.

Northern Transvaal Chamber of Industries: P.O.B. 933, Pretoria; f. 1929; Dir. J. G. TOERIEN; 200 mems. (secondary industries).

Orange Free State Chamber of Industries: P.O.B. 1140, Bloemfontein; Pres. D. S. POOLEY.

Pietermaritzburg Chamber of Industries: P.O.B. 365, Pietermaritzburg; f. 1910; Secs. Messrs. Deloitte and Co.; 64 mems.

Southern African Breweries Institute: 2 Jan Smuts Ave., Braamfontein, Johannesburg; Dir. J. A. H. VAN NIEKERK.

South African Brick Association: Paillard House, cnr. Smit and De Beer Sts., Braamfontein, Transvaal; Dir. P. J. REYNOLDS.

South African Cement Producers' Association: P.O. Box 2832, Johannesburg; Dir. V. L. HOURELD.

South African Dried Fruit Co-op. Ltd.: P.O.B. 508, Wellington.

South African Fish Canners' Association (Pty.) Ltd. P.O.B. 2066, Pearl Assurance House, Foreshore, Cape Town; f. 1953; Chair. A. F. LEES; Man. P. J. O'SULLIVAN; 15 mems.

South African Foreign Trade Organization—SAFTO: Netherlands Bank Bldg., 80 Fox St., P.O.B. 9039, Johannesburg; f. 1963; Chief Exec. W. B. HOLTES; 400 mems.

South African Institute of the Boot and Shoe Industry, Inc.: P.O.B. 2240, Port Elizabeth; f. 1939; 305 mems.; publs. on technology of shoe manufacture (educational); Hon. Sec. K. W. T. RICHES.

South African Lumber Millers' Association: P.O. Box 1602, Johannesburg; f. 1941; Dir. D. H. ELOFF; 120 mems.

South African Oil Expressers' Association: P.O.B. 17222, Hillbrow, Johannesburg; f. 1937; Sec. J. W. H. FICK; 14 mems.

South African Soap Detergent and Candle Manufacturers' Association: P.O.B. 17222, Hillbrow, Johannesburg; f. 1928; Sec. J. W. H. FICK; 24 mems.

South African Sugar Association: P.O.B. 507, Durban; Gen. Man. P. SALE.

South African Tanners' Association: P.O.B. 2221, Port Elizabeth; f. 1944; (regd. 1946); Secs. Midland Chamber of Industries; 15 mems.

South African Tyre Manufacturers' Conference: P.O.B. 7490, Johannesburg; Sec. W. S. KIRK.

South African Wool Board: P.O.B. 1378, Pretoria; f. 1946; Chair. GIDEON J. JOUBERT; Man. Dir. S. P. VAN WYK; the Board consists of 16 members. They are 10 representatives of woolgrowers and six appointed by the Minister of Agriculture. One scientific adviser is a co-opted member.

South African Wool Combers Trade Association: Secs. Midland Chamber of Industries, P.O.B. 2221, Port Elizabeth; f. 1953.

South African Wool Commission: f. 1960, to stabilize wool prices.

South African Wool Textile Council: Secs. Midland Chamber of Industries, P.O.B. 2221, Port Elizabeth; f. 1953.

Transvaal Chamber of Industries: P.O.B. 4581, Johannesburg; f. 1910; Dir. I. G. MURRAY; 900 mems.

EMPLOYERS' ORGANIZATIONS

Association of Balanced Feed Manufacturers: Siems House, Wolmarans St., Braamfontein, Johannesburg; Sec. J. W. H. FICK.

Associated Commercial Employers: P.O.B. 1042, Johannesburg; f. 1944; Sec. K. J. DEWAR; 11 mem. associations.

Association of Electric Cable Manufacturers of South Africa: P.O.B. 1338, Johannesburg; 7 mems.

Association of Manufacturers of Gates, Fences, Wire Products and Light Metal Sections: P.O.B. 1536, Cape Town; Sec. J. F. ROOS.

Bespoke Tailoring, Dressmaking and Fur Garment Employers' Association: P.O.B. 9478, Johannesburg; f. 1933; Sec. B. KIEL; 398 mems.

Boatbuilders' and Shipwrights' Association of South Africa P.O.B. 1536, Cape Town; Sec. J. F. ROOS.

Building Industries Federation (South Africa): P.O.B. 11359, Johannesburg; f. 1904; Dir. G. DE C. MALHERBE, B.ECON.; 3,186 mems.; publs. *South African Builder* (monthly), *Building and Allied Trades Official Handbook* (annually).

Bus Owners' Association: 7 Stratford Rd., Durban; f. 1931; Sec. R. MAHABEER; 170 mems.

Business Equipment Association of South Africa: Allied Building, cnr. Bree and Rissik Sts., P.O.B. 4581, Johannesburg; f. 1936; Chair. T. K. BARR; 61 mems.

Cigar and Tobacco Manufacturers' Association: 73 Carlisle St., Durban; f. 1942.

Dairy Products Manufacturers' Association: P.O.B. 265, Pretoria; f. 1945; Sec. P. H. LISHMAN; 59 mems.

Electrical Engineering and Allied Industries' Association: P.O.B. 1338, Johannesburg; f. 1936; 216 mems.

Employers' Association of the Cinematograph and Theatre Industry of South Africa: 501-503 H.M. Buildings, Joubert St., Johannesburg; f. 1945; Sec. J. A. PERL.

Engineers' and Founders' Association (Transvaal, Orange Free State and Northern Cape): P.O.B. 1338, Johannesburg; f. 1945; 503 mems.

Grain Milling Federation: P.O.B. 8609, Johannesburg; f. 1944; Sec. J. BARENDSE.

Iron and Steel Producers' Association of South Africa: P.O.B. 1338, Johannesburg; 11 mems.

Light Engineering Industries Association of South Africa: P.O.B. 1338, Johannesburg; f. 1936; 234 mems.

Master Diamond Cutters' Association of South Africa: 510 Diamond Exchange Building, cnr. De Villiers and Quartz Sts., Johannesburg; f. 1928; 44 mems.

Motor Industries Federation: P.O.B. 3478, Johannesburg; f. 1910; Dir. R. G. DU PLESSIS; 5,500 mems.; publ. *The Automobile in South Africa.*

Motor Transport Owners' Association of South Africa: 501-502 Sanlam Bldgs., 29 Loveday St., Johannesburg; f. 1941; Sec. J. J. WEDDERBURN.

National Association of Biscuit Manufacturers of South Africa: P.O.B. 3137, Cape Town; f. 1927; Sec. P. H. COATES; 5 mems.

National Association of Grain Milling Employers: P.O.B. 8609, Johannesburg; f. 1945; Sec. J. BARENDSE; 96 mems.

National Federation of Hotel and Accomodation Establishments (Non-Liquor) of South Africa: Protea Assurance Building, 102 St. George's St., Cape Town; f. 1941; Sec. A. SEBBA.

Newspaper Press Union of South Africa: P.O.B. 10537, Johannesburg; f. 1882; Pres. L. E. A. SLATER; Sec. G. G. A. UYS; 168 mems.

Non-ferrous Metal Industries' Association of South Africa: P.O.B. 1338, Johannesburg; f. 1943; 30 mems.

Plastics Manufacturers' Association of South Africa: P.O.B. 1338, Johannesburg; f. 1948; 82 mems.

Precision Manufacturing Engineers' Association: P.O.B. 1338, Johannesburg; f. 1942; 92 mems.

Radio, Appliance and Television Association of South Africa: P.O.B. 1338, Johannesburg; f. 1942; 93 mems.

Sheet Metal Industries' Association of South Africa: P.O.B. 1338, Johannesburg; f. 1948; 151 mems.

Society of Automotive Importers, Assemblers and Distributors of South Africa: 134 London House, 21 Loveday St., Johannesburg; f. 1949; Pres. J. COBB; 62 mems.

South African Agricultural and Irrigation Machinery Manufacturers' Association: P.O.B. 1338, Johannesburg; f. 1944; 38 mems.

South African Association of Shipbuilders and Repairers: P.O.B. 1338, Johannesburg; 20 mems. Also at P.O.B. 1536, Cape Town; Sec. J. F. Roos.

South African Brewing Industry Employers' Association: P.O.B. 4581, Johannesburg; f. 1927; Sec. M. E. ROBERTSON; 2 mems.

South African Electroplating Industries' Association: P.O.B. 1338, Johannesburg; f. 1942; 18 mems.

South African Federation of Civil Engineering Contractors: P.O.B. 1, Halfway House, Tvl.; f. 1940; Dir. K. LAGAAY; 140 mems.; publ. *The Civil Engineering Contractor* (monthly), circ. 2,000.

South African Fruit and Vegetable Canners' Association (Pty.) Ltd.: 810-812 Tulbagh Centre, Hans Strijdom Ave., Cape Town; f. 1953; Sec. G. S. GLENDINING; 27 mems.

South African Insurance Employers' Association: P.O.B. 1141, Johannesburg.

South African Master Dental Technicians' Association: P.O.B. 9478, Johannesburg; f. 1946; Sec. W. A. DAVIDSON (Pty.), Ltd.

South African Ophthalmic Optical Manufacturers' Association: P.O.B. 4581, Johannesburg; f. 1945; Secs. Transvaal Chamber of Industries; 24 mems.

South African Radio and Television Manufacturers' Association: P.O.B. 1338, Johannesburg; 17 mems.

South African Reinforced Concrete Engineers' Association: P.O.B. 1338, Johannesburg; f. 1944; 53 mems.

South African Tube Makers' Association: P.O.B. 1338, Johannesburg; f. 1942; 14 mems.

South African Wire and Wire-rope Manufacturers' Association: P.O.B. 1338, Johannesburg; f. 1943; 4 mems.

Steel and Engineering Industries' Federation of South Africa: P.O.B. 1338, Johannesburg; f. 1947; 2,000 mems.

Sugar Manufacturing and Refining Employers' Association: 1100 Norwich Union House, Durban Club Place, Durban; f. 1947; Sec. D. R. WOODROFFE.

Tobacco Employers' Organisation: P.O.B. 4581, Johannesburg; f. 1941; Sec. Mrs. M. ROBERTSON; 3 mems.

Transvaal Coal Owners' Association: P.O.B. 1197, Johannesburg; f. 1907; Man. Dir. A. D. TEW.

TRADE UNIONS

The Industrial Conciliation Act of 1956 provides for the registration of Trade Unions and Employers' Organizations, for the establishment of Industrial Councils on which employers and employees have equal representation and for the settlement of disputes by conciliation and arbitration. The Act provides for the setting up of racially separate Trade Unions. In cases where separate Unions cannot be formed the mixed Unions must divide into separate branches for each race, while the Union Executive must be composed of white members only. The same act also prohibits the affiliation of Trade Unions with political parties. The Native Labour (Settlement of Disputes) Act, 1953, prohibits strikes by African workers and gives the Native Labour Officer ultimate authority in settling disputes involving such workers. African trade unions are not officially recognized by the Government. The only trade union federation with a high proportion of African members, the South African Congress of Trade Unions (f. 1955), which is completely non-racial, has been severely hampered by government bannings and detentions under the Suppression of Communism Act. The Trade Union Council of South Africa (TUCSA), which lost 14 member trade unions during 1968 after it reaffirmed its policy on African workers, decided in February 1969 to debar Africans from membership.

South African Confederation of Labour—SACL: P.O.B. 31105, Braamfontein; f. 1957 (reconstituted 1968); allows affiliation by Federations as well as individual white unions; largest co-ordinating body for the labour movement, representing approx. 200,000 workers; Pres. IVAN D. MARTIN; Hon. Sec. C. P. GROBLER.

COMMITTEES

Confederation of Metal and Building Unions: P.O.B. 9692, Johannesburg; 75,500 mems. in 8 organizations; Chair. E. H. McCANN.

Electricity Supply Commission Unions' Joint Committee: 803 Amaleng, 8 de Villiers St., Johannesburg; f. 1959; 47,785 mems. in 7 organizations; Chair. B. NICHOLSON; Gen. Sec. R. F. BUDD.

Federation of Mining Unions (FMU): 803 Amaleng, 8 de Villiers St., P.O.B. 9692, Johannesburg; f. 1937; 35,000 mems. in 6 organizations; Chair. R. F. BUDD; Sec. B. NICHOLSON.

Federation of Salaried Staff Associations of S.A.: P.O.B. 61069, Marshalltown, Transvaal; f. 1959; 24,000 mems. in five associations; Pres. C. J. PRETORIUS.

Garment Workers' Unions' Consultative Committee: P.O.B. 7288, Johannesburg; f. 1960; 42,321 mems. in four unions; Chair. ANNA SCHEEPERS; Gen. Sec. JOHANNA CORNELIUS.

National Industrial Council for the Iron, Steel, Engineering and Metallurgical Industry: 412 B.P. Centre, Kerk St., Johannesburg; Parties to the Council: 33 employer organizations and 10 trade union organizations; Gen. Sec. W. R. GLASTONBURY.

National Liaison Committee of Engineering Trade Unions: Plein St., Johannesburg; 70,000 mems.; 7 organizations; Chair. E. H. McCANN; Gen. Sec. W. BORNMAN.

Pulp and Paper Industries' Joint Committee: 803 Amaleng, 8 de Villiers St., Johannesburg; f. 1958; 37,567 mems. in four unions; Chair. T. P. MURRAY; Gen. Sec. R. F. BUDD.

South African Council of Transport Workers—SACTW: 202 Vulcan House, 88 Anderson St., Johannesburg; 6,000 mems. in 8 affiliates; Sec. A. H. HAMMON.

S.A. Federation of Leather Trade Unions: 22 Trades Hall, Kerk St., Johannesburg; 18,000 mems. in 8 unions; Pres. L. ALLEN; Sec.-Treas. L. C. M. SCHEEPERS.

FEDERATIONS

Coordinating Council of South African Trade Unions—CCSATU (*Die Koordinerende Raad van Suid Afrikaanse Vakverenigings*): 273 Pretorius-straat, P.O.B. 978, Pretoria; f. 1948; 72,000 in 16 unions; Chair. L. J. VAN DEN BERG; Sec. J. A. VAN WYK; publ. *S.A. Worker.*

Federal Consultative Council of South African Railways and Harbours Staff Associations—FCC: 40 Ameshoff St., Braamfontein; 82,987 mems. from 7 unions; Chair. I. D. MARTIN; Sec. J. R. BENADE.

Trade Union Council of South Africa—TUCSA: P.O.B. 5592, Johannesburg; f. 1954; 194,288 mems. from 69 unions; Pres. L. C. SCHEEPERS; Gen. Sec. J. ARTHUR GROBBELAAR.

African Leather Workers' Benefit Fund: P.O.B. 3039, Port Elizabeth; Sec. F. J. J. JORDAAN; 4,000 mems.

PRINCIPAL REGISTERED TRADE UNIONS

Amalgamated Engineering Union of South Africa: 8 de Villiers Street, P.O. Box 1168, Johannesburg; f. 1890; Sec. E. H. McCANN; 25,000 mems.; publ. *The Metal Worker* (monthly).

Amalgamated Society of Woodworkers: P.O. Box 1095, Johannesburg; f. 1881; Sec. H. B. BULL; 3,000 mems.

Amalgamated Union of Building Trade Workers of South Africa (Executive Council): 107-110 Vulcan House, 88 Anderson St., P.O.B. 5378, Johannesburg; f. 1916; Sec. E. SCOTT; 10,000 mems.

Artisan Staff Association: "Lowliebenhof", 193 Smit Street, Johannesburg; f. 1924; represents artisans and trade hands of the South African Railways, Airways and Harbours; Pres. J. ZURICH; Sec. C. P. GROBLER; 20,000 mems.

Bank Employees' Union: P.O.B. 1647, Pretoria; 5,000 mems.; Sec. J. P. STEYN.

European Liquor and Catering Trades Employees' Union: 508 Scott's Bldgs., Plein Street, Cape Town; f. 1960; Chair. J. J. FOURIE; Gen. Sec. Mrs. N. G. FORSYTH; 875 mems.

Federation of Furniture and Allied Trade Unions: P.O.B. 2040, Johannesburg; f. 1959; Sec. J. F. KLOPPER; 7,000 mems.

Food and Canning Workers' Union: 101/104 City Centre, 18 Corporation Street, Cape Town, P.O. Box 2678; f. 1941; 8,837 mems.; Gen. Sec. Mrs. LIZ ABRAHAMS.

Garment Workers' Union of S.A.: Garment Centre, 75 End Street, P.O. Box 6779, Johannesburg; f. 1928; Pres. ANNA SCHEEPERS; Sec. JOHANNA CORNELIUS; 11,000 mems.

Garment Workers' Union of Western Province: P.O.B. 3259, Cape Town; 40,000 mems.; Sec.-Treas. LOUIS A. PETERSEN.

Hotel, Bar and Catering Trade Employees' Association: 309 Exchange Bldg., St. George's St., Cape Town; Sec. M. BARNETT; 1,000 mems.

Johannesburg Municipal Transport Workers' Union: 2nd Floor, Vulcan House, 88 Anderson St., Johannesburg; Gen. Sec. D. J. SCHUTTE; 1,500 mems.

Ironmoulders' Society of South Africa: P.O.B. 3322, Johannesburg; f. 1896; Gen. Sec. C. H. CROMPTON; 2,425 mems.

Mine Surface Officials' Association of South Africa: P.O.B. 6849, Johannesburg; f. 1919; Sec. R. H. BOTHA; 8,500 mems.; publ. *M.S.O.A. Journal.*

Mineworkers' Union: P.O.B. 2525, Johannesburg; f. 1903; Sec. P. J. PAULUS; 17,000 mems.; publ. *The Mineworker* (fortnightly).

Motor Industry Combined Workers' Union: 112 Vulcan House, 88 Anderson St., Johannesburg; f. 1960; 7,033 mems.; Pres. H. FABE; Gen. Sec. R. C. WEBB; publ. *Newsletters.*

Motor Industry Employees' Union of South Africa: 11 Biccard St., Johannesburg; f. 1939; Gen. Sec. P. J. PIENAAR; 20,196 mems.

Motor Transport Workers' Union: 315 Dalbree House, 300 Bree St., Johannesburg; f. 1934; Gen. Sec. G. H. VAN DER WALT; 1,100 mems.

National Union of Clothing Workers: P.O.B. 7288, Johannesburg; 4,000 mems.; Sec. Mrs. L. MVUBELO.

National Union of Distributive Workers: Boston House, Cape Town; f. 1936; Gen. Sec. J. R. ALTMAN; Pres. M. KAGAN; 14,500 mems.; publ. *New Day* (bi-monthly).

National Union of Furniture and Allied Workers of South Africa: Meubel Sentrum, cnr. Eloff St. and Anderson St., Johannesburg; Pres. W. J. HOLMES; Sec. C. A. BOTES; 7,100 mems.

National Union of Leather Workers: P.O.B. 3039, Port Elizabeth; Sec. F. J. J. JORDAAN; 18,000 mems.

National Union of Liquor and Catering Trades Employees: P.O.B. 290, Durban; f. 1953; 15,000 mems. in six affiliated unions; Chair. W. CRAWFORD; Sec. L. NELSON.

National Union of Operative Biscuit Makers and Packers of South Africa: P.O.B. 4141, Cape Town; 1,200 mems.; Sec. A. SOLOMON.

Operative Bakers', Confectioners' and Conductors' Union: P.O.B. 3259, Cape Town; Sec. F. W. McLEOD.

Postal and Telegraph Association of South Africa: P.O.B. 9186, Johannesburg; f. 1902; Gen. Sec. L. J. VAN DER LINDE; 12,000 mems.

Running and Operating Staff Union: 40 Ameshof St., Braamfontein, Johannesburg; 12,000 mems.; Gen. Sec. and Editor J. R. BENADÉ.

South African Association of Municipal Employees: P.O.B. 62, Pretoria; f. 1921; Gen. Sec. J. T. SMIT; 32,000 mems.

South African Boilermakers', Iron and Steel Workers', Ship Builders' and Welders' Society: 3rd Floor, Vulcan House, 88 Anderson St., P.O.B. 9645, Johannesburg; f. 1916; Sec. T. P. MURRAY; 25,000 mems.; publ. *The Crucible* (monthly).

South African Electrical Workers' Association: 6th Floor, Amaleng, No. 8 de Villiers St., Johannesburg; f. 1937; Gen. Sec. R. COWLEY; 15,000 mems.

South African Engine Drivers', Firemen's and Operators Association: 507-510 Vulcan House, 88 Anderson St., Johannesburg; f. 1894; Sec. KENNETH WILLEM DU PREEZ; 4,538 mems.

South African Footplate Staff Association: 105 Simmonds St., P.O.B. 31100, Braamfontein, Johannesburg; Pres. L. J. JOUBERT; Sec. S. STEYN; 10,000 mems.

South African Hairdressers' Employees' Industrial Union: 42 Harvard Buildings, 49 Joubert St., Johannesburg; f. 1943; Sec. J. DANIEL; 4,000 mems.

South African Iron, Steel and Allied Industries Union: 430 Church St. West, P.O.B. 19299, Pretoria; f. 1936; Sec. W. BORNMAN; 34,000 mems.

South African Postal Association: P.O.B. 2004, Johannesburg; f. 1092; Gen. Sec. T. P. VAN NIEKERK; 4,100 mems.; publ. *Postal Journal*.

South African Railways and Harbours Employees' Union: Atkinson Building, Strand St., Cape Town; f. 1924; Gen. Sec. J. H. COETZEE; 8,300 mems.; publ. *Emplo Review* (monthly).

South African Railways and Harbours Salaried Staff Association: P.O.B. 6753, Johannesburg; f. 1918; Gen. Sec. F. A. SMIT; 24,000 mems.

South African Railways Police Staff Association: P.O.B. 31308, Braamfontein, Johannesburg; 2,321 mems.; Sec. B. J. S. REINECKE.

South African Reduction Workers' Association: P.O.B. 7060, Johannesburg; Gen. Sec. H. MALLET-VEALE; 3,300 mems.

South African Society of Bank Officials: P.O.B. 31537, Braamfontein; f. 1916; Sec. T. M. M. ALEXANDER; 18,000 mems.

South African Teachers' Association: 24 Grove Buildings, Grove Ave., Claremont, Cape Town; 2,000 mems.

South African Theatre and Cinema Employees' Union: P.O.B. 8752, Johannesburg; Sec. A. E. NICHOLSON; 1,731 mems.

South African Typographical Union: S.A.T.U. House, 166 Visagie Street, P.O. Box 1993, Pretoria; f. 1898; Sec. E. VAN TONDER; 23,000 mems.

Teachers' Educational and Professional Association: Cape Town; 2,000 mems.; Sec. A. I. JACOBS.

Textile Workers' Industrial Union (S.A.): P.O.B. 4141, Cape Town; f. 1934; 4,080 mems.; Gen. Sec. N. J. DANIELS.

Tobacco Workers' Industrial Union: Oxford St., Oudtshoorn; Sec. J. J. BOTES.

Tramway and Omnibus Workers' Union: P.O.B. 1562, Cape Town; f. 1916; Sec. D. C. BENADÉ; 1,600 mems.

Transvaal Leather and Allied Trades Industrial Union: 102/5 Vulcan House, 88 Anderson St., P.O.B. 3400, Johannesburg; Sec. L. C. SCHEEPERS; 3,000 mems.

Underground Officials' Association of South Africa: P.O.B. 5965, Johannesburg; f. 1918; 9,000 mems.; Sec. J. J. G. GREYLING.

Western Province Building Workers' Union: P.O.B. 2013, Cape Town; 3,000 mems.; Sec. J. DOHERTY.

Witwatersrand Tea Room, Restaurant and Catering Trade Employees' Union: P.O.B. 6041, Johannesburg; Sec. Mrs. M. YOUNG; 1,000 mems.

MAJOR INDUSTRIAL COMPANIES

The following are 25 of the 100 top companies (supplement to *Financial Mail*, March 26th, 1970).

African Explosives and Chemical Industries Ltd.: P.O.B. 1122, Carlton Centre, Johannesburg; f. 1924; cap. R.86,250,000.

Manufacture of explosives, industrial chemicals and plastics.

Chair. H. F. OPPENHEIMER; Man. Dir. A. R. MILNE; 16,900 employees.

Anglo-Alpha Cement Ltd.: P.O.B. 6810, 222 Smit St., Braamfontein, Johannesburg; f. 1934; cap. R.12,859,584.

Production of cement, lime and limestone products for use mainly in the building industry and in agriculture.

Chair. B. L. BERNSTEIN; Man. Dir. H. BYLAND; 1,500 employees.

CNA Investments Ltd.: P.O.B. 9380, Johannesburg; cap. R.2.637m.

Holding company for Central News Agency Ltd. and other subsidiaries responsible for the distribution of literature, business equipment and stationery.

Chair. A. H. MACINTOSH; Sec. J. P. LOWMAN.

Consolidated Textile Mills Ltd. (Frame Group): P.O.B. 17, Jacobs, Natal; f. 1930.

Group of companies in South Africa and Rhodesia producing clothing and textiles.

Chair. P. FRAME; Man. Dir. M. ULFANE; over 22,000 employees.

Greatermans Stores Ltd.: P.O.B. 5460, 220 Commissioner St., Johannesburg; cap. R.5m.

The group is actively engaged in retailing and operates 10 department stores, 110 supermarkets, 35 cash stores, and a chain of discount stores.

Pres. N. H. HERBER; Vice-Pres. J. R. PRICE; 10,000 employees.

Hubert Davies and Co. Ltd.: P.O.B. 1386, 1 Main St., Johannesburg; f. 1891; cap. R.9,260,625..

Manufacturers and installers of mechanical, electrical, earthmoving, mining, food machinery and general equipment; design and construction of complete plants for the processing industries.

Chair. B. C. SMITHER; Man. Dir. R. ARNOLD; 3,800 employees.

Huletts Corporation Ltd.: P.O.B. 248, 213 West St., Durban; f. 1892; cap. R.36,100,000; the group owns among others the following subsidiaries:

Huletts Sugar Ltd.: Management company.

Huletts Refineries Ltd.: Sugar refinery.

The Natal Estates Ltd.: Sugar Mill and cane estates.

Huletts Plantations Ltd.: Timber plantation.

Chair. C. J. SAUNDERS; Man. Dir. Dr. C. VAN DER POL; 22,487 employees.

Illovo Sugar Estates Ltd.: P.O.B. 3130, Albany House West, Victoria Embankment, Durban; f. 1906; cap. R.5,200,000.

Operation of three sugar mills in Natal, responsible for 11 per cent of South African sugar production.

Man. Dir. J. P. WILLSHER; 1,560 employees.

The Imperial Cold Storage and Supply Co. Ltd.: P.O.B. 420, 171 Jacob Maré St., Pretoria; f.1902; cap. R.6,913,800.

Processor, distributor, manufacturer of meat products, milk and milk products, ice cream, fish and foodstuffs.

Chair. I. J. D. WENTZEL; Man. Dir. Dr. F. J. VAN BILJON; 13,750 employees.

Irvin and Johnson Fish Products Ltd.: P.O.B. 4804, I & J House, Davison St., Woodstock, Cape Town; f. 1937.

Processing and marketing, locally and overseas, of canned, smoked and frozen fish products.

Gen. Man. C. K. OWEN; 1,500 employees.

LTA Ltd.: P.O.B. 312, De Korte St., Johannesburg; f. 1965; cap. R.6m.

Group of companies manufacturing equipment for building and civil engineering industry and carrying on related business.

Chair. Dr. HENRY OLIVIER; Man. Dir. M. T. RIDLEY; 17,957 employees.

National Amalgamated Packaging Ltd.: P.O.B. 7698, Maraisburg Rd., Johannesburg; f. 1968; cap. R.8,934,741.

Manufacturers of corrugated and cardboard containers, paper sacks, suitcases, twines, cordage, natural and synthetic fibres, also lithographic printers.

Chair. and Man. Dir. ARON FRUMAN; 7,621 employees.

O.K. Bazaars (1929) Ltd.: P.O.B. 3171, O.K. Bldgs., Eloff, Pritchard and President St., Johannesburg; f. 1929; cap. R.8,033,000.

Operation of 160 branches of a chain store selling domestic items.

Pres. Dr. SAM COHEN; Chair. L. M. MILLER; Man. Dir. and Deputy Chair. STANLEY COHEN; 18,000 employees.

Plate Glass Bevelling and Silvering Co. and M. Lubner (Pty.) Ltd.: 337 Marshall St., Johannesburg; f. 1898; subsidiary of Plate Glass and Shatterprufe Industries Ltd.; cap. R.25m.

Manufacture of laminated safety glass and fibre glass; operation of glass processing operations and merchandising companies.

Chair. MORRIS LUBNER; Deputy Chair. BERNARD BRODIE; 12,300 employees.

The Premier Milling Co. Ltd.: P.O.B. 1530, Johannesburg; f. 1913; cap. R.12,829,680.

Milling combine with wheat and maize mills, bakeries, provender mills, edible oils and fats, fresh and frozen chickens, sugar mills and pharmaceutical division.

Chair. J. BLOOM; 17,000 employees.

Pretoria Portland Cement Co. Ltd.: P.O.B. 3811, Johannesburg; f. 1892; cap. R.23,591,000.

Manufacture and sale of Portland cement and other cementitious products. Investments in certain associated interests of building activity.

Man. Dir. A. GRANT; 1,700 employees.

Protea Holdings Cape (Pty.) Ltd.: P.O.B. 3839, 30 Auckland St., Paarden Eiland, Cape Town; f. 1963.

Chair. L. A. BEARD; Vice-Chair. B. D. PFAFF; Man. Dir. A. L. RABIE; 102 employees.

The South African Breweries Ltd.: P.O.B. 1099, 2 Jan Smuts Ave., Johannesburg; f. 1895; cap. £14,891,279.

Brewing and marketing of beer in South Africa, and in Rhodesia through partly-owned subsidiaries; operating commercial hotels, producing and marketing food products.

Chair. F. J. C. CRONJE; Man. Dir. R. J. GOSS; 6,000 employees in wholly-owned subsidiaries alone.

South African Distilleries and Wines Ltd.: P.O.B. 184, Stellenbosch; c/o Oude Meester, Coetzier St., Stellenbosch, Cape Province; f. 1953; cap. £4,050,000.

The company falls within the Oude Meester Group with wholesale interests in distilling and brewing companies and bottle stores.

Chair. Prof. J. P. YEATS; Sec. A. F. W. HARRISON.

South African Pulp and Paper Industries Ltd.: P.O.B. 10246, Unicorn House, 70 Marshall St., Johannesburg; f. 1936; cap. R.27,249,782.

SAPPI and Associates supply fine writing and printing papers to the trade, as well as industrial and binding boards to the shoe, motor and travel industries; and kraft liner, sack and bag krafts to the packaging industry.

Man. Dir. M. E. O'HARA; 11,000 employees.

Stewarts and Lloyds of South Africa Ltd.: P.O.B. 74, cnr. Voortrekker St. and Rhodes Ave., Vereeniging; f. 1902; cap. R.11,855,266.

Holding company for companies distributing industrial metal products, e.g. irrigation equipment, mining equipment; contracting and design services.

Man. Dir. T. M. KING; 8,000 employees.

L. Suzman Ltd.: P.O.B. 2188, cnr. Juta and Henri Streets, Braamfontein, Johannesburg; f. 1889; cap. R.2,127,254.

Wholesale distribution of tobacco products, groceries and fancy goods; operating 23 branches in South Africa.

Man. Dir. S. SUZMAN; 1,275 employees.

The Tongaat Sugar Co. Ltd.: P.O.B. 5, Maidstone, Natal; f. 1970; cap. R.14,423,156; (formerly The Tongaat Sugar Co. Ltd.; f. 1918); f. 1970.

Sugar milling and cane growing, manufacture of building products, property development, electrical engineering, feed manufacture.

Chair. of Group C. J. SAUNDERS; Man. Dir. A. D. HANKINSON; total no. of employees for group approx. 14,500.

The Union Steel Corporation (of South Africa) Ltd.: P.O.B. 48, General Hertzog Rd., Vereeniging, Transvaal; f. 1911; cap. R.15m.

Manufacture of special and commercial quality steels, castings, copper and aluminium conductor and associated products.

Chair. Dr. M. D. MARAIS; Gen. Man. Dr. F. P. JACOBSZ; 6,300 employees.

Williams, Hunt South Africa Ltd.: P.O.B. 5317, cnr. of Crystal Rd., and La Rochelle Rd., Springfield, Johannesburg; f. 1945; cap. R.4,820,000.

Holding and property owning company; subsidiary companies deal in the sale and service of motor vehicles, sale of garage equipment, engines, farm and irrigation equipment.

Chair. Dr. H. KHAZAM; 4,000 employees.

MINING COMPANIES

Anglo American Corporation of South Africa Ltd.: 44 Main St., Johannesburg; cap. R.74,065,000; market value of equity cap. R.733,485,000.

Head of a group comprising a large number of companies which the Corporation administers but which are not always subsidiaries in the statutory sense. These are mainly finance and investment companies, and mining, industrial and other operating companies. The Corporation also has substantial investments in a number of companies which it does not administer, e.g. De Beers Consolidated Mines and Charter Consolidated. Mining companies produce gold, uranium, diamonds, tin and coal in South Africa, copper and lead and zinc in Zambia.

Chair. H. F. OPPENHEIMER.

Charter Consolidated Ltd.: 44 Main St., Johannesburg; issued cap. £26,189,699.

Mining and finance company interested in mining and industrial companies producing diamonds, gold, tin and copper in South Africa.

Chair. S. SPIRO, M.C.; Vice-Chair. Sir PHILLIP OPPEN-HEIMER; Man. Dir. M. B. HOFMEYER.

Gold Fields of South Africa Ltd.: 75 Fox St., Johannesburg; cap. £16.4m.

The company administers nine producing gold mines in the Transvaal.

Chair. A. LOUW.

De Beers Consolidated Mines Ltd.: 36 Stockdale St., Kimberley; cap. R.21,013,000; market value of equity cap. R.1,890,916,000.

Group of diamond mining companies and allied interests.

Chair. H. F. OPPENHEIMER; Dir. A. WILSON; 16,469 employees.

General Mining and Finance Corporation Ltd.: 6 Holland St., Johannesburg; cap. R.10,500,000.

Administration of companies engaged in platinum, gold, uranium, coal and base mineral mining in South Africa and South West Africa. Participates in a consortium for oil prospecting in Angola.

Chair. W. B. COETZER; Man. Dir. Dr. W. J. DE VILLIERS.

Palabora Mining Co. Ltd.: Unicorn House, 70 Marshall St., Johannesburg; cap. R.28,315,500; 30 per cent beneficial interest held by Rio Tinto Zinc Corporation.

Mining of copper in South West Africa, with by-products of magnetite and vermiculite; copper refining.

Chair. R. W. WRIGHT; Man. Dr. E. S. W. HUNT.

Rio Tinto Holdings Ltd.: Holding company for the Rio Tinto Zinc group's interests in southern Africa, through:

Rio Tinto Management Services South Africa (Pty.) Ltd.: Unicorn House, 70 Marshall St., Johannesburg; f. 1957.

Management and service company for group companies whose interests include copper and magnetite mining at Phalaborwa, Transvaal, and prospecting for uranium and diamonds.

TRANSPORT AND TOURISM

TRANSPORT

RAILWAYS

South African Railways and Harbours Board: Union Bldgs., Pretoria; Chair. Minister the Hon. B. J. SCHOEMAN, M.P.; Deputy Minister the Hon. J. W. RALL, M.P.; Railway Commissioners Dr. J. H. BOTHA, P. J. C. DU PLESSIS, C. V. DE VILLIERS; Gen. Man. (Johannesburg) J. G. H. LOUBSER; Deputy Gen. Mans. (Johannesburg) J. M. OELOFSEN, Dr. D. J. COETSEE.

With a few minor exceptions the South African Railways and Harbours Administration owns and operates all the railways in the Republic and in South West Africa. The Administration also operates an extensive network of road transport services, which serves primarily to develop rural areas, but also acts as feeder to the railways. The fleet consists of some 43 vessels, mainly tugs and dredgers, which does not include minor harbour craft. The Administration spent approximately R.197 million on railway improvements during the year ending March 31st, 1971. This is part of the modernization programme which started just after the war.

TRACK MILEAGE:

Owned and operated by South African Railways:

1. In Republic, 19,776 kilometres.

2. In South West Africa, 2,340 kilometres.

Privately-owned lines operated by South African Railways, 48 kilometres.

The electrified distance totals 4,387 kilometres.

ROADS

NATIONAL TRANSPORT COMMISSION

P.O.B. 415, Pretoria; responsible for location, planning, design, construction and maintenance of national roads.

There are approximately 1,500 km. completed national roads, and approximately 318,700 km. provincial roads of all categories. Of the 320,000 km. of rural roads, about 35,000 km. are tarred.

MOTORISTS' ORGANIZATION

The Automobile Association of South Africa: A.A. House, 42 de Villiers St., Johannesburg; f. 1930; Pres. BRIAN KELLY; Chair. E. P. NUPEN; Dir.-Gen. E. P. TURK; publ. *The Motorist* (every 3 months), circ. 500,000.

SHIPPING

South African Shipping Board: Secretariat: Dept. of Commerce, Private Bag 84, Pretoria; f. 1929; an advisory body to the Ministry of Economic Affairs upon any matter connected with sea transport to, from or between any of the Republic ports, particularly with regard to freight rates.

The principal harbours of the Republic are at Cape Town, Mossel Bay, Port Elizabeth, East London and Durban; South-West Africa, Walvis Bay.

The principal shipping services are as follows:

Bay of Bengal/Africa Line (the Bank Line Ltd.): Gen. Agents: John T. Rennie and Sons (Pty.) Ltd., P.O.B. 1006, Durban; cargo service between South and East Africa, India and Bangladesh.

Blue Star Line (South Africa) (Pty.) Ltd.: P.O.B. 4446, Cape Town; f. 1952; cargo and limited passenger services to Australia, New Zealand, the Far East and South America; Gen. Man. G. G. H. JEFFERYS.

British India Steam Navigation Co. Ltd.: P.O.B. 1060, Durban; regular cargo and passenger services to East Africa, India and the Persian Gulf.

Christensen Canadian African Lines: P.O.B. 38, Cape Town; cargo and passenger services to Eastern Canada and to West, South and East Africa.

Clan Line Steamers Ltd.: P.O.B. 4459, Cape Town; services to the U.K., West Coast ports and Mauritius.

Companhia Colonial de Navegação: General Agents: Freight Services Ltd., P.O.B. 49, Cape Town; passenger and cargo services to Portugal and East Africa.

Compass Line (Pty.) Ltd.: P.O.B. 4446, Cape Town; f. 1969; monthly sailings between South Africa and Australia, in both directions, with limited passenger accommodation; Dir. G. G. H. JEFFERYS.

Ellerman and Bucknall (Proprietary) Ltd.: P.O.B. 39, Cape Town; freight services to and from U.K., Belgium, Holland and Germany, and coastal services in Southern Africa.

Farrell Lines: Gen. Agents: John T. Rennie and Sons (Pty.) Ltd., P.O.B. 1006, Durban; regular services between U.S. North Atlantic ports and South and East Africa.

Hain Nourse Management Ltd.: Agents: Freight Services Ltd., P.O.B. 49, Cape Town.

Hall Line Ltd.: P.O.B. 39, Cape Town; services to and from U.K. and South and East Africa.

Harrison Line (Thos. & Jas. Harrison Ltd.): Gen. Agents: John T. Rennie & Sons (Pty.) Ltd., P.O.B. 1006, Durban; cargo services to and from U.K., Europe, South and East Africa.

Houston Line Ltd.: P.O.B. 4459, Durban; cargo services to U.K. and Europe.

Interocean Lines (Pty.) Ltd.: P.O.B. 1548, Durban; representing Royal Interocean Lines; Managing Agents for Capricorn Lines and Safocean; Durban Agents for Christensen Canadian African Lines and Koninklijke Nedlloyd Mercury Shipping Co. Ltd.; regular fast cargo services between Africa (East, West and South) and the Far East, Australia, New Zealand, South America and the Persian Gulf.

Lauro Lines: Gen. Agents: John T. Rennie and Sons (Pty.) Ltd.; P.O.B. 4847, Cape Town; passenger service to United Kingdom, Italy, Mediterranean ports, Australia and New Zealand.

Lloyd Triestino Line: P.O.B. 1729, Cape Town; regular frequent services for passengers and cargo from Italy to East Africa, Pakistan and India via South Africa. Also serves Australia.

Lykes Bros., S.S. Co. Inc.: P.O.B. 1337, Durban, freight and limited passenger services to U.S. Gulf ports and East Africa.

Mitsui O.S.K. Lines Ltd.: P.O.B. 974, Durban; cargo services to and from Japan, Hong Kong, Malaya, Mauritius, East, South, West Africa and South America.

Nedlloyd SA (Pty.) Ltd.: P.O.B. 2124, Cape Town; passenger and cargo services to France, Belgium, Holland, Germany, the Pacific ports of Canada, the U.S.A., Italy and Spain.

Oriental African Line (the Bank Line Ltd.): Gen. Agents: John T. Rennie and Sons (Pty.) Ltd., P.O.B. 1006, Durban; monthly cargo service between Far East and South Africa.

Moore McCormack Lines Inc.: P.O.B. 998, Durban; cargo/passenger services to U.S. Atlantic ports.

Shaw Savill Line: P.O.B. 4847, Cape Town; passenger and cargo services to U.K., Australia and New Zealand.

South African Lines Ltd.: P.O.B. 2334, Cape Town; cargo services to South and South-East African ports and Continental ports, also U.K.

South African Marine Corporation Ltd.: P.O.B. 2171, Cape Town; incorporating Springbok Shipping Co. Ltd.; services to U.S.A. Atlantic and Gulf ports, U.K., Europe, Japan and South Africa; Man. Dir. M. DE W. MARSH.

Transatlantic S.S. Co. Ltd. of Gothenburg: P.O.B. 640, Cape Town; passenger and cargo services to Scandinavian and Baltic countries, and to Australia.

Unicorn Shipping Lines (Pty.) Ltd.: 4th Floor, Standard House, Smith St., Durban, P.O.B. 2161; regular scheduled sailings between South Africa and South West African coast ports; also to Angola and the Indian Ocean islands, Mauritius, Reunion, Madagascar, Comores and the Seychelles.

Union-Castle Mail Steamship Co. Ltd.: P.O.B. 7, Cape Town; services to U.K., Europe and South and East African ports.

West Coast South America Line: Gen. Agents: John T. Rennie and Sons (Pty.) Ltd., P.O.B. 1006, Durban; cargo service every second month from India, Bangladesh and Ceylon to South Africa and the West Coast of South America, Punta Arenas northwards to Guayaquil.

CIVIL AVIATION

All civil aviation in South Africa is controlled by the Minister of Transport under the Aviation Act of 1962. The National Transport Commission is responsible for licensing and control of air services. Executive and administrative work of the National Transport Commission is carried out by the Department of Transport.

Director of Civil Aviation: Private Bag X193, Pretoria; Dir. L. C. DU TOIT.

South African Airways (S.A.A.): South African Airways Centre, Johannesburg; f. 1934; Chief Exec. J. ADAM. There are daily passenger services linking all the principal towns of South Africa—Pretoria, Johannesburg, Durban, East London, Port Elizabeth, Cape Town, Bloemfontein, Kimberley, Upington, Keetmanshoop and Windhoek; regular services to Salisbury and Bulawayo in Rhodesia; eight services per week between Johannesburg and Lourenço Marques in partnership with DETA, and four per week to Gaborone and three per week to Francistown, five per week to Blantyre in partnership with Air Malawi, six per week to Manzini in partnership with Swazi Air, two per week to Tananarive in partnership with Air Madagascar and four times per week to Mauritius. South African Airways operates regular services to Brussels, London, Paris, Frankfurt, Zurich, Rome, Athens, Madrid, Lisbon, Las Palmas, Luanda, Perth, Sydney, Amsterdam, Luxembourg and Vienna. A once-weekly service to New York via Rio de Janeiro commenced in February 1969; a second frequency between Johannesburg and Rio de Janeiro was introduced in 1972; operates eight Boeing 707, nine Boeing 727, six Boeing 737, three HS 748, five Boeing 747B; unduplicated route mileage 100,830.

COMAIR (Commercial Airways (Pty.) Ltd.): Hangar No. 4, Rand Airport, P.O.B. 2245, Johannesburg; flies daily DC-3 schedules from Rand Airport to Welkom, Phalaborwa and Skukuza, and operates safaris to Kruger Park in conjunction with its scheduled services.

Namakwaland Lugdiens (Edms) Bpk.: P.O.B. 28, Springbok C.P., and 1917 Sanlam Centre, Cape Town; internal services.

Trek Airways (Pty.) Ltd.: 87 Rissik St., P.O.B. 2758, Johannesburg; non-scheduled flights to Europe.

FOREIGN AIRLINES

The following foreign airlines also operate services to South Africa, Johannesburg being the principal centre: Air Madagascar, Air Malawi, Alitalia, BOAC, Botswana National Airways, DETA, El Al, Iberia, KLM, Lesotho Airways, Lufthansa, Olympic Airways, PAA, Qantas, Sabena, SAS, Swazi-Air, Swissair, TAP, UTA and Varig.

TOURISM

South African Tourist Corporation: 8th Floor, President Centre, 265/9 Pretorius St., Private Bag X164, Pretoria; 10 brs. in 9 countries; Dir. T. C. OWEN.

ATOMIC ENERGY

Atomic Energy Board: Private Bag 256, Pretoria; f. 1948; 12 mems.; Pres. Dr. A. J. A. ROUX; publ. *Annual Report, Nuclear Active* (half-yearly), *Isotope* (quarterly).

The National Nuclear Research Centre: Pelindaba, Private Bag 256, Pretoria; f. 1961; 20 MW O.R.R. type research reactor (SAFARI-I) critical 1965; 3MeV Van de Graaff accelerator.

National Institute for Metallurgy: 1 Yale Road, Milner Park, Johannesburg; f. 1966; includes a pilot plant for the production of nuclear-grade uranium metal and compounds. The Institute is concerned with all aspects of mineral processing, both fundamental and applied. It is the home of the Extraction Metallurgy Division of the Atomic Energy Board and is thus responsible for all work on the processing of raw materials for nuclear power; Dir. Gen. Dr. R. E. ROBINSON; publs. *Minerals Science and Engineering, Annual Report, NIM Abstracts.*

South Africa is a founder member of the International Atomic Energy Agency. Plans were recently announced for the construction of the country's first nuclear power station in the Western Cape.

EDUCATION

There are three separate systems of education which are run by different and unco-ordinating departments. Although by law all white children are required to learn both official languages, the principle that every child should be taught in its own language is carried as far as possible so that even Afrikaans and English-speaking children generally attend separate schools.

White Education

In January 1968 the Department of Education, Arts and Science was divided into two independent departments both under a central Ministry of National Education; the Department of Higher Education, which deals with secondary and specialized education, and the Department for Cultural Affairs, which is responsible for the promotion of adult education, foreign relations in educational matters, and the care of libraries in Government departments. Primary education and Teacher Training Institutions are the responsibility of the Administrator and Executive Committee of the Provincial Councils, assisted by the Director of Education.

The Central Government subsidizes the Provinces to the extent of 50 per cent of their total expenditure on education; the other 50 per cent is obtained from direct provincial taxation.

It is compulsory for all white children to attend school between the ages of seven and fourteen years; 90 per cent attend state-controlled schools, the remainder private schools mostly run by the Roman Catholic and Anglican Churches.

In the last few years emphasis has been laid on extending and expanding the courses offered to students in secondary schools and commercial, technical, agricultural and domestic science courses are provided. To matriculate at the end of secondary school, students have to offer two languages, mathematics or a science, and three other subjects.

Bantu Education

The Bantu Education Act of 1943 transferred the great majority of African schools, previously state aided but under the management of about forty Churches and Missions, to state control; in 1958 African education was centralized in the new Department of Bantu Education; and in 1963 the Transkeian Education Department was founded with its own Minister of Education to be responsible for all educational services in that area. From 1968 to 1970 separate Departments of Education and Culture were set up in various African territories. These education departments have taken over the general administration of education, while professional standards and supervision remain in the hands of the central Department of Bantu Education. School attendance is not compulsory. The curriculum is geared to the practical needs of the Bantu, and control of the schools is in many areas in the hands of the parents themselves who make up the school committees and boards. According to official estimates, more than 20,000 Africans have obtained the Matriculation Certificate, the same one as in the white schools, up to the present time.

Coloured and Indian Education

By the Coloured Persons Act of 1963, the Department of Coloured Affairs has full control of education, and professional and administrative services have been created. Churches and Missions from all over the world still have the management of a large number of schools, about two-thirds of the total number for coloured people, and teach about half the number of children at school as given by the Bureau of Statistics. The Department of Indian Affairs controls and administers the education for Indian children, and relies largely upon the work of the churches.

University Education

The ten Universities for white people are autonomous institutions subsidized by the state to over 63 per cent of their annual expenditure. They have well-equipped departments for teaching and research in the arts and sciences as well as for professional training in medicine, dentistry, veterinary science, agriculture, engineering, economics, geology, law, education and divinity.

By the University Apartheid Act, 1959, entry to the Universities of South Africa has been progressively restricted to Europeans; the majority of non-white students enrol at the University of South Africa which provides tuition by correspondence. In 1970 it awarded 21,886 degrees and diplomas. The University College at Fort Hare serves only the African population, and it is the Government's intention to increase the number of University Colleges specifically for the Africans which would provide courses suited to their opportunities. Three new University Colleges have been created to serve the non-white population: one in the Mtunzini District of Natal, and at Pietersburg and the other at Bellville. In 1960 a University College for the Indian population was opened in Durban.

LEARNED SOCIETIES

GENERAL

Royal Society of South Africa: c/o University of Cape Town, Rondebosch; f. 1877, Royal Charter 1909; 1 honorary and 89 ordinary Fellows, 264 mems.; publ. *Transactions.*

President: N. SAPEIKA, PH.D., M.D.

Vice-Presidents: W. J. LUTJEHARMS, S. R. NAUDÉ, M.SC., LL.D., PH.D.

Hon. Secretary: A. V. HALL, M.SC., PH.D., F.L.S.

Hon. Treasurer: J. STAZ, L.D.S., R.D.S.

Africa Institute, The: cnr. van der Walt and Skinner Streets, P.O.B. 630, Pretoria; f. 1960; the Institute is for the collection and dissemination of information and research on all matters especially affecting the African continent, to attend conferences on African matters and to investigate matters *in loco*; Dir. Prof. J. H. MOOLMAN; Head of Research Prof. G. M. E. LEISTNER; Sec. P. W. ESTERHUYSEN; publs. *Africa Institute Bulletin* (monthly), *Africa, Maps and Statistics* (series of 10 publs.), *Communications of the Africa Institute* (19 issues published), *Africa at a Glance, Occasional Papers* (33 issues published), *Southern Africa Data* (6 issues published), *South African Journal of African Affairs* (annual).

Suid-Afrikaanse Akademie vir Wetenskap en Kuns (*South African Academy of Science and Arts*): Engelenburghuis, Hamilton St., Pretoria; f. 1909; for the advancement of the Afrikaans language, literature, art, science and technology; 374 mems., 1,238 assoc. mems.; Chair. Prof. H. L. DE WAAL; Sec. D. J. VAN NIEKERK; publs. *Tydskrif vir Geesteswetenskappe, Tydskrif vir Natuurwetenskappe Nuusbrief, Tegnikon* (quarterlies), *Jaarboek.*

ARCHITECTURE AND TOWN PLANNING

Institute of S.A. Architects: Transvaal Provincial Institute, 60 Biccard St., P.O.B. 31265, Braamfontein, Johannesburg; f. 1911; 1,100 mems.; Sec. Mrs. W. COFORD.

South African National Society, The: P.O.B. 3691, Cape Town; f. 1905 to promote interest in and appreciation of the countryside, to preserve as far as possible from destruction all ancient monuments and specimens of old Colonial architecture and historic interest in South Africa; 135 mems.; plus 2 life mems.; Pres. Lt.-Col. C. GRAHAM BOTHA, V.D., LL.D.; Vice-Pres. Dr. F. W. F. PURCELL, WILLIAM FEHR; Hon. Sec. and Treas. Miss GERTRUDE F. KINCAID; publs. *Year Book* and *Annual Report;* brs. of the Society at Durban, Pietermaritzburg and Grahamstown.

THE ARTS

Federasie van Afrikaanse Kultuurvereniginge (F.A.K.) *Association of Afrikaans Cultural Societies*): P.O.B. 8711, Christiaan de Wet Building, 95 Simmonds St., Johannesburg; f. 1929; 2,500 affiliated Afrikaans cultural societies; Chair. Dr. D. P. M. BEUKES; Sec. Dr. A. M. VAN DEN BERG; publ. *Lectures, Handhaaf* (monthly).

South African Association of Arts: Old Netherlands Bldg., 2 Church Square, Pretoria; encouragement of the arts, nationally and internationally.

BIBLIOGRAPHY, LIBRARY SCIENCE AND MUSEOLOGY

South African Library Association (Suid-Afrikaanse Biblioteekvereniging): c/o Ferdinand Postma Library, Potchefstroom University, Potchefstroom; f. 1930; 1,179 mems.; Pres. C. H. VERMEULEN, HON. B.A.; Vice-Pres. Prof. J. G. KESTING, M.A., DIP.LIB. (U.C.T.), F.S.A.L.A.; Hon. Sec. C. J. H. LESSING, HON. B.A., M.A.(BIBL.), U.D.L.(P.U.), A.S.A.L.A.; publs. *South African Libraries (Suid-Afrikaanse Biblioteke)* (quarterly), *Newsletter (Nuusbrief)* (monthly) and a few irregular publications.

South African Museums' Association: c/o South African Museum, P.O.B. 61, Cape Town; f. 1936; 276 mems.; Hon. Sec. Miss E. M. SHAW; publ. *Samab* (4 times a year).

ECONOMICS, LAW AND POLITICS

Economic Society of South Africa, The: P.O.B. 929, Pretoria; f. 1925 to promote the thorough discussion of, and research into economic questions, in particular those affecting South Africa; 500 mems.; Sec. Prof. F. J. DU PLESSIS; publ. *The South African Journal of Economics* (quarterly); brs. in Bloemfontein, Cape Town, Durban, Johannesburg, Port Elizabeth, Stellenbosch and Pretoria.

Institute of Bankers in South Africa: P.O.B. 61510, Marshalltown, Transvaal; f. 1904; 14,200 mems.; publ. *South African Banker* (quarterly); Sec.-Gen. P. KRAAK, F.I.B.S.A.

South Africa Foundation: P.O.B. 7006, Johannesburg; f. 1959 to promote international understanding of South Africa; 5,000 mems.; Dir. L. B. GERBER; publ. *South Africa International* (independent foreign affairs quarterly).

South African Institute of International Affairs: Jan Smuts House, P.O.B. 31596, Braamfontein, Johannesburg; f. 1934 to facilitate the scientific study of international questions, particularly African questions; 994 mems.; library of 8,500 vols.; Chair. LEIF EGELAND; Dir. C. J. A. BARRATT.

HISTORY, GEOGRAPHY AND ARCHAEOLOGY

Genealogical Society of South Africa: 40 Haylett St., Strand; f. 1963; 300 mems.; Chair. R. F. M. IMMELMAN; Hon. Sec. Dr. J. HEESE; publ. *Familia* (quarterly).

Heraldry Society of Southern Africa: P.O. Box 4839, Cape Town; f. 1953; 110 mems.; Chair. Dr. C. PAMA; Hon. Sec. J. J. SCHEEPERS; publ. *Arma* (quarterly).

South African Archaeological Society: P.O.B. 31, Claremont, Cape Town; f. 1945; 1,000 mems.; Sec. J. RUDNER; publ. *South African Archaeological Bulletin* (half-yearly).

South African Geographical Society: P.O.B. 31201, Braamfontein, Transvaal; f. 1917; 350 mems.; Pres. Prof. R. J. DAVIES; Hon. Sec. Mrs. J. POWERS; publ. *South African Geographical Journal* (bi-annually).

Van Riebeeck Society: c/o South African Library, Cape Town; f. 1918; 1,500 mems.; publishes South African Historical Documents; Chair. F. R. BRADLAW; Hon. Sec. Mrs. M. ASHWORTH; publ. 1 volume annually.

INTERNATIONAL CULTURAL INSTITUTES

British Council: British Embassy, 6 Hill St., Pretoria; Rep. D. E. FREAN, O.B.E.

Nederlands Cultuurhistorisch Instituut: University of Pretoria, Pretoria; f. 1930; offers books and information on Dutch culture, history and art; 200 mems.; library of 20,000 vols., 75 periodicals; Dir. Prof. Dr. G. VAN ALPEN, D.LITT.; publ. *Mededelingen* (6 a year).

LANGUAGE AND LITERATURE

Classical Association of Johannesburg: University of the Witwatersrand, Johannesburg; 50 mems.; Pres. Prof. S. DAVIS; Sec. A. E. THORPE.

Classical Association of South Africa: f. 1956; 240 mems.; Chair. Prof. C. P. T. NAUDE, c/o Rand Afrikaans University, P.O.B. 524, Johannesburg; Sec. Dr. W. J. HENDERSON; publs. *Acta Classica* (quarterly), *Akroterion* (annual).

English Academy of Southern Africa: Ballater House, 35 Melle St., Braamfontein, Johannesburg; f. 1961; to preserve English as a cultural and educational medium.

Federasie van Rapportryekorpse: P.O.B. 6772, Christiaan de Wetgebou, 203 Simmondsstraat 95, Braamfontein, Johannesburg; f. 1961; 403 brs.; Chair. Prof. Dr. M. J. SWART; Sec. H. S. HATTINGH; publ. *Annual Journal*.

SCIENCE
General

Associated Scientific and Technical Societies of South Africa: 2 Hollard St., Johannesburg; P.O.B. 61019, Marshalltown, Transvaal; f. 1920; affords facilities of all kinds including accommodation and secretariat for Societies and corporately represents the views of these Societies: *Full Member Societies* with total membership of over 16,500 comprise: S.A. Inst. of Mechanical Engrs.; S.A. Inst. of Mining & Metallurgy; Geological Society of S.A.; S.A. Assoc. for the Advancement of Science (Witwatersrand Centre); Inst. of Land Surveyors of the Transvaal; S.A. Inst. of Electrical Engrs.; S.A. Chemical Inst.; S.A. Inst. of Assayers and Analysts; Inst. of Certificated Mechanical & Electrical Engrs., S.A.; S.A. Inst. of Civil Engrs.; S.A. Inst. of Chemical Engrs.; Mine Ventilation Soc. of S.A.; Inst. of Mine Surveyors of S.A. *Affiliated Societies* with total membership of over 5,000 comprise: Natal Inst. of

Engrs.; Eastern Province Soc. of Engrs.; Engineers' Assoc. of S.A.; S.A. Sugar Technologists' Assoc.; S.A. Mathematical Soc.; S.A. Inst. of Physics; S.A. Inst. for Production Engrg.; S.A. Inst. of Agricultural Engrs.; Royal Aeronautical Soc. (S.A. Div.); Inst. of Land Surveyors of Natal; Zoological Soc. of Southern Africa; S.A. Inst. of Forestry; S.A. Veterinary Asscn.; Inst. of Land Surveyors of the O.F.S.; Pres. R. C. J. GOODE; Man. ERIC BODEN; publ. *Annual Proceedings.*

South African Association for the Advancement of Science: P.O.B. 6894, Johannesburg; f. 1903; 1,024 mems.; Joint Hon. Gen. Secs. A. V. BOYD, M.SC., P. L. LE ROUX, B.SC., S.O.D.; Asst. Gen. Secs. The Associated Scientific and Technical Societies of South Africa; publs. *South African Journal of Science (Suid-Afrikaanse Tydskri vir Wetenskap)*.

Biological Sciences

Botanical Society of South Africa: Kirstenbosch, Newlands, C.P.; f. 1913; 6,111 mems.; aims to promote public interest in the development of the National Botanic Gardens of South Africa at Kirstenbosch and elsewhere; Pres. DUDLEY R. D'EWES; Sec. and Treas. Miss M. DYSSELL; publs. *Journal* (annual), *Veld, Flora* (quarterly).

South African Biological Society (Suid-Afrikaanse Biologiese Vereniging): P.O.B. 820, Pretoria; f. 1907; 140 mems.; Pres. Prof. D. M. JOUBERT; Hon. Sec. J. W. MORRIS; publ. *Journal* (annual).

South African Ornithological Society: P.O.B. 3371, Cape Town; f. 1930; 2,300 mems.; Pres. Prof. G. J. BROEKHUYSEN; Hon. Sec. G. D. UNDERHILL; publs. *The Ostrich, The Bokmakierie* (both quarterly).

Wild Life Protection and Conservation Society of South Africa: P.O.B. 1398, Johannesburg; f. 1902; conservation of fauna and flora; 10,000 mems.; publ. *African Wild Life* (quarterly).

Medicine

Medical Association of South Africa: Permanent Buildings, Paul Kruger St., Pretoria, P.O.B. 1521, Pretoria; f. 1927; 7,600 mems.; library incorporated into the libraries of all the medical schools in the country; Chair. of Council J. K. BREMER, F.R.C.S.; Gen. Sec. C. E. M. VILJOEN, M.B., CH.B.; publs. *South African Medical Journal* (weekly), *South African Journal of Laboratory and Clinical Medicine* (quarterly), *South African Journal of Obstetrics and Gynaecology* (quarterly), *South African Journal of Nutrition* (twice yearly), *South African Journal of Radiology* (twice yearly).

South African Nutrition Society: c/o National Food Research Institute, P.O.B. 395, Pretoria; f. 1955; 135 mems.; Pres. Dr. A. R. P. WALKER; publ. *South African Journal of Nutrition* (quarterly supplement to *South African Medical Journal*).

Physical Sciences

Astronomical Society of Southern Africa: c/o S.A. Astronomical Observatory, P.O.B. 9, Cape Town; f. 1922; Pres. K. J. STERLING; Hon. Sec. T. W. RUSSO; 400 mems.; publs. *Notes* (monthly), *Handbook* (annually); local centres at Cape Town, Johannesburg, Bloemfontein, Durban and Pretoria.

Geological Society of South Africa: P.O.B. 61019, Marshalltown, Transvaal; f. 1895; 1,000 mems.; Hon. Sec. Dr. D. R. HUNTER; Asst. Secs. The Associated Scientific and Technical Societies of South Africa; publs. include *Quarterly News Bulletin, Transactions of the Geological Society of South Africa*.

RACE RELATIONS

South African Bureau of Racial Affairs (SABRA): P.O.B. 2768, Pretoria; f. 1948; research on race relations; bi-annual congress; Dir. Dr. C. JOOSTE; publ. *Journal of Racial Affairs* (quarterly).

South African Institute of Race Relations: P.O.B. 97, Johannesburg; f. 1929; 4,313 mems., 72 affiliated bodies; Pres. D. C. GRICE; Dir. F. J. VAN WYK; publs. *Race Relations News* (monthly), other occasional publs.

TECHNOLOGY

Cape Chemical and Technological Society: P.O.B. 2645, Cape Town; f. 1905; 120 mems.; Sec. Dr. M. B. HANLEY, PH.D.

Institute of Transport (*Southern Africa Division*): P.O.B. 1787, Johannesburg; f. 1926; 600 mems.; Chair. A. M. CONRADIE, F.C.I.T.; Hon. Sec. E. C. CURTIS, M.C.I.T.; publs. *Journal*, *African Transport Review* (twice-yearly).

Institution of Certificated Mechanical and Electrical Engineers, South Africa: P.O.B. 61019, Marshalltown, Transvaal; f. 1911; 1,600 mems.; Secs. The Associated Scientific and Technical Societies of South Africa; publs. *Journal, The Certificated Engineer.*

South African Institute of Assayers and Analysts: Kelvin House, 2 Hollard St., P.O.B. 61019, Marshalltown, Transvaal; f. 1919 to uphold the status and interests of the profession of assaying in all its branches; 210 mems.; Pres. A. M. McDONALD; publ. *Bulletin* (quarterly).

South African Institute of Electrical Engineers: P.O.B. 61019, Marshalltown, Transvaal; f. 1909; 2,935 mems.; Pres. I. R. G. STEPHEN; Secs. The Associated Scientific and Technical Societies of South Africa; publ. *Transactions* (monthly).

South African Institute of Mining and Metallurgy: Kelvin House, Hollard St., P.O.B. 61019, Marshalltown, Transvaal; f. 1892; 1,670 mems.; Pres. Dr. J. P. HUGO; publ. *Journal.*

South African Institution of Civil Engineers: P.O.B. 61019, Marshalltown, Transvaal; f. 1903; 4,229 mems.; Pres. J. P. KRIEL; publ. *The Civil Engineer in South Africa* (monthly).

South African Institution of Mechanical Engineers: P.O.B. 61019, Marshalltown, Transvaal; f. 1892; 2,500 mems.; Secs. The Associated Scientific and Technical Societies of South Africa; publ. *Journal* (monthly).

RESEARCH INSTITUTES

(*see* also under Universities)

GENERAL

South African Council for Scientific and Industrial Research: Scientia, P.O.B. 395, Pretoria; f. 1945; Pres. Dr. C. V. D. M. BRINK; Vice-Pres. Dr. F. J. HEWITT, Dr. P. J. RIGDEN, Dr. J. F. KEMP; Sec.-Treas. J. H. VISAGIE; mems.: Prof. A. J. BRINK, Prof. C. A. DU TOIT, F.R.S., G. C. V. GRAHAM, Dr. B. GAIGHER, Dr. A. J. A. ROUX, Dr. H. J. VAN ECK, Dr. J. N. VAN NIEKERK, Prof. E. T. WOODBURN, J. D. ROBERTS, Dr. P. J. RIEKERT, J. W. SHILLING. The Council has the following departments and offices:

Administrative Services Department, Pretoria.
Technical Services Department, Pretoria.
Information and Research Services, Pretoria.
Estates Department, Pretoria.
C.S.I.R. Western Cape Regional Office, P.O. Box 288, Bellville, C.P.
C.S.I.R. Natal Regional Office, P.O. Box 1, Congella, Natal.
C.S.I.R. Eastern Cape Regional Office, P.O.B. 1124, Port Elizabeth, C.P.
Office of the South African Scientific Counsellor, 6th Floor, Chichester House, 278-282 High Holborn, London, WC1V 7HE, England.
Office of the South African Scientific Counsellor, Embassy of the Republic of South Africa, 3051 Massachusetts Ave., N.W., Washington, D.C. 20008, U.S.A.
Office of the South African Scientific Counsellor, Embassy of the Republic of South Africa, Heumarkt 1, 5 Cologne, German Federal Republic.
Office of the South African Scientific Attaché, Embassy of the Republic of South Africa, 38 Rue de Bassano, Paris 8e, France.

National Physical Research Laboratory (CSIR): P.O.B. 395, Pretoria; maintains fundamental standards of physical quantities for the Republic of South Africa; specialist divisions and sections on acoustics, optics, spectroscopy, crystallography, electron microscopy, mass spectrometry, cloud physics, high pressure physics, physical oceanography, infra-red and raman spectroscopy, geophysics, and air pollution; conducts research in co-operation with other scientific institutions and for industrial firms on contract basis; Dir. Dr. A. STRASHEIM.

National Chemical Research Laboratory (CSIR): P.O.B. 395, Pretoria; research into raw materials and their processing by industry and acts as non-profit-making research institute for industry; divisions include macromolecular chemistry, inorganic chemistry, organic chemistry, biochemistry, analytical chemistry, a chemical engineering group, a corrosion group, and a Bantu beer unit; Dir. Dr. P. C. CARMAN.

National Building Research Institute (CSIR): P.O.B. 395, Pretoria; wide research on national problems of the building and construction industry; divisions include soil mechanics, structural engineering, drainage, fire, and concrete engineering, environmental engineering, architecture, methods and applied economics, evaluation and performance criteria, inorganic materials, organic materials and building research application; Dir. Dr. T. L. WEBB.

National Institute for Telecommunications Research (CSIR): P.O.B. 3718, Johannesburg; study of radio wave propagation and measurement of atmospheric radio noise; radio astronomy; study of lightning with radio and radar; radar studies of clouds and precipitation; development of electromagnetic system of distance measurement and position fixing; ionospheric research; development of specialized terminal equipment; the use of radio as an essential part of other programmes, e.g. space research; operates the Radio Space Research Station at Hartebeesthoek, Transvaal, on the basis of a contract between the U.S. National Aeronautics and Space Administration and the CSIR; Dir. R. W. VICE.

National Mechanical Engineering Research Institute (CSIR): P.O.B. 395, Pretoria; practical problems of engineering industry and research into fundamental technical problems peculiar to South Africa; undertakes research work for industry on a contract basis; research departments: material, strength, rock, process, fluid and heat mechanics, mine equipment, civil engineering hydraulics, aeronautics and fibre research; Dir. Dr. H. G. DENKHAUS.

National Institute for Personnel Research (CSIR): P.O.B. 10319, Johannesburg; major fields of research: applied psychology, psychometrics, physiological psychology, experimental psychology, developmental and comparative psychology, social psychology, industrial psychology, psychometrics, neuropsychology, psychology of learning, industrial ethnology; Dir. D. J. M. VORSTER.

National Institute for Water Research (CSIR): P.O.B. 395, Pretoria; fundamental and applied research into biological, bacteriological, biochemical and technological aspects of water supply, waste water treatment, effluent re-use or disposal; regional laboratories are located in the Provinces of Natal, Orange Free State and the Cape and in South-West Africa (Namibia); Dir. Dr. G. J. STANDER.

National Food Research Institute (CSIR): P.O.B. 395, Pretoria; research in the fields of food processing, packaging and preservation; food flavour, the composition of foods, particularly indigenous foods and the utilization and biological evaluation of nutrients; Dir. J. P. DE WIT.

National Research Institute for Mathematical Sciences (CSIR): P.O.B. 395, Pretoria; *Mathematical Sciences Research Department:* pure and applied mathematics, physical and engineering applications; numerical analysis, digital computer application in the solution of scientific, and information processing problems and in the numerical control of machine tools; mathematical and applied statistics, biostatistics; operations research; Dir. Dr. A. P. BURGER.

National Electrical Engineering Research Institute (CSIR): P.O.B. 395, Pretoria; process control, data processing, computer technology; semiconductor analysis and technology; application of electronics to research; medical electronics; development and maintenance of electronic instruments; research on lightning, surges on transmission lines, earth resistivity and thermal conductivity, the application of semiconductors in heavy current engineering, the properties and performance of insulation materials; Dir. Dr. J. D. N. VAN WYK.

National Institute for Road Research (CSIR): P.O.B. 395, Pretoria; divisions include treated materials, soil engineering, pavement engineering, maintenance and construction, traffic and safety, research application and information, road economics; Dir. S. H. KÜHN.

National Institute for Textile Research (CSIR): P.O.B. 1124, Port Elizabeth; est. 1951; registered as a non-profit-making company in 1953; transferred to CSIR in August 1964; National Institute 1971; research on wool processing (scouring, carding, gilling and combing, drawing, spinning, knitting, weaving, dyeing and finishing), improvement of current methods of processing, introduction of easy-care properties into end-commodities manufactured from animal and natural fibre/synthetic blends; Dir. Dr. D. P. VELDSMAN.

Air Pollution Research Group (CSIR): P.O.B. 395, Pretoria; studies the type and concentration of pollutants and dispersion processes; Head Dr. E. C. HALLIDAY.

Timber Research Unit (CSIR): P.O.B. 395, Pretoria; research into timber engineering, pulp and paper, as well as techno-economic studies; Head Dr. D. L. BOSMAN.

South African Astronomical and Magnetic Observatories: *see* Research Institutes, Physical Sciences.

Co-operative industrial research is subsidized through autonomous research institutes, registered as non-profit-making companies and controlled by industrial subscribers:

Fishing Industry Research Institute, Cape Town.
Leather Industries Research Institute, Grahamstown.
South African Paint Research Institute, Grahamstown.
Sugar Milling Research Institute, Durban.

The following research units and groups (mainly at universities) are supported by way of grants:

Air Pollution, Carbohydrates, Cosmic Rays, Chromatography, Geo-chemistry, Magnetism, Desert Ecology, Marine, Natural Products, Oceanography, Palynology, Solid State Physics, Mammals, Calculus of Variations, Polyene Chemistry, Hydrology.

Publs. *C.S.I.R. Annual Report, Scientiae* (monthly), *C.S.I.R. Library Information and Accessions* (quarterly), *TI—Technical Information for Industry* (monthly), *Register of Current Scientific Research at South African Universities* (annual), *C.S.I.R. Research Briefs* (4-monthly), *Radio Propagation Predictions for Southern Africa* (monthly), *Bulletin of Ionospheric Characteristics observed at Johannesburg and Cape Town* (monthly), National Institute for Personnel Research: *Psychologia Africana* (irregular), *C.S.I.R. Research Review* (biennial), National Building Research Institute: *Information Sheets* (every two months), National Institute for Road Research: *VIA* (twice yearly), C.S.I.R. Timber Unit: *Houtim* (quarterly), *Scientific Research Organizations in South Africa, Scientific and Technical Societies in South Africa, Scientific and Technical Periodicals Published in South Africa, Current Literature on Water* (fortnightly), *Calendar of South African Scientific and Technical Meetings* (annually), South African Wool Textile Research Institute: *SAWTRI Bulletin* (quarterly).

GENERAL

AGRICULTURE AND VETERINARY SCIENCE

Directorate of Agricultural Research (Pretoria): Dept. of Agricultural Technical Services, Private Bag 116; cultural research; Senior Deputy Sec. Dr. W. A. VERBEEK; publs. *Agricultural Science in South Africa:* (i) *Agroplantae* (plant sciences), (ii) *Agroanimalia* (animal sciences), (iii) *Agrochemophysica* (chemical and physical sciences), (iv) *Phytophylactica* (plant protection sciences and microbiology), all quarterly); *Onderstepoort Journal for Veterinary Research* (bi-annually), *Bothalia* (annually), *Botanical Survey Memoirs* (bi-annually), *Flowering Plants of Southern Africa* (bi-annually), *Flora of Southern Africa* (annually), *Technical Communications* (monthly), *Agricultural Research* (in four parts, quarterly), *Entomology Memoirs* (bi-annually), scientific pamphlets, monthly popular science publications, irregular publications, etc.; the Directorate controls the following specialized and regional research institutes:

Animal Husbandry and Dairy Research Institute: Private Bag 177, Pretoria; f. 1962; performance and progeny testing of and fundamental research on breeding, nutrition and physiology of farm animals; Dir. Dr. J. H. HOFMEYR.

Botanical Research Institute: P.O.B. 994, Pretoria; Botanical surveys, classification of plants and study of morphology, taxonomy and ecology of South African flora; administers the National Herbarium at Pretoria; Dir. Dr. L. E. W. CODD.

Citrus and Subtropical Fruit Research Institute: P.O. Nelspruit; Research on citrus and subtropical fruit for the entire Republic; Dir. Dr. J. H. GROBLER.

Fruit and Food Technology Research Institute: Private Bag, Stellenbosch; research on deciduous fruit under winter rainfall conditions and food technology research; Dir. Dr. P. G. MARAIS.

Horticultural Research Institute: Roodeplaat, Private Bag 293, Pretoria; research on horticulture (deciduous fruits, vegetables and ornamental plants) under summer rainfall conditions; Dir. E. STRYDOM.

Plant Protection Research Institute: Private Bag 134, Pretoria; Fundamental and applied research on plant pathology, microbiology and taxonomy of insects; economic zoology, toxicology of insecticides and biology and control of insect pests; Dir. Dr. B. K. PETTY.

Soils and Irrigation Research Institute: Private Bag 79, Pretoria; Classification and mapping of soils; chemical research; analysis of soils, water, rock, plant materials, fertilizers, weedicides, insecticides and fungicides; Dir. Dr. J. H. GROBLER.

Tobacco Research Institute: Kroondal, Rustenburg; research on culture and technology of tobacco; Dir. J. F. PEENS.

Veterinary Research Institute: Onderstepoort, Pretoria; research on animal diseases (infectious and functional, including disease caused by malnutrition); production of vaccines and remedies; biological evaluation of dips and remedies offered for registration; Dir. Dr. K. WEISS.

Viticultural and Oenological Research Institute: Nietvoorby, Stellenbosch; Research on viticulture and wine technology; Dir. Dr. J. A. VAN ZYL.

Regional Research Institutes: Transvaal (Private Bag 180, Pretoria), Highveld (Private Bag 804, Potchefstroom), O.F.S. (Bloemfontein-Glen), Karoo (Middelburg, C.P.), Natal (Private Bag 9021, Pietermaritzburg), Eastern Cape (P.O.B. 233, Queenstown), Winter Rainfall (Stellenbosch, C.P.), S.W. Africa (Private Bag 13184, Windhoek); Institute for Crops and Pastures (Private Bag 116, Pretoria).

Forest Research Institute: P.O.B. 727, Pretoria; f. 1919; headquarters of the Research Branch of the Dept. of Forestry of the Republic of South Africa; research undertaken at the institute and in field stations includes timber technology, silviculture, hydrological and tree-breeding research; Chief Officer E. K. MARSH; publs. *Forestry in South Africa*, bulletins, papers, etc.

South African Society of Dairy Technology: Dept. of Dairy Science, University of Pretoria; f. 1967; approx. 600 mems.; Pres. P. H. LISHMAN; publ. *South African Journal of Dairy Technology* (quarterly).

MEDICINE

Natal Institute of Immunology: P.O.B. 2356, Durban; f. 1968; (Division of the Natal Blood Transfusion Service); classified as one of the research institutes of the University of Natal; it has 8 research divisions; library of 650 vols.

South African Institute for Medical Research: Hospital Street, P.O. Box 1038, Johannesburg; 42 brs. at provincial hospitals throughout the Republic; f. 1912; objects: medical research into the causes and methods of prevention of human diseases; the Institute works in association with the Medical School of the University of Witwatersrand; a School of Pathology has been established for pre- and post-graduate students; Chair. Board of Management P. H. ANDERSON; Dir. J. H. S. GEAR, B.SC., M.B., B.CH., D.P.H., D.T.M.&H., DIPL.BACT.; publ. *Annual Report*.

South African Medical Research Council: P.O.B. 70, Tiervlei, C.P.; f. 1969; Pres. Prof. A. J. BRINK; Vice-Pres. Dr. J. DE V. LOCHNER; publ. *Annual Report*.

NATURAL SCIENCES
Biological Sciences

Municipal Botanic Gardens (*Parks, Recreation and Beaches Department, Durban Corporation*): 70 St. Thomas' Rd., Durban; f. *ca.* 1853; for the propagation and development of ornamental and useful plants, shrubs, trees, etc., and as a place of instruction in botany, horticulture and the related subjects; Dir. Parks, Recreation and Beaches T. A. LINLEY, F.I.P.R.A.(S.A.), A.I.P.R.A.; Curator, Durban Botanic Gardens E. R. THORP, A.I.P.R.A.(S.A.).

National Botanic Gardens of South Africa: Head Office: Kirstenbosch, Newlands, Cape Province; Regional Gardens at Worcester, Betty's Bay, Bloemfontein, Harrismith, Pietermaritzburg, Nelspruit; f. 1913; Dir. Prof. H. B. RYCROFT; objects: scientific and educational; the collection, cultivation, display and study of the indigenous flora of South Africa; the preservation of the native vegetation of Southern Africa; publ. *Journal of South African Botany* (quarterly).

National Zoological Gardens of South Africa: P.O.B. 754, Pretoria; f. 1899; Dir. Dr. D. J. BRAND, M.SC., PH.D., F.Z.S.; publ. *Zoon* (quarterly).

Physical Sciences

Boyden Observatory: P.O.B. 334, Mazelspoort, Bloemfontein; f. 1891; is maintained by the following associates: the Smithsonian Institution and Harvard College, U.S.A., Armagh Observatory, Northern Ireland, Dunsink Observatory, Irish Republic, Council of German Observatories, Royal Observatory of Belgium for Belgium Astronomical Observatories, and the Council of the University of the Orange Free State; photoelectric photometry, spectroscopy, interferometry, photography, variable star survey, southern sky patrol; Dir. Prof. A. H. JARRETT.

Geological Survey of South Africa: Private Bag 112, Pretoria; f. 1912; applied and fundamental geological research; mapping; staff of 333; library of 3,600 vols. and 52,200 periodicals; Dir. Dr. J. F. ENSLIN; publs. *Bibliography* (annually), *Annals* (annually), *Bulletins, Memoirs, Sheet Maps* (all irregular).

Leiden Southern Station: P.O. Box 13, Broederstroom; Superintendent D. F. STEVENSON.

Magnetic Observatory of the S.A.C.S.I.R.: P.O.B. 32, Hermanus; f. 1932, transferred from Cape Town 1940; studies of geo-magnetism, seismology, cosmic rays; library; Head A. M. VAN WIJK; Senior Research Officer G. L. M. SCHEEPERS; publs. *Magnetic Bulletin* (monthly), *Cosmic Ray Bulletin* (monthly), *Magnetic Observations at Hermanus* (annually), *Magnetic Observations at Tsumeb* (annually), *Geomagnetic Secular Variation Observations in Southern Africa*.

Radcliffe Observatory, Pretoria: first established 1772, at Oxford (England), transferred to Pretoria in 1937; the telescope of this observatory is employed on direct photography, spectroscopic and photo-electric work, and is among the largest telescopes in the Southern Hemisphere; Observer A. D. THACKERAY, M.A., PH.D.

Radio Space Research Station: P.O.B. 3718, Johannesburg, Transvaal; f. 1961; established in co-operation with the U.S.A.; include satellite tracking and data acquisition facilities and Deep Space Station; library of about 500 vols. and 30 periodicals; Dir. D. HOGG.

South African Astronomical Observatory: headquarters Cape Town, outstation Sutherland, Cape; f. 1972 by a merger of the Royal Observatory and the Republic Observatory in Johannesburg; maintained jointly by the Council for Scientific and Industrial Research of S.A. and the British Science Research Council; equipment includes a reversible 6-inch transit circle; 40-inch, 30-inch, 20-inch and 18-inch reflectors; 24-inch, 18-inch and 13-inch refractors; an automatic Lyot Hα Heliograph; an 8-inch astrometric camera; the Observatory specializes in astrometric and photometric work; the Observatory controls the emission of wireless time signals; Dir. Sir RICHARD WOOLLEY, O.B.E., F.R.S.

South African Atomic Energy Board: Private Bag X256, Pretoria; f. 1949; activities include Chemistry, Extraction Metallurgy, Geology, Isotopes and Radiation, External Relations, Life Sciences, Physical Metallurgy, Physics, Reactor Development, Instrumentation and Licensing; Pres. Dr. A. J. A. ROUX; publs. *Annual Report, Nuclear Active* (every 6 months).

South African Chemical Institute: Kelvin House, 2 Hollard St., Johannesburg; P.O.B. 61019, Marshalltown, Transvaal; f. 1912; 900 mems.; publs. *Journal* (3 times yearly) and *South African Chemical Processing* (bi-monthly).

South African Institute of Physics: c/o P.O.B. 395, Pretoria; f. 1955; 320 mems.; Pres. Dr. A. STRASHEIM; Sec. Dr. W. L. RAUTENBACH.

RELIGION, SOCIOLOGY AND ANTHROPOLOGY

Human Sciences Research Council (HSRC): Private Bag X41, Pretoria; est. 1969 as a corporate body, incorporating the National Council for Social Research (f. 1946) and the National Bureau of Educational and Social Research (f. 1929). The HSRC controls all matters with regard to research and development in the field of human sciences, including the humanities and social sciences. It undertakes, promotes and finances research as approved by the Minister of National Education and advises the Minister on research to be undertaken. It also co-operates with persons and authorities in other countries and acts as liaison between the Republic and other countries in connection with research in human sciences. The Council awards bursaries and grants for research and controls the following research institutes: Institute for Educational Research, Institute for Manpower Research, Institute for Psychometric Research, Institute for Sociological Research, Institute for Statistical Research, Institute for Languages, Literature and Arts, Institute for Communication Research, Institute for Historical Research, Institute for Research Development, Institute for Information and Special Services; Pres. Dr. P. M. ROBBERTSE; Vice-Pres. Dr. A. J. v. ROOY and Dr. J. D. VENTER; Sec. Miss K. M. HENSHALL; publs. *HSRC Annual Report, Humanitas, Journal for Research in the Human Sciences, Research Bulletin* (10 issues per year), *Directory of Research Organizations in the Human Sciences, Research Reports.*

Institute for the Study of Man in Africa: Room 257, Medical School, Johannesburg; f. 1960; the Institute has been established to perpetuate the work of Prof. Raymond A. Dart on the study of man in Africa, past and present, in health and disease; the Institute is to be based on a Museum of Man in Africa and serves as a centre of anthropological and medical field work; it functions partly through the auspices of the University of the Witwatersrand; through its Kalahari Research Committee it has sponsored a programme of research on the Kalahari Bushmen; Pres. Prof. L. W. LANHAM.

TECHNOLOGY

Division of Sea Fisheries: Beach Road, Sea Point, Cape Town; f. 1895; fisheries research and administration; Dir. B. DE JAGER; publs. annual reports, investigational reports, fisheries bulletins.

National Institute for Metallurgy: Private Bag 7, Auckland Park, Johannesburg; f. 1934; library of 11,000 vols.; research on concentration and processing of minerals; Dir. Dr. R. E. ROBINSON; publs. *NIM Abstracts, Minerals Science and Engineering.*

South African Bureau of Standards: Private Bag 191, Dr. Lategan Rd., Groenkloof, Pretoria; f. 1945; 1,000 mems.; draws up national standards, specifications, codes of practice, administers the SABS mark scheme; library of 10,000 books; Dir. Gen. R. F. J. TEICHMANN; publ. *Bulletin.*

LIBRARIES AND ARCHIVES

Bethlehem

Bethlehem Regional Library (Bethlehem Streekbiblioteek): Private Bag, Bethlehem; Regional Librarian Miss M. C. BOTHA.

Bloemfontein

Bloemfontein Regional Library (Bloemfonteinse Streekbiblioteek): P.B. X0606; Regional Librarian Miss D. DU TOIT, B.A.

Free State Provincial Library Service (Vrystaatse Provinsiale Biblioteekdiens): P.B. X0606; f. 1948; consists of Central Organization and Regional Libraries at Bloemfontein, Kroonstad and Bethlehem, serving 170 libraries and depots; book stock 800,000; Chief Librarian A. CORNELISSEN, B.A., HIGH.DIPL.LIB.; publ. *Annual Report, Free State Libraries.*

Public Library: P.O.B. 1029; f. 1875; Copyright, Legal Deposit, National Drama library, and Public library; 204,635 vols.; Librarian P. J. VAN DER WALT; publ. *Catalogue of the National Drama Library.*

University of the Orange Free State Library: Bloemfontein; f. 1906; the collection includes rare pamphlets and other early South African publications of the Dreyer-Africana Collection; 140,000 vols. (1,200 magazines); Librarian F. J. POTGIETER, B.COM., DIPL.BIBL.U.P., B.A.(HONS.), A.S.A.L.A.

Benoni, Transvaal

Benoni Public Library: P.O.B. 403; f. 1923; 75,600 vols.; Librarian Miss J. M. DUBBELD, B.A.(HONS.), U.D.B., A.S.A.L.A.

Boksburg

Boksburg Public Library: Box 210; 64,000 vols.; Librarian Miss M. EGAN, F.S.A.L.A.

Cape Town

Cape Provincial Library Service: P.O. Box 2108, Cape Town; f. 1945; consists of Central Library, Cape Town, 18 regional libraries serving 241 affiliated municipal public libraries and 372 library depots in Cape Province; Dir. G. R. MORRIS, B.A.(HONS.), F.S.A.L.A.; Librarians Miss J. TE GROEN, Mrs. M. B. GERTZ.

Cape Town City Libraries: 30 Chiappini Street; f. 1952; 850,000 vols.; central library and 40 suburban branches, travelling and hospital library services; Librarian Mr. C. H. VERMEULEN; publ. *Basic Children's Books* (with annual supplements).

Library of Parliament: Parliament House; f. 1857; 200,000 items, including Government documents and the Mendelssohn Library of Africana, which contains 45,000 vols. on Africa, especially South Africa; Librarian J. C. QUINTON.

Library of the Royal Society of South Africa: c/o University of Cape Town, Rondebosch; f. 1877; Librarian Assoc. Prof. F. C. M. MATHIAS, M.A., PH.D., D.SC., F.R.SS.AF.

South African Library: Queen Victoria St.; f. 1818; contains rare book collections, including Grey, Dessinian and Fairbridge collections; the library is a Legal Deposit National Reference and Research Library in the Humanities; 510,000 vols.; Dir. A. M. LEWIN ROBINSON, B.A., PH.D., F.L.A.; publs. *Quarterly Bulletin, Grey Bibliographies, Reprint Series.*

University of Cape Town Library: Private Bag, Rondebosch; f. 1829; 535,000 vols., incl. medical library of 66,773 vols.; music library of 8,425 vols., 29,183 items of printed music, and 8,476 records; architectural library of 13,124 vols., 4,600 slides, 42,185 plans; law library of 13,642 vols., incl. Van Zyl collection of Roman Dutch law; education library of 17,998 vols.; McGregor collection of modern English Poetry; Sibbett collection of Rhodes pictures; Crawford collection of mathematical monographs; Ballot collection of 18th century Dutch books; Bowle-Evans collection of English literary works, 1780-1830; MSS. collection of letters and documents by prominent South African literary and public figures; 13,218 serials; Silverman Collection of Hebraica; Rudyard Kipling collection; medical history collection; South African music manuscripts: Duncan Macmillan Collection of South African illustrations; Jack MacLean Memorial Collection of travel literature; Africana (about Central and Southern Africa); Sir Baldwin Walker MSS. collection and H. C. Willis books, both on naval history; also a school of librarianship for training librarians; Librarian Miss L. E. TAYLOR, B.A. (HONS.), F.S.A.L.A.; publs. *U.C.T. Bibliographical Series, Varia Series.*

Durban

Durban Municipal Library: City Hall, P.O.B. 917, Durban; f. 1853; 570,000 vols.; special collections of Africana and Shakespeareana; 7 br. libraries and 9 depot libraries; Librarian P. M. E. VAN ZYL, B.A., H.DIP.LIB., F.S.A.L.A.

Natal College for Advanced Technical Education Library: P.O.B. 953, Berea Rd., Durban; f. 1907; the collection includes sections on engineering, chemistry, commerce, fine arts, economics, travel and history, biography, English, Afrikaans and Dutch literature; 14,502 vols., about 139 periodicals; Librarian Miss C. A. VOLKER, A.S.A.L.A.

University of Natal Library.

Durban Campus: King George V Ave.; Librarian F. SCHOLTZ, B.A.(HONS.), F.S.A.L.A.

Howard College: King George V Ave.; f. 1922; 108,000 vols.; Powell Collection of Early Science and Technology and Webb Collection of works by African Bantu and Negroes; Deputy Librarian E. W. O. PUGSLEY, F.S.A.L.A.

City Building Branch: Warwick Avenue; f. 1936; 25,000 vols.; comprises a library for the departments of Commerce, Accountancy and Law; Assistant Librarian Mrs. R. B. BENENDE, B.A., F.S.A.L.A.

Medical School Branch: Umbilo Road; f. 1951; 21,000 vols.; Powell Cancer Research Library; Assistant Librarian Miss C. B. MAGUIRE, A.L.A.

Killie Campbell Africana Library: 220 Marriot Rd.; f. 1935; 35,000 vols.; Assistant Librarian Miss E. M. VAN DER LINDE, B.A.(HONS.), F.S.A.L.A.

Pietermaritzburg Campus: P.O.B. 375; f. 1909; 113,000 vols.; Librarian R. A. BROWN, M.A., F.S.A.L.A.

East London

East London Municipal Library Service: Buxton St., P.O.B. 652; f. 1876; 25,000 mems.; 120,000 vols.; Librarian Miss M. H. VAN DEVENTER, F.S.A.L.A.

Fort Hare

University of Fort Hare Library: f. 1916; 83,000 vols.; contains the Howard Pim Library of Africana; Librarian M. SPRUYT, B.A., LL.DRS., DIP.(LIBR.).

Germiston

Germiston (Carnegie) Public Library: P.O.B. 246; f. 1909; 3 brs.; 70,000 vols.; Chief Librarian Miss M. KORB.

Grahamstown

Grahamstown Public Library: Free Municipal Library; P.O.B. 180; f. 1842; 71,849 vols.; Librarian Mrs. C. M. C. LLOYD.

Rhodes University Library: Rhodes University; f. 1904; 200,000 vols.; Librarian F. G. VAN DER RIET, M.A., DR. DE L'UNIV. DE PARIS, A.B.L.S.

Johannesburg

Johannesburg Public Library: f. 1890; 1,314,831 vols.; Librarian Miss A. H. SMITH, M.A., F.S.A.L.A.; publs. *Annual Report, Index to S.A. Periodicals* (annual), *Municipal Reference Library Bulletin* (monthly), bibliographies (occasional).

Library of the South African Association for the Advancement of Science: c/o University Library, Jan Smuts Ave., Johannesburg; f. 1903; 10,000 vols.

Library of the South African Institute of Race Relations: P.O.B. 97; f. 1929; 4,000 vols.; valuable archival and documentary material; newspaper clippings from 1930; microfilming service; bibliographies on race relations; Librarian Mrs. J. EDWARDS.

Library of the University of Witwatersrand: Jan Smuts Ave., Johannesburg; f. 1922; 500,000 vols., including 90 incunabula and other early printed books; Medical Library of 50,000 vols.; Law Library of 12,500 vols.; special collections; works in co-operation with the Department of Bibliography, Librarianship and Typography; Librarian J. W. PERRY, M.A., F.L.A.

Kimberley

Kimberley Public Library: P.O.B. 627; f. 1882; approx. 80,000 vols.; Librarian (vacant).

Kroonstad

Kroonstad Regional Library (*Kroonstad Streekbiblioteek*): Private Bag, O.F.S.; Regional Librarian Miss M. F. B. BOTHA.

Pietermaritzburg

Natal Provincial Library Service: Private Bag 9016; f. 1952; consists of central organization and reference library at Pietermaritzburg; four regional offices for north coast, south coast, midlands and northern areas, serving 40 public libraries, 130 library depots, 24 school libraries and 25 non-white library depots; 11 travelling libraries; 836,000 vols.; Dir. C. J. FOURIE, M.A.; publ. *Libri Natales* (monthly).

Natal Society Public Library: P.O.B. 415, Pietermaritzburg, Natal; f. 1851; lending, reference and copyright depts.; children's br. library and non-European branch library; 150,000 vols.; Librarian Miss URSULA JUDD, B.A., F.L.A.; publ. *Natalia* (annual).

University of Natal Library: Pietermaritzburg Section; *see under* Durban.

Port Elizabeth

Port Elizabeth Municipal Library Service: P.O.B. 66; f. 1965; 260,000 vols.; City Librarian ALFRED PORTER, F.L.A.

University of Port Elizabeth Library: P.O.B. 1600; f. 1964; 115,000 vols., 2,500 current periodicals; Librarian J. C. CRONJE, B.A., F.S.A.L.A.

Potchefstroom

Potchefstroom University for Christian Higher Education Libraries: f. 1921; 304,493 vols., 3,521 current periodicals; Librarian Prof. H. C. VAN ROOY, M.A., B.L.S., F.S.A.L.A.; publs. *Union Catalogue of Theses and Dissertations of South African Universities*, *Abstracts of Theses and Dissertations accepted for higher Degrees in the Potchefstroom University*, *Accession List*.

Pretoria

Central Agricultural Library: Private Bag 116; f. 1910; 49,944 vols., 1,831 current periodicals; Librarian P. J. STEYNBERG.

Department of National Education Library: Oranje-Nassau Bldg., Schoeman St.; 66,000 vols.; special collections: adult education, education, library science, philology, psychology, domestic science; Librarian Mrs. A. LOUBSER.

Human Sciences Research Council Library: S.A. Agricultural Union Bldg., Schoeman St., Pretoria, Private Bag X41; f. 1969; approx. 30,500 vols.; 730 current periodicals (titles); reference service; collection on human and social sciences; Librarian J. FOURIE, B.A.

South African Council for Scientific and Industrial Research (S.A.C.S.I.R.) Library: P.O.B. 395; f. 1945; 101,650 vols., 4,350 current periodicals; scientific and technical collections; 5 brs.; Librarian Mrs. J. I. SNYMAN, F.S.A.L.A.; publs. *Periodicals in South African Libraries* (jointly with Human Sciences Research Council), *Library Information and Accessions*.

State Library: P.O.B. 397, Pretoria; f. 1887; the library is a National Library and Legal Depository library, and Depository library for U.S. Government and UN publications; 617,000 vols.; responsible for the Joint Catalogue of Books in South African Libraries; National and Inter-library Loans centre; Dir. H. J. ASCHEN-BORN, M.A., PH.D., HIGH.DIPL.LIBR.; publs. *South African National Bibliography*, *State Library Bibliographies*, *State Library Contributions to Library Science: Monographs on Printing in South Africa*, *Reprint Series*, *Annual Report*.

Transvaal Education Library Service: 328 Van der Walt St.; f. 1951; Dir. Miss C. F. M. VAN WYK; comprises *Education Library Division:* f. 1910; professional library and bibliographical research service for the teaching profession of the Transvaal and the Transvaal Education Dept.; 114,000 vols., 1,000 current periodicals; Div. Dir. Miss K. E. CROSS, F.S.A.L.A.; and *School Library Division;* f. 1951; 30,000 vols.; Div. Dir. Miss H. E. VAN HEERDEN; publs. Education Library Division: *Book Catalogue* 1969 (with annual supplements), *Bibliographies on school subjects*, *List of periodicals* 1966 (with annual supplement, circulated five-yearly); School Library Division: *Book Guide*, *Selection of Books and Periodicals in Print Suitable for the School Library* (bi-annually).

Transvaal Provincial Library: Private Bag 288, Pretoria; f. 1943; consists of Central Organization and Reference Library at Pretoria; 19 Regional Libraries; entire province served by 125 affiliated public libraries and 587 depots; 2,654,800 vols.; Dir. S. C. J. VAN NIEKERK, B.A., F.S.A.L.A.; Chief Librarians E. A. BORLAND, B.A., F.S.A.L.A., B. FOUCHÉ.

University of Pretoria Libraries: f. 1908; 418,199 vols., 248,122 pamphlets, Govt. publs., periodicals, etc., 4,200 gramophone records, 13,305 sheet-music; Main Library (Merensky Library), Macfadyen Library, Central Medical Library, Basic Medical Science Library, Music Library, Students' Library—Veterinary Science; Special Collections: Africana, Goethe, Jacob de Villiers, J. Roos, J. du Plessis, Brand, Luther, F. van der Merwe; Librarian A. J. VAN DEN BERGH, B.A., DIP.BIBL.

University of S. Africa, Sanlam Library: P.O.B. 302; f. 1947; 350,000 vols., 3,200 current periodicals; Science library, Music library and Law library specializing in Foreign and Comparative Law; brs. in Cape Town and Windhoek; Librarian J. WILLEMSE, M.A., T.H.O.D., F.S.A.L.A.; publ. *Mousaion* (irregular).

Government Archives: Private Bag 236, Union Buildings, Pretoria; Dir. of Archives for the Republic of South Africa and the territory of South-West Africa Dr. J. H. ESTERHUYSE; Deputy Dir. J. F. PRELLER; administers the following depots:

Cape Archives: Private Bag 9025, Queen Victoria St., Cape Town; Chief Archivist Miss J. H. DAVIES.

Transvaal Archives: Private Bag 236, Union Buildings, Pretoria; Chief Archivist J. H. SNYMAN.

Orange Free State Archives: Private Bag X0504, Elizabeth Street, Bloemfontein; Senior Archivist Dr. C. J. BEYERS.

Central Archives: Private Bag 236, Union Buildings, Pretoria; Chief Archivist J. H. SNYMAN.

Natal Archives: Private Bag 9012, Pietermaritz Street, Pietermaritzburg; Senior Archivist Dr. B. J. T. LEVERTON.

Archives Repository of the Transkei: c/o Dept. of Finance, Umtata; Archivist A. F. DE VILLIERS.

S.A.D.F. Archives: Defence Headquarters, Pretoria; Senior Archivist Maj. H. J. BOTHA, S.S.O.

Record Management Section: Union Building, Pretoria; Chief Archivist J. H. CILLIERS.

Publications Section: Private Bag 9025, Cape Town; Chief Editor Dr. A. J. BÖESEKEN.

State Historians: Pretoria; Dr. J. A. MOUTON, Dr. J. H. BREYTENBACH.

The administration of the Director of Archives also embraces the following: Historical Monuments Commission; S.A. War Graves Board; Heraldry Section;

Foundation Simon van der Stel; the periodical *Historia*.

Stellenbosch

Library of the University of Stellenbosch: University of Stellenbosch, Private Bag 5036, Van Ryneveld Street; f. 1900; 386,000 vols., 5,224 current periodicals; 5 brs.; Librarian F. DU PLESSIS, F.S.A.L.A.; publ. *Annals of the University of Stellenbosch* (irregular).

MUSEUMS AND ART GALLERIES

Bloemfontein

National Museum: P.O.B. 266; f. 1877; Institute for Zoology, Palaeontology, Archaeology, Local History, Anthropology and Ethnography; the unique Florisbad human fossil skull and Diarthrognathus housed here; library of 1,500 vols., 1,400 serial titles; Dir. J. J. OBERHOLZER, M.SC.; publs. *Researches of the National Museum, Memoirs*.

Cape Town

Cape Town Castle Museum: Cape Town Castle.

Michaelis Collection: The Old Town House, Greenmarket Square; f. 1917; Dutch and Flemish paintings and graphic art of the 16th–18th centuries; Dir. W. H. GRAVETT.

South African Museum: P.O.B. 61, Cape Town; f. 1855; anthropology, archaeology, ethnology, geology, zoology, palaeontology; Dir. Dr. T. H. BARRY; publs. *Annals of the South African Museum, Reports*.

South African Cultural History Museum: P.O.B. 645, Cape Town; Dir. Dr. WOLFGANG SCHNEEWIND.

Koopmans de Wet House (Branch of S.A. Cultural History Museum): 35 Strand Street; specimen of old Cape Dutch house displaying rare period furniture, silver, glass, china and pictures, and illustrating the conditions of domestic life in South Africa in the 18th and 19th centuries.

William Fehr Collection: The Castle, Cape Town; f. 1965; antique Cape furniture, silver, copper, glass, and Africana oils (Rust en Vreugd, Buitenkant St.; collection of Africana prints; Dir. Dr. J. J. P. OP'T HOF; publs. *Rust en Vreugd, Treasures at the Castle*.

South African National Gallery: Government Ave.; f. 1871; collections of South African art through the centuries, 16th to 20th century European art; Dir. Prof. MATTHYS BOKHORST, D.LIT.ET PHIL. (LEIDEN).

Durban

Durban Museum and Art Gallery: City Hall, Smith St.; f. 1887; South African fauna, flora, ethnography, archaeology; paintings, graphic art, porcelain, sculptures, local history; Dir. P. A. CLANCEY; Scientific Officer F. L. FARQUHARSON, M.SC.; Curator (Art) Miss E. S. J. ADDLESON, B.A.; Curator (Local History) Mrs. D. H. STRUTT, A.M.A.; publ. *Novitates*.

Local History Museum: Old Court House, Aliwal St.; f. 1966; local and Natal historical collections; Dir. P. A. CLANCEY, A.M.A.; Curator of Local History Mrs. D. H. STRUTT, A.M.A.

East London

East London Museum: Upper Oxford St.; f. 1931; zoology, mammalogy, ornithology, ethnology, entomology, conchology, botany, archaeology and history; houses first Coelacanth caught in 1938; Chair. Board of of Trustees G. G. SMITH; Dir. Dr. M. COURTNAY-LATIMER.

Franschhoek

Huguenot Memorial Museum: Lambrechts St., P.O.B. 37, Franschhoek; f. 1967; research into Cape Huguenot history, exhibition of over 400 Huguenot pieces and documents; 450 mems.; Chair. S. F. DU TOIT; Curator Mrs. E. LE ROUX; publ. *Bulletin of the Huguenot Society of South Africa*.

Grahamstown

Albany Museum: f. 1855; archaeology, entomology, freshwater ichthyology, local history; houses Municipal Art Collection; maintains school service throughout the province; Dir. C. F. JACOT-GUILLARMOD; publ. *Cape Provincial Museums Annals* (jointly with 4 other museums, irregularly).

Johannesburg

Africana Museum: Public Library, Market Square; f. 1935; history and ethnology of Africa south of the Zambezi; Dir. Miss ANNA H. SMITH; publs. *Africana Notes and News* (quarterly), *Annual Report*, catalogues of special exhibitions, Frank Connock publications.

Bernberg Museum of Costume: 1 Duncombe Ave., Forest Town; f. 1972; br. of the Africana Museum; costumes and accessories dating from 1750.

James Hall Museum of Transport: Pioneers' Park, Rosettenville Rd., La Rochelle, Johannesburg; br. of the Africana Museum; f. 1964; history of transport in South Africa excluding rail transport.

Museum of South African Rock Art: Zoological Gardens, Jan Smuts Ave.; f. 1969; br. of the African Museum; open air display of rock engravings.

Photographic Museum: 17 Empire Rd., Parktown; f. 1969; br. of the Africana Museum; history of photography, particularly in South Africa.

Geological Museum: Public Library, Market Square; f. 1890; economic geology especially of Southern Africa, gemmology, mineralogy, physical geology and petrology, South African stratigraphy and archaeology; Dir. Miss A. H. SMITH.

Municipal Art Gallery: Joubert Park; f. 1911; European and South African painting and sculpture, print collection, textiles, Oriental ceramics; Dir. Miss P. M. ERASMUS.

Museum of the History of Medicine: P.O.B. 1038, Johannesburg; f. 1962; attached to the University of the Witwatersrand; collection of medical and surgical instruments; library of 3,000 vols. including many books written and autographed by S.A. doctors; Hon. Dir. Dr. C. ADLER, M.B., B.CH.; Hon. Curator Mrs. E. B. ADLER, B.A.

Kimberley

Alexander McGregor Memorial Museum: P.O.B. 316; f. 1907; geology; archaeology of N. Cape; zoology; Herbarium; ethnological collection housed in Duggan-Cronin Bantu Gallery, f. 1936; Dir. R. LIVERSIDGE; publs. _Cape Provincial Museums Annals_ (jointly with 4 other museums).

Kingwilliamstown

Kaffrarian Museum: 3 Lower Albert Rd.; f. 1898; contains the largest collection of mammals in the Republic of South Africa; also collections of Eastern Cape ethnological material and material associated with early European settlement; Acting Dir. DEREK M. COMINS; Sec. Mrs. M. TURNER; publ. _Annual Report; Cape Provincial Museums Annals_ (jointly with 4 other museums).

Pietermaritzburg

Natal Museum: 237 Loop St.; f. 1904; extensive natural history exhibits, especially the collections of African animals, birds, shells and insects; ethnology; Hall of Natal's history, research in Diptera, Arachnida, Mollusca and Reptiles; Dir. J. A. PRINGLE; publ. _Annals of the Natal Museum._

Tatham Art Gallery (Municipal): City Hall; f. 1903; 19th century and modern graphic art of the British and Foreign Schools; 19th and 20th century paintings, British and French Schools; Curator V. T. L. LEIGH.

Port Elizabeth

Port Elizabeth Museum, Snake Park and Oceanarium: Humewood; f. 1885, moved 1959; Research on marine biology, herpetology, ornithology and local history; library of 20,000 vols.; Museum; whale skeletons, shells and general marine life; fossils, geology, birds and local history; Snake Park: African and worldwide collection of reptiles; Oceanarium: local fish, sea birds, seals and dolphins; Dir. J. R. GRINDLEY, PH.D.; Curator Snake Park J. N. WEIMANN; Curator Oceanarium C. K. TAYLER; publ. _Cape Provincial Museums Annals_ (jointly with 4 other museums).

Pretoria

Municipal Art Gallery: Arcadia Park; f. 1964; South African art, international 20th century graphics; Dir. A. J. WERTH; publ. _Bulletin_ (quarterly).

Museum of Science and Industry: P.O.B. 1758; f. 1960; art, education, science, history, biography, travel; Curator V. C. WOOD; publs. _Lantern_ (quarterly), _Spectrum_ (quarterly).

National Cultural History and Open-Air Museum: P.O.B. 3300; f. 1964; formerly part of the Transvaal Museum; comprises Old Museum (Boom St.), Voortrekker Monument Museum, and Paul Kruger House Museum; Dir. Mrs. K. ROODT-COETZEE.

Transvaal Museum: Paul Kruger Street, P.O. Box 413; f. 1893; from 1964 a Natural History museum only; taxonomy, ecology, zoo-geography, with main emphasis on Southern Africa; primates, including fossil ape-man (Australopithecus); library of 26,000 vols.; Dir. C. K. BRAIN, PH.D., F.Z.S.; publs. _Memoirs, Annals, Annual Report, Bulletin._

Stellenbosch

Stellenbosch Museum: f. 1965; Curator M. J. LE ROUX, B.A.; comprises:

Grosvenor House: Drostdy St.; built _c._ 1800; over 500 exhibits, Cape furniture, Cape silver and other household articles.

Old Arsenal: The Braak; built 1777; exhibition of 18th-century cannon and other firearms and weapons; also articles relating to the military history of the town.

Schreuder House: Van Ryneveld St.; built 1709; exhibitions of Cape country-made furniture and folk art; to open 1973.

UNIVERSITIES

UNIVERSITY OF CAPE TOWN

P.O.B. 594, RONDEBOSCH, CAPE TOWN

Telephone: 694351.

Founded as South African College 1829, established as university 1918.

Language of instruction: English; Academic year: March to December (two terms).

Chancellor: H. F. OPPENHEIMER, M.A., D.ECON., LL.D.
Principal and Vice-Chancellor: Sir RICHARD LUYT G.C.M.G., K.C.V.O., D.C.M., M.A.

Number of teaching staff: 500.
Number of students: 7,790.

ATTACHED INSTITUTES:

Abe Bailey Institute of Inter-racial Studies: Rondebosch; f. 1968 from funds provided by the Abe Bailey Trust, to promote good relations between the peoples of South Africa; research in race and language group relations; Dir. Prof. H. W. VAN DER MERWE.

Fishing Industry Research Institute: Rondebosch; f. 1946; financed by industry, the C.S.I.R. and the Admin. of South-West Africa (Namibia); Dir. G. M. DREOSTI.

Institute Oceanoofgraphy: Rondebosch; f. 1963 to co-ordina activitteies in branches of marine research; controlled by a Board on which other university institutes and research departments are represented.

Percy Fitzpatrick Institute of African Ornithology: Rondebosch; affiliated to U.C.T. in 1960 to promote studies in African ornithology and to provide advanced teaching in this field; Dir. J. WINTERBOTTOM.

Southern Universities Nuclear Institute: Faure; f. 1961 by the Universities of Cape Town and Stellenbosch to provide advanced research facilities to university staff and postgraduate students; main research facility is a 5.5 MeV Van de Graaff accelerator with pulsed ion source; Chair. of Board of Govs. Sir R. LUYT; Chief Scientist Dr. I. J. VAN HEERDEN.

UNIVERSITY OF DURBAN-WESTVILLE

(Formerly University College, Durban)

PRIVATE BAG 4001, DURBAN

Telephone: 858271.

Founded 1960, for Indian students; Language of instruction: English; State control; Academic year: February to December (four terms).

Chancellor: Prof. A. J. H. VAN DER WALT, D.PHIL., D.LITT. ET PHIL.

Vice-Chancellor and Rector: Prof. S. P. OLIVIER, B.A., M.ED., D.PHIL.

Number of teachers: 225.
Number of students: 2,041.

UNIVERSITY OF FORT HARE
PRIVATE BAG 314, ALICE, CAPE PROVINCE
Telephone: Alice 281.
Telegraphic Address: Hoof, Fort Hare.

Founded 1916, since 1959 for Xhosa students and Africans from Transkei; Language of instruction: English; Academic year: February to November (four terms).

Chancellor: Dr. P. E. ROUSSEAU.

Chairman of Council and Vice-Chancellor: Prof. J. J. GERBER.

Rector: Prof. J. M. DE WET, M.SC., PH.D.

Number of teachers: 107, including 33 professors.
Number of students: 615.

THE UNIVERSITY OF NATAL
PIETERMARITZBURG AND DURBAN, NATAL
Telephone: 35-2461.
Language of instruction: English.

Founded 1910, Formerly a Constituent College of the University of South Africa; assumed university status 1949.

Chancellor: Dr. G. G. CAMPBELL, M.B., CH.B., F.R.C.S., HON. LL.D.

Chairman: L. S. ROBINSON.

Vice-Chancellor and Principal: Prof. F. E. STOCK, O.B.E., M.B., D.T.M. & H., F.R.C.S., F.A.C.S.

Number of lecturers: 649, including 82 professors.
Number of students: 7,171.

RESEARCH INSTITUTES:

Institute for Parasitology.
Director: R. ELSDON-DEW, M.B., CH.B., M.D., F.R.S.S.AF.

Institute for Social Research: Durban; f. 1953.
Director: (vacant).

Meyrick Bennett Children's Centre.
Director: (vacant).

Natal Institute of Immunology.
Director: B. G. GROBBELAAR, M.D., B.CH.

Oceanographic Research Institute.
Director: A. E. F. HEYDORN, PH.D.

South African Paint Research Institute: Durban; f. 1948.
Director: D. W. EVANS, PH.D.

Sugar Milling Research Institute: Durban; f. 1948.
Director: M. MATIC, DIP.ING.CHIM., PH.D.

Wattle Research Institute: Pietermaritzburg; f. 1946.
Director: Prof. S. P. SHERRY, M.A., PH.D.

UNIVERSITY OF THE NORTH
P.O. SOVENGA, PIETERSBURG
Central Telephone: Sovenga 33/34.

Founded 1959 to serve the Tsonga, Sotho and Venda peoples.

Languages of instruction: English and Afrikaans; State control; Academic year: March to November (two semesters).

Chancellor: Dr. W. W. M. EISELEN.

Rector: Prof. J. L. BOSHOFF.
Number of teachers: 98.
Number of students: 811.

UNIVERSITY OF THE ORANGE FREE STATE
(Formerly University College of the O.F.S.)
P.O.B. 339, BLOEMFONTEIN, O.F.S.
Telephone: 89881.

Founded 1855. Formerly a Constituent College of the University of South Africa, Pretoria. Granted independent status 1949.

Principal language of instruction: Afrikaans.

Chancellor: C. R. SWART, B.A., LL.B., LL.D.(H.C.).

Vice-Chancellor and Rector: Prof. B. KOK, M.A., LITT.DOCTS., D.LITT.

Number of lecturers 321.
Number of students 3,858.

ATTACHED INSTITUTES:

Institute of Social and Economic Research.
Director: D. J. G. SMITH, D.S.C.

Institute for Contemporary History.
Director: O. GEYSER, M.A., D.PHIL.

UNIVERSITY OF PORT ELIZABETH
P.O.B. 1600, PORT ELIZABETH, CAPE PROVINCE
Telephone: 2-7961.
Founded 1964.

Languages of instruction: Afrikaans and English; Academic year: February to November (two semesters).

Chancellor: The Hon. B. J. SCHOEMAN, M.P.

Vice-Chancellor and Principal: Prof. Dr. E. J. MARAIS, D.SC.

Number of teachers: 186.
Number of students: 1,602.

ATTACHED INSTITUTES:

Conservatoire of Music.
Director: J. H. POTGIETER, D.MUS., U.T.L.M., U.P.L.M.

Institute for Planning Research.
Director: J. F. POTGIETER, M.A., D.PHIL.

S.A. Wool Textile Research Institute.
Director: D. P. VELDSMAN, M.SC., D.SC.

University Clinic.
Director: W. D. PIENAAR, M.A., PH.D.

University C.S.I.R. Research Unit for Oceanography.
Chief Research Officer: J. P. A. LOCHNER, PH.D.

POTCHEFSTROOM UNIVERSITY FOR CHRISTIAN HIGHER EDUCATION
(Formerly Potchefstroom University College for C.H.E.)
POTCHEFSTROOM, TRANSVAAL
Telephone: Potchefstroom 3361.

Founded 1869; incorporated in University of South Africa as Constituent College 1921; assumed full university status as Potchefstroom University for Christian Higher Education, March 1951.

Principal language of instruction: Afrikaans.

Chancellor: The Hon. J. DE KLERK, LL.D.

Vice-Chancellor and Principal: Prof. H. J. J. BINGLE, M.ED., D.PHIL.

Chairman of the Senate: A. A. VENTER.

Vice-Chairman of the Senate: Prof. H. C. VAN ROOY, M.A., F.S.A.L.A., B.L.S.

Number of lecturers: 344, including 82 professors.
Number of students: 5,377.

ATTACHED CONSERVATORY AND INSTITUTES:

Conservatoire of Music.
Head: Prof. J. J. A. VAN DER WALT, M.MUS., D.PHIL.

Institute of Botanic Research.
Head: Prof. M. C. PAPENDORF, M.SC., PH.D.

Institute of Economic Research.
Head: Prof. D. P. ERASMUS, D.COM.

Institute of South African Music.
Head: Prof. J. J. A. VAN DER WALT, M.MUS., D.PHIL.

Institute of Zoological Research.
Head: Prof. P. A. J. RYKE, D.SC.

Institute of Physical Research.
Head: Prof. M. A. DU T. MEYER, M.SC., D.SC.

Research Institute of Co-operatives.
Head: Prof. D. J. VILJOEN, D.COMM.

Institute of Automation.
Head: Prof. A. J. E. SORGDRAGER, M.COM., D.ECON., B.A., A.C.W.A., M.B.I.M., F.C.M.A., A.I.C.B., A.S.A.I.M.

National Institute for the Small Trader.
Head: Prof. N. J. SWART, M.COM., PH.D.

Institute of African and Bantu Studies.
Head: Prof. J. H. COETZEE, M.A., D.PHIL.

Institute of Psychological and Educational Services and Research.
Head: Prof. T. A. VAN DYK, M.A., D.LITT. ET PHIL.

Institute of Regional Planning.
Head: Prof. Dr. F. J. POTGIETER, M.A., D.PHIL.

Institute of Linguistic and Literary Research.
Head: Prof. H. VENTER, M.A., D.LITT.

Institute of Physiological Research.
Head: Prof. P. J. PRETORIUS, D.SC.

Institute of Sport.
Head: P. MALAN, B.SC.

Institute for the Advancement of Calvinism.
Head: Prof. S. C. W. DUVENAGE, M.A., M.DIV., TH.D., D.LITT. ET PHIL.

Centre for International Politics.
Head: Prof. C. P. VAN DER WALT, D.PHIL.

Institute for Afrikaans National Culture and Folklore.
Head: Prof. C. N. VENTER, M.SOC.SC., D.PHIL.

Institute of Communication Research.
Head: Prof. G. J. POTGIETER, M.A., D.PHIL.

Research Unit for Chemical Kinetics.
Head: Prof. J. A. VAN DEN BERG, D.SC.

Institute of Cardiac Research.
Head: (vacant).

Institute for Pedology.
Head: Prof. H. J. V. M. HARMSE, M.SC., PH.D.

Institute of Industrial Pharmacy.
Head: Dr. A. P. G. GOOSENS, D.SC.

INSTITUTIONS IN CO-OPERATION WITH THE UNIVERSITY:

Theological School of the Reformed Church in South Africa.
Rector: Prof. S. T. VAN DER WALT, TH.D.

Potchefstroom College of Education.
Rector: Prof. C. P. VAN DER WALT, M.A.

UNIVERSITY OF PRETORIA
HILLCREST, PRETORIA
Telephone: 74-6071.
Telegraphic Address: Puniv, Pretoria.

Founded as Transvaal University College 1908. Granted Charter as University of Pretoria 1930.

Private control: Language of instruction: Afrikaans; Academic year: February to December (two semesters).

Chancellor: The Hon. Dr. H. MULLER, M.A., D.LITT.

Vice-Chancellor and Rector: Prof. E. M. HAMMAN, LL.D.

Number of teachers: 872.
Number of students: 13,418.

ATTACHED INSTITUTES:

Veterinary Research Institute: Onderstepoort.

Margaretha Mes Institute of Plant Physiology: c/o University of Pretoria.

Financial Analysis Bureau of the University's Institute of Business Administration: P.O.B. 486, Pretoria.

RAND AFRIKAANS UNIVERSITY
P.O.B. 524, JOHANNESBURG
Telephone: 44-7151.

Founded in 1966; the first students were enrolled in 1968.

State control; Language of instruction: Afrikaans; Academic year: January to November.

Chancellor: The Hon. N. DIEDERICHS, M.A., D.LITT. ET PHIL.

Vice-Chancellor: Prof. G. VAN N. VILJOEN, M.A., LL.B., D.LITT. ET PHIL.

Number of teachers: 145.
Number of students: 1,216.

RHODES UNIVERSITY
(Formerly Rhodes University College)
P.O.B. 94, GRAHAMSTOWN
Telephone: Grahamstown 2023.
Telegraphic Address: Rhodescol.
Founded 1904.

Language of instruction: English; Academic year: March to November (four terms).

Chancellor: W. J. BUSSCHAU, M.COM., D.PHIL.

Chairman of the Council: The Hon. Mr. Justice J. D. CLOETE, B.A., LL.B., Q.C., S.C.

Principal and Vice-Chancellor: J. M. HYSLOP, M.A., PH.D., D.SC., LL.D., F.R.S.E.

Number of teachers: 188, including 42 professors.
Number of students: 2,150.

ATTACHED INSTITUTES:

Institute for the Study of English in Africa (I.S.E.A.): f. 1964; Dir. Prof. W. R. G. BRANFORD.

Institute of Social and Economic Research (I.S.E.R.): f. 1954; Dir. Prof. D. H. HOUGHTON.

Rhodes Institute for Freshwater Studies: f. 1967; Dir. Prof. B. R. ALLANSON.

J. L. B. Smith Institute of Ichthyology: f. 1968; Dir. Mrs. M. M. SMITH.

Leather Industries Research Institute: f. 1941; Dir. Prof. S. G. SHUTTLEWORTH.

UNIVERSITY OF SOUTH AFRICA

P.O.B. 392, PRETORIA

Telephone: 482811, Pretoria.

Telegraphic Address: Almamater, Pretoria.

Founded 1873, Royal Charter 1877.

Since 1946 the University has been a correspondence and examining institution, accepting only external students; multi-racial, bilingual Afrikaans and English.

Academic year: February to November (four terms).

Chancellor: Dr. F. J. DE VILLIERS, M.SC., PH.D., D.SC., F.R.I.C.

Vice-Chancellor and Principal: Prof. VAN WIJK, M.A.

Number of lecturers: 510.
Number of students: 29,152.

INSTITUTES:

Bureau for Market Research.

Bureau for University Research.

Institute of Foreign and Comparative Law.

UNIVERSITY OF STELLENBOSCH

STELLENBOSCH, CAPE PROVINCE

Telephone: 2222.

Telegraphic Address: University.

Incorporated 1918.

Language of instruction: Afrikaans. Academic year: February to December (four terms).

Chancellor: The Rt. Hon. B. J. VORSTER, LL.B., HON. DR. PHIL.

Vice-Chancellor: Rev. J. S. GERICKE, B.A., HON.D.TH.

Principal: Prof. J. N. DE VILLIERS, M.B., CH.B., F.R.C.O.G.

Number of teachers: 567.
Number of students: 8,100.

ATTACHED INSTITUTES:

Bureau of Economic Research.

Southern Universities Nuclear Research Institute.

Transport Economics Research Centre.

Research Institute for Fruit and Food Technology.

Research Institute of Viticulture and Enology.

UNIVERSITY OF THE WESTERN CAPE

PRIVATE BAG, P.O. KASSELSVLEI, BELLVILLE

Telephone: 97-6161/2/3/4/5.

Founded 1960, for Coloured, Griqua and Malay students.

State control; Languages of instruction: Afrikaans and English; Academic year: February to December (four terms).

Chancellor: Dr. I. D. DU PLESSIS, M.A., B.ED., PH.D.

Vice-Chancellor and Rector: Prof. N. SIEBERHAGEN, M.A., D.PHIL.

Number of teachers: 91 full-time, 22 part-time.
Number of students: 1,254.

ATTACHED INSTITUTE:

Bureau for Research in the Social Sciences.

UNIVERSITY OF THE WITWATERSRAND

2 JAN SMUTS AVE., MILNER PARK, JOHANNESBURG, TRANSVAAL

Telephone: 724-1311.

Founded 1922.

State subsidized, but functions under its own charter. Language of instruction: English; Academic year: February to November.

Chancellor: The Hon. O. D. SCHREINER, M.C., M.A., HON. LL.D.

Vice-Chancellor and Principal: Prof. G. R. BOZZOLI, D.SC.(ENG), F.I.E.E., PR.ENG.

Library: *see* Libraries.

Number of teachers: 756.
Number of students: 9,782.

ATTACHED INSTITUTES:

Bernard Price Institute of Geophysical Research: f. 1936.
Director: Prof. L. O. NICOLAYSEN, M.SC., PH.D.

Bernard Price Institute of Palaeontological Research: f. 1949.
Director: S. H. HAUGHTON, D.SC., F.R.S., F.G.S., F.R.S.S.AFR.

Economic Geology Research Unit.
Director: D. A. PRETORIUS, M.CS. (ENG.).

Ernest Oppenheimer Institute of Portuguese Studies.

Graduate School of Business Administration.
Director: Prof. S. BIESHEUVEL, M.B.E., M.A., PH.D.

Institute of Management Accounting.
Prof. T. W. McRAE, B.SC.ECON., C.A.

Institute for Adult Studies.

Institute of Mathematics.
Chairman: Prof. D. S. HENDERSON, M.A., PH.D.

Nuclear Physics Research Unit.
Director: Prof. J. P. F. SELLSCHOP, M.SC., PH.D.

Speech, Voice and Hearing Clinic.
Director: Prof. MYRTLE ARON, PH.D.

Solid State Physics Research Unit.
Director: Prof. F. R. N. NABARRO, M.B.E., M.A., D.SC., F.R.S.

Dental Research Unit.
Director: Prof. D. H. RETIEF, M.SC., B.DS.

Urban and Regional Research Unit.
Director: Prof. T. J. D. FAIR, M.A., PH.D.

UNIVERSITY COLLEGE OF ZULULAND

PRIVATE BAG, KWA-DLANGEZWA, VIA EMPANGENI, NATAL

Telephone: Kwa-Dlangezwa 5.

Founded 1960 for Zulu and Swazi students.

Chancellor: Dr. T. F. MULLER, M.SC., D.COM.

Rector: Prof. J. A. MARÉ, S.T.D., LL.DRS.

Number of teachers: 98.
Number of students: 815.

TECHNICAL COLLEGES

CAPE COLLEGE FOR ADVANCED TECHNICAL EDUCATION
LONGMARKET ST., P.O.B. 652, CAPE TOWN
Telephone: Cape Town 2-1035.
Telegraphic address: Teccom, Cape Town.
Founded 1923.
Languages of instruction: English and Afrikaans.
Director: R. McClelland, b.sc., b.ed., b.a., b.com.(s.a.), f.c.i.s., m.r.s.h.
Number of teachers: 130 full-time, 300 part-time.
Number of students: 10,000.

COLLEGE FOR ADVANCED TECHNICAL EDUCATION
PRIVATE BAG 6011, PORT ELIZABETH
Founded 1925.
Rector: S. D. Van Der Merwe, m.a.
Number of students: 3,500.

EAST LONDON TECHNICAL COLLEGE
EAST LONDON
Founded 1926.
Principal: I. Steyl, b.com., m.ed., ph.d.
Number of staff: 40 full-time.
Number of students: 72 full-time, 2,650 part-time.

FREE STATE TECHNICAL COLLEGE
PRIVATE BAG XO52, BLOEMFONTEIN

KROONSTAD TECHNICAL COLLEGE
PRIVATE BAG 22, KROONSTAD

M.L. SULTAN TECHNICAL COLLEGE
CENTENARY ROAD, DURBAN
Founded 1946, for Indian students.
Rector: Dr. A. Solomon, b.sc., d.ed.
Number of teachers: 346.
Number of students: 6,111, including part-time.
The College has a branch at Pietermaritzburg and conducts part-time classes at Stanger, Verulam, Tongaat, Clairwood, Mt. Edgcombe, Port Shepstone, and Chatsworth.

NATAL COLLEGE FOR ADVANCED TECHNICAL EDUCATION
P.O.B. 953, DURBAN
Founded 1907.
President of Council: G. G. Campbell, ll.d. (edin. and natal), m.b., f.r.c.s.(edin.), hon.f.r.s.s.a.

Director: A. Pittendrich, b.sc., b.com., b.ed.
Number of lecturers: 146 full-time, 300 part-time.
Number of students: 9,000.

NORTHERN CAPE TECHNICAL COLLEGE
PRIVATE BAG 31, KIMBERLEY

ORANGE FREE STATE GOLDFIELDS TECHNICAL COLLEGE
PRIVATE BAG 21, WELKOM, ORANGE FREE STATE

PIETERMARITZBURG TECHNICAL COLLEGE
PRIVATE BAG 9032, PIETERMARITZBURG
Principal: G. W. Stewart, m.sc.

PRETORIA COLLEGE FOR ADVANCED TECHNICAL EDUCATION
420 CHURCH ST. EAST, PRETORIA
Telephone: 2-5231, 2-1136.
Telegraphic Address: Teknikol.
Founded 1906.
Director: Dr. A. J. van Zyl, m.ed., ph.d.
Number of lecturers: 215 full-time, 368 part-time.
Number of students: 17,926.

Department of Technology consisting of Divisions of Mechanical, Electrical and Civil Engineering, Physical Sciences and Pharmacy, Biological Sciences; S.A. Defence Force Technical Training Institute, Lyttleton; Departments of Commerce and Management, Home Economics, Adult and Visual Education, Physical Education, Health and Recreation; Music; Art; Secretarial (day and evening classes); Teacher Training, Languages and Communication.

VAAL TRIANGLE COLLEGE FOR ADVANCED TECHNICAL EDUCATION
PRIVATE BAG, VANDERBIJLPARK

WITWATERSRAND COLLEGE FOR ADVANCED TECHNICAL EDUCATION
ELOFF ST., P.O.B. 3293, JOHANNESBURG
Founded 1925.
President: H. C. Morcombe.
Director: C. A. J. Bornman.
Number of teachers: 176 full-time, 170 part-time.
Number of students: 2,508 full-time, 6,891 part-time, 9,909 correspondence.

THE BANTU HOMELANDS

AREA	POPULATION (1970)
57,933 sq. miles	7,034,125

PLANS FOR DEVELOPMENT

(For the position of Africans before 1951 *see* earlier section, The Constitution.)

The Bantu Authorities Act, 1951, disestablished the Natives' Representative Council, which had refused to meet since 1949, and created in the Bantu homelands tribal, regional and territorial authorities which have administrative, executive and judicial functions and which are intended to form the basis for political development to full autonomy. The United Transkeian Territories General Council (UTTGC) or *Bunga* voted in 1955 to accept in principle the Bantu Authorities system, and in the following year it transformed itself into the Transkeian Territorial Authority. (For further developments in the Transkei *see* below, The Transkei.)

The Commission on the Socio-Economic Development of the Bantu Areas, which was set up in 1950 under the chairmanship of Prof. F. Tomlinson to prepare a long-term plan for "separate development", submitted its report to the Government in October 1954. It found that of the 13 per cent of the total land area of the Republic which forms the Native Reserves some 30 per cent of the land was badly eroded and a further 44 per cent moderately eroded. It also reported that per capita income had declined over the previous twenty years and that only the earnings of Africans in white areas had maintained Africans in the Reserves at subsistence level. It therefore recommended that some 50 per cent of the existing population in the Reserves be removed from agricultural land and 50,000 jobs a year be created for 25 years in the Reserves outside agriculture (in commerce and manufacturing). (Between mid-1959 and mid-1966, it has been estimated, only a few thousand new jobs were created by the Bantu Investment Corporation.) The Commission also proposed that white capital be allowed to invest in the development of the Reserves, given the paucity of resources available to Africans themselves. The Government preferred to accept a minority view on the Commission and rejected this proposal, establishing what later became the Bantu Investment Corporation with an initial capital of £500,000. The Government made it clear that industrial development in the Reserves was to be left to Africans themselves when it stated that development depended on the principle of "self-aid". From 1956 on the Government also followed a policy of building up border industries. Generous incentives, like the reduction of the minimum wage, were offered to white industrialists to move their concerns to the white fringes of the borders with the Reserves, where it was assumed, though not realised in practice, that African workers would be able to cross the borders back to their homes at reasonable intervals.

The total expenditure the Tomlinson Commission recommended to develop the Reserves and to achieve parity between whites and Africans in the white areas by the year 2000 was £104 million. Between 1956 and 1961 the Government actually spent £7.9 million on development in the Reserves. The first "development plan" for the Reserves allocated R.114,342,000 for the period 1961–66 (*see* table below). Nearly R.76 million was for "houses and development of villages". These were the townships for the workers in the white border industries or for Africans evicted from their previous homes in "white" areas and "resettled" in the Reserves. Much of the remainder of the total expenditure was earmarked for improving the badly eroded soil. In the second "development plan", 1966–71 (*see* table below), the two largest items were "physical development" and "education". The first item, allotted R.162 million, again largely consisted, as far as can be ascertained, of the costs of resettlement. (By early 1969 the Government stated that about 900,000 "redundant, non-economically active Bantu in our white areas" had been "eliminated" and settled elsewhere since 1959, and that at least 216,000 had been resettled in the Johannesburg area alone.) The second item, education (R.163 million), largely corresponded with the total expenditure planned for all Bantu education in the Republic in that period.

APARTHEID LEGISLATION

The Bantu Self-Government Act, 1959, which repealed the Representation of Natives Act, 1936, thus abolishing the limited representation of Africans in Parliament and the Cape Provincial Council, accepts the natural division of the African population into eight national units in the Republic and its vicinity. These units, beginning with a system of tribal, regional and territorial authorities may eventually become self-governing in their respective areas, although this does not necessarily mean that there will be eight territorial authorities or regional parliaments. The Act also provides for appointment of Commissioners-General to represent the Government at each of these national units and to aid the Bantu rulers in achieving this end. The Transkei Territorial Authority was set up in 1960 and those for people of the Ciskei and the Tswanas (Western Transvaal and Northern Cape) were established in 1961. In January 1962 it was announced that the Xhosa nation of the Transkei would be the first of the Bantu peoples to qualify for self-government—the next step to independence. The new Transkei Constitution was agreed to in March 1962. (*See* below, The Transkei.)

In January 1967 it was announced that the North Sotho people, living in the northern Transvaal, would have five departments of government to control the affairs of their Homeland. Matters passing from the control of the Republic Government were education, finance, justice, public works, agriculture, forestry and community development. Later it was announced that detailed attention was also being given to the transfer of management and administrative powers to the Tswana people, the Xhosa of the Ciskei, the South Sotho, the Venda and the Tsonga.

On February 3rd, 1971, the Bantu Homelands Constitution Bill was introduced in the House of Assembly. It empowered the South African Government to grant self-government, on a similar basis to that already granted to the Transkei, to any African area which had a Territorial Authority at its request. The bill provided for such territories to have their own national anthems and flags. They would be prevented, however, from maintaining an army or any similar institution. No diplomatic or consular relations with foreign countries were to be entered into, nor could they construct factories for the production of arms or explosives. They would be unable to legislate on such matters as transport, posts and telecommunications, matters of finance including currency, customs and excise duties, nor could they control the entry of any citizens other than their own into their areas.

Under this Act, Tswanaland was granted an elected Legislative Assembly on April 30th, 1971 at the request of Chief Lucas Mangope who became Chief Minister, when it became the territory of Bophuthatswana. The Ciskei was granted a similar Legislative Assembly on August 1st, 1972 with Chief Justice Mabandla as Chief Minister. In October, 1972 the same form of "self-government" was granted to Lebowa, with Chief M. M. Matlala as Chief Minister.

The removal of all representatives of non-Whites from Parliament and the establishment of separate non-White authorities has been accompanied by legislation (mostly passed since the advent of the National Party to power in 1948) designed to enforce separation between the different racial groups.

By the Natives Land Act, 1913, and the Natives (Urban Areas Consolidation) Act, 1945 (and amendments), Africans may not acquire urban land, being limited to land in the reserved areas, which constitute about 14 per cent of the total land area of the Republic. The Population Registration Act of 1950 requires every person over 16 to carry an identity card signifying the holder's racial group, which is determined by local race-classification boards, chaired by magistrates. Personal relationships between people of different racial groups are regulated as criminal offences under the Prohibition of Mixed Marriages Act, 1949, and the Immorality Act, 1957, while total residential separation of Whites, Asians, Coloureds and Africans in urban areas is enforced by the Group Areas Act, 1950 (amended and consolidated 1957), and the Natives (Urban Areas Consolidation) Act, 1945, which also limit Asians to trading in Asian areas only. In addition these acts lay down that no African may stay in an urban area for more than 72 hours without the permission of the local Native Labour Officer. Entry into an urban area by an African is, in any case, regulated by the pass system, whose basis is the Natives (Abolition of Passes and Co-ordination of Documents) Act, 1952, and which requires an African to hold a permit to enter an urban area (where he must have secured employment) and a permit to leave his previous area. The Native Labour Officer is also, under the Native Labour (Settlement of Disputes) Act, 1953, supreme in handling industrial disputes involving African workers. The same Act prohibits strikes by Africans; while the Native Building Workers Act, 1951, and the Industrial Conciliation Act, 1956, established the principle of job-reservation (already effective in the mining industry) by which skilled work is mainly reserved for Whites.

Separate public amenities, which need not be of equal quality, are provided for under the Reservation of Separate Amenities Act, 1953, and the prevention of joint worshipping by Whites and Africans is a provision of the Native Laws Amendment Act. Education of the African, and the training of his teacher, is completely state-controlled.

A number of Acts, notably the Bantu Administration Act, 1927, as amended, and the Native (Urban Areas Consolidation) Act, 1945, as amended, render Africans liable to executive and administrative decisions without provision for recourse to the law courts for possible redress. In addition political and trade union organization by Africans has been made impossible (as has any effective non-African opposition organization) by laws like the Suppression of Communism Act, 1950, as amended, the General Law Amendment Act, 1963, and the Criminal Procedure Act, 1965, as amended, which give the President and Minister of Justice wide discretionary powers that cannot be challenged in a court of law. The Suppression of Communism Act defines communism as any doctrine

expounded by Lenin, Trotsky, the Comintern or the Cominform, or a "doctrine which aims at bringing about any political, industrial, social or economic change within the Union by the promotion of disturbances or disorder, by unlawful acts or omissions or by means which include the promotion of disturbance or disorder, or such acts or omissions or threat".

THE RESERVES: FIVE-YEAR PLAN 1961-66
(Rand)

Houses and Development of Villages .	75,949,500
Staff Accommodation, Stores and Workshops	2,122,900
Roads and Bridges . . .	3,349,650
Irrigation	6,945,200
Dams and Boreholes . . .	3,946,040
Contour Banks and Grass Strips . .	1,150,000
Afforestation	8,999,108
Fencing	9,901,332
Fibre Cultivation . . .	1,777,703
Dipping Tanks	156,600
Auction Pens for Stock . . .	44,236
TOTAL . . .	114,342,269

BANTU HOMELANDS: FIVE-YEAR PLAN 1966-71
ESTIMATED EXPENDITURE
(Rand '000)

Physical Development . . .	162,539
Economic Development . . .	39,474
Education	163,575
Grants to Bantu Local Authorities .	6,630
Compensation and Transport . .	6,549
Land and Equipment Purchases .	50,000
Roads	2,394
TOTAL (incl. others) . .	490,000

ORGANIZATION

Minister of Bantu Administration and Development, and Bantu Education: M. C. BOTHA.

Director of Bantu Development: L. A. PEPLER, B.SC.AG.

Commissioners General:

Transkei, Ciskei: J. H. ABRAHAM.

KwaZulu: H. TORLAGE.

Lebowa: W. W. M. EISELEN.

VhaVenda: M. D. C. DE WET NEL.

Gazankulu: Prof. E. F. POTGIETER.

Bophuthatswana: Dr. I. S. KLOPPERS.

Basotho Quaqwa: N. C. VAN R. SADIE.

Chief Ministers and Chief Executives of the Homelands:

The Transkei (Xhosa): Chief KAIZER MATANZIMA.

The Ciskei (Xhosa): Chief J. K. M. MABANDLA.

Kwazulu (Zulu): Chief GATSHA BUTHELEZI.

Lebowa (Sepedi): Chief M. M. MATLALA.

Vhavenda (Venda): Chief P. MPHEPHU.

Gazankulu (Shangaan): Prof. H. W. E. NTSANWISI.

Bophuthatswana (Tswana): Chief L. M. MANGOPE.

Basotho Quaqwa (Seshoeshoe): Chief W. MOTA.

THE TRANSKEI

AREA AND POPULATION

AREA (sq. miles)	POPULATION (1970)
15,831	1,751,142

† Including 9,556 whites, 7,645 coloureds, 10 Asians (Capital Umtata).

Flag: The flag of the Transkei consists of equal horizontal stripes, green, white and ochre.

BUDGET, 1970–71
(Rand '000)

REVENUE		EXPENDITURE	
Domestic	5,696	Agriculture . . .	6,669
Republican Government . .	18,248	Education . . .	7,783
		Works . . .	4,878
		Interior . . .	5,351
TOTAL	23,944	TOTAL (inc. others) . .	26,261

Budget: (1968–69) Revenue R.20,496,000; Expenditure R.19,977,000.
(1969–70) Revenue R.20,344,000; Expenditure R.23,570,000.
(1971–72) Revenue R.31,676,000; Expenditure R.32,381,000.

CONSTITUTION

Although the *Bunga* had voted to accept the Bantu Authorities system in 1955, the imposition of this system, along with other grievances such as soil conservation schemes and increased taxation, resulted in violent opposition by the people, beginning in February 1960. There was a full-scale revolt in East Pondoland, and in November the Government introduced a state of emergency which has been in force ever since. No meeting can take place without the permission of the Bantu Commissioner; free speech is restricted; entry and exit in the Transkei is strictly controlled; chiefs have the power to apprehend persons described as "communists" by the Minister of Bantu Administration. (For definition of communism *see* Apartheid Legislation above). In January 1961 the Government stated that 4,769 Africans had been arrested in Pondoland and 2,067 actually tried; 25 Africans had been murdered in Pondoland, two of whom were chiefs; and 15 Africans had been killed by the police in "self-defence". Most of the troops were withdrawn in May 1961.

Despite the state of emergency in the first Bantustan election ever held, the elections in the Transkei in November 1963, 38 of the 45 elected members supported the anti-Government chief, Victor Poto, and only 7 the pro-Government candidate, Kaizer Mantanzima. However, when the full Assembly, including 64 chiefs, met, Mantanzima was elected Chief Minister, by 54 votes to Poto's 49. The 14 chiefly votes of East Pondoland are thought to have been crucial. The Paramount Chief there, Botha Sigcau, was the first chief to accept the Bantu Authorities and was given police protection during the revolt.

The Constitution of the Transkei was promulgated in the South African Parliament in May 1963, and came into force in December of the same year. The main provisions are:

Legislative Assembly: Consists of the four Paramount chiefs of the Transkei, the 60 chiefs holding office in the nine regional authority areas, and 45 members who are elected by all Transkeian subjects whether resident in the territory or in South Africa or South West Africa. The Chief Minister and the five Ministers are elected by secret ballot by the members of the Legislative Assembly.

The Legislative Assembly has the power to make laws in connection with the various government functions it controls. The laws then go to the Commissioner-General for submission, through the Minister for Bantu Administration and Development, to the State President. The State President may either give his assent or refer the bill back to the Legislative Assembly.

The Legislative Assembly meets at least once every year, and subject to the provisions of the act granting the Transkei self-government, "there will be freedom of speech and debate in the assembly". Subject to standing rules and orders, debates are to be conducted in public.

Powers: The Transkei Government has control over its own affairs apart from foreign affairs, defence, internal security, part of the administration of justice and economic development. There are ministries of finance, justice, the interior, education, agriculture and forestry, roads and works.

Under the section listing the "classes of matters" over which the Transkei Government has no power are: "The control, organization, administration, powers of entry into and presence in the Transkei of any police force of the Republic charged with the maintenance of public peace and order and the preservation of internal security and the safety of the Transkei and the Republic".

Personnel: Some white employees of the Republican Government have been placed at the disposal of the Transkeian Government but they will remain on the establishment of the Republican Government. They will be progressively replaced by suitable Bantu employees of the Transkei Government (of a Civil Service of 2,820 posts, 2,740 were filled by Bantu in 1966).

Zoning of Areas: The Constitution provides for the zoning of towns and villages in the Transkei under the jurisdiction of municipalities, village management boards, or local boards, for occupation and ownership by the Bantu. This provision was put into effect in 23 Transkei towns and villages, or in certain parts of them, in January 1966.

Justice: An elaborate system of courts provides for the administration of justice in the Transkei. It includes courts under the jurisdiction of the Republican Government. The jurisdiction of any court transferred to the Transkei does not include jurisdiction over anybody who is not a Transkei citizen.

The State President may constitute a high court of the Transkei similar in function, constitution and jurisdiction to the Supreme Court of South Africa. Appeals go from the High Court of the Transkei to the Appellate Division of the Supreme Court of South Africa. The Transkei High Court is to take over the functions of the Bantu appeal and divorce courts. It is also involved in matters of Bantu law and custom.

Finance: The Transkei Government is financed by various forms of revenue including taxation of all Xhosa, both inside the Transkei and outside. In addition to this, the Republican Government grants the Transkei enough money (about R13 million a year) to cover the administration of all departments handed over to the Transkei.

THE GOVERNMENT

THE CABINET
(*November* 1972)

Chief Minister and Minister of Finance: Chief KAIZER MATANZIMA.

Minister of the Interior: Chief JEREMIAH D. MOSHESH.

Minister of Agriculture and Forestry: N. P. BULUBE.

Minister of Education: Miss S. N. SIGCAU.

Minister of Justice: Chief GEORGE M. MATANZIMA.

Minister of Roads and Works: C. M. C. NDAMSE.

LEGISLATIVE ASSEMBLY
(Second Election, October, 1968)

Elected Members: 45 (Transkei National Independence Party 28, Democratic Party 14, Independents 3).

Chairman: Hon. M. H. CANCA.

Deputy Chairman: Hon. M. E. DYARVANE.

Members: Chief MBUNGWA LANGASIKI, Chief MAKOSONKE SIGCAU, Chief JONGILIZWE NTOLA.

Non-Elected Members: Four Paramount Chiefs, 60 office-holding Chiefs in nine Regions (56 of the 64 Chiefs support the ruling party).

POLITICAL PARTIES

Transkei National Independence Party: f. 1964; accepts policy of apartheid; aims at Transkeian independence and called for complete independence in its 1968 election manifesto, won 7 of 45 elected seats in Assembly in 1963 elections and 28 in 1968; Leader Chief KAIZER MATANZIMA.

Democratic Party: f. 1964; rejects apartheid in favour of the Transkei's status as a province within South Africa, with equal rights for both races in the Republic; won 38 of 45 elected seats in Assembly in 1963 and 14 in 1968; Leader KNOWLEDGE GUZANA.

Transkei People's Freedom Party: Umtata; f. 1966; aims at immediate independence from the Republic; Leader S. M. SINABA.

RELIGION

Church of the Province of South Africa: Bishop of St. John's Rt. Rev. JAMES LEO SCHUSTER, M.A., Bishopsmead, Umtata.

Roman Catholic Church: Bishop of Umtata (Province of Durban) Rt. Rev. HENRY CARLEN, C.M.M.

RADIO

Radio Bantu: broadcasts in Zulu, Xhosa, Southern Sotho, Northern Sotho, Tswana, Tsonga, Venda, Ndonga, Kuanyama, Nama/Damara and Herero.

FINANCE

Xhosa Development Corporation: P.O.B. 618, East London; Man. Dir. F. MARITZ; cap. R.27.7m.

Barclays National Bank Ltd.: Umtata.

Standard Bank of South Africa Ltd., The: Umtata.

TRADE AND INDUSTRY

DEVELOPMENT ORGANIZATIONS

Bantu Investment Corporation of S.A. Ltd.: P.O.B. 213, Pretoria; f. 1959 to develop Bantu areas; Chair. Dr. S. P. DU TOIT VILJOEN; Man. Dir. Dr. J. ADENDORFF.

Transkei Industrial Development Corporation: P.O.B. 103, Umtata; f. 1965; controlled by S.A. Government; intended to establish finance and develop industries in Transkei.

EDUCATION

In 1971 there were 1,679 state schools together with 38 private schools controlled by the church. Of the state schools, 1,602 are primary, 52 are secondary, 14 are high schools, four are vocational schools and five are schools for teacher training.

OTHER BANTU AUTHORITIES

The Ciskei, Bophuthatswana and Lebowa homelands have 'self-government' and the KwaZulu, Venda, Gazankulu (Shangaan) and Basotho Qwaqwa homelands are being given the same institutions by stages. The Venda and Kwa Zulu Territorial Authorities have recently become Legislative Assemblies. The South African Government has similar plans for the homelands in South-West Africa (Namibia), and in June 1972 it announced that the Owambo homeland would become self-governing in 1973.

SELECT BIBLIOGRAPHY

ACOCKS, J. P. H. *The Veld Types of South Africa.* Pretoria, 1953. (Union of South Africa, Dept. of Agriculture, Division of Botany, Botanical Survey Memoir No. 28.)

BENSON, M. *South Africa: The Struggle for a Birthright.* Harmondsworth, Penguin, 1966.

BOARD, C. "Southern Africa" in HODDER, B. W., and HARRIS, D. R. (Eds.), *Africa in Transition—Geographical Essays.* London, 1967.

BUREAU OF CENSUS AND STATISTICS. *Statistical Year Book.*

BUNTING, B. *The Rise of the South African Reich.* London, Penguin, 1969.

CARTER, G. M. *The Politics of Inequality—South Africa since 1948.* London, Thames and Hudson, 1959.

COLE, MONICA M. *South Africa.* London, Methuen, 1961.

DE KIEWIET, C. W. *A History of South Africa.* London, Oxford University Press, 1941.

DESMOND, Father C. *The Discarded People.* Penguin, 1971.

DOXEY, G. V. *The Industrial Colour Bar in South Africa.* Cape Town, Oxford University Press, 1961.

DU TOIT, A. L. *The Geology of South Africa.* Edinburgh, 1954.

FEIT, E. *African Opposition in South Africa—The Failure of Passive Resistance.* The Hoover Institution of War, Revolution and Peace, Stanford University, California.

FEIT, E. *Urban Revolt in South Africa, 1960–64. A Case Study.* 1971.

FIRST, RUTH ET AL. *The South African Connection.* London, Temple Smith, 1972.

GREEN, L. P., and FAIR, T. J. D. *Development in Africa: A study in regional analysis with special reference to Southern Africa.* Johannesburg, 1962.

HANCE, W. A., KUPER, L., McKAY, V. and MUNGER, E. (Eds.). *Southern Africa and the United States.* New York, London, Columbia University Press, 1968.

HERIBERT, A. *South Africa: Sociological Perspectives.* Oxford University Press, 1971.

HOBART HOUGHTON, D. *The South African Economy,* Oxford University Press, London, 1967.

HORWITZ, R. *The Political Economy of South Africa.* London, Weidenfeld and Nicholson, 1967.

HURWITZ, N., and WILLIAMS, D. *The Economic Framework of South Africa.* Shuter and Shuter, Pietermaritzburg, 1962.

KING, L. C. *South African Scenery.* 3rd edn., 1963.

KRUGER, D. W. *The Age of the Generals.* Johannesburg, Dagbreek Book Store, 1958.

KRUGER, D. W. (Ed.). *South African Parties and Policies 1910–1960, a select source book.* Cape Town, Human and Rousseau, 1960.

LUTHULI, A. *Let My People Go.* London, Collins, 1963.

MARQUARD, L. *The People and Policies of South Africa,* London, Oxford University Press, 4th edn., 1969.

MAYER, P. (Ed.). *Xhosa in Town.* (3 vols.), Cape Town, Oxford University Press.

MBEKI, G. *South Africa: The Peasants' Revolt.* London, Penguin African Library, 1964.

NIDDRIE, D. L. *South Africa: Nation or Nations?* Princeton, Van Nostrand, 1968.

PATTERSON, S. *The Last Trek—a Study of the Boer People and the Afrikaner Nation.* London, Routledge and Kegan Ltd., 1957.

POLLOCK, N. C., and AGNEW, S. *An Historical Geography of South Africa.* London, 1963.

RANSFORD, O. *The Great Trek.* John Murray, 1972.

REPUBLIC OF SOUTH AFRICA BUREAU OF STATISTICS POPULATION CENSUS, 6th September 1960, Vol. 1: *Geographical distribution of the population.* Pretoria, 1963.

ROBERTSON, J. *Liberalism in South Africa 1948–1963.* Oxford University Press, 1971.

ROUX, E. *Time longer than Rope.* Madison, University of Wisconsin Press, 1964.

SIMONS, H. J. and R. E. *Class and Colour in South Africa 1850–1950.* Penguin Books, 1969.

SOUTH AFRICAN INSTITUTE OF RACE RELATIONS. *A Survey of Race Relations in South Africa, 1971.* Johannesburg, 1972.

SOUTH AFRICAN RESERVE BANK. Quarterly Bulletin.

SPENCE, J. E. *The Strategic Significance of Southern Africa.* London, Royal United Service Institution, 1970.

THOMPSON, L. M. *The Unification of South Africa 1902–10.* Oxford, Clarendon Press, 1960.

TROUP FREDA. *South Africa.* London, Eyre Methuen, 1972.

UNESCO. *Apartheid, its effects on education, science, culture and information. 1972.*

VAN DER MERWE, C. R. *Soils groups and Sub-groups of South Africa.* Pretoria, 1941.

VAN DER MERWE, H. W. and WELSH, D. *Student Perspectives on South Africa.* London, Rex Collings, 1972.

VOTCHER, W. H. *White Laager: The Rise of Afrikaner Nationalism.* London, Pall Mall, 1965.

WALKER, E. A. *A History of Southern Africa.* London, Longmans, Green Co., 3rd edn., 1957.

WALSHE, P. *The Rise of African Nationalism in South Africa.* 1971.

WELLINGTON, J. H. *Southern Africa: A geographical study.* (2 vols.), London, 1955.

WILSON, M., and THOMPSON, L. (Eds.). *The Oxford History of South Africa.* 2 vols., Oxford, Clarendon Press, 1969–71.

South West Africa (Namibia) and Botswana.

South West Africa

(NAMIBIA)

PHYSICAL AND SOCIAL GEOGRAPHY

John Amer

South West Africa (Namibia) is a vast territory of 317,827 sq. miles lying across the Tropic of Capricorn. It is bordered by South Africa on the south and south-east, by Botswana on the east and Angola on the north, and the narrow Caprivi Strip between the two latter countries in the north-east extends South West Africa to the Zambezi River and a common border with Zambia.

PHYSICAL FEATURES

A plain, varying in width from 40 to 100 miles, extends 1,000 miles along the entire Atlantic seaboard. This is an arid region known as the Namib Desert where mean annual rainfall is less than 4 in.; long lines of huge sand dunes are common and it is almost devoid of vegetation. Behind the coastal plain the Great Escarpment rises to the plateau which forms the rest of the country. Part of the Southern African plateau, it has an average elevation of 3,600 ft. above sea-level but towards the centre of the country there is a rise to altitudes between 5,000 and 8,000 ft. A number of mountain masses rise above the general surface throughout the plateau. Eastwards the surface slopes to the Kalahari Basin and northwards to the large, flat, swampy Etosha Pan. Much of South West Africa's drainage is interior to the Kalahari. There are no perennial rivers within the country apart from those like the Okavango and the Cuando which cross the Caprivi Strip. The Orange River, forming the southern border, and the Cunene and Zambezi which form parts of the northern border are also permanent.

Temperatures of the coastal areas are modified by the cool Benguela Current, whilst altitude modifies plateau temperatures (cf. Walvis Bay: January 66°F., July 58°F.; and Windhoek (5,600 ft.): January 75°F., July 57°F.). Mean annual rainfall over the plateau increases northwards from less than 4 in. on the southern border to over 20 in. in the north-east. Most of the rain falls during the summer but it is unreliable and years of drought may be experienced. Grasslands cover most of the plateau; they are richer in the wetter north but merge into poor scrub in the south and east.

POPULATION AND RESOURCES

With the exception of ports and mining centres in the Namib and small numbers of Bushmen in the Kalahari these regions are largely uninhabited. Most of the population (an estimated 746,328 in 1970) live on the plateau. Over half the total population and about two-thirds of the African population live in the better-watered northern third. This includes 342,455 Owambo, who form the largest single ethnic group, and 49,577 Kavango as well as considerable numbers of East Caprivians and Kaokovelders. Almost the entire European population of 90,658 live in the southern two-thirds of the plateau, chiefly in the central highlands around Windhoek, the capital, together with the other main ethnic groups, the Damara, Herero and Nama.

South West Africa possesses scattered deposits of valuable minerals. Of particular importance are the rich surface deposits of alluvial diamonds along the coastal plain. A variety of other minerals are also produced, including lead, zinc, copper, vanadium, manganese, tin and rock salt.

RECENT HISTORY

Ruth First

GERMAN RULE AND THE MANDATE

South West Africa was colonized by Germany in 1884, during the "scramble for Africa" of the European powers. In the ensuing years white settlement encroached on African lands, especially in the southern half of the territory, and led to wars against conquest by the Herero in 1904, and by the Nama, whose resistance lasted until 1907. During the war against the Herero the brutal "extermination order" of General von Trotha cost about 65,000 lives. Only an estimated 15,000 of these formerly prosperous cattle-farmers survived, and the Herero population today is smaller than it was at the beginning of the century before the conquest. Defeated in war, the African tribes found their land and cattle confiscated and their labour conscripted as a tiny settler community secured the best farmlands of the territory.

When the First World War broke out in 1914, South African armies under Generals Louis Botha and J. C. Smuts invaded and occupied South West Africa in the name of the Allied cause. The League of Nations founded in 1920 after the Versailles Peace Conference decided that the former German colonies should not be distributed as spoils of war but should form a "sacred trust of civilization"; and a mandate system was devised whereby the German colonies were placed under the control of mandatory states, whose administration was to be supervised by the Permanent Mandates Commission of the League. The Union of South Africa was appointed the mandatory over South West Africa with a "C" class mandate. This was granted because of South West Africa's contiguity to South Africa and allowed that the mandated territory be administered as an integral part of South Africa, but subject to safeguards in the interests of the indigenous population: the mandatory power was to promote to the utmost the moral well-being and social progress of the inhabitants of the territory. It was also to make annual reports on its administration, and on the measures taken to carry out its obligations.

The mandate period lasted from 1919 to the end of the Second World War. It was during this period that South Africa not only took over but extended the system of land deprivation and segregation begun under German rule; she also entrenched vigorous discrimination against Africans in political, social and economic life. In 1933 the South African government pressed for the incorporation of the territory into South Africa, but this was never agreed to by the Mandates Commission. The latter was critical of the South African administration on a succession of issues, but had no power to enforce its strictures.

INTERNATIONAL ACTION ON S.W.A.

After the Second World War the League of Nations was superseded by the United Nations, and the mandate system by the trusteeship system. Alone of the mandatory powers South Africa refused to submit a trusteeship agreement for South West Africa. From 1946 onwards South West Africa has been a point of dispute between South Africa and the world organization. The South African government questioned the right of the United Nations to enquire into and control the manner in which South West Africa and its inhabitants were governed, and argued that the mandate had expired with the demise of the League and that South Africa's sovereignty over the territory was unrestricted. When South Africa refused to submit reports on her administration, the United Nations established the Special Committee on South West Africa and, from 1961 onwards, the Committee of 24 to compile reports. The International Court of Justice at The Hague was asked on three separate occasions for advisory opinions on the status in international law of the former mandate. Judgements were given in 1950, in 1955, and again in 1956. Their tenor was that South Africa was not legally obliged to place the territory under the UN trusteeship system, but that she was not competent to alter unilaterally the legal status of the territory.

In 1960 Ethiopia and Liberia, the two African members of the United Nations who had also been members of the League, invoked a compulsory jurisdiction of the International Court. They asked the Court to declare that the system of *apartheid*, under which South West Africa was governed, was inconsistent with South Africa's obligations in terms of the mandate. It was six years before the Court gave its decision on the case. In July 1966 it decided, by the casting vote of the Court President, that it was not necessary to go into the allegations concerning *apartheid* because Ethiopia and Liberia had no standing before the Court—this despite the fact that the Court had found in 1962 by a majority of 8 to 7 that the two states were entitled to bring the case and that the Court could proceed to examine the merits of the issue. The Court thus never dealt with the substantive accusations made against South Africa's administration of the territory.

Despite the inconclusiveness of the Court decision the 1966 session of the UN General Assembly resolved that South Africa should be stripped of her mandate over the territory, and that the responsibility for it should be assumed by a UN-appointed Council. The eleven-nation Council set up in terms of this resolution was to arrange for the transfer of the administration. In June 1968 the General Assembly adopted a resolution sponsored by African and Asian members to rename the territory Namibia, but UN action on the former mandate has otherwise remained limited to moral assertion. The first report of the Council for Namibia admitted this, and said that South African opposition had prevented it from taking over the administration of the territory. The Council called for Security Council action, since the latter alone has authority under the Charter to take decisive action in furtherance of UN resolutions, but proposals for Security Council action have failed to win the support of the big powers in the Council.

INCORPORATION INTO SOUTH AFRICA

The culmination of these long years of argument over the international responsibility for the former mandate was to prove demonstrably the hiatus between moral assertion and effective action by the world body. During 1968 and 1969 South Africa proceeded to complete the incorporation of South West Africa into the Republic. By mid-1968 South Africa already controlled South West African defence, foreign affairs, police, African administration, customs and excise, immigration and transport. The South West Africa Affairs Act of 1969 authorized South Africa to take control of revenue, commerce and industries, labour, mining and health. The territory was reduced to the status of a fifth province of the Republic. The South West Africa Legislative Assembly (elected by an exclusively white voters' roll) was left with only minor functions like roads, licensing, local authorities and white education. The major revenues of the territory, including taxes and mining duties previously controlled by the territory's legislature, are now paid directly to the Republic's central government.

The police and military forces of South West Africa are integrated with those of South Africa. African administration is under the control of the Chief Bantu Commissioner for South West Africa, an official of the South African Department of Bantu Affairs and Development. The South African government has extended to the territory the security laws in force in the Republic, which empower, among other things, the detention of political suspects for indefinite periods of time, without their recourse to *habeas corpus*.

In 1962 a government commission, generally referred to as the Odendaal Commission, was appointed to define the geographic, economic and political aspects of *apartheid* in South West Africa. It recommended the establishment of ten "Homelands", eight of them for Africans. It is estimated that once constituted the Homelands (or Bantustans) will occupy 39.6 per cent of the territory, while the exclusively white area will cover 44.1 per cent. It has also been calculated that 28.67 per cent of the African population will be required to move from existing areas under the new plan. In March 1967 the creation of the first Bantustan of Owamboland was announced. A tribal authority was installed, its powers limited to the passing of enactments relating to education, justice, community affairs and finance, and all requiring the approval of the South African government. Provision for these local powers is in the Development of Self Government for Native Nations of South West Africa Act.

Steps towards the creation of new Bantustans were next taken, in July 1971, in Kavango, the region to the east of Owamboland; and, in March 1972, in East Caprivi, where Legislative Councils composed of tribal representatives were constituted. Preparations were also afoot to establish a Damaraland Bantustan.

AFRICAN OPPOSITION

The electorate of the territory is exclusively white and both the governing National Party, and the opposition United South-West Africa Party—which can return members to the South African parliament—support the official policy of segregation or *apartheid*. The two African nationalist movements are the South West African People's Organisation (SWAPO) and the South West African National Union (SWANU), which came into existence after the Second World War and echoed the grievances earlier expressed by tribal opposition to government policy, first German, and then South African. The fate of the African people, they argued, had been one of repeated uprooting from ancestral homelands to ever more desolate parts of the country. During the late 1940s, when the issue of South West Africa was already before the United Nations, and the South African administration claimed that there was no further land available for African land settlement, white settlement absorbed an extra eighth of the country. Over the years Africans clamoured for redress of their grievances, principal among which were the alienation of their land, the operation of the contract labour system, restrictions on freedom of movement and related civil liberties, the reservation to the white minority of the bulk of the country's resources and economic, social and educational opportunity, and the consequent poverty and underdevelopment of the African areas. For two decades, from 1946 to 1966, the African organizations petitioned the United Nations and waited patiently for the world body to act.

In October 1966, shortly after the judgement of the International Court failed to find on the merits of *apartheid*, SWAPO announced that it would launch an armed struggle for the liberation of the territory. Several actions were reported between armed African guerrilla groups and the South African security forces. In 1967 thirty-five Africans were brought to trial on charges of terrorist activity. Twenty of the accused men were sentenced to life imprisonment, nine to 20 years' imprisonment, and the remainder to shorter periods. On appeal the defence argued against the competence of a South African court to try South West African nationals, but the judgement ruled that the anti-terrorist act passed by the South African Parliament applied to the mandated territory.

Several other political trials followed. During 1972 there were confrontations between guerilla groups and the South African armed forces, notably in the sensitive Caprivi Strip, the tongue of land which links South West Africa with Botswana and Zambia.

In June 1971 the International Court of Justice delivered an advisory opinion sought by the Security Council that was explicit both as to South Africa's status in relation to its administration of Namibia, and on the obligations of UN member states in their dealings with South Africa over Namibia. The Court found that "the continued presence of South Africa being illegal, South Africa is under obligation to withdraw its administration from Namibia immediately, and thus put an end to its occupation of the Territory". Member-states are "under obligation to recognise the illegality of South Africa's presence in Namibia and the invalidity of its acts on behalf of or concerning Namibia, and to refrain from any acts and in particular any dealings with the government of South Africa implying recognition of the legality of, or lending support or assistance to, such presence and administration".

South Africa rejected the Court's opinion. Inside Namibia this government reaction provoked a number of protest actions by local leaders and communities, churchmen and students, which culminated, towards the end of 1971 and the beginning of 1972, in a prolonged and extensive strike of contract workers, which shut down the large Tsumeb mine and smelter complex, diamond, copper, lead and zinc mines, and brought the railways and the fishing and construction industries in Walvis Bay and Windhoek respectively to a standstill. More than a strike against the contract labour system, this was part of a general protest against South Africa's occupation. The government responded by arresting and prosecuting the alleged strike leaders; by instituting slight adjustments to the system of labour recruitment which, however, left the essentials of the system unchanged; and by declaring a state of emergency in the territory's northern areas to which the strikers had been repatriated en masse and where a number of acts of civil disobedience against the authorities ensued. In January 1972 South African Defence Force troops were sent into the territory but even after this there were several renewed outbreaks of the strike.

On February 4th, 1972, the Security Council, meeting in Addis Ababa, adopted Resolution 309 on Namibia which requested its Secretary-General Dr. Kurt Waldheim, in consultation with a group composed of representatives of Argentina, Somalia and Yugoslavia, to initiate contacts "with all parties concerned ... so as to enable the people of Namibia to exercise their right to self-determination and independence". Dr. Waldheim's visit to South Africa in March 1972 was the first move in this attempt to end the deadlock between South Africa and the United Nations. Reporting to the Security Council within the six month deadline set for the first stage of the consultation, Dr. Waldheim indicated that little progress had been made in narrowing the differences between the United Nations and the South African conception of the meaning of self-determination and independence. Nonetheless it was decided to extend the mandate of the Secretary-General for a further six months and to appoint a UN representative to continue the consultation. SWAPO's reaction to this development was to stress that any further prolongation of the mediation effort would be unacceptable, and to point to the danger of a permanent procrastination which would be in the interests of South Africa's continuing occupation of the territory; also to point out that any interim action by the South African Government in pursuance of its Bantustan policy would be contrary to the spirit of the negotiation attempt.

ECONOMY

Ruth First

South West Africa's economy, like its system of administration, is divided into two distinct sectors. In the south, or the Police Zone, which is the area of white settlement together with a number of segregated Reserve areas for Africans, is the modern, commercialized sector of economic activity, including the wealthy mining areas. In the northern areas, inhabited by the majority of the African population, the economy is almost entirely a subsistence one, expanding hardly at all by comparison with the economic prosperity of the southern sector. Agriculture, mining, industry and services in the south are dependent upon the African labour which is recruited under contract from the northern areas, and from the Reserves in the south. Perhaps one quarter of the adult male population of Owamboland, the largest African Reserve in the north, works as contract labour in the south at any one time. Of the labour employed in agriculture and fishing, 70 per cent is that of Africans from the northern sector.

Contract labour is recruited at a fixed rate for the job for temporary periods of between 6 and 18 months, and provides the only employment for men outside the boundaries of the Reserves. Under this system the breaking of a labour contract is a criminal offence, and trade unionism and strikes are outlawed.

PRIMARY PRODUCTION

The modern sector of the economy is based largely on primary production, of which the principal products and exports are diamonds, copper and other base minerals, fish and livestock. The mining industry is the largest single contributor to exports, the gross national product and the revenue of Namibia. In 1970 revenue from mineral sales totalled R 130 million compared to R 115 million in 1965. It is also the mining industry which attracts overseas investment. Out of a total of R 50 million invested in fishing, mining and manufacturing by overseas (as distinct from South African) capital in 1967, 60 per cent went into the mining sector alone. In the same year South Africa invested R 29 million in the mining sector, which gave a combined overseas and South African investment figure of R 59 million. As of 1972 there were 18 companies engaged in mining production, all of them located in the southern zone. Diamonds have long been the mainstay of the mining industry and in 1962 South West Africa ranked fifth in the world as a producer of diamonds. Ninety-eight per cent of the territory's diamond output was produced by Consolidated Diamond Mines of S.W.A. Ltd., which is a subsidiary of De Beers Consolidated Mines, owned primarily by South African and European capital. The Marine Diamond Corporation dredges the seabed from specially equipped barges.

In 1966 the pattern of mineral production was as follows: diamonds R 84.7 million (66 per cent), blister copper R 19.2 million (15 per cent), refined lead R 12.3 million (10 per cent), and zinc, vanadium, and lithium ores R 10.9 million (8 per cent), which gave a total of R 127 million. From 1970 a significant new trend became evident, namely the decline in the total mineral production figure of the proportion of diamonds and the increase in the proportion of base minerals. Out of the total of R 130 million, diamonds accounted for R 70 million (54 per cent) and base minerals of all kinds R 60 million (46 per cent). The expansion in base metal production is due to the extension of already established companies like the Tsumeb corporation, and the opening of new mines by international mining companies. Much of the vast mineral output comes from the Tsumeb Corporation which is the largest mining company in the territory after Consolidated Diamond Mines. The largest share in this company is held by American Metal Climax. Other companies with an interest in the corporation are Union Corporation (of South Africa) and the Newmont Mining Corporation which owns 29 per cent of the Tsumeb Corporation and manages the Tsumeb mine itself. Between 1966 and 1971 four new mines have been opened, three to mine copper at Kranzburg, Oamites and Onganja, and a zinc mine at Rosh Pinah. Copper is currently the major object of prospecting activity. Of the 18 mining companies engaged in mining production, 10 are South African controlled, three are British controlled, three American, one West German and one Canadian controlled. Approximately 40 companies are prospecting for minerals and oil, on and off-shore. In 1970 Rio Tinto Zinc announced that it would proceed with its uranium development plant at Rossing. While the governments of the United States and West Germany have announced that in accordance with United Nations resolutions they will not supply export credits or guarantees to companies, the governments of Britain, France and Canada have made no comparable moves.

In 1963 the principal consumers of South West African mineral exports were the United States, Belgium, West Germany, South Africa and the United Kingdom.

By 1964 the fishing industry was second only to mining as the territory's principal economic asset and source of export earnings. Originally based on the fishing of lobster and white fish for unprocessed, and mainly local, consumption, the industry is now based on the large-scale production and processing of sardines, which provide over 90 per cent of the total fishing revenues. The rise of the fishing industry has been an important stimulus to manufacturing, which has expanded rapidly in response to the need for processing larger quantities of fish for meal, oil and canning. A substantial amount of South African capital is invested in the fishing industry, for South African companies control most of the industry either directly or through subsidiaries.

The most important agricultural industries are the karakul (Persian lamb) industry, the meat and livestock industry and dairy farming. South West Africa is the world's principal exporter of karakul pelts. The territory's surplus of slaughtered stock is exported to South Africa. Of the territory's total value of dairy products, about 40 per cent is shipped to South Africa.

ESTIMATED GROSS VALUE OF
AGRICULTURAL PRODUCTION: 1965

Product	Rand	%
Animal Husbandry		
Cattle		
Beef . . .	24,945,976	56.2
Breeding . .	215,166	0.5
Dairy Products . .	2,041,200	4.6
Sheep		
Pelts . . .	14,027,414	31.6
Breeding . .	33,117	0.1
Wool . .	1,079,727	2.4
Mutton . .	970,596	2.2
Hides and Skins .	376,631	0.8
Pigs . . .	351,720	0.8
Agriculture		
Cash Crops . .	230,001	0.5
Horticulture . .	120,000	0.3
Total . .	44,391,548	100

Source: South West Africa Survey, 1967, p. 63.

As a result of the phenomenal development of mining and fishing, the proportion of agricultural exports dropped from about 28 per cent in 1963 to 17 per cent in 1965, while minerals and mineral products rose from 53 to 60 per cent of total exports, and fishery products from 18 to 23 per cent.

The following are figures of the Gross Domestic Product for 1965, and the percentage distribution of the various sectors of the economy:

GROSS DOMESTIC PRODUCT 1965

	Rand (million)	%
Agriculture . . .	36.0	16.8
Fishing . . .	6.8	3.2
Mining . . .	99.7	46.6
All Other Sectors . .	71.4	33.4

Source: South West African Survey 1967, p. 61.

The manufacturing industry is confined to the processing of perishable goods for consumption and for export to South Africa, to finishing and assembling material obtained from South Africa, or to specialized repair and small scale production work. The 1963-64 industrial census showed a total of 212 establishments employing 8,400 persons in all, and yielding a net output of R18 million.

Between 1946 and 1962 the average rate of growth of domestic product was estimated to be more than 8 per cent a year. But the estimates of South West Africa's domestic product do not include production for own consumption outside the commercialized sector, and of the population of 526,000, 350,000 Africans live in the subsistence sector of the economy. The value of African subsistence production is almost an unknown quantity. It was calculated in 1951 to be less than 3.5 per cent of domestic product that year. More recent figures are not available. As for per capita income, South African official figures give the average annual income of the non-white population in the northern zone as R 61, and the average annual income of whites as R 1,602. The disparities in the productive processes in the two sectors are reinforcing, not diminishing the existent disparities in wealth and income. There are also glaring race discrepancies in wages. In mining for instance, white miners earned an average of R2,452 in 1962, while the non-white average was R202.9.

Since the incorporation in 1955 of most of South West Africa's statistics into those of South Africa, capital movement cannot be accurately charted. Foreign capital controlled 61.4 per cent of the mining industry in the mid-1960s, and foreign capital invested in the fish processing and manufacturing industries, as well as mining, amounted to R49 million or 53 per cent of the total invested in these industries, but the respective shares of South African and South West African capital are not easily established.

TRADE

The collection of separate trade statistics for South West Africa was suspended in 1957, and it is thus not possible to obtain comprehensive information on trade flows between the territory and any other country. In 1954 the most important source of imports was South Africa, and the trend has probably continued; in that year 80 per cent of total imports originated in South Africa. By 1961 the Federal Republic of Germany had replaced the United Kingdom as the second largest exporter to the territory; German imports consisted primarily of manufactured goods. The United States and the United Kingdom were the most important sources of exports.

Highly significant in the South West African economy is the gap between the gross domestic product and the gross national income, which latter does not include the proportion of domestic output accruing to foreign capital. The following figures were given by the Odendaal Commission Report (page 327):

PERCENTAGE OF G.D.P. ACCRUING TO FOREIGNERS

Years	%
1946–50 . .	16.3
1951–55 . .	32.4
1956–60 . .	35.8
1961–62 . .	32.0

Taking an average for the years 1958 to 1962, the share of the G.D.P. accruing to foreigners is more than 37 per cent. Foreign earnings are highly significant in the country's economy, but so too is the tremendous proportion of out-flowing foreign earnings.

Recent development schemes in the territory include a joint South African-Portuguese government scheme for a hydroelectric and irrigation project on the Kunene River which links Angola and South West Africa; and also oil exploration which was begun in 1968 and has been intensified in recent years.

The development plan has earmarked considerable sums for water and power resources and for communications, but future projects will reinforce the present inbalance in the infrastructure which has concentrated nearly all on the railways, harbours and air transport facilities, as well as water resources, in the southern Police Zone. For instance, of the £78 million earmarked for the first five year development plan, £20 million was allocated as compensation for white farmers; £20 million for road development largely in the southern zone; and £25 million for the Kunene River scheme which will lead to some improvements in the irrigation of the northern African reserves, but which will principally serve the industrial areas and the Tsumeb mining complex in the south. The African reserves remain areas of bare subsistence, several of them, by admission of the Odendaal Commission Report, unlikely ever to be self-supporting.

STATISTICAL SURVEY

AREA AND POPULATION

(1960 census and 1970* census)

AREA (sq. miles)	AFRICAN RESERVES (sq. miles)	TOTAL POPULATION	WHITES	AFRICAN	COLOUREDS	WINDHOEK (capital)
317,725	81,500	526,004	73,464	428,575	23,963	35,916 (whites 19,200)
317,827	84,774	746,328	90,658	627,395	28,275	64,700 (whites 35,700)

The principal port, Walvis Bay, is an enclave of South Africa. The summer capital is Swakopmund.

* Preliminary.

PRINCIPAL TRIBAL DIVISIONS

(1970 census*)

Owambo	.	.	.	342,455
Damara	.	.	.	64,973
Herero	.	.	.	49,203
Nama.	.	.	.	32,853
Kavango	.	.	.	49,577
East Caprivians	.	.	25,009
Bushmen	.	.	.	21,909
Rehobothers	.	.	16,474

*Preliminary.

The Owambo, who have some agriculture, form the chief source of labour in the Territory. The Bushmen are still primitive hunters while the other tribes are mainly semi-nomadic cattle raisers and stock hands.

HOMELANDS

HOMELAND				AREA (hectares)
Owamboland	.	.	.	5,607,200
Kavango	.	.	.	4,170,050
Kaokoland	.	.	.	4,898,219
Damaraland	.	.	.	4,799,021
Hereroland	.	.	.	5,899,680
East Caprivi	.	.	.	1,153,387
Tswanaland	.	.	.	155,400
Bushmenland	.	.	.	2,392,671
Rehoboth Gebied	.	.	1,386,029
Namaland	.	.	.	2,167,707
TOTAL	.	.	.	32,629,364

AGRICULTURE

LIVESTOCK

			1966	1967	1968	1970*
Cattle	.	.	2,261,000	2,196,792	1,407,658	1,662,000
Sheep	.	.	4,067,542	3,802,415	3,678,733	3,738,000
Goats	.	.	1,513,059	1,423,249	552,465	518,000

* Estimate.

LIVESTOCK PRODUCTS

('000 R.)

			1968	1969
Karakul Pelts	.	.	19,156	21,900
Beef Cattle	.	.	23,354	22,856
Beef Cattle slaughtered locally			3,440	6,077
Small Stock exported	.		1,715	1,689

DAIRY PRODUCE

('000 lb.)

			1968	1969
Butterfat	.	.	3,486,936	2,577,509
Butter	.	.	4,250,616	3,135,357
Cheese	.	.	254,820	150,455
Casein	.	.	524,526	382,278

KARAKUL PELTS
(Exports)

	NUMBER	RANDS MILLION
1968 . . .	4,870,248	27.1
1969 . . .	5,323,774	31.6
1970 . . .	5,148,396	29.8

FISHERIES

	1967	1968	1969
Canned Pilchards (short tons) .	81,000	60,000	66,800
Fish Meal (short tons) . .	189,386	262,208	224,669
Fish Oil (centals) . . .	37,684	67,324	44,342
Rock Lobster (short tons) . .	1,771	3,027	2,666

1969: Total value of catch R.36,303,000; Total catch 943,000 tons.

MINING

		1968	1969	1970	1971
Copper	'ooo metric tons	30.2	25.5	22.8	25.3
Lead	,, ,, ,,	60.9	75.7	70.5	73.2
Zinc	,, ,, ,,	24.1	33.0	46.1	50.6
Iron Ore . . .	'ooo tons	8,102.0	n.a.	n.a.	n.a.
Tin	metric tons	730	73.0	73.0	70.0
Diamonds . . .	'ooo carats	1,722.0	n.a.	n.a.	n.a.

Finance: *Currency:* South African currency is used throughout the territory. *Budget* (1966–67): Revenue R.115,370,000, Expenditure R.113,047,000.

External Trade: Total Mineral exports: (1963) R.65m., (1964 R.93m., (1965) R.115m., (1966) R.128m., (1970) R.130m. Two-thirds of the total is accounted for by diamonds, some of which are mined off-shore.
Exports to U.K.: (1967) £21,343,000; (1968) £24,464,000; (1971) £23,341,522; Imports from U.K.: (1967) £2,135,000; (1968) £1,478,000; (1971) £1,656,288.

Transport: *Roads* (1966): Registered vehicles 41,526; *Shipping* (*Walvis Bay*) (1965): Passengers 1,062, Freight 1,231,767 tons; (1966) Freight 1,187,824 tons; *Civil Aviation* (1966): To Republic of S. Africa 21,842 passengers, from Republic of S. Africa 21,769 passengers; 2,662 arrivals on international flights, 8,402 departures.

EDUCATION
Schools—1966

	PRIMARY AND SECONDARY
European	69
Coloured	57
African	417

Source: Bureau of Statistics, Pretoria.

ADMINISTRATION

The administration of South West Africa was vested by Mandate of the League of Nations, dated December 17th, 1920, in the Government of South Africa. The Territory was granted a constitution in 1925. The government consists of an Administrator appointed by the State President of the Republic, a Legislative Assembly of eighteen elected members and an Executive of four members chosen by the Assembly from its own ranks. The Parliament of the Republic is the supreme legislative authority and the Republic government is the chief executive authority. The South West Africa Legislative Assembly has wide powers except in matters of defence, railways and harbours, civil aviation, native affairs and certain legal affairs.

In 1949 the South African Parliament passed the South West African Affairs Amendment Act by which South West Africa was authorized to elect six members to the South African House of Assembly, and two members to the South African Senate. Two further senators are appointed by the State President. Non-Whites are not part of the Electorate for the South West Africa Legislative Assembly.

In October 1966 South Africa's security and apartheid laws were applied to the Territory, retrospective to 1950. The Development of Self-Government for Native Nations Act of 1968, provided for the establishment of Bantustans, and the South West Africa Affairs Act of 1969, removed control over all the major areas of administration from the Legislative Assembly to the relevant ministries in Pretoria. Its effect was to incorporate the territory as a fifth province of South Africa.

The tribal areas, including Owamboland, occupy about a quarter of the total land area in the north of the Territory. The other three-quarters of the land, including that containing most of the mineral resources, is occupied by the White population, with the exception of some small African reserves. Land in the northern tribal areas can be allocated by the Government for European settlement, provided land of equivalent value is reserved for Africans in compensation, but non-Whites cannot purchase land in White locations. Permission to enter such locations is given only to non-Whites contracted as labourers for a set period. Permits are also required by non-Whites to travel from one non-White area to another and to reside anywhere in the Territory, including the tribal areas. Any breach of these regulations is treated as a criminal offence. In the tribal areas the Commissioners, responsible to the Administrator, have ultimate authority over the non-White population and over their chiefs and headmen, who are paid allowances by the Government.

The United Nations have made annual recommendations that, as a former League of Nations Mandate, South West Africa should be placed under United Nations Trusteeship.

In 1950 the International Court of Justice advised that South Africa was not under a legal obligation to place South West Africa under the trusteeship system of the United Nations Organization. However, the court proceeded to hold unanimously that the mandate survived the dissolution of the League of Nations. It held further that the United Nations had, on the dissolution of the League of Nations, became vested with supervisory powers in respect of the mandate.

This opinion was followed by two further advisory opinions in 1955 and 1956, both of them concerned with the interpretation of the 1950 opinion.

In 1960 the governments of Ethiopia and Liberia, acting in the capacity of states which were members of the former League of Nations, brought before the International Court of Justice various allegations of contraventions of the League of Nations mandate for South West Africa by the Republic of South Africa. Final judgement was given on 18th July, 1966, when the International Court rejected the application of the plaintiff states on the grounds that they could not be considered to have established any legal rights or interests in the subject matter of their claims on South West Africa.

In 1966 the UN General Assembly terminated the League of Nations mandate and established the Council for Namibia which was entrusted with the task of recommending means by which the territory should be administered, and of acting as a government during an interim period before Namibian independence. The South African Government, which does not recognize the Council, refused to allow it to enter the territory.

In June 1971 the International Court of Justice in an advisory opinion ruled that South Africa's presence in the Territory was illegal and that she should withdraw immediately. In December 1971 there was a widely observed strike in Windhoek of Owambo contract labourers. The strikers were sent home, mainly to Owamboland in the north of the Territory and the widespread outbreaks of opposition to the Government that followed led to a declaration of a state of emergency in Owamboland. No visitors or reporters were allowed into the area and many Africans were killed and arrested.

HOMELANDS

The Odendaal Commission in 1964 recommended setting up ten Homelands for the major non-White peoples. But with the exception of the Owambo and Rehobothers, the majority of each African group actually resides outside the area of their homeland. In 1970, out of 64,973 Damara, 7,736 lived in Damaraland.

The Owambo Legislative Council of up to 42 members (nominated by the territory's seven tribal authorities) was formally opened in October 1968. There is also a seven-man Executive Council. In 1970 Kavango also obtained a Territorial Authority, and in 1972 the East Caprivi Legislative Council was formally opened. In June 1972 it was announced that the Owambo homeland would be given "self-government" in 1973. In September 1972 the Chairman of the Damara Council of Headmen, Mr. Justus Garoeb, said that the Damaras were unwilling to request or accept a Legislative Council.

(*January* 1973)

Administrator: B. J. van der Walt.

Executive Committee: D. F. Mudge, Adv. E. van Zijl, J. W. F. Pretorius.

Legislative Assembly: E. T. Meyer (Chairman).

ELECTION, APRIL 1970

The National Party won all 18 seats in the Legislative Assembly.

POLITICAL PARTIES

EUROPEAN

National Party: P.O.B. 354, Windhoek; organized on a federal basis with the National Party in the Republic of South Africa; Leader A. H. du Plessis, m.p.; Sec. A. J. Louw; won all six seats in the South African Parliament and all 18 in the Legislative Assembly of S.W. Africa in the elections of March 30th, 1966, and subsequently of April 1970.

United South West Africa Party: f. 1927; official Opposition Party; organized on federal basis with United Party in Republic of South Africa; Leader Adv. J. P. DE M. NIEHAUS; Chair. G. M. T. KIRSTEN; Sec. C. J. VAN DEN BERG.

COLOURED

South West Africa Coloured People's Organisation: f. 1959; 4,000 mems. (estimate).

AFRICAN

South West African People's Organisation of Namibia: f. 1958; P.O.B. 1071, Windhoek; formerly Ovambo People's Organisation; aims at removal of racial discrimination and full and unconditional independence for Namibia as one unitary state; Pres. SAM NUJOMA (*based in Dar es Salaam*); Vice-Pres. BRANDON SIMBWAYE (*in restriction since* 1964); Chair. DAVID MERERO; 150,000 mems.

South West Africa National Union: supported by Pan-African Congress; the acting president, GERSON VEIL, was imprisoned in 1967.

JUDICIAL SYSTEM

The Territory is divided into 18 magisterial districts and three detached assistant magistracies. Owamboland, the Kaokoveld and the Okavango Native Territory are separate magisterial districts under the control of the Minister of Bantu Administration and Development. Some magistrates are also Bantu affairs commissioners and such hold courts in cases solely affecting Africans. From the Magistrates Courts appeal lies to the Supreme Court of South Africa (South West Africa Division) which has jurisdiction over the whole of South West Africa.

The Supreme Court of South Africa (South West Africa Division):

Judge-President: Hon. F. H. BADENHORST.

Puisne Judge: Hon. G. G. HOEXTER.

Master: K. J. WATTRUS.

Registrar: M. VAN DER WESTHUYZEN.

Attorney-General: S. C. TERBLANCHE, S.C.

RELIGION

The Europeans and substantial numbers of the African and coloured populations are Christians. The principal missionary societies are Lutheran (321,000 adherents), Roman Catholic (46,000 adherents) and Anglican (5,000 adherents).

EVANGELICAL LUTHERAN
NON-WHITE CHURCHES

Ovambokavango Church: Bishop L. AUALA, Oniipa, P.O. Ondangwa.

Rhenish Mission Church: P.O.B. 5069, Windhoek; f. 1967; Pres. Prases Dr. L. DE VRIES; publ. *Immanuel* (monthly).

WHITE CHURCH

German Evangelical Lutheran Church in South West Africa: President: Rev. Landespropst K. KIRSCHNEREIT, P.O.B. 233, Windhoek.

ANGLICAN

Province of South Africa, Diocese of Damaraland: Rt. Rev. COLIN O'BRIEN WINTER, M.A., Church of St. Edmund the King, Lombard St., London, E.C.3. Exiled from Namibia.

ROMAN CATHOLIC

Keetmanshoop Vicariate: Rt. Rev. EDWARD SCHLOTTERBACK, O.S.F.S., P.O.B. 88, Keetmanshoop.

Windhoek Vicariate: Most Rev. Bishop RUDOLF KOPPMANN, O.M.I., D.D., Titular Bishop of Dalisanda, P.O.B. 2328, Windhoek.

THE PRESS

Allgemeine Zeitung: P.O.B. 2127, Windhoek; f. 1915; daily; German; Editor K. DAHLMANN; circ. 5,200.

Immanuel: Evangelical Lutheran Church in South West Africa (Rhenish Mission Church), P.O.B. 54, Karibib; f. 1961; Lit. Sec. U. POENNIGHAUS; monthly; circ. 3,500.

Namib Times: P.O.B. 706, Walvis Bay; bi-weekly (Tues. and Fri.); English, Afrikaans, German; Editor P. VINCENT.

Official Gazette of South West Africa: Secretary for South West Africa, P.O.B. 292, Windhoek; fortnightly; Government publication.

Die Suidwes Afrikaner: P.O.B. 337, Windhoek; Tues. and Fri.; Editor J. A. ENGELBRECHT.

Die Suidwester: P.O.B. 766, Windhoek; f. 1945; Mon.–Fri.; Afrikaans; Man. F. L. VAN ZIJL.

Windhoek Advertiser: P.O.B. 2127, Windhoek; f. 1919; English; daily; circ. 3,512.

PUBLISHERS

Deutscher Verlag (Pty.) Ltd.: P.O.B. 56, Windhoek; f. 1939; newspaper publishers.

John Meinert (Pty.) Ltd.: P.O.B. 56, Windhoek; f. 1924; newspaper publishers.

RADIO

Radio R.S.A.: P.O.B. 4559, Johannesburg; f. 1966; external short wave service of South African Broadcasting Corporation, broadcasting in English, Afrikaans, French, Portuguese, German, Dutch, Swahili, Chichewa and Tsonga to Africa, the Middle East, Europe, North America, Madagascar, Mauritius and Australasia. Transmitted from international short-wave station at Bloemendal, nr. Johannesburg.

FINANCE

BANKING

Barclays National Bank Ltd.: Chief Office in South West Africa; P.O.B. 195, Windhoek; Regional Gen. Man. I. A. C. VAN NIEKERK; 18 brs.

Land and Agricultural Bank of South Africa: Private Bag 13208, Branch Office, Windhoek; f. 1922; Man. F. NEETHLING.

Nedbank Ltd.: P.O.B. 370, Windhoek.

Prifinger and Roll (Pty.) Ltd. P.O.B. 7, Windhoek; f. 1933.

Standard Bank of South Africa Ltd.: Chief Office in South West Africa: Windhoek.

Volkskas Ltd.: Chief Office in South West Africa: P.O.B. 2121, Windhoek.

INSURANCE

African Life Assurance Society Ltd.: Windhoek; Man. B. T. HATTINGH.

Employers Liability Assurance Corporation Ltd.: Continental Buildings, Kaiser Str., Windhoek; Man. H. A. EICHBAUM.

Mutual and Federal Insurance Co. Ltd.: P.O.B. 151, Windhoek; Man. A. J. VAN RYNEVELD.

Protea Assurance Co. Ltd.: Windhoek; Man. I. N. MARTIN.

Prudential Assurance Co.: P.O.B. 365, Windhoek.

TRADE AND INDUSTRY

ADVISORY BOARDS

Various Advisory Boards have been established by the Administration to advise it on the development of industries, and to promote them. The most important are the Karakul Industry Advisory Board, the Diamond Board and the Fisheries Development Board.

LABOUR ORGANIZATIONS

SWANLA, the South West African Native Labour Association at Grootfontein, and the recruiting organization to obtain African labour from the north under contract for mines, fisheries and farms, was abolished as from January 31st, 1972. It was replaced by South African government recruiting stations at Ondangua in Owamboland, and Runtu in Kavango.

TRANSPORT

RAILWAYS

South African Railways: railways in South West Africa are administered by South African Railways. The main lines are from De Aar in the Republic of South Africa to Luderitz on the coast, Windhoek—Walvis Bay and Tsumeb. Total rail tracks are 2,340 route kilometres.

ROADS

There are about 34,000 miles of roads, of which some 21,000 are maintained by the South West Africa Administration. More than 69 Railway Motor Services operate over 5,366 miles of road.

SHIPPING

Walvis Bay and Luderitz are the only ports. Walvis Bay harbour has been extended.

CIVIL AVIATION

Suidwes Lugdiens (Edms) Bpk.: P.O.B. 731, Windhoek; f. 1946; subsidiary of Safmarine; Man. Dir. A. LOMBARD; fleet of one DC-4, two DC-3, one Cessna 402, two Cessna 310, three Aztec, five Twin Commanche, one Cessna 206, one Beaver, one Commache.

South African Airways provide a service three times a week between Cape Town and Windhoek and daily between Windhoek and Johannesburg. D.T.A. (Angola) also serves Windhoek.

EDUCATION

The South African Government took over the control of education in 1921, but large-scale educational developments in the main areas of African settlement only began after 1964, with the initiation of a five-year development programme of more advanced schools, hostels and teacher training facilities. Expenditure in 1966–67 amounted to more than R.1.3 million in the areas of the non-white groups. The last three years have seen some ambitious building schemes, and the training centre near Windhoek providing for high school and technical education and teacher training is nearing completion, while work on a similar centre for Owamboland has begun. All government teaching institutions function in accordance with the Bantu Education Act of 1953, whose terms were extended to Namibia by an Act of Parliament of 1970. This is geared to the policy of separate development with separate facilities for different ethnic groups. In 1970–71, expenditure on education for non-white groups was R.2.5 million.

LEARNED SOCIETIES AND RESEARCH INSTITUTES

Desert Ecological Research Unit of the South African Council for Scientific and Industrial Research: Namib Desert Research Station, P.O.B. 953, Walvis Bay; f. 1963; carries out exploration and research in Namib Desert, and basic and applied research on desert conditions in general and on nature conservation in the desert; library of 500 vols.; Dir. M. K. JENSEN; publ. *Madoqua Series II* (Scientific papers).

Institute of South West African Architects: P.O.B. 1478, Windhoek; f. 1952; 87 mems.; Pres. H. E. STABY; Sec. Mrs. R. COHEN.

South West African Association of Arts: Windhoek.

S.W.A. Scientific Society/S.W.A. Wissenschaftliche Gesellschaft/S.W.A. Wetenskaplike Vereniging: P.O.B. 67, Windhoek; f. 1925; ornithology, spelaeology, botany, archaeology, herpetology, astronomy; 700 mems. and 200 exchange mems.; library of 3,697 vols.; Pres. Dr. W. H. ARNDT; Sec. Dr. H. J. RUST; publs. *Mitteilungen/Newsletter/Nuusbrief, Mitteilungen der Ornithologischen Arbeitsgruppe* (monthly), *Journal* (annually), and others irregularly.

LIBRARY

Government Archives: Private Bag 13250, Windhoek; f. 1939; library of about 2,000 vols.; Chief S. J. SCHOEMAN.

MUSEUMS

Lüderitz Museum: P.O.B. 512, Lüderitz; f. 1966; incorporates finds of Friedrich Eberlanz of archaeological, herpetological, botanical and mineralogical interest, incl. Bushman Stone Age tools; Supervisor Mrs. A. DYCK.

State Museum: P.O.B. 1203, Windhoek; f. 1958; natural history, cultural history; library of 2,500 vols. and 300 journal titles; Dir. C. G. COETZEE, M.SC., H.ED.; publs. *Cimbebasia, Memoirs.*

Swakopmund Museum: P.O.B. 56, Strand Street, Swakopmund; f. 1951; natural history, mineralogy, marine life, history; Chair. Dr. A. M. WEBER; library of 2,500 books and newspapers; publs. *Nachrichten* (quarterly), *Bibliotheka, Namib und Meer* (annual).

COLLEGE

Technical High School: Private Bag 12014, Windhoek; f. 1972; technical education and teacher training; for whites.

SELECT BIBLIOGRAPHY

DE BLIG, H. J. "Notes on the Geography of South West Africa", *Journal of Geography*. October 1958, pp. 333–341.

FIRST, RUTH. *South West Africa*. Harmondsworth, Penguin, 1963.

GREEN, L. F., and FAIR, T. J. D. *Development in Africa, A Study in Regional Analysis with special reference to Southern Africa*. Johannesburg, W.U.P., 1962.

LOGAN, R. F. "South West Africa", *Focus*. November, 1960, pp. 1–6.

WELLINGTON, J. H. *Southern Africa: A Geographical Study*, (2 vols.). London, 1955.

Spanish Sahara

René Pélissier

PHYSICAL AND SOCIAL GEOGRAPHY

Spanish Sahara (Sahara Español) occupies a slice of the western Sahara desert. It is a destitute and entirely artificial political unit. Its neighbours are, to the north, Morocco; to the east, for a few kilometres, Algeria; and to the east and south, Mauritania, which girds the country as far as the southern fishing port of La Güera. The total area is approximately 266,000 sq. km. Two districts, Norte or Sekia el Hamra (82,000 sq. km.), and Sur or Río de Oro (184,000 sq. km.) compose the only African province of Spain. The capital is Al-Aaiún (El-Aaiún). It is made up on the whole of an extensive, sterile rocky plain, slowly rising to the east, and known as the Hammada. The Reg is a stony, alluvial plain, while the Erg is a sandy expanse of dune interspersed with salty depressions known as *Sebkhas*. The north is chiefly made up of the forbidding Hammada. The provincial capital, Al-Aaiún, is on the left bank of the dry Sekia/El-Hamra wadi on the Hammada. Its population was 24,048 in 1970. It is a brand-new desert city, built entirely by the Spaniards, who have made it their main administrative, military and population centre. Mildly booming, it has road connexions with the Muslim city of Smara, which is now chiefly a garrison for the Spanish Foreign Legion. More than 2,000 people (mostly soldiers) live in this outpost, which has all the trappings of a pre-war French *Beau Geste* film. Further south, the only reliefs of the Río de Oro are the Tiris plateau which covers most of the southern part of the district. East of Villa Cisneros, which ranks as the second centre of

Spanish habitation (population 5,454 in 1970), are the *mesetas* of El Ataf and Nekyir, from which a mountainous range branches off toward the south. The Adrar Sutuf is a black granite area of 400 m. in height. Permanent rivers are absent. The Sekia el Hamra waters some oases close to Al-Aaiún. Rainfall is so erratic and insufficient that it can be absent during successive years. In 1958, Villa Cisneros registered a rainfall of approximately o.6 mm. The climate is arid, with some spectacular temperature variations, ranging from 32°F. at midnight to 149°F. at 3 p.m. on the Tiris plateau. Water is the main factor in the life of the nomadic inhabitants, who rely on scarce wells to sustain their sheep, goats and camels. The population in 1970 was 59,793 Saharans and 16,299 Europeans. Perhaps as many as 50,000 nomads enter Spanish Sahara during the rainy season, and the European population is swollen by about 10,000–15,000 Spanish soldiers. The sedentary and semi-sedentary African population may have been about 35,000 in 1972.

Main tribes are the R'gibat, Uld Delim, Izargien, and Arosien. Most of them are of white Berber or Arab stock, with a certain mixture of Negro blood in some tribes. The Spanish government tries hard to win their allegiance by granting them all facilities to settle in and around military posts and ports. Tradition is still very strong in spite of a visible European influence. Spanish and Arabic are the written languages, Hassanya is the spoken language of the Muslim population, and Islam is the religion of all non-Spanish inhabitants.

RECENT HISTORY

In 1884 Spain nominally annexed the Saharan coast from Cape Bojador down to Cap Blanc. Some desultory exploration was conducted in the interior in 1886, but for decades Spain held nothing but the fort of Villa Cisneros, which was merely a depot for military offenders. The desert was the scene of traditional tribal feuds. Sheikh Ma-el-Ainin attempted to give the nomads both spiritual and political cohesion, and founded Smara in 1900. A French column destroyed his city. Meanwhile, Franco-Spanish conventions of 1900, 1904 and 1912 drew the frontiers of the Spanish zone of influence. A rather remarkable man, Sub-governor Bens (1903–25), did what he could to extend his penal settlement by occupying coastal points such as Cape Juby (1916) (now Moroccan Tarfaya), and La Güera (1920). Smara was occupied only in 1934. The Spanish civil war destroyed whatever development had been envisaged in this largely unexplored

desert. Some scientific explorations were made, however, and General Franco visited the Sahara in 1950. Officially, Spanish Sahara was to play the part of the military shield of the Canary Islands against an improbable invasion from Africa. In 1957 Moroccan irregulars, helped by the Tekna (belonging to the then Spanish protectorate of southern Morocco), R'gibat and other tribes, attacked Spanish inland posts, including Smara. All had to be hastily evacuated and Spanish Sahara was no longer Spanish, except for Al-Aaiún, Villa Cisneros and one or two coastal posts. Combined Franco-Spanish operations were mounted to defeat the rebels in January and February of 1958, with operations ending in March. To offset the loss of the protectorate of Southern Morocco (Tarfaya), retroceded to the Sultan after the Sintra agreement of April 1st, 1958, Madrid united Sekia el Hamra and Río de Oro into the province of the

Spanish Sahara. Since then, the country has been peaceful, except for some forays in 1961 and minor troubles in the capital in 1970. For practical purposes it is a military colony, and while Saharans are represented in the Spanish *Cortes* by three *Procuradores* and have elected representatives in the provincial *Yemáa* (President, Jatri Uld Said Uld Yumani) and the local *Cabildo* (President, Seila Uld Abeida). Spain is more strongly entrenched in the desert than ever, and is patiently building a pro-Spanish Saharan nationalism to oppose the Moroccan claims, Mauritanian counter-claims and Algerian pressure. Pressure from Morocco, Mauritania and Algeria has continued on the diplomatic level but Spain is easily parrying moves to hold a UN-sponsored referendum in Sahara. One of the thorniest points of contention is the question of whether the nomads should be allowed to vote as they are supposed to nurture anti-Spanish feelings. Some of the R'gibat chieftains have been expelled in recent years and a secret organization, Morehob (the "Blue Men") was formed in Morocco by Spanish Saharan exiles. Autonomy within the Spanish state seems to be the goal envisaged by whatever is left of the *Africanista* establishment. In 1972, the Governor-General was General Fernando de Santiago y Diaz de Mendivil.

ECONOMY

There is no Spanish Saharan economy to speak of, since extreme aridity, underpopulation and general poverty and backwardness make the Saharan province a ward of the Spanish state, which hopes nevertheless to recover its investments in political quiescence and more tangible rewards when the phosphate deposits sited at Bucraa (Bu-Kra) are fully exploited. 1,700 million tons are known to exist, and probable reserves are fixed at 10,000 million tons. A state-controlled company, Fosfatos de Bucraa, S.A., formerly the Empresa Nacional Minera del Sahara S.A. (ENMINSA), has been established, and has constructed a 3,500 m. loading pier at Al-Aaiún beach to handle up to 2,000 tons of phosphate an hour. A 60-mile conveyor brings the ore from Bucraa. This project, which is of world significance, could well outclass Moroccan competitors and is the strongest trump-card of Spain in her Saharan province. In April 1972 the first 6,000 tons were loaded at Al-Aaiún beach but it is unlikely that the target of three million tons was reached by 1972.

Fishing is the only other economic activity at present, with 6,661 tons being caught in 1969. Main fishing ports are La Güera, directly opposite the Mauritanian port Nouadhibou, formerly Port Etienne, and Villa Cisneros. Most fishermen come from the Canary Islands, which play a decisive part in the development of the province as purveyors of labour and technical skills. Agriculture is nominal (650 palm trees in 1969) and while iron ore deposits, and probably oil, exist, they are not developed either for economic reasons or for political expediency. Livestock is entirely Saharan-owned and comprised 56,287 camels, 145,408 goats and 17,975 sheep in 1970. Production of electric power was 5,508,000 kWh. in 1970. A minor building boom has become essential to house nomads, military personnel and technicians and labourers from other countries. 499 buildings were completed in 1968. Transport is still underdeveloped; there were 4,500 vehicles in 1970. Passengers disembarked in 1969 were 11,229; embarked 7,513. Freight entered was 108,423 tons; embarked 16,007 tons. 47,064 air passengers entered the country in 1969, and 47,821 left it. The tourist trade tries to divert a trickle of Scandinavian tourists to Al-Aaiún, where a *parador* (state-owned de luxe hotel), reported to be inadequate, caters for one-day excursionists from Las Palmas. 21,163 tourists came to the country in 1971.

In short, this poor desert country has its economic future pinned on phosphates, while its political course is still uncertain. Massive help from external sources will in any case be essential before it has the makings of an autonomous or independent state.

STATISTICS

Area: 266,000 square km. (approx.) (Río de Oro 184,000 sq. km.; Sekia el Hamra 82,000 sq. km.).

Population (1970): non-Europeans 59,793, Europeans 16,299 (also 15,000 Spanish soldiers). Al-Aaiún (capital) 24,048 (12,238 non-Europeans, 11,810 Europeans); Villa Cisneros 5,454; the number of nomads entering the territory during the rainy season is indeterminable.

Agriculture (1969): 650 palm trees.

Livestock (1970): 56,287 camels, 145,408 goats, 17,975 sheep, 400 cows, 2,397 asses.

Fishing (1969): Weight of catch 6,661 tons.

Industry (1970): Production of electric energy: 5,508,000 kWh.

Finance: Spanish currency: 100 céntimos = 1 peseta. Exchange rates: £1 sterling = 149.025 pesetas (December 1972); 1,000 pesetas = £6.710. U.S. $1 = 63.59 pesetas (September 1972); 1,000 pesetas = $15.73.

Budget (1972): Expenditure 1,214,783,421 pesetas. The territory receives substantial aid from Spain.

Development: The territory's extensive phospate deposits are being developed by Spain.

External Trade (1970): Imports ('ooo pesetas): 388,302 (Foodstuffs 127,095, Manufactures 261,207; Exports are negligible).

Transport: *Roads:* 6,500 km. roads and tracks; *Shipping* (1969): Passengers disembarked 11,229, freight entered 108,423 tons; *Civil Aviation* (1969): Passengers entered 47,064, Passengers leaving 47,821; Freight (metric tons), unloaded 13,999, loaded 16,077.

Tourism (1971): 21,163 tourists.

Education (1972): *Pre-primary:* 368 pupils; *Primary:* 3,405 Spanish, 614 Saharan pupils; 84 Spanish and 60 Saharan teachers; *Secondary:* about 1,500 pupils at Al-Aaiún and Villa Cisneros.

THE GOVERNMENT

Spanish Sahara was recognized as a Province in 1958. It is divided into two regions: Sekia el Hamra (82,000 sq. km.) and Río de Oro (184,000 sq. km.). A **Yemáa** (*General Assembly*) of 103 members (Pres. JATRI ULD SAID ULD YUMANI) and a **Cabildo** (*local council*) (Pres. SEILA ULD ABEIDA) are the main representative bodies of the province. The province is represented in the Spanish *Cortes* by 6 *procuradores*.

There was an election to the General Assembly in January 1971.

Governor-General: Gen. FERNANDO DE SANTIAGO Y DÍAZ DE MENDIVIL.

Director-General for Promotion of the Sahara: D. EDUARDO JUNCO MENDOZA (resident in Madrid).

Religion: Muslim; the Europeans are nearly all Catholics.

Mining: Phosphate deposits at Bucraa estimated at 1,700 million tons are exploited by Fosfatos de Bucraa, S.A., a state-controlled company. In April 1972 the first shipment of phosphate ore was loaded at Al-Aaiún. Production is expected to reach a yearly rate of 2.6m. tons in 1973.

Radio: *Radio Sahara*, Apr. 7, Al-Aaiún; government station; Dir. EDUARDO GONZÁLEZ RUIZ.

Radio Villa Cisneros, Apt. 60, Villa Cisneros; government station; Dir. E. PONCE RAMOS.

Television: retransmission stations in Al-Aaiún and Smara.

Transport: Airfields at Villa Cisneros (the chief seaport) and Al-Aaiún, with passenger services to Madrid and Las Palmas operated by Iberia. There are also landing-strips at La Güera, Hagunía, Auserd, Aargub, Bir Enzarán, Anech and Agracha. A 3,500 metre loading pier has been constructed at Al-Aaiún to handle up to 2,000 tons of phosphates an hour from 1972 onwards. A 60-mile conveyor will bring the phosphate ores from the mines at Bucraa.

SELECT BIBLIOGRAPHY

(For works on Spanish Africa generally *see* Equatorial Guinea Select Bibliography, p. 277.)

F. HERNÁNDEZ PACHECO, and J. MA CORDERO TORRES, *El Sahara Español*. Madrid, 1962

SERVICIO INFORMATIVO ESPAÑOL. *España en el Sahara*, Madrid, 1968.

INSTITUTO DE ESTUDIOS AFRICANOS. La Acción de España en Sahara, Madrid, 1971.

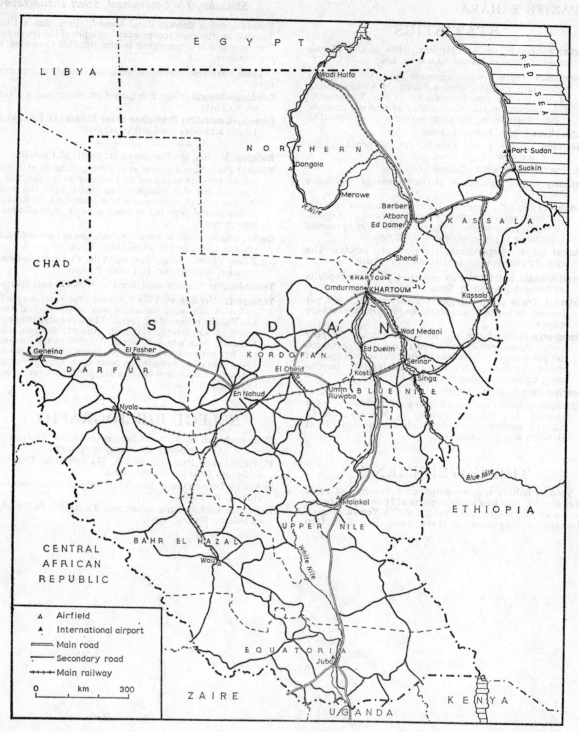

Sudan

Sudan

PHYSICAL AND SOCIAL GEOGRAPHY

L. Berry

THE NILE

The Democratic Republic of the Sudan is the largest state in Africa (2,500,000 sq. km.), stretching across nearly 18° of latitude and from sub-equatorial forest to some of the driest desert in the world. These vast spaces of contrasting terrain are, however, linked by the unifying Nile. Any account of Sudan should perhaps start with the river, so vital is it to the republic. The Nile enters Sudan from Uganda in the south and the "Bahr el Jebel" is fed by a number of streams draining the south-west of the country. Some miles north of Mongalla, the river enters the Sudd region where seasonal swamps cover a large part of the area. The White Nile drains the Sudd region northward, though half of the flow is lost by irrigation in the Sudd. The Blue Nile drains a large part of the Ethiopian Highlands and joins the White Nile at Khartoum. The two rivers are very different. In August the Blue Nile is in flood and, rising seven metres above its low level, makes up nearly 90 per cent of the total discharge at Khartoum (7,000 cu. m. per sec.). At low water the more regularly flowing White Nile provides 83 per cent of the discharge and the Blue Nile is reduced to a mere 80 cu. m. per second. North of Khartoum the Nile is the focus of most agricultural activity and pump irrigation along its banks provides a green strip through the desert to Wadi Halfa and Lake Nasser. The Atbara, which is the only tributary north of Khartoum, flows for about six months of the year and then dries up into a series of pools.

PHYSICAL FEATURES

Away from the Nile Sudan is mainly a plainland and plateau country, although there are a number of important mountain ranges such as the Imatong and the Nuba Mountains (rising to over 1,500 m.) in the south; Jebel Marra, a largely extinct volcano (over 3,500 m.) in the west; and the Red Sea Hill ranges (over 2,000 m.) in the north-east. Elsewhere the plainlands, diversified in places by smaller hill ranges, slope gently to the north and towards the Nile.

CLIMATE

Sudan has a range of tropical continental climates, with a marked climatic gradient from south to north and from the Ethiopian plateau north-westwards. In the south the rainy season lasts up to eight months, producing over 1,000 mm. of precipitation, while at Atbara, north of Khartoum, there is a one-month rainy season in August and only 50 mm. of rainfall. In the north high summer temperatures are common, mean daily maxima reaching about 104°F. in Khar-

toum in May and June, though there is usually a marked diurnal range (about 68°F.). In the south temperatures are lower (average daily maxima 86°F.), the hottest months being February and March.

VEGETATION AND SOILS

Vegetation types are related to the climatic gradient. Tropical rain forest is found only in the uplands of the extreme south; and the south-east is dominated by a wooded-grassland complex, which merges northwards in Kordofan, Darfur and Blue Nile Provinces to a "low woodland savannah", dominated by acacia and with large areas of short grassland. Northward is a gradation through semi-desert to desert. The pattern is broken in the south by the large swamp grasslands of the Sudd area.

In the south-east areas from east of Khartoum to Juba alkaline clay soils dominate, and the south-western part of the country has red latosols, but elsewhere soils are predominantly sandy with pockets and strips of finer materials along the water courses.

POPULATION

The population of Sudan, projected from the 1956 census, was about 16,000,000 in 1971 and seems to be increasing rapidly. The total is small in relation to the size of the country, but there is a very uneven distribution, with over 50 per cent of the people concentrated in 15 per cent of the total national area. High densities occur along the Nile and around Khartoum, but parts of Kordofan near the railway line, the Nuba mountains and parts of Bahr el Ghazal and Darfur have average densities of 15 per sq. km. with much higher local concentrations. The people of northern Sudan are of mixed Arabic and African origin and traditionally are nomadic or semi-nomadic; in the south Nilotic peoples predominate, the Nuer, the Dinka and the Shilluk being the most important.

The major towns are the provincial centres, with the three towns of Khartoum, Omdurman and Khartoum North forming by far the largest urban centre. The Khartoum urban complex, with a population of about 700,000, is the main industrial, commercial, communication and administrative centre, and handles 90 per cent of the external trade. Of the other towns Atbara the centre of the railway industry, Wad Medani, first town of the Gezira, El Obeid and Juba, are the most important. Sudan has a well-developed railway system which now provides good links with the most populated parts of the country. The road system is poorly developed, and outside the main towns well maintained roads are rare, except in the extreme south.

RECENT HISTORY

Muddathir Abdel Rahim*

THE CONDOMINIUM

The scramble for Africa which dominated the closing decades of the nineteenth century convinced the British government that, in order to safeguard Britain's interests in Egypt and to ward off the Italians, the Belgians and, above all, the French from the upper reaches of the Nile, it was necessary that the Sudan be brought under British control. Since this would have brought Britain in direct conflict with the French and other European powers in central Africa, however, the British government decided that the conquest should be done in the name of the Khedive and Egypt who, it was contended, were now in a position to reaffirm their control over what was described as Egyptian territory which had been temporarily disrupted by the Mahdist rebellion. The reconquest, as it was called, was as unpopular with the Egyptian nationalists as the policy of evacuation which had been imposed on Egypt after the fall of Khartoum to the Mahdi in 1885. In spite of opposition, the reconquest was executed by combined Egyptian and British forces under the general command of Gen. Herbert Kitchener. It took three years: from 1896 to 1898 when, on September 2nd, the last of the Mahdist forces were destroyed in the battle of Omdurman.

The Anglo-Egyptian Agreement of 1899 laid the foundations of the new régime in the Sudan. The important, but thorny question of sovereignty over the country was however deliberately left out of the Agreement. For, from Britain's point of view, the acceptance, as binding law, of the theory that the new régime was a restoration of the Ottoman—Egyptian régime overthrown by the Mahdi was undesirable because it would have left Britain without legal basis for its presence in the Sudan, while the alternative— the theory that Britain was sovereign or had a share in sovereignty over the Sudan—would have aroused the hostility, not only of the Egyptians and the Sultan, but also of the French and the other European powers, and was therefore similarly undesirable. While emphasizing the claims which accrued to Britain by virtue of her participation in the reconquest, therefore, the Agreement was silent as to the juridical positions of the two conquering powers in the Sudan. This allowed Britain considerable scope for political and diplomatic manoeuvre. Thus, when the French questioned Britain's presence in the Sudan the British government insisted that it was acting on behalf of the Khedive; when the Egyptian nationalists raised the same question they were reminded of Britain's role in the reconquest; and when they protested their inferior position in the administration of the country, though they had contributed the larger share of men and money during the reconquest and almost all the expenses of the administration, Britain maintained that this was only fair as the country was reconquered

in the name of Egypt which, however, was unable to govern itself let alone the Sudan. This was perhaps illogical but from a practical point of view, it made little difference so long as Britain was in effective control of Egypt as well as the Sudan. After Egypt's independence in 1922 however, and especially after the abolition of the Caliphate, in whom sovereignty over the Sudan had theoretically resided during the Ottoman-Egyptian régime, the silence of the Agreement as to the subject of sovereignty became a source of increasing embarrassment to Britain.

The juridical dispute aside, the Agreement established in the Sudan an administration which was nominally Anglo-Egyptian but was actually a British colonial administration. Like the Ottoman-Egyptian administration it was headed by a Governor-General in whom all civil and military authority was vested. He was appointed by Khedivial decree but on the recommendation of the British government, without whose consent he could not be dismissed. Nothing was mentioned in the Agreement about his nationality but it is not surprising that all the Governors-General of the Sudan—like the Province Governors and District Commissioners who assisted them—were British. The British character of the régime became more obvious after 1924, when the Egyptian troops, officers and civilians who had hitherto acted as intermediaries between the British and the Sudanese were evacuated from the Sudan following the murder in Cairo of Sir Lee Stack, the then Governor-General of the Sudan and Sirdar (i.e. C.-in-C.) of the Egyptian Army. The administration of the country was until then based on the principle of Direct Rule and was, especially before the First World War, carried out along military lines. This was necessitated by the fact that resistance to the new régime did not cease after the battle of Omdurman and risings against it occurred annually. By the end of the war, however, the process of pacification, except in the south, was completed, and the last stronghold of Mahdism was taken when, in 1916, Sultan Ali Dinar of Darfur was killed and his Sultanate made a province of the Sudan.

INDIRECT RULE

The evacuation of the Egyptians from the Sudan in 1924 was generally unpopular with the Sudanese, especially the non-Mahdists and the small but influential educated class, who sympathized with the Egyptians on grounds of common language and religion, and saw in Egypt a natural ally against the British. Demonstrations were therefore organized in order to show solidarity with the Egyptians, and a Sudanese battalion mutinied and clashed with British troops. The rising was however ruthlessly crushed. Relations between the Sudan government and educated Sudanese deteriorated rapidly and a period of intense bitterness began which lasted well into the 1930s and was much aggravated by the depression and the subsequent retrenchment of salaries.

---

* For the 1973 edition, certain revisions have been made to this article by the Editor.

It was against this background that Indirect Rule, through the agency of tribal sheikhs and chiefs, was introduced, which soon replaced Direct Rule as the guiding principle in administration. Tribalism, which had been greatly weakened during the Mahdiyya, was revived and encouraged not only for purposes of administrative decentralization but also, and more importantly, as an alternative to bureaucratic government which necessitated the creation and employment of more and more educated Sudanese. These, because of their education, however limited, were politically more conscious than tribal leaders and therefore more difficult to control. Simultaneously with the stimulation of tribalism and tribal institutions therefore, training centres such as the military college were closed down; courses for training Sudanese administrators were discontinued; and harsh discipline which "savoured strongly of the barracks" was introduced in the Gordon College—an elementary institution which had been opened in 1902 for the training of artisans and junior officials. In general, the period from 1924 to the mid-thirties may be described as the golden age of Indirect Rule, or Native Administration; but from the point of view of education—always, under the British, closely connected with policy and administration—it was, in the words of a distinguished British scholar, "a period of utter stagnation". Economically however it was notable for the development of the Gezira scheme, whose cotton crops were largely responsible for the growth of the government's revenue from £1,654,149 in 1913, when the budget was balanced for the first time since the reconquest, to over £S4 million in 1936 and nearly £S46 million in 1956. Today the scheme covers over 1,500,000 acres and is the basis of the country's prosperity.

The introduction of Native Administration in the Northern Sudan after 1924 was paralleled in the south, by the launching of the government's new "Southern Policy". Until then official policy in the south was, apart from the maintenance of law and order, largely limited to the provision of various forms of assistance to Christian missionary societies which, in the words of an official Annual Report, worked for the proselytization of the population and "teaching these savages the elements of common sense, good behaviour, and obedience to government authority". After the rising of 1924 which, incidentally was led by an officer of southern (Dinka) origin, the "Southern Policy" was introduced. It had two main objectives: the prevention of the spirit of nationalism, which had already taken root in Egypt, from spreading across the Northern Sudan to the south and to other East African "possessions"; and the separation of the three southern provinces from the rest of the country with a view to their eventual assimilation by the government of neighbouring British territories which, it was hoped, would then emerge as a great East African Federation under British control. Accordingly, Muslim and Arabic speaking people in the south, whether they were of Egyptian, northern Sudanese or west African origins, were evicted from the region while stringent systems of permits and "Closed Districts" were introduced to prevent others from entering. Southerners, on the other hand, were discouraged from visiting or

seeking employment in the north, and those among them who had adopted the Muslim religion or used Arabic names, clothes or language were persuaded, by administrative means (which sometimes involved the burning of Arab clothes) to drop them and use, instead, Christian, English or native equivalents. Whereas education was then stagnating in the north and had so far been neglected in the south it was now enthusiastically supported by the government—but along lines calculated to eradicate all traces of Islamic and Arabic culture, and thus gradually sever relations between the northern and southern provinces.

TOWARDS SELF-GOVERNMENT

As may be expected the Southern Policy, like Native Administration, was most unpopular with the nationalists who, by the mid-1930s, had recovered from the shocks they had suffered after the failure of 1924. Encouraged by the challenge which the Axis powers were then presenting to Britain and by the restoration of Egypt's position in the Sudan in 1936, itself largely the result of the changing international scene, they began to mobilize themselves and prepared to resume their offensive. The Graduates' Congress, representing the *literati* of the country, was established early in 1938. Stimulated by the war, the Atlantic Charter and the open competition of the Egyptian and Sudan governments for their sympathy and support, the graduates, in 1942, submitted to the government a famous Memorandum in which they demanded, *inter alia*, the abolition of the Closed Districts Ordinance; the cancellation of subventions to missionary schools and the unifications of syllabuses in the north and the south; an increase in the share of the Sudanese in the administration of their country and the issue of a declaration granting the Sudan the right of self-government directly after the war. The government rebuffed the graduates by refusing to receive their Memorandum but nevertheless proceeded to react, on the local level, by the gradual transformation of Native Administration into a modern system of local government and, in central government administration, by launching, in 1943, an Advisory Council for the Northern Sudan which was replaced, in 1948, by a Legislative Assembly for the Sudan as a whole. The development of local government, however, was a very slow process (the first comprehensive local government Ordinance being promulgated as late as 1951); and it was in any case peripheral to the main wishes of the nationalists. The Advisory Council and the Legislative Assembly on the other hand failed to satisfy them because among other things, they had very little power to exercise (in the case of the Council no power at all), while their composition, largely based on the principle of appointment rather than free elections, only partially reflected political opinion in the country.

The limitations of the Council and the Assembly notwithstanding, the promulgation of these institutions had the effect of accentuating differences within Congress and eventually splitting it into two rival groups. Some worried about Egypt's continued claims over the Sudan, and feeling that independence could best be achieved by co-operating with the government, thought that Congress should participate in the

Council and the Assembly however defective they were. This group, led by the Umma Party, was supported by the Mahdists, and their motto was "The Sudan for the Sudanese". Others being more distrustful of the British, felt that independence could best be achieved through co-operation with Egypt which was an Arabic-speaking and Muslim neighbouring country and, like the Sudan, despite its formal independence, a victim of British imperialism. They therefore stood for "The Unity of the Nile Valley" and, supported by the Khatmiyya, the chief rival of the Mahdists among the religious fraternities, boycotted both the Council and the Assembly.

In the meantime successive negotiations between the British and Egyptian governments led from one deadlock to another and the unhappy schism between "the Unionists" and "the Independence Front" continued until the outbreak of the Egyptian Revolution in July 1952. The new régime promptly disowned the king and the Pasha class with whom "The Unity of the Nile Valley under the Egyptian Crown" was a basic article of political faith, and thus cleared the way for a separate settlement of the Sudan question. Neguib, Nasser and Salah Salem, all of whom had served in the Sudan and knew the Sudanese well, then staged a diplomatic *coup* which put the initiative in their hands.

The British had consistently justified their continued presence in the Sudan in terms of their desire to secure self-determination for the Sudanese as opposed to imposing on them a unity with Egypt which many Sudanese were prepared to resist by force of arms if necessary. Having got rid of the king the new Egyptian régime now declared that it was equally willing to grant the Sudanese the right of self-determination. On the basis of this declaration an Anglo-Egyptian Agreement was signed in 1953. This Agreement provided, among other things, for the Sudanization of the police and the civil service and the evacuation of all British and Egyptian troops in preparation for self-determination within a period of three years. Elections, held under the supervision of an international commission, resulted in the victory of the National Unionist Party, whose leader Ismail El Azhari became the first Sudanese Prime Minister in January 1954 and proceeded to put the terms of the Agreement into effect. The Egyptians had supported the NUP during the elections and it was naturally expected that Azhari would try to lead the country in the direction of union with Egypt. However, by the time the Sudanization programme was completed and the Egyptian and British troops had left the country, it was clear that he stood for independence. Several reasons led to this apparent reversal of attitude. Among these was the fact that the overwhelming majority of the NUP had looked upon solidarity with the Egyptians as a means for achieving the independence of the Sudan. Besides, the official opening of Parliament of March 1st, 1954, witnessed a violent demonstration by the Mahdists of their determination to split the country if the government wanted to lead the Sudan along the path of unity with Egypt rather than independence. Several people were killed and the ceremony to which guests from many countries,

including Gen. Neguib, had been invited, was postponed. It then became obvious that independence would not only satisfy the aspirations of the Sudanese but would also save the country from civil war. One thing, however, could still frustrate the country's progress to independence: namely the mutiny of southern troops at Juba in August 1955. This was the prelude to an attempted revolt in the south in which nearly three hundred northern Sudanese officials, merchants and their families were massacred. The disorders, except for some sporadic outbursts, did not spread to the two provinces of Upper Nile and Bahr El Ghazal but were centred in Equatoria. Order was restored in due course but the political problem of the south which, springing from the geographic and social differences between the northern and southern provinces, had been greatly accentuated by the "Southern Policy" of the British administration, continued to present a serious challenge to the Sudanese and the unity of the Sudan. Before they could vote for independence southern members of Parliament insisted that their request for a federal form of government be given full consideration. This they were duly promised.

The agreement had prescribed a plebiscite and other protracted procedures for self-determination. Azhari, supported by all Sudanese parties, decided to side-step these arrangements, and on December 19th, 1955, Parliament unanimously declared the Sudan an independent republic and, at the same time, resolved that a committee of five elected by Parliament to exercise the powers of the Head of State in place of the Governor-General. Faced with this *fait accompli* Britain and Egypt had no choice but to recognize the Sudan's independence, which was formally celebrated on January 1st, 1956.

THE INDEPENDENT SUDAN

During its fifteen years as an independent country the Sudan has had four régimes: a civilian parliamentary régime, which lasted until November 1958; a military régime, which, under Gen. Ibrahim Abboud, continued in office until it was overthrown by a "civilian *coup*" in October 1964; a second civilian régime, which was then ushered in and lasted until May 1969 when the existing régime of Gen. Jaafar Nemery came to office. Successive governments under all four régimes have been faced, above all, by three major problems: that arising from the country's dependence in one cash crop, i.e. cotton; the problem of the southern Sudan which was inherited from the British colonial régime; and the search for a permanent constitution for the country.

Throughout the greater part of the first régime the Sudan was governed by an improbable Mahdist-Khatmiyya coalition which, led by Abdalla Khalil, replaced Azhari and the non-sectarian rump of his NUP shortly after independence. During this period the Sudan established itself in the international field, joining the UN, the Arab League and, later on, the OAU. Internally, social services were expanded; the University College of Khartoum was raised to full university status, railway extensions in the Blue Nile south of Sinnar and in Darfur were completed; and the first stages of the Managil extension began operating, in July 1958, with a gross irrigable area of 200,000 acres. But serious economic and financial problems arising from rapid expansion on the one hand and difficulty in selling cotton crops on the other began to face the country. Politically the unnatural coalition was strained by serious differences between the Mahdist Umma Party and the Peoples Democratic Party, the political organ of the Khatmiyya. Thus, during the Suez crisis, the PDP felt that Egypt should have been given greater support than the Prime Minister was prepared to give, while some Umma spokesman accused the PDP of softness towards, if not actual complicity with, Egypt when a minor border dispute arose between the two countries in February 1958. And whereas the Umma Party favoured a presidential form of government, with Sayyid Abdel Rahman al-Mahdi as first president, the PDP and the Khatmiyya could not agree. A third difficulty arose from the deteriorating financial and economic situation which, having initially resulted from failure to dispose of the cotton crop of 1957, was compounded by exceptionally poor crops in 1958. With the country's reserves falling rapidly severe and unpopular restrictions had to be imposed and, the Prime Minister felt, foreign aid had to be sought. But the PDP, already worried by what it considered was the unduly pro-western policy of Abdalla Khalil, opposed acceptance of American aid. Elections, held in February 1958, resulted in no change and the already strained coalition was returned to power. The president of the Umma Party, Sayyid Siddiq al-Mahdi, then sought an alliance with Azhari's NUP. But this was unacceptable to the Prime Minister who was the secretary of the Umma Party. Khalil—who was the Minister of Defence as well as Prime Minister and who had been an army officer—then started consultations with senior army officers about the possibility of a military *coup*.

ABBOUD'S MILITARY GOVERNMENT

The *coup* was launched on November 17th, 1958. To the people in general it came as a relief after the wrangling and differences of the parties. The two Sayyids, al-Mahdi and al-Mirghani, gave their blessing to the régime on the understanding that the army would not stay in power longer than was necessary for the restoration of stability. Gen. Abboud assured the country that his aim was the restoration of stability and sound administration at home and the fostering of cordial relations with the outside world, particularly Egypt.

In the economic field a good start was made by following a realistic cotton sales policy which ensured the sale of both the carry-over from past seasons and the new crop. Loans from various international institutions and aid from the U.S.A., the U.S.S.R. and elsewhere were successfully negotiated. The money was used to finance such projects as the completion of the Managil extension and the construction of the

Roseires Dam on the Blue Nile, and the Khashm al-Girba Dam on the Atbara. The latter was used for the purpose of irrigating an area for the resettlement of the people of Halfa whose ancient town had been submerged by waters of the High Dam at Aswan.

But discontent soon began to grow. Prompting this was the feeling that too many officers—encouraged by the absence of democratic procedures of control and accountability—had become corrupt and used public funds for private gain. The result was that when the country was again gripped by financial and economic difficulties in 1964 the public was convinced that this could not be accounted for in terms of the poor cotton crop of that year, nor in terms of over-ambitious economic development schemes; they no longer trusted the government. In the field of administration other than financial a system of provincial administrations not unlike Pakistan's "Basic Democracies" was introduced in 1961 and this was crowned in 1962 by the creation of a Central Council which met for the first time in November 1963. While these arrangements, aimed at the training of the people in self-government, were in principle acceptable to most Sudanese, the actual working of the system—very much under the control of military personnel—not only failed to win the politically sophisticated but also alienated the civil service and professional administrators, many of whom were involved in friction with army officers. Thus when the civil service was called to join the judiciary, university staff, workers and others in the general strike which followed the outbreak of the revolution in October 1964, the response was both complete and enthusiastic.

THE CIVILIAN COUP

The immediate cause of the revolution was the government's heavy-handed administration in the south. This was based on the mistaken idea that the problem of the southern Sudan was a military, not a political, problem and that it was mainly the result of the activities of the missionaries who had participated in the implementation of the "Southern Policy" of the British administration. But the expulsion of missionaries in February 1964 dramatized the problem for the outside world rather than helped to solve it, while military action against both the *Anya Nya* rebels and the civilian villagers who were sometimes obliged to give them food and shelter had the effect of forcing thousands of southerners to live as refugees in neighbouring countries and convinced many that the only solution of the problem was for them to have a separate and independent state in the south. Concerned for the unity of the country, politicians, university students and others started campaigning for the view that the country could not be saved except by the removal of the military from authority and the restoration of democratic government. Orders forbidding public discussion of the southern problem and other political matters were issued but were defiantly disregarded by students. On October 21st the police, determined to break up such a discussion, opened fire on the students within the precincts of the University. One student died and the revolution was thereby set in motion. A general strike brought the country to a standstill and Gen. Abboud was forced to start negotiations with a Committee of Public Safety, to which he subsequently agreed to surrender political power. His decision was partly dictated by the fact that the army was known to be divided and that the younger officers especially were reluctant to open fire on unarmed civilian demonstrations with whom they generally sympathized.

A transitional government in which all parties including, for the first time, the Communist Party and the Muslim Brotherhood, were represented, was sworn in under Sirr al-Khatim al-Khalifa, an educationalist with a good record of service in the south, as Prime Minister. As a result of the inclusion as ministers of representatives of the communist-dominated Workers' and Tenants' Trades Unions and certain front organizations, the cabinet as a whole was dominated by the Communist Party.

After restoring the freedom of the press, raising the ban on political parties and starting a purge of the administration (which was subsequently abandoned on account of its being carried along personal and partisan lines) the new government turned to the most important problem facing it: the problem of the southern Sudan.

One of the first acts of the government had been a declaration of a general amnesty in the south. On March 16th, 1965, a round table conference in which northern and southern parties participated was opened in Khartoum. It was also attended by observers from seven African countries. The northern parties proposed to set up a regional government in the south which would, among other things, have its own parliament, executive and public service commission. The southern parties which attended the conference were divided. Some wanted federation; others a separate state; while the unionists (who were not represented in the conference because the two other groups would boycott the conference if they were allowed to participate) favoured the *status quo*. The conference failed to reach a general agreement on the constitutional future of the country and the subject was then referred to a Twelve Man Committee on which all parties—except the unionists—were represented. But agreement was reached on a constructive programme of immediate action which included the repatriation of refugees and the restoration of order, freedom of religion and unrestricted missionary activity by Sudanese nationals and the training of southerners for army, police and civil service.

Externally, the transitional government supported national liberation movements in Southern Arabia, Congo (K.) and among the Eritreans in Ethiopia. But this, like the purging of the administration, was controversial and was especially disliked by the Umma Party and the NUP who, together with the Islamic Charter Front (at the core of which was the Muslim Brotherhood) formed a front against the more left-wing PDP and the Communist Party. As a result of mounting pressure on the part of the former elections were held in June 1965. They were boycotted by the PDP but were heavily contested by all other

parties. The Umma Party won 76 seats, the NUP 53, the Communists 11 (out of the 15 seats in the graduates' constituency) and the Islamic Charter Front 7. For the first time tribal groups fought elections, winning 21 seats: 10 for the Beja and 11 for the Nuba of Kordofan.

COALITION GOVERNMENT AGAIN

The new government had to be a coalition. This was formed by the Umma and the NUP with Muhammad Ahmad Mahgoub (Umma) as Prime Minister and Azhari the permanent President of the Committee of Five which collectively acted as Head of State.

To pacify the Ethiopian and Chad governments, both of whom had been provoked by the policy of the transitional government with regard to liberation movements in their territories, Mahgoub hastened to affirm his government's adherence to the Accra pledges of non-interference and signed a border pact with Ethiopia in June 1966. This was followed by a number of visits to neighbouring countries with a view to confirming the new government's position in this respect and, at the same time, making arrangements whereby the return of Sudanese refugees from these countries would be facilitated.

Internally, the government ran into a number of difficulties. In July 1965 there was serious rebel activity at Juba and Wau, and large numbers of southerners were killed in the course of reprisals by government troops. Subsequently there were severe difficulties in retaining southern representatives in the government. Personal animosity between Azhari and Mahgoub led to a crisis within the coalition in October which was only solved by the mediation of the young Umma Party President, Sadiq al-Mahdi. Government policies meanwhile became increasingly right-wing, and in November 1965 the Communist Party was banned and its members unseated from the Assembly. This was contested in the courts which, in December 1966, ruled that it was illegal. But the Constituent Assembly, acting in its capacity as constitution-maker, overruled the courts' judgement. A crisis in which the judiciary and the Assembly confronted one another was thereby precipitated, but this was finally resolved in favour of the Assembly.

In the meantime a serious split was developing between the right wing of the Umma Party, led by Imam al-Hadi (Sadiq's uncle) which supported Premier Mahgoub, and the younger and more moderate elements who looked to Sadiq for more effective leadership. Sadiq, however, was reluctant to accept the Premiership not only on account of his young age (30), but also because failure (which was likely, in view especially of the mounting financial and security problems of the country) would prejudice his political future. But events and the pressure of his supporters finally obliged him to change his mind. After a heavy defeat in a vote of censure, on July 25th, 1966, Mahgoub resigned and Sadiq was then elected Prime Minister.

Sadiq's government was also a coalition of Umma and NUP but included, as Minister of Finance, an able expert of Khatmiyya background, Hamza Mirghani, who had been Principal Under-Secretary of the Ministry of Finance and a senior official at the IBRD. There were also two southern Ministers.

With the help of stringent controls and loans from the IBRD and IMF the economy gradually began to recover and the country's reserves of foreign currency, which had dropped to £S13 million, began to improve. Meantime the Twelve Man Committee had made considerable progress towards the settlement of the southern problem on the basis of regional government. A "Parties Conference" continued the Committee's work and, in April 1967, submitted a report in which it also recommended a regional solution. By this time the long-awaited supplementary elections in the south had been held, bringing 36 members to the Constituent Assembly of whom 10, led by William Deng, represented SANU, the leading southern party. It was now possible to speed up the process of drafting the permanent constitution and the settlement, *inter alia*, of the southern problem.

The relative success of Sadiq's government, however, coupled with the announcement that he would stand for the Presidency under the proposed constitution, resulted in the break-up of the coalition between his wing of the Umma Party and the NUP whose leader, Azhari, like the leader of the Ansar, Imam al-Hadiq, also aspired to the Presidency. Thus, on May 1967, Sadiq was defeated in the Assembly and Mahgoub was once again elected Premier.

Under his leadership the new coalition of NUP and al-Hadi's branch of the Umma Party pursued a vigorous foreign policy, particularly in the Middle East after the Six Days War. As a result the first Arab Summit Conference after the war was convened in Khartoum (August 1967) and Mahgoub, together with Iraqi and Moroccan colleagues, was subsequently entrusted with the task of finding a formula for the settlement of the Yemeni dispute. Deterioration of relations with Western Powers, culminating in severence of diplomatic relations with the U.K. and the U.S.A. after the June War, was accompanied by the development of closer relations with the eastern bloc, and the conclusion of an arms deal with the U.S.S.R. resulted in the lifting, without formal announcement, of the ban which had previously been imposed on the Sudanese Communist Party. The internal affairs of the country, particularly the already precarious financial situation, had in the meantime been somewhat neglected. The result was that when the Constituent Assembly was reconvened after the prolonged recess which followed the outbreak of hostilities in the Middle East, the opposition, under the vigorous leadership of Sadiq al-Mahdi and William Deng (who, together with the ICF, now formed the New Forces Congress), was able to defeat the government on several occasions. This, together with the growing PDP and Communist opposition to the Draft Permanent Constitution based on Islam, regionalism and a strong executive on the presidential model, induced the government to dissolve the Constituent Assembly on January 7th, 1968, following a mass resignation of the government members in the

Assembly. Sadiq and his allies contested the constitutionality of this act in the courts. Before any judgement was pronounced, however, new elections were held in April, which were contested for the first time since 1958 by the PDP, now merged with the NUP in the new Democratic Unionist Party. This won the largest number of seats, 101, followed by Sadiq's Umma, who won 38, and al-Hadi's Umma, with 30 seats. As the DUP did not command a majority on its own, a new coalition, also with Imam al-Hadi's faction of the Umma Party, and under the leadership of Mahgoub, was formed when the Assembly was convened on May 27th.

Mahgoub's third government, however, was unable to improve the economic and financial situation while the situation in the southern provinces continued to deteriorate. Mahgoub, moreover, fell ill and the situation was aggravated by the cabinet crisis of April-May over the reallocation of ministerial responsibilities between the Umma and Democratic Unionist Parties. The result was the bloodless *coup* of May 25th, 1969, when the government was overthrown by a group of officers and civilians led by Col. (later Maj.-Gen.) Jaafar al-Nemery.

REVOLUTIONARY GOVERNMENT

The new régime which was thereby ushered in declared that it was committed to a policy of "Sudanese socialism" and gave the country the new name of the "Democratic Republic of the Sudan". Pending the promulgation of the new constitution, power was vested in a Revolutionary Council which consisted of military officers and a predominantly Civilian Council of Ministers which included several members of the Communist Party. Initially, Babiker Awadalla, the former Chief Justice, was Prime Minister and, as such, the only civilian member of the Revolutionary Council—but he was subsequently replaced as Prime Minister by Gen. Nemery, who also became Chairman of the Revolutionary Council.

All political organizations were dissolved after the *coup* and several former ministers were tried on charges of bribery and corruption, rumours of which had been rife before the *coup*. Banks and several companies have since been nationalized. The property of certain persons, including the Mahdi family, was confiscated. Following an attempt on the life of Gen. Nemery the chief source of opposition to the régime, the Imam al Mahdi and his supporters, based on Abu Island in the White Nile, was crushed in March 1970. Since then the régime has been able to turn more of its attention to the reshaping of the economy and administration in the light of its professed policy of Sudanese socialism. Considerable attention has been given to the problem of the southern Sudan in particular.

In June 1969 Gen. Nemery declared his government's policy of solving the problem by granting regional autonomy to the southern provinces and a Ministry for Southern Affairs was created to spell out the details of this policy. Mr. Joseph Garang, who was a Catholic Southern Sudanese and a member of the

Communist Party, was the Minister in charge of Southern Affairs, until his execution in July 1971 for taking part in the abortive *coup*. Several southerners have been appointed to ministerial, ambassadorial and other posts, while funds have been set aside for development and reconstruction in the southern provinces. Three Ministers from the South were included in the cabinet formed in August 1971, perhaps to mollify southerners upset by the execution of Joseph Garang.

In fact by far the most crucial development in Sudan's internal affairs since July 1971, was the conclusion of the Addis Ababa Agreement of March 1972. Among other things, this provided for the return and rehabilitation of southern Sudanese refugees abroad, the reintegration of Anya Nya rebels into the Sudanese armed forces and the establishment of administratively autonomous institutions for the southern provinces within the boundaries of the Sudan. By early 1972 the southern question was successfully resolved, all hostilities having ceased. The Ministry of Southern Affairs was dismantled and replaced by the Supreme Executive Council for the Southern Region, with the ex-Minister at its head. The former commander of the rebel forces, Major-General Lagadu, was given the same rank in the Sudanese army.

In the field of foreign affairs, one of the first decisions taken by the régime was to recognize the German Democratic Republic. This was followed by the forging of closer diplomatic and trade relations with China, the U.S.S.R. and eastern Europe. In the Middle East the régime's policy has, above all, been characterized by its militant support for the Arab cause over the Palestine question and, until recently, by close co-operation with Libya and the U.A.R. in particular. More recently, Gen. Nemery personally participated in the resolution of the Jordanian crisis, and in November 1970 it was declared that Presidents Nemery, Sadat and Gaddafi had decided to unite the Sudan, Libya and the U.A.R. into one federal state. The scheme was soon shown to be abortive, however, as Sudan's foreign policy became more African and less Arab-orientated in 1972. With the settlement of the Southern problem, the border with Uganda was re-opened in May and a defence pact signed with General Amin in June. When, however, Sudan prevented Libyan aircraft from delivering arms to Uganda during the conflict with Tanzania, relations with Libya and the U.A.R., now Egypt, deteriorated to the point where Sudanese troops were withdrawn from the joint Arab forces at Suez, and Egyptian university teachers expelled from Khartoum. The incorporation of the non-Muslim former Southern rebels into the Sudanese body politic has evidently influenced Sudan's continental stance. To the West, Sudan has maintained friendly

relations with the Chad Government and patrolled the frontier against incursions by the Chad Liberation Front (FROLINAT).

Since the 1969 *coup* there have been various reported attempts to overthrow the régime. For some time the chief source of opposition was the Mahdi family, whose property was confiscated after the *coup*. In March 1970 a rebellion led by the Imam al Mahdi from his stronghold of Aba Island in the White Nile was crushed by the government with many deaths, including that of the Imam. Later it was the communists who were accused of working against the government. Three ministers and thirteen army officers were dismissed in November 1970 for sympathizing with the Sudanese Communist Party, and the party's secretary-general was arrested. In February 1971 President Nemery expressed his intention of destroying the party, but it was the communists who moved first to remove him. On July 19th, 1971, a section of the army, led by communists, overthrew the Nemery régime, and Col. Babakr al Nur was proclaimed head of state. However, while Col. al Nur and his assistant, Maj. Farouk Hamadallah, were returning from London to take command of the revolution, the BOAC plane carrying them was forced to land in Libya. They were taken off, and the Libyan Government later handed them over to President Nemery, who had regained power in a counter-*coup* three days after being ousted. A massive purge of communists followed, and fourteen people were executed almost immediately. Apart from Maj. Hachem al Atta, who set the *coup* in motion in Khartoum, and the two leaders back from London, the Communist Party's Secretary-General, Abdel Khalik Mahgoub, the Secretary-General of the Federation of Sudanese Workers' Union, Shafieh Ahmed el Sheikh, and Joseph Garang, were all eliminated after hurried and secret trials before a military tribunal. The purge brought condemnation in unusually forthright terms from the Soviet and East European governments, though diplomatic relations have so far remained intact. President Nemery received strong support from President Sadat of Egypt, and the alliance of Sudan, Egypt and Libya drew closer until relations worsened in 1972.

In an election held in October 1971 to confirm Gen. Nemery's nomination as President, Nemery received almost four million votes, with only 56,000 "no" votes. A new government was formed, the Revolution Command Council was dissolved, and the Sudanese Socialist Union was recognised as Sudan's only political party. The new People's Assembly, some of whose members were elected in October, was convened, with Nemery as its chairman, to frame a new permanent constitution.

ECONOMIC SURVEY

Ali Ahmed Suliman

THE MAIN CHARACTERISTICS
OF THE ECONOMY

It hardly needs stating that Sudan is an agricultural and pastoral country. Agriculture, including livestock and forestry products, contributed more than 50 per cent of the gross domestic product in 1962–63. Animal wealth, though very undeveloped, contributes about 10 per cent of the G.D.P., while the share of forestry products in the G.D.P. is about the same. However, the contribution of fish and marine products is only about 2 per cent. The significance of agriculture in the Sudanese economy is also reflected in the distribution of manpower among the different economic sectors. About 85 per cent of those economically active (according to 1955–56 figures) are engaged in primary production. Manufacturing industries contributed only about 2 per cent of the G.D.P. up to 1962–63, while the share of minerals is less than 1 per cent. No important minerals have yet been found in Sudan in significant enough quantities to be exploited economically. In the late 1960s agriculture contributed about 40 per cent, while manufacturing contributed much less than 10 per cent of G.D.P. Sudan not only depends on agriculture, but on one main crop for its exports. In fact the share of extra-long staple cotton in the exports of Sudan reaches more than 70 per cent in some years. Such dependence on one major export crop, with wide fluctuations in price and quantity exported, has caused political, as well as economic, instability.

Furthermore, about 48 per cent (on 1962–63 figures) of the G.D.P. is produced in the traditional sector, and about 25 per cent, it is estimated, is produced and consumed in the subsistence sector. With such a traditional agricultural sector it is not surprising that Sudan has a low per capita income, which was only U.S. $97 in 1963–64, rising a little to $104 by 1968–69. For the last ten years or so the Sudanese economy has been growing at an annual rate of about 4 per cent, while the population has been growing annually at a rate of about 2.8 per cent.

The average density of population in Sudan is low and there is no population pressure on the available resources at present. Open unemployment is very insignificant. In fact, Sudan suffers from a shortage of labour, particularly during the cotton-picking season. Sometimes this problem is solved by immigrant labour from neighbouring countries. The Sudan is a large country with large unproductive areas. Unfortunately it is these vast unproductive parts which are close to the Red Sea, whereas the more productive regions are separated from the sea and from Port Sudan by distances ranging between 500 and 1,500 miles. Their remoteness was a major factor in retarding economic development in the past. For the present, inadequacy of transport is one of the important bottle-necks in the economy.

Perhaps one of the most striking features of the Sudanese economy is the dominant role which is played by the public sector in all important economic activities. The government, aside from its day-to-day administrative, financial and fiscal efforts, owns the majority of modern capital establishments in the economy. In the ten-year plan the share of the government was £S337 million out of the total investment of £S565 million. In the period 1955/56–1962/63 the share of the government in gross fixed capital formation ranged between a half and two-thirds. The government is not only the chief investor in public utilities, but it is the main promoter of industries such as sugar, cotton-ginning, food-processing, tanning and printing. Governmental efforts to develop the country have expanded to such an extent that all large hotels in the various parts of Sudan are owned and managed by the government. With the nationalization of all commercial banks and several leading commercial firms in May and June 1970 the economic significance of the public sector has become even greater.

AGRICULTURE

The availability of water is the governing factor for agriculture in Sudan. In most parts of the rainlands of Sudan drinking water for humans and animals is a crucial factor, especially before the rainy season, when land is prepared for cultivation, and after it during harvest time. However, land does not impose any constraint on the agricultural development of the country. The cultivable land is estimated to be about 200 million feddans (one feddan = 1.038 acres). Only about 8 per cent of this cultivable land is being utilized in agriculture, and less than four million feddans are under irrigation. Half of this area is in the Gezira scheme (with its Managil extension), and the rest is irrigated by the flood waters of two small rivers in eastern Sudan, Gash and Baraka, by the flood waters of the Nile and by pumps.

Prior to the Nile Waters agreement of 1959 the distribution of water between Sudan and the U.A.R. was governed by the Nile Waters agreement of 1929, which allocated four milliard cubic metres to Sudan. However, with the 1959 agreement and the construction of the Roseires and Khashm el Girba dams, the water problem has been solved. Sudan is now entitled to draw 18.5 milliard cubic metres at Aswan High Dam or the equivalent of about 20.5 milliard cubic metres in Sudan, and the way has been opened for considerable expansion of irrigated agriculture. At present Sudan is drawing about half of its entitlement—about ten milliard cubic metres annually—but with the development of new areas along the White and Blue Nile, Atbara River and the Main Nile, as well as the intensification of the Gezira scheme by reducing fallow, and its diversification by such crops as wheat, groundnuts and *philipesara* vegetables, Sudan is expected to utilize all its entitlement within

the coming five years or so. One of the main development projects in Sudan is the Rahad project, which
will need about four milliard cubic metres of water for
an area of about half a million feddans. The Sukki
project, which has also started, may reach an area of
170,000 feddans, while the pump-irrigated areas of the
Northern Province may increase by about 165,000
feddans within a few years to come.

In spite of the significant role played by irrigation
(particularly gravity irrigation) in the economic development of Sudan, the rainlands are more important. In 1970–71 the total cropped area of main
crops increased by 4.9 per cent from the previous
year's level of 9,820,793 feddans to 10,305,118
feddans. Rain-grown and flooded areas under cultivation both decreased from 7,900,000 and 150,000
feddans in 1969–70 to 2,400,000 and 130,000 respectively in 1970–71. The total area under irrigation
continued to increase and reached 2.8 million feddans
in 1970–71. With the exception of cotton, pulses and
a proportion of groundnuts, Sudan's foodstuffs and
most exported agricultural products come from
the rainlands. In fact Sudan is self-sufficient in
the essential foods: millet, meat, edible oils and salt.
However, the output per feddan in the rainlands is
low. Rainlands agriculture is a somewhat risky
business and to some extent this has probably
deterred investment and modernization. The government has already taken steps to encourage large
farming units and agricultural mechanization. This
type of cultivation is mainly practised in the Gedaref
area, in Kassala Province and the Dali and Mazmoum
regions of the Blue Nile Province. The total area has
increased considerably since 1955–56. In peak years,
the total area reaches about 1.5 million feddans. The
area shows considerable fluctuations, which are
mainly due to changes in the prices of durra. In these
areas durra is the main crop, but sesame and American
cotton are also grown.

The agricultural sector of the Sudan does not face
any serious land tenure problems. The rainlands, in
particular, are very free from such problems, and also
enjoy the advantage of relatively low production
costs. The present government has already started an
anti-thirst campaign and has promised the economic
and social development of those areas. The Ten-Year
Plan (1961/62–1970/71) was more concerned with the
modern sector and the irrigated lands.

Sudan has animal wealth which contributes about
10 per cent of G.D.P. annually. It was estimated in
1970–71 as 12.6 million cattle, 10.6 million sheep,
7.4 million goats and 2.5 million camels. Its annual
share in Sudan's exports (animals, hides and skins)
was about 4 per cent between 1969 and 1971.

In the year 1962–63 forest reserve estates, which are
completely owned by the government, increased by
7,000 feddans to a total of 2,574,000 feddans. Beside
gum arabic, the other important forest products are
the various types of timber which are processed by
the forest department of the ministry of agriculture.
In 1968–69 the forest department produced 112,000
railway sleepers, 390,000 poles and 4,500 tons of sawn
timber. The main consumer of these products is the
government itself.

Sudan is rich in fish and other aquatic resources.
The inland fisheries cover more than 20,000 sq. km.,
while marine fisheries extend for a distance of about
700 km. along the Red Sea. It is estimated that the
annual total value of the output of fish and aquatic
resources in Sudan is about £S10 million. The output
of fish from the Nile is 60,000 tons annually but only
a small percentage of this wealth is utilized at present.
Since the actual output of fish from inland fisheries is
estimated at around 20,000 tons annually, therefore
about 40,000, valued at £S4 million, are wasted.

The contribution of fisheries to Sudan's exports is
small. The share of salted fish and shells (mother of
pearl and torchus) is much less than 1 per cent of the
total exports.

Cotton is the most important crop in Sudan from
the economic point of view. It is the major export
crop, the chief exchange earner and the main generator
of income in the Sudan. A proportion of it is consumed
locally by the textile industry. Its average share of
exports over the five years 1965–69 was 53 per cent,
not including its by-products, and 63 per cent including them. The cotton is of two types: long-staple
varieties, Skallarides and its derivatives (commonly
known as *Sakel*), and short-staple varieties, which are
mainly American types and are consumed locally.
The *Sakel* varieties are exclusively for export and are
grown in the large schemes of the Gezira and the Gash
and Tokar deltas, while the American types are grown
in the rainlands of Equatoria, the Nuba mountains,
Gedaref and also in some of the pump schemes in the
Northern Province. The volume of output of the
American types fluctuates more than the *Sakel*, but
is generally increasing at a faster rate. In 1970–71 the
total production of *Sakel* was 618,314 tons, while the
total production of American types was 108,212 tons.

Durra includes various types of sorghum millets. It
is the most important staple food in Sudan and is
mainly grown in the rainlands. Sudan produces
annually about 1.5 million tons of durra, which is
usually sufficient for domestic consumption. It is not
an export crop, though in good years some is exported,
as, for example, in 1962–63, when 68,635 tons were
exported. In bad years the government may need to
import some durra. However, there are still no adequate storage facilities for offsetting bad years against
good years. So far there are only two grain silos in
Sudan with a storage capacity of 150,000 tons.

With urbanization and social development the consumption of bread made out of wheat flour is increasing by about 10 per cent annually. There seems
to be a shift in consumption from *kisra* made out of
durra to bread made out of wheat. Wheat is grown
mainly as a cash crop. A small proportion of rural
people use wheat flour in their diet. To meet the
rapidly expanding demand of the urban population
the government is growing wheat in the Gezira scheme
and other suitable areas. It is also paying a subsidy
to encourage its production and at the same time keep
the price of bread reasonably low. The government
buys a ton of wheat from the farmer at £S38 and then
sells it to the flour mills at £S28.7.

Sudan gums have been known in trade for at least two thousand years. Gum arabic, which constituted about 10 per cent of Sudan's exports in 1969 and 9 per cent in 1970 was for many years the second export crop, until overtaken by groundnuts in 1971. It is the most important forest product and, though collected in the traditional sector, it is a purely cash crop. It is almost entirely exported, as the confectionery industry manufactures only a very small percentage of it. Sudan is the world's largest source of gum arabic, producing about 92 per cent of the total world consumption (1962–66). Two types of gum are produced in Sudan, *Hashab* from *Acacia Senegal* and *Talh* from *Acacia Seyal*. The former is of a superior quality. The annual production of *Hashab* gum in normal years ranges between 40,000 and 50,000 tons and that of *Talh* between 2,000 and 4,000 tons. Kordofan and Darfur provinces in western Sudan are the main production centres. The chief market for gum is at El Obeid in Kordofan Province, where it is sold by auction. In order to stabilize the price of gum, the government formed the Gum Traders' Association in 1962 which was made responsible for buying any gum left in the market at a price not less than 288 piastres per kantar.* A levy of 35 piastres was paid by exporters on every kantar of gum exported, to enable the Gum Traders' Association to pay the minimum price. This system was an improvement on previous methods but it was not satisfactory. In September 1969 the government formed the Gum Arabic Company Ltd., a public concession company in which government participation is 30 per cent of the capital. The company is now handling all the gum trade of Sudan with the objectives of promoting it, maximizing the returns to the country and to the producer and stabilizing gum prices.

INDUSTRY

Industrialization usually starts in one of two basic ways, either with the processing of exports which were previously exported in their crude form, or with the manufacturing of import substitutes for an expanding home market, a surplus perhaps being exported later.

The ginning of cotton encouraged the beginning of industry in Sudan early in this century. With the expansion of cotton production the number of ginning factories have increased until the Gezira Board alone has the largest ginning enterprise under single management in the world. The processing of cotton has not gone beyond ginning. Cotton seeds are partly decorticated, while the exports of cotton-seed oil and oil cakes are increasing. Groundnuts are also shelled for export. In 1969 24,685 tons were exported in shell, while 57,456 tons were exported shelled. Minerals (copper, iron, mica and chromite), which constitute less than 1 per cent of exports, are exported in the crudest form.

However, the story of import substitution is different. This type of industry, though of more recent origin than the industries which process for export,

has made more progress, and is expected to play a more important role in the economic development of the country. With the exception of the soap, soft drinks and oil-pressing industries, large industries manufacturing import substitutes started only after 1960. The government was not involved in any industry until 1959, with the exception of the Zande scheme, which involved a cotton mill at Nzara for promoting the social development of the Zande tribe. From 1960 the involvement in industry began to increase and in 1962 the government formed an industrial development corporation to look after the large factories of the public sector. By 1968 the Industrial Development Corporation was managing nine manufacturing factories, in which the government has invested £S23.7 million. There are also factories in the public sector managed by the ministries, such as the government printing press and the mint.

The first factory to be established was the Guneid sugar factory, which, in response to the great increase in the consumption of sugar in the 1950s, came into production in November 1961 with a capacity of 60,000 tons of refined sugar annually. A second factory was needed to meet the local demand and in 1963 Khashm el Girba sugar factory was started, with a capacity similar to that of Guneid. In addition to a tannery, opened in November 1961, the government also has five food processing plants: one cannery and one date factory in Kareima, another cannery in Wau, an onion dehydrating plant in Kassala and a milk factory in Babanousa. What is very striking about these food processing industries is that the supply of raw materials is not high enough to match the productive capacity, and therefore, the weakness in these factories is not technical but agricultural.

The private sector has also played an important role in the industrial development of this country. In the period 1960–69 the private sector invested £S35.9 million in industries of which £S16.1 million was Sudanese and £S19.8 foreign capital. The foreign capital is mainly savings of foreign residents accumulated from the profits of the import and export trade. The bulk of the investment has gone into the textile, soap, oil-pressing, footwear, soft drinks, printing, packing, flour, and knitwear industries.

The government has encouraged industrialization in Sudan by various means. The Approved Enterprises (Concessions) Act, 1959, gave generous concessions to infant industries. The Organisation and Promotion of Industrial Investment Act, 1967, has been even more generous to industry. It gives exemption from the business profits tax for a number of years, depending on the size of the invested capital, allows very high rates of depreciation, gives very fair treatment to losses, reduces import duties on imported machinery and materials, protects domestic production by high tariffs and import restrictions and allocates building lands at reduced prices. In addition to this, the Industrial Bank, which was established in 1961, assists in the financing of private industrial enterprises with up to two-thirds of the capital required. By the end of 1968 the value of loans given by the bank amounted to £S3.9 million. In 1972 the Ministry

---

* Gum is weighed in small kantars. Cotton is weighed in big kantars. 1 small kantar = 44.928 kilogrammes. 1 big kantar = 141.523 kilogrammes.

of Industry brought in new legislation to encourage industrial investment. The new act is very similar to that of 1967. However, the Organization and Promotion of Industrial Investment Act of 1967 seems to favour large-scale investment, since under it enterprises whose capital is £S one million or more are exempted from the Business Profits Tax for ten years, while under the 1972 act they are exempted for the first five years and during the second five years, 10 per cent of the profits only are free from taxation.

FOREIGN TRADE

The value of Sudan's exports rose from £S63.4 million in 1960 to £S114.4 million in 1971, while the value of imports rose from £S63.7 million to £S115.4 million. Thus both exports and imports rose by 50 per cent, greater increases in exports occurring more recently, so that although Sudan has faced a deficit every year since 1960, the balance of payments has now become a less serious problem. This must be due at least in part to the Government's policy of clamping down on imports and encouraging exports. There are import restrictions and high import duties on a large number of goods, but export taxes are light and no licence is required for export, with the exception of goods consumed locally and in short supply.

Merchandise trade dominates the current account, while the net balance on the invisible account is usually negative.

Sudan's main exports are primary agricultural products, and since the establishment of the Gezira scheme in 1925, cotton has dominated. Between 1960 and 1971 the share of lint cotton alone ranged between 46 and 65 per cent. In 1971 the U.S.S.R. was the largest buyer of Sudan's cotton, followed closely by India, the People's Republic of China, whose share had doubled since the previous year, and the EEC. In the last ten years, due to the expansion of production in the traditional sector, the relative importance of oil seeds as exports has increased and in 1971 groundnuts formed the second most important export crop with the average of about 8 per cent of exports. The EEC is the largest buyer of Sudan's groundnuts (60 per cent). The east European countries buy about 20 per cent of the groundnuts and the rest go to various west European countries. Gum arabic was overtaken in importance by groundnuts in 1971 to become the third export product, making up 7 per cent of total exports.

The major imports are vehicles, transport equipment, machinery, appliances and textiles. The growth of industries which are manufacturing import substitutes has affected the pattern of imports since the mid-1960s. The imports of sugar, footwear and cigarettes are declining in relative and absolute terms

Perhaps a more striking change has taken place in the pattern of suppliers and buyers, if the late 1960s are compared with the early 1950s. The U.K. used to be the largest seller and buyer from the Sudan (30–40 per cent before independence). In 1971 only 4.5 per cent of Sudan's exports went to the U.K., and only

12.6 per cent of imports were brought from the U.K. However, the U.K. continues to have a large share of Sudan's imports of machinery, appliances, vehicles, transport equipment, chemicals, pharmaceutical products and cigarettes. Trade with socialist countries has been increasing since independence, and especially in recent years, as a result of several bilateral agreements. In 1960–69 the Sudan signed agreements with Bulgaria, Czechoslovakia, the German Democratic Republic, Yugoslavia, Hungary, Poland, China and others. The share of socialist countries in Sudan's trade is about 20 per cent of both exports and imports. Trade with the Arab countries has been expanding in recent years and exports to them have reached about 10 per cent, but imports from these countries form a smaller percentage. The Arab countries are a good market for Sudan's animals. Trade between the Sudan, Egypt and Libya is developing further as a result of an agreement on economic integration signed in May 1970. Furthermore, the summit conferences of east and central African heads of state and governments may increase trade between Sudan and east and central African countries in the near future.

FOREIGN AID 1960–1969

The Ten-Year Plan of Economic and Social Development, 1961/62–1970/71, was the country's first experience in planning, although there had been three previous attempts to develop Sudan in a systematic manner: 1946–51, 1951–56 and the Managil extension programme. In contrast to the Ten-Year Plan, the development programmes were not comprehensive, being concerned only with some projects in the public sector and depending on finance from savings of the public sector.

The total gross investment of the plan was estimated to be £S565 million, of which 40 per cent (£S228 million) was to be sponsored by the private sector and 60 per cent (£S337 million) by the public sector. Out of the total investment £S415.9 million was to be financed by domestic savings and £S219.7 million from foreign financial assistance. The £S415.9 would consist of £S219.7 million public savings and £S196.2 million private savings.

The amount of foreign aid which was actually received in the period 1960–69 did not fall very much short of the target of the plan. While £S150 million of foreign aid was forecast for the period 1961/62, 1970/71, £S141 million of aid in the form of grants, long-term and medium-term loans and in kind was received in the period 1960–69. However, in spite of the small difference between projected and realized foreign aid, the plan could not be properly implemented, mainly because of a shortage of domestic and foreign finance.

The Khashm el Girba and Roseires dams could not be utilized fully because the lack of finance prevented the associated works being completed. Additional reasons, such as wastage and corruption, also contributed to hampering the completion of projects of the public sector. Foreign aid of about £S60 million was needed in 1970 to complete the basic association projects, which will enable Sudan to utilize its investment reasonably well.

It is clear from the sources of foreign aid over the period 1960–69 that the International Bank for Reconstruction and Development has played an important part in the financing of development projects in Sudan. About 16 per cent of all foreign aid in the 1960–69 period has come from it. The Bank has financed very vital projects such as the Roseires Dam, mechanized farming, Sudan Railways extension and dieselization, and the Managil Extension. American aid, mainly given in non-project commodities, has also been important, constituting about 14 per cent of the total between 1960 and 1969. American aid to Sudan ceased when Sudan severed diplomatic relations with the U.S.A. in June 1967. Cumulative withdrawals up to the end of 1967 totalled £S23.3 million.

Aid to Sudan from Yugoslavia included a tannery, a cardboard factory and three ships, which constitute the Sudan Shipping Line. The U.S.S.R. has provided Sudan with two grain elevators, factories for processing agricultural and dairy products, a hospital and veterinary laboratories. Federal Germany also played an important role in financing the economic development of Sudan between 1960 and 1969 by contributing to the financing of the Roseires Dam; and credit from German firms helped in financing the Guneid and Khashm el Girba sugar factories.

The June War (1967), which brought about closer relations between the Arab countries, has increased the flow of Arab aid to Sudan. By the end of 1969 the drawings on Arab aid had reached £S42.4 million—more than 30 per cent of the total foreign aid received between 1960 and 1969. In addition to this Sudan received £S15 million from the United Arab Republic, not as aid, but as compensation for the resettlement of Halfa town, caused by the construction of the Aswan High Dam.

The financing of public sector projects has mainly come from various governments, but firms have also played a part. For example, Italian contractors granted a credit of £S2.6 million to cover a part of the cost of the construction of Khashm el Girba dam and three Fokker aeroplanes were obtained on a three-year credit from the suppliers.

During 1960–69 the Sudan government obtained short-term loans from the IMF and some Dutch commercial banks. The Dutch commercial banks provided £S0.9 million to finance about 90 per cent of the cost to the Sudan government of importing telecommunication equipment from Holland.

There is no information about foreign loans to the private sector, but the two textile mills in the country were financed by foreign loans from the U.S.A. and Japan.

At the end of 1969 the net foreign debt outstanding in respect of government loans amounted to £S109.3 million. This figure includes £S18 million representing obligations to the IMF, but it excludes the amounts received under the different American aid programmes, before such aid was stopped in 1967. At the end of 1971 the net foreign debt in respect of government loans amounted to £S110.6 million.

Repayment of loans in 1969 amounted to £S10.9 million, of which £S6.7 million was for principal and £S3.9 million was interest. In 1968 and 1969 the Sudan Government secured sizeable short-term and medium-term loans which had the effect of increasing the debt servicing burden immediately. The ratio of debt servicing to export proceeds rose from 6.9 per cent in 1967 to 12.5 per cent in 1969. In 1971 it reached 20 per cent. Such a high ratio of debt servicing indicates that the Sudan has reached a critical limit.

The total amount of external resources received in 1970 amounted to £S12.8 million compared to £S26.1 in 1969. In 1971 the total amount of external resources received amounted to £S10.8 million. This sum includes £S2.7 million of Sudan's allocation of Special Drawing Rights (short-term loan from the IMF), and the drawing of £S100,000 on suppliers' credit.

PUBLIC FINANCE

The Sudan government, like governments in many other underdeveloped countries, depends heavily on indirect taxes as a major source of revenue. In the fiscal year 1969–70 indirect taxes contributed 44 per cent of the central government's revenue, while in 1968–69 they yielded about 50 per cent. In these two years the relative share of indirect taxes declined because of increased import restrictions, and also because of the increased revenue from direct taxes and proceeds from government agricultural enterprises, particularly in 1969–70. The main source of revenue from indirect taxation is import duties. Because of balance of payments deficits in recent years the government has been trying to restrict imports of consumer goods, particularly luxuries, and those which bear the highest rates. Excise duties are growing in importance because of the growth of industries producing import substitutes. Thus, the share of excise duties in revenue from indirect taxation, 5 per cent in 1964–65, rose to 18 per cent in 1966–67. This change is also reducing the rate of increase of revenue from indirect taxation. Excise duties are of lower rates than import duties on the same goods, and they are more difficult to collect.

The revenue from export taxes declined from £S3.8 million in 1966–67 to £S3 million in 1969–70. The majority of export taxes, which were an important feature of the tax system of Sudan, were cancelled, together with royalties, in November 1968, with the exception of those on gum and cotton, in an attempt to encourage exports. This action has not proved effective and the revenue of the government from export taxes has been greatly reduced. The taxes were reintroduced in November 1969, but at lower rates.

The revenue from direct taxes was about 13 per cent of the total revenue of the central government in 1969–70, having been 2.7 per cent in 1963–64. The present direct taxes of Sudan (1969–70) are: income taxes, an emergency tax and a stamp duty. The income taxes comprise a personal income tax on monetary earnings, fringe benefits and interest; a business profits tax; and a tax on income from rent (as laid down by the Income Tax Act, 1967). The top rate is 50 per cent, when total income reaches £S25,000. Dividends are not normally taxable in the Sudan, since companies pay a business profits tax; shareholders do not pay an income tax on their dividends. Nevertheless, a holding company which receives dividends from its subsidiaries pays a business tax on aggregate profits, after getting a tax credit for the tax paid by the subsidiary. An emergency tax was introduced in August 1969 to absorb part of the wage and salary increases given to employees in the public sector in 1968 by the previous government. The yield of the emergency tax is estimated to be £S7 million in 1969–70. Stamp duty is considered as a direct tax in Sudan and its revenue is less than £S2 million.

In addition to the revenue from taxation, fees, charges and profits from agricultural enterprises, the central government may borrow internally to meet current expenditure. Under the Bank of Sudan Act, 1959, amended in 1962, the government, its boards and agencies, are permitted to borrow from the Central Bank up to 15 per cent of the ordinary revenue of the government, defined to include the central government, provincial and local government bodies, government boards, government banks and enterprises owned by the government or in which the government participates. For the fiscal year 1967–68 the maximum limit of such borrowing was fixed at £S21.4 million, while the total advances from the Central Bank at the end of June 1968 amounted to £21.2 million. The revenue for the fiscal year 1968–69 for all the units in the public sector was estimated at £S171,878,116, and the maximum limit of borrowing by the government from the Central Bank was fixed at £S24.5 million, while the actual borrowing of the government during that fiscal year was £S24.3 million.

Furthermore, according to the Treasury Bill Act, 1966, the government may borrow by means of treasury bills, provided that the value of such bills outstanding at any time shall not exceed £S5 million. The bulk of treasury bills have already been bought by the commercial banks. At the close of 1968 the value of commercial banks' holdings of treasury bills amounted to £S4.85 million, and £S150,000 was held by other financial institutions in the private sector.

Since the mid-1960s the Sudan government has been finding it more and more difficult to make all its local cash payments, whether wages and salaries or payment to contractors, in time. This seems to be the result of two main factors: underestimation of expenditure and ineffective financial control of government accounts. This problem of the illiquidity of the public sector has forced the government to seek various ways to increase revenue and reduce expenditure, but it has not yet been solved.

The expenditure of the central government has been rising very fast since independence in 1956. In 1949 the total current expenditure of the central government was £S10 million; by 1969–70 it was £S142 million, an increase of more than fourteen times in a period of twenty years. Besides the rise in prices and the normal expansion in government

services, increased expenditure on education, national defence and the rise in wages and salaries of the employees of the public sector have accentuated the rate of increase of the total current expenditure in recent years. The expenditure of the Ministry of Defence increased from £S14.1 million in 1965–66 to £S30 million in 1969–70, while the expenditure of the Ministry of Education increased from £S5.8 million in 1965–66 to £S9.8 million in 1969–70. This increase is a direct result of the continued crisis in the Middle East and a strong popular demand for more education. In 1968 the government raised the wages and salaries of its employees by 5–15 per cent and thus wages and salaries amounted to 41 per cent of the expenditure of the Central Government for 1968–69.

LABOUR AND WAGES

The number of persons five years of age and over reported in the 1955–56 census, as mainly engaged in economic activity, was 3,800,000 out of a population of 10.2 million. In addition, it is estimated, on the basis of detailed tabulations of the census returns, that 1,116,000 persons, whose main activity was not economic, took part in subsidiary economic activity. So the total number engaged to any degree in economic activity is approximately 4,916,000 or 48 per cent of the population. Sudan's labour force is overwhelmingly male. Men make up 56 per cent of the total economically active population, women 24.7 per cent, boys 14.4 per cent and girls 4.9 per cent.

Of all the males and females in the labour force 86.7 per cent are primary producers, 3.3 per cent secondary producers and 10 per cent tertiary producers. All these percentages of sex and industrial distribution of the Sudan's labour force have not, it is thought, changed very much since 1955–56.

Beyond 1956 it is difficult to get any reasonably accurate data in order to assess the labour situation in Sudan. However, the number of wage-earners at present is estimated to be about one million—excluding agricultural workers. About half a million workers are engaged in the public sector and about the same number are employed by the private sector.

Until about 1965 one of the country's major problems was considered to be the shortage of skilled workers. There was heavy dependence on expatriates of Greek and Armenian descent, who filled a high proportion of skilled jobs and managerial and executive posts.

However, by 1965 the major development projects were finished. The most important factories in both private and public sectors, as well as Khashm el Girba and Roseires dams, were finished by that year. In the early 1960s institutes of technical education and training centres were established and by 1965 their graduates could meet the demand for skilled labour. The Khartoum Senior Trade School was opened in 1960 to teach electronics, commerce, electrical installation, machine shop, automobile and diesel mechanics, carpentry, cabinet making, brickwork and draughtsmanship. The Khartoum Technical Institute (Polytechnic) was opened in 1950, but the total enrolment was only 25 in 1950–51. At that time it taught only civil engineering. By 1960 the enrolment had risen to 569 and the institute syllabus included courses in civil engineering, mechanical and electrical engineering, surveying, secretarial work and commerce. An up-grading centre was established in Khartoum in 1960 by the Labour Department to improve the skills of workers already employed in both public and private sectors, and an apprenticeship centre was also established in Khartoum by the government, with German aid, in 1962. Another apprenticeship centre was established in Kosti in 1967.

In fact, after 1965, unemployment began to appear among skilled workers in the towns, and some economists and businessmen began to believe that the shortage of skilled workers was no longer a serious problem to the industrialization of Sudan. Sudan has already started to export skilled workers, clerical staff and teachers to the Arab countries.

The only available figures on unemployment come from the registrations at employment exchanges in major towns. In 1967–68 31,919 were registered as unemployed. In 1970–71 registered unemployment totalled 58,022. However, it is obvious that this figure does not represent total open unemployment in Sudan. Not all the workers register themselves when they are unemployed, particularly unskilled workers. On the other hand, some workers may register more than once, while, when other workers find a job, neither they nor their employers report to the employment exchanges. Therefore, the present figures of unemployment in Sudan should be viewed with great caution.

There is no legal minimum wage in Sudan. However, in the public sector the minimum monthly wage paid for permanent employment is £S11.8, while it is about £S6 in the private sector. The daily minimum wage ranges between 25 and 50 piastres, depending on the region and the season. During the cotton-picking season in the Gezira the daily minimum wage may rise as high as 50 piastres per day. Wages and salaries are higher in the public sector than in the private sector, with the exception of modern and large firms in the private sector, who only employ a very small percentage of the labour force engaged in the modern sector.

Although wages in the public sector are higher than wages in the private sector, they have declined in real terms over the last twenty years or so. At best, money wages increased by 40 per cent between 1951 and 1970. A wage increase was given in 1965 and 1968, but the cost of living increased by at least 70 per cent between 1951 and 1970, and therefore real wages declined by about 30 per cent in that period. Most wages in the private sector have lagged behind wages in the public sector.

PLANNING AND DEVELOPMENT

The first development plan was a ten-year plan, 1961–62 to 1970–71. Then a five-year plan 1970–71 to 1974–75 was published in 1970 and later in the year it was revised. Because of nationalization, the share of the public sector in investment increased from £S200 million to £S215 million. The private sector's share in capital investment has been fixed at £S170 million. The major targets of the plan are: to increase G.D.P. at an average rate of 7.6 per cent annually; to increase the revenue of the Government to £S953 million compared to £S516.5 million for the previous five years; to increase the share of commodity production to 65 per cent in 1974–75 as against 61.1 per cent in 1969–70; to increase industrial production by 57.4 per cent, and to increase the volume of agricultural production by 60.8 per cent.

The general aim of the plan is to promote welfare through an increase in productivity, realization of full employment and an expansion of public services. The number of projects in the plan for the public sector was 276, of which 239 projects have actually been started. In 1970–71 40 projects (17 per cent of the total planned) were completed.

In the Development Budget for 1970–71 £S18.3 million was approved for development expenditure. However, only £S13.1 million was spent in that fiscal year on economic development, so that in financial terms the plan was only implemented by about 70 per cent in its first year. Poor execution of the development plan during 1970–71 was most apparent in the Ministry of Industry (37 per cent), the Ministry of Animal Resources (41.4 per cent), and the Agricultural Development Corporation (38.7 per cent). There is no information as to the fulfilment of the plan by the private sector, but the latter has not been very active in Sudan for the last three years or so.

POWER AND TRANSPORT

The installed generating capacity of the Sudan in 1970 was 96,685 kW. thermal and 29,220 kW. hydro. The total power generated in 1969 was 310,051,000 kWh. The number of consumers is 68,529 residential and commercial, 558 agricultural and 844 industrial. All the main towns of Sudan are supplied with electricity and some of the small towns which lie near to the transmission lines, such as Kamlin, also enjoy this facility. Seventeen towns in Sudan are provided with electricity.

The volume of electricity used by industry is 118,200,000 kWh., while the volume of electricity used by agriculture for pumps is 26,200,000 kWh. The electricity consumption of industry does not include that of ginning factories, the large oil mills and Guneid and Khashm el Girba sugar factories. All these generate their own electricity from by-products. The grain silos at Gedaref and Port Sudan have their own generating sets.

Sudan depends mainly on railways for transport. Steamers and motor transport play only a secondary role. All-weather roads are very limited. The total length of asphalt main roads in Sudan is 208 miles, of which Khartoum Province has 178 miles. The length of cleared tracks covered with gravel is 3,210 miles. The length of just cleared tracks is 7,810 miles and these make up the main network of roads in Sudan. However, they are usually impassable immediately after the rains. Road bridges cross the Blue and White

Niles at four points, and four dams on the river also carry traffic.

The rail transport facilities are still far from adequate. In 1969–70 the railway network was 4,756 km. In 1970 the average density of railways for the whole country is only 1.9 km. per 1,000 sq. km. The river fleet comprises 386 low-speed old steamers of various types. River transport is mainly used between Kosti and Juba (1,435 km.) and between Dongola and Kareima (187 km.); these routes are navigable all year round. The total length of the river navigation routes is about 2,445 km., of which 1,723 km. are open all the year and the rest are seasonal. River transport between Wadi Halfa and Shellal, which lies partly on Lake Nasser, is under development at present. As far as sea transport is concerned, the government company, the Sudan Shipping Line, owns four dry cargo ships of 5,000 tons each. At present, only 5 per cent of exports and imports are carried by domestic vessels. Two additional dry cargo ships of 20,000 tons each, which are being built in Yugoslavia, were to be delivered in 1972–73.

The government-owned Sudan Airways, formed in 1947, operates internal and international services. It connects Khartoum with twenty important Sudanese towns as well as with Europe, the Middle East and Africa. In 1968–69 it carried 122,574 passengers and 1.8 million ton/km, while in 1970–71 it carried 65,116 passengers and 3.3 million ton/km.

STATISTICAL SURVEY

AREA AND POPULATION

Total Area	Arable Land	Pasture	Forest	Total Population (July 1st, 1971)
967,500 sq. miles*	71,000 sq. kilometres	240,000 sq. kilometres	914,999 sq. kilometres	16,087,000

* 2,505,813 sq. kilometres.

PROVINCES
(1971)

	Area (sq. miles)	Population		Area (sq. miles)	Population
Bahr el Ghazal	82,530	1,499,000	Khartoum	8,097	922,000
Blue Nile	54,880	3,315,000	Kordofan	146,930	2,954,000
Darfur	191,650	1,779,000	Northern	184,200	1,190,000
Equatoria	76,495	1,369,000	Upper Nile	91,190	1,346,000
Kassala	131,528	1,712,000			

PRINCIPAL TOWNS

Town	Population (1971)
Khartoum (capital)	280,431
Omdurman	273,268
El Obeid	76,420
Wadi Medani	79,364
Port Sudan	116,366
Khartoum North	138,014
Atbara	58,939

Because of the flooding of the Wadhi Halfa and adjacent areas by the Aswan High Dam, over 50,000 inhabitants have been resettled in Khashm el Girba, on the Atbara River.

TRIBAL DIVISIONS
(1956 Census)

	'000	%
Arab	3,989	39
Southerners (Nilotic, Nilo-Hamitic, Sudanic)	3,056	30
Western People	1,315	13
Nuba	573	6
Beja	646	6
Nubiyin	330	3
Miscellaneous	94	1

The remaining 2 per cent was made up of 260,000 foreigners.

Births and Deaths (1966): Registered births 143,052 (birth rate 10.1 per 1,000); registered deaths 13,416 (death rate 1.0 per 1,000). Birth registration is believed to be about 20 per cent complete and death registration 5 per cent complete. UN estimates for 1965–70 put the average annual birth rate at 48.9 per 1,000 and the death rate at 18.4 per 1,000.

Employment (1970): Total economically active population 5,016,000, including 4,007,000 engaged in agriculture (ILO and FAO estimates).

AGRICULTURE

COTTON CROP

(1 feddan = 1.038 acres = 4,201 sq. metres)

	Area (feddans)			Production (tons)		
	1968–69	1969–70	1970–71	1968–69	1969–70	1970–71
Long Staple	775,159	824,662	828,306	548,707	566,667	618,314
Medium Staple	138,917	138,041	184,953	78,361	82,234	89,675
Short Staple	240,867	295,208	200,729	28,548	33,583	18,537
Total	1,154,943	1,257,911	1,213,988	655,616	682,484	726,526

Production of lint (metric tons): 184,000 in 1968; 225,000 in 1969; and 225,000 in 1970.

OTHER CROPS
(metric tons)

	1968	1969	1970	1971
Wheat	88,000	123,000	115,000	135,000
Maize	16,000	36,000	23,000	40,000*
Millet	267,000	384,000	460,000	450,000*
Sorghum (Durra)	870,000	1,499,000	1,529,000	1,500,000*
Rice	1,000	3,000	6,000	7,000*
Sugar Cane†	969,000	939,000	780,000*	750,000*
Potatoes	25,000*	26,000*	26,000*	26,000*
Sweet Potatoes and Yams	11,000*	11,000*	12,000*	n.a.
Cassava (Manioc)	132,000	140,000	140,000	n.a.
Onions	18,000	20,000*	20,000*	n.a.
Dry Beans	4,000	6,000	6,000*	6,000*
Dry Broad Beans	13,000	11,000	12,000*	13,000*
Chick-Peas	2,000	2,000	2,000*	2,000*
Other Pulses	42,000*	43,000*	40,000*	46,000*
Oranges and Tangerines	1,000*	1,000*	1,000*	1,000*
Dates	70,000	72,000*	72,000*	n.a.
Bananas	10,000*	10,000*	10,000*	n.a.
Groundnuts (in shell)	197,000	383,000	353,000	353,000*
Cottonseed	334,000	421,000	420,000	433,000*
Sesame Seed	122,000	201,600	282,000	271,000
Castor Beans	15,000	12,000	18,000	18,000*

1968: Mangoes 15,000 tons; Guavas 4,000 tons.

* FAO estimate.   † Crop year ending in year stated.

LIVESTOCK
('000)

	1968–69	1969–70	1970–71
Cattle . . .	13,326	13,500*	13,650*
Sheep . . .	12,678	13,000*	13,200*
Goats . . .	10,036	10,050*	10,100*
Pigs . . .	6*	7*	7*
Horses . . .	20*	20*	19*
Asses . . .	610*	630*	640*
Camels . . .	2,918	3,000*	3,100*
Chickens . . .	18,200*	18,500*	18,800*

* FAO estimate.

Source: FAO, *Production Yearbook 1971.*

LIVESTOCK PRODUCTS
(FAO estimates, metric tons)

	1968	1969	1970
Cows' Milk	1,330,000	1,350,000	1,360,000
Sheep's Milk . . .	120,000	125,000	130,000
Goats' Milk . . .	425,000	440,000	450,000
Beef and Veal . . .	129,000	142,000	140,000
Mutton, Lamb and Goats' Meat . .	64,000	71,000	72,000
Poultry Meat . . .	10,000	10,000	10,000
Edible Offal . . .	40,000	43,000	43,000
Other Meat . . .	52,000	54,000	56,000
Tallow . . .	6,000	6,000	6,000
Hen Eggs . . .	16,200	16,400	16,700
Cattle Hides (salted) . .	11,760	11,840	11,760
Sheep Skins (dry) . .	2,760	3,120	3,280
Goat Skins (dry) . .	360	368	360

1971 (metric tons): Cows' Milk 1,370,000; Sheep's Milk 140,000; Goats' Milk 450,000; Hen Eggs 17,000.

Source: FAO, *Production Yearbook 1971.*

FORESTRY
ROUNDWOOD REMOVALS
(cubic metres)
Twelve months ending June 30th

1966–67	20,984,000
1967–68	20,982,000

Source: FAO, *Yearbook of Forest Products.*

TIMBER PRODUCTION

	Unit	1965–66	1966–67	1967–68	1968–69
Railway Sleepers . . .	number	90,000	86,300	86,000	112,049
Poles	,,	51,497	89,379	394,929	390,000
Bamboo Canes . . .	,,	250,890	164,661	258,368	350,000
Firewood . . .	cu. metres	78,826	82,466	105,894	107,697
Other Sawn Wood . .	,, ,,	3,500	3,700	3,434	3,502

GUM ARABIC PRODUCTION
(tons)

Season	Gum Hashab	Gum Talh	Total
1965–66 . .	47,960	2,444	50,404
1966–67 . .	42,713	2,296	45,009
1967–68 . .	58,896	2,649	61,545
1968–69 . .	40,955	4,592	45,547
1969–70* . .	30,000	4,000	34,000

* Estimates.

FISHING
(metric tons)

	1967	1968
Inland waters . . .	19,200	20,700
Sea	800	800
Total Catch .	20,000	21,500

Source: FAO, Yearbook of Fishery Statistics.

MINING
PRODUCTION

	Unit	1966	1967	1968	1969
Iron Ore*	'ooo tons	14	39	—	850
Manganese Ore* . . .	tons	2,500	1,500	5,000	850
Chromium Ore* . . .	,,	25,000	17,391	22,086	23,944
Gold	ounces	—	111	29	
Magnesite . . .	tons	4,000	4,000	7,000	1,000
Unrefined Salt . . .	'ooo tons	57	43	50	51

1971: Salt 63,000 tons.

* Figures relate to gross weight. Metal content (in metric tons) was as follows:

Iron: 20,000 in 1966; 7,000 in 1967.

Manganese: 600 in 1966; 600 in 1967; 2,000 in 1968; 340 in 1969; more than 500 in 1970.

Chromium oxide: 10,100 in 1966; 9,043 in 1967; 11,485 in 1968; 12,451 in 1969; 13,866 in 1970.

INDUSTRY
PRODUCTION

	Unit	1965–66	1966–67	1967–68	1968–69
Cement	'ooo tons	73.2	101.1	128.7	140.7
Flour of Wheat . . .	,, ,,	44.1	39.9	48.8	51.5
Sugar	,, ,,	25.0	71.1	93.3	90.8
Soap	,, ,,	18.8	18.8	18.4	18.2
Wine	'ooo litres	1,254.8	1,650.9	1,634.6	1,453.8
Beer	,, ,,	7,487.5	7,778.7	7,447.6	7,159.1
Cigarettes	'ooo kilos	535.0	647.4	660.9	532.9
Matches	billion	3.1	3.9	4.0	3.9
Shoes	million pairs	7.2	8.2	9.5	10.7
Textiles	yards	79,503.0	56,170.0	93,122.0	101,350.0
Alcohol	'ooo litres	457.0	542.1	552.6	464.0
Oil	'ooo tons	—	17.0	36.0	46.0

PETROLEUM PRODUCTS
(metric tons)

	1967	1968	1969	1970
Motor Spirit	82,000	62,000	70,000	90,000
Naphtha	34,000	12,000	25,000	26,000
Jet Fuels	57,000	70,000	} 76,000	82,000
Kerosene	19,000	53,000		
Distillate Fuel Oils	428,000	184,000	234,000	234,000
Residual Fuel Oils	233,000	195,000	224,000	239,000
Liquefied Petroleum Gas	1,000	1,000	2,000	2,000

Source: United Nations, *Statistical Yearbook 1971.*

ELECTRICITY OUTPUT

Year	Installed Capacity (kW.)	Units Generated ('000 kWh.)	Units Sold ('000 kWh.)
1967 . .	91,976	317,865	254,468
1968 . .	97,412	333,795	293,851
1969 . .	130,893	528,176	430,173
1970 . .	116,966	392,421	367,900

FINANCE

1,000 milliemes = 100 piastres = 1 Sudanese pound.

Coins: 1, 2, 5 and 10 milliemes; 2, 5 and 10 piastres.

Notes: 25 and 50 piastres; £S1, £S5 and £S10.

Exchange rates (December 1972): £1 sterling = 817.54 milliemes; U.S. $1 = 348.214 milliemes.
£S100 = 122.32 sterling = $287.18.

BUDGET ESTIMATES FOR CURRENT REVENUE AND EXPENDITURE
(£S, twelve months ending June 30th)

Revenue	1969–70	1970–71	Expenditure	1969–70	1970–71
Direct Taxation . .	17,500,000	18,870,000	Ministry of Agriculture and Forests . .	3,558,739	3,655,280
Indirect Taxation . .	63,201,000	73,636,797	Ministry of Communications and Tourism	4,239,999	4,258,324
Fees and Charges, etc. .	8,129,786	10,289,597	Ministry of Education .	9,803,319	8,667,390
Proceeds from Government Enterprises . .	42,395,227	43,542,204	Ministry of Health . .	6,585,877	7,910,532
Interest and Dividends .	1,217,037	1,169,460	Ministry of Works Works	3,826,839	2,046,554
Pension Contributions .	1,373,964	1,554,000	Mechanical Transport .	2,434,941	2,494,414
Reimbursement and Inter-Departmental Services .	7,203,271	7,208,673	Ministry of Irrigation .	3,852,513	4,037,261
Other Sources . .	1,093,435	1,745,629	Department of Stores and Equipment .	1,104,171	915,310
			Other Ministries and Departments* .	65,083,411	77,558,732
			General administration .	40,623,911	38,781,043
			Koranic Studies . .	—	91,520
			Total Expenditure	141,113,720	150,416,360
			Surplus . .	1,000,000	7,600,000
Total Revenue .	142,113,720	158,016,360		142,113,720	158,016,360

* Includes the Ministry of Defence (£S31.0 million in 1969–70, £S37.7 million in 1970–71); the Ministry of Local Government (£S16.9 million in 1969–70, £S17.9 million in 1970–71); and the Ministry of the Interior (£S7.8 million in 1969–70, £S8.7 million in 1970–71).

Five-Year Plan (1970–75): £S217.3 million capital investment by public sector.

NATIONAL ACCOUNTS
(£S'000)

	1968	1969
Wages and Salaries . .	366,460	286,948
Operating Surplus . .	125,791	186,676
Domestic Factor Income .	492,251	473,624
Wages and Salaries Paid Abroad (net) . .	−2,412	−1,500
Property and Entrepreneurial Income Paid Abroad (net) .	−3,689	−1,600
Indirect Taxes . .	59,960	88,242
Less Subsidies . .	−3,742	−9,027
National Income at Market Price . . .	542,369	550,739
Other Current Transfers to the Rest of the World (net) .	−1,616	−1,100
National Disposable Income .	540,752	549,639
National Disposable Income per capita (£S) . .	37.3	37.9

FIVE-YEAR PLAN 1970/71–74/75

The Plan has as its main objectives a sustained annual growth rate of the G.N.P. of 7.6 per cent; the raising of per capita income to £S46.6 by 1974/75; increasing agricultural output by 60.8 per cent; increasing the level of investment in education and culture by 60 per cent, in health by 82 per cent and in public utilities by 58 per cent; developing urban and rural water networks; increasing livestock production by 75.5 per cent; increasing the volume of trade by value to £S340 million.

TOTAL INVESTMENT, BY PUBLIC SECTOR BY 1974/75
(£S '000)

Agriculture	80,000
Industry and Power . . .	49,200
Transport and Communications .	29,630
Education and Culture . .	14,580
Health and Public Utilities .	21,420
Central Administration . .	6,440
Technical Assistance and Grants .	9,800
Unallocated and Others . .	3,930
TOTAL . . .	215,000

RESOURCE ALLOCATION BY YEAR
(£S million)

	1970/71	1971/72	1972/73	1973/74	1974/75	TOTAL
Internal	158.0	166.0	179.0	194.0	211.0	908.0
Foreign Loans . .	18.7	22.5	23.5	25.2	19.7	110.0
Total	176.7	188.5	202.5	219.2	230.7	1,018.0
Ordinary Expenditure . .	140.7	147.0	155.8	160.3	166.6	770.4
Capital Investment . .	36.0	41.5	44.5	48.0	45.0	215.0
Total . . .	176.7	188.5	200.3	208.3	211.6	985.4
BALANCE . . .	—	—	2.6	10.9	19.1	32.6

BALANCE OF PAYMENTS ESTIMATES
(£S million)

	1970–71	1971–72*
Receipts:		
Cotton exports . .	61.3	47.2
Other exports . .	45.3	41.7
Invisible . . .	16.4	13.8
Foreign loans . .	12.1	11.8
Other short-term capital .	18.0	10.0
	153.1	124.5
Payments:		
Government imports .	43.8	28.4
Private sector imports .	75.3	68.7
Invisible . .	27.4	23.7
Repayments of capital .	11.5	7.0
	158.0	127.8
Deficit . . .	4.9	3.3

* July to April

EXTERNAL TRADE

(£S million)

	1966	1967	1968	1969	1970	1971
Imports*	77.5	74.3	89.7	92.5	108.3	123.7
Exports†	70.7	74.6	80.8	85.6	101.6	114.5

* Excluding crude petroleum (£S4,210,000 in 1970).   † Excluding camels (£S3,410,000 in 1969).

PRINCIPAL COMMODITIES

(£S '000)

IMPORTS	1969	1970	1971
Sugar	2,715	5,143	9,247
Tea	2,210	4,955	4,004
Coffee	453	1,907	1,635
Wheat Flour	1,125	657	226
Textiles	16,561	15,119	26,462
Clothing	749	672	911
Footwear	585	127	102
Sacks and Jute	2,611	3,013	3,694
Cement	47	33	70
Fertilizers	1,397	1,658	1,937
Machinery, Apparatus, Vehicles	22,790	28,788	23,312
Tyres	1,485	1,384	1,937
Petroleum Products	8,809	9,025	8,918
Pharmaceuticals	2,200	3,387	2,760
Iron and Steel	4,594	4,612	4,794

EXPORTS	1969	1970	1971
Animals	2,332	2,317	1,959
Cotton, Ginned	49,498	65,052	69,424
Cotton Seed	1,489	1,728	1,422
Cotton Seed Oil	920	771	4,501
Durra	43	60	1,136
Groundnuts	5,991	5,466	9,324
Gum Arabic	8,699	8,969	8,425
Oilseed Cake	3,879	n.a.	n.a.
Sesame	8,017	5,087	7,996
Hides and Skins	1,803	1,590	1,806

COTTON EXPORTS BY COUNTRIES

(tons)

	1969	1970	1971
German Federal Republic	21,034	15,769	13,328
India	29,913	30,462	37,001
Italy	28,596	28,509	13,620
Japan	15,663	15,900	11,260
United Kingdom	15,038	14,670	10,581
People's Republic of China	13,735	17,821	35,221
United States	935	2,388	2,549
U.S.S.R.	8,319	57,564	39,158
Romania	6,126	2,221	7,437
France	2,925	7,006	4,834
Netherlands	859	1,006	328
Hungary	3,124	4,981	4,983
Poland	4,839	4,999	6,593
TOTAL (all countries)	172,425	203,296	206,903

PRINCIPAL COUNTRIES
(£S '000)

	IMPORTS				EXPORTS			
	1968	1969	1970	1971	1968	1969	1970	1971
Belgium	1,830	2,094	2,076	2,046	2,206	1,957	1,996	2,046
China, People's Republic .	5,993	4,876	4,030	8,073	4,838	6,430	6,000	11,026
France	3,325	3,351	1,716	4,060	2,061	1,307	2,223	3,390
German Federal Republic .	4,647	5,771	7,802	6,662	12,256	10,142	9,855	8,236
India	9,342	9,063	14,226	21,126	7,946	10,133	14,226	12,425
Italy	4,990	4,327	2,430	2,334	9,713	10,777	10,190	9,436
Japan	8,113	7,153	5,629	4,737	6,652	8,010	9,250	8,191
Netherlands . . .	2,346	3,512	2,892	3,264	4,276	3,359	3,319	3,900
Poland	1,498	1,789	1,916	2,052	1,786	1,544	1,660	2,039
U.S.S.R. . . .	6,223	4,486	8,328	8,885	4,818	3,389	17,242	17,648
Egypt	3,516	3,848	5,323	6,390	2,402	3,914	4,981	6,358
United Kingdom . .	15,831	16,944	17,929	14,599	4,800	5,762	5,834	5,153
U.S.A.	1,945	2,605	2,822	2,883	2,760	3,010	4,026	4,301
Yugoslavia . . .	639	770	1,140	2,223	831	989	986	1,005
Others	19,471	21,887	30,774	34,377	13,489	14,901	9,827	28,736
TOTAL . .	**89,709**	**92,476**	**108,338**	**123,661**	**80,834**	**85,624**	**101,609**	**114,454**

TRANSPORT

RAILWAYS
(1968–69)

Number of Passengers ('000) .	3,548
Freight ('000 tons) . .	2,669

ROADS
(1969)

Passenger Vehicles . . .	29,094
Goods Vehicles . . .	21,413
Motor Cycles . . .	1,973

SHIPPING

	1966	1967	1968	1969	1970
Number of Ships calling at Port Sudan	1,223	1,004	845	770	760
Total Inward Tonnage . .	1,427,743	1,528,183	1,594,019	1,582,369	1,845,215
Total Outward Tonnage . .	941,317	866,948	952,449	950,975	1,014,757

CIVIL AVIATION
(Sudan Airways—International Traffic)

	1965	1966	1967	1968	1969
Number of Passengers . .	45,793	50,673	31,367	36,975	65,293
Freight (kg.) . . .	492,871.2	402,227.8	501,231.5	344,338	837,966

EDUCATION
(1969)

	TEACHERS	STUDENTS		
		BOYS	GIRLS	TOTAL
Pre-Primary	266	7,927	7,958	15,885
Primary	12,370	410,023	200,775	610,798
Secondary: General . . .	9,030	126,617	45,869	172,486
Vocational . . .	151	1,181	—	1,181
Teacher-Training . .	156	1,439	852	2,291
Tertiary	1,107	10,304	1,387	11,691

Source: United Nations, *Statistical Yearbook 1971.*

Source: Department of Statistics, H.Q. Council of Ministers, Khartoum, except where otherwise stated.

THE CONSTITUTION

In December 1955 a Transitional Constitution was adopted, under which the highest authority was vested in a Supreme Commission of five members, who were responsible for appointing the Prime Minister and his Cabinet from amongst the members of Parliament.

This Transitional Constitution was suspended following the military *coup d'état* of 1958, but the provisional Government which took office after the overthrow of the military regime in October 1964, announced its intention of governing under the terms of the 1955 Constitution.

The Constituent Assembly, whose term had been extended in 1968, was abolished by the new regime in May 1969.

A Provisional Constitution was introduced by the Revolutionary Command Council in August 1971. A People's Assembly. including various categories of the people's working forces, has been called to draft and ratify a permanent constitution. It had not been finalized by

January 1973. The provisional Constitution states that the President of the Sudanese Democratic Republic will be elected for a maximum term of six years and will be Supreme Commander of the Armed Forces. He is empowered to appoint two or more Deputies.

Under the Regional Constitution for the Southern Sudan, the three southern provinces form a single region, with its own regional executive in Juba headed by a president who is also a Vice-President of the whole Republic. The regional executive will be responsible for all matters outside national defence, external affairs, communications, currency and foreign trade regulation. The regional President will be appointed by and responsible to a regional People's Assembly, although, pending the election of such an assembly, he was initially appointed by Pres. Nemery after consulting representative southern Sudanese. The Constitution can be amended only by a four-fifths majority of the central People's Assembly, where southerners will be proportionally represented.

THE GOVERNMENT

President: Maj.-Gen. JAAFIR AL NEMERY (*elected October* 1971).

First Vice-President: Maj.-Gen. MUHAMMAD AL-BAQIR AHMAD.

Vice-President and President of the High Executive Council for the Southern Region: ABEL ALIER.

COUNCIL OF MINISTERS
(*January* 1973)

Prime Minister and Minister of Defence: Maj.-Gen. JAAFIR AL NEMERY.

Minister of Foreign Affairs: MANSOUR KHALID.

Minister of Interior: Maj.-Gen. MUHAMMAD AL-BAQIR AHMAD.

Minister of Justice: AHMAD SULAIMAN.

Minister of Planning: Dr. LAWRENCE WOLWOL.

Minister of Public Service and Administrative Reform: ABDUL RAHMAN ABDULLAH.

Minister of Local Government: Dr. JAAFIR MUHAMMAD ALI BAKHIT.

Minister of Housing and Public Utilities: MUBAREK SINADAH.

Minister of Health: Maj. ABU AL-QASIM MUHAMMAD IBRAHIM.

Minister of Communications: BASHIR ABBADI.

Minister of the Treasury: IBRAHIM ELIAS.

Minister of National Economy: IBRAHIM MONEIM MANSOUR.

Minister of Industry: MOUSSA AWAD BALLAL.

Minister of Transport: AHMED EL AMIN HUMMEIDA.

Minister of Agriculture: WADI HABASHI.

Minister of Natural Resources: ABDALLAM EL HASSAN.

Minister of Irrigation and Hydroelectric Power: YAHYA ABDUL-MAJID.

Minister of Education: Dr. MOHAMMED KHER OSMAN.

Minister of Information and Culture: OMAR AL-HAJJ MOUSA.

Minister of Youth, Sport and Social Affairs: Col. SALAH ABDEL AAL.

Minister of Religious Affairs and Waqfs: AWN AL-SHARIF QASIM.

Minister of Higher Education and Scientific Research EL KHITM EL KHALIFA.

Minister of State for Presidential Affairs: MAHDI MUSTAFA AL-HADI.

Minister of State for Council of Ministers Affairs: Dr. BAHA IDRIS.

Minister of State for Local Affairs: SAMUEL LOBAI.

HIGH EXECUTIVE COUNCIL FOR THE SOUTHERN REGION

There are eleven Regional Ministers.

President: ABEL ALIER.

Secretary-General: CLETO HASSAN.

EMBASSIES ACCREDITED TO SUDAN

(In Khartoum unless otherwise stated)

Algeria: Junction Mek Nimr St. and 67th St., P.O.B. 80; *Ambassador:* ABDEL AZIZ BEN HUSAIN.

Austria: Cairo, Egypt.

Belgium: St. 3, New Extension, P.O.B. 969; *Chargé d'Affaires a.i.:* GUY EID.

Bulgaria: El Mek Nimr St. South 7, P.O.B. 1690; *Chargé d'Affaires a.i.:* NIKOLA NIKOLOV.

Central African Republic: Africa Rd., P.O.B. 1723; *Ambassador:* GILBERT BANDIO.

Chad: St. 47, New Extension; *Ambassador:* EL HADJ ABDERAHMAN MOUSSA.

China, People's Republic: 69 31st St., P.O.B. 1425; *Ambassador:* YANG SHOU-CHENG.

Czechoslovakia: 1, 5GE, Khartoum Central, P.O.B. 1047; *Ambassador:* MIROSLAV NOVOTNÝ.

Egypt: Mogram St.; *Ambassador:* MOHAMMED EL TABIE MOHAMMED.

Ethiopia: 6, 11A St. 3, New Extension, P.O.B. 844; *Ambassador:* DAWIT ABDOU.

France: 6H East Plot 2, 19th St., P.O.B. 377; *Ambassador:* HENRI COSTILHES.

Germany, Democratic Republic: P4(3)B2, Khartoum West, P.O.B. 1089; *Ambassador:* KURT BOETTGER.

Germany, Federal Republic: 53 Abdel Rahman El Mahdi St., P.O.B. 970; *Ambassador:* MICHAEL JOVY.

Greece: Block 74, 31st St., P.O.B. 1182; *Ambassador:* NICOLAS KARANDREAS.

Hungary: Block 11, Plot 12, 13th St., New Extension, P.O.B. 1033; *Ambassador:* LAJOS BENCEKOVITS.

India: El Mek Nimr St., P.O.B. 707; *Chargé d'Affaires:* N. K. GHOSE.

Iraq: St. 5, New Extension; *Ambassador:* (vacant).

Italy: 39th St., P.O.B. 793; *Ambassador:* CARLO DE FRANCHIS.

Japan: 14-16, Block 5HE, P.O.B. 1649; *Chargé d'Affaires a.i.:* SHIGERU NOMOTO.

Jordan: 25 7th St., New Extension; *Chargé d'Affaires:* ADLI EL NASIR.

Korea, Democratic Republic: 2-10 BE, 7th St., New Extension, P.O.B. 332; *Ambassador:* KIM DOK SU.

Kuwait: 9th St., New Extension; *Ambassador:* JASIM MOHAMMED BORSULY.

Lebanon: 60 St. 49; *Ambassador:* BULIND BEYDOUN.

Libya: Africa Rd. 50, P.O.B. 2091; *Ambassador:* YOUNIS ABU AGEILA EL OMRANI.

Netherlands: P.O.B. 391; *Chargé d'Affaires a.i.:* J. W. BERTENS.

Niger: St. 1, New Extension, P.O.B. 1283; *Ambassador:* EL HAG OMAROU ADAMOU.

Nigeria: P.O.B. 1538; *Ambassador:* EL HAJI NUHU MOHAMMED.

Pakistan: 29, 9AE, St. 3, New Extension, P.O.B. 1178; *Ambassador:* S. A. H. AHSANI.

Poland: 73 Africa Rd., P.O.B. 902; *Chargé d'Affaires:* JAN KLIOSZEWSKI.

Qatar: St. 15, New Extension; *Ambassador:* ALI ABDUL RAHMAN MUFTAH.

Romania: St. 47, Plot 67, P.O.B. 1652; *Ambassador:* (vacant).

Saudi Arabia: Central St., New Extension, P.O.B. 852; *Ambassador:* ABDALLAH EL MALHOUG.

Somalia: Central St., New Extension; *Ambassador:* ABDULLAHI FARAH ALI.

Spain: 52 39th St., P.O.B. 2621; *Chargé d'Affaires a.i.:* JULAIN AYESTA.

Switzerland: Cairo, Egypt.

Syria: 3rd St., New Extension; *Ambassador:* CHTEIOUI MAHMOUD SEIFO.

Tanzania: Cairo, Egypt.

Turkey: 71 Africa Rd., P.O.B. 771; *Ambassador:* BESIR BALCIOGLU.

Uganda: Cairo, Egypt.

United Arab Emirates: St. 3, New Extension; *Ambassador:* MOHAMMED ALI EL SHURAFA.

United Kingdom: New Abulela Bldg., P.O.B. 801; *Ambassador:* R. G. A. ETHERINGTON-SMITH.

U.S.S.R.: B1, A10 St., New Extension, P.O.B. 1161; *Chargé d'Affaires a.i.:* BORIS SAVOSTIANOV.

U.S.A.: Gumhouria Ave.; *Ambassador:* CLEO NOEL, Jr.

Vatican: El Safeh City, Shambat, P.O.B. 623; *Apostolic Pro-Nuncio:* UBALDO CALABRESI.

Yemen Arab Republic: St. 35, New Extension; *Ambassador:* MOHAMMED ABDUL WASSE.

Yemen, People's Democratic Republic: Cairo, Egypt.

Yugoslavia: St. 31, 79-A, Khartoum 1, P.O.B. 1180; *Ambassador:* LJUBOMIR DRNDIĆ.

Zaire: Gumhouia Ave.; *Ambassador:* MATONDA SAKALA.

Sudan also has diplomatic relations with Afghanistan, Argentine, Brazil, Cameroon, Canada, Chile, Cyprus, Denmark, Finland, Guinea, Indonesia, Malaya, Mali, Mauritania, Norway, Sri Lanka, Senegal, Sweden, Democratic Republic of Viet-Nam, and Zambia.

PEOPLE'S ASSEMBLY

Under the Provisional Constitution of August 1971 a People's Assembly was called to draw up a permanent constitution.

Speaker: Dr. EL NAZEER DAFA'ALLA.

Secretary-General: MOHAMMED AHMED SULIMAN.

The Regional Constitution for the Southern Sudan envisages a regional People's Assembly for the south.

POLITICAL PARTY

Sudanese Socialist Union: Khartoum; f. 1971; inaugural conference held Jan. 1972; Sudan's only recognized political party; consists of National Conference, Central Committee, Political Bureau and Secretariat-General.

Political Bureau: Maj.-Gen. JAAFIR AL NEMERY,* Maj.-Gen. MOHAMMED EL BAGHIR AHMED,* ABEL ALIER, Maj. ABUL GASIM MOHAMMED IBRAHIM,* Dr. GAAFER MOHAMMED ALI BAKHEIT,* Dr. MANSOUR KHALID,* PETER GATKOUTH,* AHMED

ABDEL HALIM,* MAHDI MUSTAFA EL HADI,* LUEGI ADOK, TOBI MADOT, HILLERI LOGALI, Dr. LAWRENCE WOL, JOSEPH ODUHO, OMER EL HAG MUSA,* IBRAHIM MONIEM MANSOUR,* SALAH ABDEL AAL MABROUK,* NIFISA AHMED EL AMIN,* EL RASHEED EL TAHER,* IZZEDIN EL SAYED,* ABDULLA EL HASSAN, WADIE HABASHI, ABDEL RAHMAN ABDALLA,* BADR EDDIN SULIMAN,* MUBARAK SINADA.*

* Member also of the Secretariat-General.

DEFENCE

Defence Budget (1971–72): £S50,050,000.

Military Service: at present voluntary, but proposals for compulsory service have been made.

Total Armed Forces: 36,300: army 35,000; navy 600; air force 7,000.

Paramilitary Forces: 3,000 (1,000 Gendarmerie, 2,000 Frontier Police).

JUDICIAL SYSTEM

The administration of justice is the function of the Judiciary, as a separate and independent department of state. The general administrative supervision and control of the Judiciary is vested in the Chief Justice.

Civil Justice: is administered by the Courts constituted under the Civil Justice Ordinance, namely the High Court of Justice—consisting of the Court of Appeal and Judges of the High Court, sitting as Courts of original jurisdiction —and Provincial Courts—consisting of the Courts of Province and District Judges.

Criminal Justice: is administered by the Courts constituted under the Code of Criminal Procedure, namely Major Courts, Minor Courts and Magistrates' Courts. Serious crimes are tried by Major Courts which are composed of a President and two members and have power to pass the death sentence. Major Courts are as a rule presided over by a Judge of the High Court appointed to a Provincial Circuit, or a Province Judge. There is a right of appeal to the Chief Justice against any decision or order of a Major Court and all findings and sentences of a Major Court are subject to confirmation by him.

Lesser crimes are tried by Minor Courts consisting of three Magistrates and presided over by a Second Class Magistrate and by Magistrates' Courts consisting of a single Magistrate, or a bench of lay Magistrates.

Local Courts: try a substantial portion of the Criminal and Civil cases in the Sudan and work in parallel to some extent with the State Courts.

Chief Justice: UTHMAN AS SAYID.

MUHAMMADAN LAW COURTS

Justice in personal matters for the Muslim population is administered by the Muhammadan Law Courts, which form the Sharia Division of the Judiciary. These Courts consist of the Court of Appeal, High Courts and Qadis' Courts, and President of the Sharia Division is the Grand Qadi. The religious Law of Islam is administered by these Courts in matters of inheritance, marriage, divorce, family relationships and charitable trusts.

Grand Qadi: Sheikh YAHYA ABDEL GASIM.

RELIGION

The majority of Sudanese are vigorous followers of Islam—it will be remembered that the Mahdi of 1896 was a religious leader—but some communities in the south remain untouched by Islam and practise animism or fertility worship. The cultural contrast between the Muhammadan north and centre, and the non-Muslim south, with differences in race, language, religion and outlook, gives rise to one principal political problem of the Sudan. It is estimated that there are more than 9 million Muslims and over 400,000 catholics.

MUSLIM COMMUNITY
(Mainly divided into the following sects:)

Qadria: Heads of important local sub-sections include:
Sheikh AHMED EL GAALI
Sheikh IBRAHIM EL KABASHI.
YOUSIF EL SHEIKH OMER EL OBEID.
KHALIFA BARAKAT EL SHEIKH.
Sheikh HAMAD EL NIL ABD EL BAGI.
Sheikh ABD EL BAGI EL MUKASHFI.

Shadhlia: Heads of local sub-sections include:
Sheikh EL MAGDOUB EL BESHIR.
Sheikh GAMAR EL DAWLA EL MAGDOUB.

Idrisia: Heads of local sub-sections include:
Sheikh EL HASSAN EL IDRISI.

Khatmiya: MUHAMMAD OSMAN EL MIRGHANI.

Sammania: Sheikh FATEH GHARIBALLA.

Ismaila: Sayed JAYAL ASFIA EL SAYED EL MEKKI.

Ansari: Sayed EL-HADI AHMED EL MAHDI.

CHRISTIAN COMMUNITIES

Coptic Orthodox Church: Bishop of Nubia, Atbara and Omdurman: Rt. Rev. BAKHOMIOS.
Bishop of Khartoum, S. Sudan and Uganda: Rt. Rev. ANBA YOUANNIS.

Greek Orthodox Church: Metropolitan of Nubia: Archbishop SINESSIOS.

Greek Evangelical Church.

Evangelical Church: Rev. RADI ELIAS.

Episcopal Church in the Sudan: Clergy House, P.O.B. 135, Khartoum; Bishop in the Sudan: The Rt. Rev. OLIVER C. ALLISON; Asst. Bishops: The Rt. Rev. YEREMAYA DOTIRO; The Rt. Rev. ELINANA NGALAMU, The Rt. Rev. BUTRUS SHUKAI, The Rt. Rev. BENJAMINA YUGUSUK.

Catholic Church:

Roman Rite:

Vicariate Apostolic of Khartoum: P.O.B. 49, Khartoum; Rt. Rev. Bishop AUGUSTINE BARONI.

Vicariate Apostolic of Wau: P.O.B. 29, Wau; Rt. Rev. Bishop IRENEUS DUD.

Vicariate Apostolic of Juba: P.O.B. 32, Juba; Rt. Rev. Mgr. SILVESTRO LAHARAYA, Apostolic Administrator.

Vicariate Apostolic of El Obeid: P.O.B. 386, El Obeid, Rt. Rev. Mgr. FRANCO CAZZANIGA, Apostolic Administrator.

Prefecture Apostolic of Malakal: P.O.B. 27, Malakal; Rt. Rev. Mgr. PIUS YUKWAN.

Maronite Church: P.O.B. 244, Khartoum; Rev. Fr. YOUSEPH NEAMA.

Greek Catholic Church: P.O.B. 766, Khartoum; Archimandrite: BASILIOS HAGGAR.

Jewish Community: Chief Rabbi: (vacant).

THE PRESS

The Press was nationalized on August 27th, 1970. A General Corporation for Press, Printing and Publications was set up with two publishing houses, the Al-Ayam (P.O.B. 363, Khartoum), and the Al-Rai Al-Amm (P.O.B. 424, Khartoum). These two houses publish all the following newspapers and magazines with the exception of those produced by other ministries.

DAILIES

Al-Ayam: P.O.B. 363, Khartoum; Arabic.

Al-Sahafa: P.O.B. 424, Khartoum; f. 1961; Arabic.

Sudan Standard: P.O.B. 424, Khartoum; English.

PERIODICALS

Huna Omdurman: f. 1942; Arabic; weekly; Sudan Broadcasting Service Magazine; published by Ministry of Communications.

Khartoum: P.O.B. 424, Khartoum; Arabic; monthly.

Nile Mirror: English; weekly; published by High Executive Council for the Southern Region.

El Rai El Amm: P.O.B. 424, Khartoum; Arabic; weekly.

Sudan Cotton Bulletin: P.O.B. 1672, Khartoum; English; approx. quarterly; published by State Cotton Marketing Corporation.

El Sudan El Gadid: P.O.B. 363, Khartoum; Arabic; weekly.

Sudanese Economist: Khartoum; English; monthly; economic and commercial review.

NEWS AGENCIES

Sudan National News Agency: P.O.B. 624, Khartoum; f. 1971; daily and weekly summaries in English and Arabic; Man. ABDUL KARIM OSMAN EL MAHDI.

FOREIGN BUREAUX

Middle East News Agency: Dalala Bldg., P.O.B. 740, Khartoum.

Tass also has a bureau in Khartoum.

PUBLISHERS

African Printing House: Press House, P.O.B. 1228, Khartoum; f. 1960; publishers of *al-Sahafa*; also African News Service; Gen. Man. ABDUL RAHMAN MUKHTAR.

Ahmed Abdel Rahman El Tikeina: P.O. Box 299, Port Sudan.

Al Avam Press Co. Ltd.: Aboul Ela Building, United Nations Square, P.O. Box 363, Khartoum; f. 1953; Man. Dir. BESHIR MUHAMMAD SAID; newspapers, pamphlets and books.

Al Salam Co. Ltd.: P.O.B. 197, Khartoum.

Central Office of Information: Khartoum; government publishing office; publications include the *Sudan Almanac*.

Claudios S. Fellas: P.O. Box 641, Khartoum.

Fuad Rashed: Wadi Halfa.

Khartoum University Press: P.O.B. 321, Khartoum; f. 1967; scholarly works; Dir. MOHD. IBRAHIM SHOUSH, PH.D.

McCorquodale and Co. (Sudan) Ltd.: P.O. Box 38, Khartoum.

Mitchell Cotts and Co. (ME) Ltd.: P.O. Box 221, Khartoum.

RADIO AND TELEVISION

Sudan Broadcasting Service: P.O.B. 572, Omdurman; a government-controlled radio station which broadcasts daily in Arabic and English; Dir. A. RAHMAN.

There are 200,000 radio receivers.

Sudan Television Service (STS): P.O.B. 1094, Omdurman; f. 1962; thirty-five hours of programmes per week; Dir.-Gen. ALI M. SHUMMO.

There are 50,000 television receivers.

FINANCE

BANKING

(cap. = capital; p.u. = paid up; dep. = deposits; m. = million)

Under the Nationalization of Banks Act 1970, all banks have been nationalized.

CENTRAL BANK

Bank of Sudan: P.O. Box 313, Khartoum; f. 1960; acts as banker and financial adviser to the Government and has sole right of issue of Sudanese banknotes; cap. p.u. £S1.5m.; Chair. AWAS ABDEL MAGEID; Deputies EL FAKI MUSTAFA, EL BAGHIR YOUSIF MUDAWI; 7 brs; publ. *Economic and Financial Bulletin* (quarterly), *Foreign Trade Statistical Digest* (quarterly), *Annual Report*.

COMMERCIAL BANKS

El Nilein Bank: P.O.B. 466, Khartoum; f. 1965 as a partnership between the Bank of Sudan and the Crédit Lyonnais; 4 branches Chair. Dr. BASHIR EL BAKRI.

Juba Commercial Bank: P.O.B. 1186, Khartoum; formerly the Commercial Bank of Ethiopia; especially concerned with the non-Muslim south and with trading relations with African countries; 2 brs.; Gen. Man. AZIZ MUSTAFA ABU EISA.

Omdurman National Bank: Khartoum; formerly the Ottoman (National and Grindlays) Bank; 10 brs; Chair. a.i. and Gen. Man. ZAKARIA MOHAMED ABDO.

People's Bank: P.O.B. 922, Khartoum; formerly the Misr Bank; 6 brs.

Red Sea Commercial Bank: Khartoum; formerly the Arab Bank; 3 brs.

State Bank for Foreign Trade: P.O.B. 1008, Khartoum; formerly Barclays Bank D.C.O.; 22 brs.

Sudan Commercial Bank: P.O.B. 1116, Khartoum; f. 1960; cap. p.u. £S1,099,611; dep. £S8,280,000; Chair. and Gen. Man. EL SHEIKH HASSAN BELAIL; 6 brs.

DEVELOPMENT BANKS

Agricultural Bank of Sudan: P.O. Box 1363, Khartoum; f. 1957; cap. £S 7m.; provides agricultural credit; Chair. and Man. Dir. SALIH MOHAMMED SALIH.

Estate Bank of Sudan: Khartoum.

Industrial Bank of Sudan: P.O.B. 1722, Khartoum; f. 1962; cap. £S 2m.

INSURANCE COMPANIES

There are over forty foreign insurance companies operating in the Sudan.

TRADE AND INDUSTRY

Sudan Gezira Board: H.Q. Barakat; Sales Office, P.O.B. 884, Khartoum; Chair. and Man. Dir. Dr. KAMAL AGABAWI; Deputy Man. Dir. MAHMOUD MOHD. ALI; Financial Controller ABDALLA IMAM; Agricultural Man. HASSAN ABDALLA HASHIM; Sales Man. BESHIR MEDANI; Sec. YOUSIF EL KARIB.

The Sudan Gezira Board is responsible for Sudan's main cotton producing area. Starting in 1911 as a company enterprise, it was nationalized in 1950 and has since then been run by a Board of Directors, consisting of 8 to 11 members. In 1969 the Revolutionary Government formed a temporary Board of Directors consisting of six officials and a tenant farmers' representative pending an extensive reorganization of the Board.

The Gezira Scheme represents a partnership between the Government, the tenants and the Board. The Government, which provides the land and is responsible for irrigation, receives 36 per cent of the net proceeds; the tenants (who numbered about 100,000 in 1971 and who do the actual cultivation) receive 49 per cent. The Board receives 10 per cent, the local Government Councils in the Scheme area 2 per cent and the Social Development Fund, set up to provide social services for the inhabitants, 3 per cent.

The total possible cultivable area of the Gezira Scheme is over 5 million acres and the total area under systematic irrigation is now almost 2 million acres. In addition to cotton, groundnuts, sorghum, wheat and millet are grown for the benefit of tenant farmers.

Publications: *Annual Report, Annual Statement of Accounts, El Gezira News Paper* (weekly), *Weekly Bulletin*.

State Cotton Marketing Corpn.: P.O.B. 1672, Khartoum, Sudan; f. June 1970; following the nationalization of all cotton exporting firms in 1970, the Corporation now supervises all cotton marketing operations through the following four main cotton companies:

Port Sudan Cotton and Trade Co. Ltd.: P.O.B. 277, Khartoum.

National Cotton and Trade Co. Ltd.: P.O.B. 1552, Khartoum.

Sudan Cotton Trade Co. Ltd.: P.O.B. 2284, Khartoum.

Alaktan Trading Co. (Sudan) Ltd.: P.O.B. 2539, Khartoum.

Offices Abroad:

Sudan Cotton Centre, 3 rue de Marche, 1204 Geneva, Switzerland.

Sudan Cotton Centre, P.O.B. 152, Osaka, Japan.

The Food Industries Corporation: P.O.B. 2341, Khartoum; produces dehydrated onion and pepper, dried vegetables, gum arabic, etc; dates, canned fruit and vegetables; wheat bran and sweets.

CHAMBER OF COMMERCE

Sudan Chamber of Commerce: P.O.B. 81, Khartoum; f. 1908; Pres. ABDEL SALAM ABOUL ELA; Hon. Treas. TH. APOSTOLOU; Hon. Sec. SAYED SALEH OSMAN SALEH.

TRADE UNIONS

FEDERATIONS

Federation of Sudanese Workers' Unions (F.S.W.U.): P.O.B. 2258, Khartoum; f. 1963; includes 135 affiliates totalling 450,000 mems.; affiliated to the International Confederation of Trade Union Federations and the All-African Trade Union Federation; Pres. AWADALLA IBRAHIM; Sec.-Gen. (vacant); publs. *Al Talia* (Arabic, weekly), *Bulletin* (English and Arabic, monthly).

Federation of Workers' Trade Unions of the Private Sector Khartoum; f. 1965; Pres. SALIH ABDEL RAHMAN.

Federation of Workers' Trade Unions of the Public Sector: Khartoum; f. 1965.

PRINCIPAL UNIONS

In 1958 all Trade Unions were dissolved, but legislation in 1961 permitted registration of Trade Unions satisfying certain conditions. The larger ones are:

Central Electricity and Water Administration Trade Union: P.O.B. 1380, Khartoum; 3,000 mems.; Pres. ALI SAID; Sec.-Gen. MAHJUB SID AHMAD.

Department of Agriculture Trade Union: Khartoum Worker's Club, Khartoum; 1,170 mems.; Pres. ABDAL-KARIM SADALLAH; Sec.-Gen. ABDULLAM IBRAHIM.

Egyptian Irrigation Department Trade Union: Khartoum; 1,210 mems.; Pres. FADL ABD-AL-WAHAB; Sec.-Gen. MUHAMMAD AL SAIYID MUHAMMAD.

Forestry Department Trade Union: c/o Forests Department, Al Suke; f. 1961; 2,510 mems.; Pres. IMAN UMAR; Sec.-Gen. MUHAMMED IBRAHIM AHMED.

Gezira Board Non-Agricultural Workers' Union: c/o Gezira Board, Wad Medani; f. 1961; 6,600 mems.; Pres. SULAYMAN ABD-AL-FARAJ; Sec.-Gen. MIRGHANI ABD-AL-RAHIM.

Khartoum Municipality Trade Union: c/o Khartoum Municipal Council, P.O. Box 750, Khartoum; 891 mems.; Pres. MUHAMMAD ABDULLAH AHMAD; Sec.-Gen. UTHMAN MUHAMMAD AL SHAIKH.

Khartoum University Trade Union: Khartoum University, P.O.B. 321, Khartoum; f. 1947; 1,400 mems; Pres. MAHJUB AHMAD AL-ZUBAYR.

Mechanical Transport Department Trade Union: Khartoum Workers' Club, Khartoum, P.O.B. 617; 2,593 mems.; Pres. MADARRI MUHAMMAD AYD; Sec.-Gen. IBRAHIM BABALLAH.

Ministry of Education Trade Union: Khartoum Workers' Club, Khartoum; 679 mems.; Pres. MUHAMMAD HAMDAN; Sec.-Gen. UTHMAN AL-SIDDIQ.

Ministry of Health Trade Union: c/o Khartoum Hospital, Khartoum; 3,592 mems.; Pres. ABDAL RAZIQ UBAYD; Sec.-Gen. IBRAHIM UMAR ALHAJ.

Ministry of Irrigation and Hydro-Electric Power Trade Union: Medani Workers' Club, Wad Medani; 15,815 mems.; Pres. YAHYA HASAN AL-RAU.

Ministry of Public Utilities Trade Union: Khartoum Workers' Club, Khartoum; 607 mems.; Pres. AWADALLAH IBRAHIM; Sec.-Gen. HASSAN ABDEL GADIR.

Posts and Telegraphs Trade Union: Khartoum Workers' Club; 700 mems.; Pres. ABD-AL-MONEIM AHMAD; Sec.-Gen. FADL AHMAD FADL.

Sudan Textile Industry Employees Trade Union: Khartoum North; f. 1968; 3,750 mems.; Sec. MUKHTAR ABDALLA.

Sudan Railway Workers' Union (S.R.W.U.): Sudan Railway Workers' Union Club, Atbara; f. 1961; 28,000 mems.; Pres. MUSA AHMED MUTTAI; Sec. MUHAMMAD OSMAN ALI EL MUDIR.

CO-OPERATIVE SOCIETIES

There are some 600 Co-operative Societies in the Sudan, of which 570 are formally registered. Of these 206 are Consumers' Societies, 152 are Agricultural Co-operative Societies, 41 General Purpose, 107 Marketing and Credit, 15 Flour Mill and 49 other types.

MAJOR INDUSTRIAL COMPANIES

The following are a few of the larger companies either in terms of capital investment or employment.

Aboulela Cotton Ginning Co. Ltd.: P.O.B. 121, Khartoum; cotton mills.

AGIP (Sudan) Ltd.: P.O.B. 1155, Khartoum; f. 1959; cap. £S808,000.
Distribution of petroleum products.
Pres. MASSIMO DEL BO; Gen. Man. LUIGI VELANI; 121 employees.

Bata Nationalized Corporation: P.O.B. 88, Khartoum; f. 1950; cap. £S1m.
Manufacturers and distributors of footwear.
Man. Dirs. BABIKER MOHD. ALI, HILARI LOGALI, ANTOUN KRONFLI; 1,300 employees.

The Blue Nile Brewery: P.O.B. 1408, Khartoum; f. 1954; cap. £S734,150.
Brewing, bottling and distribution of beer.
Man. Dirs. IBRAHIM ELYAS, HUSSEIN MOHAMED KEMAL, OMER EL ZEIN SAGAYROUN; 336 employees.

The Central Desert Mining Co. Ltd.: P.O.B. 20, Port Sudan; f. 1946; cap. £S150,000.
Prospecting for and mining of gold, manganese and iron ore.
Dirs. ABDELHADI AHMED BASSHER, ABU-BAKR SAID BAASHER; 274 employees.

Sudan Tobacco Co. Ltd.: P.O.B. 87, Khartoum; production of tobacco products.

TRANSPORT AND TOURISM

TRANSPORT

RAILWAYS

Sudan Railways: Atbara; Gen. Man. ABDEL MONEIM ABBAS.

The total length of railway in operation is about 4,756 route-kilometres. The main line runs from Wadi Halfa, on the Egyptian border to El Obeid, via Khartoum. Lines from Atbara and Sennar connect with Port Sudan on the coast. Since independence two new lines have been built, one from Sennar to Roseires on the Blue Nile (225 km.), opened in 1954, and one from Aradeiba to Nyala, in the south-western province of Darfur (689 km.), opened in 1959. A railway branching from this line, at Babanousa, to Wau in Bahr el Ghazal province (445 km.) has now been completed.

ROADS

Ministry of Communications: P.O.B. 300, Khartoum; Dir. of Works IBRAHIM MOHD. IBRAHIM.

Roads in the Northern Sudan, other than town roads, are only cleared tracks and often impassable immediately after rain. Motor traffic on roads in the Upper Nile Province is limited to the drier months of January–May. There are several good gravelled roads in the Equatoria and Bahr-el-Ghazal Provinces which are passable all the year round, but in these districts some of the minor roads become impassable after rain.

The through route from Juba to Khartoum is open from mid-November to mid-April.

Over 30,000 miles of tracks are classed as "motorable", but only 208 miles are asphalt.

INLAND WATERWAYS

Ministry of Communications: P.O.B. 300, Khartoum.

The total length of navigable waterways served by passenger and freight services is 4,068 km. From the Egyptian border to Wadi Halfa and Khartoum navigation is limited by cataracts to short stretches but the White Nile from Khartoum to Juba is navigable at almost all seasons. The Blue Nile is not navigable.

The Sudan Railways operate 2,500 km. of steamer services on the navigable reaches of the Nile, touching Juba, Gambeila, Wau, Shellal (in Egyptian territory), and Dongola. These services connect with the Egyptian main railway services and the Nile river services of Kenya and Uganda.

The construction of the Egyptian High Dam has flooded the Wadi Halfa. Sudan and Egypt operate river services in the Wadi Halfa/Aswan reach by deep-draught vessels suitable to sail in the big lake thus created.

SHIPPING

Sudan Railways: Atbara; responsible for operating Port Sudan.

Port Sudan, on the Red Sea, 490 miles from Khartoum, is the only seaport. There are eleven fully equipped berths. with a total length of 5,718 feet, and two secondary berths, There are also two berths with a total length of 1,200 feet.

River Navigation Corporation: Khartoum; f. 1970; jointly owned by the Egyptian and Sudan governments; operates services between Aswan and Wadi Halfa.

Sudan Shipping Line: P.O.B. 426, Port Sudan; f. 1960; four vessels operating between the Red Sea, North Europe and the United Kingdom; Gen. Man. YOUSIF BAKHEIT ARABI.

CIVIL AVIATION

Sudan Airways: Gamhuria Ave., P.O.B. 253, Khartoum; f. 1947; this airline is owned by the Sudan Government; regular services throughout the Sudan and external services to Aden, Chad, Egypt, Ethiopia, Greece, Italy, Lebanon, Libya, Saudi Arabia, and the U.K.; Charter and Survey based at Khartoum; fleet of 2 Comet 4C, 7 Fokker Friendship F-27A, 1 DC-3, and 3 Twin Otters; Gen. Man. M. E. ABDEL DAYEM.

The Sudan is also served by the following foreign airlines: Aeroflot, Alitalia, Balkan, BOAC, EgyptAir, Ethiopian Air Lines, Interflug, Lufthansa, MEA, Saudia Airlines and Swissair.

TOURISM

Sudan Tourist Corporation: P.O.B. 2424, Khartoum; Dir. ABDUL RAHMAN I. KEBEDA.

EDUCATION

The education system in Sudan has been under review since 1972, and new laws governing education are being drafted for inclusion in the new Constitution. Recent education policy has aimed to help make attainable the ideals of the new Socialist State established after the May (1969) Revolution. The administrative machinery of supervision and control is conducted through the Ministries of Education and Higher Education. General Policy is executed through different technical and administrative bodies under the control of the Ministry. A technical "professional" Inspectorate at headquarters is responsible for the day-to-day application of curricula in the Higher Secondary Schools and similar Inspectorates exist at provincial levels for Primary and General Secondary Schools.

Under the new Five-Year Plan 1970/71–1974/75, education is being reconstructed and all curricula revised to relate the educational system more effectively to the new economic and social needs of the country. While the duration of formal schooling remains the same as before, i.e. 12 years, the Primary Level (*see* below) has been lengthened by two years; the six years secondary stage has been into a lower level or General Secondary and an upper level or Higher Secondary, each of three years duration. The Higher Secondary Level is in turn divided into an Academic and a Vocational/Technical/Higher Secondary stage, the latter being one year longer than the former. In 1970/71 £S20.92 million was allocated for education representing 18.4 per cent of the National Budget. Over the whole Plan period, i.e. 1970/71–1974/75, £S9,800,000 has been granted to the Ministries of Education and Higher Education and Scientific Research representing 4.9 per cent of the total Five-Year Development Budget.

Pre-Primary Education. With the exception of a few pilot projects, pre-primary education is still in the hands of voluntary bodies, e.g. Christian Mission schools. However, attempts are being made to bring these under the control of the Ministry of Education.

Primary Education. Several important developments have taken place in primary education. The most important are those in connection with the implementation of the New Plan including the extension of this level from four to six years and the expansion of classes; the completion of a scheme to raise all rural subgrade (3 year) schools to the level of primary (6 year) schools. By September 1970 a total of 615 such schools, of which 208 were girls schools, had been raised to the level of 6-year primary schools and had nearly 2,900 teachers. As regards the curricula, notable features included the introduction of "Environmental Studies", "Citizenship Education" and "National Subjects" comprising civics, history and geography.

Academic Secondary and Vocational Education. Two essential developments have taken place: firstly the introduction of the "Selective System" whereby students in the two final years specialize in one of three alternative groups of subjects: Literary, Science and Mathematics or Commercial subjects. The second change is that students sit only for those subjects included in their specialization whether literary, scientific or commercial. New curricula changes include the introduction of New Mathematics projects, Sociology and Psychology at the Higher Secondary level and French as an alternative foreign language.

Technical Education. In March 1970 a scheme for the reorganization of Technical Education was officially announced. The new system comprises schools for un-skilled workers, skilled workers, technical assistants, technicians and professional engineers, etc. Higher Technical education is provided at the Khartoum Technical Institute and in other new post-secondary, two-year institutions, for different technical and vocational specializations throughout the country. Agricultural education is being stressed and new agricultural schools and institutes are being built.

Higher Education. The Policy regarding Higher Education has been guided by three main principles: co-ordination and centralization. With regard to the University of Khartoum, the Amended Law (1970) was passed which included basic changes in the role and administration of the University, for example, the Head of State now becomes the Chancellor with the right to appoint the Vice-Chancellor, greater participation by students and the public has been granted in the running of the University's internal affairs and more democratic means are utilized in the running of academic affairs including departments.

Teacher Training. A number of crash programmes for training new teachers have been implemented following the introduction of the New Plan. The raising of the status of subgrade schools to primary schools status has created the need for at least 2,000 primary teachers who would be in charge of teaching the additional fifth class in the new primary schools. Student teachers are hence selected from the Secondary School Certificate holders.

Adult and Non-Vocational Education. Projects for increasing literacy among adults have been in progress for several years. Experiments in the improvement of syllabuses have begun and new Adult Education curricula will be introduced and taught in the teacher training institutes.

LEARNED SOCIETIES AND RESEARCH INSTITUTES

Agricultural Research Corporation, Ministry of Agriculture: P.O.B. 126, Wad Medani; f. 1919; 116 specialists; includes the following sections: Agronomy and Plant Physiology; Botany and Plant Pathology; Entomology (pest control, etc.); Cotton Breeding; Cereal Breeding; Soil Science; Horticultural Research; also directs four Regional Research Stations at Wad Medani (Gezira), Ed Damer (Hudeiba), Abu Naama (Kenana), and Yambio (Equatoria); and six sub-stations; library (*see* below); Dir. OSMAN MUHAMMAD SALIH, M.SC.

American Cultural Center: Qasr Ave., Khartoum; library of 8,000 vols.

Antiquities Service: P.O.B. 178, Khartoum; f. 1939; Acting Commissioner for Archaeology and Chief Inspector of Antiquities NAJM ED DIN SHAREEF; Acting Curator AKASHA MUHAMMAD ALI; Anthropologist ABDALLA KURDI; library: *see* Libraries; publs. *Kush* (journal of the Antiquities Service) (annual), occasional papers.

Association of African Universities: Secretariat c/o University of Khartoum, Khartoum; f. 1967; to promote exchanges, contacts and co-operation between African universities and to encourage international academic contacts; to study and make known educational and related needs in Africa and co-ordinate means whereby these needs may be met; to organize conferences and seminars; Pres. Dr. MUHAMMAD EL FASI; Exec. Vice-Pres. and Acting Sec.-Gen. Dr. E. N. DAFALLA; Vice-Pres. Dr. T. TSHIBANGU.

British Council: Central Office, 45 Sharia Gamaa, Khartoum (P.O.B. 1253, Khartoum); cultural and educational activities; library: *see* Libraries; centres and libraries at Wad Medani (8,800 vols.), El Obeid (5,400 vols.), Omdurman (8,400 vols.) and El Fasher (3,300 vols.); Rep. M. S. DALZIEL.

Centre Culturel Français: P.O.B. 1568, Khartoum; Dir. L. JARNO.

Educational Documentation Centre: P.O.B. 2490, Khartoum; f. 1967; documentation of information and educational information and exchange; library of 13,000 vols.; access to Ministry library of 4,000 vols.; Dir. IBRAHIM M. S. SHATIR; publs. *Documentation Bulletin*, reports and researches.

Forest Research and Education Institute: P.O.B. 658, Khartoum; f. 1962; Dir. A. A. BAYOUMI.

Geological Survey Department: P.O.B. 410, Khartoum; applied research and surveys; library of 3,000 vols.; Dir. ABDEL LATIF WIDATALLA.

Industrial Research Institute: P.O.B. 268, Khartoum; f. 1965 by the Government with assistance from the UN Development Programme; performs tests, investigations, analysis, research and surveys; offers advice and consultation services to industry; Dir. A. G. SULIMAN.

Institute of Public Administration: P.O.B. 1492, Khartoum; f. 1960; a joint undertaking between the UN and the Sudan, to provide practical and academic training for government officials; to conduct studies on current administrative problems and to produce manuals and other documents on administrative operation in the Sudan; library of 5,000 vols.; Dir. GALOBAWI MUHAMMAD SALIH, M.A.

Ministry of Animal Resources, Research Division: P.O.B. 293, Khartoum, Sudan; Dir. of Research Dr. MUHAMMAD EL TAHIR ABDEL RAZIG, DIP.VET.SC., M.SC., PH.D.; Senior Veterinary Research Officer Dr. AMIN MAHMOUD EISA, B.V.SC., M.SC.

National Council for Research: P.O.B. 2404, Khartoum; f. 1970; has five sub-councils: Economic and Social Research Council, Medical Research Council, Agricultural Research Council, Animal Wealth Research Council, and a Council for Industrial and Scientific Research. In the near future it will absorb all the other national research institutes. Sec.-Gen. Dr. EL SAMMANI A. YACOUB, DIP.PHYS., PH.D.

Philosophical Society: P.O.B. 526, Khartoum; f. 1946; covers many subjects, including archaeology, ethnology, economics, sociology and natural history; publs. *Sudan Notes and Records, Proceedings of Annual Conferences.*

Soviet Cultural Centre: P.O.B. 359, Khartoum; Library of 9,800 vols.; Dir. Dr. SHOTA GOURGALLASHIVILI.

Sudan Medical Research Laboratories: P.O.B. 287, Khartoum; f. 1935.

> *Director:* MAHMOUD ABDEL RAHMAN ZIADA, D.K.S.M., M.C.PATH.
>
> *Bacteriologist:* AHMED MAHMOUD ABBAS, D.M.S., DIP. BACT.
>
> *Government Analyst:* JOSEPH ZAKI, B.SC., D.C.C., L.R.I.C.
>
> *Pathologist:* ESSAYED DAOUD HASSAN, D.M.S., M.C.PATH., PH.D.
>
> *Medical Entomologist:* Dr. OSMAN M. ABDEL NOUR, DIP.SC., PH.D.
>
> Library (*see* below).

LIBRARIES

Antiquities Service Library: P.O.B. 178, Khartoum; f. 1946; embodies Flinders Petrie Library; 6,000 vols. excluding periodicals; Librarian Mrs. AWATIF AMIN BEDAWI.

Bakht er Ruda Institute of Education Library: Khartoum; central library, postal library for teachers.

British Council Library: 45 Sharia Gamaa, Khartoum; f. 1963; 8,086 vols.; Librarian P. E. LYNER.

Central Records Office: Council of Ministers, P.O.B. 1914, Khartoum; f. 1949; 4,000,000 documents covering Sudanese history since 1870; library of 5,500 vols.; Dir. Dr. M. I. A. ABU SALEEM.

Flinders Petrie Library: Sudan Antiquities Service, P.O.B. 178, Khartoum; f. 1946; number of vols. 4,932.

Geological Survey Library: P.O.B. 410, Khartoum; f. 1904; 2,000 vols.; publs. *Annual Report, Bulletin.*

Gezira Research Station Library: Wad Medani; 6,500 vols. on agricultural topics.

Khartoum Polytechnic Library: P.O.B. 407, Khartoum; f. 1950; 10,000 vols. on technical subjects; Librarian GABIR ABDUL RAHIM.

Library of the University of Khartoum: P.O.B. 321, Khartoum; f. 1945; contains 200,000 vols. and receives 4,000 periodicals and journals; includes a special Sudan and African collection; acts as a depository library for UN, FAO, ILO, WHO and UNESCO publications; both are under the general charge of the University Librarian ABDEL RAHMAN EL NASRI.

Omdurman Public Library: Omdurman; f. 1951; 17,650 vols.

Research Division Library: Ministry of Agriculture, Wad Medani; f. 1931; approx. 6,500 vols., 13,710 pamphlets, 250 current journals; Librarian S. A. MOHAMED.

Sudan Medical Research Laboratories Library: P.O.B. 287, Khartoum; f. 1904 (as part of Wellcome Tropical Research Laboratories); 7,000 pamphlets, 6,000 vols.

Wellcome Chemical Laboratories Library: Chemical Laboratories, Ministry of Health, P.O.B. 303, Khartoum; f. 1904; Librarian, Government Analyst; 1,600 pamphlets, 2,500 vols.

MUSEUMS

Ethnographical Museum: Khartoum; f. 1956; collection and preservation of ethnographical objects; Curator Dr. LUTHER STEIN.

Merowe Museum: Merowe, Northern Province; antiquities and general.

Sheikan Museum: El Obeid; archaeological and ethnographic museum.

Sudan Natural History Museum: University of Khartoum, P.O.B. 321, Khartoum; f. 1920; transferred from the Ministry of Education to the University of Khartoum, and reorganized 1956; Keeper Dr. FAYSAL T. ABUSHAMA, M.SC., PH.D.; Curator MUHAMMAD A. AL RAYAH.

Sudan Museum: P.O.B. 178, Khartoum; f. 1905; Departments of Antiquities and Ethnology; Dir. NAGM EL DIN M. SHARIF; Curator Sayed AKSHA MUHAMMAD ALI; publs. *Report on the Antiquities Service and Museums, Kush* (annually), occasional papers, museum pamphlets, etc.

UNIVERSITIES
THE UNIVERSITY OF KHARTOUM
P.O.B. 321, KHARTOUM

Telephone: 72271

The University of Khartoum came into being on July 24th, 1956, having developed immediately from the University College of Khartoum which had, in turn, been established in 1951 by the fusion of the Gordon Memorial College (f. 1903), and the Kitchener School of Medicine (f. 1924). The University grants its own degrees in all Faculties. The language of instruction is English except in the departments of Arabic and Sharia Law.

Chancellor: Maj.-Gen. JAAFIR AL NEMERY, President of the Republic.

Vice-Chancellor: Prof. MUSTAF HASSAN ISHAG, PH.D.

Number of teachers: 358.
Number of students: 2,600.

ATTACHED INSTITUTES:

Arid Zone Research Unit: f. 1961; scientific investigations into problems of the fauna, flora and geology of the arid regions of the Sudan; Sec. M. O. EL MUBARAK, M.SC., PH.D.

Computer Centre: f. 1967; Man. J. BEGGS.

Hydrobiological Research Unit: f. 1951; scientific investigations into the problems of the hydrobiology of the Nile, with special reference to inland fisheries; financed by the Government; Research Officer B. HAMMERTON, B.SC., M.I.BIOL.

National Building Research Station: f. 1962 to promote and conduct research in problems related to design, construction and performance of buildings in the Sudan; Acting Dir. ADAM MADIBBO, M.SC., PH.D.

Sudan Research Unit: f. 1964 to promote and co-ordinate interdisciplinary research on the Sudan; Dir. YUSUF FADL HASSAN, PH.D.; publs. *Bulletin of Sudanese Studies* (Arabic), *Sudan Notes and Records* (English).

University Farm: Shambat; experimental agriculture; Dir. MOHAMMED SHAZALI OSMAN, M.SC., PH.D.

CAIRO UNIVERSITY—KHARTOUM BRANCH*
P.O.B. 1055, KHARTOUM

Founded October 1955, as a branch of Cairo University.

Vice-Chancellor: Prof. MUHAMMAD TULBA AWEIDA, PH.D.
Registrar: MUHAMMAD SABRI EL SAADI, LL.B.

Number of teachers: 80.
Number of students: 5,100.

ATTACHED INSTITUTE:

Higher Institute of Statistics: f. 1969; offers two-year postgraduate course; 10 teachers, 150 students; Dir. A. M. SHAFIE, M.SC., PH.D.

* A number of Egyptian teachers were withdrawn in September 1972.

COLLEGES AND INSTITUTES
KHARTOUM POLYTECHNIC
(Formerly Khartoum Technical Institute)
Box 407, Khartoum.

Telephone: 72324.

Founded 1950.

Principal: ABDALLA RABIH.

Library of 10,600 vols.
Number of teachers: 115.
Number of students: 883 (full-time); 3,000 evening.
Courses are offered to the level of Higher National Certificate and K.P. Advanced Diploma.

KHARTOUM NURSING COLLEGE
P.O.B. 1063, KHARTOUM

Founded 1956.

Principal: FAWZIA MUHAMMAD ABDEL HALIM, M.SC.

Three-year post-secondary courses.

Number of teachers: 11.
Number of students: 65.

SENIOR TRADE SCHOOL
P.O.B. 22044, KHARTOUM

Founded 1960.

Principal: MUSTAFA MUHAMMAD ALI, B.SC.

Three-year post-secondary courses in a variety of technical subjects.

Number of teachers: 66.
Number of students: 202.

SHAMBAT INSTITUTE OF AGRICULTURE
P.O.B. 71, NORTH KHARTOUM

Founded 1954.

Administered by the Ministry of Agriculture; offers three-year courses in general agriculture.

Principal: MUTWALI AHMED AL HOWERIS.

Library of 6,000 vols.
Number of teachers: 18.
Number of students: 150.

COLLEGE FOR ARABIC AND ISLAMIC STUDIES, OMDURMAN
P.O.B. 328, OMDURMAN

Founded 1912, achieved university status in 1965 but reverted to a college in 1970.

Offers three-year course in Arabic and Islamic studies. Departments of Islamic Law, Principles of Religion, and Islamic Studies.

Registrar: MUHAMMAD ABU BAKR ABDALLAH.

Library of 20,000 vols.
Number of teachers: 53.
Number of students: 625.

COLLEGE OF FINE AND APPLIED ART
KHARTOUM

Founded 1946 as Higher School of Arts and Crafts. Attained present status 1971.

Courses in Graphic Design and Printing, Calligraphy, Sculpture, Ceramics, Painting, Industrial Design, History of Art, Drawing, General Studies.

Principal: S. A. GADDAL.

Number of teachers: 28.
Number of students: 160.

SELECT BIBLIOGRAPHY

GENERAL

ABDEL RAHIM, MUDDATHIR. *Imperialism and Nationalism in the Sudan: A Study in Constitutional and Political Developments 1899–1956.* London, Oxford University Press, 1969.

AMMAR, ABBAS, and others. *The Unity of the Nile Valley: its Geographical Basis and its Manifestations in History.* Cairo, 1947.

BARBOUR, K. M. *The Republic of the Sudan: A Regional Geography.* London, University of London Press, 1961.

BASHIR, M. D. *The Southern Sudan: Background to Conflict.* London, 1968.

BONN, GISELA. *Das doppelte Gesicht des Sudan.* Wiesbaden, F. A. Brockhaus, 1961.

DUNCAN, J. S. R. *The Sudan, a record of Achievement.* Edinburgh, 1952.

FAWZI, S. ed DIN. *The Labour Movement in the Sudan, 1946–55.* London, R.I.I.A., 1957.

GAITSKELL, ARTHUR. *Gezira: A Story of Development in the Sudan.* London, Faber, 1959.

HENDERSON, K. D. D. *The Sudan Republic.* London, Benn, 1965.

HERZOG, ROLF. *Sudan.* Bonn, Kurt Schroeder, 1958.

HILL, R. L. *A Bibliography of the Anglo-Egyptian Sudan from the earliest times to 1937.* Oxford, 1939.

A Bibliographical Dictionary of the Anglo-Egyptian Sudan. New edition, London, Frank Cass, 1967.

HODGKIN, R. A. *Sudan Geography.* London, 1951.

HOLT, P. M. *The Mahdist State in the Sudan 1881–1898.* 2nd ed., 1970.

KNIGHT, R. L., and BOYNS, B. M. *Agricultural Science in the Sudan.* 1950.

LEBON, J. H. C. *Land Use in Sudan.* Bude, U.K., Geographical Publications Ltd., 1965.

NASRI, A. R. EL-. *A Bibliography of the Sudan 1938–1958.* Oxford University Press, 1962.

NEWBOLD, Sir D. *The Making of the Modern Sudan: the Life and Letters of Sir Douglas Newbold.* London, Faber and Faber, 1953.

ODUHO, JOSEPH, and DENG, WILLIAM. *The Problem of the Southern Sudan.* Oxford University Press, 1963.

SAID, BESHIR MOHAMMED. *The Sudan: Crossroads of Africa.* London, The Bodley Head, 1966.

SUDANESE GOVERNMENT. *Ten Year Plan of Economic and Social Development 1961-62—1971-72.* Khartoum, Ministry of Finance and Economics, 1962.

TOTHILL, Dr. J. D. *Agriculture in the Sudan.* London, 1948.

HISTORY

ABBAS, MEKKI. *The Sudan Question: the Dispute about the Anglo-Egyptian Condominium, 1884–1951.* London, 1952.

ARKELL, A. J. *Outline History of the Sudan.* London, 1938.

CHURCHILL, WINSTON L. S. *The River War.* Ed. 1915, London; reprinted by Universal Publishers, New York, 1964.

COLLINS, ROBERT O. *The Southern Sudan 1883–1898.* Yale University Press, 1962.

COLLINS, ROBERT O., and TIGNOR, R. L. *Egypt and the Sudan.* New York, Prentice, 1967.

CORBYN, E. N. *Survey of the Anglo-Egyptian Sudan, 1898–1944.* London, 1946.

FABUNMI, L. A. *The Sudan in Anglo-Egyptian Relations.* Longmans, London, 1965.

HASAN, YUSUF FADL. *The Arabs and the Sudan.* Edinburgh, Edinburgh University Press, 1967.

HENDERSON, K. D. D. *Survey of the Anglo-Egyptian Sudan, 1899–1944.* London, 1946.

HOLT, P. M. *The Mahdist State in the Sudan: 1881–98.* Oxford, 1958.

A Modern History of the Sudan. London, 1962.

MACMICHAEL, Sir H. A. *A History of the Arabs in the Sudan* (2 vols.). Cambridge, 1922; reprinted London, Frank Cass, and New York, Barnes & Noble, 1967.

The Anglo-Egyptian Sudan. London, 1935.

The Sudan, London, 1954.

SABRY, M. *Le Soudan Egyptien, 1821–98.* Cairo, 1947.

SANDERSON, G. N. *England, Europe and the Upper Nile.* Edinburgh, Edinburgh University Press, 1965.

SHIBEIKA, MEKKI. *The Sudan in the Century 1819–1919.* Cairo, 1947.

British Policy in the Sudan: 1882–1902. London, 1952.

The Independent Sudan: The History of a Nation. New York, 1960.

THEOBALD, A. B. *The Mahdiya: A History of the Anglo-Egyptian Sudan, 1881–1899.* New York, 1951.

OFFICIAL PUBLICATIONS

BRITISH FOREIGN OFFICE. *Sudan: report by the Gov.-Gen. on the Administration, Finances and Conditions of the Sudan in 1945.* London, Cmd. 7316, H.M.S.O., 1948.

Documents concerning Constitutional Developments in the Sudan, and the Agreement between the U.K. and the Egyptian Government concerning Self-Government and Self-Determination for the Sudan, Feb. 1953. London, Cmd. 8767, H.M.S.O. 1953.

Egypt and the Sudan. London, Cmd. 2269, H.M.S.O., 1924.

SUDAN GOVERNMENT. *Sudan: a record of Progress, 1898–1947.* London, Sudan Agency, 1947.

Swaziland

PHYSICAL AND SOCIAL GEOGRAPHY*

John Amer

The Kingdom of Swaziland is one of the smallest political entities in Africa. With a compact area of only 6,704 sq. miles it straddles the broken and dissected edge of the South African plateau, surrounded by South Africa on the north, west and south, and separated from the Indian Ocean on the east by the Mozambique coastal plain.

PHYSICAL FEATURES

From the High Veld on the west, averaging 3,500 to 4,000 ft. in altitude, there is a step-like descent eastwards through the Middle Veld (1,500 to 2,000 ft.) to the Low Veld (500 to 1,000 ft.). To the east of the Low Veld the Lebombo Range, an undulating plateau between 1,500 and 2,700 ft., presents an impressive westward-facing scarp and forms the fourth of Swaziland's north-south aligned regions. Drainage is by four main systems flowing eastwards across these regions: the Komati and Umbeluzi Rivers in the north, the Great Usutu River in the centre, and the Ngwavuma River in the south. The eastward descent is accompanied by a rise in temperature and by a decrease in mean annual rainfall from between 45 to 75 in. in the High Veld to between 20 and 30 in. in the Low Veld, but increasing again to about 33 in. in the Lebombo Range. The higher parts receiving over 40 in. support temperate grassland whilst dry woodland savanna is characteristic of the lower areas.

RESOURCES AND POPULATION

Swaziland's potential for economic development in terms of its natural resources is out of proportion to its size. The country's perennial rivers represent a high hydroelectric potential and their exploitation for irrigation in the drier Middle Veld and Low Veld has already begun in a number of large schemes. The well-watered High Veld is particularly suitable for afforestation and over 200,000 acres have been planted with conifer and eucalyptus since the 1940s. Swaziland also possesses considerable deposits of asbestos, high-grade iron ore and coal.

A complex pattern of land ownership with Swaziland European holdings intricately interwoven throughout the country is partly responsible for considerable variations in the distribution and density of the population. The 10,000 Europeans, 2.3 per cent of the population, own most of the 44½ per cent of Swaziland in private hands. Fifty-three per cent is in the possession of the single Swazi tribe, to which most Africans belong, and has densities some six times greater than the European-held areas. Forty-two per cent of the African population of 421,000 (1971) live in the Middle Veld, Swaziland's most densely peopled region with an average of 100 per sq. mile but exceeding 500 per sq. mile in some rural areas. The Middle Veld has some of the country's best soils and its commercial centre, Manzini (population 6,000). The capital Mbabane, located in the High Veld, is the only town with a population exceeding 10,000 (13,800 in 1966). Despite some very high densities population pressure on the land is not excessive and the development of Swaziland's economic potential could probably absorb the 20,000 Swazi migratory labourers at present employed in South Africa.

* *See* map on p. 758.

RECENT HISTORY

Jack Halpern

Swaziland, which was the last directly-administered British colony in Africa before achieving independence on September 6th, 1968, is probably unique in its practical, and to a lesser extent in its constitutional, political structure. For in Swaziland the now 73-year-old King Sobhuza II has demonstrated that it is possible to use a very firmly entrenched tribal structure in order to create mass backing for an apparently modern political party which, however, remains fundamentally the instrument of the traditionalist King. At the same time, the King, whose small country is wedged between and significantly dependent upon South Africa and Portuguese-ruled Mozambique, has made skilful political use of the local but overwhelmingly pro-South African white minority (some 10,000 compared with 420,000 Swazi). In order to back demands for freedom from colonial rule he offered them special political privileges, only to subsequently reinforce his own position by adopting a "one man–one vote" pre-independence constitution which, within a legal framework of non-racialism, deprived the whites of political—though by no means of their overwhelming economic—strength and special privileges.

The Swazi were welded into what has become a highly cohesive nation by Mswati, a nineteenth century chief. Caught up, like other groups, first in inter-African warfare and also, and more importantly,

883

in the wider conflict between Britain and the Boers in South Africa, the Swazi were finally brought under British rule in 1903 only because a reluctant British government felt obliged to prevent the land locked Transvaal Republic, under President Kruger, from using Swaziland to break through to the sea in what is now Mozambique.

Two issues which have since dominated Swazi political life stem from this period: the ownership of land, and of the minerals which have long been known to lie beneath it. From the moment when he was enthroned as Ngwenyama (Lion or King) of the Swazi in 1921, Sobhuza II has waged an unceasing political and legal campaign to regain control of concessions profligately granted by one of his ancestors, Mbandzeni, and largely recognized by Britain—despite the Swazi tribal law that all land belongs in perpetuity to the nation and only its use can be temporarily assigned.

In other respects, however, the British colonial administration left the government of the Swazi almost wholly in the hands of the chieftainship, all of whom owe a semi-religious allegiance to the Ngwenyama. In theory, he is advised by the Libandla or national gathering, which the British recognized through the Swazi National Council. In practice, effective power passed to the Standing Committee of the S.N.C., whose members are appointed by the King and paid from the Tribal Treasury, and more especially to its full-time officials.

Though geographically part of South Africa, Swaziland long remained a politically and economically stagnant backwater, with the Swazi politically motivated solely by their resistance to the physical incorporation into the Union, which the very small and largely Afrikaner minority strongly desired.

Until 1964 this white minority had its affairs regulated by an European Advisory Council, which was set up in 1921. This grouped the white settlers and absentee landlords together into a coherent conservative political force, long led by Mr. Carl Todd. They exerted a strong influence in the modern political life of Swaziland, which effectively began only in 1960. On the Swazi side, prolonged British pressure led to a Swazi Treasury and Swazi Courts being established in 1950, but both served in practice to increase the power of the S.N.C., of its own executive and "civil servants" and, therefore, of the Ngwenyama, who until shortly before independence saw modern African or multi-racial political parties and "one man–one vote" as the greatest danger facing the Swazi. Here one can read "the King's own role and power" for "the Swazi".

In 1960 the Swaziland Progressive Party (SPP) was formed out of the earlier Swaziland Progressive Association which, intended to be non-political, had been founded with the approval of the British Administration and the Ngwenyama to provide a sort of social talking-shop for the small number of young and better-educated Swazi who could not be accommodated in the tribal structure.

Due to prolonged British neglect, and despite the efforts of religious missions, the Swazi have one of the lowest literacy rates in Africa—barely 30 per cent —and an estimated 78 per cent suffer from malnutrition. Preventable diseases are endemic whilst health services are grossly inadequate. The present government is making some efforts to improve this state of affairs, especially with outside assistance from UN bodies like the WHO and FAO and charities such as Oxfam and Freedom from Hunger.

These problems have, however, been at least partly reinforced by the shortage of good farming land held—through the King—by the Swazi (*see* Swaziland Economy); the rudimentary state of rural communications, agricultural extension services and credit; and by the corruption of many chiefs and some members of the S.N.C. The Ngwenyama, whilst himself above this, has in the past been criticized for being slow to stamp out known corruption, and this has probably had a long-term political effect in providing some sympathy for opposition and reformist political parties.

The European Advisory Council took the initiative in 1960 in calling for the establishment of a Legislative Council, and this was taken up, though for different reasons, by the SPP. The Ngwenyama himself also made this demand, in effect supporting—despite British opposition to his "racial federation"— a 50–50 representation for the whites and, in order to prevent the growth of political parties amongst them, for "traditionally chosen" Swazi. Nevertheless, when Britain agreed to the setting up of a Constitutional Committee at the end of 1960, consisting of representatives of the E.A.C. and S.N.C., the Ngwenyama included, as individuals, three leaders of the SPP: its founder, Mr. J. J. Nquku, Dr. Ambrose P. Zwane and Mr. O. M. Mabuza.

When it became clear to them that the Ngwenyama was primarily concerned with retaining control of land—some of which had been bought back from whites through a national levy paid into a Lifa Fund— and when Mr. Nquku was suspended, the SPP withdrew from the Committee. It subsequently split into three factions, headed respectively by the three delegates. Later, Dr. Zwane's section of the SPP changed its name to the Ngwane National Liberatory Congress (NNLC). Meanwhile, a further party was formed, the Swaziland Democratic Party (SDP), led by Mr. Simon Nxumalo and later by Dr. Allen Nxumalo, and joined by a handful of white liberals.

A Constitutional Conference took place in London in 1963, with representatives of the S.N.C., the E.A.C., Simon Nxumalo of the SDP and Mr. Nquku, recognized as the only representative of the fragmented SPP. Deadlock was reached, primarily because the then Conservative British government insisted that control of mineral rights, which constituted a major source of revenue, must rest with a representative elected legislature and not with the traditional Swazi hierarchy headed by the Ngwenyama.

Mr. Duncan Sandys, then Colonial Secretary, left mineral control theoretically in the hands of the legislature but effectively in British hands when he promulgated a constitution in 1963. This constitution, however, providing for largely racial representation, gave totally disproportionate weight to the small white community, and militated against the modern parties by providing for predominantly rural, i.e. chieftainship-controlled, constituencies. The King, after the U.K. government rejected a petition, solidly supported by a tribally organized referendum on mineral rights, had a royalist party formed, the Imbokodvo or Grindstone which, in alliance with the white United Swaziland Association, swept the boards at the 1964 elections. The NNLC gained, mainly in urban areas, 12 per cent of the overall votes, despite claims of intimidation by chiefs, but no seats, The Ngwenyama had, in all this, the benefit of a plan drawn up by a leading white South African lawyer with intimate Afrikaner government connections.

Between 1962 and 1963, the discontent of the very poorly paid, fed and housed Swazi workers on timber plantations and at the Havelock Asbestos Mine fermented into strikes which culminated in a largely successful general strike in May 1963. This, largely led by Mr. Dumisa Dlamini, who emerged as a leading lieutenant of the NNLC's Dr. Zwane, was broken with the help of a battalion of British troops who were air-lifted in from Kenya, and who were only finally withdrawn in 1967.

Though the Ngwenyama's prestige had been shaken by his failure to cope with the general strike, after 1963 he shrewdly exploited the conflict between Britain's desire to be rid of colonial responsibility for Swaziland and her need to leave behind a passably democratic form of government.

The Imbokodvo—whose leader, and now Swaziland's Prime Minister, Prince Makhosini Dlamini, made the party's nature clear by proclaiming, during an election campaign, that "It is the King, not I, who leads his people"—realized that it could, through its control by land-allocating chiefs of most Swazi, afford to accept "one man—one vote". It did so, dispensed with its white allies, and took up a Pan-African stance, demanding immediate independence. A new constitution, explicitly stated to serve as the basis for independence, was worked out by the Administration and representatives of the Legislative Council, thus excluding the NNLC. With agreement reached on all but mineral rights, and with Dr. Nxumalo's SDP having joined the Imbokodvo, as had Mr. Simon Nxumalo, the once fiery Mr. Dumisa Dlamini and other prominent NNLC leaders, elections took place in 1967. A remarkable and much criticized feature of the constitution is that it provides for a unique system of having eight constituencies each electing three members on an "all or nothing" basis and so delimited as to neutralize urban areas, where the NNLC is strong, by joining them with large rural areas. Thus, though the NNLC won 20 per cent of the total vote, it gained no representation in the legislature and was excluded from the final independence conference held in London in 1967. Rejecting Dr. Zwane's demands for single-member constituencies and fresh pre-independence elections without chiefly interference, the British

Government—now Labour—also performed an astonishing volte-face and gave in to Sobhuza II over the control of minerals.

The constitution with which Swaziland entered independence also maintains the S.N.C. and entrenches other substantial and absolute powers for the King: *inter alia* the appointment of one fifth of the Assembly and half of the Senate and the blocking of changes in constitutionally entrenched clauses, even if the changes have received the requisite 75 per cent of votes in a national referendum. The major entrenched clauses include methods of constitutional change, fundamental rights, and the establishment of the monarchy and the powers of the King.

When excluded from the 1967 Constitutional Conference, Dr. Zwane of the NNLC and Mr. Mabuza of the Swaziland United Front (SUF) warned that the King's entrenched powers and three-member constituencies in particular "left no course for democratic change within the composition of Parliament except by revolutionary methods". The only concession made on the constitution by the Imbokodvo was to make provisions for defeated parliamentary candidates to be nominated to the Assembly.

Until 1971, however, the NNLC remained the only serious opposition to the Imbokodvo. Mr. Nquku's SPP is a minuscule rump: it received 56 votes in the 1964 and only 37 votes in the 1967 elections, or less than 0.1 per cent of the poll, and Mr. Mabuza's SUF gained less than 0.3 per cent. As urbanization grows and education spreads, the semi-socialist and Pan-Africanist outlook of the NNLC could make an increased appeal, especially to ordinary Swazi discontent at their being the poorer in their mineral-rich but foreign-exploited homeland of what are, in Disraeli's phrase, "Two Nations". In 1971 a serious split occurred in the NNLC, with Dr. Zwane being expelled by a vote of five of its eight branches and replaced by a "collective leadership" of four members. Both Dr. Zwane and the "collective leadership" subsequently sought a governmental ruling on which faction constituted the legitimate NNLC. None of this helped to strengthen the opposition to the Imbokodvo in the general elections which were held in May 1972, although the results showed gains for Dr. Zwane's section of the NNLC, which won three seats from the Imbokodvo; this was considered to be a serious setback for the ruling party. Meanwhile, the Imbokodvo Government has placed considerable domestic emphasis on localization of the civil service at all but the most specialized levels and on countering increasingly voiced resentment of racialistic attitudes "imported" by white South African tourists attracted by gambling at a flourishing casino and the legality of sexual intercourse with African women—both being pleasures forbidden them in their Calvinistic, *apartheid*-dedicated Republic.

The Swaziland Government has set up a commission to study sexual immorality, the maintenance of illegitimate children and juvenile delinquency. The Prime Minister, Prince Makhosini, has publicly urged anyone suffering from racial discrimination to complain to government officials.

To underpin the localization of the civil service, the emphasis in secondary and university education has been made heavily functional. In lower schools, stress is being laid on rural and practical training, but a shortage of suitably qualified teachers persists.

The cabinet was reshuffled in 1971, but a serious conflict subsequently developed between Prince Makhosini and the Minister of Finance, Mr. Leo Lovell. The conflict, which nearly led to Mr. Lovell's resignation, apparently arose over his not being fully consulted over a measure to control land speculation by aliens, though he agreed with the measure in principle. This crisis left Mr. Lovell, a former Labour Party M.P. in South Africa, uncomfortably isolated. The most significant cabinet changes were Mr. Z. A. Khumalo's move from Foreign Minister to Deputy Prime Minister, and the taking over of the new Ministry of Justice by Senator Polycarp Dlamini, long an *éminence grise* in royalist politics. Senator Dlamini retained his position after the 1972 election, though R. P. Stephens took over the Ministry of Finance from Lovell, who left the cabinet.

The Imbokodvo government has, since independence, joined both the UN and the OAU, has made definite efforts to gain acceptance by other African governments, and has vigorously rejected any Bantustan idea. At the UN, Swaziland's ambassador has promised support for any resolution which opposes racial discrimination, and Swaziland has supported, to the surprise of many, the UN position on Namibia (South West Africa).

The Swaziland Government has, however, repeatedly ruled out any use of force against South Africa. Having also opposed the continued sale of arms by the Western countries to South Africa, the Imbokodvo Government has publicly based its stand amongst the non-aligned nations and at the OAU on the "dialogue" aspect of the Lusaka Manifesto.

Mr. Vorster, the South African Prime Minister, had talks with Prince Makhosini in Cape Town in 1971, in which the possible extension of South Africa's railway system into Swaziland was discussed. Prince Makhosini stressed publicly that South Africa had often proved "a friend indeed" to Swaziland. For the time being, however, no decision on exchanging diplomatic missions was taken.

On the diplomatic front Swaziland has, however, persuaded Zambia to establish relations on the basis of non-resident High Commissioners, and an Imbokodvo fraternal delegate has attended a conference of Zambia's ruling party, UNIP. In return, an official Zambian delegation has paid a goodwill visit to Swaziland. The Swaziland Government also attached considerable political importance to the

undertaking by the Special Commonwealth Assistance Plan of a limited technical aid programme, and to the successful renegotiation in 1971 of R. 10.9 million United Kingdom budgetary and development aid for the next three years, with R. 405,000 being a budgetary grant.

The Prime Minister has visited Nigeria and Mauritius, joining with the latter in appealing for the Indian Ocean to be kept as a nuclear-free zone. In keeping with the Imbokodvo's understandably firm anti-communist stand—which led Swaziland to vote against the admission of the People's Republic of China to the UN, Prince Makhosini has also visited South Korea.

Nearer home, discussions initiated by Botswana's President, Sir Seretse Khama, designed to resolve the crisis caused in Lesotho by the refusal of its Prime Minister, Chief Leabua Jonathan, to accept defeat at the polls, were frustrated by the Imbokodvo Government of Swaziland. (*See* Botswana, page 176 and Lesotho, page 461.)

Still nearer home, however, relations with Swaziland's immediate neighbour, the Portuguese colony of Mozambique, have been increasingly lauded. Swaziland's Minister of Agriculture, opening the Swaziland pavilion at the Lourenço Marques Exhibition in 1971, described relations as "close and vital" and thanked Portugal for training Swazi railway staff and for help in combating cattle disease. The Imbokodvo may prove not to be as monolithic as it seems, for the absorption of "Young Turks" like Simon Nxumalo, Dumisa Dlamini and Dr. Allen Nxumalo could have a progressive effect. But the Government, whilst it refused until 1972 to recruit strategic personnel from South Africa, has made clear its close adherence to South Africa. It has tightened up considerably on both the admission and limitations of even what it calls "genuine" refugees from South Africa and Mozambique. One recent case was the refusal of political asylum to Mr. Leonard Nikane who, having already entered Swaziland, was declared a prohibited immigrant. He was then placed under detention but apparently not returned to South Africa, whose police wanted to arrest him on political charges. At a UN meeting on refugees, held in Lusaka in 1970, Swaziland's Foreign Minister vigorously defended his country's record.

Prime Minister Prince Makhosini said not long after taking office that he would expect aid from South Africa if Swaziland were attacked by guerrillas or if guerrillas used the country as a route to attack South Africa or Mozambique. It could be that serious political change will occur only when the King dies, but no one can say with confidence who and what will succeed King Sobhuza II.

ECONOMY

B. D. Giles

The Kingdom of Swaziland is the smallest but economically the most advanced of the three former High Commission Territories in southern Africa. Its development to date has been markedly dualistic. Small areas of considerable prosperity and advanced technology are surrounded by a primitive peasant agriculture based on family homesteads rather than on villages.

RELATIONS WITH SOUTHERN AND EAST AFRICA

Like Lesotho and Botswana, Swaziland forms part of the South African customs and monetary area. A brief outline of these arrangements has been given in the article on the economy of Lesotho. In many other ways its connections with the Republic are similar to those of the other two countries. Its fiscal system resembles that of South Africa; there is some co-operation in marketing agricultural products; and about 7,000 Swazi are recruited each year for work in gold mines and collieries in the Republic.

Swaziland is landlocked and bordered by South Africa to the south, west and north, but there is a frontier with Mozambique to the east. Relatively easy access to the world overseas is available through this Portuguese territory. The Swaziland railway, completed in 1964, was built to carry iron ore from the Ngwenya mine near Oshoek in the west for export to Japan through Lourenço Marques, the last fifty miles of the journey being over the Mozambique railway system. There is a rail spur to the recently established Matsapa industrial area near Manzini, and it is reported that a rail link with South Africa is under discussion. Because of its communications and direct trade with the outside world Swaziland may well feel that it can look for useful economic links with countries other than the Republic of South Africa. Trade talks have already taken place with the East African Community and with Zambia.

ECONOMIC GROWTH

Growth in recent years has been substantial. National income accounts are available only from 1965–66 to 1968–69. That only a small increase in G.D.P. from R 50.2 million to R 57.0 million is shown suggests that the problems of estimation have not yet been overcome; there appears to be a conflict with other indicators of growth which are probably more reliable. Between 1961 and 1968 the value of iron ore production rose from nil to R11.8 million, coal from R 3,000 to R 249,000. Between 1963 and 1969 installed electricity generating capacity went up from 1.4 MW to 23.5 MW and sales rose from 10.4 million kWh. to 55.1 million kWh. The value of exports increased from R 12.7 million in 1961 to R 56 million in 1971, major contributions to this rise being made by asbestos, citrus and canned fruits, sugar and

molasses, iron ore and wood and wood pulp. In addition, appreciable quantities of asbestos, butter, rice, tobacco, cotton, wool and mohair were exported. Between 1950 and 1968 the irrigated area increased from 5,000 to 70,000 acres, and a pre-investment survey of another large area is approaching completion A proposal to build a very large thermal power station for the sale of electricity to South Africa is being investigated by consultants.

These figures for production and export reflect the fact that Swaziland has attracted a great deal of foreign capital during the last decade. The Commonwealth Development Corporation has made substantial investments in a variety of projects related to agriculture and forestry, and this together with other official grants and loans made Swaziland's per capita receipts of aid from Britain the highest in Africa in the mid-1960s. There have also been substantial private inflows for manufacturing, mining, commerce and plantations, but the size of the aggregate cannot be estimated from published information. Swaziland has made appreciable headway through the exploitation of its resources of raw materials for export by foreign enterprise. There is, however, a healthy lack of complacency. The Minister of Finance has said that although 1970 was a relatively good year it revealed that "the fundamental problems of stimulating investment and strengthening the agricultural sector still remain". The Government is not entirely happy with the pattern in the past and a ministerial statement has expressed an intention to develop the processing of raw materials within the country instead of increasing exports of unprocessed commodities.

Complete accounts for the balance of payments are not available—the *de facto* monetary union with South Africa makes it difficult to disentangle some items. Trade figures show that Swaziland has a substantial surplus on commodity trade, with exports of R 56 million and imports of R 47.8 million in 1971. Less than 20 per cent of exports go to South Africa and about 25 per cent go to the United Kingdom. The pattern of the overall balance of payments is a matter for conjecture. There appear to be substantial inflows of funds from the trading surplus, aid, long-term capital movements and receipts under the customs agreement with South Africa, and the banks—Barclays International and Standard—have local advances about equal to local deposits. What is on the other side of the account is not clear. Profits paid abroad are not the whole story. Repatriation of capital or hoards of cash deserve consideration. The 1969 revision of the Customs Agreement increased revenue from this source from R 2.0 million in 1968–69 to R 8.5 million in 1970–71, and a British grant in aid of the ordinary budget is no longer needed. A substantial inflow of other development aid continues, mainly from the United Kingdom.

With its varied export trade, its membership of both the Commonwealth and the Southern African Customs Union, Swaziland may be significantly affected by Britain's entry into the European Economic Community. The precise form of relationship with the EEC has not yet been determined, and the problem of choice may be complex. Swaziland is a member of both the International and the Commonwealth Sugar Agreements and there has been some concern over the implications for this product which accounts for ever 20 per cent of its exports.

FUTURE DEVELOPMENTS

The educational system has only recently begun to develop. Although the base is growing, the system is still very thin at the top. In 1971 there were over 70,000 pupils in primary schools and about 9,000 in secondary schools, but entrants for matriculation are generally few, and even fewer obtain first-class certificates. Most students for first degrees go to the University of Botswana, Lesotho and Swaziland at Roma in Lesotho. It seems probable that in the course of the next decade or so there will be such a marked increase in the output of graduates and diplomates that some difficulties of absorption may be experienced, although there are a large number of Europeans in managerial and administrative positions who might be replaced by Swazi. Localization of the civil service has proceeded rapidly since independence.

To some extent Swaziland's economic growth in some sectors may be due to the fact that 45 per cent of the land is held on freehold terms by non-Swazi. By no means all of this is well developed, but it has attracted some external capital and enterprise. The history of land tenure is complex. The "title-deed" land figured prominently in the negotiations with Britain at independence, and the problem has since been reviewed by a land mission, which reported in 1969. The report formed the basis of negotiations with the British Government. Manufacturing was given further encouragement in 1971 through the establishment of the National Industrial Development Corporation and the Small Scale Enterprises Development Company to assist with finance, premises and equipment.

The ambitious Post-Independence Development Plan was published in July 1969 for implementation by 1973–74. In essence it consists of a public investment programme totalling over R 23 million, for most of which loans and grants will be sought from a variety of sources. For many people the criterion by which it will be judged will be its degree of success in spreading the benefits of development more widely. There is no doubt that the economy of Swaziland is on the move, but the rate of advance and participation in the benefits of growth have been very uneven.

STATISTICAL SURVEY

AREA AND POPULATION

Area: 6,704 square miles.

POPULATION
(1966 Census)

	MALE	FEMALE	TOTAL
Africans . . .	172,291	190,076	362,367†
Europeans . .	4,370	3,617	7,987
Other Non-Africans .	2,134	2,083	4,217
Absentees* . .	13,512	7,055	20,567
TOTAL‡ . .	192,307	202,831	395,138

* Mainly Africans working in South Africa.

† 1971 estimate: 421,000 Africans.

‡ Excluding 126 persons (108 males, 18 females) in transit.

EMPLOYMENT

About 60,000 people are in paid employment. This figure, which includes self-employed, is just over 30 per cent of the working-age population—people between 15 and 64—which at the 1966 census was 183,000.

Main Towns (1966 population): Mbabane (capital) 13,803; Manzini 6,081.

RECRUITMENT FROM SWAZILAND FOR MINING IN SOUTH AFRICA

	TOTAL PERSONNEL	
	GOLD MINES	COAL MINES
1968 . . .	7,505	324
1969 . . .	7,941	326
1970 . . .	9,035*	291
1971 . . .	6,653*	312

*Includes 215 persons recruited in 1970 and 180 in 1971 for platinum mines.

Source: Mine Labour Organization.

Births and Deaths: Average annual birth rate 52.3 per 1,000; death rate 23.5 per 1,000 (UN estimates for 1965–70).

AGRICULTURE

CROPS
(metric tons)

	1968	1969	1970
Maize . . .	52,000	58,000	58,000
Rice . . .	6,000	8,000	6,000*
Cotton . . .	3,000	2,000	2,000*

* FAO estimate.

Source: United Nations, *Statistical Yearbook 1971.*

PRODUCTION OF PROCESSED AGRICULTURAL PRODUCTS

	Units ('000)	1968	1969	1970	1971
Sugar Products:					
Sugar, milled	metric tons	149.5	153.6	156.5	176.0
Molasses . . .	,, ,,	41.4	42.8	40.2	44.8
Cotton Products:					
Cotton Lint	,, ,,	1.0	1.4	0.9	2.1
Cotton Seed	,, ,,	1.5	2.8	1.8	6.2
Fruit Products:					
Canned Fruit	kg.	6,047.3	5,291.4	*	*
Jams and Juices . . .	,,	n.a.	28.6	*	*
Meat Products:					
Canned Meat	,,	266.6	213.7	392.9	355.5
Offal	,,	990.2	913.9	730.1	564.3
Other Meat	,,	4,086.6	2,831.3	2,784.2	3,435.2
Dairy Products:					
Butter	,,	160.2	106.1	29.9	n.a.
Wood Products:*					
Sawn Timber . . .	cu. metres	n.a.	57.4	75.5	78.7
Boxes and Woodwork . . .	,, ,,	n.a.	12.3	11.8	10.6
Mine Timber . . .	,, ,,	n.a.	49.4	47.0	18.7
Block Board . . .	sq. metres	86.5	129.7	173.8	400.3
Poles	cu. metres	n.a.	5.8	10.3	11.4
Wattle	metric tons	2.4	1.8	n.a.	1.8
Eucalyptus Oil . . .	litres	n.a.	n.a.	8.2	37.2

* By agreement with the companies concerned the quantities of wood pulp and canned fruit are no longer published. The estimated production of chemical wood pulp (in metric tons) was: 90,000 in 1968; 95,000 in 1969; 98,000 in 1970.

LIVESTOCK

		1970	1971
Cattle		568,369	571,785
Goats		259,047	261,534
Sheep		39,749	43,089
Horses		2,270	2,172
Mules		370	273
Donkeys		14,704	15,078
Poultry		359,043	399,309
Pigs		11,460	11,369

MINERAL PRODUCTION

		Unit	1968	1969	1970	1971
Chrysolite Asbestos	. .	'ooo metric tons	36.2	36.4	32.8	38.1
Iron Ore*	. . .	,, ,, ,,	2,342.3	2,294.5	2,295.1	2,312.4
Coal	. . .	,, ,, ,,	105.3	114.7	138.2	150.5
Pyrophyllite	. . .	,, ,, ,,	0.7	0.5	0.2	0.2
Barytes	. . .	,, ,, ,,	0.9	0.5	0.2	n.a.
Kaolin	. . .	,, ,, ,,	2.2	1.5	1.4	2.1
Quarried Stone	. .	'ooo cu. metres	49.6	51.6	42.1	23.3

* Figures relate to gross weight. The metal content (in 'ooo metric tons) was: 1,499 in 1968; 1,469 in 1969; and 1,469 in 1970.

FINANCE

South African currency: 100 cents=1 rand.

Coins: 1, 2, 5, 10, 20 and 50 cents; 1 rand.

Notes: 1, 5, 10 and 20 rand.

Exchange rates (December 1972): £1 sterling=1.8387 rand; U.S. $1=78.29 South African cents.

100 rand=£54.392=$127.73.

BUDGET

Twelve months ending March 31st

(Rand)

Revenue	1969–70	1970–71	Expenditure	1969–70	1970–71
Customs and Excise . .	7,534,135	6,731,283	Public Debt . . .	862,573	887,421
Income Tax . .	4,233,788	4,615,233	Statutory Expenditure .	653,952	742,768
Taxes and Duties . .	742,367	1,029,899	Civil List . . .	60,755	61,763
Licences . .	366,232	416,376	Parliament . . .	92,606	119,069
Earnings of Departments .	1,552,343	1,543,199	Prime Minister . .	685,490	919,603
Reimbursements and Loan			Police . . .	788,607	931,272
Repayments . .	202,610	186,459	Deputy Prime Minister .	831,813	981,700
Land and Minerals . .	241,445	271,753	Finance, Commerce and In-		
Judicial Fines . .	52,268	51,959	dustry . . .	2,399,833	3,531,414
Miscellaneous . .	621,322	488,513	Local Administration .	614,551	693,296
Loans . . .	—	325,916	Education . . .	2,468,449	2,623,204
			Health . . .	1,084,937	1,320,590
	15,546,450	15,660,590	Works, Power and Communi-		
			cations . . .	1,924,859	1,920,867
Overseas Service Aid Scheme	288,764	—	Agriculture . . .	1,555,573	1,586,465
U.K. Grant-in-Aid .	428,500	—	Judiciary . . .	76,751	92,505
			Law Office . . .	37,313	33,743
IMF . . .	—	821,428	Public Service Commission .	14,625	30,470
			Audit . . .	34,205	38,213
			Overseas Service Aid Scheme	281,835	—
			Other Provisions . .	48,907	64,903
			Appropriation for Capital		
Capital Revenue . .	—	1,956,034	Budget . . .	2,280,413	1,640,034
Total . . .	16,263,714	18,438,052	Total . . .	16,798,047	18,219,300

1972–73 Budget: Balanced at R20,355,000.

NATIONAL ACCOUNTS

Twelve months ending June 30th.

Gross Domestic Product (million rand): 50.2 in 1965–66; 54.9 in 1966–67; 53.4 in 1967–68; 57.0 in 1968–69.

BALANCE OF PAYMENTS
(million Rand)

	1967–68			1968–69		
	Credit	Debit	Balance	Credit	Debit	Balance
Merchandise:						
Export f.o.b., Imports c.i.f. . . .	39.7	32.6	7.1	40.6	32.4	8.2
Travel	0.9	2.3	−1.4	2.1	2.1	—
Investment Income . . .	0.1	8.0	−7.9	0.3	6.4	−6.1
Dividends	—	3.8	−3.8	0.3	5.6	−5.3
Interest	0.1	4.0	−3.9	—	0.8	−0.8
Earnings of Branches .	—	0.2	−0.2	—	—	—
Other Services . . .	0.5	1.6	−1.1	0.9	8.7	−7.8
Transfer Payments . . .	7.2	0.4	6.8	6.1	0.5	5.6
Government . . .	6.9	0.4	6.5	5.9	0.5	5.4
Private	0.3		0.3	0.2	—	0.2
TOTAL	48.4	44.9	5.4	50.0	50.1	−0.1

BRITISH AID
('000 Rand)

	1966–67	1967–68	1968–69	1969–70	1970–71
Grants-in-Aid . . .	1,200	1,760	3,296	428	—
Development Aid . .	1,603	3,315	1,634	1,863	n.a.
OSAS	64	240	378	289	218
Other Technical Assistance .	113	n.a.	690	418	n.a.
TOTAL . .	2,980	5,315	5,998	2,998	n.a.

EXTERNAL TRADE
(Rand)

	1968	1969	1970	1971
Imports . . .	34,104,000	38,000,000	42,749,000	47,824,000
Exports . . .	42,106,000	48,000,000	50,202,000	56,034,000

PRINCIPAL COMMODITIES
(1971—'000 Rand)

IMPORTS		EXPORTS	
Food	4,605	Sugar	12,503
Beverages and Tobacco . . .	2,544	Citrus Fruit	4,338
Crude Materials . . .	625	Iron Ore	12,112
Fuels, Oils and Fats . . .	3,892	Woodpulp	9,567
Chemicals . . .	4,337	Asbestos	5,904
Machinery and Transport Equipment	13,620	Wood and Wood Products . .	3,439
Manufactures classified by material .	7,942	Meat and Meat Products . .	1,819
TOTAL (incl. others) . .	47,800	TOTAL (incl. others) . .	56,034

Principal Countries: The United Kingdom and South Africa have traditionally been Swaziland's principal trade partners, taking respectively R 12,631,000 and R 10,563,700 of Swazi exports in 1970. However, with the increase in iron ore production, Japan has become an important client, taking the whole of Swaziland's iron ore exports, valued at R 11,031,000 in 1970, among total exports to Japan of R 12,071,000 in that year.

TRANSPORT

ROADS

MOTOR VEHICLES IN USE

	1967	1968	1969
Passenger Cars	4,300	4,100	4,300
Commercial Vehicles	3,200	3,500	3,300

Source: United Nations, *Statistical Yearbook.*

EDUCATION

(1971)

	SCHOOLS	TEACHERS	PUPILS
Primary	366	1,895	71,455
Secondary	54	448	9,001
Teacher Training Colleges	2	n.a.	332
Technical and Vocational Training	3	n.a.	299
Universities	1	n.a.	198*

* Including students at universities abroad.

THE CONSTITUTION

The 1967 constitution, which gave the country internal self-government, was designed to take Swaziland into independence with only a few alterations, and these were agreed to by both the British and Swaziland Governments at the Independence Conference held in London in February 1968.

The constitution seeks to maintain a non-racial state in which everyone will be treated equally without discrimination, regardless of race, colour or creed, and securing to everyone freedom and justice and inviolability of their property.

The King of Swaziland, called the *Ngwenyama* (the Lion) in siSwati, is Head of State. If the King is absent from Swaziland or incapacitated, the Queen Mother—*Ndlovukazi* (She-Elephant)—acts in his place. Succession is governed by Swazi law and custom. The executive

authority is vested in the King and exercised through a Cabinet presided over by the Prime Minister and consisting of him, the Deputy Prime Minister and up to eight other ministers.

Parliament consists of the Senate and the House of Assembly. The House of Assembly has the exclusive power to initiate legislation on taxation and financial matters. Parliament has no power to legislate in respect of Swazi law and custom, unless authorized by the Swazi National Council. The Senate has power to initiate legislation on matters other than taxation and finance and Swazi law and custom.

The Swazi National Council, which consists of the King, the Queen Mother and all adult male Swazi, advises the King on all matters regulated by Swazi law and custom and connected with Swazi traditions and culture.

THE GOVERNMENT

King of Swaziland: H.M. SOBHUZA II, K.B.E.

CABINET

(*December* 1972)

Prime Minister: Prince MAKHOSINI JAMESON DLAMINI.
Deputy Prime Minister: Dr. ZONKE AMOS KHUMALO.
Minister of Finance: ROBERT P. STEPHENS.
Minister of Local Administration: Prince MASITSELA DLAMINI.
Minister of Works, Power and Communications: Dr. ALLEN NXUMALO.

Minister of Health and Education: Dr. P. S. P. DLAMINI.
Minister of Agriculture: ABEDNEGO K. HLOPHE.
Minister of Tourism, Industry, Mines and Tourism: SIMON S. NXUMALO.
Minister for the Civil Service: KHANYAKWEZWE H. DLAMINI.
Minister of Justice: Senator POLYCARP MAFELETIVEN DLAMINI.
Minister of State for Foreign Affairs: STEPHEN MATSEBULA.
Minister of Commerce and Co-Operatives: Prince MFANA-SIBILI DLAMINI.

DIPLOMATIC REPRESENTATION

EMBASSIES AND HIGH COMMISSIONS ACCREDITED TO SWAZILAND

(In Mbabane unless otherwise stated)

(E) Embassy; (HC) High Commission.

Canada: Cape Town, South Africa (HC).

China (Taiwan): P.O.B. 56 (E); *Ambassador:* Lo MING-YUAN.

India: Blantyre, Malawi (HC).

Israel: Lusaka, Zambia (E).

Portugal: Morris St. (E); *Ambassador:* João MARAIS DA CUNHA MATOS.

Switzerland: Pretoria, South Africa (E).

United Kingdom: Allister Miller St. (HC); *High Commissioner:* ERIC LE TOCQ.

U.S.A.: Allister Miller St. (E); *Ambassador:* C. J. NELSON.

The following countries also have diplomatic relations with Swaziland: Austria, Belgium, France, Federal Germany, Iran, Italy, Japan, Republic of Korea, Netherlands and Zambia.

PARLIAMENT

THE SENATE

Consists of 12 members, 6 appointed by the King and 6 elected by the members of the House of Assembly.

HOUSE OF ASSEMBLY

Consists of 24 elected members, 6 members appointed by the King, and the Attorney-General, who has no vote.

ELECTIONS (May 1972)

	No. of Votes	No. of Seats
Imbokodvo National Movement	164,493	21
Ngwane National Liberatory Congress	38,276	3

POLITICAL PARTIES

Imbokodvo National Movement: P. B. Mbabane; f. 1964; Leader Prince MAKHOSINI DLAMINI.

Ngwane National Liberatory Congress: P.O.B. 326, Mbabane; f. 1962; opposed to white settlers and to the "African Feudalist alliance" which it sees as represented by the Imbokodvo Party; Pres. Dr. AMBROSE P. ZWANE. (The Congress split into two rival factions during 1971, but it is Dr. ZWANE's section which is represented in the House of Assembly. The rival section is led by Mr. SAMKETI).

Swaziland Progressive Party: P.O.B. 6, Mbabane; f. 1929 as Swazi Progressive Association; Pres. J. J. NQUKU.

Swaziland United Front: P.O.B. 14, Kwaluseni; f. 1962; offshoot of Mr. Nquku's party; Leader O. M. MABUZA.

JUDICIAL SYSTEM

The Judiciary is headed by the Chief Justice. There is a High Court (which is a Superior Court of Record) with five subordinate Courts in all the administrative districts, and there is a Court of Appeal which sits at Mbabane.

There are 17 Swazi Courts, including two Courts of Appeal and a Higher Court of Appeal, which have limited jurisdiction on civil and criminal cases. They have no jurisdiction over Europeans.

Chief Justice: Sir PHILIP PIKE.

RELIGION

About 40 per cent of the adult Swazi hold traditional beliefs. Nearly all the rest of the adult population is Christian.

ANGLICAN

CHURCH OF THE PROVINCE OF SOUTH AFRICA

Bishop of Swaziland: Rt. Rev. A. G. W. HUNTER, P.O.B. 118, Mbabane.

ROMAN CATHOLIC

Bishop of Manzini and Swaziland: Rt. Rev. G. M. CASALINI, P.O.B. 19, Manzini.

PRESS AND RADIO

Times of Swaziland: P.O.B. 28, Mbabane; f. 1897; English; weekly; Editor J. SPICER; circ. 6,700.

Umbiki: Broadcasting House, Morris St., P.O.B. 464, Mbabane; f. 1968; siSwati; fortnightly; Swaziland Government Information Services.

Swaziland Broadcasting Service: P.O.B. 338, Mbabane; f. 1967; broadcasts on the medium-wave in English and siSwati 6.30–8 a.m., 11 a.m.–1.45 p.m. and 5.30–9.15 p.m. Dir. D. T. NKOSI. Radio listeners also tune in to stations in South Africa and Mozambique.

Number of radio sets (1972): 35,000.

FINANCE

BANKING

Barclays Bank International Ltd.: Head Office, London; 6 brs.; 8 agencies; Swaziland Man. A. G. TUCKER.

Standard Bank Ltd.: Head Office: London; brs. in Mbabane and Manzini; sub-branch Big Bend; 11 agencies.

TRADE AND INDUSTRY

Swaziland Citrus Board: P.O.B. 343, Mbabane; f. 1956 for development of citrus industry.

Swaziland Co-operative Rice Co. Ltd.: handles rice grown in Mbabane and Manzini areas.

Swaziland Tobacco Co-operative Co.: P.O. Box 2, Goedgegun; handles all tobacco crops.

There are 18 registered trade unions.

TRANSPORT

RAILWAY

Construction of a railway line from the iron ore deposits at Bomvu Ridge, near Mbabane, to the border to link with the Portuguese East Africa railway system was completed in 1964, and a spur line to serve Matsapa Industrial Area near Manzini in 1965. The main traffic is iron ore, which is being exported to Japan through Lourenço Marques, and wood pulp and sugar.

Swaziland Railway Board: Mbabane; f. 1963; Chair. J. C. CATER.

ROADS

Ministry of Works, Power and Communications: P.O.B. 58, Mbabane, Permanent Sec. A. R. V. KHOZA.

Most roads are of gravel surface and 100 miles of tarred trunk roads had been laid by the end of 1968, mostly on a new 112-mile trans-territorial highway. Good road connections exist with Lourenço Marques, Piet Retief, Carolina, Breyten and Ermelo. There are about 800 miles of main roads and 700 miles of branch roads.

CIVIL AVIATION

The main airport, Matsapa, has a 4,800-ft. runway and can take twin-engined and some four-engined aircraft. Scheduled flights are in operation by South African Airways from Durban and Johannesburg and by D.E.T.A. from Lourenço Marques. There are about 20 privately owned grass landing strips distributed throughout the country, used by light aircraft.

Swazi-Air Ltd.: P.O.B. 552, Manzini; f. 1965; national airline; until 1971 a subsidiary of National Airways Corp. of South Africa; services to Johannesburg, Durban and neighbouring territories; fleet of one DC-4 and three DC-3; Chair. P. WILHELMI; Gen. Man. T.J. GERABHTY.

EDUCATION

RESEARCH INSTITUTES

Agricultural Research Station: P.O.B. 4, Malkerns; f. 1959; general research on crops; 10 research sections; library of 3,000 vols.; Chief Research Officer P. A. JONES, O.B.E., M.A.

Lowveld Experiment Station: P.O.B. 53, Big Bend; Irrigation Research Officer in Charge D. F. H. GILES.

Geological Survey and Mines Department: P.O.B. 9, Mbabane; f. 1942; activities include the mapping of the territory (now completed on a scale of 1 : 50,000), the investigation of mineral occurrences by prospecting, detailed mapping and diamond drilling, mine and quarry inspections, control of explosives and prospecting; small library; Dir. D. R. HUNTER, PH.D., M.SC., F.G.S., M.I.M.M.; Senior Geologist J. G. URIE, M.SC.; publs. *Annual Reports, Bulletins.*

Mpisi Cattle Breeding Experimental Station: Mpisi; to improve indigenous Nguni cattle; Dir. Dr. A. C. YENN, O.B.E.

Swaziland Sugar Association: P.O.B. 131, Big Bend; Extension Research Officer H. K. DURANDT.

LIBRARIES

Central Library: Manzini; f. 1972; operates the Swaziland National Library Service.

There are Public Libraries at Mbabane, Manzini, Goedgegun and Hlatikulu.

UNIVERSITY

THE UNIVERSITY OF BOTSWANA, LESOTHO AND SWAZILAND

SWAZILAND CAMPUS, P.O. LUYENGO

Part I studies for degrees in Humanities, Social and Economic Studies and Science. Part II studies are undertaken at the Roma (Lesotho) campus. Two-year diploma course in Agriculture. Part II studies in Agriculture to commence in 1974; Agricultural Research Centre.

Chancellor: H.M. King MOSHOESHOE II.
Pro-Vice-Chancellor: Prof. S. M. GUMA, M.A., D.LITT. ET PHIL.
Dean, Faculty of Agriculture: R. W. BELL, B.SC., D.T.A.
Dean, Faculty of Science: R. A. L. SULLIVAN, M.A., PH.D.

Number of teachers: 36.
Number of students: 227.

SELECT BIBLIOGRAPHY

Basutoland, Bechuanaland Protectorate, and Swaziland: Report of an Economic Survey Mission. London, H.M.S.O., 1960.

DUNDAS, Sir C., and ASHTON, H. *Problem Territories of Southern Africa, Basutoland, Bechuanaland, Swaziland.* Cape Town, S.A. Institute of International Affairs, 1952.

GREEN, L. P., and FAIR, T. J. D. *Development in Africa: A Study in Regional Analysis with special reference to Southern Africa.* Johannesburg, W.U.P., 1962, pp. 162–180.

"Preparing for Swaziland's Future Economic Growth". *Optima,* December 1960, pp. 194–206.

KUPER, HILDA. *The Swazi: A South African Kingdom.* Holt, Rinehart and Winston, 1963.

MARWICK, BRIAN ALLAN. *The Swazi.* London, Oxford University Press, 1940.

SWAZILAND CENSUS 1966. *Report on the 1966 Swaziland population census.* Mbabane, 1968.

For works on the former High Commission territories generally *see* Botswana, Select Bibliography, p. 191.

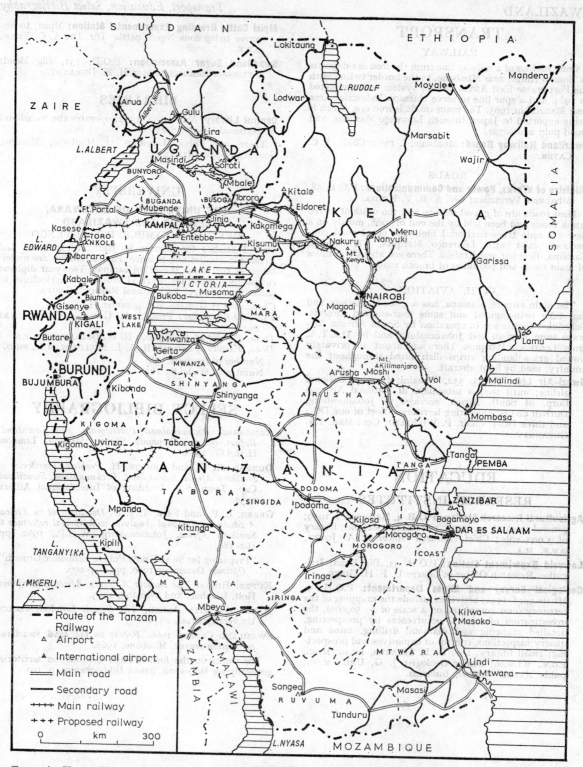

Tanzania, Kenya, Uganda. At a meeting of Presidents Amin of Uganda and Mobutu of Zaire in October 1972, it was decided that Lake Albert should be renamed Lake Mobutu Sese Seko and Lake Edward should be renamed Lake Idi Amin Dada.

Tanzania

PHYSICAL AND SOCIAL GEOGRAPHY

L. Berry

The 342,171 sq. miles (874,423 sq. km.) of the United Republic of Tanzania have a wide variety of landforms, climates and peoples; and the country includes the highest and lowest parts of Africa—Mt. Kilimanjaro (19,520 ft./5,950 m.) and the floor of Lake Tanganyika (1,175 ft./358 m. below sea level). The main upland areas occur in a northern belt—the Usambara, Pare, Kilimanjaro and Meru mountains; a central and southern belt—the Southern Highlands, the Ugurus and the Ulugurus; and a north-south trending belt, which runs southwards from Ngorongoro Crater. The highest peaks are volcanic, though block faulting has been responsible for the uplift of the plateau areas. Other fault movements have resulted in the depressed areas of the rift valley(s); and Lakes Tanganyika, Nyasa, Rukwa, Manyara and Eyasi occupy part of the floor of these depressions. Much of the rest of inland Tanzania is made up of gently sloping plains and plateaux broken by low hill ranges and scattered isolated hills. The coast includes areas with sweeping sandy beaches and with developed coral reefs, but these are broken by extensive growth of mangroves, particularly near the mouths of the larger rivers.

With the exception of the high mountain areas, temperatures in Tanzania are not a major limiting factor for crop growth, though the range of altitude produces a corresponding range of temperature regimes from tropical to temperate. Rainfall is variable, both from place to place and time to time, and is generally lower than might be expected for the latitude. About 21 per cent of the country can expect with 90 per cent probability more than 30 in. (750 mm.) of rainfall, and only about 3 per cent can expect more than 50 in. (1,250 mm.). The central third of the country is rather dry (less than 20 in./500 mm. of rain), with evaporation exceeding rainfall in nine months of the year. For much of the country most rain falls in one rainy season, December–May, though two peaks of rainfall in October–November and April–May are found in some areas. Apart from the problem of the long dry season over most parts of the country, there is also a marked fluctuation in annual rainfall from one year to the next, and this may be reflected in the crop production and livestock figures. Nineteen sixty-nine was a particularly dry year for parts of inland Tanzania.

The surplus water from the wetter areas drains into the few large perennial rivers of the country. The largest river, the Rufiji, drains the southern highlands and much of southern Tanzania. With an average discharge of 43,050 cu. ft. per sec. (1,133 cu. m. per sec.) it is one of the largest rivers in Africa, and has major potential for irrigation and hydro-electric power development. The Ruvu, Wami and Pangani also drain to the Indian Ocean, from re-

spectively the Uluguru Mountains, the Uguru Mountains and the Kilimanjaro, Pare and Usambara mountains. The Pangani has already been developed for hydro-electric power, which supplies Arusha, Moshi, Tanga, Morogoro and Dar es Salaam. Apart from the Ruvuma, which forms the southern frontier, most other drainage is to the interior basins, or to the Lakes Tanganyika, Victoria and Nyasa.

The most fertile soils in Tanzania are the reddish-brown soils derived from the volcanic rocks, though elsewhere *mbuga* and other alluvial soils have good potential. The interior plateaux are covered with red and yellow tropical loams of moderate fertility. The natural vegetation of the country has, of course, been considerably modified by human occupation. In the south and west-central areas there are huge tracts of Miombo woodland covering about 30 per cent of the country, while on the uplands are small but important areas of tropical rain forest (0.5 per cent of the country). Clearly marked altitudinal variations in vegetation occur around the upland areas and some distinctive mountain flora is found. Tanzania is, of course, well known for its game reserves, mostly set up since independence, where almost the complete range of African wildlife can be seen.

Tanzania has a population of more than 13 million people, most of whom are Africans, though people of Indian ancestry make up a significant part of the urban population. Tanzania is one of the least urbanized countries, less than 6 per cent of the population living in towns, of which Dar es Salaam (273,000), Tanga (61,000), Arusha (32,000), Moshi (27,000), Mwanza (35,000) are the most important. Although nowadays the nation has replaced the tribe as the unit, tribal differences continue to have some significance. There are over 120 tribes in Tanzania, the largest of which are the Sukuma and the Nyamwezi.

The main features of the pattern of population distribution are, firstly, sharp discontinuities in density with a number of densely populated areas separated from each other by zones of sparse population; secondly, the comparatively low density of population in most of the interior of the country; and thirdly, the way in which in most parts of the country rural settlements tend to consist of scattered individual homesteads rather than nucleated villages, which are relatively rare.

Highest population densities, reaching over 650 per sq. mile (250 per sq. km.), occur on the fertile lower slopes of Mt. Kilimanjaro and on the shores of Lake Nyasa. Most other upland areas have relatively high densities, as well as the area south of Lake Victoria known as Sukumaland. This problem of the scattered nature of the rural population has been a focus of development effort, and attempts at both capital-intensive villagization and the formation of co-operative nucleated villages (*ujamaa* villages) have been made. There are now over 1,000 *ujamaa* (Swahili: "familyhood") villages in the country.

Considerable variation in the pattern of development occurs within Tanzania. In some areas agriculture is becoming much more orientated towards cash crops, though very large areas are still primarily devoted to subsistence production. In such a large country distance to market is an important factor, and in the present and subsequent development plans major attempts are being made to improve the main and subsidiary communication networks. The TanZam

road and railway will be an important addition, leaving only the far west and the south-east without good surface links to the rest of the country.

Dar es Salaam, the capital city, is the main port, dominant industrial centre, and the focus of government and commercial effort. It has been growing at an annual rate of 10 per cent and attempts are being made to decentralize industrial development to other towns, particularly, in the current five-year plan, to Tanga, where sisal processing and steel rolling plants are being constructed. Arusha is growing rapidly, partly because of its new status as headquarters of the East African Community and partly because of its dominant role in the growth of the tourist industry.

RECENT HISTORY

John Lonsdale

For few African countries is the pre-colonial period of greater relevance to recent history than for the United Republic of Tanzania, formed in 1964 between the Republic of Tanganyika and the revolutionary régime in the former island sultanate of Zanzibar. The nineteenth-century history of the area was fashioned by the extension of the caravan trade from Zanzibar into the far interior, to the eastern Congo and Buganda, the major artery lying close to the present central railway. The Sultan of Oman had transferred his capital to Zanzibar, in consolidation of his commercial hegemony over the east coast of Africa. Clove plantations were then developed on the off-shore islands with slave labour from the mainland; Indian traders extended long-term credit for inland ventures. Slaves were sold all round the Indian Ocean, to the Mauritius sugar planters in particular, and gradually superseded ivory in importance until, in 1873, an Anglo-Zanzibar treaty prohibited the slave trade when at its peak. In 1890 a British protectorate was proclaimed over the sultanate, partly as a culmination of increasing British involvement in Zanzibari affairs, partly in reaction to the recent German acquisition of the Tanganyikan mainland. In the interior itself the long-distance trade had fostered the militarization and enlargement of many African polities; firearms were a major import item. More significant for the future, the Swahili language of the coast was fast becoming the commercial *lingua franca* over all that was to become Tanganyika, and beyond; Islam also spread along the trade routes; and porters from several inland peoples established what was to become a tradition of inter-tribal mobility.

GERMAN EAST AFRICA, 1885-1916

In 1885 Bismarck's Germany declared a protectorate over a limited area of the mainland, in support of the German East Africa Company. Three years later the company was all but expelled by a joint Arab and African rising at the coast, and the German

government was obliged to take over in 1891 in order to save the position. But it was not until 1898 with the death of Mkwawa, chief and resistance leader of the Hehe people, that German rule was finally secure. Thereafter the German period was marked by four phases of policy. Until about 1902 emphasis was laid upon European agricultural settlement in the northern highlands behind the port of Tanga which, economically, seemed to be a failure. Then the government adopted a scheme for the peasant cultivation of cotton from the west African colony of Togo. Much compulsion was used; the African peasantry reaped little if any reward; and they rose in revolt. The Maji Maji rising of 1905–06 was unique in eastern Africa for its trans-tribal character and resilience; it covered almost the whole country south of Dar es Salaam. With the famine that came in its wake it cost some 75,000 African lives, and it also caused a major change in German policy. In this third phase a new governor, von Rechenberg, concluded that security lay in a contented peasantry. He therefore built the central railway inland to Tabora to facilitate—and to be financed by—the export of traditional African crops such as peanuts and coffee. But by 1914 the settlers, encouraged by a boom in sisal and rubber, had regained the initiative; politically, they had won more than their counterparts in Kenya were ever to do, an elected majority on the Governor's Council. Their ascendancy was demolished by the First World War, but other German legacies remained. African commercial agriculture was established, and so too was Swahili, encouraged both by official education policy and by the creation of an African subordinate bureaucracy, transferable throughout the territory.

TANGANYIKA UNDER BRITISH MANDATE AND TRUSTEESHIP, 1919-61

After a resourceful defensive campaign conducted by General von Lettow-Vorbeck, the British and their allies had gained control of most of German East Africa by 1916. Rwanda and Burundi had fallen to the Belgians from the Congo and were then excised from the territory that became known as Tanganyika, and over which the British were allocated a League of Nations Mandate.

The economic history of Tanganyika between the wars was dismal. German settlers were expelled after the war, and others were slow to take up their estates. Not until 1924 did domestic exports exceed the 1913 figure; the uncertainties of the 1930s depression were increased by suspicions of a British intention to hand the territory back to Germany in appeasement of Hitler. African cash crops on the other hand did well in the few areas which were suitable; against European opposition, coffee production expanded among the Chagga on Mount Kilimanjaro and the Haya west of Lake Victoria. And two trends in African politics were of the utmost importance for the future.

First, there was an early development of territorial political consciousness among African civil servants. The British had taken over the German system of a subordinate bureaucracy, staffing it with a small cohesive group of mission adherents who had been educated in English at Zanzibar. By 1940 this minority and its successors in the Tanganyika African Association (TAA), founded in 1929, had a practical experience of political unity not shared by their counterparts in Kenya until 1944 or even later in Uganda. Secondly, partly in defence against this élite group, partly from ideological conviction, the British administration instituted, from about 1925, a system of indirect rule, under which material progress and political responsibility were to be mediated by the tribal chiefs. His dedication to this philosophy stiffened Governor Sir Donald Cameron in his opposition to the "closer union" schemes of the Colonial Secretary, Leopold Amery, and the Kenya settlers. But by the Second World War official enthusiasm for indirect rule was on the wane. The "native authorities" did not seem able to inspire economic progress, and where Africans did successfully engage in commercial production, as among the Chagga, their farmers' organizations clashed with the chiefs.

After the war Tanganyika was the scene of intensive efforts to stimulate the economy. In part this signalled Britain's long-term commitment to prepare for independence, as required by the United Nations' Trusteeship Council. More important was the need to reconstruct the devastated metropolitan economy. Thirty-six million pounds were spent on the disastrous "groundnut scheme"; not one ounce of cooking fat was produced for the British housewife. Strict land usage rules involving soil conservation and cattle limitation were introduced in the African areas, while on the other hand white farming was further encouraged. In the interests of development Tanganyika was now declared to be a "multi-racial", rather than African, country, yet in 1950, as against an African population of some eight million, there were only 17,000 Europeans and 55,000 Asians.

African opposition centred on these three issues. In many areas peasants resisted the land usage rules. In 1951 the eviction of 3,000 Africans to make way for white farms aroused opinion throughout the territory, and the creation of multi-racial local government councils in almost exclusively African areas was opposed. The United Nations—and its periodical visiting missions—provided a useful forum for protest, though more important was the long tradition of the TAA, converted by its president, Julius Nyerere, into the Tanganyika African National Union in 1954. TANU thus inherited the legitimacy of a central organization to which many local groups were already affiliated. It was also aided in its quest for unity by the wide use of Swahili and the absence of any predominant tribe. Comparatively speaking TANU was strong—as demonstrated by its sweeping victory in the first general elections held in 1958 and 1959. The unofficial M.P.s were divided equally into ten of each race, in accord with the prevailing concept of multi-racial parity, but even the Europeans and Asians owed their success to TANU support. Decolonization here would not be hindered by British concern for the minorities. Faced also with a still threatening rural discontent, the British could only hand over power as swiftly as possible. But when independence came in December 1961—the earliest in East Africa and in the poorest territory—TANU's weaknesses were only too apparent. Thanks to the legacy of indirect rule, democratic local government was ill-developed, and the institutional vacuum had to be filled from limited party resources. In addition it was apparent even at this point that TANU's two main supports in opposition, the flourishing producers' co-operatives and the trade unions, might now become its chief rivals in government.

REVOLUTION IN ZANZIBAR AND UNION WITH TANGANYIKA

The British had taken complete control over the Sultan's administration soon after the assumption of the Protectorate in 1890. The Arab community, which in 1963 numbered about 50,000 in a total population of 300,000, moved increasingly into the new bureaucracy, losing much of their former economic dominance to the Asian community, about 20,000 strong. At the same date the African population was divided into about 180,000 Shirazis or long-term residents, many of whom, on the northern island of Pemba especially, enjoyed congenial relations with the Arabs; and 50,000 "Mainlanders", both descendants of former slaves and more recent immigrants. In the mid-1950s a number of Arabs decided that their survival depended upon their assuming the leadership of Zanzibari nationalism, thus forestalling the coalescence of African consciousness. Assisted by appeals to Islamic unity, good organization, the support of many Shirazis and disunity among the Mainlanders, the Sultan's government was still in control when independence came in December 1963.

But riots after the 1961 elections when, on a conservative estimate, nearly 70 Arabs had been killed, had revealed the depth of communal feeling, which was exacerbated by retrenchment of social services immediately before independence, forced by declining clove prices. The government further weakened its position by dismissing many policemen of mainland origin whose loyalties appeared doubtful. In January 1964 an armed revolution, led by the Uganda-born Messianic figure "Field Marshal" Okello and a band of ex-policemen, overthrew the government. About 5,000 Arabs were killed in the aftermath, a further 5,000 went into exile and the remainder were dispossessed. Since Okello had had no political organization behind him he turned to the recently formed Umma party, a radical group of both Arabs and Africans which had been planning a revolution of its own. They soon dismissed Okello and consolidated previous links with the mainland. Western governments hesitated in recognizing the new régime, which soon received considerable East German and Chinese help for its socialist programme. It is probable that this development persuaded Tanganyika's President Nyerere to unite with Zanzibar in April 1964—the island régime needed some moderating influence. Zanzibar's President, Abeid Karume, leader of the Afro-Shirazi Party and associated with the Umma group, became the United Republic's First Vice-President (the Second being Nyerere's own deputy, Rashidi Kawawa). But the Act of Union was an enabling act or declaration of intent, and so far the Zanzibari leaders have chosen to work out their revolution in considerable independence from the mainland.

THE POLITICS OF SOCIALISM, 1961-71

A week after the Zanzibar revolution Tanganyika's tiny army had mutinied and deported its British officers. For a few days it held the government to ransom until the mutineers were disarmed by British marines. The army was then disbanded and a new one recruited, largely from the ranks of the TANU Youth League. The soldiers, though representing no one but themselves, in a sense represented everybody in demanding higher pay and rapid Africanization of top posts. The mutiny brought to a head the uncertainties of the first years of independence and helped to determine the subsequent new course.

At independence TANU appeared to have lost momentum. There was little party ideology save a desire for Africanization, on which Nyerere wished to proceed more slowly than some of his colleagues. He resigned his Premiership barely a month after independence, nominating Kawawa in his stead, in order to deal with both problems—the organization of the party and its programme. His thoughts on the latter were evident sooner, although his pamphlet, *Ujamaa, the Basis of African Socialism*, was less of a socialist blueprint than an assertion of traditional African communitarian values. The inauguration of a Republic in December 1962 gave evidence of some revitalization of the party. In a straight fight Nyerere won 97 per cent of the popular vote for the Presidency, but barely a quarter of those eligible had voted. With the object of increasing political participation and thus a sense of national integration and purpose

Nyerere ordered a commission of enquiry into the possibility of setting up a one-party state. Hitherto Tanganyika had been such by accident rather than by design, and its "Westminster" conventions demanded parliamentary disciplines for which there was no need. The political competition which was lacking must be supplied within a legal one-party context.

Meanwhile, a number of convergent problems were coming to a head. Relations between government and unions, which were also the most strident in demanding rapid Africanization, were soured as the latter forced up wage rates to such an extent that employment actually declined. Some of their leaders compromised themselves during the mutiny, and the government seized the opportunity to create an umbrella union organization whose officials were government nominees and under which the right to strike was curtailed. In the agricultural sector, which occupied 95 per cent of Tanganyika's 11 million people, the co-operative movement was expanded so fast that managerial probity and competence suffered. Village settlement schemes to develop fresh land ran up impossible debt burdens.

The foreign investment required for the development plan was not forthcoming, for Tanganyika, or Tanzania as she had become in 1964, had little to attract private investors. And inter-governmental aid was jeopardized from three directions. The United States and the western world in general were nervous of the Zanzibar situation, and were antagonized by Tanzania's objections to the Belgian operation in Congo (Leopoldville) in late 1964. East Germany's strong representation on Zanzibar caused West Germany to withdraw its defence aid to the mainland after the union; Nyerere insisted that it withdraw the rest. Then a British loan was frozen when, in December 1965, Tanzania honoured the Organization of African Unity's resolution that African states sever diplomatic relations in protest against Britain's equivocal handling of Rhodesia's unilateral declaration of independence. Above all Nyerere was increasingly convinced that the wide gap between the country's élite and the mass of the peasantry critically reduced the latter's readiness to make sacrifices in the cause of development. His view was confirmed when, in the first one-party election of 1965, half the eligible population both voted and rejected a large number of party officials.

Both external and internal pressures were pushing TANU in the direction to which Nyerere was philosophically inclined, a socialist strategy of development. A decision was precipitated in October 1966 by the refusal of university students to take part in the national service scheme. Early in 1967 TANU accepted a new programme, known as the Arusha Declaration, which was later amplified in a series of pamphlets by the President. The two main themes were egalitarianism and self-reliance. All party leaders were required to divest themselves of private sources of income; rural development must come not through large farms but community villages; the small urban sector must not exploit the countryside; the education system was to be completely reorganized in order to serve the mass of the population rather than train a privileged few. Commercial banks and many industries were immediately nationalized, but the rest of the programme was much more difficult to implement, for it flew in the face of the existing trends of social change.

Opposition has not been lacking. Despite the rapidly rising price of cloves in world markets, the revolutionary régime on Zanzibar has never felt secure. While his drives against Arab and Asian economic dominance won him much local popularity, the benefits of redistribution were largely appropriated by Karume himself; he was thus obliged to rely on an increasingly arbitrary rule to maintain his position. His régime survived two plots against it in 1969 and 1971, but Karume himself was assassinated in April 1972. While his killers appeared to be motivated by personal grievances, suspicion also fastened upon former leaders of the Umma party, including Abdul Rahman Babu who had until recently been a Minister in the Union Government. Babu and others were detained on the mainland. President Nyerere has been under pressure to hand them to the island authorities for trial, the more especially since Aboud Jumbe, Zanzibar's new ruler and thus Tanzania's Vice-President, appears—in contrast to his predecessor—to favour a strengthening of Union ties. But former Ministers suspected of complicity in the 1969 plot were summarily executed on being returned to Zanzibar. Nyerere has been reluctant to expose Babu to similar risk, however much he may want to strengthen his own influence over Zanzibar and so hope to moderate the excesses of the island's Revolutionary Council.

There has been political conflict on the mainland too, not so much in Parliament—the general elections for which in 1970 demonstrated a significantly increased support for government over those of 1965—as in the much more powerful party organs. The old conflict between Nyerere and TANU's secretary-general, Oscar Kambona, culminated in the conviction on treason charges of a small group which included a former Minister and two army officers. Two of the defendants were later released after a hearing in the East Africa Court of Appeal. Meanwhile, tensions of more recent origin between "right" and "left" within TANU were sharpened by a series of external crises. The Portuguese involvement in Guinea's insurrection, the new British willingness to sell arms to South Africa, the *coup* in neighbouring Uganda and increasing pressure on Zambia from the white régimes of southern Africa could all be construed as a linked assault on some of the African states most militantly involved in Pan-African liberation, amongst whom Tanzania was clearly

numbered. Ex-President Obote was given asylum immediately after the Uganda *coup* in January 1971. Within a month TANU's radicals had secured assent to the "Dar Declaration", a more clearly socialist formulation than that issued at Arusha in 1967. This attacked the "bureaucratic" tendencies of TANU's moderates, called for more political education and, in imitation of Guinea, for a people's militia.

Since then, Tanzania has moved further along its chosen socialist path. Property rented out for profit has been nationalized—an issue which caused temporary difficulties with Britain, which was dissatisfied with compensation arrangements for the owners, many of them being Asian holders of British passports. The few remaining white settlers have been given due notice to turn their farms into co-operatives or to leave. Much administrative effort has been devoted to the creation of co-operative or *Ujamaa* villages; by 1972 an estimated 12 per cent of the population was living in such settlements. But the programme has enjoyed its greatest success in the poorer, dry areas, where peasants have perhaps been attracted more by the promise of government water pumps than by co-operative farming; the murder of a Regional Commissioner in late 1971 appeared to be evidence of opposition to the programme in the wealthier farming areas. The most significant reforms have been those in the government structure, where there has been a degree of decentralization. This is in marked contrast to most other African countries, and points to the growing maturity of Tanzanian institutions. The creation of a Prime Minister (a post held by the former Second Vice-President, Kawana) and the revival of the office of Foreign Minister have removed large responsibilities from Nyerere's shoulders.

Ever since General Amin's *coup* there has been intermittent conflict with Uganda, fanned by Uganda's territorial claims on the Tanzanian border area west of Lake Victoria, Tanzania's continuing refusal to recognize the legitimacy of the military régime, and by her acceptance of refugees from Amin's purges. In September 1972 Ugandan exiles loyal to ex-President Obote launched an abortive invasion from across the Tanzanian frontier, perhaps hoping to profit by the confusions caused by Uganda's decision to expel its non-citizen Asians. Tanzanian assistance, no matter how reluctant, had clearly been provided, and Amin retaliated with air strikes against the lake-shore towns of Bukoba and Mwanza. Nyerere resisted pressures to extend the conflict. Faced as he is with the ever-present threat of trouble on his southern frontier with Mozambique, it is clearly in his interest that the peace agreement, negotiated through the good offices of Somalia, should be firm enough to insulate Tanzania from whatever future troubles may be generated within Uganda.

ECONOMY

John Loxley

A cursory glance at statistical data relating to Tanzania would suggest that the country has much in common with most other developing economies and this is indeed the case. What is perhaps unique about Tanzania is the way in which she has set about tackling the development problem.

Since February 1967 the Tanzania government has been actively pursuing policies designed to promote socialism and self-reliance. These goals formed part of TANU's platform even before independence but the main stimuli for the movement from statements to action were the bitter experiences of the first five years of independence. During this time the reliance on foreign and domestic private investment and on foreign aid led not only to underfulfilment of plan targets but also to increasing evidence of class formation and economic stratification and to a realization that Tanzania's freedom to pursue an independent and non-aligned foreign policy would need to be seriously curtailed if aid targets were to be achieved. Instability in the markets for some of Tanzania's main export crops and a hitherto unsuspected capacity of the economy to raise domestic savings to a very high proportion of G.D.P. further underscored the wisdom of the attempt to progressively reduce the relative importance of the external sector which is implicit in the policy of self-reliance. No discussion of the Tanzania economy would be complete without this preface since current economic developments must be assessed from the point of view of their contribution to the attainment of these twin goals of socialism and self-reliance.

POPULATION

In 1972 Tanzania had an estimated population of 13,996,000, of which about 44 per cent were under the age of fifteen. The population growth rate is estimated at 2.7 per cent per annum, the crude birth rate at about 48 per thousand and the crude death rate at about 21 per thousand. Infant mortality appears to have declined significantly in recent years from 190 per thousand in 1957 to about 160 in 1967. These population characteristics are, on the whole, typical of many developing countries.

Tanzania is a very large country covering 342,171 sq. miles (about the same size as Nigeria) and has therefore a relatively low population density of about 40 per sq. mile. This in itself means very little since it hides large regional inequalities in population distribution. At one extreme Zanizbar had a density of 347 per sq. mile in 1971 while at the other Ruvuma Region had only 11.7 people per sq. mile. In general the population is concentrated in a few dense pockets widely scattered through the country and transportation is a major problem. This geographical distribution was to a large extent the outcome of a colonial pattern of agriculture which encouraged cash crop production in those areas enjoying fertile soils and a good rainfall record. Less than 6 per cent of the total population lives in the ten largest urban centres although the growth rate of these centres (projected at 8.4 per cent on average in the next five years) far exceeds that of total population. The largest single concentration of population is in Dar es Salaam (272,821) which is not only the administrative capital but also the major port outlet and hence commercial centre of Tanzania. Until recently almost all the nation's industrial development was also concentrated there but government is now deliberately locating most new industries elsewhere in order to reduce regional income disparities.

NATIONAL INCOME, ITS GROWTH AND DISTRIBUTION

The Gross Domestic Product at current factor cost was calculated in 1971 at 8,704 million shillings (one shilling being equal to 14 U.S. cents), about 30 per cent of which derives from the subsistence sector. The average rate of growth of G.D.P. during the First Five-Year Plan period, 1964–69, was between 5 and 5.25 per cent, while the Second Five-Year Plan envisages a 6.7 per cent growth target. The pattern of income distribution inherited from colonial times was one of great inequality both between income groups and between different regions and districts of the country and hence the crude mean income figure of sh. 623 per head is as meaningless as the average population density figures. Government efforts to rectify income inequality between groups have taken the form of progressive taxation, income reductions for civil servants, restraint on income growth for all other employees, and price control; while regional inequalities have for the first time received considerable attention in the Second Five-Year Plan. The nationalization of the major means of production in February 1967 and the gradual extension of the public sector since that date not only allows the government direct control over the wages and salaries of more than 50 per cent of all employees but also places the bulk of the nation's investible surplus in public sector hands and should, therefore, permit more equitable regional allocation of investments than was the case in the past.

AGRICULTURE AND EXPORTS

The agricultural sector is the backbone of the economy accounting for 40 per cent of monetary and subsistence G.D.P. and for almost 80 per cent of exports. The vast majority of the population are outside the employment sector, relying on peasant agriculture for their living. Total wage employment in 1971 was estimated at only 400,000 for the whole economy. Twenty-seven per cent of these are employed on large agricultural estates, so recorded non-agricultural employment accounts for just over 2 per cent of the total population or, more appropriately, for only 3.8 per cent of those over the age of fifteen years.

In 1970 total exports (including those to the rest of East Africa) were valued at sh. 1,837 million, equivalent to 22 per cent of total G.D.P. and of this three crops (coffee, cotton, and sisal) accounted for 40 per cent and five crops (the above three plus cloves and cashew nuts) accounted for 52 per cent. Exports are now much more diversified than they were in 1962 when coffee and sisal alone accounted for 52 per cent of the total. This development is the outcome of deliberate government policy for it was the over-reliance on a limited number of crops with basically unstable markets that caused so many problems in the early years of the First Five-Year Plan. In particular, too much emphasis was placed on sisal, the output of which was forecast to reach 270,000 tons by 1970 for an export value of sh. 486 million. In fact the volume of sisal exports declined steadily from 209,000 tons in 1964 to 169,000 tons in 1969 and

export prices fell dramatically (by 56 per cent) so by the latter date the value of exports had slumped to sh. 160 million. As a result total employment in the estate agriculture sector fell by 54,000 jobs or by one third between 1964 and 1968. Coffee output has been closer to plan targets (of 49,000 tons by 1970) but unit export prices have fallen steadily since 1964 so that a 50 per cent rise in export volume has led to only a 16 per cent rise in export value. Recently the sharp reduction in the Brazilian crop due to frost and disease has had the effect of raising the coffee price, giving Tanzania coffee a brighter immediate future but not significantly improving long run prospects for the crop. Cotton output has also expanded since 1964 (by 25 per cent) but has been accompanied by large weather-induced annual fluctuations—the record crop of 1966 being 48 per cent higher than that of 1964 and 11 per cent higher than that of 1969. Prices too have varied but on the whole have been below their 1964–65 level, the net result being that export proceeds rose by only 19 per cent between 1964 and 1969.

Table 1

VALUE OF EXPORTS 1964 AND 1970

(sh. million)

DOMESTIC EXPORTS	1964	%	1970	%
Sisal	437	30.1	179	10.5
Cotton	198	13.6	247	14.6
Coffee	221	15.2	312	18.4
Cashew nuts . . .	66	4.5	115	6.8
Tea	31	2.1	42	2.5
Tobacco	1	—	45	2.6
Cloves	43	3.0	109	6.4
Meat and Meat Products . .	43	3.0	35	2.0
Hides and Skins . . .	21	1.4	27	1.6
Oil Seeds, Nuts, etc. . .	61	4.2	36	2.1
Diamonds	136	9.3	161	9.5
Petroleum	—	—	111	6.5
Other	193	13.3	270	16.0
TOTAL . . .	1,456	100.0	1,689	100.0

EXPORTS TO THE REST OF EAST AFRICA	1964	1970
Food Products	26.7	36.0
Tobacco	5.7	14.7
Vegetable Oils	11.6	13.1
Chemicals	1.5	4.1
Cotton Goods and Clothing . .	8.9	10.7
Footwear	7.2	1.9
Other Manufactures . . .	28.0	21.1
Other	17.8	35.9
TOTAL . . .	107.4	147.5
GRAND TOTAL, EXPORTS .	1,563.4	1,836.5

Agricultural diversification has, therefore, received a good deal of attention in recent years and the need for it has been rendered even more important by the knowledge that diamond production, the largest source of non-agricultural domestic export earnings (10 per cent of total exports in 1970) has been declining. Cashew nuts, tea and tobacco have all shown large increases in output since the beginning of the First Five-Year Plan and collectively their export value in 1969 was two and a half times that of 1964. The improvement in clove export performance in 1969 was, however, unexpected and is unlikely to last long.

Fluctuations in agricultural output are just as much a feature of production for the local market as they are of the export sector and the need for diversification is as pressing from a dietary and local income point of view as it is from a stabilization of export earnings viewpoint. Maize is the major food crop, the bulk of it being produced for subsistence. Only a small proportion of total output is marketed for consumption by towns, deficit areas and export markets, but large variations in annual production cause the marketed surplus to show even greater proportionate fluctuations and frequently maize needs to be imported. A new storage programme is being implemented in the Second Five-Year Plan which is designed to facilitate a more rational stock, export and import policy. Output of paddy and sugar have been rapidly expanding in recent years so that self-sufficiency was achieved in both in 1969. Wheat production presently satisfied about 50 per cent of total requirements but is scheduled to cater for 85 per cent by 1974. Steps are also being taken to improve the quality and quantity of marketed meat and meat products, largely by introducing better quality stock, by disease control and by more rational geographical specialization in animal husbandry. Fish, fruit, and vegetable production and marketing has previously been neglected but cold storage, grading, packing and transportation needs are now being investigated. A major aim is to replace imports of these commodities currently costing the country over sh. 13 million annually.

SOCIALISM AND THE RURAL AREAS

Running parallel with the government's attempts to raise and to diversify agricultural output is the much more ambitious, and in the long run undoubtedly more important, policy of socializing the agricultural sector. Taking socialism to the rural areas will not be an easy task. The Tanzanian peasantry are not blatantly oppressed by landlordism, usury, land fragmentation or shortage, and land alienation has never been a major problem. The mass of the peasants will not be easily mobilized to change their way of living. But the party and government are concerned over the mounting evidence of growing economic stratification in rural areas, unequal distribution of land, the growth of non-customary land markets, the increasing use of wage labour (unofficially it is estimated that 500,000 people are employed in agriculture outside the "estate" sector), and the relatively low productivity and poverty of most farmers. The aim of the government's policy of rural

socialism is therefore not only to prevent the growth of rural class formation, it is also to boost agricultural output by increasing farm size in order to reap economies of greater specialization and scale. The provision of social and economic services to the rural population will also be much cheaper if the population organizes itself into larger groups.

Originally, in the First Five-Year Plan, the government attempted to "transform" agriculture through the creation of village settlement schemes. This policy proved to be a failure because the schemes were highly capital intensive and mechanization proved to be uneconomic. Planning of the schemes was very poor and in general there was too much central government participation in capital, manpower and decision-taking and far too little enthusiasm and involvement on the part of the peasants.

Since 1967 government has reaffirmed its determination to build rural socialism but is now using a different strategy to achieve this. State farms have a limited but important role to play in the new approach. The Tanzania Sisal Corporation was established in 1967 when private estates producing about 60 per cent of Tanzania's total sisal output were nationalized. Its main function will be to plan the orderly contraction of sisal production and diversification to other crops so as to gradually redeploy its 15,000 workers. Government also controls most of the sugar industry and ten per cent of the acreage under tea. New state farms are being established to produce crops which benefit from mechanized, large scale production, and the Second Five-Year Plan envisages 29 covering well over 125,000 acres. Ten of these will produce wheat, nine will be cattle ranches, and four rice farms. Others include a vineyard, dairy ranches, oilseeds and coconut plantations. Their impact on the rural population will, however, be very small as they are highly capital intensive and employ very few workers.

The main thrust of the government's attempt to socialize agriculture will be concentrated on encouraging the growth of *ujamaa vijijini*—literally "familyhood villages", the basic appeal of which is supposed to lie in the traditional extended family system upon which, as the Second Five-Year Plan states, "with its emphasis on co-operation and mutual respect and responsibility, a society will be built in which all members have equal rights and equal opportunities, where there is no exploitation of man by man, and where all have a gradually increasing level of material welfare before any individual lives in luxury." In order to ensure both a swift and a widespread growth of *ujamaa* villages the government has adopted the "frontal" approach "mobilizing the full range of governmental and political institutions behind the principles of *ujamaa*." But government and party involvement, while being quantitatively larger than in previous settlement efforts, will be of a distinctly different qualitative nature. It will be essentially educational since the basic ideology of *ujamaa* must be made known to and understood by the peasantry. The establishment of villages cannot be expected to be spontaneous but at the same time government is not prepared to coerce peasants and neither is it prepared to play the dominant role in creating villages. Rather, it intends to act as a catalyst persuading peasants of the benefits of *ujamaa* through education. It will also render modest material assistance and help in the economic and organizational planning of villages but this will only be in response to peasant initiative, not in place of it. Emphasis of government technical and advisory staff on assisting the progressive individual farmer, a policy advocated in Kenya and Uganda as well as in Tanzania and one which many feel has assisted the growth of rural class formation, will now cease and all central government resources will be redirected towards the *ujamaa* effort.

So far about 2,700 *ujamaa* villages have been established with a total population of 839,000, but it is true to say that *ujamaa* has not made any significant inroads into areas where rural capitalism is most deeply entrenched, i.e. in the most prosperous densely populated peasant farming areas. As one would expect, it has been received with most enthusiasm and least resistance in relatively poor, land abundant areas, and while there is much to be said for experimenting with *ujamaa* in these parts of the country before tackling the more difficult areas, the latter will soon need to be faced and it is there that the policy may encounter hostility.

The major problems so far have been the absence of a well trained dedicated and disciplined party cadre through which to re-educate the peasantry both ideologically and practically towards *ujamaa*, and the lack of research into possible co-operative farming systems for the various areas currently untouched by *ujamaa*. Some attention is now being paid to both these problems but no action has so far been taken against the many local and foreign privately owned estates producing coffee, wheat, sisal, tea, tobacco, and sugar, but will need to be if the peasants are to be convinced of the sincerity of the government's concern for income and wealth inequalities.

INDUSTRY AND THE STRUCTURE OF IMPORTS

The manufacturing sector of the economy is still very small accounting for only 10.2 per cent of total G.D.P. but it has been growing consistently for the last few years at between 10 and 15 per cent per annum and employs 55,000 workers or about 14 per cent of the total labour force. Until recently the country's industrial strategy was essentially one of import substitution in the field of consumer goods and the major contributors to industrial output are food processing, beer, cigarette and textile producing plants. The establishment and expansion of these industries helped reduce consumer goods imports by 15 per cent between 1966 and 1970 and the proportion of consumer goods imports to total imports from 48 per cent in 1962 to 30 per cent in 1970. But the more readily identifiable opportunities in this sector have now been more or less exhausted. More basic import substituting industries such as oil refining (using imported crude oil and

exporting a large proportion of the output to Zambia), cement, paint, metal processing and saw milling industries were established prior to 1969 and the Second Five-Year Plan envisages increasing emphasis on this type of industry. Indeed 63 per cent of the total industrial investment expenditure of sh. 1,934 million over the Plan period will be concentrated on basic industries such as fertilizer, tyre, kenaf bag, paper, bicycle and wood production. These industries tend to be rather capital intensive and hence no more than 38,000 additional jobs will be created by the planned investment expenditure in the industrial sector (and only 20,000 of these by the end of the Plan period).

A major impetus to the growth of basic industry is likely to be the existence of the East African Common Market which potentially more than trebles the market for Tanzanian producers. It can be seen from Table 1 that manufactured consumer goods are already important in Tanzania's export trade with the rest of East Africa but at the same time Tanzania imports three times as much from Kenya and Uganda as she sells to them and the bulk of her purchases are manufactured goods, many of which are produced locally but less competitively. In order to encourage a more acceptable distribution of industry within the East African market Tanzania has for the last three years been permitted to impose transfer taxes on manufactured goods originating in Kenya and Uganda and this has the effect of giving additional protection to local manufactures of the same type, thereby encouraging the growth of their output. No critical survey has yet been conducted to test the impact of transfer taxes but it is evident that one effect is to encourage duplication of plant with possible loss of economies of scale which might have been derived from a more rational location of larger plants serving the East African market as a whole. If basic industries, which generally operate economically only at a fairly large minimum scale size, are to be encouraged in Tanzania, it is imperative that investment plans be co-ordinated very closely with those of Kenya and Uganda to avoid duplication.

Location of industrial activity within Tanzania has been equally controversial, since Dar es Salaam has received by far the greatest share. In the Second Five-Year Plan it has been deliberate policy to locate 81 per cent of industrial investment and 76 per cent of the planned employment increase outside the capital.

This location policy is facilitated by public sector domination of the manufacturing industry and of the investments scheduled for the Second Five-Year Plan. In 1967, as a result of the Arusha Declaration, the government, through the National Development Corporation, acquired a 60 per cent holding in the larger manufacturing companies. Private investment has since still been welcome on a minority basis in factories "on which a large section of the people depend for their living or which provide essential components of other industries", but on a majority basis in other areas. The N.D.C. does not appear to have experienced difficulty in finding foreign minority equity partners and it certainly cannot be argued that nationalization has had the effect of frightening away foreign private capital—there was relatively little finding its way to Tanzania before 1967. In fact, between Independence (1961) and 1966 there was a net outflow of private long-term capital.

TOURISM

It has been estimated that net foreign exchange earnings from tourism reached sh. 60 million in 1970. The main attractions to tourists are the many excellent game parks, the tropical beaches and Mount Kilimanjaro, and Tanzania's industry is closely connected to Kenya's by tourist circuits encompassing the main attractions of both countries. The Second Five-Year Plan envisages a 20 per cent per annum growth in foreign visitors raising net foreign earnings to somewhere in the region of sh. 100 million per annum.

The public sector has a firm hold over the tourist industry through the Tanzania Tourist Corporation which owns most of the country's international standard hotels and which plans to spend sh. 160 million on hotels in the coming five years. In the last two years licensing measures have been introduced to prevent Nairobi tour operators reaping most of the benefits of the many tourist trips to Tanzania which start and end in Nairobi.

BANKING

All foreign commercial banks were nationalized in 1967 when the National Bank of Commerce took over their business. The N.B.C. has been highly successful and since compensation talks reached amicable agreement it has enjoyed normal relationships with all foreign banks. The N.B.C. has not only rationalized the structure of commercial banking—closing down surplus offices, opening 100 new branches and mobile agencies in rural areas, standardizing internal procedures and establishing its own course—it has also created two specialized institutions; a hire purchase company and a medium and long term investment bank, to fill gaps left in the credit structure by the previous private companies. Insurance was also fully nationalized after the Arusha Declaration thereby cutting off a significant source of capital outflow from the economy (non-reinsurance outflows have been estimated at sh. 44 million between 1964 and 1966). Since Independence the government has introduced agricultural credit schemes, a national provident fund (which adds over sh. 60 million to government finance every year) and a National Housing Corporation for medium and low cost housing.

Since 1966 Tanzania has had its own Central Bank. Prior to that date Tanzania shared a common currency with Kenya and Uganda which was administered by the East African Currency Board. Tanzania is a member of the IMF.

TRADE

After the Arusha Declaration the State Trading Corporation was established to take over the import, export, and wholesale trade of the country but to-date it handles only 10 per cent of total exports, only

slightly more than 20 per cent of total imports and a distinct minority of wholesale turnover. Admittedly other public sector bodies (marketing boards, the N.D.C. and co-operatives) are also engaged in these fields but private interests are still important. The retail trade sector is almost entirely in private hands.

On the third anniversary of the Arusha Declaration the President reaffirmed the government's determination to place all but retail trade in the hands of the public sector, and gave a 12-month deadline in which this should be accomplished. There are doubts as to whether S.T.C. is organizationally capable of achieving this target as manpower constraints are liable to be crucial and some partnership, agency or management arrangements will almost certainly need to be made with private sector traders.

The direction of Tanzania's trade has been changing since Independence and in particular Britain's share is falling. Until 1970 it was still the largest buyer and seller accounting for 22 per cent of imports (26 per cent in 1962) and 24 per cent of exports (32 per cent in 1962). On the import side Britain was followed in importance by the EEC countries as a group, Kenya, Japan, N. America and China, which in 1971 became Tanzania's principal supplier; on the export side by other sterling area countries and the EEC, N. America, India and Hong Kong. An important task of the S.T.C. will be to find more attractive non-traditional markets and, on the import side, to use bulk buying to achieve economies. Breaking down irrational brand preferences will not be an easy task but is essential if the fragmented domestic market is to be consolidated and stock holding to be minimized.

No serious attempt has yet been made to socialize the retail sector with its thousands of small shops. General encouragement is given to workers' groups, co-operatives and local councils and in some areas limited progress has been made, particularly with confined lines. The co-operative movement is one of the largest in the world with 1,670 societies belonging to 40 unions and a turnover of sh. 520 million, but it concentrates almost entirely on the marketing of export (and some local) cash crops. While some unions have successfully moved into the wholesale trade on a large scale, societies have not been successful in developing retail business due to the acute shortage of suitably trained manpower at their disposal.

TRANSPORT AND COMMUNICATIONS

The main emphasis of the First Five-Year Plan was on improving north-south communications between Kenya, northern Tanzania and the capital. After the illegal régime's unilateral declaration of independence in Rhodesia, communications between Zambia and Tanzania were given top priority and this policy will continue during the Second Five-Year Plan period. Initially emergency arrangements were made to supply goods by road and for this purpose a special company, the Zambia-Tanzania Road Services was established by the two governments in conjunction with an Italian firm. This soon became the largest transporting company in Africa operating 450 of the 2,000 lorries serving the Zambia/Tanzania route. The opening of the sh. 336 million Italian built Tazama pipeline in September 1968 reduced the need for road transport since it can carry most fuels and oils, but the demands being made upon the road were still too large for the original murram structure and hence the whole road is now being rebuilt from Morogoro to the Tanzania border and this will absorb sh. 394 million or 50 per cent of the total expenditure on roads in the Second Five-Year Plan. This road, together with the Tanzania-Zambia railroad on which building work is due to start this year, will allow landlocked Zambia to switch her lines of communication away from the racist régimes to the south and east. The railroad, including rolling stock, is estimated to cost about sh. 3,000 million over the period 1970–76, a cost to be shared by Tanzania and Zambia and largely initially financed by Chinese loan commitments.

In addition to communications with Zambia, the Second Five-Year Plan provides for the expansion of feeder road communications and a new international airport to support the tourism drive in northern Tanzania.

PUBLIC FINANCE, FOREIGN AID AND INVESTMENT

Three major lessons concerning public finance were learned in the First Five-Year Plan period. The first of these was that foreign aid was not as easy to come by as had been imagined. The second was that the limited aid that was forthcoming frequently carried a very high price in terms of Tanzania's freedom to conduct an enlightened foreign policy, and the third was that the government was capable of mobilizing far more local resources than it had ever imagined. The Plan projected a total central government expenditure of sh. 2,040 and envisaged that 78 per cent of this would be financed from foreign aid, sh. 1,430 in loans and sh. 160 in grants. By the end of the Plan period total expenditure barely reached sh. 1,800 million and foreign financing accounted for only about a third of this (loans about sh. 560 million and grants about sh. 40 million). Locally raised resources, at sh. 1,200 million were therefore almost three times their planned level. The underfulfilment of overall expenditure targets was partly due to problems concerning aid but mainly due to manpower bottlenecks in project preparation and implementation.

During this period Tanzania lost over sh. 150 million in aid firstly by breaking off diplomatic relations with Britain as a result of the latter's failure to end the Rhodesian rebellion, and secondly by upsetting West Germany by accepting a permanent trade delegation of the German Democratic Republic. Tanzania's refusal, in 1967, to continue paying the pensions of British civil servants who had worked for the British Protectorate government in Tanganyika before internal self-government also prompted further aid reprisals by Britain although the latter subsequently conceded that such pensions should indeed be properly regarded as obligations of the British Government and not of the former colonies and dependencies.

Tanzania's attitude towards aid is now more circumspect. As the President has said, "we have firmly rejected the proposition that without foreign aid we cannot develop. We shall not depend upon overseas aid to the extent of bending our political, economic or social policies in the hope of getting it. But we shall try to get it in order that we may hasten our economic progress."

The Second Five-Year Plan reflects this cautious approach. Total central government spending is planned at sh. 3,055 million and 57 per cent of this will be financed internally, leaving sh. 1,600 to be found from overseas and most of this is already assured. Out of total investment expenditure of sh. 8,085 million government and other public sector bodies will account for 72 per cent and the private sector for the rest; the latter investing essentially in house and office building, transport equipment and the construction industry—the main areas still open to private capital.

Presently gross fixed capital formation is equivalent to 22 per cent of monetary G.D.P., a significant improvement over the 1964 level when it was equal to only 15 per cent of G.D.P. The Second Five-Year Plan aims to raise it even further to about 25 per cent. Increased mobilization of domestic savings through public sector financial institutions has been partly responsible for this improved performance and recurrent budget surpluses have also helped. Recent budgetary reforms have been instrumental in improving both the income elasticity of the tax structure and its equity. Sales taxation was introduced in 1969 partly to offset the fall in import duties due to the growth of domestic import substituting industries and partly to offset reduced rural taxation. High rates of sales, excise and consumption taxes have been imposed on luxury goods while necessities have been exempted. Taxation of rents and increased estate duties were announced this year. Pay as you earn was introduced in 1966 in respect of income tax and was extended to surtax in 1971 and at the same time new measures designed to ensure much prompter payment of tax by companies and self-employed took effect. Import duties are still the most important source of recurrent revenue accounting for an estimated 27 per cent in 1969–70 followed by consumption and excise duties (23 per cent) and income and personal taxes (22 per cent). Total recurrent revenue stands at approximately 29 per cent of G.D.P., and must grow at about the same rate as monetary G.D.P. (7.6 per cent per annum) during the Second Plan if it is to finance recurrent expenditure, itself growing at 7.5 per cent, *and* contribute sh. 620 million to the central government development budget as planned.

CONCLUSION

In the last five years the Tanzanian government has made considerable progress in raising the domestic surplus and since 1967 has taken steps to bring this increasing quantity of investible resources under public sector control. How best to use this surplus in order to reduce the proportionate influence of the external sector has already been given some thought, and basic industry is being expanded. But the export sector is still dominant and will be for many years to come. Agricultural diversification for both the home and foreign markets is essential if steady growth of

national income and the investment surplus is to be assured. This growth has to be achieved simultaneously with what amounts to the most fundamental structural re-organization of the rural sector since the arrival of foreign capitalism in Tanzania, and it is in this interim period of *ujamaa* village expansion that Tanzania's socialist policy will receive its severest test.

STATISTICAL SURVEY

AREA AND POPULATION

AREA (square miles)		POPULATION (1967 Census—Private Households)	
Mainland . .	341,150	African . . .	11,481,595
Zanzibar and Pemba.	1,021	Asian . . .	75,015
Water . . .	20,650	Arabs . . .	29,775
Lake Victoria .	13,450	European . .	16,884
Lake Tanganyika .	5,150	Others . . .	839
Lake Rukwa .	1,100	Not Stated . .	159,042
TOTAL . .	362,821	TOTAL . .	11,763,150

1967 Census: Total population 12,313,469 (Mainland 11,958,654; Zanzibar and Pemba 354,815); 1972 estimate of total population 13,996,000.

Principal Tribes of Tanganyika (1957 census): Sukuma 12.45%, Nyamwezi 4.13%, Makonde 3.80%, Haya 3.70%, Chagga 3.62%, Gogo 3.41%, Ha 3.30%, Hehe 2.86%, Nyakusa 2.50%, Nyika 2.41%, Luguru 2.30%, Bena 2.23%, Turu 2.23%, Sambaa 2.21%, Zaramo 2.09%.

Chief Towns: (1967) Dar es Salaam (capital) 272,821, Tanga 61,058, Mwanza 34,861, Arusha 32,452; (1970) Dar es Salaam 343,911.

REGIONS OF TANGANYIKA
(1967 Census)

REGION	POPULATION	REGION	POPULATION
Arusha . . .	610,474	Mtwara . . .	1,041,146
Coast . . .	784,327	Ruvuma . . .	393,043
Dodoma . . .	709,380	Shinyanga . .	899,468
Iringa . . .	689,905	Singida . . .	457,938
Kigoma . . .	473,443	Tabora . . .	562,871
Kilimanjaro . .	652,722	Tanga . . .	771,060
Mara . . .	544,125	West Lake . .	658,712
Mbeya . . .	969,053		
Morogoro . .	685,104		
Mwanza . . .	1,055,883		

EMPLOYMENT

	1969	1970*	1971*
Agriculture, Forestry and Fishing . .	112,888	107,368	109,692
Mining and Quarrying	5,919	6,096	5,552
Manufacturing	40,323	43,746	54,714
Construction	52,767	54,569	52,658
Electricity and Water . . .	9,755	11,296	10,618
Commerce	19,072	20,617	22,508
Transport and Communications . .	32,398	33,813	39,984
Finance	4,257	4,835	5,681
Services	90,556	93,295	100,505
TOTAL	367,935	375,635	401,912

* Provisional.

Total Labour Force (1967 census): Tanganyika had an economically active population of 5,577,569 (2,911,773 males; 2,665,796 females).

AGRICULTURE

LAND USE, 1966
('ooo hectares)

Arable Land	10,734
Under Permanent Crops . .	968
Permanent Meadows and Pastures . .	44,754
Forest Land	31,074
Other Land	1,092
TOTAL LAND AREA	88,622
Inland Water . . .	5,348
TOTAL AREA . .	93,970

Source: FAO, *Production Yearbook 1971.*

PRINCIPAL CASH CROPS*

	1969		1970		1971†	
	Production ('ooo tons)	Value (million sh.)	Production ('ooo tons)	Value (million sh.)	Production ('ooo tons)	Value (million sh.)
Sisal	209.3	185.2	202.2	157.3	181.1	141.9
Cotton‡ . . .	69.4	223.3	76.4	244.6	66.0	220.0
Coffee . . .	46.1	169.8	49.7	266.3	45.8	231.3
Groundnuts . .	7.8	7.3	6.2	6.6	8.1	8.3
Cashew Nuts . .	114.6	106.6	111.0	102.6	126.3	115.7
Tea	8.8	55.9	8.5	51.7	10.5	61.6
Tobacco . . .	11.7	47.9	11.0	49.3	11.9	49.2
Pyrethrum Extract .	3.8	14.4	2.3	8.6	3.7	13.2

* Cotton, cashew nuts and tobacco based on crop year, others based on calendar year.
† Provisional.
‡ Figures attribute quantity to cotton lint and value to seed cotton.

LIVESTOCK
('000)

	1967–68	1968–69	1969–70	1970–71
Cattle	12,345	12,862	13,206	13,300*
Sheep	2,828	2,825	2,823	2,800*
Goats	4,374	4,417	4,456	4,450*
Pigs	19	20	21	22*
Asses	160	160	160	160*
Poultry	19,372	20,049	20,405	20,600*

* FAO estimate.

Source: FAO, Production Yearbook 1971.

LIVESTOCK PRODUCTS
(metric tons)

	1968	1969	1970	1971
Cows' Milk	640,000	691,000	709,000	720,000*
Goats' Milk	48,000	46,000	48,000	50,000*
Beef and Veal† . . .	103,000*	121,000*	127,000*	128,000*
Mutton and Lamb† . .	29,000	27,000	27,000	27,000*
Hen Eggs	13,600	14,100	14,400	15,000*
Cattle Hides . . .	20,244*	23,919*	22,890*	n.a.
Sheep Skins . . .	1,478*	1,575*	1,590*	n.a.
Goat Skins . . .	3,400*	3,000*	3,000*	n.a.

* FAO estimate.

† Meat from indigenous animals only, including the meat equivalent of exported live animals.

Source: FAO, Production Yearbook 1971.

FORESTRY
ROUNDWOOD PRODUCTION
(cubic metres)

1968 . .	29,477,000
1969 . .	30,525,000

OTHER FOREST PRODUCTS
(metric tons)

	1968	1969
Bark and Other Tanning Materials . . .	10,115	11,340
Materials for Plaiting (non-bamboo) . .	59	59
Natural Gums, Resins, etc. (non-rubber) . .	206	454
Waxes . . .	318	680

Source: FAO, Yearbook of Forest Products.

ZANZIBAR—CLOVE SHIPMENTS
(million shillings)

	1969	1970	1971
India . .	0.1	0.2	2.9
U.S.S.R. . .	2.8	—	—
Pakistan . .	0.7	0.4	0.2
Indonesia . .	80.3	1.4	107.4
United Kingdom . .	1.2	0.9	—
Sudan . .	0.1	0.4	0.5
Japan . .	1.6	1.8	0.8
Hong Kong . .	4.6	15.3	18.0
Singapore . .	50.9	81.7	45.9
Kuwait . .	1.1	0.9	1.1
TOTAL (inc. others)	152.3	109.4	179.0

FISHING
(metric tons)

	1967	1968	1969	1970
Inland Waters	99,000	120,100	123,200	166,400
Indian Ocean	29,400	32,000	27,000	28,600
TOTAL CATCH . . .	128,400	152,100	150,200	195,000
Value of Landings (T£'000) . .	4,440	4,910	4,747	5,608

Source: FAO, *Yearbook of Fishery Statistics.*

MINING

	1969		1970		1971	
	Production	Export Value (million sh.)	Production	Export Value (million sh.)	Production	Export Value (million sh.)
Diamonds ('000 grammes) .	155.5	141.7	141.6	106.2	167.4	134.5
Gold ('000 grammes) . .	498.1	4.7	244.4	2.3	5.2	0.05
Salt (tons)	33,015.0	3.9	41,944.0	2.6	37,278.0	4.4
Tin Concentrate (tons) .	175.0	2.3	215.0	6.4	195.0	3.2

INDUSTRIAL PRODUCTION

	UNIT	1969	1970	1971
Beer	'000 litres	33.1	38.6	44.9
Textiles	'000 sq. metres	46.3	58.4	63.1
Cigarettes	million	2.3	2.6	2.9
Paints	'000 litres	1.6	1.6	1.8
Plywood	'000 sq. metres	975.0	1,122.0	1,119.0
Sisal Twine	tons	18.2	20.4	23.1

FINANCE

100 cents = 1 Tanzanian shilling.
Coins: 5, 10 and 50 cents; 1 shilling.
Notes: 5, 10, 20 and 100 shillings.
Exchange rates (December 1972): £1 sterling = 16.80 Tanzanian shillings; U.S. $1 = 7.143 Tanzanian shillings.
100 Tanzanian shillings = £5.952 = $14.00.
(*Note:* In this survey the term "Tanzanian £" is used to denote amounts of 20 Tanzanian shillings, equivalent to £1.19 sterling.)

BUDGET

RECURRENT REVENUE AND EXPENDITURE
(million sh.)

REVENUE	1968–69	1969–70	1970–71
Recurrent Revenue			
Direct Taxes . .	338.6	352.0	442.4
Indirect Taxes . .	660.8	827.1	921.8
Income from Property	93.7	116.2	111.9
Miscellaneous .	164.2	130.7	146.7
Revenue and Capital Transfers . .	12.5	150.9	60.2
TOTAL .	1,269.8	1,576.9	1,683.0

EXPENDITURE	1968–69	1969–70	1970–71
Recurrent Expenditure			
Economic Services .	267.6	307.2	349.4
Social Services . .	333.6	434.5	501.6
General Administration . .	368.6	480.0	533.0
Other Purposes .	216.2	305.0	247.4
Total Recurrent Expenditure	1,186.0	1,526.7	1,631.4
Surplus . . .	83.8	50.2	51.6
TOTAL .	1,269.8	1,576.9	1,683.0

DEVELOPMENT REVENUE AND EXPENDITURE
(million sh.)

REVENUE	1968–69	1969–70	1970–71
Development Revenue			
External Sources			
Loans . . .	122.7	121.5	269.7
Grants . . .	0.1	0.4	0.1
Internal Sources			
Loans . . .	132.5	230.7	250.0
Grants . . .	4.2	3.9	3.8
Surplus from			
Recurrent Budget .	83.8	50.2	51.6
Other . . .	117.2	203.8	253.9
TOTAL .	460.5	610.5	829.2

EXPENDITURE	1968–69	1969–70	1970–71
Development Expenditure			
Economic Services .	343.4	343.5	585.2
Social Services	57.7	81.3	111.2
General Administration	59.4	94.7	132.8
TOTAL .	460.5	610.5	829.2

SECOND FIVE-YEAR DEVELOPMENT PLAN
(1969–74)
TOTAL CONTRIBUTION BY SECTORS (million sh.)

Central Government	3,055
State Organization Co-operatives .	2,300
TOTAL PUBLIC SECTOR . .	5,355
East African Community . .	580
Private Sector . . .	2,150
TOTAL . . .	8,085

DISTRIBUTION OF CENTRAL GOVERNMENT EXPENDITURE

	SH.	PERCENTAGE DISTRIBUTION
Communications and Works.	922,359,270	30
Agriculture . . .	631,000,000	21
Lands . . .	309,485,000	10
Education . . .	296,922,300	10
Rural Development . .	185,648,000	6
Defence . . .	107,168,200	4
Health . . .	97,734,590	3
Home . . .	71,000,000	2
Commerce and Industry .	32,147,240	
Central Establishments .	30,000,000	
National Service . .	25,000,000	
Information . .	16,750,000	
Devplan . . .	12,240,000	4
Foreign . . .	10,924,000	
Judiciary . . .	1,070,000	
Second Vice-President's Office	392,000	
President's Office .	159,100	
SUB-TOTAL . .	2,750,000,000	
TanZam Railway (Local costs)	305,000,000	10
GRAND TOTAL .	3,055,000,000	100

DISTRIBUTION OF STATE (PARASTATAL) INVESTMENT PROGRAMME

	MILLION SH.	PERCENTAGE DISTRIBUTION
Industry . . .	783	35
Electricity Supply . .	457	20
Housing . . .	362	16
Agriculture . . .	307	13
Tourism . . .	235	10
Others . . .	156	6
TOTAL . .	2,300	100

GROSS DOMESTIC PRODUCT
(at current factor cost—million shillings)

	1970	1971
Agriculture	3,378	3,324
Mining	108	122
Industry	794	893
Construction	387	465
Electricity, Water . . .	83	92
Commerce and Trade, Hotels .	1,107	1,192
Transport and Communications .	713	800
Finance, Insurance, etc. . .	844	922
Public Administration and Other Services	819	1,025
GROSS DOMESTIC PRODUCT	8,222	8,704

BALANCE OF PAYMENTS
(Current Account—million shillings)

	1969		1970		1971	
	Credit	Debit	Credit	Debit	Credit	Debit
Goods and Services:						
Merchandise	1,754.0	1,790.1	1,809.7	2,359.6	1,945.8	2,810.4
Freight and transport . . .	242.8	93.6	328.7	112.5	452.9	103.5
Travel	83.8	80.3	96.0	91.3	98.1	153.7
Investment income . . .	76.0	96.6	76.6	101.5	67.4	87.7
Government transactions n.e.s. .	40.0	27.1	32.4	22.9	47.8	31.5
Other services . . .	49.4	69.0	83.0	77.7	80.6	116.9
Total	2,246.0	2,156.7	2,426.4	2,765.5	2,692.6	3,303.7
Transfer Payments . . .	213.4	152.6	265.8	177.1	260.8	208.4
CURRENT BALANCE . . .	2,459.4	2,309.3	2,692.2	2,942.6	2,953.4	3,512.1

EXTERNAL TRADE*
(million shillings)

	1969	1970	1971
Imports . .	1,419	1,939	2,414
Exports . .	1,667	1,689	1,735

*Excluding trade with Kenya and Uganda in local produce and locally manufactured goods.

PRINCIPAL COMMODITIES

IMPORTS	1969	1970	1971	EXPORTS	1969	1970	1971
Transport equipment .	196	288	370	Coffee beans . . .	257	312	227
Machinery other than electric . . .	154	346	400	Raw cotton . . .	235	247	245
Electrical machinery . .	70	100	154	Diamonds . . .	178	161	209
Iron and steel . .	67	107	191	Sisal . . .	160	179	134
Chemicals . . .	62	92	109	Cloves . . .	152	109	179
Crude petroleum . .	59	72	112	Cashew nuts . .	119	115	120
Food . . .	51	48	79	Distillate fuels . .	46	47	64
Cotton fabric . .	50	26	11	Tea . . .	48	42	49
Clothing . . .	42	34	27				

PRINCIPAL COUNTRIES

IMPORTS	1969	1970	1971	EXPORTS	1969	1970	1971
China . . .	79	265	601	China . . .	78	59	84
France . . .	46	64	38	Federal Germany .	68	79	69
Federal Germany .	111	181	181	Hong Kong . .	103	127	132
India . . .	48	55	51	India . . .	132	122	144
Iran . . .	104	108	138	Japan . . .	82	96	46
Italy . . .	77	109	125	United Kingdom .	429	371	424
Japan . . .	130	143	151	U.S.A. . . .	126	162	135
Netherlands . .	66	83	105	Zambia . . .	105	119	139
United Kingdom . .	387	411	487				
U.S.A. . . .	83	167	105				

INTER-EAST AFRICAN TRADE

	IMPORTS FROM KENYA AND UGANDA	EXPORTS TO KENYA AND UGANDA
1968 .	302	91
1969 .	291	104
1970 .	335	148
1971 .	311	196

TRANSPORT
EAST AFRICAN RAIL TRAFFIC

	UNIT	1969	1970	1971*
Goods Traffic . . .	million ton-miles	581	645	682
Passengers . .	'000	3,110	3,160	3,200
Rolling Stock:				
Locomotives . . .	number	155	155	149
Carriages . . .	,,	116	111	111
Wagons† . . .	,,	3,307	3,334	3,348

Source: E.A. Railways and Harbours.   * Provisional.

† This is the basic Tanzanian stock. In addition, other units are in constant circulation between the three East African countries and are consequently available for use in Tanzania.

ROAD TRAFFIC
LICENSED MOTOR VEHICLES

	1969	1970	1971*
Motor Cars	29,912	32,362	34,410
Light Commercial Vehicles . .	12,201	13,899	15,282
Private Motor Cycles . . .	7,975	9,028	9,957
Lorries and Trucks . . .	11,478	12,525	14,320
Government Vehicles . . .	4,868	6,629	7,852
Tractors, Tankers, etc. . .	4,699	4,389	4,961
Others	3,844	6,595	7,582
TOTAL	74,977	85,427	94,364

* Provisional.

SEA TRAFFIC*

	1969	1970	1971
Number of Ships	1,694	1,651	1,326
Net Registered Tonnage ('ooo tons) .	5,850	5,601	5,176
Number of Passengers† . . .	30,769	31,351	45,976
Cargo Handled ('ooo deadweight tons):			
Imports	1,497	1,765	2,207
Exports	1,040	1,092	1,041
Total‡	2,555	2,867	3,256

* Through Dar es Salaam, Tanga and Mtwara.
† Including embarked and disembarked.
‡ Including export/import transhipment.

CIVIL AIR TRAFFIC

	1969	1970	1971
Ton-km. sold ('ooo)	90,195	100,112	106,356
Passengers carried ('ooo) . . .	450	511	564
Passenger km. ('ooo) . . .	698,197	800,144	860,575
Mail ton-km. ('ooo) . . .	3,145	2,884	3,445
Cargo ton-km. ('ooo) . . .	26,061	28,198	27,685
Passenger load factor (%) . .	46.6	45.3	41.7
Gross Revenue (million sh.) . .	330	320*	340*

* Provisional.

TOURISM

	HOTELS	BEDS
1968	76	3,155
1969	80	3,623
1970	100	5,445
1971	103	5,460

Tourist Arrivals (1970): 640,057.

EDUCATION

TANGANYIKA

(1970)

	SCHOOLS	TEACHERS	PUPILS
Primary . .	4,030	17,790	827,974
Secondary . .	100	1,650	31,217
Vocational . .	3	145	1,546
Teacher Training .	22	306	4,092
University . .	1	308	2,060

Zanzibar (1966): Primary pupils 35,000, Secondary pupils 1,700.

Source: Central Statistical Bureau, Dar es Salaam.

THE CONSTITUTION

Tanganyika became a Republic, within the Commonwealth, on December 9th, 1962, with an executive President, elected by universal suffrage, who is both the Head of State and Head of the Government. A presidential election will be held whenever Parliament is dissolved. Tanzania is governed as a democratic society in which the Government is responsible to a freely-elected Parliament, representative of the people, and in which the courts of law are independent and impartial.

The structure of the legislative, executive and judicial organs of the Government are set out in the Interim Constitution of 1965, which made provisional constitutional arrangements for the Union between Tanganyika and Zanzibar.

The legislative powers are exercised by a Parliament of the United Republic, which is vested by the Constitution with complete sovereign powers, and of which the present National Assembly is the legislative house. The Assembly also enacts all legislation concerning the mainland. Internal matters in Zanzibar are the exclusive jurisdiction of the Zanzibar executive and the Revolutionary Council of Zanzibar.

The National Assembly comprises 107 Elected Members, 20 *ex-officio* Members (the Regional Commissioners) 15 National Members elected by statutory bodies, 10 Members appointed by the President, up to 32 Members of the Zanzibar Revolutionary Council, and up to 20 other Zanzibar members appointed by the President in agreement with the President of Zanzibar. Provision is made for the total to reach 204 members.

The President has no power to legislate without recourse to Parliament. The assent of the President is required before any Bill passed by the National Assembly becomes law. Should the President withhold his assen and the Bill be re-passed by the National Assembly by a two-thirds majority, the President is required by law to give his assent within 21 days unless, before that time, he has dissolved the National Assembly, in which case he must stand for re-election.

To assist him in carrying out his functions the President appoints two Vice-Presidents from the elected members of the National Assembly. The First Vice-President is also the President of Zanzibar. The Second Vice-President, who is chosen from the elected members of the National Assembly, is the leader of Government business in the Assembly. The Vice-Presidents and ministers comprise the Cabinet, which is presided over by the President.

The independence of the judges is secured by provisions which prevent their removal, except on account of misbehaviour or incapacity, after investigation by a judicial tribunal. The Interim Constitution also makes provision for a Permanent Commission of Enquiry which has wide powers to investigate any abuses of authority.

Members of Parliament are elected for five years unless the President dissolves Parliament at an earlier date. Appointed members of Parliament hold their seats until dissolution unless their appointments are revoked by the President. The President must stand for re-election each time Parliament is dissolved. The Presidential candidate is chosen by an electoral convention of TANU and the Afro-Shirazi parties. Their choice is then presented to the people for confirmation by a yes-no vote. If the convention's first choice is rejected by a majority of the voters, another candidate must be chosen and submitted to the vote

Mainland Tanzania is divided into 107 constituencies, although for the 1970 elections another 13 are being created. In each of these areas TANU, the official party, puts forward two candidates chosen by the TANU membership. Then all adult citizens of the area, whether TANU members or not, vote to decide which of the candidates will represent them in Parliament. The constitution of TANU is incorporated as part of the Interim Constitution.

The National Executive of TANU is the supreme policy making body of the Party and the Government subject only to approval of a biannual National Conference, but it is the role of the National Assembly to translate party policy into legislation. The assembly deliberates independently and has on occasion amended or refused to approve government proposals.

The National Executive is a parallel body to the National Assembly and its members are democratically chosen by party members throughout the country. Both National Executive and National Assembly members are paid at the same rate from government funds.

The Afro-Shirazi party plays a similar role in Zanzibar and Pemba, giving effect to its policies through the Zanzibar Revolutionary Council.

The Constitution also makes provision for the attainment of citizenship in accordance with the principles already approved by the National Assembly.

The Constitution can be amended by an act of the Parliament of the United Republic, when the proposed amendment is supported by the votes of not less than two thirds of all the members of the Assembly.

ARUSHA DECLARATION

The Arusha Declaration of February 1967 (approved by the National Executive Committee of TANU at the end of January) laid down that every TANU and Government leader must be a peasant or a worker; that no such leader should hold shares or directorships in any company; that no leader should receive two or more salaries; and that no leader should own houses rented out to others. In addition, the Declaration urges the Government to take further steps in the implementation of the policy of socialism, especially in ensuring that the major means of production are under the control and ownership of the peasants and workers (through the Government and the co-operatives); to put emphasis on national self-reliance rather than depending on foreign loans and grants for development, and to put great emphasis on raising the standards of living of the peasants.

THE GOVERNMENT

HEAD OF STATE
President: Mwalimu JULIUS K. NYERERE.

THE CABINET
(January 1973)

President and Minister of Regional Administration and Rural Development: Mwalimu Dr. JULIUS K. NYERERE.

First Vice-President: ABOUD JUMBE.

Second Vice-President and Prime Minister: RASHIDI M. KAWAWA.

Minister of Foreign Affairs: JOHN W. S. MALECELA.

Minister of Agriculture and Land Reform: MUHSIN BIN ALI.

Minister of Commerce and Industry: THABIT KOMBO.

Minister of Communications and Works: JOB LUSINDE.

Minister of Defence and National Service: EDWARD SOKOINE.

Minister of Economic Affairs and Development Planning: WILBERT CHAGULA.

Minister of Finance: CLEOPA MSUYA.

Minister of Health: HASSAN MWINYI.

Minister of Home Affairs: SAIDI MASWANYA.

Minister of Information, Broadcasting, Tourism and Natural Resources: PILI KHAMIS.

Minister of Labour and Social Welfare: ALFRED TANDAU.

Minister of Lands, Housing and Urban Development: MUSOBI MAGENI.

Minister of National Education: SADI DI BABUAI.

Minister of Natural Resources and Tourism: HASNU MAKAME.

Minister of Water Development and Power: ISAELI ELINEWINGA.

Minister for State Affairs: HASSAN MOYO.

JUNIOR MINISTERS

Office of the Second Vice-President and Prime Minister: PATRICK QORRO, MUSSA MASOMO.

Foreign Affairs: TAWAKALI KHAMIS TAWAKALI.

Defence and National Service: GEOFFREY MHAGAMA.

Communications and Works: ROBERT NG'ITU.

Health: MUSTAFA NYANG'ANYI.

TANGANYIKA AFRICAN NATIONAL UNION (TANU)

TANU on the mainland and the *Afro-Shirazi Party* in Zanzibar and Pemba determine the broad lines of Government policy.

President: Mwalimu JULIUS K. NYERERE.

National Executive: supreme policy-making body of the Government and subject only to approval of bi-annual National Conference; Party headed by President; chooses Party leadership, with the exception of the President, who is selected by an electoral convention.

DIPLOMATIC REPRESENTATION

EMBASSIES AND HIGH COMMISSIONS ACCREDITED TO TANZANIA

(In Dar es Salaam unless otherwise stated)

(E) Embassy; (HC) High Commission

Algeria: P.O.B. 2963, 34 Upanga Rd. (E); *Ambassador:* PAHR GAID.

Australia: P.O.B. 2996, 4th Floor, Barclays Bank Bldg., Independence Ave. (HC); *High Commissioner:* H. W. BULLOCK.

Austria: Nairobi, Kenya (E).

Belgium: Nairobi, Kenya (E).

Brazil: (E); *Ambassador:* A. F. TEXEIRA DE MESQUITA.

Bulgaria: P.O.B. 9260, Plot No. 232, Malik Rd., Upanga (E); *Ambassador:* BECHO STAMBOLIEV.

Burundi: P.O.B. 2752, 397 United Nations Rd., Upanga (E); *Ambassador:* PROTAIS MANGONA.

Cameroon: Addis Ababa, Ethiopia (E).

Canada: P.O.B. 1022, Gailey and Roberts Bldg. (1st Floor), Independence Ave. (HC); *High Commissioner:* J. A. IRWIN.

China People's Republic: P.O.B. 1649, Plot No. 77, Upanga (E); *Ambassador:* LI YAO-WEN.

Cuba: Kampala, Uganda (E).

Czechoslovakia: P.O.B. 3054, Jubilee Mansion, 69 Upanga Rd. (E); *Ambassador:* R. REZEK.

Denmark: Nairobi, Kenya (E).

Egypt: P.O.B. 1668, 21 Garden Ave. (near Pamba House) (E); *Ambassador:* MOHAMED FOUD EL BIDEWY.

Ethiopia: Nairobi, Kenya (E).

Finland: Addis Ababa, Ethiopia (E).

France: P.O.B. 2349, Standard Bank Bldg. (3rd Floor), Azikiwe St., City Drive (E); *Ambassador:* JEAN DESPARMET.

German Federal Republic: P.O.B. 2590, Standard Bank Bldg., Azikiwe St., City Drive (E); *Ambassador:* NORBERT HEBICH.

Guinea: P.O.B. 2969, 10 Luthuli Road (E); *Ambassador:* DAMOO SAHKO.

Hungary: P.O.B. 672, 20 Ocean Rd. (E); *Ambassador:* MIKLOS BARD.

India: P.O.B. 2684 (HC); *High Commissioner:* V. C. VIJAYARAGHAVAN.

Indonesia: P.O.B. 572, 299 Upanga Rd. (E); *Ambassador:* Brig.-Gen. OTTO ABDULRAHMAN.

Israel: P.O.B. 2474, Standard Bank Bldg. (1st Floor), Azikiwe St., City Drive (E); *Ambassador:* Maj. ARMON SCHLOMO.

Italy: P.O.B. 2106, Nanji Stores Bldg., Independence Ave. (E); *Ambassador:* VITTORIO ZADOTTI.

Ivory Coast: Addis Ababa, Ethiopia (E).

Jamaica: Addis Ababa, Ethiopia (E).

Japan: P.O.B. 2577; *Ambassador:* KENZO YOSHIDA.

Korean Democratic People's Republic: P.O.B. 2690, Plot 297, Upanga Rd. (E); *Ambassador:* SONG GI JAI.

Lesotho: (HC); *High Commissioner:* P. A. MABATHOANA.

Liberia: Nairobi, Kenya (E).

Mali: P.O.B. 1206, No. 9 Independence Ave. (E), *Chargé d'Affaires:* ARMANO SANGARE.

Mongolia: (E); *Ambassador:* BALJINGUIN LOTCHIN.

Morocco: Addis Ababa, Ethiopia (E).

Netherlands: P.O.B. 1174 (E); *Ambassador:* A. M. BRINK.

Norway: Nairobi, Kenya (E).

Pakistan: (HC); *High Commissioner:* BASHIR AHMED.

Poland: P.O.B. 2188, 4 Upanga Rd. (E); *Ambassador:* JAN WITEK.

Romania: P.O.B. 590, Plot 3, Bagamoyo Rd.; *Ambassador:* ION DRÎNCEANU.

Rwanda: P.O.B. 2468, Baumann House, Obote St., Kampala, Uganda (E), *Ambassador:* ALPHONSE M. KAGENZA.

Somalia: P.O.B. 2031, Karimjee Bldg., Plot No. 2 (First Floor), Independence Ave. (E); *Ambassador:* ABDUL-RAHMAN HUSSEIN MOHAMED.

Spain: P.O.B. 842; *Chargé d'Affaires:* EMILIO CASSINEL.

Sudan: P.O.B. 2266, "Albaraka", 64 Upanga Rd. (E). *Ambassador:* NUR ALI SULIEMAN.

Sweden: P.O.B. 9274, Dalgety Bldg., Second Floor, Independence Ave. (E); *Ambassador:* SUEN FREDERICK HEDIN.

Switzerland: P.O.B. 2454, Tancot House, City Drive (E); *Ambassador:* LUCIEN MOSSAZ.

Syria: P.O.B. 2442, 28 Garden Ave. (E); *Chargé d'Affaires:* NAIM KADDAH.

Turkey: Addis Ababa, Ethiopia (E).

U.S.S.R.: P.O.B. 1905, Plot No. 73, Kenyatta Drive (E); *Ambassador:* ANDREI M. TIMOSCHENKO.

United Kingdom: P.O.B. 9200, Permanent House (HC); *High Commissioner:* A. R. H. KELLAS.

U.S.A.: P.O.B. 9123, Standard Bank Bldg. (4th Floor), Azikiwe St., City Drive (E); *Ambassador:* W. BEVERLY CARTER, Jr.

Vatican: *Apostolic Nuncio:* Mgr. FRANCO BRAMBILLA.

Viet-Nam, Democratic Republic: P.O.B. 2194, Plot 79, Upanga (E); *Ambassador:* LE THANH TAM.

Yemen, Peoples Democratic Republic: (E); *Ambassador:* ABDUL BARI KASSIM.

Yugoslavia: P.O.B. 2838, Plot No. 276, East Upanga Area (E); *Ambassador:* ZIVOJIN LAKIC.

Zaire, Republic of: P.O.B. 975, Upanga Rd., Plot No. 291A (E); *Ambassador:* MWENDA ODILON.

Zambia: P.O.B. 2525, Plot 291, Upanga (HC); *High Commissioner:* R. S. MAKASA.

Tanzania also has diplomatic relations with the Cambodian National United Front, Cyprus, Greece and Sierra Leone.

REGIONAL COMMISSIONERS

Arusha: A. W. MWAKAN'GATA, M.P.

Coast: PETER KISUMO, M.P.

Dodoma: K. Y. KOMBA, M.P.

Iringa: M. N. KISSOKY, M.P.

Kigoma: P. J. NDOBHO, M.P.

Kilimanjaro: JACOB NAMFUA, M.P.

Lindi: N. A. KIONDO, M.P.

Mara: A. L. S. MHINA, M.P.

Mbeya: P. S. SIYOVELWA, M.P.

Morogoro: A. A. N. LYANDER, M.P.

Mtwara: CHEDIEL MGONJA, M.P.

Mwanza: A. O. A. MUHAJI, M.P.

Ruvuma: H. M. MKWAIA, M.P.

Shinyanga: M. M. SONGAMBELE, M.P.

Singida: M. NNAUYE, M.P.

Tabora: P. N. MGAYA, M.P.

Tanga: J. W. L. MAKINDA, M.P.

West Lake: LAWI SIJAONA, M.P.

PARLIAMENT

NATIONAL ASSEMBLY

Elected Members: 120.

Nominated Members: The President may nominate up to 30 members; 20 from Zanzibar and 10 from the mainland. To date (August 1972) 10 have been nominated from Zanzibar and 10 from the mainland.

Ex-Officio Members: 20. The majority of ex-officio members are the Regional Commissioners.

National Members: 15.

ELECTIONS, OCTOBER 1970

PARTY	SEATS
Tanganyika African National Union* (TANU)	207

32 members represent the Zanzibar regional assembly.

* Two candidates may contest each seat.

POLITICAL PARTIES

Tanganyika African National Union (TANU): P.O.B. 9151, Dar es Salaam; f. 1954; aims to develop a socialist democratic state by self-help at all levels; over 1,500,000 mems.; since Arusha Declaration of February 1967 leaders must be workers or peasants and members must be fully dedicated to the objects and beliefs of the Party; Pres. JULIUS K. NYERERE.

There are also organizations for the Party Elders, for the women (UWT), for youth (TYL) and for parents (TAPA); and the co-operatives and the trade union are also affiliated.

Afro-Shirazi Party: P.O.B. 389, Zanzibar; f. 1957; mainly African party, dominant in the Zanzibar Revolutionary Council; est. mems. 100,000; Pres. ABOUD JUMBE.

DEFENCE

Of a total armed force of 11,100, the army numbers 10,000, the navy 600 and the air force 500. Military service is voluntary.

JUDICIAL SYSTEM

Under a Bill introduced into the Assembly in December 1969 chiefs are no longer permitted to exercise any power under traditional or customary law.

From the beginning of 1970 People's Courts have been established in Zanzibar. Magistrates are elected by the people and have two assistants each.

The Court of Appeal for East Africa: P.O.B. 30187, Nairobi; Pres. Mr. Justice C. D. NEWBOLD, C.M.G.; Vice-Pres. Mr. Justice W. A. H. DUFFUS; Justices of Appeal J. F. SPRY, E. J. E. LAW; Registrar R. GAFFA. Hears appeals from Uganda, Kenya and Tanzania.

Permanent Commission of Enquiry: P.O.B. 2643, Dar es Salaam; Chair. Chief E. A. M. MANG'ENYA; Sec. H. K. KATUA.

The High Court: Has final jurisdiction in both criminal and civil cases, subject only to the right of appeal to the East African Court of Appeal. Its headquarters are at Dar es Salaam but it holds regular sessions in all Regions. It consists of a Chief Justice and eight Puisne Judges.

Chief Justice: Mr. Justice AUGUSTINE SAIDI.

Judges: Mr. Justice M. C. E. P. BIRON, Mr. Justice M. P. K. KIMICHA, Mr. Justice A. E. OTTO, Mr. Justice E. A. L. BANNERMAN, Mr. Justice H. G. PLATT, Mr. Justice G. ONYIUKE, Mr. Justice L. B. DUFF, Mr. Justice O. T. HAMLYN, Mr. Justice N. S. MNZAVAS, Mr. Justice Z. N. EL-KINDY.

Registrar: L. M. MAKAME.

Senior Deputy Registrar: D. R. MAPIGANO.

District Courts: These are situated in each district and are presided over by either a Resident Magistrate or District Magistrate. They have limited jurisdiction and there is a right of appeal to the High Court.

Primary Courts: These are established in every district and are presided over by Primary Court Magistrates. They have limited jurisdiction and there is a right of appeal to the District Courts and then to the High Court.

RELIGION

ANGLICAN

Archbishop:
Province of Tanzania: Most Rev. JOHN SEPEKU, Bishop of Dar es Salaam; P.O.B. 25 016, Ilala, Dar es Salaam.

Bishops:
Central Tanganyika: Rt. Rev. YOHANA MADINDA. P.O.B. 15, Dodoma, Tanzania.

Masasi: Rt. Rev. G. HILARY CHISONGA, Private Bag, Masasi, Tanzania.

Morogoro: Rt. Rev. GRESFORD CHITEMO, P.O.B. 320, Morogoro, Tanzania.

Ruvuma: Rt. Rev. MAURICE D. NGAHYOMA, P.O.B. 7, Songea, Tanzania.

South-West Tanganyika: Rt. Rev. JOHN RICHARD WORTHINGTON POOLE-HUGHES, P.O. Box 32, Njombe Tanzania.

Victoria Nyanza: Rt. Rev. MAXWELL L. WIGGINS, B.A., L.TH. P.O.B. 278, Mwanza, Tanzania.

Western Tanganyika: Rt. Rev. MUSA KAHURANANGA, P.O.B. 13, Kasulu, Tanzania.

Zanzibar and Tanga: Rt. Rev. YOHANA JUMAA, P.O.B. 35, Korogwe, Tanzania.

ROMAN CATHOLIC

The Catholic Church was established in Tanganyika in 1868.

Archbishop:

Dar es Salaam: Cardinal LAUREAN RUGAMBWA, P.O.B. 167, Dar es Salaam.

Bishops:

Arusha: Rt. Rev. DENNIS VINCENT DURNING, P.O.B. 3044, Arusha.

Dodoma: Rt. Rev. MATHIAS ISUJA, P.O.B. 922, Dodoma.

Iringa: Rt. Rev. MARIO MGULUNDE, Tosamaganga, P.O.B. 133, Iringa.

Mahenge: Rt. Rev. Fr. the Vicar Capitular, P.O. Mahenge.

Mbulu: Most Rev. NICODEMUS B. HANDO, Bishop's House, Dareda, P.O.B. 97, Babati.

Morogoro and Zanzibar: Rt. Rev. ADRIAN MKOBA, P.O.B. 640, Morogoro.

Moshi: Rt. Rev. JOSEPH SIPENDI, P.O.B. 3011, Moshi.

Nachingwea: Rt. Rev. B. RALPH COTEY, P.O.B. 43, Masasi.

Ndanda: Rt. Rev. VICTOR HAELG.

Njombe: Rt. Rev. RAYMOND MWANYIKA, P.O.B. 54, Njombe.

Same: Rt. Rev. Mgr. HENRY WINKELMOLEN, P.O.B. 8, Same.

Songea: Rt. Rev. JAMES KOMBA, P.O.B. 152.

Tanga: Rt. Rev. MAURUS KOMBA, P.O.B. 1108, Tanga.

Archbishop:

Tabora: Most Rev. MARKO MIHAYO, Private Bag, P.O. Tabora.

Bishops:

Bukoba: Rt. Rev. GERVASIUS NKALANGA, Bishop's House, P.O. Private Bag, Bukoba.

Kigoma: Rt. Rev. ALPHONSI NSABI, Bishop's House, P.O.B. 71, Kigoma.

Mbeya: Rt. Rev. JAMES SANGU, P.O.B. 179, M bey a.

Musoma: Rt. Rev. JOHN JAMES RUDIN, P.O.B. 93, Musoma.

Mwanza: Rt. Rev. RENATUS BUTIBABAGE, P.O.B. 1421, Mwanza.

Rulenge: Rt. Rev. CHRISTOPHER MWOLEKA, Postal Agency Rulenge, via Bukoba.

Shinyanga: Rt. Rev. EDWARD ALOYSIUS MCGURKIN, P.O.B. 47, Shinyanga.

Singida: Rt. Rev. BERNARD MABULA, P.O.B. 171, Singida.

Sumbawanga: Rt. Rev. KAROLI MSAKILA, P.O.B. 34, Sumbawanga.

There are some 2,228,600 Roman Catholics in Tanzania.

LUTHERAN

Evangelical Lutheran Church in Tanzania: P.O.B. 3033, Arusha; 568,444 mems.; Head: Bishop STEFANO R. MOSHI, D.D. (HON.); Exec. Sec. JOEL NGEIYAMU.

Bishops:

Northern Diocese: Bishop S. R. MOSHI, P.O.B. 195, Moshi.

North-Eastern Diocese: Bishop S. KOLOWA, P.O.B. 10, Lushoto.

North-Western Diocese: Bishop J. KIBIRA, P.O.B. 98, Bukoba.

GREEK ORTHODOX

Archbishop of East Africa: NICADEMUS OF IRINOUPOULIS, Nairobi. (Province covers Kenya, Uganda and Tanzania.)

There are also Muslim, Moravian and animist communities. Islam is the dominant religion in Zanzibar.

THE PRESS

DAILIES

Adal Insaf: P.O.B. 385, Dar es Salaam; English, Gujarati and Swahili.

Daily Nation: P.O.B. 3505, Dar es Salaam; f. 1960; English; local edition of Kenya newspaper; Chief Editorial Representative in Tanzania: OMAR AL-MOODY; circ. 75,000.

Daily News: P.O.B. 9033, Dar es Salaam; f. 1972; TANU Newspaper; Editor-in-Chief Pres. JULIUS NYERERE; Man. Editor S. MDEE; circ. 23,108.

Kipanga: P.O.B. 199, Dar es Salaam; Swahili; Publr. Information and Broadcasting Services.

Ngurumo: P.O.B. 937, Dar es Salaam; Swahili; Editor S. B. THAKER; circ. 15,000.

Uhuru: P.O.B. 9221, Dar es Salaam; official organ of TANU; Swahili; Editor B. MKAPA; circ. 15,000.

Zanzibar News Service: P.O.B. 1188, Zanzibar; English and Swahili.

Zanzibar Voice: P.O.B. 40, Zanzibar; evening; English and Gujarati; Sales Man. Z. E. KASSAM.

SUNDAY PAPERS

Mzalendo: P.O.B. 9221, Dar es Salaam; f. 1972; weekly organ of TANU in Swahili.

Sunday Nation: P.O.B. 3505, Dar es Salaam; local edition of Kenya newspaper; Editorial Rep. OMAR AL-MOODY; circ. 60,000.

Sunday News: P.O.B. 9033, Dar es Salaam; f. 1954; Editor-in-Chief Pres. JULIUS NYERERE; Editor (vacant); circ. 22,789.

WEEKLIES, MONTHLIES, QUARTERLIES AND OTHERS

The African Review: P.O.B. 35042, Dar es Salaam; f. 1971; politics etc.; quarterly.

Ecclesia: P.O.B. 167, Dar es Salaam; f. 1954; monthly; religious; Editor Fr. NOVATUS KAVELAARS; 5,900 copies.

Gazette of the United Republic: P.O.B. 2483, Dar es Salaam; weekly; official Government publication.

Government Gazette: P.O.B. 261, Zanzibar; f. 1964; official announcements; weekly.

Ija Webonere (*Come and See*): P.O.B. 98, Bukoba; f. 1954; monthly; religious, Editor P. B. TIBAIJUKA, 2,000 copies.

Kiongozi (*The Leader*): P.O.B. 9400, Dar es Salaam; f. 1950; incorporated Ecclesia 1971; Swahili, fortnightly; Editor C. H. B. HAKILI; circ. 25,000.

Kweupe: P.O.B. 222, Dar es Salaam; Swahili; Publr. Information and Broadcasting Service; 3 issues weekly.

Mwenge (*Firebrand*): P.O.B. 1, Peramiho; f. 1937; monthly, Editor JOHN MAHUNDI; circ. 12,800.

Mwongozi: P.O.B. 568; f. 1942; in English, Arabic and Swahili; weekly; 2,000 copies.

National Weekly: Dar es Salaam; weekly; English; circ. 5,000.

Nchi Yetu: P.O.B. 9033, Dar es Salaam; f. 1964; Swahili weekly.

News Review: P.O.B. 9142, Dar es Salaam; weekly.

Nyota Afrika: P.O.B. 9010, Nairobi; f. 1963; Swahili; monthly; circ. 50,000.

Spotlight on South Africa: Dar es Salaam; organ of the African National Congress (South Africa).

Taifa Tanzania: P.O.B. 9010, Nairobi, Kenya; weekly; Man. Editor BOAZ OMORI (*banned November* 1968).

Tanganyika Post: P.O.B. 520, Arusha; English; fortnightly.

Tanzania Trade and Industry: P.O.B. 234, Dar es Salaam; English; quarterly.

Ukulima wa Kisasa: P.O.B. 2308, Dar es Salaam; f. 1955; Swahili; monthly; agricultural; Editor C. C. RWECHUNGURA; circ. 35,000.

Ushirika: Co-operative Union of Tanzania, P.O.B. 2567, Dar es Salaam; weekly.

Young Africa: P.O.B. 908, Dar es Salaam; f. 1952; weekly; Editor E. E. KAHAN.

There are in all about 20 monthly local newspapers published in vernacular (mostly Swahili) edited by Africans.

NEWS AGENCIES

FOREIGN BUREAUX

Novosti: P.O.B. 2271, Dar es Salaam; Chief V. P. SIDENKO; publishes Swahili weekly: *Urusi Leo*.

Četeka, Prensa Latina, Reuters and Tass (Dar es Salaam and Zanzibar) also have bureaux in Tanzania.

PUBLISHERS

Longman Tanzania Ltd.: P.O.B. 3164, Dar es Salaam.

Oxford University Press: P.O.B. 21039, Maktaba Rd., Dar es Salaam.

Tanzania Publishing House: P.O.B. 2138, Dar es Salaam; f. 1966; 60 per cent owned by National Development Corporation of Tanzania; publishes educational and general books in Swahili and English·

RADIO

Radio Tanzania: P.O.B. 9191, Dar es Salaam; f. 1956; Dir.-Gen. M. KIAMA.

Broadcasts in Swahili on nine wavelengths and in English and other languages on four wavelengths.

Radio Tanzania Zanzibar: P.O.B. 1178, Zanzibar; f. 1964; Broadcasting Officer OMAR M. OMAR.

Broadcasts in Swahili on two wavelengths.

There are 200,000 radio sets in use.

FINANCE

BANKING

On February 6th, 1967, all banks in Tanzania were nationalized.

CENTRAL BANK ORGANIZATIONS

Bank of Tanzania: P.O.B. 2939, Mirambo St., Dar es Salaam; f. 1966 when assumed functions of East African Currency Board; sole issuing bank; government-owned; Gov. E. I. M. MTEI, Man. Dir. I. K. MARTIN; cap. 20m. sh.

East African Currency Board: P.O.B. 3684, Nairobi, Kenya; f. 1919 and in process of liquidation, its functions having been assumed by the central banks of Kenya, Tanzania and Uganda; Chair. D. A. OMARI, M.B.E.; Sec. H. R. HIRST, C.B.E.

OTHER STATE BANKS

The National Bank of Commerce: P.O.B. 1255, Dar es Salaam; f. 1967, by Act of Parliament, to take over branches in Tanzania of National and Grindlays Bank Ltd., Standard Bank Ltd., Barclays Bank D.C.O., Algemene Bank Nederland N.V., Bank of India Ltd., Bank of Baroda Ltd., Commercial Bank of Africa Ltd., National Bank of Pakistan and Tanzania Bank of Commerce; on October 24th, 1970, the business of the National Co-operative and Development Bank was absorbed by the N.B.C. under a Presidential Decree of October 10th; 36 branches, 2 sub-branches and 89 agencies throughout Tanzania; cap. p.u. 50m. sh.; gen. res. 47m. sh.; total dep. 1,779m. sh.; all types of banking business transacted locally and through agents and correspondents throughout the world; Chair. AMON JAMES NSEKELA; Gen. Man. SAIDI KASSIM.

People's Bank of Zanzibar: P.O.B. 1173, Forodhani, Zanzibar; f. 1966, state-controlled private concern; Chair. and Man. ERNEST C. WAKATI.

Tanganyika Post Office Savings Bank: P.O.B. 9300, Dar es Salaam; f. 1927; dep. 54m. sh.; provides banking facilities for small depositors in mainland Tanzania.

Tanzania Investment Bank: P.O.B. 9373, Dar es Salaam; f. 1970; cap. 108.3m. sh.; provides medium and long-term finance and technical assistance for economic development; Chair. and Man. Dir. G. F. MBOWE; Gen. Man. C. KAHANGI.

In 1971 provision was made to set up a Rural Development Bank, with authorized capital of 100m. sh., for financing agricultural and small-scale industrial programmes in rural areas.

INSURANCE

National Insurance Corporation: Dar es Salaam; f. 1966; nationalized 1967; handles all types of insurance business.

Some forty foreign insurance companies are represented in Tanzania.

TRADE AND INDUSTRY

CHAMBERS OF COMMERCE

Arusha Chamber of Commerce and Agriculture: P.O.B. 141. Arusha; f. 1948; Pres. H. V. Sparrow.

Bukoba Chamber of Commerce: P.O.B. 196, Bukoba.

Dar es Salaam Chamber of Commerce: Box 41, Dar es Salaam; f. 1919; 180 mems.; Pres. J. T. Lupembe, M.P

Dar es Salaam Merchants' Chamber: Box 12, Dar es Salaam.

Indian Chamber of Commerce: Box 543, Tanga.

Iringa Chamber of Commerce and Agriculture: Box 262, Iringa.

Mbeya Chamber of Commerce: P.O.B. 176, Mbeya.

Morogoro Chamber of Commerce and Agriculture: P.O.B. 98, Morogoro; 35 mems.; Pres. L. Holgate.

Moshi Chamber of Commerce and Industry: Box 280, Moshi; 38 mems.

Mtwara District Chamber of Commerce and Agriculture: P.O.B. 113, Mtwara.

Mwanza Chamber of Commerce and Industry: Box 296, Mwanza.

Southern Province Chamber of Commerce and Agriculture: P.O.B. 15, Lindi.

Tanga Chamber of Commerce: Box 331, Tanga; Secs. A. L. Le Maitre, o.b.e., L. E. Le Maitre.

Tanganyika Association of Chambers of Commerce: P.O.B. 41, Dar es Salaam.

MARKETING AND PRODUCER ASSOCIATIONS AND BOARDS

The Copra Board: f. 1950; administers the proceeds of a cess on exported copra products for the benefit of the copra industry.

Lint and Seed Marketing Board: Dar es Salaam; Gen. Man. J. F. Robinson.

Tanganyika Sisal Marketing Association Ltd.: Hospital Rd., P.O.B. 277, Tanga; f. 1948; Exec. Chair. A. K. E. Shaba; Sec. J. M. Bakampenja.

Tanganyika Pyrethrum Board: P.O.B. 41, Dar es Salaam.

Tanganyika Tea Growers' Association: P.O.B. 2177, Dar es Salaam; Chair. D. I. C. Hopkins; Sec. A. J. Foster.

DEVELOPMENT CORPORATIONS

Tanganyika Agricultural Corporation: P.O.B. 9113, Dar es Salaam; f. 1955; statutory body to take over the work of the Overseas Food Corporation and undertake commercial, development and settlement projects; Chair. H. M. Lugusha; Chief Executive Officer A. T. P. Seabrook.

Commonwealth Development Corporation: London and Dar es Salaam; finances agricultural and industrial development projects.

National Development Corporation of Tanzania: P.O.B. 2669, Dar es Salaam; f. 1965; government-owned; initial cap. 20m. sh.; Chair. P. Bomani, m.p.; Gen. Man. C. G. Kahama, m.p.

Tanganyika Development Finance Company Ltd.: P.O.B. 2478, Dar es Salaam; f. 1962; issued share cap. £2,000,000 taken up equally by the National Development Corporation of Tanzania, the Commonwealth Development Corporation and agencies of the Federal German and Netherlands Governments; to assist economic development; Man. M. A. Boyd.

Economic Development Commission: Dar es Salaam; f. 1962; Government-owned; to plan the development of the country's economy.

Mbeya Exploration Co.: financed jointly by the Commonwealth Development Corpn., and Messrs. Billiton to develop pyrochlore reserves in the Southern Highlands Province.

Tangold Mining Co.: P.O. Musoma; f. 1953; financed by Commonwealth Development Corpn. and New Consolidated Gold Fields Co.; gold mining in Musoma district; Gen. Manager C. J. McFarlane.

EMPLOYERS' ASSOCIATION

Federation of Tanganyika Employers: P.O.B. 2971. Dar es Salaam; f. 1960; Exec. Dir. P. Webster.

TRADE UNIONS

Minimum wages are controlled by law and there is also compulsory arbitration under the Trades Disputes (Settlement) Act. This Act makes strikes and lockouts illegal unless the statutory conciliation procedure has been followed. In 1964 the existing 13 trade unions were dissolved by legislation and the National Union of Tanganyika Workers (NUTA) was substituted. Wage increases are to be linked with productivity. In early 1969 NUTA had some 269,500 members.

NUTA agreements with some companies provide for a closed shop and membership is compulsory after a probation period. In other companies NUTA membership is voluntary.

National Union of Tanganyika Workers: Dar es Salaam; f. 1964; sole Trade Union organization, no international affiliation; about 240,000 mems.; Chair. N. Kazimoto; Gen. Sec. Alfred Tandau; Deputy Gen. Sec. C. Tungaraza.

INDUSTRIAL SECTIONS

East African Community Workers' Section: P.O.B. 2128, Dar es Salaam; Asst. Gen. Sec. K. Y. Vumu.

Transport, Mines and Domestic Section: P.O.B. 15380, Dar es Salaam; Asst. Gen. Sec. A. R. Bukuku.

Central and Local Government Workers' Section: P.O.B. 5376, Dar es Salaam; Asst. Gen. Sec. E. J. Mashasi.

Agricultural Workers' Section: P.O.B. 2087, Tanga; Asst. Gen. Sec. H. K. M. Naftal.

Dockworkers' and Seafarers' Section: P.O.B. 353, Tanga; Asst. Gen. Sec. T. C. Mabonesho.

Teachers' Section: Asst. Gen. Sec. M. P. Besha.

PRINCIPAL UNAFFILIATED UNIONS

African Medical Workers' Union: P.O. Box 719, Dar es Salaam; Pres. John S. Kianoo; Gen. Sec. Idi S. Msangi; 1,540 mems.

Tanganyika Railway Asian Union: P.O.B. 20525, Dar es Salaam, Pres. Fakir Chand, Hon. Gen. Sec. N. K. Karmali, 997 mems.

Workers' Department of the Afro-Shirazi Party: P.O.B. 389, Vikokotoni, Zanzibar; f. 1965; Pres. Mohamed Mfaume Omar; Sec. Khamis Abdulla Ameir.

CO-OPERATIVES

The co-operative movement plays a central role in the Tanzanian economy handling almost all of the country's exports (except sisal) and a substantial portion of the domestic economy. By far the largest portion of its activities are involved with the marketing of agricultural produce but the co-operative movement has made some preliminary incursions into the transport, wholesale, and retail field and has been granted exclusive import licences in some commodities.

The movement is composed of some 1,670 primary marketing societies under the aegis of about 40 co-operative unions. The Co-operative Union of Tanganyika is the national organization (affiliated with the ruling TANU party) to which all unions belong.

Co-operative Development Office: Zanzibar; f. 1952; encourages and develops co-operative societies.

Co-operative Union of Tanganyika Ltd.: P.O.B. 2567, Dar es Salaam; f. 1962; a Co-operative Bank and the Co-operative Supply Association were formed in 1962; Sec.-Gen. JOHN A. MHAVILLE, M.P.; 700,000 mems.

PRINCIPAL SOCIETIES

Bukoba Co-operative Union Ltd.: P.O.B. 5, Bukoba; 74 affiliated societies; 75,000 mems.

Kilimanjaro Native Co-operative Union Ltd.: f. 1932; 42 affiliated societies; 40,208 mems.

Tanganyika Co-operative Trading Agency Ltd.: 16 mems. representing 153 societies; 162,413 mems.

Zanzibar State Trading Corporation: P.O.B. 26, Zanzibar; state enterprise since 1964, sole exporter of cloves, markets clove oil, chillies, cocoa, lime juice, lime oil and clove pomanders, sole shipping agent for the port of Zanzibar; Gen. Man. ALI BIN AMEIR.

MAJOR INDUSTRIAL COMPANIES

The following are some of the largest companies in terms either of capital investment or employment.

Agip (Tanzania) Ltd.: P.O.B. 2038, Dar es Salaam; f. 1966; cap. 13.8m. sh.; government holds 50 per cent of shares. Distribution and marketing of petroleum products; refining of petroleum products from imported crudes through same group's affiliated refinery in Dar es Salaam; oil prospecting.

Man. Dir. C. E. BORRAZZI; Sec. M. SPAGNOLETTO; 125 employees.

B.A.T. Tanzania Ltd.: P.O.B. 9114, Dar es Salaam; f. 1965; cap. 48m. sh.; National Development Corporation holds 60 per cent of shares.

Manufacture and marketing of cigarettes.

Chair. C. L. G. KAHAMA; Gen. Man. D. S. DUNBAR; 752 employees.

Esso Standard Tanzania Ltd.: P.O.B. 9103, Dar es Salaam; f. 1966; cap. U.S. $770,000.

Import and distribution of crude and refined petroleum products.

Man. Dir. G. C. BICKNELL; 124 employees.

Friendship Textile Mill Ltd.: P.O.B. 2669, Dar es Salaam; f. 1966; cap. 20,000 sh; wholly owned by National Development Corporation.

Textile manufacturing; 634 employees.

Mwanza Textiles Ltd.: P.O.B. 1344, Mwanza; f. 1966; cap. 20m. sh.

Spinners, weavers, dyers and printers of textiles; 1,200 employees.

National Textile Industries Corporation Ltd.: P.O.B. 9211, Dar es Salaam; f. 1970; authorized cap. 10m. sh; wholly owned subsidiary of National Development Corporation.

Sole importer of textiles and textile articles; distribution of locally produced textiles and textile articles.

Gen. Man. I. THORSTEINSSON; Sec. G. W. HARTLEY; 450 employees.

The State Trading Corporation: P.O.B. 883, Dar es Salaam; f. 1967; company created by statute and wholly government-owned.

Distribution of general merchandise, agricultural machinery and textiles; shipping agencies and port services.

Chair. D. A. NKEMBO; 1,900 employees.

Tanganyika Packers Ltd.: P.O.B. 452, Dar es Salaam; f. 1947; cap. 16,479,240 sh.; N.A.F.C.O. owns 51 per cent of shares.

Cattle slaughtering and meat canning; 1,200 employees.

Tanzania Breweries Ltd.: P.O.B. 9013, Dar es Salaam; f. 1934; cap. 18,501,700 sh; National Development Corporation holds 51 per cent of shares.

Manufacture and distribution of beer.

Gen. Man. D. L. V. HODGE; 540 employees.

Tanzania Portland Cement Co. Ltd.: P.O.B. 1950, Dar es Salaam; f. 1959; cap. 30m. sh; National Development Corporation owns 50 per cent of shares.

Manufacture of Portland cement; capacity 400,000 tons per annum.

Gen. Man. M. H. FROEHLICH; 540 employees.

Williamson Diamonds Ltd.: P.O. Mwaduwi; f. 1942; cap. 12m. sh; National Development Corporation owns 50 per cent of shares.

Diamond mining; 2,500 employees.

TRANSPORT AND TOURISM

TRANSPORT

RAILWAYS

East African Railway Corporation: P.O.B. 30121, Nairobi, Kenya; self-financing corporation within the East African Community; Chair. D. W. NABUDERE; Dir. Gen. Dr. E. N. GAKUO.

TANZANIAN LINES	MILES
Tanga–Moshi	219
Moshi–Arusha . . .	53
Dar es Salaam–Kigoma . .	779
Mnyusi–Ruvu . . .	117
Kilosa–Kidatu . . .	68
Tabora–Mwanza . . .	236
Kaliuwa–Mpanda . . .	131

Tanzania-Zambia Railway Authority: c/o Ministry of Communications, P.O.B. 2581, Lusaka; head office is in Dar es Salaam; work on the 287-mile railway began in October 1970 and is due to be finished in 1976.

ROADS

A network of passenger and goods road services (2,611 miles) is operated in the Southern Highlands, providing a link with Zambia, and there is a through service to Nairobi in Kenya.

MILEAGE (1968)	
Bitumen	1,052
Engineered Gravel . .	671
Earth	8,654
TOTAL . .	10,377

Zanzibar has 387 miles of road, of which 276 miles are bitumen surfaced, and Pemba has 227 miles, 81 of which are bitumen surfaced. A new road is being built between Zambia and Tanzania with aid from U.S.A., the World Bank Group and the Government of Sweden.

INLAND WATERWAYS

Lake marine services operate on Lakes Tanganyika and Victoria. Steamers connect with Kenya, Uganda, Zaire, Burundi and Zambia.

SHIPPING

East African Harbours Corporation: P.O.B. 9184, Dar es Salaam; responsible for the harbours functions formerly exercised by the East African Railways and Harbours; Chair. P. K. KINYANJUI.

Harbours: Dar es Salaam (seven deep-water berths), Mtwara (two deep-water berths), Tanga (lighterage). A new anchorage is being built at Dar es Salaam for giant oil tankers and should be finished in May 1972. Tanzania Government steamers run between Zanzibar, Pemba and Dar es Salaam.

British India Line: Dar es Salaam, Zanzibar and Tanga; runs joint alternating regular fortnightly services with Union Castle to U.K. East Coast ports; British India alone runs regular monthly service to India.

Canadian City Lines: Dar es Salaam. Tanga and Mtwara; services to Canadian ports.

Christensen Canadian African Lines: P.O. Box 1906, Dar es Salaam; direct service to and from Canada and Great Lakes ports via South African ports.

Clan Line: Dar es Salaam; mainly cargo services to the United Kingdom.

Cie. Maritime Belge: Dar es Salaam; cargo services to European continental ports.

D.O.A.L. (Deutsche Ost Afrika Linie): Dar es Salaam; services to Europe.

Farrell Lines: Dar es Salaam and Zanzibar; monthly services to North Atlantic and U.S.A. East Coast ports.

Harrison Line: Dar es Salaam; services to Europe.

Indian African Line: Dar es Salaam and Zanzibar; mainly cargo services to India, Ceylon and Burma.

Koninklijke Nedlloyd nv.: P.O.B. 1906, Dar es Salaam; round-Africa services to and from European continental ports.

Lloyd Triestino Line: Cargo and passenger service between Italy and East Africa; Agent Mitchell Cotts & Co. (E.A.) Ltd.

Lykes Lines: Dar es Salaam and Zanzibar; services to U.S.A. Gulf ports via South African ports.

Maritime Co. of Tanzania Ltd.: P.O.B. 277, Dar es Salaam; brs. at Tanga and Mtwara; a subsidiary of Ellerman Lines (Mid-Africa) Ltd.; agents for Mitsui O.S.K., Svedel, Canadian City, Southern and Sovereign Marine Lines (*q.v.*).

Mitsui O.S.K. Lines: Dar es Salaam, Tanga and Mtwara; services to and from Japan, Hong Kong and other Far Eastern ports.

Moore-McCormack Line: Robin Line Service, Dar es Salaam; services to and from U.S.A. and Atlantic ports; Agent Mitchell Cotts Group.

Nedlloyd Line: P.O.B. 1906, Dar es Salaam; serves U.S. Pacific ports and Vancouver.

Nippon Yusen Kaisha Line: Regular monthly service between Far East, Japan and East Africa; Agent Mitchell Cotts Group.

Oriental Africa Line: Dar es Salaam and Zanzibar; cargo services to South Africa, Malaya, Singapore, Indonesia, Hong Kong and Japan.

Osaka Shosen Kaisha: Dar es Salaam; services to Japan, Hong Kong, Malaya, South Africa and South America.

Scandinavian East Africa Line: Dar es Salaam and Zanzibar mainly cargo services to Scandinavian and Baltic ports.

Southern Lines: Dar es Salaam, Tanga and Mtwara; Coastal and Red Sea ports service.

Sovereign Marine Lines: Dar es Salaam, Tanga and Mtwara; services to Houston, New Orleans and New York.

Svedel Lines: Dar es Salaam, Tanga and Mtwara; services to and from Hamburg, Breman, Rotterdam and Antwerp.

Swedish East Africa Line: Dar es Salaam; regular services to Scandinavian, Baltic and North French ports.

Union Castle Line: Dar es Salaam and Zanzibar; runs joint alternating regular fortnightly services with British India to U.K. East Coast ports.

CIVIL AVIATION

East African Airways Corporation: Airways Terminal, Tancot House, P.O.B. 543, Dar es Salaam; P.O.B. 773, Zanzibar.

Tim Air Charters (Tanganyika) Ltd.: P.O.B. 804, Dar es Salaam; Piper dealers for Tanzania; 10 charter aircraft.

Tanzania is also served by the following airlines: Air Comores, Air Zaire, Air France, Air Madagascar, Alitalia, B.O.A.C., Ethiopian Airlines, K.L.M., Lufthansa, P.A.A., Sabena, Swissair, T.W.A. and Zambia Airways.

TOURISM

East Africa Tourist Travel Association: Headquarters P.O.B. 2013, Nairobi, Kenya.

Tanzania Tourist Corporation: Headquarters P.O.B. 2485, Dar es Salaam; offices at IPS Bldg., Maktaba/Independence Ave.

EDUCATION

Most schools receive state aid, the remainder being organized by missions and other voluntary agencies. There are not yet enough schools to provide universal primary education. A National Examination Certificate has taken the place of the East African Certificate of Education. According to the Directorate of Education, over 200,000 people attend adult education classes.

LEARNED SOCIETIES

British Council, The: Independence Ave., P.O.B. 9100, Dar es Salaam; Rep. I. H. WATTS.

East African Literature Bureau, Tanzania: P.O.B. 1408, Dar es Salaam; f. 1948; Dir. N. L. M. SEMPIRA; Senior Book Production Officer N. SHERALY.

Goethe-Institut: P.O.B. 9510, Dar es Salaam; f. 1962; German classes, library and cultural programme.

Historical Association of Tanzania: P.O.B. 35032, Dar es Salaam; f. 1966; 1,000 mems.; Pres. J. E. F. MHINA; Sec. Dr. I. K. KATOKE.

Tanzania Library Association: P.O.B. 2645, Dar es Salaam; f. 1965; a branch of the East African Library Association; Chair. F. K. TAWETE; Sec. H. A. MWENEGOHA; publ. *Someni*.

Tanzania Society, The: Box 511, Dar es Salaam; a non-political society catering for the geographical, ethnological, historical, and general scientific interests of Tanzania; publ. *Tanzania Notes and Records* (biannually).

RESEARCH INSTITUTES

Forest Department Headquarters: P.O.B. 426, Dar es Salaam; forestry surveying, mapping, management and economics; library of 1,500 vols.; Chief of Forestry D. R. LYAMUYA.

Institute of Swahili Research: P.O.B. 35091, Dar es Salaam; initiates fundamental research and co-operates with Governments and other public authorities and organisations; promotes the standardisation of orthography and the development of language generally; preparing new standard dictionary; Dir. G. A. MHINA; publs. *Swahili* (biannual), Supplements.

Livestock Research and Training Institute: Private Bag, Mpwapwa, Dodoma; f. 1905; Breeding and nutrition of livestock and training for Assistant Veterinary Field Officers; Dir. R. A. CHIOMBA, B.VSC., M.SC.; publ. *Progressive Stockman* (quarterly).

Mineral Resources Division: Ministry of Commerce and Industries, Mineral Resources and Power, P.O. Box 903, Dodoma; f. 1925; regional mapping, mineral exploration and assessment; supporting laboratory facilities; library of 3,150 text books, 1,200 bound volumes; reprints and maps; Commissioner G. LUENA; publs. *Bulletin, Memoirs, Annual Report, Geological Maps*.

Silviculture Research Institute: P.O.B. 95, Lushoto; f. 1951; Officer in Charge P. E. KIMARIYO; publs. *Technical Notes, Tanzania Silviculture Research Notes*.

Sisal Research Station (Mlingano): Ministry of Agriculture and Co-operatives, Tanzania, Private Bag, Ngomeni, Tanga; f. 1935; research on cultivation of sisal and other crops; Senior Research Officer N. J. MUKURASI.

REGIONAL INSTITUTES:

East African Community: P.O.B. 1001, Arusha; f. 1967; Sec.-Gen. C. G. MAINA; Uganda, Kenya and Tanzania participate on an equal partnership basis.

The East African Community administers the following research services in Tanzania (*see also* Kenya and Uganda):

East African Marine Fisheries Research Organisation: P.O. Box 668, Zanzibar; f. 1950; research into fishing methods and the migration, feeding and breeding habits of fish of the East African coast; Dir. B. E. BELL; publ. *Annual Report*.

East African Institute of Malaria and Vector-borne Diseases: Amani, Tanga; f. 1949; investigation into human vector-borne diseases, especially malaria and onchocersiasis; Dir. P. WEGESA; publ. *Annual Report*.

East African Institute for Medical Research: P.O.B. 162, Mwanza; f 1949; investigations into various tropical diseases with emphasis on bilharziasis, and hookworm in East Africa; Dir. Dr. V. M. EYAKUZE; publ. *Annual Report*.

Tropical Pesticides Research Institute: P.O.B. 3024, Arusha; f. 1962; research into tropical pests, including medical and veterinary carriers of disease, insect pests and weeds in agricultural crops; Dir. Dr. M. E. MATERU; publ. *Annual Report*.

LIBRARIES

Agricultural Department Library: P.O.B. 159, Zanzibar; agriculture in general; 1,100 vols., 50 periodicals.

British Council Libraries: P.O.B. 9100, Dar es Salaam; f. 1952; 9,684 vols.; 2,784 mems.; Librarian M. NURSE; branch: Moshi, P.O.B. 426, Moshi; f. 1957; 7,201 vols., 2,055 mems.

Ladha Maghji Indian Public Library: P.O. Box 70, Mwanza; 3,000 vols.; Librarian C. B. VYAS.

Museum Library: P.O. Box 116, Zanzibar; free public lending service; 3,000 vols. and 41 periodicals.

National Archives Division: Office of the Second Vice-President, P.O.B. 2006, Dar es Salaam; f. 1963.

Tanzania Information Services Library: Dar es Salaam; reference books on Tanzania.

Tanzania Library Service: P.O.B. 9283, Dar es Salaam; f. 1964; operates the following services: **National Central Library,** Dar es Salaam; public libraries in Arusha, Bukoba, Iringa, Kibaha, Korogwe, Moshi, Mwanza, Shinyanga and Tanga; rural library extension service in three regions; school mobile service; nationwide postal and loan-collection services; total stock: 330,000 vols.; Dir. E. E. KAUNGAMNO, B.A., M.L.S.

U.S. Information Service Library: Independence Avenue, P.O.B. 9170, Dar es Salaam; f. 1959; 5,000 vols.

The University Library: P.O.B. 9184, Dar es Salaam; f. 1961; 120,000 vols.; Librarian M. MUAA.

Zanzibar Government Archives: P.O.B. 116, Zanzibar; history and administration; 3,500 vols.; Archivist SAIS HILAL EL-BAULY.

MUSEUMS

National Museum of Tanzania: P.O.B. 511, Dar es Salaam; f. 1937 as King George V Memorial Museum, name changed 1963; ethnography, archaeology and history; houses the *Zinjanthropus* skull and other material from Olduvai and other Early Stone Age sites; also houses reference library; village museum and mobile museum for Education Service; Chair. K. J. CHANDE; Curator F. T. MASAO.

Zanzibar Government Museum: P.O. Box 116, Zanzibar; local collection, items relating to exploration in East Africa; library; Archivist and Curator SAIS HILAL EL-BAULY.

UNIVERSITY AND COLLEGES
UNIVERSITY OF DAR ES SALAAM
P.O.B. 35091, DAR ES SALAAM

Telephone: 53611.

Founded 1961; University status 1970.

Language of Instruction: English; Academic year: July to March (three terms).

Chancellor: President JULIUS K. NYERERE.
Vice-Chancellor: PIUS MSEKWA.
Chief Academic Officer: Prof. I. N. KIMAMBO.
Chief Administrative Officer: A. C. MWINGIRA.

Number of teachers: 308.

Number of students: 2,060.

Publications: *Calendar, Prospectus, Report on Research, Annual Report.*

DEANS:

Faculty of Law: Prof. P. L. U. CROSS, B.L.
Faculty of Arts and Social Science: Dr. J. F. RWEYEMAMU, PH.D.
Faculty of Science: Prof. A. S. MSANGI, PH.D.
Faculty of Medicine: Prof. A. M. NHONOLI, M.D., F.R.C.P.
Faculty of Agriculture: H. O. MONGI, M.SC.

College of National Education: P.O.B. 533, Korogwe, Tanga Region; 121 students; Principal F. D. NTEMO.

Commercial School: Dar es Salaam; f. 1965; six teachers.

Dar es Salaam Technical College: P.O.B. 20571, Dar es Salaam; f. 1956.

Kivukoni College: P.O.B. 9193, Dar es Salaam; f. 1961; eight-month residential courses for adults in Politics, Economics, History, Sociology, Public Administration and Industrial Relations; controlled by independent governing council and subsidized by the Tanzanian Government; Principal I. ELINEWINGA; 120 students; publ. *Mbioni* (monthly).

St. Philip's Theological College: Kongwa; f. 1920; the theological college of the Dioceses of Central Tanganyika, Victoria Nyanza, Morogoro and Western Tanganyika; Principal Rev. F. NTIRUKA.

Usambara Trade School: Lushoto; f. 1961; 70 students.

SELECT BIBLIOGRAPHY

(For works on Kenya, Tanzania and Uganda generally *see* Kenya Select Bibliography, p. 460.)

BIENEN, H. *Tanzania: Party Transformation and Economic Development*. Princeton, New Jersey, 1967; expanded edition, 1970.

CLIFFE, L. (Ed.). *One Party Democracy*. Nairobi, East African Publishing House, 1967.

CLIFFE, L., and SAUL, J. *Tanzania Socialism—Politics and Policies: An Interdisciplinary Reader*. Nairobi, East African Publishing House (in press).

DRYDEN, STANLEY. *Local Administration in Tanzania*. Nairobi, East African Publishing House, 1968.

The Economic Survey and Annual Plan, 1970–71. Dar es Salaam, Government Printer, 1970.

HOPKINS, RAYMOND F. *Political Roles in a New State: Tanzania's First Decade*. New Haven, Yale University Press, 1971.

ILIFFE, J. *Tanganyika under German Rule, 1905–12* Cambridge University Press, 1969.

KIMAMBO, I. N., and TEMU, A. J. (Eds.). *A History of Tanzania*. Nairobi, East African Publishing House, 1969.

LIEBENOW, J. GUS. *Colonial Rule and Political Development in Tanzania*. Nairobi, East African Publishing House, 1972.

LISTOWEL, J. *The Making of Tanganyika*. London, Chatto and Windus, 1965.

LOFCHIE, M. *Zanzibar: Background to Revolution*. Princeton, New Jersey; London, Oxford University Press, 1965.

NYERERE, J. K. *Freedom and Unity, a selection from writings and speeches, 1952–65*. London and Nairobi, Oxford University Press, 1967.

NYERERE, J. K. *Freedom and Socialism, a selection from writings and speeches, 1965–67*. Dar es Salaam and London, Oxford University Press, 1968; this contains the Arusha Declaration and subsequent policy statements.

STEPHENS, HUGH, W. *The Political Transformation of Tanganyika: 1920–67*. New York, Washington, Praeger; London, Pall Mall; 1968.

SVENDSEN, K. E. (Ed.). *The Economy of Tanzania*. Tanzania Publishing House (in press).

Tanganyika First Five-Year Plan, 1964–69. Dar es Salaam, Government Printer.

Tanzania Second Five-Year Plan for Economic and Social Development, July 1969–June 1974. Vols. I, II and III.

TORDOFF, W. *Government and Politics in Tanzania*. Nairobi, East African Publishing House, 1967.

Uchumi, The Journal of the Economic Society of Tanzania, Vol. I, Nos. 1 and 2.

YAFFEY, M. H. *Balance of Payments Problems of a Developing Country: Tanzania*. Munich, IFO Institute, 1970.

Togo

PHYSICAL AND SOCIAL GEOGRAPHY*

R. J. Harrison Church

The Republic of Togo, a small state of west Africa situated east of Ghana, has an area of 21,620 sq. miles (56,000 sq. km.), and comprises the eastern two-thirds of the pre-1914 German colony of Togo. From a coast-line of 35 miles (56 km.) Togo extends inland for about 335 miles (540 km.). The total population was 1,956,000 at the 1970 census, giving a higher than average density for this part of Africa. The very literate Ewe are the leading people in the south; many also live in Ghana, the eastern part of which was part of German Togo. In northern Togo are many different peoples; among them the Kabre are notable for their terracing of hillsides and intensive agriculture.

The coast, lagoons, blocked estuaries and Terre de Barre regions are identical to those of Dahomey, but calcium phosphate, the only mineral Togo produces, is quarried north-east of Lake Togo. The Lama swamp is absent in Togo, and Precambrian rocks with rather siliceous soils occur northward, first in the Mono tableland and then in the Togo-Atacora mountains. The latter are, however, still well wooded and planted with coffee and cocoa. North again is the Oti plateau, with infertile Primary sandstones, in which water is rare and deep down. On the northern border are granite areas, remote but densely peopled, as in neighbouring Ghana and Upper Volta. Togo's climate is similar to that of Dahomey, except that Togo's coastal area is even drier (Lomé: annual rainfall 30.8 in./782 mm.). Thus Togo, though smaller in area than Dahomey, is physically, as well as economically, more varied than its eastern neighbour.

* See map on p. 364.

RECENT HISTORY

E. Y. Aduamah†

THE SCRAMBLE

The turn of the twentieth century saw the creation of German Togo to fill the so-called blank space on the map between the Volta and Dahomey. By the pressure and persistent encouragement of Britain and France the export slave trade and the wars among the natives had ceased and they were establishing them-selves in legitimate trade, particularly in palm-oil. At the same time the rival European nations had resolved their own differences: the Danes sold their Keta possession to Britain in 1850, the Spaniards and the Portuguese abandoned their claims at Whydah in 1852 and 1887 respectively, and Germany reached the final boundary agreements with Britain's Gold Coast to the west and France's Dahomey to the east in 1897 and 1899 respectively.

THE COLONIAL PERIOD

German administration met with fierce resistance. Its extension from the coast inland was therefore slow and had to await an increase in personnel and military expeditions to suppress all opposition.

The period of peace from 1902 was marked by accelerated social and economic development which included the abolition of domestic slavery, the pro-vision of hospitals and a resolute attack on infectious diseases. In Togo, which the Germans referred to as their model colony (though the smallest of the German African possessions), the government steadily de-veloped the agricultural resources through scientific cultivation and reafforestation. This made it possible for Togo to dispense with financial subsidy from Germany. The government built excellent roads and a harbour and breakwaters at the capital Lomé, and also laid down an efficient telegraph system, a direct radio circuit to Germany and three railways to open up the interior.

Germany provided greater material benefits in the 30 years of her administration than Britain provided over a much longer period for her colony. But the Togolese, weighing the comparatively restricted interference of Britain against the harshness, forced labour and direct taxes of Germany, troubled their government with petitions calling for improvement in the administration, took to large-scale migration into the Gold Coast, and welcomed the British forces with open arms at the outbreak of war in 1914. Encircled by British and French colonies and a sea commanded by British shipping, and with only a small police force, Togo could offer no effective oppo-sition to the Franco-British attack of 1914. Within three weeks the Germans, after blowing up their huge £250,000 wireless station at Kamina, were compelled to surrender unconditionally. This was the first victory of the Allies in the First World War.

Before a peace settlement Lomé and the west of Togo were provisionally under British administration

† For the 1973 edition, revisions have been made to this article by KAYE WHITEMAN and the Editor.

while the French controlled the east. Through the Treaty of Versailles the division changed and France received the larger part of Togo (20,463 sq. miles) including Lomé and the railways that she had taken. The British sphere amounted to 13,041 sq. miles in area. Germany renounced sovereignty over her colonies and Britain and France were, with effect from 1922, to act as mandatory powers in their respective territories on behalf of the League of Nations.

British Togo was administered as though it were part of the Gold Coast, the northern section being treated as part of the Northern Territories and the southern as part of the Eastern Province of the Gold Coast Colony. Elected local government was developed in the villages and districts, and petty kingdoms which in German times existed in the southern part of the territory were in the 1930s amalgamated into states. Each state had a State Council which carried on local administration under the supervision of the District Commissioners.

French Togo had its budgetary autonomy and a separate administration, except between 1934 and 1937 when as an economy measure some senior civil servants in Togo or Dahomey served in both territories, and the Commissioner of Togo was also the head of Dahomey. The French did not promote the use of the vernaculars, nor did they give much authority to the chiefs, unlike the British.

Soon after the Mandates System was imposed some southern, Ewe chiefs protested against it. Like the colonial boundaries, it ignored natural divisions, splitting the Ewe into three sections, viz. (i) the Ewe section of Togo under French mandate, (ii) the Ewe section of Togo under British mandate and (iii) the Ewe section of the Gold Coast Colony. The demands of the chiefs for reunification could not be met, but some of the difficulties were removed by the two governments, and the people were, after 1926, allowed to use their farms across the border.

After the Second World War the Mandates System was in 1946 superseded by the Trusteeship System of the United Nations. The period immediately after the war saw a political movement in the two Togos, which, unlike the times of the illiterate chiefs, were led by intellectuals making use of youth movements, political parties, and the press to put their views across. Along with the movements for Ewe national unity there now emerged other movements for the unification of the two sections of Togo and others still which wanted the individual Togos to develop along separate ways. The results of a plebiscite conducted under UN supervision in British Togo in May 1956, however, showed the inhabitants in favour (against Ewe opposition) of union with the Gold Coast.

INDEPENDENT TOGO

The introduction in 1955 of a new statute and the subsequent transfer of all powers to a new government except defence, foreign affairs, and currency had among other political measures given French Togo a large measure of internal autonomy. In April 1958 elections for a new legislative asembly held under United Nations supervision were won by M. Sylvanus Olympio's party, the *Comité de l'unité togolaise* (CUT). He thereupon became Premier, and a year later, following the country's achievement of independence on April 27th, 1960, he was elected the first President of Togo.

Togo had remained primarily dependent on small-scale agriculture, and she had to balance her ordinary budget with a French subsidy, which for the year 1958, for instance, was 20 per cent. By careful management, however, Olympio's government achieved a favourable budget and trade balance for the first time since the end of German rule. By 1960 Togo was entirely independent of French subsidy. The government nevertheless faced much opposition from other political parties in the country, whose leaders included M. Nicolas Grunitzky (Prime Minister from 1956 to 1958 under the former French trusteeship) and M. Antoine Meatchi. Special problems had also arisen over some 600 ex-servicemen who had served in France on individual enlistments and had after the Franco-Algerian war been disbanded and repatriated to Togo. The government could not satisfy the demands of all these men for re-employment in view of the financial burden that expansion of the Togolese army would impose. On January 13th, 1963, President Olympio's government was overthrown in a military rising and he himself was shot dead.

This affair brought M. Nicolas Grunitzky back to head the government. To reconcile the whole nation Grunitzky formed a coalition government of all the political parties. This dragged on unsteadily amidst opposition from the party of the late President Olympio, and dissension in the Cabinet led to the resignation of two Ministers—M. Benoit Malou (Education) and M. Pierre Adossama (Labour)—the dismissal of the entire Cabinet, and the assumption of full powers by the President and the Vice-President, M. Antoine Meatchi. The government was also threatened by several plots, the most serious being that led by Dr. Noe Kutuklui, a supporter of the late President, in November 1966. To prevent a possible civil war the army, led by their Commander, Lieut.-Colonel Etienne Eyadéma, assumed control in a *coup* on January 13th, 1967.

MILITARY GOVERNMENT

The Government was dismissed, the Constitution abolished and the National Assembly dissolved. For three months the country was governed by a Committee of National Reconciliation, and thereafter a new government was formed with Eyadéma as President of the Republic. All political parties were dissolved, so that they should not disrupt Eyadéma's project of unifying the nation. Eyadéma became a General, Togo's first, in December 1967, and has consolidated his position. He has continually announced his intention of re-establishing civilian government, and a Constitutional Committee was inaugurated in October 1967, charged with drawing up a new constitution. The committee consisted of the President and his Government, five lawyers, three representatives of religious communities (Catholic, Protestant and Muslim) and ten others chosen for their experience in politics or economics. On the first anniversary of the *coup* the President announced that there were no longer any political prisoners or political refugees and army rule could end. A year later he reiterated this, and announced that political activities were now permissable. The new constitution had been completed and only awaited ratification by a referendum, after which elections would be held. The referendum did not take place, however, as massive popular support was expressed for the President. In August he proposed the founding of the Movement of the Togolese National Rally, a party of national unity. Backed by the chiefs, a constitutive congress was held and the *Rassemblement du Peuple Togolais*, Togo's sole political party, was founded with Eyadéma as its president.

The policy of unity and reconciliation was given further emphasis on the third anniversary of the *coup*, by now a national holiday, when Eyadéma released several political prisoners. An attempt had been made on his life in 1967 by a gendarme, who was sentenced to death, but later pardoned. However on August 8th, 1969 a serious plot was discovered, and over twenty-people were arrested, including several leading political figures. Kutuklui, who was alleged to have been involved, escaped. Those arrested were brought to trial before a specially established Court of State Security, where three of the four defence lawyers appointed by the court refused to plead because they resented government interference in the judiciary. Sanctions were taken against seven trial judges, who were accused of "showing solidarity" with the defendants, and it is suspected that the prison sentences passed on the plotters were arranged by the Government in order to intimidate its opponents.

Public sympathy was not with the plotters, and Eyadéma has continued to receive massive demonstrations of public support. Each announcement that the army's "mission" has been accomplished has provoked pleas for his continued rule. The RTP's first congress, held in November 1971, reinforced the President's position; it opposed constitutionalization of the government and asked for a referendum. This was held in early January 1972, and the question of whether Eyadéma should remain as President of the Republic received an overwhelming "yes" vote of 867,941 as against 878 "noes", in an almost 99 per cent poll.

Eyadéma's position now seems quite secure, and his party, which has established itself in every town and village, has a strong following. Its principles are national unity, and development in every sphere of economic and social life, and it is significant that

Eyadéma has felt sufficiently confident to make membership, since August 1971, purely voluntary. His early fear of vengeance from Olympio's supporters was proved well-founded by the plot of August 8th, 1970, and those involved received harsh punishment, but after the referendum the survivors were pardoned and three of the seven trial judges reinstated. Several former members of Olympio's government have joined the RPT, and Eyadéma's policy of reconciliation seems to have been effective. He has also significantly reduced the inequalities between north and south, although northerners tend to dominate in the army.

FOREIGN RELATIONS

On achieving independence Togo suffered constant harassments from Ghana. President Kwame Nkrumah of Ghana had assisted Togo in 1958 in her political campaigns for independence. His aim was not, however, to develop social and economic co-operation for the benefit of the two countries, but to bring about the integration of Togo into Ghana. Failing this objective Nkrumah then used trade embargoes and border closures against Togo. A few weeks before Olympio's assassination a verbal conflict and the exchange of strongly-worded notes had developed between Ghana and Togo, the former alleging Togolese support for plots by Ghanaian refugees in Togo against the Ghana government, and the latter alleging Ghanaian complicity in previous attempts on President Olympio's life. President Nkrumah was the first to recognize the new military government when recognition was difficult. Since the fall of the Nkrumah Government in 1966 relations have improved, and from 1973 Togo and Dahomey are to obtain electricity from the hydro-electric plant at Ghana's Volta dam. An agreement was signed in 1969 to prevent smuggling and illegal immigration.

Partly of Portuguese ancestry, Olympio was educated at German, English and French schools, and he declared a policy of neutrality to enable Togo to act independently in world affairs. Under him Togo chose to remain outside the French Community. Reluctantly he signed a defence pact with France under which France guaranteed Togo's territorial integrity. Under Grunitzky Togo's dependence on France increased. In July 1963 Grunitzky signed seven conventions and agreements with France covering diplomatic, economic, monetary, defence, judicial, cultural and technical matters. In 1966 Togo became a member of both OCAM and the Conseil de l'Entente, which also includes Ivory Coast, Niger, Upper Volta and Dahomey. She is also a member of the Organization of African Unity. Apart from France, Togo receives aid mainly from Germany and the United States. A commercial and friendship treaty was signed with the U.S. in 1966. The £7.7 million deep harbour opened at Lomé in April 1968 was financed with a loan from Federal Germany.

ECONOMY

Samir Amin*

EARLY ECONOMIC EXPANSION

German Togoland, like the neighbouring Gold Coast, went through its economic "miracle" at a very early stage—before 1914. At the outbreak of the First World War its exports were worth £500,000. The ratio of the value of exports to the gross domestic product was already almost the same as in 1970. In that period too, tax revenue already made up about 5 per cent of G.D.P. More or less the same proportion was maintained for the whole inter-war period, and it did not increase until after the Second World War, when it reached about 9 per cent in 1959, on the eve of independence.

The revenue raised by taxation, relatively large for that epoch, made it possible to finance the country's infrastructure without resort to German capital. It also brought about the highest level of educational development in Africa. With 13,700 pupils in 1914 (9 per cent of those of school age) German Togoland had an enormous advantage over the other west African countries. In 1912 Southern Nigeria, with eight times the number of inhabitants, had only three times as many children in school, and Senegal, with twice the population, reached that figure only in 1938.

Togo's "miracle" was due to the rapid development of the plantation economy in the south of the country. There were both German plantations (13,000 hectares in 1914) and native-owned ones, which the colonial power had considerably helped to develop on modern capitalist lines with private ownership of the land. During the First World War the Togolese managers on German plantations appropriated the land, thus preventing its seizure by the victorious British and French. This appropriation gave rise to a middle class of Togolese planters.

The Anglo-French partition of the country after 1918 served only to accentuate the absurd aspect of the colonial boundaries, which were drawn up with no regard for ethnic considerations.

POST-WAR DEVELOPMENT AND RECENT GROWTH

Between 1920 and 1940 Togoland had hardly developed at all. Thus in 1949, the volume of exports was still much the same as it had been during German times; but the post-war period up to independence was one of relatively swift development. The index of the volume of exports rose from 100 in 1949 to 224 in 1954. This was due to a greatly increased investment in infrastructure during the time that FIDES was in operation. The rate of growth for exports between 1948 and 1960 was 7 per cent. This was the second phase of Togo's development, characterized by an increase in the population growth rate and by increasing urbanization.

*For the 1973 edition, revisions have been made to this article by the Editor.

Although the population grew from 700,000 in 1920 to only 1,420,000 in 1960, it had reached 1,956,000 by 1970, and is now increasing at a rate of 2.6 to 2.7 per cent a year. The rate of urbanization also continues to rise: in 1965 the population of Lomé and its suburbs was 126,000, and that of the other towns (almost all in the south) was 128,000—the total percentage of town-dwellers being more than 15 per cent.

Between 1920 and 1948 the Gross Domestic Product at fixed prices had increased from 15,000 million francs CFA to about 20,000 million (at 1965 value), giving a very poor growth rate of 1.5 per cent per annum. From 1948 to 1960, on the other hand, growth was again rapid, as it had been before 1914—5.3 per cent per annum. It dropped after 1960 and, despite the stimulus it received from phosphate mining after 1963, barely kept pace with the rate of growth of the population. However it increased during the first development plan to 7 per cent per annum between 1966 and 1970 and it is expected that this rate will be maintained or even improved.

THE DOMINANCE OF AGRICULTURE

Annual production by the plantation economy does not, on average, exceed 30,000 to 40,000 tons of coffee and cocoa, and about 15,000 tons of palm nuts—the three chief agricultural commodities. These are grown mainly in the south where agriculture is already highly commercialized. In 1970 there were about 300,000 plantation workers and the revenue from the three plantation crops was about 3,200 million francs CFA; thus the per capita income in this area is about 11,000 francs CFA. In the country as a whole agriculture is varied, but not yet well developed or well organized. Cotton and groundnuts are grown in the north but so far have shown a poor financial return. The first plan introduced a semi-public finance and administrative organization, *Société régionale d'aménagement et de développement* (SORAD) in each of the five regions. They are controlled by the Minister of Rural Economics and each is subdivided to reach all local concerns. During the first plan the increase in food production could not keep pace with population growth, and the second aims to intensify agriculture in order to feed the home market and allow eventually for exports. Irrigation is a priority and a project is under way in the Sio-Haho and Lake Togo valley. Cultivation of cocoa, coffee and cashew nuts is to be expanded, and in the north new crops such as cane sugar, tobacco and soy beans are being introduced. Grants from the EDF will enable plantations of cotton and 3,000 hectares of new oil-palm groves. In 1970 agriculture employed 86 per cent of the active population and provided only 46 per cent of the G.D.P. It continues, however, to be the most important motive force to the economy and provides the major part of exports. In 1970 cocoa and coffee together accounted for nearly 60 per cent of total exports.

With agriculture accounting for 46 per cent of total production, income from the agricultural sector (mainly that of plantation-owners) was about 3,000–4,000 million francs CFA in 1970, which compared favourably with that of the richest plantations in the Ivory Coast. This income is enjoyed by a few thousand families, the Ewe bourgeoisie.

The development of phosphates, the construction of the port of Lomé, and infrastructural developments have encouraged greater economic activity, which has resulted in a larger business turnover. It increased by 8 per cent a year at current prices (5 per cent at fixed prices) from 1963 to 1968.

Phosphate mining has since 1963 been important to the economy and the main source of growth in exports, accounting for 30 per cent of exports in 1970. In 1971 reserves were estimated at 12 million metric tons to be extracted at an annual rate of 600,000 tons. In addition further phosphate deposits were discovered in 1971 at Aveta, conveniently near Lomé, and exploitation will begin in 1973. Also at Aveta are 200 million tons of limestone suitable for cement production. This will be West Africa's first multinational industry, involving the Ivory Coast, Upper Volta, Ghana and Togo. Prospecting for petroleum began in 1968.

Almost all Togo's industry, which is so far on a small scale, has evolved since independence. Products include palm oil, cotton textiles, beer, manioc flour and starch, confectionery, shoes, plastics and furniture. The Benin brewery was enlarged in 1971 to allow a 25 per cent increase in capacity to 200,000 hl. per annum, while the textile factory will be able to increase output from 8 million metres in 1970 to 15 million in 1975. Recent additions include a match factory, a salt works based on the salt marshes and an oxygen plant. A factory for detergents, soap and paints is under construction, and 25 projects provided for in the second plan include flour milling, canning of fruit and fruit juice, freezing of meat, and production of cocoa butter, cattle cake, pharmaceuticals and phosphate fertilizers. Electricity is produced by a national company with a capacity of nearly 12,000 kW. Production in 1970 reached 29.5 million kWh., six times that of 1960; industrial production more than doubled this figure.

Industrial and commercial activity on modern capitalist lines is still very limited. In 1970 Togo had only 25,000 wage- or salary-earners, most of whom were in the civil service. As a result income from activities other than agriculture and mining (phosphates) did not exceed 7,400 million francs CFA, and this figure in fact includes the revenue from small private enterprise, particularly shopkeepers and artisans. The profits from processing industries, excluding handicrafts, were no more than 1,000 million francs CFA. The profits of private enterprise would thus be about 4,700 million francs CFA for the foreign sector; phosphates 1,500 million francs CFA; building and industry 1,000 million francs CFA; and firms, banking and insurance 2,200 million francs CFA. The income of the African sector would be about 2,000 million francs CFA, mainly from road transport and small trading.

INVESTMENT AND PUBLIC SPENDING

Investment in the infrastructure, which had been significant between 1890 and 1914, dropped during the inter-war years and only improved subsequently because of funds from external sources, on which Togo now came to rely. Between 1946 and 1960 foreign capital was earmarked entirely for the development of the infrastructure, 65 per cent of which it financed. Investment in the infrastructure increased again after independence and its importance has been recognized in the two development plans, as a necessary basis for future growth.

The total value of basic capital expenditure financed by the current budget rose to 6,900 million francs CFA (current) between 1960 and 1969. The amount of foreign capital in public investment also increased: 4,100 million francs CFA (current) represented French foreign aid until 1967 inclusive; 3,100 million francs CFA came from the EEC for the same period and 4,500 million francs CFA from Federal Germany. Thus the average annual total, taking into account other smaller contributions, was 2,000 million francs CFA (current) for the ten-year period from 1960 to 1970 and represents on average 8.3 per cent of the G.D.P. Togo's public finances were not, as formerly, in balance during most of this period, in spite of increased taxation, but have been since 1968. Further tax reforms coinciding with the second development plan should ensure increased revenue, and national savings have been encouraged by the creation of two new finance institutions: *Société nationale d'investissements* and *Immobilière de Togo*.

PLANNING AND THE BALANCE OF PAYMENTS

Togo's first five-year development plan (1966–70) budgeted for 28,600 million francs CFA of investment, of which 20,000 million was public investment: rural development 5,100 million; communications 8,200 million; town planning 1,700 million; health, education and administration 3,500 million; and industry 1,400 million. Adjustments in 1970 provided for total investments of 40,700 million francs CFA, of which 62 per cent was for the infrastructure, 14 per cent for the rural sector and ten per cent for industry. This first plan aimed above all to provide the bases for future development. Its first year passed without any obvious results, but as a whole it proved surprisingly successful. In 1968, following years of bad deficits, the budget was balanced for the first time without foreign aid, leaving 88 million francs CFA surplus, which in 1969 rose to 758 million. The Gross Domestic Product, which was intended to grow by 5.3 per cent per annum, in fact increased by 7 per cent at current prices, as did the national revenue. Satisfactory results were obtained in all sectors, with annual growth rates of 7.2 per cent in the rural sector, 9 per cent in industry and 8 per cent in transport.

Togo was still far from economic independence and the second development plan (1971–75) follows the same general lines as the first. It budgets for total investments of 75,890 million francs CFA, of which 23 per cent is to be financed by internal public funds and 54 per cent by foreign grants and loans, while 12 per cent each is expected from national and foreign private sources. Rural development will account for 11,177 million francs CFA, communications and transport 26,947 million, town planning and tourism 11,057 million, health, education and administration 8,225 million and trade and industry 15,536 million. It envisages an average annual increase in the G.D.P. of 7.7 per cent and in the state budget of 12.6 per cent, which would raise the latter from 7,980 million francs CFA in 1970 to 14,400 million by 1975. Major projects include completion of the deep-water port at Lomé, improvement of communications, especially the north-south road, and the re-orientation of education and training to meet the country's needs.

There are several major obstacles to development, not least the country's long, narrow shape, which makes communication difficult and inhibits the spread of industry to areas further from the coast. In addition the primary sector is overdominant, involving 80 per cent of the active population, while producing only 44 per cent of the Gross Domestic Product. It will be some time before Togo becomes self-sufficient, and

development would be impossible without foreign aid, both financial and technical.

The balance of payments is maintained only with foreign aid. During the first ten years of independence the annual average value of exports was 6,500 million francs CFA and of imports 9,300 million francs CFA (of which 1,000 million was due directly to capital expenditure by the mining industry). The first plan succeeded in its aim to cover 85 per cent of the value of imports by exports, although both increased during the five years, reaching 17,928 million and 15,176 million francs CFA respectively in 1970. The value of exports dropped however in 1971, while that of imports continued to rise. Public receipts (expenditure of embassies, etc.) and private receipts (e.g. tourism), which totalled about 1,500 million francs CFA in 1970, exceeded the equivalent expenditures by about 800 million francs CFA. Public resources were about 3,400 million francs CFA and private capital about 2,000 million (half from phosphates, the other half gross investment by the foreign sector). The national debt continues to be small, as Togo has received most of its aid in the form of grants. Gross transfers abroad of profits and foreign savings are probably about 2,400 million francs CFA, or about half of the gross profit from foreign-owned business.

STATISTICAL SURVEY

AREA AND POPULATION

Census of March-April 1970, provisional results

AREA	POPULATION
56,000 sq. km.	1,955,916

MAIN TRIBES
(1964)

Ewe . . .	185,000
Ouatchi . . .	152,000
Kabre . . .	236,000

PRINCIPAL TOWNS
(1970)

Lomé (capital) . .	94,800	Tsevie . . .	9,200
Sokodé . . .	14,700	Bassari . . .	9,200
Palimé . . .	11,900	Mango . . .	7,800
Anécho . . .	10,400	Taligbo . . .	5,900
Atakpamé . .	9,200	Bafilo . . .	5,400

Births and Deaths (1968): Registered births 71,930 (birth rate 40.7 per 1,000); registered deaths 14,444 (death rate 8.2 per 1,000). Registration is not, however, complete. UN estimate for 1965–70 put the average annual birth rate at 50.9 per 1,000 and the death rate at 25.5 per 1,000.

ECONOMIC ACTIVITY
(1966 estimates)

Agriculture	741,000
Commerce	78,000
Industry	31,200

AGRICULTURE
LAND USE, 1965
('000 hectares)

Arable Land	2,113
Under Permanent Crops . .	47
Permanent Meadows and Pastures . .	200*
Forest Land	530*
Other Areas	2,710†
TOTAL	5,600

*Data taken from the world forest inventory carried out by the FAO in 1963.

†Of which an estimated 1,300,000 hectares is land considered capable of cultivation.

Source: FAO, *Production Yearbook 1971.*

PRINCIPAL CROPS
('000 metric tons)

	1968	1969	1970	1971
Maize	120*	125	100*	100*
Millet, Sorghum and Fonio . .	193	160	130*	130*
Rice	17	21	22	22*
Sweet Potatoes and Yams . .	1,160*	1,150	1,152*	n.a.
Cassava (Manioc) . . .	1,120*	1,150	1,170*	n.a.
Dry Beans	17	25	19*	20*
Other Pulses	8*	8*	7*	7*
Palm Kernels† . . .	12.9	18.8	16	17*
Groundnuts (in shell) . . .	18	18	18	18*
Cottonseed	4	10	12	12*
Cotton (Lint) . . .	2	5	6	6*
Castor Beans . . .	—	—	1	1*
Copra	0.5	1.0	1*	1*
Coffee	16.8	13.8	13.2	13.2
Cocoa Beans‡ . . .	18.0	18.4	24.0	26.0

Coconuts: 18 million nuts in 1968; 21 million in 1969. Palm oil (1968–71): 2,800 metric tons each year (FAO estimate).

* FAO estimate.   † Exports only.

‡ Twelve months ending September of year stated. 1971–72: 26,000 metric tons.

Source: FAO, *Production Yearbook 1971.*

LIVESTOCK
ANIMALS REGISTERED FOR TAXATION
(FAO estimates—'000)

	1968	1969	1970
Cattle . . .	175	180	190
Pigs	217	220	224
Sheep . . .	575	570	570
Goats . . .	570	574	580

Poultry (1968): 1,875,000 (official estimate).

Source: FAO, *Production Yearbook 1971.*

LIVESTOCK PRODUCTS
(FAO estimates—metric tons)

	1968	1969	1970	1971
Cows' Milk	13,000	14,000	14,000	15,000
Beef and Veal* . . .	4,000	4,000	4,000	4,000
Mutton, Lamb and Goats' Meat* .	3,000	3,000	3,000	3,000
Pork*	3,000	3,000	3,000	3,000
Poultry Meat	3,000	3,000	3,000	n.a.
Other Meat	4,000	4,000	4,000	n.a.
Hen Eggs	1,200	1,400	1,500	1,800
Cattle Hides	190	220	210	n.a.

* Meat from indigenous animals only, including the meat equivalent of exported live animals.

Source: FAO, *Production Yearbook 1971.*

FORESTRY
ROUNDWOOD REMOVALS
(cubic metres)

1967	. .	1,110,000
1968	. .	1,150,000
1969	. .	1,185,000

Source: FAO, *Yearbook of Forest Products.*

Fishing (1967–70): Total catch 8,000 metric tons (sea 5,000; inland 3,000) each year (FAO estimate).

MINING
(metric tons)

	1967	1968	1969	1970
Natural Phosphate Rock . . .	1,140,000	1,375,000	1,473,000	1,508,000
Phosphate Lime . . .	866,648	1,044,448	n.a.	n.a.

INDUSTRY

	1967	1968	1969
Beer (hectolitres) . . .	36,000	51,020	80,490
Electric Energy (million kWh.) .	47.8	48.8	57.0

FINANCE

100 centimes = 1 franc de la Communauté Financière Africaine.

Coins: 5, 10 and 25 francs CFA.

Notes: 50, 100, 500, 1,000 and 5,000 francs CFA.

Exchange rates (December 1972): 1 franc CFA = 2 French centimes;
£1 sterling = 593.625 francs CFA; U.S. $1 = 255.785 francs CFA.
1,000 francs CFA = £1.685 = $3.91.

GENERAL BUDGET ESTIMATES
(million francs CFA)

REVENUE	1969	1970	1971	EXPENDITURE*	1969	1970	1971
Taxes on Income .	791.2	1,485.0	1,904.0	Interest on Public Debt . . .	162.8	193.5	208.7
Other Direct Taxes .	37.3	14.2	14.0	Subsidies to Enterprises .	233.2	217.6	253.6
Import Duties .	1,840.1	1,850.0	2,100.0	Transfers to Income Account of Households .	123.5	198.9	269.3
Export Duties .	432.0	525.0	615.0	Current Transfers to Local Governments	45.1	139.2	36.4
Other Indirect Taxes	3,042.8	2,830.0	3,385.0	Current Transfers to Abroad . .	226.0	247.0	271.1
Other Receipts .	1,275.0	1,276.0	1,982.1	Current Expenditure on Goods and Services (net) .	5,873.3	5,950.2	7,265.0
				Gross Fixed Capital Formation . .	754.5	1,033.8	1,696.0
TOTAL .	7,418.4	7,980.2	10,000.1	TOTAL .	7,418.4	7,980.2	10,000.1

*Expenditure includes (in million francs CFA):

	1969	1970	1971
Education . .	1,161.5	1,114.8	1,436.5
Public Health .	601.8	640.3	684.4
Social Services .	205.6	151.7	114.3
Defence . .	779.6	849.1	897.2

Capital Budget (1971): 1,355 million francs CFA, of which Communications 426.2 million; Administration 222.2 million; Rural Development 220.4 million; Health, Education, Information, Sport, etc. 330.5 million; Industry 155.7 million.

1972 estimate: General Budget balanced at 12,283 million francs CFA.

Source: Banque centrale des Etats de l'Afrique de l'Ouest.

SECOND FIVE-YEAR PLAN, 1971–75
(million francs CFA)

REVENUE*		INVESTMENT	
Internal Sources:		Administration and Public Services .	2,943.7
Public	20,000	Transport and Communications .	26,946.6
Investment Budget	6,000	Town Planning and Tourism . . .	11,057.0
National Finance Institutions . .	14,000	Rural Economy	11,176.8
Private	9,800	Trade and Industry	15,536.2
Togolese Nationals	3,525	Education	3,059.0
Foreigners	6,275	Health	2,222.1
External Sources:		Other Social and Cultural Projects .	2,949.4
Public	36,000		
Grants	26,000		
Loans	10,000		
Private	10,000		
Shares	2,500		
Credits	7,500		
TOTAL	75,800	TOTAL	75,889.8

*Figures are approximate.

Currency in Circulation (April 30th, 1972): 5,703 million francs CFA.

NATIONAL ACCOUNTS
(million francs CFA)

	1963	1964	1965	1966
Economic Activity at Current Producers' Values:				
Agriculture, hunting, forestry and fishing .	17,437	18,682	19,818	22,988
Mining and quarrying	889	1,715	2,477	3,377
Manufacturing	1,414	1,511	2,357	5,306
Electricity, gas and water	766	773	1,000	1,484
Construction	1,054	1,289	1,527	1,531
Wholesale and Retail Trade . .	2,988	3,863	4,857	6,127
Transport and communications . .	1,615	2,219	2,428	2,718
Finance and business services . .	979	1,160	1,401	1,375
Social and personal services . .	946	583	786	732
Public administration and defence .	2,228	2,914	3,143	3,473
Gross Domestic Product at Factor Cost .	30,316	34,710	39,795	49,111
Net indirect taxes	2,781	3,721	3,679	3,974
Gross Domestic Product at Purchasers' Values	33,097	38,431	43,474	53,085

EXTERNAL TRADE
(million francs CFA)

	1964	1965	1966	1967	1968	1969	1970	1971
Imports .	10,286	11,100	11,668	11,133	11,623	14,572	17,928	19,455
Exports .	7,448	6,679	8,872	7,894	9,549	11,477	15,176	13,626

PRINCIPAL COMMODITIES

IMPORTS	1967	1968	1969
Food and Live Animals	1,549	1,326	1,816
Fish, fresh and simply preserved . .	364	198	419
Cereals and preparations . . .	377	333	453
Sugar and honey	268	319	293
Beverages and Tobacco . . .	988	862	1,366
Alcoholic beverages	326	334	441
Tobacco and manufactures . .	650	514	902
Cigarettes	513	467	849
Petroleum Products	495	526	668
Chemicals	837	1,015	1,048
Medicinal and pharmaceutical products .	309	397	443
Basic Manufactures	3,873	4,090	4,818
Woven cotton fabrics . . .	2,098	2,191	1,972
Lime, cement, etc.	252	278	375
Iron and steel	400	328	497
Machinery and Transport Equipment . .	2,240	2,572	3,309
Machinery (non-electric) . . .	884	1,005	1,454
Electrical machinery, appliances, etc. .	470	516	482
Road motor vehicles . . .	771	922	1,203
Passenger cars . . .	334	188	468
Lorries and trucks . .	298	347	472
Miscellaneous Manufactured Articles . .	756	704	914
TOTAL (incl. others) . . .	11,133	11,620	14,567

EXPORTS	1967	1968	1969	1970
Coffee (green and roasted) . .	838	1,602	1,749	2,657
Cocoa Beans . . .	2,349	2,314	4,063	6,336
Oil-seeds, Oil-nuts, etc. . .	671	860	747	n.a.
Groundnuts (green) . .	140	164	188	219
Palm nuts and kernels . .	427	573	481	656
Raw Cotton (excl. linters) . .	355	340	154	323
Natural Calcium Phosphates .	3,032	3,237	3,356	3,720
Chemicals . . .	60	114	72	n.a.
Woven Cotton Fabrics . .	186	169	192	n.a.
Diamonds (non-industrial) . .	0	370	725	277
Machinery (non-electric) . .	123	306	97	n.a.
TOTAL (incl. others) .	7,894	9,550	11,476	15,176

1971 (million francs CFA): Phosphates 4,787; Cocoa 4,246; Coffee 2,436.

COUNTRIES

IMPORTS	1967	1968	1969	1970
China, People's Republic . . .	563	553	405	n.a.
France	3,268	3,663	4,657	5,283
Germany, Federal Republic .	1,171	831	984	1,455
Ghana	533	371	371	653
Italy	257	557	774	673
Japan	1,400	1,316	1,045	1,067
Netherlands	447	521	812	1,303
U.S.S.R.	176	148	349	377
United Kingdom . . .	901	1,040	1,779	2,424
U.S.A.	451	516	754	1,022
Venezuela	230	255	234	n.a.
TOTAL (incl. others) .	11,133	11,620	14,567	17,928

EXPORTS	1967	1968	1969	1970
Australia	395	117	0	n.a.
Belgium/Luxembourg . .	540	634	1,124	1,039
France	2,995	3,678	3,913	4,284
Germany, Federal Republic .	837	1,001	1,795	3,040
Italy	426	310	390	609
Japan	342	422	439	400
Netherlands	1,372	2,233	2,714	3,933
U.S.S.R.	49	1	256	873
United Kingdom . . .	240	459	306	361
TOTAL (incl. others) .	7,894	9,550	11,476	15,176

Source: mainly *Overseas Associates, Foreign Trade* (Statistical Office of the European Communities, Luxembourg). The totals for 1968 and 1969 differ slightly from those given in the summary table, which are provided by the national statistical authority.

TRANSPORT

RAILWAYS

	1968	1969	1970
Passengers ('000) . .	1,645	1,727	1,609
Passengers—km. (million) .	78.9	86.5	84.1
Freight ('000 tons) . .	121	124	110
Freight (million ton—km.)	12	13	12.4
Total receipts (million francs CFA)	343	372	383

INTERNATIONAL SEA-BORNE SHIPPING

	1969	1970
Vessels Entered . .	504	524
Displacement ('000 net tons) .	1,489	1,477
Freight Unloaded ('000 metric tons)	233	255
Freight Loaded ('000 metric tons)	1,544	1,576
Passenger Arrivals . .	646	181
Passenger Departures . .	535	127

ROADS
MOTOR VEHICLES IN USE

	1966	1967	1968	1969
Passenger Cars	3,500	4,800	5,800	5,900
Commercial Vehicles . .	3,800	4,000	4,400	4,500

CIVIL AVIATION

	1970	1971
Aircraft Arrivals and Departures	1,760	1,821
Freight Unloaded (tons) . .	475	498
Freight Loaded (tons) . .	263	450
Passenger Arrivals . .	12,870	16,249
Passenger Departures . .	13,315	16,528

EDUCATION
(1971–72)

	NUMBER OF SCHOOLS	NUMBER OF TEACHERS	NUMBER OF PUPILS
Primary .	934	4,403	257,877
Secondary .	71*	778	24,521
Technical .	19†	214	2,506
Higher (University)	1	93	1,369‡

*Includes four *lycées* and six colleges.

†Including one *lycée* and four colleges.

‡In addition 689 students study abroad.

THE CONSTITUTION

The Constitution promulgated in May 1963 was suspended in January 1967. A Constitutional Committee began meeting in October 1967 to draft a new constitution which was completed in 1969 but has not been promulgated.

THE GOVERNMENT

HEAD OF STATE

President: Maj.-Gen. ÉTIENNE EYADÉMA.

THE CABINET
(*December* 1972)

Minister of National Defence: Maj.-Gen. ÉTIENNE EYADÉMA.

Minister of Public Health: Lt.-Col. ALBERT DJAFALO ALIDOU.

Minister of Justice and Guardian of the Seals: Maj. JANVIER CHANGO.

Minister of Foreign Affairs: JOACHIM HUNLEDÉ.

Minister of Public Works, Transport and Mines: ALEX MIVEDOR.

Minister delegated to the Office of the Interior: BARTHÉLÉMY LAMBONY.

Minister of National Education: BENOÎT MALOU.

Minister of Finance and the Economy: JEAN TEVI.

Minister of the Civil Service, Labour and Social Affairs: NANAMALÉ GBEGBENI.

Minister of Information, Press and Radio: FRÉDÉRIC ALI DERMANE.

Minister of Rural Economy: LOUIS AMEGA.

Minister of Youth, Sport, Culture and Scientific Research: MATHIEU KOFFI.

Secretary of State for Trade, the Plan and Industry: HENRI DOGO.

Secretary of State for Public Works, charged with Posts and Telecommunications: LAURENT GABA.

High Commissioner for Tourism: MICHEL AHYI.

ECONOMIC AND SOCIAL COUNCIL

An advisory council was created in 1967 and has been active since March 1968. Its 25 members include five trade unionists, five representatives of industry and commerce, five representatives of agriculture, five economists and sociologists, and five technologists.

President: GERVAIS DJONDO.

DIPLOMATIC REPRESENTATION
EMBASSIES ACCREDITED TO TOGO
(In Lomé unless otherwise stated)

Belgium: Abidjan, Ivory Coast.

Canada: Accra, Ghana.

China: People's Republic: *Ambassador:* CHI PENG-FEI.

Czechoslovakia: Accra, Ghana.

Denmark: Accra, Ghana.

Egypt: Angle blvd. Circulaire et route d'Anèche; B.P. 8; *Chargé d'Affairs:* RIAD MOAWAD.

France: rue Colonel Derroux; *Ambassador:* JEAN-PIERRE CAMPREDON.

Gabon: Abidjan, Ivory Coast.

Germany, Federal Republic: rue d'Aflao, B.P. 289; *Ambassador:* GERHARD SOHNKE.

Ghana: Tokoin—route de Palimé; *Ambassador:* WILLIAM LIX TSITSIWU.

Haiti: Dakar Senegal.

Hungary: Accra, Ghana.

India: Lagos, Nigeria.

Israel: 22 Ancien blvd. Circ., B.P. 1025; *Ambassador:* YEHOSHOUA RASH.

Italy: Abidjan, Ivory Coast.

Japan: Abidjan, Ivory Coast.

Korea, Republic of: Abidjan, Ivory Coast.

Lebanon: Accra, Ghana.

Liberia: Accra, Ghana.

Netherlands: Abidjan, Ivory Coast.

Nigeria: P.O.B. 1189; *Chargé d'Affaires a.i.:* M. TUNAU.

Pakistan: Accra, Ghana.

Poland: Lagos, Nigeria.

Spain: Abidjan, Ivory Coast.

Switzerland: Accra, Ghana.

Tunisia: Abidjan, Ivory Coast.

Turkey: Accra, Ghana.

U.S.S.R.: route d'Atakpamé, B.P. 634; *Ambassador:* PETER K. SLYUSARENKO.

United Kingdom: Angle blvd. Circ. et blvd. de la République; *Ambassador:* FRANK SMITHERMAN.

U.S.A.: rue Victor Hugo, B.P. 852; *Ambassador:* DWIGHT DICKINSON.

Republic of Vietnam: Abidjan, Ivory Coast.

Yugoslavia: Accra, Ghana.

Zaire: *Ambassador:* ITSINDO BOSILA MPELA.

Togo also has diplomatic relations with the Congo People's Republic.

NATIONAL ASSEMBLY

The National Assembly was dissolved in January 1967. Elections were then promised within three months, but none have so far been held and a new constitution has yet to be promulgated.

POLITICAL PARTY

Rassemblement du peuple togolais (RPT): Lomé; f. 1969; holds a Congress every three years, and its central committee meets at least every three months; Pres. Maj.-Gen. ÉTIENNE EYADÉMA; Sec. MICHEL EKLO.

Political Bureau: Maj.-Gen. EYADÉMA, Lt.-Col. ALBERT DJAFALO, EDOUARD KODJO, HENRI DOGO, GERVAIS DJONDO, BENOÎT BÉDOU, JOACHIM HUNLEDÉ, BENOÎT MALOU, LOUIS AMEGA, BARTHÉLÉMY LAMBONY, Prof. VALENTIN MAWUPE-VOVOR, ALPHONSE KORTHO, Prof. JEAN KEKEH, FOUSSENI MAMA, NANAMALÉ GBEGBENI.

DEFENCE

The total armed forces number 1,500 men, divided between the infantry and two para-military gendarmeries; in addition there is a small air force, a medical unit and a signals unit.

Chief of the Armed Forces: Maj.-Gen. ÉTIENNE EYADÉMA.

JUDICIAL SYSTEM

The independence of the judiciary is assured by the Conseil Supérieur de la Magistrature, set up in 1964, consisting of the President as Chairman, the Minister of Justice, the President and Vice-President of the Supreme Court, one Deputy, two Magistrates, and another person chosen for his "independence and competence".

Cour Suprême: Lomé f. 1964; consists of four chambers: constitutional, judicial, administrative and auditing; Pres. Dr. VALENTIN VOVOR.

CRIMINAL LAW

Cour d'Appel: Lomé; f. 1961; Pres. THÉODORE ACOUETEY.

Tribunal Correctionnel: Lomé and three other centres.

Tribunal de Simple Police: Lomé and seven other centres.

Cour de Securité de l'Etat: f. Sept. 1970 to judge crimes against internal and external state security.

CIVIL AND COMMERCIAL LAW

Cour d'Appel: Lomé; f. 1961; Pres. M. PUECH.

Tribunal de Droit Moderne: Lomé; sections at Sokodé, Anécho and Atakpame.

Tribunal Coutumier de Premier Instance: Lomé and seven other centres.

ADMINISTRATIVE LAW

Tribunal Administratif: Lomé.

LABOUR LEGISLATION

Tribunal de Travail: Lomé.

RELIGION

It is estimated that 76 per cent of the population follow traditional Animist beliefs, 19 per cent are Christians (with Roman Catholics comprising 16 per cent of the total population) and 5 per cent are Muslims.

Roman Catholic Missions: In the archdiocese of Lomé there are over 5,407 mission centres; publ. *Présence Chrétienne* (fortnightly, circ. 2,500).

Archbishop of Lomé: B.P. 348, Lomé; Mgr. ROBERT DOSSEH ANYRON.

Bishop of Sokodé: B.P. 55, Sokodé; Mgr. CHRÉTIEN BAKPESSI MATAWO.

Bishop of Dapango: Mgr. BARTHÉLÉMY HANRION, D.F.N.

Bishop of Atakpamé: B.P. 11, Atakpamé; Mgr. BERNARD OGUKI-ATAKPAH.

Protestant Missions: There are about 170 mission centres with a personnel of some 230, run by European and American societies.

PRESS

DAILIES

Togo-Matin: Lomé; f. 1967; independent.

Togo-Presse: EDITOGO, B.P. 891, Lomé; f. 1962; French; political, economic and cultural; official government publication; Editor POLYCARPE JOHNSON; circ. 10,000.

PERIODICALS

Akuavi: Lomé; produced by women's organization; French; Dir. NABÉDÉ PALA.

Bulletin de la Chambre de Commerce: B.P. 360, Lomé; monthly.

Bulletin de Statistiques: B.P. 118, Lomé; published by Service de la Statistique Générale, Ministère des Finances et des Affaires Économiques; monthly.

Espoir de la Nation: EDITOGO, B.P. 891, Lomé; produced by Ministry of Information; monthly; Dir. M. AWESSO; circ. 3,000.

Gamesu: Lomé; produced by Ministries of Education and Social Affairs; local language.

Image du Togo: Lomé; monthly; circ. 2,000.

Le Lien: Office of Education, Lomé; cultural; monthly; circ. 600.

Présence Chrétienne: B.P. 1205, Lomé; f. 1960; French; Roman Catholic fortnightly; Dir. R. P. ALEXIS OLIGER, O.F.M.; circ. 2,500.

NEWS AGENCIES

FOREIGN BUREAUX

Agence France-Presse: B.P. 314, Lomé; Chief JEAN MARIE WETZEL.

D.P.A. also has a bureau in Lomé.

RADIO

Radiodiffusion du Togo: B.P. 434, Lomé; f. 1953; Government station; programmes on four wavelengths in French and vernacular languages; Dir. PROSPER AMOUZOUGAH; Tech. Dir. LUCIEN POENOU.

There are 45,000 radio sets.

FINANCE

(cap. = capital; dep. = deposits; m. = million).

BANKING

CENTRAL BANK

Banque Centrale des Etats de l'Afrique de l'Ouest: B.P. 120, Lomé; Head Office 29 rue de Colisée, Paris 8e, France; f. 1955; the bank of issue in Togo and several other West African states; cap. and reserves 3,547 m. francs CFA; Manager M. PEBAYLE.

NATIONAL BANKS

Banque Togolaise de Développement: B.P. 65, Lomé; f. 1967; cap. 300m. francs CFA; Dir.-Gen. BAWA MANKOUBI.

Union Togolaise de Banque: B.P. 359, Lomé; f. 1964 by Deutsche Bank A.G., Crédit Lyonnais and Banca Commerciale Italiana; Pres. DJIBO BOUKARY; Gen. Man. PÉDRO D'ALMEIDA.

FOREIGN BANKS

Bank of Ghana: rue du Commerce, Lomé; Head Office P.O.B. 2674, Accra, Ghana; f. 1957; cap. 4 m. new cedis; Gov. J. H. FRIMPONG-ANSAH.

Banque Internationale pour l'Afrique Occidentale: B.P. 346, Lomé; Head Office 9 avenue de Messine, Paris 8e, France; f. 1965; cap. 66.2 m. French francs; 53 branches in West and Central Africa; Pres. and Man. Dir. P. ROQUES.

Banque Nationale de Paris: Succursale de Lomé, 9 rue du Commerce, B.P. 363; Head Office P.O.B. 229-09, 16 Boulevard des Italiens, Paris 9e, France; f. 1966; cap. 325 m. French francs; Dir. and Gen. Man. P. LEDOUX.

Caisse Centrale de Coopération Economique: Avenue de la Victoire, B.P. 33, Lomé.

INSURANCE

Some thirty of the major French and British insurance companies are represented in Lomé.

TRADE AND INDUSTRY

CHAMBER OF COMMERCE

Chambre de Commerce, d'Agriculture et d'Industrie du Togo: Ave. Albert-Sarraut, B.P. 360; f. 1921; Pres. ALBERT DJABUKA; Sec. Gen. Mme. TRÉNOU; publ. *Bulletin Mensuel.*

TRADE UNIONS

The central bodies of the Togolese trade unions were dissolved in January 1973 and a committee was set up in preparation for a single trade union body.

MARKETING BOARD

Office des Produits Agricoles du Togo (OPAT): Angle rue Branly et ave. numéro 3, Lomé, B.P. 1334; f. 1964; controls prices and export sales of coffee, cocoa, cotton, ground nuts, palm oil, copra, kapok, karite and castor oil, and is the sole exporter of these products; promotes development in agriculture, finances research and grants loans; is supervised by the Minister of Trade and Industry.

MAJOR INDUSTRIAL COMPANIES

Brasserie du Bénin: B.P. 896, Lomé; f. 1964; cap. 375 m. francs CFA.

Brewing of beer and manufacture of soft drinks.

Pres. Dir.-Gen. JOACHIM HAASE.

Ciments de l'Afrique de l'Ouest (CIMAO): B.P. 1687, Lomé; f. 1968; cap. 1,000 m. francs CFA.

Cement factory in process of construction; production of clinker and cement.

Pres. E. DE NATTES; Dir. CLAUDE LAMBERT; 300 employees.

Compagnie du Bénin: B.P. 115, Anecho; f. 1950; cap 275 m. francs CFA, partly state-owned.

Manufacture of manioc flour and tapioca.

Dir. JEAN MICHEL BLOUZARD.

Compagnie Togolaise des Mines du Bénin (COTOMIB): B.P. 379, Lomé; f. 1954; cap. 2,938,950,000 francs CFA.

Mining of phosphate at Hahotoé.

Dir. MAX ROBERT.

Industrie Textile Togolaise (ITT): B.P. 1179, Lomé; f. 1962; cap. 250 m. francs CFA, partly state-owned.

Spinning, weaving, printing and dyeing of textiles.

Pres. Dir.-Gen. GUNTHER FRAUENLOB; Dir. ROBERT BIEDERMANN; 570 employees.

Société Nationale pour le Développement de la Palmeraie et des Huileries (SONAPH): Lomé; f. 1968; cap. 160 m. francs CFA; state-owned.

Cultivation of palms and production of palm-oil and palmettoes.

Dir.-Gen. ERNEST GASSOU.

Société Togolaise de Gaz (TOGOGAZ): f. 1971; cap. 80 m. fr. CFA.

Production of oxygen and acetylene.

Société Togolaise de Marbrerie: B.P. 2.1045; f. 1968; cap. 350m. francs CFA.

Quarrying of terrazzo stone and marble; manufacture of bricks and ceramics.

Pres. HENRI DOGO; Dir.-Gen. JEAN LADENT; 325 employees.

The United Africa Company—Togo S.A.: B.P. 345, Lomé; Dir. M. TOKPANU.

TRANSPORT

RAILWAYS

Chemin de Fer Togolais: B.P. 340, Lomé; f. 1905; total length 498 km., metre gauge, including three lines from Lomé—to Palimé (119 km.), to Anécho (44 km.) and to Atakpamé and Blitta (276 km.); Dir. W. RÖHR.

ROADS

There are approximately 1,662 km. of main roads, of which 170 km. are bitumized and 5,357 km. of "dry season" roads. Principal roads run from Lomé to the borders of Ghana, Nigeria, Upper Volta and Dahomey, and it is intended that the whole length of the north-south route be bitumized by 1975.

SHIPPING

The Port of Lomé completed a new deep water harbour in April 1968 which gives it a handling capacity of 400,000 tons and enables 1.5 million tons of goods to pass through per annum.

Société Navale Chargeurs Delmas Vieljeux: Lomé, avenue Gallieni, B.P. 34.

Holland West Africa Line: c/o S.C.O.A., B.P. 347.

John Holt and Co. Ltd.: B.P. 343, Lomé; merchandise importers; Lloyds agents.

Jugolinija: SOCOPAO, B.P. 821.

Société Navale de L'Ouest: S.O.A.E.M., B.P. 207.

CIVIL AVIATION

The main airport is at Tokoin near Lomé, and there are smaller ones at Sokodé, Sansanné-Mango, Dapango, Atakpamé.

Air Afrique: Togo has a 7 per cent share; *see* under Ivory Coast.

Air Togo: 1 ave. de la Libération, B.P. 1090, Lomé; f. 1963; scheduled services between Lomé and Lagos; fleet of one Beech Queen Air A80; Gen. Man. ADE AMADOU.

Lomé is also served by U.T.A.

POWER

Compagnie Energie Electrique du Togo (CEET): B.P. 42, Lomé; f. 1963; cap. 602 m. francs CFA; production and distribution of electricity; Dir. FRANCISCO LAWSON.

Communauté électrique du Bénin: Lomé; f. 1967 as a joint venture to draw electricity from Ghana's Volta Dam; production should start in 1973.

TOURISM

Office National Togolais du Tourisme: B.P. 1177, Lomé; Dir. M. AGHEKODO.

CULTURAL ORGANIZATIONS

Ministry of National Education: Lomé; in charge of promoting cultural activities.

Comité National des Foires et Expositions: Ministry of Commerce, Industry and Tourism, Lomé; in charge of overseas representation of Togo's cultural achievements; Pres. JEAN AGBÉMÉGNAN; Sec.-Gen. SIMON AYIVOR.

THEATRE GROUP

Groupement du Théâtre et du Folklore Togolais (G.T.F.T.): Direction de la Jeunesse et des Sports, Lomé; f. 1962; comedy and African ballet; Dir. MATHIAS AITHNARD.

EDUCATION

Mission schools still play an important part in education in Togo, and educate about half of the pupils. Forty-four per cent of the children between the ages of six and eighteen years attend school (50 per cent of those between six and fourteen years), and the Government aims to raise the figure to 61 per cent by 1975. Wide disparities exist throughout the country, especially between north and south, and whereas 18 per cent of the children in Mango are at school, 99 per cent are at school in the capital, Lomé. As part of the current five-year development plan, the Government hopes to build 1,944 new primary classes to counteract the disparity. In addition a literacy programme has been drawn up, as 80 per cent of the productive population is illiterate. Secondary and higher education are to be given a more technological orientation, and the university is being expanded to this end.

LEARNED SOCIETIES AND RESEARCH INSTITUTES

Institut Togolais des Sciences Humaines: B.P. 1002, Lomé; f. 1960; a Service de Documentation Générale was created in 1937, to carry out documentation in museums, archives and scientific collections for the advancement of knowledge and study of problems of interest to the territory and to stimulate and assist works relating to varied local activities. This service was taken over by the Institut Français d'Afrique Noire (IFAN) in 1945, and includes publication of scientific reports, organisation of exhibitions, courses and conferences, care of ancient monuments and historic sites, encouragement of indigenous artists and craftsmen, the application of rules concerning excavations and the export of ethnographic objects or indigenous works of art, and protection of fauna and flora. The local centre of IFAN in Togo is the Institut Togolais des Sciences Humaines-Bibliothèque Nationale (INTSHU-BN), and includes departments of anthropology, archaeology, prehistory, history, ethnography, human geography, linguistics, sociology; Dir. KWAOVI GABRIEL JOHNSON.

Alliance Française: Lomé; f. 1947.

American Cultural Center (USIS): Angle Rue Pelletier et Rue Vauban, B.P. 852, Lomé; reading room, library of 3,000 vols.; cultural activities; Dir. VINCENT ROTUNDO.

Association togolaise d'échanges culturelles avec l'étranger (*Togolese Association for cultural exchanges with foreign countries*): Lomé; Pres. SANVI DE TOVE (President of the Legislative Assembly); Sec. M. ADOSSAMA (Director of Cabinet of the Ministry of Economic Affairs).

Compagnie Française pour le Développement des Fibres Textiles (CFDT): B.P. 6, Atakpamé.

Goethe-Institut: B.P. 914, Lomé; f. 1961; Dir. Dr. PETER M. KUHN.

Institut de Recherches Agronomiques Tropicales et des Cultures Vivrières (IRAT): Dir. M. DELCASSO.

Institut de Recherches du Coton et des Textiles Exotiques: Station Anie-Mono, B.P. 1, Anie par Lomé; f. 1948; Dir. M. COÛTEAUX; publs. *Rapports annuels Coton et Fibres Tropicales.*

Office de la Recherche Scientifique et Technique Outre-Mer Centre O.R.S.T.O.M. de Lomé: B.P. 375, Lomé; f. 1949; pedology, geography, sociology, hydrology, geophysics, Oceanography; library; Dir. A. LE COCQ.

Service des Mines du Togo: Lomé.

LIBRARIES

Bibliothèque Nationale-Institut Togolais des Sciences Humaines: B.P. 1002, Lomé; German and French archives; *c.* 5,500 vols.; Dir. KWAOVI GABRIEL JOHNSON.

Bibliothèque du Ministère de l'Intérieur: Lomé; Librarian KWAOVI GABRIEL JOHNSON.

UNIVERSITY

UNIVERSITÉ DU BÉNIN

B.P. 1515, LOMÉ

Telephone: 3105-3500 Lomé

Founded 1965 as a College: university status 1970.

Language of instruction: French; Academic year November to June (three terms).

Rector: GABRIEL JOHNSON.

Library of 5,000 vols.
Number of teachers: 93.
Number of students: 1,369.

Schools of Law and Economic Science, Medicine, Science, Arts and Technology.

Ecole Nationale d'Administration: ave. de la Libération, Lomé; f. 1958; provides training for Togolese civil servants; approx. 50 students; library of over 1,000 vols.; Dir. FOUSSÉNI MAMA; Sec.-Gen. NICOLAS ADJETEY.

Technical College: Sokodé; apprentice training.

SELECT BIBLIOGRAPHY

ADUAMAH, E. Y. *Traditions from the Volta Basin 1–12.* Legon Institute of African Studies, unpublished, 1963–64.

AMENUMEY, D. E. K. *The Ewe People and the Coming of European Rule 1850–1914.* London, unpublished M.A. thesis, 1964.

CORNEVIN, R. *Histoire du Togo.* Paris, 1959.
Le Togo. Collection Que sais-je? Paris, Presses Universitaires de France, 1967.

HARRISON CHURCH, R. J. *West Africa.* London, Longmans, sixth edn., 1968, chapter 24.

"Nkrumah and the Togoland Question", *The Economic Bulletin of Ghana*, Vol. XII, No. 2/2. Accra, 1968.

"The Pre-1947 Background to the Ewe Unification Question", *The Transactions of the Historical Society of Ghana*, Vol. X. Accra, 1969.

Thompson, Virginia. *West Africa's Council of the Entente.* Ithaca and London, Cornell University Press, 1972.

The Records of United Nations on Togo.

Togoland Report, 1947–155. London.

Uganda

PHYSICAL AND SOCIAL GEOGRAPHY*

B. W. Langlands

Uganda, a republic within the Commonwealth, obtained independence in 1962. Located on the eastern African plateau, it is at least 500 miles (about 800 km.) from the Indian Ocean. The total area is 91,452 sq. miles (236,860 sq. km.) but 17 per cent of this is made up of freshwater lakes, of which Lakes Victoria, Albert† and Edward† are shared with neighbouring states. These lakes and most of the rivers form part of the basin of the upper Nile, which has its origin in Uganda, where the river leaving Lake Victoria is harnessed for hydroelectricity (Owen Falls dam).

Of the land area (excluding open water) 84 per cent forms a plateau at between 3,000 and 5,000 ft. (900–1,500 m.), with a gentle downwarp to the centre to form Lake Kyoga. The western arm of the east African rift system accounts for the 9 per cent of the land area at less than 3,000 ft. (900 m.) and this includes the lowlands flanking the rift lakes (Edward and Albert) and the course of the Albert Nile at little more than 2,000 ft. (620 m.). Mountains of over 7,000 ft. (2,100 m.) occupy 2 per cent of the land area and these lands are above the limit of cultivation. The highest point is Mount Stanley, 16,763 ft. (5,109 m.), in the Ruwenzori group on the border with Zaire, but larger areas of highland are included in the Uganda portion of the volcanic mass of Mount Elgon, near the Kenyan border. The remaining 5 per cent of the land area lies at an altitude of 5–7,000 ft. (1,500–2,100 m.) in both the eastern and western extremities which form the shoulders to their respective rift valley systems or in the foothills of the mountains already referred to. At this altitude the country is free of malaria and contains some of the most heavily populated regions.

Geologically the great proportion of the country is made up of Precambrian material, largely of gneisses and schists into which granites have been intruded. In the west, distinct series of metamorphosed rocks occur, largely of phyllites and shales, and in which mineralized zones contain small quantities of copper, tin, wolfram and beryllium. In the east old, possibly Cretaceous, volcanoes have been weathered away to form carbonatite rings with extensive deposits of magnetite, apatite and crystalline limestone. The apatite provides the basis for a superphosphate industry and the limestone for a cement industry, both at Tororo.

The economy of the country depends upon agriculture and this in turn depends upon climate. Since Uganda is located between 1° 30′ S. and 4° N., temperature varies little throughout the year, giving the country an equatorial climate modified by altitude. Rainfall is greatest bordering Lake Victoria and on the mountains, where small areas have over 80 in. (2,000 mm.). The high ground of the west, the rest of the Lake Victoria zone, and the eastern and north-central interior all have over 50 in. (1,250 mm.). Only the north-east (Karamoja) and parts of the south (east Ankole) have less than 30 in. (750 mm.). But total amounts of rain are less significant agriculturally than the length of the dry season. For much of the centre and west there is no more than one month with less than 2 in. (50 mm.) and this zone is characterized by permanent cropping of bananas for food, and coffee and tea for cash crops. To the south the dry season increases to three months (June to August); in the north it increases to four months (December to March) and in the north-east the dry season begins in October. Where the dry season is marked, as in the north and east, annual cropping of finger millet provides the staple food and cotton the main cash crop. In the driest parts pastoralism predominates, possibly with a little sorghum cultivation.

Western Uganda, where there is a greater range of different physical conditions, and generally where population densities are below average, shows a great variation of land use, with tropical rain forest, two game parks, ranchlands, fishing, mining and the cultivation of coffee and tea. The north and east is more monotonous, savannah-covered plain with annually sown fields of grain and cotton. Most of the country's coffee comes from the Lake Victoria zone (*robusta*) and Mount Elgon (*arabica*). In a situation in which less than 10 per cent of the able-bodied males are engaged in paid employment, the economy depends very heavily upon smallholding peasant production of basic cash crops.

The population at the last census in 1969 was 9,548,847 and showed a 3.8 per cent per annum increase since 1959. This high rate of increase was in large part due to a decrease in infant mortality, to international immigration of labourers and political refugees, and to a possible under-counting in 1959. Only about 7 per cent of the population lives in towns of over 1,000 people. Kampala (330,700), the capital and main commercial centre, and Jinja (52,500), an industrial town, are the only urban centres of any significance. In 1959 about two-thirds of the population, mainly in the centre and south, were Bantu-speaking, a sixth Nilotic-speaking and a sixth Nilo-Hamitic (Paranilotic). In 1969 there were 74,000 people of Indian and Pakistani origin, mainly in commerce, and 9,500 Europeans, mainly in professional services. Since the decision of August 1972 to expel non-citizen Asians, both these totals have dropped considerably.

---

*See map on p. 896.

†The Presidents of Uganda and Zaire agreed in 1972 that Lake Albert should be renamed Lake Mobutu Sese Seko and Lake Edward should become Lake Idi Amin Dada.

RECENT HISTORY

John Lonsdale

For centuries Uganda has been a cultural and linguistic frontier zone between the Nilotic-speaking peoples of the north and the Bantu of the south; the former have tended to be herdsmen, the latter cultivators. There has been much intermingling between them, the resulting diversity giving rise to Uganda's chief distinction in east Africa, a series of centralized kingdoms. The oldest of these, Bunyoro, was founded in the fifteenth century and it spawned the others by secession, including its most formidable rival, Buganda. To the north, the more exclusively Nilotic peoples had more slender governmental structures. By the nineteenth century Buganda was the dominant force in the area. But in the 1870s, Kabaka Muteesa I of Buganda, the thirtieth king of his line, was under threat from an Egypt intent on controlling the Nile headwaters. Not only did he then welcome British Protestant and French Catholic missionaries as diplomatic allies, but their teaching was attractive to young courtiers as an aid to promotion; Islam was already established. The cohesion and skills of the new Christian groups soon upset the traditional factional balance between the chiefs through which the Kabakas had manipulated power. After many had been martyred by Muteesa's son Mwanga in 1885, and after a period of civil war, the Christian parties effected an oligarchical revolution by 1890; Mwanga was their puppet. But the Christians were divided by denomination; the Protestants welcomed the assistance of Captain (later Lord) Lugard of the Imperial British East Africa Company. Thereafter a close Anglo-Ganda alliance grew out of their mutual insecurities, threatened as they were by monarchical reaction within, and from a resurgent Bunyoro, which also succoured the Ganda Muslim party, from without.

THE UGANDA PROTECTORATE, 1893-1962

The Company was bankrupted by war and the high cost of porterage from Mombasa. The British government assumed responsibility, declaring a Protectorate over Buganda in 1893. The kingdom provided a firm base for British expansion over the rest of modern Uganda; Buganda expanded too under the British wing. Territory was involved when Buganda was allotted some of the most fertile areas of Bunyoro, known later as the "Lost Counties"; elsewhere the expansion was indirect. Ganda soldiers gave way to Ganda administrative agents, many of whom were not replaced by local chiefs for a decade or more. Ganda priests often preceded European missionaries in establishing schools in unevangelized areas; they took their denominational divisions with them. Ganda political institutions were also exported as the British set up local administrations. Uganda's subsequent history has been dominated by the twin desire of her peripheral kingdoms and districts both to emulate Buganda and to set a limit to that kingdom's pretensions.

Buganda's special status was confirmed by the 1900 Agreement. This established a quasi-diplomatic relationship between the Protectorate and kingdom governments, the interpretation of which was the source of much future conflict. Internally, the Agreement confirmed the Christian oligarchs in power, especially the Protestants among them. They were awarded large official estates; previously they had governed people, now they owned land. The full significance of this change did not become apparent until later, when a market in land was established through the introduction of cash crops, cotton and coffee, the former in 1904. Protectorate land policy was undecided between the alternatives of encouraging European plantations or African peasant agriculture. By the early 1920s the question was decided by a slump in coffee prices which ruined the planters, many of whom had suffered earlier from the failure of rubber. But by this time African production, mainly of cotton, accounted for 80 per cent of Uganda's exports; thereafter Africans also took increasingly to coffee. This success story, paralleled only by cocoa in the Gold Coast, had owed much to the initial enthusiasm of the Ganda chiefs and their authority over the peasantry. Other areas of southern Uganda also adopted the same two crops—a similar extension in the north did not come until much later—but Buganda never lost its economic lead. European and Asian capital thereafter concentrated on the marketing of African produce rather than direct production.

The inter-war years saw increasing strain between the British and the chiefs. There was one adventitious source of conflict, Buganda's acute fear of the threatened extension of Kenya settler power during the discussions on closer union. The other strains were more fundamental. The Protectorate government was increasingly critical of the chiefs on both economic and administrative grounds. The chiefs took too much of the peasants' surplus production and their jealously guarded privileges limited the powers of officials at a time when the purposes of government were expanding. British concern was strengthened by a rash of economic discontent among the Ganda tenantry. The unrest came to a head in the late 1940s, with riots in Kampala. What was significant about these outbursts was their royalist sentiment; the peasants looked to the Kabaka, now Frederick Muteesa II, to bring the overmighty chiefs to heel, to undo the oligarchic revolution. The leaders of the unrest had only minimally exploited similar discontents outside Buganda. The Ganda chiefs had kept the Protectorate government at a distance; it appeared therefore that problems could best be resolved by reform within the kingdom. By this time the other areas were also developing a strong tradition of local government, in which elective representation was increasing. Each kingdom, each district, was a political arena in its own right. The only grievance common to all Uganda was the alien hold over the marketing and processing of cotton, and government began to hand these over to African co-operative societies in the 1950s. Moreover, the Legislative Council was not a focus of African concern; it had never enjoyed much prominence, and by 1950 the eight African councillors balanced the European and Asian representatives together. Under the vigorous governorship of Sir Andrew Cohen, it was increasingly evident that Uganda would be allowed to develop as an African state. There was no call for a united nationalist front; but there was every reason for dissension over the relationship between Buganda and Uganda as a whole.

The long crisis on this issue started to unroll in 1953. Cohen then appeared to secure Buganda's agreement to a future unitary state by giving the kingdom more internal responsibility. But before the year was out he had exiled the Kabaka to England; for Muteesa II had gone back on his agreement through fresh fears of an East African Federation. Public opinion in Buganda was solidly behind the king. By the time he returned, two years later, Britain had committed itself firmly to Uganda's future as an African state, something on which there had been much ambivalence; Buganda was also to develop as a constitutional monarchy. It did not do so, thanks to the Kabaka's popular esteem. The Lukiiko, the Buganda Council, was full of king's men. These contemplated Buganda's diminished role within a self-governing state with alarm. The other districts were equally determined that Buganda's privileges should not continue. But the districts were themselves internally divided, in large measure due to the export of the Ganda convention that Protestants should receive a greater share in political office than Catholics, although the latter were in a numerical majority. By 1960 two parties had crystallized on these differences; the Uganda People's Congress (UPC) was a coalition of Protestant "district establishments", the Democratic Party (DP) enlisted the Catholics. Neither could make much headway in Buganda against the opposition of the Lukiiko, which in December 1960 went to the lengths of announcing Buganda's secession and independence. This the British ignored.

Buganda had attempted to boycott the registration of voters for the first nation-wide elections held in the following year. But 4 per cent of Buganda's voters did register; they were DP supporters. The DP thus won the elections, although the UPC had won a plurality of votes outside Buganda. The Lukiiko was appalled at the prospect of the DP's leader, Benedicto Kiwanuka, both Catholic and commoner, as Prime Minister; but the fact that he was also a Ganda raised hopes that, after all, the kingdom might have a leading role still to play. A British commission of enquiry then accepted that Buganda should have a federal status within independent Uganda, with the option of indirect elections to the National Assembly through the Lukiiko; the other three kingdoms, Ankole, Bunyoro and Toro, would enjoy a quasi-federal status. Buganda had got what it wanted. The way was open

for an alliance with Milton Obote's UPC. Both the Kabaka Yekka ("the King Alone"), the party of royalists which virtually monopolized the Lukiiko, and the UPC had good reason to combine against the DP government. In the final election before independence the UPC won most of the seats outside Buganda; the Lukiiko returned KY men for all the Buganda seats. Obote thus led Uganda to independence in October 1962 at the head of a UPC–KY alliance which was also, more fundamentally, a coalition of district notables and traditional rulers. This position seemed to be reinforced when, a year later, Uganda became a Republic. The Kabaka was elected President.

REVOLUTION FROM ABOVE

The alliance between Buganda and the UPC was soon under strain. Buganda's sense of being the dominant partner in the coalition was undermined from three directions. First, the financial arrangements between the national and the Buganda government were soon proved to be unsatisfactory; they were also ill-defined. Many social services were imperilled within the kingdom; there was much argument with the central government on means to make good the deficits. Secondly, the UPC had, by the middle of 1964, gained an overall majority in Parliament, through DP and KY respectively crossing the floor and defecting. Obote extinguished the KY elements from government. Then, in late 1964, he conducted a referendum in Bunyoro's "Lost Counties", in which there was an overwhelming vote for their return to Bunyoro—a further defeat for Buganda.

The struggle between Buganda and Uganda as a whole now moved into the arena of the UPC itself. The party had never been well organized; its cohesion was now further diluted by its access of numbers in Parliament. There was also room for disagreement between the older politicians from the districts and younger, more ideologically orientated men who had recently been recruited to the party's central offices. It was in this situation that some Ganda politicians sought to resurrect the kingdom's fortunes by infiltrating the UPC. Not only did Obote begin to feel insecure personally, it was by now apparent that Uganda's strong regional loyalties were a hindrance to coherent development planning. Events rapidly moved to a crisis, assisted by uncertainties on Uganda's borders. Southern Sudanese rebels on the northern border were a constant security threat; in the south-west there were large numbers of Tutsi refugees; but the chief complication was in the west, where the Congo rebels were active adjacent to Uganda's frontier.

It was in connection with the last that the crisis finally broke. In February 1966 a KY member accused government ministers of smuggling gold from the Congo; his motion, an indirect attack on Obote, was passed almost unanimously in Parliament. It looked as if the Prime Minister must fall from power. But a few days later he executed his own *coup*, arresting five of his Ministers at a Cabinet meeting. He continued to move swiftly, suspending the constitution and taking full executive powers. In April he introduced a new constitution, with himself as President. The federal status of Buganda and the other kingdoms was abolished, as were all official estates in the hands of chiefs. Buganda's reaction came in the following month. The Lukiiko demanded that the central government leave Buganda's soil. Three days later, amid rumours that the Ganda were taking to arms, the regular army stormed the Kabaka's palace. There were heavy casualties on both sides, but the Kabaka himself escaped to exile in England, this time to die. Buganda was subsequently divided into four districts and placed under a state of emergency.

A unitary state had been restored, but at considerable cost in human life and in enduring resentment against the army. A second Republican constitution was introduced in 1967, after long and open public debate. The four kingdoms were abolished, and the central government was accorded increased control over local government generally. But Obote had yet to find the key to greater popular support and a national sense of direction. Late in 1969 he introduced his Common Man's Charter in the clear hope that a "move to the left" would reduce the economic differentials on which regional conflict had thrived. But even as he did so, Obote was wounded in an assassination attempt—not the first—and in consequence the opposition parties were banned. In 1970 the new economic policy took form in plans for a 60 per cent controlling government interest in large-scale commerce, banking and plantations. An electoral commission also proposed a new, one-party, system which was designed to reduce the tribal element in voting preferences and to give more representation to the Nilotic north, Obote's home area. Elections were announced for April 1971, the first since 1962.

They were never held. In January 1971, while Obote was at the Singapore Commonwealth Conference, in the van of African protest against British willingness to sell arms to South Africa, his chief of defence staff, Major-General Amin, seized power. The *coup* is best understood in the perspective of the relations existing between government and army ever since the mutiny of 1964. The army had never been properly disciplined; rather, it had been bought off by rapid expansion and large pay rises. Obote had then tried to counter the army's new strength by creating special security forces; and it is probable that the army officers saw the "move to the left" and the electoral reforms as a further threat to their status.

Since the *coup*, power has passed yet more decisively into the army's hands, with the dissolution of parliament and all local councils, and with the police and civil administration demoralized by periodic purges. But it was already a divided army, and it was now torn apart as Amin sought to consolidate his hold by turning upon those troops who came from Obote's tribe, the Lango, and its neighbours, the Acholi. Thousands were killed or fled to the Sudan and Tanzania; they were replaced by recruits from Amin's own West Nile district and, according to some reports,

from among the rebel forces in the southern Sudan. The command structure was upset by the rapid promotion of men whose loyalties appeared to be guaranteed by their tribal or religious affiliation. Amin's co-religionists, the Muslims, may now hold more power in Uganda than at any time since the 1880s, but established national institutions have been virtually destroyed.

The new régime initially enjoyed considerable goodwill. Internally, Obote's rule had been unpopular with many, and Buganda in particular was reconciled to Amin's still "northern" leadership by his restoration of the late Kabaka's remains from England. Abroad, Tanzania's hostility was more than compensated by scarcely-veiled British satisfaction that Amin's perceptions of international politics and his views on capital appeared to be considerably more conservative than Obote's.

This goodwill was soon dissipated. Buganda was disillusioned by Amin's continuing refusal to restore the kingdom. The people of Uganda as a whole had to endure an increasingly assertive and undisciplined soldiery. Development and welfare expenditure was cut as military appropriations expanded. For all Amin's personal popularity with ordinary Ugandans, his régime grew the more brutal and erratic as its troubles multiplied. The Asian community, which had been subject to political attacks at least since 1945 and to restrictive trade licensing since 1969, suffered a crescendo of verbal harrassment from late in 1971. Ugandans who were believed to be critical of the Government continued to disappear. Early in 1972 there was a major reversal of foreign policy when Amin expelled the Israeli military mission—first invited in by Obote—and aligned himself with the pan-Islam of Libya's Colonel Gaddafi, who seemed readier than Israel to finance Uganda's military expenditure.

Then, in August 1972, Amin announced that African refugees within Uganda's borders would have to be repatriated, that Obote's programme of nationalization would be resumed, and that all non-citizen Asians—perhaps 50,000 people, though estimates have varied widely—must leave within three months. Most of them flew to Britain, which at Independence ten years earlier had admitted ultimate responsibility for those who chose not to take Ugandan citizenship. It was apparently with some reluctance that Amin refrained from expelling those who did have Ugandan citizenship as well. Amid the confusion that attended these moves Ugandan exiles, supporters of ex-President Obote, invaded from across the Tanzanian border. They were repulsed, but not before the crisis was internationalized through the arrival in Uganda of Libyan military aid. The outlook both for Uganda and for its relations with Tanzania must remain very uncertain, with its commercial sector in the doldrums of an enforced take-over and with the equivocations of the peace agreement between the two neighbouring states affording to Amin ample pretext for further diversionary military adventures.

ECONOMY

Y. Kyesimira*

AREA AND POPULATION

The area of Uganda is 91,000 sq. miles, of which 16,000 sq. miles consist of open water. The results of the last census, held in August 1969, revealed that the population of Uganda was 9.5 million, giving a density of about 127 persons per sq. mile of land area. The 1969 census results also indicate that the rate of population growth has been high, since in 1959 the census showed a total population of only 6.5 million. The growth rate was thus 3 per cent per annum. This high rate of population increase is explained partly by the improvement in the collection of statistics, and partly by the increased inflow of immigrants from the Sudan, Rwanda and Zaire arising out of unsettled political conditions which prevailed for some time in those countries after 1959. But perhaps the most significant factor affecting population growth has been a fall in the death rate consequent upon the improvement of health facilities all over the country since independence in 1962.

As one would expect the highest rate of increase in population has been recorded in the Western Region (bordering on Rwanda and Zaire) and the Northern Region (bordering on the Sudan) with increases of 54.3 per cent and 52.3 per cent respectively over this period. The Buganda Region recorded the lowest increase (24 per cent) and the Eastern Region 35 per cent. It is also to be expected that better coverage of the population census would affect the Northern and the Western Regions more than the other two Regions. Overall the population of Uganda is estimated to have increased by 46 per cent between 1959 and 1969.

GROSS DOMESTIC PRODUCT

Between 1963 and 1971 Uganda's Gross Domestic Product (at constant 1966 purchasers' values) increased from 5,272 million shillings to 7,400 million shillings, an overall rise of more than 40 per cent. The G.D.P. for 1969 alone was 11 per cent higher than the previous year's figure. This increase in G.D.P. was largely due to the excellent performance of the agricultural sector; there was a bumper coffee crop and cotton output also showed a significant increase over the previous year. There was also a sharp rise in the output of the food processing industry. However, the rate of economic growth has slowed considerably since then, with a rise in G.D.P. (assuming constant prices) of less than 1.5 per cent in 1970, followed by a further 1.7 per cent in 1971. These small increases failed to keep pace with population growth, so the country's output per head actually decreased in 1970 and 1971.

Events of 1969 also varied from the trend of the

* For the 1973 edition, revisions to this have been made by the Editor.

previous years when G.D.P. was growing very slowly, especially since 1965. There are two main explanations for this. First, quota restrictions on Uganda's main export, coffee, which have forced her to sell substantial quantities of her coffee outside the quota, combined with official discouragement of further planting of the crop, have resulted in a slowing down of the rate of growth of Uganda's exports and hence of the whole economy, since exports generate a significant proportion of the G.D.P. in the monetary sector.

Secondly, the intensive efforts made so far to develop the economy have not yet produced their full benefits. A lot of investment has gone into building up the economic and social infrastructure, such as roads, hospitals and schools, and will begin to bear fruit only in the long run. There has also been substantial investment geared to the diversification of the economy in the field of agriculture as well as industry, but here again we cannot expect such investment to produce significant results immediately. What this means is that during the 1970s Uganda may hope to reap the benefits of most of this investment so that G.D.P. will be expected to grow at a much higher rate in the second half of the decade (other things, of course, being equal).

AGRICULTURE

Agriculture is by far the most important sector in the economy of Uganda, generating as it does one-third of Uganda's monetary income and 50 per cent of total income (inclusive of subsistence income). It is also the most important export sector and in addition provides a livelihood for nearly 90 per cent of the total population of Uganda. The development of the whole economy is therefore very much influenced by the performance of the agricultural sector. Within the monetary sector the main cash crops are coffee and cotton, although tea production has expanded very fast of late. In addition there has been, since independence, an ambitious programme of developing the livestock industry, and this is beginning to bear fruit. However, cotton and coffee continue to dominate the monetary sector and between them they generate about 35 per cent of all the monetary income earned from agriculture. The unfortunate fact is that coffee export is subject to the International Coffee Agreement quota, and the market for cotton is severely restricted because of competition from synthetic fibres. The policy of diversifying the agricultural base of the economy is largely influenced by these circumstances.

On the other hand it will be quite unrealistic to expect rapid development of the agricultural sector. The problem has still to be faced of reaching more than a million small-scale farm families who dominate agricultural production of coffee and cotton. With the exception of tea and sugar the production of other agricultural commodities is mainly concentrated in the hands of peasant producers.

EXPORT SECTOR

The four leading export commodities for Uganda are coffee, cotton, copper and tea. Between them, they constitute about 90 per cent of Uganda's domestic exports (outside East Africa) with coffee alone accounting for 56 per cent of Uganda's export earnings in 1970. It is significant to note that this dependence on these four exports has not decreased over the years, and this is an indication of the difficulty Uganda faces in diversifying her exports. Thus for a long time to come coffee will continue to be Uganda's most important export while the contribution of cotton is perhaps likely to stagnate or even fall. Since 1964 greater emphasis has been placed on tea production, especially on outgrower farms in Buganda and the Western Region. The response from the farmers has been encouraging and there has been a persistent increase in tea exports every year, but its share in total exports is still less than 10 per cent. It also looks as though in the near future, tea exports may be subject to an international quota system, although Uganda's potential as a tea grower is far from being fully tapped. In reality tea growing by the African small grower is still in its infancy and requires a lot of encouragement.

In the early 1960s copper exports rose fairly fast, but there has been a tendency to levelling off, so that in recent years its share in total exports has not been rising fast. The whole output of this mineral is exported to Japan under a long-term agreement. As far as cotton is concerned the efforts to raise output have not been attended with a lot of success. A record output was achieved in 1965–66 at 445,000 bales but since then there has been a tendency for output to fall rather than rise. In the 1971/72 season, farmers sold 403,505 bales to the Lint Marketing Board. Exports of cotton have also been affected by the establishment of local textile mills which use locally produced cotton, so that there is no automatic relationship between production and exports.

In summary, it can be safely asserted that, with the exception of tea, there has been no significant increase in the volume of Uganda's leading exports. The tremendous efforts which have gone into increased production and diversification of agriculture have been of an import-substitution nature (especially in the livestock field) and thus have not yet affected Uganda's domestic exports to any great extent.

EAST AFRICAN TRADE

Uganda is a partner in the East African Community with Kenya and Tanzania. The Treaty for East African Co-operation which governs the functioning of the Community came into existence in December 1967. Since the formal coming into effect of this Treaty Uganda's exports to her two partner states have shown a marked tendency to fall rather than rise. Total export earnings from trade with Kenya and Tanzania fell sharply in 1971 to 176 million shillings, their lowest level for eight years. This was partly due to tensions between the Ugandan and Tanzanian governments.

In contrast to this trend, Uganda's imports from her partners have risen since the signing of the Treaty. In 1971 the total cost of imports from Kenya and Tanzania reached a record 420 million shillings, compared with 331 million shillings in 1967. This indicates that Uganda has not done well within the Community as far as trade is concerned. This trend is also in contrast with Uganda's past performance in the early 1960s when her exports to her partners were rising every year.

These trends in part reflect the fact that under the provisions of the Treaty Tanzania can impose transfer taxes (to a maximum of 50 per cent of the external tariff) on manufactured goods originating from Uganda. This has adversely affected Uganda's exports of textiles to Tanzania, whose total value fell from Sh.16.4 million in 1967 to Sh.2.8 in 1969. Kenya also has been successful in increasing her sugar production, and in addition has diverted her purchases of tobacco from Uganda to Tanzania. Uganda has had to struggle to sell the same commodities outside East Africa.

SOCIAL AND ECONOMIC POLICY

In December 1969 the Delegates Conference of the ruling party, the Uganda Peoples Congress (UPC) adopted, as its guiding policy, a document entitled the Common Man's Charter. This document made it clear that the economy of Uganda was to be organized along socialistic lines, and called for state participation in a number of important enterprises as well as the nationalization of other types of property.

In pursuit of this policy the government acquired 60 per cent of the shares of a number of enterprises, including commercial banks, oil companies and large plantations. In addition only state corporations were to be allowed to participate in the export and import trade, and an Export and Import Corporation was set up for the purposes of implementing this policy. In a large number of cases negotiations on the terms of government participation, as well as the method of compensation, had already been concluded at the time of the *coup d'état* in January 1971.

After the *coup* the policy of state participation was reviewed. It was announced that in commercial banks, insurance companies and the sugar and steel industries the Government intended to take 49 per cent rather than 60 per cent participation. In August 1972, though, General Amin announced that the former government's nationalization programme would be resumed.

STRUCTURAL CHANGE

As already pointed out, Uganda's share of inter-Community trade has fallen even in absolute terms since 1966, and this is one of the major factors underlying the slow growth rate of the manufacturing sector, especially in the case of textiles and fertilizers. Secondly, the domestic demand for manufactures has not been as buoyant as had been expected because of the slow growth of consumption expenditure reflecting a high rate of savings. It is also probable that increased consumer prices consequent upon the imposition of a sales tax have affected the growth of demand for manufactured goods. This sector has therefore been characterized by surplus capacity for some major commodities so that, overall, inadequate capacity is not a major explanation for the slow growth of the sector. Investment is nevertheless being undertaken in other lines of production; in particular every effort is being made to diversify the agricultural sector itself through the encouragement of other enterprises such as tea and livestock production.

EMPLOYMENT

In contrast to the period 1958–62, when total employment declined, the period since 1963 has seen a rise in employment every year. The average increase per annum was 4.8 per cent, but the greatest increase was recorded between 1966 and 1969, when total employment rose from 246,000 to 295,000. The total in 1970 was more than 312,000.

This increase in employment has not, however, been sufficient to absorb every person looking for a job. In particular the problem of finding either paid employment or self-employment for the school leaver still exists. There has also been a tendency for unemployment to become apparent as a result of migration to the cities in search of a better life.

Recorded earnings have risen at a higher rate than employment; on the average these have risen by 8.9 per cent per annum since 1963 compared to 4.8 per cent for total employment.

INDUSTRIALIZATION

The strategy set out for industrialization in Uganda's Second Five-Year Plan was based on import substitution. In Uganda's situation this strategy does not hold out much promise for accelerating the pace of industrialization because of the small size of the domestic market. In the past import substitution was viewed on an East African basis since industries set up in Uganda had access to the markets of Kenya and Tanzania without many obstacles. This was definitely

the case with Uganda's textiles. However, the Treaty for East African Co-operation empowers Tanzania to impose transfer taxes on manufactured goods produced in Uganda if she is planning to produce goods of a similar description within three months of the imposition of the tax, or is already producing goods of a similar description at the time of the imposition of the tax. It would also seem that Kenya has been active in cultivating new markets for her products as well as consolidating her import-substitution policy. This has also adversely affected Uganda's exports of manufactured goods to that country.

It appears therefore that at this stage of Uganda's development an aggressive export policy is a prerequisite for accelerating the rate of industrialization. This policy should be directed towards Uganda's partners in the East African Community as well as her other neighbours. In this respect Uganda's landlocked position may prove an advantage, since she could have access to markets for her products on all sides. The poor state of communication may not make this an immediate possibility but in the long run this advantage should be exploited.

ECONOMIC DEVELOPMENT

Uganda's Third Five-Year Development Plan, covering 1971–76, was published early in 1972. Among its proposals, aimed at developing all sectors of the economy, are the following specific goals: 1. The rapid, steady and sustained expansion of production per head of population; 2. a most rapid and orderly Ugandanization of the economy; 3. a more equitable distribution of income and wealth, particularly by rural development; 4. increasing employment opportunities.

The monetary Gross Domestic Product is planned to grow at 5.6 per cent per annum in real terms, with the industrial sector growing at 7.6 per cent. According to the Plan, the number of Ugandans in paid employment will grow to 380,000 by 1976, and effective Ugandanization of all paid jobs will be achieved by 1981.

STATISTICAL SURVEY

AREA AND POPULATION

AREA (sq. km.)*			POPULATION (Census of August 18th, 1969)†					
Total	Land	Water	Total	African	Asian‡	Arab	European	Others
236,860	197,400	39,459	9,548,847	9,456,466	74,308	3,238	9,533	5,302

* *Source:* Lands and Surveys Department.

† Includes 13,796 people enumerated in Karasuk, a part of Kenya (*see* footnote to table below).

‡ Defined as persons from India and Pakistan (including Bangladesh) only. Other persons from non-Arab countries in Asia are included among "Others".

MID-YEAR POPULATION
(estimates)

1970 . . .	9,806,400
1971 . . .	10,127,400
1972 . . .	10,461,500

POPULATION BY REGIONS AND DISTRICTS
(1969 Census)

DISTRICT	POPULATION						LAND AREA (sq. km.)	DENSITY (per sq. km.)
	African	Asian*	Arab	European	Others	Total		
West Mengo . . .	510,277	1,913	24	1,055	229	513,498	4,613	111
East Mengo† . .	846,986	3,918	244	230	205	851,583	13,117	65
Masaka . . .	637,018	3,231	9	223	115	640,596	9,852	65
Mubende . . .	329,998	827	32	59	39	330,955	9,820	34
Kampala City . .	293,328	31,505	352	4,293	1,222	330,700	170	1,948
TOTAL BUGANDA REGION .	2,617,607	41,394	661	5,860	1,810	2,667,332	37,572	71
Teso . . .	565,936	3,555	370	216	551	570,628	10,983	52
Bugisu . . .	397,453	209	39	72	116	397,889	2,479	161
Bukedi . . .	524,723	1,808	123	194	242	527,090	3,900	135
Busoga . . .	889,989	5,393	780	116	597	896,875	8,799	102
Sebei . . .	64,432	7	—	19	6	64,464	1,738	37
Karamoja‡ . .	283,776	113	12	153	13	284,067	27,186	10
Jinja Municipality† .	43,281	8,523	59	417	229	52,509	45	1,164
Mbale Town . .	18,374	4,664	163	158	185	23,544	24	966
TOTAL EASTERN REGION‡.	2,787,964	24,272	1,546	1,345	1,939	2,817,066	55,155	51
Kigezi . . .	646,726	682	147	209	224	647,988	4,988	130
Ankole . . .	859,113	1,558	64	258	152	861,145	15,697	55
Toro . . .	567,907	1,804	332	905	566	571,514	12,928	44
Bunyoro . . .	350,286	1,293	58	143	123	351,903	16,302	22
TOTAL WESTERN REGION .	2,424,032	5,337	601	1,515	1,065	2,432,550	49,915	49
West Nile . . .	572,289	903	211	231	128	573,762	10,377	55
Madi . . .	89,842	74	22	24	16	89,978	4,668	19
Acholi . . .	462,095	1,229	3	419	98	463,844	27,675	17
Lango . . .	502,637	1,099	194	139	246	504,315	12,038	42
TOTAL NORTHERN REGION.	1,626,863	3,305	430	813	488	1,631,899	54,758	30
UGANDA TOTAL‡ . .	9,456,466	74,308	3,238	9,533	5,302	9,548,847	197,400	48

* Defined to cover only persons whose ethnic origins are in India or Pakistan (including what is now Bangladesh). This definition was not followed strictly as the total includes, among others, 18 nationals of Japan.

† Njeru Town, in East Mengo District, is included in Jinja Municipality.

‡ Population includes 13,796 people enumerated in Karasuk, a part of Kenya which was administered by Uganda at the time of the census. The administration of Karasuk has since reverted to Kenya.

Source: Ministry of Planning and Economic Development, *Quarterly Economic and Statistical Bulletin.*

AFRICAN POPULATION BY NATIONALITY
(1969 Census)

	MALE	FEMALE	TOTAL
Uganda	4,462,898	4,507,394	8,970,292
Rwanda . . .	108,826	53,127	161,953
Kenya	68,889	48,744	117,633
Sudan	34,639	30,601	65,240
Zaire	39,380	24,618	63,998
Burundi . . .	30,730	9,294	40,024
Tanzania . . .	22,454	11,164	33,618
Others . . .	711	362	1,073
Not Stated . .	1,336	1,299	2,635
TOTAL . .	4,769,863	4,686,603	9,456,466

MAIN TRIBES OF UGANDA
(1959 Census)

TRIBE	MALE	FEMALE	TOTAL
Baganda . . .	508,735	536,143	1,044,878
Iteso	257,134	267,582	524,716
Basoga . . .	246,182	255,739	501,921
Banyankore . .	253,993	265,290	519,283
Banyaruanda . .	212,434	166,222	378,656
Bakiga . . .	220,936	238,683	459,619
Lango	180,694	183,113	363,807
Bagisu . . .	163,923	165,334	329,257
Acholi . . .	141,643	143,286	284,929
Lugbara . . .	116,114	120,156	236,270
Banyoro . . .	93,907	94,467	188,374
Batoro . . .	103,436	104,864	208,300
Karamojong . .	63,747	67,966	131,713
TOTAL (incl. others) .	3,236,902	3,212,656	6,449,558

EUROPEAN POPULATION
(1969 Census)

NATIONALITY	MALE	FEMALE	TOTAL
Uganda . . .	150	97	247
United Kingdom .	3,102	2,943	6,045
U.S.A. . . .	524	508	1,032
Italy . . .	451	299	750
Germany . . .	138	126	264
France . . .	51	54	105
Belgium . . .	37	26	63
Kenya . . .	24	10	34
Tanzania . . .	1	1	2
Others . . .	544	417	961
Not Stated . .	13	17	30
TOTAL . .	5,035	4,498	9,533

OTHER NON-AFRICANS
(1969 Census)

NATIONALITY	ASIANS*			ARABS			OTHERS		
	Male	Female	Total	Male	Female	Total	Male	Female	Total
Uganda . . .	14,108	11,549	25,657	1,151	972	2,123	2,113	2,019	4,132
United Kingdom .	18,647	17,946	36,593	108	73	181	148	163	311
India . . .	4,666	4,224	8,890	21	19	40	152	143	295
Pakistan . .	137	116	253	2	—	2	7	6	13
Kenya . . .	851	917	1,768	111	68	179	56	37	93
Tanzania . .	349	384	733	29	16	45	21	28	49
Portugal . .	14	8	22	5	4	9	4	—	4
Japan . . .	13	5	18	—	—	—	11	4	15
Arab Countries .	9	3	12	382	189	571	54	49	103
Others . .	117	106	223	43	37	80	133	110	243
Not Stated . .	65	74	139	4	4	8	20	24	44
TOTAL .	38,976	35,332	74,308	1,856	1,382	3,238	2,719	2,583	5,302

* Defined as persons from India or Pakistan (including Bangladesh).

PRINCIPAL TOWNS
(1969 census)

Kampala (capital) . . .	330,700
Jinja and Njeru . . .	52,509
Bugembe Planning Area . .	46,884
Mbale	23,544
Entebbe	21,096
Gulu	18,170

Births and Deaths: Average annual birth rate 43.2 per 1,000; death rate 17.6 per 1,000 (UN estimates for 1965–70). These estimates, prepared before the final results of the 1969 census were known, assume an average natural increase rate of 25.6 per 1,000 each year. More recent official estimates, though, put the annual rate of population increase at 3.3 per cent (33 per 1,000).

EMPLOYMENT
(1970)
TOTAL EMPLOYEES

	PRIVATE INDUSTRY	PUBLIC SERVICES	TOTAL
Agriculture	44,224	7,045	51,269
Cotton Ginning . . .	6,587	—	6,587
Coffee Curing	5,113		5,113
Forestry, Fishing and Hunting . .	557	2,951	3,508
Mining and Quarrying . . .	7,855	43	7,898
Manufacture of Food Products . .	15,218	—	15,218
Miscellaneous Manufacturing Industries .	24,413	309	24,722
Construction	14,855	32,801	47,656
Commerce	14,981	156	15,137
Transport and Communications . .	4,856	8,102	12,958
Government	—	21,428	21,428
Local Government . . .	—	23,623	23,623
Educational and Medical Services . .	31,861	30,054	61,915
Miscellaneous	12,328	2,876	15,204
TOTAL . .	182,848	129,388	312,236

The total includes 298,598 Africans (of whom 46,000 were born outside Uganda). In addition more than 3,000,000 Africans not in employment are economically active in agriculture.

AGRICULTURE

LAND USE, 1967
('ooo hectares)

Arable Land	3,772
Under Permanent Crops	1,116
Permanent Meadows and Pastures . .	5,000
Forest Land	9,172*
Other Land	305
TOTAL LAND AREA . .	19,365
Inland Water	4,239
TOTAL AREA . .	23,604

*Data taken from the world forest inventory carried out by the FAO in 1963.

Source: FAO, *Production Yearbook 1971.*

PRINCIPAL CROPS
('ooo metric tons)

	1968	1969	1970	1971
Maize	333	338	335	335*
Millet	626	630	630*	630*
Sorghum	254	332	332*	332*
Rice (Paddy)	3	3	6	6*
Sugar Cane†	1,672	1,550*	1,700*	1,700*
Potatoes	23*	23*	24*	24*
Sweet Potatoes and Yams .	666	710*	710*	n.a.
Cassava (Manioc) . . .	1,945	2,321	2,150*	n.a.
Onions	10*	10*	10*	n.a.
Dry Beans	260*	260*	260*	270*
Dry Peas	2	4*	4*	4*
Pigeon Peas	27	50	34*	40*
Cow Peas	64	56	70*	63*
Groundnuts (in shell) . .	234	234	234	234*
Cottonseed	169	187	172	196
Cotton (Lint)	77	85	75	69
Sesame Seed	23	23*	23*	23*
Castor Beans‡	2	2	3	3*
Coffee	147	225	204*	210*
Tea	15.2	17.6	18.2	18.0
Tobacco	4.6	3.5	5.2	3.7

* FAO estimate.   † Crop year ending in year stated.   ‡ Exports only.

Source: FAO, *Production Yearbook 1971.*

LIVESTOCK
('ooo)

	1968–69	1969–70	1970–71
Cattle	3,857	4,145	4,400*
Sheep	766	855	880*
Goats	1,873	1,911	1,940*
Pigs	53	68*	77*
Asses	17*	17*	16*
Chickens . . .	9,500*	10,000*	10,200*

*FAO estimate.

Source: FAO, *Production Yearbook 1971.*

LIVESTOCK PRODUCTS
(FAO estimates, metric tons)

	1968	1969	1970
Cows' Milk . .	251,000	258,000	275,000
Goats' Milk . .	10,000	11,000	12,000
Beef and Veal .	52,000	53,000	57,000
Mutton and Lamb† .	9,000	10,000	10,000
Poultry Meat . .	5,900	6,200	6,500
Edible Offal . .	12,700	13,900	14,100
Other Meat . .	12,000	12,000	12,000
Hen Eggs . .	8,700*	9,000*	11,000
Cattle Hides . .	9,790	9,980	10,690
Sheep Skins . .	520	533	598
Goat Skins . .	1,280	1,409	1,435

1971 (FAO estimates, metric tons): Cows' milk 293,000;
Goats' milk 12,000; Hen eggs 11,200.

* Official estimate.

† Including goats' meat.

Source: FAO, *Production Yearbook 1971.*

FORESTRY
(Twelve months ending June 30th)
ROUNDWOOD REMOVALS
(cubic metres)

1966–67 . .	10,936,000
1967–68 . .	11,040,000
1968–69 . .	11,264,000

Source: FAO, *Yearbook of Forest Products.*

SAWNWOOD PRODUCTION
(cubic metres)

	1968–69	1969–70	1970–71
Broadleaved (hard wood)	58,726	62,634	69,057
Coniferous (soft wood) .	2,594	2,310	4,086

FISHING
(inland waters)

	1967	1968	1969	1970
Total Catch (metric tons) . .	99,600	108,400	125,300	129,000
Value of Landings (U£'000) . .	3,708	6,127	6,525	6,950

Source: FAO, *Yearbook of Fishery Statistics.*

MINING
EXPORTS
(metric tons)

	1968	1969	1970
Copper Ore*	15,200	16,500	17,600
Tin Concentrates* . . .	172	166	111
Tungsten Concentrates* . .	92	110	153
Salt (unrefined) . . .	4,000	5,000	3,000
Natural Phosphate Rock . . .	160,000	368,000	300,000

* Figures relate to the metal content of ores and concentrates.

INDUSTRY

	Unit	1968	1969	1970
Raw Sugar . . .	metric tons	150,000	151,000	154,000
Beer . . .	hectolitres	203,000	227,000	n.a.
Cigarettes and Cigars . .	million	1,035	1,124	1,060
Woven Cotton Fabrics* . .	million metres	45	43	n.a.
Cement . . .	metric tons	155,000	177,000	189,000
Crude Steel . . .	,, ,,	21,000	n.a.	n.a.
Blister Copper . . .	,, ,,	15,600	16,600	17,000
Electric Energy . . .	million kWh.	731	731	734

* After undergoing finishing processes.

Source: United Nations, *Statistical Yearbook 1971.*

FINANCE

100 cents = 1 Uganda shilling.

Coins: 5, 10, 20 and 50 cents; 1 and 2 shillings.

Notes: 5, 10, 20 and 100 shillings.

Exchange rates (December 1972): £1 sterling = 16.8084 Uganda shillings; U.S. $ = 7.143 Uganda shillings.

100 Uganda shillings = £5.949 = $14.00.

(*Note:* In this survey the term "Uganda £" is used to denote amounts of 20 Uganda shillings, equivalent to £1.19 sterling.)

BUDGET

(million shillings, twelve months ending June 30th)

Revenue	1968–69	1969–70	1970–71*	Expenditure	1968–69	1969–70	1970–71*
Income Tax	171.78	205.78	241.00	Education	274.01	322.47	381.01
Other Direct Taxes	0.03	—	—	Public Health	215.62	159.78	149.65
Export Duties	137.43	201.23	252.70	Other Social Services	40.94	60.16	95.76
Import Duties	284.05	248.60	260.50	Agriculture	90.94	133.18	163.79
Other Indirect Taxes	343.78	376.56	431.02	Tsetse Control	8.60	8.59	9.61
Other Receipts	282.57	193.56	179.76	Roads	86.07	87.58	119.87
Contributions from Local Funds	3.11	8.83	12.11	Other Economic Services	177.08	149.16	222.92
				General Administration	222.82	349.19	511.31
Total Revenue	1,222.75	1,234.56	1,377.09	Defence	144.06	170.82	147.57
Deficit	288.86	427.54	674.94	Contributions to Local Governments	25.12	26.83	31.06
				Public Debt Service	44.59	82.93	99.03
				Other Expenditures	179.76	111.41	120.45
Total	1,511.61	1,662.10	2,052.03	Total	1,511.61	1,662.10	2,052.03

* Estimates.

Figures represent cash transactions and cover both recurrent and non-recurrent items in the budget. Recurrent expenditure (in million shillings) was: 1,008.66 in 1968–69; 1,189.35 in 1969–70; and 1,291.91 (estimated) in 1970–71. Non-recurrent expenditure (including development) was: 502.95 in 1968–69; 472.75 in 1969–70; and 760.12 (estimated) in 1970–71.

1971–72: Recurrent expenditure 1,253,753,000 shillings.

1972–73: Recurrent expenditure 1,429,685,000 shillings.

DEVELOPMENT PLAN

Third Five-Year Plan (1971–76): Total investment is provisionally set at 7,700 million shillings, with spending in the public sector at 1,600 million shillings, over half of which is to be financed from local resources. G.D.P. is planned to rise in real terms at 5 per cent annually.

DEVELOPMENT BUDGET

(1970–71)

REVENUE					million shillings	EXPENDITURE					million shillings
Grants from Abroad	.	.	.	.	16.3	General Services	.	.	.	.	101.0
Miscellaneous	.	.	.	.	31.1	Community Services	.	.	.		100.6
						Education	.	.	.	.	63.6
						Health	.	.	.	.	58.4
						Other Social Services	.	.	.		23.9
						Economic Services	.	.	.		240.3
						Other Items	.	.	.	.	112.7
TOTAL	.	.	.		47.4	TOTAL	.	.	.		700.5

Currency in Circulation (March 31st, 1972): 639 million Uganda shillings.

NATIONAL ACCOUNTS

GROSS DOMESTIC PRODUCT
million shillings (current prices)

	1968	1969	1970	1971
Monetary Sector:				
Agriculture	1,396	1,691	2,021	2,022
Forestry, fishing and hunting	114	123	155	146
Mining and quarrying	106	145	144	129
Manufacturing	599	686	774	778
Electricity	82	84	90	97
Construction	102	124	116	122
Transport and communications	258	269	263	309
Government	382	385	447	512
Miscellaneous services	649	738	767	853
Trade	916	989	1,051	1,189
Non-Monetary Sector:				
Agriculture	1,638	1,821	2,224	2,629
Forestry, fishing and hunting	144	152	191	229
Construction	28	30	31	33
Owner-occupied dwellings	212	242	254	268
GROSS DOMESTIC PRODUCT AT FACTOR COST	6,626	7,479	8,528	9,316

BALANCE OF PAYMENTS
(million shillings)

	1969			1970 (provisional)		
	Credit	Debit	Net	Credit	Debit	Net
Goods and Services:						
Merchandise exports (f.o.b.) . . .	1,569.1	—	1,569.1	1,864.7	—	1,864.7
Merchandise imports (c.i.f.) . . .	—	1,419.8	−1,419.8	—	1,462.7	−1,462.7
Merchandise (net)	149.3	—	149.3	402.0	—	402.0
Freight and insurance	3.4	2.9	0.5	—	—	—
Other transportation . . .	19.8	54.1	− 34.3	20.2	66.1	− 45.9
Travel	137.4	106.8	30.6	141.9	142.9	− 1.0
Investment income . . .	26.2	151.8	− 125.6	20.7	128.1	− 107.4
Other government services . .	52.8	60.8	− 8.0	49.0	66.2	− 17.2
Other services . . .	14.2	53.8	− 39.6	15.1	61.0	− 45.9
Total Services	253.8	430.2	− 176.4	246.9	464.3	− 217.4
Total Goods and Services . . .	1,822.9	1,850.0	− 27.1	2,111.6	1,927.0	184.6
Transfer Payments:						
Private	40.8	75.5	− 34.7	30.0	79.6	− 49.6
Official	57.4	39.4	18.0	50.2	39.2	11.0
Total Transfers	98.2	114.9	− 16.7	80.2	118.8	− 38.6
BALANCE ON CURRENT ACCOUNT . .	—	—	− 43.8	—	—	146.0
Capital Account:						
Private	173.7	219.7	− 46.0	19.0	278.6	− 259.6
Public (Central government) . .	222.4	52.2	170.2	168.7	62.8	105.9
BALANCE ON CAPITAL ACCOUNT . .	—	—	124.2	—	—	− 153.7
Combined Current and Capital . .	2,317.2	2,236.8	80.4	2,379.5	2,387.2	− 7.7
Net Errors and Omissions . . .	—	—	− 10.4	—	—	—
Balance (net monetary movements)* .	—	—	70.0	—	—	− 7.7
of which:						
IMF accounts		3.3	− 3.3		14.3	− 14.3
Monetary authorities . . .	57.9	67.3	− 9.4	107.1	85.1	22.0
Commercial banks . . .	—	57.3	− 57.3	8.3	8.3	—

* Excluding Special Drawing Rights on the International Monetary Fund (Credit 38.4 million shillings in 1970).
Source: Bank of Uganda.

EXTERNAL TRADE*
(U£'000)

	1966	1967	1968	1969	1970	1971
Imports	42,898	41,292	43,795	45,462	43,265	68,100
Exports	67,120	65,550	66,347	70,595	87,650	84,000

* Excluding trade in local produce and locally manufactured goods with Kenya, Tanganyika and (since 1968) Zanzibar.
Source: United Nations, *Monthly Bulletin of Statistics.*

INTER-COMMUNITY TRADE
(U £'ooo)

	IMPORTS FROM KENYA AND TANZANIA	EXPORTS TO KENYA AND TANZANIA
1968 . .	14,989	10,679
1969 . .	16,829	9,516
1970 . .	18,179	12,043

COMMODITIES
('ooo shillings)

RETAINED IMPORTS*	1968	1969
Food	95,993	120,568
Beverages and Tobacco . . .	9,440	11,638
Crude Materials, inedible, except fuels .	28,881	32,755
Mineral Fuels, Lubricants and Related materials	71,316	81,571
Animal and Vegetable Oils and Fats .	14,541	13,711
Chemicals	121,709	122,670
Manufactures	354,410	372,858
Machinery and Transport Equipment .	321,882	343,575
Miscellaneous Articles	111,221	113,930
Other Transactions	29,092	19,182
TOTAL	1,158,486	1,232,459

* Sum of net imports and transfers from Kenya and Tanzania, minus re-exports.
1970: Total retained imports 1,212,593,000 shillings.

EXPORTS*	1968	1969	1970†
Raw Sugar	2,317	17,609	4,281
Coffee (not roasted)	715,020	779,929	1,014,464
Tea	74,258	93,067	94,558
Oilseed Cake and Meal, etc. . . .	31,800	38,680	n.a.
Tobacco	2,661	16,908	7,475
Hides and Skins (undressed) . . .	20,385	26,686	26,706
Oilseeds, Nuts and Kernels . . .	8,385	8,639	7,137
Raw Cotton	295,674	250,955	350,985
Tin Ores and Concentrates . . .	3,535	2,759	n.a.
Tungsten Ores and Concentrates . .	1,460	2,700	n.a.
Papain, Crude	7,690	6,471	2,207
Copper and Alloys, Unwrought . .	111,490	120,280	165,543
TOTAL (incl. others) . . .	1,309,419	1,397,700	1,758,718

* Excluding re-exports and inter-Community trade.   † Provisional.

PRINCIPAL COUNTRIES*
('ooo shillings)

IMPORTS	1968	1969	1970
Belgium/Luxembourg	14,650	12,615	11,096
Canada	10,755	7,122	9,805
China, People's Republic . . .	20,597	17,921	16,099
Denmark	7,893	10,914	10,206
France	31,431	27,072	31,588
Germany, Federal Republic . . .	95,018	86,447	79,013
Hong Kong	18,566	15,651	16,850
India	33,116	37,490	33,311
Israel	9,035	9,209	15,710
Italy	47,211	44,556	44,936
Japan	94,395	123,592	99,787
Netherlands	22,132	21,888	25,804
Pakistan	13,713	25,930	22,105
Sweden	13,785	18,466	14,416
Switzerland	13,804	11,260	7,675
U.S.S.R.	7,158	8,229	8,289
United Kingdom	292,655	312,258	278,425
U.S.A.	38,673	37,645	51,526
TOTAL (incl. others) . .	876,247	910,083	865,290

EXPORTS†	1968	1969	1970
Australia	45,129	51,046	43,497
Canada	66,126	56,138	49,678
China, People's Republic . . .	34,852	8,889	10,907
Germany, Federal Republic . . .	55,772	44,824	80,257
Greece	727	247	44,444
Hong Kong	21,935	55,880	62,356
Hungary	—	20,485	32,520
India	63,514	48,413	75,429
Israel	18,711	21,513	16,285
Japan	156,525	222,588	205,937
Netherlands	36,128	32,786	32,015
Poland	4,484	16,959	35,522
Romania	3,072	25,445	26,108
Spain	9,398	13,609	50,972
Sudan	25,548	17,981	37,316
Sweden	13,870	16,054	47,777
Thailand	19,820	20,957	7,885
U.S.S.R.	8,204	15,868	20,844
United Kingdom	302,342	315,798	358,949
U.S.A.	327,648	330,747	362,472
TOTAL (incl. others) . .	1,309,419	1,456,470	1,758,718

* Excluding inter-Community trade.   † Excluding re-exports.
Source: Annual Trade Reports.

TOURISM

TOURIST ARRIVALS BY COUNTRY OF RESIDENCE

	1968	1969	1970
Germany, Federal Republic . . .	2,023	2,517	2,897
India	1,727	2,025	2,333
Italy	1,049	2,000	1,788
United Kingdom	10,114	12,585	10,754
U.S.A.	7,507	11,474	10,940
Others	5,716	7,266	6,675
Unspecified	25,827	36,113	44,976
TOTAL	53,963	73,980	80,363

Source: United Nations, *Statistical Yearbook.*

TRANSPORT

Railways: (*see* Tanzania chapter).

ROADS

	CARS	COMMERCIAL VEHICLES	OTHER VEHICLES
1968 .	25,609	15,534	6,815
1969 .	28,236	13,758	6,765
1970 .	29,120	13,993	7,306

CIVIL AVIATION

TOTAL SCHEDULED SERVICES*

	1968	1969	1970
Kilometres Flown ('000) . . .	5,209	6,096	6,340
Passenger-km. ('000) . . .	222,189	233,428	267,630
Cargo ton-km. ('000) . . .	7,529	8,847	9,626
Mail ton- km. ('000) . . .	1,000	1,045	961

* Including one-third of the traffic of the East African Airways Corporation and Caspair Ltd., which operate services on behalf of Kenya, Tanzania and Uganda.

EXTERNAL AIR TRAFFIC

	PASSENGERS		FREIGHT (kg.)	
	Arrival	Departure	Unloaded	Loaded
1968 . .	26,129	26,947	581,704	1,118,521
1969 . .	33,876	37,675	774,166	1,546,820
1970 . .	34,901	40,280	1,151,200	1,414,817

EDUCATION
(1970—Aided Schools only)

	NUMBER OF ESTABLISHMENTS	NUMBER OF TEACHERS	NUMBER OF PUPILS
Primary	2,755	21,471	720,127
Senior Secondary . . .	73	1,816	40,697
Vocational Secondary . .	14	114	1,524
Technical Secondary . .	5	113	1,451
Teacher Training . . .	26	298	4,450
Technical and Commercial Colleges .	2	83	1,272
University	1	350	1,949

Higher Education Abroad (1972): 1,804.

Source (unless otherwise stated): Statistics Division, Ministry of Planning and Economic Development, Entebbe.

THE CONSTITUTION

Uganda achieved independence on October 9th, 1962, as a dominion with a federal structure. A year later, on October 9th, 1963, the country became a republic, with a nominal President and an executive Prime Minister. The Constitution was suspended on February 24th, 1966, by the Prime Minister, Dr. Milton Obote, who abolished the office of President in the following month. A provisional Constitution, which ended the federal system and introduced an executive President, came into force on April 15th, 1966, but was replaced by a new definitive Constitution on September 8th, 1967. According to this, the Republic of Uganda has an executive President who is Head of State, Leader of the Government and Commander-in-Chief of the Armed Forces. The Parliament is the supreme legislature, and consists of the

President and a National Assembly of 82 elected members. The Constitution provides for some specially elected members as may be required to give the party having the greatest numerical strength of elected members a majority of not more than ten of all the members of the National Assembly.

There are 18 Administrative Districts of Acholi, Ankole, Bugisu, Bukedi, Bunyoro, Busoga, East Mengo, Karamoja, Kigezi, Lango, Madi, Masaka, Mubende, Sebei, Teso, Toro, West Mengo and West Nile.

This Constitution was not revoked by Maj.-Gen. Amin, but in February 1971 he ordered the suspension of Uganda's legal system, and the concentration of legislative powers in his own hands, with the assistance of a Council of Ministers nominated by him.

THE GOVERNMENT

HEAD OF STATE
President: General IDI AMIN DADA.

CABINET
(*January* 1973)

Minister of Internal Affairs: General IDI AMIN DADA.

Minister of Agriculture, Forestry and Co-operatives: FABIAN L. OKWAARE.

Minister of Foreign Affairs: WANUME KIBEDI.

Minister of Commerce and Industry: WILSON LUTARA.

Minister of Animal Husbandry, Game and Fisheries: (vacant).

Minister of Public Services and Local Administration: J. M. BYAGAGAIRE.

Minister of Labour: (vacant).

Minister of Health: Dr. J. M. GESA.

Minister of Mineral and Water Resources: ERNEST WILSON ORYEMA.

Minister of Community Development and Culture: (vacant).

Minister of Finance, Planning and Economic Development: EMANUEL B. WAKHWEYA.

Minister of Education: E. RUGUMAYO.

Minister of Information: WILLIAM NABURI.

Minister of Justice: P. J. NKAMBO MUGERWA.

Minister of Works and Housing: J. M. N. ZIKUSOKA.

Minister of Defence: A. C. K. OBOTH-OFUMBI.

Minister of Tourism: (vacant).

Minister of Power and Communications: Lt.-Col. OBITRE-GAMA.

DIPLOMATIC REPRESENTATION

HIGH COMMISSIONS AND EMBASSIES ACCREDITED TO UGANDA

(In Kampala unless otherwise indicated)

(HC) High Commission; (E) Embassy.

Algeria: Dar es Salaam, Tanzania (E).

Australia: Nairobi, Kenya (HC).

Austria: Nairobi, Kenya (E).

Belgium: Nairobi, Kenya (E).

Burundi: P.O.B. 4379 (E); *Ambassador:* PROTAIS MANGONA.

Canada: Nairobi, Kenya (HC).

China, People's Republic: 41 Prince Charles Drive, P.O.B. 4106 (E); *Ambassador:* KO PU-HAI.

Czechoslovakia: P.O.B. 522 (E); *Chargé d'Affairs:* MILOSLAV STAROSTA.

Denmark: Nairobi, Kenya (E).

Egypt: P.O.B. 4280 (E); *Ambassador:* SALAH EL-DIN MOHAMED SABER.

Ethiopia: Nairobi, Kenya (E).

Finland: Addis Ababa, Ethiopia (E).

France: Ottoman Bank Bldg., First Floor, P.O.B. 3533 (E); *Ambassador:* ALBERT THABAULT.

German Federal Republic: Embassy House, P.O.B. 7016 (E); *Ambassador:* Dr. WILHELM KOPS.

Ghana: Ambassador House, P.O.B. 4062 (HC); *High Commissioner:* Brig. A. A. CRABBE.

Guinea: Dar es Salaam, Tanzania (E).

Hungary: Nairobi, Kenya (E).

India: Bank of India Bldg., P.O.B. 7040 (HC); *High Commissioner:* DHARMA DEVA.

Italy: Agip House, P.O.B. 4646 (E); *Ambassador:* Dr. RENZOL ROMANELLI.

Ivory Coast: Addis Ababa, Ethiopia (E).

Japan: Nairobi, Kenya (E).

Korea, Republic: Baumann House, P.O.B. 3717 (E); *Ambassador:* YOO DONG HAN.

Lesotho: Nairobi, Kenya (HC).

Liberia: Nairobi, Kenya (E).

Morocco: Addis Ababa, Ethiopia (E).

Netherlands: Nairobi, Kenya (E).

Nigeria: Ambassador House, P.O.B. 4338 (HC); *High Commissioner:* MBOM J. ETUK.

Norway: Nairobi, Kenya (E).

Pakistan: Nairobi, Kenya (HC).

Poland: 36 Windsor Crescent (E); *Ambassador:* Dr. E. HACHULSKI.

Rwanda: Baumann House, P.O.B. 2468 (E); *Chargé d'Affairs:* E. TANGISHAKA.

Senegal: Addis Ababa, Ethiopia (E).

Somalia: Nairobi, Kenya (E).

Sudan: Embassy House, P.O.B. 3200 (E); *Ambassador:* Maj.-Gen. MOHAMMAD ABDUL QADIR.

Sweden: Nairobi, Kenya (E).

Switzerland: Nairobi, Kenya (E).

Tunisia: Addis Ababa, Ethiopia (E).

Turkey: Nairobi, Kenya (A).

U.S.S.R.: Room C408, Amber House, P.O.B. 7022 (E); *Ambassador:* A. V. ZAKHAROV.

United Kingdom: 10/12 Parliament Avenue, P.O.B. 7070 (HC); *High Commissioner:* A. H. BRIND (acting).

U.S.A.: Embassy House, P.O.B. 7007 (E); *Ambassador:* THOMAS PATRICK MELADY.

Vatican: P.O.B. 7177; *Apostolic Pro-Nuncio:* LUIGI BELLOTTI.

Yugoslavia: P.O.B. 4370 (E); *Ambassador:* MIRKO KALEZIC.

Zaire: 32 Jinja Road (E); *Chargé d'Affairs:* MOKOLO YABO MOKWELA.

Zambia: Nairobi, Kenya (HC).

Uganda also has diplomatic relations with Jordan and Saudi Arabia.

Uganda also has diplomatic relations with Botswana, Brazil, German Democratic Republic, Greece, Jordan, Libya, Mali, Saudi Arabia, Spain and Swaziland.

PARLIAMENT

The National Assembly was dissolved on February 2nd, 1971, when Gen. Amin declared himself Head of State and took over all legislative powers.

POLITICAL PARTIES

These were suspended after the *coup* of January 1971.

DEFENCE

There is a total armed force of 9,000, comprising 8,550 army personnel and 450 air force personnel. The police force consists of 7,000, including 800 para-military. Military service is voluntary.

JUDICIAL SYSTEM

The Court of Appeal for East Africa: P.O.B. 30187, Nairobi; Pres. Mr. Justice W. A. H. DUFFUS; Justices of Appeal J. F. SPRY, E. J. E. LAW, LUTTA A. MUSTAFA; Registrar T. T. M. ASWANI. Hears appeals from Uganda, Kenya and Tanzania.

The High Court: f. 1902; it has full criminal and civil jurisdiction over all persons and matters in the country.

Appeals from the High Court of Uganda lie to the Court of Appeal for East Africa, except in constitutional matters.

The High Court consists of a Chief Justice and 14 Puisne Judges.

Magistrates' Courts: Their present status and rights are established under the Magistrates' Courts Act of 1970.

The country is divided into magisterial areas, presided over by a Chief Magistrate. Under him there are Magistrates Grades I, II, and III with powers of sentence varying accordingly. The Magistrates preside alone over their courts and have limited jurisdiction. Appeals lie to the Chief Magistrate's Court, and from there to the High Court.

Chief Justice: (vacant).

Puisne Judges: K. T. FUAD, J. W. MEAD, R. E. G. RUSSELL, L. P. SALDANHA, E. E. YOUDS, Y. V. PHADKE, A. W. K. MUKASA, S. MUSOKE, S. W. W. WAMBUZI, E. A. OTENG, M. SAIED.

RELIGION

About a half of the African population is Christian. There is a Muslim minority and the remainder follow various forms of traditional religion.

CHRISTIANS
ROMAN CATHOLICS

Archbishop: Archbishop of Kampala: EMMANUEL NSUBUGA, P.O.B. 14125, Kampala, Uganda.

There are nearly 3 million Roman Catholics in Uganda.

Bishops:

Arua: Rt. Rev. ANGELO TARANTINO, P.O.B. 135, Arua.

Fort Portal: Rt. Rev. VINCENT J. McCAULEY, P.O.B. 214, Fort Portal. Auxiliary Bishop: Rt. Rev. S. MAGAMBO.

Gulu: Rt. Rev. Dr. CYPRIAN KIHANGIRE, P.O.B. 200, Gulu.

Hoima: Rt. Rev. EDWARD BAHARAGATE, P.O.B. 34, Hoima.

Jinja: Rt. Rev. J. WILLIGERS, P.O.B. 673, Jinja.

Kabale: Rt. Rev. B. HALEM'IMANA, P.O.B. 200, Kabale.

Lira: Rt. Rev. C. ASILI, P.O.B. 168, Lira.

Masaka: Rt. Rev. ADRIAN K. DDUNGU, P.O.B. 70, Masaka.

Mbarara: Rt. Rev. JOHN KAKUBI, P.O.B. 184, Mbarara.

Moroto: Rt. Rev. S. MAZZOLDI, P.O.B. 46, Moroto.

Toro: Rt. Rev. Mgr. SERAPIO B. MAGAMBO.

Tororo: Rt. Rev. JAMES ODONGO, P.O.B. 933, Mbale.

ANGLICANS

Archbishop: Archbishop of Uganda, Rwanda, Burundi and Boga-Zaire; Most Rev. ERIC SABITI, P.O.B. 14123, Kampala.

There are about 1.8 million Anglicans in Uganda.

Bishops:

Ankole: Rt. Rev. AMOS BETUNGURA, P.O.B. 14, Mbarara.

Boga-Zaire: Rt. Rev. P. B. RIDSDALE, E.A.Z. Boga, P.O.B. 154, Bunia, Zaire.

Bukedi: Rt. Rev. YONA OKOTH, P.O.B. 170, Tororo.

Bunyoro-Kitara: Rt. Rev. YOSTASI RUHINDI, P.O.B. 20, Hoima.

Burundi: Rt. Rev. YOHANA NKUNZUMWAHI, E.A.B. Buye, B.P. 58, Ngozi, Burundi.

Busoga: Rt. Rev. CYPRIAN BAMWOZE, P.O.B. 1658, Jinja.

Kampala: Archbishop of Uganda, Rwanda, Burundi and Boga-Zaire, Most Rev. ERIC SABITI, P.O.B. 14123, Kampala.

Kigezi: Rt. Rev. FESTO KIVENGERE, P.O.B. 65, Kabale.

Madi and West Nile: Rt. Rev. SILVANUS G. WANI, P.O.B. 370, Arua.

Mbale: Rt. Rev. ERISA MASABA, P.O.B. 473, Mbale.

Namirembe: Rt. Rev. Dr. DUNSTAN K. NSUBUGA, P.O.B. 14297, Kampala.

Northern Uganda: Rt. Rev. JANANI LUWUM, P.O.B. 232, Gulu.

Ruwenzori: Rt. Rev. YONASANI RWAKAIKARA, P.O.B. 37, Fort Portal.

Rwanda: Rt. Rev. ADONIYA SEBUNUNGURI, E.A.R. B.P. 61, Kigali, Rwanda.

Soroti: Rt. Rev. ASANASIO MARAKA, P.O.B. 107, Soroti.

West Buganda: Rt. Rev. STEPHEN TOMUSANGE, P.O.B. 242, Masaka.

THE PRESS

DAILIES

Munro (*Your Friend*): P.O.B. 14125, Kampala; f. 1911; Luganda; Roman Catholic; Editor Rev. F. CLEMENT KIGGUNDU; circ. 18,000.

Obugagga Bwa Uganda (*Wealth of Uganda*): P.O.B. 15025, Kampala; f. 1956; Luganda; Editor D. KIWANUKA; circ. 10,000.

Omukulembeze (*The Leader*): P.O.B. 7142, Kampala; f. 1963; government owned; general news and sport; Editor ALONI LUBWAMA; circ. 8,000.

The People: P.O.B. 5965; f. 1964; government daily; Editor ATEKER EJALU.

Ssekanyolya: P.O.B. 84; Luganda; f. 1965; circ. 10,000.

Taifa Empya (*Modern Uganda*): P.O. Box 1986, Kampala; f. 1953; Luganda; Editor MARK KIWANUKE ZAKE; circ. 12,000.

Uganda Argus: P.O.B. 20081, Kampala; f. 1955; English; Independent; Editor MAURICE WOOD; circ. 27,000.

Uganda Eyogera: P.O.B. 15001, Kibuye; f. 1953; Luganda; Editor A. D. LUBOWA; circ. 12,000.

WEEKLIES AND THRICE WEEKLIES

Dbembe (*Freedom*): P.O.B. 14089, Mengo; f. 1960; Luganda; thrice weekly; Editor OBADIA TOMUSANGE; circ. 6,000.

Dwon Lwak (*Voice of the People*): P.O.B. 7142, Kampala; f. 1964; government publication; Editor P. ORYANG; circ. 7,000.

Kodheyo (*What News*): P.O.B. 92, Jinja; f. 1954; Luganda; weekly (Wed.); Editor S. K. MENHA; circ. 5,000.

Mugambizi (*Preacher*): P.O.B. 64, Masindi; Runyoro; weekly; Editor A. G. K. RWAKAIRA; circ. 2,000.

Mwebembezi (*The Leader*): P.O.B. 7142, Kampala; f. 1963; weekly; Editor C. B. ISINGOMA; circ. 3,000.

Taifa Uganda: P.O.B. 1986, Kampala; f. 1961; weekly; Man. Editor M. KIWANUKA-ZAKE.

Voice of Islam: P.O.B. 243, Kampala; English; weekly; Editor H. IBRAHIM.

FORTNIGHTLIES

Ageeteeraine (*Unity*): P.O.B. 150, Mbarara; Runyankore/Rukiga; f. 1959; Editor Rev. B. CLECHET; circ. 7,500.

Apupeta (*News*): P.O.B. 7142, Kampala; f. 1945; government publication; Editor F. A. OTAI; circ. 10,000.

Dwan Lotino (**The Voice of Youth**): P.O.B. 200, Gulu; supplement to Lobo Mewa; monthly; circ. 4,000.

Erwom K'iteso (*Teso News*): P.O. Box 3025, Mbale Ngora; f. 1957; Roman Catholic; Ateso; Editor Fr. MICHAEL EKUMU; circ. 5,620.

Lobo Mewa (*Our Land*): P.O.B. 200, Gulu; f. 1952; Lwo; fortnightly; Catholic; Editor Rev. Fr. GONZALEZ; circ. 12,000.

MONTHLIES

Agata e Bukedi: P.O. Box 249, Mbale; f. 1959; Luganda; Editor C. J. GIZAMBA; circ. 5,000.

Agafa e Masaba: P.O. Box 249, Mbale; f. 1959; Luganda; Editor C. J. GIZAMBA; circ. 5,000.

Agari Ankole (*News from Ankole*): P.O. Box 6, Mbarara; Runyankore; Editor Community Development Officer, Ankole; circ. 3,000.

Amut (*News*): P.O. Box 49, Lira; f. 1953; Lango; Editor Y. W. APENYO; circ. 4,000.

Leadership: P.O.B. 3872, Kampala; f. 1957; English; Editor Rev. A. DALFOVO; circ. 10,000.

Lok Mutime (*What has Happened*): P.O. Box 70, Gulu; f. 1957; Lwo; circ. 2,500.

Musizi: P.O.B. 14152, Mengo, Kampala; f. 1955; Roman Catholic; Luganda; Editor Fr. J. M. KISABWE; circ. 30,000.

The Nile Gazette: P.O.B. 3230, Kampala; f. 1958; English; Editor Rev. Fr. ALBERT DALFOVO; circ. 5,500.

OTHERS

E.A. Journal of Rural Development: Dept. of Rural Economy, P.O.B. 7062, Kampala; Editor Prof. V. F. AMANN; circ. 1,000; twice a year.

Uganda Dairy Farmer: Kampala.

NEWS AGENCIES
FOREIGN BUREAUX

Novosti and Tass have bureaux in Kampala and Reuters, AP and UPI are represented.

PUBLISHERS

Longman Uganda Ltd.: P.O.B. 3409, Kampala.
Uganda Publishing House: Kampala.

RADIO AND TELEVISION

RADIO

Radio Uganda: Ministry of Information, Broadcasting and Tourism, P.O.B. 2038, Kampala; transmits daily programmes in English, Luganda, Luo, Runyoro/Rutoro and Ateso and Runyankore/Rukiga, Lusoga, Lumasaba, Lunyole/Lusamia/Lugwe, Ngakarimojong Madi, Alur, Kupsabiny, Lugbara, Hindustani; weekly broadcasts in Kumam and Kakwa; Chief Engineer H. F. HUMPHREYS; controller of Programmes R. SEMPER.

There are an estimated 260,000 radio receivers.

TELEVISION

Uganda Television Service: P.O.B. 4260, Kampala; f. 1963; commercial service operated by the Ministry of Information and Broadcasting; transmits over a radius of 50 miles from Kampala; 5 relay stations have been built, others are under construction; Controller of Programmes (vacant); Controller of Engineering J. M. A. OBO (acting); Commercial Man. KAGIMU-MUKASA (acting).

There are an estimated 15,000 television receivers.

FINANCE

BANKING

CENTRAL BANK

Bank of Uganda: P.O.B. 7120, Parliament Avenue, Kampala; f. 1966; bank of issue; authorized cap. Sh. 40m.; dep. Sh. 532m.; Gov. S. M. KIINGI; Gen. Man. D. K. TAMALE.

STATE BANKS

Uganda Commercial Bank: P.O.B. 973, Kampala; f. 1965; cap. p.u. Sh. 30m.; dep. Sh. 335m. (Sept. 1972); 17 brs.; Man. Dir. E. A. ODEKE; Deputy Man. Dir. C. M. KABENGE, A.C.I.S., A.C.C.S.

Uganda Co-operative Ltd. Development Bank: P.O.B. 6863, Kampala; f. 1970; cap. Sh. 45m.

REGIONAL BANK

East African Development Bank: P.O.B. 7128, Kampala; f. 1967; provides financial and technical assistance to promote industrial development within the East African Community and to make the economies of the three members more complementary in the industrial field; authorized cap. Sh. 400m.; funds committed for investment (July 1972) Sh. 158m.; Dir.-Gen. and Chair. IDDI SIMBA; publs. *Guide to Investors, Annual Report.*

FOREIGN BANKS

Bank of Baroda (Uganda) Ltd.: Head Office: P.O.B. 7197, Kampala; brs. at Jinja and Mbale; merged with Bank of India (Uganda) Ltd. in August 1972; Man. Dir. N. B. DESAI.

Barclays Bank of Uganda Ltd.: Head Office: 16 Kampala Rd., Kampala; brs. at Fort Portal, Jinja, Kabale, Kampala (4), Kilembe, Masaka, Mbale, Mbarara, Tororo and 27 agencies.

Commercial Bank of Africa Ltd.: Dar es Salaam, Tanzania; Embassy House, Parliament Avenue, P.O.B. 4224, Kampala.

Grindlays Bank (Uganda) Ltd.: Head Office: 45 Kampala Rd., Kampala; 50 brs. in Uganda; Gen. Man. I. G. PEGGIE.

Libyan Arab Uganda Bank for Foreign Trade and Development: f. 1972; majority Libyan shareholding.

Standard Bank Uganda Ltd.: P.O.B. 311, Kampala; f. 1970; associated bank of the Standard Bank Ltd., three other branches in Kampala, and others at Jinja and Mbale; Chair. J. A. HARKNESS.

INSURANCE

East Africa General Insurance Co. Ltd.: 14 Kampala Rd., P.O.B. 1392, Kampala; life, fire, motor, marine and accident insurance; cap. authorized Sh. 5m.; cap. p.u. Sh. 2,694,600; appropriated by the State in 1972, to be placed in African ownership.

Uganda American Insurance Co. Ltd.: f. 1970; auth. cap. Sh. 10m.

About six of the leading insurance companies are represented in Uganda.

TRADE AND INDUSTRY

CHAMBERS OF COMMERCE

Jinja Chamber of Commerce and Industry: P.O.B. 167, Jinja; f. 1925; 75 mems.; Pres. B. M. DUNGU, M.B.E.; Vice-Pres. F. J. HUNT; Hon. Sec. S. C. BAXI.

Mbale Chamber of Commerce: P.O.B. 396, Mbale; Pres. J. S. PATEL; Sec. K. K. MISTRY.

National Chamber of Commerce and Industry: P.O.B. 2369, Kampala.

Tororo Chamber of Commerce: P.O.B. 198, Tororo; f. 1959; Pres. A. WALKER; Sec. A. C. RIDDLE.

DEVELOPMENT CORPORATIONS

National Housing Corporation: Ambassador House, P.O.B. 659, Kampala; f. 1964; Govt. agent for building works; aims to improve living standards, principally by building residential housing; Chair. J. BIKANGAGA; Chief Exec. A. S. N. KIWANA.

Uganda Development Corporation Ltd.: 9–11 Parliament Ave., P.O.B. 442, Kampala; f. 1952; Chair. S. NYANZI; publ. *Crane* (Jan. and June).

TRADE UNIONS

The Government is proposing to introduce a law creating a single national trade union with existing unions becoming branches of it.

Uganda Trades Union Congress: P.O. Box 2889, Kampala; affiliated to the ICFTU; about 102,000 mems. and 23 affiliated unions; Pres. H. LUANDE; Gen. Sec. D. G. NKUUTE.

Principal Affiliate:

National Union of Plantation and Agricultural Workers: P.O.B. 4327, Kampala; f. 1952; 31,450 mems.; Pres. SILAS EDYAU; Gen. Sec. R. N. IMANYWOHA.

Federation of Uganda Trade Unions: P.O.B. 3460, Jinga; f. 1964; 20,000 mems.; Pres. E. R. KIBUKA; Sec. J. W. TWINO.

Principal Affiliate:

Uganda Public Employees Union: P.O.B. 3460, Kampala; f. 1961; 17,000 mems.; Pres. Z. BIGIRWENKYA; Gen. Sec. E. KIBUKA.

MARKETING AND CO-OPERATIVE SOCIETIES

Lint Marketing Board: P.O.B. 7018, Kampala; statutory authority for sale of all cotton lint and cotton seed. Sales of lint to countries with State-controlled economies negotiated directly by the Board, but for others lint is sold through auction to members of East African Cotton Exporters Ltd., P.O.B. 3980, Kampala; Chair. J. M. BYAGAGAIRE; Sec. E. J. H. KITAKA-GAWERA.

Coffee Marketing Board: P.O.B. 7154, Kampala; statutory authority for sale of all processed coffee produced in Uganda. Sales of coffee to ICA quota and non-quota markets are made directly by the Board. Chair. R. J. MUKASA; Sec. B. S. LUKWAGO.

There are 2,500 co-operative unions including the following:

Bwavumpologoma Growers' Co-operative Union Ltd.: P.O. Box 501, Masaka; f. 1953; 100 mem. socs.; Pres. JOSEPH MWANJE; coffee, cotton and agricultural produce marketing association.

Bugisu Co-operative Union Ltd.: 2 Court Road, P.O. Mbale; f. 1954; handles the Bugisu *Arabica* crop; 83 mem. socs.

East Mengo Growers' Co-operative Union Ltd.: P.O.B. 7092, Kampala; f. 1968; general products growers union; 137 mem. socs.; Chair. D. MAWEJJE.

Masaka District Growers' Co-operative Union Ltd.: P.O. Box 284, Masaka; f. 1951; 200 coffee-growing societies; Pres. A. KIWANUKA; Gen. Man. ALLEN M. KERA.

Mubende District Co-operative Union: coffee growers' association.

Nkoba Za Mbogo Farmers' Co-operative Association: coffee growers' association.

Wamala Growers' Co-operative Union Ltd.: P.O.B. 99, Mityana; f. 1968; general products growers' union; 75 mem. socs.; Chair. C. SEMPALA.

West Mengo Growers' Co-operative Union Ltd.: P.O.B. 7039, Kampala; f. 1948; general products growers' union; 105 mem. socs.; Chair. B. K. KAUMI.

MAJOR INDUSTRIAL COMPANIES

The following are some of the largest companies in terms either of capital investment or employment. In May 1970 the Government acquired a 60 per cent share holding in all major industries, banks and large companies, and in Autumn 1972 all firms owned by non-citizen Asians were appropriated pending transfer of ownership to Ugandans.

The African Textile Mill Ltd.: P.O.B. 242, Mbale; f. 1970; cap. Sh. 11,250,000. Uganda Development Corporation owns 60 per cent of shares.

Manufacture of textiles; operation of a textile mill.

Alliance Oil Mill Industry: P.O.B. 353, Mbale.

B.A.T. Uganda Ltd.: P.O.B. 7100, Kampala; first factory opened 1928; tobacco manufacture and curing.

Gen. Man. R. D. H. ROBINSON; 600 employees.

Brooke Bond Oxo Ltd. (Uganda): Kampala; tea-blending and packaging.

Man. Dir. Y. B. S. MASEMBE.

East African Distillery: P.O.B. 3221, Kampala; production of spirits.

Mulco Textiles Ltd.: P.O.B. 472, Jinja; f. 1963; cap. Sh. 22m.

Manufacturers of cotton textiles.
1,500 employees.

Nyanza Textile Industries Ltd.: P.O.B. 408, Jinja; manufacture of textiles.

Steel Corporation of East Africa Ltd.: P.O.B. 1023, Jinja.

Tororo Industrial Chemicals and Fertilisers Ltd.: P.O.B. 254; f. 1962; cap. Sh. 7,400,000; Uganda Development Corporation owns Sh. 6,400,000.

Manufacture of single superphosphate fertiliser, sulphuric acid and insecticide.

Man. Dr. R. HARRISON; 250 employees.

Uganda Bata Shoe Co. Ltd.: P.O.B. 422, Kampala.

Uganda Metal Products and Enamelling Co. Ltd.: P.O.B. 3151, Kampala; f. 1956; cap. £225,000. Wholly owned subsidiary of Uganda Development Corporation.

Manufacturing of enamelware, furniture, beds, etc.

Gen. Man. J. B. KASUJJA; approx. 450 employees.

TRANSPORT AND TOURISM

TRANSPORT

RAILWAYS

See East African Railways (Kenya Chapter).

ROADS

The road network is good by the standards of tropical Africa. The Ministry of Works maintains 520 miles of tarmac road and 2,444 miles of all-weather murram road. The African Local Governments maintain a further 4,418 miles of all-weather murram roads and 3,882 miles of lesser dirt roads. A new 39-mile bitumen road from Lira to Kamdini will be built in 1971. In 1967 The International Development Association granted Uganda a credit of $5 million for road development.

INLAND WATERWAYS

Regular steamer services operate on Lake Victoria.

CIVIL AVIATION

Uganda's international airport is at Entebbe, on the shores of Lake Victoria some 25 miles from Kampala. Distances within the country are too short for air transport to be used to advantage in general, but there are several small airstrips.

East African Airways Corporation (EAAC): Head Office Sadler House, Koinange St., P.O.B. 41010, Nairobi, Kenya; joint national airline for Uganda, Kenya and Tanzania (*see* under East African Community and Kenya).

The following foreign airlines also serve Entebbe: Aeroflot, Air Zaire, Air India, Alitalia, BOAC, British Caledonian, Caspair (an EAAC associate), Ethiopian Airlines, Lufthansa, PAA, Sabena, SAS, Sudan Airways and TWA.

TOURISM

Uganda Tourist Association: P.O.B. 1542, Kampala.

EDUCATION

LEARNED SOCIETIES

Association for Teacher Education in Africa: Makerere University, Kampala; f. 1970.

British Council, The: P.O.B. 7014, National Cultural Centre, Kampala; Representative for Uganda Dr. R. WRIGHT; Regional Office for Western Region: P.O.B. 28, Fort Portal.

Uganda Society: P.O.B. 4980, Kampala; f. 1933; premises in the Uganda Museum Education Building, Kira Rd., Kampala; membership open to persons of all races and institutions, to promote interest in literary, historic, scientific and general cultural matters, discovering and recording facts about the country, arranging lectures and establishing contacts; reference library and lending library 6,000 vols. and periodicals; publ. *The Uganda Journal*.

U.S. Information Service: P.O.B. 7186, Kampala; f. 1957; library of 6,500 vols.; Dir. CHARLES D. EARLES.

RESEARCH INSTITUTES

Animal Health Research Centre: P.O.B. 24, Entebbe; f. 1926; research and field work in animal diseases, husbandry and nutrition; herbarium; library of 10,900 vols.; Chief Veterinary Research Officer A. K. OTENG; Librarian S. S. SENTAMU; publs. numerous research papers and *Annual Report*.

Child Nutrition Unit: Medical Research Council, Mulago Hospital, P.O.B. 6717, Kampala; Dir. Dr. R. G. WHITEHEAD. (*See also under* Medical Research Council, Great Britain).

Cotton Research Station (Namulonge): (*Cotton Research Corporation*): P.O.B. 7084, Kampala; pure and applied aspects of cotton culture and technology; library of 4,000 vols.

Geological Survey and Mines Department: P.O.B. 9, Entebbe; f. 1919; library of 22,900 vols.; Commissioner C. E. TAMALE-SSALI, B.SC., D.I.C., A.I.M.M., F.G.S.

Government Chemistry Analytical Laboratory: P.O.B. 2174, Kampala; forensic investigations, chemistry and bacteriology of foods and water, identification and assay of drugs, general analytical work excluding analysis of soils, fertilizers, ores and metals.

Kawanda Agricultural Research Station: P.O.B. 7065, Kampala; f. 1937; soil and agricultural research; herbarium, soil samples and collection of insects; open to visitors by invitation and appointment; library of 10,520 vols.; Chief Research Officer (vacant).

REGIONAL INSTITUTES:

East African Community: c/o P.O.B. 30005, Nairobi, Kenya; f. 1967; Sec.-Gen. C. G. MAINA; Kenya, Uganda and Tanzania participate on an equal partnership basis.

The East African Community administers the following research services in Uganda (*see also* Kenya and Tanzania):

East African Freshwater Fisheries Research Organization: P.O.B. 343, Jinja, Uganda; f. 1948; hydrobiological and fisheries research; library of 500 vols;. Dir. M. J. MANN (acting); publ. *Annual Report*.

East African Trypanosomiasis Research Organization: P.O.B. 96, Tororo; f. 1949; tsetse and trypanosomiasis research and reclamation (human and animal); Dir. Dr. R. ONYANGO; publ. *Annual Report*.

East African Virus Research Institute: P.O.B. 49, Entebbe; f. 1949; investigation into the properties, relationships and epidemiology of yellow fever and other anthropod-borne viruses; Dir. M. C. WILLIAMS; publ. *Annual Report*.

Makerere Institute of Social Research: P.O.B. 16022, Kampala; f. 1950; conducts independent research into social, political and economic problems of East Africa; 4 full-time Fellows, 45 Associates, University staff in Departments of Economics, Political Science, Rural Economy and Extension, Sociology, Social Work and Social Administration; library of 6,000 vols., 450 current periodicals and extensive pamphlets, etc.; Chair. Dr. V. F. AMANN; Sec. for Research S. N. WAKABI-KIGUWA, B.A.; Sec. P. B. MPINGA; Librarian S. BERMAN, M.S.L.S.; publs. *East African Studies*, *East Africa Linguistic Studies* (occasional), working papers, USSC Conference papers (triennial), *Policy Abstracts and Research Newsletter*, library catalogues.

LIBRARIES

British Council Library: National Cultural Centre, P.O.B. 7014, Kampala; f. 1963; 7,395 vols.; also at Fort Portal (19,938 vols.).

Cabinet Office Library: P.O.B. 5, Entebbe; f. 1920; for government officials and for research workers; 1,404 vols.; publ. *Catalogue*.

Cotton Research Corpn. Library: P.O.B. 7084, Kampala: specialized library for research students.

Makerere University Main Library: P.O.B. 7062, Kampala; 220,000 vols., 150,000 periodicals; special collections of East Africana; deposit collections of Uganda publications, U.N. and specialized agencies; Librarian T. K. LWANGA, B.SC., A.L.A.

Makerere University, Albert Cook Library: Makerere Medical School, P.O.B. 7072, Kampala: approx. 30,000 vols., 650 periodicals, covering all medical subjects, especially East African and tropical medicine; publs. *East African Medical Bibliography* (monthly), *Library Bulletin and Accessions List* (irregularly).

Public Libraries Board: Salisbury Rd., P.O.B. 4262, Kampala; f. 1964 to establish, equip, manage and maintain libraries in Uganda; 17 branch libraries, a mobile library and a postal service are administered; Librarian M. E. C. KIBWIKA-BAGENDA, A.L.A. (acting); publs. *Bi-Monthly Accessions, Annual Report*.

The Secretariat Library: The Secretariat, P.O. Box 5, Kampala; intended to be a comprehensive collection concerning Uganda, also has main works on East Africa, Africa and the British Commonwealth; available to students at the discretion of the Chief Secretary.

MUSEUMS

Entebbe Botanic Gardens: P.O.B. 40, Entebbe; f. 1898; native and exotic plants; Curator D. B. EDWARDS; publ. *Index Seminum* (annual).

Forest Department Library and Herbarium: Forest Office, P.O. Box 31, Entebbe; f. 1904; 11,000 specimens; specialised library open to students by special arrangement with the Chief Conservator of Forests.

Forest Department Utilisation Division and Museum: P.O.B. 1752, Kampala; f. 1952; collection of Uganda timbers; entomology section; preservation, seasoning and woodworking tests; logging and milling research; small specialized library.

Game and Fisheries Museum, Zoo, Aquarium and Library: P.O. Box 4, Entebbe; collections of heads of game animals, reptiles, fish and butterflies, hunting and fishing implements and weapons; library of approx. 1,100 vols.

Geological Survey Museum and Library: P.O. Box 9, Entebbe; about 37,500 specimens of rocks and minerals, library of over 9,850 vols. and 3,850 periodicals.

Uganda Museum: P.O. Box 365, Kampala; ethnology; archaeology, palaeontology; science and industry pavilion; special collection of African musical instruments; centre for archaeological research in Uganda; Curator C. M. SEKINTU.

Folk Museums: at Soroti for the Iteso and at Mbarara for the Banyankole Peoples.

National Park Museums: at Mweya in Queen Elizabeth National Park and at Paraa in Murchison Falls, National Park.

UNIVERSITY AND COLLEGES

MAKERERE UNIVERSITY

P.O. BOX 7062, KAMPALA

Telephone: 42471.

Founded as technical school 1922, became University College 1949, attained University Status 1970.

Language of instruction: English; Academic year: July to March (three terms).

Chancellor: His Excellency President Gen. IDI AMIN DADA.
Vice-Chancellor: F. K. KALIMUZO, B.A., DIP.ED.
Chairman of Council: Dr. I. K. MAJUGO, DIP.MED.(E.A.).
Secretary to Council: M. K. SOZI, M.A.
Academic Registrar: B. ONYANGO, M.A.
Bursar: (vacant).
Librarian: T. K. LWANGA, B.SC., A.L.A.

Number of teachers: 350.
Number of full-time students in residence: 3,501.

DEANS:

Faculty of Arts: Prof. B. W. LANGLANDS (acting).
Faculty of Social Sciences: Y. KYESIMIRA.
Faculty of Agriculture: Prof. K. OLAND.
Faculty of Science: Prof. T. R. C. BOYDE.
Faculty of Education: Prof. A. WANDIRA.
Faculty of Medicine: Prof. J. S. W. LUTWAMA, M.B., CH.B., D.P.H., D.I.H., D.C.H. (Eng.), D.AD.M.C.H., M.R.C.P.
Faculty of Law: Prof. V. S. MacKINNON.
Faculty of Veterinary Science: Prof. R. H. DUNLOP.
Faculty of Technology: Prof. K. EVERALD.

ATTACHED INSTITUTES AND SCHOOLS:

National Institute of Education: f. 1964; corporate body representing the Ministry of Education, Teacher Training Colleges of Uganda, Makerere University Faculty of Education; co-ordinates and encourages teacher training, promotes educational research, gives information and advice on new methods and materials, organizes in-service training and one year advanced diploma courses for teachers; Dir. W. SENTEZA KAJUBI, M.A.; Librarian Mrs. M. O. MUTIBWA, B.A.; publs. *Journal, Newsletter.*

East African School of Librarianship: f. 1963 to train librarians for all parts of East Africa; Dir. S. S. SAITH, M.A., DIP.LIB., F.L.A.

Institute of Statistics and Applied Economics: a joint enterprise of the Government of Uganda and the United Nations Development Programme; 3-year degree courses; Project Man. S. R. A. RAO, M.SC. (acting).

Margaret Trowell School of Fine Art: diploma and degree courses at both undergraduate and graduate levels; Principal (vacant).

Centre for Continuing Education: f. 1953, reorganized into three divisions: Extra Mural Department, Correspondence Courses and Mass Media Division (courses may lead to external degree of Makerere University or London University), Adult Studies Centre (one-year post secondary school courses); shorter courses are also arranged both at the Centre and up-country; Dir. D. N. OKUNGA, M.SC.(ED.).

UGANDA TECHNICAL COLLEGE

P.O.B. 7181, KAMPALA

Telephone: 51281.

Founded 1954; formerly Kampala Technical Institute.

Principal: J. L. P. VERLEY, C.ENG., F.E.A.I.E., M.I.E.E.
Registrar: J. B. KISUULE, M.L.
Senior Librarian: H. M. KIBIRIGE, B.A., A.L.A.

Number of teachers: 68.
Number of students: 718.

HEADS OF DEPARTMENTS:

Department of Civil Engineering and Building: C. NTAMBI, H.N.D., CERT.ED. (acting).
Department of Electrical Engineering: A. G. JINHA, B.SC. (acting).
Department of Mechanical Engineering: H. A. F. SABRI, DIP.AUTO.ENG., DIR.ENG., A.M.I.M.I. (acting).
Department of Science and Mathematics: M. L. SAPIRO, M.SC., PH.D., F.C.S. (acting).
English and Liberal Studies Section: T. BANERJEE, M.A. (acting).
Industrial Ceramics Section: S. EKORA-OGWANG (acting).

SELECT BIBLIOGRAPHY

(For works on Kenya, Tanzania and Uganda generally *see* Kenya Select Bibliography, p. 460.)

Annual Reports. Entebbe, Department of Agriculture, Government Printer.

Annual Trade Report of Kenya, Uganda and Tanzania. Mombasa, East African Community, 1970.

APTER, D. E. *The Political Kingdom in Uganda.* Princeton, New Jersey, and London, Oxford University Press, 1961.

Atlas of Uganda, 2nd edition. Entebbe, Lands and Surveys Department, 1967.

Background to the Budget, 1969–70 and 1970–71. Entebbe, Government Printer.

BEATTIE, J. *The Nyoro State.* Oxford, Clarendon Press, 1971.

FALLERS, L. (Ed.). *The King's Men.* London, Oxford University Press, 1964.

The Government Accounts of Uganda, 1959–60 to 1964–65. Entebbe, Government Printer.

INGHAM, K. *The Making of Modern Uganda.* London, Allen and Unwin, 1958.

Industrial Production Survey, 1967. Entebbe, Government Printer.

JAMESON, J. D. (Ed.). *Agriculture in Uganda.* London, Oxford University Press, 1971.

LEYS, C. T. *Politicians and Policies.* Nairobi, East African Printing House, 1967.

LOW, D. A., and PRATT, R. C. *Buganda and British Overrule.* London, Oxford University Press, 1960.

Quarterly Economic and Statistical Bulletin, December 1969. Entebbe, Government Printer.

Second Five-Year Plan 1966–67 to 1970–71: Supplement of Projects. Entebbe, Ministry of Planning and Economic Development, 1969.

Treaty for East African Co-operation. Nairobi, East African Common Services Organization, June 1967.

Uganda Statistical Abstract 1969. Entebbe, Government Printer.

Work for Progress: Uganda's Second Five-Year Plan 1966–71. Entebbe, Government Printer, 1966.

Upper Volta

PHYSICAL AND SOCIAL GEOGRAPHY*

R. J. Harrison Church

Like Niger and Mali, the Republic of Upper Volta is a landlocked state of west Africa and is situated north of the Ivory Coast, Ghana and Togo. Upper Volta has an area of 105,839 sq. miles (274,122 sq. km.), and in 1971 had an estimated population of 5,426,000. Although under one-quarter the area of Mali, Upper Volta has about the same population. It is, in fact, over-populated, and there is much emigration to the far richer Ivory Coast and Ghana to work on farms, in industries and the service trades. The main ethnic groups are the Bobo in the south-west, and the Mossi and Gourma in the north and east respectively. Along the northern border are nomadic Fulani.

Towards the south-western border with Mali there are Primary sandstones, terminating eastward in the Banfora escarpment. As in Guinea, Mali and Ghana, where there are also great expanses of these rocks,

their residual soils are poor and water percolates deeply within them. Although most of the rest of Upper Volta is underlain by granite, gneisses and schists, there is much loose sand or bare laterite; consequently, there are extensive infertile areas. Moreover, annual rainfall is only some 25–45 in. (635–1,145 mm.), and comes in a rainy season of at the most five months. Water is scarce except by the rivers or in the Gourma swampy area; by the former the simulium fly, whose bite leads to blindness, is common, and in the latter the tsetse, which can cause sleeping sickness in man and beast. Given the grim physical environment, the density of population in the north-central Mossi area is remarkable. The area is, in fact, one of the oldest indigenous kingdoms of west Africa, dating back to the eleventh century, and always resistant to Islam.

* *See* map on p. 364.

RECENT HISTORY*

Michael Crowder and Donal Cruise O'Brien

(Revised for this edition by KAYE WHITEMAN)

Independence was accorded in 1960 to a government formed by the *Union démocratique voltaïque*, with Maurice Yaméogo as President. The government was autocratic in style, making opposition parties illegal shortly after independence, but there remained much hostility to the régime as the economic situation (already poor) declined. A single list election in 1965 gave Yaméogo's party 99 per cent of the popular vote, but opposition then erupted in the streets of the capital. Civil servants and trade unionists had been alarmed by projected austerity measures which would have cut their salaries, and found allies among radical students who opposed the régime's dependence on France.

In January 1966, after mass demonstrations and with the prospect of a general strike, the military intervened to restore order and depose Yaméogo with general popular support. The constitution was suspended and a government formed under Lt.-Col. (now Gen.) Sangoulé Lamizana. The new government then successfully implemented the austerity measures which had brought down Yaméogo, helping to redress a poor budgetary position in the years after 1966. Initially, when the military came to power, they envisaged returning power to a new civilian administration fairly soon, and initiated round-table talks between the parties to that end, but the serious obstacles to party reconciliation and the real threat

of violence caused the army to announce in December 1966 that it would stay in power for four years, during which time it would restore health to the economy.

Ex-President Yaméogo, who had been kept under house arrest, was eventually tried and jailed for embezzling £1,200,000 from the Solidarity Fund of the Council of the Entente, the regional organization sponsored by the Ivory Coast. Although amnestied in 1970 by the military government, he was not allowed civil rights and was unable to participate in the political revival of that year. He went to the Ivory Coast, where President Houphouët-Boigny had already welcomed his children. After prolonged consultation and three months' work by a constitution commission, under the President of the Supreme Court, a Constitution was drawn up in April 1970, which provided for a return to quasi-civilian rule for the next four years. There was to be an elected parliament and a civilian Prime Minister, but General Lamizana was to remain in office as President and the Government was to include five military members out of a total of fifteen. The President retained some overall executive power, and thus the army would act as the arbiter of a civilian régime.

The new constitution was not very well received by

* For the period before independence *see* Recent History of Dahomey, p. 282.

the major political parties, especially the UDV, now under the leadership of Gérard Kango Ouédraogo and Joseph Ouédraogo, but after obtaining some minor changes, they called on their supporters to approve it in the referendum of June 14th, 1970, and it duly received the support of more than 80 per cent of the electorate.

The autumn of that year saw active political campaigning, the three main parties being the UDV, the *Parti de Regroupement Africaine*, which was strong in the western part of the country, and the *Mouvement de Libération Nationale*, a radical grouping led by Professor Joseph Ki-Zerbo. The latter two had been banned by the Yaméogo régime. The elections held in December resulted in an Assembly consisting of 37 UDV deputies, as against 12 PRA, six MLN and two independents. Only half the electorate voted. The UDV formed a government, and after a struggle for leadership between the party's President and its Secretary-General, the former, Gérard Ouédraogo, became Prime Minister. The Government included two PRA ministers, but the MLN remained in opposition, forming the only parliamentary opposition in francophone Africa. Since the creation of the new

government in January 1971 there have been various reports of friction between civilians and soldiers, especially as there is an army officer at the Finance Ministry, acting as a continued curb on the politicians. The politicians complain that real power is still held by the army. However, the situation may be changed by 1974, when the constitution has to be reviewed, and the possibility of a total withdrawal of the army from politics has to be considered.

[Upper Volta's role in world affairs is necessarilly small, but under the military government its foreign policy became slightly more active; in 1970 Voltaic votes at international forums showed a "progressive" attitude to questions of African liberation and to the Middle East. The present government has reverted to a more moderate policy and is even pro-Israel. It supports the OAU, the Council of the Entente and OCAM. However on the question of dialogue with South Africa, which it was expected to support because of the Prime Minister's close association with Houphouët-Boigny, it has remained uncommitted, possibly because of Lamizana's opposition. Lamizana has been officially recognized by France since 1971, and France has promised to increase aid. *Editor*.]

ECONOMY

Samir Amin*

Upper Volta is the Ivory Coast's source of labour. Since 1950, when the development of the Basse Côte began to increase rapidly, Upper Volta has supplied most of the manual labour for the plantation economy of the Ivory Coast and, later, for Abidjan's light industry. Upper Volta has provided 800,000 "temporary" and "permanent" immigrants to west coast countries such as the Ivory Coast and Ghana. Taking into account a natural population growth rate in Upper Volta of about 2.2 per cent per year, this migration has considerably reduced the growth rate of the population remaining behind, which grew from 4.4 million in 1960 to only 5.5 million in 1971.

If the Voltaic labour force has significantly contributed to the Ivory Coast's miraculously high growth rate, Upper Volta has, for its part, paid the price of almost total stagnation. The inland state of Upper Volta was created in 1947 simply as a colonial administrative unit, separate from the Ivory Coast, and it became independent in 1960. It has so far had a slow-moving subsistence economy, and for this reason is less well integrated into the world trading system than any other west African state.

President Maurice Yaméogo's government took over the administration of the new state after refusing to join the large Mali Federation planned in 1959. The establishment of this apparently unviable state was only made possible by extensive French aid. When this was reduced, the régime soon faced serious diffi-

culties. In 1965 the government planned to reduce the salaries of civil servants and was consequently overthrown in the *coup d'état* led by Gen. Lamizana.

THE TRADITIONAL ECONOMY

National accounts exist for the years 1954-59 and for 1964. According to the later ones the Gross Domestic Product was about 56,000 million francs CFA, of which 68 per cent was attributable to the traditional economic sector. This consists of agriculture and stock rearing, 32,300 million francs CFA (57 per cent of G.D.P.); and handicrafts, building and service industries, 6,100 million (11 per cent of G.D.P.).

Agricultural production is almost entirely at subsistence level. Estimated production of millet and sorghum is about one million metric tons, of maize about 40-130,000 metric tons, and of rice about 35,000 tons. Some small improvements in productivity have undeniably been brought about by the rural training policy. But on the whole the policy of "modernization" by extending the use of draught animals has failed, as is shown by its slow progress. This failure cannot be attributed to bad organization of the training programme, for its roots go much deeper. Draught ploughing requires more land and more labour. However, the distribution of population, which is relatively dense on the central Mossi plateau (35 persons per sq. km.) means that any intensification of agriculture would badly damage the soil, bearing in mind the need for fallow periods. The Bobo and Sénoufo regions to the west of the country are less densely populated,

* For the 1973 edition, revisions have been made to this article by the Editor.

and here better results have been achieved. But since draught ploughing also requires much more labour, and since there is no market for its production in the case of millet and only limited returns in the case of cotton and groundnuts, there is no real economic incentive to modernize.

The efforts made by French organizations towards rural improvement and the introduction of export crops (SATEC in the case of groundnuts, and CFDT in the case of cotton) certainly produced results. Production of cotton lint rose steadily from about 3,000 tons in 1961 to 11,000 tons in 1970; however, although groundnut production averaged over 125,000 tons annually through most of the 1960s, it had dropped to only 68,000 tons by 1970. Other crops are sesame seed (about 6,000 tons a year) and karité nuts (about 10,000 tons a year). But prices paid for these products were heavily subsidized compared with world prices, the proportions in any one year varying between 5 and 18 per cent for groundnuts, 8 and 20 per cent for cotton and around 30 per cent for karité nuts.

Stock rearing is carried on in thinly populated areas in the north and east. There were an estimated 2.9 million head of cattle and 4.6 million sheep and goats in 1970–71.

The combined value of subsistence agriculture, handicrafts and the traditional building and service industries increased from 29,200 million francs CFA in 1960 to 32,300 million in 1970 (at 1964 prices). On the other hand, the value of the four main industrial and export commodities (vegetable oils and cotton) grew from 400 million francs CFA to 1,500 million between 1960 and 1970 at the high rate of increase of 14 per cent per annum. The value of stock rearing grew from 6,400 million francs CFA in 1960 to 8,600 million in 1970 (at 1964 prices). Altogether the value of the traditional economic activities increased from 36,000 million francs CFA in 1960 to 38,400 million in 1964 (this figure being taken from the national accounts for that year) and to 42,400 in 1970 (at 1964 prices), giving a real annual growth rate of 1.7 per cent.

THE MODERN ECONOMY

The value added at factor cost (i.e. the value of the manufacturing or servicing processes added to raw material costs) rose to 11,700 million francs CFA in 1964 for the modern economy and has therefore remained small. This added value is distributed as shown in table 1.

In 1964 the urban population was not more than 270,000 inhabitants (100,000 in Ouagadougou, 50,000 in Bobo-Dioulasso and 120,000 in the six smaller towns). compared with a rural population of 4,340,000. Thus the urban per capita product is 67,000 francs CFA as against 8,900 for the rural sector.

The urbanization of Upper Volta increased the population of the towns from 220,000 in 1960 (5 per cent of the total population), to 360,000 in 1970 (7.2 per cent of the total). Industrial activity is still rudimentary. There are a few cotton ginneries (capacity 14,000 tons), a rice mill (capacity 3,000 tons), a brewery and soft drink factory (capacity 60,000 hectolitres of beer and 50,000 hectolitres of soft drinks), a bicycle assembly works (capacity 35,000 units), a tannery (capacity 175,000 skins) and a shoe factory (capacity 800,000 pairs). A few other projects are slowly being realized, such as a sugar refinery at Banfora (where sugar cane is grown); a small textile mill of 1,000 tons capacity at Koudougou, which has been established under the name of VOLTEX in association with German capital supplied by the Kreditanstalt; a small match factory; and a brickworks. There used also to be a small gold mine at Pourra which produced one ton a year until 1966, when it ceased to function. Mining of manganese is to begin at Tambao (250,000 tons per year) where the Japanese are actively involved.

The exploitation of manganese at Tambao has been a priority for some time together with the project to extend the railway, and both have been taken over since 1971 by the Liptako-Gourma development authority, which was set up jointly by Upper Volta, Mali and Niger. In addition to manganese, further deposits of which exist at Ansanga (Niger), phos-

Table 1*

ADDED VALUE

('000 million francs CFA)

	WAGES AND SALARIES	OVERHEADS AND PROFITS	ADDED VALUE	%
Industry and Power . . .	0.7	0.6	1.3	11
Building and Public Works . .	1.3	0.4	1.6	14
Transport and Telecommunications .	1.1	0.8	1.8	15
Commerce	0.9	4.9	5.8	50
Private Services . . .	0.2	1.0	1.2	10
+ Indirect Taxes . . .			5.6	
= Added Value at Market Price .			17.3	
Administration . . .			6.4	

* Figures rounded in some cases.

phates have been found at Tilemi, where a fertilizer industry is to be set up, limestone at Tin Hrassan, where a cement works is planned, and iron and kaolin at Sey. Prospecting continues for copper and uranium, traces of which have already been found, and for other minerals and petroleum. The Niger river between Timbuktoo and Niamey is to be developed for shipping, and dams and reservoirs are to be built to enable the irrigation of crops, watering of livestock, and fishing, and to provide hydro-electric power for the proposed new industries. In addition to the railway extension, an inter-state road network is envisaged. These development plans are to be financed by equal contributions from each of the countries involved and by large amounts of aid. Their fulfilment will take several years, but should prove very valuable.

The poor state of Upper Volta's infrastructure makes industrial competition with the Ivory Coast difficult. It is true that the railway line, which has since 1934 linked Ouagadougou to the coast, is to be extended as far as the Niger border, with a branch line to Tambao and the manganese mine, a total distance of 360 km.; and that the road network of 16,000 km. is far from negligible. But electric power is still very expensive, being supplied by a few small thermal power stations (production in 1961: 9.6 million kWh.; in 1970: 26.3 million). The level of education has been raised significantly since independence, the number of children in primary and rural schools growing at a rate of 6 per cent p.a. from 60,000 in 1961 to 102,180 in 1971. The percentage of children in school grew from 7.5 to 11 per cent of those of school age. Secondary education spread even faster, the number of pupils multiplying two-and-a-half times in eight years, so that there were more than 8,700 in 1970. There are also a considerable number of Voltaic students in higher education, and the country is far from being under-represented in the region in terms of potential and actual trained personnel. However, economic stagnation makes the effective employment of such trained personnel impossible, and they are mostly obliged to emigrate.

The foregoing factors suggest that the modern sector of the economy was all but stagnant during the first ten years of independence. Industry, although it has had a relatively high growth rate (7 per cent a year) represents only 11 per cent of the production of the modern sector. Construction and public works have experienced a limited expansion in relation to the investments effected (public and private) which amounted to about 6,500 million francs CFA in the last part of the 1960s, compared with 4,000–5,000 million francs CFA in the early years. The index of business activity worked out by B.C.E.A.O. was completely stationary until 1969, which, since prices have risen, indicates a corresponding decline in the real volume of sales. Commerce itself, and the transport system linked to it, represents two-thirds of the added value in the modern economy. The real product of this economy grew from 11,000 million francs CFA in 1960 to only 13,000 million in 1970 (at 1964 prices) giving a growth rate of 2 per cent per annum, com-

pared with growth in the urban population of over 5 per cent. The reduction in the number of wage-earners outside the government sector between 1962 and 1965 has added to fears of stagnation of the "modern" economy and of increased unemployment.

GROWTH, INVESTMENT, ADMINISTRATION AND PUBLIC FINANCE

Between 1960 and 1970 G.D.P. increased from 47,000 million francs CFA to 55,000 million (at 1964 prices). The annual growth rate of 1.8 per cent exceeded the growth rate of the population resident in Upper Volta by only 0.5 per cent or less. The level of gross investments at current prices grew from 4,500 million francs CFA to 6,500 million between 1960 and 1970, or from 4,500 million to 5,000 million at constant prices, an extremely poor performance. The first four-year plan (1967–70) envisaged 33,000 million francs CFA of investments, almost all from external sources, distributed in "traditional" proportions, which would have given a modest growth rate of 4 per cent a year.

The policy by which the infrastructure is financed made sense in the context of a large territory like former French West Africa, where the wealthy and viable regions financed the administration and development of the backward ones, but it is impracticable in the context of a small independent country. It can do nothing but create insoluble difficulties for the treasury and is no guarantee of growth.

These are the permanent financial problems affecting independent Upper Volta. Current expenditure increased from 6,500 million francs CFA in 1961 to 8,100 million in 1966—a growth rate of 5 per cent a year, allowing for price rises. This was modest but was still enough to create insuperable problems for the Yaméogo régime, whose downfall resulted. The deflation brought about by the succeeding government (reduction in expenditure to 7,100 million francs CFA and then to 7,300 million a year in 1967 and 1968) could not be maintained, and in 1970 expenditure reached the record level of 8,900 million francs CFA. This is not in fact a great deal—15 per cent of G.D.P. It seems wrong to speak of "civil-service inflation" in connection with this austere country, since the number of public employees increased from 11,000 to only 13,000 between 1962 and 1965 during a period of "heavy expenditure". With wages frozen for a long period and then reduced by the Lamizana government, it is more accurate to talk of strict austerity which has been the price of maintaining a state which is economically scarcely viable.

In this under-commercialized economy, taxable resources are so scarce that local finances have never really achieved a structural equilibrium. The deficit was permanent until 1966, varying yearly between 1,000 and 3,000 million francs CFA and covered by current foreign aid. The military régime has certainly succeeded in getting rid of this deficit by reducing expenditure and by a significant raising of taxation, which grew from 12 per cent of G.D.P. in 1960 to 14 per cent after 1966.

Table 2
GROWTH OF EXPORTS AND IMPORTS

	1954	1959	1960	1962	1965	1968	1970
Exports:							
Livestock (at 1959 prices)	2.0	2.3	2.4	2.5	2.7	2.9	3.2
Livestock (at current prices)	1.9	2.3	2.4	2.7	3.0	3.5	4.0
Other Exports (at current prices)	0.2	0.6	0.6	1.0	1.5	1.5	1.9
Total Exports (at current prices)	2.1	2.9	3.0	3.7	4.5	5.0	5.9
Imports (at current prices)	5.7	6.5	8.0	8.6	9.2	10.1	10.7
Trade Deficit ('000 million current)	3.6	3.6	5.0	4.9	4.7	5.1	4.8
Exports as Percentage of Imports	37	45	38	43	49	50	55

The commercial infrastructure itself is extremely inadequate. Here as in Congo (Brazzaville) the state—quite independently of its ideological bias—has had to intervene since 1960 to alleviate the lack of private enterprise in many regions. The *Office de commercialisation des produits de Haute-Volta* (OFCOM), formed in 1960 to collect produce, the *Caisse de stabilisation des prix de Haute-Volta* (CSPHV), formed in 1961 to subsidize marketing, and the *Coopérative de consommation de Haute-Volta* (CCHV), formed in 1962 to supply the villages with essential consumer goods, have been running at a loss. This loss, which is not attributable simply to administrative inefficiency, amounted to 465 million francs CFA between 1961 and 1967, after which date the *Société voltaïque de commercialisation* (SOVOLCOM) replaced the first and the last of these organizations combined.

THE BALANCE OF PAYMENTS AND EXTERNAL TRADE

Upper Volta's external trade is still largely unknown. Until 1960 cattle exports made up the major part of the export trade and during the next ten years their export rate grew by 3 per cent a year, from 90,000 head in 1954 to 100,000 head in 1959, and to 140,000 in 1970. Export of sheep and goats increased from 180,000 to 200,000 and 280,000 head respectively. At 1959 real prices (18,500 francs CFA a head for cattle, 2,100 francs CFA for sheep and goats), the net value of live animals exported grew from 2,000 million francs CFA in 1954 to 3,200 million in 1970. In 1954 real current prices were probably about 20 per cent lower than those of 1959; they have since increased by about 25 per cent. The agricultural exports (of vegetable oils and cotton) are well known. The latter made headway after 1960, largely due to cotton. The small gold exports ceased after 1966. Imports, including re-exports, are better known; they increased at an annual rate of 3 per cent between 1962 and 1968 (*see* table 2).

The current trade deficit appears to have been relatively stable; it was about 3,600 million francs CFA in the last years before independence and stabilized at about 5,000 million francs CFA during the decade 1960–70. The deficit corresponds roughly with the amount of external aid.

The other elements of the balance of payments are well known. Official external aid (development aid, subsidies and loans to the Treasury, and technical assistance less the Voltaic contribution) grew to 13,200 million francs CFA for the period 1959–63, and stabilized between 4,100 million and 5,000 million francs CFA between 1964 and 1968. In fact, less than 60 per cent of this amount is actually used for development. Added to these public funds are the 5,000 million francs CFA a year in pensions paid by France to the 2,000 Voltaic veterans, the revenue remitted home by temporary emigrants (2,500 million francs CFA), and the miscellaneous expenditure by embassies, tourists, etc. (500 million francs CFA). On the other side we should deduct net private transfers (about 4,000 million francs CFA), the trend of net external assets being slightly favourable (with an increase of 1,340 million francs CFA from 1962 to 1968).

The result arrived at is reasonably comparable with that obtaining in other west African countries. About 1,500 million francs CFA would represent savings sent out by the 5,000 Europeans in the country, 1,000 million the profits of private companies, and 1,500 the profits of individual Lebanese and white small traders.

Table 3
BALANCE OF PAYMENTS:
MEAN ANNUAL 1960–70
(*over 11 years in current '000 million francs CFA*)

Revenue:		
External Official Aid		4.5
Development Aid	2.6	
Technical Assistance (net)	0.7	
Treasury Loans	1.2	
Various External Receipts		5.0
Military Pensions	2.0	
Emigrant Remittances	2.5	
Embassies, etc.	0.5	
Private Foreign Capital		(0.6)
TOTAL		10.1
Expenditure:		
Commercial Deficit		5.0
Current External Expenditure		1.0
Public	0.5	
Private	0.5	
Private Transfers		(3.9)
Growth of External Assets		0.2

STATISTICAL SURVEY

AREA AND POPULATION

AREA	POPULATION
(sq. km.)	(1970 estimate)
274,122	5,426,000

PRINCIPAL TOWNS
(1970 estimates)

Ouagadougou (capital)	11,000	Kaya . . .	17,609
Bobo-Dioulasso . .	78,478	Ouahigouya . .	18,988*
Koudougou . .	41,200	Banfora . .	8,500

* 1972 estimate.

MAIN TRIBES
(1970 estimates)

Mossi	2,604,480
Fulani	542,600
Lobi	379,820
Mandingo	374,394
Bobo-Dioulasso . . .	363,542
Sénoufo	298,430
Gourounsi	287,578
Bissa	255,022
Gourmantché . . .	244,170
Others	75,964

Births and Deaths: Average annual birth rate 49.4 per 1,000; death rate 29.1 per 1,000 (UN estimate for 1965–70).

EMPLOYMENT
Economically active population (1969)

TOTAL	MEN	WOMEN
2,792,051	1,319,783	1,472,051

More than 88 per cent of the labour force is in agriculture (FAO estimate for 1970).

AGRICULTURE

LAND USE, 1970
('000 hectares)

Arable Land	5,315
Under Permanent Crops . .	62
Permanent Meadows and Pastures .	13,755
Forest Land . . .	4,101
Other Land	4,147
TOTAL LAND AREA . .	27,380
Inland Water . . .	40
TOTAL AREA . .	27,420

Source: FAO, *Production Yearbook 1971.*

PRINCIPAL CROPS
(metric tons)

	1968	1969	1970	1971
Maize	137,000	60,000	55,000	42,000
Millet and Fonio	377,000	392,000	389,000	397,000
Sorghum	530,000	547,000	563,000	576,000
Rice (Paddy)	40,000	34,000	34,000	37,000
Sweet Potatoes and Yams . .	50,000	50,000*	52,000*	n.a.
Cassava (Manioc) . . .	40,000	41,000*	42,000*	n.a.
Cow Peas	96,000*	94,000*	96,000*	85,000*
Other Pulses	75,000	80,000*	80,000*	80,000*
Groundnuts (in shell) . .	92,000	71,000	68,000	68,000*
Cottonseed	16,000	18,000	16,000	23,000
Cotton (Lint)	11,000	12,000	11,000	15,000
Sesame Seed	7,900	3,800	6,300	6,300*
Tobacco	800*	800*	800*	800*

* FAO estimate.

Source: FAO, *Production Yearbook 1971.*

LIVESTOCK
(FAO estimates—'ooo)

	1968–69	1969–70	1970–71
Cattle . .	2,700	2,800	2,900
Sheep . .	1,800	1,900	2,000
Goats . .	2,500	2,600	2,650
Pigs . .	137	139	141
Horses . .	72	71	70
Asses . .	185	190	190
Camels . .	6	6	7

Chickens (1967–68 to 1970–71): 10,000,000 each year (official estimate).

Source: FAO, *Production Yearbook 1971.*

LIVESTOCK PRODUCTS
(FAO estimates—metric tons)

	1968	1969	1970	1971
Cows' Milk	70,000	73,000	75,000	77,000
Goats' Milk	18,000	19,000	20,000	21,000
Beef and Veal* . . .	28,000	29,000	30,000	32,000
Mutton, Lamb and Goats' Meat* .	13,000	14,000	14,000	14,000
Pork*	4,000	4,000	4,000	4,000
Horse Meat	2,300	2,300	2,300	n.a.
Poultry Meat	7,300	7,200	7,900	n.a.
Edible Offal	5,000	5,000	5,000	n.a.
Other Meat	2,000	2,000	2,000	n.a.
Hen Eggs	2,900	3,100	3,200	3,300
Cattle Hides	2,232	2,250	2,250	n.a.
Sheep Skins	120	126	180	n.a.
Goat Skins	366	360	357	n.a.

* Meat from indigenous animals only, including the meat equivalent of exported live animals.

Source: FAO, *Production Yearbook 1971.*

FORESTRY
ROUNDWOOD REMOVALS
(cubic metres)

1967	.	.	3,592,000
1968	.	.	3,677,000
1969	.	.	3,767,000

Source: FAO, *Yearbook of Forest Products.*

FISHING
(metric tons)

1967	.	.	4,500
1968	.	.	4,500
1969	.	.	5,000

Source: FAO, *Yearbook of Fishery Statistics 1970.*

MINING
GOLD
(kilogrammes)

1964	.	.	1,034
1965	.	.	1,011
1966	.	.	567

1967–70: No figures available.
Source: United Nations, *Statistical Yearbook.*

INDUSTRY

	Unit	1968	1969	1970	1971
Soap	metric tons	2,350	2,711	2,301	2,786
Groundnut Oil	,, ,,	559	630	377	884
Karité Butter	,, ,,	868	1,222	945	843
Oil Cakes	,, ,,	851	n.a.	454	1,167
Beer	hectolitres	45,275	57,923	59,243	65,194
Soft Drinks	,,	17,771	23,198	28,334	32,704
Electric Power	'000 kWh.	22,753	25,194	27,164	32,719

FINANCE

100 centimes = 1 franc de la Communauté Financière Africaine.
Coins: 1, 2, 5, 10, 25 and 100 francs CFA.
Notes: 50, 100, 500, 1,000 and 5,000 francs CFA.
Exchange rates (November 1972): 1 franc CFA = 2 French centimes.
£1 sterling = 593.625 francs CFA; U.S. $1 = 255.785 francs CFA.
1,000 francs CFA = £1.685 = $3.91.

PUBLIC FINANCE 1966–70
(current million francs CFA)

STATE BUDGET	ACTUAL			ESTIMATED		
	1966	1967	1968	1969	1970	1971
Ordinary Revenue . .	7,584	7,639	8,927	9,645	n.a.	10,515
Extraordinary Revenue* . .	1,002	187	104	112	n.a.	—
Current Expenditure . .	8,068	7,108	7,288	8,223	8,853	9,572
Capital Expenditure . .	642	487	706	808	904	943
Surplus or Deficit . .	—160	231	362	—	—	—

* Mainly external.
Source: Bulletins B.C.E.A.O., No. 154, 167 and 170.

DEVELOPMENT PLAN 1967–70
(million francs CFA)

EXPENDITURE		BUDGET	FUNDS RECEIVED	ACTUAL
Rural Development	.	8,900	4,600	4,300
Modern Sector	. .	6,000	4,800	4,200
Infrastructure	.	11,900	8,100	5,800
Social Sector	.	4,800	4,400	4,000
Research	. .	2,000	1,700	1,500
TOTAL	.	33,600	23,600	19,800
Provision within the plan		33,600	22,400	18,700
Provision outside the plan		—	1,200	1,100

REVENUE		BUDGET	ACTUAL
State and Communes	. .	2,600	1,800
Private	. . .	6,700	5,200
Foreign Aid	. . .	23,700	12,700

Second Development Plan (1972–75): Investment 62,133,000 million francs CFA; Rural Development 31.8 per cent, Modern Sector 20.4 per cent, Infrastructure 28 per cent.

EXTERNAL TRADE
('000 francs CFA)

		1966	1967	1968	1969	1970	1971
Imports	. .	9,293,000	8,970,300	10,119,100	12,450,000	12,963,073	13,899,000
Exports	. .	3,869,000	4,429,300	5,290,300	5,329,275	5,055,452	4,408,000

PRINCIPAL COMMODITIES
(million francs CFA)

IMPORTS		1969	1970	1971
Food, Beverages and Tobacco	.	2,417	2,526	2,402
Petrol and Oil	. .	841	1,168	1,173
Other Raw Materials	.	951	832	n.a.
Cotton, Textiles and Clothing	.	1,491	1,008	1,399
Iron, Steel and Metal Products	.	1,019	1,044	760
Vehicles and Parts	.	1,506	1,626	1,649
Electrical Equipment	.	447	599	659
Other Machinery	. .	1,423	1,324	1,275

EXPORTS		1969	1970	1971
Live Animals	. .	1,967	1,578	1,602
Hides and Skins	. .	121	75	27*
Meat	. .	217	204	n.a.
Cotton Fibre	. .	1,487	1,298	834
Cotton Seed	. .	106	194	n.a.
Groundnuts (shelled)	.	231	318	447
Karité Nuts	. .	444	528	113*
Sesame Seed	. .	111	251	n.a.
Fruit and Vegetables	. .	268	205	n.a.

* January–July.

PRINCIPAL COUNTRIES

IMPORTS		1969	1970	1971
Belgium and Luxembourg	.	249	289	143
France	. . .	5,673	5,852	6,224
Rest of Franc Zone†	.	3,512	3,371	3,382
Federal Germany	. .	751	785	765
Netherlands	. .	376	392	473
U.S.A.	. . .	542	590	605

EXPORTS		1969	1970	1971
France	. . .	705	624	983
Rest of Franc Zone*	. .	2,436	1,976	1,936
Ghana	. . .	581	507	447
Italy	. . .	155	454	440
Japan	. . .	226	782	200

*About half of the franc zone trade is with the Ivory Coast.

TOURISM

	1970	1971
Tourist Arrivals . . .	4,331	6,369

TRANSPORT

RAILWAYS

	1968	1969	1970	1971
Passengers Carried	2,510	2,478	2,565	2,046*
Passenger-km. ('000) . .	541,000	522,000	380,942	454,854
Freight Carried ('000 metric tons) .	700	774	756	611*
Ton-km. ('000)	345,000	394,000	303,409	331,643

* January–September.

CIVIL AVIATION

	1969	1970	1971*
Aircraft Arrivals and Departures . .	2,544	2,690	2,422
Passenger Arrivals . .	13,394	15,983	16,140
Passenger Departures .	11,514	12,295	14,446
Freight Unloaded (tons) .	527	747	845
Freight Loaded (tons) .	317	410	459

* January to September.

ROADS

	1968	1969	1970	1971
Cars	5,217	5,824	6,428	7,063
Buses	117	144	156	162
Lorries	5,461	6,136	6,755	7,289
Tractors	368	389	415	318
Motor-bicycles . . .	1,128	1,292	1,393	1,459

EDUCATION

(1969–70)

	NUMBER OF SCHOOLS		NUMBER OF STUDENTS	
	Public	Private	Public	Private
Primary . . .	573	22	99,460	2,842
Country Schools . .	700	—	26,360	—
Secondary . .	18	17	5,454	3,271
Technical . . .	1	11	549	792
Teacher Training . .	5	1	298	—

Students Abroad: 581.

THE CONSTITUTION

By a constitutional referendum held on June 14th, 1970, the new constitution drawn up by the government was approved by 98.41 per cent of the votes.

The introduction proclaims the country's attachment to democracy, human rights, and African Unity. The President will be elected for five years by direct universal suffrage, and he may be re-elected but may not hold more than two consecutive mandates. However, as a transitional measure, for the first four years he will be the senior ranking army officer, which is Gen. Lamizana; and soldiers will constitute one-third of the government, which may not have more than fifteen members and will have a Prime Minister at its head.

The President ensures respect for the Constitution, the continuity of the State, and the regular running of the government. He presides over the Council of Ministers only as an exceptional measure when necessary. All acts of the President must be countersigned by the Prime Minister and the relevant Ministers; the President is Chief of the Army and President of the Higher Council of Defence.

The people exercise their sovereignty through elected representatives and through referenda. Political parties and groupings may take part in elections for which the country is divided into eleven districts represented by fifty-seven deputies. The office of deputy is unpaid, but indemnities will be granted during sessions. Deputies may not keep their parliamentary mandate if called to ministerial office.

The Parliament consists of a single National Assembly, which votes laws and taxes and controls the action of the government. The government is headed by a Prime Minister, elected by the National Assembly at the suggestion of the President. Ministers and Secretaries of State are appointed and dismissed by the President at the suggestion of the Prime Minister, who presides over the Council of Ministers and directs the work of the government.

THE GOVERNMENT

HEAD OF STATE
General Sangoulé Lamizana.

COUNCIL OF MINISTERS
(*December* 1972)

Prime Minister and Minister of Veteran Affairs: Gérard Kango Ouédraogo.

Minister of the Interior and Security: Capt. Gabriel Somé.

Minister of Justice: Malick Zoromé.

Minister of Foreign Affairs: Dr. Joseph Conombo.

Minister of National Defence: Daouda Traoré.

Minister of Finance and Trade: Maj. Tiemoro Marc Garango.

Minister of Social Affairs: Yaya Konaté.

Minister of Public Works, Transport and Town Planning: Francois Lompo.

Minister of Planning, Industry and Mines: Edouard Yaméogo.

Minister of Agriculture: Capt. Antoine Dakouré.

Minister of Civil Service and Labour: Victor Ouédraogo.

Minister of National Education and Culture: Charles Tamini.

Minister of Public Health and Population: Dr. Ali Barraud.

Minister of Information: Maj. Bila Zagré.

Minister of Youth and Sports: Capt. Felix Tientaraboum.

Minister of Posts and Telecommunications: Dr. Youl Tigaret.

UPPER COUNCIL OF THE ARMED FORCES

Since 1966 the army has had the power to assume responsibility for making a final decision on State matters. It acts through a council consisting of army officers in the government, the Chief of Staff, staff-officers and regimental commanding officers. Its president is the Minister of National Defence.

DIPLOMATIC REPRESENTATION

EMBASSIES ACCREDITED TO

UPPER VOLTA

(In Ouagadougou unless otherwise stated)

Algeria: Abidjan, Ivory Coast.

Austria: Dakar, Senegal.

Belgium: Abidjan, Ivory Coast.

Bulgaria: Accra, Ghana.

Canada: Abidjan, Ivory Coast.

Egypt: B.P. 668; *Chargé d'Affairs:* MOHAMED A. ABDEL-SALAM.

Ethiopia: Abidjan, Ivory Coast.

France: B.P. 504; *Ambassador:* RAOUL DELAYE.

Gabon: Abidjan, Ivory Coast.

Germany, Federal Republic: B.P. 600; *Ambassador:* MICHAEL SCHMIDT.

Ghana: B.P. 212; *Ambassador:* CHRISTIAN CHARLES LOKKO.

Guinea: Bamako, Mali.

Hungary: Accra, Ghana.

India: Dakar, Senegal.

Israel: B.P. 97; *Ambassador:* YAAKOU DECKEL.

Italy: Abidjan, Ivory Coast.

Japan: Abidjan, Ivory Coast.

Korea, Republic: B.P. 618; *Chargé d'Affaires:* HAYSON KIM.

Lebanon: Abidjan, Ivory Coast.

Mali: Abidjan, Ivory Coast.

Mauritania: Abidjan, Ivory Coast.

Morocco: Abidjan, Ivory Coast.

Netherlands: Abidjan, Ivory Coast.

Nigeria: B.P. 132; *Chargé d'Affaires:* A. A. AJAKAIYE.

Pakistan: Accra, Ghana.

Romania: Brussels, Belgium.

Senegal: Bamako, Mali.

Spain: Abidjan, Ivory Coast.

Switzerland: Abidjan, Ivory Coast.

Tunisia: Abidjan, Ivory Coast.

United Kingdom: Abidjan, Ivory Coast.

U.S.A.: B.P. 35; *Ambassador:* DONALD B. EASUM.

U.S.S.R.: B.P. 643; *Ambassador:* YAKOV LAZAREV.

Viet-Nam, Republic of: Abidjan, Ivory Coast.

Yugoslavia: Bamako, Mali.

Upper Volta also has diplomatic relations with the Ivory Coast, the Democratic People's Republic of Korea, Liberia and Luxembourg.

NATIONAL ASSEMBLY

The Assembly was prorogued for five years in November 1960, and further prorogued after the military coup of January 1966. However, in December 1970 elections were held for the National Assembly in which 57 seats were contested. The result was as follows:

UDV	. . . .	37
PRA	. . . .	12
MLN	. . . .	6
Independents	. . .	2

The Assembly meets for only three weeks in every year.

Master of the National Assembly: JOSEPH OUÉDRAOGO.

POLITICAL PARTIES

Union démocratique voltaïque (UDV): Ouagadougou; National section of the Rassemblement Démocratique Africain (R.D.A.); President GÉRARD KANGO OUÉDRAOGO; Sec.-Gen. JOSEPH OUÉDRAOGO.

Mouvement de libération nationale (MLN): Ouagadougou; the first Congress was held in July 1970; Sec. Gen. Prof. JOSEPH KI-ZERBO; publ. *L'Eclair* (weekly).

Parti du regroupement africain (PRA): Ouagadougou; Sec.-Gen. LAOUSSÉNI-OUÉDRAOGO.

Groupement d'action populaire (GAP): Ouagadougou; f. 1966; a religious break-away faction from the UDV, but will support that party in the elections; Pres. MASSA NOUHOUN SIGUÉ; Sec.-Gen. SAÏDOU OUÉDRAOGO.

Union pour la nouvelle république voltaïque (UNRV): f. 1970; break-away faction from PRA; Pres. BLAISE BASSOLETH; Sec.-Gen. GANSONRÉ BAKARY TRAORÉ.

Parti travailliste voltaïque (PTV): Sec.-Gen. GEORGES KABORÉ.

DEFENCE

The armed forces total 1,800, of which the army comprises 1,750 and the air force 50. There is a gendarmerie of 1,050 men and a National Guard of 1,200. The civil police numbers 400.

Chief of Staff: Lieut.-Col. BABA SY.

JUDICIAL SYSTEM

There is a Supreme Court with four chambers (Constitutional, Judicial, Administrative and Fiscal). There are also a Court of Appeals, two Courts of First Instance and seven sections of those courts.

In 1967 a Special Tribunal was set up under the jurisdiction of the Minister of Justice, to try crimes against internal and external security, crimes of embezzlement of public funds, corruption and theft.

Supreme Court: Ouagadougou; Pres. CHARLES TRAORÉ SÉRIBA.

RELIGION

Most people follow Animist beliefs. There are about million Muslims and some 220,000 Catholics.

Roman Catholic Church: There are 85 parishes with 104 African priests and 350 non-African priests.

Archbishop of Ouagadougou: H. E. Cardinal PAUL ZOUNGRANA; B.P. 90, Ougadougou.

Bishop of Bobo-Dioulasso: Mgr. ANDRÉ DUPONT; B.P. 149, Bobo Dioulasso.

Bishop of Koudougou: Mgr. ANTHYME BAYALA.

Bishop of Koupéla: Mgr. DIEUDONNÉ YOUGBARÉ.

Bishop of Nouna: Mgr. JEAN LESOURD.

Bishop of Ouahigouya: Mgr. DYONYSIUS TAPSOBA; B.P. 33, Ouahigouya.

Bishop of Fada N'gourma: Mgr. MARCEL CHAUVIN.

Bishop of Diébougou: Mgr. JEAN BAPTISTE SOMÉ.

Bishop of Kaya: Mgr. CONSTANTIN GUIRMA.

PRESS

DAILY

Bulletin Quotidien d'Information: B.P. 507, Ouagadougou; f. 1957; publ. by the Service d'Information; simultaneously published in Bobo-Dioulasso.

Bulletin Quotidien d'Information de la Chambre de Commerce: B.P. 502, Ouagadougou.

PERIODICALS

Bulletin Douanier et Fiscal: B.P. 502, Ouagadougou; monthly.

Bulletin mensuel de statistique: B.P. 374, Ouagadougou; published by National Statistics Office; monthly.

Carrefour Africain: B.P. 368, Ouagadougou; f. 1960; weekly; government sponsored; Editor in Chief ALPHONSE YAOGHO.

Journal Officiel de la République de Haute-Volta: Ouagadougou, B.P. 294; weekly.

PRESS AGENCIES

Agence Voltaïque de Presse (A.V.P.): Ouagadougou; f. 1963 under UNESCO auspices.

Agence France-Presse: B.P. 391, Ouagadougou; Chief of Bureau BERNARD LOTH.

Tass also has a bureau in Ouagadougou.

RADIO AND TELEVISION

RADIO

Radio-Haute-Volta: B.P. 511, Ouagadougou; f. 1959; services in French and 13 vernacular languages; Dir. of Radio and Television PIERRE BARRY; Dir. of Programmes KARIM KONATE. There is a second station at Bobo-Dioulasso.

There are 88,000 radio sets.

TELEVISION

Voltavision: B.P. 511, Ouagadougou; f. 1963; government-owned; transmissions on two days a week; public viewing centres have been set up; Dir. of Programmes O. SANOGOH.

There are about 3,000 television receivers.

FINANCE

BANKS

CENTRAL BANK

Banque Centrale des Etats de l'Afrique de l'Ouest: 29 rue du Colisée, Paris; Ouagadougou, B.P. 356; f. 1960; Manager KASSOUM CONGO; publs. *Notes d'information et statistiques* (monthly), *Rapport d'activité* (annual).

Banque Internationale pour l'Afrique Occidentale: 9 ave. de Messine, Paris; Ouagadougou, B.P. 362; branch at Bobo Dioulasso.

Banque Nationale de Développement (B.N.D.): Ouagadougou, B.P. 148; f. 1961; cap. 355m. C.F.A.; Dir.-Gen. E. ZOMA.

Banque Nationale de Paris (BNP): 16 blvd. des Italiens, Paris; Ouagadougou, ave. Binger, B.P. 8.

Caisse Centrale de Coopération Economique: 233 blvd. Saint-Germain, Paris; Ouagadougou, ave. de l'Indépendance, B.P. 529.

INSURANCE

Caisse de Compensation des Prestations Familiales: B.P. 333, Ouagadougou.

Several French insurance companies are also represented.

TRADE AND INDUSTRY

CHAMBERS OF COMMERCE

Chambre de Commerce d'Agriculture et d'Industrie de la Haute-Volta: B.P. 502, Ouagadougou; Pres. ANDRÉ AUBARET; publ. *Bulletin d'Information, Courrier consulaire.*

Jeune Chambre Economique Voltaïque: Ouagadougou; Pres. R.-G. TRAORÉ.

CHIEF INDUSTRIAL ORGANIZATION

Syndicat des Commerçants, Importateurs et Exportateurs: B.P. 552, Ouagadougou; mems. are commercial employers.

CO-OPERATIVE

SOVOLCOM: Ouagadougou; f. 1967 by the amalgamation of the Coopérative Centrale de Consommation and the government Office de Commercialisation; aims to supply peasants and sell their harvests.

TRADE UNIONS

Comité inter-syndical: Pres. SALIF OUÉDRAOGO.

Out of a total of 33,000 wage earners, trade union membership is about 12,500.

Confédération Africaine des Travailleurs Croyants (CATC): B.P. 445, Ouagadougou; f. 1950; 3,000 mems. in 10 affiliated unions; Pres. JOSEPH OUÉDRAOGO; Sec.-Gen. LUCIEN ZONGO.

Confédération nationale des travailleurs voltaïques (CNTV).

Fédération syndicale du commerce et de l'industrie.

Organization Voltaïque des Syndicats Libres (OVSL): B.P. 99, Ouagadougou; f. 1960 as Union Nationale des Syndicats des Travailleurs de Haute Volta; 2,500 mems. in 7 affiliated unions; affiliated to Int. Confed. of Free Trade Unions; Sec.-Gen. FRANÇOIS DE SALLES KABORE.

Union Syndicale des Travailleurs Voltaïques (USTV): B.P. 381, Ouagadougou; f. 1958 as Union Générale des Travailleurs d'Afrique Noire; 4,300 mems. in 14 affiliated unions; affiliated to the All-African Trade Union Federation; Sec.-Gen. ZOUMANA TRAORÉ.

There are nine unaffiliated unions.

MAJOR INDUSTRIAL COMPANIES

Brasseries de Haute-Volta (BRAVOLTA): B.P. 304, Bobo-Dioulasso; f. 1960; cap. 450m. francs CFA.
Brewing of beer and manufacture of soft drinks.
Dir.-Gen. ROBERT BAILLY.

Grands Moulins Voltaïques: Banfora; f. 1969; cap. 133m. francs CFA.
Flour-milling, manufacture of animal feed.
Dir.-Gen. ROGER URBAIN; Local Dir. M. LE MAOULT.

Société des Huiles et Savons de Haute-Volta (CITEC-Huilerie): B.P. 150, Bobo-Dioulasso; f. 1941; cap. 305m. francs CFA.
Manufacture of oils, fats and soaps.
Pres. Dir.-Gen. P. SEGARD; Dir. J. M. MORIN; 100–250 employees (seasonal).

Manufacture Voltaïque de Cigarettes (MAVOCI): B.P. 94, Bobo-Dioulasso; f. 1967; cap. 100m. francs CFA.
Manufacture of cigarettes.
Dir. LEFRANC MORIN; Man. Dir. M. COUTURIER; 40 employees.

Société Voltaïque de Textiles (VOLTEX): B.P. 105, Koudougou; f. 1968; cap. 400m. francs CFA of which 43 per cent state-owned.
Weaving, spinning, dyeing and printing of textiles.
Pres. Dir.-Gen. MAX LAVRIL; Dir. CLAUDE BAUDUIN; 450 employees.

TRANSPORT AND TOURISM

TRANSPORT

RAILWAY

La Régie du Chemin de Fer Abidjan-Niger: B.P. 192, Ouagadougou; Head Office: Abidjan, Ivory Coast; 1,771 km. of track linking Ouagadougou via Bobo-Dioulasso with the coast at Abidjan (Ivory Coast); 517 km. of this railway are in Upper Volta.

It is planned to build, with Japanese aid, a 360 km. extension to the Niger frontier and a branch line to the Tambao manganese deposits near the Mali frontier.

ROADS

Compagnie Transafricaine: Bobo Dioulasso, B.P. 91.

Ghana-Upper Volta Road Transport Commission: Accra; set up to implement 1968 agreement on improving communications between the two countries.

There are 4,451 km. of inter-state roads, 1,995 km. of general roads (open all year), 2,445 km. of local roads and 8,100 km. of tracks, motorable in the dry season only.

CIVIL AVIATION

Air Afrique: Upper Volta has a 7 per cent share; *see* under Ivory Coast.

Air Volta: rue Binger, B.P. 116, Ouagadougou; f. 1967; government airline with a monopoly of domestic services; fleet of one Piper Navajo, one Cherokee 6; Pres. F. LOMPO; Dir.-Gen. Adjoint R. MINGUEZ.

International services are also provided by Air Mali and U.T.A.

TOURISM

Office National du Tourisme de la Haute-Volta: B.P. 624, Ouagadougou; Dir. PIERRE BANDÉE.

POWER

Société Voltaïque d'Electricité (VOLTELEC) S.A.: B.P. 54, Ouagadougou; f. 1968; cap. 80m. francs CFA of which 80 per cent state-owned.
Production and distribution of electricity and water.
Dir. ROGER BECQUET.

EDUCATION

Education is free but not compulsory with about 11 per cent of children receiving some schooling. Although the number of children at school increases yearly, the population is growing at a comparable rate.

A rural radio service is being established to further general and technical education standards in rural areas. Primary education is lacking in both quantity and quality, whereas secondary education is lacking mainly in quality. In 1971 there were 344 graduates from secondary schools. Upper Volta's major needs is for higher education. Since 1969 Ouagadougou has had a *Centre d'Enseignement Supérieur*, but its facilities are limited, and a national university, though expensive, is considered a priority.

Government grants are available for higher education in France and Senegal.

RESEARCH INSTITUTES

Bureau de Recherches Géologiques et Minières: B.P. 386, Bobo-Dioulasso; Dir. M. RIEDEZ.

Centre Technique Forestier Tropical: Section de Haute-Volta, B.P. 303, Ouagadougou; f. 1963; research in silviculture and soil erosion; Dir. J. GALABERT.

Centre Voltaïque de la Recherche Scientifique: B.P. 6, Ouagadougou; f. 1950; 1968 incorporated into Ministère de L'Education Nationale; basic and applied research in humanities and natural sciences; library of 3,500 vols.; Dir. MARCEL POUSSY; publs. *Notes et Documents Voltaïques* (quarterly), *Recherches Voltaïques.*

Compagnie Française pour le Développement des Fibres Textiles (C.F.D.T.): B.P. 317, Ouagadougou; br. at Bobo-Dioulasso.

Direction de la Géologie et des Mines (D.G.M.): B.P. 601, Ouagadougou; f. 1961; Dir. P. OUÉDRAOGO; publ. *Rapport Annuel.*

Institut de Recherches Agronomiques Tropicales (I.R.A.T.): B.P. 596, Ouagadougou; f. 1924; research on cereals and general agronomy; stations at Saria and Farako-Ba; Dir. M. POULAIN; publ. *Rapport Annuel.*

Institut de Recherches du Coton et des Textiles Exotiques (I.R.C.T.): P.O.B. 267, Bobo-Dioulasso; f. 1961; Dir. H. CORRE.

Institut de Recherches pour les Huiles et Oléagineux (I.R.H.O.): Niangoloko, par Bobo-Dioulasso; f. 1949; research into oil-bearing plants; Dir. J. HALLE.

Office de la Recherche Scientifique et Technique Outre-Mer Mission Entomologique O.R.S.T.O.M. auprès de l'O.C.C.G.E., Centre Muraz: B.P. 171, Bobo-Dioulasso; f. 1947; medical entomology and parasitology; library; Dir. J. MOUCHET.

Office de la Recherche Scientifique et Technique Outre-Mer Centre O.R.S.T.O.M. à Ouagadougou: B.P. 182, Ouagadougou; hydrology, sociology, geography; library; Dir. H. BARRAL.

COLLEGES

CENTRE D'ENSEIGNEMENT SUPÉRIEUR

B.P. 21, OUAGADOUGOU

Telephone: 23-92.

Founded 1969.

President: GÉRARD RIOU.
Registrar: Mme G. TRAORE.
Librarian: Mme ANAYAN.

Number of books in library: 4,096.
Number of teachers: 30.
Number of students: 345.

CONSTITUENT INSTITUTES:

Collège Littéraire Universitaire.

Institut Universitaire de Pédagogie.

Institut Universitaire de Technologie.

Centre Voltaïque de la Recherche Scientifique.

Centre d'Etudes Economiques et Sociales d'Afrique Occidentale: B.P. 305, Bobo-Dioulasso; f. 1960; courses include sociology, political economy, African history, journalism, social psychology, social legislation, philosophy and population statistics; library of 4,500 vols. and 120 reviews; Dir. P. BUIJSROGGE; publ. *Construire Ensemble* (bi-monthly).

SELECT BIBLIOGRAPHY

(For works on the former A.O.F. states generally, *see* Dahomey Select Bibliography, p. 297.)

KARGOUBOU, SIBIRI. *Géographie de la Haute-Volta.* Ouagadougou, Ecole nationale d'administration.

HARRISON CHURCH, R. J. *West Africa.* London, Longmans, sixth edn., 1968, chap. 16.

DE WILDE, JOHN, et al. *Agricultural Development in Tropical Africa.* Johns Hopkins Press, 1967.

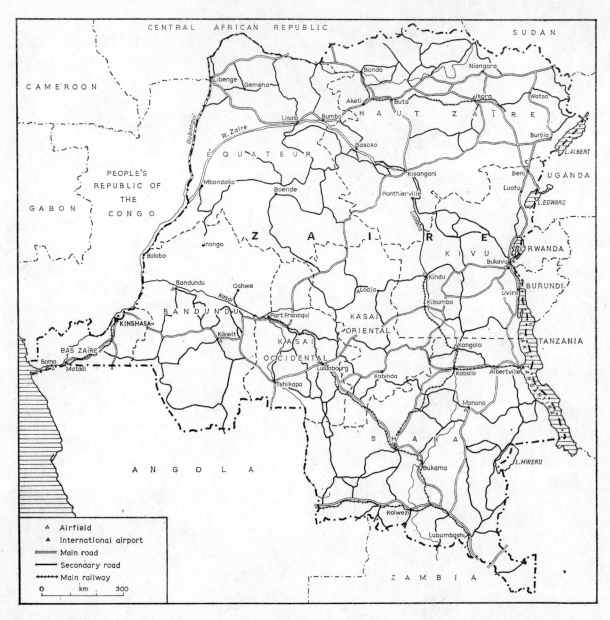

Zaire. At a meeting of Presidents Mobutu of Zaire and Amin of Uganda in October 1972, it was decided that Lake Albert should be renamed Lake Mobutu Sese Seko and Lake Edward should be renamed Lake Idi Amin Dada.

Republic of Zaire

PHYSICAL AND SOCIAL GEOGRAPHY

Pierre Gourou

HISTORICAL BACKGROUND

The Democratic Republic of the Congo (now Zaire) was the successor to the Belgian Congo, which in turn had been preceded by the Independent State of the Congo. The architect of the Independent State was Leopold II, King of the Belgians, whose geographical outlook developed at a time when people divided up the earth's surface in terms of river basins. He thus tried to unite the whole basin of the River Congo (now called the Zaire) under his authority. He did not achieve this entirely and had to leave pieces of land to Portugal (north of Angola), to France (Middle Congo, Oubangui-Chari), to Great Britain (north of northern Rhodesia), and to Germany (German East Africa with the basin of Lake Tanganyika); but to compensate for this he crossed the frontiers of the Congolese basin, and extended his territories as far as Lakes Edward and Albert (in fact into the Nile basin).

In the main Leopold II achieved his overall objectives; he was fortunate in realising the two operations most necessary to the success of his enterprise. Firstly, he managed, despite Portugal and France, to obtain an outlet on the Atlantic; and secondly he managed to grab upper Katanga away from the British. The development of the Belgian Congo and the Democratic Republic of the Congo would have been very different without the free outlet to the sea, and above all, without the copper riches of Katanga, which had no more reason to be included within the boundaries of the Independent Congo State than within those of Northern Rhodesia (present day Zambia).

PHYSICAL FEATURES

Thus the Republic of Zaire comprises first and foremost the basin of the River Zaire. This basin had a deep tectonic origin; the continental shelf of Africa had given way to form an immense hollow, which drew towards it the waters from the north (Ubangi), from the east (Uele, Arruwimi), from the south (Lualaba, that is the upper branch of the River Zaire; Kasai, Kwango). The crystalline continental shelf levels out at the periphery into plateaux in Shaba (formerly Katanga) and the Zaire-Nile ridge. The most broken-up parts of this periphery can be found in the west, in the lower Zaire (where the river cuts the folds of a Precambrian chain by a "powerful breach"), and above all in the east. Here, as a result of the volcanic overflow from the Virunga, they are varied by an upheaval of the rift valleys (where Lakes Tanganyika, Kivu, Edward* and Albert* now are) which carried the Precambrian shelf more than 5,000 m. into Ruwenzori.

* *See* note to map opposite.

The internal part of the Zairian basin conceals the basement (which, however, is not very far below) under the deposits said to be of the Karoo and Kalahari age. It is not a landscape of lakes (the only lakes here, Tumba, Leopold II (now Lake Maidombe), Mai and Ndombe are collections of water, which have flooded a network of valleys, owing to an alluvial dam), but one of horizontal terraces. The sections that have been flooded and are easily flooded cover a small area.

With an area of 2,345,000 sq. km., Zaire is the second largest country south of the Sahara. Despite its immense size, it does not present any really noteworthy points of relief, a considerable natural advantage. Lying across the Equator, Zaire has a really equatorial climate in the whole of the central region. It has an average temperature of 79°F. in the coastal and basin areas, and 64°F. in the mountainous regions. Rainfall is plentiful in all seasons. In the north (Uele) the winter of the northern hemisphere is a dry season; in the south (Shaba) the winter of the southern hemisphere is dry. The only part that is too dry (less than 800 mm. of rain per annum), is on the bank of the lower Zaire, but this only applies to an extremely small area.

The climate is favourable for agriculture and of course woodland (with the exceptions that have just been made). Evergreen equatorial forest covers approximately one million sq. km. in the equatorial and sub-equatorial parts. In the north as in the south of this evergreen forest, tropical forests appear, with many trees that lose their leaves in the dry season. Vast stretches from the north to the south, probably as a result of frequent fires, are covered by sparse forest land, where trees grow alongside grasses (*biombo* from east Africa), and savannah dotted with shrubs.

Although favourable on account of its warmth, and rainfall, the climate has indirect effects that are not quite so fortunate. There are vast stretches of Zaire where the soil is leached of its soluble elements by the heavy, warm rainfall. In addition the germs and carriers of malaria, sleeping sickness, filariasis, bilharziasis, and ankylostomiasis flourish in a warm, rainy climate.

NATURAL ADVANTAGES

However, having said this, the natural advantages of Zaire are immense. It possesses a great stretch of land that opens up immense areas to human activity; its climate is favourable to profitable agriculture; the forests, if rationally exploited could yield excellent results; the abundance of water will one day be useful to industry and will improve agriculture; the network of waterways is naturally navigable; and lastly there is considerable mineral wealth. The Zaire River carries the second largest volume of water in the world, the average flow to the mouth being 40,000 cu. metres per second. The flow is maintained because the river is fed alternately by rains from the northern and southern hemispheres. The shallows are not very marked. Upstream from Kinshasa one of the most beautiful navigable waterways in the world opens up. Downstream the river is cut by rapids. A descent of 280 m., with an average flow of 40,000 m. per second, opens up enormous possibilities for power generation, some of which will be realized at Inga. Indeed, the hydroelectric resources are considerable in the whole of the Zaire, since at the periphery of the navigable basin the rivers which already carry a large volume of water become waterfalls.

The major exports of Zaire derive from the exploitation of its mineral resources. Copper comes from upper Shaba, with other metals—tin, silver, uranium, cobalt, manganese and tungsten. Diamonds are mined in Kasai, and tin, colombite, etc. in the east around Maniema. In addition, many other mineral resources (iron, bauxite, etc.) are waiting to be exploited.

POPULATION

Given its political origins, Zaire has neither an ethnic nor a linguistic homogeneity. Its population is divided among numerous groups, which the external boundaries break up. The Kongo people are divided between Zaire, Congo (Brazzaville), Cabinda and the rest of Angola; the Zande between Zaire and Sudan; the Chokwe between Zaire and Angola; the Bemba between Zaire and Zambia; and the Alur between Zaire and Uganda. Even within its frontiers the ethnic and linguistic geography of Zaire is very varied. The most numerous people are the Kongo; the people of Kwangu-Kwilu, who are related to them; the Mongo with their many subdivisions, who live in the great forest: the Luba, with their close cousins the Lulua and Songe; the Bwaka; and the Zande. The majority speak Bantu languages, of which there is a great variety. However, the north of Zaire belongs linguistically to Sudan. The extreme linguistic variety of Zaire is maintained to some extent by the ability of the people to speak several languages, by the existence of "intermediary" languages (a Kongo dialect, a Luba dialect, Swahili and Lingala) and by the use of French.

About 80 per cent of the population of 21.6 million is rural. The average density of population is thin, (seven people to the sq. km.), and is unequally distributed. The Great Forest has only 3–4 people to the sq. km., with stretches of several tens of thousands of sq. km. practically deserted, and this is not because the area cannot accommodate more people. But it is clear that the population (with the exception of some Pygmies) cannot increase in density as long as the forest is preserved. Indeed, certain areas belonging to the forest belt but partly cleared for cultivation, although they have no particular natural advantages, have 10–20 people to the sq. km.; one such area is the land of the Ekonda, who are part of the Mongo people near Lake Tumba.

At the northern edge of the Great Forest the population density increases a little (10–20 people to the sq. km.), particularly among the Bwaka, and is then reduced to one or two in the extreme north of the country. A small stretch of relatively high population extends from Kongo to Luba country through Kwango-Kwilu. Certain parts of Mayombé (lower Zaire) have 100 people to the sq. km. The south of the republic is sparsely populated (1–3 people to the sq. km.). Shaba would be deserted, had not the mining centres attracted immigrants, particularly the Luba. Kinshasa (1.3 million people) has an overwhelming importance as an urban centre. Lubumbashi has 318,000 people while the other large towns (Kisangani, Mbuji-Mayi, Bukavu and Kananga) have populations of between 150,000 and 200,000.

RECENT HISTORY*

Roger Anstey

(Revised for this edition by KAYE WHITEMAN)

THE INDEPENDENT STATE

At the close of the nineteenth century Belgium was not yet a colonial power. Appearances might suggest otherwise—many Belgians were employed in the Congo, and Leopold II of Belgium was sovereign of the territory: but he was sovereign purely in a personal capacity, and ruled not over a conventional colony but over the *Etat indépendant du Congo*. This unusual situation had arisen because Leopold, by the time he ascended the throne in 1865, was convinced that the acquisition of colonies was a key to national prosperity but was at the same time aware that his country had no wish to undertake what it saw simply as the burden of empire. In the acquisition of a colony by his own endeavour and from his own resources, and in the subsequent bequeathing of that colony to a Belgium belatedly aware of the value of empire, Leopold would do his duty by his country, would strengthen the prestige of the Coburg house, and would find for his talents a field of action far more interesting than anything available to him as constitutional monarch of a second-class European power.

---

* This survey also covers Ruanda-Urundi up to independence.

From 1876 onwards, therefore, having failed to acquire territory in several other parts of the globe, Leopold turned to the Congo and in the following eight years, with H. M. Stanley as his principal agent, created a chain of stations along the Congo River and some of its affluents. Increasingly aware that the private association through which he undertook this work, the *Association internationale du Congo*, had no clear diplomatic standing, Leopold, by masterly diplomacy, obtained in 1884–85 the recognition by the powers of his association as a state. Possessed of a territory eighty times the size of Belgium, Leopold soon found that the slowly developing trade of the Congo left his private fortune still heavily burdened. It was the booming demand for wild rubber, following on the development of rubber tyres, that was Leopold's salvation, for he was able by a variety of expedients to monopolize the collection of rubber. He thus restored both his and the state's finances and made a handsome profit. The way might well seem to have been clear for the full realization of Leopold's hopes, but the very success of the rubber policy was to force Leopold to a premature making-over of his colony to Belgium. The methods used in the collection of rubber frequently involved quite ghastly atrocities. News of these led to the so-called Congo Reform campaign in Britain and the United States, as well as in Belgium, and to Anglo-American diplomatic pressure for the Congo Independent State to be made over to Belgium. Belgium could in some sense be made accountable: Leopold could not. Eventually, in 1908, the Congo became a Belgian colony.

BELGIAN RULE

In an important sense Belgium was thus a reluctant colonial power, a nation which had assumed the charge of empire out of a sense of national obligation and which had no habits of imperial rule to draw upon. But at the same time Belgium was a nation which owed her sure, if modest, stature in the world to the commercial and industrial achievements of her people. It was wholly natural, therefore, that she should hope that the development of the Congo's resources might yield a profit. Alongside these considerations and assumptions was the belief that Europe had a civilizing and christianizing mission in Africa, a task which in the Congo should as far as possible be entrusted to Catholic missions, since Belgium was predominantly a Catholic country. Also influencing Belgium's conduct in the Congo was the extreme pragmatism and distrust of theorizing which seems to be a characteristic of Belgians. As a Belgian scholar, Professor Malengreau has said, "Belgians are a people without imagination, a people who do not dream, a people whose thoughts are fixed on reality and do not go beyond it, but who make reality yield up useful fruits. A people who do not create but who utilize, who invent little but who make better use of the inventions of others than the inventors themselves." These then, rather than any defined national purpose, were the determinants of Belgian policy in the Congo.

In the early years of Belgian rule attention was primarily given to preventing the recurrence of the kind of abuses that had so marred the career of the Independent State—by, for instance, cutting down the size of the territorial concessions made to large companies—and to extending some kind of administrative structure over the vast area of the Congo. However no radical departures were made. If the powers of the big concessionary companies were limited, it was still to them that the colonial administration looked to develop the Congo's economy; if an attempt was made to improve "native administration", as it was called in the colonial era, the earlier assumption that one found who was the chief of a particular group, invested him with a certain authority and used him as the bottom rung of the administration, was retained.

World War I affected the Congo in a number of ways. The thinning out of the ranks of the Belgian administrators, due to the German occupation of most of Belgium and to the call for men to serve with the Belgian Congo force which took part in the conquest of German East Africa, proved to any thus far unconvinced that the basis of a sound native administration had not been laid. At the same time the cry for an increased mineral production to assist the allied war effort involved the beginnings of an age and sex imbalance in areas subject to the operations of the recruiters of labour for the mines of Katanga and elsewhere. The successful conclusion of the war led to Belgium being made the mandatory power for two territories—Ruanda and Urundi—formerly provinces of German East Africa. From 1925 this new acquisition was united with the Congo for purposes of administration, an arrangement which was continued when the United Nations succeeded the League of Nations as the mandatory, or trusteeship, authority after the Second World War.

THE PATTERN OF ADMINISTRATION

The inter-war years saw the *ad hoc* responses of the first decade of Belgian rule developed into more considered policies. Indeed, although the Second World War had important repercussions in the history of the Belgian Congo, it was not really a turning-point, for the policies laid down in the 1920s mostly lasted into the 1950s or even right through to independence. In the important field of native administration the new Minister of the Colonies, Louis Franck (appointed in 1918) was quick to realise the disarray into which administration had fallen. He saw that both the administration and Congolese society were being fragmented by the recognition of a very large number of *chefferies*, or chiefdoms, especially as it was quite clear that in very many cases these *chefferies*, numbering no less than 6,095 in 1917, did not correspond to traditional groupings, or were groupings over which a chief had been recognized who possessed no traditional authority. Franck stated that "The *chefferies* are too small, many chiefs lack all authority. The means of obtaining obedience formerly possessed by the chief have disappeared. The time is not far distant when, if we are not careful, in many regions, the collapse of indigenous authority will be complete."

His solution was to initiate a restructuring of native administration. The legislative basis was a decree of 1926 on *Tribunaux indigènes* and another of 1933 on *Circonscriptions indigènes*, but the process of reform in fact preceded the decrees in a number of areas. The essence of the reform was that *chefferies* which had been wrongly constituted, or which were too small to be viable, were to be amalgamated into new administrative entities called *secteurs*. The chiefs of the *chefferies* which ceased to exist would be members of the new council of the *secteur*, save for the most suitable one who would become the chief of the *secteur*. This chief would be given increased administrative authority, whilst the viability of the *secteur* would be built up by locating at its headquarters a dispensary, a school and above all a native tribunal. Here customary law would be administered in civil and criminal matters and, by express authorization, statutory offences might also be tried. In Ruanda-Urundi Belgium acted rather differently. She followed German practice and continued to extend to the Mwami of Ruanda and the Mwami of Urundi recognition as paramount chiefs, subject to instructions conveyed to them through Presidents acting as their advisers. Subordinate chiefs were appointed by the appropriate Mwami with the approval of the President.

It was intended that the launching of the new *secteurs* should be carried out with great care and tact so that they would not be seen by chiefs and people just as imposed groupings. In practice this happy result sometimes happened, but it seems that more often a busy administrator lacked the time and the insights to carry the people with him in what was in any event a delicate and difficult task. All too often an African with experience of European ways, perhaps a former clerk, or sergeant in the *Force publique*, was appointed chief. Of course, precisely because of his understanding of European ways he was valued by the administrator, but because he usually lacked any position in traditional society there was a clear balance of disadvantage in making such an appointment. All in all native policy from the 1920s onwards seems in its application usually to have enshrined a concern for closer regulation of traditional life rather than concern for a restructuring of local government which would *also* satisfy the people themselves. This tendency was accentuated by administrative economies of 1933, necessitated by the depression. These reduced the number of administrative officers and so left those who remained both with less time to make the thorough investigation which was supposed to precede the creation of *secteurs* and under greater pressure to appoint as chiefs men who would accept the role of mouthpiece of the administration.

LABOUR POLICY

Implied in this concern to nominate chiefs who would carry out the orders of the administrator was a positive concern to intervene in traditional life.

Such a concern was a most important characteristic of Belgium's presence in the Congo and was such as to have particularly important effects owing to the relatively low population—perhaps 9 million at the commencement of Belgian rule rising to about 13 million by 1960. The most overt type of European intervention in traditional ways was, however, that of the large European companies, especially the mining and plantation companies. From the early twentieth century the rich mineral deposits of Katanga in particular had been a lure, and the extraction of copper and other minerals led to the appearance of mining townships and involved considerable demands for labour. By the 1920s a serious population imbalance was apparent in a number of districts and this led the administration to attempt to restrict recruitment from the villages. Real change, however, began with the initiation by the *Union Minière* in 1925 of the so-called stabilized labour policy. The aim of the policy was to obtain a permanent work force which would necessarily be more efficient than what amounted to short-term levies. To persuade men to sign on for a minimum of three years, conditions and amenities were vastly improved and, above all, encouragement was given to the workmen to bring their wives and families with them. In economic terms the new policy paid off handsomely, and by the 1950s the rate of voluntary renewal of contracts was such that the *Union Minière* usually recruited the few new workmen that it needed from the families of older employees. Other large companies followed suit so that pleasant *cités des travailleurs* adjoining mine or plantation became a feature of the Congo scene.

Although the motives behind the stabilized labour policy were economic, its result was a highly significant achievement in controlled acculturation. There is considerable evidence, not least in steadily increasing readiness to re-engage, that this kind of paternalism met a real need of the African confronted with a new work situation and more complex relationships with other Africans as a result of his departure from the life of the tribe, and with new relationships with Europeans. Exposed to both the best and the worst of European values, he had to make a daily blend of European and traditional ways.

THE MISSIONS AND EDUCATION

European administration and European economic enterprise were two obvious agencies of change. Less overt, but more fundamental change was brought by the Christian missions and the schools which they established. Assessment of the missionary impact is profoundly difficult, for receptivity to Christianity and western education could cover a wide range from full and meaningful acceptance to a superficial tasting which was not in any serious sense acceptance of the new, and which left dissatisfaction with the old. Conceptually, there was bound to be tension between western, Christian individualism and the essentially corporate nature of African life; between a culture which makes a distinction between the natural and the supernatural order and one which does not; between a culture characterized by great technological sophistication and one whose technology was much inferior. Some indication of the cultural stress implicit in such a confrontation is given by the emergence in the 1920s of prophet movements, and especially Kimbanguism—named after Simon Kimbangu, the founder—which were both a protest against the inadequacies of traditional religion and Christianity, and also some kind of synthesis of them.

The administration, the big companies, and the missions were thus a kind of triune power, and they particularly exemplified the intervention and change which flowed from the presence of Belgium in the Congo. It has already been said that the process of acculturation was probably least difficult in the controlled environment of the *cités des travailleurs* of the large companies. Many more Congolese, however, were subject to European influences in—from the perspective of traditional life and custom—much more disturbing ways. The peasant who remained in his village was increasingly subject to European intervention. Because of the conviction imbued by the depression and made explicit by Leopold III, when as heir-apparent he toured the Congo, that the economy rested too much on mineral extraction and too little on peasant agriculture, a policy of encouraging peasant agriculture by compulsory crop production was taken very seriously from 1933 onwards. During the Second World War compulsion became even more onerous with the clamant need to augment by every possible means the supply of primary agricultural produce. Even after the war the so-called *paysannat indigène* scheme, whereby peasants were to be resettled in such conditions that production for the market could yield them a really good living, beneficial though its intentions were, involved major intervention. Pressures on life in the bush were an important cause of drift to the towns.

THE EFFECTS OF URBANIZATION

It was in the towns that the various changes stemming from the Belgian presence were least controlled and most apparent. Here the African was involved in a whole series of different relationships— with other Africans and with Europeans. He was more likely to marry a girl from another tribe, and away from the enveloping influence of the two families the marriage was much less the traditional alliance between two groups and more an individual compact. His friendships, especially if he became educated, were not confined to members of his own tribe living in the town. He was necessarily more aware of the political, technological and cultural dominance of Europeans and, in so far as he himself progressed up the educational ladder, was himself entering the culture of the colonizer. Nor was the number of town dwellers small. The population of Leopoldville (now Kinshasa) increased from 40,000 to 325,000 between 1938 and 1955 and that of Stanleyville (Kisangani) from 12,500 to 55,000 in the same period. By the end of 1958 nearly a quarter of the population of the Congo, a high figure, lived away from the villages in the bush.

It is particularly in the context of urbanization that the emphasis of this study must change, for in the last years of Belgian rule politics and the nationalist movement must claim our major attention, activities which germinated in the towns in the years after the Second World War. It is perhaps easier to understand this if we realize not only that it was in the towns that the Congolese most often made his entry into the culture of the colonizer but that it was inevitably a partial and frustrating entry. Malinowski pointed out thirty years ago how the African who adopted European ways was, by the fact of a colonial situation, denied full admission to European culture. In politics, in commerce, in the army or police, in the drawing room, there was eventually a threshhold which he could not cross—otherwise the colonizer would be yielding up power. Naturally, it was the better educated Congolese who became most aware of this threshhold and it was precisely this class of *évolués*, as they are termed in French-speaking Africa, who constituted the van of the nationalist movement.

In the early post-war years Belgium sought to meet the situation of this class by creating a special status for it. It was originally intended that a small but growing number of *évolués* would, by a process termed *immatriculation*, be given the same legal status as Europeans. In the event two things happened: the *évolués* themselves seem to have assumed that the new status would apply to nearly all of their number, whilst the scope of *immatriculation* was so whittled down as to make it scarcely worth coveting. For the *évolués* there was therefore a double disappointment, and though there is substantial evidence of a continuing *évolué* attachment not only to the culture of the colonizer but also to his rule, there was from the mid-1950s a transition to political activity as the means of obtaining both a personal and a national emancipation.

THE GROWTH OF NATIONALISM

External forces and influences played an important part in the launching and development of the Congolese nationalist movement and, indeed, in determining the Belgian response to it. The first call to action was a manifesto from a Belgian academic, Professor Van Bilsen, in 1955, calling for Congolese independence in thirty years. It is interesting to reflect upon how timetables of this kind were so soon reduced to a nonesense all over Africa: Van Bilsen seems indeed to have named such a period purely in order to secure a hearing for his case from a nation whose pragmatism and distrust of the long view had prevented it from noticing that African nationalism was now a fact of life. The next five years saw the rapid growth of the nationalist movement. Some parties evolved naturally from ethnic cultural associations, the ABAKO (*Alliance des Ba-Kongo*) party being the most notable example. Many other parties made an implicit or explicit ethnic appeal— in the absence of any developed national feeling one assumes that, in a period when the pillars of the colonial universe were shaking and an alternative seat of authority had to be sought, the instinctive recourse was to the ethnic group. Some parties, however, were regional parties, either because they got only that far along their professed road to becoming national parties, or because a group of tribes united to resist another tribe which they believed to be dominating them. CONAKAT (*Confédération des associations tribales du Katanga*) was a primary example of the latter. Against all the odds there were two serious national parties, the most significant of which was the *Mouvement national congolais* of Patrice Lumumba. This party gained meaningful support in four of the Congo's six provinces and appears to have owed its success to Lumumba's charisma and, paradoxically, to his flair for making profitable tactical alliances with small ethnic parties.

Once serious party rivalries started in 1957–58, a process of escalation began as parties felt the need to maintain their appeal by outbidding their rivals. The economic recession of the later 1950s led to unemployment and greater opportunity for the parties, whilst such external events as De Gaulle's visit to nearby Brazzaville in 1958, when he offered to the French Congo either autonomy within the French Community or complete independence, had a considerable influence. At the same time the nationalist movement elsewhere in Africa was gathering pace, and it must have struck the government in Brussels that the two major colonial powers, Britain and France, were not seriously resisting its pressure. The United States, moreover, the major power in NATO, was still in a position to allow itself the luxury of anti-colonial pronouncements. By the middle of 1959 the colonial administration was beginning to lose control in a few regions, and an understandable loss of nerve and of will had its culmination when Belgium agreed at the Brussels Round Table Conference in January 1960 to Congolese independence on June 30th of that same year.

Belgium can not be blamed for doing in 1960 what the major colonial powers had earlier decided they must do. More positively, she presumably reasoned that the economic interests of Belgian companies, the livelihood of Belgian planters, the labours of missionaries and teachers, would be assured because an independent Congo could not manage without them. Less charitably, it must be said that Belgium left the Congo and Ruanda-Urundi, when her turn for independence came almost as a foregone conclusion two years later, ill-prepared for independence. The fact that instances of humiliation of Africans could intermittently take place in the Congo in the late 1950s, when their perpetrators elsewhere in Africa would have been put on the next boat home, is one indication of Belgium's failure to think ahead. This involved her also in failure to prepare Congolese to take over authority, by not admitting them on any significant scale to a growing share in it whilst Belgium still ruled. Nevertheless Belgium did a number of very valuable things in the Congo especially in the realm of economic development and welfare, whilst she presided over an extensive missionary work and a massive programme of primary education. Too many of her nationals may have exhibited a racial arrogance very late in the day, but by 1960 there was of course a sense in which nothing a colonial power could do could possibly be right.

INDEPENDENCE AND REBELLION

The confrontation between the Belgians' view of their rule in the Congo, and how the Congolese saw it was clearly demonstrated in two speeches made on the occasion of the transfer of power on June 30th, 1960. King Baudouin praised the Belgian record on the Congo and the Christian mission of his grandfather, while Patrice Lumumba, the first Prime Minister, condemned both. This confirmed in the minds of the Belgians that Lumumba was not to be trusted, a lack of confidence that played an important role in the crisis that followed.

The uneasy euphoria of independence lasted only five days, before a mutiny in the *Force Publique*, the 25,000-man army (later the National Army), burst the bubble. There had been no concession to the idea of independence in the force, and General Janssens, the Belgian Force Commander, detecting signs of real discontent, attempted vainly to keep control by lecturing that for the force "before independence equals after independence". The mutiny took first of all the form of attacks on European officers and soon spread to all Europeans, a manifestation perhaps of a racial frustration built up by Belgian attitudes over the years.

On July 7th, Lumumba removed General Janssens and his staff, and a mass exodus of Europeans began. The next day the Belgians flew in paratroops to protect their compatriots, and on July 11th Moise Tshombe declared the independence of Katanga (now Shaba). It was these two key events that brought in the United Nations, at Patrice Lumumba's request, and effectively internationalized the crisis. UN troops from several countries, such as Sweden, India, Pakistan and a number of African states, replaced the Belgians, and a vast UN technical assistance programme was begun to try effectively to equip the Congo to survive as a modern state.

Lumumba's own troops were able to crush very bloodily a similar secession in Kasai, but were unable to penetrate Katanga. Indeed, for two and a half years the central government and the whole UN operation was bedevilled by the Katanga secession. Although it had been declared by the provincial Premier, Moise Tshombe, there were powerful western business interests behind him, notably the *Union Minière du Haut-Katanga* (UMHK). Belgian policy itself was ambivalent, helping the new state internally with military, technical and financial assistance, but opposing it externally. There was no Belgian recognition, and at the UN they spoke in favour of reintegration of Katanga into the Congo, although not by force. The British Conservative Government was covertly sympathetic to Katanga, as were the French. Whether or not these powers helped Tshombe to put together the force of mercenaries, which, with the Katanga gendarmerie enabled him to defy the central government and its ramshackle and ineffectual army, their international posture was certainly of assistance.

In September Lumumba clashed with President Kasavubu and they both tried to dismiss each other, only to be both dropped by Col. Joseph-Désiré Mobutu who staged a "neutralizing" *coup*. In fact this operated against Lumumba, and helped lead to the events including his escape and imprisonment which ended with his eventual murder in Katanga in January 1961 in circumstances from which the authorities in both Léopoldville and Elisabethville emerge with obloquy. The UN troops were hamstrung by a Security Council resolution inhibiting them from intervening in internal politics. It took the bitter reaction from Afro-Asian states to Lumumba's murder to reinforce the resolution so that the UN could take action.

Even so it took three military operations, from September 1961 to January 1963 to crack Tshombe's power. During the first, the UN Secretary-General, Dag Hammarskjöld, was killed in an air crash, but his successor, U Thant, realized even more than Hammarskjöld did that UN prestige depended on successfully ending the secession. The essential factor however, was the weight the Kennedy government in the U.S., sensitive to Third World opinion, cast behind the UN. U Thant was determined to pull out the UN troops, for the health of the organization and they left on June 30th, 1964, regardless of the fact that a serious grass-roots rebellion had broken out in the north and east of the country.

Based on Stanleyville (now Kisangani), the old alternative headquarters of Lumumba and his successor Gizenga, the rebellion was led by a remnant of Lumumba's party. Aspiring to be revolutionary, the leadership lost control and the followers reverted to traditional practices and magic. The brutality this sometimes produced was more than matched by that of the Congolese army. With half the country out of Léopoldville's control, Mobutu and his group, still the real arbiters of power, ditched Premier Cyrille Adoula (who had been a compromise candidate placed by the UN), and invited Tshombe to become Prime Minister.

The reason for this strange reversal of fortune was the belief that Tshombe's mercenaries were probably the only force which could prevent a complete victory for the rebels. So it proved to be, although the Congolese army was able to win some victories on its own, and the *coup de grace* in Stanleyville was in fact delivered by a Belgian-American landing attempting to rescue European hostages.

Although the rebellion continued to rumble on, its back had been broken. There was much resentment from other African states at the way the rebellion

had been crushed, and Tshombe was still a controversial figure. Moreover, he was engaged in a power struggle with Joseph Kasavubu, the President. The risk of new conflict, and the need to stop further African support for the rebels were the main reason for the definitive seizure of power by Lieut.-Gen. Mobutu in a bloodless *coup* on November 24th, 1965.

CONSOLIDATION UNDER MOBUTU

In his seven years as President, Mobutu has above all offered authority, and with it peace, which has come as a welcome antidote to the troubled first five years of independence. If he has ruled through fear rather than love, he has also eclipsed all his political rivals. The toughest was Tshombe, whose mercenaries and Katangese gendarmes staged two attempts to bring him back. Tshombe and Kasavubu are now dead; other old enemies (and friends) are retired, in business, or in prison. Most of those now in politics are of the younger generation, especially drawn from the universities, who played little role in the 1960–65 turbulences. As a result, Mobutu's dictate has been total.

From the 1966 nationalization of the *Union Minière* and the 1967 monetary reform (which provided the base for economic recovery) to the setting up of a single party, the Popular Movement of the Revolution (MPR), Mobutu has decisively imposed his image. Although he sometimes seemed without ideology, he has of late adopted a stringent form of nationalism he calls "authenticity". This led to the change of name from the Congo to Zaire (after the old Portuguese name for the river) and the obligatory dropping of Christian names in favour of African names, which brought Mobutu into conflict with the Catholic church. In general, however, Mobutu has substantial western support, principally because of his undisputed control. Relations with the Belgians were considerably improved in 1969–70, and were capped by a visit by King Baudouin ten years after independence, but there have been ups and downs since then.

From the beginning, Mobutu tried to avoid Tshombe's error and stuck to a "mainstream" African foreign policy, but he is still suspect in some quarters that cannot forget the role he played in destroying Lumumba, and feel he is too dependent on the United States. He has certainly been circumspect in developing relations with communist powers that backed Lumumba and the various Stanleyville régimes. If anything, Zaire's influence in Africa is still not proportionate to its size and wealth, although aspects of Mobutu's style of government have been emulated by other African rulers.

ECONOMY

Jean Louis Lacroix

(Revised for this edition by ALAN RAKE.)

Zaire forms an important economic complex in the centre of Africa. Its gross domestic product was $1,300 million in 1959 and increased to $2,140 million in 1970. Though the real volume of the national product increased by 7 per cent from 1966 to 1968, the nominal value increased far more sharply and indicates inflation, changes in the tax system and rising wage levels.

When Zaire became independent in 1960 administrative disorganization and political troubles profoundly dislocated the economy. In 1961 and 1962, at the time of the Katangese secession, production fell dramatically. Recovery which started in 1963 was hindered by the rebellions which shook the northeast of the country between mid-1964 and mid-1965. It was only in 1966 that the G.D.P. reached the 1959 level.

There is still considerable uncertainty in some of the G.D.P. estimates—especially in agricultural production and even more in population estimates. It should be noted that the rate of population growth established in 1956 at 2.3 per cent per year, is a weighted average between the rate of growth in the rural areas of 1.8 per cent and in the towns of between 3.7 per cent and 4.3 per cent.

Since 1960, political troubles and the falling standards of health and hygiene in the rural areas have undoubtedly resulted in a rising death rate and hence a slackening in the rate of population increase. On the other hand the drift towards the urban centres has increased the weight of those groups, where a natural rate of growth of some 4 per cent already exists. If the rate of growth established by the surveys in 1956–57 still holds at 2.3 per cent, the population of Zaire should have reached 18.6 million by 1972. However, estimates were revised after a survey in July 1970 showed a population of 21.6 million. The amended figures assume an annual population growth of 4.2 per cent, the highest natural increase rate in the world.

A recent survey has shown that in Kinshasa 52 per cent of the population is less than 15 years old and that 21 per cent is less than 5 years old* Zaire's average population density is still relatively low, being 9.2 people per sq. km. in 1970. The population of Kinshasa was estimated at 1.6 million in 1972.

ECONOMIC DEVELOPMENT

The Zairian economy went through a period of fundamental expansion before 1930. In the period between 1920 and 1930 the G.D.P. of the money economy (not counting subsistence production) grew at the fantastic rate of 12.2 per cent per year.

---

* *Etude socio-démographique de Kinshasa en 1967, Rapport général et résultats par commune.* Institut National des statistiques, Office national de la recherche et du developpement, Kinshasa, October 1969.

The big depression of the 1930s temporarily interrupted this growth, but recovery came rapidly and proceeded with scarcely any setbacks until 1958, apart from a brief recession in 1939 and 1945.

Between 1945 and 1957 the monetary G.D.P. grew at the exceptionally rapid average rate of 8.1 per cent. Until 1946 at least, it was the increase in exports which was the main reason for the economic growth of Zaire. Between 1920 and 1946 the rate of growth of exports and of the G.D.P. were closely correlated and during the whole period at least 45 per cent of the monetary G.D.P. went in exports. This reveals the open nature of the Zairian economy— an important characteristic.

The Zairian exports which play such an important part in the G.D.P. are essentially exports of primary agricultural products (oil-palm, coffee, cotton, timber, rubber, etc.) and minerals (copper and associated metals, diamonds, tin ore and gold).

Thus Zaire's economy reveals a second essential characteristic as an exporter of primary products of a relatively diverse nature. Though these characteristics still existed on the eve of independence, it can be seen that the economic structure of the country gradually changed after 1946–47. From 1947 onwards the rate of growth of the G.D.P. has always been larger than that of exports. Between 1950 and 1958 the volume of exports went up 40.3 per cent, or an average of 4.2 per cent per year, while the G.D.P. rose by 55.3 per cent or 5.7 per cent per year on average. The difference is due to the development of a sector of industry aimed at the internal market. The importance of this manufacturing sector is still relatively low, but its rate of growth is far higher than that of the traditional sectors. Between 1950 and 1958 industrial production for the home market went up by 2.78 times, revealing a rate of growth of 13.5 per cent per year.

Industry produces mainly consumer products such as drinks, cigarettes, textiles, soap and metal furniture and certain supplies for the construction industry such as cement, concrete products and metal products; or for the mines—explosives and chemicals. It does not produce supplies for industry such as steel, plastics, chemicals, paper and cartons, nor machinery or motors except for some river transport barges.

Towards the end of the 1950s the rhythm of economic expansion slackened and, after reaching a peak in 1957, the G.D.P. diminished in 1958. This is explained by a number of different factors: (i) the increase in exports of primary products both agricultural and mineral fell in the industrial countries for well known reasons. At first the Zairian economy reacted by diversifying the range of primary product exports, but this became increasingly difficult because the list of products in which Zaire has a comparative advantage on world markets, such as palm oil products, copper and diamonds, is obviously restricted; (ii) the increase in production for the home market took over the running from exports as the main factor in economic expansion, but it also ran into difficulties. The possibilities of import substitution in consumer goods were gradually exhausted. As industrial expansion continued there was a growing demand for intermediate goods (whether primary or ancillary products) which either had to be imported or drawn from goods that would otherwise have been exported, and as the rate of growth of these imports was far higher than those of traditional exports, this meant that industrial expansion was possible only at the expense of the balance of trade.

Agricultural production for the home market, whether of food or cash crops, was stimulated by the demand of the urban centres and factories. The increase in agricultural production for the home market depends entirely on increased production by peasant farmers as the large private plantations specialize in export crops. But peasant farming uses traditional techniques over large land areas and the returns per man and per acre are low. The land area devoted to food production for the urban areas is limited by transport costs and this puts pressure on the prices of traditional foodstuffs, which are often heavy products with a low unit value. This leads to the gradual abandonment of the fallow land system which in turn causes lower yields. Thus the growing demand in the urban centres finally leads to imports of agricultural products, whether these are costly products that can bear the increased transport costs or whether the import costs are compensated by the low cost per unit in the supplier country, as in the U.S.A. In Kinshasa, for example, since 1956 there has been a partial substitution of bread for cassava in the average citizen's diet.

Thus those factors that gave the Zairian economy a special dynamism in the 1950s gradually lost their effect. Since 1956–57 expansion has necessitated profound changes in the economic structure through: (i) the establishment of industry producing intermediate goods such as paper, chemicals and steel and machinery; (ii) the modernization of production and distribution systems of peasant agriculture. But this transformation of the structure of the economy scarcely began because political changes had to take priority.

In 1960 independence threw a spotlight on another obstacle in the path of economic expansion, and that was the almost total lack of managerial talent with any higher education and the fact that the new political authorities were not sufficiently trained to take on the responsibilities of government.

From 1960 to 1967 numerous other factors altered the economic structure of Zaire. Insecurity in certain regions led to lower production for the home market; monetary chaos, caused by big deficits in public spending, brought dramatic internal inflation. As the rate of exchange adjusted itself slowly in compensation, agricultural and mining exports were discouraged. Internally the industrial expansion, stimulated by inflation at home, was checked by

exchange control and import licensing. The monetary confusion also led to the unproductive sectors of the economy making a larger contribution to the overall national income.

In June 1967 there were financial reforms and a massive devaluation of Zairian currency. This resolved the currency question. Thus 1968 saw the fundamental reorganization of the Zairian economy followed by a new burst of expansion.

Table 1
EMPLOYMENT—LARGE FIRMS (1968)*

Agriculture	363,698
Extractive industry and metallurgy .	56,694
Manufacturing and food industry . .	34,989
Chemicals and steel construction . .	15,729
Construction	15,050
Transport and communications . .	60,067
Commerce, banks and other services .	29,467
TOTAL	575,694

* National Bank of Zaire and IRES.

The labour market in Zaire, particularly in the urban centres, has been dislocated by the sudden arrival of a massive new generation which has reached working age. The employment situation is worsening and one can no longer talk of a shortage of workers as one did in the 1950s. Instead Zaire, like most other developing countries, is short of qualified personnel. This situation is demonstrated by looking at the position of foreign personnel employed.

The public sector employed nearly 12,000 foreign personnel in 1960; this fell to 2,000 after independence though it was not possible to replace all foreigners by nationals with the same qualifications. According to a survey by the National Bank, the number of expatriates employed by large and medium-scale enterprises was 16,000 in 1959 and fell to 10,856 in 1967. There were 27 salaried Africans per foreigner in 1959 and 30 per foreigner in 1967.

Zaire has had a considerable drive in training local personnel over the last few years. There has also been an effort to tackle the educational system by training teachers, improving their average qualifications and by adapting primary education to the needs of the majority.

AGRICULTURE

Agriculture has suffered more than any other economic sector as a result of the political and economic disorders which have shaken Zaire since 1960. Marketed agricultural production fell almost 40 per cent between 1959 and 1967, and its share of the gross domestic product of the money economy fell from 21 per cent to 13.13 per cent in 1968.

There has been no recent survey into the agricultural production of the subsistence sector. The basic reason for the agricultural recession, which perhaps explains the magnitude of the peasant uprisings, is the fall in real rural incomes caused by inflation. While the increase of the volume of currency in circulation pushed up prices of manufactured consumer goods, the prices of agricultural export products were determined by world market prices and by official rates of exchange which followed prices upwards only after considerable delays, and then at a slower rate than internal price levels. This is why there was, at first, a considerable fall in peasant production for export, particularly in cotton and to a lesser extent in palm products.

In those parts of the country with a relatively high population density, the palm plantations are operated by independent peasants who cut the fruit and sell it to the oil mills. In the areas where there is less population pressure, production is in the hands of foreign companies which run both the plantations and the mills and use a wage-earning labour force. In the first category the falling buying power of the income received by independent peasants resulted in a fall in volume of fruit delivered to the mills; in the second category the gradually increasing production costs caused the companies to abandon their marginal plantations.

Ebony wood and rubber, also products of foreign companies for export, reached a production index level of 70 in 1966 compared with 100 in 1959. Before 1960 tea and coffee was largely in the hands of foreign settlers and small companies. Production here, largely in the east of the country, was maintained at a high level, partly because these producers lived near to the frontiers and were able to sell their crops illegally to foreign markets, receiving foreign currency in exchange and then changing this inside Zaire at advantageous rates.

This reduction in production of export crops, and fall in peasant buying power, caused a gradual disappearance of organized markets in the rural areas, and this in turn led to a return to subsistence production, especially as there was no longer the stimulus of manufactured goods on show in the local markets. But whenever peasants were paid sufficient for their produce to meet the rising prices of manufactured goods there was an immediate response in agricultural production. This was shown clearly in the Bas-Zaire region, where food production was stimulated by the growing needs of Kinshasa, the main source of monetary expansion.

Agricultural cash crop exports in general rose during the 1967–69 period, immediately after the 1967 currency reforms, but progress was still slow compared with the rapid growth in the power, mining and industrial sectors. After 1969 growth tailed away to a period of stagnation, and imports of agricultural foodstuffs, which could have been locally grown, were on the increase. The main bottlenecks were poor transport and communications systems, inadequate organization of marketing, and prices that were too low to encourage increased peasant production.

MINES AND NON-FERROUS METALS*

The mining and non-ferrous metal industries in Zaire started in the inter-war period. Although production was stimulated by the Second World War, it was not until 1950 and the Korean war that mining in Zaire suddenly took off. Though there was a recession in 1957 and 1958, production in 1959 was 60 per cent higher than in 1950. Copper and associated minerals, diamonds and manganese ore provided the basis for this expansion. Cassiterite production went ahead less fast, mainly because of the restrictions imposed by the International Tin Agreement, and because reserves in certain deposits were declining. Between 1950 and 1960 production of fine gold did not vary much, holding an average of about 11,000 kilogrammes a year. Copper production increased from 176,000 tons in 1950 to 280,000 tons in 1959.

Progress in the production of capital intensive industrial machinery in the 1950–59 period was boosted still further by the introduction of new techniques in treating of concentrates and the building of enriching plants for manganese ore and for the production of electrolytic zinc. This process started in 1953 and produced 55,000 tons of metal in 1959. Manganese mining went ahead still faster. Though it only started in 1950, by 1959 350,000 tons of ore were produced. Progress in copper and cobalt took a new leap forward in 1960 with new electrolysis plants at Luilu, near Kolwezi, which have proved very profitable.

Before independence the mining industry accounted for about 17 per cent of national production in the money sector. Since 1959 mining has dropped 30 per cent in terms of added value to factor cost, even though there is still more mining activity today than there was in 1959. This is the result of the indirect taxes of 1966 and 1967. The volume of minerals produced has scarcely increased but forms an important part of national production at current prices because, as it is entirely exported, it has received the full benefit of changing exchange rates. Thus mining accounted for 7.8 per cent of production in 1966 and 11.2 per cent in 1961, inclusive of export tax.

Diamond prices rose by 17 per cent between 1966 and 1968, but prices of other minerals fell by 5.6 per cent. Copper extraction produced 5 per cent more in volume and now forms 14.7 per cent of the national product compared with 10 per cent in 1966. After a sharp drop in 1967, zinc production grew by 3 per cent, and cobalt production has still to reach the 1966 levels.

Due to devaluation the whole mineral sector earned more in local currency, and its contribution to the domestic product increased from 12 per cent to 17.2 per cent. Copper prices trended lower between 1966 and 1968, but prices of most minerals of interest to the Zairian economy changed very little.

---

* Some information comes from E. Van der Straeten's *Histoire économique et grands travaux* (Académie royale des sciences d'outre mer white book).

INDUSTRY

Unlike the other productive sectors, industrial production increased between 1958 and 1966. Over the whole of this period the monetary expansion upheld demand and allowed industrial production to rise 30 per cent above the 1958 level. Industry's contribution to the G.D.P. therefore improved. But the rate of growth of industrial production is still lower than it was in the 1950s. In addition, the inflationary process has aggravated the structural imbalance of the industrial sector. In the 1956-57 period efforts were concentrated in the production of consumer goods, and local industry became more than ever dependent on imports of supplies and machinery.

After the financial reforms of 1967, real incomes in the urban centres were reduced and imported products became more competitive. This led to a fall in industrial production of 9 per cent. Nevertheless the recession affected different sectors unequally, some like food processing, plastics, basic chemicals and building materials improving over 1966.

By 1968 the improved agricultural incomes opened up the rural markets once again. As manufacturing industry's production only increased by 1.92 times from 1966 to 1968—or 2.23 times in respect of the whole gross domestic product of the money sector—the contribution to the G.D.P. actually fell from 6.7 per cent to 4.9 per cent. On average, factory prices of manufactured goods were multiplied 2.23 times after devaluation, while prices as a whole increased 2.51 times between 1966 and 1968. It was also noticeable that capital goods prices increased more than consumer goods.

The long-term expansion of Zaire's industry depends on solving the problems posed first in 1956–57: how to reduce dependence on imports and re-orientate in favour of producing supplies such as chemicals, fertilizers, paper, rubber and steel.

The projects which will come as a result of the Inga hydroelectric project will produce goods of this type. Financing of these new industrial investments cannot depend entirely on foreign capital, nor on domestic finance from existing industry, yet Zaire has no medium- or long-term credit agency.

The construction industry made dramatic progress between 1966 and 1968, increasing by 20 per cent in volume when investment began to flow. The value added to the G.D.P. increased in current prices from 2.4 per cent to 2.6 per cent, though prices in the construction sector did not rise as much as the average internal price level. On the other hand private building which does not figure in the total aggregates, has fallen by about 15 per cent since 1966, though the nominal value increased from 4.2 million zaires ($8.4 million) in 1966 to 7.75 million ($15.5 million) in 1968.

POWER

Oil

The search for petroleum has been going on since 1958 but it has still not been discovered in commercial quantities. A new oil agreement was made on October 14th, 1969. The SOREPZA Group (50 per cent Fina, 25 per cent Mobil Exploration and 25 per cent Shell) has been prospecting over 4,700 square kilometres on a strip of land parallel to the coast. First traces of oil were found at Lindu in 1963. A further show was found in May 1972 on the third hole drilled.

Gulf began drilling offshore in December 1970 and announced that it had struck oil in its first well near Moanda but further holes drilled were dry. Thus traces have been found both onshore and offshore, but the companies are working on such a small (50 mile) stretch of coastline that they are unlikely to find commercial quantities in the area, though the proximity of the neighbouring Cabinda field in Angola gives some ground for hope. The refinery opened on the coast in 1968 is working to capacity and a second refinery is being planned.

Coal

Zaire has two coalfields in operation; the Lukuga basin, near to Kalemie on the edge of Lake Tanganyika, produces a coal that has a high clinker content and is not good for making coke. Proved reserves amount to about 50 million metric tons. A local clinker factory takes most of the production at a rate of 1,000 tons a month. The Luena basin in Shaba produces more poor quality non-coking coal. Reserves are estimated to be about 5 million tons, and outlets to the railway, copper foundry and clinker plant are limited and declining because of competition from oil. The two coalfields have produced between 100,000 and 110,000 tons per year on average since 1960.

Nuclear Energy

There is a source of fissionable material in the uranium deposits at Shinkolobwe in Shaba, but mining was stopped in 1961. Assured reserves amount to only 1 million tons, and theoretical reserves to 5 million, but this seems modest compared with those in other African countries such as Niger and Gabon.

Hydroelectric Power

Zaire's main power resources are hydroelectricity. It has the highest hydroelectric potential of the African continent, at about 103 million kW. At Inga alone, upstream on the Zaire from Kinshasa, there is a theoretical potential of 30,000 MW, approximately the equivalent of all power used in the United Kingdom. Installed capacity in Zaire was 689 MW at the end of 1967 or 6.7 per cent of the gross theoretical potential of the country. This power from hydroelectric sources should be added to that of the thermal stations, giving a total of 766,470kW. Seventy-four per cent of this power is installed in Shaba for use in copper refining and 13.8 per cent in the Bas-Zaïre to cope with Kinshasa's industrial demands.

Power supplies in Shaba have risen according to the demands of the copper mining and refining industries. These used 2,075 GWh. in 1965 out of a total hydroelectric production of 2,178 GWh. in Shaba. Production of copper should go up by 30 per cent between 1968 and 1975 and this will have to be supplied by further hydroelectric developments at Lualaba, or by importing power from Zambia.

In the Kinshasa region there is a rapid increase in demand and the long term solution will be through the Inga complex. Inga phase I is already in operation (following the official opening on November 24th, 1972) with two of the first six generators functioning. A third and fourth are planned for July and August 1973 and the last two early in 1974.

The Zaire government is fully committed to Inga phase II which will add a further 1,000 MW to the dam's output by July 1976. Inga phase III could add a further 1,700 MW and the government has announced plans to take this power down 1,800 kilometres of high tension power lines to meet the power shortage on the Shaba copperbelt.

TRANSPORT

The structure of Zairian transport is shown on the map on page 988 and is detailed on page 1,017. This transport system gave Zaire two main export routes which suited the colonial economy exporting primary and semi-finished products, but it also provided two main routes connecting the east and west and favoured the development of regional markets. This development of a large, open, internal market meant that the system was fully utilized both ways and led to the establishment of a permanent road network linking the areas of high population density, near to the main river-rail systems. Much development is now taking place along these lines.

EXTERNAL TRADE

Like most developing countries Zaire is an exporter of primary products, but its economy is not based on one crop alone. Before 1960 exports of minerals and crops were relatively diversified. But the agricultural economic crisis caused by inflation and political instability have given an added importance to copper and associated products within the export category.

Since 1966 prices of agricultural products have been dropping. Oil palm products were hit in 1968 and 1969 by the surplus of oils and fats on world markets. Over-production was also the fate of *robusta* coffee. Palm oil prices fell by 20 per cent in the first half of 1969, having earlier recovered by 25 per cent due to a fall in copra oil production. Cocoa prices reflected world shortages, but the Zairian crop was poor mainly due to bad weather. Rubber prices responded to an increase in world demand in the first half of 1969.

The price index of most products of interest to the Zairian economy followed world trends, rising by 8 per cent in 1968 after falling by 7 per cent in 1967 and rising again by 9 per cent in the first half of 1969. This was largely caused by the rise in the price of copper, which now plays a dominant part in external trade. Prices of cash crops have, in fact, been gradually declining since 1965. Apart from

minor fluctuations copper prices continued to rise in 1968 and the first half of 1969. They continued to rise to a peak of £720 a ton for cash wirebars in London in April 1970 and fell to £423 a ton in December the same year. In 1969 copper provided 63 per cent of the budget revenue, in 1970 this fell to 55 per cent and by 1971 about 50 per cent of the budget. Export earnings followed an almost exactly parallel downward trend, though Zaire still received 65 per cent of its export value from copper in 1970. The fall in exports and budgetary receipts was caused almost entirely by the collapse in the copper price, for production has been gradually expanding from 326,000 metric tons in 1968 to 406,000 in 1971.

Zinc prices were also firm in 1968 and 1969. Tin also benefited later from a rise in demand. For most of 1968 New York tin prices were lower than in 1967 owing to over-production, despite major buying operations by the International Tin Council. But in the last third of 1968, production was better balanced and demand was rising—stimulated by uncertainty concerning major producer countries—and this pushed prices to new high levels.

Zairian exports, registered by importing countries, grew by 10.5 per cent between 1966 and 1968, increasing from $570 million to $629.9 million. This was caused mainly by improved mineral prices and by increases in the volume of agricultural exports.

Exports reached a peak in 1970 of $742 million, according to official figures from Kinshasa, dropping back in 1971 to $684 million. This was almost entirely due to the fall in the world copper price. Copper is easily the leading export, totalling $494 million in 1970, followed by diamonds ($46 million), coffee ($39 million) and cobalt ($34 million). Most exports in the 1966–72 period went to the EEC countries which took 82 per cent of exports in 1971 compared with 80.8 per cent in 1966. The Belgo-Luxembourg economic union took 53 per cent in 1971 compared with 54.3 per cent in 1966. This shows that there was scarcely any change at all among the principal trading partners. The two countries that have rapidly increased imports from Zaire over the last three years are Italy, which takes 4.8 per cent and Japan, 4.5 per cent. Both expanded from a very low base level.

Imports, as shown in the statistics of the industrialized countries, shot ahead when the 1967 currency reforms began to work their way through the system, rising from $310 million in 1968, to a peak of $626 million in 1971. The trend for 1972 shows a marked decline following the credit squeeze, strict import regulations and tighter exchange control imposed during the year. The major import growth in 1969 came in machinery and transport equipment, but in the two following years there was a disturbing growth in food, drink and petroleum products, indicating a boom in consumer demand.

Zairian imports come from a variety of sources. In 1958 imports from Belgium were only 36 per cent of total imports. This was due to the monetary autonomy of the country and free trade in the Zaire basin which was first introduced by the Berlin treaty. At that time the other main suppliers were the U.S.A. (15 per cent) and Federal Germany (9 per cent). Between 1958 and 1968 imports from the U.S.A. increased with the rise in American aid to Zaire and in 1963 they reached a level of 33 per cent. But, when the volume of aid slackened, imports tended to flow back to the traditional commercial channels. By 1970 55.5 per cent of imports came from the EEC (23 per cent of this total from Belgium and Luxembourg) and 13.6 per cent from the next biggest supplier, the U.S.A.

FINANCE

Before 1960 the Congolese franc was on parity with the Belgian franc and 50 Congolese francs equalled $1. The Congolese franc was an independent currency backed by its own gold and foreign exchange reserves. This was a very different situation to the one that applied to the ex-French colonies and the Franc Zone. The stability of Congolese currency depended entirely on the country's own balance of payments, there being no support from the Belgian treasury. This led to devaluation of the Congolese franc in 1961 and further devaluation in 1963, when a dual exchange rate was introduced.

Then the exchange rate of the Congolese franc, on the free market, moved even further from the official exchange rate and further adjustments became necessary. Immediately before the monetary reforms in 1967, the index of the rate of exchange on the free markets was 1,230 (1960=100) compared with the official rate of 300 to 350.

The monetary reform of June 1967 brought in the new currency. It was also guaranteed by a new line of stand-by credit of $27 million. This immediately gave investors confidence and guaranteed the currency against speculation. The new zaire was equivalent to two U.S. dollars or 1,000 old Congolese francs. The reforms had the intention of draining the reserves of the unproductive sectors, such as commerce and speculation, to the advantage of the productive sectors, such as agriculture and mining. At first this brought an improvement in government finances, but there has been a continual struggle to keep up with the growth of government expenditure and to divide it according to the plans laid down by the treasury and the budgets.

The objective in June 1967 was to raise sufficient revenue to do away with the additional revenue brought in by the dual rate of exchange and also the deficit financing of expenditure. Measures taken to this end, by increasing indirect taxes and by reforming the system of direct taxation, between the beginning of 1968 and 1969, brought spectacular increases in revenue. This increased flow was assisted by the recovery of foreign trade and by price rises in non-ferrous metal exports. In the first half of 1969 revenue increased still further reaching 220 million zaires in 1969 ($440 million). To the internal revenue must be added revenue from external transfers, mainly in the form of grants-in-aid which helped to strengthen state finances still further.

Public expenditure, in this improved situation, increased considerably between 1966 and 1968. Total volume went up 2.8 times in two years, increasing from 79.9 million zaires, to 222.4 million. What is more, there was a considerable shift from current to capital expenditure, much more being spent on investment.

There was also a fall in public debt. On the eve of independence national debt was $890 million or nearly 68 per cent of the annual national product. External debt in foreign exchange alone was $493 million. Half of this debt was guaranteed and had been continually serviced by Belgium since June 1960. The other half was consolidated for 40 years at an annual rate of interest of 3.5 per cent with interest payments divided between the two countries, as laid down in the Belgo-Congolese agreements of March 1965. A small surplus of revenue over state expenditure was achieved, for the first time in ten years in 1968. Such a drain on the productive resources of the economy is in danger of affecting growth, if unproductive expenditure is not reduced within the shortest possible time.

But the recovery in the balance of payments in the years of the high copper price in 1968–70, suddenly went into reverse as copper prices plummeted in the last quarter of 1970. The trade balance declined from a record of $239 million surplus in 1969 to only $58 million in 1971. The overall payments balance, with services and invisibles included, went into deficit in 1970 and was $186.4 million in deficit by 1971.

TOURISM

[Tourism developed rapidly between 1958, when 12,000 visitors were recorded, and 1970, when there was a total of 38,000. In 1971, the number of visitors increased to 63,307. Forty per cent of the total were Belgians, followed by French, Zambians, Americans and British. Most visited were Kinshasa, Kivu and Shaba. In 1971 Zaire had about 50 international standard hotels, containing about 4,200 beds. The aim was to have 100,000 visitors a year by 1975, involving the doubling of the hotel capacity. Kinshasa's 260 room luxury Continental Hotel, jointly owned by Pan Am and the Zairian Government (49 per cent share), was completed in September 1971. A new tourism promotion company was established by Air Zaire and Tanganyika Concessions Ltd. with the aim of promoting the industry in the Upper Zaire and Kivu Provinces. *Editor.*]

FOREIGN AID

Foreign aid by international organizations and various foreign governments plays an important role. But the volume has been reduced considerably during the last four years and the pattern has changed radically.

In 1968 foreign aid amounted to $60 million compared with $73 million in 1967, $87 million in 1966 and nearly $100 million in 1965. In the first half of 1969 it was estimated at $26 million. Foreign aid declined up to 1970 as the balance of payments was strong, but since then Zaire has had to borrow more abroad to make up for its balance of payments deficits. In 1971 the United Nations Development Programme, the World Bank and European Development Fund channelled large amounts into Zaire. Capital inflows in that year alone were $170 million including $70m. of Eurodollar borrowings ($50 million of this especially designated to subsidise the budget). In 1966 nearly half of this aid, or $23.8 million out of the total of $46.6 million, came in the form of free grants. In 1968 and the first half of 1969 this aid was mostly in the form of loans. This fall in the volume of aid and its changing character is largely due to the United States. Its assistance fell from $43.9 million in 1966 to $19.5 million in 1968 and $3.3 million in the first half of 1969. This is not only due to

the United States' own policies to protect its balance of payments, but also to Zairian policies.

Co-operation aid by Belgium dropped from $24.4 million in 1966 to $20.6 million in 1968 and UN aid also fell from $8.7 million in 1966 to $7.1 million in 1968. Assistance personnel was also reduced even more radically than finance, showing that average salaries of technical assistance personnel have risen partly due to a rise in the qualifications of personnel employed. Secondary and university education continue to absorb more than half of the total personnel employed. To compensate for this fall in foreign technical assistance, Zaire has been recruiting a growing number of technical assistants of its own, particularly teachers and magistrates. Teachers under Zairian government contracts have increased from 1,373 in 1967–68 to 2,000 in 1969–70.

STATISTICAL SURVEY

AREA AND POPULATION

Region				Area (sq. km.)	Population (July 1970)	Density (per sq. km.)
Bandundu	.	.	.	295,658	2,600,556	8.6
Bas-Zaire	.	.	.	53,920	1,504,361	27.6
Equateur	.	.	.	403,293	2,431,812	6.0
Haute-Zaire	.	.	.	503,239	3,556,419	6.6
Kasai Occidental	.	.	.	156,967	2,433,861	15.5
Kasai Oriental	.	.	.	168,216	1,872,231	11.1
Kivu	.	.	.	256,662	3,361,883	13.1
Shaba (formerly Katanga)	.	.	.	496,965	2,753,714	5.5
Kinshasa (city)*	.	.	.	9,965	1,323,039	132.7
Total	.	.	.	2,344,885	21,637,876†	9.2

* Including the commune of Maluku, with an area of 7,948.8 sq. km. and a population of only 14,678.

† Including 932,402 foreigners.

Source: Institut National de la Statistique, *Bulletin Trimestriel des Statistiques Générales.*

Total Population (July 1st, 1971): 22,477,000.

PRINCIPAL TOWNS
(with 1970 population)

Kinshasa (capital)	.	.	1,323,039	Likasi	.	146,394
Kananga (formerly Luluabourg)	.	428,960	Bukavu	.	134,861
Lubumbashi	.	.	318,000	Kikwit	.	111,960
Mbuji-Mayi	.	.	256,154	Matadi	.	110,436
Kisangani	.	.	229,596	Mbandaka	.	107,910

1972: Kinshasa 1,623,760 (provisional estimate).

AGRICULTURE

LAND USE, 1962
('ooo hectares)

Arable and Under Permanent Crops . .	7,200
Permanent Meadows and Pastures . .	65,500
Forest Land	129,141*
Other Areas	32,700
TOTAL	234,541

* Data taken from the world forest inventory carried out by the FAO in 1963.

Source: FAO, *Production Yearbook 1971.*

PRINCIPAL CROPS
('ooo metric tons)

	1968	1969	1970	1971
Wheat	3	3	3	3*
Maize	250	350	350*	350*
Millet and Sorghum . .	18	30	38*	38*
Rice (Paddy)	130	130	140*	140*
Sugar Cane[1] . . .	395	421	420	500*
Potatoes	50*	15	30*	30*
Sweet Potatoes and Yams .	300*	350	350*	n.a.
Cassava (Manioc) . .	10,772	10,000	10,000*	n.a.
Onions (dry) . . .	17	15	15*	n.a.
Tomatoes	24*	25	25*	n.a.
Cabbages	5*	5	5*	n.a.
Dry Peas and Other Pulses .	80*	80*	80*	80*
Oranges and Tangerines .	75*	90	90*	90*
Grapefruit . . .	8*	8	8*	8*
Other Citrus Fruit . .	6*	5	5*	5*
Bananas	60*	80	80*	n.a.
Pineapples . . .	27*	28	28*	n.a.
Palm Kernels . . .	125	128	130	130
Groundnuts (in shell) . .	200*	200	200	200*
Cottonseed . . .	24	32	32	34*
Cotton (Lint) . . .	12	16	17	17*
Sesame Seed . . .	4*	3.5	5*	5*
Coffee	60	66	72	67.5
Cocoa Beans[2] . . .	4.9	4.5	5.0	5.0
Tea	4.5	4.5	4.7*	4.7*
Tobacco	2.5*	2.0	2.0*	2.0*
Knaf	6	6	6*	6*
Natural Rubber[3] . .	40.9	36.5	32.3	35.0*

Palm oil ('ooo metric tons): 196 in 1968; 179 in 1969; 180 in 1970; 200 in 1971.

* FAO estimate.
[1] Crop year ending in year stated.
[2] Twelve months ending in September of year stated. 1971–72: 5,000 metric tons.
[3] Exports only.

Source: FAO, *Production Yearbook 1971.*

LIVESTOCK
('000)

	1968–69	1969–70	1970–71
Cattle . . .	887	900*	930*
Sheep . . .	564	570*	575*
Goats . . .	1,545	1,600*	1,650*
Pigs . . .	433	442*	450*
Poultry . . .	5,400*	5,500*	5,600*

* FAO estimate.

Source: FAO, *Production Yearbook 1971.*

LIVESTOCK PRODUCTS
(FAO estimates, metric tons)

	1968	1969	1970
Cows' Milk . .	18,000	18,000	19,000
Beef and Veal .	16,000	18,000	18,000
Mutton and Lamb* .	6,000	6,000	6,000
Poultry Meat .	4,000	4,000	4,000
Edible Offal . .	4,500	4,000	4,000
Other Meat . .	120,000	120,000	120,000
Hen Eggs . .	4,100	4,200	4,200

1971 (FAO estimates): Cows' Milk 19,000 metric tons; Hen Eggs 4,400 metric tons.

* Including goats' meat.

Source: FAO, *Production Yearbook 1971.*

FORESTRY
('000 cubic metres)

ROUNDWOOD REMOVALS

	Fuel Wood	Other Wood	Total
1967 . .	10,000	1,500	11,500
1968 . .	10,000	1,600	11,600
1969 . .	10,000	1,600	11,600
1970 . .	10,000	1,600	11,600

SAWNWOOD PRODUCTION

1967 . . .	142
1968 . . .	145
1969 . . .	150
1970 . . .	150

Source: FAO, *Yearbook of Forest Products.*

FISHING
(metric tons)

	1967	1968	1969	1970
Inland Waters	80,800	97,800	100,000	110,000
Atlantic Ocean . .	12,400	12,400	12,000*	12,000*
Total . . .	93,200	110,200	112,000*	122,000*

* FAO estimate.

Source: FAO, *Yearbook of Fishery Statistics 1970.*

MINING

	Unit	1968	1969	1970	1971
Copper ore	metric tons	326,078	364,237	385,679	406,813
Tin Concentrates . . .	,, ,,	6,742	6,647	6,447	6,127
Manganese ore* . . .	,, ,,	321,841	311,429	346,950	329,066
Coal	,, ,,	72,260	84,235	101,739	112,438
Zinc Concentrates . .	,, ,,	119,297	95,503	105,082	130,675
Cobalt Ore . . .	,, ,,	10,401	10,576	12,085	11,215
Industrial Diamonds . .	'000 carats	11,353	11,621	12,438	12,004
Gem Diamonds . .	,, ,,	551	1,802	1,649	n.a.
Silver	kilogrammes	66,533	49,349	53,145	51,105
Gold	,,	5,341	5,510	5,509	5,361

* Figures relate to gross weight. The metal content (in metric tons) was: 181,180 in 1968; 165,000 in 1969; 156,000 in 1970.

INDUSTRY

BASE METALS
(metric tons)

	1968	1969	1970	1971
Copper (unwrought): Smelter . .	327,094	340,093	385,500	n.a.
Refined . .	238,412	236,053	274,615	279,097
Zinc (unwrought)	62,574	63,732	63,744	62,674
Cobalt Metal	10,160	n.a.	n.a.	8,092
Tin (unwrought)	1,922	1,881	1,396	1,394

Lead (unwrought): 1,037 metric tons in 1967.

OTHER PRODUCTS

	Unit	1968	1969	1970	1971
Cigarettes	millions	2,972	3,478	4,261	3,416
Beer	'ooo hectolitres	2,233	2,706	3,334	3,811
Aerated drinks . . .	,, ,,	302	322	391	501
Sugar	metric tons	38,408	36,015	42,539	44,333
Margarine	,, ,,	1,700	2,051	2,578	3,896*
Sulphuric Acid . . .	,, ,,	129,000	126,000	136,000	141,000
Explosives	,, ,,	3,159	5,273	6,389	6,600
Fibro-cement products .	,, ,,	1,711	1,506	11,265	18,412
Cement	,, ,,	294,148	322,002	354,605	455,081
Motor Spirit . . .	,, ,,	81,000	104,000	120,000	n.a.
Kerosene	,, ,,	58,000	68,000	71,000	n.a.
Distillate Fuel Oils .	,, ,,	138,000	164,000	181,000	n.a.
Residual Fuel Oils .	,, ,,	264,000	316,000	294,000	n.a.
Bottles	'ooo units	18,500	12,488	23,300	25,037
Plain Textiles . . .	'ooo sq. metres	55,570	64,430	55,133	45,361
Printed Textiles . .	,, ,, ,,	36,490	36,620	37,152	37,400
Blankets	'ooo units	1,611	1,300	1,749	2,004
Electricity . . .	million kWh	2,860	2,912	2,751	3,185

* Estimate.

FINANCE

10,000 sengi = 100 makuta (singular, likuta) = 1 zaire.

Coins: 10 sengi; 1 likuta, 5 makuta.

Notes: 10, 20 and 50 makuta; 1 and 5 zaires.

Exchange rates (December 1972): £1 sterling = 1.174 zaires; U.S. $1 = 50 makuta.

100 zaires = £85.16 = $200.00.

Budget (1970 estimates): Revenue and Expenditure balanced at 215m. zaires.

RESERVES AND CURRENCY

('000 zaires at June 30th)

	1967	1968	1969	1970	1971
Gold Reserves	1,790	6,160	21,433	27,644	25,050
Currency in Circulation . .	36,755	45,600	56,320	65,984	83,833

1972 (May 31st): Gold Reserves 27,485,000 zaires; Currency in Circulation 87,820,000 zaires.

NATIONAL ACCOUNTS

GROSS DOMESTIC PRODUCT

('000 zaires at 1968 prices)

Economic Activity	1968	1969	1970
Monetary Sector:			
Agriculture	89,760	88,250	95,670
Mining	76,310	79,300	81,730
Metallurgy	108,010	118,750	128,040
Manufacturing	36,000	40,440	48,340
Energy	7,400	8,350	9,000
Building and public works .	16,040	21,700	34,200
Transport and telecommunications .	38,350	41,420	44,560
Commerce	82,300	90,400	105,900
Banks, insurance and other services .	70,800	79,240	88,990
Sub-total (at factor cost) . .	524,970	567,850	636,430
Indirect taxation . . .	53,160	69,130	73,060
Sub-total (market prices) .	578,130	636,980	709,490
Administration	43,300	42,870	43,990
State education	16,900	18,760	21,290
Defence	9,800	10,190	11,680
Total Monetary Product . .	648,130	708,800	786,450
Non-Monetary Sector:			
Agriculture	71,300	72,800	74,000
Construction	6,700	8,250	10,000
Gross Domestic Product . .	726,130	789,850	870,450

Source: Banque du Zaïre, Annual Report.

NATIONAL INCOME
(million zaires)

	AT 1968 PRICES			AT CURRENT PRICES	
	1968	1969	1970	1969	1970
Gross Domestic Product	726.1	789.9	870.5	897.8	1,025.4
Less: Net transfers abroad of interest and investment income . . .	7.3	10.8	17.2	10.8	17.2
Net transfers abroad of private income	27.5	31.7	34.8	31.7	34.8
Gross National Product	691.3	747.4	818.5	855.5	973.4
Less: Indirect taxation, net of subsidies .	143.8	171.9	190.7	191.9	216.0
Amortizations	83.5	86.9	94.0	90.1	102.0
National Income	464.0	488.6	533.3	573.3	655.4
Less: Direct taxation . . .	31.1	58.9	49.2	69.1	60.4
NATIONAL DISPOSABLE INCOME . .	432.9	429.7	484.6	504.2	595.0

Source: Banque du Zaïre, Annual Report.

EXPENDITURE ON GROSS DOMESTIC PRODUCT
(million zaires)

	1968	1969	1970
Government Final Consumption Expenditure .	140.1	196.8	277.2
Private Final Consumption Expenditure . .	306.2	423.3	575.2
Increase in Stocks	0.4	—	0.1
Gross Fixed Capital Formation . . .	139.5	216.7	330.6
Exports of Goods and Services . . .	292.2	364.0	453.4
	878.4	1,200.8	1,636.5
Less: Imports of Goods and Services . .	156.9	321.4	564.7
GROSS DOMESTIC PRODUCT (at purchasers' values) *of which:*	721.5	879.4	1,071.8
NATIONAL INCOME (in market prices) . .	577.2	747.7	934.0

Source: United Nations, *Monthly Bulletin of Statistics.*

EXTERNAL TRADE
RECORDED TRANSACTIONS
(million zaires)

	1965	1966	1967	1968	1969	1970	1971*
Imports: Merchandise . .	160.7	171.6	128.1	154.8	205.1	266.5	313.4
Exports: Merchandise . .	168.0	232.4	217.9	252.5	322.3	367.7	342.4
Gold . .	0.7	1.6	2.6	2.1	2.4	3.2	

* Provisional estimate.

TRANSACTIONS REPORTED BY TRADING PARTNERS
(merchandise only—million zaires)

	1965	1966	1967	1968	1969	1970
Imports . . .	137.0	145.8	128.7	160.4	202.5	250.5
Exports . . .	192.8	261.0	237.8	289.0	363.5	406.5

Source: International Monetary Fund, *International Financial Statistics.*

COMMODITIES
('000 zaires)

IMPORTS	1969	1970	EXPORTS	1969	1970
Fish and Fish Products . .	6,944	8,257	Coffee	12,945	19,318
Dairy Produce . . .	2,741	4,498	Raw Cotton . . .	1,662	2,048
Cereals and derivatives . .	9,030	13,825	Rubber	8,135	6,379
Coal, Coke, etc. . . .	5,000	2,910	Palm Oil	9,635	14,091
Petroleum Products . . .	10,650	15,470	Palm Kernel Oil . .	4,992	6,304
Medicinal and Pharmaceutical			Copper	214,716	246,751
Products	4,690	8,580	Diamonds . . .	17,082	22,973
Rubber Articles . . .	4,603	6,370	Gold	2,411	3,194
Paper and Paperboard . .	3,737	5,707	Cobalt	12,270	16,895
Printed Cotton Cloth . .	8,318	8,813	Zinc (unrefined) . .	6,952	8,366
Clothing	2,983	4,555	Tin (unrefined) . .	3,097	1,977
Iron and Steel Bars and Sections .	2,752	6,307	Cassiterite . . .	8,247	7,555
Iron and Steel Plates and Sheets .	3,632	6,606			
Non-Electrical Machinery . .	24,372	34,335			
Electrical Machinery . .	13,011	16,350			
Railway Equipment . .	7,851	3,802			
Road Vehicles . . .	27,653	32,917			
Aviation Equipment . .	8,340	2,123			
TOTAL, including others .	205,130	266,491	TOTAL, including others .	324,657	370,896

COUNTRIES
('000 zaires)

IMPORTS	1969	1970	EXPORTS	1969	1970*
Belgium/Luxembourg . .	48,451	65,172	Belgium/Luxembourg . .	140,260	158,602
France	15,888	21,615	France	22,571	25,695
Germany, Federal Republic .	20,456	27,613	Germany, Federal Republic .	7,099	9,640
Italy	9,776	14,449	Italy	39,500	42,212
Japan	14,280	17,958	Netherlands . . .	7,731	7,595
Netherlands . . .	13,160	11,112	United Kingdom . .	28,410	26,815
United Kingdom . .	12,784	19,362	U.S.A. . . .	6,167	6,299
U.S.A. . . .	26,124	28,493	Others . . .	8,109	9,161
			Unspecified . .	64,810	84,858
TOTAL (incl. others) .	205,130	266,491	TOTAL . .	324,657	370,877

* Excluding re-exports, valued at 18,800 zaires.

TOURISM

	1970	1971
Tourist arrivals . .	38,348	63,307

TRANSPORT

RAILWAYS
(1971)

	C.F.M.K. Network	B.C.K. Network
Freight carried ('ooo tons) .	1,825	4,957
Freight ('ooo ton-km.) .	511,182	1,971
Passengers ('ooo) .	1,372	2,636
Passenger-km. ('ooo) .	158,137	592,763

ROADS

	1967	1968*	1969*
Passenger Cars .	43,500	46,100	55,800
Commercial Vehicles .	23,200	26,200	43,100

* Provisional estimates.

Source: United Nations, *Statistical Yearbook.*

SHIPPING
(1971)

	MATADI	BOMA
Number of ships entering .	512	270
Number of ships departing .	513	274
Freight entering ('ooo tons) .	541	46
Freight departing ('ooo tons) .	932	69

	KINSHASA
Freight entering from Zaire Basin (tons) .	289,596
Freight leaving for Zaire Basin (tons) .	235,587
Freight entering from Kasai Basin (tons) .	389,832
Freight leaving for Kasai Basin (tons) .	210,163

CIVIL AVIATION
SCHEDULED SERVICES

	1968	1969	1970
Kilometres Flown ('ooo) .	8,984	10,051	12,689
Passenger-km. ('ooo) .	330,881	367,214	464,826
Cargo ton-km. ('ooo) .	9,708	11,234	14,848
Mail ton-km. ('ooo) .	1,019	1,254	1,282

Source: United Nations, *Statistical Yearbook 1971.*

EDUCATION
(1970–71)

	SCHOOLS	TEACHERS	PUPILS
Primary .	4,756	69,999	3,088,011
Secondary .	1,201	11,755	253,234
Vocational .	n.a.	n.a.	n.a.
Higher .	33	1,386	12,363

Sources (unless otherwise stated): Institut National de la Statistique, Office Nationale de la Recherche et du Développement, B.P. 20 Kinshasa; Département de l'Economie Nationale, Kinshasa, Institut de la Statistique.

THE CONSTITUTION

A new constitution was adopted by national referendum in June 1967.

The Republic of Zaire is defined as a united, democratic and social state, composed of eight administrative regions and the city of Kinshasa.

HEAD OF STATE

The President of the Republic is elected for a seven-year term by direct universal suffrage. Candidates must be natives of Zaire and aged over 40. Under the Constitution, the Head of State is also the Head of the National Executive Council and acts as the chief executive, controls foreign policy and is Captain-General of the armed forces and the gendarmerie.

EXECUTIVE POWER

The programme and decisions of the National Executive Council are determined by the President and carried out by the Councillors who are heads of their departments. The National Executive Council is dissolved at the end of each Presidential term, though it continues to function until a new National Executive Council is formed. The members of the National Executive Council are appointed or dismissed by the President.

LEGISLATURE

Parliament consists of a single Chamber, the National Legislative Council, elected for five years by direct, universal suffrage with a secret ballot. Elections were held in 1970. The National Legislative Council will consist of the President, two Vice-Presidents and four Secretaries. The members of the National Executive Council have the right, and if required the obligation to assist at the meetings of the National Legislative Council. It will meet twice yearly, from April to July, and from October to January.

POLITICAL PARTIES

In May 1970 it was resolved that the MPR should be Zaire's only party.

REGIONAL GOVERNMENTS

The governors of the eight regions are appointed and dismissed by the President.

CONSTITUTIONAL COURT

The Constitutional Court consists of nine counsellors, three named by the President, three proposed by the National Legislative Council, and three proposed by the Supreme Court of Magistrates. The Counsellors have the right to judge all matters of dispute concerning the present Constitution.

JUDICIARY

The judiciary is wholly independent of the legislature and the executive. It is responsible to the Courts and Tribunals which apply statute and common law. The chief organs of justice are the Supreme Court of Justice, the Courts of Appeal, Military Courts and Tribunals.

FUNDAMENTAL RIGHTS AND DUTIES

All citizens are equal before the law, irrespective of social class, religion, tribe, sex, birth or residence. Every person shall enjoy the rights of personal respect, protection of life and inviolability of person. No person may be arrested or detained except within the prescribed form of the law. All citizens are entitled to freedom of expression, conscience and religion. Military service is obligatory, but can be replaced by alternative forms of public service under the conditions fixed by law. All natives of Zaire have the right and duty to work, and can defend their rights by trade union action. The right to strike is recognized and is exercised according to laws.

THE GOVERNMENT

HEAD OF STATE

President: General MOBUTU SESE SEKO.

NATIONAL EXECUTIVE COUNCIL

(January 1973)

COUNCILLORS

Head of National Executive Council, Councillor in charge of Defence, Ex-Servicemen and Planning: Gen. MOBUTU SESE SEKO.

Councillor in charge of Interior: KITHIMA BIN RAMAZANI.

Councillor in charge of Foreign Affairs and International Co-operation: NGUZA KARL L'BOND.

Councillor in charge of Justice: NZONDOMYO A' DOKPE LINGO.

Councillor in charge of Information: SAKOMBI INONGO.

Councillor in charge of Finance: BARUTI WA NDWALI.

Councillor in charge of National Economy: NDONGALA TADI LEWA.

Councillor in charge of Mines: UMBA DI LUTETE.

Councillor in charge of Agriculture: KAYINGA ONSI NDAL.

Councillor in charge of Commerce: NAMWISI MA NKOYI.

Councillor in charge of National Education: MABOLIA INENGO TRA BWATO.

Councillor in charge of Public Works: ENGULU BANGA-BONGO BAKOKELE LOKONGA.

Councillor in charge of Land: KABWITA NYAMABU.

Councillor in charge of Power: MUNUTU KAKUBI TSHIONDO KABAZA WA MINTENGE.

Councillor in charge of Public Health: KALONDA LOMEMA.

Councillor in charge of Transport and Communications: EKETEBI MOYIDIBA MONDJOLOMBA.

Councillor in charge of Social Affairs: KPARAGUME ATOLOYO.

Councillor in charge of Labour: BINTU'A TSHIABOLA.

Councillor in charge of Posts and Telecommunications: Mme MATAA NKUMU WA BOWANGO ANGANDA DIOWO.

Councillor in charge of Culture and Arts: BOKONGA EKANGA BOTOMBELE.

Councillor in charge of Youth and Sports: SAMPASSA KAWETA MILOMBE.

Assistant Councillor in charge of Foreign Affairs and International Co-operation: ININGA LOKONGO L'OME.

Assistant Councillor in charge of Agriculture: D'ZBO KALOGI.

Assistant Councillor in charge of National Education: ILOO LOKWA BOSSIYO.

President of the Public Administration Commission: KASONGO MUTWALE.

POLITICAL BUREAU OF THE M.P.R.

Gen. MOBUTU SESE SEKO	BULUNDWE KITONGO	M. KITEWA	M. KABIMBI
BO-BOLINKO LOKONGA	M. NZONDOMIO	M. MAKANDA	M. NDATABAYI
MADRANDELE TANZI	M. ILEO	M. PINDA	MPANU-MPANU BIBANDA
KITHIMA BIN RAMAZANI	LUTAY KANZA	M. NGUZA KARL L'BOND	

DIPLOMATIC REPRESENTATION

EMBASSIES ACCREDITED TO ZAIRE

(In Kinshasa unless otherwise stated)

Belgium: Bldg. Le Cinquantenaire, Place Braconnier, B.P. 899; *Ambassador:* (vacant).

Bulgaria: B.P. 967; *Ambassador:* (vacant).

Burundi: B.P. 1483; *Ambassador:* JEAN-MARIE DERY.

Cameroon: B.P. 3636; *Ambassador:* JEAN-CLAUDE NGOH.

Canada: B.P. 8341; *Ambassador:* (vacant).

Central African Republic: B.P. 7769; *Ambassador:* (vacant).

Chad: B.P. 9343; *Ambassador:* (vacant).

China Republic (Taiwan): B.P. 8939; *Ambassador:* (vacant).

Congo, People's Republic: B.P. 9328; *Ambassador:* APOLLINAIRE BAZINGA.

Czechoslovakia: B.P. 8242; *Ambassador:* (vacant).

Dahomey: 11 ave. Cpt. Joubert, B.P. 3265; *Ambassador:* (vacant).

Denmark: B.P. 1446; *Ambassador:* (vacant).

Egypt: B.P. 8838; *Ambassador:* GAMAL EL DINE.

Ethiopia: B.P. 8435; *Ambassador:* BEKERE ABERRA.

Equatorial Guinea: *Ambassador:* CLEMENTE ATEBA.

France: 3 ave. Tilkens, B.P. 3093; *Ambassador:* CLAUDE CHAYET.

Gabon: B.P. 9592; *Ambassador:* (vacant).

Germany, Federal Republic: 201 ave. Astrid, B.P. 4800; *Ambassador:* GÜNTHER FRANZ WERNER.

Ghana: B.P. 8446; *Ambassador:* Gen. H. D. TWUM-BARINA.

Greece: B.P. 478; *Ambassador:* (vacant).

Guinea: *Ambassador:* AHMADOU TITIANE SANO.

India: B.P. 1026; *Ambassador:* (vacant).

Israel: B.P. 8624; *Ambassador:* SHIMON MORATT.

Italy: 8 ave. Costermans, B.P. 1000; *Ambassador:* (vacant).

Ivory Coast: 68 ave. Valcke, B.P. 8935; *Ambassador:* (vacant).

Japan: B.P. 1810; *Ambassador:* HIROSHI UCHIDA.

Kenya: B.P. 9667; *Ambassador:* (vacant).

Korea, Republic: B.P. 628; *Ambassador:* (vacant).

Liberia: B.P. 8940; *Ambassador:* JENKINS COOPER.

Morocco: B.P. 912; *Ambassador:* ABDELAZIZ BINNANI.

Netherlands: 11 ave. Ponthier, B.P. 3106; *Ambassador:* M. VERDONCK HUFFNAGEL.

Nigeria: B.P. 1700; *Ambassador:* (vacant).

Poland: B.P. 7769; *Ambassador:* (vacant).

Romania: B.P. 2242; *Ambassador:* (vacant).

Rwanda: B.P. 967; *Ambassador:* (vacant).

Senegal: B.P. 7686; *Ambassador:* PASCAL ANTOINE SANE (also accred. to Gabon).

Somalia: Dar es Salaam, Tanzania.

Spain: B.P. 8036; *Ambassador:* LUIS DEPETROSO.

Sudan: B.P. 7347; *Ambassador:* SALAH EL DIN BABIR ZARROUG.

Sweden: B.P. 3038; *Ambassador:* HENRIK RAMEL.

Switzerland: B.P. 8724; *Ambassador:* J. P. EDMOND WEBER.

Tanzania: B.P. 1612; *Ambassador:* M. TIBAN.

Togo: *Ambassador:* ALEX SEIBUO NAPO.

Tunisia: B.P. 1488; *Ambassador:* MOHAMED AMAMOU.

Uganda: B.P. 1036; *Ambassador:* EDOUARD LORIKA ATHIYO.

U.S.S.R.: B.P. 1143; *Ambassador:* M. LAVROV.

United Kingdom: 9 ave. Beernaert, B.P. 8049; *Ambassador:* MARK ALLEN (also accred. to Burundi).

U.S.A.: 310 ave. des Aviateurs, B.P. 697; *Ambassador:* SHELDON B. VANCE.

Vatican: 81 rue Martin Rutter; *Nuncio:* Mgr. BRUNO TORPIGLIANI.

Vietnam, Republic: B.P. 9316; *Ambassador:* (vacant).

Yugoslavia: B.P. 619; *Ambassador:* ESAD CERIC.

Zambia: B.P. 1144; *Ambassador:* (vacant).

Zaire also has diplomatic relations with Argentina, Austria, China (People's Republic), Cyprus, Lebanon, Luxembourg, Norway and Turkey.

PRESIDENT AND NATIONAL ASSEMBLY

PRESIDENTIAL ELECTION
(October 1970)

Total Registered Voters	.	.	.	10,101,330
Total Votes Cast	.	.	.	10,131,828
For General Mobutu	.	.	.	10,131,669
Against	.	.	.	157

The results show a 99.9985 per cent vote in favour of Gen. Mobutu, the sole candidate.

NATIONAL ASSEMBLY
(Legislative Elections, November 14th–15th, 1970)

Total Registered Voters	.	.	.	9,854,517
Votes for Party Candidates	.	.	.	9,691,132
Votes Against	.	.	.	72,378
Spoiled or Blank Papers	.	.	.	91,007

All 420 seats in the National Assembly were won by the MPR, the sole party.

President of the National Assembly: BOBOLIKO LOKONGAI.

REGIONAL GOVERNMENTS

Under the Loi Fondamentale there were 6 provinces in the Republic. This number was changed to 21 by a law promulgated in August 1962, and finally reduced to 8 by presidential decree from January 1967. These provinces were renamed "regions" in July 1972. Regional government is in the hands of a Governor and 6 Councillors.

REGION	GOVERNOR	REGION	GOVERNOR
Shaba . . .	DUGA KUGBETOLO	Lower Zaire .	Mme. MADIMBA NZUZI
Kivu . .	M. NDEBO	Equator .	NGOMA NTOLO MBWANGI
Upper Zaire .	GEYORO TEKULE	Eastern Kasai .	M. MUZAGBA
Bandundu . .	M. MULENDA SHAMWANGE MUTEBI	Western Kasai .	M. TAKIZALA

Governor of Kinshasa: (vacant) (responsible directly to the Ministry of the Interior).

POLITICAL PARTY

Mouvement populaire de la révolution (MPR): Kinshasa; f. 1967; stands for national unity, opposition to tribalism, and African socialism; political bureau of 15 members; Leader President MOBUTU; Sec. MADRANDELE TANZI.

DEFENCE

The strength of the armed forces is about 50,000, nearly all of whom are in the army, and the rest in the small navy and air force.

Chief of Staff: Lt.-Col. ANTOINE BUMBA.

JUDICIAL SYSTEM

Under the terms of the 1967 Constitution there is a Supreme Court at Kinshasa, two Courts of Appeal at Kinshasa and Lubumbashi; eight Tribunals of First Instance in each region.

SUPREME COURT
First President: MARCEL LIHAU.
Second President: GUY BOUCHOMS.
Prosecutor-General: LÉON LOBITSH.

Advocate-General: VALENTIN PHANZU.
Secretary: JUSTIN-MARIE MBEMBA, B.P. 7016, Kinshasa-Kalina.

APPEAL COURTS
Kinshasa: Pres. TRIDON LUBAMBA.
Kisangani: Pres. ANDRÉ MOISE.
Lubumbashi: Pres. EVARISTE KALALA-ILUNGA.

RELIGION

AFRICAN RELIGIONS
About half the population follow traditional beliefs, which are mostly animistic.

CHRISTIANITY

ROMAN CATHOLIC CHURCH
Archbishop of Bukavu: ALOIS MULINDWA, B.P. 3.324 Bukavu.

SUFFRAGAN BISHOPS
Butembo-Beni: EMMANUEL KATILIKO.
Goma: JOSEPH BUSIMBA.
Kasongo: TIMOTHÉE PIRIGISHA.
Kindu: ALBERT ONYEMBO.
Uvira: DANILO CATARZI.

Archbishop of Mbandaka: PIERRE WIJNANTS, B.P. 1064, Mbandaka.

SUFFRAGAN BISHOPS
Basankusu: GUILLAUME VAN KESTER.
Bikoro: CAMILLE VANDEKERCKHOVE.
Bokunga-Ikela: JOSEPH WEIGL.
Budjala: FRANÇOIS VAN DEN BERGH.
Lisala: LOUIS NGANGA.
Lolo: IGNACE JOSEPH WATERSCHOOT.
Molegbe: JOSEPH KOSENGE.

Archbishop of Lubumbashi: EUGENE KABANGA, B.P. 72, Lubumbashi.

SUFFRAGAN BISHOPS
Kalemie-Kirungu: JOSEPH MULOLWA.
Kamina: BARTHÉLÉMY MALUNGA.
Kilwa: JOSEPH ALAIN LEROY.
Kolwezi: VICTOR PETRUS KEUPPENS.
Kongolo: JÉROME NDAYE.
Manono: GÉRARD KABWE.
Sakania: PIERRE-FRANÇOIS LEHAEN.

Archbishop of Kinshasa: H.E. Cardinal JOSEPH MALULA, B.P. 8431, Kinshasa.

SUFFRAGAN BISHOPS
Boma: RAYMOND NDUDI.
Idiofa: EUGENE BILETSI.
Inongo: LEON LESAMBO.
Kenge: FRANCISCUS HOWNEN.
Kikwit: ALEXANDRE MBUKA-NZUNDU.
Kisantu: PIERRE KIMBONDO.
Matadi: SIMON N'ZITA.
Popokabaka: PETRUS BOUCKAERT.

Archbishop of Kisangani: AUGUSTIN FATAKI, B.P. 505, Kisangani.

SUFFRAGAN BISHOPS
Bondo: EMMANUEL MARCEL MBIKANYE.
Bunia: GABRIEL UKEC.
Buta: JACQUES MBALI.
Doruma-Dungu: GUILLAUME VAN DEN ELZEN.
Isangi: LODEWIJK ANTOON JANSEN.
Isiro-Niangara: FRANÇOIS ODDO DE WILDE.
Mahagi-Nioka: THOMAS KUBA.
Wamba: GUSTAVE OLOMBE.

Archbishop of Kananga: MARTIN BAKOLE, B.P. 70, Kananga.

SUFFRAGAN BISHOPS
Kabinda: MATTHIEU KANYAMA.
Kole: VICTOR VAN BEURDEN.
Luebo: FRANÇOIS KABANGU.
Luisa: GODEFROID MUKENGE.
Mbuji-Mayi: JOSEPH NKONGOLO.
Mweka: MARCEL EVARISTE VAN RENGEN.
Tshumbé: ALBERT YUNGU.

CHURCH OF CHRIST IN ZAIRE
Eglise de Christ au Zaïre: B.P. 3094, Kinshasa-Ngombe; f. 1902 (as Zaire Protestant Council); Pres.-Gen. Rev. I. B. BOKELEALE. There are 57 Zairian Protestant Communities with some 5m. mems.; Depts.: Evangelization and the Life of the Church, Protestant Education Bureau, Medical Dept., Christian Education, Youth, Women and Family Life, Inter Church Aid and Development, Chaplaincies to the Zairian Armed Forces and the Force of Gendarmes.

ANGLICAN CHURCH
(Province of Uganda)
Diocese of Boga-Zaire: Bishop: The Rt. Rev. PHILIP RIDSDALE, B.P. 154, Bunia.

OTHER RELIGIONS
Muslims . . 115,500
Jews . . 1,520

There are 143 Baha'i centres of worship in Zaire.

THE PRESS
(French language, unless otherwise stated)

DAILIES

Documentation et Information Africaine: B.P. 2598, Kinshasa I.

Elima: ave. Kasavubu, B.P. 10.017, Kinshasa I; f. 1928; independent; Editor PASCAL KAPELLA; circ. 25,000.

Elombe: ave. de l'Université, B.P. 11498, Kinshasa I; Editor THU-RENÉ ESSOLOMWA.

Monano: B.P. 982, Kisangani; f. 1969; Editor FRÉDÉRIC-MARTIN MONZEMU; circ. 5,000.

Mwanga: B.P. 2474, Lubumbashi; published by La Presse Zairoise, S.Z.A.R.L.; circ. 20,000.

Nyoto: 10eme Rue, B.P. 1366, Lisete-Kinshasa; f. 1963; published by Société d'Edition Etoile du Zaire; circ. 25,000.

Salongo: Blvd. du 30 Juin, B.P. 78, Kinshasa VII; pro-governmental; Editor GABRIEL MAKOSSO.

Taifa: 490 ave. Mobutu, B.P. 525, Lubumbashi; f. 1927; independent; Editor JAQUES TSHILEMBE; circ. 10,000.

WEEKLIES

Afrique Chrétienne: B.P. 7653, Kinshasa I; Publisher Soc. Miss. St. Paul; Dir. L. KALONJI; circ. 50,000.

Actualités du Kivu: B.P. 475, Bukavu.

Dimukai: B.P. 1375, Mbuji Mayi.

Echo du Kasai Occidental: B.P. 1670, Kananga.

Epanza: 1 ave. Bangandanga, B.P. 8205, Kinshasa.

Le Zaïre: ave. Buskadingi, Grand Marché, B.P. 8203, Kinshasa I.

M'Bandaka: P.O.B. 349, Mbandaka; f. 1947; French and Lingala.

Michezo: Stade 20 Mai, B.P. 7853, Kinshasa.

Nkumu: ave. Badjoko 340, Matonge/Kinshasa; Editor GASTON N'SENGI BIEMBE.

La Semaine: rue de Luvungi 87, Kinshasa; Editor EMILE SOLET.

Tabalayi: 31 bis, rue Doruma, B.P. 6250, Kinshasa.

Uhaki-Verité: P.O.B. 1454, Lubumbashi; f. 1946; Swahili and French; Editor JULIUS KANSO MULENGA; circ. 6,000.

Ukweli: 373 avenue Mahenge, B.P. 4425, Lubumbashi; f. 1959; Editor PASCAL HAMICI; circ. 12,000.

FORTNIGHTLIES

Zaire Magazine: P.O.B. 8246, Kinshasa; f. 1960; official publication formerly published under the title *La Voix du Congolais:* also replaces *Nos Images:* illustrated; publ. in French-Lingala, French-Kikongo, French-Kiswahili, French-Tshiluba; circ. 10,000.

Nature, Parcs et Jardins: P.O.B. 3220, Kinshasa; Kalina; f. 1938; journal of the Société Congolaise des Sciences Naturelles.

PERIODICALS

Aequatoria: B.P. 276, Mbandaka; f. 1937; scientific native questions; Editor G. HULSTAERT, M.S.C.

Afrique et l'Europe: rue d'Itanga 81, Kinshasa.

Aliazo: B.P. 8085, Kinshasa; Editor ANDRÉ MASSAKI.

Asco: B.P. 8037, Kinshasa; Editor NSIALA ZINDUKA.

Les Bantous et la Culture: 20 rue Balari, Kinshasa-Bandalungwa; Editor SEBASTIEN NANGI.

Le Bon Berger: rue de Bosobolo 47, Kinshasa; Editor M. BAVELEDY.

Centre Afrique: Direction de l'Imprimerie Nationale Congolaise, Kinshasa.

Chambre du Commerce et d'Industrie: Bukavu.

Zaïre Afrique: B.P. 3375, Kinshasa; monthly; economic and cultural; organ of Centre d'Etudes pour l'Action Sociale; Editors RENE BEECKMANS, FRANCIS KIKASSA.

Zaire News Letter: American Baptist Foreign Mission Society, B.P. 4728, Kinshasa II; f. 1910; English; Editor Mrs. WESLEY H. BROWN.

Conscience: rue Bakongo 17, Kinshasa; Editor TSHIALA MWANA.

Dionga: 2eme Rue Dima, Immeuble Amassio, B.P. 8031, Kinshasa.

Le Drapeau Zaïroise: B.P. 235, Kinshasa XI; Editor D. B. KATHALAY.

Les Droits de l'Homme: Africaine Import-Export, B.P. 991, Kinshasa, Editor JEAN-MARIE MALENGE.

Echos du Bas-Zaïre: Avenue Kabambare No. 23, Kinshasa; Editor RAYMOND BIKEBI.

Energie et Progrès: blvd. du 30 Juin, INSS Building, B.P. 500, Kinshasa I.

Equateur Mabenga: B. P. 243, ave. de Budja No. 45, Mbandaka; Editor JOSEPH BESEMBE.

Espoir: B.P. 903, Kinshasa; Editor SAKOU MAMBA.

Etudes Zaïroises: c/o Institut National d'Etudes Politiques, B.P. 2307, Kinshasa; Editor LOUIS MANDALA.

Le Flambeau: ave. Mangembo 106, Kinshasa; Editor CAMILLE LOBOYA.

Flash: B.P. 7969, Kinshasa; Editor JOSEPH FRANSSEN.

Le Grand Combat: B.P. 1129, Kinshasa; Editor PASCAL MVUEMBA.

Indépendance: B.P. 8201, Kinshasa; Editor ANTOINE KIWEWA.

Kibanguisme: 56 ave. d'Opala, Kinshasa; Editor P. LOSOLO.

Kin Malebo: B.P. 768, Kinshasa; Editor FRANÇOIS-FERDINAND DIATAKO.

Lokole Lokiso: B.P. 245, Mbandaka; Editor PAUL NGOI.

Longle: B.P. 5835, Kinshasa.

Le Matin: B.P. 1301, Kinshasa; Editor IGNACE BOLENGE.

Maro: B.P. 1466, Kinshasa; general commercial.

Le Messager du Salut: 275 ave. du Plateau, B.P. 8636, Kinshasa; journal of the Salvation Army; monthly; French, Lingala and Kikongo.

Misamu Gifumzi Gydu: B.P. 2186, Kinshasa; Editor NABOTHE NZAMBA.

Mission des Noirs: B.P. 8029, Kinshasa; Editor SIMON PIERRE M'PADI.

Mokano: Ministry of Information, B.P. 8246, Kinshasa.

Monaco: ave. Borns 9, Wangata, Kinshasa; Editor PAUL EBAKA.

Mondo: B.P. 8085, Kinshasa; Editor EMMANUEL KOUN ZIKA.

Mon Opinion: rue Van Eetevelde 15/A, Kinshasa; Editor CESAIRE KATEMBABISU.

Notre Combat: E.N.D.A., Kinshasa; Editor BONAVENTURE BIBOMBE.

Nsamu Mbote: Baptist Mid Mission, B.P. 18, Kikwit; Editor H. EICHER.

Le Porte Feuille: B.P. 3473, Kinshasa-Kalina.

Présence Universitaire: Lovanium, Kinshasa; Editor FELIX MALU.

Le Progrès: B.P. 7074, Kinshasa; Editor ADRIEN MOKESE.

Réalités: Institut Enseignement Médical, Kinshasa; Editor MICHEL NGOMA NGIMBI.

La Revue Juridique du Zaïre: Société d'Etudes Juridiques du Katanga; B.P. 510, Lubumbashi; f. 1924.

Solidarité Africaine: ave. Mgr. Kimbondo 488, Kinshasa, Bandalungwa; Editor F. KIMWAY.

Le Travailleur de l'Angola: Quartier Mongo 35/E, Kinshasa; Editor FERDINAND MAVUNZA.

Tribune Zaïroise: Kananga; Editor MEDARD OLONGO.

Tribune du Travailleur: U.N.T.C., Kinshasa; Editor VALENTIN MUTHOMBO.

Unidade Angolana: ave. Tombeur de Tabora 51, Kinshasa; Editor MARIO DE ANDRADE.

Voici l'Heure: ave. Kaviakere 3144, Kinshasa; Editor ROGER KASSONGO.

Voir et Savoir: 16 ave. Bangala, Kinshasa; Editor (vacant).

La Voix de la Nation Angolaise: rue d'Itanga No. 56, Kinshasa; Editor ROBERTO HOLDEN.

La Voix de l'Orphelin: rue Tshuapa 58, Kinshasa; Editor JULES PANDAMARE.

La Voix du Kwilu: Kikwit; Editor VALÈRE NZANBA.

Le Vrai Visage: 43 ave. des Colons, Kinshasa; Editor FRANÇOIS KUPA.

NEWS AGENCIES

Agence Zaïre-Presse (AZAP): B.P. 1595, Kinshasa; f. 1957; official agency; Dir.-Gen. M. ELEBE-MA-EKONZO.

FOREIGN BUREAUX

Deutsche Presse-Agentur and Reuters have offices in Kinshasa.

RADIO AND TELEVISION

Radiodiffusion-Télévision Nationale Zaïroise (RTNZ): B.P. 3171, Kinshasa-Kalina; f. 1940; regional stations at Kinshasa, Kisangani, Bukavu, Kananga, Mbandaka, Bakwanga, Mbuji-Mayi and Lubumbashi. Broadcasts in French and African languages; Dir. A. KIBONGUE.

    International Service: B.P. 7699; Kinshasa broadcasts in French, English, Spanish, German and Portuguese; Chief A. KONGO.

TV-College: B.P. 7074, Collège S. François de Sales, 1700 avenue Wangermée, Lubumbashi; f. 1947; religious, educational; services in French, Swahili, Kibemba,

radio services suspended 1968 but television service continues in collaboration with RTNZ; Dir.-Gen. M. SALESIENS.

Radio Léo: B.P. 3165, Kinshasa; f. 1937; religious, educational; owned and operated by Collège Albert; services in French; Dir.-Gen. P. WART.

Radiodiffusion Ufac: B.P. 97, Lubumbashi; services in French, English, Kiswahili.

La Voix de la Fraternité Africaine: Lubumbashi; f. 1965.

In 1971 there were 75,000 radio licences and 7,050 television licences.

FINANCE

(cap.=capital; dep.=deposit; m.=million; res.=reserves)

BANKING

CENTRAL BANK

Banque Nationale du Zaïre: B.P. 2697, Kinshasa; f. 1961; cap. 1m. Zaires, res. 7.8m. Zaires; Gov. SAMBWA PIDA NBAGUI; Dir.-Gen. M. BARUTI.

COMMERCIAL BANKS

Banque Commerciale Zaïroise S.Z.A.R.L.: ave. des Wagenias, B.P. 2798, Kinshasa; f. 1909; cap. 1.4m. Zaires; 29 brs.; Man. Dirs. E. BONVOISIN, J. VERDICKT, M. H. DELVOIE.

Banque de Kinshasa: ave. Tombalbaye, Pl. du Marché, B.P. 2433, Kinshasa; br. in Lubumbashi; cap. and res. 1,764,135 Zaires, dep. 21,095,220 Zaires.

Banque de Paris et des Pays-Bas: Bldg. Unibra, ave. Col. Ebeia, B.P. 1600, Kinshasa.

Banque du Peuple: Blvd. du 30 Juin, Kinshasa.

Banque Internationale pour l'Afrique au Zaïre (BIAZ): ave. de la Douane, B.P. 8725, Kinshasa.

Banque Zaïroise pour le Développement: Kinshasa; f. 1966; Gov. M. MUSHIETTE.

Barclays Bank S.Z.A.R.L.: Head Office: 191 ave. de l'Equateur, B.P. 1299, Kinshasa; f. 1951; subsidiary of Barclays Bank International Ltd.; br. in Lubumbashi; cap. and res. 13,000 Zaires, dep. 1,408,610 Zaires (Dec. 1967); Chair. Vicomte OBERT DE THIEUSIES; Man. Dir. M. J. ST. C. DYER.

Caisse d'Epargne du Zaïre: ave. Prince Charles, Kalina-Kinshasa, B.P. 8147; f. 1950; Dir.-Gen. VICTOR MAKUNGU.

Compagnie Immobilière du Zaïre "Immozaire": P.O.B. 332, Kinshasa; f. 1962; cap. 150m. Zaires; Chair. A. S. GERARD; Man. Dir. M. HERALY.

Crédit Commercial Africain: Kinshasa.

Crédit Foncier de l'Afrique Centrale: B.P. 1198, Kinshasa; f. 1961; cap. 40,000 Zaires.

Crédit Foncier du Nord Est: Bukavu; f. 1961; cap. 10m. Zaires.

Crédit Hypothécaire du Nord Est: Bukavu; f. 1961; cap. 15m. Zaires.

Société de Crédit aux Classes Moyennes et à l'Industrie: B.P. 3105, Kinshasa-Kalina; f. 1947; cap. 500m. Zaires.

Société de Crédit Foncier: Lubumbashi; f. 1961.

Société Zaïroise de Banque S.Z.R.L.: blvd. 30 Juin, B.P. 400, Kinshasa; cap. 0.6m. Zaires; taken over by government in August 1971.

Société Zaïroise de Financement et de Développement (SOFIDE): f. 1970; cap. $4m.; partly state-owned; Pres. E. MAMBU.

Union Zaïroise de Banques S.A.R.L.: 19 ave. de la Nation, Kinshasa; f. 1929; cap. 800,000 Zaires; dep. 11.75m.; Dir.-Gen. GERARD GODEFROID.

INSURANCE

FOREIGN COMPANIES

All foreign insurance companies were closed by presidential decree from December 31st, 1966.

TRADE AND INDUSTRY

CHAMBERS OF COMMERCE

Chambre de Commerce de Boma: Boma.

Chambre du Commerce de l'Equateur: B.P. 127, Mbandaka; f. 1926; 64 mem. societies; Pres. J. BOSEKOTA.

Chambre du Commerce, de l'Industrie et de l'Agriculture de l'Ituri: Bunia; f. 1932; Pres. LOUIS BEAUTHIER; Sec. HENRI GROVEN; publ. monthly bulletin in French.

Chambre de Commerce, d'Industrie et d'Agriculture du Kasai à Kananga: P.O.B. 194, Kananga; f. 1946; publ. monthly bulletin.

Chambre du Commerce et de l'Industrie du Shaba: B.P. 972, Lubumbashi; f. 1910; Pres. S. MAWAWA; Sec. A. HISETTE; 225 mems.; publ. monthly bulletin in French.

Chambre de Commerce et d'Industrie de Bukavu: P.O. Box 321, Bukavu; f. 1931; Chair. PH. MOREL DE WESTGAVER; Sec. R. BASTIN; publ. *Monthly Bulletin.*

Chambre de Commerce et d'Industrie de Kinshasa: P.O.B. 7247, 10 avenue des Aviateurs, Kinshasa; f. 1921; Pres. H. T. TUMBA; Sec. J. M. VAN LEEUW; 400 mems.; publ. bulletin in French.

Chambre de Commerce de Matadi: B.P. 145, Matadi; f. 1959; Chair. CH. VAN GOETHEM; Vice-Pres. A. WYNANT-VERPEUT; Sec. H. WAGEMANS; 103 mems.; publ. monthly *Bulletin.*

Chambre du Commerce, de l'Industrie et de l'Agriculture: P.O.B. 358, Kisangani; f. 1939; Pres. G. AUTRIQUE 250 members; publ. monthly bulletin in French.

Chambre du Commerce et de l'Industrie du Tanganyika: B.P. 228, Kamina; 43 mems.; Pres. G. HOSLI; Sec. O. MUKALA.

DEVELOPMENT

MINERALS

La Générale des Carrières et Mines du Zaïre (GÉCAMINES): Lumbumbashi; f. 1967; fully nationalized 1968; took over assets in the Congo of Union Minière du Haut Katanga; production (1970): 385,460 metric tons of copper; Pres. D. KANDOLO; Administrateur Dir.-Gen. P.-CH. DE MERRE.

PETROLEUM

Société Zaïre-Italienne de Raffinage (SOZIR): B.P. 1478, Kinshasa; f. 1963 by agreement between Zairian Government and Italian ANIC; cap. 4,400m. Zaires; 500 employees.

POWER

Societa Italo-Zairese Attività Industriali—SIZAI: avenue Costermans 10, Kinshasa; f. 1963 to advise the Zaire Government on development of the power potential of the Inga rapids; ownership: IRI (Italian state (60 per cent, Impresa Astaldi Estero 40 per cent; first contract awarded 1968 to Impresa Astaldi Estero for creation of a dam on the Van Duren tributary (now called Fwamalo) to produce power through two 58 MW. stations by 1972; four more generators will be added later to total 300 MW. output; SIZAI is now studying the development of a second power plant and an industrial area related to the project, which would include a steel plant.

Société Nationale d'Electricité (SNEL): 49 blvd. du 30 Juin, B.P. 500 Kin I, Kinshasa; state-owned; Gen. Man. M. MUTONDO.

TRADE ASSOCIATIONS

Association des Entrepreneurs du Zaire (ADEZ): B.P. 2361, Kinshasa.

Association Belgo-Zairoise du Textile (ABZT): B.P. 3097, Kinshasa.

Fédération des Entreprises du Zaire (FEZ): B.P. 8634, Kinshasa; f. 1943; Pres. MARCEL MAYNE; Gen. Rep. in Kinshasa JEAN JONCKHEERE.

MEMBERS

Association des Entreprises de l'Equateur (ADEQUA): B.P. 1052, Mbandaka.

Association des Entreprises de l'Est du Zaïre (AEEZ): B.P. 2467, Bukavu; Pres. M. GUERIN.

Association des Entreprises de l'Ouest du Zaïre (AEOZ): B.P. 8634, Kinshasa; 163 mems.

Association des Entreprises du Kasai (A.E.Kas.): B.P. 649; Kananga; Pres. M. BRUYNEEL.

Association des Entreprises du Shaba (ADES): B.P. 2056, Bâtiment Immokat, ave. H. du Kasai, Lubumbashi; 104 mems.; Dir. B. GUILLAUME.

Association des Entrepreneurs du Zaïre (ADEZ): c/o Sesomo, B.P. 2361, Kinshasa.

Association Belgo-Zaïroise du Textile (ABZT): B.P. 3097, Kinshasa.

Fédération d'Entreprises du Zaïre (FEZ): 82 blvd. du 30 Juin, B.P. 8634, Kinshasa.

TRADE UNIONS

Union Nationale des Travailleurs Zaïrois (UTZ): B.P. 8814, Kinshasa; f. 1967 as the sole syndical organization; Sec.-Gen. ANDRÉ BO-BOLIKO; publs. *Notre Droit, Formation.*

Principal Affiliated Unions:

Alliance des Prolétaires Indépendants du Zaïre (APIZ): 2 avenue de la Kéthule, B.P. 8721, Kinshasa; f. 1946; 6,400 mems.; Sec. JOSEPH KIMPIATU.

Centrale des Enseignants Zaïrois (CEZ): B.P. 8814, Kinshasa; f. 1957; 18,000 mems.; Sec. FERDINAND TOTO-ZITA; Publ. *Pedagogia.*

Centrale des Mines et Métallurgie: B.P. 8814, Kinshasa; f. 1965; 24,000 mems.; Sec. SEBASTIEN KALAIA.

Centrale des Plantations et Alimentation: B.P. 8814, Kinshasa; f. 1962; 24,000 mems.; Sec. DONAT MUTUMBO..

Centrale des Services Publics: B.P. 8814, Kinshasa; f. 1957, 12,000 mems.; Sec. CAMILLE IFELO.

Centrale des Travailleurs du Transport: B.P. 8814, Kinshasa; f. 1959; 38,000 mems.; Sec. JEAN LUYEYE.

Fédération Nationale des Agents sous Contrat de l'Etat (FNACE): B.P. 970, Kinshasa; f. 1964; 20,000 mems.; Pres. A. LINGULU; Sec. M. MONTINGIA.

Fédération Nationale des Employés Commerciaux et Cadres (FNECC): B.P. 970, Kinshasa; f. 1961; Pres. FRANÇOIS TOKO.

Fédération des Ouvriers des Mines du Zaïre (FOMIZ): Kisangani; f. 1964; Sec.-Gen. THOMAS KALOMBO.

Syndicat du Bâtiment du Zaïre (SYBAZ): Ngiri-Ngiri, Kinshasa; f. 1961; Pres. JOSEPH MULOWAYE; Sec. ALPHONSE KADIMA.

Syndicat National des Travailleurs Zaïrois (SNTZ): 398 avenue van Eetveld, B.P. 2077, Kinshasa; f. 1959; 2,000 mems.; Pres. ALPHONSE KITHIMA.

TRADE FAIR

Kinshasa International Trade Fair: Kinshasa; held annually in July.

MAJOR INDUSTRIAL COMPANIES

The following are some of the largest companies in terms either of capital investment or employment.

Brasseries, Limonaderies et Malteries du Zaïre (BRALIMA): B.P. 7246, 912 ave. Olsen, Kinshasa; f. 1926; cap. 1,350,000 Zaires.
Production of beer, soft drinks and ice.
Pres. of Administrative Council THOMAS TUMBA; Dir. ACHILLE DESCAMPS; 2,100 employees.

CIBA S.Z.R.L., Zaire: B.P. 3674, Lubumbashi; subsidiary of CIBA A.G., Basle.
Distribution of pharmaceutical products.

Société Commerciale et Minière du Zaïre S.A.: B.P. 499, Kinshasa; subsidiary of Lonrho Limited.
Engineering, motor trade, insurance, assembly and sale of earth-moving equipment.

Société Zaïro-Italienne de Raffinage (SOZIR): B.P. 1478, Kinshasa; f. 1963; cap. 4,400m. Zaires.
Oil refinery.
500 employees.

Société Zaïroise des Pétroles Shell: B.P. 2799, 1513 blvd. du 30 juin, Kinshasa; f. 1929; cap. 1,100,000 Zaires.
Import and distribution of petroleum products.
Pres. Dir.-Gen. H. J. E. BECKER; 603 employees.

Société de Recherche et d'Exploitation des Pétroles au Zaïre (SOREPZA): B.P. 700, Kinshasa.
Mining of petroleum oil.

BAT Zaire S.A.R.L.: B.P. 621, Kinshasa; wholly owned subsidiary of British American Tobacco Company Ltd., London.
Manufacture of tobacco products.

Société Générale des Carrières et Mines du Zaïre (GÉCAMINES): blvd. du 30 juin, Kinshasa; nationalized mining company; cap. 104,700m. Zaires.
Major Zairian producer of copper and associated metals.

IBM-Zaire, S.Z.A.R.L.: B.P. 7563, 6 ave. du Port, Kinshasa; f. 1954; cap. 50,000 Zaires.
Sale and maintenance of computers and business machines and associated materials.
Dir.-Gen. ROGER MAZUIR; 200 employees.

Société Minière du Tenke-Fungurume: f. 1970 by international consortium comprising Charter Consolidated of London, Government of Zaire, Amoco Minerals, Mitsui of Japan, Bureau de Recherches Géologiques et Minières de France and Léon Tempelsman and Son (U.S.A.).
Copper mining.

Les Margarineries et Savonneries Zaïroises: B.P. 8914, 1 ave. Banning; f. 1922; subsidiary of Unilever Zaire; Manufacture of vegetable oil products.
Pres. E. F. J. CHAVASSE; 1,200 employees.

Société Minière de Bakwanga (MIBA): B.P. 8633, 12 ave. des Aviateurs, Kinshasa; Congolese Government owns 50 per cent of share capital; produces 60 per cent of world's industrial diamonds.

Les Plantations Lever du Zaïre: B.P. 8611, 16 ave. Van Gèle, Kinshasa; f. 1911; subsidiary of Unilever Zaire.
Plantations of oil palm and cocoa, and livestock farming.
Pres. L. CÉSAR; 21,000 employees.

Compagnie Sucrière du Zaïre: B.P. 10, Moerbeke-Kwilu, Lower Zaire; f. 1961; cap. 1,200,000 Zaires.
Manufacture of sugar, alcohol and carbon dioxide.
Pres. ROBERT LIPPENS; Dir. GUY DUEZ; 4,466 employees.

TRANSPORT AND TOURISM

RAILWAYS

Total length of railways: 5,174 km., including 500 km. of electrified rail. A link between Ilebo and Matadi is planned. The Zaire system is also linked to Lobito via the Benguela Railway, and Beira via Zambia, Rhodesia and Mozambique.

Compagnie des Chemins de Fer Kinshasa-Dilolo-Lubumbashi (KDL): P.O.B. 297, Lubumbashi; administers the following sections: Sakania Border–Bukama 710 km.; Bukama–Ilebo 1,123 km.; Tenke-Dilolo-Border 522 km.; Kamina–Kabongo 201 km. Of these 2,556 km., 859 km. are electrified; in the near future the non-electrified lines will be equipped with Diesel engines. Pres. J. NGALULA.

Soc. Zaïroise des Chemins de Fer des Grands Lacs (formerly *C.F.L.*): B.P. 230, Kamina, Shaba; f. 1965; administers the Kisangani–Bubundu, Kindu–Kamina and Kabalo–Kasongo lines; rail services, 1,086 km.; river and Lake Tanganyika services; Pres. L. POSCOL; Man. M. GODEFROID.

Office d'Exploitation des Transports au Zaïre (OTRAZ): Regd. Office: blvd. du 30 juin, Kinshasa; operates the Kinshasa–Matadi rail link; Pres. P. KABASUBABO.

Chemin de Fer de Matadi-Kinshasa (C.F.M.K.): Head Office: P.O.B. 98, Kinshasa; length of track, 366 km.

Chemin de Fer du Mayumbe (C.F.M.): Administrative offices in Boma; length of track, 140 km.; Dir. A. DOVELLE.

Soc. des Chemins de Fer Vicinaux du Zaïre (C.V.Z.): 5 rue de la Science, 1040 Brussels, Belgium; Zaire office: Aketi; length of track, 1,020 km.

Benguela Railway Co.: Rua do Ataide 7, Lisbon 2, Portugal; Lubumbashi; 781 ave. du Kasai, B.P. 1047; 2,093 km. to Lobito on Angolan coast.

ROADS

There are approximately 145,213 km. of motor roads in Zaire (approx. 94,300 cars and lorries in 1971). In general road conditions are poor, owing to inadequate maintenance since 1958.

Road Transport

Chief companies are:

Soc. Zaïroise des Chemins de Fer du Grand Lac (*see* Railways above): Road services between Cisumbura and Kigali and from Samba to Tongoni.

OTRAZ: Head Office: P.O.B. 98, Kinshasa; regular service between Kalunda (Uvira) and Bukavu (140 km.), Boma and Tshela (140 km.); Pres. L. M. CARLOS.

C.V.Z.: 5 rue de la Science, Brussels; Road Management: Isiro, Upper Zaire; passenger and goods service in the Upper Zaire and Kivu provinces; network of 14,973 km.

INLAND WATERWAYS

For over 1,600 km. the River Zaire is navigable. Above the Stanley Falls the Zaire changes its name to Lualaba, and is used for shipping on a 965-km. stretch from Bubundu to Kindu and Kongolo to Bukama. (There is a railway from Matadi, the principal port on the lower Zaire, to Kinshasa.) The total length of inland waterways is 16,400 km.

Soc. Zaïroise des Chemins de Fer du Grand Lac (*see* Railways above): River Lualaba services, Bubundu–Kindu and Kongolo–Malemba N'kula; Lake Tanganyika services, Kamina – Kigoma – Kalundu – Moba–Mpulungu.

Zaire Network: services on the Luapula and Lake Mweru.

East African Railways and Harbours: services on Lake Mobutu Sese Seko.

Office d'Exploitation des Transports au Zaïre (OTRAZ): River Communications Office: boulevard du 30 juin, Kinshasa; passenger, mail and cargo services over 12,000 km.

SHIPPING

The principal seaports are Matadi, Banana and Boma on the lower Zaire. Matadi is linked by rail with Kinshasa. Much of the mineral trade is shipped from Lobito in Angola, however, and does not pass through Zaire's ports.

Compagnie Maritime Belge: B.P. 264, Matadi, and P.O.B. 33, Boma; weekly service Antwerp to Matadi and Boma, monthly service New York and Gulf ports to Matadi and Boma.

Compagnie Maritime du Zaïre: Matadi, P.O.B. 9496, Kinshasa; f. 1967; managed by Compagnie Maritime Belge; services to Antwerp, North Continental Range to East Africa, U.S.A., Mediterranean ports to West Africa; Chair. LIONDJO FATAKI.

Office d'Exploitation des Transports au Zaïre (OTRAZ): blvd. du 30 juin, Kinshasa; administers the port of Matadi.

CIVIL AVIATION

There are international airports at Kinshasa, Lubumbashi and Kamina.

Air Zaire, SARL: 4 ave. du Port, B.P. 10120, Kinshasa; f. 1960; national airline; Pres. JACQUES MASSANGU.

Agence et Messageries Aeriennes Zaïroises (AMAZ) S.P.R.L.: P.O.B. 671, Kinshasa, charter and regular services, Man. Dirs. J.-J. KANOE, R. LINARD, P. DAUISTER.

Foreign Airlines

Air France, Air Afrique, Alitalia, B.O.A.C., East Africa Airways, Iberian, K.L.M., P.A.A., Sabena, Swissair and U.T.A. provide services to Kinshasa.

TOURISM

Bureau International du Tourisme et des Echanges pour les Jeunes (BITEJ): Kinsako, Kinshasa; f. 1967; travel organization for young people in Zaire and abroad.

Commissariat Général au Tourisme de la République du Zaïre: 54 ave. Lothaire, B.P. 9502, Kinshasa.

CULTURAL ORGANIZATION

Centre Culturel du Zaïre: Balari No. 20, Bandalungwa, Kinshasa; aims to promote Bantu culture; publ. *Académie des Arts et Métiers*.

EDUCATION

LEARNED SOCIETIES AND RESEARCH INSTITUTES

Alliance Française: B.P. 2-289, Kinshasa.

Centre d'Etude des Problèmes Sociaux Indigènes (C.E.P.S.I.): B.P. 1873, Lubumbashi; f. 1946; to study problems arising from the social evolution of the inhabitants of Zaire.

Goethe-Institut: B.P. 7465, Kinshasa; f. 1962; Dir. HELMUT SCHMIDT.

Institut Géographique du Zaïre: 106 blvd. du 30 Juin, B.P. 3086, Kinshasa-Kalina; f. 1949; geodetic, topographical and cartographical studies; staff of 334; small library; Dir.-Gen. RENÉ KISUMUNA; Sec. L. DEGLAS.

Institut de Médecine Tropicale: Kinshasa; f. 1899; biochemical and clinical research; the Inter-African Permanent Bureau for tsetse sickness and trypanosomiasis is housed in the same building; Dir. Dr. SRIJN.

Institut National pour l'Etude et la Recherche Agronomique (INERA): B.P. 2015, Kisangani; f. 1933 to promote the scientific development of agriculture.

Institut pour la Recherche Scientifique en Afrique Centrale (I.R.S.A.C.): Lwiro, D.S. Bukavu; f. 1947; principal stations are at Lwiro, D.S. Bukavu (botany, zoology, medicine, sociology and seismology), Mabali, on Lake Tumba (botany, climatology), and Lubumbashi (biochemistry, parasitology); library of 4,300 vols.; Dir.-Gen. Dr. P. KUNKEL; publs. *Rapport Annuel, Chronique de l'I.R.S.A.C.*

Institut de la Conservation de la Nature: B.P. 4019, Kinshasa II; name changed 1969 from *Institut des Parcs Nationaux*; protection of national parks and conservation of the environment; Dir. Dr.Sc. J. VERSCHUREN.

Office National de la Recherche et du Développement: 33 ave. du Comité Urbain, B.P. 3474, Kinshasa/Kalina; f. 1967; applied research in science and technology; 690 mems.; library of 2,000 vols.; Pres. J. ILEO; Sec.-Gen. F. MALU; publs. _Revue NEM, Revue Dombi,_ bulletin of current research results.

Service Géologique: B.P. 898, 44 avenue des Huileries, Kinshasa 1; f. 1939; staff of 250 undertake mineral exploration and geological mapping; library of 7,000 vols.; Dir. GABRIEL DEMBE; publ. _Bulletin et Mémoire._

U.S. Information Center: coin des Avenues Charles de Gaulle et Kasavubu, Kinshasa.

LIBRARIES AND ARCHIVES

Archives de Zaïre: 10 blvd. Léopold II, B.P. 3090, Kinshasa: f. 1949.

Bibliothèque Centrale de l'Université Nationale, Campus de Kinshasa: B.P. 125, Kinshasa XI; f. 1954; 300,000 vols.; Chief Librarian F. J. LEROY, S.J.

Bibliothèque Centrale de l'Université Nationale, Campus de Kisangani: B.P. 2012, Kisangani; 26,000 vols.; Chief Librarian Miss M. WILLEMS.

Bibliothèque Centrale de l'Université Nationale, Campus de Lubumbashi: P.O.B. 2896, Lubumbashi; f. 1955; 60,000 vols.; Librarian JEAN ETÈVENAUX.

Bibliothèque Publique: B.P. 410, Kinshasa; f. 1932; Librarian B. MONGU; 24,000 vols.

MUSEUMS

Institut des Musées Nationaux: B.P. 4249, Kinshasa II; formerly **Musée de la Vie Indigène;** Dir.-Gen. L. CAHEN.

Musée Régional: B.P. 739, Lubumbashi, Katanga.

There are museums at Kisangani, Mbadaka and Kananga.

UNIVERSITIES

UNIVERSITÉ NATIONALE, CAMPUS DE KINSHASA
B.P. 125, KINSHASA, XI

Telephone: 30-123.

Founded 1954.

The University was founded by the Université Catholique de Louvain in collaboration with the Government; reorganized 1971.

Language of instruction: French; Academic year: October to July.

President: Mgr. J. A. MALULA, Archbishop of Kinshasa.

Vice-President: A. NDELE.

Rector: Mgr. T. TSHIBANGU.

Vice-Rector: A. ELUNGU.

Secretarys-General: M. PLEVOETS, A. MPASSE.

Librarian: E. NEVEN.

Number of teachers: 369.
Number of students: 3,612.

Publications: _Lovanium_ (irregular), _Studia Universitatis Lovanium_ (irregular), _Cahiers Economiques et Sociaux_ (quarterly), _Cahiers des Religions Africaines_ (weekly), _Etudes d'Histoire Africaine_ (yearly).

DEANS:

Faculty of Theology: A. VANNESTE.

Faculty of Medicine: J. BOUCKAERT.

Faculty of Law: J. VERHAEGEN.

Faculty of Philosophy and Letters: H. SILVESTRE.

Faculty of Sciences: J. CHARETTE.

Faculty of Economic and Social Sciences: M. NORRO.

Polytechnic Faculty: A. GUISSARD.

Faculty of Agricultural Sciences: A. PIETERS.

Faculty of Psychological and Pedagogic Sciences: L. MISSINNE.

ATTACHED INSTITUTES:

Institut de recherches économiques et sociales (I.R.E.S.): B.P. 257, Kinshasa XI; Dir. H. LECLERQ.

Centre d'études des littératures romanes d'inspiration africaine (CELRIA): B.P. 126, Kinshasa XI; Dir. V. BOL.

Centre d'études de droit comparé africain (CEDCA): B.P. 202, Kinshasa XI.

Centre d'études des religions africaines: B.P. 756, Kinshasa XI; Dir. V. MULAGO.

Centre TRICO (Recherches atomiques): B.P. 184, Kinshasa XI; Dir. F. MALU.

Bibliotheque Centrale: (_see_ Libraries).

UNIVERSITÉ NATIONALE, CAMPUS DE LUBUMBASHI
B.P. 1825, LUBUMBASHI

Telephone: 5404-7.

Founded 1955; reorganized 1971.

Language of instruction: French; State control; Academic year: October to July (October–February, March–July).

Rector: RENÉ DEKKERS.

Vice-Rector: M. NGOMA.

Secretary-General: A. MAKANDA.

Librarian: JEAN ETÈVENAUX.

Number of teachers: 261.

Number of students: 2,952.

AFFILIATED INSTITUTES:

Centre d'Etudes des Sols de l'Afrique Centrale: includes Chemistry, Microbiology, Zoology, Botany, Geomorphology, Physics, Agronomy.

Centre de Recherches d'Hydrobiologie Fondamentale et Appliquée.

UNIVERSITÉ NATIONALE, CAMPUS DE KISANGANI

B.P. 2012, KISANGANI
Telephone: 2923.

Founded 1963; reorganized 1971
(formerly Université Libre du Congo).

State control; Language of instruction: French; Academic
year: October to July (two terms).

Rector: Dr. L. MOLET.
Vice-Rector: KOLI ELOMBE MOTOKUA.
Administrative Secretary: Dr. M'VUENDY MABEKI NTU.
Secretary of Academic Affairs: Dr. MPIUTU NE MBODI.
Librarian: M. E. WILLEMS.

Number of teachers: 101.
Number of students: 1,001.

COLLEGES

(As a result of the reform in higher education most of the
following institutions are now part of the National
University).

Centre National de Formation Météorologique: Kinshasa;
f. 1960; courses in meteorology and weather fore-
casting; library of 8,500 vols.; 5 teachers, 22 students;
publs. *Meteo-Zaïre* and *Ionosphere* (both monthly);
Dir. M. CLEREBAUT.

Ecole d'Art: B.P. 58, Mushenge, Kasai; f. 1951; general
four-year training in Bakuba sculpture; aims to preserve traditional art; museum and library of 300 vols.;
3 teachers, 40 students; Dir. Fr. L. HERBERS, C.J.;
publs. *National Geographique, Afrique Chrétienne,
Nieuwe Revue, Elsevier, Eléments d'Art Bakuba.*

Ecole Nationale d'Administration—E.N.D.A.: Dépêche
Spéciale, Binza-Kinshasa; f. 1960 by the UN Legal
Advisory Commission, Congolese Government and
Ford Foundation to train Congolese for the magistracy
and public administration.

Rector: A. WEMBI.
Secretary-General: MPIA NDA-NGYE.
Director of Studies: M. BOUTEILLE.
Librarian: C. TSHIAMALA.

Library of 40,000 vols.
Number of teachers (full-time): 30.
Number of students: 550.

Publication: *Revue Zaïroise d'Administration* (quarterly).

Ecole Nationale des Postes et Télécommunications: B.P.
7248, Kinshasa; f. 1967; trains personnel in technical,
operator and postal skills at all levels; helped by UN
Special Fund; Dir.-Gen. V. MUKADI; 56 teachers, 322
students; library of 3,700 vols.

Institut National des Mines: B.P. 3131, Bukavu; f. 1962;
4-year courses in mining and geological engineering;
library of 4,000 vols.; 28 teachers, 140 students;
Dir.-Gen. J.-P. MBOMA-MUYOLO; Sec.-Gen. J.-L.
OSUNGU.

**Institut National des Bâtiments et des Travaux Publics
(I.N.B.T.P.):** B.P. 8815, Kinshasa Binza; f. 1961;
courses for building and public works engineers;
library of 9,000 vols.; 37 teachers, 173 students; Dir.-
Gen. J. ALBINI; Sec.-Gen. N. FATAKI.

Institut National d'Etudes Politiques: B.P. 2307, Kinshasa
I; f. 1960; correspondence and evening courses, documentation centre, specialized library; 50 teachers, 561
students; Pres. Dr. NGWETE; Dir.-Gen. Dr. MANDALA;
publs. *Etudes Zaïroises, Vie du Tiers-Monde, Informations Civiques.*

Institut Pédagogique National: Djelo, Binza, Kinshasa;
f. 1961 with the help of technical and financial aid by
UNOC (UN Operations in the Congo); 50 students have
started two-year courses to train as secondary school
teachers and education officers; also short courses for
primary school teachers.

Institut National des Travaux Publics, Section: B.P. 8249,
Kinshasa I; f. 1962; 5-year diploma courses in architecture; Dir. Fr. C. VANDERMEEREN; 23 teachers.

Institut Supérieur des Arts Plastiques—ISAP: Académie
des Beaux-Arts, B.P. 8249, Kinshasa; f. 1967; 4-year
diploma courses in painting, sculpture or ceramics;
Dir. Fr. J. CORNET; 12 teachers.

National Academy of Music and Dramatic Art: Kinshasa;
f. 1968; courses in music, speech and drama and oral
literature; 350 students.

SELECT BIBLIOGRAPHY

ACHERSON, NOEL. *The King Incorporated: Leopold II in the Age of Trusts*. London, Allen & Unwin, 1963.

ANSTEY, ROGER. *King Leopold's Legacy: The Congo under Belgian Rule*, 1908–1960. London, O.U.P. for the I.R.R., 1966.
"The Congo Rebellion", *The World Today*, April 1965.

BUSTIN, E. "The Congo", in CARTER, G. M. (Ed.), *Five African States*. New York, Cornell U.P., 1963.

COOKEY, S. J. S. *Great Britain and the Congo question*, 1892–1913. London, Longmans, 1968.

GÉRARD-LIBOIS, JULES. *Katanga Secession*, trans. by Rebecca Young. Madison and London, University of Wisconsin Press, 1966.

GILLE, A. "La Politique indigène du Congo-Belge et du Ruanda-Urundi", in *Encyclopédie du Congo Belge*, III, pp. 709–48.

GOUROU, PIERRE. *La Population du Congo*. Paris, Hachette, 1966.

HOSKYNS, CATHERINE. *The Congo since Independence, January 1960–December 1961*. London, O.U.P. for Royal Institute of International Affairs, 1965.

KANZA, THOMAS. *Conflict in the Congo. The Rise and Fall of Lumumba*, Harmondsworth, Penguin, 1972.

LACROIX, J. L. *Industrialisation au Congo*. Kinshasa, Institut des recherches économiques et sociales, 1965. *Les poles du développement*. Kinshasa, IRES, 1966.

LEMARCHAND, RENÉ. *Political Awakening in the Belgian Congo: the Politics of Fragmentation*. Berkeley and Los Angeles, University of California Press, 1964.

LOUIS, WM. R., and STENGERS, J. *E. D. Morel's History of the Congo Reform Association*, Oxford, Clarendon Press, 1968.

LUMUMBA, PATRICE. *Congo My Country*. London, Praeger, 1963.

PONS, V. G., XYDIAS, NELLY, and CLEMENT, P. "Social Effects of Urbanization in Stanleyville, Belgian Congo: Preliminary Report of the Field Research Team of the International African Institute", forming Part III of FORDE, DARYLL (Ed.), *Social Implications of Industrialization and Urbanization in Africa South of the Sahara*, pp. 229–492. Paris, UNESCO, 1956.

SLADE, RUTH. *English-Speaking Missions in the Congo Independent State* (1878–1908). Brussels Académie Royale des Sciences Coloniales, 1959.
King Leopold's Congo. London, O.U.P. for the I.R.R., 1961.

TURNBULL, C. M. *The Lonely African*. London, Chatto & Windus, 1963.

VERHAEGEN, B. *Rebellions au Congo*, Vol. 1. Brussels, Etudes du CRISP (1967).

WEISS, HERBERT F. *Political Protest in the Congo: the Parti Solidaire Africain during the Independence Struggle*. Princeton, Princeton University Press, 1967.

YOUNG, CRAWFORD. *Politics in the Congo: Decolonization and Independence*. Princeton, Princeton University Press, 1965.

For the detailed study of recent Zaire history *see* the annual collection of documents, together with the commentary, published by the Centre de Recherche et d'Information Socio-Politique (CRISP), Brussels, starting with *Congo 1959*.

Zambia

PHYSICAL AND SOCIAL GEOGRAPHY

D. Hywel Davies

Zambia, an independent republic within the Commonwealth since 1964, occupies tropical high plateau country in south-central Africa. Situated far inland and served by tenuous transportation links with foreign seaports to east, west and south, it is poorly located for selling copper, its only significant export, and for importing essential capital and consumer goods. Forming the head of a southward-thrusting wedge of truly independent black states, Zambia is equally vulnerable geopolitically, her opposition to white-ruled southern Africa tempered by present, if fast diminishing, dependence upon southern-controlled routes and hydroelectricity, and by military weakness. Zambia's non-aligned and non-racial policies rest upon ideological conviction, sharpened by geographical confrontation, and find expression in accelerated trade re-orientation from traditional southern to developing northern routes.

PHYSICAL FEATURES

Gently undulating plateaux, mostly between 915 and 1,500 metres m.s.l. and separated by gentle slopes or dissected escarpment zones, dominate the scenery. Mantled with thickly accumulated debris and mostly clothed with secondary woodland of stunted, mixed deciduous and evergreen trees, these surfaces represent ages of gradation, interspersed with periods of uplift accompanied by warping. Wide shallow basins with lakes, swamps and grassy plains, and isolated hills and ranges, break the monotony, as do more recently incised river valleys. In the west unconsolidated Kalahari sands were deposited by wind in great depth. Certain areas also developed rift block valleys at lower elevation, particularly along the Luangwa and middle Zambezi and their subsidiary valleys.

Three-quarters of Zambia drains to the Zambezi. From the Barotse floodplain the river flows south and then east along the Rhodesian border, plunging over the Victoria Falls to enter a gorge section now largely occupied by the 274-km., man-made Lake Kariba. The Kafue river drains the Copperbelt, flowing south through swamp, game park, floodplain and, finally gorge section to the Zambezi. The Kafue supplies much water for mines and towns of the railway zone (the remainder coming from boreholes). The other main tributary, the Luangwa, flows through its drier, undeveloped rifted valley and another game park. Northern Zambia mostly drains to the Congo, from the Chambeshi river in the north-east, through the Bangweulu lake, *sudd* and swamp complex, and north via the Luapula river. Zambian rivers show marked seasonal discharge variation, with February–May peaks after the rains take effect and October–

November low water before they begin. Disrupted by rapids and falls, they are little used for commercial navigation. Important plateau features are *dambos*—shallow, linear, moisture-retaining concavities that provide dry-season water and thus influence rural settlement patterns.

Soils are widely infertile—over-mature on much of the plateau, eroded and immature in escarpment zones, virtually worthless on Kalahari sands. Yet much plateau country supports traditional shifting cultivation, basically because of overall sparse population. Along the railway in Southern Province, and also in Eastern Province, fertile red clays and red-brown loams support commercial farming with crops such as maize, tobacco and groundnuts. But, in general, accessibility has been more critical locationally than soil quality.

NATURAL RESOURCES

Zambia, with a 70 per cent rural population, has as its basic resource land, most of which is still used traditionally. Notwithstanding widespread poor soils, tropical valleys and ameliorated plateau climates, with their ample sunshine, permit cultivation of various tropical, sub-tropical and temperate crops, including maize, cassava, groundnuts, millet, various fruits and vegetables, cotton, tobacco and sugar. Native cattle can be herded in most areas free of tsetse fly, while small herds of mixed Angoni-European breeds thrive on commercial farms. With little irrigation developed and rainfall totals (increasing northward from 60 to over 140 cm.) generally sufficient, it is the long dry season that principally limits farming.

The major rivers and lakes support subsistence and haphazardly commercial fishing, but little commercial navigation. However, water resources are vital for power production for mines and towns. Today most electricity comes from the Kariba Dam (shared with Rhodesia); future needs will increasingly be met from the all-Zambian Kafue Dam which was opened in 1971, expansion at Kariba and more small plants.

Zambia has various minerals, mostly in limited quantities. These include cobalt, manganese, silver, iron, limestone, clays and building sands. The recently developed Maamba coalfield (Zambezi Valley) enabled Rhodesian imports to be claimed as phased out during 1970. Lead and zinc mining at Kabwe (Broken Hill) is ailing but remains important. Copper, however, totally dominates mining and the national economy, accounting in 1971 for 93 per cent of domestic exports. Zambia was formally the world's third largest copper producer, but fell back to fourth place in 1970, when production dropped to 684,000 metric tons.

The major geographical division in the country remains that between the colonially developed, central "line of rail", including the Copperbelt, Broken Hill mine, the capital city (Lusaka), the commercial farming zone and all sizeable towns, and the still barely developing "bush" of the country's vast flanking "wings".

POPULATION AND CULTURE

According to 1972 figures, 4,515,000 people occupy some 290,000 sq. miles at an average density of only six per sq. km. Seventy per cent live in rural Zambia, where remote tracts are virtually unpopulated while limited areas exceed their carrying capacity under traditional cultivation. One-third live in urban centres on the line of rail, the largest being the three cities, Lusaka (estimated population 347,900 in 1970), Kitwe and Ndola. With rising expectations, larger centres are growing too quickly through migration, and mushrooming peri-urban shanty settlements indicate growing social problems, for rural migrants lack skills for urban jobs, even where these are available.

Over 98 per cent of the people are African, still largely illiterate, and divided by many tribal groupings and tongues of the Bantu group. Europeans, nearly all contract expatriates, form the main minority group of around 50,000, and there are an estimated 12,000 Asians. All minorities live overwhelmingly in towns, exercising a considerable, but relatively declining, influence in business, commerce and the civil service.

As a result of prolonged mission activity, most Africans are Christians, but increasing autonomy characterizes the churches today. Asians are mostly Hindus or Moslems.

The most pressing human resource problem is to harness the small, scattered, parochially divided and under-educated manpower for national development. Solving this problem is rightly accorded considerable developmental priority, but the low baseline imposed by colonial neglect makes this a formidable task: it is, however, a prerequisite for effectively harnessing Zambia's substantial physical resources.

RECENT HISTORY

Andrew D. Roberts

The Republic of Zambia came into existence in 1964, when independence was granted to the British Protectorate of Northern Rhodesia. This had been administered by the Colonial Office since 1924; before that, the territory had been administered for a quarter of a century by the British South Africa Company. The subjection of what is now Zambia to colonial rule was a late phase in the expansion of British power in southern Africa, and throughout most of its colonial history the territory was closely linked to the economic and political institutions of Rhodesia and South Africa.

THE BRITISH SOUTH AFRICA COMPANY

The main impetus to British intrusion north of the Zambezi came from the South African millionaire Cecil Rhodes. Rhodes wanted to see the high plateaux of central and eastern Africa under British rule and settlement; he also wanted to annex to his personal mining empire the copper deposits of Katanga, and the gold deposits between the Limpopo and Zambezi. The British government, concerned as it was with maintaining British supremacy at the Cape, was anxious to prevent the Boers, Portuguese or Germans from creating hostile alliances further north. Thus in 1889 it granted a Charter to Rhodes's newly-formed British South Africa Company, giving it powers to make treaties and conduct administration north of the Limpopo. In 1890 the Company occupied the eastern part of what became Southern Rhodesia, south of the Zambezi, and meanwhile it had obtained treaties and concessions from various African chiefs north of the Zambezi. Rhodes's agents were unsuccessful in

Katanga, which fell instead to King Leopold II of Belgium, but their agreements elsewhere served to place most of what became Northern Rhodesia firmly within a British sphere of influence.

The Company's most important agreements in Northern Rhodesia were with Lewanika, King of the extensive Lozi kingdom on the upper Zambezi. In order to secure protection both against Portuguese and Ndebele, and against rivals at home, Lewanika had made a concession in 1890, whereby he expected to receive British military, financial and technical aid in return for granting limited rights over mineral deposits and Lozi external relations. A British Resident did not arrive until 1897, but in 1900 a new treaty provided the Lozi kingdom with an important degree of internal autonomy, even though this was somewhat reduced in later years. In the north and east, Company claims had to be made good in a number of minor battles, for their only treaties were with chiefs of no great importance. On the plateau south of Lake Tanganyika, the dominant power were the Bemba, whose chiefs had traded much in ivory and slaves. Their political unity, however, fluctuated considerably, and in 1897–99 Company officials contrived to subdue them after a few skirmishes with border chiefs. East of the Luangwa river, conflict was precipitated by the demands of white settlers in the nearby British Central Africa Protectorate (later Nyasaland), and in 1898 a Company force marched against the Ngoni of Chief Mpezeni. These warriors offered united resistance, but their tactics proved ineffective against artillery and machine guns.

The British South Africa Company did little with

Northern Rhodesia, and it derived small profit from its administration of the territory. Prospectors located several surface deposits of copper (most of which had previously been exploited by Africans), but the costs of transport to the coast inhibited small-scale operations, while the large investments needed for profitable development went instead to more payable workings in Katanga. It was in fact these mines which proved the most dynamic new influence on Northern Rhodesia up to the 1920s. By 1909 a railway had been built across the territory into Katanga, which thus gained its first rail link with the coast—through the Rhodesias. The Katanga mines exported their copper south to Beira; they obtained coke from Wankie; and they were supplied with maize and beef by the white farmers who settled in a tsetse-free belt along the railway north of the Zambezi. A few other whites settled in Ngoni country, where they raised tobacco, but in general white enterprise was of no great significance. The revenues of the Company administration were heavily dependent on taxing the African population, who with few or no opportunities to earn cash near home were induced to seek work in the mines of Katanga, Southern Rhodesia and South Africa. Here and there, especially in the remoter areas, the imposition of tax provoked small-scale African resistance, in face of which Company officials often resorted to violence. It was not until about 1910 that their authority was recognized throughout Northern Rhodesia.

More effective opposition to Company rule came from the white settlers, who resented the Company's restrictive policies on land and mineral rights. By 1921 the European population had risen to 3,500, but they were represented in government only through an Advisory Council. Their leaders opposed the imposition of income tax in 1920, but this measure itself reflected the Company's financial difficulties (which had been increased by defence costs during the First World War). In 1924 the Company transferred its administrative responsibilities in Northern Rhodesia to the Colonial Office. A Legislative Council was now set up, effectively excluding Africans.

THE COPPERBELT

The first ten years of Colonial Office rule witnessed the exploitation on a large scale of the mines generally known as the Copperbelt. The rapid growth of electrical and automobile industries caused a sharp rise in world demand for copper, and geologists began intensive prospecting in Northern Rhodesia. In the late 1920s, huge ore-bodies of copper sulphide were discovered far below the surface at Mufulira, Roan Antelope and Nkana, while a large oxide deposit was found near the surface at Nchanga. The first two mines were opened up by Rhodesia Selection Trust, mostly with American capital; the other two, by the Anglo-American Corporation based in South Africa. The Depression delayed development, but by 1935 the copper industry was firmly established. (Ten years later it was contributing about one-eighth of the non-communist world's total product.) By 1937 there were nearly 20,000 Africans working on the Copper-

belt; skilled labour was provided by Europeans, who numbered about 4,000.

This rapid industrial expansion had profound social and political effects. It reinforced the character of Northern Rhodesia as a vast labour reserve. Most rural areas suffered impoverishment through the absence of able-bodied men in the mines, both within and outside the territory. At the same time, racial conflict sharply increased: for the first time, large numbers of Africans were living and working alongside Europeans in towns within Northern Rhodesia. Africans began to be aware of themselves, not simply as tribesmen, but as an indispensable labour force, with common economic interests. There was a glaring disparity in the treatment of white and black labour, especially since both the mining companies and the government were at pains to discourage long-term African settlement in towns. In 1935 Africans went briefly on strike at three mines; as yet, they lacked the organization for sustained industrial action, but they alarmed European mine-workers into forming an all-white trade union. When this white union struck in 1940, African miners struck again and achieved a modest wage increase. The Government would still not allow African unions, and in the absence of any other effective negotiating machinery Africans formed "welfare societies" throughout the Copperbelt and in towns along the railway line. These were mostly led by an élite of clerks and foremen, but they provided forums for discussing workers' problems; exerted pressure on local authorities; and built up a network of communications which soon extended throughout the territory. In 1946, delegates from both urban and rural areas met in Lusaka (the territorial capital since 1935) and formed a Federation of Welfare Societies.

In 1945 the Second World War ended; a Labour government came to power in Britain; and the pace of political change began to increase. A strike by African railway workers in the same year demonstrated yet again the need for effective machinery for industrial negotiation; African trade unions were eventually authorized; and in 1949 African mine-workers combined in a single union. This showed its strength in a prolonged but peaceful strike in 1952, which resulted in substantial wage increases. Meanwhile, the constitutional future of the territory was being hotly debated. Many Europeans were impatient to throw off Colonial Office rule. Elected members of the Legislative Council were still in a minority, and it seemed that settler control could only be achieved if Northern Rhodesia was amalgamated or federated with the settler government of Southern Rhodesia. And Europeans, no less than Africans, resented the fact that Britain, by taxing the mining companies, had drained millions of pounds out of Northern Rhodesia while making negligible grants for development—despite its great mineral wealth, the territory had been starved of the most basic social services.

NORTHERN RHODESIA CONGRESS

Most Africans, however, opposed any closer links with Southern Rhodesia, precisely because they saw clearly that such links would be used to establish

settler control north of the Zambezi. In particular they
feared that land would be alienated on a large scale, as
it already had been in the south. In the 1940s and
early 1950s these fears provided Africans throughout
Northern Rhodesia with a common political cause. In
1948 the Federation of Welfare Societies was transformed into an expressly political body, the Northern
Rhodesia Congress. Between 1951 and 1953, under the
leadership of Harry Nkumbula, Congress campaigned
vigorously against Federation, and it had the support
of most chiefs, even though these were agents of the
colonial administration. But in 1951 a Conservative
government took office in Britain. This was, for
various reasons, more willing than its Labour predecessor to increase the power of white settlers in
central Africa. In 1953, against the wishes of most
Africans in Northern Rhodesia, the territory was
joined in a Federation with Southern Rhodesia and
Nyasaland.

THE CENTRAL AFRICAN FEDERATION

At first, the Central African Federation seemed
indeed to further the interests of Europeans in
Northern Rhodesia. In the early 1950s the copper
industry enjoyed an economic boom; the Federation
attracted new investment; and both jobs and wages
for Europeans increased considerably. By 1958 they
numbered 72,000, while unofficials gained a majority
in the Governor's Executive Council. But by this time
it was clear that Federation worked mainly to the
advantage of Europeans in Southern Rhodesia, who
dominated the mainly white Federal Parliament. The
grandiose Kariba dam, with its power station on the
south bank of the Zambezi, plainly expressed this
preponderance. As early as 1959 the Northern
Rhodesia Minister of Finance (a British civil servant)
complained of the unequal distribution of Federal
revenues; it was estimated that in the past six years
Northern Rhodesia had suffered a net loss of over fifty
million pounds to the Federal Government. And while
Europeans might still tolerate Federation as a means
of blocking African political advance, Africans in
Northern Rhodesia gained neither economic nor
political advantages. In a few areas, close to towns,
African cash crop production increased, but in general
rural poverty was scarcely alleviated. On the Copperbelt, slight improvements were made in conditions
and opportunities for African workers. Against strong
European opposition, some of the jobs which had
hitherto been reserved for whites were opened to
Africans. But African education, the key to African
advance, continued to be grossly neglected; in 1958,
in a population of perhaps three million, there were
less than a thousand African children in secondary
schools, only one of which provided for entrance to
university.

INDEPENDENCE

During the first few years of Federation, the
Northern Rhodesia African National Congress (as it
had been renamed in 1951) suffered from a temporary
loss of popular support and from uncertainty as to its
own goals, now that Federation was a fact. But in
1958 Nkumbula's leadership was challenged by the

secession from Congress of a group of young radicals,
led by a former schoolteacher, Kenneth Kaunda.
These men aimed at destroying Federation and
transforming Northern Rhodesia into an independent
African state, to be called Zambia. Their new party
was banned in 1959, and Kaunda himself was gaoled;
but on his release a few months later he at once took
over the leadership of a new party, the United
National Independence Party (UNIP). In 1962, following a massive campaign of civil disobedience
organized by UNIP, the British government introduced a constitution for Northern Rhodesia which
would create an African majority in the legislature.
UNIP agreed to participate in the elections and
consequently formed a coalition government with
what remained of Congress. The Federation was thus
doomed, and it was formally dissolved at the end of
1963.

Early in 1964 another election was held, on a wider
franchise; this enabled Kaunda to form an all-UNIP
government with substantial control of internal
affairs. Independence was granted on October 24th,
1964, though during the intervening months the new
government had to confront two sources of African
opposition. In Barotseland, the traditional ruling
élite had retained an exceptional degree of autonomy
under colonial rule, and it was with some reluctance
that the paramount chief accepted subordination to a
popularly elected African government. And in the
Northern Province, the government had to suppress
armed resistance by members of the Lumpa Church,
which since its foundation by Alice Lenshina ten
years earlier had tended increasingly to oppose all
outside interference in its affairs.

The main task facing the new Republic of Zambia
was to break loose from the massive industrial
complex of white-dominated southern Africa, which
was to a large extent responsible for Zambia's major
internal weaknesses: an economy in which great
mineral wealth contributed very little to overall
national development, and a shockingly inadequate
educational structure. At independence, there were
less than a hundred Zambian graduates. In 1965 the
University of Zambia was founded; technical education rapidly expanded; while secondary schools were
started all over the country. On the eve of independence, the government obtained the mineral rights
whereby the British South Africa Company had—on
a very dubious legal basis—exacted massive royalties
from the mining companies. Rhodesia's unilateral
declaration of independence in November 1965 and
the subsequent imposition of international sanctions
stimulated Zambian efforts to reduce dependence on
imports from the south. The Maamba mine, in
Zambia's Southern Province, has replaced Wankie as
Zambia's main source of coal and coke. A new hydro-
electric scheme is in operation on the lower Kafue
river, while at Kariba a second power station is to be
built on Zambian soil. Moreover, Zambia has
strengthened her links with East Africa: there is now
a pipeline, and a new tarmac road, from the Copperbelt to Dar es Salaam, on the east coast; and Zambia
is collaborating with Tanzania and the People's

Republic of China in building a railway between these two points. Since 1969, the Zambian Government has further increased its economic freedom of action by acquiring a 51 per cent holding in mining and other industries. Wholesale and retail trade, once dominated by expatriates, especially Asians, are now largely confined to Zambian citizens, of whom very few are Asian.

Nevertheless, Zambia continues to depend heavily on economic links with the south, while copper remains virtually the only source of foreign exchange. These factors are crucial to recent Zambian politics. The numerous whites who remained after independence were content to withdraw to the sidelines. But the relative absence of conflict between black and white in Zambia has been bought at a price: for instance, the most significant wage award to African workers in 1966 widened the gap between them and the far more numerous subsistence farmers, as well as the many unemployed. Plans for rural development have met with little success; the drift to the towns continues; and though UNIP was returned to power in 1968 it had lost much of the respect and support it enjoyed in 1964. The drastic fall in copper prices since 1970 has obliged the Government to cut back expenditure in nearly all fields, especially in education and development projects, thus lowering employment prospects for the swelling number of graduates and secondary-school leavers. Imports from or through South Africa and Rhodesia are once again preferred to goods imported by the more expensive East African route. At the same time, the new railway scheme commits Zambia to buying Chinese manufactures which will at least partly compete with Zambia's own infant manufacturing sector. And Zambia's continuing support for guerrillas operating in Rhodesia and Mozambique makes her an obvious target for counter-subversion by agents, black or white, of white southern Africa.

These circumstances have given rise to political unrest. The Government has felt obliged to rebuke student critics on various occasions; it briefly closed the University in 1971; and later that year it secured the dismissal of an outspoken Zambian newspaper editor. In the middle of 1971 the former Vice-President, Simon Kapwepwe, left UNIP to form the United Progressive Party; this was involved in local but violent clashes with UNIP members, and many UPP followers were soon detained without trial. In February 1972 the UPP was banned, and Kapwepwe himself was imprisoned without trial, though by September most of the other detainees had been released. Meanwhile, the Government had set up a Commission to advise on the form of a new constitution, under which Zambia would become a one-party state. A remnant of the old ANC survives under Nkumbula and has much support in southern Zambia, but it is likely that the Government will obtain the two-thirds majority in Parliament needed to change the constitution. During November 1972 the Government announced that Zambia would become a one-party state before the end of the year. [Sweeping changes in the country's political system were debated by Parliament in December, and Zambia finally became a one-party state in the same month. *Editor.*]

ECONOMY

Richard Jolly*

ECONOMY

Since independence in October 1964, and thanks to copper, the Zambian economy has been one of the richest and fastest growing of sub-Saharan Africa. Gross domestic product in real terms increased by an estimated 13 per cent per annum from 1964 to 1969, the result of real output expanding by 5½ to 6 per cent per annum and an improvement in the terms of trade due to higher copper prices of 7 per cent per annum. Estimated G.D.P. per capita in 1969 was just over K280, or about U.S. $400 for a population of 4,057,000 (1969 Census figure). But fluctuations around this high trend have also been considerable. G.D.P. in 1970 was estimated to have fallen by 3 per cent, the result of the Mufulira mine disaster and the restrictive impact of the 1969 budget.

*Although the author has been employed by the Government of Zambia, the views expressed in this article are his personal views and not necessarily those of the Government of Zambia.

ECONOMIC STRUCTURE

Copper mining is the country's most important economic activity, providing more than 40 per cent of G.D.P., 95 per cent of exports and 60 per cent of government revenue. Owing to this predominance of the copper industry and an uneven distribution of fertile soil, the Zambian economy has an extremely dualistic structure, characterized by large disparities of income and living standards between mining and other workers, expatriates and Zambians and between persons on the "line of rail" and those scattered in other parts of the country. Agriculture officially accounts for only about 6 per cent of G.D.P., although recent unofficial estimates of subsistence output would increase agriculture's share in 1971 to about 15 per cent. The share of manufacturing output has greatly increased from under 6 per cent in 1964 to nearly 10 per cent of G.D.P. in 1971.

Zambia is the most highly urbanized country of middle Africa. By 1972 almost one third of its total population lived in the towns of 20,000 or more, mainly split between the capital, Lusaka (347,900 population in 1972) and the Copperbelt towns (Ndola 201,300 and Kitwe 251,600, being the largest). In total, about two-fifths of the total population is grouped along the line of rail, stretching from Livingstone through Lusaka to the Copperbelt. Off the line of rail, the country is very sparsely populated, even in comparison with the low average density of total population of only 14 per sq. mile. The African population is estimated to be increasing by 2.9 per cent per annum, though the number of non-Africans has fallen from 87,000 in 1963 to 58,000 in 1972. Total urban population grew at 8 per cent per annum from 1963 to 1969.

About 10 per cent of the total population have wage-earning jobs, again one of the highest proportions in Africa. Estimated employment in June 1971 was 396,000 of whom about 27,000 were non-Africans. Because of the backwardness of secondary and higher education before independence, the major proportion of the higher-level skilled and professional jobs are still filled by expatriates, in spite of strong government pressures to Zambianize as quickly as possible. Services, construction, mining and manufacturing are, in order, the sectors providing most of the enumerated wage-earning employment.

GROWTH AND DEVELOPMENT

Since 1938, the first date for which national income estimates are available, G.D.P. at constant prices has grown at an astonishingly high rate of around 10 per cent per annum, though in cycles fluctuating with the price and output of copper. The boom of 1948 and 1952, fuelled by high prices resulting from the Korean War, was followed by ten increasingly lean years, the result of Zambia being linked in unwanted Federation with Rhodesia and Nyasaland. Under the Federal constitution, the lion's share of taxation from the copper mines was channelled to Rhodesia, which also benefited by having the Federal capital and the bulk of industrial development. Moreover, in this period, African education and agriculture remained territorial responsibilities, cut off from Federal funds and lacking the priority and resources needed for rapid development.

With the break-up of Federation in December 1963, Zambia regained control over copper taxation and the right to set tariffs in accord with her own needs. A few hours before independence, ten months later, agreement was reached with the British South Africa Company, which returned to the Zambian Government revenue from copper royalties, then totalling roughly K20 million per year. These changes, combined with rising copper prices, meant that government revenue in Zambia more than quadrupled during the first four years of independence, providing government with unprecedented resources for development projects.

U.D.I.

The dislocations of U.D.I., the unilateral declaration of independence by Rhodesia in 1965, created serious problems and costs for several years in Zambia. Transportation, already under strain to meet the growing needs of post-independence expansion, was thrown into confusion by attempts to switch external trade to northern routes and retaliatory measures of various sorts by the Rhodesian government. This necessitated many millions of capital expenditure by Zambia on new transport links as well as raising recurrent costs. In addition, copper output was some 15 per cent less in 1966 than in 1965, primarily due to shortages of coal and transport dislocations arising from U.D.I. Only in 1969 did copper output surpass the levels of 1965, and then partly by exporting concentrates stockpiled from ore unable to be smelted in 1966 and 1967.

INSTITUTIONAL CHANGES

In the eight years since independence Zambia has effected major changes in economic structure and control of the economy. Under the philosophy of humanism, the President in April 1968 invited 26 major companies to accept a 51 per cent shareholding interest by the Government. (These are usually described as the Mulungushi Reforms.) In August 1969, at Matero, the President announced 51 per cent government participation in the mining industry, the terms and details for which were negotiated in the following months. In November 1970 the President announced similar measures covering the banks and other financial institutions, though these measures were largely abandoned in July 1971, and left to apply only to certain financial institutions. Government control of these major industries is formally vested in ZIMCO, the Zambia Industrial and Mining Corporation, and run by three parastatal organizations, MINDECO, the Mining Development Corporation, INDECO, the Industrial Development Corporation and FINDECO, the Financial Development Corporation. Although these corporations accept the need to implement government economic strategy, a strong emphasis has been put on management according to sound commercial principles.

CONSTRAINTS TO DEVELOPMENT

Besides U.D.I., the three major constraints to development since independence have been scarcity of skilled and educated manpower, the limitations of transport capacity, both external and internal, and, for the first few years, the shortage of construction capacity. In addition, the rapid increase in real and money wages of the urban employed, both Zambian and expatriate, has greatly increased consumption and imports, slowed the growth of employment and output and has increasingly left the rural population worse off relative to the urban population than they were in 1964. This has widened the rural-urban gap and accelerated migration to the towns.

The shortage of skills has been very severe, the result of there being only about 100 Zambians with degrees and barely 1,000 with secondary school certificates at independence. After independence Zambia embarked on an unprecedented programme of expansion. Under the Transitional Development

Plan (1965–mid-1966) Zambia greatly increased primary enrolments, tripled secondary school intake in two years and founded the University of Zambia, which quadrupled enrolments in its first four years. By 1971 the University enrolled 1,560 students and the secondary schools over 54,000. Technical training has been vastly expanded. These programmes will go far to provide the skilled and educated manpower needed in the 1970s both to Zambianize existing posts and provide for further economic expansion. But because of the time lags between enrolling students and their graduation, educational expansion since independence made little impact on the situation initially, causing the Zambianization programme to rest heavily on accelerated training, promoting under-qualified persons, withdrawing skilled manpower from the rural areas and continuing to rely on almost as many expatriates as were employed at independence.

Until 1968, transport constraints were extremely serious, externally and internally, by air, road or railway. Externally, the transport situation was eased by the building of the Great North Road, the opening of an oil pipeline to Tanzania in 1968, the construction of a main road eastwards from Lusaka to Malawi and making extremely rapid progress by the construction of a railway to the north, being built with the help of the Chinese and financed by a Chinese interest-free loan to Zambia and Tanzania, of an amount reported to be K287 million. Internally, feeder road communications are still inadequate, particularly in the rainy season (December to March), though an all-weather road is under construction to Mongu in the Western Province.

High and rapidly increasing wage rates have for many years exerted great pressure on consumption and imports. Since independence, the annual increase in earnings has accelerated, averaging 15 per cent per annum for Africans and 8 per cent per annum for non-Africans over the period 1964 to 1970 when price increases averaged only 5 per cent per annum. By 1970, average earnings for Africans in wage-earning employment were estimated to be about K865 and for non-Africans about K5160. Zambia had thus become a high wage and high cost economy, with serious implications for the level of government revenue from the mining industry, the recurrent cost of government services, the prospect for new industries, particularly in the export or import-substitution field, the growth of employment and the distribution of incomes between the wage earners, the urban unemployed and rural farmers. In 1969 at Kitwe, the President made a strong call for a wages and incomes policy. Some action was taken in 1970 to implement an incomes policy but it is too early to judge how effective this will be in changing the long-term trend.

FOREIGN EXCHANGE AND THE BALANCE OF PAYMENTS

Although copper exports by value increased rapidly between 1964 and 1969 they turned down slightly in 1970 (with lower copper prices) and sharply in 1971 and 1972 (with continuing low copper prices

and reduced output). The net surplus on current account, which had been positive every year since independence except 1968 (and nearly K340 million in 1969) was turned into an estimated net deficit of K160 million in 1971. Besides reflecting changes in copper price and output, this reversal also shows the effects of the $2\frac{1}{2}$-fold increase in imports between 1964 and 1971 and the even faster rise in net invisible payments abroad. Investment income transferred abroad remained high but apparently steady, but there was a sharp increase in other transfers (largely but not only compensation payments for the mining industry). By June 1972, Zambia's net foreign exchange assets which in 1970 had been at a level well in excess of one years' imports had fallen to about K100 million and were still declining. Import controls were introduced together with exchange controls affecting borrowing, travel allowances, personal remittances and, in September 1972, additional restrictions on the remittance overseas of foreign dividends (with the mining companies exempted). Meanwhile the beneficial effects of linking the kwacha to the dollar in December 1971 (involving a measure of *de facto* devaluation for Zambia) were largely nullified through the floating of the pound. Once again there was a tendency within Zambia to put too much emphasis on dealing with this by reducing government expenditure instead of by reducing private consumption of imports particularly of the better-off urban population or by other direct measures to reduce foreign exchange outflow.

PLANNING

Since 1964 Zambia has completed three development plans: the Emergency, the Transitional and the First National Development Plan 1966–70. The First National Development Plan was extended a further 18 months to deal with carry-overs and the Second National Development Plan commenced in January 1972.

The main points of development strategy set out in the 1972–76 Second National Development Plan are:

(i) The expansion of agricultural production as a top priority with the aim to improve income and nutritional standards of the population, cut imports of food substantially, expand economically justified exports and provide industrial inputs.

(ii) The increase of agricultural output and efficiency of production in the traditional farming sector as the most direct way of contributing to the solution of employment and income distribution problems between urban and rural areas.

(iii) Expansion and diversification of industry and mining including processing of copper on an enlarged scale.

The Plan also outlines programmes for education, health, housing, transportation, as well as new administrative structures for implementation. The concept of Intensive Development Zones will be used to stimulate a wider pattern of regional and rural development. Overall, the Second National Development Plan envisages that G.D.P. will grow at nearly 7 per cent per annum from 1972–76, thus raising per capita G.D.P. to about K300 in 1976 (measured at 1969 prices).

PERFORMANCE IN KEY ECONOMIC SECTORS

Mining

Copper accounts for 96 per cent of Zambia's mineral production. Other traditional mineral products are zinc, lead, cobalt and amethyst, though in the last few years coal and limestone have been added.

The mining industry in Zambia was developed by two major groups, Zambian Anglo American and Roan Selection Trust, which first became involved in Zambia in the 1920s. Production rose from virtually nothing before 1930 to 719,000 metric tons of copper in 1969 falling to 633,000 metric tons in 1971, mainly from the effects of the Mufulira disaster. Production at peak in 1969 was about 13 per cent of world production and made Zambia the third largest producer in the world. Except for a small amount processed as wire, all of Zambia's production is exported, mainly to England, Japan and West Germany.

In August 1969, President Kaunda announced that he was asking the owners of the mines to invite government to join their mining enterprises to the extent of 51 per cent participation by the state. Negotiations to effect this proposal were largely completed by the end of the year. The agreement reached on the re-organization of the copper industry contains five major elements:

(i) 51 per cent government participation;

(ii) replacement of the mineral royalties and export levies which were solely based on output and price with a mineral tax based on profit;

(iii) a management agreement with the two companies for at least the next ten years;

(iv) replacement of the companies' mining rights in perpetuity with 25 year leases for their present operations and special three year licences for explorations in presently unutilized areas;

(v) an arrangement for paying compensation based on book value at the time of take-over, with compensation payments to be completed in eight years for RST and 12 years for Zambian Anglo-American.

On the Zambian side, the Government, agreed to a new statutory board, MINDECO (the Mining Development Corporation) to represent its interests in management and future planning of the mines.

The new agreements were generally welcomed by all parties and hailed as measures which would provide the basis for future stability and future expansion of the mining industry. By mid-1970, copper output in 1975 was conservatively projected to be at least 950,000 short tons. In the short run, the generally optimistic future prospects have been offset by the mining disaster of September 1970. This extensively flooded the workings of Mufulira mine, killed about 90 men, has substantially reduced copper output and, with the fall in price, also reduced export earnings and government revenue in 1971 and 1972.

Agriculture

Zambian agriculture is, in effect, split into three sectors: production by a few hundred large commercial farmers, mainly expatriates, who in 1970 still produced about half the total marketed agricultural output; emerging Zambian farmers; and a mass of traditional farmers, scattered throughout the country, producing at low levels of productivity and selling little to the market. Statistics on the latter two groups are extremely inadequate, but information suggests that output per head has grown only slowly since independence. Main crops include maize, groundnuts, sorghum, millet and beans.

In recent years, the government has allocated substantial financial resources to the rural sector, in the form of direct expenditures on agricultural extension and production units, loans and other support for co-operatives, and extensive agricultural subsidies of various sorts. In spite of these efforts, the impact so far has been small, largely due to the lack of skilled manpower in the agricultural sector, inadequate marketing and transport facilities and, ironically, the fact that rapid developments in the urban sector have caused a high proportion of the younger and better educated to migrate to the towns. Production of cotton, poultry and sugar has, however, increased, and there was a marked recovery of marketed crop production, paticularly maize, in 1971, and a very large surplus of maize in 1972.

Manufacturing

Since independence, manufacturing output has grown by an average of about 20 per cent per year, under the stimulus of the rapidly expanding local market and the opportunities for import substitution forfeited during the years of Federation. In 1968 the government announced that the state would take a 51 per cent equity interest in 26 key industries, an arrangement implemented through INDECO, the government-owned Industrial Development Corporation. The assets of INDECO companies in mid-1971 totalled K133 million. Large industrial projects in preparation included an oil refinery, an iron and steel mill and a car assembly plant.

Transportation

Since the unilateral declaration of independence by Rhodesia in 1965, Zambia has allocated enormous resources to orienting her trade away from the traditional routes to the south. At independence, before U.D.I., virtually all of Zambia's foreign trade was carried on routes to the south. By 1969 this had been reduced to less than two-thirds of imports and less than three-fifths of exports.

Power

In 1971 the consumption of electric power in Zambia was about 4,400 million kWh., about 90 per cent of which was used by the copper industry. Roughly one-third of Zambia's power requirements are at present generated in Zambia itself, two-thirds coming from the generating installations on the Rhodesian side of the Kariba Dam. Earlier, the dependence on Kariba was much greater, which led Zambia to undertake several major power developments: two hydro-electric stations at Victoria Falls (capacity 100 MW); and the construction of a new hydro-electric station at Kafue, partly built with Yugoslavian aid, to have an installed capacity of 600 MW. In addition, Zambia has decided to proceed as soon as possible with constructing a power station on the Zambian side of the Kariba Dam, to add another 600 MW installed capacity by 1975.

STATISTICAL SURVEY

AREA AND POPULATION

AREA (sq. miles)	POPULATION (June 30th, 1972)		
	Total	African	Others
290,586	4,515,000	4,457,000	58,000

LAND DISTRIBUTION

(1968—'000 acres)

State Land	11,726
Freehold and Leasehold . . .	6,172
Townships	205
Protected Forest Areas and Forest Reserves	2,512
Under Tribal Occupation . . .	1,408
Inundated by Water . . .	375
Unalienated	1,053
Reserves	35,656
Trust Land	107,363
Western Province	31,231
TOTAL	185,975

CHIEF TOWNS

(POPULATION 1972)

Lusaka (capital) .	.	347,900	Luanshya . . .	110,500
Kitwe .	.	251,600	Kabwe (Broken Hill) .	83,100
Ndola .	.	201,300	Chililabombwe	
Chingola .	.	130,000	(Bancroft) . .	57,500
Mufulira .	.	124,100	Livingstone . .	49,700

Births and Deaths: Average annual birth rate 49.8 per 1,000; death rate 20.7 per 1,000 (UN estimates for 1965–70).

EMPLOYMENT
(1971)

	AFRICANS	OTHERS
Agriculture, Forestry and Fisheries	38,740	580
Mining and Quarrying . .	52,800	5,360
Manufacturing	39,020	3,000
Construction	63,140	2,730
Electricity and Water . .	3,590	450
Distribution and Catering . .	33,350	4,580
Transport and Communications .	21,010	1,570
Business Services . .	8,610	1,950
Community and Social Services .	78,740	6,320
TOTAL . . .	339,000	26,540

AGRICULTURE
LAND USE, 1962
('ooo hectares)

Arable and Under Permanent Crops . .	4,800
Permanent Meadows and Pastures . .	33,800
Forest Land	34,000
Other Areas	2,661
TOTAL . . .	75,261

Source: FAO, *Production Yearbook.*

PRINCIPAL CROPS
(metric tons)

	1968	1969	1970	1971
Maize	590,000*	655,000*	550,000*	750,000*
Millet and Sorghum . .	260,000*	280,000*	250,000*	250,000*
Sugar Cane† . . .	183,000	180,000	350,000*	322,000
Potatoes	2,000*	3,000	3,000	3,000*
Sweet Potatoes and Yams .	13,000*	13,000*	13,000*	n.a.
Cassava (Manioc) . . .	145,000	145,000	143,000	n.a.
Groundnuts (in shell) . .	47,000	62,000	42,000	103,000
Cottonseed . . .	3,000	5,000	5,000	5,000
Cotton (Lint) . . .	1,000	3,000	2,000	3,000
Tobacco	6,700	5,300	5,100	6,500

* FAO estimate.   † Crop year ending in year stated.

Source: FAO, *Production Yearbook 1971.*

TOBACCO

	UNIT	1969	1970	1971
Virginia Flue-cured:				
Crop sold	'ooo lb.	11,074	10,571	13,745
Value	K'ooo	3,904	3,001	4,306
Burley:				
Crop sold	'ooo lb.	529	561	855
Value	K'ooo	122	143	218
Turkish:				
Crop sold	'ooo lb.	166	19	10
Value	K'ooo	32	4	2

LIVESTOCK

FAO estimates ('000—)

				1968–69	1969–70	1970–71
Cattle	.	.	.	1,519*	1,550	1,600
Sheep	.	.	.	29	28	28
Goats	.	.	.	175	180	185
Pigs	.	.	.	96	100	105
Poultry	.	.	.	6,700	6,800	6,900

* Official estimate.

Source: FAO, *Production Yearbook 1971.*

LIVESTOCK PRODUCTS

(FAO estimates—metric tons)

					1968	1969	1970	1971
Cows' Milk	.	.	.	.	65,000	68,000	70,000	72,000
Beef and Veal*	.	.	.	.	23,000	24,000	27,000	27,000
Pork*	.	.	.	.	4,000	5,000	5,000	5,000
Poultry Meat	.	.	.	.	8,000	9,000	10,000	n.a.
Edible Offal	.	.	.	.	4,400	4,400	4,400	n.a.
Hen Eggs	.	.	.	.	7,300	8,000	8,400	8,700
Cattle Hides	.	.	.	.	4,221	4,423	4,893	n.a.
Sheep Skins	.	.	.	.	19	19	19	n.a.
Goat Skins	.	.	.	.	153	159	162	n.a.

Butter and Cheese: No recorded production since 1967.

* Meat from indigenous animals only, including the meat equivalent of exported live animals.

Source: FAO, *Production Yearbook 1971.*

FORESTRY

(cubic metres)

ROUNDWOOD REMOVALS

1967	.	.	4,054,000
1968	.	.	4,022,000

SAWNWOOD PRODUCTION

1967	.	.	39,000
1968	.	.	45,000
1969	.	.	45,000
1970	.	.	45,000

Source: FAO, *Yearbook of Forest Products.*

FISHING

(inland waters)

			1967	1968	1969	1970
Total Catch (metric tons)	.	.	38,500	41,300	44,000	48,400
Value of Landings ('000 kwacha)	.	.	2,215	2,358	2,400	3,000

Source: FAO, *Yearbook of Fishery Statistics 1970.*

MINING
(metric tons)

	1968	1969	1970
Coal . . .	573,000	397,200	623,000
Cobalt Ore . .	1,344	1,811	2,400
Copper Ore* .	684,858	719,467	684,064
Gypsum . .	1,075	n.a.	n.a.
Lead Ore . .	22,700	22,900	27,100
Manganese Ore .	13,444	—	—
Silver† . .	23.9	42.8	47.6
Tin Concentrates .	24	24	24
Zinc Ore* . .	67,200	68,160	64,700
Limestone Flux and Calcareous Stone .	716,000	n.a.	n.a.
Gold (kg.) . .	156	282	364

* Figures relate to the content of concentrates.
† Recovery from refinery slimes.

Source: mainly United Nations, *The Growth of World Industry.*

1971: Coal 812,100 metric tons.

INDUSTRY
SELECTED COMMODITIES
(metric tons)

	1968	1969	1970
Raw Sugar . .	22,000	30,000	40,000
Sulphuric Acid .	17,000	14,000	15,000
Cement . .	212,000	331,000	377,000
Copper (unwrought):			
Smelter* .	664,914	747,483	683,371
Refined .	571,902	642,823	580,127
Lead (primary) .	21,887	23,008	27,205
Zinc (primary) .	53,215	50,167	53,456
Cobalt Metal . .	1,197	n.a.	n.a.
Electric Energy (million kWh.)† .	659	693	949

* Including some production at the refined stage.
† Net production, i.e. excluding station use.

Source: mainly United Nations, *The Growth of World Industry.*

1971 (metric tons): Refined copper 534,600; primary lead 27,700; primary zinc 57,000.

FINANCE

100 ngwee = 1 kwacha.
Coins: 5 and 10 ngwee.
Notes: 20 and 50 ngwee; 1, 2 and 10 kwacha.
Exchange rates (December 1972): £1 sterling = 1.679 kwacha; U.S. $1 = 71.43 ngwee.
100 kwacha = £59.55 = $140.00.

BUDGET
(K million)

REVENUE	1971	1972
Recurrent Revenue:		
Company and Income Tax .	165.9	109.4
Customs and Excise . .	73.0	85.5
Mineral Royalties and Copper Export Tax . .	70.0	24.5
Interest	18.9	0.4
Other Items . . .	18.0	49.4
TOTAL (incl. other itmes) . .	345.8	274.3

EXPENDITURE	1971	1972
Development and Finance, National Guidance and Development Planning . . .	10.2	8.6
Zambia Police . . .	12.0	13.4
Provincial and Local Government .	15.6	8.4
Trade, Industry and Mines . .	2.2	7.0
Health	20.5	20.1
Power, Transport and Works .	41.8	26.8
Education	54.9	51.6
Rural Development . .	38.2	28.9
Constitutional and Statutory .	109.5	106.7
TOTAL (incl. others) . .	329.2	296.9

SECOND NATIONAL DEVELOPMENT PLAN

1972–76

	K million
Economic Facilities, Transport . . .	716.5
Industrial, Mining Development . .	655.0
Social Facilities	314.9
Education	117.5
Agriculture and Lands . . .	152.5
TOTAL	1,956.4

Currency in Circulation (June 30th, 1972): 59,310,000 kwacha.

CONSUMER PRICE INDEX

	HIGH INCOME GROUP		LOW INCOME GROUP	
	All Items	Food	All Items	Food
1969 . .	100.0	99.7	100.0	99.9
1970 . .	105.0	103.0	102.6	102.1
1971 . .	110.8	109.4	108.8	108.8
June 1972 .	118.7	121.6	114.7	114.6

NATIONAL ACCOUNTS

(K'000 at factor cost)

	1966	1967	1968	1969
GROSS DOMESTIC PRODUCT (at factor cost) .	644,500	751,100	795,700	990,100
of which:				
Agriculture, Forestry and Fishing . .	60,500	66,300	65,700	73,700
Mining and Quarrying . . .	240,100	254,600	251,900	397,600
Manufacturing	60,200	73,200	76,200	82,200
Trade	78,300	96,000	114,500	96,500
Finance, Insurance, and Real Estate .	26,700	34,700	39,500	64,900
Transport and Communications . .	32,400	49,400	48,100	51,000
Construction	54,000	55,900	63,100	66,900
Government Administration and Services.	35,700	97,200	124,100	142,000
Income Paid Abroad	− 58,000	− 50,600	− 52,100	− 47,300
GROSS NATIONAL INCOME . . .	586,500	700,500	743,600	942,800
Balance of Imports and Exports of Goods and Services.	−120,300	−58,900	−74,100	−431,800
TOTAL AVAILABLE RESOURCES . . .	466,200	641,600	669,500	511,000

GROSS DOMESTIC PRODUCT AT PURCHASERS' VALUES
(K million)

	1968	1969	1970
Agriculture, Hunting, Forestry and Fishing .	64.3	68.6	72.4
Mining and Quarrying	389.9	615.8	438.9
Manufacturing	105.8	113.9	128.5
Electricity, Gas and Water . . .	12.6	14.2	15.6
Construction	62.3	67.5	87.5
Wholesale and Retail Trade, Restaurants and Hotels	130.3	104.0	111.7
Transport, Storage and Communications .	48.4	44.1	57.6
Other Producers and Services* . .	175.8	212.0	233.9
GROSS DOMESTIC PRODUCT . . .	989.4	1,240.1	1,146.1
of which: NATIONAL INCOME (in market prices) .	878.0	1,116.0	1,032.0

* Including import duties.

Source: United Nations, *Monthly Bulletin of Statistics.*

BALANCE OF PAYMENTS
(K million)

	1968			1969		
	Credit	Debit	Balance	Credit	Debit	Balance
Goods, Services and Transfer Payments:						
Merchandise f.o.b. . . .	534.0	371.1	162.9	852.6	325.3	527.3
Travel, transport, freight, insurance .	4.5	76.8	−72.3	4.8	76.8	− 72.0
Investment income . . .	7.4	59.5	−52.1	16.3	63.8	− 47.5
Government and other services .	6.0	22.4	−16.4	5.3	23.8	− 18.5
Private transfer payments . .	2.0	26.7	−24.7	2.2	54.4	52.2
Government transfer payments .	5.1	5.3	− 0.2	5.5	4.3	1.2
TOTAL	559.0	561.8	− 2.8	886.7	548.4	338.3
Capital Transactions:						
Private	58.1	38.4	19.7	42.1	197.4	−155.3
Government	35.1	14.9	20.2	17.6	10.0	7.1
Monetary movements* . .	36.5	43.4	− 6.9	8.3	127.3	−119.0
Net Errors and Omissions . .	—	30.2	−30.2	—	60.8	− 60.8

* Includes foreign government securities held by the Zambian Government and reserve position in the IMF.

EXTERNAL TRADE
(K'ooo)

	1965	1966	1967	1968	1969	1970	1971*
Imports . . .	210,742	246,112	306,261	325,173	311,773	339,473	393,820
Exports . . .	380,294	493,458	470,009	544,416	766,489	714,800	484,890

* Provisional.

COMMODITIES
(K'ooo)

IMPORTS	1969	1970	1971*
Food . . .	30,411	} 31,300	40,332
Beverages and Tobacco .	2,196		
Crude Materials, inedible .	4,494	5,277	7,809
Mineral Fuels, Lubricants and Related Materials .	35,581	35,184	35,965
Animal and Vegetable Oils and Fats . .	2,881	4,456	4,515
Chemicals . .	22,562	26,021	32,726
Manufactured Goods .	62,791	74,979	85,114
Machinery and Transport .	123,041	131,716	159,952
Miscellaneous . .	25,613	30,540	27,407
Others . . .	2,203	—	—
TOTAL . . .	311,773	339,473	393,820

EXPORTS	1969	1970	1971*
Copper . . .	724,500	681,400	450,300
Zinc . . .	12,403	10,961	11,536
Lead . . .	6,061	4,872	4,558
Cobalt . . .	4,536	6,343	3,709
Tobacco . .	3,163	3,152	3,511
Maize . . .	374	n.a.	n.a.
Timber . . .	666	528	424
TOTAL (incl. others) .	766,489	714,800	484,890

* Provisional.

PRINCIPAL COUNTRIES
(K'ooo)

IMPORTS	1969	1970	1971*
Australia . . .	5,798	n.a.	n.a.
France . . .	5,161	n.a.	n.a.
Germany, Fed. Repub. .	12,151	16,999	17,953
Iran . . .	8,061	n.a.	n.a.
Italy . . .	6,769	n.a.	n.a.
Japan . . .	22,588	21,802	26,855
Kenya . . .	6,293	n.a.	n.a.
Rhodesia . .	21,772	23,195	21,021
South Africa . .	74,723	61,725	58,586
United Kingdom . .	71,390	80,559	97,557
U.S.A. . . .	30,083	32,439	40,177
TOTAL (incl. others)	311,773	339,473	393,820

EXPORTS	1969	1970	1971*
Brazil . . .	9,013	n.a.	n.a.
China, People's Repub. .	10,572	n.a.	n.a.
France . . .	69,994	n.a.	n.a.
Germany, Fed. Repub. .	96,071	84,152	45,523
Greece . . .	10,535	n.a.	n.a.
India . . .	14,505	n.a.	n.a.
Italy . . .	80,122	n.a.	n.a.
Japan . . .	180,316	166,459	99,668
South Africa . .	8,157	8,458	10,447
Spain . . .	11,281	n.a.	n.a.
Sweden . . .	17,941	n.a.	n.a.
Switzerland . .	10,482	n.a.	n.a.
United Kingdom . .	198,028	160,075	78,962
U.S.A. . . .	8,691	1,441	4,558
TOTAL (incl. others)	766,489	714,800	484,890

* Provisional.

TRANSPORT

ROADS
NEW REGISTRATION OF MOTOR VEHICLES

	1968	1969	1970	1971*
Passenger Cars .	7,240	6,246	5,984	5,681
Vans and Trucks .	5,071	4,797	5,213	6,779
Motor Cycles and Scooters . .	2,197	1,682	1,657	1,421

* January–November.

Motor vehicles in use (1968): 48,200 passenger cars; 25,900 commercial vehicles.

CIVIL AVIATION

	1968	1969	1970	1971
Aircraft arrivals　.　.　.	25,023	23,964	22,036	26,836
Passenger arrivals　.　.　.	192,400	227,700	256,100	300,500
Passenger departures　.　.	186,000	226,600	256,100	301,400
Freight loaded (metric tons)　.	1,396	1,959	1,917	2,538
Freight unloaded (metric tons)　.	3,922	6,828	8,242	10,155

EDUCATION
(1969)

	NUMBER OF INSTITUTIONS	NUMBER OF PUPILS			NUMBER OF TEACHERS
		Male	Female	Total	
Primary　.　.　.	2,550	367,986	293,295	661,281	13,569
Secondary　.　.　.	114	32,575	15,582	48,157	2,071
Trades and Technical　.	18	444	2	446	n.a.
Teacher Training　.	9	1,340	849	2,189	n.a.
University　.　.　.	1	1,093	205	1,298	n.a.

Source: Central Statistical Office, Lusaka.

THE CONSTITUTION

In the late nineteenth century North-Western and North-Eastern Rhodesia were included in a Charter granted to the British South Africa Company, whose administration was officially recognized by two Orders-in-Council in 1899 and 1900. In 1911 the two territories were amalgamated under the name of Northern Rhodesia, which continued to be administered by the Company until 1924, when it was taken over by the Crown. In the same year Orders-in-Council created the office of Governor of Northern Rhodesia, constituted an Executive Council, and made provision for the constitution of a Legislative Council. In 1935 the capital was moved from Livingstone to Lusaka.

In 1953 Northern Rhodesia became part of the Federation of Rhodesia and Nyasaland, but its Protectorate status and separate government were preserved and retained. Following the Victoria Falls Conference of July 1963, at which the dissolution of the Federation was agreed, a new constitution came into effect on January 3rd, 1964, immediately after the dissolution of the Federation on December 31st, 1963.

In October 1964, Northern Rhodesia became an independent Republic within the Commonwealth and adopted the name of Zambia. The Constitution of January 1964, was amended to include the following provisions:

The President: The President of the Republic of Zambia will be Head of State and Commander-in-Chief of the Armed Forces. A candidate for the Presidency must be a Zambian citizen, a qualified voter, and at least thirty years old. Election of the President will take place at the same time as that of members to the National Assembly. Each candidate for election to the National Assembly will declare in advance which presidential candidate he supports. Each voter will thus simultaneously vote for parliamentary and presidential candidates.

The Vice-President: Appointment will be by the President; the Vice-President will be leader of the National Assembly.

The Cabinet: The Chairman will normally be the President. The Cabinet will also include the Vice-President and not more than 14 members, appointed by the President from among the members of the National Assembly and removable by the President.

Legislature: Parliament will consist of the President and a National Assembly of 105* elected members. The President will have power to nominate up to five additional persons as special members of the National Assembly. Though not a member of the National Assembly, the President will have power to address it at any time. The normal life of Parliament is five years, though the National Assembly has power to vary this in special circumstances. To become law, a Bill will require presidential assent. If the President returns a Bill, it shall not again be presented for assent within six months unless it has the support of two-thirds of all members. If this occurs the President shall either dissolve Parliament or give his assent within 21 days.

The Judiciary: The Chief Justice and all other Judges will be appointed by the President.

House of Chiefs: The Constitution provides for a House of Chiefs numbering 26 provincial chiefs. The President will assume the powers, formerly vested in the Governor.

Citizenship: Automatic citizenship shall be granted to people born in Zambia and to former British-protected persons who were born in Zambia immediately before independence day. Commonwealth or Irish Republic citizens, or citizens of African countries which grant citizenship by a comparable process to Zambians may become citizens by registration.

Bill of Rights: A Bill of Rights will safeguard the rights of individuals and the interests of minorities.

* Originally 75 elected members (amended 1968).

AMENDMENTS

On November 16th, 1972, it was officially announced in a White Paper that Zambia would become a one-party state before the end of the year. The President would retain full executive powers, and would appoint a Prime Minister to head government administration and parliamentary business. The National Assembly will consist of 125 elected members, 10 members nominated by the President, and a Speaker. There will be no institutional representation, and the House of Chiefs will be retained.

The Party will be administered by a Secretary-General appointed by the President. Under the new system of one-party participatory democracy, civil servants and members of the armed forces will be free to stand in parliamentary elections and to belong to the Party. The present structure of provincial and district administrations with cabinet ministers, permanent secretaries and district governors as the main officers will be maintained. In the interests of decentralization, local authorities will be given more powers.

Membership of the Party is voluntary, but open only to Zambian citizens of not less than 18 years of age who fulfil party conditions. The qualifying period for Zambian citizenship has been increased from five to ten years.

THE GOVERNMENT

President: Dr. KENNETH DAVID KAUNDA.

THE CABINET

(*January* 1973)

President: Dr. KENNETH D. KAUNDA.

Vice-President and Minister of National Guidance and Development: M. MAINZA CHONA.

Minister of Foreign Affairs: ELIJAH H. K. MUDENDA.

Minister of Provincial and Local Government and Culture: PETER W. MATOKA.

Minister of Home Affairs: LEWIS CHANGUFU.

Minister of Defence: A. GREY ZULU.

Minister of Transport, Power and Works: FWANYANJA M. MULIKITA.

Minister of Labour and Social Services: WILSON M. CHAKULYA.

Minister of Finance: JOHN M. MWANAKATWE.

Minister of Education: WESLEY P. NYIRENDA.

Minister of Rural Development: REUBEN C. KAMANGA.

Minister of Information, Broadcasting and Tourism: SIKOTA WINA.

Minister of Trade and Industry: ACKSON J. SOKO.

Minister of Lands and Natural Resources: SOLOMON KALULU.

Minister of Mines and Mining Development: HUMPHREY MULEMBA.

Minister of Legal Affairs and Attorney-General: FITZPATRICK CHUULA.

Minister of Health: ALEXANDER B. CHIKWANDA.

Secretary-General to the Government: AARON M. MILNER.

MINISTERS FOR PROVINCES

Eastern Province: WILLIAM NKANZA.

Central Province: P. M. KAPIKA.

Copperbelt Province: ALEX SHAPI.

Western Province: JOSEPHAT B. SIYOMUNJI.

Luapula Province: SAMUEL C. MBILISHI.

Southern Province: ANDREW B. MUTEMBA.

North-Western Province: JETHRO M. MUTI.

Northern Province: PIUS K. KASUTU.

DIPLOMATIC REPRESENTATION

HIGH COMMISSIONS AND EMBASSIES ACCREDITED TO ZAMBIA

(In Lusaka, unless otherwise stated)

(HC) High Commission; (E) Embassy.

Australia: Dar es Salaam, Tanzania (HC).

Austria: Nairobi, Kenya (E).

Belgium: (E); *Ambassador:* PIERRE VAN HAUTE.

Botswana: Stand 2419, Stanley Rd., P.O.B. 1910 (HC); *High Commissioner:* E. ONTUMETSE.

Brazil: Nairobi, Kenya (E).

Bulgaria: Dar es Salaam, Tanzania (E).

Burundi: Dar es Salaam, Tanzania (E).

Canada: (HC); *High Commissioner:* Mr. BROADBRIDGE.

Chile: Chester House, North Wing, Cairo Rd. (E); *Ambassador:* Dr. HERNA SAN MARTIN FERRAIRI.

China, People's Republic: (E); *Ambassador:* LI CHIANG-FEN.

Czechoslovakia: Plot 2278, Independence Ave., P.O.B. 59 (E); *Chargé d'Affaires:* E. KUKAN.

Denmark: (E); *Ambassador:* HANS KUHNE.

Ethiopia: Nairobi, Kenya (E).

Finland: Dar es Salaam, Tanzania (E).

France: Unity House, corner of Stanley Rd., and Jameson St., P.O.B. 62 (E); *Ambassador:* Count DE LA VILLESBRUNNE.

Germany, Federal Republic: 350 Independence Ave., P.O.B. RW 120 (E); *Ambassador:* KARL-HEINZ WEVER.

Guinea: Dar es Salaam, Tanzania (E).

Hungary: Dar es Salaam, Tanzania (E).

India: Stand No. 117A, Livingstone Rd., P.O.B. 2111 (HC); *High Commissioner:* A. M. THOMAS.

Israel: Anchor House, Edinburgh Square, P.O.B. 1973 (E); *Ambassador:* G. ELRON.

Italy: Woodgate House, Cairo Rd., P.O.B. 1046 (E); *Ambassador:* GIROLAMO TROTTA.

Ivory Coast: Kinshasa, Zaire (E).

Jamaica: Nairobi, Kenya (HC).

Japan: (E); *Ambassador:* NOBUYASU NISHIMIYA.

Kenya: (HC); *Ambassador:* LEO PIUS ODERO.

Korea, Democratic Republic: (E); *Ambassador:* KIM SONG GUK.

Liberia: Nairobi, Kenya (E).

Netherlands: 20 Maxwell Rd., P.O.B. 1905 (E); *Ambassador:* Dr. BEERLAERTS VAN BLOCKLAND.

Nigeria: (HC); *High Commissioner:* E. GANA.

Norway: Nairobi, Kenya (E).

Pakistan: Dar es Salaam, Tanzania (E).

Peru: (E); *Chargé d'Affaires:* CESAR ESPEJO ROMERO.

Poland: Dar es Salaam, Tanzania (E).

Romania: (E); *Ambassador:* AUREL ARDELEANU (also accred. to Botswana).

Senegal: Addis Ababa, Ethiopia (E).

Sierra Leone: Addis Ababa, Ethiopia (HC).

Somalia: Nairobi, Kenya (E).

Spain: Dar es Salaam, Tanzania (E).

Sri Lanka: Nairobi, Kenya (HC).

Swaziland: Nairobi, Kenya (HC).

Sweden: Anchor House, Cairo Rd., P.O.B. 788 (E); *Ambassador:* FRITZ IWUO DOLLING.

Switzerland: Dar es Salaam, Tanzania (E).

Syria: Dar es Salaam, Tanzania (E).

Tanzania: (HC); *High Commissioner:* O. M. KATIKAZA.

Trinidad and Tobago: Addis Ababa, Ethiopia (HC).

Turkey: Nairobi, Kenya (E).

U.S.S.R.: 2 Shakespeare Court, Shelley Rd., P.O.B. 2355 (E); *Ambassador:* D. Z. BELOKOLOS.

United Kingdom: Stand 5000, Waddington Rd., P.O.B. RW 50 (HC); *High Commissioner:* J. S. R. DUNCAN, C.M.G., M.B.E.

U.S.A.: Independence Ave., and David Livingstone Rd., P.O.B. 1617 (E); *Ambassador:* Miss JEAN MARY WILKOWSKI.

Vatican: Prince George Rd., P.O.B. 1445 (Apostolic Nunciature); *Papal Nuncio:* Mgr. LUCIANO ANGELONI.

Yugoslavia: Plot 4048, Sandwick Rd., Sunningdale, P.O.B. 1180 (E); *Ambassador:* KEMAL SEJFULA.

Zaire: Plot 1124, Wavell St., P.O.B. 1287 (E); *Ambassador:* BARNABE-ROGER NYARANDE.

Zambia also has diplomatic relations with Cuba and Guyana.

PARLIAMENT

NATIONAL ASSEMBLY

There are 105 members elected on a single electoral roll. Following the establishment of a one-party state with UNIP as the sole party the number of members of the National Assembly is to be increased to 136.

Speaker: ROBINSON NABULYATO.

Leader of the House: MAINZA CHONA.

(Elections, December 1968)

PARTY	SEATS
United National Independence Party (UNIP) .	81
African National Congress	23
Independent	1
Nominated	5

HOUSE OF CHIEFS

22 Provincial Chiefs and four Chiefs representing Barotseland.

POLITICAL PARTIES

United National Independence Party (UNIP): f. 1959; the only legal party in Zambia since it became a one-party state in December 1972; Leader Dr. KENNETH KAUNDA; Gen. Sec. M. MAINZA CHONA.

The following political parties existed before December 1972:

African National Congress: P.O.B. 1005, Lusaka; f. 1944; Leader HARRY NKUMBULA; Deputy Leader NALUMINO MUNDIA; Gen. Sec. MUNGONI LISO.

United Progressive Party: f. August 1971; Pres. SIMON KAPWEPWE; Vice-Pres. ALFRED CHAMBESHI; the Zambia National Democratic Union (f. 1969) later merged with the UPP.

Democratic People's Party: f. 1972; opposed to the creation of a one-party state; Pres. FOUSTINO LOMBE.

DEFENCE

Of a total armed force of 5,500, the army consists of 4,500 and the air force 1,000. The police numbers 6,250, and consists of two battalions. Military service is voluntary.

Commander of the Army: Col. CHINKULI.

Commander of the Air Force: Wing Comdr. PETER ZUZE.

JUDICIAL SYSTEM

The law is administered in Zambia by a High Court, consisting of a Chief Justice and five Puisne Judges. Resident Magistrates' Courts are also established at various centres. The Local Courts deal mainly with customary law, though they have certain statutory powers in addition. A Zambian Court of Appeal was set up early in 1964.

Chief Justice: The Hon. Justice BRIAN DOYLE.

Puisne Judges: Mr. Justice PICKETT, Mr. Justice RAMSAY, Mr. Justice EVANS, Mr. Justice MAGNUS, Mr. Justice GODFREY MUWO.

Justice of Appeal: (vacant).

Registrar of the High Court: J. J. HUGHES.

RELIGION

United Church of Zambia: Synod Headquarters, P.O.B. RW 122, Lusaka; f. 1965; Pres. Rev. J. MWAPE; Gen. Sec. D. M. MUSUNSA.

> **Church of Scotland:** Mem. of United Church of Zambia; Correspondent, Clerk of Synod, U.C.C.A.R., P.O.B. 1777, Kitwe; missions at Mwenzo, Chitambo and Copperbelt.

The United Church of Zambia was formed by union of the British Congregational Church (formerly London Missionary Society, now Congregational Council for World Mission), the Church of Scotland, the British Methodist Church (Methodist Missionary Society), the Reformed Churches of France and Switzerland (formerly the Paris Evangelical Missionary Society, now the Evangelical Community for Apostolic Action), and the United Church of Canada.

ANGLICANS
PROVINCE OF CENTRAL AFRICA

Archbishop of Central Africa: Most Rev. DONALD S. ARDEN, Kasupe, Malawi.

BISHOPS IN ZAMBIA

Central Zambia: Rt. Rev. J. CUNNINGHAM (Ndola).

Lusaka: Rt. Rev. F. MATAKA (Lusaka).

Northern Zambia: Rt. Rev. J. MABULA (Mufulira); publ. *Zambia Diocesan Leaflet.*

Roman Catholic Church: P.O.B. RW 3, Lusaka; f. 1897; publs. *Cengelo, The Sun.*

METROPOLITAN ARCHBISHOPS

Lusaka: Most Rev. EMMANUEL MILINGO (Lusaka).

Kasama: Most Rev. CLEMENT CHABUKASANSHA, P.O.B. 66.

SUFFRAGAN BISHOPS

Chipata: Rt. Rev. MEDARD J. MAZOMBWE, P.O.B. 103.

Livingstone: Rt. Rev. TIMOTHY PHELIM O'SHEA, P.O.B. 138.

Mansa: Rt. Rev. ELIAS MUTALE, P.O.B. 36.

Mbala: Rt. Rev. ADOLF FURSTENBERG, P.O.B. 55.

Monze: Rt. Rev. JAMES CORBOY, P.O.B. 195.

Ndola: Rt. Rev. NICHOLAS AGNOZZI, P.O.B. 244.

Solwezi: Rt. Rev. ABDON POTANI, P.O.B. 33.

African Methodist Episcopal Church: P.O.B. 1478, Lusaka; part of the 17th district of the church; 86 churches under 11 presiding elders in 1965.

Reformed Church of Zambia: P.O.B. 13, Chipata; African successor to the Dutch Reformed Church mission.

Brethren in Christ Church: P.O.B. 115, Choma.

Seventh Day Adventists: P.O.B. 13, Chisekefi.

Salvation Army: Work in Zambia under control of Command H.Q.; P.O.B. RW 193, Lusaka; Social Service Centre: P.O.B. 75, Ndola; runs Chikankata hospital Leprosarium and Chikankata Secondary School, Caanga Clinic and a training college in Lusaka.

Watchtower Bible and Tract Society (Jehovah's Witnesses): P.O.B. 1598, Kitwe; 57,000 active members and about 100,000 adherents in Zambia where the proportion of witnesses to the total population is higher than in any other country.

Muslims: There are about 6,000 members of the Muslim Association in Zambia, and these include a number of Africans.

There are several small Christian communities in Zambia. Some of these are influenced by earlier "Watchtower" movements, and often preserve certain features of traditional African religion. In rural areas many Africans still follow traditional beliefs, though these have declined in the face of modern social and political change.

THE PRESS

DAILY

Times of Zambia. The: P.O.B. 69, Ndola; f. 1943; English; Editor VERNON MWAANGA; circ. 50,000.

Zambia Daily Mail: P.O.B. 1421, Lusaka; f. 1968; Editor-in-Chief VINCENT MIJONI; owned by government-controlled Zambia Publishing Co. Ltd., predecessor African Mail, f. 1960; owned by Zambian government; publ. by Zambia Publishing Co. Ltd., P.O.B. 1059, Lusaka.

PERIODICALS

African Adult Education: P.O.B. 2379, University of Zambia, Lusaka.

African Social Research: P.O.B. 2379, University of Zambia, Lusaka.

Cengelo: Roman Catholic newspaper; P.O.B. 992, Ndola.

Farming in Zambia: P.O.B. RW 197, Lusaka; publ. by Ministry of Rural Development; Editor D. C. MARSHALL.

Intanda: P.O.B. 182, Livingstone; f. 1958; general; fortnightly; published by Zambia Information Services; English and Chitonga; circ. 7,500.

Icengelo: Chifuba Rd., P.O.B. 992, Ndola; Bemba; monthly; published by the Franciscan Fathers; Editor Fr. LUIGI POLICARPO, O.F.M. CONV.

Liseli la Zambia: P.O.B. 80, Mongu; publ. by Zambia Information Services; Lozi; fortnightly.

Livingstone Mail, The: P.O.B. 97, Livingstone; f. 1906; Man. Dir. F. HEWER; English; weekly.

Lukanga News: P.O.B. 919, Kabwe; publ. by Zambia Information Services; English, Bemba, Lenje, Soli and Tonga; fortnightly.

Medical Journal of Zambia: P.O.B. 717, Lusaka; twice a month.

Miner, The: P.O.B. 25, Kitwe; f. 1966; general; fortnightly; house organ of Anglo American Corporation Ltd.; English and Chibemba; illustrated; Editor C. Y. KATEBE; circ. 42,000.

Mufulira Mirror: P.O. Box 67, Mufulira; f. 1963; general; fortnightly; Editor A. MAHLANGU.

Ngoma News: P.O.B. RW 20, Lusaka; English; fortnightly.

Roan Antelope: Luanshya Division, Luanshya; f. 1952; English; illustrated; fortnightly; Editor ABBY RUSIKE.

Sun: Roman Catholic magazine; P.O.B. 8067, Lusaka.

Sunday Times of Zambia: P.O.B. 69, Ndola; f. 1965; Sundays; English; Editor-in-Chief VERNON MWAANGA; circ. 40,875.

Tsopano (*Now*): P.O.B. 202, Chipata; f. 1958 as Nkhani Za Kum'Mawa; name changed 1964 and 1967; fortnightly; published by Information Services, Nyanja and English; circ. 12,000.

Z.: P.O.B. RW 20, Lusaka; f. 1969; English; monthly; published by Zambia Information Services; Editor D. SIMPSON; circ. 10,000.

Zambia Advertiser: P.O.B. 208, Ndola; f. 1935; Editor M. R. THOMPSON.

Zambia Farmer: P.O.B. 717, Ndola; official journal of the Virginia Tobacco Association of Zambia and the National Agricultural Marketing Board; monthly.

Zambia Government Gazette: P.O.B. 136, Lusaka; f. 1911; English; weekly; printed by Government Printer J. E. HARPER.

Zambian Industrial Directory: P.O.B. 717, Ndola; annual.

Zambia Law Journal: P.O.B. 2379, University of Zambia, Lusaka.

Zambian Motor News: Lusaka; official journal of the Motor Trade Association of Zambia; monthly.

Zambia Museums Journal: P.O.B. 498, Livingstone; f. 1970; yearly; Editor Director, Livingstone Museum

The Zambian Review: P.O.B. 717, Ndola; publ. by Associated Reviews; monthly.

PRESS AGENCIES

Agence France-Presse: P.O.B. RW 157, Lusaka; Chief CHRIS PARKER.

FOREIGN BUREAUX

D.P.A. and Reuters have bureaux in Lusaka.

PUBLISHERS

Astonian Press: P.O. Box 394, Lusaka.

Associated Reviews Ltd.: P.O.B. 717, Ndola; periodicals.

B. & T. Directories Ltd.: P.O.B. 1659, Ndola; publs. *Zambia Directory, Livingstone Directory, Lusaka Directory, Ndola Directory, Copperbelt Directory.*

Heinrich Printing and Publishing Co.: Kitwe.

Kabwe Press Ltd.: P.O.B. 131, Kabwe.

Kingstons Limited: P.O.B. 651, Lusaka.

National Educational Publishing Company: P.O.B. 2664, Lusaka.

Oxford University Press: P.O.B. 2335, Lusaka.

The White Fathers: P.O.B. 36, Mansa.

Zambian Advertiser Ltd.: P.O. Box 208, Ndola.

Zambia Publishing Co. Ltd.: P.O.B. 1059, Lusaka; f. 1960; publs. *Zambia Daily Mail*; Man. Dir. ALAN WATERIDGE.

RADIO AND TELEVISION

RADIO

Zambia Broadcasting Services: P.O.B. RW15, Ridgeway, Lusaka; P.O.B. 748, Kitwe; f. 1966 in succession to Zambia Broadcasting Corp.; manages sound broadcasting and puts out contracts for TV services; services in English and seven Zambian languages; Dir. ALICK NKHATA.

In 1971 there were 80,000 radio receivers.

TELEVISION

Television Zambia: P.O.B. RW15, Lusaka; P.O.B. 1100, Kitwe; programme contractors; studios in Kitwe and Lusaka; also runs educational programmes; Controller G. J. WYKES; taken over by the government, April 1967.

In 1971 there were 18,500 television receivers.

FINANCE

Originally, in November 1970, it was announced that the Zambian Government was to take a majority interest in all banks operating in Zambia, and was to take over completely building society and insurance operations. However, the banking proposals were later modified, so that only the already state-owned National Commercial Bank Ltd., together with the Commercial Bank of Zambia Ltd., have the Government as majority shareholder, through FINDECO. The foreign-owned banks have had to become incorporated in Zambia, as from January 1st, 1972. In addition, capitalization of banks has to consist of not less than K500,000 in the case of any commercial bank wholly or partly owned by the Government and not less than K2 million in the case of any other commercial bank. Furthermore, at least half the directors of these latter banks have to be established residents of Zambia.

State Finance and Development Corporation (FINDECO): P.O.B. 1930, Lusaka; f. 1971; responsible for Zambia's state banking, investment, insurance, building society and industrial financing interests; authorized cap. K50 million; Man. Dir. G. F. MUNKONGE.

Up to April 1972, FINDECO financed the Zambianization of small businesses, and now aims at encouraging import substitution, earning foreign exchange and creating employment. It is setting up an Investment Information Bureau to assist investors and promote industrial consciousness among Zambians.

BANKING

(cap. =capital; dep. =deposits)

Bank of Zambia: P.O.B. 80, Lusaka; f. 1964; central bank; cap. K2m.; dep. K54m. (end 1971); Gov. B. R. KUWANI.

COMMERCIAL BANKS

Commercial Bank of Zambia Ltd.: P.O.B. 2555, Lusaka; f. 1965; cap. K2m., p.u. K500,000, dep. K72m. (March 1972); brs. at Kitwe, Livingstone, Lusaka and Ndola.

National Commercial Bank Ltd.: P.O.B. 2811, Lusaka.

FOREIGN BANKS

Barclays Bank of Zambia Ltd.: Head Office: P.O.B. 1936, Lusaka; mem. of the Barclays Group; Chair. and Man. Dir. J. H. C. WHICKER; Gen. Man. K. H. DICKENSON; 28 brs. and 17 subsidiary offices.

Grindlays Bank International (Zambia) Ltd.: Head Office: Woodgate House, Cairo Rd., P.O.B. 1955, Lusaka; fully owned subsidiary of National and Grindlays Bank Ltd., London; nine brs., at Chingola, Kabwe, Kafue, Kitwe, Lusaka (2), Mkushi, Mufulira and Ndola; Chair. A. N. L. WINA; Gen. Man. D. C. HERNAMAN.

Standard Bank Zambia Ltd.: Head Office: P.O. Box 2238, Lusaka; brs. in all main towns; Man. Dir. D. W. BLOXAM.

STOCK EXCHANGE

Zambia Stock Exchange Council: P.O.B. 3300, Lusaka; f. 1971.

INSURANCE

Zambia State Insurance Corporation Ltd.: 1st Floor, Kafue House, Cairo Rd., P.O.B. 894, Lusaka; took over all insurance transactions in Zambia on January 1st, 1972.

TRADE AND INDUSTRY

CHAMBERS OF COMMERCE

Kitwe and District Chamber of Commerce and Industry: Baynard's Bldg., Oxford Ave., P.O.B. 672, Kitwe; 160 mems.; Sec. D. D. TRENT.

Livingstone Chamber of Commerce and Industry: P.O.B. 493, Livingstone; f. 1920; approx. 90 mems.; Pres. D. D. STEYN; Sec. Mrs. O. S. WOODS.

Lusaka Chamber of Commerce and Industry: P.O.B. 844, Lusaka; 180 mems.; Pres. B. J. SHARMA; Sec. L. R. EDWARDS.

Ndola and District Chamber of Commerce and Industry: P.O.B. 6041; f. 1930; 136 mems.; Pres. P. J. REDFERN; Sec. I. K. MEHTA.

INDUSTRIAL AND COMMERCIAL ASSOCIATIONS

Commercial Farmers' Bureau of Zambia: P.O.B. 395, Lusaka; 485 mems.; Pres. A. R. B. LANDLESS; Sec. Mrs. E. M. M. SAUNDERS.

Copper Industry Service Bureau Ltd.: P.O.B. 2100, Kitwe; formerly Chamber of Mines; f. 1941.

Zambian Industrial and Commercial Association: P.O.B. 844, Lusaka; 800 mems.; Pres. M. L. SANDERSON; Sec. L. R. EDWARDS.

STATUTORY ORGANIZATIONS

INDUSTRY

Zambia Industrial and Mining Corporation (ZIMCO): P.O.B. 1935, Lusaka; established by government to hold its mining and industrial portfolio; holds 51 per cent of shares in all mining enterprises; Chair. President KAUNDA; Man. Dir. A. SARDANIS; operates through INDECO and MINDECO which are wholly-owned subsidiaries.

Industrial Development Corporation of Zambia Ltd. (INDECO): P.O.B. 1935, Lusaka; f. 1960; cap. p.u. K32.6m; initiates and operates industrial projects, handles government investments in industry and commerce; consists of a group of over 80 subsidiaries and associates; Chair. A. SARDANIS; publ. *Enterprise* (quarterly).

Consumer Buying Corporation of Zambia Ltd.: P.O.B. 2162, Ndola; f. 1968; partially owned subsidiary of INDECO; undertakes wholesale trade; took over the Booker Group shops and stores 1968; Bookers (Zambia) Ltd. provide management services.

Mining and Development Corporation Ltd. (MINDECO): P.O.B. 90, Lusaka; controls administration of mines, handles other industrial projects; Chair. A. SARDANIS; Man. Dir. B. C. MULAISHO.

AGRICULTURE

Department of Co-operatives: P.O.B. 1229, Lusaka; Dir. S. B. MWAMBA; under Ministry of Rural Development.

Department of Community Development: P.O.B. 1958, Lusaka; under Ministry of Rural Development.

Rural Development Corporation of Zambia Ltd.: P.O.B. 1957, Lusaka; f. 1969; formerly The Agricultural Development Corporation of Zambia Ltd., f. 1968; cap. K30m.; Man. Dir. B. P. KAPOTA.

National Agricultural Marketing Board of Zambia: P.O.B. 122, Lusaka; Gen. Man. R. B. BANDA.

Cold Storage Board: P.O.B. 1915, Lusaka; Gen. Man. S. N. E. CHEMBE.

Dairy Produce Board: P.O.B. 124, Lusaka; Exec. Chair. DUNSTAN KAMANA.

Tobacco Board: P.O.B. 1963, Lusaka; Exec. Chair. W. R. MWONDELA.

TRADE UNIONS
(minimum membership, 1,000)

The Civil Servants' Association of Zambia: P.O.B. RW 12, Ridgeway, Lusaka; f. 1919; 1,500 mems.; Chair. J. A. JARVIS; publ. *Newsletter*.

Zambia Congress of Trade Unions: P.O.B. 652, Kitwe; f. 1965; 16 affiliated unions; 141,977 mems.; Pres. N. L. ZIMBA; Vice-Pres. L. MULIMBA; Gen. Sec. B. R. KABWE.

Principal Affiliates:

Airways and Allied Workers' Union: P.O.B. 272, Lusaka; Pres. M. E. MWINGA; Gen. Sec. S. K. KONGWA.

Hotel Catering Workers' Union of Zambia: P.O.B. 1627, Kitwe; 8,000 mems.; Pres. R. KASOKOLO; Gen. Sec. E. J. BANDA.

Mine Workers' Union of Zambia: P.O.B. 448, Kitwe; Pres. D. MWILA; Gen. Sec. E. S. THAWE.

National Union of Building, Engineering and General Workers: P.O.B. 1515, Kitwe; 12,000 mems.; Pres. F. CHILUBA; Gen. Sec. B. SITALI.

National Union of Commercial and Industrial Workers: 87 Gambia Ave., P.O.B. 1735, Kitwe; 16,000 mems.; Pres. G. B. ZULU; Gen. Sec. J. W. MUSONDA.

National Union of Plantation and Agricultural Workers: P.O.B. 529, Kabwe; 4,500 mems.; Pres. I. B. IKOWA; Gen. Sec. S. C. SILWIMBA.

National Union of Postal and Telecommunication Workers: P.O.B. 751, Ndola; 1,300 mems.; Pres. Mr. SAMPA; Gen. Sec. G. J. TITIMA.

National Union of Public Services Workers: P.O.B. 2523, Lusaka; Gen. Sec. W. H. MBEWE.

National Union of Teachers: P.O.B. 1914, Lusaka; 2,120 mems.; Pres. N. L. ZIMBA; Gen. Sec. M. MUBITA.

National Union of Transport and Allied Workers: P.O.B. 2431, Lusaka; Pres. J. FULILWA; Gen. Sec. B. DAKA.

Zambia Electricity Workers' Union: P.O.B. 859, Ndola; Pres. Mr. NGOMA; Gen. Sec. F. MWANZA.

Zambia Railways Amalgamated Workers' Union: P.O.B. 302, Kabwe; 5,950 mems.; Pres. E. J. MWANSA; Gen. Sec. A. H. SIMWANZA.

Zambia Typographical Union: P.O.B. 1439, Ndola; Pres. N. TEMBO; Gen. Sec. B. M. ZAZA.

Zambia Union of Financial Institutions: P.O.B. 1174, Lusaka; Gen. Sec. E. NKOLE.

Zambia United Local Authorities Workers' Union: P.O.B. 575, Ndola; Pres. H. BWEUPE; Gen. Sec. S. LUNGU.

University of Zambia Staff Association: P.O.B. 2379, Lusaka; Pres. M. MULIZWA; Gen. Sec. Mr. CHIPOTE.

Principal Independent Unions:

Zambian African Teachers' Association: Lusaka; Pres. M. M. KAUNDA.

Zambian African Mining Union: Kitwe; f. 1967 by the merger of the *African Mine Workers' Trade Union,* the *Mines Staff Association* and the *Mines African Police Association;* 40,000 mems.

MAJOR INDUSTRIAL COMPANIES

The following are some of the largest companies in terms either of capital investment or employment.

Chilanga Cement Ltd.: P.O.B. 99, Chilanga; P.O.B. 2639, Lusaka.
Manufacture of cement.

The Dairy Produce Board of Zambia: P.O.B. 124, Kwacha House, Cairo Rd.; f. 1964; state organization.
Purchase of dairy products, supply to retailers, manufacture and marketing of milk products.
Chair. R. C. KAMANGA, M.P.; Gen. Man. D. N. MUTTENDANGO; 756 employees.

Dunlop Zambia Ltd.: P.O.B. 1650, Ndola; f. 1964; cap. K2.2m.
Manufacture and distribution of motor vehicle tyres; distribution of imported products.
Man. Dir. G. C. STRIVENS; 500 employees.

Kafue Textiles of Zambia Ltd.: P.O.B. 131, Kafue; nationalized company.
Manufacture of twills, drills, poplins and sailcloth.

Lever Brothers (Zambia) Ltd.: P.O.B. 1570, Ndola.
Manufactures soaps, detergents, toilet preparations and edibles.
Man. Dir. A. T. MACKIE.

Lonrho Zambia Ltd.: P.O.B. 2568, Lusaka; subsidiaries include National Breweries Ltd., Zambia Newspapers Ltd.
Mining, engineering, manufacturing, motor trade, building.

National Breweries Ltd.: P.O.B. 2699, Kitwe; f. 1968; subsidiary of Indeco Breweries Ltd. which own 51 per cent of shares.
Operates 14 breweries.
Chair. B. G. MOYO; Gen. Man. J. M. MUFALALI; 470 employees.

Nchanga Consolidated Copper Mines Ltd.: P.O.B. 1986, Lusaka; cap. K253,973,000; state owned; Anglo American Corpn. (Central Africa) Ltd. participates.
Mining and processing of 401,000 metric tons of copper,

83,000 metric tons of lead and zinc and 2,000 metric tons of cobalt p.a.
Man. Dir. Dr. Z. J. DE BEER; 30,000 employees.

Nitrogen Chemicals of Zambia Ltd.: P.O.B. 2843, Lusaka; f. 1968; cap. K11.1m.
Production of ammonium nitrate and explosives.
Chair. A. D. ZULU; Gen. Man. Dr. R. VISCONTI; 720 employees.

Roan Consolidated Mines Ltd.: P.O.B. 1505, Mpelembe House, Broadway, Ndola; cap. K121,260,000; state owned.
Copper mining; Man. Dirs. J. L. REID, E. C. BROMWICH.

Roberts Construction Co. (Zambia) Ltd.: P.O.B. 354, Kitwe; f. 1954; cap. K547,000.
Building, civil and mechanical engineering.
Dir. and Man. W. J. R. NOWSON; 2,000–4,000 employees (seasonal).

Zambesi Sawmills (1968) Ltd.: P.O.B. 41, Livingstone; nationalized sawmill.

Zambia Breweries Ltd.: P.O.B. 91, Ndola, 74 Independence Ave., Lusaka; f. 1963; cap. K5,600,000; state enterprise.
Brewing, bottling and distribution of lager beers; 1,700 employees.

The Zambia Broken Hill Development Co. Ltd.: P.O.B. 1986, Lusaka; cap. K6,500,000; state owned; Anglo American Corpn. (Central Africa) Ltd. participates.
Mines about 23,000 metric tons of lead and 27,000 metric tons of zinc p.a.; mines cadmium and silver.
Chair. H. F. OPPENHEIMER; 3,500 employees.

TRANSPORT

In January 1971 a new state company, the National Transport Corporation Ltd., was formed to run INDECO's transport holdings. Zambia Railways, Zambia Airways and Zambia-Tanzania Road Services are to form part of the corporation.

RAILWAYS

Zambia Railways: Head Office: P.O.B. 935, Kabwe; Gen. Man. H. J. FAST.
Total mileage in Zambia 650 miles.

Tan Zam Railway Authority: P.O.B. 1784, Lusaka; construction of the line from Kapiri Mposhi, south of Lusaka, to Dar es Salaam began in 1970 with Chinese aid, and should be completed in five years.

ROADS

There is a total of 34,653 kilometres of which 6,233 are main roads. The main arterial roads run from Beit Bridge to Tunduma (the Great North Road), through the copper mining area to Chingola and Chililabombwe (the Zaïre Border Road), from Livingstone to the junction of the Kafue River and the Great North Road, and from Lusaka to the Malawi border (the Great East Road).

Indeco Transport Ltd.: P.O.B. 1935, Lusaka; state-owned freight and passenger transport service.

Zambia-Tanzania Road Services: P.O.B. 2581, Lusaka; f. 1966; 500 trucks operating between Dar es Salaam, Tunduma (Tanzanian border), the Copperbelt and Lusaka; cap. K4m.

INLAND WATERWAYS

Zambezi River Transport Service Ltd.: P.O.B. 177, Livingstone; operates a passenger and goods service from Livingstone to Senanga. The route is by road to Mambova, thence by barge to Katima Mulilo, and by road to Senanga.

CIVIL AVIATION

A new international airport, 14 miles from Lusaka, was opened in 1967.

Zambia Airways Corporation: City Airport, Lusaka, P.O.B. 272; f. 1967; management by Alitalia until 1976; internal services and flights to Kenya, Tanzania, Botswana, Cyprus, Malawi, Mauritius, Italy and U.K.; fleet of DC-8, two BAC 1-11 and four H.S. 748; Chair. S. C. KATILUNGU; Gen. Man. G. FRARACCI.

The following foreign airlines serve Zambia: Air Zaire, Air Malawi, Alitalia, BOAC, Botswana Airways, British Caledonian, East African Airways and UTA.

TOURISM

In 1971 the number of tourists visiting Zambia totalled 70,352, a 49.8 per cent increase on the 46,950 visitors in 1970.

Zambia National Tourist Bureau: P.O.B. 17, Lusaka; established a Tour Operations Unit at the beginning of 1968.

National Hotels Corporation Ltd.: P.O.B. 3200/3210, Lusaka.

POWER

Zambia Electricity Supply Corporation (ZESCO): P.O.B. 40, Lusaka; a government-controlled corporation which has recently taken over the three main public electricity undertakings and all the municipal electricity undertakings. Main sources of power are the 600 MW Kafue Gorge hydro station and the 108 MW Victoria Falls hydro station, together with power purchased from the Central African Power Corporation's grid supplied by Kariba; the 200 MW Kariba South hydro station will be augmented in 1975 by the 600 MW Kariba North station at present under construction. A further 300 MW extension to Kafue Gorge is also being planned for completion in 1977; Gen. Man. ENAR ESKILSSON.

EDUCATION

In 1969–70 there were 621,500 pupils at primary schools and 48,000 at secondary schools. There are Teacher-Training Colleges and Technical Colleges and the University of Zambia accepted its first students in 1966. Agricultural research for Central Africa is centred at Mount Makulu near Lusaka, while veterinary research is carried on at Mazabuka Research Station. English is to become the medium of instruction in all schools.

LEARNED SOCIETIES AND RESEARCH INSTITUTES

Agricultural Research Council of Zambia: Mount Makulu Research Station, P.O.B. 2218, Lusaka; f. 1967; Chair. Dr. S. SILANGWA; Dir. Dr. C. J. ROSE.

British Council, The: P.O.B. 3571, Lusaka; Rep. J. LAWRENCE; also at P.O.B. 415, Ndola; Regional Dir. E. C. PUGH; library of 15,000 vols.; 3,000 mems.

Central Fisheries Research Institute: P.O.B. 100, Chilanga; f. 1965; hydrobiological research directed towards increasing fish production; library of 4,000 vols.; Project Man. L. S. JOERIS; publs. *Puku, Fisheries Research Bulletin, Fisheries Statistics, Annual Report.*

Central Veterinary Research Station: P.O.B. 50, Mazabuka; f. 1926; directed by the Ministry of Rural Development; general veterinary diagnosis and research; Chief Veterinary Research Officer Dr. M. A. Q. AWAN, M.SC., PH.D., M.I.BIOL. (acting).

Division of Forest Products Research: P.O.B. 388, Kitwe; f. 1963; controls research by the government's Forest Department to promote the Zambian timber industry; Dir. A. A. WOOD; publs. *Bulletin, Records* (irregular).

Division of Forest Research: Forest Department, P.O.B. 2099, Kitwe; f. 1956; silvicultural research, indigenous forests and woodlands and plantations; tree breeding and selection; utilization research; staff of 20, professional and technical; Chief Forest Research Officer D. E. GREENWOOD; library of 1,650 vols. and current periodicals; publs. Research pamphlets and bulletins.

The Engineering Institution of Zambia: P.O.B. 1400, Kitwe; f. 1955; 350 mems.; Pres. D. C. GREENFIELD; Vice-Pres. R. H. ARNOLD; publs. *Journal* (quarterly), *Yearbooks.*

Geological Survey of Zambia (Ministry of Mines and Mining Development): P.O.B. RW 135, Ridgeway, Lusaka; f. 1951; research centre, statutory depository for mining and prospecting reports; the library contains approx. 16,500 vols.; Dir. A. R. DRYSDALL; qualified staff of 40; publs. *Annual Report, Records, Bulletins, Memoirs, Reports, Occasional Papers, Economic Reports, Annotated Bibliography and Index of the Geology of Zambia,* and maps.

Institution of Mining and Metallurgy: P.O.B. 450, Kitwe; f. 1950; local section of Institution of Mining and Metallurgy, London; 305 mems.; Chair. R. V. C. BURLS; Hon. Sec. W. G. WATTS.

International Red Locust Control Organisation for Central and Southern Africa: P.O.B. 37, Mbala; f. 1971; to prevent plagues of Red Locust by controlling incipient outbreaks and to carry out research; member countries: Botswana, Kenya, Lesotho, Malawi, Swaziland, Tanzania, Uganda, Zambia; Dir. K. W. KUHNE; publs. *Annual Report, Scientific Papers.*

Mount Makulu Central Agricultural Research Station: P.O.B. 7, Chilanga; f. 1952; Headquarters of Research Branch of Department of Agriculture, Ministry of Rural Development; research on soils, soil classification, vegetation types and land classification; agronomy; chemistry; ecology; entomology; pasture research; phytosanitary services; plant breeding; plant pathology; seeds services; stored products entomology; cotton breeding and entomology; main crops under investigation: maize, groundnuts, cotton, tobacco, pastures and pasture legumes, beans, etc.; library of 5,000 vols., 10,000 reports, 10,000 reprints; Deputy Dir. of Agriculture (Research) J. B. M. VOGT; Chief Research Officer M. MUMBA; publs. *Annual Report, Mount Makulu Notes and Research Memoranda.*

National Council for Scientific Research: P.O.B. RW 166, Ridgeway, Lusaka; f. 1967; statutory body to advise the government on scientific research policy, to promote and co-ordinate research and to collect and disseminate scientific information; Chair. S. M. KAPWEPWE; Sec.-Gen. Dr. GAMAL GAD.

National Food and Nutrition Commission: P.O.B. 2669, Lusaka; f. 1967; statutory body to improve the nutritional status of the people of Zambia; 98 mems.; Chair. Prof. L. K. H. GOMA; Exec. Sec. A. P. VAMOER.

Pneumoconiosis Medical and Research Bureau: Independence Ave., P.O.B. 205, Kitwe; f. 1950; research on pneumoconiosis and related chest diseases; Dir. Dr. G. H. FLETCHER; Deputy Dir. Dr. R. Z. PTASZYNSKI.

Institute for African Studies, University of Zambia (*formerly* Rhodes-Livingstone Institute): P.O.B. 900, Lusaka; f. 1937; the Institute is a recent merger of the Institute for Social Research and the Centre for African Studies and remains the research arm of the School of Humanities and Social Sciences; Dir. Prof. J. VAN VELSEN; publs. *African Social Research, Journal* (six-monthly), *Zambian Papers, Communications* and *Bulletins* (annually), *Monographs* (irregular).

The Wildlife Conservation Society of Zambia: P.O.B. 10, Lusaka; f. 1953; 1,500 mems.; Pres. Lt.-Col. R. A. CRITCHLEY; Sec. Mrs. E. CRITCHLEY; publ. *Black Lechwe* (quarterly).

Zambia Operational Research Group: P.O.B. 172, Kitwe; f. 1968; Chair. J. D. SANDY.

Zambia Library Association: P.O.B. 2839, Lusaka; Chair. L. Z. CHEELO; Hon. Sec. F. Y. TEMBO; publ. *Zambia Library Association Journal* (quarterly).

Zambia Medical Association: P.O.B. 789, Lusaka.

LIBRARIES AND MUSEUMS

Zambia Library Service: P.O.B. 802, Lusaka; f. 1962; maintains 750 library centres, 2 mobile libraries, 6 regional libraries, 1 branch library and a central library with 300,000 vols.; aims to provide a countrywide free public library service; Librarian L. E. MUKWATO; publs. *Bulletin* (quarterly), *Directory of Library Centres* (annually), *Buyers' Guide to Library Equipment* (twice a year).

British Council Library: P.O.B. 415, Capital House, Buteko Ave., Ndola; f. 1951; 15,300 vols.

Lusaka Public Library: P.O.B. 1304, Lusaka; f. 1943; 70,000 vols.; Librarian F. K. MULENGA, B.S., M.S.L.

Ndola Public Library: P.O.B. 388, Independence Way, Ndola; central library and four brs., school library service, 50,000 vols.; Librarian P. C. KULLEEN.

National Archives of Zambia: P.O.B. RW 10, Ridgeway Lusaka; f. 1947; covers national literature from earliest times to the present day in the forms of national archives, historical MSS., microfilms, cartographic, philatelic, currency, pictorial and printed publication collections; depository and lending library of about 11,500 vols. and 1,000 periodicals; Dir. P. M. MUKULA, B.A.; publs. *Bibliography, Annual Report.*

National Museums of Zambia: P.O.B. 498, Livingstone.

The Livingstone Museum: Mosi-oa-Tunya Rd., Livingstone; f. 1934; ethnology of the peoples of Zambia; archaeology, history and natural history of Zambia; autograph, letters and relics of David Livingstone; early maps of Africa; library specializing in archaeology, history, ethnography and Africana; Dir. Dr. LADISLAV HOLY; publ. *Zambia Museum Journal,*

Zambia Museum Papers, Robins Series of Monographs.

Open Air Museum: Curator A. VRYDAGH.

UNIVERSITY

THE UNIVERSITY OF ZAMBIA

P.O.B. 2379, LUSAKA

Telephone: Lusaka 74030.

Founded 1965.

Academic year: June to March (three terms).

Chancellor: Dr. KENNETH KAUNDA.
Vice-Chancellor: Prof. L. K. H. GOMA, B.SC., M.A., PH.D.
Pro-Vice-Chancellor: Prof. J. D. OMER-COOPER, B.A., M.A.
Chairman of the Council: DAVID A. R. PHIRI, B.LITT.
Registrar: E. A. ULZEN, B.A., P.C.E.
Librarian: W. H. JOHNSONS, M.SC. (acting).

Number of books in library: approx. 300,000.

Number of teachers: 260.

Number of students: 1,568.

Publications: *African Social Research, Zambian Papers, Communications, Bulletin.*

DEANS:

Natural Sciences: P. W. MILES, M.SC., PH.D.
Humanities and Social Sciences: Prof. MARY E. DUREN, B.A., M.S.
Education: P. CROSS, B.A.
Law: Prof. B. O. NWABUEZE, LL.B.
Engineering: Prof. B. FERGUSSON, PH.D.
Medicine: Prof. J. L. BROADBENT, M.D., CH.B.
Agriculture: Prof. H. BERINGER, PH.D.

ATTACHED INSTITUTES:

Department of Correspondence Studies: Dir. A. A. YOUSIF, B.A. (acting).

Department of Extra-Mural Studies: Visiting Dir. A. A. YOUSIF, B.A.

Institute for African Studies: *see* Research Institutes.

Rural Development Studies Bureau: Dir. Prof. D. H. EVANS, M.SC.

COLLEGES

Evlyn Hone College of Further Education: P.O.B. 29, Lusaka; f. 1963.

Principal: S. J. KAZUNGA, B.A.

The library contains 13,000 vols.

Number of students: 650 (full-time), 1,000 (part-time).

Natural Resources Development College: P.O.B. C.H.99, Chelston, Lusaka; f. 1964.

Principal: A. HAMAAMBA.
Vice-Principal: J. R. BIRD.
Librarian: E. W. TANKERSLEY.

The library contains 6,000 vols.
Number of teachers: 30.
Number of students: 350.

Northern Technical College: P.O.B. 1563, Ndola; f. 1964.
  Principal: T. E. ASHTON, B.SC., A.M.I.MIN.E., C.ENG.
  Registrar: M. J. MUMBATI, M.I.S.M.
  Librarian: W. P. KATETE (acting).
  The library contains 9,100 vols.
  Number of students: 1,000.

Zambia College of Agriculture: P.O.B. 53, Monze.

Zambia Institute of Technology: P.O.B. 1993, Kitwe; f. 1970.
  President: I. T. GOODINE, C.D., C.ENG., B.SC., B.ED.
  Registrar: M. A. H. BOND, M.A.
  Librarian: Mrs. B. JOHNSON.
  Library of 6,400 vols.
  Number of teachers: 53.
  Number of students: 430.

SELECT BIBLIOGRAPHY

ALLAN, W. *The African Husbandman*. Edinburgh, Oliver and Boyd, 1965.

BALDWIN, R. E. *Economic Development and Export Growth*. University of California, 1966.

BALLANTYNE, A. O. (Ed.). *Soils of Zambia*. Mount Makulu Research Station, Zambia, 1968.

BARBER, W. J. *The Economy of British Central Africa: A Case Study of Economic Development in a Dualistic Society*. Oxford University Press, 1961.

BOSTOCK, M. and HARVEY, C. *Economic Independence and Zambian Copper. A case study of foreign investment*. London, Pall Mall, 1972.

CLEFF, EDWARD. *Race and Politics: Partnership in the Federation of Rhodesia and Nyasaland*. Oxford University Press, 1960.

DAVIES, D. HYWEL (Ed.). *Zambia in Maps*. London, University of London Press (in press).

Economic Report. Zambian Ministry of Finance (annual).

ELLIOTT, CHARLES. *Constraints to Development in the Zambian Economy*. Oxford University Press (in press).

EPSTEIN, A. L. *Politics in an Urban African Community*. Manchester University Press, 1958.

GANN, L. H. *A History of Northern Rhodesia: early days to 1953*. London, Chatto and Windus, 1964.

GOVERNMENT OF THE REPUBLIC OF ZAMBIA. *First National Development Plan 1966–70*. Lusaka, Government Printer, 1966.
  Census of Population and Housing 1969. Central Statistical Office.

GRAY, RICHARD. *The Two Nations: Aspects of the Development of Race Relations in the Rhodesias and Nyasaland*. Oxford University Press, 1960.

HALL, R. *Zambia*. London, Pall Mall Press, 1965.
  The High Price of Principles. London, Hodder and Stoughton, 1969.

HAZELWOOD, A., and HENDERSON, R. F. *Nyasaland: the Economics of Federation*. Blackwell, 1960.

KAUNDA, KENNETH. *Zambia Shall Be Free*. London, Heinemann, 1963.

KAY, GEORGE. *A Social Geography of Zambia*. London, University of London Press, 1967.

MEEBELO, H. S. *Reaction to Colonialism: a Prelude to the Politics of Independence in Northern Zambia 1893–1939*. Manchester, Manchester University Press, 1971.

Monthly Digest of Statistics. Central Statistical Office.

MULFORD, DAVID. *Zambia, the Politics of Independence, 1957–1964*. Oxford University Press, 1967.

ROBERTS, ANDREW D. "The Political History of Twentieth Century Zambia" in Ranger, T. O. (Ed.) *Aspects of Central African History*. London, Heinemann, 1968.

ROTBERG, ROBERT I. *The Rise of Nationalism in Central Africa*. Harvard University Press, 1966.

PART FOUR
Other Reference Material

WHO'S WHO IN AFRICA SOUTH OF THE SAHARA

A

Abbadi, Bashir Ahmed, D.SC.; Sudanese politician; b. 1936, Omdurman; ed. Univ. of Khartoum and North-western Univ., U.S.A.
Lecturer, Faculty of Eng., Univ. of Khartoum, Head, Dept. of Mechanical Eng. 70-71; mem. Board of Dirs. Sudan Railways 68-69, Chair. 69-70; Minister of Communications Oct. 71-.
Ministry of Communications, Khartoum, Sudan.

Abbas, Major-Gen. Khalid Hassan; Sudanese army officer and politician.
Member, Revolutionary Command Council May 69-72; Chief of Gen. Staff Oct. 69-June 70; Minister of Defence 69-72, also Vice-Pres. of Sudan 71-72; mem. Political Bureau, Sudanese Socialist Union 71-72; mem. Free Officers Group; led del. to Peking 71.
c/o Ministry of Defence, Khartoum, Sudan.

Abdelahi, Mohamed Mokhtar Ould Cheik; Mauritanian politician.
Former Amb. to Spain; Minister of Foreign Affairs April 70-71; now Minister of Industrial Devt.
Ministry of Industrial Development, Nouakchott, Mauritania.

Abdul Maliki, Alhaji, C.B.E.; Nigerian civil servant; b. 1914; ed. Katsina Training Coll.
Teacher, Okene Middle School 34-35; Supervisor, Native Administration Works 36-39; Provincial Clerk 39-40; Chief Exec. Officer, Igbirra Administration 40-55, Admin. Sec. 55; mem. House of Assembly and House of Reps. 52-55; Commr. of Northern Nigeria in the United Kingdom 55-58, of Federation of Nigeria 58-60, High Commr. 60-66; Amb. to France 66-70; mem. Nigerian Port Authority, Northern Region Production Board and King's Coll. Advisory Board.
c/o Ministry of Foreign Affairs, Lagos, Nigeria.

Abdulla, Rahmatalla, M.A.; Sudanese diplomatist; b. 1922; ed. Trinity Coll., Cambridge.
Ambassador to India and Japan 56-60, to Nigeria 60-61, to France, Netherlands, Belgium, Switzerland and Spain 61-65; Minister of Nat. Educ. 64-65; Deputy Under-Sec. for Foreign Affairs 65-67; Amb. to France, Netherlands, Switzerland and Spain 68-70, to Zaire 70-72; Perm. Rep. to UN April 72-; del. to many int. confs.
Permanent Mission of Sudan to United Nations, 757 Third Avenue, 12th Floor, New York, N.Y. 10017, U.S.A.

Abdullah, Abdel Rahman; Sudanese politician; b. 1932, Abu Hamad; ed. Khartoum Univ. Coll.
Joined Ministry of Interior, Sub-Mamour 56; Inspector, Tokar district, later of Kassala Province; joined Halfa People's Settlement Comm. 59; Dir. Inst. of Public Admin. 63-65; Dir. African Admin. Training and Research Inst., Morocco 65; Dir. Nat. Inst. of Public Admin., Libya; Deputy Minister of Local Govt. Aug. 71; Minister of Public Service and Admin. Reform Oct. 71-.
Ministry of Public Service and Administrative Reform, Khartoum, Sudan.

Abebe, Lt.-Gen. Ablye; Ethiopian politician; b. 1916; ed. Haile Sellassie I Military Acad.
Aide to Emperor Haile Sellassie 40-42; Gov.-Gen. Walaga 42; Officer Commdg. First Army Div. 43; Vice-Minister of War 44-48, Minister 48-55; Amb. to France 55-58; Minister of Justice 58-59; Rep. to Eritrea 59-62; Pres. Senate 62-.
The Senate, Addis Ababa, Ethiopia.

Abraham, H.E. Ato Amanuel; Ethiopian educationist, diplomatist and politician; b. 1913; ed. Tafari Makonnen School, Addis Ababa.

Headmaster, Asba-Tafari School, Harar Province 31-35; Sec. Ethiopian Legation, London 35-42; Dir.-Gen. Ministry of Foreign Affairs 43-44, Ministry of Educ. 44-47; Del. to San Francisco Conf. on Int. Org. 45; Del. to UN, New York 47, 49 and 50, special mission to Iran and Indonesia 49; Minister to India 49-52; Amb. to Italy 52-55, to the United Kingdom 55-59, concurrently Minister to the Netherlands 56-59; Chief of Political Affairs, Private Imperial Cabinet 59-61; Minister of Posts, Telegraphs and Telephones 61-66, of Communications 66-69, of Mines 69-.
P.O. Box 1329, Addis Ababa, Ethiopia.

Abrahams, Peter; South African writer; b. 1919, Transvaal; ed. St. Peter's, Johannesburg.
Editor of *West Indian Economist;* now living in Jamaica.
Publs. *Tell Freedom* (autobiography), *Dark Testament* 42, *Song of the City* 45, *Mine Boy* 54, *Wild Conquest* 51, *Path of Thunder* 52, *Return to Gold* 53, *A Wreath for Udomo* 56, *Jamaica* 57, *A Night of Their Own* 65.
Kingston, Jamaica.

Acheampong, Col. Ignatius Kutu; Ghanaian army officer; b. 23 Sept. 1931, Kumasi; ed. St. Peter's Catholic School, Kumasi, R.C. School, Ejisu, Cen. Coll. of Commerce, Agona Swedru and Mons Officer Cadet School, U.K.
Former labourer, schoolteacher and secretary; Principal, Western Commercial Inst., Achiase, Vice-Principal, Agona Swedru Coll. of Commerce and Tutor, Kumasi Commercial Coll. 49-51; commissioned into Ghanaian army 59; Chair. Nat. Redemption Council, Commr. for Defence, Finance and Econ. Affairs Jan. 72-, for Public Relations May 72-, C.-in-C. of Ghana Armed Forces April 72-.
National Redemption Council, Accra, Ghana.

Achebe, Chinua, B.A.; Nigerian writer; b. 16 Nov. 1930; ed. Government Coll., Umuahia, and Univ. Coll., Ibadan.
Producer, Nigerian Broadcasting Corpn., Lagos 54-58, Regional Controller, Enugu 58-61, Dir. *Voice of Nigeria*, Lagos 61-66; Rockefeller Fellowship 60-61; UNESCO Fellowship 63; Foundation mem. Soc. of Nigerian Authors; Editorial Adviser African Writers' Series (Heinemann) 62-72; Chair. Citadel Books Ltd. (Publishers), Enugu 66-; Senior Research Fellow, Inst. of African Studies, Univ. of Nigeria, Nsukka 67-; American speaking tour 70; mem. E. Central State Library Board 71-; Nigerian Nat. Trophy 60; Margaret Wrong Memorial Prize 59; Jock Campbell *New Statesman* Award 65; Hon. D.Litt.
Publs. *Things Fall Apart* 58, *Longer at Ease* 60, *Arrow of God* 64, *A Man of the People* 66, *Chike and the River* 66, *Beware, Soul Brother and other Poems* 71, *Girls at War* 72.
Institute of African Studies, University of Nigeria, Nsukka, East Central State, Nigeria.

Acutt, Sir Keith (Courtney), K.B.E.; British mining executive; b. 6 Oct. 1909.
War service 39-45; Joint Deputy Chair. Anglo-American Corpn. of South Africa Ltd.; Chair. Rand Selection Corpn. Ltd., Wankie Colliery Co.; Dir. De Beers Consolidated Mines Ltd.; Dir. other finance and mining companies.
44 Main Street, Johannesburg, South Africa.

Adade, Nicholas Yaw Boafo, B.SC., B.COM., B.I., LL.B.; Ghanaian barrister and politician; b. 1927, Wenchi; ed. Govt. School, Juaso, Ash-Akim, Accra Acad., Univ. Coll. of Gold Coast and Lincoln's Inn, London.
President, Nat. Union of Gold Coast Students, Ghana 52-53; practised law at Kumasi 57-64; Editor, Ghana Law Reports Nov. 64-June 67; mem. Nat. Liberation Council Legal Cttee. 66-67; Chair. Nat. Liberation Council Cttee. on Management Agreements 66-68; Sec. Ghana Bar Asscn.

66-69; mem. Gen. Legal Council Nov. 66-; Dir. Ghana News Agency April 67-March 68; Dir. Ghana Commercial Bank Feb. 68-April 69; Attorney-Gen. and Minister of Justice 69-71; Minister for Local Admin. and the Interior Jan. 71-Jan. 72; Pres. Asian African Legal Consultative Cttee.
P.O. Box 25, Konongo, Ashanti Akim, Ghana.

Adama, Bukari Kpegla; Ghanaian politician; b. 15 Nov. 1925, Busa.
Field Assistant in medical field units 45-54; elected M.P. (Northern People's Party) for Wala South 54; attended parliamentary course, Westminster, London, 57; Opposition Chief Whip 54-65; in exile in Upper Volta 66; mem. Electoral Comm. 66-68; mem. Constituent Assembly Dec. 68-Aug. 69; M.P. (Progress Party) for Wa Aug. 69; Minister of State for Parliamentary Affairs 69-71; Minister of Defence Feb. 71-Jan. 72.
29, 6th Avenue, Accra, Ghana.
Telephone: Accra 22670.

Adama-Tamboux, Michel; Central African Republic diplomatist, politician and educationist; b. 3 Dec. 1928, Zémio; ed. Ecole Normale, Mouyoundi, Ecole Normale Supérieure, Saint-Cloud, France.
Assistant to Dir. of European School, Bangui 49, subsequently Asst. Dir. and Dir. of regional schools at Bossangoa, Bambari and Grimari; Inspector of Primary Educ. 60; Territorial Adviser, Legislative Assembly of Ubangi Shari (fmr. name of Central African Repub.) 57; mem. Cttee. to draft Central African Repub. constitution 58; Chair. Legislative Comm. on Institutions and Admin. 59; Econ. and Social Adviser 59-64; Pres. Legislative Assembly 60; Pres. Nat. Assembly (following independence) 60-66; Vice-Pres. Mouvement de l'Evolution Sociale de l'Afrique Noire (MESAN) 62-66; rep. to many int. confs. and mem. many econ. and political missions; Perm. Rep. to UN Aug. 70-; Grand Officier, Ordre du Mérite Centrafricain, Légion d'Honneur; Grand Croix, Ordre du Mérite de Tunisie; Commdr., Palmes Académiques Françaises, Mérite Agricole.
Permanent Mission of the Central African Republic to United Nations, 386 Park Avenue South, Room 1614, New York, N.Y. 10017, U.S.A.

Adebayo, Maj.-Gen. Robert; Nigerian army officer; b. 1928; ed. Christ's School, Ado-Ekiti, and Eko Boys' High School, Lagos.
Joined Army 48; commissioned in England 53, returned to Nigeria 54, Capt. 57, Maj. 60, Lieut.-Col. 62, Col. 64; A.D.C. to Gov.-Gen. 57-58; served in UN Peace Keeping Force (Congo) 61-63; Chief of Staff of Nigerian Army 64-65; Mil. Gov. of W. Nigeria 66-71; Commdt. Nigerian Defence Acad., Kaduna 71-; mem. Supreme Mil. Council.
Nigerian Defence Academy, Kaduna, Nigeria.

Adebo, Simeon Olaosebikan; Nigerian lawyer and diplomatist; b. 5 Oct. 1913, Abeokuta, Nigeria; ed. King's Coll. Lagos, London Univ. and Gray's Inn, London.
Permanent Sec. to Ministry of Finance, W. Nigeria 57-59, to Treasury 59-60; Head of Civil Service and Chief Sec. to Govt. of W. Nigeria 61-62; Amb., Perm. Rep. of Nigeria to the United Nations 62-67; UN Under-Sec.-Gen. and Exec. Dir. of UN Inst. for Training and Research 68-72; Chair. Wages and Salaries Comm. July 70; Pres. Soc. for Int. Devt. 66-67, 67-68; nine hon. degrees.
Fowotade House, Oke-Ilewo Road, Ibara, Abeokuta, Nigeria.

Adedeji, Adebayo, PH.D.; Nigerian economist; b. 21 Dec. 1930, Ijebu-Ode; ed. Ijebu-Ode Grammar School, Univ. Coll., Ibadan, Univ. Coll., Leicester and Harvard Univ.
Assistant Sec., Ministry of Econ. Planning, W. Nigeria 58-61, Principal Asst. Sec. (Finance) 62-63; Deputy Dir. Inst. of Admin., Univ. of Ife 63-66, Dir. 67- (on

leave of absence 71-74); Prof. of Public Admin., Univ. of Ife 68- (leave of absence 71-74); Fed. Commr. for Econ. Devt. and Reconstruction 71-; mem. Nigerian Inst. of Management; Pres. Nigerian Econ. Soc.; Vice-Pres. African Asscn. for Public Admin. and Management, Asscn. of Schools and Insts. of Admin.; Hon. M.P.A.
Publs. *A Survey of Highway Development in Western Nigeria* 60, *Nigerian Federal Finance: Its Development, Problems and Prospects* 69.
Federal Ministry of Economic Development and Reconstruction, P.M.B. 12558, Lagos, Nigeria.

Adekunie, Brig.-Gen. Benjamin A. M.; Nigerian army officer.
Lieutenant-Colonel June 67; Commander, Third Marine Commandos, Nigerian Army; Dir. of Training and Planning at Supreme Mil. H.Q. May 69-; Mil. Commdt. Port of Lagos May 70-; Acting Brig.-Gen. 72.
c/o Supreme Military Headquarters, Lagos, Nigeria.

Ademola, Rt. Hon. Sir Adetokunbo Adegboyega, P.C., K.B.E., C.F.R.; Nigerian lawyer; b. 1 Feb. 1906; ed. St. Gregory's Grammar School, Lagos, King's Coll., Lagos, Cambridge Univ. and Middle Temple, London.
In Crown Law Office, Lagos 34-35; Admin. officer, Enugu 35; in private practice as barrister and solicitor, Lagos 36-39; Magistrate in Nigeria 39-49; Puisne Judge, Nigeria 49-55; Chief Justice, Western Region 55-58; Chief Justice, Supreme Court 58-Feb. 72 (retd.); Chair. Census Board 72-; mem. Int. Comm. of Jurists, Int. Olympic Cttee.; Hon. Bencher, Middle Temple 59.
15 Ikoyi Crescent, Lagos, Nigeria.

Aderemi, Sir Adesoji, the Oni of Ife, K.C.M.G.; Nigerian administrator; b. 1889; ed. St. Philip's School, Ife.
Served with Nigeria Railway Dept. 09-21; Oni of Ife 30-; mem. Nigerian Legislative Council 47; Del. African Conf., London 48; Pres. Western Region House of Chiefs 51-63; mem. Nigerian House of Reps. 51-54; Central Minister without Portfolio 51-55; Del. to Nigerian Constitution Conf. 57 and 58; Gov. Western Region of Nigeria 60-62; mem. Nigerian Cocoa Marketing Board 47-51; Dir. Nigerian Produce Marketing Co. Ltd. 47-51.
The Afin, Ife, Western Region, Nigeria.

Adetoro, Joseph Eyitayo, M.ED., PH.D.; Nigerian politician and former university lecturer; b. 16 Dec. 1933, Mopa, Kabba Province, Kwara State; ed. Kaduna Coll., Govt. Coll. of Technology, Zaria, Univ. Coll., Ibadan, London Univ., Keble Coll. Oxford, Univs. of Birmingham and Alberta.
Lecturer in English, Vice-Principal, Senior English and Geography Master, Kiriji Memorial Coll., Igbajo; Lecturer in English, Dept. of Extra-Mural Studies, Univ. of Ibadan 59-63; Lecturer in Faculty of Educ., Univ. of Lagos 63-67; mem. Fed. Exec. Council 67-; Fed. Commr. for Health 67-71, for Industries 71-; Chair. St. John Council of Nigeria; C.St.J. 70.
Publs. *A Primary History Course for Western Nigeria, A Primary History of Nigeria, A School History for Nigeria, Handbook of Education in Nigeria;* Social Studies series: *The Family; The School; The Community.*
Federal Ministry of Industries, Lagos, Nigeria.

Adomakoh, Albert, M.A.; Ghanaian banker, economist and lawyer; b. 8 April 1924; ed. Downing Coll., Cambridge.
Barrister-at-Law; Sec. Bank of Ghana 57-62; Postgraduate, London School of Econ. 61-62; Man. Dir. and Chair. Nat. Investment Bank 62-65; Gov. Bank of Ghana 65-68; Commr. (Minister) for Agriculture March 68-Aug. 69; Asst. Dir.-Gen. FAO; Dir. Dept. of Investments, Africa and the Middle East, IBRD June 70-; mem. Econ. Cttee. of Nat. Liberation Council; mem. Univ. Council, Legon, Volta River Authority, Nat. Advisory Cttee.

Publ. *The History of Currency and Banking in West African Countries* 62.
Department of Investments, International Bank for Reconstruction and Development, Washington, D.C., U.S.A.

Adoula, Cyrille; Zaire politician; b. 13 Sept. 1921, Kinshasa (then Leopoldville); ed. secondary school.
Worked for private firms in Congo 41-52; Congo Central Bank 52-56; trade union activities 56-60; Minister of Interior 60-61; Prime Minister 61-64; Amb. to Belgium, Luxembourg and EEC 66, to U.S.A. Nov. 66-69; fmr. Minister of Foreign Affairs, later seriously ill in Switzerland.
c/o Ministry of Foreign Affairs, Kinshasa, Zaire.

Adu, Amishadai Larson, C.M.G., O.B.E., G.M.(GHANA), M.A.; Ghanaian public servant; b. 1914, Anum, Ghana; ed. Achimota School, Ghana, Queen's Coll. Cambridge and Imperial Defence Coll., London.
Science Master, Achimota School 39-42; joined Colonial Admin. Service, Gold Coast 42, Joint Sec. Cttee. on Constitutional Reform (Coussey Cttee.) 49; Commr. for Africanization, Gold Coast Civil Service 50-52, Dir. of Recruitment and Training 52-55; Sec. for External Affairs Gold Coast 55-57, Perm. Sec. Ministry of External Affairs, Ghana 57-59; Sec. to Cabinet, Ghana 59-61; Sec. Nat. Council for Higher Educ. and Research, Ghana 61-62; Sec.-Gen. East African Common Services Org. 62-63; Regional Rep. UN Technical Assistance Board and Dir. Special Fund Programmes in E. Africa 64-65; Deputy Sec.-Gen. Commonwealth Secretariat, London 66-Oct. 70; Dir. Consolidated African Selection Trust Oct. 70-.
Publ. *The Civil Service in Commonwealth Africa* 69.
Office: Consolidated African Selection Trust, Accra, Ghana; Home: P.O. Box 20, Aburi, Ghana.

Adwok, Bong Gicomeko, Luigi; Sudanese schoolmaster and public servant; b. 1929; ed. Rumbek Secondary School and Inst. of Education, Bakht Er Ruda.
Schoolmaster 52-58; mem. Parl. March-Nov. 58; Headmaster Tembura Intermediate School 63-64; elected mem. Supreme Council of State Dec. 64, re-elected June 65, resigned June 65; mem. Central Exec. Cttee. Southern Front Party 64-67; mem. Sudan Constituent Assembly 67-69; mem. for Educ., High Exec. Council for the Southern Region April 72-.
High Executive Council for the Southern Region, Juba, Sudan.

Afanasenko, Yevgeni Ivanovich; Soviet politician; b. 17 April 1914, Budishche Village, Byelorussia; ed. Herzen Pedagogical Inst., Leningrad.
Secondary school teacher 38-41; Soviet Army 41-46; mem. C.P.S.U. 43-; Head of Educ. Dept., Frunze Reg., Moscow 48-50; party work 50-56; Head of Org. Dept., Moscow City Cttee., C.P.S.U. 54-55, Sec. City Cttee. 55-56; Minister of Educ. for the R.S.F.S.R. 56-66; Amb. to Rwanda 66-; Candidate mem. Central Cttee. of C.P.S.U. 61-66; Deputy to U.S.S.R. Supreme Soviet; Order of Lenin, Order of Red Banner of Labour, Order of Red Star.
U.S.S.R. Embassy, P.O. Box 40, Kigali, Rwanda.

Afewerk, Teklé; Ethiopian artist; b. 1932, Ankober, Shoa; ed. Balabat School, Haile Sellassie I Secondary School, London Univ.
Commissioned to design stained glass windows for Africa Hall, Headquarters of Econ. Comm. for Africa (ECA), Addis Ababa 60; works include frescoes, mosaics, murals, sculpture, drawings and designs for Ethiopian stamps; one-man exhbns. Addis Ababa 61, Washington and New York and U.S.S.R. 64; exhbns. and lectures in Dakar, Senegal, Turkey, Congo and Egypt; First Haile Sellassie I Prize for Fine Arts 64; Commdr., Order of Merit (Senegal),

Officier, Art et Lettre (France), Order of Menelik (Ethiopia), Order of Cynil and Methodius 1st Class.
Villa Alpha, P.O. Box 5651, Addis Ababa, Ethiopia.

Afrifa, Lieut.-Gen. Akawasi Amankwa, C.V., D.S.O.; Ghanaian army officer and politician; b. 24 April 1936; ed. Adisadel Coll., Mons Officer Cadet School and Royal Military Acad. Sandhurst, England.
Second Lieut. 60; in command of rifle platoon, Congo 60; Lieut. 61, Platoon Commdr. 5th Infantry Battalion, Tamale, Ghana 61; infantry courses in U.K. 61, later served again in Congo; 1st Brigade H.Q., Ghana 62, then 2nd Brigade, Kumasi; Maj. Aug. 65; mem. Nat. Liberation Council in charge of Finance 66; Chair. Nat. Liberation Council April 69; Chair. Presidential Comm. Sept. 69-Sept. 70; Lieut.-Gen. Aug. 70; mem. Council of State 71-72; arrested Jan. 72.
Publ. *The Ghana Coup.*
c/o Ministry of Justice, Accra, Ghana.

Agama, Dr. Gotfried K.; Ghanaian politician.
Former lecturer in Econ., Univ. of Ghana; Parl. Opposition leader Nov. 69-70; research at Princeton Univ. 70; Chief Research Officer, Ghana Cocoa Marketing Board July 72-; M.P. for Tongu South.
Cocoa Marketing Board, Accra, Ghana.

Ahanda, Vincent de Paul; Cameroonian diplomatist and politician; b. 24 June 1918; ed. Mission Catholique de Mvolyé, Yaoundé, Petit Séminaire St. Joseph, Akono and Grand Séminaire St. Laurent, Yaoundé.
Civil Servant, Cameroon 40-56; Deputy to Legis. Assembly 56; Minister of Youth and Sport and Nat. Educ. 57; Amb. to Fed. Repub. of Germany 60-62, to Belgium, Luxembourg and Netherlands and Perm. Rep. to EEC 62-65; Prime Minister of East Cameroon 65-66; Pres., Dir.-Gen. of Soc. Nat. "Les Argiles Industrielles du Cameroun" Aug. 67-; Officier, Ordre de la Valeur Camerounaise; Commandeur de l'Ordre National de la République de Tunisie; Grand Croix de l'Orde de Mérite du Grand Duché de Luxembourg.
"Les Argiles Industrielles du Cameroun", B.P. 248, Yaoundé, Cameroon.

Ahidjo, Ahmadou; Cameroonian politician; b. Aug. 1924; ed. Ecole Supérieure d'Administration, Yaoundé.
Began his career in radio administration; elected as Rep. to Representative Assembly of Cameroon 47; fmr. Sec. of Assembly, Pres. Admin. Affairs Comm., Vice-Pres.; Counsellor Assembly of the French Union 55-58, fmr. Sec.; Pres. Territorial Assembly of Cameroon 56-57; Minister of the Interior 57-59; Deputy Prime Minister 57-58; Prime Minister 58-59; Prime Minister and Minister of the Interior, independent state of Cameroon Jan.-May 60; Pres. of Cameroon May 60-61, of the Fed. of Cameroon 61-72, of the United Repub. of Cameroon 72-; Pres. Groupe d'Union Camerounaise; Chair. Assembly of OAU 69; Pres. Council of Heads of States, UDEAC 70; Titulaire Etoile-Noire du Bénin.
Présidence de la République, Yaoundé, United Republic of Cameroon.

Ahin, Etienne; Ivory Coast politician; b. 1934, Adjamé-Bingerville; ed. Law Faculty, Dakar, Senegal and Nat. School of Taxation, Paris.
Trainee taxation insp. Nov. 58, Insp. Nov. 60-61; Chief Insp. Registration Dept., Bouaké 61-67; Dir. of Budget Feb. 67-Jan. 70; Minister of People's Educ., Youth and Sport Jan. 70-.
Ministry of People's Education, Youth and Sport, Abidjan, Ivory Coast.

Ahmad, Maj.-Gen. Mohammed al-Baqir; Sudanese army officer and politician; b. 1927, El Sofi; ed. Commercial Secondary School, Khartoum, Military Coll. and Cairo Univ.

Commissioned 50; Chief of Staff, Southern Command 58; Mil. Gov. Upper Nile Province 59; Mil. Attaché, London 60-67; Dir. of Training and Chief of Staff, Southern Command 68; Commdr. Mil. Coll. 68-69; Under-Sec. Ministry of Defence June-Dec. 69; First Deputy Chief of Staff of Armed Forces Dec. 69-June 70, Chief of Staff 70-71; Minister of the Interior Oct. 71-; First Vice-Pres. May 72-; mem. Political Bureau, Sudanese Socialist Union; mem. Council, Univ. of Khartoum; del. to several int. confs.; several decorations.
Ministry of the Interior, Khartoum, Sudan.

Ahmed, Jamal Mohamed, B.LITT.; Sudanese writer and former diplomatist; b. 14 April 1917; ed. Gordon Coll., Khartoum, Univ. Coll., Exeter, and Balliol Coll., Oxford.
Teacher, Sudan Govt. Schools 39-44; mem. Publications Bureau, Ministry of Educ., Sudan 46-49; Warden, Univ. Coll., Khartoum 50-56; Sudan Foreign Service 56-, Amb. to Iraq 56-59, to Ethiopia 59-64; Perm. Rep. to UN 64-65; Amb. to U.K. 65-67; Perm. Under-Sec., Ministry of Foreign Affairs 67-69; Amb. to U.K. 69-70; decorated by Iraq, Jordan, Syria, Ethiopia, Zaire, Niger and Bulgaria.
Publs. *Intellectual Origins of Egyptian Nationalism* 61; trans. of Federaiist papers (Beirut), *Africa Rediscovered* (trans.), *Readings in African Affairs, African Tales.*
c/o Ministry of Foreign Affairs, Khartoum, Sudan.

Ahomadegbé Tometin, Justin; Dahomeyan politician; b. 1917; ed. William-Ponty School, Dakar, and School of Medicine, Dakar.
Medical work, Cotonou, Porto Novo 44-47; mem. Gen. Council, Dahomey 47, Sec.-Gen. Bloc Populaire Africain; Sec.-Gen. Union Démocratique Dahoméenne (UDD) 56; mem. Grand Council, A.O.F. 57; mem. Dahomey Legislative Assembly 59, Pres. 59-60; medical work 60-61; imprisoned 61-62; Minister of Health, Public Works and Nat. Educ. 63; Vice-Pres. of Dahomey, Pres. of Council of Ministers and Minister in Charge of Interior, Defence, Security and Information 64-65, also in charge of the Plan 65; mem. Presidential Council 70-72, Pres. May-Oct. 72.
c/o Presidential Council, Porto Novo, Dahomey.

Ahouanmenou, Michel; Dahomeyan diplomatist and politician; b. 23 Dec. 1916, Porto Novo.
Principal schoolmaster; mem. ruling cttee., PRA Sept. 58-April 59; Pres. PRD Sept 59-March 60; Territorial councillor, later M.P., for Porto Novo March 52-Jan. 64; Senior councillor to French West Africa (the A.O.F.) May 57-April 59; fmr. Pres. Cttee. for Econ. Affairs, High Council of the A.O.F.; mem. Constituent State Assembly Jan.-April 59; Rep. to Senate of French Community April 59-Jan. 61; Sec. of State for Youth and Sport Jan.-Nov. 60; Minister of Nat. Educ. and Culture Dec. 60-Sept. 63; Minister of Nat. Educ. and Youth Sept. 63-Oct. 63; Dir. Cabinet of the Pres. of the Repub. 64-66; Dir. of Youth and Sport 66-67; Amb. to France 67-71, to U.K. 69-71; Minister of Foreign Affairs 71-Oct. 72; under house arrest following *coup* Oct. 72.
c/o Ministry of Foreign Affairs, Porto Novo, Dahomey.

Akassou, Djamba; Cameroonian politician; b. 1926, Yagoua.
Commercial stock-breeder and territorial councillor; M.P. for Diamaré March 52-May 57, for Mayo-Danai April 60-April 64; Pres. U.A.M.P.T. April-Nov. 61; Sec. of State attached to the Presidency, in charge of Information, Posts and Telecommunications Feb. 58-May 59; Minister of Posts and Telecommunications May 59-Oct. 61; Fed. Minister without Portfolio Oct. 61-July 64; Minister attached to the Presidency July 64-.
Offices of the President, Yaoundé, United Republic of Cameroon.

Aké, Siméon; Ivory Coast lawyer and diplomatist; b. 4 Jan. 1932; ed. Univs. of Dakar and Grenoble.
Chef de Cabinet to Minister of Public Service, Ivory Coast 59-61; First Counsellor, Ivory Coast Mission to UN 61-63; Dir. of Protocol, Ministry of Foreign Affairs 63-64; Amb. to U.K., Sweden, Denmark and Norway 64-66; Perm. Rep. of Ivory Coast to UN Sept. 66-; Officer of Nat. Order of Republic of Ivory Coast.
Permanent Mission of Ivory Coast to United Nations, 46 East 74th Street, New York, N.Y. 10021, U.S.A.

Akenzua II, Oba Omonoba Ukuakpolokpolo, C.M.G.; traditional monarch (Oba) of Benin, Nigeria; b. 1899, Benin City, Mid-Western State; *s.* of Oba Eweka II; ed. Benin Govt. School, King's Coll., Lagos.
Transport clerk, Benin Native Authority, 21-24; confidential clerk to his father 24; ascended throne April 33; nominated mem. Western House of Assembly 47, later mem. Nigerian Legislative Council; mem. Western Nigeria House of Chiefs 51-; Cabinet Minister without Portfolio 55-62; Pres. Mid-Western House of Chiefs 63-Jan. 66; Chancellor, Ahmadu Bello Univ., Zaria March 66-May 72.
Residence of the Oba, Benin City, Western Nigeria.

Aklilou Abte-Wold, Teshafi Teezaz, L.en D.; Ethiopian politician; b. 12 March 1912; ed. French Lycée, Alexandria, Univ. of Paris and Ecole des Sciences Politiques, Paris.
Chargé d'Affaires, Ethiopian Legation, Paris 36-40; Vice-Minister of the Pen 42-43; Vice-Minister (and acting Minister) for Foreign Affairs 43-49; Minister for Foreign Affairs 49; Acting Chief Del., San Francisco Conf. 45 and Ethiopian signatory UN Gen. Assembly from 1st to 7th session and 10th Session; mem. Consultative Cttee. for Legislation 43-; Pres. Board of Educ. 47-; mem. Board of Dirs. State Bank of Ethiopia; Chief Del. of Ethiopia, Suez Conf., London 56; Deputy Prime Minister and Minister for Foreign Affairs (with the title of Blattenguetta) 58-60; Prime Minister and Minister of the Pen 61-63; Prime Minister 63-; awards include Grand Officer Légion d'Honneur; Grand Officer of Trinity (Ethiopia); Grand Cordon of Menelik II (Ethiopia), Ismail (Egypt), El Sol del Peru; Order of Orange Nassau, Flag of Yugoslavia, St. George (Greece) and the Aztec Eagle (Mexico); Grand Cross Orders of the North Star (Sweden), Dannebrog (Denmark), St. Olav (Norway), Merit (Germany); Hon. G.C.V.O.
Prime Minister's Office, P.O. Box 1031, Addis Ababa, Ethiopia.

Akoto, Paul Yao; Ivory Coast educationist and politician; b. 12 April 1938, Sakasso (Bouake); ed. Ecole Normale Supérieure, Saint Cloud.
Teacher of natural sciences, Ecole Supérieure, Abidjan 66-68, concurrently Technical Adviser, Ministry of Nat. Educ.; Asst. Dir.-Gen. of Educ. 68-69; Dir.-Gen. of Educ. 69-71; mem. Political Bureau 69-; Minister of Nat. Educ. Dec. 71-; Chevalier de l'Ordre de l'Etoile Equatoriale du Gabon; Officier de l'Ordre National de Côte d'Ivoire; Grand Officier de l'Ordre National du Sénégal.
Ministère de l'Education Nationale, B.P. 1716, Abidjan, Ivory Coast.

Akufo-Addo, Edward, M.O.V., M.A.; Ghanaian lawyer; b. 1906; ed. Presbyterian Church Seminary, Akropong, Achimota School, St. Peter's Coll., Oxford, and Middle Temple, London.
Member Legis. Council, Ghana 49-50; mem. Coussey Constitutional Comm., Ghana 49; Judge of Ghana Supreme Court 62-64; Chair. Political Cttee. of Nat. Liberation Council 66; Chair. Board of Dirs. Ghana Commercial Bank 66; Chair. Constitutional Comm., Ghana 66; Chief Justice of Ghana Sept. 66-70; Pres. of Ghana Sept. 70-Jan. 72; Chair. Gen. Legal Council, Ghana 66-70; Chair. Council of Univ. of Ghana 66; mem. London Inst. of World Affairs; Hon. Fellow St. Peter's Coll., Oxford.
Yeboaa Buw, 46/5 Nima Road, Ringway Central, Accra, Ghana.
Telephone: 63534.

Akwei, Richard Maximilian; Ghanaian diplomatist; b. 1923; ed. Achimota Coll., Accra, London Univ. and Christ Church, Oxford.
Administration Officer, Ghana Civil Service 50-56; Ghana Diplomatic Service 56-; attached to U.K. High Comm., Ottawa 56-57; First Sec., Washington 57-60; Dir. W. European and E. European Depts. Ministry of Foreign Affairs, Accra 60-64; Amb. to Mexico 64-65; Perm. Rep. to UN, Geneva, and Amb. to Switzerland 65-67; Perm. Rep. to UN, N.Y. 67-72; Amb. to People's Repub. of China Sept. 72-; Ghana Rep. at numerous int. confs.
Embassy of Ghana, Peking, People's Republic of China.

Ali Aref Bourhan; French Somali politician; b. 1934.
Member Territorial Assembly French Somaliland 57-, Vice-Pres. 58; Vice-Pres. Council of Govt., Pres. 67-; Minister of Public Works and the Port 60-66; mem. Econ. and Social Council, Paris 63-66; Chevalier Légion d'Honneur, Chevalier de l'Etoile Noire.
Presidency of Council of Government, B.P. 9, Djibouti, French Afar and Issa Territory.

Alidou, Barkire; Niger politician; b. 1925, Niamey; ed. Frederic Assomption Teachers' Training Coll., Katibougou, Mali.
Former elementary school teacher and headmaster; Chef de Cabinet, Minister of the Interior 59-61; Sec.-Gen. of Nat. Defence Feb. 62-Oct. 64; Dir. of Defence Oct. 64-Nov. 65; Minister of Econ. Affairs, Commerce and Industry Nov. 65-Jan. 71; Minister of Justice Jan. 71-; mem. Political Bureau, Parti Progressiste Nigérien (PPN); Gen. Treas. Political Bureau, PPN; Titular Judge, Court of State Security; Pres. Office Africain et Malgache de la Propriété Industrielle (OAMPI); Dir. Air Afrique.
Ministry of Justice, Niamey, Niger.

Alier, Abel, LL.M.; Sudanese politician; b. 1933, Bor District, Upper Nile Province; ed. Univs. of Khartoum, London, Yale.
Former advocate; District Judge in El Obeid, Wad Medani and Khartoum until 65; participant in Round Table Conf. and mem. Twelve Man Cttee. to Study the Southern problem 65; mem. Constitution Comms. 66-67, 68; fmr. mem. Law Reform Comm. and Southern Front; Minister of Housing May-June 69, of Supply and Internal Trade July 69-July 70, of Works July 70-July 71, of Southern Affairs July-Oct. 71, concurrently Vice-Pres. of Sudan Oct. 71-; Pres. High Exec. Council for the Southern Region April 72-; mem. Board of Dirs., Industrial Planning Corpn.; mem. Nat. Scholarship Board.
High Executive Council for the Southern Region, Juba, Sudan.

Alifa, Mahamat Douba; Chad politician; b. 10 Sept. 1929, Boussa.
Member of the Nat. Political Bureau, Parti progressiste tchadien (PPT); First Vice-Pres. Nat. Assembly; Minister of the Interior Oct. 68-.
Ministry of the Interior, Fort-Lamy, Chad.

Aliey, Col. Alphonse; Dahomeyan army officer and politician; b. 9 April 1930; ed. primary schools at Lomé, Togo, and Military School in Ivory Coast.
Joined 5th Senegalese Rifle Regt., Dakar; served in Indo-China 50-53, Morocco 55-56, Algeria 59-61; returned to Dahomey 61; Second-Lieut. Dahomeyan Army 61, Capt. 62, Major 64, Lieut.-Col. 67, Chief of Staff 67; Pres. of Dahomey Dec. 67-68; Sec.-Gen. for Nat. Defence 70-72.
Carré 181-182, B.P. 48, Cotonou, Dahomey.

Alliali, Camille; Ivory Coast lawyer and diplomatist; b 23 Nov. 1926; ed. Dakar Lycée and Lycée Champollion, Grenoble.
Former Advocate, Court of Appeal, Abidjan; mem. central cttee. of Parti démocratique de Côte d'Ivoire (PDCI); Vice-Pres. Nat. Assembly, Ivory Coast 59; Senator of French Community 59-61; Amb. to France 61-63; Minister of Foreign Affairs 63-66; Keeper of the Seals and Minister of Justice 66-; Commander, Légion d'Honneur, etc.
Ministry of Justice, Abidjan, Ivory Coast.

Amin, Samir, D.ECON.; Egyptian economist; b. 4 Sept. 1931, Cairo; ed. Univ. of Paris.
Senior Economist, Econ. Devt. Org., Cairo 57-60; Technical Adviser for Planning to Govt. of Mali 60-63; Prof. of Econs., Univs. of Poitiers, Paris and Dakar; Dir. UN African Inst. for Econ. Devt. and Planning 70-.
Publs. *Trois expériences africaines de développement, Mali, Guinée, Ghana* 65, *L'Economie du Maghreb* (2 vols.) 67, *Le développement du capitalisme en Côte d'Ivoire* 68, *Le Monde des affaires sénégalais* 68, *Maghreb in the Modern World* 70, *L'Accumulation à l'échelle mondiale* 70, *L'Afrique de l'Ouest bloquée* 71.
African Institute for Economic Development and Planning, B.P. 3186, Dakar, Senegal.

Amin Dada, Gen. Idi; Ugandan army officer and Head of State; b. 1925.
Joined King's African Rifles 46; Commdr. of the Army 64-71; leader of military coup d'état which deposed Milton Obote Jan. 71; Head of State, Minister of Defence, and Chief of Armed Forces Feb. 71-; Chair. Defence Council 72-; awarded eight highest mil. decorations of Uganda.
Office of the Head of State, Kampala, Uganda.

Amissah, John Kodwo, J.C.D., D.C., C.S.; Ghanaian Roman Catholic ecclesiastic; b. 27 Nov. 1922, Elmina; ed St. Peter's School, Kumasi, St. Teresa's Seminary at Amisano, St. Augustine's Coll., Pontifical Urban Univ., Rome.
Ordained as priest Dec. 49; taught at St. Teresa's Minor and Major Seminary 50-51 and 54-57; named Auxiliary Bishop June 57; Archbishop of Cape Coast and Metropolitan of Ghana Dec. 59-70; Chair. first Pan-African Symposium of Catholic Episcopal Confs., Kampala 69; First Councillor, Standing Cttee., Symposium of Episcopal Confs. of Africa and Madagascar (SECAM) 69-; Chair. Univ. Coll. of Cape Coast 69-; mem. Council of State 69-; awarded Grand Medal.
c/o Archbishop's House P.O. Box 112, Cape Coast, Ghana.

Amponsah, Reginald Reynolds; Ghanaian politician; b. 30 Dec. 1922, Mampong-Ashanti; ed. Presbyterian Schools, Mampong-Ashanti and Kumasi Methodist Schools at Obuasi and Bekwai, Achimota School, Inst. of Art, Industry and Social Science, Achimota, N. Staffs. Technical Coll., Stoke-on-Trent, England, and Royal Coll. of Art, London.
Teacher, Enchi 46; studied industrial design, ceramics and educ., England 47-51; Educ. Officer, Kumasi 51-53 District Educ. Officer 53; Liaison Officer for Cocoa Marketing Board scholars in Europe, Stuttgart 53; later became Gen. Sec. of Nat. Liberation Movement (NLM); then Gen. Sec. of United Party; political detainee 58-66; then mem. Political Cttee. of Nat. Liberation Council; mem. Constituent Assembly; Chair. Ghana Airways until 69; Chair. African Aviation Fed. 70; Foundation mem. Progress Party 69- (banned 72); mem. Parl. for Mampong North; Minister of Lands and Mineral Resources, Nat. Forestry and Nat. Wildlife Trust 69-71; Minister of Educ. and Sport Jan. 71-Jan. 72.
c/o Ministry of Education and Sport, Accra, Ghana.

Andriamahazo, Brig.-Gen. Gilles; Malagasy army officer; b. 1919, Fort-Dauphin, Tuléar Prov.; ed. Ecole Supérieure de Guerre, Paris.
Promoted to rank of Col.; then Inspector of Infantry and Artillery, Gen. Staff Headquarters at the Presidency; Brig.-Gen., Inspector-Gen. of the Armed Forces 70-;

Mil. Gov. of Tananarive May 72-; Minister of Territorial Admin. May 72-.
Ministère de l'Aménagement du Territoire, Tananarive, Madagascar.

Andriamanjato, Rev. Richard; Malagasy ecclesiastic and politician; b. 31 July 1930; ed. Montpellier and Strasbourg, France.
Pastor, Ambohitantely Church, Tananarive; Pres. Asscn. of Malagasy Students in France 56-57; leader Congress for Independence Party (AKFM) 59-; Mayor of Tananarive 59-; Deputy for Tananarive, Malagasy Nat. Assembly 60-; Chair. All Africa Conf. of Churches 70; Dr. h.c. (Debrecen Theological Acad., Hungary) 72.
c/o Parti du Congrès de l'Indépendance de Madagascar, 43 ave. Maréchal Foch, Tananarive, Malagasy Republic.

Andrianada, Jacques; Malagasy lawyer; b. 1 Aug. 1924, Angohely, Diégo-Suarez Prov.; ed. Inst. des Hautes Etudes d'Outre-Mer, Paris.
Permanent Sec., Ministry of Justice, Adviser to the Supreme Court until 72; Minister of Justice, Keeper of the Seals May 72-.
Ministry of Justice, Tananarive, Madagascar.

Angaine, Jackson Harvester; Kenyan politician; b. 1908, Central Province; ed. Alliance High School, Kikuyu and Natal Univ.
Worked as accountant, later businessman; now farmer in Meru District; elected to Legislative Council 61; Asst. Minister for Tourism, Forests and Wild Life 62; later Asst. Minister for Educ.; Minister for Lands and Settlement 63-.
Ministry for Lands and Settlement, Nairobi, Kenya.

Anin, Patrick Dankwa, M.A., LL.B.; Ghanaian judge; b. 27 July 1928, Bekwai, Ashanti; ed. Prince of Wales Coll., Achimota, Selwyn Coll., Cambridge, and London School of Economics.
Called to Bar, Middle Temple 56, called to Gold Coast Bar 56; fmr. Dir. Bank of Ghana; mem. Electoral Comm. 66-67; Commr. for Communications July 67-Feb. 68, Commr. for External Affairs Feb. 68-Sept. 69; Justice of Appeal Sept. 69-71; Supreme Court Judge 71-72; Chair. Bribery and Corruption Comm.
P.O. Box 119, Accra, Ghana.

Ankrah, Lieut.-Gen. Joseph Arthur; Ghanaian army officer; b. 18 Aug. 1915, Accra; ed. Wesley Methodist School, Accra, and Accra Acad.
Comes from Ga tribe, S. Ghana; Warrant Officer II, Infantry and Staff, Second World War; commissioned 47; Battalion Commdr., later Brigadier, Kasai Province, Congo 60-61, awarded Ghana Mil. Cross; Deputy Chief of Defence Staff, Ghana 61-July 65; Chief of Defence Staff and Chair. Nat. Liberation Council, Ghana, Feb. 66-April 69; Officer Order of the Volta, Grand Cordon Most Venerable Order of Knighthood of the Pioneers (Liberia).
c/o House D594/3 Asylum Down, Accra, Ghana.
Telephone: Accra 24583.

Annorkwei II, Nene, Q.M.C.; Ghanaian chief; b. 1900; ed. Wesleyan School, Accra.
Entered Nigerian civil service as Treasury Clerk 19; transferred to Gold Coast 30; promoted to Accountant 44; elected Manche of Prampram 48; appointed Treas. of Provincial Council, Eastern Province, and mem. Council's Standing Cttee. 48; later Pres. Joint Provincial Council of Chiefs (representing Eastern and Western Regions); Chair. Ghana Museum and Monuments Board 57-; Queen's Medal for Chiefs 56.
Manche of Prampram, Prampram, Ghana.

Anthony, Seth Kwabla; Ghanaian diplomatist; b. 16 June 1915; ed. Achimota Coll., Ghana.
Former teacher, Achimota Coll.; Ghanaian Army 39-45;

Admin. Service, Gold Coast 46, District Officer in Ashanti 46-51; Asst. Sec. Ministry of Defence and External Affairs, Gold Coast 52-54; Senior Asst. Sec. Ministry of Interior 54-56; Counsellor and Chargé d'Affaires, Ghana Embassy, Washington 56-59; Acting Perm. Rep. of Ghana to UN 56-57; Counsellor, Paris 59, then Perm. Rep. to UN, Geneva, and Consul-Gen., Switzerland; High Commr. to India 62-66, concurrently accred. to Afghanistan 62-66, to U.K. 66-July 70; High Commr. to Canada July 70-.
Ghana High Commission, Suite 810, 85 Range Road, Ottawa, Ontario, Canada.

Apithy, Sourou Migan; Dahomeyan politician; b. 8 April 1913; ed. Ecole Libre des Sciences Politiques, Ecole Nat. d'Organisation Economique et Sociale.
Deputy of Dahomey to French Constituent Assemblies 45-46; mem. Nat. Assembly 46-58; del. to seventh and eighth sessions UN 53; mem. Grand Council French West Africa 47-57; Pres. Gen. Council Dahomey 55-57; Prime Minister Provisional Govt. 58-59; Minister without Portfolio 60; Vice-Pres. and Minister of the Plan and Development 60; Ambassador of Dahomey to France, U.K., and Switzerland to 63; Minister of Finance, Economy and the Plan 63-64; Pres. of the Republic of Dahomey 64-Nov. 65; mem. Presidential Council 70-72; under house arrest following _coup_ Oct. 72; Commdr. de la Grande-Comore.
Publ. _Au Service de mon Pays._
Porto Novo, Dahomey, West Africa.

Appiah, Joe; Ghanaian lawyer and politician.
Worked as lawyer, later politician; formed Opposition Nat. Liberation Movement Feb. 55; imprisoned 60-62; mem. Political Cttee. July 66-69; goodwill Amb. to U.S.A. and U.K. Sept. 66; Leader, Nationalist Party with M.K. Apaloo May 69, merged to form United Nat. Party (UNP) July 69; defeated in elections Aug. 69; Pres. Ghana Bar Asscn.; Chair. opposition Justice Party Oct. 70-72; Roving Amb. for Nat. Redemption Council July 72-.
Office of the National Redemption Council, P.O. Box 1627, Accra, Ghana.

Arboussier, Gabriel Marie D'; Senegalese politician; b. 14 Jan. 1908; ed. Collège des Dominicains, Sorèze, Lycée de Toulouse and Faculty of Law, Univ. of Paris.
Governor's Office, Dakar 37-41, Head of Office, Yako 41-43; Head of Political Office for Ivory Coast 43-44; Deputy for French Equatorial Africa to French Constituent Assembly 45-47; organizer of Conf. at Bamako, which formed RDA (Rassemblement Démocratique Africain) 46, Gen. Sec. 49-50; Rep. for Ivory Coast in Assembly of French Union 47-53, Vice-Pres. 47-50; Rep. of Niger at Grand Council of French West Africa 56-60, Vice-Pres., later Pres.; Minister of Justice and Keeper of The Seals, Senegal 60-62; Amb. to France 63-64, concurrently Perm. Del. to UNESCO; Exec. Dir. UN Inst. for Training and Research 65-68; Amb. to Fed. Repub. of Germany, Austria and Switzerland 68-; Consultant to Pontifical Comm. for Studies on Justice and Peace 67; Grand Croix de l'Ordre National du Sénégal, Commdr. Légion d'Honneur and other decorations; Hammarskjöld Prize 67.
Embassy of Senegal, Bonn-Center, Bonn, Federal Republic of Germany; 102 avenue des Champs-Elysées, Paris 8e, France; and 32 Victor Hugo, Dakar, Senegal.

Argod, Hubert Aymard, DIP. SC. POL.; French diplomatist; b. 28 Aug. 1914, Bourg-de-Peage (Drôme); ed. Ecole des Roches, Ecole Libre des Sciences Politiques, Paris.
Diplomatic Service 41-; French Provisional Govt., Algiers; First Sec. French Del. to UN, New York 46; First Sec., Beirut 47-50, High Comm. in Germany 51; European Affairs Dept., Ministry of Foreign Affairs 52, Tunisian and Moroccan Affairs Dept. 56-58, Head, Levant Desk 58-61; First Counsellor, Tunis 61; Amb. to Chad 61-62; Minister-

Counsellor, Algiers 62; Deputy High Rep., Algiers 63; Amb. to Cambodia 64-68, to Senegal and Gambia 69-; Officier, Légion d'Honneur, Croix de Guerre (39-45).
French Embassy, 1 rue Thiers, Dakar, Senegal.

Arikpo, Okoi, PH.D.; Nigerian politician; b. 1916 Ugep, E. Nigeria; ed. Nigeria, and Univ. of London.
Teacher, Univ. of London 49-51; mem. E. Nigeria House of Assembly 52, later mem. Fed. House of Reps. until 54; later Minister of Lands and Mines; scientist and teacher 61-67; Fed. Commr. for Trade June 67-Sept. 68; Fed. Commr. for External Affairs Sept. 68-; Sec. Nigerian Univ. Comm.
Federal Ministry for External Affairs, Lagos, Nigeria.

Arkhurst, Frederick Siegfried; Ghanaian journalist and diplomatist; b. 13 Oct. 1920; ed. Mfantsipim School, Cape Coast, and Univ. of Aberdeen, Scotland.
Eisenhower Fellowship in U.S.A. 54; Attaché, British Embassy, Rome 55-56; Public Relations Officer, Gold Coast Office, London 56-57; Second Sec. Ghana High Comm., London 57; First Sec. Perm. Mission of Ghana to UN 57-59, Counsellor 59-60; mem. Secr. UN Econ. Comm. for Africa 60-62; Principal Sec. Ministry of Foreign Affairs 62-65; Faculty Fellow, Center for International Affairs, Harvard Univ. 62-63; Perm. Rep. to UN 65-67; Asst. Dir. for African Programs, Adlai Stevenson Inst. of Int. Affairs 67-.
c/o Robie House, 5757 South Woodlawn Avenue, Chicago, Ill. 60637, U.S.A.

Arriaga, General Kaúlza de; Portuguese army officer; b. 18 Jan. 1915, Oporto; ed. Univ. of Oporto, Portuguese Mil. Acad. and Portuguese Inst. for Higher Mil. Studies.
Instructor, Field School for Mil. Engineers 39-45; attended Gen. Staff Course 45-49; Lisbon Mil. H.Q. and Army Gen. Staff 49-50; at Min. for National Defence and Rep. of Minister of Defence in Tech. Comm. for External Econ. Cooperation 50-53; Head of Office of Minister of Nat. Defence and Min. of Defence Rep. at Tech. Comm. for External Cooperation and Nuclear Energy Board 54-55; Under-Sec. of State for Aeronautics, later Sec. 55-62; High Command Course 63-64; Brigadier 64; Prof. of Strategy and Tactics, Inst. for Higher Mil. Studies 64-66; Chair. Nuclear Energy Board 67-; General 68; Commdr. all Portuguese Ground Forces in Mozambique 69-70; C.-in-C. Portuguese Forces in Mozambique 70-; mem. Overseas Council 65-69; Chair. Exec. Cttee. Soc. Portuguesa de Exploração de Petróleos (ANGOL) 66-69; Pres. Equestrian Fed. 68-; several Portuguese and foreign decorations.
Publs. include works on engineering, atomic energy and military affairs.
c/o Ministry of Defence, Lisbon, Portugal.

Arteh Ghalib, Omar; Somalian diplomatist and politician; b. 1930, Hargeisa; ed. St. Paul's Coll., Cheltenham and Bristol Univ., England.
Teacher 51-53; Vice-Principal, Sheikh Intermediate School 54-58; Principal, Gabileh Intermediate School 58-60; Asst. District Commr. Hargeisa 60; District Commr. Erigavo 60-61; First. Sec. Moscow 61; mem. UN Special Cttee. on S.W. Africa 62; Counsellor, del. to UN 62-64; Amb. to Ethiopia 65-68; attended OAU Council of Ministers, Summit Conf. in Cairo, Accra and Addis Ababa 64-66; Pres. Somali Officials Union 60; elected mem. Nat. Assembly 69-; Sec. of State for Foreign Affairs Oct. 69-; attended OAU Summit Conf. in Addis Ababa 70, and Non-Aligned States Summit Conf. in Lusaka 70.
Ministry of Foreign Affairs, Mogadishu, Somalia.

Aschenborn, Hans Jürgen, M.A.BIBL., D.PHIL., F.S.A.L.A.; South African librarian; b. 19 Aug. 1920, Windhoek, S.W. Africa; ed. Univ. of S. Africa and Univ. of Pretoria.
Merensky Library, Univ. of Pretoria 49-51; head of various depts., Transvaal Provincial Library Services 51-53;

Lecturer in Library Science, Univ of Pretoria 53-59; Joined The State Library, Pretoria 59, Dir. 64-; John Harvey Medal 64.
Publs. *Stimmen deutscher Dichter* 49, *Titelbeskrywing* 56, *Sachkatalogisierung seit Trebst* 57, *Staatsbiblioteek der Z.A.R.* 70.
State Library, Box. 397, Pretoria; Box 15294 Lynn, East Pretoria, South Africa.
Telephone: 28661 (State Library); 722460.

Ashley-Lassen, Napoleon Richard Yawovi; Ghanaian air force officer; b. 29 March 1934, Port Harcourt, Nigeria; ed. Zion Coll., Keta.
Troop leader, Recce Squadron 58-59; Platoon Commdr., 1st Battalion Ghana Regiment July-Oct. 59; Deputy Flight Commdr., Takoradi Station, Ghana Air Force 60-63, Commdr. No. 2 Squadron 63-65; Commdg. Officer 67-68; Acting Commdr., Ghana Air Force March-April 68, Commdr. 68-72; Chief of Defence Staff, Ghana Armed Forces Jan. 72-; mem. Nat. Redemption Council Jan. 72-.
Ministry of Defence, Burma Camp, Accra, Ghana.

Asika, Ukpabi; Nigerian politician and former university lecturer; b. 1936; ed. Univ. Coll., Los Angeles.
Former lecturer in political science, Ibadan Univ., Gov. East-Central State 67-; Sole civilian mem. of Supreme Military Council of Nigeria April 70-.
Publ. *No Victors, No Vanquished* 68.
Office of the Governor, Enugu, East-Central State, Nigeria.

Assila, Major James; Togolese army officer and politician; b. 1932, Nuatja.
Joined the French Army 51; served in Indochina 54-56, in Algeria 56-57; trainee at EFORTEM until 62; Commandant, second Togolese battalion; Minister of the Interior April 67-Jan. 72.
c/o Ministry of the Interior, Lomé, Togo.

Atta, William Ofori; Ghanaian politician; b. 10 Oct. 1910; ed. Achimota School, Gold Coast, Queen's Coll. Cambridge, London School of Economics, and Gray's Inn, London.
Taught history, Achimota School 39-43; State Sec. Akim Abuakwa, later State Treas. 43-47; Head of Abuakwa State Coll. 47; mem. Ghana Congress Party after 47; mem. Volta River Project Del. to Canada 55; mem. Nat. Cttee. of Volta River Project; politically detained 59, 63, 64; Chair. Cocoa Marketing Board 66-68; mem. Political Cttee., Nat. Liberation Council 66-67; mem. Constitutional Comm. 67-68; mem. Constituent Assembly 69, Nat. Assembly 69-72; Minister of Educ., Culture and Sport 69-71, of Foreign Affairs Jan. 71-Jan. 72; politically detained Jan.-Feb. 72.
P.O. Box 207, Accra, Ghana.

Audu, Ishaya Sha'aibu, M.B., B.S., D.CH., F.R.C.P.(.E), D.T.M. & H., F.M.C.; Nigerian paediatrician and University official; b. 1 March 1927, Zaria; ed. St. Bartholomew's School, Wusasa, Zaria, Univs. of Ibadan, London and Rochester.
Physician at King's Coll. Hospital, London and Univ. Coll. Hospital, Ibadan 54-58; house officer, senior house officer, then registrar of paediatrics; consultant physician-paediatrician, Govt. of Northern Nigeria, and personal physician to the Premier 60-62; lecturer, senior lecturer, Assoc. Prof. of Paediatrics, Univ. of Lagos 62-66; Deputy Chair. Lagos Univ. Hospital Teaching Board of Management 62-66; mem. Council, Lagos Univ. Medical Coll. 62-66; Visiting Assoc. Research Prof., Univ. of Rochester 64-65; Vice-Chancellor, Ahmadu Bello Univ. and Prof. of Medicine 66-; mem. Exec. Cttee., Int. Paediatric Asscn.; Ware Prize in Pathology, Univ. of London 52; Hon. L.H.D. (Ohio) 68, Hon. D.Sc. (Nsukka) 71.
Publs. *Medical Education in Nigeria: Facing Realities,*

NBC *October Lectures* 69, and over twenty contribs. to learned journals.
Vice-Chancellor's Lodge, Ahmadu Bello University, Zaria, Nigeria.

Awadalla, Babikir, BAR.-AT-LAW; Sudanese politician; b. 1917, El Citaina, B.N. Prov.; ed. Intermediate School, Rufaa and School of Law, Gordon Coll., Khartoum.
Sharia Court Judge 45-47; District Judge (second class) 47-49; District Judge (first-class) 49-54; resigned to become Speaker of the Sudanese House of Reps. 54-57; Judge of the Supreme Court 57-; Chief Justice Oct. 64-May 67; Prime Minister May-Oct. 69; Minister of the Exterior May 69-July 70, of Justice Oct. 69-71, and Deputy Prime Minister June 70-71; First Vice-Pres. Oct. 71-May 72.
c/o Office of the First Vice-President, Khartoum, Sudan.

Awolowo, Chief Obafemi, B.COMM. (HONS.), LL.B. (LOND.), B.L., LL.D., D.SC., D.LITT. (Ashiwaju of Ijebu Remo, Losi of Ikenne, Lisa of Ijeun, Apesin of Oshogbo, Odole of Ife, Ajagunla of Ado Ekiti, Odofin of Owo and Obong Ikpan Isong of Ibibioland); Nigerian politician; b. 6 March 1909, Ikenne; ed. London Univ.
Teacher 28-29; Stenographer 30-34; Newspaper Reporter 34-35; engaged in motor transport and produce buying 36-44; Solicitor and Advocate, Supreme Court of Nigeria 47-51; Minister of Local Govt. and Leader of Govt. Business Western Region 52-54; co-founder and first Gen. Sec. of Egbe Omo Oduduwa, a Yoruba cultural movement; founder and Fed. Pres. of Action Group of Nigeria; Premier, Govt. of the W. Region of Nigeria 54-59; Leader of the Opposition in Fed. Parl. 60-May 62, detained May 62-Nov. 62, on trial for treasonable felony and conspiracy Nov. 62-Sept. 63; sentenced to 10 years' imprisonment Sept. 63; given free pardon and released Aug. 66; elected Leader of Yorubas Aug. 66; Chancellor of Univ. of Ife, Nigeria 67-; Vice-Chair. Fed. Exec. Council and Fed. Commr. of Finance June 67-June 71.
Publs. *Path to Nigerian Freedom, Awo* (autobiography), *Thoughts on Nigerian Constitution, My Early Life, The People's Republic, The Strategy and Tactics of the People's Republic of Nigeria;* various pamphlets.
c/o P.O. Box 136, Ibadan, Nigeria.
Telephone: Ibadan 20087.

Awuku-Darko, Samuel Wilberforce; Ghanaian accountant and politician; b. 23 May 1924, Afransu Shum, E. Region; ed. Presbyterian Middle Boys' Boarding School, Akropong-Akwapim, Prince of Wales Coll. and Trinity Coll., Sutum.
Second Div. clerk, Income Tax Dept., Ghanaian Civil, Service 44-50; articled clerk, Casseton, Elliot and Co., Chartered Accountants, Accra 50-57; Inc. Accountant 57, later Fellow, Inst. of Chartered Accountants; privately employed 59-69; Pres. Inst. of Chartered Accountants 67-69; Minister of Works Sept. 69-72, and of Housing Jan. 71-Jan. 72; Chair. Board of Govs., Suhum Secondary Technical School 66-.
c/o Ministry of Works, Accra, Ghana.

Ayarna, Alhaji Imoru; Ghanaian businessman and politician; b. 11 Nov. 1924; ed. Native Authority School, Bawku, Govt. Boarding School, Tamale, Wolsey Hall Coll., Oxford.
Native administration clerk 45-50; mem. Legislative Assembly, Ministerial Sec., Minister of Agriculture and Natural Resources 51-54; businessman 55-69; founder and leader, People's Action Party 69-72.
Publ. *The Northerners' Future in the Balance* 52.
House No. 136, East Cantonments, P.O. Box 14, Accra, Ghana.
Telephone: 77285-75422.

Ayé, Hippolyte, D. en MED.; Ivory Coast politician; b. 1932, Anoumako, Abidjan; ed. Faculty of Medicine,

Toulouse, Ecole Nat. de Santé Publique, Rennes and Paris, France.
Member, later Vice-Pres., Econ. and Social Council 63-66; Asst. lecturer in hygiene and public health, Ecole des Sages Femmes d'Abidjan 63-66; Asst. Head of clinical dept., Faculty of Medicine, Abidjan 66-69; Asst. Head of clinical dept., Centre hospitalier et universitaire, Pathology Service Oct. 66-; Pres. WHO Gen. Assembly May 70; Minister of Health and Population Jan. 70-; mem. French and Ivory Coast Comm. on Higher Educ. 64-.
Ministry of Health and Population, Abidjan, Ivory Coast.

Ayodo, Samuel Onyango, B.SC.(EDUC.); Kenyan politician; b. 1930, Kabondo, S. Nyanza; ed. Makerere Coll., Uganda, and Union Coll., Neb., U.S.A.
Teacher 56-59; African elected mem. for South Nyanza 59-61, 61-63; mem. House of Reps. for Kasipul/Kabondo 63-69; Minister for Local Govt. 63-64; Minister for Natural Resources 64-66, concurrently for Tourism and Wildlife 64-69; Chair. Kuja Crafts Ltd., Nairobi; Elder of the Golden Heart of Kenya, Grand Band of the Star of Africa (Liberia), Grand Cordon, Star of Honour (Ethiopia).
Kuja Crafts Ltd., P.O. Box 49176, Nairobi; Home: P.O. Box 44609, Nairobi, Kenya.
Telephone: 22177.

Ayouné, Jeane-Rémy; Gabon administrator and politician; b. 5 June 1914, Assewé, Ogowe; ed. Catholic mission and seminaries in Libreville and Brazzaville.
Worked in French Equatorial African Admin., Libreville 34-37; head of Audit Bureau, Dept. of Finance, Cabinet of the Gov.-Gen., Brazzaville 37-46; Editor, Press and Information Service, Cabinet of the Gov.-Gen. 46-53; Sec. of Inspection Dept., Acad. of Libreville 53-56; mem. Del. of A.E.F. to Paris 56-57; head, Press and Information Bureau, Cabinet of High Commr. to Congo (Brazzaville) 57; trainee, Quai d'Orsay and E.N.A. 57-60; Second Counsellor, French Embassy in Fed. Repub. of Germany 60-61; 1st Amb. of Gabon to Fed. Repub. of Germany March 61-March 64; Sec.-Gen. of Govt. March 64-Dec. 66; Minister of Civil Service and Technical Admin. Co-operation Dec. 66-July 68; Minister of Foreign Affairs 68-71, concurrently of Co-operation 70-71; Minister of Justice and Keeper of the Seals June 71-Oct. 72; Pres. Gabonese Chamber of Commerce Oct. 72-.
Chambre de Commerce du Gabon, Libreville, Gabon.

Azikiwe, Rt. Hon. Nnamdi, P.C., M.A., M.SC., LL.D., D.LITT.; Nigerian politician; b. 16 Nov. 1904; ed. Lincoln and Pennsylvania Univs.
Former Instructor in History and Political Science Lincoln Univ., Pa.; fmr. Gov. Dir. African Continental Bank Ltd.; Chair. Associated Newspapers of Nigeria Ltd., African Book Co. Ltd.; Pres. Nat. Council of Nigeria and the Cameroons; Vice-Pres. Nigerian Nat. Democratic Party; elected mem. of Legislative Council of Nigeria 47-51; mem. Brooke Arbitration Tribunal 44, Nigerianization Comm. 48, MacDonald Arbitration Tribunal 48; mem. Western House of Assembly 52-53, Eastern House 54-59; former Minister of Local Govt., Eastern Region, and Minister of Internal Affairs 55-57; Premier, Eastern Nigeria 54-59; Pres. Fed. Senate 60; Gov.-Gen. and C.-in-C. Fed. of Nigeria 60-63, Pres. of Nigeria 63-66; Chancellor and Chair. Council of the Univ. of Nigeria 62-66; Chancellor, Univ. of Lagos 71-.
Publs. *Liberia in World Politics* 34, *Renascent Africa* 37, *The African in Ancient and Medieval History* 38, *Land Tenure in Northern Nigeria* 42, *Political Blueprint of Nigeria* 43, *Economic Reconstruction of Nigeria* 43, *Economic Rehabilitation of Eastern Nigeria* 55, *Zik: a Selection of Speeches* 61, *My Odyssey* 70, *Military Revolution in Nigeria* 72.
Onuiyi Haven, P.O. Box 7, Nsukka, Nigeria.

B

Baah, Maj. R. M.; Ghanaian army officer; b. 21 May 1938, Dormaa Ahenkro, Brong-Ahafo Region; ed. Royal Officers' Specialist Training School, Accra, Mil. Acad., Dehra Dun, India.
Commissioned Regular Infantry Officer, Ghana Army 62; held various posts including Instructor, Ghana Mil. Acad. and Training School, Acting Commdg. Officer, 5th Infantry Battalion, Staff Officer to Defence Adviser, Ghana High Comm., London, Asst. Defence, Armed Forces Attaché, Ghana Embassy to U.S.A.; Commr. for Lands, Mineral Resources Jan.-Oct. 72, for Foreign Affairs Oct. 72-; mem. Nat. Redemption Council 72-.
Office of the National Redemption Council, P.O. Box 1627, Accra, Ghana.

Babiiha, John Kabwimukya, DIP. VET. SC.; Ugandan politician; b. 17 April 1913, Toro; ed. St. Leo's High School, Virika, St. Joseph's Coll., Mbarara, St. Mary's Coll., Kisubi, Makerere Univ. Coll., Kampala and Pretoria Univ. (External Div.).
Assistant Veterinary Officer 38-45; Asst. Treas. Toro District Admin. 46-53; Uganda Legislative Council 54-61; mem. Parl. 62-66; Minister of Animal Industry, Game and Fisheries 62-; Vice-Pres. of Uganda 66-71; mem. American Veterinary Medicine Asscn. 64; Knight Order of Stars of Queen of Sheba (Ethiopia), Order of the Leopard (Zaire), Knight Order of Grand Cross of Pope Pius IX (Vatican), Int. Order of the Lion, Independence Medal 62, and other awards.
Publ. *The Bayaya Clan in Western Region* 57.
P.O. Box 18, Fort Portal, Uganda.

Babu, Abdulrauman Mohammed; Tanzanian politician; b. 1924, Zanzibar; ed. Makerere Univ. Coll. and London Univ.
Worked with Zanzibar Clove Growers' Asscn.; later bank clerk, London; mem. ZNP 57-; founded Umma Party 63; Minister of Defence and External Affairs 64-65, concurrently Minister of State; Minister for Commerce and Co-operatives 65-67; Minister for Health 67-68; Minister for Commerce and Industries 68-Nov. 70; Minister of Econ. Affairs and Devt. Planning Nov. 70-Feb. 72; detained 72.
c/o Ministry of Economic Affairs and Development Planning, Dar es Salaam, Tanzania.

Badarou, Dr. Daouda; Dahomeyan surgeon and politician; b. 7 Jan. 1929, Porto Novo; ed. Dakar and Univ. of Paris.
Qualified as surgeon 61; fmr. mem. Exec. Council, OMS; Minister of Public Health and Social Affairs Dec. 65-Dec. 67; mem. Bureau Nat. de l'Union pour le Renouveau du Dahomey (URD); Minister of Foreign Affairs 68-71; Amb. to France 71-.
Embassy of Dahomey, Paris, France.

Badiane, Emile; Senegalese politician; b. 1915, Tendieme; ed. Ecole Normale William-Ponty.
Former teacher; headmaster 36-47; trainee, Blanchot Coll. 47; teacher at Sedhiou 47-51, headmaster 51-58; Sec.-Gen. for Org. and Propaganda Feb. 59-July 60, then Assoc. Admin. Sec. Union Progressiste Sénégalaise (UPS); Territorial Councillor for Ziguinchor, then Deputy March 52-; mem. Fed. Constituent Assembly of Mali Jan. 59-April 59; Sec. of State to the Presidency, responsible for Information, Radio and Press April 59-March 60; Minister of Technical Instruction and the Formation of Cadres Sept. 60-Feb. 70; Minister of Co-operation Feb. 70-.
Ministry of Co-operation, Dakar, Senegal.

Bagaragaza Thaddé; Rwandan politician; b. 6 June 1936, Muvumo Buimba; ed. Mission School, Rulindo, Petit Séminaire, Kabgayi, Grand Séminaire, Nyakibanda and Lovanium Univ., Leopoldville.

Chief of dept. of Social Affairs Jan. 61-May 61, Sec.-Gen. May 61; Minister of Social Affairs and Information Oct. 61-63; Minister of Nat. Planning, Int. Co-operation and Technical Assistance 63-Oct. 69; Pres. Legislative Assembly Oct. 69-.
Office of the President of the Legislative Assembly, Kigali, Rwanda.

Bakala, Adrien; Congolese diplomatist; b. 1935, Mouyondzi; ed. Univ. de Caen and Inst. des Hautes Etudes d'Outre-Mer, Paris.
Director of Admin., Social and Cultural Affairs, Ministry of Foreign Affairs of Congo 65; Sec.-Gen., Ministry of Foreign Affairs 65-68; Deputy Head of Congolese Del. to UN Gen. Assembly 66, Head 67-68; Perm. Rep. to UN 69-70; Amb. to Egypt 71-.
Congolese Embassy, 12 Midan el Nasr, Dokki, Egypt.

Bako, Alhaji Audu, N.P.M., C.P.; Nigerian police officer and military governor; b. 1924, Kaduna; ed. Kaduna Govt. School and Zaria Middle School.
Law instructor, Police Coll. 46-49; Prosecuting Officer 49-54; Asst. Superintendent of Police in command of various divs. and formations 55, subsequently Senior Supt. of Police in charge of Admin., Kaduna Headquarters; Asst. Commr. of Police in charge of Kano and Katsina Provinces 63; Deputy Commr. of Police, F Dept., Kaduna H.Q.; now Mil. Gov., Kano State of Nigeria; War Medal, Defence Medal, Meritorious Service Medal 61, several Police Commendation Certificates.
Publs. *A History of Native Authority Police, The Police and Army, Guide to Native Authority Police, Niger Coast Constabulary. Metamorphosis of a Constable (From Constable to Military Governor), Father's Guide on Kaduna Settlement.*
4 Ahmadu Bello Way, Kaduna, Nigeria.

Bakri. Bashir el-; Sudanese diplomatist; b. 1918; ed. Univs. of Cairo, Oxford and Paris.
Member of many Sudanese dels to UN and other international centres; Foreign Ministry 56; Amb. to France 57, Belgium 57, Netherlands 59, Spain 60-61, Nigeria 61-65; Chair. El Nilein Bank 64-71.
c/o El Nilein Bank, P.O. Box 466, Parliament Street, Khartoum, Sudan.

Balancy, Pierre Guy Girald, C.B.E.; Mauritius journalist and diplomatist; b. 8 April 1924, Mauritius; ed. Royal Coll., Port Louis, and Bhujoharry Coll.
Member of Mauritius Legis. Assembly 63-68; Municipal Councillor 63-64; Parl. Sec., Ministry of Educ. and Cultural Affairs 64-65; Minister of Information, Posts and Telegraphs 65-67, of Works 67-68; Founder and Editor-in-Chief *L'Express* (daily newspaper) 63-64; Sec. Cercle Littéraire de Port Louis 62; mem. Action Sociale 59-60; mem. Directing Cttee. French Cultural Centre 57-62; Editor *Escales* (quarterly literary review) 54-60; Perm. Rep. of Mauritius to UN April 68-June 69; Amb. of Mauritius to U.S.A. July 68-, concurrently High Commr. to Canada Jan. 70-.
2308 Wyoming Avenue, N.W., Washington D.C. 20008, U.S.A.
Telephone: 387-5978.

Ball, Alan Hugh; British business executive; b. 8 June 1924, England; ed. Eton Coll.
Joined Lonrho Ltd. 47, Chair. and Joint Man. Dir. 61-72, Exec. Deputy Chair. 72-.
Lonrho Ltd., Cheapside House, Cheapside, London, E.C.2; Home: The Old Mill, Romsbury, Wilts., England.
Telephone: 01-606-8131 (Office).

Ballal, Musa Awad, M.B.A.; Sudanese politician; b. 20 Jan. 1931, Elfashir; ed. Univ. of Khartoum and Univ. of Pennsylvania, U.S.A.
Director, Devt. and Productivity Centre, Khartoum 67-70;

Deputy Man. Dir. Industrial Devt. Corpn. 70-71; Sec.-Gen. Industrial Production Corpn. 71, Supreme Authority for Public Corpns. 71; Minister of Supply 71-72; Minister of Industry and Mining 72-.
Publs. _Industrialization and the Social Progress in the Rural Areas of the Sudan_ 71, _The Problems of Industrialization in the Southern Sudan_ 71.
Ministry of Industry and Mining, P.O. Box 2184, Khartoum; Home: 3 Baladia Avenue, Khartoum, Sudan.

Ballinger, Violet Margaret Livingstone, B.A., M.A.; South African politician (wife of William Ballinger, _q.v._); b. 1894, Scotland; ed. Holy Rosary Convent (Port Elizabeth), Huguenot Coll. (Wellington), Rhodes Univ. (Grahamstown) and Somerville Coll., Oxford.
Settled in South Africa 04; elected to Union Parl. 37, returned unopposed 42, re-elected 48, returned unopposed 54 as Native Rep. for Cape Eastern; parl. seat abolished by Bantu Self-Government Act 59; mem. South African Liberal Party 53- (1st Pres.); Dyason Memorial Lecturer, Inst. Int. Affairs, Australia 60; Assoc. Fellow, Nuffield Coll., Oxford 61; fmr. Senior Lecturer in History, Witwatersrand Univ.; Hon. LL.D. (Cape Town and Rhodes Univs.).
Publs. _Influence of Holland on Africa, Britain in South Africa, Bechuanaland and Basutoland_ (with W. G. Ballinger), _From Union to Apartheid—A Trek to Isolation_ 70.
8 Firdale Road, Newlands, Cape, South Africa.

Ballinger, William George; South African (b. British) politician (husband of Margaret Ballinger, _q.v._); b. 1894; ed. Glasgow Univ. and Elsinore Coll., Denmark.
Town and Parish Councillor, Motherwell (Scotland) 22-28; Adviser on African Trade Union, Industrial and Co-operative Organizations; Adviser British Workers' Del. I.L.O. Confs. Geneva 35 and 36; Senator (Rep. of Transvaal and O.F.S. Africans) 48-60; seat abolished by Bantu Self-Government Act 59; Research student, Queen Elizabeth House, Oxford 61; Hon. Sec. Non-European Progress Trust, Cape Town.
Publs. _Race and Economic Contacts, Britain in South Africa, Bechuanaland and Basutoland_ (with Margaret Ballinger).
8 Firdale Road, Newlands, Cape, South Africa.

Balogun, Kolawole, Chief **Balogun of Otan,** LL.B.; Nigerian lawyer, politician and diplomatist; b. 1926; ed. Govt. Coll., Ibadan.
On staff of _Nigerian Advocate_, later radio announcer, then Asst. Editor _West African Pilot;_ legal studies in London 48-51, called to the Bar 51; Sec. London branch Nat. Council of Nigeria and the Cameroons (NCNC) 51; Nat Sec. NCNC 51-57; mem. of Fed. Parl. 54; Fed. Minister without Portfolio, later Fed. Minister of Information; resigned from govt. 58; Nigerian Commr. in Ghana 59-60, High Commr. 60-61; Chair. Nigerian Nat. Shipping Line 62-65; Commr. for Econ. Planning and Social Devt., Mil. Govt. of W. Nigeria 67, for Educ. 68-70; Chair. Sketch Group of Newspapers, Ibadan 71-.
Sketch Publishing Co. Ltd., New Court Road, Ibadan, Western Nigeria.

Bamba, Nanlo, L. en D.; Ivory Coast lawyer and politician; b. 15 Nov. 1916, Bouaké; ed. Ecole Normale William-Ponty.
Served in the French Colonial Admin., Paris 47-51, Ivory Coast 52-54; substituted as Public Prosecutor in Cotonou 54-55; Justice of the Peace in Bondoukou 55-56; trainee of ENFOM 56-58; Deputy Public Prosecutor, then examining magistrate in Abidjan 58; Chef de Cabinet 59-61; Dir. Nat. Police Force Feb. 60-Jan. 61; Assoc. Dir. Cabinet of Félix Houphouet-Boigny, Pres. of the Repub. Aug. 61-Feb. 63; Keeper of the Seals and Minister of Justice Feb. 63-Jan. 66; Minister of the Interior Jan. 66-.
Ministry of the Interior, Abidjan, Ivory Coast.

Bamigboye, Lieut-Col. David L.; Nigerian politician and army officer; b. 7 Dec. 1940, Omu-Aran, Ilorin; ed. Igbaja Primary School of Sudan Interior Mission, Ilorin Middle School, Govt. Coll., Zaria.
Attended Mil. Acad., Kaduna April 60-Oct. 60; attended Mons Officer Cadet Training School, Aldershot, England Oct. 60-March 61, commissioned as second lieut. March 61; served in the third battalion March 61-62; promoted to lieut. 62, to capt. 63, to major 66; served in H.Q. Second Brigade, Apapa Feb. 64-April 67, later at No. 2 H.Q. Area Command, Ibadan; now Gov. Kwara State; awarded UN medal for services with the UN in Zaire.
Office of the Governor, Ilorin, Kwara State, Nigeria.

Banana, Rev. Canaan Sodindo; Rhodesian ecclesiastic; b. 5 March 1936, Bulawayo; ed. Tegwani Secondary School, Epworth Theological Coll.
Chaplain, Tegwani High School 65-66; Chair. Bulawayo Council of Churches 69-70, Southern Africa Urban Industrial Mission 70-; Vice-Pres. African Nat. Council 71-.
Methodist Community Centre, Taylor Avenue, Makokoba, Bulawayo; Home: Room 99, New Luveve, Bulawayo, Rhodesia.

Banda, Aleke Kadonaphani; Malawian journalist and politician; b. 19 Sept. 1939; ed. United Missionary School, Que Que and Inyati School, Bulawayo.
Secretary Nyasaland African Congress (N.C.A.), Que Que Branch 54; Gen. Sec. S. Rhodesia African Students Asscn. 57-59; arrested and detained in Rhodesia 59, deported to Nyasaland; Founder-mem. Malawi Congress Party (M.C.P.), Sec.-Gen. 59; Editor Nyasaland Trade Union Congress newspaper _Ntendere Pa Nchito_ and mem. T.U.C. Council 59-60; Personal Political Sec. to Dr. Hastings Banda 60-; Sec. M.C.P. Del. to Lancaster House Conf. resulting in self-govt. for Malawi 60; Sec. to subsequent confs. 60, 62; Man. Editor _Malawi News_ 59-66; Dir. Malawi Press Ltd. 60; Dir.-Gen. Malawi Broadcasting Corpn. 64-66; Nat. Chair. League of Malawi Youth and Commdr. Malawi Young Pioneers 63-; Dir. Reserve Bank of Malawi 65-66; Minister of Devt. and Planning 66-67, of Econ. Affairs (incorporating Natural Resources, Trade and Industry, and Devt. and Planning), and Minister of Works and Supplies 67-68, of Trade and Industry (incorporating Tourism, Information and Broadcasting) 68-69; Minister of Finance, Information and Tourism 69-Feb. 72; now Minister of Trade, Industry and Tourism.
Ministry of Trade and Industry, P.O. Box 944, Blantyre, Malawi.

Banda, Hastings Kamuzu, PH.B., B.SC., M.B., CH.B., M.D., L.R.C.S.; Malawian doctor and politician; b. 1905, Kasungu District; ed. mission school, Edinburgh Univ. and in U.S.A.
Worked in gold mine; spent twelve years in U.S. in study and medical practice; medical practice in Willesden, England 39-54, in Kumasi, Ghana 54-58; returned to Nyasaland to take up leadership of Malawi Congress Party 58-; detained during declared state of emergency March 59-April 60; Minister of Natural Resources, Survey and Local Govt; 61-63; Prime Minister of Nyasaland 63-July 64, of Malawi July 64-July 66; Pres. of Repub. of Malawi July 66- (Life Pres. Sept. 70-), also Minister of External Affairs, Defence, Agric. and Natural Resources, Public Works and Supplies, Justice; Chancellor, Univ. of Malawi 65-.
State House, Zomba, Malawi.

Bandawe, Gamaliel Petro; Malawian diplomatist; b. 16 March 1932; ed. Univ. of Delhi, India.
Co-operative inspector, trade union inspector and township sec., Zambia 57-61; Admin. Officer, Ministry of External Affairs 64; First Sec., Malawi High Comm., Ghana 64-65; Admin. Officer, Senior Asst. Sec. and later Under-Sec. of Office of Pres. of Malawi 66-70; Perm. Sec., Ministry of

Local Govt. 70-71; High Commr. to Kenya 71-72; Deputy Perm Rep. to UN April-Sept. 72, Perm. Rep. 72-.
Permanent Mission of Malawi to United Nations, 777 Third Avenue, 24th Floor, New York, N.Y. 10017, U.S.A.

Bangui, Antoine; Chad politician; b. 22 Sept. 1933; ed. Central African Republic and Ecole Polytechnique, France.
Former teacher at Barthélemy Boganda Secondary School, Bangui; later taught physics and mathematics at Bongor Modern Coll.; Minister of Nat. Educ. March 62-Aug. 62; Minister of Public Works Aug. 62-Jan. 64; Amb. to Italy and Fed. Repub. of Germany Jan. 64-April 66; Minister of State attached to the Presidency with responsibility for Co-ordination April 66.
c/o Office of the Presidency, Fort-Lamy, Chad.

Bank-Anthony, Sir Mobolaji, K.B.E.; Nigerian business executive; b. 11 June 1907; ed. Methodist Boys High School, Lagos, Church Missionary Society Grammar School, Lagos, and Ibeju-Ode Grammar School.
Postal Clerk, Nigerian Post and Telegraph Dept. 24; later built up palm oil business and after Second World War built up construction, haulage and cinema companies; Fellow Inst. of Directors, London.
Executive House, 2A Mill Street, P.O. Box 75, Lagos, Nigeria.

Bankole-Jones, Sir Samuel, Kt.; Sierra Leonean judge; b. 23 Aug. 1911; ed. Methodist Boys' High School, Freetown, Fourah Bay Coll., and Middle Temple, London.
Teacher, Methodist Boys' High School, Freetown 32-34; called to the Bar 38; part-time lecturer in law and public admin., Fourah Bay Coll. 38-49; police magistrate 49-59; puisne judge 59-63; Chief Justice of Sierra Leone 63; Pres. of Sierra Leone Court of Appeal 65; Acting Gov.-Gen. Aug.-Oct. 65; Chancellor, Univ. of Sierra Leone 69-; Judge of Supreme Court 71-72; Legal Consultant 72-; Hon. D.Litt. 70.
c/o Supreme Court, Freetown, Sierra Leone.

Bannerman, E. A. L.; Ghanaian judge; b. 22 Aug. 1915.
Private legal practice 39-44; District Magistrate 44-57; Senior Magistrate 57-60; Justice of the Supreme Court Aug. 70; Acting Chief Justice Aug. 70-March 71; Chief Justice of Ghana March 71-72.
c/o Ministry of Justice, Accra, Ghana.

Barcougne, Courmo; Niger economist and politician; b. 1916, Say; ed. William-Ponty School, Dakar, and French Dept. of Overseas Studies, Paris.
Secretary-General, Parti Progressiste Nigérien (PPN) 46-55, Sec. Politique, PPN 55-; Minister of Finance and Econ. Affairs Dec. 58-Nov. 65; fmr. Pres. Banque Centrale des Etats de l'Afrique de l'Ouest (BCEAO); Minister of Finance Nov. 65-Jan. 70; Minister of Foreign Affairs Jan. 70-71.
c/o Ministry of Foreign Affairs, Niamey, Niger.

Barnard, Christiaan Neethling, M.D., M.S., PH.D.; South African heart surgeon; b. 1922, Beaufort West, Cape Province; ed. Univ. of Cape Town.
Graduated as doctor 46; intern, Groote Schuur Hospital, Cape Town 47; then spent two years in general practice in Ceres; then Senior Resident Medical Officer, City Fever Hospital, Cape Town; returned to Groote Schuur Hospital; then Charles Adams Memorial Scholar, Univ. of Minnesota, concentrating on cardiothoracic surgery; on return to Groote Schuur Hospital concentrated on open-heart operations and cardiac research; Head of Cardiac Research and Surgery, Univ. of Cape Town; developed the Barnard Valve, for use in open-heart surgery; performed first successful open-heart operation in South Africa; performed first successful heart transplant operation in world 67; Hon. Dr. Univ. of Cape Town.
Publ. *One Life* (autobiography, with C. B. Pepper) 70.

Department of Surgical Research, U.C.T. Medical School, Observatory, Cape, South Africa.
Telephone: 55-1358.

Barnes, Nathan; Liberian diplomatist, b. 14 April 1914; ed. Cape Palmas Seminary.
Liberian Revenue Service 37-44; County Attorney, Maryland County, Liberia 44, Circuit Judge 45-56; Minister to Italy 56; Ambassador to Italy 56-60; Perm. Rep. to UN 60-; Knight, Grand Band Humane Order African Redemption; Grand Commdr. Star of Africa.
Permanent Mission of Liberia to the United Nations, 235 East 42nd Street, New York, N.Y., U.S.A.

Baroum, Jacques; Chad politician; b. 13 July 1932; ed. Coll. de Bongor, Ecole des cadres supérieurs, Lycée Savorgnan-de-Brazza, Brazzaville, and Université de Paris à la Sorbonne.
Doctor, Hospital of Fort-Lamy 62-64; Minister of Public Health and Social Affairs 64; mem. Political Office of the Progressive Party 63; Minister of Foreign Affairs 64-May 71, of Health and Social Affairs May 71-.
P.O. Box 784, Fort-Lamy, Chad.

Barry-Battesti, Ange-François; Ivory Coast politician and educator; b. 11 Feb. 1932, Séguéla; ed. Univs. of Dakar, Poitiers, Grenoble.
Lecturer in geography at technical secondary school in Abidjan 61-65, headmaster 65-69; Minister of Technical Educ. and Professional Training Jan. 70-.
Ministry of Technical Education and Professional Training, Abidjan, Ivory Coast.

Bashford, Thomas Henry Patrick; British farmer and politician; b. 9 Oct. 1915, Greenwich, England; ed. Shooter's Hill Open Air School, Woolwich Polytechnic.
Settled in Africa 37; war service, Middle East, Italy 39-45; Sec. Rhodesia Nat. Industrial Council 46; Asst. Sec. Nat. Building and Housing Board 47-49; farmer 49-; formed Centre Party 68, now Pres.; founder mem. Nat. Affairs Asscn., Inter-Racial Asscn. (now defunct).
Publs. regular articles in Centre Party journal.
Centre Party, P.O. Box 1450, Salisbury; Home: St. Brendans Farm, P.O. Box 126, Karoi, Rhodesia.

Basson, Jacob Daniel du Plessis ("Japie"); South African politician; b. 1918, Paarl, Cape Province; ed. Stellenbosch Univ.
Political sec. and journalist in Repub. and S.W. Africa 39-50; mem. S. Africa Parl. for Namib, S.W. Africa 50-59 (Nat. Party of S.W.A.); expelled from Nat. Party Caucus over differences concerning Govt.'s race policies 59; Independent M.P., leading extra-Parl. Political Group (The Nat. Union) 59-61; merger of Nat. Union with United Party (official opposition party) 61; M.P. (United Party) for Bezuidenhout, Johannesburg 61-; Shadow Minister of Foreign Affairs.
House of Assembly, Cape Town; P.O. Box 66123, Broadway, Johannesburg, South Africa.

Batawangele, Losembe (Mario Cardoso); Zaire diplomatist; b. 29 Sept. 1933; ed. Univ. de Louvain, Belgium.
Teacher 53-54; Applied Psychology and Educ. Studies, Univ. of Louvain 54-58; Technical Assistance Officer of UN, New York; Perm. Rep. of Congo to UN 60-62; Chargé d'Affaires, Washington 62-65; Amb. to U.K. 66-68; Amb. to Morocco 68-March 69; Minister of Nat. Educ. March 69-Dec. 70; Minister of Foreign Affairs 70-Feb. 72.
c/o Ministry of Foreign Affairs, Kalina-Kinshasa, Zaire.

Bayero, Alhaji Ado; Emir of Kano; Nigerian administrator; b. June 1930; ed. Kofar Nudu Elementary School, Kano Middle School, and Inst. of Administration, Ahmadu Bello Univ.
Former Chief of Police, Kano Emirate; mem. N. House of Assembly; fmr. Amb. to Senegal; Emir of Kano 63-; Chancellor, Univ. of Nigeria, East Central State 66-.
Univ. of Nigeria, Nsukka, East Central State, Nigeria.

Beadle, Rt. Hon. Sir (Thomas) Hugh (William), P.C., Kt., C.M.G., O.B.E.; Rhodesian politician and judge; b. 6 Feb. 1905; ed. Univ. of Capetown and Queen's Coll., Oxford.
Advocate, Bulawayo 30-39; Royal West African Frontier Force, Gold Coast 39-40; Deputy Judge Advocate-Gen. S. Rhodesian Forces, and Parl. Sec. to Prime Minister 40-46; M.P. 39-50; Minister of Justice, Internal Affairs, Health, Education, S. Rhodesia 46-50; Judge of High Court, S. Rhodesia 50-61, Chief Justice 61-; Hon. Fellow Queens Coll., Oxford 66.
Chief Justice's Chambers, High Court, Bulawayo, Rhodesia.

Beavogui, Louis Lansana; Guinean politician; b. 1923; ed. West African Medical School, Dakar.
Former Asst. Medical Officer, Gueckedou, S. Guinea; later Medical Officer, Kissidougou, later becoming Mayor; Minister of Trade, Industry and Mining, Guinea 57-58, of Econs. 58-61, of Foreign Affairs 61-69, of Econ. Affairs 69-72; Prime Minister, in charge of the Army, Foreign Affairs, Planning, Finance Control and Information April 72-.
Office of the Prime Minister, Conakry, Guinea.

Beb a Don, Philémon Louis Benjamin, D. en D., DR. POL. SC.; Cameroonian diplomatist; b. 15 Aug. 1925, Kiki, Bafia; ed. Lycée d'Aix-en-Provence and Univs. of Aix-en-Provence, Toulouse and Paris.
With local civil and financial admin. 45-48; studied law and political science, Paris 48-57; Principal Civil Administrator, Acad. of Int. Law, The Hague 57; Chief of Staff of Ministry of Econ. Affairs 57-58; Cameroonian mem. of French Del. to Int. Conf. on Coffee, Rio de Janeiro 58; Head, Dept. of Legal Affairs, Ministry of Interior 58-60; Deputy Head of Dept., Ministry of Foreign Affairs 60-61; Diplomatic Adviser to Pres. of the Repub. July 60-; Counsellor Embassy in France 61-62; Amb. to France 62-67, to Fed. Repub. of Germany 67-72, to Switzerland, Yugoslavia 68-72; Dir. of the Cabinet 72-; several national and foreign decorations.
Publs. various articles in law journals.
Office of the President, Yaoundé, United Republic of Cameroon.

Bédié, Henri Konan, L. en D., D. ès SC.; Ivory Coast economist and politician; b. 1934; Dadiékro; ed. Poitiers Univ., France.
Worked as civil servant in France 59; Counsellor at the French Embassy, Washington March 60-Aug. 60; founded Ivory Coast mission to the UN 60; Chargé d'affaires for Ivory Coast to U.S.A. Aug. 60-Dec. 60, Amb. Dec. 60-Jan. 66; Minister Del. for Econ. and Financial Affairs Jan. 66-Sept. 68, Minister Sept. 68-; mem. Bureau Politique, Parti Démocratique de la Côte d'Ivoire (PDCI); Pres. OAMPI (Office africain et malgache de la propriété industrielle).
Ministry of Economic and Financial Affairs, Abidjan, Ivory Coast.

Behiery, Mamoun Ahmed, B.A.; Sudanese banker; b. 1925; ed. Victoria Coll., Alexandria and Brasnenose Coll., Oxford.
Former Deputy Perm. Under-Sec. Ministry of Finance and Econs.; fmr. Chair. Sudan Currency Board; Gov. Central Bank of Sudan 59-63; Gov. IMF and IBRD for Sudan; Chair., Cttee. of Nine preparing for African Devt. Bank 63; Minister of Finance and Econs. 63-64; Pres. African Development Bank 64-70; Chair. Nat. Technical Planning Cttee. 62.
c/o Ministry of Finance, Khartoum, Sudan.

Bénard, Jean Pierre, L. ès L.; French diplomatist; b. 29 Feb. 1908; ed. Lycée Janson-de-Sailly and Univ. de Paris à la Sorbonne.

Journalist, Agence Havas, Washington 34-36, Chief, News Service, Middle East and Cairo 36-39; Diplomatic Service 45-, Counsellor, U.S.A. 45-54; Dep. Dir. NATO Information Div. 55-57; Minister, Tunisia 57-60; Amb. to Fed. Repub. of Cameroon 60-65, to Ethiopia 65-71; Dir. of Cabinet of Sec. of State for Foreign Affairs 71-72; Pres. GERDAT Oct. 72-; Officier, Légion d'Honneur.
Ministère des Affaires Etrangères, quai d'Orsay, Paris 7e, France.

Bezaka, Alexis; Malagasy politician; b. 8 March 1916, Ambatokintana Mananara; ed. Petit Séminaire d'Ambihipo, Tananarive, Grand Séminaire d'Ambatorika.
Priest 37-39; mem. Rep. Council (Mouvement Démocratique de la Rénovation Malgache) 45-47; imprisoned 47-56; First Deputy Mayor of Tamatave 56, Mayor 59-64; mem. Rep. Assembly 57; Minister of Public Health 57-58; resigned from govt. 58; Deputy 60-65; now Pres. Parti Démocrate Chrétien Malgache (PDCM).
123 rue de 12e Bataillon Malgache, Tananarive, Madagascar.

Bigirwenkya, Zerubaberi Hosea Kwamya, B.A.; Ugandan civil servant; b. 24 May 1927, Masindi; ed. King's Coll., Budo, Makerere Univ., Kampala and Inst. of Educ., Univ. of London.
Community Devt. Officer in charge of Bunyoro, Masaka and Mubende Districts 54-61; Principal Asst.Sec.,Ministry of Community Devt. 60-61; Under-Sec., Ministry of Agriculture and Co-operatives June 62; Perm. Sec., Ministry of Animal Industry, Game and Fisheries Sept. 62-May 63; Perm. Sec., Ministry of Foreign Affairs 63-67; Sec.-Gen. East African Community 68-71; Perm. Sec. Office of the Pres. and Sec. to the Cabinet, Govt. of Uganda 71-; Pres. East African Management Foundation.
P.O. Box 7168, Kampala, Uganda.
Telephone: Kampala 41218 (Office); Kampala 42784 (Home).

Bihute, Donatien; Burundi international financial official; b. 22 Oct. 1940, Rugombo; ed. St. Esprit Coll., Bujumbura and Univ. of Fribourg, Switzerland.
With Banque d'Emission du Rwanda et du Burundi 60; Dir.-Gen. of Finance 65; Minister of Finance and Econ. Affairs and Gov. for Burundi, IMF 66-67; Attaché, Banque de Crédit de Bujumbura 68; Alt. Exec. Dir. IBRD, IFC and IDA 68; Exec. Dir. IBRD, IFC and IDA Nov. 70-.
International Bank for Reconstruction and Development, 1818 H Street, N.W., Washington, D.C. 20433, U.S.A.

Bingle, Hendrik Johannes Jacob, B.A., M.ED., D.PHIL.; South African university rector; b. 15 Aug. 1910, Colesberg, Cape Province; ed. High School, Steynsburg, and Potchefstroom Univ.
Teacher, various schools 32-44; Senior Lector, Faculty of Educ., Univ. of Potchefstroom for Christian Higher Educ. 45-49, Prof. 50-63, Dean of Faculty of Educ. 51-61, now Rector of Univ.; Dir. Helpmekaar Study Fund for Transvaal; mem. S.A. Akad. vir Wetenskap en Kuns; mem. Regional Council, Potchefstroom Coll. of Educ.; Chair. Gov. Body of Gymnasium High School; mem. Governing Body Ferdinand Postmas Huishoudskool; mem. Council Bantu Univ. of North, Indian Coll., Durban, Univ. of S. Africa, Rand Afrikaans Univ.; mem Anti Communistic Council; mem. State Pres. Comm. on Univs., Comm. of Univ. Principals; Chair. Directorate African Express; mem. Human Sciences Research Council; Chair. Afrikaanse Calvinistiese Beweging.
Publs. Various publs. in Afrikaans in connection with education.
The Rector, Potchefstroom University for Christian Higher Education, Potchefstroom; 1 Calderbank Avenue, Potchefstroom, South Africa.

Biobaku, Saburi Oladeni, C.M.G., B.A., M.A., PH.D.; Nigerian historian and university official; b. 16 June 1918; ed. Government Coll., Ibadan, Higher Coll., Yaba, Univ. Coll. Exeter, Trinity Coll. Cambridge and Inst. of Historical Research, London.
Master, Govt. Coll., Ibadan 41-44; Educ. Officer 47-50; Asst. Liaison Officer for Nigerian Students in U.K., Colonial Office, London 51-53; Registrar, Univ. Coll., Ibadan 53-57; Sec. to Premier and Exec. Council, W. Nigeria 57-61; Pro Vice-Chancellor, Univ. of Ife and Dir. Institutes of African Studies and of Public Admin. 61-65; Vice-Chancellor Designate, Univ. of Zambia Feb.-March 65; Vice-Chancellor Univ. of Lagos 65-72, Prof. and Dir. of African Studies 65-; Dir. Yoruba Historical Research Scheme 56-; Chair. Cttee. of Vice-Chancellors, Nigeria 67-70; Vice-Chair. Standing Cttee., *Encyclopaedia Africana* 67-; mem. Exec. Board, Asscn. of African Univs. 67-; Pres. Historical Soc. of Nigeria 68-; created Are of Iddo, Abeokuta 58; Hon. Fellow, W. African Asscn. of Surgeons 68.
Publs. *The Origin of the Yoruba 55, The Egba and their Neighbours 57, African Studies in an African University 63.*
The Chalet, Mile 2, Owode Road, Abeokuta, Nigeria.
Telephone: Abeokuta 206.

Biya, Paul, L. en D.; Cameroonian politician; b. 13 Feb. 1933, Muomékoa, Dia-et-Lobo; ed. Lycée Louis-le-Grand. Paris, Inst. des Hautes Etudes d'Outre-mer, Faculté de Droit and Inst. d'Etudes Politiques, France.
Official, Presidency of the Republic Sept. 62-Dec. 64; Dir. de Cabinet, Ministry of Nat. Educ. Jan. 64-July 65; Sec.-Gen. Ministry of Nat. Educ., Youth and Culture July 65-Dec. 67; Dir. de Cabinet to the Pres. of the Repub. Dec. 67-Jan. 68; Minister of State and Sec.-Gen. to the Presidency of the Repub. Aug. 68-; Chevalier, Ordre de la Valeur Camerounaise and other decorations.
Office of the President, Yaoundé, United Republic of Cameroon.

Blundell, Sir Michael, K.B.E.; Kenyan farmer and politician; b. 7 April 1907, London; ed. Wellington Coll.
Emigrated to Kenya 25; served in Royal Engineers (Col.) 39-45; Comm. for European Settlement 46-47; Chair. Pyrethrum Board of Kenya 49-54, Allsopps African Investments 49-54; mem. Kenya Legislative Council for Rift Valley Constituency 48-58, 61-63; specially selected mem. under Lennox-Boyd Constitution for Kenya, April 58-61; Acting Leader, European Elected mems. 51, Leader 52; Minister on Emergency War Council 54; Minister of Agriculture 55-59, 61-62; Leader New Kenya Party 59-63; Chair. Egerton Agricultural Coll. 62-72, E. A. Breweries Ltd. 64-, Uganda Breweries Ltd. 65-; Dir. Barclays Bank Int. Ltd. (Kenya) 69-.
Publ. *So Rough a Wind* 64.
P.O. Box 100, Nakuru, Kenya.
Telephone: Bahati 219 and Nairobi 20962.

Boaten, Frank E.; Ghanaian diplomatist; b. 17 Dec. 1923; ed. Prince of Wales Coll., Achimota, Univ. Coll. of the Gold Coast (Ghana) and Univ. of London.
First Sec., New Delhi 57-59; Counsellor, Moscow 60; Principal Sec., Ministry of Foreign Affairs 66-71; Visiting Fellow, Queen Elizabeth House and Senior Assoc. mem. St. Anthony's Coll., Oxford 71-72; Perm. Rep. to UN Sept. 72-; has attended numerous int. confs.
Permanent Mission of Ghana to United Nations, 150 East 58th Street, New York, N.Y. 10022, U.S.A.

Boissier-Palun, Léon Louis; Senegalese international lawyer and diplomatist; b. 29 June 1916; ed. Lycée Faidherbe and Bordeaux Univ.
Officer Troupes Coloniales, Second World War; Deputy Senegal Assembly; Senator French Community; Pres. Comm. for Economic Affairs and Planning of Senegalese

Legislative Assembly; High Counsellor, Pres. Grand Council of French West Africa 52-57; Minister for Econ. Affairs responsible for inter-territorial relations in Senegal 57; Administrator of the Banking Inst. for the issue of French currency in French West Africa and Togoland; Amb. to United Kingdom 60-66, to Austria, Norway, Sweden and Denmark 61-66, to Switzerland 64-66, to France 66; Pres. Econ. and Social Council, Dakar 64-72; co-founder Bloc Démocratique Sénégalais; Commdr. Légion d'Honneur, Grand Croix, l'Ordre Nat. du Sénégal, Hon. K.B.E., Knight of Sovereign Military Order of Malta.
67 avenue Victor Hugo, Paris 16e, France; Ile de Gorée, Dakar, Senegal.
Telephone: 5534675.

Bokassa, Lt. Gen. Jean Bédel; Central African Republic army officer and politician; b. 22 Feb. 1921; ed. Ecole Sainte Jeanne-d'Arc, M'Baiki, Ecole Missionnaire, Bangui, and Ecole Missionnaire, Brazzaville.
Joined French Army 39, rose to Captain 61; organized army of Central African Repub.; C.-in-C. Central African Repub. Army Jan. 63-; Pres., Prime Minister, Central African Repub. Jan. 66-, Minister of Defence 66-, of Justice 66-70, of Information 70-, of Agriculture and Stock-breeding Aug. 70-, of Public Health and Population Jan. 71-; Pres. MESAN Feb.-June 70; Légion d'Honneur, Croix de Guerre.
Office of the President, Bangui, Central African Republic.

Bokhorst, Matthys, LITT.D., D.PHIL.; South African art historian; b. 28 Aug. 1900, Rotterdam, Netherlands; ed. Rotterdam, Leyden Univ. and Switzerland.
Professor of Netherlands Cultural History and Dir. Neths. Inst. Pretoria Univ. 29-51; Editor *Nederlandse Post* 51-; Pres. South African Asscn. of Arts 51-58; Chair. Govt. Art Advisory Comm. 52-68; Dir. Michaelis Art Gallery 56-64; Dir. South African National Gallery 62-; mem. Exec. Council of South African Museums Asscn. 58-, Pres. 71-; mem. Nat. Arts Comm. 68-.
Publs. *Nederlands-Zwitserse Betrekkingen voor en na 1700* 30, *Kultuur van een Waterland* 37, *Handvest der Vryheid* 44, *Die Kuns van'n Kwarteeu* 54, *Art at the Cape* 64, *The S.A. National Gallery* 65.
"Het Trappenhuis", Talma Road, Muizenberg, Cape Town, South Africa.
Telephone: 85345.

Bomani, Paul; Tanzanian politician; b. 1 Jan. 1925, Musoma; ed. Ikizu Secondary School.
Employee, Williamson Diamonds Ltd. 45-47; Asst. Sec., later Sec. Mwanza African Traders' Co-operative Soc.; Organizer, Lake Province Growers' Asscn. 52; studied Co-operative Development at Loughborough Coll. 53-54; mem. Legislative Council 55; Man. Victoria Fed. of Co-operative Unions Ltd. 55; Minister of Agriculture, Tanganyika 60-62, Minister of Finance 62-64, Minister of Finance of Tanzania 64-65; Minister for Econ. Affairs and Devt. Planning 65-67, June 67, of Commerce 67; Gov. of World Bank for Tanzania 67-Nov. 70; Minister of Commerce and Industries Nov. 70-Feb. 72.
c/o Ministry of Commerce and Industries, Dar es Salaam, Tanzania.

Bomboko, Justin; Zaire politician; ed. Brussels Univ.
Member, Union Mongo Party, Equator Province; Minister of Foreign Affairs, Lumumba cabinet, June 60, Ileo cabinet, Sept. 60; mem., Congolese Comm. set up to co-operate with UN July 60: Leader, Col. Mobutu's governing College of High Commissioners, with responsibility for Foreign Affairs, Sept. 60; Minister of Foreign Affairs 61-63, 65-71, of Justice 63-65, of Foreign Trade Oct. 67-70; Amb. to U.S.A. 69-70; charged with treason Oct. 71.

Bongo, Albert Bernard; Gabonese politician; b. 30 Dec. 1935, Lewai, Franceville; ed. primary school at Bacongo (Congo P.R.) and technical coll., Brazzaville.

Civil servant; served Air Force 58-60; entered Ministry of Foreign Affairs 60; Dir. of Private Office of Pres. Léon Mba 62, in charge of Information 63-64, Nat. Defence 64-65; Minister-Del. to Presidency in charge of Nat. Defence and Co-ordination, Information and Tourism 65-66; Vice-Pres. of Govt. in charge of Co-ordination, Nat. Defence, Plan, Information and Tourism 66-67; Vice-Pres. of Repub. March-Dec. 67; Pres. of Repub. of Gabon, Prime Minister, Minister of Defence and Information, Minister of Planning Dec. 67-, of the Interior Dec. 67-Dec. 70, Minister of Development Dec. 70-, of Mines Dec. 70-June 71, Minister of Territorial Admin. Feb. 72-; Founder and Sec.-Gen. Parti Démocratique Gabonais 68; High Chancellor, Ordre Nat. de l'Etoile Equatoriale; Grand Cross, Ordre Nat. de Côte d'Ivoire, Ordre Nat. du Niger; Commdr., Ordre Nat. Français du Mérite; Officer du Mérite Combattant; Grande Croix Ordre Nat. Tchadien, du Léopard, de la Valeur du Cameroun, du Mérite Centrafricain; Grand Officier Ordre Nat. République Guinée.
Boîte Postale 546, Libreville, Gabon.
Telephone: 26-90.

Boni, Alphonse; Ivory Coast judge and politician; b. 8 Jan. 1909, Tiassale.
Worked in public prosecutor's office, Toulouse, France, later in colonial admin; held legal posts in Togo, Mali and Senegal; Public Prosecutor, Brazzaville 52-58; Minister of Justice 59; Pres. Supreme Court Feb. 63-; Pres. State Security Court; mem. Bureau Politique du Parti Démocratique de Côte d'Ivoire (PDCI).
B.P. V-30, Abidjan, Ivory Coast.

Boolell, Satcam, LL.B.; Mauritius lawyer and politician; b. 11 Sept. 1920, New Grove; ed. Mauritius, London School of Econs., Lincoln's Inn, London.
Civil Servant 44-48; practising barrister, Mauritius 52-59; mem. Legislative Council for Moka Flacq (Independent) 53; joined Labour Party 55, mem. Exec. Cttee. 55; mem. Legislative Assembly for Montagne Blanche 59, 63, for Montagne Blanche and Grand River South East 67; Pres. Mauritius Arya Sabha 56-62; Minister of Agriculture and Natural Resources 59-67, of Educ. and Cultural Affairs 67-68, of Agriculture, Natural Resources and Co-operative Devt. 68-; has represented govt. at many int. confs., participated in constitutional confs. leading to independence 61, 65; founder, _The Nation_ (daily newspaper).
Ministry of Agriculture, Natural Resources and Co-operative Development, Port Louis, Mauritius.

Boteti, Col. Lazare-Jacques; Zaire army officer.
Ambassador to Israel until 72; Chief of Gen. Staff Sept. 72-; Life Fellow, Hon. Trustee, Inst. for Int. Sociological Research 71.
General Staff Headquarters, Kinshasa, Zaire.

Botha, Johan Samuel Frederick, B.ECON.; South African diplomatist; b. 18 Feb., 1919, South Africa; ed. Univ. of Stellenbosch and Univ. of South Africa.
Served, S. African Army 40-45; Second Sec., S. African Embassy, Washington 49-54, Ottawa 54-57; Perm. Rep. to UN 57-59; Asst. Sec., Dept. of Foreign Affairs, Pretoria 59-62; Consul-Gen., Tokyo 62-64; Minister, S. African Embassy, Washington 64-67; Deputy Sec. for Foreign Affairs 67-71; Amb. to U.S.A. 71-.
South African Embassy, 3101 Massachusetts Avenue, N.W., Washington, D.C. 20008, U.S.A.
Telephone: 232-4400.

Botha, Matthys Izak, B.A., LL.B.; South African diplomatist; b. 1913, Bloemfontein; ed. Selborne Coll., London and Univ. of Pretoria.
Department of Finance 31-44; Dept. of Foreign Affairs 44-, Washington 44-51, New York 51-54; Head of Political Div., Dept. of Foreign Affairs, Pretoria 55-58; Minister, Switzerland 59-60; Minister, London 60-62; Perm. Rep. to UN 62-70; Amb. to Canada 70-.

South African Embassy, 15 Sussex Street, Ottawa 2, Ont., Canada.
Telephone: (613) 749-5977.

Botha, Michiel Coenraad; South African politician; b. 14 Dec. 1912, Lindley, O.F.S.; ed. Univ. of Stellenbosch, Pretoria Univ. and Univ. of Cape Town.
Teacher, Transvaal schools 35-36; Lecturer, Pretoria Technical Coll. 37-43; Sec. Afrikaanse Taal-en Kultuur-vereniging 43-53; mem. Parl. 53-; later Deputy Minister of Bantu Admin. and Devt.; Minister of Bantu Admin. and Devt., and Minister of Bantu Educ. 66-; Nat. Party.
Ministry of Bantu Education, Pretoria, South Africa.

Botha, Pieter Willem, M.P.; South African politician; b. 12 Jan. 1916, Paul Roux district, O.F.S.; ed. Univ. of Orange Free State.
Member of Parl.; Chief Sec. Cape Nat. Party 48-58; fmr. Deputy Minister of the Interior; Minister of Community Devt., Public Works and Coloured Affairs 61-66, of Defence 65-; Leader Nat. Party in Cape Province Nov. 66-.
Ministry of Defence, Pretoria, South Africa.

Botha, Hon. Stephanus Petrus, B.COM.; South African politician; b. 5 May 1922, Lusaka, N. Rhodesia; ed. Paarl Boys' High School.
Joined Dr. Anton Rupert's Technical Industrial Investment Organization, became financial organizer; estab. Soutpansberg Regional Devt. Soc. 57, Chair. and Hon. Pres.; M.P. for Soutpansberg; Chair. Nat. Party's Land Group; Sec. Water Affairs Group; Deputy Sec. Study Group on Bantu Affairs; mem. Bantu Affairs Comm. 66-; mem. Exec. Cttee. of Nat. Party in Transvaal; Deputy Minister of Water Affairs 66-68; Minister of Water Affairs and of Forestry 68-; Dir. Volkskas Ltd., Rondalia Ltd., Alt. Trustee Dagbreek Trust.
Ministry of Water Affairs, Pretoria, South Africa.

Botokeky, Laurent; Malagasy politician; b. 5 Dec. 1919, Bosy, Morondava; ed. schools at Tuléar and Tananarive and Ecole Normale Supérieure de St. Cloud.
Worked as teacher; mem. Provincial Assembly of Tuléar 57; mem. French Senate, and Malagasy Nat. Assembly 58; Mayor, Belo-on Tsiribina; Sec. of State for the Interior Feb. 59; Sec. of State for Educ. 59; Minister for Educ. May 59; M.P. for the Province of Tuléar Sept. 60; Minister for Cultural Affairs 65-72; Treas.-Gen. of the ruling cttee. of the PSD, resigned from PSD July 72; mem. Int. League against racism and anti-semitism; Officer of the Mérite Sportif.
c/o Ministry of Cultural Affairs, Tananarive, Madagascar.

Bottomley, Sir James Reginald Arthur, K.C.M.G., M.A.; British diplomatist; b. 12 Jan. 1920, London; ed. Kings Coll., Wimbledon, Trinity Coll., Cambridge.
Military Service 40-46; joined Dominions Office (now Foreign and Commonwealth Office) 46; overseas service, South Africa 48-50, Pakistan 53-55, U.S.A. 55-59, Malaysia 63-67; Deputy Under-Sec. of State 70-72; Amb. to South Africa 73-; mem. British Nat. Export Council 70-71, British Overseas Trade Board 72, Cttee. on Invisible Exports 70-72, Governing Body, Inst. of Devt. Studies 70-72.
Embassy of the United Kingdom, Cape Town and Pretoria, South Africa.

Bouazo-Zegbeni, Edmond; Ivory Coast politician; b. 30 March 1935, Azaguié; ed. School of Journalism, Paris and Nat. School of Administration.
Former Sec. for Foreign Affairs; Technical Counsellor 61-63; Minister of Press and Information Nov. 67-.
Ministry of Press and Information, Abidjan, Ivory Coast.

Boukar, Abdoul; Chad diplomatist; b. 1934; ed. Chad and Ecole Nationale d'Administration, Paris.
Teacher and mem. business firm, Chad 53-59; First Sec. French Embassy, Kano (Nigeria) 60-61; Amb. to Nigeria

61-64; Amb. to U.S.A. 64-68, concurrently Perm. Rep. to UN 64-68; Exec. Sec. Union des Etats de l'Afrique Centrale (UEAC) 68-69; Amb. to U.S.S.R. 69-.
Embassy of Chad, Ul. Elizarovoi 10, Moscow, U.S.S.R.

Boumah, Augustin; Gabonese politician; b. 7 Nov. 1927; Libreville.
Directeur de cabinet, Ministry of Labour 63; fmr. Dir. Gabonese School of Admin.; Minister of Youth, Sports and Cultural Affairs Jan. 67-April 67; Minister of Justice and Keeper of the Seals April 67-Sept. 67; mem. Exec. Cttee., Parti Démocratique Gabonais (PDG); Minister of the Interior Sept. 67-68, of Finance and the Budget July 68-72; Minister of State at the Pres. in charge of Planning, Devt. and Territorial Admin. Feb. 72-.
Office of the President, Libreville, Gabon.

Boye, Ibrahima; Senegalese judge; b. 29 March 1924, Saint Louis; ed. Univ. de Montpellier.
Attorney-at-Law, Court of Appeals, Nîmes, France; later mem. Public Prosecutor's Office at Court of Appeals of Montpellier; later French Judge, Guinea, Pres. of Colonial Court of Appeals, Dahomey; Examining Magistrate, Cotonou and Abidjan; Justice of the Peace, Agbonville, Ivory Coast; Technical Adviser in Ministry of Justice, Senegal 60, later Dir. of Cabinet and Justice of Supreme Court; Attorney-Gen., Senegal 61-; Chair UN Comm. on Human Rights 67-; Amb. and Perm. Rep. of Senegal to UN 68-71; mem. UN Security Council 68-69, Pres. July 69; Vice-Pres. UN Gen. Assembly 70; Amb. to U.S.S.R., concurrently to Poland, Hungary, Romania, Bulgaria Sept. 71-.
Publs. works on human rights.
Senegalese Embassy, 12 Ul. Donskaya, Moscow, U.S.S.R.
Telephone: 236-70-24.

Bozzoli, Guerino Renzo, PR.ENG., D.SC.(ENG.) (RAND), F.I.E.E.; South African university administrator; b. 24 April 1911, Pretoria; ed. Sunnyside School and Boys' High School, Pretoria, and Witwatersrand Univ.
Assistant Engineer South African Broadcasting Corpn. (S.A.B.C.) 34-36; Junior Lecturer, Dept. of Electrical Engineering, Witwatersrand Univ. 36, Lecturer 39, Senior Lecturer 42, Prof. and Head of Dept. 48-; Dean, Faculty of Engineering 54-57, 62-65, Deputy Vice-Chancellor 65-68, Vice-Chancellor and Principal, Univ. of Witwatersrand 69-, mem. Council S.A. Inst. of Electrical Engineers 46-62, Pres. 55, Chair. Advisory Cttee., Telecommunications Research Lab. 48-67; mem. Advisory Cttee., Nat. Physical Research Lab., C.S.I.R. 58-62; mem. Prime Minister's Scientific Advisory Council 63-66; mem. Board Nat. Inst. of Metallurgy 67-; Pres. Associated Scientific and Technical Socs. of S.A. 69-70; Hon. F.S.A.I.E.E.; mem. various comms. and cttees. etc.
University of the Witwatersrand, Jan Smuts Avenue, Johannesburg; Home: Savernake, 13 Jubilee Road, Parktown, Johannesburg, South Africa.

Braham, Maloum Ould; Mauritanian politician; b. 1932, Eidjikda; ed. Rosso and William-Ponty School.
Teacher at Nema 51-54, Boutilimit 54-56; Headmaster Tidjikja and Kiffa 57-63; Inspector for Primary Educ. 63-66; Minister of Foreign Affairs Feb. 66-Oct. 66; Minister of Rural Economy 66-67, of Commerce, Transport and Tourism 67-68; Guardian of the Seals and Minister of Justice 68-.
Ministry of Justice, Nouakchott, Mauritania.

Briggs, Wenike, LL.B.; Nigerian politician; b. 10 March 1918, Abonnema, River State; ed. Nyemoni School, Abonnema, King's Coll., Lagos, Regent Street Polytechnic, London and Univ. of Sheffield (external student).
Postal Clerk, Dept. of Posts and Telegraphs; Customs Official, Dept. of Customs and Excise 42; Sub-editor *Daily Service* 45; founder and editor *The Nigerian Statesman* 47; studied in U.K. called to the Bar, Gray's Inn, London

59; mem. House of Reps 59-; Fed. Commr. for Educ. 66-71, for Trade 71-.
Ministry of Trade, Lagos, Nigeria.

Brodie-Mends, Theophilus Doghan; Ghanaian politician; b. 26 Nov. 1929, Sekondi, W. Region; ed. Mfantsipim School, Cape Coast, Marx School, London, Univ. Coll., London and Middle Temple.
Worked as journalist 47-52; Sub-Editor, *Star of West Africa;* called to the Bar 60; Pres. Ghana Students' Union of G.B. and Ireland 52-57; Vice-Pres. West African Students' Union (WASU); mem. Boards of Govs., Mfantsipim School, Cape Coast, and Mfantsiman Girls' Secondary School, Saltpond, C.O.S. Board 66, Board of New Times Ltd.; Central Regional Devt. Cttee., and Constituent Assembly; Counsel, Univ. Coll. Cape Coast; Chair. Management Cttee. of the Cape Coast Municipal Council; M.P. for Cape Coast (Progress Party); Minister of Information 69-Jan. 71; Minister of Lands and Mineral Resources 71-Jan. 72.
c/o Ministry of Lands, Accra, Ghana.

Brookes, Edgar Harry, M.A., D.LITT.; South African author; b. 4 Feb. 1897, Smethwick, England.
Professor of Public Admin. and Political Science, Univ. of Pretoria 20-33; Principal, Adams Coll., Natal 34-45; Senator representing Africans of Natal and Zululand in Union Parl. 37-52; mem. Perm. Native Affairs Comm. 45-50; Pres. S.A. Inst. of Race Relations 32-33, 46-48, 59-60; S.A. Del. to L.N. 27, and to UNESCO 47; Prof. of History and Political Science, Univ. of Natal 59-62; Nat. Chair. Liberal Party of South Africa 63-68.
Publs. *History of Native Policy in South Africa* 24, *Native Education in South Africa* 29, *The Colour Problems of South Africa* 33, *The House of Bread* (poems) 44, *The Bantu in South African Life* 46, *South Africa in a Changing World* 53, *The Native Reserves of Natal* 56, *Civil Liberty in South Africa* 58, *The City of God* and *Politics of Crisis* 60, *Power Law, Right and Love* 63, *A History of Natal* (with C. de B. Webb) 65, *A History of the University of Natal* 67, *Apartheid: A Documentary Study of Modern South Africa* 68.
15 Elgarth, St. Patrick's Road, Pietermaritzburg, Natal, South Africa.
Telephone: 22714.

Brooks, Angie Elizabeth, LL.D.; Liberian lawyer and UN official; b. 24 Aug. 1928, Virginia, Montserrado County; ed. Shaw Univ., N.C., Howard Univ., Univs. of Wisconsin, London and Liberia.
Counsellor-at-law, Supreme Court of Liberia 53; Asst. Attorney-Gen. 53-58; Asst. Sec. of State 58-71; Prof. of Law, Liberia Univ. 54-58; Vice-Pres. Int. Fed. of Women Lawyers 56-58, Pres. 64-67; Liberian Del. UN Gen. Assembly 54-; Vice-Chair. Fourth UN Cttee. 56; Vice-Pres. Cttee. on Information from Non-Self-Governing Territories 61; Chair. Fourth Cttee 61; Chair. UN Comm. for Ruanda-Urundi 62; Chair. of UN Visiting Mission to Trust Territory of Pacific Islands 64; Vice-Pres. Trusteeship Council 65, Pres. 66; Pres. XXIVth Session UN Gen. Assembly 69-70; Pres. Congress on Adoption and Placement, Milan Sept. 71.
c/o United Nations, First Avenue, New York, N.Y.C., U.S.A.

Brown, Peter McKenzie; South African politician; b. 1924; ed. Michaelhouse, Cambridge Univ. and Univ. of Cape Town.
Natal Health Comm. 51; organized inter-racial discussion group which became South African Liberal Asscn.; mem. Liberal Party 53-64, Deputy Nat. Chair. 57-59, Nat. Chair. 59-64; detained under State of Emergency March-June 60; confined to Magisterial District of Pietermaritzburg since 64.
268 Longmarket Street, Pietermaritzburg, Natal, South Africa.

Bruce, Noel Hugh Botha, I.D., F.I.B.S.A.; South African. banker; b. 13 Nov. 1921, Fauresmith, O.F.S.; ed. Outeniqua High School, George Rondebosch High School, Capetown and Univ. of S. Africa.
With S. Africa Reserve Bank 38-55; Chief Cashier, Bank of Rhodesia and Nyasaland 56-65; Gov. Reserve Bank of Rhodesia 64-; Registrar of Banks and Financial Institutions, Rhodesia 64-65; Trustee, Post Office Savings Bank; mem. Prime Minister's Econ. Council; Dir. Ipcorn Ltd.; Chair. Nat. Arts Foundation; has served on many govt. comms.
Publs. various articles in economic and scientific journals.
Blue Gums, Radnor Road, Emerald Hill, Avondale, Salisbury (P.O. Box 1283, Salisbury), Rhodesia.
Telephone: 35807, 28791.

Bryceson, Derek; Tanzanian farmer and politician; b. 30 Dec. 1922, Hankow, China; ed. St. Paul's School, London and Trinity Coll., Cambridge.
Pilot, R.A.F. Voluntary Reserve 40-43; farmer, Kenya 47-52, Tanganyika 52-60; Asst. Minister of Social Services 57-58; mem. of Parl. 58-; Minister of Mines and Commerce July 59-60, of Health and Labour 60-62, of Agriculture 62-64, of Health 64-65, of Agriculture, Food and Cooperatives Sept. 65-Feb. 72; Dir. Tanzania Nat. Parks July 72-.
Old Bagamoyo Road, Dar es Salaam, Tanzania.

Bubiriza, Pascal; Burundi diplomatist; b. 1932, Rugari, Muhinga, Burundi; ed. Groupe Scolaire of Astrida, Ruanda (now Rwanda).
Secretary of Service of Justice and Litigation of Ruanda-Urundi, Usumbura 55-57; Territorial Agent, Territory of Muchinga, Burundi 58-60; Asst. Provincial Administrator, Province of Bubanza 60-61, Deputy Public Prosecutor, Usumbura 61; Chef de Cabinet to Prime Minister of Burundi 61-62; Perm. Rep. to UN 62-63; Minister of Interior, Burundi 63-64; Amb. to Ethiopia 65-67; Amb. to U.S.S.R. 67-69; Minister of Communications and Aeronautics 69-72.
c/o Ministry of Communications and Aeronautics, Bujumbura, Burundi.

Buliro, Joshua Davies, B.A.; Kenyan civil servant; b. 1932, Kenya; ed. Ebwali School, Kakamega Govt. School, Maseno Secondary School (all in Kenya) and Makerere Univ. Coll. Uganda.
Joined Shell Oil Co. as Junior Exec. 56, later Operations Asst., Asst. Operations Man., Sales Promotion and Sales Rep.; joined Kenya Civil Service 62, Asst. Sec. 62-64; Senior Asst. Sec. 64; Asst. Sec.-Gen. Org. of African Unity Sept. 64-.
Office: OAU General Secretariat, P.O. Box 3243, Addis Ababa, Ethiopia; Home: Ebwali, Emmutete, Bunyore, P.O. Box 57, Maseno, Kenya.

Bull, Benjamin Pinto; Portuguese Guinea nationalist leader.
Former school teacher, Dakar; later Pres. União dos Naturais de Guiné Portuguesa (U.N.G.P.); led amalgamation of U.N.G.P. with Frente para a Libertação e Independência da Guiné Portuguesa (F.L.I.N.G.) 63; Pres. F.L.I.N.G. 66-.
Portuguese Guinea.

Busia, Kofi Abrefa, M.A., D.PHIL.; Ghanaian university teacher and politician; b. 1913; ed. Mfantsipim (Cape Coast), Achimota Coll., London and Oxford Univs.
Awarded Carnegie Research Fellowship, Oxford Univ. 45; Admin. Officer, Gold Coast Govt. 47-49; fmr. Prof. Sociology, Univ. Coll. of Ghana; fmr. Leader of the Opposition, Ghana Parl.; fmr. Leader of United Party; Visiting Prof. Northwestern Univ. 54, Wageningen Univ. (Netherlands) 56-57, Visiting Fellow Nuffield Coll., Oxford 55; Prof. of Sociology, Inst. of Social Studies, The Hague 59-61; Prof. of Sociology and Culture of Africa, Univ. of Leiden

60-61; Visiting Prof. Collège de Mexico, Mexico City 62; Exec. mem. Int. Sociological Asscn. 53-60; returned to Ghana 66; Chair. Nat. Liberation Advisory Cttee. 66-72; founded Progress Party, Ghana 69, Leader 69-72; Prime Minister Sept. 69-72, also Minister of Econ. Planning and Information Jan. 71-72.
Publs. include *Position of the Chief in the Political System of Ashanti* 51, *Self-Government, Education for Citizenship, Industrialisation in West Africa* 55, *Challenge of Africa* 62, *Purposeful Education for Africa* 64, *Africa in Search of Democracy* 67.
Oxford, England.

Buthelezi, Gatsha; South African (Zulu) chief.
Elected leader of Zululand territorial authority June 70-; mem. Zulu royal household.
c/o Ministry of Bantu Administration and Development and Bantu Education, Pretoria, South Africa.

Butler, Frederick Guy, D.LITT.; South African university professor; b. 1918, Cradock, Cape Province; ed. Rhodes Univ., Grahamstown, and Brasenose Coll., Oxford.
War service Egypt, Lebanon, Italy, U.K. 40-45; Oxford 45-47; lecturer in English, Univ. of Witwatersrand 48-50; Prof. of English, Rhodes Univ. 52-; Editor *New Coin* (poetry quarterly).
Publs. *Stranger to Europe* (poems) 52, 60, *The Dam* (play) 53, *The Dove Returns* (play) 56, *A Book of South African Verse* 59, *South of the Zambesi* (poems) 66, *Cape Charade* (play) 68, *When Boys Were Men* 69, *Take Root or Die* 70.
c/o Rhodes University, Grahamstown, South Africa.
Telephone: 3823.

C

Cabou, Daniel, L. en D.; Senegalese economist and politician; b. 16 June 1929, Mandina, Senegal; ed. Lycée Vollenhoven, Dakar, Univ. de Dakar, Lycée Louis le Grand, Paris and Ecole Nat. de la France d'Outre Mer, Paris.
Responsible for liaisons with the Grand Council of the French African Community in the Cabinet of Xavier Torre, Sec.-Gen. of the French African Community 56-57; Chef de Cabinet for Pierre Lami, Head of Senegalese Territory 57; Technical Councillor for Mamadou Dia; Pres. Council of Ministers 59; Dir.-Gen. Entente Coopérative Sénégalaise (ENCOOP) 59; Gov. Fleuve region March 60-Dec. 61; Dir. de Cabinet for André Peytavin, Minister of Finances Dec. 61-Nov. 62; Sec. of State for Public Works, responsible for Hydraulics, Housing, and Urban Devt. Nov. 62-Dec. 62; Sec. of State for Finance and Econ. Affairs Dec. 62-Dec. 63; Minister of Finance Dec 63-Feb. 64; Minister of Commerce, Industry and Labour Feb. 64-March 68; Minister responsible for the Gen. Secretariat of the Presidency March 68-March 70; Minister of Industrial Devt. 70-72; Deputy Gov. Central Bank of West African States July 72-.
Banque Centrale des Etats de l'Afrique de l'Ouest, B.P. 3159, Dakar, Senegal.

Cabral, Amilcar; Portuguese Guinea politician; b. 1924, Bafata, Guinea; ed. Gil Eanes High School, São Vicente and Instituto Superior de Agronomia, Lisbon.
With Agostinho Neto (*q.v.*) and Mario de Andrade founded Centro de Estudos Africanos, Lisbon 48; worked for Portuguese admin. in Guinea 52-55; completed agricultural census of Guinea 54; worked on sugar estate in Angola 56-58; founder and leader of Partido Africano da Independência da Guiné e Cabo Verde (PAIGC) 56-; founding mem. (with Agostinho Neto) of Movimento Popular de Libertação de Angola (MPLA) 56; after Pidgiguiti massacre in Guinea began organizing PAIGC for armed struggle 59; led

PAIGC into direct military action against Portuguese 63. Publs. *Acerca duma classificação fitossanitária do armazenamento* 58, *Condições fitossanitárias de produtos ultramarinos em armazens do Porto de Lisboa (Alcântara-Norte)* 60, *The Facts about Portugal's African Colonies* (under pseudonym Abel Djassi) 60, *Le développement de la lutte de libération nationale en Guinée 'portugaise' et aux Iles du Cap Vert en 1964-65, Revolution in Guinea: An African People's Struggle* 70, *Libération Nat. et Culture* 70, *Our People are Mountains* 72, and many articles on agronomy, and the liberation struggle.
[Assassinated 20.1.73]

Camara, Andrew David; Gambian politician; b. 1923, Mansajang.
Teacher in govt. and mission schools 48-58; entered politics 58; mem. House of Assembly (Independent) 60-; Minister of Educ. 63; now Minister of Foreign Affairs; Vice-Pres. of the Gambia Sept. 72-.
Office of the Vice-President, Bathurst, The Gambia.

Camara, Ousmane; Senegalese politician; b. 1933, Kaolack; ed. Lycée Faidherbe, St. Louis, Dakar Univ., Centre Nat. d'Etudes Judiciaire, Paris.
Adviser to Supreme Court until 64; Dir. Nat. Security 64-70; Minister of Labour and Civil Service March-Dec. 70, of Information in charge of Assembly Relations Dec. 70-.
Ministry of Information, Dakar, Senegal.

Campbell, Evan Roy, C.B.E., P.S.C.; Rhodesian farmer and business executive; b. 2 Sept. 1908, Grahamstown, South Africa; ed. St. Andrews Coll., Grahamstown, Potchefstroom Agricultural Coll.
Farmer, Umvukwes, Southern Rhodesia 31-35, Inyazura 35-; Army service 40-45; mem. Rhodesia Tobacco Asscn. 46-50, Vice-Pres. 50-52, Pres. 52-58; Chair. Tobacco Export Promotion Council 58-63, Standard Bank Ltd., Albatros Fisons Fertilizers Ltd., Rhodesia Tea Estates Ltd., Metal Box Co. of C.A. Ltd., Manica Trading Co. of Rhodesia Ltd., Fisons Pest Control (C.A.) (Pvt.) Ltd., Central African Branch of Inst. of Dirs. 65-; High Commr. of Southern Rhodesia in U.K. Dec. 63-June 65; Dir. Sable Chemical Industries Ltd., Discount Co. of Rhodesia Ltd. and other cos. 65-; Dir. Rhodesian Promotion Council 65-.
Courtney Rise, Addington Lane, Highlands, Salisbury, Rhodesia.
Telephone: Salisbury 882715.

Carney, David, PH.D., D.P.A.; Sierra Leone economist' administrator and teacher; b. 27 May 1925, Freetown; ed. Fourah Bay Coll., Sierra Leone, Univ. of Pennsylvania and School of Advanced Int. Studies, Johns Hopkins Univ., U.S.A.
Lecturer, Fourah Bay Coll., Sierra Leone 45-47; Statistician, Dept. of Statistics, Govt. of Nigeria, Lagos, and Lecturer, Extra-Mural Dept., Univ. of Ibadan 48-52; Headmaster, Ghana Nat. Coll. Cape Coast, Ghana 52-53; Lecturer, Lincoln Univ., Franklin and Marshall Coll., Pa., Fairleigh Dickinson Univ., N.J. 53-58; Econ. Affairs Officer, Dept. of Econ. and Social Affairs, UN 58-60; Asst. Prof. of Econs., Antioch Coll., Yellow Springs, Ohio 60-61; Econ. Adviser, Govt. of Sierra Leone 61-63; UN African Inst. for Econ. Devt. and Planning, Dakar, Senegal 63-70, Project Man, Dir. April 67-70; Chair. Comm. on Higher Educ., Sierra Leone 69, E. African Community 70-; Deputy Chief Economist, E. African Common Market Secr. 70-.
Publs. *Government and Economy in British West Africa* 61, *A Ten-Year Plan of Economic and Social Development for Sierra Leone 1962/3-1971/2* 62, *Patterns and Mechanics of Economic Growth* 67; papers in national and int. journals.
East African Community, P.O. Box 1003, Arusha, Tanzania.

Chagula, Dr. Wilbert K.; Tanzanian professor.
Principal, Univ. Coll., Dar es Salaam; Pres. East African Acad.; Minister of Water Devt. and Power Nov. 70-72, of Econ. Affairs and Devt. Planning Feb. 72-.
Ministry of Economic Affairs, Dar es Salaam, United Republic of Tanzania.

Chango, Maj. Janvier; Togolese army officer and politician.
Commandant, Group I of Nat. Police Force, Minister of Nat. Defence; Minister of Justice, Keeper of the Seals Aug. 69-.
Ministry of Justice, Lomé, Togo.

Changufu, Lewis; Zambian politician; b. 1927, Kasama; ed. locally and by correspondence.
Entered politics 50; fmr. mem., African Nat. Congress 58; restricted 59; attended course in public relations and leadership, U.S.A.; Parl. Sec. to Prime Minister's Office 64-Jan. 65; Minister of Information and Postal Services Jan. 65-Dec. 66; Nat. Chief Trustee, United Nat. Independence Party (UNIP), mem. Central Cttee. June 71-; Minister of Home Affairs Dec. 66-Sept. 67; Minister of Labour Sept. 67-Dec. 68; Minister of Labour and Social Services Dec. 68, later Minister of Transport; Minister of Home Affairs Jan. 70-.
Ministry of Home Affairs, Lusaka, Zambia.

Chapman Nyaho, Daniel Ahmling, C.B.E., M.A., LL.D.; Ghanaian teacher, public servant and business executive; b. 5 July 1909, Keta; ed. Bremen Mission School (Keta), Achimota Coll., Univ. of Oxford, Columbia Univ. and New York Univ.
Teacher Govt. Senior Boys' School, Accra 30, Achimota Coll. 30-33, 37-46; Gen. Sec. All-Ewe Conf. 44-46; Area Specialist, UN Secr. Dept. of Trusteeship and Information from Non-Self-Governing Territories 47-54; mem. Board of Management of UN Int. School, New York 50-54, 58-59; Sec. to Prime Minister and Cabinet, Gold Coast 54-57; Head of Ghana Civil Service 57; Amb. to U.S.A. and Perm. Rep. to UN 57-59; Chair. Mission of Ind. African States to Cuba, Dominican Repub., Haiti, Venezuela, Bolivia, Paraguay, Uruguay, Brazil, Argentina, Chile 58; Headmaster Achimota School 59-63; Vice-Chair. Comm. on Higher Educ. in Ghana 60-61, mem. Interim Nat. Council of Higher Educ. and Research, Ghana 61-62; Fellow Ghana Acad. of Arts and Sciences; mem. UN Middle East/North Africa Technical Assistance Mission on Narcotics Control 63; First Vice-Chair. Governing Council UN Special Fund 59; Dir. UN Div. of Narcotic Drugs 63-66; mem. Political Cttee. of Nat. Liberation Council 67; mem. Board of Trustees, Gen. Kotoka Trust Fund; Amb., Ministry of External Affairs 67; Exec. Dir. Pioneer Tobacco Co. Ltd. (British-American Tobacco Group) 67-70, Dir. 70-; Dir. Standard Bank Ghana Ltd. 70-; mem. Nat. Advisory Cttee., Nat. Redemption Council 72-; Chair. Arts Council of Ghana 68-69, Volta Union; Chair. of Council, Kumasi Univ. of Science and Technology 72; Hon. LL.D.; Danforth Visiting Lecturer Asscn. of American Colls. 69-70.
Publs. *Our Homeland* (Book I—*A Regional Geography of South-East Gold Coast*) 45, *The Human Geography of Eweland* 45.
Office: Tobacco House, Liberty Avenue, P.O. Box 5211, Accra; Home: 7 Ninth Avenue, Tesano, Accra, Ghana.
Telephone: 21111 (Office); 27180 (Home).

Chidzanja, Richard B.; Malawian (Chewa) politician; b. 5 May 1921.
Worked as teacher; entered politics 50; mem. local councils; arrested 59; Minister of Local Govt. 64; Minister of the Central Region; Deputy High Commr. in Kenya until Jan. 69; Minister of Natural Resources Jan. 69-72, of Agriculture Oct. 69-72, of Transport and Communications Feb. 72-.
Ministry of Transport and Communications, P.O. Box 587, Blantyre, Malawi.

Chiepe, Miss Gaositwe Keagakwa Tibe, M.B.E., B.SC., M.A.; Botswana diplomatist; b. Serowe; ed. primary school in Serowe, secondary school in Tigerkloof, S. Africa and Univs. of Fort Hare and Bristol.

Education Officer, Botswana 48, Senior Educ. Officer 62, Deputy Dir. of Educ. 65, Dir. of Educ. 68; High Commr. in U.K. 70-, concurrently accredited to Sweden, Norway, Denmark, Fed. Germany, France and Nigeria; Hon. LL.D. (Bristol).

Botswana High Commission, 3 Buckingham Gate, London, S.W.1, England.

Telephone 01-828-0445.

Chipunza, Chad Magumise, B.A.; Rhodesian politician, farmer and businessman; b. 1925, Rusape; ed. teacher training college.

Headmaster, Highfield North School, Salisbury 51-54; Exec. Officer Capricorn Africa Soc. 55-57; Mem. of Parl. (United Federal Party) for Harare 58-63, Party Whip, subsequently Parl. Sec. to Minister of External Affairs until Dec. 63; Senior Lecturer, Domborhawa Training Centre 64-65; mem. of Parl. for Bindura 65-; Leader of Official Opposition in Parl. (United People's Party) 66-69, re-elected Leader of Opposition (Nat. People's Union) 69-; mem. Board of Govs. Bernard Mizeki Coll.

No. 34 Marimba Park, Salisbury, Rhodesia.

Telephone: 29291.

Chiwanda, Albert B. J.; Malawian politician; b. 14 March 1933; ed. Henry Henderson Inst., Malamulo Mission.

Worked as carpenter, Org. Sec. Msasa branch of Nyasaland African Congress; Chair. Mapanga branch of Malawi Congress Party 60-62; mem. Blantyre District Council July 62, Chair. Jan. 63-; Chair. Malawi Congress Party 62-; M.P. for Mwanza-Neno 64-Oct. 68; Minister of State in the President's Office Nov. 69-Nov. 71.

c/o Office of the President, Blantyre, Malawi.

Chona, Mathias Mainza, BAR.-AT-LAW; Zambian politician; b. 21 Jan. 1930, Nampeyo, Monze; s. of Chief Chona; ed. Chona Out School, Chikuni Catholic Mission, Munali Govt. School, Lusaka and Gray's Inn, London.

Interim Pres. UNIP (United Nat. Independence Party) 59-60, Vice-Pres. 60-61, Gen. Sec. 61-69, mem. UNIP Interim Exec. Cttee. 69-71, UNIP Central Cttee. 71-; M.P. for Livingstone 64, for Kaoma (Mankoya) 68; Minister of Justice 64; Minister of Home Affairs 64-66; Minister for Presidential Affairs 67; Minister without Portfolio 68; Minister for Central Province, Minister without Portfolio, Minister of Provincial and Local Govt. and Amb. to U.S.A. (also accred. to Chile) 69-70; Vice-Pres. of Zambia Oct. 70-, also Minister of Nat. Guidance and Devt. 71-; mem. OAU Comm. of Mediation, Conciliation and Arbitration 66-71, Pres. 71-; Sec.-Gen. 3rd Non-Aligned States Conf., Lusaka 70; del. to numerous int. congresses including independence constitutional confs.

Publ. *Kabuca Uleta Tunji* 52 (novel, Margaret Wrong Medal 56).

P.O. Box 208, Lusaka, Zambia.

Cisse, Jeanne Martin; Guinean diplomatist; b. April 1926, Kankan; ed. Teacher Training College.

Teacher 45-54, Headmistress 54-58; active mem. Democratic Party of Guinea and Guinean Teachers' Trade Union 58-72; Sec.-Gen. All-African Women's Org. 62-72; mem. Cen. Cttee. Democratic Party of Guinea; 1st Vice-Pres. Nat. Assembly; Perm. Rep. to UN 72-; Médaille d'Honneur du Travail, Médaille Compagnon de l'Indépendance.

Permanent Mission of Guinea to United Nations, 295 Madison Avenue, New York, N.Y. 10017, U.S.A.

Cisse, Moustapha; Senegalese politician; b. 27 Aug. 1930, Pire; ed. teacher training coll., Algiers.

Secretary, Movement for Arab Educ. 60-Dec. 61; Deputy lecturer in Arabic to Ministry of Nat. Educ. Dec. 61-Sept. 68; Sec.-Gen. Nat. Fed. of Moslem Asscns. in Senegal Dec.

62-; counseller to the Amb. to Saudi Arabia Sept. 68-May 70; Amb. to Mali May 70-71; now Amb. to Saudi Arabia, accred. to Egypt 72-; mem. Nat. Council, Union Progressiste Sénégalaise (UPS).

Embassy of Senegal, Jeddah, Saudi Arabia.

Cloete, (Edward Fairley) Stuart (Graham), F.I.A.L.; South African soldier, farmer and author; b. 23 July 1897, Paris; ed. Lancing Coll., England.

Army officer 14-25, Coldstream Guards, retd.; farming and ranching in South Africa 23-35.

Publs. *Turning Wheels* 37, *Watch for the Dawn* 39, *Yesterday is Dead* 40, *Hill of Doves* 41, *The Young Men and the Old* (poems) 41, *Congo Song* 43, *The Third Way* 46, *African Portraits, The Curve and the Tusk* 53, *The African Giant* 55, *Mamba* 56, *The Mask* 57, *Gazella* 58, *The Soldier's Peaches* (short stories) 59, *The Fiercest Heart* 60, *The Silver Trumpet* 60 and *The Looking Glass* 63 (short stories), *Rags of Glory* 63, *The Honey Bird* 64, *The 1001 Nights of Jean Macacque* 65, *The Abductors* 66, *The Writing on the Wall* (short stories) 69, *South Africa* 69, *How Young They Die* 70, *Three White Swans* (short stories) 71, *A Victorian Son* (autobiog. 1897-1922) 72, *More Nights* 73, *The Gambler* 73, *The Mill of God* (short stories).

P.O. Box 164, Hermanus, South Africa.

Clutton-Brock, (Arthur) Guy; British and Rhodesian (dual nationality) agriculturist and social worker; b. 5 April 1906, Northwood, Middx.; ed. Rugby School and Magdalene Coll., Cambridge Univ.

Cambridge House University Settlement 27-29; Rugby House Settlement 29-33; Borstal Service 33-36; Principal Probation Officer, Metropolitan Area of London 36-40; Head Oxford House, University Settlement 40-45; Youth and Religious Affairs Officer, British Military Govt., Berlin 45; with Christian Reconstruction in Europe 46; farm labourer in U.K. 47-48; Diocesan Agricultural Officer, Mashonaland (Southern Rhodesia) and Dir. of Farm Activities, St. Faith's Mission, Rusape (Southern Rhodesia) 49-59; briefly detained by Rhodesian Govt. on declaration of emergency Feb. 59; Hon. Dir. Bamangwato Development Asscn., Bechuanaland Protectorate 61-62; Field Officer of the African Development Trust 62-65; retired 66; founder mem. Cold Comfort Farm Soc.; deported to England Feb. 71.

Publ. *Dawn in Nyasaland* 59.

Gelli Uchaf, Llandyrnog, Denbigh, Wales.

Cluver, Eustace H., K.ST.J., E.D., M.A., M.D., B.CH., D.P.H., F.R.S.H.; South African emeritus professor of preventive medicine; b. 28 Aug. 1894; ed. Victoria Coll., Stellenbosch, and Oxford Univ.

Rhodes Scholar to Oxford 14; fmr. Prof. of Physiology Witwatersrand Univ. Medical School, Sec. for Public Health, Dir. S. African Inst. for Medical Research Johannesburg; Prof. of Medical Educ. and Dean Faculty of Medicine, Univ. of Witwatersrand.

Publs. *Medical and Health Legislation in the Union of South Africa* 49 (2 edn. 61), *Social Medicine* 51, *Recent Medical and Health Legislation* 55, *Public Health in South Africa* (6th edn.) 59.

Mornhill Farm, Walkerville, Transvaal, South Africa.

Telephone: Walkerville 1212.

Coetzee, Blaar; South African politician; b. 14 May 1914, Hopetown, S.A.; ed. Stellenbosch Univ.

Started publishing business in Johannesburg 43; M.P.C. for Port Elizabeth 43-48; M.P.C. for Parktown and M.E.C. for Transvaal 48-53; M.P. for Noordrand 53-57; M.P. for Vereeniging 58-61, 61-66, 66-; Deputy Minister of Bantu Admin. and Bantu Educ. 66-68; Minister of Community Devt. and of Public Works 68-72; Amb. to Italy Aug. 72-.

c/o Department of Foreign Affairs, Union Building, Pretoria, South Africa.

Coetzee, Johannes Petrus, B.SC.; South African business executive; b. 25 April 1918, Magaliesburg, Transvaal; ed. High School, Rustenburg and Univ. of the Witwatersrand.
Works Man., Amcor Works, Meyerton 57; Gen. Man. Feralloys Ltd., Cato Ridge, Natal 58-62; Gen. Man. Armament Board 63-65, Man. Dir. 65; Production Man. Amcor Group 65-66; Asst. Gen. Man. Iscor 66-68, Gen. Man. 68-71, Dir. and Gen. Man. 71-.
South African Iron and Steel Industrial Corporation (ISCOR) Ltd., P.O. Box 450, Pretoria; Home: 115 Drakensberg Drive, Waterkloof Park, Pretoria, South Africa.

Collin, Jean, L. en D.; Senegalese politician; b. 19 Sept. 1924, Paris, France.
Chief administrator, French Overseas Territories; Chief Information Service and Dir. Radio-Dakar 48; posted to Cameroon 51-56; Dir. of Cabinet of Mamadou Dia, Vice-Pres. then Pres. of the Council 57-58; Gov. of Cap-Vert March 60-Dec. 60; Sec.-Gen. of the Govt. Dec. 60-Aug. 64; Gen. Commr. of the Govt. to the Supreme Court 60; Perm. Sec. to the Higher Council for Defence June 61-May 63; Sec.-Gen. to the Presidency of the Repub. May 63-Feb. 64; Minister of Finance and Econ. Affairs 64-71, of Interior 71-; mem. Int. Monetary Fund March 68-71.
Ministry of Interior, Dakar, Senegal.

Condat, Georges Mahaman; Niger diplomatist; b. 23 Oct. 1924, Maradi.
Deputy from Niger, French Nat. Assembly 48, 56; Territorial Counsellor of the Niger and Pres. Niger Territorial Assembly 56-58; Del. to Dahomey 61-62; Amb. to Fed. Germany, Belgium, Netherlands, Luxembourg and EEC 62-64; Dir. of Admin. and Consular Affairs, Foreign Service of Niger 64-70; Amb. to U.S.A. and Canada July 70-72; Perm. Rep. to UN 70-72.
c/o Ministry of Foreign Affairs, Niamey, Niger.

Conradie, Alex Marais, M.A., B.C.L., Q.C.; South African lawyer and airline executive; b. 21 Oct. 1910, Cape Town; ed. Univ. of Cape Town, and Univ. of Oxford (Rhodes Scholar).
Advocate, Cape Town 34-35; Public Prosecutor, Magistrates' Courts 35-38; Junior Professional Asst., Office of Govt. Law Adviser 38-39; Advocate, Transvaal Div. of Supreme Court 39-40; Legal Adviser, Dept. of Defence 40-41; Dept. of Justice 41-44; Law Adviser and Legal Draftsman 44-45; Chief Legal Officer, S. African Railways 45 (also responsible for legal affairs of S. African Airways); mem. Legal Cttee., Int. Air Transport Asscn. 49-, Chair. 62-64; Chief Exec. South African Airways 66-; corporate mem. Chartered Inst. of Transport.
Publ. *The Carriage of Goods by Railway in South Africa.*
South African Airways, S.A. Airways Centre, Johannesburg, South Africa.

Coulibaly, Mamadou; Ivory Coast economist and politician; b. 10 Oct. 1910; ed. Dakar.
Headmaster in Bingerville; mem. Social Affairs Cttee., French Union Assembly 49-56; rep. of Democratic Party in Legislative Assembly 59, Deputy in Nat. Assembly 60; mem. Senate, French Community 59-61; mem. Bureau Politique du Parti Démocratique de Côte d'Ivoire; now Pres. Advisory Economic and Social Council.
Advisory Economic and Social Council, Abidjan, Ivory Coast.

Coulibaly, Sori; Mali diplomatist; b. 1925.
Served French Foreign Ministry, Paris; fmr. Sec.-Gen. Ministry of Foreign Affairs, Mali; Perm. Rep. to UN 62-66; Amb. to U.S.S.R. 67-68; Technical Adviser for Foreign Affairs at the Presidency 68-69; Minister of Foreign Affairs 69-Sept. 70; Minister of Public Service and Labour Sept. 70-.
Ministry of Public Service and Labour, Bamako, Mali.

Craig, Rev. Robert, M.A., B.D., S.T.M., PH.D., D.D.; British ecclesiastic and university administrator; b. 22 March 1917, Markinch, Fife, Scotland; ed. St. Andrews Univ. and Union Theological Seminary, N.Y.
Assistant Minister, St. John's Kirk, Perth 41-42; British Army Infantry Chaplain 42-47; Prof. of Divinity, Natal Univ., S. Africa 50-57, Dean of Coll. 53-54; Prof. of Religion, Smith Coll., Northampton, Mass., U.S.A. 58-63; Prof. of Theology, Univ. Coll. of Rhodesia 63-69, Vice-Principal 66-69, Principal 69-70; Principal and Vice-Chancellor, Univ. of Rhodesia 70-; Hon. D.D. (St. Andrews Univ.) 67.
Publs. *The Reasonableness of True Religion* 54, *Social Concern in the Thought of William Temple* 63, *Religion: Its Reality and its Relevance* 65, *The Church: Unity in Integrity* 66, *Religion and Politics: A Christian View* 72.
The Principal's Lodge, University of Rhodesia, P.O. Box MP. 167, Mount Pleasant, Salisbury, Rhodesia.
Telephone: Salisbury 36635.

Crawford, Sir Frederick, G.C.M.G., O.B.E.; British company director and former colonial administrator; b. 9 March 1906, Norham-on-Tweed, Northumberland; ed. Hymers Coll., Hull, and Balliol Coll., Oxford.
Cadet, Tanganyika 29, Asst. District Officer 31, District Officer 41; seconded to East Africa Governors Conf. 42-43 and 45-46; Econ. Sec. N. Rhodesia 47, Dir. of Development 48-50; Gov. and C.-in-C. Seychelles 51-53; Deputy Gov., Kenya 53-57; Gov. of Uganda 57-61; Dir. Anglo-American Corpn. of South Africa Ltd., and other companies.
Anglo-American Corpn., P.O. Box 1108, Salisbury, Rhodesia.
Telephone: 61431 and 33569.

D

Dacko, David; Central African Republic politician; b. 1930; ed. Ecole Normale, Brazzaville.
Minister of Agriculture, Stockbreeding, Water and Forests, Central African Govt. Council 57-58; Minister of Interior, Economy and Trade, Central African Provisional Govt. 58-59; Premier, Central African Repub. 59-66, Minister of Nat. Defence, Guardian of the Seals 60-66; Pres. of Central African Repub. 60-66; mem. Mouvement pour l'Evolution Sociale de l'Afrique Noire (MESAN); under house arrest July 69-.
Bangui, Central African Republic, Equatorial Africa.

Daddah, Abdallah Ould; Mauritanian diplomatist; b. 25 April 1935; ed. Lycée Wan Wollenhoven and Université de Paris.
Former Directeur de Cabinet, Ministry of Foreign Affairs; Sec.-Gen. Ministry of Foreign Affairs 62-64; Amb. to France, concurrently accred. to U.K., Italy and Switzerland 64-66; Amb. to U.S.A. and Perm. Rep. to UN 66-70; Minister of Equipment April 70-; Commandeur du Mérite Nat. Mauritanien.
Ministry of Equipment, Nouakchott, Mauritania.

Daddah, Moktar Ould, LIC. EN DROIT; Mauritanian politician; b. 20 Dec. 1924, Boutilmit; ed. Blanchot School, Saint-Louis, Univ. of Paris.
Interpreter; studied law; with firm Boissier Palun, Dakar; territorial councillor 57; Premier, Islamic Republic of Mauritania 58-; Pres. of the Republic 61-; Pres. Org. Commune Africaine et Malgache 65; Chair. OAU 71-72; Sec.-Gen. Parti du Peuple Mauritanien.
Office of the President, Nouakchott, Mauritania.

Dadzie, Emmanuel Kodjoe, LL.B.; Ghanaian diplomatist and lawyer; b. 16 March 1916, Sekondi; ed Achimota Coll., London and Lincoln's Inn, London.
Served in Gold Coast Civil Service 36-42; Royal Air Force 42-47; in private legal practice, Accra 51-59; Head, Legal and Consular Services Div., Ministry of Foreign Affairs 59; Amb. to Romania 62-66; Resident Rep. of Ghana to

IAEA 63-66; mem. Board of Govs. 63; Amb. to France and Perm. Rep. to UNESCO 65-67; Amb. Ministry of Foreign Affairs, Accra 68-; del. to various UN, OAU and other int. confs. and several sessions of UN Gen. Assembly.
Ministry of Foreign Affairs, Accra, Ghana.

Dafaalla, El Nazeer, D.K.V.S., DIP.BACT., A.F.R.C.V.S.; Sudanese university professor; b. 1922; ed. Khartoum and Manchester Univs.
Government Veterinary Officer, Khartoum, Malakal and Nyala 46-50; research in England on anaerobic bacteria 50-52; Research Officer, Ministry of Agriculture 52-54, Senior Research Officer 55-56; Senior Lecturer, Univ. of Khartoum 56-57, Dean Faculty of Veterinary Science 58-60; Deputy Vice-Chancellor 60-62, Prof. of Bacteriology and Vice-Chancellor 62-68; Chair. Peoples Council Oct. 72-; Pres. Round Table Conf. for Southern Sudan; member FAO Int. Panels of Experts, Nat. FAO Cttee., and various foreign socs; mem. Admin. Board Int. Asscn. of Univs.; Exec. Vice-Pres. of Asscn. of African Univs.; mem. Exec. Cttee. Sudan Veterinary Asscn. 47-; Chair. Editorial Board, *Sudan Journal of Veterinary Science and Husbandry*; mem. Advisory Panel of Experts on the Emergency Control of Livestock Diseases, Rome May 67; Hon. Fellow, Hanover Univ.; Hon. D.Sc. (Charles Univ., Prague).
Publs. many papers on veterinary bacteriology.
Peoples Council, Khartoum, Sudan.

Dakouré, Capt. Antoine; Upper Voltan army officer and politician; b. 26 Nov. 1936, Ouagadougou.
Former officer of military engineering; Chief, military cabinet of Maurice Yaméogo March 65-Dec. 65; responsible to H.Q. for the instruction and formation of cadres March 63-March 65; Sec. of State for Information, Youth and Sports. Jan. 66-April 67; Minister of Agriculture and Stock-breeding April 67-, also of Waters, Forests and Tourism.
Ministry of Agriculture and Stock-Breeding, Ouagadougou, Upper Volta.

Damas, Georges; Gabonese politician; b. 18 Nov. 1902, Libreville; ed. Catholic Mission School, Libreville and Quai d'Orsay.
Bank Clerk 24-39; accountant to a shipping co. 40-46; adviser to Privy Council of the French Gov.; Municipal Councillor for Libreville Nov. 56-; rep. of Gabon to the Econ. and Social Council of France 59; composed the Gabon Nat. Anthem *La Concorde* 60; Amb. to Belgium, Netherlands and Luxembourg 61-64, to Fed. Repub. of Germany 63-64; Pres. Nat. Assembly April 64-.
National Assembly, Libreville, Gabon.

Dambe, A. M.; Botswana politician; b. 1911, Mswazi, Ngwato Area; ed. Dombodema, Tiger Kloof, Tati Training Inst. and Adams Coll.
Teacher, Dombodema and Serowe, later headmaster, Tati District; served with H.C.T. corps in Middle East, later Sergeant; Treas. B.P. Teachers' Asscn.; mem. Legislative Assembly March 65-; Minister of Mines, Commerce and Industry March 65-April 66; Minister of Home Affairs April 66; Minister of Works and Communications until 70; then Minister of Agriculture.
c/o Ministry of Agriculture, Gaborone, Botswana.

Dandobi, Mahamane; Niger author and politician; b. 1923, Guéchémé; ed. Ecole Normale William-Ponty.
Administration clerk; fmr. M.P. for Dogondoutchi and fmr. Vice-Pres. Nat. Assembly; fmr. Senator of the French West African Community; Asst. Sec.-Gen. Political Bureau, Parti progressiste nigérien (P.P.N.); Pres. Soc. Nat. des Transports Nigériens (S.N.T.N.); Dir. Niger Nat. Troupe 58; Minister of Justice Nov. 65-Jan. 70; Minister of Public Health Jan. 70-Jan. 71; Minister of Public Works and Town Planning 71-72, of Rural Economy Aug. 72-.
Publ. *Kabrin Kabra* (play).
Ministry of Rural Economy, Niamey, Niger.

Daoudou, Sadou; Cameroonian politician; b. 1926, Ngaoundéré; ed. Bongo.
Regional admin. official 48-58; Chef de cabinet to P.M. 58-60; M.P. for Adamaoua to Nat. Assembly April 60-April 64; Sec. of State for Information for East Cameroon May 60-June 61; Minister of State in charge of Armed Forces June 61-.
Ministry of Armed Forces, Yaoundé, United Republic of Cameroon.

Darman, Ahmed, PH.D.; Somali diplomatist; b. 16 June 1930, Mogadishu; ed. Teacher Training Coll., Italy, and Univ. of Rome.
Headmaster, Ministry of Educ. 48-55; Sec. in Nat. Assembly 56-57; served in Presidency, Council of Ministers 57-61; transferred to Ministry of Foreign Affairs 61; Counsellor, Somali Perm. Mission to UN 63-65; Consul-Gen., Aden 65-68; Amb. to People's Repub. of Yemen 68, to Tanzania 68-70, to Ethiopia 70-.
Somali Embassy, P.O. Box 1006, Addis Ababa, Ethiopia.

Dart, Raymond Arthur, M.SC., M.D., CH.M.; Australian anatomist; b. 4 Feb. 1893, Toowong, Brisbane, Queensland; ed. Queensland and Sydney Univs.
House Surgeon, Royal Prince Alfred Hospital, Sydney 17-18; Capt. Australian Army Medical Corps 18-19; Senior Demonstrator in Anatomy, Univ. Coll., London 19-20; Fellow Rockefeller Foundation 20-21; Senior Demonstrator in Anatomy and Lecturer in Histology, Univ. Coll., London 21-22; Prof. of Anatomy 23-59, Dean Faculty of Medicine 25-43, Univ. of the Witwatersrand, Johannesburg; mem. Int. Comm. on Fossil Man 29-; Fellow Royal Soc. of South Africa 30-, mem. Council 38; mem. Board South African Inst. for Medical Research 34-46; mem. South African Medical Council 34-48; mem. S. African Nursing Council 44-50; Pres. S. African Soc. of Physiotherapy 59-68, Anthropological Section, Pan-African Congress of Prehistory 47-51, Vice-Pres. 59-63; Pres. S. African Asscn. for the Advancement of Science 52-53, Pres. Anthropological Section 25, Gold Medallist 39; Guest Lecturer, Viking Fund Seminar, N.Y. 49; Lowell Lecturer, Boston Oct. 49; John Hunter Memorial Lecturer, Sydney 50; Robert Broon Memorial Lecturer (Durban) 51; Senior Capt. Scott Medal, South African Biological Soc. 55; Hon. D.Sc. (Natal, Witwatersrand and La Salle Univs.); Viking Medal and Award for Physical Anthropology (New York) 57; Woodward Lecturer (Yale) 58; Simon Biesheuvel Medal 63; South African Nursing Asscn. Gold Medal 70; Silver Medal, Medical Asscn. of South Africa 72; Pres. Asscn. Scientific and Technical Socs. of S. Africa 63-64; Fellow Inst. Biology, London 64; Drennan Memorial Lecturer (Cape Town) 66; United Steelworkers Prof. of Anthropology Inst. of Man, Insts. for the Achievement of Human Potential 66-.
Publs. include: *Australopithecus Africanus: the Man-Ape of South Africa* 25, *Racial Origins in the Bantu speaking Tribes of South Africa* 37, *African Serological Patterns and Human Migrations* 51, *The Osteodontokeratic Culture of Australopithecus Prometheus* 57, *Adventures with the Missing Link* 59, *Africa's Place in the Emergence of Civilization* 60, *Beyond Antiquity* 65.
20 Eton Park, Eton Road, Sandhurst, Johannesburg, South Africa.

Davin, Jean; Gabonese diplomatist; b. 23 March 1922, Libreville.
Director of External Relations, Ministry of Foreign Affairs 60-61, Sec.-Gen. 61-64; Counsellor, Bonn 64-65; Deputy Rep. to EEC 65-66; has represented Gabon at OAU confs. and many inter-governmental meetings; mem. Gabon del. to UN Gen. Assembly 63, 64; del. to ECOSOC sessions, Geneva 65, 66; Perm. Rep. to UN 69-.
Permanent Mission of Gabon to the United Nations, 866 UN Plaza, New York, N.Y. 10017, U.S.A.

Debebe, Habte Yohannes; Ethiopian banker; b. 26 Dec. 1926; ed. Haile Sellassie I Secondary School, Addis Ababa, Rosenberg Coll., St. Gallen, Switzerland, St. Christopher's Coll., London, Guildford Technical Coll., England, and London School of Economics.

Joined State Bank of Ethiopia 47, scholarships abroad 47-50, Exchange Control Dept., State Bank of Ethiopia 50-60, Deputy Exchange Controller 55-60; guest official, Bank of England 61; Supervisor, Foreign Branch, State Bank of Ethiopia (Banking Div.) 61-63; Founder, Man. Dir. and Alt. Chair. Addis Ababa Bank S.C. 63-; Vice-Chair. Nat. Textiles S.C.; Dir. Ethiopian Publishing S.C., Blue Nile Insurance Corpn., Soc. du Tedj de Saba, Addis Shekla S.C.; Leader Ethiopia Trade Del. to Banding Conf. 59; Vice-Pres. Addis Ababa Chamber of Commerce, Ethiopian Bankers' Asscn.; mem. Exec. Cttee. Int. Christian Fellowship; Hon. Consul-Gen. of Denmark in Ethiopia.
Addis Ababa Bank S.C., P.O. Box 751, Addis Ababa, Ethiopia.

de Garang, (Enok) Mading; Sudanese politician; b. 1 Jan. 1934, Kongor, Bor; ed. Malek Atar Intermediate School, Rumbek Secondary School, Manchester Coll. of Science and Technology, Inst. of Educ., London Univ.
Managing Editor, *Malakal* 63-65; Deputy Dir. Africa Literature Centre, Kitwe, Zambia 67-69; Dir. Southern Sudan Asscn., Editor *Grass Curtain* 70-72; Principal Political Rep. abroad for Sudanese Liberation Movt. 69-72; Negotiator for SLM, Addis Ababa Peace Talks 72; mem. for Information, Culture, Youth, Tourism, Sports and Social Services, High Exec. Council for the Southern Region April 72-.
Ministry of Information, P.O. Box 126, Juba; Home; Bor. District, Upper Nile Province, Sudan.

De Graft Johnson, E. V. C.; Ghanaian politician.
Former Dir. Black Star Line (Ghana's state-owned shipping corpn.); fmr. Amb. to the Netherlands; Leader, All People's Party May 69-July 69; Leader, All People's Republican Party July 69-70, merged to form Justice Party 70.
Justice Party, Accra, Ghana.

de Guingand, Major-General Sir Francis W., K.B.E., C.B., D.S.O.; British business executive and fmr. army officer; b. 28 Feb. 1900, London; ed. Ampleforth Coll., Royal Military Coll., Sandhurst.
Joined Army 20, served in King's African Rifles 26-31; Military Asst. to Sec. of State for War 39-40; Dir. Military Intelligence, Middle East 42; Chief of Staff 8th Army 42-44, 21st Army Group 44-45, retd. 47; Dir. Rothmans of Pall Mall London 61-; Chair. Rothmans in S. Africa 61-.
Publs. *Operation Victory* 47, *African Assignment* 53, *Generals at War* 64.
P.O. Box 52056, Saxonwold, Johannesburg, South Africa. Telephone: 42-8203.

de Jongh, Theunis Willem, M.SC., M.A., D.COM.; South African banker; b. 15 Dec. 1913, Gouda; ed. Stellenbosch, Pretoria and Columbia Univs.
Chief Statistician, Industrial Devt. Corpn. of S. Africa 42-45; Head, Econ. Research, S. African Reserve Bank 46-62, Exec. Asst. 62-67, Gov. and Chair. 67-; Chair. Nat. Finance Corpn. of S. Africa 67-; Alt. Gov. IBRD, IFC and IDA 67-; mem. of Prime Minister's Econ. Advisory Council 67-.
Publ. *An Analysis of Banking Statistics in South Africa.*
South African Reserve Bank, P.O. Box 427, Pretoria, 134 Eastwood Street, Arcadia, Pretoria, South Africa. Telephone: 2-9581 (Office); 74-2231 (Home).

de Klerk, Jan; South African politician; b. 22 July 1903, Burgersdorp; ed. Potchefstroom Univ.
Started teaching 22; Principal of Primrose Afrikaans School, Germiston 32-45; Sec. of Witwatersrand section of National Party 46-48, of Transvaal section 48-; mem.

Transvaal Provincial Council 49-54, Exec. Cttee. 49-54; Minister of Labour and Public Works 55-58; Minister of Labour and Mines 58-61, of Interior and Mines Jan.-Aug. 61, of Interior, Labour and Immigration Aug.-Nov. 61, of Interior, Educ. Arts and Science Nov. 61-66, of Educ., Arts and Science (now Nat. Educ.), and Information 66-69; Pres. of the Senate 69-; Chancellor, Potchefstroom Univ.
The Senate, Cape Town, South Africa.

Delius, Anthony Ronald St. Martin, B.A.; South African journalist; b. 11 June 1916; ed. St. Aidans Coll., Grahamstown, Rhodes Univ., Grahamstown.
Served with S.A. Mil. Intelligence; helped found *Saturday* (now *Evening*) *Post*, Port Elizabeth 47; *Cape Times*, Cape Town 50-65; Talks writer, External Services (Africa Section), BBC 68-; South African Poetry Prize 59.
Publs. *Young Traveller in South Africa* 47, *Unknown Border* (poems) 54, *The Long Way Round* (travel) 56, *The Last Division* (satire) 59, *The Fall* (play) 60, *A Corner of the World* (poems) 61, *The Day Natal Took Off* 62, *Black Southeaster* (poems) 65.
c/o BBC, Bush House, Strand, London, W.C.2, England.

Deressa, Yilma, B.SC.; Ethiopian politician; b. 21 Sept. 1907, Chata, Wallega; ed. Menelik School, Addis Ababa, Victoria Coll., Alexandria, Egypt, London School of Economics and Georgetown Univ., U.S.A.
Director-General, Ministry of Finance 40, Vice-Minister, Ministry of Finance 42-48; Minister of Commerce and Industry and Pres. Planning Board 48-52; Amb. to U.S.A. 52-58; Minister of Foreign Affairs 58-60; Minister of Finance 60-69; Acting Minister of Mines and State Domain 61-63; Chair. Board of Governors, Haile Selassie I Univ., Addis Ababa 62-69; Gov. Int. Bank for Reconstruction and Development and assoc. orgs. 62-69; Minister of Commerce, Industry and Tourism 69-71; Crown Counsellor 71-; Ethiopian and foreign decorations.
P.O. Box 1769, Addis Ababa, Ethiopia.

Deshields, McKinley A., Liberian lawyer and politician; b. 23 Feb. 1909, Monrovia; ed. Coll. of W. Africa and Univ. of Liberia.
Former Sec., Gen. Post Office; Admin., Treasury and Bureau of Mines; fmr. Major, Liberian Army; Postmaster-Gen. 53-; Sec.-Gen. True Whig Party.
Ministry of Posts and Telecommunications, Monrovia, Liberia.

De Souza, Lieut.-Col. Paul-Emile; Dahomeyan army officer and politician.
Former Chief of Mil. Cabinet of the Presidency; Head of State and Minister of Defence Dec. 69-May 70; C.-in-C. of the Army July 70-72.
c/o Army Headquarters, Cotonou, Dahomey.

De Souza, Wilfrid; Dahomeyan diplomatist; b. 18 April 1935; Ouidah; ed. Univ. of Paris.
Diplomatic intern, French Ministry of Foreign Affairs and French Embassy, Vienna 60; Second Sec. Embassy of Dahomey, Bonn 61-64; First Sec., Paris 64-68; Sec.-Gen. Dahomey Ministry of Foreign Affairs (with rank of Minister Plenipotentiary) 68-70; Chief, Dahomey del. to Franco-Dahomey Comm. on Econ. Co-operation 67; del. to various int. confs. including sessions of Council of Ministers of OAU, and UN Gen. Assembly; Perm. Rep. to UN 70-.
Permanent Mission of Dahomey to United Nations, 4 East 73rd Street, New York, N.Y. 10021, U.S.A.

De Wet, Carel, B.SC., M.B., B.CH.; South African physician, politician and diplomatist; b. 25 May 1924, Memel, Orange Free State; ed. Vrede High School, Orange Free State, Pretoria Univ., and Univ. of Witwatersrand.
Medical practice, Boksburg, Transvaal, Winburg, Orange Free State, and Vanderbijlpark, Transvaal; Mayor of Vanderbijlpark 50-52; mem. Parl. 53-63; Amb. to U.K.

64-67, Sept. 72-; Minister of Planning and Mines 67-May 70, of Mines and Health 68-72.
South African Embassy, Trafalgar Square, London, W.C.2, England.

Dia, Amadou Cissé; Senegalese doctor and politician; b. 2 June 1915, Saint-Louis; ed. Dakar School of Medicine.
Chief physician, Kaolack 40-59; fmr. mem. Bloc Démocratique Sénégalais (B.D.S.); fmr. mem. directing cttee. P.F.A. and of Fed. Assembly of Mali 59; Asst. Sec. for Propaganda 59-60, for Org. July 60-Feb. 62; Sec.-Gen. Union Progressiste Sénégalaise (U.P.S.) 62-; Sec. of State for Commerce and Industry March 60-May 61; Minister of Health and Social Affairs May 61-Nov. 62; Minister of Technical Co-operation Nov. 62-Dec. 62; Minister of Armed Forces Dec. 62-March 65; Minister of the Interior March 65-June 68; Minister Del. to the Presidency, responsible for relations with Assemblies and for Religious Affairs June 68; M.P. Jan. 68-; Pres. Nat. Assembly Feb. 68-.
National Assembly, Dakar, Senegal.

Dia, Mamadou; Senegalese politician; b. 1910.
Councillor, Senegal 46-52; Grand Councillor, French West Africa 52-57; Senator for Senegal 49-55; Deputy to Nat. Assembly, Paris 56-59; Deputy to Legislative Assembly, Senegal 59; Vice-Pres., Council of Ministers Senegal 57-58, Pres. 58-59; Vice-Pres., Mali Fed. 59-60; Pres. Council of Ministers, Senegal 60-62, concurrently Minister of Defence and Security 62; Govt. overthrown Dec. 62, sentenced to life detention May 63, sentence reduced to 20 years imprisonment April 72; Chevalier, Palmes Académiques.
Publs. *Réflexions sur l'économie de l'Afrique Noire* 53, *Contributions à l'étude du mouvement cooperatif en Afrique Noire* 57, *L'économie africaine* 57, *Nations africaines et solidarité mondiale* 60.
Dakar, Senegal.

Diagana, Sidi Mohamed; Mauritanian teacher and politician; b. 1929, Kaédi; ed. Ecole normale William-Ponty.
Teacher, then headmaster until 65; Municipal Councillor for Kaédi 66; Minister of Health, Labour and Social Affairs Jan. 65-Feb. 66; Minister of Construction, Public Works, Transport, Posts and Telecommunications Feb. 66-Oct. 66; Minister of Equipment Oct. 66-Jan. 68; Minister of Finance Jan. 68-April 70; Minister of Industrialization and Mines April 70-71, of Defence Aug. 71-.
Ministry of Defence, Nouakchott, Mauritania.

Diakité, Moussa; Guinean government official; b. 1927; ed. Ecole Primaire Supérieure, Ecole Technique Supérieure.
Treasury 54; Deputy Mayor of Kankan 56; Vice-Pres. Grand Council of West Africa 58; Sec. of State, Grand Council of West Africa 58; Gov. Central Bank of Guinea and Minister of Finance 60-63; Minister of Foreign Trade and Banking 63-68; Sec. of State for Industry, Mines and Power 68-71; Minister of the Interior June 72-; Compagnon de l'Indépendance.
Ministry of the Interior, Conakry, Republic of Guinea.

Diakité, Capt. Yoro; Mali army officer and politician.
Former Dir. Mil. School at Kati; First Vice-Pres. Mil. Cttee. of Nat. Liberation and Prime Minister Provisional Govt. Nov. 68-Sept. 69; Prime Minister Sept. 69-70; Minister of Transport, Telecommunications and Tourism Sept. 69-Sept. 70; Minister of the Interior, Security and Defence Sept. 70-Jan. 71, of Defence 71; sentenced to forced labour for life July 72.
c/o Military Committee of National Liberation, Bamako, Mali.

Diallo, Abdoulaye; Niger diplomatist; b. 1924, Debere-Talata; ed. Teachers' Coll., Katibougou.
Held various teaching posts and headmasterships 47-58; Sec. School Inspection Board 56-57; Chief of Cabinet of

Minister of Educ. 58-61, Dir. of Cabinet 61-68; Sec. for External Relations, Nat. Workers Union of Niger 60-67; Commr.-Gen. for Devt. 68-72; Perm. Rep. to UN Oct. 72-; has served as Alt. Gov. IBRD and AfDB.
Permanent Mission of Niger to United Nations, 866 United Nations Plaza, Suite 570, New York, N.Y. 10017, U.S.A.

Diallo, Boubacar; Mali politician and diplomatist.
Former Sec.-Gen. U.N.T.M.; Amb. to Senegal and Mauritania July 67-Nov. 68; Minister of Public Service and Labour Nov. 68-70; Amb. to Egypt 71-, accred. to Libya, Ethiopia, Sudan, Kuwait.
Embassy of Mali, 4 Sharia Margil, Zamalek, Cairo, Egypt.

Diallo, El Hadj Saifoulaye; Guinean politician; b. 1923, Diari Village; ed. Ecole Nationale d'Administration, Dakar.
Mayor of Mamou, Deputy to French Nat. Assembly and Pres. Territorial Assembly of Guinea until independence 58; helped found Democratic Party of Guinea, mem. Political Bureau, Political Sec. till 63, Head, Comm. for Org. and Political Control till 67, Chair. Social Comm. 67; Pres. Nat. Assembly 58; Minister of State for Finance and Planning 63; Minister of Foreign Affairs May 69-72; Minister to the Presidency April 72-.
Office of the President, Conakry, Guinea.

Diallo, Madi; Mali diplomatist; b. 1928, Kayes; ed. Ecole Nat. de la F.O.M.
Directeur de Cabinet, Sec. of State for Labour and Social Affairs 60-Jan. 61; Dir. de Cabinet, Ministry of State in charge of the Civil Service Jan. 61-Oct. 62; Dir. de Cabinet, Ministry of Justice Oct. 62-63; Insp. Admin. Affairs Oct. 63-Dec. 64; Gov. Mopti Region Dec. 64-Nov. 68; Dir. de Cabinet, Ministry of the Interior, Defence and Security Dec. 68-Aug. 69; Amb. to France, also accredited to Switzerland, Spain and Italy Aug. 69-.
Embassy of Mali, 89 rue Cherche-Midi, Paris 6e, France.

Diarra, Lt. Oumar Baba; Mali politician; b. 30 Dec. 1929; ed. Ecole normale, Bamako, and Univ. de Montpellier.
Formerly worked in Office of Overseas Scientific Research, Paris; later Directeur de Cabinet to Minister of Public Works, Mali, concurrently Prof. of Political Econ. and Public Law, Nat. School of Admin., Mali; Sec. of State for Labour and Social Affairs 59, then Sec. of State for Public Works and Labour, Minister of Labour 66, now Vice-Pres. Military Cttee. for Nat. Liberation; Pres. Fourth Session UN Econ. Comm. for Africa 62; mem. Mali Del. Int. Labour Conf., Int. Labour Office (ILO) 59, Pres. Comm. on Apartheid 64; Vice-Pres. African Regional Conf. of ILO, Addis Ababa 64; Pres. of Council of Admin., ILO 65-66; Minister of Finance and Commerce Sept. 70-.
Ministry of Finance and Commerce, Bamako, Mali.

Diawara, Ange; Congolese politician.
First Vice-Pres. Nat. Revolutionary Council (C.N.R.) Aug. 68-Dec. 68; mem. C.N.R. 69-72; mem. Political Bureau of Congolese Workers' Party (P.C.T.) for Devt. and first Commissar, Nat. People's Army until 72; Minister of Devt. in charge of Water Resources, Forests, Equipment and Agriculture 70-72; sentenced to death *in absentia* March 72.

Diawara, Mohamed Tickoura, L. ès sc.; Ivory Coast politician; b. 23 May 1928, Dori, Mali; ed. Statistics Inst., Paris Univ. and Econ. Devt. Inst., World Bank, Washington.
Chef de Cabinet, Minister of Econ. Affairs 58-59; Dir. de Cabinet for Minister of Finance and Econ. Affairs Aug. 61-Nov. 62; Gen. Admin. for Planning Nov. 62-Jan. 66; Pres. Bureau Nat. d'Etudes Technique du Développement (BNETD); Minister Del. for Planning Jan. 66-Sept. 68, Minister of Planning Sept. 68-.
Ministry of Planning, Abidjan, Ivory Coast.

Dibba, Sherrif Mustapha; Gambian politician; b. 1937; ed. govt. and mission schools.

Clerk, United Africa Co. -59; mem. Nat. Assembly (People's Progressive Party) 60-; Minister of Local Govt. until 66, of Works and Communications 66; Minister of Finance until Oct. 72, concurrently of Trade and Devt. until 70; Vice-Pres. 70-72; Minister Plenipotentiary, Amb. Extraordinary to EEC Oct. 72-.

Gambian Embassy, Brussels, Belgium.

Diederichs, Nicolaas, M.A., D.LITT. et PHIL.; South African economist and politician; b. 17 Nov. 1903, Ladybrand, Orange Free State; ed. Boshof High School, Grey Univ. Coll., Univs. of Munich, Cologne and Leiden.

Former Chair. Econ. Inst., Decimal Coinage Comm; fmr. Prof. Free State Univ.; M.P. for Randfontein 48-58, Losberg 58-; Minister for Econ. Affairs 58-67, also Minister of Mines 61-64; Minister for Econ. Affairs 66-67, of Finance 67-; Chancellor Randse Afrikaanse Universiteit 68; Hon. D.Comm. (Univ. of Orange Free State).

Publs. *Vom Leiden und Dulden, Die Volkebond, Nasionalisme as Lewensbeskouing, Die Kommunisme* and numerous articles and brochures.

Union Buildings, Pretoria, Republic of South Africa.

Dieng, Diakha; Senegalese international official; b. 16 Aug. 1933, Saint Louis; ed. Lycée Faidherbe, St. Louis, Université de Dakar, Université de Paris à la Sorbonne, and Ecole des Impôts, Paris.

Registry Officer, France 60, Dakar 61; Counsellor, later First Counsellor, Embassy of Senegal, Brussels 62-63; First Counsellor, Embassy of Senegal, Paris 63-64; Sec.-Gen. Union Africaine et Malgache de Coopération Economique (U.A.M.C.E.), Yaoundé 64-65, Organisation Commune Africaine et Malgache, Yaoundé (O.C.A.M.) 64-68; Amb. to U.A.R. 68-70, concurrently accredited to Syria, Sudan, Jordan; Dir. de Cabinet, Minister of Foreign Affairs 70-71; Dir. de Cabinet, Prime Minister April 71-; Chevalier, Ordre National Sénégalais and numerous other foreign awards.

Prime Minister's Office, Dakar, Senegal.

Diete-Spiff, Lieut.-Commdr. Alfred Papapreye; Nigerian army officer; b. 30 July 1942, Nembe; ed. St. Luke's School, Nembe, St. Barnabas School and St. Joseph's Coll., Sassie-Buea, Cameroon.

Meteorological officer, Lagos Airport; Merchant seaman, Elder Dempster Lines; served with Nigerian Navy; attended Britannia Royal Naval Coll., Dartmouth, England 62-66; Lieut., Nigerian Navy; Mil. Gov., Rivers State May 67-; Acting Lieut.-Commdr. July 67-.

Office of the Military Governor, Port Harcourt, Nigeria.

Diguimbaye, Georges; Chad politician; b. 16 Oct. 1935, Fort-Lamy; ed. Bongor Modern Coll. and Paris.

Headmaster in Bongor; Asst. Dir. for Planning and Devt, and Pres. Chad Devt. Bank Nov. 62-Feb. 63; Dir. for Planning and Devt., Gen. Commissionership for Planning Feb. 63-Feb. 65; Gen. Commr. for Planning Feb. 65-April 66; Sec.-Gen. to the Presidency Jan-April 66; Minister of Planning and Co-operation April 66-71; mem. Nat. Political Bureau; arrested March 72; Officer Nat. Order of Chad, Officer of Merit, Cameroon.

c/o Ministry of Planning and Co-operation, Fort-Lamy, Chad.

Dike, Kenneth Onwuka, M.A., PH.D.; Nigerian historian; b. 17 Dec. 1917; ed. Dennis Memorial Grammar School (Onitsha), Achimota Coll. (Ghana), Fourah Bay Coll. (Sierra Leone), Univs. of Durham, Aberdeen and London.

Lecturer in History, Univ. Coll. Ibadan 50-52, Senior Lecturer 54-56, Prof. History 56-60, Principal 58-60; Vice-Chancellor, Univ. of Ibadan 60-Dec. 66; Senior Research Fellow, West African Inst. of Social and Econ. Research 52-54; Founder-Dir. Nigerian Nat. Archives 51-64; Chair. Nigerian Antiquities Comm. 54-; Pres.

Historical Soc. of Nigeria 55-69; Dir. Inst. of African Studies, Univ. of Ibadan 62-67; Chair. Planning Cttee., Univ. of Port Harcourt 67-70; Prof. of History, Harvard Univ., U.S.A. 70; Fellow Royal Historical Soc.; Hon. LL.D. (Aberdeen, Leeds, Northwestern, London, Columbia, Princeton, Ahmadu Bello Univs.); Hon. D.Litt. (Boston and Birmingham), Hon. D.Sc. (Moscow).

Publs. *Report on the Preservation and Administration of Historical Records in Nigeria* 53, *Trade and Politics in the Niger Delta 1830-1895* 56, *A Hundred Years of British Rule in Nigeria* 57, *The Origins of the Niger Mission* 58; numerous articles in learned journals on Nigerian and West African history.

P.O. Box 59, Awka, Via Enugu, Eastern Region, Nigeria.

Dikko, Dr. Russell Aliyu Barau; Nigerian politician; b. 15 June 1912, Zaria; ed. King's Coll., Lagos and Univ. of Birmingham, England.

Medical practitioner; Junior Medical officer Jan. 40-41; Medical Officer 41-Nov. 53; Senior Medical Officer Nov. 53; Principal Medical Officer, Endemic Diseases Div., N. Nigeria 53-60, Curative Service Div. 60-62; Perm. Sec. Ministry of Health 62-67; Commr. for Health; mem. Fed. Exec. Council June 67-; Fed. Commr. for Mines and Power June 67-71, for Transport 71-; mem. N. Cultural Soc., Kaduna, African Games' Club, Red Cross of Nigeria.

Federal Commission for Transport, Lagos, Nigeria.

Dillon, Ian Birt Harper, I.D.; Rhodesian politician; b. 18 April 1915, Salisbury; ed. Gatooma and Hartley Schools and St. George's Coll., Salisbury.

Mine manager 54-59; Councillor, Belingwe/Shabani Road Council 54-59; M.P. for Shabani Constituency 58-; Chief Govt. Whip 62-64; Parl. Sec. (subsequently Deputy Minister) to Minister of Mines and Lands 64-68; Minister of Mines Jan. 69-; Patron, Rhodesian Gemmological Asscn. 70-; Hon. Fellow, South African Inst. of Mining and Metallurgy 72-.

Ministry of Mines, P/Bag 7709, Causeway; Home: 92 Baines Avenue, Salisbury, Rhodesia.

Diomande, Loua; Ivory Coast politician; b. 13 Feb. 1926, Man.

Worked in admin. of France Outre-Mer (F.O.M.); territorial councillor for Man; Deputy, Parti Démocratique de Côte d'Ivoire (P.D.C.I.) 58-60; Minister of the Civil Service May 57-April 59; Minister responsible for relations with Conseil de l'Entente Jan. 61-Feb. 63; Minister Del. for the Civil Service and Information Feb. 63-Aug 64; Minister of the Civil Service Aug. 64-Jan. 70; Minister of Tourism Jan. 70-71; now Minister of State in charge of Nat. Assembly.

Office of the Minister of State, National Assembly Buildings, Abidjan, Ivory Coast.

Diop, Abdourahmane, L. en D.; Senegalese politician; b. 1917, Dakar.

Secretary to clerks and public prosecutor, Tribunal of Dakar; trainee advocate, Montpellier Bar 51-53; advocate in Dakar 53; Pres. Order of Barristers 61-63; Minister of Civil Service and Labour Dec. 63-March 68; Pres. Comm. for Programmes and Practical Activities, B.I.T.; Minister of Justice and Guardian of the Seals March 68-72.

c/o Ministry of Justice, Dakar, Senegal.

Diop, Alioune; Senegalese publisher and writer; b. Saint Louis, Senegal.

Teacher of Literature 37; Chef de Cabinet to High Commr., Dakar 46; Senator of French Repub. 46-48; Organizer of Int. World Congress of Black Writers and Artists 56; Sec.-Gen. Société Africaine de Culture 57-; Leader of Senegalese Cultural Del. to Nigeria March 65; Pres. Int. Congress of Africanists 70-; Founder and Dir. Présence Africaine 47; Pres. World Festival of Negro Art.

42 rue Descartes, Paris 5e, France.

Diori, Hamani; Niger politician; b. 16 June 1916; ed. Victor Ballot School, Dahomey, and Ecole William-Ponty, Senegal.
Deputy, Niger Territory, French Nat. Assembly 46-51, 56-58; Vice-Pres. Nat. Assembly 57; Prime Minister, Republic of the Niger 58-60; Pres. of the Republic of Niger 60-, Council of Ministers 60-, also Minister of Foreign Affairs; mem. Rassemblement Démocratique Africain (RDA); Pres. Conseil de l'Entente; Chair. OCAM 67-Jan. 70.
Bureau du Président, Niamey, Niger, West Africa.

Diouf, Abdou, L. en. D, L. ès sc.; Senegalese politician; b. 7 Sept. 1935, Louga; ed. Dakar and Paris.
Joined Union Progressiste Sénégalaise (U.P.S.) 61; now mem. Political Bureau and Deputy Admin. Sec. U.P.S.; Dir. of Technical Co-operation and Minister of Planning 62; Dir. de Cabinet of Pres. of the Repub. 63-Aug. 64; Asst. Sec.-Gen., then Sec.-Gen. to Govt. Aug. 64; fmr. Chair. Council of Ministers Org. of Senegal River Basin States; Minister of Planning and Industry March 68-Feb. 70; Prime Minister Feb. 70-.
Office of the Prime Minister, Dakar, Senegal.

Djermakoye, Issoufou Saidou; Niger politician; b. 1910 July 1920; ed. Niger and France.
Counsellor, French Union 47-57; Senator to French Senate 57; Vice-Pres. Council of Ministers of Niger 58; Minister of Justice 59; Perm. Rep. of the Repub. of Niger to UN 61-62; Minister of Justice 63-65; Under-Sec. in charge of Trusteeship Affairs, UN 67-68, Under Sec.-Gen. 68-.
United Nations Secretariat, New York City, N.Y.; and 118 East 76th Street, New York, N.Y. 10021, U.S.A.

Djidingar, Michel; Chad politician; b. 1931, Tandjile.
Farmer; Territorial Councillor, then M.P. for Logone March 57-; Rep. of Chad to Senate of the French Community June 59-Jan. 61; Minister of Finance March 52-April 66; Minister of Posts and Telecommunications April 66-72, of Public Works Oct. 66-72; now Minister of State in charge of Agriculture.
c/o Ministry of Agriculture, Fort-Lamy, Chad.

Dlamini, Rt. Hon. Prince Makhosini; Swazi politician; b. 1914, Enhletsheni; ed. Franson Christian Memorial School, Swazi National School, Matsapa, and Umphumolo Training Inst., Natal.
Headmaster, Bethel Mission School and teacher, Franson Christian High School; teacher, Matsapa Swazi Nat. High School 43-46; Principal, Swazi Nat. School, Lobamba 46-47; Chair. later Sec.-Gen. Hlatikulu Branch, Swaziland Teachers' Asscn.; became farmer 47; mem. Swazi Nat. Council 47; Rural Devt. Officer 49-62; Chief of Enkungwini 50; acted as Sec. to Swazi Nation several times 50-; travelled to Europe 59-60; Leader Imbokodvo Nat. Movement 64-; mem. Swazi Legislative Council 64; mem. Self-Govt. Cttee. 65-66; Prime Minister April 67-.
Office of the Prime Minister, Mbabane, Swaziland.

Dlamini, Mboni Naph; Swazi diplomatist; b. 1928; ed. Matsapha National High School, Swaziland, Basutoland Teacher Training Coll. and Univ. of Oxford.
Headmaster, Ntshanini School, Swaziland 63-67; Counsellor, Swazi Mission at UN 68-70; Perm. Rep. to UN May 70-72.
c/o Ministry of Foreign Affairs, Mbabane, Swaziland.

Dlamini, Prince Mfanasibili; Swazi politician; b. 1939, Manzini District; ed. Florence Mission School, Lozitha Central School and Matsapa Swazi Nat. School.
Between schooling employed as gatekeeper, Swaziland Canners, Malkern Valley; later worked in coal mines, Natal; after leaving school became weigh-bridge clerk, Mhlume Sugar Co. 63; mem. Swazi Nat. Council 63; mem. Legislative Council 64; public admin. course, U.K. 66; mem. Govt. Cttee. for new constitution 65; Minister of

Local Admin., Swaziland 67-72, of Commerce and Co-operatives May 72-; Imbokodvo Party.
Ministry of Commerce, Mbabane, Swaziland.

Dlamini, Polycarp Ka-Lazarus, O.B.E.; Swazi politician; b. 1 July 1918, at Enginamadolo Royal House; ed. Matsapa Nat. School, Natal Univ. Coll. and Univ. of S. Africa.
Clerk-interpreter, Magistrate's Court, Barberton, S. Africa 42-43; with mail-order firm, Durban 44-46; Social Welfare and Probation Officer, S. African Dept. of Social Welfare 47-51; studied for degree 47-57; Sec. to Swazi Nation 52-64; studied local govt., U.K. 61; mem. Legislative Council 64; mem. Exec. Council in charge of Educ. and Health 64-65, of Educ. 65; Minister for Works, Power and Communications 67-71, for Justice 71-.
Ministry for Justice, Mbabane, Swaziland.

Doke, Clement Martyn, M.A., D.LITT.; British philologist; b. 16 May 1893, Bristol; ed. Transvaal Univ. Coll., Pretoria, and London Univ.
Missionary S. African Baptist Missionary Soc. 14-21; Lecturer in Bantu Languages, Univ. of Witwatersrand, Johannesburg 23; Prof. and Head of Dept. of Bantu Studies 31-53; Editor *South African Baptist* 22-47; Joint Editor *Bantu Studies* 31-41 and *African Studies* 42-53; has conducted research trips to Lamba, Ila, Shona, the Bushman tribes, etc.; Pres. Baptist Union of S. Africa 49-50; Acting Principal, Baptist Theological Coll. of Southern Africa 51 and 55; Hon. D.Litt (Rhodes), Hon. LL.D. (Witwatersrand).
Publs. *Ukulayana Kwawukumo* (translation of New Testament in Lamba) 21, *Lamba Folklore* 27, *Text Book of Zulu Grammar* 27, *Unification of the Shona Dialects* 31, *The Lambas of Northern Rhodesia* 31, *Comparative Study in Shona Phonetics* 31, *Bantu Linguistic Terminology* 35, *Text Book of Lamba Grammar* 38, (with the late Dr. B. W. Vilakazi) *Zulu-English Dictionary* 48, *The Southern Bantu Languages* 54, *Textbook of Southern Sotho Grammar* 57 (with the late Dr. S. M. Mofokeng), *English-Zulu Dictionary* 58 (with the late Dr. D. McK. Malcolm and J. M. A. Sikakana), *Amasiwi Awalesa* (trans. of Bible in Lamba) 59, *Contributions to the History of Bantu Linguistics* 61 (with D. T. Cole), *English-Lamba Vocabulary* 63.
5 Recreation Road, Alice, Cape Province, South Africa. Telephone: Alice 92.

Dombo, Simeon Diedong; Ghanaian politician; b. 1923, Duori, Lawra District, Upper Region; ed. Lawra Primary Boarding School, Tamale Middle Boys' School and Govt. Teacher Training Coll., Tamale.
Teacher 47-50; became Chief of Duori (Duori Na) 49; Rep. Lawra Confederacy State Council in N. Territorial Council 50-54, Territorial Council, Legislative Assembly 51-54; M.P. for Jirapa-Lambussie and Leader of Opposition 54-56, Deputy Leader of Opposition 56-64; in detention 64-66; Minister of Interior 69-71; Minister of Health 71-Jan. 72.
c/o Ministry of Health, Box M 44, Accra, Ghana.

Dos Santos, Marcelino; Mozambique poet and nationalist leader; b. 1931; ed. Lisbon and Paris.
Secretary of External Affairs, Presidential Council of Frente de Libertação de Moçambique (FRELIMO) Feb. 69-; Vice-Pres. FRELIMO May 70-; audience with Pope Paul VI, Rome, July 70.
P.O. Box 15274, Dar es Salaam, Tanzania.

Duomro, Col. Jacques; Chad army officer; b. 1919, Fort-Lamy.
Served with Senegalese Artillery Regiment, French Army 38-39, French Sixth Colonial Infantry Regiment 39-61; Sub-Lieut. 55; transferred to Chad Armed Forces 61; attended general staff course 62; Adjutant to Chief of Chad Gen. Staff; Chief of Gen. Staff Jan. 64-Dec. 71; Pres. Chad

Ex-servicemen's Asscn., Commdr. Nat. Order of Chad, Commdr. Order of Civil Merit, Croix de Guerre.
c/o General Staff Headquarters, Fort-Lamy, Chad.

Duminy, Jacobus Petrus, B.SC., M.A.; South African university professor and administrator; b. 16 Dec. 1897, Bellville, Cape; ed. Cape Town Univ., Oxford Univ., and Univ. of Paris.
Professor of Mathematics, Univ. of Pretoria 30-42; Principal, Pretoria Technical Coll. 42-58; Principal and Vice-Chancellor, Univ. of Cape Town 58-67; Pres. S.A. Asscn. for the Advancement of Science 62; First Vice-Pres. Rotary International 69-70; Hon. LL.D. Natal, Rhodes.
The Cotswolds, Kenilworth, Cape, South Africa.
Telephone: 71-0507.

Duncan, John Spenser Ritchie, C.M.G., M.B.E.; British diplomatist; b. 26 July 1921.
Sudan Political Service 41-56; H.M. Forces 41-43; Foreign Office 56-57; Joint Services Staff Coll. 57-58; Political Agent, Doha 58-59; British Information Services, New York 59-63; Consul-Gen., Muscat 63-65; Head of Personnel (Operations) Dept., Foreign Office 66-69; Minister, Canberra 69-71; High Commr. in Zambia 71-.
British High Commission, Stand 5000, Waddington Road, P.O. Box RW 50, Ridgeway, Lusaka, Zambia.

du Plessis, Abraham Hermanus, B.ADMIN.; South African farmer and politician; b. 28 Aug. 1914, Cape Prov.; ed. Upington High School and Univ. of South Africa.
Member Legislative Assembly, South West Africa 48-69, Exec. Cttee. 50-69; mem. Parl. 69-; Deputy Minister of Finance and Econ. Affairs 70-72; Minister of Public Works and Community Devt. July 72-.
Central Government Building, Vermeulen Street, Pretoria, South Africa; and Elisenheim, P.O. Box 3145, Windhoek, South West Africa.

Dupont, Clifford Walter, I.D., M.A.; Rhodesian solicitor, farmer and politician; b. 6 Dec. 1905, London; ed. Bishops Stortford Coll., and Clare Coll., Cambridge.
Solicitor, London 29-39, 45-48; Royal Artillery, rose to Major 40-45; emigrated to Rhodesia 48; M.P. in Fed. Assembly 58-62; mem. S. Rhodesian Parl. 62-; Minister of Justice and Minister of Law and Order, S. Rhodesia 62-64; Minister without Portfolio June-Aug. 64; Deputy Prime Minister and Minister of External Affairs 64-65; Deputy Prime Minister and Minister of External Affairs and of Defence 65; appointed Head of State (with title of "Officer Administering the Govt.") by Prime Minister of Rhodesia, Mr. Ian Smith Nov. 65; appointed Acting Pres. of Rhodesia March-April 70; Pres. of Repub. of Rhodesia April 70-; Grand Master, Legion of Merit 70.
Office: Government House, Salisbury; Home: P.O. Box 2078, Salisbury, Rhodesia.

Duval, Charles Gaëtan, BAR.-AT-LAW; Mauritius politician; b. 9 Oct. 1930; ed. Royal Coll., Curepipe, Lincoln's Inn, London and Faculty of Law, Univ. of Paris.
Entered politics 58; mem. Town Council, Curepipe 60, re-elected 63, Legislative Council, Curepipe 60, re-elected 63; mem. Municipal Council, Port Louis 69-; mem. "Le Centre Culturel Français"; Chair. Town Council, Curepipe 60-61, 63-Feb. 68; Rep. Curepipe at Nice 60; Minister of Housing, Lands and Town and Country Planning 64-Nov. 65; attended London Constitutional Conf. 65; Leader, Parti Mauritien Social Démocrate (P.M.S.D.) 66-; first M.L.A. for Grand River North-West and Port Louis West 67; Leader of the Opposition 67-Nov. 69; Minister of External Affairs, Tourism and Emigration Dec. 69-; Mayor, City of Port Louis 69-71, Lord Mayor 71-; Grand Officier, Ordre Nat. du Tchad.
City Hall, Port Louis; Ministry of External Affairs, Port Louis; Grand Gaube, Port Louis, Mauritius.

Edu, Chief Alhaji Shafi Lawal; Nigerian businessman and administrator; b. 1913, Epe, Lagos State; ed. Epe Govt. School and privately.
Worked as teacher; clerk, African Oilnut Co. 36; local manager, Holland W. Africa Lines—45; ship's chandler 45, later food contractor for Nigerian Army, Lagos; mem. W. House of Assembly 51-54, later mem. for W. House of Reps. -54; Vice-Pres. Lagos Chamber of Commerce and Industry 58-63, Pres. 63; Commr. in charge of Health, W. Nigeria 62; Vice-Pres. Commonwealth Chamber of Commerce 65-66, Pres. 66; Pres. Asscn. of Chambers of Commerce, Industry and Mines of Nigeria; Dir. Nigerian Oil Refinery Co., Palm Lines and Ports Authority; mem. of Board, Mercantile Bank of Nigeria 72-.
Association of Chambers of Commerce, Industry and Mines of Nigeria, P.O. Box 109, Lagos, Nigeria.

Effiong, Lieut.-Col. Phillip; Nigerian army officer; b. 1926, Uyo Province, South-Eastern State.
Lieutenant-Colonel in Fed. Army, later Maj-Gen. in Biafran forces; took over from Gen. Ojukwu as leader of Biafra and negotiated surrender Jan. 70; reported under house arrest, Calabar April 70-July 70; dismissed from Army Nov. 71.

Efon, Vincent; Cameroonian politician; b. 28 Aug. 1927, Mbos; ed. Paris, Toulouse.
Directeur de Cabinet, Minister of Nat. Educ. July 60-July 62; Chief, Produce Dept. 62-63; Asst. Dir., then Dir. Econ. Orientation March 63-Jan. 66; Dir. of Foundation Products 66-67; Dir. CHOCOCAM and Soc. Franco-Camerounaise des Tabacs (SFCT); Minister of Commerce and Industry May 67-Aug. 68; Minister of Planning and Devt. 68-70, of Transport 70-72, of Foreign Affairs July 72-.
Ministry of Foreign Affairs, Yaoundé, United Republic of Cameroon.

Egeland, Leif, M.A., B.C.L.; South African diplomatist and businessman; b. 19 Jan. 1903, Durban; ed. Durban High School, Natal Univ. Coll., and Trinity Coll., Oxford.
Rhodes Scholar for Natal 24, Harmsworth Scholar, Middle Temple 27; Barrister 30; Fellow, Brasenose Coll. 27-30; Advocate, Supreme Court S. Africa 31; M.P. Durban 33-38, Zululand 40-43; with 6th S. African Armoured Div., Middle East 43; Union Minister to Sweden 43-46, to Neths. and Belgium 46-48; High Commr. for Union of South Africa in London 48-50; S. African Del. to San Francisco Conf. 45; leader of S. African Del. to Final Assembly LN, Geneva 46; S. African Del. to First and Third Gen. Assemblies of UN, Paris, to Paris Peace Conf. 46 and Pres. Comm. for the political and territorial questions in the draft Peace Treaty with Italy at that Conf.; Dir. Cape Asbestos Insulations Pty. Ltd.; Dir. Johannesburg Consolidated Investment Co., S. African Breweries Ltd., Rhodesian Breweries Ltd., Goodyear Tyre & Rubber Co. (S.A.) Ltd., Johannesburg Local Board of Natal Building Soc.; Chair. Standard Gen. Insurance Co. Ltd., Smuts Memorial Trust; Dir. Standard Bank Investment Corpn.; Nat. Chair. South African Inst. of Int. Affairs; Hon. Bencher Middle Temple; Hon. LL.D. (Cambridge Univ.); Commdr. with Star, Order of St. Olav (Norway).
Home: 97 Fourth Road, Hyde Park, Johannesburg; Office: c/o P.O. Box 590, Johannesburg, South Africa.
Telephone: 421642 (Home); 838-5981 (Office).

Eglin, Colin Wells, B.SC.; South African quantity surveyor; b. 14 April 1925, Cape Town; ed. De Villiers Graaff High School, Villiersdorp, Univ. of Cape Town.
Member for Pinelands (United Party), Provincial Council 53; mem. Parl. (UP) 58; major role in organizing Progressive Party (split from UP); Chair. PP, Cape Province 60, Nat. Exec. Chair. 66, Leader Feb. 71-.

Publs. *Betrayal of Coloured Rights, Forging Links in Africa, Priorities for the Seventies, New Deal for the Cities.*
Bernard James and Partners, 800 African Life Centre, St. George's Street, Cape Town; Home: 10 Southway, Pinelands, Cape Town, South Africa.

Ekangaki, Nzo; Cameroonian politician; b. 1934, Nguti (Kumba); ed. Ecole Normale Hope Waddle, Calabar, Nigeria, Univ. Coll. of Ibadan, Nigeria, London Univ., England and Oxford Univ.
Represented Nigeria at UN conferences as student; worked in local govt.; studied at Inst. Goethe, Ebersberg-bei-München and Bonn Univ., Fed. Germany; mem., Legislative Assembly, West Cameroon 61; Deputy to Nat. Fed. Assembly 62; Deputy Minister of Foreign Affairs 62-64; Minister of Health 64-65; of Labour and Social Security 65-72; Sec.-Gen. OAU June 72-.
Publs. *An Introduction to East Cameroon* 56, *To the Nigerian People* 58.
OAU, P.O. Box 3243, Addis Ababa, Ethiopia.

Eke, Abudu Yesufu, M.A.; Nigerian educational administrator; b. 7 Sept. 1923, Benin City; ed. Higher Coll., Yaba, Univ. Coll., Ibadan and Sidney Sussex Coll., Cambridge.
Various posts in Public Relations Dept. 48-54; Information Officer, Fed. Information Services 54-55; Asst. Registrar, Univ. Coll., Ibadan 55-58; Principal Information Officer, subsequently Chief Information Officer, Western Nigeria Information Services 59-61; Registrar, Univ. of Ife 61-62; Commr. for Information, W. Region Govt. June-Aug. 62; Registrar, Univ. of Lagos 62-71; Commr. for Finance, Midwest State Govt. 67-71; Fed. Commr. for Educ. 71-.
Publs. *History of Group Divergence in Physical Anthropology, One Nigeria* (one-act play), *Problems of Decolonization in Africa, The Future of the OAU.*
Federal Ministry of Education, Lagos; Home: 6 James George Street, Alagbon Close, Ikoyi, Lagos, Nigeria.

Eklou, Paulin; Togolese politician; b. 19 Feb. 1928, Central Togo; ed. Montpellier Univ., Nat. Inst. of Econ. and Financial Sciences.
Worked in Central Bank, Paris; practical overseas training, Brazzaville and Cotonou; Head, Econ. Planning Dept. of Togo 62; involved in attempted coup Nov. 66; released from Mango Prison Jan. 67; responsible for Commerce, Industry and Tourism in Cttee. of Reconciliation Jan. 67-April 67; Minister of Commerce, Industry, Tourism and Planning April 67-Aug. 69; Minister of Rural Economy Aug. 69-Jan. 72.
c/o Ministry of Rural Economy, Lomé, Togo.

Ekra, Matthieu; Ivory Coast politician; b. 27 Feb. 1917, Bonoua; ed. Ecole Normale William-Ponty.
Held several posts in the admin. of fmr. French West Africa; worked in railways and finance admins., later in road transport dept., Guinea; founded first branch African Dem. Rally (RDA) Kankam, Guinea 46; Sec.-Gen. RDA 46-47; mem. Man. Cttee. Ivory Coast Dem. Party 47; spent three years in preventive detention 49-52; Municipal Councillor for Abidjan 56; M.P. 59-; Minister of Civil Service and Information Jan. 61-Feb. 63; Amb. 63-64; Minister of Information March 65-Jan. 70; Minister of State Jan. 70-June 71; Minister of State for Tourism June 71-.
Office of the Minister of State for Tourism, Abidjan, Ivory Coast.

Ekwensi, Cyprian; Nigerian (Ibo) author and pharmacist; b. 1921, Minna, Northern Nigeria; ed. Achimota Coll., Ghana, School of Forestry, Ibadan, and Univ. of London.
Former lecturer in English and science; lecturer in pharmacy in Lagos; pharmacist, Nigerian Medical Corpn.; Head, Features Dept., Nigerian Broadcasting Corpn.; fmr. Dir. of Information, Fed. Ministry of Information; now Chair. East Central State Library Board.

Publs. *People of the City* 54, 63, *The Passport of Mallam Ilia* 60, *The Drummer Boy* 60, *Burning Grass* 62, *Jagua Nana* 61, *An African Night's Entertainment* 62, *Beautiful Feathers* 63, *Lokotown and Other Stories.*
P.O. Box 317, Enugu, Nigeria.

Elias, Ibrahim; Sudanese economist and politician b. 29 Aug. 1923, Omdurman; ed. Gordon Memorial Coll., Khartoum, Queen's Univ., Belfast and Manchester Univ.
Schoolmaster 49-56; trade officer, Ministry of Commerce, Industry and Supply 56-62; Asst. Man. Dir. Sudan Industrial Bank 62-65; Asst. Under-Sec., Ministry of Econs. 65-69; Gen. Man. Gulf Fisheries, Kuwait 69-70; Man. Dir. Blue Nile Brewery, Khartoum, and Chair. Leather and Plastic Industries Corpn. 70-72; Minister of the Treasury Oct. 72-.
Publ. *Studies in Sudan Economy* 69.
P.O. Box 1017, Omdurman, Sudan.
Telephone: 70288, 74077 (Office): 54516 (Home).

Elias, Taslim Olawale, Q.C., B.A., LL.M., PH.D., LL.D.; Nigerian lawyer and politician; b. 11 Nov. 1914; ed. C.M.S. Grammar School, Lagos, Igboli Coll., Lagos, Univ. Coll., London, Cambridge Univ. and Inst. of Advanced Legal Studies, London.
Yarborough Anderson Scholar of Inner Temple 46-49; called to the Bar 47; Simon Research Fellow, Univ. of Manchester 51-53; Oppenheim Research Fellow, Inst. of Commonwealth Studies, Nuffield Coll. and Queen Elizabeth House, Oxford 54-60; Visiting Prof. in Political Science, Delhi Univ. 56; mem. Del. to Nigerian Constitutional Conf., London 58; Fed. Attorney-Gen. and Minister of Justice, Nigeria 60-66, Attorney-Gen. Oct. 66-, Commr. for Justice June 67-; Chief Justice, Supreme Court Feb. 72-; mem. UN Int. Law Comm. 61-; mem. Governing Council, Univ. of Nigeria 59-66; Gov. School of Oriental and African Studies, London Univ. 58-61; Chair. UN Cttee. of Constitutional Experts to draft Congo Constitution 61, 62; Gen. Reporter Int. Law Comm. (ILC) 65-70, Chair. 70; mem. Int. Law Asscn. 65-; Prof. of Law and Dean of Faculty of Law Univ. of Lagos, Nigeria April 66-; Chair. Cttee. of UN Conf. on Law of Treaties 68, 69; Pres. Nigerian Soc. of Int. Law; Chair. African Inst. of Int. Law; Assoc. mem. Inst. of Int. Law 69-; Chair. Governing Council, Nigerian Inst. of Int. Affairs 72-; Hon. LL.D. (Dakar); D.Litt. (Ibadan) 69.
Publs. *Nigerian Land Law and Custom* 51, *Nigerian Legal System* 54, *Ghana and Sierra Leone: Development of their Laws and Constitutions* 62, *British Colonial Law: A Comparative Study* 62, *Government and Politics in Africa* 2nd edn. 63, *Nature of African Customary Law* 2nd edn. 62, *Nigeria: Development of its Laws and Constitution* 65; Co-author of *British Legal Papers* 58, *International Law in a Changing World* 63, *Sovereignty Within the Law* 65, *African Law: Adaptation and Development* 65, *Law, Justice and Equity* 67, *Nigerian Press Law* 69, *Nigerian Prison System* 68; Gen. Editor *Nigerian Law Journal* 68-, many articles.
20 Ozumba Mbadiwe, Victoria Island, Lagos, Nigeria.
Telephone: 27549.

Enahoro, Chief Anthony; Nigerian politician; b. 22 July 1923, Uromi Ishan Division, Mid-Western State; s. of late Chief Okotako Enahoro; ed. Govt. Schools, Uromi and Owo and King's Coll., Lagos
Journalist 42-50; Editor *Southern Nigeria Defender* 44-46, *Daily Comet* 46-49, concurrently Assoc. Editor *West African Pilot*; Editor-in-Chief *Morning Star* 50; foundation mem. Action Group, Sec. and Chair. of Ishan Div. Council; mem. Western House of Assembly and Fed. House of Reps. 51, later Minister of Home Affairs (Western Region); moved motion for self-government and attended all constitutional talks preceding independence 60; detained during Emergency period in Western Nigeria 62, fled to Britain 63; extradited from Britain and imprisoned in Nigeria for

treason; released by Mil. Govt. 66; Leader of Mid-West del. to *ad hoc* Constitutional Conf. and mem. *ad hoc* Constitutional Cttee. 66; Fed. Commr. for Information and Labour June 67-.
Publ. *Fugitive Offender* (autobiography).
c/o Federal Ministry for Information and Labour, Lagos, Nigeria.

Endeley, E. M. L., O.B.E.; Nigerian medical doctor and politician; b. 1916, Buea (then in Nigeria); *s.* of late Chief Mathias Liffafe Endeley; ed. Buea Govt. School, Catholic Mission, Bojongo, Govt. Coll. Umuahia, Higher Coll., Yaba.
Qualified as doctor 42; entered Govt. service 43; served Lagos, Port Harcourt, etc.; in charge of Cottage Hospital, Buea; trade union leader 47; formed Cameroons Nat. Fed. (afterwards Kamerun Nat. Congress) 49; mem. House of Reps. and Council of Ministers 52-54; Minister without Portfolio; Minister of Labour; First Premier, Southern Cameroons 55-59; Pres. Bakweri Co-op. Marketing Union 55; led South Cameroons Del. to Constitutional Conf., London 57; Leader of the Opposition 59-61; Leader Nat. Convention Party (later Cameroon People's Nat. Convention Party), West Cameroon 61-66; Asst. Treas. and mem. Cameroon Nat. Union Political Bureau 66-; Parl. leader, Cameroon Nat. Union Party, W. Cameroon Legislative Assembly 66-72.
P.O. Box 5, Buea, United Republic of Cameroon.
Telephone: Buea 24226.

Engone, Jean; Gabonese politician; b. 1 Jan. 1932; ed. Lycée Léon Mba, Libreville, Lycée de Châteroux, Indre (France) and Inst. des Hautes Etudes d'Outre-mer, Paris.
Civil Admin., Libreville Prefecture, Gabon 60; Asst. Dir., then Dir. of Civil Service 60-62; attached to the Presidency, and Sec.-Gen. of Nat. Assembly 62-63; Dir. of Public Health Sept. 63; Minister of Finance 64-65; Minister of Foreign Affairs March 65-68; Dir. of Devt. Bank of Gabon 68-70; Minister and Amb. in Geneva, Switzerland 70-; decorations from China, Ivory Coast, Central African Repub. and Spain.
Ambassade du Gabon, Geneva, Switzerland; also c/o Ministère des Affaires Etrangères, B.P. 389, Libreville, Gabon.

Engura, Yokosafate Atoke; Ugandan diplomatist; b. 1919, Inomo, Lango District, Uganda; ed. secondary and higher schools, Uganda.
Hospital pharmacist, Kampala 45-51; local govt. posts 47-52; one of founders and mem. Uganda Nat. Congress 52-; organizer of Uganda Nat. Congress in Lango District 52-56; political prisoner 56-59; Head of Lango District 60; Vice-Pres. of Uganda Nat. Congress 59; Amb. to U.S.S.R. 64-70; Minister of Culture and Community Devt. 71-72.
c/o Ministry of Culture, Kampala, Uganda.

Enwonu, Benedict Chuka, M.B.E.; Nigerian sculptor; b. 1921; ed. Holy Trinity School, Onitsha, Govt. Colls. Umu-Ahia and Ibadan, Univ. Coll., London.
First One-Man Show, Lagos 42; on the strength of this he was given a special scholarship by Shell-Mex to study in England; rep. UNESCO Exhbn., Paris 46; first One-Man Exhbn., London 48; subsequent exhbns. 50, 52, 55; exhbn. U.S. 50; commissioned to execute statue of H.M. Queen Elizabeth, doors, panels and Speaker's chair, Lagos House of Representatives, and the group *The Risen Christ* for the Chapel, Univ. Coll., Ibadan; Art Adviser to the Fed. Govt. of Nigeria 68-72; Prof. of Fine Arts, Univ. of Ife 72-; his works have been purchased by H.M. Queen Elizabeth, the late Sir Jacob Epstein and others; R. B. Bennett Empire Art Prize 57.
University of Ife, Ile-Ife, Nigeria.

Escher, Alfred Martin, DR.JUR.; Swiss diplomatist; b. 23 March 1906; ed. Univs. of Zürich, Berlin and Kiel, Acad. for Int. Law, The Hague.

Entered service of Fed. Political Dept. 31; Attaché, Bangkok 32; Sec. of Legation, Warsaw 35, Berlin 39; First Sec., Berlin 41, Ankara 41; Consul, Baghdad 42; Athens 44; Counsellor, London 45; Commr. Int. Cttee. of the Red Cross for Refugees in Palestine 48; Minister to Iran 51-54, concurrently to Afghanistan 53-54; mem. Neutral Nations Supervisory Comm. for Armistice Korea 54; Minister to Italy 55-57, Amb. to Italy 57-59; Amb. to Fed. Repub. of Germany May 59-64, to Austria 64-; UN Rep. to Namibia (South West Africa) Sept. 72-.
c/o Office of the UN Secretary-General UN Headquarters, New York, N.Y., U.S.A.

Eshun, Isaac; Ghanaian journalist; b. 1924, Kumasi; ed. Wesley Coll., Kumasi.
Teacher 47-49; *Ashanti Times* 50-51; *Daily Graphic* 51-64, Ed. 59-63; Dir. Ghana News Agency 60-63, 67-; Exec. Dir. Ghana Graphic Co. Ltd. 60-64; Public Relations Man., Pioneer Tobacco Co. 64-; Chair. of Board Cadco (Ghana) Ltd. (State-owned advertising agency) 67-; Dir. Ghana Tobacco Co. Ltd. 69-; Dir. Pioneer Tobacco Co. 69-.
Pioneer Tobacco Company, P.O. Box 11, Accra, Ghana.

Esono-Mica, Prim José; Equatorial Guinea diplomatist; b. 16 Dec. 1940, Bisun (Niefang); ed. Martin Luther King School, Santa Isabel.
Deputy to Parl. 68, Sec. to Parl. 69; Perm. Rep. to UN Feb. 71-.
Permanent Mission of Equatorial Guinea to United Nations, 440 East 62nd Street, Apt. 6D, New York, N.Y. 10022, U.S.A.

Esuene, Brig. Udoakaha Jacob; Nigerian army officer; b. 1936, Afaha Eket, Eket; ed. Qua Iboe Mission Secondary School, Etinian, Govt. Teacher Training Coll., Uyo, and Mons Officer Cadet School, Royal Military Acad., Sandhurst, Small Arms School, Hythe and School of Infantry, Warminster, England.
Teacher 55-58; joined army 58; transferred to Nigerian Air Force and was attached to German Air Force Establishment for Training 63-65; Commanding Officer, Air Force Base, Kaduna July 65-Jan. 66; Senior Air Operations Officer, Air H.Q., Lagos Feb. 66-May 67; Mil. Gov. South-Eastern State May 67-.
Government House, P.M.B. 1056, Calabar; Home: Afaha Eket, Eket, Nigeria.

Etiang, Paul Orono, B.A.; Ugandan diplomatist; b. 15 Aug. 1938, Tororo; ed. Busoga Coll. and Makerere Univ. Coll.
District Officer, Provincial Admin. 62-64; Asst. Sec., Ministry of Foreign Affairs 64-65; Second Sec., Uganda Embassy, Moscow 65-67; mem. Uganda Mission to UN 67-68; First Sec. 68; High Commr. to U.K. June 69-71.
c/o Ministry of Foreign Affairs, Kampala, Uganda.

Etoungou, Simon Nko'o; Cameroonian diplomatist and politician; b. 14 Feb. 1932; ed. secondary and post-secondary schools, and diplomatic training in France.
Head of Office in Ministry of Econ. Planning 56-57; Cabinet Attaché, Ministry of Finance 58-59; First Sec., Cameroon Embassy, Paris 60; Minister-Counsellor 60-61; Amb. to Tunisia 61-64; led numerous Cameroon dels. 63-64; concurrently Amb. to Algeria July-Nov. 64; Amb. to U.S.S.R. 64-65; Minister of Foreign Affairs 65-66, 68-June 70; Minister of Finance 66-68; Knight of Nat. Order of Merit (Cameroon), and decorations from Senegal, Tunisia, Fed. Repub. of Germany and Gabon.
c/o Ministry of Foreign Affairs, Yaoundé, United Republic of Cameroon.

Eyadema, Gen. Etienne Gnassingbe; Togolese army officer and politician; b. 1935, Pya, Lama Kara District, Served with French Army 53-61, especially in Indo-China, Dahomey, Niger and Algeria; commissioned 63; Army

Chief-of-Staff (Togo) 65-; seized power Jan. 67; Pres. of Togo and Minister of Defence April 67-; Pres. Rassemblement du peuple togolais Nov. 69-72.
Office of the President, Lomé, Togo.

Eyebu-Bakand'asi, Ipoto; Zaire diplomatist; b. 8 Aug. 1933, Kinshasa; ed. Inst. Universitaire de Hautes Etudes Internationales, Geneva.
Director of Cabinet of Minister of Foreign Affairs of the Congo (Leopoldville) 60-63; OAU assignments 64, 65; Deputy to Special Commr. for Cen. Basin of Congo 65; Technical Adviser, Ministry of Foreign Affairs 66; Counsellor, London 66; Amb. to Algeria 67-69, to India 70, to Ethiopia 70-72; Perm. Rep. to UN Sept. 72-.
Permanent Mission of Zaire to United Nations, 400-402 East 51st Street, New York, N.Y. 10022, U.S.A.

F

Fakhreddine, Mohamed; Sudanese diplomatist; b. 12 Oct. 1924; ed. Gordon Memorial Coll., Khartoum, and Univ. of Durham.
Chief of Protocol, Head of UN Section, Ministry of Foreign Affairs, Khartoum 56-58; Counsellor, London 58-60; Amb. to Pakistan and Afghanistan 60-64; Amb. to Pakistan, Afghanistan and People's Republic of China 64-65; Perm. Rep. to UN 65-71; Under-Sec. of Foreign Affairs 71-.
Ministry of Foreign Affairs, Khartoum, Sudan.

Fall, Medoune; Senegalese diplomatist; b. 21 July 1919, St. Louis, Senegal; ed. Ecole Supérieure, Dakar.
Secretary, Territorial Assembly, Senegal 52-56; Dir. of Social Insurance, Louga 56-59; District Chief, Podor and Bambey 59-60; Head, Diourbel Regional Devt. Assistance Centre 60-61; Gen. Dir. Nat. Board for Farm Produce Purchases, later Gov. of Diourbel Region 61-63; Amb. to France 64-66, concurrently to Spain, and Rep. to UNESCO 65-66; Amb. to Belgium and Perm. Rep. to EEC 66-68; Amb. to U.S.S.R. 68-71, concurrently to Poland; Perm. Rep. to UN 71-.
Permanent Mission of Senegal to the United Nations, 51 East 42nd Street, New York, N.Y. 10017, U.S.A.

Farah, Abdulrahim Abby; Somali diplomatist; b. 1919; ed. Univ. of Exeter and Balliol Coll., Oxford.
Ambassador to Ethiopia 61-65; Perm. Rep. of Somalia to the UN 65-72; Rep. of Somalia on UN Security Council 70-72; Chair. UN Special Cttee. on Apartheid 69-72; Commr. for Technical Co-operation, UN Oct. 72-.
Office of Technical Co-operation, United Nations Secretariat, New York, N.Y. 10017, U.S.A.

Faruk, Usman; Nigerian police officer and politician; b. 1 Jan. 1935, Pindinga, Gombe Div.; ed. Bauchi Middle School, Govt. School, Zaria, Agricultural School, Samaru, Zaria and S. Police Coll., Ikeja.
Served with police force 58-; Senior Detective Course, Wakefield, England 61; Gazetted Officers' Course, Police Coll., Scotland 64; Chief Supt. of Police; Mil. Gov. of N.W. State May 67-.
Office of the Military Governor, Sokoto, Nigeria.

Ferguson, Clarence Clyde, Jr., D.I.L.; American diplomatist and professor of law; b. 4 Nov. 1924, Wilmington, N.C.; ed. Ohio State Univ., Harvard and Havana Univs.
Called to Bar 51; teaching fellow, Law School 51-52; associated with Baltimore, Paulson and Canudo 52-54; Asst. U.S. Attorney 54-55; Professor of Law, Rutgers Univ. 55-63, Howard Univ. 63-June 70; U.S. expert, UN Sub-Comm. on Discrimination 64-; U.S. Amb. to Uganda 70-72; Deputy Asst. Sec. for African Affairs, Dept. of State 72-; fmr. Special Co-ordinator for Relief to Civilian Victims of the Nigerian Civil War; Hon. LL.D.
Publs. *Desegregation and the Law* 57, 62, 70, *Trial Presenta-* tion 57, *Enforcement Judgements and Liens* 61, *Secured Transactions* 61, *Racism and American Education* 70, numerous articles and book reviews.
Department of State, Washignton, D.C. 20521, U.S.A.

Foccart, Jacques; French civil servant; b. 31 Aug. 1913; ed. Collège de l'Immaculée Conception, Laval.
Exporter; Adviser, Rassemblement du Peuple Français (R.P.F.) Group, Council of the Republic 52-58; Sec.-Gen. R.P.F. 54; Technical Adviser, Gen. de Gaulle's Office (Pres. of the Council) 58-59; Technical Adviser in Secretariat-Gen. of Presidency of Republic 59; Sec.-Gen. Presidency for French Community and African and Malagasy Affairs 61-69, June 69-; Officier, Légion d'Honneur, Croix de Guerre 39-45, Rosette de la Résistance.
Secretariat-Général pour la Communauté et les Affaires Africaines et Malgaches, 138 rue de Grenelle, Paris 7e, France.

Fofana, Dr. Bénitiéni; Mali physician and politician.
Minister of Health and Social Affairs Feb. 69-; Pres. Org. for Co-operation and Co-ordination in the Fight against Endemic Diseases (OCCGE).
Ministry of Health and Social Affairs, Bamako, Mali.

Foncha, John Ngu; Cameroonian politician; b. 21 June 1916.
Member House of Assembly 51-65; Prime Minister and Minister of Local Govt., Southern Cameroons 59-61; Prime Minister, Western Cameroon 61-65; Vice-Pres., Fed. Republic of Cameroon 61; Leader, Kamerun Nat. Democratic Party (KNDP) 55-66; Chair. Cameroon Nat. Union (UNC) 66-72.
Union nationale camerounaise, Yaoundé, United Republic of Cameroon.

Fonlon, Bernard Nsokika, PH.D.; Cameroonian politician; b. 19 Nov. 1924, Nsau; ed. Nat. Univ. of Ireland, Oxford Univ.
Responsible for mission to Presidency of the Repub. until 64; M.P. to Nat. Fed. Assembly 62-64; Asst. Minister of Foreign Affairs July 64-Jan. 68; Minister of Transport, Posts and Telecommunications Jan. 68–June 70; Minister of Public Health and Population 70-71.
c/o Ministry of Public Health and Population, Yaoundé, United Republic of Cameroon.

Forna, Alpha George Sembu; Sierra Leonean politician; b. 11 April 1932; ed. Fourah Bay Coll., Univ. Coll., Sierra Leone, London and Antwerp.
Assistant Social Devt. Officer, Ministry of Social Welfare 55-58; Diamond Valuer, London 58-62, Sierra Leone 62-69; Minister of Transport and Communications 69; Minister of Finance 70-71; Minister of Agriculture and Natural Resources 71-.
P.O. Box 788, 121 Wilkinson Road, Freetown, Sierra Leone.
Telephone: 8234 (Home); 2756 (Office).

Forster, Isaac; Senegalese international judge; b. 14 Aug. 1903; ed. Lycée Hoche, Versailles, and Univ. of Paris.
General State Counsel's Dept. for French West Africa 30; Deputy Judge, Dakar 33, Deputy to Prosecutor, Conakry, Guinea 33; Judge, St. Denis, Réunion, then Madagascar 41; Judge of Court, Guadeloupe 45, French West Africa 47; Pres. of Chamber, Dakar 57; Sec.-Gen. of Govt. Senegal 58-60; Prosecutor-Gen., Dakar 59; First Pres. Supreme Court of Senegal 60-64; Judge, Int. Court of Justice, The Hague 64-; assoc. mem. Inst. of Int. Law; numerous decorations.
International Court of Justice, The Hague, Netherlands.

Fouché, Jacobus Johannes, D.M.S.; State President of the Republic of South Africa; b. 6 June 1898, Wepener, O.F.S.; ed. Victoria Coll., Stellenbosch.

Member of Parl. for Smithfield 41-50, for Bloemfontein West 60-68; Administrator, Orange Free State 51-59; Minister of Defence 59-66, of Agricultural Technical Services and Water Affairs 66-68; State Pres. of South Africa 68-; Decoration for Meritorious Service 71.
Office of the State President, Pretoria, Transvaal, Republic of South Africa.
Telephone: 74-3131.

Fouché, Dr. Jacobus Johannes, B.A., LL.D.; South African company director and diplomatist; b. 4 Sept. 1921, Bloemfontein; *s.* of State President J. J. Fouché (*q.v.*); ed. Rouxville High School and Univ. of Stellenbosch.
Member of Parl. 50-64; Leader Nasionale Jeugbond 46-56; mem. Provincial Head Cttee. Nationalist Party, mem. Fed. Council Nationalist Party until 64; Amb. to Netherlands 64-67.
13 Welgevallen Street, Welgelegen, Stellenbosch, C.P., South Africa.
Telephone: Stellenbosch 4401 (Office); Stellenbosch 4006 (Residence).

Fourie, Bernardus Gerhardus, M.A., B.COM.; South African diplomatist; b. 1916, Wolmaransstad; ed. Pretoria and New York Univs.
On staff of Berlin Embassy 39, Brussels 40, London High Comm. 39, 40-45; Del. to San Francisco Conf. 45, UN Prep. Comm. and 1st Gen. Assembly 46; with Dept. of External Affairs Int. Orgs. Div. 52-57, Asst. Sec. African Div. 57-58; Perm. Rep. to UN 58-62; Under-Sec. African Div., Dept. of Foreign Affairs 62-63; Sec. for Information 63-66; Sec. for Foreign Affairs 66-.
Department of Foreign Affairs, Private Bag 141, Union Buildings, Pretoria, Republic of South Africa.
Telephone: Pretoria 2-5431.

Frank, Antonio; Central African Republic politician.
Former primary school teacher; Head of Teaching Dept. of the First Degree April 63-Nov. 66; Sec. of State for Nat. Educ., in charge of Youth, Sports, Art and Culture Jan. 67-Feb. 69; Minister of Nat. Educ. Feb. 69-Sept. 69; Minister of Labour Sept. 70-Jan. 71.
c/o Ministry of Labour, Bangui, Central African Republic.

Freed, Louis Franklin, M.A., D.PHIL., M.B., C.H.B., M.D., D.P.M., D.P.H., D.T.M. and H., D.PHIL., D.LITT. ET.PHIL., D.I.H., F.R.S.S.A.F., F.S.S., F.R.A.I., F.R.G.S., F.R.C.PSYCH.; South African medical psychologist; b. 1903, Libau, Balticum; ed. Univs. of St. Andrews, Pretoria, Witwatersrand, Stellenbosch, Orange Free State and South Africa.
Former South African Editor of *International Journal of Sexology*; former Medical Officer, Tara Neuro-Psychiatric Hospital, Johannesburg 57; Medical Officer, Sterkfontein Mental Hospital, Krugersdorp 56-57; Lecturer on Social Medicine 49-; Lecturer in Dept. of Psychiatry and in Dept. of Sociology, Univ. of Witwatersrand, Johannesburg 53-; Guest Lecturer, Inst. of Criminology, Cambridge, Inst. of Criminology, Hebrew Univ. of Jerusalem, Oxford Univ. Mental Health Soc. 65; D. Phil. Univ. of Orange Free State 58; fmr. mem. New York Acad. of Sciences, S. African Asscn. for the Advancement of Science, Exec. Cttee. of Convocation, Univ. of Witwatersrand; Pres. Mental Health Soc., Witwatersrand, Exec. Cttee. South African PEN, Exec. Cttee. of Inst. for the Study of Man in Africa, Exec. Cttee. Inst. of Adult Educ., Exec. Cttee, Johannesburg Youth Council, Exec. Cttee. S. African Nat. Epilepsy League; mem. S. African Council of Mental Health 72; medical sociologist, Tara Neuro-Psychiatric Hospital, Johannesburg.
Publs. *The Problem of European Prostitution in Johannesburg* 49, *Sex Education in Transvaal Schools* 38, *The Philosophy of Sociological Medicine* 48, *Findings of an Investigation into a Group of Patients presenting the Symptoms of Schizophrenia* 53, *The Social Aspect of Venereal Disease* 51, *The Psychosociology of Neoplasia* 58, *A Metho-*

dological Approach to the Problem of Mental Disorder 56, *The Use of Methodological Principles in the Investigation of a Case of Trichomoniasis* 57, *The Problem of Crime in the Union of South Africa: An Integralistic Approach, An Enquiry into the Causality of Cancer* (with G. Giannopoulos), *Cancer-Killer No. 1* 60, *The Problem of Alcoholism: An Integralist Approach* 61, *A Critical Analysis of R. F. A. Hoernle's Contributions to Philosophy with Special Reference to his Synoptic Treatment of Diverse Dimensions of Reality* 65, *The Problem of Suicide in Johannesburg Examined from the Standpoint of Incidence, Causality and Control* 67, *The Psychopath: A Social Challenge, A Case of Temporal Lobe Epilepsy, The Social Aspects of Alcoholism* 68, *Aspects of Human Disorganization* 69, *Medico-social Aspects of Epilepsy* 69, *The Phenomenon of Guilt and Guilt Feelings: The Buberian Approach* 72.
15 Lystanwold Road, Saxonwold, Johannesburg, South Africa.
Telephone: 23-0009 (Office); 41-8877 (Home).

Fugard, Athol; South African actor and playwright.
Publs. *The Blood Knot, Hello and Goodbye, People are Living Here, Boesman and Lena* 70.
P.O. Box 5090, Walmer, Port Elizabeth, South Africa.

G

Gabre-Sellassie, Zewde, M.A., PH.D.; Ethiopian diplomatist; b. 12 Oct. 1926, Metcha, Shoa; ed. Haile Sellassie I Secondary School, Coll. des Frères and St. George School, Jerusalem, Coll. des Frères and American Mission, Cairo, Univ. of South West of England, Exeter, Oxford Univ. and Lincoln's Inn, London.
Economic Attaché, later Head of Press, Information and Admin. Div., Ministry of Foreign Affairs 51-53; Dir.-Gen. Maritime Affairs 53-55; Deputy Minister, Ministry of Public Works, Transport and Civil Aviation 55-57; Gov. of Addis Ababa 57-59; Amb. to Somalia 59-60; Minister of Justice 61-63; Senior mem. St. Anthony's Coll., Oxford 63-71; Perm. Rep. to the UN Sept. 72-; Visiting Lecturer, Univ. of Calif., U.S.A. 65; Officer of Menelik II (Ethiopia); Grand Cross, Order of Phoenix (Greece), of Istiqlal (Jordan); Grand Officer, Flag of Yugoslavia, Order of Merit (Fed. Repub. of Germany); Commdr., Order of St. Olav (Norway), of Orange-Nassau (Netherlands).
Permanent Mission of Ethiopia to the United Nations, 866 United Nations Plaza, New York, N.Y. 10017; and 29 Hereford Road, Bronxville, New York, N.Y. 10708, U.S.A.

Gamedze, Dr. A. B., M.A.; Swazi teacher, theologian and diplomatist; b. 3 April 1921, Shiselweni District; ed. at Mhlosheni and at Matsapa, Swaziland, at Umphumulo Inst., Natal, Adams Coll., Natal, and Wheaton Coll., Ill., U.S.A.
Head Teacher, Jerusalem School 42, transferred to Franson Christian High School 43; Head Teacher, Makhonza School 46-47; started first rural market for Jerusalem and New Haven Farmers Asscn.; at Wheaton Coll., Ill., studying educ., Christian educ. and theology 47-51; Lecturer, Evangelical Teacher Training Coll., Natal 51-56; Editor *Africa's Hope* 55-61; Pres. African Teachers' Christian Fellowship 56; ordained Minister of Evangelical Church 56; assisted Organizing Insp. of Religious Educ. in Secondary Schools, Transvaal 58; Lecturer in Divinity and Educ. and Chaplain of Univ. of Fort Hare 60-61; joined staff of Franson Christian High School 62; Superintendent (Grantee) of all Evangelical Church Schools 62-65; Vice-Pres. Evangelical Church; Vice-Pres. Swaziland Conf. of Churches 64; Senior Liaison Officer, Swaziland 65-67; mem. Senate 67-; Minister of Educ., Swaziland 67-71; High Commr. in U.K., concurrently Amb. to

France, Belgium and Fed. Germany 71-; Editor *Imbokodvo Bulletin*; Hon. LL.D. Wheaton Coll., U.S.A. 68.
Swaziland High Commission, 58 Pont Street, London, S.W.1, England.

Gandar, Laurence; South African journalist; ed. Univ. of Natal.
Formerly Asst. Editor *Pretoria News* and *Natal Daily News*; Editor-in-Chief *Rand Daily Mail* 57-69; Dir. Minority Rights Group, London 69-71.
14 Randolph Crescent, London, W.9, England.

Garango, Maj. Marc Tiémoko, L. en D.; Upper Voltan army officer and politician; b. 27 July 1927, Gaoua; ed. Univs. of Dakar, Paris, Aix-en-Provence.
Completed mil. training at Bingerville, Ivory Coast; served in French Army in Indochinese and Algerian campaigns; promoted to Lieut. 61, Capt. 63; Supply Officer, Upper Volta Army 65-66; Minister of Finance and Commerce Jan. 66-; Amb. to China (Taiwan) June 66; Past Pres. Banque Centrale des Etats de L'Afrique de l'Ouest; Pres. Nat. Monetary Cttee. (BCEAO); Gov. Int. Monetary Fund (IMF).
Ministry of Finance and Commerce, Ouagadougou, Upper Volta; 29 rue du Colisée, Paris 8e, France.

Garba, Dicoh, D.M.V.; Ivory Coast veterinarian and politician; b. 4 July 1937, Béoumi; ed. Lycée Pierre de Fermat, Toulouse, Ecole Nat. Vétérinaire, Lyon, Univ. de Lyon.
Assistant Dir. Maritime and Lagoon Fisheries 66-68, Dir. 68-69; Minister of Animal Production Jan. 70-.
Ministry of Animal Production, Abidjan, Ivory Coast.

Garba, John Mamman; Nigerian civil servant and diplomatist; b. 1918; ed. Igbobi Coll., Yaba, Agricultural School, Zaria and London School of Economics.
Department of Agriculture, Nigeria 37-56; Asst. Sec. Office of Nigerian Commr., London 57-58; Second Sec. Office of U.K. High Commr., Ottawa 58; Acting Senior Asst. Sec., Office of Nigerian Commr., London 58-59; Asst. Pilgrim Officer, Nigerian Pilgrim Office, Khartoum 59-60; Chargé d'Affaires, later Minister, Washington, D.C. 60-61; Acting Deputy Perm. Sec., Ministry of Finance, Nigeria 61, Deputy Perm. Sec. 62; Deputy Sec. to Council of Ministers 63; Exec. Dir. Int. Bank for Reconstruction and Development, Int. Development Asscn., and Int. Finance Corpn. 63-66; Amb. to Italy 66-72, concurrently accredited to Greece, Cyprus and Spain 69-72, to U.S.A. June 72-.
Embassy of Nigeria, Washington, D.C., U.S.A.

Gardiner, Robert Kweku Atta, M.A., B.SC.; Ghanaian civil servant and international administrator; b. 29 Sept. 1914, Kumasi; ed. Fourah Bay Coll., Sierra Leone, Selwyn Coll., Cambridge, and New Coll., Oxford.
Lecturer in Econs., Fourah Bay Coll. 43-46; Area Specialist UN Trusteeship Dept. 47-49; Dir. Dept. of Extra-Mural Studies, Univ. Coll., Ibadan, Nigeria 49-53; Dir. Dept. of Social Welfare and Community Development, Ghana 53-55; Chair. Kumasi Coll. of Technology Council, Ghana 54-58; Perm. Sec. Ministry of Housing Ghana 55-57; Establishment Sec. and Head of Civil Service 57-59; Deputy Exec. Sec. UN Econ. Comm. for Africa, Addis Ababa 59-60; mem. UN Mission to the Congo 61; Dir. Div. of Public Admin., UN, New York 61-62; Officer-in-Charge, UN Operations in the Congo 62-63; Exec. Sec. UN Econ. Comm. for Africa, Addis Ababa 61-; BBC Reith Lecturer 65; Gilbert Murray Memorial Lecturer, OXFAM, Oxford 69; J. B. Danquah Memorial Lecturer, Ghana 70; Chair. Commonwealth Foundation; Vice-Chair. Board of Dirs. Int. Inst. for Environmental Affairs; numerous hon. degrees.
Publs. *The Development of Social Administration* (with H. O. Judd), *A World of Peoples*.
Economic Commission for Africa, P.O. Box 3001, Addis Ababa, Ethiopia.

Gaseitsiwe, Bathoen Seepapitso, C.B.E.; Botswana politician; b. 18 May 1908, Botswana; ed. Tigerkloof and Lovedale (South Africa).
Paramount Chief of Banwaketse 28-69; Chair. African Advisory Council 37-47, 49-58; mem. Legislative Council and Exec. Council 61; Dir. Botswana Meat Comm. 65-69; mem. Univ. of Bechuanaland, Basutoland and Swaziland; Chair. Univ. of Botswana, Lesotho and Swaziland 67-69; Dir. Botswana Exploration and Mining Co. 68-; Chair. Botswana Nat. Museum and Art Gallery 68-; mem. Parl. 69-; Pres. Botswana Nat. Front 70-.
Mepakon, P.O. Box 100, Kanye, Botswana.

Gasim, Osman Abu al, PH.D.; Sudanese politician; b. 1930, Omdurman; ed. Omdurman, Wadi Sayedna Secondary School and Faculty of Agriculture.
Assistant agricultural insp. 53-56; study course, UN 56-59; Lecturer, later Principal, Shambat Agricultural Inst. 59-63; studied in U.S.A. 63-67; Asst. Under-Sec. Ministry of Agriculture 67-March 69; Dir. Baghdad Univ. Project, UN March 69-May 69; Minister of Co-operation and Rural Devt. May 69-.
Ministry of Co-operation and Rural Development, Khartoum, Sudan.

Gaye, Amadou Karim, D.M.V.; Senegalese politician; b. 8 Dec. 1913, Saint-Louis; ed. Paris.
Served in the Senegalese veterinary service; fmr. Capt. of the Reserve; Gen. Counsellor of Senegal 46-52; Deputy of Union Progressiste Sénégalaise (U.P.S.) March 59-, Asst. Sec. for Propaganda, U.P.S. July 60-; Minister of Educ. and Culture Jan. 59-April 59; Minister of Planning April 59-March 60; Minister Del. to the Presidency, responsible for Devt. and Technical Co-operation Sept. 60-May 61; Minister of Assistance and Technical Co-operation May 61-March 65; Minister of the Armed Forces March 65-June 68; Minister of Foreign Affairs 68-72; Pres. Econ. and Social Council June 72-.
Economic and Social Council, Dakar, Senegal.

Gbedemah, Komla Agbeli; Ghanaian politician; b. 1913; ed. Adisadel Coll., Cape Coast and Achimota Coll.
First Vice-Chair, Convention People's Party, was responsible for organising general elections 51; Minister of Health and Labour 51-52; Minister of Commerce and Industry 52-54; Minister of Finance 54-61, of Health 61; Minister of State for Presidential Affairs 60-61; fmr. Gov. for Ghana, Int. Bank Reconstruction and Development; fmr. Pres. World Asscn. of World Federalists; Leader, Nat. Alliance of Liberals 69-; banned from taking seat in Parl. Nov. 69; Roving Amb. for Nat. Redemption Council until July 72; also farmer and business executive.
Denkudi Lodge, 3 First Rangoon Close, Box 5810, Accra North, Ghana.

Gerdener, Theo J. A.; South African politician; b. 19 March 1916, Cape Town; ed. Univ. of Stellenbosch.
Former mem. editorial staff, *Die Burger* and *Die Huisgenoot*; free-lance journalist 49-; leader, Nat. Party, Natal Provincial Council 54; Dir. and editor *Die Nataller* (Afrikaans newspaper), Durban 54-59; Senator 61; Administrator of Natal 61; Deputy Minister of Bantu Devt. May 70; Minister of the Interior Nov. 70-June 72; formed Action South and Southern Africa (ASASA) 72.
Pretoria, South Africa.

Gibbs, Rt. Hon. Sir Humphrey Vicary, P.C., K.C.M.G., G.C.V.O., O.B.E.; b. 22 Nov. 1902; ed. Eton Coll., and Trinity Coll., Cambridge.
Farmer, Bulawayo 28-; Gov. Rhodesia (fmrly. S. Rhodesia) 60-June 69; Acting Gov.-Gen. Fed. of Rhodesia and Nyasaland 63; Hon. LL.D. (Birmingham), Hon. D.C.L. (E. Anglia).
P/Bag 5583W, Bonisa Farm, Bulawayo, Rhodesia.

Gichuru, James Samuel; Kenyan teacher and politician; b. 1914, Thogoto, Kiambu District; ed. Church of Scotland Missionary School, Kikuyu High School and Makerere Coll., Uganda.
Teacher, Kikuyu High School 35-40; Headmaster, Church of Scotland Mission School, Dagoretti, 40-50; Pres. Kenya African Union 44-47; Chief, Dagoretti location 50-52; under restriction order during state of emergency 55-60; Teacher, Roman Catholic Secondary School, Githunguri 58-60; Pres. Kenya African Nat. Union (KANU) 60-61, Vice-Pres. 66-; M.P. 61-; Minister of Finance April 62-63, of Finance and Econ. Planning 63, and Dec. 64; mem. of Govs. Kenyatta Foundation 66; Vice-Pres. for Central Province 66-69; Minister of Defence Dec. 69-.
Ministry of Defence, Nairobi; Thogoto, Kiambu, Kenya.

Gillet, Jean-François; French lawyer and administrator; b. 1923; ed. Secondary School, Limoges, and Univ. of Poitiers.
Barrister, Limoges Appeal Court 45-49; Gen. Sec. Grand Council of French Equatorial Africa 49-59; Gen. Sec. Chief of State's Conf., Equatorial Africa 59; mem. Board of Dirs. of the Equatorial Transport Agency 59-; Admin., Central African Higher Educ. Foundation 62-; Auditor Central Bank of Equatorial Countries and Cameroon 63-; Technical Adviser to the Gen. Sec. of Central African Econ. and Customs Union 66; several decorations.
Conférence des Chefs d'Etat de L'Afrique Equatoriale, P.O. Box 970, Bangui, Central African Republic.

Gizenga, Antoine; Zaire politician; b. 1925; ed. Congolese Seminary.
President, Parti de la Solidarité Africaine (P.S.A.); del. Brussels Round Table Conf. on Congolese independence, Dec. 59; Deputy Premier, Lumumba Cabinet June 60; dismissed by Pres. Kasavubu, Sept. 60; Pres. Orientale Province 60-62; Pres. P.S.A. 59-62; Deputy Premier, Congolese Repub. Aug. 61-Jan. 62; arrested Feb. 62; on Bolabemba Island at mouth of River Congo Feb. 63-June 64; founded United Lumumbist Party 64; mem. Senate; later went to Moscow 66.
Kinshasa, Zaire.

Gomwalk, Joseph Dechi, B.SC.; Nigerian police officer and military governor; b. 13 April 1935, Amper, Pankshin Div.; ed. Sudan United Mission Schools, Amper and Gindiri, Gindiri Secondary School, Nigerian Coll. of Arts, Sciences and Technology, and Univ. Coll., Ibadan.
Research Officer, Veterinary School, Mando Road, Kaduna June-Sept. 61; Northern Nigeria Admin. Service Oct. 61-Sept. 65; Fed. Admin. Service Nov. 65-Feb. 66; Nigerian Police Force 66; Mil. Gov. Benue-Plateau State May 67-.
Governor of Benue-Plateau State, Jos, Nigeria.

Gordimer, Nadine; South African writer; b. 20 Nov. 1923; ed. convent school.
Recipient of W. H. Smith Literary Award 61, Thomas Pringle Award (English Acad. of S.A.) 69, James Tait Black Memorial Award 72.
Publs. *The Soft Voice of the Serpent* (stories), *The Lying Days* (novel) 53, *Six Feet of the Country* (stories) 56, *A World of Strangers* (novel) 58, *Friday's Footprint* (stories) 60, *Occasion for Loving* (novel) 63, *Not For Publication* (stories) 65, *The Late Bourgeois World* (novel) 66; co-Editor *South African Writing Today* 67, *A Guest of Honour* (novel) 70, *Livingstone's Companions* (stories) 72.
7 Frere Road, Parktown, Johannesburg, South Africa. Telephone: 31-4369.

Goryunov, Dmitry Petrovich; Soviet journalist and diplomatist; b. 30 Sept. 1915, Kovrov, Vladimir; ed. Higher Party School.
Worked as lathe-turner in Kovrov and Ivanovo 30-40; mem. C.P.S.U. 40-, mem. Central Auditing Comm.; Editor youth paper *Lelinetz* 34; Leader, Ivanovo District Komsomol Cttee. (youth org.) 40-42; in charge of propa-

ganda, Central Cttee. H.Q. of Komsomol, Moscow 42-45; training at Party school 46-49; Editor *Komsomolskaya Pravda* 49-57; Asst. Editor *Pravda* 57-60; Dir.-Gen. *Tass* Agency 60-67; Amb. to Kenya 67-; Deputy to Supreme Soviet U.S.S.R. until 70; Alt. mem. of C.P.S.U. Central Cttee.; Order of Red Banner of Labour.
U.S.S.R. Embassy, P.O. Box 30049, Nairobi, Kenya.

Gowon, Gen. Yakubu; Nigerian army officer and Head of State; b. 19 Oct. 1934, Lur Pankshin Div., Benue Plateau State; ed. St. Bartholomew's School, Wusasa, Zaria, Govt. Coll., Zaria, Royal Military Acad., Sandhurst, Staff Coll., Camberley and Joint Services Coll., Latimer, England.
Adjutant, Nigerian Army March 60; with UN peace-keeping force, Congo 60-61, 63; Staff Officer, Army Head-quarters 61; promoted Lieut.-Col. and appointed Adjutant-Gen. Nigerian Army June 63; Commdr. 2nd Battalion 66; Chief of Staff 66; Head of Fed. Mil. Govt. and C.-in-C. of Armed Forces of Fed. Repub. of Nigeria Aug. 66-; Maj.-Gen. and Pres. Supreme Mil. Council June 67, concurrently Minister of Econ. Devt., Agriculture and Natural Resources; Gen. 71.
Supreme Headquarters, State House, Dodan Barracks, Lagos, Nigeria.

Graaff, Sir de Villiers, Bart., M.B.E., M.P.; South African politician; b. 8 Dec. 1913; ed. Univs. of Cape Town, Oxford and Leyden (Holland).
Served Second World War; M.P. 48-April 58, June 58-; Chair. United Party, Cape Province 56-58; Leader of the Opposition (United South African Nat. Party) 56-.
De Grendel, Pte. Bag G.P.O. Cape Town, Cape Province, South Africa.

Graham-Douglas, Nabo Bekinbo, LL.M., PH.D.; Nigerian lawyer; b. 15 July 1926, Abonnema; ed. Kalabari Nat. Coll., Buguma, Univ. Colls., Exeter and London, Inst. of Advanced Legal Studies, London.
Private practice, Legal Adviser to several Nigerian cos., Dir. B.P. Nigeria Ltd. until 66; Attorney-Gen., Eastern Nigeria March-Sept. 66; detained by rebels during Civil War 66-68; Envoy of Nigerian Govt. to U.K., U.S.A. to explain Civil War issues 68; Rivers State Attorney-Gen., Commr. for Justice 69-72; Fed. Attorney-Gen., Commr. for Justice Feb. 72-; Bencher, Head of Nigerian Bar, Chair. Gen. Council; mem. several legal cttees., Nigerian del. to 23rd UN Gen. Assembly, led del. to 6th UN Legal Cttee. 68; Sir Archibald Bodkin Prize, Bracton Prize (Exeter Univ.).
Publs. *Triumph or Turpitude? An Account of a Personal Involvement in the Nigerian Crisis 1966-1970, Forensic Aspects of Nigerian Land Law* 72, and several lectures on legal topics and social topics.
Federal Ministry of Justice, Marina, Lagos; and Orubibi Polo, Abonnema, Nigeria.

Grant, Walter Lawrence, D.SC., M.SC., C.E. & M.I.MECH.E., A.F.R.AE.S., M.(S.A.)I.M.E.; South African engineer; b. 22 Aug. 1922, Potchefstroom, Transvaal; ed. Witwaters-rand Technical Coll., Univs. of the Witwatersrand and Pretoria.
Head, Thermodynamic Div., Nat. Mechanical Eng. Research Inst. (N.M.E.R.I.), S. African Council for Scientific and Industrial Research (C.S.I.R.) 52-57, Dir. N.M.E.R.I. 57-59; Chief Engineer, S.A. Atomic Energy Board 59-64, Deputy Dir.-Gen. and Dir. of Reactor Eng. 64-67; Dir.-Gen. S.A. Atomic Energy Board 67-70, Deputy Pres. 70-71; Gen. Man. Uranium Enrichment Corpn. of S. Africa Ltd. 71-; Gold Medal, Inst. of Mechanical Eng. 58, Havenga Prize 66, Hendrik Verwoerd Award 71, and other awards.
Publs. 18 scientific publs. 53-70.
Uranium Enrichment Corporation of S.A. Ltd., P.O. Box 4587, Pretoria, Transvaal, South Africa.
Telephone: 79-4441 (Ext. 288).

Graylin, John Cranmer, C.M.G.; British (Rhodesian) lawyer and politician; b. 12 Jan. 1921; ed. Mid-Essex Technical Coll., Chelmsford, England, and Law Society School of Law, London.

Royal Air Force, Second World War; Solicitor 49; settled in N. Rhodesia 50; law practice, Livingstone 51-; Livingstone Municipal Councillor 52; mem. Fed. House of Parl. 53-63; Deputy Chair. of Cttees. 54; Minister of Agriculture 59-August 63 (resigned); Chair. Tobacco Export Promotion Council of Rhodesia 64-67; Chair., Nat. Export Council 67-69, Agricultural Assistance Board 68, Transportation Comm. 68-69, Transport Advisory Council 69; mem. Board Agric. Finance Corpn., Agric. Research Council; mem. Immigration Advisory Council; Chief Exec. Asscn. of Rhodesian Industries 69-.

Drew Road, Glen Lorne, Salisbury, Rhodesia.

Greatbatch, Sir Bruce, K.C.V.O., C.M.G., M.B.E.; British colonial administrator b. 10 June 1917, Warwicks.; ed. Malvern Coll. and Brasenose Coll., Oxford.

Appointed to Colonial Service, N. Nigeria 40; war service with Royal W. African Frontier Force 40-45; resumed colonial service, N. Nigeria 45, Resident 56, Sec. to Gov. and Exec. Council 57, Senior Resident, Kano 58; Sec. to Premier of N. Nigeria and Head of Regional Civil Service 59; Deputy High Commr. in Kenya 64; Gov. and C.-in-C. of the Seychelles and Commr. for the British Indian Ocean Territory 69-.

Government House, Victoria, Mahé, Seychelles; c/o National Provincial Bank Ltd., Cornmarket Street, Oxford, England.

Greene, James Edward; Liberian lawyer and politician; b. 6 July 1915, Greenville, Sinoe County; ed. St. Paul's High School, Greenville, Liberia Coll. (now Univ. of Liberia).

Teacher, Sinoe High School 41-49, Principal 49-52; joined 3rd Infantry Regiment, Liberian Army, Commdg. Officer 50-52; rank of Lt.-Col. 42, Col. 50; Superintendent, Sinoe County 52-61, Senator 61-72; Vice-Pres. of Liberia 72-; Nat. Vice-Chair., True Whig Party 63-67, Nat. Chair. 67-72; mem. Board of Trustees, Univ. of Liberia 62-; mem. Liberian Masonic Soc.; govt. del. to many int. confs.; Hon. LL.D. (Univ. of Liberia) 56; Grand Commdr., Order of the Star of Africa, Most Venerable Order of the Pioneers, Knight Commdr., Humane Order of African Redemption; Distinguished Service Award, and decorations from Cameroon, Gabon, Ivory Coast, Mauritania, Zaire and Fed. Repub. of Germany.

Office of the Vice-President, Monrovia, Liberia.

Greenfield, Julius Macdonald, C.M.G., Q.C., LL.B., B.C.L.; British (Rhodesian) lawyer and politician; b. 13 July 1907, Boksburg, Transvaal, S. Africa; ed. Milton School, Bulawayo, and Univs. of Cape Town and Oxford.

Rhodesian Rhodes Scholar 29; admitted to practise as advocate of High Court of S. Rhodesia 33, practised at Bulawayo till 50; elected to S. Rhodesia Parl. (United Party) 48; Minister of Justice and Internal Affairs 50-53; elected to Parl. of Fed. of Rhodesia and Nyasaland (Fed. Party) 53; Minister of Home Affairs and Educ. 53-55; Minister of Educ. and Law 55-58; Minister of Law 58-62, of Law and Home Affairs 62-63; returned to law practice 64; Puisne Judge of High Court of Rhodesia 68-.

P.O. Box 535, Bulawayo, Rhodesia.

Telephone: 88060.

Grimes, Joseph Rudolph, B.A., LL.B., M.I.A.; Liberian lawyer, diplomatist and politician; b. 31 Oct. 1923, Monrovia, Liberia; ed. Coll. of West Africa, Liberia Coll., Law School Harvard Univ. and Columbia Univ.

Cadet. Bureau of Public Health and Sanitation 38-42; Clerk, Exec. Mansion 42-47; Counsellor, Dept. of State 51-56; Dir. Louis Grimes School of Law, Liberia Univ. 54-58; Under-Sec. of State 56-60, Sec. of State 60-Jan. 72;

mem. Liberian Del. to Asian African Conf., Bandung 55, to Heads of African States Conf. 61, to 16th Session of UN Gen. Assembly; Most Venerable Order of the Pioneers, Knight Great Band, Humane Order of the African Redemption and other honours.

c/o Department of State, Monrovia, Liberia.

Grobbelaar, James Arthur; South African trade union leader; b. 24 Aug. 1925, Pretoria; ed. Pretoria Junior High School and Observatory Boys' High School, Cape.

Boilermaker by trade; Branch Official of S. African Boilermakers' Soc. 49-55, Nat. Organizer 55-59, Area Sec. 59-62, Admin. Sec. 62-64; Gen. Sec. Trade Union Council of S. Africa 64-.

Trade Union Council of South Africa, 4th Floor, Vulcan House, 88 Anderson Street, P.O. Box 5592, Johannesburg; Home: 48 Judith Road, Emmarentia, Johannesburg, South Africa.

Guede, Jean Lorougnon, L. ès sc., D. ès sc.; Ivory Coast politician; b. 25 Aug. 1935, Dalon; ed. Lyon, Paris.

Research chief, l'Office de la Recherche Scientifique et Technique Outre-Mer (ORSTOM); Deputy and Vice-Pres. Nat. Assembly 60-; Minister of Nat. Educ. Jan. 70-June 71, of Scientific Research June 71-; mem. Ruling Cttee. PDCI—RDA.

Ministry of Scientific Research, Abidjan, Ivory Coast.

Guillabert, André; Senegalese lawyer, politician and diplomatist; b. 15 June 1918; ed. Lycée Faidherbe, St. Louis-du-Sénégal, Faculté des Lettres, Bordeaux, and Faculté de Droit, Toulouse.

Lawyer, Dakar Court of Appeal 45-; Vice-Pres., Conseil Général du Sénégal 47-52; First Vice-Pres. Territorial Assembly, Senegal 52; Counsellor, Assembly of French Union 57-58; Senator (France) 58-59, Senator (French Community) 59-61; Vice-Pres. Constituent Assembly, Senegal 58-59, First Vice-Pres. Legislative Assembly 59, Nat. Assembly 60-62; Amb. to France 60-62, 66-; Minister of Foreign Affairs, Senegal 62; Keeper of the Seals and Minister of Justice 62-63; Deputy and Vice-Pres. Nat. Assembly, Senegal 63-66; Grand Officier Légion d'Honneur and many other decorations.

Ambassade du Sénégal, Square Pétrarque 2, Paris 16e, France; 47 avenue de la République, Dakar, Senegal.

Guissou, Henri; Upper Voltan diplomatist; b. 1910; ed. Ecole Primaire Supérieure, Ouagadougou, Ecole Normale William-Ponty, Dakar-Gorée.

Accountant, Office of Public Works, Abidjan 35-38; Head of Temporary Financial Office, Bobo-Dioulasso 42-43; Counsellor-Gen. of Upper Volta 48; Senator of Ivory Coast 47-48; Deputy of Upper Volta 48-56; Deputy to Nat. Assembly from Upper Volta 59; Amb. to France 61-63, 66-Oct. 72, to Fed. Repub. of Germany 64-66.

c/o Ministère des Affaires Etrangères, Ouagadougou, Upper Volta.

Gumane, Paulo; Mozambique nationalist leader.

Deputy Sec.-Gen. Frente de Libertação de Moçambique (F.R.E.L.I.M.O.) 62; expelled 62; reconstituted, with David Mabunda, União Democrática Nacional de Moçambique, Cairo May 63; now Pres. Comissão Revolucionário de Moçambique (C.O.R.E.M.O.).

Lusaka, Zambia.

Gusau, Alhaji Yahaya, O.B.E.; Nigerian politician; b. 1916, Gusau, Sokoto Province, N.W. State; ed. Gusau, Sokoto, Katsina Higher Coll. and Inst. of Educ., London Univ., England.

Teacher, Middle School, Kano and Bauchi Middle School, Govt. Coll., Kaduna and Zaria; Counsellor in charge of Educ., Sokoto Native Admin. 51; mem. House of Assembly and House of Reps. 52, resigned May 55; Educ. Officer 55-58; Sec. to Exec. Council of N. Nigeria 59-61; Perm. Sec. to Ministry of Internal Affairs 61, later to Ministry of

Justice; Provincial Sec. for Zaria Province 63; Perm. Sec.
to Ministry of Town and Country Planning 63-67; Fed.
Commr. for Econ. Devt., Agriculture and Natural
Resources 67-June 70; Dir. Nigerian Tobacco Co. 70-;
Chair. Kaduna Textiles Ltd. 70-, Northern States Market-
ing Board 70-, Nigeria Civil Aviation Training Centre;
mem. N.W. State Public Service Comm. June 72-.
Northern States Marketing Board, Yakubu Gowon Way,
Kaduna; Home: 6 Dawaki Road, G.R.A., Kaduna,
Nigeria.

H

Haak, Jan Friedrich Wilhelm; South African lawyer
and politician; b. 20 April 1917, Prince Albert; ed. Prince
Albert School and Univ. of Stellenbosch.
Attorney, Bellville, Cape Town 45-48; Advocate, Cape
Bar 60; Mayor of Bellville 49-51; M.P. 53-; Deputy
Minister of Econ. Affairs 61-64, Deputy Minister of Mines
June 62-64, Deputy Minister of Planning Dec. 62-64;
Minister of Mines and Planning Aug. 64-67, of Econ.
Affairs Jan. 67-May 70; mem. Chief Council of Nationalist
Party 51-; Dir. Iron and Steel Corpn. of S.A. and assoc.
companies, Trust Bank, Fed. Chem. Industries.
Governor Street 8, Welgemoed, Bellville, Republic of
South Africa.
Telephone: 973569.

Habte, Aklilu, PH.D.; Ethiopian educationist and uni-
versity administrator; b. 2 Sept. 1929, Addis Ababa;
ed. Univ. Coll. (now Haile Sellassie I Univ.), Univ. of
Manitoba, Canada, and Ohio State Univ., U.S.A.
Lecturer, Univ. Coll., Addis Ababa 58, Dean of Arts 61,
Dean of Educ. 62, Asst. Academic Vice-Pres. 64, Assoc.
Academic Vice-Pres. and Assoc. Prof. 67; Pres. Haile
Sellassie I Univ. (formerly Univ. Coll.) 69-.
Publs. papers on education, particularly Ethiopian
education.
Haile Sellassie I University, P.O. Box 1176, Addis Ababa,
Ethiopia.

Hag-Ali, Nasr el-, B.A.; Sudanese university official;
b. 1907; ed. Gordon Memorial Coll. and American Univ.
of Beirut.
On staff of Gordon Memorial Coll. 35-47; Vice-Principal,
Inst. of Educ., Ruda 47-51; Asst. Dir. (Personnel), Ministry
of Education 52-54, Dep. Dir. 54-56, Dir. 56-58; Vice-
Chancellor, Univ. of Khartoum 58-62; mem. Board of
Dirs., Barclays Bank Int. Ltd., Khartoum 62-; Assoc.
Univ. of London Inst. of Educ. 50; Hon. LL.D. Univ.
of Khartoum 67.
c/o Barclays Bank International Ltd., Gamhouria Avenue,
Khartoum, Sudan.

Haibak, Mokhtar Ould; Mauritanian politician.
Pres. Dir.-Gen. Soc. for the Equipment of Mauritania
(S.E.M.); Econ. and Financial Councillor to the Pres. of
the Repub. 64-68; mem. Econ. and Social Council May
67; Minister of Planning and Rural Devt. 68-70, of
Finance 70-Aug. 71; sentenced to 18 months imprisonment
for corruption June 72.
c/o Ministry of Finance, Nouakchott, Mauritania.

Haile, Dr. Minassie; Ethiopian diplomatist and politician.
Former Political Adviser to Emperor; later Amb. to
U.S.A.; Minister of Foreign Affairs Aug. 71-.
Ministry of Foreign Affairs, P.O. Box 393, Addis Ababa,
Ethiopia.

Haile Sellassie I, His Imperial Majesty; Emperor of
Ethiopia, K.G. (original name Ras Tafari Makonnen);
b. 23 July 1892.
Proclaimed Regent and Heir to Imperial Throne 16;
invested with Grand Cordon of the Order of Solomon;

took Ethiopia to League of Nations 23; proclaimed
abolition of slavery 24; proclaimed King 28; proclaimed
Emperor after death of Empress Zauditu 30; established
Constitution 31; following invasion by Italy 35 forced
to quit Addis Ababa 36; appeared personally before
League of Nations 36; lived in England till 40; rallied
refugee patriots in Kenya and Sudan and crossed the
frontier 41; reinstated in capital 41; reorganized Govt.,
reopened Parl., reinstituted State Bank of Ethiopia 42;
proclaimed new currency, established airlines, opened
roads, reorganized army, navy and air force, built numerous schools, expanded industry and agriculture, founded
the Univ. Coll. of Addis Ababa and other colleges, organized a judiciary system, codified law and revised the
Constitution 55, entered into diplomatic relations with most
of the important nations of the world; secured reintegration of Eritrea 52; Grand Cross of the Order of the Legion
of Honour; of the Annunsiata; of Leopold, Belgium; of the
Lion d'Or de la Maison de Nassau, Luxembourg; Nether-
lands Order of Orange-Nassau; Danish Order of the
Elephant; Brazilian Order of San Sebastian Guillaume;
Mexican Order of the Aztec Eagle, Order of Military
Merit of the Federal Republic of Germany; Order of the
Star of Yugoslavia; Order of Military Merit of France;
Order of Mohammed Ali of Egypt; Swedish Order of the
Seraphim; Norwegian Order of St. Olaf; Greek Order of the
Saviour; Order of Merit of the Italian Repub.; Order of
Suvorov U.S.S.R.; 1st Class Mil. Order of the White Lion
Czechoslovakia; Ribbon of the Grand Cross of the Three
Orders Portugal; Sudan Order of the Republic 1st Class;
K.G., G.C.B. (Hon.); G.C.M.G. (Hon.); G.C.V.O. (Hon.);
LL.D. (Hon.) Cantab., Columbia, Howard, McGill,
Montreal, Michigan, Athens, Laval, Banaras, Moscow,
Charles; D.C.L. (Hon.) Oxford; Hon. LL.D. (Ag.) Bonn.
Publ. *My Life and Ethiopia's Progress* 72.
The Imperial Palace, Addis Ababa, Ethiopia.

Hamoni, Mohamed Lemine Ould; Mauritanian lawyer
and politician; b. 1923; ed. schools at Atar and Boutilimit,
Mauritania and Institut des Hautes Études, Paris.
Civil servant 60-62; Commissaire Gen. of Plan 63-65; Pres.
of Supreme Court of Mauritania 65-66; Minister of Justice
and the Interior 66-67; Pres. Econ. and Social Council 67-;
Contrôleur d'Etat, with rank of Minister 68-.
Assemblée Nationale, Nouakchott, Mauritania.

Harlley, John Willie Kofi; Ghanaian politician and for-
mer police officer; b. 9 May 1919, Akagla, Volta Region;
ed. Presbyterian School, Akropong-Akwapim, Anloga
Presbyterian School and Accra Acad.
Interpreter, District Magistrate's Court, later at Supreme
Court, Accra; joined Ghana Police Service May 40, Insp.
Nov. 52-April 53, Asst. Supt. April 53-July 57, Deputy
Supt. July 57-Nov. 57, Supt. Nov. 57-July 59, Chief
Supt. July 59-Aug. 60, Asst. Commr. Aug. 60-Jan. 65,
Commr. Jan. 65-Feb. 66, Insp.-Gen. Feb. 66-Sept. 69;
fmr. Head of Special Branch; Deputy Chair. Nat. Libera-
tion Council (N.L.C.) Feb. 66-June 66; Minister of Interior
and Information, Secretariat and Depts. under N.L.C.
June 66-March 67; Minister of External Affairs, con-
currently with other appointments March 67-June 67;
Minister of External and Internal Affairs and Chieftaincy
Affairs Secretariat June 67-Feb. 68; Minister of Interior
Feb. 68-April 69; Minister of Interior and Chieftaincy
Affairs April 69; Deputy Chair. Presidential Comm. until
Sept 70; retd. from Police Service Sept. 69; Officer, Order
of the Volta (O.V.).

Harriman, Leslie Oriseweyinmi; Nigerian diplomatist;
b. 9 July 1930, Wari; ed. Govt. School, Benin, Govt. Coll.,
Ibadan, Edo Coll., Benin, Univ. Coll., Ibadan, Pembroke
Coll., Oxford, England and Imperial Defence Coll.,
London.
Manager, Unilever, Lagos 55-58; Second Sec. British

Embassy, Spain 58-59; Counsellor and Acting High Commr. for Nigeria in Ghana 61-63; Deputy Perm. Sec. Ministry of External Affairs 65-66; High Commr. to Uganda 66-69, to Kenya 66-70; Amb. to France April 70-. Embassy of Nigeria, 49 avenue Kléber, Paris 16e, France; Home: 22 avenue du Parc St. James, (92) Neuilly-sur-Seine, France.

Hartwell, Dulcie Marie; South African trade union leader; b. 1915; ed. Public Schools in Transvaal and Dominican Convents at Newcastle, Natal, Pietersburg, and Boksburg.
Dress machinist in clothing factories and Chair. Dress-makers' Branch; Vice-Pres. of Garment Workers' Union of South Africa 33-37; Asst. Gen. Sec. of the Union 37-39; Sec. Unemployment Insurance Fund for the Clothing Industry 39-50; Sec. Medical Aid Soc. for Clothing Industry 41-50; Joint Gen. Sec. S.A. Trades and Labour Council 51-53, Gen. Sec. 53-54, when this was dissolved Gen. Sec. of the S.A. Trades Union Council 55-61; hon. mem. S.A. Boilermakers, Iron and Steel Workers and Ship Builders' Soc. 55-; Sec. Nat. Union of Commercial Travellers 65-67; Sec. Witwatersrand Branch Nat. Union of Distributive Workers 67-, also Vice Pres. 70-.
Douglas Court, 62 Noord Street, Johannesburg, Transvaal, South Africa.

Haskins, James George, O.B.E., J.P.; Botswana politician; b. 24 April 1914, Bulawayo, Rhodesia; ed. Plumtree School.
Worked as business trainee, J. W. Jagger and Co. Ltd. 35-42; served with South African Service Corps and 4th Battalion (Wits.) Reserve Brigade 42-46; Vice-Chair. European and mem. Joint Advisory Councils 48-61; mem. Legislative Council 61-64 (Batawana-Chobe constituency); fmr. mem. Exec. Council, Constitutional Cttee. on Self-Govt., Rhodesia Railways Central Consultative Cttee.; later Botswana Rep. and mem. Rhodesia Railways Board 57-61; fmr. Chair. Finance and Public Accounts Cttees., Francistown Agricultural Soc.; del. to Commonwealth Parliamentary Asscn., U.K. 63; Trustee, Botswana Nat. Sports Appeal Fund; specially elected mem. Nat. (fmrly. Legislative) Assembly March 66-; Minister of Commerce, Industry and Water Affairs, of Finance Oct. 69-June 70; Minister of Agriculture June 70; now Minister of Works and Communications; Treas. Botswana Democratic Party; Hon. life mem. Botswana Red Cross Soc.
Ministry of Works and Communications, P. Bag 7, Gaborone; and c/o J. Haskins and Sons (Pty.) Ltd., Haskins Street, P.O. Box 1, Francistown; Home: 292/3 North Ring Road, Gaborone, Botswana.

Hassan, Moulaye al-; Mauritanian diplomatist; ed. Inst. of Admin. Studies, Faculty of Law, Univ. of Dakar.
Chief of Protocol, Ministry of Foreign Affairs 60-68; Consul-Gen. Mali 68-70; Amb. to Ivory Coast 70-71; Perm. Rep. to UN Sept. 71-; del. to UN Gen. Assembly 68.
Permanent Mission of Mauritania to United Nations, 8 West 40th Street, 18th Floor, New York, N.Y. 10018, U.S.A.

Hassan, Brig. Usman Katsina; Nigerian army officer; b. 1933, Katsina, N. Nigeria; ed. Kaduna Coll., Nigerian Coll. of Arts, Science and Technology, Regular Officers' Training School, Ghana, Royal Military Acad., Sandhurst, England, Cadet School, Aldershot, England.
Enlisted in army 56; commissioned 58; Chief of Staff until Feb. 72; now studying at Royal Coll. of Defence Studies, London.
Royal College of Defence Studies, Seaford House, 37 Belgrave Square, London, S.W.1, England.

Hawkins, Roger Tancred Robert; Rhodesian politician; b. 1915, Letchworth, England; ed. England.
Mined on smallworkings 36-39; commissioned 40, served with 1st Battalion, Northern Rhodesia Regiment in

East Africa and Burma; foundation mem. of Rhodesian Front Party; M.P. for Charter Constituency 64-; mem. Exec. Cttee. of Rhodesian Chamber of Mines 64-66; fmr. Chair. Rhodesian Mining Fed.; fmr. Pres. Gwanda and South Western Districts Regional Devt. and Publicity Asscn.; fmr. mem. Gwanda Town Management Board, Mining Affairs Board, Mining Promotion Council; mem. cttee. to consider establishment of school of mines, Bulawayo; Minister of Roads and Road Traffic and Transport and Power April 70-.
Ministry of Roads and Road Traffic and Transport and Power, Salisbury, Rhodesia.

Haydon, Walter Robert, C.M.G.; British diplomatist; b. 29 May 1920; ed. Dover Grammar School.
H.M. Forces 39-45; served Berne 46-47, Foreign Office 47-48, Turin 48-52; Vice-Consul 50; Vice-Consul, Sofia 52-53; Second Sec., Bangkok 53-56; First Sec. and Head of Chancery, Khartoum 58-61; First Sec. (Public Relations), U.K. Mission to UN, New York 61; Counsellor, Washington 65-67; Head of News Dept., Foreign and Commonwealth Office 67-71; High Commr. in Malawi 71-.
British High Commission, P.O. Box 479, Blantyre, Malawi.

Hein, Jacques Paul, M.A.; Mauritius lawyer and businessman; b. 2 Oct. 1924; ed. Royal Coll., Curepipe, Oxford Univ., and Middle Temple, London.
Soldier, British army (Royal Fusiliers) 44-47, attached to Mauritius forces in Middle East 46; called to the Bar 50; Man. Sec., Réunion Sugar Estate 57-69; Pres., Albion Dock 65-69; Pres., Mauritius Lawn Tennis Asscn. several times; Attorney-Gen. Dec. 69; Minister of Justice Nov. 70-.
Office of the Attorney General, Port Louis, Mauritius.

Henries, Richard Abrom, B.A., LL.D., D.C.L.; Liberian politician and administrator; b. 16 Sept. 1908, Monrovia; ed. Liberia Coll. (now Univ. of Liberia).
Professor of Mathematics, Liberia Coll. 32; Chief Clerk, Commonwealth District of Monrovia (Monrovia City Council) 33-34, Treasury Dept. 34-38; Supervisor of Schools, Sinoe and Maryland Counties 38-43; mem. House of Reps. (True Whig Party) 43-, Speaker 51-; Local Chair. TWP 44-46, later Leader of TWP Org., now TWP Legal Adviser; Pres. Board of Trustees, Univ. of Liberia 52-; Pres. Liberian Group, Inter-Parl. Union 58-, Liberian Nat. Bar Asscn. 59-; Henries Law Firm; has represented Liberia abroad; awarded all Liberian decorations including Grand Cordon, Venerable Order of the Pioneer, and numerous foreign decorations.
Publs. *Liberia, the West African Republic, The Liberian Nation.*
Office of the Speaker, House of Representatives, Monrovia, Liberia.

Hertzog, Albert, B.A., B.C.L., LL.D.; South African advocate and politician; b. 14 July 1899, Bloemfontein; s. of Gen. J. B. M. Hertzog; ed. Stellenbosch, Amsterdam, Oxford and Leyden Univs.
Member of the Council of the Univ. of S. Africa 36-39; mem. Pretoria City Council 44-51; elected M.P. for Ermelo 48, 53, 58, 61 and 66; foundation mem. of Afrikaanse Pers Beperk and Volkskas Beperk; Minister of Posts and Telegraphs, and of Health 58-68; Leader Herstigte Nasionale Party Oct. 69-.
Publ. *Saaklike Reg en Eiendom.*
10 Edward Street, Waterkloof, Pretoria, South Africa.

Heyns, Ockert Stephanus, M.A., D.SC., F.R.C.O.G., F.I.C.S.; South African obstetrician and gynaecologist; b. 27 Nov. 1906, Paarl, Cape Province; ed. Univs. of Cape Town, London and Edinburgh, Queen's Univ. (Belfast), and Univs. of Manchester and Witwatersrand.
Senior Lecturer, Univ. of Witwatersrand 39, Prof. of Obstetrics and Gynaecology 47-67, with accompanying clinical posts of Chief Obstetrician and Gynaecologist; Prof. Emer. 68-, and Hon. Consultant to Hospital;

Research in three phases: (i) bony pelvis, (ii) uterine action, (iii) abdominal decompression in labour and pregnancy (improving foetal development); Academician, South African Acad.; Corresp. mem. Soc. Royale Belge; Havenga Prize; David Hillman Fellow; Int. Soc. of Reproductive Biology.

Publs. include monograph on abdominal decompression, book on "Decompression Babies".

Whiteleaf, Hermanus, South Africa.

Telephone: Hermanus 276.

Hlophe, Abednigo Kuseni; Swazi politician; b. 13 Jan. 1922, Lozitha; ed. Zombode and Matsapa Nat. School and St. Chad's Coll., Natal.

Worked as teacher, Zombode; employed by Malaria Control Unit, Swaziland Medical Dept. and by Johannesburg City Council; clerk to the standing cttee. of the Swazi Nat. Council; fmr. Private Sec. to the Ngwenyama; Swazi Nat. Rep., Swaziland Constitutional Cttee. 61-63; del. Constitutional Confs. in London Jan. and July 63; elected to Nat. Roll seat, Manzini Constituency June 64; mem. for Local Admin. and Social Devt., Exec. Council 64-65, mem. for Urban Affairs 65; attended Independence Conf. 68; now Minister of Agriculture.

Ministry of Agriculture, Mbabane, Swaziland.

Holas, B. (Théophile); French ethnologist; b. 28 Sept. 1909; ed. Univ. de Paris à la Sorbonne.

Directeur, Centre des Sciences humaines, Abidjan; Curator, Nat. Museum of Ivory Coast; scientific missions in Africa, North and South America, Far East and Oceania; mem. Acad. des Sciences d'Outre-Mer, Int. African Inst., London, Soc. des Gens de Lettres, Paris; Commdr. de l'Ordre Nat. and several other awards.

Publs. *Mission dans l'Est libérien* 52, *Les masques kono* 52, *Le Culte de Zié* 55, *Les Sénoufo* 57, *Cultures matérielles de la Côte d'Ivoire* 60, *Changements sociaux* 61, *Les Toura* 62, *La Côte d'Ivoire: passé, présent, perspectives* 64, *La sculpture Sénoufo* 64, *Les religions de l'Afrique noire* 64, *La séparatisme religieux en Afrique noire* 65, *Industries et cultures en Côte d'Ivoire* 65, *Arts de la Côte d'Ivoire* 66, *Craft and Culture in the Ivory Coast* 68, *L'image du monde bété* 68, *Les dieux d'Afrique noire* 68, *La pensée africaine* 72.

B.P. 1600, Abidjan, Ivory Coast; and 12 rue Vavin, Paris 6e, France.

Holloway, J. E., B.A., D.SC.(ECON.); South African businessman and diplomatist; b. 4 July 1890, Hopetown District; ed. Victoria Coll., Ghent Univ. and London School of Economics.

Lecturer Grey Univ. Coll. 19; Lecturer and later Prof. of Econs., Transvaal Univ. Coll.; Dean Commerce Faculty of Univ. of South Africa 21-25; Dir. of Census and Statistics 25-33; Chair. Native Econ. Comm. 30-32 and Customs Tariff Comm. 34-35; mem. S.W. Africa Comm. 35-36; Adviser Ottawa Conf. 32, World Econ. Conf. 33, Imperial Conf. 37, Montreal Conf. 58; Econ. Adviser to Treasury 34-37; Perm. Head of Treasury 37-50; Del. Monetary Conf. Bretton Woods 44; Chair. Cttee. Gold Mining Taxation 45; Alternate Gov. Int. Monetary Fund 48-52; Leader, South African Del., Int. Conf. on Trade and Employment, Geneva 47, Havana 48; fmr. Dir. (now cons.) of Barclays Bank Int. Ltd. (South African Board); Dir. African Batignolles Construction (Pty.) Ltd., French Corpn. of S.A. Ltd., Swiss-Union Trust for S.A. (Pty.) Ltd., Anglo-Alpha Cement Ltd.; Consultant, Union Corpn. Ltd.; Chair. S.W. Africa Financial Comm. 51; Univs. Financial Comm. 51-53 and Comm. on univ. facilities for non-Europeans 53-54; mem. Comm. regarding Europeans in Transkei, Pretoria Univ. Council, S.A. Foundation; Amb. to U.S.A. 54-56; High Commr. in U.K. 56-58; Leader, South African Trade Mission to Europe 61; Hutchinson Research Medallist; Hon. LL.D. and D.Comm.

Publs. *The Debacle of Money, Gold or Authoritarian Money?*

Apartheid—A Challenge (also in French and Dutch) and articles on monetary systems and race relations in various journals.

Union Corporation Buildings, 74 Marshall Street, Johannesburg; Home: 1 Rockridge Road, Parktown, Johannesburg, South Africa.

Telephone: 838-8281 (Office).

Horton, Alexander Romeo; Liberian banker; b. 20 Aug. 1923; ed. B.W.I. Inst. Coll. of West Africa, Morehouse Coll., Atlanta, U.S.A. and Wharton School of Finance and Commerce, Pennsylvania Univ.

Founder and Pres. Bank of Liberia 54-; Asst. Econ. Adviser to Liberian Pres. 54-64; Chair. Steering Cttee. of Conf. of African Businessman 60; Chair. ECA Cttee. of Nine African Countries on Development Bank for Africa 62-63; Sec. of Commerce and Industry, Liberia 64-68; Chair. Monrovia Bankers' Asscn.; has attended numerous int. confs.; Hon. LL.D. (Atlanta); decorations include Knight Commdr. Order of African Redemption, Officier Nat. Order of Ivory Coast, Grand Commdr. Order of Star of Africa, Grand Band Order of Star of Africa, Grand Cross Order of Orange Nassau.

The Bank of Liberia, P.O. Box 131, Monrovia, Liberia.

Horwood, Owen Pieter Faure, B.COM.; South African economist and politician; b. 6 Dec. 1916, Somerset West; ed. Boys' High School, Paarl, Univ. of Cape Town.

Associate Prof. of Commerce, Univ. of Cape Town 54-56; Prof. of Econs., Univ. Coll. of Rhodesia and Nyasaland 56-57; Prof. of Econs., Univ. of Natal 57-65, Principal, Vice-Chancellor 66-70; Senator, Dir. of Cos. 70-; Minister of Indian Affairs and Tourism 72-; Pres. Econ. Soc. of South Africa 64-65; Chair., mem. several govt. comms. including Sugar Industry Comm. 67-69, Universities Comm. 68-72; Gen. Editor, *Natal Regional Survey Publs.* 58-69.

Publs. *Economic Systems of the Commonwealth* (co-author) 62, and numerous articles on economics and finance in professional journals.

Private Bag X364, Pretoria; Home: Bryntirion, Pretoria, South Africa.

Houphouët-Boigny, Félix; Ivory Coast politician; b. 18 Oct. 1905, Yamoussoukro; ed. School of Medicine, Dakar.

Doctor, Medical Assistance Service 25-40; Canton Chief 40; Pres. Syndicat Agricole Africain 44; mem. Constituent Assembly 45-46; mem. Nat. Assembly Nov. 46-, re-elected 51 and 56; successively Territorial Councillor for Korhogo, Pres. Territorial Assembly, Ivory Coast, Grand Conseiller for French West Africa; Minister attached to the Prime Minister's Office 56-57; Minister of Health 57-58; Minister of State (Pflimlin Cabinet) May 58, (de Gaulle Cabinet) June 58-Jan. 59, (Debré Cabinet) Jan.-May 59; Pres. Assembly, Ivory Coast Repub. 58-59; Minister-Counsellor to French Govt. 59-60; Pres. Council May 59-Nov. 60; Pres. of the Repub. Nov. 60-, fmrly. Minister of Foreign Affairs 61, and of Interior, Educ. and Agriculture 63; now Pres. Council of Ministers, Minister of Defence 63-, concurrently of Nat. Educ. 71-72; Pres. Parti Démocratique de la Côte d'Ivoire.

Présidence de la République, Abidjan, Ivory Coast, West Africa.

Howman, John H.; Rhodesian lawyer and politician; b. 11 Aug. 1918, Selukwe; ed. Plumtree School, Bulawayo. Partner, Coghlan, Welsh & Guest (law firm); mem. of Parl., Minister of Information, Immigration and Tourism Sept. 68; Minister of Foreign Affairs, Defence and Public Service 68-.

Ministry of Foreign Affairs, Salisbury, Rhodesia.

Human, Cornelis J. F.; South African businessman; b. 1922; ed. Reitz High School and Stellenbosch Univ.

Worked as clerk, Federale Volksbeleggings Beperk 47,

later Sec. Johannesburg Branch, Gen. Man. 59-66, Man. Dir. 66-; Trustee, Nat. Botanical Gardens of South Africa, South African Nature Foundation and South African Foundation; Pres. Die Afrikaanse Handelsinstituut, mem. Atomic Energy Board and Board of Stellenbosch Univ.
"Alvista", Camp's Bay, South Africa.

Hunlédé, Joachim, L. en D.; Togolese politician; b. 2 Feb. 1925, Anécho.
Assistant Insp. of schools, Northern Togo, then teacher at Ecole Normale d'Atakpamé 53-56; worked for French Overseas Territories Admin. 58; Asst. Admin. Mayor, Lomé; Chief, admin. subdivision of Tabligbo; Admin. Mayor of Tsévié; Amb. to France, U.K., EEC Sept. 60-July 65; High Commr. for Planning Sept. 65-April 67; Minister of Foreign Affairs April 67-.
Ministry of Foreign Affairs, Lomé, Togo.

Hurd, John Gavin, A.B., LL.B.; American diplomatist; b. 2 July 1914, Sacramento, Calif.; ed. Harvard Univ.
Associated with law firm, Pillsbury, Madison and Sutro, San Francisco, Calif. 37-39; worked in Land and Legal Dept. and Employee and Personnel Dept., Standard Oil Co. of California 39-41; U.S. Navy 41-46; Commdr. U.S.N. Reserve (retd.); partner, Killam and Hurd Ltd., independent oil producer, cattle rancher and investments 46-; U.S. Amb. to South Africa Sept. 70-.
American Embassy, Pretorius Street, Pretoria, South Africa.

Hussein, Abdirizak Haji; Somali politician; b. 1920.
Joined Somali Youth League 44, Pres. 55-56; Minister of Interior, later of Works and Communications 60-64; Prime Minister 64-67; Pres. Univ. Inst., Mogadishu.
University Institute, Mogadishu, Somalia.

I

Ibingira, Grace S., LL.B.; Ugandan diplomatist; b. 23 May 1932; ed. Mbarara High School, King's Coll., Budo, Univ. of Wales and King's Coll., London.
Called to Bar, Middle Temple 59; practised law in Uganda as advocate of the High Court until 62; Minister of Justice 62; Minister of State and Sec.-Gen., Uganda People's Congress 64-66; detained without trial 66-71; Perm. Rep. to UN July 71-.
Permanent Mission of Uganda to United Nations, 801 Second Avenue, New York, N.Y. 100017, U.S.A.

Ibrahim, Major Abu al-Qassim Mohammed; Sudanese army officer and politician; b. 1937, Omdurman; ed. Khartoum Secondary School and Military Coll.
Commissioned 61; mem. Revolutionary Council 69; Minister of Local Govt. 69; Asst. Prime Minister for Services July 70; Minister of Interior Nov. 70; Minister of Health Oct. 71-.
Ministry of Health, Khartoum, Sudan.

Ibrahim, Sir Kashim, K.C.M.G., C.B.E.; Nigerian politician; b. 10 June 1910; ed. Bornu Provincial School, Katsina Teachers' Training Coll.
Teacher 29-32; Visiting Teacher 33-49; Educ. Officer 49-52; Central Minister of Social Service 52-55; Northern Regional Minister of Social Development and Surveys 55-56; Waziri of Bornu 56-62; Gov. of Northern Nigeria 62-66; Chair. Nigerian Coll. of Arts, Science and Technology 58-62, Provincial Council of Ahmadu Bello Univ. 61-62; Adviser to Mil. Gov. of Northern Nigeria 66; Chancellor, Ibadan Univ. 67-; Grand Cross Order of the Niger.
Publs. *Kanuri Reader Elementary I-IV*, *Kanuri Arithmetic Books I-IV for Elementary Schools.*
University of Ibadan, Ibadan, Western Nigeria, Nigeria.

Idzumbuir, Théodore; Zaire diplomatist; b. 9 Nov. 1930; ed. Lovanium-Kisantu Inst., Mayidi Seminary and Inst. of International Studies, Geneva.
Minister Plenipotentiary, Perm. Rep. of the Dem. Repub. of Congo (now Zaire) to the UN 63-71; Vice-Pres. UN Gen. Assembly 67; Nat. Order of Leopard 66.
c/o Ministry of Foreign Affairs, Kinshasa, Zaire.

Ignacio-Pinto, Louis, D. en D., D. ès L.; Dahomeyan diplomatist and judge; b. 1903; ed. Ecole St. Gènes, Bordeaux and Univs. of Bordeaux and Paris.
Officer-Cadet 31-32; engaged in starch manufacture 33-36; junior counsel, Paris Court of Appeal 37-39; war service in Lorraine 39-40; Counsel, Conakry 40-46; resistance worker; Rep. of Dahomey to French Senate 46-56; Vice-Pres. Comm., France d'Outre Mer 46-56; Minister of Econs. Commerce and Industry, Dahomey 57-58; Minister of Justice 58-59; returned to legal profession 59; Counsellor, French Embassy, Vatican City 60; Ambassador of Dahomey to UN, New York 60-67, Amb. of Dahomey to U.S.A. 60-67; Pres. of Supreme Court of Dahomey 67-; Judge, Admin. Tribunal of UN; Judge Int. Court of Justice 70-.
International Court of Justice, The Hague, Netherlands.

Ike, Vincent Chukwuemeka; Nigerian academic official; b. 28 April 1931, Ndikelionwu, Awka, Eastern Nigeria; ed. Govt. Coll. Umuahia, Univ. Coll. Ibadan and Stanford Univ., U.S.A.
Various teaching posts, Nigeria 50-51, 55-56; Hon. Regional Organizing Sec., Student Christian Movt. of Nigeria 55-56; Admin. Asst., Asst. Registrar, Univ. of Ibadan 57-60; Deputy Registrar, Univ. of Nigeria, Nsukka 60-63; Registrar, Univ. of Nigeria, Nsukka 63-71; Registrar, West African Examinations Council, Accra, Ghana Aug. 71-; Chair. Planning and Management Cttee., Univ. of Nigeria, Jan.-Nov. 70; Dir. The Daily Times of Nigeria Ltd.; Nat. Patron, World Univ. Service, Nigeria; official of other orgs.
Publs. *Toads for Supper* (novel) 65, *The Naked Gods* (novel) 70; short stories.
The West African Examinations Council, Headquarters Office, P.O. Box 125, Accra, Ghana.

Ikonga, Auxence; Congolese politician.
Former prefect of Sangha; fmr. Dir., Gen. Admin.; fmr. Dir. Cabinet of Ministry of Foreign Affairs; Amb. to U.A.R. Nov. 66-June 69; Minister of Equipment, responsible for Agriculture, Water Resources and Forests June 69-70, of Foreign Affairs 70-72; Amb. to France Oct. 72-.
Embassy of People's Republic of the Congo, 57 bis, rue Scneffer, Paris 16e, France.

Ileo, Joseph; Zaire politician; b. 15 Sept. 1921, Kinshasa; ed. philosophy and sociology in Europe.
Held post in African Territories Div. of Belgian Gov.-General's Office; active in movement for independence, signatory of the "Memorandum of the Sixteen" 58; formed Congolese Nat. Movement Party with Patrice Lumumba; joined Abako Party 59; former Editor *The African Conscience;* Head of Congolese Senate July 60-Sept. 60; Premier Sept. 60-Aug. 61; Minister of Information and Cultural Affairs Aug. 61-62; Minister without Portfolio in charge Katangese Affairs 63-64; mem. of the Political Bureau and Pres. of the Nat. Research Office.
B.P. 3474, Kinshasa, Zaire.
Telephone: 2452.

Isong, Clement Nyong, PH.D.; Nigerian banker; b. 20 April 1920, Ikot Osong, S.E. Nigeria; ed. Methodist Coll., Uzuakoli, Univ. Coll., Ibadan, Iowa Wesleyan Coll. and Harvard Univ.
Primary school teacher 40, headmaster 41-45; secondary school master 46-51; Asst. Economist 57; Lecturer, Univ. Coll., Ibadan 58; Sec. Central Bank of Nigeria 61-62; Adviser, African Dept., Int. Monetary Fund, Washington,

D.C. 62-67; Gov. Central Bank of Nigeria 67-; Alt. Gov. for Nigeria, Int. Monetary Fund; Chair. Board of Dirs., Central Bank of Nigeria; Chair. Bankers Cttee. Meeting. Office: Central Bank of Nigeria, Tinubu Square, Private Mail Bag 12194, Lagos; Home: 6 Queen's Drive, Ikoyi, Lagos, Nigeria.

Issaka, Amadou; Niger politician; b. 1924, Kantché. Chief of Kantché District; Regional Councillor 46, Territorial Councillor, Zinder 46-52, Magaria 57; M.P. for Magaria 58-65; mem. Niger Assembly 58; Senator of the French Community 59-60; Minister of the Civil Service and Labour Nov. 65-Jan. 70; Minister of Justice Jan. 70-Jan. 71; Minister-Del. to Presidency of Repub. 71-72; Minister of Econ. Affairs, Commerce and Industry Aug. 72-. Ministry of Economic Affairs, Commerce and Industry, Niamey, Niger.

J

Jack, Alieu Sulayman; Gambian politician; b. 1922, Bathurst; ed. R.C. mission school. Joined Civil Service 39; mem. Bathurst Town Council 50; Speaker (Pres.), House of Assembly until 72; Minister of Works and Communications April 72-. Ministry of Works and Communications, Bathurst, The Gambia.

Jamal, Amir Habib, B.COMM.(ECON.); Tanzanian politician; b. 26 Jan. 1922, Dar es Salaam; ed. primary school, Mwanza, secondary school, Dar es Salaam, and Univ. of Calcutta, India. Elected mem. Tanganyika Legislative Council 58; Minister of Urban Local Govt. and Works 59, of Communications, Power and Works 60; Minister of State, President's Office, Directorate of Devt. 64; re-elected M.P. 65; Minister of Finance 65-72, of Commerce and Industry 72-. 109c Msasani, P.O. Box 234 Dar es Salaam, United Republic of Tanzania.

Japhet, Siméon; Malagasy doctor and politician; b. 17 Feb. 1906, Tamatave Province; ed. Tamatave School of Medicine. Served as doctor, Medical Assistance Service; mem. Social Democratic Party 56-; municipal councillor, Tamatave 59; mem. Upper House Oct. 60-; Vice-Pres. of the Senate May 64-Dec. 64; Pres. of the Senate Dec. 64-. Office of the President, Tananarive, Malagasy Republic.

Jawara, Hon. Sir Dawda Kairaba, Kt., M.P., M.R.C.V.S., D.T.V.M.; Gambian politician; b. 11 May 1924, Barajally, MacCarthy Island; ed. Muslim Primary School, Methodist Boys' Grammar School, Bathurst, Achimota Coll. and Glasgow Univ. Veterinary Officer, Kombo St. Mary 54-60; Leader, People's Progressive Pty. 60-; Minister of Educ. 60-61; Premier 62-63; Prime Minister 63-70; Pres. of Repub. of Gambia April 70-; numerous decorations. State House, Bathurst, The Gambia.

Johnson, Brig. Mobolaji Olufunso; Nigerian army officer; b. 9 Feb. 1936, Lagos; ed. Methodist Boys' High School, Lagos, Officer-Cadet Training School, Ghana, Mons Officers' Cadet School, Aldershot, England, Zaria Military Depot and Royal Military Acad., Sandhurst, England. Enlisted in army March 58; Mil. Gov. Lagos State May 67-; Lt.-Col. June 67, Col. March 68, Acting Brig.-Gen. Oct. 72. c/o Ministry of Defence, Lagos, Nigeria.

Jonathan, Chief Joseph Leabua; Basuto politician; b. 30 Oct. 1914; ed. Mission School, Leribe. Worked in mines in South Africa 34-37; returned to Basutoland 37; Court Pres. 38; entered politics 52; mem. District Council 54; mem. Nat. Council 54; mem. Panel of 18 56-59; founded Basutoland Nat. Party 59, Leader 59-; mem.

Legislative Council 60-64; Del. at Constitutional Conf. 64; Prime Minister of Basutoland (now Lesotho) and Minister of External Affairs 65-, also Minister of Defence, Internal Security and Chief of Electoral Affairs March 70-. Prime Minister's Office, P.O. Box 527, Kaseru, Lesotho.

Jones, Ernest Cyril Brieley; Liberian administrator and politician; b. 1896; ed. Tuskegee Institute, Tuskegee, Alabama, U.S.A. Vocational Arts Instructor, Prairie View State Coll., Texas, U.S.A. 21-22; Dir. of Trades School, St. John A & I School, Robertsport, Liberia 22-25; Asst. Plantations Man. Firestone Plantations Co., Liberia 26-28; engaged in private enterprise 28-31; entered politics and apptd. a County District Commr. 32, First Class District Commr. 37, Provincial Commr. 44; Chief of the Bureau of Tribal Affairs 46; Asst. Sec. of Interior 48; Cabinet Minister, Sec. of Defence 49-60; Amb. to Ivory Coast Repub. 60-69; Chair. Exec. Immigration Comm., Monrovia; Knight Commdr. Star of Africa (Liberia); Commdr. Star of Benin (France); mem. National True Whigs Party. Liberian Embassy, 17 ave. Chardy, Abidjan, Ivory Coast Republic.

Jooste, Gerhardus Petrus, M.A.; South African diplomat; b. 5 May 1904, Winburg, O.F.S.; ed. Univ. of Pretoria. Entered Union Public Service 24; apptd. Private Sec. to Hon. N. C. Havenga, Minister of Finance 29; joined Dept. of External Affairs 34; Sec. of Legation and Chargé d'Affaires a.i., Brussels 37, Chargé d'Affaires to Belgian Govt.-in-Exile, London 40-41; Head of Econ. Div., Dept. of External Affairs, Pretoria 41, Head of Political and Diplomatic Div. 46; Amb. to U.S.A. and Permanent Del. to UN 49-54; Alternate Del. UN Gen. Assembly, Paris 48, Leader S. African Del., N.Y. 49, Leader and Deputy Leader, N.Y. 50, Deputy Leader, Paris 51-52, 58, N.Y. 58, Leader, N.Y. 52, 53, 54 and 63; High Commr. in Great Britain 54-56; Sec. for External Affairs, Pretoria 56; Ex-officio mem. of Atomic Energy Board 56-66; Sec. for Foreign Affairs 61-66; Special Adviser on Foreign Affairs to the Prime Minister and Minister of Foreign Affairs July 66; mem. Comm. Water Matters 66-; Deputy Leader UN Gen. Assembly, N.Y. 66; Chair. State Procurement Board 68-71. 851 Government Avenue, Arcadia, Pretoria, Republic of South Africa. Telephone: 33091, Ext. 1 (Office); 74-5464 (Home).

Joosub, Hajee Ebrahim; South African administrator; b. 1923, Pretoria; ed. Govt. Indian School and in India. Worked in family business; first Minister of Indian Affairs 61; mem. Exec. Cttee. of the South African Indian Council 63; first Chair. S.A. Indian Council 68; controls 28 companies in S.A. and neighbouring states; Chair. Pretoria Indian Commercial Asscn. Pretoria Indian Commercial Association, Pretoria, South Africa.

Joseph, Helen; South African welfare worker; b. 1905, England. Taught in India, South Africa 31; served as Welfare Officer in WAAF during World War II; worked with Nat. Memorial Health Foundation, Cape Prov. 45-52; Sec. Medical Aid Soc. Garment Workers' Union, Johannesburg 52-66; Sec. Fed. of South African Women; Vice-Pres. Congress of Democrats; Organizer, Congress of People 55; charged with treason 56; acquitted 61; first South African to be put under house arrest 62-67, 67-. Publ. *Tomorrow's Sun.* 35 Fanny Avenue, Norwood, Johannesburg, South Africa.

Jumbe, (Mwinyi) Aboud; Tanzanian politician; b. 1920, Zanzibar; ed. secondary school, Zanzibar and Makerere Univ. Coll., Uganda. Teacher 46-50; leader, Zanzibar Nat. Union 53; fmr. mem. Zanzibar Township Council; mem. Afro-Shirazi Party

(ASP) 60-, later Organizing Sec., Head April 72-; mem. Nat. Assembly (ASP) 61-; Opposition Whip 62-64; Minister of Home Affairs Jan. 64; Minister of State, First Vice-President's Office 64-72, concurrently responsible for Ministry of Health and Social Services 64-Sept. 67; First Vice-Pres. April 72-; Chair. Zanzibar Revolutionary Council April 72-.
Office of the First Vice-President, Dar es Salaam, United Republic of Tanzania.

Juxon-Smith, Brig. Andrew; Sierra Leone army officer; b. 1933; ed. Royal Mil. Acad., Sandhurst, U.K., and Joint Services Staff Coll., U.K.
Creole from Freetown; has served with a British Regiment; Chair. Nat. Reformation Council, Sierra Leone, March 67-April 68; charged and convicted of treason 70, death sentence repealed 71.
c/o 24 Wilberforce Road, via Congo Cross, Wilberforce, Freetown, Sierra Leone.

K

Kabanda, Pierre Célestin; Rwandan diplomatist; b. 1936; ed. Petit Séminaire de Kabgayi, Grand Séminaire de Nyakibanda, and Univ. of Lovanium, Kinshasa.
Formerly in charge of Legislative Bureau of Office of Pres. of Rwanda; Sec.-Rapporteur of Cabinet; Amb. to U.S.A. and Canada 64-69; Perm. Rep. of Rwanda to UN 66-69; Amb. to France Oct. 69-, concurrently to Spain Dec. 69-, to Italy Jan. 70-, Perm. Del. to UNESCO May 70-.
Embassy of Rwanda, 17 rue Marguerite, Paris 17e, France.

Kachingwe, Joe; Malawi diplomatist; b. 1931; ed. St. Francis Xavier Univ., Canada.
Served in Malawi High Comm., London; First Sec., Malawi Legation, Pretoria 67; later High Commr. in Kenya; Amb. to S. Africa July 71-.
Embassy of Malawi, Pretoria, South Africa.

Kadji, Grah; Ivory Coast civil engineer and politician; b. 1932, Sassapou; ed. Coulommiers, Lille and Ecole Nat. des Ponts et Chaussés, Paris, France.
Departmental Dir. Public Works Sept. 65-July 66; Dir.-Gen. of Public Works July 66-Jan. 70; Minister of Public Works and Transport Jan. 70-.
Ministry of Public Works and Transport, Abidjan, Ivory Coast.

Kahangi, Christopher, B.COMM.; Tanzanian international bank official; b. 20 June 1937, Tanzania; ed. Univ. of Ireland, Dublin, and Mass. Inst. of Technology.
Ministry of Commerce and Industries, Tanzania, until Sept. 67, Chief Industrial Officer 65-67; training in bank credit at Union Bank of Los Angeles, U.S.A. Sept. 67-March 68; Alt. Exec. Dir. World Bank April 68-Oct. 68, Exec. Dir. World Bank Nov. 68-Nov. 70; Gen. Man. Tanzania Investment Bank Nov. 70-; Founder mem. and later Sec. Nat. Small Industries Corpn. 66.
c/o P.O. Box 9373, Dar es Salaam, Tanzania.

Kaka, Noma; Niger teacher and politician; b. 1920, Doutchi; ed. Ecole Normale William-Ponty.
Former headmaster; M.P. for Koni 59-65; Senator of the French Community 59-61; fmr. Grand Counsellor for French West Africa; Pres. State Security Court Oct. 64-; Minister of Nat. Defence Nov. 65-Jan. 71; Minister of Rural Economy Jan. 71-72, of Mines, Geology and Water Aug. 72-; Econ. Sec. Political Bureau of Parti progressiste nigérien (PPN).
Ministry of Mines, Niamey, Niger.

Kaleo, Jatoe; Ghanaian teacher, farmer and politician; b. July 1928, Kaleo Village; ed. Wala Native Authority Primary Boarding School, Tamale Middle Boarding School, Tamale Govt. Teacher Training Coll.

Assistant Treas. Wala Native Authority 46; Headmaster, Kaleo Primary Day School 49-50, Naro Primary Day School 53; mem. Nat. Assembly 54, mem. Nat. Assembly for Wala North 56; M.P. 69-; Minister of Labour, Social Welfare and Co-operatives 69-71, of Transport and Communications 71-72.
c/o Ministry of Transport and Communications, Accra, Ghana.

Kalonji-Ditunga, Albert; Zaire politician; b. 1929; ed. secondary and technical schools.
Mulopwe of the Baluba tribe in Kasai Province; teacher of agronomy; insurance broker; mem. Legis. Council, Brussels 59-60; nat. legislator 60; supported Congolese Nationalist Movement 58; Pres. MNC-Kalonji 59-; ruler of S. Kasai 60-62; detained by Central Govt. 62; released and reached S. Kasai Sept. 62; in exile 62-64; Minister of Agriculture (Congo) 64-65; now Pres. of Néon Africa SPRL (Gen. Trade, Import and Export, Ice Industry).
MNC-Kalonji Party, P.O. Box 1736, Kinshasa, Zaire.

Kalule-Settala, Laurence; Ugandan politician; b. 1924; ed. St. Mary's Coll., Kisubi, Makerere Univ. Coll. and Hull Univ., England.
Teacher 50-53; mem. Progressive Party; mem. Buganda Lukiko 62-; Minister of Community Devt. 63, of Industry and Communications 63-64; Minister of Finance 64-71; Acting Prime Minister 65.
Kampala, Uganda.

Kamaliza, Michael Marshall Mowbray; Tanzanian trade unionist and politician; b. 1929, Likoma, Nyasaland; ed. mission school, Likoma.
Treasurer, Tanganyika Federation of Labour (TFL) 52-57; Gen. Sec. Transport and General Workers' Union 57-60; Pres. TFL 60-64; Gen. Sec. Nat. Union of Workers' Congress (NUTA) 64-; Vice-Pres. All Africa Trade Union Fed. (AATUF); Minister of Labour 65-June 67; arrested Oct. 69, sentenced to 10 years imprisonment Feb. 71, sentence reduced July 71.

Kamanda, Jacques Gerard, L. EN D.; Zaire lawyer and administrator; b. 10 Dec. 1940, Kikwit; ed. Coll. St. Ignace de Kinati, Coll. Notre Dame de Mbansa Boma, Univ. Lovanium, Kinshasa and Brookings Inst., Washington, D.C.
Lawyer, Court of Appeal 64-; Legal Adviser, Féd. congolaise des travailleurs 64-65; Prof. Inst. nat. d'études politiques 65-66; Legal Adviser to Presidency of Repub. 65-66, Sec.-Gen. 66-67; Principal Adviser with responsibility for legal, administrative, political and diplomatic affairs to Presidency of Repub.; Dir. de Cabinet to Sec.-Gen. of Org. of African Unity 67-72, Asst. Sec.-Gen. Aug. 72-; Assoc. mem. Office nat. de la recherche scientifique du Congo; Vice Pres. Congolese section, Soc. africaine de la culture; del. to several int. confs.
Publs. *Essai de critiques du système de la criminalité d'emprunt* 64, *Négritude face au devenir de l'Afrique* 67, *L'Université aujourd'hui en Afrique* 69, *L'Intégration juridique et le développement harmonieux des nations africaines* 69, *L'Incidence de la culture audio-visuelle sur le phénomène du pouvoir* 70, *Les Organisations africaines Vol. I: L'OUA ou la Croisade de l'Unité africaine* 70, *Vol. II* 70.
OAU General Secretariat, P.O. Box 3243, Addis Ababa, Ethiopia; B.P. 9312, Kinshasa 1, 221 Avenue de Gerbéra, Zaire.

Kamanga, Reuben Chitandika; Zambian politician; b. 26 Aug. 1929, Chitandika Village, Chipata District, Eastern Province of Zambia; ed. Munali.
Imprisoned several times for political reasons 52-60; lived in Cairo 60-62; Deputy Pres. United Nat. Ind. Party; fmr. Minister of Labour and Mines; Minister of Transport and Communications 64; Vice-Pres. 64-67; Leader of House, Legislative Assembly 64; Minister of Foreign Affairs 67-69;

Minister of Rural Devt., Agriculture, Natural Resources and Land 69-
Ministry of Rural Development, Mulungushi House, P.O. Box RW197, Lusaka, Zambia.

Kambona, Oscar; Tanzanian politician; b. 1928; ed. Middle Temple, London.
Former schoolmaster; Org. Sec. Tanganyika African Nat. Union (T.A.N.U.) 54-56; studied law, Middle Temple, London 56-60; Sec.-Gen. T.A.N.U. 60-67; Minister of Educ., Tanganyika 61-62, of Home Affairs 62-63, of Foreign Affairs and Defence 63-64, of External Affairs Tanzania 64-65, of Regional Admin. 65-67, of Local Govt. and Rural Devt. 67; resigned June 67, left Tanzania for U.K. Aug. 67; charged with treason Nov. 69.
67 Prince of Wales Road, London, N.W.5, England.

Kandolo, Damien; Zaire administrator; b. 10 Sept. 1923; ed. primary and secondary school, Univ. of Brussels.
Began his career as an administrator 40; Sec. Services Administratifs Provinciaux 52; Chef de Bureau aux Affaires Extérieures 60; Chef de Cabinet under Pres. Lumumba 60; Dept. of the Interior (with M. J. Nussbaumer) 60, 62-64; Sec.-Gen. for the Interior 61; Chef de Cabinet Aug. 61; participation in organizing Congrès Nat. 63; Sec.-Gen. Ministry for Land, Mines and Power Aug. 64; Asst. Rep. of Groupe Cominière 65; Pres. Conseil d'Administration de TCC 66; Admin. Air-Congo 66; Admin. and Pres. of Gecomines (Gen. Congolese Mines) 68-; del. to several int. confs.; Chevalier, Ordre Nat. du Léopard; Officier, Ordre du Mérite du Sénégal and various other foreign awards.
Gecomines, B.P. 450, Lubumbashi, Zaire.

Kane, Falilou; Senegalese diplomatist; b. 14 July 1938, Joal; ed. Collège Blanchot, Saint-Louis, Lycée Van Vollenhoven, Dakar, and Faculty of Law and Econs., Univ. of Dakar.
Ministry of Foreign Affairs, Senegal 60-, successively Head of Div. of UN Affairs, Int. Orgs. and Gen. Affairs, Div. of Political Affairs, concurrently Technical Adviser to Minister of Foreign Affairs; Technical Adviser in Ministry of Justice Nov.-Dec. 62; Dir. of Political, Cultural and Social Affairs, Ministry of Foreign Affairs; Minister at Perm. Mission of Senegal to UN 66; Minister, Embassy of Senegal, Washington until Dec. 67; Sec.-Gen. Org. Commune Africaine et Malgache (OCAM) April 68-; has taken part in numerous int. confs.; decorations from Morocco, Upper Volta, Cameroon, Chad and Zaire.
Organisation Commune Africaine et Malgache, B.P. 437, Yaoundé, United Republic of Cameroon.

Kano, Alhaji Aminu; Nigerian politician and author; b. 9 Aug. 1920, Kano; ed. Shahuchi elementary School, Middle School, Kano, Kaduna Coll. and Univ. of London.
Teacher of History and English 42-46; Head of Teachers' Coll., Sokoto 48-50; Sec.-Gen. Northern Teachers' Asscn. 48-53; formed Northern Elements Progressive Union (N.E.P.U.), Life Pres. 59-; mem. of Parl. 59-64; Leader N.E.P.U. del. to constitutional confs. London and Lagos 53, 54, 55, 57, 58; Leader Nigerian del. to UNCTAD 64; Chair. UN Cttee. of 75 on UNCTAD; Patron, Afro-Asian Solidarity Org.; Fed. Commr. for Communications June 67-71; Fed. Minister of Health Oct. 71-; mem. American Soc. of Int. Law; Officer, Grand Cross of Independence (Equatorial Guinea).
Publs. *Kai Waye a Kasuwar Kano* (play), *Karya Fure Ta Ke Ba Ta Yaya* (play), *Alfiyya* (Hansa songs), *Motsi Ya Fi Zama* (travels), *Politics and Administration in Post War Nigeria*, *Three Lectures of Aminu-Kano*.
Federal Ministry of Health, Lagos; Home: 12A Lugara Avenue, Lagos, Nigeria.

Kapwepwe, Simon; Zambian politician; b. 12 April 1922; ed. Lubwa Mission.
Former teacher 45-51; studied in India and United States;

Treas. African Nat. Congress 56-58, Zambia Nat. Congress 58; National Treas., United Nat. Independence Party 60-67; mem. Parl. 62-71; fmr. Minister of Agriculture; Minister of Home Affairs Jan.-Oct. 64; Minister of Foreign Affairs Oct. 64-Sept. 67; Vice-Pres. of Zambia Sept. 67-Nov. 70; Minister of Provincial and Local Govt. Jan. 70-July 71, also of Culture Nov. 70-July 71; formed United Progressive Party Aug. 71, party banned Feb. 72; arrested Feb. 72, released Jan. 73.
Publs. *Tunyongandimi* 59, *Shalapo Chanichandala* 60, *Ubutungwa mu Jambo Jambo* (political fiction) 67.
United Progressive Party, Lusaka, Zambia.

Karanja, Dr. J. N., PH.D.; Kenyan diplomatist; b. 5 Feb. 1931; ed. Alliance High School, Kikuyu, Makerere Coll., Univ. of Delhi and Princeton Univ.
Lecturer in African Studies, Fairleigh Dickinson Univ., New Jersey, U.S.A. 61-62; Lecturer in African and Modern European History, Univ. of East Africa 62-63; High Commr. for Kenya in U.K. 63-70, also accred. to Holy See 66-70; Vice-Chancellor, Univ. of Nairobi 70-.
University of Nairobi, Nairobi, Kenya.

Karefa-Smart, John Musselman, B.A., B.SC., M.D., C.M., D.T.M., M.P.H., F.R.S.H., F.A.P.H.A., F.R.S.A.; Sierra Leonean politician and physician; b. 17 June 1915, Rotifunk; ed. Fourah Bay and Otterbein Colls., McGill and Harvard Univs.
Lecturer, Union Coll., Bunumbu 36-38; ordained Elder of Evangelical United Brethren Church 38; Medical Officer, R.C.A.M.C. 43-45; Sierra Leone Missions Hospitals 46-48; Lecturer, Ibadan Univ. Coll. (Nigeria) 49-52; Health Officer, WHO 52-55; Leader Del. to WHO 56 and 59; mem. House of Reps. 57-64; Minister of Lands and Survey 57-59; Africa Consultant, World Council of Churches 55-56; Minister for External Affairs 60-64; Asst. Prof. Columbia Univ. 64-65; Asst. Dir.-Gen. World Health Org., Geneva 65-70; political detainee, Sierra Leone 70-71; Visiting Prof. of Int. Health, Harvard Univ. 71-; Commdr. Order of Star of Africa (Liberia); Knight Grand Band, Order of African Redemption (Liberia); Grand Cordon, Order of the Cedar (Lebanon); Hon. LL.D. (Otterbein); Hon. LL.D. (McGill); Hon. LL.D. (Boston); Nat. Leader, United Democratic Party.
Publ. *The Halting Kingdom* 59.
55 Shattuck Street, Boston, Mass., U.S.A.

Kassum, Al Noor, BAR.-AT-LAW; Tanzanian administrator and lawyer; b. 11 Jan. 1924, Dar es Salaam; ed. Aga Khan School, Dar es Salaam, Muncaster School, Ashford, Middx., England.
Private law practice, Dar es Salaam 54-61; mem. Parl., Chief Whip of Tanganyika African Nat. Union Parl. Party 59-65; Junior Minister, Ministry of Educ. and Information 61-64, Ministry of Industries, Mineral Resources and Power 64-65; Senior Liaison Officer, UNESCO Bureau of Int. Relations and Programmes, Paris 65-67; Dir. UNESCO New York Office 67; Sec. Econ. and Social Council, UN Dept. of Econ. and Social Affairs 67-70; Deputy Gen. Man. Williamson Diamonds Ltd. (Tanzania) 70-; East African Minister for Finance and Admin. 72-; mem. East African Legislative Assembly.
East African Community, P.O.Box 3081, Arusha, Tanzania.

Katenga-Kaunda, Reid Willie; Malawi diplomatist; b. 20 Aug. 1929, Ndola, Zambia; ed. Union Coll., S.A., Inst. of Public Admin., Blantyre-Limbe, Admin. Staff Coll., Henley-on-Thames, and Trinity Coll., Oxford.
Executive Sec. Kotakota Produce and Trading Soc. Ltd. 52-62; District Chair. Malawi Congress Party, Kotakota District 60-61; Councillor, Nkhata Bay District Council 62-63; District Commr., Karonga 64-65; Senior Asst. Sec. Ministry of External Affairs 66; M.P., Parl. Sec. and Junior Minister 66-68; Under-Sec. Office of the Pres. and Cabinet 68-69; High Commr. to U.K., also accred. to

Netherlands and the Vatican 69-71, 72-; Malawi Independence Medal; Malawi Repub. Medal.
Malawi High Commission, 47 Great Cumberland Place, London, W1H 8DB, England.

Kaunda, Dr. Kenneth David; Zambian politician; b. 28 April 1924; ed. Lubwa Training School and Munali Secondary School.
Schoolteacher at Lubwa Training School 43, Headmaster 44-47; Sec. Chinsali Young Men's Farming Asscn. 47; welfare officer, Chingola Copper Mine 48; school teaching 48-49; Founder-Sec. Lubwa branch, African Nat. Congress 50, district organizer 51, provincial organizer 52, Sec.-Gen. for N. Rhodesia 53; broke away to form Zambia African Nat. Congress 58; Pres. United Nat. Independence Party 60-; Minister of Local Govt. and Social Welfare, N. Rhodesia 62-64; Prime Minister of N. Rhodesia Jan.-Oct. 64; Pres. Pan-African Freedom Movement for East, Central and South Africa (PAFMECSA) 63; First Pres. of Zambia Oct. 64-, and Minister of Defence 64-70; Minister of Foreign Affairs 69-Nov. 70, also of Trade, Industry, Mines and State Participation 69-; Chair. Mining and Industrial Devt. Corpn. of Zambia April 70-; Chair. Org. of African Unity (OAU) and Non-Aligned Nations Conf. Sept. 70-71; Order of the Collar of the Nile; Knight of the Collar of the Order of Pius XII, Order of the Queen of Sheba; Chancellor, Univ. of Zambia 66-; Hon. Dr. of Laws (Fordham Univ., Dublin, Windsor (Canada) and Sussex Univs. and Univs. of York and Chile).
Publs. *Black Government* 61, *Zambia Shall be Free* 62, *A Humanist in Africa* (with Colin Morris) 66, *Humanism in Zambia and its Implementation* 67.
State House, P.O. Box 135, Lusaka, Zambia.
Telephone: 50122 (Lusaka).

Kawawa, Rashidi Mfaume; Tanzanian politician; b. 1929; ed. Tabora Secondary School.
Former Pres. of the Tanganyikan Fed. of Labour; Minister of Local Govt. and Housing 60-61; Minister without Portfolio 61-62; Prime Minister Jan.-Dec. 62, Vice-Pres. Dec. 62-64; Second Vice-Pres., United Republic of Tanzania 64-, Prime Minister Feb. 72-; Vice-Pres. of TANU (Tanganyika African Nat. Union) and mem. TANU Central Cttee. and TANU Nat. Exec. Cttee.
Office of the Prime Minister, Dar es Salaam, Tanzania.

Kawusu Conteh, Sheku Bockari; Sierra Leonean politician; b. 1928; ed. Koyeima Govt. Secondary School.
Secretary, Koinadugu District Council 56-59; Town Clerk, Bo Municipality 62, 65-68; Exec. Officer, Gen. Govt. 64-65; M.P. 67-; Deputy Minister, Prime Minister's Office 68-69; Minister of Housing and Country Planning 69-70; Resident Minister for the Southern Province 70-71; Acting Prime Minister Sept. 70; Minister of Interior May 71, now of Lands and Mines.
Ministry of Lands and Mines, Freetown, Sierra Leone.

Kayanda, David Mathew; Kenyan diplomatist; b. 1930; ed. Alliance High School (Kikuyu).
Government employee, Kitale 51; East African Branch, Royal Dutch Shell Co. 52-56; mem. African Advisory Council, Mombasa 57, Councillor 58; mem. Mombasa Municipal Council 58-63; Deputy Mayor of Mombasa 61-62, Mayor and Chair. Mombasa Cttee. of Social Services and Welfare 62-63; Amb. to U.S.S.R. 66-71.
c/o Ministry of Foreign Affairs, Nairobi, Kenya.

Kayibanda, Grégoire; Rwandan journalist and politician; b. 1 May 1924; ed. Kabgayi and Nyakibanda, Ruanda (Rwanda since 1962).
Teacher Kigali 49-53; Information Officer Kabgayi 53-55; Editor *L'Ami* 53-55, *Kinyamateka* 55-58; Founder Ruanda Co-operative Movement 52, Hutu Social Movement 57, Democratic Republican Movement 59; Pres. TRAFIPRO Co-operative, Kabgayi; Pres. Democratic Republican

Movement; President of Ruanda Oct. 60-June 62, Rwanda July 62-.
Kavumsburg/Gitarama B.P. 54, Rwanda, Central Africa.

Kayukwa-Kimoto, Ferdinand; Zaire diplomatist; b. 9 Aug. 1935, Luena, Katanga; ed. Inst. St. Boniface, Lubumbashi, Univ. Lovanium, Kinshasa, and Univ. Libre de Bruxelles.
President-General of Gen. Union of Congolese Students 61-65; Dir. of Political Affairs, Ministry of Foreign Affairs 65-67; Adviser, then Principal Adviser to Pres. of Republic on Political, Juridical and Admin. Questions 67-69; Amb. to Senegal 71-; mem. Congolese Dels. to UN and OAU; Officier Ordre Nat. de la Côte d'Ivoire.
Publ. *Naissance des perspectives nationals dans les milieux congolais.*
Embassy of the Republic of Zaire, Imm. Daniel Sorano, 2e étage, B.P. 2251, Dakar, Senegal.

Kaziende, Léopold; Niger teacher and politician; b. 1912, Kaya, Upper Volta; ed. l'Ecole Normale William-Ponty, Daliar-Gorée, Ecole Normale Supérieure, St. Cloud.
Headmaster at Maradi-Filingué 39-40; teacher in Niamey 44-46; Pres. and Gen. Dir. Air Niger; Admin. Air Afrique; Minister of Public Works Dec. 58-Nov. 65; Minister of Public Works, Transport, Mines and Urban Devt. Nov. 65-Jan. 71; Minister of Econ. Affairs Jan. 71-; awarded Nat. Orders of Niger, France, Tunisia, Upper Volta, and Belgium.
Ministry of Economic Affairs, Niamey, Niger.

Kebbédé, Gabré; Ethiopian soldier; b. 23 June 1916.
Commander Ethiopian Expeditionary Force in Korea 51-52; Commdr. UN Forces in Congo 62-63; Chief of Staff Ethiopian Army 61-; Gov. Province of Bale; Minister of Defence 66-.
Ministry of Defence, Addis Ababa, Ethiopia.

Keita, Modibo; Mali politician; b. 4 June 1915; ed. William-Ponty Lycée, Dakar.
Conseiller Général, French Sudan; Sec.-Gen. Union Soudanaise; Councillor, Union Française 53-56; Deputy to French Nat. Assembly from Sudan 56-58, Vice-Pres. 56; Pres. Constituent Assembly, Dakar 58-60; Président du Conseil, Sudanese Repub. Mali Fed. 59-60, Mali 60-Nov. 68; Pres. of Mali 60-Nov. 68, Minister of Nat. Defence 61-Nov. 68; Lenin Peace Prize 62.
Bamako, Mali, West Africa.

Keita, Moussa Léo; Mali diplomatist; b. 1 July 1927; ed. Ecole Normale de Katibougou, and foreign service training courses in Paris, Geneva and New York.
Assistant Sec.-Gen., Ministry of Foreign Affairs 61, Head of Office 61-62, Sec.-Gen. 62-64; Amb. of Mali to the U.S.A., Brazil, Canada, Haiti 64-69, and Perm. Rep. to UN and Amb. to Cuba 66-67; Amb. to Egypt Sept. 69-71.
c/o Ministry of Foreign Affairs, Bamako, Mali.

Kelfa-Caulker, Richard Edmund, B.A., M.A.; Sierra Leonean diplomatist; b. 14 March 1909; ed. Sierra Leone, Otterbein Coll., Ohio, Oberlin Graduate School and Teachers Coll., Columbia Univ.
Headmaster, Albert Academy, Sierra Leone to 59; Commr. to the United Kingdom 59, Acting High Commr. 61; Amb. to U.S.A. 61-63; Amb. and Perm. Del. UN 63-64; High Commr. in U.K. 64-66; Amb. to Liberia Aug. 69-.
152 Benson Street, Monrovia, Liberia.

Kellas, Arthur Roy Handasyde, C.M.G., M.A.; British diplomatist; b. 6 May 1915, Aberdeen, Scotland; ed. Aberdeen Grammar School, Aberdeen Univ., Balliol Coll. (Oxford Univ.), Ecole des Sciences Politiques, Paris.
Joined Diplomatic Service 39; served in British Army Parachute Regiment 39-44; Third Sec. British Embassy, Iran 44, Counsellor 58; First Sec. British Legation, Finland 49, British Embassy, Egypt 52, Iraq 54; Imperail

Defence Coll. (now Royal Coll. of Defence Studies) 63; Counsellor, Consul-Gen., Tel-Aviv 64; Amb. to Nepal 66-70, to People's Repub. of Yemen 70-72; High Commr. to Tanzania 72-.
British High Commission, P.O. Box 9200, Dar es Salaam, Tanzania; and c/o Foreign and Commonwealth Office, King Charles Street, London, S.W.1, England.

Kenyatta, Mzee Jomo (Johnstone); Kenyan politician; b. 20 Oct. 1891; ed. Dagoretti Scottish Mission and London School of Economics.
Worked for Nairobi Municipality; returned to Kenya from studies in London 46; Pres. Kenya African Union 47; convicted of managing Mau Mau movement and sentenced to imprisonment 53, released April 59, restricted to Lodwar April 59-April 61; restricted to Maralal April-Aug. 61; Pres. Kenya African Nat. Union (KANU) Aug. 61-, Leader KANU Del. to London Constitutional Conf. Feb.-March 62; mem. Legislative Council 62-; Minister of State for Constitutional Affairs and for Econ. Planning April 62-63; Prime Minister also Minister for Internal Security and Defence and Foreign Affairs 63-64; Pres. 64-, also C.-in-C. of the Armed Forces; Hon. Fellow, London School of Econs.; Hon. LL.D. (East Africa).
Publs. *Facing Mount Kenya, Kenya: the Land of Conflict, My People of Kikuyu, Harambee!*
Office of the President, P.O. Box 30510, Nairobi; State House, P.O. Box 530, Nairobi, Kenya; Home: Gatundu, Kenya.

Keutcha, Jean; Cameroonian civil servant; b. June 1923, Bangangté; ed. Ecole Supérieure d'Agriculture de Yaoundé.
Chef de Cabinet, Minister of State with Special Responsibilities 57, subsequently Chef de Cabinet, Sec. of State with responsibility for Information, Posts and Telecommunications; Asst. to Chief of Bamiléké Region 59; Sub-Prefect, Bafoussam 60; Prefect of Mifi, subsequently of Menoua 62-64; Sec. of State for Public Works 64, subsequently Sec. of State for Rural Devt. and Sec. of State for Educ.; Minister of Foreign Affairs 71-72, of Agriculture Jan. 72-; Commdr. Ordre Camerounais de la Valeur, Grand Croix, Légion d'Honneur, Grand Officier de l'Ordre National Gabonais, etc.
Publ. *Le Guide Pratique pour la Taille du Caféier Arabica.*
Ministère de l'Agriculture, Yaoundé, United Republic of Cameroon.

Kgabo, E. M. K.; Botswana politician; b. 1925, Kweneng; ed. Kanye.
Secretary of School Cttee., Bakwena admin., later Treas., councillor and mem. of Licensing Board; J. P. 64; attended seminar on Co-operatives, German Fed. Repub. May-June 64; mem. Legislative Assembly March 65-; Parl. Sec. March 65-Oct. 66; attended UN seminar on devt. financing Aug.-Dec. 65, seminar in Addis Ababa, Ethiopia Jan.-Feb. 66; Minister of Local Govt. and Lands Oct. 66-.
Ministry of Local Government and Lands, Gaborone, Botswana.

Khalid, Mansour, LL.D.; Sudanese diplomatist and lawyer; b. 17 Jan. 1931, Sudan; ed. Univs. of Khartoum, Pennsylvania and Paris.
Began his career as an attorney, Khartoum 57-59; Legal officer, UN, N.Y. 62-63; Deputy UN resident rep., Algeria 64-65; Bureau of Relations with Member States, UNESCO, Paris 65-69; Visiting Prof. of Int. Law, Univ. of Colorado 68; Minister of Youth and Social Affairs, Sudan 69-71; Chair. of Del. of Sudan to UN Gen. Assembly, Special Consultant and Personal Rep. of UNESCO Dir.-Gen. for UNWRA fund-raising mission 70; Perm. Rep. to UN for Sudan 71; Minister of Foreign Affairs Aug. 71-.
Ministry of Foreign Affairs, Khartoum, Sudan.

Khalifa, Ser el Khatim, G.C.M.G.; Sudanese educationalist and politician; b. 1 Jan. 1919; ed. Gordon Coll., Khartoum.
Former teacher, Gordon Coll., Khartoum and Bakhter-

Ruda Inst.; Head Khartoum Technical Inst. 60-64, 65-66; Deputy Under-Sec. Ministry of Educ. 64; Prime Minister 64-65; Amb. to Italy 66-68, to U.K. 68-69; Adviser to Minister of Higher Educ. and Research 72-.
Ministry of Higher Education and Research, Khartoum, Sudan.

Khalil, Mohamed Kamal, El-Din; Egyptian diplomatist.
Formerly Dir. of Research Dept., U.A.R. Ministry of Foreign Affairs; Chargé d'Affaires, London 60-61; Dir. North American Dept., U.A.R., Ministry of Foreign Affairs 61-64; Amb. to Jordan 64-66, to Sudan 66-71.
Publ. *The Arab States and the Arab League* (2 vols) 62.
c/o Ministry of Foreign Affairs, Cairo, Egypt.

Khama, Sir Seretse, K.B.E., B.A., M.P.; Botswana politician and farmer; b. 1 July 1921; ed. Fort Hare Univ., Witwatersrand Univ., South Africa, Balliol Coll., Oxford.
Legal studies, London; son of Sekgoma II (d. 25), Chief of Bamangwato Tribe, Bechuanaland Protectorate; his uncle, Tshekedi Khama, Regent of Bamangwato Tribe in Seretse Khama's minority 26-50; dispute over Chieftancy of Bamangwato Tribe resulted in Seretse Khama's banishment 50; returned to Bechuanaland and renounced all claim to Chieftancy 56; Pres. Bechuanaland Democratic Party; mem. Legislative Council and Executive Council 61-65; mem. Legislative Assembly and Prime Minister of Bechuanaland 65-66; mem. of Parl. and Pres. of the Republic of Botswana 66-; Hon. LL.D., Hon. LL.B.
Private Bag 1, Gaborone, Botswana.

Khazali, Alimamy; Sierra Leonean politician; b. 14 June 1918, Port Loko; ed. Bo Govt. School.
Worked in Civil Service 40-64, including Chief Clerk Provincial Admin., Sec., Treasurer Kenema District Council, Electoral Commr. Northern Prov., Chief Electoral Commr. of Sierra Leone; worked in diamond business; Minister of Devt. 70-71, of Information and Broadcasting 71-72; mem. Cen. Cttee., All People's Congress Party; mem. Commonwealth Parl. Asscn., Inter-Parl. Union.
c/o Ministry of Information and Broadcasting, Lightfoot-Boston, Freetown, Sierra Leone.

Kiano, Julius Gikyono, M.A., PH.D.; Kenyan politician; b. 1926, Weithaga, Kenya; ed. Makerere Univ. Coll., Antioch Coll. (U.S.), Stanford Univ. and Univ. of California.
Lecturer in Econs. and Constitutional Law at Royal Technical Coll., Kenya 56-58; African elected mem. Legis. Council for Central Province South 58-60; Minister for Commerce and Industry 60; mem. Legis. Council for Fort Hall 61; mem. Kenya Advisory Council on Technical Educ. and Vocational Training; mem. Indian Govt. Cultural Scholarships Cttee.; Chair. Nairobi Welfare Soc.; Minister for Educ. 66-69, for Local Govt. Dec. 69-; Chair. Kenya African Nat. Union (KANU), Muranga District.
Ministry for Local Government, Nairobi, Kenya.

Kibaki, Mwai, B.A., B.SC.(ECON.); Kenyan politician; b. 1931, Othaya, Kenya; ed. Makerere Univ. Coll.
Lecturer in Econs. at Makerere Univ. Coll. 59-60; Nat. Exec. Officer Kenya African Nat. Union 60-62; elected by Legislative Council as one of Kenya's nine reps. in Central Legis. Assembly of East African Common Services Org. 62; mem. House of Reps. for Nairobi Doonholm 63-; Parl. Sec. to Treasury 63; Asst. Minister of Econ. Planning and Devt. 64-66; Minister for Commerce and Industry 66-69; Minister of Finance Dec. 69-Oct. 70; Minister of Finance, Econ. Planning and Devt. Oct. 70-.
Ministry of Finance, Economic Planning and Development, Nairobi, Kenya.

Kibedi, Wanume, LL.B.; Ugandan lawyer and politician; b. 3 Aug. 1941, Busesa; ed. Busoga Coll. and Univ. of London.
Articled with Waterhouse and Co., London 61-66, qualified solicitor 66; worked in office of Attorney-Gen., Uganda 68; Partner, Binaisa and Co. (advocates) 69-70; Minister

of Foreign Affairs Feb. 71-; del. to UN Gen. Assembly 71.

Ministry of Foreign Affairs, P.O. Box 7048, Kampala, Uganda.

King, Charles Tyrell O'Connor, B.A.; Liberian lawyer and civil servant; b. 1906; ed. Coll. of West Africa and Liberia Coll. (now Univ. of Liberia).

County Attorney, Montserrado County 42-44; Asst. Sec. of State 44-48; Judge 6th Judicial Circuit Court, Montserrado County 48-50; Admin. Asst. to Pres. of Liberia 50-55; Perm. Rep. to UN 55-59; Amb. to Nigeria 61-68, to France 68-72, to Ethiopia Sept. 72-; Chair. UN Comm. on Togoland under French Admin.; Commdr. Légion d'Honneur, Knight Crown of Italy, Order of Orange Nassau, and Liberian decorations.

Liberian Embassy, Addis Ababa, Ethiopia.

Kironde, Apollo K.; Ugandan diplomatist; b. 1915; ed. King's Coll., Budo, Makerere Coll. Kampala and Adams Coll. Natal, and Univ. of S. Africa (Fort Hare).

Teacher, King's Coll., Budo 43-50; Middle Temple, London 50-52; legal practice, Uganda 52-55; Asst. Minister of Social Services 55-58; Minister of Works and Transport 58-60; Founder, United Nat. Party 60, merged with Uganda Nat. Congress (U.N.C.) 61, Leader U.N.C. 61-; fmr. Amb. to U.S.A.; Perm. Rep. to UN 62-67; Special Asst. in African Problems, Dept. of Political and Security Council Affairs, UN 67; High Commr. in Canada 64-67; Minister of Planning and Devt. 71-72, of Tourism June-Dec. 72.

c/o Ministry of Tourism, Kampala, Uganda.

Kiwanuka, Kabimu Mugumba Benedicto, LL.B.; Ugandan barrister-at-law and politician; b. 1922; ed. Pius XII Univ. Coll., Basutoland, London Univ., Gray's Inn, London.

Called to the Bar 56, Pres.-Gen., Uganda Democratic Party; Minister without Portfolio and Leader of the House April-July 61; Chief Minister of Uganda July 61-Feb. 62; Prime Minister of Uganda March-May 62; arrested Dec. 63, charges subsequently withdrawn; arrested again Dec. 64, charges withdrawn; arrested Dec. 69 and detained; freed Jan. 71; Chief Justice of Uganda June 71-72; arrested Sept. 72; *believed to be dead.*

Ki-Zerbo, Joseph; Upper Voltan historian and politician. Director of Educ., Ouagadougou 65-; Leader Nat. Liberation Movt. 71-; Sec. Afro-Malagasy Council for Higher Educ. (CAMES); currently editing UNESCO *History of Africa Vol. 1.*

Ministère de l'Education Nationale, Ouagadougou, Upper Volta.

Kochman, Mohamed Nassim; Mauritanian lawyer, diplomatist and international banker; b. 25 Oct. 1932; ed. Van Vollenhoven Lycée, Dakar, Senegal, Marcel Gambier Coll., Lisieux, France, Caen Univ. and Inst. of Political Studies, Grenoble, France.

Lawyer, Court of Appeal, Dakar 58-61; First Sec., Embassy of Mauritania, Washington, and Mauritanian Perm. Mission to UN 61; First Counsellor, later Chargé d'Affaires, Washington 62-64; Head, Perm. Mission of Mauritania to UN 63-64; Alt. Dir. Int. Bank for Reconstruction and Devt. (IBRD), Int. Finance Corpn. (IFC), and Int. Devt. Asscn. (IDA) 62-64; Exec. Dir. for Cameroon, Central African Republic, Chad, Congo P.R., Dahomey, Gabon, Ivory Coast, Malagasy Republic, Mali, Mauritania, Mauritius, Niger, Rwanda, Senegal, Somalia, Togo, Upper Volta and Zaire, IBRD, IFC and IDA 64-; del. to UN Gen. Assembly 61-63, rep. to several int. confs.; awarded numerous decorations including Grand Officer, Nat. Order of Senegal 68; Officer, Order of Nat. Merit (Mauritania) 70; Commdr., Nat. Order (Ivory Coast).

International Bank for Reconstruction and Development, 1818, H. Street, N.W., Washington, D.C. 20433, U.S.A.

Koinange, Mbiyu, M.A., E.G.H., M.P.; Kenyan politician; b. 1907, Njunu, Kiambu District; ed. Buxton School, Mombasa, Alliance High School Kikuyu, Ohio Wesleyan Univ., Columbia Univ. New York and post-graduate work.

Founder Kenya Teachers Coll., Githunguri 39, Principal 48; Co-founder Kenya African Union 46, Rep. in Europe 51-59; Dir. for Eastern, Central and South Africa, Bureau of African Affairs, Ghana 59-60; fmr. Sec.-Gen. Pan African Freedom Movement for East, Central and South Africa (PAFMECSA); Minister of State for Pan-African Affairs, Kenya 63-65; Minister for Educ. 65-66; Minister of State, Office of the Pres. 66-69; Minister of State for Foreign Affairs 69-.

Ehothia Farm, Limuru, P.O. Box 9799, Nairobi, Kenya. Telephone: Riara Ridge 239.

Kok, Benedictus, M.A., H.E.D., D.LITT.; South African university official; b. 15 Dec. 1907, Heilbron; ed. Frankfurt High School, Grey Univ. Coll., Univs. of Amsterdam and Utrecht.

Teacher at Parys, Orange Free State 29, 34-37; Prof. of Afrikaans, Grey Univ., Bloemfontein 41-67; Principal, Univ. of Orange Free State Nov. 67-; founder and Chair. The Free State Music Soc., Chair. The Free State Eisteddfod, Chair. Joint Matriculation Board of South Africa, mem. Exec. Cttee. Performing Arts Council of the Orange Free State (P.A.C.O.F.S.), Chair. Opera Cttee. of P.A.C.O.F.S., mem. South African Acad. for Arts and Science.

Publs. *Die Vergelyking in die Afrikaanse Volkstaal, D. F. Malherbe—die Mens en sy Kuns* (co-author), *Kruim en Kors* (co-author).

P.O. Box 339, Bloemfontein; Home: 1 Stewart Crescent, Bloemfontein, Orange Free State, Republic of South Africa.

Kolo, (Alhaji) Sule D., B.SC.(ECON.); Nigerian diplomatist; b. 1926, Jos; ed. London Univ., Imperial Defence Coll. (now Royal Coll. of Defence Studies).

Counsellor, Nigerian High Comm., London 62; Perm. Sec. Ministry of Defence 63; Perm. Sec. Ministry of Trade 66; Amb. to Switzerland, Austria and Turkey and Perm. Rep. to the European Office of the UN 66-70; Chair. Gen. Agreement on Tariffs and Trade (GATT) 69-; High Commr. to U.K. 70-; Hon. F.R.Econ.S., Franklin Peace Medal 69.

Nigeria House, 9 Northumberland Avenue, London W.C.2, England.

Telephone: 01-839 1244.

Kombo, Sheikh Thabit; Tanzanian (Shirazi) politician; b. 1904.

Worked on ships and as railroad engineer; shopkeeper, Shirazi Co-operative, Zanzibar Town; leader, Shirazi Asscn.; Sec.-Gen. Afro-Shirazi Party (ASP); now Minister of Commerce and Industry.

Ministry of Commerce and Industry, Dar es Salaam, Tanzania.

Koroma, Sorie Ibrahim; Sierra Leonean politician; b. 30 Jan. 1930, Port Loko; ed. Govt. Model School, Freetown, Bo Govt. School and Co-operative Coll., Ibadan, Nigeria. Worked in Co-operative Dept. 51-58; in private business 58-62; First Sec.-Gen. Sierra Leone Motor Owners' Transport Union 58; M.P. 62-65, 67-; Deputy Mayor of Freetown 64; Minister of Trade and Industry 68-69; Minister of Agriculture and Nat. Resources 69-71; Vice-Pres. of Sierra Leone and Prime Minister April 71-, later Minister of the Interior; Vice-Chair. FAO Conf., Rome; del. to OAU Summit Conf., Addis Ababa 71, Rabat 72; decorations from People's Repub. of China, Ethiopia, Lebanon and Liberia.

Office of the Prime Minister, Freetown, Sierra Leone.

Kouandété, Lieut. Col. Maurice; Dahomey army officer and politician; b. 1939; ed. Ecole de Guerre, Paris.
Director of Cabinet of Head of State 67-69; Head of State and Head Provisional Govt. Dec. 67; Chief of Staff of Dahomey Army July 69-June 70; leader of coup which overthrew Pres. Zinsou Dec. 69; mem. of Directory (three man body ruling Dahomey), Minister of the Economy, Finance and Co-operation 69-70; arrested 70; Deputy Sec.-Gen. for Nat. Defence Aug. 70-72; arrested Feb. 72, sentenced to death May 72.
c/o Ministry of National Defence, Cotonou, Dahomey.

Krüger, Christian Martin, D.SC.ENG. (RAND), DR.ING.E.H. (AACHEN), D.ENG.H.C. (RAND); South African engineer and director of companies; b. 1 May 1905, Johannesburg; ed. Ermelo and Middelburg High Schools, Transvaal and Univ. of the Witwatersrand, Johannesburg.
With South African Iron and Steel Industrial Corpn., Ltd. (ISCOR) 31-69, Technical Asst., Roll Designing Section 33-34, Roll Designer 34-38, Man. Rolling Mills Div. 38-48, Mills Consultant, ISCOR 48-52, Technical Man. 52-53, Gen. Works Man. 53-55, Gen. Man. 55-69, Dir. 59-69, Man. Dir. 64-69, retd. 69; Dir. various companies; Hon. Prof. of Metallurgy and Metallurgical Engineering, Univ. of Pretoria 64-70; Gold Medal of Honour for Scientific Achievement in the Field of Engineering, Akademie vir Wetenskap en Kuns 59; Hon. Vice-Pres. Iron and Steel Inst. (England) 65-.
210 Anderson Street, Brooklyn, Pretoria, South Africa. Telephone: 74-2086; 745030 (Office).

Kwapong, Prof. Alex. A.; Ghanaian professor; b. 1927; ed. Presbyterian junior and middle schools, Akropong, Achimota Coll. and King's Coll., Cambridge.
Visiting Prof., Princeton Univ. 62; Pro Vice-Chancellor and Head of Classics Dept. Ghana Univ.; mem. Political Cttee. 66-; Vice-Chancellor, Ghana Univ.
University of Ghana, P.O. Box 25, Legon, nr. Accra, Ghana.

Kyari, Brig. Abba; Nigerian army officer; b. 1938, Dewa, Republic of Niger; ed. Damasak Elementary School, Bornu Middle School, Zaria Govt. Coll., Rost Teshi, Ghana, Mons Officer Cadets' School (U.K.), School of Infantry, Warminster (U.K.), Army Mechanical Transport School, Bordon, Hants. (U.K.) and U.S. Army Artillery and Missile School, Fortsill, Okla.
Mechanical Transport Officer, Nigerian Army Supply and Transport Co., Kaduna 61-63; Battery Commdr. 64-66; Commanding Officer, 5th Battalion, Nigerian Army Sept. 66-May 67; Mil. Gov. North Central State May 67-; Acting Brig.-Gen. Oct. 72.
Government House, P.M.B. 2001, Kaduna, Nigeria.

L

Labidi, Abdelwahab; Tunisian financier; b. 22 April 1929; ed. Coll. Sidiki, Tunis, Institut des Hautes Etudes, Tunis, Faculty of Law, Paris Univ.
Former Gen. Man. Banque de Tunisie; Insp. Gen. Banque Nat. Agricole de Tunisie; Man. Soc. Tunisienne de Banque; Man. Dir. Nat. Devt. Bank of Niger 64-69; Vice-Pres. African Devt. Bank June 69-Sept. 70, Pres. Sept. 70-; Chevalier, Ordre Nat. de la République de Tunisie; Officier, Ordre Nat. de la République du Niger.
African Development Bank, B.P. 1387, Abidjan, Ivory Coast.

La Guma, Justin Alexander (Alex); South African author and journalist; b. 20 Feb. 1925, Cape Town; ed. Trafalgar High School, Cape Town, Cape Technical School, Cape Town, and London School of Journalism.
Member of Communist Party 48-50; mem. Nat. Exec.

Coloured People's Congress 55-; banned from gatherings in S. Africa and South West Africa 62; under house arrest Dec. 62; detained in solitary confinement 63, 66; left S. Africa in exile Sept. 66; now freelance writer and mem. Editorial Board, Afro-Asian Writers' Bureau 68-; Afro-Asian "Lotus" Award for Literature 70.
Publs. *A Walk in the Night* 62, *And a Threefold Cord* 65, *The Stone Country* 68, *In the Fog of the Season's End* 72 (novels).
36 Woodland Gardens, London, N.10, England.

Lamana, Abdoulaye; Chad politician; b. 1935; ed. Inst. des Hautes Etudes d'Outre-Mer, Paris.
Director of Finance, Govt. of Chad 62-64; Minister of Economy and Transport Jan. 64-71, and Finance 68-71; Pres. Coton Tchad 71-; Ordre National du Tchad.
Coton Tchad, B.P. 15, Fort-Lamy, Chad.

Lambo, (Thomas) Adeoye, O.B.E., J.P., M.D., F.R.C.P., D.P.M.; Nigerian neuro-psychiatrist; b. 29 March 1923, Akeokuta; *s.* of the late Chief D. B. Lambo; ed. Baptist High School, Akeokuta, and Birmingham Univ.
Medical Officer Nigerian Medical Services 50-; Govt. Specialist-in-charge, Aro Hospital for Nervous Diseases; Consultant Physician, Univ. Coll., Ibadan; Prof. and Head of Dept. of Psychiatry and Neurology, Univ. of Ibadan 63, Dean of Medical Faculty 66; mem. Exec. Comm. World Fed. for Mental Health 64; Chair. Int. Coll. of Tropical Medicine; mem. Scientific Advisory Panel, Ciba Foundation 66; convened first Pan-African Conf. of Psychiatrists 61; founded Asscn. of Psychiatrists in Africa 61; Vice-Chancellor, Univ. of Ibadan 68-71; Asst. Dir.-Gen. World Health Org. 71-; Chair. Scientific Council for Africa, UN Advisory Cttee. for Prevention of Crime and Treatment of Offenders; mem. Exec. Cttee. Council for International Org. for Medical Sciences, UNESCO; mem. Royal Medico-Psychological Asscn. Great Britain; Chair. W. African Examinations Council 69-71; Vice-Chair. UN Advisory Cttee. on the Application of Science and Technology to Devt. 70-71; mem. Scientific Cttee. for the Centre for Advanced Study in Developmental Science 70-; WHO Advisory Cttee. on Medical Research 70-71; Hon. D.Sc., Hon. LL.D.; Haile Selassie I Laureate for African Research 70.
Publs. numerous articles in various medical journals.
World Health Organization, 1211 Geneva 27, Switzerland. Telephone: 34-60-61.

Lamizana, General Sangoule; Upper Voltan army officer and politician; b. *c.* 1916, Dianra, Tougan, Upper Volta.
Served in French Army in Second World War, and later in Indo-China; Chief of Staff, Army of Upper Volta 61, Lt.-Col. 64; Pres., Prime Minister, Minister of Defence, War Veterans, Foreign Affairs, Information, Youth and Sports, Upper Volta Jan. 66; Pres. of Republic, Pres. of Council of Ministers 67-; Brig.-Gen. 67, Gen. 70; Grand Croix, Ordre Nat. de Haute-Volta, Légion d'Honneur; Croix de Guerre, Croix de Valeur Militaire, and several other foreign decorations.
Office of the President, Ouagadougou, Upper Volta.

Lamptey, J. Kwesi; Ghanaian politician; b. 10 May 1909, Sekondi; ed. Mfantsipim School, Exeter and London Univs.
Deputy Chair. Convention People's Party (C.P.P.); Editor-in-Chief, *Gold Coast Leader* 50-52; mem., Legislative Assembly for Sekondi-Takoradi 51, resigned 52; Ministerial Sec., Ministry of Finance 51, resigned 52; M.P. for Sekondi (Progress Party); Minister of Defence Sept. 69-70; Minister of the Interior 70-71; Minister responsible for Parl. Affairs Jan. 71-Jan. 72; fmr. Asst. Headmaster, Fijai Secondary School, Sekondi.
Sekondi, Ghana.

Lansana, General Diane; Guinean army officer and politician.
Former Gov., Kankan and N'Zerekore regions; Major-Gen., Guinean battalion attached to UN in Congo 60; Gov., Labe

Region Minister of Defence 65; mem., Guinean Democratic Party's Nat. Political Bureau; fmr. Minister of the People's Army until Jan. 68; Minister in charge of the Defence of the Revolution Jan. 68-March 68; Minister of the People's Army, in charge of Nat. Defence, the Militia and Nat. Service March 68; fmr. Minister of the Interior until April 70; Minister of Social Welfare April 70-April 72; Perm. Ministerial Sec., Political Bureau of Guinean Democratic Party, Inspector Planning Cttee. May 72-.
Parti démocratique de Guinée, Conakry, Guinea.

Lardner-Burke, Hon. Desmond William; Rhodesian politician and lawyer; b. 17 Oct. 1909, Kimberley, South Africa; ed. St. Andrew's Coll., Grahamstown, South Africa.
Attorney with Coghlan and Welsh, Bulawayo 33-41; Senior Partner, Danzeger and Lardner Burke, Gwelo 41-; Dir. of various companies; M.P. for Gwelo 48-53 and 61-; Minister of Justice, Law and Order 64-; Pres. of Law Soc. 55-56.
Publ. *Rhodesia: The Story of the Crisis* 66.
8 Richmond Road, Highlands, Salisbury, Rhodesia.
Telephone: 24199.

Lawrence, Hon. Harry Gordon, Q.C., B.A., LL.B.; South African lawyer and politician; b. 17 Oct. 1901, Rondebosch, Cape; ed. Rondebosch and Univs. of Cape Town and South Africa.
Called to Bar Cape Town 26; M.P. for Salt River 29-38, for Woodstock 38-43, Salt River 43-61; joined United Party 33; Minister of Labour Union Govt. 38-39, of Interior, Internal Security, Information and Public Health 39-43; Minister of Welfare and Demobilisation Nov. 43-45, Minister of Justice and of Social Welfare and Demobilisation Nov. 45-47, Minister of Justice, of Interior and Demobilisation 48 until defeat of Govt. May 48; South African Rep. at Commonwealth Conf. on Japanese Peace Treaty Aug.-Sept. 47, led South African del. to UN, New York, Sept.-Nov. 47; resigned from United Party Sept. 59; elected Nat. Chair. and Parl. Leader, Progressive Party Nov. 59; defeated as Progressive Candidate Oct. 61; Dir. Consolidated Diamond Mines of South West Africa, Western Holdings, Springbok Colliery; Coronation Medals 37, 53.
The Cotswolds, Kenilworth, Cape Province; and Temple Chambers, Wale Street, Cape Town, S. Africa.
Telephone: 77-3278 and 41-0019.

Lawrence, J. Dudley; Liberian lawyer and diplomatist; b. 19 April 1909.
Ministry of Foreign Affairs 28-; Clerk to Supreme Court, Administrative Officer, Elections Comm. 41-49; Chief of Protocol, Dir. Int. Confs. 49-52; Minister to Spain 52-54, Ambassador 54-56, Ambassador to France 56-64; concurrently Minister to Holy See 56-72, Ambassador to Switzerland 61-72, and to U.K. 64-72; mem. Liberian Del. to UN 51-58, Chair. 55; Great Band of the Order of African Redemption, Knight Grand Commander of the Order of Pioneers, Grand Cross of Civil Merit (Spain), Grand Cross of St. Gregorius Magnus (Vatican), Grand Officer, Legion of Honour (France), Golden Grand Cross of Honour (Austria), Grand Cross National Order of Merit (France), Commdr. National Order (Madagascar), Grand Cross of Pian Order, First Class (Vatican).
c/o Ministry of Foreign Affairs, Monrovia, Liberia.

Laye, Camara; Guinean writer; b. 1924, Kouroussa; ed. Conakry and Paris.
Worked as civil servant; left Guinea 66, worked in Paris; now Researcher, Institut Fondamentale d'Afrique Noire (IFAN), Dakar.
Publs. *L'Enfant Noir* (African Child) 53, *Le Regard du Roi* (The Radiance of the King) 55, *Dramouss* (Dream of Africa) 67, and several short stories in *Black Orpheus*.
Institut Fondamentale d'Afrique Noire, Dakar, Senegal.

Lechat, Eugène Bernard; Malagasy politician; b. 21 May 1919, Hesloup (Orne), France; ed. Ecole Normale d'Instituteurs de l'Orne.
Assistant Dir. and Dir. of Regional Schools and Secondary Education in Madagascar 51-57; Conseiller Gén. Province of Fianarantsoa 57-; mem. Representative Assembly of Madagascar 57-59; fmr. mem. Perm. Comm. and Comm. of Social Affairs and Labour; Senator June 58-July 59; Dep. to Malagasy Nat. Assembly Oct. 58-; Minister of Public Works, Equipment and Transport, and with responsibility for Posts and Telecommunications May 59-Sept. 65; Minister of Equipment and Communications Sept. 65, Minister of State for Public Works and Communications until 71; Fifth Vice-Pres. 71-; Commdr. de l'Ordre National Malgache; Chevalier, Légion d'Honneur and other awards from Malagasy Repub., France and Liberia.
Office of the Fifth Vice-President, Tananarive; Home: 33 rue Georges V. Faravohitra, Tananarive, Madagascar.

Lemma, H.E. Ato Menasse; Ethiopian banker; b. 24 March 1913, Cairo, Egypt; ed. in Egypt.
Joined Bank of Ethiopia 34; served in armed forces 39-41; Sec.-Gen. for Province of Harrar 41-43; Dir.-Gen. in Ministry of Finance 43-49; Gov. for Ethiopia, IMF and IBRD 49-; Vice-Minister, Ministry of Finance 49-58; Minister of State 58-59; Minister of Mines and State Domains 59; Auditor-Gen. 59-60; Acting Gov. State Bank of Ethiopia and Chief of Finance and Planning Div., Ethiopian Cabinet 60-63; Gov. Nat. Bank of Ethiopia 64-.
National Bank of Ethiopia, Haile Selassie I Square, P.O. Box 5550, Addis Ababa, Ethiopia.

Lewis, Geoffrey Whitney, A.B.; American diplomatist; b. 20 May 1910; ed. Harvard University and Trinity Coll. Cambridge.
Assistant Dean Harvard Coll. 33-37; Principal of Private School 37-41; Officer U.S. Army 41-47, Colonel Army Reserve 47-56; U.S. Department of State 47-56; First Sec. U.S. Embassy, Karachi 56-58, Paris 58-61; Deputy Chief of Mission, Amman 61-65; Amb. to Mauritania 65-67, to Central African Republic 67-71.
Department of State, Washington, D.C., U.S.A.

Lewis, Neville, R.P.; South African painter; b. 8 Oct. 1895; ed. S. African Coll. School, Slade School, London.
Served First World War France, Belgium, Italy; painted native life S. Africa, portraits Spain, U.S.A. and England; works acquired by Tate Gallery, Nat. Gallery of Modern Art Madrid, Imperial War Museum, and Oldham, Manchester, Liverpool, Sheffield, Belfast, Leeds, Bradford, Birmingham and other Municipal Galleries, S.A. National Gallery, Johannesburg Art Gallery, Durban Art Gallery; mem. Royal Society Portrait Painters, New English Art Club; official artist to S. African Defence Force 40-43.
Works include portraits of Gen. Smuts, Solly Joel, Sir Winston Churchill, the King of Spain, the King of Greece, F.M. Viscount Alexander, F.M. Viscount Montgomery, Lord Tedder, Albert Luthuli, Sobhuza II King of the Swazis, and many well-known South Africans.
42 Rowan Street, Stellenbosch, South Africa.

Lihau-Kanza, Mme Sophie; Zaire politician.
Minister of State for Social Affairs Oct. 66-, concurrently Minister of State for Community Devt. Oct. 67-March 69, for Labour March 69-.
Ministry of Social Affairs, Kinshasa, Zaire.

Lisette, Gabriel; Chad politician; b. 2 April 1919; ed. Lycée Carnot (Point-a-Pitre, Guadeloupe), Lycée Henri IV (Paris) and Ecole Nat. de la France d'Outre-mer.
Admin. France d'Outre-mer 44-46; Dep. from Chad to Nat. Assembly, Paris 46-51, 56-59; Territorial Councillor, Chad 52-59; Pres. Chad Govt. Council 57-58; Deputy Chad Legislative Assembly 59-60; Pres. Council of Ministers,

Repub. of Chad 58-59, Vice-Pres. 59-60; Minister-Counsellor to French Govt. 59-60; Admin.-in-Chief of Overseas Affairs (France); Mayor of Fort-Lamy 56-60; French Govt. Perm. Rep. Econ. Comm. for Latin America (ECLA); Pres. Mutualité d'Outre-mer et de l'Extérieur 63; mem., Cttee. Nationale pour la Campagne Mondiale contre la Faim; fmr. Vice-Pres. Rassemblement Démocratique Africain (R.D.A.); fmr. Joint leader Parti Progressiste Tchadien; First Citizen of Honour of Chad; Officier Légion d'Honneur; Commdr. Ordre Nat. de la République de la Côte d'Ivoire.
3 boulevard des Courcelles, Paris 8e, France.

Lissouba, Pascal, D. ès sc.; Congolese politician; b. 15 Nov. 1931, Tsinguidi, Congo Brazzaville; ed. secondary education in Nice, France, Ecole Supérieure d'Agriculture, Tunis, and Faculty of Sciences, Paris.
Former agricultural specialist; Prime Minister of Congo (Brazzaville) Dec. 63-66, concurrently Minister of Trade and Industry and Agriculture; Prof. of Genetics, Brazzaville 66-71, concurrently Minister of Planning 68; Minister of Agriculture, Waterways and Forests 69; Dir. Ecole Supérieure des Sciences, Brazzaville 71-.
Ecole Supérieure des Sciences, B.P. 69, Brazzaville; and B.P. 717, Brazzaville, People's Republic of the Congo.

Logali, Hilary Nyigilo Paul; Sudanese politician; b. 1931, Juba, Equatoria Province; ed. Khartoum Univ., Yale Univ. Official with Ministry of Finance; Sec.-Gen. Southern Front 64-; Minister of Public Works, then of Communications 65; Minister of Labour and Co-operatives 67-69; fmr. Man. Dir. Bata Nationalized Corpn.; apptd. to rank of Minister 71-; mem. for Finance, Econ. Planning and Agriculture, High Exec. Council for the Southern Region April 72-.
Regional Ministry of Finance and Economic Planning for the Southern Region, Juba, Sudan.

Louw, Dr. Martinus Smuts (Tinie); South African businessman; b. 15 Aug. 1888, Ladismith, Karoo; ed. Stellenbosch Univ.
Teacher, Pietermaritzburg, Ladybrand, later Vice-Principal; teacher in Paarl; joined South African Nat. Life Assurance Co. Ltd. (S.A.N.L.A.M.) June 18 as asst. to actuary; attended Edinburgh Univ., Britain 19-20; appointed actuary, S.A.N.L.A.M. 21, later Manager; Man. Dir. Nov. 46-Dec. 49; ordinary Dir. Dec. 49-66; actuary and Gen. Man., African Homes Trust Assurance Co. 35-45; Hon. Vice-Pres. S.A.N.L.A.M. 66-70, Hon. Pres. 70-; connected with the founding of Federale Volksbeleggings Beperk, Bonusbeleggingskorporasie van Suid-Afrika Beperk Sentrale Nywerheidsaksepbank Beperk and Federale Mynbou Bpk; first Man. Dir. of Bonuskor; Chair. Bonuskor and Saambou 47-70; fmr. Dir.Industrial Devt. Corpn.; fmr. Chair. Central Accepting Bank, Coloured Investment Corpn.; fmr. Dir. Santam; fmr. mem. Council for Scientific and Industrial Research, Board of Stellenbosch Univ., Trustee of South Africa Foundation and Nat. Cancer Soc.; fmr. Pres. Inst. for Admin. and Commerce; Foundation mem., later Pres., Afrikaans Chambers of Commerce; fmr. mem. Prime Minister's Econ. Advisory Council; awarded Frans du Toit Prize 61, Hendrik Verwoerd Prize 65.
c/o Bonuscor, Sanlam Centre, Heerengracht, Cape Town, South Africa.

Lovell, Leopold, B.A., LL.B.; Swazi (British) advocate; b. 1907 Willowmore, S. Africa; ed. Grey Inst., Port Elizabeth, Rhodes Univ. Coll., Grahamstown, and Univ. of S. Africa.
Judge's Registrar, Grahamstown 28-29; Attorney, Benoni, Transvaal 31-61; M.P. (Labour Party), Benoni 49-58; Attorney, Swaziland 61-66; Advocate of Swaziland High Court 67; M.P. and Minister for Finance, Swaziland 67-May 72.
Scott Street, Mbabane, Swaziland.

Luande, H.; Ugandan trade unionist and politician. Former mem., banned Democratic Party (D.P.); M.P. for Kampala East; mem., Uganda People's Congress (U.P.C.); Pres., Uganda Trades Union Congress.
Uganda Trades Union Congress, P.O. Box 2889, Kampala, Uganda.

Lubega, Mathias K. L.; Ugandan diplomatist; b. 26 Dec. 1933; ed. St. Henry's School, Kitovu, Makerere Univ. Coll., England and U.S.A.
Joined diplomatic service 62; Second Sec., Uganda High Comm. in Ghana 64-66; with Ugandan mission to UN 66-68; Dep. Perm. Sec., Foreign Ministry 68-June 69; Amb. to U.S.S.R. June 69-.
Ugandan Embassy, Per. Sadovskikh 5, Moscow, U.S.S.R.

Lukakamwa, Lt.-Col. Samuel Eli; Ugandan army officer and diplomatist; b. 14 Jan. 1941, Butiti; ed. Mons Officer Cadet School, U.K., Nakuru Mil. Training School, Kenya and Staff Coll., Camberley, U.K.
Commissioned, Uganda Army 63; High Commr. to U.K. 71-72.
c/o Ministry of Foreign Affairs, Kampala, Uganda.

Luke, Desmond Edgar Fashole, M.A.; Sierra Leonean diplomatist and barrister; b. 6 Oct. 1935, Freetown; ed. Prince of Wales School, Freetown, King's Coll. Taunton, England, Keble Coll. Oxford and Magdalene Coll. Cambridge.
United Nations Human Rights Fellow, research in India 64; Amb. to Fed. Repub. of Germany 69-, concurrently accredited to Netherlands, Belgium, Luxembourg 70-, to France, Perm. Rep. to EEC 71-; leader of del. to Int. Atomic Energy Agency Conf., Vienna 70.
Embassy of Sierra Leone, 53 Bonn-Bad Godesberg, Ubierstrasse 88; Home: 53 Bonn, Johanniterstrasse 30, Federal Republic of Germany.

Lukindo, Raphael; Tanzanian diplomatist; b. 1933, Kizara; ed. Tanganyika, Makerere Coll., Uganda and Cambridge Univ., England.
First Regional Officer, Dar es Salaam, later in Mzizima District 60-61; joined diplomatic service 62; Second Sec., Tanganyika Embassy to German Federal Republic April 64-Jan. 65; Asst. Sec., Foreign Ministry Feb. 65-Oct. 65; Embassy Counsellor in U.S.A. 65-67; Embassy Counsellor in German Federal Republic 67-68; Amb. to U.S.S.R also accred. to Poland. Nov. 68-.
Embassy of Tanzania, Ulitsa Pyatnitskaya 33/35, Moscow, U.S.S.R.

Lupe Baraba, Elia; Sudanese politician; b. 1924, Yei; ed. Loka Intermediate School, Nabumali High School, Uganda, Sudan Police Coll., Hendon Police Coll., U.K.
Police Inspector 52, Chief Police Inspector 54; Asst. District Commr. 57; mem. Parl. 58-; coffee farmer; joined South Sudanese Liberation Movt. in exile 62; mem. for Public Service, High Exec. Council for the Southern Region 72-.
High Executive Council for the Southern Region, Juba, Sudan.

Lurie, Richard; South African stockbroker; b. 1918. Joined Johannesburg Stock Exchange 46; mem. Exchange Cttee. 60-70, Vice-Pres. 70-72; Pres. Johannesburg Stock Exchange June 72-; fmr. Chair. Wit Industrials.
Johannesburg Stock Exchange, P.O. Box 1174, Johannesburg, South Africa.

Lusaka, Paul John Firmino; Zambian diplomatist; b. 10 Jan. 1935, Broken Hill; ed. Univ. of Minnesota, Univ. of Basutoland and McGill Univ.
Graduate Asst. Lecturer, Univ. of Basutoland 60; Deputy High Commr. to U.K. 66; Amb. to U.S.S.R. 68-72, also

accred. to Yugoslavia, Romania, Czechoslovakia; Perm. Rep. to UN June 72-.
Permanent Mission of Zambia to the United Nations, 641 Lexington Avenue, New York, N.Y. 10022, U.S.A.

Lusinde, Job Malecela; Tanzanian politician; b. 1930, Kikuyu, Dodoma; ed. Alliance Secondary School, Dodoma, Govt. Secondary School, Tabora and Makerere Coll., Uganda.
Teacher, Makerere Coll. and Alliance Secondary School, Dodoma; Exec. Officer, Ugogo Council, Dodoma; Chair., Dodoma Town Council 60; Pres., Tanganyika African Parents Asscn.; M.P. for Dodoma North, Tanzania Nat. Assembly; held portfolios for Local Govt. and Home Affairs; Minister for Communications and Works 61-62; Minister for Home Affairs 62-Sept. 65; Minister for Communications and Works Sept. 65-June 67; Minister for Communications and Transport 67-, for Labour 67-70.
Ministry for Communications and Transport, Dar es Salaam, Tanzania.

Luttig, Hendrik Gerhardus, M.A., D.LITT. ET PHIL.; South African diplomatist; b. 26 Oct. 1907, Wepener, Orange Free State; ed. Wepener High School, Grey Univ. Coll., Bloemfontein (now Univ. of Orange Free State) and Univ. of Leiden, Netherlands.
Member staff Africana Museum, Johannesburg 33-34; Principal of a Correspondence Coll. 34-49; mem. Parl. for Mayfair 49-65; Amb. to Austria 65-67, to U.K. 67-72.
c/o Ministry of Foreign Affairs, Pretoria, South Africa.

Luyt, Sir Richard Edmonds, G.C.M.G., K.C.V.O., D.C.M.; b. 8 Nov. 1915, Cape Town, South Africa; ed. Diocesan Coll., Rondebosch, Univ. of Cape Town, and Trinity Coll., Oxford.
Colonial Service, N. Rhodesia 40; War Service 40-45; Colonial Service, N. Rhodesia 45-53; Labour Commr., Kenya 54-57; Perm. Sec., Minister and Sec. to Cabinet, Kenya Govt. 57-62; Chief Sec. Govt. of N. Rhodesia 62-63; Gov. and Commdr.-in-Chief, British Guiana 64-66; Gov.-Gen. of Guyana May-Oct. 66; Principal and Vice-Chancellor Univ. of Cape Town 68-.
University of Cape Town, Rondebosch, Cape, South Africa.
Telephone: 69-4351.

Lwango Birhwelima, Kashamwuka; Zaire politician.
Vice-Minister of Finance, Budget and Portfolio Oct. 67-March 69; Minister of State for Justice March 69-Aug. 69; Minister of State for Nat. Econ. Aug. 69-Oct. 70; Minister of External Trade 70-71, of Urbanization and Property July 71-Feb. 72.
c/o Ministry of Urbanization, Kinshasa, Zaire.

M

Mabandla, Chief Justice Thandathu; South African (Ciskeian) politician; b. 16 June 1926, Rwarwa, Alice; ed. Macfarlane St. Barnabas Missionary School, Keiskammahoek, Rabula and Lovedale Coll.
Teacher, Ncera Higher Primary School 52-60; became Chief of Bhele Tribe 59; Chief Exec. Councillor, Ciskeian Territorial Authority 68; Chief Minister and Minister of Finance, Ciskeian Legis. Assembly Aug. 72-.
Chief J. T. Mabandla, Chief Minister, Ciskeian Government, Private Bag 426, King William's Town; Zwelitsha, King William's Town, South Africa.

Mabuza, Obed Mpangele Lokotwako; Swazi accountant and politician; b. 16 June 1916, Manzini, Mafutseni Area; ed. Nazarene Mission School, S.A.G.M. School, Mbabane, Swazi Nat. School, Matsapha, Sastri Coll., Durban, Univ. of S. Africa and Natal Univ.

Army service 40-46; Nat. Councillor 47-61; Sec. Swazi Commercial Amadoda 57-61; Sec. Progressive Party 61-65; Leader 65-66; Chair. Swaziland United Front 66-70; Senior Rep. and Chair. Unvikeli Wabantu Nat. Movement Co-operative Soc. 64-70; now Chair. Swaziland United Front of Political Parties and Chair. Joint Council of Swaziland Political Parties; rep. of Swaziland United Front in independence talks, London 68.
Office: P.O. Box 471, Manzini; Home: P.O. Box 14 Kwaluseni, South Africa.

McCann, H. E. Cardinal Owen, D.D., PH.D.; South African ecclesiastic; b. 26 June 1907, Cape Town; ed. St. Joseph's Coll., Rondebosch and Pontificium Collegium Urbanianum de Propaganda Fide.
Ordained priest 35; Titular Bishop of Stettorio 50; Archbishop of Cape Town 51-; named Asst. at the Papal Throne 60; created cardinal 65; Hon. D. Litt. (Univ. of Cape Town).
Archdiocesan Chancery, Cathedral Place, 12 Bouquet Street, Cape Town, South Africa.
Telephone: 452419.

MacDonald, Rt. Hon. Malcolm John, O.M., P.C., M.A.; British diplomatist; b. 17 Aug. 1901, Lossiemouth, Scotland; *s.* of James Ramsay MacDonald (fmr. British Prime Minister); ed. Bedales and Oxford Univ.
Labour M.P. for Bassetlaw Div. of Notts 29-31, and National Labour 31-35 and for Ross and Cromarty 36-45; Parl. Under-Sec. of State for Dominion Affairs in First and Second Nat. Govts. Aug. and Nov. 31-June 35; Sec. of State for the Colonies in reconstructed Cabinet June-Nov. 35; Sec. of State for Dominion Affairs Nov. 35-May 38; Sec. of State for the Colonies May-Oct. 38; Sec. of State for Dominion Affairs and Colonies Oct. 38-Jan. 39, for Colonies Jan. 39-May 40; Min. of Health May 40-Feb. 41; High Commr. in Canada 41-46; Gov.-Gen. of the Malayan Union and Singapore May-July 46; Gov.-Gen. of Malaya and British Borneo 46-48; Commr.-Gen. for U.K. in South-East Asia 48-55; High Commr. in India 55-60; Chancellor Univ. of Malaya 49-61; Co-Chair. Int. Conf. on Laos 61-62; Governor of Kenya Jan.-Dec. 63, Gov.-Gen. Dec. 63-Dec. 64; Visitor, Univ. Coll., Nairobi 63-64; High Commr. in Kenya 64-65; Special Rep. of British Govt. in a number of Commonwealth countries in East and Central Africa 65-66, in Africa 66-69; Special Envoy to Khartoum Nov. 68, Mogadishu Dec. 68; Chancellor, Univ. of Durham 71-; Senior Research Fellow, Univ. of Sussex 71-.
Publs. *Down North* 45, *The Birds of Brewery Creek* 47, *Borneo People* 56, *Angkor* 58, *Birds in my Indian Garden* 61, *Birds in the Sun* 62, *Treasure of Kenya* 65, *People and Places* 69, *Titans and Others* 72.
Raspit Hill, Ivy Hatch, Sevenoaks, Kent.
Telephone: Plaxtol 312.

Machel, Samora Moisés; Mozambique nationalist leader; b. 1933, Gaza province.
Trained as male nurse; joined Frente de Libertação de Moçambique (FRELIMO) March 63; sent to Algeria for military training, organized training camp programme; leader of guerrilla army of FRELIMO 64; mem. Central Cttee., Sec. of Defence 66-, mem. FRELIMO Council of Presidency April 69-, Pres. May 70-.
Publs. Speeches.
FRELIMO Representation in Tanzania, P.O. Box 15274, Dar es Salaam, Tanzania.

Macias Nguema, Francisco; Equatorial Guinean politician; b. 1922 Msegayong, Rio Muni mainland; ed. Catholic Schools in Rio Muni.
Coffee planter 44-; entered Colonial Admin. 44; entered politics 63; Vice-Pres. Admin. Council 64-68; Pres. of the Repub. (Life Pres. July 72) and Minister of Defence Oct.

68-; mem. Popular Idea of Equatorial Guinea (IPGE) Party.

Office of the President, Santa Isabel, Fernando Póo, Equatorial Guinea.

Maga, Hubert; Dahomeyan politician; b. 1916; ed. Ecole Normale de Gorée.

Headmaster of school at Nabitingou until 51; Gen. Counsellor of Dahomey 47; Grand Counsellor of Art 48-57; Deputy for Dahomey to French Nat. Assembly 51-58; Under-Sec. for Labour, Gaillard Cabinet; Minister of Labour in Dahomey 58-59, Premier 59-63, Pres. 60-63; under restriction Dec. 63-Nov. 65; mem. Presidential Council until Oct. 72, Head of State, Minister of Interior and of Defence May 70-May 72; under house arrest Oct. 72; mem. Dahomeyan Democrat Group; awards incl. Mérite Sociale and Etoile Noire de Bénin.

Cotonou, Dahomey.

Mahdi, Saadik El (Great grandson of Imam Abdul-Rahman El-Mahdi); Sudanese politician; b. 1936; ed. Comboni Coll., Khartoum and St. John's Coll., Oxford.

Son of the late Siddik El Mahdi; Leader, Umma Mahdist Party 61-; Prime Minister 66-67; arrested on a charge of high treason 69; exiled April 70; now living in Egypt.

Publ. *Problems of the South Sudan.*

Cairo, Egypt.

Mahgoub, Mohammed Ahmed; Sudanese lawyer and politician; b. 1908; ed. Gordon Coll. and Khartoum School of Law.

Practising lawyer; fmr. mem. Legislative Assembly; accompanied Umma Party Del. to United Nations 47; mem. Constitution Amendment Comm.; non-party candidate in Gen. Election 54; Leader of the Opposition 54-56; Minister of Foreign Affairs 56-58, 64-65, Prime Minister 65-66, May 67-May 69; practising solicitor 58-64.

Publ. several vols. of poetry (in Arabic).

Khartoum, Sudan.

Maiga, Diamballa Yansambou; Niger politician.

Minister of the Interior 62-.

Ministry of the Interior, Niamey, Niger.

Maina, Charles Gatere, B.A.; Kenyan civil servant; b. 1 March 1931, Nyeri; ed. in Kianjogu, Tumutumu, Kagumo and Makerere.

Teacher 59-61; District Educ. Officer 62; Provincial Educ. Officer 62-64; Asst. Chief Educ. Officer 64-66; Deputy Sec. for Educ. 66-68; Principal, Kenya Inst. of Admin. 68-71; mem. Council, Univ. Coll., Dar es Salaam 69-70, Univ. of Nairobi 69-; mem. Agricultural Educ. Comm. 67, Working Party on Higher Educ. in E. Africa 68; Sec.-Gen. E. African Community June 71-.

East African Community, P.O. Box 1001, Arusha, Tanzania.

Telephone: 2240.

Majekodunmi, Chief The Hon. Moses Adekoyejo, C.M.G., LL.D., M.A., M.D., F.R.C.P.I., M.A.O., D.C.H., L.M.; Nigerian doctor and politician; b. 17 Aug. 1916, Abeokuta; s. of Chief J. B. Majekodunmi, Otun of the Egbas; ed. Abeokuta Grammar School, St. Gregory's Coll., Lagos, Trinity Coll., Dublin.

House Physician, Nat. Children's Hospital, Dublin 41-43; Medical Officer, Nigeria 43-49; Senior Specialist, Govt. Maternity Hospital, Lagos 49-59; Senior Specialist Obstetrician, Nigerian Federal Govt. Medical Services 49-60; Senator and Leader of Senate 60-66; Minister of State for the Army 60; Fed. Minister of Health 61-66; Fed. Minister of Health and Information 65; Admin. for W. Nigeria 62; Pres. 16th World Health Assembly 63; Internat. Vice-Pres., 3rd World Conf. on Medical Education, New Delhi 66; Medical Dir. and Chair., Board of Govs., St. Nicholas Hospital, Lagos 67-.

Publs. *Premature Infants: Management and Prognosis* 43,

Partial Apresia of the Cervix Complicating Pregnancy 46, *Sub-Acute Intussusception in Adolescents* 48, *Thiopentone Sodium in Operative Obstetrics* 54, *Rupture of the Uterus Involving the Bladder* 55, *Effects of Malnutrition in Pregnancy and Lactation* 57, *Medical Education and the Health Services: A Critical Review of Priorities in a Developing Country* 66; *Behold the Key* (play) 44.

3 Kingsway, Ikoyi, Lagos, Nigeria.

Telephone: 22450.

Major, Taylor E.; Liberian engineer and administrator; b. 24 Nov. 1918, Greenville, Sinoe County; ed. Liberia Coll. and Howard and Cornell Univs., U.S.A.

Enrolling clerk, Liberian Senate 42-43; Asst. Commr. of Communications and Chief Telephone Engineer 51-63; Commr. of Communications and Telephone Engineer 63; Chair. of Board, Public Utilities Authority 61-; Consultant and Adviser, Dept. of Nat. Planning and Econ. Affairs 67-; Sec. of Public Utilities 69-.

Secretary of Public Utilities Authority, Monrovia, Liberia.

Majugo, Dr. Ivan Kamugasa, Ugandan medical doctor; b. 20 June 1918, Buhanika; ed. Hoima Central School, King's Coll., Budo and Makerere Coll. (now Univ.), Kampala.

Worked in Uganda Govt. Hospitals 43-53; private medical practice 53-64; activities in the work of Uganda People's Congress and Chair. Bunyoro Region; Dep. Chair Uganda Public Service Comm. 64-67; Chair. Makerere Univ. Coll. Council 67-70, Chair. Makerere Univ. Council July 70-; Minister (with responsibility for Common Market and Econ. Affairs), E. African Community 67-70.

Makerere University, P.O. Box 7062, Kampala; Home: P.O. Box 8, Hoima, Uganda.

Makasa, Robert; Zambian politician.

Church Elder, Church of Scotland (now United Church of Zambia), Lubwa 47; Chair. Chinsali Branch, African Nat. Congress 50-52; Pres. Northern Prov., ANC (N. Rhodesia) 53-59; Pres. Luapula Prov., Zambian ANC 60; mem. Parl. for Chinsali North 63-; Parl. Sec. Ministry of Agriculture 63; Resident Minister for Northern Prov. 64-66; Minister of State, Ministry of Foreign Affairs 67; Minister of North Western Prov. 68; Amb. to Ethiopia 68-69; Minister of Luapula Prov. 70-72; High Commr. to Tanzania 72-.

Zambian High Commission, P.O. Box 2525, Plot 291, Upanga, Tanzania.

Makonnen, H.E. Lidj Endalkachew, M.A.; Ethiopian politician; b. 1927; ed. Haile Selassie I Secondary School, Addis Ababa and Oriel Coll., Oxford.

Ministry of Foreign Affairs 51-58, Acting Head Dept. of Protocol 52-53, Chief of Protocol 53-56, Asst. Minister 56-57, Vice-Minister 57-58; Vice-Minister of Social Affairs 58-59; Ambassador to the U.K. 59-61; Minister of Commerce and Industry 61-66; Chair. Board of Govs., Univ. Coll. Addis Ababa 59, Nat. Coffee Board 62; Perm. Rep. to UN 66-69; Minister of Posts and Telecommunications 69-; candidate for post of UN Sec.-Gen. 71; numerous decorations.

Ministry of Posts and Telecommunications, Addis Ababa, Ethiopia.

Malecela, John William Samuel; Tanzanian diplomatist and politician; b. 1934; ed. Bombay Univ. and Cambridge Univ.

Administrative Officer, Civil Service 60-61; Consul in U.S.A. and Third Sec. to the UN 62; Regional Commr., Mwanza Region 63; Perm. Rep. to the UN 64-68; Amb. to Ethiopia 68; East African Minister for Communications, Research and Social Services, East African Community 69-70, for Finance and Admin. 70-72; Minister of Foreign Affairs Feb. 72-; Order of Merit of First Degree (Egypt); First Order of Independence (Equatorial Guinea).

Ministry of Foreign Affairs, Dar es Salaam, Tanzania.

Malherbe, Ernst G., M.A., PH.D.; South African education-
ist; b. 8 Nov. 1895, Luckhoff, Orange Free State; ed.
Stellenbosch and Columbia Univs.
Studied Oxford, The Hague, Amsterdam, Germany;
Fellow, Teachers' Coll., Columbia Univ. 23-24; South
African rep. British Assch. Centenary Meeting, Lon-
don 31; fmrly. teacher Cape Town Training Coll.;
Lecturer in Educational Psychology, Stellenbosch Univ.;
Senior Lecturer in Education, Cape Town Univ.; Chief
Investigator, Education Section, Carnegie Poor White
Research Comm. 28-32; mem. Govt. Comm. to Investi-
gate Native Education in South Africa 35; Dir. Nat.
Bureau of Educational and Social Research for South
Africa 29-39; Dir. of Census and Statistics for Union 39-45;
Lt.-Col. Dir. Army Educ. Services 40-45; Dir. Military
Intelligence Union Defence Forces 42-45; Principal and
Vice-Chancellor Univ. of Natal 45-65; Pres. S. African
Asscn. for the Advancement of Science 50-51; Pres. South
African Inst. of Race Relations 66-68; Hon. M.A. (Sydney);
Hon. LL.D. (Cambridge, Queens, Melbourne, McGill, Cape
Town, Natal, Rhodes, Witwatersrand, St. Andrews).
Publs. *Education in South Africa 1652 to 1922* 25, *Education
and the Poor White* 32, *Education in a Changing Empire* 32,
Educational Adaptations in a Changing Society (Editor) 37,
Entrance Age of University Students in Relation to Success
38, *Educational and Social Research in South Africa* 39, *The
Bilingual School* 43, *Race Attitudes and Education* 46, *Our
Universities and the Advancement of Science* 51, *Die
Outonomie van ons Universiteite en Apartheid* 57, *Education
for Leadership in Africa* 60, *Problems of School Medium in a
Bilingual Country* 62, *The Need for Dialogue* 67, *Education
and the Development of South Africa's Human Resources* 67,
The Nemesis of Docility 68, *Bantu Manpower and Education*
69; articles in *Chamber's Encyclopaedia, Standard En-
cyclopedia of Southern Africa*, and diverse journals and
year books.
By-die-See, Salt Rock, Umhlali, Natal, S. Africa.
Telephone: Umhlali 103.

Malinga, Norman M.; Swazi diplomatist; b. 17 Nov.
1938, Zombodze; ed. Mphumulo Teacher Training Coll.,
Natal and Columbia Univ., U.S.A.
School teacher 62-65; Librarian, Warden, Staff Training
Inst., Swaziland 65-68, Asst. Establishment Officer 68;
Asst. Sec. Dept. of Foreign Affairs 68-70; Swaziland
Counsellor in East Africa 70-71; Dir. of Broadcasting and
Information 71-72; Perm. Rep. to UN 72-.
Permanent Mission of Swaziland to United Nations, 860
United Nations Plaza, Suite 420, New York, N.Y. 10017,
U.S.A.

Malloum, Col. Félix; Chadian army officer; b. 1932,
Fort-Archambault (now Sarh); ed. Military Schools,
Brazzaville, Fréjus, Saint-Maixent.
Served in French Army, Indochina 53-55, Algeria; joined
Chad Nat. Army; Lieut.-Col. 61, Capt. 62, Col. 68; fmr.
Head of Mil. Corps at the Presidency; Chief of Staff of the
Army Dec. 71-Sept. 72; C.-in-C. of the Armed Forces
Sept. 72-.
General Staff Headquarters, Fort-Lamy, Chad.

Malula, H.E. Cardinal Joseph-Albert; Zaire ecclesiastic;
b. 17 Dec. 1917, Kinshasa (then Léopoldville); ed. Petit
Séminaire, Bolongo, Grand Séminaire, Kabwe.
Vicar in Parish of Christ-Roi; Auxiliary Bishop of Léopoldville 59-64; Archbishop of Kinshasa 64-; cr. Cardinal
69; Pres. Univ. of Lovanium.
B.P. 8431, Kinshasa 1, Zaire.

Mamoudou, Maidah; Niger politician; b. 1924; Tessoua,
Maradi District; ed. Frédéric Assomption School, Kati-
bougou, Mali.
Former Teacher; Minister of Agriculture 59-60; Minister of

Educ. 60-63, of Rural Economy 63-71, of Foreign Affairs
71-72; Minister-Del. to the Pres. Aug. 72-.
Office of the President, Niamey, Niger.

Manambelona, Dr. Justin; Malagasy physicist; b. 31 May
1925, Mananjary, Fianarantsoa Prov.; ed. Tananarive,
Univ. of Paris.
Secretary-General Scientific Research Dept., Univ. of
Paris, then Prof. of Biophysics until 72; Minister of Culture
May 72-.
Ministère des Affaires Culturelles, Tananarive, Madagascar.

Mancham, Hon. James Richard Marie, F.R.S.A.; Sey-
chelles lawyer and politician; b. 11 Aug. 1939; ed. Univ.
of Paris and Middle Temple, London.
Called to the Bar, Middle Temple 61; mem. Legislative
Council of the Seychelles 61; mem. Gov. Council 67;
founder and leader Social Democratic Party 64-; mem.
Legislative Assembly 70-; Chief Minister, Council of
Ministers Nov. 70-.
Publ. *Reflections and Echoes from Seychelles.*
The White House, Bel Eau, Victoria, Mahé, Seychelles.

Mandefro, Ayalew; Ethiopian diplomatist; b. 4 June
1935, Harrar; ed. Ras Mekonnen Elementary School,
Harrar, General Wingate Secondary School, Univ. Coll. of
Addis Ababa and Tufts Univ., U.S.A.
Joined Ministry of Foreign Affairs 58; Private Sec. to
Minister of Foreign Affairs 61-64; Asst. Minister in charge
of American and Press Dept., Ministry of Foreign Affairs
64; Amb. to Somalia 70-; mem. Ethiopian del. to UN Gen.
Assembly 64, 66, 68, to OAU Ministerial Confs. 64-68;
Officer, Order of the Star of Honour of Ethiopia, Officier,
Légion d'Honneur (France).
P.O. Box 455, via Mogadishu, Somalia; P.O. Box 5513, Addis
Ababa, Ethiopia.

Mandela, Nelson Rolihlahla; South African lawyer and
politician; b. 1918; ed. Fort Hare, Univ. of the Witwatersrand.
Son of Chief of Tembu tribe; legal practice, Johannesburg
52; Nat. organizer African Nat. Congress (A.N.C.); on trial
for treason 56-61 (acquitted 61); arrested 62, sentenced to
five years imprisonment Nov. 62; on trial for further
charges Nov. 63-June 64, sentenced to life imprisonment
June 64.
Publ. *No Easy Walk to Freedom* 65.
Robben Island, nr. Cape Town, South Africa.

Mandi, André Fernand; Zaire diplomatist; b. 1934,
Upoto, Equatorial Province of the Congo; ed. Jesuit Coll.,
Congo, Dept. for Admin. Studies, Univ. of Lovanium
Kisanti and Université Libre de Bruxelles.
Joined Civil Service 52; served, Dept. of Statistics 52-57;
Sec. of State for Foreign Affairs 60; subsequently Minister
to Rome; Amb. to Romania and Yugoslavia; Amb. to
France 69-71; Perm. Rep. to UNESCO 70-71; del. to
various int. confs. including Council of Ministers of OAU;
Perm. Rep. to UN Aug. 71-72.
c/o Ministry of Foreign Affairs, Kinshasa, Zaire.

Manfull, Melvin Lawrence, A.B.; American diplomatist;
b. 24 Feb. 1919; ed. Weber Coll., Univ. of Utah, American
Univ., Washington.
National Inst. of Public Affairs 41-42; Officer, U.S. Naval
Reserve 42-45; U.S. Dept. of State 46-52, 57-62; Exec. Sec.
Del. to NATO and other regional orgs., Paris 52-57;
Counsellor for Political Affairs, Saigon 62-65; Imperial
Defence Coll. (now Royal Coll. of Defence Studies),
London 66; Deputy Chief of Mission, Brussels 67-70; Amb.
to Central African Repub. 71-.
American Embassy, place de la République, B.P. 924,
Bangui, Central African Republic.

Mangope, Chief Lawrence Lucas Manyane; South
African (Tswana) politician; b. 23 Dec. 1923, Motswedi,
Zeerust; ed. St. Peter's Coll. and Bethel Training Coll.

Teacher, Motswedi Secondary School 53-59; became Chief 59; Vice-Chair. Tswana Territorial Authority 61; Chief Councillor and Chair, Tswana Exec. Council 68; Chief Minister and Minister of Finance, Bophuthatswana Legis. Assembly June 72-.

Chief Minister, Bophuthatswana Government, Private Bag 5, Mafeking; Montshiwa Township, Mafeking, South Africa.

Mangwazu, Timon Sam; Malawi diplomatist; b. 12 Oct. 1935, Kasungu; ed. Inyati Boys' Inst. (London Missionary Society) Bulawayo, Tegwani Methodist Secondary School, Plumtree, Rushkin and Brasenose Colls., Oxford.

Nyasaland Civil Service 56; Sec.-Gen. Nyasaland African Civil Servants Association 61; Asst. Registrar of Trade Unions 63; First Sec. British Embassy in Vienna 64; Amb. of Malawi to German Fed. Repub., later accred. to Norway, Sweden, Denmark, Netherlands, Belgium, Switzerland, Austria 64-67; Malawi High Commr. in U.K. 67-69, concurrently Amb. to Holy See, Portugal, Netherlands and Belgium; reading Econs. and Politics at Brasenose Coll., Oxford 69-71; Malawi Independence Medal; Malawi Repub. Medal, Knight Commdr. Cross of Order of Merit of Federal Republic of Germany.

c/o Ministry of Foreign Affairs, Blantyre, Malawi.

Manuwa, Chief the Hon. Sir Samuel Layinka Ayodeji, Kt.; The Iyasere (Chief) of Itebu-Manuwa, The Obadugba of Ondo, The Olowa Luwagboye of Ijebu Ode, C.M.G., O.B.E., C.ST.J., LL.D., D.SC., D.LITT., M.D., CH.B., F.R.C.S., F.R.C.P., F.A.C.S., F.A.C.P., F.R.S. (Edin.); Nigerian surgeon and medical administrator; b. 4 March 1903, Ijebu Ode, Western Nigeria; ed. King's Coll., Lagos, Edinburgh and Liverpool Univs.

Medical Officer and Senior Surgical Specialist British Colonial Medical Service 27-48; Deputy Dir. Medical Services 48-51, Dir. 51, Insp.-Gen. 51-54; Chief Medical Adviser to Fed. Govt. of Nigeria 54-59; mem. Western Nigeria House of Assembly 48-51; mem. Legislative and Exec. Councils 51-52; mem. Governor's Privy Council 52-54; mem. Fed. Privy Council 54-60, Public Service Comm. 54-; Pro-Chancellor and Chair. of Council, Univ. of Ibadan 67-; Fellow, Royal Soc. of Arts, London, American Public Health Asscn.; mem. New York Acad. of Sciences; mem. World Health Organization Expert Panel on Public Health Admin. and Advisory Cttee. on Medical Research; Pres. World Fed. for Mental Health 65-66; Past Pres. Asscn. of Physicians of W. Africa; Past Pres. Asscn. of Surgeons of W. Africa; Commdr. Order of St. John; John Holt Medal of Liverpool Univ. for Services to Tropical Medicine.

Publs. *History of the Development of our Knowledge of the Endocrine Organs* 24, *Hernia in the West African Negro* 29, *Chronic Splenomegaly in West Africa, Spinal Anaesthesia* 34, *Lymphostatic Verrucosis* 35, *Porocephalosis* 47, *The Estimation of Age in Nigerian Children* 57, *Principles of Planning National Health Programmes in Under-Developed Countries* 61, *Mental Health Programmes in Public Health Planning* 63, *Mental Health is Common Wealth* 67, *The Training of Senior Administrators for Higher Responsibilities in the National Health Services of Developing Countries* 67, *Mass Campaign as an Instrument of Endemic Disease Control in Developing Countries* 68.

Federal Public Service Commission, Lagos; Pro-Chancellor's Lodge, The University of Ibadan, Ibadan; 2 Alexander Avenue, Lagos, Nigeria.

Telephone: 53588 (Lagos); 62550 (Ibadan).

Marchand, Jean Marie Michel Guy; Mauritius accountant and politician; b. 1926, Port Louis; ed. Couvent de Bon Secours, Port Louis, Visitation Roman Catholic Aided School, Vacoas and St. Joseph Coll., Curepipe.

Member, Parti Mauricien Social Démocrate (P.M.S.D.) Regional Cttee. for Vacoas 53-; P.M.S.D. Exec. Cttee.

59-; Legislative Council 63; mem., Town Council, Vacoas/Phoenix 63; Pres. 64; first M.L.A. for Curepipe and Midlands (P.M.S.D.) 67-69; mem., Municipal Council, Port Louis 69-; Minister of Commerce and Industry Dec. 69-.

Ministry of Commerce and Industry, Port Louis, Mauritius.

Maree, Willem Adriaan, B.A.; South African politician; b. 7 Aug. 1920; ed. High School, Brandfort (Orange Free State), and Univ. of Pretoria.

Nat. Party Organizer 43-45; farmer 45-48; M.P. Newcastle 48-; mem. Native Affairs Comm. 54; Minister of Bantu Educ. 58-66, of Indian Affairs Aug. 61-66, and of Forestry 64-66; Minister of Community Devt., Public Works, Social Welfare and Pensions 66-68; Chair. Drakensberg Press, Durban; Gov. SABC.

P.O. Box 2969 Pretoria, Republic of South Africa.

Margai, Sir Albert Michael, Kt.; Sierra Leone lawyer and politician; b. 10 Oct. 1910; ed. Catholic Schools, Bonthe and Freetown, and Middle Temple, London.

Nurse and Druggist 32-44; called to the Bar 47; mem. Sierra Leone Protectorate Assembly 49, Sierra Leone Legislative Council 51; Minister of Education and Welfare, and Local Government 51-57, of Finance 62-64; Prime Minister of Sierra Leone 64-March 67; mem. Sierra Leone People's Party 51-58; Founder-mem. People's Nat. Party 58; Knight of the Grand Cross of St. Gregory the Great.

Freetown, Sierra Leone.

Mariam, Tashoma Haile, B.C.L.; Ethiopian diplomatist; b. Dec. 1927; ed. Univ. Coll. of Addis Ababa and McGill Univ., Canada.

Codification Dept., Ministry of Justice, Addis Ababa 59-60; Dir.-Gen. of Legal Div., Private Cabinet of Emperor Haile Selassie 60-64; Attorney-Gen. 64-65; Ambassador to U.S.A. 65-67; Pres. of the Supreme Court 68-; mem. UN Comm. of Enquiry into Congo 61.

The Supreme Imperial Court, Addis Ababa, Ethiopia.

'Maseribane Chief Sekhonyana Nehemia; Basotho Chief; b. 4 May 1918; ed. Eagles Park Coll., Basutoland. Prominent Trader in Quthing District; descendant of First Paramount Chief of Basutoland, Chief Moshoeshoe I, Chief of Mount Moorosi; mem. Econ. Planning Council of Basutoland; Pres. Basuto Courts 47, and Assessor to Basutoland High Court; mem. Econ. Mission to U.S.A. 62; Prime Minister of Basutoland May-July 65, Deputy Prime Minister and Minister of Internal and External Affairs, and Leader of the House July 65-Jan. 66; Deputy Prime Minister and Minister of Internal Security and Home Affairs Jan. 66-March 70; Minister of Agriculture March 70-; Deputy Prime Minister Aug. 71-; Vice-Pres. Nat. Party.

Ministry of Agriculture, Maseru, Lesotho.

Masire, Dr. Quett K. J.; Botswana politician; b. 23 July 1925; ed. Kanye and Tiger Kloof.

Founded Seepapitso Secondary School 50; reporter, later dir., *African Echo* 58; mem., Bangwaketse Tribal Council, Legislative Council; fmr. mem., Exec. Council; foundation mem., Botswana Democratic Party (B.D.P.), Sec. Gen. and Editor of party newspaper *Therisanyo*; mem., Legislative (now Nat.) Assembly March 65; Dep. Prime Minister March 65-Aug. 66; attended Ind. Conf., London Feb. 66; Vice-Pres. and Minister of Finance April 66, now Vice-Pres. and Minister of Finance and Devt. Planning.

Office of the Vice-President, Gaborone, Botswana.

Massamba-Debat, Alphonse; Congolese politician; b. 1921; ed. Teacher Training Coll., Brazzaville.

Teacher, primary school, Fort Lamy, Chad 40; Sec.-Gen. Asscn. des Evolués du Tchad 45-47; Headmaster, primary schools, Mossendjo and Brazzaville; fmr. mem. Congo Progressive Party; mem. Democratic Union for Defence of Interests of Africa (U.D.D.I.A.) 56-; Asst. to Minister of Educ.; mem. Legislative Assembly 59-61, Pres. 59-61;

fmr. Minister of Planning and Equipment; Head of Provisional Govt. and Minister of Defence Aug.-Dec. 63; Pres. 63-68, assumed full powers Aug.-Sept. 68; arrested Oct. 69.
Brazzaville, People's Republic of Congo.

Maswanya, Saidi Ali; Tanzanian politician; b. 1923, Usungu, Tabora District; ed. Govt. Secondary School, Tabora.
Served with Uganda and Tanganyika Police; District Sec. of Tanganyika African Nat. Union (T.A.N.U.) at Shinyanga 56-58; Chair., T.A.N.U., Western Province 58-59; Dep. Organizing Sec.-Gen. of T.A.N.U. 59-60, and to T.A.N.U. Exec. Cttee. 61; Dep. Mayor, Dar es Salaam 60; Minister without Portfolio 62; Minister of Health; Minister of Agriculture, Forests and Wildlife until Sept. 65; Minister of Lands, Settlement and Water Devt. Sept. 65-June 67; mem. Parl. for Urambo 70-; Minister for Home Affairs 70-.
Ministry for Home Affairs, Dar es Salaam, Tanzania.

Matante, Philip Parcel Goanwe; Botswana politician. Leader, Opposition Party (Botswana People's Party), Nat. Assembly.
Botswana People's Party, Gaborone, Botswana.

Matanzima, Chief Kaizer; South African (Transkei) lawyer and politician; b. 1915; ed. Lovedale Missionary Institution and Fort Hare Univ. Coll.
Chief, Amahale Clan of Tembus, St. Marks' District 40; mem. United Transkeian Gen. Council 42-56; Perm. Head Emigrant Tembuland Regional Authority and mem. Exec. Cttee. Transkeian Territorial Authority 56-58; Regional Chief of Emigrant Tembuland 58-61; Presiding Chief Transkeian Territorial Authority 61-63; Chief Minister of Transkei and Minister of Finance 63-.
Office of the Chief Minister, Umtata, Transkei, South Africa.

Matenje, Dick Tennyson; Malawian educationist and politician; b. 29 Jan. 1929, Blantyre; ed. Henry Henderson Inst., Blantyre Secondary School, Domasi Teachers' Coll., Univs. of Bristol, Ottawa, British Columbia.
Teacher 51-62; District Educ. Officer Aug-Dec. 62; studied educ. systems in Australia 62-63; Lecturer, Soche Hill Teachers' Coll. Aug-Dec. 63; Headmaster, Soche Hill Secondary School Jan.-Aug. 64; Secondary Schools Staffing Officer, Ministry of Educ. 69-71; Principal, Domasi Teachers' Coll. March-Dec. 71; mem. Parl. 71-; Junior Minister, Ministry of Trade and Industry Jan. 72, Minister Feb.-April 72; Minister of Finance April 72-.
Ministry of Finance P.O. Box 53, Zomba; and Bemvu Primary School, P.O. Ncheu, Malawi.

Matoka, Peter Wilfred; Zambian politician and diplomatist; b. 8 April 1930, Nswanakudya Village, Mwinilunga, North-Western Province; ed. Mwinilunga Lower Middle School, Munali Training Centre, Munali Secondary School, Fort Hare Univ. Coll. and American Univ., Washington, D.C.
Civil Servant 55-63; Minister of Information and Postal Services 64-65, of Health 65-66, of Works 67, of Power, Transport and Works 68; Minister for Luapula Province 69; High Commr. of Zambia in U.K. 69-Nov. 70; concurrently accredited to the Vatican; Minister of Southern Province Nov. 70-June 71; Minister of Health May 71-Feb. 72, of Local Govt. and Housing Feb. 72-; Knight of St. Gregory (Vatican) 64; Knight, Egypt and Ethiopia.
Ministry of Local Government and Housing, Livingstone, Zambia.

Matsebula, Mhlangano Stephen; Swazi business executive and politician; b. 16 July 1925, Maphalaleni, Mbabane; ed. High School.
Regional Sec. Swazi Commercial Amadoda; Exec. mem.

Imbokodvo Nat. Movt.; mem. House of Assembly 67-; Minister of State for Foreign Affairs May 72-.
Leisure interests: handicrafts, reading, football.
Department of Foreign Affairs, P.O. Box 518, Mbabane, Swaziland.

Mayaki, Adamou; Niger agricultural engineer and diplomatist; b. 1919, Filingué, Niger.
Member Territorial Council, Niger 52; mem. Grand Council of French W. Africa 52-58; mem. Council of French Union 53-58; Minister for Econ. Affairs 58-60, Industry and Commerce 61-63, Foreign Affairs 63-65; Amb. to U.S. and Canada 66-; Perm. Rep. to UN 68-70.
c/o Ministry of Foreign Affairs, Niamey, Niger.

M'Bahia Ble, Kouadio; Ivory Coast politician and fmr. teacher; b. 19 Dec. 1928, Sinzekro; ed. William-Ponty School, Sebikhotane, Senegal.
Former teacher, later Vice-Principal, Bonake School 50-53; Dir. of schools 53-56; responsible for Ivory Coast students in France 56-57; territorial councillor for Bonake March 57-; mem., Political Office of Parti Démocratique de la Côte d'Ivoire (P.D.C.I.); mem., Constituent Assembly 58-April 59, Legislative Assembly April 59-; Treas., Legislative Assembly Dec. 59-Feb. 63; Minister of Youth and Sports Feb. 63-Sept. 63; Minister of the Armed Forces, Youth and Civic Services Sept. 63-Sept. 68; Minister of the Armed Forces and Civic Services Sept. 68-.
Ministry of the Armed Forces and Civic Services, Abidjan, Ivory Coast.

Mbanefo, Sir Louis Nwachukwu, Nigerian lawyer and administrator; b. May 1911, Onitsha, E. Nigeria; ed. London Univ. and Middle Temple.
Private law practice, Nigeria; mem., Nigerian Legislative Council 49-51; judge of Supreme Court, Nigeria 52-59; Chief Justice of E. Nigeria 59-70; knighted 61; judge, International Court at The Hague 62-; fmr. mem. Board of Educ., Nigerian Coal Board, E. Nigeria Devt. Board; fmr. Chair., Comm. to review govt. service salaries 59; Leader of Biafran del. to negotiate peace, London May 68, Kampala peace talks 68; Leader, peace del. Jan. 70; arrest reported June 70; Chair. Ibadan Univ. Council; Chancellor, Niger Diocese, Anglican Mission in Nigeria; mem. Nigerian Olympic Cttee., British Commonwealth Games; Fellow (London Univ.).
International Court of Justice, The Hague, Netherlands.

Mbekeani, Nyemba Wales; Malawi diplomatist; b. 15 June 1929, Blantyre; ed. Henry Henderson Inst. and London School of Economics.
Chief Clerk, Municipality of Blantyre and Limbe 45-58; Company Exec. 60-61; Asst. Town Clerk, Blantyre 63; High Commr. of Malawi in U.K. 64-67; Amb. to Vatican 66-67; Perm. Rep. to UN, Amb. to U.S.A. 67-72; Amb. to Ethiopia Sept. 72-.
Malawian Embassy, Ras Desta Damtew Avenue, P.O. Box 2316, Addis Ababa, Ethiopia.

Mbilishi, Samuel; Zambian politician.
Ambassador to U.S.A. May 66-Feb. 68; Minister of State for Home Affairs Feb. 68-Oct. 69; Cabinet Minister for N. Province Oct. 69-72, for Luapala Prov. Feb. 72-.
Office of the Minister of Luapala Province, Lusaka, Zambia.

Mbita, Maj. Hashim Iddi; Tanzanian journalist and army officer; b. 2 Nov. 1933, Tabora; ed. Govt. Town School, Tabora Govt. Senior Secondary School, East African School of Co-operatives, Kabete, Kenya, American Press Inst. (Columbia Univ., New York), Mons Officer Cadet School, Aldershot, England.
Assistant Co-operative Inspector 58-60; Public Relations Officer 60-62; Press Officer 62-64; Senior Press Officer 64-65; Press Sec. to the Pres. 66-67; Publicity Sec. Tanganyika African Nat. Union 67-68, Nat. Exec. Sec. 70-72;

Army Officer 69; Exec. Sec. OAU Liberation Cttee. Aug. 72-.
Liberation Committee, P.O. Box 1767, Dar es Salaam, Tanzania.

Mboua, Marcel Marigoh; Cameroonian politician; b. 1921, Batouri.
Worked as teacher; mem., Territorial Assembly of French Cameroons; Minister of Labour and Social Affairs 57-58; Pres. Exec. Cttee., Cameroon Nat. Union Aug. 66; Pres. Nat. Fed. Assembly 62-, became Nat. Assembly 72.
c/o National Assembly, Yaoundé, United Republic of Cameroon.

Mbouy-Boutzit, Edouard-Alexis; Gabonese politician; b. 3 Oct. 1933, Lambaréné; ed. Poitiers and Caen Univs., France.
Assistant dir., O.A.M.P.I., Yaoundé; Sec.-Gen. to the Presidency of the Republic (Gabon) until 69; Sec. of State to the Presidency of the Republic responsible for Planning and Devt. Feb. 69-March 69; Minister of Econ. Affairs, Trade, Industry and Devt. 69-72, of Mines, Industry, Energy and Water Resources Sept. 72-.
Ministry of Mines and Industry, Libreville, Gabon.

M'bow, Amadou-Mahtar, L. ès L.; Senegalese educationist; b. 20 March 1921, Dakar; ed. Faculté des Lettres, Univ. de Paris.
Professor, Coll. de Rosso, Mauritania 51-52; Dir. Service of Elementary Educ. 53-57; Minister of Educ. and Culture 57-58; Prof. Lycée Faidherbe, St. Louis 58-65; Ecole Normale Supérieure, Dakar 65-66; Minister of Educ. 66-68; Minister of Culture, Youth and Sport 68-70; Asst. Dir.-Gen. for Educ., UNESCO Nov. 70-; Commdr. Ordre national (Ivory Coast), Commdr. des Palmes académiques (France), Officier, Ordre du Mérite (Senegal).
Publs. numerous monographs, articles in educational journals, textbooks, etc.
127 rue de Longchamp, 75116 Paris, France.
Telephone: 553-23-11.

Mensah, Joseph Henry, M.SC.; Ghanaian politician; b. 31 Oct. 1928; ed. Achimota Coll., Univ. Coll. of Gold Coast (now Univ. of Ghana), London School of Econs. and Stanford Univ.
Assistant Insp. of Taxes 53; Research Fellow, Univ. Coll. of Gold Coast 53-57; Lecturer in Economics Univ. of Ghana 57-58; Economist, UN H.Q., New York 58-61; Chief Economist, Principal Sec. and Exec. Sec of Nat. Planning Comm. Ghana 61-65; Economist, UN Dir., Div. of Trade and Econ. Co-operation, and Econ. Comm. for Africa (ECA) 65-May 69; Commr. of Finance April 69-July 69; M.P. for Sunyani (Progress Party) 69-72; Minister of Finance and Econ. Planning Sept. 69-Jan. 71, of Finance Jan. 71-Jan. 72.
c/o Ministry of Finance, Accra, Ghana.

Mgonya, Chediel Yohane; Tanzanian polititican; b. 1934 Vudee, Paree District; ed. Govt. Secondary School, Tabora, Makerere Coll., London Univ. and Cambridge Univ.
Served as Admin. Officer, local govt. 59-62; Foreign Service Officer, Tanganyika UN Mission, New York July 62-Aug. 64; Senior Asst. Sec., Ministry of Foreign Affairs 64-Sept. 65; Minister of Community Devt. and Nat. Culture Sept. 65-June 67; leader, Tanzanian del. to UN 66-67; Min. of State June 67, later Minister of State for Foreign Affairs until Nov. 68; Minister of Nat. Educ. Nov. 68-72.
c/o Ministry of National Education, Dar es Salaam, Tanzania.

Mhando, Stephen; Tanzanian politician; b. 1918, Tanga; ed. King's Coll., Budo, Uganda, Tabora Secondary School and Makerere Coll.
Teacher in govt. schools 39, later Inspector of schools

(Swahili), Head of Swahili dept., Chang'ombe Teacher's Coll. and Reader in Swahili, Humboldt Univ., Berlin; Editor, *Ngurumo, The Nationalist, Uhuru* and *Mfanyakazi*; Chair., Central Negotiating Council, Arbitration Tribunal; Man. Dir., Tanganyika Sisal Marketing Asscn.; Pres., Tanganyika African Teacher's Asscn., African Govt. Servants' Asscn. and Tanganyika African Asscn.; Gen. Sec., Tanganyika African Nat. Union (T.A.N.U.) 56-58; Minister of State for Foreign Affairs Nov. 68-Nov. 70; Minister of State Nov. 70-71; Chair. Nat. Swahili Council; mem. Univ. Coll. Council; Nat. mem. Nat. Assembly.
c/o National Assembly, Dar es Salaam, Tanzania.

Miadana, Victor; Malagasy politician; b. 1920, Ambodimandresy, Antsohihy, Majunga Province; ed. Ecole Régionale d'Analalava, Ecole Le Myre de Vilers and Ecole Normale de Nice, France.
Member, Provincial Assembly of Diego-Suarez March 57, later Pres., Council of the Province; Pres., temporary Bureau of the Parti Social Démocratique (P.S.D.) Aug. 57; Pres., P.S.D. Fed., Province of Diego-Suarez; M.P., Nat. Assembly (for Diego-Suarez) Oct. 58-; Mayor of Mandritsara Dec. 64; M.P. for Majunga Province Aug. 65-; Sec. of State, Ministry of Finance, responsible for the Economy June 59-Oct. 60; Sec. of State for the Budget Oct. 60-Jan. 63; Minister of Finance Jan. 63, of Finance and Commerce Aug. 65-70; Minister of Finance until 72, concurrently Vice-Pres. Oct. 70-72, in charge of Planning.
c/o Ministry of Finance, Tananarive, Madagascar.

Micombero, Col. Michel; Burundian army officer and politician; b. 1940; ed. Catholic Colls. of St. Esprit, Bujumbura, and Military Acad., Brussels.
Recalled from Brussels Mil. Acad. when Burundi became independent 62; Chief of Staff 62; later Minister of Nat. Defence; Chief of Secs. of State 65-66; Col. 66; Prime Minister July 66-; Pres. Nov. 66-.
Office of the President, Bujumbura, Burundi.

Migolet, Stanislas-Jean: Gabonese politician; b. 1920, Koula-Moutou: ed. R.C. Mission school, Mbigou.
Worked as clerk to the Admin. 41-47; served in Gen. Council 47-52; Vice-Pres. of the Territorial Assembly 52-57; Minister of the Interior 57-58; Minister of Labour and Social Affairs 58-60; Minister of the Interior and Nat. Security 60-61: Pres., Nat. Budgetary and Finance Comm. 61-64; Minister of the Interior 64; Minister of State for Public Works until July 68; Minister of the Interior July 68-Dec. 69; Minister of State for Labour and Social Insurance responsible for Relations with the Nat. Assembly, concurrently Deputy Vice-Pres. Dec. 69-.
Ministry of Labour and Social Insurance, Libreville, Gabon.

Milner, Aaron, Zambian politician.
Minister of State for the Cabinet and Civil Service; Minister of State for Presidential Affairs Sept. 67-Jan. 70; Minister of Transport, Power and Works Jan. 70-Nov. 70; Sec. Gen. to Govt. Nov. 70-, concurrently Minister of Provincial and Local Govt. and Culture Aug. 71-.
Ministry of Provincial and Local Government, Lusaka, Zambia.

Mirghani, Abdel Karim, B.A., Sudanese politician and diplomatist; b. 1 Jan. 1924; ed. Omdurman Intermediate School, Gordon Memorial Coll., Univ. of Bristol.
Sub-mamour 46-48; teacher in nat. schools 48-53; joined Ministry of Foreign Affairs 56 as Chargé d'Affaires in London, later Head Political Section, Khartoum; mem. Sudan del. to the Admission of Sudan to the UN 56; Deputy Perm. Rep. of Sudan to UN, N.Y. 58-60; Amb. of Sudan to India, Japan, Ceylon 60-64; Minister of Commerce, Industry, Supply and Co-operation 64; Amb. to Italy 65, to Greece 66, to U.A.R. 68; Minister of Econs. and Foreign

Trade May 69; Minister of Planning Oct. 69-Sept. 70; Amb. to Greece 70-.
Embassy of Sudan, Athens, Greece.

Mkwawa, Chief Adam Sapi, O.B.E.; Tanzanian politician and administrator; b. 1920, Iringa; ed. Govt. Secondary School, Tabora and Makerere Univ. Coll., Uganda.
Paramount Chief of the Hehe 40-62; mem., Tanganyika Legislative Council 47; Speaker, Nat. Assembly 62-; Chair. Board of Trustees of Tanganyika's Nat. Parks; Chair., Electoral Comm.
National Assembly, Dar es Salaam, Tanzania.

Mobutu, Gen. Sese Seko; Zaire politician; b. 14 Oct. 1930; ed. Léopoldville and Coquilhatville.
Sergeant-Major, Accountancy Dept., Force Publique, Belgian Congo 49-56; course at Institute of Social Studies, Brussels; journalist, Léopoldville; mem. Mouvement National Congolaise; del. Brussels Round Table Conf. on Congo Independence 59-60; Sec. of State for Nat. Defence, Lumumba cabinet, June 60; Chief of Staff, Congo Army, July 60; took over supreme power in name of army and suspended all political activity for three months Sept. 60; appointed a College of High Commrs. to take over govt.; Maj.-Gen. and C.-in-C. of Congolese Forces Jan. 61-65, Lt.-Gen. and Pres. of Congo (now Zaire) Nov. 65-, also Pres. of Cabinet Oct. 66-, concurrently Minister of Foreign Affairs and Nat. Defence; Hon. LL.D. (Duquesne Univ.) 70, Order of the Source of the Nile (Uganda) 72.
Office of the President, Kinshasa, Zaire.

Mogami, Thebe D.; Botswana diplomatist; b. June 1942; ed. Univ. of Botswana, Lesotho and Swaziland, and Columbia Univ., New York.
Assistant Sec. Office of the Pres. 68-71, Under-Sec. for External Affairs 71-72; Perm. Rep. to UN July 72-; del. to several OAU confs.
Permanent Mission of Botswana to United Nations, 866 United Nations Plaza, Room 511, New York, N.Y. 10017, U.S.A.

Mohammed, Mrs. Bibi Titi; Tanzanian politician; b. 1925.
Leader, Women's Section of Tanzania African Nat. Union (TANU); arrested Oct. 69, Dar es Salaam, accused of treason and sentenced to life imprisonment, released Feb. 72.
Dar es Salaam, Tanzania.

Moi, Daniel Arap; Kenyan politician; b. 1924, Sacho, Baringo district; ed. African Mission School, Kabartonjo, A.I.M. School and Govt. African School, Kapsabet.
Teacher 45-57; Head. Teacher, Govt. African School, Kabarnet 46-48, 55-57, Teacher Tambach Teacher Training School, Kabarnet 48-54; African Rep. mem., Legislative Council 57-63; Chair. Kenya African Democratic Union (KADU) 60-61; mem. House of Reps. 61-; Parl. Sec., Ministry of Educ. April-Dec. 61; Minister of Educ. Dec. 61-62, Local Govt. 62-64, Home Affairs 64-67; Pres. Kenya African Nat. Union (KANU) for Rift Valley Province 66-67; Vice Pres. of Kenya Jan. 67-, concurrently Minister of Home Affairs; mem. Rift Valley Educ. Board, Kalenjin Language Cttee.; Chair. Rift Valley Provincial Court.
Office of the Vice-President, Nairobi, Kenya.

Mokhehle, Ntsu, M.SC.; Basotho politician; b. Dec. 1918, Teyateyaneng district; ed. St. Matthew's Secondary School, Grahamstown, and Univ. Coll. of Fort Hare, Eastern Cape, South Africa.
Began writing for *The Comet*, political Basotho paper 37; expelled from Univ. Coll. of Fort Hare for having planned several strikes 42; joined Lekhotla La Bafo, a Basotho nationalist movement, and returned to Fort Hare 44; became active mem. African Nat. Congress Youth League in South Africa; returned to Basutoland 49; Pres. Basutoland Teachers Asscn.; founded Basutoland Congress Party

(then called Basutoland African Congress) 52; Pres. Congress Party 52-; Principal, Maseru Higher Primary School 53; founded (with Bennet Makalo Khaketla) *Mohlabani—The Warrior* 55; attended first All African People's Conf. and elected mem. Steering Cttee., Accra 58; travelled to Ghana and Guinea 59; leader of Parl. Opposition (Congress Party), Lesotho 65; arrested on charges of inciting public violence Jan. 67, sentenced to two years' suspended sentence July 67; arrested and gaoled following Nat. Election Jan. 70, released June 71.
c/o Congress Party, P.O. Box 111, Maseru, Lesotho.

Molapo, C. M.; Lesotho diplomatist.
Private Sec. to the Prime Minister until 69; joined Diplomatic Service; now High Commr. to U.K. concurrently Amb. to Austria, France, Fed. Repub. of Germany, Netherlands, Sweden, Switzerland, also Perm. Rep. to UNESCO.
Lesotho High Commission, First Floor, 16A St. James's Street, London, SW1A 1EU, England.

Molapo, Mooki Vitus; Lesotho diplomatist; b. 2 June 1937; ed. Inkamana High School, Natal, Pius XII Coll., Univ. of South Africa, Univ. of Dar es Salaam, and Univ. of West Indies, Trinidad and Tobago.
Teacher, Maseru secondary school 65; Information Officer, Dept. of Information, Maseru 66; Chief announcer, Radio Lesotho 66-67; First Sec. Lesotho Embassy, Washington 67-70; Chief of Protocol, Ministry of Foreign Affairs 70-71; Perm. Rep. to UN Sept. 71-; del. to Gen. Assembly 69-, and rep. at many other int. confs.
Permanent Mission of Lesotho at United Nations, 806 United Nations Plaza, Room 533-535, New York, N.Y. 10017, U.S.A.

Molefhe, Topo James; Botswana diplomatist; b. 1927, Mafeking, S. Africa; ed. Fort Hare Coll. and Univ. of London.
Teacher, S. Africa and Botswana 50-63; taught at Teacher Training Coll., Serowe, Botswana 63; Vice-Principal Teacher Training Coll., Lobatsi, Botswana 66; Asst. Sec. Dept. of External Affairs 66; Private Sec. to Pres. of Botswana 67; Perm. Rep. to UN 68-72.
c/o Ministry of Foreign Affairs, Gaborone, Botswana.

Monday, Horace Reginald, C.B.E.; Gambian diplomatist; b. 26 Nov. 1907, Bathurst; ed. Methodist Mission Schools, Bathurst and correspondence course (London School of Accountancy).
Clerk 25-48; Asst. Accountant, Treasury 48-52; Accountant and Storekeeper, Marine Dept. 53-54; Accountant Gen. to The Gambia Govt. 54-65; Chair. Gambia Public Service Comm. 65-68; Dir., Gambia Currency Board 64-68; Pres., Gambia Red Cross Soc. 67-68; High Commr. to U.K. 68-71; Chair. Bathurst City Council 71-, Gambia Utilities Corpn. 72-; Commdr. Nat. Order of Republic of Senegal.
City Council, Bathurst, The Gambia.

Mondjo, Nicolas; Congolese diplomatist; b. 24 June 1933, Fort-Rousset, French Equatorial Africa; ed. Inst. des Hautes-Etudes d'Outre Mer, Paris.
Former Dir. of Admin., Ministry of the Interior; Amb. to France; Perm. Rep. to EEC; Minister of Foreign Affairs 68-69; Dir. of Cabinet of Pres. of Repub. 69-70; Perm. Rep. to UN June 70-; del. to 22nd, 23rd sessions of UN Gen. Assembly; del. to various int. confs.
Permanent Mission of the People's Republic of the Congo at United Nations, 4444 Madison Avenue, Room 1604, New York, N.Y. 10022, U.S.A.

Monguno, Alhaji Sheltima Ali; Nigerian educationist and politician; b. 1926, Monguno, Bornu Province; ed. Bornu Monguno elementary school, Bornu middle school, Bauchi Teachers' Training Coll., Nigerian Coll. of Arts, Sciences and Technology, Zaria, and Univ. of Edinburgh.
Teacher in primary and secondary schools 47-58; Educ.

Sec. Northern Nigeria 59; M.P. 59-; Counsellor for Educ. Bornu Native Authority 61-65; Minister of State in charge of Nigerian Air Force April-May 65; Minister of Internal Affairs May 65-66; Chair. Bornu Local Educ. Cttee. and Counsellor for Works and Social Welfare 66-67; Fed. Commr. for Industry June 67-71, and Trade Sept. 67-71; Commr. for Mines and Power Oct. 71-; Leader Nigerian Del. to UNCTAD II, New Delhi 68, and other int. confs.
Ministry of Mines and Power, Lagos, Nigeria,

Moshoeshoe II, King, (Constantine Bereng Seeiso); King of Lesotho (Basutoland); b. 2 May 1938; *m.* Princess Tabitha Masentle, *d.* of Chief Lerotholi Mojela, 1962; ed. Roma Coll., Lesotho, Ampleforth Coll. and Corpus Christi Coll., Oxford.
Paramount Chief of Basutoland 60; King (since restoration of Lesotho's independence) 66-; children: Prince Letsie David, Principal Chief-designate of Matsieng and heir apparent to the throne, b. 17 July 1963; Prince Seeiso Simeone, b. 16 April 1966; Princess Sebueng, b. 24 Dec. 1969; exiled from Lesotho April 70; returned Dec. 70 as Head of State.

Mouknass, Hamdi Ould; Mauritanian lawyer and diplomatist; b. 1935, Port-Etienne.
Member, political office of Parti du peuple mauritanien (P.P.M.) June 66-; Govt. Commr. Court of State Security 66-; High Commr. for Youth and Sport Feb. 66- Jan. 68; Social Chargé d'Affaires Oct. 66-Jan. 68; Minister for Youth, Cultural Affairs and Information Jan.-July 68; Minister for Foreign Affairs July 68-April 70, 71-; Minister of Nat. Defence April 70-71.
Ministry of Foreign Affairs, Nouakchott, Mauritania.

Mouradian, Jacques, L. ès L., L. en D., L.O.; French diplomatist; b. 14 Dec. 1910, Conches; ed. Lycée St. Louis, Sorbonne and Ecole des Langues Orientales, Paris.
Government admin. posts in Africa; Inspector-Gen. of Admin. and French Resident Commr. in New Hebrides 65-69; High Commr. of France in the Comoro Islands Nov. 69-; Officier, Légion d'Honneur, Croix de Guerre, Médaille des Evadés.
Publs. *L'Islam devant le Monde Moderne, L'Islam dans l'Afrique Occidentale, Les prolégomènes d'IBN-KHAL-DOUN* (under pseudonym A. Gouily).
Résidence du Haut Commissaire, Moroni, Comoro Islands; 10 rue de la Terrasse, Paris 17e, France.

Mousa, Omer el Haj; Sudanese army officer and politician; b. 1924, El Kawa; ed. Gordon Memorial Coll., Military Coll.
Joined the Co. Commdrs. course 53, staff course 63; worked in the Eastern, Western, Northern Commands, and the Signal Corps; later Dir. Armed Forces Admin.; Brig. 65; Dir. Gen. Staff Jan. 65-May 69; Minister of Nat. Guidance Oct. 69-71, of Information and Culture 71-; mem. Gen. Secr., Politburo, Cen. Cttee., Sudanese Socialist Union; Sec. of Information and Guidance, SSU; Chair. High Council for the Promotion of Arts and Literature.
Ministry of Information and Culture, Khartoum, Sudan.

Mphahlele, Ezekiel; South African author; b. 17 Dec. 1919, Marabastad; ed. teacher training and private study.
Teacher of English and Afrikaans, Orlando, Johannesburg till 57; Fiction Editor *Drum* magazine 55; Lecturer in English Literature, Dept. of Extra-Mural Studies, Univ. Coll. Ibadan, Nigeria 57; Dir. African Programme for the Congress for Cultural Freedom, Paris; has lectured at Cultural Centre, Nairobi and Univ. of Zambia; now lecturing at Univ. of Colorado.
Publs. include *Man Must Live, The Living and the Dead* (short stories); *Down Second Avenue* (autobiography), *The Wanderers* 72.
c/o Faber and Faber, 3 Queen Square, London, WC1N 3AU, England.

Msonthi, John Dunstan; Malawi politician; b. 12 Jan. 1928, Ntchisi District; ed. Catholic Secondary School, Zomba and St. Xavier's Coll., Bombay.
Detained during State of Emergency for 14 months and sent to Rhodesia 59; returned to teaching after release; elected M.P. for Nkhotakota 61; Minister of Trade and Industry 62-64; Minister of Transport and Communications 64; concurrently Minister of Educ., later Minister of Labour and Minister of Works and Supplies; Minister of Trade and Industry; now Minister of Educ.; Leader of House of Assembly 69.
Publ. *Kali Kokha N'Kanyama.*
Ministry of Education, Lilongwe, Malawi.

Mtei, Edwin Isaac Mbiliewi; Tanzanian politician; b. 1932, Moshi; ed. Makerere Univ. Coll., Uganda.
Management trainee, East African Tobacco Co. 57-59; entered govt. service 59; responsible for Africanization and training in the Civil Service; worked with East African Common Services Org. until 64; Principal Sec. to Treasury 64; Gov., Bank of Tanzania June 66-.
P.O. Box 2939, Mirambo Street, Dar es Salaam, Tanzania.

Mubiru, Joseph M., M.A., F.I.B., F.I.B.A.; Ugandan banker and business consultant; b. 29 Jan. 1929, Uganda; ed. Univ. of Kerala, India and New York Univ., U.S.A.
Economist, UN Econ. Comm. for Africa 62-64; Gen. Man. Uganda Credit and Savings Bank 64-65; Man. Dir. Uganda Commercial Bank 65-66; Gov. Bank of Uganda 66-71; founder of Uganda Commercial Bank and Bank of Uganda; financial and business consultant to Madhvani Group and other business firms 71-; arrested 72; Knight of St. Gregory.
c/o J. M. Mubiru Associates, AGIP Bldg., 9 Kampala Road, P.O. Box 5991, Kampala, Uganda.

Mudenda, Elijah Haatukali Kaiba; Zambian agriculturist and politician; b. 6 June 1927; ed. Makerere Univ. Coll., Uganda, Fort Hare Univ. Coll. and Cambridge Univ.
Plant Breeder with British admin. until 62; mem. Legislative Assembly 62-64; Parl. Sec. for Agriculture 62-64; mem. Zambian Parl. 64-; Minister of Agriculture 64-67, of Finance 67-68, of Foreign Affairs Dec. 68-69, of Development and Finance 69-Oct. 70; Minister of Foreign Affairs Oct. 70-.
Ministry of Foreign Affairs, Lusaka, Zambia.

Mukasa, Roger Joseph; Ugandan business man; b. 1926; ed. Makerere Univ. Coll., Univ. of Wales and Univ. of Cincinnati, Ohio, U.S.A.
Teacher 51-55; worked for Shell Co., Uganda; Asst. Sec., Coffee Marketing Board 61, Dep. Chair 63-64; Pres., Inter-African Coffee Org. 64-65; Chair., Int. Coffee Council 65-66; Chair., Uganda Coffee Marketing Board 63-.
Coffee Marketing Board, P.O. Box 2853, Kampala, Uganda.

Mulamba, Gen. Nyunyi Wa Kadima (Léonard); Zaire army officer and politician; b. 1928, Kananga (Luluabourg); ed. Military School, Luluabourg.
Commissioned 54; Maj. and Deputy Dir. of Cabinet, Ministry of Defence 61-64; Lt.-Col. 62; Col., Chief of Staff and Commr. of Eastern Province (now Haut Zaire) after re-occupation of Kivu Province 64-65; Prime Minister 65-Oct. 66; Pres. Société Nationale d'Assurances (SONAS) 66; Amb. to India 67-69; Amb. to Japan 69-; also accred. to Repub. of Korea 71-; Mil. Medal, Cross of Bravery, Commdr., Ordre de la Couronne (Belgium), Grand Officier, Ordre Nat. du Léopard (Zaire), Ordre du Mérite (Central African Repub.).
Embassy of Zaire, Tsurumi Bldg., 1-1 Tomigaya 1-chome, Shibuya-ku, Tokyo; Residence: 1-29-14 Fukazawa, Setagayaku, Tokyo, Japan.

Mulder, Hon. Cornelius Petrus, B.A., PH.D.; South African politician; b. 5 June 1925, Warmbaths, Transvaal; ed. Univs. of Potchefstroom and Witwatersrand.

Teacher Randgate Afrikaans Medium and Secondary Schools 46-52; at Riebeeck Secondary School, Randfontein 52-58; M.P. April 58-; Asst. Information Officer of Nat. Party 66-67, Chief Information Officer July 67-68; Minister of Information, of Social Welfare 68-, of Immigration 68-72, of the Interior and Pensions Aug. 72-; Leader, Nat. Party of Transvaal Sept. 72-; Mayor of Randfontein 53, 57; Chair. Divisional Cttee. of Nat. Party at Randfontein and Pres. of Transvaal Municipal Asscn. 55; mem. of numerous parl. select cttees.
Ministry of Information, Pretoria, Transvaal, South Africa.

Muliro, Masinde; Kenyan politician; b. 1922, Matili, Kimili, Bungoma District, W. Province; ed. Busoga Coll., Mwiri, St. Mary's School, Yala, Tororo Coll., Uganda and Univ. of Cape Town, South Africa.
Teacher, African Girls' High School, Kikuyu and Siriba Teachers' Training Coll.; mem. Legislative Council for Nyanza North 57-61, mem. for Elgon Nyanza 61-; mem. House of Reps. for Trans Nzoia 63-69, for Kitale East 69-; Minister of Commerce, Industry and Communications 61-63, of Co-operatives and Social Services, 69-; Chair. Maize and Produce Board 65, Cotton Seed and Lint Marketing Board.
Ministry of Co-operatives and Social Services, P.O. Box 30547, Nairobi, Kenya.

Muller, Hilgard, D.LITT., LL.B., M.P.; South African politician and diplomatist; b. 4 May 1914, Potchefstroom, Transvaal; ed. Pretoria Univ., Oxford Univ., Univ. of South Africa.
University lecturer 41-46; Partner, Dyason, Douglas, Muller and Meyer, Pretoria 47-; elected mem. Pretoria City Council 51; Mayor 53-55; Nat. Party M.P. for Pretoria East 58-60; Amb. to the U.K. 61-64; Minister of Foreign Affairs 64-; Chancellor, Univ. of Pretoria 64-; Dir. of various companies; mem. Acad. of Science and Arts; D.Phil. (h.c.)
Publs. *Christians and Pagans from Constantine to Augustus, Merkwaadige figure uit die Oudheid,* other books on history and biography; numerous literary articles.
Ministry of Foreign Affairs, Pretoria, South Africa.

Muller, Stephanus Louwrens, LL.B.; South African politician; b. 27 Sept. 1917, Cape Prov.; ed. Cape Tech. Coll. Practised law 49-56; mem. Cape Provincial Council 56-59; Chair. Cape Provincial Council 59-60; M.P. for Ceres, Cape Province 61-; Deputy Minister of Justice, Police and Prisons 66; Deputy Minister of Police, Finance and Econ. Affairs 66-68; Minister of Police and of the Interior 68-70; Minister of Econ. Affairs and Police May 70-; Nat. Party.
Ministry of Economic Affairs and Police, Pretoria, South Africa.

Muller, Thomas Frederik; South African businessman; ed. Ermelo High School, Univ. of the Witwatersrand and Birmingham Univ., England.
Employed by Rand Leases Mine of Anglo-Transvaal group of companies 37-57; Mine Man., Virginia Mine 49-55; Asst. Consulting Engineer, Head Office 55-57; Technical Man., Federale Mynbou Beperk Feb. 57-58, Gen. Man. 58-61, Man. Dir. July 61-; Man. Dir. Gen. Mining and Finance Corpn. Ltd. Oct. 63-71; Chair. South African Steel Corpn. (ISCOR) 71-; Chair. Buffelsfontein, Stilfontein, S. Roodepoort and W. Rand Consolidated Gold Mines, Trek-Beleggings (Pty.) Ltd.; fmr. Pres. Chamber of Mines of S. Africa, Afrikaanse Handelsinstituut; mem. Board of Trans-Natal Coal Corpn., Prime Minister's Econ. Council; Hon. D.Comm. (Potchefstroom).
Publs. Several papers on mining matters, especially on shaft-sinking at Virginia and Merriespruit Mines.
ISCOR, P.O. Box 450, Pretoria; Home: 17 Molesey Avenue, Auckland Park, Johannesburg, South Africa.
Telephone: 39151 (Office); 31-2182 (Home).

Mulli, Henry Nzioka, B.SC., DIP.ED.; Kenyan educationist, politician and diplomatist; b. 24 Sept. 1925; ed. Alliance High School, Kikuyu, Makerere Univ. Coll., Fort Hare Univ. Coll. and Oxford Univ.
Analytical Chemist, Govt. of Tanganyika 51-53; Head of Science Dept., Machakos High School 57-60; Parl. Sec. for Defence 62-63; Ambassador to People's Republic of China 64-65, to U.A.R. 65-68; Amb. to Somali Democratic Republic until Sept. 70; Amb. to Fed. Repub. of Germany Sept. 70-.
Embassy of Kenya, Bad Godesberg, Hohenzollernstrasse 12, Federal Republic of Germany.

Muna, Hon. Solomon Tandeng; Cameroonian politician; b. 1912, Ngen-Mbo, Momo Division; ed. Teacher Training Coll., Kumba and Univ. of London Inst. of Education.
Member of Parliament for Bamenda District 51; Eastern Nigeria Minister for Public Works 52; Minister of Works, subsequently Minister of Commerce and Industries, Minister of Finance, Southern Cameroon Region; Minister of Transport, Mines, Posts and Telecommunications of Cameroon 61-68; fmr. Minister in E. Nigeria; Prime Minister of West Cameroon Jan. 68-; Vice-Pres. March 70-72; Minister of State at the Presidency July 72-; fmrly. Chair. Board of Dirs., Cameroon Railways, Chair. Higher Cttee. on Cameroon Ports; has represented Cameroon at various int. confs.; Commdr., Ordre de la Valeur du Cameroun; Ordre du Sénégal; Grand Cordon, Ordre de L'Etoile d'Afrique (Liberia); Officier, Légion d'Honneur; Grand Officier de l'Ordre de la République Tunisienne.
Office of the President, Yaoundé, United Republic of Cameroon.

Mundia, Nalumino, M.B.A.; Zambian politician; b. 1927, Munyama, Kalabo District; ed. Munyama Paris Missionary School, Lukona Boarding School, Sefula Normal School, Munali Secondary School, Shri Ram Coll. of Commerce, Univ. of Delhi, India, and Graduate School of Business Administration, Atlanta Univ., Georgia, U.S.A.
Teacher, Gloag Ranch Mission, Bulawayo, S. Rhodesia; Holy Family Mission, Caprivi Strip; Founder mem., Deputy Nat. Treasurer, Dir. of Elections, United Nat. Independence Party (UNIP) 60-66; Minister of Local Govt., Minister of Commerce and Industry; Minister of Labour and Social Devt. 64-Jan. 66; M.P. for Kabwe (Broken Hill) until March 67; leader, banned United Party (UP) until Aug. 68; detained and restricted Aug. 68-Nov. 69; elected M.P. for Libonda, Barotse Province, African Nat. Congress; Deputy Pres. African Nat. Congress (ANC) Nov. 69, party banned Dec. 72.
c/o African National Congress Headquarters, Lusaka, Zambia.

Mungai, Njoroge, M.D.; Kenyan politician and doctor; b. 1926 Dagoretti, Kikuyu; ed. Presbyterian Church Elementary School, Kikuyu, Alliance High School, Fort Hare Univ. (S. Africa), Stanford Univ., Calif., and Columbia Univ. Presbyterian Medical Center, N.Y.
Bus driver, Kenya, before going to Fort Hare Univ.; Intern King's County Hospital, New York 58; returned to Kenya and practised medicine at private clinics in Thika, Riruta and Embu and ran mobile clinic; mem. Nat. Exec. KANU, Chair. Thika branch of KANU; mem. House of Reps. 63-; Minister for Health and Housing 63-65; Minister of Defence 65-69; Minister of Foreign Affairs 69-; mem. Kenya Educ. Fund Cttee., Nat. Nutritional Council; fmr. Pres. Kenya Medical Asscn.; personal physician to Pres. Jomo Kenyatta.
Ministry of Foreign Affairs, P.O. Box 30551, Nairobi, Kenya.

Munufie, Akumi Ameyaw, BAR.-AT-LAW; Ghanaian barrister and politician; b. 2 Dec. 1929, Techiman, Brong Ahafo; ed. Wenchi Methodist School, Livingstone Coll., Akropong, Akwapim, and Holborn Coll. of Law, London.

Teacher, Techiman Methodist School; private law practice 63-69; Minister of Rural Devt. Sept. 69-Jan. 72.
c/o Ministry of Rural Development, Accra, Ghana.

Munyenyembe, Rodwell Thomas Changara; Malawian educationist and politician; b. 21 Jan. 1936; ed. Livingstonia Secondary School, Domasi Teacher Training Coll., Inst. of Otology and Laryngology (London Univ.).
Member of Parl. (Malawi Congress Party) 71-; Minister of Information and Broadcasting 72-; attended seminars in Kenya, Denmark 68; mem. of Parl. del. to U.K. 72.
Ministry of Information and Broadcasting, P.O. Box 494, Blantyre; also Karopa Primary School, P.A. Nthalire, P.O. Chitipa, Malawi.

Murumbi, Joseph; Kenyan politician; b. 18 June 1911; ed. Bangalore and Bellary, S. India.
Staff of Admin. of Somalia 41-51; Asst. Sec. Movement for Colonial Freedom 51-57; Press and Tourist Officer, Moroccan Embassy, London 57-62; Treas. Kenyan African Nat. Union (KANU) 62; mem. Kenya House of Reps. 63-; Minister of State in Prime Minister's Office 63-64; Minister of External Affairs 64-66; Vice-Pres. of Kenya 66-Dec. 66; Chair. Rothmans of Pall Mall (Kenya) Ltd. Sept. 66-; Dir. of other Kenya companies.
P.O. Box 1730, Nairobi, Kenya.
Telephone: Nairobi 61397.

Musatov, Leonid Nikolayevich; Soviet diplomatist; b. 22 July 1921, Ust-Ureu, Ulyanovsk Region; ed. Ulyanovsk Pedagogic Inst.
Member C.P. of Soviet Union 40-; worked for Young Communist League 39-40; Army Service 40-46; Party official 46-62; Sec. Ulyanovsk Regional Cttee., C.P. of Soviet Union 57-62; Counsellor, Second African Dept., Ministry of Foreign Affairs 64; Counsellor-Minister, Soviet Embassy, Conakry 64-65; Amb. to Mali 65-; Red Banner of Labour, Badge of Honour, etc.
U.S.S.R. Embassy, Bamako, Mali.

Muzorewa, Abel Tendekayi, M.A.; Rhodesian ecclesiastic; b. 14 April 1925, Old Umtali; ed. Old Umtali Secondary School, Nyadiri United Methodist Mission, Central Methodist Coll., Fayette, Missouri, Scarritt Coll., Nashville, Tenn., U.S.A.
Pastor, Chiduku North Circuit 55-57; studied in U.S.A. 58-63; Pastor, Old Umtali Mission 63; Dir. of Youth Work, Rhodesia Annual Conf. 65; Jt. Dir. of Youth Work, Rhodesia Christian Council 65; Travelling Sec. Student Christian Movt. 65; Resident Bishop, United Methodist Church (Rhodesia Area) 68-; Pres. African Nat. Council 71-, All Africa Conf. of Churches; Hon. D.D. (Central Methodist Coll., Missouri) 60.
Publ. *Manifesto for African National Council* 72.
United Methodist Church, P.O. Box 8293, Causeway, Salisbury, Rhodesia.

Mwaanga, Vernon Johnson; Zambian diplomatist; b. 1939; ed. Hodgson Technical Coll., Lusaka, Stanford Univ., U.S.A. and Oxford Univ., U.K.
Joined Zambian independence movement 60; mem. United Nat. Independence Party 61-, later Regional Party Sec., Monze and Come Areas; Deputy High Commr. for Zambia in U.K. 64-65; Ambassador to U.S.S.R. 65-68; Perm. Rep. to UN 68-71; Chief Editor, *Times of Zambia* Jan. 72-.
P.O. Box 394, Lusaka, Zambia.

Mwanakatwe, John Mupanga, B.A., BAR.-AT-LAW.; Zambian politician; b. 1926, Chinsali; ed. Munali Secondary School, Adam's Coll., South Africa.
Former secondary school teacher and headmaster; Minister of Educ. Jan. 64-Sept. 67; Minister of Lands and Mines Sept. 67-Dec. 68; Sec.-Gen. to Govt. Jan. 69-Oct. 70; Minister of Finance Oct. 70-.
Publ. *Growth of Education in Zambia since Independence* 69.
Ministry of Finance, P.O. Box RW 62, Lusaka, Zambia.

Mwemba, Joseph Ben; Zambian teacher and diplomatist; b. 28 July 1917, Monze; ed. Univ. Coll., Fort Hare, South Africa, Teachers' Coll., Muncie, Ind., U.S.A., and American Univ., Washington, D.C.
Primary school teacher 47-48, Secondary school teacher 52-60; Man. of Schools 61-62; Educ. Officer 63; Admin. Officer, Ministry of Finance 64-65; Perm. Sec., Ministry of Educ. 65-66; Perm. Rep. to UN 66-68; Commr. for Technical Educ. and Vocational Training 68-69; Deputy Sec. Nat. Provincial Fund 69-; Pres. Northern Rhodesia Teachers' Asscn. 53-60; UNIP Parl. Candidate 64.
Publs. *Mubekwabekwa, Mukandeke.*
P.O. Box 2144, Lusaka, Zambia.

Mwendwa, Eliud Ngala; Kenyan politician; b. 1925, Kitui; ed. Kagumo Teacher Training Coll.
Teacher at Govt. African School, Kitui 47-52; head teacher Matinyani D.E.B. Intermediate School 53-57; teacher at Mutene Teacher Training Coll. 59-61; mem. Legislative Council for Kitui 61-; Minister for Health and Housing 63; Minister for Labour and Social Services 63-65; Minister for Commerce, Industry and Co-operative Devt. 65-66; Minister for Power and Communications 66-69; Minister of Labour 69-; Chair. Kenyan African Nat. Union (K.A.N.U.) in Kitui.
Ministry of Labour, Nairobi, Kenya.

N

Nabwera, Burudi; Kenyan politician and diplomatist; b. 1927; ed. Maseno School, Makerere Univ. Coll., London School of Economics and Political Science.
Teacher 54-56; Research Asst., Kenya Ministry of Home Affairs 57-58; London School of Economics 58-61; Organiser Kenya African Nat. Union (K.A.N.U.) 61-63, K.A.N.U. Nat. Headquarters Official 63; Perm. Rep. of Kenya to the UN 63-69; Amb. to U.S.A. 64-69; Asst. Minister for Foreign Affairs 69-.
Ministry of Foreign Affairs, P.O. Box 30551, Nairobi; Shivagala School, Kabras, P.O. Box 274, Kakamega, Kenya.
Telephone: 27411 (Nairobi).

Naicker, Gangathura Mohambry; South African doctor; b. 1910, Durban, Natal; ed. Edinburgh Univ.
President, Natal Indian Congress 45-63; Pres. South African Indian Congress 54-63; arrested five times 46-60 for opposing measures discriminating against Indian community and non-European Community; arrested during 1961 emergency and placed under banning order 61-73.
Publ. *Historical Synopsis of Anti-Indian Legislation in South Africa* 45.
26 Short Street, Durban, Natal, South Africa.
Telephone: 23408.

Namwizi, Wa Koyi; Zaire politician.
Minister of Economy March 69-Aug. 69; Minister of Finance Aug. 69-Sept. 70; Minister of Finance 70-72, of Trade Feb. 72-.
Ministry of Trade, Kinshasa, Zaire.

Nana Opoku Ware II, Matthew; Ghanaian ruler (The Asantehene); b. 1919; successor and nephew of Sir Osei Agyeman, Prempeh II; ed. England.
Former barrister; fmr. Commr. for Communications; named Amb. to Rome 70; King of the Ashantis July 70; mem. Council of State Jan. 71-.
Asantehene's Office, Manhyia, Kumasi, Ashanti, Ghana.

Nany, Alfred; Malagasy politician; b. 1916.
Entered admin. and financial services 34; Provincial councillor for Majunga 52-58; M.P., Malagasy Assembly

58-; mem., Social Democratic Party; Vice-Pres., Malagasy Nat. Assembly Oct. 60, Pres. Nov. 60-.
National Assembly, Tananarive, Madagascar.

Natai, Jean-Jacques; Malagasy politician; b. 16 March 1917, Moramanga; ed. Coll. Saint-Michel, Ecole des Frères d'Andohalo and Ecole de Médecine de Tananarive.
Civil servant, Moramanga and Majunga; private medical practice at Majunga; founding mem., Parti Social Démocrate until Sept. 72; Vice-Pres., Provincial Council 57-58; Pres. Provincial Council 58-June 59; Sec. of State and Head of Majunga Province June 59; Sec. of State for Agriculture, Rural Expansion and Provisions, responsible for the devt. of the W. Zone until Aug. 67; Minister of Agriculture, Rural Expansion and Provisions Aug. 67-71, of Labour and Social Affairs 71-72.
c/o Ministry of Labour and Social Affairs, Tananarive, Madagascar.

Naudé, Stefan Meiring, M.SC., PH.D.; South African physicist; b. 31 Dec. 1904, De Doorns; ed. Univs. of Stellenbosch, Berlin and Chicago.
Instructor Univ. of Chicago 29-30, Research Fellow 31; Senior Lecturer in Physics, Univ. of Cape Town 31-33; Prof. of Experimental Physics, Univ. of Stellenbosch 34-45; Dir. Nat. Physical Laboratory, Pretoria 46-50; Vice-Pres. Council of Scientific and Industrial Research 50-52, Pres. 52-71; Scientific Adviser to Prime Minister 71-; Chair. Scientific Advisory Council; Fellow, Royal Soc. of South Africa; mem. Suid Afrikaanse Akademie vir Wetenskap en Kuns; mem. American Physical Soc., Deutsche Physikalische Gesellschaft, South African Asscn. for the Advancement of Science, Advisory Univs. Cttee. Armaments Board, Council Univ. of Pretoria, Int. Rotary, Associated Scientific and Technical Socs.; Nat. Chair. Simon van der Stel Foundation, Chair. Foundation for Educ., Science and Technology; Trustee, South African Foundation; Hon. D.Sc., Hon. LL.D.
Home: 420 Friesland Avenue, Lynnwood, Pretoria; Office: Council for Scientific and Industrial Research, P.O. Box 395, Pretoria, Republic of South Africa.
Telephone: 74-6011.

Naudé, Willem Christiaan, D.COMM.; South African diplomatist; b. 5 May 1909; ed. Boys High School, Stellenbosch and Stellenbosch and London Univs.
Diplomatic service in London, Geneva, Washington; Consul-Gen. Lourenço Marques 51-54; Del. to UN 53, 59, 63, 65; Leader, South African Dels. to GATT, Geneva, 54-57, 66, 68, 70, to ICEM 56-57, to UNCTAD II, New Delhi, 68; Minister Switzerland 56-57; Under-Sec. for External Affairs 57-59, Deputy Sec. 59-60; Amb. to United States 60-65; Principal Deputy Sec. for Foreign Affairs 65-66; Amb. Perm. Rep., Geneva 66-71; Amb. to EEC 71-.
South African Delegation to EEC, 28 rue de la Loi, Brussels, Belgium.

Ndabakwaje, Libère; Burundian politician; b. 29 May 1938.
Former Sec.-Gen. to the Presidency until Dec. 69; Minister of Foreign Affairs and Co-operation Dec. 69-71; imprisoned Aug. 71.
c/o B.P. 721, Bujumbura, Burundi.

Ndayiziga, Marc; Burundi civil engineer and politician; b. 30 June 1939, Musema; ed. primary and secondary schools and Ecole Polytechnique de Bruxelles.
Engineer, Ministry of Public Works, Transport and Equipment 68, Technical Adviser 69; Minister of Public Works, Transport and Equipment Aug. 69-.
B.P. 1860, Bujumbura, Burundi.

Ndegwa, Duncan Nderitu, M.A.; Kenyan banker; b. 11 March 1925, Nyeri District; ed. Alliance High School, Kikuyu, Makerere Univ. Coll., Uganda and Univ. of St. Andrews, Scotland.

Statistician, East African High Comm. 56-59; Asst. Sec. Kenya Treasury 59-63, Deputy Perm. Sec. 63; Perm. Sec. and Head of Civil Service 63-66; Sec. to Cabinet 63-67; Gov. Central Bank of Kenya and Alt. Gov. IMF 67-; Chair. Comm. of Enquiry (Public Service Structure and Remuneration Comm.) 70; Chief of the Burning Spear.
P.O.B. 20423, Nairobi, Kenya.

N'dia Koffi, Dr. Blaise; Ivory Coast politician; b. 28 Dec. 1912, Pakonabo; ed. Dakar School of Medicine, Senegal.
Held several medical posts in Ivory Coast and Upper Volta; Dir., Treichville Hospital and Ivory Coast Nurses' School 57-59; M.P., Parti Démocratique de la Côte d'Ivoire (P.D.C.I.) April 59-Feb. 63; Minister of Public Health and Population Feb. 63-70; Minister of State 70-; Dir. Soc. du Palace de Cocody (S.P.D.C.).
Office of the Minister of State, Abidjan, Ivory Coast.

Nègre, Louis; Mali banker and politician.
Governor of Bank of Mali; Vice-Pres. African Devt. Bank; Minister of Finance Sept. 66-Jan. 69, of Finance and Commerce Jan. 69-Sept. 70; Pres. Council of Ministers UDEAO 69-.
African Development Bank, B.P. 1387, Abidjan, Ivory Coast.

Nemery, Maj.-Gen. Jaafar Mohammed al-; Sudanese army officer and political leader; b. 1 Jan. 1930, Omdurman; ed. Sudan Military Coll.
Former Commdr. Khartoum garrison; campaigns against rebels in Southern Sudan; placed under arrest on suspicion of plotting to overthrow the government; Chair. Revolutionary Command Council (RCC) until 71 and C.-in-C. of Armed Forces May 69-; Prime Minister Oct. 69-; Minister of Foreign Affairs Oct. 69-70, of Econ. and Planning Nov. 70-Aug. 71; Minister of Planning Aug. 71-; Pres. of Sudan Oct. 71-.
Office of the President, Khartoum, Sudan.

Nendaka, Victor; Zaire politician; b. 14 April 1924, Buta.
Former Vice-Pres., Nat. Congolese Movement; worked in insurance and in travel agency; Chief, Sûreté Nationale; mem., Congolese Nat. Convention 65; Minister of the Interior July 65-Nov. 65; Head, Congolese Democratic Front (F.D.C.) 65; High Commr. of E. Congolese Province of Maniema Oct. 65; Minister of Transport and Communications Nov. 65-Sept. 66; Minister of Transport and Trade Sept. 66-Oct. 67; Minister of Trade and Telecommunications Oct. 67-Aug. 68; Minister of Finance Aug. 68, dismissed Aug. 69; Amb. to Fed. Repub. of Germany Aug. 69-June 70; arrested and charged with treason Oct. 71.

Nene, Azzu Mate Kole; Paramount Chief of the Manya Krobos (King of the Krobos); b. 1910; s. of Sir Emmanuel Mate Kole.
Member, Political Cttee., Nat. Liberation Council July 66-, Constitutional Comm. Nov. 66-.
Private Sec. to the Paramount Chief of the Manya Krobos, Residence of the Paramount Chief, Odumase Krobo, Ghana.

Neto, Antonio Agostinho, M.D.; Angolan physician, poet and politician; b. 1922; ed. protestant school, Luanda, and Univs. of Coimbra and Lisbon.
Colonial Health Service, imprisoned four times 52-60; mem. Movimento Popular de Libertação de Angola (M.P.L.A.) 57, Pres. 60-; qualified as Doctor 58; imprisoned Cape Verde Islands, later Portugal 60-62; escaped July 62; Vice-Pres. Conselho Supremo de Libertação de Angola 72-.
Publs. *Colectanea de Poemas* 61, *Dry Eyes* (poems).
B.P. 2353, Brazzaville, People's Republic of the Congo.

Newsom, David Dunlop, A.B., M.S.; American diplomatist; b. 6 Jan. 1918; ed. Richmond Union High School and Calif. and Columbia Univs.
Reporter, *San Francisco Chronicle* 40-41; U.S. Navy 41-45; Newspaper publisher 45-47; Information Officer, U.S. Embassy, Karachi 47-50; Consul, Oslo 50-51; Public Affairs

Officer, U.S. Embassy, Baghdad 51-55; Dept. of State 55-59; U.S. Nat. War Coll. 59-60; First Sec. U.S. Embassy, London 60-62; Dir. Office of Northern African Affairs, State Dept. 62-65; Amb. to Libya 65-69; Asst. Sec. of State for African Affairs 69-; Dept. of State Meritorious Service Award 58; Nat. Civil Service League Career Service Award 71.
Department of State, Washington, D.C., U.S.A.

Ngaiza, Christopher Pastor; Tanzanian diplomatist; b. 29 March 1930, Bukoba; ed. Nyakato Secondary School, Tabora Secondary School, Makerere Univ. Coll. and Loughborough Co-operative Coll., England.
Local Courts Magistrate 52; private business 53-54; Sec.-Manager Bukoba District Bahaya Co-operative Store Ltd. 55-57; student Loughborough Co-operative Coll. 57-59; Rep. and Coffee Auctioneer, Bukoba Native Co-operative Union Ltd. 59-61; Counsellor for Tanganyika, Perm. Mission to UN, New York 61-62; Counsellor, Tanganyika High Comm., London 62-64; High Commr. of Tanzania in U.K. 64-65; Amb. to Netherlands 65-67; mem. East African Common Market Tribunal 68-69; High Commissioner for Tanzania in Zambia 69.
c/o Ministry of Foreign Affairs, Dar es Salaam, Tanzania.

Ngala, Ronald; Kenyan politician; b. 1923; ed. Makerere Coll., Uganda.
Teacher, then headmaster various schools 46-55; Sec. Kenya Nat. Party 59-60; mem. cttee. of newly-formed Kenya African Nat. Union March 60; Leader Coast African Political Union May 60; founder mem. and Leader Kenya African Democratic Union 60-64; Vice-Pres. Kenya African Nat. Union 66-; Minister of Labour and Social Security 60; Minister of Educ. and Leader of Government Business April 61-Nov. 61; Minister of State for Constitutional Affairs and Admin. April 62-63; Pres. Coast Regional Assembly, Mombasa, Kenya 63-66; Chair. Maize Marketing Board 65-66; Minister of Co-operatives and Social Services 66-69; Minister of Power and Communications 69-72; resigned from Nat. Exec. Cttee. of Kenya African Nat. Union March 69; Chair. African elected mems. del., Kenya Conf., London 60.
[*Died, 25 December* 1972.]

Ngei, Paul, B.SC. (ECON.); Kenyan politician; b. 1923, Machakos, Kenya; grandson of Akamba Paramount Chief Masaku; ed. Makerere College, Kampala.
Army service, Second World War; founded *Wasya wa Mukamba* newspaper and Swahili magazine *Uhuru wa Mwafrika* 50; Deputy Gen. Sec. Kenya African Union 51-52; imprisoned and under restriction for connection with Mau-Mau 53-61; Pres. Kenya African Farmers' and Traders' Union 61; founded African Peoples' Party 62; Chair. Maize Marketing Board 63-64; Minister for Co-operatives and Marketing 64-65; Minister for Housing and Social Services 65-66; Minister for Housing 66-; Managing Dir. Akamba Carving and Industrial Company.
Ministry of Housing, Nairobi, Kenya.

N'Gom, Doudou; Senegalese politician.
Former Sec.-Gen. Nat. Union of Senegalese Workers (U.N.T.S.) until June 69; Minister of Technical Teaching and Training Feb. 70-.
c/o Ministry of Education, Dakar, Senegal.

Ngom Jua, Augustine; Cameroonian politician; b. Nov. 1924; ed. St. Anthony's School, Njinikom, Elementary Training Centre, Kake-Kumba, and Govt. Teacher Training Coll., Kumba.
Teacher, Bafut Catholic School 40-42; Headmaster, Muyuka Catholic School 46-47, Catholic School, Dikome 49-50, Catholic School, Njinikom 51; Sec. Kom Improvement Asscn. 52; Chair. Regional Consultative Cttee., Enugu 53; mem. House of Assembly 54-57; Minister of Educ. and Social Services 59; Sec. of State for Finance and

Deputy Minister of Health 61-62; Prime Minister of West Cameroon May 65-67; Grand Order of Valour (Cameroon), Knight Commdr. Humane Order of African Redemption (Liberia), Great Cross Second Class of the Order of Merit of the Fed. Repub. of Germany, Order of Commdr. (Tunisia), Grand Officer of the Nat. Order of Senegal.
Buea, United Republic of Cameroon.

Ngon, Bernard Bidias À.; Cameroonian politician; b. 1938, Tchékane, Bafia; ed. Ecole Nat. d'Administration, Inst. des Hautes Etudes d'Outre-Mer and Faculty of Law and Political Sciences, Yaoundé.
Attached to the Presidency 67-; Minister of Finance 68-72; Pres. Consultative Cttee. 70; Chevalier, Ordre de la Valeur Camerounaise.
c/o Ministry of Finance, Yaoundé, United Republic of Cameroon.

Ngouabi, Major Marien; Congolese army officer and Head of State; b. 1938, Ombele, Fort-Rousset; ed. Ecole Interarmes de Coëtquidan.
Former Commdr. Brazzaville Paratroop Battalion; reduced to the ranks 66, but later Head of Gen. Studies Bureau of Gen. Staff; arrested July 68; Chief of Gen. Staff Aug. 68-; Head of Nat. Revolutionary Council Aug. 68-; Head of State Jan. 69-; Pres. Political Bureau of the Congolese Workers' Party (PCT) and of its Central Cttee.; Chair. Council of State Jan. 70-.
Office of the Head of State, Brazzaville, People's Republic of Congo.

Ngoubou, Dr. Benjamin; Gabonese politician; b. 23 July 1925; ed. Univ. of Lyons, France.
Former head of maternity and gynaecology dept., Libreville hospital; Minister of Labour and Social Affairs Jan. 67; fmr. Minister of Nat. Educ. until Dec. 69; Minister of Transport and Civil Aviation Dec. 69-April 70; Minister of Health and Population April 70-71; Minister of the Civil Service and Admin. Reforms June 71-.
Ministry of Civil Service and Administrative Reforms, Libreville, Gabon.

Ngoyi, Mrs. Lilian; African politician; b. 24 Sept. 1911; ed. in Transvaal.
Machinist in clothing factory; mem. African Nat. Congress 52-, Nat. Exec. 54, Head of A.N.C. Women's League; mem. Nat. Exec. Fed. of South African Women 54-, Nat. Pres. 56-; on trial for treason 56-61 (acquitted 61); detained without trial for five months 60; banned from attending gatherings 62-; detained 71 days without trial 63; confined to Orlando for five years 63; arrested 64, banned and confined in Johannesburg for further five years 68-Oct. 72.
9870B Nkungu Street, Orlando West 2, P.O. Phirima, South Africa.

Nguema Ndong, François, L. ès sc.; Gabonese politician and engineer; b. 16 May 1934, Melene/Oyem; ed. Collège Technique de Narbonne, Lycée de Clermont-Ferrand, Univ. de Clermont-Ferrand and Ecole Nat. Supérieure des Mines, Paris.
Assistant Dir. of Mines of Repub. of Gabon Oct. 63; Dir. of Mines and Geology March 64; Dir. Ciments Portland Gabonais 64-66; Pres. Dir. Gen. Société Gabonaise de Recherches et d'Exploitations Minières (Sogarem) 64-69; Minister of Mines, Water Resources and Power Feb. 69-71; Minister of State for Agriculture, Livestock, Scientific Research and Environment 71-72, for Environment and Forestry Sept. 72-; Officier, Ordre Nat. de l'Etoile Equatoriale, Ordre Nat. du Mérite Français.
Ministry of the Environment, Libreville, Gabon.

Ngugi Wa Thiong'o (James Ngugi); Kenyan novelist; b. 1936, Limuru; ed. Makerere Univ. Coll., Uganda and Leeds Univ., England.
Admin. Sec. Kenya Nat. Assembly 63-; Lecturer in

Literature, Nairobi; Makerere Visiting Prof. of English, Northwestern Univ. 70-71.
Publs. *The Black Hermit* (play) 62, *Weep Not Child* 64, *The River Between* 65, *A Grain of Wheat* 67, *Homecoming* (essays) 72.
c/o Heinemann Educational Books (African Writers Series), 48 Charles Street, London W1X 8AH, England.

Nicol, Davidson S. H. W., C.M.G., M.A., M.D., PH.D. (CANTAB.); Sierra Leonean doctor and educationist; b. 14 Sept. 1924, Freetown; ed. Prince of Wales School, Freetown, Cambridge Univ., London Hospital.
Research Asst. and Demonstrator in Physiology, London 50-52; lecturer in Physiology and Biochemistry, Ibadan 52-54; medical research and teaching, Cambridge 54-59; Fellow, Christ's Coll., Cambridge; Senior Pathologist, Sierra Leone Govt. 58-60; guest lecturer numerous American univs.; Principal, Fourah Bay Coll., The Univ. Coll. of Sierra Leone, Freetown 60-67; Vice-Chancellor, Univ. Sierra Leone 66-68; Chair. Conf. on Inter-Univ. Co-op. in W. Africa 61; Needs and Priorities Cttee., Univ. of E. Africa 63; Sierra Leone Nat. Library Board; attended WHO Annual Meetings 59, 60, UNESCO Conference on Higher Education 63, OAU Defence Commission 65, Commonwealth Prime Ministers Conf. 65; Pres. Sierra Leone Nat. Red Cross Soc. 63-65, West African Science Asscn. 63-65; Dir. Central Bank Sierra Leone 63-, Davesme Corpn.; Perm. Rep. to UN Dec. 68-71; High Commr. to U.K. and Amb. to Norway, Sweden and Denmark 71-72; Exec. Dir. UN Inst. for Training and Research 72-; Fellow, Royal Coll. of Pathologists; mem. UN Security Council 70-71; Chair. UN Cttee. on Colonialism 70; Vice-Pres. Royal African Soc. 72-; Hon. Fellow (Christ's Coll., Cambridge Univ.) 72; Hon. D.Sc. (Newcastle upon Tyne, and Kalamazoo Coll., Michigan, U.S.A.); Hon. LL.D. (Leeds).
Publs. *The Structure of Human Insulin* 60, *Africa, A Subjective View* 64, *African Self-Government 1865: The Dawn of Nationalism* 70.
c/o UNITAR, UN Headquarters, New York, N.Y., U.S.A.

N'Jie, Pierre Saar; Gambian lawyer and politician; b. 1909; ed. R.C. mission school and Lincoln's Inn, London, England.
Private law practice until 54; Minister of Education and Social Welfare; M.P. (United Party, U.P.) 60-; Chief Minister 61-62; Leader of Opposition, dismissed May 70; Chair., U.P. until 70.
United Party, P.O.B. 63, Buckle Street, Bathurst, The Gambia.

Njine, Michel; Cameroon diplomatist; b. 1 Jan. 1918. Cameroon Admin. Service 37; Counsellor of Territorial Assembly of Cameroon 52; Deputy of Legis. Assembly 56; Minister of Public Works, Transportation and Mines 57-58; Deputy Prime Minister in Charge of Nat. Educ., Youth and Sports 58-60; Dir. Cameroon Nat. Office of Tourism 60-62; Amb. to Ivory Coast 62-65, to German Fed. Repub. 65-67; Perm. Rep. to UN 67-.
Permanent Mission of Cameroon to the United Nations, 866 United Nations Plaza, New York, N.Y. 10017, U.S.A.

Njoku, Eni, M.SC., PH.D.; Nigerian university teacher and administrator; b. 6 Nov. 1917, Ebem Ohafia; ed. Ebem Ohafia primary school, Hope Waddell Coll., Calabar, Yaba Higher Coll. and Univ. of Manchester, England.
Teacher, Hope-Waddell Secondary School 40-42; Clerk (Army) Training School 42-44; studied in Manchester 44-48; Lecturer, Univ. of Ibadan 48-52; Minister for Mines and Power, Govt. of Nigeria 52-53; Senior Lecturer, Prof. of Botany, Univ. of Ibadan 53-62; Vice-Chancellor and Prof. of Botany, Univ. of Lagos 62-65; Visiting Prof. of Botany, Michigan State Univ. 65-66; Vice-Chancellor, Univ. of Nigeria 66-70; Prof. of Botany, Univ. of Nigeria 66-; mem. House of Reps. 52-53, Senate 60-62; Chair. Electricity

Corpn. of Nigeria 56-62; Pres. Science Asscn. of Nigeria 59-60; mem. Commonwealth Scientific Cttee. 61-66; mem. UN Cttee. on Application of Science and Technology to Devt. 64-69; mem. Provisional Council of Univ. of Zambia 64-65; mem. Superior Academic Council of Univ. of Lovanium (Kinshasa) 63-66; Hon. D.Sc. (Univ. of Nigeria), Hon. LL.D. (Michigan State Univ.).
Publs. *Plant Life in a Tropical Environment* 54 and numerous research articles in botanical journals.
University of Nigeria, Nsukka, East Central State; Home: Ebem Ohafia, East Central State, Nigeria.

Njonjo, Charles, B.A.; Barrister-at-Law; Kenyan politician; b. 1920, Kabete, Kenya; ed. Fort Hare Univ. (South Africa), Univ. Coll. Exeter (U.K.), King's Coll., Budo, Uganda, London School of Economics, Gray's Inn.
Assistant Registrar-General, Kenya 55-60; Crown Counsel 60-61; Senior Crown Counsel 61-62; Deputy Public Prosecutor 62-63; Attorney-General 63-.
Attorney-General's Office, Nairobi, Kenya.

Njoroge, Ng'ethe; Kenyan diplomatist; ed. Alliance High School, and at Busonga, Wilberforce and Dayton Coll., Ohio, and Boston Univ.
Assistant Sec. Ministry of Lands and Settlement 63-64; Senior Asst. Sec. Ministry of Foreign Affairs 64, later Head, Africa and Middle East Desk, Ministry of Foreign Affairs; then Counsellor, Bonn; High Commr. in U.K. 70-; mem. Kenya Del. to UN Gen. Assembly 64, 65, 66.
Kenya High Commission, 45 Portland Place, London, W.1, England.

Nkama, Moto; Zambian politician and diplomatist; b. 1937, Mufulira; ed. Mufulira Mine Upper Primary School, Kasam School, Eagle's Peak Coll. and Roma Coll., Lesotho and Inst. for Commonwealth Studies, Oxford.
Worked in Mufulira Mine Welfare Dept. 61; election Supervisor, United Nat. Independence Party (UNIP) 62; Deputy Dir. of elections Aug. 62; Regional Sec. UNIP 62-63; First Sec. and Counsellor, United Nations 64-68; mem. UN Council for Namibia (South West Africa) 68; Private Sec. to Pres. Kaunda 68; M.P. 68-; Asst. Minister for the Copperbelt and Minister of State for Foreign Affairs 68-69; Minister of State in charge of Cen. Province 69, for Foreign Affairs 69-70; Amb. to Fed. Repub. of Germany 70-71; Minister for Cen. Province 71; Amb. to France Jan. 72-.
Zambian Embassy, Paris, France.

Nkambo Mugerwa, Peter James; Ugandan lawyer and politician; b. 10 Jan. 1933; ed. King's Coll., Budo, Makerere, Makerere Univ., Trinity Coll., Cambridge and Gray's Inn, London.
Lecturer in Law, Univ. Coll., Dar-es-Salaam 62-64; Solicitor-Gen., Uganda 64-71; Attorney-Gen. and mem. Council of Ministers 71-; mem. African Inst. of Int. Law, American Soc. of Int. Law, Uganda Law Reform Cttee., Uganda Law Council, OAU Reconciliation Comm.
Office of the Attorney-General, Kampala, Uganda.

Nkomo, Joshua; Rhodesian politician; b. 1917; ed. Adam's Coll., Natal, Univ. of S. Africa, Johannesburg.
Welfare Officer, Rhodesia Railways, Bulawayo, then Organizing Sec., Rhodesian African Railway Workers' Union 45-50; Pres. African Congress; employed in insurance and real estate; Pres.-Gen. African National Congress 57; lived abroad when African National Congress banned 59; elected Pres. Nat. Dem. Party Aug. 60; returned to S. Rhodesia; Pres. Zimbabwe African People's Union (ZAPU) 61-; imprisoned 63-64; banished to Nuanetsi area April 64, to Gonakudzingula Restriction Camp, near Mozambique border Nov. 64- (and for a further five years Dec. 68-).

Nkumbula, Harry; Zambian politician; b. 1916; ed. Makerere Univ. Coll., Uganda and London School of Economics, England.

Teacher, Copper Belt 34; mem., Kitwe African Soc.; mem., Africa Cttee., London; salesman 50-51; entered politics 51; Pres., N. Rhodesia African Nat. Congress; imprisoned 55; Minister of African Educ. in coalition govt.; joint leader of opposition, resigned Aug. 65; Pres., Zambian Opposition Party, African Nat. Congress (ANC) 68-, party banned Dec. 72; restricted Feb. 72.

c/o African National Congress, P.O. Box 1005, Lusaka, Zambia.

Nkunabagenzi, Fidèle; Rwandan diplomatist; b. 1 Jan. 1932, Rubayi-lez-Shangi; ed. Univ. of Louvain.

Worked in Secretariat of UN Econ. Comm. for Africa 63-65; Sec.-Gen. Ministry of Planning June-Nov. 65; Sec.-Gen. Ministry of Int. Co-operation; fmr. Alt. Gov. IBRD; fmr. Pres. of Board, Bank of Rwanda; Perm. Rep. to UN 69-.

Publs. *Rwanda Politique 1958-60, Evolution de la Structure Politique du Rwanda.*

Permanent Mission of Rwanda to the United Nations, 120 East 56th Street, Room 630, New York, N.Y. 10020, U.S.A.

Nkweta, Lucas Zaa; Cameroonian agronomist and diplomatist; b. 17 Jan. 1929; ed. Umuahia Coll., E. Nigeria, School of Agriculture, Ibadan, and Univ. Coll., Ibadan.

Former agronomist, Cameroon Devt. Corpn., and fmr. Principal Agricultural Officer, W. Cameroon Govt.; First Sec., Cameroon Embassy, London 63; Consul-Gen., Lagos 64-65; Amb. to U.K. 65-; Chevalier de l'Ordre de la Valeur.

Embassy of Cameroon, 84 Holland Park, London, W.11, England.

Telephone: 01-727 0771.

Noumazalay, Ambroise; Congolese politician; b. 23 Sept. 1933, Brazzaville; ed. Mathematics Faculty, Univ. of Toulouse, France.

First Sec., Nat. Revolutionary Movement (M.N.R.); Dir. of Econ. Affairs 64-66; Prime Minister and Minister of Planning May 66-Jan. 68; mem., Nat. Revolutionary Council (C.N.R.) Aug. 68-Oct. 68; Sec., Org. Cttee. of the C.N.R. Aug. 68-Oct. 68; Minister of State in charge of Planning Aug. 68-Dec. 68; Minister of State responsible for Agriculture, Water Resources and Forests Dec. 68-June 69; Second Sec., responsible for the Execution of the Plan April 70-71; sentenced to life imprisonment March 72.

c/o Office of the Second Secretary, Brazzaville, People's Republic of the Congo.

Nsanze, Terence; Burundian diplomatist; b. 2 Feb. 1937, Burundi; ed. Georgetown Univ., Washington, D.C., and City Univ. of New York.

Chief Editor and Man. of newspaper *Ngondozi* 61; mem. Burundi Del. to IVth Special Session of UN 62; First Counsellor, Perm. Mission to UN 64-65; Counsellor of Prime Minister at Second Conf. of Non-Aligned Countries, Cairo 64; Perm. Sec. of OAU at UN 65-; Amb. and Perm. Rep. to UN 65-; Del. of Burundi to Special Political Comm. at XXth Session of UN 65.

Publs. *Burundi—A New, Friendly and Progressive Nation in the Heart of Africa* 64, *The Birth of the Republic of Burundi, Masterpiece of the New Elite* 68, *Burundi au carrefour de l'Afrique* 70.

Permanent Mission of the Republic of Burundi to the United Nations, 485 Fifth Avenue, New York, N.Y. 10017, U.S.A. Telephone: 867-0881.

Nsubuga, Mgr. Emmanuel; Ugandan ecclesiastic; b. 1916; ed. seminaries in Buganda.

Ordained priest 46; Vicar-Gen., Rubaga Archdiocese 61, later Vicar Capitular; Archbishop of Kampala Aug. 66-.

Archdiocese of Kampala, P.O. Box 14215, Kampala, Uganda.

Ntende, Elizaphan Kawanguzi Kalange; Ugandan business executive; b. 1931; ed. Makerere Univ. Coll.

Cadet labour officer, Labour Dept. 55-56; salesman, Shell Co., Uganda, later supervisor, sales promotion supervisor and trade relations officer 56-63; Chair. Uganda Lint Marketing Board 63-67; private business (dir. of 14 companies) 67-; mem. E. African Legis. Assembly 68-, E. African Univ. 69-70, Uganda Export Promotion Co. 69-70; Rotary Int. District Gov. 72-73.

Publ. *Uganda Cotton* 66.

P.O. Box 4196, Kampala, Uganda.

Nteppe, Raymond; Cameroonian politician and diplomatist.

Ambassador to U.S.S.R. Nov. 65-June 70; Minister of Foreign Affairs June 70-Jan. 71; Minister at the Presidency Jan. 71-72.

c/o Office of the President, Yaoundé, United Republic of Cameroon.

Ntiro, Sam; Tanzanian artist and diplomatist; b. 1923; ed. Makerere Coll., Kampala, and Slade School of Fine Art, London.

Lecturer, Dept. of Fine Art, Makerere Coll., Kampala, Uganda 55-61; Tanganyika Foreign Service 61-64, Acting High Commr. in London 62-63, High Commr. 63-64; on special duty, Ministry of External Affairs, Dar es Salaam March-Oct. 64; Head of Art Dept., Nat. Teachers' Coll., Kyambogo, Kampala, Uganda March 65-June 66; Warden, Livingstone Hall, Makerere Univ. Coll., Kampala, Uganda June 66-67; Commr. for Culture in Tanzania 67-; exhibition of paintings, London 67.

P.O. Box 521, Moshi, Tanzania.

Ntonya, Frank Wyllie; Malawi diplomatist; b. 1938; ed. Haile Sellassie Univ., Addis Ababa, Ethiopia, and Columbia Univ., U.S.A.

Second Sec., Malawi Mission in London, later First Sec.; then First Sec., Malawi Legation, Pretoria, South Africa; now Chief of Protocol, Ministry of External Affairs.

Ministry of External Affairs, P.O. Box 943, Blantyre, Malawi.

Nwako, M. P. K.; Botswana politician; b. 1922, Ngwato Area; ed. Tiger Kloof.

Treasurer, Bakwena and Bamangwato Tribal Admins. 48-54; Sec.-Treas., Moeng Coll. 54-64; served on African Council; fmr. Dep. Chair., Wages Board, B.P. Abattoirs; mem., Legislative (now Nat.) Assembly March 65-; Minister of Agriculture March 65-Oct. 66; Minister of State for External Affairs Oct. 66-Oct. 69; Minister of Health, Labour and Home Affairs Oct. 69-.

Ministry of Health, Labour and Home Affairs, Gaborone, Botswana.

Nxumalo, Allen Mkaulo Malabane; Swazi politician; b. 14 Feb. 1921; ed. Matsapa Swazi Nat. School, Inkamana, Fort Hare Univ., Coll. and Witwatersrand Univ., South Africa.

Former mem., first nat. exec., A.N.C. Youth League, later Chair., Western areas of Johannesburg; fmr. Chair., Non-European Scholarship Trust Fund, Witwatersrand Univ.; fmr. Zulu script corrector, Union Coll.; fmr. machine operator, Krugersdorp; fmr. asst. librarian, Witwatersrand Univ. Library; teacher, Zombode Nat. School and Swazi Nat. School, Matsapa 43-44; fmr. teacher, Mpono Primary School; worked at Baragwanath Provincial Hospital, South Africa; Medical Officer, Mbabane Govt. Hospital; fmr. Pres., Swaziland Civil Servants' Asscn.; Vice-Pres., later Pres., Swaziland Democratic Party; mem., Swazi Nat. Council and Central Educ. Advisory Board; Minister of Health, also responsible for Educ. 71-72, of Labour, Power and Communications May 72-; M.P. for Mlumati.

Ministry of Labour, Mbabane, Swaziland.

Nxumalo, Simon Sishayi; Swazi politician; b. July 1936, Nkambeni, Lowveld; ed. Nkambeni and Mbuluzi elementary schools, Manzini Central School, St. Joseph's Mission and Matsapa Swazi Nat. High School.

Teacher, Nkambeni and Mhlambanyati Schools 54-58; worked in Johannesburg gold mines 58-60; licensed speculator and dealer in livestock, Swaziland 60-62; fmr. mem., cttees. on chieftaincy of Nkambeni; founder mem., Sebeneta Nat. Inst. 61; founder mem., Swaziland Democratic Party 62; attended constitutional talks, representing alliance of Swazi political parties and trade union movement 63; Dir., Sebeneta Nat. Inst. 65; King's Envoy to African govts. 65; M.P. (Imbokodvo) 67-; Deputy Minister of Finance, Commerce and Industry 67-68; Minister of Commerce, Industry and Mines 68-72, of Industry, Mines and Tourism 72-; Chief Scout 72-.
Ministry of Industry, Mines and Tourism, P.O. Box 451, Mbabane, Swaziland.

Nyagah, Jeremiah Joseph Mwaniki; Kenyan politician; b. 1920, Central Province; ed. Alliance High School, Makerere Coll. and Oxford Univ.
Teacher, Intermediate Schools and Teacher Training Coll.; secondary schools and Teacher Training Coll. teacher 54-56; Asst. Education Officer; mem., Legislative Council 58-60, 61-; Dep. Speaker 60; mem., House of Representatives 63-; Junior Minister, Ministry of Works, Communications and Power 63-64; Junior Minister, Ministry of Home Affairs 64-66; Vice-Pres. for Kenyan African Nat. Union (K.A.N.U.) E. Region March 66-; Minister of Education May 66-Jan. 68; Chair. Nat. Library Service Board April 66-; Minister of Natural Resources Jan. 68-Dec. 69; Minister of Information Dec. 69-Oct. 70; Minister of Agriculture and Animal Husbandry Oct. 70-; mem. Boards of Govs. of many schools, Univ. Coll. Council, Nairobi, E. African Univ. Council, Boy Scouts' Training Team.
Ministry of Agriculture and Animal Husbandry, P.O. Box 30028, Nairobi, Kenya.

Nyamoya, Albin; Burundian politician; b. 1917, Bururi Province; ed. Ecole Supérieure, Astrida (now Butare, Rwanda).
Qualified as veterinary surgeon; held various posts at the Ministry of Agriculture and Stockbreeding, Ruanda-Urundi 45-61, Minister of Agriculture and Stockbreeding 61-62; Minister of Interior and Information, Burundi 62-63; Prime Minister and Minister of State 64-65; Minister of State 65-66; Deputy to Nat. Assembly 63-66; various posts in Ministry of Agriculture and Stockbreeding 66-72, Minister 71-May 72; Prime Minister and Minister of the Interior July 72-; Nat. Exec. Sec. Unity and Nat. Progress Party.
Office of the Prime Minister, Bujumbura, Burundi.

Nyamweya, James; Kenyan politician; b. 28 Dec. 1927; ed. King's Coll., London and Lincoln's Inn, London.
Legal Assistant in Ministry of Legal Affairs, Kenya 58-59; Advocate, Private Legal Practitioner, Supreme Court of Kenya 59-63; Founder-mem. and mem. Central Exec. Cttee. Kenya African Nat. Union (K.A.N.U.) 59-63; Chair. Kisii 62-64; Parl. Sec. to Ministry of Justice and Constitutional Affairs 63, and in the Office of the Prime Minister 64-65; Minister of State, Provincial Admin. Civil Service, Office of the Pres. 65-66; Leader of Govt. Business in the House of Representatives May-Dec. 66; Minister of State, Foreign Affairs, Office of the Pres. and Leader of Govt. Business in Nat. Assembly Jan. 67, Minister of Power and Communications until Dec. 69, Minister of Works Dec. 69-; Hon. LL.B., London, Hon. LL.D.
Ministry of Works, P.O. Box 30260, Nairobi, Kenya.
Telephone: 26411.

Nyerere, Julius Kambarage, M.A.; Tanzanian politician; b. 1922, Butiama, Lake Victoria; s. of Chief Nyerere Burito; ed. Musoma Native Authority Primary School, Tabora Govt. Senior Secondary School, Makerere Coll., Uganda and Edinburgh Univ.
Teacher, St. Mary's Roman Catholic School, Tabora 46-49;

student at Edinburgh Univ. 49-52; teacher, St. Francis' Roman Catholic Coll. 53-55; Founder-Pres. Tanganyika African Nat. Union (T.A.N.U.) 54-; Elected mem. Tanganyika Legislative Council 58, leader Elected Members Org. 58-60; Chief Minister 60-61; Prime Minister May 61-Jan. 62; Pres. of Tanganyika Dec. 62-64, of Tanzania 64-; Minister of External Affairs Dec. 62-March 63, Sept. 65-72, also of Regional Admin. and Rural Devt.; Chancellor, Univ. of East Africa June 63-.
Publ. *Freedom and Unity—Uhuru na Umoja* 67, *Freedom and Socialism—Uhuru na Ujamaa* 68, *Ujamaa: Essays on Socialism* 69, Swahili transls. of *Julius Caesar* and *The Merchant of Venice* 69.
State House, Dar es Salaam, Tanzania.

Nyirenda, Wesley; Zambian politician; b. 23 Jan. 1924; ed. Church of Scotland Mission School, Lubwa and South Africa.
Worked as teacher; Principal, secondary school 60-61; M.P. 61-64; Dep. Speaker 64, later Speaker, Nat. Assembly; Minister of Education Dec. 68-.
Ministry of Education, Lusaka, Zambia.

Nylander, C. T.; Ghanaian educationalist and politician; b. 30 Sept. 1905; ed. Accra Methodist and Govt. Schools in Kumasi, and Accra Govt. Training Coll.
Government schoolteacher 26; Asst. Educ. Officer 52; elected to Legislative Assembly as mem. for Dangbe-Shai 54 and for Ga 56; Parl. Sec. Ministry of the Interior 56; Minister of Educ. 57-59; Minister of Health and Social Welfare 59; Minister of State for Defence 59-60; Chair. of Library Services, Ghana 60-61; High Commr. in Canada 61-64; Amb. to Yugoslavia 64-66, to Liberia 66-68; Patron, Co-founder, Inst. of Business Educ. 70; Grand Cross of African Redemption 68.
Wetse Kojo Str., Korle Gonnio, P.O. Box 1260, Accra, Ghana.

O

Obitre-Gama, Ernest; Ugandan army officer; b. Nov. 1940, Olevu Maracha, West Nile District; ed. Busoga Coll., Mwiri.
Joined Uganda Army 64, held various army posts until 69; Commandant, Paratroopers' School, Entebbe 69-71; Minister of Internal Affairs 71-; Uganda Repub. Medal 72.
Ministry of Internal Affairs, P.O. Box 7191, Kampala, Uganda.

Obote, (Apollo) Milton; Ugandan politician; b. 1924. Labourer, clerk, salesman, Kenya 50-55; founder-mem. Kenya African Union; mem. Uganda Nat. Congress 52-60; mem. Uganda Legislative Council 57-; founder and mem. of Uganda People's Congress 60-; Leader of the Opposition 61-62; Prime Minister 62-66; Minister of Defence and Foreign Affairs 63-65; assumed full powers of Govt. Feb. 66-; Pres. of Uganda April 66-Jan. 71; in exile in Tanzania.

Odaka, Sam Ngude; Ugandan politician; b. 1933; ed. Makerere Univ. Coll.
Executive of Standard Oil Co. 55-62; Municipal Councillor for Kampala 57-59, for Jinja 59-62; Dir., Uganda Electricity Board 59-62; M.P. and spokesman for health and water resources, Uganda People's Party Opposition 61; Parl. Sec. for Finance 62; later Dep. Minister of Foreign Affairs, Minister of State for Foreign Affairs 64-66, Minister of State in the Office of the Prime Minister Feb.-May 66; Minister of Foreign Affairs April 66-Jan. 71.
Kampala, Uganda.

Odelola, Amos Oyetunji, B.SC., M.A.; Nigerian economist; b. 4 March 1927, Modakeke, Ife; ed. Oduduwa Coll., Ife, Univ. of Hull, England, and Yale Univ., U.S.A.
Agricultural Asst., Dept. of Agriculture, Nigeria, then Statistical Asst., Dept. of Statistics; then Admin. Officer,

W. Nigerian Govt.; Special Asst. to Sec.-Gen., Comm. for Technical Cooperation in Africa (CCTA) 63-64, Acting Sec.-Gen. 64-65; Exec. Sec. Scientific, Technical and Research Comm. of Org. for African Unity (OAU) (successor to CCTA) 65-.
Scientific, Technical and Research Commission of Organization for African Unity, Nigerian Ports Authority Building, P.M.B. 2359, Marina, Lagos, Nigeria.

Odero-Jowi, Joseph; Kenyan diplomatist; b. 15 Aug. 1929, S. Nyanza, Kenya; ed. Delhi School of Econs., Univ. of Delhi.
Worked in Secrs. of UN Econ. Comm. for Africa, Addis Ababa and Econ. and Social Council, N.Y. 60; Lecturer, African Labour Coll., Kampala, Uganda; mem. Kenya House of Reps. 63; Asst. Minister of Labour 63, of Finance 66; Minister for East African Community in charge of Admin. and Finance; Exec. Dir. EMCO Steel Works, Kenya Ltd. and other Madhvani Groups in Kenya; Perm. Rep. to UN Oct. 70-.
Permanent Mission of Kenya at United Nations, 866 United Nations Plaza, Room 486, New York, N.Y. 10017, U.S.A.

Odesanya, M. A.; Nigerian judge and administrator.
Judge of High Court of W. Nigeria May 67-; Pres., Org. of African Unity (OAU), Conciliation, Mediation and Arbitration Comm. Sept. 67-.
Organization of African Unity, P.O. Box 3243, Addis Ababa, Ethiopia.

Odinga, A. Oginga; Kenyan politician; b. 1911; ed. Alliance High School, Kikuyu, and Makerere Coll.
Former teacher; mem. Central Nyanza African District Council, Sakwa Location Advisory Council 47-49; mem. Legislative Council 57-; Vice-Pres. Kenya African Nat. Union (KANU) 60-66, founded Kenya People's Union 66 (party banned Oct. 69); Minister for Home Affairs 63-64; Vice-Pres. of Kenya Dec. 64-April 66; arrested Oct. 69; released March 71; rejoined KANU Sept. 71.
Publ. *Not Yet Uhuru* 67.
c/o KANU, P.O. Box 12394, Nairobi, Kenya.

Oduho, Joseph Haworu; Sudanese politician; b. 1928, Lobira, Torit District; ed. Okaru Intermediate School, St. Aloysius Senior Secondary School, Nyapea (Uganda), Rumbek Secondary School, Inst. of Educ., Bakht-Er-Ruda.
Teacher 52-59; Headmaster, Palotaka Intermediate School 60; imprisoned during revolt of Equatorial Corps Sept. 55, released Jan. 56; fled Sudan 60; Founder Pres. Sudan African Nat. Union (SANU), organized Anya-Nya Org. (Mil. Wing, SANU) 62-63, Political Adviser 68-71; imprisoned in Uganda 63-64; Pres. Azania Liberation Front 65-67; mem. Parl. March-Nov. 68; mem. for Housing and Public Utilities, High Exec. Council for the Southern Region April 72-; mem. Political Bureau, Sudanese Socialist Union 72-.
Publ. *Problem of Southern Sudan* (co-author) 63.
Regional Ministry of Housing and Public Utilities, P.O. Box 134, Juba; and c/o Local Government Inspector, P.O. Torit, Sudan.

Ogbemudia, Col. Samuel Osaigbovo; Nigerian army officer; b. 17 Sept. 1932, Benin; ed. Govt. School, Victoria and W. Boys' High School, Benin.
Enlisted in army 53; trained at Teshi, Ghana 57-59, and Nevhervon, Salisbury, Rhodesia 59-60; attended Officer-Cadet School, Aldershot, England 60-62, United States Army Special Warfare School, Fort Bragg, S. Carolina 62-63; served with UN in Congo and Tanzania 63-64; Instructor, Nigerian Military Training Coll. 64; Chief Instructor 65; Brigade-Major 66; Military Admin. of Mid-West Sept. 67-Nov. 67; Lieut.-Col. and Military Gov. of Mid-Western State Nov. 67-; Col. Aug. 69.
Office of the Military Governor, Benin, Nigeria.

Ogbu, Edwin Ogebe; Nigerian diplomatist; b. 28 Dec. 1926; ed. Bethune-Cockman Coll., Florida, and Stanford Univ., California, U.S.A.
Assistant Sec. Ministry of Finance, Kaduna 57; Sec. Students Affairs, Nigerian High Comm., London 60; Sec. Fed. Public Service Comm. 60-62; Perm. Sec. Fed. Ministry of Works 62-63, Fed. Ministry of Finance 63-66, Fed. Ministry of External Affairs 66-68; Perm. Rep. to UN 68-, also High Commr. to Barbados, Jamaica, Trinidad and Tobago and Guyana 70-; Chair. UN Special Cttee. on Apartheid Oct. 72-.
Permanent Mission of Nigeria to the United Nations, 757 Third Avenue, New York, N.Y. 10017, U.S.A.

Ohin, Alexandre John, M.D., F.A.C.S., F.I.C.S.; Togolese surgeon and diplomatist; b. 20 March 1920, Anécho, Togo; ed. Univ. of Dakar School of Medicine, Univ. of Calif., Washington Univ. School of Medicine (Homer G. Phillips Hospital) and New York Acad. of Medicine.
Intern, Resident and Chief Resident Surgeon, Homer G. Phillips Hospital, Washington Univ. School of Medicine 54-60; Research Fellow in Surgical Metabolism, Wash. Univ. School of Medicine 56-57; Staff mem., Research Fellow in Surgical Metabolism, Albert Einstein Coll. of Medicine, New York City 60-61; Surgeon, Chief Surgeon, Nat. Hospital Centre of Togo 61-67; mem. Expert Advisory Board on Cancer for WHO 67-; Asst. Sec. Asscn. of Surgeons of West Africa 65-; Minister of Health and Justice, Togo 67; Vice-Pres. 23rd, Gen. Assembly of UN; Amb. to U.S.A. and Canada, and Perm. Rep. to UN June 67-71; regular guest at Nat. Cancer Inst., Bethesda, U.S.A.; Officier de l'Ordre National du Mono (Togo).
Publs. several articles in American medical journals.
c/o Ministry of Foreign Affairs, Lomé, Togo.

Ojukwu, General Chukwuemeka Odumegwu, M.A.; Nigerian army officer and politician; b. 4 Nov. 1933; ed. C.M.S. Grammar School and King's Coll., Lagos, Epsom Coll., U.K., Lincoln Coll., Oxford, Eaton Hall Officer Cadet School, U.K. and Joint Services Staff Coll., U.K.
Administrative Officer, Nigerian Public Service 56-57; joined Nigerian Army 57; at Nigerian Army Depot, Zaria 57; army training in U.K. 57-58; joined 5th Battalion Nigerian Army 58; Instructor, Royal West African Frontier Force Training School, Teshie 58-61; returned to 5th Battalion Nigerian Army 61; Maj. Army H.Q. 61; Deputy Asst. Adjutant and Quartermaster-Gen. Kaduna Brigade H.Q. 61; Congo Emergency Force 62; Lieut.-Col. and Quartermaster-Gen. 63-64; Commdr. 5th Battalion, Kano 64-66; Mil. Gov. of E. Nigeria 66-67; proclaimed Head of State of Republic of Biafra (E. Region of Nigeria) May 67-Jan. 70; sought political asylum in Ivory Coast Jan. 70. ordered to leave Oct. 70.

Okero, Isaac Edwin Omolo; Kenyan politician; b. 1931, Ulumbi, Nyanza Province; ed. Makerere Univ. Coll., Uganda, Univs. of Bombay and Leiden and Middle Temple, London.
State Counsel, Kenya 62-63, Deputy Public Prosecutor 63-65; Commr.-Gen. of Customs and Excise, E. African Community 65-69; M.P. 69-; Minister of Health 69-; Vice-Chair. Customs Co-operatives Council.
Ministry of Health, Nairobi, Kenya.

Okezie, Dr. Josiah Onyebuchi Johnson, L.S.M., F.M.C.G.P.; Nigerian physician and politician; b. 26 Nov. 1924, Umuahia-Ibeku; ed. Higher Coll., Yaba, Achimota Coll., Ghana, Yaba Coll. of Medicine, Univ. Coll., Ibadan and Royal Coll. of Surgeons (U.K.).
Assistant Medical Officer, Nigerian Civil Service 50-54; Founder and Medical Supt. Ibeku Central Hosp., Umuahia-Ibeku 58-69; Snr. Medical Officer in charge of Queen Elizabeth Hosp., Umuahia-Ibeku 70; Assoc. Editor, *The Nigerian Scientist* 61-62; Sec. E. Nigerian Science

Asscn. 61-63; mem. Nigerian Medical Council 65-66; mem. E. Nigeria House of Assembly 61-66; Leader, Republican Party 64-66; Rep. of E. Central State, Fed. Exec. Council 70-; Fed. Commr. for Health 70-71; Fed. Commr. for Agriculture and Natural Resources 71-.
Publs. *The Evolution of Science* 59, *Atomic Radiation* 61.
Federal Ministry of Agriculture and Natural Resources, 34/36 Ikoyi Road, Lagos, Nigeria.

Okigbo, Dr. Pius; Nigerian diplomatist and economist. Former Amb. to European Common Market; Econ. Adviser, Exec. Council, Biafra June 67; Leader, Biafran del., Addis Ababa peace talks 69; arrested at Enugu May 70; imprisoned in Lagos, released Sept. 71.

Okunnu, Lateef Olufemi, LL.B., B.L.; Nigerian barrister and politician; b. 19 Feb. 1933, Lagos; ed. King's Coll., Lagos and Univ. Coll., London.
Civil Servant, Posts and Telegraphs Dept. 53; Teacher of history, King's Coll., Lagos 53-56; Publicity Sec. Cttee. of African Orgs., London 58-60; Editor *Nigerian Bar Journal* 64-68; mem. Exec. Cttee. Nigerian Bar Asscn. 64-68; Legal Adviser, Nat. Sports Council of Nigeria; Federal Commr. for Works and Housing July 67-; Leader of Nigerian del. to peace talks in Niamey, Addis Ababa and Monrovia 68-69; Commdr., Nat. Orders of Dahomey, Niger.
Federal Ministry for Works and Housing, Tafawa Balewa Square, Lagos; Home: 97 Warneman Street, Yaba, Nigeria.

Olang, Most Rev. Festo Habakkuk; Kenyan ecclesiastic; b. 11 Nov. 1914, Maseno; ed. Maseno School, Alliance High School and Wycliffe Hall, Oxford.
Member of staff, Maseno School 36, Butere School 39; ordained deacon 45, ordained priest 50; Rural Dean of Central Nyanza 51-55; Asst. Bishop of Mombasa 55; Bishop of Maseno 60; Archbishop of Kenya and Bishop of Nairobi June 70-.
Bishopsbourne, Nairobi, Kenya.

Olivier, Stephanus Petrus, M.ED., D.PHIL.; South African university administrator; b. 21 Jan. 1915, Pearston; ed. Gill Coll., Somerset East, Stellenbosch and Potchefstroom Univs. and Univs. of London and South Africa.
School teacher, Salisbury, Rhodesia 38-46; Prof. of Educ. and Dean of Faculty of Educ., Univ. of Cape Town 50-60; Rector, Univ. Durban-Westville 61-; mem. S. African Acad.
Publs. in Afrikaans: *Social Studies Handbook, Church in Rhodesia, Pioneer Treks to Rhodesia;* numerous articles on educ. and culture.
University of Durban-Westville, Private Bag 4001, Durban; Home: 8 Maryvale, Westville, Natal, South Africa.

Ollenu, Nii Amaa; Ghanaian judge and politician; b. May 1906, Labadi, Accra; ed. Labadi Basel Mission School, Accra High School and Middle Temple, London.
Teacher, Accra High School 29-37; called to the Bar 40; mem., Accra Town Council 44-50; Governor's nominee to Legislative Council 46-50; mem., Coussey Cttee. on Constitutional Reforms 49; High Court Judge 56-62; Chair., Comm. of Inheritance 59; Supreme Court Judge 62; Hon. Prof. of Law, Univ. of Ghana, Legon 62-63; Vice-Pres., Int. African Law Asscn. 63; Commr., Enquiry into Trade Malpractices Oct. 67; Speaker, Nat. Assembly Sept. 67-72; Acting Pres. Oct. 70-72; Exec. mem. World Alliance of Reformed Churches; Pres. Int. African Law Asscn. 70.
Publs. *The Law of Succession in Ghana, The Influence of English Law on West Africa, Land Law of Ghana.*
35th Circular Road, Cantonments, Accra, Ghana.

Omaboe, Emmanuel Noi, B.SC.(ECON.); Ghanaian business executive and former politician; b. 29 Oct. 1930, Amanokrom; ed. Accra Acad., Univ. Coll. of Ghana and London School of Economics.

Economics Research Fellow, Univ. of Ghana 57-59; Govt. Statistician, Central Bureau of Statistics 60-66; Chair. Econ. Cttee. of Nat. Liberation Council 66-69; Commr. for Economic Affairs 67-69; now Chair. and Man. Dir. E.N. Omaboe Associates Ltd. (business, investment and econ. consultants); Dir. Barclays Bank Int. Ltd., Ghana; Grand Medal 68.
Publs. *Internal Migration Differentials from Conventional Census Questionnaire Items* (with B. Gil) 63, *Study of Contemporary Ghana* (with Birmingham and Neustadt) 66.
E.N. Omaboe Associates Ltd., P.O. Box 6251, Accra, Ghana.

Omari, Dunstan Alfred, M.B.E., B.A., DIP. ED.; Tanzanian business executive and former civil servant; b. 1922, Newala; ed. St. Joseph's Secondary School, Chidya, St. Andrew's Secondary School, Minaki, Makerere Univ. Coll. and Univ. of Wales (Aberystwyth).
Education Officer (Broadcasting Duties) 53-54; District Officer 55-58, District Commr. 58-61; Tanganyika High Commr. in the U.K. 61-62; Perm. Sec., Prime Minister's Office, and Sec. to the Cabinet, Tanganyika 62; Perm. Sec., President's Office, and Sec. to the Cabinet, Tanganyika 62-63; Sec.-Gen. East African Common Services Org. 64-67, 67-68 (now called East African Community); Chair. East African Currency Board 64-; mem. Presidential Comm. of Inquiry into the Structure and Remuneration of Public Service in Kenya 70-71; Chair. East African Railways Salaries Review Comm. 71-72.
Publ. *Talks on Citizenship* 54.
P.O. Box 25015, Nairobi, Kenya.
Telephone: Nairobi 64120.

Omwony, Maurice Peter; Kenyan international finance official; b. 31 Dec. 1933; ed. Aligarh and Delhi Univs., India.
Associate mem. British Inst. of Personnel Management 63-; Personnel Man. African Posts and Telecommunications Corpn. 68-; Exec. Dir. IMF 70-.
International Monetary Fund, 19th Street, N.W., Washington, D.C. 20431, U.S.A.

Onana-Awana, Charles; Cameroonian politician; b. *c.* 1923; ed. Ecole Supérieure, Yaoundé and Ecole Nationale de la France d'Outre-Mer, Paris.
With the Ministry of Finance 43-57; Head, Office of Deputy Prime Minister for the Interior 57-58; Asst.-Dir. Office of Prime Minister Feb.-Oct. 58; Perm. Sec. French Cameroons, Paris 58-59; Minister of Finance 60-61; Del. to the Presidency in charge of Finance, the Plan and Territorial Admin. 61-65; Sec.-Gen. Union Douanière et Economique de l'Afrique Centrale 65-70; Minister of Planning and Territorial Improvement June 70-72, of Finance July 72-; fmr. Dir. Banque Centrale de l'Afrique Equatoriale et du Cameroun; fmr. Gov. Int. Monetary Fund; Officier Ordre de la Valeur, Cameroon; Commdr. Légion d'Honneur, Ordre de la Rédemption Africaine, Ordre Tchadien.
Ministry of Finance, Yaoundé, United Republic of Cameroon.

Onyeama, Charles D., LL.B.; Nigerian judge; b. 5 Aug. 1917, Eke, Enugu; *s.* of Chief Onyeama; ed. King's Coll., Lagos, Achimota Coll., Gold Coast, Univ. Coll., London and Brasenose Coll., Oxford.
Cadet Admin. Officer, Nigeria 44; mem. Legislative Council of Nigeria and Eastern House of Assembly 46-51; mem. Nigerianization Comm. and mem. Gen. Conf. and Constitutional Drafting Cttee. 48-50; Chief Magistrate, Nigeria 52-56; Acting High Court Judge, W. Nigeria 56-57; High Court Judge, Lagos 57-64; Acting Chief Justice, Lagos High Court 61 and 63; Justice of Supreme Court of Nigeria 64-66; Judge Int. Court of Justice, The Hague 66-.
International Court of Justice, Peace Palace, The Hague Netherlands.
Telephone: 39-23-44.

Onyonka, Zachary; Kenyan politician; b. 1938.
Former Prof. of Econs., Univ. Coll., Nairobi; Minister of
Econ. Planning and Devt. Dec. 69-Oct. 70; Minister of
Information and Broadcasting Oct. 70-; mem. Kenya
African Nat. Union (KANU).
Ministry of Information and Broadcasting, Nairobi,
Kenya.

Oppenheimer, Harry Frederick, M.A.; South African
industrialist; b. 28 Oct. 1908, Kimberley; ed. Charterhouse
and Christ Church, Oxford.
Chairman, Anglo-American Corpn. of South Africa Ltd.,
De Beers Consolidated Mines Ltd.; Chair., Dir. of 68 or
more subsidiary and other companies; M.P. 47-58;
Chancellor, Cape Town Univ. 67-; Hon. D.Econ. (Natal);
Hon. LL.D. (Leeds, Witwatersrand and Rhodes).
Brenthurst, Federation Road, Parktown, Johannesburg,
South Africa.

Ordia, Abraham; Nigerian sports administrator; ed.
Finchley Grammar School, England.
Worked in hospital as mental health specialist in Friern
Barnet, Hull, Oldham, Manchester and East Grinstead;
now Sec.-Gen., Nat. Sports Council of Nigeria, Pres.
African Sports Council and Pres. Supreme Council for
Sport in Africa.
African Sports Council, Yaoundé, Cameroon.

Osman, Abdool Hack, Bar.-at-Law; Mauritius politician;
b. 1925, Port Louis; ed. Grammar School, Port Louis and
Middle Temple, London.
Elected mem., Legislative Council for Phoenix 59, re-
elected 63; Minister of Information, Posts, and Telegraphs
and Telecommunications 62-65; Minister of Housing,
Lands and Town and Country Planning 61-65; attended
Commonwealth Parl. Course, London 61, London Consti-
tutional Conf. 65; Attorney-Gen. 65-68; Minister of Works
June 68-, concurrently Minister of Communications
March 69-Nov. 69; Pres., Comité d'Action Musulman
(C.A.M.) 61-; Third mem. Legislative Assembly for La
Caverne and Phoenix 67-.
Ministry of Works, Port Louis, Mauritius.

Osman, Hassan Mutwakil Mohamed; Sudanese cotton
executive; b. Jan. 1918; ed. Coll. of Agriculture, Sudan.
Agriculturalist with Sudanese Dept. of Agriculture 42-48;
Senior Officer Atbara Dairy 48-50; Insp. of Mechanized
Crop Production 50-51; Insp. of Agriculture, Sennor and
Fung Districts 51-54; Govt. Soil Conservation Officer
54-57; Asst. Dir. of Agriculture, Dept. of Agriculture
59-62, Deputy Dir. 63-65, Dir. 66; Man. Dir. Sudan Gezira
Board 66-; mem. Council, Univ. of Khartoum, Board of
Faculty of Agriculture, and Khartoum Technical Inst.
Sudan Gezira Board, Barakat, Blue Nile Province, Sudan.

Osman Daar, Aden Abdulla; Somali businessman and
politician; b. 1908; ed. Government School, Somalia.
Member Somalia Territorial Council 51-55, Vice-Pres.
53-55; Pres. Somali Youth League 54-56, 58-59; Pres.
Legislative Assembly 56-60, Constituent Assembly 60;
Pres. of the Somali Republic 61-67; Life Deputy in Nat.
Assembly 67-.
c/o National Assembly, Mogadishu, Somalia.

Osogo, James Charles Nakhwanga, M.P.; Kenyan
teacher and politician; b. 10 Nov. 1932, Bukani; ed. Port
Victoria Primary School, St. Mary's High School, Yala,
Railway Training School, Nairobi and Kagumo Teachers'
Training Coll.
Teacher, Sigalame School 55, Withur School 56, Barding
School 57. Ndenga School 58, Port Victoria School 59;
Headmaster Kibasanga School 60, Nangina School 61-62;
Vice-Chair. Kenya Nat. Union of Teachers, Central
Nyanza 58-62; mem. Kenya House of Representatives
63-; Asst. Minister, Ministry of Agriculture 63-66;

Minister for Information and Broadcasting 66-69; Minister
of Commerce and Industry 69-, also acting Minister of
Agriculture May 70; Chair. Kenya Youth Hostels Asscn.
64-70, Patron 70-; Elder, Order of the Golden Heart
(Kenya), Order of the Star of Africa (Liberia), Grand
Cordon of the Star of Ethiopia, Grand Cross of the
Yugoslav Flag.
Ministry of Commerce and Industry, P.O. Box 30430,
Nairobi; M.P. for Busia South, P.O. Port Victoria, via
Kisumu, Kenya.

Ouattara, Brig.-Gen. Paul Thomas D'Aquin; Ivory
Coast army officer.
Second class private, French Army; served in Second
World War and in Indochina campaign; Major 54; Chief of
Gen. Staff, Ivory Coast 61-64; Lieut.-Col. 64-66; Brig.-Gen.
Aug. 66-; Dir., Political Dept., Org. of African Unity
(OAU).
c/o Organization of African Unity, P.O. Box 3243, Addis
Ababa, Ethiopia.

Ouedraogo, Gerard Kango; Upper Voltan politician.
Former Amb. to U.K.; Pres. Union Démocratique Vol-
taïque; Prime Minister Feb. 71-.
Office of the Prime Minister, Ouagadougou, Upper Volta.

Ouko, Robert John; Kenyan administrator; b. 31
March 1932, Kisumu; ed. Ogada School, Kisumu, Nyangori
School, Kakamega, Siriba Coll., Haile Selassie I and
Makerere Univs.
Teacher 52-55; worked in Kisii District, Ministry of
African Affairs 55-58; Asst. Sec. Foreign Affairs Dept.,
Office of the Prime Minister 62-63, Senior Asst. Sec. 63;
Perm. Sec. Ministry of Foreign Affairs 63-64, Ministry of
Works 65-69; East African Minister for Finance and Admin.
69-70, for Common Market and Econ. Affairs Nov. 70-;
Pres. African Asscn. for Public Admin. and Management;
mem. East African Legislative Assembly; Hon. LL.D.
(Pacific Lutheran Univ.) 71.
Publs. essays on administration in professional journals.
East African Community Common Market Secretariat,
P.O. Box 1003, Arusha, Tanzania.

Ousmane, Sembene; Senegalese writer; b. 1923; ed.
Primary School.
Plumber, bricklayer, apprentice mechanic; served in
Europe in Second World War; docker in Marseilles; studied
film production in U.S.S.R.; first prize for novelists at
World Festival of Negro Arts, Dakar 67; Dir. film
Mandabi 69.
Publs. *Le Docker Noir* 56, *O pays, mon beau peuple* 57,
Les Bouts de Bois de Dieu 60, *Vehi Ciosare* 65.
c/o Nouvelles Editions Latines, rue Palatine 1, Paris 6e,
France.

Owusu, Victor; Ghanaian politician; b. 26 Dec. 1923,
Agona-Ashanti; ed. Univs. of Nottingham and London.
Called to the Bar, Lincoln's Inn 52; practising barrister
52-67; M.P. for Agona-Kwabre 56-61; Attorney-Gen. 66-
April 69, concurrently Minister of Justice July 67-April 69;
Minister of External Affairs 69-71; Attorney-Gen. and
Minister of Justice Feb. 71-Jan. 72; Chair. Univ. Council,
Univ. of Ghana, Legon Nov. 70-; fmr. Nat. Vice-Chair. for
Ashanti Progress Party.
c/o Ministry of Justice, P.O. Box M.60, Accra, Ghana.

Oyono, Ferdinand Leopold; Cameroonian author and
diplomatist.
Former Amb. to Liberia; Amb. to Belgium, also accred. to
Luxembourg and the Netherlands Oct. 69-Sept. 70; Amb.
to Italy Sept. 70; now Amb. to France.
Publs. *Une Vie de Boy* 56, *Le Vieux Nègre et la Médaille* 67,
Le Pandemonium.
Cameroonian Embassy, 147 bis, rue de Longchamp,
Paris 16e, France.

P

Pascal, Chabi Kao; Dahomeyan politician; b. 10 March 1935, Parakou; ed. Teachers' Training Coll., Dabou, Ivory Coast, Univ. of Aix-Marseille and Paris Centre of Financial, Economic and Banking Studies, France.
Secretary-General, Banque Dahoméenne de Développement; Minister of Labour; Minister of Finance May 70-72.
c/o Ministry of Finance, Porto Novo, Dahomey.

Patassé, Ange; Central African Republic politician; b. 25 Jan. 1937; ed. French Equatorial Coll.
Agricultural inspector 59-65; Dir. of Agriculture 65; Minister of Devt. 65; Minister of State for Transport and Power March 69-Feb. 70, concurrently Minister of State for Devt. and Tourism Sept. 69-Feb. 70; Minister of State for Agriculture, Stock-breeding, Waters and Forests, Hunting, Tourism, Transport and Power Feb.-June 70; Minister of State for Devt. June-Aug. 70; Minister of State for Transport and Commerce 70-72, for Rural Devt. May 72-; Pres. Soc. Franco-Centrafricaine des Tabacs, Union Cotonnière Centrafricaine 70.
Office du Président, Bangui, Central African Republic.

Paton, Alan Stewart, B.ED., B.SC.; South African writer and politician; b. 11 Jan. 1903, Pietermaritzburg, Natal; ed. Pietermaritzburg Coll. and Natal Univ.
Teacher 24-36; Principal Diepkloof Reformatory for African Juvenile Delinquents, Johannesburg 36-48; Pres. Liberal Party of South Africa till 68; started a new magazine *Reality* 69; Hon. L.H.D. (Yale Univ.); Hon. D.Litt. (Kenyon Coll., Univ. of Natal, Trent, Harvard and Rhodes Univs.); Hon. D.D. (Edinburgh Univ.) Freedom Award 60; Award from Free Acad. of Art, Hamburg 61.
Publs *Cry, The Beloved Country* 48, *Too Late the Phalarope* 53, *The Land and People of South Africa* 55, *South Africa in Transition* 56, *Hope for South Africa* 58, *Debbie Go Home* (short stories) 61, *Hofmeyr* 65, *Instrument of Thy Peace* 68, *The Long View* 68, *Kontakion for You Departed* 69, musical *Mkhumbane* (Village in the Gulley).
P.O. Box 278, Hillcrest, Natal, Republic of South Africa.
Telephone: Durban (Natal) 788920.

Peal, Samuel Edward; Liberian diplomatist; b. 3 Feb. 1923; ed. Central Nat. School, White Plains, and Liberia Coll.
Former Town Clerk, Millsburg; Foreign Service, Paris, London, Hamburg; fmr. Amb. to Netherlands, to Guinea; now Amb. to U.S.A.; numerous decorations.
Embassy of Liberia, Washington, D.C., U.S.A.

Pelser, Petrus Cornelius, B.A., LL.B.; South African politician; b. 28 Feb. 1907, Reddersburg, O.F.S.; ed. Paarl Gimnasium, Univ. of South Africa (private study) and Univ. of the Witwatersrand.
Joined Public Service 25; Dept. of Mines 25-37, Dept. of Commerce and Industry 37-43; Attorney, Klerksdorp 43; mem. Provincial Council, Klerksdorp 50; mem. Parl. 53-; Deputy Chair. of Cttees., House of Assembly 62-66; Deputy Speaker and Chair. of Cttees, 66; Minister of Justice and Prisons Sept. 66-; Nat. Party.
Ministry of Justice, Union Buildings, Pretoria, South Africa.

Pepler, L. A.; South African administrator; b. 16 Aug. 1908, Bloemfontein.
Civil Service 31-; Dept. of Native Affairs 49-; Dir., Bantu Agriculture 56; Dir. Bantu Devt. 61-66, Bantu and Physical Devt. of Bantu Homelands 66-71; Senior Deputy Sec., Planning of Bantu Homelands 71-.
Department of Bantu Administration and Development, Pretoria; Home: William Street 466, Brooklyn, Pretoria, South Africa.

Perraudin, Most. Rev. André; Swiss (Catholic) ecclesiastic; b. 7 Oct. 1914, Bagnes, Switzerland; ed. Fribourg.

Entered Order of White Fathers 34, ordained 39; served Kiganda (Burundi) 47, Kibunbu 48, Nyakibanda (Rwanda) 50; Rector of Seminary, Nyakibanda 52; Vicar Apostolic, Kabgayi 55; Archbishop of Kabgayi 59-; received Papal Pallium 60; Pres. of Episcopal Conf. of Rwanda and Burundi.
Publs. include: *Super Omnia Caritas* 59, *Le Rwanda au seuil de son indépendance* 60, *L'attitude des Chrétiens face aux événements actuels, Les laïcs et le Concile*, etc.
Archevêque de Kabgayi, B.P. 715, Kigali, Rwanda.

Philip, Kjeld, DR.ECON.; Danish economist and politician; b. 3 April 1912, Copenhagen; ed. Copenhagen Univ.
Instructor Aarhus Univ. 37-43 and Prof. of Social Politics and Public Finance 43-49, Prof. of Econs. and Social Politics, Stockholm Univ. 49-51; Prof. of Economics, Univ. of Copenhagen 51-57, 64, 66-69; Minister of Commerce 57-60; Minister of Finance 60-61; Minister of Econ. Affairs 61-64; Chair. Co-ordination Cttee. 55; Dir. Inst. of History and Econs. 56-60; UN Senior Econ. Adviser to Prime Minister of Somalia 65; Chair. Comm. on East African Co-operation 65-67, Danish Board for Technical Co-operation with Developing Countries 68-; Industrialization Fund for Developing Countries 68-; Adviser to ILO 69-71; leader, team studying African econ. co-operation, Econ. Comm. for Africa.
Publs. *En Fremstilling og analyse of Den danske Kriselovgivning* 31-38, 39, *Bidrag til Laeren om Forbindelsen mellem, det offentliges Finanspolitik og dem okonomiske Aktivitet* 42, *Staten og Fattigdommen* 47, *La Politica Financiera y la Actividad Económica*, Madrid 49, *Intergovernmental Fiscal Relations* 53, *Skattepolitik* 55, second edn. 65.
Rungstedvej 91, DK-2960 Rungsted Kyst, Denmark.

Phillips, John Frederick Vicars, D.SC., F.R.S.E., F.R.S.S.AFR.; South African ecologist, conservationist and agriculturist; b. 15 March 1899, Grahamstown, S. Africa; ed. Dale Coll., King William's Town, South Africa, and Univ. of Edinburgh.
Initiated research into indigenous forests, Knysna, S. Africa 22-27; ecologist and later Dep. Dir. Tsetse Research, Tanganyika Territory; Prof. of Botany, Univ. of Witwatersrand, Johannesburg 31; Gen. Man., later Joint Gen. Man. and Chief Agricultural Adviser to Overseas Food Corpn. (East African Groundnuts Scheme) 48; Consultant in Agriculture to FAO and Int. Bank of Reconstruction and Development; British Gov. Econ. Survey Mission of High Comm. Territories, Southern Africa 59; Chair. Cttee. of Enquiry into African Educ., Nyasaland 61; Prof. of Agriculture, Univ. Coll., Ghana and Adviser in Agricultural Educ. to Ghana Ministry of Education 52-60; Chair. Cttee. reporting on development of economic resources in Southern Rhodesia 60-62; co-ordinating agro-economic aspects of the Tugela Basin 63-68; Visiting Prof. Univ. of Pa. 66; Leader of UN Survey Team, Socio-economy of Hill Tribes, Thailand 67-69; Consultant in applied ecology and devt., Messrs. Loxton, Hunting Associates; Pres. South African Asscn. of Advanced Science 69; Chair. Aircraft Operating Co. Technical Services, South Africa; Corresp. mem. Sociedade de Estudos Moçambique; Hon. Senior Research Fellow, Applied Ecology, Univ. of Natal; Hon. D.Sc. Rhodes Univ.
Publs. *The Forests of George, Knysna and the Zitzikama: A Brief History of their Management, 1778-1939, Agriculture and Ecology in Africa* 59, *Kwame Nkrumah and the Future of Africa* 60, *Development of Agriculture and Forestry in the Tropics: Patterns, Problems and Promise* 61 (2nd edn. 66).
c/o University of Natal, P.O. Box 375, Pietermaritzburg, Natal; Home: 'Green Shadows', P.O. Sweetwaters, Natal, South Africa.
Telephone: (University) 21043; (Home) 25063.

Phiri, Amock Israel, M.A.; Zambian diplomatist; b. 25 Oct. 1932, Israel Village, Chipata.
Lecturer in Sociology, Univ. of Zambia 67-69; mem. Parl. and Chair. Public Accounts Cttee. Nov. 68-March 69; Minister of State, Ministry of Nat. Guidance March-Dec. 69; Minister of State for Information, Broadcasting and Tourism Jan.-Dec. 70; High Commr. to U.K. and Amb. to the Holy See Oct. 70-.
Zambian High Commission, 7-11 Cavendish Place, London, W.I, England.
Telephone: 01-580-0691.

Pickard, Sir Cyril Stanley, K.C.M.G.; British diplomatist; b. 18 Sept. 1917, London; ed. Alleyn's School, Dulwich, and New Coll., Oxford.
Ministry of Home Security 39; Royal Artillery 40-41; Office of Minister of State, Cairo 41-45; UNRRA Balkan Mission 44, later with UNRRA in Germany; Home Office 45-48; Commonwealth Relations Office (CRO) 48-; Office of U.K. High Commr. in India 50-52; Official Sec. to Office of U.K. High Commr. in Australia 52-55; Head, S. Asia and Middle East Dept., CRO 55-58; Deputy High Commr. in New Zealand 58-61; Asst. Under-Sec. of State, CRO 62-66; Acting High Commr., Cyprus 64; High Commr. in Pakistan 66-71, in Nigeria 71-.
British High Commission, Lagos, Nigeria.

Pierre, James Alexander Adolphus; Liberian lawyer; b. 18 July 1908, Harford, Grand Bassa County; ed. Bible Industrial Acad., Cuttington Coll. and Divinity School.
Counsel, later judge; mem. Supreme Court; Attorney-General until 71; Chief Justice of the Supreme Court April 71-.
Temple of Justice Building, Monrovia, Liberia.

Pike, Sir Philip Ernest Housden, Kt.; British barrister-at-law; b. 6 March 1914, Jamaica; ed. De Carteret School and Munro Coll., Jamaica, and Middle Temple, London.
Crown Counsel, Jamaica 47-49; Legal Draftsman, Kenya 49-52; Solicitor-Gen., Uganda 52-58; Attorney-Gen., Sarawak 58-65; Chief Justice, High Court in Borneo 65-68; Judge, High Court of Malawi Aug. 69-Feb. 70, Acting Chief Justice Feb.-Aug. 70; Chief Justice of Swaziland Nov. 70-Dec. 72; Panglima Manku Negara (Malaysia) 68; Panglima Negara Bintang Sarawak 65; Queen's Counsel (Uganda) 53, (Sarawak) 58.
Little Commons, Mullion, Nr. Helston, Cornwall, England.

Pirbhai, Count Sir Eboo, Kt., O.B.E.; Kenyan company director; b. 25 July 1905; ed. Duke of Gloucester School, Nairobi.
Representative of Aga Khan in Africa; mem. Nairobi City Council 38-43; mem. Legislative Council, Kenya 52-60; Pres. Muslim Asscn.; Pres. Aga Khan Supreme Council, Africa; granted title Count by Aga Khan 54; mem. other official bodies; Brilliant Star of Zanzibar 56.
P.O. Box 898, Nairobi; and 12 Naivasha Avenue, Muthaiga, Nairobi, Kenya.

Plantey, Alain Gilles; French government official; b. 19 July 1924, Mulhouse; ed. Univs. de Bordeaux and Paris à la Sorbonne.
Staff of Council of State 49; French del. to UN 51-52; Master of Requests Council of State 56-; Legal Adviser Org. for European Econ. Co-operation (OEEC) 56-57; Prof. Ecole Royale d'Administration Cambodia 57; Gen. Sec. *Agence France-Presse* 58; Asst. Sec.-Gen. for the Community and African and Malagasy Affairs at the Presidency 61-; French Amb. in Madagascar 66-72; Council mem. Museum Nationale d'Histoire naturelle; numerous decorations.
Publs. *La Réforme de la Justice marocaine* 49, *La Justice Répressive et le Droit Pénal Chérifien* 50, *Au Coeur du Problème Berbère* 52, *Traité Pratique de la Fonction*

Publique 56, 63 and 71, *La Formation et le Perfectionnement des Fonctionnaires* 57, *La Communauté* 59.
6 avenue Sully-Prudhomme, Paris 7e, France.
Telephone: 555-26-49.

Porter, Arthur T., M.A., PH.D.; Sierra Leonean professor and administrator; b. 1924; ed. Fourah Bay Coll., Sierra Leone, Cambridge Univ., Inst. of Educ., London, Boston Univ., U.S.A.
Worked in Dept. of Social Anthropology, Edinburgh Univ. 51-52; Lecturer in History, Fourah Bay Coll. 52-56; research in African Studies, Boston Univ. 56-58; Prof. of Modern History, Fourah Bay Coll., later Vice-Principal 60-64; Principal, Univ. Coll., Nairobi 64-70; UNESCO Educ. Planning Adviser, Kenya 70-; Vice-Chancellor, Univ. of Sierra Leone 72-; Fellow, Royal Soc. of Arts, London 72; Phi Beta Kappa Soc. (Boston Univ.) 72; Hon. D.Hum.Litt. (Boston Univ.) 69, Hon. Dr.Iur. (Royal Univ. of Malta) 69.
Publ. *Creoledom.*
University of Sierra Leone, Freetown, Sierra Leone; and c/o Ministry of Education, P.O. Box 48823, Nairobi, Kenya.

Poto Ndamase, Paramount Chief Victor; South African (Transkei) politician; b. 1898; ed. Buntingdale Inst., Mission Schools at Clarkebury, Queenstown and Leribe and Fort Hare Univ. Coll.
Paramount Chief of West Pondoland 18-; fmr. mem. Pondoland Gen. Council, United Transkeian Gen. Council, Bantu Representation Council, Transkeian Territorial Authority; defeated candidate in elections for Chief Minister of Transkei 63.
The Great Place, Nyandeni, P.O. Libode, Transkei, South Africa.

Q

Qassim, Awn al-Sharif, M.A., PH.D.; Sudanese politician; b. 15 Oct. 1933, Halfaiat al Molook; ed. Univs. of Khartoum, London and Edinburgh.
Lecturer, School of Oriental and African Studies, London Univ. 59-61; Lecturer, Dept. of Arabic, Univ. of Khartoum 61-64; Senior Lecturer 69, Dir. Translation Section 69-70; Minister of Waqfs and Religious Affairs Oct. 71-.
Ministry of Waqfs and Religious Affairs, Khartoum, Sudan.

Quaison-Sackey, Alexander, M.A.; Ghanaian diplomatist; b. 9 Aug. 1924; ed. Mfantsipim School, Exeter Coll. Oxford, London School of Economics and Lincoln's Inn, London.
Former teacher at Mfantsipim School and with Gold Coast Secretariat; Labour Officer Gold Coast 52-55; Attaché British Embassy, Rio de Janeiro 56; Head of Chancery and Official Sec. Ghana High Commission, London 57-59; Perm. Rep. of Ghana to UN 59-65; Minister of Foreign Affairs 65-66; Vice-Pres. UN Gen. Assembly 61-62, Pres. UN Gen. Assembly 64-65; Amb. to Cuba 61, to Mexico 62; under house arrest 66, released June 66; Hon. LL.D. (Univ. of Calif.) 65.
Publ. *Africa Unbound* 63.
Alcumbia Lodge, P.O. Box 104, Winneba, Ghana.

Quarshie, Richard Abusua-Ye-Dom, BAR.-AT-LAW; Ghanaian barrister and politician; b. 6 March 1918. Ewusiadje; ed. Achimota Coll. and Lincoln's Inn, London.
Served in Political Admin., Ghanaian Civil Service 40-45, Labour Dept. 46-56, Ministry of External Affairs 56-61; fmr. Sec., Congo Co-ordination Cttee.; Resident-Dir., C.A.S.T. 63-; Commr. for Trade and Industries April-July 69; M.P. (Progress Party) Aug. 69-; Minister of Trade and Industries including Tourism Sept. 69-Jan. 72.
c/o Ministry of Trade and Industries, Accra, Ghana.

Quenum, Dr. Alfred Auguste; Dahomeyan physician; b. 1926, Ouidah; ed. African School of Medicine and Pharmacy, Dakar, and Faculty of Medicine, Univ. of Bordeaux.

Formerly at Centre d'Etudes Nucléaires, Saclay; later Dakar Faculty of Medicine; del., Sixteenth World Health Assembly 63, WHO Regional Cttee. for Africa; mem. WHO cttee. on Professional and Technical Education of Medical and Auxiliary Personnel; Prof. of Histology and Embryology, Dakar Faculty of Medicine 62-64; Regional Dir. for Africa, World Health Org. 65-; Prof., Faculty of Medicine and Pharmacy, Dakar 66-; mem., Council of Lovanium Univ., Kinshasa, W. African Biological Soc., Medical Soc. of French Speaking W. Africa.
World Health Organization Regional Office for Africa, P.O. Box 6, Brazzaville, People's Republic of the Congo.
Telephone: 30-72, 73, 74.

R

Rabemananjara, Jacques: Malagasy politician; b. 23 June 1913.
Joined French Admin. 39; in France during Second World War, became known as novelist and poet; Deputy for Madagascar in French Nat. Assembly 46; later Sec.-Gen. Democratic Movement for Malagasy Renovation (M.D.R.M.); detained in France after Madagascar uprising 47; Minister of Econ. Affairs, Madagascar 60-65, of Agric., Land and Food 65-67; Minister of State for Foreign Affairs 67, and Social Affairs; Vice-Pres. Oct. 70; concurrently Minister of State for Foreign Affairs and Social Affairs; in charge of Cultural Affairs and Public Health; Vice-Pres. and in charge of Foreign Affairs, Cultural Affairs, Information, Tourism and the Traditional Arts June 71-72; mem. Exec. Cttee. Soc. Africaine de Culture.
Publs. include plays: *Les Dieux Malgaches* 47, *Rites Millénaires* (poems) 55, *Lamba* (poem) 56, *Les Boutriers de l'Aurore* 57, *Agape des Dieux-Tritiva* 62; poems: *Sur les Marches du Soir* 42, *Antsa* 56.
c/o Ministry of Foreign Affairs, Tananarive, Madagascar.

Rabetafika, Joseph Albert Blaise, L. ès L.; Malagasy diplomatist; b. 3 Feb. 1932, Tananarive.
Teacher in U.K., France and Madagascar 53-59; joined Ministry of Defence, France 60; mem. Madagascar del. to independence negotiations with France 60; Counsellor in charge of cultural affairs and information, Madagascar diplomatic mission, France 60-63; Perm. del. to UNESCO, Paris 61-63; Head, Del. to IBE Confs., Geneva 61-63; mem. del. to UN Gen. Assembly 62-69; Perm. Rep. to UN 69-.
Permanent Mission of Madagascar to the United Nations, 301 East 47th Street, New York, N.Y. 10017, U.S.A.

Rakotomalala, H.E. Cardinal Jerome; Malagasy ecclesiastic; b. 15 July 1914, Sainte-Marie, Madagascar; ed. Petit et Grand Séminaires.
Ordained 43; Vicar at Cathedral, Tananarive, and Teacher of Science and Mathematics, Grand Séminaire 44-47; Dir. of Missionary District of Ambohimiadana 47-53; Dir. Ecole normale des Instituteurs, Tananarive 53-59; Vicar-Gen. to Archbishop of Tananarive 59-60; Bishop 60, and Archbishop of Tananarive 60-; cr. Cardinal 69; Commandeur de l'Ordre national malgache; Officier de la Légion d'Honneur; Ordre militaire du S. Sauveur et de Sainte Brigitte (Sweden).
Archevêché, Andohalo, Tananarive, Madagascar.

Rakotomalala, Joël; Malagasy army officer; b. 29 March 1929, Tandrano-Ankazoabo, Tuléar Prov.; ed. Ecole de Formation des Officiers Ressortissants des Territoires d'Outre-Mer, Fréjus, Ecole d'Application de l'Infanterie, Saint-Maixent, Ecole d'Application de Transmission, Montargis, France.
Commander, Signalling Corps, Malagasy Army 61-67; assigned to Gen. Staff Headquarters; Deputy Commdr. 2nd Combined Regiment, Fianarantsoa until 72; Minister of Information May 72-.
Ministry of Information, Tananarive, Madagascar.

Ramanantsoa, Maj.-Gen. Gabriel; Malagasy army officer; b. 13 April 1906, Tananarive; ed. Lycée de Tananarive, de Marseille, Ecole Speciale Militaire, Saint-Cyr, Inst. des Hautes Etudes de Défense Nationale.
Assistant to Chief Officer Ecole Mil. Preparatoire des Enfants de Troupe 32; assigned to Colonial Infantry Regiment of Morocco, French Army 31, 35-36; rank of Capt. 40; returned to Madagascar, organized Ecole Supérieure d'Educ. Physique, Fianarantsoa 41, 43-46; Dept. of Colonial Troops, Ministry of Defence, Paris 46, 53-59; in charge of War Veterans, Mil. Office of French High Comm., Madagascar 48-53; served with French Army in Viet-Nam 53; Lt.-Col., Col. 59, Brig.-Gen. 61, Maj.-Gen. 67; participated in Franco-Malagasy negotiations for independence 60; Chief of Gen. Staff of the Malagasy Armed Forces; Prime Minister, Minister of Defence, Minister of Planning May 72-; Head of Govt. Oct. 72-.
Présidence de la République, Tananarive, Madagascar.

Ramangasoavina, Alfred, D. en D.; Malagasy politician; b. 2 Nov. 1917, Moramanga; ed. Ecole Le Myre, Vilers and School of Political Sciences, Paris, France.
Served in Malagasy admin. 39-47; lawyer, Tananarive Appeal Court, Paris Appeal Court 52-54; served at Central Treasury for Overseas France 54-56; worked in Madagascar Exchange Office; municipal councillor for Tananarive 56; Finance Minister 57-58; Minister of Equipment 58-59; Minister of Industry and Planning 59-60; Deputy for Tananarive Province (Social Democratic Party) Sept. 60-; Minister of Justice Oct. 60-Dec. 69; Minister of Information, Tourism and Traditional Arts Dec. 69-Sept. 70; Minister of State for Commerce, Supply, Industry and Mines Sept. 70-71; Vice-Pres. and in charge of Public Health and Population, Public Works and Communications, Women's Advancement, and the Protection of Children 71-72; mem. UN Int. Law Comm., del. to ILO and other int. confs.; Commdr. Etoile Royale de la Grande Comore, Grand Officer, Nat. Order of Ivory Coast, Commdr. Ordre de la Valeur, Cameroon.
c/o Ministry of Public Health, Tananarive, Madagascar.

Ramaroson, Albert Marie; Malagasy economist; b. 17 Sept. 1925, Ambositra, Fianarantsoa Prov.; ed. Ecole Nat. des Impôts, Paris, Inst. d'Etudes du Développement Economique et Social (Univ. of Paris), Ecole Pratique des Hautes Etudes, Paris.
Inspector of Taxes; Inspecteur d'Etat, Head of Dept. Public Inspection Office until 72; Minister of Finance and the Economy May 72-.
Ministry of Finance and the Economy, Tananarive, Madagascar.

Ramathan, Mustapha, B.COM.; Ugandan diplomatist; b. 29 Jan. 1936, Bombo; ed. in Uganda and Cairo.
Headmaster of secondary school in Bombo 60-63; Deputy Sec. Uganda Lint Marketing Board 68-; Amb. to U.S.A. June 71-.
Embassy of Uganda, 5909 16th Street, N.W., Washington, D.C. 20011, U.S.A.

Ramgoolam, Sir Seewoosagur, Kt., L.R.C.P., M.R.C.S.; British (Mauritius) physician and administrator; b. 18 Sept. 1900; ed. Royal Coll., Mauritius and Univ. Coll. London.
Municipal Councillor 40-53, 56; Dep. Mayor of Port Louis 56, Mayor 58; mem. Legislative Council 48-; mem. Exec. Council 48-; Liaison Officer for Educ. 51-56; Ministerial Sec. to the Treasury 58-60; Minister of Finance 60-61, Leader of the House 60-, Chief Minister and Minister of Finance 61-64; Premier 64-; also Minister of Finance 64, now Minister of Defence, Security, Information and Broadcasting; Chair, Board of Dirs. *Advance* (daily); Pres. Indian Cultural Asscn.; Editor *Indian Cultural Review*.
Government House, Port Louis, Mauritius.
Telephone: 2-0460.

Ramphul, Radha Krishna; Mauritius diplomatist; b. 4 Jan. 1926, Curepipe; ed. London School of Econs., and Lincoln's Inn, London.
Manager, Choisy Estate, Sec. Dir. Ramphul Ltd. Mauritius 45-50; Dir. private firm in London 55-69; Perm. Rep. to UN 69-.
Permanent Mission of Mauritius to UN, 301 East 47th Street, Suite 3c, New York, N.Y. 10017, U.S.A.

Raoul, Major Alfred; Congolese army officer and politician; b. 1930; ed. Military Acad., Saint-Cyr, France.
Adjutant to C.-in-C. of Congolese Armed Forces 63-65; Dir. of Corps of Engineers 65; Sec. in charge of Defence, Directorate of Nat. Revolutionary Council Aug. 68; Prime Minister of Congo (Brazzaville) Aug. 68-Dec. 69, concurrently Minister of Defence Sept. 68-Jan. 69, concurrently Minister of State Planning and Admin. Sept.-April 70, Minister of Trade, Industry and Mines April 70-71; Head of State Sept. 68-Jan. 69; Vice-Chair. Council of State Dec. 69-Dec. 71; sentenced to 10 years imprisonment March 72; mem. Political Bureau of Congolese Workers' Party (PCT); 2nd Sec. Central Cttee. of PCT.
Brazzaville, People's Republic of Congo.

Raphaël-Leygues, Jacques; French diplomatist and former politician; b. 13 Dec. 1913.
Head Commr. Nat. Marine; with Office of Pres. of Council 38-39; Army service 39-45, in Indochina 45-50; Councillor for French Union 50-58; Peace Missions to Far East 52-54; Dep. to Nat. Ass. 58-62, Vice-Pres. of Cttee. for Foreign Affairs 59-62, Vice-Pres. of Nat. Assembly 62; Mayor and Gen. Councillor Villeneuve-sur-Lot; Ambassador to Ivory Coast 63-; Commdr. Légion d'Honneur; Lauréat de l'Académie Française.
Publs. Plays: *Saigon 46, Grand Chef Blanc*; Poetry: *Retour de Mer, Mers indiennes, Minuit à quatre.*
Ambassade de France, B.P. 1393, Abidjan, Ivory Coast; 6, avenue Frédéric-Le-Play, Paris 7e, France.

Rasidy, René; Malagasy politician; b. 5 July 1927, Bevahona, Antsohihy District; ed. Teachers' Training Coll., Caen, France.
Inspector of primary education; founder mem., Madagascar Social Democratic Party 56; provincial councillor for Majunga 57-58; deputy, Malagasy Assembly 58-; Sec. of State for Farming June 59-60; Minister of Agriculture 60-Aug. 65; Minister of Mines and Industry Aug. 65-Sept. 70; Minister of Information, Tourism and Traditional Arts 70-72.
c/o Ministry of Information, Tourism and Traditional Arts, Tananarive, Madagascar.

Ratsimamanga, Albert Rakoto, D.SC., D.MED.; Malagasy diplomatist; b. 28 Dec. 1907; ed. High School (S.P.G.) Tananarive and Univ. of Paris.
Research Dir. Centre Nat. de la Recherche Scientifique; Dir. Ecole Pratique des Hautes Etudes; Ambassador of Malagasy Repub. to France 60-, to German Fed. Repub. 61-68, to Sierra Leone Nov. 71-; mem. Exec. Council, UNESCO 60, Vice-Chair. 62; corresp. mem. of Académie des Sciences, Institut de France 66; Grand Officier Légion d'Honneur, etc.
Major works: Thèse sur l'Anthropologie de Madagascar, Travaux sur la Biochimie de la Surrénale, Hormones Steroidiques et Vitamines Hydrosolubles, Etudes expérimentales sur l'Action antituberculeuse et anti-lépreuse des phtalydrazides, Cicatrisants Triterpenoïdes
Embassy of the Malagasy Republic (Madagascar), 1 boulevard Suchet, Paris 16e, France.
Telephone: 870-1817.

Ratsimandrava, Lt.-Col. Richard; Malagasy army officer; b. 21 March 1931, Tananarive; ed. Lycée Galliéni, Tananarive, Ecole Speciale Mil. Interarmes de Coëtquidan, Ecole des Officiers de la Gendarmerie Nat. Française, Melun, France.

Served with French Army, Morocco, Algeria 54-60; commissioned in Malagasy Army 60; rank of Gendarmerie Capt. 62, Lt.-Col. 68; Commdr. of the Gendarmerie 69-; Minister of the Interior May 72-.
Ministry of the Interior, Tananarive, Madagascar.

Ratsiraka, Capt. Didier; Malagasy naval officer; b. 4 Nov. 1936, Vatomandry; ed. Coll. Saint Michel, Tananarive, Lycée Henri IV, Paris, Ecole Navale, Lanveuc-Poulmic (France), Ecole des Officiers "Transmissions", Les Boumettes, and Ecole Supérieure de Guerre Navale, Paris.
Had several naval postings 63-70; Mil. Attaché, Malagasy Embassy, Paris 70-72; Minister of Foreign Affairs May 72-.
Ministère des Affaires Etrangères, Tananarive, Madagascar.

Rawiri, Georges; Gabonese government official and diplomatist; b. 10 March 1932, Lambaréné, Gabon; ed. Protestant school, Ngomo and Lycée Jean-Baptiste Dumas, Ales.
Head, Technical Centre, Garoua Radio Station 57, Libreville Radio Station 59; a founder of Radio Gabon 59; Dir. Radiodiffusion Gabonaise 60, Radio-Télévision Gabonaise 63; Counsellor for Foreign Affairs 63; Minister of Information, Tourism, Posts and Telecommunications 63-64; Minister of State and Amb. to France 64-71, also accred. to Israel, Italy, Spain, U.K., Malta (65-71), and Switzerland (67-71); Minister of Foreign Affairs and Co-operation June 71-; Grand Officier de l'Ordre de l'Etoile Equatoriale and decorations from Mauritania, France, Malta, and the Ivory Coast; Médaille d'Or des Arts, Sciences et Lettres; Grand Officier de l'Ordre Int. du Bien Public.
Ministère des Affaires Etrangères et de la Co-opération, B.P. 2245, Libreville, Gabon.

Razafimbahiny, Jules Alphonse; Malagasy economist and diplomatist; b. 19 April 1922; ed. Institut du Droit des Affaires de la Faculté de Droit, Paris, and Institut des Hautes Etudes Politiques, Paris.
President of Comm. of Overseas Countries associated with Econ. and Social Council of Common Market and EURATOM, Brussels 58-59; Technical Counsellor to Minister of State for Nat. Economy, Madagascar 60-61; First Sec.-Gen. OAMCE (Org. Africaine et Malgache de Co-opération Economique) 62-64; Amb. to U.K., Italy, Greece and Israel 65-67; Sec. of State for Foreign Affairs (Econ. and African Affairs) 67-69; Amb. to U.S.A. 70-; Pres. Admin. Council Société d'Energie, Madagascar, Pan-African Inst. of Devt.; mem. of Board, Coll. of Econ. and Social Sciences (Paris); mem. Editorial Board, Soc. for Int. Devt., Washington, D.C.; Commdr. Ordre Nat. (Chad, Mauritania, Madagascar, Zaire, Green Crescent of the Comoro Islands; Officier Ordre Nat. (Upper Volta and Gabon); Grand Cross, Order of Saint Sylvester (Vatican); Nat. Order (Italy).
Ministère des Affaires Etrangères, Tananarive, Madagascar.
Telephone: 21198.

Razafindralambo, Edilbert Pierre, D. EN D., L. ès. L.; Malagasy judge; b. 1921, Tananarive; ed. Tananarive European Primary School, Lycée Galliéni, Tananarive, and Univs. of Paris and Cambridge.
Teacher, Michelet Coll. 40-46; student at Sorbonne 46-48, Paris Faculty of Law 46-50; Pres. Nat. Student Asscn. of Madagascar 48-50; Barrister, Paris Court of Appeal 49-60; Deputy Public Prosecutor, Tananarive Court of Appeal 60-61; Public Prosecutor, Malagasy Supreme Court 61-62; Pres. of Chamber of Cassation, Supreme Court 63-67; Chief Justice of Supreme Court 67-; Chair. Malagasy Del., UN Conf. on Law of Treaties, Vienna 68-69; Prof. of Law, Univ. of Tananarive 61-; Gen. reporter, Cttee. of Experts on Applications of Conventions and Recommendations of ILO 64; Arbitrator, IBRD, ICAO, Int. Arbitration,

Geneva; Officer of Malagasy Nat. Order; Officer of French Nat. Order of Merit, of Green Crescent of Comoro Islands.
Publs. *Flagrant Infraction in French, English and Czechoslovak Law* 55, *Swedish Machinery of Control of the Administration and the Judiciary* 62, *Malagasy Civil Procedure* 63, *Malagasy Private International Jurisprudence* 64, *Malagasy Supreme Court* 68, *The Ombudsman and the Protection of Human Rights* 67.
Supreme Court of Madagascar, P.B. 391, Tananarive; Home: 2 rue Amiral de Hell, P.B. 391, Tananarive, Madagascar.

Rebocho Vaz, Lieut.-Col. Camilo Augusto de Miranda; Portuguese army officer and administrator; b. 7 Oct. 1920, Avis; ed. Univ. de Coimbra, Escola do Exército, Lisbon and Inst. de Altos Estudo Militares, Lisbon.
Military service in Portugal, Azores and Angola; 2nd Commdr., Infantry Regt., Luanda, Angola 60; Commdr. of anti-terrorist activities 61; Gov. District of Uige, Angola 61-66; Gov.-Gen. of Angola 66-72; numerous military and civil decorations.
Publs. *Quatro Anos de Governo no Distrito do Uige, Angola 1967, Ángola 1969, Dois Anos de Governo.*
c/o Ministry of Defence, Lisbon, Portugal.

Reinhardt, John Edward, M.S., PH.D.; American teacher and diplomatist; b. 8 March 1920, Glade Spring, Va.; ed. Knoxville Coll., Univs. of Chicago and Wisconsin.
Instructor in English, Knoxville Coll. 40-41, Fayetteville State Coll. 41-42; U.S. Army 42-46; graduate student 46-50; Prof. of English, Virginia State Coll. 50-56; Visiting Prof. of English, Atlanta Univ. 53; Asst. Cultural Officer, American Embassy, Philippines 56-58; Dir. American Cultural Center, Kyoto, Japan 58-62; Dir. of Field Programs, American Embassy, Tokyo 62-63; Cultural Attaché, Teheran 63-66; Deputy Asst. Dir. of U.S. Information Agency (for Far East) 66-68, (for Africa) 68-70, (for Far East) 70-71; Amb. to Nigeria 71-.
American Embassy, Lagos, Nigeria.
Telephone: 57320, Ext. 60.

Resampa, André; Malagasy politician; b. 24 June 1924, Mandabe, Mahabo district.
Secretary-interpreter; clerk, Dept. of Justice; mem., Provincial Assembly of Tuléar 52-57; mem. Representative Assembly 57-58; Deputy, Nat. Assembly Oct. 58-; Minister of Social Affairs, Education and Health 58-59; mem., Council of Inst. des Hautes Etudes, Tananarive 59-60; Minister of State for the Interior 59-71; Sec.-Gen. Social Democratic Party (PSD), Vice-Pres. 70-71; resigned from party June 72; detained on charge of treason 71, released 72; Pres. Nat. Cttee. for a New Repub. (CNRN) Aug. 72-; Sec.-Gen. Malagasy Socialist Union Sept. 72-.
Assemblée Nationale, Tananarive, Madagascar.

Retta, Ato Abbebe, G.C.V.O.; Ethiopian diplomatist and politician; b. 27 Sept. 1909; ed. Ethiopian schools and colls. in various monasteries, Ethiopia and abroad.
Principal Private Sec. to Gov.Gen. of Wag 29-32; joined Emperor's entourage in Great Britain during Italian occupation; after restoration, was for four years Counsellor of Ethiopian Legation, London; returned to Ethiopia, becoming mem. Govt. as Head of Ministry of Public Health; Minister to Great Britain 48-49, Ambassador 49-56 concurrently Minister to Norway, Sweden, Denmark and Neths.; Minister of Commerce 56-58; Minister of Public Health 58-66; Minister of Commerce and Industry 66-68, of Agriculture 68-.
Ministry of Agriculture, Addis Ababa, Ethiopia.

Richardson, Philip Arthur, C.B.E.; British overseas civil servant; b. 16 Feb. 1918, Woodford, Essex; ed. Rugby School, Queens' Coll., Cambridge, and Middle Temple, London.
Administrative Cadet, Nigeria 40; Sec. to Govt. of Kingdom

of Tonga 47-50; Sec. to Govt. of British Solomon Islands Protectorate 50-53; Colonial Office 53-55; Admin. Officer, Nyasaland Protectorate 55-59, Senior Admin. Officer 59-61, Under-Sec. 61-64; Sec. for External Affairs, Malawi 64-67; Chargé d'Affaires, Malawi Legation, South Africa 67-71; Commdr. Order of Menelik II (Ethiopia) 65; Grand Commdr. Order of Brilliant Star of Repub. of China 67.
150 Outeniqua Avenue, Waterkloof Park, Pretoria, South Africa.

Ringadoo, Veerasamy, BAR.-AT-LAW; Mauritius politician; b. 1920, Port Louis; ed. Port Louis Grammar School and London School of Economics, England.
Called to the Bar 49; elected Municipal Councillor 56; elected Mem. Legis. Council for Moka-Flacq 51-67; Minister for Labour and Social Security 59-64; Minister for Educ. 64-July 67; Minister of Agriculture and Natural Resources July 67-June 68; attended London Constitutional Conf. 65; First mem., Legislative Assembly (MLA) for Quartier Militaire and Moka 67- (Lab.); Minister of Finance June 68-; Officer, Ordre National Malgache.
Ministry of Finance, Port Louis, Mauritius.

Rive, Richard Moore, M.A., B.ED.; South African teacher and writer; b. 1 March 1931, Cape Town; ed. Trafalgar High School, Hewat Coll., Cape Town, Univ. of Cape Town and Columbia Univ., New York.
Fulbright Travelling Fellowship, Columbia Univ. Recruitment Fellowship, and Heft Int. Fellowship, Columbia Univ. 65-66; Senior Teaching Asst., South Peninsula High School, Cape Town 66-; Asst. Editor *Contrast* (literary quarterly); Writer of the Year (South Africa) for *The Visits* (short story) 70; Winner of BBC Playwriting Competition with *Make Like Slaves* 71; has lectured and broadcast in numerous countries; works translated into German, Swedish, Russian, Danish, Norwegian, Italian, French, Portuguese, Amharic, Dutch, Flemish and Serbo-Croat.
Publs. *African Songs* (short stories) 63, *Emergency* (novel) 64, *Quartet* (short stories) 64, *Modern African Prose* 64, *The Visits* (short story) 70, *Make Like Slaves* (play) 71; also stories, essays and plays in numerous magazines.
2 Selous Court, Rosmead Avenue, Claremont, Cape Town, South Africa; also Longwall Annexe 3, Magdalen College, Oxford, England.

Roberto, Holden; Angolan nationalist leader; b. 1925, São Salvador, Northern Province; ed. the Congo.
Worked in Finance Dept., Belgian Admin., Leopoldville, Stanleyville and Bukavu; founded União das Populacões de Angola (U.P.A.) 54; travelled widely in Africa and Europe; attended first and second All African Peoples Confs. Accra 58, Tunis 60; elected to the Steering Cttee., Tunis; founded *La Voix de la Nation Angolaise*, a fortnightly newspaper; assumed leadership of guerrilla liberation operations in Angola; made several trips to U.S.A. 61; became leader of Frente Nacional de Libertação de Angola (F.N.L.A.) when U.P.A. merged with Partido Democrático Angolano (P.D.A.) March 62; Premier of Angolan govt. in exile, Governo Revolucionário de Angola no Exílio (G.R.A.E.) 62-; (recognition of G.R.A.E. as govt. in exile by OAU's African Liberation Cttee. withdrawn July 68). Pres. Conselho Supremo de Libertação de Angola 72-.
Kinshasa, Zaire.

Robinson, Sir Albert Edward Phineas, Kt., M.A.; British (Rhodesian) business executive; b. 1915; ed. Durban High School and Stellenbosch, London, Cambridge and Leiden Univs.
Barrister-at-Law, Lincoln's Inn; Imperial Light Horse, N. Africa 40-43; mem. Johannesburg City Council and Leader United Party 45-48; United Party M.P., South African Parl. 47-53; resident in S. Rhodesia 53-; Dir. Banks, Building Socs., several financial and industrial cos. 53-61; Chair. Central African Airways Corpn. 57-61; mem. Monckton Comm. 60; High Commr., Fed. of Rhodesia and

Nyasaland in the U.K. 61-63; Chair. Johannesburg Consolidated Investment Co. Ltd. Nov. 71-, Rustenburg Platinum Mines Ltd.; Exec. Dir. Anglo-American Corpn. of S. Africa Ltd.; Dir. Anglo-American Corpn. Rhodesia Ltd., Zambian Anglo-American Ltd.
P.O. Box 2341, Salisbury, Rhodesia; P.O. Box 590, Johannesburg, South Africa.

Robinson, Robin Edmund, PH.D.; South African chemical engineer; b. 6 Nov. 1929, Bloemfontein; ed. St. John's Coll., Johannesburg and Univ. of the Witwatersrand.
Research Officer, Govt. Metallurgical Lab., Johannesburg 50; Head of Chem. Engineering Section, Central Metallurgical Lab., Anglo-American Corpn. of South Africa Ltd. 54-61; Dir.-Gen. Nat. Inst. for Metallurgy, Johannesburg 61-; Dir. Extraction Metallurgy Div., S.A. Atomic Energy Board 61-; Hon. Prof. Univ. of Witwatersrand; Past Pres. S.A. Chem. Inst.
Office: c/o National Institute for Metallurgy, Private Bag 7, Auckland Park, Transvaal; Home: 50 Young Avenue, Houghton, Johannesburg, South Africa.

Rostain, Claude-François; French diplomatist; b. 1916; ed. Ecole Nat. de la France d'Outre-Mer.
Administrator, Indo-China; private sec. to the delegate to Tonkin, French High Comm.; dir. de cabinet, French High Comm. in Laos; dir.; Bureau of International Affairs 56-59; responsible for the Communauté and African and Malagasy Affairs, Gen. Secr. 60-64; Amb. to Togo 64-69; Amb. to Niger April 70-.
Embassy of France, B.P. 240, Niamey, Niger.

Rouamba, Tensoré Paul; Upper Voltan diplomatist; b. 28 March 1933, Ouagadougou; ed. Univs. of Bordeaux, Grenoble and Paris.
Former mem. Constitutional Chamber of Supreme Court of Upper Volta; fmr. Asst. Prof., Centre of Tropical Geography, Univ. of Abidjan; Prof. at Normal School, Ouagadougou 63-65; Perm. Rep. to UN 66-72; Amb. to U.S.A. and Canada 66-72, to Nigeria Nov. 72-.
Embassy of the Republic of Upper Volta, Lagos, Nigeria.

Rouch, Jean Pierre, D. ès L., Ingénieur Civil; French anthropologist and film-maker; b. 31 May 1917; ed. Lycée Henri IV, Ecole National des Ponts et Chaussées, Centre Nat. de la Recherche Scientifique.
Engineer, worked in Niger 41-42; served with Free French 42-45; studied anthropology 45-48; made first descent of River Niger by canoe 46-47; set up Niamey branch of Inst. Français d'Afrique Noir (IFAN), Dir. 62-; teacher, Musée de l'Homme, Paris; Chevalier, Légion d'Honneur.
Films: *Magiciens noirs, Initiation à la danse des possédés, Circoncision* (Grand Prix, Biarritz 49), *Les Fils de l'Eau, Jaguar, Les Maîtres fous* (Grand Prix, Venice 57), *Moi un Noir* (Prix Louis Delluc 58), *La Pyramide humaine* 59-60, *Chronique d'un été* (with Edgar Morin) 60-61, *Monsieur Albert, Prophète, La Punition* 63, *Ceux qui parlent français* (Special Prize, Venice) 63, *La Chasse au lion, à l'arc et aux flèches* 65, *Paris vu par* . . . . 65.
Publs. *Les Songhay, Religion et Magie des Songhay, Histoire des Songhay.*
Musée de l'Homme, place du Trocadéro, Paris 16e, France; Institut français d'Afrique noir, Niamey, Niger; and 4 rue de Grenelle, Paris 6e, France.

Roux, Abraham Johannes Andries, DR. ENG., D.SC., B.SC.; South African nuclear scientist; b. 18 Oct. 1914, Bethlehem, Orange Free State; ed. Univ. of the Witwatersrand.
Lecturer, Dept. of Mechanical Engineering, Witwatersrand Univ. 39-44; Senior Lecturer, Stellenbosch Univ. 44-46; Principal Research Officer, Nat. Building Research Inst., Council for Scientific and Industrial Research (C.S.I.R.) 46-52, Officer in Charge C.S.I.R. Mech. Engineering Research Unit 52, Nat. Physical Research Lab.

52-55, Dir. Nat. Mech. Engineering Research Inst., C.S.I.R. 55-57, Vice-Pres. C.S.I.R. 57-60; Part-time Dir. Atomic Energy Research Programme 56-59, Dir. of Research, Atomic Energy Board 59-60, Dir. Atomic Energy Board 60-64, Dir.-Gen. June 64-Oct. 67, Chair. Nov. 67-70, Pres. 70-; Chair. Nat. Inst. for Metallurgy 67-, UCOR 70-; mem. Board of C.S.I.R. 66, Board of Dirs. Nuclear Fuels Corpn.; mem. Univ. Advisory Cttee. 66, Scientific Advisory Council of the Prime Minister 68; D.Sc. h.c.
Publs. *Mechanical Engineering Research in South Africa* 52, *Mechanical Engineering in Relation to Industry* 55-57, *Developments in the Field of Nuclear Power and their Impact on South Africa* 58, *The Atomic Energy Research and Development Programme of South Africa* 59, *Science, Industry and the Professional Society* 60, *The First Reactor Installation of the Republic of South Africa* 62, *South Africa's Programme of Nuclear Research* 62, *The Scope of Research and Development in the Field of Radioisotopes and Nuclear Radiation in South Africa* 64, *Nuclear Engineering in South Africa* 64, *Power Generation in South Africa with Special Reference to the Introduction of Nuclear Power* (Co-author) 66, *Nuclear Energy in South Africa* 67, *Energy for the Coming Century—Nuclear Energy* 69, *Policy Aspects of the Introduction of Nuclear Power in South Africa* (Co-author) 69.
Atomic Energy Board, Private Bag X256, Pretoria, Transvaal, South Africa.
Telephone: 79-4441, Ext. 200.

Rugambwa, H. E. Cardinal Laurian; Tanzanian ecclesiastic; b. 12 July 1912, Bukongo; ed. Rubya Seminary, Katigondo Seminary, De Propaganda Fide Univ., Rome.
Ordained priest 43; missionary work in East Africa; studied canon law in Rome 48-51; Bishop of Rutabo 52; cr. Cardinal by Pope John XXIII 60; transferred to Bukoba Diocese 60, to Dar es Salaam Archdiocese 69.
Archbishop's House, P.O. Box 167, Dar es Salaam, Tanzania, East Africa.
Telephone: Dar es Salaam 22031.

Rupert, Anthony Edward, M.SC.; South African business executive; b. 4 Oct. 1916, Graaff-Reinet; ed. Volks High School, Graaff-Reinet, and Univs. of Pretoria and South Africa.
Lecturer in Chemistry, Pretoria Univ. 39-41; Founder, Chair. and Managing Dir. Rembrandt Group of Companies (tobacco) 48-; Dir. Carreras Ltd., London, Rothmans Tobacco Holdings Ltd., London 50-; Chair. Technical and Industrial Investments Ltd., Historical Homes of S. Africa Ltd.; Pres. Nat. Devt. and Management Foundation of S. Africa; Fellow, Int. Acad. of Management; Hon. Prof. in Business Admin., Univ. of Pretoria; Hon. Industrial Adviser to Govt. of Lesotho; Pres. S.A. Wildlife Foundation; mem. Exec. Council World Wildlife Fund; Dir. S. African Reserve Bank; Hon. Fellow, Coll. of Medicine of South Africa; mem. S.A. Chem. Inst., S. African Acad. of Arts and Sciences, S. African Inst. of Management; Hon. D.Sc. (Pretoria); Hon. D.Comm. (Stellenbosch).
Publs. *Progress through Partnership, Leaders on Leadership.*
Office: Alexander Street, Stellenbosch; Home: 13 Thibault Street, Mostertsdrift, Stellenbosch, South Africa.
Telephone: Stellenbosch 2331 (Office).

Rwetsiba, William Wycliffe, B.SC.; Ugandan administrator; b. 1922, Mbarara; ed. King's Coll., Budo, Makerere Univ. Coll., Kampala and Queen's Univ., Belfast.
Teacher 45-60; Parl. Sec. Ministry of Natural Resources 58-61; Under-Sec. Ministry of Educ. 61-62; Perm. Sec. Ministry of Animal Industry, Game and Fisheries 62-63, Ministry of Educ. 63-71; East African Minister for Communications, Research and Social Services 71-; mem.

Ugandan Legislative Council 58-61, East African Legislative Assembly.
East African Communications Secretariat, P.O. Box 1002, Arusha, Tanzania.

S

Sabir, Mohi Aldin, PH.D.; Sudanese politician; b. 1919, Dalgo; ed. Cairo Univ., Bordeaux Univ., France and Sorbonne Univ.
Director, Ministry of Social Affairs 54; Editor-in-Chief, *Sot Es Sudan* and *El Istglal*, Man. *El Zaman;* Head, Social Sciences Dept., Regional Centre for Social Devt. at Siras Llyan; mem. Constituent Assembly 68-; Minister of Educ. 69-.
Publs. several books in Arabic on civilization and devt. in Arab countries.
Ministry of Education, Khartoum, Sudan.

Safo-Adu, Kwame, M.B.B.S.; Ghanaian medical doctor and politician; b. 23 Dec. 1932, Pasuro, Kumasi; ed. Methodist Mission School, Kumasi, Achimota Coll., Ghana Univ., King's Coll., London and Cambridge Univ., England.
Demonstrator in physiology and pharmacology, King's Coll. Medical School 57-60; Lecturer in pharmacology and therapeutics, Ibadan Medical School 62-65; Senior Lecturer, Ghana Medical School 65; fmr. Chair. Advisory Cttee., Ashanti Region Centre for Civic Educ.; Pres. Ashanti Youth Asscn. 68; Minister of Agriculture Sept. 69-Jan. 72.
c/o Ministry of Agriculture, Accra, Ghana.

Safronchuk, Vasily Stepanovich; Soviet diplomatist; b. 16 Feb. 1925, Lozovatka, Dnepropetrovsk region, Ukraine; ed. Moscow Inst. of International Relations.
Lecturer, researcher at Moscow Inst. of Int. Relations 55-59; First Sec. Counsellor at Soviet Embassy in U.K.; Deputy Chief Second European Dept. Foreign Ministry; Amb. to Ghana 67-.
U.S.S.R. Embassy, Ring Road East, P.O. Box 1634, Accra, Ghana.

Sahnoun, Hadj Mohamed, M.A.; Algerian diplomatist; b. 8 April 1931; cd. Lycée of Constantine, Univ. de Paris a la Sorbonne and New York Univ.
Director of African, Asian and Latin American Affairs Ministry of Foreign Affairs 62-63, of Political Affairs 64; Del. to UN Gen. Assembly 62-63, 64-65; Asst. Sec.-Gen. Org. of African Unity (OAU) 64-.
Publ. *Economic and Social Aspects of the Algerian Revolution* 62.
OAU, P.O. Box 3243, Addis Ababa, Ethiopia.

Salim, Salim Ahmed; Tanzanian diplomatist; b. 1942, Zanzibar; ed. Lumumba Coll., Zanzibar and Univ. of Delhi.
Publicity Sec. of UMMA Party and Chief Editor of its official organ *Sauti ya UMMA* 63; Exec. Sec. United Front of Opposition Parties and Chief Editor of its newspaper; Sec.-Gen. All-Zanzibar Journalists Union 63; Amb. to United Arab Repub. 64-65; High Commr. to India 65-68; Dir. African and Middle East Affairs Div., Ministry of Foreign Affairs 68-69; Amb. to People's Repub. of China and Democratic People's Repub. of Korea June-Dec. 69; Perm. Rep. to UN Feb. 70-; fmr. del. of Tanzania at UN Gen. Assembly and other int. confs.
Permanent Mission of Tanzania at United Nations, 800 Second Avenue, 3rd Floor, New York, N.Y. 10017, U.S.A.

Sall, Abdul Aziz; Mauritanian politician and administrator; b. 1 Jan. 1924, M'Bout.
Worked as book-keeper, writer and in gen. admin.; Sec.-Gen. Del. from Mauritania to Dakar 60; First counsellor, Amb. to U.S.A. 61-65; Sec.-Gen. Council of Ministers

65-68; Dir. de Cabinet, Pres. of the Repub. Nov. 66-July 68; Minister of the Interior July 68-71; mem. Political Office, Parti du peuple mauritanien (P.P.M.); Pres. Parl. Group P.P.M. Dec. 68-.
Parti du peuple mauritanien, B.P. 61, Nouakchott, Mauritania.

Sall, Amadou Clédor; Senegalese politician and administrator.
Governor of Siné-Saloum, later of Cape Verde Region; Minister of the Interior June 68-71, of Justice, Keeper of the Seals June 72-.
Ministry of Justice, Dakar, Senegal.

Samantar, Mohamed Said; Somali diplomatist; b. 1928; ed. Istituto Magistrale, Istituto Universitario di Diritto ed Economia di Mogadiscio, and Univ. of Rome.
Officer of Public Admin. in Somalia 50-59; Officer of Somali Ministry of Foreign Affairs 63-64; Political Counsellor, Somali Embassy in Brussels 64-66; First Counsellor, Somali Embassy in Rome 66-70; Amb. to the Repub. of Italy 70-.
Embassy of Somalia, Via dei Gracchi 305, Rome, Italy.

Sandoungout, Marcel; Gabonese trade unionist and diplomatist; b. 25 Oct. 1927.
Former trade unionist, Gabon; fmr. Chef de Cabinet to Minister of Planning for Agriculture; Chief, Div. for Int. Orgs., Ministry of Foreign Affairs 60; mem. Nat. Assembly 61, Chair. Cttee. for Foreign Affairs and Defence, 61, 62; Del. to Defence Council of African and Malagasy Union 61, 62; Minister of Health and Social Affairs May-Dec. 62, for Public Works, Tourism and Posts and Telecommunications 63-64; Amb. to German Fed. Repub., Belgium, Netherlands, Norway, Denmark, Sweden and Luxembourg 64-66; Perm. Rep. to GATT and EEC 64-66; Perm. Rep. to UN 67-68; Amb. to Dahomey Oct. 69, to Senegal Nov. 69; now Amb. to France.
Ambassade du Gabon, Paris, France.

Santos e Castro, Fernando A.; Portuguese administrator and agricultural engineer; b. 1912, Funchal, Madeira; ed. Luanda, Angola.
Worked in Ministry of Agriculture; Chair. Lisbon Municipal Council; Gov.-Gen. of Angola Oct. 72-; has represented Portugal in many int. orgs.
Palácio do Governador-Geral, Luanda, Angola.

Sapeika, Norman, M.D., PH.D., F.R.S.S.AF.; South African professor of pharmacology; b. 17 Jan. 1909, Oudtshoorn; ed. Boys High School, Kimberley and Univ. of Cape Town.
Wernher Beit Asst. in Pharmacology, Univ. of Cape Town 33-47, Senior Lecturer 44-55, Assoc. Prof. 56-65, Prof. of Pharmacology 65-; Pres. Royal Soc. of S. Africa 72-; Pres. Athenaeum Trust 70-; mem. Drugs Control Council 66-71.
Publs. *Actions and Uses of Drugs* 43, 9th edn. 72, *Food Pharmacology* 69, and chapters in books.
Department of Pharmacology, Medical School, University of Cape Town, Observatory, Cape Town, South Africa.
Telephone: 554707.

Sarakikya, Maj.-Gen. Marisho Sam Hagai; Tanzanian army officer; b. 1934, Meru; ed. Govt. Secondary School, Tabora and Military Acad., Sandhurst, England.
Private, Tanganyika King's African Rifles 58; Chief, Tanzania People's Defence Forces (T.P.D.F.) 64-; Maj.-Gen. July 69-.
c/o Ministry of Defence, Dar es Salaam, United Republic of Tanzania.

Sardanis, Andreas Sotiris; Zambian company director; b. 13 March 1931, Cyprus; ed. Cyprus.
Emigrated to Zambia 50; managerial posts in trading and transport undertakings 50-62; Chair. and Man. Dir. Industrial Devt. Corpn. June 65-April 70; Perm. Sec.

Ministry of Commerce, Industry and Foreign Trade 68; later Perm. Sec. Ministry of Trade, Industry and Mines, and Perm. Sec. Ministry of Devt. and Finance; Man. Dir. Zambia Industrial and Mining Corpn. Ltd. and Chair. of its subsidiaries, Indeco Ltd. and Mindeco Ltd. April 70-Dec. 71; Perm. Sec. Ministry of State Participation April 70-Dec. 70; Joint Man. Dir. of new co. to streamline Lonrho's interests W. of the Zambesi Jan.-May 71; Man. Dir. Sardanis Assocs. Ltd. (consultancy and investment group) 71-.
London: Sardanis Associates Ltd., Excel House, 42 Upper Berkeley Street, London, W1H 7PL, England; Lusaka: Sardanis Associates (Zambia) Ltd., P.O. Box 2943, Lusaka, Zambia.
Telephone: 73027 (Lusaka).

Savimbi, Dr. Joseph; Angolan nationalist leader; ed. Univ. of Lausanne.
Former Sec.-Gen. União das Populações de Angola (U.P.A.); Foreign Minister of Governo Revolucionário de Angola no Exílio (G.R.A.E.) 62-July 64; resigned from G.R.A.E. at OAU meeting, Cairo July 64; studied at Univ. of Lausanne 64-65; moved to Lusaka; founded União Nacional para a Independência Total de Angola (U.N.I.T.A.) near Luso, March 66; Pres. U.N.I.T.A. March 66-; expelled from Zambia 67; went to Cairo; reported back in Angola 68.
Angola.

Sawadogo, Abdoulaye; Ivory Coast agriculturalist and politician; b. 17 Feb. 1933, Kayes; ed. Nat. Agricultural School, Montpellier, France and Paris.
Agricultural expert, specializing in tropical agronomy; Insp. Caisse Nat. du Crédit Agricole (C.N.C.A.) 59-61; technical councillor 61-62; Dir. de Cabinet, Ministry of Agriculture Jan. 62-Sept. 66; Minister Del. of Agriculture Sept. 66-Sept. 68; Minister of Agriculture Sept. 68-.
Ministry of Agriculture, Abidjan, Ivory Coast.

Schlesinger, John Samuel; South African business executive; b. 1923; ed. Michaelhouse and Harvard Univ.
United States Army Air Corps, Second World War; Pres. Schlesinger Org. (real estate) 49-, developments in Johannesburg, Durban, Cape Town and Port Elizabeth; Chair. African Life Assurance Soc. Ltd., African Guarantee and Indemnity Co. Ltd., African Consolidated Investments Corpn. Ltd., African Amalgamated Advertising Ltd., African Realty Trust Ltd., African Caterers Ltd.
Schlesinger Organization, P.O. Box 1182, Johannesburg, South Africa.

Schoeman, Barend Jacobus, M.INST.T.; South African politician; b. 19 Jan. 1905, Johannesburg; Forest Secondary School, Johannesburg.
Leader Witwatersrand Nat. Party 40-; fmr. Minister of Labour, Minister of Public Works, Minister of Forestry; Nat. M.P., Maraisburg 48-; Minister of Labour and Public Works 50; Minister of Transport 54-; Leader, Nat. Party in Transvaal; Chancellor, Univ. of Port Elizabeth.
Ministry of Transport, Pretoria, Republic of South Africa.

Schonland, Sir Basil Ferdinand Jamieson, Kt., M.A., PH.D., F.R.S., C.B.E.; South African physicist; b. 5 Feb. 1896, Grahamstown; ed. St. Andrews Coll. and Rhodes Univ. Coll., Grahamstown, and Gonville and Caius Coll., Cambridge.
Lecturer, later Prof. of Physics Univ. of Cape Town 22-37; Dir. Bernard Price Inst. of Geophysics and Carnegie Price Prof. of Geophysics Witwatersrand Univ. 37-54; Deputy Dir. Atomic Energy Research Establishment, Harwell 54-58, Dir. 58-60; Dir. of Research Group of which Harwell forms a part 60-61 (retd.); Halley Lecturer Oxford 37; Supt. Army Operation Research Group, Ministry of Supply 41-44; Brigadier (Scientific Adviser) to C.-in-C. 21st Army Group B.L.A. 44; Pres. S.A. Council Scientific

and Industrial Research 45-50; Chree Lecturer Physical Soc. of London 43; F.R.S. South Africa; Hughes Medal 45; Elliott-Cresson Medal Franklin Inst. of Philadelphia 50; Faraday Medal of Inst. of Electrical Engineers 62; Chancellor Rhodes Univ. 51-63, Pro-Chancellor Univ. of Southampton 60; Hon. Sc.D. (Cambridge, Cape Town, Rhodes, Southampton); Hon. LL.D. (Natal); Hon. Fellow Gonville and Caius Coll. 59.
Publs. *Atmospheric Electricity* 32, *The Lightning Discharge* (Halley Lecture) 37, *The Flight of Thunderbolts* 50, *The Atomists 1805-1933* 68.
The Down House, Shawford, near Winchester, Hants., England.
Telephone: Twyford 2221.

Scott, Rev. Moses N.C.O., D.D.; Sierra Leonean ecclesiastic; b. 1911; ed. London Coll. of Divinity.
Served as curate, Grappenhall, Cheshire; Bishop of Sierra Leone 61-; Archbishop of the Province of West Africa (Anglican) July 69-.
Archbishop of the Province of West Africa, Bishopscourt, P.O. Box 128, Freetown, Sierra Leone.

Seck, Assane, L. ès L.; Senegalese professor and politician; b. 1 Feb. 1919, Inor; ed. Ecole Normale William Ponty.
Former Prof. of Literature, Dakar; Minister of Cultural Affairs June 66-March 68; Minister of People's Educ. and Culture March 68-June 68; Minister of Nat. Educ. June 68-.
Ministry of National Education, Dakar, Senegal.

Segal, Ronald Michael, B.A.; South African author; b. 14 July 1932, Cape Town; ed. Univ. of Cape Town and Trinity Coll., Cambridge.
Director, Faculty and Cultural Studies, Nat. Union of South African Students 51-52; Pres. Univ. of Cape Town Council of Univ. Socs. 51; won Philip Francis du Pont Fellowship to Univ. of Virginia (U.S.A.) 55 but returned to South Africa to found *Africa South* (quarterly) 56; helped launch economic boycott April 59; banned by South African Govt. from all meetings July 59; in England with *Africa South in Exile*, April 60-61; Gen. Editor Penguin African Library 61-; Hon. Sec. South African Freedom Asscn. 60-61; Convenor, Int. Conf. on Econ. Sanctions against South Africa 64, Int. Conf. on S.W. Africa 66; Visiting Fellow, Center for the Study of Democratic Insts. (Santa Barbara) 73.
Publs. *The Tokolosh* (a fantasy) 60, *Political Africa: A Who's Who of Personalities and Parties* 61, *African Profiles* 62, *Into Exile* 63, *Sanctions Against South Africa* (Editor) 64, *The Crisis of India* 65, *The Race War* 66, *South West Africa: Travesty of Trust* (Editor) 67, *America's Receding Future* 68, *The Struggle Against History* 71.
The Old Manor House, Manor Road, Walton-on-Thames, Surrey, England.
Telephone: Walton-on-Thames 27766.

Segokgo, M. K.; Botswana politician; b. 1928, Tlokweng, Gaborone; ed. Gaborone and Kanye Teacher Training Coll.
Head teacher, Batlokwa Nat. School; asst. master, St. Joseph's Coll.; elected to Batlokwa Tribal Council 61; mem. cttee. to study unified teaching service 62; elected to Legislative (now Nat.) Assembly March 65-; Parl. Sec. April 65-Oct. 66; Asst. Minister of Finance Oct. 66-69; Minister of Finance 69-Oct. 69; Minister of Commerce, Industry and Water Affairs Oct. 69-.
Ministry of Commerce, Industry and Water Affairs, Gaborone, Botswana.

Seid, Joseph Brahim; Chad lawyer and politician; b. 1927; ed. Univ. of Lyons, Ecole Nationale de la France d'Outre-Mer, Univ. of Paris.
Magistrate, Moundou, Chad; mem. of Chad Del. to UN 60;

High Rep. of Chad in Paris with rank of Amb. 61-65; Minister of Justice April 66-.
Ministry of Justice, Fort-Lamy, Chad.

Selem, Kam; Nigerian police officer; b. 1924, Dikwa, North-Eastern State; ed. Dikwa Elementary School and Bornu Secondary School.
Enlisted in Nigeria Police Force as beat constable April 42; trained at Police Coll., Kaduna: Detective, Kano until April 50; Sub-Insp. of Police April 50-53, Asst. Supt. 53-55, Deputy Supt. 55-59; attended Officers' Course, Ryton-on-Dunsmore, U.K. 56; Supt. of Police 59-60, Chief Supt. 60-Dec. 61; attended senior officers' course, Scottish Police Coll. 60; Asst. Commr. of Police Dec. 61-March 62; Deputy Commr. March 62-Sept. 62; Commr. of Police in command of Northern Region Sept. 62-July 65; Deputy Insp.-Gen. July 65-Sept. 66, Insp.-Gen. Sept. 66-; mem., Supreme Mil. Council and Fed. Exec. Council Jan. 66-; Fed. Commr. for Internal Affairs June 67-; Pres. Nigeria Branch of Int. Police Asscn.; mem. Int. Asscn. of Chiefs of Police; Defence Medal; Colonial Police Long Service Medal, Queen's Police Medal for distinguished service, Nigerian Independence Medal, Nigeria Police Medal for Meritorious Service, Nigeria Police Long Service Medal 72.
Force Headquarters, The Nigeria Police, Moloney Street, Lagos; Home: The Inspector-General's Lodge, Onikan, Lagos, Nigeria.

Selormey, Maj. Anthony Hugh; Ghanaian army officer and politician; b. 2 March 1937, Dzolukope, Volta Region; ed. local Catholic Mission School, Bishop Herman Secondary School, Kpandu, and Ghana Military Acad., Teshie.
Joined Ghana Army 61, commissioned 62; has attended mil. courses in U.K. and U.S.A.; has been Support Troop Leader, Sabre Troop Leader, Intelligence Officer and Commanding Officer, 2nd Recce Regiment in Ghana Army; Instructor, Ghana Mil. Acad., Teshie for three years; now C.O. Recce Regiment, Accra., mem. Nat. Redemption Council and Commr. for Transport and Communications.
Ministry of Communications, P.O. Box M.38, Accra, Ghana.

Semega-Janneh, Bocar Ousman, M.B.E.; Gambian diplomatist; b. 21 July 1910; ed. Mohammedan Primary School and Methodist Boy's High School.
Joined Gambia Surveys Dept. 31, Senior Surveyor 48, Dir. 53-66; mem. Bathurst City Council 51-67, Mayor 65-67; High Commr. to Senegal 67-71, also accred. as Amb. to Mali, Mauritania, Guinea and Liberia and High Commr. to Sierra Leone 69-71; High Commr. to U.K. 71-, also accred. as Amb. to Fed. Germany, France, Belgium, Sweden, Switzerland and Austria; del. to UN Gen. Assembly 68-; Grand Officer, Order of Merit (Senegal, Mauritania).
Gambia House, 28 Kensington Court, London, W.8, England.

Seminega, Fulgence, LL.D.; Rwandan lawyer; b. 21 Nov. 1936, Kibande, Biumba Region; ed. St. Esprit Coll., Bujumbura, Burundi and Namur and Louvain Univs.
President of the Supreme Court 63-.
Supreme Court of Rwanda, Nyabisindi, Rwanda.

Sène, Alioune; Senegalese diplomatist and politician.
Former Dir. de Cabinet to Pres. of the Repub.; Sec. of State to Presidency in charge of Information until Jan. 70; Amb. to Lebanon June 65-Feb. 70; Minister of Culture and Information Feb. 70-Dec. 70; Minister of Culture Dec. 70-; mem. Nation and Devt. Club.
Ministry of Culture, Dakar, Senegal.

Senghor, Léopold Sédar; Senegalese writer and politician; b. 9 Oct. 1906; ed. Lycée de Dakar, Lycée Louis le Grand, Paris and Paris Univ.
Teacher, Lycée, Tours 35-44, Lycée Marcelin Berthelot,

Paris 44-48; mem. Constituent Assemblies 45-46; Deputy from Senegal to Nat. Assembly 46-58; Prof., Ecole Nat. de la France d'Outre-Mer 48-58; Sec. of State, Présidence du Conseil 55-56; mem. Consultative Assembly, Council of Europe; Pres. Fed. Assembly, Mali Fed. of Senegal and Sudan 59-60, Pres. Senegal Repub. 60-, also Minister of Defence 68-; leader, Union Progressiste Sénégalaise, nat. party of Parti Fédéraliste Africain (PFA); Chair. OCAM April 72-; mem. Inst. Français, Acad. des Sciences morales et politiques 69-; Dag Hammarskjöld Prize 65; Peace Prize of German Book Trade, Frankfurt.
Publs. *Chants d'ombres* (poems) 45, *Hosties noires* (poems) 48, *Chants pour Naëtt* (poems) 49, *Ethiopiques* (poems) 56, *Nocturnes* (poems) 61, *Langage et poésie négro africaine* 54, *L'Apport de la poésie nègre* 53, *Esthéthique négro-africain* 56.
Office of the President, Dakar, Senegal, West Africa.

Seydou, Amadou; Niger scholar and diplomatist; b. 1928, ed. Dakar, Inst. des Hautes Etudes, Algiers, Al Azhar Univ., Cairo and Univ. of Paris.
Former teacher, founded Nat. School of Medersa 60; Chargé d'Affaires, Niger Embassy, Paris 60-61, Amb. to France 61-66, concurrently to U.K. 64-66; Dir. Dept. of Culture, UNESCO Oct. 67-; Commandeur Légion d'Honneur.
UNESCO, 7-9 place de Fontenoy, Paris 7e, France.

Shagari, Alhaji Shehu Usman Aliu; Nigerian educationist and politician; b. 1925, Shagari; ed. Middle School, Sokoto, Kaduna Coll., Teacher Training Coll., Zarta.
Science Teacher, Sokoto Middle School 45-50; Headmaster, Argungn Senior Primary School 51-52; Senior Visiting Teacher, Sokoto Prov. 53-58; mem. Fed. Parl. 54-58; Parl. Sec. to the Prime Minister 58-59; Fed. Minister of Econ. Devt. 59-60, of Establishments 60-62, of Internal Affairs 62-65, of Works 65-66; Sec. Sokoto Prov. Educ. Devt. 66-68; State Commr. for Educ., Sokoto Prov. 68-70; Fed. Commr. for Econ. Devt. and Reconstruction 70-71, for Finance 71-.
Publ. *Wakar Nijeriya* (poetry) 48.
Federal Ministry of Finance, Mosaic House, Lagos; Home: 6A Okoli'e Eboh Street, Ikoyi, Lagos, Nigeria.

Shako, Juxon Levi Madoka; Kenyan politician; b. 1918, Taita district; ed. Alliance High School.
Teacher, Teachers' Training Centre, Machakos, teacher and headmaster at various schools 37-52; joined provincial admin. 52; Asst. District Officer 53-55; District Asst., Kisii/Kakamega Districts 59-60; District Officer Jan. 61-62; District Commr. for Kitui 62-Jan. 63; Senior District Commr. Jan. 64-Jan. 66; Amb. to Fed. Repub. of Germany and to France Jan. 67; Perm. Sec. Ministry of Defence; Chair. E. African Harbours Corpn. 68-69; Minister for Tourism and Wildlife Dec. 69-.
Ministry of Tourism and Wildlife, P.O. Box 30027, Nairobi, Kenya.

Sherman George Flamma, D.S.O., B.A.; Liberian educationalist and diplomatist; b. 28 Aug. 1913, River Cess, Grand Bassa County; ed. Coll. of West Africa and Liberia Coll.
Teacher, Bassa High School 39-41, Principal 42-44; Supervisor of Schools 44-52, Gov. Grand Bassa County 52-56; Asst. Sec. Public Works and Utilities 56; Consul-Gen., London 56-60; Amb. to Ghana 60-70; Chief, Special Mission to the Congo 60-61; Dean of Diplomatic Corps 63-; Sec. of Educ. Feb. 70-; Grand Medal of the Order of the Volta (Ghana), Grand Medal of the Pioneers, Grand Commdr. Star of Africa, Order of African Redemption.
Department of Education, Monrovia, Liberia.

Shilling, John Woollerton; South African mining official; b. 9 June 1913, S. Africa; Kingswood Coll., Grahamstown, C.P.
Member of Side Bar 34-39; Legal Adviser, Transvaal and O.F.S. Chamber of Mines 46-53; Dir./Man. Anglo-American

Corpn. of S. Africa Ltd.; Chair. of several gold mining companies in Anglo-American group; Chair. Nuclear Fuels Corpn. of S. Africa Ltd.; Pres. S. African Chamber of Mines.

Office: P.O. Box 61587, Marshalltown, Transvaal; Home: 80 South Avenue, Athol, Sandton, Johannesburg, South Africa.

Telephone: 838-8111 (Office); 40-4473 (Home).

Siad Barre, Maj.-Gen. Muhammad; Somalian army officer.

Commander-in-Chief of the Armed Forces; Pres. of the Supreme Revolutionary Council since the coup of Oct. 69-.

Supreme Revolutionary Council, Mogadishu, Somalia.

Sidikou, Abdou; Niger pharmacist and diplomatist; b. 1927; ed. William-Ponty School and African School of Medicine and Pharmacy, Dakar, and Univ. of Paris.

Director of Laboratory, French Sudan 49-52; Seine Hospital 56-57; Chief Pharmacist, Niamey Hospital 57-59; Dir. de Cabinet to Minister of Health, Niger 59-60; later Sec.-Gen. of Foreign Affairs 61-62; Amb. to U.S.A. and Perm. Rep. to UN 62-64; Amb. to Benelux, Fed. Germany and Perm. Rep. to EEC, Brussels 64-66; Sec. of State for Foreign Affairs 67-69; Sec. of State to the Presidency Jan. 70-Jan. 71.

c/o The Presidency, Niamey, Niger.

Sijaona, Lawi Nangwanda; Tanzanian politician; b. 1928, Mnima, Newala District; ed. St. Andrew's Coll., Minaki.

Worked in public relations; Editor, *Habari za Leo;* Exec. Officer and Clerk of Newala Local Council until 55; Chair. Lindi Town Council; Parl. Sec. to Ministry of Local Govt. 61-62, Treasury 62; Minister of Nat. Culture and Youth; Minister of Lands, Settlement and Water Devt.; Minister of Home Affairs Sept. 65-June 67; Minister of State, Office of the Second Vice-Pres. June 67-Oct. 68; Minister of Health and Housing Oct. 68; Minister of Health and Social Welfare until 72; Chair. Tanzania Youth League Central Cttee.

c/o Ministry of Health and Social Welfare, Dar es Salaam, Tanzania.

Simango, Rev. Uria; Mozambique nationalist leader.

Vice-President Council of Frente de Libertação de Moçambique (F.R.E.L.I.M.O.) 62-Feb. 69; Co-ordinator of triumvirate of F.R.E.L.I.M.O. Feb. 69- Nov. 69; suspended from Council Nov. 69; expelled from Tanzania Feb. 70.

Simba, Iddi, B.SC., C.E.R.; Tanzanian banking official; b. 8 Oct. 1935, Usumbura; ed. Panjab Univ., Pakistan, and Univ. of Toulouse, France.

Agricultural Field Officer, Ministry of Agriculture 61-62; Asst. Dir. of Planning, Ministry of Econ. Affairs and Planning; Alt. Exec. Dir. IBRD 66-68; Chair. and Dir.-Gen. East African Devt. Bank Feb. 68-; Fellow, Int. Bankers' Asscn., and Econ. Devt. Inst. (IBRD).

Publs. *Planning of a typical peasant farm to meet complete dietary and cash needs of a five-member peasant family 62, The use of a national centre for the collection of Agricultural Statistics in the planning of peasant agriculture in Tanzania 64.*

East African Development Bank, P.O. Box 7128, Kampala, Uganda.

Telephone: Kampala 30021.

Sinada, Mubarak; Sudanese politician; b. 1919, Omdurman; ed. Omdurman Intermediate School, Gordon Coll., Administration School.

Worked as Clerk 41-47, Sub-Mamor 48-52, Mamor 52-54, Deputy District Commr. 54, District Commr. 55, Deputy Gov. 66; later Lands Commr.; Minister of Housing 69-71, of Housing and Public Utilities Oct. 71-.

Ministry of Housing, Khartoum, Sudan.

Sinzogan, Lt.-Col. Benoit; Dahomeyan army officer and politician.

Former Aide-de-camp to Gen. Soglo; Minister of Foreign Affairs Dec. 67-July 68; Dir. Nat. Police Force Sept. 68-; promoted to Lt.-Col. July 69; mem. of three-man ruling cttee. and co-head of state Dec. 69-70; Minister of Foreign Affairs, Justice and Nat. Educ. Dec. 69-May 70; Chief of Staff of Nat. Gendarmerie Aug. 70.

Cotonou, Dahomey, West Africa.

Sissoko, Souleymane Ibrahim; Ivory Coast politician; b. 1914, Kani, Séguéla.

Head of Accounts Dept., Ministry of Posts and Telecommunications, fmr. French West Africa, Dakar 54-59; Head of Postal Services 60-May 62; Head of Inspection May 62-63; Dir. Office of Posts and Telecommunications 63-Sept. 64; Sec. of State for Posts and Telecommunications Aug. 64-Jan. 66; Minister of Posts and Telecommunications Jan. 66-.

Ministry of Posts and Telecommunications, Abidjan, Ivory Coast.

Sisulu, Walter Max; South African politician; b. 1912; ed. mission school.

Worked as a gold miner on the Rand; later in a Johannesburg bakery; mem. African Nat. Congress (A.N.C.) 40-, Sec.-Gen. 49-54; on trial for treason 56-61 (acquitted 61); on trial for organizing national strike 61, sentenced to six years' imprisonment; found guilty of sabotage and sentenced to life imprisonment June 64.

Robben Island, nr. Capetown, South Africa.

Sithole, Rev. Ndabaningi; African (Rhodesian) clergyman and politician; b. 1920; ed. Waddilove Inst., Marandellas and Newton Theological Coll., U.S.A.

Teacher 41-55; U.S.A. 55-58; Ordained at Mount Silinda Congregationalist Church 58; Principal, Chikore Cen. Primary School; Pres., African Teachers Asscn. 59-60; Treas. Nat. Dem. Party (N.D.P.) 60, Del. to Fed. Review Conf. London Dec. 60; fmr. Chair. Zimbabwe African People's Union (Z.A.P.U.) S. Rhodesia, Pres. July-Aug. 63; Leader Zimbabwe African Nat. Union (Z.A.N.U.) Rhodesia Aug. 63-; sentenced to 12 months imprisonment Dec. 63, sent to Wha Wha Restriction Camp May 65; tried and sentenced to six years hard labour for incitement to murder Ian Smith Feb. 69.

Publ. *African Nationalism* 59, 67.

c/o Zimbabwe African National Union (Z.A.N.U.), Dar es Salaam, Tanzania.

Skeen, Brig. Andrew, O.B.E.; Rhodesian politician and diplomatist; b. 3 Oct. 1906, Deshali, India; ed. Wellington Coll. and Royal Mil. Coll., Sandhurst.

British Army Service 26-47, war service France, Middle East, N. Africa, India, Burma; Pres. Manicaland Publicity Asscn.; Commr. Rhodesian Forestry Comm.; Rhodesian Tourist Board, Labour Conciliation Boards, Umtali Odzi Road Council, Vumba Town Planning Authority; Chair. Manicaland Div. Rhodesian Front Party; High Commr. for Rhodesia in London 65; mem. Rhodesian Parl. 66-; Independence Commemorative Decoration (Rhodesia).

Publ. *Prelude to Independence.*

Las Anod Farm, Box 277, Umtali, Rhodesia; 19 Granta Road, Vainona, P.O. Borrowdale, Salisbury, Rhodesia.

Telephone: Umtali 2283-13; Salisbury 882097.

Slater, Richard Mercer Keene, C.M.G.; British diplomatist; b. 27 May 1915, India; ed. Eton and Magdalene Coll., Cambridge.

Indian Civil Service (Punjab Comm.) 39-47; joined British Diplomatic Service 47; served Karachi 47-49, Foreign Office 49-52, Lima 52-54, Moscow 54-56, Imperial Defence Coll. 57, Foreign Office 58-59, Rangoon 59-62, Foreign Office 62-66; Amb. to Cuba 66-69; High Commr. in Uganda 70-72, concurrently Amb. to Rwanda 70-72.

c/o Foreign and Commonwealth Office, King Charles Street, London, S.W.1, England.

Smith, Ian Douglas; Rhodesian politician; b. 8 April 1919; ed. Chaplin School, Gwelo, Rhodesia and Rhodes Univ., Grahamstown, S. Africa.
Royal Air Force 41-46; farmer; mem. S. Rhodesia Legislative Assembly 48-53, 62-, Parl of Fed. of Rhodesia and Nyasaland 53-61; fmr. Chief Whip United Fed. Party; foundation mem. and Vice-Pres. Rhodesian Front 62, Pres. 64-; Deputy Prime Minister and Minister of Treasury S. Rhodesia Dec. 62-April 64; Prime Minister of Rhodesia April 64-.
8 Chancellor Avenue, Salisbury, Rhodesia; Gwenoro Farm, Selukwe, Rhodesia.

Snelling, Sir Arthur Wendell, K.C.M.G., K.C.V.O.; British civil servant and diplomatist; b. 7 May 1914, London; ed. Univ. Coll., London.
Study Group Sec. Royal Inst. of Int. Affairs 34-36; appointed to Dominions Office 36; Private Sec. to Parl. Under-Sec. of State 39; Joint Sec. U.K. Del. Int. Monetary Conf., Bretton Woods 44; Deputy High Commr. in New Zealand 47-50, in South Africa 53-55; Asst. Under-Sec. of State, Commonwealth Relations Office 56-59; High Commr. in Ghana 59-61; Deputy to Perm. Under-Sec. Foreign and Commonwealth Office 68-69; Amb. to South Africa 70-72, retd.
c/o Foreign and Commonwealth Office, King Charles Street, London, W.C.1, England.

Sobhuza II, H.R.H. King; King (Ngwenyama) and Head of State of Swaziland; b. 22 July 1899; s. of King Bhunu.
Installed as ruler 21; led deputation to London to petition against land lost under the Partitions Proclamation of 1907 Dec. 22; petitioned King George VI of England 41; officially recognized by Britain as King and Head of State April 67; founder mem. Nat. Imbokodvo Party 64.
Official Residence of the Ngwenyama, Lozithehlezi, Swaziland.

Sobukwe, Robert Maugatiso; South African politician; b. 1924; ed. Univ. Coll of Fort Hare.
Former Lecturer, Witwatersrand Univ., Johannesburg; fmr. mem. Africa Nat. Congress; Pres. South African Pan Africanist Congress 59-; in detention March 60-63, 63-May 69; now restricted to Kimberley; refused permission to leave S. Africa July 70.
Kimberley, South Africa.

Socé, Ousemane; Senegalese novelist; b. Saint-Louis.
Publs. *Karim* (novel) 35, *Mirages de Paris* (novel) 55.
c/o Nouvelles Editions Latines, Paris, France.

Soglo, Gen. Christophe; Dahomeyan army officer and politician; b. 1909.
Joined French Army 31, 2nd Lt. Second World War; later fought in Indo-China becoming Capt. 50, Maj. 56; Col. of Armed Forces of Dahomey 61, Gen. 64; Head of Provisional Govt. Oct. 63-Jan. 64; Chief of Staff, Dahomeyan Army Jan. 64-Dec. 65; Pres. of the Repub. and Prime Minister Dec. 65-67, also Minister of Defence and for Rural Devt. Dec. 66-67.
Cotonou, Dahomey.

Soko, Hosea Josias; Zambian politician.
Former Amb. to U.S.A.; Amb. to U.S.S.R. May 66-July 68; High Commr. to Kenya July 68-Jan. 69, to Uganda Jan.-March 69, to U.K. March 69; Chair., Zambian Nat. Coal Board; Gen. Man. United Bus Co. of Zambia Ltd. Aug. 71-.
Zambian National Coal Board, Lusaka, Zambia.

Soyinka, Wole, B.A.; Nigerian playwright and lecturer; b. 13 July 1934, Abeokuta; ed. Univ. of Ibadan, Nigeria, and Univ. of Leeds, England.
Worked at Royal Court Theatre, London; Research Fellow in Drama, Univ. of Ibadan 60-61; Lecturer in English, Univ. of Ife 62-63; Senior Lecturer in English, Univ. of Lagos 65-67; political prisoner 67-69; Dir.

School of Drama, Univ. of Ibadan 69-72; Research Prof. in Dramatic Literature, Univ. of Ife 72-; Artistic Dir. Orisun Theatre, 1960 Masks; Literary Editor Orisun Acting Editions; Prisoner of Conscience Award, Amnesty International, Jock Campbell-*New Statesman* Literary Award 69.
Publs. plays: *The Lion and the Jewel* 59, *The Swamp Dwellers* 59, *A Dance of the Forests* 60, *The Trials of Brother Jero* 61, *The Strong Breed* 62, *The Road* 64, *Kongi's Harvest* 65, *Madmen and Specialists* 71, *Before the Blackout* 71; novels: *The Interpreters* 64, *The Forest of a Thousand Demons* (trans.), *The Man Died* 72 (non-fiction); poems: *Idanre and Other Poems* 67, *A Shuffle in the Crypt* 72.
Department of English Literature, University of Ife, Ile-Ife, Nigeria.

Spínola, António Sebastião Ribeiro de; Portuguese army officer; b. 11 April 1910, Estremoz; ed. Mil. Schools, Lisbon, Univ. of Lisbon.
Promoted to rank of Capt. 44, Maj. 56, Lt.-Col. 61, Col. 63, Brig. 66, Gen. 69; held various posts in Portuguese Army; Deputy Commdr., later Commdr. 2nd Lancers Regiment 61; Commdr. 345th Cavalry Group, Angola 61-64; Provost Marshal 64-65; High Command Course 65-66; Cavalry Inspector 66-67; Deputy Commdr. Nat. Republican Guard 67-68; Gov., C.-in-C. of the Armed Forces of Portuguese Guinea May 68-; Dir. Sociedade Hípica Portuguesa (Equestrian Soc.) 40-44, Pres. 67; mem. Board of Dirs., Siderurgia Nacional (Nat. Steel Works Co.) 55-64; Commdr., Order of Aviz 59, Gold Medal for Exemplary Conduct 65, of Military Merit with Laurels 72, and many other military decorations.
Publs. *Por Uma Guiné Melhor* (For a Better Guinea) 70, *Linha de Accão* (Line of Action) 71, *No Caminho do Futuro* (On the Path to the Future).
Palácio do Governo, Bissau, Portuguese Guinea; Home: Rua Rafael de Andrade 25-1°, Lisbon, Portugal.

Spiro, Sidney, M.C.; South African business executive; b. 1914, South Africa; ed. Grey Coll., Bloemfontein and Cape Town Univ.
Joined Anglo American Corpn. S.A. Ltd. 53, Exec. Dir. 61; Vice-Chair. and Man. Dir. Charter Consolidated Ltd. 69, Chair. and Man. Dir. Jan. 71-Oct. 72.
Charter Consolidated Ltd., 40 Holborn Viaduct, London, EC1 1PIAJ; 43 Lowndes Square, London, SW1 X9JL, England.

Stanley, Henry Sydney Herbert Cloete, C.M.G.; British diplomatist; b. 5 March 1920; ed. Eton and Balliol Coll., Oxford.
Commonwealth Relations Office 47; served in Pakistan 50-52, Swaziland and S. Africa 54-57, U.S.A. 59-61, Tanganyika 61-63, Kenya 63-65; Insp. H.M. Diplomatic Service 66-68, Chief Insp. 68-70; High Commr. to Ghana 70-.
British High Commission, Barclays Bank Building, High Street, P.O. Box 296, Accra, Ghana.

Stevens, Siaka Probyn; Sierra Leone politician; b. 24 Aug. 1905, Moyamba; ed. Albert Acad., Freetown, and Ruskin Coll., Oxford (47-48).
Court Messenger Force 23-30; railway worker, rising to Station Master, later mine worker with Sierra Leone Devt. Co. (DELCO) 30-43; Sec. Marampa Mineworkers Union 43, later Gen. Sec. United Mineworkers Union; mem. Protectorate Assembly, Bo 45; at Ruskin Coll. Oxford 47-48; mem. Legis. Council 51-57, Minister of Lands, Mines and Labour 51; Founder mem. Sierra Leone Org. Soc., later Sierra Leone People's Party; Deputy Leader People's Nat. Party 58-60; Leader All People's Congress 60-; political imprisonment 61; Mayor of Freetown 64-65; Prime Minister March 67; in exile 67-68; Prime Minister April 68-71, also Minister of Defence and Interior April 70-71; Pres. Repub. of Sierra Leone April 71-; Minister of

Public Service and Police March 72-; Dr. h.c. of Civil Law (Univ. of Sierra Leone) 69.
Office of the President, State House, Freetown, Sierra Leone.

Stradling, Rt. Rev. Leslie Edward, M.A., D.C.L.; British ecclesiastic; b. 11 Feb. 1908; ed. Oxford Univ., Westcott House, Cambridge.
Curate in London 33-38, Vicar 38-45; Bishop of Masasi 45-52, of S.W. Tanganyika 52-61, of Johannesburg, South Africa 61-.
Publs. *A Bishop on Safari* 60, *"The Acts" through Modern Eyes* 63, *An Open Door* 66, *A Bishop at Prayer* 71.
Bishop's House, 4 Crescent Drive, Westcliff, Johannesburg; also P.O. Box 31792, Braamfontein, Transvaal, South Africa.
Telephone: 725-1910.

Strauss, Hon. Jacobus Gideon Nel, Q.C., B.A., LL.B.; South African lawyer and politician; b. 17 Dec. 1900; ed. Univ. of Cape Town.
Private Sec. to Prime Minister 23-24; admitted to Johannesburg Bar 26; M.P. for Germiston District 32-57; Minister of Agriculture and Forests in Smuts Cabinet 44; Leader of Opposition 50-56; resigned from United Party 59.
Schöne-Brunnen Stud Farm, Box 509, Krugersdorp, Transvaal, Republic of South Africa.
Telephone: 622-2118.

Sukati, John Brightwell Mfundza, B.E.M.; Swazi politician; b. 11 Nov. 1915, Ezabani, Manzini district; ed. Zombodze and Matsapa Swazi Nat. Schools.
Worked at Havelock Mines 40; Induna-in-Charge of Swazi Regts', Pioneer Corps, later Sergeant-Maj. 40-49; rural devt. Officer, Dept. of Agriculture 49-64; mem. Legislative Council 64-; mem. House of Assembly 67-; Deputy Prime Minister 67-71; Minister of Power, Works and Communications 71-May 72; Pres. Commdr., Swazi Regt.
c/o Ministry of Power, Mbabane, Swaziland.

Sukati, Samuel Thornton Msindazwe, M.B.E., B.A.; Swazi diplomatist; b. 11 June 1910, Manzini District; ed. school at Zombodze and Lovedale Inst., Cape Province, South Africa.
First Swazi Revenue Clerk, Swaziland Govt. 35; Senior Liaison Officer between Swazi King and Central Govt. 44; First Establishment Officer, Swaziland Govt., and first Swazi to be in Senior and Pensionable Service 50; attended Overseas Civil Service Course, London School of Econs. 55; Chair. Council of Univ. of Botswana, Lesotho and Swaziland 66; First Speaker House of Assembly 67; Amb. of Kingdom of Swaziland to U.S.A. and High Commr. in Canada 68-, concurrently Perm. Rep. to UN 68-70; mem. UN Cttee. for Elimination of all forms of racial discrimination 69-; Certificate of Honour and Badge 45; Hon. LL.D. 68.
Embassy of Kingdom of Swaziland, 441 Van Ness Centre, 4301 Connecticut Avenue, N.W., Washington, D.C. 20008; Home: 4517 28th Street, N.W., Washington, D.C. 20008, U.S.A.
Telephone: 362-6683 (Chancery); 362-4458 (Home).

Suliman, Ahmed; Sudanese diplomatist and politician; b. 1924; ed. Faculty of Law, Cairo Univ.
Minister of Agriculture 64; Deputy to Constituent Assembly; fmr. Chair. Sudan Peace Cttee.; Amb. to U.S.S.R. 69; Minister of Econs. and Foreign Trade Oct. 69-June 70; Minister of Industry and Mining June 70-Oct. 71; Minister of Justice Oct. 71-; has attended many int. confs. sponsored by World Peace Council and Afro-Asian People's Solidarity Org.
Ministry of Justice, Khartoum, Sudan.

Sutherland, Efua; Ghanaian poetess and playwright; b. Cape Coast, Ghana; ed. Cambridge Univ., England.
Teacher, established school in Transvolta; prose writer but mainly poetess; now occupied with school of drama, Univ. of Ghana.
Publs. *Playtime in Africa* 62, *Foura* (play) 62, *Adufa* (play) 62, *New Life at Kyerefaso* (prose poem).
c/o University of Ghana (School of Drama), P.O. Box 25, Legon, nr. Accra, Ghana.

Suzman, Helen, B.COM., M.P.; South African politician; b. Germiston, Transvaal; ed. Parktown Convent, Univ. of Witwatersrand.
Assistant statistician, War Supplies Board, 41-44; part-time lecturer, Dept. of Econs. and Econ. Hist., Univ. of Witwatersrand 44-52; now M.P. for Houghton and only parl. rep. of the Progressive Party; mem. South African Inst. of Race Relations.
The House of Assembly, Cape Town, Cape Province, South Africa.

Swart, Charles Robberts, B.A., LL.B., D.M.S.; South African lawyer, journalist and politician; b. 5 Dec. 1894, Morgenzon; ed. Grey University College, Bloemfontein, Univ. of South Africa and Columbia Univ., New York.
Advocate Supreme Court of South Africa 19-48; fmr. Organizing Sec. Nat. Party of Orange Free State 19-28; Leader Nat. Party of O.F.S. 40-59; fmr. mem. Fed. Nat. Party Council; fmr. Lecturer in Law and Agricultural Legislation; M.P. for Ladybrand 23-38, Winburg 41-59; Minister of Educ., Arts and Science 49-50; Minister of Justice 48-59; Deputy Prime Minister and Leader, House of Assembly 54-59; Gov. Gen. 60-61; State Pres. Repub. of South Africa 61-67; Chancellor, Univ. of Orange Free State 51-; Hon. Col. Oos-Vrystaat Regt. 53-, Regt. Univ. Oranje-Vrystaat 62-; Hon. LL.D. (Univ. of Orange Free State, Rhodes Univ. and Potchefstroom Univ.); Hon. Fellow, Coll. of Physicians, Surgeons and Gynaecologists of S. Africa; Hon. mem. S. African Acad. of Science and Art; Hon. Fellow, S. African Inst. of Architects; Hon. Pres. Automobile Asscn. S. Africa; Life Patron-in-Chief Voortrekker Youth Movement; Justice Medal 72; freeman of numerous S. African towns.
Publs. *Kinders van Suid-Afrika* 33, *Die Agterryer* 39.
P.O. Box 135, Brandfort, Orange Free State, Republic of South Africa.

Sylla, Djim; Mali public servant; b. 1933; ed. Bamako and Ecole Nat. de la France Outre-mer, Paris.
Served in French admin. of Upper Volta 56-57; Dir. de Cabinet to Abdoulaye Diallo as Minister of Labour, Soudan 57-59; Head of Civil Service, Soudan 59-60; Dir. de Cabinet to Dr. Seydou Kouyate as Minister of Planning 60-62, then of his successor Jean Marie Kone 62-65, Administrator of Devt. Plan; Co.-Sec. Council of Asscn. between EEC and African-Malagasy States 65-.
Council of Association to the EEC, 23 rue Beau-Site, Brussels 5, Belgium.

T

Tadjo Ehué, Joseph, D.SC.(ECON.); Ivory Coast teacher and politician; b. 5 Jan. 1930, Maféré; ed. Paris.
Professor of Higher Educ. at Ecole d'Agronomie, Ecole Nat. d'Admin., Ecole de Statistique 65-; Minister of the Civil Service Jan. 70-; Pres. Comm. des Affaires Economiques et Financières du Conseil Economique et Social, Société de Construction et d'Exploitation du Pont de Moossou (S.C.E.P.O.M.), Comm. de Financement et de l'Equilibre; Commandeur, l'Ordre Nat. de la République Tunisienne.
Ministry of the Civil Service, Abidjan, Ivory Coast.

Tali, Alhaji Yakubu, Tolon Na; Ghanaian Chief and diplomatist; ed. Achimota.
Teacher, Northern Territories 38-47; Tali Na (Chief of Tali) 47-53; Tolon Na (Chief of Tolon) 53-; Chair. Dagomba Native Authority Council 49, later Dagomba District Council; mem. Gold Coast Legislative Assembly, later Ghana Legislative Assembly 51-, fmr. Deputy Speaker; Pres. Northern Territories Council 53-; High Commr. of Ghana in Nigeria 65-67; Ghana Mission to UN 61-62, 69-70; Amb. to Yugoslavia, Bulgaria and Romania 70-72; High Commr. to Sierra Leone 72-; Northern People's Party.
Ghanaian High Commission, Freetown, Sierra Leone.

Tamba-Tamba, Victor; Congolese politician.
Secretary for Org., Steering Cttee. of Nat. Revolutionary Council (C.N.R.) Oct. 68-; Sec. of State for Transport and Public Works Jan. 70-April 70; Sec. of State in charge of Devt., Posts and Telecommunications, Civil Aviation, Tourism, Town Planning and Housing April 70-.
Office of the Secretary of State for Posts and Telecommunications, Brazzaville, People's Republic of the Congo.

Tambo, Oliver; South African politician; b. 1917; ed. Anglican mission schools and Univ. Coll. of Fort Hare, Cape Province.
Teacher, Secondary School; Solicitor, Johannesburg, 51-60; banned from attending meetings 54-56 and for five years 59-64; arrested on treason charges 56, charges withdrawn 57; Deputy Pres. African Nat. Congress 58-67, Pres. 67-; escaped to London 60; mem. del. of exiled reps. of S. African parties to Third Conf. of Independent African States, Addis Ababa 60; attended UN Gen. Assembly (15th Session) 60; Head, External Mission of African Nat. Congress of South Africa.
African National Congress of South Africa, P.O. Box 2239, Dar es Salaam, Tanzania; and Africa Unity House, 3 Collingham Gardens, London, S.W.5, England.

Tamboura, Amadou, L. en D.; Upper Voltan international civil servant; b. 31 Dec. 1933; ed. primary schools in Djibo and Ouahigouya, Bamako Lycée in Mali, and Univs. of Dakar and Paris.
Customs Inspector 62; envoy to GATT 63; Div. Insp. of Customs and First Counsellor to Embassy of Upper Volta in Brussels 64; Chief, Third Div. Ouagadougou Customs; Sec.-Gen. Customs Union of States of West Africa until 72, of Communauté Economique de l'Afrique de l'Ouest 72-.
Communauté Economique de l'Afrique de l'Ouest, B.P. 28, Ouagadougou, Upper Volta.

Tandau, Alfred Cyril; Tanzanian trade unionist and politician; b. 1936, Mbuli, Mbinga District; ed. Old Moshi Secondary School, Kasubi Secondary School, Uganda.
Bank Clerk, fmr. Barclays Bank D.C.O. (now Barclays Int. Ltd.) 57-59; Branch Sec., Regional Sec. Transport and Gen. Workers' Union (Tanganyika) Sept. 57, Financial Sec. 59-62; Deputy Sec.-Gen. TFL March-Aug. 62, Acting Sec.-Gen. 62-64; Deputy Sec.-Gen. NUTA (Nat. Union of Tanganyika Workers) 64-68, Sec.-Gen. 69-; Gen. Man. Friendship Textile Mill 68-69; Minister of Labour and Social Welfare Feb. 72-.
Publs. *History of TFL and Formation of NUTA, One Union, One Aim.*
P.O. Box 9014, Dar es Salaam; also P.O. Box 15359, Dar es Salaam, Tanzania.

Tanoe, Appagny; Ivory Coast diplomatist; b. 1 Oct. 1929; ed. Univ. de Bordeaux.
Former Head Doctor, Centre Hospitalier, Abidjan; Vice-Pres. Econ. and Social Council of the Ivory Coast 61-64; Amb. to France 65-.

Embassy of the Ivory Coast, 102 Avenue Raymond-Poincaré, Paris 16e, France.

Tarka, Joseph Sarwuuan; Nigerian politician; b. 10 July 1932, Igbor, Tiv Division; s. of late Chief Tarka Nachi, fmr. District Head of Mbakov; ed. Gboko Primary School, Katsina-Ala Middle Secondary School and Bauchi Teachers' Training Coll.
Teacher, Provincial Secondary School, Tiv Native Admin.; Pres. United Middle Belt Congress (U.M.B.C.); elected mem. House of Reps. 54-; Shadow Minister of Commerce and Industry; mem. Accounts Cttee. 58; del. Nigerian Constitutional Conf. 57-58, Pan-African Conf. 59; del. N. Region, All Nigeria Constitutional Conf. 66; mem. Fed. Exec. Council June 67-; Commr. for Transport and Aviation June 67-71, for Posts and Telecommunications Nov. 71-.
Federal Ministry for Posts and Telecommunications, Lagos, Nigeria.

Taswell, Harold Langmead Taylor, M.COM.; South African diplomatist; b. 14 Feb. 1910, Cape Town; ed. Christian Brothers Coll., Pretoria, and Univ. of Cape Town.
Department of External Affairs 35-, Berlin 37-39, London 39, The Hague 40, New York 40-46; Consul, Elisabethville 46-49; Int. Trade and Econ. Section, Dept. of External Affairs, Pretoria 49-51; First Sec., Wash. 51-56; Consul-Gen., Luanda, Angola 56-59; High Commr. of S. Africa in Fed. of Rhodesia and Nyasaland 59-61, accredited Diplomatic Rep. 61-63, accredited Diplomatic Rep. in S. Rhodesia 63-64; Head, Africa Div., Dept. of Foreign Affairs, Pretoria 64; Amb. to U.S.A. 65-71, to UN, Geneva 71-.
Permanent Mission of South Africa, 114 rue du Rhône, 1204 Geneva, Switzerland.

Taya, Sid'Ahmed Ould; Mauritanian diplomatist; b. 1936, Atar; ed. Inst. des Hautes Etudes d'Outre-mer, Paris.
Primary school teacher 56-61; Asst. Editor *Mauritanie Nouvelle* (newspaper) 61; Dir. Cabinet of Minister of Construction and Public Works 61; entered diplomatic service as Counsellor, Washington 65; Sec.-Gen. Ministry of Foreign Affairs Dec. 65; Amb. to Algeria 67-69; Dir.-Gen. Air Mauritanie 69-70; Perm. Rep. to UN May 70-71.
c/o Ministère des Affaires Etrangères, Nouakchott, Mauritania.

Taylor, Catherine Dorothea; South African politician; b. 4 Feb. 1914, Birmingham, England; ed. St. Michael's School, Bloemfontein, St. Mary's Diocesan School, Pretoria, Bristol Univ. and Univ. of Tours.
Member, Cape Provincial Council 54-63, Chief Whip 56-60, Chair. 60-61; Deputy Leader, United Party 61-63; mem. Parl. 63-; mem. Cape School Board 54-66, Cape Hospital Board 54-60; Nat. Convenor Public Affairs and Legislation, South African Fed. of Business and Professional Women's Clubs 64-68; Chair. several school cttees.; has lectured extensively in U.K. and U.S.A.; Hon. Pres. Wynberg Sports Club 71-.
"Van-My-Lewe", St. Alban's Close, Bishops Court, Cape Province, South Africa.

Taylor, Most Rev. Robert Selby, M.A., D.D.; South African (Anglican) ecclesiastic; b. 1 March 1909, England; ed. Harrow School, St. Catharine's Coll., Cambridge, and Cuddesdon Theol. Coll.
Ordained deacon 32, priest 33; Curate, St. Olave's York 32-34; Missionary, N. Rhodesia 35-41; Bishop of N. Rhodesia 41-51, of Pretoria 51-59, of Grahamstown 59-64; Archbishop of Cape Town and Metropolitan of Church of Province of S. Africa 64-; Sub-Prelate, Order of St. John 60; Hon. Fellow, St. Catharine's Coll. Cambridge 64-; Hon. D.D. (Rhodes Univ., Grahamstown) 66.
Bishopscourt, Claremont, Cape Town, South Africa.

Taylor-Kamara, Ismael Byne; Sierra Leonean diplomatist; b. 1913, Mabanta, Kase Chiefdom; ed. Methodist Boys' High School and Fourah Bay Coll., Freetown.
Entered Sierra Leone Civil Service 37-46; called to the Bar, Lincoln's Inn, London 49; in private practice as solicitor and advocate in Sierra Leone 50-57; mem. Sierra Leone Public Service Comm.; mem. Parl. 57; Minister of Trade and Industry 57-62; First Chair. Sierra Leone Electricity Corpn.; Notary Public 68; Perm. Rep. to UN Sept. 71-; mem. del. to constitutional talks prior to independence of Sierra Leone 58, 60.
Permanent Mission of Sierra Leone at United Nations, 919 Third Avenue, 22nd Floor, New York, N.Y. 10022, U.S.A.

Tchanqué, Pierre; Cameroonian civil servant; b. 16 Dec. 1925, Douala; ed. Univ. de Paris.
Former Dir. of Public Accounts; Sec.-Gen. Ministry of Finance; Dir. Société Nationale d'Investissement du Cameroun; Pres. of Council, CIMENCAM; dir. of various companies; Sec.-Gen. Union Douanière et Economique de l'Afrique Centrale (UDEAC) July 70-; Officier et Chevalier de l'Ordre National (Cameroon) and decorations from Tunisia and Fed. Germany.
Union Douanière et Economique de l'Afrique Centrale (UDEAC), B.P. 969, Bangui, Central African Republic.
Telephone: 28-08.

Tchoungi, Simon Pierre; Cameroonian doctor and politician; b. 28 Oct. 1916; ed. Ecole Primaire Supérieure, Centre Médicale, Ayos, Ecole de Médecine, Dakar, and Univ. de Paris à la Sorbonne.
Former Dir. of Office, Ministry of Public Health and Population, then of Ministry of Public Works; Dir. Int. Relations, Ministry of Public Health and Population 59-60; Dir. of Public Health for Cameroon 61-; Minister of Public Health and Population 61-64; Minister of Nat. Economy 64-65; Sec. of State to the Presidency 65; Prime Minister of East Cameroon 65-72; numerous decorations.
B.P. 1057, Yaoundé, United Republic of Cameroon.

Teelock, Leckraz, C.B.E., M.B., CH.B., D.T.M., L.M.; Mauritius diplomatist; b. 4 March 1899, Mauritius; ed. Royal Coll. of Mauritius and Univ. of Edinburgh.
Member Legislative Council of Mauritius 59-63; Commr. for Mauritius in U.K. 64-March 68; High Commr. to U.K. March 68-, Amb. Extraordinary and Plenipotentiary to the Holy See, Belgium, EEC.
Mauritius High Commission, Grand Buildings, Northumberland Avenue, London, W.C.2, England.
Telephone: 01-930 2895.

Tejan-Sie, Sir Banja, K.C.M.G.; Sierra Leone public official; b. 7 Aug. 1917, Moyamba, S. Province; ed. Bo school, Prince of Wales School, Freetown, and London School of Econs.
Station clerk, Sierra Leone Railway 38-39; Nurse, Medical Dept. 40-46; Council of Legal Educ. 47-51, called to Bar, Lincoln's Inn 51; Nat. Vice-Pres., Sierra Leone People's Party 53-56; mem. Keith Lucas Comm. on Electoral Reform 54; Police Magistrate, E. Province 55, N. Province 58; Hon. Sec. Sierra Leone Bar Asscn. 57-58; Senior Police Magistrate, Provinces 61; Speaker of House of Reps. 62-67; numerous official visits to other countries; Chief Justice 67-68; Acting Gov.-Gen. April 68-70, Gov.-Gen. 70-April 71; Grand Band of Order of Star of Africa (Liberia) 69; Special Grand Cordon of Order of Propitious Clouds (Repub. of China) 69.
14B Syke Street, Freetown, Sierra Leone.

Telli Boubacar, H.E. Diallo; Guinean international official; b. 1925, Poredaka, Mamou district; ed. Lycée de Dakar, Lycée Louis Le Grand, Paris, Faculté de droit, Sorbonne, L'Ecole Nationale de la France d'Outre-Mer.
Called to the Bar 51; Asst. Public Prosecutor, Senegal 54,

later with Court of Cotonou, Dahomey and Court of Appeal, Dakar; served on staff of French High Commr., Dakar; Sec.-Gen. Grand Council, French West Africa 57-58; Amb. to U.S.A. 58-61 and Perm. Rep. to the UN 58-64; Vice-Pres. 17th Session of UN Gen. Assembly 61-62; Chair. special Cttee. on Apartheid of UN Gen. Assembly 63-64; Sec.-Gen. Org. of African Unity Aug. 64-72; Minister of Justice Aug. 72-.
Ministry of Justice, Conakry, Guinea.

Tembo, John Zenas Ungapake; Malawi politician; b. Sept. 1932; ed. senior primary school, Kongwe, Mlanda School, Ncheu, Blantyre Secondary School and Roma Univ. Coll., Basutoland.
Worked for Colonial Audit Dept., Zomba 49-March 55; studied at Roma Univ. Coll. 55-58; fmr. mem. African Students' Rep. Council; attended course for educational diploma, Salisbury, Rhodesia Dec. 58-Nov. 59; teacher Kongwe Secondary School 59-61; mem. Legislative Council for Dedza 61-62; Parl. Sec. for Finance 62-64; M.P. for Dedza North 64, resigned May 70; Minister of Finance 64-68, concurrently Minister of Trade, Industry, Devt. and Planning 64-68; Minister of Trade and Finance Dec. 68-Aug. 70; Gov., Reserve Bank of Malawi Aug. 70-.
Reserve Bank of Malawi, Blantyre, Malawi.

Tessemma, H.E. Ato Getahoun; Ethiopian politician and diplomatist; b. 1911; ed. Ethiopia, Egypt, Lebanon.
Fought with guerrillas during Italian occupation; Dir.-Gen. Ministry of Pensions 41-42; Dir.-Gen. Ministry of Interior 42-43; First Sec., Washington 43-47; Perm. Rep. UN 47-48; Vice-Minister, Commerce and Industry 48-58, Agriculture 58; Minister of Public Health 58; Amb. to U.S.S.R. 59-60, to India 60-62; Minister of Nat. Community Devt. 62-71, concurrently Minister of Social Affairs 66-71; Minister of Interior 71-; Pres. ILO Conf. 67; Grand Officer of the Collar of Ethiopia, Liberation Medal, Patriots Medal.
Ministry of Interior, Addis Ababa, Ethiopia.

Tévoédjré, Albert, D. ès SC. ECON. et SOC., L. ès L.; Dahomeyan politician and international civil servant; b. 1929, Porto Novo; ed. Toulouse Univ., Fribourg Univ., and Institut Universitaire des Hautes Etudes Internationales, Geneva, Sloan School of Management, Mass. Inst. of Technology.
Assistant teacher, Lycée Delafosse, Dakar 52-54; teacher in France 57-58; teacher Lycée Victor Ballot, Porto Novo 59-61; Asst. Sec.-Gen. Nat. Syndicate of Teachers, Dahomey 59, Dahomeyan Democratic Resettlement Oct. 60-; Sec. of State for Information 61-62; Sec.-Gen. Union Africaine et Malgache (UAM) 62-63; founder-mem. Promotion Africaine (soc. to combat poverty in Africa); Prof. in charge of Research, Center for Int. Affairs (Harvard Univ.) 64-65; joined Int. Labour Office 65; Regional Co-ordinator for Africa March 66-69, Asst. Dir.-Gen. Jan. 69-; fmr. Chief Editor *L'Etudiant d'Afrique Noire*.
Publs. *L'Afrique Revoltée* 58, *Pan-Africanism in Action* 65, *La Formation des cadre africains en vue de la croissance économique* 65, *L'Afrique face aux problèmes du socialisme et de l'aide étrangère* 66, etc.
Bureau International du Travail, Geneva; also Le Manoir des Amadies, 1245 Collonge-Bellerive, Switzerland.
Telephone: 32-62-00 (Office); (022) 52-33-86 (Home).

Thema, B. C., M.B.E.; Botswana politician; b. 1912, Ngwaketse; ed. Ngwaketse and Tiger Kloof Teachers' Training Coll.
Founded Tshidi Barolong Secondary School 46; teacher 46-55; Principal, Moeng Coll. 55-64; studied privately 37-47; fmr. Gen. Sec. Cape Teachers' Union and mem. Fed. Council of African Teachers' Asscns.; mem. Legis. Assembly (now Nat. Assembly) March 65-; Minister of Labour and Social Services March 65-Oct. 65; Minister of Finance Nov.

65-April 66; Minister of Educ., Health and Labour April 66-Oct. 69; Minister of Educ. Oct. 69-.
Ministry of Education, Gaberone, Botswana.

Thiam, Doudou; Senegalese politician; b. 3 Feb. 1926; ed. Lycée Van Vollenhoven, Dakar, and Poitiers Univ. Former Magistrate, Senegal; helped draft Constitutions of Repub. of Senegal and of Mali Fed.; fmr. Minister of Finance, Econ. Affairs and Planning, Mali Fed. Minister of Foreign Affairs, Senegal Aug. 60-63; State Minister in Charge of Foreign Affairs and Relations with the Assemblies 63-68; Pres. Council of Ministers for Org. of African Unity 63-64; Mayor of Mbake; mem. UN Int. Law Comm. Publs. *Le Problème de la Citoyenneté française dans les territoires d'outre-mer, La Politique étrangère des Etats africains.*
68 rue Wagane Diouf, Dakar, Senegal, West Africa.

Thiam, Habib, L. en D.; Senegalese politician; b. 21 Jan. 1933, Dakar; ed. Faculty of Law and Economics, Paris. Directeur de Cabinet Dec. 60-Dec. 62; Sec. of State in charge of Planning and Devt. Dec. 62-Dec. 63; Minister of Planning and Devt. Dec. 63-March 68; Minister of Rural Devt. March 68-.
Ministry of Rural Development, Dakar, Senegal.

Thierry-Lebbe, Alexis; Ivory Coast politician; b. 22 March 1920, Fresco.
Worked as teacher, later in civil admin.; Dir., Ministry of Public Affairs 58-; attended course on public affairs, Paris; fmr. Prefect for South; Sec. of State for the Interior Aug. 64-Jan. 66; Minister of Animal Production Jan. 66-Jan. 70; Minister of Town Planning Jan. 70-; mem. Exec. Cttee., Parti Démocratique de la Côte d'Ivoire (P.D.C.I.).
Ministry of Town Planning, Abidjan, Ivory Coast.

Tibandebage, Andrew Kajungu; Tanzanian diplomatist; b. *c.* 1921, Kasheshe; ed. Makerere Coll. and London Univ. Inst. of Education.
Schoolteacher St. Mary's, Tabora 45-54, Headmaster, Bugene Middle School, Karagwe 55; Head of Mathematics Section, St. Thomas More Secondary School, Ihungo, Bukoba 56-61; Ministry of External Affairs 62-; Counsellor in London 62; Head Tanganyika Embassy to Fed. Germany 62-63, Amb. 63-64; Amb. of Tanzania to the Congo (Kinshasa) 64-67; Principal Sec. at Ministry of Information and Tourism 67-68; Tanzanian Amb. to France 68-70; Asst. to Pres. of Tanzania (Foreign Affairs) 70-72; Amb. to Zaire (also accred. to Burundi and Rwanda) 72-.
B.P. 1612, Kinshasa, Zaire.

Tobias, Philip Vallentine, PH.D., D.SC., F.R.S.S.A.F., F.L.S., M.B.B.CH.; South African professor of anatomy; b. 14 Oct. 1925, Durban; ed. St. Andrew's School, Bloemfontein, Durban High School, Univ. of the Witwatersrand and Emmanuel Coll., Cambridge.
Lecturer in Anatomy, Univ. of Witwatersrand 51-52, Senior Lecturer 53, Prof. and Head of Anatomy Dept. 58-; founder mem. Inst. for the Study of Man in S. Africa, Anatomical Soc. of Southern Africa, S. African Soc. for Quaternary Research; mem. numerous int. asscns.; Fellow, Royal Anthropological Inst. of Great Britain and Ireland, Royal Soc. of S. Africa; Vice-Pres. and acting Exec. Pres. S. African Asscn for the Advancement of Science; Pres. Royal Soc. of S. Africa 70-72; British Asscn. Medal 52; Simon Biesheuvel Medal 66; S. Africa Medal 67. Publs. *Man's Anatomy* (with M. Arnold) 67, *Olduvai Gorge Vol. II* 67, *Man's Past and Future* 69, *The Brain in Hominid Evolution* 71, many articles in scientific journals. Department of Anatomy, University of the Witwatersrand Medical School, Hospital Street, Johannesburg; 602 Marble Arch, 36 Goldreich Street, Hillbrow, Johannesburg, South Africa.
Telephone: 724-1561 (Office); 44-7211 (Home).

Todd, Reginald Stephen Garfield, D.D.; Rhodesian rancher and politician; b. 13 July 1908, Invercargill, New Zealand; ed. Otago Univ., Univ. of Witwatersrand, and Glen Leith Theological Coll.
Worked with Thomas Todd & Sons Ltd., Invercargill, N.Z.; Supt. Dadaya Mission, Southern Rhodesia 34-53; M.P. 46-58; Pres. United Rhodesia Party 53-58; Prime Minister 53-58; Minister of Labour 54-58; Minister of Native Educ. 55-57; Minister of Labour and Social Welfare 58; founded (with Sir John Moffat) Central Africa Party 58, Pres. 59-60; founded New African Party July 61; Dir. Hokonui Ranching Co. Ltd.; restricted to his ranch for 12 months Oct. 65; imprisoned Jan. 72, under house arrest Feb. 72-; Hon. LL.D.
P.O. Dadaya, Rhodesia.
Telephone: 01222 Shabani.

Togbe, Jacques Dabra, LIC. EN DROIT; Togolese international official; b. 3 May 1930, Akloa, Akposso District; ed. Petit Séminaire Sainte Jeanne d'Arc, Ouidah, Dahomey, Lycée Bonnecarrère, Lomé, Collège Victor Ballot, Porto Novo, Dahomey, Univ. of Montpellier, Inst. des Hautes Etudes d'Outre-Mer, Paris.
Factory Inspector, Head of Labour Inspection and Social Laws Dept. 65-68; Dir.-Gen. of Labour, Manpower and Social Security 68-72; Perm. Rep. to UN April 72-; mem. Political Bureau, Rassemblement du Peuple Togolais (RPT); Asst. Sec.-Gen. RPT 69-71; mem. Social Security Comm., Int. Labour Org. (ILO) 69-; del. to Int. Labour Conf. 64-, to numerous ILO regional confs.; Prof. of Social and Labour Law, Ecole Nat. d'Administration Togolaise 65-72; Officer, Order of the Leopard (Zaire).
Permanent Mission of Togo to the United Nations, 800 Second Avenue, New York, N.Y. 10017, U.S.A.

Tolbert, Stephen A.; Liberian politician; b. 16 Feb. 1922, Bensonville; brother of W. R. Tolbert (Pres. of Liberia) *q.v.*; ed. Liberia Coll. (now Univ. of Liberia), Howard Univ., Washington and Univ. of Michigan, U.S.A.
Former Organizer and Dir., Nat. Forest Service; Asst. Sec., later Sec. of Agriculture and Commerce; Pres., Meesurada Group of Companies; fmr. Chair. of Board Liberia Produce Marketing Corpn., Agriculture Credit Corpn.; Dir. Bank of Liberia, Liberia Devt. Corpn., Liberian Devt. Bank and numerous other companies; del. to various OAU, ILO and FAO confs.; Sec. of the Treasury Jan. 72-; decorations, from Govts. of Liberia, Ivory Coast, U.K., Guinea, Senegal, Austria, Madagascar and Taiwan.
The Treasury, Monrovia, Liberia.

Tolbert, William Richard, Jr.; Liberian politician; b. 13 May 1913; ed. Liberia Coll. (now Univ. of Liberia). Liberian Treasury 35-, Disbursing Officer 36-43; mem. of House of Reps. 43-51; Vice-Pres. of Liberia 51-71, Pres. 71-; Pres. of the Senate; Pres. Baptist World Alliance 65-66; Hon. mem. American Int. Acad.; Hon. D.C.L. for Africa 65-70; fmr. Chair. Board of Dirs., Bank of Liberia; Hon. mem. American Int. Acad.; Hon. D.C.L., Hon. D.D. (Liberia); numerous Liberian and foreign decorations.
The Executive Mansion, Monrovia, Liberia.

Tombalbaye, François; Chad politician; b. 15 June 1918. Former businessman, school official; Territorial Councillor 52, 57-59; mem. Grand Conseil 57-59, Vice-Pres. 57-58; Prime Minister 59-60, Minister of Justice 59-62, of Defence 60-62; Pres. of Council of Ministers 60-; Pres. of the Repub. 62-; Sec.-Gen. Parti progressiste tchadien (P.P.T.); Pres. OCAM Jan. 70-72; Grand Croix de la Légion d'Honneur, Grand Croix de l'Ordre National Gabonais.
Office of the President, Fort-Lamy, Chad.

Touré, El Hadj Abdoulaye, M.D.; Guinean diplomatist and doctor of medicine; b. 16 Dec. 1923, Kankan; ed. School of Medicine and Pharmacy, Dakar.
Practised medicine in Niger, Congo (Brazzaville), Central African Repub. and Ballay Hospital, Conakry; Chief Physician in Beyla, Kankan and Siguiri regions; Sec.-Gen. Jeunesse démocratique africaine 46; fmr. Sec. Exec. Cttee., Democratic Party of Guinea, Kankan; Deputy Mayor of Kankan 55, Mayor of Siguiri 56-59; Gov. of Pita 58; Dir.-Gen. Information Service of the Repub. of Guinea; Pres. Union des Radiodiffusions et Télévisions nationales africaines; del XVI session of UN Gen. Assembly and many int. confs.; Perm. Rep. to UN 69-72.
c/o Ministère des Affaires Etrangères, Conakry, Guinea.

Touré, Ismaël; Guinean politician; b. 1925; ed. in France.
Head, Kankan Meteorological station; mem. Kankan Municipal Council 56; mem. Faranah Territorial Assembly; Minister of Works 57-59, of Posts, Telegraphs and Transport 59-61; Minister of Public Works and Transport 61-62; Minister of Econ. Devt. 63-68; Minister of Finance 68-, concurrently of the Economy with responsibility for Industry, Mines, Power, Banks and Public Works April 72-; led Guinea del. to All-African People's Conf. 60; del. to UN 60, 61; mem. Political Bureau Parti Démocratique de Guinée.
Ministère des Finances, Conakry, Guinea.

Touré, Mamoudou, L. EN D., PH.D.; Mauritanian diplomatist and administrator; b. 1928; ed. Univs. of Dakar and Paris and Ecole Nationale de la France d'Outre-Mer.
Served in Admin. of French Overseas Territories, Paris 57-58; Counsellor and Head of Service de Pays et Territoires d'Outre-Mer associés, Secr. of EEC Council of Ministers, Brussels 58-61; Amb. to France, U.K., Fed. Germany, Belgium, Spain and EEC 61-62; Sec.-Gen. Comm. for Technical Co-operation in Africa, Lagos 62-63; Consultant for co-ordination of bi-lateral programmes, UNICEF 63-65; Dir. UN African Inst. for Econ. Devt. and Planning, Dakar 65-66; Amb. to Fed. Germany, Belgium, Luxembourg and Netherlands 66-70; Minister of Planning 70-71; Dir. African Dept. IMF 71-.
International Monetary Fund, 19th and H Streets, N.W., Washington, D.C. 20431, U.S.A.

Touré, Sekou; Guinean trade unionist and politician; b. 9 Jan. 1922; ed. Ecole Coranique, French Guinea Primary Schools, Ecole Professionnelle Georges Poiret, Conakry.
Entered Post and Telecommunications Service, French Guinea 41; Sec.-Gen. Syndicat du Personnel des P.T.T., mem. Comm. Consultative Fédérale du Travail, mem. Guinea Comm. Consultative Territoriale, Comms. Mixtes Paritaires et Administratives 45; Comptable, Trésoreries (Cadre Supérieur), Sec.-Gen. Syndicat des Employés du Trésor 46: founder-mem. Rassemblement Démocratique Africain (RDA) 46; Sec.-Gen. Union Territoriale, Confédération Générale du Travail (CGT) 48; Sec.-Gen. CGT Co-ordination Cttee., French West Africa and Togoland 50; Sec.-Gen. Guinea Democratic Party 52-; Territorial Counsellor 53; Pres. Confédération Générale des Travailleurs d'Afrique Noire (CGTA) 56, Mayor of Conakry, Deputy from Guinea to French Nat. Assembly 56; mem. Comité Directeur Fédéral, Union Générale des Travailleurs de l'Afrique Noire (UGTAN) Jan. 57-; Territorial Counsellor, Conakry, Grand Counsellor, French West Africa, Vice-Président du Conseil, Govt. of Guinea May 57; Vice-Prés. RDA Oct. 57; Président du Gouvernement (Head of State), Republic of Guinea (upon declaration of independence following referendum) Oct. 58- (re-elected 61, 63, 68); Lenin Peace Prize 60.
Présidence de la République, Conakry, Guinea.

Towett, Taita Arap; Kenyan politician; ed. Govt. African School, Kabianga, Alliance High School, Makerere Coll., Uganda and Univ. of South Africa.

Worked for African District Council of Kericho; attended course in public and social admin., South Devon Technical Coll., Torquay, England 55; mem. for Kipsigis, Legislative Council 61-; Minister of Labour and Housing April 61-62; Minister of Lands, Survey and Town Planning 62-Dec. 69; Minister of Educ. Dec. 69-.
Ministry of Education, Nairobi, Kenya.

Townsend, Edison Reginald; Liberian journalist; b. 23 July 1920, Schieffelin, Marshall Territory; ed. Lott Carey Mission School, Brewerville, Liberia Coll. High School, Univ. of Washington, and Michigan State Coll
Worked as journalist; Press Sec. to Pres. Tubman 54; Chief of Bureau of Information, later Liberian Information Service, later Dept of Information and Cultural Affairs; mem. Liberian cabinet; Minister of State for Presidential Affairs Jan. 72-.
Office of the President, Monrovia, Liberia.

Tra, Vanie Bi, L. en D.; Ivory Coast politician; b. 1936, Vouéboufla, Zuéneula; ed. Dakar, Senegal, Montpellier, France and Univ. of Paris.
Public prosecutor, Daloa 64-65, Bouaké 65-66, Abidjan 66-67, 67-; Minister of Labour and Social Affairs Jan. 70-.
Ministry of Labour and Social Affairs, Abidjan, Ivory Coast.

Traore, Col. Moussa; Mali army officer and politician; b. 25 Sept. 1936, Kayes; ed. Training Coll., Fréjus, Cadets Coll., Kati.
Became N.C.O. in French Army; returned to Mali 60; promoted Lieut. 64, Col. 71; at Armed Forces Coll., Kati until 68; leader, Military Cttee. for Nat. Liberation, Commdr. in Chief of the Armed Forces; Pres. of Mali 68-; Pres. Conf. of Heads of State, UDEAO 70.
Office of the President, Bamako, Mali.

Traore, Seydou; Mali diplomatist; b. 3 Feb. 1927, Sofara; ed. Ecole Nationale de France d'Outre-Mer and Orientation à la Fonction Internationale, Paris.
Technical Adviser, Ministry of Commerce 60; Dir. of Econ. Affairs 61; Technical Adviser, Ministry of Foreign Affairs 62, Chief Legal Div. 63, Head Econ. Div. 64; Dir. of Cabinet of Minister for Co-operation and Technical Assistance 64; Amb. to Belgium, Sweden, Fed. Germany and EEC 68-69; Amb. to U.S.A. Oct. 69-, Perm. Rep. to UN June 70-; del. to UN Gen. Assembly 62, 63, ECOSOC meetings 62, UNCTAD meetings 64, 68 and sessions of the Council of Ministers of OAU.
Permanent Mission of Mali at the United Nations, 111 East 69th Street, New York, N.Y. 210021, U.S.A.

Tredgold, Rt. Hon. Sir Robert Clarkson, P.C., K.C.M.G., Q.C.; Rhodesian lawyer and politician; b. 1899; ed. Hertford Coll., Oxford.
Served First World War; called to Bar, Inner Temple 23; practised Southern and Northern Rhodesia; M.P. for Insiza District 34-43; Minister of Justice and Defence S. Rhodesia, 35-43; Minister of Native Affairs 41-43; High Court Judge 43-50; Chief Justice 50-55; Chief Justice Fed. of Rhodesia and Nyasaland 55-60; mem. Commonwealth Judicial Cttee. Privy Council.
Publ. *The Rhodesia that was My Life* 68.
Tynwald South, Salisbury, Rhodesia.

Treurnicht, Andries Petrus, M.A., PH.D.; South African politician; b. 1921, Piketberg; ed. Piketberg High School, Stellenbosch and Cape Town Univs., Stellenbosch Theological Seminary.
Minister, Dutch Reformed Church 46-60; Editor *Die Kerkbode* 60-67, *Hoofstad* 67-71; mem. Parl. for Waterberg 71-.
Publs. several publications on religious topics.
383 Bergkaree Avenue, Lynnwood, Pretoria, South Africa.

Tseghe, Yohannes, M.SC.; Ethiopian politician; b. 20 Dec. 1928, Gore; ed. Seattle Pacific Coll., Seattle, Wash., and Univ. of Washington, Seattle.

Adviser, Ministry of Public Health 54-58; Dir.-Gen. for Basic Health Services 58-61; subsequently Asst. Minister for Basic Health Services, Vice-Minister for Public Health 61-66; Chair. Advisory Board of Health 56-62; Minister of State for Public Health 66-70; has led dels. to various int. confs., including World Health Assembly and other WHO confs.; Vice-Chair. Exec. Board, UNICEF 66, Chair. Admin. Budget 67-68; Perm. Rep. to UN 70-72.
c/o Ministry of Foreign Affairs, Addis Ababa, Ethiopia.

Tshibangu, Muyembe Kanza; Zaire politician.
Minister of Posts and Telecommunications Oct. 67-March 69; Minister of Energy March 69, fmr. Minister of Justice; Minister of Power until Oct. 72.
c/o Ministry of Power, Kinshasa, Zaire.

Tsiebo, Calvin; Malagasy politician; b. 12 July 1902, Andoharana, Beraketa, Tuléar; ed. Mission schools.
Lieutenant-Governor Native Admin. 25-37, Local Admin. 37-49, Gov. 49-56; Admin. Sec. Madagascar 56-57; Provincial Counsellor Tuléar 57-58; Deputy Provincial Govt. 58-60; Pres. Nat. Assembly 60; mem. Exec. Bureau Social Democratic Party; Vice-Pres. Madagascar 60-65, 65-, concurrently Minister of Social Affairs, Admin. Co-ordination and Labour; in charge of Equipment, Justice, Information, Tourism and Traditional Arts; Vice-Pres. and also in charge of Agriculture, Rural Devt., Mines, Industry, Trade, Food Supply, Labour and Justice 71-72; Grand Officier Légion d'Honneur and numerous other honours.
c/o Office of the Vice-President, Tananarive, Madagascar.

Tsiranana, Philibert; Malagasy politician; b. 1910; ed. Univ. of Montpellier.
Teaching until 55; mem. Majunga Provincial Assembly, Pres. 56; mem. fmr. Malagasy Rep. Assembly 52-58; Deputy from Madagascar to French Nat. Assembly 56-59; Prime Minister, Malagasy Repub. 58-April 59, Pres. of the Cabinet May 59-72; Pres. (Head of State) 60-Oct. 72; in charge of Rural Animation, Co-operation, Civil Service and the Advancement of Women and Children Oct. 70.
c/o Présidence de la République, Tananarive, Madagascar.

Tutuola, Amos; Nigerian writer; b. 1920, Abeokuta, W. Nigeria; ed. Mission Schools.
Worked on father's farm; trained as coppersmith; served with R.A.F. Second World War; Nigerian Broadcasting Corpn., Ibadan 45-.
Publs. *The Palm-Wine Drinkard* 52, *My Life in the Bush of Ghosts* 54, *Simbi and the Satyr of the Dark Jungle* 55, *The Brave African Huntress* 58, *The Feather Woman of the Jungle* 62, *Ajaiyi and His Inherited Poverty* 67.
c/o Nigerian Broadcasting Corporation, Broadcasting House, Ibadan, Nigeria.
Telephone: 22661/26.

U

Usher Assouan, Arsene, B.A.; Ivory Coast lawyer and politician; b. 1930; ed. Bordeaux and Poitiers Univs.
Lawyer, Court of Appeals, Poitiers 55-56; Cabinet attaché of M. Houphouet-Boigny 56; Asst. Dir. Caisse des Allocations Familiales 57-59; Conseiller Général 57-59; Deputy Vice-Pres. Nat. Assembly 59-60; Lawyer, Court of Appeals Abidjan 59; Head, Ivory Coast Perm. Mission to UN 61-67; Minister of Foreign Affairs 67-; mem. UN Security Council 64-67.
Ministry of Foreign Affairs, Abidjan; and Cocody-Abidjan, Ivory Coast, West Africa.

Usman, Brig. Musa; Nigerian air force officer; b. 1940, Enugu; ed. Ibadan Goodbye School, Kaduna St. Michael School, Zaria Military Training School, Ghana Accra Regular Officers' Special Training School, Officer Cadet

School, Aldershot, England, Royal Mil. Acad. Sandhurst, and Army Infantry School, Georgia, U.S.A.
Served in Congo in UN Peace Keeping Force; later C.O. of Nigerian Air Force, Kaduna; Mil. Gov. of N.E. State of Nigeria 67-; Acting Brig.-Gen. Oct. 72.
Office of the Governor of N.E. State, Maiduguri, Nigeria.

Uys, Dirk Cornelis Hermanus; South African farmer and politician; b. 15 May 1909; ed. Bredasdorp High School and Stellenbosch Univ.
Farmer 31-; fmr. Dir. several Agricultural Co-operatives; fmr. mem. Wheat Industries Control Board; M.P. 48-; Minister of Agricultural Econ. and Marketing 58-66, of Agricultural Credit and Land Tenure 66-68, of Agriculture 68-72.
c/o Ministry of Agriculture, Pretoria, South Africa.

Uys, Johann Kunz, B.COMM.; South African diplomatist; b. 14 June 1907, Swellendam; ed. Stellenbosch Univ.
Entered Dept. of External Affairs 28; served Washington 33-37; Dept. of External Affairs 37-38, The Hague 38-40, Netherlands Govt., London 40-41; Sec. Industrial and Agricultural Requirements Comm., South Africa 41-43; Consul Elisabethville, Belgian Congo 43-46, during which time also served as Acting Consul-Gen. Léopoldville and Acting Commr. Nairobi; First Sec., The Hague 46-49; Counsellor, Dept. of External Affairs, Head of Econ. Int. Trade and Gen. Sections, Dept. of External Affairs 49-54; High Commr. in Australia 54-57; Amb. to German Fed. Repub. 57-60; Deputy Sec. for Foreign Affairs 60-65; Amb. to German Fed. Repub. 65-68, to Australia 69-71.
c/o Ministry of Foreign Affairs, Pretoria, South Africa.

V

van der Merwe, Schalk Willem, M.B., CH.B.; South African medical practitioner and politician; b. 18 Sept. 1922, Citrusdal, Cape Prov.; ed. Paarl Hoer Jongenskool, Univs. of Cape Town and South Africa.
Practised as Gen. Practitioner, District Surgeon at Keimoes, Cape Prov. 47-66; mem, Parl. 66-; Deputy Minister of the Interior, Social Welfare and Pensions and Coloured Affairs 70-72; Minister of Health, Coloured Relations and Rehoboth Affairs Aug. 72-.
Ministry of Health, Private Bag X399, Pretoria, South Africa.

van der Spuy, Johannes Petrus; South African politician; b. 24 Nov. 1912, Reitz, O.F.S.; ed. Univ. of Stellenbosch and Univ. Coll. of Orange Free State.
Teacher, Dewetsdorp 35, Boshof 35-43; Lecturer in Afrikaans, Pretoria Tech. Coll. 43-45; cultural org. work, Asscn. of Afrikaans Cultural Socs. (F.A.K.) 46-61; M.P. for Westdene 61-66, Johannesburg West 66-67; Senator 69-; Amb. to Austria 67-69; Minister of Nat. Educ. 69-; Nat. Party.
Ministry of National Education, Pretoria, South Africa.

Van der Wath, Johannes Gert Hendrik; South African administrator; b. 4 Nov. 1903, Ladybrand, O.F.S.; ed. Ficksburg Secondary School, Glen Coll., Normal Coll., Bloemfontein, and Univ. of Halle, Germany.
Farmer (Karakul Stud); M.P. for Windhoek, concurrently mem. Fed. Board of Nat. Party and leader of Nat. Party in S.W. Africa until 68; Deputy Minister for S.W. African Affairs 61-68; Administrator of S.W. Africa 68-.
South West Africa House, P.O. Box 2114, Windhoek, South West Africa.

Vasey, Sir Ernest Albert, K.B.E., C.M.G.; Kenyan financial consultant; b. 27 Aug. 1901;
Nairobi Town Council 39-50; mem. Kenya Legislative Council 45, mem for Health and Local Govt 50-51, for Educ. Health and Local Govt. 51-52; Minister for Finance

and Devt. 52-59; Minister for Finance, Tanganyika 60-62, Financial and Econ. Adviser, World Bank Devt. Service 62-66, Resident Rep., IBRD in Pakistan 62-66; 2nd Class Brilliant Star of Zanzibar, Hilal-i-Azam of Pakistan 66.
Publs. *Report on African Housing* 50, *Economic and Political Trends in Kenya* 56.
P.O. Box 14235, Nairobi, Kenya.

Viljoen, Hon. Marais; South African politician; b. 2 Dec. 1915, Robertson; ed. Jan Van Riebeeck Secondary School, Cape Town, and Univ. of Cape Town.
Manager, *Die Transvaler Boekhandel* 40-43; Organizer, Nat. Party 43-51, Information Officer 51-53; mem. Transvaal Provincial Council for Pretoria 49-53; mem. Parl. for Alberton, Transvaal 53-; Deputy Minister of Labour and of Mines 58-62; Deputy Minister of Interior, Educ., Arts and Science, of Labour and of Immigration 62-66; Minister of Labour and of Coloured Affairs 66-69; Minister of Labour, of Coloured Affairs and of Rehoboth Affairs June 69-May 70; Minister of Labour and the Interior May-Dec. 70, of Labour, Posts and Telegraphs Dec. 70-.
Office: Private Bag X117, Pretoria; Home: Bryntirion 20, Pretoria, South Africa.

Vincent, Olatunde Olabode; Nigerian banker; b. 16 May 1925, Lagos; ed. C.M.S. Grammar School, Lagos, Chartered Inst. of Secs., London, Univ. of Manchester, and Admin. Staff Coll., Henley, England.
Nigerian Army 42-46; Financial Sec.'s Office 47-65; Fed. Ministry of Finance 56-61; Asst. Gen. Man. Central Bank of Nigeria 61-62, Deputy Gen. Man. 62, Gen. Man. 63-66; Vice-Pres. African Devt. Bank 64-; Lecturer in Econs., Extra-Mural Dept., Univ. Coll. of Ibadan 57-60; mem. Lagos Exec. Devt. Board 60-61; mem. Cttee. which set up Nigerian Industrial Devt. Bank; Dir. Nigerian Industrial Devt. Bank 64-66; mem. Cttee. of Nine which set up African Devt. Bank; mem. Soc. for Int. Devt.; Econ. Adviser, African Church (Inc.), Lagos.
African Development Bank, B.P. 1387, Abidjan, Ivory Coast.

von Hirschberg, C. F. G.; South African diplomatist; b. 13 Jan. 1926; ed. Univ. of Cape Town.
Entered foreign service 48; served in London 52-57, Vienna 57-62; served in Dept. of Foreign Affairs, Pretoria 62-67; Head UN and Int. Orgs. Div. 66-70; mem. S. African del. to gen. confs. of IAEA 57-61, alt. Gov. 57-62; del. to UN Gen. Assembly 67; Perm. Rep. to UN Oct. 70-.
Permanent Mission of South Africa at the United Nations, 300 East 42nd Street, 17th Floor, New York, N.Y. 10017, U.S.A.

Vorster, Balthazar Johannes, B.A., LL.B.; South African lawyer and politician; b. 13 Dec. 1915, Jamestown, Cape Province; ed. Sterkstroom High School and Stellenbosch Univ.
Member Parl. for Nigel 53; Deputy Minister of Educ. Arts, Science, Social Welfare and Pensions 58-61; Minister of Justice Aug. 61-66; Minister of Justice, Police and Prisons 66; Prime Minister 66-; Leader Nat. Party 66-; Chancellor Univ. of Stellenbosch 68-.
Union Buildings, Pretoria; Groote Schuur, Cape Town; Libertas, Bryntirion, Pretoria, Republic of South Africa.
Telephone: 699-121; 743151.

W

Wallot, Jean-Marie; Central African Republic politician.
Former Sec. of State to the Presidency in charge of Internal and External Trade; Minister of Commerce Feb. 70-Aug. 70; Minister of Public Works and the Civil Service Aug. 70-Jan. 71; Sec. of State to the Presidency Jan. 71-.
c/o The Presidency, Bangui, Central African Republic.

Waring, Frank Walter, B.A., B.COM.; South African politition; b. 7 Nov. 1908, Kenilworth, Cape Prov.; ed. S. African Coll. School and Cape Town Univ.
Grain Broker; M.P. for Orange Grove, Johannesburg 49-72; has held portfolios of Information, Tourism, Forestry, Sport and Recreation, Indian Affairs at various times 61-72; retd.; Nat. Party.
Box 2090, Johannesburg, South Africa.

Weeks, James Milton; Liberian politician; b. 15 Nov. 1921, Croizerville; ed. Liberia Coll., and London School of Economics.
Former teacher and bank clerk; senior exec. Bank of Liberia 56; assigned to Treasury, Nat. Production Council and Budget Bureau; Dir. Bureau of Econ. Research and Statistics Oct. 59-65; Dir. Nat. Planning Agency May 62-65; Acting Sec. to Treasury 65-Aug. 66; First Sec. of Planning and Econ. Affairs Aug. 66; Sec. of the Treasury (Minister of Finance) Feb. 67-Jan. 72.
c/o Office of the Secretary of the Treasury, Monrovia, Liberia.

Weeks, Rocheforte L., LL.M.; Liberian lawyer and politician; b. 15 Aug. 1923, Crozierville; ed. Liberia Coll. (now Univ. of Liberia), and Howard and Cornell Univs., U.S.A.
Admitted to Montserrado County Bar Asscn. 55; Counsellor at Law, Supreme Court of Liberia 56; Instructor, Univ. of Liberia Law School 55-59; Pres. Univ. of Liberia 60-72; Sec. of State (for Foreign Affairs) Jan. 72-; Sec. Liberian Del. to UN Gen. Assembly 54-55; Special Consultant to UNESCO for conf. on Devt. of Higher Educ. in Africa; Pres. Int. Asscn. of Univ. Presidents 71; fmr. del. to various int. confs. and mem. numerous nat. and int. orgs.; decorations include Grand Commdr., Order of Star of Africa and Order of Merit of Fed. Repub. of Germany; Hon. doctorate (Univ. of Liberia) 59.
Ministry of Foreign Affairs, Monrovia, Liberia.

Welensky, Rt. Hon. Sir Roy (Roland), K.C.M.G.; Rhodesian politician; b. 20 Jan. 1907, Salisbury; ed. Primary School, Salisbury.
Worked for Rhodesia Railways (beginning as fireman and engine driver) 24-53; M.L.C. Northern Rhodesia 38-53; mem. Exec. Council 40-53; Dir. of Manpower 41-46; Leader of the Unofficial Mems. 46-53; Deputy Prime Minister Fed. Govt. of Rhodesia and Nyasaland 53-56, Minister of Transport 53-56, of Posts 53-56; Prime Minister and Minister of External Affairs 56-63, of Defence 56-59; Pres. United Fed. Party 56-63; Leader New Rhodesia Party Aug.-Dec. 64.
Publ. *Welensky's 4,000 Days* 64.
82 Queen Elizabeth Road, Greendale, P.O. Box 804, Salisbury, Rhodesia.
Telephone: 23338.

Wetmore, Robert Bernard Norton, M.B.E.; Rhodesian (retired) civil servant and diplomatist; b. 31 Aug. 1911, Beira, Mozambique; ed. Prince Edward School, Salisbury.
Government Service (Treasury) 29-37; Man. Southern Rhodesia Publicity Office, Johannesburg 37-42, Supply Office 42-46; Asst. Food Controller, Salisbury 47-50; Sec. at High Comm., Pretoria 51-55; Consul-Gen. in Mozambique 55-57; Counsellor for Rhodesia and Nyasaland Affairs, British Embassy, U.S.A. 57-62; Under-Sec. External Affairs, Salisbury 62-64; accredited Diplomatic Rep. for Rhodesia in South Africa 64-65; Sec. for External Affairs 65-67.
2 Wetmore Close, Highlands, Rhodesia.
Telephone: 42656 (Home).

Wey, Vice-Admiral Joseph Edet Akinwale, O.F.R., Nigerian naval officer and marine engineer; b. 7 March 1918, Calabar; ed. Holy Cross School, Lagos, Methodist School, Ikot Ekpene and St. Patrick's Coll., Calabar.

Engineer Cadet-in-Training, Nigerian Marine 39; Marine Engineer Second Class 50-56; Sub-Lieut. Engineer, Nigerian Navy 56-59; First class Marine Engineer 59-; Lieut. 58, Lieut.-Commdr. 60; transferred to Exec. Branch and promoted Commdr. 62; Commanding Officer of Base and Naval Officer in Charge, Apapa 62-63; Capt. and Chief of Naval Staff 63; served in India 64; Commodore and in command, Nigerian Navy March 64-; Rear-Admiral 67-71; mem. Supreme Mil. Council and Fed. Exec. Council; Commr. for Establishments and Service Matters; also Acting Commr. for Labour 71-; Vice-Admiral 71-.
Nigerian Naval Headquarters, Ministry of Defence, Lagos, Nigeria.

Williams, Sir (Arthur) Leonard, G.C.M.G.; British politician and Governor-General; b. 22 Jan. 1904; ed. Holy Trinity Church of England Elementary School, Birkenhead, and Labour Coll. London.
Member, Liverpool and N. Wales District Council, Nat. Union of Railwaymen 20-21, Sec. Birkenhead and District Joint Cttee. 23-24; Tutor, Liverpool Labour Coll. 24-26; Tutor-Organizer, Nat. Council of Labour Colls. 26-36; Labour Parl. Candidate, Southport 29, Winchester 35; Sec. Leeds Labour Party 36-42; Regional Organizer, E. and W. Ridings of Yorkshire 42-46, Asst. Nat. Agent 46-51, Nat. Agent 51-59, Nat. Agent and Deputy Gen. Sec. 59-62, Gen. Sec. 62-68; Gov.-Gen. Mauritius 68-72; Editor *Leeds Weekly Citizen* 37-44, *Labour Organiser* 52-62. [*Died, 27 December 1972*].

Wina, Sikota; Zambian politician; b. 1931; ed. Fort Hare Univ., South Africa.
Worked in Information Dept., N. Rhodesia Govt.; Editor, Copper Belt newspaper; Publicity Dir. United Nat. Independence Party (U.N.I.P.); fmr. Parl. sec. for Local Govt.; Minister of Health; Minister of Local Govt. and Housing; Acting Minister of Foreign Affairs until Dec. 68; Minister of Information, Broadcasting and Tourism Dec. 68-; Govt. Chief Whip; Chair. Zambia Publishing Co. March 69-.
Ministry of Information, Broadcasting and Tourism, Lusaka, Zambia.

Wrathall, John James; Rhodesian chartered accountant and politician; b. 28 Aug. 1913, Lancaster, England; ed. Lancaster Royal Grammar School, England.
Worked in Income Tax Dept., Southern Rhodesia 36-56; Sec. of public co. 47-49; private practice, Bulawayo 50-63; mem. Parl. 63-, Deputy Speaker Jan.-Oct. 63; Minister of Health and Educ. 63-64, of Finance and Posts 64-; Deputy Prime Minister 66-; Independence Decoration.
Ministry of Finance, Salisbury; Home: Northward, 4 Chancellor Avenue, Salisbury, Rhodesia.

Y

Yacé, Philippe; Ivory Coast politician; b. 23 Jan. 1920; ed. William-Ponty School, Dakar.
French Army 40-45; mem. Democratic Party of Ivory Coast (P.D.C.I.) 46-, Sec.-Gen. 59-; mem. Territorial Assembly, Ivory Coast 52-58; Deputy to Ivory Coast Constituent Assembly 58-59; Senator of the French Community 59-61; Pres. Nat. Assembly, Ivory Coast 60-; Pres., High Court of Justice 63-; Pres. Parl. Conf. of EEC and African States 69-; Grand Officier, Légion d'Honneur, Grand Officier, Ordre National de la République de la Côte d'Ivoire.
Assemblée Nationale, Boulevard de la République, Abidjan, Ivory Coast.

Yaguibou, Télesphore; Upper Voltan diplomatist; b. 18 Oct. 1933, Po; ed. Faculties of Law and Econs., Dakar and Paris and Inst. des Hautes Etudes d'Outre-Mer, Paris.

Judge, Court of First Instance, Bobo-Dioulasso 66-67; Sec.-Gen., Govt. of Upper Volta and Council of Ministers 67-71; responsible for relations between Govt. and Parl. 71-72; Perm. Rep. to UN Sept. 72-; fmr. del. to confs. of OAU and OCAM.
Permanent Mission of Upper Volta to United Nations, 866 Second Avenue, 6th Floor, New York, N.Y. 10017, U.S.A.

Yaméogo, Antoine W.; Upper Voltan financial official; b. 17 Jan. 1928, Kondougou; ed. Univ. de Bordeaux, Ecole Nationale des Impôts, Paris, and Univ. de Paris.
Inspector of publicly controlled financial bodies, France, Senegal, Mauritania and Upper Volta 55-59; Dir. of Treasury, later Commr. for Upper Volta Devt. Plan 59-61; Minister of Nat. Economy, Upper Volta 61-62; Economist with Int. Monetary Fund (IMF) 63-64, Alternate Exec. Dir. 64-66, Exec. Dir. 66-.
International Monetary Fund, Washington, D.C. 20431; 1614 Tuckerman Street, N.W., Washington, D.C., U.S.A. Telephone: DUI-2866 (Office); 882-6401 (Home).

Yaméogo, Maurice; Upper Voltan politician; b. 31 Dec. 1921; ed. High School.
Member of Grand Council French W. Africa 47, Minister of Agriculture 55, of Interior 56, Premier 58-60; Pres. Council of Ministers 60-66, Minister of Defence 65-66; Pres. of the Repub. 60-66; mem. Rassemblement Démocratique Africain (RDA); on trial for embezzlement April 69; sentenced to 5 years hard labour May 69, sentence reduced to 2 years Aug. 69, released Aug. 70.
Ouagadougou, Upper Volta, West Africa.

Yassein, Mohamed Osman, B.SC.; Sudanese international civil servant; b. Nov. 1915, Berber; ed. Khartoum School of Administration and London School of Economics.
Joined Sudanese Political Service 45; Liaison Officer in Ethiopia 51-52; Gov. Upper Nile Province 53-55; Perm. Under-Sec. of Foreign Affairs 56-65; mem. Sudanese Del. to UN 56; Del. to Ind. African States Conf., Monrovia 59, to Accra Conf. on Positive Action for Peace and Security in Africa 60, to Independent African States Conf., Léopoldville 60, to Arab League 62; Special Adviser to UN on training of diplomatists 61-62; Special Envoy to Ethiopia and Somalia on border dispute 63; mem. African Unity Org. Comm. for Conciliation and Arbitration between Algeria and Morocco 63-64; organized first African Ministers of Finance Conf., Khartoum 63; mem. and Adviser, Round Table Conf. on Southern Sudan 65; mem. Int. Political Science Conf. 65; Hon. mem. Int. Inst. of Differing Civilization 66; UN Consultant with ECA 66; UN Special Adviser to Govt. of Zambia on Civil Service Structure 66-67, of Southern Yemen on Public Admin. 68-69, of Yemen Arab Repub. on Public Admin. 69; Resident Rep. UN Devt. Programme, Amman, Jordan 69-; Kt. Great Band of Humane Order of African Redemption, Liberia, Grand Officer, Order of Menelik II, Republican Order, Egypt, Star of Yugoslavia.
Publs. *The Sudan Civil Service* 54, *Analysis of the Economic Situation in the Sudan* 58, *Problems of Transfer of Power— The Administration Aspect* 62, *Germany and Africa* 62, *Melut Scheme—an experiment in social development in developing countries* (article) 65, *The Poet's Ballet* (in Arabic) 66, *The Social, Economic and Political Role of Urban Agglomerations in Developing Countries* (article) 67, *The Reform of the Machinery of Government in the Sudan* (in Arabic) 71, *The Diplomat in Developing Countries* 71.
United Nations Development Programme in Jordan, P.O. Box 565, Amman, Jordan; Home: P.O. Box 2201, Khartoum, Sudan.

Yifru, H.E. Ato Ketema; Ethiopian government official; b. 11 Dec. 1929; ed. Haile Sellassie Secondary School, Addis Ababa and Boston Univ., U.S.A.
Italian Dept., Ministry of Foreign Affairs 52-53; Dir.-Gen.

American and Asian Sections, Ministry of Foreign Affairs 53-56, Asst. Minister and Head of Dept. of Asian and American Affairs 56-58; Ministry of The Pen 58-61, Vice-Minister 60-61; Minister of State for Foreign Affairs 61-66; Minister of Foreign Affairs April 66-71; Minister of Commerce, Industry and Tourism 71-; Grand Officer of Order of Menelik II and other decorations.
Ministry of Commerce, Addis Ababa, Ethiopia.

Z

Zakara, Mouddour; Niger politician; b. 1916, Diguina, Filingué Region; ed. Niamey Coll.
Head of Imanan Canton; Territorial Adviser, Tahona Département 57-58; Sec. of State for the Interior 58-63, in charge of Saharan Affairs 58; Minister of Posts, Telephones and Telecommunications 63-70, of Finance Jan. 70-.
Ministry of Finance, Niamey, Niger.

Zhiri, Kacem; Moroccan diplomatist; b. 25 March 1920; ed. Inst. of Higher Studies, Rabat.
Detained for activities in independence movement of Morocco 36, 44, exiled and detained 52; fmr. Man. daily newspapers *Al-Maghrib* and *Al Alam*; Gen. Dir. Broadcasting Station of Morocco 56-59; Amb. to Senegal 60-61, to Yugoslavia 62-64, to Algeria 64-65; Dir. of Information, Ministry of Foreign Affairs 66; Perm. Del. of League of Arab States to UN, Geneva 66-68; Minister of Secondary and Technical Educ. 68-69; Amb. to Mauritania 70-72, to People's Repub. of China 72-; Founder, Free School in Al-Jadida; Moroccan and Yugoslav decorations.
Publs. *Biography of Mohammed V* 56, *The Gold of Sous* (novel) 55, Political commentaries 56-58, Social and historical studies.
Kilomètre 3, 3,300 Route des Zaers, Rabat, Morocco.

Zinsou, Emile Derlin; Dahomeyan doctor and politician; b. 23 March 1918; ed. Ecole Primaire Supérieure, Ecole Africaine de Médecine, Dakar and Univ. de Paris à la Sorbonne.
Represented Dahomey in French Nat. Assembly; fmr. Vice-Pres. Assemblée de l'Union française, Senator, Territorial Council; fmr. Minister of Economy and of The Plan; fmr. Amb. to France; Pres. Supreme Court of Dahomey; Minister of Foreign Affairs 61-63, 65-67; Pres of Dahomey 68-69; numerous decorations include Commdr. Ordre Nat., Dahomey, Grand Officier Légion d'Honneur.
Paris, France.

Zoa, Mgr. Jean, DR.THEOL.; Cameroonian ecclesiastic; b. 1924, Saa; ed. Parish School, Efok, Petit Séminaire d'Akono, Grand Séminaire de Mvolyé, Coll. de Propaganda Fide, Rome.
Ordained priest 50; Vicar, Ombessa (Bafia) 53-57; Parish priest, Sacred-Heart Paris (Yaoundé) 57-58; Dir. of Operations, Archdiocese of Yaoundé 58-61; Archbishop of

Yaoundé 61-; founder Nova et Vetera Coll.; Adviser, Council for the Laity; 2nd Vice-Pres., Symposium of Episcopal Confs. of Africa and Madagascar; mem. Perm. Secr. of Synod, of Council, 24 pour la Congrégation pour l'Evangélisation des Peuples; Officier, Légion d'Honneur, Commdr., Ordre de la Valeur (Cameroon).
Archevêché, B.P. 207, Yaoundé, Cameroon.

Zoungrana, H.E. Cardinal Paul; Upper Voltan ecclesiastic; b. 3 Sept. 1917; ed. l'Institut Catholique de Paris, and Université Pontificale Gregorienne.
Ordained priest 42; mem. Missionary Soc. of the White Fathers; Archibishop of Ouagadougou 60-; created Cardinal 65; Pres. Symposium of Episcopal Confs. of Africa and Madagascar (SECAM).
Archbishop's House, B.P. 90, Ouagadougou, Upper Volta.
Telephone: 27-92.

Zulu, Rt. Rev. Alphaeus Hamilton, B.A., L.TH.; South African ecclesiastic; b. 29 June 1905, Nqutu; ed. St. Chad's Training Coll., Ladysmith, Fort Hare Univ. and St. Peter's Theological School.
Principal, Umlazi Mission School 24-35; Asst. (Anglican) Priest, St. Faith's Church, Durban 40-52, Rector 53-60; Bishop Suffragan, Diocese of St. John's Transkei 60-Sept. 66; Bishop of Zululand Oct. 66-; Pres. World Council of Churches 68-.
Box 147, Eschowe, South Africa; Home: Bishop's House, Gezinsila, Eschowe, South Africa.
Telephone: Eschowe 147 (Office); Eschowe 673 (Home).

Zulu, Alexander Grey; Zambian politician; b. 3 Feb. 1924, Chipata, Eastern Province; ed. Mafuta Lower Primary School and Munali Secondary School.
Water Devt. Asst., Northern Rhodesia 50-53; Bookkeeper/Man., Kabwe Co-operative and Marketing Union 53-62; Parl. Sec., Northern Rhodesia 63; Minister of Commerce and Industry 64; Minister of Transport and Works 64; Minister of Mines and Co-operatives 65-67; Minister of Home Affairs Aug. 67-Jan. 70; Minister of Defence Jan. 70-.
Ministry of Defence, The Secretariat, Independence Avenue, P.O. Box RW17, Ridgeway, Lusaka, Zambia.

Zwane, Ambrose Phesheya, M.B., B.CH.; Swazi medical practitioner and politician; b. 30 April 1924, Manzini, Swaziland; ed. St. Joseph's Catholic Mission, Manzini, Inkamana R.C.S., Vryheid, Natal, S. African Native Coll., Fort Hare, and Univ. of Witwatersrand.
As a child, looked after cattle at Bulunga, Manzini, Swaziland; House physician, Charles Johnson Memorial Hospital 52; Medical Officer, Anglican Mission Hospital 53-59; Medical Officer, Swaziland Colonial Admin. 59-60; Gen. Sec. Swaziland Progressive Party (S.P.P.) 60-61, split with S.P.P. 61; Pres. Ngwane Nat. Liberatory Congress 62-; publishes two newspapers *Kusile Ngwane* (monthly) and *Ngwane Forum* (monthly).
Ngwane National Liberatory Congress, P.O. Box 326, Mbabane, Swaziland.

Calendars, Time Reckoning, and Weights and Measures

THE MUSLIM CALENDAR

The Muslim era dates from July 16th, A.D. 622, which was the beginning of the Arab year in which the *Hijra*, Muhammad's flight from Mecca to Medina, took place. The Muslim or Hijra Calendar is lunar, each year having 354 or 355 days, the extra day being intercalated eleven times every thirty years. Accordingly the beginning of the Hijra year occurs earlier in the Gregorian Calendar by a few days each year. The Muslim year 1394 A.H. begins on January 24th, 1974.

The year is divided into the following months:

1. Muharram	30 days		7. Rajab	30 days	
2. Saphar	29 ,,		8. Shaaban	29 ,,	
3. Rabia I	30 ,,		9. Ramadan	30 ,,	
4. Rabia II	29 ,,		10. Shawwal	29 ,,	
5. Jamada I	30 ,,		11. Dulkaada	30 ,,	
6. Jamada II	29 ,,		12. Dulheggia	29 or 30 days	

The Hijra Calendar is used for religious purposes throughout the Islamic world.

PRINCIPAL MUSLIM FESTIVALS

New Year: 1st Muharram. The first ten days of the year are regarded as holy, especially the tenth.

Ashoura: 10th Muharram. Celebrates the first meeting of Adam and Eve after leaving Paradise, also the ending of the Flood and the death of Hussain, grandson of Muhammad. The feast is celebrated with fairs and processions.

Mouloud (*Birth of Muhammad*): 12th Rabia I.

Leilat al Meiraj (*Ascension of Muhammad*): 27th Rajab.

Ramadan (*Month of Fasting*): Begins 1st Muharram.

Id ul Fitr or **Id ul Saghir** or **Küçük Bayram** (*The Small Feast*): Three days beginning 1st Shawwal. This celebration follows the constraint of the Ramadan fast.

Id ul Adha or **Id al Kabir** or **Büyük Bayram** (*The Great Feast, Feast of the Sacrifice*): Four days beginning on 10th Dulheggia. The principal Muslim festival, commemorating Abraham's sacrifice and coinciding with the pilgrimage to Mecca. Celebrated by the sacrifice of a sheep, by feasting and by donations to the poor.

Hijra Year				1392		1393		1394	
New Year	.	.	.	Feb. 16th,	1972	Feb. 6th,	1973	Jan. 24th,	1974
Ashoura .	.	.	.	Feb. 25th,	,,	Feb. 15th,	,,	Feb. 2nd,	,,
Mouloud .	.	.	.	April 26th,	,,	April 16th,	,,	April 4th,	,,
Leilat al Meiraj	.	.	.	Sept. 8th,	,,	Aug. 27th,	,,	Aug. 5th,	,,
Ramadan begins	.	.	.	Oct. 9th,	,,	Oct. 1st,	,,	Sept. 17th,	,,
Id ul Fitr	.	.	.	Nov. 8th,	,,	Oct. 30th,	,,	Oct. 17th,	,,
Id ul Adha	.	.	.	Jan. 15th,	1973	Jan. 7th,	1974	Dec. 24th,	,,

Note: Local determinations may vary by one day from those given here.

THE ETHIOPIAN CALENDAR

The Ethiopian Calendar is solar, and is the traditional calendar of the Ethiopian Church. New Year (*1st Maskarem*) usually occurs on September 11th Gregorian. The Ethiopian year 1965 began on September 11th, 1972.

The year is divided into thirteen months of which twelve have thirty days each. The thirteenth and last month (*Paguemen*) has five or six days, the extra day occurring on leap years. The months are as follows:

1. Maskarem	8. Maiza
2. Tikimit	9. Ginbat
3. Hidar	10. Sene
4. Tahsas	11. Hamle
5. Tir	12. Nahasse
6. Yekatit	13. Paguemen
7. Megabit	

The Ethiopian Calendar is used for all purposes, religious and secular, in Ethiopia.

STANDARD TIME

Behind G.M.T.	Greenwich Mean Time (G.M.T.)	One Hour Ahead of G.M.T.	Two Hours Ahead of G.M.T.	Three Hours Ahead of G.M.T.	Four Hours Ahead of G.M.T.
Cape Verde Is.: 2 hrs. Guinea (Bissau): 1 hr. Liberia: 45 mins.	Algeria Ascension The Gambia Ghana Guinea Ivory Coast Mali Mauritania Morocco St. Helena São Tomé and Príncipe Senegal Sierra Leone Spanish Sahara Togo Tristan da Cunha Upper Volta	Angola Cameroon Central African Republic Chad Congo (Brazzaville) Dahomey Equatorial Guinea Gabon Niger Nigeria Tunisia Zaire—western section	Botswana Burundi Egypt* Lesotho Libya Malawi Mozambique Rhodesia Rwanda South Africa South West Africa Sudan Swaziland Zaire—eastern section Zambia	Comoro Is. Ethiopia French Terr. Afar and Issa Kenya Madagascar Somalia Tanzania Uganda	Mauritius Réunion Seychelles

* Egypt observes summer time, the only country in Africa to do so.

WEIGHTS AND MEASURES

Principal weights and units of measurement in common use as alternatives to the Imperial and Metric systems.

WEIGHT

Unit	Country	Metric Equivalent	Imperial Equivalent
Frazila	Tanzania (Zanzibar)	15.87 kilos.	35 lb.
Metir or Netir	Ethiopia	0.454 kilos.	1 lb.
Pound (Dutch)	South Africa	0.494 kilos.	1.09 lb.
Wakiah	Tanzania (Zanzibar)	280 grammes	0.988 oz.

LENGTH

Unit	Country	Metric Equivalent	Imperial Equivalent
Busa	Sudan	2.54 cm.	1 in.
Cubito	Somalia	55.88 cm.	22 in.
Foot (Cape)	South Africa	31.5 cm.	12.4 in.
Foot (French)	Mauritius	32.5 cm.	12.8 in.
Kadam or Qadam	Sudan	30.48 cm.	12 in.
Pouce	Mauritius	2.54 cm.	1 in.
Senzer	Ethiopia	23.114 cm.	9.1 in.

1134

CAPACITY

Unit	Country	Metric Equivalent	Imperial Equivalent
Ardeb	Sudan	198.024 litres	43.56 gallons
Balli	South Africa	46 litres	10.119 gallons
Cabaho	Ethiopia	5.91 litres	1.3 gallons
Corde	Mauritius	3.584 cubic metres	128 cubic ft.
Gantang	South Africa	9.2 litres	2.024 gallons
Kadah	Sudan	2.063 litres	3.63 pints
Keila	Sudan	16.502 litres	3.63 gallons
Kuma	Ethiopia	5 litres	1.1 gallons
Messe	Ethiopia	1.477 litres	2.6 pints
Mud or Muid	South Africa	109.1 litres	24 gallons
Ratel	Sudan	0.568 litre	1 pint

AREA

Unit	Country	Metric Equivalent	Imperial Equivalent
Are	Mauritius	0.01 hectare	0.0247 acre
Darat or Dural	Somalia	8,000 sq. metres	1.98 acres
Feddan	Sudan	4,201 sq. metres	1.038 acres
Gasha	Ethiopia	40 hectares	99 acres
Morgen	South Africa	0.857 hectare	2.117 acres

METRIC TO IMPERIAL CONVERSIONS

Metric Units	Imperial Units	To Convert Metric into Imperial Units Multiply by:	To Convert Imperial into Metric Units Multiply by:
Weight			
Gramme	Ounce (Avoirdupois)	0.035274	28.3495
Kilogramme (Kilo.)	Pound (lb.)	2.204622	0.453592
Metric ton	Short ton (2,000 lb.)	1.102311	0.907185
	Long ton (2,240 lb.)	0.984207	0.016047
	(The short ton is in general use in the U.S.A., while the long ton is normally used in Britain and the Commonwealth.)		
Length			
Centimetre	Inch	0.3937008	2.54
Metre	Yard (=3 feet)	1.09361	0.9144
Kilometre	Mile	0.62137	1.609344
Capacity			
Cubic metre	Cubic foot	35.315	0.0283
	Cubic yard	1.30795	0.764555
Litre	Gallon (=8 pints)	0.219976	4.54596
	Gallon (U.S.)	0.264178	3.78533
Area			
Square metre	Square yard	1.19599	0.836127
Hectare	Acre	2.47105	0.404686
Square kilometre	Square mile	0.386102	2.589988

Primary Commodities of Africa

AGRICULTURAL

Cashew (*Anacardium occidentale*)

This is a spreading evergreen tree up to 12 metres in height, native to tropical America. The seeds are the source of cashew nuts, produced by shelling the roasted fruits. They are used in confectionery and dessert, and yield an edible oil which is, however, not economical to produce. The shells also yield an oil which is used commercially as a wood preservative, in varnishes, cable insulation and an additive with tung oil.

Mozambique and Tanzania are the chief African producers. For production and export figures, *see* statistical section for these countries.

Cassava (Manioc, Tapioca) (*Manihot esculenta*)

Cassava is made from the root tubers of a shrub, 1 to 5 metres in height, which has latex in all parts. It is a member of the family of Euphorbiaceae. There are two varieties, bitter and sweet cassava, sometimes considered as two separate species, *M. utilissima* and *M. dulcis* or *aipi*. The tubers may be eaten raw if of the sweet variety; they may be boiled and pounded to make a paste, made into flour, or dried and stored. Cassava is the chief or second staple throughout the tropics in Africa; there is a certain amount of interfrontier trade within the continent.

About half of world acreage is estimated to be in Africa. The chief exporter of cassava is Madagascar. The United States of America and Europe import most, which is sold as tapioca. Production figures below refer to fresh cassava, but may not be accurate since it is a subsistence crop.

PRODUCTION
('000 metric tons)

	1969	1970
WORLD TOTAL	90,819*	92,222*
Africa	35,653*	37,157*
Leading African Producers:		
Angola	1,590	1,600
Burundi	1,024	1,577
Central African Republic	1,000*	1,000*
Ghana	1,320	1,596
Madagascar	1,253	1,218
Mozambique	2,100*	2,100*
Nigeria	6,800*	7,300*
Tanzania	1,300*	1,500*
Togo	1,150	1,170*
Uganda	2,321	2,150*
Zaire	10,000	10,000*
Leading non-African Producers:		
Brazil	30,074	29,464
Indonesia	11,034	10,451

*FAO estimate.

Clove (*Eugenia caryophyllus*)

This tree is a small evergreen up to 14 metres high, and cloves are its dried, unopened flower-buds. They are used as spices, and clove oil, produced by distillation of cloves, flower stalks and leaves, is used in perfumes and toiletries.

In the nineteenth century, cloves were transplanted from Mauritius to Zanzibar, which is now the world's leading producer. With Madagascar, the island produces most of the cloves entering world trade.

Between 1930 and 1962 average annual exports of cloves from Zanzibar were 10,188 metric tons. For further production figures, *see* statistical sections of Madagascar and Tanzania.

Cocoa (*Theobroma cacao*)

This small tree, 6 to 14 metres high, is thought to have originated in south and central America. Its roasted seed (bean) is pounded and may be mixed with sugar to make cocoa powder and chocolate. The previously extracted fat is made into cocoa butter and the shell is used as stock feed or manure.

Ghana is the world's largest producer and cocoa provided more than two-thirds of the country's export earnings in 1970. Recorded world trade in cocoa beans during 1971 totalled 1,207,000 metric tons, of which 940,000 tons (more than 75 per cent) were exported from African countries. The world's three leading exporters were Ghana (344,170 tons), Nigeria (271,836 tons) and the Ivory Coast (146,939 tons). The seven major producers in 1970/71 and 1971/72 were Brazil, Cameroon, the Dominican Republic, Ecuador, Ghana, Ivory Coast and Nigeria.

PRODUCTION OF DRIED COCOA BEANS
Twelve months ending September 30th
('000 metric tons)

	1970/71	1971/72 (provisional)
WORLD TOTAL	1,495.0	1,549.0
Africa	1,084.7	1,119.6
Leading African Producers:		
Cameroon	112.0	120.0
Equatorial Guinea	30.0	32.0
Ghana*	396.2	437.0
Ivory Coast	179.6	220.0
Nigeria*	307.8	248.0
São Tomé and Príncipe	10.0	10.0
Togo	28.0	32.0
Leading non-African Producers:		
Brazil†	181.6	192.0
Dominican Republic	35.0	42.0
Ecuador	61.0	60.0

* Purchases for export.

† Estimates by FAO Cocoa Study Group.

Source: FAO, *Cocoa Statistics*, October 1972.

1136

Cocoa is underproduced globally, and world prices fluctuate, making its market position unstable. However, recent talks between the major producing and major consuming countries, held under the auspices of UNCTAD, have not resulted in the formation of an international agreement.

The production figures relate to cocoa beans fermented and dried.

Coffee (*Coffea*)

This is an evergreen shrub or small tree between 5 and 10 metres high. The dried seeds (beans) are roasted, ground and brewed. Coffelite, a type of plastic, is also made from the bean. The varieties of chief economic importance are *C. arabica* (native to Ethiopia), which accounts for 75 to 80 per cent of world production, and *C. canephora*, also known as *robusta*, which accounts for all but one per cent of the rest.

Africa comes second to Latin America as a producer. In the last decade African coffee was about 23 per cent of the world total and, of this, 75 per cent was the *robusta* variety.

Coffee prices are controlled under the International Coffee Agreement of 1959, renewed in 1968.

PRODUCTION OF GREEN COFFEE BEANS
('000 metric tons)

	1970	1971 (provisional)
WORLD TOTAL . . .	3,910.0*	5,170.0*
Africa . . .	1,298.9*	1,331.0*
Leading African Producers:		
Angola . . .	204.0	210.0*
Cameroon . . .	81.0	88.5
Ethiopia . . .	205.0	215.0
Ivory Coast . .	240.0	249.0
Kenya . . .	58.7	60.0
Madagascar . .	66.6	65.5
Tanzania . . .	64.2	64.0*
Uganda . . .	204.0*	210.0*
Zaire . . .	72.0	67.5
Leading non-African Producers:		
Brazil† . . .	754.8	1,665.5*
Colombia . . .	570.3	520.0
Indonesia . . .	184.8	180.0*
Mexico . . .	183.9	192.0

* FAO estimate.

† Data officially reported in terms of dry cherries have been converted into clean coffee at 50 per cent.

Copra

This is the dried kernel of the coconut, and is the source of coconut oil. It is used in the manufacture of margarine and cooking fat, soap and detergents. *Coir* (husk fibre) is another product of the coconut, and is used in mattresses and rope-making, etc.

The Philippines is the world's largest producer and exporter. The U.S.A. is the largest importer.

Production figures for copra relate only to quantities traded, no allowance being made for copra treated for oil by primitive methods.

COCONUT PRODUCTION
(million nuts)

	1969	1970
WORLD TOTAL . . .	29,312*	29,614*
Africa . . .	1,429	1,512*
Leading African Producers:		
Ghana . . .	168	201
Mozambique . .	380*	407*
Nigeria . . .	200*	200*
Tanzania . . .	300	321
Leading non-African Producers:		
India . . .	5,779	5,780*
Indonesia . . .	5,536	5,807
Philippines . .	7,745	7,814

* FAO estimate.

COPRA PRODUCTION
('000 metric tons)

	1970	1971 (provisional)
WORLD TOTAL . . .	3,352.7*	3,747.8*
Africa . . .	119.9*	127.1*
Leading African Producers:		
Comoro Islands . .	4.4	5.2
Ivory Coast . .	6.9	7.7
Mozambique† . .	60.0	62.0
São Tomé and Príncipe .	4.5	6.0*
Seychelles . . .	4.8	4.8*
Tanzania . . .	28.0	30.0*
Leading non-African Producers:		
India . . .	280.0	280.0
Indonesia . . .	694.0	730.0
Philippines . .	1,325.0	1,626.0

* FAO estimate.

† Exports of copra and coconut oil in copra equivalent.

Cotton (*Gossypium*)

The seed of the commercial cotton tree bears a lint or growth of hair on its epidermis. This collapses on drying and forms a ribbon which can be detached and spun. Cotton is classified by length, the staple length being the measure of the length of fibre of a sample of raw cotton. This length determines the texture of the resulting yarn, the longer the staple, the finer and stronger the textile. Staple lengths are between ⅝ in. and 2 in. and are classified as short, medium, long and extra long. Cotton textiles are made into clothes, household articles and cable insulation. The seed also bears a short fuzz, known as cotton linters, which is used to make paper, cotton wool, surgical lint and rayon.

In spite of competition from artificial fibres, world consumption of cotton continues to rise, largely due to the demand from communist countries, which are the chief markets for Sudanese cotton. Cotton marketing in Sudan, Tanzania and Uganda is under government control; until September 1970 world production was subject to the GATT Long Term Arrangement regarding International Trade in Cotton Textiles.

PRODUCTION OF COTTON LINT
('ooo metric tons, excluding linters)

	1970	1971 (provisional)
WORLD TOTAL . .	11,522*	11,980*
Africa . . .	1,318*	1,329*
Leading African Producers:		
Egypt . . .	509	536
Mozambique . .	46	40
Nigeria . . .	91	40
Rhodesia . .	43	43*
Sudan . . .	225	228
Tanzania . .	71	75
Uganda . .	75	69
Leading non-African Producers:		
China, People's Republic	1,518	1,518
India† . . .	954	1,127
U.S.S.R. . . .	2,343	2,380
U.S.A. . . .	2,213	2,280

* FAO estimate.

† Estimates by the International Cotton Advisory Committee.

Cottonseed (*Gossypium*)

The production of this oilseed depends on the volume of cotton for fibre cultivated. It can be a valuable subsidiary cash crop. The oil is mainly used to make margarine and cooking fat, and the residual

PRODUCTION
('ooo metric tons)

	1970	1971 (provisional)
WORLD TOTAL . . .	21,362*	22,365*
Africa . . .	2,414*	2,335*
Leading African Producers:		
Egypt . . .	884	865*
Mozambique . .	93	80
Nigeria . . .	180	80
Rhodesia . .	86	86*
Sudan . . .	420	428*
Tanzania . .	120	128
Uganda . .	165	147
Leading non-African Producers:		
China, People's Republic	3,036	3,036
India† . . .	1,908	2,428
U.S.S.R. . . .	4,547	4,716
U.S.A. . . .	3,713	3,850

* FAO estimate.

† Estimates based on lint data published by the International Cotton Advisory Committee.

oilcake is used as fodder and fertilizer. The seed itself may be used for fertilizer or fuel.

In 1968 cottonseed accounted for 12 per cent of total vegetable oil supplies. Recently, about 13 per cent of world cottonseed oil supplies has entered world trade every year.

Groundnut (**Peanut, Monkey Nut**) (*Arachis hypogaea*)

This is not a true nut, but the pod or legume of the plant which ripens underground. The plant is an erect or trailing, hairy annual herb. It was introduced from south America, and resembles the indigenous African Bambarra groundnut, which it now outnumbers. The nut is consumed by the grower or exported for its oil; groundnuts are the second largest world source of vegetable oil. Other products are oil cake (human or animal food), peanut butter and salted peanuts.

Groundnuts are the most important of Africa's oil seeds and form the chief export crop of Senegal and Niger. Nigeria, South Africa and Sudan are also important exporters. Most African countries grow the nut as a subsistence, particularly storage, crop, and for this reason published figures do not indicate total crops. Recorded production fell steadily between 1967 and 1970, but there was a recovery in 1971.

Groundnuts are a small farmer's crop, and may be marketed through cooperatives or through State Marketing Boards, as in the case of Nigeria. The African Groundnut Council (*see* p. 145) advises producing countries on marketing policies. Western Europe, particularly France, is Africa's largest market.

PRODUCTION OF GROUNDNUTS
(in shell, 'ooo metric tons)

	1970	1971 (provisional)
WORLD TOTAL . .	17,626*	18,259*
Africa . . .	4,339*	5,175*
Leading African Producers:		
Cameroon . .	190	209
Niger . . .	200	240
Nigeria . . .	780	900
Senegal . . .	583	960
South Africa . .	318	404
Sudan . . .	353	381
Uganda . . .	234	234*
Zaire . . .	180	180
Leading non-African Producers:		
China, People's Republic	2,650	2,700
India . . .	6,110	5,712
U.S.A. . . .	1,351	1,362

* FAO estimate.

Maize (**Indian Corn, Mealies**) (*Zea mays*)

Maize is the third most important cereal crop, after wheat and rice. Two main varieties are dent maize and flint maize. The former is high in soft starch and is the chief variety grown in South Africa.

Sweet corn, popcorn and hybrid maize are also common, hybrids being grown in Zambia and Rhodesia. Most of the maize entering international trade is for animal fodder, but maize in Africa is a subsistence crop and production figures do not give a precise idea of total harvests. Marketing boards in the main exporting countries, e.g. South Africa and Kenya, stabilize prices.

PRODUCTION
('ooo metric tons)

	1970	1971 (provisional)
WORLD TOTAL . . .	259,783*	304,236*
Africa . . .	19,077*	22,306*
Leading African Producers:		
Angola . . .	456	400*
Egypt . . .	2,397	2,342
Ethiopia . . .	950*	971
Kenya . . .	1,500	1,400*
Malawi . . .	900*	1,100*
Nigeria . . .	1,220*	1,220*
Rhodesia . . .	700*	1,179
South Africa . . .	6,133	8,600
Tanzania† . . .	650	541
Zambia . . .	550*	750*
Leading non-African Producers:		
Brazil . . .	14,216	14,307
China, People's Republic	29,000*	29,500*
U.S.A. . . .	104,131	140,728

* FAO estimate.

† Maize grown alone and mixed with other crops.

Millet and Sorghum

Millet and sorghum are cereals grown chiefly as feed for livestock and poultry in Europe and North America, but are used to a large extent as food in Asia, Africa and the U.S.S.R.

Data on millet relate mainly to the following: cattail millet (*Pennisetum glaucum* or *typhoides*), also known as pearl millet or, in India and Pakistan, as "bajra"; finger millet (*Eleusine coracana*), known in India as "ragi"; bread millet (*Panicum miliaceum*), also called proso; foxtail millet (*Setaria italica*), or Italian millet; and barnyard millet (*Echinochloa crusgalli*), also often called Japanese millet.

Sorghum statistics refer mainly to the several varieties of *Sorghum vulgare* known by various names, such as kafir or kafircorn, milo, feterita, durra, jowar, sorgo, maicillo, etc. Other species included in the table are Sudan grass (*S. sudanense*) and Columbus grass or sorgo negro (*S. almum*). The use of grain sorghum hybrids has resulted in a considerable increase in yields in recent years.

Wherever possible, statistics are given separately for millet and sorghum, but many countries, especially in Africa, do not make any distinction between the two grains in their reports; in such cases, combined figures are given. Together, millet and sorghum comprise Africa's most important cereal crop, grown in many countries where rain is not plentiful. The main producing region is West Africa.

Sorghum, sometimes called Guinea corn, was first cultivated in Sudan. Durra is the most common variety in East Africa and kafircorn (*caffrorum*) in Southern Africa.

Millet and sorghum are grown as subsistence crops in Africa, so much of the quantity produced is not covered by the statistical reporting services.

PRODUCTION
('ooo metric tons)
M = Millet; S = Sorghum; U = Unspecified (only combined figures reported)

	1970	1971 (provisional)
WORLD TOTAL: M .	21,232*	17,440*
,, ,, S .	43,840*	50,199*
,, ,, U .	28,608*	30,444*
Africa: M . .	5,763*	5,558*
,, S . .	8,414*	9,396*
,, U . .	5,805*	6,625*
Leading African Producers:		
Chad: U . .	610	700*
Egypt: S . .	874	854
Ethiopia: U† . .	2,630	2,680*
Mali: U‡ . .	600	900
Niger: M . .	901	800
,, S . .	337	300
Nigeria: M . .	2,800*	2,800*
,, S . .	3,500*	3,500*
Senegal: U‡ . .	405	650
South Africa: M . .	15*	15*
,, ,, S . .	445	650
Sudan: M . .	460	325
,, S . .	1,529	2,152
Uganda: M . .	630*	630*
,, S . .	332*	332*
Upper Volta: M‡ . .	389	397
,, ,, S . .	563	576
Leaning non-African Producers:		
China, People's Republic: U . .	22,000*	23,000*
India: M . .	12,074	8,500*
,, S . .	8,188	7,800*
U.S.A.: S . .	17,690	22,743

* FAO estimate.

† Including teff (*Eragrostis abyssinica*).

‡ Including fonio.

Oil Palm (*Elaeis guineensis*)

This is a native of west Africa. The entire fruit is of use commercially; palm oil is made from its pulp, and palm kernel oil from the seed. The former is used mainly in the manufacture of edible fats and the latter for detergents and soaps, as well as fats. The oil palm is the staple of Dahomey's economy.

PRODUCTION OF PALM KERNELS
('ooo metric tons)

	1970	1971 (provisional)
WORLD TOTAL	1,143.0*	1,219.0*
Africa	767.0*	800.0*
Leading African Producers:		
Cameroon	56.0	58.0
Dahomey	94.3	80.0*
Ghana	37.0	37.0
Ivory Coast	26.0	30.0
Nigeria	270.0	320.0
Sierra Leone[1]	60.0	52.0
Zaire	130.0	130.0
Leading non-African Producers:		
Brazil[2]	180.9	185.0*
Indonesia[3]	48.0	53.0
West Malaysia[3]	87.2	118.8

* FAO estimate.

[1] Exports only.   [2] Babassu kernels.
[3] Production on estates only.

PRODUCTION OF PALM OIL
('ooo metric tons)

	1970	1971 (provisional)
WORLD TOTAL	1,774.0*	2,038.0*
Africa	1,056.0*	1,118.0*
Leading African Producers:		
Angola	38.0	38.0*
Cameroon	54.0	56.0
Dahomey	45.0	47.0
Ghana	60.0	60.0
Ivory Coast	52.4	70.0
Liberia	41.2*	41.2*
Nigeria	488.0	500.0
Sierra Leone	53.0	60.0
Zaire	180.0	200.0
Leading non-African Producers:		
Indonesia†	216.8	248.0
West Malaysia†	402.5	550.8

* FAO estimate.   † Production on estates only.

PRODUCTION OF PALM KERNEL OIL
('ooo metric tons)

	1969	1970
Africa	605*	767*
Leading African Producers:		
Cameroon	52	56
Dahomey	56	60
Nigeria	177	305
Sierra Leone	49	59
Zaire	128	130

* FAO estimate.

Source: UN Economic Commission for Africa, *Survey of Economic Conditions in Africa 1971.*

Pyrethrum (*Chrysanthemum cinerariaefolium*)

The plant is a perennial herb, 30–60 centimetres high. The flowers contain toxic substances known as pyrethrins which are used in the manufacture of insecticides in the form of aerosol sprays, repellent creams, dips, etc. In spite of its advantages over the more toxic D.D.T. and other chlorinated hydrocarbons, the pyrethrum industry is threatened by the prevalence on the market of such "synthetic" insecticides, which are economically produced by the large chemical companies.

Kenya is the largest world producer. Pyrethrum is also produced in Tanzania and Zaire.

PRODUCTION

Kenya: 1967, 11,105 metric tons; Tanzania: 1967, 6,600 tons.

Rice (*Oryza sativa*)

A variant of this species, *O. glaberrima*, is widely cultivated in Africa, as well as *O. sativa*. The former is native to Africa, but now both are widespread. Wild rice is also consumed at village level. Unhusked rice is known as paddy; after removal of the husk it is called brown rice; in its common European form the outer layer of the grain is removed (milled rice) and it may be further treated or glazed. The bulk of international trade is in the long and medium grain varieties.

Rice in Africa is largely a subsistence crop and only about 10 per cent enters international trade. About 90 per cent of Africa's rice exports are from Egypt. In 1970 African countries imported a total of 834,400 metric tons. Africa's main rice importer is Senegal.

Methods of cultivation differ widely and are frequently low in productivity. Rice is a staple food in Madagascar, Tanzania and many west coast areas.

The West African Rice Development Association has been formed by producing states with the aim of improving yields in the sub-region. (*see* p. 141).

PRODUCTION OF PADDY RICE
('ooo metric tons)

	1970	1971 (provisional)
WORLD TOTAL	308,218*	306,955*
Africa	7,422*	7,592*
Leading African Producers:		
Egypt	2,605	2,534
Guinea	400	400*
Ivory Coast	316	310*
Madagascar	1,865	1,873
Nigeria	550	550*
Sierra Leone	425	460
Tanzania	182	185*
Zaire	175	204
Leading non-African Producers:		
China, People's Republic	102,000*	104,000*
India	63,672	64,000*

* FAO estimate.

Rubber (Para Rubber) (*Hevea brasiliensis*)

This tree was introduced from Brazil to Africa via the east in the early twentieth century. The tree is the source of 90 per cent of the world's natural rubber. Latex, produced in all parts of the tree, is extracted by tapping and rubber is made from this.

Rubber is a plantation crop. Africa produced less than 7 per cent of the world's rubber in 1971.

In 1944 the International Rubber Study Group was formed by the chief importing and exporting countries to regulate the market by supplying advice and information about supply and demand, and to develop production.

PRODUCTION OF NATURAL RUBBER
('000 metric tons)

	1970	1971
WORLD TOTAL . . .	2,897.5	3,002.5
Africa	213.0	194.8
Leading African Producers:		
Cameroon* . .	12.2	12.8
Ivory Coast* . .	10.9	11.8
Liberia* . . .	83.4	74.2
Nigeria* . . .	59.3	50.2
Zaire* . . .	40.0	40.0
Leading non-African Producers:		
Indonesia . . .	780.0	834.0
West Malaysia . .	1,215.7	1,276.3
Thailand† . . .	287.2	316.3

* Exports only.

† Exports plus estimated consumption.

Source: mainly International Rubber Study Group, *Rubber Statistical Bulletin, October 1972.*

Sesame Seed (Beniseed) (*Sesame indicum*)

Sesame is an erect annual herb, 1 to 2 metres tall. The edible seeds yield a semi-drying oil which is used in the manufacture of cooking oil, margarine and

SESAME SEED PRODUCTION
('000 metric tons)

	1970	1971 (provisional)
WORLD TOTAL . . .	2,078.0*	1,937.0*
Africa . . .	486.0*	467.0*
Leading African Producers:		
Egypt . . .	20.0	21.0
Ethiopia . . .	70.0*	70.0*
Nigeria† . . .	20.0	10.0
Sudan . . .	282.0	271.0
Uganda . . .	23.0*	23.0*
Leading non-African Producers:		
China, People's Republic .	365.0	365.0
India . . .	568.4	459.4
Mexico . . .	162.5	186.0

* FAO estimate.

† Commercial production only.

other edible fats, in soaps and paints, and as a vehicle (synergist) for pyrethrum in aerosol sprays.

The plant is thought to be native to Africa, and is widely cultivated there.

Sisal (Agave sisalana)

The leaf tissue of this plant yields hard, flexible fibres which are suitable for making rope and twine, cord matting, padding and upholstery. Sisal accounts for two-thirds of world production of hard fibres. Agricultural twine is the main usage.

Hard fibres have declined in output over the last few years because of competition from nylons and other synthetics. For example, Kenya exported 55,870 metric tons, valued at U.S. $9,372,000, in 1966, but exports fell in 1967 to 41,805 metric tons, worth only $5,833,000.

The FAO Study Group on Hard Fibres was established to look into falling prices and the generally critical state of the world industry. In recent years producers have been operating a quota system to improve the pricing structure of the crop.

PRODUCTION
('000 metric tons)

	1969	1970
WORLD TOTAL . . .	635.0*	625.0*
Africa . . .	392.0*	381.0*
Leading African Producers:		
Angola . . .	67.5	68.4
Kenya . . .	49.6	48.0
Madagascar . .	29.5	26.3
Mozambique . .	28.5	29.0
Tanzania . . .	209.3	202.0
Leading non-African Producer:		
Brazil . . .	185.0*	190.0*

* FAO estimate.

Sugar

This is the product either of sugar beet (*Beta vulgaris*) or sugar cane, a giant perennial grass of the genus *Saccharum*. Until seedling canes were introduced about 1920, all cultivated canes were ascribed to one species, *S. officinarum*. Generally speaking, cane sugar is exported from producing countries in the raw state, while beet sugar is refined in the country of origin, and almost all the latter is consumed domestically. Sugar is the staple of Mauritius' economy.

As well as providing sugar, quantities of cane are grown in some countries for seed, feed, fresh consumption, the manufacture of alcohol and other uses.

World prices are determined by various international agreements such as the 1969 International Sugar Agreement which excludes the United States

and the EEC, and the Commonwealth Sugar Agreement, as well as by the policies of the EEC and COMECON. Of relevance to Africa is the OCAM Sugar Agreement, in terms of which each member has to make a contribution to a fund which helps to provide a guaranteed sugar price in each member country. In 1970 Senegal withdrew from this pact.

Production data for sugar cane and sugar beets cover generally all crops harvested, except crops grown explicitly for feed. The third table covers the production of raw sugar by the centrifugal process. Figures listed under split years relate to harvests and sugar production corresponding to the sugar campaign starting any time between March of one year and February of the following year, unless otherwise indicated.

PRODUCTION OF CENTRIFUGAL SUGAR
(raw value, '000 metric tons)

	1969/70	1970/71
WORLD TOTAL: Cane	43,188*	42,551*
Beet	29,276*	29,500*
Africa: Cane	4,563*	4,353*
Beet	133*	176*
Leading African Producers:		
Egypt: Cane	491	515
Kenya: Cane[1]	141	147
Mauritius: Cane	669	576
Morocco: Beet	117	163
Mozambique: Cane	224	284
Réunion: Cane	260	218
Rhodesia: Cane	127	142
South Africa: Cane	1,622	1,399
Swaziland: Cane	157	170
Uganda: Cane[1]	166	154
Leading non-African Producers:		
Brazil: Cane[2]	4,543	5,431
Cuba: Cane	8,533	5,924
India: Cane[3]	4,637	4,098
U.S.S.R.: Beet	8,853	9,293
U.S.A.: Cane[4]	2,045	2,192
Beet[4]	3,021	2,911

* FAO estimate.

[1] Calendar year referring to the second part of the split year.

[2] Years from June to May.

[3] Includes sugar (raw value) refined from gur.

[4] Calendar year referring to the first part of the split year.

SUGAR CANE PRODUCTION
('000 metric tons)

	1969/70	1970/71 (provisional)
WORLD TOTAL	595,358*	585,482*
Africa	46,074*	43,499*
Leding African Producers:		
Egypt	6,975	7,000*
Kenya	1,451	1,750
Mauritius	5,824	5,120
Mozambique	2,100*	2,730*
Réunion	2,437	1,937
South Africa†	14,788	12,144
Swaziland	1,429	1,550*
Uganda	1,700*	1,700*
Leading non-African Producers:		
Brazil	75,247	79,753
Cuba	64,000*	49,000*
India	135,024	128,769

* FAO estimate.   † Cane crushed for sugar.

Sweet Potatoes and Yams

Sweet potatoes (*Ipomoea*) and yams (*Dioscorea*) are important root crops in many tropical and subtropical countries. They do not belong to the same

SUGAR BEET PRODUCTION
('000 metric tons)

	1969/70	1970/71 (provisional)
WORLD TOTAL	219,416*	228,151*
Africa	1,047*	1,258*
Leading African Producers:		
Algeria	899	1,114
Morocco	114	114*
Leading non-African Producers:		
U.S.S.R.	71,158	78,324
U.S.A.	25,162	23,930

* FAO estimate.

PRODUCTION
('000 metric tons)

	1969	1970
WORLD TOTAL	136,812*	147,713*
Africa	21,685*	23,505*
Leading African Producers:		
Burundi	874	1,082
Dahomey	599	605
Ghana	1,305	1,617
Ivory Coast	1,541	1,572
Nigeria	12,500*	13,500*
Togo	1,150	1,152*
Uganda	710*	710*
Leading non-African Producers:		
China, People's Republic	93,600*	103,200*
China, Republic (Taiwan)	3,702	3,441
Indonesia	3,021	3,029

* FAO estimate.

botanical family but are frequently reported together. Like cassava, much of the crop is grown on small plots and consumed locally, mainly in West Africa. For this reason, production figures are not very reliable for many countries.

Tea (*Camellia sinensis*)

Cultivated tea is a low spreading bush, between 0.5 and 1.5 metres high. Black tea is made from its withered, rolled, fermented and dried leaves. Tea may be of the Assam or China variety, or a hybrid, such as Darjeeling.

In 1971, Africa produced nearly 9 per cent of the world's tea. Tea provided nearly a quarter of Malawi's export earnings in 1969. Mauritius, in an attempt to diversify its single crop economy, is increasing its acreage under tea, and in 1970 produced 3,500 metric tons.

Tea is no longer controlled by an international agreement, although the International Tea Committee remains in existence. In 1969 the FAO Consultative Committee on Tea was formed, with the responsibility of maintaining tea prices through a quota system.

PRODUCTION OF MADE TEA
('000 metric tons)

	1970	1971 (provisional)
WORLD TOTAL . . .	1,293.0*	1,310.0*
Africa . . .	116.6*	116*
Leading African Producers:		
Kenya . . .	41.1	38.0
Malawi . . .	18.7	18.6
Mozambique . . .	17.0	16.5
Tanzania . . .	8.3	10.5
Uganda . . .	18.2	18.0
Zaire . . .	4.7*	4.7*
Leading non-African Producers:		
China, People's Republic .	172.0*	173.0*
India . . .	421.8	432.6
Sri Lanka (Ceylon) . .	212.2	217.8

* FAO estimate.

Tobacco (*Nicotiana tabacum*)

The leaf of the plant is dried or "cured" by one or more different processes such as fire-curing or flue-curing. Marketed tobaccos vary considerably, depending on the soil and climatic conditions, hybridization and selection of the plants, as well as on methods of curing the leaf. Flue-cured is the chief variety entering world trade, though Malawi exports mainly fire-cured.

Rhodesia exported 95 per cent of her crop before sanctions were established, and much of it is now stored. Uganda has a small but growing production of flue-cured. In 1969 tobacco provided more than a third of Malawi's total export revenue. African tobacco is generally bought and sold by auction in the producing countries.

PRODUCTION
(farm sales weight, '000 metric tons)

	1970	1971 (provisional)
WORLD TOTAL . . .	4,690.0*	4,610.0*
Africa . . .	206.0*	213.0*
Leading African Producers:		
Malawi . . .	19.0	22.3
Nigeria . . .	12.0	17.5
Rhodesia . . .	62.3	62.3
South Africa . . .	33.9	34.0*
Tanzania . . .	15.3	15.3*
Leading non-African Producers:		
China, People's Republic .	785.0*	785.0*
U.S.A. . . .	865.4	774.0

* FAO estimate.

Wheat (*Triticum vulgare*)

There are three main varieties, based on the suitability of the grain for bread-making. These are hard, semi-hard and soft, the latter being the least suitable. A fourth very hard type, *T. durum*, is grown in north Africa and the Mediterranean and is suitable for making pasta.

Except in South Africa, wheat yields are low because of low rainfall and backward methods of farming.

Until 1968 world trade in wheat was controlled by an International Wheat Agreement. The International Grains Arrangement then replaced its functions until 1971, when another International Wheat Agreement (in force until June 30th, 1974) took effect. African parties to the Agreement are Egypt, Kenya, Libya, Nigeria and Tunisia.

Production figures for wheat include the output of spelt, except for the U.S.S.R.

PRODUCTION
('000 metric tons)

	1970	1971 (provisional)
WORLD TOTAL . . .	318,588*	353,707*
Africa . . .	8,080*	9,319*
Leading African Producers:		
Algeria . . .	1,435	1,600*
Egypt . . .	1,519	1,729
Ethiopia . . .	840*	876
Kenya . . .	205	210*
Morocco . . .	1,901	2,300
South Africa . . .	1,396	1,620
Sudan . . .	115	135
Tunisia . . .	450	600
Leading non-African Producers:		
China, People's Republic .	31,000*	32,000*
India . . .	20,093	23,247
U.S.S.R. . . .	99,734	98,700
U.S.A. . . .	37,291	44,620

* FAO estimate.

Sources for Agricultural Tables (unless otherwise indicated): FAO, *Production Yearbook 1971* (Rome, 1972); FAO, *Monthly Bulletin of Agricultural Economics and Statistics*, 1972 issues.

MINERALS

Aluminium

The chief commercial source of aluminium is bauxite ore. The ore is washed and purified after mining, and the aluminium content is reduced in the form of compounds (alumina) which are converted to metallic aluminium by electrolysis. The ratio of bauxite to alumina is approximately 2 : 1. Because of the high cost of electrolytical reduction alumina is generally exported to refineries in the consuming countries. An exception is the alumina refinery in Guinea which treats locally mined metal. The industrial uses of aluminium are legion, due to its high strength in comparison with its weight, its resistance to corrosion and its electrical conductivity.

Guinea is Africa's major producer and is thought to have 20 per cent of world reserves of a very high-grade ore. There are indications of large-scale developments around Sengeredi, in Guinea's Boké region, where mine production could be starting in 1972, with an eventual target output of 6.6 million tons a year by the mid-1970s. There are plans to establish a refinery in Malawi by means of a consortium including the British government and Lonrho (Aluminium Corporation of Malawi).

PRODUCTION OF BAUXITE
(crude ore, '000 metric tons)

	1969	1970
WORLD TOTAL . . .	53,810	59,050
Africa . . .	3,162	3,440
Leading African Producers:		
Ghana . . .	246	342
Guinea* . . .	2,459	2,642
Sierra Leone . .	449	449
Leading non-African Producers:		
Australia . . .	7,921	9,388
Jamaica† . . .	10,319	12,010
Surinam . . .	6,236	6,011
U.S.S.R.* . . .	5,000	5,000

* *Source:* U.S. Bureau of Mines.

† Dried equivalent of crude ore.

Asbestos

This is a fibrous mineral, of which the most important type is chrysotile. After mining, rock particles are removed by crushing, and the asbestos fibres are divided mechanically and graded into lengths. Asbestos is used chiefly as an insulating material on account of its sound- and heat-resistance, and its extreme hardness.

PRODUCTION OF NON-FABRICATED ASBESTOS
(fibres and powder, '000 metric tons)

	1969	1970
WORLD TOTAL[1] . .	3,730.0	3,820.0
Africa[2] . . .	380.0	405.0
Leading African Producers:		
Rhodesia . . .	79.8	79.8
South Africa[3] . .	258.2	287.4
Swaziland . . .	36.5	32.4
Leading non-African Producers:		
Canada . . .	1,461.7	1,500.5
China, People's Republic[4]	160.0	170.0
U.S.S.R.[4] . . .	1,000.0	1,040.0

[1] Excluding Bolivia, Ethiopia, North Korea, Madagascar, the Philippines, Portugal and Romania.
[2] Excluding Ethiopia and Madagascar.
[3] Excluding asbestos powder.
[4] *Source:* U.S. Bureau of Mines.

Chromium

This is a rare mineral, derived from the ore chromite. Most chromite ores are not adaptable to concentration processes. The ore is smelted in an electric furnace and marketed in the form of ferrochrome. The major use of chromite is an alloy in steels such as stainless steel. It is tough and resistant to most forms of corrosion. It is used also as a refractory mineral and in chemical compounds for dyeing, tanning and bleaching. Chrome plating is popular.

PRODUCTION OF CHROMIUM ORE
(chromic oxide content, '000 metric tons)

	1969	1970
WORLD TOTAL* . . .	2,550.0	2,840.0
Africa . . .	900.0	1,000.0
Leading African Producers:		
Madagascar . .	18.6	43.4
Rhodesia† . .	n.a.	n.a.
South Africa . .	538.8	642.5
Sudan . . .	12.5	13.9‡
Leading non-African Producers:		
Turkey . . .	259.3	294.9
U.S.S.R. . . .	710.0	735.0

* Excluding Bulgaria, Romania and North Viet-Nam.
† Production was 281,100 metric tons in 1965.
‡ *Source:* U.S. Bureau of Mines.

Coal

Coal is a mineral of organic origin, formed from the remains of vegetation over millions of years. There are several grades: *anthracite*, the hardest coal, with the highest proportion of carbon, which burns smoke-free;

bituminous and *sub-bituminous coal,* used for industrial power; some is made into coke when the volatile matter is driven off by heating; *lignite* or brown coal, the lowest grade and nearest to the peat stage. Coal gas is made from brown coal, but is not widely used for energy except in the U.S.S.R.

Coal is South Africa's only indigenous source of energy; she exports anthracite to the European Coal and Steel Community and Japan. Rhodesia's production, which was 3.9 million tons of all grades in 1965, has fallen since the imposition of sanctions, and Zambia, which formerly imported all of its coal for the copper industry from Rhodesia, announced in June 1970 its intention to become self-sufficient in the near future. Production there began in 1966 and reached 800,000 tons in 1971.

In Nigeria, coal production fell to almost nothing during the civil war (1967-70) but the Okpara Mine is now being renovated and the pre-war output of 600,000 tons per year may be re-established.

PRODUCTION OF HARD COAL
('000 metric tons, excluding lignite)

	1969	1970
WORLD TOTAL . . .	2,066,400	2,126,000
Africa	57,370	59,600
Leading African Producers:		
Morocco . . .	361	433
Mozambique . .	277	351
Rhodesia* . .	3,332†	3,360
South Africa . .	52,752	45,612
Zambia . . .	397	623
Leading non-African Producers:		
China, People's Republic*	330,000	360,000
U.S.S.R. . . .	425,795	432,715
U.S.A. . . .	513,436	541,562

* *Source:* U.S. Bureau of Mines.
† Sales only.

Cobalt

The presence of cobalt is usually associated with other ores; in the case of African cobalt it is copper. It is found in very weak concentration, usually about one ton per 500 tons of ore. The ore must be crushed and ground after mining and subject to flotation process to obtain the concentrate. Cobalt is used industrially in its mineral form as an alloy to make heat-resistant steels, and to resist friction and rust in steels. It is also used to make magnets, and in its compound form has minor uses as pottery stain, in printing inks, paints, for colouring glass, and as a catalyst in the petroleum industry.

Africa is already a major producer in the non-communist world. It is hoped that mines at Kilembe in Uganda will become productive in the near future.

The bulk of production is handled by sole agents in London and Belgium who supply most of the American, European and Far Eastern markets.

PRODUCTION OF COBALT ORE
(cobalt content, metric tons)

	1969	1970
WORLD TOTAL . . .	17,107	20,040
Leading African Producers:		
Morocco . . .	1,466	604
Zaire . . .	10,576	12,085
Zambia . . .	1,811	2,400
Leading non-African Producers:		
Canada . . .	1,477	2,371
Finland . . .	1,537	2,124

Source: United Nations, *The Growth of World Industry.*

Copper

The ores containing copper are mainly copper sulphide or copper oxide. They are mined both underground and by open cast or surface mining. After break-up of the ore body by explosives, the lumps of ore are crushed, and the resulting concentrate is subjected to a flotation process by which copper-rich granules are extracted. These are dried, smelted, refined and made into blister copper, which is further refined to 99.98 per cent purity by electrolysis. The anodes are then cast into convenient shapes for handling. Copper is soft and ductile, resists corrosion and is the best conductor of electricity. Its industrial uses are mainly in the electrical industry (45 per cent) and the building and chemical industries. In the latter cases it is in alloy form. Bronze and brass are copper alloys used for decorative purposes.

PRODUCTION OF COPPER ORE
(copper content, '000 metric tons)

	1969	1970
WORLD TOTAL . . .	5,930.0	6,300.0
Africa . . .	1,271.0	1,286.0
Leading African Producers:		
Rhodesia[1,2] . .	19.0	20.4
South Africa . .	125.6	148.2
South West Africa[3] .	n.a.	n.a.
Uganda[4] . .	16.5	17.6
Zaire . . .	356.9	385.7
Zambia[4,5] . .	719.5	684.1
Leading non-African Producers:		
Canada . . .	520.0	611.2
Chile . . .	700.0	710.0
U.S.S.R.[2,6] . .	900.0	n.a.
U.S.A.[7] . . .	1,401.2	1,560.0

[1] Shipments.
[2] *Source:* U.S. Bureau of Mines.
[3] Production was 37,300 metric tons in 1966.
[4] *Source: World Metal Statistics.*
[5] Content of concentrates.
[6] Primary metal production.
[7] Production calculated as recoverable.

Mineral production in Zambia increased at a rapid rate in the 1960s, particularly after 1965, helped by high world prices for copper, the staple of Zambia's economy. Africa's copper output declined in 1971, when Zambia's production was reduced as a result of the Mufulira mine disaster in 1970. There has also been a steep fall in copper prices since the middle of 1969, because of a widening gap between supply and demand. However, both Zaire and Zambia have announced plans to increase production substantially over the next few years. The target for Zambia is more than 900,000 tons (by 1975) and for Zaire 460,000 tons (by 1974).

The world marketing of primary copper is carried out through the London Metal Exchange. The Inter-governmental Council of Copper Exporting Countries met in 1970 to discuss the formation of a buffer stock to help stabilize world prices, as in the case of tin.

A copper project at Akjoujt, in Mauritania, reached the production stage in 1971. There is a copper and nickel project in Botswana, where mining is due to begin when facilities are completed. Copper deposits have also been discovered recently in Ethiopia.

Diamonds

The primary source of diamonds is a rock called kimberlite, occurring in volcanic pipes which may be from a few square feet to several acres in area, and volcanic fissures which are considerably smaller. Chrome diopside is an accessory mineral. Not all kimberlites contain diamonds, and in ore which does, the ratio of diamond to waste is usually between 15 and 30 to one million parts. Open cast mining is the commonest, but diamonds are recovered also by

PRODUCTION OF UNCUT DIAMONDS
(gem and industrial stones, '000 metric carats)

	1969	1970
WORLD TOTAL . . .	45,290	47,430
Africa	37,460	38,930
Leading African Producers:		
Angola . . .	2,022	2,396
Central African Republic .	535	494
Congo (Brazzaville)* .	n.a.	n.a.
Ghana . . .	2,391	2,550
Ivory Coast† . .	202	213
Liberia‡ . .	836	826
Sierra Leone† .	1,989	1,955‡
South Africa . .	7,863	8,122
South West Africa† .	2,024	2,200
Tanzania . .	777	708
Zaire* . .	13,423	14,086†
Leading non-African Producers:		
U.S.S.R.† . .	7,500	7,850
Venezuela . .	194	500†

* Exports of diamonds from Congo (Brazzaville) totalled 5,300,000 metric carats in 1968. It has been reported that this trade relates to diamonds originating in Zaire and illegally imported into Congo (Brazzaville). The production figures for Zaire apparently exclude these smuggled diamonds.

† *Source:* U.S. Bureau of Mines.

‡ Exports only.

underground and alluvial mining. The diamond is separated from its ore by careful crushing and processes such as gravity concentration. Stones are of two sorts: gem qualities, which are superior in terms of colour, quality or shape, and industrial qualities, about 75 per cent of the total, which are used for high precision machining or crushed into an abrasive, boart. Gem qualities are used for jewellery.

Africa is by far the major producing region for natural diamonds. Zaire's production, from Eastern Kasaï, is mainly of low-value crushing boart (about 83 per cent of the total) and higher quality industrial diamonds (about 15 per cent). A diamond project in Botswana has recently reached the production stage.

The Central Selling Organization is a London-based company with associated South African companies which contracts to sell on behalf of producers and handles more than 85 per cent of world production. Gem stones are sold at regular sales known as sights.

Synthetic diamonds are produced by a method which simulates the geological formation of diamonds, but the stones are always small.

Gold

Gold minerals are commonly found in quartz and may occur in alluvial deposits, or in rich thin underground veins. In South Africa gold occurs in sheets of low-grade ore (reefs) which may be as much as 4,000 feet below ground level. A chief requisite for economic mining at such depth is a plentiful supply of low-paid labour. Gold is associated with silver which is its commonest by-product. Uranium oxide is another valuable by-product, particularly in the case of South Africa. Depending upon its associations, gold is broken down by cyaniding, or concentrated and smelted.

The chief use of gold is as bullion in reserve for bank notes issued. Jewellery and the arts account for 54 per cent of its industrial use. The dental, electrical and electronics industries account for the rest. The industrial uses are generally increasing and in 1968 non-monetary uses took 1,600 metric tons.

PRODUCTION OF GOLD
(fine gold content, kilogrammes)

	1969	1970
WORLD TOTAL* . . .	1,260,000	1,280,000
Africa . . .	1,017,000	1,043,000
Leading African Producers:		
Ethiopia . .	1,319	n.a.
Ghana . .	22,001	21,892
Rhodesia . .	14,930	n.a.
South Africa . .	969,341	1,000,417
Zaire . .	5,516	5,509
Leading non-African Producers:		
Canada . .	79,162	72,736
U.S.A. . .	53,400	56,390

* Excluding the U.S.S.R. and the People's Republic of China.

The gold industry faces the disadvantages of a stable world price and rising production costs. This applies particularly to South Africa, which produces over half the world's gold and 95 per cent of that mined in Africa. In December 1969 an agreement was formed between South Africa, the U.S.A. and the IMF concerning the marketing of gold. The South African authorities agreed to sell newly-mined gold on the free market except when the free market price fell to $35 an oz. or less. In the latter case the IMF would purchase newly-mined gold to supply South Africa's balance of payments needs. Provision was also made for South Africa to sell other gold to the IMF if a further need for foreign exchange was experienced. The increased official gold price of $38 per troy ounce could encourage additional output in 1972.

Iron Ore

The chief economic iron-ore minerals are magnetite and haematite. Iron ore agglomerate is treated straight after mining to improve its physical characteristics by a number of processes, one of which is *sintering*. The reduction of treated iron ore to pig-iron is achieved through smelting with coke and limestone. The proportion of ore to pig-iron yielded is usually about 2 : 1. Cast iron, wrought iron and steel are obtained from pig-iron, the latter by alloy with carbon. Other steels (e.g. stainless) are made by the addition of ferro-alloys such as chromium, cobalt and manganese.

Iron ore is found throughout southern and western Africa. In Liberia a new pelletizing plant with a capacity of 2 million tons was finished in 1971, and

PRODUCTION OF IRON ORE
(iron content, '000 metric tons)

	1969	1970
WORLD TOTAL . . .	392,200	418,800
Africa . . .	35,800	37,000
Leading African Producers:		
Algeria . . .	1,599	1,546
Angola . . .	3,396	3,752
Liberia . . .	14,786	15,388
Mauritania* . .	5,229	5,923
Sierra Leone . .	1,402	1,355
South Africa . .	5,594	5,869
Swaziland . .	1,469	1,469
Leading non-African Producers:		
Australia . . .	24,842	32,732
Canada† . . .	22,347	29,687
U.S.S.R. . . .	100,985	106,058
U.S.A.‡ . . .	52,513	53,308

* Exports only.

† Shipment from mines.

‡ Shipment of usable iron ore excluding manganiferous iron ores containing 5 per cent or more of manganese.

new discoveries of about 550 million tons of ore were reported. In Mauritania the present development plan includes a project to increase the production capacity to 12 million tons per year.

Lead

The principal lead ore is galena or lead sulphide. After mining, the rock containing the ore is crushed and ground, and the galena is extracted by flotation. The concentrate is then burned to form lead oxide which is smelted to yield impure metallic lead, often containing traces of gold and silver. This impure lead is refined and marketed with 99.99 per cent purity. For most mechanical applications the lead must be alloyed with small quantities of other metals. In addition, appreciable tonnages of lead chemicals (red lead, white lead) are produced annually. The car battery is the largest user of lead (about 800,000 tons a year). Cable sheathing, sheet and pipe metal, solder and printing metal are other large users.

PRODUCTION OF LEAD ORE
(lead content, '000 metric tons)

	1969	1970
WORLD TOTAL . . .	3,260.0	3,380.0
Africa . . .	212.0	213.0
Leading African Producers:		
Algeria[1] . . .	7.9	6.5
Morocco[1] . . .	80.0	84.5
South West Africa[1,2] .	75.7	70.5
Tunisia[3] . . .	23.9	22.0
Zambia[2] . . .	22.9	27.1
Leading non-African Producers:		
Australia[1] . . .	452.0	457.4
Canada . . .	300.1	357.9
U.S.S.R.[4,5] . . .	440.0	440.0
U.S.A.[6] . . .	461.8	518.7

[1] Content of concentrates.

[2] *Source: World Metal Statistics.*

[3] Content of concentrates, excluding mixed concentrates.

[4] Primary metal production.

[5] *Source: U.S. Bureau of Mines.*

[6] Production calculated as recoverable.

Manganese

This is obtained from a number of ores such as hausmannite and manganite. The ore is usually washed or hand-sorted and then furnaced with iron ore to make ferromanganese (80 per cent manganese) in which form it is chiefly used as an alloy in steel, manganese steel being particularly hard and tough. Almost 95 per cent of manganese produced is thus used. Electrolytic manganese is used to make stainless steel and in the aluminium industry. A minor use of the metal is in dry-cell batteries, paints and varnishes and in ceramics and glass making.

	1969	1970
WORLD TOTAL . . .	7,200.0	7,400.0
Africa	2,200.0	2,400.0
Leading African Producers:		
Angola . . .	11.9	9.4
Botswana . .	9.0	16.3
Gabon . . .	711.0	729.0
Ghana . . .	159.7	191.3
Ivory Coast . .	57.7	10.4
Morocco . . .	68.1	59.6
South Africa . .	1,044.2	1,177.7
Zaire . . .	165.0	156.0
Leading non-African Producers:		
Brazil . . .	884.8	n.a.
India . . .	586.0	644.0
U.S.S.R. . .	2,386.2	2,446.1

Petroleum

Crude oils, from which petroleum fuel is derived, consist essentially of a wide range of hydrocarbon molecules which are separated by distillation in the refining process. Refined oil is treated in different ways to make the different varieties of fuel. Over four-fifths of total world oil supplies are used as fuel for the production of energy in the form of power or heating.

Oil prospecting in Africa is widespread, both inland and offshore, all along the West African continental shelf and coast from Angola to Spanish Sahara. During 1970 a total of 263 "wildcat" wells were completed in Africa, with a success rate of about 14 per cent (33 oil and three gas discoveries). Commercially exploitable wells have been discovered in Ghana and Zaire. The Cabinda enclave of Angola started producing in 1968 and is far from its full potential. In 1970, African oil, exclusive of natural gas liquids, amounted to 13 per cent of the world total. Countries where reserves are known to exist but which do not yet produce are Cameroon, Dahomey, Mozambique, Senegal and Swaziland. Madagascar's first oil discovery was announced in August 1971.

The eight largest producing companies, which include Standard Oil Company of New Jersey (Esso) and Royal Dutch/Shell, are associated for production and marketing purposes. Smaller companies, sometimes nationally based in the producing countries, are however developing; Nigeria, for example, is planning to launch a state-owned company. In 1960, the Organization of Petroleum Exporting Countries was set up to maintain prices in the producing countries. Attempts to establish quotas have not been wholly successful. The southern African countries are not members, though Nigeria has sent observers to meetings.

Nigeria's oil production, from the Niger delta, was hit badly during the civil war but, since the end of

hostilities, output has been increasing at an extremely high rate. The oil produced, being of low sulphur content and high quality, is much in demand on the European market. Nigeria now ranks ninth in the world among producing countries.

PRODUCTION OF CRUDE PETROLEUM

('000 metric tons, including shale oil)

	1970	1971 (provisional)
WORLD TOTAL . . .	2,278,400	2,377,000*
Africa[1] . . .	294,300	n.a.
Leading African Producers:		
Algeria . . .	47,281	36,350
Angola . . .	5,065	5,830
Egypt[1] . . .	16,410	14,700
Gabon . . .	5,423	5,785
Libya . . .	161,708	132,400
Nigeria . . .	54,203	76,370†
Tunisia . . .	4,151	4,090
Leading non-African Producers:		
Iran . . .	191,740	227,750
Kuwait[2] . . .	137,398	146,785
Saudi Arabia[2,3] .	176,850	223,415
U.S.S.R.[4] . . .	352,574	376,990
U.S.A. . . .	475,346	466,705†
Venezuela . . .	193,873	185,770

[1] Excluding production in the Israeli-occupied Sinai peninsula, estimated (in '000 metric tons) at 2,500 in 1969; 4,500 in 1970.

[2] Excluding the Neutral Zone, jointly shared by Kuwait and Saudi Arabia.

[3] *Source:* Arabian American Oil Company.

[4] Including gas condensates.

* Excluding China. Production in 1970 (in '000 metric tons) totalled 24,000 in the People's Republic (*Source:* U.S. Bureau of Mines) and 90 in Taiwan.

† Excluding shale oil, of which 1970 production (in '000 metric tons) was: Nigeria 100; U.S.A. 60.

Phosphates

Phosphorus is obtained chiefly from various kinds of rock and pebble, e.g. phosphate rock and apatite. Some 80–85 per cent of the phosphorus thus produced is used in the manufacture of fertilizers. Other important uses are the manufacture of detergents and animal feed supplements. It is also used to make insecticides and matches, and in ceramics.

Africa accounts for nearly a quarter of world output, though most of the continent's production is concentrated in North Africa, where the largest deposits are in Morocco. Deposits have been found at Cabinda and exploitation is planned. Huge reserves have been found at Rio de Oro in Spanish Sahara, which the Spanish Government hopes to exploit from 1972. New deposits are also being developed in Egypt.

PRODUCTION OF NATURAL PHOSPHATE ROCK
('ooo metric tons, including apatite)

	1969	1970
WORLD TOTAL . . .	82,670	85,070
Africa	19,500	20,100
Leading African Producers:		
Morocco . . .	11,294	11,424
Senegal . . .	1,035	998
South Africa . .	1,679	1,685
Togo	1,473	1,508
Tunisia . . .	2,599	3,021
Leading non-African Producers:		
Nauru[1,2] . .	2,198	2,200
U.S.S.R.: Apatite[2] .	10,500	10,900
Phosphate rock[2] .	8,750	9,500
U.S.A. . . .	34,224	35,143

[1] Exports during 12 months ending June 30th of year stated.

[2] *Source:* U.S. Bureau of Mines.

Platinum

This is one of a group of related metals, including iridium and osmium. In the production of platinum these are usually alloyed. Platinum is a common by-product of the electrolytic refining of metals such as nickel and chromite. Platinum is a precious metal; it is very hard and heavy, and its white colour makes it popular in jewellery. It is used also in the electrical, chemical and dental industries. The U.S.S.R. is the largest world producer.

PRODUCTION OF PLATINUM ORE, 1968
(platinum content, kilogrammes)

African Producers:	
Ethiopia . .	8
South Africa . .	27,900

Source: U.N. Economic Commission for Africa, *Statistical Yearbook 1970.*

Silver

Much of the silver mined is derived from gold, lead, copper and tin ores, and cobalt is also associated with it. There are also straight silver ores such as native silver and argentite. Methods of recovery depend upon the composition of the silver-bearing ore. About 10 per cent of new production is made into coins. The rest is either hoarded or used for decoration or in industry, e.g. the photographic industry.

In 1969, new mine production was responsible for somewhat less than half the available silver in the free world. The rest was obtained through imports, salvage and coinage melting and the release of silver by the American General Services Administration. Much is hoarded by speculators and on the commodity exchanges.

PRODUCTION
(silver content of ores, metric tons)

	1969	1970
WORLD TOTAL* . .	8,900.0	9,200.0
Africa . . .	280.0	280.0
Leading African Producers:		
Morocco . .	26.8	n.a.
South Africa . .	103.7	109.7
South West Africa .	39.6	n.a.
Zaire . . .	61.7	53.1
Zambia† . .	42.8	47.6
Leading non-African Producers:		
Canada . . .	1,354.0	1,387.7
Mexico . . .	1,334.5	1,332.4
Peru . . .	1,073.9	1,217.3
U.S.A. . . .	1,234.0	1,371.3

* Excluding the People's Republic of China, the U.S.S.R. and the Communist countries of Eastern Europe.
† Recovery from refinery slimes.

Tin

Tin occurs mainly in the equatorial zones of Asia and Africa. Cassiterite is the chief tin-bearing ore, and the metal is associated with tungsten, silver and tantalite. Mined ore is subjected to concentration processes to obtain tin-in-concentrate, in which form it is generally exported. The chief industrial applications of tin are due to its resistance to corrosion, formability, solderability and low cost. Its main uses are: as a coating for a baser metal (tin-plating), as an alloy (tin-lead solder, bronze, pewter, bearing and printing metal), and as a chemical compound (in paints, electroplated coatings, plastics and disinfectants). Of these uses, tin-plate is the largest and takes up about 45 per cent of world production.

PRODUCTION OF TIN CONCENTRATES
(tin content, metric tons)

	1969	1970
WORLD TOTAL* . .	179,500	185,700
Africa . . .	20,400	19,400
Leading African Producers:		
Nigeria . . .	8,741	7,959
Rhodesia . . .	610	610
Rwanda . . .	1,340	1,340
South Africa . .	1,823	1,986
South West Africa .	730	730
Zaire . . .	6,647	6,447
Leading non-African Producers:		
Bolivia . . .	30,047	30,100
Indonesia . . .	16,542	19,092
Malaysia . . .	73,325	73,794
Thailand . . .	21,092	21,779

* Excluding the U.S.S.R., East Germany, North Viet-Nam and the People's Republic of China.

Much of the world's trade in tin is covered by the Fourth International Tin Agreement of 1971, one of the world's most important price stabilization arrangements. The Agreement includes a pact with the IMF under which the Fund may assist producing countries which contribute to the buffer stock which regulates supply. The governing body of the Agreement is the International Tin Council, based in London. Nigeria and Zaire are the only African parties to the Agreement, which expires in 1976.

Tungsten

Two main groups of ores contain tungsten, wolframite and scheelite. These occur in veins of quartz and may be associated with tin. Tungsten minerals, usually very low in concentration, must be separated out by gravity concentration and flotation. Because of its high melting point (the highest of any metal), tungsten is used as an alloy with steel to make high-speed tools and armaments. The metal filaments in light bulbs are of pure tungsten, and the chemical form has many industrial applications where heat resistance is essential, e.g. in ceramics.

China and the communist world have the largest reserves of tungsten ores, and Africa is relatively poor in them. Most of the tungsten entering world trade is in the form of concentrates, and trade in the pure metal is small.

PRODUCTION OF TUNGSTEN CONCENTRATES
(tungsten trioxide content, metric tons)

	1969	1970
WORLD TOTAL	40,460	42,980
Africa	750	850
Leading African Producers:		
Rwanda	319	n.a.
South West Africa*	n.a.	n.a.
Uganda	110	153
Zaire	148	220
Leading non-African Producers:		
China, People's Republic†	10,100	10,100
U.S.S.R.†	8,200	8,500
U.S.A.	3,949‡	4,636

* Production was 106 metric tons in 1966 (*Source:* U.S. Bureau of Mines).
† *Source:* U.S. Bureau of Mines.
‡ Shipments from mines.

Uranium

Uranium occurs in pitchblend ores, and may be mined by open-cast methods or underground. It is also found in association with gold-bearing ores. South Africa, one of the leading nations in reserves of fissionable ores, produces uranium oxide (yellow-cake) as a by-product of gold mining. It is produced by concentrating plants from the slimes left after the extraction of gold. This production makes gold-mining particularly profitable. Uranium is chiefly valuable as a fuel for the production of nuclear energy. In July 1970 the Prime Minister of South Africa announced that a new method for the enrichment of uranium and its conversion into fuel had been discovered locally, but details of this have not yet been made public. In 1965, Africa's share of world

resources was estimated by the European Nuclear Energy Agency to be about 25 per cent. In 1968 Africa produced 13.7 per cent of the world total.

The U.S.A. and Canada are the largest producers. The two main producers south of the Sahara are South Africa and Gabon. However, an important deposit in Niger has been brought into production, and workable deposits have been found in the Central African Republic. In South West Africa (Namibia) a German firm (Urangesellschaft m.b.H.) and Rio Tinto Zinc are planning to exploit large-scale deposits of uranium oxide. Uranium has also been discovered in Somalia.

PRODUCTION
(tons)

	1968	1969
South Africa	3,514	3,902
Gabon	1,371	491
Madagascar	21*	n.a.
World Production	29,000	25,000

* Uranium content of uranothorianite.

Zinc

In many mines lead and zinc are co-products of the same ore (galena), and zinc may be in the form of zincblende. It may also be associated with silver, gold or copper. Complex zinc ores are concentrated by flotation processes and treated by electrolysis and roasting. Secondary production from scrap plays a significant role in the markets for both lead and zinc. The chief industrial uses of zinc are in the motor car industry, in galvanizing, brass making and die casting.

Africa has small reserves of zinc (about 5.3 per cent of world reserves).

PRODUCTION OF ZINC ORE
(zinc content, '000 metric tons)

	1969	1970
WORLD TOTAL[1]	5,400.0	5,480.0
Africa	305.0	285.0
Leading African Producers:		
Algeria[2]	20.9	17.0
Morocco[2]	32.4	15.8
South West Africa[2,3]	70.0	n.a.
Zaire[2]	99.9	105.1
Zambia[2,4]	68.2	64.7
Leading non-African Producers:		
Australia[2]	509.9	489.1
Canada	1,194.2	1,239.2
U.S.S.R.[3,5]	610.0	n.a.
U.S.A.[5]	501.8	484.6

[1] Excluding Czechoslovakia, Romania and North Viet-Nam.
[2] Content of concentrates.
[3] *Source:* U.S. Bureau of Mines.
[4] *Source:* World Metal Statistics.
[5] Production calculated as recoverable.

Sources for Mineral Tables (unless otherwise indicated): United Nations, *Statistical Yearbook 1971*; U.N., *Monthly Bulletin of Statistics*, 1972 issues.

───────────

We acknowledge with many thanks the assistance of the following bodies in the preparation of this section:

The International Rice Research Institute, the Cotton Research Corporation, the International Rubber Study Group, the International Wheat Council, De Beers Consolidated Mines Ltd., the Institute of Petroleum, the Copper Development Association, the International Tin Council, the Asbestos Information Committee, the Lead Development Association, the Tin Research Institute and the Cobalt Information Centre.

Research Institutes

Associations and Institutions Outside Africa South of the Sahara Studying Africa*

(See also Regional Organizations in Part II)

ALGERIA

Centre de Recherches Africaines: Faculté des Lettres, Université d'Alger, 2 rue Didouche Mourad, Algiers.

AUSTRALIA

Australian Institute of International Affairs: 177 Collins Street, Melbourne; f. 1932; 1,561 mems.; brs. in all States; Pres. Prof. JOHN ANDREWS; Hon. Sec. Miss NANCE DICKINS; publ. *The Australian Outlook* (three times yearly).

AUSTRIA

Afro-Asiatisches Institut in Wien (*Afro-Asian Institute in Vienna*): A-1090 Vienna, Türkenstrasse 3; f. 1959; cultural and other exchange between Austria and African and Asian countries, lectures, economic and social research, seminars; library of *c.* 1,000 vols.; Gen. Sec. A. GRÜNFELDER.

Österreichische Forschungsstiftung für Entwicklungshilfe (*Austrian Research Institute for Development Aid*): A-1090 Vienna, Türkenstrasse 3/III; f. 1967; research, documentation and information on development aid and developing countries, particularly relating to Austria; library of 7,000 vols.; Pres. Prof. Dr. K. M. ZACHERL; Dir. Dr. H. MILLENDORFER; publs. *Internationale Entwicklung* (quarterly).

Österreichische Gesellschaft für Aussenpolitik und Internationale Beziehungen (*Austrian Society for Foreign Policy and International Relations*): A-1010 Vienna, Josefsplatz 6; f. 1958; lectures, discussions; 380 mems.; library of 2,200 vols., press cuttings; Pres. Dr. G. FÜRSTENBERG; Sec.-Gen. Dr. JOSEF SCHONER; publ. *Österreichische Zeitschrift für Aussenpolitik* (six times yearly).

Österreichisches Institut für Entwicklungshilfe und technische Zusammenarbeit mit den Entwicklungsländern (*Austrian Institute for Development Aid and Technical Co-operation with the Developing Countries*): Vienna I, Grillparzerstrasse 14; f. 1963; projects for training of young people; Pres. Dr. FRANZ-JOSEF MAYER-GUNTHOF and Prof. FRITZ KLENNER.

BELGIUM

Académie Royale des Sciences d'Outre-Mer: Koninklijke Academie voor Overzeese Wetenschappen: 1 rue Defacqz, 1050 Brussels; f. 1928; the promotion of scientific knowledge of overseas areas, especially those with particular development problems; Pres. M. J. OPSOMER; Perm. Sec. Prof. P. STANER; 11 hon. mems., 43 mems., 62 assocs., 50 corresps.

Centre d'Étude et de Documentation Africaines (CÉDAF): 7 place Royale, 1000 Brussels; f. 1970; Dir. B. VERHAEGEN; publ. *Bulletin de CÉDAF*.

Centre de Formation (Section Enseignement pour Etrangers): Ministère des Affaires Etrangères et du Commerce Extérieur, 183-185 ave. Louise, Brussels 5; the School provides free training for candidates preparing for posts in Africa and language training for students from developing countries; library collections of books and documents on the overseas territories; Dir. E. NYS, rue Emile Banning 108, Brussels 5.

Centre International de Documentation Economique et Sociale Africaine: 7 place Royale, 1000 Brussels; f. 1961 to collect and co-ordinate documentation on economic and social subjects concerning Africa with a view to furthering the progress of the continent in these fields; 92 institutions are mems.; Pres. Dr. G. JANTZEN; Sec.-Gen. Dr. J. B. CUYVERS; publs. *Bibliographical Index-cards, Bulletin, Bibliographical Enquiries*.

Centre pour l'Etude des Problèmes du Monde Musulman Contemporain (*Study Centre for Problems of the Contemporary Muslim World*): 44 ave. Jeanne, 1050 Brussels; f. 1957; Scientific Dir. Prof. A. ABEL; publ. *Correspondance d'Orient—Etudes* (bi-annual).

Institut d'Etude des Pays en Développement (*Study Institute of Developing Countries*): Catholic University of Louvain, 2A Van Even Straat, 3000 Louvain; f. 1961; Pres. Prof. F. BEZY (French); Prof. L. BAECK (Flemish).

Institut pour la Recherche Scientifique en Afrique Centrale (I.R.S.A.C.) (*Institute for Scientific Research in Central Africa*): 1 rue Defacqz, 1050 Brussels; and Lwiro, Bukavu (Zaire); f. 1947 to conduct scientific research in Central Africa, with special reference to Zaire; the principal fields of research investigation are in biology, physics and human sciences; there are two research centres in Africa at Lwiro (Zaire) and Mabali (Lake Tumba); Sec.-Gen. L. SOYER; Dir. Dr. P. KUNKEL; publs. *Rapport Annuel, Folia Scientifica Africae Centralis* (quarterly review), *Bulletin des Stations séismologiques de l'I.R.S.A.C., Bulletin de la Station ionosphérique, Observations radio-électriques de la station de Radio-astronomie*.

Institut Royal des Relations Internationales: 88 ave. de la Couronne, 1050 Brussels; f. 1947; Pres. Baron JEAN-CHARLES SNOY ET D'OPPUERS; Vice-Pres. and Treas. Prof. PIERRE ANSIAUX (Senator); Dir.-Gen. Prof. EMMANUEL COPPIETERS, DR.ECON., DR.JUR., M.SC.(ECON.); research in international relations, international economics, international law and international politics; specialized library containing 10,000 vols. and 300 periodicals; archives; lectures and conferences are held; publs. *Chronique de Politique Etrangère* (bi-monthly), *Internationale Spectator, Tijdschrift voor Internationale Politiek* (semi-monthly), *La Belgique et les Nations Unies, La crise du système de sécurité collective des Nations Unies, 1946–47, La Belgique et l'aide économique aux pays sous-développés, Consciences tribales et nationales en Afrique Noire, Le rôle proéminent du Secrétaire général dans l'opération des Nations Unies au Congo, Les conséquences d'ordre interne de la participation de la Belgique aux Organisations internationales*.

Institute for Developing Countries—State University Centre of Antwerp: Kasteel Den Brandt, Villa La Chapelle, Beukenlaan 12, Antwerp; f. 1920; fmrly. the *Institut Universitaire des Territoires d'Outremer*; Pres. Dr. J. RENS; Admin. Dir. Prof. G. SCHMIT.

Koninklijk Museum voor Midden-Afrika—Musée Royal de l'Afrique Centrale: Steenweg op Leuven 13, 1980 Tervuren, near Brussels; f. 1898; Dir. L. CAHEN; large collections in the fields of prehistory, ethnography, native arts and crafts; geology, mineralogy, palaeontology; zoology (entomology, ornithology, mammals,

---

* For Research Institutes in countries in Africa South of the Sahara, see entries under individual countries.

reptiles, etc.); history; economics; library of 40,000 vols., and 3,500 periodicals; 37 scientific staff; publs. *Annales du Musée Royal de l'Afrique Centrale*, and miscellaneous publications.

Société Belge d'Etudes Géographiques (*Belgian Society for Geographical Studies*): Blandynberg, 2 Ghent; f. 1931; Pres. G. POLSPOEL; Sec. M. E. DUMONT; centralizes and co-ordinates geographical research in Belgium and the Congo; 325 mems.; publ. *Bulletin* (twice a year).

Union Royale Belge pour le Congo les Pays d'Outremer: formerly Royal Union Coloniale Belge; 34 rue de Stassart, Brussels; f. 1912; Chair. ALBERT COFFIN; Gen. Sec. LÉON MOREL; 200 mems.; publ. *Bulletin* (monthly).

BRAZIL

Instituto Brasileiro de Relacões Internacionais (*Brazilian Institute of International Relations*): Praia de Botafogo 186, Gr.B. 213, Rio de Janeiro, GB.; f. 1954; 1,500 vols.; Exec. Dir. CLEANTHO DE PAIVA LEITE; Sec. CEZAR C. HAROUCHE; publs. *Revista Brasileira de Política Internacional* (quarterly).

BULGARIA

Research Centre for Asia and Africa: Dept. of Philosophy, Economics and Law, Bulgarian Academy of Sciences, 7 Noemvri 1, Sofia; f. 1967; Dir. Acad. E. KAMENOV.

CANADA

Canadian Association of African Studies: f. 1971; Sec.-Treas. Dr. D. R. F. TAYLOR, Department of Geography, Carleton University, Ottawa, K1S 5B6; publ. *Canadian Journal of African Studies.*

Canadian Council for International Co-operation (*Conseil canadien pour la coopération internationale*): 75 Sparks St., Ottawa, Ontario, K1P 5A5; f. 1968 (formerly Overseas Institute of Canada, f. 1961); information centre for international development and forum for voluntary agencies; 300 individual mems., 65 organizational mems.; Pres. J. MAGWOOD, Q.C.; Exec. Dir. A. ARCHER; publs. *Informadev* (monthly), *Film Catologue*, Dossier Series, Bibliographies, Action Manuels, Surveys, Directories, Fact Sheets.

Canadian Institute of International Affairs: 31 Wellesley St. East, Toronto 284; f. 1928; affiliate of R.I.I.A., London; 3,000 mems. in 23 brs.; Dir.-Gen. JOHN W. HOLMES; Exec. Dir. ROBERT W. REFORD; Sec. Miss EDNA A. NEALE; publs. *International Journal* (quarterly), *Annual Report, Behind the Headlines, Contemporary Affairs, International Canada, Canada in World Affairs* (every two years) and special research projects.

Centre for Developing Area Studies (*Centre d'études pour les régions en voie de développement*): McGill University, 3437 Peel St., Montreal 112, Quebec.

Institute for International Co-operation (*Institut de coopération internationale*): f. 1968; an attached Institute of University of Ottawa, Ottawa, Ont., K1N 6N5; Dir. Prof. L. SABOURIN.

International Development Research Centre (*Centre de recherches pour le développement*): 2197 Riverside Drive, Ottawa.

CHILE

Instituto de Estudios Internacionales de la Universidad de Chile (*Institute of International Studies*): Casilla 14187, Sucursal 21, Santiago; f. 1966; postgraduate international, political and economic studies; Dir. CLAUDIO VÉLIZ; publ. *Estudios Internacionales* (quarterly).

PEOPLE'S REPUBLIC OF CHINA

Chinese People's Institute of Foreign Affairs: Peking; Hon. Chair. CHOU EN-LAI; Pres. CHANG HSI-JO; Sec.-Gen. WU MAO-SUN.

Institute of International Relations: Dept. of Philosophy and Social Sciences of Chinese Acad. of Sciences, Peking.

CUBA

Instituto de Política Internacional (*Institute of International Politics*): Ministry of Foreign Affairs, Havana; f. 1962; 11 mems.; Principal Officers Dr. FERNANDO ALVAREZ TABÍO, Dr. JUAN B. MORÉ BENÍTEZ, Dr. ELOY G. MERINO BRITO, Dr. MARIANO RODRÍGUEZ SOLVEIRA, Dr. JULIO LE RIVEREND BRUSSONE; publ. *Política Internacional* (quarterly review).

CZECHOSLOVAKIA

Institute of International Politics and Economics: Prague 1, Vlašská 19; Dir. Dr. ANTONÍN SNEJDÁREK.

DENMARK

Institute for Development Research: 5 Sct. Annae Plads, 1250 Copenhagen; f. 1969; to promote and undertake research in the economic and social development of developing countries; Dir. Prof. T. KRISTENSEN; publs. *Den Ny Verden* (quarterly), *Newsletter* (English, irregular).

Det Udenrigspolitiske Selskab (*Foreign Policy Society*): Vandkusten 8, DK-1467 Copenhagen K; f. 1946; studies, debates, courses and conferences on international affairs; Dir. JOHAN WILHJELM; publs. *Fremtiden, Udenrigspolitiske Skrifter, Økonomisk Krønik.*

FRANCE

Académie des Sciences d'Outre-mer: 15 rue La Pérouse, Paris 16e; f. 1922; 100 members attached to sections on Geography, Politics and Administration, Law, Economics and Sociology, Science and Medicine, Education; Pres. PIERRE LEGOUX; Permanent Treas. R. BARGUES; Perm. Sec. OSWALD DURAND; publ. *Comptes Rendus.*

Association d'Etudes et d'Information Politiques Internationales: 86 blvd. Haussmann, Paris 8e; f. 1949; Dir. G. ALBERTINI; publs. *Est & Ouest* (Paris, twice monthly), *Documenti sul Comunismo* (Rome), *Este y Oeste* (Caracas).

Centre d'Etudes de Politique Etrangère: 54 rue de Varenne, Paris 7e; publ. *Politique Etrangère.*

Centre de Recherches Africaines: (an Institute of the University of Paris), 17 rue de la Sorbonne, Paris 5e.

Centre des Hautes Etudes Administratives sur l'Afrique et l'Asie Modernes: (an affiliated Institute of University of Paris), 13 rue du Four, Paris 6e; Dir. G. R. MALÉCOT; publs. *L'Afrique et l'Asie* (quarterly), *Cahiers de l'Afrique et l'Asie* (irregular), *Langues et Dialects d'Outre-Mer* (irregular), *Recherches et Documents de CHEAM* (irregular).

Ecole des Hautes Etudes Internationales: 44 rue de Rennes, Paris 6e; f. 1924; Pres. J. ROLLAND; Dir. A. LE JULES.

Institut Européen des Hautes Etudes Internationales (*European Institute of Higher International Studies*): (an affiliated Institute of the University of Nice), Palais de Marbre, ave. de Fabron, Nice.

Musée de l'Homme: Palais de Chaillot, Paris 16e; f. 1878; library of 250,000 vols.; ethnography, anthropology, prehistory; Admin. Dir. LIONEL BALOUT; publs. *Revue* (quarterly), *Objets et Mondes*.

Office de la Recherche Scientifique et Technique Outre-Mer: 24 rue Bayard, 75008 Paris; f. 1943, reorganized 1960; autonomous national institution, financially independent; centres in Africa: Cameroon, Central African Republic, Congo Republic, Ivory Coast, Senegal, Chad, Togo, Dahomey, Gabon, Upper Volta, Madagascar; Pres. ANDRÉ VALABREGUE; Dir.-Gen. Prof. GUY CAMUS; Sec.-Gen. JEAN SEVERAC.

Société des Africanistes (CSSF): Musée de l'Homme, place du Trocadéro, Paris 16e; f. 1931; 300 members; Sec. Mme G. DIETERLEN; publ. *Journal de la Société des Africanistes*.

Société Française d'Histoire d'Outre-Mer (formerly Société de l'Histoire des Colonies Françaises): B.P. 107-01, 43 rue Cambon, Paris 1er; f. 1913; Hon. Pres. ROBERT DELAVIGNETTE; Pres. HUBERT DESCHAMPS; Vice-Pres. GABRIEL DEBIEN, Mlle BLANCHE MAUREL; Sec.-Gen. CARLO LAROCHE; publ. *Revue Française d'Histoire d'Outre-Mer* (quarterly), also books occasionally.

U.E.R. Oriental and North African Languages and Civilizations: Université de Paris I, rue des Ecoles, Paris 5e.

FEDERAL REPUBLIC OF GERMANY

African Studies Centre: I.F.O. Institute for Economic Research, 8000 Munich 86, Poschingerstrasse 5.

Deutsche Afrika Gesellschaft: Bonn, Markt 10-12; publ. *Afrika Heute* (monthly).

Deutsche Gesellschaft für Auswärtige Politik e.V. (*German Society for Foreign Affairs*): Bonn, Adenauerallee 133; f. 1955; 1,150 mems.; discusses and promotes research on problems of international politics; research library of 24,000 vols.; Pres. Dr. Dr. h.c. GÜNTER HENLE; Exec. Vice-Pres. Dr. GEBHARDT VON WALTHER; Dir. Research Institute, Prof. Dr. KARL CARSTENS; publs. *Die Internationale Politik* (yearbook), *Europa-Archiv*, *Zeitschrift für internationale Politik* (fortnightly).

Deutsches Institut für Afrika-Forschung e.V. (*German Institute of African Studies*): 2 Hamburg 1, Klosterwall 4; f. 1963; research, discussion groups, international contact with organizations and individuals with specialized knowledge of African affairs; library of 12,000 vols.; Chair. Prof. Dr. ALBERT KOLB; publs. *Hamburger Beiträge zur Afrika-Kunde, Afrika Spectrum, Dokumentationsdienst Afrika*.

GERMAN DEMOCRATIC REPUBLIC

Department of African and Near Eastern Studies: Karl-Marx University, 701 Leipzig, Peterssteinweg 8; Dir. Prof. Dr. G. BREHME.

Institut für Internationale Beziehungen, Deutsche Akademie für Staats- und Rechtswissenschaft "Walter Ulbricht" (*Institute for International Relations*): 1502 Potsdam-Babelsberg, August Bebelstr. 89; f. 1964; training in international law and international relations; Dir. Prof. Dr. GERHARD HAHN; publs. *Deutsche Aussenpolitik* (bi-monthly), *German Foreign Policy* (every two months), *Referatezeitschrift Völkerrecht und internationale Beziehungen, Blickpunkt Weltpolitik* (five to seven times a year).

GUYANA

Guyana Institute of International Affairs: 154 Charlotte St., Lacytown, Georgetown; Dir. DONALD A. B. TROTMAN; publs. *International Affairs Quarterly, Selected Sketches on Current World Situations*.

HUNGARY

Centre for Afro-Asian Research of the Hungarian Academy of Sciences: Budapest 126, P.O.B. 36; f. 1963; library of 18,000 vols.; Dir. Prof. J. BOGNÁR; publ. *Studies on Developing Countries*.

INDIA

Indian Council of World Affairs: Sapru House, Barakhamba Rd., New Delhi 1; f. 1943; non-governmental institution for the study of Indian and international questions; 1,500 mems.; library of 125,000 vols., 1,500 periodicals; Pres. Dr. H. N. KUNZRU; Sec.-Gen. S. L. POPLAI; over 50 publs., periodicals *India Quarterly* (1944-), *Foreign Affairs Reports* (monthly, 1952-).

Institute of Afro-Asian and World Affairs: 14 Theatre Communication Bldg., Connaught Circus, New Delhi; publ. *Afro-Asian and World Affairs* (quarterly).

International Council for Africa: 5 Balwantray Mehta Lane, New Delhi; publ. *Africa Quarterly*.

INDONESIA

Indonesian Institute of World Affairs: c/o University of Indonesia, Djakarta; Chair. Prof. SUPOMO; Sec. Mr. SUDJATMOKO.

ISRAEL

Afro-Asian Institute for Co-operative and Labour Studies: P.O.B. 16201, Tel-Aviv; f. 1960 to teach development, co-operation and labour problems to African and Asian trade unionists, co-operative workers, government officials and teaching staff of universities and colleges; French-speaking course Jan. to April, English-speaking course Aug. to Nov., 50 students each course; special courses on selected subjects May-July; library of 7,500 vols.; 2,450 graduates from 85 countries; Chair. E. ELATH; Principal A. EGER.

Institute of Asian and African Studies: Hebrew University of Jerusalem, Jerusalem; f. 1926; studies of medieval and modern languages, culture and history of Middle East, Asia and Africa; Dir. Prof. GABRIEL BAER; irregular publications.

International Institute for Development, Co-operative and Labour Studies: f. 1971 by the Afro-Asian Institute; Principal A. EGER.

Israel Oriental Society, The: The Hebrew University, Jerusalem; f. 1949; aims to promote interest in and knowledge of life in the Middle East, Asia and Africa; arranges lectures and symposia to study all aspects of contemporary Middle Eastern, Asian and African affairs; Pres. E. ELATH; publs. *Hamizrah Hehadash* (*The New East*) (quarterly 1950–70), *Oriental Notes and Studies* (scientific monographs 1951–66); *Asian and African Studies* (annual 1965-71); *Journal* (three times a year).

Shiloa Center for Middle Eastern and African Studies: Tel-Aviv University, Ramat-Aviv, Tel-Aviv.

ITALY

The Bologna Center School of Advanced International Studies of the Johns Hopkins University: Via Belmeloro 11, 40126 Bologna: f. 1955; objective: graduate work in international affairs; Dir. SIMON H. SERFATY; 19 teachers, 100 students; publs. *Bologna Center Catalogue, Alumni Newsletter.*

Istituto Affari Internazionali: viale Mazzini 88, 00195 Rome; Dir.-Gen. ALTIERO SPINELLI.

Istituto Italo-Africano: via Ulisse Aldrovandi, 16 Rome; Sec.-Gen. Ambassador PAOLO TALLARIGO; publs. *Africa* (quarterly), *La Voce dell'Africa* (monthly).

Istituto per gli Studi di Politica Internazionale: via Clerici 5, Milan; f. 1934 for the promotion of the study and knowledge of all problems concerning international relations; seminars at post-graduate level; library of 40,000 vols.; Pres. Prof. DINO DEL BO; Gen. Dir. Dott. GIOVANNI LOUBETTI; publs. *Relazioni Internazionali* (weekly), *Annuario di Politica Internazionale* (yearly) and series of books.

JAPAN

Institute for the Study of Languages and Cultures of Asia and Africa: Tokyo University of Foreign Studies, 51 Nishigahara, 4-chome, Kita-ku, Tokyo; f. 1964; 30 researchers, 34 administrators, 16,532 vols.; Dir. M. OKA; publs. *Journal of Asian and African Studies* (annually), *Newsletter* (thrice yearly).

Nippon Kokusai Seiji Gakkai (*The Japan Association of International Relations*): Hosei University, Fujimi-cho, Chiyoda-ku, Tokyo; f. 1956; 512 mems.; Pres. H. KAMIKAWA; publ. *International Relations* (quarterly).

THE NETHERLANDS

Afrika Instituut: Prinses Beatrixlaan 7, 's Gravenhage; publ. *Afrika* (monthly).

Afrika-Studiecentrum: Stationsplein 10, Leiden; f. 1947 to promote study of Africa, especially in the humanities; to promote the co-operation of all Dutch institutions engaged in the study of Africa; to promote the spread of academic knowledge about Africa; Dir. Prof. J. F. HOLLEMAN; Sec.-Gen. G. W. GROOTENHUIS; publ. *Kroniek van Afrika* (quarterly), *Documentatieblad* (monthly).

Nederlandsch Genootschap voor Internationale Zaken (*Netherlands Institute of International Affairs*): 2 Alexanderstraat, The Hague; f. 1945; 900 mems.; research on international issues; lectures; library of 6,500 vols.; Sec.-Gen. J. L. HELDRING; publs. *Internationale Spectator* and *Wereldwijzer.*

NEW ZEALAND

New Zealand Institute of International Affairs: P.O.B. 196, Wellington; f. 1934; Pres. ALEXANDER MACLEOD; Dir. KEN KEITH; publs. numerous books and pamphlets.

NORWAY

Norsk Utenrikpolitisk Institutt (*Norwegian Institute of International Affairs*): Bygdöy Allé 3, Oslo 2; f. 1959; information, publication and research in international relations; Pres. PAUL THYNESS; Dir. Dr. JOHN SANNESS; Sec. HARALD NJÖS; publs. *Internasjonal Politikk* (quarterly), *Economics of Planning* (Scandinavian journal of Eastern economies with emphasis on theoretical problems).

PAKISTAN

Pakistan Institute of International Affairs: Strachen Road, Karachi; f. 1947; to study international affairs and to promote the scientific study of international politics, economics and jurisprudence; library 15,000 vols.; 400 mems.; Pres. The Minister of Foreign Affairs; Sec. KH. SARWAR HASAN; publs. *Pakistan Horizon* (quarterly); books and monographs.

POLAND

Centre of African Studies: University of Warsaw, Krakowskie Przedmiescie 26-28, Warsaw; f. 1962; Dir. Prof. Dr. BOGODAR WINID; publs. *Africana Bulletin* (English, French, semi-annual), *Przeglad informacji o Afryce* (quarterly), *Informatory Problemone* (series), *Informatory Regionalne* (series).

Polish Institute of International Affairs: Warsaw, Warecka 1a; f. 1947; library of 90,000 vols.; Dir. RYSZARD FRELEK; publs. *Sprawy Międzynarodowe* (monthly), *Zbiór Dokumentów* (monthly, in Polish and French), *Polish Perspectives* (monthly, in English, French and German), *Zbiór Umów Międzynarodowych Polskiej Rzeczypospolitej Ludowej* (Polish International Agreements, annual), *Yearbook of International Law* (in English), *Studies on Developing Countries* (in English), *Studies on International Relations* (in English).

PORTUGAL

Junta de Investigações do Ultramar—JIU (*Overseas Research Council*): Ministério do Ultramar, 7° piso, Restelo, Lisbon 3; f. 1936; Pres. Dr. JUSTINO MENDES DE ALMEIDA; Vice-Pres. Dr. RAIMUNDO BRITES MOITA; Sec. Dr. JOSÉ J. FERRAZ; publs. *Anais; Memórias; Estudos, Ensaios e Documentos; Garcia de Orta* (series); *Estudos de Ciências Políticas e Sociais; Bibliografia Científica da Junta de Investigações do Ultramar;* geographical maps and plans of the overseas provinces.

Museu Etnográfico do Ultramar (*Overseas Ethnographical Museums*): Rua das Portas de Santo Antão, Lisbon; f. 1875; native arts, arms, clothing, musical instruments, statutes of navigators and historians, relics of voyages of discovery, scientific instruments; Dir. Prof. ANTÓNIO DE ALMEIDA.

SINGAPORE

Singapore Institute of International Affairs: c/o Roy H. Haas, Dept. of Political Science, University of Singapore, Bukit Rimah Rd., Singapore 10; Pres. GEORGE G. THOMSON.

SPAIN

Instituto de Estudios Africanos (*Institute of African Studies*): Castellana 5, Madrid; f. 1945; 20 mems.; Dir. EDUARDO JUNCO MENDOZA; Sec. JOAQUÍN VENTURA BAÑARES; publs. *Africa* (monthly), *Collección Monográfica Africana* (irregular).

Instituto de Estudios Políticos (*Institute of Political Studies*): Plaza de la Marina Española 8, Madrid; f. 1939; the Institute organizes lectures and seminars on political, economic, administrative and social questions; library of 20,000 vols., access to the Senate Library of 100,000 vols.; Dir. LUIS LEGAZ LACAMBRA; Sec.-Gen. MANUEL SOLANA SANZ; Pres. of Permanent Commission LUIS LEGAZ LACAMBRA; publs. *Revista de Estudios* (6 issues yearly), *Política Internacional* (6 issues yearly), *Revista de Administración Pública* (every 4 months), *Revista de Politica Social* (quarterly), *Revista de Economía Política* (every 4 months).

SRI LANKA

Ceylon Institute of World Affairs: c/o Mervyn de Silva, 82B Ward Place, Colombo 7; f. 1957; Pres. Maj.-Gen. ANTON MUTTUKUMARU.

SWEDEN

Institutet för internationell ekonomi (*Institute for International Economic Studies*): Fack, S-104 05 Stockholm 50 (attached to the University of Stockholm); f. 1962; Dir. ASSAR LINDBECK.

Nordiska Afrikainstitutet (*The Scandinavian Institute of African Studies*): Box 345, S-751 06 Uppsala; f. 1962; documentation and research centre for current African affairs, library, publication work, lectures, seminars and courses; 12 mems.; library of 15,000 vols., 1,800 periodicals; Dir. Prof. CARL GÖSTA WIDSTRAND; Admin. Sec. K. E. ERICSON; publs. *Annual Seminar Proceedings, Research Reports, Africana, Newsletter*.

Utrikespolitiska Institutet (*The Swedish Institute of International Affairs*): Wenner Gren Center, 166 Sveavägen, 113 46 Stockholm; f. 1938; object: to promote the studies of international affairs; Pres. Dr. KURT SAMUELSSON; Man. Dir. Dr. ÅKE SPARRING; publs. *Världspolitikens dagsfrågor, Strategisk bulletin, Archives 69, Internationella studier, Kalendarium*.

SWITZERLAND

Institut Africain de Genève: 24 rue Rothschild, 1202 Geneva; f. 1960; lectures on African geography, history, culture, economic and sociological problems; introductory and advanced seminars, research; Dir. PIERRE BUNGENER; Dir. of Studies RENÉ WADLOW; 14 teachers; library; publ. *Genève-Afrique* (half-yearly).

Institut Universitaire de Hautes Etudes Internationales (*Graduate Institute of International Studies*): 132 rue de Lausanne; f. 1927; a research and teaching institution studying international questions from the juridical, political and economic viewpoints; Dir. Dr. J. FREYMOND.

Schweizerisches Institut für Auslandforschung (*Swiss Institute of International Studies*): (an attached Institute of St. Gall Graduate School of Economics, Business and Public Administration), Münstergasse 9, 8001 Zurich; Exec. Dir. Prof. D.Dr. F. A. LUTZ; Pres. of the Board Dr. R. LANG.

U.S.S.R.

Institute of Africa: attached to the Department of Economics, U.S.S.R. Academy of Sciences, Starokonyushenny per. 16, Moscow; Dir. V. G. SOLODOVNIKOV.

Institute of International Relations: Metrostroyevskaya 53, Moscow; Dir. B. P. MIROSHNICHENKO.

Scientific Council on Problems of Africa: Section of Social Sciences of U.S.S.R. Academy of Sciences, Leninsky prospekt 14, Moscow; Chair. V. G. SOLODOVNIKOV.

UNITED KINGDOM

The Africa Bureau: 48 Grafton Way, London, W1P 5LB; f. 1952; aims: to improve understanding in Britain about current African events and problems; to promote British policies that will assist social and economic development in Africa; to oppose racial tyrannies in Africa; to promote the achievement of non-discriminatory majority rule in Africa; Chair. Sir BERNARD DE BUNSEN; publ. *X-Ray* (monthly).

African Studies Association of the United Kingdom: c/o Centre of West African Studies, University of Birmingham, P.O.B. 363, Birmingham, B15 2SD; f. 1963 to advance academic studies relating to Africa by providing facilities for the interchange of information and ideas; holds inter-disciplinary conferences and symposia; 500 mems.; Hon. Pres. Prof. J. D. HARGREAVES; Hon. Treas. H. P. WHITE; Hon. Sec. Dr. R. P. MOSS; publ. *Bulletin* (three times a year).

African Studies Group: Department of History, King's College, Aberdeen University; f. 1966; Chair. Prof. J. D. HARGREAVES; Sec. Dr. R. C. BRIDGES.

Centre of African Studies: attached Institute of the University of Cambridge; Dir. J. R. GOODY, SC.D.

Centre of African Studies: University of Edinburgh, Edinburgh, Scotland.

Centre of West African Studies: associated Institute of the University of Birmingham, P.O.B. 363, Birmingham, B15 2TT; Dir. Prof. J. D. FAGE, M.A., PH.D.

International African Institute: 210 High Holborn, London, WC1V 7BW; f. 1926; information centre on African ethnology, linguistics and social studies; conducts research programmes, holds seminars and conferences; library of 6,000 vols.; mems.: 2,500 in 97 countries; Chair. Sir ARTHUR SMITH; Admin. Dir. Prof. DARYLL FORDE; publ. *Africa* (quarterly).

Overseas Development Institute: 10-11 Percy St., London, W1P 0JB; f. 1960 to act as a research centre and forum for the discussion of development issues and problems; the Institute publishes its research work in the form of pamphlets and books; library of over 8,000 vols.; Chair. Lord SEEBOHM; Dir. ANTONY TASKER, C.B.E.; Dir. of Studies ROBERT WOOD.

Project Planning Centre for Developing Countries: an attached Institute of the University of Bradford, Bradford, Yorks., BD7 1DP.

Royal African Society: 18 Northumberland Ave., London, WC2N 5BJ; f. 1901; 1,000 mems.; Pres. (vacant); Sec. Miss H. HEATHER; publs. *Journal* (quarterly), *African Affairs*.

Royal Commonwealth Society: 18 Northumberland Ave., London, W.C.2; f. 1868; 30,000 mems.; Chair. of Central Council Lord ASTOR OF HEVER; Sec.-Gen. A. S. H. KEMP, O.B.E.; publ. *Commonwealth* (bi-monthly).

Royal Institute of International Affairs: Chatham House, 10 St. James's Square, London, S.W.1; f. 1920 to facilitate the scientific study of international questions; mems., all categories, approx. 3,000; Pres. The Rt. Hon. the EARL OF AVON, K.G., M.C., PHILIP NOEL-BAKER, Sir ANDREW MACFADYEAN; Chair. Lord TREVELYAN, G.C.M.G., C.I.E., O.B.E.; Dir. ANDREW SHONFIELD; Dir. of Studies J. E. S. FAWCETT, D.SC.; Admin. Dir. Mrs. MARGARET CORNELL; affiliated Institutes in Canada, Australia, New Zealand, India, Pakistan, Singapore, Nigeria, Trinidad and Tobago, Guyana and Sri Lanka; publs. *British Year Book of International Law* (annually), *International Affairs* (quarterly), *The World Today* (monthly), individual studies, *Memoranda*, and study group reports (irregularly).

School of African and Asian Studies: University of Sussex, Falmer, Brighton, Sussex; Dean D. F. POCOCK, M.A., D.PHIL.

School of Oriental and African Studies: Malet St., London, WC1E 7HP; a school of the University of London; f. 1916; Dir. Prof. C. H. PHILIPS, M.A., LL.D., D.LITT., PH.D.; Sec. J. R. BRACKEN, M.A., B.LITT.; library of 350,000 vols.; number of teachers, 197, including 47 professors; number of students, 836; publs. *The Bulletin, Calendar, Annual Report, Journal of African History* (quarterly).

School of Oriental and African Studies Library: University of London, Malet St., WC1E 7HP; f. 1916; over 350,000 vols. and pamphlets and 1,900 MSS. dealing with Oriental and African languages, literatures, philosophy, religions, history, law, cultural anthropology, art and archaeology, social sciences; Librarian B. C. BLOOMFIELD, M.A.

UNITED STATES OF AMERICA

Africa Studies and Research Centre: Cornell University, Ithaca, N.Y. 14850; Dir. J. E. TURNER, M.A.

African American Institute: 345 E. 46th St., Room 815, New York, N.Y. 10017; publ. *Africa Report* (monthly).

African Bibliographic Center: P.O.B. 13096, Washington, D.C. 20009; f. 1963; indexing and information service on African affairs; Exec. Dir. DANIEL G. MATTHEWS; publs. *Current Bibliography of African Affairs* (every 2 months), *African Bibliographic Center News*, other irregular publs. in Special Bibliographic Series and Current Reading List Series.

African Studies Association: 218 Shiffman Center, Brandeis University, Waltham, Mass. 02154; f. 1957; 2,100 mems.; encourages research and collects and disseminates information on Africa; Pres. I. WALLERSTEIN; Sec. J. DUFFY; publs. *Review, Issue, Newsletter.*

African Studies Center: Boston University, 10 Lenox St., Brookline, Mass. 02146; f. 1953; research and teaching on literature, law, anthropology, economics, sociology, history and political science of Africa; library of 30,000 vols.; Dir. Dr. A. A. CASTAGNO; publs. *International Journal of African Historical Studies* (quarterly), *Boston University Papers on Africa* (irregular).

African Studies Center: University of California, Los Angeles, Calif. 90024; f. 1959; centre for co-ordination of scholarship on Africa in the social sciences and humanities, and for graduate training on Africa; Dir. BONIFACE I. OBICHERE; publs. *African Arts* (quarterly), *Studies in African Linguistics* (three times yearly), *Ufahamu: Journal of the African Activists Association* (three times yearly), *African Religious Research* (three times yearly), *Occasional Papers Series*, also books.

African Studies Center: Michigan State University, East Lansing, Mich. 48823; f. 1960; Dir. Dr. ALFRED E. OPUBOR; publs. *African Studies Review, Rural Africana, African Urban Notes.*

African Studies Committee: Southern Illinois University, Carbondale, Ill. 62901; f. 1961; Chair. Dr. J. E. REDDEN.

African Studies Program: Howard University, Washington, D.C. 20001; f. 1959; Dir. P. CHIKE, PH.D.; publ. *Newsletter* (bimonthly).

African Studies Program: University of Wisconsin, 1450 Van Hise Hall, 1220 Linden Drive, Madison, Wis. 53706.

American Society of African Culture: 401 Broadway, New York, N.Y. 10013; f. 1957; 300 mems.; affil. with the Société Africaine de Culture, Paris; exists to establish channels of communication for the recognition and development of African culture; Pres. SAUNDERS REDDING; Exec. Dir. CALVIN H. RAULLERSON; publ. *African Forum* (quarterly).

Brookings Institution: 1775 Massachusetts Ave., N.W., Washington, D.C. 20036; f. 1927; 127 professional mems.; 45,000 vols.; research, education, and publishing in the fields of economics, government, and foreign policy; Pres. KERMIT GORDON; publs. *Annual Report, Brookings Bulletin* (quarterly), *Brookings Papers on Economic Activity* (3 times a year), *Research Reports, Reprint Series* (irregular).

Center for International Studies: Massachusetts Institute of Technology, Cambridge, Mass. 02139; Dir. E. B. SKOLNIKOFF, PH.D.

Center for the Study of Democratic Institutions: Box 4068, Santa Barbara, Calif. 93103; f. 1959; 100,000 mems.; Chair. ROBERT M. HUTCHINS; Pres. HARRY S. ASHMORE; Sec. and Treas. GARY M. CADENHEAD; publ. *The Center Magazine.*

Center for the Study of Developing Nations: an organized research unit of the University of California, Santa Barbara, Calif. 93106.

Center of International Studies: Princeton University, Princeton, N.J. 08540; Dir. C. E. BLACK, PH.D.

Council on Foreign Relations Inc.: 58 East 68th St., New York, N.Y. 10021; f. 1921; 1,500 mems.; Chair. DAVID ROCKEFELLER; Pres. BAYLESS MANNING; Sec. FRANK ALTSCHUL; publs. *Foreign Affairs* (quarterly), *United States in World Affairs* (annual), *Documents on American Foreign Relations* (annual), *Political Handbook of the World* (annual), also many publs. on specific international questions.

Institute of African Studies: affiliated to Columbia University, Morningside Heights, New York, N.Y. 10027; Dir. HOLLIS R. LYNCH.

Institute of International and Intercultural Studies: University of Connecticut, Storrs, Conn. 06268; Dir. J. N. PLANK, PH.D.

Institute of International Studies and Overseas Administration: University of Oregon, Eugene, Ore.; Dir. JOHN GANGE.

Institute of World Affairs, Inc.: Hadden Campus, Twin Lakes, Salisbury, Conn. 06068; f. 1924; summer seminar for advanced students interested in international affairs or planning an academic career in some phase of public service, provides some scholarship assistance; 2,000 graduate mems.; Pres. Mrs. DANA C. BACKUS; Exec. Dir. JOHN BENJAMIN SCHMOKER.

International Research Institute: American Institutes for Research, 10605 Concord St., Kensington, Md. 20795; f. 1946; research on human resources in developing countries, human relations, role of attitudes and values in social change and economic development; Dir. Dr. PAUL SPECTOR.

Library of International Relations: 660 North Wabash Ave., Chicago, Ill. 60611; f. 1932; non-profit institution supported by voluntary contributions; founded to stimulate interest and research in international problems; 500 mems.; has a specialized collection of 300,000 books, documents and pamphlets, and more than 1,000 magazines and newspapers coming from all over the world; holds Round Table discussions for members; conducts seminars on special areas; offers documentary film programmes; offers special services to businesses and to academic institutions; Pres. EVEN T. COLLINSWORTH, Jr.; Sec. ELOISE RE QUA; Research Associate HAROLD NADEAU; publ. *International Information Notes* (monthly).

Program of African Studies: Northwestern University, 1813 Hinman Ave., Evanston, Ill. 60201; f. 1948; attached to Northwestern University, supported by the Ford Foundation and the Office of Education as well as the University; 35 faculty mems., 150 students; Dir. Prof. GWENDOLEN M. CARTER; publs. *Reprint Series, Reports.*

School of Advanced International Studies: Johns Hopkins University, Baltimore, Md. 21218; Dean F. O. WILCOX, PH.D., DR.SC.POL.

School of International Affairs: Columbia University, Morningside Drive, New York, N.Y. 10027; Dean HARVEY PICKER, B.A., M.B.A., D.SC.

The Adlai Stevenson Institute of International Affairs: Robie House, 5757 South Woodlawn Ave., Chicago, Ill. 60637; f. 1967; Pres. WILLIAM R. POLK; Dir. of Studies PETER DIAMANDOPOULOS; Dir. of Admin. SUMNER RAHR.

University Center for International Studies: Mervis Hall, University of Pittsburgh, Pittsburgh, Pa. 15213; a coordinating centre for international research and information retrieval at the University of Pittsburgh; Dir. CARL BECK; Co-Dir. PAUL WATSON; publs. *International Newsletter, Newssheet, Historical Methods Newsletter, Peasant Studies Newsletter, Canadian-American Slavic Studies Journal, Cuban Studies Newsletter,* and occasional papers.

Woodrow Wilson School of Public and International Affairs: Princeton University, Princeton, N.J. 08540; Dean J. P. LEWIS, M.P.A., PH.D.

YUGOSLAVIA

Institute for Developing Countries: attached to the University of Zagreb, Zagreb, Ul. 8, maja 82.

SELECT BIBLIOGRAPHY (PERIODICALS)

ACTIVADADE ECONÔMICA DE ANGOLA. Direcção Provincial dos Serviços de Economia e Estatística Geral, Governo Geral de Angola, Luanda, Angola; thrice yearly.

AFRICA. B.P. 1826 Dakar, Senegal; economic development of Tropical Africa; six times yearly.

AFRICA. Instituto de Estudios Africanos, Castellana 5, Madrid, Spain; monthly.

AFRICA. Instituto Italo-Africano, via Ulisse Aldrovandi, 16 Rome, Italy; quarterly.

AFRICA. International African Institute, 210 High Holborn, London, WC1V 7BW, England; quarterly.

AFRICA CONFIDENTIAL. 33 Rutland Gate, London, S.W.7, England; news and analysis of contemporary African politics and economics; fortnightly.

AFRICA CONTEMPORARY RECORD. Rex Collings Ltd., 6 Paddington St., London, W.1, England; annual documented survey.

AFRICA DIARY. F-15, Bhagat Singh Market, New Delhi 1, India; f. 1961; weekly.

AFRICA DIGEST. Africa Publications Trust, 48 Grafton Way, London, W1P 5LB; six times yearly.

AFRICA EDUCATION BULLETIN. UNESCO Regional Centre for Educational Information and Research, P.O.B. 2739, Accra, Ghana; f. 1963; irregular.

AFRICA INSTITUTE BULLETIN. Africa Institute, P.O.B. 630, Pretoria, South Africa; f. 1961; English and Afrikaans editions; political and economic; ten issues yearly.

AFRICA KENKYU. Journal of African Studies, Japanese Association of Africanists, Department of Geography, Faculty of Science, University of Tokyo, Tokyo, Japan; annual or twice yearly.

AFRICA QUARTERLY. Indian Council for Africa, 5 Balwantray Mehta Lane, New Delhi, India.

AFRICA REPORT. 866 United Nations Plaza, New York, N.Y. 10017, U.S.A.; nine per year.

AFRICA RESEARCH BULLETIN. Africa Research Ltd., 1 Parliament St., Exeter, England; f. 1964; monthly bulletins on (a) political and (b) economic subjects.

AFRICA-TERVUREN. Amis du Musée Royal de l'Afrique Centrale, 13 chaussée de Louvain, Tervuren, Belgium; f. 1961; African ethnology, history and archaeology; quarterly.

AFRICA TODAY. Africa Today Associates, Graduate School of International Studies, University Park Campus, Denver, Colo. 80210, U.S.A.; f. 1954; Exec. Editor EDWARD A. HAWLEY; quarterly.

AFRICAN AFFAIRS. Royal African Society, 18 Northumberland Ave., London, WC2N 5BJ, England; f. 1901; social sciences and history; covers the whole of Africa; quarterly; Editors ALISON SMITH and ANTHONY ATMORE.

AFRICAN ASSOCIATION REVIEW. African Association, 5 Ahmed Hishmat St., P.O.B. 1615, Zamalek, Cairo, Egypt; studies in African politics; English and Arabic parallel editions; monthly.

AFRICAN DEVELOPMENT. African Buyer and Trader, Wheatsheaf House, Carmelite St., London, E.C.4, England; f. 1965; Editor ALAN RAKE; monthly.

AFRICAN FORUM. American Society of African Culture, 401 Broadway, New York, N.Y. 10013, U.S.A.; 4–6 Oil Mill St., Lagos, Nigeria; quarterly.

THE AFRICAN HISTORIAN. Historical Society, University of Ife, Ile-Ife, Nigeria; African history, particularly Nigeria; annual.

AFRICAN LANGUAGE REVIEW. Frank Cass and Co. Ltd., 67 Great Russell St., London, WC1B 3BT; f. 1962; Editor DAVID DALBY; annual.

AFRICAN NOTES. Institute of African Studies, University of Ibadan, Ibadan, Nigeria; thrice yearly.

AFRICAN SOCIAL RESEARCH. Institute for African Studies, University of Zambia, P.O.B. 900, Lusaka, Zambia; Editors Prof. J. VAN VELSEN and M. E. KASHOKI; twice yearly.

AFRICAN STUDIES. University of the Witwatersrand, Johannesburg, South Africa; study of African administration, culture and languages; in English and Afrikaans; quarterly.

AFRICAN STUDIES REVIEW. African Studies Association, 218 Shiffman Humanities Center, Brandeis University, Waltham, Mass. 02154, U.S.A.; thrice yearly.

AFRICAN WORLD. St. Bride Foundation Institute, Bride Lane, London, E.C.4, England; f. 1902; monthly.

AFRICANA BULLETIN. Centre of African Studies, University of Warsaw, Warsaw 64, Poland; f. 1964; articles in English or French; Editor Dr. BOGODAR WINID; twice yearly.

AFRICASIA. 32 rue Washington, 75008 Paris, France; f. 1969; information, analysis and opinion; fortnightly.

AFRIKA. Prinses Beatrixlaan 7, 's Gravenhage, Netherlands; publ. by Afrika Instituut; monthly.

AFRIKA. Afrika-Verlag, 8 Munich, Kolombus Str. 20, Federal Republic of Germany; review of German-African relations; English and French editions; Editor Dr. HERBERT SCHROEDER; six times yearly.

AFRIKA HEUTE. Deutsche Afrika Gesellschaft e.V., Bonn, Markt 10-12, Federal Republic of Germany; politics, social and cultural affairs in Africa; monthly.

AFRIKA SPECTRUM. Deutsches Institut für Afrika-Forschung, 2 Hamburg 1, Klosterwall 4, Federal Republic of Germany; in German, English and French; thrice yearly.

AFRIQUE. Société Internationale de Publications Commerciales, Culturelles et Artistiques, 21 rue Barbet de Jouy, 75007 Paris, France; political, economic, social and cultural aspects of French-speaking Africa; monthly.

AFRIQUE ACTUELLE. O. Bhély-Quenum, 19 rue Greneta, 75002 Paris, France; monthly international African news magazine.

AFRIQUE CONTEMPORAINE. Centre d'Etudes et de Documentation sur l'Afrique et l'Outre-Mer, 31 quai Voltaire, 75007 Paris, France; documents on Black Africa and Madagascar; six times yearly.

L'AFRIQUE ET L'ASIE. Centre des Hautes Etudes Administratives sur l'Afrique et l'Asie Moderne, 13 rue du Four, 75006 Paris, France; quarterly.

AFRO-ASIA. Centro de Estudos Afro-Orientais, Universidade Federal de Bahia, Avenida Leovigildo Filgueiras 69, Salvador, Bahia, Brazil; f. 1965; history, politics, etc. of African and Asian countries; twice yearly.

AFRO-ASIAN AND WORLD AFFAIRS. Institute of Afro-Asian and World Affairs, 14, Theatre Communication Building, Connaught Circus, New Delhi 1, India; quarterly.

AFRO-ASIAN ECONOMIC REVIEW. Afro-Asian Organization for Economic Co-operation, Chamber of Commerce Building, Mindan El Falakry, Special P.O. Bag, Cairo, Egypt; monthly.

ASIA AND AFRICA TODAY. Institute of Asian Peoples and Institute of Africa, U.S.S.R. Academy of Sciences, Moscow, U.S.S.R.; scientific, social and political; monthly.

ASIA AND AFRICA REVIEW. Independent Publishing Co., 38 Kennington Lane, London, S.E.11, England; political, cultural and trade review; monthly.

BIBLIOGRAFIA CIENTÍFICA DA JUNTA DE INVESTIGAÇÕES DO ULTRAMAR. Centro de Documentação Científica Ultramarina, Junta de Investigações do Ultramar, Avenida da Ilha da Madeira, Restelo, Lisbon 3, Portugal; annual.

BOLETIM CULTURAL DA GUINÉ PORTUGUESA. Centro de Estudos da Guiné Portuguesa, Museu da Guiné Portuguesa, Caixa Postal 37, Bissau, Portuguese Guinea; quarterly.

BOLETIM GERAL DO ULTRAMAR. Agência Geral do Ultramar, Praça do Comércio, Lisbon, Portugal; articles summarized in French and English; monthly.

BULLETIN DE MADAGASCAR. Direction de la Presse, Ministère de l'Information, Place de l'Indépendance, B.P. 271, Tananarive, Madagascar; economic, social, cultural, linguistic studies; Editor M. RANDRIAMAROZAKA; every two months.

BULLETIN OF THE ABERDEEN UNIVERSITY AFRICAN STUDIES GROUP. Aberdeen African Studies Group, Dept. of History, King's College, Aberdeen, Scotland; f. 1967; contains bibliographical information; irregular.

BULLETIN OF INFORMATION ON CURRENT RESEARCH ON HUMAN SCIENCES CONCERNING AFRICA. Centre International de Documentation Économique et Sociale Africaine, 7 place Royale, 1000 Brussels, Belgium; French and English; twice yearly.

BULLETIN OF THE INTERNATIONAL COMMITTEE ON URGENT ANTHROPOLOGICAL AND ETHNOLOGICAL RESEARCH. International Committee on Urgent Anthropological and Ethnological Research, International Union of Anthropological and Ethnological Sciences, Universitätstrasse 7, 1010 Vienna 1, Austria; f. 1958; annual.

BULLETIN OF THE SCHOOL OF ORIENTAL AND AFRICAN STUDIES. School of Oriental and African Studies, University of London, London, W.C.1, England; f. 1917; three issues annually.

BULLETIN OF THE SOCIETY FOR AFRICAN CHURCH HISTORY. Department of Religious Studies, University of Aberdeen, Aberdeen, AB9 2UB, Scotland; f. 1963; Editor A. F. WALLS; annual.

CAHIERS AFRICAINS D'ADMINISTRATION PUBLIQUE. Centre Africain de Formation et de Recherche Administratives pour le Développement, B.P. 310, Tangier, Morocco; French and English editions; twice yearly.

CAHIERS D'ETUDES AFRICAINES. Ecole Pratique des Hautes Etudes, VIe Section, Division des Aires Culturelles, 20 rue de la Baume, 75008 Paris, France; quarterly.

CAHIERS ECONOMIQUES ET SOCIAUX. Institut de Recherches Economiques et Sociales, Université Lovanium, Kinshasa XI, Zaire; in French or English; particularly about Zaire; quarterly.

CAHIERS O.R.S.T.O.M. Office de la Recherche Scientifique et Technique Outre-Mer, Service Central de Documentation, 70 route d'Aulnay, 93140 Bondy, France; publs. 9 separate series; quarterlies on entomology and parasitology, hydrobiology, hydrology, oceanography, human sciences, pedology; twice yearly: geology; irregulars: biology, geophysics.

CANADIAN JOURNAL OF AFRICAN STUDIES. Committee on African Studies in Canada, Loyola College, 7141 Sherbrooke West Street, Montreal, Quebec, Canada; twice yearly.

COLLECIÓN MONOGRÁFICA AFRICANA. Instituto de Estudios Africanos, Castellana 5, Madrid, Spain; irregular.

CONNAISSANCE DE L'AFRIQUE. Cercle Universitaire "Connaissance de l'Afrique", 54 rue des Entrepreneurs, 75015 Paris, France; co-operation and development; six times yearly.

COOPÉRATION ET DEVELOPPEMENT. Bureau de Liaison des Agents de Coopération Technique, 54 rue des Entrepreneurs, 75 Paris 15e, France; developmental aspects of technical aid, new ways of teaching and training in Africa and Madagascar; six times yearly.

CURRENT BIBLIOGRAPHY OF AFRICAN AFFAIRS. African Bibliographic Center, P.O.B. 13096, Washington, D.C. 20009, U.S.A.; f. 1962; coverage of published and unpublished material on African affairs; every two months.

DEVELOPING ECONOMIES. Institute of Developing Economies, 42 Ichigaya Hommura-cho, Shinjuku-ku, Tokyo 162, Japan; f. 1962; English language; quarterly.

DOKUMENTATIONDIENST AFRIKA. Deutsches Institut für Afrika-Forschung e.V., 2 Hamburg 1, Klosterwall 4, Federal Republic of Germany.

EAST AFRICA JOURNAL. East African Institute of Social and Cultural Affairs, P.O.B. 30492, Uniafric Building, Koinange St., Nairobi; special literary issue in January; monthly.

EAST AFRICAN STUDIES. East African Institute of Social Research, Makerere University College, Kampala, Uganda; irregular.

ECONOMIC AND FINANCIAL REVIEW. Central Bank of Nigeria, P.M.B. 12194, Tinubu Square, Lagos, Nigeria; economy and finances of Nigeria; quarterly.

ECONOMIC BULLETIN FOR AFRICA. Economic Commission for Africa, Addis Ababa, Ethiopia; twice yearly.

ECONOMIC BULLETIN OF GHANA. Economic Society of Ghana, P.O.B. 22, Legon; quarterly.

ETHIOPIA OBSERVER. P.O.B. 1896, Addis Ababa, Ethiopia; Ethiopian social, economic and cultural problems; quarterly; Dir. R. PANKHURST.

EURAFRICA ET TRIBUNE DU TIERS MONDE. Chambre de Commerce et d'Industrie pour le Marché Commun Eurafricain, 55 rue Bosquet, 1060 Brussels, Belgium; political and economic relations between Europe and Africa, particularly Zaire; monthly.

EUROPE FRANCE OUTREMER. 6 rue de Bassano, 75016 Paris, France; f. 1923; economic and political material on French-speaking states of Africa; monthly.

FRANCE-EURAFRIQUE. 9 rue Bourdaloue, 75009 Paris, France; political, economic and cultural development of Africa (particularly French-speaking); monthly.

GENÈVE-AFRIQUE. Institut Africain de Genève, 24 rue Rothschild, 1202 Geneva, Switzerland; twice yearly.

INDEX TO AFRICAN EDUCATIONAL JOURNALS. UNESCO Regional Centre for Educational Information and Research in Africa, P.O.B. 2739, Accra, Ghana; f. 1967; twice yearly; English and French editions.

INDO-AFRICAN TRADE JOURNAL. Africa Publications (India), 9-M Bhagat Singh Market, New Delhi 1, India; f. 1965; monthly.

INTER-AFRICAN LABOUR INSTITUTE BULLETIN. Inter-African Labour Institute, B.P. 2019, Brazzaville, P.R. of Congo; quarterly review of labour problems in Africa; French and English editions.

INTERNATIONALES AFRIKA FORUM. Weltforum Verlags G.m.b.H., 8 Munich 19, Hubertusstrasse 22/II, German Federal Republic; f. 1965; monthly.

DER ISLAM. D2 Hamburg 13, Rothenbaumchaussee 36, German Federal Republic; three issues annually.

ISLAMIC QUARTERLY. The Islamic Cultural Centre, Regent's Lodge, 146 Park Rd., London, N.W.8, England; f. 1954; quarterly.

ISLAMIC REVIEW. Woking Muslim Mission and Literary Trust, 18 Eccleston Sq., London, S.W.1, England.

ISSUE. African Studies Association, 218 Shiffman Humanities Center, Brandeis University, Waltham, Mass. 02154, U.S.A.; a quarterly journal of Africanist opinion.

JEUNE AFRIQUE. Presse Africaine Associée, 51 av. des Ternes, 75017 Paris, France; f. 1960; weekly.

JOURNAL DE LA SOCIÉTÉ DES AFRICANISTES. Société des Africanistes, Musée de l'Homme, Palais de Chaillot, place du Trocadéro, 75016 Paris, France; some articles in English; twice yearly.

JOURNAL OF AFRICAN HISTORY. School of Oriental and African Studies, University of London, Malet St., London, WC1E 7HP, England; four times yearly.

JOURNAL OF AFRICAN LANGUAGES. A-633 Wells Hall, Michigan State University, East Lansing, Mich. 48823, U.S.A.; f. 1962; Editor IRVINE RICHARDSON; thrice yearly.

JOURNAL OF ASIAN AND AFRICAN STUDIES. Department of Sociology and Anthropology, York University, Toronto 12, Canada.

JOURNAL OF DEVELOPMENT STUDIES. Frank Cass and Co. Ltd., 67 Great Russell St., London, WC1B 3BT; f. 1964; Editors JOHN PEEL, MICHAEL LIPTON; 3 issues yearly.

JOURNAL OF ETHIOPIAN STUDIES. Institute of Ethiopian Studies, Haile Sellassie I University, Box 1176, Addis Ababa, Ethiopia; f. 1963; social and cultural anthropology, literature, history; twice yearly.

JOURNAL OF IMPERIAL AND COMMONWEALTH HISTORY. Frank Cass and Co. Ltd., 67 Great Russell St., London, WC1B 3BT; f. 1972; Editor TREVOR REESE; 3 issues yearly.

JOURNAL OF MODERN AFRICAN STUDIES. Prof. David Kimble, University of Botswana, Lesotho and Swaziland, P.O. Roma, Maseru, Lesotho; political and economic; quarterly; Editors DAVID and HELEN KIMBLE.

JOURNAL OF PEASANT STUDIES. Frank Cass and Co. Ltd., 67 Great Russell St., London, WC1B 3BT; f. 1973; quarterly.

JOURNAL OF RACIAL AFFAIRS. South African Bureau for Racial Affairs, P.O.B. 2768, Pretoria, South Africa; in Afrikaans and English; Man. Editor Dr. C. J. JOOSTE; quarterly.

JOURNAL OF RELIGION IN AFRICA. Department of Religious Studies, University of Aberdeen, Aberdeen, AB9 2UB, Scotland; f. 1967; Editor A. F. WALLS.

JOURNAL OF THE ISRAEL ORIENTAL SOCIETY. The Hebrew University, Jerusalem, Israel; three issues per year.

KRONIEK VAN AFRIKA. Afrika-Studiecentrum, Stationsplein 10, Leiden, Netherlands; quarterly.

LEEDS AFRICAN STUDIES BULLETIN. African Studies Unit, University of Leeds, Leeds, England; twice yearly.

MARCHÉS TROPICAUX ET MEDITERRANÉENS. 190 blvd. Haussmann, 75008 Paris; f. 1945; specializes in economics; Editor-in-Chief PIERRE CHAULEUR; weekly.

MONDO AFRO-ASIATICO. Via Marianna Dionigi 17, Rome, Italy; economic, political and cultural; articles in Italian and English or French; ten times yearly.

NARODY ASII I AFRIKI (Istoriya, Ekonomika, Kultura). 13 Khohlovsky per., Moscow 109028, U.S.S.R.; Akad. Nauk S.S.S.R., Institut Vostokovedeniya, Institut Afriki, Moscow, U.S.S.R.; f. 1955; bi-monthly; Editor-in-Chief Prof. I. S. BRAGINSKY.

NATIONS NOUVELLES, OCAM, B.P. 437, Yaoundé, Cameroon; f. 1964; articles on French-speaking Africa; Editor KANE FALILOU; every two months.

NIGERIAN OPINION. Nigerian Current Affairs Society, Faculty of Social Sciences, University of Ibadan, Ibadan, Nigeria; monthly.

NOTES AFRICAINES. Institut Fondamental d'Afrique Noire, University of Dakar, B.P. 206, Dakar, Senegal; quarterly.

ODU. A Journal of African Studies, Institute of African Studies, University of Ife, Ibadan, Nigeria; irregular.

OPTIMA. Anglo-American Corporation of South Africa, 44 Main Street, Johannesburg, South Africa; political, economic, social, cultural and scientific aspects of African development; quarterly.

PENANT. Documentation Africaine, 57 ave. d'Iéna, 75016 Paris, France; review of law in African countries; quarterly.

POUNT. Société d'Etudes de l'Afrique Orientale, B.P. 677, Djibouti, French Territory of the Afar and Issa; f. 1966; history, ethnology, social psychology, sociology and linguistics in Afar and Issa Territory; quarterly.

RECHERCHES AFRICAINES (formerly *Etudes Guinéennes*). Institut National de Recherches et de Documentation de Guinée, Secrétariat d'Etat à la Présidence de l'Information du Tourisme et de l'I.N.R.D.G., B.P. 561, Conakry, Guinea; quarterly.

REMARQUES AFRICAINES. Revue Panafricaine de Documentation; J. Ceulemans, 16 rue aux Laines, 1000 Brussels, Belgium; f. 1959; fortnightly.

RESEARCH REVIEW. Institute of African Studies, University of Ghana, Legon, Ghana; thrice yearly.

REVUE DES ETUDES ISLAMIQUES. Librarie Orientaliste Paul Geuthner, 12 rue Vavin, 75006 Paris, France; f. 1927; ed. H. LAOUST.

REVUE FRANÇAISE D'ETUDES POLITIQUES AFRICAINES. Société Africaine d'Edition, B.P. 1877, Dakar, Senegal; f. 1969; political; Editor PHILIPPE DECRAENE; monthly.

RHODESIANA. Rhodesiana Society, P.O.B. 8268, Causeway, Salisbury, Rhodesia; twice yearly.

SIERRA LEONE STUDIES. Department of Modern History, Fourah Bay College, Freetown, Sierra Leone; twice yearly.

SUDAN NOTES AND RECORDS. P.O.B. 555, Khartoum, Sudan; incorporating the proceedings of the Philosophical Society of the Sudan; Editor YUSUF FADL HASAN; Semi-annually.

A SURVEY OF RACE RELATIONS IN SOUTH AFRICA. South African Institute of Race Relations, P.O.B. 97, Johannesburg, South Africa; yearly.

TANZANIA NOTES AND RECORDS. Tanzania Society, National Memorial Museum, P.O.B. 511, Dar es Salaam, Tanzania; twice yearly.

TRANSAFRICAN JOURNAL OF HISTORY. Journals Department, East African Publishing House, P.O.B. 30571, Nairobi, Kenya; f. 1971; twice yearly.

UGANDA JOURNAL. Uganda Society, Kampala, Uganda; history, literature, local ethnology; twice yearly.

ULTRAMAR. Procuradoria dos Estudantes Ultramarinos, Avenida da Republica 84-6e, Lisbon 1, Portugal; quarterly.

LA VOCE DELL'AFRICA. Instituto Italo-Africano, via Ulisse Aldrovandi, 16 Rome, Italy; monthly.

DIE WELT DES ISLAMS. Publ. E. J. Brill, Oude Rijn 33a, Leiden, Netherlands; f. 1913; contains articles in German, English and French; Editor Prof. Dr. O. SPIES.

WEST AFRICA. Overseas Newspapers (Agencies) Ltd., Cromwell House, Fulwood Place, London, W.C.1; f. 1917; published in London and Lagos, Nigeria; Editor D. M. WILLIAMS; weekly.

X-RAY. The Africa Bureau, 48 Grafton Way, London, W1P 5LB, England; f. 1971; a monthly bulletin of current affairs in southern Africa.

THE ZAMBIA JOURNAL. Livingstone Museum, P.O.B. 498, Livingstone, Zambia; twice yearly.

ZAMBIAN PAPERS. Institute for African Studies, University of Zambia, P.O.B. 900, Lusaka, Zambia; Editors Prof. J. VAN VELSEN and M. E. KASHOKI; annual.

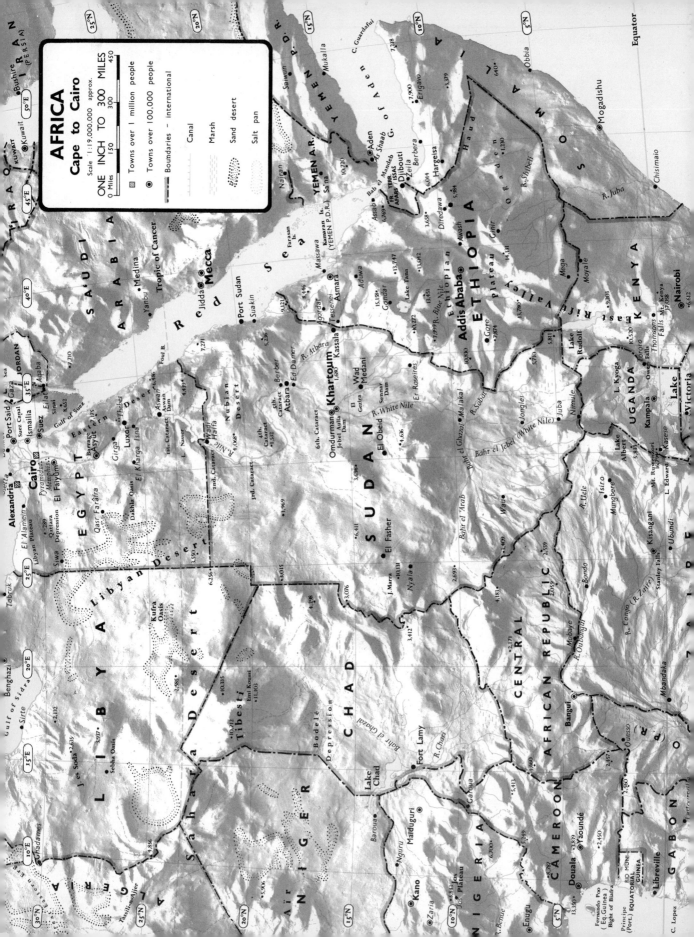

AFRICA
Cape to Cairo

Scale 1:19,000,000 approx.

ONE INCH TO 300 MILES
0 Miles   150   300   450

Towns over 1 million people
Towns over 100,000 people
Boundaries – international

Canal
Marsh
Sand desert
Salt pan